DEFINITIVE COUNTRY

THE EMPLOYEES OF DELTA AIR LINES
CONGRATULATE BARRY McCLOUD FOR HIS
SPECIAL EFFORTS IN COMPLETING

DEFINITIVE COUNTRY

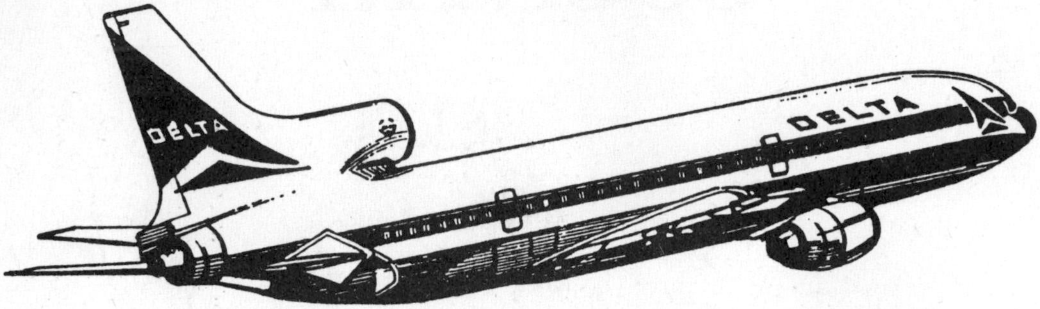

DELTA AIR LINES

YOU'LL LOVE THE WAY WE FLY

TODAY'S COUNTRY SOUND
HAS NO BOUNDARIES, AND IT WAS OUR
SINCERE PLEASURE TO HELP COORDINATE
THE WORLDWIDE TRANSPORTATION
REQUIREMENTS NECESSARY TO COMPLETE
THE PROJECT.

DEFINITIVE COUNTRY

The Ultimate Encyclopedia of Country Music and Its Performers

Barry McCloud

with

Ivan M. Tribe, Charles K. Wolfe, James I. Elliott, William K. McNeil, Janet Bird, Lesley-Anne Peake, Steve Morewood, Dale Vinicur, Steve Eng, and Bonnie Bucy

A PERIGEE BOOK

A Perigee Book
Published by The Berkley Publishing Group
200 Madison Avenue
New York, NY 10016

Book design by Barry McCloud
Cover design by One Plus One Studio

The author gratefully acknowledges permission to reprint the poem on Pop Stoneman and the autoharp by Garrison Keillor on p. 777, used by pemission of Garrison Keillor.

First edition: July 1995

Published simultaneously in Canada.

Library of Congress Cataloging-in-Publication Data

McCloud, Barry.
Definitive country: the ultimate encyclopedia of country music and its performers / Barry McCloud — 1st ed.
"A Perigee book."
Includes discographies
ISBN 0-399-51890-8 (hardcover)
ISBN 0-399-52144-5 (trade paperback)
1. Country music—bio-Bibliography—Dictionaries. I. Title
ML102.C7M33 1994 94-28400
781.642'03—dc20 CIP
MN

Printed in the United States of America

10 9 8 7 6 5 4 3 2 1

Contents

Contributors

IMT	Ivan M. Tribe, Professor of History at Rio Grande University. Among his many published works is a recent definitive work on the Stoneman Family. Member of the Board of Advisers of the IBMA.
CKW	Charles K. Wolfe, Professor of English at Middle Tennessee State University. One of the most respected music writers in the world, whose latest book is on Leadbelly. Also a member of the Board of Advisers of the IBMA. He has been nominated for a Grammy Award for his liner notes on three occasions.
WKM	William K. McNeil, Folklorist and Curator of the Ozark Folk Museum.
JIE	James I. Elliott, Associate Professor at Belmont University. He is also an award-winning Christian songwriter, Professional Manager for Ricky Skaggs and writer for Crook and Chase.
JAB	Janet Bird, Director of Marketing and Administration for Bumper Books (Europe) Ltd., based in the U.K.
LAP	Lesley-Anne Peake, freelance writer, TV link-person, script writer. One-time columnist of the *Nashville Banner*.
DV	Dale Vinicur, freelance writer who wrote with Lycretia Williams the biography of Hank and Audrey Williams *Still in Love With You.*
SE	Steve Eng, freelance writer and author of *Satisfied Mind*, the biography of Porter Wagoner.
SM	Steve Morewood, freelance writer on Country music and European political economics, based in the U.K.
BB	Bonnie Bucy, freelance journalist, former manager of David Allan Coe and Johnny Rodriguez and long-time publicist for *Hee Haw*.

All entries without credits were written by Barry McCloud.

Photographs are courtesy of Alan Mayor, Country music's premier photographer, Ivan M. Tribe, John Morris (of Old Homestead Records), and Barry McCloud, and thanks to the record companies, management companies and countless performers.

Acknowledgments

I would like to thank all my writers, but especially Dr. Ivan Tribe for his support over and above the call of duty. (If I could hand out knighthoods, then you would receive one.) I thank all the record companies who have given their support over the ten years of putting together this work, in particular: Debbie Bellin (Atlantic), Jackie Proffett (Arista), Greg McCorren (BMG), Mike Rogers and Robin Christian (CBS), Sarah Brosmer and Pam Russell (MCA), Charlotte Pennington (Step One), Bev Paul (Sugar Hill), Yumi Kimura and Susan Niles (Warner Brothers), Tor (Flying Fish), Troy (Curb), Sandy Neese and Juanita Duthie (Mercury), Scott (Giant), Mark Pucci (Capricorn), Ken Erwin (Rounder), the staff at BNA, all at Rebel, County, Soundwaves, CMH, Hightone, Dejadisc, Rykodisk, Elektra-Asylum, Decca and Polydor. Thanks also to Bruce Greenberg and Cathy Gurley (Liberty Records).

Additionally, I want to thank all the performers, songwriters and sidemen, current and not so current, and their families, managers, agents and publicists who have given their time and cooperation, many of whom are now dear friends. In particular, I wish to thank them for their help in getting chart placings, which come from no one source, but are based on average placings. I want to thank my researchers, Shannon Parkes and Eric Daniel Nicholls, also Ronnie Pugh at the Country Music Foundation and Don Butler at the GMA Resource Center. Also gratitude goes to the organizations and their staffs who have helped me along the way, and these include ACM, ASCAP, AMA, BMI, BCMA, CMA, CRIA, CARAS, SESAC, TNN, CRIA, RIAA, CMAA, IBMA, Grand Ole Opry, CMT, Americana, NSAI, NARAS, CCMA, IFCO, American Awards, RPM, Tennessee State Archives and the GMA. Thanks also to my friends at the radio stations, who have helped in locating performers no longer in the public gaze. Special thanks are due to Ed Benson and Jeff Green at the CMA for continued support, and to The Johnson Girls (IFCO) for their help and friendship.

I wish to thank those artists and performers who participated in the project, in particular Little Jimmy Dickens, Steve Wariner, Vern Gosdin, Buddy Emmons, Larry McNeely, Mike Auldridge, Patsy Stoneman, Harold Bradley, Vassar Clements, Frank Wakefield, and especially Billy Walker for his help in getting me to the U.S.A. I also thank the late Vic Willis for his help.

I would like to give thanks to my agent, Ann Tanenbaum, and her trusty lieutenant, Bill Mogan (William the Peacemaker), for their support. Thanks to Janet Bird for years of support and to Lesley-Anne Peake, Bonnie Bucy and Jay Serra for wading in when the waters started rising, to Tony Ashley at Delta Air Lines for getting me back and forth to Nashville in the early days, and to Sleep Country, Nashville, for letting me get at least some sleep. Thanks to Mark Wachter and David McClatchey at Inacomp for assisting in getting the computer hardware and software together. Personal thanks are due to my attorney, J. Richard Villarin, for his friendship and Marty Stuart stories. Thanks to Andy Smith for his scanning work.

Finally, my thanks go to the Lord God for giving me the strength to continue when the storm clouds gathered and allowing me to complete this work. This work is dedicated to my late parents, whose support allowed me to fulfill this dream. I miss you guys! It is also dedicated to my sons, Elliott, Alex and David, without whom nothing else matters.

Introduction

When I started researching this book in 1986, it would have been almost impossible to have forecast the impact that Country music would have at the end of that decade and into the 90's. From being a form of music that deejays would introduce with a "hee haw," it has become one of the most potent and respected. Where albums sold 20,000 units, if they were successful, we now have artists like Garth Brooks selling in the multi-millions.

Country music has gone through many changes since the early days of string bands. It hasn't so much diluted, although that has happened at certain times; it is more a case of fanning out. In the 90's, there is room for all types of Country music from Pop-Country, through Pure Country, Country Rock, Western Swing, Cajun, and even a renewed interest in Western music. In producing this book, I've looked at all the pioneers who believed in their music as well as the sidemen who backed the stars and the songwriters, without whom there would be no music. Some only made it to local fame while others have gone on to be international stars. Some branched out into movies, while others finished their days as organizational figures; sadly some have long been forgotten. I have also looked at the new pioneers who are currently carving out careers and crossing borders undreamed of at the start of the century.

Country music has come a long way from being a purely domestic music, what Jimmie Fadden of the Nitty Gritty Dirt Band once told me was "American music." It is now to be found in Canada, Australia, Europe, Japan, South America and Africa. This is only natural; after all, the foundation for the music comes from the different ethnic and national groupings that found their home in the U.S.A. While gathering the often abused and down-trodden refugees from war-torn nations, the U.S.A., personified as "Liberty," also gathered together all the music heritage of these peoples.

I hope that in reading or browsing through this work, you, dear reader, will feel the desire to go to a record store, an antique mall or a garage sale and try to discover some of the music from the past, while you still continue to discover the fine sounds being made by the history makers of today and the stars of tomorrow.

Barry McCloud
Nashville, December 1994

Reflections on Country Music

I consider myself Country. I was raised in West Virginia. I know what we listened to when I was a child: the Grand Ole Opry. It was fiddles and banjos and mandolins. It was a Bluegrass kind of music that we were listening to. That I consider Country music.

When I came to the Opry (Mr. Acuff brought me there), I considered Mr. Acuff . . . Country music, Ernest Tubb . . . Country music, Eddy Arnold . . . Country music.

What it means to me is . . . I was raised on it. My people played guitars and banjos. I can never remember a time when there wasn't a guitar or banjo. So I decided at an early age that's what I wanted to do. Dreaming of the day I would come to the Grand Ole Opry. As a youngster just out of high school, I worked in various radio stations around the country, playing just basic chords on the guitar. There was no programming like today; no disc jockeys.

I met Mr. Acuff in Cincinnati and he let me be a guest on his show; he liked what I did. A couple of years later I was in Saginaw, Michigan, and he was there in concert and he gave me the shock of my life when he asked me if I would like to come onto the Opry. A couple of weeks later, I got a phone call to do a guest spot. I came, I was accepted by the audience and I did another guest appearance in about a month. Then they asked me if I'd like to stay. After a couple of hit records, I had to establish a style. I did that accidentally when we got the twin guitar sound on *Sleeping at the Foot of the Bed.*

Country music is everything to me. I live it, I love it. It's a part of Little Jimmy Dickens. Do shows for people; I love to entertain. I love to talk and visit with folks.

—Little Jimmy Dickens

• • •

Country music in my opinion is listened to by more people than any other music in the world. It's loved by more people. It makes you feel in love; it makes you stay in love. It's something to dance to. Country music is something to laugh about, something to cry about. Country music is a must, that's the way I feel about it.

Country music's been my whole life since I was a kid. For the last twenty years, I wake up every morning and think about it. I go to bed thinking about it and sometimes I wake in the middle of the night thinking about it. I'm either writing or arranging a song I've just got through with or I'm out on the road performing or I'm writing with somebody, all the time. I'm sorta married to it, you might say. I make my living with it; I do everything with it.

I'm real happy I'm in the Country music business and I'm having a real fine time doing it. I love my fans and I think they love me. I got some diehard fans out there that I'm proud of. It don't happen to everybody and I didn't realize it for a long time. I just always took it for granted but just lately I've learned about the friends I have made.

—Vern Gosdin

• • •

Saturday night listening to the radio . . . clear channel 650 WSM, Nashville, Tennessee . . . The Grand Ole Opry! What a great memory! It was always exciting trying to guess which Country star would be coming out next. As a kid, I would imagine it was *me* being introduced by Mr. Roy Acuff, the King of Country Music, making my debut on that Ryman stage! I could almost feel those spotlights pick me up as I made my way out.

My interest and love for Country music came naturally, having parents who loved it and, particularly, a father who was a very gifted and talented musician and writer.

My dream *did* come true in 1973 as I performed for the first time on the Ryman stage with "Miss Country Sunshine," Dottie West, right around the time I moved to Nashville at the ripe old age of 17. This began my Country music career. I am very grateful I had the chance to taste that particular era of Country music working for and traveling the world with Dottie West, Bob Luman and later, the one person who gave me that chance to make records, my hero and mentor, Chet Atkins. Oh, what valuable lessons to learn at such an early age!

Country music's appeal is its honesty and simplicity; coming straight from the heart and speaking directly *to* and *about us* all. It is the music and voice of common, working people.

Although the Country music business (like our own culture) may have changed quite a bit over the years—fads come and go—it will always cycle back to those *real,* honest lyrics reflecting our own struggles, victories and everyday experiences. My personal hope is that the heritage of Country music will always be remembered, and those artists, musicians and writers who blazed trails for us all will never be forgotten.

I can't help thinking, right now, there's a young kid out there somewhere, listening to the Opry, dreaming his or her own Country Dreams!

—Steve Wariner

Commonly Used Phraseology

A & R
The A & R Department is basically the department within a record company that looks after the actual selection of songs and recording of albums and singles. Originally the head of A & R and his assistants produced the recordings. In modern times, the specialized record producer has evolved. Often they operate outside of the record company as an independent production company. It is often said (in humor) that A & R men have "no ears." Although this is true within some major companies, the advent of independent producers has in fact ensured that most producers are now musically and technologically sound.

BASEMENT LEVEL
This is the area of the chart below the Top 80.

CHART TOPPER
This is a record that reaches No.1.

COVER
This is a recorded version of a song. To the songwriter this is referred to as a cut.

DEMO
This is a demonstration recording of a song. Often produced on 8-track. Demos are either "full band" or "guitar/vocal."

EPONYMOUS
Album of the same name as the artist.

GIG
Live booking. This normally refers to a club booking as opposed to a concert date.

HOUSE BAND
Resident band at a venue.

HYPE (1)
To illegally promote a record into the charts.

HYPE (2)
To inflate a career by wild claims in the media.

LOWER ENTRY
Top 70 through Top 80.

MAJOR HIT
A chart position up to the Top 30.

MASTER
A master recording. Normally this was on 24-track but in recent times, studio sizes have increased to 96-tracks and above.

MINOR HIT
A record that charts Top 40 to Top 60.

PLUGGER
Someone who promotes a song or record. Sometimes called a pitcher or pitchman.

SESSIONMAN
Musician who plays on a recording session. In Nashville, the top players are called the A-Team.

SIDEMAN
Musician in a band.

SUB
To deputize for another musician in a band. In the U.K., this would be called "depping."

TO CHART
To make an appearance on the charts.

TRACK
A single 45 recording or selection from an album.

Organizational List

ACM	Academy of Country Music
AMA	American Music Awards
BCMA	British Country Music Association
BPI	British Phonographic Industry
CARAS	Canadian Academy of Recording Arts and Sciences
CMA	Country Music Association
CMAA	Country Music Association of Australia
CMF	Country Music Foundation
CRIA	Canadian Record Industry Association
IBMA	International Bluegrass Music Association
IFCO	International Fan Club Organization
MCN	Music City News
NARAS	National Association of Recording Arts & Sciences
NARM	National Association of Rack Merchandisers
NSAI	Nashville Songwriters Association International
PRS	Performing Rights Society
RIAA	Record Industry Association of America
TNN	The Nashville Network
UA	United Artists Records
WB	Warner Brothers Records

A

NATHAN ABSHIRE

(Fiddle, Accordion)

Date of Birth: June 27, 1913
Where Born: Nr. Gueyden, Louisiana
Married: Unknown
Children: Adopted son Ray
Date of Death: May 13, 1981

Cajun accordionist ***Nathan Abshire***

Although Nathan Abshire made his professional debut at the age of 8 at La Sakke de Tee-Gar Guidry dance hall in Marmentan Cove, Louisiana, he never made a living from music and for most of his working life, he held a menial job at the town dump in Basile.

Beginning as an accordion player, he made his first record in the early 1930s with Happy Fats & the Rainbow Ramblers. Backed by the now-named Rayne-Bo Ramblers, he recorded for Bluebird in 1936 and the following year, as Nason Absher, he did likewise in the Bluebird 2000 series. Following ten years of relative obscurity because of a diminishing interest in his accordion, he took up the fiddle.

After serving in the military, Nathan was booked for a one-day-a-week engagement at Quincy Davis' Avalon Club in Basile. Resuming his recording career, in 1949, he cut *Pine Grove Blues* backed by *Kaplan Waltz* for the D.T. label. He followed up with a re-recording of *French Blues*, which he had originally cut for Bluebird. *Pine Grove Blues*, which Nathan would record on many occasions, this time featured the vocals of Roy Broussard.

In 1950, George Khoury started his Khoury and Lyric labels and for Khoury, Nathan cut his most successful recordings, *La Valse de Holly Beech* and *Shamrock Waltz*, featuring the fiddle playing of Dewey Balfa. For the remainder of the 50's, he played fiddle at local dances. He also cut sides for various small labels, including Swallow, where he recorded with the Balfa Brothers.

In the early 60's, he recorded for Jay Miller's Kajun label, and the tracks cut included *Popcorn Blues*, *Hey Mom*, a new version of *Pine Grove Blues*, *Jolie Catlin*, *La Banana au None Adam* (featuring vocals by Robert Bertrand), *The La La Blues*, *Mardi-Gras Song* (vocals by Dewey Balfa), *Gabriel Waltz*, *Dreamers Waltz* and *Trouble Waltz*.

His later Swallow recordings showcase Nathan Abshire at his very best and include *Tramp sur la Rue*, *Lemonade Song*, *A Musician's Life*, *Offshore Blues*, *Valse de Bayou Teche*, *Games People Play* (a 1970 single) and yet another recording of *Pine Grove Blues*.

With the revitalized interest in Folk and Cajun music in the 70's, Nathan found himself in demand playing to festival and college audiences. In 1972, he again worked with the Balfa Brothers on the album ***The Cajuns*** for Sonet Records. In 1975, he starred in the PBS documentary, *Good Times Are Killing Me*, about the Cajuns. Then, just as his career was starting to take off, it slumped as alcoholism took over. He cut some sides for Folkways and La Louisienne, which lacked quality. He also played local dates and had an afternoon program on a Lake Charles radio station.

On May 13, 1981, in Mamou, Louisiana, Nathan Abshire's life came to an end. He was a fine Cajun musician who has left behind a legacy of many excellent albums. His career, limited by his own private life, nonetheless contributed music that is still vibrant in the 90's.

RECOMMENDED ALBUMS:

"A Cajun Legend—The Best of Nathan Abshire" (Swallow)
"The Cajuns" (Sonet)(1972) [Also features the Balfa Brothers]
"The Good Times Are Killing Me" (Swallow) [With the Balfa Brothers]
"Jay Miller Sessions, Vol. 13" (Flyright) [With the Pinegrove Boys. These are the Kajun recordings]
"Louisiana Cajun Music Special" (Ace) [Various artists]

ACADEMY OF COUNTRY MUSIC

In 1964, Eddie Miller, Tommy Wiggins (the publisher of *D.J.'s Digest*) and Mickey and Chris Christiansen got together with the aim of promoting greater acceptance in the western states of Country and Western music and to "create a framework for like-minded to meet and for greater recognition of performers and executives." It was chartered as a non-profit-making organization and initially known as the Country and Western Academy.

There was so much enthusiasm for the new body that the first awards event was held later that year at the Red Barrel Nightclub in Los Angeles, with *D.J.'s Digest* underwriting the cost of the event, and was emceed by Tex Williams.

The following year, the second awards dinner was sponsored by *V.I.P.* magazine. By now, membership was on the increase and a Board of Directors was set up, chaired by Dick Schofield. Their first mandate was to decide which direction should be taken in promoting the acceptance of Country music. It was decided to introduce a dues system, with the result that when the first official awards show was held at the Hollywood Palladium in February 1966, the Academy could afford to sponsor itself. Tex Williams was elected President, a post he held through 1968. The second Annual Awards Dinner was held on March 6, 1967, at the Beverly Hilton in Beverly Hills, California.

In 1968, an office was opened at the Crossroads of the World in Los Angeles and Fran Boyd became Executive Secretary (a post she continues to hold in 1994). A year later, the Academy became an international body and made plans to televise the awards show. In 1972, this became a reality. Two years later, the awards show debuted on ABC-TV, under the guidance of Gene Weed. In 1979, Dick Clark of *American Bandstand* fame became involved, and the show moved to NBC prime time. Produced by Gene Weed and Al Schwartz and directed by Gene Weed, the awards show has led the field in its time block for nine straight years.

Members of the Academy who were especially active included Cliffie Stone, Bill Boyd and Johnny Bond. The awards are voted on by the members, with the exception of the Pioneer Award and the Jim Reeves Memorial

Award, the recipients of which are chosen by the Board of Directors. The Pioneer Award was created in 1968 "for the recognition of outstanding and unprecedented achievement in the field of Country music." The Jim Reeves Memorial Award was created in 1969 and is "presented annually to an individual, not necessarily a performing artist, who has made substantial contributions towards the international acceptance of Country music during the preceding calendar year."

The Academy is now involved in a year-round cycle of activities and events geared to promote Country music. They have a research project entitled "What's This Country All About." The Academy's 1994 President was Ken Kragen and Tim DuBois was Vice-President. Robert Romeo served as Board Chairman and Bill Boyd was Executive Director.

THE ACADEMY OF COUNTRY MUSIC, PO Box 508, Hollywood, CA 90078.
Telephone: 213-462-2351/Fax: 213-462-3253

ROY ACUFF

(Singer, Songwriter, Fiddle, Music Publisher, Yo Yo Exponent)

Given Name: Roy Claxton Acuff
Date of Birth: September 15, 1903
Where Born: Maynardville, Tennessee
Married: Mildred Louise Douglas
Children: Roy Jr.
Date of Death: November 23, 1992

When Roy Acuff died, radio station WSM, the flagship station for the *Grand Ole Opry*, interrupted its regular programming and devoted the next two days to the music and memories of the man called "The King of Country Music." Singers ranging from George Jones to Garth Brooks called in to pay tribute to Mr. Roy and talked about how much he had influenced them. Fans called in to share their memories of meeting him in the past, or of special shows they had seen during the almost sixty years Acuff had been performing. It was a tribute unparalleled in Nashville and justly so. In many ways, Acuff was Country music's most important stylist and was a major influence on younger singers like Hank Williams, Lefty Frizzell, the Louvin Brothers and George Jones.

Though he had ceased having hit records decades ago, his continued presence as the Grand Master of the *Grand Ole Opry* had given him a platform from which he could influence the music as a publisher, as a media pioneer, as a songwriter, as a national spokesman and in later years, a defender of older traditions. Along the way, he also gave to the music some of its best known and most enduring songs.

Mr. Roy was born in Maynardville, a hamlet of some 200 in Union County, about 25 miles north of Knoxville, near the Smoky Mountains. He grew up in modest circumstances even though his father had attended a local college—rare in those days in east Tennessee—and served both as a lawyer and as a preacher at the local Baptist church. In the rural area where he grew up, Mr. Roy remembered hearing old mountain singers, keening the old ballads unaccompanied in a high, forceful style that marked his notion of music forever. His father taught him to play his instrument next to the family Victrola, to the accompaniment of records by Uncle A.M. Stuart and the Skillet Lickers.

He also attended church singing school, although as a boy, the young Roy was more interested in baseball and fighting. "There was nothing I loved as much as a physical fight," he said. After the family moved to Knoxville, he was routinely involved in good ball games and routinely thrown into jail for fighting. He was a good enough ball player to get invited for a tryout at a Major League training camp, but fate intervened. A 1929 fishing trip to Florida resulted in severe sunstroke, followed by a nervous breakdown. Once recovered, he decided baseball was out and so apprenticed himself to a local medicine show man, Doc Hauer.

***Roy Acuff** with **DeFord Bailey**, on the stage of the Grand Ole Opry, celebrating DeFord's 70th birthday*

Traveling around the country as the show's entertainment, Roy learned to work a crowd, to be a showman, to sing loudly (there were no mikes in those days), to do imitations (train whistles were a specialty) and even to balance things on his nose. All this experience led to a job with a local band, The Tennessee Crackerjacks, playing on Knoxville's WROL, who were soon dubbed The Crazy Tennesseans. "Mostly we fiddled and starved," Acuff recalled.

This all changed one day when Roy, for 50 cents cash, got a fellow radio performer to write out for him the words to an old Gospel song called *The Great Speckle* [sic] *Bird*, a strange allegorical song that had been associated with the then-popular Church of God sect. After Roy started singing it, he became a sensation all over east Tennessee and he was invited to record for the ARC label, then providing records to many of the country's leading chain stores. A trip to Chicago yielded some twenty sides, including *The Great Speckled Bird*, another local song called *The Wabash Cannonball* (on which Acuff did not sing, but just did the train whistle), *Steamboat Whistle Blues* and even a brace of off-color songs like *When Lulu's Gone*, released under the name the Bang Boys.

Although there was some reluctance on the part of the *Grand Ole Opry* management, Roy was invited to try out for the show in 1938 and sang *The Great Speckled Bird.* Cards flooded in and he was hired, after the *Opry* bosses changed his band's name to the Smoky Mountain Boys. In 1939, he re-formed his band, bringing in Pete Kirby, or Bashful Brother Oswald, to play Dobro and sing high harmony. An amazing string of hit records followed in the early 1940's, making Roy and his sound into a national phenomenon; they included *Beneath That Lonely Mound of Clay* (1940), *The Precious Jewel* (1940), *The Wreck on the Highway* (1942), *Fire Ball Mail* (1942), *Wait for That Light to Shine* (1944) and *Two Different Worlds* (1945).

During WWII, his shows routinely attracted 15,000 fans and he was as popular with servicemen as Benny Goodman and Frank Sinatra. A well-known story tells of American Marines in the Pacific who heard Japanese soldiers taunting them by shouting, "To hell with Babe Ruth! To hell with Roy Acuff!" In 1942, in part to preserve his own publishing rights to songs that were even being put on V-discs, Acuff joined with veteran songwriter and WSM staffer Fred Rose to open the first modern publishing company in Nashville to specialize in Country music, Acuff-Rose.

Almost immediately it was successful and Rose never had to touch the seed money Roy had advanced. By the late 1940's, it had become the home base for the sensational songs of Hank Williams, the Louvin Brothers and later, artists like Don Gibson, the Everly Brothers and Roy Orbison. Acuff-Rose still exists today as a major Nashville force and member of the Opryland Music Group.

During 1944, Roy had three major hits on the Country charts, with *The Prodigal Son* (also a Pop cross-over), *I'll Forgive You, But I Can't Forget* (another Pop cross-over) and the flip side, *Write Me Sweetheart*, on OKeh Records. In 1947, his Columbia release *Jole Blon* reached the Top 5; the following year, *Waltz of the Wind* reached the Top 10. His other record successes that year were *Unloved and Unclaimed/This World Can't Stand Long*, *The Tennessee Waltz* and *A Sinner's Death*. Mr. Roy was absent from the charts for a decade, but in 1958, on Acuff-Rose's Hickory label, he had a Top 10 hit entitled *Once More*. He followed up with two further Top 20 singles, *So Many Times* (1958) and *Come and Knock* (1959).

Roy, whose touring had included doing package tours with Elvis Presley in the 50's, decided by the 1970's, to come off the road. He returned to the older traditional roots and in 1971 he participated on the Nitty Gritty Dirt Band album ***Will the Circle Be Unbroken*** and saw his audience expand dramatically.

His later years saw him survive the death of his beloved wife, Mildred, in 1981, as well as the deaths of many of his key band members, like fiddler Howdy Forrester and pianist Jimmie Riddle. In addition, he saw the land near his house on the Cumberland River converted into a huge new complex called Opryland, and he entertained President Richard Nixon during the opening ceremonies for the New Opry House in 1974, demonstrating his legendary skill with a yo-yo, as well as balancing his fiddle on the end of his nose. He had his final chart entry in 1987, with Charlie Louvin on the inspirational *The Precious Jewel* on Hal Kat Records.

Towards the end of his life and in failing health, he moved into a specially built home a few yards from the Opry's front door, where he sat, greeted friends and fans and served his final years as the music's most legendary elder statesman. His famed dressing room at the *Opry* remained his other location to meet friends, fans and fellow musicians. CKW

RECOMMENDED ALBUMS:

"Songs of the Smoky Mountains" (Capitol)(1955) [Re-issued by Stetson UK in the original sleeve (1987)]
"The Great Roy Acuff" (Capitol)(1964) [Re-issued by Stetson UK in the original sleeve (1988) and also on (Harmony)(1965)]
"Greatest Hits Vol. 1" (double)(Elektra)(1976)
"Greatest Hits Vol. 2" (double)(Elektra)(1979)
"Country Music Hall of Fame's Roy Acuff & His Smoky Mountain Boys (Songs of the Smoky Mountains)" (Capitol)(1979)
"1936-1939 Steamboat Whistle Blues" (Rounder Special Series)(1985)
"Mountain Memories" (double)(Hickory)
"Historic Edition" (Columbia)
"All Time Country & Western Hits" (Series of seven albums)(Decca)(July, 1960-August, 1966)

ROY ACUFF, JR.

(Singer, Guitar, Drums)

Given Name:	**Roy Neal Acuff**
Date of Birth:	**July 25, 1943**
Where Born:	**Nashville, Tennessee**
Married:	**1. Quinny (m. 1961) (div.)**
	2. Aubrey Chestain (div.)
	3. Susan
Children:	**Roy Neal, Jr., Alex Wolfgang**

Being the son of such a famous father can carry mixed blessings if you are trying to carve out a career for yourself in the entertainment business. However, Roy Neal plowed his own furrow, achieving a moderate level of success.

After graduating from high school in 1962, he worked as a guide at the family's Dunbar Cave. The following year, he became interested in music and learned to play guitar and dabbled with drums. By 1964, he was working in the shipping department of Acuff-Rose Music, but the following year, he was heard singing by producer Don Gant, who had him make a private demo recording. Wesley Rose liked what he heard and signed Roy, Jr. to the company's Hickory Records.

His first session for the label was on September 30, 1965, when he recorded *Baby Just Said Goodbye* and one of his father's standards, *Wabash Cannonball*. On October 23 of that year, he made his professional debut on the *Grand Ole Opry* and sang his new single and encored with the flip side. The following year, he had three singles on the charts: *Stand Tall*, *Victim of Life's Circumstances* and *Lament of the Cherokee Reservation*.

Touring and recording without further success, Roy, Jr. decided to call it a day in 1976 and took over the promotion department at Hickory Records, where he stayed until 1982, just after his mother died, when he quit the business. Being a gifted artist, he resumed painting and in 1990, he had a showing at a gallery in Florida. Roy, Jr. is an animal lover and cares deeply for the environment.

RECOMMENDED ALBUMS:

"Roy Acuff, Jr." (Hickory) (1970)
"California Lady" (Hickory/MGM) (1974)

ACUFF-ROSE GROUP OF PUBLISHERS

Roy Acuff discovered there was money to be made in music publishing when he sold 100,000 copies of a songbook he compiled. He resisted the offers of major publishers from New York who wanted the rights to his songs. Acuff needed a partner who knew the business of music publishing and found that person in Fred Rose.

Rose was a successful songwriter and piano player who was working at WSM Chicago. He had played Pop music in that city and recorded for Brunswick Records. Rose was a prolific composer with many Pop hits to his credit, including *Red Hot Mama*, *Be Honest with Me* and *Deed I Do*. Acuff scored a radio hit with Rose's *Pins and Needles*. Although Rose was initially hesitant to go into business with Acuff, the persistence of the *Opry* star won him over.

Acuff-Rose Publications was established in October, 1942 with the songs of Roy Acuff and his $25,000 investment. The operation was launched from Rose's house and was a success almost immediately. Fred Rose also contributed many songs to the company that became big hits, including *Faded Love*, *Roly Poly*, *Winter Roses*, *Take These Chains from My Heart*, *Deep Water*, *Fireball Mail* and *Blue Eyes Crying in the Rain*.

In 1945, Fred persuaded his son Wesley to leave his accounting job with Standard Oil in Chicago to run the business affairs of Acuff-Rose. In 1948, Fred Rose signed a young songwriter from Alabama named Hank Williams to the company for a $50 a month advance on royalties. Williams added songs to Acuff-Rose Publications that became Country music classics and generated millions of dollars, including *I'm So Lonesome I Could Cry*, *Your Cheatin' Heart*, *Honky Tonk Blues*, *I Can't Help It If I'm Still in Love with You* and *Cold, Cold Heart*. Fred Rose was also instrumental in securing Hank Williams a contract with Sterling Records.

One of Acuff-Rose's most lucrative copyrights was Redd Stewart and Pee Wee King's *Tennessee Waltz*. It was a hit for both Pee Wee King and Cowboy Copas in 1948. The song, inspired by Bill Monroe's *Kentucky Waltz*, was recorded by Pop singer Patti Page in 1950. Her version shot to the top of the Pop chart and by 1951 had sold nearly 5 million copies, earning Acuff-Rose and the songwriters a reported $330,000.

The tremendous success of *Tennessee Waltz* by Patti Page was the result of Fred Rose's friendship with Columbia Records'

New York executive Mitch Miller. As director of A & R for Columbia Records Miller was responsible for finding songs for many major Pop stars. The Acuff-Rose-New York connection resulted in a series of Pop hits, including the No.1 *Cold Cold Heart* by Tony Bennett, Top 3 *Half as Much* by Rosemary Clooney and the Top 3 hit *Jambalaya* by Jo Stafford.

Wesley Rose assumed leadership of Acuff-Rose Publications when his father died in 1954. In addition to maintaining steady growth for the company, Wesley co-founded the Country Music Association. Rose was also very active in the community, lending his support and guidance to the Nashville Symphony, Belmont University, First American Bank, Vanderbilt University and the Nashville Area Chamber of Commerce.

As well as Hank Williams, Acuff-Rose's main writers throughout the 50's were Mel Foree, Vic McAlpin, Johnnie & Jack, Wilma Lee Cooper, Ira and Charlie Louvin and Leon Payne. During the 60's, the company's principal songwriters included Don Gibson, John D. Loudermilk, Boudleaux and Felice Bryant, Roy Orbison, the Everly Brothers and Liz Anderson. Writers in the 70's included Dallas Frazier and Whitey Shafer.

Acuff-Rose Music was purchased by Opryland USA in 1985 and the 20,000 copyrights became the anchor for the Opryland Music Group. Former RCA Records executive Jerry Bradley was hired the following year to manage the company. Bradley brought publishing veteran Jerry Flowers to the company and together they sought new ways to increase the use of the Acuff-Rose songs. The popularity of the copyrights in Europe encouraged the expansion of Country Music Television (also owned by Opryland parent company, Gaylord) to expand into those markets. In England, the BBC produced a two-hour radio special to commemorate Acuff-Rose's 50th Anniversary entitled *The Nashville Dream*, that was hosted by Emmylou Harris.

Opryland Music Group signed several new songwriters in the 90's and the result was a series of hit songs. One of the new writers was RCA Records artist Aaron Tippin, who reached No.1 with *There Ain't Nothin' Wrong with the Radio* (co-written with Buddy Brock). Other No.1 songs followed, including Alan Jackson's *Love's Got a Hold on You* (written by Carson Chamberlain and Keith Stegall), *If I Didn't Have You* (Randy Travis) written by Skip Ewing and Max D. Barnes, *(Without Me) What Do I Do with Me* written by David Chamberlain, Royce Porter and L. David Lewis and recorded by Tanya Tucker, and Collin Raye's *Love Me*, written by Skip Ewing and Max T. Barnes.

The historic songs of Acuff-Rose have been included in many of Hollywood's biggest movies including *Another 48 HRS*, *Bull Durham*, *Steel Magnolias*, *Mississippi Burning*, *Pretty Woman* and *Honeymoon in Las Vegas*. Advertisers who have licensed some of the classic songs to promote their products include Goodyear, Kraft, Jell-O, Quaker Oats, Chrysler and Frito-Lay.

With the advent of the performance rights organization Broadcast Music Incorporated (BMI), Acuff-Rose Publications became the BMI affiliated company, while Milene Music affiliated with ASCAP. BMI has awarded Acuff-Rose more than 40 "Million Air" awards signifying one million performances of a song. Included in the prestigious list are Jimmy Dean's *Big Bad John*, Hank Williams' *Honky Tonk Blues* and *I Can't Help It (If I'm Still in Love with You)*, Don Gibson's *Sweet Dreams*, Hank Locklin's *Send Me the Pillow You Dream On* and the Whitey Shafer-Lefty Frizzell composition, *That's the Way Love Goes*.

More than a dozen of the Acuff-Rose songs have generated two million performances and they include *Cathy's Clown* by Don Everly, *Oh Pretty Woman* by Roy Orbison and Bill Dees and four Hank Williams songs: *Cold Cold Heart*, *I'm So Lonesome I Could Cry*, *Jambalaya* and *Your Cheatin' Heart*. Roy Orbison and Joe Melson wrote two songs with three million performances: *Blue Bayou* and *Crying*. *Tennessee Waltz* by Redd Stewart and Pee Wee King also has generated three million performances as well as the Eddie Miller, Dub Williams and Robert Yount song, *Release Me*. The Acuff-Rose song with an all-time high of four million performances is the Don Gibson classic, *I Can't Stop Loving You*.

Acuff-Rose Publications was the first music publishing company dedicated to Country music. It was the first successful music business in Nashville not affiliated with WSM or the *Grand Ole Opry* and it became the cornerstone of the Country music empire that has been built in Nashville. Acuff-Rose also made history as the first publisher to print its own songbooks and sheet music in Nashville. The company established its own recording studio and was the first publisher to form a record company, Hickory Records, which released product by Roy Acuff, Don Gibson, Sue Thompson, Ernest Ashworth, Bob Luman, Leona Williams, Redd Stewart and Acuff-Rose writers including Mickey Newbury. The label ceased during 1979. Opryland Music Group would operate 16th Avenue Records during the middle 80's, which released product by Charley Pride and Neal McCoy (then billed as McGoy). JIE

DERROLL ADAMS

(Singer, Songwriter, Banjo, Harmonica)
Given Name: **Derroll Lewis Thompson**
Date of Birth: **November 25, 1925**
Where Born: **Portland, Oregon**
Married: **Div. 4 times**

Many performers become legends in their own lifetime, but Folk-Country singer Derroll Adams has attained a reputation that is so apocryphal that it's difficult to separate truth from fiction.

Derroll's unique life is almost certainly a result of his upbringing. His father, Tom, was an ex-vaudeville juggler who got drunk so often that Derroll's mother, Gertrude, left him. She remarried, but left her second husband because he took a belt buckle to Derroll. She finally settled down with George Adams, an inventor and salesman from Washington, D.C., who studied at night school to get an engineering degree.

Derroll spent much of his childhood traveling around the West with his mother and stepfather. George worked on the Bonneville Dam power line, but picked fruit when times were bad. Derroll became interested in music after hearing the *Grand Ole Opry* on the car radio and soon his mother bought him a harmonica. He was also influenced by the western genre and when, at last, the family settled down, he began wearing cowboy outfits.

Following the bombing of Pearl Harbor in 1941, Derroll, then only 16, falsified his age and enlisted in the U.S. Army at the end of December. Gertrude and George found him and allowed him to stay, but the army said no and he was discharged. The next year, he was married for the first time, to a fellow student, and enlisted in the Coast Guard.

He had a nervous breakdown and attacked one of his officers with a knife and was placed in a hospital on Treasure Island, San Francisco. With his earring, the medicos must have thought that a real pirate was among them. Discharged again, he returned home and bought a banjo to while away the hours until full recovery. However, because he taught himself, his tuning was not conventional.

Whether he had recovered or not is contentious, because he started art studies at Reed College's Museum Art School in Portland. He was also getting into drugs and had joined the Vedanta Society. He had even grown a beard, which, coupled with the earring, reinforced his buccaneering look. Still only in his early 20's, he embraced Marxist doctrine. Derroll's playing had improved and he was an avid student of such greats as Josh White. He was adept enough to sing and play at Henry Wallace's Progressive Party rallies, supporting Wallace's 1948 presidential bid.

By now, he had left two wives and had remarried. En route to Mexico, where Adams intended to study art, it was discovered that his third wife was pregnant. They settled in San Diego, California, where he worked driving Marines during the Korean War and truck driving for Max Factor. Thanks to the help of another truck driver, World Folk Artists started to get Adams gigs. Derroll had ceased to be a political activist and concentrated on singing and art.

Moving to Topanga Canyon near Los Angeles was the catalyst for his career. Here he met several Country-Folk performers, most importantly, Woody Guthrie and Ramblin' Jack Elliott. He was asked by Elmer Bernstein to play banjo for the soundtrack for the movie *Durango* in 1957. The year before, Jack Elliott had gone to England and in 1957, he invited Derroll to follow. By now Derroll was between marriages, so he went. In London, he and Jack recorded ***The Rambling Boys***, a 10" album for Topic. They became very popular in the burgeoning English Skiffle and coffee bar scene and when they toured Europe, their fame spread.

Adams then left Jack and started drinking heavily. Sobering up, he moved to Paris, where he was married for a fourth time, to the daughter of a French aristocrat, who disowned her on hearing of the marriage. The couple moved to Brussels, Belgium, where the new Madame Adams built a successful interior decorating company. In 1958, Derroll appeared at the World's Fair (Expo) in Brussels with Jack Elliott and was very well received. From then until 1966, he dropped out of playing and helped his wife run her firm. When that marriage broke up, he resumed performing. He returned to London, where he befriended one of the new generation of folkies, Donovan. He continued with phases of performing and inactivity.

To describe Adams' singing voice is difficult. It is somewhere between John Wayne's talking voice and Pete Seeger's singing voice. He is important not just to Folk but also to Country, because, especially when he performs in tandem with Jack Elliott, there are hints of the string band sound of the Bristol Sessions. However, his lyrics sometimes offended and although now, in an enlightened 90's, they would be shrugged off, some audiences were genuinely outraged.

RECOMMENDED ALBUM:
"The Rambling Boys" (Topic UK)(1957) [With Ramblin' Jack Elliott]

J.T. ADAMS

(Singer, Songwriter)

Given Name:	**James Taylor Adams**
Date of Birth:	**July 17, 1926**
Where Born:	**Virginia**
Married:	**Judy**
Children:	**Carol, Holly, John, Joel**

J. T. Adams and his group, the Men of Texas, recorded some of the best Gospel music to be released on a mainline Country label. A graduate of North Texas State University at Waco and East Texas State Teachers College, he was signed to the Republic label in 1952 and initially released *My God Is Real/Dear Lord, Remember Me*, which remained one of his most popular records. Through 1953 to 1955, he continued issuing singles and the two EPs, *Songs of Faith* and *Christmas Time.*

In 1971, he became the Director of Music and Youth at the First Baptist Church, Sulphur Springs, Texas. He is still active in Gospel music in Greensboro, North Carolina.

RECOMMENDED ALBUMS:
"Songs of Faith" (Republic)
"Voices Skyward" (Word)[Also on Wrangler]
"J. T. Adams & the Men of Texas" (Wrangler)

EDDIE ADCOCK

(Singer, Songwriter, Banjo, Guitar)

Given Name:	**Edward Windsor Adcock**
Date of Birth:	**June 21, 1938**
Where Born:	**Scottsville, Virginia**
Married:	**1. Mildred**
	2. Martha Hearon
Children:	**Eddie, Beatrice, Dennis**

Though many fans associate him primarily with Bluegrass, Eddie Adcock has always been willing and able to extend his boundaries. From his long tenure with the Country Gentlemen all the way up to his 1990's band, his guitar and banjo work has reflected a cornucopia of musical genres, including Folk, Country, Rock, Jazz and Blues. A typical set is likely to include the old New Orleans standard *Make Me a Pallet on the Floor*, The Allman Brothers' *Midnight Rider*, or Dylan's *Tonight I'll Be Staying Here with You.* The common thread that runs through all different songs is quality, taste and innovation.

Eddie grew up on a farm near Scottsville, Virginia, selling a calf to buy his first five-string banjo. He began performing with his brother Frank, singing Gospel music in rural churches and over the radio stations in Charlottesville. While a teenager, he helped form the James River Playboys and began to expand his horizons, and when working at a theater in Scottsville, he got to see most of the big touring Country acts of the day, such as the Bailes Brothers and Wilma Lee and Stoney Cooper.

A family crisis led to his leaving home when he was 14 and for the next seven years he used his muscular physique to forge a career as a semi-professional boxer. Later he got into drag racing, using his car called Mr. Banjo to pile up 34 straight wins and set two track records at Manassas, Virginia. With these and other jobs, such as auto mechanic, sheet metal worker, dump truck driver and auto parts salesman, Eddie was able to continue with his music. In 1953 he took a job with Smokey Graves and his Blue Star Boys at WSVS radio in Crewe, Virginia. This led to stints as a sideman with Mac Wiseman, Bill Harrell and finally Buzz Busby, in Washington, D.C.

*Bluegrass star **Eddie Adcock***

In 1957, while Eddie was working as a janitor in Annandale, Virginia, Bill Monroe called him to offer a job with the Blue Grass Boys, but these were lean times, even for Monroe, and soon Eddie had to quit to become a sheet metal worker. Soon after, John Duffey, Charlie Waller and Jim Cox talked him into joining their new band, the Country Gentlemen. Eddie stayed for 12 years and became a prime architect of the distinctive Folk-Bluegrass sound and of what became the most popular of the second generation Bluegrass bands. His influence on the Country Gentlemen was profound and he especially encouraged them to seek out new and unusual songs and to experiment with progressive arrangements.

By the late 60's, he was anxious for even more musical experimentation and he moved to California. There he started a Country-Rock band, the Clinton Special, and played electric guitar under the pseudonym Clinton Codack.

They recorded one single for MGM's Rocky Ridge label, *Just as You Are I Love You/Blackberry Fence*. The topside was included in the 1971 movie *The Horsemen*, starring Omar Sharif. Interestingly, the flip-side was written by master songwriter Dewayne Blackwell, when he was age nine! Eventually, though, Eddie came back east and started his own group, IInd Generation, with former Gentleman Jimmy Gaudreau, Bob White, Wendy Thatcher and for a time, Tony Rice. After three albums for the traditional Rebel label, they sought new horizons and eventually they worked for a time with David Allan Coe.

In 1973, Eddie met Martha Hearon and invited her to become a member of IInd Generation. She was a South Carolina native, the daughter of a successful farmer who was a singer himself and who had once been offered a job with Kay Kyser, the big band leader. Her background was in Classical and Folk music and she was fascinated with the music Eddie was making. Soon the pair had married and Martha was developing her skills as a songwriter, singer and promoter. Moving to Tennessee about 1980, the couple eventually started to tour as a trio with bass player Missy Raines. A string of brilliant cds emerged in the early 90's, as well as a clutch of awards and such popular songs as *Missy's Dog*. Eddie also found time to appear with the all-star band, the Masters, touring internationally and appearing on network TV shows including *The Tonight Show*. CKW

RECOMMENDED ALBUMS:

"Eddie Adcock and the Talk of the Town" (CMH)(1987)(Cassette)
"Eddie Adcock and His Guitar" (CMH)(1988)(Cassette)
"The Acoustic Connection" (CMH)(1988)(Cassette)
"Dixie Fried" (CMH)(1991)

ALABAMA

Formed: 1969 as Young Country/1972 as Wildcountry/1977 as Alabama

Members:

Randy Owen	**Lead Vocals, Rhythm Guitar**
Jeff Cook	**Vocals, Lead Guitar, Keyboards, Fiddle, Bass Guitar**
Teddy Gentry	**Vocals, Bass Guitar**
Mark Herndon	**Drums, Percussion**

The heyday of the band concept was back in the early days of Country music, when groups such as the Gully Jumpers and the Beverly Hillbillies achieved fame. Then, except for occasional albums recorded, with the blessing of their boss, by bands such as the Buckaroos and the Strangers, the groups played backup for a featured singer. With the advent of Alabama, the band concept followed in its wake and continues unabated.

Randy (b. December 14, 1949, Fort Payne, Alabama) and Teddy (b. January 22, 1952, Fort Payne, Alabama), who are first cousins, grew up more like brothers, on small cotton farms on Lookout Mountain in Dekalb County. They learned to play guitar together and sang in church together before they reached age six. Randy's grandfather Gladstone Owen had played guitar and Randy's mother, who worked in a textile mill, sang and played piano at local Gospel revivals; she bought him his first Gretsch guitar. Teddy was brought up by his grandfather, after his parents divorced. His grandfather raised seven children single-handedly.

***Alabama**, who re-introduced the group concept to Country music*

Throughout the 60's, Randy and Teddy played separately, in a variety of local and family bands, performing everything from Pop to Bluegrass. One of the bands Teddy played in while in high school was the Sand Mountain Chicken Pluckers, which won a trophy in a "Battle of the Bands" at Dekalb Theater. At high school, they met another cousin, Jeff Cook (b. August 27, 1949, Fort Payne, Alabama), a multi-instrumentalist. Jeff's father was a car salesman and better off. Jeff had already played in various bands—the first being a Rock band, the Viscounts, when he was 13—and by the time he was 14, he had become a Rock'n'Roll deejay. At the time the cousins met, Jeff had his own band, J.C. and the Chosen Few.

They joined forces, as Young Country, in 1969 and their first paying gig was a high school talent contest. Singing a Merle Haggard song, they won two tickets and gas money to the *Grand Ole Opry*, where they shook hands backstage with Lester Flatt. Randy went to Jacksonville State University, where he got a bachelor's degree in English. Jeff obtained an electronics degree at Alabama Technical College and landed a job with the government, in Anniston, Alabama, while Teddy became a carpet layer, ran a theater and worked in a grocery store and on his grandfather's farm.

In order to keep the band together, they all moved to Anniston, getting jobs laying carpet and hanging drywall. They moved into a $56.00-a-month apartment, where they labored over their harmonies. In 1972, they became Wildcountry and along with drummer Bennett Vartanian they played weekends at Canyon Land Amusement Park in Little River Canyon. In March 1973, much to their families' displeasure, they decided to turn professional. Randy's father was so incensed that for three months he refused to talk to his son. They moved to Myrtle Beach, South Carolina, and got a regular booking playing for tips at a beachside bar called the Bowery. They started to write and play some of their own material, including *Tennessee River* and *My Home's in Alabama*. After Vartanian, the band went through four other drummers, until Rick Scott came on board in 1974 and stayed until 1979.

Renamed Alabama, they landed a one-record deal in 1977, with GRT in Nashville, and had their first taste of Country chart success with *I Wanna Be with You Tonight*, which reached the Top 80. As the band was now doing over 300 gigs per year through the Southeast, the guys pooled their funds and bought a Dodge van, The Blue Goose. They borrowed $4,000 from a Fort Payne bank and recorded and pressed their own records to sell at live dates. At this point Randy, Teddy and Jeff incorporated the band. When GRT folded, they found that because of complications in the contract, they were stopped from recording anything for two years and they then had to raise money to buy themselves out.

They then lost Rick Scott and on April 1, 1979, Mark Herndon (b. May 11, 1955, Springfield, Massachusetts) replaced him. For some time, there was a visible gap between the three cousins and Herndon in terms of band membership equality, although it is without a doubt his Rock edged drumming that has given Alabama its distinctive sound. Mark, a qualified pilot, is the son of a Marine fighter pilot and grew up on air bases. His experience up to joining Alabama had been with Rock bands.

That year, the band got together enough money for an album and hired an independent Atlanta promotion man for $1,000 to get airplay on a single cut, *I Wanna Come Over*. They followed up with hundreds of hand-written letters to Country radio Program Directors and deejays. The single was picked by Dallas-based MDJ Records and reached No.33. The following year, *My Home's in Alabama*, also on MDJ, reached the Top 20 and on the strength of that, they got a spot on that year's *New Faces* show at the Country Music Seminar at Nashville's Hyatt Regency Hotel. There they were spotted by RCA and immediately signed to the label.

Shortly after signing to RCA, their manager, Larry McBride, was jailed for a 1978 fraud and they severed connections with him. They were initially produced by Harold Shedd, who had originally connected with the band in 1979. They then began a run of No.1 Country hits, that is truly amazing and may never be surpassed. Beginning with their first RCA single, in 1980, *Tennessee River*, they had a run of 21 No.1 hits, through to 1987, broken only by the 1982 Christmas single, *Christmas in Dixie*. In addition to this, nine of their singles crossed over to become Pop successes.

Their No.1 hits were: 1980: *Tennessee River, Why Lady Why*; 1981: *Old Flame, Feels So Right, Love in the First Degree*; 1982: *Mountain Music, Take Me Down, Close Enough to Perfect*; 1983: *Dixieland Delight, The Closer You Get, Lady Down on Love*; 1984: *Roll On (Eighteen Wheeler), When We Make Love, If You're Gonna Play in Texas (You Gotta Have a Fiddle in the Band)/I'm Not That Way Anymore, (There's a) Fire in the Night*; 1985: *There's No Way, Forty Hour Week (For a Livin'), Can't Keep a Good Man Down*; 1986: *She and I, Touch Me When We're Dancing, You've Got "The Touch."*

Their summer 1987 hit, *Tar Top* (Randy Owen's nickname), reached No.7 and then they were off on another run of 6 No.1 hits into 1989; these were: 1987: *Face to Face* (with K.T. Oslin guesting); 1988: *Fallin' Again, Song of the South*; 1989: *If I Had You, High Cotton, Southern Star*. In 1990, they had three more hits with *Pass It on Down* (No.3) and the two No.1 records, *Jukebox in My Mind* and *Forever's as Far as I Go*. They continued with another No.1 in 1991, with *Down Home* and followed-up with the Top 3 single *Here We Are*, which was written by Beth Nielsen Chapman and Vince Gill. They wrapped up the year with the Top 5 single *Then Again*. They had four major successes in 1992, with two No.2 hits, *Born Country* and *Take a Little Trip*, another No.1, *I'm In a Hurry (and Don't Know Why)* and the Top 3 record, *Once Upon a Lifetime*.

As well as this phenomenal success with singles, they have had an equally impressive run with their albums, all of which have enjoyed long stays on the Country and Pop album charts. Their debut album, ***My Home's in Alabama,*** was released in 1980 and reached Platinum status in 1982; by 1986, it had sold over 2 million copies. This was followed by ***Feels So Right*** in 1981, which went Platinum that year and by 1985 had sold over 4 million copies. In 1982, they released ***Mountain Music***, which by the following year had gone Platinum and by 1985 had sold more than 4 million copies.

Their 1983 album, ***The Closer You Get***, went Platinum that year and triple Platinum by 1985. In 1984, Alabama released *Roll On*, which also went Platinum the same year and by 1989, it had reached sales of over 3 million. Their album ***40 Hour Week*** was released in 1985 going Platinum before year end and double Platinum by 1989. They also released a seasonal album, ***Alabama Christmas***, which also went Platinum before Christmas. RCA put out ***Alabama's Greatest Hits***, in 1986, which went Platinum that year and had reached sales of over 3 million by 1989. The video ***Alabama's Greatest Video Hits*** also went Platinum in 1986, the same year it was issued. ***The Touch,*** which was released in 1987, went Platinum the same year; ***Alabama Live*** and ***Just Us***, released in 1988, went Gold that year, with the former going Platinum, in 1993. ***Southern Star***, the 1989 album, also went Gold the year of issue and Platinum in 1993. Their 1990 album, ***Pass It Down***, became a major seller, going Gold during the year of release and reaching Platinum status in 1993. Both ***Greatest Hits Volume II*** and ***American Pride*** were Certified Gold in 1992, the latter being Certified Platinum in 1993. In 1994, Alabama released their album ***Cheap Seats***.

In 1981, they were scheduled to appear in concert in Fort Payne. Some of the proceeds were to go to local schools. However, the promoter failed to deliver and the following year Alabama started what was to become the annual Alabama's June Jam. It started as a one-day concert and has grown into a 10-day festival. The proceeds from these events have helped thousands of needy people.

Alabama is one of the most honored acts in Country music. To make the list of their awards easier to read, it appears at the back of this book; see Awards Section.

RECOMMENDED ALBUMS:

"My Home's in Alabama" (RCA Victor)(1980)
"Feels So Right" (RCA Victor)(1981)
"Mountain Music" (RCA Victor)(1982)
"The Closer You Get" (RCA Victor)(1983)
"Roll On" (RCA Victor)(1984)
"40 Hour Week" (RCA Victor)(1985)
"Alabama's Greatest Hits" (RCA Victor)(1986)
"The Touch" (RCA Victor)(1986)
"Just Us" (RCA Victor)(1987)
"Alabama Live" (RCA Victor)(1988)
"Southern Star" (RCA Victor)(1989)
"Pass It Down" (RCA)(1990)
"Greatest Hits II" (RCA)(1991)
"American Pride" (RCA)(1992)
"Cheap Seats (RCA)(1994)

ALABAMA BOYS, The

Formed:	**1934**
Members:	
Don Ivey	**Guitar, Piano**
Eldon Shamblin	**Guitar**
Charlie Laughton	**Trumpet**
Ray DeGeer	**Saxophone**
Harley Huggins	**Lead Vocals, Guitar**

The Alabama Boys, who hailed from Oklahoma and Texas, maintained a close relationship with Bob Wills and the Texas Playboys. Don Ivey had played piano with Wills but decided to quit to form his own band. Producing their version of Western Swing using a horn section, the band became regulars on KVOO Tulsa; as their popularity increased, Allen Franklin, the station's Program Director, became their manager. At this point, Don Ivey left, no doubt feeling supplanted as band leader. They operated alongside Wills' Texas Playboys, who also played on the station and performed at Tulsa's Playmore Ballroom while Wills played at Cain's Dancing Academy, in the same city.

Due to the pressure of work at KVOO, Franklin gave up being manager and in 1937 the band appointed Dave Edwards, a businessman from Ponca City. Edwards decided not just to manage the band, but also to front it as Dave Edwards and his Alabama Boys. At this stage, the band started to fall apart, with Shamblin, Laughton and DeGeer leaving to join Bob Wills.

The remnants of the band, now without horns, went to Dallas in December 1937 to record for Decca. The material had been chosen in advance by the label's A & R man, Dave Kapp, and he refused to let them record some of the songs they had selected. In addition, Huggins was physically unable to sing; and after the session, morale was at rock bottom and the band broke up. The members joined either Johnny Lee Wills' band or Bob Wills' Texas Playboys.

On reflection, it seems that if Don Edwards had been content just to manage the band, then they would probably have continued and built a reputation as strong as the Texas Playboys or the Musical Brownies.

RECOMMENDED ALBUM:

"Dave Edwards And His Alabama Boys" (Texas Rose)(1983) [Part of the Western Swing series.]

BUDDY ALAN

(Singer, Songwriter, Guitar)

Given Name:	**Alvis Alan Owens**
Date of Birth:	**May 23, 1948**
Where Born:	**Mesa, Arizona**
Married:	**Jane**
Children:	**Paul, Douglas**

The son of Country stars Buck and Bonnie Owens, Buddy Alan decided not to trade on the family name and instead used his nickname and middle name. He grew up in Bakersfield, California, where Buck and Bonnie were carving out their names. From an early age, Buddy was exposed to Rock'n'Roll as well as Country and by age 14, he had formed his first band, a Rock group, the Chosen Few, that played local dances and shows. However, as he reached his late teens, he became interested in Country music

After the break- up of his parents' marriage and Bonnie's re-marriage to Merle Haggard, he lived with his mother until he moved to Arizona in 1965 to attend Arizona State University. He became a deejay on a Phoenix country music station and attended an electronics school, where he earned a first class radio license.

The turning point in his Country music career was in 1965, when Buck called him on stage to sing a Christmas song. He was scared, but the audience got behind him and demanded an encore. In 1969, he got a job at a Country music nightclub and after a summer tour with the Buck Owens Show, he fully committed to music. He became a member of Buck Owens' All American Show and toured with his father, all the time growing in stature, both literally and metaphorically. As a result, he started headlining his own shows and made regular appearances on *Hee Haw* for over seven years as a soloist and back-up musician.

In 1968, he signed to Capitol; his first release was a duet with Buck Owens, *Let the World Keep on a Turnin'*, which made the Top 10. Later in the year, he released his first solo single, *When I Turn Twenty One*, a song written by Merle Haggard, which just scraped into the Top 60. His releases for 1969 included chart success with *Lodi* and *Big Mama's Medicine Show*, which both peaked in the Top 25. That year, he released his first album, ***Wild, Free and Twenty One***.

Throughout 1970, he continued to reach the lower rungs of the singles list with *Santo Domingo*. At the end of the year, he teamed up with Buckaroo lead guitarist Don Rich and produced a Top 20 hit with *Cowboy Convention*. That same year, he was named "Most Promising Male Artist" by the ACM.

His chart entries from 1971 through 1975 attained only modest showings. Only *Too Old to Cut the Mustard* (1971), another duet with Buck Owens (as Buck & Buddy), made the Top 30. During his eight year career with Capitol, he released seven albums, but never achieved the acclaim that he deserved. He produced many fine sides and had a good vehicle with *Hee Haw*.

In 1978, he moved back to Arizona where he attended college. He returned to radio as Buddy Alan Owens and is currently Music Director of KNIX and KCW in Tempe, Arizona. He was voted "Music Director of the Year" by *Billboard* in 1988, 1989, 1991 and 1992 and was chosen by *Gavin* magazine as "Musical Director of the Year" in 1992 and 1993.

RECOMMENDED ALBUMS:

"Buddy Alan and Don Rich—We're Real Good Friends" (Capitol)(1971)

"The Best of Buddy Alan" (Capitol)(1972)

SUSIE ALLANSON

(Singer, Actress, Piano)

Date of Birth:	**March 17, 1952**
Where Born:	**Las Vegas, Nevada**
Married:	**Ray Ruff (div.)**

Susie Allanson's professional career got under way in 1970 with music just as far removed from Country as you could get. She was a member of the U.S. road version of Galt McDermott's controversial musical, *Hair*. Up to that point she had been an usher for the *Merv Griffin Show* in Los Angeles.

She came from a Country background; and when Susie was in first grade, her grandmother taught her piano and she sang in the church choir. Her passion was horse riding and over the years she broke both collarbones, dislocated her hip, and suffered three concussions and a broken neck. As happens when you fall that often, something tells you to get your kicks elsewhere and it was towards singing she turned.

After a year in *Hair*, she joined the cast of the original U.S. company of Tim Rice and Andrew Lloyd Webber's *Jesus Christ Superstar*, remaining in the cast for for 18 months, singing on the U.S. album and appearing in the movie.

In 1975, she moved to southern California and auditioned for a project at the time of the Bicentennial. Ray Ruff, who was running the project, was so impressed with her that he took over her management and proposed marriage. She accepted both. Ray Ruff had been around the business for many years and took over the arranging and production of her career.

The following year, ABC released her eponymous debut album, from which came the single *Love Is a Satisfied Woman/Me & Charlie Brown* without causing too much interest. At the beginning of 1977, *Baby Don't Keep Me Hangin' On* was released on Ruff's Oak label. Curb Records took notice when the single attracted attention and signed her. Through their agreement with Warner Brothers Records, they took over the single and it became a Top 30 hit.

Warner/Curb released the album ***We Belong Together*** in 1978. It was produced in Hollywood with a much sparser sound than most Nashville recorded albums. From this came her first Curb single, which was prereleased, and Bobby Lee Springfield's *Baby, Last Night Made My Day*, which followed its predecessor into the charts; then, *Maybe Baby*, the Buddy Holly classic, went Top 10 and the title track reached No. 2, making it four in a row during 1978. The album went to No.1 and so the label plundered it for another release; this time, another Bobby Lee Springfield song, *Back to the Love*, which climbed into the Top 20.

In 1979, Curb switched her to Elektra/Curb, which was a strange move. Elektra had started out as a Folk, Folk-Country and Folk-Rock label with performers such as Judy Collins, Tom Paxton and the Doors. However, it had been expanding in Country, with performers such as Carmol Taylor, Melba

Montgomery and the Hagers. Susie brought out a new album, ***Heart to Heart,*** and carried on with her chart success. She had major chart hits in 1979 with *Words* and *Two Steps Forward and Three Steps Back*. Her next single just scraped into the charts and the follow-up, *I Must Be Crazy*, only made it into the Top 40.

Curb switched her once again, this time to United Artists/Liberty/Curb with the resultant ***Susie*** album in 1980; however, she had no better chart success and *While I Was Making Love* and *Dance the Two Step* were only minor hits. The following year found her with two Top 50 records, *Run to Her*, a female version of the Bobby Vee hit *Run to Him,* and *Love Is Knockin' at My Door*.

In 1986 and 1987, she was back in the charts through two singles on TNP/Enigma, *Where's the Fire* and *She Don't Love You*, neither of which climbed above the Top 70 mark.

Susie possesses a voice similar in tone to Cyndi Lauper's. It is not a Country voice in the conventional sense, being slightly "little girlish and whispery" with traces of the stage musical tonality.

RECOMMENDED ALBUMS:
"We Belong Together" (Warner/Curb)(1978)
"Heart to Heart" (Elektra/Curb)(1979)
"Susie" (Liberty/Curb)(1980)

ALLEN BROTHERS, The

AUSTIN ALLEN
(Singer, Banjo, Guitar, Tenor Banjo)
Given Name: Austin Ambrose Allen
Date of Birth: February 7, 1901
Date of Death: 1959

LEE ALLEN
(Singer, Guitar, Kazoo, Piano)
Given Name: Lee William Allen
Date of Birth: June 1, 1906
Date of Death: 1980's
Both Born: Sewanee, Tennessee

One of the most popular brother duets of the 1920's and 1930's, Lee and Austin Allen, "the Chattanooga Boys," distinguished themselves for their lively, up-tempo songs, which were strongly influenced by the Blues and old-time vaudeville of their native southern Tennessee area. Unlike the sentimental and Gospel songs favored by groups like the Blue Sky Boys, the Allen Brothers' repertoire was full of topical songs, double entendre Blues, rowdy "hokum" songs and comedy pieces. Their 36 sides issued between 1926 and 1934 included more than a few influential pieces, not the least of which was *A New Salty Dog*, which remained in print for years after the Allens themselves retired.

The Allens were born on Monteagle Mountain, about 50 miles north of Chattanooga, and grew up in a setting that was part sophisticated and part traditional. Their father was a sawmill worker and their mother was a trained violinist who also knew a plethora of old ballads. As boys, the Allens attended the prestigious St. Andrews School on the Mountain and were there at the same time as Father Flye, later immortalized by fellow Sewanee resident James Agee.

By 1923, the brothers had started traveling, making music on circuits that extended as far north as West Virginia. Lee Allen recalled that some of their best audiences were in remote coal mining camps where the only way in was by narrow gauge company railway. During this period, they collected dozens of songs from white and black sources and started writing their own material, much of which was filled with references to their Chattanooga area home.

In 1926, they began recording for Columbia and their first release, a version of *Salty Dog Blues,* called *Bow Wow Blues,* did quite well. This relationship ended, though, when Columbia executives mistakenly issued their Chattanooga Blues in the 1400 "Race" series instead of the 1500 "Hillbilly" series.Though they were intrigued that their Blues sounded authentic enough to fool a veteran music executive, the brothers were upset and threatened a lawsuit if the disc was not withdrawn.

The action never came to a head and the Allens moved their business to Victor. There they encountered Ralph Peer, who started to have his own success with Jimmie Rodgers, a white man who could sing the Blues. Peer immediately saw similar potential in the Allens and began recording their repertoire of good-time songs. In their personal appearances, the Allens often did slower, more sentimental songs as well as the uptempo ones, but much to their frustration, Peer was soon insisting that they stick only to Blues for their Victor sessions.

The Victor years extended from 1928 until 1932 and produced such hits as *Skippin' and Flying,* in 1928 (a version of the Molly and Tenbrooks song); *Jake Walk Blues* (1930; about the Jamaica Ginger poisoning scare); *Chain Store Blues* (complaining of the new supermarket chains growing up); *Maybe Next Week Sometime* (later redone by Hank Williams); *Roll Down the Line* (1930), the well known coal mining song, and others. *Price of Cotton Blues* (1930) was a topical song about the fall of the cotton market in which the brothers sang, "Guess I'll have to go to bootlegging, brother, I can't raise cotton."

As the Depression deepened, the brothers tried their hand at legitimate theater, appearing for a time in a play called *Bushwhacker,* but soon found that even their best-selling records were selling only 4,000 copies, hardly enough to support a family. In 1933, Austin moved his family to New York, where he worked for a time as a radio announcer. Lee remained in Tennessee and went into construction work. They did a final session for ARC in 1934, on which they redid some of their big hits, but the sales were still disappointing. Austin eventually drifted into construction and engineering work and died in Williamston, South Carolina, in 1959.

In the late 1960's, Old-Time music fans rediscovered the bouncy music of the Allens and several albums of their work were issued. Lee Allen was located and encouraged to come out of retirement to make music; he did make a few appearances around his home town of Lebanon, Tennessee, before his own death in the 1980's. CKW

RECOMMENDED ALBUMS:
"The Chattanooga Boys" (Old Timey)
"Sweet Rumors" (Rounder)
"Clara's Boys" (Rounder)

DEBORAH ALLEN

(Singer, Songwriter, Guitar)
Given Name: Deborah Lynn Thurmond
Date of Birth: September 30, 1953
Where Born: Memphis, Tennessee
Married: Rafe VanHoy

This talented lady with dark smoldering eyes came to public attention in 1979, when she was chosen by Mary Reeves (Davis) to dub her voice onto three Jim Reeves tracks. The result was three singles released on RCA: *Don't Let Me Cross Over* (1979), *Oh How I Miss You Tonight* (1979) and *Take Me in Your Arms and Hold Me* (1980) (for which she got label credits).

Although this was her first foray into recording, Deborah was already a music veteran. While still at school in Memphis, she sang with a group called the Hightides. Her first "real" job was singing back-up to Roy Orbison. The story goes that she approached him in a restaurant without realizing who he was, but she thought by his appearance he must be in the music business. However, Deborah was smart and when he told her that he was in entertainment she told him that she was a singer. This is known as chutzpah. Her first session for The Big O netted her $90.

She worked at Opryland on the "General Jackson" showboat and was chosen to ac-

Deborah Allen with Porter Wagoner

company Tennessee Ernie Ford as a singer and dancer when he visited Russia. Jim Stafford took her out to California to appear on his TV show and as opening act on his gigs and she stayed in Los Angeles for two years.

The album she recorded for Capitol in 1980, ***Trouble in Paradise***, yielded the Top 20 single *You (Make Me Wonder Why)*. She then signed to RCA, releasing a mini album, ***Cheat the Night*** (1983), which gave her three major self-penned singles hits, *Baby I Lied* (Top 5), *I've Been Hurt Before* (Top 3) and *I Hurt for You* (Top 10). After the release of a full album, ***Let Me Be the First*** (1984), she suddenly vanished from the performance scene. However, encouraged by Shel Silverstein and in partnership with her equally talented husband, Rafe VanHoy, she has carved out a meritorious career as a songwriter. She has penned some memorable hits. Her songs have been recorded by many big names including *Don't Worry 'Bout Me Baby* (Janie Frickie), *You Do It* (Sheena Easton) and *Can I See You Tonight* (Tanya Tucker).

For a lady who claims to be influenced by Patsy Cline, Deborah also displays the ability to sing more rocky material. At the beginning of 1993, she re-emerged with a new album, ***Delta Dreamland***, on the Giant label. The initial single, which was accompanied by a raunchy concept video, was entitled *Rock Me*.

She may have been one to watch in 1982, but most decidedly, the ensuing decade has seen her grow into a mighty talent and a future star. However, at the end of 1993, Deborah and Rafe separated and it must be hoped that it won't have a negative effect on her.

RECOMMENDED ALBUMS:
"Trouble in Paradise" (Capitol) (1980)
"Let Me Be the First" (RCA) (1984)
"Delta Dreamland" (Giant)(1993)
Plus the tracks recorded with Jim Reeves

JULES ALLEN

(Singer, Guitar)
Given Name: Jules Verne Allen
Date of Birth: 1883
Where Born: Waxahachie, Texas
Date of Death: 1945

Jules Allen ranks a close second to Carl T. Sprague in significance among early cowboy singers. Like his predecessor, Allen performed his material in a plain style to the accompaniment of his own guitar, with additional instrumentation on a few cuts. Allen also sang his songs on radio stations in Dallas, San Antonio and Los Angeles.

Details of Allen's life are sketchy, to say the least. Born in Waxahachie, Texas, he had actual experience as a working cowhand from the age of 10 until 1907. According to at least one source, Allen also spent some time in law enforcement and may have been a Texas Ranger. He served in the Army during WWI; he spent the 20's and 30's carving out a career of sorts as a radio cowboy vocalist at various stations in Texas and California, sometimes using such pseudonyms as "Shiftless" and "Longhorn Luke."

Jules Allen's prime importance derives from the two dozen songs he recorded for Victor in 1928 and 1929. Some of the songs Jules sang had been previously recorded by Carl Sprague, but more often than not, his recordings were the first. These included excellent versions of such traditional ballads as *Home on the Range*, *Little Joe, The Wrangler*, *Zebra Dun* and *The Cowboy's Dream*. Lesser known Allen classics included *'Long Side the Santa Fe Trail*, *Days of Forty-nine*, *A Prisoner for Life* and the song about the life of a ranch cook, *Punchin' the Dough*.

Allen is also important because of his book about the life and music of his one-time occupation. In 1933, he wrote *Cowboy Lore*, which was published by the Naylor Company of San Antonio and went through at least three printings, most recently in 1971.

In addition to several reissue anthologies that included some of his recordings, an entire album of his work appeared in Germany in the early 70's. IMT

RECOMMENDED ALBUM:
"Jules Allen the Texas Cowboy" (Folk Variety) (1971) [And Bear Family Germany]

RED ALLEN

(Singer, Guitar, Songwriter)
Given Name: Harley Allen
Date of Birth: February 12, 1930
Where Born: Perry County, Kentucky
Married: 1. Clara (div.) 2. Betty
Children: Deloris, Devona, Debra, Cathy (dec'd), Mark, Michael, Ronnie, Greg, Harley, Jr., Neil (dec'd)
Date of Death: April 3, 1993

Born in the heart of Appalachian Kentucky, Red Allen had a voice that personified "the high lonesome sound," making him an ideal Bluegrass lead singer. Although few of his solo recordings appeared on major labels, he managed to gain considerable respect for his vocal talents and attract a wide following. Seldom based in Nashville, Red divided his most productive musical years between his adopted hometown of Dayton, Ohio, and the Washington, D.C., area, both fertile territories for Bluegrass music.

As a child, Red listened to local musicians and folks like Charlie Monroe, whose radio programs from WNOX Knoxville were beamed into the hollow where he was reared. As he later told an interviewer, "I just naturally fell into music." After joining the U.S. Marine Corps, at age 17, Red served 2 years and then moved to Dayton, where he found work in a refrigerator factory.

Numerous Appalachians had settled in the Dayton area during the 40's, including several aspiring musicians, among the most talented being Red Allen, banjoist Noah Crase, mandolinist Frank Wakefield and the Osborne Brothers. They worked on such local radio stations as WPFB in nearby Middletown and formed bands which played in local bars and nightclubs. Red made his first recordings about 1954, on a small Kentucky label with a band that included Crase on banjo. When the latter left for another job, Red joined forces with the Osborne Brothers who had recently split from Jimmy Martin. Together they developed an outstanding vocal trio with Bluegrass accompaniment. They played on the *Wheeling Jamboree* and signed to MGM, recording such Bluegrass classics as *Ruby, Are You Mad at Your Man*, *Once More*, *Wild Mountain Honey* and *Ho, Honey Ho*. Red remained with the Osbornes until 1958 and then dropped out of music for a time.

Allen and his wife divorced in 1959 and the following year he moved to the Washington, D.C., area, where he did some of his best recordings. He and Frank Wakefield formed the Kentuckians, who over the years included such members as the Yates Brothers (Bill and Wayne), Porter Church, Bill Emerson and after Wakefield left, David Grisman. The band recorded albums for Folkways, Melodeon and County, as well as scattered singles on Starday and Rebel, including Red's acclaimed arrangements of *Beautiful Blue Eyes* and *Thinking Tonight of My Blue Eyes*.

Red left Washington for Nashville in 1967 as a temporary replacement for Lester Flatt, who was recuperating from a heart attack. In 1968, he and J. D. Crowe formed the Kentucky Mountain Boys, working at the Holiday Inn in Lexington, Kentucky and recording their widely hailed ***Bluegrass Holiday*** album, originally released on the Lemco label.

After a year, Red Allen returned to Dayton, where he assembled a band built around his four sons who had grown to adolescence. As Red Allen and the Allen Brothers, he again affiliated with the WWVA *Wheeling Jamboree* and recorded albums for Lemco and King Bluegrass Records. The Allen Brothers also recorded on their own, usually in a more progressive style of Bluegrass.

Red rejoined Folkways in 1979, cutting a pair of albums, one of them a tribute to the then recently deceased Lester Flatt that included instrumental support from several veterans of the Nashville Grass. Over the span of his recording career, Red Allen also had two more albums released in Japan. He continued to work, though less actively, at clubs and festivals from his home base in Dayton into the 80's, but in 1993, he died of cancer.

Red's recorded work from the 50's and his solo work from the 60's represents some of the best hard-driving Traditional Bluegrass made. IMT

RECOMMENDED ALBUMS:

"Bluegrass Country" (County)(1966)
"Red Allen and the Kentuckians" (County)(1967)
"Red Allen, Frank Wakefield and the Kentuckians" (Folkways)(1964)
"The Solid Bluegrass Sound of the Kentuckians" (Melodeon)(1965)
"The Kentucky Mountain Boys: Bluegrass Holiday" (Lemco)(1969) [Later released as (King Bluegrass) and (Rebel)].

REX ALLEN

(Singer, Guitar, Fiddle)
Given Name: Rex Allen
Date of Birth: December 31, 1920
Where Born: Willcox, Arizona
Married: Bonnie Linder
Children: Rex Jr., Curtis, Mark, Bonita

Rex Allen has the honor of being the last of the Hollywood singing cowboys. Known as the Arizona Cowboy, he starred in 19 pictures for Republic between 1950 and 1954. Over a period of decades, he also enjoyed a number of hit records and made several albums of western songs.

Rex grew up in Cochise County, Arizona, where his fiddle-playing father got Rex a guitar at age 11 to back him at dances. He soon started singing as well and landed his first radio job at KOY Phoenix shortly after finishing high school. He joined the rodeo circuit for a time, but when he got injured while riding a bull, in 1943, he returned to radio, working at WTTM in Trenton, New Jersey. From there, he went to the Sleepy Hollow Ranch gang in Pennsylvania. In the summer of 1945, Lulubelle and Scotty heard him performing at an outdoor park and suggested that he audition for WLS and the *National Barn Dance*.

In Chicago, Rex became a popular figure at the *Barn Dance*, made some transcriptions for M. M. Cole and in 1946 became one of the first Country-Western artists to sign with Mercury Records. He had several releases on the label before *Afraid* hit the charts in the summer of 1949. Shortly after, he recorded some duets with Pop-Country singer Patti Page.

Later that year, he went to Hollywood and Republic pictures, taking a CBS Network radio program with him. Like Gene Autry, Rex came to movies after success on the *Barn Dance*. Rex's first feature film, *The Arizona Cowboy*, was finished in the spring of 1950. From then through February 1954, when he finished *Phantom Stallion,* Rex starred in 19 musical westerns with such sidekicks as Fuzzy Knight, Buddy Ebsen and especially Slim Pickens (who later became a regular on *Hee Haw*). Critics have generally held *Rodeo King and the Senorita* (1951), with Mary Ellen Kay as leading lady, to be his strongest performance.

Rex had a major record success in 1951, when his Mercury recording *Sparrow in the Tree Top* was a Top 10 Country hit and crossed over to the Pop Top 30. During the early 50's Rex switched to Decca Records and in 1953 enjoyed his biggest hit with *Crying in the Chapel,* which made the Top 5 in the Country chart and Top 10 on the Pop chart. Later in the decade, he concentrated on albums of Western songs before returning to Mercury. In the meantime, he made 39 episodes of a television drama, *Frontier Doctor.*

With Mercury, Rex Allen had a pair of minor hits, *Marines Let's Go* and *Tear After Tear*, in 1961 and 1964 respectively. In between, he scored in a big way in 1962, with *Don't Go Near the Indians*, which made the Top 10 on the Country chart and Top 20 on the Pop chart. Rex had a final appearance on the charts

The last of the singing cowboys, ***Rex Allen***

in 1968 with *Tiny Bubbles,* in a second stint with Decca. He also recorded, primarily albums, on such labels as Buena Vista, Disneyland and JMI over the years. European labels such as Bear Family, Cowgirlboy and Stetson have reissued some of his best material. His career went through still another phase as a narrator for many Walt Disney nature films and TV programs, as well as lending his voice to the sound tracks of various Disney cartoons.

In recent years, Rex Allen has become something of an elder statesman among cowboy singers. His oldest son, Rex Allen, Jr., has carved out his own musical niche, while the senior Allen has a museum in Willcox and in 1989, was honored by the Governor of Arizona for his dedication to the state. He also attends an occasional Western film fair where he is a favorite with both old and new fans of the genre. (See Movie Section) IMT

RECOMMENDED ALBUMS:

"Under Western Skies" (Decca)(1956) [Reissued by Stetson UK in original packaging (1987)]
"Mister Cowboy" (Decca)(1959)
"Rex Allen Sings 16 Favorites" (Buena Vista)(1961)
"Faith of a Man" (Mercury)(1962)
"Rex Allen Sings and Tells Tales" (Mercury)(1962)
"Smooth Country Sound of Rex Allen" (Decca)(1968)
"The Touch of God's Hand" (Decca)(1968)
"Golden Songs of the West" (Vocalion)(1970)
"Favorite Songs" (Disneyland)(1970)

REX ALLEN, JR.

(Singer, Songwriter, Guitar)
Given Name: Rex Allen, Jr.
Date of Birth: August 23, 1947
Where Born: Chicago, Illinois
Married: Judy Wright (m. 1967)
Children: Wyatt, twins Cody and Logan

It can be very hard to be the son of a famous father unless you are imbued with talent yourself. In Rex Jr.'s case, lightning has struck twice. He possesses a deep, fruity baritone voice that comes into full effect in songs like *The Streets of Laredo.*

From age 6 he traveled with his father, beginning professional life as a member of the Townsmen, a Californian folk trio. He then put together Saturday's Children, which headlined several TV shows. When he signed to Liberty/United Artists as a writer/artist, he became the youngest writer in the label's history.

During 1967-1969, Rex, Jr. served in the military, with part of the time in Special Services. He then came to Nashville and appeared on CBS-TV's *Newcomers*. He released an album, ***Today's Generation,*** for Shelby Singleton's SSS label and released singles on JMI Records. Then in 1973, he signed to Warner Brothers Records. His first single that year was *The Great Mail Robbery*, which only reached the Top 70, but stayed on the charts for nearly three months. His next release, *Goodbye*, in 1974, made it to the Top 20, but for the next two years, his records hovered around the Top 30 at best. During that time, he released two albums, ***Another Goodbye Song*** (1974) and ***Ridin' High*** (1975).

A turning point in Rex Jr.'s career came in May 1976, when he climbed to the Top 20 with *Can You Hear Those Pioneers,* featuring backing vocals from father Rex and the Sons of the Pioneers. *Teardrops in My Heart* also went Top 20, but *Two Less Lonely People*, which charted in November, went up into the Top 10. He continued his Top 10 run in 1977 with Wayland Holyfield's *I'm Getting Good at Missing You (Solitaire), Don't Say Goodbye* and *Lonely Street. No, No, No (I'd Rather Be Free), With Love* (both 1978) and *Me and My Broken Heart* (1979) climbed into the Top 10, while his other chart entries all made it into the Top 20.

However, between 1980 and 1983, when he left the label, only two singles went Top 20: *It's Over* and *Cup of Tea*, a duet with Margo Smith, both in 1980. One of the most interesting albums released on the label was the 1982 concept album, ***The Singing Cowboy*** which included the chart single, *Last of the Silver Screen Cowboys*, featuring Rex Allen and Roy Rogers. That year, Rex Jr.'s song *Arizona* was made the official state song by the Senate and House of Representatives of the State of Arizona. His band, named for the song, is called Arizona.

After departing from Warner, he went to the independent label Moonshine and chalked up some more middle level hits, the most successful being the Top 20 *Dream on Texas Ladies* and *Running Down Memory Lane* (Top 30) in 1984. Three years later he scored a major success with his appearance at the Wembley Festival. Returning home, he found

Famous son of a famous father, ***Rex Allen, Jr.***

himself with another hit on TNP, *We're Staying Together*, which, although only reaching No. 59, still showed that Rex Allen, Jr. had his fans.

In 1988, he retired from the business for a year on legal advice because of contractual problems and turned to running the video department he had donated to Baptist Hospital, Nashville. He is now a resident performer on the *Statler Brothers TV Show* on TNN; however, this is not his first taste of series TV, as he had co-hosted 52 episodes of *Nashville on the Road* with Jim Stafford.

RECOMMENDED ALBUMS:

"Best of Rex Allen, Jr." (Warner Brothers)(1977)
"Oklahoma Rose" (Warner Brothers)(1980)
"The Cat's in the Cradle" (Warner Brothers)(1982)
"The Singing Cowboy" (Warner Brothers)(1984)

ROSALIE ALLEN

(Singer, Yodeler, Guitar)

Given Name: **Julie Marlene Bedra**
Date of Birth: **June 27, 1924**
Where Born: **Old Forge, Pennsylvania**
Married: **Unknown**
Children: **Dorothy**

In the decade following WW II, in an era when more female vocalists were coming to the forefront, Rosalie Allen gained some renown as a Country singer-cowgirl yodeler and deejay. In many respects, Rosalie was a younger, Eastern U.S. version of Patsy Montana in the genre. Moreover, her career is one of several that illustrate the attractions that some persons of East European descent had for a musical type generally identified with Anglo-Celtic Americans.

Like many other singers of her generation, Rosalie came from a large family that encountered difficult times in the Great Depression. As early as age 9 she was working part-time as a dishwasher to help pay her own way. Inspired by the sounds of radio performers, Miss Bedra learned to play her brother's guitar and taught herself to sing and yodel like the airwaves cowgirls, much against her mother's wishes. She landed her first radio job in Wilkes-Barre, Pennsylvania, and then went to WORK York, Pennsylvania, as a vocalist with Shorty Fincher's Prairie Pals. Having won a yodeling contest in 1939 that dubbed her "Queen of the Yodelers," she used this title throughout her career. Rosalie moved to New York City in 1943; there she began working with radio veteran Denver Darling's group, the Swing Billies, and later she worked with Zeke Manners and met her future duet partner, Elton Britt.

In 1945, Rosalie signed with RCA Victor and had a hit record with a revival of the Patsy Montana favorite of a decade earlier, *I Want to Be a Cowboy's Sweetheart*, and also *Guitar Polka*, both ranking in the Top 5. Over the next several years, she had a number of other memorable solo releases, usually backed by a lively studio group called the Black River Riders. Notable titles included Red River Dave's anti-hate song *Hitler Lives*, *Rose of the Alamo*, *He Taught Me How to Yodel* and Jenny Lou Carson's *Station L-O-V-E Signing Off*.

Rosalie Allen also recorded a number of duets with Elton Britt, including a cover of the Chickie Williams song-recitation *Beyond the Sunset—Should You Go First*, which was the only one of the several versions to be listed in the *Billboard* charts and is credited to Allen and Britt and the Three Suns. Their most successful duet, *Quicksilver*, reached the Country Top 3. *Mocking Bird Hill*, *Tennessee Yodel Polka* and the inspirational Stuart Hamblen composition, *It Is No Secret (What God Can Do)*, rank among their other duet offerings. Rosalie appeared in Soundies from 1943 through 1945 and also appeared in the 1949 movie *Village Barn*.

Allen's performing activity was generally confined to New York, Pennsylvania and adjacent states. She had her own television show in the Big Apple for a time and a deejay program, *Prairie Stars* (1944-1946), for many years over WOV, which made her the city's only Country record spinner for a while. She also had her own Country TV show in New York City from 1949 through 1953. As a sideline, she opened the first Country record shop, Rosalie Allen's Hillbilly Music Center, providing a retail outlet for Country fans in New York City. During the late 40's and early 50's, she wrote columns for *National Jamboree*, *Country Song Roundup* and *Hoedown*.

In the mid-50's, after leaving RCA Victor, Rosalie shared half of an album with Elton

Britt on the New York based Waldorf label (later re-released on Grand Award) which proved to be her last recordings and on which New Jersey based Country band leader Smokey Warren furnished accompaniment. These offerings included such standards as *Columbus Stockade Blues*, *Jealous Heart* and a memorable yodeling specialty, *Ding Dong Polka*.

In recent years Rosalie has lived in quiet retirement. Two compilations of her RCA material have appeared on German collector-oriented labels, while several of the Allen-Britt duets appear on Elton Britt's RCA Victor albums and reissues. IMT

RECOMMENDED ALBUMS:

"Starring Elton Britt and Rosalie Allen" (Grand Award)(1966)
"Queen of the Yodelers" (Cattle Germany LP)(1983)
"The Cowboy's Sweetheart" (Cowgirlboy Germany)(1990)

SHELLY LEE ALLEY

(Singer, Songwriter, Fiddle)

Given Name:	**Shelly Lee Alley**
Date of Birth:	**July 6, 1894**
Where Born:	**Alleyton, Texas**
Married:	**Unknown**
Children:	**Shelly Lee Alley, Jr., Clyde Brewer (stepson)**
Date of Death:	**1964**

Shelly Lee Alley with his band the Alley Cats were counted among the fine Western Swing bands on the Texas scene in the 30's and 40's.

A native of the community of Alleyton, Texas, Shelly Lee Alley had the ability to read music as a child, which later helped him become leader of the base orchestra during his WWI service in a San Antonio army camp. In the 20's, he led several small orchestras that played on several Texas radio stations including KRLD Dallas.

Alley's major interests in those days were in Pop and Jazz combos and he appeared as a member of one such group called the Dixie Serenaders at WFAA Dallas as early as January 1923. This preference began to change with the success of the Jimmie Rodgers Victor rendition of his song *Travelin' Blues,* which sold over 31,000 copies (big sales for the Depression-impacted times of 1931-32); a number on which Shelly Lee and his brother Alvin had played fiddles. Later, he worked for Bewley's Best Flour as a member of the Chuck Wagon Gang at WBAP Fort Worth before the Carter Quartet took that name and program more or less permanently.

Around 1936, Alley organized the Alley Cats, a Western Swing unit that worked primarily out of Houston and Beaumont on various radio stations and played dances in the area. Between 1937 and 1940, the Alley Cats had several sessions for the American Record Corporation with fifty-four sides being released primarily on the Vocalion label. *Houston Blues* and *Alley Cat Stomp* are typical of his repertoire. Among those who served apprenticeships in the Alley Cats were Ted Daffan (b. 1912) and Leon Selph (b. 1914), who later led bands of their own. Shelly Lee also had a session for Bluebird in 1941 with one single being released prior to WWII. In addition, Alley wrote several songs recorded by Jimmie Davis in this period.

For a time during WWII, Alley disbanded his own group and worked with a band in Beaumont known as Patsy and the Buckaroos. Later, he re-formed the Alley Cats and cut a single for a local label, Globe. Apparently Shelly dissolved his outfit about 1946, but remained semi-active as a musician, once helping Benny Hess do a session for Jet Records. He also continued songwriting, turning out, among others, several fine sacred numbers following his own conversion in the early 50's. A stepson, Clyde Brewer, remained active as a Western Swing and Country musician for many years after Shelly Lee's retirement and death. To date, three of his recordings with the Alley Cats have appeared on various Western Swing anthology albums. IMT

JOE ALLISON

(Singer, Songwriter, Deejay, TV Personality, Scriptwriter, Record Producer, Industry Executive)

Given Name:	**Joe Marlon Allison**
Date of Birth:	**October 3, 1924**
Where Born:	**McKinney, Texas**
Married:	**1. Audrey (div.)** **2. Rita**
Children:	**Gregory Joe, Brian James, Mark Woodward**

To a lot of people outside of the center of Country music, Joe Allison is best known as the writer of Jim Reeves' monster hit, *He'll Have to Go*. However, Joe is one of Country music's most talented, multi-faceted personalities.

He went to college in Texas and then joined the U.S. Air Force at the end of WWII. He became a commercial artist before entering showbiz as a radio broadcaster, breaking into Country music when he joined Tex Ritter in 1945 as a performer. He traveled all over the U.S. with Ritter and then rejoined radio as one of the foremost Country deejays. In 1945, he was at KMAC San Antonio and he had his first chart success the following year, when Tex Ritter took the Allison song *When You Leave Don't Slam the Door* into the Top 3 on the Country chart.

During 1947, Joe moved on to WDIA Memphis, but 1949 found him at WMAK Nashville and then, in 1950, he relocated to Nashville to become the deejay and host on his own daily show on WSM and WSIX. The show became the vehicle for many of Country music's biggest names and musicians, including the Everly Brothers, Anita Kerr (whom Joe considers to be one of the few musical geniuses he has met), Chet Atkins, Grady Martin, Walter Haynes, Brenda Lee, Jackie DeShannon and Ray Edenton.

Joe moved to Los Angeles in 1952. There

Industry veteran ***Joe Allison***

he took over from Tennessee Ernie Ford on his daily radio program on KXLA. During the early 50's, Allison became involved with the fledgling WSM-TV out of Nashville, as well as *Town Hall Party* on KTTV in California. By 1957, he started his own TV show, *Country America*, on Channel 7 (ABC-TV) out of Los Angeles. This was a highly rated show for three years and was screened immediately after the *Lawrence Welk Show*. Among the artists starting their careers on *Country America* were Jerry Wallace, Randy Sparks, Billy Strange (considered by Joe the best singer he was ever involved with), Gordon Terry, Glen Campbell and Dave Burgess.

During the same period, Joe chalked up several songwriting hits, often co-written with his first wife, Audrey. These included a pair of Faron Young successes, *Live Fast, Love Hard, Die Young* and *It's a Great Life (If You Don't Weaken)*, both in 1955. Teen idol Tommy Sands had his first hit in 1957 with Allison's *Teen-Age Crush*. Two years later, Jim Reeves cut *He'll Have to Go*; and a year later, Jeanne Black retorted with *He'll Have to Stay* to chalk up double hits with essentially the same song.

During 1952, "Uncle" Joe hosted *The*

Jamboree on KTSA out of San Antonio, Texas. As a radio programming consultant, Allison promoted the format for Country radio that became the norm in the 70's and helped shape radio stations such as KRAK Sacramento, KAYO Seattle, KSAY San Francisco, WJRZ Newark and WWVA Wheeling. He was also heavily involved in developing the Country Music Association and produced influential trade shows in New York, Detroit, Chicago and Nashville for executives in the advertising industry, leading directly to Country music being played nationwide. Additionally, he was involved in the pre-sell of WJJD in Chicago in 1962, for persuading the City of Nashville to donate the land on which the Country Music Museum now stands and for selling the CMA Awards Show concept to the networks. For these efforts, he was presented the 1964 CMA President's Award as "the individual who contributed most to the CMA in a single year."

In 1960, Joe was responsible for creating the first Country department, for Liberty Records, which led to the discovery and development of new artists such as Willie Nelson, Ray Sanders, Hank Cochran, Warren Smith, Billy Strange, Floyd Tillman and Rex Allen, Jr. He was behind the reunion of Bob Wills and Tommy Duncan after a 15-year separation. At the same time, Joe became the General Manager of Central Songs, also in 1960, and worked with Harlan Howard, Tommy Collins, Ned Miller, Bobby Bare, Charlie Williams, Billy Mize, Dallas Frazier and Buck Owens.

In 1967, Joe became an independent producer and was behind Jody Miller's *He Walks Like a Man*, Roy Clark's *Tips of My Fingers* and Hank Thompson's *Where Is the Circus*. He later transferred Clark and Thompson to Dot Records and continued to produce a string of hit albums and singles for both of them. In 1969, Roy Clark had a Top 60 hit with the Allison-Red Lane song, *Love Is Just a State of Mind*.

Joe moved from California to Nashville in 1970 and took over as head of the Country department of Paramount Records. While there, Roy Clark, Hank Thompson, Joe Stampley and Tommy Overstreet had hit records. Two years later, Joe became head of the Capitol Country department and helped develop Red Steagall, Dick Curless and Connie Cato. He was reunited with his former boss Tex Ritter and produced Ritter's last album, ***Tex Ritter: An American Legend***. He left Capitol in 1974 to become an independent producer once again and cheered himself with another Jim Reeves hit cut, *I'd Fight the World* (which had originally charted a decade earlier for Hank Cochran).

The following year, he decided to leave the business and for the next thirteen years, he was involved in buying and selling antiques and paintings, until a heart attack in 1988 persuaded him to really retire.

Joe was inducted into the D.J. Hall of Fame in 1976 and the Nashville Songwriters Hall of Fame, two years later. His legacy to Country music is incalculable. He has served in executive offices as one of the founders and Board Directors of the CMA, Board Director of the Country Music Academy (later the ACM), a member of the Board of Governors of NARAS, a member of the advisory board of the Tennessee Performing Arts Council and President of the Nashville Songwriters Association.

AMAZING RHYTHM ACES, The

Formed:	**1974**
Members:	
Russell Smith	**Lead Vocals, Guitar**
Jeff Davis	**Bass Guitar**
Butch McDade	**Drums**
Billy Earhart III	**Keyboards**
Barry Burton	**Guitar, Dobro (left 1977)**
James Hooker	**Piano**
Duncan Cameron	**Guitar (joined 1977)**

Jeff Davis and Butch McDade had previously toured and recorded with Jesse Winchester. They got together in Memphis with Russell Smith, Billy Earhart and Barry Burton, where Smith and McDade discovered a common interest in the music of Blues giant B. B. King. As a group, they didn't know what they wanted to play, but they knew what they didn't want to play and that was no Disco and no Heavy Metal; instead they opted for a more Country-Rock sound. They had the usual teething problems putting a band together, but by 1974 James Hooker, piano, had been added and the group settled in.

In 1975, they signed to ABC Records and their first album, ***Stacked Deck,*** was well received. They hit the Country charts with two singles from the album, *Third Rate Romance* (Top 20) (a Russell Smith song) and *Amazing Grace (Used to Be Her Favorite Song)* (Top 10).

In 1976, they won a Grammy Award for "Best Country Vocal Performance by a Group," for Russell Smith's *The End Is Not in Sight (A Cowboy Tune),* which came from the second album, ***Too Stuffed to Jump*** (which has a most imaginative sleeve design built around a frog on a wooden motorcycle). Their next album, ***Toucan Do It Too,*** was released in 1977, but did not garner the same acclaim as its predecessors. That same year, Burton left and was replaced by Duncan Cameron who had been playing guitar since the age of 15 and was formerly a member of Dan Fogelberg's group, Fool's Gold. Cameron would later go on to play with Sawyer Brown.

The following year saw a new album, ***Burning the Ballroom Down,*** the last engineered and produced for the group by the now departed Burton. They now enlisted producer Jimmy Johnson who was out of Rick Hall's Muscle Shoals Studio. This was a good move, as Johnson released a lot of the musical inhibitions that were present in the earlier recordings. It was as if their stage act had at long last been captured on vinyl. The album ***The Amazing Rhythm Aces*** was the result. It was and is still a good album, but in many ways, like the Aces themselves, it was a decade too early. Country music was going through a "Pop" period and R & B was looking toward Eric Clapton and bluesier performers or toward the emerging Disco sounds. The pleasure of the album is accentuated by the presence of Joan Baez and Tracy Nelson and the Muscle Shoals Horns. A classic case of a brilliant album at the wrong time.

The Aces moved on to Columbia with an eponymous album in 1979, and then to Warner Brothers with ***How the Hell Do You Spell Rhythum,*** but by now, the party was over. Russell Smith went on to a successful writing career and a blossoming solo performing one. The already departed Burton went on to become Judy Rodman's lead guitarist. Billy Earhart joined Hank Williams, Jr.'s Bama Band and Duncan Cameron became Bobby Randell's replacement in Sawyer Brown. If they had a fault, it was, to paraphrase Lonnie Mack, "They were too R & B for Country and too Country for R & B."

RECOMMENDED ALBUMS:

Now is the time to dig these out and re-listen.
"Too Stuffed to Jump" (ABC)(1976)
"The Amazing Rhythm Aces" (ABC)(1979)

AMERICANA TELEVISION NETWORK

(TV Cable Channel)

Launched in April 1993, Americana Television Network, based in Branson, Missouri, was carried daily during prime time hours on Nostalgia Television. It later launched on its own and began broadcasting 24 hours in January 1994. Programming is back-to-basics music: Country, Bluegrass, Jazz, Blues and Gospel, lifestyle pieces, outdoors and sports shows, travel, crafts and folk arts.

According to Stan Hitchcock, Chairman,

President and CEO of Americana, the idea of a network carrying an eclectic blend of roots-type programming came during his 8 years as Senior Vice President of Country Music Television. "A broad-based concept of programming," said Hitchcock, "is not an easy thing. I've found, though, people who liked Blues also like Gospel. That's what Americana is, it's Country music, but it's also roots music. It's American music: Country, Gospel, Bluegrass, Blues, Folk, Mountain. It's this eclectic mix of music that all has roots in America." The 24-hour network claims 2.9 million subscribers (first quarter, 1994) and is currently available in 13 states.

Programs currently airing include:

• *Backstage Pass,* hosted by Billy Parker and Jim Kalal. The hosts wander around and behind the scenes in Branson, Missouri, getting the inside scoop on various Branson headliners.

• *Americana's Featured Documentaries.* Unique views of Country life, characters and time-honored crafts. The common theme in these stories relates to the quest for simplicity in life within a world growing more complicated.

• *Americana Sampler.* Runs through the programming each day providing viewers with an eclectic taste of all the music Americana offers. Interwoven with music videos are special segments from Americana's various programs. Also featured are special mini-documentaries spotlighting master craftsmen, scenic and historic spots and out-of-the-way characters.

• *Outdoors Across America.* A 22-Saturday afternoon package of programs providing visual footage of America's fishing, hunting and family vacation spots. Individual programs include *Anglers in Action,* with Jimmy Rogers, *Americana Outdoors,* hosted by former Oakland Raiders quarterback Daryle Lamonica, *Freshwater Adventures, On the Line,* Billie Westmoreland's *Fishing Diary* and Charlie West's *Outdoor Gazette.*

• *Americana Roadshow.* Focuses on various American celebrations, exploring why we celebrate and how the events happen.

• *Old Country Church.* Tours country churches around America, showcasing Gospel music. Segments include conversations with people who worship in these churches, church choirs and local church singers as well as known and emerging Gospel artists.

• *Reno's All Time Music Festival.* Showcases acoustic music. Brothers Dale and Don Wayne Reno team up with today's instrumentalists in the Super Pickers portion. The show received a nomination for the cable industry's Cable Ace Award for "Outstanding Music Series" before Americana went 24-hours.

• *Stan Hitchcock's Heart to Heart,* hosted by Stan Hitchcock. Features one-on-one interviews with Country music stars, performers and creators of Folk Music. The show originated on Country Music Television in the 80's.

• *Chuck's Country Lightning.* A one-hour video and interview show featuring the latest Top 5 playlists, videos with breakout potential and concert information. Hosted by Chuck Long, the show is the third version of a show Long started in Los Angeles in 1988.

• *Love and Romance.* Omaha, Nebraska, VJ Pam Kalal offers advice on matters of the heart for those who call in and allow her to read their personal messages to loved ones on the air. In between, spotlighted videos run the gamut of romantic music.

• *Storyteller's Theatre.* Cameras take to the back roads to find people who give spark to the art of storytelling. Show also features people who relate folk stories and oral histories of true American legends.

• *Americana Digest.* Pirie Jones and Chuck Long produce this magazine-format show, traveling around the country discovering entertaining news and bits of American music. Show tapings often take place in rustic lodges and feature regular guests: Bob Phillips, with his *Life in Texas* series, Wade Henderson with *Life in Louisiana* vignettes, Nancy Jay with movie reviews and Earl Ziff with reports from New York.

• *Americana Branson Jam.* Jim Stafford and Russian comedian Yakov Smirnoff host this showcase for the new seasons of shows in Branson, Missouri, as well as touring artists who play Branson. All shows emanate from Branson's largest theater, the Grand Palace.

• *After Hours.* Guest stars jam together, bringing Country, Folk and Blues to a relaxed setting on an empty stage after hours.

• *Night Air.* Crossing musical formats from Jazz to Folk to Country, music videos are interspersed with intimate commentary from an unseen mystery deejay along with surprise drop-in visits from the security guard, pizza boy, a news reporter and his nagging ex-wife. The anonymous host occasionally catches artists in spontaneous phone interviews that give listeners a glimpse of their favorite entertainer.

• *Kid Vid Block.* Music, storytelling and adventure are the focus of these programs designed exclusively for children, focusing on their point of view. Action-packed adventures, tales of mystery and intrigue, imaginative arts and crafts projects and videos created especially for children round out the package.

• *River City Folk.* This is the first-ever TV version of the National Public Radio series by the same name. This version, hosted by Omaha Folk singer Tom May, features a half hour of acoustic singers, songwriters and Folk musicians from all over North America. The shows are produced at the University of Nebraska at Omaha. In between musical sessions May engages the guests in conversation. LAP

BILL ANDERSON

(Singer, Songwriter, Guitar, Harmonica)

Given Name:	**James William Anderson III**
Date of Birth:	**November 1, 1937**
Where Born:	**Columbia, South Carolina**
Married:	**1. Bette Rhodes (div.)** **2. Becky**
Children:	**Terri Lee, Jennifer, James William IV**

Bill Anderson first found success in Country music as a songwriter. He began writing while working as a disc jockey in Commerce, Georgia. In 1958, he penned *City Lights,* which became a No.1 hit for Ray Price, and by year's end, he began his own recording career with *That's What It's Like to Be Lonesome* for Decca.

Although he was born in South Carolina, Bill grew up in Georgia towns: Commerce and the Atlanta suburb of Avondale. As a high school student, he began writing songs and formed his own band. He continued songwriting while attending the University of Georgia at Athens and in 1959 he graduated with a B.A. degree in journalism. After working as a sportswriter for the *Dekalb New Era,* he then moved to one of the nation's leading newspapers, becoming a correspondent for the *Atlanta Constitution.*

The 1960's proved to be a stellar decade for Anderson's recording and songwriting, with a record 24 songs making the national charts. In 1960, his recording of *Tips of My Fingers* and *Walk Out Backwards* reached Top 10. In addition, Jim Reeves had a Top 3 hit with the Anderson composition *I Missed Me.* The following year, *Po Folks* reached the Top 10 and brought the young singer an invitation to join the *Grand Ole Opry.*

Bill reached the top of the charts for the first time as an artist with his 1962 single, *Mama Sang a Song* and crossed over to the Pop Top 90. The following year, *Still* shot to No.1 on the Country charts and crossed over to become a Top 10 Pop hit.

Commenting on the 30-year anniversary of

his signature song, Bill related, on TNN's *Crook and Chase*, the lasting impact it has had. To this day, people tell him stories of how the song affected their marriage or how they were separated or divorced, and the song got them back together. There's hardly a concert that goes by, or a time he visits the fans, that somebody doesn't come by to tell him a story of how *Still* affected their lives. This makes him realize what a tremendous responsibility he has when he makes a record. It was around this time that he was dubbed "Whispering Bill" because of his style of vocal delivery.

He continued his Top 10 hits with *8 x 10* (also a Pop hit)(1963) and the 1964 successes, *Five Little Fingers*, *Me* and *Three A.M.* In addition to his own chart success that year Anderson provided a No.1 song for Connie Smith, *Once a Day*, after he helped her land a contract with RCA Records, and another for Lefty Frizzell, *Saginaw, Michigan*, co-written with Don Wayne.

During the second half of the decade, Bill Anderson placed *Bright Lights and Country Music* on the Country charts in 1965 and the following year scored big with the Top 5 *I Love You Drops* and the No.1 hit *I Get the Fever.* To round off the decade, he had the Top 5 *Get While the Gettin's Good*, the Top 10 *No One's Gonna Hurt You Anymore* (both 1967), *Wild Weekend*, *Happy State of Mind* (both Top 3, 1968) and the No.1 *My Life (Throw It Away If I Want To)* and the Top 3 *But You Know I Love You* (both in 1969). With his enormous success in Country music came a syndicated TV show and appearances in five mid- 60's movies, *Forty Acre Feud*, *Las Vegas Hillbillies*, *Road to Nashville*, *Country Music on Broadway* and *From Nashville with Music*.

As Country music grew and embraced more styles in the 1970's, Bill proved he had staying power. He placed more than 20 songs on the Country charts, including *Love Is a Sometimes Thing* (Top 5), *Where Have All the Heroes Gone* (Top 10) (both 1970), *Always Remember* (Top 10), *Quits* (Top 3, 1971), *All the Lonely Women in the World* (Top 5), *Don't She Look Good* (Top 3) (both 1972), *If You Can Live With It (I Can Live Without It)*, *The Corner of My Life* (both Top 3), *World of Make Believe* (No.1) (all 1973), *Every Time I Turn the Radio On* (Top 10, 1974), *Peanuts and Diamonds* and *Liars One, Believers Zero* (Top 10, 1976), *Head to Toe* (Top 10, 1977) and the Top 5 *I Can't Wait Any Longer* (1978).

In addition to his solo career, Bill recorded a string of popular duets between 1966 and 1975. He scored five hits with fellow *Opry*

***Bill Anderson** made more hits than he stopped*

star Jan Howard, including the No.1 *For Loving You* in 1967 and the Top 5 releases, *If It's All the Same to You* (1969), *Someday We'll Be Together* (1970) *and Dis-Satisfied* (1971). Bill reached the Top 10 with Mary Lou Turner on *Sometimes* (1975) and *That's What Made Me Love You* (1976). Other duet partners included David Allan Coe, on *Get a Little Dirt on Your Hands* in 1980, and Roy Acuff, on *I Wonder If God Likes Country Music* in 1989.

In the 1980's, Bill Anderson became a television producer and host. He helped develop a Country music talent show called *You Can Be a Star* for The Nashville Network that was hosted by Jim Ed Brown. Anderson hosted the Country music quiz game show, *Fandango*, also on TNN and became the first (and only) Country artist to host a network game show with ABC-TV's *The Better Sex.* He also appeared on the network soap opera *One Life to Live*. Other TV appearances included hosting *Backstage at the Grand Ole Opry* and regular appearances on *Nashville Now*, both on TNN.

Bill Anderson has received numerous awards for his songwriting and recording success. The music licensing agency BMI has honored him with more than 50 songwriter awards. He is the recipient of more than 15 trade magazine awards, including 5 "Male Vocalist" honors, a "Record of the Year" award in 1963 and accolades as the "Top Songwriter" 1963-1965. A *Billboard* magazine poll chose Bill as one of the "Three Greatest Country Music Songwriters." He was elected to the Nashville Songwriters Hall of Fame in 1975, and the Georgia Music Hall of Fame inducted him in 1985.

Bill has written his autobiography and continues to make regular appearances at the *Grand Ole Opry* and tours with his band, Po Folks. He is also the spokesman for a restaurant chain that bears the name of his 1961 hit, *Po Folks*. In 1992 Anderson received a second BMI songwriter award for *Tips of My Fingers* when Steve Wariner's version of the song became a big hit. JIE

RECOMMENDED ALBUMS:

"The Bill Anderson Story" (double)(MCA)(1972)
"Bill Anderson Greatest Hits Vol. 2" (MCA)(1973)
"For Loving You" (MCA)(1969) [With Jan Howard]
"Billy Boy and Mary Lou" (MCA)(1977) [With Mary Lou Turner]
"Southern & Fried" (Southern Tracks)(1983)
"Best of Bill Anderson" (Curb)(1991)(cd)

JOHN ANDERSON

(Singer, Songwriter, Guitar, Harmonica)

Given Name:	**John David Alexander**
Date of Birth:	**December 13, 1954**
Where Born:	**Orlando, Florida**
Married:	**Jamie Adkison (m. 1983)**
Children:	**Brionna-Cheri (stepdaughter)**

John Anderson is the man who worked as a laborer on the construction of the Grand Ole Opry House roof and has since built a career as one of Country music's outstanding performers and songwriters. When he debuted on the stage of the *Opry*, he told the audience "Now that I'm here, I just pray the roof doesn't fall in."

He was taught his first guitar chords by a friend of his sister, Donna, when he was 7. By the time he was 12, he had bought a Gibson guitar from the money he had earned working in the orange groves in Apopka, Florida. While in seventh grade, he joined a rock band, the Weed Seeds, which later called itself the Living End, playing material by Hendrix, Steppenwolf and the Rolling Stones. He switched to Country music because his sister, Donna, a very fine songwriter, was in a Country band playing to sell-out crowds around central Florida. He started to listen to George Jones, Merle Haggard and Hank Williams and was hooked.

John came to Nashville in his VW in 1971 and arrived at Donna's apartment flat broke; the first song he wrote after arriving in Nashville was the aptly titled *Long Cold Winter.* Eventually, though, he signed to Nashville publisher Al Gallico as a writer. Following an initial single on Ace of Hearts Records, *What Did I Promise Her Last Night* in 1974, John signed to Warner Brothers three years later. In 1980, he was nominated as "Best New Artist" by the ACM.

His big breakthrough came in 1980-1981 with the success of *1959* and the Billy Joe Shaver song *I'm an Old Lump of Coal (But I'm Gonna Be a Diamond Someday)* which went Top 5 and was nominated as CMA's "Song of the Year." It was the song John sang when he debuted on the *Grand Ole Opry* that same year. He had two further Top 10 hits in 1981, *Chicken Truck/I Love You a Thousand Ways* and *I Just Came Home to Count the Memories.* His first single the following year was *Would You Catch a Falling Star*, which went Top 10. He hit No.1 that year, with *Wild and Blue* from the album of the same name, his fourth for Warner Brothers, which went Gold in 1984.

But it was 1983 that made everyone aware of John Anderson. *Swingin'* (pronounced "swangin"), written by John and frequent co-writer Lionel Delmore, became the biggest selling single in Warner Brothers' history. It resulted in John winning several awards that included the CMA "Song of the Year" (1983), *Music City News* "Song of the Year" (1983) and CMA's coveted "Horizon Award." The same year, he had *Goin' Down Hill* (Top 5) and another No.1 with *Black Sheep.* His two 1984 successes were *Let Somebody Else Drive* (Top 10) and the Top 3 single *She Sure Got Away with My Heart.*

John's string of hits continued, but at a less successful level. His major hits from 1985 through 1986 were *It's All Over Now* and *Down in Tennessee* (both 1985) and the Top 10 single, *Honky Tonk Crowd* (1986). In 1987, he moved to MCA, where he was produced by Jimmy Bowen, but success eluded him; he only had a medium sized hit with Waylon Jennings on *Somewhere Between Ragged and Right.* Even a move to the short-lived Universal label was unproductive.

However, you can't keep a good man down. In 1992, he signed to BNA Entertainment, a new Nashville label, and under the guiding hand of James Stroud, John emerged from the wilderness with the superb album ***Seminole Wind***, which took everyone by storm. The first single, *Straight Tequila Night*, went to No.1 and the follow-up, *When It Comes to You*, was written by and featured guitarist extraordinaire Mark Knopfler of Dire Straits and Notting Hillbillies fame. John performed the song at the PNE Arena in Vancouver with Dire Straits. As he went on stage with Knopfler, John said to him, "I'll back off my hot licks for you, Mark." Hot licks apart, John is a good musician, playing not only guitar, but also a pretty mean harmonica. The title track of this new album also went to No.1 and in February, 1993, the album itself went Platinum. John Anderson was truly back. His 1993 album, ***Solid Ground***, did not sell nearly as well as its predecessor.

John and his family live on a 350-acre farm near Smithville, Tennessee, where he indulges his passion for gardening on a one-acre plot growing vegetables and grapes. The gardening is in the blood: his father, George, was Landscape Superintendent for the University of Central Florida. In addition, John is a very keen fisherman.

John Anderson, *who went from working on the Opry roof to working on the Opry stage*

At a time when there are Merle Haggard and George Jones clones around by the tour bus load, John Anderson stands as an original.

RECOMMENDED ALBUMS:

"John Anderson's Greatest Hits" (Warner Brothers)(1984)
"Tokyo, Oklahoma" (Warner Brothers)(1985)
"Blue Skies Again" (MCA)(1987) [John's first digitally recorded album]
"10" (MCA)(1988)
"Seminole Wind" (BNA)(1992)
"Solid Ground" (BNA)(1993)

LIZ ANDERSON

(Singer, Songwriter, Guitar)

Given Name:	**Elizabeth Jane Haaby**
Date of Birth:	**March 13, 1930**
Where Born:	**Roseau, Minnesota**
Married:	**Casey Anderson (m. 1946)**
Children:	**Lynn**

Quite often, Liz Anderson is dismissed by Country books as being only the mother of Lynn Anderson. This is unfair as Liz Anderson wrote many memorable songs that were converted into hit recordings.

She grew up in a rural area of Minnesota near the Canadian border, in a family that was poor and very religious. They had a mandolin and when she was eight, she sang in church. The family moved to Grand Forks, North Dakota, when she was 13. She was married just after her 16th birthday and had Lynn a year later. Casey was still in the Navy; in May 1951, when he was back in civilian life, they moved to California, where he was to attend jet engine school. They were very short of money when they arrived, and he started to sell cars. That year, Liz studied at a Redwood City, California, business college and worked initially as a secretary.

They moved to Sacramento and in 1957, Liz started to write songs with Casey's encouragement. He was a member of the Sheriff's Posse, which was planning to take part in the National Centennial Pony Express Celebration. He suggested to Liz that she write a song in honor of the Pony Express. She did; it was named official song and gained her a Medal of Honor. One of Jack's co-workers was Jack McFadden, who was trying to make his way in the music business. He successfully pitched Liz's *I Watched You Walking* to Del Reeves. Reeves would go on to record two more Anderson songs, *I Don't Wonder* and *Be Quiet Mind.*

In 1964, Roy Drusky recorded *Pick of the Week* which became a Top 15 hit. The following year, Merle Haggard had a Top 10 hit with *(My Friends Are Gonna Be) Strangers.* Liz received a BMI Award for it at the 1965 DJ Convention in Nashville. During that visit, Chet Atkins signed her to record her debut album, ***(My Friends Are Gonna Be) Strangers*** and daughter Lynn was signed to Chart Records.

Liz's initial two singles for RCA fared very well, but it was her third, *The Game of Triangles*, with Bobby Bare and Norma Jean, that hit the Top 5. Six months later, in April 1967, she repeated this with *Mama Spank.* The rest of her singles for RCA also achieved middle level acclaim. In 1968, she just missed the Top 20 duetting with Lynn on *Mother May I.* She continued to rack up minor successes and then in 1970, she made the Top 30 with *Husband Hunting* from the album of the same name.

In 1971, she moved to Epic, but by then her career was on the wane and the four singles that charted got no higher than the Top 60. However, by then her songs had been recorded by many of Country's cream and she had been presented with BMI Awards for 1964, 1965 and 1967 and an ASCAP Award for 1967. She had been in the Top 5 for 1967 Grammy Awards for "Best Country Vocal Performance, Female" and "Best Country Vocal Performance by a Group,"and she and Casey had set up Greenback Music.

Among her songs recorded were *The Fugitive*, co-written with Casey, which was a

No.1 hit for Merle Haggard in 1966; *Guess My Eyes Were Bigger Than My Heart*, Conway Twitty's first country hit, the same year; *Beggars Can't Be Choosers* (LaWanda Lindsey); and *Too Many Dollars* (Connie Eaton). Liz also wrote her daughter's first hit, *Ride, Ride, Ride,* and her 1970 hit *Big Girls Don't Cry.* Liz served as Vice-President of the Nashville Songwriters Association International.

RECOMMENDED ALBUMS:

"(My Friends Are Gonna Be) Strangers" (RCA Camden)(1966)
"Liz Anderson Sings" (RCA)(1967)
"Cookin' Up Hits" (RCA)(1967)
"Liz Anderson Sings Her Favorites" (RCA)(1968)
"Like a Merry-Go-Round" (RCA)(1968)
"Liz Anderson Country Style" (RCA)(1969)
"If the Creek Don't Rise" (RCA)(1969)
"Husband Hunting" (RCA)(1970)

LYNN ANDERSON

(Singer, Guitar, Songwriter)

Given Name:	**Lynn Rene Anderson**
Date of Birth:	**September 26, 1947**
Where Born:	**Grand Forks, North Dakota**
Married:	**1. Glenn Sutton (m. 1968)(div.)**
	2. Harold "Spook" Stream (m. 1979)(div.)
Children:	**Lisa Lynn, Gray, Melissa**

A case of lightning striking twice. Lynn is the daughter of songwriters Casey and Liz Anderson. She has proven to be an enduring performer who always delivers. In the memory is 1970, when she played the Wembley Festival and gave her all, no one realizing that she was pregnant. She came off stage and collapsed.

While she was still a child, her family moved to Redwood City, California and then to Sacramento. She learned guitar before reaching her teens and as a young girl enjoyed singing and dancing. In 1965, although still at American River College, she joined *Country Corners* in Sacramento, staying on it until the following year. She came to Nashville with her parents when Liz was collecting a BMI Award for *Strangers* (the first hit for Merle Haggard).

During the Disc Jockey Convention at a get-together at a friend's house, Lynn sang with her mother. Slim Williamson of Chart Records heard them and invited Lynn to record for the label. Her presence on the label would help elevate it to a major independent record company. Her first single with Jerry Lane was *For Better or for Worse*, at the end of 1965. The following year, she released her first solo single, *In Person.*

In 1967, Lawrence Welk invited her to join his TV show. That same year, she was made "Most Promising Female Vocalist" in a *Cash Box* deejay poll, made her debut on the *Grand Ole Opry* and released her first album, ***Ride, Ride, Ride***. The following year, she married songwriter/producer Glenn Sutton; in 1968, Lynn was named ACM's "Best Female Vocalist" and she left the Welk Show. As her recording career started to blossom, she began to appear on major country shows such as *Mid-Western Hayride* and *Gene Autry's Melody Ranch.*

Star singer and horse rider ***Lynn Anderson***

Lynn stayed with Chart until 1970 and produced a string of chart hits including the Top 5 singles *If I Kiss You (Will You Go Away)* and *Promises, Promises* (both 1967). In 1968, she released the Top 10 single *No Another Time* and *Big Girls Don't Cry* (1968). The following year, she had the Top 3 single *That's a No-No.*

She also produced another nine albums for the label. In 1968, there were ***Promises, Promises*** and ***Big Girls Don't Cry***; 1969 saw ***The Best of Lynn Anderson***, ***With Love from Lynn*** and ***At Home with Lynn Anderson.*** Her final year with the label had releases on ***Songs That Made Country Girls Famous***, ***Uptown Country Girl***, ***Songs My Mother Wrote*** and ***I'm Alright.*** Chart released three more albums, including a double, during 1971 and 1972 after she had left the label: ***Lynn Anderson with Strings*** and two greatest hits albums.

He first single for Columbia was in 1970. *Stay There, Till I Get There* was written by Glenn Sutton. However, it was her fourth single that turned Lynn into an international star. The Joe South song *(I Never Promised You a) Rose Garden* earned her a slew of honors. It was a No.1 record on both the Pop and Country charts and reached No. 3 on the UK national charts. The ***Rose Garden*** album was released in 1971 and both single and album went Gold. Lynn won a Grammy in 1970 for "Best Country Vocal Performance, Female." She was ACM's "Top Female Vocalist" and CMA's "Best Female Vocalist" in 1971. The album marked Glenn taking over the production reins on Lynn's product; 1970 also marked Lynn being invited by President Nixon to attend a celebrity breakfast. She has now sung for three Presidents and Queen Elizabeth II.

During this time, she was on the road supporting her record success, backed by her group, the Country Store, and appearing on all the major network shows as well as being seen on *Hee Haw* and the *Opry.* Lynn and her daughter Lisa were shown on a national Christmas Seal Poster.

She stayed with Columbia until 1981 and had many fine hits that included the Top 10 hits (1971) *You're My Man* (No.1), *How Can I Unlove You* (No.1) (1972), *Cry, Listen to a Country Song* and *Fool Me* (1973), *Keep Me in Mind* (No.1), *Top of the World* and *Sing About Love* (1974), *Talkin' to the Wall* and the No.1 *What a Man, My Man Is* (1975) and *Isn't It Always Love* (1980). She had less successful hits that have since gone on to become classics, including *Wrap Your Love All Around Your Man* (1977) and *Even Cowboys Get the Blues* (1980).

In 1983 she moved to the short-lived independent label Permian where she cut the prophetic album ***Back***. From that she had a Top 20 hit with *What I Learned from Loving You* and the Top 10 duet with Gary Morris, *You're Welcome to Tonight.* In 1984, she cut a one-off single for MCA and then for two years, her recording activities were on a back burner. Then in 1986 she signed with Mercury and her career once more took off. She also duetted with Ed Bruce on his RCA track *Fools for Each Other*, which achieved Top 20 status.

At Mercury she debuted with the superb album ***What She Does Best.*** She proved that she was still a force to be reckoned with. She had chart hits with *Didn't We Shine* (1986), *Read Between the Lines* (1987) and her reworking of *Under the Boardwalk* (1988), and a Top 50 entry with the album title track. She received the accolade of *Record World's* "Country Artist of the Decade." She had her own hour-long prime time TV network special. She appeared in an episode of *Starsky and Hutch* and was in the NBC Movie of the Week, *Country Gold.*

That is the Country music side of Lynn Anderson. But there is so much more to her. She is an expert horse rider (a talent passed on to her daughter Lisa, who is an award winning rider), gourmet cook and stock car driver, and there is also the Lynn Anderson with a public conscience.

In 1966, she was California Horse Show Queen at the State Fair in Sacramento. She is the Youth Advisor for the Tennessee Quarter Horse Association. She has won over 100 trophies and 600 ribbons, two regional championships and a reserve championship at the Junior Grand National Horse Show at San Francisco's Cow Palace. During their marriage, she and Glenn raised quarterhorses and cutting horses that were award winners. She was inducted into the Western Hall of Fame.

She is an adept cook and won the Southern Gourmet cooking contest in Dallas to benefit the March of Dimes. Linking her interests to her charitable work, she works with disabled children in a therapy program using animals to help the children cope with their disabilities.

She is also interested in psychics and appears on a cable TV show extolling the virtues of a psychic phone-in number. Let's hope the prognostication is that Lynn will continue her career for many years to come, because there's still a lot of Country in her.

RECOMMENDED ALBUMS:

Lynn is one of the most popular artists for compilations, and collections of her work occur on many labels including K-Tel, Time/Life, Pickwick, Album Globe, Showcase and the UK label Country Store.

"The Best of Lynn Anderson" (Chart)(1969)
"Songs My Mother Wrote" (Chart)(1970)
"Rose Garden" (Columbia)(1970)
"The World of Lynn Anderson" (double)(Columbia)(1971)
"Lynn Anderson's Greatest Hits" (Columbia)(1972)
"Lynn Anderson's Greatest Hits Vol. 2" (Columbia)(1976)
"Outlaw Is Just a State of Mind" (Columbia)(1979)
"Even Cowboys Get the Blues" (Columbia)(1980)
"Back" (Permian)(1983)
"What She Does Best" (Mercury)(1988)
"Lynn Anderson's Greatest Hits" (Columbia)(1992) [Re-issue of 1972 album]

Daniel Ray Andrade, refer HANK THE DRIFTER

ANDY ANDREWS

(Comedian, Author)
Given Name: Andy Andrews
Date of Birth: May 22, 1959
Where Born: Birmingham, Alabama
Married: Polly

Wherever Andy Andrews has entertained, from college campuses to the White House, from television shows to Las Vegas clubs, he is known as a comedian who is "clean" and he is famous for his top parental sayings.

He was once a student himself at Alabama's Auburn University, studying veterinary medicine. His professors were shocked when, after studying for two and a half years and always getting excellent grades, he decided to quit after writing jokes in class. So, instead of working toward his degree, he decided to try and be a comedian. The parting words of his tutors were, "You'll be back." He has been back! But that was to do concerts at that college three times.

Andy's first professional performance was at a local pizza outlet when friends dared him to do his routine. He got up on a chair, did his act, and the manager paid him by giving them free pizzas. He does not limit his act to one kind of venue. On the contrary, he plays about anywhere from cruise ships to conventions, and his appeal reaches all ages and types of people.

For two years in a row, he was voted "Comedian of the Year" by the National Association of Campus Activities. He was also given their highest honor when he was voted "Entertainer of the Year," voted on by 1,000 colleges and universities nationwide. The 1988 cassette *Andy Andrews Live at Caesars, Tahoe*, was the first live tape recorded by a comedian at Caesars and is selling very well around the country. This followed his video for children, *Off the Road wth Andy Andrews*, produced by Opryland USA Home Video. His book, *Storms of Perfection* (published by Lightning Crown), is a great success. It tells of how rejection has not deterred any of the famous people whose letters are reproduced in the book.

An audio cassette of a motivational speech, also entitled *Storms of Perfection*, was released in 1992. During that year, he released another cassette, *Burn the Boats*, which explores the message of commitment. Andy has also written monthly articles for various Country music magazines. Volume 2 of *Storms of Perfection* (Lightning Crown) was published in 1994. That year, *Country America* magazine, to which Andy contributes, released a collection of his articles under the name of *Andy Andrews' Tales from Sawerton Springs.*

*Funny man **Andy Andrews***

Andy Andrews' rapport with his audience is quick as he blends jokes, impressions and observations of everyday life. He has a natural charm and a true love for people. He says, "I watch people laugh, for a living." JAB

RECOMMENDED ALBUM:

"Andy Andrews Live at Caesars, Tahoe" (1988)

ANGLIN BROTHERS, The

Formed: 1933
RED ANGLIN
(Singer)
Given Name: Van Buren Anglin
Date of Birth: April 20, 1910
Date of Death: 1975
JIM ANGLIN
(Singer, Songwriter, String Bass)
Given Name: James London Anglin
Date of Birth: March 23, 1913
Date of Death: January 21, 1987
JACK ANGLIN
(Singer, Guitar, Songwriter)
Given Name: Jack Anglin
Date of Birth: May 13, 1916
Date of Death: March 8, 1963
All Born: Franklin, Tennessee

Although the Anglin Brothers are one of the lesser brother acts of the 30's, they still have considerable significance as predecessors of the highly successful team of Johnnie and Jack. Furthermore, Jim Anglin had a later career as a songwriter that merits considerable attention. As a musical group, the Anglins fit within the spectrum of what might be termed the Delmore tradition.

The Anglins came from a large family of eight boys and two girls who, although born in Tennessee, grew up in Athens, Alabama. As youngsters they became friends with the Delmore Brothers and were influenced by their style, even before Alton and Rabon turned professional. In 1930, the Anglin family moved to Nashville and in 1933, when the Delmores came to radio station WSM and the *Grand Ole Opry*, Red, Jim and Jack decided to follow a musical career and formed a vocal trio, with Jack playing guitar and Jim on string bass. Jack had the most talent and duetted with both Red and Jim.

The Anglins did their first radio work in the mid-30's for WSIX, then one of Nashville's smaller stations. They did not get paid, but soon landed a paying job at WAPI in Birmingham on the recommendation of the Delmores. They remained there for about two years and gained sufficient stature to take the nickname "the South's Favorite Trio." While at WAPI, they were invited to recording sessions held in San Antonio by the American Record Corporation. The Anglins waxed their numbers on November 5, 1937. One side of their initial release was *They Are All Going Home But One,* their most requested radio favorite, originally popularized by the Chicago based team of Karl and Harty.

The following year, the brothers moved to WMC Memphis, but did not do as well as in Birmingham. They did have a second recording opportunity at Columbia, South Carolina on November 12, 1938. Although the boys cut a total of 34 masters, only 14 were released. All appeared on the Vocalion label, some under the artist credit of Anglin Twins or Anglin Twins and Red. After Memphis, they worked for a brief period at WSB Atlanta and for a longer stint at WWL New Orleans. In the spring of 1940, they moved to Charlotte, but disbanded shortly afterwards when Red became one of the first men drafted following the Selective Service Act of 1940.

WWII took the Anglin Brothers along different paths. Unfortunately, Red sustained injuries in the Allied invasion of France and never resumed his career. He died in 1975. Jim wrote several good songs such as *Beneath That Lonely Mound of Clay* and *Stuck Up Blues*, which he sold to Roy Acuff. He served in the Pacific during the war; afterward he sold more songs to Acuff and wrote many more which were recorded by both Kitty Wells and Johnnie and Jack, including such hits as *One by One*, *Ashes of Love* and *Let Your Conscience Be Your Guide*. During this time, Jim worked first for Tennessee Light and Power and later the Sho-Bud Guitar Company. Originally, Jim aspired to be a serious fiction writer in the manner of a William Faulkner or an Ernest Hemingway, but wound up being one of the best country songwriters of the 40's and 50's.

Jack Anglin teamed up with his brother-in-law Johnnie Wright, whom he had known since the WSIX days as co-leader of the Tennessee Mountain Boys when they were known as Johnnie and Jack. They worked together until Jack entered the service in 1943 and again from 1946, having a string of hits on RCA Victor in the early 50's. They remained a team until Jack's death in an automobile crash in 1963 (see Johnnie and Jack).

Although the work of the Anglin Brothers is often considered little more than a footnote to that of the more widely known Johnnie and Jack, two of their Vocalion sides appeared on Yazoo and Library of Congress anthologies during the 70's. At the end of the decade, Old Homestead issued a collector's edition containing all their released songs. IMT

RECOMMENDED ALBUM:
"The South's Favorite Trio" (Old Homestead)(1979)

CHUBBY ANTHONY

(Fiddle, Guitar, Banjo)
Given Name: **Donald Lee Anthony**
Date of Birth: **December 20, 1935**
Where Born: **Lincolnton, North Carolina**
Married: **Daisy**
Date of Death: **February 5, 1980**

A Bluegrass fiddler of high quality, Chubby Anthony worked with the Stanley Brothers on many of their recordings during 1956-1961. He also played as a sideman with Cousin Wilbur (Westbrooks), Ken Clark, the Lilly Brothers and especially Charlie Moore. After some years out of music, he organized Big Timber Bluegrass, a Florida-based band that was quite active in the late 70's. Surviving Anthony's death, Big Timber continued as a Bluegrass group for another decade

Chubby grew up near Shelby, North Carolina and began indicating a serious interest in music from the age of 6. He showed his principal talents on fiddle, but also became proficient on both banjo and guitar; by his later teens, Chubby was playing professionally. In early 1956, he worked with Cousin Wilbur on a daily TV show in Asheville as part of a band that also included Buck Trent. Switching to the Stanley Brothers, the young fiddler did his first of nine sessions as a Clinch Mountain Boy in Nashville for Mercury on July 16, 1956. When the Stanleys moved to Live Oak, Florida, in 1958, Chubby went along, subsequently making his permanent home in the Sunshine State when he married and settled in the town of Willborn in 1962.

Although he traveled some with Charlie Moore and Bill Napier's Dixie Partners in the early 60's, Anthony made no recordings with them. After several years of relative musical inactivity, he emerged to fiddle on Charlie Moore's 1976 album, ***Wheeling***. The following year, Anthony came out with a solo fiddle album and organized Big Timber Bluegrass. This group cut a pair of straight Bluegrass albums for Old Homestead which were favorably reviewed and well received. Big Timber twice won awards as Florida's best Bluegrass band.

Unfortunately Chubby's health began to fail. In June 1979, he entered a hospital, suffering from kidney failure. Other problems complicated his difficulties and Chubby passed away the following February. Big Timber Bluegrass survived Chubby Anthony's demise. Banjo picker Jim Free took over as leader,and Tommy Cordell, a fine West Virginia fiddler, moved south and joined them. Promoted by Glen Odom, who had helped them during Chubby's lifetime, the band remained active through the 1980's. IMT

RECOMMENDED ALBUMS:
"Fiddlin' Chubby Anthony" (Old Homestead)(1978)
"Chubby Anthony and Big Timber: The Best of Bluegrass" (Old Homestead)(1979)
"Chubby Anthony and Big Timber: Love and Life" (Old Homestead)(1980)
"Big Timber Bluegrass on My Mind" (A & O)(1985)

TONY ARATA

(Singer, Songwriter, Guitar)
Given Name: **Anthony Michael Arata**
Date of Birth: **October 10, 1957**
Where Born: **Savannah, Georgia**
Married: **Jaymi (m. 1985)**
Children: **Kate (b. July 6, 1992)**

If Country music fans hadn't previously heard of Tony Arata, they certainly had after Garth Brooks recorded his song *The Dance*. As well as being a No.1 hit for 3 weeks in 1990, it was nominated for a Grammy Award in 1990 and won "Song of the Year" in 1991 from the ACM. It was the most performed song of 1990, and the video won "Best Video" honors in 1990 and 1991 from the CMA, the ACM and the TNN/Music City Awards. In addition, it was nominated for the CMA "Song of the Year" award in 1991.

Tony graduated from Georgia Southern University, Statesboro, Georgia, in 1980 with a degree in journalism. He had played and continued to be in several regional bands playing everything from Bluegrass to Pop to Rock'n'Roll. He made his professional debut in 1975, playing in Uncle Ralph's Pub in Statesboro with Mel Bordello and the New Hash Boys, a Bluegrass band. From 1978 through 1982, he had his own backing group, Handpicked, and he made his radio debut in Fort Myers, Florida, in 1985.

He was playing in the Atlanta area when a tape of some of his songs fell into the hands of Don Tolle. Tolle had just started Noble Vision Records and had signed Jim Glaser. Tony was signed to Tolle's publishing company and his songs started appearing on Jim's albums. To date, Jim has recorded six of Tony's songs: *Stand by the Road*, *Pretend*, *You Were Gone Before You Said Goodbye*, *Don't Let Her See Me Fall*, *I'll Be Your Fool Tonight* and the highly successful 1983 hit *Man in the Mirror*.

Tony had two chart singles as an artist for Noble Vision, *Come on Home* (1984) and *Sure Thing* (1985). Both peaked in the 70's. He recorded an album for MCA/Noble Vision in 1986, ***Changes***, which was recorded at Bennett House, Franklin, Tennessee.

The following year, he and his wife decided to make the move to Nashville. Don Tolle also made the move and tied in his publishing with Dennis Morgan; as a result Tony signed with MorganActive Songs and Pookie Bear Music in 1989.

Garth Brooks has now recorded two more Arata songs: *Same Old Story*, which appeared on his 1990 album, ***No Fences***, and *Face to Face* from the 1992 album, ***The Chase***. Suzy Bogguss cut Tony's song *Part of Me* on her 1991 release, ***Aces***. 1992 was a good year for Tony as his credibility and reputation as a writer got around. Delbert McClinton recorded *I Used to Worry,* one of the few songs Tony has co-written; Dan Seals, no slouch as a writer, cut *Slower*; the Oak Ridge Boys did *Standing by the River*, and Jo-El Sonnier celebrated his new marriage by including *Someday I Will Lead the Parade*, which Tony had written with Scott Miller, on his ***Hello Happiness Again*** album. To round the year off, David Slater, enjoying a second lease on recording life, cut *One of My Reasons*.

Tony maintains a second career born out of his interest in journalism. He currently serves as editor for a trade journal and has his own free-lance copywriting service.

RECOMMENDED ALBUM:

"Changes" (MCA/Noble Vision)(1986)

Plus read liner credits and grab a listen to any Tony Arata song.

AMEDEE ARDOIN

(Singer, Songwriter, Accordion)

Date of Birth:	**ca. 1896**
Where Born:	**L'Anse Rougeau, between Eunice and Mamou, Louisiana**
Date of Death:	**November 9, 1941**

Within Cajun circles, the name of Amedee Ardoin is greatly respected. He is often affectionately given the sobriquet "Tite Negre" or little black fellow. Born of black Louisiana Creole stock, who had been brought as slaves from Avoyelles Parish near Bayou Teche, the family took its name from the family who initially raised them. When Amedee was still a child, his family moved to work on the Rougeaus' farm in L'Anse de Rougeau near Basile.

Amedee, and his brother, Austin, moved to L'Anse aux Vaches and gathered around him a coterie of musicians that included accordionist Adam Fontenot, fiddle player Alphone LaFleur and from Bellaire Cove, fiddler Douglas Bellars. They played primarily white dances because these paid better and they could get between $2 and $2.50 per night. It was not unusual for Amedee to sing and play from 8 p.m. until 2 a.m. He always carried a lemon in his pocket to care for his throat, as he was particularly proud of his singing voice.

He spent a lot of his younger years traveling around working for his board and keep. It was not unusual for him to be seen with his accordion in a flour sack with a goose or a wolf balanced atop it. He had a unique way of playing that was often copied. He would place a towel on his knee to play. He always played either a Monarch or Sterling-made instrument with the bellows made out of paper.

Whilst working as a sharecropper on the farm of Oscar Comeaux near Chataignier, in 1921, he met Dennis McGee, a notable white fiddle player from Eunice. They played neighborhood house dances (known as fais do-dos). In 1928, they won an accordion and fiddle contest in Opelousas. When Comeaux sold his farm, the two musicians moved to Celestin Marcantel's farm near Eunice. Because Marcantel was so fond of music, he would drive Ardoin and McGee to dances in the area in his buggy.

In 1929, with Marcantel's help, Amedee and Dennis recorded for Columbia. As well as playing with McGee, Amedee also worked with fiddle player Sady Courville from Eunice; they played at Abe's Palace in Eunice every Saturday night for some three years. During the time that Sady played second fiddle, Shelby Vidrine would play lead fiddle.

On December 9, 1929, in New Orleans, he cut six sides for Columbia: *Taunt Aline*, *Two Step de Mama*, *Madam Archen*, *Two Step de Prairie Soileau*, *La Valse ah Abe* and *Two Step de Eunice*. On these tracks he was billed as Armadie Ardoin and Dennis McGee played fiddle. On November 20, 1930, McGee and Ardoin recorded a further six sides in New Orleans for Brunswick with equal billing; Amedee is actually credited as being Anda Ardoin. The sides recorded were *Amadie Two Step*, *La Valse a Austin Ardoin*, *Blues de Basile*, *La Valse a Thomas Ardoin*, *Two Step D'Elton* and *La Valse de Gueydan*. The following day they recorded four more tracks: *Valse a Alcee Poulard*, *One Step d'Oberlin*, *Valse des Opelousas* and *One Step de Chameaux*.

Amedee Ardoin and Dennis McGee cut six sides for Bluebird at the Texas Hotel, San Antonio, on August 8, 1934. These sides were *Les Blues de Voyage*, *La Valse de Amities*, *Les Blues de Crowley*, *Oberlin*, *Sunset* and *Tout que Reste c'est Mon Linge*. Later that year, Amedee traveled to New York City and on December 22, he recorded a final 12 sides: *Tostape de Jennings*, *La Midland Two-Step*, *La Valse de Chantiers Petroliperes*, *Valse Brunette*, *Tortope d'Osrun*, *La Valse de Ballard*, *La Turtape de Saroied*, *Valse de la Pointe d'Eglise*, *Les Blues de la Prison*, *Valse de Mon Vieux Village*, *St. Dur d'Etre Seul* and *Aimez-Moi Ce Soir*. Fourteen of his recordings for these various labels have been collected onto one album by Old Timey Records.

There are conflicting stories as to how Amedee Ardoin died. It is known that he died in Pineville Mental Institution. One story says that his whiskey was poisoned by a jealous black fiddle player. However, the more likely cause was that he died from a beating. It would appear that while he was playing a local dance, a daughter of the owner of the land on which the dance was held lent him a handkerchief to wipe his face. Some people who didn't live in the area objected to a black man using a white woman's handkerchief and followed him home and beat him up. It is also believed that he was beaten but that it didn't kill him, and that he died from alcoholism in the Louisiana State Institution for the Mentally Ill in Pineville.

Amedee left behind a wealth of recorded music. In 1980, he, along with another Cajun musician, Joseph Falcon, was honored at the Second Arcadiana Day at the Arcadian Village in Lafayette.

RECOMMENDED ALBUMS:

"1st Black Zydeco Recording Artist" (Old Timey)

Other tracks have been re-released on Arhoolie.

AREA CODE 615

Formed:	**1969**
Members:	
Wayne Moss	**Guitar/Bass Guitar**
Mac Gayden	**Lead Guitar, Vocals**
David Briggs	**Keyboards**
Norbert Putnam	**Bass Guitar, Cello**
Kenny Buttrey	**Drums**
Charlie McCoy	**Harmonica**
Weldon Myrick	**Steel Guitar**
Bobby Thompson	**Banjo, Guitar**
Buddy Spicher	**Fiddle, Viola, Cello**

Back in 1969, Moss, Gayden, Briggs, Putnam and Buttrey were in Moss' Cinderella studio in Madison, Tennessee, discussing the possibilities of getting into Pop music. They decided to elicit the help of McCoy, Myrick, Thompson and Spicher, all well-established Country session players. Experimenting, the Country players started to play Rock'n'Roll, but that didn't happen and when the rhythm players went Country, it was nothing special. It was then decided that each musician should play in his natural style and find a song that could accommodate it. The "right sound" happened when Buddy Spicher and Bobby Thompson came in with an arrangement of Lennon and McCartney's *Hey Jude*. Elliott Mazer, a New York record producer, happened to be in Nashville, heard them and recommended them to Polygram.

On their eponymous first album on Polydor they covered established songs. The record was very well received and as a result, a second album, ***A Trip in the Country***, was released in 1970. One track from this album, *Stone Fox Chase*, a tour de force from Charlie McCoy, was lifted and became the theme for the UK's BBC-TV Rock program *The Old Grey Whistle Test*, which started in 1971 and ran for many years.

Polydor was ever hopeful that the band would tour, but the band's members were equally adamant that they wouldn't. They were all session men with commitments in Nashville. In 1970, they made their solitary concert appearance when they appeared in San Francisco at the Fillmore West for four days with Country Joe and the Fish and the Sons of Champlin.

After the band had "dissolved," many of its members surfaced in the Moss-driven Barefoot Jerry. Polydor put the two albums together in a double package, which was released in 1974.

RECOMMENDED ALBUM:

"Area Code 615"/"A Trip in the Country" (double) (Polydor)(1974)

ARKIE THE ARKANSAS WOODCHOPPER

(Singer, Guitar, Piano)

Given Name: **Luther William Ossenbrink**
Date of Birth: **September 21, 1915**
Where Born: **Knobnoster, Missouri**
Married: **Vera Firth (m. 1937)**
Date of Death: **June 23, 1981**

Arkie the Arkansas Woodchopper was a radio personality, singer, square dance caller, emcee, and humorist, known for his long tenure at Chicago's WLS *Barn Dance*. Although WLS publicists billed him as a "Country boy from the Ozarks," he was actually a flatlander from the middle part of Missouri, near Sedalia. As a boy, he learned music by playing guitar and fiddle for local square dances, getting a princely $4.00 for six hours a dance. He also became expert in such rural pleasures as bee trees, coon hunting, hunting, fishing and running dogs—knowledge he used to great advantage in his radio monologues, skits and songs.

His radio debut occurred in 1928, on KMBC Kansas City, where he played for nearly 2 years on Sears programs. He joined the *National Barn Dance* in 1929, and he spent most of his career as a regular, so much so that by 1954 he was being referred to as "Old Man Barn Dance." He stayed with the show through its time on WLS (until 1960) and its reincarnation on WGN (1960-1970).

In 1937, he married Vera Firth of Perry County, Illinois, and settled into a comfortable life around Chicago. Other *Barn Dance* members recall that Arkie was easy-going and relaxed on the air, and an easy target to tease. They often managed to break him up on the air. For example, the Maple City Four would get down on all fours like a drove of pigs and Ralph Emerson would wave his arms and chase them right in front of Arkie.

His recording output was relatively small, and consisted primarily of a series of late 1930's and early 1940's sides for ARC and Columbia. The vocals were pieces like *Little Blossom, Mrs. Murphy's Chowder, Cowboy Jack* and *Little Green Valley*. In 1940, M. M. Cole issued an entire songbook featuring Arkie's square dance calls, one of the few such tomes ever released. In 1941, he issued a square dance album that featured his calling to fiddle tunes like *Arkansas Traveler* and *Sally Goodin*. Though he toured with many on the *Barn Dance*, Arkie preferred to work with Guy Colby's square dance group, and with Lulu Belle Wiseman and Salty Holmes. CKW

ARMSTRONG TWINS, The

LLOYD ARMSTRONG
(Vocals, Mandolin)
FLOYD ARMSTRONG
(Vocals, Guitar)

Date of Birth: **January 24, 1930**
Where Born: **DeWitt, Arkansas**

A promotional sheet for Cliffie Stone's *Dinner Bell Roundup Gang* from KXLA Los Angeles in 1950 described the Armstrong Twins as "Arkansas boys who sing from the heart." In many respects, the Armstrongs represented the tail end of that tradition of great harmony duets that dominated much of the Country scene in the 1930's and on into the next decade as well. Lloyd and Floyd hit their peak in the late 40's and early 50's on the West Coast at a time when many of the great duets of the past, with the exception of the Louvins, were starting to end their careers. Since most of the other great harmony teams flourished in Appalachian states, the thriving of the Twins in areas otherwise dominated by Western Swing and Honky-Tonk musicians makes their experience somewhat unique.

Their parents moved from the small town of DeWitt into Little Rock in 1933, and the twins made their first radio appearance two years later. By the time they reached age 9, they had a regular show. As they grew older, they developed excellent harmonies, with Lloyd playing mandolin, and Floyd the guitar as accompaniment. They generally favored songs that had been popularized by the Monroe, Callahan or Bolick (Blue Sky Boys) Brothers, later adding numbers associated with the Bailes Brothers, early Bluegrass bands and other duet acts.

By 1946, the boys had two daily programs on KLRA and also appeared on the *Arkansas Jamboree* on Saturday nights with Alma "Little Shoe" Crosby, Charlie Dial, Frank Dudgeon and others. By then, their younger sister, Patsy, sometimes joined them for a song. They sometimes appeared on the other major Little Rock station, KARK, and played live shows throughout the state.

The following year, the twins opted to try their luck in California. A friend of their mother knew T. Texas Tyler and got them a guest spot on his program that led to a contract with 4 Star Records. Soon they had their own program on KXLA and a spot on Cliffie Stone's *Mid-day* show as well. The boys also did personal appearances in the traditional western dance halls where they played between sets of Swing bands such as those of Spade Cooley.

Over a period of five years, they recorded a dozen or so single releases. Their discs often tended to be covers of songs associated with other duet acts or early Bluegrass bands, but the twins also waxed original mandolin instrumentals and some light-hearted numbers such as Carolina Cotton's *Three Miles South of Cash* and *Beetle with the Boogie Beat*.

In 1952, the Armstrongs relocated to Odessa,Texas, where they had both radio and TV programs. Later they toured extensively with Johnny Horton and worked on KWKH's *Louisiana Hayride* out of Shreveport. Returning to California near the end of the decade, they worked on the *Town Hall Party* in Compton. They then returned to Little Rock and dropped out of music for several years, except to record a single on Wayne Raney's Rimrock label.

In 1979, Chris Strachwitz of Arhoolie Records, an admirer of the Armstrongs since he heard them on radio in the late 40's, reissued an album of their original numbers on his Old Timey label. This led to the "rediscovery" of the twins, their subsequent appearance on several major folk festivals and a brand new album, released in 1980. As the decade passed they worked with less frequency as serious health problems plagued Floyd Armstrong.

IMT

RECOMMENDED ALBUMS:
"Hillbilly Mandolin" (Old Timey)(1979)
"Just Country Boys" (Arhoolie)(1980)

BILLY ARMSTRONG

(Fiddle, Singer, Sousaphone)
Given Name: **William Russell Armstrong**
Date of Birth: **March 18, 1930**
Where Born: **Streator, Illinois**
Married: **Annetta Hatzold (m. 1969)**

A fiddle player's fiddle player. Billy Armstrong was the ACM's "Fiddle Player of the Year" for 13 straight years, from 1965 through 1977. He is a master of his instrument and he also plays the sousaphone!

He made his professional debut in 1943 with Bob Lively's Dude Ranch Cowboys in Costa Mesa, California. Four years later, he formed his own group, Billy Armstrong and the Westerners. The band comprised Don Hoag (drums), Bobby Wagoner (guitar) and Billy Strange (guitar). In 1948, he was playing on *Spade Cooley Presents* at the Old Rancho Ballroom in Los Angeles; the following New Year's Eve he auditioned for Tommy Duncan's Western All Stars, replacing "Lefty" Joe Holley, who was a great influence on Billy. Holley was what is known as a "gouger"—that is, he digs into his fiddle—and Billy emulated this style. Duncan wanted a musician proficient on electric fiddle. Billy bluffed his way through and in a few days tried to adjust to the amplified fiddle. He played badly but Duncan could see through to Billy's real ability. He stayed with them until the band broke up in Lubbock, Texas, the following year. He appeared on several of Duncan's recordings on the Intro label.

Billy returned to Los Angeles where he joined Hi Busse & the Frontiersmen, with whom he stayed until 1951. He then moved over to Tex Wallace at the Hitchin' Post in Gardena, California. He didn't stay with them very long and at the end of the year formed the Westernaires in order to play the B & J Ranch in Long Beach. They became so popular that they also broadcast on station KXLA Pasadena. In 1953, the Western Corral opened in Long Beach and Billy and the band moved over. The band went through some line-up changes and now included Tommy Duncan's brother Glynn on bass, and Hank Cochran on fiddle and sax. They stayed together until 1957, by which time the audiences had started to dwindle.

At this point, Billy joined Hank Thompson's Brazos Valley Boys as a replacement for Curley Lewis. He knew Hank's music, having played on several of his early recordings, and he stayed with Hank for six months, but then traveling proved too much. He returned to Los Angeles, where he joined Cliffie Stone's *Hometown Jamboree*. Then Billy joined another swing giant, Tex Williams. Here he put down some roots, and from 1958 through 1963 he was part of Tex's band, the Western Caravan, playing Williams' new club, The Village, in Newhall, California. During 1959, Billy cut two singles: *Gloria/Sleeping at the Foot of the Bed* for Wildcat and *If You Leave While I'm Sleeping/Heartbreak Valley* for Toppa.

After leaving Tex Williams at the end of a U.S. tour, Billy rejoined Hi Busse & The Frontiersmen, accompanying Dale Robertson, Fess Parker, Milburn Stone and the cast of *Bonanza*. During a concert at the Astrodome in Houston, Lorne Greene stopped the show to announce to the 50,000 strong audience that Billy had won his first ACM award. Always on the move, Billy was with the Gene Davis band in the television series *Star Route*. He cut one of his rare singles during 1965, when he recorded the classic fiddle tune *Orange Blossom Special/The High Cost of Leaving*. In October of 1966, he joined the Sons of the Pioneers, singing lead and alternating tenor with Lloyd Perryman. He had to learn about trio singing the hard way. He also had to change his fiddle style to one nearer to Hugh Farr's. He toured the Orient with the Sons of the Pioneers. He had been offered the gig back in 1963, but had reluctantly turned it down. He never recorded with them during his stay. In 1969 he married Annetta.

In April 1972, after 6 years with the Sons of the Pioneers he joined the Chapparrel Brothers. Billy was about to enter a fruitful time for his solo recording. During the 70's he recorded three albums for Hillside: the 1976 release, ***World's Greatest Fiddle Player***, was repackaged and retitled ***Mr. Fiddle*** by Westwood Records when it was released in the U. K.; his other Hillside albums were ***The Best of Billy Armstrong*** and ***Billy Don't Sell Your Fiddle***. He obviously took his own advice because he was next found aboard a tour ship entertaining the shipboard passengers.

RECOMMENDED ALBUMS:
"World's Greatest Fiddle Player" (Hillside)(1976) [As "Mr. Fiddle" (Westwood UK)]
"Billy Don't Sell Your Fiddle" (Hillside)
"The Best of Billy Armstrong" (Hillside)

EDDY ARNOLD

(Singer, Songwriter, Guitar, Harmonica, Yodeler)
Given Name: **Richard Edward Arnold**
Date of Birth: **May 15, 1918**
Where Born: **Nr. Madisonville, Tennessee**
Married: **Sally Gayhart**
Children: **Richard E. (Dickie), Jo Ann**

Eddy Arnold has enjoyed immense popularity as a Country and a Pop artist and throughout his long career has never suffered a low spot. His easy listening style has appealed to a broad spectrum of listeners and his achievements can only be truly appreciated by looking at statistics. Some, shown here from the Country charts: He is the No.1 selling performer, having had 28 No.1 hit singles between 1945 and 1968; he is the Country artist with the most charted singles; and he has spent more weeks at No.1 than any other Country artist.

He grew up on a farm and attended a one-room school. When he was age 10, he was taught guitar by his mother and listened to his father play fiddle and sing bass. The following year his father died and Eddy left school early to help on the farm. As soon as he was able, he began playing at square dances and earned 75 cents a night.

He made his radio debut on a Jackson radio station then went to St. Louis, spending some time playing in small night clubs with fiddler Speedy McNatt. Then he got a radio spot on WMPS Memphis, where he stayed for six years, becoming an audience favorite.

When WWII broke out in Europe, Eddy was booked to go on the Camel Caravan, sponsored by R. J. Reynolds and featuring the *Grand Ole Opry's* Pee Wee King's Golden West Cowboys, Redd Stewart, Minnie Pearl and San Antonio Rose. They entertained the troops all over the U.S. and also in Panama from the summer of 1941 through December 1942.

Eddy then became the featured singer with the Golden West Cowboys on the *Grand Ole Opry*. Known early on as the "Tennessee Plowboy," a sobriquet he later tried to shake off, Eddy sang initially like Gene Autry but later changed to sound more like Pete Cassell.

In 1944, Eddy cut his first single, *Mommy Please Stay Home with Me* for RCA Victor, where he was guided through most of his early recordings by the label's head of A & R, Steve Sholes.

The following year, he left Pee Wee and went solo and got married. His very first chart single, *Each Minute Seems a Million Years*, was a Top 5 entry in 1945 on RCA's Bluebird label. The next year saw the start of his meteoric record career. *All Alone in This World Without You* went Top 10; *That's How Much I Love You* went to Top 3 in the charts and stayed there for 16 weeks selling

650,000 copies, with the flip-side, *Chained to a Memory,* also reaching the Top 3.

Eddy's amazing success continued into 1947. He had back-to-back No.1s with *What Is Life Without Love* and *It's a Sin*, the latter being at the top for 5 weeks; the flip-side, *I Couldn't Believe It Was True,* went Top 5. He followed with the No.1 record of the 40's, *I'll Hold You in My Heart (Till I Can Hold You in My Arms).* It was at the top for 21 weeks out of a total 46 weeks on the charts and was Certified Gold. It crossed over onto the Pop chart's Top 30. The last hit of the year was *To My Sorrow*, which went Top 3.

A similar situation followed in 1948. Eddy started with *Molly Darling*, which went Top 10, and followed it with another Gold record, the chart topper *Anytime*, which stayed at the top for 9 weeks and went Top 20 on the Pop chart. The flip-side, *What a Fool I Was*, also reached the Top 3 and went Top 30 on the Pop list. Eddy then had three No.1's in a row: *Bouquet of Roses*, which stayed at the top for 19 weeks out of 54 weeks on the charts, crossed over to the Top 15 on the Pop charts and went Gold; the flip-side, *Texarkana Baby*, a three week chart topper; and *Just a Little Lovin' (Will Go a Long, Long Way)*, which stayed at No.1 for 8 weeks, went Top 25 on the Pop chart and also went Gold. The flip-side of the last named, *My Daddy Is Only a Picture*, also went Top 5. He closed out the year with the No.1 *A Heart Full of Love (For a Handful of Kisses)* which was backed by the Top 3 *When I Turned and Slowly Walked Away*, a Pop Top 30 success. Eddy now had a backing band, the Tennessee Plowboys, and his first manager was Colonel Tom Parker, later to become notorious as the manager of Elvis Presley. He had star billing on all the Country radio shows and was in great demand.

He wrapped up the decade with a clutch of major hits in 1949, beginning with a Top 10 single, the re-released *Many Tears Ago*. He then spent 12 weeks at No.1 with *Don't Rob Another Man's Castle* (Pop Top 25), of which the flip-side, *There's Not a Thing (I Wouldn't Do for You)* went Top 3. After this came *One Kiss Too Many*, a 3-week chart topper and a Pop Top 25 success; the Top 3 *The Echo of Your Footsteps;* and *I'm Throwing Rice (at the Girl I Love)*, another No.1, which stayed at the top for 4 weeks and went Pop Top 20 single and was coupled with the Top 10 *Show Me the Way Back to Your Heart*. He finished off the year with the double-sided seasonal success *C-H-R-I-S-T-M-A-S* and *Will Santy Come to Shanty Town*, both going Top 10; *There's No Wings on My Angel* (Top 10); and the No.1 *Take Me in Your Arms and Hold Me*.

During the 50's, Eddy Arnold toured every state in the U.S. and also many overseas countries. He was given star guest spots on all the major network TV shows of the time such as *Arthur Godfrey's Talent Scouts* and the *Perry Como Show*. He became the first Country star to have his own network syndicated TV show, *Eddy Arnold Time,* on NBC and then ABC.

He continued his chart success in the first half of the 50's with an unbroken string of Top 10 singles, although through 1954 he had no further crossover hits. His 1950 hits were *Mama and Daddy Broke My Heart; Little Angel with the Dirty Face*; the flip-side, *Why Should I Cry?; Cuddle Buggin' Baby*; the flip-side, *Enclosed, One Broken Heart*; *Lovebug Itch;* and the flip-side, *Prison Without Walls.*

In 1951, he had the 11 week No.1 *There's Been a Change in Me, May the Good Lord Bless and Keep You,* the No.1 *Kentucky Waltz,* the 11 week No.1 *I Wanna Play House With You*, the flipside, *Something Old, Something New*, *Somebody's Been Beating My Time* and *Heart Strings*. The following year he had *Bundle of Southern Sunshine*, the flip-side, *Call Her Your Sweetheart*; two No.1's, *Easy on the Eyes* and *A Full Time Job*; *Older and Bolder*; and *I'd Trade All of My Tomorrows (For Just One Yesterday).*

He started off 1953 with 3 weeks at the top with *Eddy's Song*, which was made up of the titles of his past hits. He followed this with *Free Home Demonstration* and the flip-side, *How's the World Treating You?,* then *Mama, Come Get Your Baby Boy.* The following year, he began with the No.1 *I Really Don't Want to Know*; *My Everything*; *This Is the Thanks I Get (for Loving You)* and the flip-side, *Hep Cat Baby*. He closed out the year with *Christmas Can't Be Far Away*, his first record not to make the Top 10.

With the arrival of the Rock'n'Roll era, Eddy found that his record career was untouched, unlike the careers of a lot of other Country singers. His Top 10 hits that year were *I've Been Thinking, In Time* and the flip-side, *Two Kinds of Love*. He followed with the No.1 record that would become his theme song, *The Cattle Call*, which also went Top 50 on the Pop chart. After this came the flip-side *The Kentuckian Song;* the No.1 *That Do Make It Nice;* its flip-side, *Just Call Me Lonesome; The Richest Man (in the World);* and the flip-side, *I Walked Alone Last Night.*

Although Eddy charted 19 singles between 1956 and 1964, his only Top 10 entries during this time were *Trouble in Mind* and *You Don't Know Me* (both 1956); *Tennessee Stud* (1959), which was also a Top 50 Pop Hit; *Tears Broke Out on Me*; *A Little Heartache* and its flip-side, *After Loving You*; the Top 5 single, *Does He Mean That Much To You?* (all 1962); and *Molly* and *I Thank My Lucky Stars* (both 1964).

Eddy was changing from the Tennessee Plowboy style to a more polished, urbane one that appealed to a broader spectrum of listeners. He developed a romantic soft sound as a crooner with the help of Roy Wiggins and his Hawaiian-chorded steel guitar. This helped him create a second wave of interest in his recording from 1965.

Between 1965 and 1969, he had a string of major singles, all of which were major Pop hits, starting with the 1965 No.1 *What's He Doing in My World*. He closed out the year with another No.1, *Make the World Go Away*, which stayed at the top for 3 weeks and crossed over to the Pop chart's Top 10. He followed with the 1966 No.1 *I Want to Go with You*, which stayed at the top for 6 weeks and was a Top 40 Pop hit. He followed with back-to-back Top 3's, *The Last Word in Lonesome* and *The Tips of My Fingers,* both of which were big Pop hits. In the fall, he had a 4-week at-the-top single, *Somebody Like Me*. His other Top 10 hits from 1967 through 1969 were *Lonely Again* (No.1), *Misty Blue*, *Turn the World Around* (No.1) and *Here Comes Heaven* (all 1967), *Here Comes the Rain, Baby*, *It's Over, Then You Can Tell Me Goodbye* (No.1), *They Don't Make Love Like They Used To* (all 1968) and *Please Don't Go* (1969).

Eddy Arnold was elected to the Country Music Hall of Fame in October 1966. He was honored as being a powerful influence in setting musical tastes. Then, in 1967, he was made "Entertainer of the Year" by the CMA, the first person named in that category. On February 23, 1970, Eddy was appearing at New York's Waldorf-Astoria when RCA Records presented him with an award to commemorate and affirm his selling of over 60 million records. This total would increase to over 85 million, ranking him among the top recording artists of all time

The Tennessee Plowboy, ***Eddy Arnold***

From 1969 to 1970, although he no longer crossed over to the Pop chart, Eddy continued to get singles into the Country chart. He had 33 chart entries, most of them in mid chart positions. At the end of 1972, he left RCA after 27 years and moved to MGM, where he had the Top 20 success *I Wish That I Had Loved You Better* in 1974. He returned to RCA in 1976 and that year had a major hit with *Cowboy*. Two years later, he had another with *If Everyone Had Someone Like You.*

At the beginning of the 80's, two singles went into the Top 10: *Let's Get It While the Gettin's Good* and *That's What I Get for Loving You* (both in 1980). Eddy has had records in the charts every decade since he began recording in the 40's.

The ACM awarded him with the "Pioneer Award" in May 1984 and he received the "President's Award" from the Songwriters Guild in January 1987. Eddy has the honor of being the only artist to receive all three of these awards. During his career, Eddy has been seen on every major network variety show, both in the U.S. and in Europe. He has hosted many television specials and when Johnny Carson was on vacation, Eddy hosted the *Tonight Show*. He narrated the NBC-TV special *Music from the Land*, a summer *Kraft Music Hall* series entitled *Country Fair* and a *Kraft Music Hall Christmas Special*.

He is a well respected businessman with wisely invested financial interests, including extensive real estate and land development, an automobile dealership, music publishing and record pressing. He is on the Board of Directors of several leading corporations and banks and is the Past President and Honorary Governor of the Nashville Chapter of NARAS. He is still what he wanted to be, a singer—so much so that in the 90's, he is still in demand on the concert stage and on television. In 1993 he released a cd box set, *Last of the Love Song Singers: Then & Now*, and he is about to publish his autobiography. JAB

RECOMMENDED ALBUMS:

"Anytime" (RCA Victor)(1955) [re-issued in the original packaging by Stetson UK(1986)]
"Praise Him, Praise Him (Fanny Crosby Hymns)" (RCA Victor)(1967) [originally released in 1958]
"The Best of Eddy Arnold" (RCA Victor)(1967)
"The Best of Eddy Arnold Vol. 2" (RCA Victor)(1970)
"The Best of Eddy Arnold Vol. 3" (RCA Victor)(1973)
"The Wonderful World of Eddy Arnold" (RCA Victor)(1975)
"Eddy Arnold's World of Hits" (double) (RCA Victor)(1976)
"Cattle Call" (RCA Victor)(1980)
"Eddy Arnold a Legendary Performer" (double)(RCA Victor)(1983)
"Collectors Series" (RCA Victor)(1985)
"The Eddy Arnold Show" (Anthology of Country Music)
"Last of the Love Song Singers: Then & Now" (cd Box Set) (RCA)(1993)

JIMMY ARNOLD

(Banjo, Fiddle, Guitar, Singer, Songwriter)

Given Name:	**James Edward Arnold**
Date of Birth:	**1952**
Where Born:	**Fries, Virginia**
Married:	**married six times**
	5. Katrina Donald (div.)
	6. Charlotte Brunt
Children:	**Amanda, Grayson, Travis**
Date of Death:	**December 26, 1992**

Jimmy Arnold was a talented artist who was almost legendary among his fellow musicians but was little known to the general public.

The only child of Doris and Lucille Arnold, Jimmy did not get his interest in music from his family. Instead, his initial exposure came from hearing the sons of neighbors practicing in their backyard. His parents purchased his first guitar but his first love was the 5-string banjo. The 9-year-old soon purchased his own instrument and at age 12 formed his own band, the Twin County Partners. This trio consisted of Jimmy, his cousin Tommy on mandolin and Wes Golden on guitar. For about a year the young Bluegrass band was something of a regional sensation, appearing on *The Don Reno Show* and other area television programs, and even making a single for Stark Records.

By the end of 1965, the Twin County Partners were history, but Arnold's music career was just beginning. He frequently performed at music festivals throughout the South, an experience that gained him valuable exposure. Unfortunately, it also introduced him to alcohol, and for the rest of his life, he would have the reputation of a hard drinker. In 1970, after graduating from high school, Arnold was invited to Nashville by Joe Greene, a fiddler and session man who met the boy at the Galax fiddlers' convention. Arnold returned after a few months and enrolled in a community college, but left after two terms. He then teamed up briefly with his old friend Wes Golden and the Virginia Cut-ups. Shortly after they cut an album for Latco Records, Arnold became a solo act again.

In the next several years Arnold joined a number of bands, including Cliff Waldron and the New Shades of Grass, Charlie Moore and the Dixie Partners, Keith Whitley and the New Tradition, among others. His heavy drinking usually led to his dismissal from these bands, but Arnold also used his time with these groups honing his skills on the fiddle and guitar. In 1974, he recorded a solo album of banjo instrumentals, ***Strictly Arnold***, that is now regarded as a classic. Three years later his album ***Jimmy Arnold Guitar*** revealed his skill on that instrument, the harmonica, and Dobro. But the recording by which he is best remembered, ***Southern Soul***, was recorded in 1983 on the edge of Chancellorsville Battlefield. This lp was an attempt to present a Civil War soldier's story through first- person songs blending fragments of Arnold's own life with that of an imaginary composite Confederate. Although a critical success, ***Southern Soul*** enjoyed only moderate commercial approval.

After ***Southern Soul*** appeared, Arnold dropped out of the music business for a time, earning his living as a tattoo artist. Unfortunately, he soon started using his tattoo parlor as a front for drug selling, an activity for which he was sentenced to jail in 1985. After his release, Arnold spent some time as a resident artist at Martin Community College in eastern North Carolina, but was soon fired. An unsuccessful tour to Australia left Arnold without even his guitar, and several unreleased sessions, one of Jimmie Rodgers' songs and another of Hank Williams', followed. In 1992, Jimmy decided to devote himself to the Pentecostal Church, frequently speaking against the evils of alcohol and drug abuse. Then, late in the year, he decided to give music another try and was booked for a solo tour in Eastern Europe. Sadly, on Christmas Day, he went to sleep and never woke up, passing away in the night from ischemic heart failure. WKM

RECOMMENDED ALBUMS:

"Strictly Arnold" (Rebel)
"Rainbow Ride" (Rebel)
"Southern Soul" (Rebel)

CHARLINE ARTHUR

(Singer, Songwriter, Guitar, Comedy)

Given Name:	**Charline Highsmith**
Date of Birth:	**September 2,1929**
Where Born:	**Henrietta, Texas**
Married:	**Jack Arthur (div.)**
Date of Death:	**1987**

If Charline Arthur didn't make it during her lifetime, part of the reason was that she went totally out of step with Country music's conservative conventions. Her temper, at best unpredictable, made her a very controversial and hard-to-manage act.

She was born the second of twelve children and when she was four, the family moved to Paris, Texas. Her father was a Pentecostal preacher who played harmonica and her mother was a conscientious churchgoer who also played guitar. She began singing in church and by the time she was in school, she and her sister Dottie were entertaining. As a youngster of 7, she collected empty soda bottles and raised $6 to buy her first guitar. When she was age 12, she wrote her first song, *I've Got the Boogie Blues*.

Her first influence was Ernest Tubb and by 1945, she was appearing on radio station KPLT in Paris. When a traveling medicine show came to town, Charline won a contest and gained a place on the show. However, as she was not yet 16, she had to get parental permission. Shortly after this, she married Jack Arthur, who played bass on all her recordings.

In 1949, after singing in clubs and honky tonks in Texas, she recorded for Bullet Records, cutting *I've Got the Boogie Blues* and *Is Love a Game*. She then moved to Kermit, Texas, where she got a job as a deejay and singer on KERB. She put together her own band and began to get a local following. As a result Charline and the band appeared on KERB 6 days a week for as many as 3 times a day. In 1950, while at the station, she recorded two sides that were released on the custom label Imperial.

Colonel Tom Parker and Eddy Arnold heard her perform and recommended her to Julian and Gene Aberbach who owned the music publishing company Hill and Range and they signed her to a publishing deal. They then introduced her to RCA Records and signed a deal on January 1, 1953. She recorded her initial RCA sides in Dallas in February and over the next three and one half years, Charline had thirteen further sessions. Musicians on the sessions included Chet Atkins, Dale Potter, Don Helms and Floyd Cramer.

As a result of recording for RCA, she appeared on the *Big D Jamboree*, in 1953, the *Louisiana Hayride* and the *Ozark Jubilee*. In 1955, she was named runner-up to Kitty Wells in the *Country & Western Jamboree* magazine annual "Deejay Choice" poll. She appeared frequently with Elvis Presley, whose mother was a great fan of Charline's big, brassy, bluesy Country voice that at times was almost a forerunner of Rockabilly. It is highly possible that Elvis was influenced by Charline's on-stage pyrotechnics. She was not one to stand still; she was the first woman in Country music to wear slacks and she took advantage of this to cavort all over the stage.

Charline also worked the *Prince Albert* segment of the *Grand Ole Opry*, where her material was vetted by Grant Turner before she could sing it, as her songs were often racy. However, at RCA she was not happy. After initially working with Steve Sholes, Chet Atkins took over as producer and he and Charline did not get on. Her contract with RCA came to an end in 1956 and the following year, she recorded for Coin, again without success, and then she and Jack separated.

She teamed up with her sisters, Dottie and Betty Sue, but by the beginning of 1960, she was penniless. She arrived in Salt Lake City where Ray Pellum, a night club owner and fan of Charline's, got her a job at a night club in Chubbuck, Idaho, where she worked for the next five years. She also recorded for Pellum's Eldorado label.

Charline moved to the West Coast in 1965 and remained there until 1978, recording for Republic, Rustic and Wytra during her stay. In 1969, she was found by Alice M. Michaels in bad shape in Pocatello and she took Charline in and became her manager. For some while, Charline played Redwood Gardens in San Jose and venues around San Francisco.

She moved back to Idaho suffering from arthritis and lived on a $335 a month disability pension. In 1986, Bear Family Records in Germany put together Charline's RCA tracks and released ***Welcome to the Club***. This contains such classics as *Burn That Candle*, *Kiss the Baby Goodbye* and *Just Look, Don't Touch, He's Mine*. She was at last happy that someone had recognized her talent and a year later, she died in her sleep.

Perhaps if she had been prepared to toe the line, Charline Arthur would have been talked of in the same breath as Wanda Jackson and Patsy Cline; instead she became a casualty of Country music.

RECOMMENDED ALBUM:

"Welcome to the Club" (Bear Family Germany)(1986)

EMRY ARTHUR

(Singer, Songwriter, Guitar)
Date of Birth: **ca. 1900**
Where Born: **Wayne County, Kentucky**
Married: **(div.)**
Date of Death: **1966**

He is remembered today by Old Time music fans and Folk song students, but in his prime, from 1928 to 1935, singer and songwriter Emry Arthur was one of the most popular and prolific early Country singers. He was one of the best singers to come from the rich Kentucky Folk tradition and one of the best to translate that tradition into commercial terms. He recorded some 78 sides for major labels like Vocalion and Decca and for the independent Paramount and Lonesome Ace labels. He was the first to record the haunting *I Am a Man of Constant Sorrow*, the Bluegrass standard made famous by the Stanley Brothers years later.

Arthur was born in the remote Elk Spring Valley in south central Kentucky, in an area rich in traditional musicians. His father was a collector of old songs and his brothers Sam and Henry (who were later to accompany him on some of his records) were skilled instrumentalists. Neighbors included Dick Burnett, Leonard Rutherford and William Rexroat, all of whom also recorded. When he was young, a hunting accident took one of his fingers, making him adopt a plain percussion guitar style that is heard on most of his records.

About 1925, young Arthur moved to Indianapolis to work in factories and do other odd jobs. An audition for Vocalion Records (then an independent company, though later a division of ARC) brought him a contract and on January 17, 1928, in Chicago, Emry and his brother Henry recorded 10 songs. Two of the cuts, jaunty versions of the old Gospel songs *Love Lifted Me* and *Shining for the Master*, became hits and within six months the company wanted more. Arthur's repertoire ranged from old Wayne County traditional songs like *Going Around the World* to old Pop songs like *In the Heart of the City That Has No Heart*.

By August 1929, though, Arthur's professional and personal life fell apart. "I had to leave everything I had," he wrote, and had to move to his brother's home in Jacksonville, Illinois. His wife sued him for divorce and his recording contract was dropped. The Depression made work hard to find and soon he was working at a chair factory in Port Washington, Wisconsin, the very company that owned Paramount Records. When his bosses discovered who he was, more recordings followed, but none were successful. A short-lived stint with the independent West Virginia label Lonesome Ace also fell through. He managed to get a last session with Decca in 1934, redoing some of his old hits and cutting new songs like *Empty Pockets Blues*. Eventually he returned to Indianapolis, where he died in 1966 CKW

RECOMMENDED ALBUM:

"I Am a Man of Constant Sorrow" (Old Homestead)

ASCAP

The American Society of Composers, Authors and Publishers is one of the three performing rights organizations in the United States. It was the first such organization to be established.

ASCAP represents songwriters and music publishers in the area of public performances. They issue "blanket" licenses to radio and television stations which allow the broadcasters to use any of the songs in the ASCAP repertoire. The broadcasters pay an annual fee for this license and the monies collected are distributed to the songwriters and publishers after ASCAP deducts its expenses. Between 1982 and 1991, ASCAP collected $2,767,939,000 in performance royalties from about 10,000 radio stations, 900 local television stations, cable providers (HBO, Cinemax, TNN, etc.) and the three major television networks (CBS, NBC, ABC).

ASCAP issues licenses not only to broadcasters, but also to more than 100,000 other users including nightclubs, hotels, restaurants, skating rinks, theme parks, circuses, jukebox operators, background music services and airlines. Colleges and universities, symphony orchestras and concert promoters must also purchase a license from ASCAP on an annual basis.

Congress paved the way for the establishment of ASCAP in 1897 when it added public performances to the U.S. copyright law. That addition to the law gave copyright owners the right to collect payment for the use of their music in hotels and restaurants. The problem copyright owners faced was a method of collecting the public performance royalties.

The move to create a performing rights society in America was helped by visiting Italian composer Giacomo Puccini. He was earning significant performance royalties in Europe for his operas *La Boheme* and *Madama Butterfly* and was surprised that no performing rights society existed in the United States. During a visit in 1910, he encouraged many well-known composers to form an organization to collect their performance royalties.

The effort to create a performing rights society was undertaken by composer Raymond Hubbell, publisher George Maxwell and attorney Nathan Burkan. They enlisted the help of popular composer Victor Herbert, who in addition to being the principal conductor of the Pittsburgh Symphony, wrote many popular operas, including *Wizard of the Nile*, *Prince Ananias* and *The Fortune Teller*. Herbert garnered the support of many important songwriters and music publishers, who established the American Society of Composers, Authors and Publishers on February 13, 1914 at the Hotel Claridge, in New York City. The founding members included legendary composer Irving Berlin.

ASCAP was structured as a nonprofit organization made up of a 12-member board of writers and a 12-member board of music publishers. The plan was to distribute all royalties collected to members after deducting expenses. Writer members paid annual dues of $10.00 and publisher members paid $50.00.

The first establishment to purchase an ASCAP license was Rectors Restaurant on Broadway in New York City. They paid an annual fee of $180.00. By the end of its first year, ASCAP had licensed about 85 hotels and restaurants. There was, however, great resistance from establishments. There were two major court cases that set precedents for ASCAP. The first was a suit filed by Victor Herbert against New York's Shanley's Restaurant and the other by John Philip Sousa against the Vanderbilt Hotel. The charges were that these businesses had violated the copyright law by not obtaining a license for the public performance of the composers' works. The cases were decided by the U.S. Supreme Court, with Nathan Burkan representing the composers and ASCAP. The opinion of the court was written by Justice Oliver Wendell Holmes, who said: "If music did not pay, it would be given up. Whether it pays or not, the purpose of employing it is profit and that is enough."

ASCAP determines the amount of payments to writers and publishers from a sampling of performances. These samples come primarily from radio and television. With an estimated 53 million hours of radio broadcasts per year, it is not possible to monitor every performance. ASCAP samples 60,000 hours per year by randomly taping radio stations around the country. This process goes on year round and provides ASCAP with an estimate of what songs are being performed on radio. ASCAP has devised a formula to credit writers and publishers for those performances and royalty payments are made four times per year. ASCAP also samples 30,000 hours per year of local television to determine payment to members for those performances. The three major television networks, ABC, NBC and CBS, provide ASCAP with a complete listing (known as a cue sheet) of all musical uses. Royalty payments for most other uses (shopping malls, nightclubs, hotels, etc.) are based upon the information ASCAP gathers from the radio and television performances.

ASCAP represents about 4,000 writers and publishers. They license every style of popular music. Country music songwriters who are ASCAP members include Alan Jackson and Garth Brooks. JIE

JOHN ASHBY

(Fiddle)

Given Name: John Chilton Ashby
Date of Birth: October 6, 1915
Where Born: Nr. Warrenton, Virginia
Married: Francis
Children: George Everett (Skipper), Barbara
Date of Death: May 11, 1979

John Ashby was a carpenter by trade. He, his brother Marshall, his cousin Moffett Ashby and two friends, Bill Robinson and Morrison Green, formed the Free State Ramblers in 1930. They played for house parties and dances locally. He won the first fiddling contest in Front Royal, Virginia; shortly after, they were invited to play the National Folk Festival in Constitution in 1938 and were invited back every year until 1943, when the festival stopped for WWII.

In 1947, the group joined Connie B. Gay's *Gay Time* on WRAL in Washington, D.C. and stayed on the show for two years. After this, John restricted his playing to local square dances and fiddlers' conventions and contests around Virginia and to music sessions with his friends and family. Both his son, Skipper, and Moffett's son, Richard (who played on the County albums), continue the musical tradition. John Ashby died in May 1979.

RECOMMENDED ALBUMS:

"Old Virginia Fiddling" (County)(1971)
"Down on Ashby's Farm" (County)(1974)[With Richard Ashby, Ronnie Poe, Ashby Kyhl and Jack Frazier]
"Fiddling by the Hearth" (County)(1979)

CLARENCE TOM ASHLEY

(Singer, Banjo, Guitar)

Given Name: Clarence Earl McCurry
Date of Birth: September 29, 1895
Where Born: Bristol, Virginia
Married: Hettie Osborne
Children: Eva (b. 1919), J.D. (b. 1921)
Date of Death: June 2, 1967

One of the best mountain singers of the century, Tom Ashley was a rare example of a veteran of the Old Time music scene of the 1920's who actually became known after he was rediscovered by the Folk revival in the 1960's. Best known for his solo recordings of *The Coo Coo Bird* and *The House Carpenter*, in 1929, Ashley was a complex and talented musician who won later fame for his work with Tex Isley, Doc Watson and other luminaries of the Folk festival circuit. He was also one of the first 1920's veterans to be extensively interviewed and provided to historians one of the first and best looks into that shadowy era.

Though he was born in Bristol, the border town that would in later years be the focus of early recording efforts, young Tom Ashley soon moved with his family to Ashe County, North Carolina and then later to Shouns,

Tennessee. He got his first instrument, a banjo, in 1903, but, like many mountain musicians, he did not get a guitar until later, in his case 1907.

By 1911 he had become accomplished enough to decide to try to make money with his music and chose the route followed by many early Appalachian musicians: the traveling rural medicine show. Ashley's first stint was with Doc White Cloud's medicine show in 1911 and for the next two decades he continued to work off and on with others, including the famous Doctor Hauer's, where he worked with a young Roy Acuff.

Ashley was married in 1914 to Hettie Osborne and in 1919 their daughter, Eva, was born. To support his young family, Ashley turned to "busking" (traveling around and playing on street corners or in railroad stations for money in the hat) with musicians like G. B. Grayson, the blind fiddler and Hobart Smith, the banjoist; both would later win fame for their recordings. Other early companions were not as well known: Dwight and Dewey Bell of West Virginia, the Cook Sisters, the Greer Sisters and others.

Then, starting in 1928, he embarked on an intense period of recording activity. Unlike some traditional musicians Ashley liked the idea of recording, was aggressive enough to pursue it and saw it as a legitimate way to make money. From 1928 through 1933, he appeared on over 70 sides, occasionally by himself but more often as a member of a string band. The first of these was a Victor band called the Carolina Tar Heels, which featured Ashley's singing with Doc Walsh and harmonica player Garley Foster. Their light, airy sound and unusual tunes made them popular and prolific recording artists. Their *Peg and Awl* was an early song about technological unemployment, as were *My Home's Across the Blue Ridge Mountains* (1929, later revived by Bluegrass bands), *Somebody's Tall and Handsome* (1929) and *There's a Man Going Round Taking Names*.

Then came the Columbia session, in which Ashley was a member of a band called Byrd Moore and His Hot Shots, followed by a 1931 job with a Victor group called the Haywood County Ramblers and a lengthy 1931 session with a large studio band called the Blue Ridge Mountain Entertainers, with Clarence Green (fiddle), Walter Davis (guitar), Gwen Foster (harmonica—no relation to Garley) and others.

In between, he cut some splendid solo sides. In Johnson City in 1929 and again in 1930, he took only his old banjo into the studio and using his odd model "sawmill" tuning, did a wonderful and definitive version of the ancient British lyric *The Coo Coo Bird*, as well as *Dark Holler Blues, Old John Hardy* and *House Carpenter*. Though the records were not spectacular sellers in the 1920's, they were later reissued (some on the famed Harry Smith Folkways set) and influenced thousands during the 1960's.

In 1933, under the name Ashley and Foster, he and Gwen Foster recorded a set of tunes for ARC that showed Ashley's mastery of white Blues: *East Virginia Blues, Rising Sun Blues, Greenback Dollar* and *Bay Rum Blues*.

The ARC records, though, sold poorly and by 1934 Ashley was working in the West Virginia coalfields and driving a freight truck for the government. Hard times, as well as the illness of his son J.D., spelled an end to touring and he soon was buying an eight-acre farm. In 1941 he felt secure enough to travel a little with Charlie Monroe (during which time he met Lester Flatt and Tex Isley), but soon turned more and more to farming and working lumber. By 1953 he had gotten pretty much out of music, but rekindled his interest by teaching his grandson Tommy some of his old songs.

In 1960, he met young Folk song collector, singer and researcher Ralph Rinzler and recorded some new sides, which were issued in two volumes by Folkways as ***Old Time Music at Clarence Ashley's***. In 1961 and 1962, he traveled to New York, appearing at Carnegie Hall, and recorded more. In 1963, he was featured at the country's largest and best Folk festivals—Newport, Chicago, Monterey and Philadelphia. More records followed and by 1966 even overseas tours of England. He died on June 2, 1967, pleased and surprised at the way his old music had survived. CKW

RECOMMENDED ALBUMS:

"Old Time Music at Clarence Ashley's" (Folkways)(1961)
"Old Time Music at Clarence Ashley's, Volume Two" (Folkways)(1963)
"Clarence Ashley and Tex Isley" (Folkways)(1966)
"Ashley and Foster" (Yazoo) [With Gwen Foster]
"Ashley and Foster" (Rounder) [With Gwen Foster]

LEON ASHLEY

(Singer, Songwriter, Guitar)
Given Name: **Leon Walton**
Date of Birth: **May 18, 1936**
Where Born: **Newton County, Georgia**
Married: **1. (div.)**
2. Margie Singleton
Children: **Leon, Jr., Tommy**

When Leon Ashley set up Ashley Records, he became the first artist to write, record, publish and distribute his own material on his own label and then have the pleasure of seeing it go to No.1 on the Country chart and cross over onto the Pop chart.

Leon was 9 years old when he made his professional debut, on WMOC Covington, Georgia, and by the time he was 11, he had his own show. He cut his first release, *He'll Never Go*, for Goldband in 1960. The following year, he signed to Imperial and released two singles, *Teen Age Angel* and *It's Alright Baby*. This was followed by another Goldband single, *Not Going Home*, the following year.

By 1964, he was on Dot for a one-off single, *You Gave Me Reason to Live*. Two years later, he teamed up with Margie Singleton on the Monument single *How Can We Divide These Little Hearts*. In 1967, Leon and Margie married and have continued a domestic and working relationship together since.

That same year, Leon set up his own label, Ashley (which was initially distributed by RCA) and the chart success that had eluded him with the other labels at last came his way. The label's third release, *Laura (What's He Got That I Ain't Got)*, leaped to No.1 and crossed over to peak at No.120 on the Pop chart. He and Margie followed with a duet, *Hangin' On*, which narrowly missed the Top 50. Leon ended the year with *Anna, I'm Taking You Home*, which went Top 30.

In 1968 he got under way with *Mental Journey* which was a Top 15 success and continued with another duet, *You'll Never Be Lonely Again*. At the end of the year, Leon made the Top 10 with *Flower of Love*. He had three solo hits in 1969: *While Your Lover Sleeps, Walkin' Back to Birmingham* and *Ain't Gonna Worry*. Of his other singles, only the 1972 record *Ease Up* made the lower levels of the Country charts. Since then, his name has been missing from the charts.

Since 1971, Leon and Margie have traveled around the States under the auspices of Linda G. Denny, their manager, and the *Country Music Spectacular*. Leon has had three distinct backing bands. In the 50's he had the original Country Boys, in the 60's, the Journeymen and since the 70's, the Strings of Nashville.

His songs have been cut by many artists, including Claude King (1967), Marty Robbins (1973) and Kenny Rogers (1976), all of whom have recorded *Laura (What's He Got That I Ain't Got)*. He has written many songs with Margie; these include *Silence*, recorded by Charley Pride in 1965, and *Don't Blow Your Horn*, recorded by the Geezinslaw Brothers in 1970.

RECOMMENDED ALBUMS:

"Laura (What's He Got That I Ain't Got)" (RCA)(1967)
"Ode to Billie Joe" (Hilltop)(1968) [With Margie Singleton]
"Mental Journey" (Ashley)(1969)
"A New Brand of Country" (Ashley)
"Ease Up—By Special Request" (Ashley)
"The Best of Leon Ashley" (Ashley)(1970)

ERNIE ASHWORTH

(Singer, Songwriter, Guitar)

Given Name:	Ernest Bert Ashworth
Date of Birth:	December 15, 1928
Where Born:	Huntsville, Alabama
Married:	Elizabeth Rose (Bettye)
Children:	Mike, Mark, Paul, Rebecca Gail

Ernie Ashworth is a civil servant who made good—a man who raced up the charts and was at one time involved with the space race. From 1948 to 1949, Ernie sang and played guitar on radio station WBHP Huntsville, during which time he was a member of the Tunetwisters, whom he left in 1950. He moved to Nashville and between 1949 and 1950, he could be found on WEKR Lafayetteville, Tennessee. He then moved on to WLAC, where he stayed until 1951, at which point he moved to station WSIX. He was with them until 1955. He first came to notice as a songwriter and more especially, he was noticed by Wesley Rose. During the 50's his songs were recorded by Little Jimmy Dickens and Carl Smith.

In 1955, Wesley Rose secured a recording deal for Ernie with MGM. Credited as "Billy Worth," he cut six singles for the label, none of which charted. The first was *Because I Cared*, in 1955, and the last *Jim, Joe and Mary*. Two years later, Ernie returned to Alabama and joined the Army's Redstone Arsenal. However, Rose didn't give up that easily, and three years later got Ernie a deal with Decca. This time, he was billed as Ernest Ashworth and he immediately had a Top 5 hit with *Each Moment (Spent with You)*. He followed up later in the year with the Top 10 *You Can't Pick a Rose in December*. The following year he made it three in a row with the Top 20 *Forever Gone*.

In 1962, still billed as "Ernest," he signed to Hickory. He hit the Top 5 with his first release, *Everybody but Me,* and followed it with the Top 10 success *I Take the Chance*. It was in 1963, with his third single, *Talk Back Trembling Lips,* a self-written song, that he scored his first and only No.1. He won the "Most Promising" category in both *Cash Box* and *Billboard* in 1963 and 1964 and in *Record World* in 1964.

On March 7, 1964, Ernie Ashworth became a member of the *Grand Old Opry*. During that year, he had a Top 10 hit with *A Week in the Country* and a Top 5 hit with *I Love to Dance with Annie*, and just missed the Top 10 with *Pushed in a Corner*.

During 1965, he made his solitary movie, *The Farmer's Other Daughter*. He continued his hits throughout 1965 and 1966 with *Because I Cared*, the Top 10 *The D.J. Cried* (1965) and *I Wish* (the first single billing him as "Ernie"), *At Ease Heart* (Top 20) and *Sad Face* (1966). In 1967, his chart success level dropped and only *A New Heart* in 1968 reached the Top 40. Then in 1970, he had his last chart entry (Top 70), appropriately titled *The Look of Goodbye*.

He signed with the independent O'Brien label, but his four releases failed to make any impression. Ernie lives on his farm in Lewisburg, Tennessee. He currently owns radio station WSLV Ardmore in Tennessee. He was an Honorary Colonel on the staff of Alabama Governor George Wallace and Tennessee Governor Ray Blanton. He was one of the select few in Tennessee to receive special tags stating that he was on the Governor's staff. He held an Official Deputy Sheriff's card and he was an Honorary Captain on the Tennessee Highway Patrol. He is a Mason and a Shriner and still plays dates around the country and appears regularly on the *Grand Ole Opry*, sporting his colorful stage attire.

RECOMMENDED ALBUMS:

"Best of Ernie Ashworth" (Hickory)(1968)
"Ernie Ashworth Sings His Greatest Hits" (Starday)(1976)
"Country Hits" (O'Brien)

ASLEEP AT THE WHEEL

Formed:	1969
Original Members:	
Ray Benson	Lead Vocals, Lead Guitar
Leroy Preston	Guitar, Drums, Vocals
Lucky Oceans	Steel Guitar, Drums
Chris O'Connell	Lead and Harmony Vocals, Guitar
Floyd Domino	Piano
Other Members:	
Danny Levin	Mandolin, Fiddle
Scott Hennige	Drums
Link Davis, Jr.	Flute, Sax
Bill Mabry	Fiddle
Johnny Gimble	Fiddle
Patrick (Taco) Ryan	Woodwinds
Tony Garnier	Bass
Chris York	Drums
Andy Stein	Fiddle
Gene Dobkin	Bass
Richard Casona	Fiddle
Billy Briggs	Sax
Ed Vizard	Sax
Billy Joor	Trumpet
Mike O'Dowd	Woodwinds
David Poe	Sax
Ammett Cobb	Sax
Bucky Meadows	Guitar
Dennis Solee	Sax
Larry Franklin	Fiddle, Guitar, Vocals
John Ely	Steel Guitar, Fender Hawaiian Guitar
Dave Sanger	Drums
Jon Mitchell	Fiddle
Current Line-up:	
Ray Benson	Lead Vocals, Lead Guitar
Tim Alexander	Piano, Accordion, Harmony Vocals
Cindy Cash Dollar	Fender Hawaiian Steel Guitar
Tommy Beavers	Drums
David Earl Miller	Bass, Harmony Vocals
Rickey Turpin	Fiddle, Electric Mandolin
Michael Francis	Sax

Asleep at the Wheel is arguably the finest band live and on record, period. Led by its founder, 6'6" Ray Benson, the group is steeped in Western Swing, but is adept at delving into material as diverse as contemporary Country songs, having the original version of Ronnie Dunn's *Boot Scootin' Boogie*, classic Country (check out their version of Ernest Tubb's *Walking the Floor over You*), through to Benson's memorable duet with Willie Nelson on *Chattanooga Choo Choo*, with all the flair that would have had Glenn Miller bursting with ecstasy.

The roots of the band go back to the occasion Ray (b. Ray Benson Siefert, March 16, 1951) met Leroy Preston, who was attending the same college in Boston (Northeastern) as Benson's sister. Ray and Leroy got together with Lucky Oceans (b. Reuben Gosfield) on Benson's rent-free 1,500- acre farm near Paw Paw, West Virginia. They formed a Country band and played bars and lodge gigs in West Virginia and it was Oceans who came up with the band's name. Soon, their line-up was augmented by singer/guitarist Chris O'Connell.

It was meeting Joe Kerr, the manager of Commander Cody and the Lost Planet Airmen, that helped the Wheel on their way. He had repeatedly tried to get the group to move to San Francisco, which they did in 1971. Initially times were tough and they managed to get a 30-day tour with Stoney Edwards for food and expenses. Jazz pianist Floyd Domino was added and at last they got a residency at the Longbranch Saloon in Berkeley. A young Huey Lewis often opened for the Wheel and they reciprocated by opening for his group, Clover, at the Lion's Share in Marin County, California.

Soon the Wheel got a large following and this led to their first album, ***Comin' Right at Ya***, on United Artists, in 1973. The following year, they decided to relocate to Austin, Texas, which remains their base. That year, they released a self-titled album for Epic, which spawned their first Country chart entry, a remake of Louis Jordan's classic *Choo Choo Ch'Boogie*, which reached the Top 70.

In 1975, the Wheel signed with Capitol and released the album ***Texas Gold***, which featured an incredibly young Lisa Silver on fiddle and Bobby Womack on trumpet. This album yielded the Top 10 hit *The Letter That*

Johnny Walker Red. The band followed up with *Bump Bounce Boogie*, which peaked at No. 31. In 1976, they had three more hits in *Nothin' Takes the Place of You*, the impeccable *Route 66* and the classic *Miles and Miles of Texas*. That year, they also released ***Wheelin' and Dealin'***, which featured a young Jo-El Sonnier on accordion, Linda Hargrove on guitar and former Bob Wills sidemen Eldon Shamblin on guitar and Tiny Moore on mandolin. They released three more albums on Capitol, ***The Wheel*** (1977), ***Collision Course*** (1978) and ***Served Live*** (1979). The 1977 album features another famous ex-Wills player, Leon Rausch, on vocals. During this time, the band had two further chart singles, *The Trouble with Lovin' Today* (1977) and *Texas Me & You* (1978). In 1977, the band was voted "Best Touring Band" by the ACM and a year later it received a Grammy Award for "Best Country Instrumental Performance" for the track *One O'Clock Jump* from ***The Wheel*** album.

In 1980, the band began to face problems. First Lucky Oceans left, and then the group found itself with debts of some $200,000. They kept alive by doing TV commercials for Budweiser and doing soundtrack work on movies such as *Liar's Moon*, Louis Malle's *Alamo Bay* (1985), in which they appeared, and *1918*. Then long-time member Chris O'Connell left to have a baby, and to make matters worse, they didn't sell records.

They released one album in 1980 for MCA entitled ***Framed,*** which was a solid Country affair, with no trace of swing in sight. In 1985, MCA-Dot released the ***Asleep at the Wheel*** album, but the band was treading water. However, in 1986 they were named National Association of Campus Activities' "Country Band of the Year." In 1985, Ray Benson produced Aaron Neville and Rob Wasserman on *Stardust* on the ***Duets*** album and a year later he did the same duties for Bruce Hornsby and Willie Nelson on *Nobody There but Me*.

Then, in 1987, Rick Blackburn signed them to Epic Records. That year, they released ***Asleep at the Wheel 10*** and found themselves back in the Country singles lists, with *Way Down Texas Way* (Top 40) and *House of Blue Lights* (Top 20) and the fall hit *Boogie Back to Texas*. The album also contained the Huey Lewis song, *I Want a New Drug*, which was produced by Lewis and Benson. They received their second Grammy for "Best Country Instrumental Performance (Orchestra, Group or Soloist)" for *String of Pars*. The line-up of the band at this time included Larry Franklin, one of the hottest fiddlers out of Texas and from a line of fiddlers including his father, Lewis, and his uncle, Major Franklin; bass player Jon Mitchell, who had played with the Austin Symphony; David Sanger, who had played in a Blues band; steelie John Ely, who had played in a Reggae band; sax player Mike Francis; pianist/accordionist Tim Alexander, who had played with Buddy Greco and Gatemouth Brown; former Wheelie Chris O'Connell on harmony vocals; and Johnny Gimble on fiddle.

Their second album for Epic, ***Western Standard Time***, was released in 1988 and led to the band receiving another Grammy Award for "Best Country Instrumental Performance (Orchestra, Group or Soloist)" for *Sugarfoot Rag*. They had three chart entries that year: *Blowin' Like a Bandit, Walk on By* and *Hot Rod Lincoln*. They were also heard on the soundtrack of the movie *Heartbreak Hotel*. In 1989, they traveled to England to appear at the Wembley Festival and were so well received that they were invited back the following year.

They moved to Arista Records in 1990 and released the memorable album ***Keepin' Me Up Nights***, which contained their version of *Boot Scootin' Boogie*. They also had two chart singles, the title track and *That's the Way Love Is*. The following year, Ray had a solo chart record entitled *Four Scores and Seven Beers Ago*, featuring the Pigskins (seven members of Arista's promotion team) and the Wheel scored with *Dance with Who Brung You*. The band released one of their finest albums in 1992, entitled ***Greatest Hits Live and Kickin'***. This was the last album for most of the line-up and the debut one for fiddle player Rickey Turpin. By 1993, Cindy Cash-Dollar was in on Hawaiian steel guitar, David Earl Miller on bass and Tommy Beavers on drums. That year, the band released their most acclaimed album, on Liberty, ***Tribute to the Music of Bob Wills and the Texas Playboys***, which featured Playboys Eldon Shamblin, Johnny Gimble and Leon Rausch, plus Chet Atkins, Marty Stuart, Lucky Oceans, Vince Gill, George Strait, Garth Brooks, Lyle Lovett, Dolly Parton, Johnny Rodriguez, Suzy Bogguss, Huey Lewis, Jody Nix, Willie Nelson, Merle Haggard, Brooks & Dunn and Riders in the Sky.

The band that once had 11 members has long since settled down to 7, but has the leadership of Ray Benson, who in some ways is comparable to Bluesman John Mayall, in always having the best musicians around him and always ensuring that when members leave, they are better for the experience. Ray leads from the front as musician, writer, producer and film producer (he produced *Wild Texas Wind)*. There may have been some 80 members past and present of Asleep at the Wheel, but they seem to produce a consistency of sound.

RECOMMENDED ALBUMS:

We suggest you listen to all of them.
"Comin' Right at You" (United Artists)(1973)
"Asleep at the Wheel" (Epic)(1974)
"Texas Gold" (Capitol)(1975)
"Wheelin' and Dealin'" (Capitol)(1976)
"The Wheel" (Capitol)(1977)
"Collision Course" (Capitol)(1978)
"Served Live" (Capitol)(1979)
"Framed" (MCA)(1980)
"Asleep at the Wheel" (MCA-Dot)(1985)
"Asleep at the Wheel 10" (Epic)(1987)

Asleep at the Wheel *under the leadership of Ray Benson (third right)*

"Western Standard Time" (Epic)(1988)
"Keepin' Me Up Nights" (Arista)(1990)
"Greatest Hits Live & Kickin'" (Arista)(1992)
"Tribute to the Music of Bob Wills and the Texas Playboys" (Liberty)(1993)
(See also Lucky Oceans.)

BOB ATCHER

(Singer, Guitar, Fiddle)

Given Name: James Robert Owen Atcher
Date of Birth: May 11, 1914
Where Born: Hardin County, Kentucky
Married: 1. Loetta Applegate (div.)
2. Marguerite Alice Whitehill
Children: Robert W., Mary C., Cecily A.
Date of Death: October 31, 1993

Through a long association with WLS and the *National Barn Dance* in Chicago, Bob Atcher gained title to being the "Dean of Cowboy Singers." More than that, however, Atcher also had good taste for other Folk material, straight Country material of his era and duet songs as well.

Born in central Kentucky's Hardin County on land that later became part of Fort Knox, Atcher's father was an Old Time fiddler; Bob and his younger brother, Randall (b. December 7, 1918), fell into music naturally. According to some early PR releases, Bob spent part of his growing-up years in North Dakota, but that appears to be the kind of vested publicity that many singers of the 40's used to identify with the cowboy image and it seems more likely that he grew up in West Point. He began his radio career at WHAS Louisville in the early 30's and from there he spent short stints at a variety of stations, including WJJD Chicago, WSB Atlanta, WCHS Charleston and WIND Gary. In 1939, he landed a steady position on WGBM Chicago, where he established a daily program broadcast over the CBS radio network. From this, he achieved wide popularity.

He also began his recording career in 1939 for the American Record Corporation with his early releases on the associated Vocalion, OKeh, Conquerer and later Columbia labels. Many of his pre-1943 recordings were duets with "Bonnie Blue Eyes" (Loetta Applegate) and a few had Randy Atcher on them as well. After a stint in the service during the latter part of WWII, Atcher returned to radio and the recording studio in 1945. His post-war Columbia efforts were nearly all solo vocals and numbers such as *I Must Have Been Wrong* and *Why Don't You Haul Off and Love Me?* all ranked on the charts.

In 1948, Bob Atcher moved to WLS and the *National Barn Dance*, where he was one of the program's top stars in its last decade. Shortly after the end of the recording ban that kept artists out of the studio through most of 1948, Atcher recorded two of the earliest 10-inch albums for Columbia, one of cowboy songs and the second of Folk songs. In 1950, he switched to Capitol, cutting eight sides, and had a single on the Tiffany label. Active on Chicago television, he won an award for the best children's program. After WLS discontinued the *National Barn Dance*, Atcher also appeared on the WGN *Barn Dance* on both radio and television during the 60's, recording with the entire cast on Kapp and cutting a new album for Columbia in 1964.

By the time Bob appeared on the WGN *Barn Dance*, his interests had broadened beyond music. He owned his own business, served on the board of directors of the Schaumburg State Bank and spent some twenty years, from 1959, as the city Mayor.

Meanwhile, brother Randy carved out his own career on radio and television in Louisville and had sessions on MGM Records. A recent reissue album in Germany included several of Bob's long out-of-print singles. IMT

RECOMMENDED ALBUMS:

"Early American Folk Songs" (Harmony)(1952) and (1964)
"Songs of the Saddle" (Harmony)(1953)(10" album)
"The Dean of Cowboy Singers" (Columbia)(1964)
"Star of the WLS National Barn Dance" (Cowgirlboy Germany)(1992)

TEX ATCHISON

(Singer, Songwriter, Fiddle, Mandolin, Guitar, Banjo)

Given Name: Shelby David Atchison
Date of Birth: February 5, 1912
Where Born: Rosine, Kentucky
Married: 1. Dolly Good (div.)
2. Gertrude
Children: Joy Ann
Date of Death: August 4, 1982

Arguably the best left-handed fiddler in the history of Country music, Tex Atchison led a long and varied career that ranged from the hills of Kentucky to the studios of Hollywood. He performed with some of the most famous figures of the 30's and 40's and appeared as an ace studio man on literally hundreds of records. He was, in a narrow sense, the Tommy Jackson of his day, but his roots were deeper and more interesting than those of Jackson. His fiddle tunes and breaks were emulated around the country and some of his songs were made into hits by people as diverse as Johnny Horton and Pearl Butler.

Atchison was born and grew up in the Ohio County area of western Kentucky, on a farm near that owned by Bill Monroe's family. Like many musicians in this remarkably rich area, he grew up hearing a wide variety of music, which gave him a complex and more sophisticated background than an average hill country fiddler. By the time he was eight, he was playing his father's fiddle and six years later he had moved into a local band that featured Old Time music, as well as Dixieland Jazz and Ragtime.

His early radio experience came from WGBF in Evansville, Indiana and WOC in Davenport, Iowa. In 1932, he joined three other friends from western Kentucky—Chick Hurt, Jack Taylor and Floyd "Salty" Holmes—and formed a hot string band that was first called the Kentucky Ramblers, but later the Prairie Ramblers. The music they produced—to judge from a remarkable series of Bluebird Records they made in 1933—was a fast, infectious blend of square dance music, Western Swing and Jazz, all taken at a breakneck tempo. Unlike many older string bands, they traded off the lead between fiddle (Tex), the mandola (Hurt) and the banjo and used the big doghouse bass to propel the rhythm. Pieces like *Tex's Dance*, *Lefty's Breakdown* and *Blue River* featured Tex's fiddle. In the fall of 1932, they joined Chicago's WLS *National Barn Dance*. The following year, Atchison entered the fiddle contest at the 1933 Chicago World's Fair and won, and also became Kentucky champion fiddler that year.

The group was soon backing up other *National Barn Dance* stars like Gene Autry and yodeler Patsy Montana. After a stint with Autry, they switched to the more smooth, sophisticated cowboy sound preferred by network radio and Hollywood. At personal appearances, they came in on horseback, delighting crowds at state fairs and outdoor shows around the Midwest. Their repertoire moved more toward *Riding Down the Canyon* and *Nobody's Darling But Mine* and they began a long, rich recording series with the American Record Company in 1935. Their backing of Patsy Montana on hits like *I Wanna Be a Cowboy's Sweetheart* (1935) gave them even more exposure.

While at WLS, Ted met Dolly and Millie Good, who were better known to millions as the Girls of the Golden West. After a short courtship, Tex and Dolly were married and started a family. In 1937, Tex also decided to strike out on his own and leave the Ramblers. He moved west to WHO in Des Moines, Iowa, and to WMBD in Peoria, Illinois, where he worked as a soloist from 1937 to 1941. As the war gradually engulfed the world, the California coast, with its thousands of defense plants and military bases, became a mecca for entertainers, and Tex soon joined the trek to Los Angeles.

After a short stint in the Navy in 1942, he joined the band of Western star Ray Whitley, best known for writing *Back in the Saddle Again,* and appeared on CBS's *Hollywood Barn Dance*. By 1945, he had joined Foy Willing's big group, Riders of the Purple Sage, and was being heard on their network program, *Eight to the Bar Ranch*. Atchison found himself now taking over more and more of the lead-singing chores for the band. During the period 1943 through 1947, he appeared in 33 Charles Starrett movies for Columbia (see Movie section). He later appeared in *Jack McCall* for Columbia National and in 1954, in the Universal production *Second Graded Sex*.

In 1946 and again in 1948, Atchison became Los Angeles champion fiddler. Along with guitarist Merle Travis, Atchison soon became one of L.A.'s most popular studio musicians. He backed up people as diverse as Jimmy Wakely and Marty Robbins, as well as playing with Spade Cooley. He recorded under his own name as a soloist for Columbia (1933), Victory, Belltone and King (1947), Imperial (1953) and Sage & Sand (1964) and he even made a series of square dance 78's for a local label that was catering to the new square dance fad springing up. One of his bigger hits was *Somebody's Rose* for King in 1947.

From 1945 through 1960, he was the leader of his own band and appeared on KXLA Los Angeles. He also got into songwriting, producing almost 100 songs that were recorded, usually by other performers. They included *Sleepy Eyed John*, later done by Johnny Horton and Bill Monroe; *The Old Kentucky Fox Chase*, done by Red Foley; *Sick, Sober and Sorry*, made into a smash by Johnny Bond, and *Honky Tonkitis*, Carl Butler's only solo chart record.

In later life, Atchison returned to his native Kentucky, where he often performed at music festivals in the area. CKW

BOBBY ATKINS

(Singer, Songwriter, Banjo, Guitar)

Given Name:	**Bobby Lee Atkins**
Date of Birth:	**May 22, 1933**
Where Born:	**High Shoals, North Carolina**
Married:	**Judy Smith**
Children:	**Charles, Bobby L., Jr., Torey, Matthew, Mark, Jason, Steve**

Bobby Atkins and the Countrymen have played a pleasing style of Country music, flavored with Bluegrass, in the Carolinas for some three decades. Over the years some high-quality musicians have worked in Bobby's band, including Tony Rice, Frank Poindexter, most of Bobby's children, and the late and legendary harmonica wizard Slim Martin (1919-1975).

Bobby Atkins grew up as part of a large musical family in Madison County, North Carolina. Bobby recalls that he and his brother, Kemp, formed a duo when both were children, his mother taught him some guitar chords, and he performed in his local elementary school as a second-grader. Although shy at first, he got over it quickly when the principal gave him 15 cents and some chewing gum. At age 16, Bobby took up the banjo after hearing and seeing Don Reno play Bluegrass-style banjo. Through the 1950's, Atkins worked in various bands, including two brief experiences with Bill Monroe in 1954 and 1958. He also spent some time as a member of Charlie Monroe's Kentucky Partners in the mid-1950's,working on radio at WPAQ Mount Airy, and on television at Winston-Salem and Greensboro.

About 1956, Bobby met Joe Stone (b.1925); they formed the Dixie Mountaineers and broadcast on radio stations in Mount Airy and Greensboro. Carlton Haney recruited them as cast members of the *New Dominican Barn Dance* at WRVA. They also managed to fit two weekly TV shows at Greensboro into their schedule for a couple of years.

About 1959, Bobby and Joe went to Odessa, Texas, where for some 14 months, they did both radio and television. Back in North Carolina, the two remained together for a time, but eventually split. Joe contented himself with a part-time musical career but Bobby preferred it as a full-time occupation.

Not long after, he had his third and longest—eight months—stint with Bill Monroe. Then, in the early 60's, Bobby formed the Countrymen, who have had regular television programs through the Carolina Piedmont section, played numerous club dates, festivals and shopping malls and appeared in a couple of motion pictures over the past 30 years. Among the more significant musicians who have worked in Bobby's band through the years have been the team of Wilma Martin and her husband, Slim, who played both fiddle and harmonica; Frank Poindexter, a superb Dobroist; and Tony Rice, who eventually went on to become a Bluegrass guitar superpicker. In recent years, Bobby's children have played key roles in his band, including daughter Torey, who has been a featured vocalist, and sons Charles, Matt and Mark, who have often played drums, guitar and mandolin, respectively. Tim Atkins, a nephew, has played bass. As of mid-1993, Bobby's band consisted of Mark Atkins, mandolin; Jason Atkins, bass; and Danny Casstevens, guitar.

Over the years Bobby Atkins and the Countrymen have recorded on several labels. Bobby once had a single on Decca. Discs made with his band have appeared on Cattle, Colony 13, Heritage, Stokes and Old Homestead. In addition, Atkins cut two albums with Jim Eanes. Bobby's band also furnished support for Slim Martin's album on Heritage and for Frank Poindexter and Joe Stone on Old Homestead. Among the several songs he has written, Bobby takes special pride in one title, *In the Good Old Days*. IMT

RECOMMENDED ALBUMS:

"Country 'n Grass" (Colony)(1974)
"Back Home in Gold Hill" (Heritage)(1976)
"A Tribute to Charlie Monroe" (Old Homestead)(1977)
"Bluegrass with a Country Flavor" (Old Homestead) (1978)
"Enough to Keep Me Dreaming On" (Old Homestead)(1980)
"Sounds of the Starlight Featuring Torey Atkins" (Old Homestead)(1981)
"Back in the Good Ole Days" (Cattle Germany)(1984)
"1968 Sessions" (Old Homestead)(1979) [with Frank Poindexter and Tony Rice]
"A Song for You" (Old Homestead)(1986)
"I've Lived a Lot in My Time' (Old Homestead)(1986)
"Jim Eanes & Bobby Atkins" (Old Homestead)(1986)
"Songs and Tunes of the 50's" (Old Homestead)(1988)
"Feelings of a Country Man" (Old Homestead)(1989)
"Dirty Rich" (Stokes)(1991)
"Heart of the South" (Rural Rhythm)(1991) [with Jim Eanes]

CHET ATKINS

(Guitar, Fiddle, Banjo, Occasional Singer, Record Producer, Industry Executive, Songwriter, Composer)

Given Name:	**Chester Burton Atkins**
Date of Birth:	**June 20, 1924**
Where Born:	**Luttrell, Tennessee**
Married:	**Leona Johnson**
Children:	**Merle W. (daughter)**

When Chet Atkins was inducted into the Country Music Hall of Fame on October 15, 1973, he was the youngest recipient of this honor. Yet he had achieved more by then than most performers could hope for.

He was influenced early on by Jimmie Rodgers and Merle Travis. Travis played the syncopated thumb and fingers roll that would in time become "Chet Atkins licks." His elder brother, Lowell, and half-brother, Jim, both played guitar and tried to dissuade Chet from playing the instrument. So this shy asthmatic child started to learn the fiddle. When he was 9, he traded an old pistol for his first guitar.

By the time he left high school, he was already a highly proficient player. He left school and home in 1941 and through some contacts of his brothers he landed a job at WNOX Knoxville, with the *Bill Carlisle Show*. He also played with the Dixie Swingers and it was with them that he made his first broadcast. While at the station, he worked with Homer and Jethro. He would be reunited with them much later. He remained at WNOX for the next 3 years and then went to WLW Cincinnati.

During 1946, he appeared on the *Grand Ole Opry* with Red Foley and made his first recordings for the Bullet label. He also appeared on WRVA Richmond, Virginia. He kept getting fired because he heard musical arrangements in a different way from the station executives and as he was too shy to stand up for what he believed in, he was shown the door. The day after his eighth dismissal, he married Leona. During 1949-1950, Chet was broadcasting on KWTO Springfield, Missouri. He had been heard by RCA Victor's head of Country music, Steve Sholes, on another Missouri station, but Sholes couldn't trace him. As luck would have it, Si Saman of KWTO had already sent a broadcast tape to Al Hindle of RCA Victor's Chicago office. Hindle sent it to Sholes and Sholes sent for Atkins. By then, he was out of KWTO and playing at KOA Denver, Colorado, with Shorty Thompson and His Rangers. Chet borrowed money on his car and went to Nashville to record.

Five of the eight sides recorded were vocals, which Chet, who does possess a pleasant "Jazzman's" voice, would rather didn't exist. In 1949, Sholes, who looked on Chet as his protege, made him the studio guitarist for all Nashville sessions. However, it was not until 1950 that Chet felt settled in Nashville, where he was taken under the wings of Mother Maybelle and the Carter Sisters as a regular on the *Grand Ole Opry*.

By 1953, Atkins had been made a consultant to RCA Victor's Nashville operation. From 1953, RCA Victor issued a regular supply of consistent instrumental albums that highlighted his playing ability. In 1955, he had his first Country hit as an instrumentalist when *Mr. Sandman* reached the No.13 position. He and Hank Snow, that other fine RCA Victor guitarist, followed this up with the duet *Silver Bell*. By now, Atkins was justly known as "Mr. Guitar."

Gibson Guitars issued the Chet Atkins Country Gent (designed by the original Gretsch Guitars designer and for which most pickers would kill) and the Chet Atkins Tennessean (for which they would at least commit grievous bodily harm). In 1955, Gretsch asked Chet to work with company craftsmen to create and endorse a guitar to his own specifications. He created 2 instruments, a Chet Atkins solid body and the more prestigious Chet Atkins hollow-bodied Model 6120.

When Sholes became head of Pop A & R in New York in 1957, Chet became full-time manager of the Nashville operation. He made an appearance at the Newport Jazz Festival in 1960 and a year later appeared at the White House and entertained President John Kennedy. In 1963 Camden released ***Guitar Genius***, on which Jim Atkins was featured on vocals.

Chet adapted the Boots Randolph saxophone classic *Yakety Sax* into *Yakety Axe* and had a Top 5 hit with it in 1965. It also made the national chart's Top 100. His 1966 album, ***Chet Atkins Picks on the Beatles***, seemed to foresee some of the Pop developments in Country music since. That same year, he appeared with the Boston Pops Orchestra under the baton of Arthur Fiedler and recorded two albums with them: ***The Pops Go Country*** (1966) and ***Chet Picks on the Pops*** (1969).

In 1968, the year Steve Sholes died, Chet was promoted to Vice-President of the Country Division. Chet established a reputation for spotting talent; he had brought on to the label Charley Pride, Waylon Jennings, Don Gibson, Connie Smith, Floyd Cramer and Bobby Bare and had nurtured their careers. He produced most of the acts going through the Nashville office, including Eddy Arnold and Elvis Presley.

In 1969, he recorded an instrumental that will always be associated with him, *Country Gentleman*. He has returned to the singles charts on infrequent occasions, but none of his successes in this area were momentous: *Prissy* in 1968 (No. 30), *Fiddlin' Around* in 1973, with Johnny Gimble (No. 75) and *The Night Atlanta Burned*, as the Atkins String Company, in 1975 (No. 77). *Frog Kissin'* (1976) made it to No. 40 and in 1980 he hit twice, with *Blind Willie* (No.83) and *I Can Hear Kentucky Calling Me* (No. 83).

During 1970-1971, he recorded five albums with Homer and Jethro under the name of the Nashville String Band; these were released through 1970-1972. After Homer's death, Chet worked on various projects with his brother-in-law, Jethro Burns. Chet's 1971 album, ***Chet, Floyd & Boots***, with Floyd Cramer and Boots Randolph, was a forerunner of the Masters' Festival that featured the trio and was organized by Chet's manager, X. Cosse.

By 1980, Atkins was urging RCA Victor to let him record a Jazz album, without positive response. He was also suffering from a recurrence of cancer of the colon (he received a letter from President Reagan welcoming him to the "semi-colons"). He was also getting sick of the state of Country music. With his new manager Fred Kewley's urging and blessing, he quit RCA Victor in 1982 and joined Columbia as a performer.

His initial album was ***Work It Out With Chet Atkins*** in 1983. His third album, ***Stay Tuned,*** was almost like a revelation. At last, Chet Atkins had grown wings and produced an album that was not Country, but a glorious fusion of Jazz and Rock. It featured Chet on duets with some of the newer guitar giants, including Dire Straits' maestro, Mark Knopfler; Earl Klugh; George Benson; Larry Carlton; and Steve Lukather. The album made the Top 20 of most Jazz charts, as did the 1986 follow-up, ***Street Dreams,*** which featured Jazz-Funk

Chet Atkins *(right) with his good buddy* ***Jerry Reed***

greats such as Harvey Mason and Ronnie Foster as well as Country pickers Terry McMillan and Mark O'Connor. Earl Klugh has said that he only wanted to play after hearing one of Chet's records on the radio. That same year, the Atkins Video Society issued a visual tutorial, *Get Started on Guitar*, which was given the thumbs-up by *Guitar* magazine.

The following year, ***Sails*** found Chet on banjo as well as guitar. The album featured bouzouki and sitar. The 1988 album, ***Chet Atkins, C.G.P.***, continued this voyage of discovery. ("C.G.P." means Certified Guitar Player.)

Over the years, Chet has returned to the roots of country with some tandem recordings including ***Home Town Guitar*** (1968) with Sonny Osborne, ***Me and Jerry Reed*** (1970), ***C.B. Atkins and C.E. Snow*** (1970) with Hank Snow, ***Me and Chet*** (1972) with Jerry Reed and ***The Atkins-Travis Traveling Show*** with Merle Travis in 1974. In 1990, he returned to Country-Fusion, releasing ***Neck and Neck*** with Mark Knopfler and in 1992 he paired up for a third outing with Jerry Reed on ***Sneakin' Around***.

For many years, Chet has had his own golf tournament, which raises a lot of money for charity. He has received numerous accolades, both from his peers and from the public at large In 1972, he was given the "Humanitarian Award" by the National Council of Christians and Jews. He has been nominated by the CMA as "Instrumentalist of the Year" every year for the last 26 years and has won it 9 times. In addition, he was the recipient of *Cash Box* and *Playboy* instrumentalist awards.

During his career, he has picked up 11 Grammy Awards. ***Chet Atkins Picks the Best*** was voted "Best Contemporary Instrumental Performance" in 1967 and the above-mentioned ***Me and Jerry Reed*** was the recipient of the "Best Country Instrumental Performance" award. In 1971, he won "Best Country Instrumental Performance" for his single *Snowbird*. ***The Atkins-Travis Traveling Show*** album received a Grammy for "Best Country Instrumental Performance" in 1974 and the following year he received the same award for the track *The Entertainer* from the album ***Chet Atkins Goes to the Movies***. He again won the award in 1976 with the album ***Chester and Lester***, which he recorded with that other guitar genius, Les Paul. In 1981, he again received the award, this time for the album ***Country—After All These Years***. In company with new guitar great Mark Knopfler, Chet received the award for *Cosmic Square Dance* from the Columbia album ***Stay Tuned.*** They were double recipients again in 1990 with their duet album ***Neck and Neck***. They received "Best Country Vocal Collaboration" (Yes, "vocal." It seems what goes around comes around) for *Poor Boy Blues* and "Best Country Instrumental Performance" for the album. In 1993, Chet was honored with the "Lifetime Achievement Award" from NARAS.

RECOMMENDED ALBUMS:

We are recommending albums that would appeal to a Country audience; however, we do recommend that you take a listen to his Columbia Jazz-Fusion albums to hear Chet Atkins in a group environment.

"Chet Atkins in Three Dimensions" (RCA Victor)(1955) [re-packaged in original sleeve by Stetson UK in 1988]
"Me and Jerry Reed" (RCA Victor)(1970) [With Jerry Reed]
"Me and Chet" (RCA Victor)(1972) [With Jerry Reed]
"C. B. Atkins and C. E. Snow" (1972) [With Hank Snow]
"The Atkins-Travis Traveling Show" (RCA Victor)(1974)
"The Night Atlanta Burned" (RCA Victor)(1975) [As the Atkins String Company]
"Chester and Lester" (RCA Victor)(1976) [With Les Paul]
"The Nashville String Band" (RCA Victor)(1979) [With Homer and Jethro]
"The First Nashville Guitar Quartet" (RCA Victor)(1979)
"Country—After All These Years" (RCA Victor)(1981)
"Collector Series" (RCA Victor)(1985)
"Neck and Neck" (Columbia)(1990) [With Mark Knopfler]
"Sneakin' Around" (Columbia)(1992) [With Jerry Reed]

RAY "DUCK" ATKINS

(Dobro, Guitar)

Given Name:	**Raymond Atkins**
Date of Birth:	**February 19, 1927**
Where Born:	**Erwin, Tennessee**
Married:	**Lois**
Children:	**three sons**

Ray Atkins was one of Country music's few Dobro pickers in the two decades after WWII. He also had a talent for doing Donald Duck imitations that contributed to his commercial potential as a sideman. "Duck" spent much of his career with three groups—Johnnie and Jack, Carl Story and Arthur "Guitar Boogie" Smith. Not satisfied with life as a sideman, Atkins initially took up deejay work, but then went into radio station management and eventually into part ownership.

A native of Erwin, Tennessee, Atkins grew up idolizing Roy Acuff's Dobro player, Bashful Brother Oswald (Pete Kirby). Ray says when he took up the instrument there were only three other Dobro pickers in the business: Oswald, Cliff Carlisle and Speedy Krise.

In 1942, Ray won a talent contest judged by Carl Story, who offered him a job, and a few weeks later, he boarded a bus for Asheville and became a Rambling Mountaineer. Later, the band moved to WNOX Knoxville, where Story got drafted into military service, but Ray remained in Knoxville working for the Morris Brothers and Buster Moore.

Early in 1946, he joined Johnnie and Jack's Tennessee Mountain Boys, who had just moved to WPTF Raleigh. Ray remained with them as they moved to WSM Nashville and KWKH Shreveport. Ray's tenure in Louisiana was frequently interrupted because his wife, Lois, was very unhappy there. This finally led him to quitting in 1951. Atkins recorded with Johnnie and Jack on Apollo, King and on three of their first four Victor sessions, including their biggest hits, *Poison Love* and *Let Your Conscience Be Your Guide*.

Back in Knoxville, Ray re-joined Carl Story's Rambling Mountaineers, staying with him through 1955 and recording on Mercury and Columbia. He remained at WNOX until 1958 as a staff musician when he joined Arthur Smith at WBT Charlotte. He worked there for 8 years, playing daily TV and also doing comedy with a duck-voiced puppet named "Quackerjack." After eight years of this, Ray went into deejay work and in 1968 became part owner of WIXE Monroe, until he retired and sold his share of the station in 1990. He has played relatively little in the last quarter century, but dusted off his Dobro long enough to cut an album for Old Homestead in 1979. Today, Ray and Lois, who had something of a career in music herself, are now retired in Mint Hill, North Carolina. IMT

RECOMMENDED ALBUM:

"Ray Atkins: Early Dobro Stylings" (Old Homestead)(1982)

MIKE AULDRIDGE

(Dobro [6 and 8-string], Guitar, Banjo, Steel Guitar, Lap Steel, Singer, Songwriter)

Given Name:	**Michael Dennis Auldridge**
Date of Birth:	**December 30, 1938**
Where Born:	**Washington, D.C.**
Married:	**Elise Fox (m. 1961)**
Children:	**Laura, Michele**

There are very few masters when it comes to playing the Dobro. The principal players have all become much sought after to enhance the finest and make it even finer. Such players include Josh Graves, Tut Taylor, Jerry Douglas and the redoubtable Mike Auldridge.

Mike was brought up in Kensington, Maryland, and began playing guitar at age 12, banjo at 16 and Dobro when age 17. He made his radio debut in 1954 as part of a local group with his brother Dave. Mike attended the University of Maryland, where he graduated with a B.A. degree in 1967. Initially, he became a commercial artist and was content to play local bookings. He made his professional debut in 1969, when he played with Bill Emerson, Cliff Waldron and the New Shades of Green. Within a year of joining the group,

Mike was being hailed as the most influential Dobro player in Bluegrass since its introduction to the genre by Buck Graves in 1955 with Flatt & Scruggs' Foggy Mountain Boys.

In 1971, Mike became a charter member of the Seldom Scene. However, this did not stop him playing on a wide selection of albums by other acts and also cutting his own albums. In 1972, he recorded the critically acclaimed ***Dobro*** for Takoma/Devi. During 1973, Mike worked with the Country Gentlemen as an occasional sideman. The following year, he released another Takoma album, ***Blues & Bluegrass***. During 1976, Mike released his eponymous album for Flying Fish and also appeared on Emmylou Harris' ***Elite Hotel***, the Starland Vocal Band's self-titled album and Jimmy Arnold's ***Rainbow Ridge***. That year, Mike learned to play steel guitar to add to his other instrumental abilities.

The following year, he released ***Old Dog*** and appeared on Jonathan Edwards' ***Sailboat***, Emmylou Harris' ***Luxury Liner*** and Linda Ronstadt's ***Simple Dreams***. In 1979, Mike released a new album, ***Slidin' Smoke***, while Takoma put together his early tracks as ***Critic's Choice***. During 1980, Mike appeared on Linda Ronstadt's ***Mad Love***. In 1982, Mike released ***Eight-String Swing*** on Sugar Hill. This album illustrated the added range that his 8-string Dobro could achieve, utilizing steel guitar licks never before achieved on the Dobro.

In 1989, Mike got together with two other Bluegrass stars, lead singer/mandolinist Lou Reid and longtime Doc Watson associate, bassist T. Michael Coleman. The resultant album, ***High Time***, also featured Alison Krauss on harmony vocals. Mike followed this with his solo album ***Treasures Untold***. That year, Mike was featured on Mary-Chapin Carpenter's ***State of the Heart***.

RECOMMENDED ALBUMS:

"Dobro" (Takoma/Devi)(1972)
"Blues & Bluegrass" (Takoma)(1974)
"Mike Auldridge" (Flying Fish)(1976)
"Old Dog" (Flying Fish)(1977)
"Slidin' Smoke" (Flying Fish)(1978)
"Eight-String Swing" (Sugar Hill)(1982)
"High Time" (Sugar Hill)(1989) [As Auldridge, Reid and Coleman]
"Treasures Untold" (Sugar Hill)(1989)
(See Seldom Scene, The)

AUSTIN

Austin, Texas, unlike Bakersfield, California, never set itself up as an alternative Nashville. Bakersfield became a bastion of hard Country, whereas Austin was to become the home of refugees from Nashville's homogeneous recordings but also, and more importantly, the location where performers who had a more Folk and Rock background could sing songs that owed more to Woody Guthrie and Cisco Houston than Country music's 3 minutes of radio airplay material.

The start of Austin as a music center can be traced back to 1962, when students and musicians such as Janis Ian began playing Country and Folk music. With the arriving theme of "make love, not war," psychedelia made its presence felt with groups that fell afoul of the Texan redneck mentality and wound up driven out or busted. These included Tex-Mex musicians such as Doug Sahm of Sir Douglas Quintet fame.

By the early 70's, a new imagery was coming to Austin in the shape of the songs of Commander Cody, Michael Murphey (then without his middle name, Michael) with his Cosmic Cowboy music, Kinky Friedman and his Texas Jewboys. They sang of the spirit of the Texas that had been evoked in Peter Bogdanovich's movie *The Last Picture Show*. Willie Nelson's return to Austin focused the attention of the media on Austin and it became the spiritual home of Outlaw Country. Nelson noted the young audiences at the Armadillo World Headquarters and let his hair grow, adopting a hippie attitude.

In 1972, Willie's Fourth of July Picnic further directed the media's attention to Austin. It has continued at its own pace to be a place to hear experimental Country, Cosmic Country or whatever name the press decide to pigeonhole Country music that is alternative to Nashville. One label, Dejadisc, is consciously promoting and recording Austin-based artists. These include Butch Hancock, Sarah Elizabeth Campbell, Don McCalister, Jr., Lisa Mednick and Ray Wylie Hubbard. The label's ***Pastures of Plenty: An Austin Celebration of Woody Guthrie*** was recorded live at La Zona Rosa.

BOBBY AUSTIN

(Singer, Songwriter, Guitar, Bass Guitar)

Date of Birth:	**May 5, 1933**
Where Born:	**Wenatchee, Washington**
Married:	**Fern**
Children:	**Linda, Bobby, Jr., Bill, Steve**

The song *Apartment #9* brought Bobby Austin into the public limelight in 1966; and the following year, Tammy Wynette made it her first chart record.

By then, Bobby was a veteran of the business, having begun entertaining at the advanced age of 5 aboard an Oklahoma-bound train. He soon acquired a guitar and started songwriting. His favorite singers early on were Hank Snow and Ernest Tubb and he formed his own band, while still a teenager in Vancouver, Washington, which entertained in the bars.

In 1955, he and his wife and family moved to Los Angeles, where his first job was as a punch press operator, initially in Glendale and then at Lockheed Aircraft in Burbank. He then became a meter reader for the city of Glendale.

His win on an L.A. TV Country music talent show singing *Wabash Cannonball* gained him a $10 wrist watch and provided a career catalyst. He was spotted by a club owner who gave him a job. From there, his reputation spread and soon he and his band were working for more money and getting more experience. He started to record for obscure labels; in 1960 he released the single *Polynesian Baby* for Challenge and garnered some attention in the U.S., particularly Hawaii, as well as in Japan.

The following year, he performed with Wynn Stewart's band in L.A. and then went to Las Vegas to open at the Nashville Nevada. He stayed in Vegas for 6 years, playing the New Frontier, the Lariat, the Eldorado and the Town Hall.

He began playing bass guitar and did some sessions for Buck Owens. This brought him to the attention of Ken Nelson, Capitol Records' famed A & R man. During an Owens session break, Nelson asked Austin to sing and as a result, signed him to the label in 1962. His initial singles through 1962 and 1963 spread the name around but did nothing else. In 1966, he released the aforementioned *Apartment #9* on the Tally label; in fact, it was the last-ever single for the label. The record peaked at No. 21 but was enough for Capitol to pull him back into the fold. The song won the ACM's "Song of the Year" in 1966, an award that went to Bobby, Fuzzy Owen and Johnny Paycheck, the writers. His next release came out on Capitol's cadet label, Tower.

In 1967, he had another hit with his co-written *Cupid's Last Arrow,* which made the Top 60. The year ended with another Top 60 entry, *This Song Is Just for You*. However, there was no consistency with his hit records and it would be two years until he charted again, this time with *For Your Love*, which had been a Pop hit for Ed Townsend over a decade earlier. One of his sides that didn't chart, but should have on the title alone, was *Tommy Jekyll and Linda Hyde*.

He left Capitol in 1970 and two years later emerged on Triune, which released *Knoxville Station*. This was picked up by Atlantic Atco as their first foray into Country music. It reached the Top 40; however, Atlantic didn't pick up his other Triune singles, but did record and release *Forgotten Footprints/Time for One More Dream* in 1973 and this spelled the end of Bobby's chart story.

RECOMMENDED ALBUMS:

"Apartment # 9" (Capitol)(1969)
"Bobby Austin" (Hurrah)
"Bobby Austin" (Syndicate)
"Bobby Austin" (Design)

HAROLD AUSTIN

(Singer, Guitar)

Given Name: Harold Eugene Austin
Date of Birth: August 3, 1944
Where Born: Sharon, Pennsylvania
Married: Judy Hagy
Children: Melissa

Harold Austin ranks along with Jimmy Martin, Del McCoury, Bill Monroe and Ralph Stanley as one of the short list of Bluegrass lead singers of the "high lonesome" variety. He cites three vocalists—Lester Flatt, Jimmy Martin and Bill Monroe—as being the prime influences on his own vocal style, along with the manner in which Carl Story and the Rambling Mountaineers approached Gospel music.

Although born in Pennsylvania, Harold Austin has lived in south central and southeastern Kentucky nearly all of his life. His preferred music has been Bluegrass for as long, too. After high school Harold attended classes at Somerset Community College and also took correspondence courses through a seminary in Louisville to prepare him for the ministry. He was pastoring a church at Walton, Kentucky, and working with a part-time band called the Kentucky Boys in 1972, when Carl Story heard him sing in a local talent contest. Soon afterwards, Carl hired Harold as lead vocalist with the Rambling Mountaineers.

Harold worked for some three years with Story, gaining a reputation as a vocalist of high quality on both solo numbers and in both duets and trios. His voice blended especially well with the leader. His experiences with the Rambling Mountaineers provided Austin an ample opportunity to display his singing prowess on the festival circuit. He also recorded with Carl on such labels as Artco, Jessup, Starday (not released) and a pair of albums for Atteiram, one of which used his own composition *Mother's Last Word* for a title cut.

He quit in the fall of 1975 to form his own group, the First National Bluegrass, a band named with the help of Bill Monroe. Musicians in Harold's group included Art Hatfield, mandolin; Argil Meeks, fiddle; and Gordon Reed, banjo.That same autumn, Harold also had the honor—albeit sad duty—of ministering at Charlie Monroe's funeral.

In 1975, Harold had already cut a solo album, for Carl Queen's Georgia-based label, Atteiram, with the aid of the Story band prior to forming First National Bluegrass. He subsequently cut two more for this label. For a couple of years in the late 1970's the band worked over a fairly wide geographic area, but did most of its playing closer to home during the 1980's.

In 1992, Harold rejoined Carl Story again and worked for him through the festival season. Meanwhile, he has also been serving the Little Cake Christian Church of Dunnville, Kentucky, as minister. He recently reactivated First National Bluegrass and was planning a new album. In 1993, Harold joined forces with the Alabama-based Sullivan Family, another respected Bluegrass group of many years' standing. IMT

RECOMMENDED ALBUMS:

"Kentucky Bluegrass Preacher Man" (Atteiram)(1975)
"Welcome to Kentucky" (Atteiram)(1977)
"He Took Your Place" (Atteiram)

AUSTRALIA, refer LEGARDE TWINS

AUTOHARP AND THE STONEMANS

By Patsy Stoneman

There are a great many things that are taken for granted in our lives; for me, one of those things has been the autoharp. I just accepted the fact that it was part of our heritage and the musical sounds that were heard almost daily in our home throughout our lives was a normal thing, as it had been in my father's and mother's homes. As a child, I would watch my father as he would carefully place his autoharp back into a table he had built to hold his harp at home, and when he would be leaving to record or to play music somewhere, he would put the harp in a case he had built for traveling, a case which would also improve the sound. I guess you could say that it might have been an early version of the resonator that is used on banjos today. That case is now on display at the Country Music Hall of Fame and Museum in Nashville, Tennessee; as well as the finger picks he invented.

I never questioned how he played; the fact he did, was enough for me. Today, scholars describe his style in this manner, and I quote, "Stoneman played the autoharp on his lap, usually on top of a special case he made to give the harp more resonance. He also frequently used an electric pick-up for added volume. His style for melody playing was the standard 'pinch' with the thumb and index finger. Stoneman played below the chord bar assembly and filled in the rhythm with an upward stroke made by the back of the index finger. He had to have a special type of pick made from spring wire in order to make this 'backward' motion of the index finger."

My dad said that as a boy, he had learned to play the autoharp by watching and listening to his aunts, uncles and cousins. Not being able to afford to order his own harp from Sears, he decided he could make one, using parts from an old piano. Although I never saw the original harp, he must have met with some success. Dad's brother Ingram was said to be a fine autoharp player, but he never took it seriously; with Daddy, all his music was a serious matter and it pleased him whenever any of us children would show any sign of carrying on the tradition he held so dear. When he was a boy there wasn't so many forms of entertainment available for children as there was for us as we grew up, so I guess it was natural that not many of his own children would take time to be as interested in the autoharp as he had been as a kid.

As he grew older and his health began to fail, I realized that someone just had to carry on his music. I knew that I could never be as good on the autoharp, jews harp nor guitar as he had been, but I needed to try. I had watched Dad tune the harp by using a D jews harp, so I tried to do the same for years. Those were the times I understood why he always tried to keep us kids from dragging his harp around as we seemed to do with all our other instruments, some of which he had made for us. An autoharp is a very sensitive instrument; I learned that the hard way. Then my nephew Van, Jr. gave me an electronic tuner—how much easier life became! I have often wished that Dad had been able to have all the modern accessories for the autoharp that are available today.

Ernest V. Stoneman began his recording career in September of 1924, and was the first to record using the autoharp, and continued to use it on most all of his recordings until he passed away in June of 1968.

Scholars and autoharp enthusiasts can read all about his career, his life and his family in the recently released book written by Dr. Ivan M. Tribe, Professor of History at the University of Rio Grande, Ohio, and published by University of Illinois Press. The book is titled *The Stonemans, An Appalachian Family and the Music That Shaped Their Lives.*

The technical aspects of the autoharp, its origin and everything pertaining to it can best be discovered by reading *The Autoharp Book,* written by Becky Blackley, and published by i.a.d. Publications, P.O. Box 504, Burbank, California 94005.

And the Music goes on.....

GENE AUTRY

(Singer, Songwriter, Guitar, Industry Executive)
Given Name: **Orvon Gene Autry**
Date of Birth: **September 29,1907**
Where Born: **Tioga, Texas**
Married: **Ina May Spivey**

Gene Autry came to epitomize the Hollywood singing cowboy. With his white hat, trusty horse, Champion, and neatly paired six-shooters, he became an American icon, revolutionized American popular culture and changed the face of Country music. His clear, mellow voice dominated the sound of the music in the 1930's and 1940's and became as recognizable as that of Bing Crosby. He gave Country music a new respectability and middle-class acceptance it had never enjoyed before and showed that it could appeal widely to people all over the world. He was not the first Country crossover artist—Vernon Dalhart has that honor—but he certainly moved Country music into the mainstream of American Pop music and along the way he introduced at least a dozen songs that have become standards.

In fact, Gene Autry had some genuine roots in the actual Old West. The Oklahoma he grew up in was barely a state, just a few years away from being known as "the Indian nations." His mother, Elnora Ozment Autry, taught him to play the guitar and he had learned to sing in his grandfather's church in Tioga, Texas. His first taste of show business came when, as a teenager, he traveled with an outfit called the Fields Brothers Marvelous Medicine Show.

By 1928 he was a brash aspiring singer, but was making his living as a telegrapher for the St. Louis and Frisco Railroad. After being encouraged by the famed humorist Will Rogers, he took one of his free employee passes and traveled to New York to try his luck. There he met two fellow Oklahomans, Johnny and Frankie Marvin, who were successful radio and record stars. The trip was largely unsuccessful.

Autry returned to Tulsa and got a job on KVOO as the Oklahoma Yodeling Cowboy. In 1929, he returned to New York where the Marvins managed to land him a record contract with RCA Victor. By this time Autry had become expert at imitating the blue yodels of Jimmie Rodgers and over the next few years he recorded dozens of songs—largely Rodgers covers—for labels like Gennett, Grey Gull, Velvet Tone and others. (His very first records on RCA included *My Dreaming of You* and *My Alabama Home*, both duets with fellow railroader and frequent singing partner Jimmy Long.)

By 1931, Autry was finding his own style and Art Satherley signed him to a contract with the ARC group of labels. The depth of the Depression was hardly a good time to be starting a career, but several factors helped Gene get the kind of national exposure he needed. One was *The National Barn Dance*, at the time the most popular Country music show in the nation. Also, the station was owned by Sears, Roebuck, which soon began featuring young Gene in the mail-order catalogs that went to every corner and every outhouse in the land. There were special "Gene Autry Round Up Guitars" for $9.98, less case; there were Gene Autry songbooks; and there were entire sections of Gene Autry records, often on Sears' special label Conqueror (a subsidiary of ARC). He also appeared on the *Conqueror Record Time Program,* also on WLS.

By 1934, "Oklahoma's Singing Cowboy," as he was now styled, was one of the most famous singers in the country, with record sales to match. Early best-sellers included *I Left My Gal in the Mountains* (1930), *That Silver-Haired Daddy of Mine* (with Jimmy Long, 1932), *Moonlight and Skies* (1932), *The Yellow Rose of Texas* (with Long, 1933), *The Death of Jimmie Rodgers* (1933) and *There's an Empty Cot in the Bunkhouse Tonight* (1933).

One of the executives at ARC was Herbert Yates, who also controlled a number of film companies that had recently been merged to form Republic Studios. Yates and his partners were trying to find a way to make the studio turn a profit and decided to revive interest in that oldest of Hollywood forms, the Western. One idea was to revive the idea of the singing cowboy hero; Art Satherley began lobbying for his new star, Autry. A singing part in a 1934 Ken Maynard film called *In Old Santa Fe* showed that Autry had real magnetism on camera—some say he stole the show from Maynard—and in 1935, he was cast in a bizarre science-fiction-cowboy serial called *The Phantom Empire*. That too was successful and by the summer of 1935 Gene was hard at work on the back lots grinding out the first of the Saturday afternoon two-reelers that would make his national reputation. In 1935, he managed to finish no fewer than four films in only four months.

His hectic schedule would continue for years and result in an amazing output: over 90 films (see movie section for full listing), a 17-year radio series called *Melody Ranch* and over 300 masters for the ARC-Columbia company between 1931 and 1957. "I knew I could make money as long as I could work," quipped Autry. He worked at songs like Billy Hill's evocative *The Last Round-up* (1934); *Tumbling Tumbleweeds*, the No.1 record for 1935; *Mexicali Rose*, the No.1 Country hit for 1936; Ray Whitley's *Back in the Saddle Again* (1939), which became the theme for *Melody Ranch*; and *You Are My Sunshine*, the No.1 for 1941. In between there were romantic film songs like *When It's Springtime in the Rockies* (1938), *Take Me Back to My Boots and Saddle* (1938) and *South of the Border* (1940) and innocuous songs like *Tweedle-O-Twill* (1942).

In 1942, Gene enlisted in the military, serving in the Army Air Corps, flying as a pilot in North Africa and the Far East. At home, he issued special song folios with photos of him dressed in his uniform.

OKeh and Columbia Records continued to release his records during his absence and between 1944 and 1945, he appeared on the Country chart's Top 10 with *I'm Thinking Tonight of My Blue Eyes* and *I Hang My Head and Cry* (both 1944) and *Gonna Build a Fence Around Texas/Don't Fence Me In, At Mail Call Today* (which stayed at No.1 for 8 weeks)/*I'll be Back, Don't Hang Around Me Anymore* and *Don't Live a Lie/I Want to Be Sure* (all 1945). He returned from the service in late 1945 to find that Roy Rogers was threatening his status as the nation's leading film cowboy. He responded by taking control of many of his production media, forming his own corporation to do films for Columbia, producing (between 1950 and 1965) over 90 television films. He also started his own record company.

He continued to appear on the Country charts with his Columbia recordings and in 1946 and 1947 he scored with *Silver Spurs (On the Golden Stairs), I Wish I Had Never Met Sunshine/You Only Want Me When You're Lonely, Wave to Me My Lady* and *Have I Told You Lately That I Love You/Someday* (all 1946) and *You're Not My Darling Anymore* (1947). He explored the world of children's culture, making children's albums, comic books and even coloring books. Two of his last giant hits were basically children's songs: *Here Comes Santa Claus* (1947), which also became a Top 10 Pop hit and went Gold, then became a hit again the following year and *Rudolph the Red Nosed Reindeer* (1948), a No.1 crossover hit that also went Gold and became a hit in 1950. His other chart hits, which were also major Pop successes, were *Buttons and Bows* (1948), *Peter Cottontail* and the Gold Certified single *Frosty the Snowman* (both 1950). His last Country chart record was *Old Soldiers Never Die*, in 1951.

Autry also acquired a chain of TV and radio stations, opened a music publishing firm, started a hotel chain and even bought a Major

***Gene Autry**, the original singing cowboy*

League Baseball team, the California Angels. In the 1980's he opened a museum devoted to Western culture near Los Angeles and was generally recognized as one of the most financially successful of Country (or Country and Western) singers. Though considered a little too slick for many hard Country purists (he often used a Lawrence Welk style muted trumpet in his arrangements), he had a vast appeal in his day and set the tone for much of the Country music of the 30's and 40's. CKW

RECOMMENDED ALBUMS:

"The Essential Gene Autry,1933-1946" (Columbia/Legacy)
"The Murray Hill Theatre Presents Gene Autry's Melody Ranch Radio Show" (4 albums)(Murray Hill)
"Back in the Saddle Again" (Harmony)(1968)
"South of the Border" (Republic)(1976)
"Gene Autry Cowboy Hall of Fame" (Republic)(1976)
"Gene Autry Live from Madison Square Garden" (Republic)(1976)
"Gene Autry Sings Songs of Faith" (Republic)(1978)
"Gene Autry—50th Anniversary" (double)(Republic)(1978)
"Gene Autry" (Columbia Historic Edition)(1982)

HOYT AXTON

(Singer, Songwriter, Guitar, Piano, Actor)
Date of Birth: March 25, 1938
Where Born: Camanche, Oklahoma

Hoyt Axton once told the writer that he had enjoyed a two-year career that had lasted for 30 years. Not true. Hoyt Axton has had a varied career that continues to provide entertainment to his fans and the general public alike.

He is the son of Mae Boren Axton, who was a teacher of English and drama in Jackson, Florida, when she decided to become a songwriter. One of her songs, *Heartbreak Hotel* became a Presley monster in 1956 and was a major contributing force in the impact of Rock'n'Roll. Hoyt learned traditional ballads from her as a child, but it was Rock'n'Roll that had the most profound effect on him.

He had taken Classical piano lessons as a child, but decided that he preferred Boogie instead. He started to play guitar while still in his teens; however, it was sports that he excelled at. He received several football scholarship offers and was a talented player while at Oklahoma State University. His music was no more to him at that stage than providing entertainment for his college friends.

He left college and entered the Navy, but by the time he had left the service, he found himself drawn more and more towards the blossoming Folk music revival. He did the rounds of the coffee houses and Folk clubs in the San Francisco and Los Angeles areas and he started to build up a following at places like the Troubadour in L.A., but the East Coast folkies considered him too conservative because of his refusal to join causes for the sake of joining them. They also didn't approve of his drinking and fast driving. However, Hoyt is a giver and was a charter member of the Bread and Roses organization founded by Mimi Farina, Joan Baez's sister, for prisoners' care. He has helped to care for three orphans, has done benefits for American Indians in need and was also affiliated with UNICEF.

Hoyt just went about his business, playing and writing. In 1962, *Greenback Dollar*, a song he had co-written with Ken Ramsey, was recorded by the Kingston Trio and became a big hit, although he only earned 1/4 cent per copy. That same year, he was signed to Horizon Records, which released ***The Balladeer*** album. A year later he released ***Thunder 'n Lightnin'*** and in 1964 he completed the trio with ***Saturday's Child.***

During that year, John Kay heard Hoyt play *The Pusher* and was so impressed that when he formed Steppenwolf, it was recorded by them and featured on their eponymous debut album in 1968. It eventually appeared on four of their albums. In addition, it was part of the soundtrack for the movie *Easy Rider*. The band also recorded Hoyt's anti-drug song *Snowblind Friend* in 1971.

In 1964, Hoyt signed to Vee-Jay Records which released no less than five albums during the year: ***Hoyt Axton Explodes***, ***The Best of Hoyt Axton, Greenback Dollar, Saturday's Child*** and ***Thunder 'n Lightnin'***. The next year, he recorded ***Mr. Greenback Dollar*** on Surrey Records. In 1966, he recorded an interesting album for Exodus entitled ***Hoyt Axton Sings Bessie Smith***, an interpretation of the legendary jazz singer's work.

Hoyt opened for Three Dog Night during 1969-1970 and they recorded his song *Joy to the World*, which became a Pop and Country No.1 and was an international hit during 1971, selling over 1 million copies. The group also recorded Hoyt's *Never Been to Spain* which was a Top 10 hit in 1972. During this period, Hoyt recorded ***My Griffin Is Gone*** (1969) for Columbia and ***Joy to the World***, with the Hollywood Living Room Band, and ***Country Anthem*** for Capitol in 1971.

He was still playing concerts around the world; in 1974, he signed to A & M Records. Two of his albums were repackaged and appeared on Vee-Jay while new product was released. In 1974, he released ***Less Than the Song*** and ***Life Machine*** with a couple of very successful singles, *When the Morning Comes* and *Boney Fingers*. Both achieved Top 10 status; the latter featured Linda Ronstadt. In 1975, he produced Commander Cody and His Lost Planet Airmen's successful album, ***Tales from the Ozone,*** and also played on it. His 1975 and 1976 albums were ***Southbound,*** which featured John Hartford and Gail Davies, and ***Fearless***. The 1976 album was dedicated to "Fearless the Wonder Dog," an 18-month-old St. Bernard. Guests on the record included the Ozark Mountain Daredevils and Nicolette Larson, as well as a Soul group, the Miracles, on the Top 20 single *Flash of Fire*. His last album for the label was the 1977 ***Road Songs***, which featured guest artists Linda Ronstadt and Ralph Mooney.That same year, he moved over to MCA Records and recorded the watershed album ***Snowblind Friend.*** The tracks included *You're the Hangnail in My Life (*not his own composition but written by Woody Bowles, now a successful Nashville manager, and Mike Montgomery), *Funeral of the King*, his version of *Never Been to Spain* and his rendition of Townes Van Zandt's *Pancho and Lefty*. Featured guests included Byron Berline and Tanya Tucker, who duetted with him on *You Taught Me How to Cry*. In 1978, he made *Free Sailin'* for MCA and then sailed off to his own Jeremiah label.

In 1979, he shook the world with the single *Della and the Dealer*. It was released on Jeremiah in the States and Young Blood in the U.K. It became one of those rare Country singles to chart in Britain. He followed this up with a Top 20 hit in the U.S., *Rusty Old Halo,* which came from the album of the same name. In 1980-1982 he released the album ***Where Did the Money Go*** (1980), which was followed by the live double album ***Hoyt Axton Live*** in 1981 and ***Pistol Packin' Mama*** in 1982.

Hoyt has also carved out a notable career as an actor, having appeared in many period pieces including the mini-series *Washington* and the movies *The Black Stallion* (1979) and *Gremlins* (1984). He doesn't consider himself an actor; most would say differently. However, he will admit to one major fault (or perhaps virtue): He loves junk food, which probably accounts for his rotundity. Just before he was to appear at the Peterborough Festival in England in 1987, he found that his case of chocolate bars, etc., had been mislaid by the airline. He had to go and find some macadamia nuts or bust. Mae Boren Axton just said to this writer, "tell him to lose weight." How can a nice man be told that?!

RECOMMENDED ALBUMS:
"Joy to the World" (Capitol)(1971)
"Fearless" (A & M)(1976)
"Snowblind Friend" (MCA)(1977)
"Hoyt Axton Live" (double)(Jeremiah)(1981)

B

BAILES BROTHERS, The

KYLE BAILES
(Vocals, Guitar, String Bass)
Given Name: Kyle Bailes
Date of Birth May 7, 1915
Married: Inez
JOHNNIE BAILES
(Vocals, Guitar, Mandolin)
Given Name: John Jacob Bailes
Date of Birth: June 24, 1918
Married: Nita
Date of Death: December, 1989
WALTER BAILES
(Vocals, Songwriter, Guitar, String Bass)
Given Name: Walter Butler Bailes
Date of Birth: January 17, 1920
Married: Frankie
HOMER BAILES
(Vocals, Fiddle, Guitar)
Given Name: Homer Abraham Bailes, Jr.
Date of Birth: May 8, 1922
Married: Mary Margaret
All Born: Kanawha County, West Virginia

The Bailes Brothers made up one of the most popular harmony duets during the middle and later 40's. Although there were four brothers, they seldom all worked together at once, more often performing in combinations of two. Their singing style was characterized by a feeling of deep emotional sincerity termed "Pentecostal" by historian Bill C. Malone. In addition, the brothers produced a large body of original song lyrics. Walter Bailes, in particular, showed keen talent for writing both secular and especially sacred material.

The Bailes Brothers were born and reared north of Charleston, West Virginia. After their minister father died in 1925, their mother, plunged into poverty, experienced a difficult time keeping the family together. But, as Walter, who immortalized her memory in his song *Give Mother My Crown,* says, "she reared her children and steered them in the proper direction." Working at a variety of odd jobs during the Great Depression, the brothers, inspired by the music they heard in churches and on local radio station WOBU (later WCHS) by such musicians as Billy Cox and Buddy Starcher, endeavored to forge careers in Country music. Although they played well, they faced several years of struggle alongside other aspiring singers, including Jimmy Dickens, Red Sovine and Skeets and Dixie (Molly O'Day) Williamson at WCHS Charleston, WPAR Parkersburg, WJLS Beckley, WWVA Wheeling and WHIS Bluefield.

Finally about 1942, Johnnie and Walter worked out a duet which found fan favor at WSAZ Huntington. They gained lasting popularity and added other musicians to their group including bass player Evelyn (Little Evy) Thomas, fiddler Del Heck and for the first time, former *Grand Ole Opry* star Fiddlin' Arthur Smith. When Roy Acuff heard them, he began to persuade *Opry* and WSM executives that the Bailes Brothers would make a hit there. As a result, Johnnie and Walter came to WSM and the *Grand Ole Opry* in October 1944, at which time mandolinist Ernest Ferguson joined them.

They remained in Nashville for a little over two years and in February 1945 began to record for Columbia. Their initial sessions produced such original songs as *Dust on the Bible*, *I've Got My One Way Ticket to the Sky*, *The Drunkard's Grave* and *I Want to Be Loved*, as well as a pair of Jim Anglin classics, *As Long as I Live* and *Searching for a Soldier's Grave*. They added more of their own numbers like *Broken Marriage Vows*, *Everybody Knew the Truth but Me* and *Ashamed to Own the Blessed Savior* to their recordings. By this time, steel guitarist Shot Jackson had joined their group and Homer Bailes, newly released from the service, had replaced Heck, and Ramona Riggins (soon to be Ramona Jones) supplanted Little Evy on bass fiddle.

When their close friend Dean Upson left WSM for KWKH Shreveport, the brothers went along and repeated the pattern of popularity they had established in Nashville. Older brother Kyle became the bass player and Charlie Cope and then Clyde Baum played mandolin, but Ernest Ferguson worked on their April 1947 Columbia session. This resulted in more originals such as *Whiskey Is the Devil* and the beautiful heart song penned by Walter's wife, Frankie, *Oh So Many Years*. In July, Walter dropped out of the group to enter the ministry and Homer Bailes became Johnnie's duet partner. Their final recordings for Columbia that December included more of their own classics, such as *My Heart Echoes*, *Will the Angels Have a Sweetheart* and *Pretty Flowers*.

In April 1948, the Bailes Brothers helped

*The **Bailes Brothers,** who normally played in duets*

found and open the *Louisiana Hayride* at KWKH. By that time, Kyle was concentrating on bookings and Tillman Franks played bass. In May, Ernest Ferguson left to rejoin the West Virginia Home Folks. Although the Baileses made no more recordings, in 1949, they did cut some radio transcription which later appeared on record. The band continued as a top act at KWKH until the end of 1949, when the original act dissolved.

Later versions of the Bailes Brothers nonetheless persisted in Country music. For instance, Homer and Kyle worked as a duet at KARK Little Rock, Arkansas, in the early 50's and later on in Ohio they cut a single for Briar Records. Johnnie and Walter got back together as a Gospel duo on radio in Texas and recorded three sessions for King in 1953. Johnnie also made some solo recordings for Decca. In the 60's, Walter, based in Alabama, made recordings with both Kyle and Homer at different times on the Loyal label. In the early 70's, Johnnie and Homer did a reunion album for Starday.

Since Homer regularly pastored a church in Roanoke, Louisiana and Johnnie managed three radio stations in rural Georgia, they seldom traveled for show dates, but Kyle, Walter and Ernest Ferguson worked churches and occasional festivals from 1977 into the 80's. Walter also preached at numerous revivals in various parts of the eastern USA and toured Holland with the team of A.G. and Kate, whom they subsequently brought to America. Walter and Kyle recorded an album for Old Homestead in 1976 and the following year all four brothers made an album of quartets for the same firm, an older sister, Minnie, joining them on a few cuts. Homer also cut a pair of solo albums and Walter did extensive recording on his own Starlit and White Dove labels (released mostly on cassette). One of his more recent efforts is a tribute song to the *Grand Ole Opry*'s "solemn old judge," George D. Hay. Various Bailes recordings have appeared both on reissue albums and anthologies. IMT

RECOMMENDED ALBUMS:

"Avenue of Prayer" (Audio Lab)(1959)
"Gospel Reunion" (Starday)(1973)
"The Walter Bailes Singers" (Starlit)(1974)
"Early Radio" (Old Homestead)(1975)
"I've Got My One Way Ticket" (Old Homestead)(1976)
"Early Radio Favorites" (Old Homestead)(1977)
"Early Radio Favorites, Vol. II" (Old Homestead)(1977)
"Four Bailes Brothers" (Original)(1978)
"Family Reunion" (Old Homestead)(1979)
"Yesteryears and Today" (White Dove)(1983)

BAILEY BROTHERS, The

CHARLIE BAILEY
(Singer, Songwriter, Mandolin, Guitar)
Date of Birth: February 9, 1916

DANNY BAILEY
(Singer, Songwriter, Guitar)
Date of Birth: December 1, 1919
Both Born: Happy Valley, Tennessee

The Bailey Brothers are among the few traditional brother duets who made the complete transition from Old Time musicians to a full-fledged Bluegrass band. As a radio team, the brothers gained a near legendary status in such locales as WNOX Knoxville, WPTF Raleigh and WWVA Wheeling. Unfortunately, the Baileys never had a really good opportunity to record for a major label in their prime years and the material they did record never had adequate distribution.

They hailed from the community of Happy Valley (later known as Pressmen's Home), in Hawkins County, Tennessee—as did famed politician-fiddlers Alf and Bob Taylor, some two generations earlier. Charlie and Danny came from a large family that had gained local renown for its members' singing abilities. Around 1936, Charlie began singing professionally when he and Charlie Cope (of the Cope Brothers) took an extended tour. After his return, Charlie and Danny formed a duo and soon began harmonizing on local radio stations in Bristol, Johnson City and Kingsport. In 1940, they moved into full-time entertainment with programs on WNOX and WROL Knoxville under the sponsorship of the Cas Walker Super Markets.

They were doing quite well and drawing large crowds to their shows, when Charlie was drafted into the U.S. Army in August 1941. This caused the brothers to miss a Bluebird recording opportunity that fall.

Meanwhile, Danny continued in Knoxville, forming a group known as the Happy Valley Boys, which included the Brewster Brothers. In 1944, they switched over to WSM Nashville and the *Grand Ole Opry*. When the army took the Brewsters, Charlie and Lester Cope came over from Knoxville and worked in Danny's band. Charlie Bailey came back from the war in 1946 and the Copes returned to WNOX.

Dissatisfied with WSM, the Baileys soon left Nashville for Albany, Georgia, where they remained for only a few months before returning to the Cas Walker shows in Knoxville. Here they took on the trappings of a full Bluegrass band with the addition of L. E. White on fiddle, Wiley Birchfield on banjo and Jake Tullock on bass. This quintet of Happy Valley Boys, augmented by Carl Butler on rhythm guitar, cut six sides for Rich-R-Tone in the fall of 1947, including the first recorded versions of J. B. Coates' *The Sweetest Gift* and the Louvins' *Alabama*. Later they did two more sides on Rich-R-Tone.

*Charlie and Danny, the **Bailey Brothers***

In January 1949, Charlie and Danny moved to WPTF Raleigh, North Carolina, where fiddler Clarence "Tater" Tate and banjo picker Hoke Jenkins joined their band. The Baileys started their own Canary label while in Raleigh, recording 9 more sides in the next three years. In January 1952, the brothers relocated to WDBJ Roanoke, Virginia, for three months and then in April they moved to WWVA Wheeling, West Virginia, where their career reached its peak. Don McHan picked banjo for their band at the *Wheeling Jamboree*. In addition, Tullock and Tate remained with the group. Tate once remarked that no group with whom he worked, including Bill Monroe's Blue Grass Boys, could draw crowds like the Baileys.

The northern climate adversely affected Danny's health and after some two years in Wheeling the brothers stopped performing together, except for a few months in Knoxville later in 1954 and again in 1957-1958. Danny remained in Knoxville more or less permanently from 1954, usually working for Cas Walker on radio and TV until the Walker program, *Farm and Home Hour*, ended in mid-1983. Danny's tenor part on the show's theme made an unforgettable impression. Charlie worked briefly at WRVA Richmond and then returned to WWVA, where he initially had a band built around some members of the McCumbee Family of Morgan County, West Virginia and later the Osborne Brothers.

Later, Jimmy Elrod, Chubby Collier and Ray Myers (the Armless Musician) worked in a unit with Charlie until the latter part of 1957. This group cut a few recordings at WWVA and also had a session for the Event label in Maine. After the Bailey Brothers split again in early 1958, Charlie went to Canada and spent six months touring extensively in the Maritime Provinces.

Charlie retired from music in February

1960 and eventually operated an exterminating business in Wilmington, Delaware. In 1970, he and Danny had a reunion concert at the Smithsonian Festival of American Folklife. Twice in the 70's, the Bailey Brothers recorded albums for Rounder, a company which also reissued most of their early Rich-R-Tone and Canary sides. They played at the 1975 old-timer reunion at Fan Fair and at a few other special events, including the 1992 Knoxville World's Fair. After Charlie retired, he moved back to rural east Tennessee, while Danny continues residing in Knoxville. IMT

RECOMMENDED ALBUMS:

Bailey Brothers:

"Have You Forgotten" (Rounder)(1974) [Re-issue of older recordings]

"Take Me Back to Happy Valley" (Rounder)(1975)

"Just as the Sun Went Down" (Rounder)(1980)

"Early Duet Stylings" (Old Homestead)(1981) [1957 and 1970 recordings]

Charlie Bailey:

"Everlasting Joy" (Old Homestead)(1975) [1955 recordings]

DEFORD BAILEY

(Harmonica, Banjo, Guitar, Composer, Singer, Yo-Yo Exponent)

Given Name: DeFord Bailey
Date of Birth: December 14, 1899
Where Born: Bellwood, Tennessee
Married: Ida Lee
Children: DeFord, Jr., Dezoral, Christine
Date of Death: July 2, 1982

Though best remembered as the first black star of the Grand Ole Opry, DeFord Bailey was far more than an obscure historical first or footnote to *Opry* history. In the fifteen years he spent on the *Opry* (1926-1941), he was one of the show's most popular performers and one of the single most influential harmonica players in Country music history. Skilled at playing Blues, Jazz and Old Time music, Bailey amazed generations of fans who saw him on *Opry* tours throughout the South and on the many WSM radio broadcasts.

Like his old friend Uncle Dave Macon, he was a vital link between the older 19th-century rural music and the modern Country styles. Though he left the *Opry* and "retired" before WWII, he did stay active in music and made a comeback of sorts in the 1970's. He even lived long enough to dictate an autobiography and preserve some of his vast, unusual repertoire for folklorists and historians. DeFord grew up in the hill country east of Nashville, in a community where he was surrounded by what he later called "black hillbilly music." His grandfather was a championship fiddler and the "Bailey Band," which included relatives and neighbors, was a regular feature in country fairs in the area. Stricken with polio at age 3, DeFord amused himself during his convalescence learning to play a little harmonica. Though he eventually survived the disease, it left him stunted and frail.

"If I'd been stout," he recalled, "I'd have laid that harp down when I was a boy." Fortunately for the musical world, he did not. Lying in bed, listening to the distant sound of trains, of birds and of coon dogs running through the woods, he became adept at doing careful and subtle imitations with his harp and merging these with the old traditional melodies his relatives played on their fiddles, banjos and mandolins.

In 1918, DeFord moved to Nashville, where he found work at a variety of menial jobs, including being a "houseboy" for wealthy white families. He found time to attend the various theaters in Nashville, where he heard Blues singers like Bessie Smith, Ma Rainey and others, and some of their songs he adapted for his harmonica. By 1925, he had gotten up enough courage to enter a harmonica contest sponsored by and broadcast on Nashville's first radio station (causing the manager to award two prizes, one for the best of "each race"). About this time, too, he got a job working as an elevator operator at the building where WSM radio was located and became friends with Dr. Humphrey Bate, a fellow harp player who led the first string band on the station. At Bate's insistence, WSM manager George D. Hay let Bailey play on the newly formed *Barn Dance* (later to be renamed *Grand Ole Opry*).

DeFord soon became a regular on the show and in 1928 appeared on the air more than any other performer. Record companies got interested in him and in 1927, he recorded for both Columbia (unissued) and Brunswick (eight sides, including his most popular numbers—*Fox Chase*, *Pan American Blues* and *Evening Prayer Blues*, all harmonica solos). The following year, he recorded for Victor at the very first Nashville session, but these records were generally flops and only three sides were even issued. The eleven sides were to constitute Bailey's total recorded output until the modern era; he felt the companies had cheated him and that his real calling was broadcasting and touring for the Opry. (In this respect, he was similar to dozens of other radio artists of the time who were successful and influential without ever having had a hit record.)

When the *Opry* organized its Artist Service Bureau in 1932, Bailey became part of the many tours organized to spotlight the show's artists. He toured with the Delmore Brothers, the Fruit Jar Drinkers, Uncle Dave Macon and later Roy Acuff and Bill Monroe. The tours were at times nerve wracking because many southern towns did not have a "colored" hotel and refused to let DeFord stay in ones used by the regular tour groups. To their credit, many of the *Opry* musicians demanded that Bailey stay with them, or helped him find other accommodations.

Audiences now began to see the harmonica wizard in person and were amazed to see that he was black. The *Opry* management had discouraged him from speaking on the air, so few listeners knew he was black and he tried to ignore the patronizing publicity that dubbed him the show's "mascot." He was always dressed in a sharp suit and stood on a Coke bottle carton, played his harp into a huge megaphone and impressed everyone.

In 1941, he was fired from the *Opry* in a complex dispute arising from the ASCAP-BMI feud; because his record company producers had copyrighted many of his songs with ASCAP and since ASCAP had banned their songs from the radio networks, DeFord was now being told he could no longer play his old favorites, like *John Henry* and *Fox Chase*. Puzzled and confused, he refused to produce "new," non-ASCAP songs and was eventually fired. For years afterwards, Bailey was bitter and refused to have anything to do with the show or its history.

In the late 1960's, he was "rediscovered" by young musicians interested in the Folk revival and he began to play a few concerts and shows. He did not record, however, and refused TV and even motion picture roles. In 1974, at the urging of a young friend named David Morton, he did agree to return to the *Opry* stage for an "Old Timers'Reunion," and in succeeding years made several other appearances. Finally defeated by failing health, he died on July 2, 1982. DeFord Jr., a fine Blues musician, carries on the musical tradition. CKW

RAZZY BAILEY

(Singer, Songwriter, Guitar)

Given Name: Rasie Michael Bailey
Date of Birth: February 14, 1939
Where Born: Five Points, Lafayette, Alabama
Married: Sandra (d. 1993)
Children: Michael, Tammy, twins Jenevra and Jenetta

Razzy Bailey was born to be a performer. He represents a unique blending of Country and Soul and in many ways, he carries the Jimmie Rodgers flame through Blues into Soul into Country.

Raised on a farm in Five Points, Alabama, he received a second-hand guitar from his father, Erastus, who played guitar and banjo and would later co-write songs with him. By the time he was 10, Razzy was recording for B & K records. Interestingly, he has always named his guitars for his mother, Adella.

In school, he joined a string band sponsored by Future Farmers of America organization. He worked on his guitar playing and became adept. When he was 15, the FFA group came in second in a contest held at Auburn University. After graduation, Razzy knew that he wanted to be a professional musician.

He started playing with a Country group in a night club on the road between LaGrange and Columbus, Georgia. After four months, the state closed the highway resulting in the closure of the club. For eighteen months in the early 60's he left off playing music because he couldn't stand Beach Music. He took jobs as a truck driver, insurance salesman and furniture salesman.

In 1966, he wrote a song entitled *9,999,999 Tears* which he took with other songs to Bill Lowery, who was then at Atlantic Records. Lowery liked what he heard, especially that song and arranged a recording session at which the studio musicians included Freddy Weller, Billy Joel and Joe South. The single didn't chart, but it was a start and it gave Razzy the impetus to try again.

In 1968 Razzy put together a trio, Daily Bread. They got a two-week engagement to play a venue in Naples, Florida and it went so well that they stayed for six months. He put out recordings on small labels such as Peach and his own Erastus. In 1972, he formed the Aquarians and in 1974 recorded *I Hate Hate* for MGM, using just his first name.

Joey Masco, who was then working for MGM, liked Razzy's material and when Masco joined RCA, he talked to Dickey Lee about it. In 1976, Dickey cut *9,999,999 Tears* and took it to No.1. That year, he scraped into the Country charts with *Keepin' Rosie Proud of Me* on Erastus. The following year, Dickey recorded another Razzy song, *Peanut Butter*, which Razzy recorded on Capricorn in 1975 as *Mr. Bailey* without success. Now Dickey's recording went to No.1.

In 1978, Razzy signed to RCA and had a Top 10 hit with *What Time Do You Have to Be Back in Heaven*, which stayed on the charts for nearly four months. He followed up with *Tonight She's Gonna Love Me (Like There's No Tomorrow)*, which also went Top 10. The following year, he reached the Top 10 with *If Love Had a Face, I Ain't Got No Business Doin' Business Today* and the Top 5 with *I Can't Get Enough of You*.

Razzy Bailey, the Country star with Soul

His success continued into the 80's with four back-to-back No.1s, *Loving Up a Storm*, *I Keep Coming Back/True Life Country Music* (both 1980), *Friends/Anywhere There's a Jukebox* and *Midnight Mauler* (both 1981). The flip-side of *Midnight Mauler*, *Scratch My Back (and Whisper in My Ear)*, was also a Top 10 entry. He closed out 1981 with another No.1, *She Left Love All Over Me*. Also in 1981, he was named *Billboard's* "Country Singles Artist" of the year.

The following year, Razzy had Top 10 hits with *Everytime You Cross My Mind (You Break My Heart)* and *Love's Gonna Fall Here Tonight* (1982) and then his success level tapered off. *After the Great Depression* (1983) and his version of Wilson Pickett's *In the Midnight Hour* (1983) were his only subsequent Top 20 entries.

In 1984, he signed with MCA and had a Top 30 with the old Eddie Floyd soul hit *Knock on Wood*. Of the remainder of his MCA releases, only his tribute to Jimmie Rodgers, *Old Blue Yodeler*, got into the Top 50. In 1987, he set up his own SOA label (Sounds of America) and the initial three releases all made the basement region of the Country charts. In 1993, ***Razzy Bailey: Fragile, Handle with Care***, his first album in three years, was released on Slammin' Discs/Sony (Canada).

The Country music world was shocked and saddened in 1993, when it was announced that Sandra, Razzy's wife, had taken her own life. Everyone's heart went out to him. Being the true professional he is, he continued to entertain his fans even at such a numbing time.

RECOMMENDED ALBUMS:

"Greatest Hits" (RCA)(1983)
"The Midnight Hour" (RCA)(1984)
"Razzy Bailey: Fragile, Handle with Care" (Slammin' Discs/Sony Canada)(1993)

BAILLIE & THE BOYS

Formed:	**1973**
Original Members:	
Kathie Baillie	**Lead Singer, Guitar, Songwriter**
Michael Bonagura	**Guitar, Vocals, Songwriter**
Alan LeBoeuf	**Bass, Vocals, Actor [left January 1989]**
New Members:	
Lance Hoppen	**Bass, Vocals**
Johnny Pearce	**Bass, Vocals**

In 1968, while still at school, Michael and Alan played together in a band called London Fog. When they went to college, they went their separate ways, Alan to Rutgers and Michael to the University of Delaware. Kathie came into the picture in 1973, when Alan and Michael were playing as a duo. A girlfriend of Kathie's gave Michael her phone number and it was love at first sight—though Michael says it was her Martin guitar that did the trick.

The trio, as it became, toured throughout the northeastern U.S. They worked as studio musicians and backup vocalists in New York with acts such as Talking Heads, the Ramones (!) and Gladys Knight and they recorded jingles for Pepsi-Cola, Burger King and Ford. During 1977, Alan landed the role of Paul McCartney in the Broadway hit musical *Beatlemania*. Also that year, Michael and Kathie became husband and wife.

The band reunited in 1980 and Kathie told the others that they should go to Nashville. Things were hard when they arrived; they had no money and Alan's wife, Linda, was still in New Jersey, where she stayed for a year. However, they were soon noticed and they landed individual songwriting contracts with Colgems-EMI Publishing. Under the name of Michael Brook, Bonagura wrote Marie Osmond's 1987 hit *There's No Stopping Your Heart*.

RCA's President, Joe Galante, spotted them; following an hour-and-a-half-long audition in his office, he signed them and assigned producers Paul Davis and Kyle Lehning to work with them. Kathie and Michael started working with ace songwriter Don Schlitz and together wrote *Oh Heart* (1987), which became a Top 10 hit. This was followed by *He's Letting Go*, which made it into the Top 20. Michael and Craig Bickhardt wrote the third single, *Wilder Days*, which peaked at No. 9. 1987 saw the release of their debut eponymous album. They have sung back-up vocals on nearly every Randy Travis recording. Kathie and Michael have a daughter, Alyssa, and Alan and Linda LeBoeuf have a daughter, Claire.

*Kathie Baillie and Michael Bonagura of **Baillie & the Boys***

Their second album, ***Turn the Tide***, produced by Kyle Lehning, came out in 1988. From this they again made the Top 5 with *Long Shot* and hung around for over six months. During 1989, they had Top 10 hits with *She Deserves You, (I Wish I Had a) Heart of Stone* and *I Can't Turn the Tide*. That year, Alan decided to leave and Baillie and the Boys became a duo. The first album recorded in this format was ***The Lights of Home*** (1990). For the fashion-conscious, it also marked a change of image for Kathie, who became much more street credible. During that year, they achieved one Top 10 record, a remake of *A Fool Such As I*. In 1991, ***The Best of Baillie and the Boys*** appeared with no mention of Alan LeBoeuf on the cd. During this year, they only managed a Top 20 success, *Treat Me Like a Stranger*.

In 1992, they left RCA when the label tried to persuade Kathie to become a solo act.

RECOMMENDED ALBUMS:

"Baillie and the Boys" (RCA Victor)(1987)
"Turn the Tide" (RCA Victor)(1988)
"The Lights of Home" (RCA)(1990)
"The Best of Baillie & the Boys" (RCA)(1991)

BILLY BAKER

(Fiddle, Banjo)
Date of Birth: July 5, 1936
Where Born: Pound, Virginia
Married: Betty
Children: Sarah

If Billy Baker hadn't become a musician, that would have been one of the biggest surprises of all time. His father, Eddie, played guitar and banjo and his mother, Esther, was also a banjo player. One of three children, Billy was encouraged from an early age to learn an instrument and become part of the family band.

By the time he was 4, he played banjo and by 6, he played fiddle. While at school, he played pie suppers with his father while his brother danced. He joined his first band when he was 12 and played with Jack, Hubert and Curtis, the Cook Brothers, on station WNBA out of Norton, Virginia, in 1951. He then joined Porter Church, of the Church Brothers, and played dates with him around Bristol, Virginia.

Billy recorded with Earl Taylor, Jack Cook, Walter Hensley and Boat Whistle McIntyre. In 1960 and 1961, they broadcast over WBMD Baltimore, Maryland. During 1963, he worked with Del McCoury and the Dixie Pals and recorded ***Del McCoury Sings Bluegrass*** on Arhoolie. He played with Bill Monroe's Blue Grass Boys the following year and by 1965, he was with the Golden State Boys on TV in Los Angeles.

Like a lot of pickers of Billy Baker's quality and flexibility, he was always in demand and on the move. By 1966, he had moved to working with Alex Campbell and Olabelle. After them, he returned to Del McCoury and the Dixie Pals, staying with them until 1969. He has lent his skills to the work of Hazel Dickens and Alice Gerrard, Frank Necessary and Al Jones, Jimmy Martin, Smiley Hobbs, Bob Goff, Buzz Busby, Walter Hensley and Cliff Walchon.

In the 70's, he commenced a relationship with John Morris' Old Homestead Records and worked with the Bluegrass Kinsmen from Virginia. Two albums were recorded on the label, ***Fiddle Classics Volume 1 and 2***, featuring Lawrence Lane and the Kentucky Grass and the Bluegrass Kinsmen respectively. During this time, he also did a lot of work with Carl Story, one the foremost Bluegrass Gospel singers.

RECOMMENDED ALBUMS:

"Fiddle Classics Vol. 1 & 2" (Old Homestead)(1979)[Two albums]
"Wise County Special" (Maggard)
"Dobro & Fiddle" (Zap)[One side Billy Baker, other side Kenny Haddock on Dobro (Zap is a subsidiary of Rebel Records/County Sales)]

BUTCH BAKER

(Singer, Songwriter, Guitar)
Date of Birth: October 22, 1958
Where Born: Sweetwater, Tennessee
Married: Suzanna
Children: Beau

Butch sang almost as soon as he could talk. The son of a Methodist circuit-riding preacher in Sevierville, Tennessee, he was 19 months old when he soloed *Precious Lord Take My Hand* in one of his father's churches. He continued this, but he was not only influenced by Gospel music, he also came under the influence of Elvis, Ray Charles, the Everly Brothers, Don Gibson and Red Foley.

He graduated from Tennessee Military Institute at the precocious age of 16 and entered the University of Tennessee at Knoxville. He majored in drama and studied under Ralph Allen, who had written the Broadway hit *Sugar Babies*. However, he found that his musical talents were often utilized and he found himself drifting from acting towards singing.

He made a trip to Nashville during his last semester at university and in the summer of 1979, he made the ultimate sacrifice: he sold his guitar to pay his fare to Nashville. Once there, he worked as a menswear salesman to earn money and sat in with various bands. His appearances at the famed Nashville Palace nightspot were so well received that he was given a nine-week engagement. He formed SRB for the booking and they remained his backing band. Butch started to get work on demo recordings for the legendary songwriters Jerry Foster and Bill Rice, as well as for CBS, Acuff-Rose and other publishers.

He signed a writing deal with Acuff-Rose and came under the guiding hand of Wesley Rose. He used his time well, learning at the feet of the greats, such as Mickey Newbury, Dallas Frazier and Whitey Shafer. In 1984, he was signed to Mercury Records and his first release, *Torture,* featured Emmylou Harris on harmonies. He followed this with the minor chart singles *Burn Georgia Burn* and *Thinking About Leaving* (1984), *That's What Her Memory Is For* and *Your Loving Side* (1986). In 1987 he had lower level entries with his version of Joe South's *Don't It Make You Wanna Go Home* and *I'll Fall in Love Again.* He still hovered around that level with his 1988 single, *Party People*.

Butch made his TV debut on *Hee Haw* and appeared in the TV movie *Country Gold* alongside Loni Anderson. In 1987, he appeared on Hank Williams, Jr.'s recording *Young Country* alongside T. Graham Brown, Steve Earle, Marty Stuart, Highway 101, Dana McVicker and Keith Whitley. The track appeared on Hank's ***Born to Boogie*** album. He had two further low level entries in 1989, with *Our Little Corner* and *Wonderful Tonight*. He duetted with another Mercury newcomer, Daniele Alexander, on the Alexander song *It Wasn't You, It Wasn't Me* in 1990; it reached the Top 40. That year, Butch released his debut album, ***We Will,*** which was produced by Harold Shedd. Since then, he has been released from the label and is busy writing and hoping for a new record deal. He regularly guests on TNN's *Morning Video* program.

RECOMMENDED ALBUM:
"We Will" (Mercury)(1990)

CARROLL BAKER

(Singer, Songwriter)
Given Name: **Carroll Ann Baker**
Date of Birth: **March 4, 1949**
Where Born: **Port Medway, Nova Scotia, Canada**
Married: **John Beaulieu (m. 1968)**
Children: **Candace**

There have been several "blue nosers" (residents of Nova Scotia) who have been successful Country musicians. Hank Snow and Anne Murray come immediately to mind. Carroll Baker is another who has built up a strong reputation in Canada since 1970.

The youngest of 6, she was brought up in a family that liked Country music (her father was an old time fiddler). She didn't. Like any youngster growing up, she was into Rock'n'Roll. When she moved with her family to Ontario, she found that she would hear a Country song and get homesick.

Pushed by her husband, she made her professional debut in 1969. He urged her to join a local bar band in Oakville, Ontario. She got the job but was fired three weeks later because they felt she hadn't progressed enough. However, fate stepped in. She was asked to join a program on a local radio station and in 1970 she was heard by a sculptor, George Petralia, who lived in Thunder Bay. He had just written a song entitled *Mem'ries of Home*. He knew that Carroll was the person who had to record it and he persuaded her to travel there. She went and the song was released on Gaiety.

Carroll worked her hardest to help get the record to radio stations and her growing fan base. She succeeded and it entered the Canadian Country charts, rose to No.14 and stayed there for 26 weeks.

In 1977, at the Juno Awards, she was named Canada's "Top Female Singer." At the awards show, she sang Conway Twitty's *I've Never Been This Far Before*. She stopped the show and shortly after was given her own CBC-TV show, *The Carroll Baker Jamboree*. In addition, she did three specials for CBC. That same year, Ed Preston signed her to RCA Canada and she released three albums for them: ***Carroll Baker***, ***Sweet Sensation*** and ***If It Wasn't for You.***

She became the first Canadian performer to headline a Country music special from the stage of the *Grand Ole Opry* with *Carroll Baker in Nashville* for CBC-TV. In 1977, she made her first appearance at the prestigious Wembley Festival and received such acclaim that she was invited back the following year. In 1979, she capitalized on this by touring the U.K. with Slim Whitman, who was then at the height of his fame in Britain. In 1981, her Excelsior single *Mama What Does Cheatin' Mean* was in the basement of the Country charts.

Ed Preston had left RCA and in 1983, he signed Carroll to his Tembo label. By now her total record sales had topped 1 million. In 1984, Tom Jones cut her song *I'm an Old Rock and Roller (Dancin' to a Different Beat),* which was a lower-level country hit for him. She again had minor success with her 1985 single for the label, *It Always Hurts Like the First Time*. She continues to release extremely good Country records for Tembo. They have all fared well in the Canadian charts, but none have crossed over to the States. In 1989, she headlined for Regent Holiday Tours *Carroll Baker's Country Cruise*, which takes in the Caribbean and presents a Country show on the high seas.

Canadian Country star ***Carroll Baker***

Since 1977, Carroll has garnered a slew of awards. She has won the Big Country Award for "Top Country Female Artist" six times. She has received the Juno Award for "Top Country Music Singer" three times. Big Country Awards in 1978 named her "Entertainer of the Year." She has won the RPM Programmer Award as "Top Country Female Artist" three times. Her album ***20 Country Classics*** (Tee Vee Records) went Platinum in 1978 and ***Carroll Baker*** (Excelsior) did the same in 1979. She has received two BMI Certificates of Honor for songwriting.

In 1980, RPM *Music Weekly* reported that Carroll had achieved 11 consecutive singles at No.1 on the Country Music Popularity Charts in Canada. That represented the period 1975-1980. She was the first recipient of the CCMA's C. F. Martin Humanitarian Award in 1991. The following year, she reached the pinnacle when she was inducted into the Canadian Country Music's Hall of Honour. In 1993, she teamed up with the grizzly bear, Jack Scott, for a remake of his old hit *Burning Bridges*.

Carroll is so superstitious that whatever new one comes up, she adds it to the list. However, judging by her success, she must have knocked wood or carried a rabbit's foot.

RECOMMENDED ALBUMS:
"Carroll Baker" (RCA Canada)
"Sweet Sensation" (RCA Canada)
"If It Wasn't for You" (RCA Canada)
"At Home in the Country" (Tembo)
"A Step in the Right Direction" (Tembo)
"Heartbreak into Happiness" (Tembo)
"Carroll Baker's Greatest Hits" (K-Tel)

KENNY BAKER

(Fiddle, Guitar)
Date of Birth: **June 26, 1926**
Where Born: **Jenkins, Kentucky**

To many casual Country and Bluegrass fans, Kenny Baker is best known as the long-time fiddler for Bill Monroe. To many fiddlers and fiddling devotees, however, he is considered to be the most influential fiddle player in modern times. His long series of solo albums for the independent County label have had immeasurable impact on contest fiddling and Bluegrass fiddling across the country. He has introduced dozens of tunes into the modern fiddle repertoire and his driving, complex style has influenced three generations.

Kenny was born and grew up in the east Kentucky coal mining town of Jenkins, a company town set up by the Consolidated Coal Company. Both his father and grandfather were traditional fiddlers, playing tunes like *Forked Deer* and *Billy in the Lowground.* By the time he was 8, young Kenny was trying to play fiddle, but soon became discouraged by his father's critical comments. He turned to guitar and played that until he joined the Navy at the age of 16. There, surrounded by people who were not so used to fiddling of any kind, he took up the instrument again and made his peace with it. After his discharge, he returned to Jenkins, took a job as an 8-dollar-a-day coal loader and played for local dances.

As he began to develop his skills, he began to listen to some of the professional fiddlers on radio and became fascinated with the work of Marion Sumner, "the biggest influence I ever had." Sumner could do traditional mountain tunes, but he was also one of a number of musicians from that area who merged traditional styles with the newer Swing and Pop music. Kenny also discovered the hot fiddle of Jazz musician Stephane Grappelli, partner to Django Reinhardt. (Unknown to Baker, other major fiddlers of the time, including great Nashville session man Tommy Jackson, were also intently studying Reinhardt and Grappelli.)

About 1953 Kenny got a job offer to play with singer Don Gibson, who was just starting to make a name for himself on the *Saturday Night Barn Dance* over WNOX Knoxville. Gibson, as well as some of his other musicians, encouraged Baker's interest in Jazz fiddle and Baker stayed with the band for four years.

During his stint in Knoxville, Kenny had been approached several times by Bluegrass star Bill Monroe about joining the Blue Grass Boys; about the time Gibson moved to Nashville, Kenny decided to try Bluegrass. "It was a big challenge, the change I had to make in my music," he recalled about his switch to Bluegrass. He managed it, though, with Monroe's encouragement, and made his recording debut with the band on December 15, 1957, playing twin fiddle with Dale Potter on a song called *Sally Joe.* A few months later he and Bobby Hicks provided the second fiddle parts for one of Monroe's most popular instrumentals, *Scotland.*

Unfortunately, the late 50's were lean times for Monroe—and for Bluegrass—and Kenny left the band twice to go back and work in the mines. By around 1967, he joined up with Monroe again, this time for a much longer stay. In 1970 he provided the fiddle parts for Monroe's album ***Uncle Pen.*** In the fall of 1967, he recorded his first solo album, for the independent Virginia label County, entitled ***Portrait of a Bluegrass Fiddler*** (released in 1969). This set the tone for a series of seven other solo LP's that followed through the next decade; many of them were recorded informally at motel rooms during festivals. The simple formula—Baker leading a crack Bluegrass band through a dozen original and traditional tunes—worked wonderfully well. Many of Kenny's albums were sold at record tables at festivals and often outsold Monroe's. Among later highlights were ***Kenny Baker Plays Bill Monroe*** (1976), in which he was joined by the Osborne Brothers.

In the 1980's Kenny left Monroe again and spent most of his time working on his farm. He did tours with an all-star group called the Masters as well as working with Josh Graves. In the 1990's he appeared on a series of tours sponsored by the National Council on Traditional Arts, Masters of the Folk Violin. He continued to record prolifically, often in company with other fiddlers like Blaine Sprouse and Bobby Hicks. CKW

RECOMMENDED ALBUMS:

"Portrait of a Bluegrass Fiddler" (County cassette)(1969)
"Frost on the Pumpkin" (County cassette)
"Highlights" (County cassette)
"Indian Springs" (Rounder) [with Blaine Sprouse]
"The Puritan Sessions" (Rebel) [with Josh Graves]

BAKERSFIELD

There was a period in the mid-60's when Bakersfield, California, like Austin, Texas, became a base for performers and writers unhappy with the Nashville scene. Located on the Kern River, in the San Joaquin Valley, it became the home and center of operations for Buck Owens. Out of him came this drive to have a location that offered more authentic Country than that then being offered in Nashville. The town became so associated with Owens that it became known as "Buckersfield."

Following the Dust Bowl period of the 1930's, many Oklahomans had moved west and settled in the area. The inhabitants were more used to the honest-to-goodness Country music experienced in Oklahoma and Texas, and this Owens provided. Among these migrants were Merle Haggard's family; following Merle's release from prison, he returned to Bakersfield. Like Owens, he strove for a harder edge to his Country, and he came under Owens' tutelage. Other performers to settle in the area included Wynn Stewart and Freddy Hart.

Because of Owens' connections and the proximity to Los Angeles, it became inevitable that these performers came to the attention of the head of A & R at Capitol, Ken Nelson, and were signed to the label.

More recently, producer/guitarist Pete Anderson has harked back to Bakersfield for his compilation albums ***A Town South of Bakersfield, Volume 1 and 2.*** Owens has become a mentor to Dwight Yoakam, and Bakersfield again surfaced as the title of their 1988 No.1, *Streets of Bakersfield.* In days when Country music is being further eroded, it can only be hoped that a new breed of performers will emerge from "Nashville West."

DEWEY BALFA/ BALFA BROTHERS, The

Formed: 1967

Original Members:

Dewey Balfa	**Vocals, Fiddle, Harmonica, Accordion, Petit Fer (Triangle), Spoons, Guitar**
Rodney Balfa	**Vocals, Guitar, Harmonica**
Will Balfa	**Second Fiddle**
Harry Balfa	**Accordion**
Burkeman Balfa	**Petit Fer (Triangle), Spoons**
Hadley Fontenot	**Accordion**

Les Freres Balfa were raised in the heart of Cajun country as part of a family of six boys and three girls born to Charles and Euna Balfa. They were born into poverty and a system of sharecropping that penalized all but the landlords. From their father, the boys learned the wealth of Cajun material that they would later put to such good use, for their music is traditional Cajun.

Dewey was early influenced by J.B. Fusilier, Leo Soileau, Harry Choates and Bob Wills as he progressed to being a superb fiddle player. During the 40's, the brothers began playing for the family parties and at local house parties. From there, they started playing in dance halls and would often play at eight dances a week. Hadley Fontenot was farming at the time, so sometimes Dewey (b. March 20, 1927, near Big Mamou, Louisiana [Bayou Grand Louise]/d. June 17, 1992), Will (d. February 6, 1979) and Harry (b. 1931) would play as a string band.

Dewey also performed with both J.Y. Sebastian from Grand Prairie and the Louisiana Rhythmaires under the leadership of Maurice Barzas and Elise Deshotel. In 1951, the brothers made their first recordings, *La Valse de Bon Baurche* and the energetic *Le Two Step de Ville Platte.* The tracks were recorded on a home recording machine and were released on George Khoury's Khoury label as a 78 single.

From the early 50's, Dewey began recording with Nathan Abshire for Khoury, Jay Miller's Kajun and Floyd Soileau's Swallow labels. Among the sides Dewey recorded with Abshire were the successful *La Valse de Holly Beech* and *Shamrock Waltz*.

In 1964, Dewey came to the attention of Ralph Rinzler, the then head of the division of arts and crafts at the Smithsonian Institute in Washington. Rinzler, the friend, mentor and discoverer of many Folk artists, came to Louisiana looking for talent for the Newport Folk Festival. Dewey became a late replacement on the festival, playing guitar with accordionist Gladius Thibodeaux, from around Point Noir, and fiddle player Louis "Vinest" Lejeune. This was the biggest crowd he had played to. He was used to 200 in an audience. Here he was faced with 17,000. However, he did not need to worry. The crowd went wild and wouldn't let the trio off stage. This surprised certain elements, who thought that the Cajuns would be laughed off stage.

Three years later, Dewey returned with Rodney (b. 1934/d. February 6, 1979), Will, daughter Nelda and Hadley Fontenot as the Balfa Brothers. They became emissaries of Cajun music and toured in Europe and appeared at festivals all over the U.S. In 1968, they appeared at Mexico City for the Olympics festival.

Dewey had been nagging Floyd Soileau to record the brothers but Floyd, on his own admission, was somewhat intransigent; for him, "Cajun" meant accordion. However, in 1967, Dewey informed Floyd that the brothers had recorded *La Valse de Bon Baurche* back in 1951; he was suddenly excited. They went in and recorded *La Valse de Bambocheurs (Drunkard's Sorrow Waltz)* with *Indian on a Stomp* as the other side. Soileau was now sold on the traditional sounds of the Balfas. An album, ***Balfa Brothers Play Traditional Cajun Music,*** was released on Swallow. It featured *T'ai Petite et T'ai Meon* and *Lacassine Special.* This album was followed by ***Balfa Brothers Play More Traditional Cajun Music***.

They made their film debut in 1972, when they appeared in and played for the Les Blank movie *Spend It All*, a study of the Cajuns in southwest Louisiana. They brought their music to a new generation, avid to enjoy the traditional sounds of their heritage.That year, they cut an album with Nathan Abshire for Sonet, ***The Cajuns***. They also shared another album with Abshire for Swallow, ***The Good Times Are Killing Me***, from the 1975 documentary of the same name.

However, the Balfas were capable of producing modern Cajun music with their nightclub orchestra. This comprised Dewey, Rod, Nathan Menard on accordion, Dick Richard (fiddle), J. W. Pelsia (steel guitar), Tony Balfa (Rod's son) on bass guitar and Austin Broussard on drums.

In February 1979, tragedy struck the Balfas, as Rod and Will were killed in an auto accident in Avoyelles Parish near Bunkie while visiting family. The following year, Dewey's wife, Hilda, died from trichinosis. Dewey soldiered on with Tony, Dick Richard, Marc Savoy and Ally Young. He continued to use the name "the Balfa Brothers" as he felt that the musicians, while not being blood brothers, were brothers in music.

Swallow released another album on the band, ***The New York Concerts***. Folkways issued a solo album of Dewey's, ***Cajun Fiddle Tunes,*** and Arhoolie released ***Louisiana Cajun Music (Under the Oak Tree)*** which features Dewey with Marc Savoy and D. L. Menard.

Dewey Balfa died in 1992, but the Balfa Brothers carry on his tradition.

RECOMMENDED ALBUMS:

"Balfa Brothers Play Traditional Cajun Music" (Swallow)(1967)
"Balfa Brothers Play More Traditional Cajun Music" (Swallow)
"The Cajuns" (Sonet)(1972)
"The Good Times Are Killing Me" (Swallow)(1975) [With Nathan Abshire]
"The New York Concerts" (Swallow)
"Louisiana Cajun Music (Under The Oak Tree)" (Arhoolie)
"Cajun Fiddle Tunes" (Folkways) [Dewey Balfa solo]

JOHN BALTZELL

(Fiddle, Composer)

Given Name:	**John Leroy Baltzell**
Date of Birth:	**September 23, 1860**
Where Born:	**Knox County, Ohio**
Married:	**Mary Amanda Whitney**
Children:	**Ada, William**
Date of Death:	**1940**

In the earliest years of Country music commercialism, traditional fiddlers received a higher proportion of attention than in later decades. Among the more frequently recorded Old Time fiddlers in those first years was John Baltzell, an aged boilermaker from Mount Vernon, Ohio. The Buckeye State musician recorded some 42 masters over a five-year period beginning in 1923, mostly for Edison. Not only was Baltzell a significant musician in his own right, but he provides an important link between 19th-century minstrel Dan Emmett and the emerging Country music industry.

Born in rural Harrison Township in central Ohio, Baltzell, the child of a shoemaker, began honing his skills on a cornstalk fiddle, but soon obtained a real one in a trade with a neighbor. From his youth into old age, he played regularly for dances and other community gatherings when asked. In 1888 John married, moved to the town of Mount Vernon and found work as a boilermaker at the Pennsylvania Railroad roundhouse and repair shops. That same year, the elderly Dan Emmett, fiddler and minstrel show pioneer, retired to his boyhood home and the two became friends and musical associates until Emmett's death in 1904.

John Baltzell's activity and fame as an Old Time fiddler remained pretty much confined to Knox County until 1922, when he won an Ohio state fiddling championship, following up with equally impressive victories in Kentucky and Indiana. He began playing regularly on WEAO radio in Columbus and also fiddled with less frequency on stations in Cleveland. At WLW Cincinnati, he won a $200 fiddle as the most popular fiddler at the station. Having retired from the railroad in 1925, he had more time to compete in contests and attracted nearly as much attention as more elderly competitors like Maine's Mellie Dunham and Tennessee's Uncle Jimmy Thompson.

John Baltzell made his initial recordings on September 7, 1923, for Edison in New York, cutting six tunes. Later, he also did sessions for OKeh, Plaza, and Victor, none of which were released. His last studio trip, in April 1928, was, like the first, for Edison. Overall, of the 42 masters cut, 32 were released, more than those of the other early artists of strictly fiddle tunes. His repertoire included tunes similar to those of Southern fiddlers, such as *Turkey in the Straw*, *Arkansas Traveler* and *Sailor's Hornpipe*. Others are more atypical, including *Flowers of Edinburgh Hornpipe*, *Electric Light Schottische* and *Tramp Waltz*. His tunes also consisted of those of his own composition, often with titles reflecting his Knox County environment, such as *Clinton Quadrille*, *Kenyon Clog*, *Ginger Ridge Quadrille* and *John Baltzell's Reel*.

From 1929, Baltzell's fame as a fiddler waned. With the advent of the Great Depression, he made no more recordings and his radio appearances ended. John then officially retired, except for playing around home with friends until his death at age 80. Unfortunately, none of his numbers have been re-issued. IMT

Bama Band refer HANK WILLIAMS, JR.

BANDANA

Formed:	**1981**
Original Members:	
Lon Wilson	**Drums, Lead Vocals**
Jerry Fox	**Bass Guitar**
Tim Menzies	**Guitar**
Joe Van Dyke	**Guitar**
Jerry Ray Johnston	**Drums, Lead Vocals**

Newer Members:

Michael Black	**Guitar**
Billy Kemp	**Guitar**
Bob Mummert	**Drums**

In the wake of Alabama's success at the beginning of the 80's, groups started to find themselves in favor. Bandana for a while enjoyed success, in the middle of that decade, through their recordings on Warner Brothers Records.

Lon Wilson and Jerry Fox met at an audition in 1980, found that they were sympathetic and decided to work together as a rhythm section for hire. They worked the clubs and developed their musical ideas. Central to their partnership was their collaboration as writers, with Lon taking on the role of lead singer.

Lon grew up in Monroe, Louisiana, learned to play drums and joined a local band. During his days at Northeast University, where he majored in marketing, he played in a Jazz group for some four years. He worked as a bank teller and also as a men's clothing salesman while playing music in his free time.

Jerry grew up in Hobart, Oklahoma, where his family owned a radio station. By the time he was 11, he was a full-time deejay on the station (outside school hours), forming his first band when he was 16. After graduating from Boston University with a degree in public relations, he worked as a news reporter and deejay and was Program Director at several New England radio stations. In 1978, he moved to Nashville to play bass guitar for Charly McClain.

In 1981, Lon and Jerry decided it was time to make a positive decision on their joint career. A diamond ring was pawned for $400, and with the money they hired a studio to record six of their jointly written songs. The response was good. First, Nashville publishers started to get interested and then the music reached Frank Jones, who was head of Warner Brothers, Nashville Division. He signed them; they brought in Tim Menzies, Joe Van Dyke and Jerry Ray Johnson and became Bandana.

Their first single, *Guilty Eyes,* was released in 1982 and reached the No. 37 spot on the Country chart. The follow-up record, *Cheatin' State of Mind,* only reached a lower-level position. *The Killin' Kind,* later in the year, attained Top 20 status. The group was nominated by the ACM as "Vocal Group of the Year." The following year they had two more hit singles: *Can't Get Over You (Gettin' Over Me)* and *Outside Lookin' In*. The latter reached No.13 on the Pop chart. *Billboard* voted Bandana one of the top five finalists in its "Talent in Action" awards and *Cash Box* included the band in its top five "Radio Programmers' Choice" awards.

In 1985, they released their eponymous album. It was co-produced by master producer Jim Ed Norman. From this came further middle-order hits, *Better Our Hearts Should Bend (Than Break)* (Top 30), *Just Another Heartache* and *Lovin' Up a Storm*. Their first chart single of 1986 was *Touch Me,* which Lonnie produced with Barry Beckett. They made a video of this song. However, major success eluded them. By 1986, Wilson and Fox had lost the other three members: Michael Black and Billy Kemp had come in on guitars and Bob Mummert on drums.

They toured until September, 1987, and then broke up. Jerry Fox left the business to become a realtor; in 1994, he formed the Fox Management Group, in Nashville. Lonnie (as he is now styled) Wilson has subsequently become an in demand Nashville session drummer and a successful songwriter signed to Zomba Music. His cuts include *There Goes My Heart Again* by Holly Dunn (1989) and *A New Way to Light Up an Old Flame* which was recorded by Joe Diffie in 1991.

RECOMMENDED ALBUM:

"Bandana" (Warner Brothers)(1985)

***Bandana**, led by Lonnie Wilson and Jerry Fox*

MOE BANDY

(Singer, Guitar)

Given Name:	**Marion Bandy**
Date of Birth:	**12 February 1944**
Where Born:	**Meridian, Mississippi**
Married:	**Margaret**
Children:	**three**

Meridian is the birth place of Jimmie Rodgers, and Moe Bandy's grandfather worked with the great man on the railroads. During his early years, Moe (nicknamed by his father) heard a lot of his grandfather's collection of records by the "Father of Country Blues" and Hank Williams. Moe was one of six children of a guitar-making father and a piano player mother.

In 1950, the family moved to San Antonio, where his father put together a Country band, the Mission City Cowboys. While at high school, Moe started rodeo performing, but later gave this up, having broken too many bones. However, in 1975, he was given the "Texas Entertainer of the Year Award" by the Rodeo Cowboys Association.

After leaving school, he became a sheet metal worker by day and a Country singer by night, clocking up over 70 hours per week. In 1964, Satin Records released his self-penned *Lonely Lady* without success. He formed his backing group, the Mavericks, in 1974, and he became a regular performer on San Antonio's TV show *Country Corner*. The group also backed other performers, including Bob Wills and Loretta Lynn.

During a hunting trip in 1972, Moe met producer Ray Baker and persuaded him to listen to some tapes that he had made. Baker agreed to produce him if Moe found the money to pay for the session. Moe pawned his furniture, but nothing happened with the records. In 1973, Moe took out a loan to pay for a session and recorded *I Just Started Hatin' Cheatin' Songs Today*. Baker released it on Footprint Records and pressed 500 copies. The record started to happen, was picked up by GRC and charted nationally, becoming a Top 20 hit, but Moe kept on as a sheet metal worker.

A succession of hits followed on GRC: *Honky Tonk Amnesia;* the Top 10 hit *It Was So Easy to Find an Unhappy Woman* (both 1974); *Doesn't Anyone Make Love at Home Anymore?*; and the Top 10 Whitey Shafer/Lefty Frizzell song *Bandy the Rodeo Clown* (both 1975).

In 1975, he signed to Columbia Records, with Baker still producing. He had immediate success with the Top 3 single *Hank Williams You Wrote My Life,* from the album of the same name. The same year he was named "Most Promising Male Vocalist" by the Academy of Country Music. In 1976, he had hits with *The Biggest Airport in the World, Here I Am Drunk Again* and *She Took More Than Her Share*. The hits continued through 1977 and 1978. There was *I'm Sorry for You My Friend* (Top 10), *Cowboys Aren't Supposed to Cry* and *She Just Loved the Cheatin' Out of Me* (1977); *Soft Lights and Country Music, That's What Makes the Jukebox Play* and the Top 10 *Two Lonely People* (1978).

In 1979, he duetted with Janie Fricke on the Top 3 release *It's a Cheatin' Situation* and it won ACM's "Song of the Year" (1980). In 1979, he also had Top 10 success with *Barstool Mountain* and the No.1 *I Cheated Me Right Out of Her*. The same year, he got together with Joe Stampley to form those good ol' boys, Moe and Joe. They chalked up some great chauvinist songs including the No.1 *Just Good Ol' Boys*, the Top 10 *Holding the Bag* (1979) and *Tell Ole I Ain't Here, He Better Get on Home* (1980), all coming from their highly successful album ***Just Good Ole Boys***. In 1980, they were made ACM "Duo of the Year" and CMA "Duet of the Year"; they repeated the ACM award in 1981.

During 1980, Moe had hits with *One of a Kind, The Champ* and back-to-back Top 10 successes *Yesterday Once More* and a duet with Judy Bailey, *Following the Feeling*. In 1981, Moe charted with duet hits with Joe, *Hey Moe Hey Joe* (Top 10) and *Honky Tonk Queen,* and two solo hits, *My Woman Loves the Devil Out of Me* and the Top 10 *Rodeo Romeo*. The following year he scored with *Somebody Soon* and the Top 5 hit *She's Not Really Cheatin' (She's Just Gettin' Even)* and closed out the year with *Only If There Is Another You.* He started off 1983 with *Only If There Is Another You* and *I Still Love You in the Same Ol' Way*; then his 1983 album, ***Devoted to Your Memory***, spawned the Top 10 duet *Let's Get Over Them Together,* with Becky Hobbs, and contained *Don't Sing Me No Songs About Texas*, with Merle Haggard. In 1984, he and Joe rocked Country music with the camp *Where's the Dress,* which so incensed Boy George's management that they sued. It seems that others felt differently; the video of the record won the 1984 award as "Best Country Video" from the New York Film Festival and the America Video Awards. That year, his only sizable solo hit was *Woman Your Love*.

In 1986, in front of a packed crowd of 51,000 fans at the Central State University Stadium in Edmond, Oklahoma, Moe signed a new recording deal with MCA/Curb Records. With this move he changed producers: gone was long-time associate Ray Baker and in came Jerry Kennedy. From here on in, his solo work seems smoother. Gone is the Honky Tonk sound of the mid-70's. That was retained for his work with Joe Stampley.

Despite that, Moe turned out hits for his new label with the same frequency, but less successfully than before. From the 1987 album, ***You Haven't Heard the Last of Me***, he had a Top 10 with *Till I'm Too Old to Die Young*. The 1988 album on Curb, ***No Regrets***, created two more Bandy hits, the patriotic Top 10 *Americana* and *I Just Can't Say No to You. Americana* was used by George Bush as his presidential theme song. Moe was invited to play at the Presidential Inauguration and was invited back to the White House twice more the next year. 1989 produced another duet with Becky Hobbs, *Pardon Me (Haven't We Loved Somewhere Before),* but it didn't chart and the album, ***Many Mansions,*** also on Curb, marked another step away from the full-bodied Honky Tonk sound towards a very nice but bland, safe sound.

Moe Bandy should be up there with the Straits and Sheltons. He is still one of the best Honky Tonk singers around. He is truly in the tradition of Lefty Frizzell. It is only when you listen to his albums with Joe Stampley that you hear what should be. He was once dubbed by a New York critic the "Jesus Christ of Country." That wasn't because of his looks, but because he sang of real life—the cheating, drinking and making up of life.

In 1991, Moe opened the 900-seater Moe Bandy Americana Theatre in Branson, Missouri, in which he performs with his Americana Band. He lists golf as his interest and he is very involved with the Children's Transplant Association of Texas; his annual Celebrity Golf Tournament each November benefits that organization.

Moe Bandy *at Wembley Festival, England*

RECOMMENDED ALBUMS:

"The Best of Moe Bandy Volume 1" (Columbia) [Contains his GRC recordings]
"Just Good Ol' Boys" (Columbia)(1980) [With Joe Stampley]
"She's Not Really Cheatin' (She's Just Gettin' Even)" (Columbia)(1981)
"Devoted to Your Memory" (Columbia)(1983)
"Hey Moe, Hey Joe" (Columbia)(1984) [With Joe Stampley]
"You Haven't Heard the Last of Me" (MCA/Curb)(1987)

R. C. BANNON

(Singer, Songwriter, Guitar)

Given Name:	**Daniel Shipley**
Date of Birth:	**May 2, 1945**
Where Born:	**Dallas, Texas**
Married:	**Louise Mandrell (m. 1979; div. 1991)**

R.C. Bannon is a singer/songwriter who has not as yet had the success that early signs indicated. Like so many Country performers, he started out singing in church (Pentecostal) when he was 4 years of age. He took part in Gospel and hymn singing as he grew older and by the time he was in high school he was also a promising guitarist.

During the late 50's and 60's, he organized several Rock and Soul bands. He moved with his family to Seattle in the mid-60's and began performing in local clubs as well as singing "the song of the hour" on a local TV show, while deejaying became his main source of income. After five years, he decided to try performing as a career. He moved to Southern California and Las Vegas and in 1973, joined Marty Robbins' band, touring around the States. Marty encouraged him to move to Nashville, but R.C. felt that he wasn't ready and went back to Los Angeles. The following year, he cut a single for Capitol, *Freedom/I Don't Want to Play Games,* which didn't make the charts.

In 1976, he finally heeded Marty's words and came to Nashville, initially working at Smuggler's Inn as a disco deejay. A meeting with songwriter Harlan Sanders led to R.C. being signed as a writer with Warner Brothers

Singer and Songwriter ***R.C. Bannon***

Music at the end of that year. The following year, he signed with Columbia Records and his first pair of singles scraped into the Country charts. The third single was a remake of Paul Anka's *It Doesn't Matter Any More,* which had been the first posthumous hit for Buddy Holly in 1959. R.C.'s version reached just under the 30 mark. During the summer, he had met Louise Mandrell at Fan Fair and they were now making wedding plans.

The next two singles, in 1978, peaked around the No. 60 level. During that year, his songs started to get cut with greater frequency. Ronnie Milsap recorded *Only One Love in My Life,* which R.C. had written with John Bettis, and then Bobby G. Rice recorded *The Softest Touch in Town,* which was written by R.C., Harlan Sanders and Kent Westberry. In 1979, the year he and Louise married, they scored with two duets on Epic: *I Thought You'd Never Ask,* which went Top 50, and their version of Peaches & Herb's Disco hit *Reunited,* which climbed to No.13. He followed this with the solo *Winners and Losers,* which reached the Top 30.

During the next year, Bannon had a Top 40 success with *Never Be Anyone Else But You,* which had been a pop smash for Ricky Nelson over 20 years earlier.

In 1981, R.C. and Louise signed with RCA and had a Top 40 hit with *Where There's Smoke There's Fire,* which came from their 1982 album, ***Me and My RC*** (with a play on the sleeve upon the soft-drink brand). This was mainly a duet album with two solo tracks apiece from the artists. Later in the year, they recorded a second album, ***You're My Superwoman, You're My Incredible Man*** but still the major hit eluded him.

Six of R.C.'s songs (mostly co-written with John Bettis) appeared on Louise's ***Too Hot to Sleep*** album in 1983, including the title track, which went Top 10. The following year, Louise's album ***I'm Not Through Loving You Yet*** contained five Bannon songs. In 1984, Gus Hardin cut his *Are We Still in Love or Just Lonely*.

Louise's Bannon-produced 1985 album, ***Maybe My Baby***, had two of R.C.'s songs on it, including the Top 10 hit *I Wanna Say Yes*. In 1991, R.C. and Louise went their separate ways, although he is still involved in a musical capacity with Barbara Mandrell's show.

RECOMMENDED ALBUMS:

"R.C. Bannon Arrives" (Columbia)(1978)
"Inseparable" (Epic)(1979) [With Louise Mandrell]
"Love Won't Let Us Go" (Epic)(1980) [With Louise Mandrell]
"Me and My RC" (RCA)(1982) [With Louise Mandrell]
"You're My Superwoman, You're My Incredible Man" (RCA)(1982) [With Louise Mandrell]
"Best of Louise Mandrell and R.C. Bannon" (RCA)(1983)

AVA BARBER

(Singer, Piano)
Date of Birth: **June 28, 1954**
Where Born: **Knoxville, Tennessee**
Married: **Roger**

Statuesque Ava Barber made her professional debut at age 10. By the time she was 15, she had become a cast member on the *Bonnie Lou and Buster* show, a syndicated TV series seen on 20 stations around the country. Because of her popularity on the show, other work came in; she performed locally at clubs and barn dances and released her debut single, *Atlanta*, on the Dogwood label.

In 1973, her mother encouraged her to try and further her career by writing to Lawrence Welk, the famed band leader, and sending details of some of her work. She did not expect to hear back from him, but several months later, she received a favorable reply when Lawrence Welk came to Nashville in August to play in a golf tournament. Ava went to see him and he auditioned her there and then in a tent that contained a piano. Afterwards, he told her that he had a Country show coming up and she would be perfect for it.

Recently married, Ava and her band drummer husband moved to Los Angeles, where she joined the *Lawrence Welk Show* in 1974 and stayed as a regular Country vocalist until 1982. She traveled with the Lawrence Welk touring show, and appeared during the late 70's on the WWVA *Jamboree* at Wheeling, West Virginia. From 1975, she was headlining in major Nevada hotels and appearing usually at Harrah's club at Lake Tahoe. That same year, she guested on *That Good Ole Nashville Music Show, Pop Goes Country* and then was featured on *Hee Haw* in 1978. She also did two guest appearances on the *Grand Ole Opry* in 1978 and 1979. In addition, she toured the U.S. and Canada at fairs and concerts and

The beautiful ***Ava Barber***

traveled to Germany, where she did 13 days in 1978 playing a Country show on military bases.

She signed to Ranwood Records in 1976, and had several chart singles. Her first three, in 1977, were *Waitin' at the End of Your Run, Your Love Is My Refuge and Don't Take My Sunshine Away*. Her highest-placed hit came in 1978; it was a Top 15 success, Gail Davies' *Bucket to the South,* which was followed by *You're Gonna Love, Love* and *Healin'*. She changed labels in 1981, to Oak, and had a chart placing with *I Think I Could Love You Better Than She Did.*

While working on the Welk show, she met Dick Dale and when the Welk show finished, they worked and toured together. During 1988, Ava recorded a single for KMI entitled *I Don't Want to Hurt That Way Ever Again,* without success. At that time, she was appearing on the *Smoky Mountain Hayride Show* in Pigeon Forge, Tennessee. In 1990, Ava and Dick opened the Rainbow Music Theater in Pigeon Forge, where she still performs. JAB

RECOMMENDED ALBUMS:

"Country as Grits" (Ranwood)(1977)
"You're Gonna Love, Love" (Ranwood)(1978)

GLENN BARBER

(Singer, Songwriter, Guitar, Dobro, 5-String Banjo, String Bass, Steel Guitar, Drums)
Given Name: **Martin Glenn Barber**
Date of Birth: **February 2, 1935**
Where Born: **Hollis, Oklahoma**
Married: **Betty Ann (m. October 1952)**
Children: **Glenn, Jr.**

During the 70's, Glenn Barber looked like he was going to be a major star. However, despite having 21 charted singles, he never reached the upper echelons.

Raised in Pasadena, Texas, Glenn started to play guitar at age 6 and has become one of the finest pickers in Texas. As he started to make his way in the music business, he was a constant winner of talent contests and had a band while in high school. At age 16, he cut his first single, *Ring Around the Moon*, for "Pappy" Dailey's Stampede label. Dailey would be very much involved in Glenn's career and managed him for 10 years through the 60's and 70's. During 1958, he cut *Hello Sadness/Same Old Fool Tomorrow* for the D label.

From 1962-1968 he was a deejay on station KIKK Houston and with his band the Western Swingmasters had a five-times-a-week show. It was not until 1964 that he first saw chart action when *How Can I Forget You* on Sims made the Top 50. He then signed to Starday and his debut single for the label was a double-sided hit, *If Anyone Can Show Cause/Stronger Than Dirt*; the flip-side made the Top 30. He stayed with Starday until 1966, but no more hits ensued. Through Dailey, he released product on United Artists in 1967, including *Most Beautiful, Most Popular, Most Likely to Succeed,* which narrowly missed the charts. He then went on to record the self-penned *You Can't Get Here from There* for Skill Records, which would later be recorded by Freddy Fender.

In 1968, he signed to Hickory and was with them until 1974, during which time he had four records make the Top 30: *Kissed by the Rain, Warmed by the Sun* (1969), *She Cheats on Me* (1970), *I'm the Man on Susie's Mind* and *Unexpected Goodbye* (both 1972). In 1969, he made his debut on the *Grand Ole Opry* and although he never became a member, he has made several appearances.

Glenn was absent from the charts between 1974 and 1977 and then had a couple of low-level entries on Groovy in 1977 and 1978. He scored in a big way on Century 21 with two Top 30 successes through 1978 and 1979, *What's the Name of That Song* and *Love Songs Just for You*. By the end of 1979, he had moved on to MMI and had a pair of low-level entries. One of these was the aptly prophetic *Everybody Wants to Disco*. By 1980, he was on Sunbird and then he was on his travels again with short stays at Tudor in 1983 and 1984 and Brylen at the end of 1984.

Glenn Barber is a creative man. As well as having musical skills, he is also an able carpenter (like his father) and built Orbit recording studio in the 70's with the help of his son. He is also a fine portrait painter who's sold many of his canvases and has now moved into murals. However, he also has one talent that is fun. He gets someone in the audience to suggest a theme for a song and he makes one up on the spot.

Glenn is still active in the 90's. He has been writing movie scripts; one of them, *Songs for Love,* which has attached to it a dozen Barber songs, is looking for production. He is also writing Gospel music of the more down-to-earth variety and an album is forthcoming soon. His song *She Cheats on Me* has been recorded by Mickey Gilley, Sue Thompson, Don Gibson, Ferlin Husky and Roy Orbison.

RECOMMENDED ALBUMS:

"Best of Glenn Barber" (Hickory)(1972)
"Glenn Barber" (MGM/Hickory)(1974)
"First Love Feelings" (Tudor)(1983)
"Saturday's Heroes Are Gone" (Tudor)(1984)
"Most Wanted Man from Tennessee" (Brylen)(1984)

FIDDLIN' BURK BARBOUR

(Fiddle)
Date of Birth: **July 20, 1910**
Where Born: **Pittsylvania County, Virginia**

Burk Barbour is yet one more example of a musician who was a child prodigy. He started playing fiddle when he was 8 years old and was winning music awards from the age of 12. A year later, he moved to Lynchburg, Virginia, where he played on various stations, especially Tri-County Network, which took in stations in Lynchburg, Danville and Roanoke.

During 1936, he played at various fiddlers' conventions including the White Top Mountain Festival. He performed with his group the Southern Serenaders and played radio stations as far away as WJJD Chicago. Here he made radio transcriptions using the name the Hired Hands.

From 1944 to 1946, Burk played fiddle with Lynn Davis and Molly O'Day and the Cumberland Mountain Folks in Beckley, Dallas and Knoxville while Skeets Williamson was in the service; he also made radio transcriptions with them.

While with the group, he also did some session work. He worked on the Bill and Cliff Carlisle session in 1945, which produced their hit record *Rainbow at Midnight*. He played again with Cliff Carlisle at RCA, when Carlisle and his group, the Buckeye Boys, recorded *The Devil's Train* and *Death by the Roadside.* When Skeets Williamson returned, Barbour continued with the the Cumberland Mountain Folks and they enjoyed the luxury of twin fiddles. Then he left the band and with Jim Eanes, Joe Johnson and Happy Bobbitt formed the Blue Mountain Boys. For the next nine months, they played WBDB in Galax and WNOX Knoxville. The band cut 32 sides for the National Record Company of New York, but only one record was released.

Shortly afterwards, he formed the Smiling

*Virginia's own **Fiddlin' Burk Barbour***

Mountain Boys, whose members included the Lilly Brothers, Lonnie Glosson and Paul Taylor. Like their predecessors, they also worked at WNOX. After about a year, Burk Barbour joined Homer & Jethro and played fiddle for them. He also worked a little with Archie Campbell but in 1948, he decided to quit being on the road and returned to Lynchburg and became a crane operator for Glamorgan.

In the early 70's he again became active and started recording again. He had albums of fiddle tunes released on Kanawha and Princess and recorded three albums with Jake and Fennie and the Hearts of Gold. In addition, he played on banjo player Troy Brammer's Dominion album, ***Bluegrass Western Swing Style***. Brammer reciprocated by playing on one of Burk's releases.

In 1985, he was still playing fiddle with Bill and Mary Reid on WLVA-TV when it commenced broadcasting. He now plays in a band called the Old Timers.

RECOMMENDED ALBUMS:

"Blue Ridge Mountain Music" (Kanawha)
"The Champ" (Princess)

BOBBY BARE

(Singer, Songwriter, Guitar)
Given Name: **Robert Joseph Bare**
Date of Birth: **April 7, 1935**
Where Born: **Ironton, Ohio**
Married: **Jeannie**
Children: **Bobby, Jr., Cari Jean (d. 1976), Sharon**

Bobby's start in life was far from easy. When he was 5 his mother died, and the family split up when his father was unable to earn sufficient to feed and clothe them. Bare's sister was put up for adoption. By the time he was 15, he was a farm worker and this was followed by a spell working in a clothing factory and selling ice cream. He built his first guitar and played for little or no money with a local Country band in Springfield, Ohio.

He moved to Los Angeles and in 1958 he recorded, under the name of Bill Parsons, a self-penned song entitled *The All American Boy,* which was an updated talking Blues. He got no interest in the song until Ohio-based Fraternity Records picked it up for an outright fee of $50, including the publishing rights. Fraternity released the single in 1959 and it became the second-largest seller in the States during December of that year, reaching the Top 3 on the Pop chart. In the U.K., it was released on the umbrella London label and reached No. 22.

But the fates stepped in: Bobby was drafted, and to add insult to injury, while he was serving his country, the label put another singer on the road as "Bill Parsons." On release from the service, he roomed with Willie Nelson, then capitalized on the success of the record and pursued a career in Pop music. He toured with Jay and the Americans, Roy Orbison and Bobby Darin. He drifted to Hollywood and cut sides for various West Coast labels. He was writing a lot and three of his songs were in the Jimmy Clanton-Chubby Checker movie *Teenage Millionaire*.

However, he realized that his heart wasn't in Pop music. He wanted to sing Country and he slowly developed his own brand of Folk-Country. The turning point was being signed by Chet Atkins to RCA in 1962. That year, he had a Top 20 hit with *Shame on You.* This was one of the first Nashville records to have horns on it. It broke into the Pop chart, reaching the Top 25.

In 1963, his version of *Detroit City,* which was written by Mel Tillis and Danny Dill, was a Top 10 Country hit and crossed over to the Pop chart. Bobby received a 1967 Grammy Award for his version as "Best Country & Western Recording." The song was subsequently a mammoth hit for Tom Jones. He followed this with another Top 10, *500 Miles from Home*. This also crossed over into the Pop chart's Top 10. This was a traditional Folk song that had been re-worked by Folk singer Hedy West and Charles Williams. 1964 was an important year for Bobby. As well as chalking up Top 5 hits with Hank Snow's *Miller's Cave* and Ian Tyson's *Four Strong Winds*, he also made his first movie appearance in the western *A Distant Trumpet*. The following year, he had a Top 10 hit with *It's Alright.* In 1966, he scored a Top 5 with *The Streets of Baltimore*.

During the 60's, Bobby's musical emphasis was much more towards Country-Folk material and he recorded material by such worthies as Bob Dylan. In 1968, he came to England for live appearances and recorded an album with the Liverpool Country group the Hillsiders, which was released as ***The English Country Side***. The following year, he had his final Top 5 entry on RCA, *(Margie's at) The Lincoln Park Inn.*

1970 saw a move from RCA to Mercury Records where he continued his hit streak with *How I Got to Memphis*, *Come Sundown* and *Please Don't Tell Me How the Story Ends*, all of which reached the Top 10. He left Mercury in 1972, and recorded ***This Is Bare Country*** for United Artists, which was released in 1976. He had already put out an album of this title for Mercury, and UA had already released an album, ***The Very Best of Bobby Bare***. That year, he was back at RCA and in 1973, he reached the Top 3 with *Daddy What If*, on which he was joined by his son, Bobby, Jr. The following year Bobby started in earnest in his collaboration with Shel Silverstein. He had recorded *Sylvia's Mother* while at Mercury but in 1973 he released a double album of Silverstein songs, ***Bobby Bare Sings Lullabys, Legends and Lies***. The album received critical acclaim and has been described as Country music's first concept album. It brought Country to areas previously undreamed of. FM stations and followers of the outlaw movement found that Bare was a force to be reckoned with.

In 1974, Bobby had his first No.1 with *Marie Laveau.* Bare and Silverstein followed up with the 1975 album ***Bobby Bare and the Family Singin' in the Kitchen***. This and its predecessor were very good vehicles for the now renowned Bare humor. However, tragedy was to strike the Bare household shortly after he recorded the above album. Cari, Bare's elder daughter, died of heart failure; she was just 15 years of age.

Bill Graham, who ran the Fillmores, signed Bare to his management company in 1977, thereby pointing him at a wider audience and in Canada he was described as the "Springsteen of Country music." High praise indeed, and as a result, Bobby found himself a great hit with campus audiences. The following year saw him once more changing labels. His first album for Columbia was the self-produced ***Bare,*** from which came his first chart single for his new label, *Sleep Tight Tonight, Goodnight Man.* This was followed in 1979 with ***Sleeper Whenever I Fall***. Bare was pleased with this album, which included songs by Rodney Crowell and Bob McDill and reworkings of the Byrds' *I'll Feel a Whole Lot Better* and the Rolling Stones' *The Last Time*.

His relationship with Silverstein continued with the 1980 live album ***Down and Dirty***. On this album are the chauvinistic *Numbers* and the clever *Tequila Sheila*, both of which show Bare's sense of fun; they were Top 20 and Top 30 entries respectively. Later that year, he released the album ***Drunk and Crazy*** and followed that with the 1981 album, ***As Is,*** which was produced by Rodney Crowell. Among the musicians featured were Albert Lee and Ricky Skaggs. Again, Bare had cast his net wide in his choice of writers. This time he included material by J. J. Cale, Townes Van Zandt and Guy Clark.

The album ***Ain't Got Nothin' to Lose*** came out in 1982 and was followed by yet another collaboration with Silverstein. ***Drinkin' from the Bottle, Singin' from the Heart*** contains some of the most delicious tracks recorded by Bare. The stand-out tracks are *The Jogger* (a sort of *Beep Beep* with Reeboks) and *The Diet Song* (try dieting after hearing it), both low-entry successes. The record sleeve has a typical picture of Bare with his ever-present cigarette drooping from his right hand. In 1985, he signed with EMI America but of the three chart entries, only *When I Get Home* climbed near the Top 50.

Over the years, Bobby Bare has recorded hits in tandem with other Country artists, most notably Skeeter Davis. They charted with *A Dear John Letter* and *Your Husband, My Wife*. The former came from their duet album, ***Tunes for Two*** (1965) and the latter was the title track of their 1970 album ***Your Husband, My Wife***. In 1966, he teamed up with Liz Anderson and Norma Jean for ***The Game of Triangles,*** which spawned the hit of the same name. Jeannie Bare, Bobby's lovely wife, shared the honors with him in 1977 with a Top 30 entry, *Vegas*. Two years later, Rosanne Cash went into the Top 20 with him on *No Memories Hangin' Round.* Bare had a hit in 1983 with Lacy J. Dalton on *It's a Dirty Job*.

Bare has always gone out of his way to help other performers and has brought many

Bobby Bare *giving a Perfect 10*

songwriters to the fore. Included in this are Waylon Jennings, whom he urged Chet Atkins to sign even though he was playing the same sort of material at the time as Bare.

He also helped Billy Joe Shaver (whom he signed to a publishing deal), Kris Kristofferson, Shel Silverstein and Mickey Newbury.

For a while he hosted *Bobby Bare and Friends* on The Nashville Network. He has appeared at the prestigious Wembley Festival in England on four occasions, 1971, 1979, 1983 and 1989 and is still very popular in the U.K. Many in the past have criticized Bobby Bare for not being really Country. From the viewpoint of the 90's, this is not valid at all. In his own words he approached country "ass-backwards from the way everyone in Nashville does," but there's no denying that in the broad spectrum of contemporary Country, Bobby Bare is an integral part.

RECOMMENDED ALBUMS:

"Bobby Bare Sings Lullabys, Legends and Lies" (RCA)(1973)
"Bobby Bare and the Family Singin' in the Kitchen" (RCA)(1974)
"This Is Bobby Bare" (United Artists)(1976)
"Down and Dirty" (Columbia)(1980)
"Encore" (Columbia)(1981)
"As Is" (Columbia)(1981)
"Drinkin' from the Bottle, Singin' from the Heart" (Columbia)(1983)
"Collector's Series" (Columbia)(1985)

BAREFOOT JERRY

Formed:	**1971**
Original Members:	
Wayne Moss	**Guitar (The one constant musician)**
Mac Gayden	**Guitar, Vocals, Keyboards**
Kenney Buttrey	**Drums**
John Harris	**Keyboards**
Other Members:	
Russ Hicks	**Guitar**
Kenny Malone	**Drums**
Bobby Thompson	**Bass**
Dave Doran	**Bass, Guitar, Vocals**
Si Edwards	**Drums**
Buddy Skipper	**Horns, Vocals, Percussion**
Terry Bearmore	**Bass, Guitar, Harmonica**
Jim Colvard	**Guitar**
Warren Hartman	**Keyboards, Horns**
Russ Hicks	**Steel Guitar, Horns**
John Moss	**Horns**
Barry Chance	**Keyboards**
Mike McBride	**Bass**

Barefoot Jerry was formed out of the remnants of Area Code 615. Guitarist Wayne Moss, born in Charleston, West Virginia, began playing with Rock and R & B groups, then played in Brenda Lee's backing band for two and a half years. He became a session man in Nashville and in 1966 played on Bob Dylan's *Blonde on Blonde* album. He went on to form the Escorts, a Rock'n'Roll band that included as members Kenney Buttrey and Charlie McCoy. They pooled their finances and set up the Cinderella Studio in Madison, Tennessee. Moss later bought them out.

Moss remained the catalyst throughout the life of the band. He was its lead guitarist, vocalist, producer and one of the writers. In 1971, Barefoot Jerry recorded its first album for Capitol, ***Southern Delight.*** The band members were Mac Gayden, who had been in Area Code 615, on guitar, vocals and keyboards; Kenney Buttrey, another 615 alumnus on drums, and keyboard player John Harris.

By 1972, the group had moved to Warner Brothers and released their eponymous album. Gayden and Buttrey had gone. In came Russ Hicks and Kenny Malone with a bunch of guests including Buddy Spicher on fiddle, and later semi-resident Bobby Thompson on bass, vocals and guitar. Russ Hicks was playing steel guitar by the time he was 13. He was discovered by Connie Smith and had toured with Ray Price, Kitty Wells and Bob Luman. Kenny Malone was a session player of some note. As well as John Harris, Moss employed Tom Knox and Dan Fickenger on keyboards.

When they signed to Monument in 1974, there were more line-up changes. On the 1974 album ***Watchin' TV***, Si Edwards helped out on drums. He had been taught to play by W. S. Holland of the Tennessee Three. Buddy Skipper came in on horns, vocals and percussion; Dave Doran played bass and guitar and sang and Fred Newell assisted on vocals, bass and banjo.

The same year, Monument re-packaged the Capitol and Warner Brothers albums into a double package, ***Grocery***. With the release of ***You Can't Get Off with Your Shoes On*** in 1975, the constant flow of members seemed to settle. Terry Bearmore came in on bass, guitar and harmonica. He was signed as a writer to Combine Music, which was the writing arm of Monument. He had worked with Dennis Linde and Brewer & Shipley. Jim Colvard was also a new member. He was, up to his death, a very much in demand session guitarist. Finally there was Warren Hartman, a multi-instrumentalist. Within the band he played piano, organ, mellotron, moog and clavinet. He had been a member of Stanley Steamer and had cut an album for MGM. He and Russ Hicks provided the horns for the band under the name of the Hendersonville Horns. With this 1975 album, the band came of age. It is interesting to note that among the dedications is one to their label boss: "Understanding & Freedom by Fred Foster." It is certain that Foster was perceptive enough to allow the band its head.

The 1976 album ***Keys to the Country*** retained the same band members and like its predecessor, featured Charlie McCoy as guest. It also introduced John Moss on horns. By 1977, the end was in sight. They delivered their final album, ***Barefootin'.*** Bearmore, Colvard and Hartman had left, and Moss soldiered on with Edwards and Hicks plus Barry Chance on keyboards, Mike McBride on bass and guests Charlie McCoy and banjoist/Dobro player Buddy Blackmon. (Buddy would go on to co-write the Randy Travis hit *1982*).

It is perhaps apposite that the band ended with a bluesy title. Their music was always a melting pot of Rock, Country and Blues, often erroneously called "Country-Rock"; they were similar, in a way, to Asleep at the Wheel and Amazing Rhythm Aces. However, whereas the Wheel has carried on, achieved the fame it deserved and turned public taste its way, and the Aces were a decade ahead of their time, Barefoot Jerry now seems to be a child of its generation, not helped by Zappa-esque and Beatles influences, which have not worn well in Barefoot Jerry's hands.

RECOMMENDED ALBUMS:

"You Can't Get Off with Your Shoes On" (Monument)(1975)
"Keys to the Country" (Monument)(1976)
"Barefootin'" (Monument)(1977)

JOHNNY BARFIELD

(Singer, Guitar)

Given Name:	**Johnny Alexander Barfield**
Date of Birth:	**March 3, 1909**
Where Born:	**Tifton, Georgia**
Date of Death:	**January 16, 1974**

A popular singer in the 1930's, Johnny Barfield is best known today for his series of Bluebird records and for being the first Country singer to use the term "boogie woogie" in a recording. He was a close friend of Rex Griffin, and was a popular radio entertainer throughout the Deep South. His high, clear tenor voice won him fans as far away as Australia, where his Bluebird records were immensely popular (some more so than in the U.S.A.), and where lp reissues of his work were in print in the 1980's. Until recently, though, little biographical information was available on him and for decades he existed only as a name in Bluebird and RCA catalogs.

Johnny grew up around Columbus, Georgia, near the Alabama line, the son of a local cotton farmer. After an early try-out for Columbia Records with his brother Coot, which resulted in none of their sides being released, Johnny met fiddler Bert Lana and became associated with the Atlantic band The Skillet Lickers. In fact, in the early 1930's, he replaced Riley Puckett in the band and performed with them over WCKY Covington, Kentucky.

By the late 1930's, he had returned to the Columbus area, playing with his band (called either the Troubadours or the Pleasant Valley Boys) over WRLB, and at various clubs and dance halls. He became close friends with Decca star Rex Griffin, known for his yodeling arrangements of *Lovesick Blues* and *Over the River,* and Johnny often appeared on shows and on the radio with him. Between August 1939 and September 1941, Johnny recorded four sessions for RCA's Bluebird label. Locally, the most popular record was *Numbers Blues*—so named because Barfield used to run numbers and make moonshine in the wide-open Phoenix City area. Another very popular piece was the sentimental *Berry Picking Time* (1940) and several Griffin compositions, including *Everybody's Trying to Be My Baby* (1939). Best known of all, though, was *Boogie Woogie* (1939), a loose, apparently improvised piece that helped initiate a long line of Country boogie songs in the next decade.

Johnny gave up singing to join the army in 1942, entered the European Theater and spent almost a year as a German POW. After he was repatriated, he returned to find that his reputation as a singer had grown considerably, and he was able to do package tours with the likes of Bill Monroe, the Duke of Paducah, Max Terhune, Rex Griffin and Lew Childre. His own venues during these later years were the Comer Auditorium and Charley's Club, both in Columbus. The local music scene, which had depended on the wide-open atmosphere of Phoenix City and its proximity to Fort Benning military base, suffered when Phoenix City was "cleaned up" in 1953. Barfield continued to play in the area, turning down an offer from the *Opry,* and even recorded on his own JB label in the late 1950's. He died January 16, 1974, almost forgotten by all except his local fans. CKW

JACK BARLOW

(Singer, Songwriter, Guitar)
Given Name: **Jack Butcher**
Where Born: **Muscatine, Iowa**
Married: **Jan (div.)**

If you are destined to be in the music industry, the call can come at any time. For Jack Barlow it was while he was farming in Muscatine that he was hired as a deejay for the local station, KWPC. He then moved to Moline and had his own show on WQUA. From there, he moved to WIRE Minneapolis. He started attending deejay conventions in Nashville, and his mind turned to the possibilities of recording.

He recorded his first single for Dial Records. This was a label with a wide-based artist roster. A lot of the artists on it were R & B, including Joe Tex, Clarence "Frogman" Henry and Bobby Marchan, but Dial also had many Country acts, such as Johnny Lee, Diana Trask and Marty Martel (Boxcar Willie). It was distributed by Mercury but the production was allied to Tree Publishing and Buddy Killen. Jack wrote (he was by then a staff writer for Tree) and recorded *I Love Country Music* in 1965. It reached No. 21 in the Cash Box chart. Jack cut one more single for the label before being picked up by Epic. The relationship lasted for two years without any major success, and in 1968 Dot Records beckoned.

With the success of his initial single, *Baby Ain't That Love,* which made the Top 40, Jack left behind his tractor and the deejay microphone and headed for Nashville. He appeared on the *Grand Ole Opry* in 1966, singing *I Love Country Music.* Jack followed with some middle to low positions and then he had a dry year in 1970. He came back in 1971 with his version of Donovan's *Catch the Wind,* which climbed to the Top 30. He then followed up with a pair of hits in the Top 50's, one of which was *They Call the Wind Maria,* from the hit film musical by Lerner and Loewe, *Paint Your Wagon*; it was particularly suited to his deep brown voice.

In 1975, Jack released a single, under the name of "Zoot Fenster," which dealt with a rather revealing photograph in the Sears catalog, *The Man on Page 602.* This novelty record on Antique reached the Top 30.

In recent times, he has been doing a lot of commercials—including ones for Dollar General Store, a sponsor of the *Grand Ole Opry*—where his resonant bass voice is as uniquely identifiable as it was on his recordings.

RECOMMENDED ALBUMS:
"Baby Ain't That Love" (Dot)(1969)
"Son of the South" (Dot) (1969)
"Catch the Wind" (Dot)(1970)
"I Live the Songs I Sing" (Antique)(1975)

RANDY BARLOW

(Singer, Songwriter, Guitar)
Date of Birth: **March 29, 1943**
Where Born: **Detroit, Michigan**
Married: **Three times**
Children: **Joe, Patricia JoAnne**

For a while during the decade from 1974 through 1983, Randy Barlow looked like he might be a major force in Country music. However, unlike his good friend, John Anderson, Randy was unable to sustain the impetus.

He is one quarter Cherokee, his grandmother being a full-blooded Cherokee named Mahalapuss. His family came from rural Missouri, Arkansas and Kentucky, and allegedly, his ancestors rode with Daniel Boone. For many years, Randy raised a prize Appaloosa stallion, Pete. Barlow knew he wanted to be a singer at age 10, playing Rhythm & Blues with local bands. By age 14, he was performing professionally. He attended Western Kentucky University, where he was a psychology major, but music was his main interest. In his senior year at college, he began booking name acts at or near the university. An argument with college officials over booking Ray Charles resulted in Randy being given an ultimatum: Drop the concert or leave college—he left college!

After leaving academe, in 1965, he headed for Los Angeles to be a stuntman, but there was a lot of competition, and Randy looked elsewhere. He joined the *Dick Clark Caravan of Stars* as a promoter, master of ceremonies, comedian and performer. He recorded for Mercury in 1968, and released the single *Color Blind/St. Clair,* which failed to make the charts.

In 1973, he was spotted by producer Fred Kelly, who became his manager. Through Kelly, he signed with Capitol, and in 1974, *Throw Away the Pages* made the Top 80. The following year, Randy moved to Gazelle, and during 1976 he had three medium-level hits, *Johnny Orphan, Goodnight My Love,* the Top 50 entry *Lonely Eyes* and the Top 20 single *Twenty-Four Hours from Tulsa.* During 1977, he had a further three middle-order successes, *Kentucky Woman, California Lady* and *Walk Away from Me.*

Randy moved over to Republic Records in 1978, and immediately had the first of three Top 10 singles. It started with *Slow and Easy* and went on to *No Sleep Tonight* and *Fall in Love with Me Tonight.* He stayed with Republic until the end of 1979 and racked up three more hits, *Sweet Melinda* (Top 10), *Another Easy Lovin' Night* (Top 25) and *Lay Back in the Arms of Someone* (Top 15). During the year, he appeared at the International Festival of Country Music at Wembley, England. Randy moved on to Paid Records in 1980 and had the Top 50 single *Willow Run.* He had three more hits on the label: *Dixie Man, Love Dies Hard* and *Try Me.* He had one Top 30 success on Jamex in 1981, entitled

Love Was Born. He returned to Gazelle in 1983 and made the lower levels of the Country charts with *Don't Leave Me Lonely Loving You.*

Randy is an expert gourmet chef, and although he hasn't had any chart records in the last decade, he is quite capable of cooking up a mess of hits.

RECOMMENDED ALBUMS:

"Arrival" (Republic)(1977)
"Fall in Love with Me" (Republic)(1978)
"Randy Barlow" (Republic)(1979)
"Dimensions" (Paid)(1981)

BENNY BARNES

(Singer, Guitar)

Given Name: Benjamin M. Barnes, Jr.
Date of Birth: 1934
Where Born: Beaumont, Texas
Married: Jeanette
Children: 5 daughters
Date of Death: 1985

In Benny's family there is oil in the blood. Both his father and grandfather worked in the oil fields; at 15, he became a roughneck and also an occasional truck driver. At the age of 19, he played guitar on a George Jones recording at Starday. In 1956, while recovering from an oil rig accident, he took a job at a local lounge. That same year, he was signed by Starday; his first single, *Once Again,* didn't do much, but Mercury bought the rights to the second single, *Poor Man's Riches,* which climbed in 1957 to No. 2 and stayed on the chart for four months.

He toured with the stars of the *Grand Ole Opry* and was a regular on the *Louisiana Hayride*. He made many appearances on the *Opry* and turned out many sides for Starday and Mercury, the most successful being *Gold Records in the Snow* (Starday, 1959).

In 1960, he quit the music business and opened a beer tavern, The Blue Lantern, in Beaumont. He ran it for some four years. In 1961, Mercury released *Yearning* and it climbed to the Top 30. During this time, he wrote *Bar with No Beer*, which, based upon an Australian folk song, would seem to have more than a passing connection to Slim Dusty's *Pub with No Beer*, which was a hit in 1959. At least the ale ran out in both songs. When Benny recorded it for Hallway in 1965, it became successful regionally and then hit nationally when leased to Kapp the following year.

Tragedy struck the Barnes household in 1966, when Benny's 4-year-old daughter was accidentally shot. The next year, financially in trouble and mentally in agony, he closed the Blue Lantern and leased another club for a year, but it didn't work out. He started playing at another Country and Western club and touring. In 1970, he moved to Whittier, California, and played one-nighters all over Southern California.

He returned to Beaumont in 1971 and built Benny Barnes' Melody Ranch. With his band, the Ranch Hands, he entertained from the beginning of 1972. The band, originally known as the Cimarron Boys, was fronted by Danny Brown, who had been with it as singer and guitarist since 1961.

After a spell at Hallway (1962-1965, initially as Ben E. Barnes), Benny signed with Pappy Dailey's Musicor label and from 1965 through 1968, he turned out regular singles, none of which achieved smash hit status. In 1968 he cut another single for Kapp, *Sweet Suzannah*, and then in 1972 released *Woman Leave My Mind Alone* on Mega.

In 1973, he returned to Starday and recorded *Chillie Smith*. In 1976, he signed to Hugh Hefner's Playboy label and released two singles, *Little Brown Paper Bag Blues* (1976) and *I've Got Some Gettin' Over You to Do* (1977), the latter scraping into the chart basement.

With his cooking group, Benny's Burners, he won the 8th Annual World Championship Barbecue Cook-off in Houston.

RECOMMENDED ALBUM:

"The Rockin' Honky Tonk Man" (Country Classics Library) [With the Echoes]

MAX D. BARNES

(Songwriter, Singer, Guitar)

Given Name: Max Duane Barnes
Date of Birth: July 24, 1936
Where Born: Hardscratch, Iowa
Married: Patsy
Children: Jenny, Patrick, Max Troy

Max D. is one of Nashville's most prolific songwriters having 14 Gold Album credits, 7 Platinum Album credits, 3 Double-Platinum Album credits, 2 Triple-Platinum Album credits, 1 Quadruple-Platinum Album credit and 6 movie soundtrack credits—and he is the recipient of 42 songwriter awards. In addition, he is a two-time winner of the CMA's "Song of the Year" award.

Max got his first guitar, from his sister Ruthie, when he was 11, while the family lived in Logan, Iowa. Soon after, his parents divorced and Max moved with his mother and two younger brothers to Omaha, Nebraska. He dropped out of school at age 16 and took a job, singing in an Omaha nightclub for two years. He formed a band, the Golden Rockets and met his wife-to-be, Patsy, who joined the band as lead singer. After the birth of daughter Jenny, they quit playing clubs. After the birth of their first son, Patrick, Max went to work for a concrete company; then, a year later, he moved to Long Beach, California, as foreman of a lamp factory.

When he quit, the company told him he could come back anytime. For the next four years, the family lived in Omaha for part of the year and wintered in California, where he sang in clubs at the weekends. He bought a nightclub near Lake Okiboji, Iowa, in 1962, but he had to sell it after eight months. He moved back to Omaha, where he drove diesels cross-country for the next nine years.

Max came to Nashville in 1971 and cut a record for the Jed label, *Ribbons of Steel/Hello Honky Tonk*. He then released a second single for Willex: *You Gotta Be Putting Me On/Growing Old with Grace*. Fellow songwriter Kent Westberry encouraged Max to move to Nashville, which he did in 1973. The following year, he became a writer for Roz-Tense Music, and Charley Pride cut two of his songs. In all, Pride has now recorded three Max D. songs: *There Ain't No Me Without You, The Man I Used to Be* and *Don't See How I Can Love You Anymore*.

Over the next couple of years, he worked through Gary S. Paxman Music and Danor Music, the latter being a company jointly owned by Troy Seals, Norbert Putnam and David Briggs. At Danor, Max co-wrote a lot with Troy Seals and had about 30 cuts by named artists. At one point, he had five songs on the charts at the same time. In 1975, his son Patrick was killed in a car accident, a tragedy that would later manifest itself in the song *Chiseled in Stone* (co-written with and a hit for Vern Gosdin in 1989).

He signed with Screen Gems-EMI in October 1976 and this led to a recording contract with Polydor. He had his first taste of personal chart success the following year, when *Allegheny Lady* made a brief visit to the charts. During the 70's, Max's major cuts were *I Can't Love You Enough* (Conway Twitty & Loretta Lynn, 1977, No. 2, featured in the movies *Six Pack* and *Steel*), *From Seven Till Ten* (Conway Twitty & Loretta Lynn, 1978, featured in the movie *Resurrection*), *Bordertown Woman* (Mel McDaniel, 1978), and *Don't Take It Away* (Conway Twitty, 1979, No.1).

Max returned to the charts with a spoken-word single on Ovation, *Dear Mr. President*. This was admitted to the National Archives of Public Broadcasting and was a part of the Teaching Global Awareness Using the Media Teacher's Manual (University of Denver). He had three further 1980 chart records on Ovation, *Mean Woman Blues*, *Cowboys Are Common as Sin* and *Heaven on a Freight Train*. In 1981, he had his final chart single for the label, *Don't Ever Leave Me Again*. That year, the UK label Country Roads released the album ***Pieces of My Life***, which also featured Patsy Barnes.

During the 80's, he had numerous chart cuts by major artists. These included *Red Neckin' Love Makin' Night* (Conway Twitty, 1981), *If You're Gonna Do Me Wrong (Do It Right)* (Vern Gosdin, 1983, co-written with Gosdin), *Way Down Deep* (Vern Gosdin, 1983), *Slow Burnin' Memory* (Vern Gosdin, 1984, co-written with Gosdin), *Thank God for the Radio* (Kendalls, 1984, No.1), *Drinkin' and Dreamin'* (Waylon Jennings, 1985, No. 2), *Who's Gonna Fill Their Shoes* (George Jones, 1985), *Ten Feet Away* (Keith Whitley, 1986), *I Won't Need You Anymore (Forever and Always)* (Randy Travis, 1987, No.1), *Everybody Needs a Hero* (Gene Watson, 1988) and *Joe Knows How to Live* (Eddy Raven, 1988, No.1). It is possible that *Way Down Deep*, which Max D. wrote with his son Max T., was the first Top 10 song co-written by a father/son combination. During this period, he received many awards including, in 1989, CMA "Song of the Year" for *Chiseled in Stone*, which he co-wrote with Vern Gosdin. The same song was named NSAI "Song of the Year." Furthermore, it was a Grammy finalist for "Song of the Year."

As the 90's rolled around, Max D. continued his winning streak. Pam Tillis had a Top 5 hit with *Don't Tell Me What to Do* (1990); Vince Gill did the same with *Look at Us* (1991) and John Anderson included *Let Go of the Stone* (1991) on his highly successful **Seminole Wind** album and took the single into the Top 10. *Look at Us* (1991), co-written with Vince Gill, became the CMA's 1992 "Song of the Year" and won the MCN's "Song of the Year" in 1993.

In addition to the songs mentioned above, Max's songs have been heard in the movies. *Can't Get the Notion in Motion* was in *The China Syndrome* (1979) and *Thanks to the Cathouse (I'm in the Doghouse)* was in *Tender Mercies* (1983). Both were sung by Max himself. Ricky Van Shelton's rendition of *Hillybilly Heart* was featured in *Next of Kin*.

On September 27, 1992, Max D. Barnes was inducted into the Nashville Songwriters Hall of Fame—something that was long overdue! Max D. has shown a consistency that even surpasses the great Harlan Howard. How he manages to turn out such quality songs is beyond even his family. His 15 BMI awards attest to his quality. Max attributes a lot of his success to his wife, Patsy, for her support and encouragement. However, the secret of Max's success lies in the fact that he still writes accessible songs for the common man. This means that he will be writing hits long after certain fashionable writers will only be memories.

Max D. Barnes *with his sister Ruthie Steele*

RECOMMENDED ALBUMS:

"Rough Around the Edges" (Ovation)(1977) [re-released in 1980]

"Pieces of My Life" (Country Roads UK)(1981)

BOBBY BARNETT

(Singer, Songwriter)

Given Name:	**Bobby Glen Barnett**
Date of Birth:	**February 15, 1936**
Where Born:	**Cushing, Oklahoma**
Married:	**Nita Joan Skelton**
Children:	**Robert V., Glen E., Matthew D., Mary Jan, plus one adopted**

Bobby Barnett was one of thirteen children born to George and Berls Barnett and soon discovered his love for Country music. When he graduated from high school in 1953, he moved to El Paso and worked at the El Paso Natural Gas Company as an engineer, but decided that he wanted to perform.

In 1960, he cut Eddie Miller's *This Old Heart*, his second single for the Muskogee, Oklahoma, label Razorback; it reached No. 24 in the Country charts and was picked up by Republic in the U.S. and Sparta in Canada. Republic released the next single, *Please Come Home/It Makes No Difference*, in 1961, but without success. Bobby then moved to Boyd Records; then Reprise bought the masters in 1962 and Bobby became only the second Country artist on the label, behind Dorsey Burnette. He released a pair of singles, *Crazy Little Lover/Last of the Angels* and *Same Old Love/Temptation's Calling*.

Bobby's success now began to happen. In 1963, he signed to Sims. He had a major hit with *She Looks Good to the Crowd*, which made it to No. 6 on one of the Country charts. He followed this up the following year with the Top 50 success *Worst of Luck*. Although his next single died, Bobby started the following year in fine form with a Top 30 record, *Mismatch*, which had been released at the end of 1964 and had *Moaning the Blues* on the flip-side.

He returned to the charts in 1967 on John Capps' K-Ark Records with *Down, Down Came My World*, following that later in the year with the low-level *The Losing Kind*.

When George Richey (now married to Tammy Wynette) went to A & R at Columbia, he called Bobby. They had met in Tucson when George was a deejay and bandleader. Richey was impressed with Bobby's soulful style and as a result signed him to the label in 1968. With his first release, Bobby had a major hit with *Love Me, Love*. It marched up to the Top 15 and reached even higher in certain charts. The next single, *Your Sweet Love Lifted Me*, was also a Top 50 success and this was followed by a record that deserved to be a bigger hit than it was, *Drink Canada Dry*.

Then all went quiet and it was not until 1978 that Bobby's name appeared in the hit lists; he scraped in with his Cin Kay recording *Burn Atlanta Down*. Three years later, he again reached the foot of the charts with a single on Marshall, *Born in Country Music (Raised on Dixieland)*.

RECOMMENDED ALBUMS:

"Bobby Barnett at the World Famous Crystal Palace, Tombstone, Arizona" (Sims)

"Lyin', Lovin' & Leavin'" (Columbia)

"Heroes, History & Heritage of Oklahoma Volume 1" (Heritage)(1974)

"Heroes, History & Heritage of Oklahoma Volume 2" (Heritage)(1985))

[About historical Oklahomans; produced by Dave Kirby]

BARRIER BROTHERS, The

HERMAN BARRIER

(String Bass, Fiddle)

Given Name:	**Herman Barrier**
Date of Birth:	**January 23, 1920**
Married:	**Irene Franklin**
Children:	**Ruby, Lulubelle, Diana, Ruth, Franklin, Joe, Herman, Jr., Roy, Ronnie**
Date of Death:	**September 5, 1988**

ERNEST BARRIER

(5-string Banjo, Mandolin)

Given Name:	**Ernest Barrier**
Date of Birth:	**January 23, 1925**
Married:	**1. Maxine Caston 2. Nancy Mason**
Children:	**Carolyn, Jesse, David, Janie, Rick**
Date of Death:	**February 3, 1994**

HENRY RAY BARRIER
(Lead Vocals, Guitar)
Given Name: Henry Ray Barrier
Date of Birth: March 4, 1939
Married: Jerrilyn
Children: Delina, Henry Ray, Jr.

All Born: Hardin County, Tennessee

The Barrier Brothers, like the Lilly Brothers and Red Ellis, helped pioneer Bluegrass music in the northern portion of the United States.

Natives of a rural area south of Savannah, Tennessee, Herman and Ernest Barrier learned to play Old-Time music as they grew up in a region near both the Tennessee River and the Mississippi-Alabama line. In the early 50's they had a radio program on a small station in Corinth, Mississippi, for a time. However, as little work was available in the region, in music or labor, the Barriers, including their parents, soon moved to South Bend, Indiana, where Ernest found steady employment as a welder and Herman as a cabinet maker.

By this time, Herman favored the bass and Ernest the 5-string banjo. As their much younger brother Henry Ray grew up, the others taught him to sing lead and play the guitar. A Missouri fiddler named Gene Dykes joined forces with the Barriers to give them a full Bluegrass band. Through their entire career, the Barriers worked almost exclusively as a weekend band playing parks, fairs, carnivals and small jamborees in Indiana and adjacent states.

By the end of the 50's, the Barrier Brothers and their Ozark Mountain Boys had several years of experience as semi-professional Bluegrass musicians. Ray Earle of Winona Lake, Indiana, had started a small record company and asked the Barriers to cut some material for him. They did two singles and an extended-play Gospel disc on Earle's Armoneer label (Ernest's daughters, Carolyn and Janie, also recorded a single).

The Barrier Brothers then landed a contract with a major firm, Philips International. Over a three-year period, the brothers recorded three albums. Unfortunately, the company chose most of the material, which tended to be largely covers of Flatt and Scruggs and Bill Monroe standards and although competently performed, did not show as much of their versatility as it might have done.

Not long after their Philips contract ended, the Barriers stopped performing as the years of grueling weekend travel had begun to take their toll on Herman's health. Herman and Ernest eventually moved back to Tennessee and Henry Ray went on to work with a variety of Country bands in northern Indiana where he still resides. Herman died on Labor Day of 1988, while Ernest worked as a self-employed welder until he retired. In July 1992, he reported that he still participated in jam sessions with local musicians from time to time. IMT

RECOMMENDED ALBUMS:
"Golden Bluegrass Hits" (Philips)(1962)
"More Golden Bluegrass Hits" (Philips)(1963)
"Gospel Songs: Bluegrass Style" (Philips)(1964)
"Pickin' and Singin'" (Old Homestead)(1977) [Taken from home recordings]

Linda Bartholomew refer LINDA HARGROVE

BASHFUL BROTHER OSWALD

(Singer, Guitar, Dobro, Banjo)
Given Name: Beecher Ray Kirby
Date of Birth: December 26, 1911
Where Born: Sevierville, Sevier County, Tennessee
Married: 1. Lola (d. 1981)
2. Euneta Phillips

For three generations, "Pete" Kirby, also known as Bashful Brother Oswald, served as the most important member of Roy Acuff's Smoky Mountain Boys. It was his Dobro that kicked off the Acuff anthems like *Great Speckled Bird* and *Wabash Cannonball*, his high mountain voice that soared above Acuff's on *Wreck on the Highway*; his exuberant horse laugh that brayed forth as the band launched into comedy numbers; his old overalls and size 44 shoes that bought down the house when he broke into an impromptu buck dance. He was the most colorful character in the Acuff band, but he was also the most skilled and influential musician. It is possible to imagine the Smoky Mountain Boys without him, but it would have been a poorer and less dynamic band and Acuff's claim to be the King of Country Music would have been much less secure.

Os was born in the same Sevier County, at the foot of the Smoky Mountains, that produced both the singers of Folksong collector Cecil Sharp and Country stars like Dolly Parton. Oswald's father was steeped in the musical vocabulary of the region and played fiddle, guitar and banjo and taught shape-note singing schools (and even wrote songs for the old Stamps-Baxter songbooks). Rural music parties were a part of young Oswald's life and by the time he was a teenager, he was playing square dances at night and working at the Appalachian Cotton Mill in Knoxville during the day.

He moved to Flint, Michigan, to find work in the Buick factory but the Depression ended this hope. However while he was up North he got work playing music over WFDF. When the station manager decided to emphasize Hawaiian music, then a national fad, Oswald bought a steel-bodied National guitar and learned how to play it from a local guitarist named Rudy Waikuiki. By 1933 he was in Chicago, working at the World's Fair and hearing an even wider variety of music at the clubs and taverns around town. By the time he returned to Knoxville, in 1934, he had become adept at using the Dobro, and had little trouble finding local bands to perform with; one was Acuff's early Knoxville band, the Crazy Tennesseans.

When Acuff got a job on the *Grand Ole Opry* and shortly thereafter re-formed his band, he quickly turned to Oswald as a replacement for his original Dobro player, Clell Summey. This was an important role, since most of Acuff's early record hits had featured the distinctive sound of the Dobro. Oddly, though, Oswald's first session on record with Acuff featured him playing the old-time clawhammer banjo. This was an ARC session held July 5, 1939, in Memphis, and featured Oswald charging through such favorites as *Ida Red.*

Soon Roy discovered that Oswald could sing as well, having been trained in the classic "open" harmony of mountain Gospel music. In 1940 he had Oswald do the famous "screaming tenor" part on the trademark *Precious Jewel*, and in 1942, Os repeated his work on the *Wreck on the Highway.* In 1943, he created his stage costume of floppy hat and old overalls; a magazine photographer was trying to get some shots of one of Acuff's horses and Oswald succeeded in calming the skittish animal while dressed informally in overalls. Acuff and the photographer were fascinated, and he asked Oswald to add the garb to his stage shows.

He had already been dubbed "Brother Oswald" as a ploy to convince conservative audiences that Os was the big brother of Rachel Veach, a young unmarried woman Acuff had added to the band, and whose presence might otherwise have been unacceptable on tour. Though Oswald performed on almost all of the dozens of records Acuff made in the 1940's, 1950's and 1960's it was not until relatively modern times that he was featured on his own cuts and albums. In the 1960's he appeared as a sideman on several Starday albums and was spotlighted on ***Bashful Brother Oswald*** in 1962.

In 1972, the Nitty Gritty Dirt Band came to Nashville to record their ***Will the Circle Be Unbroken*** set and as they cut tracks with Acuff, became fascinated with Oswald and eventually featured him on several songs. That same year veteran guitarist and Dobroist Tut

Taylor produced a superb solo album of Oswald's Dobro music, ***Brother Oswald,*** on the then new Rounder label. A series of three other lp's soon followed, including two with fellow Smoky Mountain Boy Charlie Collins, with whom Oswald was now often working dates in the new Opryland theme park.

The 1980's saw a number of significant changes in Oswald's life. As Roy Acuff moved toward retirement and began to cut back his activities, Oswald found himself lionized by young Dobro players who were fascinated with his style, and who credited him with keeping the instrument alive during the dark days of the 1950's when the *Opry* was putting pressure on him to electrify his instrument. His wife of forty-five years, Lola, died in 1981 after a long illness, but he refused to let it sour him on life. He carried on with his music and remarried in 1983. When Acuff himself died in 1992, Oswald and Charlie Collins continued to perform on the *Opry* as a duo, keeping alive the old Smoky Mountain songs and the classic sound of the older music. CKW

Pete Kirby, aka ***Brother Bashful Oswald***

RECOMMENDED ALBUMS:

"Bashful Brother Oswald" (Starday)(1962)
"Brother Oswald" (Rounder)(19772)

DR. HUMPHREY BATE

(Singer, Harmonica, Piano, Physician)
Date of Birth: May 25, 1875
Where Born: Castallian Springs, Sumner County, Tennessee
Married: Unknown
Children: Alcyone (Beasley), Buster
Date of Death: June 12, 1936

A mainstay and founding father of the *Grand Ole Opry*, Dr. Humphrey Bate and his band, the Possum Hunters, routinely opened the *Opry* at 8:00 o'clock with *There'll Be a Hot Time in the Old Town Tonight* during the first ten years of the show. Though overshadowed by the more colorful *Opry* pioneers like Uncle Jimmy Thompson and Uncle Dave Macon, Dr. Bate and his band were the first people to actually broadcast Country music from Nashville. The "Solemn Ol' Judge," George Hay, referred to Bate as "the Dean of the Opry," and recent research has revealed just how accurate this assessment was.

Dr. Bate's band had in fact been a fixture of middle Tennessee since before the turn of the century, usually performing as Dr. Bate's Augmented String Orchestra. It was the idea of Hay and *Opry* publicists to rename the band the Possum Hunters, and pose them in a cornfield with hound dogs for publicity photos. The basic band included Dr. Bate on harmonica and occasionally vocals, Oscar Stone on fiddle, Burt Hutcherson on guitar, Bill Barret on fiddle and Walter Ligget on banjo.

The band was hardly the collection of rustics that publicity made them out to be. Dr. Bate was a genuine practicing physician, a graduate of the Vanderbilt Medical School and a veteran of the Spanish-American War, who went to Florida each winter to fish. He liked a wide variety of music, especially the band of John Philip Sousa, and often played light classical music on his harmonica.

Bate learned many of his tunes—which are quite rare and unusual—from an old exslave on his father's farm when Bate was only a boy. He formed his first band before 1900, and it included a cello as well as a banjo and guitar (later bands included a doghouse bass, played with a bow). By the days of WWI, he was running two or three separate little bands, including a special Hawaiian band playing at socials, on steamboat excursions down the Cumberland River, and even between shows at the local movie houses then running silent films. As a result of these varied venues, his music soon was a remarkable cross-section of nearly every type of turn-of-the-century Folk, Pop and Parlor music.

Unfortunately, Dr. Bate's splendid band left us only a handful of recordings, the results of a single session for Brunswick-Vocalion in Atlanta in 1928. Of the 12 numbers cut, some have a distinct Blues influence: *Goin' Uptown, Old Joe* and *Take Your Foot Out of the Mud and Stick It in the Sand.* (Bate grew up in the same general area as DeFord Bailey, the Opry's other great harmonica player, and shared some of the repertory known by Bailey and his family.) Another favorite was *How Many Biscuits Can You Eat*, which would in later years become a theme song for Flatt and Scruggs, and *My Wife Died on Saturday Night*, which became an *Opry* favorite. Pieces like *Greenback Dollar* and *Eighth of January* showed off the band's complex and invigorating ensemble sound, and are considered today some of Country's very best early string band recordings.

In 1931, Dr. Bate led one of the first tour groups to go out from the *Opry*, into the wilds of Wisconsin and Illinois. He became close friends with Judge Hay and approved the attempts to make the *Opry* grow into something more than a radio show. As his health began to fade in the mid-1930's, Dr. Bate told Hay, "It is my wish to die in the harness." He passed away in early 1936, the night before the *Opry* moved to its new home on Fatherland Street.

His funeral services were held in the front yard of his house at Castallian Springs, where hundreds of friends and patients paid homage to the genial country physician. His band, the Possum Hunters, continued on the *Opry*, and his daughter, Alcyone Bate Beasley, remained a regular at the station into the 1970's. CKW

PHIL BAUGH

(Guitar, Composer)
Given Name: Philip Roland Baugh
Where Born: Marysville, California
Married: Unknown
Children: Phillip R., Jr., Tiffany, Heather
Date of Death: November 4, 1990

Phil Baugh's distinctive electric-guitar playing made him one of Nashville's premier session musicians in the 70's and 80's. He played on hundreds of hit records for artists including Janie Fricke, Moe Bandy, Johnny Rodriguez, and Sammi Smith. His trademark note-bending technique was especially prominent on the George Jones classic *He Stopped Loving Her Today.*

Phil grew up in Northern California, where there were many transplanted Oklahomans and Texans who brought their Country music with them. He developed an interest in the guitar as a child and first performed in churches. Eventually he worked in bands that played for dances and in nightclubs. Phil was making a living as a long-distance truck driver at that time but he always carried a guitar and amplifier in the passenger seat on his cross-country travels.

Ray Price gave Phil his first major break in the music business. His guitar work with Price led to his own recording contract with Dallas-based Longhorn Records, in 1964. Baugh teamed with Vern Stovall to record an album titled ***Country Guitar.*** The record produced two Top 10 singles, *Country Guitar* and *One Man Band*. In 1965 Baugh was voted "Best

Guitarist" by the ACM and named "Outstanding Instrumentalist of the Year" by *Billboard*, and "Instrumentalist of the Year" by *Cash Box* magazine.

In 1969 and 1970 Baugh returned to the Ray Price band as lead guitarist. In 1971, he moved to Dallas and quickly became the city's favorite studio player. In addition to frequent jingle sessions, Baugh also played on some record projects. He was re-united in Dallas with Merle Haggard at the Sumet-Bernet studio where Haggard was recording. Baugh had played on several of Haggard's earlier hits including *Swinging Doors* in 1966. Also in Dallas, Baugh recorded instrumental albums for Toro Records and the A & B label.

When Baugh's father died in 1975, he used his share of the estate settlement to move to Nashville. It did not take him long to break into studio work and he soon became a favorite of many producers. It was his invention, the "Phil Baugh Pedal," that helped give his guitar playing a unique sound. Baugh spent twenty years developing the unit to bend the strings on an electric guitar to produce sounds similar to a pedal steel guitar. His creation contained six foot pedals that raised and lowered the pitch of each string.

In 1980 Baugh formed a recording and performing group called the Superpickers. The members were Nashville's favorite studio players, including Buddy Emmons, steel; Buddy Harmon, drums; Henry Stryzlecki, bass; Willie Rainsford, piano; and Terry McMillian, harmonica and percussion. The group served as the house band for the syndicated television show *That Nashville Music,* and other television specials, including one for Tammy Wynette.

In addition to studio work and live performances, Baugh also found success as a record producer in the early 80's. The artists he produced included Sammi Smith, Jimmie Rodgers, and Allen Frizzell. A 1985 heart attack slowed Baugh down but he continued his television work in the late 80's on the Nashville Network's *Church Street Station.* Health problems continued to plague Baugh and he died on November 4, 1990, at age 53. JIE

RECOMMENDED ALBUM:

"Country Guitar" (Longhorn)(1965) [with Vern Stovall]

Norma Jean Beasler refer NORMA JEAN

PAPPY GUBE BEAVER

(Singer, Guitar, Harmonica)

Given Name: **Parlin Kenneth Beaver**
Date of Birth: **March 7, 1919**
Where Born: **Newport, Tennessee**
Married: **Mildred**
Children: **Eddie, Jo Ann, Marilyn, Jerry**

When Roy Acuff's stellar career rose to its heights in the early 40's, record companies began to look for other strong-voiced, traditionally-based singers. One who came quite close to filling the bill was another East Tennessean known as Pappy Gube Beaver. His early recordings showed that he had both power and potential in his vocal range.

A native of Cocke County, Tennessee, Gube learned to play Old-Time music, mostly on guitar and harmonica, from his parents and from Carter Family records they had in their home. Because of his small stature as a child, his mother nicknamed him "Gube" (a derivative of "goober," or peanut). As a teenager, Gube worked for the Civilian Conservation Corps and after his marriage in 1940 went to work at WROL radio in Knoxville for Cas Walker, the local supermarket magnate and politician. It was Walker who added the "Pappy" to Gube's nickname, after the birth of Beaver's first child.

Gube soon had his own radio show at WBIR in Knoxville and as WWII gas rationing limited his traveling to personal appearances, he drove a taxi to supplement his income. Shortly after the war ended, he signed with Capitol Records and did a pair of sessions for them, assisted by several local musicians including a young Chet Atkins on fiddle. Gube's trademark song, *You Can Be a Millionaire with Me*, had originally been written and recorded by the duo of Grady and Hazel Cole for Bluebird in 1939. Although Gube sang in a style not unlike that of Roy Acuff, it was sufficiently his own to avoid being labeled an Acuff copyist. He did record covers of a pair of Acuff sacred songs, *Automobile of Life* and *I'm Dying a Sinner's Death*, but other titles such as *The Straight and Narrow Way*, *Cruel Hearted Girl* and *The Great Judgment Day* fell outside the Acuff mold.

In spite of the popularity of his Capitol discs, Gube did little to advance his career. He alternated radio appearances with taxi driving and periodic drinking binges. He went on one such drinking spree after driving a passenger all the way to Greenville, South Carolina, and found himself thrown into jail. While incarcerated, he got religion and subsequently told his employer Cas Walker that he should "stop singing for the Devil and start singing for the Lord."

Gube continued to sing Gospel songs on commercial radio, and also organized his family into a group which sang at revivals.

Later he became a minister and worked tent revivals and preached in a store-front church, the Bible Church of God in Knoxville. He also had religious radio programs on WKXV. Although small in stature, Reverend Beaver has become a near legend in East Tennessee for his enthusiastic preaching style where the spirit sometimes moves him to stand on his head or climb poles in tent revivals. Reverend Beaver has also become known for the colorful words and phrases he uses in his ministry.

To date, none of his eight original recordings for Capitol has been re-issued. IMT

Beef Eaters refer BYRDS

MOLLY BEE

(Singer, Yodeler, Dancer, Actress)

Given Name: **Molly Beachboard**
Date of Birth: **August 18, 1939**
Where Born: **Oklahoma City, Oklahoma**
Married: **Three times**
Children: **Bobbi Jo, Malia**

Molly Bee is another example of precocious stardom. Her early years spent yodeling and singing on the farm were similar to those of a lot of Country performers. She was raised in Beltbuckle, Tennessee; then her family moved to Tucson, Arizona, where her career started in earnest. Her mother took her to see Rex Allen and told her to sing for him. The blond-haired, blue-eyed youngster sang *Lovesick Blues* and not long after, at the ripe old age of 10, debuted on Allen's radio show.

The following year, Molly's family moved to Hollywood and at the age of 11, she became a regular on Cliffie Stone's Los Angeles-based TV show, *Hometown Jamboree*. She stayed with the Jamboree until she reached her late teens. The show was often referred to as "the Molly Bee Show." At the same time, she was also appearing on TV on the *Pinky Lee Show,* which she joined when 13 and remained on for three years.

In 1952, she had signed to Capitol Records and her first single was *Tennessee Tango*. At the end of that year, she was highly successful with *I Saw Mommy Kissing Santa Claus*. Among her successes the following year was a duet with Tennessee Ernie, *Don't Start Courtin' in a Hot Rod Ford,* which was somewhat forward for a 13-year-old to sing.

After leaving Pinky Lee, she signed with the Tennessee Ernie Ford daytime TV show as a regular member. As her career blossomed, she was seen on other shows. At her live performances, during the 50's, she was drawing record-breaking crowds.

In 1958, Molly released the album ***Young***

Romance and also had an EP of the same title taken from it. She had two more singles that year, *Don't Look Back* and *5 Points of a Star*. She became a cast member of *Swingin' Country* along with Roy Clark and Rusty Draper during the late 60's. The show was nationally shown and gave her even greater exposure. She became a great circuit attraction in Las Vegas in the 60's and played most of the major showrooms, singing and dancing.

During that decade, she added acting to her other talents. She made her stage acting debut in the musical *The Boy Friend* at the Garden Court Theater in San Francisco. She appeared in *Finian's Rainbow* with Alan Young and *Paint Your Wagon* with Buddy Ebsen. She also appeared in two movies, *Chartreuse Caboose* (1960) and *The Young Swingers* (1963).

During 1962 to 1964, she released several singles for Liberty Records, none of which made any dent on the national charts, although *She's New to You* (1963) was a regional hit. In 1965 she signed to MGM Records and her initial single for them was *Keep It a Secret/Single Girl Again*. Later that year, she released *I'm Gonna Change Everything/ Together Again*. Both of these singles could be found on her 1965 album, ***It's Great...It's Molly Bee***. The following year, her most successful MGM release was *Losing You/Miserable Me*. It was strange to see Molly singing *Miserable Me* with a big smile on her face! Later that year, she released *How's the World Treating You/It Keeps Right on a Hurtin'*. She rounded off 1966 with *A World I Can't Live In*.

Molly started 1967 with the release of another fine recording, her version of *Almost Persuaded* with the flip-side *Heartbreak USA*. This was followed by *I Hate to See Me Go*. On the other side was her rendition of the Hank Williams classic *You Win Again*. That same year, there was another album, ***Swingin' Country,*** and she toured Japan. *Fresh Out of Tryin'* was to be her last MGM release.

It's Great...It's **Molly Bee**

By now, Molly had been through two marriages and was having problems with her third. She had a drug problem that was in danger of wrecking her career; a story not unfamiliar with child stars. Molly was determined that the business had to take a back seat and she was equally certain that she had to work on her life and get it sorted out. She wanted to spend time with her two daughters and try to save her marriage.

In 1975, she signed to Cliffie Stone's Granite label and released a new album, ***Good Golly Ms. Molly*** which was issued in the UK by Pye. She proved that the old magic was still there and that the public still wanted her with the chart single *She Kept on Talkin'*. She followed this up with three more singles for the label, *Right or Left at Oak Street* (No. 83), *California Country* and *I Can't Live in the Dark Anymore*, the last two not charting. In 1982, Accord released Molly's album ***Sounds Fine to Me***.

RECOMMENDED ALBUMS:
"Young Romance" (Capitol)(1958)
"It's Great...It's Molly Bee" (Capitol)(1965)
"Swingin' Country" (MGM)(1967)
"Good Golly Ms. Molly" (Granite)(1975)
"Sounds Fine to Me" (Accord)(1982)

PHILOMENA BEGLEY

(Singer)
Date of Birth: **October 20, 1954**
Where Born: **Pomroy, County Tyrone, Northern Ireland**
Married: **Tom**
Children: **Mary Aiden, Carol**

Known as "Ireland's Queen of Country Music," Philomena Begley has made a firm imprint on the Irish, British and European markets.

The fourth of eight children, Philomena enjoyed a typical Irish upbringing with a love for Country music instilled in her from an early age. It also helped that her mother sang while her father played accordion. Philomena was influenced by Hank Williams and as a child she won ten shillings (75 cents) singing a duet with another girl in Clarrie Hayden's Travelling Show.

Working in Fishers Hat Factory in Cookstown, County Tyrone during the day, Philomena joined the Old Cross Ceila Band to occupy her at night. In the process she gained a husband (a band member) and cut her first record, *My Little Son* (1968). Reflecting the increasing popularity of Country music in Ireland, the band's name was changed to the Country Flavour, resulting in the band making a greater impact. In 1971 the band made the Irish Top 10 with *Here Today, Gone Tomorrow* and *Never Again*.

This success encouraged Begley to form her own band, the Ramblin' Men, a connection which would last for 10 years and spur many Irish hits. Among them were *Ramblin' Man*, a cover of *Blanket on the Ground* (which Philomena took to No. 5, while Billie Jo Spears only took her original to No.11), *Wait a Little Longer, Once Around the Dance Floor* and *Whiskey Drinkin' You*. There were also duet successes with fellow Irishman Ray Lynam, including *You're the One I Can't Live Without* and *My Elusive Dreams*. In addition, the duo released two albums. More recently Philomena has duetted with rising Irish singer Mick Flavin, enjoying a single success with *'Til a Tear Becomes a Rose* and cutting an album with him, ***In Harmony***. Among her many notable albums is ***Country, Scots and Irish***, in which she combined songs from or about the two countries.

Philomena first visited the United States in 1977, appearing in Boston, New York and Chicago. Her impact was such that the following year, while visiting Nashville, Porter Wagoner invited her to guest on the *Grand Ole Opry*. In addition, he also produced several singles and albums recorded in his Fireside Studios in Nashville, including ***Philomena's Country***. Philomena has also appeared on the International Show at Fan Fair. She was also a regular performer at the prestigious Wembley Country Music Festival in England and has also been in demand over the years to support American Country acts whenever they played Britain and Ireland; among these have been Don Williams and Glen Campbell. In January 1984, Philomena signed with Ritz Records, Ireland's premier Country label, and has released a series of albums. In addition, K-Tel released her collection, ***The Best of Philomena Begley***, and it achieved Platinum status.

Philomena has also toured extensively as the top of the bill in Country clubs, both in her native Ireland, and across the UK. Europe has also been graced with her talents and in October 1992, Philomena participated in a two-hour special on the satellite radio program, Quality Europe FM, whose potential audience is 150 million people. There was a tremendous response, with phone requests from all over the Continent to hear her material.

Philomena has appeared extensively on Irish TV, has made a live video and received numerous awards for her achievements. During 1983 she received the European Gold Star Award in Holland. Perhaps the most significant accolade was the British Country Music Association award in November 1992 in recognition of Philomena Begley's contribution to the development of Country music in Britain.

Philomena Begley's success is in large part due to her ability to handle a wide range of material, whether it be original songs or covers given the Begley treatment. She's been in the business for over 30 years and retirement is still far from the horizon. When she's not touring or recording, Philomena relaxes on her family farm. SM

RECOMMENDED ALBUMS:
"You're in My Heart" (Ritz UK)(1984)
"Philomena's Country" (Ritz UK)(1984) [Originally released on Top Spin UK]
"The Best of Philomena Begley" (Ritz UK)(1984)
"More About Love" (Ritz UK)(1987)
"Silver Anniversary Album" (Ritz UK)(1988)
"Reflections" (K-Tel)(1990)

CARL BELEW

(Singer, Songwriter, Guitar)
Given Name: Carl Robert Belew
Date of Birth: April 21, 1931
Where Born: Salina, Oklahoma
Married: Kate May
Children: Robert, Gene
Date of Death: October 31, 1990

Although he sought fame as a performer, it is as a songwriter that Carl Belew is best remembered, leaving a legacy of classic songs.

Carl grew up in Salina and at age 15, became a plumber and subsequently worked in construction; however, he was intent on making it in the music business. In 1955, Marvin Rainwater got him a recording session on Four Star Records (best known for the early recordings of Patsy Cline) and the following year Carl appeared on *Town Hall Party* in Compton, California, and the Los Angeles-based *Cliffie Stone Show*. During 1957 he gained a spot on the *Louisiana Hayride*.

The following year Belew's true vocation became apparent when his composition *Stop the World (and Let Me Off)* became a Top 10 hit for Johnnie and Jack. That same year, Carl appeared on the televised Ozark Jubilee. After delving into Rockabilly material, Carl's *Lonely Street* was pitched to Andy Williams, who took it into the U.S. Pop Top 5 in 1959. It quickly became a standard, recorded by countless artists, among them Gene Vincent, Rex Allen Jr. (Top 10, 1977/8), and Patsy Cline. Both these songs earned Carl BMI Awards.

In 1959 there came another classic from the Belew pen entitled *Am I That Easy to Forget*; a song that was inspired by the imaginary situation of his own 30-year marriage

Never easy to forget, ***Carl Belew***

coming to an end. In 1960 the song was a No. 25 Pop hit for Debbie Reynolds and eight years later, Engelbert Humperdinck took it to the Top 3 on the British charts. Countless singers have recorded their versions, including Skeeter Davis, Jim Reeves, Orion, Don Gibson and Leon Russell. In 1965, Eddy Arnold took *What's He Doing in My World* to No.1. *That's When I See the Blues (in Your Pretty Brown Eyes)* was a posthumous hit for Jim Reeves, in 1968.

Carl himself was a respectable singles artist. He signed with Decca in 1958 and his longest chart run (20 weeks), predictably enough, was with *Am I That Easy To Forget*, a Top 10 in 1959. He followed this, in 1960, with the Top 10 release, *Too Much to Lose*.

In 1962, he moved to RCA Victor and *Hello Out There* gave him his second and final Top 10 record. He had Top 25 success with *In the Middle of a Memory*. Although he didn't write it, Carl had the original release of *Crystal Chandelier* (written by Ted Harris), later an overseas hit for Charley Pride. Carl's version peaked at No.12 in 1965. Although he continued to chart, his records only reached the lower levels. In 1971, a duet success with Betty Jean Robinson, *All I Need Is You,* could only reach No. 51. Three years later came Carl's final single, *Welcome Back to My World*, on MCA, but it only made the Top 60.

Among other charted versions of Carl's songs are Waylon Jennings and Susan Raye, who both had Top 20 hits with *Stop the World (and Let Me Off)* in 1965 and 1974 respectively. LaWanda Lindsey reached the Top 30 with *Hello Out There* and Jerry Wallace had a low-level entry with *Even the Bad Times Are Good*, both in 1974.

In his later years, Carl Belew was plagued by ill health and he ultimately succumbed to cancer. SM

RECOMMENDED ALBUMS:
"Am I That Easy to Forget" (RCA Victor)(1964)
"Country Songs" (Vocalion)(1966)
"Twelve Shades of Belew" (Decca)(1968)
"When My Baby Sings His Song" (Decca)(1972) [With Betty Jean Robinson]

BELLAMY BROTHERS, The

HOWARD BELLAMY
(Singer, Songwriter, Guitar, Banjo, Mandolin)
Date of Birth: February 2, 1946
Married: Ilona
Children: Cheyenne
DAVID BELLAMY
(Singer, Songwriter, Guitar, Banjo, Accordion, Piano, Omnicord, Mandolin, Fiddle)
Date of Birth: September 16, 1950
Married: Janet
Children: Jesse, Noah, Cole, Dustin
Both Born: Darby, Florida

The Bellamy Brothers have become the most successful duo in the history of Country music with their bright, breezy and uplifting style of delivery. Over a period of time, the brothers were exposed to a series of influences which were eventually reflected in their musical outpourings. Their father, Homer, frequently performed traditional Country material around the house and in a Western Swing band at weekends, and his sons' first public appearance was with him at the 1958 Rattlesnake Round-Up in San Antonio, Florida.

What was to make Howard and David's music distinctive was their willingness to be influenced by other musical forms besides mainstream Country. At an early age, they were inspired by Jamaicans from the nearby Caribbean Islands who sang all day when they came each year to pick the orange crop. Their sister also brought home Elvis and Everly Brothers records, while later on the Bellamys were receptive toward the Beatles and R&B. Later still, Merle Haggard and George Jones provided their foremost Country influences.

Howard and David received little formal musical training but nevertheless came to master a wide range of instruments. Their singing talents emerged at fraternity parties at the University of Florida in Gainesville, which represented their first paid work for their music. Both brothers earned degrees, Howard in veterinary medicine, David in psychology.

The brothers joined a series of bands including the Accidents (David) and in 1968 tried their luck in Atlanta, where they helped form Jericho, honing their versatile approach in response to the varying demands of club audiences. They then returned home to recuperate and develop their songwriting. From the beginning, David was the more prolific and commercial songwriter. It was his composition, *Spiders and Snakes*, inspired by farm experiences, which finally gave the duo the financial security to pursue a musical career uninhibited by the necessity to hold down day-time jobs. Fortuitously, in 1973, the brothers met a man who knew singer Jim Stafford, then recording in Los Angeles and seeking material. Stafford was so enthralled with the song that, after some adjustments to accommodate his humorous delivery, it became his next single, selling 3 million copies.

The brothers then moved to Los Angeles in search of a recording contract and were signed up by Warner/Curb, in 1975. Their first release, *Nothin' Heavy*, a David Bellamy song, did nothing chart-wise. They became friendly with a member of Neil Diamond's band, drummer Dennis St. John. One day he brought along a song written by Diamond's roadie, Larry E. Williams. Howard and David needed little persuading that *Let Your Love Flow* was an ideal vehicle and it became their second single. It became a No.1 Pop hit and just failed to reach the Country Top 20. It also proved to be a monster hit in Europe, staying at the top of the West German charts for a month, going Gold in Scandinavia and Silver in Britain.

Their debut album, of the same name, enjoyed similar success, achieving Platinum status in Britain, Diamond in Scandinavia and Gold in West Germany. When the single began to take off in Europe, the Bellamy Brothers embarked on a promotional tour and they were to stay, intermittently, for the next two years, riding the crest of their new-found popularity. Staying in Europe enabled them to pay off accumulated debts due to mismanagement, leading the Bellamys to let their mother, Frances, control the financial side. In 1977, their album ***Plain & Fancy*** went Gold in both Norway and Sweden.

1978 was a seminal year. It marked the time when the Bellamys returned to their homeland and tired of life in the L.A. fast lane, to their family's farm in Darby, Florida, where they still reside. Their second post-return single, *Slippin' Away*, provided their first Top 20 Country hit and marked a move in a more definite Country direction. They closed out the year with another Top 20 Country hit, *Lovin' On*.

In 1979, the witty *If I Said You Had a Beautiful Body Would You Hold It Against Me*, inspired by Groucho Marx, was the song that was to become the first of the brothers' many Country chart toppers (it also went Top 40 on the Pop chart) as well as providing them with a second international hit. Ironically, their record company did not at first feel the song was worthy of a single release. They were persuaded after it began taking off in Ireland on an independent label and it eventually went Silver in Britain. They closed out the year with the Top 5 *You Ain't Just Whistlin' Dixie*. That year, *Cash Box* named them "New Vocal Group of the Year" and they were nominated for a Grammy Award as "Best Country Performance by Duo or Group."

The Bellamys started 1980 with back-to-back No.1 Country hits, *Sugar Daddy* and *Dancin' Cowboys* and followed-up with the Top 3, *Lovers Live Longer*. That year, they were named CMA's "Most Promising Group of the Year." They started out 1981, with another No.1, *Do You Love As Good As You Look*. Their next single, *They Could Put Me in Jail*, just failed to make the Top 10, but their fall single, *You're My Favorite Star*, went Top 10. Their year-end seasonal single *It's So Close to Christmas (And I'm So Far from Home)*, also managed to reach the Top 70. That year, they were nominated for the CMA's "Vocal Group of the Year" award.

At the end of 1981, Curb moved the Bellamy Brothers to Elektra for distribution. Their first single under this connection, *For All the Wrong Reasons*, went to No.1. It was followed by the highly inventive *Get into Reggae Cowboy*, which just missed the Top 20. They ended the year with another No.1, *Redneck Girl*. In 1982, the Bellamy Brothers were nominated for the ACM's "Vocal Duo of the Year." This was a nomination they would receive in 1984 through 1987, without winning. During 1983, the Bellamy hits were *When I'm Away from You* (No.1), *I Love Her Mind* (Top 5) and the Top 15 *Strong Weakness*, the title track of their 1982 very Floridian-covered album. *Billboard* named them "Top Country Duo" for both Singles and Albums. The CMA nominated them for "Top Vocal Group" and they received Lifetime Membership of the Federation of International Country Air Personalities.

In 1984, Curb/MCA distributed the Bellamys' releases and continued their success. That year, they had the Top 5 *Forget About Me* and the Top 10 *World's Greatest Lover*. Their album ***Restless*** went Gold in both Austria and Germany. The following year, they started off with the No.1 *I Need More of You*, which earned a "No.1 Award" from the CMA. This was followed by *Old Hippie*, which appealed to Vietnam vets, went Top 3 and earned for them the "Creative Genius Award" from the NSAI. They closed out the year with *Lie to You for Your Love*, which did the same. Their ***Greatest Hits*** album went Gold in Austria and the following year was their first Certified Gold album in the U.S. In addition, *I Need More of You* became a Gold single in Austria.

The Bellamys' first hit of 1986 was the Top 3 *Feelin' the Fire* and then they teamed up with the Forester Sisters for the No.1 *Too Much Is Not Enough*. This was followed by another No.1 for Howard and David, *Kids of the Baby Boom*, which hit home with its mixture of optimism and pessimism of a generation mingling with the gloom after the utopian promise of the early 60's. They followed with another very inventive song that didn't find radio favor, *Country Rap*.

The Bellamy Brothers stayed with Curb/MCA until 1990 and their major suc-

David and Howard, the ***Bellamy Brothers***

cesses were *Crazy from the Heart* (Top 3, 1987), *Santa Fe* (Top 5), *I'll Give You All My Love Tonight* and *Rebels Without a Clue* (both Top 10, all 1988), *Big Love* (Top 5) and *You'll Never Be Sorry* (Top 10) (both 1989). In 1990, they once again teamed up with the Forester Sisters on John Hiatt's *Drive South* (which would be a Top 3 hit, two years later, for Suzy Bogguss). Their last big hit was the Top 10 single, *I Could Be Persuaded*.

After one album with Atlantic, ***Rollin' Thunder*** (notable for Howard and David's co-writing with songwriter Don Schlitz), which yielded two chart singles, the most successful being the Top 50 *She Don't Know That She's Perfect*, the Bellamy Brothers signed with Jupitor Records. ***The Latest and the Greatest*** (1992) was not only produced by the Bellamys but also came out on their new label, Bellamy Brothers Records, as did their first album of new material, ***Rip Off the Knob*** (1993).

In a sense the brothers had come full circle since their beginning, finally gaining full control of their productions, but independent status has also diminished the success of their singles, although *Cowboy Beat*, which went Top 25, showed that indies can still make it.

David explains the Bellamy Brothers' success in terms of them meeting traditional and progressive Country halfway. "We don't go too far either way. We're not a traditional group, but we like traditional music and certainly aren't intimidated by doing it, while the progressive stuff comes pretty naturally to us. So we just stay in the crack." SM

RECOMMENDED ALBUMS:

"Greatest Hits" (Warner/Curb)(1982) [Re-released as "Greatest Hits Volume I" by Curb Records]
"Country Rap" (Curb/MCA)(1986)
"Greatest Hits, Volume Two" (Curb/MCA)(1986)
"Crazy from the Heart" (Curb/MCA)(1987)
"Rebels Without a Clue" (Curb/MCA)(1988)
"Greatest Hits Volume III" (Curb/MCA)(1989)
"Rollin' Thunder" (Atlantic)(1991)
"The Latest and the Greatest" (Bellamy Brothers) (1992)
"Rip Off the Knob" (Bellamy Brothers)(1993)

BOYD BENNETT

(Drums)
Date of Birth: December 7, 1924
Where Born: Muscle Shoals, Alabama

Boyd Bennett and his music rank as marginally Country in a manner somewhat similar to that of Bill Haley. His earliest and best-known discs were released in the latter days of King Records' legendary 500 series, but his biggest recognition came in the Pop field.

Boyd grew up near Nashville and secured some of his professional experience in music as a drummer and vocalist in a group led by WSM staff band leader Francis Craig. Shortly after, Boyd entered the military during the latter part of WWII. At the end of hostilities, he got a job at a radio station and organized a small dance band called the Southlanders. Boyd described this unit's style as leaning towards Western Swing. In 1952, Boyd signed with King Records and his initial session took place that December. One side of his first release, a Country number called *Time*, met with modest success, but the next year, he began restyling his band for more appeal to a youthful audience, renaming them the Rockets (this was about the time that Haley's Saddlemen became the Comets).

In January 1955, the Rockets cut *Seventeen*, which Bennett and co-writer John Young had penned about the latter's teenage daughter. Despite producer Syd Nathan's initial reluctance to even release it, *Seventeen* rose to No. 5 on the Pop charts and provided King with one of its all-time best-sellers. A number of established Pop artists quickly covered the number ultimately pushing writer-sale royalties to some 3 million. The follow-up, *My Boy Flat-Top*, with vocals by a band member known as Big Moe (James Muzey), also crashed the Pop Top 40 listings. They had one more Pop chart single in 1956, with their version of Carl Perkins' *Blue Suede Shoes*, but it only reached the Top 70. Bennett and the Rockets recorded several more numbers with King through January 1958, and while some did quite well, such as *High School Hop* and *Hit That Jive, Jack*, none ever quite had the impact of *Seventeen*. Boyd's band also backed Moon Mullican on the 1956 session which produced his Rockabilly classic *Seven Nights to Rock*. Ironically, the Rockets themselves did not really play the primitive type of Rockabilly which collectors would later treasure.

After leaving King, Boyd signed with Mercury and had a minor hit with *Boogie Bear* in the latter part of 1959. He was acutely aware that he was several years older than most of the emerging Rock'n'Roll superstars and with a sharp mind for business, opted to get out of music while ahead of the game. He already owned three night clubs and became part owner of a TV station.

In 1967, Bennett started a company called Hardcast Manufacturing which in recent years has made parts for the air-conditioning industry. In 1988, when an album of his King sides was released in Denmark, researcher Adam Komorowski reported that Boyd was more or less retired from music except for an occasional charity benefit appearance with Ray Price when Price does a show in the Dallas area, where Boyd now resides. IMT

RECOMMENDED ALBUMS:

"Seventeen Partners" (King)(1958)
"Boyd Bennett and His Rockets: Seventeen" (Sing Denmark)(1988)

MATRACA BERG

(Singer, Songwriter, Keyboards, Guitar)
Date of Birth: February 3, 1964
Where Born: Nashville, Tennessee

It seems impossible to think of Matraca Berg being anything but a singer or songwriter or musician. Being the daughter of Nashville session singer and songwriter Icee Berg and having songwriter/guitarist Dave Kirby as a stepfather and Patsy Cline as a third cousin, Matraca was exposed to the music industry from a very young age.

Matraca's father deserted Icee when it was discovered she was pregnant. This abandonment has instilled a resentment within Matraca, which often surfaces in her songs. When she was still in her teens, her mother took her around the music publishing houses, showing off Matraca's skill as a songwriter. Matraca met Bobby Braddock at Tree Publishing, and he suggested that they write together. Their first song together, *Faking Love,* was recorded by T. G. Sheppard and Karen Brooks in 1982 and became a No.1 Country hit the following year. However, success brought pressures in itself for the then 18-year-old writer, and she relocated to Louisiana, where she became the keyboard player for the Rock-orientated Kevin Stewart Band.

However, two years later, Matraca was back in Nashville, looking after her younger brother and sister following the death of their mother. To make matters worse, Matraca's own marriage broke up. She continued writing songs for others without ever contemplating a singing career, often not even singing on her own song demos. In 1986, Tanya Tucker released Matraca's *Girls Like Me*, which became the title song of her album that year. In 1987, Reba McEntire had a No.1 hit with Matraca's *The Last One to Know.* Although that song was written with Jane Mariash, a lot of Matraca's songs are written with Ronnie Samoset. Highway 101 cut the first of three Berg songs that year, *Bridge Across Forever*. They went on to record *Somewhere Between Gone and Goodbye* in 1988 and *If Love Had a Heart* the following year. In 1988, Joe Galante put Matraca on *Signatures II*, the second album in RCA's songwriters' series, where she sang *Your Baby Ain't a Baby* and *Lying to the Moon*. Also in 1988, Tom Wopat cut Matraca's *Bad Love Blues* and the Forester Sisters recorded *You Love Me*.

In 1990, Matraca released her debut album,

Lying to the Moon, which climbed into the Country Albums Top 50. She had her first taste of Country Single chart success with *Baby, Walk On*, which went Top 40. She followed up with *The Things You Left Undone*, which reached the same position. She had three further chart entries in 1991 with *I Got It Bad* being the most successful. The follow-up, *Must Have Been Crazy,* is a song in which she looks back at the time she spent on an analyst's couch, exorcising the pain suffered by being in love with one person, following the break-up of her marriage. She ended the year with *It's Easy to Tell*.

Matraca has not sampled the delights of major stardom as a performer, but her future albums may unlock the key.

RECOMMENDED ALBUM:

"Lying to the Moon" (RCA)(1990)

SHIRLEY BERGERON

(Steel Guitar, Guitar, Singer, Songwriter)

Given Name: **Shirley Ray Bergeron**
Date of Birth: **November 16, 1933**
Where Born: **Point Noir, Church Point, Louisiana**
Married: **Lee Audrey**
Children: **Ruby, Janet, Phyllis**

Like many Cajun musicians, Shirley is known only within his area of music and within his own locale. His father, Alphee Bergeron (1912-1980), was for many years a very respected accordion player. Over the years, Alphee had played with Nathan Abshire, Happy Fats and Mayeuse Lafleur and had his own band, the Veteran Playboys, which had broadcast over KSIG Cowley, KSLO Opelousas, KEUN Eunice, and KVPI Ville Platte. He had recorded for Brunswick prior to WWII and had cut one single, *Chinaball Special/Eunice Waltz,* for Feature.

Shirley joined his father's band and became one of the most popular local musicians. He was playing dances every night of the week during the late 40's. He regularly broadcast on KSLO.

When Rock'n'Roll started to become a major force, gigs started to drop off and Shirley was only getting Saturday dates. However, in 1960, his career started to take off. He recorded *J'ai Fait Mon Edée* for Lanor, a label owned by his old school friend Lee Lavergne. Also playing on the single were his father and the Veteran Playboys. He followed this single with *Chez Tanie* and in 1963, *French Rocking Boogie*. Shirley's first album, ***The Sounds of Cajun Music,*** was very well received. ***Cajun Style Music,*** his second album, did not sell well, and for a while he decided to retire from music. He returned to playing locally on a part-time basis. He became an insurance salesman and then worked as a bank officer. In 1994, it was discovered that Shirley had cancer and he was finally forced to give up music.

RECOMMENDED ALBUMS:

"The Sounds of Cajun Music" (Lanor)
"Cajun Style Music" (Lanor)

BYRON BERLINE

(Fiddle, Singer, Mandolin, Guitar, Sousaphone)

Date of Birth: **July 6, 1944**
Where Born: **Caldwell, Kansas**

If ever there was the title of "Renaissance man fiddle player," then Byron Berline would capture the crown. Probably more than any other Country-based fiddler, he has played on albums as diverse as Jazz, Blues, Country-Rock and Pop. The only other fiddle player to come anywhere near his range is Vassar Clements. In addition, Byron has scored and appeared in several movies, and like Clements, is a multi-instrumentalist.

As a child, Byron was raised on a farm in Oklahoma, just over the state line from Caldwell. His father, Lue, was a very adept Old-Time fiddle player, who set about teaching Byron, then age 5, to play the fiddle perfectly. Byron's mother, Elizabeth, played piano and his brother played guitar. Practicing in the bathroom, under his father's strict tutoring and assisted by a family friend, Frank Mitchell, who was a direct influence on Byron's style, the young Berline was soon being taken around fiddling contests.

At high school, he played sousaphone in the band, and also was a fine track and field athlete. In 1962, he went to the University of Oklahoma on a football scholarship; however, during the first season he suffered a broken thumb and was on the sick list for six weeks. He switched to field events, specializing in javelin, throwing a personal best of 221 feet 5 inches. While at university, he also played in a Folk group.

In November 1963, on the day that President Kennedy was assassinated, the Dillards were entertaining on campus. One of Byron's friends encouraged Doug Dillard to listen to Byron play. Dillard invited young Berline to play with the group for one number, and he wound up playing for two hours. While in college, he played with the Cleveland Country Ramblers, and for two years, they performed on a TV program sponsored by Garrett Household Furniture. By the following year, the Berline career started in earnest, when he was the starring attraction on the Dillards' ***Pickin' and Fiddlin'*** and he won the National Fiddle Championship in Missoula, Montana.

In 1965, he played at the Newport Folk Festival, and again won the National Fiddle Championship, this time in Weiser, Idaho. While at Newport, he met Bob Dylan and Bill Monroe. There he jammed with Monroe, who told him that he wanted Byron to play with the Blue Grass Boys.

Byron graduated in 1967, with a B.A. degree in education, and the intention of becoming a coach at a junior high in Garland, Texas. However, fate now stepped in twice. First, Bill Monroe was as good as his word, and in March of that year, Byron became a Blue Grass Boy, replacing Richard Greene, and made his debut on the *Grand Ole Opry*. Then, six months later, he was drafted into the U.S. Army. He did his basic training at Camp Polk, Louisiana. After five weeks, he was asked by the sergeant whether he knew anything about music. He was then put in charge of a daily family show. As there wasn't a fiddle in camp, he arranged for his old friend Alan Munde (later of Country Gazette fame) to bring him one. Byron's music went over well with the Colonel, a Roy Acuff fan.

The day before Byron left the service, in 1969, he was contacted by Doug Dillard to become a part of the Dillard and Clark Expedition, with Gene Clark. By this time, Kenny Baker had become the fiddler with Monroe. Byron moved to Los Angeles and stayed with Dillard and Clark until 1971, when the group broke up. He recorded the album ***Through the Morning*** while with the group, and also appeared on other albums. These included ***Gilded Palace of Sin*** (Flying Burrito Brothers, 1969), ***Silent Song Through the Land*** (Ron Davies)(on which he played mandolin), ***Copperfields*** (Dillards) and ***Burrito De Luxe*** (Flying Burrito Brothers), all in 1970, and ***Byrdmaniax*** (The Byrds), ***Rotten to the Core*** (Crabby Appleton), ***Last of the Red Hot Burritos*** (Flying Burrito Brothers) and ***Barry McGuire & The Doctor*** (Barry McGuire), all in 1971. In addition, Byron again won the National Fiddle Championship, in 1970, in Weiser.

While with Dillard and Clark (and its successor, Dillard Expedition), he scored the ABC Movie of the Week, *Run Simon Run*. This led to him scoring many other movies. He was in the process of putting Country Gazette together when he was approached in 1971 to tour with the Flying Burrito Brothers, playing a Bluegrass segment in the middle of each concert with Roger Bush and Kenny Wertz. They formed themselves into Country Gazette (see separate entry). In 1972, Byron played on sessions for Stephen Stills' Manassas (***Manassas***) and Rick Roberts (***Windfalls***).

During 1973, as well as appearing on Country Gazette's ***Don't Give Up Your Day Job*** and ***Bluegrass Special,*** Byron also guested on Doug Dillard's ***Dueling Banjos***, the soundtrack album of *Pat Garrett and Billy the Kid* (for which he provided some of the music), Deke Leonard's ***Iceberg,*** Ian Matthews and Southern Comfort's ***Valley Hi*** and Gram Parsons' ***GP***. Byron appeared on Country Gazette's 1974 album, ***Banjo Sandwich*** and his playing was heard on Bert Jansch's ***L.A. Turnaround,*** Deke Leonard's ***Kamikazee***, the Nitty Gritty Dirt Band's ***Stars & Stripes Forever*** and Bill Wyman's ***Monkey Grip***. Byron also played on Gram Parsons' ***Grievous Angel*** album, released in 1974.

He left Country Gazette during 1975, as he was tired of touring, and decided he wanted to stay home home with his family in L.A. and concentrate on writing, session work and movie assignments. He scored his first major motion picture, *Stay Hungry*, that year, for director Bob Rafelson.

When he put together Sundance, in 1975, Byron pulled in Dan Crary (whom he had met in 1974) on guitar, Jack Skinner (bass, banjo), John Hickman (banjo, guitar, mandolin), Allen Wald (guitar) and Skip Conover (Dobro, guitar), to form the line-up. The group remained together until 1978, although it underwent some changes when Skinner left in 1976, to be replaced by Vince Gill (guitar), Mark Cohen (drums) and Joe Villegas (bass). The following year, Hickman also went his merry way. During their existence, Byron Berline & Sundance recorded one eponymous album for MCA, released in 1976.

While with Sundance, Byron continued to do session work and appeared on The Band's ***Northern Lights, Southern Cross***, Dillard and Clark's ***Gene Clark & Doug Dillard*** and Emmylou Harris' ***Pieces of the Sky*** (playing mandolin) (all 1975). In 1976, Byron sessioned on American Flyer's eponymous album, Jonathan Edwards' ***Rockin' Chair***, Lawrence Hammond's ***Coyote Dream***, Emmylou Harris' ***Elite Motel*** (playing mandolin again), Chris Hillman's ***Slippin' Away***, Kristofferson's ***Surreal Thing*** and James Taylor's ***The Best of.*** The following year, he played on Olivia Newton-John's ***Making a Good Thing Better*** and Arlo Guthrie's ***The Best of.*** He also got together with Mark O'Connor and Sam Bush for an in-concert recording, released on O'Connor's own label.

Byron was approached by a Japanese promoter to play in Japan. However, he could only afford three musicians, and so he was joined by Crary and Hickman. The result was so good that Berline, Crary, Hickman stayed together, recording three albums for Sugar Hill. At the same time, Byron formed the L.A. Fiddle Band, which is still in existence, and features three fiddles, a banjo, guitar, bass and Dobro. He released the album ***Live at McCabe's*** on Takoma (as a part of Country Gazette) and ***Dad's Favorites*** on Rounder, and worked on sessions for Rodney Crowell's ***Ain't Living Long Like This*** and Randy Meisner's self-titled album. He also appeared in the movie *Every Which Way But Loose*, with Clint Eastwood.

In 1979, he played on Doug Dillard's ***Heaven*** and toured with Dillard's band. He also played on Michael (Martin) Murphey's ***Peaks, Valleys, Honky Tonks & Alleys***. He, Crary and Hickman formed a production company called BCH. In 1980, Byron did the honors on Dillard's ***Jackrabbit!***, the Doobie Brothers' ***One Step Closer*** and Elton John's ***21 at 33.*** He also recorded the solo album ***Outrageous*** for Flying Fish, on which he was accompanied by Crary, Hickman, James Burton, Albert Lee, Vince Gill, Jay Dee Manes, Skip Conover, John Hobbs, Lee Sklar and Mark Cohen. That year, he appeared in four movies, *Brubaker* (with Robert Redford), *Any Which Way You Can*, *Bronco Billy* (both with Clint Eastwood) and *Urban Cowboy* (with John Travolta). He continued his association with rock stars in 1981, when he appeared on Rod Stewart's ***Tonight I'm Yours***. That year, he and the L.A. Fiddle Band released a self-titled album on Sugar Hill.

Byron appeared on the pivotal 1984 Chris Hillman album, ***Desert Rose***, which would lead to the formation of the Desert Rose Band. Then Berline and Hickman put together a set of fiddle-banjo duets for the 1986 released album ***Double Trouble***, which was a mix of covers and original material. In 1988, Berline, Crary, Hickman renamed themselves BCH; the group comprised Berline, Crary, Hickman and Steve Spurgin, who had started to play bass in the group in 1988. Spurgin is also a fine singer, drummer (he played drums in Sundance) and songwriter. That year they released the Sugar Hill album ***Now They Are Four.***

In 1990, they added mandolinist and guitarist John Moore, who had been a member of the L.A. Fiddlers since 1988, and California was created. The band's debut album, *Traveler,* was released in 1992 and before the year was out, California was named "Instrumental Group of the Year" by the International Bluegrass Music Association (IBMA).

RECOMMENDED ALBUMS:

"Byron Berline, Sam Bush & Mark O'Connor" (O'Connor)(1976)
"Byron Berline & Sundance" (MCA)(1976)

Byron Berline *(center back) with the other members of* ***California***

"Live at McCabe's" (Takoma)(1977) [With Country Gazette]
"Dad's Favorites" (Rounder)(1977)
"Outrageous" (Flying Fish)(1980)
"Byron Berline with the L.A. Fiddle Band" (Sugar Hill)(1981)
"Berline, Hickman, Crary" (Sugar Hill)(1981)
"Night Run" (Sugar Hill)(1984) [As Berline, Crary, Hickman]
"Double Trouble" (Sugar Hill)(1986) [With John Hickman]
"BCH" (Sugar Hill)(1986)
"Now They Are Four" (Sugar Hill)(1990) [As BCH]
"Traveler" (Sugar Hill)(1992) [As California]

ROD BERNARD

(Singer, Guitar)
Date of Birth: August 12, 1940
Where Born: Opelousas, Louisiana

Rod Bernard made his professional debut at the tender age of 10 when he appeared on the Saturday morning show on KSLO Opelousas sponsored by Dezauche's Red Bird Sweet Potatoes. He found himself a sponsor in Main Motors Company, and got his own afternoon show. Early in his life, Rod was exposed to Cajun music through his grandfather, who owned a nightclub in Port Barre near Opelousas. Rod used to sneak over there to watch the acts that included Jimmy C. Newman. When Rod was 12, he became a deejay on KSLO. However, he moved with his parents to Winnie, Texas, in 1954, and there met Huey Meaux, the great producer of Cajun music. At the time Huey was the barber in Winnie.

Rod returned to Opelousas and resumed his deejay job. While still in high school, he formed the Twisters. They cut two records for Jake Graffagzino's Carl label and then recorded *This Should Go On Forever* for Jin. Rod had heard the writer King Karl (Bernard Jolivette) sing this song at the Moonlight Inn and after Karl had failed to record it, Rod persuaded him to teach it to him. Floyd Soileau, who owned Jin, got Rod and the Twisters into the studio. The band comprised Marion Presley (piano), Charles Boudreaux (trumpet), brother Rick Bernard (bass) and Ray Thomasine (drums). Because they were not used to studio conditions additional musicians were brought in. They were Al Foreman (lead guitar) and Bobby McBride (bass) and Rick switched to guitar. Rod developed a nose bleed and had to finish the session with a towel around his face.

Rod took a box of records to Huey Meaux who ran a French music show on KPAC Port Arthur. Huey got it played all over East Texas. He took a copy to J. P. Richardson (The Big Bopper) who was the first to play it at KTRN Beaumont, Texas. The record took nearly seven months to break, but when it started to happen, it was leased to Argo (a subsidiary of Chess) for national distribution. It reached the Pop chart Top 20. Rod appeared on Dick Clark's *American Bandstand* performing the song, only after changing some of the lyrics, because it was felt that one line, "If it's a sin to really love you then a sinner I will be," was immoral, and "sin" became "wrong." Incidentally, when it was first released by Jin, *Cash Box* named it the worst record they had heard, and yet when Argo released it, it became the Hit of the Week. Chess took an option on the follow-up, *You're On My Mind,* and Rod signed a management deal with Bill Hall.

As a result of this chart activity, he signed to Mercury. Although he recorded some 40 sides for Mercury, only the first, *One More Chance,* made the Pop charts (No. 74) and in all only five singles were released. Most of them were teen fodder. In 1962, his contract with Mercury came to an end and he went down to Beaumont and recorded for Bill Hall's Hall-Way Records. His sides here included *I Might As Well*, *Loneliness*, *Forgive*, *Fais Do-Do*, *Colinda* (which was a regional hit) and *Boss Man's Son*. Legendary albino bluesmen Johnny and Edgar Winter played guitar and sax on most of Rod's recordings at Hall-Way.

He then went into the Marines in 1962. Upon his release, he returned to deejaying and became Musical Director of KVOL and WLFY-TV in Lafayette. He confined his musical activities to the Shondels, a group he had formed with Warren Storm and Skip Stewart in 1963. They appeared on KLFY-TV. Twelve Rock'n'Roll songs from the TV show were released as ***Saturday Hop*** in 1965 on the La Louisienne label. The Shondels also released the single *Our Teenage Love* for Teardrop.

In the mid-60's, Rod and Carol Ranchou of La Louisienne launched the Arbee label which was distributed nationally by Scepter. It had one hit single, *Recorded in England*, so called because as a deejay, he seemed to be getting records with "made in Britain" stamped on the label.

In 1967, he moved to the Tri-State area and attended the University of Evansville for two years as a music major. In 1979, he moved to Fresno, California. The 70's were more or less uneventful with just the occasional album release on Jin. One of these, ***Country Lovin'***, sold 15,000 copies, but ***Boogie in Black and White,*** which Rod recorded with Clifton Chenier, was not so successful. He cut a series of singles for Jin, including *Big Mamou* and a duet with Chenier of the old standard *Shake, Rattle and Roll*. In 1979, he cut his first Country single, *Love Me Tonight,* which got to No. 4 on the Country Comer list of *New York Entertainment* magazine.

Rod Bernard stands astride various musical forms and falls into the area that Tony Joe White has made popular, Swamp Rock; a blend of Rock, Country and an essence that is pure Louisiana.

RECOMMENDED ALBUMS:

"Rod Bernard" (Jin) [contains Hall-Way recordings]
"Country Lovin'" (Jin)
"Louisiana Swamp-Rock from the Jin & Hallway Labels" (Ace) [Various Artists; includes Rod Bernard]
"This Should Go on Forever and Other Bayou Classics" (Crazy Cajun)

Delia Bell refer BILL GRANT AND DELIA BELL

TOOTSIE BESS

(Owner of "Tootsie's Orchid Lounge")
Given Name: Hettie Louise
Date of Birth: 1915
Where Born: Hohenwald, Tennessee
Married: Big Jeff Bess
Date of Death: February 18, 1978

This lady became more of a legend than some of the performers who passed through the equally legendary portals of "Tootsie's Orchid Lounge." The bar is situated on Broadway just a few paces from the back door of the former home of the *Grand Ole Opry*, the Ryman Auditorium.

It was at Tootsie's where hopefuls would gather to meet, show off their new songs and make one beer last all night. These included Willie Nelson and Hank Cochran. Tootsie herself was diminutive but full of life. She would financially help those she felt genuinely wanted to make their way in Country music. However, she was also armed with a diamond-headed three-inch hat pin that Charley Pride had given her for jabbing slow drinkers.

In 1975, she appeared in a semi-autobiographical role in the movie *W.W. and the Dixie Dancekings*.

BEVERLY HILL BILLIES, The

Formed: 1930
Members have been:
Glen Rice (Organizer)
Leo Mannes (Zeke "Craddock" Manners)
Tom Murray
Cyprian Paulette (Ezra Longnecker)
Henry Blaeholder (Hank Skillet)
Aleth Hansen (Lem H. Giles, H.D.)
Ashley Dees (Jad Scroggins)
Hubert Walton
Marjorie Bauersfeld (Mirandy)
Stuart Hamblen (Dave Donner)
Curt Barrett (Gabe Hemmingway)
Jimmy Baker (Elton Britt)
Charlie Quirk (Charlie Slater)
Shug Fisher (Aaron Judd)
Ken Carson (Kaleb Winbush)
Wesley Tuttle
Chuck Cook
Len Dossey
Norman Hedges
Eddie Kirk
Curley Bradley
Lloyd Perriman
Hubert Flatt
"Squeak" McKinney

In the wake of the Great Depression, Raymond S. MacMillan, owner of MacMillan Petroleum Corporation and radio KMPC Los Angeles, Glen Rice, the station manager at KMPC, and John McIntire, the station's staff announcer, dreamed up the idea of the Hill Billies, going against the trend of having western names. He built the group around accordion player Leon Mannes, who became known as Zeke Manners. Mannes was not a regular performer. In fact, he was discovered when he had stopped at the station on the way back from the beach and was playing children's parts to help out on a show. It was agreed that Tom Murray and Cyprian Paulette, then appearing on KFI's *Saturday Night Jamboree,* should join the group. Rice created a publicity campaign stating that strange, primitive musicians had been found in Beverly Hills.

On April 6, 1930, the Hill Billies made their debut on KMPC, dressed as they thought hillbillies should be dressed. Their act was part music and part comedy. Within a few days, Henry Blaeholder joined them; this foursome is generally considered to be the Original Beverly Hill Billies. Shortly afterwards, Aleth Hansen was added. Another early member was Ashley Dees, who replaced Murray.

In June 1930, Hubert Walton, a 14-year-old yodeler, was added for a 6-week stay. Later that year, the group was augmented by Marjorie Bauersfeld. About the same time Marjorie arrived, so did the young yodeler Jimmy Baker (Elton Britt). Before the year was out, Stuart Hamblen had joined. However, he stayed for only a short while and was replaced by Curt Barrett. Another 1930 joiner was Charlie Quirk.

Shortly after their formation, the Hill Billies signed to Brunswick. Several of their early songs were written by the "Happy Chappies," Nat Vincent and Fred Howard. The Hill Billies also appeared in several movies alongside Jackie Oakie, Charles Starrett, Ray Whitley, Gene Autry and Tex Ritter (see Movie section). They also appeared with Smith Ballew in both movies and on tour.

In September 1932, the group left KMPC and went initially to KTM. They then split into two groups, each claiming to be the original one. At KMPC, Zeke Manners put together a replacement group, Zeke and His City Fellers. At the time, Manners was at the Salvation Army in L.A. In late 1932, Glen Rice re-formed the group and took it to San Francisco. The line-up was Shug Fisher, "Squeak" McKinney, Ken Carson, Curly Bradley, "Ezra" Paulette, Lloyd Perriman and Hubert Flatt.

In 1963, former members Dees, Hansen, Quirk and Barrett sued and won a settlement from the TV producers of *The Beverly Hillbillies* for name infringement.

RECOMMENDED ALBUMS:

"Those Fabulous 'Beverly Hillbillies'" (Rar-Arts)(1961)
"Those Authentic 'Beverly Hillbillies'" (Rar-Arts)(1961)
[Three albums]

Craig Bickhardt refer SKO/SKB

BIG SLIM, THE LONE COWBOY

(Singer, Songwriter, Guitar)

Given Name:	**Harry C. McAuliffe**
Date of Birth:	**May 9, 1903 or 1899 or 1904**
Where Born:	**Bluefield, West Virginia**
Married:	**Martha**
Children:	**Harry Jr. (Billy), Phyllis, Roy, Kenneth**
Date of Death:	**October 13, 1966**

Big Slim, the Lone Cowboy became one of the WWVA *Jamboree*'s most memorable stars in the generation when he first came to Wheeling radio in 1937, after some earlier experience over the airwaves in Pittsburgh. During that time, he helped popularize a number of significant traditional songs like *Patanio, The Pride of the Plains, The Roane County Prisoner, Billy Vernero* and that song of English music-hall origins, *Footprints in the Snow.* Slim also holds a share of the composer credits on some memorable lyrics such as *When They Found the Atomic Power, Moonlight on My Cabin, There Ain't Nobody Gonna Miss Me When I'm Gone* and especially *Sunny Side of the Mountain.* Slim was a man of mystery in many respects; his influence in show business transcended his own career in large part because of the impact he had on two proteges, Hawkshaw Hawkins and Hank Snow.

By his own claim, Big Slim was born adjacent to East River Mountain near the city of Bluefield on the West Virginia state line, although some of his contemporaries considered him a Pennsylvanian. He claimed to have worked as a cowboy in Wyoming and also wrote that he fired and engineered on the railroad prior to entering radio in 1929. Some of this may reflect the kind of image that radio cowboys liked to create for themselves, but there can be no doubt that he learned a great deal about training horses and the use of the bullwhip. He not only used horses and whips in his stage act, but taught these skills to Hawkshaw in later years.

After varied radio experiences at KDKA and KQV in Pittsburgh, Big Slim went to Wheeling late in 1937 as a temporary replacement for a member of the Doc Williams band. He remained at WWVA, off and on, for the rest of his life. Although he left the station from time to time, Slim always returned to its friendly confines and a warm welcome from his fans. Slim's popularity tended to be concentrated in the northeastern U.S. and eastern Canada. He aspired to appear in western films and may have had some actual experience as a rodeo rider, but Big Slim apparently failed to gain much attention when he once visited Hollywood.

Perhaps because he spent so much of his career at WWVA, a station whose management did not encourage recording activity, his appearances on disc seem rather sparse for an artist of his stature. He did an initial session for Decca as Big Slim Aliff in December 1936, recording four songs. A decade later, Slim cut another half-dozen titles on the obscure Dixie label, and six more for the Johnstown, Pennsylvania firm Page Records about 1949. In the late 50's, he did an extended-play 45 rpm disc for Audiosonic.

*WWVA's **Big Slim, The Lone Cowboy***

In his twilight years, Slim made three albums for the Canadian company Arc, which received some mail order sales in the U.S. as a WWVA special offer. He died in upstate New York, but his body was returned to Wheeling for funeral and burial. Twenty years after his death, Old Homestead released an album containing most of his earlier sides. Doc Williams has kept Big Slim's Arc material available via cassette. IMT

RECOMMENDED ALBUMS:

"Sunny Side of the Mountain" (Old Homestead)(1986)
"Big Slim, the Lone Cowboy" (Arc)(1960)
"Big Slim's Old Favorites" (Arc)(1961)
"On Tour with Big Slim, the Lone Cowboy" (Arc)(1962)

BILLY HILL

Formed:	**1989**
Members:	
John Scott Sherrill	**Guitar, Vocals**
Dennis Robbins	**Guitar, Vocals**
Bob Dipiero	**Guitar, Vocals**
Martin Parker	**Drums**
Reno Kling	**Bass Guitar**

Billy Hill was a short lived Country-Rock band that recorded one album for Reprise in 1989. Their album was entitled ***I Am Just a Rebel*** and produced the Top 30 hit single *Too Much Month at the End of the Money.*

The nucleus of this group emerged in the late 70's in the popular Nashville nightclub band known as Wolves in Cheap Clothing. In 1987, Dennis Robbins joined the foursome as a vocalist and electric guitarist. In addition to their live performances, group members Scott Sherrill, Robbins and Dipiero had found success as songwriters (often writing together) and studio musicians. Billy Hill members' writing credits include the Oak Ridge Boys' *American Made*, Highway 101's *(Do You Love Me) Just Say Yes* and *Cry, Cry, Cry*, John Anderson's *Wild and Blue*, Reba McEntire's *Little Rock*, and Steve Earle's *Nowhere Road.*

Unlike most Country albums recorded in the 24-track studios on music row, the Billy Hill album was produced in the home studio of group member Bob Dipiero. The band spent about two months recording the album in Dipiero's 12-track demo studio.

The group had fun naming the band with the variation of the term "hillbilly." They created a fictional character they called Billy Hill whom they featured on their album cover. In the liner notes they provided the history of the questionable Southern gentleman. Billy Hill was said to have been born on a mountaintop in Tennessee, the greenest state in the land of the free. His father was killed in a bar when he was only 3, but nobody seemed to remember what year that was, so speculations on Billy's age range from "pretty old" to "just a kid." Billy served in Vietnam, worked on a shrimp boat off the coast of Texas, in a steel mill in Ohio, as a park ranger in North Carolina and as a bat boy in St. Louis. He played music in Alabama with a band called Thunderbolts and ended up in the Death Valley desert, where he recorded an album called ***Poultry in Motion*** which influenced all the members of Billy Hill.

At the end of 1989, the band had a Top 60 success with a reprise of the Four Tops hit, *I Can't Help Myself (Sugar Pie Honey Bunch).* After one album and a tour, Billy Hill disbanded in 1991. Dennis Robbins then recorded as a solo artist for Giant Records in 1992 (see separate entry). He, Bob Dipiero (who is married to Pam Tillis) and John Scott Sherrill continued their successful songwriting careers and Martin Parker and Reno Kling resumed their studio and record production work in Nashville. JIE

RECOMMENDED ALBUM:
"I Am Just a Rebel" (Reprise)(1989)

BINKLEY BROTHERS, The

AMOS BINKLEY
(Banjo)
Given Name: Amos Binkley
Date of Birth: 1895
GALE BINKLEY
(Fiddle)
Given Name: Gale Binkley
Date of Birth: 1896
Both Born: Cheatham County, Tennessee

For many years, Amos and Gale Binkley led the *Grand Ole Opry* string band called the Dixie Clodhoppers. Unlike many of the hell-for-leather hoedown bands on the show, the Binkleys had a precise, almost polite sound that resembled that of Charlie Poole as much as anyone. For most of its tenure on the Opry, the band was basically a string trio consisting of the two brothers and their long-time friend, guitarist Tom Andrews. Gale, the fiddle player, had the reputation of being a careful and meticulous musician, admired for his tone and noting technique, qualities that befitted his vocation as a watch repairman and jeweler. Tom Andrews was from Franklin, Tennessee, and was a friend of fellow *Opry* stars Sam and Kirk McGee. Though generally overlooked by official histories of the *Opry* (including George D. Hay's), the Binkleys were important figures on early Nashville radio and they made the first hit record to be recorded in Nashville.

The Binkleys made their debut on the *Opry* on October 30, 1926, with their Barn Dance Orchestra, though guitarist Andrews had appeared with numerous pick-up bands before then. During 1927 and 1928, the band, which George D. Hay had renamed the Dixie Clodhoppers, appeared about once a month on WSM, but jumped ship to the rival station WLAC in 1929-1931. By 1932, they had returned to the Opry, playing in the regular rotation until August 1939, when they dropped out. (Their slot was taken by the young Bill Monroe.)

The Brothers seldom played music full-time. By day, they worked in their watch-repair and jewelry store in the old Arcade in downtown Nashville. For a time, the brothers used as their vocalist a Lebanon, Tennessee, native named Jack Jackson. Billed as "The Strolling Yodeler," Jackson had been appearing as a soloist on both WSM and WLAC. With his good looks, his styled pompadour hairdo and his clear well-trained voice, he had attracted a considerable local following. A newspaper of the time referred to him as "perhaps the most popular radio entertainer in the south." (He later recorded solo sides for Columbia.)

The Binkleys and Jackson joined forces in the fall of 1928 for a series of Victor recordings and stage appearances. They were among the first, if not the first, musicians to record in Nashville, in October 1928. Six sides were released, of which two were bona fide hits: *I'll Rise When the Rooster Crows* and *Give Me Back My Fifteen Cents*. The former became a favorite in Old-Time music. It stayed in print well into the lp reissue era, and was still performed in the 80's by TNN star David Holt. CKW

BOB BISHOP

(Singer, Songwriter, Guitar, Steel Guitar, Bass Guitar, Drums, Actor)
Given Name: Bishop Milton Sykes
Date of Birth: August 6, 1928
Where Born: Henry County, Tennessee
Married: Hazel Marion
Children: Deborah Susan, Beverly Ann

Bob Bishop was raised on a farm and came into music at an early age. His father died in an accident during the Depression and his older brother Freeman moved to Detroit to work for the government work program, WPA, in the mid-30s. From Detroit he sent for his family.

In 1945, Bob made his debut on WXYZ Detroit and then went on to broadcast on WJR and WWJ-TV, also in Detroit. He formed a singing group, the Saddleridge Buckaroos, which sang Sons of the Pioneers songs. In 1949, having just passed his 21st birthday, Bob moved to California, where he did nightclub shows until 1953. That year, he returned to Michigan.

Nashville beckoned in 1954 and he stayed there for eight months but did not get his big break. He then moved to Rockford, Illinois, to work for a friend in a car dealership by day and sing in a band at night. Three weeks later, Chet Atkins called and offered him a job singing on WSIX-TV Nashville's *Homefolks* show, and then Marty Robbins entered the scene and hired Bob as a guitarist. With Marty, he made his *Grand Ole Opry* debut in 1955.

Bob recorded as "Bobby Sykes" for Decca and Epic at the end of the 50's, and then in 1961 moved on to Columbia. Bob recorded for the Sims label in 1966, under the name of "Johnny Freedom." The circumstances of this recording as recounted by Bobby are bizarre. Marty Robbins had written and recorded two songs entitled *Ain't I Right* and *My Own Native Land,* but because the subject matter was so contentious, and political, Marty's label, Columbia Records, refused to allow him to release the single. It was, of course, when the Vietnam War was at its height and the songs mentioned politicians, albeit not by name. As a result, Marty took his band in the studio and Bob handled vocals. The record went to No.1 in Philadelphia; questions were asked in Congress, and at least one radio station playing the record was burned down, with others under threat of having their license revoked. Bob continued playing with Marty and was a featured singer, taking the baritone part in the Marty Robbins Trio. He also acted as Marty's booking agent. During the 60's, he appeared in 6 movies, five with Marty Robbins; they included *Hell on Wheels*, *From Nashville with Love* and *Guns of a Stranger*.

Bob then met Red Foley and they became close friends. In 1968, Bob had a Top 50 hit with the self-penned *Roses to Reno* on ABC Records. He released two more singles for the label, neither of which made an impression on the charts. Then in 1969, he released the album ***Somewhere in the Country***, for ABC. Bob subsequently signed with the independent label JMI, again calling himself "Bobby Sykes," and released an album in 1974 of Red Foley classics entitled ***The Rhythm of Red***. A single, *Sugarfoot Rag/Foggy River,* was issued at the same time, without success.

Bob became a member of Hank Snow's Rainbow Ranch Boys in 1986 and stayed with them until he was diagnosed with cancer in 1993 and retired from music. It can only be hoped that this very nice man makes a speedy recovery.

RECOMMENDED ALBUMS:
"Somewhere in the Country" (ABC)(1969)
"The Rhythm of Red" (JMI)(1974)

CLINT BLACK

(Singer, Songwriter, Guitar, Bass Guitar, Harmonica)
Given Name: **Clint Patrick Black**
Date of Birth: **February 4, 1962**
Where Born: **Long Branch, New Jersey**
Married: **Lisa Hartman**

When Clint was scheduled to appear at the Houston Livestock Show and Rodeo in February 1990, all 48,000 tickets were sold within 48 hours. Just a year before, Clint Black was unknown as a Country music performer, except in Houston, which he considers his home town. He played the clubs on the Houston circuit for six years before making it into the big time.

He was actually born in New Jersey, where his father, a steel worker, was on a 6-month contract. Clint's mother, pregnant at the time, visited her husband and gave birth to Clint Patrick. By the time he was 2 months old, the family had returned to Houston. Clint grew up with horses, farms and pastures and fished for bass and catfish on the Buffalo bayou along with his three older brothers. They were all musical and they sang at backyard barbecues and family picnics. Clint was impressed with the singing of Merle Haggard and learned to play harmonica after "borrowing" one from one of his brothers when he was 13. Clint's songwriting career began when he was only 15, and in the same year, he went out on gigs with his older brother Kevin, singing harmonies and playing bass.

In 1981, Clint got a solo spot at Houston's Benton Springs Club singing Folk and Texan material. While singing on the Houston club circuit in the mid-80's, Clint met Hayden Nicholas and they wrote (and still write) songs together, and recorded demos on Hayden's 8-track machine which he kept in his garage. Clint also worked as a construction worker.

Through a promotion man, a tape of Clint's songs was given to Bill Ham, ZZ Top's manager, who had wanted a Country act for years but had never found the right artist. Bill came to see Clint and a management deal followed, in 1987. Bill Ham advised Clint to concentrate on songwriting and build up his catalog. By 1988, Clint was signed to RCA Records in Nashville.

The debut single and video of *A Better Man* were released in March 1989, and the record became a No.1 hit. Black caused a stir by being the first new Country male artist in 15 years to debut with a No.1 single. This led to Clint's debut on the *Grand Ole Opry*, in April of that year. ***Killin' Time,*** Clint's debut album, was released in May 1989 and was Certified Gold in September 1989, Platinum in January 1990 and Double Platinum in October 1990. The album topped the Country Album chart for 17 weeks and narrowly missed the Pop Albums Top 30. It revealed a traditional Country singer, who was walking a contemporary line without watering down the end result to please radio stations. Here was a singer who could write songs with more than three chords. Clint's next two singles, *Killin' Time* and *Nobody's Home,* went to No.1 that year. Some impressive awards came his way during 1989. These included the 1989 CMA "Horizon Award" and Cashbox's 1989 Nashville Music Awards as "Best New Male Vocalist" and "Best New Act of the Year."

In 1990, *Walkin' Away* also went to the top and although *Nothing's News* reached No. 3 in *Billboard, R & R* made it a No.1, and therefore, Clint became the first artist in the history of Country music to achieve five No.1 singles from a debut album. *Killin' Time* and *Walkin' Away* were also released in video form. Clint closed out the year with the Top 5 release *Put Yourself in My Shoes*, from his second album, which had the same name. This album, released that year, was Certified Double Platinum less than a year after release, reaching No.1 on the Country Album chart and Top 20 on the Pop Album chart.

Clint was named the first recipient of NSAI "Songwriter/Artist of the Year" in 1990 and the same year received the ACM Awards for "Album of the Year" (***Killin' Time***); "Single of the Year" (*A Better Man*); "Best New Male Vocalist" and "Best Male Vocalist," TNN/Music City News Awards' "Star of Tomorrow" and "Album of the Year" and the CMA's "Male Vocalist" and "Best New Touring Artist" awards.

Clint's success started, he acquired a brand new Silver Eagle tour bus and averaged 550 miles a day, touring extensively. He opened for such acts as Dwight Yoakam, the Judds and Randy Travis among others. Clint spent most of 1990 on tour as a special guest of Alabama. In addition, he did many talk shows and TV specials.

Clint Black *with his friend in the white hat, the legendary* ***Roy Rogers***

In 1991, *Loving Blind* went to No.1, *One More Payment* went Top 5 and *Where Are You Now* also went to No.1. In addition, Clint hit the Top 50 with *Hold On Partner*, a duet track with Roy Rogers taken from Roy's tribute album. Other special events in 1991 came when he was inducted as the 66th member of the *Grand Ole Opry*, was co-host of the ACM awards on NBC-TV and began a Canadian tour in March, co-headlining with Reba McEntire.

A surprise marriage to former *Knots Landing* star Lisa Hartman made the news. They met on New Year's Eve and in a short while were married.

Then Clint took a seven-month hiatus from recording, so as to get his battery recharged and get his enthusiasm back into top gear. His third album, ***The Hard Way***, the first in two years, was released in July 1992 and was Certified Platinum by October, reaching No. 2 on the Country Album chart and Top 10 on the Pop Album chart. The radio deejays decided that they would play *This Nightlife*, a cut from the album; however, it only reached No. 61. The "official' single," *We Tell Ourselves*, became No.1 in the charts. This was followed by *Burn One Down,* which went Top 5. That year had the longest tour yet, with 150 dates from June 1992 till March 1993—including a trip to Somalia on a USO tour for the troops, on which he was accompanied by his wife.

During 1993, his fourth album, ***No Time to Kill,*** was released and went Platinum before year end. During that year, Clint appeared on the tribute album to the Eagles, ***Common Thread: The Songs of the Eagles***, singing *Desperado*. In 1994, Clint was paired with the Pointer Sisters for the Don Covay song *Chain of Fools* on the concept album ***Rhythm, Country and Blues***. The track, more than any other, reveals Clint's talent as a singer and more especially as a fine harmonica player.

JAB

RECOMMENDED ALBUMS:

"Killin' Time" (RCA)(1989)
"Put Yourself in My Shoes" (RCA)(1990)
"The Hard Way" (RCA)(1992)
"No Time to Kill" (RCA)(1993)

JEANNE BLACK

(Singer)
Given Name: Gloria Jeanne Black
Date of Birth: October 25, 1937
Where Born: Pomona, California

Jeanne was one of the few performers to get a hit record with an "answer" song. *He'll Have to Stay* was the response to Jim Reeves' hit *He'll Have to Go*. In May 1960, Jeanne's single on Capitol went to No. 4 on the Pop chart and No. 6 on the Country lists.

She had been on the Country scene since 1956, when she began appearing as the vocalist for Cliffie Stone on the *Hometown Jamboree* TV show out of Anaheim in California. At the time, she was still attending Chaffey Junior College in Ontario, California. In 1957, she appeared on the *Lawrence Welk Show* on ABC-TV. She stayed with the Jamboree until 1958, by which time she had begun to appear at night-spots in Las Vegas, such as the Showboat Hotel and at Lake Tahoe's Wagonwheel.

In 1959, she left Cliffie Stone's band and joined Billy Strange. The following year, she signed to Capitol and released her debut single, the aforementioned *He'll Have to Stay*. However, despite releasing other singles, try as she might she couldn't emulate those heady heights. In 1962, she teamed up with her sister, Janie, as Jeanne and Janie but record success failed to return.

RECOMMENDED ALBUM:

"A Little Bit Lonely" (Capitol)(1960)

BLACKWOOD BROTHERS, The

Formed: 1934
ROY BLACKWOOD
(Baritone Vocals)
Given Name: Roy E. Blackwood
Date of Birth: December 24, 1900
Where Born: Fentress, Mississippi
Married: Susie Jane
Children: R.W., Cecil
Date of Death: March 21, 1971
DOYLE BLACKWOOD
(Bass Vocals)
Given Name: Doyle J. Blackwood
Date of Birth: August 22, 1911
Where Born: Ackerman, Mississippi
Married: Lavez C. Hawkins
Children: Terry, Karen
JAMES BLACKWOOD
(Lead Vocals)
Given Name: James Webre Blackwood
Date of Birth: August 4, 1919
Where Born: Ackerman, Mississippi
Married: Miriam Lee Grantham
Children: James Webre, Jr., William LeRoy (Billy)
R.W. BLACKWOOD
(Tenor Vocals)
Given Name: Ronald Winston Blackwood
Date of Birth: October 23, 1921
Where Born: Ackerman, Mississippi
Married: Unknown
Children: Robbie
Date of Death: June 24, 1954
CECIL BLACKWOOD
(Baritone Vocals)
Given Name: Cecil Stamps Blackwood
Date of Birth: October 28, 1934
Where Born: Ackermann, Mississippi
Married: Barbara Doris
Children: Cecil Mark, Regina Monnette
JAMES BLACKWOOD, JR.
(Baritone, Lead Vocals)
Given Name: James Webre Blackwood, Jr.
Date of Birth: July 31, 1943
Where Born: San Diego
Married: Katherine Mona
Children: Dana Le
Other Members: Don Smith (Bass Vocals), Bill Lyles (Bass Vocals), Bill Shaw (Tenor Vocals), J.D. Sumner (Bass Vocals), Hylton Griswold (Piano), Wally Varner (Piano), Billy "Mr. Gospel Drums" Blackwood (Drums), Peter Kaups (Piano), Larry Davis (Bass Guitar)

For many years, the Blackwood Brothers defined Southern Gospel quartet music. They were in the 1950's the best known quartet, the most recorded quartet, and the quartet that inspired a young Elvis Presley. Though dogged by tragedy and at times controversy, the Blackwood Brothers used promotional and organizational techniques that, in a very real sense, brought Southern Gospel music into the 20th century. They also founded a dynasty which continues to the 1990's.

The patriarch of the family, Roy, was born to Mississippi delta sharecroppers in 1900; his brothers Doyle and James followed in 1911 and 1919. By the time James had been born, their mother had been saved at a brush arbor meeting, and Gospel music had taken on a real significance in the family's rural lifestyle. Roy married in 1919, and in 1921 his first child, R.W., was born. A second, Cecil, followed in 1934. In that year, too, the first Blackwood quartet was formed, consisting of Roy, Doyle, James, and 13-year-old R.W. Of these, Doyle was probably the most musical. His early influences included the *Grand Ole Opry*'s Vagabonds and Mississippi's favorite son, Jimmie Rodgers.

As early as 1926 Doyle and James had started singing duets at local church gatherings and schoolhouse programs. For a year, starting in 1933, the pair joined with a local singing school teacher named Ray to form the Choctaw County Jubilee Singers. In the meantime, Roy, who had been traveling through the South preaching, decided to return home. Doyle had found his way to Birmingham, where he had tried singing with another quartet, but by 1934 he too had returned home. All the members were in place for the formation of the family quartet.

The Depression caused the family to abandon its quartet for a time, but by 1937 they had reunited and were broadcasting over WHEF, Kosciusko, Mississippi. In November 1937 they moved to a much larger station, WJDX, in Jackson, where they sang Pop and Country as well as Gospel. By April 1939, their popularity had grown to where they were able to move to the 50,000-watt powerhouse KWKH in Shreveport. There the Gospel song publisher V.O. Stamps heard them and contacted them, asking them to go to work for the huge Stamps-Baxter publishing company, then the South's largest Gospel publishers. Part of the offer was that Stamps would provide them with a regular full-time pianist to accompany them. The Blackwoods agreed.

In July 1940, Stamps sent them to KMA in Shenandoah, Iowa—far from the southern base for Gospel, but at a station that was known nationwide for its successful mail order sales. The war years caused a temporary break-up of the group, and James (the second youngest) had to take on many management chores. After the war, Doyle dropped out of the group, to be replaced by California bass singer Don Smith. The quartet also decided to drop their Stamps-Baxter affiliation in 1946, and to start up their own record company. Their broadcasts from Iowa reached a huge new audience, and by 1948, they were so popular that Doyle had to return and start a second quartet, the Blackwood Gospel Quartet. In the original group, meantime, Bill Lyles was now singing bass, and the Jazz-flavored Hilton Griswold was playing piano.

It was at this point that the Brothers made a momentous decision: they would relocate to Memphis, closer to their home base. In August 1950, they made the move. Roy, now nearing 50, opted to retire from performing, as did Doyle; this left, of the original four, only James and his nephew R.W. A twice daily program on WMPS Memphis helped spread their music, as did a new record contract with RCA Victor, and a series of "All Night Sings" at the local auditorium. One of their first RCA sides (recorded Jan. 4, 1952) was *Rock My Soul* and this hit was followed by *Swing Down*

Chariot and *Have You Talked to the Man Upstairs,* in which the Blackwoods combined older Country harmony styles with their own adaptations from black Gospel traditions. By 1954, they were gaining a national reputation, and in mid-June appeared on Arthur Godfrey's national TV show. Then tragedy struck. Two weeks later R.W. and Bill Lyles were killed in a plane crash.

Devastated, the Blackwoods vowed never to sing again. Gradually, though, they overcame their grief and regrouped. Bass singer J.D. Sumner was hired to replace Bill Lyles, and soon the Blackwoods were back before audiences in local auditoriums. One of their biggest fans became young Elvis Presley, who hung around backstage at the all-night sings; at one point, Presley even auditioned for a group led by Cecil Blackwood, the Songfellows, but was told he didn't understand harmony well enough.

Through the 1950's and 1960's, the Blackwoods did a long series of albums for RCA, and then later for Skylite. They joined forces with another popular quartet, the Statesmen, to form Stateswood Music, and to buy out several of the old Gospel song publishing companies. In the early 1990's, James Blackwood, who was inducted into the Gospel Music Hall of Fame in 1974 and is known as "Mr. Gospel Singer of America," was still very actively performing, and the Blackwoods still existed as a quartet—though with numerous personnel changes.

Throughout their lengthy career, the Blackwood Brothers have won a slew of awards. James Blackwood won a Dove Award as "Male Vocalist of the Year" in 1969, 1970, 1972 through 1975 and 1977. The group won a Dove award as "Male Group of the Year" in 1973 and 1974 and the "Associate Membership Award" in 1974, 1976 and 1977. In addition, in 1970, they won a Dove for "Album of the Year" for ***Fill My Cup, Lord***. The Blackwood Brothers have also garnered eight Grammy Awards: "Best Sacred Recording (Musical) for ***Grand Old Gospel*** (1966), "Best Gospel Performance" for ***More Grand Old Gospel*** (1967) and for ***In Gospel Country*** (1969) (all with Porter Wagoner) and "Best Gospel Performance" for ***Love*** (1972), ***Release Me (From My Sin)*** (1973), ***Lift up the Name of Jesus*** (1979), ***We Come to Worship*** (1980) and ***I'm Following You*** (1982). CKW

RECOMMENDED ALBUMS:

"Grand Old Gospel" (RCA Victor)(1966) [With Porter Wagoner]
"More Grand Old Gospel" (RCA Victor)(1967) [With Porter Wagoner]
"In Gospel Country" (RCA Victor)(1969) [With Porter Wagoner]
"Fill My Cup, Lord" (RCA Victor)(1970)

*Gospel music stars the **Blackwood Brothers***

"Love" (RCA Victor)(1972)
"Release Me (From My Sin)" (RCA Victor)(1973)
"Lift up the Name of Jesus" (Skylite)(1979)
"We Come to Worship" (Voice Box)(1980)
"I'm Following You" (Voice Box)(1982)

NORMAN BLAKE

(Singer, Songwriter, Guitar, Banjo, Mandolin, Dobro)
Date of Birth: March 10, 1938
Where Born: Chattanooga, Tennessee
Married: Nancy Short

Norman Blake can best be described in musician's parlance as being "tasty"—not a flashy player, but one adept at guitar, Dobro, mandolin and fiddle. Norman came from a railroad family. One house he lived in overlooked the Southern Railroad tracks, and his songs often contain railroad themes.

He attended high school in Rising Fawn, Georgia, and Trenton, North Carolina. When he was 16, he left school and joined the Dixieland Drifters, playing mandolin. They debuted on WNOX Knoxville's *Tennessee Barn Dance*. In 1956, he left to join banjo player Bob Johnson as the Lonesome Travelers. In the late 50's, they added another banjo player, Walter Forbes, and recorded two albums for RCA of Old-Time tunes. In 1959, Norman joined Hylo Brown and the Timberliners but still appeared with Johnson during the several occasions he appeared at the *Grand Ole Opry*.

During 1960, Norman continued with Hylo Brown and appeared on the WWVA *Wheeling Jamboree* playing Dobro and mandolin and also toured with June Carter. The following year he was drafted and sent to Panama where he served his time as a radio operator on the Panama Canal. While in the U.S. Army, he formed a Bluegrass band, the Kobbe Mountaineers. The group was voted best group in the Caribbean Command and Norman received the accolade as best musician. While on leave in 1962, he recorded ***12 Shades of Bluegrass***.

The year 1963 was a busy one for Norman. He was discharged from the Army, became a guitar teacher and joined Johnny Cash as a regular sideman. In addition, he married Nancy and settled in Chattanooga. When Bob Dylan made his historic ***Nashville Skyline*** album, in 1969, it was to Norman Blake that he turned. Norman moved to Nashville that year to be with Cash for his CBS-TV show. This was a good move, because he found himself in demand. Blake joined Kris Kristofferson, playing guitar and Dobro in his touring band, and then did similar duties for Joan Baez, in whose band he also played mandolin. He also recorded with both of these artists.

He went on to join John Hartford's Aero-Plane. This was a meeting of minds with musicians with similar uncompromising tastes. The band didn't last long but Norman stayed with Hartford as backup musician for eighteen months. Norman started his on-off-on connection with Rounder Records with the 1972 album ***Back Home in Sulphur Springs***. He still continued his session work and in 1973, appeared on the milestone album by the Nitty Gritty Dirt Band, ***Will the Circle Be Unbroken***. The same year, he went on the road with the Bluegrass group Red, White and Blue(grass) Band.

In 1974, Norman was joined musically by his talented wife, Nancy (credited initially as Nancy Short), who had been with Natchez Trace, and Norman's solo albums from then on in are enhanced by her cello, fiddle and guitar work. In 1974, Norman moved over to another fine independent label, Flying Fish, for his next album, ***The Fields of November***. In 1975 and 1976, Blake continued his prolific output. Flying Fish albums released were ***Norman Blake Super Jam Session*** which featured like-minded pickers (among others, Tut Taylor, Vassar Clements, Jethro Burns and Sam Bush; 1975) and ***Old and New*** (1976). In addition, Norman cut an album for County Records in 1976, ***Norman Blake and Red Rector (Guitar & Mandolin)***.

Norman's last album for Flying Fish was ***Blackberry Blossom***, in 1977. It represents a virtual tour de force by Norman and Nancy. The twosome increased to a trio when James Bryan joined them on fiddle. He had played on the ***Old and New*** album, had toured with Bill and James Monroe and had acted in loco parentis for Kenny Baker on the *Grand Ole Opry*. The threesome, under the name of the Rising Fawn String Ensemble, brought out an album of the same name in 1979. During the end of the 70's and into the 80's, Norman released several albums on Rounder and also County and Takoma. There was the re-issued 1972 album, ***Full Moon on the Farm (Whiskey Before Breakfast)*** (Rounder), ***Darlin' Honey*** (County), ***Live at McCabe's*** (Takoma), and ***Directions*** (Takoma).

He continued his association with Rounder during the 80's and produced consistently high-quality recordings, including ***Original Underground Music from the Mysterious South*** (1983), ***Nashville Blues*** (1984) and ***Lighthouse Blues*** (1985) and an album with guitarist Tony Rice, ***Blake & Rice***. Nancy recorded a solo album for Rounder entitled ***Grand Junction***. With the advent of the cd, Rounder released ***The Norman and Nancy Blake Compact Disc,*** and this medium's clarity could only but enhance the pure sounds produced.

Norman Blake is a musician who has been single-minded about what he plays and as a result with whom he plays. This is perhaps the secret of producing music over a period of time that bridges Folk and Country but never betrays either. His is not the music of the contemporary charts but a deep-rooted traditional sound that harkens back to English Folk ballads and American Bluegrass via Scotland and Ireland.

RECOMMENDED ALBUMS:

Basically all of the above-mentioned are worth spending time with, and then spending some more time enjoying.

ARTHUR BLANCH

(Singer, Songwriter, Guitar)
Where Born: **Tamworth, New South Wales, Australia**
Married: **Berice**
Children: **Jewel Evelyn**

Of all the Country and Bush performers to emerge from Australia, the Blanch family has made the biggest impression in the U.S. Daughter Jewel is married to Barry Coburn, also from Australia, and together they run the highly successful 1010 Music Group, which managed Holly Dunn and Alan Jackson.

Arthur was born and raised on the family sheep farm, 50 miles north of Tamworth. As a youngster, he would hurry home from school and listen to Country music on the radio. His mother and father were professional musicians, playing piano and violin. His father, a good singer, encouraged Arthur to vocalize. While away at boarding school, he entertained his fellow students. After he had finished school, Arthur caught rabbits and got enough money to buy a mail-order guitar.

Soon he was entertaining locally, and then he made his first broadcast on 2TM Tamworth. Len Wynn from 2NZ Inverell helped Arthur to cut some acetates and played them on the air. He won on Australia's Amateur Hour and this success led to professional bookings. Arthur's next step forward was on a talent quest run by 2LM Lismore's celebrated *Radio Ranch Club*. Many of the staff announcers on the show chose to adopt the dress and speech of the American "hillbilly" rube, which most people found unfunny. The show also produced its own magazine, *Spurs*, which was widely distributed.

In 1952, Arthur won the talent quest at the Federalette Theatre. The concert went out live on radio. Part of the prize was an audition with EMI Records. However, Tim McNamara offered Arthur a deal with Rodeo Records.

Arthur recorded six sides, including two of his own songs. He played various Sydney shows, including Sydney Town Hall, and then after his marriage to Berice in February 1954, he returned to the New England Ranges, where he bought his own place, named Harmony Hills. He now sang as a solo and also in tandem with Berice. He had three regular radio shows, and recorded a series for ABC in Tamworth. He and Berice sang at the ABC studios at the Royal Easter Show. The singles Arthur released for Rodeo, *Headin' Back Home/Sister of Sioux City Sue, Broken Dreams/Shearin' Time* and *Golden Rocket/It Makes No Difference Now*, were all successful. He also appeared on the first Harmony Trail concert, organized by radio 3SR Shepparton (the show ran for eight years).

Following the birth of Jewel, Arthur and Berice auditioned successfully for a TV station in Brisbane. They moved to Brisbane (naming their house Harmony Hill) and worked the clubs and hotels on the Gold Coast. At the age of 3, Jewel made her debut on a Christmas TV special. The family moved to Sydney and played the clubs and appeared on national TV shows such as *6 O'Clock Rock* and *Bandstand*. Arthur released a single on Columbia, *The Strange Little Girl*, which made the Top 40. At age 4, Jewel released the single *I Wanna Stay on Jumbo*, a song written by Arthur and Jim Wesley.

Arthur released two more singles on Rodeo, *Our Best Friend/Television on the Telephone* and *China Doll/Keep It a Secret*. The family recorded their first album, ***Meet the Blanch Family***, for the W & G label, from which came the single *For Pete's Sake Pete/Choctaw Joe*. Among the musicians on the album was U.S. West Coast steel guitarist Speedy West, who encouraged them to come to the U.S.

They went to Nashville at the end of 1963 and stayed for a year, making a lot of contacts. They played some shows and did some TV, and then recorded a single for Dot, *Maker of Raindrops and Roses/Sing a Little*. They then returned to New South Wales; and for 4 years they worked the clubs and TV, and recorded a second album for W & G, ***Walking in the Sunshine***. In 1968, they traveled as the starring act on the SS *Australia*'s world cruise. After the trip ended, they chose to return to the U.S. This time, they stayed in Nashville for 10 years, working with a lot of the major acts, and appearing with Ralph Emery on WSM's *Opry Place*. Jewel began appearing as a child actress on TV and in films. Because Jewel was so busy, and Berice was with her, Arthur started to play solo again. He refused to play long-term bookings in Las Vegas, to be near the family.

In 1978, Mike Curb approached Arthur to record for his MC label. Arthur's debut single, *The Little Man's Got the Biggest Smile in Town*, reached the Top 75. At the same time, Jewel signed with RCA Victor, and her single *So Good* got to the Top 70. She followed up early in 1979 with *Can I See You Tonight*, which climbed to No. 33. Arthur again hit the charts during the fall of 1979, with *Maybe I'll Cry Over You*, which reached No. 82.

The family visited Tamworth for the Australian Country Music Awards, and became homesick. They returned to Australia in 1979 and decided to stay. Arthur recorded a 4-track EP, with the Bushmen, entitled *Country Round Up*, for Festival Records. They settled in Brisbane, in 1980, but Jewel returned to Nashville, with her husband, in the 80's. Arthur and Berice have subsequently moved back to Nashville.

RECOMMENDED ALBUMS:

(No releases in the U.S.)
"Meet the Blanch Family" (W & G)
"Walking in the Sunshine" (W & G)

Jewel Blanch refer ARTHUR BLANCH

JACK BLANCHARD & MISTY MORGAN

JACK BLANCHARD
(Singer, Songwriter, Piano, Saxophone)
Date of Birth: **May 8, 1942**
Where Born: **Buffalo, New York**
MISTY MORGAN
(Singer, Songwriter, Piano, Organ)
Date of Birth: **May 23, 1945**
Where Born: **Buffalo, New York**

Jack and Misty may not be clones of one another, but they share many similarities. They both came from Buffalo, New York, and were born in the same hospital, Millard Fillmore. Both were born in May and have blue eyes and brown hair. In addition, they both have parents named John and Mary and sisters named Virginia. They also both moved to Ohio when young. When they met, they were both playing clubs in Hollywood, Florida and were assumed to be brother and sister, even though, since 1963, they were actually husband and wife.

Misty started playing piano at the age of 9. After a year of lessons, she carried on playing by ear. She joined various small groups and then moved to Cincinnati before moving on to Florida. Jack had played piano and saxophone in bands for many years as well as doing solo piano work and comedy. It was not until the couple had been married for five years that they teamed up. At one time, they were so strapped for cash that Jack played a department store Santa Claus while Misty was Santa's helper.

Although Jack's recording career began in 1959, it was not until 1969 that Jack and Misty appeared on the Country charts with their Top 60 entry *Big Black Bird (Spirit of Our Love)* on Wayside. However, it was the following year that they hit the big time with *Tennessee Bird Walk,* which was a Country No.1 and a Top 30 Pop hit. They followed this up with *Humphrey the Camel* which made the Top 5 on the Country lists and crossed over onto the Pop Top 80. Their final single for Wayside was the Top 30 Country hit *You've Got Your Troubles (I've Got Mine).*

In 1971, they moved over to Mega and had a Top 30 hit with *There Must Be More to Life (Than Growing Old).* They wrapped up the year with the No.15 hit *Somewhere in Virginia in the Rain.* 1972 got under way with the Top 40 hit, *The Legendary Chicken Fairy.* All of these songs were Jack Blanchard compositions. By 1973, Jack and Misty had moved over to Epic and had scored with the Top 30 single *Just One More Song.* From here on in, their records hovered around the Top 50 mark. In 1977, they moved to United Artists but chart success eluded them. A move to the Autumn Hill label in 1979 and Nu Sound Records in 1980 did nothing to correct this. Jack and Misty have subsequently divorced.

RECOMMENDED ALBUMS:

"Birds of a Feather" (Wayside)(1970)
"Two Sides of Jack & Misty" (Mega)(1972)

RED BLANCHARD

(Singer, Songwriter, Guitar)

Given Name:	**Donald F. Blanchard**
Date of Birth:	**July 24, 1914**
Where Born:	**Pittsville, Wisconsin**
Married:	**Sally**
Children:	**Donald, Jr., Colleen Donna, Laura Lee**

Red Blanchard is primarily known for his long association with the *National Barn Dance*, being connected with the program from the early 30's through the show's demise in 1969. He did, however, appear on a variety of other programs on stations in his native Wisconsin and in Iowa. He first came to WLS, original home of the *National Barn Dance,* in 1931 when he was only 17 years old. During his early years on the program he was a member of Rube Tronson's Texas Cowboys, a band consisting of fiddle, banjo, guitar, accordion, drums, and clarinet. Later, for four years, he was a member of the Sage Riders, a western group composed of Don White, Ray Klein, and Dolph Hewitt, in addition to Red who usually provided the comic relief for the group.

Although Blanchard was not a prolific recording artist he appeared on four labels, Columbia, Kapp, Dot, and Kahill, with his best selling sides being made for Dot and Kahill. His two most popular recordings were *Open the Door, Richard* and *Oklahoma Hills* (a duet with Dolph Hewitt). He also tried his hand at songwriting and penned numbers like *She Went and Gone Away, Too Many People,* and *I'm Lonesome in the Saddle (Since My Old Horse Died).*

Blanchard moved to WGN when that station took over the *National Barn Dance* in 1960, and in 1963 he became part of the television version of the show. When the program folded in 1969 Blanchard busied himself with various business enterprises. He, Dolph Hewitt, and several other partners owned radio stations in St. Charles, Ottawa, and Dixon, Illinois. WKM

RECOMMENDED ALBUM:

"Saturday Night at the Old Barn Dance" (Kapp)(1965)

BLUE BOYS, The

Formed:	**1958**
Members:	
Royce Morgan	**Guitar**
Billy "Kraut" Harlan	**Bass**
Jimmy Day	**Steel Guitar**
Peewee Kershaw	**Drums**
Leo Jackson	**Guitar**
Dean Manuel	**Piano**
Bud Logan	**Bass, Lead Vocals**
Bunky Keels	**Piano**
Jimmy Orr	**Drums**

The Blue Boys, the most famous of Jim Reeves's bands, was named after the song *Blue Boy* that was a major hit for Reeves in the late 50's. Reeves's original band was called the Wagon Masters but, after Porter Wagoner's arrival in Nashville, in 1957, Reeves decided that name would be more appropriate for Wagoner's group.

The original Blue Boys were Billy "Kraut" Harlan, Royce Morgan, Jimmy Day and Peewee Kershaw. Lead guitar player Leo Jackson, who had been with Reeves for some time, was called into military service shortly before the Blue Boys were formed. Harlan had a good friend, Royce Morgan, that he recommended to Reeves. Since Harlan had been preparing Morgan for the potential opening, Morgan had rehearsed every Reeves song he could find. Thus, it was an easy matter for him to step in when the call came to join the Blue Boys.

The original band was together less than a year before being disbanded. Reeves later reorganized the Blue Boys but with different personnel, including Leo Jackson who by then was back from the U.S. Army. This version of the band remained together for more than 7 years, continuing for three years after Reeves' death in a plane crash on July 31, 1964. Piano player Dean Manuel, who died in the crash with Reeves, was replaced by Bunky Keels and this last version of the Blue Boys recorded four albums before finally calling it quits in 1968. They had two minor Country chart singles, *My Cup Runneth Over* (1967) and *I'm Not Ready Yet* (1968). Jimmy Day went on to became a famed steel player (see separate entry) while Bud Logan sang duets with Wilma Burgess on Mary Reeves' Shannon label in the early 70's, their most successful single being the 1973 *Wake Me into Love*. He then became a very successful record producer with artists such as John Conlee. WKM

RECOMMENDED ALBUMS:

"We Remember Jim Reeves" (RCA Victor)(1965)
"Sounds of Jim Reeves" (RCA Victor)(1966)
"The Blue Boys in Person" (RCA Victor)(1967)
"Hit After Hit" (RCA Victor)(1967)

BLUE SKY BOYS, The

BILL BOLICK
(Singer, Mandolin)

Given Name:	**William A. Bolick**
Date of Birth:	**October 28, 1917**

EARL BOLICK
(Singer, Guitar)

Given Name:	**Earl A. Bolick**
Date of Birth:	**November 16, 1919**
Married:	**Elizabeth Geraldine**
Children:	**William Steven, Joseph Alan, stepson: Gerald Glenn Reagan**
Both Born:	**Hickory, North Carolina**

*Bill and Earl Bollick, the **Blue Sky Boys***

The Blue Sky Boys came perhaps closer than anyone in Country music history to perfecting the harmony duet. While the piercing harmonies of the earlier Monroe Brothers and the later Louvin Brothers may be better known than the smoothness of Bill and Earl's vocal blend, their quality seems unequaled. Through the duo's radio work in the Carolinas and Georgia and their Bluebird and Victor recordings, earned the Blue Sky Boys a legendary status which has hardly diminished among fans of traditional Country sounds.

Natives of East Hickory, North Carolina, Bill and Earl Bolick grew up in the traditional, music-rich Piedmont Country that flowered in the 30's. As the two brothers began to sing duets, they experimented with both two guitars and a guitar-mandolin combination, eventually settling on the latter. Bill got into radio first in 1935, working for a few months in a band that included Homer and Arthur Sherrill and Lute Isenhour. After a few months with the Crazy Hickory Nuts at WWNC Asheville, Bill returned to Hickory. That fall he and Earl along with Homer Sherrill, calling themselves the JFG Coffee Boys, went back to Asheville and another radio program. This time they stayed in radio although they soon left to work for Crazy Water Crystals at WGST Atlanta as the Blue Ridge Hillbillies. In June 1936, Bill and Earl came back to North Carolina. Sherrill remained in Atlanta and hired the duo of Shorty and Mack to replace the Bolick brothers.

When Bill and Earl returned to North Carolina, Eli Oberstein of RCA was conducting sessions for Bluebird Records. The brothers cut their first 10 of the 124 numbers they would make over the next fifteen years. Since there were so many brother groups recording already, they came up with the name the Blue Sky Boys, which they used thereafter on radio as well. In February 1937, the Bolicks returned to WGST Atlanta for another six months. They enjoyed two more stints at that station covering most of 1938 and 1939 and a final post-war residency from March 1946 until February 1948. In between times, they had shorter stays in Raleigh (1939-41, 1948-49, and 1950-61); Greenville (1941); Bristol (1949); Rome, Georgia (1949-50); and Shreveport (1950).

Although the brothers are remembered primarily as a duet, at times they carried a third musician, usually a fiddler, who sometimes sang on some trio numbers. After Homer Sherrill left in 1937, this third person included Richard "Red" Hicks, Sam "Curley"' Parker, Joe Tyson, and Leslie Keith. The Blue Sky Boys' prewar discs were duets with only mandolin and guitar, but Parker and Keith fiddled on some of their postwar Victor sessions. From about 1938 until the duo dissolved in February 1951, Earl Bolick also portrayed a comic character, "Uncle Josh," on their radio and stage shows.

The musical repertoire of the Blue Sky Boys included a goodly share of traditional and Victorian ballads as well as sacred songs. They also did some covers of newer numbers in a traditional style including two of their most popular post-war sides, the Karl and Harty song *Kentucky* and the Bailes Brothers Gospel classic *Dust on the Bible*. Folk scholars came to admire the Bolicks' pleasing harmonies and their renditions of such traditional ballads such as *Banks of the Ohio* and *Hills of Roane County*.

WW II interrupted the career of the Blue Sky Boys from August 1941 until March 1946 when they returned to the airways. They seem to have lost much of their enthusiasm for show business during the war even though they returned to it and enjoyed some of their biggest records in the late 40's. Nonetheless, Honky Tonk styles gained in popularity at the expense of their traditional approach to music and Earl became increasingly desirous of getting out of entertainment. Accordingly, the Bolicks disbanded in February 1951.

In some forty years of musical retirement, the Blue Sky Boys have had a few forays into reunion activity. Earl and his wife settled in the Atlanta area where he worked at Lockheed Aircraft. Bill attended Lenoir-Rhyne College for three years and then took a job with the postal service in Greensboro. In 1962, Starday released an album of their radio transcription material and they cut a pair of albums for that label, one of sacred songs, and another one for Capitol. They made a few concert appearances as well, one of which later appeared on a live album. In the mid-70's they cut an album for Rounder and played a few Bluegrass festivals.

Their last public concert took place at Duke University in April 1975. Bill eventually retired and moved back to Hickory while Earl resides in Tucker, Georgia. Since the early 60's, old Blue Sky Boys recordings have been available in the reissue market, some recent releases being in compact disc form.

IMT

RECOMMENDED ALBUMS:

"Together Again" (Starday)(1963)
"Precious Moments" (Starday and Pine Mountain)(1964)
"Blue Sky Boys" (RCA Camden)(1964)
"The Blue Sky Boys (Bill and Earl Bolick)" (Bluebird)(1976)
"The Blue Sky Boys" (Rounder)(1976)
"Collector's Items" (Provincia)(1980)
"The Blue Sky Boys in Concert, 1964" (Rounder)(1989)
"There'll Come a Time/Can't You Hear the Nightbird Crying?" (Blue Tone)(1991)
"Within the Circle/Who Wouldn't Be Lonely" (Blue Tone)(1992)
"Blue Sky Boys on Radio, Volume One" (Copper Creek)(1993)
"Blue Sky Boys on Radio, Volume Two" (Copper Creek)(1993)

BLUEGRASS ALLIANCE, The

Formed:	**1967**
Members:	
Lonnie Peerce	**Fiddle**
Dan Crary	**Guitar**
Tony Rice	**Guitar**
Curtis Burch	**Guitar**
Courtney Johnson	**Banjo**
Sam Bush	**Mandolin, Fiddle**
Ebo Walker	**Mandolin**

Although it was together less than five years during the late 60's and early 70's, the Bluegrass Alliance is an important group in the popularization of so-called progressive Bluegrass. Headquartered in Louisville, Kentucky, the band originally centered around the traditional fiddling of Lonnie Peerce and the work of Bluegrass guitar legend Dan Crary. However, as new members joined the Alliance moved farther and farther away from classic Bluegrass, experimenting with modern songs and jazzy stylings. Crary left and was succeeded by Tony Rice and, later, Curtis Burch.

The person generally considered most responsible for the band's shift in focus, however, is Sam Bush, a mandolin and fiddle player, who joined in 1970. Bush is known not only for his wild, lengthy improvisations but for his constant experimentation with various forms of music. It was after his arrival that the Bluegrass Alliance had its biggest hit with *One Tin Soldier*. This song, also known as *The Legend of Billy Jack*, was performed by the quintet Coven as background music in the 1971 movie *Billy Jack*.

Progressive Bluegrass group the ***Bluegrass Alliance***

The Bluegrass Alliance's version did not sell as well as the original recording by the Original Caste, but it was highly influential among young Bluegrass musicians in the early 70's.

In 1972, musical differences with Peerce led to the departure of Bush, Johnson, Walker, and Burch. They formed the New Grass Revival, a group that some consider the quintessential progressive Bluegrass band. The Bluegrass Alliance survived the departure of Bush, and the others, its last album being released in 1982, but its days of glory ended a decade earlier.

RECOMMENDED ALBUMS:

"The Bluegrass Alliance" (American Heritage)(1971)
"Tall Grass" (Bridges)(1973)

BLUEGRASS CARDINALS, The

Formed:	**1974**
Current Members:	
Don Parmley	**Banjo, Baritone Vocals**
David Parmley	**Guitars, Lead & Harmony Vocals**
Larry Stephenson	**Mandolin, Guitar, Tenor Vocals**
Mike Hartgrove	**Fiddle, Harmony Vocals**
Dale Perry	**Bass Guitar, Bass Vocals**
Former Members:	
Norman Wright	**Mandolin, Lead Guitar, Lead & Harmony Vocals**
John Davis	**Acoustic Bass, Harmony Vocals**

The Bluegrass Cardinals have become Bluegrass music's aristocracy. Don Parmley formed the group in 1974 with his 15-year-old son, David, while working as a studio musician on *The Beverly Hillbillies* TV series in Los Angeles. Don came from Monticello, Kentucky, where he had played with the Golden State Boys (with Vern and Rex Gosdin) and its successor, the Hillmen (1962-63), which also included Chris Hillman. Except for the theme song, which was played by Earl Scruggs, all the banjo playing heard on *The Beverly Hillbillies* was Don's.

In 1976, the Cardinals moved to Virginia to get closer to the bookings in the eastern states. Their music is a blend of traditional and contemporary Bluegrass but all the time utilizing traditional acoustic instrumentation. They were the first Bluegrass act to record Gospel music in a cappella style. That year, they released their first eponymous album for Briar. But in true string band tradition, they moved on to another label for their second album. Rounder issued their 1977 album, ***Welcome to Virginia.***

Their connection with CMH Records during 1978 through 1982 produced five excellent albums: ***Livin' in the Good Old Days*** (1978), ***Cardinal Soul*** (1979), ***Live & on Stage*** (1980), ***Sunday Mornin' Singin'*** (1980) and ***Where Rainbows Touch Down*** (1982). In addition, they appeared on the 1978 double album ***Tennessee Mountain Bluegrass Festival*** **and** ***Lester Flatt's Greatest Performance*** (1979). On this album they sang two songs which were released as a single. On their live 1980 double album their guests were Buddy Spicher, Don Reno and Chubby Anthony.

In 1982, Larry Stephenson recorded a solo album for Outlet, on which Don helped out on vocals and David added guitar and vocals. In 1983, the Bluegrass Cardinals moved over to another prestigious independent label, Sugar Hill Records. ***Cardinal Class*** was the initial release and was acknowledged as a recording of special merit by *Stereo Review*. In their review of the album, the magazine pointed out that unlike some Bluegrass bands, the Bluegrass Cardinals don't just throw the sound out, they have dynamics and finesse. Also, it was pointed out that the emphasis was more on vocals and harmonies than instrumentals.

The Bluegrass Cardinals*, led by banjoist Don Parmley*

The Bluegrass Cardinals went back to basics for their 1984 outing, ***Home Is Where the Heart Is***, producing an album that would please traditionalists and Newgrass fans. The following year, they returned to Gospel for the inspirational ***The Shining Path***.

All of the Cardinals' albums blend their expert musicianship with three-part and Gospel quartet harmonies. Dave Parmley and Larry Stephenson are probably the finest Bluegrass singers in the business.

RECOMMENDED ALBUMS:

"The Bluegrass Cardinals" (Briar)(1976)
"Welcome to Virginia" (Rounder)(1977)
"Livin' in the Good Old Days" (CMH)(1978)
"Cardinal Soul" (CMH)(1979)
"Live & on Stage" (double)(CMH)(1980)
"Sunday Mornin' Singin'" (CMH)(1980)
"Where Rainbows Touch Down" (CMH)(1982)
"Cardinal Class" (Sugar Hill)(1983)
"Home Is Where the Heart Is" (Sugar Hill)(1984)
"The Shining Path" (Sugar Hill)(1985)

BMI

BMI was formed in 1939 by 600 broadcasters as a non-profit agency to ensure that all people who created music would receive compensation for their works and to create a competitive force in music licensing. Prior to BMI's formation, the primary licensing body, the American Society of Composers, Authors and Publishers (ASCAP), founded in 1914, comprised only 140 publishers and 1,100 writers.

To gain admission to the organization, a writer had to have five published hit songs. With admission requirements this tough, a majority of writers were precluded from collecting fees for their works and only about 15 publishers dominated the majority of songs played on network radio. By 1939, radio had become the primary form of family entertainment and three networks, NBC, CBS and Mutual Broadcasting System, dominated the airways.

In 1932, ASCAP negotiated an agreement with the radio industry that established fees based on a percentage of advertising time sales. The proposed increase in those fees, considered explosive by the radio industry, led to a confrontation between ASCAP and the radio industry. While networks dominated the airwaves, music publishing firms were increasingly controlled by motion picture companies. Many writers, however, did not fit into the interests of Hollywood, particularly those writers of the Blues, Ragtime, Jazz, and Country music traditions.

The *Grand Ole Opry* was the main source of public access Country performers had, and many well-known Country stars including Gene Autry and Jazz talents like Jelly Roll Morton were rejected for membership in ASCAP for years. BMI entered the scene of this tightly controlled industry during the fall of 1939, precipitated by the upcoming expiration of the five-year contract with ASCAP in which radio had agreed to pay 5% of its annual advertising sales revenues toward licensing fees for music. A special group of radio industry leaders met in Chicago during the fall of 1939 to consider forming a new licensing body to be called Broadcast Music, Inc. The charter was drawn up by Sidney M. Kaye, an upcoming young copyright attorney. The charter called for broadcasting companies to pledge sums of 50% of their 1937 ASCAP payments as capital and operating funds for the new organization, which would operate on a non-profit basis, the main purpose being to provide an opportunity for those writers and publishers unable to gain entry to ASCAP to share performance rights revenue and to provide an alternative source for broadcasters and other users of music.

The BMI charter was filed on October 14, 1939, and offices opened in New York City February 15, 1940. In March of 1940, ASCAP's newly proposed contract called for a 100% increase in the rates radio stations were paying over the previous year. Between 1931 and 1939, licensing payments from radio had risen from $960,000 to $4.3 million, a 448% increase. By the end of 1940, 650 broadcasters had signed licenses with BMI and by the time ASCAP's contract expired only 200 stations continued to use its catalog.

During this time, as ASCAP and radio stations hammered out a new agreement, BMI began building its own catalog. A number of major publishers joined and BMI set up its own publishing company, which was later sold. BMI also began "fronting" aspiring publishers with advances to start their own companies. During this 11-month battle between ASCAP and the networks in 1941, BMI built up a base of support. Sydney M. Kaye became VP and General Counsel, and later CEO, and Carl Haverlin, who began as Director of station relations, was made President in 1947. Robert Burton became House Counsel in 1941, then was promoted to Director of publisher relations, later becoming VP of domestic performing rights, then later President. George Marlo, who started in promotion of the publishing wing, later directed writer relations, and Russell Sanjek directed public relations.

As musical technologies have progressed, the copyright, originally designed to protect printed copies of musical compositions, has expanded to include mechanical rights (the right to reproduce musical works on sound recordings) and the synchronization, or sync, right (the right to record music in timed relation to a film or video soundtrack). It is the performing right that BMI administers that has become a central component in the economy of the music industry. BMI licenses radio and television stations, low-power television stations, radio and television networks, PBS, NPR, cable program services and other users of music.

There are four kinds of BMI licenses specifically designed to serve the needs of broadcasters, covering all programming: a blanket license, a per program license, a license for non-commercial broadcasters and a special license for non-commercial educational broadcasters. The performing right entitles the holder of a musical copyright to receive payment for almost any performance of the composition. BMI acquires these performing rights from copyright holders and collects the license fees on their behalf from users of the composition.

As no copyright holder could collect or negotiate with the thousands of enterprises that rely on music as part of their business, BMI, in effect, serves as the middleman between the owners and users of music. Payment to writers and publishers is based mainly on broadcast performances. With over 10,000 radio stations in the United States it is considered safe to assume that what is being played on the airwaves reflects what is being played by other music users. Since keeping track of performances of music played in bowling alleys, nightclubs, restaurants and the like is next to impossible, a system known as "logging," which incorporates a daily census from users such as cable suppliers, radio and television networks, and tracking all performances of syndicated shows and films via the 120 regional issues of *TV Guide*, is used. Logging of local radio and television is done on a scientific sampling basis to reflect all locations, sizes and types of stations. That sample is multiplied to reflect the national picture, and between the census and the sampling system BMI currently analyzes over 6 million broadcast hours per annum. BMI's logging procedure was designed by Paul Lazerfield of Columbia University's Office of Radio Research.

BMI pays its writers and copyright owners according to a published royalty schedule, and is the only performing rights organization to make such a schedule available to its songwriters, composers and publishers. From the beginning BMI has had an "open door" policy to all creators of music; any bona fide writer can join. There are no restrictions in the admissions process and no up-front fees. With BMI's "open door" policy to writers of all genres of music, and the increasing popularity and sales of Country music, in 1958 BMI became more committed to Country music, and established a branch office in Nashville.

In the beginning, the Nashville office was run by one person, Frances Williams (now BMI President Frances Preston), who originally ran the office out of her home. "During that first year," Frances recalls, "I used to have to meet with writers in coffee shops, because I didn't have an office and a lot of the writers were working downtown at the WSM studios. So, I signed many of the first people at the Clarkston Coffee Shop next door to WSM, because I would meet them after they came off the radio shows.

"When we opened our first real office, it was located in the Life and Casualty Tower, Nashville's first skyscraper. We signed everybody, I mean, they came in from far and near to join BMI. When the first statements started coming in, some writers came in almost crying, saying, 'You know, this is the first time I've ever received any money like this, the very first time.'

"In those early days, Country songwriters didn't know music as an industry. It was strictly an art form. They wrote their songs and kept them in shoeboxes. They wrote about their everyday lives. They didn't think about writing a song as a way to make money. If you had told Hank Williams, when he was just starting out, that somebody wanted to record his song, he would have paid them to do it." This confidence in Nashville's Country music soon paid off.

By 1969, over 600 radio stations were playing Country music full-time, compared with only 81 stations in 1961. As the music industry economics increased and music became an international enterprise, BMI began establishing working relationships with songwriters, composers and publishing rights societies abroad. This dealt with both the acquisition of United States rights in foreign works and collection of royalties for foreign use of BMI works.

Today, BMI has agreements with 40 foreign performing rights organizations. In addition to American repertoire, broadcasters with BMI licenses have access to the catalogs of these organizations throughout the world, and copyright holders may collect royalties from worldwide distribution of their material. A key BMI leader in the effort to increase international ties was Jean Geiringer, who joined the organization in 1941 and was appointed VP for foreign relations in 1961. Due to the efforts of this Austrian-born composer, reciprocal licenses were established with all major performing rights societies in Western Europe, Scandinavia, Japan and Latin America. The foreign associations were facilitated in Europe by Bob Musel, who ran the London office BMI established in the late 50's.

BMI Canada was formed in 1941, as a subsidiary, under the management of Harold Moon. In 1975, BMI divested itself of all ownership in the organization, and it became the Canadian owned and operated Performing Rights Organization-Canada. BMI today represents approximately 100,000 songwriters, composers and music publishers who own copyrights.

The organization is involved in every genre of musical entertainment from Country to Rhythm & Blues to Rock'n'Roll to Gospel. As new technologies developed, log usages which didn't exist during the first part of BMI's existence began to develop. FM, TV, cable TV and musical theater all became part of the repertoire throughout the 60's, 70's and 80's. BMI today is developing new marketing campaigns as the definition of a "primary user" of music expands from the traditional users, such as restaurants and bars, to include categories such as aerobics and health clubs, shopping malls, banks and other service institutions.

As the company begins its second half century of operation, perhaps its 1940 policy statement best reflects its purpose: "a means of giving to you who make up the musical public an opportunity to grow familiar with the work of composers who have not been previously privileged to put their music before you."

With the creation of BMI a free, unrestricted, and competitive market has been maintained both among the users of music and those who create it. Among BMI's most successful Country writers contemporarily are Vince Gill, Paul Overstreet, Paul Kennerley and Bob McDill. LAP

GINGER BOATWRIGHT

(Singer, Songwriter, Guitar, Piano)

Given Name: Ginger Kay Hammond
Date of Birth: September 21, 1944
Where Born: Columbus, Mississippi
Married: 1. Grant Boatwright (div.)
2. C.C. Kuhn, Jr.
Children: Danae

Since her arrival on the Bluegrass scene in 1966, the highly attractive, voluptuous and talented Ginger Boatwright has become one of the favorites on the festival circuit. Possessing a rich vocal tone and being an adept flat-picker, Ginger is also a natural communicator and loves the interplay between herself and her audience.

Coming from a musical family, Ginger was exposed to singing at home and at reunions. As a child, she was diagnosed as having viral polio, but thankfully survived. When she was 10, her father, rhythm guitarist Hap Hammond, and a few friends put together a band, the Magic Circle Ramblers. This gave Ginger her first taste of Bluegrass music, up close. Ginger has a reputation as an expert on Martin guitars and remembers that her father bought a Martin guitar from a member of Bob Wills' Texas Playboys. She even remembers that it was a Herringbone.

She attended Birmingham Southern Conservatory of Music, Alabama, studying piano. She attended the University of Alabama, Birmingham on a double scholarship. She had also received an approach from Birmingham Southern College, also with a double scholarship, each of the scholarships being in oratorical speaking; however she majored in history and sociology.

While at college Ginger started to play guitar. In 1966, while in the audience at the Lowenbrau House in Birmingham, she was invited on stage by singer/guitarist Grant Boatwright. They soon formed a duo, Grant and Ginger, and played professionally. They soon became a trio, when Ginger's cousin Dale Whitcomb joined them. In 1969, it was discovered that Ginger had a rare form of cancer and its treatment meant that she had to leave college just six hours short of gaining her degree. She also had to give up a job in Birmingham, where she was training to be a juvenile probation officer. The formation of the trio Grant, Dale and Ginger, led to the creation of Red, White & Blue(grass) and Ginger's marriage to Grant.

While with the group, she signed to GRC Records as a solo act and had success with the single *The Lovin's Over* in 1972. That year, Ginger bought the music venue the Pickin' Parlor in Nashville. When the group moved to Mercury, Ginger also had a solo contract, but without notable success. The group broke up in 1979; Ginger and Grant subsequently divorced and then her house burned down, with the resulting loss of 300 albums.

Ginger put together the Bushwackers, an all-female Country/Bluegrass group with banjoist Susie Monick. The other members of the quartet were April Barrows (bass guitar) and Ingrid Reese (fiddle and guitar). The group was active on the college circuit and released one self-named album that was produced by Vassar Clements. Among the featured players on the album was Ingrid's father, the legendary Woody Herman.

After two years, the Bushwackers split up and at the same time (1981), Ginger closed the

Pickin' Parlor. She felt like calling it a day musically, then Rodney Dillard told her that his brother Doug was putting a new band together and she was invited to join. At the time, Ginger had applied and been accepted for a job as a senior court supervisor in Nashville. However, when she met Doug Dillard, she had no doubts about joining the group. As of this writing, she remains an active member of the group.

Ginger's strengths are not just her singing and playing, but also her great rapport with an audience; she is the perfect front-person. Apart from music and Martin guitars, the other love of Ginger's life is her "protector," the redoubtable Shar-Pei (dog), Rufus Duvall Dawg. She has now added another "protector" to her life, as in 1994 she married C. C. Kuhn, Jr.

RECOMMENDED ALBUMS:

"The Bushwackers" (Laser Lady)
"What's That" (Flying Fish) [As the Doug Dillard Band]
"Fertile Ground" (Flying Fish)

DOCK BOGGS

(Singer, Banjo)
Given Name: Moran Lee Boggs
Date of Birth: February 7, 1898
Where Born: West Norton, Virginia
Married: Sara
Date of Death: February 7, 1971

Dock Boggs played a fine traditional brand of Old-Time banjo and sang in an equally fine manner. He had a unique picking style and also sang in an unusual way that made his music distinctive. Boggs spent much of his adult life working in the coal mines of southwest Virginia and adjacent parts of Kentucky and West Virginia, picking and singing professionally off-and-on in the later 20's and after he retired in the eight years prior to his death.

A native of Wise County, Virginia, Moran Boggs grew up as the youngest child in a large family of mountaineers. The industrial revolution came to that section of Appalachia with the dawning of the new century and at age 12, he went to work as a "trapper" in the coal mines for seven cents an hour. He also began to play banjo, developing a style which showed more African-American influence than most mountain banjoists. Several other members of his family also played music and Dock learned many song lyrics from his brother-in-law Lee Hunsucker. With the passing of time, Boggs graduated to more adult forms of mine labor. He married in 1918, but like many young men in the mountains, continued to pursue something of a rounder lifestyle, or, as he phrased it, lived like a "rambling man."

In February 1927, Brunswick Records conducted local auditions of mountain musicians in the Norton Hotel. Only the Dykes Magic City Trio and Dock Boggs sufficiently impressed the talent scouts to receive an invitation to go to New York for sessions. On March 10, Boggs recorded eight numbers while the Dykes Fiddle Band cut some fourteen sides over a three-day period. Dock's most memorable songs tended to be white-Blues items like *Down South Blues*, but he also did old ballads such as *Pretty Polly* and *Danville Girl*. G. H. "Hub" Mahaffey of the Magic City Trio provided rhythm guitar accompaniment on five of the cuts.

Two years later, Boggs cut four more songs for The Lonesome Ace, a short-lived local label initiated by a Richlands, Virginia, businessman named William Myers. Emry Arthur assisted on these masters, which were pressed by Paramount and became extremely rare through a combination of poor distribution and deepening Depression which soon drove the firm into bankruptcy. Boggs, who performed some music on a semi-professional basis in the late 20's, continued working in the mines and for some years he gave up music entirely.

In 1954, the mine where Dock was working shut down and the middle-aged mountaineer found himself permanently unemployed. However, he and Sara managed to survive through frugal living until Dock became eligible for Social Security. In 1963, Mike Seeger, familiar with Dock's old records, located him in Norton after a diligent search. Dock had only recently resumed playing banjo again for his own amusement. Seeger persuaded Dock to record again and he subsequently cut two albums for Folkways and one for Asch, as well as an interview album. Dock also appeared at several Folk-revival festivals, including those at the University of Chicago; Asheville, North Carolina; Newport, Rhode Island and Whitesburg, Kentucky.

A dozen years after Dock's death, Mike co-produced a reissue album for Folkways containing all twelve of his original recordings from 1927 and 1929. More recently a nephew, Johnny Hunsucker, has cut an album for Heritage of music in the Dock Boggs style.

IMT

RECOMMENDED ALBUMS:

"Dock Boggs: Legendary Singer & Banjo Player" (Folkways)(1964)
"Dock Boggs: Volume 2" (Folkways)(1966)
"Dock Boggs: Volume 3" (Asch)(1970)
"Dock Boggs: His Original Recordings" (Folkways)(1983)

NOEL BOGGS

(Steel Guitar)
Given Name: Noel Edwin Boggs
Date of Birth: November 14, 1917
Where Born: Oklahoma City, Oklahoma
Married: Helen M.
Children: Noel Paul Richard, Sandra K., Debra S.
Date of Death: August 31, 1974

Noel Boggs was one of Country music's finest steel guitarists. He was born into hard times. By the time he was age 10, the U.S. was drifting towards the Great Depression. Living in Oklahoma was tough and music seemed to be the only way to get out of the poverty trap. While at junior high school, Noel took a twelve-lesson course in the fundamentals of music at the princely sum of 25 cents per lesson; he practiced hard.

During 1935 and 1936, while still attending senior high school, Noel started to work for WKY, KOMA and KEXR radio stations in Oklahoma City. In 1936, he joined Hank Penny's Radio Cowboys and toured the south and east. He and Penny owned only one suit each so they swapped clothes to appear better off. During 1936 and 1937, Noel appeared on radio WWL New Orleans as a staff musician. He did the same duties for WAPI and WBRC in Birmingham. In 1937, he returned to Oklahoma City and joined WKY as performer on the early morning show. He also appeared at Salathiel's Barn in Oklahoma City during that year. During this period, he started recording with Wiley and Gene. In 1941, he formed his own band and for three years played the Rainbow Room, Oklahoma City. He also played with Jimmy Wakely during the pre-WWII period.

Boggs was a great fan of Leon McAuliffe and this was mutual. Their knowledge of one another's work went back to 1935 and in 1944, when McAuliffe left Bob Wills' Texas Playboys to form the Cimarron Boys, Noel Boggs became his replacement. As a member of the Texas Playboys, he met guitarists Jimmy Wyble and Cameron Hill. They formed a fast friendship and their musical input helped create Western Swing's distinctive sound. While with Wills, Boggs appeared on many of the Tiffany Transcriptions and was on the Columbia recordings of *Texas Playboy Rag* (originally a solo vehicle for Noel Boggs), *Roly Poly*, *Stay a Little Longer* and *New Spanish Two Step*.

In 1945, Noel left Wills and re-formed a group to undertake an extended booking at the Hollywood Palladium. When that was over, Noel rejoined Wills. He left in 1946 to join another King of Swing, Spade Cooley.

He was with Spade Cooley's Dance Band until 1954.

Noel had become good friends with Jazz guitar giant Charlie Christian and they played together; this helped shape the style of Boggs' musical output. He, Wyble and Hill took the Christian solos on Benny Goodman tracks and re-arranged them into three-part harmonies or three-part leads; in fact, any variant they could think of.

Noel Boggs was known as a man with a great sense of humor and a generous person. When steelie Speedy West was trying to break into the business and had first arrived in Los Angeles, he couldn't afford a telephone. Noel was getting more work than he could handle, so he passed work on to Speedy. Noel was always pulling stunts on other musicians. One time while with Cooley, he put a live lobster inside the piano just before a performance and wired up six musicians' chairs. The lobster grounded the circuits and as a result there were musicians and music everywhere.

In 1955, at age 38, Noel suffered the first of what was to be a series of heart attacks. He wasn't able to work for three months and although he formed the Noel Boggs Quintet in 1956, he never really recovered. The four musicians supporting him in the quintet included Billy Armstrong and Harrell Hensley.

During his life, Noel appeared on some 2,000 commercial recordings as a soloist, with Bob Wills, Spade Cooley, Jimmy Wakely, Hank Penny, Bill Boyd, Sheb Wooley, Les Anderson, Merle Travis and the Cass County Boys. He worked on radio with Rex Allen, Roy Rogers, Gene Autry and the Sons of the Pioneers. He made regular television appearances with Spade Cooley and on Jimmy Wakely's network show.

Super steel guitarist ***Noel Boggs***

His motion picture work included solo work in Paramount and Columbia movies. He also created special sound effects and appeared in various movies, including *Rhythm Roundup*, *Blazing the Western Trail, Lawless Empire* (1945), *Frontier Frolic* (a musical short with Bob Wills and various of the Texas Playboys)(1946), *Everybody's Dancin'* (Lippert)(1950) and *Out West Teenagers* (Monogram)(1950).

Noel played many of the nightspots in Las Vegas, Reno and Lake Tahoe and undertook U.S.O. tours including one to Alaska and the Orient for five months. His business interests included ownership of Delphine Marine on Redondo Beach, California.

His final days were sad ones. He was estranged from his wife and children; overwork, alcoholism and a heart attack finally brought an end to this talented man's life. However, humor prevailed. At the funeral, a friend recounted how Noel had traveled home laid out in a hearse. Every time they came to an intersection, he would rise in the coffin. Noel had specified that he didn't want sad organ music at his funeral; he wanted good steel music, so they played his records. He was buried in Granada Hills, California.

RECOMMENDED ALBUMS:
Noel Boggs Quintet:
"Western Swing" (Repeat)(1965)
"Any Time" (Repeat)(1968)
"Magic Steel" (Shasta and Vintage Classics)
Featuring Noel Boggs:
"Western Swing and Pretty Things" (Shasta) [Jimmy Wakely album]
"Tobacco State Swing" (Rambler) [Hank Penny & his Radio Cowboys album]
"Tiffany Transcriptions Volume 1" (Kaleidoscope) [Bob Wills & His Texas Playboys album]
"Spade Cooley Volumes 1 and 3" (Club of Spade)
"Bill Boyd 1943-1947" (Texas Rose)(1985)
"Country Boogies Wild & Wooley" (Bear Family Germany)(1985)

SUZY BOGGUSS

(Singer, Songwriter, Yodeler, Guitar)
Given Name: **Susan Kay Bogguss**
Date of Birth: **December 30, 1956**
Where Born: **Aledo, Illinois**
Married: **Doug Crider**

Suzy Bogguss has always had an independent spirit. She built her career by being on the road for five years, working from a camper, taking any singing job she could find, with only her German Shepherd dog Duchess for company. She was her own booking agent and manager. She played coffee houses, nightclubs, resorts, hotels and colleges and traveled throughout the Midwest, the Northeast and Canada.

The youngest of four children, Suzy remembers, as a child, listening to her parents' records of Eddy Arnold. She also enjoyed dressing up and wearing flowers in her hair. She made her first public appearance when she was age 5 singing in the Aledo Presbyterian Church Angel Choir. After graduating from Illinois State University, where she obtained a BA degree in art, she intended to be a metalsmith and design and make jewelry, but after sharing a house with drama and music majors, Suzy learned a lot about guitar and realized that music could be her career. She began singing whenever she could and during her five years of traveling, she began attracting larger and larger audiences and playing bigger and better venues. As a result of this, she was asked by the Peoria PBS affiliate to appear in a special it was producing. The response to her performance was very good and she found herself hosting and starring in two more one-hour shows.

Soon Suzy was in demand and was opening for such acts as Dan Seals and Asleep at the Wheel, traveling to Mexico and touring throughout the West. She decided one day in 1985 to go to Nashville. She set off for Music City where she soon got a job singing in a local restaurant, supplementing her income with studio session work. Suzy recorded a low budget album at Wendy Waldman's studio. She circulated copies of the tape and some Nashville magazines extolled her talents. In 1986, she signed for the tourist season as the headlining act at Dolly Parton's musical theme park, Dollywood, taking her album with her to sell.

Meanwhile her tape was brought to the attention of Jim Fogelsong, then president at Capitol Records, Nashville, who within days of hearing it initiated a recording contract. Suzy was soon asked to appear on TNN's *Nashville Now*. After the show, Chet Atkins, who was one of the guests, invited her to open his concert at the Ordway Theater in St. Paul, Minnesota.

Suzy's first two singles for Capitol in 1987, *I Don't Want to Set the World on Fire* and *Love Will Never Slip Away*, reached the Country Top 70. *I Want to Be a Cowboy's Sweetheart*, in 1988, showcased Suzy's yodeling ability, but only made the Top 80. Her first album ***Somewhere Between*** in 1989 was produced by Wendy Waldman. That year, the title track went Top 50, *Cross My Broken Heart* went Top 15 and *My Sweet Love Ain't*

The very talented ***Suzy Bogguss***

Around went Top 40. Suzy was named "Best Female Artist" by ACM, during the year.

During 1990, her two singles, *Under the Gun* and *All Things Made New Again,* flopped and only reached the Top 75. They both came from her second album, ***Moment of Truth,*** which was released that year. Suzy started off 1991 with the Top 15 *Hopelessly Yours*, a duet with Lee Greenwood from his album ***A Perfect 10***. She followed with the Top 15 *Someday Soon*. Her third album, ***Aces***, released in 1991, went Gold the following year. Then success came her way in a big way, when *Outbound Plane* and *Aces* both went Top 10. These were followed by *Letting Go* and *Drive South*, which went Top 10 and Top 3 respectively. ***Voices in the Wind*** was the next album, released in 1992, and went Gold in 1993. In November 1992, she won the prestigious CMA "Horizon Award." She attended the awards ceremony with her husband, Doug, and because of a mix-up, almost didn't sing her song when she only had about three minutes to change instead of twenty.

Her successes in 1993 were *Heartache* (Top 25), *Just Like the Weather* (Top 5) and *Hey Cinderella* (Top 5). That year, she released her next album, ***Something Up My Sleeve***. Suzy has recently branched out into the fashion scene with a line of designer jackets. She is also one of the "unofficial contestants" in the "who wears the shortest skirts" contest in Country music. JAB

RECOMMENDED ALBUMS:

"Somewhere Between" (Capitol)(1989)
"Moment of Truth" (Capitol)(1990)
"Aces" (Liberty)(1991)
"Voices in the Wind" (Liberty)(1992)
"Something Up My Sleeve" (Liberty)(1993)

Bill & Earl Bolick refer BLUE SKY BOYS

EDDIE BOND

(Singer, Deejay)

Given Name:	**Edward James Bond**
Date of Birth:	**July 1, 1933**
Where Born:	**Memphis, Tennessee**
Married:	**Gladys Rebecca**
Children:	**Eddie James Jr., Becky Louise, Lisa Karen**

Eddie Bond started his career in Country music in 1955, playing on the KWAM Memphis *990 Jamboree*, KWBQ-TV Memphis and WHHM Memphis. He also worked on KWKH *Louisiana Hayride* out of Shreveport with Elvis Presley and Johnny Horton. Eddie formed his own band, the Stompers, and when he decided to do some Rockabilly, he added a drummer to the line-up.

Eddie auditioned for Sam Phillips at Sun Records, but Phillips said that Eddie's voice was too mediocre for rock'n'roll and that he wouldn't make it. Sam Phillips changed his mind later and Eddie recorded a lot of Country and some Gospel on the Phillips label but in 1956, Eddie moved to Mercury Records.

On this label, he recorded some Rockabilly singles like *Rockin' Daddy, Boppin' Bonnie* and on Diplomat, Eddie cut *Monkey and the Baboon.*

Great instrumentation made them excellent records; among the musicians playing on these sides were such top sessionmen as Chip Young, Hank Garland and James Wilson. In addition, John Hughey, a great steel guitarist, was also present and he continued to play with Eddie into 1962, when the sessions with Phillips were finally recorded and a remake of *Rockin' Daddy* was included.

Most of the material was Gospel and these sessions were used for an album. Although Eddie almost had a hit with *Rockin' Daddy*, he just didn't have the personality or the good management to make it to the top. He continued to work, appearing on WSM *Grand Ole Opry, Big D Jamboree*, Dallas and also doing a regular spot in 1966 on WABQ-ABC-TV *Country Shindig*.

He remained in Memphis and later became a deejay and TV personality. He also owned Tab, Millionaire and Diplomat labels and he recorded on these and about twenty others, like Advance, Frontier and Western Lounge. He was a familiar figure in Memphis and in 1974, Eddie Bond ran for Sheriff.

JAB

RECOMMENDED ALBUMS:

"Eddie Bond Sings the Greatest Country Gospel Hits" (Phillips International)(1961)
"Favorite Country Hits from Down Home" (Millionaire)(1967)
"Eddie Bond Sings the Legend of Buford Pusser" (Enterprise)(1973)

JOHNNY BOND

(Singer, Songwriter, Guitar)

Given Name:	**Cyrus Whitfield Bond**
Date of Birth:	**June 1, 1915**
Where Born:	**Enville, Oklahoma**
Married:	**Dorothy Louise Murcer**
Children:	**Sherry Louise, Jeannie Anne, Susan Paulette**
Date of Death:	**June 22, 1978**

Johnny Bond spent much of his career as an associate of movie cowboys such as Gene Autry and Jimmy Wakely, yet he managed to carve out an identity for himself. Bond had a string of recordings on Columbia and later Starday that demonstrated a flair for Country, Western and novelty material. He also wrote songs of quality ranging from the Western classic *Cimarron (Roll On)* to the Bluegrass standard *I Wonder Where You Are Tonight.*

Johnny was born and reared in rural south-central Oklahoma. Although he played a horn in the high school band, his heart lay with the guitar and music of Jimmie Rodgers, Milton Brown and the Light Crust Doughboys. After getting out of school, Johnny journeyed to Oklahoma City hoping to find success in radio. After some months, he formed a trio with Jimmy Wakely and Scotty Harrell, known as the Bell Boys from their Bell Clothing Company sponsorship on radio. They favored Gene Autry and Sons of the Pioneers songs while playing daily shows at local station WKY and making transcriptions for KVOO Tulsa. In 1939, after they appeared in the film *Saga of Death Valley* with Roy Rogers for Republic Pictures, the boys began to get serious notions about moving to Hollywood permanently. In late May, 1940, Johnny, Jimmy Wakely and Dick Reinhart left for California, where in September they went to work for Gene Autry's *Melody Ranch* CBS radio program.

Johnny soon broadened his activities in the Los Angeles area. While remaining a regular on the *Melody Ranch* show until its cancellation in 1956, he also appeared in 38 motion pictures through 1947. In most of those films, he took the role of a supporting musician with such singing cowboy heroes as Gene Autry, Tex Ritter and Wakely (who soon became a star in his own series at Monogram), or in a musical sequence starring an action-oriented star like Charles Starrett or Johnny Mack Brown. Cast members often doubled as ordinary cowpokes, posse members or supporters of the lead figure who had a minimal speaking role, but were always handy whenever the script demanded musical scenes (see Movie section).

Not long after helping Jimmy Wakely on his first Decca session in August 1940, Johnny Bond secured a solo contract with Art Satherley. He did his initial recordings in August, 1941, with his first cut being *Those Gone and Left Me Blues*. Johnny remained with OKeh and Columbia where he had the 1947 Top 5 hits *Divorce Me C.O.D.*; *So Round, So Firm So Fully Packed* and *The Daughter of Jole Blon*. In 1948, he went Top 10 with *Oklahoma Waltz* and in 1949 charted with *Till the End of the World* and *Tennessee Saturday Night*. The following year, Johnny had a Top 10 hit with *Love Song in 32 Bars*. On most of these hits he was backed by his Red River Valley Boys.

Through August 1957, he had a total of 123 released numbers. His more memorable songs included the anti-Hitler novelty *Der Fuehrer's Face, I'll Step Aside, Cimarron* and *Sick, Sober and Sorry*; the latter was a Top 10 hit in 1951. In addition to *Melody Ranch*, Bond worked as a regular on the *Hollywood Barn Dance* for many years from 1943 and the *Town Hall Party* in Compton, California, on both radio and television from 1953 until the program ended on January 14, 1961. Johnny also appeared with Gene Autry on most of his tours during the 40's and 50's.

After his Columbia contract ended, Johnny had a brief liaison with Gene Autry's Republic label in 1960, but then signed with Starday with whom he remained through 1971. During that time, Johnny released 14 albums. His 1964 recording of *Ten Little Bottles*, a novelty drinking song (originally cut for Columbia in 1951) went Top 3 in the charts the following year and became his biggest hit. In 1965, Gene Autry revived *Melody Ranch* for a Los Angeles television station and Johnny went back to work for him on this program as both a performer and scriptwriter for another five years.

During the last decade of his life, Johnny continued in music but also spent more time in prose writing. In 1969, he joined Merle Travis in a tribute album to the Delmore Brothers released on Capitol and following his Starday contract did albums on Lamb and Lion and for Jimmy Wakely's Shasta label. Beginning in 1970, Johnny started writing a still unpublished biography of Gene Autry and following Tex Ritter's death in 1974, he authored a creditable biography entitled *The Tex Ritter Story* (1975) and his own *Reflections* (1976). Later in 1976, in company with the Willis Brothers, Johnny made two CMH albums featuring songs that had been written for and/or performed in musical Westerns. At the time of his death, Johnny and Ken Griffis were at work on a book about Western music. IMT

RECOMMENDED ALBUMS:

"Johnny Bond's Best" (Harmony)(1964)
"Bottled in Johnny" (Harmony)(1965)
"That Wild, Wicked but Wonderful West" (Starday)(1961)
"Live It Up and Laugh It Up" (Starday)(1962)
"Songs That Made Him Famous" (Starday)(1963)
"Ten Little Bottles" (Starday)(1965)
"Famous Hot Rodders I Have Known" (Starday)(1965)
"The Best of Johnny Bond" (Starday)(1969)
"Here Come the Elephants" (Starday)(1971)
"The Singing Cowboy Rides Again" (CMH)(1977) [With the Willis Brothers]
"The Return of the Singing Cowboy" (CMH)(1977) [With the Willis Brothers]
"Rare Country, Western & Rockabilly Songs" (Cowgirlboy Germany)(1992)

BONNIE LOU

(Singer, Yodeler, Guitar, Fiddle)

Given Name:	**Mary Kath**
Date of Birth:	**October 27, 1924**
Where Born:	**Towanda, Illinois**
Married:	**1. Glenn Ewins (dec'd.)**
	2. Milt Okum
Children:	**Connie Ewins**

For a time in the mid-50's, Bonnie Lou ranked among the top female Country vocalists. She carried on the tradition of the Midwestern-based yodeling cowgirl set by Patsy Montana and the Girls of the Golden West.

Bonnie Lou was born and reared in the farm country of central Illinois, where she learned to yodel from her Swiss grandmother, but she was undoubtedly influenced by the Girls of the Golden West, who were then broadcasting over WLS radio. She became interested initially in the violin but became more serious about the guitar at age 11. After winning a local talent contest, she set her heart on a radio career and began at WMBD Peoria in 1939. A year later, she moved to WJBC Bloomington, which was nearer her home. In 1942, the young high school graduate landed a position at a major station, KMBC Kansas City. There she became a regular on the *Brush Creek Follies*, both as a member of the Rhythm Rangers and as a solo under the name of "Sally Carson," a pseudonym owned by the station.

In the spring of 1945, Bill McCluskey

The Tennessee Wig Walk girl, ***Bonnie Lou***

needed another girl singer at the powerful WLW station in Cincinnati and hired her in May after hearing her transcribed version of *Freight Train Blues*, complete with yodeling. Since she needed a new name, McCluskey created "Bonnie Lou," who joined the *Midwestern Hayride* on WLW while it was playing a show in Newark, Ohio.

The attractive girl quickly won her way into the hearts of fans with her singing and yodeling, both on her own and with a group called the Trailblazers. In 1947, Bonnie returned to Bloomington and WJBC for a time, but then came back to the Queen City to stay. She remained on the *Midwestern Hayride* for the duration of the show, which for a time after 1948 was on both radio and TV. During the 50's, the *Louisiana Hayride* served as a summer replacement show on the NBC Network in various time slots. This provided Bonnie with additional audience exposure.

Bonnie Lou initiated her recording career for King in 1953, with her first release, *Seven Lonely Nights*, which climbed to the Top 10 on the country charts. Later that year, she followed it with a novelty number, *Tennessee Wig Walk*, which did even better, reaching the No.6 slot. Bonnie had a total of twenty-four songs released on King, including *Papaya Mama* and *Teen Age Wedding*, but none had quite the impact of her two major hits. However, Bonnie Lou's appeal to Hayride audiences continued undiminished and she continued to be a headline act on the show through 1966.

She also worked as a regular vocalist on WLWT daytime TV. Ruth Lyons, a pioneer figure in variety talk show TV, became a virtual institution on the Queen City with her *50/50 Club,* and Bonnie Lou sang on the show. She helped cut a Christmas album on Ruth's Can-dee label around 1961. She also appeared on the *Paul Dixon Show* until the program terminated with Dixon's death in 1974. When Ruth retired in 1967, Bob Braun took over her show and Bonnie Lou continued with him. In her performances on these shows, Bonnie Lou moved towards a more Pop-Country direction. She had acquired some experience singing with a dance band in Bloomington and this undoubtedly worked to her advantage on these variety-oriented packages.

In 1945, Bonnie Lou had married a newly returned war veteran, Glenn Ewins. He was later killed in an automobile accident and she subsequently married Milton Okum, a furniture retailer from suburban Cheviot. Although Bonnie Lou has appeared on occasional shows in the Cincinnati area and on local TV commercials within the last decade, she is now retired and the Okums divide their time between Ohio and Florida. IMT

RECOMMENDED ALBUM:

"Bonnie Lou Sings" (King)(1958)

BONNIE LOU & BUSTER

Formed: 1946

BONNIE LOU

(Singer, Songwriter, Guitar)
Given Name: Margaret Bell
Date of Birth: June 4, 1927
Where Born: Asheville, North Carolina

BUSTER

(Singer, Songwriter, Guitar, Mandolin, Banjo, Fiddle)
Give Name: Hubert R. Moore
Date of Birth: October 28, 1920
Where Born: Bybee, Tennessee

This is a husband-wife team with experience in Country music that extends back to the mid-40's. Both have deep Appalachian roots and have spent their careers entertaining in an area extending from Georgia to West Virginia. Their music, a blend of Old-Time, Traditional Country, Bluegrass and hillbilly comedy has pleased both dedicated and casual fans alike.

Buster Moore received his nickname early in life because he weighed 10 pounds at birth. Traditional music had always been popular in mountainous Cocke County, Tennessee, where he grew up working on his father's farm and attending school in nearby Newport. He learned to play the mandolin and other string instruments. He especially liked the sounds of the Monroe Brothers and Mainer's Mountaineers and they influenced his music considerably. After Buster finished high school, he moved to Knoxville and found work in a grocery store but hoped to land a job at either WNOX or WROL radio. Finally, he and Eddie Hill formed a group which successfully auditioned at WNOX.

When WWII Selective Service began to take its toll on band members, Buster went across the mountains and worked in Carl Story's Rambling Mountaineers at WWNC until he too received his draft notice. While in Asheville, he made the acquaintance of two musically aspiring teenagers, Lloyd and Margaret Bell.

Returning to the mountains after his discharge from the Army, Buster rejoined Carl Story at Asheville, but soon went back to WROL as leader of a band called the Dixie Partners which included Ray "Duck" Atkins, Wiley Morris, Willie Brewster and a guy known as "Panhandle Pete," the one-man band. When Wiley Morris was temporarily sidelined, Buster got his new bride, Margaret, to fill in for him. She proved so popular that she was kept in the act. Buster renamed her Bonnie Lou (not to be confused with the one of *Midwestern Hayride* fame). After a time, Bonnie Lou & Buster left Knoxville and worked briefly in Greenville, South Carolina, before having a longer stay at WRAL and then WPTF in Raleigh, where Lloyd Bell, Art Wooten and Carl Butler worked in their band.

In 1948, Bonnie Lou & Buster returned to Knoxville and the next year they cut four sides for Mercury Records including a cover of Molly O'Day's *Teardrops Falling in the Snow* and Mac Odell's *Wolves in Sheep's Clothing*, both with Speedy Krise on Dobro. Then, the duo went to Memphis where they joined up with Buster's old partner, Eddie Hill, for a year.

Buster considered leaving show business at this point and even took a J. C. Penney store management position briefly, but he and Bonnie soon went to WSVA Harrisburg, Virginia, for eleven months. They did quite well with a group called the Tennessee Sweethearts, but then the station's new owner put all the entertainers on notice.

The couple then went to WCYB Bristol where they combined with Homer Harris (the Seven Foot Cowboy) and his trained horse, Stardust. In 1953, WJHL-TV in Johnson City went on the air and Bonnie Lou & Buster had a three-day-a-week program for a time and then went to a daily morning show. In addition to Harris and Lloyd Bell, their ensemble usually included a steel player and a fiddler.

In the early 60's, Bonnie Lou & Buster made a Gospel album for Waterfall Records. They remained in Johnson City for nine years until they began working on a group of stations for Jim Walter that covered homes from Columbia, South Carolina to Bluefield, West Virginia. In 1963, this became the syndicated *Jim Walter Jubilee*, which cut down on the amount of traveling that this schedule had re-

*Husband and wife **Bonnie Lou & Buster***

quired. Most of their shows, which some stations still carried into the early 80's, were taped at WATE-TV in Knoxville. In 1970, they appeared in the movie *A Walk in the Spring Rain,* which starred Ingrid Bergman and was filmed largely in Gatlinburg, Tennessee.

In 1972, they inaugurated the *Smoky Mountain Hayride*. This is a live Country music show which runs nightly at the Pigeon Forge, Tennessee, Coliseum during the tourist season. Here Bonnie Lou & Buster, together with Lloyd Bell, Don McHan, Louie Roberts, Little Roy Wiggins and others, present an appealing program that has won favor with mountain tourists for some twenty-one seasons. This gives casual fans an opportunity to hear a variety of quality Country music and to see Buster do his comic characterization of the brash but bumbling "Humphammer." Bonnie Lou & Buster continue to make recordings, mostly for sale at the *Smoky Mountain Hayride.* IMT

RECOMMENDED ALBUMS:

"Hymn Time" (Waterfall)(1963)
"Bonnie & Buster Sing Country, Bluegrass & Gospel" (Angel)(1977)
"Bonnie Lou & Buster with Lloyd Bell Sing Gospel" (Bonnie Lou & Buster)(1982)
"Smoky Mountain Hayride Show" (Green)(1983)
"Bonnie Lou & Buster with Lloyd Bell: Gospel Country" (Tandem)(1984)
"Bonnie Lou & Buster with Lloyd Bell: Gospel '88" (Crystal)(1988)
"Bonnie Lou & Buster with Lloyd Bell: Gospel '91" (Crystal)(1991)

CLAUDE BOONE

(Singer, Songwriter, Guitar, Bass Fiddle, Electric Bass)
Given Name: Claude Boone
Date of Birth: February 18, 1916
Where Born: Yancey County, North Carolina
Married: Grace
Children: five

Claude Boone sustained one of the longest careers in Country music, extending for half a century from the mid-30's. This achievement becomes even more remarkable when one considers that it has nearly all been spent outside Nashville. Much of Claude's work originated in Knoxville, but he was also a significant figure in Asheville and Charlotte. His music ran the gamut from Old-Time to Bluegrass to Honky-Tonk Country.

Claude was born and reared in the mountain country of western North Carolina about twenty-five miles north of Asheville, a region steeped in traditional music. The sounds of Jimmie Rodgers proved a greater inspiration to Claude in his youth, although both the Rodgers and the mountain sounds could be heard in Claude's music as the years passed. Claude began his professional career in his late teens when he went to WWNC Asheville and joined Cliff Carlisle's band. He remained with the Carlisle entourage until 1938. During that time, he backed Cliff on his Bluebird and Decca records and also did a few duets with Cliff as well as with Walter Hurdt, Joe Cook and Leon Scott. Claude also released a solo rendition of *The Hobo Blues*. As Scott and Boone, the Elk Mountain Boys, the duo cut ten sides for Decca in a style somewhat similar to Wade Mainer and Zeke Morris vocally and the Delmore Brothers instrumentally.

When Cliff Carlisle went to WCHS Charleston, West Virginia, Claude accompanied him but soon returned to Asheville where he joined the newly arrived Carl Story's Rambling Mountaineers. Claude would be associated with Carl in one way or another for the next 25 years, except for a period during the war when he served in the U.S. Navy and a short stint working at WNOX Knoxville with Buster Moore and Eddie Hill. After the war, Claude returned to the Rambling Mountaineers and they spent the next two decades working from bases in either Asheville or Charlotte but mostly Knoxville. Claude played either rhythm guitar or bass fiddle on all of Story's Mercury and Columbia recordings as well as on many of the Starday and small label discs that Carl's group often made. Claude sang various parts and some solos on the Rambling Mountaineer recordings and even composed a few of the songs, including one of the band's more memorable numbers, *Why Don't You Haul Off and Get Religion*. In 1949, Claude had his own solo contract with Mercury, cutting six sides with instrumental support from Jethro Burns on mandolin, Homer Haynes on guitar and young Anita Carter on bass fiddle. During his time with the rambling Mountaineers, Claude also played a comedy character named "Homeless Homer."

While continuing to work personal appearances with the Story group into the mid-60's, Claude also became a staff musician on the *Cas Walker Show* at WBIR-TV Knoxville. He remained a stalwart on this daily early morning program for more than twenty years until it ended in 1983. By that time, Claude was content to retire to his home in suburban Strawberry Plains and spend more effort at his favorite pastime of fishing. Over the years, Claude has written several Country standards, such as *Have You Come to Say Goodbye*, *You Can't Judge a Book By Its Cover* and *Wedding Bells*. However, it seems to be generally acknowledged that Claude bought *Wedding Bells* from Arthur Q. Smith. One could certainly term it a wise investment since the hit versions, first by Hank Williams and then Margaret Whiting and Jimmy Wakely, paid sufficient royalties that Claude purchased a home with his checks. Certainly, over the years, Claude Boone gained a reputation as one of the finest, most even-tempered and likable fellows in the music business. MCA Japan reissued an anthology containing one of the Scott and Boone duets and the Library of Congress Bicentennial series contained one of his Mercury solo efforts. Many of his recordings with Carl Story have also remained available. IMT

RECOMMENDED ALBUMS:

(See Carl Story)

DEBBY BOONE

(Singer)

Given Name: **Deborah Ann Boone**
Date of Birth: **September 22, 1956**
Where Born: **Leonia, nr. Hackensack, New Jersey**
Married: **Gabriel Ferrer**
Children: **Jordan, Gabrielle and Dustin (twins)**

A third-generation performer in the Country music field, Debby Boone is the third daughter of her famous father Pat Boone and the granddaughter of one of the most popular Country music performers, Red Foley. She became very successful in her own right for a short while.

Brought up in a Christian environment, Debby and her sisters harmonized together. Around the end of the 60's, Pat and Shirley Boone and Debby and her sisters became part of the Boone Family and in 1969, the family toured Japan. They appeared all around the Los Angeles area, singing at such venues as Disneyland and Knotts Berry Farm. They also appeared on many network shows and traveled around the country giving concerts. Later the girls formed a Gospel quartet called the Boones.

When Debby was 21, she set off on her own, signing a record contract with Warner/Curb. Her very first record, *You Light Up My Life*, became a smash hit in 1977; in October that year it went Gold and the following month it was Certified Platinum. The album of the same name also went Gold in October and by December was Certified Platinum. It reached No.1 on the Pop chart, staying at the top for 10 weeks and crossed to the Country Top 5.

The song became the year's best selling single and won a Grammy as the "Best Song of the Year" for its writer, Joe Brooks. Debby also won a Grammy as the "Best New Artist of the Year" for 1977 and was also named ACM's 1977 "Top New Female Vocalist." The next year, Debby was in such demand she appeared all over the the U.S. in concerts and TV shows.

During 1978, she had three middle-order singles, of which the most successful was *God Knows*. In 1979, she had success with *My Heart Has a Mind of Its Own,* which peaked just below the Country Top 10, and *Breakin' in a Brand New Heart*, which went Top 25. Both these songs had been Pop hits for Connie Francis.

Debby started 1980 with her first No.1 on the Country chart, *Are You on the Road to Lovin' Me Again*. The follow-up, *Free to Be Lonely Again*, went Top 15. Of Debby's two Country chart placings in 1981, *Perfect Fool* was the more successful, reaching the Top 30.

Debby continued in the Gospel field, winning another Grammy award in 1980, for the "Best Inspirational Performance" for her album ***With My Song I Will Praise Him***, on the Lamb and Lion label. In 1984, she won a Grammy with Phil Driscol for "Best Gospel Performance by a Duo or Group" for *Keep the Flame Burning,* a track from Debby's Lamb and Lion/Sparrow album, ***Surrender***.

She is married to Gabriel Ferrer, the son of Rosemary Clooney and Jose Ferrer, and they have three children. In 1989, Debby recorded the album ***Home for Christmas***, which includes her duetting with Rosemary Clooney on *White Christmas*.

RECOMMENDED ALBUMS:

"The Pat Boone Family" (Word)
"You Light Up My Life" (Warner)(1977)
"Surrender" (Lamb & Lion/Sparrow)(1983)

LARRY BOONE

(Singer, Songwriter, Guitar)

Date of Birth: **June 7, 1956**
Where Born: **Cooper City, Florida**
Married: **Lynn**

A college sports injury opened the door to a career in Country music for Larry Boone. Attending college on a baseball scholarship, Larry aspired to play professionally like his father. When he severely damaged a knee playing a pick-up football game, he turned his attention to music.

Larry learned to play guitar from his mother, Marie, when he was growing up in Cooper City. Music was still primarily a hobby for him in high school, but he performed publicly while attending Florida Atlantic University in Boca Raton, Florida. He performed at nightclubs and restaurants while studying physical education and journalism. He made his professional debut in 1976 at Chuck's Steak House in Plantation, Florida, where he played for three years. His music included material by Jim Croce, Gordon Lightfoot and John Denver. One day, Gordon Lightfoot was in the restaurant and tipped Larry $100.

In 1980, following graduation, Larry moved to Nashville and supported himself as a substitute teacher. He also played music for tourist tips at the Country Music Wax Museum on Music Row. Larry developed his songwriting skills by teaming up with veterans like Sonny Throckmorton and Bob McDill. He also struck a successful writing partnership with brothers Paul and Gene Nelson.

Gene Ferguson, a former record company executive turned manager, took an interest in Larry and helped him to get his first song recorded. Ferguson managed John Anderson and Charly McClain and convinced Charly to record a song Larry had co-written, *Meet You in the Middle of the Bed.* This led to MTM signing him to a writer's contract.The following year, Charly cut another song that Larry had co-written with Dave Gibson, *Until I Fall in Love Again.* This became a minor hit in 1985, when it was cut by Marie Osmond.That same year, Keith Whitley had a low-level success with another Boone co-write, *I've Got the Heart for You.*

Singer/Songwriter ***Larry Boone***

During the next two years, his songs were recorded by nearly 40 artists including *Love Is the Only Way Out* by William Lee Golden and *12:05* by Lacy J. Dalton, both in 1986. John Conlee's 1987 recording of *American Faces* was featured on NBC-TV during the 1988 Olympics.

During 1986, Larry signed with Mercury Records and after releasing five moderately successful singles, he debuted with his self-titled album. Until then, his most successful single had been *Stranger Things Have Happened* (1987), which was not one of his compositions. He at last hit the Top 10, with *Don't Give Candy to a Stranger*, in 1988. This was one of those clever songs that use a play on words, with which Country music abounds. Larry followed this with *I Just Called to Say Goodbye Again*, which made the Top 20. This track came from his second album ***Swingin' Doors, Sawdust Floors***, released in 1989. In 1988, *Billboard* named Larry one of Country music's Top 10 new artists (Singles and Albums) and *Cash Box* named him "Breakout Artist of the Year" and "Top New Male Vocalist." Larry again hit the Top 20 with his remake of the Faron Young hit *Wine Me Up.* That year, he provided Don Williams with the Top 10 hit *Old Coyote Town,* and Kathy Mattea scored a No.1 with Larry's *Burnin' Old Memories*. That year, Larry was nominated in the "Favorite New Country Artist" category for the fan-voted American Music Awards.

Larry's third album was entitled ***Down That River Road*** and contained the memorable song *Everybody Wants to Be Hank Williams (But Nobody Wants to Die)*, which deserved to go higher than its Top 75 placing. George Strait chose Larry's *Beyond the Blue Neon* as the title track for his 1990 album. In 1991, Larry moved to Columbia Records and charted with *I Need a Miracle* and *To Be with You*. In 1993, Larry's debut album for Columbia, ***Get in Line***, produced a Top 70 chart entry with the title track. JIE

RECOMMENDED ALBUMS:

"Larry Boone" (Mercury)(1988)
"Swingin' Doors, Sawdust Floors" (Mercury)(1989)
"Down That River Road" (Mercury)(1990)
"Get in Line" (Columbia)(1993)

PAT BOONE

(Singer, Songwriter, Actor, Author)

Given Name:	**Charles Eugene Boone**
Date of Birth:	**June 1, 1934**
Where Born:	**Jacksonville, Florida**
Married:	**Shirley Foley**
Children:	**Cheryl Lynn (Cherry), Linda Lee, Deborah Ann (Debby), Laura Gene (Laury)**

Pat Boone is the great-great-grandson of the legendary pioneer, Daniel Boone. During the 50's and 60's, Pat was the All American Superstar, with a string of Pop chart hits, selling around 45 million records. His record successes were only bettered during the 50's by Elvis Presley.

Pat was one of of four children and his family moved to Nashville when he was one year old, so he considers himself to be a Tennessean. At the age of 10, he was already entering amateur talent shows. He worked as an emcee on a high school talent revue on radio, which led to a winning appearance on the *Ted Mack Amateur Hour.* While at David Lipscomb High School, he excelled as an all-around sportsman and was also President of the student body and Shirley, who later was to become his wife, was secretary. She is the daughter of Country legend Red Foley. At this time, Pat had his own show, *Youth on Parade* on WSIX Nashville.

Pat and Shirley eloped when Pat was in his first year at college, and the couple moved to Denton, Texas. To make ends meet while he studied, Pat ran a show for WBAP-TV at a salary of $44.50 a week. Encouraged by his fans to audition for *Arthur Godfrey's Talent Scouts*, he tried out and became a winner. This led to a recording contract with Dot Records in 1954. Pat was signed by Randy Wood, who sent him to Chicago to record. *Two Hearts* became a Top 20 hit, followed by the million selling No.1 Pop hit, *Ain't That a Shame* (1955) (also a Top 10 hit in the U.K.), followed by the Top 10 *At My Front Door (Crazy Little Mama)*. Pat ended the year with the Top 20 Pop success, *Gee Whittakers!*

Pat opened his 1956 account with the now classic *I'll Be Home*, which reached the Top 5 and became his first No.1 in Britain, staying at the top for 6 weeks. The flip-side, a somewhat homogenized version of Little Richard's *Tutti Frutti*, also made the U.S. Pop Top 15. Pat followed with his second No.1, *I Almost Lost My Mind.* His recording of *Friendly Persuasion (Thee I Love)* was featured on the soundtrack of Gary Cooper's movie *Friendly Persuasion.* It reached the Top 5, while the flip-side, *Chains of Love*, went Top 10. The top-side gave Pat a Top 3 single in Britain. He ended the year with another No.1, *Don't Forbid Me*, which reached No.2 in the U.K. That same year, the American Broadcasting Company signed Pat to his first television series, *The Pat Boone Chevy Showroom*. This made him the youngest performer on air to have a network show. Other shows followed, including a daily 90-minute syndicated segment for Filmways.

Given a regular cast status on the *Arthur Godfrey Show*, Pat moved to New Jersey and continued studying at Columbia University. He then signed a million-dollar contract with 20th Century-Fox and began his movie career, starring in 15 motion pictures including *Bernardine* (1957), *April Love* (1957), *Journey to the Center of the Earth* (1959) and *Yellow Canary* (1963).

During 1957, Pat continued to rack up Pop hits starting with *Why Baby Why* (Top 5) and continuing with *Love Letters in the Sand* (No.1 for 7 weeks) coupled with the Top 15, *Bernardine*. Again, the top-side reached No.2 in the U.K. This was followed by the double-sided hit, *Remember You're Mine* (Top 10)/*There's a Gold Mine in the Sky* (Top 15). The coupling went Top 5 in Britain. He closed out the year with *April Love* which went to No.1, where it stayed for 6 weeks. It also went Top 10 in Britain. That year, his younger brother, known as Nick Todd, chalked up two Pop chart entries, *Plaything* (Top 50) and *At the Hop* (Top 30), both on Dot Records.

Pat graduated in 1958, magna cum laude, majoring in speech and English. By this time, he and Shirley were the parents of four daughters. That year he had a double-sided Top 5 hit with *A Wonderful Time Up There/It's Too Soon to Know*, both sides of which charted in the U.K., reaching No.2 and No.7 respectively. The top-side was the first major indicator of Pat's Christian beliefs. He then went Top 5 with *Sugar Moon* (Top 10 in the U.K.) and followed with the Top 10 *If Dreams Come True*. He then found that his singles, although charting, were not nearly as successful. During 1959 through 1960 his biggest hits were *Twixt Twelve and Twenty* (Top 20, 1959) and *(Welcome) New Lovers* (Top 20, 1960). In 1960, his album ***Pat's Greatest Hits*** was Certified Gold.

Pat bounced back in 1961 with a "tragedy" song, the melancholic *Moody River*, which went to No.1. Pat followed up with the Top 20 hit *Big Cold Winter*. The following year, in Britain, he also enjoyed a resurgence with the Top 5 *Johnny Will*. Later that year, Pat had his last major hit, the wonderfully manic *Speedy Gonzales*, which featured Robin Ward. This reached the Top 10 in the U.S. and No.2 in Britain.

Another indicator of Pat's beliefs had surfaced when he wrote lyrics to Ernest Gold's theme music for the movie *Exodus* and released it as *The Exodus Song (This Land Is Mine)*, in 1961. A committed Christian, his faith brought him through a bad patch in the mid-60's, when he had a financial crisis due to bad investments and in addition, his marriage was floundering. He read a book called *The Cross and the Switchblade*, by David Wilkerson, and was so impressed by it that he made a film about it. Pat began to work more and more on religious projects. In 1973, he toured Britain with a concept of Christian fellowship called *Come Together*. As a musical, with Christian groups participating, it was a huge success.

In 1968, Pat formed the Boone Family with his wife, Shirley, and their children, and they toured Japan and made several albums, including many Country-Gospel albums with the First Nashville Jesus Band on labels such as Word, DJM and Pat's own Lamb & Lion.

Pat wrote his first book, called *Twixt Twelve & Twenty*, a guide for teenagers. It sold more than 800,000 copies (and Pat owns up to buying one of them), with all royalties donated to the Northeastern Institute of Christian Education. Other books followed: *A New Song*, with over one million sales, has been published in five different languages; *The Honeymoon Is Over* was published in 1977; *Pray to Win* and *Pat Boone: The Family Scrapbook*, both published in 1980, were well received. Pat recorded a cassette of *Pray to Win* and it has been a great success in colleges, libraries and at home.

Not to forsake his Country roots, Pat also recorded a couple of Country albums. He signed with Melodyland (renamed Hitsville) in 1975 and had five Country chart entries, of which the most successful was the 1976 single, *Texas Woman* (released on Hitsville), which went Top 40. The following year, Pat's daughter Debby began a solo career and carried on the Country music tradition to the third generation.

In the sports world, Pat is active playing in and organizing tournaments for the benefit of charitable causes. For several years Pat has hosted the Telethon for the National Easter Seals Society, raising millions of dollars. Although the Telethon is an annual event, Pat works throughout the year for it, traveling all over the country for press conferences, interviews and benefit concerts. He is in demand as a speaker at Christian functions and at other organizations like Teen Challenge, YMCA, etc.

Pat has had innumerable honors heaped upon him. In 1979 the Israel Cultural Award was presented to him in recognition of his artistry and humanitarianism. His rendition of *Exodus* seems to have become the second Israeli National Anthem. He did a Royal Command Performance in Bangkok on the King's birthday and was a guest of Ronald Reagan in 1981 at the Inaugural Ball. Pat was invited to speak at the famous 4th of July celebration at Aalborg in 1981 by Queen Margrethe of Denmark.

Pat is the president of KDOC, Channel 56, Orange County, a television station, for which it took many years to get the license. The Christian Broadcasting Network and Procter and Gamble gave Pat and Shirley a contract to do a 30-minute cable TV show, *Together Shirley and Pat Boone*. Thirteen shows have already been completed. *The Pat Boone Radio Show,* which began in 1983, is broadcast on 130 stations all around the country. This is a show rather like the old *Arthur Godfrey Show. Pat Boone USA* became a daily show on national syndicated TV. Most shows are taped at Knotts Berry Farm in Buena Park, California. Another show Pat introduced to CBN Cable Network is *Gospel Gold,* a Gospel video network show.

Writing books, recording albums on his Lamb and Lion label and working for charity makes it difficult for Pat to find time for his grandchildren (they call him "Daddy Pat"). He is not slowing down and is not ready to retire yet, nor ready to relax in his home in Hawaii, but he seems to be busier and more energetic than ever. JAB

RECOMMENDED ALBUMS:

"I Love You More and More Each Day" (MGM)
"The Pat Boone Family" (Word)
"The Family Who Prays" (Lamb and Lion)
"Texas Woman: The Country Side of Pat Boone" (Hitsville)
"Pat Boone and the First Nashville Band" (MGM)
"All the Hits" (Topline UK)(1986)

TONY BOOTH

(Singer, Songwriter, Guitar, Bass Guitar)
Date of Birth: **February 7, 1943**
Where Born: **Tampa, Florida**
Married: **Rose**
Children: **Danny, Jeanene, Todd**

Tony came to public attention during the 70's, as a member of Buck Owens' Buckaroos. However, he had been building a career long before that.

When he was 14, Tony won a nationwide talent contest for guitar playing in New Port Richey, Florida. Although a left-hander, he played guitar right-handed. His early and continuing influence is Ray Price. He attended the University of New Mexico, majoring in music with the intention of becoming a school teacher.

He soon decided to make music his full-time business and got his first job with the Mel Savage Band at the Club Chesterfield in Albuquerque, New Mexico, and from there, Tony traveled with Jimmy Snyder playing venues such as Caravan East in Albuquerque and Mr. Lucky's in Phoenix, Arizona. He put together a band, Modern Country, in 1968 and played in Las Vegas, then the Westerner and Palomino in California. At the latter, Modern Country, then renamed the Tony Booth Band, became the house band.

On the recording front, he cut a single, *Big Lonely World*, for K-Ark and then moved on to BUB Records. In 1970, MGM gave him his first taste of chart success with Merle Haggard's song about inter-racial love, *Irma Thompson*. There was one more single that year that didn't chart and an album. By now, Tony had become a part of Buck Owens' organization and was signed to Capitol. In 1971, his debut single, *Cinderella*, made the Top 50. The ACM that year made him their "Most Promising Male Vocalist." In 1970 through 1972, the ACM voted the Tony Booth Band the "Band of the Year." The line-up included Jay Dee Maness (later with the Desert Rose Band) and Tony's younger brother, Larry. During the time Tony was at the Palomino, it was ACM's "Country Nightclub" award winner.

1972 was the year in which Tony really came into his own. He had three Top 20 hits starting off with *The Key's in the Mailbox*, continuing through *A Whole Lot of Something* and rounding off with *Lonesome 7-7203*. During the following year, he had five records on the Country chart. *When a Man Loves a Woman (The Way I Love You)* was just under the Top 30 and the other four, *Loving You, Old Faithful, Secret Love* (once a Doris Day hit) and *Happy Hour,* all peaked in the Top 50.

In 1974, he had three chart entries, two at the bottom level and one sandwiched between them, in the Top 30. That one was a reworking of Jim Croce's great song *Workin' at the Car Wash Blues*. He had two more singles that did nothing and by the end of 1975, he was off the label.

Tony's next and final appearance on the chart was in 1977 when the United Artists single *Letting Go* just scraped in. In the 90's, he could be found playing in Gene Watson's band.

RECOMMENDED ALBUMS:

"On the Right Track" (MGM)(1970)
"The Key's in the Mailbox" (Capitol)(1972)
"Lonesome 7-7203" (Capitol)(1972)
"Workin' at the Car Wash Blues" (Capitol)(1974)

MARIE BOTTRELL

(Singer, Songwriter)
Given Name: **Marie Diane Bottrell**
Date of Birth: **January 16, 1961**
Where Born: **London, Ontario, Canada**
Married: **Peter (div.)**

Marie Bottrell, who is greatly influenced by Dolly Parton, is a Canadian who just had to sing. By the time she was 11, she had joined her first Country band which was a family affair consisting of her brother Glen playing lead guitar and fiddle and older sister Sandra on bass and sister-in-law Darlene on drums.

In 1978, when just 16, Marie signed to MBS Records out of St. Elmira, Ontario. That same year she released the album ***Just Reach Out & Touch Me***, from which came the title track and *Always Having Your Love*. She quit school the next year while in 11th grade to concentrate on her blossoming career. That year, Marie reached the Canadian charts with three singles, *This Feeling Called Love, Oh Morning Sunshine Bright* and *The Star*.

In 1980, Marie released her second album for MBS, entitled ***Star***. This was to be an important year for Marie. She was nominated for "Outstanding New Artist in Canada" and won "Outstanding Performance by a Female Vocalist" at RPM's Big Country Awards. She also received the Canadian Radio Programmers' Award for "Outstanding New Artist" and was nominated for a Juno Award for "Top Country Female Artist." Marie's Canadian chart successes that year were *Walk Back*, which was also released in Germany, *Flames of Evil Desire* and *The Ballad of Lucy Jordan*. Marie had just one chart entry in Canada during 1981, *Wonderin' If Willy*.

In 1981, Marie signed with RCA Canada and signed a songwriter's deal with RCA's Dunbar Music. The following year, she released the album ***A Night Like This***. Marie had two singles on the Canadian charts, *Lay Your Heart on the Line* and *Does Your Heart Still Belong to Me*. That year, she was nominated for the CCMA's "Top Country Female Vocalist in Canada," for a Juno Award for "Top Country Female Vocalist" and won the Radio Programmers Music Poll as "Number One Country Female Vocalist in Canada." She began working closely with various Nashville-based writers.

In 1983, she had a new album, ***Everybody Wants to Be Single*** (recorded in Nashville) from which came the Canadian hit singles *Only the Names Have Been Changed* and the album title track. Marie was nominated for a Juno Award as "Top Country Female Vocalist" and was chosen as "Female Vocalist of the Year" in the *Country Music News* Fan Awards. She also received nominations from the CCMA as "Female Vocalist of the Year," for "Best Album" and as "Songwriter of the Year."

During 1984, she toured with Lee Greenwood and won "Female Vocalist of the Year," "Album of the Year" and "Entertainer of the Year" awards in the *Country Music News* Fan Awards. She also won the Radio Programmers Award for "Female Vocalist of the Year." She was also named the CCMA's "Female Vocalist of the Year." She also received a PRO Awards' "Award of Distinction." Marie's single hits that year were *Lovers Moon* and *Until Forever*.

In 1985, Marie released the album ***Girls Get Lonely Too*** and had a hit single with *Premeditated Love*. Marie retained her crown as the CCMA's "Female Vocalist of the Year." The next three years were not good ones for Marie, as she shopped for a new label and cut back on touring to concentrate on her songwriting. She had two Canadian hits with *Hopelessly Romantic* and *Girls Get Lonely Too*, in 1986.

Marie teamed up with Dan Paul Rogers, in 1989, for the chart hit *Lover's Game*, which received a CCMA nomination for "Duo of the Year." In 1991, she went with Tony Migliori's Cardinal Records and released the single *Lasso Your Love*. She also sang on the soundtrack of the Canadian movie *Border Town Cafe*. The following year, *I Don't Give Up So Easy* went to No.1 on the *Country Music News* Chart. That year, she received a CCMA nomination along with Tracey Prescott and Anita Perras (as Treeo) for "Vocal Collaboration of the Year" for *Snowflake* on Sony Canada.

RECOMMENDED ALBUMS:

"Just Reach Out & Touch Me" (MBS Canada)(1978)
"Star" (MBS Canada)(1980)
"A Night Like This" (RCA Canada)(1982)
"Everybody Wants to Be Single" (RCA Canada)(1983)
"Girls Get Lonely Too" (RCA Canada)(1985)

RORY MICHAEL BOURKE

(Songwriter, Singer, Guitar)
Given Name: **Rory Michael Bourke**
Where Born: **Cleveland, Ohio**
Married: **Rita**
Children: **Allison, Kelley**

Rory Bourke was born and raised in Cleveland, the son of an advertising copywriter. He graduated from Mount Saint Mary's College in Emmitsburg, Maryland, and worked briefly for the New York Central Railroad.

Rory's first job in the music business was in promotion for Mercury Records. The label moved him to Nashville in 1969 and promoted him to National Sales and Promotion

Manager. He left the security of the label to pursue his dream of being a songwriter.

After writing songs for about a year without success, Rory began to seriously doubt his songwriting future. A devout Catholic, Rory often visited his church to pray and one day asked God for a sign to show him whether he should keep writing songs. Five of his songs were recorded the next week, and before long, he was offered a writing contract with major publisher Chappell Music.

Rory began co-writing with some of Nashville's finest tunesmiths, including Charlie Black, Tommy Rocco and Sandy Pinkard. He began to amass a host of hits, including five for Anne Murray. The radio favorites provided by Rory include *Shadows in the Moonlight, A Little Good News, Another Sleepless Night, Lucky Me* and *Blessed Are the Believers*.

Female vocalists especially were attracted to the songs he wrote. Janie Fricke had a hit with his *Let's Stop Talkin' About It* and Gail Davies hit the Top 10 with *Round the Clock Lovin'*. *Baby I Lied* became a hit for Deborah Allen and Jennifer Warnes racked up a hit with Rory's Pop flavored *I Know a Heartache When I See One*.

Rory not only wrote hits for women, he wrote songs about women that became hits. Charlie Rich's recording of his *The Most Beautiful Girl* became one of the singer's signature songs. The Bellamy Brothers added to their list of hits with *Do You Love as Good as You Look*, as did Ronnie Milsap with *Where Do the Nights Go* and Don Williams with *I Wouldn't Be a Man*. George Strait had a chart topper with Rory's *You Look So Good in Love*.

In the early 90's, a host of artists recorded Rory's songs including Ricky Van Shelton, Steve Wariner, Shenandoah, Baillie and the Boys, Dan Seals, Riders in the Sky, Don Williams, Lee Greenwood, Shelby Lynne, Mike Reid and Sweethearts of the Rodeo. Lee Roy Parnell included four of Rory's songs on his 1992 ***Love Without Mercy*** album. One of those songs was *Tender Moment,* which became a hit in 1993. Parnell also included the Bourke song *Fresh Coat of Paint* on his 1993 album ***On the Road***.

Among Rory's accolades are three ASCAP "Country Songwriter of the Year" Awards.

JIE

JIMMY BOWEN

(Industry Executive, Record Producer, Singer, Songwriter, Bass)

Given Name:	**James Albert Bowen**
Date of Birth:	**November 30, 1937**
Where Born:	**Santa Rita, New Mexico**
Married:	**Ginger**
Children:	**Christian**

Jimmy Bowen is currently the President of Liberty Records and as such, is one of the most successful record producers and industry executives in popular music. With artists such as Garth Brooks, Tanya Tucker and Suzy Bogguss under his wing, he has also ensured that with him at the helm, his label is among the most influential.

Jimmy initially entered the music industry as a performer. He attended West Texas College in Canyon, Texas, and then in 1955 sang and played standup bass in the Rhythm Orchids, a group that included Buddy Knox, Don Lanier and Dave Alldred (Dickie Doo). Initially they were a Country band until one night a local drummer, Don Mills, sat in. Don played on some cardboard boxes and the group suddenly became a Rockabilly group.

Jimmy and Buddy visited Norman Petty's recording studio in Clovis, New Mexico, in 1956. Until then, the studio was used as a recording facility for the Norman Petty Trio. Bowen and Knox persuaded him to let them record. They cut two sides, *I'm Stickin' with You*, a Knox-Bowen composition on which Bowen sang lead, and Buddy's *Party Doll*. They initially released the sides on their own Blue Moon label, then formed Triple-D and pressed another 2,500 singles. Lanier's sister sent a copy to music publisher Phil Khal, and he and his partner, Morris Levy, then formed Roulette and released the record. *I'm Stickin' with You* coupled with *Ever Lovin' Fingers* was released by Jimmy Bowen and Jimmy's *My Baby's Gone* was the flipside of Buddy's *Party Doll*. Both records sold over a million in 1957.

Jimmy also had a Pop hit with *Warm Up to Me Baby* in 1957. He was featured in the 1957 movie *Jamboree* singing *Cross Over*. During 1958, he charted with *By the Light of the Silvery Moon*. He released one single during 1959, *You're Just Wasting Your Time/Walkin' on Air* before deciding to call it a day as a performer.

During this time, Jimmy made his first visit to Nashville and ran into trouble with the Country music establishment, because he used drums, which was still frowned on. During 1959, Jimmy moved to Colorado Springs, Colorado, and worked as a deejay. By the end of the year, he relocated to Los Angeles, where he signed to the American Music Publishing Company as a staff writer and worked closely with fellow songwriter Glen Campbell. Jimmy later became professional manager of the company.

At the end of 1961, Jimmy moved over to Chancellor Records and ran the West Coast office. At the time, their roster included teen idols Frankie Avalon and Fabian. In 1963, he relocated to Reprise Records' A & R Department, where he produced Jack Nitzsche's *The Lonely Surfer*. A year later, he started a production relationship with Dean Martin. Together, they recorded 26 hit singles including *Everybody Loves Somebody Sometime*, 15 Gold albums and 5 Platinum albums. While at Reprise, as the Jimmy Bowen Orchestra, Jimmy cut some singles from 1964 through 1967.

He also worked with Frank Sinatra and produced *It's My Life* (after making Sinatra resing his vocals) and *Strangers in the Night*. Jimmy left Reprise in 1968 to form his own Amos Productions. Here he recorded the early sides by Kenny Rogers and the First Edition, Kim Carnes, Mason Williams, Glenn Frey and Don Henley. The company closed its doors two years later and he resumed production work with Dean Martin and Glen Campbell.

In 1974, Jimmy became President of MGM Records, but a year later Polygram phased out the label. Somewhat disillusioned with what was going down in Los Angeles musically, Jimmy moved to Nashville. He had found this a happy hunting ground for songs for Martin and so in 1976 he moved to Eureka Springs, Arkansas, and commuted to Nashville. He started working with Tompall Glaser at the Glaser Brothers studio and learned about the music business in Nashville from him. He also produced sides on Roy Head, Red Steagall and Mel Tillis. He also went out into the field to find out why people did or did not buy Country records.

By 1978, Bowen had acted as Vice President and General Manager at MCA, which was going through a problematic stage. However, by the end of the year he had taken over at Elektra/Asylum's Nashville office as Vice President and General Manager. He told his bosses that he would give them a $30 million operation in four years. He missed by one million. While at the label, he added to the artist roster that had consisted of Eddie Rabbitt, by bringing in Conway Twitty, Crystal Gayle, Hank Williams, Jr., the Bellamy Brothers, Eddy Raven and Kieran Kane. When the label merged with Warner Brothers in January 1983, he switched to Warner's Nashville operation with the same title.

By 1984, MCA was in serious trouble in Nashville. Their ranking among the other labels had dropped and although the acquisition of ABC/Dot had increased their success rate, they needed leadership help. Bowen became President of MCA's Nashville operation and Executive VP of the company. He turned the company around within a year. In

1985, MCA was named "Label of the Year" and George Strait became *Billboard*'s "Top Singles Artist."

In 1987, Jimmy Bowen produced 23 Top 20 singles including 11 No.1s and 6 Top 5 albums including 3 No.1s. That year the label was named *Billboard*'s "Top Singles Label" and "Top Album Label." Under his guidance, sales tripled and MCA's market share soared from 12% to 20% and then up to 28%.

At the end of 1988, Jimmy set up Universal Records, which was marketed by MCA, but problems dogged it and when at the end of the following year he left to become the President of Capitol Nashville, his artist roster went with him. In 1992, he changed the name of the company to Liberty Records so as to emphasize the autonomy of the label.

Jimmy has made changes that are sometimes controversial, but all the time he has striven for technical improvements such as his insistence that all his product is recorded digitally. He has played a major role in the formation of the Nashville Music Association, now renamed the Nashville Entertainment Association. He has also strengthened the infrastructure at Liberty so as to bring his label to the forefront; not as a Country label but as a Nashville one.

BRYAN BOWERS

(Singer, Songwriter, Autoharp, Guitar, Dulcimer, Mandocello, Mandola)

Given Name: **Bryan Benson Bowers**
Date of Birth: **August 18, 1940**
Where Born: **Yorktown, Virginia**
Married: **(div.)**
Children: **Sean Camile**

If the title "King of the Autoharp" belonged to anyone, then Bryan Bowers has this accolade. His style is unlike that of any other players. He uses a 5-finger picking technique as opposed to a back and forth strum. Bryan's popularity on the Folk club circuit and his virtuoso mastery of his instrument has led to him becoming a charter member of *Frets* magazine's "First Gallery of the Greats."

As a child, Bowers listened to old call-and-answer songs of the field workers and gandy dancers which gave him a great base for his musical development. In high school, he played on the basketball team (he's 6'4") and received an athletics scholarship from Randolph Macon College in Ashland, Virginia. Shortly after, both his parents died and three hours short of taking his degree in Spanish, he dropped out. At the same time (the late 60's), he started playing guitar, which helped to alleviate his suicidal thoughts. Shortly after that, he took up the autoharp after being introduced to it by Dr. Rollie Powell, a friend from Virginia. He had tried dulcimer, slide guitar and mandocello, but immediately decided that the autoharp was for him.

In 1971, he moved to Seattle and played for pennies as a street singer and passed the hat around in bars. He then moved on to Washington, D.C. in his 1966 Chevy panel truck known as "Old Yeller." He managed to get a regular spot at the Childe Harold club, where he played between the sets for some money and food. At another club, The Cellar Door, he met the Dillards and played *The Battle Hymn of the Republic* for them to demonstrate the autoharp. They were so impressed that they invited Bryan to travel with them to the Berryville Bluegrass Festival. During their second encore, they introduced Bowers to the audience and the audience was captivated.

In 1977, Bryan signed with Flying Fish Records and debuted with ***The View from Home*** album. His recording career has been intermittent but he has subsequently produced further fine albums on Flying Fish: ***Home, Home on the Road*** (1980), ***By Heart*** (1984) and ***For You*** (1990).

Bryan's induction to *Frets'* "First Gallery of the Greats" followed five years of winning the magazine's "Stringed Instrument, Open Category" in the readers' poll. This distinction puts Bryan alongside such greats as Chet Atkins, David Grisman, Stephane Grappelli, Itzhak Perlman, Tony Rice, Rob Wasserman and Mark O'Connor. He currently plays at festivals and on the campus circuit, where his mix of zaniness and reverence delights his audiences.

RECOMMENDED ALBUMS:

"The View from Home" (Flying Fish)(1977)
[Features Steve Goodman, Sam Bush, Claudia Schmidt and Mike Auldridge]
"Home, Home on the Road" (Flying Fish)(1980)
[Features Sam Bush and the Seldom Scene]
"By Heart" (Flying Fish)(1984)
"For You" (Flying Fish)(1990)

MARGIE BOWES

(Singer, Guitar)

Date of Birth: **March 18, 1941**
Where Born: **Roxboro, North Carolina**
Married: **Doyle Wilburn**
Children: **Sharon Rene**

The Pet Milk Company's nationwide talent search helped launch several Country singers on a successful career and Margie Bowes was one. She was already a seasoned performer in 1958, when she entered the contest in Nashville and won it, and later that year, she was signed to Hickory Records.

Margie started to entertain while she was still in elementary school and by the time she was 13, she was appearing on WDVA *Virginia Barn Dance*, Danville, and WRXO Roxboro as well as TV and radio from WFMY Greensboro, North Carolina, and radio and TV in Roanoke, Virginia, and Durham, North Carolina.

Her first single in 1958, *Won'cha Come Back to Me/One Broken Heart*, created interest but didn't chart; neither did her second single, *One Time Too Many/Violets and Cheap Perfume*. During that year, she made her debut on the *Grand Ole Opry*. It was with her third single, *Poor Old Heartsick Me*, that she hit the Top 10. The follow-up single, *My Love and Little Me*, peaked in the Top 15. Margie released three further singles, none of which did very much.

She then moved to Mercury and her initial single in 1961, *Little Miss Belong to No One,* leveled out just below the 20 slot, but her other singles for the label didn't fare as well. By 1963, she was with Decca and the following year she had two more charted records, *Our Things* (Top 40) and *Understand Your Gal* (Top 30). The latter was an answer to Johnny Cash's *Understand Your Man*.

She continued releasing singles on Decca throughout the 60's with none charting. Her final single for the label was *Go Woman Go/I Have What It Takes* in 1969. During this time, she also appeared on *Jubilee U.S.A.* and in the movie, *Golden Guitar*.

RECOMMENDED ALBUMS:

"15 Country Greats" (Hickory)(1960)
"Country Boys, Country Girls" (Mercury)(1962)
"Margie Bowes Sings" (Decca)(1967)
"Today's Country Sound" (Decca)(1969)

ROGER BOWLING

(Singer, Songwriter, Guitar)

Given Name: **Roger Dale Bowling**
Date of Birth: **1943**
Where Born: **Harlan, Kentucky**
Married: **Miss Tricia**
Children: **Roger Dale, Jr. ("The Rock")**
Date of Death: **December 26, 1981**

Roger Bowling had the potential of becoming one of the major songwriters and performers in Country music. However, his premature death robbed the musical world of one of its finest people and talents.

Although born in Kentucky, Roger always considered Idaho his adopted state. It was as a songwriter that he initially made his mark. He first came to Nashville in 1970, but, after a three-month stay, realized that his songs weren't good enough. He returned in 1974, and through Larry Butler, he got Del Reeves to record his song *Pour It All on Me*, which was a Top 70 single for Reeves. The story of how Roger got his songs recorded is so unlikely that it could be a fairy tale. It appears he was playing poker with record producer Larry Butler and had won $4,000 from him. Butler was about to get remarried and didn't have the money. So Larry agreed to record some of Roger's songs so as to wipe out the debt. The artist chosen was Kenny Rogers, who at the time was not the superstar he is now, and not much became of them.

Roger's song *Blanket on the Ground* became a No.1 song through another Butler-produced act, Billie Jo Spears, in 1975, and was one of those rare Country songs to become a major hit in the U.K. That same year, Freddie Hart had a Top 5 hit with Roger's *I'd Like to Sleep Til I Get Over You* and Billie Jo Spears followed up with *Stay Away from the Apple Tree*, which went Top 20. Also, in 1975, Roger began his own recording career when he had the single for United Artists, *Jukebox Girl*.

The following year, Roger had a second single, *You've Got a Lovin' Comin'*, which had been recorded, without success, by Moe Bandy. It was not a particularly successful year for Roger, although Kenny Rogers' recording of *While the Feeling's Good* made the Top 50.

In 1977, Kenny Rogers took *Lucille*, a song Roger had written with Hal Bynum, to the No.1 position on the Country charts and the No. 5 spot on the Pop lists, going Gold in the process. Again he broke through in Britain, where the song reached No.1. The song was named both ACM and CMA "Single of the Year" and "Song of the Year" and also won a Grammy award for Kenny Rogers for "Best Country Vocal Performance, Male." That year, George Jones and Tammy Wynette reached the Top 5 with Roger's *Southern California* and Dottie West's single of *Every Word I Write* went Top 30.

In 1978, Billie Jo had a Top 20 hit with two other Bowling songs, *Lonely Hearts Club* and *'57 Chevrolet*. That year, Roger debuted as an artist on the Country charts with the basement entry *Dance with Molly*, on the Louisiana Hayride label. He followed up with *A Loser's Just a Learner (On His Way to Better Things)*, which fared only slightly better. The next year, the Bowling song *Coward of the County* became another monster hit for Kenny Rogers. It stayed atop the Country charts for 3 weeks, reached Top 3 on the Pop lists, went Gold and went to No.1 in the U.K. This time, his co-writing partner was the celebrated Billy Edd Wheeler, with whom Roger wrote several memorable songs. The song was named *Music City News*' 1980 "Single of the Year."

In 1980, Roger moved to NSD Records, where he came under the guidance of Joe and Betty Gibson. During that year, Roger hit the charts four times with *Friday Night Fool, The Diplomat, Long Arm of the Law* and the Top 30 single, *Yellow Pages*. That year, Roy Clark reached No.21 with the Bowling-Wheeler song *Chain Gang of Love*. The following year, Roger had his sole taste of major label success, with the Top 50 Mercury single *Little Bit of Heaven*. That year, Rex Allen, Jr. and Margo Smith duetted on yet another version of *While the Feeling's Good*, which went Top 30.

Roger was dropped by Mercury and he returned to NSD, where he released the 1982 single *A Good Bartender* and a non-Bowling song, *Then I'll Stop Loving You*. That year, Roger discovered that he was dying from a brain tumor. He did not tell his wife or child, and carefully arranged to take his life on the day after Christmas Day, 1982, so as not to let his family suffer, during his almost certain suffering.

In 1983, NSD released ***Then I'll Stop Loving You***, the album that the sparkling, bearded Roger Bowling, performer, never had during his lifetime, with tributes from some of his co-writers, Hal Bynum, Billy Edd Wheeler, Paul Richey and Glenn Sutton, and the artists he helped make stars, Kenny Rogers and Billie Jo Spears, as well as his family.

RECOMMENDED ALBUM:

"Then I'll Stop Loving You" (NSD)(1983)

DON BOWMAN

(Singer, Songwriter, Guitar, Comedy)
Date of Birth: August 26, 1937
Where Born: Lubbock, Texas

There are funny men and there are *funny* men and then there is Don Bowman. Billed as "The World's Worst Guitar Picker," he has been known to play his instrument like a fiddle. He is also sometimes acknowledged as the world's worst Country singer.

Don started singing in church while still a boy. His early ambition was not to be run over by a truck. As he grew, and he did, he became a local deejay and also picked cotton, which probably sounded better than his pickin' guitar. He also sold hubcaps. It can't be ascertained whether they were new ones or ones taken from someone's car.

In 1960, Don became a deejay in San Diego and then moved on to San Francisco, Minneapolis-St. Paul and then finally to WKDA Nashville. It was in Nashville that he came to the attention of Chet Atkins, who signed him to RCA Victor in 1964 and produced his records.

Don hit the charts in July with *Chet Atkins, Make Me a Star* and, by golly! he did. The single rose to the Top 15 and stayed on the chart for four months. He would never achieve that level of personal chart success again. However, in 1965, Bobby Bare recorded *Just to Satisfy You*, which Don co-wrote with Waylon Jennings. Willie and Waylon had a No.1 hit with the song in 1982 and five years later, Barbara Mandrell recorded it. Bowman was one of those who urged Chet Atkins to sign Waylon Jennings.

Don's next artist success came in 1966 when his parody on Red Sovine's *Giddy-Up Go*, entitled *Giddyup Do-Nut*, made the Top 50. He had four more charted records in the 70's, including *Surely Not* (1966), *For Loving You* with Skeeter Davis in 1968, *Folsom Prison Blues #2*, also in 1968, and *Poor Old Ugly Gladys Brown*, in 1969 with assistance from Willie, Waylon and Bobby Bare. During 1974, Jim Stafford hit the Pop Top 10 with *Wildwood Weed*, which Stafford had written with Don. In 1979, Don surfaced on the Lone Star label with the almost autobiographical ***Still Fighting Mental Health***.

To get the full taste of Don Bowman, his albums are essential listening. As a parodist he is in the same league as Homer & Jethro and Ben Colder.

RECOMMENDED ALBUMS:

"Our Man in Trouble" (RCA Victor)(1964)
"Fresh from the Funny Farm" (RCA Victor)(1965)
"The Best of Country Comedy" (RCA Victor)
"Funny Way to Make an Album" (RCA Victor)(1966)
"Don Bowman Recorded Almost Live" (RCA Victor)(1967)
"From Mexico with Laughs" (RCA Victor)(1967) [Features the Tijuana Drum & Bugle Corps]
"Funny Folk Flops" (RCA Victor)(1968) [With Skeeter Davis]
"Support Your Local Prison" (RCA Victor)(1969)
"Whispering Country" (RCA Victor)(1970) [A send-up of Bill Anderson]
"The All New Don Bowman" (RCA Victor)(1972) [Featuring Farley McCluth and Ralph Emery]
"Still Fighting Mental Health" (Lone Star)(1979)

BOXCAR WILLIE

(Singer, Songwriter, Guitar)
Given Name: Lecil Travis Martin
Date of Birth: September 1, 1931
Where Born: Sterratt, Texas
Married: Lloene ("Miz Box") (m. 1964)
Children: Tammy, Lorri and Larry (twins)

On Saturday, April 14, 1979, a dishevelled figure in overalls and battered hat, with a two-day growth of beard and an old jacket, came on to the stage at the International Country Music Festival, Wembley, England as an unknown. He left the stage to the most rapturous applause. A star had been born. Boxcar Willie had become an overnight sensation after pounding the roads and the boards for 30 years.

Boxie had been born into the world of trains, hobos and Country music and the family home was six feet from the railroad tracks. He started to perfect his now famous whistle from the age of two. His father played fiddle and young Lecil was raised on the music of Jimmie Rodgers, Ernest Tubb and Roy Acuff. He would later be influenced, like all real Country singers, by Hank Williams.

By the time he was 16, Boxie was performing regularly on the *Big D Jamboree* in Dallas. He decided to join the U.S. Air Force and became a C5 pilot. He must have felt like a sky hobo as he clocked up 10,000 flying hours. On leaving the Air Force, he helped start the *Cowtown Hoedown,* a radio show that came out of Forth Worth, Texas. However as rock'n'roll crept into the show and Country music diminished, he got disillusioned.

In 1960 he became "Marty Martin" and started to formulate the hobo character that would become "Boxcar Willie." He had been up in Lincoln, Nebraska, when he saw a hobo who looked like Willie Nelson emerge from a boxcar. As a result he wrote a song, *Boxcar Willie*.

He became a deejay on Corpus Christi radio in Texas, but in 1976, with the help of his wife and family, he decided that he had to stake all on his hobo character. The first year

The legendary ***Boxcar Willie***

was tough, with "Miz Box" being the main breadwinner. Then fate stepped in when George Jones was sick and couldn't play his Possum Holler Club in Nashville. Boxie was called in to replace him and during his act, he was spotted by Scottish booking agent Drew Taylor. Taylor signed Boxie for a Scottish tour and the rest reads like a storybook.

Boxie toured Britain every year through to 1980 and appeared at the Wembley Festival again in 1980, 1981, 1988 and 1989, always to a standing ovation. In 1981, Boxcar Willie became the 60th member of the *Grand Ole Opry*. His album ***King of the Road*** was marketed through TV by Suffolk Marketing and has sold in excess of two million copies. He has received Platinum albums for it in the U.K., Canada and the U.S. In 1981, his name and a bronze star were embedded in the Country Music Hall of Fame's Walkway of the Stars. In the same year, he was given the *Music City News* Award as the "Most Promising New Artist." Not bad for a 50th birthday present. He appeared regularly on *Hee Haw* and made guest appearances in two movies, the 1982 TV-movie *Country Gold* and *Sweet Dreams*, the 1985 biopic about Patsy Cline. His hobo hat and overalls now hang alongside Hank Snow's Nudie suit in the Country Music Hall of Fame.

Among Boxie's other honors is being made the World Ambassador for the Hobos. He received this accolade at a worldwide hobo convention in Britt, Iowa, in 1981. This is an appropriate honor for a man of honor. Well remembered is his gesture towards Billy Walker during a badly judged cessation of Billy's act at the 1989 Wembley Festival by an overofficious stage manager. Boxie told promoter Mervyn Conn that he would not go on unless Billy did an encore during his set.

Of note to followers of interesting facts is that the bass guitarist in Boxie's Texas Trainmen at the 1988 Wembley Festival was none other than the legendary ex-Texas Playboy Leon Rausch, who sang a couple of numbers.

Boxcar Willie is an important part of Country music. The fact that only one of his singles, *The Man I Used to Be* (1983), has made the Top 50 is irrelevant. In times when some Country artists barely qualify to be in Country music, Boxie stands resolutely as the true traditional Country performer. Country music is secure in the hands of America's favorite hobo.

RECOMMENDED ALBUMS:

"King of the Road" (Suffolk Marketing/Main Street/Warwick (UK))(1982)

"Last Train to Heaven" (Main Street)(1982)

"Live in Concert" (Hallmark)(1984)

"The Boxcar Willie Collection" (Double)(The Collector Series UK)(1986)

And if you can get it!

"Jamboree U.S.A. (Boxcar Willie Live, June 13, 1981, Capitol Music Hall, Wheeling, West Virginia)" (double)(Star Fleet CSF-17-1981)(1981) [Issued as a promotional album]

BOY HOWDY

Formed: **1990**

Members:

Jeffrey Steele	**Vocals, Bass Guitar**
Cary Parks	**Guitar, Mandolin, Harmony Vocals**
Larry Parks	**Guitar, Fiddle, Harmony Vocals**
Hugh Wright	**Drums, Harmony Vocals**

During the 1990's, a lot of new groups have emerged in Country music. From first hearing, it was apparent that several were not going to make it, because either they were session men, who got together, but would be lured back by the money and independence that session playing afforded, or they would be songwriters, who would soon realize that ensemble performing was not for them. There was a third breed, and that is the group that looks like it will succeed, because there is some pedigree in their make-up. Such a group is Los Angeles-based Boy Howdy, who purvey "L.A. Hip."

Jeffrey Steele (b. August 27, 1961, Burbank, California) was influenced by Lennon & McCartney, Willie Nelson, Hank Williams and Kristofferson and by the time he was 17, he was touring with Jimmy Ordge. On returning to LA, Jeffrey led and played in various bands and then came to the notice of producer Pete Anderson, the man behind the desk for Dwight Yoakam. As a result, Steele performed his own song *Driftin' Man* on the Anderson-produced compilation ***A Town South of Bakersfield, Vol. 2.*** In 1990, Jeffrey's song *Where Fools Are Kings* appeared on the Steve Wariner album ***Laredo***. Jeffrey also appeared in an episode of TV's *Murder She Wrote*.

Brothers, Cary (b. March 15, 1956, Stockton, California) and Larry (b. June 3, 1959, Stockton, California) Parks were born to play music. Their father, Ray Parks, was a well-known Bluegrass fiddler, and formed the group Vern and Ray, which also boasted Herb Pederson, who would later sing on Boy Howdy's debut single. Cary has played with Country-Rockers Randy Meisner (ex-Eagles and Poco) and Rick Roberts (ex-Flying Burrito Brothers).

Drummer Hugh Wright (b. December 18, 1951, Keokuk, Iowa) has been playing since age 15 and was professionally trained. He received a degree at the University of Iowa School of Music. He has played a wide variety of styles and among the performers he has backed is legendary Bluesman John Lee Hooker.

These four musicians found themselves playing together on a club date and as the chemistry was there, they decided to form a band. As Boy Howdy, they became a popular live act and debuted on KZLA Burbank, California. Blending Country and Rock in the tradition of Creedence Clearwater Revival and the Eagles, with an emphasis on the strong songs of Steele, the guitar work of the Park brothers and tight harmonies, they soon began recording in LA. Their first single, *When Johnny Comes Marchin' Home Again*, was released in early 1991, and was timely with the Gulf War. That year, they signed with Curb Records and were chosen by the LA Chapter of the California Country Music Association as "Best Vocal Group" with Jeffrey being named "Best Male Vocalist of the Year." He was also chosen as "Best Bassist" and Wright was named "Best Drummer." In addition, the group was named "Best Non-Touring Band" by the ACM.

In 1991, they released their first album, ***Welcome to Howdywood***, which was produced by Chris Farren, in California, and they made their debut on the Country singles chart with *Our Love Was Meant to Be*, which reached No.43. During 1992, they appeared in the George Strait movie *Pure Country* and then, later in the year, Hugh Wright was seriously injured while assisting at the scene of an auto crash. In 1993, the band released their second album, ***Boy Howdy***. During the year, they had singles success with *A Cowboy's Born With a Broken Heart* and the title track from their 6-track mini album, ***She'd Give Anything***. This album has proven to be the breakthrough that the group needed and it has scurried up the Country Album chart in 1994.

RECOMMENDED ALBUMS:

"Welcome to Howdywood" (Curb)(1991)
"Boy Howdy" (Curb)(1992)
"She'd Give Anything" (Curb)(1994)

Playing their brand of "L.A. Hip" Country, ***Boy Howdy***

BILL BOYD

(Singer, Guitar)

Given Name: **William Lemuel Boyd**
Date of Birth: **September 28, 1914**
Where Born: **Fannin County, Texas**
Date of Death: **December 7, 1977**

The Country side of Western Swing was nowhere more convincingly demonstrated than in Bill Boyd's band, the Cowboy Ramblers. While groups like Bob Wills' Texas Playboys made serious incursions into Pop music and Swing, with large ensembles and horn sections, Bill Boyd's band retained the rural Southwest string band flavor, and managed to maintain a large and loyal audience for over two decades and to produce some of the best-known and longest hits of the genre.

Like many settlers in Texas, the parents of Bill Boyd and his younger brother Jim originally came from middle Tennessee. By 1903, they had established a ranch and cotton farm near the town of Ladonia. This gave the Boyd boys some real experience not only at picking cotton, but also riding, roping and other cowboy duties. When they sang of the cowboy life later on the radio, they did so with conviction.

At night, ranch hands often relaxed by playing music and the two Boyds usually joined in; both parents were also decent singers. As early as 1926, while they were still in their teens, Bill and Jim were considered good enough to perform over station KFPM in nearby Greenville. By 1929, the family moved to Dallas and the brothers got a taste of city life. Bill enrolled in Dallas Technical High School, joined a band and met a young fiddle player named Art Davis.

As he worked at various menial jobs and watched the Depression deepen, Bill continued to dream of making a living with his music. The local live radio scene in Dallas was booming and Bill soon plugged into it. After a period at WFAA with a pick-up band, he formed the first edition of the Cowboy Ramblers in 1932, and began to work over station WRR. A charter member was brother Jim on bass, another was fiddler Art Davis and tenor banjo player Walter Kirkes rounded out the band. By working steadily throughout the radio day and by acting as his own salesman to line up sponsors, Bill was soon able to make a living wage.

The district manager for RCA Victor Records heard them on air and arranged a recording contract in 1934. The band headed for San Antonio and did a series of sides for the Bluebird label, sides that ranged from fiddle instrumentals like *The Lost Wagon* to lively Western songs like *The Strawberry Roan* and *I'm Gonna Hop off the Train*. Both the latter sold very well, and the next year saw another session and an even bigger set of hits: *Under the Double Eagle* in an arrangement that was copied for generations and was still used by Willie Nelson's band in the 1980's, *Going Back to My Texas Home* and a version of *Desert Blues* called *The Windswept Desert*.

RCA soon learned that Bill's band had a popular sound and began scheduling regular sessions. By 1938, the group had grown to ten pieces and was including some important Western Swing pioneers including fiddlers Carroll Hubbard and Kenneth Pitts, pianist Knocky Parker, and banjo player Marvin "Smoky" Montgomery. At other times, fiddler Jesse Ashlock, electric steel guitarist Wilson "Lefty" Perkins and fiddler Cecil Brower were members of the band and recorded with it. Over the years, the Cowboy

Ramblers cut some 229 sides for RCA Victor; later hits included *Wah Hoo* (1936), *Fan It* (1936), *Beaumont Rag* (1937), *La Golondrina* (1938), *New Spanish Two-Step* (1938) and *Lone Star Rag* (1949).

During all this recording, the band was invited to Hollywood to make films, and eventually appeared in six features for PRC in the 1940's (see Movie section) including *Texas Manhunt*, *Raiders of the West* and *Prairie Pals*. Brother Jim continued to act as a sort of assistant director for the band, filling in when Bill was away and later recording with his own group, the Men of the West. By the 1950's, the live music scene on Dallas radio was drying up, and both brothers had to take jobs as deejays in the new Country music world of records and rock'n'roll. Bill died in 1977 and his brother Jim followed in 1993.

CKW

RECOMMENDED ALBUMS:
"Bill Boyd—1943-1947" (Texas Rose)
"Bill Boyd's Cowboy Ramblers" (double)(Bluebird)

BOYS FROM INDIANA, The

Formed 1973

AUBREY HOLT
(Guitar, Bass, Vocals)
Given Name: Aubrey Lee Holt
Date of Birth: August 15, 1938
Where Born: Milan, Indiana
Married: Thelma
Children: Carla, Brent, Anita, Tony, Margie, Rhonda

JERRY HOLT
(Bass, Vocals)
Given Name: Jerry Ray Holt
Date of Birth: August 15, 1941
Where Born: Cincinnati, Ohio
Married: Rose
Children: Jeffrey, Gregory, Laura, Stanley

TOMMY HOLT
(Mandolin, Bass, Guitar, Vocals)
Date of Birth: July 17, 1949
Where Born: Hamilton, Ohio
Married: Joyce

HARLEY GABBARD
(Dobro, Banjo, Fiddle, Guitar, Vocals)
Given Name: Harley Royce Gabbard
Date of Birth: December 31, 1935
Where Born: West Harrison, Indiana
Married: Josephine
Children: Randy, Harlan

Other Members:
Banjo: Rod Case, Noah Crase, Jeff Murray
Fiddle: Randall Collins, Glenn Duncan, Sam Jeffries, Paul Mullins, Bill Thomas, Steve Williams
Mandolin: Frank Godbey

Although of Kentucky ancestry, the main core of the Boys from Indiana consisted of the three Holt brothers and their favorite uncle, Harley Gabbard, having spent most of their lives in the Midwest while creating some of the most original traditional Bluegrass of the past decades. Highlighted by the many fine compositions of the band members—especially guitarist Aubrey Holt—and a well-paced stage show, the Boys nearly always delight their audiences. Their songs, almost without exception, bring a degree of freshness to such time-honored Bluegrass themes as family, home, lost love, a musician's life, patriotism and traditional values.

The Holt brothers and Harley Gabbard all grew up in rural Indiana about fifty miles west of Cincinnati. Taught some of the fundamentals of traditional music from childhood, they supplemented them with inspiration from the *Grand Ole Opry*. Bill Monroe, Lester Flatt, Earl Scruggs, and Hank Williams all caught their attention. Before Aubrey was out of his teens, he and his mother's brother, Harley Gabbard, formed a Bluegrass band which recorded a few sides for both Excellent and Starday, one of the latter being *Family Reunion*, which Carl Story and the Rambling Mountaineers covered on Mercury, turning it into a minor Bluegrass classic. Meanwhile, the Gabbard and Holt band had limited commercial success and subsequently dissolved.

Harley, who had initially played banjo, switched to Dobro, working as a session musician and sideman for such folks as the Osborne Brothers, J.D. Jarvis and the Goins Brothers. He also did a few solo recordings on the Vetco label, featuring his deep voice that is strongly reminiscent of Johnny Cash. Aubrey kept writing songs and taking them to Music City, where publishers told him that they were too nostalgic and traditional for the Nashville Sound.

In 1973, Aubrey and Harley got together the Boys from Indiana with the addition of Jerry Holt on bass, Paul "Moon" Mullins on fiddle, and Noah Crase on banjo. Their initial recording effort was a Gospel album for Jewel, with *We Missed You in Church Last Sunday* as the title cut. It contained several of Aubrey's original songs. The follow-up album, for King Bluegrass, also contained several original songs, most notably *Atlanta Is Burning*, a Civil War ballad, and *My Night to Howl*, a Honky-Tonk flavored number. Aubrey's original songs and the tight vocal trios of him, Jerry and Harley quickly made the Boys from Indiana a popular act on the festival circuit. They released three more King Bluegrass albums in the later 70's, each containing at least six of Aubrey's numbers, and an original tune or two by Crase and Mullins. Some of his more memorable numbers included *One More Bluegrass Show, You Can Mark It Down, Bluegrass Music Is Out of Sight, Play Hank's Songs Once Again, Carolina Jane,* and *Shaking the Grate*. After the demise of King Bluegrass Records, Rebel kept the ***Atlanta Is Burning*** album in print, and re-released highlights from the other three albums as ***Best of the Boys from Indiana***.

By 1979, the band experienced some changes in personnel, but their vocal sound re-

*The Holt Brothers and uncle, Harley Gabbard, the **Boys from Indiana***

mained intact. First, Crase and then Mullins departed, to be replaced by Rod Case and Billy Thomas, respectively. Also Tommy Holt joined the band, after completing his military service. By this time the group had begun to develop thematic concepts which they worked into their shows, the most notable being a 20-minute segment devoted to the pioneers of Bluegrass. Another thematic set which found favor with fans was patriotic in nature and entitled ***Tribute to the American Soldier***. Throughout the 80's, the band had six albums released on their own Old Heritage label and did another one for Carl Queen of Atteiram, released in 1985. Their most recent effort, a cd on Rebel, contains eight of Aubrey's originals and songs like *Call This Country Boy Home* and *Will Heaven Be Like Kentucky*, indicating that his fertile mind is far from exhausted.

In addition to being favorites on the Bluegrass festival circuit for nearly 20 years, the Boys from Indiana have worked numerous clubs, guested on the *Grand Ole Opry* several times and in 1989 entertained President Bush at the White House. A recent conversation with Aubrey Holt suggested that Jerry, Tommy and perhaps Harley intended to get off the road for a while. Aubrey expected to continue singing and writing songs in some manner, taking a just pride in his contributions to Bluegrass and Country music. In 1994, he had both Gospel and Christmas albums on the drawing board. IMT

RECOMMENDED ALBUMS:

"We Missed You in Church Last Sunday" (Jewel)(1973)
"Atlanta Is Burning" (King Bluegrass) and (Rebel)(1975)
"Best of the Boys from Indiana" (Rebel)(1980)
"An American Heritage: A Tribute to the Pioneers of Bluegrass Music" (Old Heritage)(1980)
"Show Me My Home" (Old Heritage)(1981)
"Did You Forget God Today" (Old Heritage)(1982)
"Showtime" (Old Heritage)(1983)
"Guide This Silver Eagle" (Old Heritage)(1985)
"Live at Gilley's (with Chubby Wise)" (Old Heritage)(1988)
"Life on the Road" (Atteiram)(1985)
"Touchin' Home" (Rebel)(1992)

JOHN BRACK

(Singer, Songwriter, Guitar)

Given Name: Hans-Heinrich Brack
Date of Birth: April 4, 1950
Where Born: Zurich, Switzerland
Married: Barbara

Known as "Mr. Swiss Country," John Brack is a popular performer on the European Country scene. John's music is down-to-earth Honky-Tonk Country and he always feels complimented whenever he is told that he sounds like he comes from the U.S. John, the son of a lawyer, had his career mapped out for him, serving a ministerial apprenticeship. His musical interests were centered on Folk, Blues, Beat and the Beatles. No one at that time could guess that John would get into Country music. He had trained as a classical singer for two years and successfully auditioned for the Zurich Opera. Then he decided to travel in the U.S.; setting off in a Buick, he covered some 11,000 miles and became hooked on Country music.

He made his professional debut in 1975 as a singer with the duo Che and Ray. By 1979, John was a finalist at the First National Country Music Festival in Zurich. The following year, he released his first album for EMI, ***Feel So Good***, on which seven of the songs were self-penned. That year, John traveled to Nashville to appear on the International concert at Fan Fair.

In 1982, John's self-titled album, which was recorded in Nashville, was released. At the Euro Country Music Festival in Holland, John won a Silver Medal and his fame spread. Two years later, John released his third EMI album, ***Country Special***, which was also recorded in Nashville. That year, he debuted at the Wembley Festival in England and with Boxcar Willie, John appeared at the International Country Music Festival in Zurich, playing to an audience of 11,000, and receiving a standing ovation.

In 1985, John released his fourth album, ***Strong Feelings***, which became Switzerland's first cd. During the year, John undertook a European tour which encompassed festivals in England (Wembley and Peterborough), Northern Ireland (Belfast), Germany (Frankfurt), Austria and Switzerland (Zurich). He also appeared on the Eurovision broadcast *Star Award* from Holland. In 1986, John released his ***By Request*** album, on which he used his own JB road band and which he produced himself. He again traveled to Nashville to appear at Fan Fair and did the festival circuit in Europe.

*Swiss Country star **John Brack***

John's most ambitious album, ***Hard Times***, was produced in Nashville by Randy Scruggs with all of the songs written by John and his long-time friend, Max Stenz. It was distributed throughout Europe. At the end of 1988, John released the seasonal album ***A Time for Feelings*** with Austrian Country music star Jeff Turner. John then signed a record deal with BMG Ariola Switzerland, on their RCA label, a major achievement for a Swiss-born act. His next album, ***Borderline***, was recorded in Nashville and produced by Randy Scruggs and John.

John's next album, ***Face to Face***, included 14 duets with Country stars such as Bobby Bare, Paul Overstreet, Stella Parton, Moe Bandy and Linda Davis. In 1992, John released ***Light in the Darkness***, a Gospel album, on which he was joined by Jeff Turner. He then had another No.1 in Switzerland entitled *High Moon*.

During 1993, John released ***Wenn Ich Traum***, an album for BMG Ariola Germany and a Swiss-German version of *Rub It In*. At the end of 1993, John undertook a 30-concert Gospel tour. The following year, John and Jeff Turner appeared at the International CSI, where John received a standing ovation. JAB/BM

RECOMMENDED ALBUMS:

(All European releases)
"Feel So Good" (EMI)(1980)
"John Brack" (EMI)(1982)
"Country Special" (EMI)(1984)
"Strong Feelings" (EMI)(1985)
"By Request" (EMI)(1986)
"Hard Times" (EMI)(1987)
"A Time for Feelings" (EMI)(1988) [With Jeff Turner]
"Borderline" (BMG Ariola/RCA)(1989)
"Face to Face" (BMG Ariola/RCA)(1991)

BOBBY BRADDOCK

(Singer, Songwriter, Keyboards)

Date of Birth: August 5, 1940
Where Born: Lakeland, Florida
Married: 1. (div.) 2. Sparky Lawrence
Children: Loren ("Jeep")

When Bobby Braddock was inducted to the Nashville Songwriters Hall of Fame in 1981, he had become one of Country music's most successful songwriters. Possessing a quirky sense of humor, Bobby has written and recorded material that includes such ditties as *Dolly Parton's Hits* and *I Lobster but Never Flounder*.

Bobby grew up in Florida, listening to Country music and R & B. His hero was Ray

Charles and he was a great admirer of John Lee Hooker, Jimmy Reed and Little Richard. During the 60's, he was greatly attracted to the Beatles. In 1964, Bobby, a talented keyboard player, joined Marty Robbins' tour band. Two years later, Marty charted Bobby's first song, *While You're Dancing*, which reached the Top 30 on the Country lists. Bobby settled in Nashville, and signed to Tree International as a staff writer, to replace Roger Miller, who had moved to the West Coast. As well as writing, Bobby played on recording sessions throughout the late 60's and, in 1967, began recording for MGM. It was with his second release, *I Know How to Do It,* that he had his first chart entry as an artist, reaching the Country Top 75.

In 1967, Bobby had a Top 10 hit via the Oak Ridge Boys recording of his *Would They Love Him Down in Shreveport*, and back-to-back Top 10 hits for the Statler Brothers, *Ruthless* and *You Can't Have Your Kate and Edith Too*, both clever plays on words. The following year, Tammy Wynette recorded the Braddock-Curly Putman song *D-I-V-O-R-C-E*, which gave Bobby his first No.1. The "letters" idea had been derived from another earlier song of his, *I L-O-V-E You (Do I Have to Spell It Out)*. The song, in parody form, was recorded in 1975, by Scottish comedian/musician/actor Billy Connelly, and went to the top of the U.K. National chart. Bobby's other big hit in 1968 was *The Ballad of Two Brothers,* recorded by Autry Inman (Top 15).

The pairing of Charlie Louvin and Melba Montgomery had a Top 20 Country hit with Bobby's *Something to Brag About* and also recorded *Did You Ever*, which in 1971 became a No.2 hit in the U.K. for Nancy Sinatra and Lee Hazelwood. George Jones recorded several Braddock songs, including *Nothing Ever Hurts Me (Half As Bad),* (1973, Top 10) and *Her Name Is...* (1976, Top 3).

One of Bobby's biggest hits came in 1975, when Tanya Tucker had a Top 20 hit with *I Believe the South's Gonna Rise Again*, which had been a low-level chart record for Bobby Goldsboro the preceding year. 1976 was a highly successful year for Braddock with major cuts such as *Come on In* (Sonny James, Top 10), *Golden Ring* (George Jones & Tammy Wynette, No.1, written with Rafe VanHoy), *Peanuts and Diamonds* (Bill Anderson, Top 10), *Thinkin' of a Rendezvous* (Johnny Duncan, No.1, written with Sonny Throckmorton). During 1976, Bobby recorded for Mercury without chart success.

Bobby also had a memorable year in 1978 with *Come on In* (Jerry Lee Lewis, Top 10), *Fadin' In, Fadin' Out* (Tommy Overstreet, No.11), *Something to Brag About* (Mary Kay Place with Willie Nelson, Top 10) and *Womanhood* (Tammy Wynette, Top 3). The following year, the Oak Ridge Boys had a Top 3 hit with *Come on In* and Tammy Wynette went Top 10 with *They Call It Making Love*. During 1979, Bobby signed to Elektra Records, where he continued to be produced by the legendary Don Gant, and had the Top 60 single *Between the Lines,* the title track of his 1979 album.

The 80's brought memorable cuts and awards for Bobby. Lacy J. Dalton had a Top 10 hit with *Hard Times* and then George Jones had one of his most memorable No.1 hits with the Braddock-Putman classic *He Stopped Loving Her Today* (which had been recorded by Johnny Russell in 1977). The song renewed Jones' career and was named ACM "Single Record of the Year" and "Song of the Year." It also became CMA's "Song of the Year" in 1980 and 1981 and "Single of the Year" in 1980. George's recording was recognized with a Grammy Award for "Best Country Vocal Performance, Male" in 1980 and the following year, *Music City News* voted the record "Single of the Year." In 1980, Bobby also had a low-level novelty chart record, *Nag, Nag, Nag*, taken from his second Elektra album, ***Love Bomb***. Bobby was inducted to the Nashville Songwriters Hall of Fame in 1981.

T.G. Sheppard recorded several Braddock songs, including *I Feel Like Loving You Again* (1981, No.1, written with Sonny Throckmorton), *Arthur and Alice* (1983) and the duet with Karen Brooks, *Faking Love* (1983, No.1, written with Matraca Berg). During 1983, Tammy Wynette had a low-level success with *Unwed Fathers*, which Bobby had written with John Prine. Gail Davies recorded the song two years later and had a Top 60 single.

Bobby hasn't been quite as successful since the mid-80's, but in 1993, his song *Nashville*, which must have touched many of the would-be's as well as being somewhat autobiographical, appeared on John Anderson's ***Solid Ground*** album.

RECOMMENDED ALBUMS:

"Between the Lines" (Elektra)(1979)

"Love Bomb" (Elektra)(1980)

HAROLD BRADLEY

(Guitar, Bass, Mandolin, Banjo)

Given Name:	**Harold Ray Bradley**
Date of Birth:	**January 2, 1926**
Where Born:	**Nashville, Tennessee**
Married:	**Eleanor Allen**
Children:	**Beverly Allen, Bari Allen**

Harold Bradley is a homegrown Nashvillian. His parents moved there in 1922 and Harold grew up with his brother Owen. When he was 12, Harold met Billy Byrd (then about 18) and played rhythm guitar to Billy's hot electric guitar licks. Harold's early influences were Charlie Christian and Django Reinhardt. However, Harold's first fascination was with the banjo and he only switched on his brother's advice. While still in high school, Harold began playing popular music in a band led by Jack Gregory. He actually became professional when he was 15. During the summer of 1943, he toured for three months with Ernest Tubb and made his debut on the *Grand Ole Opry*. While at high school Harold was adept enough at baseball to be offered a professional baseball contract by the Chicago Cubs.

During and after WWII, Harold spent two years (1944-1946) in the U.S. Navy. At this point, he still preferred a career in baseball, but strained eyesight, from working a code-breaking machine that decoded Japanese military codes, as well as a chipped bone in the arm put an end to that aspiration.

After discharge, Harold enrolled at George Peabody College in Nashville under the G.I. Bill. He was there from 1946 through 1949 as a music major. While there, he played with a dance band and began recording both Pop and Country music. During 1946-1948, he was much in demand and played with Eddy Arnold, Pee Wee King (with whom he had made his first recording session on December 17, 1945) and Bradley Kincaid. His record credits include sessions with Teresa Brewer, Brook Benton, Patti Page, Connie Francis, Brenda Lee and the Everly Brothers. In addition, Harold can be heard on recordings by Burl Ives, Red Foley, Anita Bryant and Ann-Margret.

Harold recorded with Hank Williams in 1946 on his Sterling Records session. He said that he knew Hank's songs would be hits because they came out of a "mean bottle." Harold was a member of the original "A Team" of session musicians. He is one of the most recorded session musicians and has proven his range of playing by appearing on sessions by Elvis Presley (he played on 12 of his million-selling records), Hank Snow and Jim Reeves. During 1950-1962, Harold played on WSM *Sunday Hoedown South*. In 1952, Harold played on Ray Anthony's hits *The Bunny Hop* and *The Hokey Pokey*.

In the early 50's, Harold and Owen started a film studio. It was not a success and they had a lot of recording equipment left over. As a result, they started a recording studio in an old house on Music Row. Later, they turned a surplus army building situated in the yard behind the house into the historic Quonset Hut Studio (it was the second recording studio in Nashville). It was to this studio that Buddy Holly came in 1956, before he found the winning formula with Norman Petty in Clovis, New Mexico. During the late 50's, Harold Bradley co-produced, with his brother Owen, 39 filmed 30-minute variety shows.

During 1962-1966, Harold recorded three albums of light Jazz renditions of popular melodies. These were *The Bossa Nova Goes to Nashville* (1963), *Misty Guitar* (1964) and *Guitar for Lovers Only* (1965). There is also one album on Harmony, *Guitar for Sentimental Lovers*.

In 1983, Harold was still going strong when he played on John Anderson's smash hit *Swingin'* and 1989 found him better than ever when he played on Alan Jackson's *Here in the Real World.*

From 1974 through 1979, Harold received the NARAS "Superpicker Award." *Who's Who in Country Music* listed him on its "Most Valuable Player" polls in 1977, 1978 and 1979. He is one of 12 musicians inducted into the Studio Musicians Hall of Fame at RCA's Studio B. He was Music Director for the PBS fund-raising telethon *Legends of Country Music* in 1985. In December 1990, Harold was elected President of the Nashville Association of Musicians Local 257 of the American Federation of Musicians. His playing can be heard on the movie soundtracks for *The Sugarland Express* (1974), *Smokey & the Bandit II* (1980) and *Sweet Dreams* (1985). He appeared briefly in the movie *Nashville* (1975).

RECOMMENDED ALBUMS:

The Columbia albums listed above make pleasant listening but are not really Country. To hear Harold Bradley, the consummate session player, look at the back of RCA and Decca albums from the 50's through the 70's and then look some more at albums from the 80's and 90's.

OWEN BRADLEY

(Piano, Organ, Trombone, Arranger, Orchestra Leader, Record Producer, Businessman, Industry Executive)

Given Name:	**Williams Owen Bradley**
Date of Birth:	**October 21, 1915**
Where Born:	**Westmoreland, Tennessee**
Married:	**Mary Katherine Franklin (m. 1935)**
Children:	**Patsy Ann, Jerry Owen**

When James Robertson arrived in Fort Nashborough in 1779 full of the pioneering spirit, there was no way that he would know that another pioneering spirit would help turn this settlement into the Country music capital of the world. Owen Bradley was that man.

Owen was born on a farm 4 miles from Westmoreland, Tennessee. At age 7, he moved to Nashville with his parents. He began his career when he was 15 years old, playing piano wherever he could, including road houses and lodge halls and later area clubs and gambling houses.

He started working at WSM radio in 1935 as a "spot man." This was a part-time job which allowed him to get his foot in the door doing whatever was needed. By 1940, this developed into a full-time job known as a "utility man." Owen's various activities included acting as an arranger, pianist, organist and trombonist. By 1947, he was made Musical Director, a position he held until 1958. Popular radio shows on which he participated included *Noontime Neighbors* and *Sunday Down South*.

During the 30's, Owen began putting together various musical groups to play private parties around town. Because the demand was so high, he decided in 1940 to put together a big band, which was known as the Owen Bradley Orchestra. This orchestra was considered the premier Nashville dance band for country club parties and other local high society events until it disbanded in 1964.

In 1947, Owen started working with Paul Cohen, the head of the Country Division of Decca Records, who worked out of New York. Owen served as an apprentice to Cohen, learning to produce records for him and eventually producing them for himself, when Cohen was unable to come to town.

In 1958, Owen left WSM to open the Nashville Division of Decca Records, where he served as Vice President. When Decca and MCA merged their companies in the mid-60's, Owen continued in his position. He retired from MCA in 1976, but during his tenure he produced, among others, Loretta Lynn, Conway Twitty, Jack Greene, Kitty Wells, Patsy Cline, Ernest Tubb, Brenda Lee, Red Foley, Bill Anderson and Webb Pierce.

In 1951, Owen and his brother, Harold, opened their first film studio on the third floor of a lodge hall at 2nd and Lindsley. Because they lost their lease, they moved their Bradley's Film Studio to a rented building in Hillsboro Village the following year. They stayed there until they opened the Quonset Hut.

In 1954, Owen and Harold purchased an old house on 16th Avenue South. A Quonset hut was attached to the house and it was opened as a recording studio in 1955. In 1957, when RCA built a studio a block away, this area became known as the now famous Music Row. Harold and Owen sold the Quonset Hut to Columbia Records in 1962, when it became known as Columbia "B" until it was closed in 1982.

In 1961, Owen purchased a farm 20 miles east of Nashville and converted an old barn into a demo studio for his son to learn a little bit about making records. Eventually, it was upgraded to a first-class facility and became known as Bradley's Barn. It burned to the ground in 1980 but a couple of years later, a

The superstar producers; left-to-right: ***Bob Beckham, Billy Sherrill, Owen Bradley, Buddy Killen*** *and* ***Larry Butler***

new structure was built in the same spot and still operates as a studio today. Owen's assistant was Harry Silverstein, who used to produce all the Bluegrass records for Decca. He tragically died in 1970 after a simple operation which resulted in him getting a blood clot.

Owen Bradley was elected to the Country Music Hall of Fame in 1971. From 1976 to the present, Owen has worked as an independent producer with such artists as Eddy Arnold, Jimmie Davis, Burl Ives, Pete Fountain and k.d. lang. He was also the Music Director for the major movies *Coal Miner's Daughter* and *Sweet Dreams*. Owen once told his son, Jerry Bradley, "Don't worry about having all the hits, just have your share."

TERRY BRADSHAW

(Singer, Songwriter)

Given Name:	**Terry Paxton Bradshaw**
Date of Birth:	**1949**
Where Born:	**Shreveport, Louisiana**
Married:	**1. Melissa Babish (div.)** **2. Jo Jo Starbuck (m. 1976)(div.)** **3. Charla Hopkins (m. 1986)(div.)**

It wasn't Mike Reid who was the first ex-jock to make it in Country music. After graduating from Louisiana Tech,Terry Bradshaw was the #1 draft pick by the Pittsburgh Steelers, where he played quarterback. He led the team to four Superbowl victories in 1974, 1975, 1978 and 1979.

While playing ball, Terry was quite successful as a Country singer. He made his professional debut on the *Old South Jamboree*, Walker, Louisiana, on February 7, 1976. That year, he signed to Mercury Records and his first success was Hank Williams' *I'm So Lonesome I Could Cry*, which reached the Top 20 on the Country chart and crossed over into the Top 100 on the Pop chart. However, he was unable to capitalize on this and the follow-up, *The Last Word in Lonesome Is Me,* only reached the 90 mark.

In 1978, Terry embarked on another career as a movie actor. He appeared in three Burt Reynolds movies, *Hooper* (1978), *The Cannonball Run* and *Smokey and the Bandit 2* (both in 1980). Terry had switched to Gospel material and signed with the Benson label by 1980 and he made the Top 75 with the title track from the album ***Until You***. He continued with Gospel material with the album ***Here in My Heart*** on Heartwarming in 1981. He then retired from recording in 1984.

Of some note are Terry's wives. Melissa Babish was a former Miss Teenage America, Jo Jo Starbuck was an Olympic ice skating champion and star of *Ice Capades* and Charla Hopkins was a law student.

RECOMMENDED ALBUMS:

"I'm So Lonesome I Could Cry" (Mercury)(1976)
"Until You" (Benson)(1981)
"Here in My Heart" (Heartwarming)(1981)

L.L.Brasfield refer UNCLE CYP & AUNT SAP

Neva Inez Brasfield refer UNCLE CYP & AUNTSAP

ROD BRASFIELD

(Comedian)

Given Name:	**Rodney Leon Brasfield**
Date of Birth:	**August 22, 1910**
Where Born:	**Smithville, Mississippi**
Married:	**1. Eliner Humphreys (div.)** **2. Cindy Rushing**
Children:	**James (adopted)**
Date of Death:	**September 12, 1958**

Born on a farm near Smithville in the northeast Mississippi hill country, Rodney found himself attracted to the theater, inspired by a much older brother, Lawrence L. "Boob" Brasfield (d. 1966) and his wife, Neva, who had traveled with various tent show dramas from the early years of the century. The younger Brasfield joined the tent show circuit about 1926, playing small parts and running errands for the other actors. Minnie Pearl recalls that he worked his way up to leading man status and that Boob was initially more the comedian while Neva specialized in playing upper-crust ladies. About 1937, Rod switched to comedy roles. More often than not, he worked with the Bisbee Comedians, a tent show repertory group owned by J.C. Bisbee, a former magician. According to Minnie, they would typically set up shows for a week in a southern town, presenting a different play nightly.

WWII apparently put an end to the Bisbee operation about 1942, and in 1944 Rod came to the *Opry*. He quickly became a favorite on the network segment. Many of his monologues concerned fictional characters who resided in Hohenwald, especially his Uncle Cyp, Aunt Sap and Rod's "gal" Susie. In his *Opry* character, Brasfield, from time to time, also displayed something of a romantic interest in Cousin Minnie Pearl. Rod spent the rest of his life sharing honors with Minnie and the Duke of Paducah as the show's premier comedians.

Although a considerable volume of Brasfield's comedy is preserved on radio transcriptions, he recorded only occasionally. A 1957 single on Hickory of a monologue titled *Rod's Trip to Chicago* was his only commercial release. He also appeared in many of the syndicated TV programs by Gannaway Productions and in a few motion pictures, including *A Face in the Crowd* (1957) and *Country Music Holiday* (1957). When he died from a heart attack in September 1958, his remains were returned to Smithville for burial. By that time, his brother Boob and sister-in-law Neva had brought Rod's Uncle Cyp and Aunt Sap characters to life in a weekly skit seen regularly on network TV's *Ozark Jubilee*.

IMT

Brazos Valley Boys refer HANK THOMPSON

THOM BRESH

(Singer, Actor, Songwriter, Guitar, Clarinet, Trumpet, Saxophone, Tuba, Trombone, Banjo, Bass, Steel Guitar)

Given Name:	**Thomas Charles Bresh**
Date of Birth:	**February 23, 1948**
Where Born:	**Hollywood, California**
Married:	**1. Merrilee** **2. Jennifer**
Children:	**David, Cathy**

Thom Bresh may qualify as being one of Country music's most versatile performers. He was only 3 years old when he sang *Your Cheatin' Heart* in a musical show at the Carriganville Movie Ranch near Barstow, California. By the age of 7, he had appeared in his first movie. He had already started playing steel guitar and now learned to play guitar. He was helped in his efforts by his father, Merle Travis, as well as Tex Williams.

He majored in music and orchestra theory, and at age 15 he replaced Roy Clark in Hank Penny's Band. When Hank retired, Thom became the headliner. Always one to keep himself busy, Thom spent his teenage years either trying to kill himself or playing music. The killing-himself bit came about when he became an actor/stuntman, billed as

The multi-talented ***Thom Bresh***

"Hollywood's Youngest Stuntman," and did this for 10 years.

He worked in a Rock band, the Crescents. They recorded, but it was at a time when the British invasion was under way. In 1970, Thom formed a road band but after several months of touring returned to Los Angeles. He appeared on stage in *Finian's Rainbow, Harvey* and *The Music Man*. He later went to Seattle, where he ran a recording studio owned by Merilee Rush. In addition, he has run a restaurant and a photographic studio. He was also co-host of TV's *Nashville Swings,* which came from Canada. Thom is a consummate impressionist and his victims include Charley Pride and Howard Cosell.

In 1972, Thom cut the one-off single *D.B. Cooper, Where Are You* for Kapp. In 1975, Thom was with MGM, where he released *You're the Best Daddy in the World* and *Soda Pop & Gumball Days*. The following year found him on the Farr label, where Thom recorded *Home Made Love*, the single and the album of the same name. The single climbed into the Country chart Top 10. *Sad Country Love Song* (1976) was a Top 20 hit and *Hey Daisy (Where Have All the Goodtimes Gone)* (1977) made the Top 40. In all these cases, he was billed as "Tom Bresh." In 1976, he was voted "Top New Male Vocalist, Singles," in *Cash Box*.

In 1977 and 1978, Thom Bresh settled down with ABC/Dot Records. *Until I Met You* was a song written by Thom as was his 1978 release *First Encounter of a Close Kind*. His other releases at ABC were *That Old Cold Shoulder* (1977), *Smoke Smoke Smoke (That Cigarette)* (1978), which was more than a salute to his old mentor Tex Williams, and *Ways of a Woman in Love*. He cut two albums for the label, ***Kicked Back*** in 1977 and ***Portrait*** a year later. However, none of his singles were any more than minor hits.

In 1982, Thom signed to Liberty Records and had a fine duet with Lane Brody, *When It Comes to Love,* which again was only a lower level entry; and alas no follow-up appeared to *I'd Love You to Want Me.*

He continues to appear on stage with Lane Brody and after appearing on Lee Greenwood's USO Tour Special for TNN, in which they were so successful, they were given their own USO TV Special.

Looking at Thom Bresh's career is somewhat frustrating. He has so much talent and so much ability, but like so many entertainers, Thom has not been able to come up with consistent chart records and thereby launch himself into Country music superstardom.

RECOMMENDED ALBUMS:
"Kicked Back" (ABC/Dot)(1977)
"Portrait" (ABC/Dot)(1978)
For Thom Bresh at his best try watching re-runs of Nashville Swings

BRIARHOPPERS, The (a.k.a. WBT BRIARHOPPERS)

Formed: 1935

Members:

Roy "Whitey" Grant	**Guitar**
Arval Hogan	**Mandolin**
Shannon Grayson	**Banjo, Mandolin**
Garnet B. Warren	**Fiddle, Saw, Mandolin**
Walden Whytsell (Don White)	**Bass, Steel Guitar**

Other members: "Big Bill" Davis (dec'd), Homer Lee Drye (dec'd), Homer Christopher (dec'd), Sam Poplin, David Deese, Cecil Campbell (dec'd), Claude Casey, Fred Kirby and Arthur Smith

From 1935 until 1951, the WBT Briarhoppers reigned as a top Country music radio unit in Charlotte, North Carolina. Their daily programs, usually sponsored by Consolidated Drug Trade Products of Chicago (makers of Peruna Cough Medicine and Tonic), attracted a wide audience for many years. Numerous musicians worked with the Briarhoppers over the years and during their peak period in the 40's, two bands kept working on the road, filling the demand for their personal appearances.

Charlie Crutchfield, a WBT announcer, assembled the original Briarhopper band with John McAllister, Clarence Etters, Jane Bartlett, Billie Burton, Thorpe Westerfield, Homer Drye and Bill Davis as the original members. Only the youthful Drye and bass player Davis remained for any significant time. Drye had sessions on both Bluebird and Decca as a solo artist and continued to use the name Homer Briarhopper for several years after he left the group.

Much more important figures included Don White, a western-style singer who worked in the group from 1935 to 1939 and Hank Warren (b. April 1, 1909, Mount Airy, North Carolina), a fine fiddler-comedian who had prior experience with the Tennessee Ramblers and the Swingbillies, who came in 1937 and has remained for the duration. The guitar-mandolin duetting of Whitey (b. April 7, 1916, Shelby, North Carolina) and Hogan (b. April 7, 1916, Shelby, North Carolina) came in 1941 after doing radio work in Gastonia and a 16-side record session for Decca in November 1939.

In 1941, Shannon Grayson (b. September 30, 1916, Sunshine, North Carolina/d. May 10, 1993), a veteran of six years as a sideman for the Carlisle Brothers, joined the group. At various times Cecil Campbell, Claude Casey, Homer Christopher, Fred Kirby, Sam Poplin and Arthur "Guitar Boogie" Smith also worked with the Briarhoppers in their radio days, as did Don White (b. September 25, 1909, Wolf Creek, West Virginia), who came back from Chicago for a while in the early 40's before returning to the Windy City. At the end of the 40's, Grayson formed his own band, the Golden Valley Boys, and had recording sessions for both RCA Victor and King.

During the 40's, the Briarhoppers tended to record as individuals rather than as a unit.

From WBT Charlotte, North Carolina, the ***Briarhoppers***

Fred Kirby cut several sides for Sonora at the end of the war, with other Briarhoppers supporting him, as they also did for Whitey and Hogan. The latter also had two sessions for DeLuxe and made one single on the Cowboy label with Grayson providing a Bluegrass banjo on one side containing their arrangement of *Jesse James*. Their best numbers on DeLuxe were covers of Molly O'Day's *Tramp on the Street* and an answer to Fred Kirby's popular hit, *There's a Power Greater Than Atomic*. On Sonora, they scored with the sentimental *Talking to Mother* and the comic *Mama, I'm Sick*.

After 1953, the Briarhoppers went into other lines of work and seldom played as a musical unit. Whitey and Hogan both became mailmen in Charlotte, while Grayson plied his trade as a cabinet maker. Warren remained with WBT and WBTV as a photographer, while White worked in private business. With traditional music and Bluegrass enjoying a modest comeback in the early 70's, Whitey, Hogan, Grayson, Warren and White regrouped and began entertaining again.

In 1977, Old Homestead released an album taken from old home recordings, transcriptions and three of Whitey and Hogan's duets from 1939. That December, John Morris of that label went to Charlotte and obtained sufficient new material for two more albums in 1981 and 1984. The Briarhoppers also cut material for the Charlotte-based Lamon Records, including two albums and a third released on cassette only.

Meanwhile, the band played numerous Bluegrass festivals, entertained school children through an arts and humanities program and played for enormous crowds at the annual Bob Evans Farm Festival held in Rio Grande, Ohio, each October. On another occasion, they journeyed to Minnesota for an appearance on National Public Radio's *Prairie Home Companion* program with Garrison Keillor. Whitey and Hogan toured the Netherlands and the entire group received prominent billing at the 1985 reunion concert of old-time Charlotte radio performers. In 1992, the retirement of Grayson, who had contracted Alzheimer's disease (subsequently passing away the following May), suggested that the Briarhoppers might not go on forever.

For the moment, however, they continued on with David Deese, former banjo picker for both Red Smiley and the Jones Brothers, as his replacement. At other times, Homer Sherrill, a veteran of the Hired Hands, has filled in for an ailing Hank Warren IMT

RECOMMENDED ALBUMS:

"Early Radio" (Old Homestead)(1977)
"Whitey and Hogan (with the Briarhoppers) Volume I" (Old Homestead)(1981)
"Whitey and Hogan (with the Briarhoppers) Volume II" (Old Homestead)(1984)
"Hit's Briarhopper Time" (Lamon)(1980)
"Hit's Briarhopper Time Again" (Lamon)(1983)
"Hit's Briarhopper Hymn Time" (Lamon)(1988)

BRISTOL SESSIONS

In Country music history, the term "Bristol Sessions" refers to two field recording sessions held in the small city of Bristol, on the Tennessee-Virginia line, in 1927 and 1928. Supervised by legendary Victor A & R man Ralph Peer, the sessions were among the first and most successful attempts by major record companies to record on location. Johnny Cash, who later married into one of the groups to record there (the Carter Family), asserted that "these recordings . . . are the single most important event in the history of Country music." Later historians have tended to agree that the sessions were surely the most dramatic and influential of all the early field sessions. They produced, among other things, the debut recordings of Jimmie Rodgers and the Carter Family, as well as influential recordings of other major figures in Old-Time music.

The genesis of the Bristol trip was a series of early attempts on Peer's part to find fresh talent for what was emerging as a Country music market. In 1925, Peer had left the OKeh company (where he had discovered and recorded Fiddlin' John Carson) and joined the Victor Talking Machine Company. He recalled later, "They wanted to get into the hillbilly business and I knew how to do it." Peer would travel through the South, looking for "hillbilly," Gospel, and Blues singers; if he recorded them, his company would take the song publishing rights. Networking through Victor dealers, Peer set up temporary studios in Atlanta and Memphis, and in early 1927 set up more in Savannah, Charlotte, and Bristol. Flanked by Kingsport to the immediate west and Johnson City to the South, Bristol formed part of an early urban conglomerate known locally as Tri-Cities; in 1927, it had a collective population of 32,000, making it the largest population center in Appalachia. It was also accessible from the mountains of Virginia, North Carolina, and Kentucky, places where, Peer was convinced, true "mountaineer melodies" were preserved.

On July 21, 1927, Peer, accompanied by his wife Anita and two engineers named Eckhart and Lynch, along with a carload of portable recording equipment recently developed by Western Electric, drove into Bristol. He leased a former furniture store at 408 State Street (the street that was the state line). On the second and third floors the team hung blankets on the wall to deaden the echo, and built a tower for the pulleys that would drive the recording turntable. Though Peer had actually lined up a number of acts in advance, he was also interested in attracting new talent, and to this end he invited a local newspaper editor to attend a session during the first week. The result was a major news story on the front page of the local paper, and a huge amount of free publicity. "This worked like dynamite," recalled Peer. "The next day I was deluged with long-distance calls from the surrounding mountain region." Peer had to schedule night sessions to accommodate all the different acts that appeared.

The first major group to record—the group Peer had actually come to Bristol to record—was the Stoneman Family from Galax, Virginia, a large string band headed by Ernest "Pop" Stoneman. Stoneman was already an experienced recording star, and was getting $100 a day for his services from Victor. Other veteran acts included the Johnson Brothers, duet singers who had worked in vaudeville and would later record again for Victor. A number of Gospel singers appeared, including Alfred Karnes, from Kentucky, who played the harp-guitar and sang definitive versions of *When They Ring Those Golden Bells*; Ernest Phipps and his group, other Kentuckians from a Holiness church who did vibrant, uptempo versions of *Do Lord, Remember Me*; and the Alcoa Quartet, from Tennessee, who sang lovely unaccompanied quartet music.

There were also several mountain string bands, such as the Shelor Family (from Virginia), the West Virginia Coon Hunters and the Tenneva Ramblers, the band that had actually come to the audition with their lead singer, Jimmie Rodgers. Benjamin Frank Shelton, a barber from Kentucky, recorded four powerful ballads with his banjo, including *Old Molly Dear* and *Pretty Polly,* that would become classics of mountain Folk music. Blind Alfred Reed, harmonica player El Watson, banjoist J.P. Nestor, and singers Mr. and Mrs. J.W. Baker rounded out the cast. During the last week of the stay, Peer auditioned a singing trio called the Carter Family (on August 1 and 2) and a young yodeler named Jimmie Rodgers (on August 4). He took six songs by the Carters and only two by Rodgers.

By the end of the two weeks, Peer shipped some 76 masters back to New York for processing. In their diversity, they represented an almost perfect cross section of early Country music. While some of the groups slipped back into the mountains never to record again, others would become stars of the early record medium. On October 7, 1927, the Bristol newspapers announced the release of Victor's "New Southern Series" of sides done locally. Peer continued to travel the South, returning the following year (1928) for an even longer session in Bristol—a session that called back some of the 1927 musicians and discovered even more new ones. Rival companies, sensing that Bristol was Victor's turf, tried their own field sessions in Johnson City (Columbia, 1928 and 1929) and Knoxville (Brunswick, Vocalion, 1929 and 1930). While they found no one to rival the Carters or Rodgers, they too produced amazing and rich results, testifying to the wealth of talent that was in the region during the formative years of Country music. CKW

RECOMMENDED ALBUMS:

"The Bristol Sessions: Historic Recordings from Bristol Tennessee" (Country Music Foundation) [Leased through RCA]

ELTON BRITT

(Singer, Songwriter, Guitar, Yodeler, Actor)
Given Name: James Britt Baker
Date of Birth: June 27, 1913
Where Born: Marshall, Arkansas
Date of Death: June 23, 1972

In the wake of Jimmie Rodgers and his "blue yodel," dozens of singers in the 1930's came forth with hopes and aspirations to Rodgers' title. One of the few who could really rival Rodgers in yodeling ability was a young Arkansas singer named Elton Britt. Throughout the 1930's and 1940's, his name was as well-known nationally as that of any Country singer and though he later became stereotyped as a slick, "drugstore cowboy" type of singer, Elton Britt was an important link between the older cowboy music and the newer West Coast styles that featured trick vocalizing and dynamic display music. Fans who saw Britt's live shows remember his high, keening falsetto, his breathtaking triple yodels and his ability to hold a note for five choruses of a song.

Britt's boyhood in Arkansas was pretty standard, and by the time he was a teenager, he had his Sears-Roebuck guitar and was absorbing local songs and radio shows. Then, in the summer of 1930, his career suddenly took a quantum leap. The Beverly Hill Billies, an early West Coast band from Los Angeles, found themselves needing to replace one of their singers, Hubert Walton. They flew to Walton's home state of Arkansas and began a talent search. It soon led them to 17-year-old James Baker and within a few days, they had

*The sky-high yodeler, **Elton Britt***

hired him and all were back on the plane to California. By the time they landed, James Baker had become "Elton Britt," and he was able to treat the crowd waiting at the airport to a good version of Rodgers' song *The Drunkard's Child*, singing from the wing of the airplane.

For a time, it looked like Britt was settling in for a career in Southern California's fledgling music scene. He worked for three years with the Beverly Hill Billies and got to know other singers like Stuart Hamblen and Patsy Montana, as well as film stars Tom Mix and Will Rogers. In 1933, he decided to move east and went to New York to join an act called Pappy, Zeke, Ezra and Elton. The next few years saw a rather intense round of commercial recording—some with the Wenatchee Mountaineers, some with Zeke Manners' Gang, some with the Rustic Rhythm Trio and some under his own name. A major hit came in 1939, when he switched to RCA's Bluebird label and recorded *Chime Bells*, a yodeling tour de force. He also began a long association with Memphis songwriter turned producer Bob Miller.

Miller had moved to New York in the 1920's to work for Columbia Records and had become the reigning purveyor of topical event songs like *Eleven Cent Cotton and Forty Cent Meat*. He was also a gifted writer of sentimental songs and soon adapted these skills to Britt's style. During WWII, Miller wrote favorites like *Rocky Mountain Lullaby*, *Buddy Boy* and *Driftwood on the River*. His biggest gift to Britt, though, was *There's a Star Spangled Banner Waving Somewhere* (1942), the most popular Country song to come out of the war and the first Country single to be Certified as a Gold Record. It was originally to be the flipside and eventually sold over 4 million copies. At the time, Britt was billed as "the Highest Yodeler in the World." In 1942, at President Roosevelt's request, Britt appeared at the White House singing this song.

Continuing to work from his base in New York, Britt soon had a national venue for his radio work, as well as major national sponsors. For a short time, he moved to the *Hayloft Hoedown* out of Boston, but soon returned to New York. In the late 1940's, he initiated a series of duets with Alabama singer Rosalie Allen, including *Quicksilver* and *The Yodel Blues*. In 1948, Britt appeared in the Western *Laramie* and followed up with *The Last Doggie* and *The Prodigal Son*. In 1951, Britt received the "Award of Esteem" from the Department of Defense.

His record work survived well into the lp era, with new albums on labels like RCA Victor and ABC-Paramount. His last serious effort was a 1968 single for RCA Victor, *The Jimmie Rodgers Blues*, a rambling cant fable about Rodgers' songs and life. Britt announced his retirement numerous times, once to run in the New Hampshire presidential primary in 1960.

Britt died at a farm in central Pennsylvania and was laid to rest at Broad Top City in that state. Unlike many singers from his era, he has not fared well with the re-issue and revival circuit; considered too sophisticated for the young fans of the Folk revival and a shade too Pop for hard Country fans, Britt's distinctive art has been undervalued and underappreciated in recent years. CKW

RECOMMENDED ALBUMS:

"Yodel Songs" (RCA Victor)(1956) [Re-issued by Stetson UK in the original sleeve (1988)]
"The Best of Elton Britt" (RCA Victor)(1963)
"The Singing Hills" (ABC-Paramount)(1965)
"The Jimmie Rodgers Blues" (Camden)(1969)
"The Best of Elton Britt, Volume 2" (RCA Victor)(1973)

LANE BRODY

(Singer, Songwriter, Guitar, Actress)
Given Name: Lynn Connie Voorlas
Date of Birth: September 24
Where Born: Oak Park, Illinois

Lane Brody is a talented and beautiful lady who made her impression on Country music in the 80's and is still a potential major act. Her musical influences are very indicative of her broadness of style. They include Elvis, Paul McCartney, Billie Holiday, Judy Garland, Aretha Franklin, Dusty Springfield, Patsy Cline, Barbra Streisand, Johnny Mathis, Linda Ronstadt and Dolly Parton.

Lane was raised in Racine, Wisconsin, and by the age of 5 had shown her love of singing. By the time she was 12, she had written her first song, *Through the Darkness*. She worked in her parents' restaurant from age 10 to 17. At 14, she was scouted by the U.S. Olympics for her ability on the balance beam, but she turned them down because she wanted to be a singer. While still in school, she formed a three-girl group. When she was 18, Lane decided to move to New York. While there, she sang in a Country group and also a multi-style group. There, she was discovered by Bobby Whiteside.

She then moved to Chicago and began a highly successful career singing jingles. She also appeared in many commercials and in print ads and packaging covers for a host of companies including Honda and Harley-Davidson. Between 1974 and 1976, she studied under Helen Espee, the Chicago voice and diction coach and from 1975 to 1978 at the Ted Liss School of Acting. In 1976, Lane started training under Mary Strong, a Milwaukee-based acting coach. Lane made her first single for GRT in 1976 under the name of Lynn Nilles, *You're Gonna Make Love to Me,* which created some interest.

In 1978, she moved to California and won $100 at the Palomino on talent night. She was offered a spot singing with the Palomino house band, the Palomino Riders.

1981 was the pivotal year for Lane. She signed to Liberty Records and had her first chart success in April 1982. *He's Taken,* produced by Mick Lloyd and written by Lane, reached the Top 60 and shortly after, *More Nights* also charted around the same level. She ended the year with a low-level duet with Thom Bresh. In 1981, she guested in the ABC-TV series *Taxi* playing Jennine and started working with one of L.A.'s top acting coaches, Jeff Corey.

Her co-written song *Over You* was specially recorded for the movie *Tender Mercies,* for which its star, Robert Duvall, received an Oscar. The song was Oscar-nominated, made the Top 15 and was on the charts in 1983 for

The super-talented ***Lane Brody***

some 5 months. Lane was nominated for ACM's "Top New Female Artist." Chips Moman became her producer, but *It's Another Silent Night* only made the Top 60. Lane came back like a racehorse in February 1984 with her next single, *The Yellow Rose* (from the NBC-TV series), which paired Lane with Johnnie Lee and was Lane and John Weilder's re-writing of the old Civil War song. With Jimmy Bowen at the production helm, this hit the No.1 slot, staying on the charts for over 5 months and earning her an initial BMI "Most Performed Song of the Year" award.

Lane's debut eponymous album produced by Harold Shedd was released in 1985 on EMI America (Liberty's name change) and spawned two chart singles, the most successful being Bobby Lee Springfield's *He Burns Me Up.* The following year, she was reunited with Johnny Lee for the Warner Brothers release *I Could Get Used to This,* which was a Top 50 success. She continued her acting with a guest appearance as Jenny Jamison, a Country singer in ABC-TV's *Heart of the City,* in which she sang three songs, including her composition *Everything but True.*

In addition to her on-screen appearances, Lane was the singing voice behind Linda Hamilton's lips in the 1982 CBS-TV Movie of the Week *Country Gold.* In another 1982 Movie of the Week, *The Gift of Life,* starring Susan Dey, Lane sang *Just a Little More Love,* which received an Emmy nomination. In 1989, Lane began dramatic studies with L.A.-based Suze Lanier.

Lane is a lady with a deep social conscience and a charitable inclination, toward both her fellow humans and four-legged friends. She is a member of many respected animal organizations. Her *All the Unsung Heroes* was performed by her as the title song of a 40-minute video documentary on the Vietnam Veterans Wall and is also played in the Smithsonian Institution and Arlington National Cemetery. The song is also part of the soundtrack cd that includes President Bush, the Oak Ridge Boys, Eddie Rabbitt, Ricky Van Shelton and Thom Bresh.

For her endeavors she has received numerous special awards including the "Special Public Service Announcement Award" in 1988 and the "Special Broadcast Award" in 1990 and 1991 from the U.S. Department of the Interior. She is a Commissioned Kentucky Colonel, Honorary Colonel in the Oklahoma National Guard, Honorary Member of the Tennessee House of Representatives, Honorary Member of the Tennessee Lieutenant Governor's Staff and an Honorary Member of the Fraternal Order of Police.

Nowadays, Lane tours mainly with the multi-talented Thom Bresh and after appearing on Lee Greenwood's USO Tour Special for TNN, in which they were so successful, they were given their own USO TV Special. For the trivia buff, Lane Brody's favorite food is bread.

RECOMMENDED ALBUMS:

"Lane Brody" (EMI America)(1985) [Lane is in good voice but the record suffers from bad mixing]

"Tender Mercies" (Liberty)(1982) [This soundtrack album contains Lane's Oscar-nominated "Over You," which was produced by her and Thom Bresh]

Kix Brooks refer BROOKS & DUNN

BROOKS & DUNN

KIX BROOKS
(Singer, Songwriter, Guitar, Piano)

Given Name:	**Leon Eric Brooks III**
Date of Birth:	**May 12, 1955**
Where Born:	**Shreveport, Louisiana**
Married:	**Barbara**
Children:	**Molly, Eric**

RONNIE DUNN
(Singer, Songwriter, Guitar)

Given Name:	**Ronnie Gene Dunn**
Date of Birth:	**June 1, 1953**
Where Born:	**Coleman, Texas**
Married:	**1. (Div.)**
	2. Janine
Children:	**Whitney, Jesse, Haley Marie**

If there are such things as marriages made in heaven, perhaps partnerships are made there, too. In the case of Brooks & Dunn, it would seem that for the first time in ages, Country music is experiencing a duo that is truly "together." They are both over six feet tall, both have fathers who come from a pipeline background, and it seems amazing that they only teamed up in 1990.

Kix Brooks grew up in Shreveport, Louisiana, and enjoyed all the variety of music indigenous to the region: Cajun, Blues, Jazz and Country. His first musical instrument was a ukulele obtained when he was 6. He lived on the same street as Johnny Horton's widow (she had also been married to Hank Williams), and seeing all the Gold records on the wall was an inspiration to the young lad. His first gig was with Johnny's daughter when he was 12. He attended boarding school and by the time his college days came around, Kix was already an established performer and worked on the Louisiana club circuit. Kix once performed for 72 nights in a row on Bourbon Street in New Orleans. At this time, he had already become serious about songwriting. Kix took a year off from college to work on the Alaska pipeline and played in Fairbanks. Later,

*Kix Brooks and Ronnie Dunn, the dynamic **Brooks & Dunn***

he played the ski resorts in Maine, the state where his sister had an advertising agency.

During a trip to Nashville, Kix met an old boarding school roommate who worked for Charlie Daniels' publishing company. Kix then decided to move to Nashville, too. He had a tough time trying to get established while doing odd jobs. Fortune was on his side when he signed a publishing contract to the new music publishing company owned by Don Gant. Formally head of ABC Records, Don helped Kix to establish himself as a songwriter and he soon had cuts by John Conlee, *I'm Only in It for the Love* (No.1, 1983), Nitty Gritty Dirt Band, *Modern Day Romance* (No.1, 1985) and Highway 101, *Who's Lonely Now* (No.1, 1990), among others. The Nashville official theme song was co-written by Kix and Chris Waters and Kix co-wrote with Pam Tillis the official Tennessee Earth Day Song. Kix signed to Avion in 1983 and charted Top 75 with *Baby, When Your Heart Breaks Down*. He recorded an album, ***Kix Brooks,*** for Capitol in 1989 and the same year had a Top 90 chart entry with *Sacred Ground*. Kix had been in Nashville for 10 years.

Ronnie Dunn is a native of Coleman, Texas. His dad played guitar and sang in a hillbilly band in his spare time. Ronnie started to play bass in high school in Port Isabel. Later, while he was studying psychiatry and theology at Abilene Christian College, Texas, with the intention of becoming a Baptist minister, Ronnie went out to play in honky-tonks, got caught and was given a choice: to stop playing there or quit college. He quit. Moving with his parents to Tulsa, Oklahoma, at the time the "Urban Cowboy" craze erupted, Ronnie obtained a job heading the house band at a huge club called Duke's Country and opened for every act that played there. A brief time was spent on Jim Halsey's Churchill label, where he had two Top 60 chart entries, *It's Written All Over Your Face* (1983) and *She Put the Sad in All Her Songs* (1984).

Ronnie's musical direction changed when a friend, Jimmy Oldecker (Eric Clapton's drummer), filled in an entry form in a grocery store and entered Ronnie for a Marlboro talent contest. They sent in a tape and Ronnie was chosen to be in the regional finals in Tulsa. Quickly putting a band together and rehearsing three songs, he won the regional finals. The overall finals were in Nashville in the Bullpen Lounge and Ronnie once again won. First prize was $30,000 and a $25,000 recording session that was engineered by Scott Hendricks (now one of Nashville's top record producers), with whom he kept in touch. Ronnie sent him his latest tunes on tape and, in turn, Scott played the tunes to Arista Nashville head Tim DuBois.

Ronnie moved to Music City, signed with Tree Publishing and began to do some songwriting with Kix. They teamed up not only to write but also to perform. Tim DuBois was impressed with their collaboration and a label deal with Arista ensued. Tim DuBois advised them to "Keep your boots on, keep your jeans on and keep it Country," a formula they adhered to. Brooks & Dunn's first single, *Brand New Man*, became a No.1 hit within 2 months of release. The second single, *My Next Broken Heart*, also hit the top spot. Their debut album, ***Brand New Man,*** was released in August 1991, and by the end of 1992 was Certified Double-Platinum and went on to Triple-Platinum status in 1993. Extensive touring, opening for such acts as Reba McEntire and Alabama, recording, songwriting, and TV appearances kept the duo very busy.

They made an appearance at the Opry House in February 1992 with Alan Jackson. Their third single, *Neon Moon,* was released in 1992 and gave them three-in-a-row No.1 hits, and then the flip-side of *Neon Moon* gave the duo their biggest hit. Ronnie Dunn's song *Boot Scootin' Boogie* stayed at No.1 for 4 weeks, crossed to the Pop Top 50 and launched a dance of the same name. The duo closed the year with the Top 10 hit *Lost and Found.*

Brooks and Dunn were named CMA "Vocal Duo of the Year" in 1992 and 1993. In February 1993 they started to do their first shows as headliners. Their album ***Hard Workin' Man*** was released in 1993 and by year-end had reached sales of over 2 million. The title track reached the Top 5 and was followed in 1993 by *We'll Burn That Bridge* (Top 3) and the No.1 *She Used to Be Mine*.

In 1994, Brooks & Dunn scored with *Rock My World (Little Country Girl)*, which made the Top 3. Radio deejays flirted with *Ride 'Em High, Ride 'Em Low*, but soon lost interest and it only reached the Top 75. However, the official next single, *That Ain't No Way to Go*, again gave Brooks & Dunn another No.1.

In 1994, Brooks & Dunn were again named the CMA's "Duo of the Year." JAB

RECOMMENDED ALBUMS:

"Brand New Man" (Arista)(1991)

"Hard Workin' Man" (Arista)(1993)

GARTH BROOKS

(Singer, Songwriter, Guitar, Actor)

Given Name:	**Troyal Garth Brooks**
Date of Birth:	**February 7, 1963**
Where Born:	**Luba, Oklahoma**
Married:	**Sandy Mahl (m. 1986)**
Children:	**Taylor Mayne Pearl, August Anna**

That Garth Brooks is the phenomenon of Country music, there is no doubt. In a form of music that had considered album sales of 20,000 for most acts as the norm, Garth has astounded the music business with album sales in the multi-millions. He has achieved album cross-over success far beyond that achieved by any other Country artist. At the same time, he has endeared himself with the Country music establishment, fans and the media. In addition, in times when it is difficult to tell if the music is Country or Pop, there is no doubt that Garth Brooks is a Country singer, who has been able to push forward the barrier without diluting the content of his material. He has also been able to live up to the comments that *Grand Ole Opry* star Billy Walker made to the writer: "There are lots of singers in Country music, but not many entertainers." Garth Brooks is most definitely an entertainer.

Garth was born one of 6 children to Troyal and Colleen Carroll Brooks. His father was a fair guitar and mandolin player who taught Garth his first chords. His mother had been a Country singer, and performed from 1957 through 1979. She recorded for Capitol Records, without any chart success, and also appeared with Red Foley on the *Ozark Jubilee*. While at high school, Garth excelled in football, basketball, baseball and track. He attended Oklahoma State University in Stillwater on a partial athletics scholarship (javelin) and majored in advertising, graduating in December 1984.

While at college, Garth played local clubs, also working as a bouncer. It was in this latter capacity that he met his future wife, Sandy Mahl, also an OSU student and rodeo rider, when he helped remove her fist from the ladies' restroom wall, after she had pitched her fist at a romantic rival.

In 1985, Garth decided to try his luck in Nashville, but returned home in 23 hours after realizing that Nashville didn't want him. He returned to Nashville with Sandy, in 1987, and they both worked for a boot store. Garth did a lot of demo singing and then signed with Bob Doyle and Pam Lewis (Doyle/Lewis Management). By 1988, he had signed with Capitol Records, where he is produced by Allen Reynolds and the following year, he released his debut, self-titled album. All at once, the Brooks star was in its ascendant. His first single, *Much Too Young (to Feel This Damn Old)*, reached the Top 10 and was followed by *If Tomorrow Never Comes*, which went to No.1. The album itself reached No. 8 on the Country Album chart and by 1990, had crossed-over to the Pop Album chart Top 20. By September 1993, the album had racked up a remarkable 5 million sales.

In 1990, Garth went from strength to strength. His opening single of the year, *Not Counting You*, reached the Top 3, but it was the follow-up, Tony Arata's *The Dance*, that caused a major stir. It went to No.1, and became much awarded. This was followed in turn by another No.1, Dewayne Blackwell and Earl Bud Lee's *Friends in Low Places*, which was likewise much awarded. The year was wrapped up by a third No.1, the magnificent *Unanswered Prayers*, which Garth wrote with Pat Alger and Larry Bastian. In September,

Country music superstar ***Garth Brooks***

Garth released his second album, ***No Fences***, and this stayed on top of the Country Album chart for 23 weeks and reached No.12 on the Pop Album chart. By May 1993, this release had sold an unbelievable 10 million copies! During the year, Garth was made a member of the *Grand Ole Opry*.

Garth continued into 1991, with two more No.1 singles taken from ***No Fences***, *Two of a Kind, Workin' on a Full House* and *The Thunder Rolls*. The third single of the year, Larry Bastian's *Rodeo*, came from the third album, ***Ropin' the Wind***. It reached No.3 and was followed by Garth's version of Billy Joel's *Shameless*. ***Ropin' the Wind*** went to No.1 on both Country and Pop Album charts, staying on top of the Country charts for 25 weeks and the Pop lists for 7 weeks. By the end of 1991, it had already sold 5 million copies, and by the end of 1992, sales exceeded 9 million. That year, Capitol Nashville released the video ***Garth Brooks***, which by October had gone Double Platinum (200,000 units) and by the end of April 1992, it had sold over 400,000 units. In 1991, Garth appeared in the *CountryWeston* episode of the comedy series *Empty Nest*.

The following year, Garth opened his singles account with *What She's Doing Now*, which stayed at the top of the Country charts for 4 weeks. That was followed into the charts a month later by *Papa Loves Mama*, which reached No.3. Then, a month after that, *Against the Grain*, the flip-side of *Shameless*, picked up enough air-play to drop it into the charts, and although it was around for 5 months, it only reached No.66. In May of 1992, *The River*, a song written by Garth and Victoria Shaw, went to No.1. Garth deliberately released his Christmas album, ***Beyond the Season***, in August, to emphasize that the spirit of Christmas should extend the entire year.

The following month, it was followed by the album ***The Chase***. The first single from ***The Chase***, *We Shall Be Free*, written by Garth and Stephanie Davis, was a comparative flop. This had nothing to do with the song, which was a brilliant piece about love and caring, but this seemed to be beyond the understanding of a lot of radio stations! It peaked at No.12, but the video did get a lot of attention. This song brought further visibility for Stephanie Davis, who had been singing and writing and most especially playing fiddle around Nashville for some years, and who has emerged as a full-blown star in her own right, and was Garth's opening act. That same year, Garth did backing vocals on Chris LeDoux's *Whatcha Gonna Do with a Cowboy*, which reached the Top 10, and Garth's connection helped finally (and belatedly) launch the LeDoux career.

We Shall Be Free was followed by yet another No.1, *Somewhere Other Than the Night*. He wrapped up the year with a single from ***Beyond the Season***, *The Old Man's Back in Town*, which reached No.48. Such is Garth's fan base that ***Beyond the Season*** had sold 2 million copies before Christmas had even arrived, and reached No.2 on both Country and Pop Album charts. ***The Chase*** did even better, selling 5 million before the year ended and attaining No.1 place on both the Country (16 weeks) and Pop (7 weeks) Album charts. His

This Is Garth Brooks NBC-TV special made network history for a Country show, with over 28 million viewers. The show was ranked in the week's Top 10, NBC's highest rating on a Friday night for more than 2 years. The video of the same name had sold over 400,000 units by the end of August.

In 1993, Garth sold out the 65,000-seater Texas Stadium in Dallas in 92 minutes and two further shows were sold out in 93 minutes and 120 minutes. This broke the attendance record set by Paul McCartney. He also issued a new album, ***In Pieces***, which at the time of writing had sold over 3 million copies. His single successes during 1993 were *Learning to Live Again* (Top 3), *That Summer*, *Ain't Going Down (til the Sun Comes Up)* and *American Honky-Tonk Bar Association* (all No.1s). However, the radio stations ruined Garth's success level when they plundered his albums for cuts such as *Dixie Chicken*, *Standing Outside the Fire*, *Callin' Baton Rouge* and *One Night a Day*, which all failed to be major successes.

Garth Brooks is many people. He is a shy man, who is also gregarious. He comes from a "loud" family, yet produces songs of utmost sensitivity. He is an introvert, who swings across his stage on a rope, like Tarzan. Most especially, he is a likable man, who in the tradition of Country music loves his fans and goes out of his way for them. One example of that was when he ran his existing fan club down, because he could no longer honor allowing them all backstage. He sent back their subscriptions and set up a new fan club, more in keeping with the amount of security necessary and the logistical situation. All the fans returned their money to rejoin.

He is also blessed with a great backing band, Stillwater, which is made up of his sister Betsy Smittle (bass guitar, backup vocals), Dave Gant (fiddle, keyboards), James Garver (lead guitar, backup vocals), Ty England (backup vocals), Steve McClure (steel guitar, guitar) and Mike Palmer (percussion). His recordings have had the added weight of lead guitarist Chris Leuzinger. In his live performances, Garth has perfected the use of the head microphone, which became popular in the early 80's through keyboardist Howard Jones. (For Garth's many awards, see Awards Section.)

RECOMMENDED ALBUMS:

"Garth Brooks" (Capitol Nashville)(1989)
"No Fences" (Capitol Nashville)(1990)
"Ropin' the Wind" (Capitol Nashville)(1991)
"Beyond the Season" (Liberty)(1992)
"The Chase" (Liberty)(1992)
"In Pieces" (Liberty)(1993)

BROTHER PHELPS

Formed: 1992

RICKY LEE PHELPS
(Singer, Songwriter, Guitar)
Given Name: Richard Lee Phelps
Date of Birth: October 8, 1953
Married: Susan
Children: Joshua Lee, Rosa Leeann

DOUG PHELPS
(Singer, Songwriter, Bass Guitar)
Given Name: Douglas Phelps
Date of Birth: February 16, 1960
Married: Kim
Children: Rachel
Both Born: Edmonton, Kentucky

By the time Ricky Lee and Doug Phelps came to depart from the Kentucky Headhunters in 1992, the Headhunters had virtually divested themselves of any Country music that had marked their debut.

The brothers therefore feeling that their road and the Headhunters were heading in different directions, decided to branch out on their own. To get their name, Ricky Lee and Doug held a nationwide competition on TNN's *Crook & Chase.* They decided on it as a tribute to their father, an Assembly of God preacher, who has always been known to his congregation as Brother Phelps.

As teenagers, they had formed their own band and therefore when they started out in 1992, there was that naturalness in their vocal harmonies that only siblings can achieve, as evidenced by the Everly Brothers, the Delmore Brothers, etc.

When Asylum Records came to Nashville, the brothers became one of the first to sign to them. Their debut album, ***Let Go***, showed that they were going to stick to a much more Country path. The title track was released as a single in the early summer of 1993 and reached the Top 10, staying on the charts for some 5 months. The follow-up, the self-penned *Were You Really Livin'*, went Top 30. They are currently working on a new album and if their performance at 1993's Fan Fair is representative, then they will have a long career.

RECOMMENDED ALBUM:

"Let Go" (Asylum)(1993)

COUSIN CECIL BROWER

(Fiddle, Songwriter)
Given Name: Cecil Lee Brower
Date of Birth: November 27, 1914
Where Born: Bowie, Texas
Married: Sibyl Knight (m. 1938/div. 1962)
Children: none
Date of Death: March, 1964

Cecil Brower had studied music and violin at the Texas Christian University and seemed on the way to a classical career when he played briefly with the Dallas Symphony Orchestra. However that all changed when he made his radio debut in 1931 with the Georgie Porgie Boys, recording a commercial for a breakfast cereal company in North Carolina. The following year, he joined Milton Brown's Musical Brownies and stayed with the band until Brown's death in an auto accident in 1936. Cecil was one of the most Jazz-influenced fiddle players at that time and greatly influenced other Brownies such as Jesse Ashlock and Cliff Bruner. He recorded with the Brownies on their second Decca session in March 1936 and is featured on *Black and White Rag*. Cecil then went on to lead the Light Crust Doughboys.

He then went on to station WRR in Dallas, where he and Sibyl married. While playing with Roy Newman's band at the station, Cecil was auditioned by Ted Fio Rito and in 1937, flew out to Los Angeles and joined Fio Rito's society orchestra. For some six months of his two-year stay with the orchestra, Cecil was playing at the Beverly Wilshire Hotel. He also appeared in two shorts with the orchestra for RKO Films. He left the orchestra in 1939 and joined Bob Wills and his Texas Playboys. He had appeared on several recordings with Wills and was with the Texas Playboys until 1941, when the band broke up with the advent of WWII. During the hostilities, Cecil was in the Coast Guard Service and didn't return to civilian life until 1946. That year, he formed his own band, Cecil Brower's Western Band, which was based in Odessa, Texas, and was resident on KECK Odessa. The band lasted until 1949, when Cecil joined Leon McAuliffe's band in Tulsa, Oklahoma. He stayed with them until 1954 when he moved to Nashville. At this time, he and Sibyl decided amicably to divorce. They remained good friends.

From 1957 to 1959, Cecil appeared on NBC-TV's *Five Star Jubilee* which had succeeded the *Ozark Jubilee*. From 1962-1964, he recorded several hoedown and square dance albums for Smash and Cumberland in Nashville. He moved to New York at the start of the 60's to appear as fiddle player on Jimmy Dean's TV Show on ABC-TV. In March, 1964, Cecil had appeared with Jimmy at a Carnegie Hall concert and after the show, they were at the Waldorf-Astoria Hotel. Cecil was playing fiddle when he collapsed and died of an ulcerated stomach. If you're gonna die anywhere then go in style!

RECOMMENDED ALBUMS:
"America's Favorite Square Dances (With Calls)" (Smash)(1962)
"America's Favorite Square Dances (Without Calls)" (Smash)(1962)
"Old Fashioned Country Hoedown" (Cumberland)(1963)
"America's Favorite Square Dances (With Calls)" (Cumberland)(1964)
"America's Favorite Square Dances (Without Calls)" (Cumberland)(1964)

Ginny Brown refer LITTLE GINNY

HYLO BROWN

(Singer, Guitar, Bass, Fiddle)
Given Name: Frank Brown
Date of Birth: April 20, 1922
Where Born: River, Kentucky

A Bluegrass and Country singer who got his nickname because of his considerable vocal range, Hylo Brown attained a wide following and moderate commercial success during the mid-to-late 1950's. Born in Johnson County, Kentucky—later the birthplace of Loretta Lynn—Brown grew up in an Appalachian region rich in musical tradition. After gaining brief radio experience in Ashland, Kentucky and Logan, West Virginia, he moved with his family to Springfield, Ohio, during WWII.

In the Buckeye State, Brown continued working as a semi-professional Country musician at WPFB Middletown and playing with Bradley Kincaid at WWSO Springfield. During that period, he wrote a song about the *Grand Ole Opry* which Jimmy Martin later recorded. In 1954, he composed a number entitled *Lost to a Stranger* which Dayton deejay Tommy Sutton believed held considerable promise. Hylo took the song to Ken Nelson of Capitol Records, who signed Hylo to a record contract. He recorded it and three others at a November session with Bluegrass accompaniment. The modest success of this and subsequent Capitol efforts like *Lovesick and Sorrow* and *The Wrong Kind of Life* enabled Brown to form a band and land a regular spot at the "World's Original Jamboree" at WWVA Wheeling.

In 1957, Brown joined Lester Flatt and Earl Scruggs as a featured vocalist with the Foggy Mountain Boys. As this group's popularity increased—at a time when many traditional acts found economic survival difficult—they formed a second unit with Brown as leader. Known as the Timberliners, this band included such noted pickers as Red Rector on mandolin, Clarence "Tater" Tate on fiddle, Jim Smoak on banjo and Joe Phillips on bass. Initially, they worked on a three-station circuit of television stations in west Tennessee and Mississippi for Martha White Mills. Several months later, they switched places with Flatt and Scruggs, traveling over a five-station chain that extended from Chattanooga, Tennessee, to a variety of locales in West Virginia. In August 1958, Hylo Brown and the Timberliners recorded an eponymous album for Capitol that is considered one of the all-time classics of traditional Bluegrass.

Soon after this, videotape and syndicated television ended the band's work for Martha White Mills as the company could now play the Flatt and Scruggs program on all the stations. Brown continued for a time with a band that included Billy Edwards on banjo and session guitarist Norman Blake on Dobro. A little later, Hylo rejoined Flatt and Scruggs as a featured vocalist. During the early 60's, he also began a liaison with Starday Records that yielded four albums of Bluegrass and a few singles with Country backing. Through most of the decade he worked as a solo act in clubs, small jamborees and schoolhouses. Beginning in 1966, he recorded six more Bluegrass albums for Uncle Jim O'Neal's Rural Rhythm label. He also did Country-backed material for smaller Nashville-based firms such as King's Music City and K-Ark.

In the 70's, Hylo relocated for a time to Jacksonville, Ohio, and did albums for companies like Jessup and Atteiram. However, by now, his voice seemed to have lost some of the power and range it had earlier, particularly in the high natural keys. Hylo continued singing for a time in clubs and did an occasional Bluegrass festival, but has become increasingly inactive in recent years.

In retrospect, Hylo Brown set the standard with his Bluegrass and Traditional recordings for Capitol. Unfortunately, he arrived on the national scene at a time when the mainstream of Country music was shifting in a direction that did not sit well with his style of singing. Hylo's generation was that of Bill Monroe, Flatt and Scruggs, the Stanleys and Red Smiley. However, by the time Hylo did his first session, they had already become fairly established. Had he received a contract with a major label four or five years earlier, he might have attained a similar legendary status. As it is, he still ranks as a significant figure.

IMT

From the Buckeye State, ***Hylo Brown***

RECOMMENDED ALBUMS:
"Hylo Brown" (Capitol)(1959) [Reissued by Stetson UK in original packaging (1988) and by Collectors Classics]
"Bluegrass Balladeer" (Starday)(1961)
"Bluegrass Goes to College" (Starday)(1962) [Re-issued on Nashville]
"Hylo Brown Meets the Lonesome Pine Fiddlers" (Starday)(1963)
"Hylo Brown & the Timberliners, 1954-60" (Bear Family Germany)(1992)

JIM ED BROWN

(Singer, Songwriter, Guitar)
Given Name: James Edward Brown
Date of Birth: April 1, 1934
Where Born: Sparkman, Arkansas
Married: Rebecca Sue Perry (Becky)
Children: Jim Ed, Jr. (Buster), Kimberly

Jim Ed came to public attention in 1954 as a member of the family group the Browns. However, his career started before that and continues to date.

He grew up on a 160-acre farm on which he helped run the family's successful sawmill business. He was a sporting young man and while at high school was President of the student body and captain of both basketball and football teams. He entered Arkansas A & M College as a forestry major and then switched to Arkansas State Teachers College to study music and voice.

While still in high school, he and his older sister, Maxine, had a radio series on KCLA in Pine Bluff, Arkansas, and became regular members of *Barnyard Frolic*. From 1954, they released five singles for the Fabor label, as Jim Ed and Maxine Brown, including *Lookin' Back to See* and *Draggin' Main Street*. On the former, which they wrote, Jim Reeves was featured on rhythm guitar and Floyd Cramer on piano. Later that year, Bonnie joined them to become the Browns (see Browns, The). Jim Ed left the group to serve in the Armed Forces.

Although the group broke up in 1967, Jim Ed had already signed two years earlier to RCA, where the Browns had scored their hits. It is stated that Maxine and Bonnie persuaded

Jim Ed Brown with Helen Cornelius

Chet Atkins to sign him, but almost certainly Chet was perceptive enough to see that Jim Ed had what it takes to make it as a solo.

His initial solo outings were as Jim Edward Brown and he struck a pattern of Top 40 hits with the 1966 release *A Taste of Heaven* going into the Top 25 and *You Can Have Her* going Top 20 the year after. In the spring of 1967, he scored his first major success with *Pop a Top,* which he followed with the Top 15 *Bottle, Bottle*. His hit records showed no popularity pattern. Some of his singles did well while others only fared so-so. His Top 20 successes from 1968 to 1970 were *The Enemy* (1968), *Man and Wife Time* (1969) and *Morning,* a Top 5 record in 1970. This last record crossed over to become a Top 50 Pop success.

In 1968, Jim Ed formed the Gems as his backing group and started a lengthy stint at the Sahara Tahoe's Juniper Lounge. The following year he became host of the syndicated TV series *The Country Place*, on which he stayed until 1970.

From 1971 to 1975, his Top 20 records were more abundant, with *Angel's Evening* in 1971, *Southern Loving*, a Top 10 entry, *Broad Minded Man, Sometime Sunshine*, another Top 10 success (all 1973) and the Top 10 single *It's That Time of Night* in 1974.

During 1976, he teamed up with Helen Cornelius and here he enjoyed his greatest success. In the summer of that year, they had a No.1 with *I Don't Want to Have to Marry You,* which was followed by the Top 3 record *Saying Hello, Saying I Love You, Saying Goodbye*. As a result, he and Helen were named CMA "Duo of the Year" the following year. There were other awards. The song *I Don't Want to Have to Marry You* won a *Music City News* "Song of the Year" award for the writers Fred Impus and Phil Sweet and the album of the same title won the "Album of the Year" award from the same magazine.

1977 yielded two more upper register hits for the duo in *Born Believer* and *If It Ain't Love by Now*. They stayed together until 1981 and between 1978 and then, they racked up another 8 hits including *I'll Never Be Free, If the World Ran Out of Love Tonight* and *You Don't Bring Me Flowers* (all 1978, the latter having been a monster hit for Barbra Streisand & Neil Diamond that year). The following year was excellent. Their three singles all charted in the Top 5. They were *Lying in Love with You, Fools* and *Morning Comes Too Early*. That year, Jim Ed had a moderate hit with *You're the Part of Me*. They rounded off their joint careers with *The Bedroom* in 1980 and *Don't Bother to Knock* in 1981.

Their split was somewhat acrimonious but seven years later they got back together briefly. Jim Ed continues to appear on the *Grand Ole Opry* and host TV game shows and talent shows. He currently operates and appears nightly, at the Jim Ed Brown Theater, located near Opryland in Nashville.

RECOMMENDED ALBUMS:

"Morning" (RCA Victor)(1971)
"Barrooms and Pop-a-Tops" (RCA Victor)(1973) [Re-released on Pickwick (1980)]
"It's That Time of Night" (RCA Victor)(1975)
"Jim Ed & Helen" (RCA Victor)(1979)
"One Man, One Woman" (RCA Victor)(1980)
"Jim Ed & Helen—Greatest Hits" (RCA UK)(1981)
"Greatest Hits—Jim Ed Brown & Helen Cornelius" (RCA Victor)(1982)

MILTON BROWN

(Singer, Bandleader)
Given Name: Milton Brown
Date of Birth: September 8, 1903
Where Born: Stephensville, Texas
Married: Mary Helen
Children: one son
Date of Death: April 18, 1936
Musical Brownies: Durwood Brown (Guitar), Jesse Ashlock (Fiddle), Wanna Coffman (Bass), Ocie Stockard (Tenor Banjo), Fred Calhoun (Piano), Cecil Brower (Fiddle), Bob Dunn (Steel Guitar), Cliff Bruner (Fiddle)

Milton Brown shares with Bob Wills the honor of being the principal creator of Western Swing music.

Born and reared on a farm some 60 miles south and west of Fort Worth, Brown and his family moved to that city in 1918. He graduated from high school in 1925 and worked as a cigar salesman until losing that position during the Great Depression. In 1930, a chance meeting with aspiring fiddler Bob Wills changed his life forever. Milton went to a dance in Fort Worth and joined in on the chorus of *St. Louis Blues* with the Wills Fiddle Band, which led to his joining the group as vocalist.

After Milton lost his job with the cigar company, the threesome of Bob, Milton and Herman Arnspiger worked in a medicine show until that fall when they landed a spot on WBAP radio as the Aladdin Laddies, sponsored by the Aladdin Lamp Company. They also began dances at a pavilion called Crystal Springs. Early in 1931, they went to work for the Light Crust Flour Company as the Light Crust Doughboys at KFJZ. Although he originally detested their "hillbilly" music, O'Daniel widely accepted it once its popularity began selling flour and he became the announcer and even wrote some songs, moved the program to WBAP and soon had it on a multistation hookup. In February 1932, the group cut a single for Victor as the Fort Worth Doughboys.

In September 1932, Brown went on his own (as did Wills subsequently) and formed the Musical Brownies, broadcasting at radio station KTAT. Initial band members included brother Durwood on guitar, Jesse Ashlock on fiddle, Wanna Coffman on bass and Ocie Stockard on tenor banjo. A little later they added Fred Calhoun on piano and Cecil Brower, who had some formal musical training, as a second fiddler. Their repertoire included many Pop and Jazz numbers. The band cut their first recordings—8 sides—for Bluebird in April 1934 and another 10 in August.

By the time of their first Decca sessions in January1935, the Brownies had added Bob Dunn on steel guitar (usually credited with being the first to use an electrified instrument in Country music). These sessions, done over several days, turned out 36 numbers and established the Brownies as probably the top group on the Texas Swing scene (Bill Boyd, Roy Newman and a revamped Light Crust Doughboys group had all recorded by now).

For their final sessions in March 1936 at New Orleans, Cliff Bruner had joined Brower as fiddler (Ashlock never recorded with the Brownies). The band cut nearly 50 songs on this trip, which was fortunate, given Milton's fatal auto crash a few weeks later. He lingered for five days after the accident before he expired. Durwood Brown kept the band together and they cut another dozen sides for Decca prior to their dissolution in 1938. Another brother, Roy Lee Brown, also had a group in the mid-40's.

Milton Brown's large recorded legacy supplemented his short career. Other Brownies like Bruner and Dunn also had significant recording careers while Ashlock and Brower worked in many later bands. Other Western Swing vocalists such as Adolph Hofner give Milton credit for influencing their style. Decca released a 10" album by Brown in their ***Dance-O-Rama*** series in 1955 and MCA a regular album in 1982, while RCA did half a compact disc in 1990. String and Texas Rose also did single album reissues while other cuts appeared on Western Swing anthologies. Texas Swing researcher Cary Ginnel has worked on a lengthy Brown biography. IMT

RECOMMENDED ALBUMS:

"Dance-O-Rama" (Decca)(1955) [Note: Re-issued as Western)
"Taking Off!" (String)(1977) [Note: Decca Masters]
"Pioneer Western Swing" (MCA)(1982) [Note: Decca Masters)
"Milton Brown and His Musical Brownies" (Texas Rose) [Note: Victor Masters]
"Easy Ridin' Papa" (Charly UK)(1987) [Note: Decca Masters]
"Under the Double Eagle" (RCA)(1990) [Note: nine by Brown and nine by Bill Boyd; compact disc & cassette)

T. GRAHAM BROWN

(Singer, Songwriter, Actor)

Given Name: Anthony Graham Brown
Date of Birth: October 30, 1954
Where Born: Arabi, Georgia
Married: Sheila (m. 1979)
Children: George Anthony ("Acme")

His T-Ness is a colorful, carefree character who can be totally outrageous. An example is the time he came on TNN's *Nashville Now* and cut off host Ralph Emery's tie. He sings with a soul-saturated voice which is projected straight from the heart. His style is Country, Soul and Rock with a touch of Rhythm and Blues.

T. dreamed of being a baseball star, and was an All-State High School pitcher and center fielder. However when he went to the University of Georgia and made the team, he found himself watching from the bench. He decided to quit the team and concentrate on music. By now he was singing at night and attending school by day. He played Beach Music as half of Dirk and Tony, a popular duo that played in Athens through the early 70's. He later fronted an eight-piece "Outlaw Country band" called Reo Diamond and sported long hair, a full beard, an earring, a tattoo and a ten-gallon hat. In 1979, he changed his image and went out as T. Graham Brown & Rack of Spam, playing Rhythm and Blues.

He moved to Nashville with his wife, Sheila, in 1982; she supported him all the way and even took two jobs so that he could "hang out" on Music Row getting to know people. T. sang during the happy hour and did a bit of hard drinking. He met Harlan Howard and managed to get some demo work. He soon began getting jingle work, singing for many major brands. In 1983, T. signed to CBS as a writer. Terry Choates, who was at Tree International, had hired T. for demo work. When Terry changed his job and became head of A & R for Capitol/EMI America, he recommended that T. Graham Brown be signed to the label. His recordings would reveal that his co-written songs would form the backbone of his success.

T.'s first single, *Drowning in Memories,* was a Country Top 40 entry in 1985. He followed this at the end of the year with *I Tell It Like It Used to Be*, which went Top 10. T. started the following year with *I Wish That I Could Hurt That Way Again*, which went Top 3, and followed up with *Hell and High Water*, which went to No.1. That year, T. quit drinking and began opening for Kenny Rogers, a gig that lasted for two years. He started off 1987 with his second No.1 hit, *Don't Go to Strangers,* and followed with the Top10 *Brilliant Conversationalist* and the Top 5 *She Couldn't Love Me Anymore*. He then went on a promotional tour of Germany and England. While in Germany, he released the single *Sittin' on the Dock of the Bay*, and Capitol issued *Rock It, Billy* in England. T.'s popularity in Germany led to *Later Train* being included on the soundtrack of the German movie *Zabou*.That year, he appeared in two movies. The first was the Richard Pryor movie *Greased Lightning*; he also appeared as a redneck hotel clerk in the David Keith movie *The Curse*, starring John Schneider.

He started off 1988 with the Top 5 *The Last Resort,* followed up with the No. 1 *Darlene* and ended up the year with *Come as You* Were, which went Top 10. That year, he landed a role in another David Keith movie, *Heartbreak Hotel*, in which his band, the Hardtops, portrayed Elvis Presley's band. The following year, T. charted with the Top 30 *Never Say Never*. That year, he became a father for the first time, with the birth of his son, George Anthony, whom he calls "Acme."

Taking no prisoners, ***T. Graham Brown***

In 1990, T. was back in favor when both *If You Could Only See Me Now* and his duet with Tanya Tucker, *Don't Go Out*, reached the Top 10. He closed out the year with a Top 20 cut from his ***Bumper to Bumper*** album, *Moonshadow Road*. That year, he made his debut on the *Grand Ole Opry*. T. also appeared in a series of commercials for Taco Bell. The following year, another cut from the album was given air play, namely, *I'm Sending One for You*, but it only reached the Top 60. T. closed out the year with the Top 40 cut *With This Ring*, which came from the album ***You Can't Take It With You***. Currently T. Graham Brown is without a label deal. JAB

RECOMMENDED ALBUMS:

"I Tell It Like It Used to Be" (Capitol)(1986)
"Brilliant Conversationalist" (Capitol)(1987)
"Come as You Were" (Capitol)(1988)
"Bumper to Bumper" (Capitol)(1990)
"You Can't Take It with You" (Capitol)(1991)

BROWN'S FERRY FOUR

Formed: 1943
Members: Grandpa Jones
Merle Travis
Alton Delmore
Rabon Delmore

Other members have included: Red Foley, Clyde Moody, Red Turner, Zeke Turner and Dolly Good, Rome Johnson, Roy Langham, Wayne Raney, Lonnie Glosson

Country's first great all-star Gospel quartet was formed during the turbulent days of WWII and existed in various forms until 1952. During that time, it recorded some 45 songs, all for the King record label out of Cincinnati. Though by modern standards (in terms of albums or cds) the total output was barely four albums' worth of music, they were influential beyond sheer numbers. Being released on 78's, then on 45's, then reissued on 45 EP's and finally albums, the group's recorded output was worn to pieces by deejays who used them for theme songs, by amateur groups who tried to copy their arrangements and by generations of fans who found their arrangements of Gospel classics built around four voices and an acoustic guitar both inspirational and appealing.

The original quartet was composed of four men who went on to become Country music legends: Louis M. "Grandpa" Jones, guitarist and singer Merle Travis and Alton and Rabon Delmore. The Delmore Brothers had pioneered close-harmony duet singing on the *Grand Ole Opry* in the 1930's.

The story of the group starts in June 1943, when they all were working over the powerful station WLW in Cincinnati. Travis was a member of a band called the Drifting Pioneers, Grandpa Jones was doing a solo act and the Delmore Brothers had their own radio slot. By 1943, WLW was starting to increase its hours of Country programming and hired George Biggar from Chicago to help out on their new show, *Boone County Jamboree*, later to become *Midwestern Hayride*, which was bidding to become a Country barn dance contender. The Drifting Pioneers had a regular half-hour spot each day singing Gospel songs, but by mid-1943, the draft and defense industries had caused the band to break up. Biggar commented to his staff that he sure could use a good, down-to-earth Country Gospel quartet in that spot. Alton Delmore heard this and responded that he used to teach Gospel singing using shape notes. In fact, as a boy growing up in Alabama, Alton had attended the old-time singing schools taught by members of the Vaughan Music Company in nearby Lawrenceburg. Both he and his brother had sung in quartets as boys.

Alton got his brother, Grandpa and Merle and talked them into trying a couple of numbers. Grandpa recalled that they went out into the hallway of the studio and tried out a few songs. Their voices blended all right, so they went in and told Mr. Biggar he had his Gospel group. "Start in the morning" was his response.

The foursome reassembled and began to think of a name. Alton's biggest hit song up to that time had been his 1933 *Brown's Ferry Blues*, named after a river crossing near where they lived in Alabama. Jokingly, Travis suggested this as a name and everybody laughed at the joke, a Gospel quartet named for an off-color song. But the more they thought about it, the more they liked it and decided to try it. It worked, Travis recalled: "Nobody ever connected it to Alton's bawdy 'two old maids lying in the sand' song."

Another problem was finding enough material to fill 30 minutes of live radio a day. This they solved by having Alton teach them songs from the old paperback shape note songbooks, and by going to a used record store to find old records by earlier Gospel groups, especially black ones, that they could copy. At first, Grandpa sang baritone, Alton lead, Rabon tenor and Travis bass. Within a few days, letters began pouring in from the farmers and factory workers who tuned in at such an early hour. Ironically, about this time, the group had to break up. Travis went into the Marines, Grandpa into the Army and Alton into the Navy. It would not be until March 1946, after the war, that this original group would get back together again. By then the Delmores were in Memphis, Grandpa in Nashville and Merle in California. Back in Cincinnati, WLW still had a radio quartet called the Brown's Ferry Four on the air. The station owned the name and could fill the slots with anybody available, which included local singers like Rome Johnson, Roy Lanham, and Dolly Good.

The original four were going to California to record for King Records and the label owner, Sid Nathan, decided to reunite them for some Gospel sides. The first two records were *Will the Circle Be Unbroken,* the old Carter Family song and *Just a Little Talk with Jesus* by black composer Cleavant Derricks. King's next problem was how to keep the group alive when it was by now basically a studio group, a common enough idea now, but novel back in 1946. Nathan flew them all back to Hollywood and in September 1946 cut 12 more sides. These included early versions of the Brumley classic *I'll Fly Away*, *If We Never Meet Again This Side of Heaven,* the old favorite *Rockin' on the Waves* and *Over in Glory Land.* Though these records continued to sell well, changes in the quartet were inevitable. After he signed with Capitol, Travis had to drop out. At the same time, Grandpa and the Delmores had hit secular records like *Mountain Dew* and *Hillbilly Boogie,* which made recording Gospel sides even more a labor of love. On one session (probably in October 1947), Travis' part was taken by another well-known star, Red Foley. This session produced *I'll Meet You in the Morning* and *Jesus Hold My Hand.* In 1948, during the recording ban, the Delmores finally began adding a version of the Brown's Ferry Four to their live stage shows, filling it out with Wayne Raney and Lonnie Glosson.

During the last few sessions, only the Delmores were constant members. They were joined in 1951 by mandolin player Red Turner from Middlesboro, Kentucky, and in 1952 by Clyde Moody, who was then a best-selling artist for King. In later years, there were spasmodic attempts to revive the group. Alton Delmore did it for several sides on the Acme label and in 1965 Grandpa Jones re-formed the group for a Monument lp. Jones has also said that the Brown's Ferry Four were a direct inspiration for the formation of the popular Hee Haw Gospel Quartet. CKW

RECOMMENDED ALBUMS:

"Sacred Songs" (King)(1957)
"Sacred Songs, Volume 2" (King)(1958)
"16 Greatest Hits" (King)(1965)
"Wonderful Sacred Songs" (King)(1977)
"16 Greatest Hits" (Starday)(1977)
"16 Greatest Hits, Volume 2" (Starday)(1977)
"24 Songs" (Pine Mountain)
"Sacred Songs" (Pine Mountain)

BROWNS, The

Formed: 1955
JIM ED BROWN
Given Name: James Edward Brown
Date of Birth: April 1, 1934
Where Born: Sparkman, Arkansas
Married: Rebecca Sue (Becky)
Children: James E., Jr., Kimberly
MAXINE BROWN
(Singer, Songwriter, Guitar)
Given Name: Ella Maxine Brown
Date of Birth: April 27, 1932
Where Born: Samti, Louisiana
Married: Tom Russell
Children: James B.
BONNIE BROWN
(Singer, Songwriter, Guitar)
Given Name: Bonnie Gean Brown
Date of Birth: July 31, 1937
Where Born: Sparkman, Arkansas
Married: Gene Ring
Children: Kelly Lea, Robin Rachelle

The brother-sister group the Browns constituted one of Country music's finest harmony teams of the 50's and 60's. The Browns grew up in rural Arkansas, where their father operated a sawmill. Their parents encouraged them in musical endeavors, and singing quickly became their strong suit as they developed excellent harmony. About 1952, they became increasingly serious about their music as Jim Ed and Maxine began to appear with some frequency on the *Barnyard Frolics* over KLRA Little Rock, as well as at smaller stations in Camden and Pine Bluff, and on TV at KLRA in the state capital. They also guested on the Ernest Tubb Record Shop show at WSM Nashville where they sang their original *Looking Back to See,* a novelty song which brought them national attention.

Independent record producer Fabor Robison signed them to a contract with his new Fabor label and they cut *Looking Back to See* for his company at the KWKH studios in Shreveport in March 1954. The song remained on the Country charts all summer, reaching the Top 10 (a Decca cover by Goldie Hill and Justin Tubb went to No. 4) and the Browns launched their professional careers by joining the *Louisiana Hayride* that fall. By this time the duet had become a trio when sister Bonnie joined them after finishing high school in 1955. At the end of the year, as Jim Edward, Maxine & Bonnie Brown, they reached the Top 10 with *Here Today and Gone Tomorrow.*

They joined the cast of the *Ozark Jubilee* in 1955, which gave them network TV exposure and the show's producer, Si Siman, helped them land a contract with RCA Victor in 1956. They soon had two more major hits with *I Take the Chance* (Top 3), and *I Heard the Bluebirds Sing* (Top 5). Jim Ed's stint in the U.S. Army interrupted the group's touring activities, but they continued to record during leaves and a third sister, Norma, filled in on personal appearances.

On June 1, 1959, as "the Browns," they waxed the inspirational, Folk-flavored *The Three Bells,* which became a super hit, spending 10 weeks at the top of the Country charts and four atop the Pop listings. It also reached the UK Top 10. This success landed them appearances on such network television programs as the *Ed Sullivan Show,* the *Jimmy Dean Show*, and *American Bandstand.* Capitalizing on the Folk boom and their crossover appeal, the Browns had 2 follow-ups that scored high with the Pop market: *Scarlet Ribbons* (1959, Top 10 Country/Top 20 Pop) and *The Old Lamplighter* (1960, Top 5 Pop/Top 20 Country). The latter was credited to "the Browns featuring Jim Edward Brown." Their 1960 version of Hank Locklin's *Send Me the Pillow That You Dream On* also did well. Later numbers continued to do well in the Country field, such as *Then I'll Stop Loving You* (1964, Top 20) and *I'd Just Be Fool Enough* and *Coming Back to You* (both 1966), but the group's cross-over appeal faded after 1961. In 1963, the Browns joined the *Grand Ole Opry.*

In late 1967, the Browns dissolved as a trio. Maxine and Bonnie both returned to Arkansas to devote more time to their families. Jim Ed, who began recording solo in 1965, remained with the *Opry* and went on to forge a successful solo career. Maxine recorded some numbers on Chart in the late 60's, having her main success with *Sugar Cane Country* in 1968. Mary A. Bufwack and Robert K. Oermann, in their book *Finding Her Voice*, described her as "the salty, good-humored alto," and report that she is writing her memoirs. Interest in the group has remained sufficiently high for Bear Family Records to re-issue their Fabor sides and some of the earlier RCA cuts. IMT

RECOMMENDED ALBUMS:

"Jim Edward, Maxine and Bonnie Brown" (RCA Victor)(1957)
"Sweet Sounds by the Browns" (RCA Victor)(1959)
"Town & Country" (RCA Victor)(1960)
"The Browns Sing Their Hits" (RCA Victor)(1960)
"Grand Ole Opry Favorites" (RCA Victor)(1964)
"Best of the Browns" (RCA Victor)(1966)
"Our Kind of Country" (RCA Victor)(1966)
"Rockin' Rollin' Browns" (Bear Family Germany)(1983)
"Looking Back to See: The Fabor Recordings" (Bear Family Germany)(1986)
(See also Jim Ed Brown.)

ED BRUCE

(Singer, Songwriter, Guitar, Actor)

Given Name:	**William Edwin Bruce, Jr.**
Date of Birth:	**December 29, 1940**
Where Born:	**Kaiser, Arkansas**
Married:	**1. Sarah (div.)**
	2. Patsy (div.)
	3. Judy ("Doggett")
Children:	**Trey, Ginnie, Anne-Marie, Beau**

If you go back into the vaults at Sun Records, you will find some great rockabilly tracks recorded by Edwin Bruce. It has been alleged that Ed was discovered by Scotty Moore and Bill Black at the Rebel Club in Osceola while in a band with Ace Cannon. This is not so as Ed was already recording for Sun before playing this club. From such a wild and rockin' beginning, young Edwin became one of the most respected Country performers around.

As a songwriter, Ed Bruce writes good melodies and intelligent lyrics. His songs, often written in collaboration with his ex-wife Patsy and Ron Peterson, have proved to be enduring. Charlie Louvin cut *Lonesome Is Me*, Tanya Tucker recorded *The Man That Turned My Mother On* and *When I Die, Just Let Me Go to Heaven*, Tex Ritter did *Working Man's Prayer* and Crystal Gayle recorded *Restless.*

The one song that has achieved classic status is *Mamas, Don't Let Your Babies Grow Up to Be Cowboys.* Originally recorded by Ed on United Artists in 1976, it went on to classic stature when cut by Waylon Jennings and Willie Nelson.

Ed's father was a part-time drummer, and singing in the family was a regular occurrence. With that sort of influence, it was not surprising that while still in high school, Ed had his own band, although he was also still deciding whether to play football or baseball. By 1957, he had already started to write songs and went to see Jack Clement at Sun and before he knew it, he was recording for the label. He was not yet 17 years of age.

Singer and Actor ***Ed Bruce***

The first song Ed had recorded by another artist was *Save Your Kisses*, which was the flip-side to Tommy Roe's 1962 smash hit *Sheila.*

In 1964, he moved to Nashville and became a member of the Marijohn Wilkins Singers. His first major Country cut was *See the Big Man Cry,* which was a hit for Charlie Louvin in 1965.

He has had his share of record success over the years. Ed signed with RCA Victor in 1966 and his first Country chart entry was the Top 60 *Walker's Woods.* In 1968, Ed moved to Monument, but he still couldn't manage to get a major chart single. In 1973, Ed signed to United Artists and in 1975, he hit the Top 20 with *Mamas, Don't Let Your Babies Grow Up to Be Cowboys.*

Ed's period at Epic Records (1977-1978) did not produce a major hit, but once Ed signed with MCA, success came his way. His major hits on the label included *Diane* and *The Last Cowboy Song* (on which he was assisted by Willie Nelson) (both 1980), *Girls, Women and Ladies* (1980), *(When You Fall in Love) Everything's a Waltz* (1981), the No.1 hit *You're the Best Break This Old Heart Ever Had* (1981), *Love's Found You and Me, Ever, Never Lovin' You* (Top 5, 1982), *First Taste of Texas* (Top 10, 1983) and *After All* (Top 5, 1983). His two major hits for his second contract with RCA are *You Turn Me On (Like a Radio)* (Top 3, 1984) and *Nights* (Top 5, 1986). In 1986, he teamed up with Lynn Anderson for the Top 50 success *Fools for Each Other.*

Ed does, however, have many strings to his bow. Not least of these is his acting. He enrolled at Memphis State University majoring in drama and speech. He became known on TV through the commercials and early morning TV series on WSM Nashville as "the Tennessean." His acting blossomed and he has now become an established actor. His credits include playing "Tom Guthrie" in the revitalized *Maverick* TV series starring James Garner. Ed wrote the theme song and sang it with Mr. Garner. He also appeared in the mini-series *The Chisholms*, the TV series *Dalton*, *Down the Long Hill* and the movie *The Last Days of Frank and Jesse James*, which also starred Kris Kristofferson and Johnny Cash.

In 1988, he seemed to find a new peace within himself when he met his present wife,

Judy. He moved to "Home at Last" ranch, where he raises Tennessee walking horses and collects vintage cars and where Judy makes the "best dips imaginable." Ed consciously cut back on his recording and performing. To his many fans and friends, this was a shame, as he still possesses a fine voice.

In 1992, Ed re-emerged with a duet entitled *The One That Got Away* with David Frizzell from David's album ***My Life Is Just a Bridge***. Ed isn't on a label now by his own choice. He plays gigs when he feels like it. He used to host *American Sports Cavalcade,* which won an Ace Award for excellence.

Ed Bruce's career is a catalog of excellence. He bothers about what he does. From his earliest mentors such as Pete Drake and under the guidance of producers such as Bob Ferguson and Larry Butler, he has developed into the archetype of good solid Country performer.

As of 1994, Ed was hosting *Truckin' U.S.A.* for the Nashville Network. Ed has said that if he had to give up everything, he would, except songwriting. He is back in the studio recording again, so perhaps the bug is still there. Perhaps it is the songwriting success of his son Trey that has spurred him (in the nicest possible way). Trey had his first No.1 as a songwriter with *Look Heart, No Hands* by Randy Travis. Still Ed probably wasn't surprised. After all, he told the writer back in 1988 with pride about his talented son.

RECOMMENDED ALBUMS:

"Rockin' & Boppin' Baby" (Bear Family Germany)
"Mamas, Don't Let Your Babies Grow Up to Be Cowboys" (United Artists)(1976)
"The Best of Ed Bruce" (MCA)(1981)
"Greatest Hits" (MCA)(1985)
"Night Things" (RCA Victor)(1986)
"Ed Bruce" (MCA)(1988)

VIN BRUCE

(Singer, Songwriter, Guitar)
Given Name: **Ervin Bruce**
Date of Birth: **April 25, 1932**
Where Born: **Cut Off, Louisiana**

Vin Bruce has been a major figure in Cajun music for some four decades. Like many second-generation Cajun performers, Vin played a combination of French Acadian and Honky-Tonk Country, being equally adept at both forms. Along the way, he earned the nickname of "King of the Cajuns" and once, won the honor of being "Citizen of the Year" in his native Lafourche Parish, Louisiana.

Vin, the son of Levy Bruce, a trapper, fisherman and Cajun fiddler, grew up with music, but came to favor the guitar. He gained early experience as a member of Dudley Bernard's Southern Serenaders and Gene Rodrigue's Hillbilly Swing Kings. When Vin was age 19, Columbia distributor Henry Hildebrand heard him sing on a New Orleans radio station and recommended him for a contract. Vin subsequently recorded several numbers at the studio at the Andrew Jackson Hotel in Nashville with a backing group that included Grady Martin. Most of the songs recorded were in English, but he also cut a couple in French, which gained considerable popularity in southern Louisiana. The biggest seller was the Cajun ballad *Dans la Louisianne,* which led to an appearance on the *Grand Ole Opry* and the formation of a fan club. This title and the flip-side, *Fille de la Ville*, were two of the last straight Cajun recordings on a major label.

For a time, it appeared that Vin might attain national popularity, but the advent of rock'n'roll terminated his Columbia career and he returned to being a local artist and making his principal living out of the livestock business. In 1961, Vin Bruce resumed recording on Floyd Soileau's Swallow label in Ville Platte, Louisiana, at the direct request of producer Leroy Martin. He cut an old love song, *Le Delaysay (The Divorcee)*, which did well in the Cajun area. This resulted in an album, ***Vin Bruce Sings Jole Blon & Cajun Classics***, which was recorded at radio station KLFT (now KLEB) in Golden Meadow. When the sessions became unproductive, Soileau called in ace fiddle player Doc Guidry and as a result 13 tracks were finished in one night. Vin's single of *Jole Blon* became a regional hit, fifteen years after Harry Choates cut his version.

Vin subsequently released another two albums and several singles. In 1969, singer Joe Barry talked Chet Atkins into signing Vin to RCA Victor. However, Vin declined as he was not prepared to return to Nashville and preferred playing in Cut Off and retaining his identity as a Cajun performer. In 1980, he played at the National Folk Festival.

While Vin Bruce has remained close to his French roots, he has nonetheless modernized considerably. His band, the Acadians, use modern electric instruments (including bass guitar played by Leroy Martin) with Doc Guidry's fiddle (since 1968) and Vin's own vocals (at times not unlike Jim Reeves), supplying the principal link with the past. In 1986, Vin's career memorabilia were added to the Country Music Hall of Fame in Nashville.

IMT

RECOMMENDED ALBUMS:

"Vin Bruce Sings Jole Blon & Other Cajun Classics" (Swallow)(1962)
"Vin's Greatest Hits" (Swallow)(1966)
"Cajun Country" (Swallow)
"Vin Sings Country" (Swallow)
"Cajun Country's Greatest" (La Louisianne)
"Country Songs from Louisiana" (Cowgirlboy Germany)(1991) [reissue of early 50's material]

AL BRUMLEY

(Singer, Guitar, Bass)
Given Name: **Albert Edward Brumley, Jr.**
Date of Birth: **October 11, 1933**
Where Born: **Stella, Missouri**
Married: **Robin Davis**
Children: **Albert E. III, Kimberly**

Al Brumley, the son of noted Gospel composer Albert E. Brumley, has spent the better part of his life following a Country music career. Al and his brothers grew up preferring Country as their music of choice. One brother, Tom, became quite well known as a steel guitarist for several different artists, most notably Buck Owens, while Al has made his contributions to the genre mostly as a vocalist.

He got his start in 1949, on radio in Joplin, Missouri, where a duo known as Cookie and Ollie had a jamboree-type show. After finishing high school, Al got work as a staff musician at KOAM Pittsburg, Kansas, where the noted radio team of Roy (McGeorge) and Lonnie (Robertson) had their home base. By the 50's, radio staff musicians were becoming a thing of the past at most locales, so when KOAM added a TV station in 1953, Al worked there, too. He spent most of 1956 and 1957 in the U.S. Navy.

After leaving the Navy, Al went to Fresno, California, and joined Dave Stogner's Rythmairs, who worked all over the San Joaquin Valley, primarily as a vocalist. The Rhythmairs had a regular program on KMJ-TV in Fresno as well as their appearance schedules. Al cut a couple of singles with 4-Star Records during his stay with the Rhythmairs, but in 1959 he went to Bakersfield, where he worked with Cousin Herb Henson on KERO-TV. During this period, Al took time out to go to Nashville where he cut a solo album for SESAC with vocal support from the Anita Kerr Singers and a Harold Bradley-backed musical combo.

Back in California, Al joined Jimmy Thomason's group for about six years. In this period, he had three single releases on Capitol with moderate success, but no real hits. In 1970, Al came to Nashville working primarily as a front act for such Country stars as Leroy Van Dyke and Johnny Russell. He kept this up for ten years, cutting a scattering of single discs during that period.

In 1980, Al went back to Missouri and began to incorporate more of his dad's music into his own repertoire. Al estimates that, during the 60's, about sixty percent of his work was in churches and another twenty percent at outdoor festivals. In 1986, he recorded a two-album set of Albert Brumley songs which have been widely sold via mail order and television ads. One album contained songs largely sentimental in nature while the other concentrated on his best-known sacred standards. The songs fit Al's light and casual, but sincere vocal style quite well, and have been warmly received.

Al opened a show in Branson, Missouri, in 1989 with brother Tom and other family members which played for four summers. In 1993, he moved the production to Eureka Springs, Arkansas, home of the *Ozark Mountain Hoedown* and a booming tourist center in its own right. One of Al's current goals is to record some additional Albert E. Brumley songs. IMT

RECOMMENDED ALBUMS:
"The Al Brumley Showcase" (SESAC)(1963)
"Albert E. Brumley's Legendary Gospel Favorites" (Memory Valley)(1986)
"Albert E. Brumley's Legendary Gospel Favorites, Vol. 2" (Memory Valley)(1986)
"Albert E. Brumley, Jr." (Memory Valley)(1988)
"Songs I've Recorded Through the Years" (Memory Valley)(1992)

ALBERT E. BRUMLEY

(Singer, Songwriter)

Given Name: **Albert Edward Brumley**
Date of Birth: **October 29, 1905**
Where Born: **Spiro, Oklahoma**
Married: **Goldie Edith Schell (m. 1931)(d. 1988)**
Children: **Bill, Al, Tom, Bob, Jackson, Betty**
Date of Death: **November 15, 1977**

Albert E. Brumley became the most celebrated writer of Gospel songs, having written more than 800 songs and hymns and Country songs that he called "memory" songs. He became the only Gospel writer to have four exclusive albums of his songs, recorded on major labels by well-known recording artists the Chuck Wagon Gang, the Statesmen Quartet, the Smitty Gatlin Trio and the Shelton Brothers Trio.

Brumley attended singing schools, music normals and from 1926 to1931, Hartford Music Institute, Hartford, Arkansas, where he studied under some of America's most eminent teachers and writers of sacred music, including Virgil O. Stamps, E.M. Bartlett, J.H. and W.H. Ruebush, Thomas Benton, Homer Rodeheaver and Dr. J.B. Herbert. Brumley was intent on becoming a teacher of music, but once married, he decided to concentrate on writing and settled down in Powell, Missouri. In 1931, he wrote a song that would become a classic, *I'll Fly Away*. Albert felt that he wasn't a great performer and being a shy person, who never liked the limelight, he was content to be a writer in Powell, among the Ozarks.

He worked long and hard on his songs, believing that success was 1 percent talent and 99 percent sweat. He opened up his own music publishing house, Albert E. Brumley & Sons, and in 1948 bought Hartford Music Co., who published *I'll Fly Away,* among other Brumley compositions. In 1966, a songbook, *The Best of Albert E. Brumley*, was published.

In 1970, Albert E. Brumley was among the initial writers inducted into the Nashville Songwriters Hall of Fame. Two years later, he was elected to the Gospel Hall of Fame. Among the songs that Brumley penned were *Turn Your Radio On, I'll Meet You in the Morning, Rank Strangers, Jesus Hold My Hand, If We Never Meet Again, God's Gentle People, I'm As Poor As a Beggar, It's an Unfriendly World, The Blood That Stained the Old Rugged Cross, I'd Rather Be an Old-Time Christian, I Cannot Find the Way Alone, I'm Bound for That City, Surely I Will Lord, He Set Me Free, I've Found a Hiding Place, I Want to Walk As Close As I Can, Did You Ever Go Sailin'?, Her Mansion Is Higher Than Mine, I'd Like to Go Back, There's a Little Pine Log Cabin* and *Nobody Answered Me*.

Albert E. Brumley died on November 15, 1977. His life story is recounted in the book *I'll Fly Away*, written by Kay Hively and Albert E. Brumley, Jr. His music is kept alive by his son Al and by the millions of people who sing his songs each week. His children have gone on to carve their own niches within the music business: Al as a performer, Tom as a famed steel guitarist, Jackson (Jack) as a manager and publisher and Bill, Bob and Betty, who run the family publishing company.

CLIFF BRUNER

(Fiddle, Songwriter)

Date of Birth: **April 25, 1915**
Where Born: **Texas City, Texas**
Married: **Ruth**

Bruner is known primarily for having the first recorded version of *It Makes No Difference Now* and for cutting *Truck Driver's Blues*, the first recorded truck-driving song, but he should also be regarded as one of the most Jazz-oriented Country fiddlers of the 30's. He started playing the fiddle at the age of 4 and 10 years later, at 14, he was hopping freight trains and going places to play his instrument. Within a few years he was a member of Dr. Scott's Medicine Show, a troupe that promoted a panacea called Liquidine Tonic. The experience was valuable primarily because it brought him into contact with Leo Raley and Cotton Thompson, two important names in the history of Texas Swing music, and also provided Cliff with a training ground as a performer.

In 1934, Cliff became part of Milton Brown and his Musical Brownies, at the time billed as the "Greatest String Band on Earth." Cliff cut 48 sides with the Brownies before Brown's death in an auto accident in April 1936. After that tragic event, Cliff moved to Houston and formed the Texas Wanderers (also known as Cliff Bruner's Boys) and in 1937 this band began a lengthy association with Decca. Their biggest hit was their 1938 recording of Floyd Tillman's *It Makes No Difference Now*. Their repertoire was a mix of traditional and contemporary numbers, with Bruner himself preferring Pop and Jazz songs from the 20's and 30's. The Texas Wanderers included a number of artists of historical importance such as Aubrey "Moon" Mullican, a highly influential Honky-Tonk pianist, and Bob Dunn, inventor of the amplified steel guitar used in Western bands.

After his tenure with Decca ended, Bruner recorded for the Ayo label. By the early 50's, he was virtually out of the music business, earning his living as an insurance salesman and executive, but still performing occasionally. He now lives near Houston. WKM

RECOMMENDED ALBUM:
"Cliff Bruner's Texas Wanderers: Western Swing Music 1937-1944" (Texas Rose) (1983)

BRUSH ARBOR

Formed: **1971**
Members:
Jim Rice **Lead Vocals, Banjo, Guitar, Steel Guitar**
Joe Rice **Mandolin, Guitar, Vocals**
Plus:
James Harrah
Mike Holtzer
Dave Rose

Brothers Jim and Joe Rice formed Brush Arbor in San Diego, California, in 1971 to enter a *Country Star* talent contest for KSON radio. They took the name of the band from the "brush arbor" revival meetings where shelters were covered with brush to protect the people from bad weather. The newly formed band beat out nearly 200 other contestants to win first place. The result was performing at a concert that featured Sonny James, Mel Tillis and Bill Anderson. The group signed a contract with Capitol Records and was invited to perform on the *Grand Ole Opry*.

Jim Rice was the group's primary songwriter and also the lead vocalist. Brother Joe handled the harmony vocals and played mandolin and guitar. Brush Arbor's self-titled debut album for Capitol was released in 1972 and it was followed that year with the ***Brush Arbor 2***. The group was very popular in southern California and were featured at many tourist attractions including Disneyland, Knott's Berry Farm, and Seaworld. That year, they debuted on the Country chart with their version of *Proud Mary*, which went Top 60.

In 1973, Brush Arbor was featured on Dean Martin's *Music Country* show and were invited by Johnny Cash to perform on his 1974 NBC-TV Special. They had their biggest singles hit in 1973 with *Brush Arbor Meeting* which included bits of *I'll Fly Away* and *Old Time Religion*, and which hit the Top 50. In 1973, the band was named "Vocal Group of the Year" and "Touring Band of the Year" by the ACM. They were also nominated for a CMA award in 1973 and performed on the awards show.

The band recorded an album for Monument in 1977 entitled ***Straight*** and had a Top 60 single, *Get Down Country Music*. They also appeared on *Hee Haw* and the *Celebration* program in Canada. In 1979, Brush Arbor left the heavy touring schedule behind and performed occasional concerts primarily in churches.

In 1993, Brush Arbor returned to the studio to record the album ***What Does It Take***, for Benson Records. JIE

RECOMMENDED ALBUMS:

"Brush Arbor" (Capitol)(1972)
"Brush Arbor 2" (Capitol)(1973)
"Page One" (Monument)(1975) [Re-issued 1976]
"Straight" (Monument)(1977)
"Hero" (Myrrh)
"Hide Away" (Myrrh)
"What Does It Take" (Benson)(1993)

BOUDLEAUX & FELICE BRYANT

BOUDLEAUX BRYANT

(Songwriter, Singer, Violin, Fiddle)

Given Name: Diadorius Boudleaux Bryant
Date of Birth: February 13, 1920
Where Born: Shellman, Georgia
Date of Death: June 25, 1987

FELICE BRYANT

(Songwriter, Singer)

Given Name: Matilda Genevieve Scaduto
Date of Birth: August 7, 1925
Where Born: Milwaukee, Wisconsin
Children: Dane Boudleaux, Del Rene

The Bryants rank among the premier songwriters in the history of popular music. To list their songs and the artists who have recorded them would take up many pages. Yet, it is not Pop or Country music to which Boudleaux tipped his hat when he started his career. He intended to have a career in classical music and from the age of 5 studied to be a concert violinist.

He looked to be well on the way when he played with the Atlanta Philharmonic for a season during 1938. However, fate works in strange ways. While in a violin maker's shop, Boudleaux fell into conversation with a man from WSB radio in Atlanta. This fellow was looking for a fiddle player for a Country band. Boudleaux had played some Country for his own amusement and decided to accept the job.

So for many years, he played Country, including a spell with Hank Penny & his Radio Cowboys, and then switched to Jazz. In 1945, while in Milwaukee, he met Felice. She was employed as an elevator attendant at the Shrader Hotel. Shortly after meeting, they decided to get married and she went on the road with him. She had already some experience of the business, having been on the radio when 5 and performed in USO shows as a teenager. She had also appeared in plays and at fairs and clubs in Wisconsin.

They started to write songs to amuse themselves, although Felice had been writing from an early age. Rome Johns, a friend and fellow performer, urged them to send some material to Fred Rose of Acuff-Rose. They sent *Country Boy*. Fred Rose liked it, bought it and so started their association with Acuff-Rose. Little Jimmy Dickens cut the song and it became a hit in 1949. At first the connection with Acuff-Rose was on a non-exclusive basis and they were also writing for Tannen Music, but in 1950 they moved to Nashville at the urging of Mr. Rose.

The Bryants' songs were recorded by all of the top names in Country music. *Hey Joe* was a 1953 Country hit for Carl Smith, and on the Pop charts, Frankie Laine turned it into a million seller that same year. For many years they provided Carl Smith with a constant and consistent supply of chart material. In 1954, they started Showcase Music but still continued their relationship with Acuff-Rose.

Eddy Arnold recorded *I've Been Thinking* and *Richest Man (in the World)* in 1955, but soon the advancing specter of rock'n'roll was appearing. The faint-hearted headed for the hills, but not Boudleaux and Felice. Undaunted, they embraced it and turned it to their advantage. They produced rock'n'roll classics that still sound fresh nearly 40 years later. In 1957, they started working with the Everly Brothers. The hits rolled in, now to an international audience: *Bye Bye Love, All I Have to Do Is Dream, Problems, Bird Dog, Poor Jenny, Take a Message to Mary* and *Wake Up Little Susie*. From 1957 to1967 they wrote exclusively for Acuff-Rose.

But it was not just the Everlys who had hits with the Bryants' songs. Buddy Holly rarely recorded other writers' material but he did select *Raining in My Heart* as one of four tracks on what would be his last recording session on October 28, 1958. In addition, the Bryants were still scoring with Country songs, including Jim Reeves' 1958 hit with their *Blue Boy*.

As the swinging 60's got under way, the hits continued to swing their way. Bob Luman had an international hit with *Let's Think About Living*. In 1961, Boudleaux had a global hit with his instrumental recording *Mexico*, which went Gold in Germany. When the Everly Brothers signed to Warner Brothers Records and started to record more self-penned songs, the Bryants just carried on as before and concentrated on the Country music market. In 1964, they scored through Sonny James' version of *Baltimore*. *Rocky Top* is a song written in 10 minutes in 1967, according to Felice, that has become a classic through its numerous renditions but most especially the recordings of Buck Owens and also the Osborne Brothers. The latter version has made it one of the most programmed Bluegrass numbers. In 1967, they switched from Acuff-Rose to their own House of Bryant (a BMI publishing house).

With the dawn of the 70's, there were new hits with new songs and new hits with songs that had been successful the first time around. In 1974, Charley Pride hit it big with *We Could,* which Felice had written. (This was not the first time that they hadn't written together. Several of the hits with the Everly Brothers had been written by Boudleaux alone and as early as 1953, he had co-written with Carl Smith on *This Orchid Means the End*.)

By 1974, it was estimated that 400 artists had recorded Bryant songs. Cristy Lane increased this with 1976 and 1977 hits on *Sweet Deceiver* and *Penny Arcade*. The latter had been a hit for Roy Orbison in 1969. Jim Capaldi, formerly with British Rock supergroup Traffic, cut another classic Boudleaux song, *Love Hurts,* in 1975 (it had originally been a hit for Roy Orbison). It reached the No.4 slot in the U.K. charts and would be a song that was destined to be recorded often with versions from Linda Ronstadt to Gary Morris. In 1978, another Brit, Leo Sayer, had a hit with *Raining in My Heart.*

The following year, the Bryants recorded an album produced by Boudleaux, for DB Records, an English company, entitled ***All I Have to Do Is Dream***. It was released in 1980. They had intended recording an entire album of new material but under the guidance of their two sons they included *All I Have to Do Is Dream, Bye Bye Love, Rocky Top* and *Raining in My Heart.*

Chart success continued for the Bryants through the 80's and although Boudleaux died in 1987, there were covers into the 90's. They will probably continue into the next century and beyond. Why? They wrote simple songs that made the foolish say "I could have written that" but of course they couldn't. It takes genius to write like that. Ask any of the songwriters who look for a hit on 16th Avenue.

The achievement of Boudleaux and Felice Bryant is astounding: an estimated 300 million records sold. More than 3,000 songs written and about 1,200 cuts. In 1972, they were inducted into the Nashville Songwriters Hall of Fame. In 1986, they were inducted into the National Songwriters Hall of Fame. In 1991, they received the ultimate accolade when they were inducted into the Country Music Hall of Fame.

Felice has written some since Boudleaux's death, but she misses the trust that she had with him and the ability that they both had of critiquing each other's work. Of taking the silliest idea and seeing where it took them. Yes, Boudleaux is sorely missed at the Rocky Top Inn in Gatlinburg, Tennessee, which they ran. However, there are still songs inside Felice to be written.

RECOMMENDED ALBUMS:

To hear their songs listen to the Cadence recordings of the Everly Brothers, listen to Carl Smith albums and too many albums by too many artists to list.

For Recordings:

"Tobacco State Swing" (Rambler) [This is Hank Penny & his Radio Cowboys' album that features Boudleaux on fiddle]

"Boudleaux Bryant's Best Sellers" (Monument)(1963)

"A Touch of Bryant" (CMH)(1980) [This is the U.S. title of DB Records' "All I Have to Do Is Dream"]

JIMMY BRYANT

(Guitar, Fiddle, Songwriter, Singer, Actor)

Given Name: Ivy James Bryant
Date of Birth: 1925
Where Born: Moultrie, Georgia
Married: 1. Gloria E. Davis (div.)
2. Patricia Murphy
Children: Jay Roy Murphy, John Clayton Murphy, Gloria Faye ("Cookie"), Patricia Ivy, Tootie, Donna Sue ("Bug"), Corrina Lynn ("Bodie"), Anne Lorraine
Date of Death: September 22, 1980

One of the finest guitarists to grace the Country stage, Jimmy was known as "the Fastest Guitar in the Country."

He started out as a fiddle player at the tender age of 5, playing hoedowns alongside his father. He and his father made a living playing on street corners, at tobacco markets and in barber shops. After his father had stopped traveling, Jimmy continued. While in Panama City, Florida, during 1936-1938, Jimmy played fiddle to Hank Williams' guitar.

Jimmy went into the Army (infantry) in 1941, where he learned to play guitar. For 18 months, he served in France and Germany. He was wounded and was transferred into Special Services. While in the forces, he first heard Django Reinhardt, who was one of the major influences on most guitarists of this period. After leaving the service in 1946, Jimmy headed to Washington, D.C., where he bought his first guitar and amplifier out of his mustering-out pay. In D.C., he played on station WRC.

Jimmy returned to Georgia, where he continued to play hoedowns. In 1947, he joined Russell "Lucky" Hayden and they traveled to Los Angeles. Hayden had played fiddle for Hopalong Cassidy (William Boyd). Tex Williams asked Bryant to play guitar and fiddle on a session for him, with the result that Bryant signed a long-term contract with Capitol.

Jimmy became a member of the Sons of the Pioneers and as such appeared in 12 Roy Rogers movies and was under contract to Republic Studios as an actor. In 1949, he joined the *Roy Rogers Radio Show* and was on the program until 1953. The following year, he became a member of Cliffie Stone's *Hometown Jubilee* from Hollywood. He stayed on the show for 11 years. At the same time, he was also a member of the *Spike Jones Show* as well as being a regular on the *Louella Parsons Show*.

When he and steel player Speedy West got together in 1953, the musical sparks flew. Their first album was ***Two Guitars Country Style*** which was originally issued as a 10" album. From 1953 through 1957, Capitol paired them for 12 singles, which resulted in them being named in 1956 as "Best Instrumental Group of Less Than Six" in a DJ Poll. Their greatest hits were *Speedin' West* (1953), *Jammin' with Jimmy, Stratosphere Boogie* and *Frettin' Fingers.* Over the years, Jimmy played on sessions for Kay Starr, Stan Kenton, the Ventures, the Monkees, Billy May, Tennessee Ernie Ford, Bing Crosby and Roy Rogers. It is therefore remarkable that he did not read music until he had become a session musician and then not comfortably. According to Speedy West, when Jimmy's 1960 album ***Country Cabin Jazz*** was about to be released, he was unwilling to have his photo taken for the cover and so guitarist Billy Strange's photo was used instead.

Jimmy Bryant was also an able songwriter. As far back as 1951, Tennessee Ernie Ford and Joe "Fingers" Carr had recorded his *Tailor Made Woman* and taken it to Top 10 status. With Speedy West, Jimmy had a taste of the Country charts in 1967 with the instrumental *Shinbone* under the name of Orville and Ivy on Imperial. In 1968, Jimmy's song *Only Daddy That'll Walk the Line* was recorded by Waylon Jennings and was a Top 3 hit that year. He had also had songs recorded by Jody Miller, Connie Smith and the Stone Poneys.

In 1966, Jimmy signed to the Imperial label. He died in 1980, after a two-year fight with lung cancer.

RECOMMENDED ALBUMS:

"Two Guitars Country Style" (Capitol)(1954) [With Speedy West]

"Country Cabin Jazz" (Capitol)(1960) [Re-issued by Stetson UK in original sleeve (1989)]

"Bryant's Back in Town" (Capitol)(1966) [Re-issued by Stetson UK in original sleeve (1992)]

"Play Country Guitar with Jimmy Bryant" (Dolton)(1967)

"For the Last Time" (Step One)(1990) [With Speedy West]

GARY BUCK

(Singer, Songwriter, Guitar, Bass Guitar, Industry Executive)

Given Name: Gary Ralph Buck
Date of Birth: March 21, 1940
Where Born: Thessalon, Ontario, Canada
Married: 1. Jean (div.)
2. Deborah Way
Children: Raymond, Trudy Lynn, Kailie, Christine, Matthew

The history of Country music is very important to Gary Buck. For several years, he worked on the establishment of the Canadian Country Music Hall of Fame. It was initially located in the Country music capital of Canada, Hamilton, and in 1988 opened its doors. Gary became President of the Hall of Fame, which in 1992 was relocated to Swift Current, Saskatchewan. Gary Buck should qualify for induction because for over 35 years he has been one of the prides of Canadian Country.

Gary made his professional debut in 1958 and the same year appeared on the Ray Koivisto *Country Caravan Show* on radio CKCY out of Sault Ste. Marie. He released his first album for Canatal Records and then in 1963, he signed with Petal Records. That year he had his first taste of chart success in the States. *Happy to Be Unhappy* made it to the Top 15 and stayed on the lists for over 4 months. At the time, Gary was still working as a cost analyst for Algoma Steel Co. When he was voted "Best Newcomer of the Year" by *Cash Box*, Gary knew that his future lay in Country music.

In 1964, Gary made his second trip into the Country charts with *The Wheel Song*. He hosted *The Gary Buck Show* on CKCO-TV in Kitchener, Ontario, from 1965 through 1967. In 1966, he moved over to the major league with Capitol Records but had no major successes although he did make a guest appearance at the *Grand Ole Opry* that year. In 1968, he joined Beechwood Music as General Manager. While with the company, he signed *Snowbird, Put Your Hand in the Hand* and *Countryfied.* However, as the publishing house was a part of Capitol Records, he felt restricted and in 1972, he set up his own Broadlands Music. He was by now producing other Canadian artists, including Tommy Hunter and Dick Damron, for his own Broadlands label. Other artists on the label included Ian Tyson and Dallas Harms. That year, *The Gary Buck Show* (eight episodes) was syndicated by CKCO-TV and shown across Canada.

Gary continued to tour with his band, Loose Change. He didn't record for his own label as a matter of deliberate policy so that the other artists could not accuse him of possible bias. In 1973, he visited New Zealand as part of the *Miss New Zealand Show*. While there, he met Maori singer/entertainer Eddie Low and they subsequently recorded the duet of *Pokarekare Ana* in 1975. During that year, he returned to New Zealand to do a TV series for South Pacific Television entitled *A Touch of Country*.

Canadian Country star ***Gary Buck***

Gary toured the U.K. to promote the Calgary Exhibition and Stampede in 1979. The following year, he visited Germany to supply the music for Calgary's successful Winter Olympics bid. On August 19, 1980, his hometown of Sault Ste. Marie named that day as Gary Buck Day in recognition of his success and endeavors. At the beginning of 1982, Gary returned to the Country charts with his Dimension recording of *Midnight Magic*. He cut back on his touring to concentrate on his CCMA work, but in 1987 Ed Preston at Tembo lured him back into the studio and the initial single from the session, *Blossom,* made its way to the top of the Canadian Country charts. He followed that in 1992 with *One Step of a Two Step*. His records are now being released on GB Records.

Over the years, Gary has won a slew of Canadian awards including being a six-time winner of the Juno/Big Country Awards "Male Vocalist of the Year" as well as "Producer of the Year" in 1975, and Broadlands was voted "Label of the Year." Gary was one of the Founding Directors of the Academy of Country Music Entertainment, which became the Canadian Country Music Association. He was elected in 1990 for a two-year term as International Director of the CMA. This was his fifth term and on two occasions in this capacity he was invited to the White House. Gary was one of five recipients of a "Medal of Worth" from the city of Sault Ste. Marie for his outstanding contributions to the music industry.

He now splits his time between Kitchener, Ontario, and Nashville, where he set up in 1991 a U.S. operations base. Broadlands International Records goes from strength to strength and had among its artists Gene Watson. Gary is also producing Billie Jo Spears, George Hamilton IV and Penny DeHaven. Among Gary's other industry involvements was his 1992 assignment as Hank Snow's literary agent for Hank's autobiography.

RECOMMENDED ALBUM:
"Gary Buck's Country Scene" (Tower)(1967)

JIMMY BUFFETT

(Singer, Songwriter, Guitar)
Date of Birth: **December 25, 1946**
Where Born: **Pasagoula, Mississippi**
Married: **1. div.**
2. Jane Slagsvole (b. 1951)
Children: **Savannah Jane**

In the words of Jimmy's 1978 double live album, *"You Had to Be There."* When listening to the idiosyncratic songs of Jimmy Buffett, it helps to be parked inside his head. In Buffett's own words, he is a "professional misfit" and he also avers that he doesn't let his education get in the way of his writing.

Jimmy inherited his twin loves of the sea and music from his much adored grandfather, Captain James Delaney Buffett. Jimmy encapsulated the stories that he heard from grandfather in the touching song *The Captain and the Kid*, written just after his grandfather died.

After graduation from high school, Jimmy went to Auburn University in Mississippi, but he paid more attention to his music than to his studying and he and some other students got involved in playing Folk music. He dropped out of university and because he didn't much like the idea of going to Vietnam, he enrolled at Pearl River Junior College in Poplarville, Mississippi, with the intention of becoming a journalist. He became a member of a Folk trio playing coffee houses and college dances as a spare-time thing.

Jimmy got married and decided to return to university to get his degree and attended the University of Southern Mississippi. He joined another Folk group, the Upstairs Alliance, and spent more time in New Orleans than at college, getting a regular gig at the Bayou Room on Bourbon Street. Despite this, in 1969, he graduated with a B.S. degree, majoring in history and journalism.

While playing gigs around New Orleans and the Gulf Coast, he met Milton Brown, who dabbled at writing and owned a small recording studio. With Brown's help, Jimmy recorded his first single, *Abandoned on Tuesday*, which was sold at gigs. Brown then got a songwriting deal with Snuff Garrett and went on to write *Every Which Way But Loose* among others.

In 1971, Jimmy moved to Nashville, found no interest in his songs and got a job with *Billboard* as a reviewer. Jimmy caught the attention of songwriter, producer and singer Buzz Cason, and in 1972, Cason recorded *Heavy Dudes and Heartaches*, a song that he had written with Jimmy, for release on Caprice. Cason also got Tompall and the Glaser Brothers to cut *The Christian* and *Tin Cup Chalice*, both of which turned up three years later on an album.

That year, Jimmy recorded an album, ***Down to Earth,*** for Barnaby (a label owned by Andy

Williams), which was released in 1972. However, the follow-up album, ***High Cumberland Jubilee***, was lost somewhere in the vaults and didn't get released until 1976, by which time Buffett was successful.

Jimmy was more than a little peeved at the situation and, in company with Jerry Jeff Walker, turned his back on Nashville and went to Miami and from there to Key West. He wrote with Jerry Jeff and their *Railroad Lady* became one of Lefty Frizzell's final chart hits. It was also recorded by Merle Haggard. Don Gant, then producing for ABC Dunhill Records, persuaded Jimmy to come back to Nashville in 1973, and the result was the splendid ***A White Sport Coat and a Pink Crustacean.*** From this, Jimmy tasted his first chart success. *The Great Filling Station Holdup* climbed into the Top 60 in the Country charts.

It was with the next album that success really came to Jimmy. ***Living and Dying in 3/4 Time*** contained the memorable *Come Monday*. Although it again only made the Country Top 60, it crossed over into the Pop Top 30 and was a turntable hit in Europe. This led to him appearing as the opening act for James Taylor, the Eagles and Linda Ronstadt.

During 1975 and 1976, he released ***A1A*** and ***Havana Daydreamin'*** (his first album on ABC) and Barnaby finally issued the album ***High Cumberland Jubilee***. Jimmy's music was also found in 1975 on the soundtrack of the United Artists movie *Rancho Deluxe,* which starred Jeff Bridges and Sam Waterston. A soundtrack album was released on UA. During that year, Jimmy put together his band, the Coral Reefer Band, with Roger Bartlett (guitar), Greg "Fingers" Taylor (harmonica, piano), Harry Dailey (bass guitar) and Phillip Fajardo (drums). Jimmy also had a medium-sized crossover hit with *Door Number Three*. However, it was the 1977 Norbert Putnam-produced album, ***Changes in Latitudes, Changes in Attitudes,*** that projected Buffett into the major artist realms. From this came the smash hit *Margaritaville*. It went into the Pop Top 10 and hung around for over five months. It was also a big Country hit and made the Top 15. The follow-up was the album's title track and was also a crossover hit. By 1977, the album had gone Platinum.

Such was Jimmy's fan base that the 1978 album ***Son of a Son of a Sailor*** went Platinum shortly after release. That year, he had a further Pop hit with the very funny *Cheeseburger in Paradise* and this was followed by the crossover hit *Livingston Saturday Night*. The year finished off with the lower level Pop single *Manana*. During the year, he released the live double album ***You Had to Be There***, which featured Jimmy in a leg cast and was recorded at the Fabulous Fox in Atlanta, Georgia, and the Maurice Gusman Cultural Center, Miami. It has to be one of the finest live productions, although it would appear to be even more pleasurable if you were "stoned." It also featured a great version of *Why Don't We Get Drunk (and Screw)*, which although not written by Jimmy has been a Buffett tour de force for many years. He was also featured in two movies that year, *FM* with Michael Brandon and *Goin' South* with Jack Nicholson.

Volcano was recorded on the island of Montserrat and released on MCA in 1979. Two singles from it made the Pop charts, *Fins* and the title track. The album went Gold soon after release. Barnaby now put all their recorded tracks together for a double album, ***Before the Salt.*** The following year, Jimmy along with so many others appeared in the watershed movie *Urban Cowboy* singing *Hello Texas*. That same year, he released the album ***Coconut Telegraph*** and had a low-level Pop chart hit, *Survive*. He returned to Nashville to record ***Somewhere Over China*** and from this came the 1981 Top 60 Pop chart single *It's My Job*.

The 1983 album ***One Particular Harbor*** included his versions of Van Morrison's *Brown Eyed Girl*, Rodney Crowell's *Stars on the Water* and Steve Goodman's *California Promises*. Jimmy had some production heavyweights at the tiller for his 1984 album ***Riddles in the Sand.*** These were Jimmy Bowen, Mike Utley and Tony Brown. Like others before, it was dedicated to Jimmy's wife Jane, whom he had married at Redstone Castle near Aspen (it is alleged that the champagne cost $3,000). Some of the drawings on the inner sleeve are by Jimmy's daughter, Savannah Jane. This was much more of a Country album and three singles went onto the Country chart, *When the Wild Life Betrays Me* (Top 50), *Bigger Than the Both of Us* (Top 60) and *Who's the Blonde Stranger?* (Top 40).

"You had to be there" says ***Jimmy Buffett***

Last Mango in Paris (yes, "Mango"!) in 1985 yielded three Country chart singles, *Gypsies in the Palace*, the Top 20 hit *If the Phone Doesn't Ring It's Me* and the Top 50 *Please Bypass This Heart*. There was also the compilation ***Songs You Know by Heart—Jimmy Buffett's Greatest Hits***, which by 1989 had gone Platinum and by 1992 had sold over 2 million copies. 1986's ***Floridays*** was somewhat low-key and has Jimmy flirting with brass and percussion (including his daughter on mini congas). His 1990 album ***Feeding Frenzy*** was a return to form that was indicated by the fact that in 1992 it was Certified Gold.

However, the biggest surprise and a true indicator of how much Jimmy is admired were the sales of his 1992 4-cd box set on Margaritaville/MCA, ***Boats, Beaches, Bars & Ballads***. This 72-song collection was Certified Platinum just months after release. The only negative comment on the sleeve photo is. . .Jimmy grow back your mustache!! In 1993, Jimmy briefly returned to the Country chart with his version of Sam Cooke's *Another Saturday Night*.

Jimmy now runs a store, Margaritaville; a label, Margaritaville (artists include the splendid Evangeline); a line of tropical clothing and, of course, his boat. In addition, he's authored two *New York Times* bestsellers, *Tales from Margaritaville* and *Where Is Joe Merchant?* Although in a different genre, Jimmy Buffett is in the same league as a storyteller as Tom T. Hall and is perhaps the nearest to Ernest Hemingway with music.

RECOMMENDED ALBUMS:

Frankly all of them!! However, the following are essential.

"You Had to Be There" (double)(ABC)(1978)

"Boats, Beaches, Bars & Ballads" (4 cd box set)(Margaritaville/MCA)(1992)

WILMA BURGESS

(Singer)

Given Name: **Wilma Charlene Burgess**
Date of Birth: **June 11, 1939**
Where Born: **Orlando, Florida**

Indirectly, Eddy Arnold was responsible for this lady's success. Until she saw him in concert, she had no thoughts at all about Country music, let alone performing it. Even after hearing him, she didn't think of making a musical career.

Wilma enrolled as a physical education major at Stetson University in Florida. Just after finishing college in 1960, a Country music songwriting friend asked her to go to Nashville to sing some of his songs for some music publishers. Charlie Lamb of Sound Format publications was more interested in her singing than the songs and brought her to the attention of Owen Bradley. In 1962, she cut a single for United Artists, *Confused/Something Tells Me* and then Bradley signed Wilma to Decca in 1964. She moved to Nashville and Charlie Lamb became her manager.

Her first single for the label was *Raining on My Pillow/This Time Tomorrow* (1964). The following year, she released *Happy Fool/You Can't Stop My Heart from Breaking* and *Closest Thing to Love/When You're Not Around* and then she had her first Top 10 record with Ray Griff's *Baby*. In 1966, she released her debut ***Don't Touch Me*** album, from which the title track became a Top 15 hit. She also had major success with *Misty Blue* (Top 5), which was the title track of her 1967 successful album, ***Wilma Burgess Sings Misty Blue***. Her other hits in 1967 were *Fifteen Days* and *Tear Time* (from the album of the same name).

In 1969, Wilma had her final major chart success for Decca with *Parting (Is Such Sweet Sorrow)*. She released two more albums for Decca, ***The Tender Lovin' Country Sound*** (1968) and ***Parting Is Such Sweet Sorrow*** (1969). She released her last single for the label, *Lonely for You*, in 1970.

She left Decca and signed to Shannon Records. The company was part of Jim Reeves Enterprises. Mary Reeves Davis, Jim's widow, had wanted to put Wilma together with Bud Logan for some time. Bud had been the leader of the Blue Boys, Jim's band. Now that Wilma was under the Shannon wing, this became a reality. Wilma's recording was now under Mary's control and was split between solos and duets with Bud.

In 1974, Wilma and Bud had a Top 20 hit with *Wake Me into Love*. Her most successful outing on the label was the Top 50 *Love Is Here*, that same year. One of the finest song stylists in the business, Wilma quit the business after unjustified, malicious rumors were made against her and she decided that she didn't need that sort of pain. During the late 80's, she opened Nashville's first women's bar. She now indulges her twin passions of golf and playing cards.

RECOMMENDED ALBUMS:

"Don't Touch Me" (Decca)(1966)
"Wilma Burgess Sings Misty Blue" (Decca)(1967) [Re-released on Coral in 1973]
"Tear Time" (Decca)(1967)
"The Tender Lovin' Country Sound" (Decca)(1968)
"Parting Is Such Sweet Sorrow" (Decca)(1969)
"Wake Me Into Love" (Shannon)(1974) [With Bud Logan]

FIDDLIN' FRENCHIE BURKE

(Fiddle, Singer)
Given Name: **Leon Bourke**
Where Born: **Kaplan, Louisiana**
Children: **two**

No, it wasn't Jimi Hendrix who was the first to play an instrument behind his head and perhaps it wasn't Fiddlin' Frenchie Burke, but there is no doubt that Frenchie caused quite a stir with his antics on stage. He played his fiddle behind his back, on top of his head or lying on stage with his bow between his legs. He plays while other people hold the bow and he runs the fiddle up and down the bow.

Frenchie was taught to play by his grandfather. The fiddle he learned on had once housed a family of mice. By the time he had reached the old age of 13, he was playing with small bands in the Kaplan area. His family moved to Port Arthur, Texas, in the early 50's and three years later, Frenchie joined the U.S. Air Force as an operating room specialist. He took first place in an Air Force talent show in the Western Group Category and Western Solo Division, becoming the first double winner in the history of the competition.

After his forces stint, Frenchie went to Houston, where he worked as a machinist by day and played with Johnny Bush, Little Jimmy Dickens and Ray Price among others by night. He did his first recording while with Bush, cutting *Warm with Love in Here*. He then formed his own band, the Song Masters. His personal recording career started in 1974 with sides for TNT Records.

In 1975, Frenchie received the *Cash Box* "Instrumentalist of the Year" award, which he was to receive again in 1981. In 1975, he released his eponymous album for 20th Century Fox. From this album there were three singles released, the most notorious being *Big Mamou* (1974), which was originally released independently in Texas, Louisiana and Oklahoma but picked up by 20th Century 10 weeks later for national distribution and went Top 40. The song was written by Frenchie, didn't feature fiddle and was about incest. On the label, he is billed as Fiddlin' Frenchie Bourque and the Outlaws. He had one other significant success on the label, the Cajun evergreen *Colinda,* which made the Top 30. He also charted at the basement level with *The Fiddlin' of Jacques Pierre Bordeaux*, both in 1975. In the late 70's, Frenchie moved to Waco, Texas, and then joined the house band at the Winchester Club, Houston. In 1978, he had more minor chart action on Cherry with *Knock, Knock, Knock*.

In the 80's, Frenchie had four albums released on Delta Records. Delta also released the single *(Frenchie Burke's) Fire on the Mountain,* which just scraped into the charts in 1981, the same year of release of ***The Best of Fiddlin' Frenchie Burke,*** which was marketed exclusively through the Nashville Network. Frenchie moved to San Antonio, where it was found that he had cancer. However, he has now recovered and is once more actively performing.

RECOMMENDED ALBUMS:

"The Best of Fiddlin' Frenchie Burke" (Delta)(1981)
"Cajun Fiddle" (Delta)(1982)
"Fiddlin' Man" (Delta)(1984)

BILLY BURNETTE

(Singer, Songwriter, Guitar)
Given Name: **William Beau Burnette III**
Date of Birth: **May 8, 1953**
Where Born: **Memphis, Tennessee**

With Billy Burnette's antecedents, it's no surprise that he has made his mark in the music industry. His father was the famed rock'n'roll and Country singer Dorsey Burnette and his uncle was another Rockabilly cat, Johnny Burnette. His cousin, Johnny's son Rocky, has also followed in the family tradition.

When he was 7, Billy cut his first record, for Dot, *Hey Daddy (I'm Gonna Tell Santa on You),* on which he was backed by Ricky Nelson's band. He was billed as Billy Beau and it was released in 1961. At the time, Dorsey was also on the label. By the time he was 11, Billy was performing all over the world as part of Brenda Lee's show. He released a single on A & M in 1964, *Little Girl Big Love*, as Young Billy Beau. He started to play guitar when he was 16. Growing up in Los Angeles, Billy was exposed to the Country sounds of the Bakersfield-based artists Buck Owens and Merle Haggard as well as Glen Campbell.

He moved to Memphis in 1969 and worked with producer Chips Moman, who had just produced Elvis' *Suspicious Minds* and *In The Ghetto*. Chips took Billy under his wing, encouraging his songwriting efforts and teaching him how to engineer sessions. Danny O'Keefe's *Good Time Charlie's Got the Blues* in 1972 was one track on which Billy drove the desk.

During this time, Billy also worked as a singer/guitarist with Roger Miller, who was one of Dorsey's closest friends. Billy moved to Nashville in 1972 to concentrate on his songwriting and cut his first eponymous album that year for Entrance Records. He worked at his craft and the cuts started to come. In 1979, Kenny Rogers' associate Kin Vassy got into the charts with Billy's *Do I Ever Cross Your Mind.* The song would surface twice again via Dolly Parton and Ray Charles. Dolly had the song as the flipside of the 1974 No.1 *I Will Always Love You* and Ray had a 1984 Top 50 entry.

In 1979, Billy signed to Polydor and released another self-named album. He followed this up later in the year with ***Between Friends***. From this, Billy had his first singles chart entry with *What's a Little Love Between Friends.* The following year, Billy signed to Columbia and released another ***Billy Burnette*** album and in 1981, ***Gimme You.*** Three singles were released during 1980 and 1981 that helped to reinforce his reputation, but didn't chart.

During 1985, Eddy Raven cut Billy's *She's Gonna Win Your Heart* and took it into the Top 10. That year, Billy racked up a pair of mid level hits on MCA/Curb. *Ain't It Just Like Love* and *Try Me.* The following year, he charted at the same level with *Soldier of Love.* As a result of this action, he was nominated by the ACM as 1986 "Top New Male Vocalist."

Then fate stepped in. Lindsey Buckingham left Rock supergroup Fleetwood Mac and Billy was asked to join the band. He toured the world (three times) with Mac and appeared on their 1988 ***Greatest Hits*** album and ***Behind the Mask,*** which was recorded in 1990. He also appeared with them in England at Wembley Arena before the Prince and Princess of Wales and played on Mac's box set compilation.

In 1992, Billy returned to the Country chart with the Top 70 single on Warner Brothers, *Nothin' to Do (and All Night to Do It).* Later that year, he signed with Nashville "newboys" Capricorn Records, which had been such a driving force in Country-Rock through the 70's and 80's with the Allman Brothers, Elvin Bishop, Wet Willie and Grinderswitch. Billy's first album for the label, ***Coming Home,*** was issued the following year and the initial single was *Tangled Up in Texas.*

RECOMMENDED ALBUMS:

"Billy Burnette" (Columbia)(1980) [Includes his version of Dorsey's "Honey Hush"]
"Coming Home" (Capricorn)(1993)

DORSEY BURNETTE

(Singer, Songwriter, Guitar, Steel Guitar, Bass)
Given Name: **William Dorsey Burnette, Jr.**
Date of Birth: **December 28, 1932**
Where Born: **Memphis, Tennessee**
Married: **Unknown**
Children: **Billy and 5 others**
Date of Death: **August 19, 1979**

Neil Diamond wrote a song, *Done Too Soon,* about celebrities who had passed on long before they should have. Dorsey Burnette was in this category. His music has often been overshadowed by the achievements of his younger brother, Johnny, but he remains a seminal figure of rock'n'roll and a fine Country singer.

Dorsey developed twin leanings toward Country music and sports from an early age. His father, Dorsey, Sr., was an avid listener to the *Grand Ole Opry* and as soon as he could drive, Dorsey would go to Nashville every Saturday to the *Opry.* He also became interested in boxing.

Both Dorsey and Johnny learned to play guitar at an early age. In 1950, Dorsey met Paul Burlison at a Golden Gloves boxing match and while they were waiting for their bouts, started talking about music. They discussed the possibilities of getting together. Dorsey had by this time considered going professional as a boxer and went to St. Louis. However, he got bloodied once too often and decided to return to playing music. By 1951, Dorsey was playing steel with Bill Black, Scotty Moore and Bud Deckleman and working at Crown Electrical, where he had been training to be an electrician since 1948.

In 1952, with Johnny's persuasion, the Burnettes got together with Paul Burlison. They brought in a piano player, Doc McQueen, and a sax player, Frenchie. They got a regular gig at the Hideaway. Their act was split into Country with the trio and Rockabilly with the full group. They were heard by Bill Bond and he arranged for the Burnette Trio to cut a single for the Von label.

By 1954, they were great friends with Elvis Presley, who also worked at Crown, and he often played with them when they did a promotional job for Airways Used Cars. Elvis referred to the two brothers as the Dalton Gang because of the scrapes they got into.

The brothers went to see Sam Phillips at Sun Records, but he turned them down because of the similarity to Presley. After seeing Elvis' debut national TV appearance in January 1956, they decided to go to New York. Through the electricians' union, Dorsey and Paul got jobs in the Big Apple.

They went for an audition for the *Ted Mack Show* and although they were told that any successful acts would have to wait six months to appear, the trio made such an impression that they were on the show the following week on April 1, 1956. They won three times in a row and qualified for the final at Madison Square Garden. Henry Jerome, Ted Mack's orchestra leader, offered to manage them.

The trio went on tour that year with the other winners from the show and found that when they returned, there were recording offers from Capitol, ABC and Coral. When they arrived for their first recording session in May, they were surprised to find a full orchestra waiting. The session did not go well and the Burnettes dispensed with the orchestra. Although *Tear It Up* and *You're Undecided* were released as their first single under the credit of the Johnny Burnette Trio, they insisted that for all future recordings they go to Nashville.

By July, they were recording at Bradley's Barn in Nashville with drummer Buddy Harman, Owen Bradley on piano and Grady Martin on rhythm guitar. For the first time, Dorsey sang lead on *Sweet Love on My Mind* and *Blues Stay Away from Me.* However, success still eluded them and then in October, they lost in the Ted Mack finals. They were booked for a three-month tour of the Northeast with Carl Perkins and Gene Vincent and signed for an appearance in the movie *Rock, Rock, Rock.*

However, pressures were starting to build. The failure of three singles and Johnny being given top billing over Dorsey created problems. Dorsey left and returned to Memphis. He cut two singles in 1956 for Abbott, *Let's Fall in Love/The Devil's Queen* and *At a Distance/Jungle Magic* and then returned to Nashville in March 1957 to record with the trio, but again nothing happened and the group split up in the fall of that year.

Dorsey followed Johnny to California, where he recorded the frenetic *Bertha Lou* and *(I'm Gonna Rock) Till the Law Says Stop.* Then his luck changed not as a performer but as a songwriter. Ricky Nelson had major hits with two songs co-written by Dorsey and Johnny, *Waitin' in School* (1957) and *Believe in What You Say* (1958). Dorsey also had a monster success with Ricky Nelson's recording of his song *It's Late* (1959). Rick also recorded Johnny's *Just a Little Too Much* in 1959. Imperial Records, no doubt hoping to capitalize on the brothers' success, issued a single in 1958 of the Burnette Brothers, *My Honey/Warm Love.*

In 1959, Dorsey cut the solo single *Try/You Came As a Miracle*. Imperial carried on and released another three singles at irregular intervals through to 1963. Dorsey had by then gone to Era Records and at last made his breakthrough into the national charts. In 1960, he scored with *Tall Oak Tree*, possibly the first contemporary song about the ecology. Era released an album, ***Dorsey Burnette's Tall Oak Tree***, to capitalize on the single. Later that year, he struck again with *Hey Little One*. The label released two more singles without further success.

In 1961, he moved over to Dot and his Country leanings, which had already surfaced during his year at Era, now gave full flight. Dot released an album, *Dorsey Burnette Sings*, but still the stardom that brother Johnny had achieved eluded him. The two brothers had an instrumental one-week chart entry that year on Infinity as "the Texans" with *Green Grass of Texas*. In 1962, Dorsey became the first Country artist on Reprise.

When Johnny drowned in a boating accident in 1964, Dorsey was shattered. The effects stayed with him for some time. During the middle and latter part of the 60's, Dorsey had a house band at the Palomino Club in Los Angeles and one of his band members was a young man soon to be Country star Johnny Paycheck. Glen Campbell, who was one of Dorsey's close friends, had a 1968 hit with the Burnette song *Hey Little One*. In 1969, Dorsey had another minor success with *The Greatest Love*

By 1972, Dorsey was with Capitol and produced a regular stream of medium sized hits through 1974, the most successful being the 1972 record *In the Spring (the Roses Always Turn Red)*, which reached the Top 30 in the Country charts and *Darlin' (Don't Come Back)* in 1973, which peaked in the Top 30. Capitol released a pair of albums, ***Here & Now*** and ***Dorsey Burnette***, with which Dorsey was not happy.

By 1975, Dorsey had gone to Melodyland, for which *Molly (I Ain't Getting Any Younger)* made it into the Top 30. His next fair sized hit came in 1977 when *Things I Treasure*, which came from the album of the same title on Calliope, reached the Top 40. The album sleeve depicts Dorsey and his family, relaxed and happy.

In 1979, Dorsey signed for Elektra and was having discussions about a Las Vegas show featuring all of his and Johnny's hits. Then on August 19, he suffered a heart attack and died, at 47 years of age. The following month, his debut single for Elektra, *Here I Go Again*, entered the Country charts and reached the Top 80. A month after that, on October 12, Dorsey's friends—and he had many, including Glen Campbell, Roger Miller, Tanya Tucker and Johnny Paycheck, among many others—paid tribute to him at a benefit concert at the Los Angeles Forum.

Dorsey Burnette's rock'n'roll contributions are as raw and dynamic as any that were produced in those heady pioneering days. His inspirational songs, such as *The Magnificent Sanctuary Band*, have often been recorded; his teen songs for Ricky Nelson still sound as fresh. His son Billy Burnette has carved out a very successful career as a performer.

RECOMMENDED ALBUMS:

"Things I Treasure" (Calliope)(1977)
"The Golden Hits of Dorsey Burnette" (Gusto)
For his rock'n'roll sides:
"The Legendary Johnny Burnette Rock'n'Roll Trio" (double)(Charly UK)(1984)
"Bertha Lou Devil Queen" (Zirkon Canada)

SMILEY BURNETTE

(Singer, Songwriter, Guitar, Accordion, played an alleged 100 instruments, Comedy Actor)

Given Name:	**Lester Alvin Burnette**
Date of Birth:	**March 8, 1911**
Where Born:	**Summum, Illinois**
Married:	**Dallas McConnell (m. October 25, 1936)**
Children:	**Linda, Steve, Carolyn, Brian (all adopted)**
Date of Death:	**February 17, 1967**

The rotund Smiley Burnette, who was known as "the poor man's Bob Hope," achieved his fame during the 30's through the 50's as a sidekick to Roy Rogers, Charles Starrett and Gene Autry. During his career, he made some 350 motion pictures and wrote over 400 songs (see Movie section).

Both of his parents were ministers in the Church of Christ. At the age of 9, he made his debut playing *The Glow Worm* at a YMCA banquet in Carthage, Illinois, playing the musical saw, for which he received the princely sum of $3.00. While at high school, he had his own band and on leaving school he had a variety of jobs, finally ending up as entertainer, announcer and handyman on WDZ Tuscola, Illinois.

***Smiley Burnette** with friend*

On Christmas Eve, 1933, Smiley was hired to appear on WLS *Barn Dance* in Chicago by Gene Autry. This was the push his career needed. He made some duet recordings for Sears Roebuck's Conqueror Records and appeared with Autry and Ken Maynard in the Mascot movie *In Old Santa Fe*. From 1935 through 1942, he appeared with Autry in some 55 musical western features for Republic under the guise of "The Frog" (who always wore a floppy black hat). For the same company, Smiley featured in his own John Paul Revere westerns from 1942 through 1945. He also appeared in the early Roy Rogers movies at Republic (Smiley named Roy's horse Trigger) and alongside Charles Starrett in around 100 of the Durango Kid westerns up to 1953. During the 50's he acted in westerns with Gene Autry for Columbia.

In 1936, Smiley married a newspaper columnist, Dallas McConnell. Together, they later produced a cookbook. Smiley's songs have been recorded by Bing Crosby, Dean Martin, Red Foley, Riders of the Purple Sage, Vaughn Monroe, Ferlin Husky and George Morgan. Smiley had a home workshop in which he repaired his musical instruments and built some of the Rube Goldberg-type contraptions which he used as instruments in his movies.

Smiley's recording career covered releases on Abbott, Capitol, Bullet and Cricket. He made appearances on the *Ozark Jubilee*, *Jubilee USA*, the *Grand Ole Opry* and the *Louisiana Hayride*. He was very active, making live appearances around the U.S. including children's rodeos, which he dubbed "Buckarodeos." Smiley died on February 17, 1967, of acute leukemia. In 1971, he was inducted into the Nashville Songwriters Hall of Fame.

RECOMMENDED ALBUM:

"Ole Frog" (Starday)(1962)

JETHRO BURNS

(Mandolin, Singer, Guitar, Composer, Comedy)

Given Name:	**Kenneth C. Burns**
Date of Birth:	**March 10, 1920**
Where Born:	**Conasauga, Tennessee**
Married:	**Louise**
Children:	**John, Terry (daughter)**
Date of Death:	**February 4, 1989**

One of the world's most respected mandolinists, Jethro Burns was equally at home playing Jazz, Bluegrass and standards and like the most superb of instrumentalists he is better listened to than talked about.

Jethro grew up in Knoxville and the first mandolin he touched belonged to his brother Aytchie. When Aytchie was out, 6-year-old Jethro would play it until he far surpassed his brother's ability. By the time he was 11, Jethro and his brother played mandolin and guitar and were able to play any kind of music, but had never played Country music. When Jethro was 12, the brothers entered an amateur talent contest to be broadcast on WNOX but did not win. However, they were chosen, along with Henry D. Haynes and another lad, to form a station band called the String Dusters. During Jethro's time with this band, it was noted that he was already beginning to make the mandolin a Jazz instrument. (From this point, see the entry for Homer & Jethro.)

During the time of their comedy duo days as Homer & Jethro, Jethro and Henry recorded two albums of instrumentals, ***Playing It Straight*** and ***It Ain't Necessarily Square,*** on RCA Victor Records, both of which have become collector's items. When Slim Whitman first began recording on RCA in 1943, three beautiful performances by Slim were enhanced by the instrumental accompaniment of Jethro Burns on mandolin and Chet Atkins (Jethro's brother-in-law) on electric guitar. These singles were *Tears Can Never Drown the Flame, I'll Never Pass This Way Again* and *Please Paint a Rose on the Garden Wall.* Jethro and Henry also formed a group with Chet Atkins called the Nashville String Band. Chet had worked with Homer and Jethro early on, when they were with WNOX.

When Henry died in 1971, Jethro continued to entertain and educate others on the mandolin. He teamed up with Ken Edison when he wrote two books on how to play mandolin called *Jethro Burns' Book 1* and *Jethro Burns' Book 2*, published by Mel Bay Publications. Jethro toured with Steve Goodman in the late 70's and has worked on various instrumental projects with Chet Atkins.

Jethro's series of Jazz lps have been greatly acclaimed and his son John can be heard playing electric guitar on these albums, continuing the family tradition.

Jethro always walked a path between Country and Jazz. His mandolin playing made him a much admired and imitated musician's musician. JAB

RECOMMENDED ALBUMS:

"Jethro Burns" (Flying Fish)(1977)
"Jethro Burns Live" (Flying Fish)(1980)
"Norman Blake—Super Jam Session" (Flying Fish)(1975) [Features Jethro Burns]
"Back to Back" (Kaleidoscope)(1980) [Jethro Burns & Tiny Moore]
"Teas for One" (Kaleidoscope)(1982)
"Old Friends" (Rebel)(1983) [Jethro Burns & Red Rector]

Burrito Brothers refer FLYING BURRITO BROTHERS

BUZZ BUSBY

(Singer, Songwriter, Mandolin)

Given Name:	**Bernarr Busbice**
Date of Birth:	**September 6, 1933**
Where Born:	**Eros, Louisiana**
Married:	**Patricia Padgett (div.)**
Children:	**two**

Of the various Bluegrass musicians who helped popularize Bluegrass in the Washington, D.C., area, Buzz Busby ranks as the first to achieve prominence in the genre. Some of his original lyrics also capture the tragedy that rural people often experience in making the adjustment to urban environments. Unfortunately, Buzz personified many of the pitfalls described in his songs and, as a result, his own career has been marked by starts, stops, reversals and interruptions. However, at his best, Busby's work in music displayed both skill and innovation.

Born in rural Louisiana, young Bernarr Busbice learned to play mandolin so he could join his brothers in a local square dance band. After graduating from high school at the top of his class, he came to Washington to work for the FBI and hopefully further his education. The local honky-tonk and musical scene soon competed for his attention and the latter quickly became dominant. Two musicians in particular caught his attention, Jack Clement and Scott Stoneman. However, during the course of the 50's, many other now noted musicians worked in combination with Busby (he shortened his name for stage purposes), including Bill Emerson, Pete Pike, Eddie Adcock and Charlie Waller among others. Buzz and Pike developed a comic duo loosely patterned after Homer and Jethro that was dubbed "Ham and Scram." Buzz and Scott Stoneman spent a stint as band members for Mac Wiseman, who worked daily radio in Baltimore in 1953. Among Buzz's foremost accomplishments in the popularization of Bluegrass in the capital was his daily half-hour television program, *Hayloft Hoedown*, which ran from September 1954 for six months on WRC-TV. For periods of a few months each, Buzz and his group, the Bayou Boys, went to WWVA Wheeling, WCOP Boston and KWKH Shreveport, but they always eventually returned to his adopted city of Washington.

The Bayou Boys cut their first record, *Cold and Windy Night*, on the Sheraton label, in Boston, when Buzz along with Clement and Stoneman worked at the *Hayloft Jamboree*. While the band worked on the *Louisiana Hayride*, Buzz did his now classic singles *Me and the Jukebox* and *Lost*, for Jiffy Records. The first, with its realistic description of honky-tonk life and the second, with the haunting fiddle of Scott Stoneman, rank as two of the best examples of original traditional Bluegrass not cut in the Bill Monroe mold. Beginning in 1957, Buzz recorded several singles for Starday, including *Where Will This End, Lonesome Wind, Going Home* and *Reno Bound*. Later, in the mid-to-late 60's, Buzz cut some singles for Rebel of newer material that included the instrumental *Mandolin Twist* and *Blue Viet Nam Skies*.

In the meantime, the lifestyles described in songs like *Me and the Jukebox* and *Lonesome Road* had become all too real for Buzz, who never could adjust well to urban life and the bar room atmosphere of a nightclub musician's economic environment. Pills, alcohol and the accidents that resulted therefrom had plagued him from the mid-50's and he found himself serving six months in prison during 1961-1962. His life continued checkered with periodic downswings and recoveries.

In the late 60's, Buzz and Leon Morris got together in a band that stayed intact long enough to record some material that eventually came out on the Rounder label. Soon, however, Buzz had more problems that eventually landed him back in prison. After release, he worked in a band with Al Jones and Frank Necessary.

By the early 80's, Buzz got himself sufficiently straight to do some recordings for Webco, a company started by his brother Wayne. The Johnson Mountain Boys accompanied him on some of his more recent efforts. However, 30 years of hard living was catching up with him and in 1984, Buzz retired on a disability pension, though he still played at a special event every now and then. In retrospect, although Busby's career has been marked by some severe ups and downs, his best moments have produced some creative, exciting and memorable music. IMT

RECOMMENDED ALBUMS:

"Honkytonk Bluegrass" (Rounder)(1974) [With Leon Morris]
"A Pioneer of Traditional Bluegrass" (Webco)(1981)
"Yesterday and Today" (Webco)(1982)

JOHNNY BUSH

(Singer, Songwriter, Guitar, Drums)
Given Name: **John Bush Shin III**
Date of Birth: **February 17, 1935**
Where Born: **Houston, Texas**
Married: **Linda**

Johnny Bush is a rarity. He is one of the few Country drummers to make it as a singer. He actually started out on guitar but never progressed on it because he didn't really want to play it.

Johnny started to play and sing while still in his teens and made his professional debut in 1952 at the Texas Star Inn, San Antonio, when he was still playing guitar and also working a day job.

He switched to drums and got a gig with a small Texas band which included Willie Nelson. During the 60's, Johnny joined Willie's touring band, the Record Men. When the band broke up, Johnny became Ray Price's drummer in the Cherokee Cowboys. He got the gig after Darrell McCall and Buddy Emmons had persuaded Price.

He stayed with Price for three years, during which time Price recorded Johnny's song *Eye for an Eye*.

Johnny had been trying to get a record deal but sounding so like Ray Price went against him. It was not for nothing that he got the soubriquet "the Country Caruso." Johnny had no joy until Willie paid for a session that yielded the album and single *Sound of a Heartache*. Originally, the single was just distributed by Stop but after it picked up local interest, the label took it and Johnny Bush on board. In 1967, he hit the charts with a low entry, *You Oughta Hear Me Cry*. The following year saw his recording career blossom as he went Top 30 with *What a Way to Live* and then hit the Top 10 with *Undo the Right*. He completed the year with the Ray Price song *Each Time*.

Honky-Tonk singer ***Johnny Bush***

Johnny started 1969 with his version of Marty Robbins' *You Gave Me a Mountain*, which was also a Pop hit for Frankie Laine. Although he had several minor hits for Stop, there was nothing higher than Top 30. In 1972, Johnny had Top 20 success with *I'll Be There* for the Million label and that year, he signed to RCA. He struck with the self-penned *Whiskey River*, which became a Top 10 hit. (Willie Nelson, who published the song, recorded it in 1979 and it became his theme song.) In 1972, Johnny suffered from a major throat problem for six months and his vocal range suffered. In 1978, he was finally diagnosed as having spastic dysphonia, an uncommon neurological disorder. RCA, in the meantime, released some tracks and Johnny produced middle-sized successes. When he moved to Gusto in 1978, things did not improve. His own label, Whiskey River, had a chart basement entry in 1979 with *When My Conscience Hurts the Most*. In 1981, Johnny moved to Delta and he scraped into the lists with a new recording of *Whiskey River*.

In 1985, Johnny met Gary Catona, an Austin voice "builder." He had experimented with a radical vocal technique. He managed to work on Johnny's voice until it was about 70% of what it used to be. Johnny's duet album with Darrell McCall, ***Hot Texas Country***, on Step One in 1986, is one that any self-respecting honky-tonker should have in their collection and definitely showed that he still had what it takes.

Johnny put together a big band, the Bandoleros, that included three fiddles, keyboard player and a horn section as well as backup singers. He started to take a new drug, Botox, and found that he could now talk, but couldn't sing. He gave up the cure; singing was more important. Johnny continued to perform around San Antonio and in February 1994, he released ***Time Changes Everything***. The tapes for the album had been held along with other tapes seized when Willie Nelson's Pedernales recording studio was taken by the IRS. After a two-year legal battle, Johnny recovered his own goods. In addition, RCA released a Greatest Hits double cd, including unreleased material. This renewed interest in Johnny Bush led to a major tour.

During his career, Johnny Bush has produced some fine Honky-Tonk albums and it may be a better idea to listen to these. His chart success has no bearing on his ability as an excellent straight ahead Country singer.

RECOMMENDED ALBUMS:
"Here's Johnny Bush" (Starday)(1972)
"Greatest Hits" (Stop)(1972)
"Whiskey River/There Stands the Glass" (RCA Victor)(1973)
"Johnny Bush & the Bandoleros Live at Dance Town, U.S.A. (in Houston, Texas)" (double)(Whiskey River)(1979)
"Live From Texas" (Delta)(1982)
"Hot Texas Country" (Step One)(1986) [With Darrell McCall]
"Greatest Hits 1968-1972" (GH)(1993)
"Whiskey River/There Stands the Glass" (Whiskey River)(1993)
"Time Changes Everything" (TCE)(1994) [Features Willie Nelson and Hank Thompson]
"Greatest Hits" (double)(RCA)(1994)

Sam Bush refer NEW GRASS REVIVAL

CARL AND PEARL BUTLER

CARL BUTLER

(Singer, Songwriter, Guitar)
Given Name: **Carl Roberts Butler**
Date of Birth: **June 2, 1927**
Where Born: **Knoxville, Tennessee**
Date of Death: **September 4, 1992**

PEARL BUTLER

(Singer, Songwriter)
Given Name: **Pearl Dee Jones**
Date of Birth: **September 30, 1927**
Where Born: **Nashville, Tennessee**
Children: **Carla, Robin**
Date of Death: **March 3, 1989**

In many ways, Carl Butler was a singer's singer. For years, he produced influential and exciting records on labels like Capitol and Columbia, yet he had relatively few major chart hits. Most fans remember him chiefly for the duet with his wife, Pearl, *Don't Let Me Cross Over*, in 1962. However, those who really know something about the roots of Honky-Tonk and Bluegrass music and those who really pay attention to vocal styles and their development remember Carl Butler as one of the finest singers of the genre. He was the first to record classics like *Linda Lou*, *I Wouldn't Change You If I Could* and *Honky Tonkitis*. He merged the Old-Time "open" mountain harmony with the newer drinking and cheating songs and was one of the first to adopt Ray Price's shuffle beat to other types of songs. He and Pearl had been among the first supporters of a young Dolly Parton, with whom they worked for years in Knoxville. Carl was also a gifted songwriter whose work was recorded by, among others, Roy Acuff, Rosemary Clooney, Carl Smith and Bill Monroe.

In 1939, Carl was playing Country dances and started to sing informally. Growing up, he heard music from both directions. From Nashville, he heard the *Grand Ole Opry* and their popular young singer Roy Acuff. He found it hard to escape the latter's influence and soon he was phrasing and pitching his voice like Acuff's. From the east, Carl heard the rich mountain sounds of the Knoxville stations and later the pre-Bluegrass sounds of the Tri-Cities area (Bristol, Kingsport, Johnson City). It was the latter that attracted him first. After a stint in WWII (serving in field hospital units in Italy, Germany and Africa), Carl returned to take a job with the Bailey Brothers. In 1947, he made his recording debut with them, singing lead on their recording of *John Henry*. Soon after, he joined the Sauceman Brothers and showed he could sing what is now called Bluegrass Gospel.

By 1950, Carl was working as a soloist on Knoxville radio and had signed a contract with Capitol. His first attempts on the label were again in the Bluegrass style and featured back-up musicians like Speedy Kreise, Jake Tullock and Tater Tate. But by 1951, Carl had moved to a sound more like that of the current rage, Lefty Frizzell: an electric guitar, a romping barroom piano and steel. One of his last Capitol releases was a song called *I Need You So* that bore composer credits to Pearl Butler. Carl had met his composer in Nashville, where she had grown up, singing in school choirs and around the house and listening to the *Opry*, and subsequently they had married.

In 1952, Carl signed with Columbia and for two decades became one of the label's most steady and dependable performers. He continued to work around Knoxville, with side trip stints at Lexington and Raleigh, and to draw on the pool of talent associated with shows like *Mid-Day Merry Go Round*, *Tennessee Barn Dance* and the *Cas Walker Show*. Like most singers, he bought some songs from the legendary Arthur Q. Smith, the song peddler who sometimes stood outside studio doors selling songs as if they were apples. In August 1954, Carl cut *I Wouldn't Change You If I Could*, a Smith song that was later picked up by Reno and Smiley and later, Ricky Skaggs. Carl showed his ability with

Carl and Pearl Butler

Gospel by recording a series of sides with the Webster Brothers. None of the early records charted, however, and Carl and Pearl had to keep looking for good songs.

They finally found their song in one by another Knoxville area veteran, Penny Jay, *Don't Let Me Cross Over*. The decision was made to cut it and Pearl, who had often sung informally with Carl around the house, decided to join in on the harmony. She later recalled that it was a session of first times. It was the first time she had ever been at a session. Frank Jones, the A & R man, had just come down from Canada and this was his first session and for Carl, it was the first time he had been allowed to choose his own musicians and his own material. Frank said he thought they would probably all lose their jobs; but they didn't. Hardly! The record reached No.1 and excited everybody. Carl and Pearl had both been fans of the Bailes Brothers and their adaptation of the Pentecostal harmony to modern themes struck a chord throughout Nashville. For a time, the Butlers were the most popular male-female team in Country music. They joined the *Grand Ole Opry* in 1962, became regular members on TV shows like that of Porter Wagoner and even appeared in a feature film, *Second Fiddle to a Steel Guitar* (1963). Through the 1960's, they had 12 chart hits, including *Loving Arms* (1963), *Too Late to Try Again* (Top 10), *I'm Hanging up the Phone* and *Forbidden Street* (both 1964), *Just Thought I'd Let You Know* (1965) and *Punish Me Tomorrow* (Top 30).

Through the 1960's and 1970's, Columbia continued to issue albums by the duo, and to re-release some of Carl's older records from the 1950's. Their later albums came out on the Chart label in 1972 and the CMH Label in 1980. In later years, Pearl and Carl pretty much retired from music, staying on their Crossover Acres ranch near Franklin, Tennessee.

Two years after Pearl's death, Carl attempted a comeback, cutting a duet single with Nancy Anne, *Cut Him Loose*, on Stop Hunger Records, but it failed to score, as he did as a solo on Castle Records. CKW

RECOMMENDED ALBUMS:

"Carl & Pearl Butler's Greatest Hits" (Columbia)(1970)
"For the First Time" (Harmony)(1971) [Carl Butler solo]
"Temptation Keeps Twistin' Her Arm" (Chart)(1972)
"Carl & Pearl Butler Honky Tonkitis" (CMH)(1980)

LARRY BUTLER

(Piano, Singer, Songwriter, Record Producer, Music Publisher)

Date of Birth: **March 26, 1942**
Where Born: **Pensacola, Florida**
Married: **Several times**
Children: **Schanda Lee**

In 1979, Larry became the first and only Nashville record producer to win a Grammy Award for "Producer of the Year." He had already won a Grammy in 1975 with Chips Moman as the writers of *(Hey Won't You Play) Another Somebody Done Somebody Wrong Song*.

His career started while he was still a child. When he was 4, he began to play piano. By the time he was 6, he had guested with the Harry James Orchestra and by the time he was 10, he had sung with Red Foley. Before he had hit his teens, he was hosting his own radio show on two local stations and co-hosting a top live TV show. In 1955, he was the winner of a five-state talent contest in classical music.

Larry joined a Florida band, Jerry Woodard and the Esquires. On a trip to Nashville, he met Buddy Killen of Tree International (Nashville's top music publishing house). Killen's encouragement brought Jerry to Nashville permanently in 1963 with $3.50 in his pockets. His piano ability soon had him in demand as a session musician and he played on Conway Twitty's *Hello Darlin'* and Bobby Goldsboro's *Honey*. In the late 60's, Larry moved to Memphis and teamed up with Chips Moman. They became part of the Rock band the Gentrys, which was formed in 1963.

In 1966, Larry co-wrote the Poppies' Pop chart success *Lullaby of Love*. One of the group was Dorothy Moore, later a major R & B star. Then Larry was signed to United Artists as a solo performer and also became pianist and musical director for Bobby Goldsboro.

Larry returned to Nashville in 1969 and joined Capitol as an in-house producer. The first single he produced for the label was Jean Shepard's *Seven Lonely Days,* which became a Top 20 hit that year. At the urging of Billy Sherrill, Larry moved to Columbia Records. He worked closely with Johnny Cash, later becoming Cash's producer, pianist, musical director and studio manager.

In 1973, Larry moved to United Artists as the head of the label's Nashville division, where he signed to the label acts such as Kenny Rogers, Crystal Gayle and Dottie West. He left the label and formed Larry Butler Productions. The artists he produced included Billie Jo Spears (*Blanket on the Ground*), Charlie Rich (*You're Gonna Love Yourself in the Morning*), Mac Davis (*It's Hard to Be Humble*), Debby Boone *(Are You on the Road to Loving Me Again*), Don McLean (*Crying*) and John Denver *(Some Days Are Diamonds*).

However, it was with Kenny Rogers that

Larry achieved his greatest success. Butler worked on *Lucille, She Believes in Me, Coward of the County* and *The Gambler* among others. He also produced Kenny's hits with Dottie West that included *Everytime Two Fools Collide* and his duets with Kim Carnes that included *Don't Fall in Love with a Dreamer.*

Larry is also a fine songwriter and in addition to *(Hey Won't You Play) Another Somebody Done Somebody Wrong Song*, he wrote or co-wrote *Only the Strong Survive* (Tammy Wynette), *Standing Tall* (Billie Jo Spears) and *What's Wrong With Us Today* (Kenny Rogers & Dottie West). During 1983, Larry took off most of the year to concentrate on his songwriting.

The following year, he formed the Larry Butler Music Group and his writers included Mickey Newbury, Dean Dillon and Julie Didier. Over the next few years, the new company had hits via *The Chair, Ocean Front Property* and *It Ain't Cool*, all with George Strait, *The Factory* (Kenny Rogers), *Shine, Shine, Shine* (Eddy Raven), *Set 'Em Up Joe* (Vern Gosdin); *Homecoming '63* and *Miami My Amy* (both Keith Whitley) and his own composition, *Wonder What You'll Do When I'm Gone,* which was cut by Waylon Jennings. He then sold the company to Frank Dileo, who was Michael Jackson's manager.

In 1992, he signed a multi-album production deal with Los Angeles label JRS Records and a production deal with Horipro, a music company headed by Bob Beckham and Ron Chancey. He continues to produce, as well as heading a guidance company that evaluates and helps new acts get started in the recording business.

RECOMMENDED ALBUMS:

As an artist:

"Larry Butler and Friends" (United Artists)

"Twelve Top Country Hits of the Year (1967)" (Imperial)(1968)

As a producer:

Listen to United Artists albums by Kenny Rogers, Crystal Gayle and Dottie West.

BILLY BYRD

(Guitar, Tenor Banjo, Mandolin, Bass Guitar)

Given Name: William Lewis Byrd
Date of Birth: February 17, 1920
Where Born: Nashville, Tennessee
Married: Glena Pearl Callis (m. 1943)
Children: Beverley Lee, Charlotte Ann, Billie June, Barbara Joan

When Billy Byrd learned guitar at the tender age of 10, he did so against the wishes of his parents, but he earned the approbation of the musical world for ignoring parental advice. His mom and dad favored classical music but Billy loved Pop music and Jazz. In 1935, Billy made his radio debut on WLAC's late-night show with his brother James (d. 1937). He worked unpaid on WSIX's *Old Country Store,* where Johnnie and Jack and Kitty Wells also performed.

In June 1938, Billy earned his first money when he was hired as a background musician on the *Grand Ole Opry* on WSM. In the same year, he started to work with Herold Goodman and the Tennessee Valley Boys and played on WSM radio as well as the Opry. Billy also played with various other bands including Pop ones. At Christmas of that year, he was about to set off on a tour of East Texas and Oklahoma with several local musicians when he split his elbow in a basketball accident. As soon as he had recovered, he started to play his first love, dance band music, with among others Owen Bradley, in clubs around Nashville.

1942 was an interesting year for Billy. He got a steady gig with Francis Craig's Orchestra at the Hermitage Hotel in Nashville and then late in the year, he joined the Navy and served as a cook on a destroyer escort ship. On September 10, 1943, Billy married his childhood sweetheart. Upon his return to civilian life, Billy went to Nashville and started playing Country music again. He spent nearly two years with Wally Fowler & His Georgia Clodhoppers, leaving the group in 1948. He then went to Louisiana with the Four Deacons and played with them on the opening of KWKH's *Louisiana Hayride* in April 1948. He also played the Hayride with Curley Williams & the Georgia Peach Pickers.

It was when he joined Ernest Tubb's Texas Troubadours during the fall of 1949 that the world became familiar with this guitar wizard. He came into the band to replace Tommy "Butterball" Page and created some of the most memorable guitar licks ever played. The most memorable one was a distinctive four-note climbing phrase that had been used by Eddie Tudor on his solitary session with E.T. on a song entitled *Try Me One More Time.* Billy Byrd made it his own and played it whenever Tubb evoked that familiar phrase "Play it pretty, Billy Byrd."

In 1959, Byrd left the Troubadours but not before playing on some memorable sessions. He can be heard on *Jealous Loving Heart, Two Glasses Joe, Answer the Phone, Half a Mind* and *Letters Have No Arms.* Billy also recorded with Eddy Arnold and Red Foley. He was on Little Jimmy Dickens' *Take an Old Tater and Wait*; he also added a certain flavor to cuts by Tex Ritter, George Hamilton IV, Cowboy Copas, Webb Pierce, Leon McAuliffe and Burl Ives.

In 1950, he designed the famed *Byrdland* guitar for Gibson with another guitar great, Hank Garland. In 1959, he moved west to Van Nuys, California, to join singer/fiddle player Gordon Terry, playing local nightclubs and doing session work on albums that included ones by Tab Hunter and Tex Ritter. After just over a year, Billy returned to Nashville, where he continued as a studio musician and got a six-night-a-week gig at Shakey's Pizza Parlor. In addition, for the next six years he was a member of the house band on *The Eddie Hill Show* on early morning TV. In 1969, E.T. invited Billy to rejoin the Texas Troubadours on the road. He stayed with them for the next year. He would return to them once more before he announced his retirement from touring, in 1973.

In 1975, Billy acquired a yellow cab and put it on the road twelve hours a day driving the 4:30 a.m. to 4:30 p.m. shift. It seemed a strange way to retire from the road! However, Billy's career found time for his own recording endeavors. In 1959, he recorded *I Love a Guitar* for Warner Brothers (which had sleeve notes by E.T.), *Lonesome Country Songs* (Reprise, 1962), *The Golden Guitar of Billy Byrd* also on Warner Brothers, 1964 and *Gospel Guitar* (Scripture) with the Ranger.

The first recording with Ernest Tubb was on November 8, 1949 and was *Tennessee Border No. 2,* which featured Tubb and Red Foley. The last Tubb session he did was on February 20, 1974 during his last tour with E.T. He cut *Anything but This* and *Don't Water Down the Bad News.* Billy also played on the famed tribute to Tubb, *The Legend & the Legacy*, that was assembled by Pete Drake.

Billy Byrd has given Country music the benefit of his talent over many years and the man who could play any string instrument (he also played tenor banjo, mandolin and electric bass) has given us a virtual treasure house of guitar pickin' and grinnin'.

RECOMMENDED ALBUMS:

Any Ernest Tubb album that Billy appeared on.

"I Love a Guitar" (Warner Brothers)(1960)

"Lonesome Country Songs" (Warner Brothers)(1962)

"The Golden Guitar of Billy Byrd" (Warner Brothers)(1964)

"Gospel Guitar" (Scripture)

JERRY BYRD

(Steel Guitar, Hawaiian Guitar)

Given Name: Jerry Lester Byrd
Date of Birth: March 9,1920
Where Born: Lima, Ohio
Married: Thelma Marie McWiley
Children: Lani Jo, Luana June

There can't be too many musicians who are hailed with near reverence, but that is the case with Jerry Byrd, who has attained that level of respect in Hawaii.

When he was a child, Jerry Byrd had a thing about Hawaiian music that has remained with him all his life. He was never happy with pedal steel guitar stylings and kept to his Hawaiian guitar ones, yet was one of the main players that made the steel guitar so much an integral part of Country music.

In the 1930's, he moved into Country music and from 1935 to 1937 was playing on WLOK Lima. In 1938, he began playing on WLW in Cincinnati. He stayed there until the next year and then moved to WHAS Louisville. Jerry became a regular member of the *Renfro Valley Barn Dance* in 1941. By 1942, he was on the move again, this time to WJR Detroit. He stayed there until 1944 when he joined Ernie Lee's Pleasant Valley Boys. He remained with Lee until 1946, taking time out to appear with Ernest Tubb and Red Foley at the *Grand Ole Opry* from 1945 through 1947.

In 1946, Jerry created his own band, the Jay-Bird Trio. A year later, he appeared in the movie *Hollywood Barn Dance*. By 1948, he had joined Red Foley's band and was a member of the elite musicians corps at King Records that included Zeke Turner (electric guitar), Louis Innis (rhythm guitar) and Tommy Jackson (fiddle). While at King, he released a pair of singles. He cut *Mountain Mambo* with the Country Cats while *Sun Shadows* was recorded under the name of Jerry Robin, again with the Country Cats.

In 1948, he made his first solo recordings for Mercury. Between 1948 and 1952, he turned out some fine 78s that included *Steelin' the Blues* (1948), *Limehouse Blues* (1950), *Wabash Blues* (1951), *Beyond the Reef* and *St. Louis Blues* (both 1952). During his stay with the label, he started to record Hawaiian tracks that were also released as singles, including *Hilo March*, *Paradise Isle* and *My Isle of Golden Dreams*. Between 1951 and 1960, Mercury released nine albums by Jerry Byrd, about half of them being his Hawaiian recordings.

Jerry became a regular with Red Foley on WLW *Midwestern Hayride* and from 1950, he was on NBC-TV's televising of the show. During 1952 to 1954, he recorded some sides for Decca with the Paradise Trio, including *Song of Love* and *Paradise Waltz*. He made some recordings for RCA Victor in 1954 and then in 1958 moved over to Fred Foster's Monument label for six albums that surfaced between 1966 and 1969. Monument also released several singles, most of which veered away from his Hawaiian music and included his version of *The Bells of St. Mary*.

From 1954 through 1956, he appeared in Nashville on WSIX-TV's *Home Folks*. He then moved to WLAC-TV's *Country Junction*, where he stayed until he became a member of Bobby Lord's TV Show Band in 1964.

After 1968, Jerry Byrd shrugged off all Country music connections and all his recorded output is of Hawaiian melodies. He moved to Hawaii, where he has now been honored with membership in the Hawaiian Music Foundation. His records have been released in Japan, South Africa, Germany, Australia, the U.K. and Italy.

RECOMMENDED ALBUMS:

Country recordings:
"Guitar Magic" (Mercury)(1954)
"Steel Guitar Favorites" (Mercury)(1958)
"Hi-Fi Guitar" (Decca)(1958)
"Admirable Byrd" (Monument)(1966) [Re-released on Vintage Classics]

Hawaiian recordings:
There are around 30 excellent albums but of note are:
"Byrd of Paradise" (Monument) [Re-released on Vintage Classics]
"Hawaiian Golden Hits" (Mercury) [With the Royal Hawaiian Guitars]
"Hawaii's Greatest Instrumentals" (Lehua) [With the New Hawaiian Band. Also on Trim Records]

ROBERT BYRD

(Fiddle, Politician)

Given Name:	**Robert C. Byrd**
Date of Birth:	**November 20, 1917**
Where Born:	**North Wilkesboro, North Carolina**
Married:	**Erma Ora James**
Children:	**Mona, Marjorie**

Best known as a powerful and prominent figure in the American political system, Robert Byrd also plays a very creditable fiddle to Old-Time and/or Bluegrass accompaniment. Traditional music and politics have often mixed quite well in the Appalachian and southern scene going at least as far back as the celebrated Tennessee governor's race of 1886 when brothers Robert L. and Alfred A. Taylor competed on the stump with both oratory and fiddle bow. Byrd represents the most recent example of a tradition that also includes such colorful individuals as W. Lee O'Daniel and Jimmie Davis. He was born in western North Carolina into the family of a furniture worker. Robert Byrd's mother died when he was still a baby and he was brought up by an aunt and uncle in Stotesbury, West Virginia. Byrd attended the local high school, graduating at the head of his class, and then worked as a butcher and meat cutter for various stores in Raleigh County, West Virginia. When WWII started, he went to Baltimore, learned the welding trade and labored in the shipyards.

After the war he and his wife went back to West Virginia and purchased a grocery store in the town of Sophia. Robert also attended classes at Concord College and, in 1946, ran successfully for a seat in the lower house of the State Legislature. After a second term, he went to the State Senate for two years. In 1952, Byrd was elected to the U.S. Congress, where he served three terms. In 1958, he won a seat in the U.S. Senate and was reelected in 1964, 1970, 1976, 1982 and 1988. He has been majority and minority floor leader and has received national fame above all else for the large number of federal tax dollars he has channeled into the Mountain State.

Byrd has also maintained his interest in traditional fiddle music. He began to play the instrument at the age of 12 and is self-taught save for a few informal lessons from his future father-in-law and listening closely to records by the Kessinger Brothers in the early 30's. He played square dances from his mid-teens. Music historian Linnell Gentry, who worked with him in the grocery, recalls Byrd trading licks and techniques with various musicians from WJLS Beckley when they stopped by the store. Fiddling played an important role in his early political campaigns where it attracted both attention and votes. As late as 1956, cartoons in Mountain State newspapers often termed him "Fiddlin' Bob Byrd" and portrayed him as such.

Byrd's fiddling also attracted attention from traditional music enthusiasts and scholars. He played for various entertainment events and parties in Washington and made a guest appearance on the *Grand Ole Opry*, recorded several reels of tape for the Library of Congress and made an album of traditional tunes and songs for County Records in February 1978. It included items like *Cumberland Gap* and *Forked Deer*, old Country numbers such as *Don't Let Your Sweet Love Die* and one newer piece, Kris Kristofferson's *Come Sundown*. James Bailey and Doyle Lawson of the Country Gentlemen accompanied him on the session.

In the 80's, Robert Byrd continued his interests in traditional music. He often twin-fiddled around the nation's capital with well-known Bluegrass sideman Joe Meadows and talked of cutting another album. Byrd also demonstrated regard for the historical development of the idiom by authoring the foreword to Ivan Tribe's book *Mountaineer Jamboree: Country Music in West Virginia* in 1984.

IMT

RECOMMENDED ALBUM:

"U.S. Senator Robert Byrd: Mountain Fiddler" (County)(1978)

TRACY BYRD

(Singer, Songwriter, Guitar)

Date of Birth:	**December 18, 1966**
Where Born:	**Vidor, Texas**
Married:	**Susan**

Tracy Byrd is among the third wave of new traditionalists that are helping to turn the tide of Pop-Country back toward pure Country.

Tracy's parents are hardcore Country fans and he visited the *Grand Ole Opry* while still being carried in his mother's arms. His father worked for 30 years with DuPont and his mother was a teacher's assistant and she drove a school bus.

Tracy attended Southwest Texas State in San Marcos and after a year of business courses transferred to Lamar University in Beaumont, Texas. He was very shy about singing in public and made his first recording in the privacy of a shopping mall "recording studio," where he put his voice onto *Your Cheatin' Heart*. He so impressed the saleswoman that she invited him to perform on a monthly amateur show. He sang *Folsom Prison Blues* and *Weary Blues from Waiting* and got a standing ovation. This persuaded him what career he should follow.

Tracy started as a solo act, while working days as a runner for a law firm and later as a house painter. He landed a job playing with Mark Chesnutt, then headlining at Cutters nightclub in Beaumont. When Mark became successful and hit the road, Tracy formed his own band and starred at the club.

After 10 months, he sortied to Nashville without success. However, on his next trip, he showcased and then, accompanied by just his guitar, Tracy auditioned for MCA's Bruce Hinton and Tony Brown. Tracy signed with MCA and Keith Steagall produced Tracy's self-named album. The first single, *That's the Thing About a Memory,* only went Top 75 in 1992, but the follow-up in 1993, *Someone to Give My Love To*, reached the Top 50.

Tracy hit pay dirt with the third single, *Holdin' Heaven*, which went all the way to No.1, with his final single of 1993, *Why Don't That Telephone Ring*, reaching the Top 40. Tracy's second album, ***No Ordinary Man***, was produced by Jerry Crutchfield and released in 1994; Tracy co-wrote two of the titles, *Redneck Roses* and the title track. During 1994, *Lifestyles of the Not So Rich and Famous* reached the Top 20. Meanwhile, Tracy and his band, Only Way to Fly, are building up a very healthy fan base.

RECOMMENDED ALBUMS:

"Tracy Byrd" (MCA)(1993)
"No Ordinary Man" (MCA)(1994)

BYRDS

Formed:	**1964**
Members:	
Roger McGuinn	**12-String Guitar, Vocals**
David Crosby	**Guitar, Vocals**
Chris Hillman	**Bass Guitar, Vocals**
Gene Clark	**Vocals, Percussion**
Michael Clarke	**Drums**
Kevin Kelley	**Drums**
Gram Parsons	**Guitar, Keyboards, Vocals**
Gene Parsons	**Drums, Vocals**
Clarence White	**Lead Guitar, Vocals**
John York	**Bass Guitar, Vocals**
Skip Battin	**Bass Guitar, Vocals**
John Guerin	**Drums**

Looking at Pete Frame's family tree of the Byrds and the Country-Rock and Folk-Rock groups they generated on the album ***The History of the Byrds***, it makes it easy to see the importance of this group. These groups have included the Flying Burrito Brothers, Country Gazette, the Eagles, Crosby, Stills, Nash & Young and Dillard & Clark.

The seed of the group was generated in June 1964, when Gene Clark saw Jim McGuinn (who re-named himself Roger in 1968, following his involvement with the Subud movement) at the Los Angeles Troubadour doing Beatles covers during his Folk act. Clark suggested they put a group together. McGuinn (b. July 13, 1942) had started his career as accompanist for the Folk group the Limeliters in 1960. After less than two months with them, he moved on and played Greenwich Village in New York as a solo Folk singer and then joined the Chad Mitchell Trio. He left them in 1962 and backed Bobby Darin for another two years. During this time, he also did session work for Tom & Jerry (Simon & Garfunkel), Judy Collins and the Irish Rovers.

Gene Clark (b. November 17, 1941/d. May 24, 1991) had been a singer and guitar player with the New Christy Minstrels for a couple of years before the fateful meeting with McGuinn. The twosome brought in David Crosby (b. August 14, 1941) to play bass and formed the Jet Set. Crosby had been playing as a solo Folk singer. The Jet Set recorded two tracks which eventually wound up on the Together label album ***Early L.A.,*** also known as ***Early Flight***.

It soon became apparent that more than a trio was needed to play the music they wanted to play and they brought in Chris Hillman (b. December 4, 1942) and Michael Clarke (b. June 3, 1943). Hillman had played with the Scottsville Squirrel Barkers and had recently been a member of the Hillmen with Vern and Rex Gosdin and Don Parmley (who would later form the Bluegrass Cardinals). Clarke hadn't played with any group before joining. Their rehearsals were recorded by their manager, Jim Dickson, and the tracks were released on Bumble Records as ***Preflyte*** that year. They released a single, *Please Let Me Love You/Don't Be Long*, on Elektra as the Beefeaters.

They signed to Columbia Records as the Byrds with Doris Day's son, Terry Melcher, as their producer. Their first single, Bob Dylan's *Mr. Tambourine Man,* was released in the spring of 1965, as Columbia publicity avers, to "bridge the gap between Bob Dylan and the Beatles." The single, featuring what was to be the trademark 12-string Rickenbacker guitar of McGuinn, became an enormous hit. It went to No.1 on the Pop chart and became an international success when it also became No.1 in the U.K. This was followed by their debut album of the same name, which was also successful.

Their next single, *All I Really Want to Do,* only reached the Top 40, but was again a major hit in Britain, where it reached No.4. In the fall, they released *Turn! Turn! Turn! (To Everything There Is a Season).* This song was a tract from the Book of Ecclesiastes that had been adapted by Pete Seeger. It went to No.1, where it stayed for three weeks.

In 1966, the Byrds released the album ***Turn, Turn, Turn*** and Gene Clark decided to leave the group as he developed a fear of flying. He joined the Gosdin Brothers, and apart from a brief return to the Byrds in 1967, the rest of his career appears in a separate entry (see Gene Clark). During the year, the group released several singles of which the most successful were *Eight Miles High* (which got banned by a lot of radio stations for alleged drug connotations), which went Top 15, and *Mr. Spaceman*, a Top 40 entry. During the late summer, they released their third album, ***Fifth Dimension***.

1967 was a mixed year for the Byrds. They started the year with the Top 30 hit *So You Want to Be a Rock'n'Roll Star* and then did a short tour of England. They then had their last major singles hit, Bob Dylan's *My Back Pages,* which went Top 30. They also released the ***Younger Than Yesterday*** album. However, in the fall, David Crosby was asked to leave, which he did, taking a large financial settlement which he spent on a yacht. Later that year, he formed Crosby, Stills & Nash with Stephen Stills and Graham Nash.

During the recording of ***The Notorious Byrd Brothers***, in 1968, Michael Clarke decided to give up music and drummer Jim Gordon completed the album. Also on the album are steel guitarist Red Rhodes and guitarist Clarence White. During the year, their ***Greatest Hits*** album was Certified Gold and would reach Platinum status in 1986. Chris Hillman's cousin Kevin Kelley, who had played with Taj Mahal's Rising Sons, joined the group as drummer.

Then Gram Parsons (b. November 5, 1946/d. September 19, 1973) came on board and persuaded the group to adopt a more Country musical stance. This led to the recording of ***Sweetheart of the Rodeo,*** which also featured as guests John Hartford, Lloyd Green, Junior Husky and Earl Ball. However, on the eve of their tour of South Africa, Parsons quit and the group's roadie, Carlos Bernal, impersonated him on the tour. Both steelie Sneaky Pete and banjo star Doug Dillard played on some gigs with the band during this time.

On their return, there was total chaos. Kelley was fired and Hillman quit and formed the Flying Burrito Brothers, allegedly unhappy with the group's management. Now only McGuinn was left. He was joined by Clarence White (b. June 4, 1944/d. July 14, 1973), Gene Parsons (b. April 9, 1944) and John York. White was already a near legend with his work with his family group, the Kentucky Colonels. York had played with Sir Douglas Quintet and had been an avid Byrds fan but became overwhelmed at playing with the group, and after recording ***Dr. Byrds & Mr. Hyde***, in 1969, he left to become a studio musician.

His place was taken by Skip Battin (b. Clyde Battin, February 2, 1934) and for over three years, the line-up was stable. They recorded ***Ballad of Easy Rider*** and ***Untitled*** (both 1970) and ***Byrdmaniax*** (1971). From the latter came *Chestnut Mare*, a U.K. Top 20 single. The group made several overseas tours including appearing at the Bath and Lincoln Festivals in Britain.

The last album they recorded together was ***Farther Along*** in 1972, then Gene Parsons left and signed to Warner Brothers Records as a solo performer. By 1973, each of the members was involved in solo projects. They recorded an eponymous album for Asylum that year, but then it was decided to fold the band after that.

McGuinn went on to be a member of Bob Dylan's Rolling Thunder Revue. In 1977, McGuinn formed Thunderbyrd. He has teamed up with former members of the Byrds Gene Clark and Chris Hillman and in 1979, they had a Top 40 hit with *Don't You Write Her Off*. Every so often, the group gets together for a reunion, including the occasion in 1990 when McGuinn, Hillman and Crosby appeared together at a tribute concert to Roy Orbison.

In 1991, the original members were inducted into the Rock and Roll Hall of Fame. According to Gene Parsons, a new tour of the U.S. is being planned.

RECOMMENDED ALBUMS:

"Mr. Tambourine Man" (Columbia)(1965)
"Turn, Turn, Turn" (Columbia)(1966)
"Fifth Dimension" (Columbia)(1966)
"Younger Than Yesterday" (Columbia)(1967)
"The Byrds' Greatest Hits" (Columbia)(1967)
"Notorious Byrd Brothers" (Columbia)(1968)
"Sweetheart of the Rodeo" (Columbia)(1968)
"Dr. Byrd & Mr. Hyde" (Columbia)(1969)
"Ballad of Easy Rider" (Columbia)(1970)
"Untitled" (Columbia)(1970)
"Byrdmaniax" (Columbia)(1971)
"Farther Along" (Columbia)(1972)
"Preflyte" (Columbia)(1972) [Originally released on Bumble (1964)]
"History of the Byrds" (CBS UK)(1973)
"The Byrds" (Asylum)(1973)
"The Byrds Play Dylan" (Columbia)(1980) [Compilation]
(See also Chris Hillman, Gene Clark, Gene Parsons, Gram Parsons, Clarence White)

C

BUDDY CAGLE

(Singer, Guitarist)

Given Name:	**Walter L. Cagle, Jr.**
Date of Birth:	**February 8, 1936**
Where Born:	**Concord, North Carolina**
Married:	**Unknown**
Children:	**Danny, Mickie**

Buddy Cagle is known today primarily for his several chart recordings in the 60's. Despite his success he had no thoughts about a career in Country music until after his discharge from the military.

Buddy grew up in the Children's Home in Winston-Salem, North Carolina, and then enlisted in the Air Force. Although he had always liked Country music and enjoyed singing, he never seriously considered becoming a professional entertainer. That all changed shortly after his discharge in the late 50's. Some friends told him he had a good voice and, with this encouragement, Buddy decided to try to find work as a singer in Southern California. He soon met other Country artists who were sufficiently impressed with his abilities that they told local record companies about him.

Wynn Stewart and Don Sessions brought Buddy to the attention of executives at Capitol, and they signed Cagle. Buddy first hit the Country chart with *Your Mother's Prayer* in 1963 and it reached the Top 30. He followed-up with Wynn Stewart's song *Sing a Sad Song*, which also reached the Top 30. Buddy disappeared from the chart for nearly two years and then reached the Top 40 with his Mercury recording *Honky Tonkin' Again*. Six months later, Buddy reached just below the Top 30 with his Imperial recording *Tonight I'm Coming Home* in 1966. The following year, he had his final chart records with Imperial, *Apologize* (Top 60) and *Longtime Traveling* (Top 75).

Buddy toured Europe three times, always to large, enthusiastic crowds, and performed on several American TV shows, In addition, Buddy frequently toured with Hank Thompson's Brazos Valley Boys. This period, however, proved to be the peak of Cagle's career rather than the beginning of a long stay in the limelight. WKM

RECOMMENDED ALBUMS:

"The Way You Like It" (Imperial)(1966)
"Mi Casa, Tu Casa" (Imperial)(1967)
"Longtime Traveling" (Imperial)(1967)
"Through a Crack in a Boxcar Door" (Imperial)(1968)

BENNY AND VALLIE CAIN

BENNY CAIN

(Singer, Mandolin)

Given Name:	**James Bennett Cain**
Date of Birth:	**May 21, 1921**
Where Born:	**New Haven, Connecticut**

VALLIE CAIN

(Singer, Guitar)

Given Name:	**Vallie R. Cave**
Date of Birth:	**July 19, 1927**
Where Born:	**Kitzmiller, Maryland**
Married:	**July 1950**
Children:	**Paul**
Date of Death:	**April 15, 1993**

Benny and Vallie Cain are a traditionally orientated husband and wife harmony duet. While they have never ascended to the high ranks of fame in the Bluegrass field, the couple deserve considerable credit for helping to popularize the music in the nation's capital. Their pleasing, but somewhat atypical, harmony blend adds a touch of uniqueness to their vocal sound.

At the age of 3, Benny Cain moved with his parents to Berkeley Springs, West Virginia, and began playing harmonica at the age of 8. Later, he began to play a little guitar and banjo, but eventually settled on the mandolin. In August 1942, young Cain joined the U.S. Navy and served four years as a gunnery officer in both Europe and the Pacific. After his discharge, Benny went to work for the U.S. Treasury in the Bureau of Alcohol, Tobacco and Firearms. He remained in the civil service until his retirement in 1985, only pursuing music as a part-time avocation.

Vallie Cave's family had moved to Berkeley Springs about 1934. In 1947, Benny met Vallie and within a few months, they had organized a band, the Country Cousins, and obtained a weekly radio program at WINC Winchester, Virginia. The couple married in July 1950 and moved to Washington, D.C. While Benny kept his day job, the Cains maintained a heavy schedule of restaurant and club appearances on week nights and often worked at parks and carnivals on weekends. The year that they married, the Cains switched from a Country to a Bluegrass instrumental format which blended well with their vocal harmony. Over the next quarter century, many well-known Bluegrass musicians worked as members of their band, the Country Clan, including Bill Emerson, Don Bryant, Johnny Whisnant, Don Stover, Scott Stoneman, Pete Kuykendall, Roni Stoneman, Don Mulkey, Tom Gray and their son, Paul Cain.

The Cains made their first recording, a single on the Adelphi label, in 1956. In 1962, they affiliated with Rebel Records, releasing three singles in the next two years. Ten additional cuts appeared on the four-album set ***Bluegrass Spectacular***, which contained a total of 70 songs and tunes, 13 by Benny and Vallie. In 1968, they did their debut album for Rebel simply titled ***Benny and Vallie Cain and the Country Clan***. Six years later, they followed with ***More of Benny and Vallie Cain***, assisted by Bill Poffinbarger on fiddle and Billy Wheeler on banjo.

In the 70's, Benny and Vallie continued their regular work at restaurants and clubs, albeit less frequently than in the two previous decades. They also worked some Bluegrass festivals. In 1982, they did a tour of Europe performing their music and in 1985, Benny retired from his position with the federal government. Over the years, Benny gained a considerable reputation as an authority on stringed instruments and also as a song collector. In 1990, Benny suffered a mild heart attack, but subsequently recovered. Benny and Vallie Cain resided in Falls Church, Virginia and were still playing an occasional weekend show date, until Vallie died in the spring of 1993. IMT

RECOMMENDED ALBUMS:
"Benny and Vallie Cain and the Country Clan" (Rebel)(1968)
"More of Benny and Vallie Cain" (Rebel)(1974)

CALAMITY JANE

Formed:	**1981**
Members:	
Pam Rose	**Vocals, Guitar, Keyboards, Bass Guitar, Banjo**
Mary Ann Kennedy	**Vocals, Guitar, Keyboards, Drums, Mandolin**
Mary Fielder	**Vocals, Guitar, Keyboards, Percussion**
Linda Moore	**Vocals, Guitar, Keyboards, Autoharp, Percussion**

This short lived all-girl group acted as a springboard for Pam Rose (b. West Palm Beach, Florida) and Mary Ann Kennedy (b. Milwaukee, Wisconsin), who went on to become one of Country music's most successful songwriting teams.

Pam Rose majored in voice and classical guitar at Florida State University. Mary Ann Kennedy majored in voice and music education at the University of Wisconsin and was a junior high choral teacher before moving to Nashville in 1978. Linda Moore (b. Nashville, Tennessee) is the daughter of bass player Bob Moore and she studied music business at Nashville's Belmont University. Mary Fielder (b. Bluffton, South Carolina) majored in voice and percussion at Florida State University. It was originally intended that Linda Hargrove and Marshall Chapman would be in the line-up with Rose and Kennedy.

The group signed to Columbia and their initial single, *Send Me Somebody to Love,* peaked just below the Top 60 in 1981. For four songwriters, it seemed strange that the follow-up was a Lennon and McCartney song, *I've Just Seen a Face.* It reached the Top 50 and stayed on the charts for a couple of months. They again chose a cover for their third single, *Walkin' After Midnight,* which also made the Top 60 in 1982.

After Mary Fielder left, Calamity Jane soldiered on as a trio. The group's final entry was the 1982 *Love Wheel,* which just scraped into the lists. The end was in sight and shortly after, they disbanded and resumed their songwriting activities.

RECOMMENDED ALBUM:
"Calamity Jane" (Columbia)(1982)

CALLAHAN BROTHERS

JOE CALLAHAN
(Singer, Yodeler, Guitar, String Bass, Comedy)

Given Name:	**Walter Callahan**
Date of Birth:	**January 27, 1910**
Date of Death:	**September 10, 1971**

BILL CALLAHAN
(Singer, Yodeler, Guitar, Bass Fiddle, Mandolin)

Given Name:	**Homer Callahan**
Date of Birth:	**March 27, 1912**
Both Born:	**Madison County, North Carolina**

The Callahan Brothers rank among the more significant duet acts of the 30's and their careers continued intermittently thereafter. Natives of the mountainous country of western North Carolina, the Callahans grew up influenced by both the traditional music of their Southern Highland homeland and early phonograph records of such pioneer figures as Ernest Stoneman, Riley Puckett, Jimmie Rodgers and especially the early yodeling duo of (Reece) Fleming and (Respers) Townsend. They utilized duet yodeling in an appearance at the Rhododendron Festival at Asheville, North Carolina, in 1933, which brought them to the attention of both the radio and record folks.

The Callahans journeyed to New York for their initial session on January 2, 1934, with the American Record Corporation. They also began radio work that same year at WWNC Asheville. While continuing to record they changed their radio base periodically to such locales as WHAS Louisville, Kentucky; WWVA Wheeling, West Virginia; WLW Cincinnati, Ohio, and KWTO Springfield, Missouri. On the record session of August 1934, their sister Alma joined them on four numbers and in December 1936, Roy ("Shorty") Hobbs picked mandolin. Well-known songs associated with the Callahan Brothers included *Little Poplar Log House, Gonna Quit My Rowdy Ways,* their country version of *St. Louis Blues* and especially *She's My Curly Headed Baby,* which attained sufficient popularity to go three versions on record and to become a standard in the field. The Callahans also did covers of many of the popular numbers introduced by other well-known duet singers of the times.

In 1940, the Callahan Brothers worked briefly at KVOO Tulsa, Oklahoma, and then went to KRLD Texas in 1941. For most of the remaining years of the 40's, the brothers headquartered at either KRLD or KWFT Wichita Falls, Texas.

The Callahans had been preceded in Texas by the brother duo of Bob and Joe Shelton, so they dropped the longer first names of Homer and Walter and took the shorter nicknames of Bill and Joe, which they used for the remainder of their careers.

In April 1941 they switched record labels,

doing a session for Decca. On these discs, Homer switched to bass fiddle while young Paul Buskirk did the mandolin work. Although they made fewer records after they went to Texas, they did make extensive transcriptions for the Sellers Company of Dallas, which were used for radio airplay.

Although they lived and worked permanently in Texas from 1941, the Callahans left long enough to make a movie, *Springtime in Texas,* with cowboy star Jimmy Wakely in 1945, with whom they then toured extensively for several months. Homer also took time out to make an extended tour of the eastern states with Ray Whitley in 1947, during which time he cut a solo disc for Cowboy Records in Philadelphia.

In 1951, the Callahan Brothers hooked up with country newcomer Lefty Frizzell and toured as his opening act for a time. However, by the 50's their music was becoming a bit dated, although they did a final session of eight sides for Columbia in October 1951 under the direction of their old boss at ARC, Art Satherly. Somewhat later, Walter Callahan returned to Asheville and entered the grocery business. Homer remained in Dallas and entered other lines of work, chiefly photography, but continued to dabble in music mostly as a bass player or comedian. For a time in the mid-60's, Walter returned to Dallas and the brothers did a few final shows together. Walter, in declining health, then returned to Asheville, where he died in 1971. Homer lives in retirement in Dallas.

Musically the Callahans were probably the ARC's chief brother duet of the 30's. The quality of their singing holds up well although most critics have not ranked them as high as the Monroe Brothers or the Blue Sky Boys. Their duet yodeling did provide them with a certain distinctness that the others lacked. The recordings of the Callahan Brothers have not been extensively reissued, but one entire album has been devoted to them and a few of their numbers have appeared on various anthologies.

IMT

RECOMMENDED ALBUM:

"The Callahan Brothers" (Old Homestead)(1975)

The Callahan Brothers from North Carolina

CAMP CREEK BOYS, The

Formed: 1930's

Members:

Fred Cockerham	Fiddle
Kyle Creed	Banjo
Paul Sutphin	Guitar
Ronald Collins	Guitar
Ernest East	Fiddle
Verlin Clifton	Mandolin
Roscoe Russell	Guitar

One of the last of the pure mountain string bands, the Camp Creek Boys came to national fame in the 1960's on the strength of recordings done for the influential independent County label. The leader was banjoist and banjo maker Kyle Creed, who named the group after the community where he grew up in the Blue Ridge Mountains—in Surrey County, North Carolina, not far from the Blue Ridge Parkway. Two other key members, fiddler (and sometime banjoist) Fred Cockerham and guitarist Paul Sutphin, were reared there too, while other members of the band were also from nearby in Surrey County.

Formed in the 1930's, the Camp Creek Boys began by playing at local dances and socials and community events like corn shuckings and barn raisings. This in turn led to local radio work and especially to appearances at the many fiddlers' conventions that began to appear in the 1930's. After live music began to decline on the radio, these Old-Time music contests and conventions became the main outlet for preserving the old ensemble sound of the classic Galax area string bands like the Camp Creek Boys. Creed, in fact, eventually settled in Galax, where he operated a store and became a central figure in the revival of interest in the music in the 1960's.

Larger than the classic three-piece (fiddle, banjo, guitar) mountain string band, the Camp Creek Boys had a sound that depended on the additional rhythm support of two guitars as well as Verlin Clifton's mandolin. People like Creed and Cockerham could still play the older form of string band music that featured only the banjo and fiddle, but the overall sound of the full ensemble is what made the band so influential in the late 1960's. Their best known tunes included *Fortune*, *June Apple*, *Cider Mill*, *Honeysuckle* and *Let Me Fall*—the last of which made it into modern Bluegrass circles. They eventually completed four albums for the County and Mountain labels.

CKW

RECOMMENDED ALBUMS:

"Blue Ridge Square Dance" (Mountain)
"June Apple" (Mountain)
"The Camp Creek Boys" (Mountain)
"The Camp Creek Boys" (County)

ALEX CAMPBELL & OLA BELLE

Formed: 1946

ALEX CAMPBELL

(Singer, Songwriter, Banjo)

Date of Birth: 1922

OLA BELLE

(Singer, Songwriter, 5-String Banjo)

Given Name: Ola Belle Campbell

Married: Bud Reed

Both Born: Lansing, Ash County, North Carolina

Alex Campbell & Ola Belle are two of the most colorful and popular entertainers in Country music with a career that has spanned over 40 years.

They were two of 13 children born to Arthur Campbell, a school teacher who turned to music and formed his own band in 1910. The family owned a store that sold record players and general merchandise. Alex and Ola Belle were raised along the banks of the New River, where, at an early age, they learned to appreciate and enjoy the Old-Time Country music and Gospel songs. Ola Belle taught Alex to play guitar when he was 10 years old.

During WWII, Alex was wounded in the invasion of Normandy Beach. He was in the same unit as Grandpa Jones and after the German surrender, the huge radio station at Munich was taken over by the Americans. They could broadcast to Russia, Britain and all over Europe. There was a dispute among the disc jockeys on what to play: Frank Sinatra, Pop or Roy Acuff. They let the audience decide by a poll and Roy won by a landslide. Alex and Grandpa Jones set up their broadcasts over a large beer hall and broadcast live as Grandpa Jones and His Munich Mountaineers, from April to December 1945, after which they came home.

When this brother and sister team organized their own Country music band in 1946, they took the name of Alex and Ola Belle and the New River Boys and broadcast over WASA in Havre de Grace, Maryland. They played mountain Bluegrass style with traditional stringed instruments. The Campbells moved to Pennsylvania and picked up a strong following in the Oxford area of that state. They were featured on many radio shows, broadcasting over WCOJ Coatesville, Pennsylvania and WBMO Baltimore, Maryland. While their transcribed shows were featured on many other radio stations in the U.S., Alex and Ola Belle wrote over 200 songs and recorded 20 albums: one of the double albums featured 19 of their original songs. In 1949, Alex and Ola Belle re-formed the band and the line-up of the New Rover Boys became Deacon Brumfield (Dobro), Ted Lundy (5-string banjo), John Jackson (fiddle) and Earl Wallace (string bass)

In 1951, Alex Campbell, Ola Belle and her husband Bud Reed established the New River Ranch near Rising Sun, Oxford, Pennsylvania, which was one of the most active of the Country music parks. They were the first to bring the big-name Bluegrass and Country stars to the area. In 1960, they transferred to Sunset Park in West Grove, Pennsylvania. They were there for 26 years, broadcasting their own regular Sunday radio show from the park. In the early 60's, they were on WWVA in Wheeling, West Virginia, broadcasting to the entire eastern U.S. and up into Canada.

In addition to radio and personal appearances, Alex and Ola Belle operated a very successful Country music record store which specialized in the mail order sale of Country and Gospel records from Oxford, Pennsylvania.

Alex has for over 40 years been an independent deejay and operated from his Campbell's Corner Store. He bought time and broadcast by remote control where he peddled his own wares, being one of the best "pitchmen" in radio. He and Ola Belle were on 200 radio stations at one time and have appeared on most TV stations and festivals.

Alex retired in 1984 but in 1990 still kept busy on radio WGCB in Red Lion, Pennsylvania, and lent a hand at Sunset Park.

JAB

RECOMMENDED ALBUMS:

"Alex Campbell & Ola Belle" (Ken-De)
"Old Time Gospel Singing" (Essgee)
"Sixteen Radio Favorites" (Starday)(1963)
"Travel On" (Starday)(1965)

ARCHIE CAMPBELL

(Singer, Songwriter, Comedy, Script Writer, Sculptor, Poet, Artist)

Given Name:	**Archie James Campbell**
Date of Birth:	**November 7, 1914**
Where Born:	**Bulls Gap, Tennessee**
Married:	**Mary Lee Lewis**
Children:	**Stephen Archie, Phillip Edward Lee**
Date of Death:	**August 29, 1987**

To many, Archie Campbell will always be remembered as one of the side-splitting team on TV's successful *Hee Haw*. Although he was one of Country music's funniest men, he was also a multi-faceted entertainer who encompassed recording artist and script writer and in addition was a highly talented sculptor, poet and artist and played off a two handicap in golf.

Archie grew up in the foothills of the Smokies, which helped him become the humanist that he became. He studied art between 1934 and 1935 at Mars Hill College in North Carolina, intending to be a commercial artist, but soon he decided that he wanted to join the entertainment business. Archie made his radio debut as an announcer on WNOX Knoxville's *Mid-Day Merry Go Round*, in 1936, alongside Roy Acuff, Pee Wee King, Eddie Hill, Homer & Jethro, the Carlisles and Chet Atkins (who became his best friend). He also appeared in the station's *Barn Dance*.

In 1937, Archie moved on to WDOD Chattanooga, Tennessee, where he stayed until 1941, when he joined the U.S. Navy. After the end of the war, Archie returned to radio, rejoining WNOX in 1949. In 1952, he had his own TV show, *Country Playhouse*, on WROL-TV Knoxville. This show, which assisted the careers of Carl & Pearl Butler, Carl Smith and Flatt & Scruggs, continued until 1958, when he moved to Nashville and the following year, Archie joined the *Prince Albert* portion of the *Grand Ole Opry*.

In 1959, Archie signed to RCA Victor, and his first single, the self-penned *Trouble in the Amen Corner*, went Top 25 on the Country chart, in 1960. In 1962, Archie signed with Starday Records, where he stayed until 1965, without any chart action. He went back to RCA and during the beginning of 1966, Archie returned to the Country chart with the Top 20 release *The Men in My Little Girl's Life*. The following year, Archie had a Top 50 hit with the novelty song *The Cockfight*.

RCA then teamed Archie with Lorene Mann, who had recently scored duet hits with Justin Tubb. During 1968, they registered three chart records with *The Dark End of the Street* (Top 25), *Tell It Like It Is* (Top 40) and *Warm and Tender Love* (Top 60). The last two songs had been hits for R & B singers Aaron Neville and Percy Sledge respectively. That year, Archie joined *Hee Haw* as performer and Chief Writer. He also got together with fellow member Junior Samples for the very funny album ***Bull Session at Bull's Creek*** for Chart Records. The following year, he again dueted with Lorene for the Top 40 *My Special Prayer*.

Although Archie only had one more hit, in 1973, *Freedom Ain't the Same as Bein' Free*, which went Top 90, most of his more memorable songs were not hits and included *Rindercella, Beeping Sleauty* and *Pee Little Thrigs*. Archie has been described as a "modern Will Rogers." That is true to a degree, but Archie had a much broader and deeper substance to his humor. He was not just a humorist, he was also a comedian; with his large cigar, he became a sort of "Country George Burns." He was also a talented after-dinner speaker.

There was also a civic side to Archie Campbell. For eight years he was a member of the Knoxville School Board and he was involved in Republican politics. He remained a talented painter and his golfing was highly rated. In 1976, Archie signed with Elektra Records and released an eponymous album. During 1984, he hosted TNN's chat show *Yesteryear in Nashville*. On June 15, 1987, Archie was struck down by a heart attack and following complications, he died in August. Both of his sons are involved in the entertainment industry with Steve running a management company and Phil starring in *Hee Haw*.

RECOMMENDED ALBUMS:

"Bedtime Stories for Adults" (Starday)(1962)
"The Grand Ole Opry's Good Humor Man" (RCA Victor)(1966)
"The Cockfight (and Other Tall Tales)" (RCA Victor)(1966)
"Kids, I Love 'Em" (RCA Victor)(1967)
"Bull Session at Bull's Creek" (Chart)(1968) [With Junior Samples]
"Archie & Lorene Tell It Like It Is" (RCA Victor)(1968) [With Lorene Mann]
"The Many Talents of Archie Campbell" (Nashville)(1968)

"The Best of Archie Campbell" (RCA Victor)(1970)
"Archie Campbell" (Elektra)(1976)

CECIL CAMPBELL

(Composer, Steel Guitar, Tenor Banjo, Guitar)

Given Name: Cecil R. Campbell
Date of Birth: March 22, 1911
Where Born: Stokes County, North Carolina
Married: Katherine
Children: Joretta Kay, Linda Lee
Date of Death: June 18, 1989

Cecil Campbell worked as a key member of the Tennessee Ramblers through much of the 30's and early 40's.

The youngest son in the large family of a tobacco farmer, Cecil remained on his dad's farm until 1932. During the later years, he developed his musical skills and performed a little on WSJS radio in Winston-Salem. His show business career really began when he visited his brother in Pittsburgh and met Dick Hartman and Harry Blair of the Tennessee Ramblers, who frequented the elder Campbell's barbershop. Cecil joined the group and played in their band from radio stations in Pittsburgh, Rochester, Charlotte and Atlanta, among other locales. He recorded many sides with them on Bluebird as Dick Hartman's Tennessee Ramblers, as Hartman's Heartbreakers and as the Washboard Wonders. Cecil also made one single with brother Ed as the Campbell Brothers. Cecil played a wide variety of instruments, but in the early days he generally favored tenor banjo or the acoustic steel guitar. After Hartman departed from the band in 1937, Jack Gillette took over the leadership with Campbell continuing as a key member.

In 1945, Cecil took over the leadership of the band, landed a new contract with RCA Victor and worked regularly at WBT Charlotte, North Carolina. By this time, he played electric steel guitar almost exclusively, often complementing it on disc. Campbell originals included *Steel Guitar Wiggle, Steel Guitar Tango, Steel Guitar Swing* and *Steel Guitar Dig.* Some of his recordings also appeared on the Palmetto and super Disc labels. In the mid-50's, Campbell signed with MGM, releasing several singles, including two with a Rockabilly flavor, *Dixieland Rock* and *Rock and Roll Fever,* which were much sought after by collectors, despite their being quite uncharacteristic of Cecil's style.

In 1963, he cut an all-original album, ***Steel Guitar Jamboree,*** for Starday. In later days, Campbell started his own label in Charlotte and Winston and recorded some singles and cassettes. He played shows in the Charlotte area for years and at the 1985 reunion of Charlotte old timers. In company with former Tennessee Ramblers Claude Casey and Don White, Cecil also appeared annually at the Western Film Fairs, held alternately at Charlotte and Raleigh, for several years up until his death. IMT

RECOMMENDED ALBUMS:
"Steel Guitar Jamboree" (Starday)(1963)
"Steel Guitar Classics" (Country Classics)(1981)

GLEN CAMPBELL

(Singer, Songwriter, Guitar, Bagpipes, Mandolin, Banjo, Actor, Author)

Given Name: Glen Travis Campbell
Date of Birth: April 22, 1936
Where Born: Delight, Arkansas
Married: 1. (div.)
2. (div.)
3. (div.)
4. Kim (m. 1983)
Children: Debby, Kelli, Travis, Kane, Nicklaus, Shannon, Ashley

According to Glen Campbell, "I am not a Country singer. I am a country boy who sings." Despite this disclaimer, Glen's music is predominantly associated with Country music, although his talents are such that he has been able to diversify.

Often wrongly described as the seventh son of a seventh son, *he* is a seventh son of a *second* son.

After his father, Wesley, ordered a $5.00 guitar from a Sears-Roebuck catalog when he was 4, Glen's prodigious talent began to blossom. He was influenced by Don Carlyle, Grady Martin, Hank Garland, Barney Kessel and most of all by Django Reinhardt. Before he was 10, Glen was extremely proficient musically and left school at the earliest opportunity to work for his uncle, Dick Bills, in his Western Swing band in Albuquerque, New Mexico.

Glen formed his own band, the Western Wranglers, for a time, touring the Southwest. In 1960, with $300 to his name, Glen moved to Los Angeles and joined the Champs for about a year. Although the group could not reproduce the success of their chart topper, *Tequila*, Glen was involved with the lesser hit *Limbo Rock*, which charted in 1962. It was at this time that Glen Campbell the vocalist began to emerge. His tenor style was influenced by a multiplicity of singers from Little Jimmy Dickens to Hank Thompson to Frank Sinatra.

In the early 60's, Glen teamed up with Jimmy Bowen to write songs and do demo sessions for a Los Angeles publishing company. Campbell mainly contributed the musical accompaniment. His singing and instrumental work attracted attention and he was soon busily involved in sessions. Glen got to back some of his idols, including Frank Sinatra, Elvis Presley and Nat King Cole. He also worked with the Righteous Brothers, Merle Haggard and Rick Nelson. One of the notable hits from this period was Sinatra's *Strangers in the Night*.

Glen also flirted with success as a singer. In 1961, he had a minor Pop hit with *Turn Around, Look at Me* on Crest, which led Capitol to sign him. His first album, ***Big Bluegrass Special***, appeared in 1962 under the credit "The Green River Boys Featuring Glen Campbell" and from this came the Country Top 20 success *Kentucky Means Paradise*. Glen then had a further minor Pop hit, *Too Late to Worry, Too Blue to Cry*, after which Glen's singing career nosedived for several years and he was out of the charts except for *The Universal Soldier*, a Top 50 Pop success in 1965. Meanwhile he recorded two guitar albums issued in 1963 with the Dillards and Tut Taylor, as the Folkswingers, and two issued in 1964 and 1965 under his own name.

Glen had been involved in several Beach Boys hits and when Brian Wilson was off the road, Glen toured with the band, playing bass. Afterward his voice contributed to their continued success, playing a part on records like *Help Me Rhonda* and *Dance, Dance, Dance*. This phase lasted until 1967.

Glen returned to the Country chart with his 1967 singles *Burning Bridges* (Top 20) and the minor success *I Gotta Have My Baby Back*. When in Nashville, Campbell discovered a John Hartford song, *Gentle on My Mind*. "It was one of those songs that makes you stop your car and listen," Glen remembers. The tune, which would be covered by over 300 artists, proved the ticket to cross-over super stardom, although it was not a big hit for Glen in the U.S., reaching only Top 70 on the Pop chart (Top 40 on reissue in 1968) and Top 30 on the Country Chart. It earned Glen a slew of awards, including Grammy Awards for "Best Country & Western Recording" and "Best Country & Western Solo Vocal Performance-Male." From the ACM Glen took the "Male Vocalist," "Single of the Year" and "Album of the Year" for ***Gentle on My Mind***. This album was Certified Gold in 1968 and by 1991 had achieved Platinum status.

Glen confirmed his success later in 1967, with the first of his successes with Jimmy Webb songs. *By the Time I Get to Phoenix* went Top 3 Country and Top 30 Pop. The single won Glen two further 1967 Grammy Awards for "Best Contemporary Male Solo Vocal Performance" and "Best Vocal Performance, Male." The album of the same name went Gold in 1968 and by 1992 had been Certified Platinum. During 1967 through 1969, Glen got involved in a studio group, Sagittarius, with Bruce Johnston, Terry Melcher, Gary Usher and Kurt Boetcher; the group had a pair of minor chart records.

Glen's major successes during 1968 were all on the Country charts and were *Hey Little One* (Top 15), *I Wanna Live* (his first No.1), *Dreams of the Everyday Housewife* (Top 3) and *Wichita Lineman* (No.1). During the year, Glen received awards from ACM as "Male Vocalist," "Song of the Year" (*Wichita Lineman*) and "Album of the Year" (for the duet album ***Glen Campbell & Bobbie Gentry***). The CMA named Glen "Male Vocalist of the Year" and "Entertainer of the Year." Glen also won a 1968 Grammy for "Album of the Year" for ***Wichita Lineman***. The album went Gold the year of release and by 1992 had been Certified Double-Platinum. That year, Glen also won the ACM's "TV Personality" as he began *The Glen Campbell Goodtime Hour*, which ran on CBS-TV. The show always opened with its genial host exclaiming, "Hi. I'm Glen Campbell!" At its height, almost 50 million people watched each week, ensuring Glen's singles and albums sold well.

1969 saw Campbell star with his hero, John Wayne, in the movie *True Grit*. Later he would joke that his acting was so bad that he earned Wayne his only Oscar. *Wichita Lineman* peaked on the Pop chart, reaching the Top 3 and earned him a Gold Record. He followed with a Top 15 Pop duet success with Bobbie Gentry, *Let It Be Me*. Then in the spring, Glen scored another monster hit with Jimmy Webb's *Galveston*. The single stayed at the top of the Country chart for 3 weeks, reached the Pop Top 5 and earned Glen another Gold single. His other major single successes were *True Grit* (Top 10 Country) and *Try a Little Kindness* (Top 3 Country). That year, the albums ***Hey Little One***, ***Glen Campbell & Bobbie Gentry***, ***Galveston*** and ***Glen Campbell—"Live,"*** were all Certified Gold. ***Galveston*** went on to reach Platinum status in 1991.

Glen's second movie, *Norwood* (1970), in which his co-star was a chicken, was disastrous and killed all ambitions to pursue a movie career. He used the proven power of TV to market himself in Britain, where he has toured on a regular basis, having racked up hits with *Wichita Lineman*, *Galveston* and *Try a Little Kindness*.

During the first half of the 70's, Glen's singles did much better on the Country chart and his major successes were: 1970: *Honey Come Back* (Top 3), *All I Have to Do Is Dream* (a Top 10 duet with Bobbie Gentry), *Everything a Man Could Ever Need* (Top 5, from the movie *Norwood*) and *It's Only Make Believe* (Top 3 Country/Top 10 Pop); 1971: *Dream Baby (How Long Must I Dream)* (Top 10); 1972: *Manhattan Kansas* (Top 10) and 1974: *Bonaparte's Retreat* (which featured Glen on the bagpipes). Glen also teamed up with Anne Murray in 1971, but their 1971 duet, *I Say a Little Prayer/By the Time I Get to Phoenix*, only reached the Top 40.

Glen's albums ***Try a Little Kindness*** and ***Glen Campbell's Greatest Hits*** were Certified Gold in 1970 and 1972 respectively. The latter would go Platinum in 1991. In 1971, Glen was again named "TV Personality" by the ACM, but in 1972, tiring of the weekly grind, he ended his CBS show. Glen made his TV movie debut in *Strange Homecomings*, during 1974. The following year, his career got a second wind from *Rhinestone Cowboy*, which topped both the Country and Pop charts and was Certified Gold. Glen received the ACM Awards for "Song of the Year" and "Single of the Year" for the record.The album of the same name also went Gold that year. Glen's other major hits in 1975 were *Country Boy (You Got Your Feet in L.A.)* (Top 3 Country/Top 15 Pop) and the medley *Don't Pull Your Love/Then You Can Tell Me Goodbye* (Top 5 Country). That year, Glen got together with Tennessee Ernie Ford for the delightful album ***Ernie Sings & Glen Picks***. In 1976, Glen's ***That Christmas Feeling*** album, which had been released in 1968, was Certified Gold.

Glen returned to the top again in 1977 with Allen Toussaint's *Southern Nights*, which went to No.1 on both Country and Pop charts and was Certified Gold. The album of the same name also went Gold that year. This was Glen's last major Pop success and from here on in, his hits were primarily Country. He stayed with Capitol until 1980 and his major successes were Neil Diamond's *Sunflower* (Top 5, 1977), *Can You Fool* (Top 20, 1978) and *I'm Gonna Love You* (Top 15, 1979).

During the early 1980's, Glen had further minor duet successes, with Rita Coolidge (*Somethin' 'Bout You Baby I Like*, 1980) and Tanya Tucker (*Dream Lover*, 1980 and *Why Don't We Sleep on It Tonight*, 1981). He also enjoyed a Top 10 single with *Any Which Way You Can*, the title song of the highly successful Clint Eastwood movie, in which he made a cameo appearance.

Glen left Capitol in 1981, one reason being their refusal to release *Highwayman* as a single. In 1982, Glen signed with Atlantic American and his major successes during his four-year stay with the label were *I Love How You Love Me* (Top 20, 1983), *Faithless Love* (Top 10, 1984), *A Lady Like You* (Top 5) and *It's Just a Matter of Time* (Top 10) (both 1985). In 1984, Glen dueted with Mel Tillis on the Top 50 *Slow Nights* from Mel's ***New Patches*** album.

In 1985, Glen celebrated his years in the music business with an HBO special, *The Silver Anniversary of the Rhinestone Cowboy*, with special guests Anne Murray, Willie Nelson, Johnny Cash, Kris Kristofferson and Mel Tillis.

Glen signed with MCA in 1987, reuniting him with Jimmy Bowen, and during a two-year stay, had major success with *The Hand That Rocks the Cradle*, a 1987 Top 10 duet with Steve Wariner, *Still Within the Sound of My Voice* (Top 5, 1988) and *I Have You* (Top 10, 1988). In 1989, Glen moved with Bowen to Universal, where he had a Top 10 single, *She's Gone, Gone, Gone*. When Bowen moved to head Capitol (later renamed Liberty), Glen moved with him, for a second period on the label, but has failed to register a major success there, his most successful single being *Unconditional Love* from the album of the same name.

By the 1990's, Campbell had shaken off the handicaps of reliance on alcohol, turning to Christianity and enjoying a stable marriage. Revitalized, he might not have repeated the success of old, but he produced some highly distinctive and heavily Country flavored albums. He has also turned out Christian material and in 1986, his Word album ***No More Night*** won a Dove Award from the GMA as "Album by a Secular Recording Artist," and in 1992, his single *Where Shadows Never Fall*, on New Haven, won a Dove Award for "Southern Gospel Recorded Song of the Year."

Glen Campbell may no longer be in the fast lane, but he's still coming up with interesting musical offerings. "I listen for chord progression, melody, a good lyric that says something, and something positive," he explains. Not everything he's done has been Country (although he's even yodeling these days!), but that is a tribute to his versatility which has taken him down several musical routes. Or as he puts it: "I think God gave me a gift to sing and play. I really don't call it Country or Pop or Rock."

In 1994, Glen produced his autobiography and it proved to be a "revelation" book and he received a lot of flack, not least of all from Tanya Tucker, with whom he's had a stormy relationship. However, Glen has been totally open about the ups and downs of his life. SM/BM

RECOMMENDED ALBUMS:

"12 String Guitar" (World Pacific)(1963) [As the Folkswingers]
"12 String Guitar, Volume 2" (World Pacific)(1963) [As the Folkswingers]
"The Astounding 12-String Guitar of Glen Campbell" (Capitol)(1964) [Re-issued in 1978]
"Gentle on My Mind" (Capitol)(1967) [Re-issued 1979]
"By the Time I Get to Phoenix" (Capitol)(1967) [Re-issued in 1980]
"Wichita Lineman" (Capitol)(1968) [Re-issued 1981]
"Hey Little One" (Capitol)(1968) [Re-issued 1982]
"Galveston" (Capitol)(1969) [Re-issued 1982]

"The Glen Campbell Goodtime Album" (Capitol)(1970)
"Glen Travis Campbell" (Capitol)(1972) [Re-released 1982]
"Rhinestone Cowboy" (Capitol)(1975) [Re-issued in 1980]
"Bloodline" (Capitol)(1976) [Re-released in 1978]
"Glen Campbell Live (at the Royal Albert Hall)" (double)(Capitol)(1977)
"Southern Nights" (Capitol)(1977)
"Highwayman" (Capitol)(1979)
"It's the World Gone Crazy" (Capitol)(1981)
"Old Home Town" (Atlantic America)(1982)
"Still Within the Sound of My Voice" (MCA)(1987)
"Light Years" (MCA)(1988) [All songs but two written by Jimmy Webb]
"Unconditional Love" (Capitol)(1991)
"Somebody Like That" (Liberty)(1993)
Glen Campbell & Anne Murray:
"Glen Campbell & Anne Murray" (Capitol)(1971) [Re-released in 1980]
Glen Campbell & Bobbie Gentry:
"Glen Campbell & Bobbie Gentry" (Capitol)(1968)
Tennessee Ernie Ford & Glen Campbell:
"Ernie Picks & Glen Sings" (Capitol)(1975)

Canadian Sweethearts refer LUCILLE STARR

ACE CANNON

(Saxophone, Composer)
Given Name: **Hubert Cannon**
Date of Birth: **May 4, 1934**
Where Born: **Grenada, Mississippi**

Although the saxophone is not an instrument usually associated with Country music, there are certain players who have established a reputation for it in Country music circles. These include Boots Randolph, Jim Horn, Maury Finney and Ace Cannon.

Ace started playing at the age of 10. During the rock'n'roll pioneering days, he was part of the blossoming Sun Records coterie and appeared with Billy Lee Riley and Brad Suggs. In 1959, he joined the original Bill Black Combo and was present on all their chart hits on Hi. He left the band in 1961 and continued with Hi. That same year, he had a major chart success with the Top 20 instrumental *Tuff.* He followed this up with a Top 40 hit, *Blues (Stay Away from Me).* Later that year, he scraped into the lists with *Sugar Blues* on the Santos label. Then in 1963 and 1964 he had further hits on Hi with *Cottonfields* and *Searchin'.* In 1974, he was the subject of a documentary film, *Ace's High.* He relocated from Longview, Texas, and started recording in Nashville in 1975. During 1977, his version of *Blue Eyes Crying in the Rain* made the Country Top 75 and was nominated for the "Best Country Instrumental Performance" Grammy Award that year. Ace is still an active musician and is often featured when rock'n'roll legends such as Carl Perkins play in concert.

RECOMMENDED ALBUM:
"Golden Classics" (Gusto)(1980)

JUDY CANOVA

(Singer, Comedy, Actress)
Given Name: **Juliette Canova**
Date of Birth: **November 20, 1916**
Where Born: **Jacksonville, Florida**
Married: **unknown**
Children: **Diane, Julietta England**
Date of Death: **August 5, 1983**

For many people, Judy Canova *was* Country. Her wide-eyed bumpkin humor embodied rural homespun values. Judy played the hayseed who won out in the end, the country innocent against the city sophisticate. She spoke with a southern drawl, which audiences seemed to enjoy and she was in the tradition of the Beverly Hill Billies (not the TV program), Minnie Pearl and Cousin Emmy. Vocally, she was in the same mold as Betty Hutton and Martha Raye, a voice that could crack glass from 50 paces! However, she also had a voice that could croon her theme song, *Go to Sleep Little Baby.* She changed this theme song during WWII to Patsy Montana's *Good Night Soldier,* revealing her tender heart.

Judy's father was a cotton broker and her mother a concert singer. Such was her clever and versatile performing character that it was totally at variance with her upbringing. Juliette wouldn't be expected to say in Judy's hillbilly way, "You're telling I." In 1930, Judy formed the Three Crackers, with her brother Leon and her sister Diane, an old-timey trio singing popular mountain songs. They also did some recordings. Their character names were Judy, Zeke and Ann and they eventually expanded into a singing and comedy act, performing on WJAX Jacksonville as the Canova Cracker Trio.

By 1934, the act had moved to New York with Leon getting top billing. They were now called Zeke and the Happiness Girls and performed in clubs like the Village Barn and Jimmy Kelly's. Judy began to show her versatility by singing lead, yodeling and telling gags. Soon she branched out on her own, appeared on Broadway, did some small film roles and then she performed in *Ziegfeld Follies of 1936.* Alongside these solo activities, she continued with the family group. Through 1936-1937, they became regulars on radio shows hosted by Edgar Bergen and Paul Whiteman. On May 3, 1939, the Canovas were chosen as one of the first Country acts to broadcast on the NBC-TV experimental transmissions.

After her successful role in the musical *Yokel Boy,* Judy was Hollywood-bound and during the 40's was a big star with Republic Films. Her movies included *Scatterbrain, The Wac from Walla Walla, Louisiana Hayride* and *Puddin' Head* (see Movie section). During the period 1943-1953, Judy had her own radio show, *The Judy Canova Show.* She attracted 18 million listeners coast-to-coast, with her jokes keeping her in the Top 10 of audience favorites. Television, of course, was a perfect medium for Judy. Variety shows such as *Cavalcade of Stars* and the *Colgate Comedy Hour* were ideal vehicles for her.

Judy's recording career continued from the early days through all her radio, TV and film success. Recording with Mercury, OKeh, Coronet, Varsity, Sterling, RCA and many other labels, her early recordings included such songs as *I've Been Hoo-Dooed, I Wish I Were a Country Girl Again* and later *My Fickle Eye, Never Trust a Man* and *No Letter Today.*

By the mid-50's, Judy had become a millionaire. This didn't stop her carrying on with her acting career. She continued taking parts in such shows as *No No Nanette* in 1971. She also appeared on TV's *Alfred Hitchcock Presents* in 1960, *Police Woman* and *Love Boat.* Judy also appeared in the 1960 movie *Huckleberry Finn.*

Judy Canova died of cancer in the summer of 1983, in Hollywood, aged 66 and was survived by two daughters, Diane, a gifted comedienne in her own right, and Julietta. Judy's ashes were interred at the famed Forest Lawn Cemetery.

Funny ladies are few and far between, especially those with a silly brand of humor. Perhaps there will never be her like again, singing old-timey songs, cracking jokes in that vaudeville hayseed style, tugging her trademark braids and ringing out her life with a cowbell. JAB

CAP, ANDY AND FLIP

Formed: **1930**
Original Members:
Cap Caplinger **Guitar**
Andrew Patterson **Vocals, Fiddle, Guitar**
Flip Strickland **Tenor Vocals, Banjo, Mandolin**
Other Member:
Milt Patterson (Replacement "Flip")

Although their fame has been confined largely to West Virginia and adjacent states, the radio trio of Cap, Andy and Flip made one of the most popular regional acts of the 1930's.

Caplinger (b. Samuel Warren Caplinger, June 16, 1889, Kanawha Station, Wood County, West Virginia/d. July 7, 1957) and Patterson (b. Andrew Patterson, August 28, 1893, Petros, Tennessee/d. November 19, 1950) both had earlier careers as recording artists and all of them played a role in the early professional career of Grandpa Jones.

Cap was born near Parkersburg, West

Virginia, and had worked in coal mines before moving to East Tennessee in 1920. There he met Patterson, who was a skilled vocalist, fiddler and guitarist. The two formed a string band in company with George Rainey and his two sons, Willie and Albert. In February 1928, they recorded nine sides for Brunswick and Vocalion (both part of ARC), in Ashland, Kentucky, under the name of Warren Caplinger's Cumberland Mountain Entertainers. Later that year, Caplinger moved to Akron, Ohio, a northern industrial city with a large population of displaced southern and mountain folk.

Patterson first joined forces with two brothers named McCartt, doing a session for Columbia Records that fall as the McCartt Brothers and Patterson. However, a few weeks later, he rejoined Cap in Akron, where they formed a group known as the Dixie Harmonizers. They played radio there and in Cleveland and recorded for Gennett. Under the name of the Pine Ridge String Band, they worked with the famous comedy team of Lum and Abner on a network radio program that originated in Cleveland. Grandpa Jones did some of his earliest work as a professional musician with their act.

In 1930, Flip Strickland (b. William Austin Strickland, November 28, 1908, Blount County, Alabama/d. July 21, 1988), who had previous radio experience, joined them singing tenor and playing both tenor banjo and later mandolin. The trio achieved great popularity in Akron and later on the West Virginia stations of WWVA Wheeling, WMMN Fairmont and WCHS Charleston. They worked for brief periods at WAIU Columbus, Ohio, and WCMI Ashland, Kentucky. Although they recorded only occasionally, they had 11 known songs on the obscure Fireside Melodies label in 1939 and 1940. They managed to exercise considerable influence as a radio act.

Cap, Andy and Flip

Cap, Andy and Flip were the first to popularize the traditional ballad *Roane County Prison* and the first to record a song about television, a sacred lyric entitled *Television in the Sky*. They also published five important songbooks during their decade of popularity. By the end of the 30s, sacred numbers dominated their repertoire.

In 1940, Flip left the act to go into the chicken farming business with his father-in-law in Cairo, West Virginia. The act continued for another decade with Andy's 16-year-old son, Milt, as the third member. By then, they were almost exclusively a Gospel act and permanently settled in Charleston. They remained there through most of the 40's. About 1945, they did a record session on the local M & L label.

They disbanded in 1949 when ill health forced Andy's retirement; he died the following year. Cap worked as a deejay, first at WKRA and then WGKV, both in Charleston. After his death, he was buried adjacent to Andy in the St. Albans, West Virginia, cemetery. Milt Patterson returned to Harriman, Tennessee, where he now lives in retirement.

Flip Strickland later returned to music, working first in Texas Ruby and Curly Fox's band at the *Grand Ole Opry* and briefly at WDBJ in Roanoke, Virginia, with Mel Steele. He left the business in the fall of 1946 and moved to Indiana shortly after and worked as a part-time musician for many years. He retired in 1973 and moved back to Alabama in 1979. After his death, his widow, Helen, took his remains back to her hometown of Gallipolis, Ohio, for burial. IMT

RECOMMENDED ALBUMS:

Although none of Cap, Andy and Flip's scarce recordings have ever been re-issued, three of Warren Caplinger's Cumberland Mountain Entertainer sides have appeared in re-issue anthologies including "Old Time String Band Classics" (County)

CAPTAIN STUBBY AND THE BUCCANEERS

Formed: 1938

Members:

Tom C. Fouts Comedy, Novelty Instruments, Musical Hat Rack, Tuned Toilet Seat (Gitarlet), Vocals

Jerald R. Richards Clarinet, Flute, Bass Clarinet, Ocarina, Tin Whistle, Vocals

Sonny Fleming Guitar, Banjo, Vocals

Peter Kunatz Accordion, Piano

Tiny Stokes Lead Vocals, Bass

Other Members: Curly Myers (Guitar, Banjo, Vocals), Chuck Kagy (Fiddle, Guitar, Mandolin), Buddy Ross (Accordion), Tony Walberg (Accordion)

Country music achieved a lot of its appeal through the bands of crazies that occasionally came into creation. Such a band was Captain Stubby and the Buccaneers, whose instrumentation included a tuned toilet seat known as a gitarlet.

This group was established in 1938 by Tom C. Fouts (b. November 24, 1918, Carroll County, Indiana). During his one-year stay at Indiana Central College in Indianapolis, Fouts formed the Rhythm Rustics with Jerald Richards (b. Freeport, Illinois), a fellow student. When they left college, the other members of the group had summer jobs and didn't want to go into music full-time. Tom and Gerry sought out Curly Myers and Tiny Stokes of the Hoosier Ramblers and formed Captain Stubby and the Buccaneers. From 1938 to 1940, they started working on radio WDAN Danville, Illinois. In 1939, they were joined by Chuck Kagy. During 1940-1944 the group was broadcasting on the WLW *Boone County Jamboree* in Cincinnati and in 1941, Kagy left and was replaced by Buddy Ross. In 1944, the Buccaneers joined the U.S. Navy, with the exception of Myers, who failed his medical. His place was taken by Sonny Fleming, a native of Paducah, Kentucky. In addition, Tony Walberg joined, replacing Buddy Ross. That year, while members of the United States Great Lakes Entertainment Division, they were all in the cast of the Warner Brothers movie *Musical Shipmates*.

They remained in uniform during 1944-1946, entertaining troops around the world. After WWII ended, the group spent three years (1946-1949) working at the Village Barn in New York. Then, in 1949, the Buccaneers moved to WLS's *National Barn Dance,* where they became fixtures for the next nine years. At the same time, Walberg left and the Buccaneers were joined by Peter Kunatz, who used the stage name Peter Kaye. This Chicago native had considerable musical experience. He

***Captain Stubby** and his Gitarlet*

spent the year 1938 studying at the Chicago Conservatory of Music while at the same time leading his own band, which was together from 1936-1941. With the addition of Kaye the best remembered group of Buccaneers—Fouts, Richards, Fleming, Kaye and Tiny Stokes—was complete.

The Buccaneers recorded for five labels, Columbia, Decca, Mercury, Rondo and Stephany, their most successful recordings being on Decca. Between 1948-1951, they recorded *Beyond the Sunset, Money, Marbles and Chalk* and *At the Rainbow's End* for Decca. Their recording of the 1936 Virgil and Blanche Brock hymn *Beyond the Sunset* was the best-selling record of their career. In 1952, they moved to Mercury, where they had some success with the song titled *Fair, Fat and Forty*. The following year they moved to Rondo and then in 1958 to Stephany, where they had another fair seller with a Fouts composition called *I Love Her Truly*. The next year, 1959, they were back with Mercury, where they had their last real commercial success with *Do You*.

In 1958, the Buccaneers moved to WBKB-TV Chicago as staff musicians as well as singing hymns on *Chicagoland's Faith* every Sunday. They remained at the station until 1966. While on WBKB, Tom had an early morning show on WLS called *Farm Special* with Charles Homer Bill that ran from 1960 to 1968. Then, for two years, 1966-1968, the Buccaneers were again on the *Barn Dance,* which, by this time, was known as the WGN *Barn Dance*. Then in 1968, Captain Stubby and the Buccaneers disbanded.

In 1968, Tom joined *Don McNeill's Breakfast Club* as performer and writer, remaining on the show until 1971. For a time, Fouts also had a syndicated show called *Captain Stubby's Special Delivery* (a talk show sponsored by Wayne Feeds), which started in 1968 and continues to date and was recorded at an independent studio in Chicago.

More recently Tom Fouts has been a popular after-dinner speaker (Wayne Feeds' Goodwill Ambassador) who also occupies himself running several farms in Cass and Carroll counties in Indiana. He currently lives in Cass County with his wife of 53 years, Eva Lou. Fleming was involved in both television and religious work (he died in 1982). Kaye maintained business interests in Allied Mills in Chicago and Purina Mills in St. Louis. Richards stayed in show business doing jingles and commercials but was also involved in the real estate business in the Chicago area. WKM/BM

RECOMMENDED ALBUMS:

"Captain Stubby and the Buccaneers Polka Album" (Columbia)(1955)
"Animal Ditties for the Kiddies"

HENSON CARGILL

(Singer, Songwriter, Guitar)
Date of Birth: **February 5, 1941**
Where Born: **Oklahoma City, Oklahoma**

Don't ever say to Henson Cargill, "Sue me," because he'll know how to do it. He comes from a long line of lawyers and politicians and at one point was destined to become a legal eagle himself. His father was a famous trial lawyer and his grandfather was a former Mayor of Oklahoma City.

However, Henson's career intentions were in ranching. He studied animal husbandry at Colorado State University, getting married in his final year. He returned to the family spread in Oklahoma to work. He had been playing guitar since he was a boy and became more interested in Country music and started to play local clubs. In addition to his ranch chores, he worked as a deputy sheriff in Oklahoma County. A meeting with Harold Gay, the leader of the Kimberlys, led to him giving up being a peace officer and joining them.

By the mid-60's, Henson was in Nashville knocking on record company doors. In 1967, Fred Foster at Monument decided to take him in. He put Henson with producer Don Law and they recorded a composition by blind songwriter Jack Moran, *Skip a Rope*. The record not only topped the Country charts for five weeks but also became a Top 25 Pop hit. The follow-up in 1968, *Row, Row, Row,* reached the Top 15, but the following year, Henson was back into the upper 10, with *None of My Business*. That year, he took over from Dean Richards as the host of Avco Broadcasting's *Midwestern Hayride* out of WLWT-TV Cincinnati. This show was syndicated as *Country Hayride*.

Henson produced a steady flow of albums at Monument, including the 1971 release ***The Uncomplicated Henson Cargill***, from which *The Most Uncomplicated Goodbye I've Ever Heard* made the Country Top 20. The following year, he moved over to Mega Records but failed to pull off another major success. By 1973, he had moved again, this time to Atlantic. He remained with them until they closed their Nashville/Country operation in 1975 (they returned over a decade later, most successfully). Henson had two Top 30 successes with them, *Some Old California Memory* in 1973 and Mac Davis' *Stop and Smell the Roses* in the following year.

For five years, Henson Cargill's name was missing from the charts and then in 1979, he chalked up another Top 30 entry with *Silence on the Line* for the independent Copper Mountain label. He followed this with the 1980 minor success *Have a Good Day*. Since then, Henson has reverted to his interest in ranching.

RECOMMENDED ALBUMS:

"Skip-a-Rope" (Monument)(1968)
"Comin' on Strong" (Monument)(1968)
"None of My Business" (Monument)(1969)
"Uncomplicated Henson Cargill" (Monument)(1970)
"On the Road" (Mega)(1972)
"Welcome to My World" (Harmony)(1972)
"This Is Henson Cargill Country" (Atlantic)(1973)

BOB CARLIN

(Banjo, Guitar, Trombone)
Given Name: **Robert Mark Carlin**
Date of Birth: **March 17, 1953**
Where Born: **New York, New York**

One of the best and most influential Old-Time banjo players, Bob Carlin has also done extensive field work on Folk music, written for numerous periodicals, produced documentary albums and done award-winning radio programs. He is a musician who has taken the traditional instrument and traditional styles and added to them his own unique musical vision. Garrison Keillor, of *Prairie Home Companion* fame, has said, "I don't particularly care for banjo. But Bob's come along and done amazing things with it, and he makes us want to listen to this instrument again." Carlin himself has noted, "The banjo is such a perfect reflection of the coming together of European and African cultures."

Carlin's interest in the banjo came from an unlikely source. Born in New York City, with both sets of grandparents natives of Russia, he was early exposed to the Folk revival movement. He recalls seeing his first banjo at a Pete Seeger concert when he was 5, and grew up listening to Folk albums by him and the Weavers. For a time, he studied Blues guitar with a group of young urban folkies that included Roy Bookbinder. He turned to the banjo when he was 16, and when his father found a local musician who was giving lessons, both father and son signed up, but Bob's father soon dropped out. Bob's real mentor, though, was Hank Sapoznick, who later worked with him on Carlin's first album, ***Melodic Clawhammer Banjo*** (1977).

The late 1970's were an intense period of learning for Bob. In a formal sense, he graduated from Rutgers (1976) with a degree in communications. Less formally, he traveled to North Carolina to study with Appalachian greats Tommy Jarrell and Fred Cockerham. Bob and Sapoznick also joined a group called the Delaware Water Gap String Band and did two lps on Adelphi with them. This was an eclectic group whose repertoire ranged from Reggae to Swing, but Carlin wanted to explore the banjo more on his own and left the band in 1980.

Carlin did his first lp for a nationally distributed label in 1981, when he recorded ***Fiddle Tunes for Clawhammer Banjo*** for Rounder. This was followed with ***Where Did You Get That Hat***, which delved more into Old-Time comic songs and older traditional tunes (1983). ***Banging and Sawing*** followed for Rounder in 1985, before he began recording on the Merimac label with ***Take Me As I Am*** (1990) and ***Mr. Spaceman*** (1992).

Carlin also produced a number of important albums of older banjo recordings, including ***Library of Congress Banjo Collection*** (1988) and ***The Banjo on* Folkways, *Volume One and Two*** (1992), the latter on Smithsonian/Folkways. Between 1983 and 1985, he used his knowledge of the Archive of American Folksong in the Library of Congress to produce *Our Musical Heritage*, a 12-part radio documentary heard widely on public radio stations. He has lectured and conducted numerous workshops, primarily in the Virginia-Carolina area, and in the 1990's served as artist in residence at a number of venues. In the 1990's he was developing a comprehensive study of the history of the banjo in American music. CKW

RECOMMENDED ALBUMS:

"Fiddle Tunes for Clawhammer Banjo" (Rounder)(1981)
"Where Did You Get That Hat" (Rounder)(1983)
"Banging and Sawing" (Rounder)(1985)
"Take Me as I Am" (Merimac)(1990)
"Mr. Spaceman" (Merimac)(1992)

BILL CARLISLE

(Singer, Songwriter, Guitar, Yodeler)

Given Name:	**William Carlisle**
Date of Birth:	**December 19, 1908**
Where Born:	**Wakefield, Kentucky**
Married:	**Leona**
Children:	**Billy, Sheila**

The younger brother of Cliff Carlisle, Bill Carlisle first established himself as a creditable white Bluesman in the 1930's, and then as a boisterous singer of novelty songs in the 1950's and 1960's. He and his family group, the Carlisles, became regulars on the *Grand Ole Opry* and remained as one of the show's veteran acts into the 1990's. Known in recent years for his antic leaping ("Jumping" Bill Carlisle) and outrageous green wigs, he has enjoyed a career that extends back to the very first decade of Country music and that embraces virtually every major genre since.

Bill followed in the footsteps of his older brother Cliff, except that whereas Cliff learned how to master the steel and Hawaiian guitars, Bill stuck with the standard model. In July 1933, Cliff, by then a veteran of the recording studio, got Bill a try-out with the ARC group of labels. The result was *Rattlesnake Daddy*, a hit record that was re-issued several times in the 1930's and emerged as a Bluegrass favorite in the 1940's. "Smilin' Bill," as he was called by the company publicists, could rip off runs on his flat-top guitar with stunning accuracy and was soon rivaling his brother in popularity on the record scene.

Like Cliff, he did excellent Rodgers-like yodels, and also like him he had a penchant for the slightly bawdy double-entendre song: titles like *String Bean Mama* (1934), *Copper Head Mama* (1934) and *Jumpin' and Jerkin' Blues* (1935) graced his release list. When he recorded for Decca in 1938 and 1939, he became more eclectic. At one particular session in July 1939, he did a bawdy song called *Sally Let Your Bangs Hang Down* with the old Gospel piece *I Dreamed I Searched Heaven for You,* back-to-back. His work for Bluebird was equally varied, though the best known records were *Bell Clapper Mama*, *The Heavenly Train* and *A Shack by the Side of the Road*—all from the mid-1930's.

Through the 1930's and 1940's, Bill moved widely from radio station to radio station, sometimes working with Cliff, sometimes with his own group. He was at WLAP Lexington, Kentucky, for a time, then at stations in Charlotte, North Carolina, Greenville, South Carolina, Louisville, Kentucky, Winston-Salem, North Carolina, KWKH Shreveport, WSB Atlanta, Memphis and WNOX Knoxville, Tennessee. It was while in Knoxville, in 1946, that Bill and Cliff (as the Carlisle Brothers) had one of their biggest hits, *Rainbow at Midnight*, on the new King label. In 1948, Bill hit the Country chart with his solo rendition of *Tramp on the Street*, which went Top 15.

As Cliff gradually drifted into retirement about 1950, Bill organized his own group, the Carlisles, and returned to Knoxville, where he did shows with Don Gibson, Chet Atkins, Homer and Jethro and others. At this time, Bill also created his jumping persona. He based it on an old comic act that he had created in the 1940's, "Hot Shot Elmer," who would disrupt live shows by jumping over chairs, tumbling off the stage and so forth.

He also began recording a string of successful novelty songs for Mercury. The first of these was *Too Old to Cut the Mustard*, an original song that Bill had written about an old mule his father had told them about. It was recorded in July 1951, with Gospel singer Martha Carson helping out on the harmony (Cliff actually sang on the session too, unacknowledged) and it became a 1952 Top 10 hit. It was followed by *No Help Wanted* (1952), with Betty Amos replacing Martha Carson, in 1953. It stayed for 4 weeks at No.1 out of 5 months on the charts. Other hits that year were another original, *Knot Hole*, which went Top 3, as did *Is Zat You, Myrtle?* one of several of Ira Louvin's first songs to be recorded. Bill & the Carlisles completed the year with *Taint Nice (to Talk Like That)*, which went Top 5. On the strength of these and other hits, the band was invited to join the *Opry* in 1953. In 1954, the Carlisles reached the Top 15 with *Shake-a-Leg* and *Honey Love*.

The Carlisles continued to record for a number of major labels, including Columbia, Hickory, Vanguard and Chart. By the1960's, Bill's children, Sheila and Billy, had joined the act and seemed destined to carry on the Carlisle brand of music for yet another generation. At the end of 1965, Bill appeared on the Country chart with *What Kind of Deal Is This*, which in 1966 reached the Top 5. Bill and the Carlisles are still firm favorites of the *Opry* crowd; although illness in 1993 looked like it *might* threaten his jumping, it didn't. CKW

RECOMMENDED ALBUMS:

"On Stage with the Carlisles" (Mercury)(1958)
"The Best of Bill Carlisle" (Hickory)(1966)
"Jumpin' Bill Carlisle" (Brylen)(1983)
"Carlisle Family—Old Time Great Hymns (Featuring Bill & Cliff)" (Old Homestead)

Bill and Cliff Carlisle

CLIFF CARLISLE

(Singer, Songwriter, Hawaiian Guitar, Steel Guitar, Dobro, Guitar, Yodeler)

Given Name:	**Clifford Raymond Carlisle**
Date of Birth:	**May 6, 1904**
Where Born:	**Mount Eden, Kentucky**
Married:	**Alice Henrietta Smith**
Children:	**Thomas Raymond, Violet Louise**

Next to Gene Autry, singer and guitarist Cliff Carlisle was probably the most prolific recording artist of the 1930's. His distinctive Jimmie-Rodgers-derived style and yodeling were heard on over 300 sides, on virtually every major label, including Gennett, Bluebird, ARC, Decca and even King. Cliff was a pioneer in adapting the steel guitar and Dobro to Country music, starting with a small standard Martin played Hawaiian-style and gradually moving up to a metal-bodied National, a Dobro, and finally to an instrument of his own design. His songs included some of the funniest and raunchiest white Blues of the age, but one of the most popular was a Dashiell Hammett-like ballad of San Francisco called *The Girl in the Blue Velvet Band*. By the end of the 1930's he had turned to sentimental and novelty songs as well as cowboy songs, often working with his little son, Tommy. Surprisingly, some of these off-color pieces were released under a pseudonym, "Bob Clifford," leaving many record buyers to think they were performed by a black artist.

By the mid-30's, Cliff was starting to work a lot with his younger brother Bill and as radio work increased, the duo began to move away from the saltier songs to sentimental pieces like *The Blind Child's Prayer* and *Valley of Peace*. Cliff's little boy, Tommy, who became known as Sonny Boy Tommy, became part of the act (though it caused problems with some states' child labor laws), making his first record in 1936. During the 1940's, the brothers generally worked together, centering their work on Knoxville and Memphis. They had their last big hit in 1946, when they charted with the Top 5 *Rainbow at Midnight* for King.

Cliff drifted into retirement in the early 1950's, though he made several lps for independent labels in the 1960's. Unlike many veterans from the 1930's, he lived to see his music rediscovered and re-issued on albums during the Folk revival of the 1960's. CKW

RECOMMENDED ALBUMS:

"Kountry Kind" (Rem)(1963)
"Maple on the Hill" (RCA Victor)(1964)
"Cliff Carlisle" (RCA Victor)(1965)
"Old Timey 1 & 2" (Arhoolie)(1965)

THUMBS CARLLILE

(Guitar, Songwriter)

Given Name:	**Kenneth Ray Carllile**
Date of Birth:	**April 2, 1931**
Where Born:	**St. Louis, Missouri**
Married:	**Virginia Boyle (m. 1955)**
Children:	**Tammy Ruth, Mary Katherine (Kathy Carllile)**
Date of Death:	**July 31, 1987**

Thumbs Carllile was a very talented musician who devised a style of playing guitar that would grace many a record and many a live performance.

Thumbs grew up on a tenanted farm in Harrisburg, Illinois, where he wore overshoes made out of discarded truck tires. When he was 8, his sister Evelyn won a Dobro for selling Cloverine salve. He borrowed the instrument so much that Evelyn hid the steel bar and so he started to play with his thumbs. His father later gave him a Sears Silvertone guitar but as Kenneth couldn't curl his short, fat fingers around the neck he wore it Dobro-style and played it as if he was playing a piano. In recent times, only the blind Canadian Blues/Rock guitarist Jeff Healy has played like this.

When he was 10, Thumbs' family moved to Granite City, near St. Louis, Missouri. He made his debut that year at the Music Box club in East St. Louis during a Ferlin Husky gig and played *Sweet Georgia Brown*. The audience was ecstatic. At 16, he was kicked out of school for "not shaving." When asked how he would make a living, he held up his thumbs. He did some gigs with Husky and then was discovered by Little Jimmy Dickens playing in a nightclub in St. Louis. It was Dickens who gave him his nickname, which he never really liked. He got the job with Little Jimmy after demonstrating that he could play both parts of Dickens' twin guitar lines on his own. Carllile performed with Dickens' Country Boys on and off from 1949 to 1952, including appearances on the *Grand Ole Opry*.

From 1952 through 1954, Thumbs was a member of the Army's Special Services. While on a base in Stuttgart, Germany, he met another recruit, Virginia Boyle, who was singing in an army show and they married in 1955. From 1954 to1957, Thumbs was a member of Bill Wimberley's Rhythm Boys. During this time, he also joined Red Foley's Troupe and became a featured musician on the *Ozark Jubilee*.

In 1961, Thumbs met Les Paul, who was excited by Virginia's songwriting and Thumbs' ability. He took them to his home in Mahwah, New Jersey, and recorded enough material for two albums. That year, Carllile released a single on Epic with Ginny O'Boyle entitled *Indian Girl, Indian Boy/Now That You're Leavin' Me*. During 1963, he became a member of the Wade Ray Five and Wade Ray's Las Vegas band.

Shortly after this in 1964, Thumbs joined Roger Miller and stayed with him for eight years. In 1964 and 1965, he appeared at the Grammy Awards show with Miller when Roger swept the board. Thumbs also appeared on Johnny Carson's *Tonight Show* on NBC-TV five times between 1961and 1968 with Miller.

During this time, Roger Miller got Thumbs signed to Smash Records. He released two albums for the label, ***Roger Miller Presents Thumbs Carllile*** and ***All Thumbs*** (both 1965). He also released one single for Smash in 1966, *My Bossa Nova/Candy Girl*. Several tracks that he recorded for Smash became popular, if not charting. These included *Let It Be Me, Caravan, No Yesterday, Theme from Picnic, Blue Skies, Stranger on the Shore* and *Hold It*.

Two years later, Carllile signed with Capitol and released the album ***Walking in Guitar Land***. No singles were released but again, certain tracks caught the public's interest. These were *It's a Good Day, Work Song* and *High Noon*. In 1980, Thumbs' daughter Kathy had a middle-order hit with *Stay Until the Rain Stops* on Frontline.

During 1986, the family moved from Chattanooga to Atlanta, where Virginia had to work in a factory making springs. Thumbs had to undergo surgery for colon cancer, which, despite fund-raisers, left the family bankrupt; a sad thing to happen to such a talented man. He started to play on WRFG Atlanta's *Sagebrush Boogie* thanks to David Chamberlain, who was a Carllile admirer. Chamberlain also arranged for him to open for guitarist Michael Hedges. On July 31, 1987, Thumbs suffered a heart attack and died.

RECOMMENDED ALBUMS:

"Roger Miller Presents Thumbs Carllile" (Smash)(1965)
"All Thumbs" (Smash)(1965)
"Walking in Guitar Land" (Capitol)(1968)
"On His Own" (Gemini)

PAULETTE CARLSON

(Singer, Songwriter, Guitar)

Date of Birth:	**October 11, 1952**
Where Born:	**Northfield, Minnesota**
Married:	**Randy Smith**
Children:	**Cali Gabriel**

Paulette Carlson is best known for her award-winning vocal work with Highway 101. Prior to joining the group, and following her departure, Carlson recorded and toured as a solo artist.

While growing up in rural Minnesota, Paulette began playing guitar as a teenager. Her father was a big Country music fan and Paulette also developed a love for the music. Following high school, Paulette performed with several Country music bands around Minnesota. She developed a large following in her home state and won Minnesota's "Female Country Vocalist of the Year" award before she moved to Nashville.

Paulette first found success in Nashville as a songwriter. She landed a job as a staff writer with the Oak Ridge Boys' Silverline/Goldmine music publishing companies, and had songs recorded by Gail Davies and Tammy Wynette. Paulette's success as a songwriter helped her land her own recording contract with RCA in the early 80's. Her early efforts as a recording artist were critically acclaimed but were commercially disappointing. Her debut single, *You Gotta Get to My Heart (Before You Lay a Hand on Me),* made a brief appearance on the charts in 1983. Paulette followed with *I'd Say Yes* and *Can You Fool*, but neither single made the Top 40.

Disappointed at her lack of airplay on her singles, Paulette returned home to Minnesota in 1985. The following year she was encouraged to give Country music another chance when she became the lead vocalist of a new group being formed, Highway 101. As a member of the group, Paulette earned a string of No.1 singles and a Gold-selling album. Both the ACM and the CMA named Highway 101 "Group of the Year," in 1987 and 1988 and 1988 and 1989 respectively.

Paulette left Highway 101 in 1991, to pursue a solo career once again. She recorded an album for Capitol entitled ***Love Goes On***, that produced the Top 20 hit, *I'll Start with You,* early in 1992. The following year, Paulette had a minor success with *Not with My Heart You Don't* and continued to perform as a solo artist.

RECOMMENDED ALBUMS:

"Love Goes On" (Capitol)(1991)

(See also Highway 101.)

JENKS TEX CARMAN

(Singer, Guitar, Hawaiian Guitar)

Date of Birth: **May 14, 1903**

Where Born: **Hardinsburg, Kentucky**

Date of Death: **February 2, 1968**

Though by most standards a decidedly minor figure in Country music history, Jenks Tex Carman was an engaging and popular showman who was extremely popular on the West Coast in the 1940's and 1950's. Best remembered for his odd Hawaiian steel guitar style and his affectation for Indian costumes, Carman left a handful of commercial records, and evidence of how one with even limited talent could sell himself through sheer showmanship and personality. Singer Johnny Western remembered that Carman wasn't a good musician but he was novel enough for people to pay attention. He'd come out with that big smile and play that Hawaiian guitar with all those flourishes and soon he'd have everybody cheering for him. It was strictly a visual act.

Whether or not Carman was actually part Cherokee, as he often claimed, and exactly when he was born were matters of mystery and speculation until a researcher traced the singer's career. Little evidence about a Cherokee background was found, but the Carman family was traced to Breckenridge County, Kentucky, where Tex was the seventh of eight children born to Alford Carman and his wife, who were farmers in the area. Like many other figures in the 1930's, Tex got his first taste of music from the Pop scene, working in vaudeville and as a leader of the Glee Quartet with the Chautauqua Bureau in Louisville. Soon he was appearing on radio stations WHAS Louisville and KMOX St. Louis.

Frank Plada, a Hawaiian steel guitarist who had recorded extensively in the 1920's, taught Carman his style of playing the guitar, which involved fretting with a steel bar and using a sharp, staccato sound. Carman's success with this style eventually took him to Los Angeles, where he billed himself as Jenks Tex Carman, the Dixie Cowboy, and worked over station KXLA in Pasadena. He signed a record contract with the local 4 Star label, saw several interesting releases, and soon found his way to TV shows like *Town Hall Party* and *Hometown Jamboree.* Through the latter show, he met Capitol talent scout Cliffie Stone, who brought Carman to the attention of Capitol's Ken Nelson.

Between April 1951 and December 1953, Carman recorded about 20 sides for Capitol, of which the most popular were *Hillbilly Hula* and *Hilo March.* This was not enough to keep him on the label, though, and he soon left to sign with local label Sage & Sand. He continued to be popular on California TV, but eventually as local programming faded in the face of network, he drifted into retirement. He died on February 2, 1968, at the age of 64. CKW

RECOMMENDED ALBUM:

"The Wreck of the Old '97" (Old Homestead)

CAROLINA TAR HEELS, The

Formed: **1928**

DOCK WALSH

(Vocals, Banjo, Guitar)

Given Name: **Doctor Coble Walsh**

Date of Birth: **July 23, 1901**

Where Born: **Wilkes County, North Carolina**

Married: **Unknown**

Children: **Drake**

Date of Death: **1967**

GARLEY FOSTER

(Harmonica, Vocals, Imitations)

Given Name: **Garley Foster**

Date of Birth: **January 10, 1905**

Where Born: **Wilkes County, North Carolina**

GWEN FOSTER

(Harmonica, Vocals)

Where Born: **probably Gaston County, North Carolina**

TOM ASHLEY (See Clarence Tom Ashley)

The Carolina Tar Heels were a successful 1920's string band which made some 40-odd sides for Victor Records and were later rediscovered in the 1960's during the Folk revival. Their performance style was distinctive in that they had no fiddle (using the harmonica as a substitute) and developed a repertoire strong in mountain Blues and unusual 19th-century songs. Their hit records included *Bring Me a Leaf from the Sea* (1927), *I'm Going to Georgia* (1927), *Roll on Boys* (1928), *Peg and Awl* (1928), and *My Home's Across the Blue Ridge Mountains* (1929).

The central figure in the band was Dock Walsh, a banjoist and singer who had recorded as a soloist for Columbia in 1925. By 1926 he was "busking" around the mills in the Gastonia area when he met Gwen Foster, a harmonica and guitar player from the area. The pair added two musicians and auditioned as a full string band for Ralph Peer in 1927; Peer decided he wanted only Walsh and Foster and signed them up, giving them the name the Carolina Tar Heels. Three sessions were done in this manner, but by late fall 1927, the pair had split up and Walsh recruited Garley Foster (no relation to Gwen) as a replacement. Garley was an old friend who was also a talented whistler and sometimes billed himself as "the Human Bird."

Starting in the fall of 1928, the band was augmented by Tom Ashley, the fine Tennessee singer and banjoist who had already recorded on his own and with Byrd Moore. Though Ashley was a superb banjo player, he played guitar and sang during the 17 titles he recorded with the Tar Heels. He left the band by mid-1929 and the band again became a duet. A few later records were issued under the name the Pine Mountain Boys, and their last session (in Atlanta, in 1932) featured the original duo of Dock and Gwen Foster.

In 1962, researchers Gene Earle and Archie Green discovered Dock and Garley and recorded an lp by them on the Folk Legacy label, which also featured Dock's son, Drake. Walsh died in 1967, Garley a few years later; Tom Ashley passed away in 1968. Little is known about the later life of Gwen Foster.

From 1931 to 1933, an entirely separate band called the Carolina Tarheels performed over WSB radio in Atlanta. This band was apparently led by Claude Davis and for a time included Hoke Rice and Curly Fox. They never recorded, however, and the only relation to the original Tar Heels was to force Walsh's band to bill themselves as "the Original Carolina Tar Heels" on the labels from their 1932 session. CKW

RECOMMENDED ALBUMS:
"The Carolina Tarheels" (Folk Legacy)
"Look Who's Comin'" (GHP and Old Homestead)

MARY-CHAPIN CARPENTER

(Singer, Songwriter, Guitar)
Given Name: **Mary-Chapin Carpenter**
Date of Birth: **February 21, 1958**
Where Born: **Princeton, New Jersey**

When Mary-Chapin Carpenter stepped up to receive her CMA "Top New Female Vocalist of the Year" award in 1990, Country music stepped onto a more literate plane. Gone was the glitz and glam, and in its place were the "Folk songs" of the new blue-collar worker and his wife, with the problems of the 90's.

Mary-Chapin, born in Princeton, New Jersey, was the third of four daughters. She moved to Japan with her parents when she was 10 and while in school there, she became interested in music and started to play guitar. They returned to New Jersey two years later. The family moved to Washington, D.C., in 1974, where Mary-Chapin discovered a thriving music scene. She graduated from Brown University, Providence, Rhode Island, with a B.A. in American civilization. During her time at university, she played at "open mic" sessions in D.C. clubs. One night, she asked for a job and got it and so began her professional life. She played in clubs and bars in the Washington area and began to get well known locally. Her friend John Jennings started making tapes of her songs, initially in his basement studio. The idea was to make a cassette to sell at gigs. At this time, Mary-Chapin met Tom Carrico (now her manager), who said he would try and shop her tape around for her.

In 1986, Mary-Chapin was awarded her first of Washington Area Music Awards. Gary Olsey, the owner of a club in Virginia, was chatting to Larry Hamby at CBS in Nashville and mentioned her name. Larry was interested and as he was about to go to Washington, asked Mary-Chapin to leave a copy of her tape at the hotel. In the meantime, Tom Carrico had been doing a good job and Rounder Records, an independent label, was interested. Larry asked Mary-Chapin not to sign until he had a chance to hear the tape. CBS signed her and acquired the master tape of her recordings.

The debut album, ***Hometown Girl***, was released on Columbia in 1987 and her songwriting abilities were acclaimed. She was again a multi-winner at the Washington Area Music Awards. Her popularity was evident in June 1988, when she performed at the Kerrville, Texas, Folk Festival and received three standing ovations.

In 1989, Mary-Chapin signed a co-publishing agreement between her own Getarealjob Music and EMI/SKB Music. She again won more awards from the Washington Area Music Awards and Columbia released her second album, ***State of the Heart,*** which she co-produced with Jennings and on which she composed 10 of the 11 songs. She began a promotional tour and also performed at the Swiss Alps Country Music Festival in Grendelwald and the Winnipeg Folk Festival. *How Do*, the first single from ***State of the Heart***, went Top 20 while the second single, *Never Had It So Good*, reached the Top 10. The album itself reached the Albums chart Top 30 and crossed over to the lower rungs of the Pop Albums chart.

1990 started well for Mary-Chapin with *Quittin' Time* going Top 10. She followed that with the Top 15 hit *Something of a Dreamer*. That year, Mary-Chapin appeared at the Wembley Festival in England. At the ACM awards, she was named "Top New Female Vocalist." She released her third album, ***Shooting Straight in the Dark***, in October 1990 and in April 1992, it was Certified Gold. The first single from it, *You Win Again*, became a Top 20 hit at the start of 1991. She was invited to be the opening act at the CMA awards show and she sang an unrecorded song that she had featured in her concerts and was given a standing ovation.

During the spring of 1991, Mary-Chapin reached the Top 15 with *Right Now*. This was followed by the Cajun-flavored *Down at the Twist and Shout*, which gave her a Top 3 placing. She won a Grammy Award for the single as "Best Country Vocal Performance, Female" and performed the song at the ceremony with her band and members of the Cajun group Beausoleil. The single was also awarded *Music Row* magazine's "Best Performance Video" award. During the year, she was nominated for the ACM "Best Female Vocalist" and the CMA "Horizon Award." A BBC-TV special with Mary-Chapin was taped in England and she appeared at New York's *Bottom Line Late Show* with Rosanne Cash and Nanci Griffith. She continued to tour the U.S., appearing with great success at festivals and clubs. The national press gave her favorable reviews and she ended the year touring Australia.

Country star ***Mary-Chapin Carpenter***

Mary-Chapin started out 1992 with Top 15 single *Going Out Tonight*. Mary released the album ***Come On Come On*** and at the end of June, within two months, it was Certified Gold. The first single from the album was *I Feel Lucky,* which reached the Top 5, and Mary-Chapin received a Grammy Award for it as "Best Country Vocal Performance, Female." She also received the CMA's "Female Vocalist of the Year" award. In the late summer, Mary-Chapin charted with *Not Too Much to Ask*, a Top 15 duet with Joe Diffie.

1993 started with the Top 5 single *Passionate Kisses*, which gave Mary-Chapin her first cross-over success, reaching the Pop Top 60 and earned her another Grammy Award for "Best Country Vocal Performance, Female." Her other chart successes in 1993 were *The Hard Way* (Top 15) and Mark Knopfler's song *The Bug* (Top 20). That year, Mary-Chapin held on to the CMA's "Female Vocalist of the Year" award and her ***Come On Come On*** album was Certified Platinum.

In 1994, Mary-Chapin scored a Top 3 hit with *He Thinks He'll Keep Her*, a song she wrote with Don Schlitz. Mary-Chapin's strength lies in the fact that she can create "Folk" songs of almost gauze-like delicacy and then release an uptempo frivolous song like *I Feel Lucky*. JAB

RECOMMENDED ALBUMS:
"Hometown Girl" (Columbia)(1987)
"State of the Heart" (Columbia)(1989)
"Shooting Straight in the Dark" (Columbia)(1990)
"Come On Come On" (Columbia)(1992)

FIDDLING JOHN CARSON

(Fiddle, Guitar, Vocals)
Given Name: **John Carson**
Date of Birth: **ca. March 23, 1868**
Where Born: **Blue Ridge, Fannin County, Georgia**
Married: **Jennie Nora**
Children: **Rosa Lee**
Date of Death: **December 1949**

Though Texas fiddler Eck Robertson has the honor of being the first southern musician to record, the colorful fiddler and singer Fiddlin' John Carson was in many ways the first full-fledged Country musician to record. Carson was a fiddler, a singer, and an all-round entertainer par excellence, and it was the unexpected success of his recordings that alerted the record companies and the media in general that there was a market for what we now call Country music.

Through his extensive recordings and personal appearances at fiddling contests, Carson became a darling of the mass media and was written about more than any other figure from the "golden age" of the 1920's. While the image presented of him, with his long coat, wide-brimmed hat, and coon dog, was not entirely accurate, it did fix the stereotype of the mountain fiddler in the minds of the American public. While the records he produced were similarly full of such stereotypes (one series of skits featured Carson as a moonshiner, and his daughter, Rosa Lee [b. 1909] as a saucy mountain wench named "Moonshine Kate"), they also preserved a rich variety of old fiddle tunes and styles. Many considered "Moonshine Kate," who was a fine singer and guitarist, as the first major female hillbilly comedy celebrity.

Carson was the son of a railroad section foreman, and was reared in remote Fannin County, not far from the Georgia-Tennessee line, in the lower Blue Ridge Mountains. Young Carson began his career as a racehorse jockey, but then turned to work in the area cotton mills, which became his livelihood for some 20 years. He also began to play the fiddle and gain a reputation at the local Atlanta fiddling contests, which began in 1913. By the end of WWI, Carson was regularly winning these contests, as well as playing for carnivals, dances, and medicine shows. Like many older southern fiddlers, he developed the ability to sing and play the fiddle at the same time, and to perform unaccompanied. When Atlanta station WSB took to the air in 1922, Carson was one of the first to perform. During his performances, Carson's wife created the rhythm accompaniment by hitting his fiddle strings with straws.

In June 1923, Ralph Peer came to Atlanta to do a field session for OKeh Records; most of the acts he recorded were local mainstream artists—dance bands, college glee clubs, and the like—but on the advice of local dealer Polk C. Brockman, Peer also recorded two sides by Carson. These were two songs that would be associated with him for the rest of his career: *The Little Old Log Cabin in the Lane*, an old 1870 song by Kentucky riverman Will S. Hays, and *The Old Hen Cackled and the Rooster's Going to Crow*, an old traditional piece. Peer thought Carson's singing was "pluperfect awful" but agreed to press up 500 copies of the record for Brockman to sell locally. Convinced that he would never hear any more about it, Peer did not even put a release number on the record. As it turned out, the records arrived in Atlanta on the eve of a major fiddling contest and Carson sold every one of them off the stage! Brockman ordered more and eventually Peer had to formally add the record to the catalog and bring Carson to New York to make more records.

From November 1923 until 1931, Carson recorded regularly for OKeh, running up over 150 sides; in 1934, he added another 20-plus sides for Victor's Bluebird series. In 1924, he started recording with a string band, the Virginia Reelers, which came to include crack local fiddlers like Earl Johnson. Carson's early hits included *You Will Never Miss Your Mother Until She Is Gone*, which was even issued in sheet music with Carson's picture on it and *Be Kind to a Man When He's Down*. Topical songs were always popular, such as *The Farmer Is That Feeds Them All* and *The Grave of Little Mary Phagan* (with vocals by "Kate"), about a local murder case, where an anti-Semitic mob hung an innocent man. Bizarre titles were a specialty, too: *If You Can't Get the Stopper Out, Break Off the Neck* and *Who Bit the Wart Off Grandma's Nose*. Carson's singing, which was heavily mannered and much more appealing to modern ears than to Ralph Peer's, was spotlighted on a number of older ballads and popular songs, such as his fiddling contest showpiece, *It's a Long Way to Tipperary*.

Like many first-generation Country stars, Carson fell on hard times during the Depression. He made no more records after 1934, and spent his later years working as an elevator operator at the Georgia State Capitol. He died in December 1949, at the age of 81. His records were rediscovered by a new generation in the 1970's, and reissued on a number of albums. His life was the subject of a major biography by Gene Wiggins, *Fiddlin' Georgia Crazy*, in 1987.

During his life, Carson was involved with political campaigns and his song *Georgia's Three-Dollar Tag* was influential in getting Governor Eugene Talmage elected. He also played a part in the election of Senator Tom Watson of Georgia, both on a Populist ticket.

CKW

RECOMMENDED ALBUMS:

"A Fiddlers Convention in Mountain City, Tennessee" (County) [Various artists]

"The Old Hen Cackled and the Rooster's Going to Crow" (Rounder)

JAMES CARSON

(Singer, Songwriter, Mandolin, Guitar, Bass)

Given Name:	**James William Roberts**
Date of Birth:	**February 10, 1918**
Where Born:	**Richmond, Kentucky**
Married:	**1. Irene (Martha Carson) (div.)**
	2. Pearl (div.)
	3. Sally
Children:	**Anne Maria, James Phillip**

James Carson was a significant figure in music who had a professional career that has spanned some six decades. However, James never quite became well known except among musicians and fans in areas such as East Tennessee, Georgia and portions of Kentucky. This circumstance resulted from his being part of a group or team during the higher points of his musical life. Ironically, James had all the ingredients needed to be a strong individual performer except for the right timing.

James entered music at an early age as the son of Phillip "Doc" Roberts, one of the most significant Old-Time fiddlers on disc during the 1924-1934 era. Doc also played mandolin and supported the vocal performances of his recording partner, Asa Martin. When James learned to play rhythm behind his dad's fiddle and to sing tenor harmony with Asa, the Fiddling Doc Roberts Trio and Martin and Roberts teams came into being for fiddle band and Old-Time singing respectively.

By the time these groups made their final recordings in 1934, James had some six years of studio experience behind him at the age of 16, including a few solo efforts on such songs as *Duvall Country Blues* and *Down and Out Blues*. In the mid-1930's, Doc and James went to Iowa and played on radio for a time, but by and large, Doc Roberts contented himself with being a farmer who cut fiddle records, and avoided the city life that full-time musicianship would have entailed. James, on the other hand, looked forward to a career in music, particularly after serving a hitch in the U.S. Navy and seeing a bit of the world. He also, during this time, developed considerable expertise on the mandolin.

When James got out of the Navy in 1939, he headed for Lexington, where his dad's one-time partner Asa Martin had a radio program on WLAP entitled the *Morning Roundup*. James joined the show and met a trio of aspiring sisters from Neon, Kentucky, named Bertha, Irene and Opal Amburgey (known on stage respectively as Minnie, Martha and Mattie). James and Irene married on June 8, 1939 and James soon accompanied the Amburgeys to WHIS Bluefield, West Virginia, where the couple sang as James and Irene.

In 1940, they moved to the *Renfro Valley*

Barn Dance and then to WSB Atlanta, where the Amburgeys became the Hoot Owl Holler Girls and somewhat later James and Irene became James and Martha, the Barn Dance Sweethearts. On the same day as the Pearl Harbor attack, December 7, 1941, the *Atlanta Journal* described them as "the most promising singing duet of home Folk songs on radio." Fulfilling that promise, James and Martha subsequently came to rank with the Blue Sky Boys as the most popular Country act in Atlanta radio history.

Overwhelmingly oriented to sacred numbers, they cut 8 sides for White Church Records about 1947 and 22 more for Capitol in 1949 and 1950. James also played mandolin on an RCA Victor session for Judie and Julie Jones in 1949. Early in 1950, James and Martha moved to WNOX Knoxville, and by the end of the year had dissolved as a team. Martha went on to enjoy a solo career (as Martha Carson). James went to WWVA Wheeling where he led the staff band and worked as part of Wilma Lee and Stoney Cooper's Clinch Mountain Clan, recording with them on Columbia.

In 1952, James returned to Knoxville, where he worked on the Cas Walker radio and TV programs until 1960 as both a solo performer and support musician. During that time, James did sessions with the Lonesome Pine Fiddlers on RCA Victor and the Masters Family on Columbia. His work with the latter involved singing lead on several of his own compositions, including *Everlasting Joy* and *I Wasn't There (but I Wish I Could Have Been)*. As a writer, he dabbled in the teen market with a song recorded by Sonny James entitled *Let's Go Bunny Huggin'*.

After 1960, James no longer worked in music full-time, but operated service stations for the Waco Oil Company. He did remain active as a part-time Gospel singer and joined Doc Roberts and Asa Martin in a reunion concert at Berea College. Having moved back to Lexington, he took a tour of the Netherlands in 1984 and served a stint as staff musician at the *Renfro Valley Barn Dance* in the late 1980's.

Carson was always under-recorded as a solo performer, but a cassette tape of new material came out in 1988. A brief anthology of his earlier work appeared on the Dutch label Strictly Country at the time of his Dutch tour and an anthology of his duets with Martha came out at about the same time. A few of his early recordings have appeared on other anthologies. By 1993, James and his wife were living in Lexington, where the retired musician was teaching a Tuesday evening Bible class. IMT

RECOMMENDED ALBUMS:

"James Carson: Historical Tracks" (Strictly Country Holland)(1984) [Note: 7" containing six songs]

"James and Martha: Early Gospel Greats" (Anthology of Country Music)(1984)

"James (Carson) Roberts: Keep Your Hands on the Plow" (cassette)(1988)

JENNY LOU CARSON

(Singer, Songwriter, Guitar)

Given Name: **Lucille Overstake**
Date of Birth: **1915**
Where Born: **Decatur, Illinois**
Married: **1. Jack Dumbald (div.)**
2. Tiny Hill (m. 1946) (div. 1949)
Date of Death: **1978**

Although responsible for some of Country music's finest songs, Jenny Lou Carson remains a little-known figure among the greats. Still using the name Lucille, she and her sisters Evelyn and Eva were collectively known as the Three Little Maids, and grew up with a musical background in the Salvation Army. One of their tour-de-force numbers was *I Ain't Gonna Study War No More*. From 1931, they were resident on the WLS *Barn Dance* out of Chicago, with Lucille providing the instrumental accompaniment. In 1933, Eva married Red Foley and the group broke up.

In 1936, Lucille moved to Memphis, having just got married to Jack Dumbald. However, in 1938, she moved back to WLS and the following year, she recorded "off-color" material as Lucille Lee. On these recordings she was backed by Patsy Montana's Prairie Ramblers under the name of the Sweet Violet Boys (Patsy was actually not allowed in the studio during the recording sessions). These songs included *Widow's Lament, I Married a Mouse of a Man, Chiselin' Daddy* and the very risque *I Love My Fruit.*

Lucille became Jenny Lou Carson during the 40's. She recorded for Decca and appeared on radio. However, it was her songwriting that brought her great fame. Jenny Lou became interested in songwriting after meeting with Fred Rose, with whom she had an affair. She worked closely with him at Acuff-Rose Music for about 10 years, although she always wrote on her own. One of Jenny Lou's earliest hits was *Never Trust a Woman*, a Top 3 Country hit in 1942 for Red Foley. In 1945, Tex Ritter had a No.2 hit with one of her finest songs, *Jealous Love*, which would be a major hit for both Al Morgan and Kenny Roberts in 1949 and a minor one for Barbara Seiner in 1979.

During 1946, Eddy Arnold had a Top 3 entry with Jenny Lou's *Chained to a Memory*. Arnold went on to successfully record several other Jenny Lou songs, including *Don't Rob Another Man's Castle, The Echo of Your Footsteps* and *C-H-R-I-S-T-M-A-S* (all 1949), *Lovebug Itch* (1950) and *I'd Trade All My Tomorrows (for Just One Yesterday)* (1952). *Don't Rob Another Man's Castle* was also a major hit for Ernest Tubb & the Andrews Sisters in 1949. Hank Snow had a No.1 hit with Jenny Lou's *Let Me Go, Lover* in 1955, which was also a minor success for Karen Kelly in 1975.

Jenny Lou was one of the most active songwriters of morale-boosting material during WWII. For her writing to servicemen during the hostilities, Jenny Lou was given the soubriquet "the Radio Chin-Up Girl." Jenny Lou's songs also achieved major Pop chart success. *Let Me Go, Lover* was a No.1 hit for Joan Weber, in 1955, and other major hit versions that year were by Teresa Brewer, Patti Page and Sunny Gale. In the U.K. it was a major hit for Irish star Ruby Murray. *Jealous Heart* was a minor success for both Tab Hunter and the Fontane Sisters (both 1958) as well as Connie Francis in 1965.

Jenny Lou stopped writing and moved to California. She was inducted into the Nashville Songwriters Hall of Fame in 1971. Jenny Lou Carson died in 1978.

MARTHA CARSON

(Singer, Songwriter, Guitar)

Given Name: **Irene Amburgey**
Date of Birth: **March 19, 1921**
Where Born: **Neon, Kentucky**
Married: **1. James Carson (div.)**
2. Xavier Cosse (d. 1993)
Children: **James, Martha**

In 1950, at the height of their popularity, James and Martha Carson, the Barn Dance Sweethearts, split up, and Martha Carson started a solo career. During the next two decades, Martha moved about as far as she could from the simple guitar-mandolin duets of the James and Martha years; she developed a dynamic, Rock-flavored Gospel style that influenced everybody from Elvis Presley on

James and Martha Carson

down. She also became one of the first Country performers to deliberately launch a career in Pop.

When she and James split (both personally and professionally), Martha was working at WNOX in Knoxville, Tennessee. She was at the time under contract, as a duet act, to Capitol for seven more years, and for a time the company refused to let her record solo, trying repeatedly to match her up with a suitable male singer. During this time, she did session work, singing on Bill Carlisle's hit *Too Old to Cut the Mustard*.

In Nashville, she met Fred Rose, who listened to her and then helped convince Capitol to give her a solo shot. In November 1951, she returned to Nashville (with back-up from Carlisle, Chet Atkins and her sister Jean Chapel) and cut her first Capitol solo, and biggest hit, *Satisfied*. She had written the Gospel song herself as a response to irate listeners who criticized her for her divorce from James.

From 1951 to 1954, Martha did over two dozen sides for Capitol, joined the *Grand Ole Opry*, and toured widely with performers like Jimmy Dickens, Faron Young, Ferlin Huskey and the young Elvis Presley. Presley often asked Martha to sing Gospel songs with him backstage and later told the Jordanaires that she had inspired his stage style more than anybody.

During this time, too, Martha remarried, to Xavier Cosse (known as X. Cosse), a Pop booker and promoter who had come to Nashville to learn Country music and work with Hank Williams and then Chet Atkins. Cosse and RCA producer Steve Sholes noted the nationwide trend for religious music in the mid-1950's Pop-flavored Gospel music and thought Martha could become a part of it. They signed her to RCA and at once did her first session in Hollywood, with a band of top studio men.

By late 1955, RCA started doing all of Martha's sessions in New York, and soon she had a string of minor hits: *Journey to the Sky*, *Let the Light Shine on Me*, *This Ole House* and *Saints and Chariot*, a combination of *Swing Down Chariot* and *When the Saints Go Marching In* that Elvis later added to his stage shows. She also signed with the William Morris Agency, and in 1957 she and Cosse relocated to New York.

A national appearance on television's *Steve Allen Show* helped spread the word even more, and soon Martha was cutting non-Gospel material by writers like Otis Blackwell. The Pop experiment won her many new fans and took her places where no Gospel singer had gone before, but by the late 50's it was collapsing. Martha and Cosse returned to Nashville and their roots. Later recordings on Decca, Cadence, and Sims were solid and well done but made little impact on the charts. By the 1990's Martha was in semi-retirement; X. Cosse, who continued to manage and promote her, died in 1993. CKW

RECOMMENDED ALBUMS:

"Journey to the Sky" (RCA Victor)(1955)
"Rock-a My Soul" (RCA Victor)(1957)
"Satisfied" (Capitol)(1960) [Re-released by Stetson UK in original sleeve (1989)]
"Martha Carson's Greatest Gospel Hits" (Gusto-Starday)(1978)

CARTER FAMILY, The

Formed: 1926

A.P. CARTER
(Guitar, Fiddle, Vocals)

Given Name: Alvin Pleasant Carter
Date of Birth: December 15, 1893
Where Born: Maces Springs, Virginia
Married: Sara Carter (div.)
Children: Gladys, Janette, Joe
Date of Death: November 7, 1960

SARA CARTER
(Guitar, Autoharp, Vocals)

Given Name: Sara Doughtery
Date of Birth: July 21, 1899
Where Born: Flatwoods near Colburn, Wise County, Virginia
Married: 1. A.P. Carter (div.) 2. Col Bayes
Children: Gladys, Janette, Joe
Date of Death: January 8, 1979

MAYBELLE CARTER
(Guitar, Autoharp, Vocals)

Given Name: Maybelle Addington
Date of Birth: May 10, 1909
Where Born: Nickelsville, Virginia
Married: Ezra J. Carter
Children: Helen, June, Anita
Date of Death: October 23, 1978

The legendary first family of Country music is remarkable in that all the hyperbole and exaggeration about them is actually well-founded. In fact, as scholars have begun to seriously explore their career and influence, it seems apparent that Country music owes even more to them than the casual fan believes. They gave to the music dozens of songs which became standards, ranging all the way from *I'm Thinking Tonight of My Blue Eyes* to *The Wabash Cannonball*.

They gave to Country music a pattern for harmony singing which still inspires singers as diverse as Vince Gill and Bill Monroe. Their melodies, among the most haunting and singable in any music, have appealed to everyone from Roy Acuff to Woody Guthrie. Maybelle's "Carter lick" on the guitar has become the most influential technique in the music's history. Their 350-plus recordings made between 1927 and 1941 form a body of collected works that reached every corner of the U.S., as well as to Australia, England, Canada and even India. And the way in which A.P. took old songs both Folk and popular and made them into something new is a process which became a standard for the industry. And though the original Carter Family broke up in 1943, their sons and daughters and cousins have carried on the music in a wonderful variety of ways.

The Carter story begins in the Clinch Mountains of southwest Virginia, just a few miles from the Tennessee line. A.P. Carter conducted singing schools for the local churches, and fiddled a bit on the side. Restless, he traveled widely and when he met his bride-to-be, Sara, he was selling fruit trees. Sara, for her part, was playing an autoharp and singing an old train wreck song called *Engine 143* that she had learned from her family.

The pair were married in 1915, and continued to make music informally in the community. In 1926, they were joined by Sara's young cousin Maybelle, who played the guitar some and sang a little. After an unsuccessful try-out for Brunswick Records (who wanted to make A.P. into a fiddler), they recorded at Ralph Peer's famed Bristol sessions in August 1927. (Contrary to popular belief, the audition was not a spur-of-the-moment bit of serendipity; Peer and A.P. had earlier corresponded and set up the audition, working through the local Victrola dealer.) The Carters cut six songs at this first session, including *The Wandering Boy*, *The Storms Are on the Ocean* and *Single Girl, Married Girl*. To Sara's surprise, it was the latter cut, a solo by her, that became the big hit and eventually got the Carters called up to New York to do follow-up records.

This second session included *Keep on the Sunny Side*, an old 1899 Sunday school song that became their theme song. They recorded *Anchored Love*, a badman ballad from West Virginia called *John Hardy Was a Desperate Little Man* and an old Civil War parlor song called *Wildwood Flower* which featured Maybelle's guitar picking and which became the most popular starter piece for Country guitar pickers. For a time, it seemed the Carters would outsell Jimmie Rodgers and certainly by the time this second batch of records hit the stores, Peer knew he had a major act on his hands.

Unfortunately, the big record success came just at the start of the Depression and the Carters were really not able to take advantage of their record hits. Instead of touring in radio and vaudeville, they remained in the mountains, doing schoolhouse shows for 15 and 25 cents a head. For a time in 1929, A.P. went north to Detroit to find work and Maybelle and her husband moved to Washington, D.C., to get work.

The legendary ***Carter Family***

For several years, the Carters got together mainly for recording sessions. Both women, who did most of the singing on the records, were busy having children and raising their families, leaving most of the career management to A.P. and Peer. This finally yielded some decent radio contracts by the mid-1930's, and in 1938 it resulted in the Carters going south to appear on the "border radio" station XERF in Del Rio, Texas. Border stations, with their transmitters across the Rio Grande in Mexico, were exempt from the federal radio regulations that limited the power of U.S. stations to 50,000 watts. The border stations often shot up to over 100,000 watts, meaning the Carters could be heard pretty much all over the United States. The result was a surge in their record sales—they had moved from Victor to ARC to Decca—and a huge rise in popularity.

Unfortunately, personalities entered into the picture again. In 1939, Sara and A.P. divorced after a number of earlier separations, and eventually Sara remarried and she and her new husband moved to California. Then in 1941, the border station went off the air for good. There was one last chance to make the big time, and the trio reunited for a short stint at Charlotte in 1941. The same week that *Life* magazine planned to run a spread on them, the Japanese bombed Pearl Harbor. Heartsick, A.P. returned to Virginia, where he spent the rest of his life running a country store. Sara retired to a peaceful life in California.

Maybelle took her daughters, Helen, June and Anita and formed a new act, Mother Maybelle and the Carter Sisters. In 1952, A.P. Carter re-formed the Carter Family with his ex-wife, Sara and their children and opened an outdoor arena in Maces Springs, called Summer Park. A tiny Kentucky label called Acme persuaded A.P., Sara, and daughter Janette to do a new series of records in the early 1950's, but they sounded outdated in the world of Hank Williams and Lefty Frizzell. The original Carter Family called it a day in 1956. A more successful comeback occurred in 1966 (after A.P. had died in 1960), when Sara and Maybelle reunited, played a number of Folk festivals and did a reunion album for Columbia. CKW

RECOMMENDED ALBUMS:

"Great Original Recordings by the Carter Family" (Harmony)(1962)
"A Collection of Favorites by the Carter Family" (Decca)(1963) [Re-issued by Stetson UK in the original sleeve (1987)]
"Carter Family in Texas" (Vols. 1-6) (Old Homestead)(1984-1986)
"Clinch Mountain Treasures" (County)(1991)
"Original Carter Family (Early Classics)" (Anthology of Country Music)
"The Original Carter Family (from 1936 Radio Transcripts)" (Old Homestead)
"All Time Favorites" (Acme)
"In Memory of A.P. Carter (Keep on the Sunny Side)" (Acme)

CARTER FAMILY, The (a.k.a. CARTER SISTERS, The)

Formed: **1943**

Members:

Mother Maybelle Carter	**Vocals, Autoharp**
Helen Carter	**Vocals, Accordion, Guitar, Autoharp**
June Carter	**Vocals, Autoharp, Guitar**
Anita Carter	**Vocals, Bass, Guitar**

After the break-up of the original Carter Family, Mother Maybelle formed a new version of the Carter Family with her daughters, as Mother Maybelle and the Carter Sisters. They began broadcasting on WRNL Richmond, Virginia, until 1946 when they joined the *Old Dominion Barn Dance* over WRVA Richmond, Virginia. They stayed there until 1947, then moved to the *Tennessee Barn Dance* on WNOX Knoxville, Tennessee, where they stayed for another year. In 1948, they recorded their first release, *The Kneeling Drunkard's Plea.* They went on to KWTO Springfield, Missouri, in 1949, where they joined the *Ozark Jubilee*.

In 1950, the group went on to the *Grand Ole Opry*, with the itinerant Chet Atkins, who had been fired from many a radio station in his attempt to play his music. He had come under the Carter wing in 1948 and stayed with them until 1951. At the time, Mother Maybelle and the Carter Sisters were singing largely Gospel material, but the marriages and divorces of Anita and June made it difficult for them to concentrate on a full-time repertoire of religious content.

In 1952, they performed on the first nationally telecast Country music TV show hosted by Kate Smith. That year, A.P. Carter re-formed the Carter Family with his ex-wife, Sara, and their children, opened Summer Park, an outdoor arena in Maces Spring and recorded for Acme. This continued until 1956 without much impact. Following A.P.'s death in 1960, Mother Maybelle and the Carter Sisters became the Carter Family. During 1956 and 1957, Mother Maybelle and the girls toured with Elvis Presley as his opening act.

During the 60's, Mother Maybelle found herself in demand as a solo performer on the emerging Folk circuit and June found her career more intertwined with her third husband, Johnny Cash. Anita began recording for RCA, where she duetted with Hank Snow on the 1951 double-sided smash *Bluebird Island/ Down the Trail of Aching Hearts*. She then become a part of the teen trio 'Nita, Rita & Ruby between 1955 and 1957. In 1968, Anita had a Top 5 single, *I Got You*, with Waylon Jennings, then went on to United Artists and Capitol, chalking up several chart hits. Helen turned to songwriting and penned Margie Bowes' 1959 hit, *Poor Old Heartsick Me*.

From 1961, the Carter Family became associated with Johnny Cash. The Carter Family recorded for Decca and Columbia, but it was while with the latter that they chalked up singles hits. This started when they backed-up Cash on his 1963 hit, *Busted*. They then had a Top 40 success, *A Song to Mama*, on which Johnny did the narration. In 1967, they left the *Grand Ole Opry* to join the *Johnny Cash Show*, appearing on his ABC-TV show from 1969. In 1972, they went Top 50 with *Travelin' Minstrel Band* and then with Cash supporting them, they had a Top 40 single, *The World Needs a Melody*. That year, they appeared on the Nitty Gritty Dirt Band's ***Will the Circle Be Unbroken*** album. Their final chart entry was in 1973, *Praise the Lord and Pass the Soup*, with Cash and the Oak Ridge Boys. That year, they were named "Favorite Group" in the Country Category of the AMA. During this time, Helen's son David, Anita's daughter Lori and June's daughter Carlene Carter became part of the road show.

Mother Maybelle Carter with daughters, June, Anita and Helen

In 1971, the Carter Family appeared on Merle Haggard's double album ***The Land of Many Churches*** along with Bonnie Owens. Following Mother Maybelle's death in 1978, Helen and Anita continued to tour and in 1988, they and June and Carlene recorded the album ***Wildwood Flower***, which was produced by Jack Clement for Mercury. In 1980, the Carter Family was named "Gospel Act of the Year" at the MCN Cover Awards. In 1992, they appeared on the Nitty Gritty Dirt Band's ***Will the Circle Be Unbroken, Vol. 2***, for which they received a Gold Record.

RECOMMENDED ALBUMS:

"The Carter Family Singing Their Favorite Carter Family Songs" (Decca)(1962) [Re-Kin the original sleeve (1989)]
"A Collection of Favorites (Folk, Country, Blues & Country Songs)" (Decca)(1963)
"Travelin' Minstrel Band" (Columbia)(1972)
"Three Generations" (Columbia)(1974)
"The Carter Sisters: Maybelle, Anita, June & Helen" (Bear Family Germany)(1982)
"Wildwood Flower" (Mercury)(1988)

ANITA CARTER

(Singer, Songwriter, Guitar,Autoharp,Guitarro,Bass)

Given Name:	**Ina Anita Carter**
Date of Birth:	**March 31, 1933**
Where Born:	**Maces Springs, Virginia**
Married:	**1. Dale Potter (div.)** **2. Donald S. Davis (div.)** **3. Donald S. Davis (re-married/div.)** **4. Robert C. Wooton (div.)**
Children:	**Lorrie Frances, John Christopher**

Anita, the youngest of the three daughters of Maybelle and Ezra Carter, made her first public appearance in 1937 with her sisters on *The Popeye Club*, on radio station WOPI Bristol, Virginia, singing *Beautiful Brown Eyes*. Two years later, the three sisters joined the Carter Family on the border station XERA out of Del Rio, Texas. In 1941, the girls joined the family on WBT Charlotte, North Carolina. Following the folding of the Carter Family, Mother Maybelle and the girls got together, in 1943, as Mother Maybelle and the Carter Sisters. (See Carter Family second entry.)

In 1951, Anita got together with Hank Snow (the Singing Ranger) and the Rainbow Ranch Boys for the double-sided Country smash hit *Bluebird Island* (Top 5)/*Down the Trail of Achin' Hearts*, on RCA Victor. In 1953-1954, Anita recorded for Columbia and then in 1955, RCA decided to promote Anita as a Pop performer as part of 'Nita, Rita & Ruby with Rita Robbins (real name Ruby Winters, the sister of Don Winters) and Ruby Wright (daughter of Kitty Wells and Johnny Wright) while also recording Anita as a solo Country singer. The group appeared on the *Grand Ole Opry* and were named "Most Promising Country Group" in the *Cash Box* Disc Jockey Poll of 1956. However, by 1957, the idea had run out of steam, as Anita was busy touring with the Carter Family. Anita went on to record for Cadence (1957), Jamie (1960) and Mercury (1963).

During the 60's, Anita did a lot of back-up work and her distinctive soprano voice could be heard on many recordings. Anita returned to RCA in 1965 and to the Country charts in 1966, with a pair of medium-sized successes, *I'm Gonna Leave You* (Top 50) and in 1967 *Love Me Now (While I Am Living)* (Top 70). In 1968, Anita teamed up with Waylon Jennings for the Top 5 duet *I Got You*. In 1968, Anita signed with United Artists and chalked up a Top 70 hit with *To Be a Child Again* and then, the following year, she teamed up with Johnny Darrell for the Top 50 *The Coming of the Roads*.

At the end of 1970, Anita signed with Capitol and the following year she had a Top 50 hit, *Tulsa County,* and followed with her final chart entry, *A Whole Lotta Lovin'*, which went Top 70. At the end of the 70's, Anita became involved in TV production and in 1979 served as talent coordinator, consultant and performer on *The Unbroken Circle: A Tribute to Mother Maybelle Carter*. In 1982, Helen served as Associate Producer on the movie *Country Gold*, in which she appeared. She also acted as talent coordinator and consultant on the 1986 CBS-TV movie, *Stagecoach*.

RECOMMENDED ALBUMS:

"Together Again" (RCA Victor)(1962) [With Hank Snow]
"Anita Carter Sings Folk Songs Old & New" (Mercury)(1963) [Re-released on Bear Family Germany (1981)]
"Anita Carter (of the Carter Family)" (Mercury)(1964)
"Just to Satisfy You" (RCA Victor)(1969) [Waylon Jennings, on which two tracks are duets with Anita Carter]
"So Much Love" (Capitol)(1972)
"Rock Love" (Bear Family Germany)(1986) [as Nita, Rita & Ruby]
"Ring of Fire" (Bear Family Germany)

CARLENE CARTER

(Singer, Songwriter, Guitar, Piano)

Given Name:	**Rebecca Carlene Smith**
Date of Birth:	**September 26, 1955**
Where Born:	**Madison, Tennessee**
Married:	**1. Joe Simpkins (m. 1970)(div.)** **2. Jack Routh (m. 1974)(div.)** **3. Nick Lowe (m. 1979)(div.)**
Children:	**Tiffany, Jackson**

With an awesome show business lineage behind her, a grandchild of the legendary Carter Family and daughter of famous Country singiers Carl Smith and June Carter, Carlene Carter set out to prove herself. She went away from Nashville to search for her musical potential. She served her apprenticeship in the Rock-Pop market and then returned to her Country roots.

When Carlene and her younger sister, Rosie, were small they didn't appreciate their family history. Carlene, while still young, was taught to play guitar by her grandmother, Maybelle Carter. Carlene made her first stage appearance when she was age 4, singing with the Carter Family and she has many memories of county and state fairs. When she was really small, she spent every weekend with her dad. Early on, they led a quiet life but when June married Johnny Cash, things changed. Many famous stars came to their house like the Monkees, Bob Dylan, Eric Clapton, Joni Mitchell and James Taylor. The children got spoiled and their lives began to be put under a microscope. Tourists took their pictures, tour buses stopped outside their house, their pocket money went up from $1 to $10. Carlene then started to realize the fame surrounding her family.

When she was 15, Carlene married and became a mother. She then went to college to major in piano. At the age of 17, she played with the Carter Family in Morgantown, West Virginia. There were around 10,000 people there. It was when Mother Maybelle Carter came on stage and got a standing ovation that Carlene realized the incredible fame of her grandmother.

Carlene married again when she was 19 and had a son. In 1978, she got a recording contract with Warner Brothers and released her debut album, ***Carlene Carter***. She had never played with a band before or been in a studio and didn't know what to expect. Her first single in 1979, *Do It in a Heartbeat,* reached the Country Top 50 and crossed to the lower rungs of the Pop chart. Carlene returned to the Country chart Top 80 in 1980 with *Baby Ride Easy*, a duet with Dave Edmunds. By this time, Carlene was in London and married to Nick Lowe, the British Rock musician, singer and producer. In 1983, Carlene had a Pop chart single, *I Couldn't Say No*, on RCA in duet with Robert Ellis Orrall. Living in London, England, Carlene pursued a Rock career working as a solo artist in Europe and had a featured role in the musical *Pump Boys and Dinettes*, which ran at the Piccadilly Theatre in London.

When Carlene's marriage crumbled in the mid-80's, she returned to her childhood home in Madison, Tennessee, and toured with her mother and two aunts Helen and Anita as the Carter Family for two years. In 1981, Carlene had met Howie Epstein when he joined Tom Petty and the Heart Breakers as bass player. When she returned to the U.S., she and Epstein decided to write and record a demo tape to try to get a record deal. At the end of 1989, Carlene dueted with Southern Comfort on their Top 30 single *Time's Up*.

When Jim Ed Norman of Warner Brothers heard the song *Get out of My Way*, he re-signed Carlene to the Warner Brothers' Reprise label and with Epstein as producer, Carlene cut her single *I Fell in Love,* which was accompanied by a music video and quickly went Top 3 in 1990. She followed this with another Top 3 single, *Come on Back*.

As her Country career took off, Carlene formed a band and went on the road, and ironically shared some dates with her step-brother-in-law, Rodney Crowell. On her album ***I Fell in Love***, Carlene wrote or co-wrote most of the songs. The album reached the Country Album chart Top 20. In 1991, both of her singles failed to register as high on the chart, with *The Sweetest Thing* going Top 25 and *One Love* reaching the Top 40.

The third generation of talent, ***Carlene Carter***

For nearly two years, Carlene had no chart action and then in 1993, she signed with Giant Records and returned to the Top 3 with *Every Little Thing*, which was accompanied by a very amusing music video. The follow-up single, *Unbreakable Heart*, just failed to make the Top 50. These all came from her critically acclaimed 1993 album ***Little Love Letters***. Her 1994 single *I Love You 'Cause I Want To* also only reached the Top 40. Then in 1994, Carlene appeared on the soundtrack album of the movie *Maverick* on Atlantic Records. Carlene and James Stroud co-produced her track on the album, *Something Already Gone*, which was released as a single and reached the Top 50. Carlene has emerged as a true heiress of the Carter and Smith heritage. JAB

RECOMMENDED ALBUMS:

"I Fell in Love" (Warner Brothers)(1990)
"Little Love Letters" (Giant)(1993)

HELEN CARTER

(Singer, Songwriter, Autoharp, Guitar, Accordion, Piano, Mandolin)

Given Name: **Helen Myrl Carter**
Date of Birth: **September 12, 1927**
Where Born: **Maces Springs, Virginia**
Married: **Glenn Jones (m. 1950)**
Children: **Glenn Daniel, Kenneth Burton (dec'd.), David Lawrence, Kevin Carter**

Helen, the eldest of the three daughters of Maybelle and Ezra Carter, was born and raised into what was destined to be the first family of Country music. She was born just one month after the first recording session of the original Carter Family in Bristol, Tennessee.

Helen made her first public appearance in 1937 with her sisters on *The Popeye Club* on radio station WOPI Bristol, Virginia, singing *Beautiful Brown Eyes*. Two years later, the three sisters joined the Carter Family on the border station XERA out of Del Rio, Texas. In 1941, the girls joined the family on WBT Charlotte, North Carolina. Following the folding of the Carter Family, Mother Maybelle and the girls got together, in 1943, as Mother Maybelle and the Carter Sisters. (See Carter Family second entry.)

Helen married pilot and inventor Glenn Jones in 1950, and their third son, David, has participated in the Carter Family. In 1951, she signed with Tennessee Records and turned out several sides, including duets with her brother-in-law Don Davis, Bob Eaton and Grant Turner. In 1952, Helen released a pair of singles for OKeh. That year, she turned out a duet with Johnny Bond called *I Went to Your Wedding*, for Columbia. During 1956 through 1958, Helen released singles for Hickory without charting. Helen turned to songwriting and penned, among many others, Margie Bowes' 1959 hit, *Poor Old Heartsick Me*. Helen teamed up with Delores Dinning of the Dinning Sisters as the Blondettes for the 1960 single *Little Butterfly/My Love (Is Many Things)*. She moved on to Starday in 1973 and recorded *The Wild Side of Life*, with the Willis Brothers and *Release Me*, with Bobby Sykes. In 1975, Helen accompanied her mother when she recorded for the Smithsonian Institution. Following the death of Mother Maybelle in 1978, Helen continued to tour with her sisters. In an attempt to preserve the music of the Carter Family, Helen has addressed school and college groups throughout the U.S.

RECOMMENDED ALBUMS:

"This Is for You Mama" (Old Homestead)(1979)
"Clinch Mountain Memories" (Old Homestead)(1993)

JOE & JANETTE CARTER

JOE CARTER

(Singer, Songwriter, Guitar)

Given Name: **Joe Carter**
Date of Birth: **February 27, 1927**
Where Born: **Maces Springs, Virginia**
Married: **(div.)**
Children: **Kim**

JANETTE CARTER

(Singer, Songwriter, Autoharp)

Date of Birth: **July 2, 1923**
Where Born: **Maces Springs, Virginia**
Married: **(Divorced twice)**
Children: **Dale, Don, Rita**

If you would like to experience how it used to be in days gone by, when music was played in rural communities, pure Old-Time Country music that came from God-fearing folk, the place to go is Maces Springs, Virginia. It is well off the beaten track and the nearest big city is Knoxville, Tennessee, 125 miles away. On Saturday nights, if you go to the Carter Family Memorial Music Center, better known locally as the Carter Family Fold, you will encounter just that. There are no blaring amplifiers and no electric instruments. The only things plugged into the wall are the microphones. The other rules are: no drinking and no profanity.

Joe and Janette are the children of the legendary A.P. Carter and Sara, who, with Sara's cousin Maybelle, were the pioneers of Country music, the original Carter Family. A.P. and Sara had three small children, Joe, Janette and Gladys, at the time they did the first recording sessions in Bristol, Tennessee, in 1927. By 1933, their marriage was in trouble, although they continued to work together. It was in 1938 that Janette was introduced to the group, then Maybelle's daughters, first Anita then June and Helen.

The Carters moved to Del Rio, Texas, to begin a series of broadcasts over XERA (where Janette made her debut in 1939, and Joe in 1940), XEG and XENT. These were Mexican border stations that had an output of 50,000 watts. The Carters recorded twice daily on their own radio program and cut many transcriptions which were mailed to other stations to be used at any time. They stayed in Texas until 1941, when they moved to station WBT in Charlotte, North Carolina. During this time Janette could be heard singing a Rex Griffin song, *Last Letter,* which was a Country hit of the 30's. Although A.P. and Sara divorced in 1939, the original Carter Family remained together as a group until 1943.

Sara had remarried and now moved to California, and A.P. moved back to open his country store at the foot of Clinch Mountain with his children. A.P., Sara, Joe and Janette began a renewed life in recording as the Carter Family, or sometimes the A.P. Carter Family and between 1952 and 1956, they recorded for a little-known label called Acme cutting some 80 songs. The pressings were inferior and the owner, Clifford Spurlock, did not really have any effective distribution. It seems the cuts were only intended for radio consumption. Their efforts had little impact and gradually they were virtually forgotten. A.P. opened Summer Park, an outdoor area for Country music, in Maces Springs, Virginia, in 1953. At this time Janette recorded her own composition *Pretty Raindrops.*

Just before A.P. died in 1960, Janette promised him she would try and carry on his work and somehow find a way to let people hear his music. He wanted to keep pure Old-Time Country music going. This promise took some time to come to fruition because Janette had her young family to raise and very little money, but in 1974, when she was 51, she decided it was now or never. She cleaned up the one-room store her father had owned in Maces Springs, put in benches to hold 200 people, booked two local musicians, notified the newspapers and prayed. Charging $1.00 admission, she took $196 on the first night. She booked hoedowns for every other Saturday, made her own posters and took them around herself and worked full-time as a school cook to raise additional funding.

After two years, taking her courage in both hands, Janette left her job and made the hoedowns weekly events. The people kept coming. Janette, Joe and Gladys (the elder sister) had always remained close. They have always lived near each other and helped one another. In 1979, Joe (a skilled carpenter) and friends built the present "Fold," which is a kind of large shed with an aluminum roof, built on a hill with seats on the slope, giving a good view of the performance and seating over 400 people. The old store has been converted to the Carter Family Museum. Janette, Joe and Gladys sponsored the First Annual Carter Family Memorial Festival, held in Hiltons, Virginia, in 1975, and it continues to date. JAB

RECOMMENDED ALBUMS:

"Carter Family Favorites" (County)
"Howdaydoo" (Traditional)
"Storms Are on the Ocean" (Birch)(1949)
"A New Branch from Old Roses" (Vecto)(1983) [Joe Carter solo]

JUNE CARTER

(Singer, Songwriter, Banjo, Autoharp, Guitar, Mandolin, Harmonica, Actress, Author)

Given Name:	**Valerie June Carter**
Date of Birth:	**June 23, 1929**
Where Born:	**Maces Springs, Virginia**
Married:	**1. Carl Smith (div.)** **2. Rip Nix (div.)** **3. Johnny Cash (m. 1968)**
Children:	**Carlene Carter, Rosie Nix, John Carter Cash**

June is a famous daughter of a famous family and the famous wife of a famous husband. The family being the Carter family and the husband Johnny Cash, and four members of her family have been elected to the Country Music Hall of Fame: mother (Maybelle Carter), husband (Johnny Cash), uncle (A.P. Carter) and aunt (Sara Carter). June carries on the tradition of being an entertainer and is not shy of offering her famous "squaw" dance to the delight of her audiences.

Born at the foot of the Clinch Mountain, June was musical as one would expect and was taught autoharp by her mother, Maybelle. June and her sisters, Helen and Anita, made their first public appearance in 1937 on *The Popeye Club* on radio WOPI Bristol, Virginia, singing *Beautiful Brown Eyes.* They also appeared together with cousin Janette Carter as part of the Carter Family in 1939.

When the original Carter Family disbanded, June, Helen and Anita joined forces with Mother Maybelle in 1943 as the Carter Sisters and toured many parts of the U.S. They appeared on various radio stations throughout the later 40's, such as WRNL (1943-46) and WRVA's the *Old Dominion Barndance* (1946-47) both in Richmond, Virginia. In 1948, they performed on KNOX Knoxville, Tennessee, where they cut their first single, *The Kneeling Drunkard's Prayer.* During the time they were on KWTO Springfield, Missouri, June recorded on RCA Victor, and on Columbia some of her discs were *Tennessee Mambo, Time's a Wastin', He Don't Love Me Anymore* and *Left Over Lovin'.* A novelty single with Homer &

June Carter** with **Waylon Jennings, Hank Williams, Jr.** and **Johnny Cash

Jethro, *Baby It's Cold Outside,* went into the Top 10 in 1949.

June made her debut on the *Grand Ole Opry* in 1950 and she remained there for many years. After the family moved to Nashville in 1952, they assumed the Carter Family name and performed on the first nationally telecast Country music TV show, which was hosted by Kate Smith. Around this time, June married the famous Country singer Carl Smith. In 1955, their daughter, Rebecca Carlene, was born. (She is now known as singer Carlene Carter.)

Although June continued to appear with the Carter Family, she wanted a career of her own and she enrolled with an actors' studio in New York and studied drama at Manhattan's Neighborhood Playhouse. She also did solo guest appearances on shows for Tennessee Ernie Ford and Jack Parr. Through June's acting training, she now began to get parts in several TV series including *Gunsmoke* and *Jim Bowie* and a part in the 1958 movie *Country Music Holiday*. She also appeared in *Little House on the Prairie*.

Following the break-up of her first marriage, June married Rip Nix and gave birth to Rosie. June joined Johnny Cash's troupe in the early 60's as a solo act. In 1964, June had a successful duet with him with *It Ain't Me Babe,* which was in the Country and the Pop charts. June toured with Johnny's show, even appearing in Liverpool, England, where the show was a smash sellout. In 1967, the Carter Family joined the *Johnny Cash Show* and Johnny and June recorded the now famous duet *Jackson,* which won a Grammy Award as "Best Country & Western Performance Duet." This was followed by another Top 10 hit in the Country charts, *Long Legged Guitar Pickin' Man.*

Johnny proposed to June on stage before a huge audience in London, Ontario, and they were married in 1968 in Franklin, Tennessee. June, a committed Christian, encouraged Johnny to cure himself of his drug habit and he renewed his interest in Christianity. The CMA voted Johnny Cash and June Carter "Vocal Group of the Year" in 1969. The following year, they released the hit record duet *If I Were a Carpenter*, another Grammy winner for "Best Country Performance by a Duo." That year, 1970, John Carter Cash was born.

In 1971, June had the solo Top 30 hit *A Good Man* and followed with several duets with Johnny. These were *No Need to Worry* (Top 15, 1971), *If I Had a Hammer* (Top 30, 1972), *The Loving Gift* (Top 30, 1973) and *Allegheny* (Top 70, 1973).

An ambition of Johnny and June was fulfilled in 1972, when they went to Israel, to work on the movie *Gospel Road*. This was a full-length film of the life and times of Jesus Christ co-written with Larry Murray and narrated by Johnny Cash. The idea had originated from a dream June had when they were visiting the Holy Land. In her dream, she saw Johnny reading about Jesus from a Bible while standing on the slopes of a mountain. June played the role of Mary Magdalene. The film was distributed by 20th Century Fox. Later it was acquired by the Reverend Billy Graham's World Wide Pictures of Burbank, California.

In 1976, June and Johnny had a Top 30 duet with *Old Time Feeling*. As a songwriter June has written or co-written many songs, including *Ring of Fire* with Merle Kilgore and *The Matador* with Johnny Cash. In 1979, she wrote her autobiography, *Among My Keidiments*, followed by a second book, *From the Heart,* in 1987.

June Carter Cash, as she has styled herself since 1971, is a very versatile lady with a warm humor and immense talent. Over the years, she has sung songs, played her autoharp, looked after her family, toured, and performed, and continues to carry on the famous family tradition. JAB

RECOMMENDED ALBUMS:

"Carryin' On" (Columbia)(1967) [With Johnny Cash/Re-issued as "Johnny Cash & His Woman" (Columbia)(1973)]
"Appalachian Pride" (Columbia)(1975)
"Gone Girl" (Columbia)(1978) [With Johnny Cash]
"Johnny and June" (Bear Family Germany) [With Johnny Cash]

MOTHER MAYBELLE CARTER

(Singer, Songwriter, Guitar, Autoharp)

Given Name: **Maybelle Addington**
Date of Birth: **May 10, 1909**
Where Born: **Nickelsville, Virginia**
Married: **Ezra J. Carter**
Children: **Helen, June, Anita**
Date of Death: **October 23, 1978**

Most of Mother Maybelle's career has been covered under the Carter Family and the successor group of the same name with her daughters, Helen, June and Anita. However, during the 60's, Mother Maybelle enjoyed a fruitful solo career.

The respect conferred on her by the college audiences of this period was almost idolatrous. This renewed interest in her work led to the reissuing of Carter Family albums. Maybelle appeared on Flatt & Scrugg's ***Songs of the Famous Carter Family***, which was released in 1961. In 1963, Mother Maybelle appeared at the Newport Folk Festival and three years later, she got together with her former sister-in-law, Sara Carter, for the album ***An Historic Reunion***, which was recorded in Nashville. In 1967, the two got together to wild acclaim at the Newport Folk Festival. The following year, Maybelle was named "Mother of Country Music" by *Music City News*.

During the 60's and 70's the autoharp was added to her already acclaimed guitar playing. As part of the original Carter Family, Maybelle was inducted into the Country Music Hall of Fame. In 1972, she was invited to appear on the Nitty Gritty Dirt Band's ***Will the Circle Be Unbroken***. Two years later, Mother Maybelle and her daughters were named "Favorite Group" in the Country Category of the American Music Awards.

After she played a wrong note on a 1976 TV program, Maybelle never played the autoharp again. That year, she made her final appearance at the Carter Family Reunion at Janette's Fold (niece Janette Carter's venue) with Sara. Maybelle was now suffering from arthritis and a form of Parkinson's Disease. She died in October 1978. In 1993, Maybelle Carter was one of the initial 30 women inducted into the Women of Virginian Historical Trail recognizing outstanding conributions to the improvement of society and to the general welfare of the state, with April 25, 1993 being proclaimed Maybelle Carter Day.

RECOMMENDED ALBUMS:

"Mother Maybelle (Queen of the Autoharp" (Kapp)(1964)
"A Living Legend" (Columbia)(1966)
"Mother Maybelle Carter" (double)(Columbia)(1973)
"Autoharp (For Students & Educators)" (Autoharp) [Narrated by Nat T. Winson, Jr., with instruction booklet]
With Sara Carter:
"An Historic Reunion" (Columbia)(1966)

Wilf Carter refer MONTANA SLIM

LIONEL CARTWRIGHT

(Singer, Songwriter, Piano, Guitar, Mandolin, Keyboards)

Given Name: **Lionel Burke Cartwright**
Date of Birth: **February 10, 1959**
Where Born: **Gallipolis, Ohio**
Married: **Cindy Stewart**
Children: **Lynn, Mason**

Lionel Cartwright has taken time to learn his trade, looking into all aspects from A to Z. His apprenticeship has ended, but he is still learning. He has said, "I want to plow new ground, take music to new places, but always retain that Country edge." Even before he left high school he was a self-taught, multi-talented musician who played 10 instruments. Lionel's career began at the age of 10, performing at hometown functions. While still at high school, he became a regular on a Country radio show at Milton, West Virginia. He worked his way through college and graduated with a degree in business administration.

He was a featured singer and musician on the popular *Country Cavalcade* show on WMNI in Columbus, Ohio. From there he went to the famous WWVA *Wheeling Jamboree* in West Virginia. He started as a back-up pianist, became a performer and went on to become the show's Musical Director. In 1982, Lionel secured a place on TNN on the Knoxville-based music and comedy series *I-40 Paradise* and the spin-off *Pickin' at the Paradise.* He was not only a performer on the series but also arranger, Musical Director and appeared in comedy sketches. In addition, he wrote and sang the theme song to both shows.

When he was in Knoxville, he met his co-writer and future wife, Cindy. Another writer he met later was Boudleaux Bryant and when he and Felice befriended Lionel, they encouraged his songwriting ambition.

Tony Brown, then a producer with MCA Records, had seen Lionel on the TV show, then saw his performance live, but decided to let him get more experience. After a couple of years performing, Lionel set off for Nashville in the fall of 1986 to visit Tony Brown, taking with him his best songs. This time, Brown considered Lionel ready and signed him to MCA.

Lionel's debut single with MCA, *You're Gonna Make Her Mine* (1988), managed a Top 50 placing and was included on his eponymous debut album (1989), which also produced three further chart singles: *Like Father Like Son* (Top 15), *Give Me His Last Chance* (Top 3) and in 1990, the Top 15 *In My Eyes*.

In 1990, his next album, ***I Watched It on the Radio***, yielded three more chart singles. Two of them reached the Top 10, *I Watched It All (on My Radio)* and *My Heart Is Set on You* and the Top 40 *Say It's Not True*. These were followed, in 1991, by Lionel's first No.1, *Leap of Faith* and *What Kind of Fool*, which reached the Top 25, both from the album ***Chasin' the Sun.*** Lionel's three 1992 releases failed to reach the upper rungs of the chart with both *Family Tree* and *Be My Angel* only reaching the Top 70 and *Standing on the Promises* getting into the Top 50. Lionel was then dropped from the label and is now pondering his future. JAB

RECOMMENDED ALBUMS:

"Lionel Cartwright" (MCA)(1989)
"I Watched It on the Radio" (MCA)(1990)
"Chasin' the Sun" (MCA)(1991)

JOHNNY CARVER

(Singer, Songwriter, Guitar)
Given Name: **John David Carver**
Date of Birth: **November 24, 1940**
Where Born: **near Jackson, Mississippi**
Married: **Pat**

During the early to mid-70's, Johnny Carver carved out a meritorious Country music career on the back of *Tie a Yellow Ribbon Round the Old Oak Tree*, a song that became synonymous with bringing home heroes and hostages.

Growing up in a rural area, Johnny lived Country music. He began singing with his family in a Gospel quartet in neighborhood churches and on the radio. He got his first guitar by borrowing $4.00 from his mother's egg money (she raised chickens) and paying her back by doing chores and mowing lawns. Johnny practiced hard to master his guitar and learned songs from the radio. He was soon confident enough to start his own band, the Capital Cowboys. They played for drive-in restaurants and soon got sponsored by a milk company and then an ice cream company. Wherever the ice cream was sold, they put on a show to draw crowds.

By the time Johnny was 16, he was playing nightclubs, but he was still in senior high school and his mother wasn't very happy. She said he could continue to play if he did the milking every morning and went to church every Sunday. As he wanted to play so much, he struggled through.

In 1969, Johnny went on the road with his band and performed at clubs and fairs all over the U.S. and in Canada. After two years, he based himself in Milwaukee where he met his wife, Pat. They moved to Los Angeles in 1965, where Johnny became the leader of the house band at the Palomino Club in North Hollywood. At this time, he also appeared regularly on TV in L.A.

Johnny achieved songwriting success when Roy Drusky had a Top 25 hit with Johnny's *New Lips*. Scotty Turner at Imperial Records suggested that Johnny go to Nashville to record for the label. Johnny's debut album, ***Johnny Carver***, was released in 1967 and at the end of that year, he debuted on the Country singles chart with *Your Lily White Hands*, which just fell short of the Top 20.

Soon, Johnny was out on the road again, opening for George Jones and Connie Smith. He appeared as a guest on the *Grand Ole Opry* but so far has not achieved his ambition, to become a member of the *Grand Ole Opry* cast. Johnny continued to have chart success with *I Still Didn't Have the Sense to Go* (Top 50, 1968), *Hold Me Tight* (Top 40), *Sweet Wine* (Top 30) and *That's Your Hang Up* (Top 50) (all 1969). During 1970, Johnny had three more chart records of which the most successful was *Willie and the Hand Jive* (Top 50).

In 1971, Johnny moved to Epic Records, where he racked up hits with *If You Think That It's All Right* (Top 40, 1971), *I Start Thinking About You* (Top 30) and *I Want You* (Top 40) (both 1972). Johnny moved to ABC Records at the end of 1972 and in the spring of the following year had his Top 5 hit with *Yellow Ribbon*. When Johnny charted Country with his version, Dawn was just making it to the top of the Pop chart with its rendition. Johnny reached the Top 5 and followed up with *You Really Haven't Changed,* which reached the Top 10.

Johnny stayed with ABC and its successor label, ABC/Dot, until the end of 1977. During this period, Johnny's major hits were *Tonight Somebody's Falling in Love* (Top 15), *Country Lullabye* (Top 30) and *Don't Tell (That Sweet Ole Lady of Mine)* (Top 10) (all 1974), *January Jones* (Top 40, 1975), *Afternoon Delight* (Top 10, 1976) and *Living Next Door to Alice* (Top 30) and *Down at the Pool* (Top 40) (both 1977). Johnny was absent from the chart between 1977 and 1980 and then he had a basement hit on Equity with *Fingertips*. The following year, he had a Top 75 success with Abba's *S.O.S.* on Tanglewood.

In 1992, Johnny could be found playing a summer season at Branson, Missouri. He is now backed by the seven-piece Nashville All-Star Band and they play music for round and square dancing, which has suddenly come back into vogue. They also include everything from Western Two-Step and the Cotton-Eyed Joe to waltzes, polkas and line dancing. JAB

RECOMMENDED ALBUMS:

"Johnny Carver" (Imperial)(1967)
"Really Country" (Imperial)(1967)
"I Start Thinking About You" (Harmony)(1973) [Epic masters]
"Tie a Yellow Ribbon Around the Old Oak Tree" (ABC)(1973)
"The Best of Johnny Carver" (ABC/Dot)(1977)

CLAUDE CASEY

(Singer, Guitar)
Date of Birth: **September 13, 1912**
Where Born: **Enoree, South Carolina**
Married: **Ruth Derrick (m. 1942)**
Children: **Leon, Michael**

A Carolina musician who cultivated a western image and style with moderate success, Claude Casey sustained a career in Country music that extended from coast to coast. Except for some side trips to Hollywood for film experience, Claude spent most of his life in the Carolinas and adjacent states. As his performing career waned, Claude became a successful radio station owner.

Growing up in the Carolina Piedmont and later Danville, Virginia, Claude Casey had frequent contact with the many traditional musicians who populated the region and aspired to make a living with this music as it evolved into a commercial genre, but he also labored in the textile mills from time to time. Claude continued in this mode for several years at various locales. In July 1937, his Claude Casey Trio made its first recordings for the American Record Corporation, but none of the six masters were released.

He had better luck in January 1938 when his small Western Swing band, Claude Casey and the Pine State Playboys, cut eight sides for Bluebird. The Playboys featured some hot fiddling and piano playing by Jimmy Rouse and Willie Coates respectively. That September, they did 10 more numbers. In between, they did daily radio programs at WFTC Kinston, North Carolina. This band broke up in 1939, but within a year, Claude had assembled a new group and was back in the studio.

In 1941, Claude landed a position at prestigious WBT Charlotte and worked not only as a solo but also with both of the popular established groups on the station, the Briarhoppers and the Tennessee Ramblers. As part of the latter band, he worked in the Republic motion picture *Swing Your Partner,* starring Dale Evans, in 1943 and did other films as well. His most prominent movie role came in *Square Dance Jubilee* for Lippert in 1949, where he sang two solo numbers.

For a time, Claude and his postwar group, the Sagedusters, did radio work at WGAC Augusta, Georgia, when the area was booming with construction of the Savannah River nuclear plant. Beginning in December 1953, he had a regular TV program in Greenville, South Carolina. In the immediate post-war years, Claude recorded for RCA Victor and closed out his disc cutting with MGM in 1953.

Claude Casey remained in music until the end of the 50's, but with the changing styles he got into radio work in 1961 when he founded WJES in Johnston, South Carolina. By the mid-80's, he increasingly turned the management over to his younger son, Mike. He never totally stopped singing, however, and performed at the 1985 reunion concert featuring many Charlotte old-timers and also at Western film fairs in Charlotte and Raleigh with fellow Tennessee Rambler alumni Don White and the late Cecil Campbell. With his good memory, congenial personality and extensive first-

Pine State Playboys leader ***Claude Casey***

hand knowledge of such musical pioneers as Emmett Miller and Charlie Poole, a trip down memory lane with Claude Casey is a rewarding experience. In 1987, Old Homestead Records released a collector's edition containing several Pine State Playboy numbers along with a few of Claude's post-war sides.

IMT

RECOMMENDED ALBUM:

"Pine State Honky Tonk" (Old Homestead)(1987)

JOHNNY CASH

(Singer, Songwriter, Guitar, Harmonica)

Given Name:	**J.R. Cash**
Date of Birth:	**February 26, 1932**
Where Born:	**Kingsland, Arkansas**
Married:	**1. Vivian Liberto (m. 1954) (div. 1966)** **2. June Carter Cash (m. 1968)**
Children:	**Tara, Kathy, Rosanne, Cindy, John**

A true Country great, Johnny Cash's deep bass voice and complementary sparse sound are at once instantly recognizable and compelling. His life has contained all the ingredients to mold a superstar of the genre: struggle, tragedy, self-destruction, happiness.

His formative influences were shaped by a hard upbringing in the Depression when he almost starved to death. Born into a large sharecropping family, he was soon hoeing and weeding cotton patches. By the time he was age 3, the family moved to Dyess, Arkansas. At 10, Johnny was employed by a road gang and two years later was hauling a nine-foot cotton sack. The Cash family also worked on the Dyess Colony Scheme to reclaim land by the Mississippi River. His mother played guitar and sang Folk songs. Johnny began writing songs by the age of 12, inspired by the Country stars he heard on radio, and his first earnings were partly spent on listening to Country tunes at the local drugstore. That year, his brother Jack was tragically killed, when he tripped across an electric saw.

At high school in Blytheville, Arkansas, Johnny sang on radio station KLCN. During the late 40's, Johnny's brother Roy led the Dixie Rhythm Ramblers. After graduating in 1950, Cash endured successive jobs in a Detroit body plant and then in an Evedale margarine firm as a floor sweeper. The outbreak of the Korean War saw Johnny enlist in the Air Force (where he adopted his first names of John Ray) that July as a military cryptographer, becoming a staff sergeant during his 4 years of service.

There was a lot of time to kill in Germany, which allowed Johnny to buy his first guitar, learn to play it, and write more songs. Among them was *Folsom Prison Blues*, which was inspired by the movie *Inside the Walls of Folsom Prison*. He also had a poem, *Hey Porter*, published in an armed forces magazine, and formed a Country group, the Landsberg Barbarians. There were also less pleasant moments. A drunken doctor, charged with removing a cyst from Johnny's cheek, left a scar, which later gave rise to the legend that it was imparted by a knife wound. A German girl also permanently impaired Johnny's hearing through poking a pencil down his left ear.

Upon his discharge, in 1954, Johnny settled in Memphis with his new wife, Texan Vivian Liberto, and became an electrical appliance salesman. Evenings were devoted to Country music, with Cash fronting a trio with two friends, Luther Perkins (electric guitar) and Marshall Grant (bass). They worked for free for station KWEM. Looking for a way out of his ill-paying day job, Cash took a radio announcing course at a broadcasting school on the G.I. Bill, and practiced in readiness for an audition at Sun Records. Johnny originally auditioned as a Gospel singer, reflecting his deep faith, only to be told bluntly by Sam Phillips that he wouldn't sell. Several further auditions followed until Phillips selected the Rockabilly-tinged *Cry Cry Cry* and *Hey Porter* as the debut release by Cash and the Tennessee Two. It sold around 100,000 copies and debuted on the Country chart in the Top 15. This led to him debuting on the *Louisiana Hayride*, and he stayed on the show for the next year.

The pattern was set for what many regard as Cash's stellar period. Perkins was an extremely limited lead guitarist, with his solos sounding much of a muchness, playing what is known as a chapel beat or boom-chicka-boom beat. His weakness was conversely Cash's strength. Johnny's strong voice and well structured songs were ideally showcased by the simple instrumental backdrop. His next single, in 1956, *So Doggone Lonesome/Folsom Prison Blues,* gave Johnny a double-sided Top 5 hit. He followed this with *I Walk the Line/Get Rhythm*, which stayed at No.1 for 6 weeks out of nearly 11 months on the charts. It also crossed over to the Pop chart Top 20. He followed with another No.1, *There You Go*, which stayed at the top for 5 weeks out of 7 months on the charts. The flip-side, *Train of Love,* also went Top 10.

In 1957, Johnny started with the Top 10 *Next in Line/Don't Make Me Go*. This was followed by the Top 3 *Home of the Blues*. The flip-side, *Give My Love to Rose*, went Top 15. That year, he made his debut on the *Grand Ole Opry*. He appeared clad all in black in contrast to the rhinestone suits favored by other performers. Thereafter he became known as "the Man in Black." Johnny had his photograph taken with Elvis Presley, Jerry Lee Lewis and Carl Perkins, which for years perpetuated the myth that he participated in the famous million-dollar session. In fact, Johnny went Christmas shopping! Johnny had the honor of being the first Sun artist to have an album released, ***Johnny Cash with His Hot and Blue Guitar*** (1957). Johnny started 1958 with what is still his biggest hit, Jack Clement's *Ballad of a Teenage Queen*. The single stayed at the top for 10 weeks and crossed over to the Top 15 on the Pop chart. The flip-side, *Big River,* also went Top 5. He then had his fourth No.1, *Guess Things Happen That Way*, another Clement song, which remained at the top for 8 weeks, and just missed the Pop Top 10. The flip-side, *Come in Stranger,* went Top 10. Johnny's other hits that year were Charlie Rich's *The Ways of a Woman in Love*, which went Top 3, and was backed by the Top 5 *You're the Nearest Thing to Heaven*. That year, Johnny appeared in the movie *Five Minutes to Live*.

Piqued at Sun for refusing to allow him to record a Gospel album, Cash moved to Columbia Records in the summer of 1958. Johnny's unreleased recordings allowed Sun to issue singles until 1961 and six albums in the six years following his departure.

His first single for Columbia was *All Over Again*, which went Top 5 and crossed over to the Pop Top 40. The flip, *What Do I Care*, went Top 10 and crossed to the Pop Top 60. Johnny's second single, *Don't Take Your Guns to Town*, in 1959, sold 500,000 copies, and went to No.1, where it stayed for 6 weeks and crossed to the Pop Top 40. His next singles were the Sun releases *It's Just About Time*, which went Top 30 Country and Top 50 Pop, followed by *Luther Played the Boogie*, which went Top 10. The flip-side, *Thanks a Lot,* also reached the Top 15. Johnny's other 1959 hits were *Frankie's Man Johnny* (Top 10/Top 60 Pop)/*You Dreamer You* (Top 15), *Katy Too* (Top 15/Top 70 Pop, on Sun), *I Got Stripes* (Top 5/Top 50 Pop)/*Five Feet High and Rising* (Top 15) and *Goodbye Little Darlin'* (Top 25, on Sun).

Johnny Cash** with **June Carter

In 1960, the Tennessee Two was enlarged by drummer W.S. Holland, to become the Tennessee Three. Johnny's Top 20 singles on the chart that year were *Straight A's in Love/I Love You Because* (Sun recording), *Seasons of My Heart* (Top 10)/*Smiling Bill McCall* and *Second Honeymoon*. That year, Johnny became very depressed over the death of Country star Johnny Horton, who was killed in an auto crash. The following year, the Cash Top 20 singles were *Oh Lonesome Me* (Sun recording) and *Tennessee Flat-Top Box*. In December that year, Johnny began working with June Carter (of the Carter Family).

His only major hit in 1962 was a reprise of Jimmie Rodgers' *In the Jailhouse Now*, which went Top 10. It was becoming obvious that this record was more than apposite. It is now clear that Johnny was experiencing severe personal problems brought on by fame. Johnny was in such demand that he was playing around 300 gigs a year. He started to take drugs back in 1959, to give him energy, and soon became addicted. The "uppers" he took to keep awake led to abnormal behavior. During 1962, Johnny played a 30-hour tour of Korea and a disastrous Carnegie Hall gig.

The following year, he teamed up with the Carter Family for Harlan Howard's *Busted*, which went Top 15. He then had another No.1, with the June Carter-Merle Kilgore song *Ring of Fire*. It stayed at the top for 7 weeks out of 6 months on the chart and went Top 20 on the Pop chart. He ended the year with *The Matador*, which reached the Top 3 and crossed to the Pop Top 40. His 1963 album ***Ring of Fire*** was Certified Gold in 1965. That year, Johnny appeared in the movie *Hootenanny Hoot*. In 1964, Johnny opened his account with *Understand Your Man* (with a similar melody to Dylan's *Don't Think Twice It's Alright*), which stayed at No.1 for 6 weeks and went Top 40 on the Pop chart. He followed this with the classic Peter Le Farge song *The Ballad of Ira Hayes* and John D. Loudermilk's *Bad News*, which went Top 10. He ended the year with a Top 5 duet with June Carter, Dylan's *It Ain't Me Babe*. His 1964 album ***I Walk the Line*** was Certified Gold in 1967. That year, Johnny performed at the Newport Folk Festival with Bob Dylan.

In 1965, Johnny was arrested by El Paso's Narcotics Squad and received a suspended jail sentence. He also smashed the footlights at the *Grand Ole Opry* and was told he wasn't welcome. Next year, he was arrested again—for picking flowers in a private garden at 2:00 a.m.—and his wife sued for divorce. Johnny's salvation came from June Carter and the Carter Family. With their help and assistance from Dr. Nat Winston, Johnny conquered his addiction and his career entered its most successful phase.

Johnny continued to have hits, but less regularly. His successes were, *Orange Blossom Special* (Top 3), *Mister Garfield* (Top 15), *The Sons of Katy Elder* (Top 10) and *Happy to Be With You* (Top 10) (all 1965), *The One on the Right Is on the Left* (Top 3/Pop Top 50), *Everybody Loves a Nut* (Top 20) and *You Beat All I Ever Saw* (Top 20). In 1966, Carl Perkins, fresh from his own woes, joined the Johnny Cash touring show. That year, Johnny broke the attendance record set by the Beatles in Liverpool, England.

1967 marked the renaissance of Johnny Cash. He and June had the Top 3 single *Jackson* and the Top 10 *Long-Legged Guitar Pickin' Man*. These were followed at year end by the Top 3 *Rosanna's Going Wild*. Then, in 1968, Johnny went behind bars again, but this time to record the epic live album ***Johnny Cash at Folsom Prison***. From this came the No.1 single *Folsom Prison Blues*, which stayed at the top for 4 weeks and crossed to the Pop Top 40. The album was Certified Gold during the year. The year ended with the Carl Perkins-penned *Daddy Sang Bass*, which went to the top of the chart and stayed there for 6 weeks and was a Top 50 Pop hit. Johnny proposed to June on stage in London, Ontario, Canada and they married in 1968 with Merle Kilgore ("the famous Johnny Cash impressionist") acting as best man. Johnny and June's wedding bands were purchased in Jerusalem and inscribed, "Me to my love and my love to me."

Johnny Cash at San Quentin in 1969 was filmed for TV and included *A Boy Named Sue*. The humorous song, ideal for a prison audience, gave Johnny his only Pop Top 10 single, reaching the Top 3; it reached No.4 in Britain. It also went No.1 on the Country chart for 5 weeks and was Certified Gold the same year as was the album. He closed out the year with *Blistered,* which went Top 5 and Top 50 Pop.

The *Johnny Cash Show* ran on ABC-TV from 1969 to 1971, with the Carter Family heavily featured. "Hello, I'm Johnny Cash" became one of the most famous opening remarks. It was even imitated by Elvis. It also became the title of his 1970 album, which went Gold the same year.

In 1970, Johnny made a much praised appearance in the movie *The Gunfight*, starring Kirk Douglas, and was the subject of a documentary (now available on video). Johnny turned to religion for sustenance, appearing with evangelist Billy Graham. That year, Johnny provided the narration for the conceptual ***A Day in the Grand Canyon,*** featuring the Andre Kostelanetz Orchestra. Johnny would later perform with John Williams and the Boston Pops Orchestra.

In 1970, Johnny's Columbia singles all made the Top 3 and were *What Is Truth* (also a Top 20 Pop hit), *Sunday Morning Coming Down* (No.1) and *Flesh and Blood* (No.1), the latter coming from the Gregory Peck movie *I Walk the Line* (in which Johnny sang five songs); in addition, the duet with June, *If I Were a Carpenter*, went Top 3. Johnny's 1970 double album ***The World of Johnny Cash*** was Certified Gold in 1971.The following year, he had success with *Man in Black* (Top 3), *Singing in Viet Nam Talking Blues*, *No Need to Worry* (with June) and *Papa Was a Good Man. A Thing Called Love*, recorded with the Evangel Temple Choir, went Top 3 and was a U.K. Top 5 hit in 1972. His other releases that year, *Kate*, *Oney* and *Any Old Wind That Blows*, also went Top 3. His 1972 album ***The Johnny Cash Portrait/His Greatest Hits, Vol. 2*** went Gold in 1977. In 1973, Johnny made a documentary and double album, ***The Gospel Road***. Columbia wasn't all that happy, leading Johnny to remark, "My record company would rather I'd be in prison than in church."

From then on, Johnny had major hits less often. Although not big hits, *Praise the Lord and Pass the Soup* (with the Carter Family and the Oak Ridge Boys) and *Pick the Wildwood Flower* (with Mother Maybelle Carter), both in 1973, were excellent releases. His major hits through 1982 were *Lady Came from Baltimore* (1974), *One Piece at a Time* (No.1 and Top 30 Pop) (1976), *I Would Like to See You Again, There Ain't No Good Chain Gang* (Top 3, with Waylon Jennings) (1978), and *(Ghost) Riders in the Sky* (Top 3, 1979). During 1974, Johnny could be seen in an episode of the mystery series *Columbo*. In 1975, Johnny wrote his autobiography, *Man in Black* (Zondervan) and appeared with June in the TV movie *Thaddeus Rose and Eddie*.

Over the years, Johnny Cash has recorded a number of exceptional concept albums. Often using narrative to link songs, he applied the sympathetic eye of the working man to themes which chronicled the American experience. ***Ride This Train*** (1960), ***Hymns from the Heart*** (1962), ***Blood Sweat and Tears*** (1963), ***Bitter Tears (Ballads of the American Indian)*** (1964) and the double album ***The Ballads of the True West*** (1965) were among the most notable earlier releases. Johnny returned to the concept album in 1972 with ***America: A 200 Year Salute in Story and Song.*** In 1980, Johnny was one of the featured artists on Paul Kennerley's concept album ***The Legend of Jesse James***. That same year, Johnny became the youngest inductee of the Country Music Hall of Fame.

In 1985, Johnny had his next No.1 with Columbia, *Highwayman*, from the album of the same name, with Waylon Jennings, Willie Nelson and Kris Kristofferson. The album also yielded the Top 20 hit *Desperados Waiting for a Train* and was Certified Gold in 1986. This was a foretaste of an artistic association that would periodically surface. After a 28-year association, Columbia, in 1986, unceremoniously dropped Johnny from the label and he signed with Mercury Records. His first album proclaimed that ***Johnny Cash Is Coming to Town*** (1987) (as if he had ever left!). Recorded with his band, it yielded the hit *The Night Hank Williams Came to Town*, which also featured Waylon Jennings. That year, Johnny wrote a biography of St. Paul, *Man in White* (Harper & Row), whose redemption paralleled his own. Ex-President Jimmy Carter tried to persuade Johnny to write the book on a word processor, without success.

In 1988, Johnny got together with Hank Williams, Jr., for the charted single *That Old Wheel*. The following year, Johnny made the Top 50 with a new version of *Ballad of a Teenage Queen* with Rosanne Cash (his daughter) and the Everly Brothers. In 1989, he got back together with Jennings, Nelson and Kristofferson for ***Highwayman II***, which yielded the Top 25 single *Silver Stallion*.

Johnny Cash's status as a Country legend has been confirmed by his innumerable appearances with other artists. He prevented Bob Dylan from being dropped by Columbia. Dylan returned the favor by giving Johnny the song *Wanted Man*. Although they recorded many songs together, only *Girl from the North Country* appeared officially on Dylan's 1969 watershed album ***Nashville Skyline***. In 1982, Johnny recorded ***The Survivors*** with Jerry Lee Lewis and Carl Perkins, a line-up which was joined by Roy Orbison for another album, ***Class of '55*** (1986).

In 1987, in a massive "catch-up," Johnny's albums ***Johnny Cash's Greatest Hits***, ***Johnny Cash at Folsom Prison*** and ***Johnny Cash at San Quentin*** were Certified Platinum and Double Platinum. While recording in Jamaica, Johnny persuaded Paul McCartney to duet with him. ***Water from the Wells of Home*** (1988) was a star-studded album that contains *New Moon Over Jamaica*, which was written by Johnny, Tom T. Hall and Paul McCartney, but which none of them claim(!), and so the royalties went to charity. In 1990, Johnny was presented with a Grammy Legend Award. In 1993, Johnny appeared with the world's premier Rock group, U2, on their album ***Zooropa***, singing *The Wanderer*. That same year, he signed with Def American (later renamed American), a move which promised to see a revival of his Rockabilly roots. The debut album, ***American Recordings,*** reached the Country Album Top 30 during the summer of 1994. (For Johnny Cash's awards, see Award Section.) SM/BM

RECOMMENDED ALBUMS:

"Johnny Cash with His Hot and Blue Guitar"(Sun)(1957)
"Ring of Fire" (Columbia)(1963)
"I Walk the Line" (Columbia)(1964)
"Bitter Tears" (Columbia)(1964) [Re-released as "Ballads of the American Indian" (Harmony)(1973)]
"Johnny Cash Sings the Ballads of the True West" (double)(1965)
"Johnny Cash's Greatest Hits, Volume 1" (Columbia)(1967)
"Carryin' On" (Columbia)(1967) [With June Carter] [Re-issued as "Johnny Cash & His Woman" (Columbia)(1973)]
"Johnny Cash at Folsom Prison" (Columbia)(1968)
"Johnny Cash at San Quentin" (Columbia)(1969)
[Above two re-released as double album (1975)]
"The Holy Land" (Columbia)(1969)
"Hello, I'm Johnny Cash"(1970)
"The World of Johnny Cash" (double)(Columbia)(1970)
"Johnny Cash & Jerry Lee Lewis Sing Hank Williams" (Sun)(1971) [Not together]

"Starportrait" (double)(CBS Germany)(1972)
"America: A 200 Year Salute in Story and Song" (Columbia)(1972).
"The Gospel Road (The Story of Jesus as Told & Sung by Johnny Cash" (Soundtrack)(double)(Columbia)(1973) [Re-issued by Priority (1982)]
"John R. Cash" (Columbia)(1974)
"A Believer Sings the Truth" (double)(Cachet)(1979) [With the Carter Family, Rosanne Cash and Rodney Crowell] [Re-released on Priority (1982)]
"The Original Johnny Cash" (Charly UK)(1980) [Sun Masters]
"The Adventures of Johnny Cash" (Columbia)(1982) [Cover photo by Marty Stuart]
"The Survivors" (Columbia)(1982) [With Jerry Lee Lewis and Carl Perkins]
"Johnny 99" (Columbia)(1983) [With June Carter, Marty Stuart and Hoyt Axton]
"Highwayman" (Columbia)(1985) [With Waylon Jennings, Willie Nelson and Kris Kristofferson]
"Class of '55" (America/Smash)(1986) [With Jerry Lee Lewis, Carl Perkins and Roy Orbison]
"Johnny Cash Is Coming to Town" (Mercury)(1987)
"1958 to 1986 The CBS Years" (Columbia)(1987)
"Classic Cash" (Mercury)(1988)
"Water from the Wells of Home" (Mercury)(1988) [With Rosanne Cash, the Everly Brothers, Emmylou Harris, Waylon Jennings, Jessi Colter, Roy Acuff, June Carter, the Carter Family, Tom T. Hall, John Carter Cash, Hank Williams, Jr., Glen Campbell and Paul & Linda McCartney]
"Highwayman 2" (Columbia)(1989) [With Waylon Jennings, Willie Nelson and Kris Kristofferson]
"Boom Chicka Boom" (Mercury)(1990)
"American Recordings" (American)(1994)

ROSANNE CASH

(Singer, Songwriter, Guitar, Piano)

Given Name:	**Rosanne Cash**
Date of Birth:	**May 24, 1956**
Where Born:	**Memphis, Tennessee**
Married:	**Rodney Crowell (m. 1979) (div. 1992)**
Children:	**Caitlin Rivers, Chelsea Jane, Carrie Kathleen**

Despite the huge shadow cast by her famous father, Johnny Cash, Rosanne has shown that she has the talent to stand alone on her own merits.

The daughter of Johnny and his first wife, Vivian Liberto, Rosanne moved with her family to California in 1959. Despite the break-up of her parents' marriage in the early 60's, Rosanne retained close ties with her father. After completing school, she and her step-sister, Rosie, joined her father on tour. He allegedly gave her a list of 100 essential Country songs that she had to know if she was to be his daughter. Over a three-year period, she progressed from tour laundress to back-up singer and occasional soloist.

Valuing her independence and not wanting to ride on her father's coattails, Rosanne broke free and moved to England in 1976, where she worked in the London office of CBS. She

Rosanne Cash** (right) with **Emmylou Harris** and **Rodney Crowell

returned to Nashville after about a year with the intention of returning to London, but Johnny decreed otherwise. She then enrolled in a drama and creative writing course at Vanderbilt University. After that came classes with the Lee Strasberg Institute in Los Angeles. Still seeking her own identity, Rosanne returned to Europe, this time to Germany, with her friend Renate Dann, who worked for Ariola Records.

At a label Christmas party, she was asked if she sang and was told to submit a demo. The Germany label signed her and the result was the "horrible" 1978 self-titled album. The venture gave Rosanne two things: first, a husband, Rodney Crowell, whom she had met at a Waylon Jennings party and second, a record deal with Columbia. Crowell had produced Rosanne's early demos and now he also produced three tracks on the first album for Columbia.

The debut album, ***Right or Wrong*** (1979), yielded three hits: the duet with Bobby Bare, *No Memories Hangin' Round*, the solo *Couldn't Do Nothing Right*, both of which went Top 20 and the slightly less successful *Take Me, Take Me*. Clearly Rosanne, with her punk-influenced look, was very different from her father. The next album, ***Seven Year Ache***, in 1981, was produced by Crowell and was Grammy nominated and went Gold in 1983. The self-penned title track provided her with her first Country chart No.1 and crossed over onto the Pop chart Top 30. Rosanne had two more back-to-back No.1's with Leroy Preston's *My Baby Thinks He's a Train* and her own *Blue Moon with a Heartache*.

Naturally, Columbia wanted a follow-up album quickly, but ***Somewhere in the Stars*** (1982), recorded when Rosanne was pregnant and feeling uninspired, was a disappointment. She still managed to chalk up two more Top 10 hits, *Ain't No Money* and *I Wonder*. Rosanne's single *It Hasn't Happened Yet*, only reached the Top 15, in 1983.

There followed a three-year hiatus before her next album, ***Rhythm and Romance***, in 1985. Rosanne's fusion of Rock and Country was underscored by the No.1 *I Don't Know Why You Don't Want Me*, which she wrote with Rodney and which won a Grammy for "Best Country Vocal Performance, Female" that year. This was followed to the top by theTom Petty/Benmont Tench song *Never Be You*. She also had Top 5 hits with *Hold On* (1985) and *Second to No One* (1986).

Two years passed before the next album, ***King's Record Shop***, named after a store in Louisville, Kentucky. Again produced by Crowell, it was well worth the wait. The album produced four straight No. 1's: John Hiatt's *The Way We Make a Broken Heart*, Johnny Cash's former hit *Tennessee Flat Top Box* (both 1987), *If You Change Your Mind* (written by Rosanne with Hank DeVito) and *Runaway Train*, which came from the pen of John Stewart (both 1988). Wedged in the middle of this was a No.1 duet with Rodney, *It's Such a Small World*, which came from his ***Diamonds and Dirt*** album. In 1988, Rosanne was named *Billboard's* "Top Singles Artist."

With the advent of 1989, Rosanne guested with the Everly Brothers on her father's remake of *Ballad of a Teenage Queen* and then she was back at No.1 with the Lennon and McCartney song *I Don't Want to Spoil the Party*, which came from the chart album ***Hits 1979-1989***, as did the next single, *Black and White*, which just made the Top 40. By 1990, Rosanne's rate of success had slowed and her marriage was coming to an end. A separation from Crowell preceded her maudlin self-produced album ***Interiors***. The single, a self-penned song, *What We Really Want*, only made the Top 40 and her only other chart success that year was a guest appearance on the Nitty Gritty Dirt Band's *One Step Over the Line* with John Hiatt.

The following year saw a separation from Crowell and the release and flop of the single *On the Surface*. Rosanne's album **The Wheel**, in 1993, marked a return to form, though it also contained some confessional material; creatively, it was much more inventive than its predecessor, mixing and matching various musical styles. Rosanne has never toured extensively, preferring to put family first. Nevertheless, she can rightly claim a leading innovative role in the "New Country" movement. Clearly, there is a lot of creative mileage left in this lady yet. SM

RECOMMENDED ALBUMS:
"Right or Wrong" (Columbia)(1979)
"Seven Year Ache" (Columbia)(1981)
"Rhythm and Romance" (Columbia)(1985)
"King's Record Store" (Columbia)(1988)
"Hits 1979-1989" (Columbia)(1989)
"The Wheel" (Columbia)(1993)

TOMMY CASH

(Singer, Songwriter, Guitar)
Date of Birth: **April 5, 1940**
Where Born: **Dyess, Arkansas**
Married: **1. Barbara Ann Wisenbaker (div.)**
2. Pamela Dyer (m. 1978)
Children: **Mark Alan, Paula Jean**

Being the brother of Country superstar Johnny Cash could have been a blessing or otherwise, but Johnny's younger brother, Tommy Cash, has managed to carve out a very successful career of his own.

Although Tommy was born into a poor sharecropper farm life, the family was close-knit and loving and one of his earliest memories is of singing and telling stories while sitting around with his mama, daddy and other family members. His nickname was Tomcat, a name reflected later in the choice of his band's name (the Tomcats, which he formed in 1970). When he was 16, he began to play guitar after watching his brother Johnny perform and was soon entertaining his fellow students. By the late 50's, he had become a deejay at KWAM Memphis.

Tommy joined the Armed Forces when he was 18, and was soon a deejay on AFN in Frankfurt, Germany, where he had his own show called *"Stickbuddy Jamboree"* (June 1959-May 1961). Tommy recalls he really enjoyed doing that show and has been back to AFN Germany since then to visit. It was during this time that he met his first wife, Barbara.

No sooner had he returned to civilian life than he found himself back in uniform because President Kennedy called up the reserves. Tommy was sent to Fort Bragg and was soon a deejay again on WFNC in Fayettville, North Carolina, until he finally left the Army in 1962.

Joining Johnny's organization, he became an executive in charge of publishing and public relations, but he soon found himself longing for the bright lights and decided to pursue a singing career. His professional debut was on a show in Montreal, Canada, with Hank Williams, Jr.

Tommy recorded his first single, *I Guess I'll Live* in 1965, on Musicor. He first hit the Country chart with the 1968 Top 50 single, *The Sounds of Goodbye*, which was released on United Artists. The following year, Tommy signed with Epic Records and that year had a Top 50 hit with *Your Lovin' Takes the Leavin' Out of Me*.

In 1970, Tommy had his biggest hit, *Six White Horses*, a tribute to John F. Kennedy, Robert Kennedy and Martin Luther King,Jr. The single reached the Country Top 5 and crossed-over to the Pop Top 80. Soon Tommy was touring, taking his band on extensive tours in the U.S. and Europe and March 1970 marked his *Grand Ole Opry* debut,when he was introduced by Roy Acuff. Tommy's other 1970 hits were *Rise and Shine* and *One Song Away*, both Top 10 entries and *The Tears on Lincoln's Face*, which went Top 40.

Tommy stayed with Epic until 1974, during which time his hit records were: 1971: *So This Is Love* (Top 20), *I'm Gonna Write a Song* (Top 30) and *Roll Truck Roll* (Top 70)(all 1971); *You're Everything* (Top 40), *That Certain One* (Top 25) and *Listen* (Top 25) (all 1972); *Workin' on a Feelin'* (Top 40) and *I Recall a Gypsy Woman* (Top 20) (both 1973) and *She Met a Stranger, I Met a Train* (Top 25)(1974).

In 1974, Tommy moved to Elektra Records and the following year, chalked up a Top 60 entry with *The One I Sing My Love Songs To.* In 1976, Tommy charted with *Broken Bones*, which was on the soundtrack of the movie *Death Riders* and was released on 20th Century Records. Tommy signed with Monument in 1977 and released the album ***New Spirit***, on which he included an updated version of his hit *Six White Horses*. Two singles from this album charted, *The Cowboy and the Lady* (Top 70, 1977) and *Take My Love to Rita* (Top 100, 1978). After Monument, Tommy signed with Indigo Records in 1983 and stayed on the label until 1984. In 1984, Tommy appeared in Britain at the Peterborough Festival. In 1990, Tommy signed with Playback Records.

Tommy Cash has written around 100 songs, some of them with his co-writer, Jim Pepper. Some have been recorded by such greats as Conway Twitty, Loretta Lynn, Jean Shepard, Kitty Wells and of course Johnny Cash.

In 1990, Tommy disbanded the Tomcats and in 1992 he appeared in Branson for 150 dates at the Jubilee Theater backed by the Ozark Country Jubilee Band, which is the permanent orchestra there. He returned to Branson for the 1993 season while also making personal appearances, and visited Germany in July 1993. Tommy and his wife Pamela, whom he met on her birthday, in 1976, fell in love at first sight. They are living happily ever after with their three dogs. Tommy was working on a new album in 1994 to be released on Playback Records. JAB

RECOMMENDED ALBUMS:
"Country Cousins" (Musicor)(1966)
"Here Comes Tommy Cash" (United Artists)(1966)
"Best of Tommy Cash" (Epic)(1972)
"Six White Horses/Your Lovin' Takes the Leavin' Out of Me" (double) (Epic)(1975)
"Only a Stone" (Elktra)(1975)
"New Spirit" (Monument)(1978)

CASS COUNTRY BOYS

Formed: **1940's**
Members:
Fred Martin **Lead Vocals, Accordion**
Jerry Scroggins **Baritone Vocals, Guitar**
Bert Dodson **Tenor Vocals, String Bass**

Although the Sons of the Pioneers will always be remembered as the premier Country and Western harmony group, there were others who also made their mark in western movies. The Cass Country Boys were among the finest. They appeared in numerous movies with Gene Autry, including *Trail to San Antone* and *Twilight on the Rio Grande* (both in 1947). They also accompanied Autry on many live appearances.

They appeared with Charles Starrett in his Durango Kid series in movies that included *Buckaroo from Powder River* (1947), *Trail to Laredo* (1948) and *The Kid from Amarillo* (1951). In the last named, the group was credited as Jerry Scroggins and the Cass Country Boys.

The group's recording career took in Columbia, Decca and ARA. They also made some excellent transcriptions for McGregor Transcriptions and appeared on Doye O'Dell's eponymous Era album. Dodson appeared on Autry's 1949 recording of *Silver Haired Daddy of Mine* and his 1950 recording of *Mississippi Valley Blues*, and the trio were present on *Children's Christmas,* an EP recorded by Gene Autry in 1956.

RECOMMENDED ALBUM:
"Melody Ranch—A Radio Western Adventure with Gene Autry" (Radiola)(1975) [Features the Cass Country Boys]

PETE CASSELL

(Singer, Guitar)
Given Name: **Peter Webster Cassell**
Date of Birth: **August 27, 1917**
Where Born: **Cobb County, Georgia**
Married: **Ruth Hamlin**
Children: **Jean, Roy William (dec'd.)**
Date of Death: **July 29, 1954**

Pete Cassell was a blind Country radio singer who gained enormous popularity with his audiences, many of whom still marvel at his uncanny ability to "put over" a song. Like many of his fellow radio artists in the 40's, Pete traveled frequently from station to station. Often he remained at the same locale for only a few months and apparently he never stayed more than two years. Cassell's peak popularity occurred during his stints in Atlanta, Wheeling, and the Washington, D.C., area. He also recorded, somewhat sparingly, between 1941 and 1949 for Decca, Majestic, and Mercury.

Like Riley Puckett, whose career sometimes paralleled his own, Pete Cassell had been accidentally blinded in infancy. Nonetheless, he managed to receive a good education at special schools in Atlanta, Macon and Pittsburgh. Although he seems to have had some attraction to the study of law, it was not as strong as the appeal of radio as a career. It is said that Pete had perfect pitch and that he was a self-taught musician. He apparently held his first radio job on the *Cross Roads Follies* at WSB Atlanta in the late 30's (he may have first played on the air via WDOD in Chattanooga), and he also worked regularly on WSB from March 1941 to 1943 when he moved to rival station WAGA for two years. He first appeared on WWVA Wheeling for a brief time about 1940 and went back for a second stint in 1945 and won that station's most popular artist honors the following year. Later in the decade he went to WARL Arlington,Virginia, and worked for the legendary promoter Connie B. Gay. In between times, Pete sang on other radio stations in such locales as Rome, Georgia; Springfield, Missouri; Scranton, Pennsylvania; and Milwaukee.

Pete did his first record session for Decca on March 12, 1941, when he cut six sides that included *Freight Train Blues* and *I Know What It Means to Be Lonesome*. After WWII, Pete made recordings for Majestic and Mercury, including numbers like *Oh How I Miss You, Where the Old Red River Flows* and *'Neath the West Virginia Sky*. He also waxed a topical ballad about the 1946 fire in Atlanta, entitled *Burning of the Winecoff Hotel*. Perhaps because of his West Virginia experiences, Pete also had a flair for recitation which he demonstrated on recordings such as *Too Many Parties and Too Many Pals* and *Waiting for Ships That Never Come In*. However, he never really had a hit record that might have propelled him to national stardom. In fact, he seems to have recorded somewhat reluctantly and to have considered phonograph discs somewhat of a threat to radio singers like himself.

Cassell's health seems not to have been especially strong. During a period of rest in Key West, Florida, he died from coronary thrombosis, a few weeks prior to his 37th birthday. His widow returned his remains to Cobb County for burial. In 1956, Pickwick Records released a budget album. Old Homestead Records has also released some of his work.

IMT

One of the best Country singers, ***Pete Cassell***

RECOMMENDED ALBUMS:

"The Legend of Pete Cassell" (Hilltop)(1965)
"Pete Cassell, Blind Minstrel" (Old Homestead)(1993)

CATES SISTERS, The/CATES, The

MARCY CATES
(Singer, Violin, Viola, Guitar, Mandolin, Piano)
Given Name: Marcy Lynn Cates
Date of Birth: September 27
Where Born: Independence, Missouri
Married: Earl Erb

MARGIE CATES
(Singer, Violin, Viola, Guitar, Mandolin, Piano)
Given Name: Anne Marjorie Cates
Date of Birth: September 6
Where Born: Independence, Missouri
Married: John Stacey

The Cates Sisters are the perfect example of brains and beauty being able to work together. They started playing and singing Country music at a young age, and then they both attended the University of Missouri at Kansas City Conservatory of Music (1966-1971), studying classical music. They each earned a bachelor of music education degree in 1969 and, two years later, they earned master of music degrees.

They decided to pursue a career in Country music and moved to Nashville, where they soon became in demand as session singers and musicians. In 1972, they joined the Jim Ed Brown Show, making their debut on the *Grand Ole Opry* that year. Within Jim Ed's show, the Cates appeared as a duo as well as working with Jim Ed as a threesome, specializing in close harmony singing. While with Brown, they appeared at the 1973 Wembley Festival in England, where they caused a sensation with their twin-fiddle version of *Orange Blossom Special*. During 1973 and 1974, the Cates recorded singles for MCA.

They stayed with Jim until 1976 and then struck out on their own. That year, they signed to Caprice Records as the Cates Sisters and had their first Country chart entry, that same year, with *Mr. Guitar*, which reached the lower rungs. Then as the Cates, they had a Top 50 entry with *Out of My Mind*. Their other major successes on the label were *I'll Always Love You* and *I've Been Loved* (both Top 30, 1977) and *Loving You off My Mind* (Top 40, 1978). At the end of 1978, as the Cates, they signed to Ovation Records, for whom they had five chart singles, the most successful being *Make Love to Me* (Top 60) and *Let's Go Through the Motions* (Top 70), both in 1979. They had their final chart record in 1980 with the Top 75 *Lightnin' Strikes*. They also cut some singles for Salute, but without success.

The Cates continue to be very busy as session singers and musicians.

RECOMMENDED ALBUMS:

"Cates Sisters" (Caprice)(1978)
"Steppin' Out" (Ovation)(1979) [As the Cates]
"That's What I Like About the South" (Music Masters)(1980) [TV Album]
"Moments" (Salute)(1992)

CATHEDRALS, The/CATHEDRAL QUARTET, The

Formed: 1964
Members:
Glen Payne Lead Vocals
George Younce Bass Vocals
Ernie Haase Tenor Vocals
Scott Fowler Baritone Vocals
Roger Bennett Piano
Past Members:
Danny Koker, Bobby Clark, Mac Taunton, George Webster, Roy Tremble, Lorne Mathews, Roger Horne, Bill Dykes, Haskell Cooley, Kirk Talley, Danny Funderburk, Gerald Wolfe, Mark Trammell

Founded in 1964 by evangelist Rex Humbard, the Cathedrals have become synonymous with Southern Gospel music. Originally known as the Cathedral Trio, Humbard put the group together to perform on his weekly TV outreach, *Cathedral of Tomorrow*, in Akron, Ohio. The new musical group gained a large following performing on the religious program that was seen around the country.

The original members of the group were lead vocalist Glen Payne, bassist George Younce, Danny Koker and Bobby Clark.

Payne, a veteran of the Stamps/Baxter School of Music, had resolved to have a Gospel career at age 12. He began his career in Gospel music when he was 17 as a member of the popular Stamps Quartet and was also a member of the Cathedral Trio. Prior to joining the Cathedrals, George Younce sang with the Gospel group the Weatherfords, with whom Rex Humbard had worked as far back as 1956.

After polishing their blend of Country influenced Gospel music for six years on the Rex Humbard TV show, the Cathedral Quartet went out on their own in 1969. Traveling initially in a converted egg truck, the group eventually moved up to the fully equipped tour buses.

By the late 70's, the Cathedrals were one of the most popular groups in Southern Gospel music. They won their first Grammy Award for "Best Gospel Performance" in 1977, an accomplishment they repeated in 1978, 1979 and 1982. Also in 1977, the Gospel Music Association honored them with Dove Awards for "Male Group of the Year" and "Best Southern Gospel Album" for ***Then...and Now***. The album also won Dove Awards that year for "Best Cover Photo or Cover Art" and "Best Graphic Layout or Design."

In 1979, Payne and Younce remained after the other members left and anchored the group through the many changes of members. In the late 70's, pianist Roger Bennett joined the group. Sharing the lead vocal duties in the 70's and 80's were Kirk Talley, Danny Funderburk, Gerald Wolfe and Mark Trammell. The Cathedrals had a steady stream of No.1 singles on the Gospel chart, including *Step Into the Water*; *Can He, Could He, Would He*; *I Can See the Hand*; *Champion of Love* and *I've Just Started Living*.

During 1986 through 1990, they were featured as an exclusive Southern Gospel group at Bill Gaither's Praise Gathering for Believers. Breaking with the tradition of recording in Nashville, the Cathedrals traveled to England in 1988 to record their ***Symphony of Praise*** album with the London Philharmonic Orchestra.

The group earned "Best Southern Gospel Music Album" awards from the Gospel Music Association in 1987 (***The Master Builder***), 1988 (***Symphony of Praise***), 1989 (***Goin' in Style***), 1990 (***I've Just Started Living***) and 1991 (***Climbing Higher & Higher***). They also garnered GMA Dove Awards for "Best Southern Gospel Song" in 1989 for *Champion of Love* and in 1991 for *I Can See the Hand*. In 1989, *Gospel Music Voice* named them "Group of the Year." *Cash Box* named their ***Goin' in Style***, the "Southern Gospel Album of the Year" in 1989.

Celebrating their 25th anniversary in 1989, the Cathedrals maintained a heavy touring schedule performing in large churches and concert halls. Also that year, they were featured on TNN's *Gospel Jubilee* music series. JIE

RECOMMENDED ALBUMS:

"Then...and Now" (Canaan)(1977)
"The Master Builder" (RiverSong)(1987)
"Symphony of Praise" (RiverSong)(1988)
"Goin' in Style" (Homeland)(1989)
"I Just Started Living" (Homeland)(1990)
"Climbing Higher & Higher" (Homeland)(1991)

CONNIE CATO

(Singer, Guitar)
Given Name: **Connie Ann Cato**
Date of Birth: **March 30, 1955**
Where Born: **Bethalte, East St. Louis, Missouri**
Married: **several times**

For a while during the 70's, Connie Cato looked like she would be, if not a queen, certainly a princess of Country music. Blonde and bubbly with a voice somewhere between Dolly Parton and Brenda Lee and an accent as sweet as molasses, she sadly failed to sustain the initial impact.

Connie was born into great hardship and never knew her father. She grew up with her mother and stepfather and attended school until the fourth grade. Her mother was continuously ill and so Connie had to be "little mother" to her three stepbrothers. It was left to her to do the laundry, cook and clean.

As Connie reached her teens, fate stepped in. She was sitting in the beauty parlor and started to sing *Ruby, Don't Take Your Love to Town*. This led to the hairdresser introducing her to someone who needed a singer for a homecoming dance. Suffering from nerves and tranquilized, she got through that first show. That led to the agent booking her for other shows.

When Connie was 15, she packed her guitar and hitched to Nashville. Her similarity to Dolly Parton worked against her until she met master songwriter Curly Putnam. Curly had come to fame as the writer of *Green, Green Grass of Home*. He arranged for Connie to record a demo and took it to booking agent Happy Wilson, who then took it to Capitol Records in Los Angeles. The label executives were interested, but shied away when they found out Connie was only 15. She returned home and started to work as a waitress and gas station attendant, performing the occasional gig whenever she could get one.

In 1972 fate stepped in again. Joe Allison, who had written *He'll Have to Go* and was a Country music producer, asked Connie to come to Nashville to try out some songs that seemed just right for her. She signed with Capitol, who obviously felt that 17 was better than 15. Her first single, *How Come You Struck the Match,* didn't light up the chart, nor did the follow-up, *Four on the Floor*. However, her third release started the chart roll for Connie. *Superskirt* was released at the end of 1973 and charted the following February. It reached the Top 40 and was on the charts for four months. The next two chart entries, *Super Kitten* and *Lincoln Autry,* were only low-level successes, but in 1975, Connie came back strongly with her version of *Hurt*, which had been a major international Pop hit for Timi Yuro in 1961.

However, after this, Connie was unable to sustain any momentum. None of her singles achieved much success. In 1980, she surfaced on MCA and had a Top 50 single entitled *You Better Hurry Home (Somethin's Burnin')* but then the chart party was over.

Connie now has her memories. Like the time Ray Pillow introduced her on the *Opry* and she sang three songs, instead of the normal one, and the crowd went wild. There are times when the music business can be a ruthless taskmaster.

RECOMMENDED ALBUMS:

"Super Connie Cato" (Capitol)(1974)
"Good Hearted Woman" (Capitol)(1975)
"Whoever Finds This, I Love You" (Capitol)(1977)

ROY LEE CENTERS

(Singer, Guitar, Banjo)
Given Name: **Roy Lee Centers**
Date of Birth: **November 8, 1944**
Where Born: **Jackson, Kentucky**
Married: **Lucille**
Children: **Lennie and two others**
Date of Death: **May 2, 1974**

Roy Lee Centers sang lead and played rhythm guitar for Ralph Stanley's Clinch Mountain Boys from early 1970 until his tragic death in 1974. Centers' tenure is especially memorable in light of the fact that his voice sounded very similar to that of Carter Stanley. Roy Lee helped put Ralph's new group on a level almost as legendary as the original Stanley Brothers. Born in the heart of feud country's "Bloody Breathitt" County, Centers grew up in a musically rich area where poverty and violence had become part of the lifestyle. Like many eastern Kentucky youth, Roy Lee moved to southwest Ohio to find employment. He also became part of the local Bluegrass scene, working with Fred Spencer under the name Lee Brothers and for Jack Lynch and the Miami Valley Boys. After Larry Sparks left Ralph Stanley's band in the fall of 1969, Joe Isaacs filled the spot temporarily until Roy Lee took it on a permanent basis. Later, Centers and his family moved to Breathitt County.

The more than four years that Roy Lee Centers spent with the Clinch Mountain Boys coincided with tremendous growth of Bluegrass festivals. Stanley fans accepted the congenial Kentuckian as the nearest humanly possible version of a second Carter Stanley. The Clinch Mountain Boys also included fiddler Curly Ray Cline, bass player Jack Cooke and for more than a year the youthful duo of Keith Whitley and Ricky Skaggs. As a result, they gained a large and loyal following on the festival circuit. They also toured Japan, where they received a tremendous welcome.

Roy Lee also recorded a great deal with the Clinch Mountain Boys. He sang lead on two albums on Jessup, six on Rebel and another one on King Bluegrass (subsequently reissued on County). A two-album ***Live in Japan*** set issued on the Seven Seas label in Japan also later appeared on Rebel. Centers played on Curly Ray Cline's albums and those of Keith Whitley and Ricky Skaggs, Lee Allen and J.D. Jarvis. Sometimes he played banjo rather than guitar, being equally skilled on both instruments.

Given the wide acceptance that Centers received, Bluegrass fans were shocked when they learned that Roy Lee had been fatally shot in one of the shooting altercations that have made his section of Kentucky notorious. The fans were even more shocked when they learned that his killing went virtually unpunished. Centers came to be a revered figure in the Bluegrass world and his childhood friend and fellow musician, Lee Allen, wrote and recorded a tribute song entitled *In Memory of Roy Lee Centers*. Vecto Records released two albums made largely from live recordings. For a time, Roy Lee's oldest son, Lennie, worked in the bands of Lee Allen and also of the Goins Brothers. IMT

RECOMMENDED ALBUMS:

"I've Lived a Lot in My Time" (Vector)(1975)

"The Early Years" (Vector)(1976)

CEE CEE CHAPMAN

(Singer, Songwriter, Guitar)

Given Name: **Melissa Carol Chapman**

Date of Birth: **December 13, 1958**

Where Born: **Portsmouth, Virginia**

Although Cee Cee Chapman has yet to have *the* big record, her discography to date has been marked by a series of fine singles. She just needs one career single to confirm what live audiences have known for some while: that she is a star-in-waiting.

Cee Cee was tutored by her father, Curtis, a 22-year career Navy man, who also played guitar. She spent her early years continuously moving around. Her mother was always singing and her grandfather could play any stringed instrument. Cee Cee sings Country, Rockabilly, Gospel and Blues and was influenced by Buck Owens, Roy Orbison, Elvis, Crosby, Stills, Nash and Young and even liked a little Bob Wills Western Swing. She also listened to Chet Atkins albums.

Cee Cee's first show business experience was in bands with her father. He thought she could be a great singer and when she was about 16, she started engagements on her own in Virginia and North Carolina. When Cee Cee was 20 years old she did a low budget vocal/guitar demo. Cee Cee sent it out to several people asking for advice and one of these people was Liberty Records' Scotty Turner, who wrote her a long letter of encouragement and suggested she send the tape to songwriter Bobby Fischer, who was looking for a new singer to produce.

When Bobby listened to it, he asked her to come and meet him. He said he liked her voice, but it took five years before anything happened. Then Bobby, with Charlie Black and Austin Roberts, wrote some songs for her and made a demo recording of her vocals. She finally signed with Fischer and came to Nashville, where the demo tapes were played to Dick Whitehead of Curb Records. He liked the songs *Santa Fe* and *End of a Heartache*.

Cee charted in 1988 with the Top 60 *Gone but Not Forgotten*, on which she was backed by her band, Santa Fe. She cut her first album, ***Twist of Fate***, in 1989. Cee Cee had her second chart record in 1989 with *Frontier Justice*, which just fell short of the Top 50. She followed this with the album title track, which made the Top 50. Her first single was flipped and the B-side, *Love Is a Liar,* made the Top 70. She released her self-named album in 1990, but none of the singles from it charted. Cee Cee was then missing from the singles charts for 3 years, but returned in 1993 with the Top 70 *Two Ships That Passed in the Moonlight*.

*Virginia's own **Cee Cee Chapman***

When Cee Cee's not on the road, she spends her time as a celebrity spokeswoman for the American Cancer Society and she enjoys golf and shopping. JAB

RECOMMENDED ALBUMS:

"Twist of Fate" (Curb)(1989)

"Cee Cee Chapman" (Curb)(cd)(1990)

STEVEN CURTIS CHAPMAN

(Singer, Songwriter, Guitar, Piano)

Given Name: **Steven Curtis Chapman**

Date of Birth: **November 21, 1962**

Where Born: **Paducah, Kentucky**

Married: **Mary Beth**

Children: **Emily, Caleb, Will Franklin**

Steven Curtis Chapman has emerged as the major male Contemporary Christian singer and songwriter of the late 80's and 90's.

He was born and raised in Paducah, Kentucky. His father owned a music store and Steve spent much of his youth learning to play a variety of instruments and became accomplished on the guitar and piano. He was also introduced to the songwriting process at an early age by his father.

Following high school Steven enrolled in pre-med studies at Anderson College in Anderson, Indiana. However, his love of music was stronger than his desire for higher education, so he headed to Nashville. He took a job performing in a Country music show at Opryland U.S.A. Steven spent his time away from Opryland writing songs and before long found success when the Gospel group the Imperials recorded one of his songs.

Steven's talent as a performer and songwriter attracted the interest of many labels and publishers and he signed with the major Christian music label Sparrow in 1987. His debut album, ***First Hand***, was released later that year and his first single, *Weak Days*, rose to No.2 on the Contemporary Christian music chart. His follow-up album, ***Real Life Conversations***, produced four radio hits, including the No.1 *His Eyes* (co-written with James Isaac Elliott). The song was named "Contemporary Recorded Song of the Year" by the GMA, earning Steven a Dove Award in 1989. He earned a second Dove Award that year as "Songwriter of the Year."

1989 was a big year for Steven with the re-

Gospel star ***Steven Curtis Chapman***

lease of his ***More to This Life*** album. The record produced four No.1 radio hits and earned Steven a record-breaking 10 1990 Dove Award nominations from the GMA. He took home 5 awards, including songwriting honors, "Inspirational Song of the Year" for *His Strength Is Perfect*, "Southern Gospel Song of the Year" for *I Can See the Hand* and "Songwriter of the Year." Steven was also named "Male Vocalist" and "Artist of the Year."

Chapman continued his reign as Contemporary Christian music's leading artist in 1990 when his ***For the Sake of the Call*** yielded 5 No.1 singles. He picked up consecutive Dove Awards as "Male Artist," "Songwriter" and "Artist of the Year." The following year, Steven earned his first Grammy award in the "Best Pop Gospel Album" category for ***For the Sake of the Call***. Chapman picked up a Dove Award in 1991 in the "songwriter" category.

"Saddle up your horses we've gotta trail to blaze..." With those opening lines from 1992's ***The Great Adventure***, Chapman set out to take his music to a wider audience. He made his first music video (of the title track) that was seen on the TNN and CMT cable TV channels. The video was honored by the GMA and *The Great Adventure* was also named "Contemporary Recorded Song of the Year" and the album, "Album of the Year." The album produced several radio hits including *That's Paradise* and *Still Called Today*.

Another major development for Steven came in 1992 when his record company was purchased by EMI/Liberty, the label of Garth Brooks. The powerful distribution network put Steven's records in the major discount chains and helped boost sales. ***The Great Adventure*** passed the 500,000 sales mark and earned Steven his first Gold Disc in 1993. It also earned a Grammy Award for "Best Pop Gospel Album." In addition, ***For the Sake of the Call*** won a Dove for "Inspirational Album."

Steven's successful tour to promote ***The Great Adventure*** became a live album and video called ***The Live Adventure***, released in 1993. It was honored with a Grammy Award and multiple awards from the Gospel Music Association. Steven also continued his reign as the GMA "Songwriter of the Year" and ***The Great Adventure*** took Dove Awards in four categories. Steven was also honored as "Songwriter" and "Artist of the Year." The *American Songwriter* magazine named Steven the "Top Professional Songwriter" in 1993.

In 1994, Steven released his seventh album, entitled ***Heaven in the Real World***. The award winning artist supported the release with a 70 city tour. Steven wrote or co-wrote all the songs on the album in the tradition of all his previous releases. Among the other artists who have recorded Steven's songs are Glen Campbell, Roger Whitaker, Sandi Patti and Billy Dean. JIE

RECOMMENDED ALBUMS:

"First Hand" (Sparrow)(1987)
"Real Life Conversation" (Sparrow)(1988)
"More to This Life" (Sparrow)(1989)
"For the Sake of the Call" (Sparrow)(1990)
"The Great Adventure" (Sparrow)(1992)
"The Life Adventure" (Sparrow)(1993)
"Heaven in the Real World" (Sparrow)(1994)
Video:
"The Life Adventure" (Sparrow)(1993)

JERRY CHESNUT

(Songwriter, Singer, Guitar)

Given Name:	**Jerry Donald Chesnut**
Date of Birth:	**May 7, 1931**
Where Born:	**Harlan County, Kentucky**
Married:	**1. Dorothy**
	2. Patricia
Children:	**Barbara, Linda, Kathy, Donna**

Jerry Chesnut made his mark on Country music as a premier songwriter, who is still providing hits for dozens of artists.

Jerry was born in the rugged hills of eastern Kentucky. He spent his early childhood in Harlan County traveling from one coal mining camp to another with his father. When he graduated from high school, Jerry joined the U.S. Air Force and did a tour of duty in Korea. Following his military service Jerry settled in Florida and found work on the railroad, eventually becoming a conductor for the Florida East Coast Railway Company.

According to Jerry, for a little excitement, he occasionally joined his friends in rustling cattle. They would travel the interstate highway in search of cows near the road. One night while on the prowl by himself, Jerry spotted a black Angus standing alone near the highway. He caught the cow, tied him up, and began to load the bovine in his pickup truck. Jerry managed to get the 1,000 pound animal in his truck but in the process pulled his back out. He learned his lesson that crime doesn't pay by spending the next six months flat on his back recuperating.

His injury proved to be a blessing in disguise. He spent much of his time listening to the radio and analyzing songs. He also experimented with writing songs and some of the ones he composed became hits a decade later.

Jerry moved to Nashville in 1958, but his early attempts to get his songs recorded were unsuccessful. To make ends meet, he worked a variety of odd jobs. He discovered he had a knack for selling vacuum cleaners door to door and so the company put him in charge of a three state region. Chesnut kept writing and pitching and after nine years in Nashville, in 1967, Del Reeves recorded his *A Dime at a Time*.

The success of the Del Reeves single began opening doors for Chesnut. The following year, Roy Drusky had a Top 20 hit with *Weakness in a Man* (which was also recorded by Brook Benton), Jerry Lee Lewis scored a hit with Chesnut's *Another Place Another Time*, which Chesnut had written during his recuperation. Porter Wagoner and Dolly Parton had a Top 10 duet with *Holding on to Nothin'* and Del Reeves had a Top 5 hit with *Looking at the World Through a Windshield*. In 1969, Johnny Darrell hit the Top 20 with *Woman Without Love*, a song that would also be recorded by Bob Luman and Brook Benton. Del Reeves had a Top 3 hit with the Chesnut song *Good Time Charlies* and George Jones hit the Top 10 with *If Not for You*.

Country songwriter ***Jerry Chesnut***

During 1969 and 1970, Jerry cut some singles for United Artists Records, including *Tiny Fingers* (1969) and *Legend of the Highway* (1970), without success. More and more artists began to record his songs, and in 1970, George Jones had a big hit with Chesnut's *A Good Year for the Roses*. The song was recorded in 1981 by British rocker Elvis Costello for his Country album, ***Almost Blue***.

Early in 1971, Tammy Wynette had a Top 5 hit with the Chesnut song *The Wonders You Perform,* and later that year Faron Young recorded Jerry's classic song *It's Four in the Morning,* which rose to the top of the charts, spending two weeks at No.1 and remaining on the chart for 5 months. Tom Jones also enjoyed a Top 30 hit with the same song, in 1985. In 1972, Johnny Cash hit the Top 3 with the Chesnut song *Oney* and Bill Anderson, no slouch himself as a songwriter, had a Top 3 hit with Jerry's *Don't She Look Good.* In addition, that year, Hank Williams, Jr., had a Top 3 success with *Pride's Not Hard to Swallow*.

Loretta Lynn had a Top 5 hit with *They Don't Make 'Em Like My Daddy* and Elvis Presley recorded *It's Midnight* in 1974, giving Jerry another Top 10 Country and Top 15 Pop hit. The following year Elvis scored another hit with Chesnut's *T-R-O-U-B-L-E.* The single did well on both the Country and Pop charts. Nearly 20 years later, in 1992, Travis Tritt resurrected the song and took it to the Top 15, while the video found favor on CMT. Tritt's version of the Chesnut song was also featured in the motion picture *Honeymoon in Vegas*. Undoubtedly the largest audience to ever hear a Chesnut composition was when Travis Tritt performed *T-R O-U-B-L-E* on network TV during the 1994 Super Bowl.

Jerry's many awards include *Billboard* magazine's 1972 "Songwriter of the Year" and "International Songwriter of the Year." In 1993 Chesnut was nominated for induction in the Nashville Songwriter's Association International's Songwriter Hall of Fame. JIE

JIM CHESNUT

(Singer, Songwriter, Guitar, Piano, Bass Guitar)
Date of Birth: **December 1, 1944**
Where Born: **Midland, Texas**
Married: **1. Linda**
2. Christine

Jim was raised in a middle class family and studied piano and singing under the tutelage of the church and local school instructors. In his late teens, he performed as a professional with the Dan Blocker Singers, a group sponsored by Blocker, who had come to fame as "Hoss" in the TV western series *Bonanza.*

During this time, Jim tried to complete his college degree, but the lure of music was too strong. To help pay the bills, he worked as a carpenter, advertising salesman, TV weatherman, cameraman, News Director, communications technician, deejay (he holds a first class broadcasting license) and aircraft mechanic.

In 1970, Jim went on the road with his first wife, Linda, as his drummer. During the next six years, they toured around the country but after the birth of their children, their marriage fell apart. During this time, Jim did achieve some sort of career breakthrough, when he wrote the score for the movie *For Such as We,* which won the 1972 Atlanta Film Festival gold medal. In addition, his song *Oklahoma Morning* was recorded by Charley Pride.

In 1977, Jim moved to Nashville. He became active in the Country Music Association and was signed by Acuff-Rose Music. That same year, he signed to ABC/Hickory Records. His initial singles fared only moderately, but in 1979, by now on MCA, he had a Top 30 chart single, *Let's Take the Time to Fall in Love Again*. The following year, he moved over to United Artists and had a Top 50 hit with *Out Run the Sun* and then in 1981, his Liberty recording *Bedtime Stories* went Top 40.

At the end of 1981, Jim decided to quit the business and started a marketing consulting firm and another producing direct mail brochures. He returned to the music business in 1987, but he is no longer trying to compete.

RECOMMENDED ALBUMS:
"Let Me Love You Now" (ABC/Hickory)(1977)
"Show Me a Sign" (ABC/Hickory)(1978)

MARK CHESNUTT

(Singer, Guitar, Drums)
Given Name: **Mark Nelson Chesnutt**
Date of Birth: **September 6, 1963**
Where Born: **Beaumont, Texas**
Married: **Tracie**

George Jones said of Mark Chesnutt, "This boy from Beaumont is a real deal." George also lent his support with some very complimentary sleeve notes on Mark's album ***Too Cold at Home***.

Mark started to play on his father's guitar when he was 5 years old (Bob Chesnutt had put out a couple of records in the 60's and 70's). Mark grew up listening and singing along to his father's Hank Williams records and also sang in the choir at high school. It was his father Bob who encouraged him every step of the way. His mom and dad used to take him around to clubs in Beaumont and since his dad knew some of the bands, Mark used to sit in with them.

Soon Mark started playing a couple of nights a week. He also did occasional trips to Dallas, Lufkin and Pasadena. He continued playing and singing for nearly 10 years, appearinging in clubs in and around Beaumont. He landed a job headlining at Cutters nightclub in Beaumont and among his band members was Tracy Byrd, soon to be a star in his own right. A number of regionally successful singles were recorded locally, six on the AXBAR label in San Antonio and two on the Cherry label in Houston.

On one of Mark's trips to Nashville, while trying to find a deal and looking for songs, he

Mark Chesnutt** (right) with another traditional star, **Joe Diffie

turned up *Too Cold at Home*, written by Bobby Harden. It was this song that was to give Mark his big break. A tape of Mark's work got to Roger Ramsey Corkhill, the regional promotions man for MCA in Houston, who took the song to Nashville and Tony Brown, MCA Records executive and producer. After flying down to see Mark perform in Beaumont, Brown signed Mark to MCA with Mark Wright producing.

Mark's first single, *Too Cold at Home,* reached the Top 3 and stayed on the chart for 5 months. Hot on its heels came his debut album of the same name, and in September 1991, this album was Certified Gold. Released at the end of 1990, Paul Craft's song *Brother Jukebox* gave Mark his first No.1 hit, in 1991. This was followed by *Blame It on Texas* (Top 5) and *Your Love Is a Miracle* (Top 3). *Broken Promise Land* was released at the end of 1991 and became a Top 10 in 1992. As a result of this success, Mark was nominated for the CMA "Horizon Award" and won the AMOA award for the "Rising Star of the Year." This award is given for across the board jukebox plays and he beat out Chris Isaak, Vanilla Ice, Timmy T and Gerardo.

Mark spent 300 days on the road with his New South Band, which set him up as an accepted Country act. Mark had a personal setback in 1991, when his father, who had been so supportive of him, died of a massive heart attack.

In 1992, Mark scored with the wonderfully inventive Bobby Braddock-Rafe VanHoy song, *Old Flames Have New Names*, which came from his second album, ***Longnecks and Short Stories***. The single went Top 5, and the album was Certified Gold less than 7 months after release. Mark's next single, *I'll Think of Something*, went to No.1 and was followed by the Top 5 hit, *Bubba Shot the Jukebox*. This last single gave Mark his first taste of cross-over success, when it reached the lower rungs of the Pop chart.

Mark started 1993 with another Bobby Harden song, *Old Country*, which went Top 5. This was followed by back-to-back No.1 hits, *It Sure Is Monday* and the title track of his next album, *Almost Goodbye*. The album was Certified Gold four months after release. In 1993, Mark was the recipient of the CMA's "Horizon Award."

Mark's next single, *I Just Wanted You to Know*, also became a No.1 in 1994 and he followed it with *Woman, Sensuous Woman*, a Gary Paxton song that had been a No.1 for Don Gibson, 20 years earlier. Mark's version reached the Top 25.

Mark Chesnutt's producer, Mark Wright, says that Mark grew up with Country in the marrow of his bones and that he has been living and breathing Country all of his life. The *L.A. Times* called him "the Best Pure Country Singer in the New Country Crop." Mark only sings Country and he is an avid collector of old Country records. JAB

RECOMMENDED ALBUMS:

"Dance Time in Texas" (Axebar)
"Too Cold at Home" (MCA)(1990)
"Long Necks and Short Stories" (MCA)(1992)
"Almost Goodbye" (MCA)(1993)

LEW CHILDRE

(Singer, Hawaiian Guitar, Trumpet, Trombone, Drums, Comedy, Yodeler)

Given Name:	**Lew Childre**
Date of Birth:	**November 1, 1901**
Where Born:	**Opp, Alabama**
Married:	**Unknown**
Date of Death:	**December 3, 1961**

When Lew Childre died in 1961, his friend Whitey Ford, the Duke of Paducah, eulogized him as "one of the greatest one-man shows in the business." Lew could play the guitar, sing, buck dance, do comedy, recite poetry, ad lib commercials and improvise dialogue. He could do it live on stage, on the air, or on transcriptions, and he could do it with a grace and panache that made him one of the most popular entertainers in the music business in the 1930's and 1940's. He was one of the last of the Old-Time entertainers who had come up through the medicine show-vaudeville-tent show circuit and made the transition to Country music, and his career ranged from the dusty Texas tent shows of Harley Sadlers and Milt Tobert to the stage of the *Grand Ole Opry*.

He did programs with a wide range of Country legends, including Wiley Walker, Floyd Tillman, Curly Fox, Bill Monroe, Bill Boyd and Stringbean. He made a bare handful of commercial records, but was one of the many musicians from his era whose reputation was established outside the recording studio and whose influence was far greater than his records indicate. Childre made his reputation with a little Spanish Martin played Hawaiian style, and with his wonderfully flexible voice that could ease into a complex yodel at the drop of a hat and with an apparently inexhaustible fund of old songs and stories.

Lew was born, as he often reminded his listeners, in Opp, Alabama, just a few miles from the Florida line, in 1901. His father was a county judge, and was not too happy when he found that his son, by the age of 8, was standing on downtown street corners doing a buck dance for any passerby who would give him a nickel. In high school young Lew acted in plays, sang Pop songs of the day and played trumpet, trombone and drums in the school band. His family wanted him to go to medical school, though, and to this end he enrolled in the University of Alabama around the close of WWI. Here he received some medical training that would serve him well later in his famous "Dr. Lew" comedy act, where he pretended to be a bogus doctor known for his "wonderful liver and lights remedy." Though he actually finished college, Lew had by then been bitten by the show business bug, and in 1923 he joined the Milt Tolbert tent show as a Pop singer. Soon he had formed his own Jazz band, the Alabama Cotton Pickers, in which he played drums. The group was popular, even made some records and included in its personnel a then-unknown young man named Lawrence Welk.

In 1925, the early boom in Country music had hit and Lew decided to try his hand at it. According to a popular legend, he bought a guitar, took off to the backwoods for a fishing trip and vowed not to come back until he had learned to play it. When he did return, Lew had devised a style that involved playing a standard guitar with a Hawaiian-type steel. Soon he was working tent shows as a soloist, and by 1930, he was broadcasting as a singer over stations in San Angelo, Texas, and Hot Springs, Arkansas. In September 1930, he made his first recordings for Gennett, a session which included one of his signature songs, *Horsie Keep Your Tail Up*. A two-year association with Wiley Walker (later to gain fame as half of the Wiley and Gene team) followed, in which the pair did shows across Texas, billing themselves as the Alabama Boys.

By 1934, Lew was a mainstay of WWL in New Orleans, and this led in 1935 to a major recording session for the ARC group of companies. Two of the releases, *Fishing Blues* and *Hang Out the Front Door Key*, were successful, but didn't capture much of the warm easygoing personality that made Lew such a radio favorite. Advertisers sensed that Lew could sell about any product he chose on radio and were clamoring for his services. By 1938, he was broadcasting alongside the Carter Family over border station XERA in Del Rio, Texas, and by the 1940's was a member of the WWVA *Jamboree* in Wheeling. In 1943, Lew had a daily radio show nationwide over the NBC Blue Network, and a year later he was doing three daily shows over WAGA in Atlanta.

Lew came to the *Grand Ole Opry* in 1945, and a year later began a fruitful partnership with Stringbean. (Unfortunately, no recordings of the comedy duets between these two masters survive.) By now Lew was producing his own transcriptions for companies like Warren Paints, General Foods, and Pepsi and raking in money from patenting a special fishing lure he had invented. An lp for Starday followed in the late 1950's—actually a good, informal, jam-session of a work, and one which really captured the informal radio style of the "Boy from Alabam." Weakened health forced Lew to retire from the *Opry* and from music in 1959, and he died two years later in Foley, Alabama. CKW

RECOMMENDED ALBUMS:

"Old Time Get-Together With Lew Childre" (Starday)(1961) [With Cowboy Copas, Josh Graves and Junior Huskey] [Re-released 1975]

"On the Air 1946, Vol. 1" (Old Homestead)

HARRY CHOATES

(Singer, Fiddle, Guitar, Steel Guitar)

Date of Birth: December 26, 1922
Where Born: Rayne, Louisiana
Married: Helen Daenen (m. 1945) (div. 1950)
Children: Edison, Linda
Date of Death: July 17, 1951

Harry Choates has achieved immortality as the man who recorded the Cajun classic *Jole Blon*. However, there are a few claimants to its writing ownership. In fact the melody of *Jolie Blonde* dates back to the last century and the probable author of the lyrics was Angelas LeJeune in the 1910's. Choates had a major hit with it, however, in 1946, when his recording on Modern Music reached the Country Top 5.

Choates was raised in Port Arthur, Texas, where he played in local barbershops for small change. In his teenage years, he had already started drinking. He joined Leo Soileau's band in Ville Platte playing guitar. Soileau, an early performer of Cajun music, was a singer and fiddle player. He recorded *Jole Blon* in 1935 as *Le Valse de Gueyden* and it is highly likely that Choates heard his version. When Choates recorded the song, he included all the whoops and calls that Soileau had used.

In 1946, Choates went solo. The success he had with *Jole Blon* gave him some sort of celebrity status and he worked the Texas honky tonk clubs as a result. However, Choates was a hell-raiser and chronic alcoholic. In July 1951, he was jailed in Austin for non-support of his wife and children. How he died remains one of Country music's mysteries. Some reports say he had delerium tremens, others that he suffered an epileptic fit and went into a coma. Still others claim that he was a victim of police brutality.

From 1955 through 1961, Starday and D Records released a series of singles. These included *Original Jole Blon* (French and English versions)/*Opelousas, Waltz/Poor Hobo, Port Arthur Waltz/Honky Tonk Boogie, Draggin' the Fiddle/Allons a Lafayette* and *Basile Waltz/Tondellay* on Starday; *Allons a Lafayette/Draggin' the Fiddle, Jole Blon/Dragging the Bow* (a re-issue of the 1946 recording), *Jole Blon/Corpus Christi Waltz, Opolousas Waltz/Poor Hobo, Honky Tonk Boogie/Port Arthur Waltz, Big Woods/Oh-Neon* on D Records.

Choates had the ability to become a major star but was obviously a troubled man. It is claimed that throughout his short life, he always played on borrowed instruments.

RECOMMENDED ALBUMS:

"Fiddle King of Cajun Swing" (Arhoolie)(1982)

"Jole Blon" (D) [Repackaged as "Original Cajun Fiddle"]

CHUCK WAGON GANG, The

Formed: 1935 as the Carter Quartet/1936 Chuck Wagon Gang

DAD CARTER
(Tenor Vocals)
Given Name: David Parker Carter
Date of Birth: September 25, 1889
Where Born: Milltown, Kentucky
Married: Carrie Brooks (dec'd.)
Children: Ernest (Jim), Clellon, Rosa, Effie (Anna), Anna (Jane), Ruth, Roy, Bettye
Date of Death: April 28, 1963

JIM CARTER
(Bass Vocals, Guitar)
Given Name: Ernest Carter
Date of Birth: August 10, 1910
Where Born: Tioga, Texas
Married: Soney
Children: Rusty

ROSE CARTER
(Soprano Vocals)
Given Name: Rosa Lola Carter
Date of Birth: December 31, 1915
Where Born: Noel, Missouri
Married: R.T. Karnes
Children: Ricki, Randy, Midgie

ANNA CARTER
(Alto Vocals)
Given Name: Effie Carter
Date of Birth: February 15, 1917
Where Born: Noel, Missouri
Married: 1. William Howard Gordon (dec'd.) 2. James H. "Jimmie" Davis
Children: Howard, Jr., Vicki, Greg Gordon

RUTH ELLEN CARTER
(Alto Vocals)
Given Name: Ruth Ellen Carter
Date of Birth: January 3, 1924
Where Born: Noel, Missouri
Married: Glenn Yates
Children: Glenn, Jr., Judith, Beverly, Roy D.

ROY CARTER
(Bass Vocals)
Given Name: Roy Carter
Date of Birth: March 1, 1926
Where Born: Calumet, Oklahoma
Married: Thada Smart
Children: Sherron, Shirley

Other significant members of the Chuck Wagon Gang at one time or another have included Eddie Carter (Tenor Vocals), Bettye Carter (Soprano Vocals), Alynn Billodeau, Ronnie Crittenden, William Howard Gordon (d. 1967)(Guitar), Patrick McKeehan, Patricia Neighbors, Ronnie Page, Harold Timmons (Piano), Debby Trusty, Howard Welborn and Greg Gordon (Guitar)

The Chuck Wagon Gang comprises a major link between the world of commercial Country music and that of sacred music in a career that spans some 60 years. They also represent a link with the older Southern singing school tradition. Although in the beginning the group also used a mandolin a little bit and in recent years has added more instrumentation, the Gang's sound in their most significant years consisted of four voices (two of each sex) and a guitar—acoustic until 1954 and electric until 1967.

David Carter was born in Kentucky and moved westward with his family as a child. In a Clay County, Texas, singing school, he met Carrie Brooks and they married in 1909. They reared a family of eight, and Carter worked as a brakeman on the Rock Island Railroad until 1927, and then the family labored in the cotton fields for some years. When one of the children fell ill, and with the family virtually penniless in 1935, Dad Carter talked the management at KFYO Lubbock into a daily radio program for a total salary of $12.50 a week, which soon became $15.00. Rose and Anna sang soprano and alto respectively, while Dad did tenor, and Jim, who played guitar, also sang bass.

Originally known as the Carter Quartet, they became the Chuck Wagon Gang in 1936 when they moved to WBAP and began shows under the sponsorship of Bewley's Best Flour. They sang a variety of songs in those early days and only gradually became a Gospel group. They actually sang more secular than sacred material on their first two sessions in 1936 and 1937 for the American Record Corporation. In 1940 and 1941 they recorded only religious songs. For several months in 1942 they moved to KVOO in Tulsa, Oklahoma, and then disbanded until after WWII.

After WWII ended, the Chuck Wagon Gang went back to WBAP for Bewley Mills and in December 1948 returned to what had become Columbia Records. Ironically, they had made few personal appearances until 1950, when Wally Fowler booked them on one of his All-Night Singing Conventions in Augusta, Georgia. The next year they gave up radio so they could tour full-time. Some changes took place from time to time. Jim Carter gave up music after 1953 and Anna's husband Howard Gordon played electric guitar for the group, serving until his death in 1967. Dad Carter retired in 1955 and was initially replaced by Eddie Carter. Roy Carter sang the bass part, as Jim had also quit singing. From the later 50's, non-family members such as Pat McKeehan also served stints with the band.

Through the years, various Carters came and went from the group. After Howard Gordon died, his son Greg took over as guitarist for a time. Rose and Anna did not always tour, but sang on all their Columbia recordings, which numbered 408 masters by the time they had completed their final session in September 1975. For some years the Gang worked in music only part-time. Rose retired, and after Anna married Jimmie Davis, she was not always available. Bettye and Ruth Ellen took over their parts. Roy Carter had studied at Abilene Christian College for both the ministry and education, and for several years he taught school and the group toured only during his vacation time. After a three-year hiatus from the studios, they began recording again, mostly on the Copperfield label.

Finally in 1987, the Chuck Wagon Gang went full-time again. Roy Carter retired from teaching and put a new quartet together with sister Ruth Ellen Yates, Pat McKeehan, who had worked with them off and on since 1957 and a New Mexico girl named Debby Trusty. In 1984, Dad Carter was elected in the Deceased Category to the Gospel Music Hall of Fame. They had also added a regular pianist, Harold Timmons, formerly of the Hemphills, in 1985. By the end of the decade they had returned to the top of the Gospel music world. From 1988 through 1993, they were named "Gospel Artist or Group of the Year" by *Music City News*. Strangely, they are yet to win a Dove Award from the GMA.

Meanwhile Ruth Ellen retired in October 1989 and a Floridian named Alynn Billodeau replaced her. Earlier that year, May Kutz had become part of their circle as a "jill-of-all-trades." In 1990, Bob Terrell's authorized history, *The Chuck Wagon Gang: A Legend Lives On*, told much of the group's complex history. Harold Timmons added much with a complete discography. In the early 90's, however, a series of changes and upheavals put the group's future in an uncertain status. IMT

RECOMMENDED ALBUMS:

"Sing the Songs of Mosie Lister" (Columbia)(1960)
"He Walks with Me" (Columbia)(1963)
"Anna Gordon of the Chuck Wagon Gang" (Columbia)(1968)
"Greatest Hits" (Columbia)(1968)
"Hallelujah" (Columbia)(1971)
"Oh What a Happy Day" (Columbia)(1973)
"Family Tradition" (CWG & Copperfield)(1979 & 1983)
"Keep on Keeping On" (Copperfield)(1983)
"A Golden Legacy" (Copperfield)(1983)
"16 Country Gospel Favorites" (Copperfield)(1984)
"Columbia Historic Edition" (Columbia)(1985)
"Homecoming" (Copperfield)(1986)
"20 Golden Gospel Greats" (Copperfield)(1987)
"An American Tradition" (Copperfield)(1988)
"Memories Made New, Vol. 1 & 2" (Associated Artists)(1989)
"An Old Fashioned Christmas at Home, Vol. 1 & 2" (Manor House)(1989)

CHURCH BROTHERS, The

BILL CHURCH
(Guitar, Vocals)
Given Name: **Williams Cears Church**
Date of Birth: **September 8, 1922**
EDWIN CHURCH
(Fiddle, Vocals)
Given Name: **Edwin Ralph Church**
Date of Birth: **July 29, 1925**
RALPH CHURCH
(Mandolin, Vocals)
Given Name: **Arthur Ralph Church**
Date of Birth: **June 28, 1928**
All Born: **Wilkes County, North Carolina**

The Church Brothers and their Blue Ridge Ramblers rank as an early and excellent, albeit somewhat obscure, Bluegrass band. Their active years as a group were relatively few and their recordings sparse and inadequately distributed. Even so, the brothers have received their share of praise from collectors and historians, and thanks to Rounder Records and writer Clarence H. Greene, the Church story is no longer lost.

The Church Brothers and their musical associates all hailed from the North Wilkesboro area of North Carolina. Bill Church gained some early experience in music working with Roy Hall and His Blue Ridge Entertainers prior to entering the service in WWII. When Bill returned from the Army, he found that two of his brothers had also taken up music along with a cousin, Ward Eller, and neighbor Drake Walsh (son of Doc Walsh of Carolina Tar Heels fame).

The three brothers, Eller and Walsh began playing on local radio station WILX as the Wilkes County Entertainers. A little later Walsh dropped out, and Garfield and Elmer Bowers joined on banjo and bass fiddle respectively. Later Johnny Nelson came in as banjo picker and Ralph Pennington played bass. In 1948, the band switched over to station WKBC in North Wilkesboro, which would be their radio home for the remainder of their career. At the time they changed stations, the group also adopted the name of the Church Brothers and Their Blue Ridge Ramblers.

The Church Brothers began their recording career for Rich-R-Tone early in 1950. A girl in North Wilkesboro named Drusilla Adams had a knack for writing lyrics and as the Churches needed new songs, the two parties struck up a partnership of sorts as various band members helped develop tunes for Drusilla's words. In addition to two releases on Rich-R-Tone, the Churches backed a vocalist named Buffalo Johnson on a pair of cuts.

Somewhat later, Noah Adams started Blue Ridge Records and the unreleased Rich-R-Tone masters were transferred to his control. The band also recorded some additional material. With all their sessions held between early 1950 and late 1952, the Church Brothers had a total of 8 sides released on Blue Ridge and 4 on Rich-R-Tone. Three unissued masters later appeared on album releases, with Bill Church writing one song and Johnny Nelson contributing an original instrumental. Except for the old favorite, *Roll in My Sweet Baby's Arms*, all the Church songs recorded were co-written by Dru Adams, who actively endeavored to promote their recordings.

Unfortunately, the Churches seem to have been only marginally interested in becoming a nationally acclaimed band, preferring not to travel long distances for show dates. The career of the Church Brothers took a new turn on January 28, 1953, when Johnny Nelson died in an automobile crash. As Ralph Church later explained to Clarence H. Green, "The Army got Ward Eller right after Johnny got killed, and then the rest of us got married; everybody went their separate ways."

At last report, Ward Eller, Edwin and Ralph Church still make their home in Wilkes County. Bill Church moved to South Carolina, where he currently resides. Ralph Pennington lived in retirement near Salisbury, North Carolina and Gar Bowers in Winston-Salem. In 1969, GHP Records of Cuxhaven, Germany, released an album containing a dozen Church Brothers masters and two with vocals by Buffalo Johnson. A decade later, Rounder released an album containing 15 Church cuts, without the two with Johnson in their Early Days of Bluegrass series. IMT

RECOMMENDED ALBUMS:

"The Church Brothers, Traditional Bluegrass" (GHP Germany)(1969)
"The Church Brothers" (Rounder)(1978)

GENE CLARK

(Singer, Songwriter, Guitar, Tambourine, Harmonica)
Date of Birth: November 17, 1941
Where Born: Tipton, Missouri
Date of Death: May 24,1991

Gene Clark is most often remembered as a founding member of the Byrds. His contribution to the ground-breaking 60's band is important, but his musical expression extended into many other areas during his career.

Born into a large family in the Ozark Mountains of Missouri, Gene learned to play guitar from his siblings. He polished his skills on the instrument during the regular back porch musical get-together. In high school Gene played in several bands, including the Surfriders when "surf" music was the rage. The next stop on his musical journey was performing in the Midwest at Folk music clubs. During one of his appearances, Clark came to the attention of Randy Sparks, who led one of the nation's most popular Folk groups, the New Christy Minstrels. Sparks offered him a job playing 12-string guitar with the group. Clark went on tour and recorded two albums with them. He played guitar on several of their hit singles, including *Green, Green, Saturday Night* and *Liza Lee*.

When Clark left the New Christy Minstrels he settled in Los Angeles, where, in 1964, he played in a band led by Jim Dickson. That same year, Gene met Jim (soon to change his name to Roger) McQuinn (who was then doing covers of Beatles songs) and David Crosby. The three became fast friends and often spent time together at West Hollywood's Troubadour Club, where McGuinn was playing. McGuinn invited Clark and Crosby to join him onstage during one of his solo performances and when the vocal blend drew rave reviews, Gene suggested they put a group together.

With a desire to combine their Folk roots with the melodic Rock sounds of the British bands (they were especially influenced by the Beatles' movie *A Hard Day's Night)* the three friends formed the Jet Set and then the Beefeaters. They added Michael Clark on drums and Chris Hillman on bass and went to work creating the Byrds sound, which was largely built around the distinctive 12-string guitar of McGuinn. They initially recorded as the Beefeaters for Elektra. When their debut album was released on Columbia in the summer of 1965, the band enjoyed instant success with the Bob Dylan song *Mr. Tambourine Man*. The Byrds released their second album late in 1965 and experienced another big hit with the title track, *Turn! Turn! Turn!* Clark supplied lead vocals to several songs on both albums and contributed his songwriting on favorites *I'll Feel a Whole Lot Better* and *Eight Miles High*. (See the Byrds.)

By early 1966, the Byrds were in great demand for concert appearances and the band toured heavily. Their success had extended around the world and their travels were often by airplane. Clark developed a fear of flying and that, coupled with the increasing demands of a hit group, eventually took its toll. At the peak of their popularity, Gene Clark left the Byrds.

Back in Los Angeles, Gene began writing songs for a solo project. He wanted to release an album that was completely written by him. He called on some old Bluegrass friends to record with him and in 1967 released ***Gene Clark with the Gosdin Brothers***. As well as featuring Vern and Rex Gosdin, the album also featured performances by Leon Russell, Glen Campbell, Doug Dillard, Clarence White, Chris Hillman and Michael Clark. The 1967 recording was one of the first to explore the "Country-Rock" sound and found an even greater audience when it was re-released, in 1972. Gene went on to form the short-lived Gene Clark Group, and then returned for a brief time to the Byrds, replacing Dave Crosby.

In 1968, Clark teamed up with Doug Dillard to form the Dillard & Clark Expedition. Dillard's Bluegrass background blended well with the Folk roots of Clark, and they threw in a little Rock for good measure. The group recorded two albums for A & M, ***Fantastic Expedition*** in 1968 and ***Through the Morning, Through the Night***, in 1969. Among other members of the Dillard and Clark Expedition was Bernie Leadon, who would go on to become a founder of the Country-Rock supergroup the Eagles. Although the group's albums were critically acclaimed, they were a commercial disappointment. Commenting on the reason Clark said, "We were just a little bit ahead of our time. No Country-Rock sold well until after 1969, and that was only after people decided that Crosby, Stills, Nash and Young were Country-Rock to some degree."

When the Dillard and Clark Expedition disbanded in late 1969, Clark left Los Angeles heading north to Mendocino, California. The change of scene sparked his creative output and he wrote material for a new solo album. He collaborated with producer/guitarist Jesse Ed Davis in the recording of the Clark ***White Light*** album.

In 1973 Clark reconnected with his former bandmates for a Byrds reunion album and tour. Gene contributed *Full Circle* and *Changing Times* to the project for Asylum Records. Although successful, the project didn't create enough interest to continue and the group members went their separate ways. Clark recorded a solo album, ***No Other***, for Asylum and then switched to RSO Records to release ***Two Sides to Every Story***.

The next group Clark joined came as the result of a performance with old friend Roger McGuinn at the Roxy in Los Angeles. Chris Hillman and David Crosby joined Clark and McGuinn onstage for an impromptu performance and the crowd went wild. The quartet repeated their performance in several other cities and discussed forming a new group; the result was McGuinn, Clark, and Hillman. (David Crosby had previous commitments.) The trio released an album on Capitol in 1979 that made the Top 10 Pop Album chart. Touring to support the album brought back all of Clark's fears, and he questioned his continued involvement in the group. When the second lp was released the name changed to McGuinn and Hillman, featuring Gene Clark. Gene contributed a couple of songs to the album but only appeared on selected dates on the following concert tour.

Clark fled Los Angeles to spend a few years in Hawaii. When he returned to California, he secured a contract with Allegiance Records. He called on old friends Chris Hillman and Herb Pederson to help him record *Firebyrd* that featured remakes of the Byrds hits *Mr. Tambourine Man* and *Feel a Whole Lot Better*. Gene Clark died from natural causes, in 1991, at the age of 49. JIE

RECOMMENDED ALBUMS:

"Gene Clark & the Gosdin Brothers" (Columbia)(1967)
"White Light" (A&M)(1972)
"No Other" (Asylum)(1974)
"Two Sides to Every Story" (RSO)(1977)
"Firebyrd" (Allegiance)
The Byrds:
"Mr. Tambourine Man" (Columbia)(1965)
"Turn! Turn! Turn" (Columbia)(1966)
"The Byrds" (Asylum)(1973)
Dillard & Clark:
"Fantastic Expedition" (A&M)(1968)
"Through the Morning, Through the Night" (A&M)(1969)

GUY CLARK

(Singer, Songwriter, Guitar)
Given Name: **Guy Clark, Jr.**
Date of Birth: **November 6, 1941**
Where Born: **Monahans, Texas**
Married: **Susanna**
Children: **Travis**

Guy Clark is widely respected as one of Country music's most gifted and introspective songwriters. His fine blending of words and music has provided hits for many artists, including Ricky Skaggs, John Conlee, Vince Gill, and Johnny Cash. Guy is also a critically acclaimed recording artist with seven albums to his credit.

Born in the small West Texas town of Monahans, Guy's earliest memories are of being raised by his grandmother. His father was in the Army and his mother worked, leaving young Guy with his grandmother. She ran the town hotel, whose residents included an old oil well driller named Jack Prigg. He had drilled wells all over the world and his exotic tales made a lasting impression on the 5 year old Guy. Prigg became the subject of one of Guy's best known songs, *Desperados Waiting for a Train*, recorded by, among others, Jerry Jeff Walker, Bobby Bare, and the Highwaymen.

When Guy's father returned from WWII, the family moved to Houston and then to Corpus Christi, where Guy's father started a law practice. Both his parents encouraged Guy to foster an interest in the arts. A regular part of the evenings at the Clark home were poetry readings. Guy immersed himself in the words of the great American poets Robert Frost and Stephen Vincent Benet. The family didn't have a record player until Guy was a teenager. His parents loved big band music, and Guy's favorites included Bill Haley, Louis Armstrong, and Little Willie John.

Guy's interest in playing music was sparked by his dad's law partner, who played guitar and sang Mexican music. Guy ventured to nearby Mexico and purchased his first guitar when he was 16. Most of the first songs he learned to play and sing were in Spanish.

After a stint at several colleges, Guy moved to Houston and befriended fellow songwriters Townes Van Zandt and John Lomax, Jr. Guy began writing songs himself and developed friendships with Blues performers Mance Lipscomb and Lightnin' Hopkins. Houston was also where Guy first performed on a regular basis at Folk clubs and coffeehouses.

In the mid-60's, Guy spent some time in San Francisco performing and repairing guitars. When he returned to Houston, he worked as an art director for a TV station. In the late 60's, Guy and his new bride, Susanna, a fellow songwriter and painter, decided to move to Los Angeles to pursue the music business. To make ends meet, Guy worked at the Dopera Brothers' Dobro factory.

Unable to afford demo recordings of his songs, Guy made appointments to perform live for publishers. When he sang a few songs for the President of Sunbury Music it earned him a contract as a staff writer. Guy was also happy to discover the company had an office in Nashville. After living less than a year in the nation's second largest city, Guy was ready to leave California. He expressed his dissatisfaction of the hectic lifestyle in *L.A. Freeway*. It became one of his first songs to be recorded when Jerry Jeff Walker included it on his MCA self-titled debut album, in 1972.

Guy and Susanna made the move to Nashville in 1971. Soon their home became a gathering place for aspiring songwriters like Texas transplant Rodney Crowell. Likening Guy to Picasso, Crowell credits Guy as his biggest songwriting influence.

After Jerry Jeff Walker recorded *L.A. Freeway* and *That Old Time Feeling*, other artists began to discover his writing. Johnny Cash charted with Guy's *Texas 1947* (1976) and *The Last Gunfighter Ballad* (1977) and David Allen Coe did renditions of *Desperados Waiting for a Train* and *Texas 1947*. Guy recalled his childhood days in West Texas for many of his compositions. *Texas 1947* recounts when the first diesel train shook the station in Guy's small hometown. He recalled the whole town waiting by the tracks to see the mammoth silver and red train speed through without even stopping.

Guy's success as a songwriter led to his own recording contract with RCA in 1975 and the release of ***Old No.1***. The album contained Guy's own version of several songs that had been recorded by others. The cover of the album was painted by wife Susanna. Guy also appeared in 1975 on the ***Kerrville Folk Festival Commemorative Live*** recording, singing *Anyhow I Love You*.

Guy recorded a second album for RCA, ***Texas Cookin'***, in 1976. He then moved to Warner Brothers and released ***Guy Clark*** (1978), ***South Coast of Texas*** (1981) and ***Better Days*** (1983). While with Warner Brothers, Guy charted with *Fool for Each Other* (Top 100, 1979), *The Partner Nobody Chose* (Top 40, 1981) and *Homegrown Tomatoes* (Top 50, 1983).

The singer/songwriter developed a loyal following but none of his albums were major commercial successes. Some of his biggest fans were fellow artists, music business insiders and music critics. His ***Better Days*** topped the list of England's *New Musical Express* newspaper's "Top 15 Country Recordings of the Year," ahead of Dolly Parton, Waylon Jennings and Willie Nelson.

While success as a recording artist continued to evade Guy, other artists continued to find good fortune with his songs. Bobby Bare scored a Top 20 hit with Guy's *New Cut Road*, in the spring of 1982. Later in the year, Guy celebrated his first No.1 when Ricky Skaggs took his *Heartbroke* to the top of the charts. The song was eventually also recorded by

One of music's greatest writers, ***Guy Clark***

George Strait, Rodney Crowell and the Marshall Tucker Band.

Guy took a hiatus from recording between 1983 and 1988 but continued to see his songs recorded by others. The masters' quartet of Johnny Cash, Willie Nelson, Waylon Jennings, and Kris Kristofferson took Guy's *Desperados Waiting for a Train* to the Top 15 as the Highwaymen in 1985. The following year, Guy's friend Vince Gill had a Top 15 hit with *Oklahoma Borderline*, written by Guy, Crowell, and Gill. Also in 1986, Ed Bruce and Lynn Anderson had a hit with Guy's *Fools for Each Other*. In early 1987, John Conlee reached the Top 10 with *The Carpenter*.

In 1989, Guy joined Sugar Hill Records and released ***Old Friends***. The album included songs written by his wife, Susanna, and fellow Texans Townes Van Zandt and Joe Ely. Guy's unique songwriting continued to draw praise as *The Washington Post* suggested that "he... captured modern Texas as well as any book Larry McMurtry has ever written."

In 1992, Pirates of the Mississippi had a Top 40 hit with *Too Much*, which Guy wrote with Lee Roy Parnell. ***Boats to Build***, Guy's seventh album, was released that year on Asylum Records (American Explorer Series). For the title track the song-poet once again drew from the well of personal history from his high school days living on the Gulf Coast of Texas. A summer job building wooden shrimp boats taught him the importance of taking pride in one's work. The attention to detail the boat carpenters took became good subject matter and a philosophy Guy applied to his songwriting.

Several of Guy Clark's admirers and colleagues joined him on the album, including Rodney Crowell and Emmylou Harris. Guy's son, Travis, made his recording debut on ***Boats to Build*** playing bass. A music video was made of the infectious track *Baton Rouge*. JIE

RECOMMENDED ALBUMS:

"Old No.1" (RCA Victor)(1975) [Re-released on Sugar Hill]
"Texas Cookin'" (RCA Victor)(1976)
"Guy Clark" (Warner Brothers)(1978)
"The South Coast of Texas" (Warner Brothers)(1981)
"Greatest Hits" (RCA Victor)(1983)
"Better Days" (Warner Brothers)(1983)
"Old Friends" (Sugar Hill)(1989) [Mother Records in Europe]
"Boats to Build" (Asylum American Explorer)(1992)

ROY CLARK

(Singer, Songwriter, Guitar, Banjo, Fiddle, Trumpet, Actor, Comedy)

Given Name:	**Roy Linwood Clark**
Date of Birth:	**April 15, 1933**
Where Born:	**Meherrin, Virginia**
Married:	**Barbara Joyce Rupard (m. 1957)**

Anyone who ever watched *Hee Haw* knows that Roy Clark is one of the most versatile performers in Country music if not in the entertainment industry period. He is also one of the nicest men in the industry and one with a big heart and a social conscience.

Roy was raised in Meherrin, Virginia, Staten Island, St. Clairsville, Ohio, and Washington, D.C. His father, Hester, was at various times a tobacco grower, sawmill worker and computer programmer for the Department of Health, Education and Welfare. He also played in local groups and his mother, Lillian, played piano. Roy's father saw that he learned to play banjo properly. However, his first instrument was a cigar box with a ukulele neck on it and four strings rigged by his father for a school band at Meherrin Elementary.

As a child, Roy had a newspaper route for the *Washington Star*. As a teenager, he worked as a car hop at a restaurant in Alexandria, Virginia. He made his first appearance in 1948, with Hester Clark's square dance band at a military service club, and his first paid job was at a similar venue a year later when he received $2.00. When he was 16, Roy was offered a try-out with the St. Louis Browns baseball team, but had to decline because he couldn't afford the fare. At the age of 17, he boxed in the light-heavyweight division in and around Washington, D.C. He won 15 straight bouts before turning to music.

At the end of the 40's, Roy won the Country Music Banjo Competition. He did it again the next year and was rewarded with an appearance on the *Grand Ole Opry*. Before he was out of his teens, Roy could play banjo, guitar and fiddle. In 1956, he guested on *Arthur Godfrey's Talent Scouts Show*. From 1960, he played with Wanda Jackson in Las Vegas and from the mid- 60s to the mid-70s, Roy had a long-term contract to play the show room at the Frontier Hotel, 12 weeks per year. He first headlined in Vegas in 1962. Roy made his debut on the *Tonight Show* in 1963 and became the first Country artist to host the show.

From 1969, Roy was co-host of *Hee Haw* on WLAC-TV with Buck Owens. Because of his heavy schedule, Roy recorded his portion in two 10-day sessions a year. He headlined at Caesar's Palace, Las Vegas, with Petula Clark. In 1976, he made a three week concert tour of Russia, playing Riga, Moscow and Leningrad. As a result, Roy was given an award as CMA "Friendship Ambassador."

Although he had recorded singles for Four Star, Coral and Debbie, Roy's solo recording career got off the ground in 1962 with his album ***The Lightning Fingers of Roy Clark*** on Capitol. With his 4th single for Capitol, *Tips of My Fingers*, Roy achieved Top 10 status and also crossed over onto the Pop charts Top 50. Although he released several singles on Capitol and its cadet label, Tower, over the next five years, only *Through the Eyes of a Fool* in 1964 and the Audie Murphy penned *When the Wind Blows in Chicago* a year later, achieved even Top 40 credit.

In 1968, Roy moved over to Dot and initially didn't fare well. Then in 1969, he had a Top 10 hit with *Yesterday When I Was Young,* which was also a Top 20 Pop hit. He didn't hit this level again until the following year, with *I Never Picked Cotton* (Top 5) and *Thank God and Greyhound* (Top 10).

In August 1972, the novelty number *The Lawrence Welk-Hee Haw Counter-Revolution Polka* hit the Top 10, followed by the No.1 hit *Come Live with Me* in 1973. That same year, Roy had a Top 30 success with the instrumental *Riders in the Sky* and then went Top 3 with *Somewhere Between Love and Goodbye*. Roy started 1974 with *Honeymoon Feelin',* which peaked in the Top 5 and *The Great Divide,* which made it into the Top 15.

In the summer of 1975, he was made happy with the Top 20 *Heart to Heart* and then in January 1976, Roy had a Top 3 hit with the song most associated with him, *If I Had to Do It All Over Again*. His label had changed from Dot to ABC/Dot and it now was going through more changes as it became ABC. The 1976 hits *Think Summer* and *I Have a Dream, I Have a Dream/Half a Love* represented his last higher order successes for some while.

Chain Gang of Love in 1979 on ABC's successor, MCA, went Top 30 and really heralded his last major hit. Roy recorded a Gospel album for Songbird in 1981, *The Last Word in Jesus Is Us*, from which the title track made the Top 75. Then he moved to long-time manager Jim Halsey's Churchill Records in 1982 and on again to Silver D. in 1986, but the hits got no higher than the 50s and 60s.

In 1984, Roy Clark, Grandpa Jones, Buck Owens and Kenny Price (supported by Charlie McCoy) formed the Hee Haw Gospel Quartet, which had an eponymous album on the Hee Haw label.

But it is not by single release success that Roy can be measured. His albums are almost entirely seamless. Although certain albums have been recommended below, any Roy Clark album will be worth having or listening to, not just for Country purists but for lovers of musical professionalism and sheer undiluted entertainment.

Roy has also appeared in an acting capacity on TV and the big screen. He appeared in

The Beverly Hillbillies playing cousin Roy and his mama, Big Mama Halsey (a not too subtle in-joke at the expense of his then manager, Jim Halsey). He was in *Matilda* (1978) with Elliot Gould, *Uphill All the Way* with Frank Gorshin, Glen Campbell, Mel Tillis and Burl Ives, and he also made an appearance in TV's *The Odd Couple* that starred Tony Randall and Jack Klugman.

In his illustrious career, Roy has achieved a lot of firsts. He was the first Country artist to be shrined in the Movieland Wax Museum in Buena Park, California. He was the first Country artist to headline a night at the Montreux International Jazz Festival. He is the only Country artist to be invited to headline the Brussels Millennium, the first Country artist to headline at MIDEM, the music industry fair in Cannes. He is also one of the few Country artists to receive a Five Star rating in the jazz periodical *Downbeat*. He is one of the few Country artists to play Madison Square Garden and was the first Country performer to begin major TV guesting abroad with the *Tom Jones Show* from London in 1969.

Over the years, Roy has chalked up a fine collection of awards. In 1969, 1970 and 1971, he was ACM "Comedy Act of the Year." He was voted "Instrumentalist of the Year" in the *Music City News* Fan Voted Poll in 1969 through 1972. ACM also voted him "TV Personality of the Year" in 1972 and in 1972 and 1973, he was ACM's "Entertainer of the Year." In 1973, the CMA made him "Entertainer of the Year." That same year he was named "Country Music Star of the Year" by the American Guild of Variety Artists. Roy and Buck Trent received the CMA award as "Instrumental Group of the Year" in 1975 and 1976. *Guitar Player* magazine awarded him the prize for "Best Country Guitarist" 1976 through 1980. He was ACM's "Lead Guitar Player of the Year" in 1977 and CMA's "Instrumentalist of the Year" 1977, 1978 and 1980. *Playboy* magazine named him "Picker of the Year" in their readers' poll for 1977, 1978 and 1979. At the 1982 NARAS awards, Roy received a Grammy for his Churchill recording of *Alabama Jubilee* as "Best Country Instrumental Performance." He had first recorded the tune on Capitol in 1964.

On top of his awards by his peers in the industry, Roy Clark has also received other citations such as the Honorary Doctorate of Humane Letters from John Brown University and from Baker University. He was named Oklahoma's Ambassador of Goodwill and has a star on Hollywood Boulevard. He was the first Country singer inducted into the Las Vegas Entertainers Hall of Fame and he is a

The multi-talented ***Roy Clark***

charter member. The Roy Clark Elementary School in Tulsa, Oklahoma, was dedicated to him in 1977. January 16, 1980, became Roy Clark Day in Virginia when he became the first native born son to be honored on one day by every governing body of that state. On November 16, 1982, Roy was inducted into the Oklahoma Hall of Fame. That same year, he was admitted to the Gibson (Guitar) Hall of Fame.

Roy Clark is someone who cares about others. He has donated a million dollars to the Children's Medical Center of Tulsa. His annual benefit concerts for the Hollenbeck Division of the Los Angeles Police Department have raised monies to build and staff the Hollenbeck Youth Center. The Roy Clark Emergency Treatment Center is a new wing at the Southside Community Hospital in Farmville, Virginia. The Lincoln County High School in Lafayette, Tennessee, has built the Roy Clark Fieldhouse at their sports facility. Roy was the visiting artist in residence at Longwood College in Farmville, Virginia.

The man who couldn't afford the fare to try out for a baseball team now is part owner of the Texas Drillers and the Texas Rangers AA Farm Club. His leisure activities are hunting, fishing, boating and photography and he loves fried chicken and spring water. He is an aviation nut and pilots his own plane. The airport in Skiatook, Oklahoma, is named after him.

In recent years, Roy, like so many Country performers, has been performing in Branson. His backing group for a long while was Rodney Lay & the Wild West and his background singers were Fanci. He became a member of the *Grand Ole Opry* in 1987.

RECOMMENDED ALBUMS:

"Roy Clark Live" (Dot)(1972)
"Entertainer of the Year" (Capitol)(1975)
"A Pair of Fives (Banjos that Is)" (Dot)(1975) [With Buck Trent re-issued on MCA]
"ABC Collection" (double)(ABC)(1977)
"Banjo Bandits" (ABC)(1978) [With Buck Trent re-issued on MCA]
"Makin' Love" (MCA)(1981) [With Gatemouth Brown]
"The Last Word in Jesus Is Us" (Sunbird)(1981)
"The Roy Clark Show Live from Austin City Limits" (Churchill)(1982)
"The Hee Haw Gospel Quartet" (Hee Haw)(1984)

SANFORD CLARK

(Singer, Songwriter, Guitar)
Date of Birth: 1935
Where Born: Tulsa, Oklahoma

On the strength of one song, *The Fool*, which had been written by Lee Hazelwood, Sanford Clark leapt into rock'n'roll history. He possessed a vocal sound that moved between Johnny Cash and Ricky Nelson.

While he was still a child, Sanford's family moved to Phoenix, Arizona, and he got his first guitar when he was 12. His early idols were somewhat diverse, being Hank Williams and Mario Lanza. After a while, he fell under the spell of Lefty Frizzell, Little Richard and Fats Domino. He was definitely not into the Swing music of Bob Wills and Hank Thompson. He played around the Phoenix area clubs until 1953, when he enlisted in the U.S. Air Force. After basic training in San Antone, he was shipped out to Johnston Island in the Pacific. Here he put together a band and they won a talent contest in Hawaii.

The Air Force then shipped him to Phoenix, where he met up with a boyhood friend, the now legendary guitarist Al Casey. Casey spoke to Lee Hazelwood, who at the time was a deejay on WTYL and budding songwriter. They went into Floyd Ramsey's tiny Audio Recorders recording studio and cut the slow Rockabilly number *The Fool*. The single was initially released in 1956 on MCI, a label owned by Ramsey drummer, Connie Conway and bass player Jimmy Wilcox.

Initially, his record did nothing until a deejay in Philadelphia heard it and called Randy Wood at Dot Records. Wood got in touch with Lee Hazelwood and the single was licensed to Dot. Interestingly, the single also gives credit to Al Casey, who played guitar on the record.

Sanford, with his leather covered guitar, and Al got out on the road. They worked with headliners as diverse as Ray Price, Gene Vincent and Roy Orbison. The single started to climb the Pop charts and peaked in the Top 10 and stayed around for about five months. It crossed over to the Country charts, where it entered and fell out after one week in the Top 15.

At the end of 1956, Sanford and Al returned to Ramsey's new studio and cut another Lee Hazelwood song, *A Cheat,* and also *Don't Cry*. The former was released, but died in the Top 75. Sanford was experiencing a lot of problems with the label and in particular Randy Wood. Wood wanted to make Clark into a clone of Pat Boone, then Dot's biggest artist. The label then sent Sanford to record material in Hollywood, but a lot of the tracks were never released at the time. They were released at a later date, and clearly show that Clark was very unhappy with the songs. He did turn out some good tracks such as *Loo Bee Doo* and *Cross Eyed Cat,* but they sank without trace.

In 1958, the team of Clark, Hazelwood and Casey left Dot and went to Jamie Records. This became fertile ground for Hazelwood and Casey because of their work with Duane Eddy. Sanford cut *Still as the Night* with Duane on lead guitar but the hits would not come. Sanford left the label in 1960 and joined 3-Trey and then Project, still without success. Now living in Hollywood, Sanford became friendly with Roger Miller, who was playing at the Palomino. Roger asked Clark to record his songs, he didn't, Roger did and the rest is musical history. In 1964, Sanford went to Warner Brothers Records, where it looked like he was going to get back into the charts with the Hazelwood song *Houston*. The record started to take off, then Dean Martin cut it for Reprise (another Warner label) and he had the hit.

In 1965, Clark left Warner Brothers and by 1967, he was reunited with Floyd Ramsey on Ramsey's Ramco label. They re-recorded *The Fool* and this time Waylon Jennings played lead guitar. Lee Hazelwood had now become a big-time producer and he pulled Sanford onto his LHI label, where he cut the album *Return of the Fool* in 1967, which was released two years later. By the 70's, Sanford had decided that he was not going to earn a full-time living out of the music business.

For many years, Sanford Clark had been involved in the construction industry. He concentrated on this increasingly, as well as the utilization of his other skill, that of blackjack player, which has earned him a pretty sum. He still occasionally records around the Phoenix area, in particular some sides for his own Desert Sun label. Was Sanford unfortunate or was he just lucky to get the one hit? On reflection it was the former. Sanford produced a lot of excellent material but a lot of the time had very bad label guidance, especially while at Dot.

RECOMMENDED ALBUMS:

"Return of the Fool" (LHI)(1969)
"The Fool" (Ace)(1983)
"Rockin' Rollin' Vol. 1 and 2" (two albums)(Bear Family Germany)(1986) [Note: Dot and Jamie Masters]

YODELING SLIM CLARK

(Singer, Songwriter, Guitar, Yodeler)

Given Name:	**Raymond LeRoy Clark**
Date of Birth:	**December 11, 1917**
Where Born:	**Springfield, Massachusetts**
Married:	**Celia Jo Roberson**
Children:	**Wilf Carter, Jewell LaVerne**

Slim Clark is one of the best singers of Cowboy and Western songs that the genre has produced, despite the fact that he has spent most of his life in New England. Like Hal Lone Pine, Dick Curless, and Gene Hooper, Clark is a product of the rural Northeast and still manages to sound authentically Country. Unlike the others, however, Yodeling Slim manifests a much greater Wilf Carter (Montana Slim) influence and remains much more Western than Country in his upbringing.

Although born in the city of Springfield, Slim moved to a farm while still an infant and he subsequently gained a great appreciation for the out-of-doors. He later claimed that he had decided by the age of 8 that his ambition was to be a cowboy singer. By the age of 13, Slim began to play guitar and sing songs learned from phonograph records. When he was about 17, someone told him he sounded like Montana Slim. He soon began listening to the Canadian singer, who quickly became Slim's idol.

By 1937, Yodeling Slim had begun playing and singing in local communities throughout central Massachusetts, and by 1941 he had regular radio programs at WKNE Keene, New Hampshire, where he remained for more than a decade. His longest broadcasting stint came at WABI Bangor, Maine, where he had both radio and television programs from 1952 to 1967.

Slim Clark began cutting for the New York-based Continental label in 1946. He had numerous singles on this label over several years and much of this material was subsequently re-released on both 10" and 12" albums on labels like Remington, Pontiac and Masterseal. His repertoire consisted of traditional cowboy and Folk songs, covers of Wilf Carter numbers and some originals of his own or co-written with Pete Roy, almost always delivered simply but effectively, with his own guitar as the only instrumental accompaniment.

*Famed Western singer **Yodeling Slim Clark***

As his name suggests, he yodeled when appropriate in a clear, crisp manner. In 1953, Slim recorded four singles for Doc Williams' Wheeling label. He also cut an album for Arc records of Canada. In 1965, Slim began a series of albums for Palomino Records, a small New Jersey-based company (later they moved to Florida) that have been of consistently high quality.

As Slim grew older, he also became a painter of considerable renown, his speciality being outdoor woodland scenes often containing white-tailed deer, although he painted a western scene to adorn the cover of one of his Palomino albums. It is his intention to carry on singing *and* painting. In recent years, Elmwood Station Music of Providence, Rhode Island, has reissued some of his earlier material on cassettes. One could sum up Slim and his work as a man of the forests who sings the songs of the plains with skill and taste. IMT

RECOMMENDED ALBUMS:

"Cowboy Songs" (Masterseal)(1957)
"The Legendary Jimmie Rodgers Songs" (Palomino)(1965)
"Yodeling Slim Clark Sings Montana Slim Songs Vol. 1" (Palomino)(1965)
"Yodeling Slim Clark Sings Montana Slim Songs Vol. 2" (Palomino)(1966)
"I Feel a Big Trip Comin' On" (Palomino)(1968)
"Yodeling Slim Clark Sings the Ballad of Billy Venero" (Palomino)(1970)
"Yodeling Slim Clark Sings Wilf Carter Songs, Volume #3" (Palomino)(1980)

LEE T. CLAYTON

(Singer, Songwriter, Guitar, Hawaiian Guitar)

Date of Birth:	**October 29, 1942**
Where Born:	**Russellville, Alabama**

Lee Clayton is the man who gave Outlaw music its name from his song *Ladies Love Outlaws*. In fact Lee T. Clayton was known as the "outlaw's outlaw."

He was raised in Oak Ridge, Tennessee, and inherited his father's love of Country music, listening to Jimmie Rodgers and Red Foley. When he was 6, he was taken to the *Grand Ole Opry* by his father. When he was 9, Mr. Clayton, Sr., gave him the option to learn to play either accordion or guitar. He chose guitar and was given a Hawaiian guitar. For 18 months, he studied, and although not overly keen, he became proficient enough to debut on a local radio station, playing Leon McAuliffe's *Steel Guitar Rag*, a year later.

He stopped playing for a while in high school but started playing again when age 16. Six months before he graduated from the University of Tennessee, he married his childhood sweetheart. He gave up playing to become "Mr. Normal." Then one day, he decided he wanted to become a pilot. His wife was studying for her Ph.D. in mathematics at the time and within a year they were divorced. In 1965, he joined the U.S. Air Force and flew a "Widowmaker." He was discharged in 1969 and never flew again. After leaving the service, Lee gravitated toward Nashville.

His serious songwriting started in 1966. *Ladies Love Outlaws,* which was cut by Waylon Jennings in 1972, was his first writing success. At that time, he was getting attention paid to his performing skills due to an article in *Rolling Stone* magazine after a concert at Griffith Springs, Texas, which also created a career boost to Billy Joe Shaver. Lee released his debut album on MCA in 1973, which did nothing. In 1974, he moved to Joshua Springs, California. Then Waylon released Clayton's *If You Could Touch Her at All*, Jerry Jeff Walker released *Won'tcha Give Me One More Chance*, Bonnie Koloc recorded *Silver Stallion* and Hoyt Axton cut *Whisper on a Velvet Night* for the *Outlaw Blues* soundtrack. It seemed that other songwriters wanted to record this songwriter's material.This was further reinforced by the fact that Tom Rush and the Everly Brothers also recorded *Ladies* and Willie Nelson had a hit with *If You Could Touch Her at All.* Waylon also recorded Lee's *Memory of You and I.* After his sojourn in Joshua Springs, Lee returned to Nashville.

In 1977, Lee signed to Capitol and the next year he released ***Border Affair*** and in 1979, ***Naked Child***. The latter featured howls from Lee's half-breed wolfdog, Elvis Firewolf!

During 1980, Lee toured the world. Upon returning to the U.S., he recorded ***The Dream Goes On***, but it was not imbued with the same Clayton feeling as the others. On the verge of making a video and releasing an initial single, he up and disappeared into the desert to get his act back together.

Bono from the Rock band U2 has said that Clayton was one Country performer that influenced him. During the 80's, Lee didn't record, but he did write two books and a stage play, *Little Boy Blue,* all based on his life.

However, 1990 saw him back in the studio. ***Another Night*** was recorded live in Oslo, Norway, with a Scandinavian band. The album was released by Provogue Music Productions. That year, Lee's song *Silver Stallion* appeared on the ***Highwayman 2*** album of Jennings, Nelson, Cash and Kristofferson. In 1994, Lee was starting to get more active and appeared at Linda Hargrove's Leukemia Concert and was planning to return to the recording studio.

RECOMMENDED ALBUMS:

"Border Affair" (Capitol)(1978)
"Naked Child" (Capitol)(1979)
"Another Night" (Provogue)(Norway)(1990)

JACK CLEMENT

(Record Producer, Recording Engineer, Studio Owner, Steel Guitar, Guitar, Dobro, Ukulele, Bass Guitar, Film Producer, Poet, Video Maker, "Professional Goofing Offer")

Given Name:	**Jack Henderson Clement**
Date of Birth:	**April 5, 1932**
Where Born:	**Memphis, Tennessee**
Married:	**1. Doris (m. & div. twice)**
	2. Sharon Johnson
Children:	**Niles, Alison**

There has to be one unanswered question in rock'n'roll circles. If there was no Jack Clement, would there have been Sun Records, and would we have ever heard of Johnny Cash, Jerry Lee Lewis or Elvis Presley? Or all the young men who, perhaps just for their allotted 15 minutes, became stars. For Jack was and still is one of the finest producer/engineers around in popular music.

"Cowboy" Jack was raised on the music of Roy Acuff, Wayne Raney and Slim Rhodes on radio WMC Memphis. He early on started playing guitar and Dobro. He got a steel guitar when he was 13. From 1948 to 1952, Jack served in the U.S. Marines. For the last two years, he was stationed in Washington, D.C., and was part of the drill team. In 1950, while still in the armed forces, he learned the banjo and worked with the Stonemans, Jimmy Dean and Roy Clark. He got a band together with Scotty and Jimmy Stoneman, Buzz Busby and Jack Clement as the Tennessee Troupers.

In 1953, with Buzz Busby on guitar, Jack formed a Bluegrass duo called Buzz and Jack, the Banjo Boys. They played on the *Wheeling Jamboree* as a comedy act for a few months and they then had a series on WWVA Boston's *Hayloft Jamboree* playing many of Jack's songs. They also played the Cellar in Boston with Ralph Jones and a bass player. Jack worked in a band playing Hawaiian music and Country later that year. He went back to college in 1954-55 and continued to play in the evenings.

In 1955, Jack returned to Memphis to thaw out from the Boston cold. He became a dancing teacher at Arthur Murray's for six months. Jack and a club-owning/truck-driving friend, Slim Wallace, purchased an old Magnacorder recording machine from deejay Sleepy Eyed John, and set up Fernwood Records. *Rock with Me Baby* by Billy Lee Riley was the intended first single for their Fernwood label and the work tape was done in Wallace's garage on Fernwood Drive in Memphis and in a rented studio at WMPS. They also cut *Think Before You Go*, but it was considered too Country, so they released *Trouble Bound* instead as the top side.

Jack played the tracks to Sam Phillips at Sun and soon both he and Riley were signed there. Phillips recognized Jack's abilities as a producer. Clement was on $60 per week, working up to $90. Jack took over the engineering and production duties at the label and also auditioned the hopefuls. Jack released two singles as an artist while at Sun, *Ten Years/Your Lover Boy* and *The Black Haired Man/Wrong*.

Jack moved on in 1959 and opened Jack Music and Summer Records. The label folded before the end of the year. However, his Fernwood Records was still in existence, and in 1961 the label released Thomas Wayne's single *Tragedy*. Fernwood also issued some solo singles by two singer/songwriters who were destined to become a major writing team, Jerry Foster and Bill Rice.

During 1960, Jack was at Echo Studios, Memphis, with Allen Reynolds and Dickey Lee when they dubbed each other "cowboy" for a recording to a friend in the armed forces; Jack's sobriquet stuck.

By 1960/1961, Jack was busy working with Chet Atkins at RCA and produced Jim Reeves. In 1961, he went to Beaumont, Texas, and worked with Bill Hall and they set up Hall-Clement Music, which signed Foster and Rice and was later sold to Polygram. Jack also produced Moon Mullican, Cliff Bruner and Rod Bernard. During 1964, Jack produced the classic Johnny Cash track *Ring of Fire*. Jack then set up his production and publishing company, Jack Music, in Nashville.

In 1965, Jack received Charley Pride's demo recording and persuaded RCA to sign him. He produced Charley's first single, *Snakes Crawl at Night*. He also produced Sheb

*The legendary "Cowboy" **Jack Clement***

Wooley, the Stonemans, Mac Wiseman, Tompall and the Glaser Brothers, Doc Watson, Louis Armstrong, Waylon Jennings and John Prine. Jack has still to complete the Armstrong project.

During 1970, Jack built the Jack Clement Recording Studio. He then got into film production and produced *Dear Dead Delilah*, which, to be charitable, "lost money." In 1972, Jack set up JMI Records and all Don Williams' early chart successes were on this label, including his 1974 Top 5 success *We Should Be Together*. Unfortunately, Jack had forgotten to sign a contract with Don and by 1974, Williams had signed with Dot. In 1976, Jack created for fun the group Peace and Quiet, which developed into the Cowboy's Ragtime Band. It had horns and played everything from Dixieland to rock'n'roll. During 1978, he revived JMI and recorded *If I Had to Do It All Over Again*, by Stoney Edwards.

That year, Jack began recording for Elektra Records and promptly entered the Country singles charts with *We Must Believe in Magic/When I Dream* and *All I Want to Do in Life* (both Top 90), the latter being the title track of his Elektra album. Elektra picked up the option for a second album, but by the 1990's, the album had still not been delivered. *When I Dream* was popular in Australia.

Jack Clement is also a songwriter of note. Among his covers are *Miller's Cave,* which has been cut by Hank Snow, Bobby Bare and Ed Bruce. Johnny Cash has recorded four of Cowboy Jack's songs, *Guess Things Happen That Way*, *Ballad of a Teenage Queen*, *Everybody Loves a Nut* and *The One on the Left Is on the Right* and George Jones recorded *A Girl I Used to Know* and *What I Had in Mind*.

In 1984, Jack produced and played rhythm guitar, Dobro and ukulele on John Hartford's sublime ***Gumtree Canoo***, on Flying Fish. As a result, he and Hartford played some gigs. During 1993, Jack produced Charley Pride's new album on Branson Entertainment. This was in part a re-recording of Charley's hits. Jack has also produced Frank Yankovic's ***Live*** album and three albums for Johnny Cash.

Jack Clement is one of the most charming, affable, knowledgeable buccaneers in the business who makes each recording stand out. Would-be producers and some of those who think they are producers should take note.

RECOMMENDED ALBUMS:

"All I Want to Do in Life" (Elektra)(1978)

[In addition, pick up any album that shows Jack Clement as Producer.]

Do listen to John Hartford's "Gum Tree Canoe" (Flying Fish)(1984) and listen to Jack's all-around work.

VASSAR CLEMENTS

(Fiddle, Viola, Cello, Bass, Guitar, Mandolin, Dobro, Tenor Banjo, Sometime Singer, Composer)

Given Name:	**Vassar Carlton Clements**
Date of Birth:	**April 25, 1928**
Where Born:	**Kinard, Florida**
Married:	**1. Jean (div.)**
	2. Millie (m. 1953)
Children:	**Terry, Renee; stepchildren: Ginger, Midge, Joey, Terri, Renee**

Vassar Clements has many sobriquets including "the philosopher fiddler" and "Superbow." Whatever one calls him, there is no doubt that he is one of the most inventive maestros of the fiddle in any form of music. Although he is primarily a Country and Bluegrass player, his Jazz stylings have made him much in demand as a session player for Rock and Pop musicians.

Vassar taught himself to play fiddle at age 7. He got together with two cousins and they formed a band. He was already so efficient as a picker that by 1949, he had appeared with Bill Monroe and his Blue Grass Boys, on the *Grand Ole Opry*. The following year, he made his recording debut with Monroe. He stayed with Bill off and on until 1956. In 1957, he became a member of Jim & Jesse's Virginia Boys, alongside Don McHan and Bobby Thompson, and stayed with them until 1961. For some while, he had a drinking problem that cut back on his playing. He returned to active playing again in 1967, when he moved to Nashville.

Vassar began recording and played tenor banjo in the Dixieland Landing Club, where he remained until 1969, when he toured with Faron Young's Country Deputies. That same year, Vassar joined John Hartford's Dobrolic Plectorial Society, alongside Norman Blake and Tut Taylor. The group continued for some 10 months and then, on its demise, Vassar joined the newly formed Earl Scruggs Revue.

In 1971, Vassar started his illustrious session career in earnest, by appearing on Gordon Lightfoot's ***Summerside of Life*** and the eponymous albums by Steve Goodman and David Bromberg. The following year, he played on Mike Audridge's ***Dobro,*** played Dobro on J.J. Cale's ***Really*** and he played with Borderline, Jim Rooney and David Sanborn.

Also in 1972, while with Earl Scruggs, Vassar recorded his own album, ***Crossing the Catskills***, for Rounder. This would be a watershed year for the many musicians, due to the Nitty Gritty Dirt Band's ***Will the Circle Be Unbroken***, and almost certainly was a springboard for Clements' career. With the help of his wife, Millie, who acts as his manager, he became established on the college circuit.

During 1973, Vassar was in great demand as a session musician and appeared on Jimmy Buffett's ***A White Sports Coat & a Pink Crustation***, the Grateful Dead's ***Wake of the Flood***, Kris Kristofferson & Rita Coolidge's ***Full Moon***, Mickey Newbury's ***Heaven Help the Child*** and Toni Brown and Terry Garthwaite's ***Cross Country***. That year, he hit the road with his own group, the Vassar Clements Band, playing a fusion of Country, Bluegrass, Jazz, Blues and Rock. This was fired by the superb double album ***Hillbilly Jazz***, which launched Flying Fish Records, and featured Dave Bromberg, D.J. Fontana and Doug Jernigan.

The following year, Vassar could be found enhancing Elvin Bishop's ***Let it Flow***, Doug Dillard's ***Douglas Flint Dillard***, Andy Fairweather Low's ***Spider Jiving***, the Grateful Dead's ***From Mars Hotel***, Gene Parson's ***Kindling*** and Corky Siegel's self-named album.

During 1974, Vassar signed with Mercury Records, and released two interesting albums the following year. ***Vassar Clements***, featuring John Hartford, the Nitty Gritty Dirt Band and Charlie Daniels, was not his finest work, however, but ***Superbow***, released later in the year, was a much better affair, and featured the superb *Orange Blossom Special* and *Yakety Bow* (his version of *Yakety Sax*). He also guested on two notable albums, Dickie Betts' ***Highway Call*** and Steve Goodman's ***Jessie's Jigs & Other Favorites***. Vassar also became part of a one-album group, Old and in the Way, which featured Grateful Dead's Jerry Garcia as well as David Grisman, Peter Rowan and John Kahn.

During 1977, Vassar released two excellent albums, which further confirmed his peerless position. ***The Vassar Clements Band*** was put out by MCA and ***The Bluegrass Session*** by Flying Fish. The latter featured Bobby Osborne and Doug Jernigan, and included five Clements originals. That year, Vassar appeared on Jerry Jeff Walker's ***A Man Must Carry On*** and Mike Auldridge's ***Blues & Bluegrass***.

Vassar emerged, in 1981, with another pair of fine albums for Flying Fish, ***Hillbilly Rides Again***, with Doug Jernigan and ***Vassar***. He also appeared on Dave Davies' second album, ***Glamor***. Vassar's next album, ***Westport Drive,*** was released in 1984, on the Mind Best label. Over the next decade, he continued his merry way, endorsing his popularity, especially in Japan.

"Superbow" ***Vassar Clements***

During 1993, Vassar worked closely with Thom Bresh in recording a tribute album to Vassar's friend and Thom's father, Merle Travis, released on Shenachie Records. Over the years, Clements has played with a wide range of performers, live and on record. Among those not so far mentioned are Steve Martin, the Monkees, Spinal Tap, Bruce Hornsby, Delbert McClinton, Shenandoah, Bela Fleck, Willie Nelson, Hank Williams, Jr., Paul McCartney, Paul Butterfield, Vince Gill, Michelle Shocked and Bonnie Raitt.

In addition, Vassar has been nominated for a Grammy Award on five occasions. He has also made three videos, ***Vassar Clements Fiddle Instruction Tapes*** (Homestead), ***Vassar Clements in Concert [Vassar Swings]*** (Shikata) and ***Vassar Clements in Concert [Ramblin' 810]*** (Shenachie).

RECOMMENDED ALBUMS:

"Hillbilly Jazz" (double)(Flying Fish)(1975)
"Superbow" (Mercury)(1975)
"The Bluegrass Session" (Flying Fish)(1977)
"Hillbilly Rides Again" (Flying Fish)(1981)
"Vassar" (Flying Fish)(1981)
"Together Again" (Flying Fish)(1982) [with Stephane Grappelli]
"Westport Drive" (Mind Best)(1984)
"Old and in the Way" (Round/Sugar Hill)(1975) [As Old and in the Way]

ZEKE CLEMENTS

(Singer, Songwriter, Guitar, Tenor Banjo, Mandolin, Fiddle, Actor, Yodeler)
Date of Birth: September 6, 1911
Where Born: Warrior, Alabama

Zeke Clements, known as the "Alabama Cowboy," will always be remembered as the voice of the yodeling Bashful, in Walt Disney's 1937 animated movie *Snow White and the Seven Dwarfs*. However, he would go on to become one of Country music's finest songwriters, being a charter inductee into the Nashville Songwriters Hall of Fame in 1971.

Zeke was raised on a farm near Warrior, Alabama, and when he was age 6, his mother died. In 1929, he traveled to Chicago to visit his uncle and auditioned for the *National Barn Dance*. Using Bradley Kincaid's guitar, he was booked for that evening's show, at the princely fee of $10. However, two years later, he decided to go on tour with Otto Gray's Oklahoma Cowboys, at $90 a week. It was at this time that he began doing comedy, as a rube.

In 1931, Zeke began the morning radio show on WSM Nashville. He then moved on to Detroit and then Cincinnati, where he formed the Bronco Busters, which included singer Texas Ruby. They moved up to Philadelphia and then to Nashville, where, in 1933, they became regulars on the *Grand Ole Opry*, with Zeke becoming one of the first performers to wear a cowboy outfit. The group also traveled to Louisville, doing a daily weekday show on WHAS. They then moved to WHO Des Moines' weekend *Iowa Barn Dance Frolic*, on a two-year contract. However, Ruby and the show's emcee, Ronald ("Dutch") Reagan, did not hit it off, and as a result, Reagan refused to do any more than the station breaks.

It was while doing the Village Barn in New York City that they were approached by a Texan who was both the owner of the major newspaper and the major radio station in Fort Worth, and encouraged them to play Texas. Texas Ruby was very keen to play the Lone Star State, and soon the group was performing regularly on WBAP Fort Worth. There they were sponsored by a big oil company, until Ruby, somewhat worse for drink, told them what she thought of them. As a result, Clements was told that *he* could stay, but not Ruby.

So the group headed out to California, where they became the featured act on *Hollywood Barn Dance*. It was while in Hollywood that Zeke auditioned for Disney. Originally Jay C. Flippen was slated to play the part of Bashful, having already done the original speaking tracks, but he was then appearing on Broadway and Clements got the job.

Zeke was involved in an auto wreck and he and Ruby split up. After the accident, Zeke began to write songs. Over a two-year period, he also appeared in a slew of Westerns, notably supporting Charles Starrett (the Durango Kid), and eventually appeared in over 100 movies. (See Movie Section.)

Zeke returned to the *Opry* in 1939, where he stayed throughout the 40's. He had his first success as a songwriter with the WWII song *Smoke on the Water*, which he co-wrote with Earl Nunn. This became a No.1 hit for Red Foley in 1944 (staying at the top for 13 weeks), and a year later, Bob Wills took it to the top and Boyd Heath reached the Top 10 with it. Clements also recorded a version, but failed to chart it. Also in 1945, Zeke formed the Liberty label in Los Angeles, with the John Daniel Quartet and Paul Howard as artists, selling the label two years later.

He moved on to KWKH's *Louisiana Hayride* and then in 1948, Zeke had a million seller, when Eddy Arnold recorded his song *Just a Little Lovin' (Will Go a Long, Long Way)*. The single stayed at No.1 for 8 weeks out of 32 weeks on the charts. It also crossed over to the Top 15 on the Pop charts. Arnold would go on to have hits with other Clements songs,*Why Should I Cry*, a Top 3 hit, in 1950 and *Somebody's Been Beating My Time*, which also reached the Top 3. The following year, Eddy also recorded Zeke's *Live and Learn*. In 1952, pop singer Eddie Fisher had a Top 20 hit with *Just a Little Lovin' (Will Go a Long, Long Way)*. Kitty Wells also recorded a pair of Zeke's songs, *There's Poison in Your Heart*, which charted Top 10 and *My Mother*. Other successful songs written by Clements include *Blue Mexico Skies*.

During the 50's, Zeke headlined his own TV variety shows on WWL New Orleans, WAPI Birmingham, WENO Madison, Tennessee, WSB Atlanta and WNAH Nashville. During the 70's, Zeke moved to Miami and played with Dixieland Jazz bands on cruise ships out of Florida.This he did for nearly 10 years, before returning to Nashville, where he currently lives.

RECOMMENDED ALBUM:

"The Man from Music Mountain" (Guest Star)

BILL CLIFTON

(Singer, Songwriter, Guitar, Autoharp)
Given Name: **William August Marburg**
Date of Birth: **April 5, 1931**
Where Born: **Riverwood, Maryland**
Married: **Sarah**
Children: **seven**

Bill Clifton and his Dixie Mountain Boys played straight Bluegrass music. However, partly because of their leader's atypical background, they helped bridge the gap between the urban Folk fans and traditional Country audiences. Bill has also become, by virtue of substantial periods of residence outside the U.S., an effective advocate and spokesman for Bluegrass over a considerable portion of the entire world.

Born William Marburg to affluent parents and raised near Baltimore, Bill gained his first fascination with hillbilly music via radio and took it to his heart. Marburg took the name Bill Clifton for stage purposes when he began to play on radio and in public about 1950. That year, Bill commenced studies at the University of Virginia, obtaining a B.A. degree in 1954 and after attending the same university's Graduate School of Business Administration, he earned an M.A. in 1959.

At college, Bill met Folk singers Paul Clayton and Dave Sadler. In 1952, the threesome made some recordings, said to be a curious blend of Old-Time and Bluegrass. The addition of banjo picker Johnny Clark to their circle shifted the group decidedly toward Bluegrass, and they cut a few sides for Blue Ridge Records. They did programs on a variety of local radio stations and briefly affiliated with the WWVA *Wheeling Jamboree*. Bill also gained the friendship of the Stanley Brothers and musical pioneer A.P. Carter, the latter then operating a country store in southwest Virginia.

Following a hitch in military service, Bill resumed his musical career, recording for both Mercury and Starday at sessions in both Nashville and Falls Church, Virginia. Over a period of seven years he had a total of five albums released on Starday and two more on the firm's budget label, Nashville.

Notable Dixie Mountain Boys on these recordings in addition to Clark included Curley Lambert of the Stanley Brothers band (Ralph Stanley picked banjo on one session), Mike Seeger of the New Lost City Ramblers, and various members of the Country Gentlemen. More than any other performer, Clifton put songs associated with the original Carter Family into Bluegrass permanently as well as other Old-Time numbers like *Little White Washed Chimney, Goodbye, Mary Dear, Living the Right Life Now,* and *Flower Blooming in the Wildwood.* Bill also had the initial recording of the ghostly *Bringing Mary Home*, which achieved Bluegrass standard status through a somewhat later version by the Country Gentlemen.

In 1963, Bill and his family moved to England. For the next four years, he remained in the U.K. playing numerous Folk clubs and also periodically visiting other Western European countries. Then in 1967, he took an administrative position in the Peace Corps and spent three years in the Philippines, visiting Australia and New Zealand at the end of his tenure. While in New Zealand, Bill recorded an album with the local Hamilton County Bluegrass Band.

Bill then returned to England, making his home in Sussex for several years. He had continued to record while abroad, sometimes returning to the U.S. for sessions. In 1976, Bill and mandolin player Red Rector cut an album in Germany while there on tour.

In 1972, Bill Clifton returned to the U.S., where he played his first Bluegrass circuit festivals (he had staged a one day event himself, in 1961). Thereafter, he began spending more time in his native land although he did not return permanently until later in the decade. Meanwhile, Bill returned to regular studio recording work, cutting two albums for County with an all-star cast of Bluegrass sidemen, and a third one featuring himself and Red Rector performing duets. Calling themselves the First Generation, Bill, Red and banjo picker Don Stover worked several festivals together in the late 70's. Clifford subsequently moved to the community of Mendota, Virginia, near Bristol and held a position in business, but still did several festivals and concert engagements annually. In 1980, he did an autoharp instrumental album on his own Elf label. In 1992, Rounder records released a compact disc containing 19 of his classic Starday masters with the Dixie Mountain Boys from 1957 and 1958. IMT

RECOMMENDED ALBUMS:

"Mountain Folk Songs" (Starday)(1959)
"Carter Family Memorial Album" (Starday)(1961)
"The Bluegrass Sound of Bill Clifton" (Starday)(1961)
"Soldier, Sing Me a Song" (Starday)(1963)
"Code of the Mountain" (Starday)(1963)
"Mountain Folk Songs" (Nashville)(1964)
"Bluegrass in the American Tradition" (Nashville)(1964)
"Come by the Hills" (County)(1975)
"Another Happy Day" (County)(1976) [With Red Rector]
"Clifton and Company" (County)(1977)
"Autoharp Centennial Celebration" (Elf)(1981)
"Bill Clifton: The Early Years" (Rounder)(1992)

CHARLIE CLINE

(Fiddle, Banjo, Mandolin, Guitar, Bass Fiddle)
Date of Birth: **May 6, 1931**
Where Born: **Baisden, West Virginia**
Married: **Lee Barnett**

Charlie Cline stands as one of the most versatile sidemen in the history of Bluegrass music. As a member of the family that founded the Lonesome Pine Fiddlers, Cline not only served as part of that pioneer group but also led a latter-day version of them. In addition, he did more than yeoman duty as a sideman for Bluegrass groups ranging from those of Bill Monroe to the Warrior River Boys over a period of four decades.

A native of the Gilbert Creek region of southern West Virginia, Charlie's brother-in-law and cousin Ezra, along with older brothers Ireland (Lazy Ned) and Curly Ray, had been part of the Lonesome Fiddlers from about 1938, a group that worked on radio at WHIS Bluefield, West Virginia. During WWII, Ned was killed in action. When the Fiddlers resumed regular daily broadcasts, Charlie, who had developed proficiency on several instruments, joined them on a regular basis.

However, neither Charlie nor Curly Ray was in the Fiddlers when they did their initial recordings for Cozy in March 1950, but both were part of the Sunny Mountain Boys when they did their session for King in July 1951, under the co-leadership of Jimmy Martin and Bobby Osborne. Charlie returned to the Fiddlers briefly before becoming a member of Bill Monroes Blue Grass Boys. Over a period of three years, 1952-1955, Charlie worked off and on with Monroe, recording some 38 songs, all on Decca. It has been said that he played every instrument at one time or another in the Monroe group except mandolin.

Charlie spent most of 1953 back with the Lonesome Pine Fiddlers working at WJR radio in Detroit and cutting 6 numbers for RCA Victor, including 2 original instrumentals, *Lonesome Pine Breakdown* and *Five String Drag*. When Ezra brought the band to Pikeville, Kentucky, in November, Charlie rejoined Bill Monroe. In 1954, Charlie did a session, playing lead guitar, with the Stanley Brothers and also another one on RCA with the Fiddlers, although he was not otherwise working with them at the time. He also worked briefly as a sideman with the Osborne Brothers, although he did not record with them.

By 1958, Charlie (electric lead guitar) and his wife, Lee (electric bass), had rejoined Ezra and Curly Ray in the Lonesome Pine Fiddlers, who were experimenting with a more modern sound and working a TV show in Huntington,

West Virginia, in addition to daily radio in Pikeville.

In 1959, Charlie and Lee became active Christians and left music, subsequently spending several years in evangelistic work, and relocating to Alabama. After Ezra retired, Charlie revived use of the name Lonesome Pine Fiddlers in the mid-70's and recorded a custom Gospel album entitled ***One of His Own***. In addition to Lee on electric bass, the revived version of the Lonesome Pine Fiddlers included Chuck Carpenter on banjo and Ed Wilson on guitar. Charlie alternated on fiddle and mandolin. He followed with two more albums for Atteiram and four for Old Homestead, with one on each label being Gospel and the others secular. On one album entitled ***Why Ray, Ralph?***, Charlie revealed a flair for comedy with his parody of brother Curly Ray's work with Ralph Stanley.

In the early 80's, Jimmy Martin urged Charlie Cline to come back to the festival circuit as a Sunny Mountain Boy, which he did. After several years with Martin, Charlie switched over to the Warrior River Boys in 1986, playing fiddle and sometimes mandolin. While with them he played on their record albums on Rutabaga and Rounder, while they backed him on a fiddle album for Rutabaga. Charlie also kept his own group together and cut at least one Gospel cassette and made a Lonesome Pine Fiddler Reunion tape with Curly Ray and the Goins Brothers.

[NB: Charlie Cline of the Lonesome Pine Fiddlers should not be confused with Charlie Cline of Myersville, Maryland, who worked with the Carroll County Ramblers, and is a quality Dobro player.] IMT

RECOMMENDED ALBUMS:

"Shalom (Peace)" (Atteiram)(1977)
"Strictly Cline" (Atteiram)(1978)
"Lonesome Pine" (Old Homestead)(1978)
"Why Ray, Ralph" (Old Homestead)(1979)
"Bushy Creek" (Old Homestead)(1981)
"Sunset Is Coming" (Old Homestead)(1983)
"Charlie Cline with the Warrior River Boys" (Old Homestead)(1988)

CURLY RAY CLINE

(Fiddle, Singer, Songwriter, Comedy)
Given Name: **Ray Cline**
Date of Birth: **January 10, 1923**
Where Born: **Baisden, West Virginia**
Married: **Verdie Jones Cline**
Children: **Ricky Ray, Timmy, Rod**

Curly Ray Cline has long been known as one of the premier fiddlers in Bluegrass music. Cline's achievement is no less significant inasmuch as he has spent his entire career as a sideman with two bands—the Lonesome Pine Fiddlers and Ralph Stanley's Clinch Mountain Boys—in more than half a century of professionalism. In addition to many recordings with these groups, the ever congenial, albeit somewhat commercial-minded musician, has cut numerous instrumental albums on his own that not only display his fiddle prowess, but also his flair for novelty vocals with just a touch of tongue-in-cheek comedy.

Born into a remote mountain community in southern West Virginia, Cline gained much of his professional inspiration from the *Grand Ole Opry*'s Fiddlin' Arthur Smith and entered the professional ranks himself at the age of 15, when his cousin/brother-in-law Ezra Cline organized the Lonesome Pine Fiddlers at WHIS radio in Bluefield around 1938. Curly Ray worked with this band for the better part of the next 28 years.

During some of the time, the Fiddlers were more of a semi-professional group than full-time entertainers, and Cline alternated between an entertainment career and laboring in the coal mines. Ironically, he had temporarily absented himself at the time the Lonesome Pine Fiddlers did their initial recordings as well as their reunion cassettes. In the band's earlier, pre-Bluegrass years, Ray and his brother Charlie sang duets in a Delmore Brothers' style. He also played fiddle on session work for such fellow mountain musicians as Jimmy Martin and Bobby Osborne, Rex and Eleanor Parker and Hobo Jack Atkins.

As the Lonesome Pine Fiddlers wound down their performing career from 1963, Curly Ray went to work for the Stanley Brothers. Carter Stanley died shortly afterward and Ray went on to become Ralph Stanley's only fiddler (to date). Cline's return to full-time musical work coincided with the resurging popularity of Bluegrass and the rise of festivals. Since Ralph Stanley has recorded frequently in the past quarter century, Ray's work with the band is on all of these albums (except for the a cappella Gospel cuts).

Curly Ray has also recorded more than a dozen albums—primarily instrumental—under his own name. In addition to standard Bluegrass fiddling, the early ones feature tunes which combined barking foxhounds and braying mules. However, when he signed with Rebel Records in 1972, Ray began to sing on one or two cuts per album. Some were original lyrics (usually parodies) concerning his family; for example, his wife, *Blue Eyed Verdie,* or his father-in-law, *Flem Jones*, while *Money in the Bank* or *Why Me, Ralph?* poked gentle fun at himself. In the early 80's, Curly Ray persisted with these numbers when he switched to other labels such as Old Homestead and recorded *Boar Hog* and Tin Ear, where he cut *Smarter than the Average Idiot* and *Just a-Hangin*.

Promoted on stage with great fanfare by Ralph Stanley, these efforts provided Cline with an image as a musician which transcends that of the average sideman. At the end of May 1993, Cline retired from his long-time association with Ralph Stanley. IMT

RECOMMENDED ALBUMS:

"Curly Ray Cline and His Lonesome Pine Fiddler" (Melody)(1969) [Re-issued on Old Homestead]
"Chicken Reel" (Rebel)(1971)
"They Cut Down the Old Pine Tree" (Rebel)(1972)
"My Little Home in West Virginia" (Rebel)(1973)
"Fishin' for Another Hit" (Rebel)(1974)
"Why Me, Ralph?" (Rebel SLP)(1975)
"Boar Hog" (Old Homestead)(1980)
"The Old Kentucky Fox Hunter Plays Gospel" (Old Homestead)(1982)
"Smarter than the Average Idiot" (Tin Ear)(1989)

PATSY CLINE

(Singer)
Given Name: **Virginia Patterson Hensley**
Date of Birth: **September 8, 1932**
Where Born: **Gore (near Winchester), Virginia**
Married: **1. Gerald Cline (m. 1953) (div. 1957)**
2. Charlie Dick (m. 1957)
Children: **Randy, Julia**
Date of Death: **March 5, 1963**

Despite her short career, Patsy Cline has assumed the legendary status of Country music's most-important-ever woman performer and the inspiration for countless female Country singers. Possessing a dynamic voice and vocal range to match, she injected hyper emotion into her best material, often so moved by the songs that she cried.

Born into a poverty-stricken family, escapism was a big part of Virginia's early years. Inspired by Shirley Temple, she won a dance competition at age 4. After her family moved to Winchester, she came under the influence of the *Grand Ole Opry* and would sing along to the WSM broadcasts. Her dream was to become a member of the cast.

Although she did not play an instrument professionally, at 8 she took piano lessons, giving her an insight into the rudiments of music. Her singing was featured in school plays and her church choir and she made some appearances in local clubs.

In 1948, when *Opry* regular Wally Fowler and his Oak Ridge Quartet played Winchester, the 16-year-old Virginia engineered a meeting. After hearing her sing, Fowler urged her to audition for the *Opry*. The trip to Nashville proved a great disappointment. The Hensley party, driven by a family friend, could only stay for a day, but the *Opry*'s Jim Denny wanted more people to hear her before a decision was made. He failed to make further contact, but Virginia was encouraged by the interest shown in her by Roy Acuff and Moon Mullican.

The next few years saw her plying her trade and developing her talent in a variety of venues, such as local taverns, beer joints, racetracks and family clubs. After a brief spell as lead singer with Gene Shiner's Metronomes, Virginia joined a local band, Bill Peer and the Melody Boys. Despite his married status, Peer and Hensley began an illicit affair. Wrongly assuming that Patricia was her middle name, Peer came up with "Patsy" as a good stage name. "Cline" came when she married Gerald Cline. Patsy soon regretted the match and went on seeing Peer.

In 1953, she made her second trip to Nashville, where Ernest Tubb's influence ensured that she appeared on ET's *Midnight Jamboree*. Another influential figure then entered the Cline story, noted booking agent and promoter Connie B. Gay. After Patsy took first prize in the Warrenton, Virginia, 4th Annual National Championship Country Music Contest in August 1954, Gay gave Cline a spot on his *Town and Country Time* syndicated radio show. Patsy earned $50 an appearance and cut her first songs, including *It Wasn't God Who Made Honky Tonk Angels.*

Next came a recording contract that was to retard rather than advance her career. A demo tape of Patsy's reached Bill McCall, owner of 4 Star Music Sales. Patsy signed a recording contract with him on September 30, 1954. The royalty rate was derisory, but Patsy hoped that the deal would boost her earnings from personal appearances. Allegedly, she received nothing. More damaging still was the little noticed stipulation that McCall could approve what Patsy recorded, which meant only the generally lamentable songs that he published.

A leasing deal was done with Decca, and Owen Bradley started producing Patsy in 1955. Her first four singles failed to chart and her career was going nowhere. Then writer Don Hecht came up with a song he had written with an electronics engineer, Alan Block. *Walkin' After Midnight* had been written for Patsy's favorite Pop singer, Kay Starr, but it had been fortuitously rejected by Kay's label, Capitol. McCall thought it ideal for Patsy and pushed her into cutting it, despite her protest that it was "nothin' but a little ole Pop song!" For the first of several times, Patsy's resistance to hit material was overcome.

Patsy successfully auditioned for the *Arthur Godfrey Talent Scouts* show. She was persuaded to ditch her cowgirl outfit for a cocktail dress. Patsy easily won the *Talent Scouts* show on January 21, 1957. This national exposure guaranteed the success of *Walkin' After Midnight,* which was a cross-over smash, reaching the Country Top 3 and the Pop Top 15, selling 750,000 copies, with the flip, *A Poor Man's Roses (or a Rich Man's Gold)* peaking in the Top 15. On the back of this success came a first album, ***Patsy Cline***.

However, Patsy, imprisoned by her 4 Star contract, failed to build on this success and she was in danger of becoming a flash-in-the-pan. All of her follow-up singles were slanted toward the Pop market and they made no impact there or in the Country market. Patsy's second husband, Charlie Dick, entered the Army and then Patsy found that she was pregnant. On his return from the service, they were so poor that only a bureaucratic mistake, which saw the Dicks receive a pile of subsistence checks, allowed them to move to Nashville.

The immortal ***Patsy Cline***

In Nashville, Charlie got work with a printing company. Patsy worked on the road, often with Faron Young and Ferlin Husky, to make ends meet. Waiting for her 4 Star deal to end, Patsy recorded less and less, so that not much material would be left for release. She also got herself a get-up-and-go manager, Ramsey Hughes (known as Randy), a guitarist, former road manager for Husky and a broker.

Patsy also ensured her material gained greater exposure through joining the regular *Opry* cast in January, 1960. At last free of McCall, all the ingredients for success were now in place. Signing with Decca, on November 16, 1960, Patsy cut the Hank Cochran-Harlan Howard song *I Fall to Pieces.* She didn't care for it and it had been turned down by several acts including Roy Drusky. The single took months to break, but when it did, it resulted in another cross-over smash, going to No.1 in the Country charts and staying on the charts for 39 weeks and peaking in the Pop Top 15.

The question now was, could Patsy follow it up? Her chances weren't helped by an almost fatal auto accident from which she took time to recuperate. However, the answer came in the form of Willie Nelson's *Crazy*. Again Patsy was not enthusiastic, not least because of Willie's semi-narrative singing style. She tried to copy it without success at one session. When someone suggested she sing it normally, only one take was required and it reached the Top 3 on the Country chart and Top 10 on the Pop lists.

Patsy's biggest hit of 1962 was another Hank Cochran song, *She's Got You*, which for five weeks topped the Country chart and peaked in the Top 15 on the Pop chart. It even made the British Pop chart, suggesting a rosy international future. She followed this up with the Top 10 hit *When I Get Thru with You (You'll Love Me Too).* She rounded off the year with *So Wrong,* which peaked in the Top 15. Two further albums were released, ***Showcase*** (1961) and ***Sentimentally Yours*** (1962).

Patsy's increasingly sophisticated image was reinforced when in November 1962 she did a stint at the Mint Casino in Las Vegas. Earlier that year, she had played the Hollywood Bowl with her favorite Country singer, Johnny Cash.

In February 1963, she cut what were to be her final recordings for a fourth Decca album slated for release in late March. With her current single, *Leavin' on Your Mind,* riding the charts, Patsy was one of many *Opry* stars to play a Kansas City benefit for the family of deejay Jack Call on March 3, 1963. She topped the bill and gave what was to be her last performance. Two days later, returning in inclement weather in her manager's private plane, Patsy perished along with Hughes, Cowboy Copas and Hawkshaw Hawkins. Country music was stunned and the *Opry* put on a tribute to the deceased stars. In June, Decca released a two-record package, ***The Patsy Cline Story***. Don Gibson's *Sweet Dream (of You)* and Bob Wills' *Faded Love,* from her last sessions, provided posthumous hits. During the rest of the 60's, three more singles charted, of which the most successful was *He Called Me Baby.*

The 70's represented a dormant period, then came an explosion of renewed interest, which has yet to play itself out. In 1981, there were just eight Cline albums. By 1993, the total had jumped to an amazing 50-plus on

14 different labels. All of this despite the fact that Patsy only recorded a little over 100 songs! The revival began in 1980, with Loretta Lynn's biopic *Coal Miner's Daughter,* in which the wonderful Beverly D'Angelo had a cameo role as Patsy. Patsy's name appeared in the Country charts with the Top 20 success *Always*. The following year produced a controversial book by Ellis Nassour, *Patsy Cline: An Intimate Biography*. That same year, Patsy's voice was electronically combined with that of Jim Reeves for two duet singles, *Have You Ever Been Lonely,* which was a Top 5 hit and *I Fall to Pieces,* which was a lesser success. A full-blown movie on Patsy was made in 1985 entitled *Sweet Dreams* with the glorious Jessica Lange in the lead role. The soundtrack, featuring Patsy with new backings, was a great success. It went Gold in both the U.S. and Britain.

In 1991, *Crazy* became a major chart success in Britain, partly because Soul singer Seal had a hit with a different song of the same title. However, such was Patsy's impact in Britain that later that year, a young lady in a TV look/soundalike program, *Thank Your Lucky Stars*, won out with her impression of Patsy. There had been other tributes to Patsy, including Loretta Lynn's 1977 album ***I Remember Patsy,*** which included a conversation with Owen Bradley. Bradley also produced k.d. lang's ***Shadowland*** album, a notable attempt to re-create the Cline sound. k.d. had paid further tribute to Patsy by calling her group the Reclines.

Interest in Patsy was maintained by the release of a definitive box set in 1991 and two videos which Charlie Dick co-produced, ***The Real Patsy Cline*** (1986), intended as a rejoinder to Nassour's book, and ***Remembering Patsy*** (1993), which contained stunning performances from a rediscovered TV show Patsy made shortly before her death. The former was Certified Gold in 1991. Also in 1993 came a second edition of Nassour's book, retitled *Honky Tonk Angel: The Intimate Story of Patsy Cline*.

Three decades after her death, Patsy is one of MCA's top five selling artists. The 1973 ***Greatest Hits*** album had been Certified Quadruple Platinum by 1991, which means it had sold over 4 million copies in 18 years!

In 1973, she became the first female performer to be elected to the Country Music Hall of Fame. The words on her grave's bronze plaque say it all: "Death cannot kill what never dies."

SM

RECOMMENDED ALBUMS:

"Greatest Hits" (MCA)(1973)
"The Last Sessions" (MCA)(1980)
"Songwriters' Tribute" (MCA)(1986)
"Live at the Opry" (MCA)(1988)
"The Patsy Cline Collection" (box set)(MCA)(1991)
Videos:
"The Real Patsy Cline" (Cabin Fever Ent.)(1986)
"Remembering Patsy" (Cabin Fever Ent.)(1993) (also Lonesome Pine Fiddlers, the)

TAMMY CLINE

(Singer, Songwriter, Guitar, Actress)
Given Name: Marilyn Margaret Cross
Date of Birth: June 16, 1953
Where Born: Hull, Yorkshire, England
Married: Rodney Bolton
Children: Melanie, Richard

Tammy Cline has been described as a "tiny pocket dynamo." Her retirement from the British Country music scene to concentrate on being a grandmother and enjoy playing golf came as a big disappointment to her long-time admirers.

She began her career while still at school, singing with a local Pop group and soon formed a Country band called Uncle Sam. After years of playing the clubs, her talent was recognized in 1981 when she was named "Best Female Country Singer" at the Wembley Festival in England and the following year, she retained her crown. She went on to win the title four times. Her Country style made her a hit and she had 30 TV appearances in 1982 alone.

After watching from the audience at Wembley in 1982, Rick Blackburn, then CBS Nashville President, was so impressed with Tammy that he flew her to Nashville to record. While there, she appeared on the *Grand Ole Opry* and appeared at venues in Nashville and Fort Worth. In 1983, Tammy put together the Southern Comfort Band and released an album on President Records, which was endorsed by the whiskey, Southern Comfort.

In 1986, Tammy joined forces with Little Ginny to form Two Hearts. In a short time, they were named "Top European Duo" in the *Country Music Round Up National Poll.* As a result, they represented Britain at Fan Fair in Nashville. They both toured with the hit production *Pump Boys and Dinettes*. In 1987, Tammy released the album ***Tammy Cline Sings the Country Greats*** for EMI's Music for Pleasure label. Two years later, Two Hearts released their eponymous album. In 1992, the duo broke up when Tammy announced her retirement.

JAB/BM

RECOMMENDED ALBUMS:

(All U.K. releases)
"Tammy Cline and the Southern Comfort Band" (President)(1983)
"Tammy Cline Sings the Country Greats" (Music for Pleasure)(1987)
"Two Hearts" (PCM)(1989) [With Little Ginny]

JERRY CLOWER

(Comedy)
Date of Birth: September 28, 1926
Where Born: Liberty, Mississippi
Married: Homerline Wells
Children: Ray, Amy, Sue, Katy

Professional entertaining and recording was a second career for humorist Jerry Clower. While growing up in rural Mississippi, Jerry developed a serious interest in agriculture and was an active member of the youth organization 4-H. His admiration for 4-H Club agent Monroe McElvin led to his first goal in life, which was to become a 4-H agent himself. Jerry joined the Navy the day after he graduated from high school. Following his discharge he attended Southwest Mississippi Junior College and then moved to Mississippi State University on a football scholarship. Having attained a degree in agriculture, Jerry fulfilled his life's ambition by serving as a 4-H agent.

Later, Jerry became a salesman for a fertilizer company. Jerry's talent for story-telling, which had been evident throughout his life, became an effective tool in selling. He began telling the farmers that he spoke to funny stories about his youth and the people with whom he grew up, as part of his sales pitch. After speaking to a farm group in Lubbock, Texas, in 1970, Jerry was urged by a deejay in the audience to make an album. The deejay taped Jerry's next talk, sent it to MCA and Jerry was offered a record deal.

Jerry's first album was ***Jerry Clower from Yazoo City, Mississippi, Talkin'***. Early in his career, Jerry appeared on the *David Frost Show* and did frequent guest spots on the *Grand Ole Opry*. He was inducted as a member of the *Opry* in 1973. Jerry makes over 200 personal appearances a year and has recorded 23 albums. All of his albums are recorded with live audiences because, Jerry says, he doesn't believe in canned laughter, as he thinks it is dishonest. Jerry's material is based on real life experiences of country living, both past and present. His stories often reflect the activities of his youth, "going to the swimming hole, playing 'gator, plowing a mule, going coon hunting, bird hunting, sawing stove wood, making molasses and all of that type of rural upbringing." "Marcel Ledbetter" and the rest of the "Ledbetter" family are characters who make frequent appearances in his stories. Other subject matter has included animals (*Dogs I Have Known*, in 1982) and truck

From Yazoo City, ***Jerry Clower***

drivers (*Runaway Truck*, 1986). His 1987 album ***Top Gum*** included a slight departure from his usual format; the title cut of the album is a rap song, which was also released as a single. In 1992, Jerry's 1979 album ***Greatest Hits*** was Certified Gold.

In 1993, Jerry signed a new eight-year contract with MCA Records. In addition to doing concerts and albums, Jerry co-hosted the nationally syndicated radio program *Country Crossroads* and a nationally syndicated TV show, *Nashville on the Road*. He has written three best-selling books, *Ain't God Good*, *Let the Hammer Down* and *Life Everlaughter*. A documentary film about him, also called *Ain't God Good*, won an award from the New York International Film Festival in the category of Ethics and Religion. Jerry was named "Country Comic of the Year" for 10 consecutive years by Country music fans and the trade publications *Billboard*, *Record World* and *Cash Box*. In 1976, he received the national "4-H Alumni" award given by the Future Farmers of America. Yazoo City, Mississippi, has recognized Jerry with the naming of Jerry Clower Boulevard. In 1979, *Music City News* named him "Comedy Act of the Year." Other honors bestowed upon Jerry include the "Christian Service Award" from the Southern Baptist Radio and Television Commission and an honorary doctor of letters degree from Mississippi College.

Jerry is a devoted family man and church member. He is very proud of the fact that his entertainment is family-oriented and G-rated. He says he thinks families need to laugh together, and as a family entertainer he loves what he does. Jerry has been an active member of the Gideon Bible Society, served as a Deacon for the First Baptist Church of Yazoo, Mississippi, and appeared in a national crusade with Billy Graham. JIE

RECOMMENDED ALBUMS:

So as not to be selective, we suggest you sample all of Jerry Clower's albums. However, like all good southern humor, not all of it crosses the Mason-Dixon Line with ease, but if you move south, you'll start enjoying the albums more and more.

HANK COCHRAN

(Singer, Songwriter, Guitar)

Given Name:	**Garland Perry Cochran**
Date of Birth:	**August 2, 1935**
Where Born:	**Greenville, Mississippi**
Married:	**1. Shirley (div.)**
	2. Jeannie Seely (div.)
	3. Susie
Children:	**Hank, Jr., Jimmy, Danny**

The mighty and inventive pen of Hank Cochran has spawned some classic songs which have made him one of Nashville's most revered songwriters. Within the hierarchy of songwriters, if Harlan Howard is the "Dean," then Hank is, at the very least, a Principal.

He lost his parents as a child, and spent several of his initial years in a Tennessee orphanage. At 10 he ran away to relatives at Hobbs, New Mexico, and earned his living as an oil field worker while laying the groundwork for a musical career. His uncle taught him the guitar. To begin with, he played Hank Williams tunes he heard on the radio, but soon felt the urge to write his own material.

With a clutch of songs to his name, he headed for California. Still earning a living from manual work, he spent much of his spare time at the Riverside Ranch, where he hung around Country acts looking for a break. It was here that he met Squakin' Deacon, who nicknamed him "Hank." One of the stars that he met was Jim Reeves, who was the entertainer for the amateur show Hank was on.

After meeting Eddie Cochran, the two formed the Cochran Brothers act in 1954 and appeared on the *California Hayride* and the *Town Hall Party* TV show. They signed to the Ekko label, for which they recorded the singles *Mr. Fiddle* and *Guilty Conscience*. They also backed Al Dexter on his reworking of *Pistol Packin' Mama*, for the same label. Their interest in Country music went out of the window after they saw Elvis in Dallas, at which point they were on that city's *Big D Jamboree*. They briefly went to Hawaii as members of Lefty Frizzell's backing band and then, their derivative single, *Tired and Sleepy*, bombed and the pair split. Hank, now married, gained regular work on the *California Hayride*.

Hank was drafted into the Army, spending his brief service of six months at Fort Ord, California. Following his discharge, he played for a time at the base's NCO club. His quick exit from the Army was due to Hank's friendship with Johnny Cash and the fact that Hank's sergeant was a Cash fan. Hank arranged a meeting between the two, and soon he was back in civilian clothes.

By now, writing had become a habit and Hank managed to gain a job as staff writer with the California branch of Pamper Music Company, which earned him $50 a week.The standard of his work was such that in October 1959, he was transferred to the Nashville division as a staff writer and song plugger. Within days of his arrival Skeets McDonald recorded Hank's *Where You Go I'll Follow*, but it was a while before big success came.

Hank started to hang out with other aspiring songwriters at Tootsie's Orchid Lounge. He befriended Harlan Howard and Willie Nelson. Indeed, when Joe Allison, head of Liberty Records Country music division, offered Hank a recording contract, he suggested Willie first and only after Willie had signed was Hank added to the roster.

One day, Hank thought up a title, *I Fall to Pieces*, and took it over to fellow Pamper writer Howard's house. They wrote the song together and Jan Howard then cut a demo. Its future didn't look too bright after Roy Drusky and Brenda Lee, among others, turned it down. Finally, Hank and Owen Bradley persuaded Patsy Cline to do it and the rest is history. That same year, Ernest Tubb charted Hank's *Through that Door*.

Hank forged a close friendship with the Clines and often gave Patsy first choice on his material. In late 1961, he was working alone at Pamper after hours when the idea hit him for another smash and he wrote it within 15 minutes. He took it over to Patsy, who was enthralled and cut it within days. *She's Got You* went to No.1. 1962 was a vintage year for Hank. Burl Ives scored with *A Little Bitty Tear* and *Funny Way of Laughing*, the latter earning a Grammy Award for Ives. Other chart hits that year included Eddie Arnold with *Tears Broke out on Me*, Shirley Collie and Willie Nelson with *Willingly*, Patti Page with *Go on Home* and in addition, Jim Reeves recorded *I'd Fight the World*. Although Reeves only cut three Cochran songs, the pair struck up a close friendship, often reviewing songs and drinking together into the small hours.

Hank signed with Liberty Records in 1962 and he had two chart hits with Harlan Howard's *Sally Was a Good Old Girl* and *I'd Fight the World*. He moved over to Gaylord the following year and charted with *A Good Country Song*. When Ray Price cut *Make the World Go Away*, he originally had doubts about releasing it, but they were dispelled when Hank mischievously suggested another singer's cut was better. The song was a 1963 Country hit for Price. Reeves cut it at his final recording session, joking that it would pay for Hank's divorce, which came through that day. Other 1963 hits for Hank included *You Comb Her Hair* by George Jones, *Your Best Friend and Me* by Mac Wiseman and *Yesterday's Memories* by Eddy Arnold.

It was Eddy Arnold, however, who made *Make the World Go Away* an international hit in 1965. Hank recorded two albums with RCA, after joining them in 1964, ***Hits from the Heart*** and ***Going in Training***, both in 1965. His second wife, Jeannie Seely, had hits with three of his tunes, during 1966, *Wanderin' Man*, *Don't Touch Me* and *It's Only Love*. *Don't Touch Me* was also a hit for Wilma Burgess, and in 1969, a Pop hit for Bettye Swann. Other 1966 hits with Cochran songs were *A Way to Survive* (Ray Price) and *I Want to Go wth You*, a No.1 for Eddy Arnold. During 1967, Hank had a low-level chart single, *All of Me Belongs to You*, which he recorded for Monument. Jeannie Seely racked up two more successes with Hank's songs, *I'll Love You More (Than You Need)* and *These Memories* (both 1967) and the following year, Dick Curless scored with *Bury the Bottle with Me*. In 1968, Hank signed with Monument and released the album ***The Heart of Hank Cochran*** that year.

Hank went on to handle the production department at Pamper. He continued to write under the Tree banner after they took over Pamper in 1969, though he was less prolific, exacerbated by all-night drinking sessions (which were not unusual at the time). He had two major successes in 1970, when Jack Greene & Jeannie Seely went Top 3 with *Wish I Didn't Have to Miss You* and Ray Price scored with *You Wouldn't Know Love*. The following year, Elvis Presley had a minor Pop hit with *It's Only Love*. Hank returned to the top of the Country charts, in 1972, via Merle Haggard's recording of *It's Not Love (but It's Not Bad)*.

During the period 1973 through 1978, his major covers decreased. In 1973, Hank had *Can I Sleep in Your Arms* by Jeannie Seely and *Satisfaction* by Jack Greene; in 1974, there was *I'd Fight the World* by Jim Reeves and *Lucky Ladies* by Jeannie Seely; 1977, *She's Got You* (No.1) and *Why Can't He Be You*, both by Loretta Lynn.

Hank Cochran-With A Little Help from My Friends (1978) was an album made with Willie Nelson, Merle Haggard, Jack Greene and Jeannie Seely. Jeannie's affecting sleeve notes hid the fact that she lived apart from Hank and divorce would soon follow. She wrote about their relationship in the satiric story *We're Still Hanging in There, Ain't We Jessi*. The album yielded two low-level chart records, *Willie* and *Ain't Life Hell*. In 1979, Cochran presented the soon influential *Austin City Limits* TV program when it started. The same year, as a result of Nelson's influence, Hank appeared in the movie *Honeysuckle Rose*, whose soundtrack included *Make the World Go Away* and a later composition, *I Don't Do Windows*. Hank also opened for Willie in the 1979-80 season. Hank had a Top 60 single in 1980, with a reprise of *A Little Bitty Tear*, on Elektra, with Willie handling harmonies. In 1981, a Nelson duet with Ray Price of Hank's *Don't You Ever Get Tired of Hurting Me* was a hit.

Compared to what had gone before, the 1980's were pretty barren, although Hank found a new songwriting partner in Dean Dillon. The liaison produced two chart toppers for George Strait, *The Chair* (1985) and *Ocean Front Property* (1987), as well as a Top 50 record, *Ashes in the Wind*, for Moe Bandy, written with Jeff Tweel, in 1988. Two of his old songs became No.1 hits in the 80's, *That's All That Matters* by Mickey Gilley (1980) and *Don't You Ever Get Tired of Hurtin' Me* by Ronnie Milsap (1989).

During May 1981, Hank and Laurence Purvis opened Cochran's Club in Nashville, but by July of that year, Hank had taken his name from the club. "The Hanktum," as he is known affectionately by his friends, now lives in virtual retirement and enjoys his hobby of deep sea fishing. Willie Nelson has said that Hank's main quality is sincerity. This comes across in his material, which also reflects the mood swings he is known for, which range from extreme happiness to great sorrow. In 1974, Hank Cochran was inducted into the Nashville Songwriters Hall of Fame.

SM/BM

RECOMMENDED ALBUMS:

"Hits from the Heart" (RCA Victor)(1965)
"Going in Training" (RCA Victor)(1965)
"The Heart of Hank Cochran" (Monument)(1968)
"Hank Cochran-With a Little Help from His Friends" (Capitol)(1978) [With Merle Haggard, Willie Nelson, Jack Greene and Jeannie Seely]
"Make the World Go Away" (Elektra)(1980)

DAVID ALLAN COE

(Singer, Songwriter, Guitar, Actor, Magician)

Given Name:	**David Allan Coe**
Date of Birth:	**September 6, 1939**
Where Born:	**Akron, Ohio**
Married:	**1. Betty (div.)** **2. (div.)** **3. (div.)** **4. Debra Lynn (div.)** **5. Jody Lynn**
Children:	**Carla Dawn and Shelley (from previous marriages), Tyler Mahan, Tanya Montana, Shyanne and Carson David (with Jody Lynn)**

Although he's trying to soften the image today, David Allan Coe professes to being the original outlaw of Country music. He could be well within his rights to make such a declaration over the titles normally assigned to such acts as Willie Nelson and Waylon Jennings, because David spent the biggest part of his first 29 years incarcerated in one form of institution or another. From the time he was 9 and sentenced to reform school to his final release from the Ohio State Penitentiary at 29, the longest period David was free was six months at a time. On his release from prison in 1967, he sported 365 blue ink tattoos scattered all over his body.

David emphasized his "outlaw" image over the next 20 years with such antics as literally riding with the infamous Outlaw Motorcycle Club; wearing earrings long before they became popular and fashionable for male entertainers; riding his Harley on stage; boasting about being a Mormon priest who practiced polygamy by having nine "wives" at once; dyeing his long, unruly hair and beard unheard of colors; dressing up in elaborate costumes such as bishop's robes and pirate drag; getting sued over fights in bars; using language on stage never used by any other Country artist and getting away with it; moving to and living in a cave in Tennessee after the IRS seized his house in Key West, Florida, and fighting a constant battle with the Nashville powers that be. Because of, or in spite of, this image, David has endured where a lot of performers have fallen by the wayside.

On his release from the Ohio State Penitentiary, David headed for Nashville, where he literally lived for a while in an old hearse he had painted up with his name on it. He would feed dimes into the parking meters so he could keep it parked in front of the Ryman Auditorium (then home of the *Grand Ole Opry*) on Saturdays where people could see it. His talent was raw at the time, but he was recognized by a few of the prominent industry leaders as having potential. Shelby Singleton, President of Plantation Records, released two albums of David's, ***Penitentiary Blues I & II***, that featured David's self-penned prison-oriented songs and garnered some attention. He toured for a while with Grand Funk Railroad. Mel Tillis gave David one of his rhinestone suits to wear and David became the first to wear such an outfit while sporting long hair and a beard. People started calling him "the Rhinestone Cowboy," which later transcended to "the Mysterious Rhinestone Cowboy" when David took to wearing a mask on stage for a time.

Approximately three years elapsed when David concentrated on his writing development and stage delivery. The writer, then a Nashville publicist and believer in David, helped him launch his own publishing company. It was in 1972 that David got his first song recorded by another artist when Billie Jo Spears charted with his *Souvenirs & California Mem'rys*. In 1973, *Would You Lay with Me (in a Field of Stone)*, a song he wrote as wedding vows for his brother, was recorded by Tanya Tucker and went No.1 on the Country chart, captured a BMI Award and was subsequentially recorded by more than 40 other artists. This success opened the floodgates and many artists began recording David Allan Coe songs, including Johnny Paycheck in 1974 with his monstrous hit on David's *Take This Job and Shove It* (recently released by New Wave group the Dead Kennedys). Other artists to record David's songs include Willie Nelson, George Jones, Johnny Cash, Leon Russell, Tammy Wynette, Waylon Jennings, Melba Montgomery and David Rodgers. He also co-wrote with Willie Nelson the music for the 1986 movie *Stagecoach*, plus wrote dozens of the songs he recorded himself.

As a recording artist, David signed with Columbia Records in 1973, an association that lasted 13 years and produced 26 albums and many singles. His first major chart success came in 1975 when his single of the Steve Goodman song *You Never Even Called Me by My Name* went Top 10 and was followed by *Longhaired Redneck*, which went Top 20. Other headliners over the next dozen years included *Willie, Waylon & Me,* which went Top 30 in 1976; his Top 50 duet with Bill Anderson in 1980 on *Get a Little Dirt on Your Hands*; his male version of *Stand by Your Man,* which went Top 90 in 1981; his Top 5 hit in 1983 of the Gary Gentry song about Hank Williams, *The Ride*; his double outings in 1984 on his own pennings of *Mona Lisa Lost Her Smile* (Top 5) and *She Used to Love Me a Lot* (Top 15); his 1985 Top 30 release of *Don't Cry Darlin'*, which featured a recitation by George Jones; his 1986 duet with Willie Nelson on *I've Already Cheated on You* and his Top 70 release in 1987 of *Tanya Montana*, written about his daughter and the only single to date to be accompanied by a video release.

In 1984, Columbia released the double-album entitled ***For the Record...The First Ten Years***. He continued putting out fine albums, including ***Son of the South*** in 1986 (which has cover photos of a beardless DAC) and features Willie Nelson, Waylon Jennings, Jessi Colter, Karen Brooks and Allman Brothers alumnus Dickey Betts. In 1987, David released what many consider his best album for the label, ***A Matter of Life...and Death***, which included songs written for each of his family members, including his father, Donald Mahan Coe, Jr., who finished out his life on the road with David and who died just three weeks before the birth of David's daughter Tanya Montana. Interestingly, the song *Jody Like a Melody* was written by David (and Jimmy Lewis) before he met his wife Jody Lynn, and in his words "But God must have heard the song because He sent this lovely girl to me and I was smart enough to marry her..."

David is also a very talented magician, a skill he has on videotape for sale; has written and published his own biography plus a novel entitled *Psychopath*; has acted in several movies, including *Stagecoach* and *The Last Days of Frank and Jesse James,* and appeared as himself in two low-budget films on the life of Elvis Presley, *The Living Legend* and *Lady Grey*. He's suffered and survived a nervous breakdown, several bouts with the IRS and total snubs and rejections from the Nashville music industry, although he packs the places he plays and has more than 43 record albums to his credit and has been cited by music critics who compare him to Richard Petty, Burt Reynolds and John F. Kennedy for "having that special charisma that captivates an audience" and for being "not just one of Country music's best entertainers, but one of music's best entertainers without regard to category."

A classic example of David's power over an audience came in 1987 during an appearance at the world famous Wembley Festival in London, England. While David was singing, the crowd went stone quiet and a stage assistant came up to David and told him he wasn't getting through to the audience, so please cut his show short and leave the stage. He did and the audience about tore the place down until Mervyn Cohn got David to come back up. The stage management had misread the crowd. They weren't bored, they were mesmerized! Conn said to David that he wanted him back the following year. However, David being David, he went back on stage, sang the first chorus line to *Take This Job and Shove It* and walked off.

The David Allan Coe of today is softer and much more family oriented. Taking a line from his *Actions Speak Louder Than Words** song from his ***Matter of Life...and Death*** album, "You can't eat the fruit while you're cussing the tree," David has cut down on a lot of things (he never did drink or do drugs), including cussing and is trying to bring his life into line. He moved his family to Branson, Missouri, for a few years, where he operated a museum. In 1993, he moved back to Nashville, where he is based. He still loves to gamble and, fortunately, a lot of his bookings take him to Las Vegas.

In 1990, David cut a collection of 20 of his own songs on his own label entitled ***1990 Songs for Sale,*** which he sold through his home marketing company. In 1993, Bear Family Records in Germany released it as a two-cd box set as well as releasing five other cds on him (two of which are among the six "naughty" albums he has recorded and which were unreleased). At the same time, Columbia released a ***Super Hits*** package, proving David still sells records. His latest self-produced album as of 1994 is entitled ***Standing Too Close to the Flames*** and features the David Allan Coe of success years doing such songs as *Lead Me Not into Temptation (I Can Get There by Myself)*. Temptations ignored or accepted, David Allan Coe is always colorful, entertaining, unpredictable, but ever persevering

BB

*©1986 Tanya Montana Music (BMI).

RECOMMENDED ALBUMS:

All are worth getting, but those below are a must:
"Penitentiary Blues" (SSS International)(1977)
"The Mysterious Rhinestone Cowboy" (Columbia)(1974) [Re-released on Bear Family Germany]
"Human Emotions" (Columbia)(1978)
"D.A.C." (Columbia)(1982)
"Hello in There" (Columbia)(1983)
"Just Divorce" (Columbia)(1984)
"Unchained" (Columbia)(1985)
"I Love Country" (CBS UK)(1986)
"Son of the South" (Columbia)(1986)
"A Matter of Life...and Death" (Columbia)(1987)
"Crazy Daddy" (Columbia)(1989)
"Super Hits" (Columbia)(1993)
"Headed for the Count" (Bear Family Germany)(1993)
"1990 Songs for Sale" (double cd)(Bear Family Germany)(1993)
"Standing Too Close to the Flames" (David Allan Coe)(1994)

PAUL COHEN

(Record Company Executive, Record Producer)

Given Name:	**Paul Cohen**
Date of Birth:	**November 10, 1908**
Where Born:	**Chicago, Illinois**
Married:	**Cecilia**
Children:	**Paul, Jr.**
Date of Death:	**April 1, 1970**

Paul Cohen was the first producer to record one of his artists in Nashville. The artist was Red Foley; the year was 1945; the location was WSM's Studio B. Cohen was the first to recognize the potential that Nashville had as a recording center.

Cohen began his career with Columbia but switched to Decca in the early 30's, where he sold records and scouted talent in the Midwest and New York from his base in Cincinnati. At the end of WWII, he was placed in charge of Decca's Country division.

Having broken the ground with the Foley session, he produced Ernest Tubb on his first session in Nashville in September 1945, and two years later, two engineers, Aaron Shelton and Carl Jenkins, opened Castle Studios on the site of the old Tulane Hotel at 8th and Church, which became the first recording studio in Nashville. Cohen stayed with Decca until 1958, during which time he had helped the careers of Red Sovine and Kitty Wells among others. In 1958, he moved from New York and based himself in Nashville and started his own Todd Records. In the 60's, Cohen ran Kapp and ABC-Paramount Records.

Although a man of judgment, he was capable of letting one get away. When Buddy Holly was recording at Owen Bradley's studio, Cohen referred to Holly as the "biggest no talent he had ever worked with." If only all performers were as untalented as Buddy Holly! Paul Cohen was President of the Country Music Association when the Country Music Hall of Fame was opened on March 31,1967. Paul Cohen died in 1970 from cancer and in 1976, six years after his death, he was inducted into the Country Music Hall of Fame.

Ben Colder refer SHEB WOOLEY

B.J. COLE

(Steel Guitar, Guitar, Dobro, Composer)

Given Name:	**Brian John Cole**
Date of Birth:	**June 17, 1946**
Where Born:	**North Enfield, Hertfordshire, England**
Married:	**Drucilla**
Children:	**Emily, Peggy**

B.J. has taken the pedal steel guitar into areas of music not usually associated with the instrument. He has played for performers as diverse as Elton John and Garth Brooks.

Inspired by British Pop instrumental stars, the Shadows, B.J. began playing guitar when he was age 12. His father always had instruments around their home and B.J. played every form of guitar including Dobro, but settled on steel guitar as his main instrument. He soon became an in-demand session player and then in 1970, he became a member of Cochise, a Rock band that recorded for United Artists during 1970 through 1972, cutting ***Cochise*** (1970), ***Swallow Tales*** (1971) and ***So Far*** (1972).

By the time he left the band in 1972, B.J. had already established himself as a respected session player, having played on Humble Pie's eponymous album (1970) and ***Rock On*** (1971), Elton John's ***Madman Across the Water*** (1971) and Nazareth's self-titled 1971 album. In 1972, B.J. recorded his solo United Artists album, ***New Hovering Dog***. B.J. continued as a session player through the 70's and 80's appearing on Roger Cooke's ***Minstrel in Flight*** (1973), Marc Bolan & T. Rex's ***Light of Love***, Ian Matthews & Southern Comfort's ***Some Days You Eat the Bear***, Procol Harum's ***Exotic Birds & Fruit***, Tim Rose's eponymous album, Al Stewart's ***Past, Present & Future*** and Jimmy Webb's ***Lands End*** (all 1974), Chris De Burgh's ***Far Beyond These Castle Walls*** (1975), Elton John's ***Single Man*** (1978), Alan Parsons Project's ***Eve*** (1979), Roy Harper's ***Unknown Soldier*** (1980), Shakin' Stevens' ***Give Me Your Heart*** (1982) and Paul Young's ***The Secret of Association*** (1985).

B.J. has toured all through Europe and has acted as a "fixer" putting bands together for visiting U.S. acts. When Garth Brooks visited the U.K., it was B.J. who arranged the band for Garth's TV appearance on BBC-TV, Pebble Mill. In recent years, B.J. has experimented with a midi interface in an ever searching quest for new sounds from his steel guitar. In reality, if B.J. ever decided to leave the U.K. for Nashville, he would be hailed as one of the most exciting players of the steel guitar, but is content at being one of the top session and touring musicians in Europe. JAB/BM

RECOMMENDED ALBUMS:

"Swallow Tales" (United Artists)(1971) [With Cochise]
"So Far" (United Artists)(1972) [With Cochise]
"New Hovering Dog" (United Artists)(1972) [U.K. Release]

T. Michael Coleman refer DOC WATSON

BIFF COLLIE

(Deejay, Singer, Trumpet, Booking Agent, Promoter)

Given Name:	**Hiram Abiff Collie**
Date of Birth:	**November 25, 1926**
Where Born:	**Little Rock, Arkansas**
Married:	**1. Marge Tillman (div.)** **2. Shirley Caddell (Shirley Collie/Shirley Nelson) (div.)** **3. Barbara**
Children:	**Sandra, Sharon**
Date of Death:	**February 19, 1992**

When Country music is examined, it is usual to look at the performers, songwriters and pickers, but the broadcasters are often overlooked. One of the most influential over the last 40 years has been Biff Collie.

Although born in Arkansas, from the time he was six weeks old, Biff called San Antonio,Texas, home. His entrance into the world of broadcasting came when he was 17 when he became a full-time deejay on KMAC San Antonio. During WWII, he was based at KBWD Browning, Texas, and in 1947, he could be found on KBKI Alice, Texas.

In 1948, Biff moved to the position of senior deejay at the prestigious KNUZ station in Houston. He then moved over to the important Houston station KPRC. At this time, he started appearing at the Magnolia Gardens. This led to his getting involved in artist booking and concert promotion. He cut his first record for Columbia, *I Don't Care Who Knows/Why Are You Blue*, in 1951. His first wife, Marge, followed suit the following year, as Marge Collie. During 1955 and 1956, Biff released four singles for Starday, none of which charted. They were *Lonely/What this Old World Needs*, *Goodbye Farewell, So Long/Look on the Good Side* (1955), *Empty Kisses/Doodle Doo* and *All of a Sudden/Joy, Joy, Joy* (1956).

By 1957, Biff had become manager and emcee of the Philip Morris Country Music Show which toured through 37 states during 1957-1958. These shows were broadcast on Mutual and CBS radio and helped spread not only Country music but also the name Biff Collie. During this time, he was also an active musician and helped bring brass into Country music.

By the 60's, he had made Long Beach, California, his base and was instrumental in elevating local station KFOX to the forefront of Southern California Country stations. For a dozen straight years, Biff was among the nation's Top 10 deejays in *Billboard* and *Music Reporter*. In 1965, he was named "Best Radio Personality" by the ACM. He was also on the Board of Directors of the CMA and in 1967 he produced the ACM's Award Show in Beverly Hills.

Biff had business interests during the 60's that included music publishing, record shops and syndicated radio shows, including *Houston Jamboree*. In 1972, he became a chart artist when his United Artists single *Miss Pauline* went Top 60 under the nom de chante Billy Bob Bowman with the Beaumont Bag & Burlap Company. In 1978, he was inducted into the DJ Hall of Fame. When Biff died in 1992, the Country music world lost one of its most knowledgeable members.

MARK COLLIE

(Singer, Songwriter, Piano, Guitar)
Given Name: **George Mark Collie**
Date of Birth: **January 18, 1956**
Where Born: **Waynesboro, Tennessee**
Married: **Anne**
Children: **Nathan**

Mark Collie has always been Country and grew up listening to radio WHBO Memphis and WSM Nashville. His influences were Jerry Lee Lewis, who encouraged him to play piano, Carl Perkins as regards electric guitar playing and Willie Nelson and Kris Kristofferson, who provided the impetus for Mark's songwriting.

Being one of six children, Mark had always enjoyed a captive audience and he loved performing with his guitar or playing piano and this love is evident in his live shows today. While he was still in school, he had a job at local radio station WAAM as a deejay and got educated on Country music. He joined his first band when he was only 12 years old and when his school days were over, he went out on the road and played in various bands all over the southeastern U.S.

Visiting his brother in Hawaii, he sang with some bands and in the end stayed for one and a half years. After he got back home, he tried to join the armed forces, only to find that he had diabetes and so was turned down. After a spell in Memphis, Mark moved to Nashville in 1982, with the encouragement of his wife, Anne. He wanted to concentrate on songwriting and become a staff writer. He had no success and was discouraged, but he started writing for himself and went out and played his songs to live audiences.

Mark played the Douglas Corner Cafe about once a month. At first there were about 15 people there but gradually more and more came, until there were about 150. Then a showcase was arranged, in 1989, and MCA/Nashville Executive Vice President, Tony Brown saw him, liked what he saw and signed him the next day.

Mark's debut single with MCA was *Something with a Ring to It*, in 1990, which got into the Top 60. Next came *Looks Aren't Everything,* which reached Top 40. These songs were from his debut album, ***Hardin County Line*** (1990), which was produced by Tony Brown and Doug Johnson. Mark had a hand in writing every song on this album. A video was made for the single, *Hardin County Line*, which was filmed in his hometown and live concert footage of Mark was shot at the nearby Crockett theater. The single only made the Top 60.

He was soon out on the road again playing dates with Reba McEntire, Conway Twitty and Charlie Daniels. As 1991 got under way, Mark had his first Top 20 hit with *Let Her Go.* Then Mark released his second album, ***Born and Raised in Black & White***. The first three singles from that were *Calloused Hands* (Top 40), *She's Never Comin' Back* (Top 30) and in 1992, *It Don't Take a Lot* (Top 70). Mark closed out the year with his most successful single, *Even the Man in the Moon Is Crying*, which went Top 5. Five of the songs were either written or co-written by Mark. In 1993, MCA released a third album, ***Mark Collie***. Mark started off 1993 with the Top 10 *Born to Love You* and then continued the year with *Shame Shame Shame Shame* (Top 30) and *Something's Gonna Change Her Mind* (Top 25).

Singer and Songwriter ***Mark Collie***

RECOMMENDED ALBUMS:
"Hardin County Line" (MCA)(1990)
"Born and Raised in Black and White" (MCA)(1991)
"Mark Collie" (MCA)(1993)

BRIAN COLLINS

(Singer, Songwriter, Guitar, Fiddle, Piano, Drums)
Date of Birth: **October 19, 1950**
Where Born: **Baltimore, Maryland**
Married: **1. Beth (div.)**
2. Cindy (div.)
3. Janie

Brian Collins was a young Country singer who looked like he might happen in a big way during the early 70's, but after a decade of hit making, disappeared from the major label scene.

Brian was born in Baltimore but brought up in Texas City, Texas. He was another Country performer who started his career at a very young age. Brian was just 11 when he became a professional entertainer. He told the owner of Duffy's Club that his gig was not to be advertised because his mother might find out that he wasn't playing football. Brian eventually told her about his musical aspirations and she encouraged him.

While in junior high school, he played some rock'n'roll with his band, the Nomads. He returned to Country but still retained a love of most music but especially R & B. In 1969, Brian met Dolly Parton at a Country show in Houston and she encouraged him to try Nashville. He eventually gave up his job in a florist's shop and arrived in Nashville with 50 cents to his name. He played with various groups and then a friend from Texas, Billy Carr, arranged for a demo session and they started to punt the tape around.

In 1971, Brian signed to Mega Records and had a Top 70 entry with *All I Want to Do Is Say I Love You.* The following year, he hit the Top 50 with his remake of Herman's Hermits' *There's a Kind of Hush (All Over the World).* In 1973, Brian moved over to Dot (later ABC/Dot) and had a Top 25 hit with *I Wish (You Had Stayed).* At year end, he charted with *I Don't Plan on Losing You*, which went Top 50 in 1974. This was followed by Brian's Top 10 recording of the Jan Crutchfield song *Statue of a Fool.* That same year, he joined Tom T. Hall and Leroy Van Dyke to perform on the UNICEF Country and Western Tour traveling to various countries to benefit the children of Bangladesh. When he appeared on the *Grand Ole Opry*, he received a standing ovation. Brian closed 1974 with the Top 25 hit *That's the Way Love Should Be*.

Through 1975 to 1977, he had a series of low-level successes. In 1978, Brian signed to RCA, but the success level didn't increase. He was absent from the chart between 1979 and 1982 and then in 1982, he had two further low-level entries with Primero Records.

Brian decided to leave Country music and entered the Christian Gospel Ministry calling himself a "born-again spirit-filled Christian." He said that he had "been called by God to help evangelize the world by sharing the Gospel of Jesus Christ in word and song."

RECOMMENDED ALBUMS:

"That's the Way Love Should Be" (ABC/Dot)(1974)
"The ABC Collection" (ABC)(1977)

TOM COLLINS

(Record Producer, Music Publisher, Arranger, Trumpet, Piano)

Given Name: Bernie Tom Collins
Date of Birth: May 30, 1942
Where Born: Knoxville, Tennessee
Married: Jennifer Jones
Children: Bradley Thomas, Courtney Paige

During the 70's and 80's, Tom Collins had a similar effect on Country music as Chet Atkins had in the 60's. There was a concerted effort to make the music more accessible to a wider audience. As the producer for, particularly, Barbara Mandrell, Ronnie Milsap and Sylvia, he became a major force within Nashville. Furthermore, his company, Collins Music, which boasted such writers as Rhonda Kye Fleming and Dennis Morgan, was to become much in demand for its catalog.

Tom began playing piano at the age of 7 and the trumpet at 13. He made his professional debut at the age of 14, as a choir director. From 1968 through 1970, he was a schoolteacher and then in 1971, he commenced his climb up the musical industry ladder. He joined Pi-Gem Publishing and two years later, he started to produce. The first track that he produced was Ronnie Milsap's *Where My Heart Is*.

In 1975, Tom became the Musical Director for the *Barbara Mandrell Show*, which was one of the most successful variety shows on U.S. TV. He set up Collins Music in 1982 and the company has received over 100 BMI and ASCAP awards for songs such as *Kansas City Lights* (Steve Wariner, 1982), *Like Nothing Ever Happened* (Sylvia, 1983), *Happy Birthday Dear Heartache* (Barbara Mandrell, 1984), *To Me* (Barbara Mandrell/Lee Greenwood, 1984) and *Crossword Puzzle* (Barbara Mandrell, 1984), *Fast Lanes and Country Music* (Barbara Mandrell, 1986), *Walk On* (Reba McEntire, 1990)and *Don't Rock the Jukebox* (Alan Jackson, 1991). Collins Music acquired the legendary Hallnote Music catalog of Tom T. Hall in 1991, further strengthening and re-affirming Tom's company as one of the major independent music publishers in the U.S.

Tom also produced what is probably Sylvia's finest album, ***Drifter***, in 1981. The following year, the Collins-produced Sylvia single *Nobody* won the BMI award for "Most Performed Song of the Year." Tom has also produced albums for Steve Wariner, Jim Ed Brown & Helen Cornelius and Irish flautist James Galway.

Tom is one of the few Nashville music business people who are internationally conscious and he can be found every January at MIDEM in Cannes furthering the commercial outlets for his catalog, which also benefits his writers.

RECOMMENDED ALBUMS PRODUCED BY TOM COLLINS:

Ronnie Milsap:
"It Was Almost Like a Song" (RCA Victor)(1977)
"Lost in the Fifties Tonight" (RCA Victor)(1986)(Grammy winner)
Barbara Mandrell:
"Spun Gold" (MCA)(1983)
"Clean Cut" (MCA)(1984)
"Sure Feels Good" (EMI America)(1987)
"I'll Be Your Jukebox Tonight" (Capitol)(1988)
Steve Wariner:
"Steve Wariner" (RCA Victor)(1982)
Sylvia:
"Drifter" (RCA Victor)(1981)
Jim Ed Brown & Helen Cornelius:
"One Woman, One Man" (RCA Victor)(1980)

TOMMY COLLINS

(Singer, Songwriter, Guitar)

Given Name: Leonard Raymond Sipes
Date of Birth: September 28, 1930
Where Born: Bethany, Oklahoma
Married: Wanda Lucille Shahan (div.)
Children: Tommy, Kimbra, Timothy

Back in the early 50's, Tommy Collins had several hit songs on Capitol Records, most of them his own compositions. In recent years, he has become known as one of the chief pioneers of the Bakersfield sound that propelled Buck Owens and Merle Haggard to superstardom. Most of the Collins hits tended to be humorous novelty songs that looked at the lighter side of romance, but he often coupled them with more serious ballads.

Born near Oklahoma City, Tommy had ample exposure to Western Swing and Honky-Tonk music in his youth. Displaying an early flair for both singing and songwriting, he appeared on some local radio shows and won a talent contest which netted him a small program on local KLPR. During 1949-1952, Tommy attended Edmond State Teachers College majoring in chemistry. During this period he recorded four sides for the Fresno, California-based Morgan label. After a short hitch in the U.S. Marines, Tommy went to California with Wanda Jackson and her parents. The Jacksons soon returned to Oklahoma, but Tommy remained in Bakersfield, where he struck up a friendship with rising young Capitol recording artist Ferlin Husky, for whom he wrote a few songs. In June 1953, Husky helped Sipes secure his own Capitol contract at which time he shortened his professional name to the more commercial-sounding Tommy Collins.

In 1954, Tommy's second release, *You Better Not Do That*, shot up to No.2, where it stayed for nearly two months and the Collins career shifted into high gear. Other successes, nearly all in the novelty vein and his own compositions, included *Watcha Gonna Do Now* (Top 5, 1954), *Untied* (Top 10), *It Tickles* (Top 5) and *I Guess I'm Crazy/You Oughta See Pickles Now* (both Top 15) (all 1955). Tommy also recorded other of his own songs that were also popular without charting and these included *Always Get a Souvenir*, *All the Monkeys Ain't in the Zoo* and *High on a Hilltop*. Buck Owens served as lead guitarist on many of Tommy's early sessions. In 1955, Faron Young had a big hit with Tommy's *If You Ain't Lovin'*.

In January 1956, Tommy had a conversion experience and subsequently began to record some sacred material, some in duet form with his wife, Wanda, but continued to do secular songs too. In 1957, Tommy decided to enter the ministry, enrolled in Golden Gate Baptist Seminary in the Bay area and from 1959, pastored churches, and continued to record for Capitol, through 1960, until his contract expired. During 1960 and 1961, Tommy attended Sacramento State College. By 1963, however, not feeling fulfilled with his ministry, Tommy returned to Bakersfield, went back to the music business, and re-signed with Capitol. In 1964, Tommy and Wanda had a duet Top 50 single called *I Can Do That*.

In 1965, Tommy Collins switched to Columbia Records and had a Top 10 hit in 1966 with *If You Can't Bite, Don't Growl*. His other Columbia chartmakers were *Shindig in the Barn* (1966), *Don't Wipe the Tears That You Cry from Him (on My Good White Shirt)/Birmingham* and *Big Dummy* (all 1967) and *I Made the First Prison Band* (1968) but only ranked as minor hits. During much of this time, he toured U.S. military bases abroad, served as an opening act for Buck Owens and later did the same for Merle Haggard. Unfortunately, Tommy's personal life began to crumble as he became increasingly dependent on alcohol and pills. Tommy and Wanda's marriage ended in 1971 and further depression took its toll on the once highly ranked singer/writer.

Slowly pulling himself together, Collins continued to write songs, including such Merle Haggard hits as *Carolyn* (1972) and *The Roots of My Raising* (1976). In all, Haggard recorded about 30 of Tommy's compositions. Tommy himself recorded an album for Starday in 1976, which included some of his songs that had hit big for others as well as humorous recitations like *Opal, You Asked Me* and *Cigarette Milner*. For a time in the mid-80's, he wrote for Sawgrass Music, turning out, among others, *New Patches*, which became a Top 10 hit in 1984 for the firm's owner, Mel Tillis. In 1987, another of Tommy's originals, *Second Chances*, went Gold as the result of being on a million-selling George Strait album. The following year, Strait had a No.1 hit with yet another revival of *If You Ain't Lovin'*, which has become a Country classic. In 1980, Merle Haggard wrote and subsequently recorded *Leonard*, a Collins tribute song which went to Top 10. During the 80's, European companies began to reissue some of his early recordings, the ultimate of which was reached in 1992, when Bear Family Records released a cd set. This renewed interest in Tommy's work led to his appearing at the 1988 Wembley Festival in England. Tommy Collins signed with Ricky Skaggs Music in 1993 and a new chapter in his writing career is about to unfold. IMT

RECOMMENDED ALBUMS:

"Words and Music Country Style" (Capitol)(1957) [Re-issued by Stetson UK in original sleeve (1988)]
"Light of the Lord" (Capitol)(1959)
"This Is Tommy Collins" (Capitol)(1959) [Re-issued by Stetson UK in original sleeve (1988)]
"Songs I Love to Sing" (Capitol)(1960)
"Let's Live a Little" (Tower)(1966)
"The Dynamic Tommy Collins" (Columbia)(1966)
"Tommy Collins on Tour" (Columbia)(1968)
"Shindig" (Tower)(1968)
"Tommy Collins Callin'" (Starday)(1976)
"Leonard" (5-cd set)(Bear Family Germany)(1992)[Containing entire Morgan, Capitol and Columbia recordings]

COLLINS KIDS

LARRY COLLINS

(Singer, Songwriter, Lead Guitar)

Given Name: Lawrence Albert Collins
Date of Birth: October 4, 1944
Where Born: Tulsa, Oklahoma
Married: Mary Jo
Children: Larissa

LORRIE COLLINS

(Singer, Songwriter, Guitar)

Given Name: Lawrencine May Collins
Date of Birth: May 7, 1942
Where Born: Tahlequah, Oklahoma
Married: Stewart Ronald Carnall
Children: Christy, Lynn

If James Dean and Elvis Presley symbolized the spirit of rebellious youth in the media culture of the 50's, the Collins Kids represented the sometimes brash but more conventional attitudes of rural and rural-in-origin youth of the same era.

Like many California Country musicians, the Collins Kids were products of Oklahoma's agrarian culture. Their dad farmed and then worked in a steel mill, while their mother sang down-home Country and Gospel songs. Family members and others viewed Lorrie as a child prodigy and at 8 years old she won a talent contest in Tulsa. Steel player extraordinaire Leon McAuliffe urged Lorrie's parents to take her to California and in 1952, Mrs. Collins took her there to sample the market. They decided to move to the coast the following year.

For his Christmas present in 1952, Larry had received a guitar and he mastered it rather quickly. Soon after their move to the West Coast, their dad told Lorrie and Larry to go into the bedroom and practice together, "and they came out as an act," their mother later recalled.

After winning a variety of talent contests, the Kids landed a regular spot on the *Town Hall Party* in February 1954, giving them a major radio and TV contract before they had reached their teens. Legendary guitarist Joe Maphis took Larry under his wing and turned a good picker into a great one.

For the next five years, Larry and Lorrie were a popular act, touring widely and appearing on several prime-time network TV shows. As Larry later recalled, "Our proud daddy drove us on cross-country tours in brand new Cadillacs." On Larry's 11th birthday, the Collins Kids had their first session on Columbia, their initial release being a novelty number called *Hush Money* about a kid brother trying to blackmail his older sister. The flipside, *Beetle Bug Bop,* had a Rockabilly flavor. In 1956, the duo joined the syndicated *Ranch Party* and stayed with the show for the next three years.

Although they have now become collector's items today, none of the Collins Kids' releases ever became major hits, although they could certainly be termed moderate successes. *Whistle Bait* and their version of *(Let's Have a) Party* constituted the Kids' best selling singles. Teenage novelty songs that fitted their image and Rockabilly-tinged material dominated their recorded repertoire. They were the ideal adolescent act for the California Country scene of that era. Their songs created an image of a wholesome, attractive teen girl and her smart-aleck brother.

Larry and Lorrie, the ***Collins Kids***

Lorrie did a few vocal solos and Larry cut some hot guitar duets with Joe Maphis played on their matching twin-neck guitars built by Semie Moseley. Like Carolina Cotton in the early 50's and the Stonemans in the 60's, the Collins Kids remained essentially a visual act, ideal for TV and live shows, but difficult to capture on record.

In the latter part of 1959, the career of the Collins Kids came to a temporary halt when Lorrie eloped. At the time, she and Ricky Nelson were engaged and it came as a bit of a shock when she and Johnny Cash's road manager, Stew Carnall, went to Las Vegas and tied the knot. However, the Kids resumed work after a few months. In 1960, they appeared in the movie *Music Around the World* for Universal. They had a final session for Columbia in June 1961, several weeks after Lorrie had given birth to her first child. Larry had a few singles on Columbia by himself and the Collins Kids undertook some tours and reunion concerts thereafter, but their days as a top entertainment act were over.

Lorrie generally devoted herself to rearing her children and raising thoroughbred horses. Larry eventually emerged as a successful songwriter. In 1972, he co-wrote with Alex Harvey the crossover hit *Delta Dawn*, which was a monster hit for a young Tanya Tucker. His other hit songs include *You're the Reason God Made Oklahoma*, which he wrote with Sandy Pinkard and was an award-winning success for David Frizzell and Shelly West, in 1981. More recently, he has earned his living as a golf pro. As a guitarist, Larry has been a great influence on surf guitarist Dick Dale. IMT

RECOMMENDED ALBUMS:

"Introducing Larry and Lorrie" (Epic)(1983) [Re-issues]
"Rockin' Rollin' Collins Kids" (Bear Family Germany)(1981) [Re-issues]
"Rockin' Rollin' Collins Kids, Vol. 2" (Bear Family Germany)(1983) [Re-issues]
"Larry Collins & Joe Maphis" (Bear Family Germany)(1983)
"Hop Skip & Jump" (Bear Family Germany)(1991) (Boxed set containing complete recordings)
"The Collins Kids at Town Hall Party" (Country Routes UK)(1990)

COLORADO

Formed: 1979
Current Members:

Geordie Jack	**Lead Vocals, Guitar, Fiddle**
Dado Duncan	**Bass Guitar, Vocals**
Gordy Davidson	**Lead Guitar, Mandolin, Vocals**
Brian Coghill	**Banjo, Steel Guitar, Accordion**
Willie Anderson	**Drums**

Former Members: Sandy Mackay (Drums), Davy Duff (d. 1984) (Bass Guitar, Pedal Steel, Vocals), Ruby Rendall (Keyboards, Guitar, Fiddle, Vocals), Alan Thompson (Keyboards), Findlay Grant (Drums), Alan Murphy (Drums)

Colorado has a unique style of Country music that incorporates a Celtic overtone. The band was first formed by a group of youngsters who had grown up together in the small village of Golspie in the far north of Scotland. The original line-up of Geordie Jack, Dado, Davy Duff and Sandy Mackay soon gained recognition on the U.K. Country scene after winning a talent competition on the Wembley stage in 1979. Their prize was to represent Britain at Fan Fair in Nashville. While in Nashville, they were invited to appear on the *Grand Ole Opry*.

They were soon in demand as a back-up band for American performers touring Europe. The British fans took this group to their hearts and by 1984, they were voted "No.1 Group" for the third straight year by the British Country Music Association.

Then tragedy struck when Davy Duff left the band in 1983 due to illness (he died in 1989). The group was devastated. They tried to overcome their loss, but the void was difficult to fill and over the next few years, the band changed its identity. First, Ruby Rendall joined, then Alan Thompson, changing the chemistry of the group. Then Sandy Mackay left and was replaced by Findlay Grant and then later, when he left, Alan Murphy joined.

Colorado continued to win national awards and they then felt that their real strength lay in their musical roots and this led to the Celtic influences. In 1986, the three remaining original members added multi-instrumentalist Brian Coghill and drummer Willie Anderson to their ranks. It is this line-up which has brought even greater fame to the group in Europe. From 1987, they became regular performers at the Wembley Festival in England. That year, they were again voted "Best British Band" by the BCMA and by 1994, they had received this title for nine straight years (1986-1994).

Their first album, ***Colorado Sings Country Music***, was released on the Big R label in 1980 and this was followed the next year by ***Tennessee Inspiration***. In 1984, they moved to the Trim Top label, where they released ***Colorado***, ***Still Burnin'*** and a live recording, ***Berwick Speedway Club Presents Colorado***. Their album ***Exclusive***, was named "Album of the Year" by *International Country Music News*, in 1988. Their other albums are ***All My Cloudy Days Are Gone*** and ***Inside Stories***. They also recorded an album under the name of Caledonia, entitled ***Across the Hills of Home***. Several of their albums were recorded in Nashville.

Colorado have appeared at the Royal Albert Hall and on countless TV and radio shows. They represent the connection between Country and Scottish music and have successfully wedded the two cultures. JAB

RECOMMENDED ALBUMS:

(All U.K. releases)
"Colorado Sings Country Music" (Big R)(1980)
"Tennessee Inspiration" (Big R)(1981)
"Colorado" (Trim Top)(1984)

The pride of Scotland, ***Colorado***

"Still Burnin'" (Trim Top)(1986)
"Berwick Speedway Club Presents Colorado" (Trim Top)(1987)
"Exclusive" (Trim Top)(1988)
"All My Cloudy Days Are Gone" (Trim Top)(1989)
"Inside Stories" (Trim Top)(1990)
As Caledonia:
"Across the Hills of Home" (Trim Top)(1990))

JESSI COLTER

(Singer, Songwriter, Piano, Guitar, Actress)

Given Name:	**Miriam Johnson**
Date of Birth:	**May 25, 1947**
Where Born:	**Phoenix, Arizona**
Married:	**1. Duane Eddy (div.) 2. Waylon Jennings**
Children:	**Jennifer Eddy, Buddy Jennings, Scooter Jennings**

Jessi Colter made her mark in both Country and Pop music as a singer, songwriter, and performer. She began recording as a teenager and wrote songs for many other Country stars. Jessi was featured on ***Wanted! The Outlaws***, in 1976, which was the first Country album to be Certified Platinum.

The sixth of seven children, Miriam Johnson was born and raised in Phoenix, Arizona. Her father was a mining engineer who was also an inventor and race car builder. Her mother sold cosmetics and ran a hotel before becoming a Pentecostal minister. Jessi started playing piano when she was 6 years old and when she was 11, she became the pianist in her mother's church.

As a teenager, Jessi decided she wanted to pursue a career in music. Feeling like she needed a better stage name than Miriam Johnson, she adopted the name of her great-great-great uncle Jesse Colter. He was a real outlaw and train robber who was a member of the Frank and Jesse James gang. Jessi inherited a little of her ancestor's wildness and slipped away from home at night to sing in the local bars. At 16, Jessi went on tour with legendary rock'n'roll guitarist Duane Eddy. They later married and in 1961, Duane produced a record on her on Jamie Records entitled *I Cried Long Enough/Making Believe* (as Miriam Johnson). The couple settled in Beverly Hills, California, and she appeared with Eddy in clubs and on TV, including Dick Clark's *American Bandstand.* When their marriage ended in divorce seven years later, Jessi returned to Phoenix.

Back in Arizona, Jessi met Waylon Jennings when he performed at the popular JD's nightclub. They became friends and Waylon invited her to record a duet with him in a Phoenix studio. By this time Jessi had proven herself as a songwriter, penning Dottie West's 1965 hit *No Sign of Living*. Her songs had also been recorded by Don Gibson and Nancy Sinatra. Jennings was impressed with Jessi's songs and her voice and helped secure a contract with RCA Records. He co-produced the album, added vocals, and wrote the liner notes. Their personal relationship blossomed during the album project and in 1969 they were married in Jessi's mother's church. The following year Jessi's album ***A Country Star Is Born*** was released. Several single releases from the lp failed to make the charts but success awaited her at another label. However, Jessi had a Top 25 hit with Waylon with Mark James' *Suspicious Minds* in 1970. The following year, they again had a duet hit with the Top 40 *Under Your Spell Again*.

Jessi Colter's career breakthrough came in 1975 when she signed with Capitol Records and recorded the lp ***I'm Jessi Colter***. Her self-penned *I'm Not Lisa* rose to the top of the Country chart and Top 5 on the Pop chart. The highly emotional song showcasing Jessi's intimate vocal capabilities received two Grammy nominations. Before the year was over, Jessi had two more hit singles, including *What's Happened to Blue Eyes* (Top 5 Country/Top 60 Pop). 1976's follow-up lp on Capitol, ***Jessi***, produced the hits *It's Morning (and I Still Love You)* (Top 15 Country) and *I Thought I Heard You Calling My Name* (Top 30). Jessi and Waylon's *Suspicious Minds* was re-released and reached the Top 3.

Jessi's best selling ***Diamond in the Rough*** album was released later in 1976. Also that year, Jessi teamed up with Waylon, Willie Nelson, and Tompall Glaser to record ***Wanted! The Outlaws*** on RCA. The album expanded the bounds of Country music and was purchased by many new fans. It became Country's best-selling album of the time, topping the 1 million sales mark and by 1985, it had sold 2 million copies. Jessi went on an extensive tour with her recording partners to promote the album.

Jessi released her fourth album for Capitol in the summer of 1977 using her given name for the title, ***Miriam***. ***That's the Way a Cowboy Rocks and Rolls*** followed in 1978 and Jessi toured with Waylon to support the release. Jessi and Waylon teamed up to record the Gold selling ***Leather and Lace*** album for RCA in 1981. The duo had two chart singles that year with the Top 20 *Storms Never Last* and the Top 10 medley *Wild Side of Life/It Wasn't God Who Made Honky Tonk Angels*. The following year, Jessi had the solo Top 70 single *Holdin' On*. In 1985, Jessi moved to the small Triad label to record ***Rock 'n' Roll Lullaby***. The album, produced by studio veteran Chips Moman, featured several Pop standards, including *Stormy Weather* and *I Can't Stop Loving You*.

In 1991 Jessi was featured in the home video *Jessi Sings Songs from Around the World Just for Kids*. The hour-long concert featured international children's favorites, including *London Bridge, La Cucaracha,* and *Old King Cole*. Waylon Jennings made a special appearance in the video reciting original poetry. JIE

RECOMMENDED ALBUMS:

"A Country Star Is Born" (RCA Victor)(1970) [Features Waylon Jennings]
"I'm Jessi Colter" (Capitol)(1975)
"Jessi" (Capitol)(1976)
"Wanted! The Outlaws" (RCA Victor)(1976) [with Willie Nelson, Waylon Jennings and Tompall Glaser]
"That's the Way a Cowboy Rocks and Rolls" (Capitol)(1978)
"Leather and Lace" (RCA Victor)(1981) [With Waylon Jennings]
"Ridin' Shotgun" (Capitol)(1981)
"Rock 'n' Roll Lullaby" (Triad)(1985)

COMMANDER CODY AND HIS LOST PLANET AIRMEN

Formed:	**1967**
Members:	
George Frayne	**Vocals/Piano**
John Tichy	**Guitar**
Bill Kirchen	**Guitar, Trombone, Vocals**
Bruce Barlow	**Bass Guitar/Vocals**
Billy C. Farlow	**Harmonica/Vocals**
Lance Dickerson	**Drums/Vocals**
Andy Stein	**Fiddle, Sax**
West Virginia Creeper	**Steel Guitar**
Bobby Black	**Steel Guitar, Vocals**

George Frayne (Commander Cody) and John Tichy put the band together in Detroit from like-minded Country-based musicians. The name of the band came from space movie characters.

They had been in college together at the University of Michigan, Ann Arbor. The music was fairly eclectic but based upon a modern Western Swing feel in the same vein as Asleep at the Wheel with a shade more anarchic tendencies. Frayne had played organ in various Detroit Rock bands. Farlow had at the time his own band, Billy C. & the Sunshine, playing white Blues. Kirchen was playing in a local band, the Seventh Seal. In 1969, at Kirchen's suggestion the band relocated to San Francisco. They started to build up a good following in California and signed to Paramount.

In 1971, they released their first album, entitled ***Lost in the Ozone***, to critical acclaim. After the release of the album, West Virginia Creeper left the band and was replaced by Bobby Black. The following year, the band had a Top 60 hit with Johnny Bond's *Hot Rod Lincoln*. Their next album, ***Hot Licks, Cold Steel and Truckers Favorites***, which was produced for just $5,000 on a four-track machine, became a watershed for the band. It captured the feel of the band to perfection.

They released two more albums for Paramount, both well received: ***Country Casanova*** (1973) and ***Live Deep in the Heart of Texas*** (1974). In 1973 they brought out their version of Tex Williams' *Smoke! Smoke! Smoke! (That Cigarette)*. Their final single, *Riot in Cell Block No. 9*, was in 1974. When ABC took over Paramount, the band felt that a move was in order.

The band moved to Warner Brothers and in 1975 brought out their eponymous album. This was the first album that experimented with trumpets (Greg Adams and Mic Gillette). The album was not a success. The follow-up, which was produced by Hoyt Axton, was a lot better. This is an album bulging with additional vocalists and musicians. During their tour of Europe (they were particularly big in France), they recorded their last album for Warner Brothers. It was a double live project, ***We've Got a Live One Here***. It marks the introduction of Norton Buffalo on harmonica and Rick Higginbottom on guitar.

At the end of the tour, Frayne broke up the band. The following year he signed to Arista for a solo album, ***Midnight Man*** (1977). He resurrected the Airman for two final albums for Arista. On the first, ***Rock'n'Roll Again*** (1977), only Barlow and Black remained of the original band. Frayne brought in a six-piece bar band from Nevada, the Sutro Symphony Orchestra. Also featured was Nicolette Larson, who had guested on ***Tales from the Ozone***.

The last album in 1978 was ***Flying Dreams*** and indeed they were. By now only Frayne and Black were left from the early days. Norton Buffalo came back, as did Nicolette Larson. Guest vocalists included Delaney Bramlett, Clydie King and Jennifer Warnes but the sound had drifted from its earlier Country pretentions. MCA, who had taken over ABC-Paramount, re-issued the early albums just to underline the band's enduring quality.

Commander Cody soldiered on and the Commander Cody Band toured Europe on several occasions opening for Led Zeppelin and reggae star Peter Tosh. In 1981, they recorded an album for German release, ***Lose It Tonight,*** which was released in the U.S. on Peter Pan. From the album came the Emmy winning MTV video *Two Triple Cheese, Side Order of Fries*, which is now in the *Rolling Stone* magazine Video Hall of Fame and the Museum of Art Video Archives. The Commander's original artwork is to be found in the book *Star Art*.

The band has appeared in the NBC series *Police Woman* and the 1976 movie *Hollywood Boulevard*. They recorded an album for Blind Pig (via Flying Fish), ***Let's Rock***, and still comprise two of the original Lost Planet Airmen, Bill Kirchen and Bruce Barlow. George Frayne is still active with a revitalized Airmen into the 90's.

RECOMMENDED ALBUMS:
"Hot Licks, Cold Steel and Truckers' Songs" (Paramount)(1972)
"Tales from the Ozone" (Warner Bros.)(1975)
"Rock'n'Roll Again" (Arista)(1977)
"Lose It Tonight" (Peter Pan)(1981)
"Let's Rock!" (Blind Pig)(1987)

COMPTON BROTHERS

TOM COMPTON
(Vocals, Lead Guitar)
Married: Liz
BILL COMPTON
(Vocals, Guitar)
HARRY COMPTON
(Vocals, 12-String Guitar, Drums)
Married: Susan

All Born: Desloge, Missouri
Other member:
Dave Murray Bass Guitar

These three brothers started as professionals when Tom was 12, Bill 11 and Harry 7. They entered a talent contest in Rangely, Colorado, and won first prize. Colorado was just one of many homes for this young trio. Their father, a pipeline construction worker, traveled with the family in a house trailer to most of the western states and as far afield as Moose Jaw in Saskatchewan in Canada.

Shortly after winning the contest, they moved back to Missouri and won some 100 first prizes in contests. Their reputation spread and soon they were booked on the prestigious *Ozark Jubilee*. However, as they got older, school and especially military service intervened. Tom and Bill both served in the Signals Corps, with Tom stationed in Germany and Bill stationed in Korea. They continued their music, playing NCO clubs. Tom was writing most of the songs at this stage and it was at this time that they met Dave Murray, who joined the brothers.

In August 1964, they entered a five-state Country music talent contest that was held in Baltimore, Maryland. They won the first prize of $500.00 and a Columbia recording contract. They released only one single, *Still Away*, on Columbia the following March. The song had been co-written by Tom while stationed in Germany. The group decided early on to incorporate comedy and impressions in the act, with Harry, in a battered old hat with a bolt through it, as the group's comedian.

In October 1965, they signed for management with Omac, the Buck Owens/Jack McFadden organization. They became regulars on the WWVA *Wheeling Jamboree*. As their career got under way, they appeared with stars such as Owens and Roger Miller and did syndicated TV appearances with Jim & Jesse.

In 1966, the group moved over to Dot and had their first chart entry at the end of that year with *Pickin' Up the Mail*. It was over a year until they charted again, this time with *Honey*. Both of these entries were in the 60s, but it was not until 1969 that the group made a major mark with their reworking of the Gene Simmons' Pop hit *Haunted House,* which reached the Top 15. They followed this with another cover, *Charlie Brown*. This novelty song had been a major Pop success for the Coasters over a decade earlier. The Comptons' version reached the Top 20. Despite several more releases, the best they could manage between 1970 and 1975 were a pair of Top 50 singles, *Yellow River* and *Claudette* in 1972. Their final chart record was in 1975, when their ABC/Dot single *Cat's in the Cradle* just scraped into the Top 100.

RECOMMENDED ALBUMS:
"On Top of the Compton Brothers" (Dot)(1968)
"Haunted House/Charlie Brown" (Dot)(1970)
"Yellow River" (Dot)(1970)

Confederate Railroad *like their women a little on the trashy side*

CONFEDERATE RAILROAD

Formed: 1987
Members:

Danny Shirley	**Lead Vocals, Guitar**
Mark Dufresne	**Drums**
Wayne Secrest	**Bass Guitar**
Chris McDaniel	**Keyboards**
Michael Lamb	**Lead Guitar**
Gates Nichols	**Steel Guitar**

When Confederate Railroad broke onto the national scene in 1992, it was with a solid background of playing the club circuit. They are the latest in a line of acts to embrace the Outlaw/Southern Rock style of Country music. They follow in the steps of the Allman Brothers, Lynyrd Skynyrd and the Marshall Tucker Band as well as Waylon Jennings and Hank Williams, Jr. There would have been a time not so long ago, when Country was less expansive, that they would have been thought of as a Rock band, but times change.

In 1982, Danny Shirley (b. August 12, 1956, Chattanooga, Tennessee) started playing around the clubs in the Southeast with his own group. Danny had played with Travis Tritt in the house band at Miss Kitty's in Marietta, Georgia. In 1984, Danny signed with the independent Amor label. Although he had five chart entries between 1984 and 1986, none rose above the Top 75 and the most successful was his initial entry, *Love and Let Love*, in 1984.

Danny's band evolved into Confederate Railroad around 1987 and they became great favorites at Miss Kitty's. They got their tape to Rick Blackburn, the head of Atlantic Records,

Nashville Division and he signed Confederate Railroad to the label in 1991. Their debut eponymous album hit the streets in 1992. Their first single, *She Took It Like a Man*, reached the Top 40 and the follow-up, *Jesus and Mama*, climbed to the Top 5. The year was completed by *Queen of Memphis*, which went Top 3 in 1993. The ACM named Confederate Railroad "New Vocal Duet/Group of the Year" in 1992.

Confederate Railroad continued in 1993 with the Top 15 *When You Leave That Way You Can Never Go Back*. However, it was the flip-side, Chris Wall's *Trashy Women*, that caught the imagination of the radio stations and the public. The single reached the Top 10 and the outrageous and sassy music video became a favorite on CMT with Danny Shirley and the band emerging as media and public favorites. Their debut album had sold over 1 million copies by the end of October 1993.

The band started 1994 with the album track *She Never Lied*, which went Top 40 and followed with the Top 10 single *Daddy Never Was the Cadillac Kind*. At the same time, Confederate Railroad released their second album, ***Notorious***, which was Certified Gold 5 weeks after release. Confederate Railroad continues to be based in Georgia.

RECOMMENDED ALBUMS:

"Confederate Railroad" (Atlantic)(1992)
"Notorious" (Atlantic)(1994)

JOHN CONLEE

(Singer, Songwriter, Guitar)

Given Name:	**John Wayne Conlee**
Date of Birth:	**August 11, 1946**
Where Born:	**Versailles, Kentucky**
Married:	**Gale (m. 1982)**
Children:	**Rebecca, Jessica, John**

With one record, *Rose Colored Glasses*, John Conlee stepped into the limelight. In the 90's, when the video is king, John would not fit into the mold of "hunk" Country star, but he possesses one of the finest and most distinctive hard-core Country voices imaginable.

John was born on a 200-acre ranch and assisted his father with raising tobacco and looking after the animals. By the time he was 9, he had started guitar lessons, but it was for nothing more than personal pleasure. On leaving high school, John trained to be a funeral home attendant and mortician. He worked at this for six years and then decided to try his hand at dealing with the living, as music called. He did and still does maintain his mortician's license.

John became a deejay on radio stations in Fort Knox, Elizabethtown and Versailles playing Pop music. In 1971, he moved to Nashville and joined Country station WLAC-FM. During his stay with the station, John began writing with Dick Kent, who was also a deejay at WLAC. Dick, who later became John's manager, introduced him to Jim Fogelsong, then at ABC/Dot. As a result, Conlee was signed to the label in 1976.

Bud Logan, a former Jim Reeves Blue Boy, was put in charge of John's record production, a position he still maintains. John's first release, the self-penned *Back Side of Thirty,* came out on Dot in the back side of the year. Although this and his next two singles started to pick up localized support, it was in 1978 on ABC that *Rose Colored Glasses* did the trick. The song was co-written with Glenn Barber and became a Top 5 hit. He followed this with the No.1 hit, a Rafe VanHoy-Don Cook song, *Lady Lay Down*. In 1979, he went from strength to strength with another No.1. This time, the re-issue of *Backside of Thirty*, making a truism of the phrase success breeds success. 1979's other hits were *Before My Time* (Top 3) and *Baby, You're Something* (Top 10). Both of these were on MCA (which had absorbed ABC). John was named ACM's "Best New Male Vocalist" that year.

As the 80's dawned so John's success continued. Both *Friday Night Blues* and *She Can't Say That Anymore* reached the Top 3 and were partly or entirely written by Sonny Throckmorton. From here on, John Conlee the songwriter fades away and he becomes the brilliant interpreter of other writers' brilliant thoughts. Most of 1981 was not particularly successful, with his two hits being *What I Had with You* (Top 15) and *Could You Love Me (One More Time)* (Top 30). However, in the summer of that year he had a monster hit with Red Lane's wonderful song, *Miss Emily's Picture*. He followed this with his version of *Busted*; Harlan Howard's song had been a hit previously for Johnny Cash and Ray Charles in 1963. John sang it with heartfelt feeling and the sleeve of the *Busted* album sums up the lyrics admirably. His next Top 10 hit came at the end of 1982 and was the classic *I Don't Remember Loving You,* written by Harlan Howard and Bobby Braddock, which deals with a man in a mentally disturbed state who cannot (or will not) remember his ex-wife and family. Its chart placing does not fairly represent the quality of the recording.

***John Conlee** is just a Common Man*

Through 1983 and 1984, he pulled off four No.1 records in a row: *Common Man*, *I'm Only in It for the Love*, *In My Eyes* and *As Long as I'm Rockin' with You*. He closed 1984 with two further Top 5 hits, *Way Back* and *Years After You*. 1985 was John's last year with MCA and he had two hits in *Working Man* (Top 5) and *Old School* (Top 10).

In 1986, he moved over to Columbia and released the album ***Harmony,*** which yielded a Top 10 hit with the title track, the No.1 single *Got My Heart Set on You*, which stayed on the charts for over five months and the wonderfully descriptive Guy Clark song *The Carpenter*. During this year, his 1981 ***Greatest Hits*** album was Certified Gold. John's second and final album for Columbia was ***American Faces,*** from which came the Top 5 single *Domestic Life*, *Mama's Rockin' Chair,* which made it to the Top 15, and *Living Like There's No Tomorrow (Finally Got to Be Tonight)* which bombed.

He moved to Opryland's new label, 16th Avenue, in 1989, and released his debut album for them, ***Fellow Travelers***. The label closed down in 1991, and for the first time in 16 years, John was without a label.

John is a performer who gives back to society. Through his efforts, the Family Farm Defense Fund was created and he became Honorary Chairman. John is on the Board of Directors of Farm Aid and through his endeavors raised $500,000 for the fund. He moved into a 32-acre farm outside Nashville on which he works when not performing. He is also the Tourist Ambassador for the state of Tennessee and an Honorary Kentucky Colonel.

RECOMMENDED ALBUMS:

"John Conlee's Greatest Hits" (MCA)(1981)
"Greatest Hits Volume 2" (MCA)(1985)
"Conley Country" (MCA)(1986)
"Harmony" (Columbia)(1986)
"Fellow Travelers" (16th Avenue)(1991)

EARL THOMAS CONLEY

(Singer, Songwriter, Guitar)

Given Name:	**Earl Thomas Conley**
Date of Birth:	**October 17, 1941**
Where Born:	**West Portsmouth, Ohio**
Married:	**Sandra**
Children:	**Tyrone, Amy**

Whereas "E.T." used to mean Ernest Tubb, to modern Country fans it refers to Earl Thomas Conley. As a youngster he had the ambition of being either the greatest actor in the world or Jesus Christ. He didn't make the first, but got the looks of the latter.

He was born, one of eight children, into a strict Baptist family. His father, a railroad man, also played banjo, guitar, mandolin,organ and piano around the house. However, his father wasn't allowed to drink in the house and so he used to sit with his brother in the car listening to the *Grand Ole Opry* and their favorites, Jimmy Martin, Bill Monroe and Hank Williams.Young Conley started to listen to Nat King Cole, Brook Benton, Little Richard, the Rolling Stones and ZZ Top among others.

Conley learned to play guitar from his father. When he was 14, he left home when his father was laid off with the advent of diesel. He went to stay with his sister, who was married to a banker, in Ohio. She put him through high school, but when he was offered a scholarship to art school, he declined even though he was particularly adept at sculpture and painting. Instead, he hitched a ride to Denver and then on the spur of the moment, enlisted in the Army.

He was shipped out to Nuremberg, Germany, where he worked as a demolition expert, tank commander and squad leader in the U.S. Corps of Engineers. During a 30-day pass, Earl Thomas married Sandra, his childhood sweetheart. In 1962, tragedy struck when E.T.'s sister was killed in an auto crash.

During his army time, he started to appreciate Country once again. On leaving the service, E.T. joined his aunt and uncle in a Gospel group. In 1968, he started writing seriously and came to Nashville, where he was ignored. Two years later, he decided to move with his family to Huntsville, Alabama, where he worked in a steel mill.

While in Huntsville, he met Nelson Larkin, who would go on to be his producer. During 1974, E.T. signed with GRT Records as Earl Conley and all four singles released scraped into the Country chart in the 70-90 area. In 1975, he got his first break when Nelson's brother Billy Larkin recorded E.T.'s song *Leave It up to Me,* which gave him his first Top 20 hit as a writer. This was followed by Mel Street's hit with E.T.'s *Smokey Mountain Memories.* Then E.T.'s idol Conway Twitty recorded *I've Hurt Her More Than She Loves Me.*

E.T. had by now moved to Nashville and formed a songwriting and production company with Nelson Larkin. As 1977 came, E.T. signed a new record deal, this time with Warner Brothers. He got into the Country chart with *Dreaming All I Do* (Top 40) and *Middle Age Madness* (Top 50). By the time of the latter, E.T. added Thomas to his stage name. At year end, E.T.'s band, the ETC Band, had a Top 30 hit with *Stranded on a Dead End Street.*

Earl Thomas then took six months off to study philosophy and to reassess his life and career. Reunited with Larkin, he signed a fresh deal with Sunbird Records. The initial single, *Silent Treatment,* made the Top 10 but the follow-up *Fire and Smoke* went to No.1. It was *Billboard's* "Song of the Year" in 1981 and soon E.T. was being signed by Joe Gallante to RCA.

His first album, ***Black Pearl***, was released on Sunbird in 1981 and was followed up with his debut on RCA, ***Fire & Smoke***. E.T. followed with *Tell Me Why* (Top 10, 1981), *After the Love Slips Away/Smokey Mountain Memories* (Top 20) and *Heavenly Bodies* (Top 10) (both 1982). In 1982, E.T. had another No.1 hit with the title track from his 1983 album ***Somewhere Between Right and Wrong***. Also from the album came the Top 3 entry *I Have Loved You Girl (But Not Like This Before)*, which he had originally cut for GRT and now re-recorded.

Then his career went onto a different plateau. He reeled off 15 straight solo No.1's and went into the record books as being the first artist in any genre to have 4 No.1 singles from one album.

The album was the 1983 release ***Don't Make It Easy for Me***. The singles were *Your Love's on the Line, Holding Her and Loving You* (1983), *Don't Make It Easy for Me* and *Angel in Disguise* (1984).

In 1984 E.T.'s new album, ***Treadin' Water,*** yielded three No.1s: *Chance of Loving You* and *Honor Bound* (both 1984) and *Love Don't Care (Whose Heart It Breaks)* (1985). In addition, E.T. had a Top 10 duet in 1984, *All Tangled up in Love*, with Gus Hardin. The inevitable ***Greatest Hits*** album followed that year and like its predecessors was successful in the album listings. It was actually "greatest hits plus" and presented E.T. with the chart topping *Nobody Falls Like a Fool* (1985) and *Once in a Blue Moon* (1986). During 1986, the album ***Too Many Times*** was shipped. In many ways this was different. Apart from the shorter haircut that E.T. sported, there was a shortage of songs written by E.T. Up to then, most of the tracks were written by him with Nelson Larkin or Randy Scruggs. The title track was a duet with soul diva Anita Pointer which went Top 3. Also the sleeve puts E.T.'s name before Larkin for the first time with regard to producer credits. However, there were another three chart toppers: *I Can't Win for Losin' You* (1986), *That Was a Close One* and *Right from the Start* (both 1987).

In 1986, E.T. again took stock of his life and career. His father had just died and then E.T. started to experience financial problems and severe vocal strain that was originally thought to be throat cancer. The volatile perfectionist started to look at himself and became more relaxed and eventually emerged to return to the studio.

Once again, he achieved the remarkable tally of four No. 1's from one album. The album was ***The Heart of It All***, released in

Earl Thomas Conley *with Soul diva* ***Anita Pointer***

1988, after this two year lay-off. This time, he was produced by Emory Gordy, Jr., and Randy Scruggs. There was a difference. A new dynamism seemed to be in his work. There were just two songs from his own pen. He started off 1988 with two No.1's from the pen of Bob McDill, *What She Is* and *We Believe in Happy Endings* (a duet with Emmylou Harris). These were followed in 1989 by *What I'd Say* and *Love Out Loud*. The year was completed by E.T.'s first failure in many years, *You Must Not Be Drinking Enough*, which went Top 30.

In 1990, E.T. achieved another feat with the release of a second volume of ***Greatest Hits***. Two singles released failed to make the No.1 slot: *Bring Back Your Love to Me* (Top 15) and *Who's Gonna Tell Her Goodbye* (Top 70) (both 1990). However, E.T. came back strongly in 1991, with *Shadow of a Doubt*, which went Top 10. He followed this with the magnificent duet with Keith Whitley, *Brotherly Love*, which went Top 3.

With ***Yours Truly***, in late 1991, E.T. produced a watershed album. Using the services of three teams of producers, Larry Michael Lee and Josh Leo, Blake Mevis and Richard Landis, he produced a first rate Country album. Country purists may say that this is E.T.'s first Country album. It was certainly his most straight ahead. His musicians included Jerry Douglas, Sam Bush, Bernie Leadon and Jimmie Fadden. One cut, *The Perfect Picture (to Fit My Frame of Mind)* is straight out of the Honky-Tonk textbook and E.T.'s *Borrowed Money* is as good a slab of Country-Rock as you'll find anywhere. However, the two singles from the album that charted, *Hard Days and Honky Tonk Nights* (Top 40) and *If Only Your Eyes Could Lie* (Top 75), showed that E.T. had reached another crisis point in his career. Since 1992, Earl Thomas Conley is without a record label.

RECOMMENDED ALBUMS:

"Greatest Hits" (RCA Victor)(1985)
"The Heart of It All" (RCA Victor)(1989)
"Greatest Hits Vol. II" (RCA)(1990)
"Yours Truly" (RCA)(1991)

COODER BROWNE

Formed: 1976
Members:
Larry Franklin Fiddle, Mandolin, Guitar, Vocals
David Haworth Piano, Vocals
Skip Tumbleson Bass, Harmonica, Vocals
Dale Bolin Percussion, Vocals

The Austin-based band got its name from an expression that emanated from Victoria, Texas, "drunker than Cooder Browne." It was a group that threatened to happen in a big way.

Larry Franklin, the group's principal writer, became interested in music at the age of 7 and learned to play fiddle from his father. Larry was Texas State fiddle champion on several occasions and in 1971, at the age of 16, he became World Champion. He played in various local bands as well as one in Germany. David's early influence was Ludwig van Beethoven. Skip was an "air-force brat" who was raised in Europe. He joined his first band in Germany as vocalist. Dale came from Lawton, Oklahoma, but moved to St. Louis and then in 1968 to Sherman, Texas, where he met Skip.

Their brand of Western Swing attracted such attention that just two years after their formation, Cooder Browne was personally signed by Willie Nelson to his Austin-based Lone Star Records. This was obviously important because it brought them into the Nelson "family" and also ensured that they had major distribution via Lone Star's association with Polygram.

Their first recordings appeared on the compilation ***Lone Star 6-Pak, Volume I***. In 1977, they were nominated for "Instrumental Group of the Year" by the Country Music Association. They recorded their initial album at Capricorn Studio in Macon, Georgia, but shortly afterward Lone Star folded. The group never got the same opportunity again. They were again nominated by the CMA, which was a surprise for a group without a label.

RECOMMENDED ALBUMS:

There are none, but they have two tracks on "Lone Star 6-Pak, Volume I" (Lone Star)(1978).

RY COODER

(Singer, Songwriter, Composer, Arranger, Record Producer, Slide Guitar, Mandolin, Banjo, Guitar, Accordion)
Date of Birth: March 15, 1947
Where Born: Los Angeles, California

During the 70's, Ry Cooder emerged as one of the most formidable sessionmen and producers to burst onto the Country-Rock and Rock scene in Los Angeles. He was acknowledged as one of the finest slide guitar players ever and his quirky adaptation of Country and Blues has made him a legend and cult hero in his own time.

Ry was given his first guitar, a Sears Silvertone tenor 4-String, when he was 3 years old and learned to play from listening to his parents' Folk records. When he was 8, he was exposed to the Blues for the first time, when his folks bought him a Josh White album. Ry worked hard and mastered White's playing style. When he was 10, his father got him a Martin guitar and tried to have him taught properly, but the lessons were not to Ry's liking and he soon stopped taking them.

By the time he was 13, Ry had taken on board all the material he could listen to. At that time, he became interested in Appalachian finger-style picking and in his quest for a teacher, gravitated to the Folk scene in L.A. and in particular, the Ash Grove. Here he studied at the feet of the masters, including the legendary Rev. Gary Davis. He would give them $5.00 to get them to play for him and then learn.

When he was 16, he was persuaded to play at the Ash Grove to tumultuous applause. Soon, he was appearing regularly, and later that year he formed a Blues duo with Jackie DeShannon, who would go on to fame as the writer of *Needles and Pins* and *Bette Davis Eyes* and who became a successful recording star. However, the duo was not successful and they went their separate ways.

Ry was continuously improving his playing and by 1964, he had mastered banjo and started on the road to being the finest bottleneck guitarist in the world. He studied Delta Blues and perfected his playing using a glass bottleneck as used by the early Bluesmen. Later that year, he met Taj Mahal and the two struck up a friendship after jamming together at the Teenage Fair in L.A. They put together a Blues-Rock band called the Rising Sons and although Columbia wanted to release an album, the project was never completed and the band broke up.

After the disbanding of Rising Sons in 1967, Cooder appeared on Taj Mahal's self-titled album and then moved on to play and arrange on the first two Buddha albums for Captain Beefheart, ***Safe As Milk*** (1967) and ***Drop out Boogie*** (1968). It was an unlikely combination, yet a look at Cooder's work shows that he has not been afraid to push back his musical boundaries.

Through arranger/producer/keyboardist Jack Nitzsche, Ry went to England, in 1969, to play on the soundtrack score for the movie *Candy*. While in the U.K., Ry got close to the Rolling Stones and appeared on their 1969 album ***Let It Bleed,*** playing slide guitar and mandolin. His revitalized style of Blues mandolin would also appear on the Stones' 1971 ***Sticky Fingers*** and John Sebastian's 1974 ***Tarzana Kid***.

1970 was a year in which Ry became more and more in demand as a session player. He appeared on Marc Benno's eponymous album, Randy Newman's ***12 Songs*** and Gordon Lightfoot's ***Sit Down Young Stranger***. In addition, with James Burton, Buddy Emmons, John David Souther, Glenn Frey, Doug Kershaw, Jim Gordon, Larry Knetchel and Joe Osborn, Ry was a part of the aggregation known as Longbranch Pennywhistle, which released one self-titled album on Amos. He also worked on the soundtrack for Mick Jagger's 1970 movie *Performance,* and released his first self-titled solo album for Reprise with the help of Van Dyke Parks and Lenny Waronker. Of particular interest on that collection was Ry's reading of the Blind Alfred Reed fiddle tune, *How Can a Poor Man Stand Such Times and Live*.

Ry spent a lot of 1971 touring with Captain Beefheart and it was not until 1972 that his new album, ***Into the Purple Valley***, was released. It entered the Pop Album charts and became a great favorite in the Netherlands, where it went Gold. Ry continued appearing on other artists' albums, and the notable ones for 1971 and 1972 were Little Feat's eponymous debut, Buffy Sainte Marie's ***She Used to Wanna Be a Ballerina,*** David Blue's ***Stories***, the Everly Brothers' ***Stories We Could Tell*** and Randy Newman's ***Sail Away***. He also teamed up with Mick Jagger, Bill Wyman, Charlie Watts (of the Stones) and Nicky Hopkins for the project ***Jamming With Edward***.

1973 saw the release of Ry's third album, ***Boomer's Story,*** which included *Maria Elena* played on a Spanish guitar, *Rally 'Round the Flag* and Dan Penn-Chip Moman's *Dark End of the Street* (which would be revitalized in 1991 by the Commitments). His 1974 album, ***Paradise and Lunch***, was wide reaching and included Gospel material as well as *Ditty Wa Ditty,* which featured legendary Jazz pianist Earl "Fatha" Hines. That year, Ry contributed to Johnny Cash's ***John R. Cash*** album.

Before the release of his next album, he traveled to meet two musicians that would greatly influence that project. He learned Hawaiian slack-key guitar from Gabby Pahinui and persuaded Warner Brothers to issue an album of Pahinui's music (***The Gabby Pahinui Hawaiian Band***). He also visited with Flaco Jiminez in Austin, Texas, and learned to play the accordion in the Jiminez style of Tex-Mex. Ry's ***Chicken Skin Music*** was released in 1976 and is largely a continuation of Cooder's desire to dig deeper into musical styles and experiment. Only one track fails miserably, that being Joe and Audrey Allison's *He'll Have to Go,* which doesn't sit right with a Tex-Mex feel.

In 1977, he put together the Chicken Skin Revue, which featured Jiminez and three Gospel singers. The response in the U.S. was surpassed by the reaction in Europe. A concert in San Francisco was recorded that year and released as ***Show Time***. The following year, Ry gave support to Rodney Crowell's album ***Ain't Living Long Like This,*** and Ry released the 20's and 30's influenced ***Jazz*** album, which tips its hat particularly at Jazz cornetist Bix Beiderbeck. Ry was involved with Jack Nitzsche again, this time on the soundtrack of the Richard Pryor movie *Blue Collar*.

Throughout 1979 and the 80's, Cooder continued producing high quality albums, most notably ***Bop Till You Drop*** (1979), which included *Little Sister,* which had been recorded by Elvis and would be a hit for Dwight Yoakam. This was the first ever digitally recorded Rock album.

In 1980, Ry released ***Borderline***, which featured John Hiatt and then he wrote the music for the soundtrack (album) for Walter Hill's movie *The Long Riders,* the story of the James-Younger Gang which starred the Carradine, Keach, Quaid and Guest brothers. The following year, Ry was back sessioning with Little Feat on their ***Hoy-Hoy!*** In 1982, Ry released his album ***The Slide Area*** and the following year, he appeared on Eric Clapton's ***Money and Cigarettes***.

During 1984, Ry was busy with the score for the highly praised movie *Paris, Texas,* which starred Harry Dean Stanton, Nastassia Kinski and Dean Stockwell. It was considered that the music was a contributing factor to the movie's success. Ry's next movie project was in 1986, when he was particularly requested by director Michelle Manning for the film version of Ross MacDonald's *Blue City* and Ry included on the soundtrack, his version of Johnny Cash's *Don't Take Your Love to Town*. That year Warner Brothers dug into the vaults and released a series of "Best of" albums that included ***Why Don't You Try Me Tonight?-The Best of Ry Cooder***.

RECOMMENDED ALBUMS:

In their way every album is of interest, but of particular note to Country music followers are these:
"Ry Cooder" (Reprise)(1970)
"Into the Purple Valley" (Reprise)(1972)
"Chicken Skin Music" (Reprise)(1976)
"Show Time" (Warner Brothers)(1977)
"The Slide Area" (Warner Brothers)(1982)
"Paris, Texas" (soundtrack)(Warner Brothers)(1985)
"Blue City" (Warner Brothers)(1986)
"Why Don't You Try Me Tonight?-The Best of Ry Cooder" (Warner Brothers)(1986)

SPADE COOLEY

(Band Leader, Fiddle, Singer, Actor)

Given Name:	**Donnell Clyde Cooley**
Date of Birth:	**December 17, 1910**
Where Born:	**Pack Saddle Creek, Grand, Oklahoma**
Married:	**1. Unknown** **2. Ella Mae Evans (m. 1945)(dec'd.)**
Children:	**2 sons, 1 daughter**
Date of Death:	**November 23, 1969**

During the 40's and 50's, Spade Cooley was the King of Western Swing on the West Coast. He fronted the largest band ever assembled in Country music. His sobriquet came about because of his luck in playing poker. That luck didn't extend to his personal life and most of the last eight years of his life were spent in prison.

When he was 4, Spade's family relocated to Oregon. Although his family was very poor, he was classically trained, playing both violin and cello in the school orchestra. This was not unexpected as both his father and grandfather were talented fiddle players. By the time he was 8, Spade had made his professional debut playing fiddle with his father.

In 1930, the family, in an attempt to get out of the poverty trap, moved to Modesto, California. Spade went to Los Angeles to try his luck there musically without success. He returned to Modesto, getting a gig in a club for $15 a night and sitting in with various bands. Down on his luck again, he returned to L.A. in 1934 and got parts as an extra in several Westerns for RKO, Universal, Warner, Lippert and Columbia and also acted as Roy Rogers' stand-in at Republic. (See Movie Section.)

Cooley toured for a while as Roy Rogers' fiddle player, and sang with the Riders of the Purple Sage. In 1941, he started his recording career while playing with Cal Shrum's band. Then in 1942, he took over leadership of the band formed by Jimmy Wakely at the Venice Pier Ballroom in Santa Monica, California. Cooley featured three fiddle players and three vocalists (Tex Williams, Deuce Spriggins and Smokey Rogers), as well as steel guitarist Joaquin Murphy.

The band moved from the Venice Pier to the Riverside Rancho in 1943 and then to the Santa Monica Ballroom. In 1945, Spade and His Orchestra signed to OKeh Records and their initial release, *Shame on You,* went to No.1 for 9 weeks and stayed on the chart for 32 weeks with the flip-side, *A Pair of Broken Hearts,* going Top 10. Spade and the band completed the year with *I've Taken All I'm Gonna Take from You,* which peaked in the Top 5. That year, Spade married his second wife, Ella Mae, who also played fiddle in the band. In 1946, he switched to Columbia but continued his chart popularity. *Detour* and the flip-side, *You Can't Break My Heart,* both reached the Top 3 and in 1947, *Crazy 'Cause*

I Love You reached the Top 5. On all these hits, Tex Williams was the featured vocalist.

However, Williams was soon to be fired because as his popularity grew, he had demanded more money. In June 1946, Cooley told him to go and Williams did, taking a lot of the band with him.

In 1947-48, Cooley made the move to TV. He appeared on KTLA Hollywood, the first commercially licensed TV station in Los Angeles on a show called The *Hoffman Hayride*. At this point, Spade started to call himself "the King of Western Swing." The band appeared in several movies at this time including *Chatterbox, The Singing Bandit, The Singing Sheriff, Outlaws of the Rockies* and *Texas Panhandle*. He also appeared in musical shorts *King of Western Swing* and *Spade Cooley and His Orchestra* in 1949. All of these appearances enhanced the band's popularity.

The *Hoffman Hayride* became the most popular Saturday night show in L.A. with an estimated three-quarters of all TV sets in the area tuned in to it. In 1950, Spade signed with Decca and in 1953, the band released four consecutive singles on the label, the sides being *Nashville Bounce, Baltimore Bounce, Rochester Reel, San Fernando Square, Jersey Jig, Santa Monica Rambler, Seattle Square* and *Y-Knot Rag*. In 1954, they issued *Anita/The Cryin' Waltz*. However, dark clouds were soon on the horizon. At the start of the 50's, Spade suffered a series of heart attacks and then musical tastes changed as the Lawrence Welk sound became the in thing. Spade's program's appeal was waning and he tried to pull back his audience. He replaced his band with an all-girl one, but that didn't work.

Spade's life was not helped by a severe drinking problem. When he was sober, he was affability itself but once drunk he was a demon. He and Ella Mae also had problems with their marriage. She had now left him, but Cooley wouldn't accept this, and had to see her. He started a business project to build a recreational park in the Mojave Desert called Water Wonderland, which was running into financial problems. On April 3, 1961, following an argument, he beat and kicked his wife to death in front of their 14-year old daughter who was forced to witness the event.

The media had a field day and on August 22, Spade was sentenced to life imprisonment. In the middle of the trial proceedings, he suffered another heart attack and was sent to the medical detention center at Vacaville. He was a model prisoner who helped fellow inmates learn to play musical instruments and played for them. Without the alcohol to ruin him, he was fine. He applied for parole and in view of his behavior, it was in the cards that when the parole board met in early 1970, it would be granted. He was given permission to entertain a 3,000-strong audience at a sheriff's benefit in Oakland, California.

He received a warm reception from the crowd. After the show, he went backstage and had another heart attack and died.

RECOMMENDED ALBUMS:

"Roy Rogers Souvenir Album" (10" album)(RCA Victor)(1952)
"Rompin' Stompin' Singin' Swingin'" (Bear Family Germany)(1983) [With Tex Williams]
"Spade Cooley Volumes 1 and 3" (Club of Spade) [With Noel Boggs]
"Historic Edition" (Columbia) [With Joaquin Murphy]
"Swingin' the Devil's Dream" (Charly UK)(1985)

RITA COOLIDGE

(Singer, Songwriter, Piano, Actress)

Date of Birth:	**May 1, 1944**
Where Born:	**Nashville, Tennessee**
Married:	**1. Kris Kristofferson (m. 1973) (div. 1980)**
Children:	**Casey (daughter)**

This part Cherokee "Delta Lady" has managed to tread lightly in Country, Rock and Pop and to rack up hits in all three genres. Her appeal has helped her to sell records throughout the world.

Rita grew up on a farm in Nashville and at age 2 started singing in a church choir with her sisters, Priscilla (who later married Booker T.) and Linda. She was taught piano at an early age. When she was 15, her family moved to Florida. She decided that she wanted to teach art, and for a while art and music co-existed. She formed the Rock band R.C. and the Moonpies, playing around the Florida area while she studied for her master's degree in fine arts at Florida State University.

However, Rita gave up her studies and went to Memphis for a year to do voice-overs on commercials and sing back-up for, among others, Delaney and Bonnie (she sang on their debut album), Eric Clapton, Dave Mason, Graham Nash and Stephen Stills. She did some session work at Sun studios and then cut a single for Pepper Records, *Turn Around and Love You/Walking in the Morning*, which did well locally.

Rita then moved to California in 1969, with Delaney and Bonnie as one of their "Friends." She toured with the group on three occasions, enhancing her reputation with her fellow performers as well as the audiences. Leon Russell wrote *Delta Lady* as a tribute to her, and Joe Cocker had a major hit with his recording of the song. By 1970, Rita had joined the Joe Cocker/Leon Russell 40-plus aggregation known as Mad Dogs and Englishmen. A double live album and a film were made of the U.S. tour. Rita also went with them when they toured Europe.

In 1970, Rita met producer David Anderle and this resulted in her being signed to A & M Records. Her eponymous album was released the following year and boasted luminaries from Country and Rock, including Ry Cooder, Chris Ethridge, Booker T., Graham Nash, Leon Russell, Stephen Stills, Clarence White and Bobby Womack. The album fared well, but it was her follow-up album, ***Nice Feelin'***, that made an impact on the charts. By now, Rita had formed the Dixie Flyers, which comprised lead guitarists Marc Benno and Charlie Freeman, Mike Utley on organ and piano, bass player Tommy McClure and drummer Sammy Creason. They played dates in Britain and Canada.

During 1971, a singular event changed Rita's life. While at Los Angeles International Airport, she met Kris Kristofferson. They instantly became friends. 1972 saw the release of Rita's most successful album, ***The Lady's Not for Sale***. Soon, Rita broke up her band and joined Kristofferson. In 1973, they married and became cast members of NBC-TV's *Music Country*. They released their first album together, ***Full Moon***, which went Gold in 1975. From it came the Grammy winning single, *From the Bottle to the Bottom*, which was named "Best Country Vocal Performance by a Duo or Group." They scraped into the Country charts with *A Song I'd Like to Sing*, which was a Pop Top 50 success and in 1974, Tom Jans' *Loving Arms* also made the Top 100. In 1973, Rita appeared in the movie *Pat Garrett and Billy the Kid*, with Kristofferson.

That same year, Rita had a new solo album, ***Fall Into Spring***, from which came the Country basement level chart entry *Mama Lou*, and then she became pregnant. On returning to active duty in 1975, Rita had two albums on the market: a solo, ***It's Only Love***, and a duet with Kris on Monument, ***Breakaway***. From the latter came the Billy Swan song *Lover Please*, which netted them their second Grammy in the same category. They also charted Country with *Rain*.

Rita made an appearance in the Streisand/Kristofferson movie *A Star is Born* in 1976. 1977 was the year Rita's career climbed another notch or two. She released the album ***Anytime...Anywhere*** (with backup vocals from Kim Carnes), which attained Platinum status that same year. However, it was the overwhelming success of her singles that suddenly made her an international star. Boz Scaggs' *We're All Alone* started the ball rolling. It reached the Pop Top 10 and was Certified Gold in 1978. In the U.K. the single also reached the national chart Top 10. The song was not Country, yet reached the Top 90 in the Country charts. *(Your Love Has Lifted Me) Higher and Higher*, her follow-up single, went Gold the year of release. ***Love Me Again***, her 1978 album, also went Gold the year of release and the title single reached the Top 70 on the Pop chart. Country listeners flipped the record and made it a double-sided hit, with *The Jealous Kind* preferred. She also charted Pop with the Boz Scaggs' song *Slow Dancer*. During that year, she made another film appearance, this time in Kris' movie *Convoy*.

The long-awaited duet album with Kris, ***Natural Act***, came out in 1978. However, the act seemed to be falling apart and Rita's 1979 single, *I'd Rather Leave While I'm in Love,* from the album ***Satisfied,*** seemed prophetic. Shortly after, her marriage to Kris ended in separation and finally divorce. This single was the only one of Rita's records that fared better in the Country charts than it did in the Pop charts, by reaching No.32 Country and No. 38 Pop.

With all the inherent trauma of a break-up, there was no album release in 1980, save for ***Greatest Hits (The Very Best Of)***. However, Rita did rack up another crossover hit with the duet with Glen Campbell *Something 'bout You Baby I Like,* on Capitol. It peaked in the Pop Top 50 and the Top 60 on the Country listings. In 1981, the new album, ***Heartbreak Radio,*** yielded another hit, *Fool That I Am,*

*Rita Coolidge with **Kris Kristofferson***

which was also a crossover success, peaking in the Top 50 on the Pop charts and Top 80 on the Country charts.

With the release of the James Bond movie *Octopussy*, Rita found herself with a new project. She sang the theme song, *All Time High*, which could be found on her album of the year, ***Never Let You Go***. The following year saw her final album for A & M, ***Inside the Fire***. Her next record appearance was in 1986, when she duetted with Rupert Holmes on *Touch and Go* for Polygram.

RECOMMENDED ALBUMS:

"Rita Coolidge" (A & M)(1971)
"Full Moon" (A & M)(1973) [With Kris Kristofferson]
"Breakaway" (Monument)(1975) [With Kris Kristofferson]
"Anytime...Anywhere" (A & M)(1977)
"Love Me Again" (A & M)(1978)
"Natural Act" (A & M)(1978) [With Kris Kristofferson]
"We're All Alone" (Hallmark UK)

COON CREEK GIRLS

Formed: 1937

LILY MAY LEDFORD
(Vocals, Banjo, Fiddle)
Given Name: Lily May Ledford
Date of Birth: March 17, 1917
Where Born: Pilot, Kentucky
Married: Unknown
Children: Benny Joe Pearson, Robert Glenn, James Preston Pennington (J.P., formerly of Exile), Barbara Ann Pennington
Date of Death: July 14, 1985

ROSIE LEDFORD
(Singer, Guitar, Banjo)
Given Name: Rosa Charlotte Ledford
Date of Birth: August 16, 1915
Where Born: Pilot, Kentucky
Married: Clarence Vernon Foley
Children: Clarence Vernon, Jr., Clyde Benjamin, Lois Faye

DAISY LANGE
(Singer, String Bass, Fiddle)
Given Name: Evelyn Lange

VIOLET KOEHLER
(Singer, Guitar, Mandolin)
Given Name: Esther Koehler

BLACK EYED SUSAN
(Vocals, String Bass)
Given Name: Minnie Lena Ledford
Date of Birth: October 10, 1922
Where Born: Pilot, Kentucky

A fixture on the *Renfro Valley Barn Dance* for over fifteen years, the Coon Creek Girls developed into one of the best known all-women string bands in early Country music. Whereas many other women performers of the 1930's tended toward sentimental or even cowboy songs (e.g. Patsy Montana, the Girls of the Golden West and the Three Little Maids), the Coon Creek Girls were distinctive because they all played their own instruments, and because they used a repertoire of southern mountain tunes. When Eleanor Roosevelt asked them to play in Washington, D.C., for King George VI and Queen Elizabeth in 1939, she chose them knowing that they reflected an authentic mountain style filtered through their own remarkable talent.

Though the personnel of the Coon Creek Girls varied over the years, the original cornerstone of the group was the remarkably talented Lily May Ledford. She was born in a beautiful but remote section of Powell County in eastern Kentucky called Big River Gorge. The seventh child of a family of ten boys and four girls, she grew up on a tenant farm, enriched by the string band music her own family made. By the time she was a teenager, she had joined her sister Rosie and brother Cayen in a band called the Red River Ramblers, which played for local square dances. Lily May learned both fiddle and banjo, picking up repertoire from her family, especially her brother Kelly. He had absorbed banjo tunes and styles while working in the mines of Pike County.

In 1936, the Ramblers auditioned for one of the WLS talent scouts who routinely made the rounds in the upland South, and Lily May was chosen to come to Chicago and appear on the WLS *Barn Dance*. There she met entrepreneur and announcer John Lair, who was fascinated with her and signed her to a five-year personal management contract. For a time, she was was a featured soloist on the *Barn Dance*, and soon became so popular that *Stand By!*, the WLS magazine, even ran a comic strip about her. When Lair moved his cast to Cincinnati, and then to Renfro Valley, he decided to form an all-girl string band around Lily May, and the Coon Creek Girls were born.

Originally, the quartet consisted of Lily May, her sister Rosie, and two new musicians from the Chicago area, "Daisy" Lange and "Violet" Koehler. By design, all the girls were given the stage names of flowers, and used as their theme tune, the old song, *You're a Flower Blooming in the Wildwood*. They made their radio and live debut on October 9, 1937, in a show from the Cincinnati Music Hall.

The girls were an immediate hit on the new *Renfro Valley Barn Dance*, and in 1938, they recorded what would become their only major label session for Vocalion (ARC). They did traditional songs like *Little Birdie* and *Pretty Polly* and uptempo efforts like *Banjo*

Pickin' Girl and *Sowing on the Mountain*. However, their real success was on radio, not records, and in touring with Lair's troupes, as the moved around the South and Midwest. The band even turned down an offer from the *Grand Ole Opry*, because they could make far more money with Lair.

By 1939 though, the original quartet split up, with Koehler and Lange leaving for other work with the Callahan Brothers' Blue Ridge Mountain Folk in Dallas. A third Ledford sister, Minnie, replaced them, under the name Black Eyed Susan. This trio, or one with other performers from Renfro Valley occasionally replacing one of the members, continued on at Renfro Valley until 1957, doing occasional recordings for the local Redbird label, and for Capitol.

Lily May Ledford pursued a solo career in later years, recording under her own name for Voyager and with a "comeback" band for County. She wrote a delightful autobiography, *Coon Creek Girl,* in 1980 and passed away in 1985. Her son, J.P. Pennington, is a popular songwriter who helped to found the Pop-Country group Exile. Violet played for a while on the *Boone County Jamboree*, eventually married one of Lily May's brothers, and settled in Berea, Kentucky. Daisy married and settled in Indiana, retiring from music, but often playing at fiddling contests. A modern Bluegrass band, the New Coon Creek Girls was formed in the 1980's and appeared on records and at numerous festivals. CKW

RECOMMENDED ALBUMS:

"Early Radio Favorites" (Old Homestead) [Most of the original Vocalion recordings from 1938]

"Lily May, Rosie & Susie" (County) [Newer recordings]

Lily May Ledford:

"Banjo Pickin' Girl" (Voyager) [New concert appearances by Lily May]

WILMA LEE AND STONEY COOPER

STONEY COOPER

(Fiddle, Singer)

Given Name:	**Dale Troy Cooper**
Date of Birth:	**October 16, 1918**
Where Born:	**Harmon, West Virginia**
Date of Death:	**March 22, 1977**

WILMA LEE COOPER

(Singer, Songwriter, Guitar, Banjo)

Given Name:	**Wilma Leigh Leary**
Date of Birth:	**February 7, 1921**
Where Born:	**Valley Head, West Virginia**
Children:	**Carolee (Carol Lee Cooper)**

Wilma Lee and Stoney Cooper rank as one of the great husband-wife teams in Country music. Although a force for tradition in the industry, they, like Roy Acuff, Molly O'Day, Johnnie and Jack, and the Louvin Brothers, helped bridge the gap between the older and newer styles. After nearly four decades of performing, half of them at the *Grand Ole Opry*, Stoney's death left Wilma to carry on the tradition.

Natives of opposite ends of mountainous Randolph County, West Virginia, Stoney hailed from a family of fiddlers while Wilma came from a family of sacred singers. After Stoney finished high school, he worked for a time as fiddler for Rusty Hiser's Green Valley Boys at WMMN Fairmont, West Virginia. In the meantime the Singing Leary Family began their musical career at WSVA Harrisonburg, Virginia. When the Green Valley Boys dissolved, Stoney came back home and soon found that the Learys needed a fiddler. Jacob Leary offered Stoney the job and Stoney and Wilma soon became both singing pals and romantic partners. After the Learys moved to WWVA Wheeling, West Virginia, the couple married in 1941 and soon embarked on their own career at a string of radio stations: KMMJ Grand Island, Nebraska; WIBC Indianapolis; WMMN Fairmont; KLCN Blytheville, Arkansas; and finally WWNC Asheville, North Carolina, in 1947.

While in Asheville, the Coopers began recording for Jim Stanton's Rich-R-Tone company, doing a second session for that firm later in the year when they relocated to WWVA *Wheeling Jamboree*, where they remained for a decade and became one of the most popular acts in the station's history. In 1949, they began a five-year association with Columbia Records that yielded most of the songs that became their musical trademarks, including *Sunny Side of the Mountain*, *Thirty Pieces of Silver*, *West Virginia Polka*, *White Rose* and those memorable accounts of the Crucifixion, *Legend of the Dogwood Tree* and *Walking My Lord Up Calvary Hill*. Like Roy Acuff's Smoky Mountain Boys and Molly O'Day's Cumberland Mountain Folks, the Coopers built their Clinch Mountain Clan around the acoustical instrumentation of Dobro, fiddle and mandolin. These were generally in the capable hands of musicians such as Will Carver, Burkett ("Josh") Graves, Tex Logan, Blaine Stewart, James Carson and Stoney himself.

In 1955, Wilma Lee and Stoney switched to the new Acuff-Rose-owned Hickory Records. In 1956, they scored two minor hits with *Each Season Changes You* and *Cheated Too*, which led to their moving to Nashville and joining the *Grand Ole Opry* in 1957. 1959 produced the Top 5 Country hits *Come Walk with Me*, *Big Midnight Special* and *There's a Big Wheel* and in 1960, they scored with the Top 20 hits *Johnny My Love (Grandma's Diary)* and *This Ole House*, with their final chart record being the 1961 Top 10 *Wreck on the Highway*. Although chart successes, none of these had the lasting impact of their earlier standards.

Stoney suffered a heart attack early in 1963, and from that point on, his health was never quite what it had been, although the Coopers kept on working. They had a total of three albums and numerous singles in their eight years with Hickory. They went to Decca in 1965, where an attempt to modernize their

Stars of the Renfro Valley Barn Dance, the ***Coon Creek Girls***

Wilma Lee and Stoney Cooper

traditional sound did not come off very well. Later recordings with Skylite, Gusto and Rounder were more satisfying in spite of Stoney's declining vigor. He finally passed away in the spring of 1977, a true gentleman of the old school.

Wilma Lee kept on going. Her band took on more of a Bluegrass sound. Although the Coopers had sometimes used a banjo earlier, Wilma nearly always had one. She completed an unfinished second album for Rounder and cut new ones for Leather and Rebel. Although she has slowed down a little in the 90's, Wilma Lee did maintain a regular touring schedule for a dozen years on her own. Moreover, daughter Carolee with her Carol Lee Singers has for many years provided vocal backup on a regular basis for nearly all the *Grand Ole Opry* acts.

IMT

RECOMMENDED ALBUMS:

"Sacred Songs" (Columbia Harmony)(1960)
"There's a Big Wheel" (Hickory)(1960)
"Family Favorites" (Hickory)(1962)
"Songs of Inspiration" (Hickory)(1963)
"Sunny Side of the Mountain" (Columbia Harmony)(1966)
"Wilma Lee and Stoney Cooper" (Rounder)(1976)
"Early Recordings" (County)(1979) [Note: Columbia Masters]
Wilma Lee Cooper only:
"A Daisy a Day" (Leather)(1980) [Re-released on Rebel]
"White Rose" (Rebel)(1981)
"Wilma Lee Cooper" (Rounder)(1981) [Six of the 11 cuts are by Wilma Lee and Stoney Cooper]

COWBOY COPAS

(Singer, Songwriter, Guitar)

Given Name:	**Lloyd Estel Copas**
Date of Birth:	**July 15, 1913**
Place of Birth:	**Adams County, Ohio**
Married:	**Edna Lucille Markins**
Children:	**Kathy Loma, Gary Lee, Michael Lane**
Date of Death:	**March 5, 1963**

Cowboy Copas emerged as one of America's ranking Country singers at the end of WWII and remained so for several years. His career took a down-swing in the later 50's but bounced back in 1960.

Copas grew up in the hilly farm country of Adams County, Ohio, near the rural communities of Blue Creek and Lynx, attending school until reaching the age of 14. He gained some of his earliest musical experience with a local string band, Fred Evans and his Hen Cacklers. "Cope," as his friends called him, became acquainted with a young fiddler from the neighboring community of Peebles, named Lester Vernon Storer, who subsequently took the name of "Natchee the Indian." They started their career on radio as the result of a dare, by going to Cincinnati and entering a contest. Somewhere along the line, the two hooked up with a promoter named Larry Sunbrock, who held a series of staged fiddling contests between the showy Natchee and such notables as Curly Fox, Clark Kessinger and Clayton McMichen.

During 1938-1940, Copas worked on various radio stations, usually for short periods. Perhaps the places where audiences got to know his voice best were those near his home territory such as WCHS Charleston, WSAZ Huntington and various stations in Cincinnati including WLW and WKRC. By 1940, he had acquired a band known as the Gold Star Rangers, consisting of Fiddlin' Red Herron and Rusty Gabbard, which played at WCHS Charleston and WNOX Knoxville.

Despite his broad range of radio experience, survival had been difficult for Copas until WWII brought an upswing in the economy. He went to WLW and joined the cast of *Boone County Jamboree,* and in 1943 Cope received an ever bigger opportunity when he replaced Eddy Arnold as lead vocalist for Pee Wee King's Golden West Cowboys at WSM and the *Grand Ole Opry.* Like Arnold, Copas used this experience to successfully re-launch his solo career. For Copas it now meant that he didn't have to starve anymore.

In 1946, Copas signed with King Records and his initial release of *Filipino Baby* became the label's first Country hit. The song dated back to the Spanish-American War and Philippine Insurrection of 1898 and had been released by Billy Cox and Cliff Hobbs in 1937, but the somewhat modernized version by Copas combined with the WWII experience gave it a whole new life. Cope became a regular on the *Grand Ole Opry* in 1946, remaining there until his death.

A string of top numbers followed on King: *Signed, Sealed and Delivered* (Top 3), *Tennessee Waltz* (Top 3), *Tennessee Moon* (Top 10) and *Breeze* (Top 15) (all 1948), *I'm Waltzing with Tears in My Eyes* (Top 15), *Candy Kisses* (Top 5) and *Hangman's Boogie* (Top 15) (all 1949) among them. His covers of *Tennessee Waltz* and *Candy Kisses* scored high in the charts.

During 1951, Copas hit the Country Top 5 again with *The Strange Little Girl* and followed it up the next year with the Top 10 *'Tis Sweet to Be Remembered.* Then he began experiencing problems finding hit records, although he continued with King through 1955. He did cut some good sacred numbers like *From the Manger to the Cross, Scarlet Purple Robe* and *The Man Upstairs,* which became classics in their own way, but did not rank as chartmakers. Furthermore, with rock'n'roll starting to appear, Cope found that his straight Honky-Tonk style did not lend itself to Rockabilly-type numbers as it did with some Country vocalists.

A brief switch to Dot didn't help, but when he went to Starday, he suddenly hit the top with a bang, in 1960. The song that did it, *Alabam,* could be considered an unlikely number, as it came straight from the realm of Old-Time music. Frank Hutchison had cut it in 1926 as *Coney Isle* and Asa Martin and Shorty Hobbs did it in 1933 under the title Copas used. It remained at No.1 for 12 weeks out of over 8 months on the chart and it also crossed-over to the Pop Top 70. He followed this with the Top 10 hit *Flat Top* and a Top 15 single, *Sunny Tennessee,* in 1961. He ended the year with a remake of *Signed, Sealed and Delivered,* which this time around made it to the Top 10.

Along with Patsy Cline, Hawkshaw Hawkins and his son-in-law, Randy Hughes, Cope journeyed back from a benefit show in Kansas City to Nashville in a small private plane which crashed near Camden, Tennessee, on March 5, 1963, killing all passengers. Hughes was the husband of Cope's daughter,

The legendary ***Cowboy Copas***

Kathy, who had recorded several duets with her dad over the years. Somewhat ironically, the last Copas hit was entitled *Goodbye Kisses.* It reached the Top 15, entering the charts seven weeks after his death. IMT

RECOMMENDED ALBUMS:

Both King and Starday kept many of Cowboy Copas' albums in print for several years following his death. Gusto reissued some of his material, in altered form, in the 70's, mostly from Starday masters.

"Cowboy Copas Sings his All-Time Hits" (King)(1957)
"Sacred Songs" (King)(1959)
"Tragic Tales of Love and Life" (King)(1960)
"Broken-Hearted Melodies" (King)(1960)
"All Time Country Music Great" (Starday)(1960)
"Inspirational Songs" (Starday)(1960)
"Opry Star Spotlight" (Starday)(1961)
"Mister Country Music" (Starday)(1962)
"The Country Gentleman of Song" (King)(1963)
"As You Remember" (King)(1963)
"Country Music Entertainer #1" (Starday)(1963)
"Beyond the Sunset" (Starday)(1963)
"The Unforgettable Cowboy Copas" (Starday)(1963)
"Star of the Grand Ole Opry" (Starday)(1963)
"Cowboy Copas and his Friends" (Starday)(1964)
"The Legend Lives On" (Starday)(1965)
"The Cowboy Copas Story" (double)(Starday)(1966)
"Tragic Romance (King)(1969) Starday masters
"16 Greatest Hits of Cowboy Copas" (Starday)

CORBIN/HANNER

Formed: 1980

BOB CORBIN
(Singer, Songwriter, Guitar, Keyboards)
Given Name: Robert Phillip Corbin
Date of Birth: April 9, 1951
Where Born: Butler, Pennsylvania
Married: Edana
Children: Cole, Jessica

DAVE HANNER:
(Singer, Songwriter, Guitar, Keyboards)
Given Name: David Nicely Hanner
Date of Birth: February 22, 1949
Where Born: Kittanning, Pennsylvania
Married: Jan
Children: Jake, Casey, Alex

When Corbin/Hanner signed to Mercury Nashville in 1991, it looked like here were two more songwriters moving over to the performing and recording side of the business. Nothing could have been further from the truth. These are two people who started singing together at the age of 14.

Corbin and Hanner first met while in high school. After watching the Beatles on the *Ed Sullivan Show*, they decided they wanted to be singers because it attracted the girls. They traveled to New York to record an album even before they could drive. After graduation, they ended up at different colleges but both gravitated to Pittsburgh, where they formed a five-piece band, Gravel. The group became very popular in the area. Bob's wife, a freelance writer, interviewed Mel Tillis, and he turned out to be very helpful. When Mel heard Bob and Dave, he signed them to his publishing company. However, they soon returned to Pittsburgh.

In 1979, they enjoyed their first taste of the charts with *America's Sweetheart* on Lifesong as Corbin & Hanner. By 1980, they were on Alfa as the Corbin/Hanner Band with Al Snyder (keyboards), Kip Paxton (bass guitar) and Dave Freeland (drums). During 1981 and 1982, they had four hits for the label, *Time Has Treated You Well, Livin' the Good Life, Oklahoma Crude* and *Everybody Knows I'm Yours.* Lifesong released *One Fine Morning* in 1982 and that was also a low-level hit. The Corbin/Hanner Band also recorded two albums for Alfa, ***Son of America*** (1980) and ***For the Sake of the Song*** (1981), before the label suddenly folded.

In 1984, they decided to come off the road and concentrate on their songwriting. Dave had a No.1 hit in 1985 via Alabama's recording of his *Can't Keep a Good Man Down* and Bob scored with the Oak Ridge Boys' cut of his *Beautiful You* in 1984 and Don Williams' 1986 recording of *I'll Never Be in Love Again.* When Harold Shedd took over the hot seat at Mercury Nashville, he rang Bob and Dave and offered them a deal. He had known them for some while and felt their presence on the label would be beneficial. Their first album, ***Black and White Photograph***, was produced by them and Shedd, and yielded the hit single *Work Song,* which has become the favorite of morning radio deejays. In 1991, they had a Top 60 single, *Concrete Cowboy.* This was followed up with their 1992 album ***Just Another Hill***. From that album, Corbin/Hanner scored with the title track (Top 75, 1992), *I Will Stand by You* (Top 50) and *Any Road* (Top 75) (both in 1993). They still call Pennsylvania home, with Bob living in Pittsburgh and Dave in Gibsonia.

RECOMMENDED ALBUMS:

"Black and White Photograph" (Mercury)(1991)
"Just Another Hill" (Mercury)(1992)

HELEN CORNELIUS

(Singer, Songwriter, Guitar, Piano, Actress, Dancer)
Given Name: Helen Lorene Johnson
Date of Birth: December 6, 1941
Where Born: Monroe City, Missouri
Married: 1. Lewis Cornelius (div.)
2. Jerry Garren (m. 1981)
Children: Joseph (Joey), Christina (Christye), Dennis (Denny)

Some Country singers just sing, some are adept musicians and some fall in the category of Renaissance men or women. Helen Cornelius is one of the latter. She possesses a delightful voice, able to play various instruments and is a capable actress and dancer.

Helen grew up on a farm in a musical atmosphere. Her brothers always had Country bands. She formed a trio with her sisters, Judy and Sharon, and their father, Joseph, encouraged the girls and provided the car to get them to gigs. Helen went solo and had a backing group, the Crossroads. She got onto the *Ted Mack Show* without having taken an audition. She so impressed the talent coordinator of the show who had heard her sing in an amateur talent contest in Quincy, Illinois, that he took this step. However, the show was terminated before she could take part in the finals.

She graduated from school in Monroe City, Missouri, when she was 17 and she married a year later. She initially worked as a secretary. During the 60's, she performed all over the Midwest and then she turned her attention to songwriting. However, it was not until 1970 that she was signed as a writer to Columbia-Screen Gems Music, within a week of submitting a tape of her songs. When the company went under, she got a contract with MCA Music after sending a tape to Jerry Crutchfield, and he got her a deal with Columbia Records.

She came to Nashville in 1973, to record two singles, *If I Go On/Tweedle Dee Dee* and *Little Sugar Plum/Patchwork Girl.* They didn't bother the charts, but John Ragsdale of Duchess Music heard her recordings and recommended her to Bob Ferguson at RCA.

In 1975, Helen released her first single for RCA, *We Still Sing Love Songs in Missouri*, without it charting. The following year, she released *Morning Made for Lovin'/Only Lovers.* That year, Bob Ferguson had an inspired thought: he put Helen together with Jim Ed Brown and then her career took off.

Their first single in 1976, *I Don't Want to Have to Marry You*, shot to the top of the charts. Helen then had her first solo chart entry, *There's Always a Goodbye.* Strangely, her solo efforts were never as successful as her duets. The next single with Jim Ed, *Saying Hello, Saying I Love You, Saying Goodbye,* climbed to the Top 3. During 1976, they started their residency on the *Nashville on the Road* TV series and the same week, Helen joined Jim Ed's road show and made her debut on the *Grand Ole Opry.*

Their three 1977 releases had mixed fortunes, *Born Believer* and *If It Ain't Love by Now* both reached the Top 15, but their Christmas song, *Fall Softly Snow*, only just got into the Top 100. During that year, Helen was named "Most Promising Female Artist" in the *Music City News* Cover Awards and the CMA named Helen and Jim Ed the "Vocal Duo of the Year."

1978 brought a further upturn in fortunes. The duet singles *I'll Never Be Free* and *If the World Ran out of Love Tonight* went Top 15 and Top 10 respectively. Helen then had a Top 30 hit with her first solo chart entry for over a year, *What Cha Doin' After Midnight, Baby.* A month later, she and Jim Ed had a Top 10 hit with *You Don't Bring Me Flowers,* which had been a No.1 Pop hit for Neil Diamond and Barbra Streisand.

The following year was a vintage one for Jim Ed and Helen. *Lying In Love with You* and *Fools* both went Top 3. Helen's solo *It Started With a Smile* settled in the Top 70 at the end of the year. They had a spring 1980 hit with *Morning Comes Too Early,* which made it to the Top 5. By then, however, the two decided to go their separate ways amidst a much publicized rift. Helen considered that she had become an extension of Jim Ed. They had two more hit singles, *The Bedroom* (1980) and *Don't Bother to Knock* (1981).

Helen moved over to Elektra Records and her release *Love Never Comes Easy* went Top 50. On June 22, 1981, Helen married Jerry Garren.

Her next hit was not until 1983, when she had a Top 70 success with *If Your Heart's a Rollin' Stone* on Americ-Can. During that year, Helen served as Arkansas spokesperson for the Cystic Fibrosis Foundation.

During 1984, Helen changed gear when she appeared as "Annie Oakley" in the road version of *Annie Get Your Gun.* She also spent part of 1984-1985 touring with the Statler Brothers. In 1985, Helen released an excellent eponymous album on MCA/Dot. On it is her solo version of *You Don't Bring Me Flowers* and *I Don't Want to Have to Marry You* plus three of her own co-written songs. In March 1988, Helen and Jim Ed got back together for a series of dates under the title of *Reunited Tour '88.* Helen now runs the Helen Cornelius Nashville South dinner theater in Gatlinburg, Tennessee.

RECOMMENDED ALBUMS:

Solo:

"Helen Cornelius" (MCA/Dot)(1985)

With Jim Ed Brown:

"One Woman, One Man" (RCA Victor)(1980)

"The Greatest Hits-Jim Ed Brown & Helen Cornelius" (RCA Victor)(1982)

CARL COTNER

(Fiddle, Arranger)

Given Name:	**Carl B. Cotner**
Date of Birth:	**April 8, 1916**
Where Born:	**Lake Cicott, Indiana**
Married:	**Juanita Dean**
Children:	**Lance W., Carl Gene, Linda Jean**

Carl Cotner is best known for his long association with Gene Autry, but his musical career went back much further. By 1934, he was already playing on WHAS Louisville. The following year, he joined Clayton McMichen's Georgia Wildcats. He appeared with them on the *Grand Ole Opry* in 1936 and stayed a member of the band until 1937. Carl appeared on their recordings on Decca in 1935. In 1937, he moved to WLW Cincinnati. While there, he studied at Cincinnati College of Music.

In 1939, Carl moved from WLW to CBS Radio with Gene Autry's *Melody Ranch.* Shortly after his arrival, Carl was made Music Director (Leader) of the Melody Ranch Band. Cotner brought a change to the Autry sound. Under his direction there were gentle guitars, violins, accordion, background steel guitar and horns.

Carl Cotner directed many of Gene Autry's TV shows in the early 50's. He appeared on recordings for OKeh and Columbia from 1939, Challenge from 1954 and RCA in 1961. With Autry, he recorded *Here Comes Santa Claus* (1948), *Rudolph the Red-Nosed Reindeer* (1949), *South of the Border* and *Mexicali Rose.* He appeared in 40 Gene Autry movies for Republic between 1939 and 1948. (See Movie Section.)

In 1964, *Melody Ranch* switched to KTLA-TV in Hollywood. Cotner was involved with Gene Autry's business affairs into the late 70's.

RECOMMENDED ALBUMS:

Refer to Gene Autry albums.

CAROLINA COTTON

(Singer, Yodeler, Actress)

Given Name:	**Helen Hagstrom**
Date of Birth:	**October 20, 1933**
Where Born:	**Cash, Arkansas**
Married:	**Bill Ates (div.)**
Children:	**two**

Carolina Cotton became Hollywood's chief cowgirl yodeler in Western and Country music motion pictures for a decade from 1944. During this time, her image as a perky, wholesome adolescent won her a broad following among the film public and through her programs on the Armed Forces Radio Network. While she recorded but sparingly, her movie appearances had sufficient lasting popularity to sustain her career through the 50's.

Born Helen Hagstrom in the northern Arkansas farm community of Cash, of Swedish parentage,while still a baby, she moved to California with her parents. A talented child, she attended a dancing school in San Francisco which led to her landing a job with Western bandleader Dude Martin at local radio station KYA. It was Martin who gave Helen her stage name of Carolina Cotton. "The Carolinas had a more positive southern image than Arkansas in California," she says. Through her work with Martin, she received an opportunity to test for a part in the Republican film *Sing, Neighbor, Sing,* which featured Roy Acuff, Lulu Belle and Scotty and several lesser-known musicians. From there, Carolina worked in other films and shorts, gaining increasingly more significant parts as time went by.

From 1945 onward, Carolina appeared mostly in Columbia Pictures. These included two with Charles Starrett, four with Ken Curtis and another one with Roy Acuff. In the winter of 1949-1950, she appeared in both of Eddy Arnold's films, *Feudin' Rhythm* and *Hoedown,* two Gene Autry flicks in 1952, *Apache Country* and the *Blue Canadian Rockies.* In Charles Starrett's *The Rough Tough West* (1952), she became a full-fledged leading lady, a saloon singer who eventually reformed Jack Mahoney and presumably lived happily ever after.

Carolina's recordings gained less attention than her motion picture career. She did a vocal side on a Mercury disc about 1945, but her first real session came in 1946, for King, when she recorded four numbers including her own trademark song, *Three Miles South of Cash in Arkansas.* After sessions with the

The delectable ***Carolina Cotton***

smaller Crystal and Mastertone labels, she went with MGM in 1950 and had several releases over the next three years, including four songs in 1951 backed by Bob Wills and His Texas Playboys. A new arrangement of *Three Miles South of Cash in Arkansas* likely constituted the most notable cut. She also recorded Soundies (film shorts) and Snader Telescriptions.

During the mid and later 50's, Carolina continued to be active as a yodeler cowgirl singer. She made numerous USO tours which included six trips to Korea, and she visited other military locales such as Alaska, Germany and Japan. In the mid-50's, she married Bill Ates, a relative of character actor Roscoe Ates, and became the mother of two children. However, the marriage did not endure. Later, Carolina went to college and followed her sister into an education career. From 1969-1974, she taught in U.S. Government schools in Central America, but since 1974, Carolina has taught elementary school in her current home of Bakersfield, California. In recent years, she has attended Western film fairs with some regularity, where she continues to impress fans with her outgoing personality and yodeling skills. IMT

RECOMMENDED ALBUM:

"Bob Wills and His Texas Playboys: Pap's Jumpin'" (Bear Family Germany)(1985) [Featuring Carolina Cotton]

COUNTRY BOYS, The

Formed: 1954

Members:

Roland White	**Mandolin, Vocals**
Clarence White	**Guitar, Vocals**
Eric White	**Bass, Vocals**
Billy Ray Latham	**Banjo, Vocals**
LeRoy Mack	**Dobro, Vocals**
Bobby Sloan	**Fiddle, Vocals**
Scotty Stoneman	**Fiddle, Vocals**

The Country Boys is another name for the Kentucky Colonels, a Bluegrass band that was very popular in the 60's. During that decade they got their greatest exposure from two 1961 appearances on *The Andy Griffith Show*. Brothers Roland, Clarence and Eric White began performing around Los Angeles in 1954 and later, they added Billy Ray Latham on banjo and LeRoy Mack on Dobro and the group found steady work. They frequently appeared on the *Town Hall Party* and *Hometown Jamboree* TV shows and within a short time acquired a reputation as Southern California's best Bluegrass band. This recognition resulted in an audition for Griffith's show, at the time one of the most popular programs on TV. In 1961, the Country Boys also performed on four sides with Griffith on an lp released that year.

Shortly after their appearances on the Griffith show, the Country Boys added a fiddler to their band, Bobby Sloan being the first and Scotty Stoneman succeeding him. In 1964, they made a highly successful East Coast tour, highlighted by a very well-received appearance at the Newport Folk Festival. This resulted in an important album on Vanguard, but the group disbanded a few years later. Roland White performed with a variety of bands, including Bill Monroe's Bluegrass Boys, Lester Flatt's Nashville Grass, Country Gazette and currently, the Nashville Bluegrass Band. Clarence went on to join the Byrds and to become a session musician playing behind such artists as Ricky Nelson and Linda Ronstadt. He also helped develop with fellow Byrd Gene Parsons the Parsons-Whites String Bender or "B Bender," a guitar mechanism that simulated the sound of a pedal steel guitar. In 1973, Clarence was killed by a hit-and-run drunk driver in a club parking lot after a show in Palmdale, California. WKM

RECOMMENDED ALBUM:

"Appalachian Swing" (Rounder)(1993)

COUNTRY GAZETTE

Formed: 1972

Original Members:

Byron Berline	**Fiddle**
Kenny Wertz	**Guitar, Vocals**
Roger Bush	**String Bass**
Alan Munde	**Banjo, Vocals**
Herb Petersen	**Guitar, Vocals**

Other Members:

Roland White	**Guitar, Mandolin, Vocals**
Dave Ferguson	**Fiddle**
Mike Anderson	**Bass Guitar**
Billy Joe Foster	**Bass, Fiddle (1984-86)**
Gene Wooten	**Dobro, Vocals**

At the end of 1971, out of the fourth incarnation of the Flying Burrito Brothers grew Hot Burrito Revue/Country Gazette. Country Gazette was the Bluegrass wing of the operation.

They got a record deal with United Artists and brought in Herb Petersen on several tracks. Alan Munde had formerly played with Jimmy Martin and Wertz had been a member of the Kentucky Colonels. Musically, they were a blend of traditional Bluegrass and Country and contemporary Country-Rock material, very much a forerunner of Newgrass in the 80's and 90's. Their first album was ***Traitor in Our Midst,*** and as with the Burritos, they were produced by Jim Dickson.

The Gazette worked that first summer at Disneyland and through contacts in Los Angeles started opening for Crosby and Nash, Don McLean and Steve Miller. They were trying very hard to bring Bluegrass to a new audience. They then went to Holland and recorded a live album which was released on the Bumble label as ***Live in Amsterdam***. Their next studio album, ***Don't Give up Your Day Job,*** came out in 1973. That year they moved to the European label Ariola and brought out ***Bluegrass Special.*** By now, Country Gazette was much more popular in Europe than in the States and was voted "Top Country Band" in the British Country Music Association Awards, and several of their albums were released in Britain and Holland.

Berline decided to leave in 1975 to form Sundance, and Roger Bush of the magnificent upturned Dali mustache also decided to leave. The band's next Ariola album was ***Live*** and included Roland White, who had come on board following the tragic death of his brother Clarence.

The Gazette's 1976 album ***Out to Lunch*** was released on Flying Fish, but just after they recorded this album, Wertz departed. The album was released in the U.K. by Transatlantic as ***Sunnyside of the Mountain***.This was the first Gazette album on which Dave Ferguson appeared playing fiddle.

The band released two albums for Ridge Runner, ***What a Way to Earn a Living*** (1977) and ***All This and Money Too*** (1979). The first featured fiddle players Richard Greene and the returning Byron Berline rather than Dave Ferguson. Flying Fish released ***American and Clean*** in 1981 and ***America's Bluegrass Band***, in 1982.

The band broke up after this, but was reactivated in 1983 with the line-up of Alan Munde (banjo, vocals), Roland White (guitar, mandolin, vocals), Mike Anderson (bass guitar, vocals) and Gene Wooten (Dobro, vocals). In 1988, the band wound down and Roland White joined the Nashville Bluegrass Band.

RECOMMENDED ALBUMS:

"A Traitor in Our Midst" (United Artists)(1972)
"Don't Give Up Your Day Job" (United Artists)(1973) [Re-issued by Liberty in 1983]
"Live" (Ariola/Transatlantic UK/Antilles Holland)(1976) [In U.K. as "Sunnyside of the Mountain"]
"Out to Lunch" (Flying Fish)(1976)
"What a Way to Make a Living" (Ridge Runner)(1977)
"All This and Money Too" (Ridge Runner)(1979)
"American and Clean" (Flying Fish)(1981)
"America's Bluegrass Band" (Flying Fish)(1982)

COUNTRY GENTLEMEN

Formed: July 4, 1957

Current Members:

Charlie Waller	**Lead Vocals, Guitar**
Jimmy Bowen	**Vocals, Mandolin (originally played String Bass)**
Greg Corbett	**Vocals, Banjo**
Ronnie Davis	**String Bass**
Former Members:	
John Duffey	**Vocals, Mandolin, Dobro (Original Member)(left 1969)**
Bill Emerson	**Vocals, Banjo (Original Member)(left 1958) (rejoined 1969-72)**
Larry Lahey	**String Bass (Original Member)(left 1957)**
Tom Morgan	**String Bass**
Jim Cox	**String Bass**
Pete Kuykendall	**String Bass, Fiddle**
Pete Kuykendall	**(as Pete Roberts) Vocals, Banjo, Guitar (1958-59)**
Roy Self	**String Bass**
Sonny Johnson	**String Bass**
Stoney Edwards	**String Bass**
Tom Gray	**String Bass (1960-64)**
Ed Ferris	**String Bass (1964)**
Ed McGlothlin	**String Bass (1964-70)**
Bill Yates	**String Bass, Vocals (1970)**
Eddie Adcock	**Vocals, Banjo (1959-70)**
Jimmy Gaudreau	**Vocals, Mandolin (1969-72)(rejoined 1981)**
Doyle Lawson	**Vocals, Mandolin (1972-79)**
Rick Allred	**Vocals, Mandolin (1979-81)**
Mike Lilly	**Vocals, Banjo**
James Bailey	**Vocals, Banjo (twice)**
Bill Holden	**Vocals, Banjo**
Kent Dowell	**Vocals, Banjo**
Norman Wright	**Vocals, Mandolin**
John Hall	**Fiddle**
Carl Nelson	**Fiddle**
Ricky Skaggs	**Fiddle**
Kenny Haddock	**Dobro**
Jerry Douglas	**Dobro**
Dick Smith	**Vocals, Banjo**
Walt Hensley	**Banjo**
Ronnie Bucke	**Drums**
Spider Gilliam	**Bass**

Formed in 1957, the Country Gentlemen quickly became the trendsetters in what became known as Progressive Bluegrass, Modern Bluegrass and Newgrass. Several of the more significant sidemen in Bluegrass music have been members of the Gents at one time or another and played a role in their development, but the principal leader has always been guitarist/lead singer Charlie Waller. Other key musicians in the group have been banjo pickers Bill Emerson and Eddie Adcock, mandolinists John Duffey and Doyle Lawson and bass players Tom Gray, Ed Ferris and Bill Yates. Among those notables who have worked shorter stints with the band are *Bluegrass Unlimited* founder Pete Kuykendall (who has played string bass, fiddle and banjo), Country star Ricky Skaggs, Jimmy Gaudreau, Country superpicker Jerry Douglas and one-time Bluegrass Cardinal Norman Wright.

From the beginning, the Country Gentlemen distinguished themselves by their sophisticated sounding vocals and choice of material from songs outside the normal perimeters, including Folk music, rock'n'roll, R & B and Modern Country, as well as standard Bluegrass.

The founder, the leader and the only constant member of the Country Gentlemen, Charlie Waller, had been born in Texas, but he grew up in Louisiana. He credits Hank Snow among his major musical influences, especially in vocal phrasing. He moved to Washington, D.C., at age 10 and got his first guitar, a $15 Stella, at this time. By the age of 13, he was playing the beer joints in D.C., as part of a trio of 13-year-olds. He played around the clubs for a while and then in 1954, he moved to Baltimore, where he joined Earl Taylor. At the same time, Charlie met Louisiana mandolinist Buzz Busby and played in Busby's band as well. The following year, Charlie joined Busby's band, the Bayou Boys, and went back to Louisiana. Here he worked at Shreveport's *Louisiana Hayride*. By the early summer of 1957, he had returned to D.C. Early that year, the Bayou Boys were involved in a car crash. The band had a regular gig at the Admiral's Grill in Bailey's Cross Roads, Virginia. Bill Emerson, the banjo player of the group, decided to put a band together to fill in while the Bayou Boys were on the mend and so the Country Gentlemen were born.

The group went through many changes until Eddie Adcock joined in 1959 and for more five years, the foursome of Waller-John Duffey-Adcock-Tom Gray remained constant. Next to Waller, the person who spent the longest time as a Country Gentleman was Bill Yates, who played bass through virtually all of the 70's and 80's. Although none of the current members, other than Waller, have much seniority, the personnel have changed less than the average long-term Bluegrass band.

The earliest Country Gentlemen records consisted of several singles and an album on Starday Records, along with three albums for Folkways, and one album on the budget Design label and another for Mercury in 1963, entitled ***Folk Session Inside***, which probably illustrated their Modern Bluegrass approach more than any other. About 1964, they began recording for Richard Freeland's Rebel label and the greatest number of their records have been for that company, including the ghostly song version of "the vanishing hitchhiker" story, *Bringing Mary Home*, which is one of the few Bluegrass singles to reach the Country charts, peaking in the Top 50, in November 1965.

Since the mid 60's, the Gentlemen have recorded numerous albums for Rebel plus a couple each for Vanguard and Sugar Hill. More than any other band, they helped popu-

***Country Gentlemen** under the leadership of Charlie Waller*

larize Bluegrass in the Washington, D.C., area through their years of steady appearances at clubs such as the Shamrock in Georgetown and the Red Fox in Bethesda, Maryland. It was after playing the latter in 1972 that Bill Emerson, who was having a second sojourn with the Gents, was shot in the arm by a gunman in a speeding car. It was during Emerson's second incumbency that the band recorded one of their most popular songs. In 1970, Emerson recommended a song he had recorded while with Cliff Waldron, the Manfred Mann composition *Fox on the Run,* and it appeared on the group's ***Sound Off*** album. From that album also came their version of the Crosby, Stills & Nash song *Teach Your Children Well,* which became "No.1 Bluegrass Song of the Year."

The Country Gentlemen have also ranked among the most popular bands on the Bluegrass festival circuit. Since the departure of Norman Wright and Bill Yates, recent combinations of the band have seen Waller supported by younger musicians of lesser stature, but their sound, like that of other Bluegrass legends, maintains a remarkable continuity.

As well as the aforementioned line-up of Waller-Duffey-Adcock-Gray, one other wielded enormous influence, that of Waller-Doyle Lawson-Bill Emerson-Bill Yates. They worked together from mid-1971 until mid-1973. Through thirty-five years of quality Bluegrass, the Country Gentlemen can undoubtably look forward to several more years as a top act on the Bluegrass circuit. IMT

RECOMMENDED ALBUMS:

"Bluegrass at Carnegie Hall with the Country Gentlemen" (Starday)(1962)
"Country Songs-Old And New" (Folkways)(1960)
"The Country Gentlemen Sing and Play Folksongs and Bluegrass" (Folkways)(1961)
"The Country Gentlemen On The Road" (Folkways)(1963)
"Going Back to the Blue Ridge Mountains" (Folkways)(1973)
"Folk Session Inside" (Mercury)(1963)
"Hootnanny" (Design)(1963)
"Bringing Mary Home" (Rebel)(1966)
"The Country Gentlemen Sing Bluegrass" (Zap)(1967)
"The Traveler (And Other Favorites)" (Rebel)(1968)
"The Country Gentlemen Play It Like It Is" (Rebel)(1969)
"The Country New Look, New Sound" (Rebel)(1970)
"One Wide River to Cross" (Rebel)(1971)
"Country Gentlemen Sound Off" (Rebel)(1971)
"The Award Winning Country Gentlemen" (Rebel)(1972)
"The Country Gentlemen" (Vanguard)(1973) [Features Al Rogers on drums!]
"The Country Gentlemen, Yesterday and Today, Volume 1" (Rebel)(1973)
"The Country Gentlemen, Yesterday and Today, Volume 2" (Rebel)(1973)
"The Country Gentlemen Live in Japan" (double)(Seven Seas Japan)(1975) [Licensed to Rebel and released in 1988]
"Joe's Last Train" (Rebel)(1976)
"Calling My Children Home" (Rebel)(1978)
"River Bottom" (Sugar Hill)(1981)
"Twenty-Fifth Anniversary" (double)(Rebel)(1982)
"Let the Light Shine Down" (Rebel)(1991)
"New Horizons" (Rebel)(1992)

COUNTRY MUSIC ASSOCIATION

Founded in 1958, the Country Music Association was the first organization of its kind to promote a specific type of music. Starting with 233 members, the organization has grown to include more than 7,000 members and 700 organizations in 31 countries. CMA was originally formed as a trade organization to help guide the development of Country music, and now enhances its development worldwide. Additionally, its objectives include demonstrating Country music as a viable medium to advertisers, consumers and the media and providing a unity of purpose for the industry. It is a nonprofit organization.

There were originally 9 directors and 5 officers, with Wesley Rose, President of Acuff-Rose Publishing, serving as CMA's first Chairman of the Board. The founding President in 1958 was broadcasting executive Connie B. Gay. Jo Walker-Meador joined the organization in 1958 as Office Manager and a short time later became the CMA's Executive Director. She served in that capacity for 33 years overseeing the expansion of the organization from a struggling entity to the large, prestigious organization it is today. She retired in 1991.

TNN executive Paul Corbin currently serves as Chairman of the Board and Dan Halyburton of KPLX radio serves as President. Ed Benson serves as Executive Director, and there are 5 staff directors: Helen Farmer (Special Projects), Tammy Genovese (Administrative Services), Teresa George (Public Relations), Jeff Green (International) and Tom Murray (Marketing/Membership).

Today, CMA has a Nashville staff of 25 and an international staff of 4. Originally there were 9 individual membership categories which have been expanded to the current 15, representing all facets of the music industry. Memberships are available to persons and organizations who are involved in Country music, directly and substantially. Annual dues for individual members are $50.00 and company membership dues range from $125.00 to $5,000. Each membership category is represented by two directors on the board, with six directors-at-large and four lifetime directors. Officers are elected by the directors each year for a one-year term. The board meets four times a year, and officers and directors serve on a gratis basis, paying all their own expenses.

The CMA awards, the first music awards to be aired on network television, are perhaps one of the greatest contributions the organization has made to the music industry. CMA awards have long been considered to be the most prestigious awards in Country music. The awards were inaugurated in 1967 and taped for TV broadcast the following year. Since 1969, the awards have been carried live. Additionally, a stereo-radio simulcast of the awards and the post-awards party have taken place since 1983. The gala is also syndicated for broadcast in Canada, and is telecast internationally.

The annual awards are presented in 12 categories to outstanding Country artists, voted upon by CMA's membership, to honor excellence in artistry. The first CMA awards in 1967 were presented at an awards banquet and show hosted by Sonny James and Bobbie Gentry. At this time CMA leadership believed this event could be used to broaden the appeal and audience of Country music. The following year board member Irving Waugh (then President of WSM, Inc.) sold the idea of a televised event to J. Walter Advertising, who took the ball and ran with it to Kraft. Kraft became the first exclusive sponsor of the awards and continued until 1987. The second annual awards were held the following year in Nashville's Ryman Auditorium and taped for rebroadcast on the "Kraft Music Hall." The event was hosted by Roy Rogers and Dale Evans.

In 1969, the event was broadcast live for the first time, with Johnny Cash dominating the evening and walking away with a record five awards, which still stands. 1970 marked the induction of a new award, "Vocal Duo of the Year," while "Comedian of the Year" was presented for the last time. By the time the fifth annual awards rolled around, the event merited an hour of its own on NBC, rather than being broadcast as part of the "Kraft Music Hall" series. In 1972, CBS-TV began broadcasting the special and has continued to do so ever since. This also marked the first year a woman, Loretta Lynn, won "Entertainer of the Year." 1973 saw Charlie Rich win three awards, and the following year Conway Twitty and Loretta Lynn won the third of their four "Vocal Duo" awards.

1975 was a first when John Denver accepted his award from Australia via satellite. 1976 saw the program expanded from 60 to 90 minutes. In 1977, Ronnie Milsap took 3 of 12 awards. 1978 marked another milestone when the program was radio-simulcast for the first time. In 1980, Barbara Mandrell and Mac Davis began serving as hosts for the first of three consecutive years. The 15th annual (1981) CMA award show marked another first in the event's history when Barbara Mandrell won a second consecutive "Entertainer of the Year" award. The same year was the first for the "Horizon Award," with Terri Gibbs walking away with the honors. In 1982, Alabama made history by becoming the first group to win "Entertainer of the Year." This was followed by CMA's 25th anniversary as music trade association (1983) and included the very first synchronized stereo-radio simulcast distributed by satellite. The three hour radio broadcast included the airing of a pre-awards show as well as a post-awards show, helping to deliver the largest audience ever. The same year also saw the introduction of the "Irving Waugh Award for Excellence," presented for the first time to the man for whom it was named.

In 1984, Alabama made unprecedented history by winning "Entertainer of the Year" for the third time. 1985 saw the first ever "Music Video of the Year" award, presented to Hank Williams, Jr., who declared to a roaring audience that he made a little audio as well. Several forms of music were "married" in the 1986 presentations as Alabama joined Pop star Lionel Richie and Ricky Skaggs teamed with Gospel singer Amy Grant. It was also the year the much touted trio of Dolly Parton, Linda Ronstadt and Emmylou Harris performed.

During the 21st special, Reba McEntire won the unprecedented fourth consecutive "Female Vocalist of the Year" award, and another milestone occurred when the CMA awards were first broadcast in Canada. 1988 saw the first two-hour awards telecast, with CMA producing its first special, in association with CBS. Another new award, "Vocal Event of the Year," was also introduced. The following year saw more musical numbers and set changes than any previous telecast. The awards were first in their time slot in the ratings game. The 24th CMA awards telecast was also first in its time slot, and the Judds claimed their seventh consecutive award since winning the "Horizon Award" in 1984. The following year the 25th annual awards show was viewed by over 33 million people and came in first in the television ratings for the week. By 1992, more than 48 million viewers were watching the event worldwide.

The list of CMA accomplishments includes a spectrum of events in Country music's history. Other major contributions to the industry are:

• International Country Music Fan Fair. Co-sponsored by the CMA and the *Grand Ole Opry*, the event is held in Nashville each June. The giant Country music festival enables Country music fans to attend a week crowded with activities ranging from meeting their favorite artists to attending live performances. 24,000 fans attended in 1992, and Fan Fair '94 sold out within a month of registration opening.

• Recognition of October as Country Music Month. Proclaimed so by Presidents Nixon, Carter, Reagan and Bush. In 1983, CMA initiated, in association with the National Association of Recording Merchandisers (NARM), an extensive merchandising campaign conducted on the rack and retail level. The campaign focuses on the CMA awards, structured to boost sales and awareness of Country music in September and October.

• The Country Music Hall of Fame. The Hall of Fame was established in 1961 to immortalize Country music's greatest contributors. The building housing the museum was erected in 1967, and since then, the CMF has operated the facility. The CMA continues to conduct the annual selection and induction into the Hall of Fame. The CMF operates a library and research facility.

• International Market Development. In 1982, CMA established an office in London to increase the popularity of Country music in Europe. In 1993, this was broadened to include the Nashville-based International Department, which functions to oversee global development of Country music. In 1994, CMA restructured its presence to include a regional representation system with offices serving the U.K./Ireland, Germany/Switzerland/Austria, the Benelux and later, Scandinavia. These offices coordinate activities including artist tours, radio airplay, licensing of the CMA awards TV broadcast and a communications network via label relations, conferences, advisory groups, research projects, databases and publications.

Additionally, the CMA works to attain positive publicity for Country music through major media outlets throughout the world.

• *Close Up* monthly magazine. Compiled and published monthly, this magazine is produced solely for CMA membership. *Close Up* features in-depth profiles of established artists and rising stars, musicians, songwriters and other industry notables as well as factual information documenting Country music. Additionally, CMA has taken an active role in legislative activities which affect the music business, and continues to do so. CMA also sponsors professional growth seminars, such as the SRO, the annual talent buyers' marketplace in October of each year. CMA compiles and disseminates research materials relating to the Country music industry. The research includes: *Close Up* magazine, *Country Radio Survey* (updated annually, the survey gives a complete listing of full- and part-time stations in the U.S. and Canada), reference guides (the guides provide detailed listings of artists, record company personnel, publishers, publications, producers, personnel managers, publicists, talent agencies and artist/label/manager/agent cross-reference) and the Simmons Study of Media and Markets. In addition, CMA presents a number of awards each year honoring excellence of achievement in the industry. The awards include: "Broadcast Personality of the Year," "Station of the Year," (in three markets), "The Connie B. Gay Award," presented to an individual who has rendered outstanding services to the CMA, the SRO Awards, honoring outstanding achievement in the touring industry, which are presented in 16 categories and a Special President's Award, presented by the acting President of CMA at his/her discretion honoring individuals making noteworthy contributions to Country music or CMA.

In 1994, while in its 36th year of operation, CMA has helped shape Country music around the world. Called by some industry leaders "the world's most active trade organization," CMA continues to be, in the 90's, a guiding light to the worldwide growth and expansion of Country music. LAP

COUNTRY MUSIC RADIO (CMR)

(European radio channel)

Country Music Radio (CMR) is the first 24-hour Country music radio station anywhere in the U.K. or Europe. It initially went on the air in May 1993 with a grand opening by Country music star Crystal Gayle which was covered live by Carlton Television in London. Caron Keating, the host of *London Tonight*, interviewed Crystal and CMR's owner, British veteran broadcaster and promoter Lee Williams and included the opening with an 8-minute feature about the huge popularity of Country music in England.

The station broadcasts on the Astra Satellite and Cable stations throughout the U.K. and 25 other countries in Europe and Scandinavia. This equates to a potential audience of 150 million and growing monthly.

CMR is based in Alton, Hampshire, and broadcasts from its studio direct to the satellite via Sky Television. Most of the cable stations now take CMR and ordinary stations around the U.K. and Europe are now taking certain programs from CMR.

The Country music content is primarily the Contemporary music from the U.S. with some Country Gold and releases from British, Irish and European Country music artists. CMR caters to all Country tastes, including Cajun, Bluegrass, Roots and Folk, Western Swing, Texan and New Beat.

On a recent survey carried out by U.K. Gold and Super Channel, CMR came ninth in Europe as the most listened to radio station out of 63 and fifth in the U.K., after only one year in operation.

The programs on CMR are presenter led and include a host of leading British, American and European personalities with 95% in the English language. The American personalities include top Country star Ricky Skaggs and his show, *The Simple Life,* plus Crook & Chase from TNN in Nashville with a four hour Country Top 40 called *The Nashville Record Review*. In addition, Jerry Foster presents *The Nashville Entertainment Connection*, a 2-hour show recorded live every week in Nashville and *Bluegrass U.S.A.*

COUNTRY MUSIC TELEVISION (CMT)

(Cable TV Channel)

Founded by entertainer Stan Hitchcock and a group of investors, Country Music Television has grown from a fledging network with few available videos to one of the fastest growing networks in the U.S., Canada and Europe, reaching over 35 million households worldwide (A.C. Nielsen 4/94, GWSC 4/94 and 2/94). The network began as CMTV, an all-Country video network, that produced its own videos from the facilities of Video World International in Hendersonville, Tennessee, a suburb of Nashville.

In 1984, Stan Hitchcock and his investors purchased the company and its 2 million subscribers and launched CMT. "At that time there were 30 major videos in existence," recalled Hitchcock. "We had a lot of artist involvement, many artist interviews and I began the program Heart to Heart [an interview program now aired on the Americana Network]. The network was not back-to-back videos at that time. We did road shows, concerts, and other programming to break up the steady flow of videos." In July 1984, CMT was launched in Canada.

Over the next decade, CMT's impact was acknowledged throughout the recording industry, as Country fans became more sophisticated and record companies acknowledged the medium as a way to break in new, lesser known artists. An indication of this can be seen today in CMT Pickhits, which are outstanding videos selected by the staff each week to receive additional play. According to CMT, in 1992, 76% of the records supported by Pickhit videos reached the Top 10 on the charts of *Radio and Records*, a music industry trade publication.

"All that happened," according to Hitchcock, "was that a window was opened for a new breed of artist that didn't have an outlet before. We also reached a new, younger audience that understood and were attuned to videos. They didn't listen to Country radio but they would see a video and stop. They might see Travis Tritt or Garth Brooks and they liked what they saw. I think it was simply having the window raised for this new breed of artists, and letting them have access. That's all they asked. When we started CMT many of the existing videos were not airable. They were of established artists. When the record industry recognized the impact of CMT, two things happened: CMT helped bring a younger audience to Country music because of video, and secondly it opened the window to feed that younger crowd with new artists and give them the ability for radio recognition. Today, it's reversed. Now it's all the younger artists and there's no room for the Ronnie Milsaps and people like that. Ten years ago this phenomenon had not happened, but the talent was there. CMT gave them that WINDOW."

In January 1991, CMT was sold to Gaylord Entertainment Company and Group W Satellite Communications. The new management reformatted CMT's music, imaging and cross-promotion with radio. In October 1992, CMT Europe was launched in the United Kingdom. In addition to the U.K., CMT Europe is available in Scandinavia, Germany, Ireland, Moscow, Latvia, the Czech Republic, Poland, Slovenia, Slovakia and Georgia. The European service provides viewers with a special mix of contemporary American and European artists. Special features of the 24-hour network include:

- CMT Countdown Show, featuring the 10 most requested videos. At year end CMT telecasts an annual 60-minute video countdown showcasing the Top 10 Country videos of the year.
- CMT Saturday Nite *Dance Ranch*, a one-hour music video series featuring dance videos, is telecast on Saturdays. CMT Europe also features a weekly CMT Countdown Show and CMT Saturday Nite *Dance Ranch*. Occasionally, CMT Europe augments its music video line-up with long form programs that promote Country music artists such as the Canadian Country Music Association awards and TNN *Music City News* awards. As of 1994, Tom Griscom is Chairman of the Board of Directors and David Hall is President. Griscom is also President of the Gaylord Communications Group (Nashville) and Hall is Senior Vice President, Cable Networks, Opryland U.S.A., Inc. LAP

COUSIN EMMY

(Singer, Songwriter, Banjo, Fiddle, Guitar, Harmonica, Tenor Guitar, Ukulele, Trumpet, Accordion, Piano, 12-String Guitar, Jew's Harp, Dulcimer, Hand Saw, Rubber Gloves, Comedy, Yodeler, Dancer, Actress)

Given Name: Cynthia May Carver
Date of Birth: 1903
Where Born: Lamb, Kentucky
Date of Death: April 11, 1980

Cousin Emmy will go down in the annals of Country music as one of the most versatile of female pioneers. Her blend of musical talent (she played at least 15 instruments) and entertainment ability should have made her a candidate for the Country Music Hall of Fame, but time has a habit of forgetting those, especially the women, that forged a path through a predominantly male preserve. With her platinum-blond hair tied in highly colored ribbons, pale face, "Martha Raye" mouth in a broad grin, attired in an ill-fitting gingham dress, white stockings and ankle boots, Cousin Emmy hammed it up on stage with such tricks as playing her fiddle with the bow passing through her legs.

Emmy was born the youngest of eight, into a poverty-stricken family. Her father was a sharecropper on a tobacco farm and the family lived in a two-room log cabin 18 miles from the nearest railroad. Her early life was spent working on the farm, but her talent for "showing off" soon manifested itself. She only ever had two weeks of education and she once stated that "I ain't educated, but I'm sincere." She learned to read by scouring mail order catalogs.

Music was in the family and she learned Folk ballads from her great-grandmother. After hearing a radio for the first time in the general store in Glasgow, Kentucky, she was determined to be an entertainer. However, when she told her mother, all she got was a whipping, but that did not deter her. Emmy had two cousins, Noble ("Uncle Bozo") and Warner Carver, who ran a band called the Carver Boys and already had a reputation on radio and records. Emmy began playing banjo with them over WHB Kansas City.

Her big break came when she attempted to get a spot on WHAS Louisville. After she had auditioned for an executive at the station, she was advised that she would be called; she wasn't. Whenever she rang, she was told that he was out. So one morning, she got to the station early and hid in the executive's restroom and challenged the man when he arrived. Because of her nerve, he gave her a spot and within two weeks, she was "the biggest thing to hit any man's radio station."

As she grew she learned to master 15 different instruments as well as having the ability to slap her hands against her cheeks and play, among others, *Turkey in the Straw*. She stayed at WHAS from 1935 until 1937, playing on the early morning show. In 1936, she became the first female to win the National Old Fiddlers' Contest in Louisville, Kentucky.

In 1937, Emmy moved to the WWVA *Midnight Jamboree* in Wheeling, West Virginia, as a part of Frankie Moore's Log Cabin Boys. It was while here that she taught Grandpa Jones how to play the 5-string banjo. While at the station, Emmy sponsored amateur shows and was responsible for helping launch acts such as the Kissinger Brothers. They, and occasionally "Uncle Bozo," became a part of her act. In 1938, Emmy left Wheeling and returned to WHAS.

About now, she began calling her band Cousin Emmy and Her Kin Folks and in October 1939, they moved to Atlanta, where they starred on the *Cross Road Follies*, which was broadcast over WSB and WAGA in Atlanta. In addition, Emmy had her own 10:30 program on Friday mornings on WSB. Among the members of the Kin Folk at that time was Tiny Stewart, who went on to be Redd Stewart, a longtime associate of Pee Wee King and with King, the writer of such classics as *Tennessee Waltz*. By the next year, they were on their travels again, playing on WHAS and Knoxville, Tennessee's WNOX.

By 1941, they were at KMOX St. Louis, Missouri, where they had a twice daily show. The show was sponsored by a hair dye and cough cure company and by the early part of 1942, Emmy and her group were making transcriptions for coast-to-coast broadcasting. Because KMOX was a 50,000-watt station, Emmy's reputation spread and by the end of 1943, she was the subject of an article in *Time* magazine. She was also heard by Professor R.M. Schmitz of the English Department of Washington University at St. Louis. He persuaded her to make some private recordings of her Folk songs and got her to perform, in 1944, at the St. Louis Museum to help illustrate his lecture on "the ballad." That year, Emmy appeared in the movie *Swing in the Saddle* for Columbia Pictures.

Emmy was a shrewd businesswoman and she ensured that her copyrights, which included the Bluegrass classic *Ruby (Are You Mad at Your Man)*, were well protected. *Ruby* went on to become a Top 60 hit for the Osborne Brothers in 1970. She remained unmarried, joking, "I ain't got no time to do no courtin'," and she learned to handle her finances herself. However, she was a highly religious person and had tithed her income as far back as the 30's.

During 1944, she played WAVE Louisville and then returned to the WSB *Barn Dance* in the fall of 1945. Her repertoire was a mix of the traditional and her originals such as *John Henry*, *Milk Cow Blues* and *Ground Hog* and of course *Ruby*. Her Kin Folk at the time consisted of Bill Drake (announcer/singer), Ruth and Jean DeVore, George Money and Jack Nichols. The following year, Emmy moved back to KMOX for a year and then in 1947, she recorded an album of 78s for Decca under the direction of Alan Lomax, the famed folklorist, entitled ***Kentucky Mountain Ballads***, from which *Ruby/The Broken Hearted One You Love* was released as a highly successful single and which also included *Free Little Bird* and *Johnny Booker*.

In 1955, having moved to the West Coast, she appeared in the movie *The Second Greatest Sex*, which was based on the classical tale of Lysistrata and was a musical dealing with women out west going on a sex strike. In 1961, Emmy was appearing at Disneyland, in somewhat different attire. According to John Cohen of the New Lost City Ramblers, she was "dressed in a white sequined dress, with a necklace that sparkled to the back row, high heels and blond hair piled on in the latest fashion. Her delivery was like Sophie Tucker from the country and she was introduced as the 'first hillbilly star to own a Cadillac.'" These Cadillacs had been used to transport adopted children and waifs and strays.

Thanks to the New Lost City Ramblers, Emmy had a comeback and in 1965, she appeared at the Newport Folk Festival, where she "stopped the show." She also appeared on a TV show, *Rainbow Quest*, with Pete Seger. During 1966, Emmy toured with the Ramblers and the Stanley Brothers in Europe. The following year, she appeared at the Ash Grove in Los Angeles, where she told the audience (according to John Cohen), "Don't give up. If you set out to do something, do it or bust, honey. Just keep on and you'll get it."

In 1968, she teamed up with the Ramblers and released the Folkways album ***The New Lost City Ramblers with Cousin Emmy***, which included *Lost John*, *Old Tim Brooks* (a variant on *Molly and Tenbrooks*), *Ruby* and *Bowling Green*. During the early 70's, Emmy appeared at various festivals including a Festival of American Folklife, in Washington, D.C. (1971), and the University of Utah at Salt Lake City (1973). Sadly, Cousin Emmy died in Sherman Oaks, California, in 1980. In 1985, *Come All You Virginia Gals* was included in the Time-Life album ***The Women***.

RECOMMENDED ALBUMS:

"Kentucky Mountain Ballads" (Decca)(1947) [Re-released on Brunswick as 2 EPs]
"The New Lost City Ramblers with Cousin Emmy" (Folkways)(1968)

COUSIN JODY

(Vocals, Comedy, Dobro, Steel Guitar)
Given Name: James Clell Summey
Date of Birth: December 11, 1914
Where Born: near Sevierville, Tennessee
Married: Marie Hill
Date of Death: 1976

Clell Summey had a face that could only belong to a funny man. A toothless grin that nowadays would be called gurnin'. It belied the talent that made him one of the greatest pioneers of the Dobro.

He began his career playing straight dance music, but in 1933, he joined the Tennessee Crackerjacks, the group formed by Roy Acuff and gave the group its distinctive sound. Mr. Roy felt that in importance Clell's Dobro came second only to his vocals. In October 1936, he traveled with the band to Chicago to record some sides for the American Recording Company. They recorded twenty songs including *The Old Speckled Bird* and *Wabash Cannonball*.

Summey was with the group when Roy Acuff made his debut on the *Grand Ole Opry* in October 1937 at the Dixie Tabernacle. He was the first person to play Dobro on the *Opry* and he helped keep a very nervous Roy Acuff from going off the rails. When Roy Acuff made his first membership appearance on the *Opry* on February 19, 1938, he was by his side. The following week, the band's name was changed to Roy Acuff and the Smoky Mountain Boys.

By late 1939, Summey along with bass player Red Jones felt that the band should play more Pop material. Mr. Roy felt differently and so Clell left the group. He started to play steel guitar and was one of the first to play it on the *Opry* when he was a member of Pee Wee King's Golden West Cowboys.

It was then that his comedy really surfaced. He joined forces with Oral Rhodes as Odie and Jody. He then joined that other crazy duo, Lonzo and Oscar and was with them for many years. For over a decade after this, Clell had his own spot on the *Opry*. He suffered with ill health in later years and died of cancer in 1976. He was described by Roy Acuff in his book *Roy Acuff's Nashville* (Perigee, 1983) as being "one mean Dobro Guitar player." That says it all.

RECOMMENDED ALBUMS:

There are no albums of Clell Summey. Suggest you listen to ARC recordings of Roy Acuff circa 1936.

Cowboy Auctioneer refer JOE CARL TAYLOR

COWBOY LOYE

(Singer, Songwriter, Guitar)

Given Name: **Loye Donald Pack**
Date of Birth: **June 3, 1900**
Where Born: **Nashville, Tennessee**
Married: **Zeta**
Children: **JoAnn, Donald, Gerald, Paul**
Date of Death: **March 15, 1941**

Cowboy Loye exemplifies the radio singer who had a wide impact on the Country music of his era without ever making a single record. In the decade prior to his death, Loye gained a large following and fans loved him and fellow musicians admired his singing. Sponsors greatly appreciated his ability to sell their products over the airwaves.

Born Loye D. Pack in Nashville, before it became the home of Country music, the man destined to become known as Cowboy Loye, like many of his generation, exhibited considerable wanderlust in his youth. During the 20's, he settled down to the life of a ranch hand in Nebraska, where he learned a wide variety of songs and ballads and also found a wife. According to the best available information, Pack initiated his radio career at York, Nebraska, in January 1929, when an announcer named Bill Tabor introduced him to listeners. From there his pathway led eastward to WAIU Columbus, Ohio, by 1931, and to WWVA Wheeling in November 1933. In his early days in Wheeling, Loye often sang and shared programs with another musician known as "Just Plain John" Oldham, but by 1936, he had gathered several performers jointly known as the Blue Bonnett Troupe (from a favorite sponsor, Blue Bonnett Crystals), which included fiddler French "Curly" Mitchell, Jake and Betty Taylor, an older fiddler known as "the Sheepherder" (James Moore), and "Radio Dot" Henderson. Leaving Wheeling in 1937 and moving to WMMN Fairmont, he worked with the three Curry sisters, known as the Blue Bonnett Girls. Grandpa Jones, who knew Loye quite well and hunted with him often, stated that while there was "nothing fancy" about him, he was quite a good singer who could sell anything.

Cowboy Loye's career came to a sudden end in early March 1941, when he went to the Cleveland Clinic for a stomach ulcer operation. He died of complications three days later on March 15 at 1:00 a.m. Ironically, the same announcer who first introduced him on radio served a similar capacity on Loye's last program. Zeta Pack took her husband's remains to Ponca, Nebraska, for burial. Like most entertainers in the Depression decade, Cowboy Loye, although idolized by tens of thousands of radio fans, never earned more than a modest subsistence for his endeavors. An examination of Pack's estate showed that his sound equipment (P.A.) and his two guitars were his most valued possessions. However, younger artists such as Wilma Lee and Stoney Cooper, Grandpa Jones, Buddy Starcher and Doc Williams, who admired his style and songs, honored his memory by continuing to sing and eventually record songs he had first popularized at WWVA and WMMN. Since Loye made no records and no transcriptions of his work are known to survive, his only other musical legacy can be found in the three printed songbooks, all treasure chests of Old-Time lyrics, that he left for posterity. IMT

Cowboy Poetry refer WADDIE MITCHELL

Cowboy Ramblers refer BILL BOYD

BILLY COX

(Singer, Songwriter, Harmonica, Guitar)

Given Name: **William Jennings Cox**
Date of Birth: **August 4, 1897**
Where Born: **Kanawha County, West Virginia**
Children: **Dorothy, Lillian, William, Jr.**
Date of Death: **December 10, 1968**

A noted vocalist and songwriter in the 1930's, Billy Cox performed some of the most original topical ballads, humorous lyrics, and love laments of the Depression era.

Young Bill learned to play the harmonica at an early age from his mother and other facets of his life from his railroading father. Later he also learned to play the guitar. He spent much of his adult life working alternately as a stationary engineer at the Ruffner Hotel or an employee of the Kelly Axe Factory, both in Charleston. Through the 20's, he sang, played guitar and harmonica at local entertainments. From 1927, he also exhibited his talents on radio at station WOBU (later WCHS), the studios of which were located in the Ruffner Hotel, where he worked.

The radio management arranged for Cox to make recordings for the Gennett label in Richmond, Indiana, his first session being on July 11, 1929. His early efforts, like those of Gene Autry, tended toward covers of Jimmie Rodgers hits, but he soon veered in the direction of more original material in the Rodgers style, and more significantly to comic songs allegedly based on his own hectic and reckless domestic life. These included such fare as *The Jailer's Daughter*, *Alimony Woman* and *Rollin' Pin Woman*. Through 1931, he released 43 sides for Gennett, many of which appeared on subsidiary labels under such pseudonyms as Luke Baldwin on Champion, Charlie Blake on Supertone and Clyde Ashley on Superior.

On August 30, 1933, Bill Cox switched companies and began recording for the American Record Corporation, an affiliation he retained through 1940. He still appeared infrequently on WCHS radio and played occasional stage shows with more active artists through central West Virginia, but made the greatest impact on phonograph record. By this time, he had acquired a sobriquet, "The Dixie Songbird." From 1936, his recording manager, Art Satherley, aware of the increasing popularity of duets, suggested that Cox bring a harmony singer to the studio with him. Although he had vocalized locally with his first cousin once removed, Woodrow "Red" Sovine, and another aspiring singer named Harry Griffith, Cox chose a young man from Cedar Grove, West Virginia, named Cliff Hobbs (1916-1961) as his duet partner on record. Hobbs generally sang the tenor part on the chorus of their recordings although he received equal billing on label credits. In all, the duo of Cox and Hobbs had some 60 released sides, mostly on OKeh, Vocalion and Conqueror, while Cox had an additional 45 solo recordings for the firm.

The Billy Cox legacy and influence rests largely on his widely varied songs. Topical numbers containing noteworthy social commentary included *N R A Blues*, *The Democratic Donkey* and *Franklin D. Roosevelt's Back Again*, the latter two penned and waxed shortly after the 1936 presidential election. He also recorded event songs written by Bob Miller, such as *The Trial of Bruno Richard Hauptmann*, *Will and Wiley's Last Flight* and *The Fate of Will Rogers and Wiley Post.* Later examples of his comic repertory are *Hitch-Hiker Blues*, *The Whole Dam Family* and *Barefoot Boys with Boots On.* He also wrote some fine love songs such as *Drift Along Pretty Moon*, *My Beautiful Blue-Eyed Blonde* and *Darling Rose Marie.*

The two songs most associated with Billy

Cox that have become all-time Country classics are *Filipino Baby* and *Sparkling Brown Eyes*. Although the former borrowed heavily from the lyrics of an 1898 composition of Charles K. Harris entitled *Mah Filipino Baby,* Cox claimed to have based it on the experiences of an uncle who had been in military service during and after the Philippine Insurrection. While the 1937 version by Cox and Hobbs made a minimal impact, slightly revised adaptations—mostly toning down some racially tinged phrases—became enormously popular during WWII. It no doubt reflected experiences with which tens of thousands of soldiers and sailors in the Pacific Theater could identify, and recordings by Cowboy Copas on King, Ernest Tubb on Decca, T. Texas Tyler on Four Star and Jim Robertson on Victor became best-sellers. Such artists as Wade Mainer, Cliff Bruner and Bill Carlisle quickly did covers of *Sparkling Brown Eyes* in the late 30's, and later recordings by Jerry and Sky (1945), Webb Pierce (1954), and Dickey Lee (1973) contributed to the song's enduring status. Tex Ritter also performed it in one of his musical western films. Sadly, Cox received little in the way of royalties from either number.

While two of his songs continued to be oft-heard by Country music fans, Billy Cox himself drifted slowly into obscurity after 1940. To some degree, he became a victim of his own apparently reckless and intemperate habits.

Some 25 years later, Ken Davidson, a Charleston resident and Old-Time music enthusiast, rediscovered the Dixie Songbird, residing in dire poverty in a run-down section of Charleston. Shortly afterward, he recorded a new album containing some of his older songs and new compositions, for Davidson's Kanawha label. Davidson also secured some monetary aid and local recognition for the aged performer before Cox's death some three years later. Several of Billy Cox's recordings have appeared on various anthologies. IMT

RECOMMENDED ALBUM:

"The Dixie Songbird" (Kanawha)(1967)

BILLY "CRASH" CRADDOCK

(Singer, Songwriter, Guitar)

Given Name:	**William Wayne Craddock**
Date of Birth:	**June 13, 1939**
Where Born:	**Greensboro, North Carolina**
Married:	**Mae**
Children:	**Billy, Jr., Steve, April**

Billy's sobriquet of "Mr. Country-Rock" is most apt, for Billy has always musically bridged Country music and rock'n'roll. He is also a consummate entertainer who is probably at his best on stage.

Billy was raised on a farm, one of 10 children of a poor family. He was taught to play guitar by his eldest brother Clarence (Chauncey), and saved up his pocket money earned by mowing his aunt's lawn to buy his first guitar when he was 11. While still at high school, Billy got together with his brother Ronald and they won a local talent contest for 13 straight weeks. While at high school, he got his nickname, "Crash," because as a running back in the football team, he used to crash through the opposition.

On leaving school, Billy and Ronald and two friends formed a Rockabilly band, the Four Rebels. During 1957, the group cut a single for Colonial and then, in 1958, they cut the single, *Ah, Poor Little Baby*, for the Date label. In 1959, a talent scout for Columbia Records spotted the band and asked Billy to come to Nashville and sign to the label. As often happens, the record company couldn't see what music Billy was into and tried to turn him into a Fabian clone. Under the names of Billy Craddock, Crash Craddock and finally Billy Crash Craddock, Columbia released seven singles, only one of which made any impression; that was the third, *Don't Destroy Me,* which charted for one week in the Pop Top 100, in 1959. Strangely, three of the singles did well in Australia.

Billy returned to Greensboro, where he worked in construction and had to suffer the jibes of his workmates. He also spent time stock car racing and working in a cigarette factory. He did some gigs around the area and then got married. This went on for some 10 years and then in 1969, he was spotted by Dale Morris, who was at the time a pharmaceutical salesman. Morris was sufficiently interested that two years later, when he and producer Ron Chancey formed the Cartwheel label, he called Billy to Nashville and cut the song *Knock Three Times*. Dawn had already entered the Pop charts with the song and would take it to No.1. Billy broke into the Pop listings with it but at a lowly level, but he did have a major Country success with it, reaching the Top 3, in 1971.

For the rest of 1971, Billy had two more major hits with the old Bobby Darin hit *Dream Lover* (Top 5) and another oldie, *You Better Move On* (Top 10), which had been a success for Arthur Alexander nearly a decade earlier. In 1972, Billy racked up a pair of biggies with *Ain't Nothin' Shakin' (But the Leaves on the Tree)* (Top 10) and the Top 5, *I'm Gonna Knock on Your Door*. Cartwheel released their penultimate single on Billy before licensing the single to ABC. *Afraid I'll Want to Love Her One More Time* seemed to fall into the cracks between the two labels and just failed to make the Top 20. Billy signed with ABC, but then it looked like the move to a major label was going to be detrimental to Billy's career, when the 1973 releases *Don't Be Angry* went Top 40 and *Slippin' and Slidin'* Top 15, respectively. However, Billy was voted *Music City News*' "Most Promising Male Artist" that year.

Then in 1973, it all came together for Billy, in a big way. *Till the Water Stops Runnin'* made it to the Top 10 and this was just a presage of the next three years. 1974 produced *Sweet Magnolia Blossom,* which reached the Top 3 and then Billy had back-to-back No.1's with *Rub It In* and *Ruby, Baby*. Both of these were big Pop hits peaking in the Top 20 and Top 40 respectively. The following year, Billy had a Top 5 record with *Still Thinking 'Bout You* and followed it with *I Love the Blues and the Boogie Woogie* (Top 10) and rounded off the year with the Top 3 smash *Easy as Pie,* which was also charted Pop. From this single on, his label had become ABC/Dot.

Through 1976, the hits came unabated. There was *Walk Softly* (Top 10), *You Rubbed It in All Wrong* (two successes on a single theme!)(Top 5) and the chart-topper *Broken Down in Tiny Pieces*. Then there was a little glitch with the next release, *Just a Little Thing,* which went Top 30, but then in June of 1977, Billy had a Top 10 success with the old Teresa Brewer hit *A Tear Fell.*

At the end of 1977, Billy left ABC/Dot for Capitol, but the old label continued to release singles and this caused confusion. Before his departure, he had a Top 10 record with *The First Time*, then in 1978, his first release for Capitol, *I Cheated on a Good Woman's Love,* made it to the Top 5, but while that was starting its ascent, ABC/Dot released *Another Woman,* which flopped at No. 92. Then in

Country-Rocker ***Billy "Crash" Craddock***

May, they released another single, *Think I'll Go Somewhere (and Cry Myself to Sleep)*, which coincided with *I've Been Too Long Lonely Baby* on Capitol. Neither single fared well.

Billy's next major hit was not until the end of 1978, when *Hubba Bubba* got into the Top 15, followed up by the 1979 Top 5 record *If I Could Write a Song as Beautiful as You*. However, with the advent of the latest rash of Pop-Country, Billy's rockier style was less in favor and from here on, only three of his singles made the Top 20, *Robinhood* (1979), *A Real Cowboy (You Say You're)* (1980) and *I Just Need You for Tonight* (1981).

By 1983, he was off Capitol and on his own Cee Cee label. In 1986, he recorded an album for a temporarily reactivated Dot that included his version of *Honey Don't* and *Three Times a Lady* as well as a re-recording of *Broken Down in Tiny Pieces*. MCA re-issued four albums that Billy had cut for the absorbed ABC/Dot label. In 1989, he came under the production guidance of Nelson Larkin and was signed to Atlantic, where he recorded the aptly titled ***Back on Track*** album. That year, Billy returned to the singles chart with the Top 70, *Just Another Miserable Day (Here in Paradise)*.

Billy "Crash" Craddock is now a performer back in vogue. At one time, he was the Rock man of Country but now that there is a more all-embracing attitude, he has become a performer who could happen all over again.

RECOMMENDED ALBUMS:

"Crash" (ABC/Dot)(1976) [Features Janie Fricke]
"Billy 'Crash' Craddock Sings His Greatest Hits Vol. 1" (MCA) [Originally released on ABC/Dot]
"Billy 'Crash' Craddock Sings His Greatest Hits Vol. 2" (MCA) [Originally released on ABC/Dot]
"Live-Billy 'Crash' Craddock" (MCA) [Originally released on ABC/Dot]
"The New Will Never Wear off of You" (Capitol)(1982)
"Greatest Hits-'Crash' Craddock" (Capitol)(1983)
"Back on Track" (Atlantic)(1989)

FLOYD CRAMER

(Piano, Organ, Synthesizer, Composer)
Date of Birth: **October 27, 1933**
Where Born: **Sampti, Louisiana**
Married: **Mary**
Children: **Dianne, Donna**

The piano sound of Floyd Cramer is as distinctive as, say, the guitar playing of Mark Knopfler, the vocals of George Jones or the dancing of Fred Astaire. His style was based on a whole-note slur using guitar-like slides to give a "lonesome" sound. He maintained that he developed the style from hearing Mother Maybelle Carter on the autoharp. However, there is also evidence that Floyd borrowed the style from songwriter Don Robertson's original demo of *Please Help Me I'm Falling*. Along with Chet Atkins, Floyd's playing can be heard with distinction on numerous RCA sessions that emanated from their Studio B.

Floyd grew up in Huttig, Arkansas, and when he was 5, his parents bought him a piano. He learned to play by ear and played a few dates while still at school. He left high school in 1951 and returned to Shreveport, where he appeared on KWKH's *Louisiana Hayride*. He toured with various performers from the show including Jim Reeves, Webb Pierce and Faron Young and was on the show when Elvis Presley made his debut. He also played some sessions for Abbott Records and in 1953, he cut his first single for the label, *Dancin' Diane / Little Brown Jug*.

Between 1952 and 1954, Floyd did session work in Nashville and came to the attention of Chet Atkins. Chet encouraged Floyd to make the move to Nashville, which he did in January 1955, becoming one of the busiest session players in town. He also played live dates with, among others, Elvis and Hank Williams, and appeared on some of the King's movie soundtracks as well as on singles such as *Heartbreak Hotel*.

Around this time, he made his debut on the *Grand Ole Opry*. He cut one album for MGM, ***That Honky-Tonk Piano***, in 1957 and then signed with RCA Victor. A year later, Floyd had his first Pop hit with *Flip, Flop and Bop* but it was not until 1960 that the impact of his playing really caused a major stir. Hank Locklin's recording of *Please Help Me I'm Falling* with that aforementioned distinctive riff went to No.1 for 14 weeks. Later in the year, Floyd had a monster hit of his own with his composition, *Last Date*. It soared to the Top 3 on the Pop charts and Top 15 on the Country lists. In 1961, Floyd followed up with another self-penned instrumental, *On the Rebound*, which provided him with his first international hit. It topped the U.K. national chart and stayed in the lists for nearly four months. His version of the Bob Wills' classic *San Antonio Rose* made the Top 10 on both the Country and Pop charts.

He continued racking up Pop hits with *Chattanooga Choo Choo* and *Hot Pepper* in 1962. He started a ***Class Of...*** series of albums in 1965, on which he released each year his versions of the year's top hits. He continued this series until 1974. To commemorate his 15 years with RCA (1974), Chet Atkins presented a surprised Floyd with an engraved metronome during a performance at the Festival of Music at Opryland.

Floyd released a notable album in 1977 entitled ***Keyboard Kick Band***, which featured him playing eight keyboards including an ARP synthesizer. Floyd's next sizable Country hit came in 1980 with his recording of the theme from the TV series *Dallas*.

From 1957 to 1981, Floyd released a constant and consistent flow of easy listening instrumental albums. He did some projects with Chet Atkins and Boots Randolph under the banner of the Masters Festival of Music and they recorded the album ***Chet, Floyd & Boots*** in 1971. He also recorded an album with Atkins and Danny Davis in 1977. Four of Floyd's albums, ***The Class of '73, Piano Masterpieces 1900-1975, The Class of '74 & '75*** and ***Floyd Cramer Country,*** were released in Quadraphonic sound.

In 1988, he released three albums on the highly successful label Step One, one of which, ***Just Me and My Piano!***, was just that. Floyd Cramer as a sessionman created a distinct sound that became a part of the new "accommodating" sound that Chet Atkins produced in the 60's, which strangely enough has worked with the developing sound of modern Country since then. As such, his relevance to Country music is more in that regard than for his solo work.

RECOMMENDED ALBUMS:

"That Honky-Tonk Piano" (MGM)(1957) [Re-packed as "Floyd Cramer Goes Honky Tonkin'" (MGM)(1964)]
"The Keyboard Kick Band" (RCA Victor)(1977)
"Collector Series" (RCA Victor)(1985)
"Country Gold" (Step One)(1988)
"Special Songs of Love" (Step One)(1988)
"Just Me and My Piano!" (Step One)(1988)

TOMMY CRANK

(Singer, Songwriter, Guitar)
Given Name: **William Thomas Crank**
Date of Birth: **April 13, 1926**
Place of Birth: **McKee, Kentucky**
Married: **1. Irma (dec'd.)**
2. Alberta
Children: **William T., Jr., Shirley, Charles, George**

Tommy Crank has spent many years of his life as a Gospel vocalist and promoter of Gospel music and singings. He has also been a minister, Gospel deejay and record producer.

A native of the same part of Appalachian Kentucky that produced such musical notables as Stringbean, Rusty Gabbard and Joe Isaacs, Tommy started singing at the age of 13 in a Gospel quartet. Three years later, the Crank family moved to Indiana, where Tommy's father was subsequently killed in an automobile accident. In 1946, Tommy organized a Country music group with some brothers named Jackson, and they played in neighborhood bars and clubs for a time.

After some of his associates met their death in a tragic accident, Crank moved back into sacred music and has remained in that field since. Relocating to southwest Ohio, an area containing numerous folks from the Kentucky hill country, he organized a group known as the Gospel Mountaineers that played in area churches for several years. During the later 50's, he remembers teaching a youthful Larry Sparks and his sister their first guitar chords.

In the late 50's, the Cranks moved to Cadillac, Michigan, to assist with an ailing relative. There Tommy pastored a church and subsequently started the IRMA record label, named for his then wife and standing for International Rural Music of America. This company produced a number of albums, chiefly of Bluegrass Gospel, for such artists as Wade Mainer, Lowell Varney, the Sons of the Gospel and Crank himself. Tommy went to WJCO Jackson, Michigan, where he worked as a Gospel deejay.

Carl Jessup started the Jessup and Michigan Bluegrass labels and Tommy helped him produce a number of Bluegrass and Gospel albums, including two by Ralph Stanley and some for Carl Story, Hylo Brown and Red Ellis, in addition to numerous other performers. Tommy recorded one album for Jessup and another for Old Homestead during this period.

In 1971, Tommy returned to southwestern Ohio, where is his own words, he has "bounced back and forth" a bit, residing for a time at West Union, but mostly in the Middletown-Lebanon area. From here he has participated in and promoted numerous Gospel sings. Through the years, Crank has sung, usually with Bluegrass accompaniment, in what might best be described as a raw primitive mountain style, somewhat reminiscent of Brother Claude Ely (a legendary figure who recorded some powerful sacred material for King in 1953 and afterward).

Since his move to the Buckeye State, Tommy has recorded for Pine Tree and has made several cassette tapes. As of May 1993, Tommy and his second wife, Alberta, were living in Middletown, Ohio, where age and health problems (he has had heart surgery) have slowed him down a little. However, he still remains active in the promotion of Gospel music and takes satisfaction in having been named a Kentucky Colonel in 1984 and honored with the nickname of "the Ole Gospel Mountaineer." IMT

RECOMMENDED ALBUMS:
"Tommy Crank Sings Bluegrass Songs" (IRMA)(1968)
"Tommy Crank and the Golden Strings" (Jessup)(1971)
"Tommy Crank Sings Revival Songs" (Old Homestead)(1972)
"Best Bluegrass Gospel" (Pine Tree)(1976)

ROY CROCKETT

(Singer, Songwriter, Guitar)
Given Name: Roy Crockett
Date of Birth: May 22, 1927
Where Born: Wayne County, West Virginia
Married: Doris Jean Rawsey
Children: Roy A., Kenneth M., Eva S., Donna G.

Roy Crockett grew up in Wayne County, which is situated between the city of Huntington and the Kentucky border. He always possessed an interest and involvement in the local musical scene, especially in Gospel music. In the early 50's, he worked in the Crockett Brothers Quartet. About 1955, the Crocketts won a talent contest that was part of a Flatt and Scruggs show at the Clark Theater in Grayson, Kentucky. Their prize included some free airtime at WCMI Ashland, Kentucky.

After Earl Scruggs suffered serious injuries in an auto accident, the Foggy Mountain Boys needed some extra help to fill out their shows and they got Roy to help with the singing on their regular Thursday evening show at WSAZ-TV and with their live performances later that night. Roy stayed on after Earl returned and for the next 8 years, whenever the group worked a date in that region, Roy was there, usually singing a hymn. While Hylo Brown and the Timberliners were on WSAZ-TV, Roy played a similar role.

In the meanwhile, Charlie Monroe and Everett Lilly came to town and initiated a similar program on rival station WHTN, recruiting Roy as a band member. However, the situation did not work out as planned and the show was soon terminated. About 1962, Roy decided to form a part-time band of his own, the Pleasant Valley Boys, which spent years playing and promoting Bluegrass in the region. Jesse McKenzie played mandolin and shared the vocal duties with Roy, who played rhythm guitar. Charlie Love of Proctorville played banjo for several years until Richard Bird replaced him. John Parog did the fiddle work, while first Don Brown and then Carl Norris played bass fiddle. Mike Johnson and Isaiah Bird also served stints with the Pleasant Valley Boys.

Over a period of several years, the band recorded a single followed by three albums. The single contained what had already become Roy's signature song, *Hide Me Rock of Ages*, which had been Roy's most requested number from the Foggy Mountain Boys days. The first album, like the single, came out on the D & R label and contained a mixture of sacred and secular songs, most of them composed by various members of the band. The second album, on Rem, was all Gospel and was also comprised mostly of original compositions. The third album, for Lemco, cut in 1972-1973, contained well-chosen, but generally not over-recorded Bluegrass standards.

The Pleasant Valley Boys played less often through the 80's, but remained on the scene until 1987. Roy, meanwhile, retired after some 20 years of employment with Haudille Industries, Inc. More recently, he has organized a Gospel group, the Inheritors, who have maintained a busy schedule in area churches. He remains a devotee of traditional Bluegrass and retains fond memories of his past involvement in the world of music. IMT

RECOMMENDED ALBUMS:
"Gospel and Bluegrass Music" (D & R)(1965)
"Gospel Songs Bluegrass Style" (Rem)(1967)
"By Popular Demand" (Lemco)(1973)

CROOK AND CHASE

LORIANNE CROOK
(Talk Show Host)
Given Name: Lorianne Lynee Crook
Where Born: Nashville, Tennessee
Date of Birth: February 18, 1957
Married: Jim Owens

CHARLIE CHASE:
(Talk Show Host)
Given Name: Charles Wayne Chase
Date of Birth: October 19, 1952
Where Born: Rogersville, Tennessee
Married: Karen
Children: David, Rachel

Millions of Country music fans have tuned in to *Crook and Chase* five nights a week to see their favorite singing stars and for the latest in Country music news. The popular show debuted on the Nashville Network in 1985 and was expanded to an hour in 1992. In 1993 the two television personalities premiered a new 90-minute show for TNN called *Music City Tonight*. This Monday-through-Friday show filled the time slot left by the retirement of Ralph Emery and his *Nashville Now* cable television program.

It was a part-time job during her last year of graduate school that changed everything for Lorianne Crook. She was working for the Nashville Sounds baseball team and was asked to do a TV commercial for a free-bat night. That exposure to the bright lights of a TV studio planted a seed that led her to seek work first as a news reporter for KAUZ-TV in Wichita Falls, Texas, in 1980. Lorianne had planned on a career as an interpreter with the Central Intelligence Agency (CIA). A magna cum laude graduate in Russian and Chinese from Vanderbilt University, Lorianne was already in the process of getting her security clearance when she made the baseball team commercial.

In 1981, Lorianne returned to Nashville to host the local entertainment show *PM Magazine*. Two years later television producer Jim Owens asked her to produce and co-host a new nationally syndicated show. Owens had also invited popular Nashville radio and television personality Charlie Chase to co-host the show he called *This Week in Country Music*. The show gained a wide national audience and became the first major outlet for Country music videos. *This Week in Country Music* offered a great opportunity for exposing Country music and helped expose many new artists such as Ricky Van Shelton, Suzie Bogguss and Vince Gill.

Lorianne married producer Jim Owens in 1985 and teamed with him to produce a variety of award-winning specials and series for TV. In 1986, they developed *Crook and Chase* for Nashville Network, combining live performances with entertainment news. The show was named "Best Entertainment News Program" in the Second Annual Readers Poll of the *Cable Guide* published in April 1988. In 1992 the same magazine named Lorianne one of the "Ten Most Beautiful Women on Cable Television."

In addition to her work with Charlie Chase, Lorianne produced a series of specials for TNN called *Celebrities Offstage*. The in-depth interviews show featured Country music's biggest stars including Alabama, Ricky Skaggs, Lorrie Morgan, Ricky Van Shelton and Reba McEntire.

Unlike his co-host, Charlie Chase always knew he wanted a career in broadcasting. He got his first job as a radio announcer when he was 13 years old in his hometown of Rogersville, Tennessee. Young Charlie rose every morning at 5:00 a.m. and rode his bike seven miles to sign the stations on the air. When the station secretary came in to work, she took him to school and picked him up in the afternoon so he could return to work at the station until sign off.

Charlie moved on to radio stations in the East Tennessee towns of Kingsport and Knoxville before moving to Nashville. After a stint at pop station WMAK, Chase became a deejay at Country music's legendary WSM. He spent nine years at the 50,000 watt home of the *Grand Ole Opry* and was a two-time finalist for the Country Music Association "Disc Jockey of the Year" award.

Lorianne Crook and Charlie Chase

In 1982, Charlie made his TV debut when WSM's TV station invited him to host their *Channel 4 Magazine*. The following year he came to the attention of producer Jim Owens, who asked Charlie to team up with Lorianne Crook for the syndicated *This Week in Country Music*. The series moved out of syndication and onto TNN in 1987 until it was canceled in 1990.

In addition to his work with Lorianne Crook, Chase hosted and produced a series of specials for TNN titled *Funny Business with Charlie Chase*. The comedy show chronicled his practical jokes on a variety of stars including Tricia Yearwood, Larry Gatlin, Clint Black, Reba McEntire and Vince Gill. Charlie continued his practical jokes as an occasional feature of TNN's *Music City Tonight*.

Charlie debuted as a recording artist with the album ***My Wife...My Life*** on Epic/Nashville in the fall of 1993. The project was a mixture of recitations and songs featuring many special guests. Chase sang *Thank God for Kids* with the Oak Ridge Boys and other selections featured Collin Raye and Garth Brooks.

Lorianne Crook and Charlie Chase also host a weekly four-hour radio countdown show. Since 1988, The *Nashville Record Review* has been heard on more than 300 radio stations in the United States, Japan and the United Kingdom. JIE

CROOK BROTHERS

Formed: 1920's

HERMAN CROOK
(Harmonica)
Given Name: Herman Crook
Date of Birth: 1899
Where Born: Scottsboro, Tennessee
Date of Death: 1988

MATTHEW CROOK
(Harmonica)
Given Name: Matthew Crook
Date of Birth: 1896
Where Born: Scottsboro, Tennessee
Date of Death: Unknown

LEWIS CROOK
(Banjo, Guitar, Vocals)
Given Name: Lewis Crook
Date of Birth: 1909
Where Born: Trousdale County, Tennessee

One of the longest-running bands in Country music history, the Crook Brothers band was a fixture on the *Grand Ole Opry* from 1926, just a few months after the show began, until 1988, when leader Herman Crook passed away—a run of some 62 years. Although they made few records—by choice—and toured very little—also by choice—their music became an important part of the *Opry*. Herman Crook's harmonica gave the band a unique sound and a distinctive role in the history of string band music

The Crook Brothers featured no fiddle at all, but the sparkling twin harmonicas of Herman and Matthew. They were real brothers, born in a rural community about 15 miles from Nashville. Both parents died when the boys were quite young, and older brothers and sisters reared them. An older brother also taught them how to play the harmonica, an instrument which was incredibly popular in middle Tennessee around the turn of the century. An uncle had a cylinder player and on it the boys heard their first records and some of their first songs.

As a young man, Herman worked at a variety of jobs in Nashville. He eventually became an expert cigar roller and soon joined his brother in playing at union halls and at local house dances in east Nashville. Like many early *Opry* stars, the Crooks first played on the small station WDAD, which took to the air before WSM. However, by summer of 1926, *Opry* manager George D. Hay had heard of the Crooks, and invited them to appear on WSM.

Like many other early *Opry* bands, the Crooks appeared on the show on alternate weeks; this left them free to work on other stations, including WBAW and WLAC (both in Nashville). They were popular enough in the late 1920's that they worked as regulars on both WSM and rival WLAC. Then, in 1927, an unusual coincidence occurred that was to have a lasting and major impact on the band. At a fiddlers' contest in Walterhill, Tennessee, Herman ran into his old friend and mentor Dr. Humphrey Bate, who had in tow a young banjoist and guitarist from his native Trousdale County. Coincidentally, his name was Lewis Crook—though he was absolutely no relation to Herman or Matthew. By the fall of 1929, Herman asked Lewis to join the band, which then included a piano player, a guitarist, and three men named Crook.

In 1928, the band participated in the famous first Nashville recording session, held by Victor. They did four instrumentals, all featuring the twin harmonica lead of Matthew and Herman: *My Wife Died on Friday Night*, *Jobbin' Gettin' There, Goin' Across the Sea* and *Love Somebody*. All sold fairly well, and were later re-issued by Montgomery Ward for their catalog sales. They would be the only records the band made until the 1960's, when they cut half of an lp for Starday.

About a year after Lewis joined the band, Matthew quit to work full-time for the Nashville police force. Unable to find a good second harmonica, Herman added a fiddle player and began designing a style that was based on the odd texture of the fiddle and harmonica playing unison lead. For a time, Kirk McGee played with the group, then he was replaced by Floyd Etheridge, who stayed with the band throughout most of the 1930's. A native of McEwen, Tennessee, Etheridge came from the same West Tennessee area that spawned fiddler Arthur Smith—in fact, he had played with Smith as a young man.

Also by the early 1930's, Lewis Crook got up enough courage to start singing on the air, and this helped the band's repertoire. Soon Lewis was singing on about half the tunes on an average set: Jimmie Rodgers hits like *Blue Yodel No.1*, Vernon Dalhart favorites like *Wreck of the Old 97* and Charlie Poole favorites like *May I Sleep in Your Barn Tonight Mister*. By the 40's, *Opry* air checks of the band show another shift had taken place: a smooth harmony trio was added, featuring father and son, Neil Matthews, Sr. and Jr. (the latter eventually became a member of the Jordanaires). These vocals, framed by Herman's warm, bluesy harmonica, helped modernize the sound of the band, and bring it into the 40's.

Through all of this, and on into the 60's, when the Crooks were rediscovered by the Folk revival, Herman insisted on seeing the music only as a hobby, and continued to work at his day job. He refused to tour, and was lukewarm about making records. In 1976, Charles Wolfe had arranged a recording date with Rounder for the band, but Herman kept finding excuses to put it off. The band was eventually combined with the remnants of the Possum Hunters, and survived on the *Opry* until Herman's death in 1988. CKW

RECOMMENDED ALBUM:

"Sam & Kirk McGee & the Crook Brothers" (Starday)(1962) [One side each]

***The Crook Brothers** band with Herman Crook on harmonica*

ROB CROSBY

(Singer, Songwriter, Guitar)

Given Name:	**Robert Crosby Hoar**
Date of Birth:	**April 25, 1954**
Where Born:	**Sumpter, South Carolina**
Married:	**Pam**
Children:	**Matthew**

Rob Crosby got his first guitar and wrote his first song when he was 9 years old. By the time he was in the fifth grade, he had a band called the Radiations that performed at school functions. In high school he continued writing and performing with a three-piece acoustic group. He drew inspiration from the songwriting of Kris Kristofferson, Bob Dylan, and Paul Simon. Rob also cites the vocal arrangements of the Beatles and Crosby, Stills & Nash as major influences.

While attending the University of South Carolina, Rob worked the nightclub circuit as a member of the band Savannah. When the group broke up he began performing as a solo artist for the college audiences. Eventually he formed the Rob Crosby Group and traveled the Southeast. The band developed a loyal following in the South Carolina cities of Columbia, Charleston and Augusta. When the group disbanded in 1974, Rob moved his family to Nashville. Two members of the group also relocated to Tennessee and they performed in Nashville clubs with Rob.

Rob landed a job as a staff writer with a small music publishing company and within the year scored a Top 30 hit in 1985 when the group Chance recorded his *She Told Me Yes*. Other artists began to record his songs, including Eddy Raven and, in 1990, Lee Greenwood, who had a major hit with Rob's *Holdin' a Good Hand*. Rob supplemented his songwriting by singing radio and TV commercials for clients such as Coors Beer and McDonald's.

Record producer Tim DuBois heard Rob perform at a songwriters night hosted by the Nashville Entertainment Association and introduced himself after the show. He told Rob he liked the songs he'd heard and would like to hear more, because he was producing a record for the group Restless Heart. Rob sent DuBois a tape and a week later got a call from DuBois' partner, Scott Hendricks, informing him they wanted to produce him. While Rob was working in the studio with Hendricks, DuBois accepted an offer to direct Arista Records' new Country Division. Rob was one of the first artists signed to the label.

Rob's debut album, ***Solid Ground***, was released in 1991, producing the hit singles *Love Will Bring Her Around* (1990, Top 15), *She's a Natural* (1991, Top 15) and *Still Burning for You*, which went Top 20 at the end of 1991. Rob wrote or co-wrote all the songs on the album. The critics applauded his sensitive lyrics directed to the female listeners. In 1992, Rob was unable to maintain his success and the first single of the year, *Working Woman*, only made the Top 30. He released his second album, entitled ***Another Time & Place***, and the first single from that, *She Wrote the Book,* only reached the Top 60. He followed that with *It's in the Blood*, which although accompanied by a good video, failed to get past the Top 50. Shortly after that, Rob was dropped from Arista and his future now has a question mark over it. JIE

RECOMMENDED ALBUMS:

"Solid Ground" (Arista)(1991)
"Another Time & Place" (Arista)(1992)

HUGH CROSS

(Singer, Songwriter, Announcer, Guitar, Banjo)
Given Name: Hugh Ballard Cross
Date of Birth: 1904
Where Born: Oliver Springs, Tennessee
Date of Death: 1970

Though he is primarily remembered today as the source for Roy Acuff's version of *Wabash Cannonball*, Hugh Cross was one of the best-known recording artists from east Tennessee in the 20's and 30's. A native of Olive Springs, a hamlet northwest of Knoxville, Cross signed a record contract with Columbia in the 20's, and soon became one of their favorite singers. His high tenor paired with the voice of Riley Puckett on the original 1927 record of *Red River Valley* (the first recording of the cowboy classic, which featured Clayton McMichen on fiddle), and his 1928 recording (as a duet with his wife) of *You're As Welcome As the Flowers in May*, sold over 74,000 copies for Columbia. Cross and Puckett cut a further seven sides together in two sessions in April and October 1928, including *Gonna Raise a Ruckus Tonight*, which was later released on Regal as by the Alabama Barn Stormers, *My Wild Irish Rose* and *Call Me Back Pal O'Mine.* As a songwriter, he was responsible for the later Roy Acuff hit *Don't Make Me Go to Bed and I'll Be Good*. It was Acuff's version of this song that turned songwriter/publisher Fred Rose onto Country music.

When he was 16, Cross joined a medicine show and by the late 1920's, he was on radio over Knoxville. From 1930 to 1933, he was a member of John Lair's Cumberland Ridge Runner on WLS' *National Barn Dance*. He toured stations as a single through the 1930's, including WWVA in Wheeling, and in 1937, he joined singer/bass player Shug Fisher in an act called Hugh and Shug's Radio Pals. This was essentially a polished string band that featured Lenny Ayleshire on accordion and Ted Grant on fiddle. They made a dozen interesting sides for Decca in 1937, including well-known pieces like *Back to the Old Smoky Mountains* and *There's a Blue Sky Over Yonder*. For many years, Cross and Fisher remained a bankable and popular radio act, later performing on WLW's Boone County Jamboree. Cross and Fisher stayed together until 1940.

Hugh Cross later did some announcing and A & R work before retiring back to Tennessee, where he died around 1970 in Oliver Springs. CKW

RECOMMENDED ALBUMS:

Hugh & Shug's Radio Pals can be heard on one track, "Sugar Babe" on:
"Western Swing and Country Jazz" (MCA Japan)
Hugh Cross & Riley Puckett can be heard on one track, "Red River Valley" on:
"Duets" (booklet notes by CKW) (Time Life CW-05)

Hugh Cross** (left) with, from left-to-right, **Linnie Ales**, **Shug Fisher** and **Lonnie Glosson

J.D. CROWE

(Banjo, Guitar, Singer, Songwriter)
Given Name: James Dee Crowe
Date of Birth: August 27, 1937
Where Born: Lexington, Kentucky
Married: Sheryl
Children: David, Stacey

J.D. Crowe, who became one of the major forces in progressive Bluegrass, first became enthused about the music after hearing Flatt & Scruggs on the *Kentucky Barn Dance* in 1950. Fascinated by the banjo, he attended the show every weekend, always sitting in the front row so he could see Scruggs play. J.D. played with local groups and then passed a summer playing with Pee Wee Lambert and Curley Parker, while also working in construction during the day.

In 1956, J.D. got his major break as a professional musician when Jimmy Martin was driving through Lexington, Kentucky, and heard the 16-year-old banjo player on a local radio station. Martin was so impressed that he drove to the station and offered Crowe a job. During his tenure with Jimmy Martin, J.D. frequently sang songs by Little Richard. He was influenced by rock'n'roll and Blues and in fact studied Blues guitar, so as to adapt the style to banjo.

J.D. left Jimmy Martin in 1962, his place being taken by Bill Emerson. J.D. then spent time performing in Lexington beer joints, later moving "uptown" to the Holiday Inn. His band, the Kentucky Mountain Boys, made three records for Lemco featuring a traditional sound on songs ranging from old Bluegrass numbers to modern Country and Rock.

In 1971, J.D. changed his band from an acoustic to an electric sound. That year, mandolinist Doyle Lawson left the group and joined the Country Gentlemen. J.D.'s group, the New South, signed with Starday in 1973, but their most important record, indeed the most influential Bluegrass album of the decade, ***J.D. Crowe and the New South***, appeared on Rounder in 1975. This band consisted of Tony Rice (guitar and lead singer), Ricky Skaggs (mandolin and tenor singer), Bobby Slone (fiddle and bass) and Jerry Douglas (Dobro). The New South performed a mixture of old Bluegrass and contemporary songs in a very sophisticated manner that at the time was considered very daring. Nevertheless, their work was not dramatically different from the blend J.D. had always sought in his music. Although the New South brought to fruition one of J.D.'s long-time desires, blending various types of music together under the general heading of

Bluegrass, the band's work did not please Bluegrass purists.

Undoubtedly, one of the major reasons J.D. utilized non-Bluegrass elements in his band's music was to give it broader appeal. He felt that hardcore Bluegrass recordings would never experience great commercial success because they were too specialized. Nevertheless, he didn't entirely forsake the traditional sound. In 1979, J.D. and the New South recorded ***Live in Japan***, during their April 18 concert at Kosei Nenkin Sho Hall in Tokyo. The line-up for the band was now Keith Whitley (lead vocals, guitar), Bobby Slone (fiddle), Jimmy Gaudreau (mandolin, tenor vocals) and Steve Bryant (bass). This album was not released until 1987.

In 1980, J.D. joined Tony Rice, Doyle Lawson, Bobby Hicks and Todd Phillips and the following year did an album simply titled ***The Bluegrass Album***, which proved sufficiently successful that several subsequent albums were issued and the band made a large number of festival and club appearances. By ***Volume V***, the line-up of the band was Crowe, Lawson, Rice, Jerry Douglas, Vassar Clements and Mark Schatz. J.D.'s 1982 album, ***Somewhere Between,*** featured Keith Whitley and from this came the single *I Never Go Round Mirrors*, which Keith would later record.

In 1983, the New South won a Grammy Award for "Best Country Instrumental Performance" for the track *Fireball*, which featured Ricky Skaggs, Jerry Douglas, Tony Rice and Todd Phillips. In 1986, J.D. and the New South released the Rounder album ***Straight Ahead*** to critical acclaim. J.D. came off the road in 1988, tired of traveling and between then and 1991, he sat in with various bands, notably Tony Rice's. In 1991, he decided to return, but said that he would not tour full-time again. WKM

RECOMMENDED ALBUMS:

J.D. Crowe and the Kentucky Mountain Boys:
"Bluegrass Holiday" (Lemco)(1968) [With Red Allen] [Re-released on King-Bluegrass]
"Ramblin' Boy" (Lemco) [Re-released on King-Bluegrass and then on Rebel as "Blackjack" in 1991]
"The Model Church" (Lemco) [Re-released on Rebel]
J.D. Crowe and the New South:
"J.D. Crowe & the New South" (Starday)(1972)
"J.D. Crowe & the New South" (Rounder)(1975)
"My Home Ain't in the Hall of Fame (Rounder)(1980)
"Somewhere Between" (Rounder)(1982)
"Straight Ahead" (Rounder)(1986)
The Bluegrass Album Band:
"The Bluegrass Album" (Rounder)(1981)
"The Bluegrass Album, Volume II" (Rounder)
"The Bluegrass Album, Volume III, California Connection" (Rounder)
"The Bluegrass Album, Volume IV" (Rounder)
"The Bluegrass Album, Volume V, Sweet Sunny South" (Rounder)(1989)

RODNEY CROWELL

(Singer, Songwriter, Guitar, Drums, Record Producer)
Date of Birth: **August 7, 1950**
Where Born: **Houston, Texas**
Married: **1. div.**
2. Rosanne Cash (m. 1979)(div. 1992)
Children: **Hannah, Caitlin Rivers, Chelsea Jane, Carrie Kathleen**

Of all Country music stars, Rodney Crowell deservedly earns the title of Renaissance man. For many years he has received plaudits for his songwriting, playing and record producing and then in the 80's he became a much lauded chart act.

Rodney has music in his genes. Both of his grandfathers were musically inclined, one being a church choir leader and the other being a Bluegrass banjoist. In addition, one of his grandmothers played guitar. His father was a full-time musician until the Depression forced him to become a construction worker, although he continued playing bars and honky tonks.

Young Crowell started playing drums in his father's band at the age of 11 and formed his first band while still in school. He played his first professional gig independent of his father, in 1965, when he formed the Arbitrators (with Rodney playing guitar), which had a girl drummer. In order to avoid being sent to Vietnam, Rodney decided to go to college.

In 1972, Rodney went to Nashville, where he met Townes Van Zandt, Guy Clark and Mickey Newbury. While playing an acoustic set at the Steak and Ale, he was spotted by Jerry Reed and his manager. Rodney sang the self-penned *You Can't Keep Me Here in Tennessee* and Reed invited him to his table and two days later, Jerry recorded the song and also signed Rodney to his publishing company.

When Emmylou Harris invited Rodney to join the Hot Band in 1975 he relocated to Los Angeles. While with Emmylou, he blossomed as a songwriter. Emmylou recorded many of Rodney's songs at this time and subsequently, including *Till I Gain Control Again*, *Ain't Livin' Long Like This*, *Leaving Louisiana in the Broad Daylight*, *Amarillo* (co-written with Emmylou), *You're Supposed to be Feeling Good*, *Ashes by Now*, *Tulsa Queen* and *I Had My Heart Set on You* (a 1986 hit). Rodney stayed with Emmylou until 1977, by which time he had become in demand.

In 1978, Rodney and his band, the Cherry Bombs, signed to Warner Brothers Records and strangely, his first hit was not his own composition. His cover of the Dallas Frazier standard, *Elvira*, just scraped in the lower levels of the charts. That year, LaCosta (Tanya Tucker's sister) charted with Rodney's *Even Cowgirls Get the Blues*. This song would be a hit again in 1980 for Lynn Anderson and in 1986 for Johnny Cash & Waylon Jennings. Rodney now got into production through his wife Rosanne's coercion and produced her 1980 album ***Seven Year Ache***. The following year, Rodney was again at the foot of the charts with his version of *(Now and Then There's) A Fool Such As I*. That year Bobby Bare had a hit with *Till I Gain Control Again*. This song would provide Crystal Gayle with a No.1 hit in 1983.

Rodney achieved a breakthrough of sorts in 1980 when *Ashes by Now* became a crossover hit, reaching the Pop Top 40 and being a lower-level Country entry. In 1981, Rodney's record *Stars on the Water* also crossed over and reached the Country Top 30. He followed this up with the Country hit *Victim or a Fool*, in 1982. While with Warner Brothers, Rodney released three albums that started to create a cult following, ***Ain't Living Long Like This*** (1978), ***But What Will the Neighbors Think*** (1980) and ***Rodney Crowell*** (1981). A fourth album was rejected by the label.

During the late 70's and 80's, Rodney's reputation as a songwriter was enhanced by major successes such as *No Memories Hangin' Round* by Rosanne Cash and Bobby Bare (1979), *Leavin' Louisiana in the Broad Daylight*, a No.1 for the Oak Ridge Boys in 1980, *Ain't No Money* by Rosanne Cash (1982), *Shame on the Moon*, a Top 3 Pop hit for Bob Seger (1982), *Long Hard Road (Sharecropper's Dream)*, a No.1 for the Nitty Gritty Dirt Band in 1984 (who had enjoyed a minor hit in 1980 with Rodney's *An American Dream*, as the Dirt Band) and *Somewhere Tonight,* a 1987 chart topper for Highway 101 co-written with Harlan Howard.

Rodney's career propulsion started with the move to Columbia in 1986. His debut album, ***Street Language***, produced by Rodney and the legendary Booker T. Jones, was critically acclaimed. The first single from it, *When I'm Free Again*, which Rodney had written with Will Jennings, made the Top 40, but the two follow-up singles in 1987 did not fare that well with John Hiatt's *She Loves the Jerk* and the Crowell-Rosanne Cash song *Looking for You* only reaching the lower levels. However, during that year, Rodney produced Rosanne's Grammy Award winning album, ***King's Record Shop***.

1988 was the decisive year. Rodney released the splendid album ***Diamonds and Dirt***, which was produced by Rodney and Tony Brown. Suddenly, Rodney was the golden boy. The first release from the album, *It's Such a Small World*, a duet with Rosanne, went to No.1 and stayed on the charts for over five months. He followed this with the melodic *I Couldn't Leave You If I Tried*, also a No.1, and made it three in a row with *She's Crazy for Leavin'*, which he had written with his old friend Guy Clark. 1989 opened up with Rodney making it four straight No.1's from the same album with *After All This Time*. ***Diamonds and Dirt*** was Certified Gold in 1990, having been nominated for three Grammy Awards and as the CMA "Album of the Year," the preceding year. He won a Grammy for *After All This Time* as "Best Country Song."

Rodney's follow-up album, the 1989 ***Keys to the Highway***, did not have quite the impact as its predecessor and two of the songs, *Many a Long and Lonesome Highway* and *Things I Wish I'd Said*, were inspired by loss of his father, James. During 1989, Rodney had a further No.1 with *Above and Beyond* and the Top 3 *Many a Long and Lonesome Highway*. Rodney started out 1990 with the Top 10 *If Looks Could Kill* and then his success level fell away. *My Past Is Present* (Top 25, 1990), *Now that We're Alone* (Top 20) and *Things I Wish I'd Said* (Top 75) (both 1991).

Rodney returned in 1992, following the painful divorce from Rosanne, with the appropriately titled ***Life Is Messy***. The album was co-produced with Bobby Colomby, Larry Klein and John Leventhal and features guests Steve Winwood and Linda Ronstadt (a former Cherry Bomb). For many the result was too emotional to bear. Rodney returned to the upper echelons of the chart with *Lovin' All Night* (Top 10) and *What Kind of Love* (Top 15); the latter was co-written by Rodney and Roy Orbison.

Rodney is a man who impresses. Well remembered is the night he made his debut on the *Grand Ole Opry* in 1989, to the great delight of the legendary Bill Monroe.

RECOMMENDED ALBUMS:

"Ain't Living Long Like This" (Warner Brothers)(1978)
"But What Will the Neighbors Think" (Warner Brothers)(1980)
"Rodney Crowell" (Warner Brothers)(1981)
"Street Language" (Columbia)(1986)
"Diamonds and Dirt" (Columbia)(1987)
"Keys to the Highway" (Columbia)(1989)
"Life Is Messy" (Columbia)(1992)

Simon Crum refer FERLIN HUSKY

JAN CRUTCHFIELD

(Songwriter, Singer, Guitar, Keyboards)

Given Name:	**Jan Lynn Crutchfield**
Date of Birth:	**February 26, 1938**
Where Born:	**Paducah, Kentucky**
Married:	**1. Helen (div.)**
	2. Mary Beatrice (Bea)
Children:	**Rose Lyn, Janalyn "Pumkin," Holly Jo**

Jan Crutchfield is one of the unsung heroes of songwriting, whose songs have been sung and recorded by the cream of Country music. Jan began writing back in the 50's and is still "current" in the 90's.

Jan started out in the music business while still a teenager. When 11, he and his elder brother Jerry sang tenor in various Gospel groups and later harmony groups in the style of the Inkspots and the Mills Brothers. Jan was at the time in the Hawkins Quartet on WKYB and WPAD Paducah and Jerry in the Melody Masters. They sent off tapes to the most important people in Country music, including Chet Atkins, Don Law, Owen Bradley and Ken Nelson. After some discussion, Chet Atkins invited them to record for RCA in 1955. They also did some back-up singing for, among others, Hawkshaw Hawkins. RCA released two singles under the name of the Country Gentlemen, including John D. Loudermilk's *A Rose and a Baby Ruth*, which was a major hit for George Hamilton IV.

However, it was felt that the name was not conducive to what they were doing and shortly after, they became the Escorts. In 1956, they auditioned in Nashville for the *Arthur Godfrey Talent Scouts Show* and went to New York for the show, which they won. It was now decision time. Jan decided that he wanted to write and make singles. He returned to Paducah but decided that he needed to be in Memphis. There he did back-up at Sun Records but couldn't make a living so he returned to Paducah.

Jan made the decision to move to Nashville in 1959 and after 6 months, Jerry moved to Nashville as well and joined Tree. Initially, Jan wrote for Tree Music and got cuts with Eddy Arnold. He then joined Pamper Music alongside Hank Cochran and Harlan Howard. Teddy and Doyle Wilburn approached him in 1961, to join their Surefire Music. Here, Jan was writing and plugging and also singing on demos for other people. In addition, he supplemented his income with records imitating the vocals of the stars.

He cut singles with Decca with Owen Bradley that included *Lost Forever* in 1968. He also recorded for Mercury and United Artists. He continued recording until the mid-70's, his last single being *Going Away Party* from the album ***Bob Wills for the Last Time***, which was produced by Tommy Allsop.

By the beginning of the 60's, Jan had remarried and decided to leave Surefire. He was asked to join Cedarwood Music, but initially decided against it. However, after Jim Denny's death and Bill Denny's arrival as company head, Jan joined as Professional Manager. He stayed there for two years.

At this point, Owen Bradley set up Forrest Hills Music and Jan joined alongside Jerry Bradley. In 1967, Wilma Burgess had a big hit with Jan's *Tear Time*. Eleven years later, the song would be recorded by Dave & Sugar and go to No.1. He then part owned Dixie Jane Music, which he later owned completely. In 1969, he rejoined Tree Music as Director, where he stayed for three years. Also in 1969, Jack Greene had a No.1 hit with Jan's *Statue of a Fool*. Jan was approached in 1972 by some investors to buy out Dixie Jane, which Jan sold in 1992. In 1974, Brian Collins had a Top 10 hit with *Statue of a Fool*.

By the late 70's, Jan put together a deal with MCA Music, where his brother worked and set up Red Angus Music. It was through this company that he had his hits with Lee Greenwood. In 1982, he was approached by Chappell Music. He set up Jan Crutchfield Music with them and stayed to 1984.

Jan then returned to Red Angus/MCA Music, but once Jerry left, he decided to move on. From then on until 1992, he didn't write much. In 1989, however, Ricky Van Shelton reprised *Statue of a Fool* and took it to the Top 3. In 1992, Jan joined up with NEM and set up Peetie Pie Music. Also in 1992, he left BMI after some 30 years and joined ASCAP.

Jan has established a very low profile, intentionally. He writes about 15 songs a year and relies on quality rather than quantity. He mainly writes on his own and shuns what he calls "writing orgies," which is three or more people writing a song. He considers that his family is the most important thing in his life and enjoys hunting (for which he goes up to his place in Paris, Tennessee) and participating in archery with his wife, Bea.

Jan is the winner of many awards, yet he is not a man that seeks them. He is a professional songwriter who knows his craft. He is outspoken about his God-given talents and quite rightly so. He has enough credentials to see off most other people who think they're writers. It is strange that Jan Crutchfield has not been inducted into the Songwriters Hall of Fame. An omission that must soon be remedied.

CUMBERLAND RIDGE RUNNERS

Formed:	**1932**
Members:	
John Lair	**Harmonica, Jug**
Linda Parker	**Vocals**
Karl Davis	**Guitar**
Hartford Taylor	**Mandolin**
Ramblin' Red Foley	**Bass, Vocals**
Doc Hopkins	**Guitar, Vocals**
Homer "Slim" Miller	**Fiddle**
Hugh Cross	**Vocals, Guitar, Banjo**

After young John Lair established himself at radio station WLS in Chicago in the early 30's, he began to recruit for the station's *National Barn Dance* a number of gifted young musicians from his native eastern Kentucky. Many came from the Renfro Valley area (where later would start his *Renfro Valley Barn Dance*), and were formed into a loose confederation called the Cumberland Ridge Runners. Though the band went through several early personnel changes, it eventually stabilized to include Linda Parker, a young singer born in Covington, Kentucky, but reared in Indiana; Karl Davis and Hartford Taylor, a guitar-mandolin duo from Mount Vernon, Kentucky; a 20-year-old from Bluelick, Kentucky, who played bass and occasionally sang, named Ramblin' Red Foley; a guitarist and vocalist from Harlan County who was reared in Renfro Valley, Doc Hopkins; and Homer "Slim" Miller, a fiddler born in Lisbon, Indiana, but reared in Renfro Valley. One final key member was Hugh Cross, from Oliver Springs, Tennessee. He was the only member who had not grown up playing Kentucky music. He had been active on records, recording as a duet partner with Riley Puckett and Clayton McMichen. Lair himself announced for the group, and occasionally played harmonica or jug.

This young, spirited group soon became the favorite on the *National Barn Dance* in the mid-30's. It was, in a sense, an all-star group, and each of its members (except for Linda Parker, who was killed in a car crash in 1936) went on to much greater fame. The band recorded some 42 songs for ARC between 1933 and 1935, and of these, only six really feature the overall band. Featured specialities included Red Foley doing *The Lone Cowboy* and *Footprints in the Snow*; Linda Parker did *Take Me Back to Renfro Valley* and *I'll Be All Smiles Tonight*; Karl and Harty did *I'm Here to Get My Baby out of Jail*, and Slim Miller did a wonderful *Rounding Up the Yearlings*.

For all practical purposes, this original band only lasted about three years, dissolving in 1935 as its members found fame on their own.

CKW

DICK CURLESS

(Singer, Guitar)

Given Name:	**Richard William Curless**
Date of Birth:	**March 17, 1932**
Where Born:	**Fort Fairfield, Maine**
Married:	**Pauline Chinnock**
Children:	**Terry Leigh**

Dick Curless is one of a small group of "Down East" Country musicians who have made a national impact. Truck-driver songs have been the mainstay of the Curless repertoire and have provided most of his best-known songs. Dick has performed as a regular on the *Wheeling Jamboree*, has toured with Buck Owens and more recently has entertained audiences in the midcontinent tourist mecca of Branson, Missouri.

Born in the potato country of northern Maine, Dick Curless got some early musical experience with a group called the Trail Blazers and in 1948 as the "Tumbleweed Kid" on the radio station in Ware, Massachusetts, where he lived for a long time. Conscripted into the Army in 1951, Dick broadened his musical resume still further via an Armed Forces Network program in the Far East, where he took the unusual sobriquet of "The Rice Paddy Ranger." Back in Maine by 1954, he worked around clubs in the Bangor area. Winning on an *Arthur Godfrey Talent Scouts* program led to some additional club dates in the Las Vegas and Hollywood areas. He made some recordings for Tiffany. However, a bout of illness forced Dick to give up music for a time.

Dick recovered and, back in Maine again, began making his mark on the local scene, often working with other Down East stars such as Gene Hooper and the duo of Lone Pine and Betty Cody. A trucker song about the lonesome stretches of road in the Maine forest country, *A Tombstone Every Mile*, became his ticket to the national Country scene. Released on Allagash Records, it was leased by Tower Records, a Capitol subsidiary and went Top 5 on the Country charts in 1965. Dick had nine more chart-making releases on Tower, of which the most successful was the follow-up *Six Times a Day (the Trains Came Down)*, which went Top 15 in 1965. Other successful releases were *All of Me Belongs to You* (Top 30, 1967) and *I Ain't Got Nobody* (Top 40, 1968).

Dick was switched to the parent Capitol label, in 1970, where he had another memorable trucker hit, *Big Wheel Cannonball*, which had been recomposed from *Washball Cannonball*. It went Top 30 and was followed during the summer of 1970 by *Hard, Hard Traveling Man*, which just failed to make the Top 30. Another notable number, *Drag 'Em off the Interstate, Sock It to 'Em J.P. Blues* dealt with the perennial problem of speed traps and reached the Top 30 at the end of 1970. In all, Dick accumulated some 22 charted numbers of which the most successful of the others were *Loser's Cocktail* and *Snap Your Fingers* (both Top 40 in 1971) and *January, April and Me* and *Stonin' Around* (both Top 40 in 1972).

That truck driving man, ***Dick Curless***

Meanwhile, Dick joined the cast of the *Wheeling Jamboree,* where he worked as a regular off and on for a decade, taking time out to tour with the Buck Owens entourage during 1966-1968. He also sang on the soundtrack of a film, *Killer's Three* in 1969. A tall man with a commanding presence, Dick became known as the "Baron of Country Music," a title reinforced by one of his minor hits from 1966 (*The Baron*). He often appeared on stage with a black patch over one eye to ease the strain on his already weakened vision.

Through the later 70's and into the 80's, Curless struggled with alcoholism, but finally conquered the problem and also became a born-again Christian. During that darker period he cut for such smaller labels as Interstate and Belmont. In 1987, he recorded an album in Norway for Rocade while on tour, which was subsequently released on Rutabaga in the U.S. In 1992, he appeared regularly in Branson on daily shows at the Cristy Lane Theater with other accomplished Country music veterans such as George Hamilton IV, Ferlin Husky and Melba Montgomery. A recent single on the Allagash label contained a tribute song to policemen slain in the line of duty, backed with one of the first published Hank Williams' compositions, *I'm Praying for the Day That Peace Will Come.*

IMT

RECOMMENDED ALBUMS:
"Songs of the Open Country" (Tiffany)(1958)
"A Tombstone Every Mile" (Tower)(1965)
"Hymns" (Tower)(1965)
"A Devil Like Me Needs an Angel Like You" (Tower)(1966)
"At Home with Dick Curless" (Tower Records)(1967)
"The Long Lonesome Road" (Tower)(1968) [Re-released on Stetson UK (1988)]
"Tombstone Every Mile" (Capitol)(1972)
"Living at the Wheeling Truck Driver's Jamboree" (Capitol)(1973)
"The Last Blues Song" (Capitol)(1973)
"Welcome to My World" (Rutabaga)(1989)
"It's Just a Matter of Time" (Stetson UK)(1990)

CURLY DAN & WILMA ANN

Formed: **1955**
CURLY DAN
(Singer, Songwriter, Guitar, Mandolin, Banjo)
Given Name: **Densile Holcomb**
Date of Birth: **September 12, 1923**
Where Born: **Clay, West Virginia**
WILMA ANN
(Singer, Songwriter, String Bass)
Given Name: **Wilma Ann Lowers**
Date of Birth: **August 11, 1924**
Where Born: **Charleston, West Virginia**
Children: **Delmas Ray, Virginia Sue, Ricky Dan**

The husband and wife team of Curly Dan & Wilma Ann Holcomb became one of the first resident Bluegrass bands in the Detroit area. Natives of rural West Virginia, the Holcombs composed a goodly number of original songs, mostly filled with nostalgia for their mountain homes, which captured the feelings of Appalachian migrants in much the same manner that Harriet Arnow's novel, *The Dollmaker,* did in serious literature. Although only a part-time band, Dan and Wilma, together with their group the Danville Mountain Boys, contributed a great deal to the development of Bluegrass music in southeastern Michigan. Their songs like *South on 23, A Visit Back Home,* and *North on 23* continue to be lyrics with which southern or mountain people transplanted to big northern cities can still readily identify.

Both Dan and Wilma grew up in rural isolated Clay County, West Virginia, noteworthy as the homeland of such celebrated archaic traditional musicians as French Carpenter, Jenes Cottrell, and Sylvia O'Brien. Dan describes his personal involvement in music as extending over "virtually all my life," including picking and singing with various neighbors and kinfolk. At age 19 he married Wilma Ann Lowers on Christmas Eve of 1942.

The years following WWII took a heavy toll on the West Virginia economy as numerous mines closed and it became virtually impossible to earn enough cash to eke out a living on the little hillside subsistence farms that dotted the state. Thousands of West Virginians trekked northward to such industrial towns as Akron, Columbus, Detroit and other cities to find work in the factories. In 1952, the Holcombs joined this movement, moving to Detroit, where Dan initially worked for the Chrysler Corporation, but he subsequently worked for some 30 years in his skilled trade of stationary engineer for the public school system in Royal Oak, Michigan. The family made their home in nearby Hazel Park and Dan began to involve himself in music almost from the time of his arrival and Wilma Ann began to play bass in 1954. The following year, they formed the Danville Mountain Boys and had their first record, *Sleep Darling/My Little Rose,* on the Fortune label, in 1956. It got quite a bit of airplay on the local Country stations and over the next decade they had additional releases on such labels as Fortune, Dearborn, Danville, and Happy Hearts.

Curly Dan & Wilma Ann first recorded their signature song *South on 23,* in 1961 on Happy Hearts. This number, about the joys of a return visit home, could be identified with by anyone who ever traveled southward from Michigan on U.S. Highway 23, whether to Clay, West Virginia, eastern Kentucky or even southern Ohio. The recording attracted sufficient attention for Starday to re-release it and another Holcomb original entitled *A Visit Back Home* on their Nashville label subsidiary. Another one of their numbers, *North on 23,* described the departure from West Virginia and the initial wonder of viewing Michigan and Detroit. Although many of Dan and Wilma's songs appear to be so personal that it is hard for others to properly sing them, that other pioneer of Bluegrass in Michigan, Red Ellis, did record two of them for Starday. In 1965, Carmon Flatt, a second cousin of the better known Lester, joined the Danville Mountain Boys, remaining a key member of the band for some 16 years.

In 1972, Dan and Wilma began recording for Old Homestead and subsequently cut 3 albums for them as well as one additional side on a single to give them a total of 40 songs on that label. In addition to Flatt, J.R. Duty picked mandolin on many of these recordings and Ricky Dan Holcomb played banjo on the third album. As with their earlier singles, a majority of the songs were originals of both a sacred and secular nature. Lonesome feelings for the old home tended to be a recurring theme in many of both Dan and Wilma's lyrics.

Curly Dan & Wilma Ann performed less often through the 1980's. Their longtime associate Carmon Flatt died and as of May 1993, Dan and Wilma retired to their Hazel Park home. Dan has experienced recurring bouts with ill health in recent years, but maintains an active interest on the musical scene. He hears one of his songs played on local public radio every now and then and hopes that other artists will someday record them. IMT

RECOMMENDED ALBUMS:
"South on 23" (Old Homestead)(1972)
"A Place on the Mountain" (Old Homestead)(1973)
"New Bluegrass Songs" (Old Homestead)(1975)

SONNY CURTIS

(Singer, Songwriter, Fiddle, Guitar)
Date of Birth: **May 9, 1937**
Where Born: **Meadow, Texas**
Married: **Louise**
Children: **Sarah**

With a career spanning four decades, Sonny Curtis has made major contributions to both Country and Rock music. While stardom as a recording artist evaded him, the brilliant songs he composed helped build careers for dozens of other artists from Buddy Holly to the Everly Brothers to Keith Whitley.

Sonny Curtis grew up near Lubbock, Texas, into a big family. He began playing guitar at an early age and by the time he was in high school was a regular performer on local radio station KDAV. Sonny befriended another aspiring musician, Buddy Holly, and Sonny played fiddle on the KDAV's popular Buddy and Bob radio show that featured Holly and Bob Montgomery. Waylon Jennings was a deejay on another radio station, KLLL, and they all often performed together at the local movie theater between films.

In 1956 Curtis joined Holly's group, the Three Tunes, as fiddle player/guitarist and background vocalist. Marty Robbins' road Manager introduced the group to Cedarwood Publishing and *Grand Ole Opry* manager Jim Denny. Denny helped Buddy Holly and the Three Tunes secure a contract with Decca Records. The group traveled to Nashville to record with the legendary producer Owen Bradley. In addition to an early version of Holly's *That'll Be the Day*, Buddy recorded Curtis' *Rock Around with Ollie Vee.* Many years later when this recording event in Nashville was portrayed in the movie *The Buddy Holly Story,* Curtis was prompted to write and record *The Real Buddy Holly Story* to set straight the many misrepresentations in the film (it was a Top 40 Country hit for Sonny in 1980). Buddy wasn't happy with the sound he got in Nashville. He felt no empathy with

Bradley and definitely didn't find any help from Decca's Paul Cohen. Buddy recorded *That'll Be the Day* with Norman Petty producing, in Clovis, New Mexico, the following year. By then Curtis was no longer working with Buddy's new group, the Crickets, but the two remained good friends until Buddy's untimely death on February 3, 1959.

When Sonny left the Three Tunes he went on the road playing guitar for Slim Whitman. Following Buddy's death, the Crickets asked Curtis to join the group as guitarist and lead vocalist. The group often performed with the Everly Brothers and Sonny became good friends with Don and Phil. In 1960 Curtis was drafted and stationed at Fort Ord. That's where he wrote *Walk Right Back* and later played the song for the Everlys. The hit-making brothers liked the song but asked Curtis to write another verse. However, the Everlys recorded the song before Sonny had a chance to write a second verse, opting to repeat the first verse.

Sonny first heard the song on Radio Luxembourg when he was stationed in Toul, France. The song became a big hit for the Everly Brothers in 1961 and the large sum of money that Curtis received encouraged him to continue his music career after his discharge. He celebrated the success of the hit and the big payday by buying a brand new Cadillac, a car he still had 30 years later. Both Perry Como and Andy Williams recorded the song, including the second verse Curtis had written. When Anne Murray scored a big hit with the song in 1979, she recorded the same version the Everlys had, repeating the first verse.

Sonny Curtis' solo recording career began in 1958 on Dot with the single *Wrong Again.* Over the next 30 years Curtis recorded for more than a dozen labels, including Viva, Capitol, A & M, Liberty, Imperial, Ovation, Coral, and Elektra. His first successful recordings were *My Way of Life* (Top 50, 1966), *I Wanna Go Bummin' Around* (Top 50, 1967), *Atlanta Georgia Stray* (Top 40) and *The Straight Life* (Top 50) (both 1968), all on Viva. He achieved occasional moderate success but dozens of other artists scored heavily with the songs he wrote. Hank Williams, Jr., recorded his *I Fought the Law,* as did rock artists Lou Reed and the Clash. Bobby Goldsboro scored with Sonny's *The Straight Life*. Rick Nelson, Glen Campbell, and Bing Crosby also recorded songs Curtis had written.

Sonny had success as a recording artist in 1970 when he was called on to write the theme song for *The Mary Tyler Moore* TV show. He wrote and recorded *Love Is All Around* after reviewing a four-page format for the show given him by the producers. The show was a major network hit for many years and continues to be seen in syndication 20 years later. The single made the Country Top 30. Sonny Curtis also wrote the theme song for the early 90's hit TV situation comedy *Evening Shade* starring Burt Reynolds.

In the early 80's, Sonny reunited with original Crickets Joe B. Maudlin and Jerry Allison to tour as part of the Waylon Jennings road show. In addition to performing several of the Crickets' hits, Curtis sang many of his own compositions backed up by Maudlin and Allison along with Jennings' band, the Waylors. In 1981, Curtis made a respectable showing with his release on Elektra, *Good Ole' Girls*, which went Top 15 on the Country chart. He followed this with the Top 40, *Married Women.* He was also in demand as a jingle singer, lending his voice to commercials for San Diego's Sea World, Anaheim's Knots Berry Farm and on a public service announcement for the U.S. Forest Service. Sonny had his last Country chart entry as an artist in 1986 with the Top 70, *Now I've Got a Heart of Gold* on 'Steem.

In the late 80's and early 90's, Curtis continued to make a strong contribution to Country music, providing the hauntingly introspective *I'm No Stranger to the Rain* for Keith Whitley. He also wrote songs for Ricky Skaggs *(He Was on to Something)* and John Schneider (*Welcome Home, An Old Rainbow, Jukebox and You*). Curtis was honored by the Nashville Songwriters Association International in 1991 when he was inducted into the prestigious Songwriters Hall of Fame. JIE

RECOMMENDED ALBUMS:

"Love Is All Around" (Elektra)(1980)
"Rollin'" (Elektra)(1981)

T. TOMMY CUTRER

(Deejay, Announcer, Singer, Politician)

Given Name:	**Thomas Clinton Cutrer**
Date of Birth:	**June 29, 1924**
Where Born:	**Osyka, Mississippi**
Married:	**1. Lucille Lang (div.)**
	2. Vicky Martin
Children:	**Richard, Gary, Tyrone, Zelicia, Zenett**

Although Osyka is in Mississippi, T. Tommy's birth occurred in the family house just across the Louisiana state line. Growing up in Osyka, T. Tommy was known by the townsfolk as Little Tom, his father, Thomas Joseph Cutrer, a logger, being Big Tom. T. Tommy's mother, Zellie, was killed in 1942, when a troop train hit the bus that she was traveling in, truly becoming a war casualty.

Former Senator ***T. Tommy Cutrer***

While in high school, Cutrer played football and his dream was to be a professional footballer or boxer. However, fate ruled against this, and a bruise that he received when playing football turned out to be osteomyelitis and he spent the next 8 months in bed. While lying there listening to the radio, he began to harbor thoughts about being a broadcaster. His first job was at WSKB McComb, Mississippi, where for three hours a day, he received 30 cents per hour of which he spent 38 cents a day on bus fares. From there, he went to WDSU New Orleans, earning $12.50 per week. However, he got himself fired after two weeks, by turning up late one morning. His next station was WNOE New Orleans and he received $16 a week.

While at WJDX Jackson, Mississippi, in 1942, Tommy met 16-year-old Sonny James. In 1943, he joined KARK Little Rock and did the announcing for *Mothers Best Flour*, starring the Rhodes Brothers. With their help, he got on WMC Memphis, where he stayed for a year, then moved to Memphis radio station WREC, where he stayed for two years, before moving on to WSLI Jackson, where he started his first band, Tommy Cutrer and the Rhythm Boys. This group lasted around two years.

After a period at KWYZ and KNUZ Houston, Tommy emerged at KCIJ Shreveport in 1952. It was here that he became the first deejay to play a Johnny Cash record on air. This later resulted in T. Tommy getting the announcing job on the Johnny Cash network TV show. During the the early 50's, Tommy recorded several singles for Capitol, RCA Victor, Mercury, Columbia, Million and Dot. He cut jukebox and Gospel material for them and also recorded for the Army and Air Force.

In 1954, thanks to the efforts of Faron Young and Webb Pierce, Jack Stapp, then WSM's Program Director, gave him a job on the station. On his way from Little Rock, Cutrer had a car crash which resulted in him losing a leg. However, he still kept the job on WSM and became an announcer on the *Grand Ole Opry*. In 1957, T. Tommy was named the "Nation's Top DJ." In 1965, he appeared in the Gemini movie *Music City USA*.

In 1976, T. Tommy ran for Congress. One of the other candidates was Al Gore, Jr., who was the victor. With Mr. Gore's support, T. Tommy ran for the State Senate on the Democratic ticket and was elected. He acted in this capacity until 1982, when he was defeated. He has been working for the International Brotherhood of Teamsters since 1981 as a field representative.

BILLY RAY CYRUS

(Singer, Songwriter, Guitar)

Given Name:	**Billy Ray Cyrus**
Date of Birth:	**August 25, 1961**
Where Born:	**Flatwoods, Kentucky**
Married:	**1. Cindy (m. 1986)(div.1991)**
	2. Leticia
Children:	**Destiny Hope,**
	Brason Chance

Billy Ray has great belief in the words of Thomas Edison that "every time you fail, you declare one other way that won't work, so you are one step closer to the one that will." He kept them in mind when his career was at its lowest ebb and he drove all night, back to the little church his granddaddy built in the 30's. When he walked in, the preacher was saying, "God loves a desperate man," and Billy Ray knelt down and prayed a desperate man's prayer and two weeks later he had his record deal.

Billy Ray became the phenomenon of the 90's. His popularity was enormous and his on-stage charisma rivaled that of Elvis. His looks epitomize the Country hunk, but his gentle way of speaking and quiet manner belie his hip swinging, dynamic stage performance. His besotted fans drive miles to see him perform; they shriek and scream as they see his muscles ripple and are carried away by his powerful Country-Rock voice.

Billy Ray learned his singing early. His father had a Gospel quartet and sometimes little Billy Ray would sing with the group. After his parents divorced and Billy Ray went through the traumas of the breakup, his mother worked as a housemaid to support them. During his school days, Billy Ray had plans to become a great baseball player and went through the usual teenage antics. He left high school before graduation and set off for California, where he stayed for six months. Then he returned and worked in a cigarette warehouse.

He was 20 when a voice inside him began telling him to buy a guitar. A local radio station was offering tickets for a Neil Diamond show and Billy decided that if he won the tickets, it would be confirmation that he should buy the guitar. He won the last two tickets and after seeing the show was inspired to follow his dream. He bought the guitar and started a band called Sly Dog. He set the band a goal that they would be playing in a bar within 10 months. Just short of that, they were playing their first gig at the Sand Bar in Ironton, Ohio, and Sly Dog started to get a following. In 1984, a fire destroyed all the band's equipment and Billy Ray took this as a sign to move on. He headed for Woodland Hills, California, put together a new band and started selling cars. He then got married to Cindy and in 1986 moved back to Flatwoods and the Ragtime Lounge in Huntington, West Virginia, became music base.

Billy Ray began trying to infiltrate Nashville, but he couldn't afford to stay in Music City. He would drive there, knock on a few doors, then drive back and play for six nights with the band and then set off again for Nashville. He did this about 42 times. Eventually, his persistence paid off. From a tape made by Billy Ray, one of his songs was cut by *Grand Ole Opry* star Del Reeves. Reeves introduced Billy Ray to Jack McFadden, his former manager. As a result Billy Ray secured a management agreement with McFadden. Booked to open a performance of Reba McEntire and Highway 101 at Louisville's Freedom Hall, he was seen by Buddy Cannon, Mercury Nashville's Head of A & R. This led to Harold Shedd, the label's VP, catching his act at Huntington, West Virginia and a recording contract was signed.

His debut single, *Achy Breaky Heart,* written by Don Von Tress, was released in April 1992 and became not only a No.1 Country hit (it stayed at the top for 5 weeks) but also became a Top 5 Pop hit and a huge international success. In addition, it became one of those rarities, a single that sells copies; in this case, it was Certified Platinum by July 1992. Part of its success was due to the Line Dance, the Achy Breaky, which had been created by Melanie Greenwood. This in turn started the

***Billy Ray Cyrus** in action*

Line Dance craze. Now new dances are being created around records with a danceable beat.

Billy Ray can be pleased his prayers were answered. His national itinerary was soon filled and he was booked to sing at the POW NMIA Rolling Thunder Ride for Freedom rally in Washington, D.C., where he sang his Vietnam-inspired *Some Gave All,* the title song of his first album. Six of the 10 songs on the album were self-penned. Released in May 1992, the album had been Certified Triple-Platinum by July 1992 and by March 1993, sales were in excess of 7 million.

Billy Ray's next single, *Some Gave All*, only reached the Top 60 and more than a few people in Country music relished what looked like a one-hit wonder situation. However, Billy Ray proved that his detractors were wrong. His subsequent singles have all been major hits and were *Could've Been Me* (Top 3/Top 75 Pop),*She's Not Crying Anymore* (Top 10/Top 70 Pop) and *Wher'm I Gonna Live?* (Top 25). Billy Ray sang the national anthem at the start of the 1992 baseball World Series. During 1992, Billy Ray's video *Billy Ray Cyrus* was Certified Triple-Platinum.

The *Billy Ray Cyrus Special—Dreams Come True* was aired on ABC network in February 1993. Billy Ray's second album, ***It Won't Be the Last***, was released in June 1993 and its title was a clarion call to the industry and some of his fellow performers who had been taking pot-shots at Billy Ray and his songwriting abilities. The public responded and the album immediately was Certified Platinum. Billy Ray's lead-off single from the album was *In the Heart of a Woman*, which went Top 3 and was also a Pop Top 80 success. This was followed by *Somebody New*, which went Top 10 in 1994. Billy Ray's video *Live on Tour* was Certified Gold during 1993. During that year, the American Music Awards named him "Favorite New Artist" and *Achy Breaky Heart* was made their "Favorite Single," both in the Country Category. Billy Ray's other 1994 chart record was the Top 15 *Words by Heart*. JAB

RECOMMENDED ALBUMS:

"Some Gave All" (Mercury Nashville)(1992)
"It Won't Be the Last" (Mercury Nashville)(1993)

D

TED DAFFAN

(Songwriter, Guitar, Steel Guitar)

Given Name:	**Theron Eugene Daffan**
Date of Birth:	**September 21, 1912**
Where Born:	**Beauregarde Parish, Louisiana**
Married:	**Fannie Mae Martin (Bobbie Daffan)**
Children:	**Dorothy Jean**

Ted Daffan has become immortal as the man who wrote what is considered to be the first trucker's song, *Truck Drivers Blues*.

He spent his childhood in Texas and graduated from Houston's Jefferson Davis High School in 1930. In 1932, Daffan led the Blue Islanders, a Hawaiian band. During 1933, he broadcast on radio station KPRC Houston. In 1934, Daffan became steel guitarist with the Blue Ridge Playboys, who had Floyd Tillman on lead guitar. Two years later, Ted joined the Bar X Cowboys, a Houston band.

In 1939, he wrote *Truck Drivers Blues*, which Cliff Bruner (with Moon Mullican on vocals) turned into a major hit. Daffan had just left the Bar X Cowboys and formed Ted Daffan's Texans. As a result of Bruner's success, Daffan and the band were signed to ARC's OKeh label. In 1940, they had a major hit with Daffan's song *Worried Mind*, which sold a staggering 350,000 copies. On the advent of WWII, Daffan disbanded the Texans.

By 1943, he was back recording again. *No Letter Today/Born to Lose* became a double-sided self-penned million seller in 1944. The vocals on the former were by Chuck Keeshan and Leon Seago and on the latter by Leon Seago. He followed these up with more highly successful recordings, *Look Who's Talkin'* (1944, also with Leon Seago singing), *Time Won't Heal My Broken Heart/You're Breaking My Heart* and *Shadow on My Heart/Headin' Down the Wrong Highway* (1945). In 1946, he had a hit with his Columbia recording of *Shut That Gate* (George Strange on vocals).

With this amount of success, Daffan reformed the Texans and they became resident at the Venice Ballroom in Los Angeles. In 1946, Daffan moved back to Arlington, Texas, and from 1948-49, Daffan and the Texans could be heard on *Town Hall Party* from Compton, California.

In 1950, Daffan released *I've Got Five Dollars and It's Saturday Night* on Columbia and then broke up the Texans and relocated to Houston in 1951. He then organized bands in the Fort Worth and Dallas locales. There followed a fruitful period for Daffan with Les Paul and Mary Ford recording *I'm a Fool to Care* in 1954 and Faron Young recording *I've Got Five Dollars and It's Saturday Night* in 1956.

Hank Snow, who recorded Daffan's *Tangled Mind*, became a partner in Ted's publishing enterprises in 1958, which was the same year Daffan received his Gold Disc for *Born to Lose*. In 1961, he was working in Houston as General Manager of a music store.

As a songwriter, often writing as Frankie Brown, Daffan has had a lot of success. *I'm a Fool to Care* was also charted by Joe Barry, Marcia Ball and Donny King and Ray Charles recorded *Born to Lose* in 1962. In 1970, Ted Daffan was among the charter members to the Nashville Songwriters Hall of Fame. He was listed in the Smithsonian Collection of Classic Country Music, and in 1982, he received a Platinum Disc for *Born to Lose*. One of his most recorded songs is *Headin' Down the Wrong Highway*, which has been cut not only by Daffan but also by Ernest Tubb, Hank Locklin, Tab Hunter, Don Gibson, Billy Walker and Billy Western.

Ted Daffan was also a pioneer in the electrification of instruments. He had a radio repair shop in Houston in which he experimented with amplifiers and other electronic gadgetry.

RECOMMENDED ALBUMS:

Ted Daffan tracks appear on the following compilations:
"Country Music South and West" (New World) [Various artists]
"Western Swing, Vol. 4" (Old Time Classics) [Various artists]
"The Smithsonian Collection of Classic Country Music" (Smithsonian Institution)(1980) [Various artists] [A box set worth getting]

PAPPY DAILEY

(Industry Executive, Record Producer)

Given Name:	**Harold W. Dailey**
Date of Birth:	**February 8, 1902**
Where Born:	**Yoakum, Texas**

Throughout the history of post-1945 recorded music, certain names stand paramount. Among these is a man who was the guiding light behind such luminaries as George Jones (whom he encouraged to sound like himself), Gene Pitney, Floyd Tillman and Arlie Duff.

During WWI, Dailey enlisted in the Marine Corps even though he was underage. On his return from the hostilities, he went into business and became successful. In addition, he was involved in the affairs of ex-servicemen and in 1931 and 1932 he was elected Commander of the American Legion.

He started his involvement with Country music and the music industry as early as 1933. However, it was not until 1953 that he became fully immersed when he and Jack Starnes set up in Beaumont, Texas, Starday Records, one of the most celebrated labels in Country music. The early recordings were made at Starnes' house. Their first major success was their fourth release, *You All Come* by Arlie Duff. By the end of 1955, they were starting to score heavily with George Jones, who had his first hit for them that year with *Why, Baby, Why*.

By this time, Starnes had left and Don Pierce had joined Dailey and would become a major force in the future of Starday. They were then approached by Mercury to produce Country material on the label and this they did until 1961, while still running Starday. One of their last produced hits under this arrangement was Jones' *Aching, Breaking Heart* (not the same one!).

In 1961, Dailey and Pierce divided the corporate assets. Dailey took the publishing wing, Starright and Pierce acquired the label, with each taking half the catalog and master recordings. Pappy had already set up his own D label in 1958 and had started to get major chart action via James O'Gwynn, Eddie Noack and Claude Gray. The label continued until 1965 and then was reactivated through 1970 and 1971.

When United Artists beckoned Dailey in

1961 as Country & Western Director, he brought George Jones with him. He had never formally managed George, but was more like a father and advisor to him. On George's insistence, Pappy signed the then unknown Melba Montgomery and ended up producing not only George on a string of hits but also the duo of George and Melba, including their 1963 smash hit, *We Must Have Been Out of Our Minds*.

When Art Talmadge and Dailey set up Musicor records in 1965, it was inevitable that Jones would soon be on the label. He made the move later that year. However, in 1971, there was a big flare-up when George, unhappy at how he'd been treated, wanted to move to Epic to record with Tammy Wynette, under the direction of Billy Sherrill. Talmadge allegedly made certain demands and the matter got out of hand. As a result Pappy Dailey and George were estranged. They did keep in contact but things were never the same.

Without George Jones and with the advent of a new generation of producers, A & R men and major corporate labels, the career days of Pappy Dailey were numbered.

KENNY DALE

(Singer, Songwriter, Drums, Guitar)

Given Name:	**Kenneth Dale Eoff, Jr.**
Date of Birth:	**October 3, 1951**
Where Born:	**Artesia, New Mexico**
Married:	**1. Kay (div.)**
	2. Judy
Children:	**Kimberly, Kara, Kelly**

During the late 70's and early 80's, Kenny Dale was one of the most popular Country music singers around. His producer, Bob Montgomery, once described him as "a sleeping giant" and although Kenny didn't get the elusive No.1 hit, he still managed to achieve some giant successes.

Although born in New Mexico, Kenny was raised in Texas. He was interested in music from an early age and his mother told him that he used to rock his high chair in time with the music he heard. He started playing drums at age 10 and played in his first group, Dougie Poo and the Punks, when 14, playing Top 20 material from a pawnshop.

Kenny played in various bands and then in 1971, he met Fiddlin' Frenchie Bourke at the Western Club in Houston. Kenny asked to go on stage to sing with Bourke's group, the Outlaws. However, he got on stage and forgot the words because of stage fright. He did redeem himself and played with the band, Bourke being the major influence in moving Kenny's style towards Country music. That year, Kenny met Terry Tyler while playing at the Cactus Club in Houston and joined Tyler's group, Terry and the Rounders, staying with them until 1973.

Kenny decided to go solo and formed Love Express. It was in 1973 that he cut his first single, *Patches*, for his own Express Records. In 1975, Kenny recorded *Somebody Help Me Get to Houston*, for Earthrider Records. While playing in Bay City, Kenny was approached by Bea Rittersbacher, who liked what he was playing and asked if she could help in any way. This led to her financing Kenny's next recording, *Bluest Heartache of the Year*, also on Earthrider. The single was produced by A.V. Mittelstedt, who would play a continuing role in Kenny's record career. When the single started to take off, Capitol Records licensed the master and during the spring of 1977, it reached the Top 15 on the Country chart.

Capitol signed Kenny to the label and their faith was paid back when *Shame, Shame on Me (I Had Planned to Be Your Man)* also went Top 15 during the fall. At the end of the year, Kenny made his debut on the *Grand Ole Opry*, an event that caused a flow of nerves when he saw, as he put it, "the little box with WSM on it." He never became a member because his booking agency, United Talent, felt it would tie down his career, a situation that Kenny regrets. The following year, Kenny's hits were *Red Hot Memory* (Top 20), *The Loser* (Top 30) and *Two Hearts Tangled in Love* (Top 20).

In 1979, Bob Montgomery began producing Kenny and the year started with the Top 20 hit *Down to Earth Woman* and then Kenny hit the Top 10 with *Only Love Can Break a Heart*, which had been a Pop hit for Gene Pitney, 17 years earlier. He wrapped up the year with another Top 15 hit, *Sharing*. 1980 was to be his final year with Capitol and his successes that year indicated a falling off with *Let Me In* going Top 20 and *Thank You, Ever-Lovin'* and *When It's Just You and Me*, both peaking in the Top 40. While with Capitol, Kenny received 5 ASCAP awards and a SESAC award for his rendition of Loretta Lynn's *I Don't Feel Like Living Today*. He also received a Gold Record from New Zealand for his album ***Greatest Hits of Kenny Dale***.

Kenny had his next chart entry on Funderburg, a version of Hank Williams' *Moanin' the Blues*, which reached the Top 70, in 1982. The following year, Kenny signed with Republic and in 1984, he charted with his self-penned *Two Will Be One*, which was a minor success. This was followed by *Take It Slow* and that was also a low-level entry. The following year, he moved to Saba, where his song *Look What Love Did to Me* was another minor success. In 1986, Kenny reached the Top 70 with *I'm Going Crazy* on San Antonio label BMG.

In 1989, Kenny recorded for Axbar, releasing four singles, *When I Be Five*, *Perfect Angel* (both self-penned), *I'm Getting Better* and *You Have My Heart*. He is currently writing a lot and working with A.V. Mittelstedt on a new cd. He gigs around the San Antonio area with his wife, singer Judy Dale.

RECOMMENDED ALBUMS:

"Bluest Heartache" (Capitol)(1977)
"Red Hot Memory" (Capitol)(1978)
"Only Love Can Break a Heart" (Capitol)(1979)
"When It's Just You and Me" (Capitol)(1981)

VERNON DALHART

(Singer, Songwriter, Harmonica, Jew's Harp)

Given name:	**Marion Try Slaughter**
Date of Birth:	**April 6, 1883**
Where Born:	**Marion County, Texas**
Married:	**Unknown**
Children:	**One daughter**
Date of Death:	**September 14, 1948**

Though he sang in a stiff, formal manner that is not appealing to modern Country fans, though he wrote very few songs and though he seldom toured or did radio, Vernon Dalhart qualifies as the first big Country star to win a national following.

He spent much of his career in the studios, creating a discography of some 5,000 releases on virtually every major label in the 1920's and 1930's; often he recorded the same songs for different companies, which issued them under one of the 135 or so pseudonyms Dalhart used. These names included Frank Evans, Vernon Dale, the Lone Star Ranger, Wolfe Ballard, Harry Harris, Tobe Little, Fred King, Bill Vernon, Tom Watson, Bob White, Jeff Calhoun, Mack Allen, Hugh Latimer, Joseph Elliott, Jep Fuller, Bob Massey, Guy Massey, Warren Mitchel, Sid Turner, Billy Stuart, B. McAfee, Carlos McAfee and Al Carver.

Dalhart was almost certainly the first Country singer to sell a million copies of a record, when he did so with *The Wreck of the Old 97*, in 1924 and 1925. Though his recording career was virtually over by 1938, his records dominated absolutely the first generation of Country music, and many of the songs he preserved have become Country and Bluegrass standards.

Though many felt Dalhart was a New York studio singer who had a feel for Old-Time songs, he really was from Texas, where his grandfather had been a Confederate veteran, a deputy sheriff and a member of the Ku Klux Klan. Dalhart's father was himself killed in a knife fight, leaving young Marion to make his way herding cows and singing at community functions.

He also learned the harmonica, and learned how to become an expert whistler. By around the turn of the century, though, he found himself living in Dallas, receiving some formal musical training at the Dallas Conservatory of Music, getting married, and starting a family. In 1910, Dalhart moved to New York City, where he found work in a music store. Later he studied light opera and sang part-time for funerals. In 1912, he appeared in opera and the following year, he appeared in *HMS Pinafore* and *Madame Butterfly*. By 1915, he was starting to record for Edison Diamond Discs and was featuring the kind of Pop vocals represented by his first release, *Can't Yo' Hear Me Calling Caroline?*

Dalhart soon attracted critical attention with his ability to mimic the "Negro dialect" in such songs, though he told an interviewer that "I never had to learn it" since he was born and brought up in the South. Possibly because of this he was asked to record *The Wreck of the Old 97* for Edison, and later for Victor, in 1924. The song had earlier been recorded by Henry Whitter, but it was Dalhart's version that took off, thereby thrusting the fledgling Country recording industry into high gear. On the other side of *Wreck* was *The Prisoner's Song*, with its famous chorus, "If I had the wings of an angel, over these prison walls I would fly." Though both songs eventually generated court cases over copyright and ownership, the public loved them. Sales eventually totaled over 25 million copies, according to some authorities.

In 1925, Dalhart recorded a series of topical "event" ballads that put Columbia's Country series on the map. These included *The Death of Floyd Collins* (about the death of a Kentucky cave explorer), *The John T. Scopes Trial* (about the evolution trial in Dayton, Tennessee), *Little Marion Parker* (a murder ballad), *Kinnie Wagner* (about a local outlaw) and *The Santa Barbara Earthquake*; many of these topicals sold over 100,000 copies, making them among the best-selling records for Columbia. Later hits for Dalhart included *My Blue Ridge Mountain Home*, a duet with Carson Robison, *The Letter Edged in Black*, *The Little Rosewood Casket*, *Golden Slippers*, *The Convict and the Rose*, *Maple on the Hill* and *The Dream of the Miner's Child*. Many of these songs were old 19th-century chestnuts, and most were recorded during the period 1926-1930.

In 1955, Victor producer Ralph Peer wrote, "Vernon Dalhart was never a hillbilly and never a hillbilly artist. Dalhart had the peculiar ability to adapt hillbilly music to suit the taste of the non-hillbilly population." Dalhart himself seemed to agree with this, and it might explain why his popularity declined after the Depression. By then, "authentic" Country singers like Jimmie Rodgers and the Carter Family were well represented on record, and the formalism of Dalhart fell out of vogue.

Though he continued to write to record companies asking for work, there was none and by 1942 Dalhart was working as a night clerk at the Barnum Hotel in Bridgeport, Connecticut —all but forgotten except by a few fans. He also worked for a time as a voice coach, giving private lessons and keeping his own voice in shape. He died of a coronary occlusion in Bridgeport on September 14, 1948. In 1981, after long lobbying by historians and fans, he was elected to the Country Music Hall of Fame. CKW

RECOMMENDED ALBUMS:

"Vernon Dalhart (The First Singing Cowboy on Records)" (Mark 56)(1978)
"Vernon Dalhart (First Recorded Railroad Songs)" (Mark 56)(1978)
"Ballads and Railroad Songs" (Old Homestead)(1980)
"The Wreck of the Old 97" and Other Early Country Hits, Vol. III" (Old Homestead)(1985)
"Old Time Songs" (Davis Unlimited)

LACY J. DALTON

(Singer, Songwriter, Guitar)
Given Name: Jill Lynne Byrem
Date of Birth: October 13, 1946
Where Born: Bloomsburg, Pennsylvania
Married: 1. John Croston (d. 1973)
2. Aaron Anderson (m. 1989)
Children: (John) Adam

Lacy J. has the resolve and determination to kick away adversities and come out on top. She possesses one of the smokiest voices in Country music. Her influences are more Folk and Rock than Country and she is also an admirer of Janis Joplin and Bob Dylan.

However, it was not Lacy J.'s original aim to become a singer. She attended Brigham Young University in Utah with the intention of becoming an artist. She went there because the fees were low. She cleaned toilets between 3:00 a.m. and 7:00 a.m. in the campus art department to get her through college. She dropped out of college and became a short-order cook for the summer in Brainerd, Minnesota. She then returned to Pennsylvania before heading out to California,where she then formed a psychedelic Rock band, Office, in the Santa Cruz area. She fronted it for three years and received record offers if she would drop the band, but she refused. The band broke up in 1970. She had married the band's manager, John Croston, but at the end of the year, not long after the break-up of the band, he collided with another person in the swimming pool and sustained head injuries. He was paralyzed for two years and then died. Lacy J. had to go on food stamps and took part-time jobs to support John while he was in hospital. A week after the accident, Lacy J. found out that she was pregnant. To make ends meet, she worked in a restaurant making crepes. Her son, Adam, was born on February 27, 1971.

She recorded an album, ***Jill Croston***, in 1978, which was released on Harbor Records. It sold almost 4,000 copies in Northern California and covered a wide musical spectrum including Rock and Country. A copy went to David Wood, an attorney friend, who had been a Country deejay. He became her first manager and having been particularly impressed with the Country numbers, arranged for her to record some demo tapes. He sent copies of the tapes to Emily Mitchell, who was at the time A & R executive at CBS Records. She parleyed with Billy Sherrill, CBS's top producer, and in 1979, she was signed to Columbia.

Sherrill insisted that she change her name and after much discussion, Jill Croston became Lacy J. Dalton. "Lacy" from a friend, "J" for Jill and "Dalton" from Karen Dalton, who had taught her to sing.

Her first album, ***Lacy J. Dalton,*** was released that year. Her co-penned *Crazy Blue Eyes* was the 1979 lead-off single and it was a creditable debut, peaking in the Top 20. As a result she was named ACM's "Best New Female Artist." She followed up in 1980 with another Top 20 hit, a new version of the Pee Wee King-Redd Stewart standard *Tennessee Waltz*. The third single, *Losing Kind of Love*, fared better. Again it was a Dalton original and it climbed to the Top 15. *Hard Times,* which came from the album of that title, followed at the end of the summer. It provided Lacy with her first Top 10 entry.

If 1980 was good, 1981 was vintage. *Hillbilly Girl with the Blues,* which was Lacy's first solo written hit, reached the Top 10, as did Lacy's follow-up, *Whisper*. The new album, ***Takin' It Easy***, was released to critical and chart acclaim. The title track scaled the heights to the Top 3 and remained on the charts for nearly five months.

With the arrival of 1982, she had a Top 5

single, *Everybody Makes Mistakes/Wild Turkey*. *Slow Down,* which went Top 15 and also showed up on the Pop chart, came from Lacy's new album, ***16th Avenue***, which was also very successful. The title track, written by Thom Schuyler, became an anthem for "all the boys and girls who make the noise" on Music Row. It reached the Top 10 and remained on the charts for almost five months.

Lacy's duet with Bobby Bare, *It's a Dirty Job,* although released as a single in 1983, later turned up on Lacy J.'s 1987 album, ***Blue Eyed Blues***. This is just one of four duet tracks on the album. The others are with David Allan Coe, George Jones and Earl Scruggs. However, the single only reached the Top 30. Lacy was back in the Top 10 with her remake of Cindy Walker's *Dream Baby (How Long Must I Dream)*, which had been a monster hit for Roy Orbison, 20 years before. The final chart record of 1983 was somewhat prophetic. *Windin' Down* only made it to the Top 60.

She didn't come on the charts for another year. In November 1984, she charted with *If That Ain't Love,* which went Top 15 in 1985 and came from ***Can't Run Away from Your Heart***, her first album in two years. The following year she appeared on a duet with George Jones, *Size Seven Round (Made of Gold)* from George's Epic album, ***Ladies Choice***. Wendy Waldman's song *You Can't Run Away from Your Heart* brought Lacy back into the Top 20 but the follow-up, *The Night Has a Heart of Its Own,* only made it to the Top 60. The first single of 1986 indicated that all was not well. *Don't Fall in Love with Me* only reached the Top 50.

In 1986, a new broom came in. Walt Aldridge, songwriter, musician and later leader of the Shooters, took over production for ***Highway Diner***. There was only one song written by Lacy on it, *Changing All the Time*. The album was recorded at Rick Hall's Fame Studios in Alabama and in many ways seemed to be the album that she was looking for. *Working Class Man*, the first single, climbed to the Top 20 but *This Ol' Town* only made it to the Top 40.

For some while, the relationship with Columbia was less than friendly and apart from the aforementioned ***Blue Eyed Blues***, which was put together by the label in lieu of a "Greatest Hits" package, no albums were released.

When Jimmy Bowen opened the ill-fated Universal label, Lacy J. Dalton again entered the recording arena. The appropriately titled album ***Survivor*** was the result. It also marked Lacy's debut as co-producer. From this came *The Heart,* which reestablished Lacy with a Top 15 hit. This was followed by *I'm a Survivor*, which went Top 20, and *Hard Luck Ace,* which peaked just below the Top 30. When the label went under, Bowen moved to take over the Nashville hot seat at Capitol and Lacy J. signed to the label.

The first album, ***Lacy J.***, came out in 1990 and marked the start of her collaboration with songwriters Even Stevens and Hillary Kanter. *Black Coffee* put her back in the Top 10 but the follow-ups did nothing. Strangely, a duet with Glen Campbell, *Shaky Ground,* did not get single release. Capitol re-released the ***Survivor*** album and then in 1991 came the album ***Crazy Love***, from which the label released the great Sterling Whipple bluesy song, *Lightnin' Strikes a Good Man*. By 1992, Capitol had become Liberty and that year they issued the album ***Chains on the Wind***.

By 1993, Lacy J. was off the label and wondering about the future. She is still in great demand as she tours the country with her band, the Dalton Gang.

RECOMMENDED ALBUMS:

"Greatest Hits" (Columbia)(1983)
"Highway Diner" (Columbia)(1986)
"I Love Country" (CBS UK)(1986)
"Blue Eyed Blues" (Columbia)(1987)
"Crazy Love" (Capitol)(1991)
"Chains on the Wind" (Liberty)(1992)

DICK DAMRON

(Singer, Songwriter, Yodeler, Guitar)
Where Born: Bentley, Alberta, Canada

Dick's claim to fame occurred in 1971 when George Hamilton IV's version of his song *Countryfied* hit the U.S. Country chart Top 50 and Dick's own version topped the Canadian charts.

While still in his teens, Dick had played rock'n'roll at local dances and on radio shows with a group that included his brother and his ex-wife. Dick decided he wanted to make a career of music and he spent the next 12 years writing and playing in Canada and the States.

After the success of *Countryfied*, due to a lack of management support and the fact that his next single took a year to be released, Dick's career started moving backward. He then had marital problems and was warned by the doctors that he had to quit drinking and taking drugs. He returned to Bentley to straighten himself out.

Dick's strengths lie in his songwriting and his stage performance. His little dance up to the microphone and his announcement, "Hi there, folks, I'm Dick Damron, your average hippie Country singer, fresh from beautiful Bentley, Alberta, the home of the Medicine Hat Marijuana Festival," have endeared him to Canadian and British Country audiences (he first toured in Britain in 1976). He was named "Top Canadian Country Singer" for 1976, 1977 and 1978 and his song *Susan Flowers* was "Canadian Country Song of the Year" in 1977.

Dick was presented with the CCMA's C.F. Martin Award in 1982 and the following year, he was voted "Vocalist of the Year (Male)" by the CCMA. In 1984, the CCMA named Dick's song *Jesus It's Me Again* as its "Song of the Year." In 1985, they made him their "Entertainer of the Year" and he became their "Instrumentalist of the Year" in 1989.

RECOMMENDED ALBUMS:

"Countryfied" (Columbia Canada)
"Soldier of Fortune" (Westwood)
"Honky Tonk Angel" (RCA Canada)

CHARLIE DANIELS/CHARLIE DANIELS BAND, The

CHARLIE DANIELS

(Singer, Songwriter, Guitar, Fiddle, Mandolin, Banjo)

Given Name:	**Charles Edward Daniels**
Date of Birth:	**October 28, 1936**
Where Born:	**Wilmington, North Carolina**
Married:	**Hazel**
Children:	**Charles William**

CHARLIE DANIELS BAND, The

Formed:	**1971**
Current Members:	
Bruce Ray Brown	**Guitar/Vocals**
"Taz" DiGregorio	**Keyboards, Vocals**
Charlie Hayward	**Bass Guitar**
Jack Gavin	**Drums, Percussion**
Carolyn Corlew	**Vocals**

Former Members:
Buddy Davis (Drums), Gary Allen (Drums), James W. Marshall (Drums, Percussion), Don Murray (Drums, Percussion), Mark Fitzgerald (Bass, Vocals), Fred Edwards (Drums, Percussion), Tom Crain (Guitar, Vocals)

At 6'4", Charlie Daniels stands like a monolith representing the true values of the U.S.A. and the fusion of honest-to-goodness Country-Rock, Southern Boogie and Blues. Always backed by a band of musicians of complementary dexterity, their leader Charlie has become a major recording and performing star.

The son of a lumberjack, Charlie was raised in North Carolina. He didn't come from a musical background. His father played some harmonica but by the time Charlie was 15, he could play guitar. He then got into mandolin and then fiddle playing. He was a member of a local Bluegrass band, the Misty Mountain

Boys, that played for square dances and school gigs. Music remained a part-time thing at that time. Charlie got a job in the creosote factory, where his father and grandfather worked. In 1958, he joined the Rockets, who played in the evenings in Jacksonville, North Carolina.

At this time, Charlie chose to be laid off at the factory so that a black family would still have a breadwinner and so he could go into music full-time. By now, he was into rock'n'roll and moved to Washington, D.C. For the next three years, the Rockets played the Washington area with sorties to other parts of the U.S. In 1959 they arrived in Fort Worth, Texas, and made their first record, *Jaguar*, for Epic. At this point, the Rockets became the Jaguars. It also marked the beginning of a relationship with producer Bob Johnston.

Apart from some time spent working in a Denver junkyard, Charlie continued with the Jaguars into the 60's. One of Charlie's songs, *It Hurts Me*, was cut by Elvis in 1963. Johnston had been keeping an eye on Charlie's progress and suggested that he come to Nashville as a sessionman. Through Johnston's involvement, Charlie played on Bob Dylan's *Nashville Skyline* (1969), *Self Portrait* and *New Morning* (both 1970) and *Dylan* (1973). He also played on Ringo Starr's *Beaucoups of Blues*, in 1970. He appeared on numerous albums throughout the late 60's and 70's, as featured guest, including three for Al Kooper, four with the Marshall Tucker Band, one each with Elvin Bishop, Grinderswitch, Michael (later Michael Martin) Murphey, Tanya Tucker, Earl Scruggs, Winter Brothers Band (Johnny and Edgar Winter) and Papa John Creach.

In 1969 Charlie produced the Youngbloods' ***Elephant Mountain***, for RCA, before being offered a solo album deal with Capitol. His eponymous album was released in 1970 and featured keyboardist Taz DiGregorio, who has continued to be with Daniels. The following year Charlie started to put together the band and signed with Kama Sutra. The label was part of the Buddah complex and seemed to be diametrically opposite to the blossoming Daniels sound, having a reputation for Soul and bubble gum music.

Charlie's first album for the label, ***Te John, Grease & Wolfman***, was released in 1972 to critical acclaim. The CDB followed this up with ***Honey in the Rock***, which yielded their first chart hit, the Talking Blues *Uneasy Rider*, which reached into the Pop Top 10 and made the bottom end of the Country chart. They would later update this song as *Uneasy Rider '88*. In 1974, the band released the album ***Way Down Yonder*** and Charlie inaugurated the Volunteer Jam at the War Memorial Auditorium in Nashville as an annual charity event.

The next year the CDB album ***Fire on the Mountain*** caught the public imagination. By June of that year, it had been Certified Gold. The single, *Texas*, made it into the Country Top 40 and the Pop Top 100. The CDB delivered one more album, ***Nightrider***, for Kama Sutra before being welcomed into the arms of Epic Records.

At Epic it was much as before. They followed *Texas* with the Top 25 hit *Wichita Jail*, from ***Saddle Tramp***, their first album for the label. However, it was in 1979, with the release of ***Million Mile Reflections***, that the whole world started to learn about Charlie Daniels and his cohorts. On the album, Charlie added James W. Marshall on drums and percussion to augment Fred Edwards.

The man . . . ***Charlie Daniels***

The Devil Went Down to Georgia was a hot fiddle number with demonic overtones and it soared to No.1 on the Country charts, Top 3 on the Pop chart, and it also was a big hit in Europe, where it was viewed in the same way as *Orange Blossom Special*, a long-time favorite. The year was drawing to a close when *Mississippi* followed and became a Top 20 hit. That year the CDB received a Grammy for "Best Country Vocal Performance by a Duo or Group." They also won an armful of trophies at the CMA Awards; Charlie garnered the CMA's "Instrumentalist of the Year," the band was named "Instrumental Group of the Year" and *The Devil Went Down to Georgia* was voted "Single of the Year." They also won ACM's "Touring Band of the Year" Award. Both the album and single were Certified Gold and the album went on to Double-Platinum status in 1986, while the single had sold a million by 1989. On the "Million Mile Reflection" tour, Charlie had a retinue of thirty-seven.

From now on, the band and in particular, Charlie himself, moved in the star arena. They were constant visitors to the charts, not always with major hits but always with great quality. The strength of the CDB has always been in their live appearances and their albums. In 1980 they scored with *Long Haired Country Boy* (Top 30) and *In America* (Top 15 Country and Pop) from the album ***Full Moon***. They finished off the year with *The Legend of Wooley Swamp*, which was a Top 40 hit on the Pop chart without repeating it on the Country chart. During that year, they repeated their award success with the CMA "Instrumental Group of the Year" and the ACM "Touring Band of the Year." ***Full Moon*** went Platinum in the year of its release. The band was one of several Country acts to appear in the movie *Urban Cowboy*.

During 1981, they released *Sweet Home Alabama*. This was a song identified with Lynyrd Skynyrd, a band that the CDB had toured with and felt close to. Charlie and Skynyrd's lead singer, Ronnie Van Zandt, were like brothers. On October 20, 1977, Ronnie was killed in a plane crash in which band members Steve and Chrissie Gaines also died. Charlie's version was the most sincere compliment that anyone could pay to the memory of the premier southern Rock band. The fact that it was not a major hit was almost irrelevant. It was the gesture that mattered.

That year, the 1976 album ***Saddle Tramp*** went Gold and in 1982, the readers of *Playboy* magazine voted the band "Country Group of the Year." The amazing sales for the band's albums continued with the 1981 album, ***Windows***, which went Gold in the year of release. In 1983, Epic released a compilation under the title ***Decade of Hits***. By 1985, this had gone Gold and by January 1989, it was Certified Platinum.

They had one of their career singles in 1986, with *Drinkin' My Baby Goodbye* from *Me and the Boys* (1985), an album with a great cover showing the band in duster coats looking real mean. The single reached the Top 10 and was on the charts for over five months. Fred Edwards left in 1986 and was replaced on drums and percussion by Jack Gavin. Jack made his recording debut with the CDB on their album ***Powder Keg***, in 1987.

It took another eighteen months before they repeated their single success but repeat it they did with *Boogie Woogie Fiddle Country Blues* from ***Homesick Heroes***, in 1988. It was also a time that the CDB toured extensively with Alabama. Charlie added to the Volunteer Jam, by having a Chili Cook-out in 1989 in Nashville with guest acts Asleep at the Wheel, Wild Rose and Mason Dixon.

In 1990, Bruce Ray Brown became the guitarist in the band, replacing longtime incumbent Tommy Crain. Bruce's first album with the CDB, ***Simple Man***, went Gold that year. The title track went Top 15, during the beginning of 1990.

During 1991, Charlie visited the site of the Berlin Wall, and this and other events were celebrated in a 90-minute video, *Homefolks and Highways*. There seemed to be more emphasis on Charlie Daniels as an individual at this point and the 1991 album, ***Renegade***, was credited to him rather than the Charlie Daniels Band, even though all the band was present. Something else had changed; up to then, most of the songs that the CDB recorded were group compositions, with the occasional Charlie Daniels song. Indeed, their strength lay in their togetherness. However, on ***Renegade***, there are four outside songs, including a version of the Derek and the Dominoes' classic, *Layla* (a Grammy winner in its acoustic form for Eric "Derek" Clapton, in 1993).

Fire on the Mountain, which had gone Gold in 1975, was Certified Platinum in 1992. This meant that the album had sold 500,000 copies between 1975-92, a remarkable feat! It is an album that continues to consistently sell eighteen years after its release. This is a testimony to the continued communication between Charlie Daniels and the "Simple Man."

In 1993 Charlie signed with Liberty Records and released ***America, I Believe in You***, from which the patriotic title track made the Top 75. This album marked the debut of vocalist Carolyn Corlew. In 1994 Charlie appeared on Mark O'Connor's ***Heroes*** album and the track *The Devil Comes Back to Georgia*, which had vocals by Johnny Cash, Marty Stuart and Travis Tritt, made the Top 60 and was nominated for a Grammy Award for "Best Country Instrumental Performance."

RECOMMENDED ALBUMS:

"Charlie Daniels" (Capitol)(1970)
"Te John, Grease & Wolfman" (Kama Sutra)(1972) [Re-issued Epic (1977)]
"Honey in the Rock" (Kama Sutra)(1973)
"Way Down Yonder" (Kama Sutra)(1974)
"Fire on the Mountain" (Kama Sutra)(1975) [Re-issued Epic (1979)]
"Nightrider" (Kama Sutra)(1975) [Re-issued Epic (1979)]
"Saddle Tramp" (Epic)(1976)
"High and Lonesome" (Epic)(1977)
"Midnight Wind" (Epic)(1977)
"Million Mile Reflections" (Epic)(1979)
"Full Moon" (Epic)(1980)
"Windows" (Epic)(1982)
"A Decade of Hits" (Epic)(1983)
"Me and the Boys" (Epic)(1985)
"Powder Keg" (Epic)(1987)
"Homesick Heroes" (Epic)(1988)
"Simple Man" (Epic)(1990)
"Renegade" (Epic)(1991)
"America, I Believe in You" (Liberty)(1993)
There is also an EP "Volunteer Jam" which was originally packed with "Fire On The Mountain" on Kama Sutra which features Dickie Betts and Toy Caldwell. There are also several live albums of the Volunteer Jams.
Charlie Daniels has been featured on other artists' albums. Worth looking for are:
"Sounds of the Western Country" (Lucky)(1979) [Chris LeDoux album]
"Buddy Spicher & Friends-Yesterday And Today" (Direct Disk)
"Anniversary Special" (Epic) [Earl Scruggs album]
"Brothers of the Road" (Arista)(1981) [The Allman Brothers album]

DARBY AND TARLTON

Formed: **mid-1920's**

TOM DARBY
(Singer, Guitar)
Given Name: **Thomas Darby**
Date of Birth: **1884**
Where Born: **Columbus, Georgia**
Date of Death: **1971**

JIMMIE TARLTON
(Singer, Steel Guitar)
Given Name: **Johnny James Rimbert Tarlton**
Date of Birth: **May 8, 1892**
Where Born: **Chesterfield County, South Carolina**
Date of Death: **1979**

Though much has been made of the Blues influence in early Country music, relatively few of the early performers actually sound like the black Bluesmen of the era. The great exception is the team of Tom Darby and Jimmie Tarlton. Best known for the huge two-sided hit of *Birmingham Jail* and *Columbus Stockade Blues,* both of which became Country music standards, Darby and Tarlton were the White Blues masters of the 1920's. From 1927 to 1933 they recorded over 60 sides for three major labels and did much to popularize the slide steel in white Country music. Their style was built around Tom Darby's lead singing and Jimmie Tarlton's slide guitar and was one of the loosest, most soulful sounds of the era.

Tarlton seems to have been the dominant member of the duo. He was the son of sharecroppers in Orange County, South Carolina, and learned to sing old ballads and to play fretless banjo from his parents. By the time he was 12, though, he was learning to play slide guitar in the open tuning he was hearing from black musicians as his family traveled around. Though he spent a stint in the textile mills he soon was drawn to "busking," traveling around playing his music on street corners, in taverns, in train stations, wherever he could pass the hat and get some change.

He traveled widely, from Oklahoma to New York, picking up songs and styles along the way. About 1922, on the West Coast, he ran into Hawaiian guitarist Frank Ferrara and learned how to use his steel slide in a more dexterous way. He brought this skill with him when he returned to the Columbus, Georgia, region to settle down.

There Tarlton met another guitarist, Tom Darby. Darby had not played much in public, but had learned a remarkable vocal style from area black musicians. Darby's parents had come from the north Georgia mountains and his family included several members who were full-blooded Cherokees. He was also a second cousin to Skillet Lickers star Riley Puckett. A local talent scout persuaded Darby and Tarlton to team up and got them an audition with Columbia Records. Their first release was a send-up on Florida land speculators called *Down in Florida on a Hog*. It was successful enough but at their next session (November 10, 1927) they produced their giant hits, *Birmingham Jail* and *Columbus Stockade Blues.* Both had traditional roots, but both were reworked by the singers to such an extent that even today it is impossible to tell how much they had created and how much they borrowed. Later, Tarlton used to tell the story that he wrote *Birmingham Jail*, in 1925, when he had been jailed in that city for moonshining. The record sold almost 200,000 copies for Columbia, making it one of the very best sellers in the company's catalog. Unfortunately, the singers had taken only the flat fee of $75 for their work and garnered none of the later profits.

A follow-up to *Birmingham Jail*, entitled *Birmingham Jail No.2*, backed with *Lonesome Railroad*, became the team's second big hit, in 1928. Later best-sellers included a pair of down-and-dirty Blues, *Travelling Yodel Blues* and *Heavy Hearted Blues*, and a strange version of the Victorian chestnut *After the Ball*. Tarlton was quite fond of adapting old and new Pop songs to their style, and even did a bluesy version of the Gene Austin 1927 hit, *My Blue Heaven*, which he called *My Little Blue Heaven*.

By late 1929, the team was having contract disagreements with Columbia and in April 1930 did their last session for the label. In the next few years, each man did separate sessions and even tried a comeback session or two, but the glory days were over. By now, the slide guitar was commonplace in the music and the pair's eccentric, rough-hewn vocals sounded dated and old-fashioned.

By 1935, both Darby and Tarlton retired from their music and entered other lines of work. In the 1960's, both were rediscovered by enthusiasts during the Folk revival. Tarlton made a brief comeback that included a new album, stints at Folk clubs around the country and interviews with folklorists. It was learned that Tarlton had tried comebacks before and had for a time appeared in a medicine show with Hank and Audrey Williams. Darby also performed a few times and there were even a few concerts with the team reunited. However, it was late for both men and neither enjoyed many fruits from this second career. CKW

RECOMMENDED ALBUM:
"Darby & Tarlton" (Old Timey)

DENVER DARLING

(Singer, Guitar)

Given Name:	**Denver Darling**
Date of Birth:	**April 6, 1909**
Where Born:	**Whopock, Illinois**
Married:	**Garnett Tucker**
Children:	**Ronnie, Susan, Tim**
Date of Death:	**April 27, 1981**

Denver Darling hailed from Illinois and achieved his greatest fame as a radio cowboy in New York City. Possessed of a pleasant voice, Darling prospered in the 40's until he developed throat problems and his desire to get out of the city caused him to curtail his career. One of the few Country artists who continued to make records during the war years, Denver's patriotic songs helped maintain morale on the home front for the duration of the armed conflict.

Darling's parents moved from his birthplace to Jewett, Illinois, during his childhood. In 1920, a neighbor showed him a few guitar chords and he soon developed musical ambitions. At the age of 20, he went to work in radio at WBOW Terre Haute, Indiana, where in 1931 he married Garnett Tucker. Between 1931 and 1937, Darling sang over various midwestern radio stations in such locales as South Bend, Tuscola, Des Moines, Chicago, Wheeling and Pittsburgh. By the fall of 1937, he arrived in New York City, which remained his primary base for the rest of his career except for a stint at WEEV Reading, Pennsylvania. In New York, his programs first originated on WOR, but he soon switched to WNEW.

In addition to daily radio, sometimes performing two and three times a day, Denver emceed and performed on shows at the Village Barn, a noted Country music nightclub where live shows were sometimes broadcast over the network. Another musician working with Darling, Silver Yodelin' Bill Jones, met Denver during his brief association with the WWVA *Wheeling Jamboree*. Additional musical associates included Vaughn Horton, Eddie Smith, Slim Duncan and Rosalie Allen, who would soon be famous in her own right.

Darling initiated his recording career with Decca in November 1941. By the time of his second session in late December, the U.S. had entered WWII and Denver began his string of patriotic songs with *Cowards Over Pearl Harbor*. Many others followed, including *The Devil and Mr. Hitler, Modern Cannonball* and *When Mussolini Laid His Pistol Down*. He also waxed a variety of other Country songs for Decca, releasing a total of 36 numbers over a period of five years. Possibly because he remained under contract for Decca, Darling's recordings for DeLuxe were initially released as Tex Grande and his Range Riders. In 1947, he did his final sessions, cutting 12 numbers on the MGM label, giving him a total of more than 80 released sides in a six year period.

By the end of the 40's, Denver Darling was becoming increasingly unhappy with living in New York City and also somewhat concerned with his throat. As a result, he and Garnett took their three children back to Jewett, Illinois, and reared them in what he considered a more wholesome environment. In the more than three decades remaining to him, Darling lived the life of a gentleman farmer. Despite the fact that Darling's WWII song repertoire could be said to have played a role as a morale booster in Country music similar to many of John Wayne's war films, none have been reissued. In 1958, the Audio Lab division of King Records released a long out of print album containing 10 of his DeLuxe masters.

IMT

RECOMMENDED ALBUM:
"Songs of the Trail" (Audio Lab)(1959)

JOHNNY DARRELL

(Singer, Songwriter, Guitar)

Date of Birth:	**July 23, 1940**
Where Born:	**Hopewell, Cleburne County, Alabama**
Married:	**Catherine E.**
Children:	**Lisa Gail**

Johnny has been the first artist to record quite a few songs that then went on to become classics. It was he who originally cut Curly Putnam's *Green Green Grass of Home*, Dallas Frazier's *Son of Hickory Holler's Tramp* and Bobby Goldsboro's *With Pen in Hand*. However, Johnny also had sizable Country hits with these songs.

When he was 14, Johnny taught himself to play guitar. When he joined the Army, he sang and played at base clubs. He moved from Atlanta, Georgia, to manage a Holiday Inn motel in Nashville in 1964 and started mixing with people in the business. Then one day in 1965, somebody suggested that he make a record. He spoke about it to Bobby Bare, who recommended Johnny to United Artists Records and came up with *Green, Green Grass of Home*. Johnny followed this with his first chart success, *As Long as the Wind Blows*, which went Top 30, in 1966 and Johnny was voted "Most Promising Male Artist" by *Cash Box*. He then had two medium sized hits in 1966 and then, in 1967, he had a Top 10 hit with Mel Tillis' *Ruby, Don't Take Your Love to Town*, 2 years before Kenny Rogers' version.

1968 got under way with Dallas Frazier's *The Son of Hickory Holler's Tramp*, which went Top 25. Johnny followed this with his monster version of *With Pen in Hand*, which went Top 3 and crossed over into the lower regions of the Pop chart. Johnny's last hit of the year was the Top 30 single *I Ain't Buying*.

Johnny started 1969 with the Top 20 *Woman Without Love* and then teamed up with Anita Carter and had a Top 50 single entitled

The Coming of the Roads. He closed out the year with two sizable hits, Mickey Newbury's *Why Have You Been Gone So Long* (Top 20) and Billy Edd Wheeler's *River Bottom* (Top 25). That year, in company with Hank Snow, Willie Nelson, Nat Stuckey and Wes Buchanan, Johnny appeared in Britain as part of the celebration for the now defunct British Country magazine, *Opry,* for its first birthday, *Opry's Party Night.*

He had three minor successes on United Artists before coming to the end of his five year stint. In 1973, Johnny returned to the charts with another minor hit, *Dakota the Dancing Bear,* on Monument. Over a year later, Johnny reappeared on the chart for a final minor hit with the standard *Orange Blossom Special* on Capricorn.

Although Johnny never sustained a successful record career, it is praiseworthy that he and his producer, Bob Montgomery, were adventurous in their choice of songs and songwriters.

RECOMMENDED ALBUMS:
"Giant Country" (United Artists)(1970)
"The Best of Johnny Darrell" (United Artists)(1970)
"Water Glass of Whiskey" (Capricorn)(1975)
"Greatest Hits" (Gusto)(1979) [Re-recorded tracks]

GAIL DAVIES

(Singer, Songwriter, Guitar)
Given Name: Patricia Gail Dickerson
Date of Birth: June 5, 1948
Where Born: Broken Bow, Oklahoma
Married: 1. Robert Hubener (div.) 2. Richard Allen (div.)
Children: Christopher Alan Scruggs (son of Gary Scruggs)

As one of the most literate and intelligent singer/songwriters in Country music, Gail Davies may not have received the full acclaim that she richly deserves.

She moved to Seattle when she was 5 years old, with her mother and two brothers, following the break-up of her parents' marriage. At age 9, she teamed up with her brother Ron, learning to sing harmony from listening to the Everly Brothers, and they recorded an album together. Gail was influenced by the Beatles, and when she left high school, she toured with a Rock band. From the mid-1960's, Gail was on the road for nine years. During that time, she got married to Jazz musician Robert Hubener and they moved to L.A. Gail attempted to become a Jazz singer, but soon returned to what she did best, Country. After she had been performing for several years she was advised by her doctor to give her voice a rest and so she turned to songwriting and learned to play the guitar. Her marriage broke up, and she soon became a fixture on the L.A. music scene.

Singer/Songwriter ***Gail Davies***

While her voice was healing, she managed to get to see someone at Lawrence Welk's Vogue Music. She rushed home, wrote some songs, then went back and got a songwriter's contract. She did some studio sessions singing back-up for Hoyt Axton and worked for some months with Roger Miller, who had heard her at the Troubadour in L.A. At this time, she became friends with singer/songwriters Ronnee Blakley, Stephen Bishop and Paul Williams. Paul was a great supporter and she would have cut his *Rainy Days and Mondays* had not the Carpenters recorded it and converted it into a huge success. Gail met her second husband, Richard Allen, when Screen Gems Music sent her to Nashville to record. Richard was a staff writer for them. Nashville turned her down saying she was "too Pop." This was a surprise and a bit of a puzzle, as she had been brought up on nothing but Country and William "Tex" Dickerson, her father, was a pioneer performer on the *Louisiana Hayride.*

After persevering for some time, Gail got her break when she was signed in 1978 to Lifesong Records (distributed by CBS) by Tommy West. Her first singles to hit the charts in 1978 were *No Love Have I* (Top 30) and *Poison Love* (Top 30). Gail's song *Bucket to the South* was a Top 15 hit for Ava Barber in 1978. In 1979, Gail had a Top 15 hit with *Someone is Looking for Someone Like You.* Gail moved to Warner Brothers in 1979 and at the beginning of 1980, she had hits with *Blue Heartache* (Top 10), *Like Strangers* (Top 25) and *Good Lovin' Man* (Top 25).

Gail had her biggest hit at the beginning of 1981 with the Top 5 *I'll Be There (If You Ever Want Me)* and followed it with *It's a Lovely, Lovely World* (Top 5) and *Grandma's Song* (Top 10). In 1982, Gail charted with *Round the Clock Lovin'* (Top 10), *You Turn Me on I'm a Radio* (Top 20) and *Hold On* (which, although released in 1982, went Top 25 in 1983). Extensive touring followed Gail's 1982 album, ***Givin' Herself Away***, and she opened for the Oak Ridge Boys a number of times.

In 1983, Gail's successes were the Top 20 hits *Singing the Blues* and *You're a Hard Dog (to Keep Under the Porch)* and in 1984, *Boys Like You* (Top 20) and *It's You Alone* (Top 60), the latter written by Gail's brother Ron. On this track Ricky Skaggs played mandolin and sang harmony. Gail finished off the year with the excellent *Jagged Edge of a Broken Heart*, her first success for her new label, RCA. Gail continued her chart run in 1985 with *Nothing Can Hurt Me Now* (Top 40), *Unwed Fathers* (Top 60) and *Break Away* (Top 15).

Gail's route into production nearly got her into trouble. She had been produced by someone who was also working with another artist and as a result burning the midnight oil. Gail requested that she produce herself. The producer said yes, the label said wait. She went ahead and used money earmarked to buy her a house. The label executives were so impressed that she got her money back and bought her house and had the record.

During 1986, Gail led a short-lived group called Wild Choir, on RCA. They had two mid-level chart singles, *Next Time* and *Heart to Heart.* Changing labels to MCA in 1989, Gail released the album ***Pretty Words***, but she only charted with two low-level singles. She then moved on to Capitol Nashville in 1990 and released two albums and when Capitol became Liberty, Gail was hired by Liberty Records as a staff producer, the label's first female staff producer in Country music. JAB

RECOMMENDED ALBUMS:
"Gail Davies" (Lifesong)(1978)
"The Game" (Warner Brothers)(1979)
"I'll Be There" (Warner Brothers)(1980)
"Givin' Herself Away" (Warner Brothers)(1982)
"What Can I Say" (Warner Brothers)(1983)
What's a Woman to Do" (RCA)(1984)
"Pretty Words" (MCA)(1989)
"The Other Side of Love" (Capitol)(1990)
Wild Choir:
"Wild Choir" (RCA)(1986)

Davis Sisters refer SKEETER DAVIS

DANNY DAVIS AND THE NASHVILLE BRASS

DANNY DAVIS

(Trumpet, Bandleader, Arranger, Singer, Songwriter, Record Producer)

Given Name: George Nowlan
Date of Birth: April 29, 1925
Where Born: Dorchester, Massachusetts
Married: Barbara

THE NASHVILLE BRASS

Formed: 1968

Danny Davis proved that there was room for brass instruments within Country music, which is primarily a string instrument style of music. Since the advent of the Nashville Brass, several Country performers have used horns, most notably Merle Haggard.

Young George Nowlan knew that he wanted to be a horn man when he was still in high school. Coming from an Irish-American background with a mother who was an opera coach, he was certain to be taught properly. He bought his first instrument by working as a delivery boy to a fruiterer in Boston. He attended the New England Conservatory of Music.

By the time he was 14, he was a soloist with the Massachusetts All State Symphony Orchestra. Then in 1940, at the tender age of 15, he was offered a gig with the legendary Jazz drummer Gene Krupa, which he willingly accepted. He went on to play with some of the greats of Jazz and Swing including Art Mooney, Bobby Byrne, Bob Crosby, Hal McIntyre and Freddy Martin. Danny started working with Vincent Lopez, who at the time was resident bandleader at the Astor Hotel in New York, a position he would hold for many years. In addition, Danny worked with Blue Barron and Sammy Kaye. While with Freddy Martin, Danny recorded the vocal *The Object of My Affection*.

In 1958, he became record producer with Joy and MGM Records. While at MGM, he produced Connie Francis on her successes, including six No.1's. He also worked with Herman's Hermits and Johnny Tillotson. He moved over to RCA in New York and produced Lana Cantrell and Nina Simone. On a trip to Nashville, Danny met Fred Rose and Chet Atkins, and it was Chet who suggested that Danny join him as his production assistant with the title of Executive A & R Producer in Nashville. This Danny did in 1965 and for some years he worked with many of the artists on the label.

Danny Davis and the Nashville Brass

Toward the end of the 60's, Danny came to Chet with the idea of adding brass to Country music. Atkins approved Danny's setting up a band with which to experiment. The first album by the Nashville Brass, ***The Nashville Brass Featuring Danny Davis Play Nashville Sounds***, was released in 1968 and caused more than a little stir in Country music circles. However, the second album, ***More Nashville Sounds*** in 1969, really got people talking.

It resulted in NARAS splitting up the "Best Country Performance, Duo or Group, Vocal or Instrumental" Grammy category. The new category, "Best Country Instrumental Performance," was awarded to the Nashville Brass that year. In every year during the period 1969-1974, the CMA voted them "Instrumental Group or Band of the Year." *Billboard* named them "Best Instrumental Group" in their Annual Country Music Awards and *Cash Box*'s nationwide DJ Poll chose them as their "Most Programmed Band" and "Top and Coming Band." They were named "Best Country Instrumental Group" by *Record World*. In 1971, the three trades were in total agreement in making them "Best Instrumental Group."

The Nashville Brass continued to put out a consistent and constant flow of albums. In 1970, they teamed up with Hank Locklin and produced an album and two medium-sized hit singles, *Please Help Me I'm Falling* and *Flying South*. In between these two singles, the Nashville Brass had charted with their version of the Country classic *Wabash Cannon Ball*. They rounded off 1970 with another instrumental, *Columbus Stockade Blues*.

During the 70's, seven of their albums were available in Quadraphonic sound: ***Travelin'*** and ***Caribbean Cruise*** (1973), ***Bluegrass Country*** and ***Latest & Greatest*** (1974), ***Dream Country*** and ***Country Gold*** (1975) and ***Texas*** (1976).

During 1977, Danny got together with Chet Atkins and Floyd Cramer for the album ***Chet, Floyd and Danny.*** Willie Nelson teamed up with Danny and the boys in 1980 and they released an excellent album and two successful singles. *Night Life* went Top 20 and *Funny How Time Slips Away* just missed the Top 40.

By the time of their next single success, Danny had left the heady heights of RCA and appeared on his own Wartrace label. *I Dropped Your Name* just scraped into the Country charts and then two years later, with Dona Mason, they charted with *Green Eyes (Cryin' Those Blue Tears)* peaking in the Top 70; however, singles were never that important to the Nashville Brass. After all, with all the success they have had with their albums for years and their appearances in Las Vegas, Branson and on network TV, they never needed singles. Danny Davis and the Nashville Brass have become a national icon that prompted Buck Owens to form the Bakersfield Brass and has also influenced the highly successful Swing Shift Band of Ray Pennington and Buddy Emmons.

RECOMMENDED ALBUMS:

"More Nashville Sounds" (RCA Victor)(1969)
"Hank Locklin & Danny Davis & the Nashville Brass" (RCA Victor)(1970)
"Latest & Greatest" (RCA Victor)(1974) [Available in Quadraphonic sound]
"Danny Davis & Willie Nelson & the Nashville Brass" (RCA Victor)(1980)
"Don't You Ever Get Tired of Hurting Me" (RCA Victor)(1984)
"Danny Davis and the Nashville Brass and Dona Mason" (JRC)

JIMMIE DAVIS

(Singer, Songwriter, Guitar, Public Official, Actor)
Given Name: James Houston Davis
Date of Birth: September 11, 1902
Where Born: Beech Springs, Louisiana
Married: 1. Alvern Adams (dec'd.)
2. Anna Carter Gordon
Children: James Williams

Jimmie Davis made a successful career for himself not only in Country and Gospel music but also in politics, serving two four-year terms as Governor of Louisiana. Jimmie had a lengthy career as a recording artist extending for a half century from 1928. He also acquired the rights of several standard Country songs, ranging from the old favorite *Nobody's Darlin' but Mine,* to the Bluegrass standards *Shackles and Chains* and *You Won't Be Satisfied That Way.* Other Davis classics include *Sweethearts or Strangers*, *There's a New Moon Over My Shoulder*, and the all-time classic *You Are My Sunshine*.

Born the son of a north Louisiana sharecropper, Jimmie Davis became the first graduate of his local high school to attend college, earning a B.A. degree from Louisiana College at Pineville in 1924. Coming back to Beech Springs, he taught school for a time and then went to Louisiana State University, where he received an M.A. in 1927. The following year Davis taught history at Dodd College in Shreveport. He also began singing one evening a week at W.K. Henderson's KWKH radio. He made a few recordings in 1928, none of which were released.

However, in 1929, Jimmie began cutting masters for Victor and had 68 sides released over the next five years, most of them excellent white Blues songs performed in a Jimmie Rodgers style. Some contained risqué and double-entendre lyrics that political opponents would later use in unsuccessful efforts to discredit him. Most of the releases, whether on Victor, Bluebird, or Montgomery Ward, did not sell well because they coincided with some of the worst years of the Great Depression. Since Davis only sang on his discs, he used other local musicians for backup, including Buddy Jones (who later had a successful solo career on Decca) and black slide guitarist Oscar Woods (who also had some memorable recording sessions on his own). *Bear Cat Mama from Horner's Corners* appears to have been Jimmie's best-seller while an early version of *Where the Old Red River Flows,* a later Davis standard, became the most memorable recording in his overall career.

In the meantime, Jimmie Davis quit teaching and took a position as clerk of the Shreveport Criminal Court. He retained this job until 1938 when local voters elected him Commissioner of Public Safety, which placed him in charge of the police department.

In 1934, Davis switched over to Decca and had his first major hit with the self-penned *Nobody's Darlin' but Mine.* He also continued some risqué numbers such as *Jelly Roll Blues* and *Bedbug Blues*, a few of them performed with Buddy Jones, who subsequently became a member of the Shreveport police force. Another of Jimmie's many Decca recordings which gained standard status, *It Makes No Difference Now,* had been purchased from Floyd Tillman. In 1940 Jimmie's co-written (with Charles Mitchell) *You Are My Sunshine*

Former Governor of Louisiana ***Jimmie Davis***

became a major hit covered by many Pop and Country artists, yielding him the signature song of a lifetime.

In 1942, Jimmie moved up the political ladder by being elected Louisiana Public Service Commissioner. That year, he appeared in the first of three movies with Charles Starrett, *Riding Through Nevada*, the others being, *Frontier Fury* (1943) and *Cyclone Prairie Ramblers* (1944).

In 1944, Jimmie was elected to his first four-year term as Governor. During his period in office, Jimmie racked up a quintet of charted sides: *Is it Too Late Now* (Top 3)/*There's a Chill on the Hill Tonight* (Top 5) in 1944, *There's a New Moon Over My Shoulder* (No.1, 1945), *Grievin' My Heart Out for You* (Top 5, 1946) and *Bang Bang* (Top 5, 1947). In 1947, Jimmie starred in *Louisiana* for Monogram, a movie largely based on his own life. He also continued with recordings. As Country music historian Ronnie Pugh points out, somewhat ironically Jimmie was never a full-time entertainer until his term as Governor expired in 1948. As a working vocalist, he initially switched to Capitol, but soon renewed his long-time association with Decca. From the early 50's when songs like *Suppertime* found favor with fans, Jimmie became increasingly associated with Gospel songs. In 1960, he went back to the Governor's Mansion for a second term. School integration constituted a hot issue in the Deep South in those years and while Davis maintained a segregationist stance, his moderate form of opposition helped Louisiana avoid much of the violent confrontations that took place in neighboring states. In 1962, Jimmie had a Top 15 chart record with *Where the Old Red River Flows.*

Retiring again in 1964, he returned to music, even more oriented toward sacred song. Throughout the 60's he turned out an average of two albums yearly. In 1965, a large tabernacle named for him was dedicated adjacent to his humble birthplace in Jackson Parish. Widowed in 1967, he married Anna Carter Gordon, long-time alto singer with the Chuck Wagon Gang, two years later. After his Decca contract expired, after some 40 years with the company, Davis remained active in the studio through the 70's with Canaan, Paula, and Plantation Records. In 1971, Jimmie was inducted into the Nashville Songwriters Hall of Fame and the following year, he was inducted into the Country Music Hall of Fame.

Much respected in Louisiana and throughout the region for his contributions to southern culture, Jimmie still gave occasional concerts going into his 90th year. Interest in white Blues music led Bear Family Records of Germany to reissue some of his early material. Later, MCA released a compact disc, mostly of representative secular sides from the 30's and 40's, in their Hall of Fame Series. IMT

RECOMMENDED ALBUMS:

"Rockin' Blues" (Bear Family Germany)(1983) [Victor cuts]
"Barnyard Stomp" (Bear Family Germany)(1988) [Victor cuts]
"Sounds Like Jimmie Rodgers" (Anthology of Country Music)(ca. 1983)
"You Are My Sunshine" (Decca)(1959)
"Suppertime" (Decca)(1960) [Re-issued on MCA in 1973]
"How Great Thou Art" (Decca)(1962) [Re-issued on MCA in 1973]
"Gospel Hour" (Decca)(1966)
"Singing the Gospel" (Decca)(1968) [Re-issued on MCA in 1973]
"Greatest Hits" (Decca)(1968) [Re-issued on MCA in 1973]
"The Country Side of Jimmie Davis" (Decca)(1969) [Re-issued on Coral in 1973]
"Songs of Consolation" (Decca)(1970) [Re-issued on MCA in 1973]
"Greatest Hits, Vol. 2" (MCA)(1974)
"Hall of Fame" (MCA)(1991)

LINDA DAVIS

(Singer, Guitar)

Date of Birth:	**November 26, 1962**
Where Born:	**Dodson, Texas**
Married:	**Lang**
Children:	**Hillary**

Hailing from the Longhorn State, Linda Davis was no stranger to the music business prior to her No.1 smash duet with Reba McEntire, *Does He Really Love You*, in 1993.

Linda began cutting her teeth on Country music when she was age 6, singing on the East Texas *Gary Jamboree* and later performing on the *Louisiana Hayride*. In 1982, Linda made the move from Texas to Music City during a time when male/female duos were particularily hot. She climbed abord this bandwagon with partner Skip Eaton as Skip and Linda. They performed on the Country Radio Seminar's New Faces Show and signed with MDJ Records. The duo had three hits in 1982: *If You Could See You Through My Eyes* (Top 70), *I Just Can't Turn Temptation Down* (Top 80) and *This Time* (Top 90).

Eventually she was back on her own again, singing in piano bars and recording jingles for Dr Pepper and Kentucky Fried Chicken. Unfortunately, Linda never managed to burst upon the scene as she wanted.

"Emotionally, it was like a rollercoaster," she said in an earlier interview, "we would just get on a little wave, and I'd think, 'O.K. this is going to do it.' Then it would peter out and we'd sit there and scratch our heards and go 'why didn't this work out?' There were so many people that tried to make it happen, I just have to realize and accept that there is a time for everything. Those moments that were dark and slow were definitely rewarded by being asked to sing with Reba on the duet, *Does He Love You*. Since then, it's really been something."

Linda signed to Epic in 1988 as a solo artist and released *All the Good Ones Are Taken*, which went Top 50. This was followed in 1989 with *Back in the Swing Again* (Top 60) and *Weak Nights* (Top 70). By the end of 1990, she was signed to Capitol and in 1991 released the Top 70 *In a Different Light*, the title track of her debut album. Linda followed up with *Some Kinda Woman* (Top 70).

The break Linda had been waiting for came in 1993 when she stepped into the spotlight with Reba McEntire when *Does He Love You* became a No.1 hit and earned for the pair the 1993 Grammy Award for "Best Country Vocal Collaboration." Following the success of this single Linda signed with Arista and recorded the album ***Shoot for the Moon***. The album went Top 30 and produced the 1994 singles *Company Time* (Top 50) and *Love Didn't Do It* (Top 60). ***Shoot for the Moon*** was produced by longtime friend John Guess and features Linda's unyielding vocal strength through a collection of numbers ranging from traditional to Country rockers.

Throughout 1994, Linda has toured with Reba McEntire. Linda credits much of her uphill struggle with having a good family life. "I believe it's going to happen," Davis said. "When they applaud me when I come out by myself, I just feel so warm, like a blanket is around me and they're giving me the acceptance that I have lived for." LAP

RECOMMENDED ALBUMS:

"In a Different Light" (Capitol)(1991)
"Linda Davis" (Liberty) (1992)
"Shoot For the Moon" (Arista) (1994)

MAC DAVIS

(Singer, Songwriter, Guitar, Harmonica, Actor)

Given Name: Scott Davis
Date of Birth: January 21, 1942
Where Born: Lubbock, Texas.
Married: 1. Sarah (div.)
2. Lise
Children: Scotty, Noah, Cody

When Mac Davis wrote and recorded *It's Hard to Be Humble* (with tongue in cheek), he could have been excused for making that boast. Mac's wonderfully varied career has covered songwriting, recording and appearing on Broadway in the title role of *The Will Rogers Follies*. He has also worked on TV, acted in movies and performed on the concert stage.

Mac sold his first song, *The Phantom Strikes Again*, in a restroom in Nashville to the manager of Sam the Sham. Later Mac became Regional Manager in Atlanta for Vee-Jay Records. Leaving in 1965, he joined Liberty. They brought him to L.A. to head Metric Music. Elvis recorded one of Mac's compositions, *A Little Less Conversation*, in 1968. He then asked Mac for material for his first Tennessee session in years. In 1969, Elvis registered a Top 40 Pop hit with Mac's *Memories* and then followed up with the song which brought Mac to prominence, *In the Ghetto*. It went Top 3, was Certified Gold and received a Grammy nomination for "Best Song." In 1970, Elvis recorded a fourth Davis song, *Don't Cry Daddy*, which went Top 15 on the Country chart and Top 10 on the Pop chart and was also Certified Platinum.

Other compositions were recorded by Lou Rawls (*You're Good for Me*), Glen Campbell (*Within My Memory*), O.C. Smith (*Friend, Lover, Woman, Wife*), Bobby Goldsboro (*Daddy's Little Man* and *Watching Scotty Grow*), and Kenny Rogers and the First Edition (*Something's Burning*). In the past, Mac also wrote as Scott Davis and Mac Scott Davis to avoid confusion with lyricist Mack David. He arranged the music for Elvis' first TV special and two of his movies as well as for Glen Campbell's movie *Norwood*.

In 1970, Mac signed to Columbia Records as an artist and had his first charted single with *Whoever Finds This I Love You* that year, reaching the Country Top 50 and the Pop Top 60. He followed up with the Top 70 Country success *I'll Paint You a Song* from the movie *Norwood*. He received a Gold Record for his 1972 single *Baby Don't Get Hooked on Me*, which was a No.1 Pop hit as well as peaking in the Top 15 on the Country charts and earned Mac a Grammy nomination for "Best Vocal Performance" and a CMA award nomination for "Best Song."

During 1973, he had success with *Dream Me Home* (Top 50), *Your Side of the Bed* (Top 40) and *Kiss It and Make It Better* (Top 30).

1974 brought *Stop and Smell the Roses*, which reached the Pop Top 10 and Country Top 40. The following year, he continued his cross-over success with *Rock 'n' Roll (I Gave You the Best Years of My Life)* (Pop Top 20/Country Top 30), *(If You Add) All the Love in the World* (Pop Top 60) and *Burnin' Thing* (Top 40). Chart placings in 1976 were *Forever Lovers* (Top 20) and *Every Now and Then* (Top 40). Mac's biggest chart record between 1977 and 1978 was the Top 50 *Picking Up the Pieces of My Life*.

Mac signed with Casablanca in 1980 and although they were not versed in the Country market, they managed to raise his record career success. In 1980, he had three consecutive Top 10 hits, *It's Hard to Be Humble* (also Pop Top 50), *Let's Keep it That Way* and *Texas in My Rearview Mirror* (also Pop Top 60). In 1981, he could boast *Secrets* (Top 50), *Hooked on Music* (Top 5) and *You're My Best Friend* (Top 5). Three more chart places appeared in 1982, *Rodeo Clown* (Top 40), *The Beer Drinkin' Song* (Top 60) and *Lying Here Lying* (Top 70).

Two more Davis singles charted in 1984, *Most of All* (Top 50) and *Caroline's Still in Georgia* (Top 80). This brought to an end Mac's liaison with Casablanca and he moved to MCA Records. In 1985, he hit the Top 10 with *I Never Made Love (Till I Made Love with You)* and had Top 40 success with *I Feel the Country Calling Me*. In 1986, he had middle-order chart singles in *Sexy Young Girl* and *Somewhere in America*.

In 1989, he duetted with Dolly Parton on *Wait 'Til I Get You Home*, which they co-wrote and which appears on Dolly's album ***White Limozeen***. They also co-wrote the title track on the album. 1991 bought Mac a Gold Record for his 1979 ***Greatest Hits*** album.

In addition to his accomplishments as a songwriter and recording artist, Mac Davis has toured the U.S. giving concert performances in such places as Las Vegas, Reno, Lake Tahoe and Atlantic City. He has hosted his own TV series, a musical variety show from 1974 to 1976 and in 1977, he did a Christmas special, *I Believe in Christmas*, for NBC. Two specials followed in 1978 and two more a year for the next three years until 1981. He was selected by the ACM as "Entertainer of the Year" in 1974 and the "Favorite Male Performer" by the People's Choice Awards. He has also starred in the movies *North Dallas Forty* (1979) with Nick Nolte and *The Sting II* (1983) with Jackie Gleason, Karl Malden and

Singer, Songwriter, Actor ***Mac Davis***

Oliver Reed, and in 1980, the TV movie *Cheaper to Keep Her*.

In 1992, Mac admitted to being an alcoholic. However, he now has this under control thanks to his own self-will and the love of his family. JAB

RECOMMENDED ALBUMS:

"Song Painter" (Columbia)(1970)
"Mac Davis Sings" (Trip)(1973)
"Greatest Hits-Mac Davis" (Columbia)(1979)
"It's Hard to Be Humble" (Casablanca)(1980)
"Who's Lovin' You" (Columbia)(1983)
"Somewhere in America" (MCA)(1986)

SKEETER DAVIS

(Singer, Songwriter)

Given Name:	**Mary Frances Penick**
Date of Birth:	**December 30, 1931**
Where Born:	**Dry Ridge, Kentucky**
Married:	**1. Ralph Emery (m. 1960)(div. 1963) 2. Joey Spampinato**
Children:	**Steve**

Known for her warm and friendly personality, Skeeter Davis has had a very successful career in Pop-Country music, being one of the finest exponents of the Nashville Sound. Her life has not always been happy, but her faith has helped her to carry on.

As a small child, Mary was given the name "Skeeter" by her grandfather, because she was "always buzzing from one place to another like a 'skeeter' (mosquito)." She was the eldest of seven children, and her early influences in music were Country, Gospel and Folk. She remembers hearing the Carter Family and always listened to the *Grand Ole Opry*.

Skeeter and her close friend Betty Jack Davis (b. March 3, 1932, Corbin, Kentucky/d. August 2, 1953) had begun singing together in high school. Both girls were committed Christians and in 1949, they formed the Davis Sisters. They performed in small clubs in Lexington, Kentucky, and soon made their debut on WLEX Lexington, in 1949, where they had their own series.

They were soon to be heard on WJR Detroit, WCOP and WKBC-TV Cincinnati. They signed to the Fortune label and also broadcast on WWVA Wheeling, West Virginia.

In 1952, Steve Sholes of RCA Victor signed the Davis Sisters to a recording contract and they cut the single *I Forgot More (Than You'll Ever Know)*, the following year. It was a smash hit reaching No.1, where it stayed for 8 weeks out of 6 months on the charts.

Then on August 2, 1953, while on the journey home from a performance on WWVA Wheeling after a night drive, their car was struck by another vehicle that crossed over the line and hit them head-on. Betty was killed outright and Skeeter was seriously injured and her recovery was slow and complicated. Skeeter was shocked and in despair and her friends began to encourage her to get out and perform again. Skeeter and Betty Jack's sister Georgia teamed up for a brief period, but Georgia's heart wasn't really in show business and so this liaison didn't last and for some years, Skeeter mourned.

Deciding to try to start a solo career, Skeeter moved to Nashville, and was taken under the wing of Chet Atkins, who was then A & R executive for RCA. To get experience as a solo artist she toured with RCA's Caravan of Stars which included Eddy Arnold and Elvis Presley. She began recording and in 1958 had a single in the Top 20, *Lost to a Geisha Girl* (the answer to Hank Loklin's *Geisha Girl*). She was also named "Most Promising Female Country Vocalist," in a *Cash Box* Survey, in 1959. She won this title again in 1960. The next single, *Set Him Free*, was released in 1959, reached the Top 5 and was Grammy nominated. Skeeter became a member of Ernest Tubb's touring show and also, in 1959, became a member of the *Grand Ole Opry*, an association that has lasted to date.

Star of the Grand Ole Opry ***Skeeter Davis***

A song Skeeter wrote herself, *(I Can't Help You) I'm Falling Too*, which was an answer song to another Hank Locklin hit, *Please Help Me, I'm Falling*, reached the Top 3, in 1960 and also crossed over to the Pop Top 40. This was followed closely by *My Last Date (With You),* which also hit both charts, reaching the Top 5 Country and the Top 30 Pop, in 1961.

That year, Skeeter charted with *The Hand You're Holding Now* (Top 15) and *Optimistic* (Top 10). In 1962, Skeeter scored with the Top 10 single, *Where I Ought to Be*. The flipside, *Something Precious*, reached the Top 25, as did *The Little Music Box*. Skeeter started 1963 with her biggest single, *The End of the World*, which reached the Top 3 on both Country and Pop charts and was a U.K. success. She followed up with *I'm Saving My Love* (Top 10 Country/Top 50 Pop) and *I Can't Stay Mad at You* (Top 15 Country/Top 10 Pop).

During this time she appeared on many TV shows and did two evangelistic TV Specials for Oral Roberts. Skeeter got the *Music Reporter* Award as "Entertainer of the Year" and the *Music Vendor* Award for "Top Female Vocalist of the Year," in 1963. Skeeter had four chart singles in 1964, of which the most successful were *He Says the Same Things to Me* (Top 15) and *Gonna Get Along without You Now* (Top 10).

In 1965, *A Dear John Letter*, a duet with Bobby Bare, reached the Top 15 and there was another Grammy nomination for the Top 30 single, *Sun Glasses.* The hits kept on with Dolly Parton's *Fuel to the Flame* (Top 15), *What Does it Take (To Keep a Man Like You Satisfied)* (Top 5), another Grammy nominee (both 1967), *There's a Fool Born Every Minute* (Top 20, 1968), *I'm a Lover Not a Fighter* (Top 10), *Your Husband My Wife* (Top 25, with Bobby Bare)(both 1970), *Bus Fare to Kentucky* (Top 25, 1971) and *I Can't Believe That It's All Over* (Top 15, 1973). In addition, she had two more low placed chart singles in 1974 and 1976. In 1976, Skeeter moved to Mercury Records after 18 years with RCA and *I Love Us* became a Top 60 single for Mercury.

During the 60's and the 70's, Skeeter toured extensively, visiting such places as Europe, Japan and Indonesia and appeared at Carnegie Hall, Wembley Festival, Royal Albert Hall, rodeos, fairs, theaters, the club circuit and radio and TV shows.

Apart from performing on the *Grand Ole Opry*, Skeeter sings in prisons and senior citizens' homes. She has a 300-acre farm in Brentwood, Tennessee, and is married to Joey Spampinato, the bass guitarist with NRBQ. He was at one time thought of as a possible replacement for Bill Wyman in the Rolling Stones and he played with Keith Richards, in Chuck Berry's backing band in the *Hail! Hail! Rock'n'Roll* movie. JAB

RECOMMENDED ALBUMS:

"Best of Skeeter Davis" (RCA Victor)(1965)
"Hand in Hand With Jesus" (RCA Victor)(1967)
"Skeeter Davis Sings Buddy Holly" (RCA Victor)(1967) [Featuring Waylon Jennings on guitar. Re-issued in the UK on Detour (1983)]
"Maryfrances" (RCA Victor)(1969)
"Down Home in the Country" (RCA Victor)(1970) [With George Hamilton IV]
"Best of Skeeter Davis Vol. 2" (RCA)(1973)
"The Best of the Best of Skeeter Davis" (Gusto)(1978)

JIMMY DAY

(Steel Guitar, Guitar)

Given Name: James Clayton Day
Date of Birth: January 9, 1934
Where Born: Tuscaloosa, Alabama
Married: Marilyn
Children: Marla

To nominate the No.1 steel player in the world would be one of the hardest jobs in the world. Some would say Buddy Emmons, some Paul Franklin, while others would nod knowingly and aver, Jimmy Day.

Jimmy started out on guitar when 12, but didn't take to it. However, three years later he saw Shot Jackson playing steel guitar with the Bailes Brothers on television and decided that this was going to be his instrument. Three years later, he auditioned for Webb Pierce's band using Shot's steel. The job with Webb meant that Jimmy started out on KWKH's *Louisiana Hayride*. It was 1951 and Webb was still selling shirts at Sears Roebuck.

Jimmy's first major recording was Webb's *That Heart Belongs to Me,* which was a 1952 No.1. At the time, Faron Young was front man for Pierce and Jimmy played on *Tattletale Tears*, *Have I Waited Too Long* and *Foolish Pride,* also in 1952. While at the *Hayride*, Jimmy played for six months with Hank Williams, who was in his post-Opry phase. Jimmy was mainly working with Red Sovine at this time but Hank also used Red's band. Hank asked Jimmy to join him but he died before that could take place. Jimmy also worked with Billy Walker, Johnny Horton and T. Texas Tyler.

In 1952, Jimmy started to work as a session man on Abbott recordings. This meant that he played on most of the sides cut by Jim Reeves while at Fabor and Abbott. Jimmy continued to record with Jim once he'd been signed to RCA. He also did some dubs on some Hank Williams tracks after the great man's death. Mitchell Torok and Jim Ed and Bonnie Brown were other artists to benefit from the Day touch. Just listen to Torok's 1953 recording of *Caribbean*—the steel player is Jimmy Day.

During 1954, Jimmy worked with Lefty Frizzell and along with Floyd Cramer, gigged with a young Elvis Presley. It was Jimmy who talked Elvis out of using steel guitar. With Cramer, Jimmy had a staff band at the *Hayride*, but in 1955, he left the show because it was getting too rock'n'roll for his liking. He moved to Nashville in December of that year and initially stayed with his good friend Floyd Cramer and his wife. Floyd was also a new boy in town. During 1955, Jimmy cut his only instrumental single for Abbott, *Rippin' Out/Blue Wind.*

He toured with Webb Pierce during 1956 and 1957 but, due to his worsening marital problems, he flipped back and forth between Nashville and Louisiana. He also yo-yoed between Ray Price's Cherokee Cowboys and Jim Reeves' Blue Boys. In 1959, Jimmy met Willie Nelson, who shortly after joined Price's band on bass (he'd never played one before!). Three years later, Nelson left Price and took Jimmy with him. Jimmy stayed with Willie's band for six months and then he joined George Jones and appeared on several albums and singles, notably, *The Race Is On*. Jimmy and George became great friends but couldn't work together because they both got drunk too much.

From George, Jimmy went on to work with Ferlin Husky. This was a good time for Jimmy, but he left for more money elsewhere and then along with Buddy Emmons played with Ray Price again, the two of them alternating between bass and steel. Then in 1966, he returned to Willie Nelson, who was then putting together the Record Men. Jimmy played alongside Wade Ray (fiddle) and Johnny Bush (drums). Jimmy stayed with Willie until 1973, while also playing certain dates with Little Jimmy Dickens. In 1973, Jimmy moved to Texas, where he stayed playing for three years. He then returned to Nashville, where he played for Charlie Louvin on live dates and at the *Opry*. In 1978, Jimmy moved back to Texas, where he has been ever since. He now plays dates with Jimmy Bush and Willie, as well as lesser known local bands.

In 1982, Jimmy was inducted into the International Steel Guitar Hall of Fame. In 1986, he was elected to the Texas Steel Guitar Hall of Fame and in 1994, he was inducted into the Texas Western Swing Hall of Fame. He is currently preparing instructional videos which will be marketed in 1995.

RECOMMENDED ALBUMS:

"Stealing Home" (Country Style) [Transcription with Leon "Shot" Jackson]
"Golden Steel Guitar Hits" (Phillips)(1962) [Also on Vintage Classics]
"All These Years" (Midland) [Released in the UK on Checkmate]
"Jimmy Day Salutes Don Helms" (Texas Musik)
" Swingin' Country Greats" (Cumberland) [With the Swingbillies]

BILLY DEAN

(Singer, Songwriter, Guitar, Fiddle, Piano)

Given Name: William Harold Dean
Date of Birth: April 1, 1962
Where Born: Quincy, Florida
Married: Cathy Massie (m. 1989)
Children: William Eli

It was Billy Dean's appearance on the *New Faces Show* at the 1991 Country Radio Seminar in Nashville that was the turning point in the direction of his career. Although he had been heard on the radio, this TV exposure put a face and personality to the voice.

Billy learned to play guitar while still in grade school and made his debut performance when he was 8 years old playing in his father's band, the Country Rock. Billy began songwriting when he was 15, and after attending college in Decatur, Mississippi, on a one-year college basketball scholarship, he began a solo act playing clubs and hotels along the Gulf Coast.

Billy was a National finalist in the Wrangler Starsearch Talent Contest and as a result performed at the Opry House. He moved to Nashville in 1980 and formed his own band. He began touring and opening for such stars as Mel Tillis, Gary Morris, Ronnie Milsap and Steve Wariner. In addition to this, he sang and acted in commercials for many major accounts.

His songwriting and singing eventually were brought to the attention of publisher and producer Jimmy Gilmer, who got Billy a songwriting contract with EMI Music and then a recording deal with Capitol Nashville/SBK Records (later SBK/Liberty). In 1989, Randy Travis recorded *Somewhere in My Broken Heart*, which was written by Billy and Richard Leigh.

Billy's first album, ***Young Man***, was released in 1990. Five of the ten songs on the album were self-penned. *Only Here for a Little While*, the song he sang on the *New Faces Show,* was his debut cut and assisted by a music video, made it to the Top 3 in 1991 and was followed by the single *Somewhere in My Broken Heart*, which also went Top 3. The latter song brought Billy the ACM Award for "Top New Male Vocalist" and "Song of the Year." Billy was also nominated for a Grammy Award for "Best Country Vocal Performance, Male" and was a finalist for the CMA's "Horizon Award."

Billy's next album, ***Billy Dean***, was released that year and went Gold in February 1992. The lead-off single, *You Don't Count the Cost* and the 1992 follow-ups *Only the Wind* and *Billy the Kid* all went Top 5, and *Somewhere in My Broken Heart* hit No.1 in 1992.

During 1992, Billy was asked to write and perform the theme song for a new children's animated series entitled, *Wild West C.O.W.-Boys of Moo Mesa*, for ABC-TV. For most of that year, he was without a manager, after forming his own company, however, he is now managed by Teri Brown.

During 1993, Billy released his third album, ***Fire in the Dark***, which was produced by Jimmy Bowen and Billy. From this album, Billy charted in 1993, with *Tryin' to Hide a Fire in the Dark* (Top 10), *I Wanna Take Care of You* (Top 25) and *I'm Not Built that Way* (Top 40). In 1994, Billy scored a Top 10 hit with *We Just Disagree* and then reached the Top 60 with *Once in a While*, a track from the MCA Soundtrack album, ***8 Seconds***. During June, 1994, Billy released his fourth album, ***Men'll Be Boys***. JAB

Billy the Kid, ***Billy Dean***

RECOMMENDED ALBUMS:

"Young Man" (Capitol Nashville/SBK)(1990)
"Billy Dean" (Capitol Nashville/SBK)(1991)
"Fire In The Dark" (SBK/Liberty)(1992)
"Men'll Be Boys" (SBK/Liberty)(1994)

EDDIE DEAN

(Singer, Songwriter, Guitar, Fiddle, Tenor Banjo)

Given Name:	**Edgar Dean Glosup**
Date of Birth:	**July 9, 1907**
Where Born:	**Posey, Texas**
Married:	**Lorene "Dearest" Donnelly**
Children:	**Donna, Edgar, Jr.**

Eddie Dean is one of the seven Hollywood "Singing Cowboys" who achieved prominence for both his musical western films (see Movie Section) and his Country vocals. While his fame and success never approached that of Gene Autry, Tex Ritter, or Roy Rogers, his career in music has extended over a lengthier period of time. Eddie started on radio in the late 20's, and 60 years later he could still warble a pretty decent song. Furthermore, as a songwriter, Dean penned one of the all time classics with his *I Dreamed of a Hill-Billy Heaven.*

Eddie came from a large family and his father was a farmer and a schoolteacher who sang. The youth learned a great deal about vocal parts and harmony and a little later received additional inspiration via the radio broadcasts of Dallas radio singer Peg Moreland, who has a vast repertoire of old ballads and other numbers. Eddie went to Chicago in 1926 hoping to land a radio program, but could get little more than guest spots. He did shorten his name for stage purposes and in 1927 obtained regular employment at KMA Shenandoah, Iowa, a station owned by the May Seed Company.

In 1929, Eddie went to WNAX Yankton, South Dakota, where his older brother Jimmy Dean (not the Jimmy Dean who had a hit with *Big Bad John*) joined him to form a duet. They later moved to WIBW Topeka, Kansas, and in late 1933 finally made it to WLS for an early morning show and the *National Barn Dance.* In 1934 and 1935, the pair recorded several duets for the ARC group of labels under Art Satherley's direction as well as a few Gospel numbers for Decca. In the latter year, the Deans went their separate ways as Jimmy shifted over to WJJD and took a dramatic role in a daytime network program entitled *Modern Cinderella.*

In 1937, Eddie Dean decided to try his luck in Hollywood, hoping to emulate the success of Gene Autry. For nearly a decade, he worked in small film roles, appearing on Judy Canova's network radio show, and cut 10 (eight released) numbers for Decca in 1941 and 1942, including *On the Banks of the Sunny San Juan*. However, Eddie's real big break came in 1944 when he got the opportunity to star in a musical western, *The Harmony Trail*, which subsequently led to a series of 19 more movies for PRC/Eagle-Lion films. The first five pictures were shot in color, featured such winsome leading ladies as Shirley Patterson and Jennifer Holt, sidekicks like Rosco Ates and Emmett Lynn, and contained three or four songs spotlighting Dean's strong voice. He continued the series through 1948 and thereafter concentrated almost exclusively on his singing career, which the reputation earned in the movies allowed him to maintain.

Eddie's recordings appeared on Majestic, Mercury, and Crystal in the late 40's. He appeared on the Country chart in 1948 with his Crystal recording of *One Has My Name (The Other Has My Heart)* (co-written with his wife). Eddie recorded for Capitol in the early 50's and his biggest number, *I Dreamed of a Hill-Billy Heaven*, hit the charts in early 1955 on the Sage and Sand label. Tex Ritter's revised 1961 version of the song even made the Top 20 on the Pop charts. *One Has My Name (The Other Has My Heart)* went to the top for fellow Western singer Jimmy Wakely. Jerry Lee Lewis had another hit with it in 1969.

From the 60's, Eddie's recordings usually appeared on budget labels like Crown and Design and in the 70's for W.F.C. and Shasta.

Throughout his career, Eddie Dean has al-

Eddie Dean *(right) with* ***Rosco Ates***

ways conducted himself in a congenial, gentlemanly, and dignified manner. During the 80's, he often guested and sang at the western film fairs with a magnificent voice that never wavered. Eddie's wife, Lorene, whom he married in 1931, often accompanied him on these appearances. In 1993, Eddie was inducted into the Cowboy Hall of Fame. IMT

RECOMMENDED ALBUMS:

"Greater Westerns" (Sage)(1956)
"The Golden Cowboy" (Crown)
"Eddie Dean Sings" (Crown)
"Sincerely, Eddie Dean" (Shasta)(1974)
"A Cowboy Sings Country" (Shasta)(1976)
"Dean of the West" (W.F.C.)(1976)
"I Dreamed of a Hillbilly Heaven" (Castle)(1981) [Recordings of singles from the 50's]

JIMMY DEAN

(Singer, Songwriter, Piano, Guitar, Accordion, Harmonica, Business Entrepreneur)

Given Name:	**Jimmy Ray Dean**
Date of Birth:	**August 10, 1928**
Where Born:	**Seth Ward, Plainsview, Texas**
Married:	**1. Sue Wittauer (div.)**
	2. Donna L. Meade (m. 1991)
Children:	**Gary, Connie, Robert**

It may sometimes be difficult to take Jimmy Dean seriously, when he doesn't take himself seriously. After all, there are no other Country performers who are producers and packers of quality meats who come and tell you about it on TV commercials. From being laughed *at* as a child, he learned the merits of being laughed *with*.

He was born into extreme poverty. His mother ran the local barbershop and was the family breadwinner. When Jimmy was old enough, he got work on farms in the area. Despite their circumstances, Jimmy's mother taught him piano when he was 10 and he started to learn to play guitar, accordion and harmonica.

When he was 16, Jimmy tried his hand at irrigation engineering but before long enlisted in the Merchant Marine for a two year hitch. Following that, he went into the U.S. Air Force. While stationed at Bolling Air Force Base near Washington, D.C., he put together the Tennessee Haymakers and played both service and civilian clubs. He left the forces in 1948, but hung around the Washington area and put together the Texas Wildcats. They were featured on WARL-TV Arlington.

By 1952, he had come under the guiding hand of the legendary promoter Connie B. Gay. He sent Jimmy on a tour of the U.S. bases in the Caribbean. That year, Jimmy cut a single for 4 Star Records, *Bumming Around*, which took some while to chart, but in 1953, reached the Top 5 on the Country charts. The follow-up, *Queen of Hearts/I'm Feeling for You*, did nothing.

Connie Gay put Jimmy on *Town and Country Time* on WMAL-TV and he started to get attention. The show was syndicated as *Town and Country Jamboree* and was broadcast every Saturday from the Capitol Arena in Washington. This led to CBS giving Jimmy his own *Jimmy Dean Show* on WTOP Washington in the 7:00 a.m. slot against NBC's Dave Garroway. However, the lack of sponsors spelled the death knell and even though there was talk about an afternoon show, nothing came of it.

In 1957, Jimmy had signed to Columbia Records and steadily released 10 singles without any chart success (imagine that happening in the 90's!). In 1961, on his way to a recording session in Nashville, Jimmy wrote his first song. The result was that *Big Bad John* (part narrative/part singing) went to No.1 Country (2 weeks) and Pop (5 weeks) and went Gold. It even went to No.2 in the U.K. national chart. It also suffered from parodies.

Jimmy followed this in 1962 with *Dear Ivan*,which reached the Top 10 on the Country chart and the Top 25 Pop. This was a narrative, as was the double sided hit *The Cajun Queen/To a Sleeping Beauty,* which hit the charts a week after *Dear Ivan*. This was remarkable for a non-vocal record. It made the Top 20 on the Country list on both sides and Top 30 Pop. In April of that year, with his other records starting to fade, Jimmy came in with another biggie. *PT109,* about President John Kennedy's wartime boat, rode the waves of a new President in office and reached the Top 3 on the Country charts and Top 10 on the national lists. He finished off the year with *Little Black Book,* which was a Top 10 hit and made the Pop Top 30.

From 1963 through 1966, he hosted the daytime *Jimmy Dean Show* on ABC-TV. From 1964 to 1966, he had an evening show, which was not quite so successful. During this time, he had three hit records. In 1964, he remade the Hank Williams classic *Mind Your Own Business,* which went Top 40 on the Country chart. A year later, he returned to the No.1 slot with *The First Thing Ev'ry Morning (and the Last Thing Ev'ry Night)*. It crossed over and made the Top 100 on the Pop chart. *Harvest of Sunshine* followed in its wake and reached the Top 40.

Jimmy moved from Columbia in 1966 and started recording for RCA. *Stand Beside Me* was a Top 10 hit and heralded a consolidation of his recording career. During 1967, he had three hits, *Sweet Misery* (Top 20), *Ninety Days* (Top 50) and *I'm a Swinger* (Top 30). The following year, he also had a triple hander of hits, *A Thing Called Love* (Top 25), *Born to Be By Your Side* (Top 60) and *A Hammer and Nails* (Top 25). He just missed the Top 50 with his 1969 entry *A Rose is a Rose is a Rose*, but in 1971 was back fighting fit with the Top 30 duet with Dottie West *Slowly.* That was followed by the solo Top 60 *Everybody Knows* and the following year, *The One You Say Good Morning To* (Top 40). In 1973 Jimmy scraped into the charts with a single for Columbia, *Your Sweet Love (Keeps Me Homeward Bound)*.

Then just when it seemed like his recording career had ground to a halt, he came back with another career single. *I.O.U.*, a narration in the *No Charge* vein, was released on GRT/Casino in 1976 and went Gold. It reached the Top 10 on the Country chart and the Top 40 on the Pop chart. Jimmy then re-recorded his 1962 hit *To a Sleeping Beauty* and the new version made it to the Top 90. To coincide with Mother's Day, Casino re-released *I.O.U.* in 1977 and once again it charted. Churchill Records had by 1983 acquired the masters and put it out again that year and once again it appeared in the lists.

Jimmy Dean is without doubt an undervalued performer. His recording career could have been more successful, it's true, but that is not always the yardstick of success. He has been an in demand entertainer for many years. His TV shows were pure cornball fun and were the forerunners of programs such as *Hee Haw*.

RECOMMENDED ALBUMS:

"Big Bad John (& Other Fabulous Songs & Tales)" (Columbia)(1961)
"Jimmy Dean's Greatest Hits" (Columbia)(1966)
"Most Richly Blessed (& Other Inspirational Songs) (RCA Victor)(1967)
"The Jimmy Dean Show" (RCA Victor)(1968)
"Everybody's Favorite" (Columbia Limited Edition)(1973)
"Jimmy Dean—I.O.U." (Casino)(1976)

Big bad ***Jimmy Dean***

PENNY DeHAVEN

(Singer, Actress)
Given Name: **Charlotte DeHaven**
Date of Birth: **May 17, 1948**
Where Born: **Winchester, Virginia**

Although top stardom has eluded Penny DeHaven to date, she is a dynamic and vivacious performer who remains on a quest for "that one big hit." A critic once described her shows as a "happiness explosion." Penny, who began her Country music career as a child in the Eastern Panhandle section of West Virginia, progressed from local shows to WWVA Wheeling's *Jamboree USA* and then to Nashville. Through 1988, she had accumulated 17 charted numbers, but the highest only reached No.20.

Penny DeHaven grew up in Berkeley Springs, West Virginia, where as a child she sang on shows featuring such local favorites as Dale Brooks and comedian Dusty Shaver, as well as serving as a cheerleader and as secretary of her high school senior class. After graduation, she became a regular on the *Jamboree* using the stage name Penny Starr.

She first hit the Country charts in January 1967 with *Grain of Salt,* a single on the Band Box label. Her stint at the *Jamboree* lasted for two years during which time, the maturing songstress became the first girl Country singer to tour combat zones in Vietnam. By 1969, Penny had moved to Nashville and signed a contract with Imperial Records as Penny DeHaven, hitting the charts three times in a 9 month period. The songs included *Mama Lou* as well as Country covers of Billy Joe Royal's *Down in the Boondocks* (both Top 40, 1969) and the Beatles' *I Feel Fine* (Top 60, 1970). When Penny switched to United Artists in 1970, she immediately had her biggest success, a duet with Country veteran Del Reeves entitled *Land Mark Tavern.* Penny opened 1971 with the Top 50, *The First Love*. Her best solo effort followed with *Don't Change on Me,* which reached No.42. Scott Turner produced both her Imperial and United Artists sides. During this period, Penny guested several times on the *Grand Ole Opry*, describing her first such experience as "my greatest thrill."

In 1973, Penny signed with Mercury and had three chartmakers, but the strongest one, *I'll Be Doggone,* topped out in the Top 70. None since has done so well, but her name periodically pops up in the Country chart listings, most recently on the Main Street label, where she had three minor hits in the early 80's, one of them a duet with Boxcar Willie. In between times, Penny recorded for Starcrest and Elektra. She recently contracted anew with Broadland International.

The stunning ***Penny DeHaven***

Despite having no really big records, the demure but dynamic Penny manages to continue attracting and exciting fans on the road. She also had small dramatic roles in five motion pictures, including *Bronco Billy* (1980) and *Honkytonk Man* (1982), singing the Cajun flavored *Bayou Lullaby* on the soundtrack of the latter Clint Eastwood favorite. DeHaven stands only an inch over five feet in height with hazel eyes and a spectacular figure. Known as "the movingest gal in Country music," she maintains an active schedule of singing at clubs, conventions, parks, and military bases abroad. In recent months Penny has provided her enthusiastic brand of entertainment at numerous sales conferences. IMT

RECOMMENDED ALBUMS:
"Penny DeHaven" (United Artists)(1972)
"Penny DeHaven" (Main Street)(1974)

DELMORE BROTHERS, The

ALTON DELMORE
(Vocals, Songwriter, Guitar, Tenor Guitar, Fiddle)
Given Name: **Alton Delmore**
Date of Birth: **December 25, 1908**
Married: **Thelma Neeley**
Children: **Lionel, Billie Anne, Norma Gail, Susan (dec'd.), Deborah**
Date of Death: **June 8, 1964**

RABON DELMORE
(Vocals, Songwriter, Tenor Guitar, Fiddle)
Given Name: **Rabon Delmore**
Date of Birth: **December 3, 1916**
Married: **Nola King**
Date of Death: **December 4, 1952**

Both Born: **Elkmont, Alabama**

The Delmore Brothers were probably the most influential, and certainly the most creative, of all the brother duet acts of the 1930's and 1940's. As singers they created some of the most complex and sophisticated harmonies, featuring a soft, close harmony and difficult, complex harmony yodels and falsetto passages. As songwriters, they produced a dozen good Country classics that are still heard today, songs ranging from their first giant hit, *Brown's Ferry Blues,* in 1933, to the rock'n'roll-flavored *Blues Stay Away from Me*, in 1949. Their style borrowed equally from the Blues and from Gospel music, and for a time in the 1930's they were the most popular Country radio stars in the nation.

The Limestone County area in northern Alabama, where the Delmores were born and grew up, was a hotbed for Gospel quartet music and singing conventions (though not for Sacred Harp music). The Delmores grew up and went to school with important Gospel figures like Jake Hess, G.T. Speer and Dwight Brock. They both attended the local singing schools, where they learned to read the seven-shape note music, to mark time and to understand harmony; in later years Alton became one of the very few members of the *Grand Ole Opry* who could notate and read music. By 1925, Alton and his mother, "Mollie," were writing Gospel songs for a local publisher, the Athens Music Company and one of these, *Bound for the Shore*, remained in his repertoire for years after. The Delmores' uncle was W.A. Williams, a well-known figure in Gospel music who penned a number of songs for the old paperback songbooks.

By 1926, when Rabon was only 10, the brothers were starting to sing the soft, intricate duets for which they became famous. They began winning local fiddle contests and on the advice of the Allen Brothers, began creating their own material and trying to get a record contract. They succeeded in 1931, when Columbia invited them to Atlanta to record two sides (*Alabama Lullaby* and *Got the Kansas City Blues*). In the depth of the Depression, though, the disc sold fewer than 500 copies and the brothers returned to their circuit of fiddling contests and small-time schoolhouse shows. They next began approaching the *Grand Ole Opry*, begging for an audition and in the spring of 1933, they finally got hired by Harry Stone, then the manager.

The Delmores' stay on the *Opry* was stormy and controversial at times, but it gained them access to a national audience. They were popular at once and soon were receiving more fan mail than anyone else on the show except Uncle Dave Macon. In December 1933, they traveled north to Chicago with the Vagabonds to record 17 songs for the RCA Bluebird label. Included were two important songs, *Brown's Ferry Blues* (named for a ferry near the boys' birthplace) and *Gonna Lay Down My Old*

The vocally harmonious ***Delmore Brothers***

Guitar. The *Opry* first paired them for tours with Uncle Dave Macon, but in 1936 switched them to Arthur Smith; they recorded with both, joining Smith for his famous *More Pretty Girls Than One* (1936). They continued their own prolific record-making, doing hits like *Southern Moon*, *When It's Time for the Whippoorwill to Sing*, *Weary Lonesome Blues* and *Fifteen Miles from Birmingham*.

In 1938, when Roy Acuff joined the *Opry*, Stone paired him with the Delmores to help him gain acceptance and familiarity with the tour audiences. This worked for a while, but later that year tensions that had been mounting between the Delmores and *Opry* management came to a head and in September 1938, the brothers left the show and pulled out of Nashville for WPTF Raleigh. A series of short stays on various stations followed, eventually leading the brothers to WLW in Cincinnati. Here they had some of their most productive years, forming the Gospel quartet the Brown's Ferry Four (with Merle Travis and Grandpa Jones) and recording for the local King label.

With the advent of WWII, Rabon was drafted for a brief time into the U.S. Navy, Alton being exempt because he had a cast in his eye. While Rabon was in the service, Alton worked solo but got himself sacked. When Rabon returned, he tried to get Alton back without success. So they moved on to WIBC Indianapolis in 1944. The following year, they moved on to WCM Memphis, Tennessee, where they met Blues harmonica player Wayne Raney.

Unlike the Bluebird sides, their King sides at this time had much more of a Blues influence: often they featured Wayne Raney or the electric guitar of Zeke Turner and pianist Henry Glover. Many were "Boogies," like *Freight Train Boogie* and *Hillbilly Boogie,* and many of them anticipated the developing sounds of rock'n'roll. During the late 40's and into 1950, the brothers appeared on the Country chart with *Freight Train Boogie* (Top 3, 1946), *Blues Stay Away from Me* (No.1, 1949) and *Pan American Boogie* (Top 10, 1950).

The brothers moved to Chattanooga in 1947, and then to WRBC Jackson, Mississippi, in 1948. They settled at KWHN (now KTCS) Fort Smith, Arkansas, where Lionel Delmore, then age 10, debuted. In 1950, the Delmores moved to XREF Del Rio, Texas. However, at this time, Alton suffered a mild heart attack and in 1951, they went to KPRC Houston, Texas. It was at this time that a legal battle ensued over the copyright of *Beautiful Brown Eyes* and Alton, without the financial wherewithal to fight the case, had to settle for a nominal payout.

Shortly after, their father died, which shook Alton in particular. Then almost immediately after that, his 3 year old daughter, Susan, died. Alton lost interest in music and resorted to drink. Rabon's marriage, always precarious, was breaking up and he tried to get his brother to move to Detroit, but Alton refused. Rabon left intent on a solo career. Alton then ran a bar but after Rabon informed him that he was ill, Alton moved to Detroit and the two performed together. Rabon was then diagnosed with lung cancer.

Following his brother's death, Alton, who had grown closer than ever to Rabon, quit music and became a mailman and salesman before continuing with his music. He recorded on his own for several small labels, including Acme, and worked in radio. He did some duo work, with Lionel taking Rabon's place and also taught guitar and wrote short stories. He died in 1964, although the cause is not clear, being either a heart attack or complications caused by a liver disorder.

Alton, the dominant member of the duo, eventually wrote over 1,000 songs in his lifetime, and saw them recorded by artists as diverse as Grandpa Jones, Tennessee Ernie Ford, Glen Campbell, Doug Sahm and Bob Dylan. Alton wrote a remarkable autobiography, *Truth is Stranger Than Publicity*. In 1971, both brothers were elected to the Nashville Songwriters Hall of Fame. CKW

RECOMMENDED ALBUMS:

"The Delmore Brothers 30th Anniversary Album" (King)(1962)
"The Best of the Delmore Brothers" (King)(1970)
"Weary Lonesome Blues" (Old Homestead)
"Singing My Troubles Away" (Old Homestead)
"Early Sacred Songs" (Old Homestead)
(See also Brown's Ferry Four.)

LITTLE JIMMY DEMPSEY

(Singer, Songwriter, Guitar)

Given Name: James Clifford Dempsey
Date of Birth: August 23, 1937
Where Born: Atlanta, Georgia
Married: Tena Carrie
Children: James Timothy

Little Jimmy Dempsey is one of those talented artists who started performing publicly at a very early age. He began entertaining at the age of 5 on various Atlanta stations. A short time later, he appeared on national programs with Bob Hope, Eddie Cantor, Phil Harris, and others—usually dressed in a tuxedo. A victim of childhood polio, Dempsey created quite a dapper image when dressed for his act. For two years, 1946-1948, Dempsey had a show on Atlanta's radio station WSB.

During the 1950's, he was the lead guitar player for the Longhorn Ranch Boys, the house band at a popular Atlanta Country music club. Then, in 1958 he became the leader of the Cherokee Country Boys and made his first appearance on records, signing with the Starday label. Jimmy left the Cherokee Country Boys in 1962 to form his own trio.

He later appeared on several other labels including Sing & Skylite, Dot, ABC Paramount, and his own JCD. His most successful recordings were an instrumental called *Bop Hop* and a song called *Rhode Island Red.* As a songwriter he is noted for humorous titles like *Bessie was a Good Old Cow*, *Betcha Can't Eat Just One* and *But First a Word from Our Sponsor*. He also wrote, or co-wrote, *Turn Around*, *Honky Tonk World*, and *I'm Gonna Pray*.

In the late 50's and early 60's, Jimmy appeared on the *Ernest Tubb Radio Program* and on the German program *American Music* and in 1968, Jimmy had his own syndicated TV show. Dempsey eventually moved to Nashville but has since moved away, just exactly where is unclear. Some sources say he is in Florida, others say he is in the Louisville, Kentucky, area. Apparently, he is semiretired from the music business. WKM

RECOMMENDED ALBUMS:

"Lots of Gospel Guitar" (Sing)
"Mr. Versatile Guitar" (World Wide)
"I'll Fly Away" (Gloryland)
"Guitar Country of Little Jimmy Dempsey" (ABC Paramount)

JIM DENNY

(Industry Executive, Booking Agent, Music Publisher)

Given Name: James Ray Denny
Date of Birth: February 28, 1911
Where Born: Buffalo Valley, Putnam County, Tennessee
Married: 1. Margaret Clement (div.) 2. Dolly
Children: J. William
Date of Death: August 27, 1963

Like so many captains of industry, Jim Denny only attended school to fourth grade but had an unassuaged appetite for reading and learning. When he first arrived in Nashville, he was still a young boy and he had several jobs including telegram boy for Western Union. He obtained a job with National Life and Accident Company, which owned WSM radio and staged the *Grand Ole Opry*.

Jim gradually climbed the promotion ladder and worked his way into the Opry organization. In 1951, he became WSM Talent Director. Three years later, he set up Cedarwood Music, which became the most important music publishing house in Nashville, until overtaken by Jack Stapp's Tree Publishing. His partners in the company were Webb Pierce and Carl Smith.

He then widened his empire by creating a booking agency, the Jim Denny Bureau. He took under his wing most of the artists he had signed while at the *Opry*. *Billboard* estimated that by 1961 the bureau was handling over 3,300 personal appearances throughout the world. Denny was a firm believer in the handshake basis of doing business and called it the "Jim Denny Deal." He was a man who was as good as his word.

On October 22, 1966, three years after his death, he was inducted into the Country Music Hall of Fame. His plaque acknowledged him as a "leader" who "served to promote, protect and encourage some of the most important artists in the industry" and confirmed that "his contribution to Country music is widely recognized, and his untimely death was a tragic loss to all."

Jim Denny's son, Bill (b. August 25, 1935, Nashville, Tennessee), followed his father into the music business. While still young, Bill worked at the *Opry* on Saturday nights and traveled with a carnival during his summer holidays. While still in high school, he worked as both a prop man and a cameraman at WSM-TV. He also worked as a deejay at Nashville radio stations WSM and WMAK.

Bill attended Vanderbilt University and majored in business administration. In 1956, he became road manager for the Philip Morris Company Music Show. He worked for a while at an advertising agency and also for Columbia Records as Nashville Studio Manager. In 1963, Bill became General Manager of Cedarwood Publishing Company. Bill served as the youngest President of the CMA during the mid-60's and was the youngest member of the Board of Trustees of NARAS.

JOHN DENVER

(Singer, Songwriter, Guitar, Actor)

Given Name: John Henry Deutschendorf, Jr.
Date of Birth: December 31, 1943
Where Born: Roswell, New Mexico
Married: 1. Annie (Anne Martell) (m. 1967)(div.1983) 2. Cassy
Children: Zachary John, Anne Kate

Friendly, humorous and good natured, John Denver likes the outdoor environment and is concerned for the beauty of nature. He is a poet who may be classed as folksy, but who has written and sung some of Country's finest songs.

He was brought up in an Air Force family. John's education was conducted in many places including Japan. His father was a pilot with three aviation world records to his credit and he passed this love of flying on to John. He was given a Gibson guitar by his grandmother and he took lessons and by the time he was in the ninth grade, he played well. He sang in the church choir in Fort Worth, Texas, and performed in school Rock bands. He also played at proms and parties. During his teens, John ran away from home to California, but became frightened and confused, and returned to Texas.

Graduating from high school, John enrolled at Texas Tech., Lubbock, as an architecture major, but spent more time making music than studying. This was the Folk era and John was influenced by Bob Dylan, Joan Baez, Tom Paxton and Peter, Paul and Mary. John sang in coffeehouses and at college functions, with the result that his studies suffered and so he dropped out of school and set off for California once more.

He managed to get a job in Los Angeles as a draftsman, while he looked for work in the music business. After a year he was singing in a Folk-oriented club, when the club owner, Randy Sparks, founder of the New Christy Minstrels, offered John a regular job performing at Leadbetters (one of his venues). This led to a position at the Lumbermill in Phoenix, where he auditioned for a place in the Chad Mitchell Trio. Chad had gone through about 200 applicants, but John got the job and toured with the trio from 1965-1969.

During this time, John began to take his songwriting seriously. In 1966, he wrote *Leaving on a Jet Plane* and played it in the trio. Peter, Paul and Mary heard them sing it and recorded it the following year, although it did not become popular until 1969, when it was played continually by a deejay in Denver, Colorado, to please his girlfriend, making it a big hit.

The remaining two members of the trio left, because of tension and personality clashes. It was later re-formed by John and renamed as Denver, Boise and Johnson (Johnson being Michael Johnson), but the trio didn't last long and disbanded.

John decided to try his luck as a solo artist. He had married by this time and with the help of his wife, Anne Martell, set off for Aspen, Colorado, in 1970, where they settled permanently and entertained in the ski resorts. The opportunity arose to perform at the Cellar Door in Washington, D.C. Here he found himself a manager, Jerry Weintraub. They got on well and Jerry arranged guest appearances for John on several shows and got him a recording contract with RCA.

John's debut album, ***Rhymes and Reasons*** (1969), included *Leaving on a Jet Plane*. The second album, ***Take Me Tomorrow***, was released in 1970 and failed to ignite the public. However, John got together with two friends from the Cellar Door days, Bill Danoff and Taffy Nivert, and sat down to complete a song they had been working on. It was the now famous *Take Me Home, Country Roads*, which rose to the Top 3 on the Pop chart and was Certified Gold. This song and *I Guess He'd Rather Be in Colorado* both appeared on the 1971 album, ***Poems, Prayers and Promises***, which also went Gold. John undertook a tour of the U.S., appearing in concerts, and then did a TV series for the BBC-2 in the U.K. With the experience he got there, he was soon appearing on U.S. TV shows and was even hosting the *Midnight Special*, chatting with the guests and also singing on the NBC musical show.

After the success of *Country Roads*, John was unable to consolidate on it with the next three minor successes. However, in 1972, he released the excellent ***Aerie*** album, which also went Gold and then he was back in the Top 10, with *Rocky Mountain High*, from the album of the same name. The album was Certified Gold that year and the following year, the album ***Farewell Andromeda*** did likewise. In 1973, RCA released ***John Denver's Greatest Hits*** and that rapidly achieved Gold status.

John was on a series called *Bighorn* about ecology and he also wrote the score for the TV drama called *Sunshine*. A single was released from this in 1974, called *Sunshine on My Shoulder* and it became John's first Pop No.1. Originally the title had been the flip-side of his minor chart record, *I'd Rather Be a Cowboy*. This became John's second Gold single.

Now a whole string of hit records followed. *Annie's Song*, written for his wife,

Anne, went to No.1 in the Pop charts and Top 10 on the Country chart and was Certified Gold. It also was a No.1 hit in the U.K. national charts. *Back Home Again* and the album of the same name completed a phenomenal year. The single peaked at No.5 in the Pop charts and gave John his first Country No.1. Both the single and the album were Certified Gold. He ended the year with *Sweet Surrender*, which made the Country Top 10 and was a Top 20 Pop hit. The track was recorded live at Universal City Amphitheater and was featured in the Disney movie *The Bears*.

During 1974, John played a dramatic role in the TV mystery series *McCloud*. The Governor of Colorado made June 24-30 "Welcome Back Home Again, John Denver" week and proclaimed him "Poet Laureate of the State." John's double live album, ***An Evening with John Denver***, was released in 1975 and Certified Gold that year. As well as *Sweet Surrender*, a second track from the album, entitled *Thank God I'm a Country Boy*, provided John with a massive hit in 1975. It topped both the Country and Pop charts and was Certified Gold. John made it two in a row when *I'm Sorry* made it to No.1 in both the Country and Pop charts. The single was Certified Gold and the flipside, *Calypso* (dedicated to Jacques Cousteau's boat), made it a double-sided success, when it reached the Top 3. During 1975, the album from which it came, ***Windsong***, also went Gold. John's next single, *Fly Away* with backing vocal by Olivia Newton-John, was not as successful and only reached the Top 20 in both charts. John had his first Christmas hit with the Pop Top 60 *Christmas for Cowboys*.

John was voted the "No.1 Selling Artist in the U.S." He was also named "Entertainer of the Year" by the CMA and received his award on satellite relay while he was in Australia on tour. His award raised some hackles among the

International star ***John Denver***

purists in Nashville. That year, *The John Denver Rocky Mountain Christmas* TV Show Special was watched by 30 million viewers and the album ***Rocky Mountain Christmas*** went Gold before the year was finished.

Then suddenly in 1976, John failed to sell singles and with the exception of *Looking for Space* (Top 30), *Like a Sad Song* (Top 40) and *Baby, You Look Good to Me Tonight* (Top 30), his 1976 offerings failed to ignite. However, the album ***Spirit*** went Platinum. Continuing to do TV shows, specials and cabaret, John also appeared in the 1977 movie *Oh, God!*, with George Burns and had a Top 40 single, *My Sweet Lady,* and a Top 30 Country hit with *How Can I Leave You Again.* His album ***John Denver's Greatest Hits, Volume II*** went Gold in 1977 and Platinum in 1981, while ***I Want to Live*** went Gold in 1977 and Platinum the following year.

In 1979, John hosted the Grammy Awards and his eponymous album was Certified Gold. Then in 1980, he hit Platinum with the album ***A Christmas Together***, in company with the Muppets, and the following year, had a Top 10 Country hit with Billy Joe Shaver's song, *Some Days Are Diamonds (Some Days Are Stone)*. The single also made the Pop Top 40. The album ***Some Days Are Diamonds***, which was produced by Larry Butler, was Certified Gold. In 1982, he had minor hits with *Perhaps Love*, on which he was joined by Placido Domingo, and *Shanghai Breezes*.

The following year, John's 1982 album ***Seasons of the Heart*** was the latest to go Gold. John released the album ***It's About Time*** and unveiled a new look. Gone were the familiar granny glasses and his overall look was of Mr. Cool. He came back into the Country chart with a duet with Emmylou Harris entitled *Wild Montana Skies*. Although he had a minor hit with Sylvie Vartan in 1984, John didn't hit the charts in a big way again until 1985, when *Dreamland Express* became a Top 10 Country record. In 1989, he was back in the Country chart in tandem with the Nitty Gritty Dirt Band on *And So it Goes*, which came from ***Will the Circle Be Unbroken, II***. From 1988, John's recordings can be found on his own label, Windstar. Since 1989, John has been absent from the charts, but is still in demand as a concert performer. JAB

RECOMMENDED ALBUMS:

"Poems, Prayers & Promises" (RCA)(1971)
"Aerie" (RCA Victor)(1971)
"Back Home Again" (RCA Victor)(1974)
"An Evening with John Denver" (double)(RCA Victor)(1975)
"Live in London" (RCA Victor)(1976)
"Some Days Are Diamonds" (RCA Victor)(1981)
"It's About Time" (RCA Victor)(1983)
"Greatest Hits" (RCA Victor)(1984)
"Greatest Hits, Volume 2" (RCA Victor)(1985)
"Greatest Hits, Volume 3" (RCA Victor)(1985)
"One World" (RCA Victor)(1986)
"Higher Ground" (RCA Victor)(1988)

JON DEREK & COUNTRY FEVER

JON DEREK

(Singer, Songwriter, Guitar)

Date of Birth:	**March 10, 1941**
Where Born:	**Harlech, North Wales**
Married:	**Sandra (m. 1969)**
Children:	**John, Mark**

COUNTRY FEVER

Formed: **1968**

Original Members:

Jon Derek	**Lead Singer, Guitar**
Albert Lee	**Lead Guitar**
Pete Oakman	**Bass Guitar**
Jed Kelly	**Drums**
Gerry Hogan	**Steel Guitar**

A very popular British Country music entertainer, both as a solo and as the leader of Country Fever, Jon Derek has had over 30 years experience on the Country music scene.

His early influence was his parents' love of Gene Autry, Jimmie Rodgers and Hank Williams. Jon learned to play guitar in the mid-50's. During the rock'n'roll era, while still at college, Jon joined a group called the Kool Kats. Jon originally had plans to be an architect. However, when Radio Luxembourg ran a talent show and Jon won, he soon forgot those plans and played in various groups.

After Jon met Gerry Hogan (then a guitarist) and the late Gordon Huntley (a famed British steel guitar player), in 1958, they formed a band. They broadcast regularly for the BBC on such programs as *Easy Beat* and *Saturday Club*, hosted by deejay Brian Matthew. Then the band backed up Jim Reeves and in 1964, went professional. They recorded for the U.K. Decca label and toured with Hank Locklin and Carl Perkins.

British Country star ***Jon Derek***

In 1968, Albert Lee, who would go on to fame as one of Country music's greatest guitarists, joined the group and then he and Jon formed Country Fever. The band's original bassist, Pete Oakman, had formerly been a member of Joe Brown's Bruvvers, and Gerry Hogan now switched to steel guitar. Over the years, Country Fever backed up U.S. Country stars such as George Jones, Bobby Bare, Slim Whitman, Marty Robbins and George Hamilton IV.

Jon Derek & Country Fever have appeared on many Wembley Festivals and Jon has also emceed the BCMA talent shows. In addition, the band has appeared at the London Palladium and the Royal Albert Hall. Jon and Country Fever have recorded for Pye, Rediffusion, Decca, Lucky, Westwood, ECM and Artistry. After 25 years, a commemorative album called ***Goin' Back*** was released and contained popular songs from Jon's repertoire, including *I'm Still Your Fool* and *Making Believe*. In the early 90's, Jon decided to perform as a solo and Country Fever has now become Wishbone. Jon is now encouraging his son, Mark, who is following in his father's footsteps as a Country singer. JAB

RECOMMENDED ALBUM:

"Goin' Back" (Artistry UK)(1993)

DESERT ROSE BAND, The

Formed: 1986

Original Members:

Chris Hillman	**Lead Vocals, Guitar, Mandolin**
Herb Pedersen	**Vocals, Acoustic Guitar, 5-String Banjo**
John Jorgenson	**Vocals, 6- & 12-String Electric Guitars**
Bill Bryson	**Bass, Background Vocals**
Steve Duncan	**Drums, Percussion, Background Vocals**
Jay Dee Maness	**Pedal Steel Guitar**

Later Members:

Tom Brumley	**Pedal Steel Guitar**
Jeff Ross	**Guitar**
Tim Grogan	**Drums**

The Desert Rose Band are the inheritors of the mantle of Country-Rock that was created by Chris Hillman among others within the Byrds, the Flying Burrito Brothers and was nurtured by Chris in the Souther, Hillman, Furay Band.

In 1982, Hillman assembled a group of star players that included fiddle player Byron Berline and steel guitarist Al Perkins. Perkins had been a member of the Souther, Hillman, Furay Band. The result was the album ***Morning Sky***. As a result of this, Hillman brought together James Burton, Bernie Leadon (ex-Eagles, Linda Ronstadt and the Nitty Gritty Dirt Band), Herb Pedersen, Jay Dee Maness and Byron Berline. The album resulting from this aggregation was entitled ***Desert Rose***. This laid the groundwork for putting together what was a Country-Rock supergroup, the Desert Rose Band.

Herb Pedersen had sung and played banjo on numerous albums by Linda Ronstadt, James Taylor, Stephen Stills, John Denver, Emmylou Harris and Buck Owens. In addition, he had sung on tracks by Kenny Rogers, Kris Kristofferson & Rita Coolidge, Anne Murray, John Prine, Johnny Rivers and the Earl Scruggs Revue. He had also played banjo on a Diana Ross single. He had been heard playing on TV themes including those for *The Rockford Files, The Dukes of Hazzard, Kojak* and *The A-Team*. In addition, he had arranged the ***Trio*** album (Dolly Parton, Emmylou Harris and Linda Ronstadt).

John Jorgenson had toured with Dan Fogelberg and Rose Maddox. He had performed with Benny Goodman (one of his idols) while his father had conducted. He was at one time the featured bassoonist for the L.A. Camerata. For the previous eight years, his day job was at Disneyland as a member of the Jazz and Bluegrass group in which he played mandolin, saxophone, clarinet and guitar.

Jay Dee Maness had recorded or played with the Byrds, Gram Parsons, Buck Owens, Ronnie Milsap, Glen Campbell, Ray Stevens, Fats Domino, Arlo Guthrie, the Carpenters and Rod Stewart. He had been heard on the movie and TV soundtracks/themes of *Urban Cowboy, The Dukes of Hazzard, Dynasty, Night Court* and *Hee Haw*. He won the ACM "Steel Player of the Year" twelve times between 1970 and 1990.

Steve Duncan had played and recorded with Roger Miller, the Burrito Brothers, Freddy Fender, John Denver, Steve Wariner and Emmylou Harris. In addition, he had co-produced Roger Miller. He had been a nominee for ACM's "Drummer of the Year."

Bill Bryson began playing Bluegrass in 1961, in Southern California. From 1974-76, he was with the Bluegrass Cardinals and from 1976 to 1978, Country Gazette. He has also worked on various movie soundtracks that included *The Long Riders* in 1980.

The Desert Rose Band were signed to MCA/Curb in 1986 and their first release was a remake of the Johnny and Jack hit *Ashes of Love*. It made the Top 30 in 1987 and was followed by their debut eponymous album. Interestingly, the sleeve says "featuring Chris Hillman, John Jorgenson and Herb Pedersen" and only they appear on the front of the cover. Their next three singles *Love Reunited* (Top 10), *One Step Forward* (Top 3) and the chart topping, *He's Back and I'm Blue* (1988) came from this album and were all co-written by Chris Hillman. In 1987 and 1988, Desert Rose Band received Grammy nominations.

In 1988, DRB released ***Running***, their second album, and this time all six members were emblazoned on the front of the sleeve. They were named ACM's "Touring Band of the Year" in 1988, 1989 and 1990. From this

Country-Rock stars the ***Desert Rose Band***

came *Summer Wind*, which went Top 3, and *I Still Believe in You*, which, in 1989, gave them their second No.1 Both were Hillman originals. They then released the John Hiatt song, *She Don't Love Nobody*, which went Top 3. The final single release from the album was the Top 15 *Hello Trouble*, which had been a hit for its co-writer, Orville Couch, back in 1963. DRB were nominated by the CMA as "Best Vocal Group" in 1989 and 1990.

Their next album, ***Pages of Life***, hit the streets in 1989 and once again only Hillman, Pedersen and Jorgenson were on the cover. In 1990, DRB hit the Top 10 with *Start All Over Again* and followed up with *In Another Lifetime* (Top 15) and *Story of Love* (Top 10). This was the Desert Rose Band's last major hit and although they charted five more times, the most successful single was *Will This Be the Day*, in 1991, which came from the 1990 album ***A Dozen Roses/Greatest Hits***.

In 1992, Jay Dee Maness, John Jorgenson and Steve Duncan left. Maness was replaced by supersteelie Tom Brumley, who had played with Buck Owens and Rick Nelson. Jorgenson was replaced by Jeff Ross, who had played with the Bellamy Brothers, Kelly Willis and West Coast cow punk group Rank and File. Duncan was replaced by Tim Grogan, a fine up-and-coming drummer. The new band recorded the albums ***True Love*** (1992) and ***Traditional*** (1993).

In 1993, the Desert Rose Band released their final album, ***Life Goes On***, but by now the steam had gone out of the band and in 1994, the group disbanded.

RECOMMENDED ALBUMS:

"Desert Rose Band" (MCA/Curb)(1987)
"Running" (MCA/Curb)(1988)
"Pages of Love" (MCA/Curb)(1989)
"A Dozen Roses/Greatest Hits" (MCA/Curb)(1990)
"True Love" (MCA/Curb)(1991)
"Traditional" (MCA/Curb)(1993)
"Life Goes On" (Curb)(1993)

AL DEXTER

(Singer, Songwriter, Guitar, Violin, Organ)

Given Name:	**Clarence Albert Poindexter**
Date of Birth:	**May 4, 1902**
Where Born:	**Jacksonville, Cherokee County, Texas**
Married:	**Frankie**
Children:	**Jimmie, Wayne, Helen Louise**
Date of Death:	**January 28, 1984**

There cannot be many people who have not heard of the song *Pistol Packin' Mama*. It was written in 1942 by Al Dexter, who recorded it in 1943. It sold three million singles in 22 months and after only seven months 200,000 copies of the sheet music were sold. Bing Crosby & the Andrews Sisters had a hit with it in September 1943 and the song was ranked as one of the top three hits of WWII. Endless parodies of the song were sung in USO and camp shows. By February 1944, Al was playing in vaudeville theaters at a salary of $3,500 a week.

In the turbulent and violent oil field days, Al Dexter was the owner of a tavern in Texas. The idea for the song came when a gun-toting woman chased her husband's girlfriend (one of Al's waitresses) through a barbed wire fence. Al wondered, "How would you talk to a woman with a gun? and I thought, 'lay that pistol down, babe, lay that pistol down.'"

Al perfected his style in the oil boom towns of East Texas in the 1920's and early 30's. He started with square dances and local parties and went on to play with a mainly black band in the dance halls of Longview, Texas. During this time, Al was writing popular songs for local bands. When the Depression hit in the 30's, he became a house painter. He then formed his own group, the Texas Troopers, who toured and became popular in East Texas. Their first recordings were made in 1934 and Al managed to get them released on a small local label. Soon OKeh and Vocalion were interested in them and some of the recordings were of original compositions by Al.

It is thought that Al was the first artist to use the phrase "Honky Tonk" in 1937 in his song *Honky Tonk Blues*. This was a term used for beer-drinking music, often raucous and rollicking, although sometimes lonely and sad. *Pistol Packin' Mama*, as well as being a Country No.1, was also a Pop chart topper in 1944 and was Certified Gold. During 1944, Al and his Troopers again hit the No.1 spot on the Country chart with *Rosalita* (the top side of *Pistol Packin' Mama* and also a Pop Top 25 hit), *So Long Pal/Too Late to Worry and Too Blue to Cry* (the latter also a Top 20 Pop hit).

In 1945, *I'm Losing My Mind Over You* went to No.1 on the Country chart and stayed there for 7 weeks with the flip-side, *I'll Wait for You Dear*, going Top 3. Al's other single that year was also a major hit with *Triflin' Gal* going Top 3 and the flip-side, *I'm Lost Without You*, reaching the Top 5. Moving from OKeh to Columbia Records in 1946, Al topped the Country chart for 16 weeks with the instrumental *Guitar Polka*, which crossed over to the Pop Top 20. The flip, *Honey Do You Think It's Wrong*, also reached the Top 3. He followed up with *Wine, Women and Song*, which stayed at No.1 for 5 weeks. The flip-side of this, *It's Up to You*, also reached the Top 3.

Al Dexter and his Troopers were still represented on the charts in 1947, when *Kokomono Island* and *Down at the Roadside Inn* both went Top 5. The following year, *Rock and Rye Rag* and *Calico Rag* both made the Top 15.

Al received a Citation of Achievement for *Pistol Packin' Mama* in 1943/1944 and the Western Motion Picture Association Award in 1943. In 1946, he was voted "Leading Artist" by the Jukebox Operators Association, and received an Oscar for *Guitar Polka*. He received 12 Gold Records for million sellers during 1943 through 1948. In the period 1940-1943, Al and the Troopers were heard on radio KFRO Longview, Texas, and during 1940-1952, they appeared at theaters, nightclubs, fairs and rodeos.

Then Al opened his own nightspot, the Bridgeport Club, in Dallas, where he performed, until he retired. He also had business interests in a motel in Lufkin, Texas, and real estate in Dallas and a federal savings and loan operation. In 1971, he was inducted into the Nashville Songwriters Hall of Fame. In a speech made at the ceremony, he recalled trying to find satisfactory recording arrangements in 1935, "and times were not so good. The record company said, they could not pay much royalty on records sold for 16 cents wholesale then, but I said I would take it, as I'm not doing much anyway now." Al Dexter died on January 28, 1984 at age 81. In the words of his first composition, he was "Going Home to Glory."

JAB

RECOMMENDED ALBUMS:

"Pistol Packin' Mama" (Harmony)(1961)
"Al 'Pistol Packin' Mama' Dexter Sings & Plays His Greatest Hits" (Capitol)(1962) [Re-issued on Stetson UK in the original sleeve (1989)]
"Al Dexter, The Original Pistol Packin' Mama" (Pickwick/Hilltop)(1968)
"Songs of the Southwest" (10" album)(Columbia)

DeZURICK SISTERS

CAROLYN DeZURICK
(Singer, Guitar)

Date of Birth:	**1919**
Married:	**Rusty Gill**

MARY JANE DeZURICK
(Singer)

Date of Birth:	**1917**
Married:	**Augie Klein**
Date of Death:	**1981**

EVA DeZURICK
(Singer)

Married:	**Ray Klein**

LORRAINE DeZURICK
(Singer)

All Born:	**Royalton, Minnesota**

The DeZuricks were among the premier yodeling groups on the *National Barn*

Dance. Always a duet act, the original pair consisted of Carolyn (guitar) and Mary Jane. They were noted for their sky-high yodels, triple-tongue yodels, machine-gun yodels and for their ability to make their yodels sound like chickens. This talent earned them the other name by which they were sometimes known, the Cackle Sisters. It also led to their being employed by the Ralston Purina Company for their *Checkerboard Square* program 1937-1941. Carolyn and Mary Jane first appeared on WLS in 1936 and although their career lasted until the early 50's, they made only three 78rpm records. A better idea of their work is contained on numerous radio transcriptions they did for the *Checkerboard Square* shows, many of which are now in the hands of collectors.

In 1941, the sisters married fellow WLS performers, Carolyn marrying Rusty Gill and Mary Jane wedding Augie Klein (with sister Eva later marrying Augie's brother, Ray). That same year, they were on the *Midwestern Hayride* and from 1944 to 1947 they were part of the cast of the *Grand Old Opry*, commuting by train to appear on each Saturday's show. They became the first females to achieve success on both the *Barn Dance* and the *Opry*.

In 1948, Mary Jane retired to bring up her family and was replaced by a younger sister, Lorraine. This new version of the DeZuricks returned to WLS, where they finished out their careers. However, Eva would also appear, if one or another of her sisters could not perform. After the sister act ended Carolyn and husband, Rusty, continued to perform, first in Dayton, Ohio, and then back in Chicago, where for several years they hosted a TV show called *It's Polka Time*.

Lorraine left show business and currently resides in Washington State, Mary Jane died in 1981 and for the past few years, Carolyn has been in ill health and is currently recovering from a stroke. WKM

Hot Country music group ***Diamond Rio***

DIAMOND RIO

Formed: **1984**
Members:

Marty Roe	**Lead Vocals, Guitar**
Jimmy Olander	**Lead Guitar, Banjo**
Gene Johnson	**Mandolin, Vocals**
Dan Truman	**Keyboards**
Dana Williams	**Bass, Vocals**
Brian Prout	**Drums**

Diamond Rio seemed to be a band that came from nowhere and went straight to the top, but in fact all members of the group had paid their dues.

Marty Roe, named for Marty Robbins, started his professional career when he was age 12 and toured with a band named Windsong. He joined the Tennessee River Boys, which evolved into Diamond Rio. Jimmy Olander had played with the Nitty Gritty Dirt Band, Rodney Crowell, Foster and Lloyd and Duane Eddy. Gene Johnson had played with David Bromberg and J.D. Crowe. He also plays fiddle and guitar and is an excellent harmony singer. Dan Truman is a classically trained pianist. He toured with the Brigham Young University's Young Ambassadors and appeared in the Soviet Union and Poland. Dana Williams is the nephew of Bluegrass legends the Osborne Brothers. He had played with Vassar Clements, Cal Smith and Jimmy C. Newman and is also an excellent harmony singer. Brian Prout had played in Country and Rock bands, including Hot Walker Band and Heartbreak Mountain. He joined Diamond Rio in 1986. His wife, Nancy, was the drummer with the all-female band Wild Rose.

As the Tennessee River Boys, they played Nashville's Opryland USA and also gigged around the country for some seven years. It was fishing that led to their signing with Arista. Marty had attended David Lipscomb College with Monty Powell (their producer). Powell had written Restless Heart's hit, *Dancy's Dream*, with Tim DuBois, who was the head of Arista in Nashville. Marty, Monty and Tim went fishing together and a deal with Arista followed. The band was renamed Diamond Rio, from a misspelled Diamond Reo truck. There had been a Rock group named "Diamond Reo" that recorded for Big Tree in 1975.

Their debut eponymous album was released in 1991. The initial single, *Meet in the Middle*, went to No.1 and put them in the record books as the first Country group to have a debut single reach the top of the charts in all the trade papers. The follow-up, *Mirror Mirror*, was a Top 3 hit. Their next single, *Mama Don't Forget to Pray for Me*, also made it into the Top 10.

In March, 1992, the album went Gold and the award nominations came flooding in. On the strength of one album, they received 1991 nominations for Grammys for "Best Country Performance by a Duo or Group with Vocal" for *Meet in the Middle* and "Best Country Instrumental Performance" for *Poultry Promenade*. They were named the ACM's "Vocal Group of the Year."

In 1992, Diamond Rio released their second album, ***Close to the Edge***. That year, both their singles made the Top 10. *Norma Jean Riley* reached the Top 3 and *Nowhere Bound* got to the Top 10. They were named the CMA's "Vocal Group of the Year" and the ACM's "Top Vocal Group."

In 1993, *In a Week or Two* reached the Top 3, *Oh Me, Oh My, Sweet Baby* went Top 5, *This Romeo Ain't Got Julie Yet* went Top 15 and *Sawmill Road* reached the Top 25. Diamond Rio retained their crown as CMA's "Vocal Group of the Year." In addition, *In a Week or Two* was Grammy nominated.

In the early 90's, it was the policy to try and cross acts over from Country into Pop. Diamond Rio made no such attempt. They play Country that is contemporary but yet retains traditional Country roots. In 1994, Diamond Rio was named the CMA's "Vocal Group of the Year."

RECOMMENDED ALBUMS:
"Diamond Rio" (Arista)(1991)
"Close to the Edge" (Arista)(1992)

HAZEL DICKENS

(Singer, Songwriter, Guitar, Bass)
Given Name: **Hazel Jane Dickens**
Date of Birth: **June 1, 1935**
Where Born: **Mercer County, West Virginia**
Married: **Joe Cohen (div.)**

A singer/songwriter whose work is rooted in traditional Folk, with elements of Bluegrass and Country, Hazel Dickens made a promise to herself early on in her career to chronicle her coal mining, working class people and their way of life through the vehicle of music. "There is no difference between my life and music," she has said, and her songs reflect her deeply felt beliefs about the plight of society's underclasses. In addition, her untamed, untrained, strong and high lonesome mountain voice adds the dimensions of authenticity and true emotion to the ideas and feelings expressed in her music.

Born the eighth of eleven children in Mercer County, West Virginia, where mining was "a family way of life and death," Hazel recalls a childhood in a mountain shack with never enough to eat, never enough fuel to keep all the stoves heated at once, never enough pencils and paper for schoolwork. A radio was one of the family's few possessions, and Hazel's father, a banjo picker and Baptist minister who hauled timber for the coal mines, would only allow them to listen to the "good" Country music performed by such traditionalists as Uncle Dave Macon, Bill and Charlie Monroe, Martha Carson, the Carter Family and Wilma Lee and Stoney Cooper.

Hazel left home at the age of 19, following her older sister to Baltimore, Maryland, where she worked at a succession of jobs in factories, and also as a waitress and sales clerk. When two of her brothers, Robert and Arnold, moved to Baltimore, they began to attend "pickin' parties" together, where Old-Time and Bluegrass music were played and where Hazel first began to sing publicly. In the early 50's, through her brother Robert, who was hospitalized with tuberculosis at the Mt. Wilson Sanatorium, she met Mike Seeger (younger brother of Folk singer/songwriter Pete), then a conscientious objector serving as a hospital attendant at the sanatorium and later a member of New Lost City Ramblers and leading light in Folk music. The two began playing music casually together, then formed a band which also included Robert and Arnold, and started performing in bars and small clubs.

There followed what Hazel calls a freelance period of playing bass and singing tenor, with Bobby Baker and the Pike County Boys and Jack Cooke's band, as part of the explosion of Bluegrass that was taking place around Baltimore and Washington, D.C. Hazel also toured as bassist with the Greenbriar Boys, one of the first urban Bluegrass revivalist bands, backing Joan Baez, in the 60's.

Then, after a brief hiatus from performing, Hazel met Alice Gerrard, a classically trained singer with a passion for Bluegrass and mountain music and the two began singing and writing together. To develop a repertoire, they attended Folk festivals to tape performances of Old-Time musicians and studied sheet music in the Library of Congress, unearthing feminist treasures from the 1930's and 40's like the Coon Creek Girls' *Banjo Pickin' Gal,* Wilma Lee's *Tomorrow I'll Be Gone,* and Bill Monroe's *True Life Blues* (written in 1945 and one of the first women's Bluegrass songs).

In the early 60's, Hazel and Alice participated in an organized tour of Folk festivals in the south, traveling by bus, visiting rural communities, and writing songs about what they had observed and experienced. They became cult figures of a sort and spokespersons for the feminist movement, although their songs related more to the trials and lives of traditional women than to the new feminist ideals of the 60's. They recorded four albums together, two for Folkways (***Who's that Knocking (& Other Bluegrass Country Music)*** in 1965 and ***Won't You Come and Sing for Me*** in 1973) and two for Rounder (***Hazel & Alice*** in 1973 and ***Hazel Dickens and Alice Gerrard*** in 1976). Their albums were significant in that they were two women singing lead (Alice) and tenor (Hazel) in a Bluegrass duet fashion reserved normally for men, and also for their revivalist selection of traditional music. The records also included a sampling of each singer's original compositions.

By the time of the completion of the second Rounder album, the partnership had been dissolved, and Hazel's solo recognition had begun with the release of Barbara Koppel's Academy Award-winning documentary on coal mining, *Harlan County, USA*, which featured four of Hazel's original songs on its soundtrack, including *They'll Never Keep Us Down* (used later by the United Mine Workers as the title song for a video on organizing), *Don't Put Her Down, You Helped Put Her There,* and *Black Lung* (written for her brother Robert, who had since succumbed to the disease). Hazel, concerned with continuing the traditions of people like Sarah Ogan Gunning and Aunt Molly Jackson, who left behind rich and powerful collections of songs about union organizing in the Appalachian coal mines, was beginning to be accepted as a writer of meaningful protest songs in her own right.

In 1981, Hazel's first solo album, ***Hard Hitting Songs for Hard Hit People***, was released by Rounder Records. It had a bare, back hills sound and, in Hazel's fashion, covered styles ranging from Old-Time traditional Carter Family tunes to modern Country music to songs of protest and pride. Two other Rounder albums followed: ***By the Sweat of My Brow*** (1983) and ***It's Hard To Tell the Singer from the Song*** (1987). Albums featuring one or more of Dickens' songs included: ***The Strange Creek Singers*** (Arhoolie, 1972), a group that included Mike & Alice Seeger, Tracy Schwartz, Lamar Greer and Hazel, as well as compilations ***Come All You Coal Miners*** (Rounder, 1973), ***They'll Never Keep Us Down*** (Rounder, 1984), and ***Don't Mourn, Organize: Songs of Labor Songwriter Joe Hill*** (Smithsonian/Folkways, 1990).

Hazel achieved further recognition from another coal mining film, *Matewan* (1987), by filmmaker John Sayles, in which she appears on camera to sing a cappella during a miner's hillside burial. Three of her original songs were featured in the soundtrack. Hazel's songs also appeared on the soundtracks of the films *With Babies and Banners* (1976) and *Coal Mining Women* (1984).

Hazel Dickens has performed at all the major U.S. Folk festivals, including Newport, Philadelphia, and the Smithsonian Festival of American Folklife, as well as touring throughout Europe, Japan, Canada and Australia. She has appeared at Lincoln Center and Madison Square Garden in New York, the Kennedy Center and White House in Washington, D.C., and at museums, universities, peace rallies, human rights demonstrations and benefits for coal miners and other union workers around the country and the world. Her songs, like *Old Calloused Hands* (written about a sister who died of cancer after a hard life), *Working Girl Blues,* and the union anthem *They'll Never Keep Us Down,* mean something. They speak of dignity and life and of the timeless struggle of all peoples for their freedom. In 1994, Hazel became the first female recipient of the IBMA's "Merit Award" for her contribution to Bluegrass. DV

RECOMMENDED ALBUMS:
"Hard Hitting Songs for Hard Hit People" (Rounder)(1981)
"By the Sweat of My Brow" (Rounder)(1983)
"It's Hard to Tell the Singer from the Song" (Rounder)(1987)
"A Few Old Memories" (Rounder)(1987) [Compilation cd from Hazel's previous Rounder albums]
With Alice Gerrard:
"Who's that Knocking (& Other Bluegrass Music)"

(Folkways)(1965)
"Won't You Come and Sing for Me" (Folkways)(1973)
"Hazel & Alice" (Rounder)(1973)
"Hazel Dickens and Alice Gerrard" (Rounder)(1976)

LITTLE JIMMY DICKENS

(Singer, Songwriter, Guitar)
Given Name: James Cecil Dickens
Date of Birth: December 19, 1920
Where Born: Bolt, Raleigh County, West Virginia
Married: 1. Connie (div.) 2. Ernestine (dec'd.) 3. Mona
Children: Pamela Jean (adopted), Lisa (Mona's daughter)

Known for his strong voice and small physical stature, Little Jimmy Dickens skyrocketed to national fame in 1949 and 1950 with a string of novelty and "heart" songs on Columbia Records that made him a major figure on the Country scene.

Jimmy was raised in a musical environment and as he recalled, there were always instruments around the house. From early on, he dreamed of being a professional performer and appearing on the *Grand Ole Opry*. He built up a decade of solid experience in radio behind him, beginning with the opening of his hometown station WJLS in Beckley, West Virginia, in April, 1939. Many of the early entertainers at Beckley went on to make a name for themselves and included Molly O'Day, Johnnie and Walter Bailes, Bob Byrd, the Lilly Brothers, but none so much as the diminutive Dickens, who worked as Jimmy the Kid and who often put the station on the air each morning by crowing like a rooster.

The redoubtable ***Little Jimmy Dickens***

When Jimmy moved northward to attend West Virginia University, he went to work at WMNN Fairmont, where he met T. Texas Tyler. The two proceeded on to WIBC Indianapolis. When Tyler entered military service, Dickens remained in Indiana for another year where he picked up *Take an Old Cold 'Tater (And Wait)*, a 1921 composition by Gospel writer E.M. Bartlet. Jimmy then went to the powerful WLW Cincinnati for a year, working on their *Boone County Jamboree* and *Midwestern Hayride*. During that time, he grew from 4'6" at the age of 21 to his full height of 4'11". In 1946, Jimmy switched to WIBW Topeka, Kansas, and then moved to WKNX Saginaw, Michigan, where Jimmy met Roy Acuff, who helped him secure a contract with Columbia Records and a position with WSM's *Grand Ole Opry*.

Jimmy did his first Columbia session in January 1949 and became an Opry member some months later. *Take an Old Cold 'Tater (And Wait)* reached the Top 10 (credited as Jimmie Dickens) some months afterward. This was followed by Boudleaux and Felice Bryant's *Country Boy*, which also went Top 10, *Pennies for Papa* (Top 15) and *My Heart's Bouquet* (Top 10).

In 1950, Jimmy scored with *A-Sleepin' at the Foot of the Bed* (Top 10) and *Hillbilly Fever* (Top 3). Jimmy was out of the chart between 1951 up to the middle of 1954. He then returned with the Top 10 hit *Out Behind the Barn*. Other novelty singles which did well included *I'm Little But I'm Loud*, *Bessie the Heifer*, *Cold Feet* and *It May Be Silly (But Ain't It Fun)*. His heart songs included *My Heart's Bouquet*, *We Could* and *I've Just Got to See You Once More*.

His use of twin electric guitars helped give him one of the more exciting band sounds in those years too. His Country Boys were one of the most highly rated backing bands in Country music. Jimmy left the *Opry* in the mid-50's to tour with the Philip Morris Caravan, but came back in the 70's and has remained there ever since. He recorded a few Rockabilly-flavored numbers in the late 50's like *Blackeyed Joe's* and *I've Got a Hole in My Pocket*, but it took a heart ballad, *The Violet and the Rose*, to propel him back into the Top 10 in 1962, after a hiatus of eight years. During 1963-1965, Jimmy's only chart records were *Another Bridge to Burn* (Top 30, 1963) and *He Stands Real Tall* (Top 25, 1965).

In 1965, Jimmy scored bigger than ever before with *May the Bird of Paradise Fly Up Your Nose*, another novelty lyric that hit the top of the Country chart and made the Top 15 on the Pop chart. A string of other humorous songs followed, such as *When the Ship Hit the Sand* (Top 30), *Who Licked the Red Off Your Candy* (Top 50) (both 1966) and *Country Music Lover* (Top 25, 1967).

Switching to Decca in 1967, Jimmy had three more minor hits of which the most successful was *When You're Seventeen* (Top 60) and three albums in as many years. In 1969, tragedy struck, as Jimmy's wife, Ernestine, was killed in an auto wreck. Jimmy switched to United Artists Records and his last singles (*Everyday Family Man* and *Try It, You'll Like It*) to hit the charts were on that label in 1971 and 1972, but were only low-level successes. Since then he did one album each with Gusto and Tater Patch as well as singles on the Little Gem label.

The comments of Marty Robbins, on his election to the Country Hall of Fame in 1982, about how folks like Little Jimmy Dickens were more deserving, probably helped create a groundswell of support for the pint-sized West Virginian who received the same honor the following year. Re-issued albums in the mid-80's brought recordings from his prime years onto the market again including one that gave just attention to his heart songs. He has continued to be active both at the *Opry* and on road shows. In May 1989, he attended a benefit in Minnesota for Boys' Camps along with Ralph Emery. Jimmy's manager of many years, Richard Davis, was piloting Jimmy back to Kansas City in Davis' plane, when the nose gear failed on landing. They both walked away unscathed, even though the plane was totaled.

Through some fifty-five years of professionalism and versatility, Little Jimmy Dickens in many respects exemplifies what Country music is all about. IMT

RECOMMENDED ALBUMS:
"Little Jimmy Dickens Best" (Harmony)(1964)
"Alone with God" (Harmony)(1965)
"Greatest Hits" (Columbia)(1966)
"Greatest Hits" (Decca)(1969)
"Columbia Historic Edition" (Columbia)(1984)
"Straight from the Heart, 1949-1955" (Rounder)(1985)

JOE DIFFIE

(Singer, Songwriter, Guitar, Bass Guitar, Drums)
Given Name: Joe Logan Diffie
Date of Birth: December 28, 1958
Where Born: Tulsa, Oklahoma
Married: 1. (Div.) 2. Debbie
Children: (Joe) Parker, Kara Elizabeth, (Justin) Tyler, (Joshua) Drew

In the 90's there was a great influx of new talent into Country music. Some should have been in Pop music, some shouldn't have bothered and some, like Joe Diffie, brought a love of the tradition and have enhanced the music. In Joe's case, not only by his music but by his obvious sense of fun.

Joe was born into a family that favored Country music. His father, Joe, played guitar and his mother, Floss, sang. Young Joe was a member of his high school Gospel group, Genesis II, and also played in a Rock group, Blitz. While living in Duncan, Oklahoma, he joined Higher Purpose, a Gospel group, and Special Edition, a local Bluegrass band.

He attended college and then worked in the Texas oil fields and later returned to Duncan to work in the foundry. Special Edition started to get a following and appeared at various festivals, including the Bill Grant Bluegrass Festival in Hugo, Oklahoma. Joe started playing Country gigs with his aunt, Dawn Anita, and his sister, Monica, and Joe had one of his early songs, *Love on the Rocks*, recorded by Hank Thompson.

Joe wanted to get to Nashville and he was able to do that, thanks to the financial assistance of his friend Cecil Petty. Joe began working for Gibson Guitars and his songwriting perseverance paid off. In 1989, Holly Dunn recorded a song Joe had written with Lonnie Wilson and Wayne Perry, *There Goes My Heart Again*, on which he sang back-up vocals. Then the Forester Sisters cut *Come Hold Me*, which was the title track of their 1989 album.

Bob Montgomery heard some of Joe's singing on demos and wanted to sign him to Epic, however, Montgomery's roster was full and he asked Joe to wait. A year later, Bob was as good as his word, as was Joe, who had been approached by every label in town.

The first single was *Home* in 1990 and it went to No.1, thus making Joe the first artist with a debut single at No.1. That year, he made his *Grand Ole Opry* debut. He followed this with the co-written *If You Want Me To* (Top 3), *If the Devil Danced (In Empty Pockets)* (No.1) and the Top 3, *New Way (To Light an Old Flame)*, which Joe also co-wrote. In addition, Joe released his debut album, ***A Thousand Winding Roads***, produced by Montgomery and Johnny Slate. He also received his first BMI Award for *There Goes My Heart Again*.

In 1991, Joe was the recipient of the *Billboard* Award for "Top Singles Artist" and also *Cash Box*'s "Male Artist of the Year" Award. The following year, his success rate continued unabated. *Is It Cold In Here,* another wonderful Country song co-written by Joe, went Top 5 and was the first single from his new album, ***Regular Joe***. This was followed to the Top 5 in 1992, by Paul Nelson-Dave Gibson's *Ships that Don't Come In*. Joe continued the year with *Next Thing Smokin'* (Top 20) and the Grammy nominated duet with Mary-Chapin Carpenter, *Not Too Much to Ask*, which came from her album ***Come On, Come On***. Although Joe's nod to Hank Williams and Merle Haggard, *Startin' Over Blues*, only reached the Top 50 in 1993, the release of his third album, ***Honky Tonk Attitude***, heralded a return to the upper levels of the chart and before the end of 1993, it had been Certified Gold. The title track reached the Top 5 and Joe and his band, Heartbreak Highway, were shown to fine effect in the performance video of the song. Joe followed this with the Top 3 single, *Prop Me Up Beside the Jukebox (If I Die)*, which also crossed over to the lower levels of the Pop chart. In 1994, Joe reached the Top 5 with *John Deere Green*, which also gave him his biggest cross-over success, when it reached the Pop Top 70. This was followed by *In My Own Backyard*, which reached the Top 25.

Joe has another side to him. He enjoys art, antiques, reading and sports. He is also very good at woodwork and makes furniture. As they say, he's a "'regular Joe."

RECOMMENDED ALBUMS:

"A Thousand Winding Roads" (Epic)(1991)
"Regular Joe" (Epic)(1992)
"Honky Tonk Attitude" (Epic)(1993)

DANNY DILL

(Singer, Songwriter, Guitar)

Given Name:	**Horace Eldred Dill**
Date of Birth:	**September 19, 1924**
Where Born:	**Carroll County, West Tennessee**
Married:	**1. Annie Lou (div.) 2. Carolyn Penick ("Doozie")**
Children:	**Ava Tyanne (Bissell)**

Danny rode into immortality on the strength of two classic songs co-written by him, *The Long Black Veil* (written with Marijohn Wilkin) and *Detroit City* (written with Mel Tillis). However, there was a lot more to Danny Dill than being a songwriter. In fact he describes himself as a "performer who wrote some songs."

Danny began singing in a church choir and started playing guitar and singing in public, while in his junior year at high school. The applause convinced him to make music his career. He hitchhiked, in 1943, to Jackson, Tennessee, and launched his career at WTJS with Zeke Martin's band (unpaid) and played schoolhouses. He appeared as a "Toby," which was a comedian with a red wig and blacked-out teeth. He appeared on radio stations in Arkansas and by 1944, Memphis and then back to Jackson and to WNOX Knoxville on the *Mid-Day Merry-Go-Round*, with Johnny Wright and Kitty Wells, Bill and Cliff Carlisle and Chet Atkins, where he played with two musicians from Jackson, playing Western music (which didn't go down too well). He moved back to Jackson, where he met his future wife, Annie Lou. Then, he moved to Arkansas and broadcast on WILO and then WREC Memphis, before returning to Jackson, where he married Annie Lou.

On December 21, 1945, he and Annie Lou got a spot on the WSM morning show (after auditioning for Jack Stapp, Grant Turner, George Hay, Harry Stone and Roy Acuff). The started on the first Monday of 1946, and then three months later, their time slot changed and they began an 11-year stint, being billed as "Annie Lou and Danny: The Sweethearts of the Grand Ole Opry," basing themselves on Lulu Belle and Scotty. Danny considered that their act was built on mistakes, which they kept in. They specialized in humorous material. They also recorded some material for Bullet Records, in 1949, and released two singles, *Dime a Dozen/My Loss Is Another Man's Gain* and *I'm in Love Up to My Ears/There's a Rainbow in Your Tears*, but were not primarily a recording act. In 1951, they cut some material, singing with Chet Atkins, who at the time could not sell records.

They began to play package shows with Eddy Arnold, Hank Williams and the Duke of Paducah. As well as performing with Annie Lou, Danny also emceed most of these shows, and by 1952, through the help and guidance of the Duke of Paducah, Danny had built up a reputation as the best emcee in the business. Danny also played rhythm guitar, at this time, on occasions for Ernest Tubb. Because Audrey Williams was the only other woman on the show, Danny and Annie Lou traveled a lot with Hank and Audrey.

By 1952, following the birth of their daughter, the couple's relationship started to fall apart and they divorced. Danny decided to try songwriting as a profession. Jim Denny, who was the Director of the *Opry*, had just formed Cedarwood Music, and Danny was signed as a writer (he was the first hired employee). He spent the next year writing songs, screening songs and plugging songs. The first major cut he had was *If You Saw Her Through My Eyes* by Carl Smith. Then Ray Price recorded the Dill-Don Davis song *Let Me Talk to You*. That same year, Danny spotted songwriter Wayne Walker, and brought him to the company.

During 1953, Danny returned to road work as a Texas Troubadour, emceeing Ernest Tubb's shows. That same year, Danny wrote *Partners*, which would become a Top 5 hit for Jim Reeves, six years later (after Annie Lou had taken the song to Chet Atkins, at RCA, Jim's label). It won a BMI Award for Danny. At the end of the year, Danny appeared as a solo, in concert, co-promoted with his friend, Shelly Snyder, under the banner of "An Evening with Danny Dill."

Danny moved to Swainesboro, Georgia, in 1954, to work as a radio announcer on WJAT. Here, he became known for his ad-lib method of reading commercials. The following year, Danny returned to Nashville, and after a short stint announcing on WENO, he returned to songwriting. In 1959, he put together the lyrics (and a melody) for *The Long Black Veil*, which Annie Lou persuaded him to take to the office. There, Marijohn Wilkin put a new melody to it and by the afternoon of the same day, Lefty Frizzell had recorded it and went on to have a Top 10 hit with it. (Marijohn played the song on a piano, to Lefty and Don Law, and it was instantly agreed to cut it.) This would later be recorded by over fifty other artists including Sammi Smith and John Anderson.

During 1960, Danny wrote another major song, *Detroit City*, with Mel Tillis. This became a Top 10 song for Bobby Bare in 1963, and for Tom Jones, in 1967. It went on to win three BMI Awards. The original version was by Billy Grammer, who came up with the "detuning" sound of the guitar riff. In 1961, he wrote *The Comeback*, which the following year, reached the Top 5 for Faron Young, and won a further BMI Award.

In 1960, he cut an album, ***Folk Songs of the Wild West***, for MGM and, in 1963, ***Folk Songs from the Country***, with songs mainly written by Danny. Shortly after recording the latter album, Danny moved to California, where he worked as a studio musician and songwriter. While there, Walter Brennan recorded Danny's narrative song *The Old Courthouse* (which Faron Young charted the following year, and which Danny still performs on stage).

During 1964, Danny went back on the road as a goodwill ambassador for the George Dickel Company for six months, singing about the story of "Stubborn George" Dickel. Then Danny quit and "went into semi-retirement, with a beer in each hand" and "sat in Country Corner, with a bunch of other drunks, telling each other how great a songwriter they were." He remained in that state until 5:30 p.m., July 18, 1974, when he had a serious automobile accident. After 22 days in intensive care, and eight more days in the hospital, Danny emerged, a non-drinker with a renewed perspective on life.

Danny was recognized by his peers, in 1975, when he was inducted into the Nashville Songwriters Hall of Fame. The following year, he was signed by his old friend, Marijohn Wilkin, to her Buckhorn Music. He went on to appear on the *Nashville Jubilee* and at the 1977 Fan Fare. He also appeared with Annie Lou, on the *Grand Ole Opry Reunion Show*.

In 1993, Danny made a momentous return to the performing arena, when he appeared on stage at the Vanderbilt Plaza Hotel in Nashville, as a "superwriter" on the NSAI Superwriters Concert, alongside Hugh Prestwood, Jill Colucci and Gary Burr, and stole the show. To most of the audience, he was unknown when he was introduced, but by the end of the evening, he had two standing ovations, and was acknowledged as one of the funniest men around.

RECOMMENDED ALBUMS:
"Folk Songs of the Wild West" (MGM)(1960)
"Folk Songs from the Country" (Liberty)(1963)

DOUG DILLARD

(Singer, Songwriter, Banjo, Guitar, Actor)
Given Name: **Douglas Flint Dillard**
Date of Birth: **March 6, 1937**
Where Born: **East St. Louis, Illinois**

Doug Dillard's importance lies in his work with the Dillards as well as the bridge that his music forms between Bluegrass, Country-Rock and Pop music and the fact that his recordings continue to break new ground musically.

Doug came from a musical family in Salem, Missouri, and early on he was playing with his father, Homer, Sr., and brothers Rodney and Homer, Jr. In 1953, Doug played banjo for the Hal Teaque Band and played on radio. Doug also attended college to study bookkeeping. During the late 50's, Doug and Rodney played with various bands. During 1956-1959, they were with the Ozark Mountain Boys and appeared on the *Ozark Jubilee*. In 1957, Doug played with the Hawthorn Brothers and then during that year and 1958, he appeared on TV with Lee Mace and the Ozark Opry.

In 1958, Doug and Rodney cut two singles for K-Ark and the following year, they recorded a Gospel EP. In 1958, they joined Joe Noel & the Dixie Ramblers and in 1960, they cut a single, *Banjo in the Hollow*, for Marlo Records. Doug and Rodney got together in 1958 and 1959 with the Hawthorn Brothers and the Lewis Brothers in a Bluegrass package.

Doug was with the Dillards from the group's start in 1962 and left in 1967. In 1963, Doug, Rodney, Dean Webb, Glen Campbell and Tut Taylor released two instrumental albums, ***12 String Guitar*** and ***12 String Guitar, Vol. 2***, on World Pacific under the name of the Folkswingers. During 1966, Doug played on the album ***Gene Clark & the Gosdin Brothers***. The following year, he played banjo on the soundtrack of the movie *Bonnie and Clyde*, with him playing all banjo tracks except *Foggy Mountain Breakdown*. In 1968, he recorded ***The Banjo Album*** for Together Records, on which John Hartford, Gene Clark and Bernie Leadon supported. In May of that year, Doug toured England as a part of the Byrds.

During the summer of 1968, Doug got together with Gene Clark (ex-Byrds) as Dillard & Clark and signed to A&M Records, releasing the album ***Fantastic Expedition***. The line-up of the group was Bernie Leadon (guitar), David Jackson (bass) and Don Beck (Dobro, mandolin). After recording the album, another former Byrds member, drummer Michael Clarke, was added for their first tour. By 1969, the line-up had changed drastically. Byron Berline had joined on fiddle, as had Donna Washburn on guitar and Jon Corneal on drums. A second album, ***Through the Morning, Through the Night***, was released that year and featured Chris Hillman and Sneaky Pete Kleinow.

By the end of 1969, Bernie Leadon had left and in 1970, Gene Clark left to go solo. Doug continued the group as Dillard and the Expedition. The line-up was Byron Berline (fiddle) and two ex-Kentucky Colonels members, Billy Ray Lathum (guitar) and Roger Bush. When Doug left the group, the remaining members formed the basis for Country Gazette.

In 1971, Doug formed Dillard & the Country Coalition with John Kurtz (drums), David Jackson (bass), Peggy Bradley (fiddle) and Dick Bradley (guitar). That year, Doug went solo and worked on the soundtrack of the movie *Vanishing Point,* which starred Barry Newman. In 1973, Doug signed with 20th Century Records, He released two albums for that label, ***Dueling Banjos*** (1973) and ***Douglas Flint Dillard—You Don't Need a Reason to Sing*** (1974). Doug then did a lot of session work playing on records by the Beach Boys, the Monkees, Glen Campbell and Harry Nilsson. Nilsson produced a single on Doug, *Goin' Down/Poor Old Slave*, but it was only released in the U.K. Doug also wrote and performed the theme song for Dean Martin's *Music Country* series.

In 1977, Doug with Rodney and John Hartford released the album ***Glitter-Grass from the Nashwood Hollyville Strings*** for Flying Fish. The following year, Doug recorded the album ***Heaven***, with Rodney producing. On this album are Byron Berline, the Dillards (Rodney Dillard, Jeff Gilkinson, Paul York and Doug Bounsall) and Dan Crary. This led to Doug forming the Doug Dillard Band featuring Byron Berline, which included Billy Constable (guitar), Ray Park (fiddle), Skip Conover (Dobro) and Bill Bryson (bass). That year, the group recorded the album ***Jackrabbit!***, which was also produced by Rodney and recorded at the 6th Annual Telluride Bluegrass and Country Music Festival in Colorado (June 22-24). Guesting on the album, which was released in 1980, is mandolinist Sam Bush. Also in 1979, Doug, Rodney and Byron appeared as members of Bette Midler's band in the much praised movie *The Rose*. August 8 that year was named "Dillard Day" in Salem, Missouri, and a reunion was held which was recorded at the Sinks and at the Dillard family house. In 1980, an album was released on Flying Fish, entitled ***Homecoming & Family Reunion*** and the event was later shown on NBC-TV's *Real People* program.

At the beginning of 1980, Doug went to Malta to work on the soundtrack of Robert Altman's movie *Popeye*, which starred Robin Williams and had songs by Nilsson. On his return, Doug re-formed the Doug Dillard Band with Ray Park, Billy Constable and bassist Larry Park. Doug also joined up with Rodney and John Hartford for the album ***Permanent Wave***. By 1985, the line-up of the group was Ginger Boatwright (guitar, vocals), Jon Yudkin (fiddle, vocals) and Kathy Chiavola (bass guitar and vocals).

In 1986, Doug released his next album for Flying Fish, ***What's That?*** The group still included Ginger, but also included Roger Rasnake (bass guitar, vocals) and David Grier (lead acoustic guitar). The line-up was still in place in 1993, when the album ***Heartbreak Hotel*** was released. The album, a collection of recorded tracks from 1986, 1988 and 1993, also included Jonathan Yudkin on fiddle and mandolin and is an excellent mix of original and cover material.

RECOMMENDED ALBUMS:

"The Banjo Album" (Together)(1969)
"Heaven" (Flying Fish)(1979)
"Jackrabbit!" (Flying Fish)(1980)
"What's That" (Flying Fish)(1986)
"Heartbreak Hotel" (Flying Fish)(1993)
Dillard & Clark:
"Fantastic Expedition" (A&M)(1968)
"Through the Morning, Through the Night" (A&M)(1969)
Dillard Hartford Dillard:
"Glitter-Grass from the Nashwood Hollyville Strings" (Flying Fish)(1977)
"Permanent Wave" (Flying Fish)(1980)

DILLARDS, The

Formed:	**1962**
Original Members:	
Doug Dillard	**Banjo, Guitar, Vocals**
Rodney Dillard	**Guitar, Dobro, Vocals**
Mitch Jayne	**Bass, Vocals**
Dean Webb	**Mandolin, Vocals**
Later Members:	
Byron Berline	**Fiddle**
Herb Pedersen	**Banjo, Vocals**
Paul York	**Drums**
Billy Ray Lathum	**Guitar**
Irv Dugan	**Bass**
Jeff Gilkinson	**Bass, Banjo, Cello, Bass Harmonica, Vocals**
Doug Bounsall	**Guitar, Mandolin, Fiddle, Vocals**
Ray Parks	**Fiddle**
Eddie Ponder	**Drums**
Joe Villegas	**Bass**
Peter Grant	**Steel, Banjo**

Doug Dillard** Band featuring **Ginger Boatwright

Doug (b. Douglas Flint Dillard, March 6, 1937) and Rodney Dillard (b. Rodney Adean Dillard, May 18, 1942) both born in East St. Louis, Illinois, came from a musical family in Salem, Missouri. They began playing and singing while still in elementary school. From the beginning, their music was always Bluegrass-orientated. Their early living-room picking included the participation of their father, Homer, Sr., and their brother Homer, Jr. Between 1956 and 1959, Doug and Rodney played in the Ozark Mountain Boys and appeared on the *Ozark Jubilee*. In 1958, Doug and Rodney recorded two singles for K-Ark Records, *Doug's Breakdown/My Own True Love* and *Mama Don't 'Low/Highway of Sorrow*. The following year, they recorded a Gospel EP for the label. During 1958 and 1959, the brothers got together with the Hawthorn Brothers and the Lewis Brothers as a Bluegrass package.

They also played with Joe Noel & the Dixie Ramblers between 1958 and 1960. In 1960, they got financial support to cut the single *Banjo in the Hollow/You're on My Mind*, for the Marlo label. John Hartford, who was a member of the group, missed the session, because he was in the Army.

Mitch Jayne (b. Mitchell Jayne, July 5, 1930, Hammond, Indiana), who was then a deejay on KSMO Salem, hosting *Hickory Hollow*, played the single and then joined the brothers at local bookings. They were soon joined by Dean Webb (b. Roy Dean Webb, March 28, 1937, Independence, Missouri), who had played with the Ozark Opry Road Show.

In 1962, the foursome of Dillard, Dillard, Jayne and Webb decided to try their luck in

Los Angeles, but broke down on the way. They arrived in Oklahoma City and worked a week at the Buddae Club where they were to receive $300. They did so well that they got a $100 bonus. They arrived in L.A. and went to the Ashgrove where they jammed with the Greenbriar Boys. They were spotted by Jim Dickson (later associated with the Byrds) and by the end of the first week, the Dillards got a deal with Elektra Records. They then were signed to appear on the *Andy Griffith Show* on TV. For three years, they played and acted on the show, portraying the somewhat mentally deficient "Darling Family."

In 1963, they released their debut album, ***Back Porch Bluegrass***. That year, Doug, Rodney, Dean, Glen Campbell and Tut Taylor released two instrumental albums, ***12 String Guitar*** and ***12 String Guitar, Vol. 2***, on World Pacific under the name of the Folkswingers. That year, the Dillards were featured guests on Judy Garland's TV special. In 1964, the group released their second album, ***Live...Almost!*** which was recorded at the Mecca in Buena Park, California. The following year, they recorded a pair of singles for Capitol, *Last Thing on My Mind/Lemon Chimes* and *Nobody Knows/Ebo Walker,* and then came ***Pickin' & Fiddlin'*** on which Byron Berline guested.

The Bluegrass establishment was getting increasingly upset at the Dillards for amplifying their instruments. In 1967, Doug and Rodney were heard on the soundtrack of the movie *Bonnie and Clyde*. The band didn't release another album until 1968, but before it was recorded Doug had left to play some dates with the Byrds in London. The new album, ***Wheatstraw Suite,*** had Herb Pedersen taking over the banjo position. Also, the Dillards added drums and this further exasperated the Bluegrass purists. The band also used the very un-Bluegrass sound of a steel guitar, which was played by Buddy Emmons.

During 1969, Mitch wrote his book *The Fish Hawk*, the rights to which were sold to 20th Century Fox in 1972 and then in 1979 went to Avco-Embassy, and the movie was released in 1980 (Mitch has since written two further books, *The $17,000.00 Privy* (1973) and *The Glory Hole War* (1980)). Also in 1969, Paul York joined the band on drums and he debuted on the Dillards' 1970 album, ***Copperfields***, which was their last for Elektra. The group recorded a pair of singles for White Whale entitled *One Too Many Mornings/Turn it Around* and *Comin' Home Again/Fields Have Turned to Brown*.

In 1971, Herb Pedersen left and was replaced by Billy Ray "Hot Rod Banjo" Lathum, who had played banjo with the Kentucky Colonels. He appeared with the Dillards on their Anthem label album, ***Roots & Branches***, in 1972. During 1971, the Dillards scraped into the Pop chart with a pre-released single, *It's About Time*. That year, the Dillards opened for Elton John on his first U.S. tour. The following year, the group recorded ***Tribute to the American Duck*** for the Poppy label.

During 1974, Rodney recorded a single for United Artists, *Stone's Throw Away/In My Life*. That year, Mitch Jayne departed (returning to KSMO in 1976), and Irv Dugan, the group's roadie, doubled on bass. Then in 1975, former Mason Williams bassist Jeff Gilkinson joined. Although Elektra released a ***Best of the Dillards*** in 1976, the group didn't record again until 1977, when they released their first album for Flying Fish (which included a music industry board game, as an enclosure), ***The Dillards vs. the Incredible L.A. Time Machine***.

During 1977, Doug and Rodney reunited with John Hartford for the album ***Glitter-Grass from the Nashwood Hollyville Strings***. Billy Ray Lathum left the group in 1978 and was replaced by Doug Bounsall, who also brought his songwriting skills to the band. The Dillards' next album, ***Decade Waltz*** (1979), was made up primarily of originals, but also included Lennon and McCartney's *We Can Work it Out*. Herb Pedersen returned and Ray Parks played fiddle and veteran session player Glen D. Hardin played keyboards on it.

August 8 that year was named "Dillard Day" in Salem and to celebrate, a reunion was held which was recorded at the Sinks and at the Dillard family house. An album was released in 1980 on Flying Fish under the title of ***Homecoming & Family Reunion*** and the event was later shown on NBC-TV's *Real People* program.

In 1980, the Dillards recorded a direct-to-disc project, ***Mountain Rock***, which marked the temporary return to the group of Billy Ray Lathum. Following the album, Paul York, considered the best drummer in Country-Rock, retired.

During 1980, Doug and Rodney and John Hartford got together again for their ***Permanent Wave*** album, which includes versions of *That'll Be the Day*, *Boogie on Reggae Woman* and *Yakety Yak*. That year, the Dillards underwent several line-up changes and Gilkinson and Bounsall left and were replaced by Joe Villegas and Peter Grant; Eddie Ponder, formerly with the Flying Burritto Brothers, replaced Paul York.

Since then, Rodney has performed with his own band, the Rodney Dillard Band, playing at the Silver Dollar City in Branson. He has released two albums on Flying Fish, ***Rodney Dillard at the Silver Dollar City*** (1985) and ***Let the Rough Side Drag*** (1992). In May 1988, the orginal line-up with actor Denver Pyle, who played "Briscoe Darling" in *The Andy Griffith Show*, got back together on TNN's *Nashville Now*.

RECOMMENDED ALBUMS:

"Back Porch Blues" (Elektra)(1963)
"Live...Almost!" (Elektra)(1964)
"Pickin' & Fiddlin'" (Elektra)(1965)
"Wheatstraw Suite" (Elektra)(1968)
"Copperfields" (Elektra)(1970)
"Roots & Branches" (Anthem)(1972)
"Tribute to the American Duck" (Poppy)(1973)
"Country Tracks/Best of the Dillards" (Elektra UK)(1976)
"The Dillards vs. the Incredible L.A. Time Machine" (Flying Fish)(1977)
"Decade Waltz" (Flying Fish)(1979)
"Mountain Rock" (Crystal Clear)(1980)
"Homecoming & Family Reunion" (Flying Fish)(1980)
(See also Doug Dillard)

CRAIG DILLINGHAM

(Singer, Songwriter, Guitar)
Date of Birth: **1958**
Where Born: **Brownwood, Texas**

When Craig Dillingham signed to MCA/Curb in 1983, he could already boast of a professional career stretching back seventeen years, although he was then only 25.

He started out at the tender age of 8, singing with his sisters as Craig and the Dillingham Sisters. He became a regular at the weekly Country music shows held at Panther Hall in Fort Worth, Texas. One evening, he approached the conductor of Ray Price's orchestra and asked if he could sing with them. Ray agreed to this and was so impressed with Craig that he incorporated him into the show, whenever school vacations permitted. Ray continued to play at the Panther and started to pick up a local following.

In June 1975, Craig became a member of KWKH's *Louisiana Hayride* in Shreveport. The following year, he was asked to perform at the Bicentennial celebration in Washington D.C. This fell on the day (May 8) that he was supposed to graduate; however, all things are arrangeable, and a Texas Senator presented Craig with his diploma during the performance.

Having left school, Craig became the regular opening act for Ray Price. In 1982, Craig decided to try to go solo. He returned to Texas and put together a band. They cut a custom single of a Dillingham song, *Song of Hello and Goodbye*. It became a jukebox favorite of a Louisiana oilman, Dennis Buckingham. Craig was introduced to him and Buckingham be-

Former Ray Price acolyte ***Craig Dillingham***

came his business manager. Buckingham contacted Los Angeles attorney David E. Wood, who had been behind Lacy J. Dalton's initial success. However, Wood had retired but said that he would listen to the tape anyway. As a result, he came out of retirement and took over Craig's personal management. Craig was then signed to MCA/Curb.

However, dreams and reality don't always go hand in hand and although five of his singles charted, none of them were big successes. *Have You Loved Your Woman Today* just missed the Top 30 and each subsequent release including the follow-up single, *Honky Tonk Women Make Honky Tonk Men* (Top 50), was placed lower and lower. Craig's final chart record, a duet with Tish Hinojosa, got stuck at the 80 mark in 1986.

Craig continues as a member of the *Louisiana Hayride*. He is still young enough to have a second bite of the cherry.

DEAN DILLON

(Singer, Songwriter, Guitar)

Date of Birth:	**March 26, 1955**
Where Born:	**Lake City, Tennessee**
Married:	**Keni**
Children:	**Jessie Jo, twins: Brass and Chance**

Dean Dillon is a perfect example of someone who wants to become a performer, then becomes a much recorded songwriter and then is able to be a performer again.

In his own words, his life has been like *Coal Miner's Daughter II.* Shortly after his birth, Dean's father left home and he has not seen him since. His mother left for five years, while she tried to make a living in Detroit, and Dean was brought up by his grandparents until she returned.

Dean got his first guitar when he was 7, but it was watching his stepfather playing, that got him hooked onto Country music. He made his first public appearance two years later, singing Merle Haggard songs. He started songwriting when he was 11 and by the time he was 15, Dean was appearing on the weekly *Kathy Hill* TV show in Knoxville, Tennessee. About that time, he won a guest appearance on a Tennessee Valley Authority show.

When he was 17, Dean left home to live in Oak Ridge, Tennessee, with his uncle, Gene, who put him through his last year of high school. He desperately wanted to live life according to Haggard.

After graduating in 1973, Dean went to Europe for a month with his high school choir and got drunk every day. A week after his return to the U.S., he hitchhiked his way to Nashville. His reception was less than welcoming; only songwriter Frank Dycus offered the hand of friendship and acted like a surrogate father. Dean met Merle Haggard and played for him. He was told by Merle that it would take seven years for Dean to become successful. As it turned out, he was almost spot-on. Over the next three years, he drifted to most parts of North America, but always returned to Nashville. During this time, he recorded a single, *Las Vegas Girl/A Perfect Way to Cry*, for Plantation Records, as "Dean Dalton."

In 1976, he returned to Knoxville to audition for Opryland USA and landed the role of "Hank Williams" in the Country Music Show. While in the show, he received great help from the Live Entertainment Department. A friend of his, Cathy, introduced him to songwriter John Schweers, who took him under his wing. He introduced Dean to Tom Collins, who was then heading Pi Gem-Chess Music and Collins signed him as a staff writer. Within three weeks, Barbara Mandrell had cut three of Dean's songs. In 1979, Dean got his first No.1, with *Lying Here in Love with You* by Jim Ed Brown and Helen Cornelius.

That same year, Jerry Bradley signed him to RCA. His debut single, *I'm Into the Bottle (To Get You Out of My Mind)*, reached the Top 30. His follow-up, *What Good is a Heart*, did a little better and *Nobody in his Right Mind (Would Have Left Her)* went Top 25. (Six years later, George Strait recorded the song and took it to No.1.) However, Dean's next five records did not occupy the same heady heights. Despite this in 1981, *Billboard* voted him "Singles Artist of the Year." That same year, Dean and Frank Dycus wrote George Strait's first hit, *Unwound.*

In 1982, Bradley hit upon pairing Dean with Gary Stewart. Either Bradley was being foolhardy or a genius. Stewart had the reputa-

Singer/Songwriter ***Dean Dillon***

tion of being a wild one. Putting together Dean Dillon (who after one of his benders had been put into an institution by Tom Collins) with the King of the Honky Tonkers caused heads to be shaken. But Bradley was right. Under the production guidance of Eddie Kilroy, they recorded the album ***Brotherly Love***. It was better received outside of the U.S. RCA persevered and in 1982, the team was back in the studio recording a mini-album, ***Those Were the Days***.

Dean's songwriting was going from strength to strength and in 1983, he had cuts from George Strait (*Marina Del Rey*), Johnny Rodriguez (*She Calls it Love*) and Hank Williams, Jr./Ernest Tubb/Waylon Jennings (*Leave Them Boys Alone*), and George Jones and David Allen Coe both recorded *Tennessee Whiskey*, which Dean wrote with Linda Hargrove.

He kept away from recording for five years, during which time he racked up a mind-blowing list of co-written songs recorded by the cream of Nashville. George Strait has recorded *The Chair, Ocean Front Property, Nobody in his Right Mind, It Ain't Cool to Be Crazy About You, I've Come to Expect It from You, If I Know Me* and *Famous Last Words of a Fool.* Vern Gosdin cut *Set 'Em Up, Joe* and *Is it Raining at Your House*; Steve Wariner recorded *By Now* and Keith Whitley had *Miami, My Amy* and *Homecoming '63*.

In 1988, he signed to Capitol and he released the album ***Slick Nickel***, from which came one of Dean's biggest hits, *I Go to Pieces* (Top 40, 1988), which was not one of his own songs, but written by Del Shannon. Dean released ***I've Learned to Live*** in 1989. The latter featured a duet with Tanya Tucker, *Don't You Even Think About Leaving* and three songs written with his old mentor, Frank Dycus. In 1991, Dean moved over to Atlantic Records which brought out his most successful album,

Out of Your Ever Lovin' Mind. From this album, *Friday Night's Woman* made the Top 40.

Dean is no longer the hell-raiser of his youthful years and he's now a happily married man with a loving family.

RECOMMENDED ALBUMS:

"Brotherly Love" (RCA)(1982) [With Gary Stewart]
"Those Were the Days" (1982) [With Gary Stewart] [Mini-album]
"Slick Nickel" (Capitol)(1988)
"I've Learned to Live" (1989)
"Out of Your Ever Lovin' Mind" (Atlantic)(1991)

Dirt Band refer NITTY GRITTY DIRT BAND

DIXIANA

Formed: 1986
Members:

Cindy Murphy	Lead Vocals, Acoustic Guitar
Mark Lister	Bass Guitar, Vocals
Phil Lister	Acoustic Guitar, Mandolin, Fiddle, Banjo, Vocals
Randall Griffith	Keyboards
Colonel Shuford	Drums

Since Alabama showed the way in the early 80's, Country performers operating under a group banner have proliferated. Some have succeeded and some have fallen by the wayside. Dixiana have a good chance of being one of those that make it. Under the production guidance of Bob Montgomery, they have been given a flying start.

Dixiana's roots lie in the musical activities of the Lister brothers. They were playing almost as soon as they could walk and for four years in the mid-70's, they hosted a TV show in Maudlin, South Carolina. Among their regular guests were Wildcountry, who, of course, went on to become Alabama.

The Listers were joined by Randall Griffith from Montgomery, West Virginia, and Colonel Shuford. However, when their lead singer left and the band was scheduled to appear on *Nashville Now*, they approached Cindy Murphy to help out. She had been a part of the family Bluegrass group, the Wooden Nickel Band. The Listers had known her since they were children. Cindy decided to leave the family group and join Dixiana.

In 1992, they signed to Epic and released their debut eponymous album. Their two initial singles, *Waitin' for the Deal to Go Down* and *That's What I'm Working on Tonight*, both made the Top 40. However, their third single, *Now You're Talkin'*, only made the Top 70 in 1993.

RECOMMENDED ALBUM:

"Dixiana" (Epic)(1992)

DIXIE GENTLEMEN, The

Formed: 1956
Members:

Jake Landers	Guitar, Vocals
Herschel Sizemore	Mandolin, Vocals
Rual Yarbrough	Banjo, Vocals

The Alabama-based Dixie Gentlemen created some of the more original and creative Bluegrass music of the early and middle 60's. They built much of it around the compositions of guitarist/lead vocalist Jake Landers (b. Jacob Landers, August 14, 1938, Lawrence County, Alabama) along with their vocal trios and the solid instrumentation of Herschel Sizemore (b. Herschel Lee Sizemore, August 8, 1935, Sheffield, Alabama) on mandolin and Rual Yarbrough (b. January 13, 1930, Lawrence County, Alabama) on banjo. The band eventually dissolved when Sizemore and Yarbrough went to work as sidemen in better-known bands but the three remained close friends and periodically got together in the studio to re-create the sound of the Dixie Gentlemen on record. In addition, the three continued to produce Bluegrass music of quality in a variety of other roles.

The Dixie Gentlemen's origins date back to 1956, when Herschel Sizemore and Rual Yarbrough met and worked in a Country band called the Alabamains. When a friend of Herschel's named Jake Landers got out of military service the following year, they formed their own group which they initially called the Country Gentlemen, but changed it to the Dixie Gentlemen after learning that another newly formed band already had a claim to the name.

For the next decade, the band remained together and active, working shows primarily in Alabama and adjacent states. They did television programs in various locales, especially at WMSL Decatur, Alabama. In addition, fiddler Vassar Clements played with them for a time, as did a lesser-known fiddler, Al Lester. The group had several bass players over the years including Billy Sizemore, Wesley Stevens, and especially Jesse Handley.

The Dixie Gentlemen first recorded in 1959, on the small Blue Sky label of St. Cloud, Florida, their first effort being a pair of Gospel songs, *Pray for Me* and *Three Steps.* Nashville fiddler Tommy Jackson needed a good Bluegrass band to accompany him on a Dot album and the Gentlemen filled the bill. They also cut a pair of albums containing Bluegrass standards on the Time label as the Blue Ridge Mountain Boys. Their crowning achievement in the studio came later in 1963 with an album on United Artists, that contained a dozen new songs, mostly written by Jake Landers, but all firmly within the Bluegrass tradition. Highlight titles included *Dear One, Will You Wait,* and *This Is the Girl I Love.* The band cut their last album as a working group in November, 1966, with Vassar Clements on fiddle and Tut Taylor on Dobro. They also backed Rual Yarbrough on a banjo album at about the same time. Rual initially released both albums on his own Tune label.

The dissolution of the Dixie Gentlemen resulted from a need for their services as sidemen in bands led by top names in the field. Late in 1967, Sizemore went to work as a mandolin picker for Jimmy Martin, and then in March, 1969, he relocated in Virginia, where he played in various bands, most notably the Shenandoah Valley Cutups and the Bluegrass Cardinals. Yarbrough also worked briefly for Martin, and then from 1969 to 1971 with Bill Monroe's Blue Grass Boys. He then got back with Landers in a group called the Dixiemen, which subsequently recorded four albums together. Jake Landers continued writing songs and did some additional recording.

In December 1972, the Dixie Gentlemen, including Vassar Clements, got together and did a reunion album for Old Homestead and nearly two decades later did another one for Rutabaga. The three core members have all recorded albums under their own names as well. IMT

RECOMMENDED ALBUMS:

"Hootenanny N' Blue Grass" (Time)(1963) [As the Blue Ridge Mountain Boys]
"Blue Grass Down Home" (Time)(1963) [As the Blue Grass Mountain Boys]
"The Country Style of the Dixie Gentlemen" (United Artists)(1963)
"Blues and Bluegrass" (Tune)(1967) [Also released on Old Homestead]
"Together Once More" (Old Homestead)(1973)
"Take Me Back to Dixie" (Rutabaga)(1992)

DIXON BROTHERS, The

DORSEY DIXON
(Vocals, Songwriter, Guitar, Fiddle)

Given Name:	Dorsey Murdock Dixon
Date of Birth:	October 14, 1897
Married:	Beatrice Moody (div.)
Children:	four sons
Date of Death:	April 17, 1968

HOWARD DIXON
(Vocals, Steel Guitar)

Given Name:	Howard Briten Dixon
Date of Birth:	June 19, 1903
Married:	Mellie
Children:	eight
Date of Death:	March 24, 1961

Both Born: Darlington, South Carolina

In the era of the mid-to-late 30's, when brother duets held an atypical high degree of popularity, the Dixon Brothers had one of the more distictinctive sounds. It was distinguished by a steel guitar lead, rather than a mandolin or twin guitars, and a harmony that has been described as raucous or reedy, as opposed to the smoothness of the Blue Sky Boys or the high pitch of the Monroes. While perhaps less appealing than some duets to listeners, the Dixons compensated for any musical deficiencies with a higher degree of original songs on a wide variety of subjects. Among other things, the Dixon originals contain more social commentary on the life and culture of textile workers than any other, with the possible exception of the David McCarn (*Cotton Mill Colic* et al.) compositions.

The Dixons were products of that period of Southern industrialization when plain-folk families forsook agricultural poverty for labor in the textile mills. Their parents became mill workers sometime prior to the birth of Dorsey and Howard and the children all went into the cotton mills at an early age. Dorsey started his labors at 12 and Howard at about 10. Both worked on the railroad during WWI, but afterwards returned to the mills, settling in East Rockingham, North Carolina. At first, they played music for local dances and then began taking their hobby more seriously when Columbia artist Jimmie Tarlton visited their community. Howard, impressed by Tarlton's steel guitar style, soon took up the instrument himself and about 1934, the Dixons began to appear on WBT Charlotte's *Crazy Barn Dance*. Initially they seem to have been a feature act within J.E. Mainer's Mountaineers, and then went, more or less, on their own. At one time, the Dixon Brothers also worked at WPTF Raleigh.

For a two and one half year period beginning in February, 1936, the Dixons recorded extensively on Bluebird, with some of their material leased to Montgomery Ward. In all, they had some 55 sides released, although a few are so rare as to be virtually non-existent. Most Dixon songs were either originals or parodies by Dorsey Dixon, who had one of the more fertile imaginations of his era. Many were of a sacred or inspirational nature, such as *Wonderful Day*, *Not Turning Backward* and *Easter Day*. Others reflect humor, including *The Intoxicated Rat*, *She Tickles Me*, *Fisherman's Luck* and *Time for Me to Go*. Some commemorate local tragedy like *Two Little Rosebuds*, *School House Fire*, *Down With the Old Canoe* and *I Didn't Hear Anybody Pray* (more commonly known as *Wreck on the Highway*). Finally there are those of a protest nature, such as *Sales Tax on the Woman*, *The Old Home Brew* and *How Can a Broke Man Be Happy*. Scholarly interest has generally centered on Dorsey's songs about life in the mills: *Weave Room Blues*, *Spinning Room Blues* and *Weaver's Life Is Like an Engine*.

In addition to their own duets, Dorsey and his wife, Beatrice, recorded six sacred songs. Howard waxed a dozen or so numbers with a friend named Frank Gerald, as the Rambling Duet, and a few more as a trio with the addition of Mutt Evans. After the brothers stopped performing as a team, Howard Dixon worked as a band member with the Wade Mainer group at WWNC Asheville.

When the Dixons ended their musical careers, both returned to jobs at the Aleo Mills in East Rockingham. After 1946, Dorsey finally did get recognition and royalties from Acuff-Rose for *Wreck on the Highway*. Howard worked in later years with a local quartet known as the Reaping Harvesters until a massive heart attack took his life. Dorsey struck up a correspondence with Australian collector-scholar John Edwards until John died in a car crash. Eugene Earl and Archie Green visited Dorsey in 1962 and made field recordings of him and his sister Nancy that subsequently appeared on a Testament album. The next year, Dorsey played at the Newport Folk Festival, from which three cuts came out on a Vanguard lp. In the mid-60's, the aging textile worker-bard suffered a heart attack and went to live with his son, Dorsey, Jr., a minister in Plant City, Florida. Almost to the end, Dorsey maintained correspondence and exchanged tapes with several collector pen-pals. All found him a deeply religious and sensitive, yet congenial friend. As the years went by, a few Dixon Brothers recordings appeared on various anthologies, and eventually entire albums containing most of their output became available on Country Turtle and Old Homestead collector editions. IMT

RECOMMENDED ALBUMS:

"Babies in the Mill" (Testament)(1965)
"Beyond Black Smoke" (Country Turtle)(1979)
"Rambling and Gambling" (Country Turtle)(1984)
"The Dixon Brothers: Volume I" (Old Homestead)(1983)
"The Dixon Brothers: Volume II" (Old Homestead)(1984)
"The Dixon Brothers: Volume III" (Old Homestead)(1986)
"The Dixon Brothers: Volume IV" (Old Homestead)(1987)

DOBRO

By Mike Auldridge

My earliest memory of hearing the word "Dobro" was when I was about 13 years old. Recording artists such as Wilma Lee and Stoney Cooper and Molly O'Day, as well as Roy Acuff and Johnnie & Jack, all still used this wonderful sounding instrument that I had always called an "Old-Time steel." This was in the early 1950's when almost all Country (or hillbilly) bands used an electric steel guitar. The modern pedal steel had yet to be invented. But these particular artists hung on to the sound of the 30's and 40's, which greatly appealed to me, (as did another form of early sounding music which would come to be known as "Bluegrass"), because I had grown up listening to my uncle Ellsworth Cozzens playing the Old-Time steel. He had recorded with Jimmie Rodgers in the late 1920's and was the family hero.

This "Old-Time steel," I soon learned, had the brand name of "Dobro," as opposed to the more familiar Gibson or Martin brands. The Dobro guitar was invented and marketed by four brothers by the name of Dopyera (later changed to Dopera) who came to California from Czechoslovakia in 1908. All the brothers were musical and played the violin and several other instruments. But John was the most inventive and was always looking for a way to amplify acoustic instruments. He succeeded in 1926 by designing a steel bodied guitar in which he installed three aluminum resonators. He and his brothers, and some other investors, formed a company called the National String Instrument Corporation, to produce this guitar and later variations that used a single resonator. These National guitars were very successful, but it was not long before there were differences among the brothers and the other investors. In 1928, John and his brothers founded another company, wholly their own, based on his new variation, which was a wooden bodied guitar with a single resonator that was invented from the original design. Not only did they use this resonator design in guitars, but also in mandolins and violins. This company was named The Dobro Corporation. Dobro means "good" in their native language and was an abbreviation of DOpyera BROthers. The two companies merged in the mid-1930's to become the National Dobro Corporation.

The metal-bodied National guitars became the instrument of choice among the Hawaiian music and Blues-style players. The more mellow-sounding wooden bodied Dobro guitar was better suited for the hillbilly bands of the era, which almost always included a steel guitar. The "steel" referred to the steel bar held in the left hand which was slid along the strings in the Hawaiian style of playing a guitar. Things started to change with the arrival of the electric pick-up in the mid-30's. Almost all steel guitarists went to the electric sound and by 1941, with the arrival of WWII and the metal shortage, National-Dobro went out of the guitar making business. A handful of players, Speedy Krise, Pete (Bashful Brother Oswald) Kirby, Shot Jackson, Ray Adkins and most notably, Buck (Josh) Graves, among very few others, carried on with the acoustically amplified Dobro.

I say most notably Josh Graves, because he joined Flatt & Scruggs in 1955 and started a revival of interest in the Dobro. This was the first time a steel guitar was used in Bluegrass music and Josh was the first to approach the steel with the attack of a banjo player. He revolutionized Dobro playing as much as Earl Scruggs had revolutionized banjo playing a dozen years prior. There was so much renewed interest, that the original Dopyera brothers went back into business in the 1960's and started the Original Musical Instrument Company (OMI). This company was recently bought by the Gibson organization. There are also at least a half dozen custom resonator-guitar manufacturers on the scene today.

I came along in the 1960's and tried to copy Graves' style but never could get that gutty, powerful Blues-based sound that was his alone, as hard as I tried. My sound was more polite and pretty and I soon resigned myself to the fact that I had to play what was in my heart and hands. I became involved as a founding member of a band called the Seldom Scene and luckily my style fit the direction the band wanted to go. I also recorded several instrumental albums where I was able to showcase my style. Over the next few years, I met Tut Taylor, who is the only Dobroist that I know of to play with a flat pick, rather than fingerpicks, which gives him a style all his own. Jerry Douglas, whom I met when he was a teenager, has become the most recorded Dobroist in the history of the instrument because he can play any style from Country to Jazz to Bluegrass . . . beautifully slow or blazingly fast. There are many, many new young players recording, standing in the wings and just walking out of the woods, with all the enthusiasm and knowledge it takes to ensure the future of the Dobro guitar.

[For biographies on Dobroists and recommended albums, see: Ray Adkins, Mike Auldridge, Bashful Brother Oswald, Jerry Douglas, Josh Graves, Lloyd Green, Shot Jackson, Tut Taylor]

DR. HOOK

Formed:	**1968 (as Dr. Hook & the Medicine Show)**
Original Members:	
Ray Sawyer	**Lead Vocals, Guitar, Percussion, Songwriter**
Dennis Locorriere	**Lead Vocals, Guitar, Songwriter, Bass Guitar, Drums**
Jay David	**Drums**
Billy Francis	**Keyboards**
George Cummings	**Steel Guitar**
Jance Garfat	**Bass Guitar, Vocals**
Later Members:	
Rik Elswit	**Lead Guitar, Vocals**
John Wolters	**Drums, Vocals**
John "Willard" Henke	**Guitar, Vocals**

It could be excused if Dr. Hook & the Medicine Show initially looked like the mouthpiece for super-songwriter Shel Silverstein. However, over the years, this seven-piece aggregation demonstrated that they were one of the finest left-field bands to emerge. Their blend of fine and often humorous songs and comedic stage act ensured that they stayed in demand as a chart act for over a decade.

Ray Sawyer (b. February 1, 1937, Chicksaw, Alabama) and Dennis Locorriere (b. June 13, 1949, New York) are definitely the front men of this group, the motivating force, and apart from Silverstein, the main writers. Sawyer, with the eye patch and the battered hat, is the one to whom the sobriquet "Dr. Hook" belongs. He started out playing guitar in honky tonks at the delicate age of 14. His hero at this time was Hank Williams, who was born in Georgiana, Alabama, which is not far from Chicksaw. After having seen a John Wayne movie, Ray decided to move to Portland, Oregon, determined to give up music and be a logger. On the way, he had an auto accident which left him with sight-loss in his right eye. He decided to stay with music and got together with Billy Francis (b. January 16, 1942, Mobile, Alabama). It was while they stopped at Transfer Station near Union City, New Jersey, to play in the bars that proliferated in the area, that they met Dennis. They started working as a trio, with Dennis, who was primarily a drummer, playing bass.

They gave a tape to someone who passed it to Ron Haffkine, who was, at that time, musical director for the Dustin Hoffman movie *Who is Harry Kellerman and Why is He Saying These Terrible Things About Me*. The music for the movie had been written by Shel Silverstein. They agreed that the group should sing the theme, *Last Morning,* for the movie. Haffkine became their manager and producer and got them their record deal with Columbia. The trio was augmented by Jay David (b. August 8, 1942), George Cummings (b. July 28, 1938), Jance Garfat (b. March 3, 1944, California) and Rik Elswit (b. July 6, 1945).

It was with their second single, in 1972, that Dr. Hook & the Medicine Show zoomed from the unknown to international fame. Silverstein's *Sylvia's Mother* climbed into the Top 5 of the Pop charts. Four months after release, the single was certified Gold and in the U.K., it reached No.2. It looked like they might be one hit wonders, when *Carry Me Carrie* only reached the bottom levels of the Pop charts. Then at the end of the year, they charted with one of their finest singles, the immensely funny *Cover of "Rolling Stone."* It climbed up to the Pop Top 10 and by April 1973, had also gone Gold.

During the remainder of 1973-1975, they

Dr. Hook with Shel Silverstein

didn't fare too well and by the time they left Columbia, with five albums under their belt, they had gone into bankruptcy. They used their pooled resources and recorded the album ***Bankrupt***. In 1975, Jay David and George Cummings left the group and were replaced by John Wolters (b. April 28, 1945, New Jersey) and John "Willard" Henke (b. April 29, 1951, Pennsylvania). The group signed to Capitol in 1976 as "Dr. Hook," and their second single did the trick. Sam Cooke's *Only Sixteen* reached the Pop Top 10 and crossed over into the Country Top 60. By May of that year, it was Certified Gold.

Dr. Hook released their second album for the label, ***A Little Bit More***, that year and it yielded two hits that were bigger in Europe than in the States. In the U.S., the title track reached the Top 15, staying on the Pop charts for nearly six months. In the U.K., where they were enjoying enormous popularity, it peaked at No.2. The flip-side, *A Couple More Years*, was also a U.S. Top 50 Country hit. They followed this with Locorriere's *If Not You*, which didn't fare that well in the Pop listings but was a Top 30 Country hit and again they did well in the U.K., where the single went Top 5.

In 1977, Ray Sawyer released his eponymous album, from which he had a 1976 Country cross-over hit, *(One More Year of) Daddy's Little Girl*. The band's next major hit came in 1978 when *Sharing the Night Together* hit the Pop Top 10 and gave them their fourth Gold Record. It also became a Top 50 Country hit.

The following year, they had one of their biggest hits when Even Stevens' *When You're in Love with a Beautiful Woman* hit the Pop chart Top 10. In The U.K. it was a No.1 success, staying in that position for 3 weeks. Both the single and the album ***Pleasure and Pain*** reached Gold Record status by the fall of 1979. Dr. Hook rounded off the year with *Better Love Next Time*, which was a U.K. Top 10 single and made it up to the Top 15 on the U.S. Pop chart.

In 1980, they had their last major hit with the Top 5 record *Sexy Eyes* which provided them with yet another Gold Record and also gave them their last big record in the U.K. That year, Dr. Hook recorded a BBC-TV special in the U.K. and the following year, Capitol released the ***Live in the UK*** album. This was their last album for the label as they had already moved over to Casablanca (Mercury in the U.K.). Their first album for that label, ***Rising***, had appeared in 1980. However, by now musical trends had started to move and they only achieved one more album, ***Players in the Dark,*** and two more medium sized hits, *Girls Can't Get It* (1980) and *Baby Makes Her Blue Jeans Talk* (1982).

Although they soldiered on, the end was in sight. By the 90's, Dennis had gone solo and was touring the U.K. successfully.

RECOMMENDED ALBUMS:

"Dr. Hook & the Medicine Show" (Columbia)(1971)
"Bankrupt" (Capitol)(1976)
"Pleasure and Pain" (Capitol)(1978)
"Sometimes You Win" (Fame UK)(1979)
"Rising" (Casablanca)(1980)
"Live in the UK" (Capitol)(1981)
"Players in the Dark" (Casablanca)(1983)
"Dr. Hook & the Medicine Show" (Pickwick UK)(1984) [Columbia masters]
"The Very Best of Dr. Hook" (Country Store UK)(1985) [Capitol masters]
"Dr. Hook-Volume 2" (Country Store UK)(1988) [Columbia masters]
NB: Country Store is available in the U.S.
Ray Sawyer:
"Ray Sawyer" (Capitol)(1977)

DR. SMITH'S CHAMPION HOSS-HAIR PULLERS

Formed:	**1926**
Members:	
Bryan Lackey	**Fiddle**
James Clark Duncan	**Fiddle**
Owen Hunt	**Fiddle**
W.P. McLeary	**Fiddle, Guitar**
Luther Walker	**Fiddle**
George Dillard	**Fiddle**
Ray Marshall	**Mandolin**
Leeman Bone	**Guitar, Vocalist**
Grayton Bone	**Vocalist**
Roosevelt Garner	**Vocalist**
Hubert Simmons	**Vocalist**
Homer T. Goatcher	**Vocalist**
J. Odie Goatcher	**Vocalist**

This band with the colorful name was led by a non-playing member, Dr. Henry Harlin Smith. Born May 16, 1881, in the Spring Creek community, three miles from Calico Rock, Arkansas, Dr. Smith was a surgeon for the Missouri Pacific Railroad.

He was also a tireless promoter of his home region, who resented the backward image that many Americans held of the White River area and was determined to do something about breaking the stereotype. Moreover, he was proud of the region's natural beauties and resources and felt they did not receive adequate promotion. Aware of the wealth of musical talent that existed in the immediate vicinity, Smith felt the best means of accomplishing both goals was through giving local musicians greater prominence. For this reason he organized a fiddle contest that was held in Calico Rock in January, 1926. From the winners of this contest, he formed the "Hoss-Hair Pullers" (the name coming from the fiddle bow, which is made of horsehair) and he soon assembled a group of vocalists that he called the Hill-Billy Quartet.

The next step was to arrange for them to play for a wide audience. Smith soon succeeded in getting them a spot on KTHS (Kum To Hot Springs) Hot Springs, Arkansas, one of the state's most powerful stations. Three nights of performances at a Hot Springs theater helped pay for the band's travel expenses.

The band's appearance on KTHS was successful, leading to return engagements. Smith himself helped their chances by inviting columnists for various papers to be guests at their performance. Some favorable columns about the "Calico Rock bunch" that resulted, did nothing to harm the band's popularity. In later performances on KTHS Smith's band was billed as the Hoss-Hair Pullers, the Hill-Billy Duet, and Hill-Billy Quartet. The band's first KTHS appearance took place March 13, 1926, their last on December 20, 1926.

The group soon tired of the long, difficult trip between Calico Rock and Hot Springs (a distance of 180 miles, which, on the primitive roads of the 1920's, was very exhausting). Moreover, having achieved a certain degree of fame, the Hoss-Hair Pullers were able to stay busy closer to home. They frequently performed in local theaters, high school chapel programs, and Missouri Pacific Railroad functions. Although the band's members made a little money from their performances, they never viewed the venture as anything more than a lark.

Historically, the band's highlight was a September 12, 1928, recording session for the Victor label in Memphis. Their six selections included religious songs, "coon songs" and Folk songs. Their records, although good musically, sold well only in Izard, the band's home county. The Hoss-Hair Pullers lasted only two years after their recording session, finally breaking up in 1930. Over the four years they were together, personnel shifted from one performance to another. At no time did the band have more than eight members, but a total of thirteen men belonged to the organization over the years of its existence. One reason why the membership kept changing was Dr. Smith's penchant for sponsoring instrumental contests and adding the winners to his group. For example, on one occasion he held a French Harp contest, the winner becoming a member of the Hoss-Hair Pullers for a couple of performances.

Dr. Smith outlasted his band by only a short time. On October 14, 1931, while driving to Little Rock, he suffered a cerebral hemorrhage. He was taken to a hospital but never regained consciousness. WKM

RECOMMENDED ALBUM:

"Echoes of the Ozarks, Volume 2" (County) [Various artists]

JOHNNY DOLLAR

(Singer, Deejay)

Given Name: John Washington Dollar, Jr.
Date of Birth: March 8, 1933
Where Born: Kilgore, Texas
Married: Unknown
Children: John Washington III
Date of Death: April 13, 1986

With a name that sounded like it had been made up especially to sing, Johnny Dollar was the real thing. The son of John Washington and Nellie Mae Morgan Dollar, John, Jr., grew up in Sheridan, Texas, and attended Schreiner's Military Academy in 1951.

In 1952, John started recording for Shelby Singleton's D Records without success. The following year, his musical career took off as he became a deejay on stations in Louisiana and New Mexico, became leader of the Texas Sons and started playing on the *Louisiana Hayride* out of KWKH Shreveport. In 1954, he left the Texas Sons and by 1955, he was playing in Martin McCullough's Light Crust Doughboys. That year he cut *Lumberjack* for Winston Records.

1959 saw him appearing on *Country Style USA*, the syndicated version of the *Big D Jamboree* out of Dallas. He completed an eight-year stint as a deejay in 1961 and it was not until 1964 that fame seemed about to look him in the eye. That year, Johnny signed with Columbia, but he had to wait until 1966 before he tasted chart success. *Tear-Talk* reached the Top 50 but fell out after two weeks. Johnny followed on its heels with *Stop the Start (Of Tears in My Heart)* which made it all the way up to the Top 15 and stayed on the charts for nearly four months. He was nominated in 1966 and 1967 for *Billboard* and *Record World*'s "Best New Artist" Award. By 1967, Johnny had moved over to Dot and had a minor success with *Your Hands*. However, by the fall of that year, he was on the move again, this time to Date. He had two Top 40 successes for them, *The Wheels Fell Off the Wagon Again* and in 1968, *Everybody's Got to Be Somewhere*. Starting with this last record, he was billed as Johnny $ Dollar. Later in 1968, he changed labels again, this time to Chart. He had a pair of "Big" hits with *Big Rig Rollin' Man* in 1968 and *Big Wheels Sing for Me* in 1969, both not being that big on the charts. His

Mr. Personality, ***Johnny Dollar***

final hit for Chart came in 1970 with *Truck Driver's Lament* which made the Top 75 and for which he reverted to Johnny Dollar.

During his life, Johnny had not been afraid of trying to make a dollar. He had worked as a truck driver, in the oil fields, in lumber yards, on a cattle ranch and in life insurance. He died in April 1986.

RECOMMENDED ALBUMS:

"Mr. Personality" (Dot)(1966)
"Johnny Dollar" (Date)(1967)
"Big Rig Rollin' Man" (Chart)(1969)
"Country Hit Parade" (Chart)(1969)

DUCK DONALD

(Vocals, Songwriter, Poet, Mandolin, Guitar, Jew's Harp, Dulcimer)

Given Name: Duckworth Bruce Andrew Donald
Date of Birth: August 18, 1951
Where Born: Montreal, Quebec, Canada
Married: Maxine McEachern
Date of Death: April 22, 1984

When a performer dies prematurely, their importance and impact can only be judged as if in a microcosm. Duck Donald was only 32 when he died, but his impact on Bluegrass was already being felt.

He was attracted to Bluegrass and referred to it as "Country music with an edge." He didn't read music but played by ear and was self-taught. He initially worked in a clothing warehouse and played in his spare time. While playing with the Bobby Cusson Trio in Montreal, he met banjo player Cathy Fink. They formed a duo and played around the country and eventually moved to Winnipeg in 1973.

They recorded their first album together, ***Kissing is a Crime***, in 1975 on the Likeable label. Three years later, Flying Fish released ***Cathy Fink and Duck Donald***. In 1980, they (with Peter Paul Van Camp) recorded the children's album ***I'm Gonna Tell***, again for Likeable.

In 1981, Cathy and Duck formed the Cathy Fink and Duck Donald Band, with Darcy Deville (guitar, fiddle, vocals) and Dave Harvey (string bass, tuba, vocals). The band broke up in 1983 and Duck continued playing with Darcy for a while. The following year, Duck died of a congenitally-caused brain hemorrhage. He is buried at the Cote de Neige Cemetery in Montreal.

RECOMMENDED ALBUMS:

All with Cathy Fink:
"Kissing is a Crime" (Likeable)(1975)
"Cathy Fink and Duck Donald" (Flying Fish)(1978)
"I'm Gonna Tell" (Likeable)(1980)

LONNIE DONEGAN

(Singer, Songwriter, Banjo, Guitar, Drums)

Given Name: Anthony Donegan
Date of Birth: April 29, 1931
Where Born: Glasgow, Scotland

Lonnie Donegan rightly earned the title "King of Skiffle music." His brand of Folk music mixed with vaudeville made him the eighth most successful artist in the British charts between 1952 and 1980. Through his playing, British audiences were made aware of the music of Woody Guthrie, Leadbelly and the whole tradition of American Folk music as well as being reminded of British Music Hall. Lonnie did run into criticism, particularly over the copyright on *Rock Island Line* (which was not credited to Leadbelly, but was acknowledged to "traditional arr. Donegan"), but Lonnie was no mere copyist. His treatment was and still is fresh.

Lonnie was the son of a fiddler with Irish descent and this accounted for his being labeled the "Irish hillbilly"' when he became successful. However, Lonnie despite his birth was a cockney through and through. He was conscripted into the British Army and played drums in an army traditional Jazz band. At the time, Ken Collyer was to traditional Jazz in London what Bill Monroe was and is to Bluegrass and John Mayall is to the Blues. All like-minded musicians hung around him and Donegan was no exception and joined Collyer's Crane River Band. Collyer also formed the first Skiffle group, which Lonnie joined on Collyer's return from New Orleans, in 1952. Skiffle's name was based upon the old black "'rent or skiffle party" music, where musicians would play to raise money to pay the rent.

Lonnie moved on to play banjo in the Chris Barber Jazz Band. Barber is one of the most respected Jazz band leaders and musicians in London and allowed Lonnie to form a Skiffle group with the band. One of the songs that Lonnie played was the aforementioned *Rock Island Line*. The song was originally recorded as part of a Chris Barber album, ***New Orleans Joys***. The track was played on BBC radio and the requests started flowing in. Decca (U.K.) released the single at the end of 1955 and it became a Top 10 hit in the U.K. in 1956 and repeated this in the Pop charts in the States on the London label. Eventually, the single would sell over a million copies worldwide. Lonnie toured the U.S. that year and left Barber to form Lonnie Donegan and his Skiffle Group.

Later in 1956, Lonnie signed to Pye Nixa (U.K.) and had a double-sided smash in the U.K. with *Lost John/Stewball*, which made it to No.2. Again the record crossed over the Atlantic and *Lost John* made the Top 70 in the U.S. on Mercury. From now on, he couldn't go wrong in the U.K.. He charted again with *Rock Island Line* and an EP, *Skiffle Session*, also made the Top 20. He rounded off 1956 with another double-sided Top 10 single, *Bring a Little Water Sylvie/Dead or Alive,* and ***Lonnie Donegan Showcase***, an album that sold so well, it appeared in the singles charts (a feat that occasionally happened in the U.K.). He made a second tour of the States to great acclaim.

1957 was a vintage year. Lonnie had a Top 5 single with Wally Whyton's *Don't You Rock Me Daddy-O* and then followed it with back-to-back No.1's with Woody Guthrie's *Cumberland Gap* and the double-sided *Gamblin' Man/Putting on the Style*. He rounded off the year with *My Dixie Darling* and *Jack O'Diamonds*.

He slipped a little in 1958 and although all his singles charted, the most successful were *Sally Don't You Grieve/Betty Betty Betty* and his version of *Tom Dooley*, which in the U.S. was a hit for the Kingston Trio. In the U.K., the Kingston Trio reached No.5 while Lonnie reached No.3.

Lonnie opened up 1959 with a hit on both sides of the "pond" entitled *Does Your Chewing Gum Lose Its Flavor (On the Bedpost Overnight)*. This was a slice of pure Music Hall fun and climbed to No.3 in the U.K. and made it to the Top 5 in the U.S. (released on Dot). Lonnie continued the successes that year with *Fort Worth Jail, Battle of New Orleans* (a U.S. hit via Johnny Horton, which also went Top 20 in the U.K.), *Sal's Got a Sugar Lip* and *San Miguel*.

Lonnie enjoyed a return of favor in a big way during 1960 with his revival of the Music Hall standard *My Old Man's a Dustman*, which gave him another No.1. He followed this with his version of *The Sloop John B* entitled *I Wanna Go Home*. Lonnie closed out the year with *Lorelei, Lively* and the beautiful Christmas calypso *Virgin Mary*. The following year, he opened his account with *Have a Drink on Me*, which was a cleaned-up version of the Leadbelly cocaine song *Have a Sniff on Me*. He followed this with his version of *Michael Row the Boat* and for the first time was outgunned by the U.S. original. The Highwaymen had taken the song to No.1 (as *Michael*) and now repeated that in Britain.

It was swan song time in 1962 for Lonnie. He had three hits, *The Commancheros, The Party's Over* and *Pick a Bale of Cotton*, and then he vanished from the charts as the onslaught of the "Liverpool Sound" of the Beatles was about to be felt. However, Lonnie continued to be extremely popular both on TV and on stage where he gave and still gives 150 percent effort.

However, it is unlikely that the Beatles would even have existed without the advent of Lonnie Donegan. When they first started, it was as the Quarrymen, a Skiffle group. Lonnie's importance to the British music scene was underlined in 1978 when he signed to Chrysalis and re-recorded many of his hits on ***Puttin' on the Style***, with guests that included Albert Lee, Ringo Starr, Elton John, Leo Sayer, Zoot Money, Michelle Phillips, Brian May and Rory Gallagher. Later in the year, Lonnie released ***Sundown*** which featured Emery Gordy, Jr., Albert Lee, Doug Kershaw and Mickey Raphael. Among the tracks are three written by Doug Kershaw including *Cajun Stripper*, as well as *Dreaming My Dreams with You* by Allen Reynolds, *The Battle of New Orleans* by Jimmie Driftwood, *Home* by John D. Loudermilk, the title track by Gordon Lightfoot and *I'm All Out and Down* by Leadbelly. Both albums were produced by the legendary Adam Faith.

Lonnie continues to entertain around the U.K. and appeared at the 1988 ill-fated Grantham Country Festival.

RECOMMENDED ALBUMS:

"An Englishman Sings American Folk" (Mercury)(1956)
"Lonnie Donegan" (Dot)(1961)
"Skiffle Folk Music" (Atlantic)
"Puttin' on the Style" (Chrysalis U.K./United Artists U.S.)(1978)
"Sundown" (Chrysalis U.K.)(1978)
"Jubilee Concert" (Dakota U.K.)(1981)

DOTTSY

(Singer)

Given Name:	**Dottsy Brodt**
Date of Birth:	**April 6, 1954**
Where Born:	**Seguin, Texas**
Married:	**Robin Dwyer**

Dottsy flitted across the Country music firmament in 1975 and by 1981 was but a memory. She left the business of her own accord, while still successful, to tend for mentally delayed children. It had always been her intention to do this and Dottsy has brought joy to others with her life.

She came from a German family and by the time she was 12, she had appeared at a firemen's convention and she had won a talent contest on radio KBER San Antonio, which had as first prize an appearance on the *Grand Ole Opry*. She started to appear in talent shows and conventions. By the time she was 14, she was a regular on a weekly San Antonio TV show.

She went to college for a while in 1972, but quit in favor of a career in music. She was playing a hotel managers' convention when she was spotted by Happy Shanahan. He took over her management. He booked her to appear at his holiday venue, Alamo Village at Brackettville, Texas, where she did five shows a day. She met Shanahan's other artist, Johnny Rodriguez, and toured with him.

In the summer of 1974, Dottsy came to Nashville and met Ron Dea, then a producer at RCA, who signed her. Her first release, *Storms Never Lie*, was written by Jessi Colter. It entered the chart and peaked in the Top 20, spending over four months on the chart. This was an auspicious start that was soon capitalized on. *I'll Be Your San Antonio Rose* fared even better, climbing to the Top 15.

In 1976, her debut album, ***The Sweetest Thing***, entered the album chart, but her singles hit a sticking point. The next two singles failed to impress, but in 1977, Dottsy came back strongly with *(After Sweet Memories) Play Born to Lose Again*, which made the Top 10. She completed the year with two medium successes, *It Should Have Been Easy* (Top 25, 1977) and *Here in Love* (Top 20, 1978).

Dottsy's successes continued with *I Just Had You on My Mind* (Top 25, 1978) and then, in 1979, *Tryin' to Satisfy You*, which was the title of her second album, climbed to the Top 15, no doubt helped by Waylon Jennings' appearance on it. That same year, Dottsy debuted at Wembley Country Music Festival in England and impressed a lot of people with her husky voice and blonde girl-next-door looks.

She chalked up two more Top 20 hits that year, *Slip Away* and *When I'm Gone*. Then she was gone. For two years, she had no further chart action. In 1981, Dottsy had two middle order entries on Tanglewood with *Somebody's Darling, Somebody's Wife* and *Let the Little Bird Fly*. Then she was gone for good.

During her career, Dottsy won several awards including, "Miss Snake Charmer" at Brackettville Lions Club Rattlesnake Round-up in Texas, in 1976. That year, Dottsy also received an ASCAP Award for *I'll Be Your San Antonio Rose* and a *Cash Box* Award for "Album of the Year by a New Female Artist." The following year, she was awarded with the Alcade Award from Del Rio, Texas, and *Cash Box*'s "Top New Female Vocalist" award.

She now works full-time with the Texas Association for Retarded Children. She has made TV and radio commercials on their behalf.

RECOMMENDED ALBUMS:

"The Sweetest Thing" (RCA Victor)(1976)
"Tryin' to Satisfy You" (RCA Victor)(1979)

CHARLIE DOUGLAS

(Deejay, Announcer)

For five glorious hours *Charlie Douglas and his Road Gang* beamed out Monday through Friday on station WWL, New Orleans, and was arguably the most listened-to truckers' radio show. For thirteen years, his show came at you wherever in the U.S. you were.

Charlie became addicted to late night radio while still a boy in Georgia. He listened to *Mr. District Attorney*, *One Man's Family* and *Grand Central Station* and nighttime broadcasters such as Hoss Allen and John R. Although Charlie began in Country radio, he switched to playing rock'n'roll in San Antonio, Buffalo, Hartford, San Diego and Miami. During his time at Buffalo, he set a roller-coaster riding record and while in Texas, he broadcast live from a hot air balloon. However, in the latter case, the show came to an undesired end when Charlie went missing for a few days, after drifting out over the Gulf of Mexico. He became the first person to broadcast live whilst parachuting from an airplane. Charlie also achieved firsts when broadcasting standing in a lion's cage and when riding on the back of a bucking Brahma bull.

In 1970, Charlie moved to WWL for his decade plus stint. He was named *Overdrive* magazine's "Trucking Disc Jockey of the Year" in 1973 and CMA's "Country Music Disc Jockey of the Year," the following year. In 1975, Charlie took his show on the road for what he called "narrow-casting" from over 40 locations over a 50 day period. The next year, Charlie was named ACM's "Disc Jockey of the Year."

In 1983, Charlie moved to Nashville where he joined the Music Country Radio Network, which had started the previous year. Douglas replaced Chuck Morgan who went off to join the Texas Rangers baseball organization. From there, Charlie moved to WSM where he still broadcasts. He has now become one of the doyens of announcers having been heard on the *Grand Ole Opry* and guesting on the 1989 Peterborough Festival in England. He is a former President of Country Radio Broadcasters and is currently on the Board of Directors of that organization. He has also made some recordings, most notably in 1980 with Dave Dudley.

RECOMMENDED ALBUMS:

"Dammit Ray, Again!" (Delta)
"Diesel Duets" (Sun)(1980) [With Dave Dudley]

JERRY DOUGLAS

(Dobro, Lap Steel, Guitar, Composer)

Given Name:	**Gerald Calvin Douglas**
Date of Birth:	**May 28, 1956**
Where Born:	**Warren, Ohio**
Married:	**Jill**
Children:	**Grant, Patricia, Olivia, Nola**

Jerry Douglas has taken Dobro playing to new heights and introduced a new generation to the traditional Bluegrass instrument. Often playing in tandem with fiddle wizard, Mark O'Connor, their interplay has become as well known in Country music as Sly Dunbar and Robbie Shakespeare in Reggae, and Jerry talks of them as "the Sweeteners" or "the Saccharin Brothers."

Jerry was first introduced to the Dobro by his father, who was a Bluegrass musician. His interest with the instrument began when he was 8 years old, living in Warren, Ohio. He attended a Flatt & Scruggs concert in 1963 and was spellbound by the Dobro playing of "Uncle" Josh Graves. The performance made such an impression on him, that Jerry converted his Silvertone guitar so he could play it with a bar like Graves. It wasn't long before Jerry was playing Dobro in his father's Bluegrass band.

Dobro wizard ***Jerry Douglas***

When Jerry was 16, the band played at a summer Bluegrass festival that featured the well-known group the Country Gentlemen. His impressive playing earned him an invitation to finish the summer season as a member of the Gentlemen, whose members at the time included Doyle Lawson. Jerry went on to work with J.D. Crowe and the New South and David Grisman and the band Boone Creek, which featured Ricky Skaggs.

Through his many years of playing the Dobro, Jerry developed a unique style highlighted by his incredible finger-picking speed combined with the precise gliding of the steel bar. His fellow musicians were so impressed with his speed and accuracy, that they gave him the nickname, "Flux." Jerry picked up on this name for the title of his debut album on Rounder in 1978, ***Fluxology***.

In 1983, he recorded another album for Rounder entitled ***Tennessee Fluxedo***. His distinctive style was first heard on Country radio via his first recordings with the Whites. *Hangin' Around* (1983) and *Pins and Needles* (1984) were among the Whites' hit singles that featured Jerry's Dobro playing.

After six years of touring and recording, he left the Whites to pursue studio session work and a solo career as an instrumentalist. He quickly became a favorite of many artists and producers and has played on albums by Kathy Mattea, Randy Travis, Emmylou Harris, Hank Williams, Jr., Ray Charles, Michael Johnson, Ricky Skaggs, Michael Martin Murphey and the Nitty Gritty Dirt Band.

His solo recording continued in 1986, when he was one of the first artists signed to MCA Master Series, a new label started by MCA/Nashville. ***Under the Wire*** was the debut Douglas album for that label and this was followed, the next year, with ***Changing Channels***. This album included guest appearances by former band-mates, Buck White and Ricky Skaggs. Jerry followed these with ***Plant Early*** in 1989 and addressed the new direction he was taking musically. "I decided I want to do my own records as if I were a vocalist, as if I were a singer with a band behind me. And instead of words, it's Dobro music, slide music, because the Dobro is so vocal-like. You can play a harmony line with a singer, and if you do it the right way, it sounds like somebody else is singing. So I thought, since there aren't words, the tunes will have to be interesting enough to carry the listeners along, to keep the imaginations working."

During the spring of 1987, Jerry and Mark appeared with Peter Rowan at the Wembley Festival in England. In the early 90's, Jerry teamed up with guitarists Albert Lee and Tal

Farlow, as part of a U.S. tour for the National Council of Traditional Arts. Jerry has also taken his brand of Dobro music around the world to various countries including Poland, Czechoslovakia and Ireland.

Jerry Douglas was named "Best Dobro Player" for five consecutive years in *Frets* magazine and was retired to their "Gallery of Greats" in 1985. He won a Grammy Award in 1983 for "Best Country Instrumental Performance" for his work as part of the New South, with J.D. Crowe, Ricky Skaggs, Tony Rice and Todd Phillips, for the track *Fireball*. In addition, he was nominated for the same award in 1986 and 1987. Between 1989 and 1993, he was the recipient of the "Speciality Instrument" Award every year from the ACM. He has recently gotten into producing other artists and one of his most memorable assignments was fellow Dobro player Sally Van Meter's 1991 album ***All in Good Time.*** Jerry can be seen each week as part of the American Music Shop band on the TNN show *American Music Shop.* In 1993, Jerry got together with guitarist Russ Barenberg and bassist Edgar Meyer to record the album ***Skip, Hop & Wobble***, for Sugar Hill. That same year, Jerry guested on the album by Russian Bluegrass band Kukuruza, entitled ***Crossing Borders.***

JIE

RECOMMENDED ALBUMS:

"Fluxology" (Rounder)(1978)
"Tennessee Fluxedo" (Rounder)(1983)
"Under The Wire" (MCA Master Series)(1986)
"Changing Channels" (MCA Master Series)(1987)
"Plant Early" (MCA Master Series)(1989)
"Skip, Hop & Wobble" (Sugar Hill)(1993) [With Russ Barenberg and Edgar Meyer]

RONNIE DOVE

(Singer, Songwriter, Guitar)
Date of Birth: **September 9, 1940**
Where Born: **Herndon, Virginia**
Married: **Unknown**
Children: **four**

Ronnie Dove is a Country music phenomenon in that while he has only had two hits on the Country charts, he has had 20 Pop hits. Remarkably, these songs have all been released on an independent label, as well.

Ronnie was born in Herndon, Virginia, but raised in Baltimore, Maryland. He grew up listening to the music of Hank Williams, Webb Pierce and Elvis Presley. Ronnie's first ambition was to follow in his father's footsteps and become a policeman. While still quite young, to help Ronnie raise money for a safety patrol, his father sponsored a Country music show featuring *Grand Ole Opry* star Ernest Tubb. Ronnie recalls his meeting with Tubb as being one of the most exciting events of his first nine years.

A few years later he was performing with a Rock vocal group in high school. His first job was working in an uncle's grocery store. Ronnie really set his sights on a music career while working as a machinist in the Coast Guard. To pass the time he would play and sing for his shipmates. Eventually they encouraged him to sing a song at a waterfront cafe in Baltimore, Maryland. One song later the owner offered him a job on his nights off. He was hired at $5.00 a night and began a career that would exceed his wildest dreams.

In 1964, he was signed with the independent Diamond label. His first recording, *Say You* (1964), was the first of an impressive roll of 20 hits on the Pop charts. Ronnie got the opportunity to meet another idol, Elvis Presley, while cutting *Say You.* Elvis was recording in another studio in the same building at the time. Ronnie's second hit, *Right or Wrong*, went Top 15. His second year with Diamond (1965) led to five more smash singles: *Hello Pretty Girl* (Top 60), *One Kiss for Old Time's Sake* (Top 15), *A Little Bit of Heaven* (Top 20), *I'll Make Your Dreams Come True* (Top 25) and *Kiss Away* (Top 25). The latter four songs were arranged by Ray Stevens. 1966 was also a good year for Ronnie, producing five more hits, all in the Top 30. He started the year with *When Liking Turns to Loving* (Top 20). This was followed by *Let's Start All Over Again* (Top 20), *Happy Summer Days* (Top 30), *I Really Don't Want to Know* (Top 20) and *Cry* (Top 20). The following year brought three more hits: *One More Mountain to Climb* (Top 60), *My Babe* (Top 50), both written and produced by Neil Diamond, and *I Want to Love You for What You Are* (Top 60).

By the end of 1967, Ronnie's incredible roll of hits was beginning to slow down, with his most successful record during that period being *Mountain of Love* (1968) (Top 70). Nearly all of Ronnie's hits on Diamond were produced by Diamond VP, Phil Kahl. In 1971, Ronnie signed with Decca Records and had two hits on the Country charts that both went Top 70: *Kiss the Hurt Away* (1972) and *Lilacs in Winter* (1973).

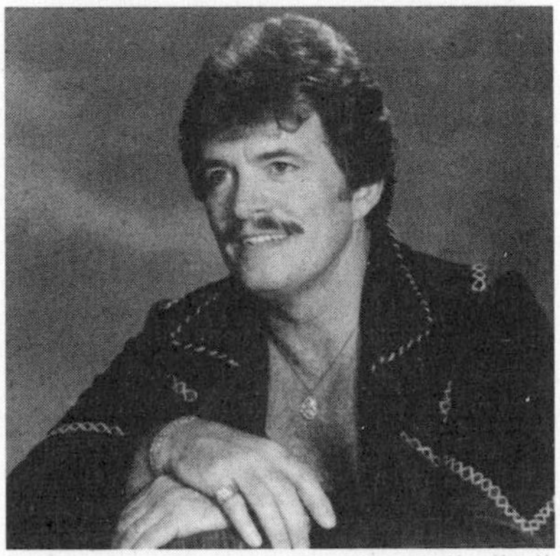

Say you, this is ***Ronnie Dove***

In 1975, Ronnie had a short-lived career with Melodyland Records, Motown's Country label. His first release, *Please Come to Nashville*, went Top 75, followed by *Things* (Top 25), the same year. In 1987, he re-signed with Diamond and released two more songs that went Top 80, *Heart*, followed by *Rise and Shine*, his final chart entry to date. Ronnie Dove has also appeared on the *Grand Ole Opry.* His television credits include the *Dick Clark Caravan of Stars, That Nashville Music, Nashville Now*, Merv Griffin and the Mike Douglas shows and *American Bandstand.* He is also a champion of causes he considers worthwhile. These include sponsorship of a golf tournament to help raise money for prisoners of war and military personnel missing in action, appearances in Johnny Lee's Pro-Am Celebrity Golf Classic, benefiting a home for the mentally handicapped in Lakeside, California, and performing at other benefits. His hobbies include golfing, swimming and woodworking. It is rare for an artist to have such an impressive list of hits on an independent label and perhaps Ronnie Dove's greatest contribution to the music industry is to prove that a major label isn't the only way to go. LAP

BIG AL DOWNING

(Singer, Songwriter, Piano)
Date of Birth: **January, 9, 1940**
Where Born: **Centralia, Oklahoma**
Married: **Unknown**
Children: **three**

Big Al Downing has had one of the most checkered careers in show business, with stardom always slightly out of reach, but he is one of the few black performers to foray across the musical spectrum of Disco, Pop, R & B, Gospel and Country.

Born in rural Oklahoma into a family of 12 children, Big Al spent his early childhood tending the horses and cattle his family raised, and singing with two brothers, his father, and a sister in a Gospel group. By the time he was 10, he was teaching himself to play on an old, upright piano that had 40 working keys. Four years later, he was performing at community functions and high school proms.

His great influence at this time was Fats Domino, and it was his impression of his idol doing *Blueberry Hill* that won him first prize at the local Coffeyville, Kansas, radio station. After the contest, Bobby Poe, a local singer who heard him play in the contest, asked him to join his band. Downing forfeited a basketball scholarship at Kansas State University and accepted Poe's offer. They played locally in Kansas, Oklahoma, in VFW halls and Country beer joints.

Big Al's break came when Country entertainer Wanda Jackson needed a back-up singer to tour with her and contacted Poe's band. While touring with Wanda, Big Al performed in all the west and midwestern states opening for Marty Robbins, Bobby Bare, Red Sovine, Pete Drake and Don Gibson. In California he played piano on one of Jackson's biggest recordings, *Let's Have a Party*, released in 1960, on which back-up was provided by Gene Vincent's Blue Caps. The single was an enormous hit in Japan and Europe, reaching No. 32 in the U.K. and Top 40 on the U.S. Pop chart.

After coming off the road, Big Al and others in the band left Oklahoma for Boston where they worked seven days a week and that included two jam sessions on Saturday and Sunday, from 1:00 p.m. until 1:00 a.m. for $90.00 a week. "That's what I really called payin' dues," recalled Downing in an earlier interview. From 1957 to 1964, Downing played with the band and had recordings released as a solo artist for White Rock, in 1958 and later Columbia and Carlton. His best effort was a cover of Marty Robbins' *Story of My Life*.

In subsequent years, Big Al embarked on tours of his own, traveling to England, Spain, Holland, Germany, Sweden, Isle of Malta, Libya, North Africa, Italy, France, Luxembourg, Greece, the Far East, Hong Kong, Singapore, Japan, the Philippines, Guam, Hawaii, and Thailand, where he played for the King.

During these overseas tours he played with Johnny Mathis, Dottie West, Lou Rawls, the Drifters and Fats Domino, his early idol. Domino recorded two songs Downing wrote, *Mary, Oh Mary* and *Heartbreak Hill*. 1973 brought a recording contract with Lenox Records, and the Top 80 Pop hit *You'll Never Miss the Water (Till the Well Runs Dry)*, a duet with Little Esther Phillips. Later, he signed with Warner Brothers.

In 1974, Al released a single, *I'll Be Holdin' On*, that made the Disco charts in America and Europe. Disco and Big Al Downing, however, were not meant to be. He had compiled a stockpile of his own songs which he presented to his producer at Warner Brothers, and Country was the consensus vote of what he did best. 1978 brought *Mr. Jones*, which charted in the Top 20, then *Touch Me (I'll Be Your Fool Once More)*, the following year which went Top 20. The song showcased his ability as a vocalist to soar, then drop to an emotional sill. The same year also produced *Midnight Lace*, charting in the 50's, and the flip-side, *I Ain't No Fool*, which reached the upper 70's. *The Story Behind the Story* charted the following year, reaching the Top 40 and then, *Bring it on Home* reached the Top 20.

Two years elapsed before he saw another hit, this time on the Team label. *I'll Be Loving You* went Top 50, followed by *Darlene*, which reached the lower 60s, both in 1982. The following year, *It Takes Love* went Top 40, followed by *Let's Sing About Love*, which peaked in the mid-60s. *The Best of Families* reached the Top 50 in 1984, and that year saw Al's final Team hit, *There'll Never Be a Better Night for Being Wrong* which only made the Top 80.

In 1987, Big Al signed with the Vine Street label which released *Oh How Beautiful You Are (To Me)* and *Just One Night Won't Do*, both which only reached the Top 70. Two years later he was signed with Door Knob Records and had the 1989 Top 100 hit, *I Guess By Now*, which was Al's only chart entree with that label.

While often compared to Charley Pride, Big Al feels this comparison is not correct. In an 80's interview he said, "When you hear Charley Pride sing, he often sounds white. When I sing there will be no way I'll be mistaken for a white. Besides, Charley sings a Honky-Tonk hillbilly style and I sing more Soul and Blues." As of 1988, Big Al was living in Massachusetts. LAP

RECOMMENDED ALBUM:

"Big Al Downing" (Team)(1983)

PETE DRAKE

(Steel Guitar, Dobro, Guitar, Record Producer, Music Publisher)

Given Name:	**Roddis Franklin Drake**
Date of Birth:	**October 8, 1932**
Where Born:	**Atlanta, Georgia**
Married:	**1. Rebecca (div.) 2. Rose Trimble**
Children:	**Johnny, Jacky Mason, Joyce, Judy, Jennifer, Janet, Lynn, Lori**
Date of Death:	**July 29, 1988**

If the sobriquets "Mr. Nice Guy" and "Renaissance Man" belong to any man in Country music, then they surely belong to Pete Drake, a consumate musician, record producer, music publisher and innovator.

Pete got his nickname when he was around age 3. The family neighbor had a pet pig named Pete and whenever the pig's name was called, Pete would appear. Pete's father was a Baptist minister. He held revival meetings almost every night and made Pete play the only two tunes he knew, *Jesus Loves Me* and *What a Friend We Have in Jesus*. By the time he was 15, his father died and the family had to move out of the church. He had to help his mother make the payments on their first house, by holding down three jobs while still at school.

He was turned on to steel guitar after hearing Jerry Byrd in 1950 and built his own pedal steel. Within a year, he was leading his own band, the Sons of the South, and playing with them on WLWA Atlanta and WTJH East Point, Georgia. The members of the band included a young Jerry Reed, Joe South, Doug Kershaw and Roger Miller (these two were in the army camp near Atlanta) and Jack Greene, who was on drums. According to Pete, they were terrible but packed in the crowd. Pete's other great influence at this time was Bud Isaacs.

Pete started to work for Wilma Lee and Stoney Cooper and moved with them to Nashville in 1959. At first, he tried to emulate the styles of Buddy Emmons and Jimmy Day, but gave it up to present his own stylings. For the first year and a half he starved, with just a few gigs from Marty Robbins and Don Gibson, before Roy Drusky and George Hamilton IV used him on sessions. He had been playing with Carl and Pearl Butler and had reverted to using C6 tuning. Roy pressured Owen Bradley to use him on a session. Roy's single *Anymore* and George's *Before the Day Ends* both went Top 5, in 1960. The word went round about Pete's skill, and as a result, he did twenty-four sessions in the next month.

During the 60s, Pete introduced the "talking guitar." This arose when he was watching some deaf neighbors and saw how they communicated. Then he saw Alvino Ray playing in a Kay Keyser movie and the idea gelled. He created the voice tube that has subsequently been used to good effect by Rock singer/guitarist Peter Frampton. The first recording that utilized it was Roger Miller's *Lock, Stock and Teardrop*, in 1963. The same year, Jim Reeves also used it on his recording *I've Enjoyed as Much of This as I Can Stand*. Pete used the talking guitar on 3,000 station identification messages.

In 1962, he cut his first album for Starday, ***For Pete's Sake***, using a standard pedal steel. This was followed by ***The Fabulous Steel Guitar Sound of Pete Drake***. A year later, Cumberland released ***Country Steel Guitar***.

Then in 1964, Pete was approached by Shelby Singleton and Jerry Kennedy to record a single, *Forever*, for Smash, a subsidiary of Mercury. After a slow start, the single took off and sold over a million, although it never charted Country. He followed up the single with the albums ***Forever*** and ***Talking Steel Guitar***.

Starday put out another album in 1965, ***The Amazing Incredible Pete Drake*** and Smash contributed ***Talking Steel & Singing Strings***. Pete owned the patent for the actuator that he used on ***Forever***.

Pete was largely instrumental in introducing the steel guitar into Rock and Pop music. For over 12 years, Pete worked on Elvis Presley sessions. He played on four albums by Bob Dylan: the 1968 album ***John Wesley Harding***, ***Nashville Skyline*** (1969), ***Self Portrait*** (1970) and ***Dylan*** (1973). In 1970, the media were excited to report that Pete had brought Ringo Starr to record in Nashville. Ringo was the first ex-Beatle to do this. The first thing Pete had to do when Ringo arrived was to take him to Ernest Tubb's Record Shop. Ringo's album ***Beaucoups of Blues*** also featured Charlie Daniels and Jerry Reed. A year later, Pete was featured on George Harrison's monster hit *My Sweet Lord*, for which Pete went to London for a week to record.

In 1970, Pete was inducted into the Walkway of Stars at the Country Music Hall of Fame. He received the "Super Picker" Award in 1975, 1976, 1977 and 1979.

Pete produced his favorite project in 1979. ***The Legend and the Legacy*** by Ernest Tubb remains one of the most remarkable recording projects ever undertaken. Remarkable, because it's an absolutely classic album, but also because it was put together without ET ever realizing that other Country music stars would be singing with him. It was released to coincide with his 65th birthday. It became Ernest Tubb's only Gold Album. Interestingly, Pete's brothers Jack and Bill were both members of the Texas Troubadours. His surprise for ET probably more than anything summed up the heart that Pete Drake had.

In 1982, Pete received a Grammy and a Dove Award as producer of B.J. Thomas' *Amazing Grace*. Pete was inducted into the International Steel Guitar Hall of Fame in 1986. He was part owner of Stop Records and First Generation Records. Over the years, he produced David Rogers, Johnny Bush, the Kendalls, B.J. Thomas, Ronnie Robbins, Freddy Weller, Bobby Vinton, Tommy James, Slim Whitman, Bjøro Håland, Boxcar Willie, Tracy Nelson, Leon Russell, Ernest Tubb, Melba Montgomery, Billie Jo Spears, George Harrison and Oak Ridge Boys.

Pete recorded sixteen of the *Grand Ole Opry* artists for First Generation. The albums were put out by Pete and then CBS picked them up for their record club. This was Pete's way of celebrating the years that he had as a sideman on the *Opry* and making sure that they weren't forgotten. He operated what he called the Drake School of Recording where he encouraged new artists. Among writers signed to his Window Music were Dottie West, Ed Bruce, Linda Hargrove and Pam Rose & Mary Ann Kennedy. He was also a great help to Sonny Throckmorton and turned Elvis on to Jerry Reed.

He had a great ability to spot a hit song. Sometimes he would take a song even if he didn't publish it and get a writer cut, because he was a nice guy. His other achievements are noteworthy. At one point, he was on 59 of the 75 singles in *Billboard*. In 1987, Pete received the Masters Award from the Nashville Entertainment Association, a SESAC "Special Achievement Honor," a NARAS "Appreciation" Award and a *Cash Box* "Instrumental" Award. Pete Drake performed on 118 Gold and Platinum albums and received several BMI and ASCAP song publishing awards for songs from his Drake Music Group.

During 1987, his health deteriorated. He was suffering with emphysema, heart trouble, diabetes and asthma. He moved to Florida for his health, but got bored because there were no studios there. Then he received his most valued award, his induction to the Steel Guitar Hall of Fame, and moved back to Nashville. He built a new studio in Berry Hill and re-opened his publishing company, ever looking for talent and "looking for the note on the steel that I haven't found." On July 29, 1988, the search ended, when Pete Drake died of complications from a lung disease.

Pete Drake left a legacy that no one has yet been worthy of taking on. His open door to talent has been replaced by "business." Most record company and publishing company executives could learn a lot from Pete's life. "Learn to play, get 'ears' but mostly get 'heart.'"

The unique ***Pete Drake***

RECOMMENDED ALBUMS:

"Forever" (Smash)(1964)
"Steel Away" (Canaan)(1968)
"The Pete Drake Show (Recorded Live from Frontier City)" (Stop)(1970)
"Golden Country Hits" (Cumberland) [Recorded as "Dean Dallas"]
Plus a whole slew of albums including the above named by Bob Dylan and recordings by Jim Ed Brown, Skeeter Davis, Roy Drusky, George Hamilton IV. Also check out records on the Stop and First Generation labels.

RUSTY DRAPER

(Singer, Songwriter, Guitar, Banjo, Impressionist, Actor)

Given Name:	**Farrell H. Draper**
Date of Birth:	**January 25**
Where Born:	**Kirksville, Missouri**
Married:	**1. Marcia Willsey (div.)** **2. Fay**
Children:	**Judy, John**

It was with one record, *Gambler's Guitar*, that Rusty Draper, known as "Ol' Redhead," went from unknown to cross-over star. In the 90's, however, his name is not spoken of despite having eleven Pop chart entries and six appearances on the Country chart.

Rusty's first glimmer of interest in the music business occurred when his father, Samuel C. Draper, who owned a local general store, presented him with a guitar at the age of 10. Two years later, young Rusty, by then dubbed "Freckles," was strumming his guitar and singing over the airwaves of WTUL Tulsa, on the *Cy Perkins Show*. It didn't hurt that Cy Perkins was in fact his uncle, Ralph Powell. It wasn't, however, a simple case of an undeserved nepotism, because within a short time Rusty landed another job on his own at WHO in Des Moines. There, he often took over for sports announcer Dutch Reagan, who would later become film star Ronald Reagan, and eventually President of the United States.

Next came another stint with his uncle in Quincy, Illinois, where he also worked with the Sons of the Ozarks, at the Congress Theater in Chicago. He also did some recording dates for RCA's Bluebird label, without success.

When Rusty was 18, he moved with his family to San Bernardino, California, having attended 18 high schools throughout the Midwest before receiving his diploma. Unable to find work, he became a Western Union messenger boy, and recalls that the highlight of his job was "delivering wires to Dorothy

Lamour's summer home where the butler would always tip me at least 50 cents."

Eager to return to show business, Rusty hocked his electric guitar to have enough money to make it to San Francisco, where he picked up pocket change, playing and singing in local bars. One of the bars where he performed was a place called The Barn, where he went to work for $45.00 a week. According to an oft repeated story, a chief petty officer in the Navy took a shine to Rusty's singing and refused to pay his $75.00 bar tab unless the owner hired Rusty to play there. Rusty got the job, the CPO paid his bill, new customers began to appear, and within a year, Rusty had quadrupled his salary and became a favorite with The Barn's patrons.

A year later Rusty landed a two-week job at The Rumpus Room. It was lucky in two respects: first, it turned into an eight-year gig, and gave him the opportunity to break into the big time and secondly, it was here he met his first wife Marcia Willsey, a statistician, whom Rusty recalls he fell in love with "at first sight." Two years later she agreed to marry him. Marcia became Rusty's manager and his career soon began to take off. He guested on the Patti Page, Ed Sullivan and Eddie Cantor shows, and hosted the *Arthur Godfrey Talent Scouts*. At one point, Rusty had the first sponsored TV show in San Francisco.

Marcia set up a tour for Rusty of the top clubs and theaters in the nation. She knew it was a gamble since he did not have a hit record, although he had just signed with Mercury Records. However, luck was with them and by January 7, 1953, one week into the tour, his *No Help Wanted* began to attract attention. In August, *Gambler's Guitar* zoomed to the million dollar sales figure, and peaked in the Top 10 on the Country charts, and made the Pop charts as well.

In 1955, Rusty had a memorable year with *Seventeen* making the Pop Top 20. It was followed by the Top 3 Pop hit *Shifting, Whispering Sands* and the year ended with *Are You Satisfied?*, which just failed to make the Top 10. During 1956 and 1957, Rusty charted Pop five more times, of which the most successful singles were *In the Middle of the House* (Top 20, 1956) and *Freight Train* (Top 10, 1957).

There were no more chart entries until 1960, when Rusty released his version of *Muleskinner Blues*, which didn't chart in the U.S., but made the Top 40 in Britain. However, the flip-side, *Please Help Me I'm Falling*, reached the U.S. Pop Top 60. The following year, *Signed, Sealed and Delivered* proved to be his final Mercury charted record, barely making the Pop Top 100.

By 1963, Rusty was signed to Monument Records and reached the Pop Top 60 with Willie Nelson's *Night Life*, his final Pop hit. Rusty returned to the Country charts, but his most successful release was the 1968 Top 60 *Buffalo Nickel*.

Rusty continued to play club dates, write songs, and make TV appearances. For seven years, he was known as the "Singing Emcee" at the Mel Hertz Club in San Francisco. His daytime musical series, *Swingin' Country*, ran for 26 weeks on NBC and he made guest appearances on *77 Sunset Strip* and *Rawhide*. It was reported in 1972 that he received a personal phone call from astronaut Gene Cernan telling him that the astronauts woke to his songs every morning on their trip to the moon.

Rusty Draper's final Country chart entry was *Harbor Lights*, in 1980 on KL Records, but it only reached the Top 90. LAP

RECOMMENDED ALBUMS:

"Something Old, Something New" (Monument)(1969)
"Rusty Draper's Greatest Hits" (Monument)
"Rusty Draper Sings Night Life" (Monument)
"Rusty Draper Plays Guitar" (Monument)
"Swingin' Country" (Monument)

DRIFTING COWBOYS BAND

Formed:	**July 14, 1949**
Original Nashville Members:	
Don Helms	**Steel Guitar, Vocals**
Bob McNett	**Guitar, Vocals**
Jerry Rivers	**Fiddle, Vocals**
Hillous B. Butrum	**String Bass**
Later Members:	
Cedric Rainwater	**String Bass**
Bobby Andrews	**String Bass, Lead Vocals**
Jimmy Heap, Jr.	**Drums**
Sammy Pruett	**Guitar**

The original Drifting Cowboys, formed in 1937, were the back-up band for Hank Williams. The group consisted of Smith "Hezzy" Adair (guitar), who was more like Hank's partner, Charley Mays (fiddle), Shorty Seals (string bass), Boots Harris (steel guitar) and Indian Joe Hatcher (guitar).

Don Helms (b. February 28, 1927, New Brockton, Alabama) joined in 1941 when he used to take his steel guitar to station WSFA Montgomery, Alabama, and publicize their regional schoolhouse shows and honky tonk dances. He left the band to work as a welder in the shipyards in Panama City, Florida. There he met Sammy Pruett (from Goodwater, near Birmingham, Alabama), who at the time was a so-so guitar player and Curly Corbin, a bass and guitar player. In 1943, Hank was again looking for musicians and hired all three. Except for a short period in the armed forces, in WWII and another period, when he joined another band (for more money) during Hank's time at KWKH's *Louisiana Hayride* (he re-joined Hank on the *Opry*), Helms was with Hank right up until Williams' death on January 1, 1953.

The bass player in the Drifting Cowboys was always the comedian dressed in baggy trousers. When Cannonball Nicholas, who was a part-time wrestler, played bass, he also acted as protector of the band and their instruments, making up with brawn what he lacked in ability.

At the end of WWII, Hank re-formed the Drifting Cowboys and Helms and Pruett returned to their old jobs, with Lum York coming in as bass player/funnyman. Bob McNett (b. October 16, 1925, Roaring Branch, Pennsylvania) had joined Patsy Montana on the *Louisiana Hayride* but just as the band broke up, he got the call to join Hank, playing lead guitar and emceeing. He was the only one of the band at Shreveport to go to Nashville.

Once in Nashville and on the *Grand Ole Opry*, Hank put the band back together and this line-up would be the one that would more or less carry on into the 90's. Jerry Rivers (b. August 25, 1928, Nashville, Tennessee) heard through the grapevine that Hank was forming the band. He was doing an early morning radio show, selling electronic parts, doing a show in the late afternoon and playing dances during the week and square dances each Saturday. So, he took his fiddle to WSM studios and asked Hank for a job. He had already passed up two opportunities to join the band in 1948, as he didn't want to leave Nashville. Hank played *Sally Goodin* and asked Jerry to play. Hank hired him there and then. Rivers recommended Hillous Butrum (b. April 21, 1928, Lafayette, Tennessee) to Hank as the bass player. Butrum had played the Opry since he was 16. Not one of the Drifting Cowboys was over 21.

When Butrum left in July, 1950 to join the Hank Snow Show, he was replaced by Howard Watts, who was better known as Cedric Rainwater, and shortly after McNett left and Sammy Pruett returned. Hank had nicknames for all the members. "Shag" was Don Helms, "Burrhead" was Jerry Rivers and "Mule" was Hillous Butrum. The line-up of Helms, Rivers, Pruett and Rainwater remained with Hank Williams until that fateful night in 1953.

Two singles were released by the Drifting Cowboys during 1953, *Corn Crib/Mud Hut* and *Canal Street Parade/Swing Shift Boogie,* and one in 1954, *Fish Tail/Rock Point*, before they called it a day. The band re-formed in 1960 and during 1968, worked a lot of dates with Hank Williams, Jr. It was interesting to note that when they played Little Rock in their opening week, they pulled the biggest audience since Hank Sr. had appeared there seventeen years earlier. MGM released an album in 1971, ***We Remember Hank Williams***. Then they went their separate ways.

In 1976, Butrum was working as talent coordinator on a film entitled *That's Country* with Lorne Greene. He decided to reunite the Drifting Cowboys for the project. The line-up was and is Don Helms, Jerry Rivers, Bob McNett, Bobby Andrews and Jimmy Heap, Jr. They then worked with Grant Turner on a series of radio shows. That year, three albums were released with the title of ***The Best of the Drifting Cowboys***, on Boll Weevil, Quality and Westwood. They also recorded an album for Epic, ***A Song for Us All***, which was produced by Charlie Daniels and featured Jim Owen. Two of the tracks made the bottom end of the Country charts during 1978, *Lovesick Blues* with Jim Owen on vocals and *Rag Mop*.

That year, the Drifting Cowboys appeared at the first Hank Williams Memorial Show from WWVA Wheeling, West Virginia. From their TV broadcasts with Ronnie Prophett on Canadian Broadcasting Company and Nashville's Fan Fare, which was aired on PBS, tracks were trawled to make up a 1979 album, ***Original Drifting Cowboys—Live***, on Westwood. They appeared at a special performance in March 1980, that honored Hank Williams' contribution to American music by the Smithsonian Institution. In 1982, Delta released the album ***One More Time Around***.

They continue to entertain in the U.S. and overseas and received a great welcome when they appeared at the International Festival of Country Music, Wembley, England, in 1982 and 1986. They have also toured Norway, Ireland, Germany and Switzerland, and have appeared with the New Orleans Pops Symphony Orchestra in a joint concert.

RECOMMENDED ALBUMS:

Listen to all Hank Williams tracks post July 14, 1949.
"We Remember Hank Williams" (MGM)(1971)
"A Song for Us" (Epic)(1977) [Features Jim Owen]
"Drifting Cowboys Tribute to Hank Williams" (Stoneway)(1979)
"The Original Drifting Cowboys—Live" (Westwood)(1971)
"Classic Instrumentals" (Delta)(1981)
"One More Time Around" (Delta)(1982)

*The legendary **Drifting Cowboys Band***

JIMMY DRIFTWOOD

(Guitar, Mouth Bow, Fiddle, Banjo)

Given Name:	**James Corbett Morris**
Date of Birth:	**June 21, 1907**
Where Born:	**Mountain View, Arkansas**
Married:	**Cleda**
Children:	**Bing, James (both dec'd.)**

In the late 1950's, a wave of "saga" or historical pseudo-Folk songs swept both the worlds of Country and Pop music. The most prominent lyric writer of these numbers was an Ozark schoolteacher who used the name "Jimmy Driftwood" and could boast of having six of his compositions on the *Cash Box* Top 40 at once, in September 1959, a rare feat by any standard. In addition, Jimmy sang a good traditional song himself and made several albums for RCA Victor and later for Monument Records. Driftwood further made use of his prominence to help develop a greater public awareness of and appreciation for the traditional music of the Arkansas Ozarks.

A native of Stone County, Arkansas, James Morris grew up with traditional music. His father, Neal H. Morris, a local singer of some renown, had been field-recorded by various folklorists. Jimmy used his own musical talents by playing at dances and made enough money working them to help finance his entering college. Like many teachers of his generation, he accumulated sufficient credits to obtain a teaching certificate, but continued taking courses until he finally obtained a degree in 1949.

Jimmy also farmed on a part-time basis. As a teacher he saw the educational value of using music and song as a means to instruct as well as to entertain. While advancing through the educational bureaucracy, Jimmy wrote songs for pedagogical purposes especially to emphasize historical events. Frequently he composed lyrics to existing tunes. For instance, *The Battle of New Orleans* used the old fiddling favorite *The Eighth of January* while *Soldier's Joy* borrowed the melody of the old hoedown of the same name.

In 1958, Jimmy signed with RCA Victor and recorded an album entitled ***Newly Discovered American Folksongs***, although most of them were re-compositions or newly written lyrics by Jimmy Driftwood (he spells it with a "y," although RCA Victor spelled it with an "ie"). One number, *Zelma Lee*, came directly or indirectly from an Uncle Dave Macon rendition of *Darling Zelma Lee* on Vocalion. *The Unfortunate Man* was a reworking of the oft-told song about the old maid and the burglar. The Kingston Trio's 1958 No.1 Pop chart hit recording of *Tom Dooley* had created a boom for Folk songs and Johnny Horton's 1959 cover of *The Battle of New Orleans* became a No.1 cross-over hit, setting off a similar fad for saga songs. Other Driftwood songs also became 1959 hits, most notably *Tennessee Stud* for Eddy Arnold, *Sailor Man* for Johnnie & Jack, *Soldier's Joy* for Hawkshaw Hawkins, and the Homer and Jethro parody *The Battle of Kookamonga*.

Driftwood's own 1959 recording of *The Battle of New Orleans* also made the Country charts, but never achieved the popularity of the Horton version. Jimmy had five more albums released on RCA Victor which found favor with fans beginning with ***The Wilderness Road***. Later albums were built around thematic concepts such as the Civil War or sea songs. Jimmy threw in a few authentic older lyrics like Henry Clay Work's *The Ship That Never Returned*, but most were his own compositions. At the height of his popularity, Jimmy appeared at Carnegie Hall and guested on the *Grand Ole Opry*, but his national following faded as the Folk music fad burned itself out in the mid-60's. Jimmy switched to Monument in 1963, subsequently cutting three albums for Fred Foster's firm.

As a crusader for Arkansas and Ozark music traditions, Jimmy helped make Mountain View something of a center for the music and culture. He organized the Rackensack Folksong Society and built Jimmy Driftwood's Barn, where he, his wife and local musicians displayed their skills. In the 70's, he cut a pair of albums on his own Rackensack label and released another which featured various Ozark musicians. In 1990, the aging Driftwood was injured in an auto wreck in Iowa, but by August 1992 at age 85 he still managed to render a song on the stage of his barn. IMT

RECOMMENDED ALBUMS:

"Newly Discovered American Folksongs" (RCA Victor)(1958)
"The Wilderness Road" (RCA Victor)(1959)
"The Westward Movement" (RCA Victor)(1960)
"Tall Tales in Song" (RCA Victor)(1960)
"Songs of Billy Yank and Johnny Reb" (RCA Victor)(1961)
"Driftwood at Sea" (RCA Victor)(1962)
"Voice of the People" (Monument)(1963)
"Down in the Arkansas" (Monument)(1964)
"The Best of Jimmy Driftwood" (Monument)(1966)
"Beautiful Buffalo River" (Rackensack)(1978)
"I Hear Your People Singing" (Rackensack)(1978)

ROY DRUSKY

(Singer, Songwriter, Guitar, Drums, Clarinet, Piano)

Given Name: **Roy Frank Drusky, Jr.**
Date of Birth: **June 22, 1930**
Where Born: **Atlanta, Georgia**
Married: **Bobbye Jean Stafford**
Children: **Roy Frank III, Tracy**

Roy is a case of a precocious talent. His mother, a church organist for over twenty years, tried to get him to take piano lessons without success, yet he started as a bandleader and drummer while still in kindergarten. However, this wasn't his first love. He was a natural athlete with a love for playing baseball (he was a second baseman). He did further the musical side of his life by eventually having lessons on both piano and clarinet.

He attended the University of Georgia and then enlisted in the U.S. Navy, where he remained for two years. While in the forces, he bought a guitar while his ship was docked in Seattle and eventually during his time aboard the USS *Toledo* in the Pacific, he graduated from being in the audience to entertaining his shipmates.

On leaving the service in 1950, Roy returned to academia and studied at Emory University, majoring in veterinary medicine. He was still a baseball nut and had a try-out with the Cleveland Indians. In 1951, Roy and some friends put together a group, the Southern Ranch Boys. It was nothing serious, but they decided to enter a talent contest sponsored by WEAS Decatur, Georgia. They won their own show on the station, which became a listener favorite. Roy was asked to become a deejay and announcer on the station. He was soon in demand and was given two TV shows on Atlanta's WLWA. He was also making personal appearances in the area.

In 1953, Roy signed with Starday, where the single *Such a Fool* caused sufficient stir for him to be signed to Columbia, in 1955. He moved to Minneapolis that year, to join KEVE as a deejay. He started headlining at the Flame Club, which was one of the most prestigious venues in the area. Word was getting out to Nashville about Roy and in 1958, Lester Vanadore, a friend of Faron Young's, heard Roy's song *Alone with You*. Faron recorded it and his single became a No.1 hit for him, staying in that position for 13 weeks and staying on the charts for seven months. Roy moved to Nashville and through the help of Vanadore and Hubert Long, met Owen Bradley. Roy was soon signed to Decca and his first release was *Just About that Time/Wait and See*.

In 1960, Roy had his first major hit with *Another*, a song written with regular co-writer Vic McAlpin. This made it to the Top 3 and stayed on the charts for nearly six months. He was invited to become a member of the *Grand Ole Opry*. In the summer of that year, he was back at that Top 3 level with another self-penned song, *Anymore*. He rounded off the year with the Top 30 duet with Kitty Wells, *I Can't Tell My Heart That*.

The following year, Roy consolidated his position as Country's finest up-and-coming male singer. *I'd Rather Loan You Out* and *Three Hearts in a Tangle* become a double-sided smash with the top side going Top 10 and the flip-side reaching the Top 3, where it stayed for four weeks and also crossed over to the Pop Top 40. He closed out the year with the Top 10 hit, *I Went out of My Way (To Make You Happy)*. Through 1958-60, Roy received three BMI Awards for *Alone with You* (1958), *Country Girl* (1959) and *Another* (1960). *Country Girl* had been another No.1 for Faron Young.

Before leaving Decca for Mercury, Roy had the Top 20 single *There's Always One (Who Loves a Lot)* and the Top 3 hit *Second Hand Rose*. He continued his winning ways at his new label with *Peel Me a Nanner* (Top 10, 1963), *Pick of the Week* (Top 15, 1964) and *(From Now on All My Friends Are Gonna Be) Strangers* (Top 10, 1965). While at Mercury, he recorded some duets with Priscilla Mitchell (Mrs. Jerry Reed). *Yes, Mr. Peters* was a No.1 single and without doubt, the most successful of a trio of chart duets.

By this time, he had taken over the Nashville hot seat for SESAC, the licensing organization, whom he helped set up. He was also producing other acts, including Pete Sayers (one of the few Englishman to make it in Nashville, and then leave it all behind and return home) and Brenda Byers. In 1965, Roy appeared in the movie *White Lightnin' Express*

The mellifluous voiced ***Roy Drusky***

and sang the title song. He later appeared in two other film efforts, *The Golden Guitar* and *Forty Acre Feud*. He was busy touring with his band, the Loners, and of course becoming a favorite on the *Opry*. Roy's successes during the second half of the 60's were *White Lightnin' Express* (Top 25, 1965), *Rainbows and Roses* (Top 20), *The World is Round* (Top 10) (both 1966), *If the Whole World Stopped Lovin'* (Top 15) and *New Lips* (Top 25) (both 1967), *Weakness in a Man* (Top 20), *You Better Sit Down Kids* (Top 30) and *Jody and the Kid* (Top 25) (all 1968) and *Where the Blue and Lonely Go* (Top 10), *My Grass is Green* (Top 15) and *Such a Fool* (Top 10) (all 1969).

During 1970, he seemed to be back at strength with three major successes via *I'll Make Amends* (Top 15), *Long Long Texas Road* (Top 5) and *All My Hard Times* (Top 10). During that year, Roy appeared at the Wembley Country Music Festival, through some insistence of the writer, but his backing band rather let him down. At this time, his major hits started to peter off and except for *I Love the Way That You've Been Lovin' Me* (Top 15, 1971), Neil Diamond's *Red Red Wine*

(Top 20), *The Last Time I Called Somebody Darlin'* (Top 25) (both 1972) and *Satisfied Mind* (Top 25, 1973), most of Roy's chart records were in the middle and lower levels.

In 1974, Roy moved over to Capitol, but that was only of interest because of his cover of Elton John's *Dixie Lily*, which hung around the charts for some three months but got no higher than the Top 50. Roy's move to Scorpion Records didn't yield any major successes.

During the 90's, Roy moved over to Country-Gospel and enjoyed something of a renaissance. His smooth style may no longer be in vogue, but Roy still possesses a fine voice. Roy Drusky is quite capable of turning out fine albums that his faithful admirers will continue to buy.

RECOMMENDED ALBUMS:

"Anymore with Roy Drusky)(Decca)(1961) [Re-packaged by Stetson UK in the original sleeve (1988)]
"The Pick of Country" (Mercury)(1964)
"All Time Country Hits" (Mercury)(1964)
"Love's Eternal Triangle" (Mercury)(1965) [With Priscilla Mitchell]
"Together Again" (Mercury)(1966) [With Priscilla Mitchell]
"Twenty Grand Country Hits" (double)(Mercury)(1969)
"All My Hard Times" (Mercury)(1970)
"This Life of Mine" (Capitol)(1976)
"Night Flying" (Scorpion)(1976)

DRY BRANCH FIRE SQUAD

Formed 1976
Current Members:
Ron Thomason Vocals, Mandolin, Guitar, Banjo, Fiddle, Drums
Mary Jo Leet Vocals, Guitar, Bass
Suzanne Thomas Vocals, Guitar, Piano, Autoharp, Old-Time Banjo
Dan Russell Vocals, Banjo
Charlie Leet Vocals, Bass, Guitar, Piano
Former Members:
John Baker (Guitar), John Carpenter (Bass), Dave Edmundson (Guitar), Dick Erwin (Bass), John Hisey (Banjo), Robert Leach (Banjo)

Despite a contemporary sounding name, the Dry Branch Fire Squad has emerged in the last decade and a half as one of the best and most tradition-orientated Bluegrass bands in the nation. Leader Ron Thomason has kept the group focused toward the more primitive forms of Appalachian sounds almost from the beginning with a particular emphasis on the word "lonesome." Thomason's carefully cultivated style of emcee work containing generous amounts of satire and parody also help make the D.B.F.S. one of the most admired acts on the festival circuit.

Ron Thomason (b. Ronald S. Thomason, September 5, 1944, Russell County, Virginia) grew up in Virginia and Ohio, the son of a Stanley Brothers fan. Regardless of his artistically-crafted hillbilly image—the accent is authentic—Ron obtained a B.A. degree from Ohio University in 1967. He has spent most of his working life as a high school English teacher/administrator. Having earlier learned to play mandolin and guitar, he settled in the Springfield area and joined a Bluegrass band whose members included Frank Wakefield. Later, he worked with Jack Casey and spent a year touring with Ralph Stanley's Clinch Mountain Boys.

Afterward, he joined Lee Allen's Dew Mountain Boys and then in 1976, he organized the Dry Branch Fire Squad. Other early members included John Baker (son of fiddler Kenny Baker) on guitar, Robert Leach on banjo and John Carpenter on bass. Mary Jo Leet (b. Mary Jo Dickman, March 28, 1947, Dayton, Ohio) did their bookings and in 1978, joined the band on quartets. From the beginning, they insisted on not being full-time musicians, in part, to make themselves less susceptible to commercial pressures. Traditionalists would hail this decision as wise, in that the group have maintained a high degree of musical integrity.

Dry Branch recorded three albums on custom labels in the late 70's before signing with Rounder. By this time, Dick Erwin and John Hisey, who would each spend roughly a decade with the group, joined on bass and banjo, respectively. The quintet of Thomason, Baker, Leet, Hisey and Erwin remained together through 1983 and cut three studio albums for Rounder, plus a live album on Thomason's Gordo label. Thomason's booklet, *Lonesome Is a Car on Blocks* (1979), sold along with records at their show dates, underscored what Bluegrass writer Art Menius described as their "quest for lonesome." During this time, the band increasingly became favorites on the festival scene, displaying a wide variety of traditional skills in their arrangements and undertaking a six-week tour of southern and eastern Asia, in addition to the U.S.A.

When John Baker departed from the group, former Hotmud Family member Dave Edmundson replaced him. This combination made three additional albums for Rounder and maintained a high degree of sound continuity. The current membership, which includes only Thomason and M.J. Leet from the earlier aggregation, is comprised of the latter's husband, Charlie Leet (b. Charles Emery Leet, September 25, 1944, Dayton, Ohio) on bass, newcomer Dan Russell (b. Danny Keith Russell, April 18, 1950, Highland County, Ohio) on banjo and Suzanne Thomas (b. January 6, Dayton, Ohio), another Hotmud Family alumnus, on guitar. To date, they have one Rounder cd to their credit.

Through their various personnel changes, the band has kept its edge on the lonesome sound, with a respect for the traditions exemplified by such musicians of earlier generations as G.B. Grayson and the first years of the Stanley Brothers. However, D.B.F.S. has not been afraid of adapting more contemporary material such as Jesse Winchester's *Brand New Tennessee Waltz*. Many of their songs, such as *Auction at the Home Place* and *Devil Take the Farmer*, reveal a social identitfication with the less fortunate segments of society.

Bluegrass favorites ***Dry Branch Fire Squad***

Offstage, Ron shows considerable pride in his Arabian horse, Saalo Supreme, who "wrote" the liner notes for one of the group's albums. Overall, one must credit Thomason's leadership for providing a cementing influence on the band, in much the same manner that Charlie Walker has done for the Country Gentlemen. As the founding generation of Bluegrass musicians, typified by Bill Monroe and Ralph Stanley, recedes from the scene in coming years, younger pickers led by such as those in the Dry Branch Fire Squad will continue to bear the torch of traditional influences. IMT

RECOMMENDED ALBUMS:

"Spiritual Songs from Dry Branch" (RT)(1977)
"Dry Branch Fire Squad" (RT)(1978)
"Dry Branch Fire Squad on Tour" (Gordo)(1979)
"Born to Be Lonesome" (Rounder)(1979)
"Antiques & Inventions" (Rounder)(1981)
"Fannin' the Flames" (Rounder)(1982)
"Good Neighbors & Friends" (Rounder)(1985)
"Golgotha" (Rounder)(1986)
"Fertile Ground" (Rounder)(1988)
"Long Journey" (Rounder)(1991)
Ron Thomason:
"The Mandolin & Other Stuff" (Kanawa)(1975)
"Branching Out" (Gordo)(1984)
"Strong at Heart" (Gordo)(1987) [With Bill Lowe]
Mary Jo Leet:
"I Love Bluegrass" (Go Go)(1989)

FRANK DUDGEON

(Singer, Guitar, Harmonica)

Given Name:	**Frank Charles Dudgeon**
Date of Birth:	**September 7, 1901**
Where Born:	**Jackson County, West Virginia**
Married:	**1. Mildred Kauffman (div.) 2. Irene Curylo**
Children:	**Gilbert, Lucille, Frank, Jr., Robert**
Date of Death:	**March 16, 1987**

Frank Dudgeon, who became known as the "West Virginia Mountain Boy," worked for nearly twenty years in radio. He sang his songs in a simple unadorned style to his own guitar accompaniment. Although he seldom recorded, his radio broadcasts and songbooks were quite popular and he counted automobile tycoon Henry Ford among his fans.

Born near Ripley, West Virginia, Frank Dudgeon was reared on a farm, but left it in his late teens for New Lexington, Ohio, where he worked for several years in a brick plant. After hearing and seeing Bradley Kincaid, who had won great acclaim as a singer of old ballads on WLS radio in Chicago, Dudgeon decided that the music of his own heritage was equally commercial. Frank secured a radio program at WAIU Columbus, Ohio. His popularity became even more widespread through stints at WWVA Wheeling and WMMN Fairmont, both in West Virginia. Staying on the move, he also appeared on stations in Fort Wayne, Indiana, and Greensburg and Uniontown, both in Pennsylvania. He did record sessions for the Starr Piano Company in 1932 and 1933, releasing a total of four singles on the Champion label at a time when record sales were very poor because of the Great Depression. Perhaps his most interesting song was a dog tribute lyric titled *Rattler*, that would later be made legendary through the work of Grandpa Jones.

West Virginia Mountain Boy ***Frank Dudgeon***

WWII disrupted Dudgeon's career as he went to work at a defense plant in Cleveland. After the war, he went to KLRA in Little Rock, Arkansas, where he worked for "Cousin Emmy" Carver's niece Alma "Little Shoe" Crosby on the *Arkansas Jamboree Barn Dance,* where he stayed for more than a year. During this time, Dudgeon started a record label called Frank's Folk Tunes and cut six songs for it with the help of his oldest son, Gilbert, on electric guitar. However, because of their limited distribution, they, too, are quite scarce. Early in 1947, he returned to WWVA and remained until the end of 1949, working as a featured act, then left music and went to work as an auto mechanic in Pittsburgh. He remained in that area for the rest of his life. IMT

RECOMMENDED ALBUMS:

The only recordings of Dudgeon to be available in recent years are a couple of tunes that appeared on the anthology Little Home in the West Virginia (Old Homestead) in 1985.

DAVE DUDLEY

(Singer, Songwriter, Guitar)

Given Name:	**David Darwin Pedruska**
Date of Birth:	**May 3, 1928**
Where Born:	**Spencer, Wisconsin**
Married:	**1. Jean (div.) 2. Marie**

Quite correctly Dave Dudley is described as the "Father of Truck Driving Songs" and the "High Priest of Diesel Country." His recording of *Six Days on the Road* remains one of the landmarks of Country music.

Dave grew up in Stevens Point, Wisconsin, and when he was11, his father bought him a guitar and Dave learned to play by watching Saturday performances at the local Fox Theatre. He played baseball for Gainsville Owls, Texas, and was a star pitcher. While recovering from an arm injury from a baseball game, he stopped by station WTWT Wausau and began playing along with the records. Vern Shepherd, the deejay, suggested he sing live on his show the following day. By 1950, he had gotten the morning show on the station called *The Texas Stranger Show*.

He then went on to head his own program on KBOK Waterloo, Iowa, DJing and singing. In 1952, he went to KCHA Charles City, Idaho, and played around other stations in the state. He set up various groups and then in 1953, formed the Dave Dudley Trio which lasted for seven years until he disbanded it. Shortly afterwards in Minneapolis, Dave formed the Country Gentlemen (not the Bluegrass band of the same name) and became resident at a new nightclub, The Gay Nineties. The group consisted of three other musicians and a female vocalist.

Dave was starting to get a fan base and as a result became a deejay on KEVE Minneapolis and was engaged as emcee at The Flame nightclub Country evening. On December 3, 1960, he was struck by a car while packing away his guitar after a late night gig at The Flame. He spent several months in hospital and was restricted to bed for six months and then only got back to work little by little.

In 1961, Dave had his first taste of chart success when *Maybe I Do*, on Vee, made the Top 30. A year later, he was into the Top 20, with his Jubilee release *Under Cover of the Night.* He decided to spend some money on making one more recording. He put down *Six Days on the Road*, a song written by Earl Greene and Carl Montgomery. Dave took it to a friend, Jim Madison, who supplied records for jukeboxes. Madison could see its potential. It was put out on Sona and then switched to Golden Wing. By the middle of 1963, Dave Dudley was a star. The single rose to the Top 3 and was just below the Top 30 on the Pop charts. He followed it up with the Top 3 hit *Cowboy Boots*.

In the fall of 1963, Dave was picked up by Mercury and they rounded off the year with another Top 10 success, *Last Day in the Mines*.

He put together a new four-piece band, the Roadruners, and from 1964, they ran with him all over the country, as the hits came building up. He had just one Top 10 hit that year, *Mad*, which like its predecessors, stayed on the charts for over 4 months. That year, he made his *Grand Ole Opry* debut.

1965 was also a sweet year for Dave Dudley. *Two Six Packs Away*, which has since become a classic, only reached the Top15, but any disappointment over that was quickly assuaged by the success of *Truck Drivin' Son-of-a-Gun* (Top 3) and *What We're Fighting For* (Top 5). The latter written by Tom T. Hall and the follow-up, Kristofferson's *Viet Nam Blues* (Top 15) were clear statements of endorsement for the U.S.'s presence in Vietnam.

Dave finished 1966 with further Top 15 hits, *Lonelyville* and *Long Time Gone*. The following year presented successes in the shape of *My Kind of Love* (Top 15), *Trucker's Prayer* (Top 25) and *Anything Leaving Town Today* (Top 15). He then seemed to get a second wind in 1968 starting with the Top 10 single *There Ain't No Easy Run* and continuing with *I Keep Coming Back for More* (Top 15) and *Please Let Me Prove (My Love for You)* (Top 10). The following year produced two big hits, *One More Mile* (Top 15) and the title track from his album ***George (and the North Woods)*** (Top 10).

His big success in 1970 was also his first and only No.1, *The Pool Shark*, which stayed on the charts for 4 months. His next two records were *This Night (Ain't Fit for Nothing But Drinking)* (Top 20) and *Day Drinkin'* (a Top 25 duet with Tom T. Hall). During the period 1971-73, Dave had major hits with *Listen Betty (I'm Singing Your Song)* (Top 15), *Comin' Down* (Top 10) and *Fly Away Again* (Top 10) (all 1971), *If It Feels Good Do It* and *You've Gotta Cry Girl* (both Top 15, 1972) and *Keep on Truckin'* (Top 20, 1973). He recorded one more duet, this time with Karen O'Donnell, *We Know It's Over*, but it only made the Top 40, in 1973.

Father of Truck Driving songs, ***Dave Dudley***

In 1973, Dave moved over to Rice Records and without major company backing, his success rate dropped. By 1975, he was back with a major label, United Artists. He had two reasonable hits with them: *Fireball Rolled a Seven* (Top 25) and *Me and My Ole C.B.* (Top 15), both in 1975. By 1978, he was back recording for Rice and then in 1980, he released another classic, *Rolaids, Doan's Pills and Preparation H*, which only reached the Top 80, but it has gone on to personify the truckers' view on life. Co-written by his wife, Mary Ann Dudley, who has written much of Dave's material, it appeared on his Sun Records album ***King of the Road***, which was pressed on gold vinyl. Likewise, Sun gave the gold treatment to two other 1980 albums of Dave's, ***Interstate Gold*** and the duet album with Charlie Douglas, ***Diesel Duets***.

Dave was given a solid gold security card by the Nashville local of the Truckers' Union in appreciation of his musical services on behalf of truckers. He has also received BMI Awards for *Cowboy Boots*, *Last Day in the Mines*, *Mad* and *Two Six Packs Away*. During 1989, Dave could be found recording for the Portland label.

Dave Dudley has a loyal following in Australia and Europe and his records still sell in Germany, Switzerland, Austria, Holland and Norway.

RECOMMENDED ALBUMS:

"Dave Dudley's Greatest Hits" (Mercury)(1965)
"Dave Dudley's Greatest Hits Vol. 2" (Mercury)(1968)
"George (and the North Woods)" (Mercury)(1969)
"The Pool Shark" (Mercury)(1970)
"Seventeen Seventy-Six (1776)" (United Artists)(1976)
"Diesel Duets" (Sun)(1980) [With Charlie Douglas]
"King of the Road" (Sun)(1980)

ARLIE DUFF

(Singer, Deejay)

Given Name:	**Arleigh Elton Duff**
Date of Birth:	**March 28, 1924**
Where Born:	**Jack's Branch nr. Warren, Texas**
Married:	**Nancye Anne White**
Children:	**Kelly O'Neal, Casey Scott, Rebecca Jo**

In 1953, schoolteacher and deejay Arleigh Duff became Country star Arlie Duff. His self-penned song *You All Come*, was coming through the airwaves and becoming a Top 10 hit for 10 weeks. The song earned him a BMI Award. However, Arlie would never repeat this and returned to playing other people's songs.

Arlie was a highly intelligent man who had attended Stephen F. Austin State College, Nacogdoches, Texas, between 1946 and 1951 and graduated with both B.S. and M.S. degrees. He taught school until his climb up the dizzy heights of stardom. He provided Starday with their first big record with *You All Come*. By 1954, he was at WFAA *Saturday Nite Shindig* out of Dallas. From there he appeared on ABC-TV's *Ozark Jubilee*, KWKH's *Louisiana Hayride*, the *Grand Ole Opry* and KOGT Orange, Texas.

That year, Arlie had moved to Decca and he produced such classic recordings as *Courtin' in the Rain* (1954) and *I Dreamed of a Hill-Billy Heaven* (1955) but neither made the charts. With the former, Arlie came up against T. Texas Tyler, who had a Top 3 hit with it, and with the latter, he was steamrollered by Eddie Dean with his Top 10 version.

DUKE OF PADUCAH, The

(Singer, Songwriter, Tenor Banjo, Comedy)

Given Name:	**Benjamin Francis Ford**
Date of Birth:	**May 12, 1901**
Where Born:	**De Soto, Missouri**
Married:	**Unknown**
Date of Death:	**June 20, 1986**

Benjamin "Whitey" Ford, best known as a comedian, experienced a lengthy career in show business. Over the decades, he graced the stage of medicine shows, vaudeville, the *National Barn Dance*, helped found the *Renfro Valley Barn Dance* and ultimately, he came to the *Grand Ole Opry*. Whitey immortalized the closing of his stage act and comedy routines with the memorable line, "I'm goin' back to the wagon, boys, these shoes are killing me."

A native of De Soto, Missouri, Ford spent most of his early years in Little Rock,

Whitey Ford, the ***Duke of Paducah***

Arkansas, where he was brought up by his grandmother. He joined the Navy in WWI, during which time he learned to play tenor banjo. Afterward, he organized a Dixieland musical combo known as Benny Ford and His Arkansas Travellers. For some years he worked medicine shows and the vaudeville stage. Whitey made his radio debut at KTHS Hot Springs, Arkansas, in 1924. Later, he toured on the most prestigious of all vaudeville circuits, the Keith-Albee theater chain, as a member of Otto Gray's Oklahoma Cowboys. With the deepening of the Great Depression, he turned increasingly to radio, working as a comedian and emcee with Gene Autry at WLS Chicago. At this locale, he took the stage name of Duke of Paducah, a rube-type character who typically appeared in a suit too small and button shoes, pretending to be something more of a sophisticate than he was. Other jokes centered on the Duke's "big fat wife."

Ford left Chicago in 1937, with John Lair and Red Foley, going to WLW Cincinnati, where he appeared on the network show *Plantation Party* and Lair's *Renfro Valley Barn Dance.* Together with Red's brother Cotton, the four began constructing the "big barn" at Renfro Valley to become the show's permanent home base in 1939. The Duke and the Foleys soon sold their interest in the show to Lair. Whitey Ford then came to the *Grand Ole Opry*, making his debut on September 19, 1942. He remained an *Opry* regular through 1959, endearing himself to audiences with his brand of rural comedy. In those days, the Duke even devised his own coat of arms containing two ears of corn, a pair of button shoes, and a wagon. Thereafter, he toured in both large and small package shows. Although noted primarily for his comedy, he usually played a tenor banjo tune or two during his stage act.

Like other Country comedians of his era, the Duke recorded sparingly, although more than his contemporary Rod Brasfield. He appeared on the fifty-two transcribed Royal Crown Cola shows with Roy Acuff in 1953. In 1961, the Duke cut an album of his humorous monologues for Starday and in 1963, he re-created the line of a side show, a fair midway, and a medicine show barker with assistance of some guest vocalists on masters extracted from the Starday files.

In later days, the Duke developed some serious talks as an after-dinner speaker on such subjects as *You Can Lead a Happy Life*, and even talked to college groups. He also published a book entitled *Funneee* (1980) that contained many of his jokes. Pleasant and well-liked by fellow entertainers and noted for his generosity to charitable causes, Ford fought a losing battle with cancer in his last years. Although confined to a nursing home, he maintained cheerful spirits to the end, giving copies of his picture and book to those who came to visit and entertain. IMT

RECOMMENDED ALBUMS:

"Button Shoes, Belly Laughs and Monkey Business" (Starday)(1961)
"At the Fair" (Starday)(1963)

JOHNNY DUNCAN

(Singer, Songwriter, Guitar)

Given Name:	**John Richard Duncan**
Date of Birth:	**October 5, 1938**
Where Born:	**Dublin, Texas**
Married:	**1. Betty Fisher (div.)**
	2. Connie Smith (not the singer)
Children:	**Angela (Anje), Lezlie, Lori, John Isaac**

For a while during the middle 70's through the beginning of the 80's, Johnny Duncan was one of the hottest acts in town. In 90's parlance, he would be called a "hunk." Standing over 6'4", he is a straight-ahead, no-nonsense Country singer.

Johnny was born on a farm into an illustrious musical family. His cousins are Jimmy Seals (of Seals and Crofts fame) and Dan Seals. He was taught to play guitar by his mother, Minnie, and along with her, his cousins and his uncle, fiddler Ben Moroney, Johnny formed a band that played small dance venues in Texas. His early icons were Merle Travis and Chet Atkins, and he hoped to be a guitarist and emulate them.

Johnny studied English at Texas Christian University and it was here that he met his wife and married her. During 1959, Johnny moved to Clovis, New Mexico, where he became a part of the Norman Petty operation. Petty had become known for his studio work with Buddy Holly. Johnny spent three years in Clovis but Petty attempted to record him as a Pop star and even took him to London, England to record, backed by banks of strings.

For a while, Johnny was a deejay on WAGG Franklin, Tennessee, before moving to nearby Nashville. There, he did a number of jobs outside the music industry including bricklaying. He appeared on Ralph Emery's early morning TV show on WSM in 1966, when he was spotted by Don Law, the veteran Columbia Records producer, who signed him to the label. Law initially put Johnny with Frank Jones, as producer.

Johnny reached the Top 60 with his 1967 release *Hard Luck Joe* and by 1968, *To My Sorrow* had given him a Top 50 hit. However, it was at the end of 1968 that he got close to the Top 20 with a duet with June Stearns, *Jackson Ain't a Very Big Town.* Columbia tried Bobby Goldsboro and Bob Montgomery as producers in an attempt to elevate his success level, but in the period 1969 through 1970, only occasional records rose above the middle and lower chart positions. These were *When She Touches Me* (Top 30, 1969), *You're Gonna Need Me* (Top 40) and *Let Me Go (Set Me Free)* (Top 30) (both in 1970). From 1969 to 1972, Johnny was a part of Charley Pride's roadshow.

Ace producer Billy Sherrill took over the reins and then Johnny's chart placings began to improve. *There's Something About a Lady* in 1971 went Top 20 and was followed by the Top 40 *One Night of Love*. Johnny wrapped up the year with the Top 15 *Baby's Smile, Woman's Kiss*. 1972 produced *Fools*, a Top 20 hit, and in 1973 Johnny had his first Top 10 record, *Sweet Country Woman.* He followed this up with *Talkin' with My Baby*, which made the Top 20. After he left Charley Pride, Johnny sang in a dinner lounge in Bowling Green, Kentucky.

In 1974, the steam seemed to go out of Johnny's recording career. He even asked Columbia to release him from his contract. The label asked for one more single. Along came *Jo and the Cowboy* which featured an un-credited, unknown Janie Fricke and was written by Johnny and Larry Gatlin. The record made the Top 30 and although the follow-up, *Gentle Fire,* bombed, in 1976, his career suddenly took off.

His next three singles benefited from the vocal harmonies of the still uncredited Janie Fricke. *Stranger*, a song written by Kris Kristofferson, went Top 5 and stayed on the charts for five months. Johnny completed the year with his first No.1, *Thinkin' of a Rendezvous*. When Johnny appeared at the *Grand Ole Opry* singing *Stranger*, he received a tumultuous reception.

1977 was a vintage year for Johnny. He started with another No.1, *It Couldn't Have Been Any Better,* and then had a Top 5 hit with *A Song in the Night*. The final hit for the year was a duet with Janie Fricke (now named), the old Jay and the Americans hit *Come a Little Bit Closer.* It went Top 5 and not only was Johnny on a roll, but it also launched Fricke as a major star.

In 1978, Johnny had another chart topper with *She Can Put Her Shoes Under My Bed (Anytime)* and followed up with *Hello Mexico (And Adios Baby to You)*, which went Top 5. Johnny's 1979 hits both went Top 10 and were *Slow Dancing* and *The Lady in the Blue Mercedes.*

However, come the 80's a decided shift of record fortune happened. All four of his 1980 releases only made the Top 20. They were *Play Another Slow Song*, *I'm Gonna Love You Tonight (In My Dreams)*, *He's Out of My Life*, another duet with Janie Fricke (which had been recorded by Michael Jackson as *She's Out of My Life*) and *Acapulco*. The following year, *All Night Long* could only make the No.40 slot and then he was gone.

He re-appeared on the Pharaoh label in 1986, but by then new heroes and new hunks had arrived and *The Look of a Lady in Love* and *Texas Moon* only made it to the lower area of the chart.

RECOMMENDED ALBUMS:

"The Best of Johnny Duncan" (Columbia)(1976)
"Johnny Duncan's Greatest Hits" (Columbia)(1978)
"In My Dreams" (Columbia)(1980)
"Nice 'n' Easy" (Columbia)(1980) [Features Janie Fricke]
[All feature tracks with Janie Fricke]

Popular Country music star ***Johnny Duncan***

TOMMY DUNCAN

(Singer, Songwriter, Piano)

Given Name: Thomas Elmer Duncan
Date of Birth: January 11, 1911
Where Born: Hillsboro, Texas
Married: Marie
Children: Unknown
Date of Death: July 25, 1967

Tommy Duncan has become synonymous with Bob Wills. For many years, he was the vocalist with the Light Crust Doughboys and the Texas Playboys. Yet, he came to the band as a Blues singer rather than a Country one.

Around the time that the Light Crust Doughboys recorded *Nancy Jane* and *Sunbonnet Sue* for Victor, W. Lee O'Daniel, the progenitor of the group, ruled that they were not to play any more dances. This created a difference of opinion between O'Daniel and Wills. Milton Brown, then the vocalist with the group, decided to quit over O'Daniel's edict.

Wills auditioned sixty-seven singers and lighted upon Tommy Duncan. Wills asked Duncan to sing *I Ain't Got Nobody*, as his audition piece. It seems that because he was such a good singer, Wills chose to overlook his background in Blues. He possessed a fluid baritone voice that was equally at home with smooth ballads and yodeling Blues.

When Wills was fired in 1933 by O'Daniel for being drunk and missing broadcasts, most of the band moved with him to Waco, with Tommy Duncan handling vocals and piano. The new band was initially known as Bob Wills and his Playboys, but by the time they were broadcasting over WKY in Oklahoma City, they had become Bob Wills and his Texas Playboys. O'Daniel, using his influence, got their show canceled after less than a week and on February 9, 1934, they started broadcasting on KVOO Tulsa, where they stayed for the next twenty-four years.

When the band moved to Tulsa, Duncan gave up the piano chores to Alton Stricklin. On April 16, 1940, the band recorded the song that would be forever associated with them, *San Antonio Rose*. It had been recorded as an instrumental back in 1938, but this time, Duncan added his mellifluous tones. A year later, Tommy appeared with the band in the movie *Go West Young Lady*.

Duncan remained with Wills until 1942, when he announced that he was joining the Army and fighting the Nazis and within a few days he had enlisted. Then other members of the band followed his example. By Christmas 1941, the band was disintegrating.

At the end of hostilities, Duncan returned to the Wills fold. He stayed with the Texas Playboys until 1948, when he decided to put his own band together. The Western All-Stars comprised several of the Texas Playboys and they recorded and toured during 1948-1949. They had one major hit, in 1949, when their Capitol recording *Gamblin' Polka Dot Blues* rose to the Top 10 on the Country charts. Tommy had first recorded this Jimmie Rodgers song with Bob Wills in 1938.

Over the next decade, Tommy recorded for Intro with the Miller Brothers Band and for Coral as a solo. In the mid to late 50's he recorded the occasional single for Cheyenne, Award and Fire. In 1960, Duncan rejoined Wills to record a series of albums for Liberty Records. By then the era of the big band had all but gone, but the albums produced during 1960-1961 (see below) are a lasting monument to the greatest association in Western Swing. After 1961, Tommy toured, usually using a support or house band to back him.

Tommy Duncan was an excellent songwriter and many of his compositions were Texas Playboy hits. Among his songs were *Time Changes Everything*, *Good Old Oklahoma*, *Stay a Little Longer*, *New Spanish Two Step* (a No.1 in the Country charts for an incredible 16 weeks and a top 20 Pop hit in 1946), *Bubbles in My Beer* (a hit in 1948), *Cindy* and *Take Me Back to Tulsa*.

Tommy released a single, *I Brought It on Myself/Let Me Take You Out*, in 1966, on Smash. In July 1967, Tommy Duncan suffered a heart attack and died.

RECOMMENDED ALBUMS:

"Mr. Words & Mr. Music" (Liberty) [With Bob Wills]
"A Living Legend" (Liberty) [With Bob Wills]
"Hall of Fame" (Liberty) [With Bob Wills]
"Together Again" (Liberty) [With Bob Wills]
"The Very Best of Bob Wills and the Texas Playboys Featuring Tommy Duncan" (Liberty UK) (1984) [Culled from the Liberty albums above]
"The Golden Era" (double)(Columbia)(1987) [Bob Wills and his Texas Playboys] [An excellent collection of unenhanced material recorded 1936-46 and put together by Bob Pinson and Michael Brooks]

UNCLE ECK DUNFORD

(Fiddle, Guitar, Singer, Comedy)

Given Name: Alex or Aleck Dunford
Date of Birth 1878
Where Born: Carroll County, West Virginia
Married: Callie Frost
Date of Death: 1953

Uncle Eck Dunford played fiddle for Ernest Stoneman and his Dixie Mountaineers. During this time, he received an individual contract with Victor and recorded a few songs, several humorous monologues and appeared in skits which featured his unique (and likely archaic) speaking voice. These skits and stories mark him among the first Country music comedians.

Dunford was born in Carroll County, West Virginia. Oral tradition has it that he was an illegitimate child. Be that as it may, Eck learned the skills of photography and was considered by his contemporaries in the Blue Ridge to have an above average education. Among other things, he could quote Shakespeare and Burns with seeming authority. In 1908, he married Callie Frost, giving his age as 30 on his marriage license application. This nuptial drew him into the extended Frost family circle that Ernest Stoneman would also enter a decade later. Unfortunately, Eck's bride died in 1921 and by all accounts left him a lonely man who sought solace in the company of family musicians and their children. He lived in a little cabin on Ballard Branch about a mile from the town of Galax and about the same distance from the Stoneman home.

Eck played a fine fiddle, and also the guitar, but his droll manner of speaking marked him as a singular individual, even in the mountain community where he lived. Once he advised an aspiring vocalist to never try singing faster than he talked. Dunford sang numbers that illustrated his dry humor, such as *Old Shoes and Leggin's*, but his monologues with their amusing vignettes of mountain life are cultural treasures. These include such tales as *My First Bicycle Ride*, *The Savingist Man on Earth* and *The Taffy Pulling Party*, all on Victor. He is also heard to good advantage on such skits as *Old Time Corn Shucking*, *Possum Trot School Exhibition* and *Serenade in the Mountains*, as well as on the Ernest Stoneman-Irma Frost rendition of *The Mountaineer's Courtship*.

After Ernest Stoneman left Galax in 1932, Dunford began a musical association with the Ward Family. With the Wards and as a member of the Ballard Branch Bogtrotters, he recorded for the Library of Congress, and in 1940, they even played on network radio. From 1935 onward, Dunford was a familiar figure at the Galax Fiddler's Convention. Kahle Brewer recalled that Dunford was quite poor in his old age and sold pencils on the streets in Galax for sustenance. Dunford remained a revered figure among local musicians. At the August 1953 Galax Convention, all participants and audience observed a moment of silence in Uncle Eck's memory, as he had passed away a few weeks earlier. The cover of the album featuring highlights of the 1978 convention contains a photo of his cabin home, which still stands on Ballard Branch.

IMT

(See also Ernest Stoneman, Stonemans, The)

HOLLY DUNN

(Singer, Songwriter, Guitar, Drums)
Given Name: Holly Suzette Dunn
Date of Birth: August 22, 1957
Where Born: San Antonio, Texas

No sooner had she left college than Holly was on a run to success. She was helped by the fact that her brother, Chris Waters, was already established as a Nashville songwriter and with her own natural talent as a performer and songwriter, she soon became an overnight success.

The daughter of a Church of Christ preacher, Holly was influenced by the music of Joni Mitchell, Jackson Brown and Carole King. From 1975 to1976, she was the lead singer with a high school group called the Freedom Folk. They represented Texas at the Bicentennial celebrations at the White House, and performed at concerts and on TV throughout the South. Holly was also a member of the Hilltop Singers, at Abilene Christian University, a USO tour group. In 1978, Christy Lane recorded *Out of Sight, Not Out of Mind*, a song Holly had written with her brother.

After graduating from college, Holly moved to Nashville, where her brother was now established as a songwriter. She worked at various jobs and then began singing lead or back-up on demos for music publishers. Holly was signed as a full-time songwriter with CBS Songs (where Chris was also signed) and filled in as a receptionist.

When the new label MTM Records came to Nashville in 1984, producer Tommy West offered Holly Dunn a contract as a songwriter and a performer when the label got going in 1986. By this time, Holly had written or co-written *I'm Not Through Loving You Yet* (Louise Mandrell, Top 10, 1984), *An Old Friend* (Terri Gibbs, 1984), *True Blue* (Sylvia, 1985), *That Old Devil Moon* (Marie Osmond, 1985) and *Daddy's Hands* (the Whites, 1985). Holly had amassed her songs during the two-year period between signing to MTM and laying down tracks for her debut album, ***Holly Dunn***. Holly had already released two singles in 1985, *Playing for Keeps* and *My Heart Holds On*, which had entered the Country chart Top 70. These were followed in 1986, by *Two Too Many* and her first Top 10 record, her version of *Daddy's Hands*, both in 1986. Holly had originally written this song for her daddy, as a Father's Day present. That year, Holly was named "Top New Female Vocalist" by the ACM in 1986 and she received two Grammy nominations, one for "Best Country Vocal Performance, Female" and one for "Best Country Song" for *Daddy's Hands*.

Country star ***Holly Dunn***

Holly started off 1987 with a duet single, *Face in the Crowd*, with Michael Martin Murphey from Murphey's ***Americana*** album, that went Top 5 and was Grammy nominated. Her next album was ***Cornerstone,*** also produced by Tommy West, and from that came *Love Somebody Like Me* (Top 3), which Holly wrote with Radney Foster and *Only When I Love* (Top 5). That year, the CMA voted Holly the prestigious "Horizon Award."

Holly started off 1988 with another Top 10 single, *Strangers Again*. She then released her third album, ***Across the Rio Grande***. This album marked Holly's producing debut and from here on, she produced all her own albums in tandem with brother, Chris. Most of the material on this and future albums would be written by the two of them with Tom Shapiro. However, the first single, *That's What Your Love Does to Me*, was written by Chick Rains and Bill Caswell and reached the Top 5. That year, she was named one of three BMI "Songwriters of the Year."

However problems were looming at MTM and when the company imploded in 1988, Holly's single *(It's Always Gonna Be) Someday* was left stranded in the Top 15. Holly then set off on an extensive tour and for 12 months, worked the country from coast to coast.

Before the year was out, she had signed to Warner Brothers Records. Her debut album on the label, ***The Blue Rose of Texas,*** yielded her first No.1, *Are You Gonna Love Me*. This was followed by the Top 5 hit, *There Goes My Heart Again*. She started off 1990 with the Top 25 *Maybe*, a duet with Kenny Rogers, taken from Kenny's album ***Something Inside So Strong***. Her next single, *My Anniversary for Being a Fool*, only reached the Top 70, but Holly came back strongly with the No.1 hit, *You Really Had Me Going*.

Her 1991 singles failed to reach the heights and *Heart Full of Love* only made it to the Top 20, while *Maybe I Mean Yes* only reached the Top 50. In 1991, Warner Brothers released Holly's compilation, ***Milestones: Greatest Hits*** album.

There had already been an influx of outside material on ***Heart Full of Love*** and this continued on Holly's 1992 album, ***Getting It Dunn***. In addition, Paul Worley was drafted in to produce. The three singles that charted in 1992, *No Love Have I, As Long As You Belong to Me* and *Golden Years*, all failed to ignite the radio stations and by 1993, Holly was looking for a new label. JAB

RECOMMENDED ALBUMS:

"Holly Dunn" (MTM)(1986)
"Cornerstone" (MTM)(1987)
"Across the Rio Grande" (MTM)(1988)
"The Blue Rose of Texas" (Warner Brothers)(1989)
"Heart Full of Love" (Warner Brothers)(1990)
"Milestones: Greatest Hits" (Warner Brothers)(1991)
"Getting It Dunn" (Warner Brothers)(1992)

Ronnie Dunn refer BROOKS & DUNN

SLIM DUSTY

(Singer, Songwriter, Guitar, Steel Guitar, Fiddle)

Given Name:	**David Gordon Kirkpatrick**
Date of Birth:	**June 13, 1927**
Where Born:	**Kempsey, Australia**
Married:	**Joy McKean (m. 1951)**
Children:	**Anne, David**

Slim Dusty is a phenomenon in Australian Country music. Everyone in Australia has heard of him and he is the proud possessor of the M.B.E. (Member of the Order of the British Empire), which is a citation awarded by the head of the British Commonwealth, H.M. Queen Elizabeth II, for distinguished service. All of his 80 albums are still available and he has been the subject of *This is Your Life* and a documovie, *The Slim Dusty Story*.

Born on Friday the 13th, the son of David (known as "Noisy Dan" and "Davey Kirk") and Mary Kirkpatrick, Slim was raised on a dairy farm at Nulla Nulla Creek, just about 300 miles north of Sydney, New South Wales. As a boy, he listened to old 78s of Jimmie Rodgers, Gene Autry, Vernon Dalhart and Carson Robison, but it was when he heard *The Drunkard's Child* being sung by an aborigine that he switched his mind to performing. When he was 11, he called himself by the good Country name of Slim Dusty. By the time he was 12, he had written his first song, *The Way the Cowboy Died*. At 14, he forced his way into Radio 2KM in Kempsey and made his first broadcast. A little while later, he started his recording career by paying for his own session. After much traveling back and forth to Sydney, he received a letter from Columbia, on October 18, 1946, offering him a recording session. He was paid $15 for recording six sides, providing he forfeited the royalties. The sides were released on Regal-Zonophone and he has been with the same label ever since (it is now known as EMI Records).

In 1950, he moved to Sydney and became a regular on Tim McNamara's 2SM Country music sessions. The following year, he married singer/songwriter Joy McKean. Up to 1953, he had been working in the building trade as a plasterer, but now he put together his own full-time show. It wasn't long before he was being called the "King of Country Music." Many of the songs that Slim recorded were written by Joy.

Between 1954 and 1957, Slim recorded thirty-six sides of his brand of bush ballads. Then in 1957, the turning point in his career came. He recorded *A Pub with No Beer*. It was originally the flip-side of *Saddle Boy*. It became the biggest seller in Australian recording history and it resulted in the first and last Gold Disc for a 78 rpm record. In Britain, it made No.3 in the Pop charts. His hits in Australia just kept right on rolling.

In 1960, Slim released his first album, ***Slim Dusty Sings,*** and in 1964, inaugurated his annual tour of Australia that takes in 30,000 miles over a 10-month period. He received his M.B.E. in 1970 and two years later received the first "Eddy" presented by the Federation of Australian Broadcasters. During 1974, Slim suffered with throat problems but these were ignored when he played to a capacity crowd of 2,700 in the Concert Hall of the Sydney Opera House in April 1975.

When the Australasian Country Music Awards were launched by Radio 2TM in 1973 (from 1976, they were taken over by the CMAA), it was soon discovered that Slim and his family were the main recipients of the Annual Gold Guitar Awards (see Awards Section). During 1979, Slim's likeness was put on a brass plaque and mounted on a granite boulder outside 2TM as the fourth person elevated to the CMAA's Roll of Renown. The following year, Slim's autobiography, *Walk a Country Mile*, was published along with a special album of the same title. In 1989, he made his first visit to Europe and the U.S.

Over the years, Slim Dusty has received numerous awards for Gold albums and singles and a Platinum award for sales in excess of one million Australian dollars. His wife, Joy, is also a multi-winner for her songs that have contributed in no small way to Slim's success, and she is also a fine guitar and fiddle player in the Slim Dusty Show. Their daughter, Anne, has also shown her skills singing on her dad's recordings and playing a nifty mandolin. Son David has also followed in his father's footsteps singing and playing guitar. Looking at Slim Dusty, you see the archetypical Australian, with his bush hat resting back on his head, with an easy smile. Slim's contribution to Country music has been immense over the nearly fifty years that he has been recording.

RECOMMENDED ALBUMS:

All Australians will probably have them and do not need us to recommend them.
In the U.S., only one album is available:
"Australia Is His Name" (Rounder)

FRANK DYCUS

(Singer, Songwriter, Guitar)

Given Name:	**Marion Franklin Dycus**
Date of Birth:	**December 5, 1939**
Where Born:	**Hardmoney, Kentucky**
Married:	**1. Dominique (div.)**
	2. Tabatha Gail Eves (div.)
	3. Lynda
Children:	**Robert Russell, Shawn Dell, Sheila Dawn, Shannon Danna**

Frank Dycus is one of the most articulate songwriters in Country music. Frank considers himself to be the "'last token hillbilly," who writes from his life's experiences with the benefit of a "beer elbow."

When he was around 8, he was considered to be studious and eagerly devoured Jack London and Ernest Hemingway. He considers himself to have been a strange boy with cross-eyes who didn't play ball. He started writing poetry to his mother when he was 14. When he was 16, he moved to California and joined the U.S. Air Force. While there, Frank met a rock'n'roll singer, Don Gonzalez, who taught him to play guitar. They put together a duo, Don and Frank. They mimicked the Everly Brothers and played dances in Washington State, Oregon and Montana. They got a spot on KPEG Spokane, Idaho. As much as Washington was "tight" on drinking and live music, Idaho was the opposite. While playing the Idaho clubs, Frank met Ray Price, Jim Reeves and Buck Owens. Buck was at that time playing in Tacoma. Frank received encouragement as a writer from Charlie Ryan, who had penned the classic, *Hot Rod Lincoln*.

Frank first came to Nashville in 1959 while still in the armed forces. He moved there in 1962, but moved back to Wichita to work for Boeing Aircraft. By now, he had gotten married and had the early morning show on KATE. He stayed in Wichita until 1967, all the time writing for Pete Drake's Window Music. He moved back to Nashville in 1967 and re-signed to Window.

Frank got to know Hap Peebles, who introduced him to Minnie Pearl and Lonzo & Oscar. Tommy Hill asked Frank to write a truck driving song for the Willis Brothers. After protesting that he couldn't write one, he was told to pretend he was a trucker. As a result Frank had his first cut, *White Lines and Road Side Signs.*

He stayed with Window until 1970, when he set up Empher Music with Larry Kingston and Roger Fox. They sent out Emphermation Sheets to the deejays about their cuts and hits, one of which was Wynn Stewart's first RCA hit, *Paint Me a Rainbow*, in 1972. That year, they sold the company to Dolly Parton and Porter Wagoner. Frank signed to Owpar, Dolly Parton's company, with whom he stayed until 1976.

By 1974, Frank was managing Porter and Dolly's Fireside Studios and it was now that Dean Dillon came into the picture. Frank sensed his ability immediately and arranged for Dean to work at the studio and also let him sleep there. At this time, Porter Wagoner took Frank into the recording studio to cut some sides. Frank decided with the engineer, Al Gore, that he would do them his way and so was created Lonesome Frank and the Kitchen Band. They used pizza boxes for drums and a tea chest bass and Porter did backup vocals on some tracks. The sides were released on the Papa Joe label and became the deejays' No.1 favorite in Oklahoma and Texas.

For the period 1975-1979, suffice it to say that Frank was not active. He traveled to Sweden in 1979 and did some recording with Abba's drummer and some local musicians. Back in the U.S., Frank cut an album with Buddy Cannon and Jimmy Darrell which was leased to Sonet in Sweden. In 1981, Frank co-wrote two hits for George Strait: *Unwound* (Top 10) and *Down and Out* (Top 20). The following year, George had another Top 10 hit with a Dycus co-penned song, *Marina Del Rey*.

Super songwriter ***Frank Dycus***

RCA wanted Frank to record a live album in 1986 but they kept changing the parameters and then Frank started to get sick. As a result, he underwent heart surgery. During 1988-1989, Frank lived in the mountains and then returned to Nashville and married Lynda, whom he had known for some fourteen years. After a lot of soul searching, during which he had decided to leave writing for good, he started a new publishing company. After looking at his row of rocking chairs outside his house in Goodlettsville, Tennessee, he wrote *I Don't Need Your Rockin' Chair*, which became a hit for George Jones in 1992, coming from the album ***Walls Can Fall***, which was named for another Dycus song.

Frank is a great encourager of new talent, but after the tragic death of his protégé, Chris Austin, in an air crash with the rest of Reba McEntire's band, he swore that he would never take on any new writer. Very shortly after, he heard Billy Yates and Frank was back in action as the "grand man" of songwriters.

E

EAGLES

When Formed:	**1971**
Members:	
Glenn Frey	**Vocals, Guitar**
Don Henley	**Vocals, Drums**
Bernie Leadon	**Vocals, Guitar, Banjo (left 1975)**
Randy Meisner	**Vocals, Bass, Guitar (left 1977)**
Don Felder	**Vocals, Guitar (joined 1975)**
Joe Walsh	**Vocals, Guitar (joined 1975)**
Timothy B. Schmit	**Vocals, Bass (joined 1977)**

The Eagles epitomize the peak of 70's West Coast Country-Rock bands that found their roots in the Byrds nearly a decade earlier. All the founding members had served their apprenticeships in star bands before forming the band in 1971.

Glenn Frey (b. November 6, 1948, Detroit, Michigan) had played with J.D. Souther as Longbranch Pennywhistle and recorded for Amos Records in 1970. While hanging out at the Troubadour in Los Angeles, he met Don Henley (b. July 22, 1947, Gilmer, Texas). Henley had started out with the Four Speeds in 1963 and then joined Felicity, which became Shiloh in 1969. This group also included Jim Ed Norman (now a famed Country record producer) and Richard Bowden (now one half of comedy duo Pinkard and Bowden) and recorded an album for Amos, produced by Kenny Rogers.

Randy Meisner (b. March 8, 1947, Scottsbluff, Nebraska) had played with the group Poor (1964-1968). In 1968, he had become a founding member of Poco. He stayed with the group until 1969 when he joined Rick Nelson's Stone Canyon Band, where he remained until 1971. Bernie Leadon (b. July 19, 1947, Minneapolis, Minnesota) began with Scottsville Squirrel Barkers in 1958. From 1964 through 1968, he was a member of Hearts & Flowers and then he moved on to Dillard & Clark from 1968 to 1969. He then became a member of Linda Ronstadt's backing group, the Corvettes, but after five months, he joined the Flying Burrito Brothers.

Frey had tried to make it as a solo performer but was dissuaded by David Geffen, who would later head Asylum Records and then his own Geffen label. Frey joined Linda Ronstadt's band and Don Henley did likewise. On their first night playing together, they made up their minds to form their own band. When Meisner and Leadon joined Linda Ronstadt, they knew that all the members were in place. Amicably, they left Linda and with the help of Jackson Browne, acquired Geffen as their manager.

The band got their songs together in Aspen, Colorado, and then went to England to record their eponymous debut album with the legendary British producer Glyn Johns. This album yielded three singles during 1972, all of which made the Pop chart: *Take It Easy* (Top 15), *Witchy Woman* (Top 10) and *Peaceful Easy Feeling* (Top 25). Immediately, it was apparent that the Eagles' releases were going to be marked by excellent melodic self-penned songs, supported by equally fine material from Jack Tempchin and Jackson Browne.

In 1973, they returned to England for their second album, ***Desperado,*** which was built around the infamous wild west Doolin-

Dalton gang. The singles released, *Tequila Sunrise* and *Outlaw,* failed to set the chart alight and only hit the lower order. They then made two dramatic changes. First, the band changed managers and enlisted the aid of Irving Azoff, and then for their all-crucial third album, the majority of the tracks were produced by Bill Szymczyk in Los Angeles (he remained their producer from then on in). This album, ***On the Border***, released in 1974, marked the debut of Don Felder as a fifth Eagle (he initially played on the album as a session man).

Felder (b. September 22, 1947, Gainesville, Florida) had played with Flow and then had worked as a session musician and engineer on records by Crosby & Nash and David Blue. The album also featured former Shiloh steel player Al Perkins. The first single, *Already Gone*, reached the Top 40 but the follow-up, *James Dean,* only got to the Top 80. However, the final single, *Best of My Love*, gave the band its first No.1 single. In 1974, the Eagles' first three albums all went Gold.

Their 1975 album, ***One of These Nights***, proved to be one of the most successful and musically dynamic Country-Rock albums, going Gold the year of release. Featured on the album were David Bromberg (fiddle) and Jim Ed Norman (piano). The title track went to No.1 and opened up their international account. This was followed by the Top 3 *Lyin' Eyes*, which also became a Country Top 10 hit and earned them a Grammy Award as "Best Pop Vocal Performance by a Duo, Group or Chorus." The final single from the album, *Take It to the Limit*, went Top 5.

After this album and during 1975, Bernie Leadon left and formed the Bernie Leadon/Michael Georgiades Band and then worked as a session musician, playing with David Bromberg, Andy Fairweather-Low, Chris Hillman, Helen Reddy, Chi Coltrane, Rita Coolidge and Stephen Stills. In 1987-1988, he was a member of the Nitty Gritty Dirt Band, replacing John McEuen. Leadon was replaced by Joe Walsh (b. Joseph Fidler Walsh, November 20, 1947, Cleveland, Ohio). Walsh played with the James Gang from 1969-1971 and then from 1972 to 1973, he was a member of Barnstorm. During 1973-1975, he had chalked up single hits on Dunhill: *Rocky Mountain Way* (Top 25, 1973), *Meadows* (Top 90, 1974) and *Turn to Stone* (Top 100, 1975). During most of 1975, he headed his own Joe Walsh Band.

In 1976, ***The Eagles' Greatest Hits*** was released and went on to be one of the biggest sellers of all times. By 1994, it had racked up sales of 14 million copies! In 1977, it was named "Favorite Album" in the Pop/Rock Category of the American Music Awards. At the end of 1976, *New Kid in Town* was released as the debut single of their ***Hotel California*** album. The single went to No.1, crossed to the Country Top 50 and was Certified Gold the following year. At the beginning of 1977, the title track also went to No.1 and went Gold that same year (and was a U.K. Top 10 single). These were followed by *Life in the Fast Lane* (Top 15) and then a year later, the Eagles charted with the seasonal *Please Come Home for Christmas*, which went Top 20. The album ***Hotel California*** had achieved Platinum status in 1976 and had sold 9 million copies by 1990, and earned them a Grammy Award as "Record of the Year" in 1977. They also earned a Grammy that year for "Best Arrangement for Voices" for *New Kid in Town.*

Randy Meisner left the group in 1977 and started a solo career, releasing his Top 20 album ***Hearts on Fire***. He has subsequently joined the re-formed Poco. He was replaced by Timothy B. Schmit (b. October 30, 1947, Sacramento, California). Schmit began with the Folk trio Tim, Tom & Ron, in 1962. The following year, he joined the Surfband Contenders and then moved on to the New Breed, who in 1968 became Glad. At the beginning of 1970, he also joined Poco, where he stayed until joining the Eagles.

The Eagles' new line-up recorded the 1979 album ***The Long Run***, on which Jimmy Buffett and sax player David Sanborn guested. The album went Platinum in 1980 and by 1990 had sold 4 million copies. In 1979, the band returned to the top of the chart with *Heartache Tonight*, which went Gold the following year and earned a 1979 Grammy Award for "Best Rock Vocal Performance by a Duo or Group." They closed out 1979 with the title track, which went Top 10. They opened 1980 with another Top 10 single, *I Can't Tell You Why*. They also released the album ***Eagles Live***, which featured J.D. Souther on vocals and guitar. At year end, they had their final single success, Steve Young's *Seven Bridges Road*, which peaked just below the Top 20 and crossed to the Country Top 60. The album had been Certified Platinum by 1981. Also in 1981, the group was named "Favorite Band, Duo or Group" in the Pop/Rock Category of the American Music Awards.

In 1982, the group decided to disband and Asylum released ***Greatest Hits Volume 2***, which went Gold in 1983. Glenn Frey went on to rack up a series of single hits on both sides of the Atlantic; for Asylum: *I Found Somebody* (Top 40), *The One You Love* (Top 15) and *All Those Lies* (Top 50) (all 1982); for MCA: *Sexy Girl* (Top 20) and *The Allnighter* (Top 60), *The Heat Is On* (from the movie *Beverly Hills Cop*) (U.S. Top 3, U.K. No.12) (all 1984), *Smuggler's Blues* (U.S. Top 15, U.K. No.22), *You Belong to the City* from the *Miami Vice* soundtrack (Top 3) (both 1985), *True Love* (Top 15, 1988), *Livin' Right* (Top 90, 1989) and *Part of Me, Part of You* (Top 60, 1991) and *I've Got Mine* (Top 100, 1992). Glenn also appeared in episodes of *Miami Vice* and *Wiseguy*.

Don Henley had his first single success in 1981 with the Top 10 duet with Stevie Nicks *Leather and Lace* on the Modern label. For Asylum, he charted with *Johnny Can't Read* (Top 50) and the Gold Certified *Dirty Laundry* (Top 3) (both 1982), *I Can't Stand Still* (Top 50, 1983), and for Geffen: *The Boys of Summer* (Top 5, 1984), *All She Wants to Do Is Dance* (Top 10), *Not Enough Love in the World* (Top 40), *Sunset Grill* (Top 25) (all 1985), *The End of Innocence* (Top 10) and *The Last Worthless Evening* (Top 25) (both 1989), *The Heart of the Matter* (Top 25), *How Bad Do You Want It* and *New York Minute* (both Top 50, all 1990) and *Sometimes Love Just Ain't Enough* (a duet with Patty Smyth, Top 3, 1992). In 1992, he got together with Trisha Yearwood for the Top 3 Country hit *Walkaway Joe*.

Timothy B. Schmit had two chart singles: *So Much in Love* from the movie *Fast Times at Ridgemont High* (Top 60, 1982) on Full Moon and the 1987 Top 25 *Boys Night Out* on MCA. He played on sessions for Elton John, Bob Seger, America, Joe Walsh, and Crosby, Stills & Nash. Joe Walsh has gone on to play on sessions for Ringo Starr, Diana Ross and Randy Newman. His singles have been *Life's Been Good* (Top 15, 1978), *All Night Long* from the movie *Urban Cowboy* (Top 20, 1980), *A Life of Illusion* (Top 40, 1981) and *Space Age Whiz Kids* (Top 60, 1983) on Asylum and Full Moon. Don Felder also went on to a solo career, and just prior to the group split, had only one single hit, *Heavy Metal (Takin' a Ride)* from the animated movie *Heavy Metal* (Top 50).

In 1993, Don Henley got together various Country artists plus members of the Eagles for a tribute album entitled ***Common Thread: The Songs of the Eagles***. The album was a phenomenal success and before year end was No.1 on both Country and Pop Album charts and had sold over 2 million copies. The sleeve annotation notes that, "A portion of the royalties from the sales are going to the Walden Woods Project, a non-profit organization founded in 1990. The purpose of the Walden Woods Project is to purchase, and thereby preserve, environmentally sensitive and historically significant forestland located near Henry David Thoreau's famed retreat at Walden Pond." The track-listing for the project is: *Take It Easy* (Travis Tritt), *Peaceful Easy Feeling* (Little Texas), *Desperado* (Clint Black), *Heartache Tonight* (John Anderson), *Tequila Sunrise* (Alan Jackson), *Take It to the Limit* (Suzy Bogguss), *I Can't Tell You Why* (Vince Gill), *Lyin' Eyes* (Diamond Rio), *New Kid in Town* (Trisha Yearwood), *Saturday Night* (Billy Dean), *Already Gone* (Tanya Tucker), *Best of My Love* (Brooks & Dunn) and *The Sad Cafe* (Lorrie Morgan). From this album, the tracks by Travis Tritt, Clint Black, Little Texas and Alan Jackson have all been Country chart hits, with Travis being the most successful, reaching the Top 25.

As a result of this renewed interest in the Eagles, Henley, Frey, Schmit and Felder have re-formed for U.S. concerts.

RECOMMENDED ALBUMS:

"The Eagles" (Asylum)(1972)
"Desperado" (Asylum)(1973)
"On the Border" (Asylum)(1974)
"One of These Nights" (Asylum)(1975)
"Greatest Hits" (Asylum)(1976)
"Hotel California" (Asylum)(1977)
"The Long Run" (Asylum)(1979)
"Eagles Live" (Asylum)(1980)
"Greatest Hits Volume 2" (Asylum)(1982)
Glenn Frey:
"No Fun Around" (Asylum)(1982)
"The Allnighter" (MCA)(1984)
Don Henley:
"I Can't Stand Still" (Asylum)(1982)
"Building the Perfect Beast" (Geffen)(1984)
"The End of the Innocence" (Geffen)(1989)
Don Felder:
"Airborne" (Asylum)(1983)
Timothy B. Schmit:
"Playing It Cool" (Asylum)(1984)
Randy Meisner:
"Hearts on Fire" (Asylum)(1979)
"One More Song" (Epic)(1980)
"Randy Meisner" (Epic)(1982)
Bernie Leadon:
"Natural Progression" (Asylum)(1977) [With Michael Georgiades]
Joe Walsh:
"But Seriously Folks" (Asylum)(1978)
"There Goes the Neighborhood" (Elektra)(1981)
"You Can't Argue with a Sick Mind" (MCA)(1981) [Originally issued on ABC (1975)]
"You Bought It—You Name It" (WEA/Full Moon)(1983)
Also:
"Common Thread: The Songs of the Eagles" (Giant)(1993)

JIM EANES

(Singer, Songwriter, Rhythm Guitar)
Given Name: **Homer Robert Eanes, Jr.**
Date of Birth: **December 6, 1923**
Where Born: **Mountain Valley, Henry County, Virginia**

Jim Eanes has been active in music since the 40's in both Country and Bluegrass, with most of his recordings falling in the latter category. His vocal approach with both forms is similar: a smooth relaxed delivery which contrasts sharply with the high lonesome sound favored by some Bluegrass singers. While never quite ranking in the star category, Smilin' Jim has been an enduring musical figure, whose career has been quite significant and spans more than a half century of professionalism.

His father played old-time banjo in a square dance group and Jim got his first guitar at the age of 9. He learned to play rhythm guitar despite an injury-related problem with the fingers of his left hand which made fretting any instrument difficult for him. After some years of playing square dances with his father and some neighbors, Jim, at 16, became a junior member of Roy Hall's Blue Ridge Entertainers at WDBJ Roanoke, Virginia. Hall was a popular figure in the region and had recorded for both the American Record Corporation (ARC) and Bluebird with a band that came close to playing Bluegrass. Eanes made no recordings with the Blue Ridge Entertainers, but did gain some valuable experience. After Hall's death in 1943, Jim returned home for a time.

After the end of WWII, Jim joined Uncle Joe and the Blue Mountain Boys, whose members included Fiddlin' Burk Barbour. They played on WHEE and WMVA, Martindale, Virginia; WBOB Galax, Virginia; and finally, WNOX Knoxville, Tennessee; and for a few months in 1948, Jim worked with Bill Monroe.

During 1949, Jim made his first recordings under his own name on Capitol. He had Homer Sherrill and Snuffy Jenkins playing fiddle and banjo, respectively. In 1951, Jim came to WBTM Danville, Virginia, and organized the Shenandoah Valley Boys, which included Hubert Davis on banjo and his brother Pee Wee on fiddle. Later musicians included fiddle players Benny Jarrell and Roy Russell, Allen Shelton on banjo and Arnell Terry on guitar. They cut several singles on the small Blue Ridge label and then signed with Decca. Here his music was given the Nashville treatment and studio musicians were used to produce a more "Country" sound although he did record some Bluegrass instrumentals.

One of Jim's Blue Ridge singles, *Missing in Action*, a Korean War song, was covered by Ernest Tubb, who had a major hit with it in 1952. Another one, *Little Brown Hand*, dealt with the then touchy subject of an interracial romance. Although none of his Decca releases made the charts, several were good sellers and they helped spread his name.

After his Decca contract expired in 1955, Smilin' Jim began recording with the Shenandoah Valley Boys for Starday, where *Your Old Standby*, recorded at his first session in December, 1956, soon became one of his trademark numbers. Alternating between Starday and Blue Ridge for the next five years, Eanes recorded several other memorable numbers including the first release of his original *I Wouldn't Change You If I Could*. It was soon covered by Reno and Smiley and, in 1982, became a No.1 hit for Ricky Skaggs. He also did Bluegrass versions of Victorian ballads like *Budded Roses, Log Cabin in the Lane* and *There'll Come a Time*.

Continuing deejay work on a variety of Virginia stations in the 60s, Eanes still did show-dates through the Old Dominion and adjacent states, recording material for local labels such as Salem and Dominion. In 1967, he recorded his first Bluegrass album for the Rebel subsidiary, Zap, ***Your Old Standby,*** and followed it with two on Rural Rhythm, ***Jim Eanes*** and ***Rural Rhythms Present Jim Eanes***. On the latter two, he was backed by Red Smiley's Bluegrass Cut-Ups. The second Rural Rhythm album is more Country than Bluegrass.

At the same time, Eanes and the Smiley group were working at the WWVA *Wheeling Jamboree*.

After Red Smiley decided to retire from music when his TV show at WDBJ Roanoke was canceled, Jim took over the band, renaming it the Shenandoah Cutups. In March 1970, the group cut a fine Bluegrass-Gospel album for County, ***The Shenandoah Valley Quartet with Jim Eanes***, but a few months later, they went their separate ways.

Eanes emceed various festivals and recorded Bluegrass albums for smaller labels like Jessup/Michigan Bluegrass, (***The Statesman of Bluegrass***) and Folly in the early 70s and a much stronger album, ***Where the Cool Waters Flow***, for Leather later in the decade.

In 1978, Jim Eanes suffered a heart attack and was out of commission for about a year, returning in 1979 to make a tour of Western

Europe. He did two more such tours in 1980 and 1982, cutting an album with the Belgian Bluegrass band Smoketown Strut during his second visit.

While, Jim has not maintained a heavy travel schedule during the 80s, he has continued to be quite active in the studios and has had releases on Webco and Rebel. In 1986, he and Bobby Atkins did an album together for Old Homestead. His most recent record, ***50th Anniversary***, was released in 1990 on Rebel as a celebration of a half century in show business. Re-issues have also made some of his best earlier efforts available.

IMT

RECOMMENDED ALBUMS:

"The Early Days of Bluegrass: Volume 4" (Rounder) [Re-issue of Blue Ridge and Rich-R-Tone singles]
"Jim Eanes: Bluegrass Special" (BS France) [French re-issue of Decca singles]
"Where the Cool Waters Flow" (Leather)(1979)
"Shenandoah Grass: Yesterday and Today" (Webco)(1983) [Mixture of older and newly recorded material]
"Log Cabin in the Lane" (Highland)(1988) [Re-issue of Starday singles]
"Jim Eanes" (Rebel)(1986-80)

STEVE EARLE

(Singer, Songwriter, Guitar, Bass Guitar, Mandolin, Harmonica, Actor)

Date of Birth: **January 17, 1955**
Where Born: **Fort Monroe, Virginia**
Married: **1. (div.)**
2. (div.)
3. Carol (m. 1981)

With only an eighth-grade education, Steve Earle composed some of Country music's most thought provoking songs of the late 80's. He has picked up a cult following, but his brushes with the law have damaged his public persona and retarded his progress.

Although he was born in Virginia, Steve's family almost immediately moved back to Texas. His father was an air traffic controller; his family moved around a lot, but by the time Steve was in second grade, they were settled in San Antonio. He started playing guitar at age 13 and, a couple of years later, started to sport long hair, but after being given a bad time by Country music fans because of his looks, he cut off his hair with a knife and began hating Country music. Steve was traveling around the Lone Star State by age 16, playing music.

By the time he was 18, Steve was married and living in Houston. While working in a car wash, he met Jerry Jeff Walker and Townes Van Zandt. In 1974, Steve moved to Nashville, where he met songwriter/singer Richard Dobson and was introduced to Guy Clark and Rodney Crowell. Steve wrote songs at night and made ends meet as a carpenter and also played bass for Guy Clark. In 1975, Steve had a small part in the Robert Altman movie *Nashville*. After several years in Tennessee, Steve got restless and returned to Texas. He continued south to San Miguel de Allende in Mexico and kept writing songs.

Following the break-up of his second marriage and running short of money, Steve moved back to Nashville in 1979. Carl Perkins then recorded Steve's *Mustang Wine*, Zella Lehr cut *Heartache to Heartache* and *Live Wire* and in 1982, Johnny Lee charted Steve's co-written song, *When You Fall in Love*.

After his third marriage and the birth of his first child, Steve worked delivering record test pressings and washing dishes as well as continuing writing. After playing in a local bar and receiving a good reaction, Steve recorded an EP, *Pink & Black*, with the help of a pair of Texans, Zip Gibson and Bullett Harris, Jr., who became the Dukes. This led to a record contract with Epic.

Epic released the singles *Nothin' But You* (1983) and *What'll You Do About Me* (1984) but both failed to break the Top 60. After one album of Rockabilly influenced songs, Steve left the label. It was producer Tony Brown's intervention that brought Steve to MCA at the end of 1985. His first charted single for MCA was the 1986 Top 40 *Hillbilly Heaven*, but it was the follow-up, *Guitar Town*, from the album of the same name, that made him a star. The album rose to the top of the chart. Steve's follow-up single, *Someday*, made the Top 30. His Country music laced with Folk and Rock drew comparisons with John Cougar Mellencamp and Bruce Springsteen. Fans and critics alike, in the U.S. and Europe, welcomed Steve Earle with open arms. He was named "Top Country Artist" in *Rolling Stone*'s Critics Poll and his music was praised in the *Village Voice*, *Time*, *Newsweek* and the *New York Times*. That year, Waylon Jennings recorded Steve's *The Devil's Right Hand* and Steve appeared at Farm Aid II playing an acoustic set with John Cougar Mellencamp's guitarist, Larry Crane.

Country-Rocker ***Steve Earle***

1987 started with another track from the debut album, *Goodbye's All We've Got Left*, which went Top 10. Earle followed up his successful debut album with ***Exit O*** that year. Breaking with Nashville tradition, he recorded the album with his touring band, the Dukes. The line-up of the group at this stage was Bucky Baxter (steel guitar, vocals), Reno Kling (bass guitar), Mike McAdam (guitars, vocals), Ken Moore (keyboards, vocals) and Harry Stinson (drums). Earle co-wrote the Top 20 radio hit, *Nowhere Road*, with Reno Kling, but all other selections were written by Steve on his own. Nearly all the songs on the album were autobiographical including the Top 40 hit, *Sweet Little '66*, about a 1966 Chevelle SS-396 that he and a friend built in high school, and *Angry Young Man*, which Earle called an updated version of Merle Haggard's *Mama Tried*. That year, Patty Loveless recorded Steve's co-written song *Some Blue Moons Ago*, on her debut album.

Steve Earle, now looking like a Hell's Angel with beard, sun shades and very long hair, continued to push the limits of Country music with 1988's Rock-influenced ***Copperhead Road***. The title track charted on many Rock stations but was not played by most Country stations. Steve traveled to London to record the Vietnam War anthem, *Johnny Come Lately*, with the Irish group the Pogues. Also featured was Telluride, made up of Mark O'Connor, Jerry Douglas, Sam Bush and Edgar Meyer. Taking up the cause of homeless children, Steve donated the songwriting royalties from his *Nothing But a Child* to the Boston-based Robert F. Kennedy Action Corps, Inc.

Earle was making headlines for more than his music in 1988 when he spent New Year's Day in a Dallas jail for punching a policeman (although he had been rendered unconscious by the officer's billy club, which had been placed across his throat). Also in 1988, Earle and his band recorded *Six Days on the Road* and *Continental Trailways Blues* for the John Hughes film *Planes, Trains and Automobiles*, which starred Steve Martin and John Candy. The former title reached the Top 30, while the latter was included on the MCA compilation ***Country & Eastern***.

The 1990 album, ***The Hard Way***, explored more social and political issues including the death penalty and abusive police. Earle's hard core fans purchased the album, but radio ignored the record. His 1991 album release, ***Shut Up and Die Like an Aviator***, was a live album that failed to produce any radio hits. In 1993, Steve got together with former Eagle Joe Walsh for a totally pointless reprise of Carl Perkins' *Honey Don't*, which was on ***The Beverly Hillbillies*** soundtrack album.

Steve Earle's unique songwriting style landed his compositions on the records of Johnny Lee, Connie Smith, Steve Wariner and Carl Perkins. In 1992, he found himself in trouble with the law again, when he failed to appear for jury duty and was charged with possession of cocaine. In 1994, Steve was involved in an auto action, from which he received lacerations and again found the police chasing him.

Steve unfortunately seems to have lost himself on his own Nowhere Road: too Rock for Country and too Country for Rock and thereby becoming a cult figure rather than a star.

RECOMMENDED ALBUMS:
"Guitar Town" (MCA)(1986)
"Early Tracks" (Epic)(1987)
"Exit O" (MCA)(1987)
"Copperhead Road" (MCA)(1988)
"The Hard Way" (MCA)(1990)
"Shut Up and Die Like an Aviator" (MCA)(1991)
"Essential Steve Earle" (MCA)(1993)

EAST TEXAS SERENADERS, The

When Formed: Around 1927
Members:
Cloet Hamman Guitar
Huggins Williams Fiddle
Henry Bogan Cello, String Bass
John Munnerlyn Tenor Banjo
Henry Lester Second Fiddle
Additional Member:
Shorty Lester Banjo

None of the members of this band ever contemplated becoming full-time musicians, yet during the 20's and 30's, they cut twenty-four sides for Columbia, Brunswick and Decca. Cloet ran a truck farm, Henry Bogan worked for the post office, Huggins worked as a florist, an undertaker and in a printing office at various times and John ran a gas station a little west of Mineola, Texas.

Hamman and Williams were born near Lindale, Texas. Hamman's father, Will, was a famous fiddle player and piano tuner and Cloet learned to play guitar by backing his father at fiddle contests. All of the Hamman family were musicians; his sister, Lola, was an acclaimed piano player and his brothers, Gaston and Clyde, played guitar and mandolin respectively. Cloet was also an adept cello player.

Huggins's father was also a fiddle player, who started out on a gourd fiddle until he bought the real thing. He had tried to prevent his children from playing, but young Williams would sneak his father's fiddle when his father was at work. Because he was left-handed, he started to play the wrong way. However, when his father found out about his son's skills, he bought him a left-handed fiddle and had him taught. He learned to play rags and songs popular at the time from a fiddle player who came from "the north," a certain Mr. Brigsley.

John Munnerlyn, who was with the band at the start but moved on to Houston, was replaced by Shorty Lester on later recordings. He was a musician known for his steady and full sound. Henry Bogan was a very adept player of the 3-string cello (pronounced "sello" in East Texas) and was equally capable of plucking and bowing his instrument.

At the time that the East Texas Serenaders got together, they were pioneering new territory. Other bands that followed would copy their style. Even the stars of Western Swing like Bob Wills and Milton Brown owed a debt to this band. Their music was a blend of ragtime, fiddle dance music and more contemporary "hits" with more than a little "palm court orchestra" sound about it.

They got their start by playing in barns and serenading the local farmers in the middle of the night. They played at house parties, Chamber of Commerce functions and any other social event. Their fame spread as far afield as Dallas, Houston and Oklahoma. Generally, they never played anywhere where strong liquor was served, although they did a six-month stint at the Ashby Cafe in Tyler, Texas. However, they were not averse to taking the odd sip to help improve their recording. In 1927, they did their Columbia recording session and the following three years they cut material for Brunswick. By the time of their final recordings for Decca, Munnerlyn had left and the two Lester brothers were brought in.

A lot of their recorded sides were written by Williams, including *The Acorn Stomp, The East Texas Drag* and *Arizona Stomp*. Hamman was also a composer and one of his tunes, *Adeline Waltz*, was a band staple. The aforementioned Mr. Brigsley also wrote songs that the band recorded, including *The Shannon Waltz* and *The Sweetest Flower Waltz*.

RECOMMENDED ALBUM:
"The East Texas Serenaders 1927-1936" (County)(1977)

EASTER BROTHERS, The

When Formed: 1953
RUSSELL EASTER
(Banjo, Guitar, Vocals)
Given Name: Russell Lee Easter
Date of Birth: April 22, 1930
Married: Myrtle Belle
Children: Russell, Jr., Roger, Linda
JAMES EASTER
(Guitar, Mandolin, Vocals)
Given Name: James Madison Easter
Date of Birth: April 24, 1932
Married: Mary Louise
Children: Jeff, Steve, Teresa
ED EASTER
(Mandolin, Banjo, Vocals)
Given Name: Edward Franklin Easter
Date of Birth: March 28, 1934
Married: Ann
Children: Bobby, Edward Arnold, Billy
All Born: Mount Airy, North Carolina

The Easter Brothers have had a quality Country-Gospel group, playing primarily with Bluegrass instrumentation, for some four decades. Based in their hometown of Mount Airy, North Carolina, the Easters have appeared on radio, television, concerts and have recorded quite extensively. The skilled instrumentation and vocal harmonies the brothers presented to their listeners have been further supplemented by a large number of outstanding original songs.

The region of Surry County, North Carolina, along with Carroll and Grayson counties, Virginia, has long been known for the quality of traditional Anglo-American musicians native to the area, extending from Ernest Stoneman and the Ward family to Tommy Jarrell. The Easter Brothers are likely the leading figures from that three county zone in traditional Gospel music. They grew to musical maturity in the period when Bluegrass instrumentation and vocal harmony were reaching maturity, and in a locale where the new form of Old-Time music achieved wide popularity. Russell Easter was the first to take up music and formed a band with fiddler Wayburn Johnson in 1947. Later as James and Ed also began to play, Russell worked with them, and in 1953 they formed a group. With the addition of a fourth member, they became the Green Valley Quartet in 1955. For several years from 1957, Ronald Thomas, who sang and played bass, occupied this position. At times they had programs over two stations in Danville and also at WPAQ in Mount Airy. By the end of the 1960's, the Easter Brothers had become familiar figures in Gospel music circles in a region that stretched from northern Georgia to southern Pennsylvania, mostly along the Blue Ridge and adjacent portions of the Piedmont. They also appeared on many TV shows, notably those of the Reverend Leonard Repass, who had a television ministry based in Bluefield, West Virginia.

The Easter Brothers made their first recordings in April, 1960, in a studio in Virginia owned by Carlton Haney, and did a second session at the King studios in Cincinnati on February 27, 1961. They recorded a total of eleven sides, but only six were released on King, all under the name of Green Valley Quartet. Don Reno, Mac McGaha, and John Palmer from the Tennessee Cut-ups assisted on one session, while Joel Martin played banjo on both, and Allen Mills, who later became leader of the Lost and Found, played bass on the other. The sides which King did not release subsequently appeared on Haney's Commandment label (later all were released on a Rebel album).

Through the remainder of the 60's, the Easters recorded several more albums for Commandment. While more often than not their music could be classified as Bluegrass-Gospel, several sides also featured electric steel guitar and other instruments not associated with Bluegrass. In 1968, the brothers cut an all-acoustic album for David Freeman's County Records which many collectors consider their finest overall effort. By this time, Russell Easter, Jr., had joined the group playing a variety of instruments but especially banjo and Dobro. Johnny Taylor and Wayburn Johnson both added to the quality of their County album.

Through the 1970's and 1980's the Easter Brothers recorded for other companies, including Old Homestead, Rebel and such Nashville firms associated with mainstream Southern Gospel such as the Benson Corporation's Life Line label, and Eddie Crook's Morningstar. At one time or another during this period, most of the Easter children worked with the group. Jeff Easter, son of James, proved excellent on harmonica and, after marrying Sheri Williamson of the Lewis Family, played with that band for a time before he and Sheri went on their own.

Among non-family members, Jimmy Edmunds of Galax, Virginia, worked on many of their albums playing fiddle and other Bluegrass instruments. Three Bluegrass albums on Rebel in the early 80's, one of them a Gospel tribute to Don Reno and Red Smiley, probably constitute the high water mark of their later disc efforts.

Over the years, several Easter Brothers songs have won them wide acclaim. Among them is *They're Holding Up the Ladder*, which has been recorded by numerous other Gospel groups including the Lewis family and *Thank You Lord for Your Blessings on Me,* which they consider their all-time biggest success. Two others with special appeal are *He's the Rock I'm Leaning On* and *A Heart that Will Never Break Again.* Others favor their earlier songs, such as *I Want My Light to Shine* and the semi-humorous recitation *That's All There Is to It,* about a fellow who keeps postponing his visit to a tent revival.

Russell Easter considers the group's peak years to be 1984 to 1987, when the brothers worked Gospel concerts over much of the eastern U.S. and in such states as Texas, Oklahoma, Missouri and Arkansas. In recent years, the three Easter Brothers along with Russell's grandson Jason Easter, who plays bass, have been the members of the traveling group. As in the earlier years, they have increasingly confined their concerts to that area extending from northern Georgia to Ohio and Pennsylvania, with many of their dates being in North Carolina and Virginia. IMT

RECOMMENDED ALBUMS:

"Let Me Stand Lord" (Commandment)(1965)
"Lord I Will" (Commandment)(1966)
"Country Hymn Time" (Commandment)(1967)
"The Easter Brothers and Their Green Valley Quartet" (County)(1968)
"From Earth to Gloryland" (Commandment)(1969)
"Hold On" (Old Homestead)(1976)
"I Feel Like Traveling On" (Rebel)(1981)
"Almost Home" (Rebel)(1981)
"He's the Rock I'm Leaning On" (Morningstar)(1981)
"Early Sessions [1960-1961]" (Rebel)(1983)
"The Easter Brothers" (Life Line)(1983)
"Hereafter" (Life Line)(1984)
"Tribute to Reno & Smiley" (Rebel)(1985)

CONNIE EATON

(Singer)

Date of Birth:	**March 1, 1950**
Where Born:	**Nashville, Tennessee**
Married:	**Cliff Williamson**

Connie was born in the year that her father, Bob Eaton, a former *Opry* performer, had his successful record *Second Hand Heart*. By the time she was 14, she was a talent to watch. *The Tennessean* newspaper named her as the discovery of 1964. She attended David Lipscomb College but was suspended for leaving the dormitory after hours. However, she redeemed herself by becoming the runner-up in the Miss Nashville beauty talent contest.

By 1968, she had won an acting award and then met Cliff Williamson, A & R man for Chart Records; they later married. Connie started to appear on TV talent shows and beat the Carpenters into second place on one. She made appearances on the *Lawrence Welk Show* and *Arthur Godfrey Talent Scouts* as well as

The Bluegrass-Gospel sounds of the ***Easter Brothers***

Hee Haw. In 1969, Connie signed with Chart Records and released her first album, ***I Got Life to Live***. It was with her third single of the year that success came her way. The song *Angel of the Morning* would later provide both Juice Newton and Merrilee Rush with major hits, but in Connie's hands, it reached the Top 40. Shortly after, she got into a duet mode, first with Tony Martin and then with actor/singer David Peel. With Peel she cut the 1970 album ***Hit the Road Jack***. The single of that name made the Top 50. The follow-up single, *It Takes Two,* had originally come out of the Motown stable via Marvin Gaye and Kim Weston. Connie and David took it into the Top 60.

Cash Box and *Record World* both voted Connie "Most Promising Female Vocalist" in 1970. She had two more solo entries on Chart, but her chart strike rate left a lot of good records not being successful. She stayed with the label until 1973 without any further action.

It was not until she moved to Dunhill Records in 1974 that she tasted a sizable hit. *Lonely Men, Lonely Women* hit the charts in 1975 and reached the Top 25 and was on the charts for some three months. Shortly afterward, Dunhill was absorbed into ABC Records and they released just one single, *If I Knew Enough to Come Out of the Rain,* which just scraped into the Top 100. Since then, Connie released sides on Musictown and Enterprise, but then she vanished from the scene.

RECOMMENDED ALBUMS:

"I Got Life to Live" (Chart)(1969)
"Hit the Road Jack" (Chart)(1970) [With David Peel]
"Something Special" (Chart)(1971)
"Connie Eaton" (ABC)(1975)

Dave Edwards refer ALABAMA BOYS

DON EDWARDS

(Singer, Songwriter, Guitar)

Given Name:	**Donald Edwards**
Date of Birth:	**March 30, 1939**
Where Born:	**Boonton, New Jersey**
Married:	**Kathy**
Children:	**Courtney, Llayne**

As a child growing up in a New England farming community, Don Edwards discovered a land far away through the books of Will James. The stories told in books like *Cowboys North and South* and *The Lone Cowboy* inspired Don to follow in the footsteps of his favorite writer in search of the Western way. He started playing guitar at age 10 and learned the songs of Gene Autry and Tex Ritter from their Western movies. He was also influenced by Jimmie Rodgers. Don left home when he was 16 and found work in the oil fields and on the ranches in Texas and New Mexico. He loved the cowboy way of life and decided to dedicate his life to singing about it.

When the amusement park Six Flags Over Texas opened in 1961, Don landed his first professional job as a singer, actor and stuntman. He performed at the theme park for the next five years and then headed to Nashville in search of a record contract. There he found little interest in Western music in the mid-60's and the time spent in Tennessee was discouraging. "I was pretty disillusioned with the whole thing. I found out talent didn't matter. Western music was totally alien and besides that, I had too many influences." Some record executives encouraged him to go to Greenwich Village, but the thought of going to New York had no appeal.

Eventually Don recorded a custom album on the Stop label that generated some regional airplay. The album was a mixture of old and new songs and included Don's first songwriting efforts. "I was doing 'put togethers,' that's what Woody Guthrie called them, when you take an old poem or something or an old forgotten song, like you make a new melody or you write music for an old poem, that's how I got into writing songs."

Don returned to Texas, settling in the Fort Worth area. In 1980, he recorded an album in Hollywood with the help of deejay friend Larry Scott at KLAC in Los Angeles. Scott arranged for many of the musicians who played on the recordings of Gene Autry and the Sons of the Pioneers to record with Don. The sessions created a lot of interest and many of Don's heroes, like Roy Rogers, Stuart Hamblen and Jimmy Wakely, visited the studio while he was recording. Don titled the album ***Happy Cowboy***, and released it on his own Sevenshoux label.

Don then released a book/cassette anthology of cowboy songs, ***Songs of the Cowboy***. This was a 24-song tribute to Jack Thorpe, the cowboy minstrel, who was the first to collect cowboy songs. Don's second book/cassette anthology of cowboy songs was ***Guitars & Saddle Songs***. The inspiration to record the traditional cowboy songs came while performing at the Cowboy Poetry Gathering in Elko, Nevada. His next release was ***Desert Nights and Cowtown Blues***. This 1990 album was made "Album of the Year" by *Song of the West* magazine Readers' Poll.

Don's 1991 album ***Chant of the Wanderer*** was the winner of the National Cowboy Hall of Fame's "Western Heritage Wrangler Award for Outstanding Traditional Western Music." While at a Cowboy Poetry Gathering in 1990, Don met Michael Martin Murphey, who had long admired Don's work. Murphey was recording his ***Cowboy Songs*** album and invited Don to sing on it. The success of the album helped Don to land a recording contract with Warner Western, a new Western music label that Warner Brothers was establishing.

Don released ***Songs of the Trail*** in 1992 and it also became the winner of *Song of the West*'s Readers' Poll for "Album of the Year." He followed this up with the 1993 album ***Going Back to Texas***. This included several new Western songs written by some of Nashville's premier writers, including Bob McDill's *Coyotes*, Alex Harvey's *Say Goodbye to Montana* and *Line Shack Blues* by Roger Brown and Luke Reed.

Two of Don Edwards' recordings are included in the Folklore Archives of the Library of Congress. JIE

RECOMMENDED ALBUMS:

"Happy Cowboy" (Sevenshoux)(1980)
"Songs of the Cowboy" (Sevenshoux) [Book/Cassette]
"Guitars & Saddle Songs" (Sevenshoux) [Book/Cassette]
"Desert Nights & Cowtown Blues" (Sevenshoux)(1990)
"Chant of the Wanderer" (Sevenshoux)(1991)
"Songs of the Trail" (Warner Western)(1992)
"Going Back to Texas" (Warner Western)(1993)

JOHN EDWARDS AND THE JOHN EDWARDS MEMORIAL FOUNDATION

John Edwards (1932-60) was an Australian record collector who developed a passionate interest in American Country music of what he called the "Golden Age" (1924-1939). He not only amassed a respectable collection of 78 rpm recordings, but also carried on correspondence with many of the Old-Time performers and published numerous biographical and discographical articles in several American, British and Australian fan magazines.

He was killed in an automobile accident on Christmas Eve, 1960, near his house in Cremorne, Australia. He had left a will instructing that his collection of records and all related materials be used for the "furtherance of serious study, recognition, appreciation and preservation of genuine Country or Hillbilly music..." and named his friend, American record collector Gene W. Earle, as executor. In 1962, Earle and other correspondents of Edwards, Archie Green, D.K. Wilgus, Fred

C. Hoeptner and Ed Kahn, formed a non-profit corporation in California, the John Edwards Memorial Foundation (JEMF), and found an amenable host at the University of California at Los Angeles in the person of Wayland Hand, Chairman of the Folklore and Mythology Center. Dr. Wilgus, the Secretary of the Foundation, was given initial responsibility for the collection. Kahn, a graduate of UCLA, became Treasurer. Earle became President and Green and Hoeptner were Vice Presidents. The officers of the Foundation donated nearly 10,000 records.

From 1964 to 1988 the JEMF devoted itself to the preservation and study of Country music and related forms of Folk-derived musical genres, including Blues, Cajun, Gospel, Western and various ethnic musics. The JEMF's activities included publishing a regular quarterly journal (the *JEMF Quarterly*), issuing an occasional Special Series of bibliographic, discographic and historical pamphlets, reprinting important articles from scholarly publications and issuing extensively documented lp sound recordings.

Over the years, the JEMF built up a major collection of sound recordings, journals, songbooks, documents and other ephemera relating to these various musical traditions. In 1988, the JEMF collection was sold to the University of North Carolina at Chapel Hill, where, as the John Edwards Memorial Collection (JEMC), it was incorporated into the Southern Folklife Collection in the Manuscripts Department of the Academic Affairs Library.

The JEMF was reorganized as the John Edwards Memorial Forum, with the primary purposes to raise funds in support of the JEMC and to support, however possible, the study of traditional, Folk and vernacular music.

When the Country Music Foundation was opened in 1964, a grant was given to copy all the original Edwards material.

[Our thanks to Norm Cohen, Executive Secretary, JEMF, for his assistance]

JONATHAN EDWARDS

(Singer, Songwriter, Guitar, Piano, Harmonica, Bass, Drums)

Given Name:	**Jonathan Edwards**
Date of Birth:	**July 28, 1946**
Where Born:	**Aitkin, Minnesota**
Married:	**1. (div.)**
	2. Deborah
Children:	**three**

Jonathan Edwards scored the biggest hit of his career by accident. While recording his debut album, ***Jonathan Edwards***, for Capricorn Records in 1971, one of the songs was accidentally erased. The recording engineer who made the mistake was fired and Edwards recorded a new song to replace the missing one. The new song, *Sunshine*, was a protest song extolling the virtues of independence and it became a Top 5 Pop hit.

The son of an F.B.I. agent, Jonathan grew up in the Washington, D.C., area, between Alexandria and Fort Vernon. As a child, he took piano lessons, but switched to guitar in high school. Jonathan drew inspiration from the soulful stylings of Ray Charles and Gladys Knight, as well as Folk artists like Peter, Paul and Mary and the Kingston Trio. The recordings of Leadbelly and Woody Guthrie helped him develop his guitar technique and the music of Donovan and Bob Dylan inspired him to take up the harmonica. Jonathan also considers that he learned his first music from his grandmother.

Jonathan studied art at Ohio University, but dropped out to pursue music back east. He started songwriting in 1967 with Malcolm McKinney. He landed in Boston and put together a band performing Electric Folk music. The band became popular all over New England performing under a variety of names, including Finite Minds, Headstone Circus and St. James Doorknob. The band recorded an album for MetroMedia Records under the name Sugar Creek.

After several years of working with the band, Jonathan decided to return to acoustic music as a solo artist. He rented a van and a P.A. system and began traveling to colleges in the New England area. He would show up unannounced, set up, and begin playing. His popularity grew and led to him opening for major acts including B.B. King and the Allman Brothers. After three years of touring, he reckoned that any airport was his home. While working with the Allmans, he came to the attention of Capricorn Records.

After the success of *Sunshine*, Jonathan moved to Atco and released ***Honky Tonk Stardust Cowboy*** in 1972. However, the album was not promoted properly and the singles from it failed to chart. During the year, he played the Bluegrass festival circuit with his band, Orphan. His third album, also on Atco, ***Have a Good Time for Me***, was released in 1973 and was supported by Jonathan's constant touring. That year, he moved to Nova Scotia to take a break from the pressures of the business. While in Canada, he received a call from a friend, Emmylou Harris, who wanted him to come to Los Angeles to sing on her ***Elite Hotel*** album. Emmylou's then husband/producer, Brian Ahern, helped Jonathan land a record deal with Reprise/Warner Brothers. The two albums he produced for the label received critical acclaim but failed to generate sufficient sales.

In 1979, Jonathan moved back to the U.S., settling in New Hampshire for two years and then moving to the Washington, D.C., area. Two years later, he released ***Jonathan Edwards Live!*** on his own Chronic

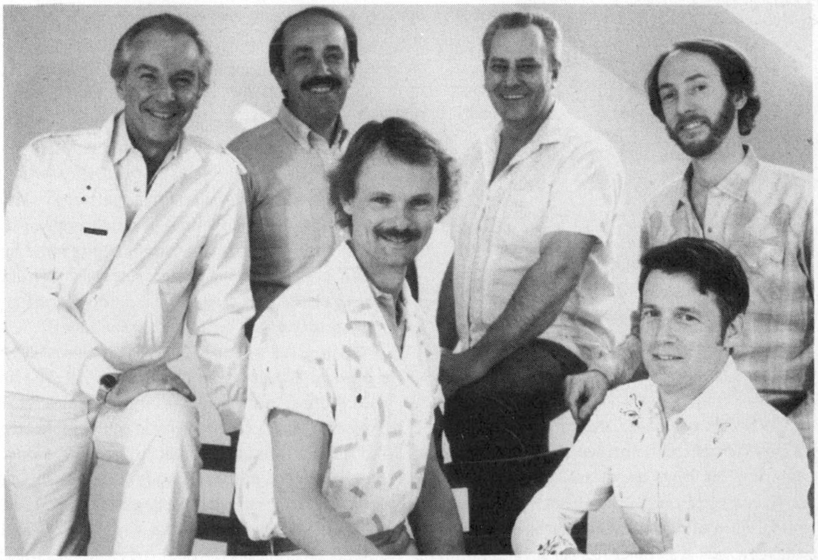

Jonathan Edwards** with the **Seldom Scene

label. In 1983, Jonathan toured the country with a production of *Pump Boys and Dinettes* with Nicolette Larsen and Henry Gross. He returned to the recording studio in 1985, when he teamed up with popular Bluegrass group the Seldom Scene. The result was the album ***Blue Ridge,*** released on Sugar Hill Records.

Singer/songwriter/record producer Wendy Waldman had utilized Jonathan's talents on one of her albums and now she encouraged him to move to Nashville. Curb Records signed him and released the album ***The Natural Thing*** in 1989. From this album came Jonathan's sole Country chart success, *We Need to Be Locked Away*, which was released at the end of 1988. Unlike most of his previous releases, Jonathan only wrote one song on the album. The public received the album well and the video, *Look What We Made (When We Made Love),* was considered to be a hit.

Although Jonathan has not returned to the charts, he can be heard singing jingles for Lowenbrau, Roy Rogers Restaurants, Kentucky Fried Chicken and Campbell's Soup. He now lives in Virginia. His current trio includes Kenny White on keyboards and Jimmy Biggins on sax, flute, piano and guitar. He also acquired producer status when he produced an album for Cheryl Wheeler.

Jonathan describes his music as Acoustic/Folk, but a listen to his albums reveals a multifaceted performer who brings to the fore all of his musical influences. JIE

RECOMMENDED ALBUMS:

"Jonathan Edwards" (Capricorn)(1971)
"Honky Tonk Stardust Cowboy" (Atco)(1972)
"Have a Good Time for Me" (Atco)(1973)
"Lucky Day" (Atco)(1974)
"Rockin' Boat" (Reprise)(1976)
"Sailboat" (Warner Brothers)(1977)
"Jonathan Edwards Live!" (Chronic)(1981)
"Blue Ridge" (Sugar Hill)(1985) [With the Seldom Scene]
"The Natural Thing" (MCA/Curb)(1989)

STONEY EDWARDS

(Singer, Songwriter, Guitar, Fiddle, Piano)
Given Name: Frenchy Edwards
Date of Birth: December 24, 1929
Where Born: Seminole, Oklahoma
Married: Rosemary

Every so often in Country music, a black performer will surface and make a major contribution. Most important among this group have been DeFord Bailey, Charley Pride, O.B. McClinton and Stoney Edwards.

Edwards was raised in rural Oklahoma of mixed heritage. His father's antecedents were Negro, American Indian and Irish and his mother's were Negro and American Indian. He grew up on a small farm with his seven siblings. When he was still young, his father left home. By the time Stoney was 13, he could play various instruments and used to play with uncles. Even at that age he was a huge Country fan and his dream was to play on the *Grand Ole Opry*. In particular he was a fan of Bob Wills.

For a while, during his formative teen years, Stoney was reunited with his father in Oklahoma City. While there, he earned his living washing dishes. He moved to California to be with one of his uncles and worked at various jobs including janitor and truck driver as well as being a cowboy and moving around the country.

He then moved back to California, where he met Rosemary, and in 1954 they married. They settled in the Bay Area of San Francisco and started raising a family. For the next fifteen years, Stoney kept music as a part-time thing. While working as a machinist in a shipyard in Richmond, California, he got a bad case of carbon dioxide poisoning. This affected his memory and for a while he didn't even recognize his wife. He had just returned to work when he had an accident at work that broke his back. The doctors warned him not to do heavy work.

He seriously contemplated leaving home, so that his wife could get welfare. He was on the verge of going when his little daughter, holding a wind-up toy, interceded. Stoney was so affected that he went off and wrote his first song, *A Two Dollar Toy*. His mind was made up. Over the next few months, he worked at his writing and playing guitar.

In 1970, Stoney was invited to play at a benefit for Bob Wills across the Bay in Oakland. He arrived late and it looked like he wasn't going to play. Tony Rose made Stoney take part of his set. He sang *Mama's Hungry Eyes* and was approached by an attorney who was in the audience who was much impressed with Stoney's performance and suggested he make contact with Capitol Records. Within the week, Stoney had made a demo recording and shortly after, he signed to the label.

His first album, ***Stoney Edwards, A Country Singer***, was released in 1971. His initial chart entry was the aforementioned *A Two Dollar Toy,* which made the Top 70. He put out another album later in the year, ***Down Home in the Country***. Slowly, he was picking up a fan base and at the beginning of 1973 *She's My Rock* sailed into the Top 20 and stayed on the charts for nearly four months. Most of his record successes were in the middle to lower end of the lists. Every so often, he produced a record that became more of a career single in spite of the lowness of its chart placing. The Dallas Frazier-Doodle Owens song *Hank and Lefty Raised My Country Soul* was such a one. It only reached the Top 40 but has become a legendary single.

In 1975, Stoney was again in the higher regions of the charts with *Mississippi You're on My Mind*, which was also the title of his 1975 album. By 1978, Stoney was off Capitol and on JMI, for whom he had the minor hit *If I Had to Do it All Over Again*, which had been a big hit for Roy Clark two years before. In 1981, he appeared on Music America with the album ***No Way to Drown a Memory***, which yielded the Top 60 single of the same name.

Health problems sidelined Stoney a lot during the 80's and after five operations, he lost the lower part of his right leg due to diabetes. He returned in 1986 with an album which featured Johnny Gimble, Ray Benson, Floyd Domino, Jimmy Day, Leon Rausch and Ralph Mooney.

RECOMMENDED ALBUMS:

"Stoney Edwards" (Capitol)(1971)
"She's My Rock" (Capitol)(1973)
"Mississippi You're on My Mind" (Capitol)(1975)
"Blackbird" (Capitol)(1976)
"No Way to Drown a Memory" (Music America)(1981)

JIMMY ELLEDGE

(Singer, Songwriter, Piano)
Date of Birth: January 8, 1943
Where Born: Nashville, Tennessee

Jimmy Elledge was a Pop singer who was discovered by Chet Atkins and signed to RCA Victor. His claim to fame is that he was the first person to record Willie Nelson's *Funny How Time Slips Away*.

He premiered on RCA with a song he wrote called *Send Me a Letter*, but he hit the Pop chart in November 1961 with the Nelson song and during the beginning of 1962 took it to the Top 15. His rendition, although produced by Atkins, was not particularly Country in feel.

Nothing was heard of Jimmy on the chart until 1975, when his 4 Star recording *One by One* scraped onto the lower rungs of the Country chart. Since then, nothing has been heard of him. WKM

RAMBLIN' JACK ELLIOTT

(Singer, Songwriter, Guitar, Actor)
Given Name: Elliott Charles Adnopoz
Date of Birth: August 1, 1931
Where Born: Brooklyn, New York
Married: June Hammerstein

Growing up in the largest metropolitan area of the United States seems an unlikely background for a Cowboy/Folk singer. The magic of television introduced young Elliott Adnopoz to the land of the Wild West with cowboys and cactus. Longing to be like the heroes portrayed on the small screen, the young city kid began calling himself "Buck Elliott." The call of the West was so strong for him that he ran away from home when he was 16 to join a traveling rodeo. He was sent home by the authorities a few months later and finished high school. Following graduation he attended the University of Connecticut and Adelphi College in New York.

Jack adopted the name Ramblin' Jack Elliott when he dropped out of college to pursue his musical dreams. Settling in New York City's musically rich Greenwich Village, Jack quickly made friends of fellow singers by visiting the Folk clubs and coffee houses. By the early 50's, Jack had developed a good friendship with Woody Guthrie. Guthrie was so impressed with his talent that he invited Jack to live with his family in Coney Island. The time spent with Guthrie had a tremendous impact on Jack, as he learned guitar playing and songwriting techniques from his hero. Following a stint as an actor and musician at Knott's Berry Farm in Southern California, Jack traveled to Europe. He became very popular in England and recorded there for Topic Records. Jack was invited to perform on many television shows and also made an appearance at the Brussels World's Fair. In the late 50's, he toured Europe with the Weavers and Pete Seeger.

After he returned to the U.S. in 1960, Jack's popularity grew following the release of his first American album in 1961, ***Jack Elliott Sings the Songs of Woody Guthrie***. He gained an ever wider audience with his 1963 performance at the Newport Folk Festival. After several more popular releases on Prestige Records, Jack signed with Vanguard in 1964. His first album for the label, entitled ***Jack Elliott***, featured one of his admirers, Bob Dylan, on the harmonica. Dylan used the pseudonym "Tedham Porterhouse." Other releases in the 60's included ***Talking Woody Guthrie*** on Delmark Records (1966) and ***Songs of Woody Guthrie*** on Prestige in 1967. The following year, Elliott produced an album for the Archive of Folk Music called ***Jack Elliott***. In 1969, Jack recorded the album ***Roll on Buddy*** with his long-time touring associate, Derroll Adams.

Ramblin' Jack's recordings were sporadic in the 70's and 80's. In 1970, he recorded ***Bull Durham Sacks & Railroad Tracks*** for Reprise. In addition to the traditional folk songs he often recorded, Elliott included new songs by several modern writers including Bob Dylan. Dylan invited Elliott to join him on his Rolling Thunder Revue in the mid-70's where Jack performed for thousands of new fans. Elliott recorded *Kerouac's Last Dream* in 1984 and later two compilations of his work appeared: ***Talking Dust Bowl—The Best of Ramblin' Jack Elliott*** (1989) and ***Hard Travelin'*** (1990). JIE

RECOMMENDED ALBUMS:

(On occasion, Elliott is spelled "Elliot" on record sleeves)
"Jack Elliott at the Second Fret" (Prestige)(1963)
"Young Brigham" (Reprise)(1968)
"Roll on Buddy" (Topic UK)(1969) [With Derroll Adams]
"Bull Durham Sacks & Railroad Tracks" (Reprise)(1970)
"The Essential Ramblin' Jack Elliott" (double)(Vanguard)(1976)
"Hard Travelin'" (double)(Fantasy)(1977)
(See also Derroll Adams)

RED ELLIS

(Singer, Guitar, Mandolin)

Given Name:	**Marvin Thrushel Ellis**
Date of Birth:	**December 21, 1929**
Where Born:	**Arkadelphia, Arkansas**
Married:	**Agee Nugent**
Children:	**Linda Carol, Marvin Lynn**

In the late 50's and early 60's, Red Ellis and Jimmy Williams recorded some excellent Bluegrass-Gospel material for Starday. Based in Michigan, Ellis and the Huron Valley Boys ranked as one of the first groups made up of southern migrants to a northern state that recorded for a Nashville company.

A native of rural southern Arkansas, young Ellis began playing the guitar at age 13 and later took up the mandolin. At age 14, his family moved to Malvern, where Red attended school. He served in the Army during the Korean War and twice suffered combat wounds. Following his recovery and discharge, the young veteran went to the Draughton School in Little Rock, where he learned the skills of sound and video engineering. Red went to Michigan in 1955 and worked at radio stations in Ann Arbor and Ypsilanti, also doing Gospel deejay shows at the latter locale from 1957.

Through contacts made on his program, Ellis became acquainted with other southern migrants who shared his musical interests, including former Stanley Brothers sideman Jimmy Williams. The two teamed up to record a pair of singles for the local Happy Hearts label and several EPs for Starday culminating in the album ***Holy Cry from the Hills***. In 1962 and 1963, Red Ellis and the Huron Valley Boys, which included skilled banjo picker Leonard Styles and mandolinist Billy Christian, did two additional albums for Starday. Their songs included Gospel standards, numbers initially popularized by the Stanley Brothers, like *Rank Stranger* and *No School Bus in Heaven*, along with originals composed by various band members. An unusual aspect of the Ellis career is that he engineered virtually all of his own recordings, except those made in 1971.

From the mid-60's, Red moved more in the direction of Country-Gospel, as he started and recorded for his own Pathways label. In this period he often worked churches and did sessions with the Crossmen, a trio comprised of Roy Maples, Everett Sanders and Blain Rhodes. Agee Ellis also recorded several vocal solos as well as duets with her husband.

In 1968, the Ellis family felt the need to return to Arkansas, where they could be near their aging parents. Red initially went to work as a radio engineer at KAMD Camden, and then to KATV Little Rock as a video engineer. His only formal foray into music came in August, 1971, when the newly formed Jessup label of Jackson, Michigan, arranged for Red and Jimmy Williams to cut a pair of reunion albums for them, which they did with instrumental backup provided by the Detroit-based Sunnysiders band. In recent years Red has only involved himself in music for his own amusement. Red and Jimmy Williams have occasionally gotten together to jam and reminisce. As of March, 1993, Red and Agee were residing in Little Rock. In 1987, Old Homestead Records assembled two albums from his more traditional sounding Pathways recordings. Rebel Records has included his original songs *Christmas Is Not Far Away* and *Home for Christmas* on their anthology album of Bluegrass holiday seasonal numbers. IMT

RECOMMENDED ALBUMS:

Red Ellis and/or Red and Agee Ellis:
"The Sacred Sound of Bluegrass Music" (Starday)(1962)
"Old Time Religion Bluegrass Style" (Starday)(1963)
"A Soldier's Dream" (Old Homestead)(1987)
Jimmy Williams and Red Ellis:
"Holy Cry from the Hills" (Starday)(1961)
"God Brings Bluegrass Back Together" (Jessup)(1971)
"Little David's Harp" (Jessup)(1975)

BROTHER CLAUDE ELY

(Singer, Songwriter, Guitar, Harmonica, Organ)

Given Name:	**Claude Ely**
Date of Birth:	**July 21, 1922**
Where Born:	**Lee County, Virginia**
Married:	**Rosey**
Children:	**Roger, Claudette, Claude, Jr.**
Date of Death:	**May 7, 1978**

Brother Claude Ely recorded some of the most powerful and emotional Gospel songs ever made. Known sometimes as the Gospel Ranger, Ely spent nearly thirty years as a minister in the Appalachian heartland of eastern Kentucky, east Tennessee, southwestern Virginia, and eventually to a migrant community in suburban Cincinnati. His early efforts on the King label—recorded during Kentucky mountain religious services—preserve some excellent and spontaneous music from the white Holiness and Pentecostal traditions.

Claude Ely was born in a mountain homestead some five miles from Pennington Gap, Virginia. At 12, physicians diagnosed him as suffering from tuberculosis, which they believed terminal, but he subsequently recovered. However, during his illness, he began to play musical instruments, although he had no prior experience. Ely subsequently worked as a coal miner and served in the U.S. Army during WWII. Afterwards, he returned home, had a conversion experience and worked in the mines until 1949, when he received a call to preach.

For the next sixteen years Brother Claude conducted numerous revivals and pastored churches in such mountain towns as Sneedville, Tennessee; Grundy, Virginia; and Cumberland, Kentucky. During his pastorate at the Free Pentecostal Church of God in Cumberland, he recorded two sessions for King Records, the first apparently taken from a remote broadcast in the church to a radio station in Whitesburg, Kentucky, on October 12, 1953, and the second from a recording made at a revival meeting in the local Letcher County Courthouse the following June. According to J. D. Jarvis, who was present, Ely initially had some reservations about commercially recording in a studio, but finally decided to permit cutting the material in an actual service and putting it on disc. A total of fifteen numbers were recorded at both services although only eight appeared on single releases, but their uniqueness has long impressed folklorists and students of Appalachian religious traditions. Brother Claude's rendition of songs like *Holy, Holy, Holy (That's All Right), There's a Leak in This Old Building* and especially *There Ain't No Grave Gonna Hold My Body Down* are outstanding and the latter number went on to become something of a standard in the Gospel field.

Claude Ely continued not only to conduct revivals and Gospel sings, but also to minister churches. In 1962 and in 1968, he again recorded for King, but this time in a more conventional studio setting. Meanwhile his pastorate took him to Charity Tabernacle in Newport, Kentucky—within the Cincinnati metropolitan area—where he spent the last thirteen years of his life. Not long after his last session at King, Brother Claude recorded an album at Rusty York's Jewel studio, backed by local Gospel musicians such as Dennis Hensley, Bill Miles, Herschel Lively, J.D. Jarvis and Herman Crisp. He released it on his own Gold Star label.

Ely suffered a heart attack in September, 1977, but seemingly recovered. At that time, he began to tape many of his own unrecorded compositions for preservation. This proved to be a wise move because he suffered a fatal heart attack the following May and died during a service at his church. His daughter assembled an album and a sermon from these home recordings and they were released on Dennis Hensley's Jordan label in 1979. Several latter-day Appalachian Gospel singers trace varying influences to Brother Claude and his music, including Robert Akers, Tommy Crank, Joe Freeman and J.D. Jarvis. Interest in his music persists and in 1993, the British label Ace released a compact disc containing his entire 1953 and 1954 sessions, including the talking, sermonettes and unreleased cuts, as well as a few of his numbers from 1962. IMT

RECOMMENDED ALBUMS:

"The Gospel Ranger" (King)(1962)
"At Home and at Church" (King)(1968)
"Child of the King" (Gold Star)(1969)
"Where Could I Go But to the Lord" (Jordan)(1979)
"Satan Get Back" (Ace UK)(1993) [King masters]

JOE ELY

(Singer, Songwriter, Guitar, Steel Guitar)
Date of Birth: September 2, 1947
Where Born: Amarillo, Texas

This is the story of the boy who wanted to join the circus and did. Joe Ely is now one of the most respected of the Texas coterie of singer/songwriters that emerged in the mid-1970's and yet still remains an underground hero apart from the mainstream of Country music.

When he was 11, his family moved to Lubbock, Texas. They were not into Country music, preferring hymns, and in fact his grandfather sang in the church choir. Joe's parents aimed him at classical music training. When he was in second grade he commenced violin lessons and then, by the time he was in fifth grade, he took steel guitar lessons from a door-to-door teacher.

After this, he took up guitar. He was influenced, early on, by the Blues and in particular the playing of Jimmie Rodgers, Bo Diddley and Robert Johnson. By the time he was 15, Joe was playing the clubs around Lubbock. He started out as a solo and, at the time he was leaving junior high school, had put his first band together, which primarily played rock'n'roll. Like a lot of performers trying to make it, Joe had secondary jobs including washing dishes.

When he was 17 and had dropped out of college, Joe headed for Dallas/Fort Worth, played the clubs and then moved to Houston and did the same. It was an event there that had a profound effect on him. He had not turned up for a gig and the club manager threatened him with violence. To make matters worse, his guitar had been stolen. He headed out for Los Angeles, arriving with only a few dollars. He walked to Venice Beach, where he managed to buy a guitar for $5.00.

He spent the next few years riding the rails, singing where he could and writing along the way. In 1969, Joe went to New York and joined a Texan theatrical group with Joseph Papp's Shakespeare Theater and stayed with them when they toured Europe in 1970. On his return to the U.S., he began alternating between Texas and New York and then suddenly while in Albuquerque, New Mexico, he joined the Ringling Brothers Circus tending the animals. He stayed there for about three months until the circus went to Lubbock, and then decided that he had received one too many kicks from the animals.

Back in Lubbock, Joe renewed his friendship with songwriter Butch Hancock and put together an acoustic band, with Jimmie Dale Gilmore, fiddler Steve Wesson and mandolinist Tony Pearson. They demoed some songs that Joe and Butch had written and headed for Nashville. They were offered a deal but felt uneasy about it. Joe returned to Texas and put together a new band, the Flatlanders, in 1972, with Jimmie Dale Gilmore, Butch and Tommy Hancock, Sylvester Wright and Steve Wesson. The band recorded the album ***One More Road***, which surfaced in 1980 on the U.K. Charly label. The band demoed some new material and a copy of their tape fell into the hands of Jerry Jeff Walker. MCA heard the tape and sent people to hear Joe at Houston's Cotton Club.

Joe's eponymous album was released in 1977 to great critical acclaim within all areas of the industry. The single from it, *All My Love*, made a low level entry on the Country chart the following year. In 1978, Joe's second album, ***Honky Tonk Masquerade***, was released. It would be listed as one of the top albums of the 70's by *Rolling Stone* magazine. Like its predecessor it served notice that Joe Ely was here to stay. He toured widely with his band comprised of Lloyd Maines (steel guitar), Steve Keeton (drums), Gregg Wright (bass guitar), Ponti Bone (accordion, piano) and Jesse Taylor (guitars). However, it was the third album, ***Down on the Drag***, in 1979, which was produced by Bob Johnston, that marked Ely's coming of age. As with the others, it had a mixture of Ely and Hancock songs but unlike the others, it was not recorded in Nashville, but Seattle.

In 1980, he brought out ***Live Shots***, which had been recorded at three venues in London, England: The Hope and Anchor, Dingwalls and the sadly missed Venue (it was released in the fall of 1981 in the States on South Coast/MCA). This album has an edge and featured New Wave group the Clash (for whom the Joe Ely Band opened in a tour of the U.K.) and also Carlene Carter. Among the tracks on the album is Butch Hancock's classic *She Never Spoke Spanish to Me Too Much* and Hank Williams' *Honky Tonkin'*. The following year, Joe released yet another fine album, ***Musta Notta Gotta Lotta***. During that year, he played the California State University at Long Beach Banjo, Fiddle and Guitar Festival and drew an amazingly agreeable reception from an audience unaware of his material.

It would be three years before Joe would release another album. In 1984 came the highly acclaimed but un-Country ***Hi Res***, which debuted the song *Cool Rockin' Loretta*. Joe's 1987 album, ***Lord of the Highway***, included the magnificent *Me and Billy the Kid* and marked a return to his Honky-Tonk roots. During 1988, Sunstorm released Joe's recordings of Butch Hancock songs culled from MCA recordings from 1977-81. That same year, Demon, in the U.K., put out ***Dig All Night***, a set of new recordings produced by Ely that featured his new band with David Grissom (guitars), Jimmy Pettit (bass guitar) and Davis McLarty (drums). This would surface initially on MCA and then Hightone in the U.S.

In 1990, MCA released Joe's second live outing, ***Live at Liberty Lunch***. It featured new versions of *Cool Rockin' Loretta, Drivin' to the Poorhouse in a Limousine* and *Me and Billy the Kid.* He returned to the studio for the 1992 release, ***Love and Danger***, which was co-produced by Tony Brown. Joe has moved a long way from his early MCA days and although the instrumental dynamism is missing without Lloyd Maines and Ponti Bone, there is an animal aggression that started with ***Live Shots***. In 1992, Joe got together with John Mellencamp, Dwight Yoakam, John Pride and James McMurtry as the Buzzin' Cousins in the movie *Falling from Grace*. They had a Top 70 Country single, *Sweet Suzanne*, which appeared on the movie's soundtrack album.

RECOMMENDED ALBUMS:

"Joe Ely" (MCA)(1977)
"Honky Tonk Masquerade" (MCA)(1978)
"Down on the Drag" (MCA)(1979)
"Live Shots" (South Coast/MCA)(1981)
"Musta Notta Gotta Lotta" (South Coast/MCA) (1981)
"Lord of the Highway" (MCA)(1987) [Re-issued on Hightone]
"Dig All Night" (Demon)(1988) [Re-issued on Hightone]
"Live at Liberty Lunch" (MCA)(1990)
"Love and Danger" (MCA)(1992)
The Flatlanders:
"One More Road" (Charly UK)(1980)

BILL EMERSON

(Singer, Songwriter, Banjo, Guitar)
Given Name: **William Hundley Emerson**
Date of Birth: **January 22, 1938**
Where Born: **Washington, D.C.**
Married: **Lola**
Children: **Michael, John, Billy**

Although Bill Emerson spent twenty years of his career in the U.S. Navy, his work prior and subsequent to his service period has made him one of the more important instrumentalists in Bluegrass music.

He began listening to Country and Bluegrass music records and determined to become a musician. In 1955, he began playing guitar and a year later he started playing what was to be his principal instrument, banjo. That year he heard Uncle Bob & the Blue Ridge Partners on WINX Rockville, Maryland, and went to the station and was asked to join them.

Later that year, Bill joined Buzz Busby and the Bayou Boys. However, in 1957, the band was involved in an auto accident, although Bill was not in that vehicle. At the time, the band had a regular booking at the Admiral Grill in Bailey's Cross Roads, Virginia. So as to keep the booking, while Buzz recovered from his injuries, Bill and fellow Bayou Boy, Charlie Waller, put together a band, which by July that year was the Country Gentlemen.

Bill recorded three singles with them for Dixie (*Goin' to the Races/Heavenwood Bound*, 1957) and Starday (*It's the Blues/ Backwoods Blues* and *High Lonesome/Hey Little Girl*, both 1958). Bill left the Country Gentlemen in the fall of 1958. He then began playing with the Stonemans on live dates. By 1960, Bill was playing with Bill Harrell, with whom he stayed for a year and then in 1962, he joined Jimmy Martin and the Sunny Mountain Boys. During this period with Martin, he recorded ***This World is Not My Home*** (1963).

Bill left Jimmy Martin in 1964 and joined Red Allen & the Kentuckians. While with the group, Bill recorded several albums as Bill Emerson and his Virginia Mountaineers. These were ***Banjo Pickin' 'n Hot Fiddlin' Country Style***, ***Banjo Pickin' 'n Hot Fiddlin' Country Style, Vol. 2***, both for Coronet and ***Bluegrass Banjo*** for Design. Bill left Red Allen in 1965 and rejoined Jimmy Martin, with whom he recorded ***Mr. Good 'n Country*** (1966) and ***Big & Country Instrumentals*** (1967). Bill left Martin in 1967 and the following year, joined forces with Cliff Waldron as Emerson & Waldron and the Lee Highway Boys (later renamed New Shades of Grass). Together, they recorded ***New Shades of Grass***, ***Bluegrass Country*** and ***Invite You to a Bluegrass Session***, all for Rebel.

By 1970, Bill was back with the Country Gentlemen, replacing Eddie Adcock. He brought with him a song that he had played with Waldron titled *Fox on the Run*. The song was written by South African Rock keyboardist Manfred Mann (who had become a star in Britain). The song became one of their biggest numbers. While with the Gentlemen, Bill recorded ***One Wide River to Cross*** (1971), ***Country Gentlemen Sound Off*** (1971), ***The Award Winning Country Gentlemen*** (1972) (all on Rebel) and ***The Country Gentlemen*** (1973, Vanguard). Bill stayed with the Country Gentlemen until 1972 and left after a bizarre shooting incident. The band was just leaving the Red Fox Inn in Bethesda, Maryland, after a show when a car sped by and someone fired a gun from it. Bill was shot in the arm and although he fully recovered, the band stopped playing clubs for a long while.

The following year, Bill joined the U.S. Navy Band with the rank of Master Chief Petty Officer. While in the forces, he formed a Country/Bluegrass band, the Country Current. Bill served his time based in Washington, D.C., playing an assortment of music and "playing guitar for 75% of the time." While in uniform, Bill continued to play on other people's albums as well as turning out a pair of duet albums with Pete Goble, ***Tennessee 1949*** (1985) and ***Dixie in***

My Eye (1988), for Webco. During the middle to late 80's, Bill guested on several Webco albums including ***Shenandoah Grass—Yesterday and Today*** by Jim Eanes, ***Stained Glass Bluegrass*** by the Busby Brothers, Larry Stevenson's ***Everytime I Sing a Love Song*** and Jimmy Gaudreau's ***Classic J.A.G.***

Bill recorded two solo albums for Rebel: ***Home of the Red Fox*** (1988) and ***Gold Plated Banjo*** (1991). In 1990, Sterling Banjo Works issued a Signature Series of the "Bill Emerson Red Fox Model" as well as a "Bill Emerson" line of banjo gear. In August 1992, Webco released Bill's ***Reunion*** album, which featured some of the lead singers with whom Bill had worked including Jimmy Martin, Charlie Waller, Red Allen, and Tony Rice. The album was nominated for an IBMA "Album of the Year" award.

Bill left the service in 1993 and since then he has released a duet album, ***Appaloosa***, with his protégé, Wayne Taylor. Bill has no aspirations to rejoin a group but has played reunion concerts with groups such as the Country Gentlemen.

RECOMMENDED ALBUMS:

"Country Banjo" (Design/Pickwick)
"Banjo Pickin' 'n Hot Fiddlin' Country Style" (Coronet) [Also released on Mount Vernon as Pickin' 'n' Fiddlin' as by Bill Emerson and the West Virginia Mountaineers]
"Banjo Pickin' 'n Hot Fiddlin' Country Style, Vol. 2" (Coronet)
"Home of the Red Fox" (Rebel)(1988)
"Gold Plated Banjo" (Rebel)(1991)
"Reunion" (Webco)(1992)
Emerson & Waldron:
"New Shades of Grass" (Rebel)
"Bluegrass Country" (Rebel)
"Invite You to a Bluegrass Session" (Rebel)
Bill Emerson & Pete Goble:
"Tennessee 1949" (Webco)(1985)
"Dixie in My Eye" (Webco)(1988)
Bill Emerson & Wayne Taylor:
"Appaloosa" (Webco)(1994)
With Scotty Stoneman:
"20 Bluegrass Fiddlin' Banjo Hits" (Country Music Legends)(1980)

RALPH EMERY

(TV Talk Show Host, Sometime Recording Artist)
Given Name: Walter Ralph Emery
Date of Birth: March 10, 1933
Where Born: McEwen, Tennessee
Married: 1. Betty Fillmore (m. 1951)(div. 1959)
2. Betty Fillmore (div.)
3. Skeeter Davis (m. 1960)(div. 1964)
4. Joy Kott
Children: Steve, Michael, Ralph, Jr.

Up to October, 1993, Ralph Emery's face was a familiar one to the millions who turned on their TV and tuned in to *Nashville Now*. As the dapper host of the show, he was totally in control, never ruffled, and his velvet glove approach to his guests put them at their ease and enveloped them in an air of sophistication. Looking in, you felt part of this intimate conversation as he introduced and chatted with his guests. This is the essence of Ralph Emery.

As a young child, he was lonely and unhappy. He was sent to his grandparents' farm to live, when he was only 4 years old, because his father was a hopeless drunk and his mother was so busy trying to make ends meet, she was slowly sinking into a nervous breakdown. So this made Ralph, although loved, a lonely and introverted boy. He became an avid listener to the radio, spending hours enjoying the *Grand Ole Opry* and looking through picture books of the stars. Later, as an insecure and awkward teenager who couldn't get a girlfriend, he retreated into the magic of radio, listening to such programs as *Captain Midnight, Jack Armstrong the All American Boy* and *Inner Sanctum*. He became a cinema usher where he could immerse himself in films.

Ralph's next job was as a stock boy at Kroger's at $11 a week. He began to save his money, then enrolled at a broadcasting school and was taught by legendary Nashville deejay John R. Ralph chose to be a broadcaster because he wanted to be someone. He worked very hard to change his speech and practiced very hard at home and at school.

He became the class star pupil and was recommended for a broadcasting job at a small station, WTPR in Paris, Tennessee, where he began working his way up the ladder. Among the positions he held in those years was as an announcer for live wrestling on TV and for high school student Pat Boone.

After working on a Louisiana station he came to Nashville and worked on WMAK but after a problem there, he was fired. Ralph was now 24 years old, and with nothing to lose, he went to WSM, the premier radio station in Nashville, looking for a job. The position that was open was for the all-night shift and as Ralph had more experience than the other applicants, he was hired at $90 a week.

Everyone who met Ralph liked him. His personality was such that they were drawn to him and in the magic of the night, Ralph built his show, learning as he interviewed new as well as established artists. He encouraged many of them to bring along guitars or to sit down at the piano and entertain, thus making his program different. The audience enjoyed this open door policy and continued to support him. They phoned in to speak to him on many subjects. The program was broadcast to thirty-eight states and for 15 years, Ralph held forth over the nighttime air waves.

Liberty Records asked Ralph to try his hand at recording and in 1961, he cut his first single, *Hello Fool*, the answer to Faron Young's *Hello Walls*. Ralph's single shot to the Top 5 on the Country chart. Ralph's next move was to TV, where he was invited to host the early morning show, *Opry Almanac*, which featured news, weather, sports, traffic reports and music. On January 1, 1972, the show became the *Ralph Emery Show* and within a few months, he finished his all-night radio show, although he subsequently took on a weekly radio program, *Take Five for Country Music*, currently entitled *Goody's Presents Ralph Emery*, which is aired over 425 stations.

In 1966, Ralph had an afternoon show called *Sixteenth Avenue*, which ran until 1969. Later he was the host of *Pop Goes Country*, a nationally syndicated weekly series which ran from 1974 until 1980. Another show Ralph did was a live Country music series called *Nashville Alive*, which was aired on Ted Turner's cable superstation WTBS and ran from 1981 to the end of 1982. No sooner had this program ceased than Ralph's most successful show, *Nashville Now*, was born just a few months after.

With a highly successful career behind him, Ralph stepped into the show that was to bring Country music to a wide audience. The show was seen by more than a million people a day and the viewers respected the friendly down-to-earth feel of the show. They also enjoyed the versatility and diversity of the guests being interviewed by Ralph. In addition, Ralph has a comic foil in the effervescent Shotgun Red, the hand puppet who has won the hearts of millions.

Honors have been heaped upon Ralph, named as the most popular personality on cable television today. In 1977, *Music City News* presented Ralph with their "Founders Award." He was placed first in three categories in a poll conducted by *Cable Guide* magazine in 1986: "Best Entertainment/Talk Show," "Best Host of a Talk Entertainment Show" and "Favorite Cable Personality." *Music City News* voted *Nashville Now* as their favorite TV series in four different years, 1985-1988. In October, 1988 he was chosen as SESAC's "Ambassador of Country Music."

The biggest thrill of his career was an all star

***Ralph Emery** (left) with Lester "Roadhog" Moran & the Cadillac Cowboys (aka the **Statler Brothers**)*

Salute to Ralph Emery during 1990, a television extravaganza, in which seventy of Country's top names paid tribute to him, as the man who had for so long given so much to their means of livelihood. Apart from his radio and TV work, Ralph has made time to serve terms as both President and Vice President of the Country Music Foundation, a Board member of the CMA, a founding member of the Nashville chapter of the American Federation of Television and Radio Artists (AFTRA) and a Director of the National Academy of Recording Arts and Sciences (NARAS).

Ralph has appeared in four movies: *The Road to Nashville, Country Music on Broadway, Nashville* and *The Girl from Tobacco Row*. After years of wearing a beard, one day in 1987 he shaved it off. In 1991 Ralph retired from his early morning TV show, and an autobiography of his life, written with Tom Clark, was published entitled *Memories*. It spent 25 weeks on the *New York Times* best-seller list. In 1993, he followed up with *More Memories*, which he also wrote with Tom Clark.

Ralph was shown at his best when interviewing the legendary Dick Clark in a one to one interview (*Ralph Emery: On the Record*) in 1992. His sympathy, rapport and understanding shone through. In April, 1993, Ralph announced that he was planning to leave *Nashville Now* on October 15. Through his Ralph Emery Television Productions, he was planning to produce specials for TNN. JAB

RECOMMENDED ALBUMS:

With Shotgun Red:

"Songs for Children" (RCA)(1989)

"Christmas with Ralph & Red" (RCA)(1989)

BUDDY EMMONS

(Steel Guitar/Singer/Composer/Lap Steel/Piano/Bass Guitar)

Given Name:	**Buddy Gene Emmons**
Date of Birth:	**January 27, 1937**
Where Born:	**Mishawaka, Indiana**
Married:	**1. Georgene (div.)** **2. Peggy**
Children:	**Larry, Buddie Gene, Tami; stepchildren: Deborah, Dianna (twins)**

Just say "Buddy Emmons" to another steel guitar player, and you see their eyes glaze over in ecstasy. Resplendent in his brown derby, he is the consummate player who is at home with Country and Swing.

He was given a 6-string lap steel when he was 11 and he was hooked. He studied at the Hawaiian Conservatory of Music, South Bend, Indiana, and by the time he was 16, he was playing in local clubs in Calumet City, Illinois, and jamming in Chicago during weekends.

In 1965, he moved to Detroit where he depped for Walter Haynes at a Little Jimmy Dickens gig. This led to him being a permanent band member of Dickens' Country Boys. As a result, he started making appearances on the *Grand Ole Opry*. He recorded three singles with the Country Boys, *Red Wing/Country Boy Bounce* (1956), *Buddy's Boogie/Raisin' the Dickens* and *I Won't Beg Your Pardon/Alone in Love* (1957) and two solos, *Cold, Rolled Steel/Flint Hill Special* (1956) and *Silver Bells/Border Serenade* (1957), all on Columbia. Buddy started making appearances with Ernest Tubb's Texas Troubadours on the *Midnight Jamboree*. In 1960, Buddy cut *Four Wheel Drive/Blue Wind* for Decca. From 1963 through 1968, he was a member of Ray Price's Cherokee Cowboys.

In 1965, he recorded his first album with that other great steelie, Shot Jackson, entitled ***Steel Guitar & Dobro Sound***, on Nashville Records. He and Shot founded the Sho-Bud Company, marketing the first pedal steel guitars with push-rod pedals. Buddy left Nashville to play bass guitar for Roger Miller in Los Angeles in 1969. He played West Coast sessions for Ray Charles, Henry Mancini and Linda Ronstadt between tours for Miller.

In 1973, Buddy split from Roger and returned to Nashville. Two years later, he started his association with Flying Fish Records. Among the albums he released on this label are ***Buddy Emmons Sings Bob Wills*** (1976), ***Buddies***, with fiddle player Buddy Spicher (1977) and ***Minors Aloud***, with Lenny Breau (1978).

Buddy has recorded for a miscellany of labels over the years, including Mercury, Starday, K-Ark, Cochise, EQ, Steel Guitar Record Club, Cumberland and Midland. In recent years, he has maintained a relationship with Ray Pennington's Step One Records. He and Ray have put together albums under the name of the Swing Shift Band with the cream of Nashville sessionmen that include Rob Hajacos, Gregg Galbraith, Bunky Keels and Jerry Kroon. This blend of nostalgia and inventiveness takes the big band sounds of the 40's and mixes them with a touch of Western Swing, a soupçon of Country ballads and smidgeon of Hot Club of France. Darting throughout is Buddy's steel and the vocals of Ray Pennington. During 1993 and 1994, Buddy has been busy touring the world with the Everly Brothers. He has also spent some of that time period writing his autobiography.

RECOMMENDED ALBUMS:

"Best of Western Swing" (Cumberland)

"Buddy Emmons Sings Bob Wills" (Flying Fish)(1976)

"Buddies" (Flying Fish)(1977) [With Buddy Spicher]

"Live from Austin City Limits" (Flying Fish)(1979) [As the Nashville Super Pickers]

"Buddy Emmons (The Black Album)" (Emmons)

For Swing fans, the Swing Shift Albums:

"Swingin' from the 40's Thru the 80's" (double)(Step One)(1984)

"In the Mood for Swingin'" (Step One)(1986)

"Swingin' Our Way" (Step One)(1990)

"Swingin' By Request" (Step One)(1992)

If you want to try and learn steel guitar:

"Learn to Play" (Emmons)

EVANGELINE

When Formed: 1988
Current Members:
Kathleen Stieffel Vocals, Acoustic Guitar
Sharon Leger Vocals, Bass Guitar, Washboard
Rhonda Bolin Lohmeyer Vocals, Guitar, Fiddle
Beth McKee Vocals, Keyboards, Accordion
Former Members:
Nancy Buchan Vocals, Fiddle, Mandolin
Dudley Fruge Drums

During the 90's, there seemed to be more groups than ever making their way to the top. However, for some reason, at a time when solo female acts are more dominant in all forms of music, all-girl groups have had difficulties making the breakthrough. Evangeline is one of the best. The band blends several influences to make it one of the most cohesive units in Country music.

They have three lead vocalists in the group: Kathleen Stieffel from Bay St. Louis, Louisiana, on the Gold Coast, who had played in various local Country bands; Sharon Leger, who brings her Cajun influence to the aggregation, had been featured on several albums by Cajun singer Bruce Daigrepont; and Beth McKee, who hails from Jackson, Mississippi, is the band's Blues exponent, having been a regular on Austin's Blues scene. In 1991, Beth toured with Fingers Taylor, who opened for Jimmy Buffett on his 1991 summer tour. Completing the line-up is Rhonda Bolin Lohmeyer from Gretna, Louisiana, who comes from a Country-Rock and Country background.

The group originally comprised Rhonda, Kathleen and Sharon. The name of the band comes from the long lost lover in the Longfellow poem about Arcadians migrating from Nova Scotia to Louisiana. After just a few rehearsals they got a gig playing a club in Bourbon Street, New Orleans, four nights a week. At this time, their line-up also included Nancy Buchan, who grew up in Wichita, Kansas, but moved to New Orleans after playing in New York and Colorado. She came from a diverse background that includes the classics, Jazz-Rock and Bluegrass. There was also one "token male" in the band, Dudley Fruge from Lake Charles, Louisiana. He had recorded and toured with Zachary Richard.

In 1988, they entered the initial Jazz Search, a talent contest sponsored by the New Orleans Jazz and Heritage Festival and Audubon Zoo. They won this and a spot on the Jazz Fest and it spurred them on to enter the Marlboro Talent Roundup and the True Value Country Music Showdown. As a result of winning the Jazz Fest, the producer, Quint Davis, booked them every year and brought them to the notice of Jimmy Buffett. After hearing them live, Buffett signed them to his new Margaritaville label that is marketed through MCA Nashville. He called in Justin Niebank to produce Evangeline. He was better known for his work with Blues artists on the Alligator label.

The debut eponymous album, in 1992, will for a long time remain one of the finest by a new group. The songs are mainly written by members of the group, but also feature material by Brendan Croker (of Notting Hillbillies), Van Morrison, Nanci Griffith (*Gulf Coast Highway,* which features a duet with Jimmy Buffett) and Jesse Winchester. One of the stand-out tracks is the Cajun tour-de-force *Bon Temps La Louisiane* by Waylon Thibodeaux and Sharon Leger. If there is one thing wrong with the album, it's the sleeve, which is so boring. Not the way to launch a new act.

By the time of their second album, ***French Quarter Moon*** (with a much more appealing sleeve), in 1993, Evangeline was down to a quartet, with Nancy and Dudley having departed. However, it was not until 1994 that the group got its first taste of singles chart success, when the Kelly Willis-Kostas song, *Let's Go Spend Your Money, Honey,* reached the Top 70.

RECOMMENDED ALBUMS:
"Evangeline" (Margaritaville/MCA)(1992)
"French Quarter Moon" (Margaritaville/MCA)(1993)

Dale Evans refer ROY ROGERS

LEON EVERETTE

(Singer, Songwriter, Guitar)
Given Name: Leon Everette Baughman
Date of Birth: June 21, 1948
Where Born: Aiken, South Carolina
Married: Kathy
Children: Tammy Lynn, Kimberley Ann, Brenton Duane

Leon Everette has one of the highest energy stage shows in Country music. His band, Hurricane, is almost certainly the most active on stage and Leon has hired fiddle players (who have included the exciting Mark Lavender), who specialize in running around the audience while sawing away.

Leon was raised in Queens, New York, and after leaving high school, he joined the U.S. Navy. He served on an aircraft carrier and while on leave in the Philippines, he bought a guitar and taught himself to play. The Navy sponsored a talent contest, which he entered and won. After leaving the Navy he married Kathy and got a job with the South Carolina Power and Gas company. He left this job when he threw a $40,000 piece of equipment into the river because "my boss told me to always do what he told me" (his boss *had* told him to to throw it into the river).

With a wife (who was seven months pregnant) and two children to care for, Leon decided to put together a band. He was soon getting booked into clubs along the South Carolina/Georgia border. Leon initially recorded for Doral Records without success. He tried to get people in Nashville interested in what he was doing. True Records in Nashville took him on in their mail room and later he was signed to the label. Leon then moved his family to Nashville. In 1977, True got him to do an Elvis tribute record called ***Goodbye King of Rock and Roll,*** which he wasn't happy about, so he tore up the contract and returned to Carolina with his family. However at year-end, True released *I Love That Woman (Like the Devil Loves Sin)*, which found Leon debuting on the Country chart in the Top 90.

As a favor to his friends from his old band, Leon did some gigs in Augusta, Georgia, where he was spotted by Carroll Fulmer, a Florida trucking executive, who was in the audience. Fulmer founded Orlando Records in 1978 and called in Jerry Foster and Bill Rice to write songs for Leon. During 1979, Orlando placed four Everette singles on the chart: *We Let Love Slip Away* (Top 90), *Giving Up Easy* (Top 90), *Don't Feel Like the Lone Ranger* (Top 40) and *The Sun Went Down in My World Tonight* (Top 50). At year-end, Leon did even better with a re-recording of *I Love That Woman (Like the Devil Loves Sin)*, which went Top 30 in 1980. He followed this in with *I Don't Want to Lose You*, which peaked in the Top 30 in 1980 and then *Over* took Leon into the Top 10.

Because of his success, Leon soon had RCA Records interested in him and he was signed to the label in 1980. At the end of the year, he charted with the RCA re-issue of *Giving Up Easy*, which reached the Top 5 in 1981. Two further hits followed in 1981, *If I Keep on Going Crazy* (Top 15) and *Hurricane* (Top 5). That year, Leon was nominated by the ACM as "Best New Male Vocalist" and

Leon's band, Hurricane, was nominated as the ACM's "Touring Band of the Year."

At the end of the year, Leon charted with *Midnight Rodeo*, which reached the Top 10 in 1982. He followed that with the Top 10 hits *Just Give Me What You Think Is Fair* and *Soul Searchin'*. His first hit of 1983 was *Shadows of My Mind* (Top 15), *My Lady Loves Me (Just as I Am)* (Top 10) and *The Lady, She's Right* (Top 10). The latter had harmony vocals from Rex Gosdin.

1984 brought *I Could'a Had You* (Top 10) and *Shot in the Dark* (Top 30). However, Leon became disillusioned by the promotional aspect of his contract with RCA and moved to Mercury Records and had three minor hits in 1985: *Too Good to Say No To*, *A Good Love Died Tonight* and *'Til a Tear Becomes a Rose*.

Leon still wasn't happy and soon asked his managers, Carroll Fulmer and Michael Jackson, to reactivate Orlando Records and get him off Mercury. They obliged and his records in 1986 on Orlando that charted were *Danger List*, *Sad State of Affairs* and *Still in the Picture*. Leon appeared at the Wembley Festival in England in 1987 and again in 1988, where he was enthusiastically applauded for his lively performance.

Since 1988, Leon and his wife have been running a shop that imports wicker and is a lace and craft supplier in their hometown of Ward, South Carolina. JAB

RECOMMENDED ALBUMS:

"Goodbye King of Rock & Roll" (True)(1977) [A tribute to Elvis]
"I Don't Want to Lose" (Orlando)(1980)
"Hurricane" (RCA Victor)(1981)
"Maverick" (RCA Victor)(1982)
"Doin' What I Feel" (mini album) (RCA Victor)(1984)
"Best of Leon Everette" (RCA)(1985)

Leon Everette and his dynamic band, Hurricane, at Wembley Festival in the U.K.

EVERLY BROTHERS,The

DON EVERLY
(Singer, Songwriter, Guitar)

Given Name:	**Isaac Donald Everly**
Date of Birth:	**February 1, 1937**
Where Born:	**Brownie, Kentucky**
Married:	**1. Sue Ingram (div.)**
	2. Venetia Stevenson (m. 1962) (div.)
	3. Karen
Children:	**Venetia, Stacy, Erin, Eden**

PHIL EVERLY
(Singer, Songwriter, Guitar)

Given Name:	**Philip Everly**
Date of Birth:	**January 19, 1939**
Where Born:	**Chicago, Illinois**
Married:	**1. Janet Bleyer (div.)**
	2. Jackie Ertell
Children:	**Jason, Christopher**

The Everly Brothers are famed for their immaculate sibling harmonies, which were honed during their childhood and gave them a string of classic hits in the late 50's and early 60's, and that made them the No.1 duo of the rock'n'roll era.

Their parents, Ike and Margaret, were Country Gospel-Folk artists and Ike was a formidable guitarist. From a young age, the boys were trained to follow in their parents' footsteps. To augment the family act, Don and Phil were quickly taught basic guitar chords (although they were both left-handed, Ike taught them to play right-handed) and when Don was age 8 and Phil age 6, they made their radio debut on KMA out of Shenandoah, Iowa, and accompanied their parents on summer tours. In 1953, the family moved to Knoxville, Tennessee, where they worked for WROL.

Perhaps because there were already several brother acts—the Bailles Brothers, the Louvin Brothers, the York Brothers, the Blue Sky Boys and the Delmore Brothers—the Everlys found it hard to get a break. When Chet Atkins invited them to Nashville, they expected much, but at the time Chet did not quite wield the clout that he would later. He did however sign Don to his publishing company, Athens Music, and in 1954, Kitty Wells cut Don's song *Thou Shalt Not Steal*, which only charted for a week. Don had two further cuts on Justin Tubb, but both releases failed to chart.

The Everlys secured a six-month recording deal with Columbia on November 8, 1955. At a session lasting just 22 minutes, they recorded 4 self-composed sides, accompanied by Carl Smith's Tunesmiths (who had traveled 200 miles to be at the session), but after the initial single, *The Sun Keeps Shining/Keep a Lovin' Me*, released on February 6, 1956, flopped, Columbia locked the other two tracks away. The four songs were released in 1981, as a retrospective.

Early in 1956, Don signed with music publishers Hill & Range. Later that year, the brothers were in Hal Smith's office at Pamper Music and he told them that the only publisher able to get a record deal was Acuff-Rose. Wesley Rose was impressed with the Everlys and allegedly bought out their Hill & Range contract. Don and Phil had already been rejected by Capitol and Cadence, but Rose was setting up a Country & Western Division of Cadence Records for Archie Bleyer, Cadence's boss. Bleyer had not been impressed with the Everlys and so Rose said that he would make up a tape and send it to Bleyer; this time Bleyer was hooked and late in 1956 the Everly Brothers signed to the label.

By now, rock'n'roll had assumed its ascendancy and it became reflected in the recordings of the Everlys. With the powerful yet simple songs of Boudleaux and Felice Bryant, their career took off in 1957 with *Bye Bye Love,* which went to No.1 (for 7 weeks) on the Country chart, staying around for 6 months, and Top 3 in the Pop list. It also broke through internationally, reaching No.6 in the U.K. The clean-cut duo quickly gained a young and loyal following. This was the beginning of a spectacular period when the combination of the Bryants' material and the Everlys' superb harmonies proved irresistible. On May 11, 1957, the Everly Brothers made their debut on the *Grand Ole Opry*.

The follow-up, *Wake Up Little Susie*, topped the Country (8 weeks), Pop (4 weeks) and R&B charts, again hanging around for six months, even though it was banned in Boston for being too suggestive. In 1958, their initial single, *This Little Girl of Mine*, was a Top 5 Country hit, but only made the Pop Top 30. The flip-side, *Should We Tell Them*, also made the Country Top 10. However, the next release, *All I Have to Do Is Dream/Claudette* (flip-side by Roy Orbison), repeated the feat of topping the Country, Pop and R&B charts. In addition, it was at No.1 for 7 weeks in Britain. This was followed to the top of the Pop chart by *Bird Dog* with the flip-side, *Devoted to You*, also becoming a Top 10 cross-over hit. They wrapped up the year with *Problems*, which made it to the Pop Top 3, but only made the Top 20 on the Country charts. During the summer, they had recorded the memorable Folk-Country album ***Songs Our Daddy Taught Us***.

Behind the scenes, all was not well. Increasingly, the Everlys wanted their artistic freedom, especially as Don was now writing more commercial material, while Rose, naturally, wanted them to continue putting out his copyrights as singles. In 1959, the single *Take a Message to Mary/Poor Jenny* was by their standards a flop, the top-side making the Pop Top 20 and the flip reaching the Top 25. However, this was followed by the first single written by Don Everly, *('Til) I Kissed You*, which became a Top 5 Pop hit and a Top 10 Country success, also reaching No.2 in the U.K. Among the musicians were their good friends Jerry Allison and Sonny Curtis from the Crickets.

Near the end of their Cadence contract, the Everlys started experimenting with strings (much as their pal Buddy Holly had) on the English-translated Gilbert Becaud song, *Let It Be Me*. This was to be their last single for the label, although Cadence released *When Will I Be Loved* (Top 10, 1960), *Like Strangers* (1960), a re-release of *All I Have to Do Is Dream* (1961) and *I'm Here to Get My Baby Out of Jail* (1962), after the duo had left.

Having sold 15 million records in the preceding three years, the Everlys signed for 10 years to the newly formed Warner Brothers Records for $1 million, a deal which Wesley Rose had negotiated. The first single, penned by Don and Phil, *Cathy's Clown*, proved to be a monster hit. It stayed on the top of the U.S. Pop chart for 5 weeks and the U.K. charts for 7 weeks. They followed-up with *So Sad (to Watch Good Love Go Bad)*(Top 10)/*Lucille* (Top 25).

In 1961, they started the year with the double-sided Top 10 hit, *Ebony Eyes/Walk Right Back*. The former, an archetypal "death" song, was written by John D. Loudermilk. The sides were reversed in Britain and reached No.1. They wrapped up the year with a song that was to prove contentious. *Temptation* had been recorded by Bing Crosby in 1934 and Wesley Rose was really against the duo recording the song. They defied him and so a premature split occurred and Jack Rael became their manager. The single failed to ignite the U.S. but did reach No.1 in Britain. During the year, they made their first concert tour of Britain, accompanied by the Crickets. As a result of the split with Rose, they found themselves cut off from the fine material of the Bryants.

At the end of 1961, the Everly Brothers were both drafted into the U.S. Marines for six months. While they were away, Warner Brothers released *Don't Blame Me/Muskrat* (two tracks of a 4-track EP), which only made the Top 20, and the immortal *Crying in the Rain* (1962), which went Top 10. Their final major hit occurred later in 1962 with *That's Old Fashioned (That's the Way Love Should Be)*. Their demise was not helped by coming off the road to avoid paying Rose commission, nor did the "British invasion," which swept away all in its path. Somewhat ironically, the Beatles had been influenced by Don and Phil!

In 1965, the Everlys staged a brief revival with *The Price of Love*, which made No.1 in the U.K., and *Love Is Strange*, which also gave them a major hit there. During this period, they were reduced to recording songs slanted at the European market, including some songs in Italian and the superb album ***Two Yanks in England***, with most of the songs written by the Hollies. The brothers, unfortunately, tended to be judged on their singles, with their many fine albums usually failing to get the credit they deserved.

They moved, before the full term of their contract, from Warner Brothers to RCA in 1968 and cut two albums. Two of the best tracks were solo vocal efforts, Don's *I'm Tired of Singing My Song in Las Vegas* and Phil's *Up in Mabel's Room*.

In 1970, the duo had their own TV special, *Johnny Cash Presents the Everly Brothers*, on which Ike came out of retirement to appear before a national audience. However, the strain between brothers was reaching a breaking point. Both had suffered marriage and drug problems and during the 1963 U.K. tour, Don had undergone a nervous breakdown. During a concert at Buena Park, California, on July 13, 1973, promoter Bill Hollingshead stopped the below-par performance and Phil stormed off the stage, smashing his guitar, leaving Don to complete the show, so ending the Everly Brothers, Chapter 1. They both carried on with solo careers.

Don had already released a self-titled album on Ode in 1971 and in 1973, Phil signed as a solo with RCA and issued the critically acclaimed ***Star Spangled Springer***, which featured Duane Eddy, Buddy Emmons, James Burton and J.D. Maness. The following year, Don released his second Ode album, ***Sunset Towers***, which was also well received by the pundits. Phil moved over to Pye that year and issued ***Phil's Diner*** (titled ***Nothing's Too Good for My Baby***, in the U.K.) and in 1975, ***Mystic Line***. Don signed with Hickory, in 1977, and released the excellent album ***Brother Jukebox***. He had three Country chart singles, of which the most successful was the 1976 *Yesterday Just Passed My Way Again*.

Phil moved on to Elektra in 1979, and released the largely self-penned ***Living Alone***. He moved on to Curb in 1980, and returned to the Country singles charts with *Dare to Dream Again* that year and the even more successful *Sweet Southern Love* the following year. In 1983, Phil traveled to England and under the guiding hand of Stuart Coleman, recorded the self-titled album for Capitol. Coleman had been very successful as the producer of British Rockabilly star Shakin' Stevens. Phil returned to the U.K. Top 10 with a duet with superstar Cliff Richard, *She Means Nothing to Me*. The album featured Mark Knopfler, Pete Wingfield, Billy Bremner and Fleetwood Mac's Christine McVie. Only one track was recorded in the States, *When I'm Dead and Gone*, which was produced by Kyle Lehning. That year, Phil had a Top 40 Country hit with a song not on the album, *Who's Gonna Keep Me Warm*.

Such was their bitterness toward each other that for nearly 10 years the Everly Brothers only met at their father's funeral. However, it was inevitable that a reunion had to take place and in June 1983, at London's Royal Albert Hall, a reunion concert took place. The occasion was captured on video and album. It is sad to note that the only comment that certain elements of the media could make was on how much weight Don had put on. For everyone else, there was joy at the fact that the harmonies were still there.

The following year ***EB84***, produced by Dave Edmunds, appeared on Mercury, and yielded a Pop Top 50 hit, Paul McCartney's *On the Wings of a Nightingale*. They released the album ***Born Yesterday*** in 1986, and it was chosen by *Time* magazine as one of the Top 10 Pop albums of the year. In 1988, they released the excellent album, ***Some Hearts***, which featured Albert Lee and for which the associate producer was drummer Larry Londin.

In 1986, the Everly Brothers were inducted into the Rock and Roll Hall of Fame. In 1990, the brothers inaugurated the Everly Brothers' Homecoming Music Festival, a benefit concert for the mining community in Muhlenberg County, Kentucky. The proceeds go to the Everly Brothers Foundation. The duo was still together in 1993 and, in company with Buddy Emmons, traveled to the U.K. for yet another tour and continued to play the U.S., including Las Vegas, in 1994.

One of the things that the Everly Brothers were responsible for was to extend sibling harmony from Country and Gospel into the still undefined realms of rock'n'roll, allowing others such as the Kalin Twins and non-fraternal groups such as the Hollies, the Searchers, the Eagles and even Simon and Garfunkel to bring melody into Rock.SM/BM

RECOMMENDED ALBUMS:

"Songs Our Daddy Taught Us" (Cadence)(1958) [Re-released on Ace UK in 1983]
"The Everly Brothers Sing Great Country Hits" (Warner Brothers)(1963)
"Two Yanks in England" (Warner Bros.)(1966)
"Roots" (Warner Bros.)(1969)
"Pass the Chicken and Listen" (RCA Victor)(1973)
"Greatest Hits" Volumes 1, 2 & 3 (Barnaby)(1978)
"Reunion Album" (Mercury/Impression UK)(1984)
"Classic Everly Brothers" (Bear Family Germany)(1991)
Solo albums:
Don Everly:
"Sunset Towers" (Ode)(1974)
"Brother Jukebox" (Hickory)(1977)
Phil Everly:
"Star Spangled Springer" (RCA Victor)(1973)
"Phil Everly" (Capitol)(1983)

SKIP EWING

(Singer, Songwriter, Guitar, Bass Guitar, Banjo)

Given Name:	**Donald Ralph Ewing**
Date of Birth:	**March 6, 1964**
Where Born:	**Redlands, California**
Married:	**1. div.**
	2. Angel
Children:	**Rebecca Lynn**

Some time ago, there was the feeling that to be a successful Country music songwriter, one had to be over 40. This view changed at the end of the 80's and with the advent of the new breed of songwriter, the reality is that they are getting younger. One of the first to emerge was the talented writer Skip Ewing.

Skip, the son of a career military man, was born in Redlands, California, but soon moved on to Charleston, South Carolina. By the time he was age 9, he no longer had a permanent home, but hailed from "everywhere." It was hearing Merle Haggard and Lefty Frizzell on his father's car radio and the family stereo that turned Skip on to Country music. Skip learned to play guitar before he was able to read. He began writing songs while still in his teens, and by the time he had finished high school, he had appeared in stage musicals and played banjo at Bluegrass festivals.

It was while playing bass guitar in The Old Country in Virginia, a show at Busch Gardens, that Skip was approached about working at Opryland. He moved to Nashville in 1984, age 19, and for two and one half years he impersonated famous Country stars at Opryland. He spent his spare time honing his skills as a songwriter and singing on demo and jingle sessions.

He then signed to Acuff-Rose Music. In 1987, he signed with MCA Records, and Jimmy Bowen, then heading MCA's Country Division, asked Skip to co-produce his own debut album, ***The Coast of Colorado***. He debuted on the Country singles chart in 1988 with *Your Memory Wins Again*, which reached the Top 20. He followed with *Don't Have Far to Fall* (Top 10) and *Burnin' a Hole in My Heart* (Top 3).

In 1989, he had two more hits from the album in *The Gospel According to Luke* (Top 10) and the title track, which got to the Top 15.

Singer/Songwriter ***Skip Ewing***

That year, Skip released his second album, ***The Will to Love*** and went back in the Top 5 with the track *It's You Again*. By 1990, his recording star had waned, and the two singles that charted, *If a Man Could Live on Love Alone* and *I'm Your Man*, only reached the Top 70. The latter was co-produced by Skip and Ricky Skaggs.

In 1991, Skip left MCA and moved to Capitol, where Jimmy Bowen was now running the show. The first album, ***Naturally***, yielded the single, *I Get the Picture*, which only reached the Top 75. The title track, promoted in 1992, also reached the Top 75. The need for drastic action was evident and when his fourth album, ***Homegrown Love***, was recorded in 1993, veteran producer Jerry Crutchfield was at the helm. In addition, for the first time, Skip recorded material not written by himself and his co-writers.

As a writer, Skip has gone from strength to strength. Often writing with Don Sampson and Red Lane, his cuts include *One Hell of a Song* (George Jones), *Have You* (Randy Travis), *Rock-a-Bye Heart* (Wild Rose), *If I Were a Painting* (both Kenny Rogers and Willie Nelson), *Autumn's Not That Cold* (Lorrie Morgan), *It Wasn't His Child* (Sawyer Brown) and *Love Me* (Collin Raye).

RECOMMENDED ALBUMS:

"The Coast of Colorado" (MCA)(1988)
"The Will to Love" (MCA)(1989)
"Naturally" (Capitol)(1991)
"Greatest Hits" (MCA)(1991)
"Homegrown Love" (Liberty)(1993)

EXILE

Formed:	**1963 as Exiles/1973 as Exile**
Members:	
J.P. Pennington	**Lead Vocals/Guitar**
Jimmy Stokley	**Vocals**
Buzz Cornelisons	**Vocals/Keyboard**
Marlon Hargis	**Keyboard/Vocals**
Sonny Lemaire	**Bass/Vocals**
Steve Goetzman	**Drums**
Les Taylor	**Lead Vocals/Guitar**
Mark Gray	**Keyboard/Vocals**
Paul Martin	**Guitar/Vocals**
Lee Carroll	**Keyboards**
Mark Jones	**Guitar/Vocals**

Exile started out in Kentucky as a Rock-orientated band called Exiles. The group was co-formed by J.P. Pennington, the son of Lily May Ledford, one of the Coon Creek Girls. In 1965, the band toured with Dick Clark and in 1973, the band was renamed Exile. They first hit the Pop chart with their Atco release, *Try It On*, which just scraped into the Top 100.

Their first major success came with the

Pop hit *Kiss You All Over*, which was written by Pop superwriters Mike Chapman and Nicky Chinn, which appeared on Micky Most's Rak label; the song was a top 10 hit in the U.K. in 1978. In the U.S., it was released on Warner Brothers and for 4 weeks it topped the Pop chart. In 1979, they had a Top 40 Pop hit with *You Thrill Me*.

After a long dry spell, the band returned to their roots in Kentucky to regroup and write music. They played in local small clubs and had a good local following. Several of the songs written and recorded then were useful to other acts; Janie Fricke recorded *It Ain't Easy Being Easy*, Dave and Sugar cut *Stay With Me* and Alabama recorded both *Take Me Down* and *The Closer You Get*. While at this stage, they honed their talents into a musical style, a high energy Southern Rock sound and set off in a new direction.

Their manager, Jim Morley, had lunch with Buddy Killen and started the ball rolling towards a recording contract with Epic Records. While they were playing at Buddy Killen's Stockyard, a night club/restaurant in Nashville, Buddy brought along Rick Blackburn of Epic Records to see them. He was convinced, they were signed and their Country career had begun; producer Buddy Killen took them into the studio. At this time, their line-up was J.P. Pennington, Les Taylor, Sonny Lemaire, Marlon Hargis and Steve Goetzman. Early that year, they recorded their debut Country single, *High Cost of Leaving*, which became a Top 30 success and led to their first album, ***Exile***, on which all ten songs bore member credits. The next two singles from the album, *Woke Up in Love* and *I Don't Wanna Be a Memory*, were No.1 hits. The second album, ***Kentucky Hearts***, released in 1984, yielded three more chart toppers, *Give Me One More Chance, Crazy for Your Love* and *She's a Miracle*. 1985 saw the release of the album ***Hang on to Your Heart***, which again gave them four No. 1 hit singles, *Hang on to Your Heart, I Could Get Used to You, It'll Be Me* and *She's Too Good to Be True*. It also yielded the Top 25 release, *Super Love*.

Exile was nominated for the CMA's "Vocal Group of the Year" in 1985, 1986 and 1987 and "Instrumental Group of the Year" in 1985. In 1986, Sonny Lemaire was named BMI "Songwriter of the Year" and that year *Radio & Records* magazine named *It'll Be Me* as its "Country Record of the Year."

The next album did not appear for another two years, although there had been some compilation albums of their hits in the interim, two on MCA/Curb and one on Epic. However, with the album ***Shelter from the Night***, things began to change. Buddy Killen, who had given them a string of No.1 hits, was strangely dumped in favor of Elliot Scheiner and this album was cut in Connecticut instead of Nashville. This was the debut album for Lee Carroll, who had replaced Marlon Hargis on keyboards in 1985. From 1987 to when they left the label in 1989, Exile racked up hits with *She's Too Good to Be True* (No.1, 1987), *I Can't Get Close Enough* (No.1), *Just One Kiss* (Top 10) and *It's You Again* (Top 25) (all 1988).

In 1989, Les Taylor left Exile after 10 years and was replaced by Mark Jones. A year later, J.P. Pennington, one of the group's mainstay songwriters, left after 27 years with the band and was replaced by guitarist Paul Martin. In 1990, Exile signed with Arista, but by the time of their debut album on the label, Mark Jones had left and appears on the album as an additional player. The group that had once been a seven-piece was now a quartet. The new album, ***Still Standing***, yielded *Nobody's Talking* (Top 3) and *Yet* (Top 10). The first single of the second album, ***Justice*** (1991), *Even Now*, reached the Top 20. During 1990, Curb released a pair of albums of Exile's early tracks. After being dropped from the Arista label in 1993, the group decided to call it a day. Steve Goetzman has now become Steve Wariner's manager. JAB

RECOMMENDED ALBUMS:

"Exile" (Epic)(1983)
"The Best of Exile" (MCA/Curb)(1985)
"Greatest Hits" (Epic)(1986)
"The Best of Exile" (Curb)(1990)
"Still Standing" (Arista)(1990)
"Justice" (Arista)(1991)
"Super Hits" (Sony)(1993)

F

BARBARA FAIRCHILD

(Singer, Songwriter, Guitar)
Date of Birth: November 12, 1950
Where Born: Knobel, Arkansas
Married: 1. (div.)
2. Randy Reinhard (div.)
3. Milton Carroll (div.)
Children: Randy Reinhard II, Tara Nevada, Randina Sierra

Barbara is another of Country music's prodigies, having made her first performance in a local school's talent contest at the tender age of 5. When she was 13, her family moved to St. Louis and by the time she was 15, she had cut her first single, *Brand New Bed of Roses*, for the Norman label and was appearing on local TV.

On finishing high school in 1968, Barbara and a friend, Ruby Van Hoy, headed for Nashville to pitch songs and try and get a record deal. She met music executive Jerry Crutchfield in a record company parking lot and he invited her in and listened to her songs. He thought she had some potential and he encouraged her to go back home and write seven more songs of the same quality. Barbara returned to Nashville two months later with fifteen songs and Crutchfield signed her as a staff writer for MCA Music. He was also impressed with her voice and took one of her songs to Billy Sherrill, Columbia/Nashville Vice President of A & R. *Love Is a Gentle Thing* landed Fairchild a recording contract with Columbia and became her first release in 1969.

The single reached the Top 70 as did the follow-up, but it introduced her to the radio deejays. As a result, her third chart entry, *A Girl Who'll Satisfy Her Man*, reached the Top 30 in 1970. Her next moderate successes came the following year with *(Loving You Is) Sunshine* and *Love's Old Song*. In 1972, Barbara had a Top 40 hit with a cover of the 1967 Petula Clark hit *Color My World*. She followed that with *Thanks for the Mem'ries*, which reached the Top 30. Late in 1972, Barbara scored the biggest hit of her career with a song from ***A Sweeter Love***, her third album. *Teddy Bear Song* became a No.1 record

Country and Gospel singer ***Barbara Fairchild***

and held the spot for two weeks. The record also crossed over to peak in the Top 40 on the Pop chart. As a result, Barbara was nominated for a Grammy Award. She also started to appear on national TV shows and had her own one-hour BBC-TV Special in the U.K.

Barbara continued her success in 1973 with *Kid Stuff*, which reached the Top 3 and also crossed-over onto the Pop charts. Her final Top 10 single, *Baby Doll*, followed in 1974. She wrapped up the year with *Standing in Your Line* (Top 20) and *Little Girl Feeling* (Top 40). Between 1975 and 1978, Barbara had 10 charted singles for Columbia, of which the most successful were *Mississippi*, which just failed to make the Top 30, and *Cheatin' Is*, a Top 20 record, both in 1976, and *Let Me Love You Once Before You Go*, which made it to the Top 25.

Barbara's reign at Country radio came to an end in 1978 when none of her releases reached the Top 40. She had received some plaudits for her work with her being named "Entertainer of the Year" for three consecutive years by the Professional International Rodeo Association. Following the break-up of her second marriage in 1979, she left the music business and moved to San Antonio, Texas, to spend time with her children.

In 1980, Barbara recorded several duets with Billy Walker on the Paid label, three of which were low level chart entries. During 1982, she married evangelical singer and songwriter Milton Carroll and returned to Nashville two years later. She attempted a come-back in 1986 with Capitol Records, where she was produced by Don Williams and Allen Reynolds, but she only managed a low level chart single from this association.

Barbara discovered a new career in Gospel music in 1989 when she was asked to join the group Heirloom. One of the members of the trio was leaving to pursue a solo career and Barbara came to join existing members Candy Hemphill and Tanya Goodman Sykes. The following year, she recorded the album ***Apples of Gold*** with the group and that produced the Gospel radio hits *Prayin' Up a Storm* and *Suffer the Little Children*. In 1991, Barbara released her first solo Gospel album entitled ***The Light.*** She wrote many of the songs on the album and had radio hits with *Turn Right and Then Go Straight* and *Mary Washed His Feet.*

In addition to her Gospel recording career, Barbara is a regular performer in Branson, Missouri. For two years, she was part of the show at the Mel Tillis Theater and in 1993, was a regular on the *Jim Stafford Show*. This lovely lady continues to record with Heirloom. JIE

RECOMMENDED ALBUMS:

"Barbara Fairchild's Greatest Hits" (Columbia)(1977)
"It Takes Two" (Paid)(1981) [With Billy Walker]
"The Biggest Hurt" (Audio)(1982)
"Apples of Gold" (RiverSong)(1990) [As Heirloom]
"The Light" (RiverSong)(1991)

RAYMOND FAIRCHILD

(Banjo, Guitar, Singer)
Date of Birth: March 5, 1939
Where Born: Cherokee, North Carolina
Married: Shirley
Children: Mary Sue, John, Zane Anthony

Some years ago, a subtitle to Raymond Fairchild's first Rural Rhythm album hailed him as "King of the Smoky Mountain Banjo Players." None could deny the accuracy of the label, because Fairchild can certainly pick the fire out of the old 5-string. A biographical article once characterized him as "someone really different." His straightforward emotionless approach to his instrument has virtually become a form of showmanship in itself.

Raymond, who is part Cherokee, was born on the eastern side of the Great Smoky Mountain National Park. His aunt played the Old-Time banjo, but Raymond developed an interest in the guitar, first taking up the Bluegrass banjo at the age of 20. From then on his commitment to the instrument was total. In the early 60's, Raymond cut his first album, ***Authentic Folk Banjo***, for Sim Records. Meanwhile, the young picker continued working with a variety of musicians in his home locality, particularly in the developing tourist center of Maggie Valley, north of Cherokee. From the mid-60's, he began recording for Uncle Jim O'Neal's Rural Rhythm label, releasing a series of primarily instrumental albums. By the early 70's, Raymond was attracting increasing attention on the festival circuit with his dynamic picking and deadpan countenance, particularly on his exciting rendition of *Whoa Mule*, where he would sometimes pick below the bridge of his banjo.

Fairchild's only weakness as a festival attraction resulted from a lack of quality vocalists among the musicians who accompanied him on the road. This situation ended in the spring of 1975 when he met Wayne and Wallace Crowe, two brothers from Clayton, Georgia, who had a fine harmony duet, and also furnished rhythm on guitar and bass, respectively. This combination provided the necessary variety that both needed and they worked together for some fifteen years. They recorded several albums for both Atteiram and Skyline, backing one another.

In 1990, Raymond and the Crowes went their separate ways and Raymond began to assemble a new band, The Maggie Valley Boys, which came to include Ricky Lee, formerly with Ralph Stanley, singing lead and playing guitar; George Hazlewood, formerly with Carl Story, singing tenor and playing mandolin; youngest son, Zane Fairchild, on lead guitar and young Shane Crowe on bass. Meanwhile, in 1989, Raymond had recorded an album with Ralph Stanley and in 1990 another one with fiddler Chubby Wise. Raymond actually did some singing as well as picking on the former effort. Hitherto silent on stage, he also began to emcee his own shows when he put his new band together. Moving into the mid-90's, Raymond Fairchild continues to be a dynamic banjo picker and in his own way both a real American original and a true mountaineer. Listening to one of his off-stage conversations about his own experiences, such as keeping rattlesnakes in his home, can be every bit as entertaining as (and more informative than) his banjo picking. IMT

RECOMMENDED ALBUMS:

"Raymond Fairchild" (Rural Rhythm) [Re-issued with varying catalog numbers (1965-1976)]
"The Maggie Valley Boys: Picking and Singing in Maggie Valley" (Atteiram)(1978)
"The Legendary Raymond Fairchild Plays Little Zane" (Skyline)(1981)
"Raymond Fairchild Plays Requests" (Skyline)(1985)
"World Champion Banjo" (Skyline)(1987)
"Me and My Banjo at Home in Maggie Valley" (Atteiram)(1989)
[See also Crowe Brothers, the]

RUBY FALLS

(Singer, Songwriter)
Given Name: Bertha Bearden Dorsey
Date of Birth: 1946
Where Born: Jackson, Tennessee
Married: Unknown
Children: Vanessa (Downs), Symona (Frizzell)
Date of Death: June 15, 1986

There have been very few black female entertainers in Country music, but Ruby Falls was among the most successful. Although, she never achieved super-stardom, she managed to have a string of middle to low-level record successes during the middle and late 70's. Unfortunately, none of the major labels took a chance on her and that was Country music's loss.

Ruby started singing in church and at local social events while still a child. She moved to Milwaukee, in her teens, and became a professional performer, appearing with local bands. In the late 60's, Charley Pride had opened the door slightly for other black Country singers and in 1974, Ruby moved to Nashville. It was soon apparent to the Nashville establishment that this was one talented lady and for a while she toured with the Justin Tubb Show. Her ability as an entertainer soon was felt among the glitter of Las Vegas, where she was very well received.

Ruby first hit the Country charts in 1975, when she scored with two low-level singles, *Sweet Country Music* and *He Loves Me All to Pieces*. The singles were on 50 States Records, as were all her chart successes. In 1976, she hit with *Show Me Where* and *Beware of the Woman (Before She Gets to Your Man)*, which also hit a basement level. The following year, she again had a low-level success with *Do the Buck Dance* and then, at last, she had a Top 40 single, *You've Got to Mend This Heartache*.

In 1978, Ruby returned to the lower levels with her remake of Fats Domino's hit *Three Nights a Week* and *If That's Not Loving You (You Can't Say I Didn't Try)*. She had her final chart entry in 1979, when *I'm Gettin' into Your Love* reached the Top 60.

Just a few weeks before her death, Ruby complained of headaches. Until then, she had enjoyed good health, but on June 15, 1986, at Vanderbilt Hospital, she succumbed to a brain hemorrhage. So a very talented and well-loved entertainer passed away. Perhaps this entry will help to rekindle an interest in Ruby Falls.

RECOMMENDED ALBUM:

"Ruby Falls—Sweet Country Lady" (50 States)(1980)

DONNA FARGO

(Singer, Songwriter, Guitar)

Given Name: **Yvonne Vaughn**
Date of Birth: **November 10, 1945**
Where Born: **Mount Airy, North Carolina**
Married: **Stan Silver (m. 1969)**

Once upon a time, there was an English teacher who became a star. Six years later, she was diagnosed with multiple sclerosis, but she fought on and continued to be a star. Over a decade later, she remains a star.

Donna, or Yvonne as she still was, had no ambitions for stardom while still in North Carolina. She entertained occasionally but nothing more. She attended High Point Teachers College in North Carolina and then set off to study at the University of Southern California. After getting her degree she headed to Los Angeles. There she became a high school teacher in Covina, California, where she progressed to become head of the English Department. It was in California that she met Stan Silver. Stan was to become a major part of Donna's career. First, he taught her how to play guitar and encouraged her to write songs. She started to get some gigs around L.A. while teaching.

She went to Phoenix in 1966, became Donna Fargo (which they thought a better stage name than her real name) and recorded her first single, *Would You Believe a Lifetime*. It started to attract attention. Her first major show was with Ray Price and she started playing around Southern California. She followed up with a new single on Ramco in 1967, *Who's Been Sleeping on My Side of the Bed*. However, the title was thought to be too racy and it was retitled *Who's Been Playin' House*. Later that year, she issued her final single on the label, *Kind of Glad I'm Me*.

Her career started moving, and in 1968, she cut *Daddy* for Challenge Records. Over a decade later, she would rerecord the song on Warner Brothers and it would become a Top 15 success. She brought out *Wishful Thinking* later that year for Ramco.

In 1969, Donna (or Donna Lisa, as Stan calls her) and Stan got married, and as the 70's beckoned, she was on the brink of stardom. Her first single for Dot Records became a monster. The self-penned *Happiest Girl in the Whole U.S.A.* was a Country No. 1 and stayed on the chart for nearly six months. It went to Top 15 on the Pop chart and was the winner of numerous awards.

Donna received the National Association of Record Merchandisers (NARM) award for "Best Selling Female Country Artist" (1972), a feat she was to repeat in 1973. She received a Gold Record for the single and a Platinum

The super talented ***Donna Fargo***

one for the album of the same name. She swept the ACM board, winning 1972 awards for "Top Female Vocalist," "Single of the Year" and "Song of the Year." The CMA gave her the award for "Single of the Year." She got the Grammy for "Best Country Vocal Performance, Female." BMI presented her with the Robert J. Burton Award for "Most Performed Song of the Year." She also received the *Billboard* Country Music Award for "Best New Female Artist." Needless to say, she quit her teaching job and that fall, she moved to Nashville.

To prove she was no one-hit wonder, Donna came back stronger than ever with her 1972 follow-up single, *Funny Face*, which was also a self-penned song. It reached No.1 on the Country chart and scaled the Pop chart to reach the Top 5. The single was Certified Gold and the Music Operators of America (Jukebox award) made it their "Record of the Year." Donna again received the BMI Robert J. Burton Award and somehow *Billboard* still voted her "Best New Female Artist." Over the years, these two hits would win four BMI Awards for over 4 million performances, having played over 100,000 hours.

Over the next two years, there was no let-up with her success rate. Her next two releases for 1973, *Superman* and *You Were Always There*, went to No.1 and in the fall of 1973 she peaked in the Top 3 with *Little Girl Lost*. 1974 was also very successful with *I'll Try a Little Bit Harder* going Top 10. Martin Cooper's *You Can't Be a Beacon (If Your Light Don't Shine)* made it to the top of the charts and *U.S. of A.* reached the Top 10. She was named *Billboard*'s "Best Female Singles Artist."

By this time, Dot had been acquired by ABC and there was a noticeable dropping off of chart placings after this event. Donna's first record of 1975, *It Do Feel Good*, went Top 10, but *Hello Little Bluebird* just made it to the Top 15. Her next three singles for the label did not fare well and in 1976, she moved to Warner Brothers Records for a reported figure of $1 million. Immediately, success came back in a big way. Her first single for the label, *Mr. Doodles*, was a Top 20 hit. *I've Loved You All the Way* went Top 15. Then just as the year was ending, she had a major hit with *Don't Be Angry*, which went Top 3 in 1977.

1977 was another vintage year with her version of *Mockingbird Hill*, which was a Top 10 hit and then came another chart topper with the narrative, *That Was Yesterday*. To round off the year, she covered *Shame on Me*, which had been a Pop hit for Bobby Bare. This time around, it made the Top 10. She won awards from *Billboard* for "Best Female Singles

Artist" and *That Was Yesterday* was named "No.1 Recitation."

The following year was one of mixed emotions. On the record front, Donna chalked up further major hits with Paul Anka's *Do I Love You (Yes in Every Way)*(Top 3) and *Ragamuffin Man* (Top 20) and *Another Goodbye* (Top 10). Unfortunately, this was the year that she was diagnosed with MS. For a while she was down, but with medical advice and Stan's support, Donna made it back. She started to listen to faith-building tapes by Kenneth Hagin, who ministered in Tulsa, and that helped.

Returning to a limited schedule in 1979, Donna immediately had another Top 10 hit in *Somebody Special*. This was followed by her re-recording of *Daddy*. For the next few years, the successes came at a less frenetic level. Instead of Top 5's and Top 10's, the singles reached the Top 50's and 60's.

Donna recorded a Gospel album, ***Brotherly Love***, for MCA/Songbird in 1981 that was very well received. In 1982, she moved over to RCA, where she had a Top 40 success with *It's Hard to Be the Dreamer (When I Used to Be the Dream)*, that year. In 1983, she was at Columbia and in 1984, Donna moved to Cleveland International. Steve Popovic, one-time head honcho at Cleveland, signed her to Mercury and then there was an upswing for her. Donna's 1986 single *Me and You* made the Top 30 and in 1987, in tandem with Billy Joe Royal, she had a Top 25 record with *Members Only*. Both of these came from her more than aptly titled ***Winners*** album. Donna moved back to Cleveland International when Popovic returned to the helm and in 1991 released *Soldier Boy*, which made the Top 75 and contained references to the Gulf War.

Donna Fargo has achieved much in her life. Her success has not been in the U.S. alone. She had chalked up Gold Discs in Australia and Canada; she is loved in Britain, where she scored resoundingly at the Wembley Festival. She has received the CMA Triple Play for songwriters who achieve three No.1 records in a 12-month period. She and Stan have run the tremendously successful Prima-Donna Entertainment Corporation, which publishes all of Donna's songs. She has won fifteen BMI Writer's Citations and fifteen Publisher's Citations. She is probably one of the most underrated writers in Country music. No doubt, one day some young singer will discover the songs of Donna Fargo.

In 1992, Donna started work on her autobiography and there has been positive talk about a movie being made. The filmmakers would be hard-pressed to find someone with her personality to play the part. She is quite capable of writing and recording another career single.

RECOMMENDED ALBUMS:

"The Best of Donna Fargo" (ABC/Dot)(1977)
"Shame on Me" (Warner Brothers)(1977)
"Donna Fargo—Her Greatest Recordings" (ABC/At Ease)(1978) [Armed Forces issue]
"Brotherly Love" (MCA/Songbird)(1981)
"Winners" (Mercury)(1986)
Any Donna Fargo album is worth listening to.

FARR BROTHERS, The

HUGH FARR

(Singer, Songwriter, Fiddle)

Given Name: Thomas Hubert Farr
Date of Birth: December 6, 1903
Where Born: Llano, Texas
Date of Death: March 17, 1980

KARL FARR

(Singer, Songwriter, Guitar)

Given Name: Karl Marx Farr
Date of Birth: April 25, 1909
Where Born: Rochelle, Texas
Married: May Barksdale
Children: Karl, Jr.
Date of Death: September 20, 1961

Hugh and Karl Farr provided the instrumentation for the Sons of the Pioneers. Their respective fiddle and guitar work not only helped illuminate that group's vocal expertise, but also set widely accepted styles and standards which other musicians emulated. More than any other fiddler, Hugh infused Jazz influences and sounds into Country music while Karl's guitar work was also much admired.

The Farrs came from small towns in central Texas where their father, originally a farmer, became a building contractor as well as a part-time musician. The elder Farr steered Hugh toward the fiddle while younger brothers Glenn and Karl took up guitars. Hugh often listened to Jazz on the radio during the 20's and that musical form greatly influenced his own style. The Farrs played a lot of house parties and square dances in central Texas until 1925 when the entire family relocated in Encino, California. Hugh worked in a club at Sherman Oaks called Mammy's Shack for three years until a fire engulfed it.

By then Hugh wanted to pursue music as a full-time occupation and he and Karl found a job with Len Nash's Country Boys. This band worked four years at KFOX radio in Long Beach, appeared regularly at a dance hall, and recorded a few sides for Brunswick including *Kelly Waltz*. During the winter of 1933-34, Hugh joined the Pioneer Trio, which consisted of Bob Nolan, Leonard Slye, and Tim Spencer, at KFWB Hollywood. This group soon changed its name to the Sons of the Pioneers. In the meantime, Karl had been working in a band called Jimmie LeFevre and His Saddle Pals, but as none of the Pioneer Trio were outstanding guitarists, Hugh urged that Karl be added, which was done in mid-1935. The Farr Brothers remained with the band through the better part of their careers, Hugh until 1958 and Karl until his death in 1961. After leaving the Pioneers, Hugh led his own group for a time, worked for Jimmy Wakely, helped form the Country Gentlemen (not the Bluegrass band of the same name), and worked with a group in New Mexico. He eventually retired to Wyoming.

On their own, the Farr Brothers recorded only four sides for RCA Victor in 1946. However, with the Pioneers, Hugh appeared on all their Decca, American Record Corporation (ARC) and RCA Victor sides through July 1957. Except for missing the first two Decca sessions, Karl worked on all of their recordings through 1961. In addition, the brothers appeared on numerous radio transcriptions that the band made, including many tunes that featured their instrumental virtuosity. They also worked in most of the motion pictures in which the Sons of the Pioneers were heard and/or seen. Some of the numbers featured on the transcriptions had been improvised on the spot! An excellent anthology of tunes taken from these programs featuring the Farr talents was assembled by Michael Mendelson and released by the John Edwards Memorial Foundation. IMT

RECOMMENDED ALBUMS:

"Texas Crapshooter" (J.E.M.F.)(1978)
(See also Roy Rogers, Sons of the Pioneers, and Movie Section)

TERRY FELL

(Guitar, Bass, Mandolin)

Given Name: Terry Fell
Date of Birth: May 13, 1921
Where Born: Dora, Alabama

Terry Fell is best known as writer of and the original artist to record the classic *Truck Driving Man*. However, for several years he did pursue a full-time career as a Country vocalist and cut some fine sides for RCA Victor and its subsidiary, X. Otherwise, Fell has spent much of his working life in the song publishing end of the business.

Born in Alabama, Terry traded a pet groundhog for his first guitar at age 9, but then had to wait three years until someone showed him the chords. Later, another person taught him mandolin as well. In 1937, he bummed his way to the West Coast and visited a half-brother in Oklahoma. A year later, Fell and his widowed mother moved to the Los Angeles area. During the 40's, he worked in a tire factory and played part-time in the Country bands of such musicians as Merle Lindsay, Billy Hughes and Johnny Tyler. Terry also cut some single records for small companies like Fargo, Memo, Courtney, and the larger 4 Star label. From the mid-40's, he also wrote songs for Sylvester Cross' American Music Company.

In 1954, Cross helped Terry secure a contract with RCA Victor, which released his first ten sides on their X label. His first release, cut on February 17, 1954, on which he was backed by the Fellers, proved most memorable. *Don't Drop It* made the Top 5 and the flip-side *Truck Driving Man* went on to become an all-time Country favorite. After RCA closed X, Terry's material was released on the parent label. During the late 50's, throat problems and dissatisfaction with performing conditions helped Fell decide to get out of the business as an artist, although he did periodically record songs on smaller labels.

In 1962, Terry moved to Nashville as a representative for American Music. Later, he worked for other publishing companies in various capacities, while continuing to write songs. Sharing credits on *You're the Reason*, a Bobby Edwards crossover hit in 1961, proved his biggest success. Today, Fell lives near Nashville in semi-retirement. Bear Family Records released a cd containing all twenty-four of his RCA masters. IMT

RECOMMENDED ALBUM:

"Truck Driving Man" (Bear Family Germany)(1993)

DICK FELLER

(Songwriter, Singer, Guitar)
Date of Birth: January 2, 1943
Where Born: Bronaugh, Missouri
Married: Gayle (m. 1984)

When the titles *Biff, the Friendly Purple Bear* and *The Credit Card Song* are mentioned, then heads nod and the name "Dick Feller" surfaces. Dick got a reputation for writing "off-the-wall" songs.

Growing up in Missouri, he wanted to be a poet, but then came up with the thought that all the great poets were dead. He visited Nashville and then moved to Los Angeles, where he played in a band by night and wrote songs when he could, demoed them and got them to publishers. Now, the strange thing about Dick Feller is that no one told him he couldn't write, at least by everyone else's rules. Mind you, they didn't tell him he couldn't play guitar because he had short fingers.

Dick returned to the Midwest where he continued to play in bands, then in 1966, he moved back to Nashville. At the time, other writers like Kris Kristofferson and Mickey Newbury were trying to make their way. Dick initially earned his living playing guitar on demo sessions and in Mel Tillis' road band, the Statesiders. He also performed at the Quality Motor Inn. Then, he signed as a songwriter with Johnny Cash's House of Cash and in 1972, he wrote Johnny's hit *Any Old Wind That Blows*. He got a cut with Tex Ritter, who recorded *The Night Ms. Nancy Ann's Hotel for Single Girls Burned Down*. In 1973, he wrote *Lord Mr. Ford* for Jimmy Dean, but then Dean stopped recording. Dick had a dream that he had taken the song to Jerry Reed. He awoke and located Reed, and sure enough he recorded it and it went to No.1. Feller and Reed started to write together and some of the output went into the movies *Smokey and the Bandit* and its first sequel; songs included *East Bound and Down* and the flip *(I'm Just A) Redneck in a Rock and Roll Bar*.

In 1973, Dick hit the charts as an artist with his United Artists narrative *Biff, the Friendly Purple Bear,* which reached the Top 25 and the Top 100 on the Pop charts. The following year, he did even better with *Makin' the Best of a Bad Situation*, on Asylum. This reached the Top 15 on the Country charts and Top 90 on the Pop listing. Dick had a second hit that year with the legendary *Credit Card Song*, which was a Top 10 Country hit, also appearing on the Pop charts. In September 1974 he made his solo debut on the *Grand Ole Opry*, having previously appeared on the show with Tillis. 1975 saw his final chart entry with *Uncle Hiram and the Homemade Beer,* which made it to the Top 50, on Asylum.

Between 1974 and 1975, Dick wrote for Jerry Reed's Vector Music and then he moved to Tree Music. In 1978, Jerry Reed had a double-sided hit with Dick's *(I Love You) What More Can I Say* and *High Rollin',* both being in the movie *High-Ballin'*. The following year, Reed did it again for Dick with *Second Hand Satin Lady (And a Bargain Basement Boy)*.

John Denver, one of the finest Folk-Country writers, recorded Dick's beautiful *Some Days Are Diamonds (Some Days Are Stone)* in 1981 and had a major Pop and Country hit with it. During the short life of Audiograph Records, Dick recorded an eponymous album for them.

RECOMMENDED ALBUMS:

"Dick Feller Wrote" (United Artists)(1973)
"No Word On Me" (Asylum)
"Some Days Are Diamonds" (Asylum)(1975)
"Children in Their Wishes, Ladies in Their Dreams" (Asylum)
"Dick Feller" (Audiograph Alive)(1984)

NARVEL FELTS

(Singer, Songwriter, Guitar, Bass Guitar)
Given Name: Albert Narvel Felts
Date of Birth: November 11, 1938
Where Born: Nr. Keiser, Arkansas
Married: Lorretta Stanfield (m. 1962)
Children: Narvel Jr. ("Bub"), Stacia

Performing a range of music from rock'n'roll to Country-Soul, Narvel Felts, who was once known as "Narvel the Marvel," has a career that has spanned over three decades.

When he was a boy, Narvel's interests were art and music. The first singer to catch Narvel's attention was Ernest Tubb. The first song Narvel can remember singing was Floyd Tillman's *They Took the Stars Out of Heaven*. He bought his first guitar from Sears Roebuck for $15.95 and taught himself to play.

In 1956, Narvel entered a talent contest at his high school in Bernie, Arkansas, singing *Blue Suede Shoes,* and won. In the audience was a deejay from station KDEX Dexter, Missouri. While Felts was listening to the radio the next day, this announcement was made: "If Narvel Felts is listening, please contact KDEX immediately." Narvel got his father to drive him to the nearest phone which was eight miles away. The result was that Narvel secured a regular Saturday afternoon radio show.

Jerry Mercer was playing with his band in a neighborhood club when Narvel introduced himself and asked if he could sit in with the band. Mercer agreed, so Narvel got up and sang a couple of songs. Jerry invited him to sing with the band again. More shows followed, giving him more and more experience in the entertainment business. At

Country star ***Narvel Felts***

the end of 1956, Jerry Mercer left the band to marry and the band became Narvel Felts and the Rockets.

A record shop owner became Narvel's first manager and he arranged an appointment with Sun Records for an audition. Feeling very scared, the 17-year-old Narvel and one of his band members set off for Memphis and the Sun studio. They auditioned for Jack Clement, who said, "Well, go home, write some songs and bring the whole band down and we'll see what we can come up with," and that is just what Narvel did. However, the resulting sessions were not released at that time.

Narvel and his band were booked into the Fox Theater in St. Louis, opening for the movie *Rock, Pretty Baby*. They were noticed by a regional promoter from Mercury, who paved the way for Narvel to record for the label. Five singles were eventually released by Mercury, but in 1959, the label let them go. With Jerry Tuttle and Leon Barnett, Narvel wrote *Three Thousand Miles*, which was released on the Pink label, and this was followed in 1960 by their version of the Drifters' hit *Honey Love*. This gave Narvel his first Pop chart entry, reaching the Top 90. As a result, as Narvel recalls, "MGM called me from New York, signed me, I got me a hot-shot New York manager, agent and all that stuff, they kept me on contract for two years and never released a record."

In January, 1961, Narvel joined the National Guard, serving six years with the Poplar Bluff, Missouri, National Guard. During this time he met and married Lorretta Stanfield and had two children. Narvel continued playing and recording and in 1973, he joined the newly formed Cinnamon label. With his second release, Mentor Williams' *Drift Away*, Narvel had his first Country chart hit when it reached the Top 10 that year. He followed with the Top 15 hits *All in the Name of Love* (1973) and *When Your Good Love Was Mine* (1974). Narvel had three more hits in 1974: *Until the End of Time* (a Top 40 duet with singer/songwriter Sharon Vaughn), *I Want to Stay* (Top 30) and *Raindrops* (Top 40). Although Cinnamon folded, Narvel signed with ABC/Dot in 1975 and the hits continued. Narvel was produced at Dot by Johnny Morris and they remained closely associated. *Reconsider Me* was released and became Narvel's biggest hit, reaching the Top 3, and at the DJ Convention during October, the single was voted by both *Billboard* and *Cash Box* as "Record of the Year." Other hits that followed were *Funny How Time Slips Away* (Top 15, 1975), *Somebody Hold Me (Until She Passes By)* (Top 10), *Lonely Teardrops* (Top 5), *My Prayer* (Top 15) (all 1976), *My Good Thing's Gone* and *The Feeling's Right* (both Top 20, 1977). Narvel's other principal hits on ABC/Dot and its successor, ABC, were *To Love Somebody* (Top 25, 1977), *Runaway* and *One Run for the Roses* (both Top 30, 1978). In 1979, ABC was taken over by MCA and in the shuffle several artists were lost; one of them was Narvel.

During the mid-70's, Narvel's road manager fired his band and started booking him as a single act, hooking him up with a group of boys who called themselves Wild-country. He played about 13 dates with them, still keeps in touch with them and wrote the liner notes on their first album. They are now called . . . Alabama. Over the years, Narvel has performed with his band, the Driftaways, touring all over the United States and Europe. He has appeared at the Wembley Festival in England in 1974 and 1979, becoming a firm favorite in Britain.

From MCA, Narvel moved to Collage (1979), GMC (1981), Lobo (1982), Compleat (1982) and Evergreen (1983). Although he continued to chart, Narvel's biggest hits were *Cry Baby* (1983), *Fool* and *Let's Live This Dream Together* (both 1984) and *Hey Lady* (1985), all Top 60 entries. His last chart record was the 1987 remake of the Percy Sledge hit *When a Man Loves a Woman*, which also went Top 60. Narvel is a great family man, a great entertainer, a man of God and since 1980, a committed Christian. He has recorded a Gospel collection, ***On the Wings of a Song,*** and a Christmas collection, ***Seasons Greetings***. In 1988, Narvel appeared at Peterborough, Britain's other main festival at the time. In the 90's, Narvel continues singing and is on the road every weekend. He still cuts records and is still enjoying his career. JAB

RECOMMENDED ALBUMS:

"Drift Away" (Cinnamon)(1973)
"Narvel Felts Greatest Hits Vol. 1" (ABC/Dot)(1976) [Re-issued on MCA]
"This Time" (Hi)(1976)
"The Very Best of Narvel Felts" (Gusto)

FREDDY FENDER

(Singer, Songwriter, Guitar)

Given Name:	**Baldemar G. Huerta**
Date of Birth:	**June 4, 1937**
Where Born:	**San Benito, Texas**
Married:	**Vangie (m. 1958, div. 1963, remarried 1964)**
Children:	**Sonny, Danny, Marla**

To a lot of people in the 90's, Freddy Fender is better known as a member of the Tex-Mex group, Texas Tornados. However, his career stretches back four decades to the days when he was still known as Baldemar Huerta and recorded for Falcon.

At age of 10, Freddy went with his family into the northern states, where they worked as casual farm laborers through Michigan, Ohio, Indiana and Arkansas. By then, Freddy was already playing a guitar of sorts. When he was 16, he dropped out of school and joined the Marines, where he stayed for three years. However, Freddy preferred playing guitar and drinking in the barracks to being a Marine.

By the late 50's, he was back in San Benito working taverns and Chicano dances. By 1958, he was cutting sides in Spanish, which were doing well in Texas and Mexico. He switched styles to a more Rockabilly feel, becoming Freddy Fender the next year, to get into the wider "gringo" market. Local club owner Wayne Duncan formed Duncan Records to give Freddy exposure. Duncan leased product to Imperial Records and Freddy's first release was *Holy One*. This started to pick up some attention outside of the area, as did the follow-up, the self-penned *Wasted Days, Wasted Nights* in 1960. He had just released *Crazy, Crazy Baby* when on May 13, the heavens descended.

He was arrested for possession of marijuana in Baton Rouge and was given a five-year prison sentence in Angola State Penitentiary along with his bass player. While an inmate, he cut several sides for Goldband, including *My Train of Love* and *Bye Bye Little Angel*. He was released in July 1963, having served three years. His parole was in part due to the intervention of the musical Governor of Louisiana, Jimmie Davis. However, a condition of the parole was that Freddy must leave the music business. He worked in a New Orleans bar with his parole officer keeping an eye on him. At the end of his parole period, Freddy tried to get his career under way again. Although he got some gigs, performing at Papa Joe's in Bourbon Street in New Orleans, recording-wise he was dead in the water.

He returned to San Benito in 1969, where he worked as an auto mechanic and for two years went back to school, resulting in him becoming a sociology major. In 1974, he was living in Corpus Christi, Texas, when he was introduced to Huey P. Meaux, who ran the Houston-based Crazy Cajun label. He recorded Freddy in a more Country style, although it would never be possible (or desired) to remove all the Hispanic feel from Fender records.

Freddy hadn't wanted to record *Before the Next Teardrop Falls* but Meaux insisted and was vindicated by his decision. Huey touted the single around but there were no buyers, possibly because he was asking too much and

Tex-Mex star ***Freddy Fender***

so it was released on Crazy Cajun. It started to gain attention locally and then Larry Baunach of ABC/Dot licensed the recording. By the end of January 1975, Freddy Fender had become a star. The record went to No.1 on both the Country and Pop charts and was Certified Gold before the end of May. By the end of August, the album bearing the same title had also achieved Gold status. Before the middle of the year, the follow-up single, *Wasted Days and Wasted Nights*, which Freddy had originally recorded for Imperial, had gone to the top of the Country charts and peaked in the Top 10 on the Pop charts. By the end of 1975, this had also gone Gold.

Before the year ended, Freddy was represented on the Country Top 10 by two more singles, one on his current label and one on GRT, who had also licensed Meaux productions. They entered the Country charts in the reverse order to their impact on the Pop ones, but irrespective *Since I Met You Baby*, the Ivory Joe Hunter classic, became Freddy's third cross-over single (Top 10 Country/Top 50 Pop) to be followed immediately by the former Doris Day hit *Secret Love*, which gave Freddy a Country No.1 and a Pop Top 20 hit. In 1975, Freddy received two accolades. The ACM named him "Most Promising Male Vocalist" and the CMA made *Before the Next Teardrop Falls* "Single of the Year."

GRT released another single at the beginning of 1976, *The Wild Side of Life*, which was a Country hit, peaking out in the Top 15. ABC/Dot swiftly released Freddy's version of the R & B ballad *You'll Lose a Good Thing* and it provided him with his third No.1 and again crossed-over to become a Top 40 Pop hit. Freddy received two Grammy nominations in 1976 for "Best Country Vocal Performance, Male" (he lost to Ronnie Milsap, who had also, at one time, been recorded on Crazy Cajun) and "Best Country Song" (*Before the Next Teardrop Falls*), for which he was outgunned by Larry Gatlin's *Broken Lady*.

1976's other hits (both cross-over) were *Vaya Con Dios* (Top 10) and *Living It Down* (Top 3). The following year got under way with a double-sided Top 5 hit, *The Rains Came/Sugar Coated Love*. The top side had been a hit for Sir Douglas Quintet and fourteen years later, Freddy would be in the Texas Tornados with ex-Sir Douglas players Doug Sahm and Augie Meyer.

From here on, Freddy's hit pace slowed down. *If You Don't Love Me (Why Don't You Just Leave Me Alone)* just missed the Top 10 and the follow-up, *Think About Me*, just made the Top 20. In 1978, only *Talk to Me* on ABC made the Top 15. Freddy left ABC in 1979 after his final entry, *Walking Piece of Heaven*, which went Top 25.

Freddy joined Meaux's new label, Starflite, (which had major distribution by Epic) and had a Top 25 hit with *Yours*. By now, Freddy had found a new interest as actor and screenwriter and appeared in the movie *She Came to the Valley* (portraying Pancho Villa) and also made an appearance in the show *Tijuana Donkey*. By 1983, he had moved to Warner Brothers Records, but only succeeded at the lower level.

During the period following his success, Freddy was having a hard time with drugs and drink and by 1985, he was having to undergo drug rehabilitation. In 1988, he appeared in the highly acclaimed Robert Redford directed movie *The Milagro Beanfield War* and a year later Freddy was in the Universal film *Always Roses*. That same year, he signed with Critique Records but nothing much happened and then in 1990, he became a member of the Texas Tornados and he had a whole new career (see Texas Tornados, for the continuation of the story). In 1994, Freddy signed with Arista Texas, Arista's new Tex-Mex label out of Austin.

RECOMMENDED ALBUMS:

"Since I Met You Baby" (GRT)(1975)
"Freddy Fender" (Pickwick)(1975)
"Your Cheatin' Heart" (Pickwick)(1976)
"Rock'N'Country" (ABC/Dot)(1976) [Worth it for the sleeve alone!]
"The Best of Freddy Fender" (ABC/Dot)(1977) [Later released on MCA]
"Merry Christmas—Feliz Navidad" (ABC/Dot)(1977)
"Texas Balladier" (Starflite)(1979)
"Existos Grandes" (Starflite)
"Live Inside Louisiana State Prison" (Power Pak)
"Love Me Tender" (Crazy Cajun)

ERNEST FERGUSON

(Mandolin, Comedy)

Given Name: **Ernest C. Ferguson**
Date of Birth: **July 16, 1918**
Where Born: **Hickman County, Tennessee**
Married: **Unknown**
Children: **John David, Danny, Tommy, Carol, Lorretta**

Ernest Ferguson is generally remembered as one of the best Country mandolin pickers of the 40's, being particularly adept at playing accompaniment for harmony duets, trios, and quartets.

Born near Bon Aqua Post Office, about 35 miles west of Nashville, Ernest moved into the city in the mid-30's, where he became acquainted with the Anglin Brothers, who were then beginning their radio career at WSIX. He recalls Jack Anglin telling him to stick with the mandolin, as guitar pickers were too common. Taking Anglin's advice, Ernest began playing on a Saturday show at WSIX, where he made the acquaintance of Johnnie Wright, forming what later became known as the Tennessee Mountain Boys, Johnnie & Jack. Paul Warren, Emory Martin and Ernest worked at WSIX through the remainder of 1940. They then moved in succession to WBIG Greensboro, WCHS Charleston, and WHIS Bluefield, the two latter locales in West Virginia, in 1941 and 1942. Ernest spent most of 1943 working in a defense plant in Charleston, but then in January 1944, Ernest rejoined Wright's group at WNOX Knoxville.

Ferguson remained in Knoxville for several months picking with Wright and his new partner, Eddie Hill. That September, he went to WSM and joined forces with the Bailes Brothers, newly arrived at the *Opry*. He remained with them during their entire sojourn at WSM. He recorded with them on Columbia and King, providing most of the instrumental leads on their sides. When they left Nashville at the end of 1946, Ernest remained and started his own booking agency, although he did two more sessions with the Bailes Brothers in 1947. When Johnnie & Jack came to WSM and needed a mandolin player, Ernest worked with them on radio but did not go out on the road except for the week they went to Ohio and provided instrumental leads on the sides of the King Sacred Quartet (Johnnie & Jack plus Clyde Moody and Ray Atkins).

In May 1948, Ernest aspired to get back into music and rejoined the Bailes Brothers in Shreveport, replacing Clyde Baum, who ironically went to work with Johnnie & Jack. He remained with the Bailes' West Virginia Home Folk until their breakup, at which time Ernest went to Washington, D.C., to join Grandpa Jones, recording two sessions with him on King. In the fall of 1950, Ernest went to work as a drywall finisher but continued as a part-time musician for the next several years as part of the Wasington-based Blue River Boys. He also revived the comedy character of "Abner Abernacky."

Ferguson eventually returned to Tennessee, settling in the town of Fairview, where he continued to labor in the drywall trade. Although out of music for some 20 years, he got back in after meeting again Walter and Kyle Bailes. Thereafter, he worked many weekend dates with the Bailes Brothers and recorded again, with both of them on their ***Reunion*** album and with Walter, alone. In the fall of 1977, Ernest cut a mandolin instrumental album for Old Homestead. A modest gentleman, who can also sing most vocal parts when needed, Ferguson is truly one of the unsung musical heroes of his generation. ITM

RECOMMENDED ALBUMS:

"Ernest Ferguson—Mandolin Album" (Old Homestead)(1977)

[See also Bailes Brothers, the, Johnnie & Jack.]

FIDDLE

By Vassar Clements

It's a pleasure to be able to write about some of these fiddle players who are my best friends. First I'd like to talk about a friend of mine called Bobby Hicks. We played twin fiddles with Bill Monroe back then. Bobby is now playing with Ricky Skaggs, playing all different types of music. You can identify Bobby's playing when you hear it on records. He can play Bluegrass, Country and Swing. I first played with him back in about 1956 or 1957 and he's one of my favorite fiddle players.

Mark O'Connor is one I've known since he was a kid. He was real good back then. Mark has taken the time to play with all kinds of violinists. He plays a lot of different syles and does a good job playing with anybody. He's an all-around great fiddle player. He learned from Benny Thomasson and he's carried on from there.

Kenny Baker is somebody I've known for a long while, even though I haven't gotten to play with him much. Anyone can tell his style of playing. His music fits with Bill Monroe as well as anyone I've ever heard. Chubby Wise was the first fiddle player I heard with Monroe when I was growing up in the 40's. He can get more tone out of one note than anyone I've ever heard.

Johnny Gimble used to play with Bob Wills and also has his own special touch. They all have an identity that separates them from the others. I recorded with Stephane Grappelli in the 80's, which was a real honor. He is one of the all-time greats. Another fiddler that has to be mentioned is Doug Kershaw. He has such a movement with his bow arm and keeps time by raising the fiddle up and down or moving the bow.

Benny Martin goes way back and uses a long bow and has played with Big Jeff Bess, Lester Flatt, Bill Monroe and Roy Acuff. Gordon Terry got identified from playing *Buckin' Mule* and that set his style. It's not the fiddles they play, it's just that they have something special about their playing.

When you're around them you know that they love to play, the same way that I love to play.

[For biographies on fiddle players see: Bobby Atkins, Kenny Baker, Vassar Clements, Doug Kershaw, Benny Martin, Johnny Gimble, Mark O'Connor, Chubby Wise and many more.]

FIELDS BROTHERS, The

When Formed: 1968

BENNIE FIELDS

(Vocals (normally Lead), Songwriter, Guitar)

Date of Birth: January 22, 1941

CLANCY FIELDS

(Tenor Vocals, Bass Fiddle, Guitar, Songwriter, Mandolin)

Date of Birth: February 11, 1950

Both Born: Kermit, Mingo County, West Virginia

Bennie and Clancy Fields led a Columbus, Ohio, based Bluegrass band for several years. The brothers, born near the Kentucky state line, played at clubs and festivals throughout Kentucky, Ohio and West Virginia.

There were 12 children in the Fields family, of which Bennie was the eighth and Clancy the youngest. Their uncle, Lundy Fields, gained some local renown as a mandolin player. Bennie sang in the church choir at the age of 12 and organized his first band at 18. It was only when Clancy joined in 1968 that the Fields Brothers as a band came into existence.

They really began to gel in 1970, when Curtis Beck joined them. Beck, a Dobro/fiddle player from Pike County, Kentucky, was raised in nearby Crum, West Virginia. When they won the band contest at the prestigious Frontier Ranch Bluegrass Festival near Columbus, Ohio, they received considerable attention.

They recorded their initial album, ***Waiting and Wondering***, in 1973 for Jessup-Michigan Bluegrass. Their banjo player was a former farm boy from Licking County, Ohio, named Dave Clark. On their second album, ***The Fields Brothers Sing of Old Kentucky and West Virginia***, released in 1974, Orville Dingess played bass and Tom Dew replaced Clark on banjo. Clancy alternated between guitar and mandolin and Beck played Dobro and fiddle. On both albums, the brothers included several original songs, mostly compositions by Bennie. Other Fields songs came from Bluegrass tradition or were Old-Time obscurities such as *Country You Blotted My Happy School Days*, which Edith and Sherman Collins had recorded for Decca in 1938.

Personal problems led to them dissolving the act in the mid-70's. Clancy later worked as a sideman with Dave Evans and River Bend and recorded with him on Evans' first Rebel album in 1981. Interestingly, their uncle, Lundy Fields, who had earlier worked with Lowell Varney, also played in Evans' band. IMT

RECOMMENDED ALBUMS:

"Waiting and Wondering" (Jessup/Michigan Bluegrass)(1973)

"The Fields Brothers Sing of Old Kentucky and West Virginia" (Jessup/Michigan Bluegrass)(1974)

CATHY FINK

(Singer, Songwriter, 5-String Banjo, Fiddle, Guitar, Button Accordion, Yodeler)

Given Name: Cathy Ann Fink

Date of Birth: August 9, 1953

Where Born: Baltimore, Maryland

Cathy was influenced by an active Folk music community when she began her professional career in Montreal in 1973 at the Yellow Door coffee house. She absorbed Folk and Old-Time styles on guitar and 5-string banjo. Cathy's yodeling and her five-string banjo stylings have become her trademarks.

She made her radio debut on CBC Canada, in 1974, and since then, she has played every major Folk festival in North America from Winnipeg to Winfield. In 1974, she teamed up with Duck Donald and they remained together until 1979. At that point, she moved to Takoma Park in Maryland and has since been a central figure in Folk, Bluegrass and Old-Time music, playing more than 5,000 shows. She has also recorded many children's albums and in the early 70's she performed in children's hospitals and day care centers. From 1983, she has been in partnership with another talented musician, Marcie Marxer, operating from their base in Silver Spring, Maryland.

She recorded her first album, ***Kissing Is a Crime***, for Likeable Records in 1975. This was followed by her duet album, ***Cathy Fink & Duck Donald***, on Flying Fish three years later. On both these albums, Dave Essig was the main producer. She released her first album of children's songs, ***I'm Gonna Tell***, in 1980, in tandem with Duck. Her next "adult" album was ***The Leading Role***, on Rounder in 1985.

The following year, Cathy started to get involved in outside productions and was responsible for Critton Hollow Stringband's ***By and By*** and Magpie's ***If It Ain't Love***. In 1987, she produced Rude Girl's ***Rude Awakening*** and ***Children of Selma***. She moved over to Sugar Hill for her own 1988 offering, ***Blue Rose***. That year, she produced another yodeling great, Patsy Montana, on her album ***The Cowboy Sweetheart***, on Flying Fish.

1989 was a particularly busy year for Cathy. She produced the Great Dreams album and released her excellent duet album, ***Cathy Fink & Marcie Marxer***. In addition, along with Marcy and Si Kahn, she issued ***The Runaway Bunny/Goodnight Moon***, which were tapes of best-selling children's books, for Harper & Row. She also released two children's videos for Homespun Video, ***Kids Guitar 1 & 2*** and ***Making and Playing Homemade Instruments***.

In 1991, Cathy continued her frenetic pace with a new solo album, ***Doggone My Time***, for Sugar Hill. That year and the next, she contributed 80 songs for the Macmillan/McGraw-Hill reading curriculum, ***A New View.*** In 1992, she produced Si Kahn's ***I Have Seen the Freedom*** and a duet album with Marcy, ***Banjo Haiku***. In 1993, she produced Kahn's children's album, ***Goodtimes and Bedtimes***. She also produced a series of children's albums for A & M Records. JAB

RECOMMENDED ALBUMS:

"Cathy Fink & Duck Donald" (Flying Fish)(1978)
"The Leading Role" (Rounder)(1985)
"Blue Rose" (Sugar Hill)(1988)
"Cathy Fink & Marcie Marxer" (Sugar Hill)(1988)
"Doggone My Time" (Sugar Hill)(1991)

SHUG FISHER

(Bass, Fiddle, Songwriter, Actor, Comedy)

Given Name:	**George Clinton Fisher**
Date of Birth:	**September 26, 1907**
Where Born:	**Tabler, Grady County, Oklahoma**
Married:	**Peggy Summers**
Date of Death:	**March 16, 1984**

Fisher got his sobriquet because his mother called him "sugar," because he was so sweet when he was a baby. His father was Scots-Irish and his mother was one-quarter Choctaw. When he was 10 years old, his family moved in a covered wagon to Pittsburg County, Oklahoma. Shortly after the move, Shug traded a saddle blanket for a "tater bug" mandolin.

By the time he was 16, he had traded this for a fiddle. His father had never mentioned his own ability on the fiddle and Shug only found out when he caught his father playing the instrument. Shug learned to play the guitar so as to back his father. Shug started to play at local square dances. He couldn't afford a fiddle case and used to carry his instrument in a pillowcase.

In 1924, he saw a medicine show and the show's "toby" impressed him. The "toby" was a comedian with a red wig and blacked-out tooth. Shug was determined that comedy mixed with music would be his route. He moved with his father and a friend to California in 1925 and took on various jobs, including stints in the oil fields as a cable and tool dresser. He moved to Poplar, in the San Joaquin Valley, California, and was asked to appear for no money on the *Fresno Bee* newspaper radio station, KMS. This taught him a lesson that he always adhered to: "My motto was, pay me something, or I don't play."

He appeared at the Hollywood Breakfast Club and then was approached in 1931 by Tom Murray, who had just left the Beverly Hill Billies and had formed the Hollywood Hillbillies. Shug learned to play bass fiddle and was among the first to make the stand-up bass work within the confines of Country music. Shug left the group and joined the revitalized Beverly Hill Billies in San Francisco. He assumed the name "Aaron Judd" within the group. He was soon on his way again and joined Stuart Hamblen's group.

In 1935, Shug teamed up with Roy Faulkner, "the Lonesome Cowboy," broadcasting from station XER Del Rio, Texas. While they were appearing in Council Bluffs, Iowa, Shug was approached by Hugh Cross, who invited him to join his organization which was sponsored by the Georgie Porgie Breakfast Food Company. Cross suggested they try a song out together. Fisher suggested *Back to Old Smokey Mountains*. Cross concurred. After they started, Shug told Cross that he wasn't singing it correctly. Cross came back saying Fisher had it wrong. When Shug asked Cross what made him think he was right, Cross countered, "'Cause I wrote it." They stayed together on WWVA *Wheeling Jamboree* and WLW *Boone County Jamboree*. They called their act at WLW Hugh and Shug's Radio Pals. By then, Shug had started songwriting.

They eventually went their own ways in 1940, at the outbreak of WWII. Shug returned to Los Angeles, where he worked for Lockheed Aircraft in Burbank on defense-related work. He also worked with the Victory Committee, entertaining defense workers.

On the mobilization of Pat Brady in 1943, Shug joined the Sons of the Pioneers for the first of three stints, as bass player and comedian, appearing on their *Lucky U Ranch* program. He stayed with them until early 1946, when Pat Brady returned from WWII and then joined Stuart Hamblen's *Lucky Stars*. In 1949, he was back with the Sons of the Pioneers when Brady left to join Roy Rogers for movie and TV work. The highlight of this association was an appearance at Carnegie Hall in 1951. By 1952, Shug was back with Hamblen.

He got together with Ken Curtis in 1953 and worked with him in movies, TV and radio. He stayed put until 1955, when he left to return to the Sons of the Pioneers. Over the years, he toured with the Sons of the Pioneers and appeared on several RCA Victor recordings with them. One of his songs, *Forgive and Forget*, appeared on an early album. He finally left the group in 1959.

He was then offered a spot on Red Foley's *Ozark Jubilee* TV show and he stayed with the show until 1961.

Shug also had another string to his bow. He was a very adept actor. He appeared in 16 movies (see Movie Section) with Roy Rogers as well as seven other movies. In 1961, he worked on the TV series *Ripcord* alongside Ken Curtis. He played Shorty Kellums in 19 episodes of the now classic TV series *The Beverly Hillbillies* and appeared alongside James Arness and Dennis Weaver in TV's *Gunsmoke*.

He died in March 1984 after a lingering illness, with his long-time friend Ken Curtis at his side.

RECOMMENDED ALBUMS:

(See the Sons of the Pioneers albums for tracks featuring Shug Fisher.)

5-STRING BANJO IN COUNTRY MUSIC

By Larry McNeely

For many years, it was written, anywhere the 5-string banjo was mentioned, that Joel W. Sweeney added the short string on the top side of the existing 4-string banjo neck, thus creating the instrument we now call the 5-string banjo, the only truly American instrument besides the dulcimer.

It's more probable that slaves, bringing a 4-string banjo with them when they were brought to America in the 1700's, had already put the short string where it is and Joel Sweeney merely added a bass string. As people have a tendency to muddle history to enhance the more popular theory, I don't suppose anyone will ever really know whose idea it was to put the short string to the banjo but I know this: 200 plus years ago, whoever did it gave us one of the most popular instruments in Country and Bluegrass music.

As no records exist of how the players then played the instrument, we will have to assume that our later style, which has been called "clawhammer," is an evolution of one of the primary picking styles. Also, classic style is an evolved form of an even more sophisticated style. (One wishing to find out more about classic style can write to the American Banjo Fraternity, c/o Norm Azinger, 271 McKinley St., Braddock Hills, PA. 15221.)

Although the banjo has always been a semi-popular instrument and used in every type of music conceivable, the 5-string banjo's popularity skyrocketed when a young man from North Carolina introduced his method or approach to the instrument; that was Earl Scruggs. In the mid-1940's, he joined Bill Monroe and the Bluegrass Boys and forever changed the course of the 5-string banjo. This hard-driving three-finger style, as it has been called, added to Monroe's high singing style, created a music style we now call Bluegrass. This music is loved and played by millions around the world.

In 1950, Earl recorded *Foggy Mountain Breakdown*, a tune he'd written, and it soon became the Bluegrass banjoist's anthem. With several other tunes also written by Scruggs, we have the basic repertory for the banjo.

At around the same time, another fine player, Don Reno from South Carolina, came up with a similar method and many have said it was just a matter of being at the right place at the right time for Earl to become the father of Bluegrass banjo. Be that as it may, Don's incredible output of instrumentals is second to none. Both Earl and Don gleaned ideas from all styles of music. The banjo was appealing to an even wider audience.

In the late 1950's, two other banjoists would develop methods employing both Scruggs' and Reno's devices but would borrow from the aforementioned classic style. Players such as Fred Van Eps, Fred Bacon and Frank Bradbury were classic players who had nothing to do with Country music but there were elements in the style that could be gleaned. The two banjoists were Bobby Thompson, from South Carolina, and Bill Keith, from Boston, Massachusetts. They both came up with styles more melodic than the basic Scruggs style with its one melody note to two or more filler or auxiliary notes. With the melding of all these styles, one could now play a fiddle tune or any tune, for that matter, stating a melody much more clearly.

To be fully appreciated, these players all have to be heard. It's fortunate that recordings of all these players are available. Scruggs', Reno's, Thompson's and Keith's methods would shape the period from 1945 to about 1980. Players such as Tony Trischka, Allen Shelton, Doug Dillard, John Hartford, Carl Jackson, John Hickman, Alan Munde, Butch Robbins, J.D. Crowe, and many more add their own ideas to the methods these four men developed. All of these contributions have been great and the banjo is more popular than ever.

We now come to the 80's and Béla Fleck, who has taken his banjo off-planet and into the 90's. His traditional playing is beyond words and he's taken the instrument into another realm. Like the first four players mentioned, Béla's contributions have already been many.

Although he now plays more Jazz than anything, Pat Cloud started out playing Bluegrass and has opened the instrument to an even wider audience.

The 5-string banjo has been heard on the original *Beverly Hillbillies* TV show, *Bonnie and Clyde*, *Deliverance* and countless other films. If someone wants to sell cars or hamburgers they'll use a 5-string banjo to grab attention. Because of its bright staccato sound, the instrument always stands out and it is the instrument that makes Bluegrass, Bluegrass.

[For the 5-string banjo's principal players see J.D. Crowe, Doug Dillard, Bill Emerson, Béla Fleck, John Hartford, Carl Jackson, Bill Keith, Larry McNeely, Earl Scruggs, Tony Trischka.]

LESTER FLATT

(Guitar, Mandolin)

Given Name:	**Lester Raymond Flatt**
Date of Birth:	**June 19, 1914**
Where Born:	**Overton County, Tennessee**
Married:	**Gladys Lee Stacy (div.)**
Children:	**Brenda (adopted)**
Date of Death:	**May 11, 1979**

Lester Flatt ranks as the all-time preeminent lead singer in Bluegrass music. Although he spent the major years of his career, from 1948 to 1969, as half of the now legendary team of Flatt & Scruggs, he also had some notable earlier experience as a sideman and led his own Nashville Grass for a decade before his death. Lester took his own group musically back to the traditional Bluegrass that had brought the team to initial prominence and recorded some fine albums chiefly for RCA Victor. He regularly performed on the *Grand Ole Opry* and appeared often on the festival circuit.

A native of the Cumberland Mountains in East Tennessee, Lester Flatt grew up with traditional music. However, he left school at an early age and worked at various jobs until 1931, when he went to work at a textile mill in Sparta, where his wife, Gladys, also labored. Both worked in mills at various locations for several years. In the meantime, Lester got a part-time job at WDBJ Roanoke with a group known as Charlie Scott's Harmonizers. Later, he worked briefly in Burlington, North Carolina, with Clyde Moody and in 1943 both Lester and Gladys went to work for Charlie Monroe's Kentucky Pardners. After a year or so, Flatt moved to Nashville, where he worked with Bill Monroe's Bluegrass Boys until February 1948, when he left to form his partnership with Earl Scruggs. After 21 years, this team dissolved over musical differences and Flatt went on his own.

Flatt's new band consisted largely of the old Foggy Mountain Boy stalwarts Paul Warren, Josh Graves, and Jake Tullock with the addition of Vic Jordan on banjo and Roland White on mandolin. He retained *Grand Ole Opry* membership and the long-time sponsorship of Martha White Mills on the early morning WSM radio show. After one badly over-produced album for Columbia, he severed that connection and recorded a traditional offering for Nugget before signing with RCA Victor. ***Flatt on Victor*** displayed a return to the musical style associated with the sounds that the older fans still treasured. He turned out five more albums and while his band went through changes, he maintained the Bluegrass styling throughout. Haskell McCormick and Kenny Ingram succeeded Jordan, and Charlie Nixon replaced Graves on Dobro. A youthful Marty Stuart took over on mandolin and former Foggy Mountain Boy Curley Seckler returned to sing tenor and play rhythm guitar. Jack Hicks and then Pete Corum played bass fiddle, and after poor health forced long-time fiddler Paul Warren out of the band, respected veteran Clarence "Tater" Tate took over.

During the early 70's, Lester also cut three albums with another legendary Bluegrass vocalist, Mac Wiseman, on RCA Victor. Leaving that label in 1975, Flatt cut excellent albums with Flying Fish and Canaan before signing with Martin Haerle's new CMH Records.

In 1975, Lester Flatt's health began to decline. However, he remained fairly active until November 1978, when he experienced some serious problems. He returned to the *Opry* in March, but then encountered even more health difficulties. When he died in May 1979, his remains were taken back to Sparta, which had been his hometown since boyhood. In 1985, Flatt & Scruggs were elected to the Country Music Hall of Fame. IMT

RECOMMENDED ALBUMS:

"Flatt Out" (Columbia)(1970)
"The One & Only Lester Flatt" (Nugget)(1970)
"Flatt on Victor" (RCA Victor)(1972)
"Kentucky Ridge Runner" (RCA Victor)(1972)
"Foggy Mountain Breakdown" (RCA Victor)(1973)
"Country Boy" (RCA Victor)(1973)
"The Best of Lester Flatt" (RCA Victor)(1974)
"Live! Bluegrass Festival" (RCA Victor)(1974)
"Flatt Gospel" (Canaan)(1975)
"Tennessee Jubilee" (Flying Fish)(1975) [With John Hartford and Benny Martin]
"Lester Raymond Flatt" (Flying Fish)(1975)
"Lester Flatt's Bluegrass Festival" (CMH)(1977) [With the Pinnacle Boys, the Lewis Family and Little Roy Lewis]
"Pickin' Time" (CMH)(1978)
"Fantastic Pickin'" (CMH)(1979)
Mac Wiseman & Lester Flatt:
"Lester 'n' Mac" (RCA Victor)(1971)
"Over the Hill to the Poorhouse" (RCA Victor)(1973)

FLATT & SCRUGGS

Formed: **1948**

LESTER FLATT
(Singer, Composer, Guitar, Mandolin)
Given Name: **Lester Raymond Flatt**
Date of Birth: **June 19, 1914**
Where Born: **Overton County, Tennessee**
Married: **Gladys Lee Stacy (div.)**
Children: **Brenda (adopted)**
Date of Death: **May 11, 1979**

EARL SCRUGGS
(Banjo, Composer)
Given Name: **Earl Eugene Scruggs**
Date of Birth: **January 6, 1924**
Where Born: **Flint Hill, North Carolina**
Married: **Louise Certain**
Children: **Randy, Gary, Steve (dec'd.)**

The team of Lester Flatt & Earl Scruggs attained more national popularity than any other Bluegrass act and ranks with that of Bill Monroe as the most influential. Although both men had earlier and later careers on their own, the three years they spent with Monroe (1945-1948) and their 21 years as a team (1948-1969) rank as most significant. Their early-morning radio show for Martha White Mills, television programs, Mercury and Columbia discs, *Grand Ole Opry* work and soundtracks (*The Beverly Hillbillies, Bonnie & Clyde*) all helped broaden the audience and thereby the appeal of Bluegrass music. Earl's banjo and Lester's guitar licks and vocal leads have set a virtual standard for quality within the idiom created by Bill Monroe.

Flatt hailed from the Cumberland Plateau region of East Tennessee and Scruggs from the North Carolina Piedmont and each had varied musical experiences prior to coming to work for Bill Monroe in 1945. Together with fiddler Chubby Wise and bassist Howard Watts (Cedric Rainwater), these five individuals, under Monroe's lead, created Bluegrass music as the term came to be understood and defined. Many elements of the form had of course existed in earlier Monroe aggregations and various Virginia-Carolina groups, but this quintet put it all together and popularized it through their radio programs, stage shows, and Columbia Records.

Flatt & Scruggs left Monroe in 1948 and soon formed the Foggy Mountain Boys. They initially worked out of radio stations such as WCYB Bristol, Virginia, WROL Knoxville, Tennessee, WDBJ Roanoke, Virginia, and WVRK Versailles, Kentucky, and recorded for two years on Mercury before signing with Columbia in 1950. Their single *'Tis Sweet to Be Remembered* became a Top 10 hit in 1952. Martha White Mills hired them for their morning radio show at WSM in 1953 and they subsequently joined the *Grand Ole Opry* as well, much to Monroe's consternation. In 1955, the band began a series of five television programs in such Appalachian locales as Chattanooga, Knoxville, Bluefield, and Huntington, again under the sponsorship of Martha White Mills.

The mountaineer audience that appreciated the music of the Foggy Mountain Boys helped sustain them through the difficult years of the later 50's, when hard-core Country acts traveled a rough road. With a band that also included fiddler Paul Warren, tenor vocal-mandolinist Curly Seckler, bass player Jake Tullock, and from 1956, Dobro player Buck Graves, the group had both quality and continuity. Earl's instrumentals like *Foggy Mountain Breakdown, Flint Hill Special,* and *Earl's Breakdown,* together with both secular and sacred vocals such as *Head Over Heels in Love, Blue Ridge Cabin Home, Give Mother My Crown,* and *Bubblin' in My Soul* became trademarks of the group. *Cabin on the Hill* remained on the *Billboard* charts for some 30 weeks.

Lester Flatt & Earl Scruggs

From 1959, the television shows went into syndication and Bluegrass of the Flatt & Scruggs variety began to gain some popularity among the college crowd as an aspect of the Folk music fad. During the early part of the 60's, Flatt & Scruggs frequently appeared on the Country chart with *Crying My Heart Out Over You* (Top 25, 1960), *Polka on a Banjo* (Top 15) and *Go Home* (Top 10)(both 1961) and *Just Ain't* (Top 20) and *The Legend of the Johnson Boys* (Top 20)(both 1962). In 1962, Flatt & Scruggs broadened their appeal still more when their music became the opening theme for the CBS-TV hit show *The Beverly Hillbillies.* Their Columbia version of *The Ballad of Jed Clampett* became the first Bluegrass song to hit No.1 (also a Pop Top 50 single) and their popularity soared. Among their other chart entries, the most successful were *Pearl Pearl Pearl,* also from *The Beverly Hillbillies* (Top 10), and *New York Town* (Top 30)(both 1963), *You Are My Flower* (Top 15), *Petticoat Junction* (Top 15) and *Workin' It Out* (Top 25)(all 1964) and *California Up Tight Band* (Top 20, 1967).

Unfortunately, this surge of strength increasingly began moving them away from the traditional Bluegrass sounds that had started their initial climb up the ladder of success. This created tension between the co-leaders, which along with other factors led to the group's dissolution in February 1969 after some 20 numbers on the charts, more than any other Bluegrass band.

After their breakup, each man formed his own group. Flatt returned to a more traditional sound with most of the old band, while Scruggs and his sons continued to experiment with progressive sounds. Interest in their earlier recordings remained high and various collector-oriented labels reissued many of their classic Bluegrass sides. In the meantime, the duo had a mild reconciliation shortly before Flatt's death in 1979. In 1985, they became the second Bluegrass act elected to the Country Music Hall of Fame and in 1991 each was inducted individually into the Bluegrass Hall of Honor.

Bear Family Records in Germany re-issued their entire recorded output on cd. IMT

RECOMMENDED ALBUMS:

Because of the complexity of Flatt & Scruggs album releases, this list includes only the original Mercury and Columbia/Harmony album releases and those from the collector oriented labels of Bear Family, Copper Creek, County and Rounder. Material on the listed Mercury and Harmony albums came from earlier singles.

"Great Original Recordings" (Harmony)(1965)
"Foggy Mountain Jamboree" (Columbia)(1957)
"Songs of the Famous Carter Family" (Columbia)(1961)
"Folk Songs of Our Land" (Columbia)(1962)
"At Carnegie Hall" (Columbia)(1963)
"Live at Vanderbilt University" (Columbia)(1964)
"Greatest Hits" (Columbia)(1966)
"Strictly Instrumental" (Columbia)(1967)
"The Story of Bonnie & Clyde" (Columbia)(1968)
"Final Fling" (Columbia)(1969)
"Columbia Historic Edition" (Columbia)(1982)
"Don't Get Above Your Raisin" (Rounder)(1979)
"The Mercury Sessions, Volume I" (Rounder)(1985)
"The Mercury Sessions, Volume II" (Rounder)(1985)
"Flatt & Scruggs, 1948-1959" (Bear Family Germany)(1992)
"Flatt & Scruggs, 1959-1963" (Bear Family Germany)(1992)
"Flatt & Scruggs, 1964-1969" (Bear Family Germany)(1993)

BÉLA FLECK

(Banjo, Slide Banjo, Electric Banjo, Nylon-Strung Banjo, Guitar, Composer)

Given Name:	**Béla Anton Leos Fleck**
Date of Birth:	**July 10**
Where Born:	**New York, New York**

There is no doubt that Béla Fleck is one of the most highly acclaimed banjo players in the world. He has managed to take the instrument to areas not even dreamed of. His work with New Grass Revival and latterly Béla Fleck and the Flecktones has enchanted audiences who would not have believed that the banjo could be taken into such diverse areas of music.

Béla was named for composer Béla Bartók and he also has a brother Ludwig (named after Beethoven); both were raised in New York City. Béla got his first banjo at the age of 15, after hearing Flatt & Scruggs' *Ballad of Jed Clampett* and Eric Weissberg/Steve Mandell's *Dueling Banjos*. After leaving the High School of Music and Art in New York, where he adapted the music of the bebop greats for banjo, he joined his first band, Boston-based Tasty Licks, recording two albums with the group and staying until their disbandment in 1979. He moved to Kentucky and then became a member of Spectrum, with whom he recorded two albums on Rounder, ***Two Hot for Words*** and ***Opening Roll***.

Within 5 years of starting to play banjo, Béla had his debut solo album, ***Crossing the Tracks***, which was named "Best Overall Album" in the *Frets* magazine Readers' Poll in 1981. His main influences are Tony Trishka, Earl Scruggs, Chick Corea, Charlie "Bird" Parker, John Coltrane, the Allman Brothers, Aretha Franklin, the Byrds and Little Feat.

Béla left Spectrum to join New Grass Revival in 1982, and stayed with them until they ceased in 1990. During this time, he was retired to the Hall of Greats by *Frets* magazine. His composition *Drive*, from the ***New Grass Revival*** album, in 1988, was nominated for a Grammy Award, one of three Grammy nominations he has received over the years. In 1989, he got together with Sam Bush (mandolin), Mark O'Connor (fiddle), Edgar Meyer (bass) and Jerry Douglas (Dobro), and recorded ***The Telluride Sessions*** under the name of Strength in Numbers. That same year he produced Maura O'Connell's ***Helpless Heart*** album.

He then formed his "fantasy band," Béla Fleck and the Flecktones. The members of the group were, initially, Howard Levy on harmonica, piano, synthesizer, pennywhistle and ocarina (left 1993), Victor Lemonte Wooten on bass guitar and brother Roy Wooten (also known as "Futureman") on a guitar shaped electronic drum known as synth-ax-drumitar. The group was formed in response to a request from PBS for Fleck to play on the *Lonesome Pine Special*, which was eventually aired in the spring of 1992. In March 1990, they released their debut self-titled album on Warner Brothers to critical acclaim. This was followed by the equally lauded 1991 release, ***Flight of the Cosmic Hippo***, from which the title track was released as a video. In 1992, they had their third album, ***Hurricane Camille***. Their fourth album, ***Ufo Tofu***, released in 1993, contained Bluegrass, Jazz, R & B and World Beat music, and featured as guests Branford Marsalis (saxophone) and Bruce Hornsby (keyboards).

Whether Béla Fleck is still a Country musician is unanswerable. His music now takes him to audiences that appreciate musicians such as Kenny G. However, his skill as a banjo player has won the admiration of greats such as legendary banjoist Earl Scruggs, even though Béla's banjo nowadays looks more like a guitar.

RECOMMENDED ALBUMS:

Béla Fleck and the Flecktones:
"Béla Fleck and the Flecktones" (Warner Brothers)(1990)
"Flight of the Cosmic Hippo" (Warner Brothers)(1991)
"Hurricane Camille" (Warner Brothers)(1992)
"Ufo Tofu" (Warner Brothers)(1993)
[See also albums by New Grass Revival post 1982 and "The Telluride Sessions" by Strength in Numbers, (1989)]

FLYING BURRITO BROTHERS

When Formed: Flying Burrito Brothers:1968-1972/Burrito Brothers: 1980-1985/Flying Brothers: 1985-1988

Original Members:	
Gram Parsons	**Lead Vocals**
Chris Hillman	**Guitar, Mandolin, Vocals**
Sneaky Pete Kleinow	**Steel Guitar, Vocals**
Chris Ethridge	**Bass**
Jon Corneal	**Drums (On first album only)**
Popeye Phillips	**Drums**
Members 1969:	
Gram Parsons	**Lead Vocals**
Chris Hillman	**Guitar, Mandolin, Bass Guitar, Vocals**
Sneaky Pete Kleinow	**Steel Guitar, Vocals**
Bernie Leadon	**Guitar, Vocals**
Michael Clarke	**Drums**
Members 1971:	
Chris Hillman	**Guitar, Mandolin, Bass Guitar, Vocals**
Al Perkins	**Steel Guitar**
Rick Roberts	**Guitar, Vocals**
Joel Scott-Hill	**Guitar, Vocals**
Alan Munde	**Guitar, Vocals**
Byron Berline	**Fiddle**
Kenny Wertz	**Guitar, Banjo, Vocals**
Roger Bush	**String Bass**
Members 1981:	
Gib Gilbeau	**Fiddle, Guitar, Vocals**
Sneaky Pete Kleinow	**Steel Guitar, Vocals**
Skip Battin	**Bass Guitar, Vocals**
Greg Harris	**Guitar, Banjo, Vocals**
Ed Ponder	**Drums**
Members Late 1981:	
Gib Gilbeau	**Fiddle, Guitar, Vocals**
John Beland	**Guitar, Vocals**
Members 1985-1988:	
Sneaky Pete Kleinow	**Steel Guitar, Vocals**
Skip Battin	**Bass Guitar, Vocals**
Greg Harris	**Guitar, Banjo, Vocals**
Jim Goodall	**Drums**

Flying Burrito Brothers was one of the first groups to pioneer the blending of Country and Rock music that was later popularized by the Eagles. (Flying Burrito Brother member Bernie Leadon became a member of the Eagles.) Although the Burritos never achieved mass popularity, the influence of the group is widespread and important in Country music.

Chris Hillman and Gram Parsons left the Byrds to form a new band in 1968. They decided to name the band after a popular Mexican food item, the burrito. They invited bassist Chris Ethridge, pedal steel guitarist Pete Kleinow and drummer Popeye Phillips to join them as Flying Burrito Brothers. The band recorded their debut album, ***The Gilded Palace of Sin***, for A & M Records in 1968. The album contained several songs that define the merging of Country and Rock music. Songs such as *Sin City, Wheels*, and *Do Right Woman* have been studied and recorded by many artists, including Dwight Yoakam and Emmylou Harris.

Parsons and Hillman shared a passion for mixing Country music themes and lyrics with Rock music's instruments and attitude. Growing up in Waycross, Georgia, Gram Parsons developed a love for Country music. He displayed musical talent early, taking piano lessons at 3 and playing the guitar by 13. As a teenager, Parsons' musical development came from playing the music of the Everly Brothers, Chuck Berry and Ray Charles. In 1965, Parsons spent one semester at Harvard before dropping out to form the International Submarine Band in Cambridge, Massachusetts. Parsons eventually moved the band to California and when the group broke up, he accepted an invitation to join the Byrds.

Chris Hillman cut his musical teeth playing Bluegrass. He sharpened his skills as a guitarist and mandolinist performing with various bands around California. Hillman was the leader of a Bluegrass group called the Scottsville Squirrel Barkers before becoming a member of the Hillmen and a founding member of the Byrds.

Sneaky Pete Kleinow's pedal steel guitar playing added distinctive Country flavor to Flying Burrito Brothers recordings. He learned to play as a teenager in Michigan, honing his skill in the Country bars. In the mid-50's, he ventured west and landed a job with Smokey Rogers' Western Swing band in San Diego, California. In the 60's, Sneaky Pete began experimenting with Rock and Jazz music and settled in Los Angeles as a member of Norm Raleigh's band. In the late 60's, he met Parsons and Hillman when he did some studio work for the Byrds.

One of the first changes in the band came when drummer Popeye Phillips left. After several temporary replacements, former Byrds drummer Michael Clarke joined the Burritos. When Chris Ethridge made his exit in 1969, Bernie Leadon stepped in. Leadon had worked previously with Hillman in his Scottsville Squirrel Barkers and with Doug Dillard and Gene Clark in their band Dillard & Clark's Expedition.

In 1970, Flying Burrito Brothers released a second album for A & M entitled ***Burrito De Luxe***. They continued to explore Country music, covering Merle Haggard's *Sing Me Back Home* and John D. Loudermilk's *Break My Mind*. Bob Dylan's *If You Gotta Go* was also included in the album. Dylan cited Flying Burrito Brothers as his favorite Country-Rock band in a *Rolling Stone* magazine interview. Other notable songs on their sophomore effort were *God's Own Singer* and the impassioned *Close Up the Honky Tonks*.

Flying Burrito Brothers developed a loyal following performing at the Troubadour and the Whiskey-A-Go-Go. In support of their recordings the band toured the U.S. to glowing reviews by the media. When Gram Parsons was injured in a motorcycle accident in 1970, Rick Roberts stepped in to take his place. After recuperating, Parsons returned to the band briefly in 1971. Rick Roberts remained in the group contributing several songs on the Burritos' third album, ***Flying Burrito Brothers***. Also in 1971, Sneaky Pete Kleinow left the band and was replaced by Al Perkins, who came from a band called Shiloh. The reorganized Flying Burrito Brothers invited three Bluegrass musicians to join the band: Byron Berline, Kenny Wertz, and Roy Bush (later the foundation of Country Gazette).

In 1972, the band released its fourth and final album, ***Last of the Red Hot Burritos***. The strain of continual personnel changes and lack of greater success led to the breakup of the band in 1972.

In 1974, A & M Records released a two record collection titled ***Close Up the Honky Tonks***. In addition to selections from earlier albums, the set contained several previously unreleased songs. Encouraged by the sales of that album, two original members, Kleinow and Ethridge, decided to re-form the group. They invited former Byrd Gene Parsons and Linda Ronstadt band member Gib Gilbeau to join them for the New Flying Burrito Brothers. The group recorded two albums for Columbia, ***Flying Again*** and ***Airborne***. By the end of the 70's, Parsons and Ethridge had left the band and John Beland, who was a member of Rick Nelson's Stone Canyon Band, teamed up with Gilbeau and Kleinow.

In 1980 the Flying Burrito Brothers had their first Country chart entry with Merle Haggard's *White Line Fever*, which came from their 1979 Regency label album, ***Live from Tokyo***. Later in 1980, the band had shortened the name to the Burrito Brothers and landed a contract with Curb Records. In 1981, their first album, ***Hearts on the Line***, produced three singles that charted nationally that year: *She's a Friend of a Friend* (Top 70), *Does She Wish She Was Single Again* (Top 20) and *She Belongs to Everyone But Me* (Top 20). These introduced the Burritos to a new generation of Country music fans. To support the album the group toured with Emmylou Harris. In 1981 the group was honored by the trade magazines *Billboard* and *Cash Box*. The Burrito Brothers' second album for Curb, ***Sunset Sundown*** in 1982, produced *If Something Should Come Between Us (Let It Be Love)* (Top 30), *Closer to You* (Top 40) and *I'm Drinking Canada Dry* (Top 40). Following the second album release, Kleinow returned to his career as an animator/special effects creator in Hollywood. He had built a reputation working on 60's TV series like *Outer Limits* and on dozens of movies, including *The Wonderful World of the Brothers Grimm*.

In the mid-80's A & M released a double retrospective album of Flying Burrito Brothers music with liner notes written by founding member Chris Hillman. John Beland and Gib Gilbeau continued to record and perform as the Burrito Brothers until 1985. In the early 90's, Beland joined the Bellamy Brothers as lead guitarist and Gilbeau concentrated on his songwriting. Both Beland and Gilbeau found success as songwriters. In addition to writing a majority of the songs they recorded as the Burrito Brothers, their songs were recorded by many other artists, including Rod Stewart, Bobby Womack and the Bellamy Brothers. In 1985, Kleinow re-formed the band with Skip Battin, Greg Harris and John Goodall. The band lasted until 1988, after which it had occasional resurrections. Gib Gilbeau's son, Ronnie, is a member of 1990's Country-Rock group Palomino Road. JIE

RECOMMENDED ALBUMS:

"The Gilded Palace of Sin" (A & M)(1968)
"Burrito De Luxe" (A & M)(1970)
"Flying Burrito Brothers" (A & M)(1971)
"Last of the Red Hot Burritos" (A & M)(1972)
"Close Up the Honky Tonks (1968-1972)" (double) (A & M)(1974)
"Flying Again" (Columbia)(1975)
"Sleeping Nights" (A & M)(1976) [With Gram Parsons]
"Live from Tokyo" (Regency)(1979)
"Hearts on the Line" (MCA/Curb)(1981) [As the Burrito Brothers]
"Sunshine Sundown" (MCA/Curb)(1982) [As the Burrito Brothers]

DAN FOGELBERG

(Singer, Songwriter, Guitar, Piano)
Date of Birth: August 13, 1951
Where Born: Peoria, Illinois

Dan Fogelberg is a singer/songwriter who bestrides Folk, Country and Rock with consummate ease and enhances any form of music he cares to dip into with equal aplomb. He defies categorizing and is able to pull together threads from an eclectic background to weave songs of stature.

He was encouraged in his musical

development by his parents. His father was a band leader (immortalized in the Fogelberg song *Leader of the Band*) and his mother was a singer. Dan took piano lessons and experimented with an acoustic slide guitar that he had received from his grandfather (for whom he was named). Dan started writing songs when age 14 and played in a selection of garage bands, but it was not until he was in his high school sophomore year that he began to emerge. While studying painting at the University of Illinois, he found himself taking up more of his time on music. He left college, in 1970, after two years, and then met Irving Azoff (who would later head MCA Records, and manage the Eagles and Joe Walsh), and they headed for the West Coast. While in L.A., Dan accompanied Van Morrison on tour. Then Azoff got a record deal for Dan, with Epic/Full Moon.

The initial album, ***Home Free*** (1973),was totally made up of Fogelberg songs, was produced in Nashville by bass player Norbert Putnam, and featured steelie Weldon Myrick and fiddle player Buddy Spicher. During 1974, Dan sang or played on other artists' albums, including Jackson Browne's ***Late for the Sky***, Roger McGuinn's ***Peace on You*** and Joe Walsh's ***So What.*** He also spent some time on a farm outside of Nashville, until 1975, when he moved to Denver, Colorado.

In 1975, Dan released his ***Souvenirs*** album, which was produced by Joe Walsh. Among the guests singing or playing were Graham Nash, Don Henley, Randy Meisner, Glenn Frey and Joe Walsh. By the following year, the album had been Certified Gold and would go on to be a Platinum seller in 1986 and then the same year reach sales of 2 million. In 1975, Dan had his first single success when *Part of the Plan* reached the Top 40 on the Pop charts. He followed this up with the album ***Captured Angel,*** on which he played most of the instruments, but it did feature John David Souther and the Hot Damn Brothers(!). The album went Gold by 1977 and sold steadily, so as to register Platinum status in 1992.

Dan Fogelberg *in concert*

His 1977 album ***Nether Lands*** marked the intial playing together of Dan and Jazz-Fusion flautist Tim Weisberg, and was co-produced by Dan and Norbert Putnam. That same year, the album had gone Gold and by 1979 had been Certified Platinum. The two got together in 1978 for the cleverly titled ***Twin Sons of Different Mothers***. This was very well received and by the end of that year, it had reached Platinum status. One of the tracks, *The Power of Gold*, became a Top 25 Pop hit. With the exception of three tracks, this album was instrumental, showing off Fogelberg's musical ability, as none of its predecessors had done. During 1979, his debut album, ***Home Free***, was Certified Gold.

However, it was Dan's next album, ***Phoenix*** (1980), that yielded his biggest Pop hit, *Longer*, which reached the Top 3 and crossed over into the lower regions of the Country chart. The follow-up single, *Heart Hotels*, reached the Top 25 on the Pop chart. The album featured some excellent horn playing from Tom Scott and Seawind's Jerry Hey and went Platinum during its year of release. As Dan turned age 30, he released the 1981 album ***The Innocent Age***, and this event manifested itself in the songs. It was also Dan's most successful in terms of singles. The classic *Same Old Lang Syne* was a pre-release in 1980 and reached the Top 10. It was followed in 1981 by *Hard to Say* and *Leader of the Band*, both Top 10 singles, as well as the Top 20 record *Run for the Roses,* in 1982.

During 1982, his label released the ***Greatest Hits*** package, and this yielded two new hits, *Missing You* and *Make Love Stay*, both of which made the Top 30. The same year, this album was Certified Gold. Dan's 1984 album, ***Windows and Walls,*** was interesting for many reasons, but most especially because the initial single, *The Language of Love*, was accompanied by Fogelberg's first video. Featured on the album were Jeff and Mike Porcaro from Toto, Timothy B. Schmit from Poco and Tom Scott. Like its predecessors, the album went Gold shortly after release. As well as *The Language of Love*, Dan also charted with *Believe in Me* that year.

High Country Snows marked a change of direction for Dan. In 1985, he had recently moved from Boulder to Colorado's San Juan Mountains and the music has a definite Newgrass feel, which was reflected by the musicians appearing on the album. These included Ricky Skaggs, Jerry Douglas, Doc Watson, Chris Hillman, David Grisman, Emory Gordy, Jr., Herb Pedersen, Marty Lewis and Jim Buchanan. The singles from the album to chart were *Go Down Easy* and *She Don't Look Back*, which entered the basement area of the Pop chart and *Go Down Easy* and *Down the Road Mountain Pass*, which entered the Country charts, the latter reaching the Country Top 40. However, for the first time, Dan's album didn't go Gold and neither did the follow-up in 1987, the hard-rocking ***Exiles***, although he did have the pleasure of seeing a collection of his black and white photographic prints released in a coffee table book.

Although a solid seller of records and a craftsman of songs (*Leader of the Band* took two years to write and *Same Old Lang Syne* eighteen months), Dan and his backing groups (Fools Gold and Mile High Band) have been criticized for their sometimes lackluster live performances. Dan normally is on stage for some two hours, often opening for himself with an acoustic set. His tearful ballads can sometimes be just too much for an audience, and although he rings the changes during his act, his music has been described as being "vanilla." However, sales in excess of 8.5 million albums have got to speak volumes that critics couldn't even begin to understand. In addition, although Dan's songs have been covered by others (e.g., Don Williams' 1990 recording of *Diamonds to Dust*), Fogelberg songs are at their best when sung by Fogelberg.

RECOMMENDED ALBUMS:

"Home Free" (Epic/Full Moon)(1973)
"Souvenirs" (Epic/Full Moon)(1975)
"Captured Angel" (Epic/Full Moon)(1975)
"Nether Lands" (Epic/Full Moon)(1977)
"Twin Sons of Different Mothers" (Epic/Full Moon)(1978) [With Tim Weisberg]
"Phoenix" (Epic/Full Moon)(1980)
"The Innocent Age" (Epic/Full Moon)(1981)
"Greatest Hits" (Epic/Full Moon)(1982)
"Windows and Walls" (Epic/Full Moon)(1984)
"High Country Snows" (Full Moon)(1985)
"Exiles" (Full Moon)(1987)

JIM FOGLESONG

(Industry Executive)

Where Born:	**West Virginia**
Married:	**Toni**
Children:	**Cindy, Jimi, Leslie, Russell**

As a Music Row executive in the 70's and 80's, Jim Foglesong helped lay the foundation for the Country music boom in the 90's. As President of Dot, ABC, MCA and Capitol Records over nearly 20 years, Foglesong signed million-selling artists Donna

Fargo, Don Williams, Barbara Mandrell, the Oak Ridge Boys, Reba McEntire, George Strait, Sawyer Brown, Suzy Bogguss, Tanya Tucker and Garth Brooks.

As a boy growing up in South Charleston, West Virginia, Jim loved to sing but planned one day to be a schoolteacher. In high school he developed an interest in journalism but also loved to play baseball. His skill at the sport earned him a tryout with the Cleveland Indians. When his dream of becoming a professional baseball player didn't pan out, Jim attended the Eastman School of Music in Rochester, New York, earning a degree in music. Following graduation, he pursued his goal of becoming a professional singer. Moving to New York City, he took a job at Chase Manhattan Bank and auditioned every chance he got. Foglesong kept his voice in shape by singing several times a week in various Brooklyn churches.

It was Jim's music education at Eastman that helped him land a job with Columbia Records. Jim had a friend who was leaving the label and told him about the opening that required reading music. In September of 1951, Jim took the job in the engineering department assisting in the transfer of the label's catalog from the 78 format to the new lp format. Following the score for each record, Foglesong made sure the engineers didn't leave out or add a beat in the process of transfer from record to tape.

The following summer, Foglesong took a leave of absence from Columbia to sing with Fred Waring's Pennsylvanians. His new wife, Toni, also went on tour as a vocalist. Six months later, Jim returned to Columbia and moonlighted as a studio singer. His session work provided a great education singing for major New York producers and backing up stars, including Dion & the Belmonts, Connie Francis and Neil Sedaka. Foglesong often worked with producer and orchestra leader Mitch Miller, noting his attention to detail. In those years before multi-track recording, Miller made sure everything was right and recorded in the first take.

In 1953, Jim was tapped by Columbia to help launch the new Epic label as coordinator of product. Initially releasing classical recordings, Foglesong persuaded the label to re-release some of Columbia's older Jazz recordings. The move proved profitable for the label and earned Foglesong the opportunity to produce some dance bands and Pop artists. He signed Bobby Vinton to Epic and produced a string of hits for Robert Goulet on Columbia.

When Steve Sholes offered him a job as an executive producer with RCA Records, in 1963, Foglesong accepted. During his tenure with the label, Jim produced a series of Gold selling Pop records for Ed Ames, including *When the Snow Is on the Roses* and *Who Will Answer*. In addition to producing records in New York and Los Angeles, Foglesong was one of the first to produce Pop music in Nashville. Jim had to get used to the unorthodox "Nashville Number System" where musicians assign each chord a number rather than using the traditional sheet music name.

In 1970, Jim moved to Nashville to become an executive at Dot Records and by 1973, he was president of the label. Under his leadership, the company experienced a tenfold increase in sales over the year prior to his presidency. One thing Foglesong did to cut costs was trim down the roster to about 20 artists. He produced Roy Clark's first No.1 record and brought the then unknown Donna Fargo to the label. In 1974, Foglesong released her *The Happiest Girl in the Whole U.S.A.* and saw combined sales of her singles and albums top the 1 million mark.

When ABC Records purchased Dot, Foglesong remained at its helm. In 1979, he was named President of MCA Records when they purchased the ABC label. During his five years of leadership at MCA, Foglesong signed Reba McEntire, George Strait and Lee Greenwood.

In 1984, Jim became the President of Capitol Records' Nashville Division. He inherited a fledgling label that was overshadowed by the other record companies in town. Jim brought the label back to life by signing the R & B-flavored T. Graham Brown and the Pop-influenced Marie Osmond. Capitol also enjoyed a Pop crossover hit with Dan Seals' *Bop* in 1986. Jim directed the eclectic label back to prominence with consistent hit makers Don Williams, Anne Murray and Tanya Tucker as well as Folk-Pop star Don McLean and acoustic-based group New Grass Revival. One of Foglesong's last signings was the artist who would take Country music to the largest audience in history, Garth Brooks.

By the early 1990's, Foglesong was no longer a Music Row executive but found himself finally a teacher. He taught courses in music business at Belmont and Vanderbilt universities in Nashville. In 1993, the Nashville Entertainment Association gave Jim Foglesong their Master Award. The award "pays homage to those individuals who pioneered the Nashville sound and whose efforts have brought this town international acclaim, prestige and respect as a major entertainment center."

JIE

BETTY FOLEY

(Singer, Guitar)

Given Name: Betty Foley
Date of Birth: February 3, 1933
Where Born: Chicago, Illinois
Married: Bentley Cummins
Children: Patrick Bentley, Clyde Foley, Charlotte Jean
Date of Death: 1990

From age 17, in 1950, Betty was a popular member of the *Renfro Valley Barn Dance*, where she stayed, singing and playing guitar, until 1954. The program ran weekly from Kentucky, and Betty's father, the famous Red Foley, had helped to establish the show, which was broadcast to many stations across the Midwest.

Her mother, Pauline, died in childbirth, and Betty was raised by her step-mother, Eva (also known as Judy Martin and a former member of the Three Little Maids), in Berea, Kentucky. Betty learned to play guitar when she was very young and by the time she had become a high school student, she was an excellent musician. While performing on the *Barn Dance* she began recording with Decca. In 1954, Betty had a Top 10 hit with *As Far as I'm Concerned,* which was a duet with Red Foley. She then had a well-received solo single, *Sweet Kentucky Rose*, which was followed in 1955 with another duet with her father, *Satisfied Mind*, which went to Top 3. She set off on a personal appearance tour and performed on national syndicated radio and TV shows. During 1956 and 1957, Betty was a cast member on the WLW *Midwestern Hayride* and also appeared on WCKY, both in Cincinnati. During 1957, she made her debut on the *Grand Ole Opry* and subsequently made several guest performances. She was named "Most Promising Female Vocalist" in the Disc Jockey Polls. 1958 saw her on the WNOX Knoxville *Tennessee Barndance*.

Betty signed with the Bandera label in 1959 and released the Top 10 single *Old Moon.* The same year, Betty started performing on KWKH's *Louisiana Hayride*, out of Shreveport. Red Foley was now the feted host of a new show on the ABC network, *Jubilee USA,* from Springfield, Missouri, and Betty was taken on as one of the regular members.

Her business interests included an involvement with Kentucky Fried Chicken. She was also a Kentucky Colonel. Betty Foley died in 1990.

JAB

RECOMMENDED ALBUM:

"Red Foley Souvenir Album" (Decca)(1958) [Features Betty Foley]

RED FOLEY

(Singer, Songwriter, Guitar, Harmonica, String Bass, Emcee)

Given Name:	**Clyde Julian Foley**
Date of Birth:	**June 17, 1910**
Where Born:	**Berea, nr. Blue Lick, Kentucky**
Married:	**1. Axie Pauline Cox (d. 1933) 2. Eva Overstake (Judy Martin)(d. 1951) 3. Sally Sweet**
Children:	**Betty, Shirley Lee, Jenny Lou, Julia Ann**
Date of Death:	**September 19, 1968**

Red Foley was one of Country music's most versatile and beloved singers and "a superstar of his time." He had a constant succession of hit records between 1944 and 1956, selling about 25 million records and remaining one of the biggest selling Country artists of all time.

A shy child, Red was happiest on his own, playing an old battered guitar given to him by his father, who ran the general store. His father also sold harmonicas and Red used to practice on them to his heart's content. His mother was proud of Red's vocal potential and hired a music coach but Red wasn't happy with this arrangement so this was abandoned. Music wasn't his only interest and he also excelled in sports, particularly basketball and track events.

Red's career dated back to a singing contest, which he won when he was 17. He was invited to Louisville to compete at the state level, but having a bit of stage fright, he faltered and had to begin again three times. However, he eventually sang the song so well that he charmed the audience and the judges and walked away with first prize. In 1930, during his time at Georgetown College, Georgetown, Kentucky, he was spotted by a talent scout from WLS in Chicago who signed him for the *National Barn Dance.* There he joined John Lair's Cumberland Ridge Runners. Red spent his time absorbing new music and preparing himself for his future success.

The legendary ***Red Foley***

Red was also impressed by the Blues and apparently learned to play bottle-neck guitar at this time from the migrating black musicians who stopped off in Chicago. In 1933, after his first wife had died in childbirth, Red married Eva Overstake, who was one of the Three Little Maids and a sister of Jenny Lou Carson, who would become a talented Country music songwriter.

Red's solo singing, his comedy and his duet singing with Lulu Belle Cooper made him more and more popular. Red stayed with the *National Barn Dance* until 1937.

In October 1937, Red Foley and John Lair founded the *Renfro Valley Barn Dance,* which started in Cincinnati, Ohio. In November 1939, it moved to Renfro Valley, Kentucky, and Red performed as a regular on the show for three years. Red's flexible baritone voice was warm and rich and he was at home with any kind of song material from sentimental ballads to boogie. He also became the first Country artist to have a network radio show, *Avalon Time*, which co-starred comic Red Skelton. His popularity ensured that he was continually performing, making personal appearances at fairs, theaters and one nighters.

From 1940-1947, WLS *National Barn Dance* once again claimed Red. From 1946, Red appeared on the NBC segment of the *Grand Ole Opry* called the *Prince Albert Show.* Red was the emcee and principal singer and also acted as straight man to such comics as Minnie Pearl and Rod Brasfield. In addition, Red did recitations. He did much to make the *Grand Ole Opry* the most famous Country radio show. He was emcee when Hank Williams appeared on the *Opry*, on June 11, 1949, the wildly cheering audience asking for more and more encores of *Lovesick Blues.* Red had to ask them to cease howling for more, and let the program proceed.

In 1951, Red's second wife, who was known professionally during her solo career as Judy Martin, committed suicide after learning of his infidelity with Sally Sweet (whom he would later marry). Red went into virtual retirement to bring up his family after the death of his wife, but he was lured back by Si Siman and John Mahaffey of RadiOzark Enterprises, who offered to build a whole show around him, and needless to say the show was a phenomenal success. The show, *Ozark Jubilee*, was networked on ABC-TV from 1954 through 1960.

Red's recording career started in 1933, when he signed to the Conqueror label and stayed with them until 1936. Decca signed Red Foley to a lifetime contract in 1941. This was the year that Red made his western movie debut in *The Pioneers*, starring Tex Ritter. During the 1940's, some of the most popular songs recorded were *Old Shep*, self-penned and a great weepy (Elvis Presley, for one, admitted being a fan of Red Foley and he later recorded the song) and *Foggy River.*

In 1944, Red spent 13 weeks at No.1 with *Smoke on the Water*, which was also a Top 10 Pop hit. The flip-side, *There's a Blue Star Shining Bright*, made the Country Top 5. He started 1945 with the Top 5 double-sided hit, *Hang Your Head in Shame/I'll Never Let You Worry My Mind* and completed it with the No.1, *Shame on You* (a Top 15 Pop hit)*/At Mail Call Today* (Top 3), on which Red was accompanied by Lawrence Welk and His Orchestra. In March 1945, Red was the first major performer to record in Nashville, in studio B at WSM, and was produced by Paul Cohen.

Red's 1946 hits were the double-sided Top 5 success *Harriet/Have I Told You Lately That I Love You*, on which Red was accompanied by Roy Ross & His Ramblers and which came from the movie *Over the Trail*, in which he appeared. From 1947 through the spring of 1949, Red recorded with his group, the Cumberland Valley Boys. The hits during this period were 1947: *That's How Much I Love You* (Top 5), *New Jole Blonde (New Pretty Blonde)* (No.1), *Freight Train Boogie* (Top 5) and *Never Trust a Woman* (Top 3); 1949: *Candy Kisses* (Top 5)*/Tennessee Border* (Top 3).

Red's other hits in 1949 were *Tennessee Polka* (Top 5)*/I'm Throwing Rice (at the Girl I Love)* (Top 15) and *Two Cents, Three Eggs and a Postcard* (Top 10). At the end of 1949, Red got together with Ernest Tubb and in 1950, their single *Tennessee Border No.2* became a Top 3 hit and its flip, *Don't Be Ashamed of Your Age*, went Top 10. Red followed these with *I Gotta Have My Baby Back/Careless Kisses* (both Top 10). This was followed by a single that became Red's trade-mark number, *Chattanoogie Shoe Shine Boy*, which stayed at the top of the Country charts for 13 weeks and at the top of the Pop chart for 8 weeks. The flip-side, *Sugarfoot Rag*, went Top 5 Country and Top 25 Pop and featured Hank Garland on guitar. After these, Red scored with the Top 10 *Steal Away.* This was followed by another No.1, *Birmingham Bounce*, which stayed at the top for 4 weeks and made the Pop Top 15. The flip-side, *Choc'late Ice Cream Cone*, went Top 5. Red's other hits that year were *Mississippi* (No.1), *Just a Closer Walk with Thee* (Top 10), *Goodnight Irene* (with Ernest Tubb, No.1 Country/Top 10 Pop) and the flip, *Hillbilly Fever No.2* (Top 10), *Cincinnati Dancing Pig* (Top 3 Country/Top 10 Pop) and *Our Lady of Fatima* (Top 10 Country/Top 20 Pop).

Red's 1951 hits were *My Heart Cries for You* (Top 10, with Evelyn Knight), *Hobo Boogie* (Top 10), *The Strange Little Girl* (Top 10, with Ernest Tubb), *(There'll Be) Peace in the Valley* (Top 5, Certified Gold) and *Alabama Jubilee* (Top 3 Country/Top 30 Pop, with the Nashville Dixielanders featuring Francis Craig on bones). *(There'll Be) Peace in the Valley*, on which Red was accompanied by the Sunshine Boys Quartet, was the first million-selling Gospel song. In 1952, Red scored with *Too Old to Cut the Mustard* (Top 5, with Ernest Tubb) and *Milk Bucket Boogie/Salty Dog Rag* (both Top 10) and in 1953, he had *Midnight* (No.1), *Don't Let the Stars Get in Your Eyes* (Top 10), *Hot Toddy* (Top 10), *No Help Wanted #2* (Top 10, with Ernest Tubb), *Slaves of a Hopeless Love Affair* (Top 10) and *Shake a Hand* (Top 10).

Red started out 1954 with the Top 10 hit *As Far as I'm Concerned*, on which he was joined by his daughter Betty Foley. This was followed by another duet, this time with Kitty Wells, on the No.1 *One By One*. The flip-side, *I'm a Stranger in My Home*, also made the Top 15. Red wrapped up the year with the Top 10 *Jilted*. In 1955, Red scored with *Hearts of Stone* (Top 5) and the double-sided hit with Kitty Wells, *As Long as I Live* (Top 3)/*Make Believe ('Til We Can Make it Come True)* (Top 10). During the end of the 50's, Red's hits were *You and Me/No One But Me* (Top 3, with Kitty Wells, 1956) and *Travelin' Man* (Top 30). Of course, during this time Red recorded dozens of albums on Decca.

In the early 60's, Red co-starred with Fess Parker in the ABC-TV series, *Mr. Smith Goes to Washington*. Red's daughter Betty Foley (Cummins) was a successful Country singer from the 1950's and his daughter Shirley Lee married Pat Boone and one of their daughters is successful Pop-Country singer Debby Boone.

Red and Ernest Tubb helped to persuade the music industry to replace the word "hillbilly" with the less derisory "Country." Red Foley was elected to the Country Music Hall of Fame in 1967, being honored as "one of the most versatile and moving performers of all time" and "a giant influence during the formative years of contemporary Country music and today a timeless legend." That year, Red enjoyed a return to the lower region of the chart with the Top 50 duet with Kitty Wells *Happiness Means You* and the flip-side *Hello Number One*, which went Top 60. At the beginning of 1968, the twosome charted with the Top 70 *Living as Strangers*.

Red died of a heart attack after a tour with WSM's *Grand Ole Opry* at Fort Wayne, Indiana. At the beginning of 1969, Red had a posthumous hit with *Have I Told You Lately that I Love You?* on which he was paired with Kitty Wells.

Red always signed off on his radio and TV broadcasts with his famous "Good night Mama, Good night Papa, Good night Red." JAB

RECOMMENDED ALBUMS:

"Red Foley Souvenir Album" (Decca)(1958) [Featuring Betty Foley] [Originally 10" album in 1951]
"Red and Ernie" (Decca)(1957) [With Ernest Tubb] [Re-issued in original sleeve by Stetson UK (1987)]
"Red Foley's Golden Favorites" (Decca)(1959)
"Company's Comin'" (Decca)(1961) [Re-issued in original sleeve by Stetson UK (1992)]
"The Red Foley Show" (Decca)(1963) [With Patsy Cline, Ernest Tubb, Kitty Wells, the Wilburn Brothers, Speedy Haworth & Uncle Cyp Brasfield][Re-issued in original sleeve by Stetson UK (1987)]
"Red Foley's Golden Favorites" (Decca)(1965)
"Red Foley" (Vocalion)(1966) [With Judy Martin]
"Red Foley's Greatest Hits" (Decca)(1968)
"Gospel Favorites" (double)(Country Music)(1976)
"Red Foley Memories" (MCA)
"The Red Foley Story" (double)(MCA) [With the Jordanaires]
"Songs of Devotion" (MCA)
"Beyond the Sunset" (MCA) [With the Jordanaires, the Anita Kerr Singers & the Sunshine Boys]
"I'm Bound for the Kingdom" (MCA)
"Tennessee Saturday Night" (Charly UK)(1984)

ALLEN FONTENOT

(Singer, Songwriter, Fiddle, Scrub-Board, Club Owner, Deejay)

Date of Birth:	**1932**
Where Born:	**Grand Prairie, Evangeline Parish, Louisiana**

Among the Cajun community, the name "Fontenot" carries quite a reputation and one of the most celebrated is fiddler Allen Fontenot. When he was age 7, Allen received a ukulele for his Christmas present. However, this wasn't to his liking and he fixed it up into a fiddle. He did this with various other non-musical pieces, such as cigar boxes, stringing them with wire and playing with a bow that would be better used to shoot arrows.

When Allen was 15, his grandfather, who also played fiddle, bought him the real thing, which came from Sears Roebuck. Like most Cajun musicians, Allen has always had a second string to his bow and was for many years a bill collector. In the early 70's, Allen put together his five-piece band, the Country Cajuns, with Leroy Veilloa (concertina), Darrel Brasseaux (drums), Hudson Dauzat (guitar) and the only non-Cajun, John Scott, on bass.

They cut a few singles and played at the annual Jazz and Heritage Festival and landed a regular Sunday morning show on WNPS radio. In 1975, they appeared in the Charles Bronson movie *Hard Times*. The group has also been featured on *Good Morning America*, *Real People* and *Austin City Limits*.

Allen, who is a chain-smoker, became a very successful deejay on station WSDL Slidell, Louisiana. In the late 70's, he opened the closest Cajun club to New Orleans, the Cajun Bandstand in the city of Kenner, which served Cajun food and at which the Country Cajuns played. The club remained open until 1982, when it was sold.

On the recording front, Allen has benefitted, as most Cajuns have, from the efforts of record entrepreneur Floyd Soileau. Allen has cut albums for Great Southern, Antilles and Delta.

RECOMMENDED ALBUMS:

"Jole Blon (& Other Cajun Honky Songs)" (Delta)(1981)
"Old Fais Do Do Songs" (Delta)(1982)

DICK FORAN

(Singer, Guitar, Actor)

Given Name:	**Nick Foran**
Date of Birth:	**June 18, 1910**
Where Born:	**Flemington, New Jersey**
Married:	**Unknown**
Children:	**John, James**
Date of Death:	**August 10, 1979**

There will always be disputation as to who was the original singing cowboy. Some say that Gene Autry was the one, others point to John Wayne (although his character, "Singing Sandy," used Smith Ballew's vocals) and yet another view is that it was Ken Maynard. However, there is a good chance that Warner Brothers created the genre with Dick Foran, but delayed releasing his initial movie until after Gene Autry had hit the silver screen.

Foran was certainly not born on the range. The son of a U.S. Senator, Arthur F. Foran, Dick was educated at Princeton but hankered after a theatrical career. Before getting into the entertainment business full-time, he worked as a seaman and a special investigator.

He possessed a voice that belonged more on Broadway than the Hollywood trail and was more of the Nelson Eddy texture and in fact during his career, he did appear on the stage. He also cut some popular music sides as Nick Foran. Two months after Gene Autry's first major movie in 1934, Nick Foran made his celluloid debut with *Stand Up and Cheer*. By the time of *Moonlight on the Prairie*, Nick had become Dick. Over the next three years, the red-headed Dick Foran turned out 12 western movies for Warner Brothers. From his 1937 movie, *Cherokee Strip*, Dick had a hit with the song, *My Little Buckaroo*.

Dick's final western was *Prairie Thunder*, at the end of 1937. Following this movie, Warner Brothers stopped the Dick Foran series of movies and he resorted to being a contract player.

In 1940, Dick signed to Universal Films and that year, he appeared in the movie *The Mummy's Hand*. The following year, he starred with Leo Carrillo and Devine in two serials and the feature movie *Road Agent*. In 1942, Dick appeared with Abbott & Costello in the movie *Ride 'Em Cowboy*, singing *I'll Remember April*.

During the 40's, Foran made singing radio transcriptions for Dr Pepper. His film output also included several non-westerns, where he

Singing Cowboy ***Dick Foran***

played the all-American college hero. In 1945, he appeared with Don Ameche and Claudette Colbert in the sophisticated comedy *Guest Wife*. In 1948, Dick appeared with John Wayne, Henry Fonda and Shirley Temple in the movie *Fort Apache*. His last major movie was *Taggart* (based on Louis L'Amour's novel of the same name), in which he appeared with Tony Young and Dan Duryea. In the late 60's, Foran appeared as "Slim" in the *Burl Ives* TV series. (See Movie Section.)

GERRY FORD

(Singer, Songwriter, Guitar, Deejay, Emcee)

Given Name:	**Gerard Corcorran**
Date of Birth:	**May 25, 1943**
Where Born:	**Athlone, Ireland**
Married:	**Joan**
Children:	**Gerard**

Gerry Ford has appeared on the *Grand Ole Opry* on 20 occasions to date, having been first introduced on the *Opry* by Roy Acuff. Gerry's career has spanned over 30 years from the time he began as an emcee/deejay in London, where as one of Britain's most respected Country singers and deejays he had the privilege of introducing Jim Reeves.

Gerry was born the fourth of five children and made his first public appearance singing *The Man from Laramie* at a local Christmas pantomime. His initiation into Country music came as he listened to the radio in Ireland, where American Country and Western singers were very popular and local showbands also performed Country songs. In 1960 he bought his first guitar and taught himself to play.

After an apprenticeship as a baker in Scotland, Gerry moved to London, where he qualified as a baker-confectioner. He also worked in the evenings as a deejay and emcee and introduced the Beatles and Gerry and the Pacemakers on their first London show. In 1961, Gerry met Joan and in 1964, they married and returned to Scotland, where Gerry became a policeman. In his off-duty time, he started performing as a singer and soon gained popularity.

Gerry made his first broadcast on Radio Clyde in Glasgow in 1974 and by April 1975, he had started *Forth Country Special* on the newly opened Radio Forth in Edinburgh. This was a one hour show which soon became two and a half hours.

The first song Gerry recorded was *Reuben James* and in August 1976, he turned professional. He worked the clubs both as a singer and a deejay and signed a 3-year contract with Emerald Records. He recorded his debut single for the label, *Which One Will It Be*. On the flip-side was one of his own songs, *You're Still Mine*. His debut album was ***These Songs Are Just for You*** (1977) and was well received by the British Country press. After putting together a package show called the *Gerry Ford Country Show*, he toured the clubs that year.

From 1978 until 1993, Gerry presented BBC Radio Scotland's *Country Corner*. When it was taken off the air, there was a hue and cry in the national and Country press, with hundreds of listeners complaining by letter petitions and by telephone, in an effort to keep the program. Some of Gerry's other popular shows have been *Ford's Country Profile*, *Waxing Eloquent* and *On the House—Country Style*. BBC Radio 2's *Country Club* invited Gerry to be a guest presenter in 1984 and on TV he interviewed Bobby Bare and Boxcar Willie on a program called *Dallas Through the Looking Glass*.

As a performer, Gerry has toured with star Country singers such as Willie Nelson, Boxcar Willie, Moe Bandy, Roy Drusky, Dottsy and his good friend Jean Shepard. He has also toured all over Europe and has regularly appeared and emceed the Wembley Festival in England. In 1988, Gerry formed his own band, which backed him until 1991, when he reverted to being a solo performer. In 1992, a 30 minute special of Gerry Ford was shown on Scottish TV. He was also featured on BBC-TV on a show called *An Evening with Daniel O'Donnell*. Gerry has also presented a Gospel special on BBC radio.

Gerry has traveled to Nashville many times over the years. He has recorded all his albums at Hilltop Recording Studios (now called Oaks Place) in Hendersonville, Tennessee. They were ***Some One to Give My Love To*** (1978) and ***With Love*** (1979), both on Emerald. He then switched to Big R Records, where he released ***On the Road*** (1981) and ***Let's Hear It for the Working Man*** (1982). He then moved labels again and went with Trim Top, releasing ***Memory Machine*** (1984), ***Thank God for the Radio*** (1986), ***All Over Again*** (1987) and ***Stranger Things Have Happened*** (1989). In 1990, Gerry released his first cd, ***16 Country Favourites (Volume I)***. This was followed by ***Better Man*** (1991), which won the "Best Album by a British Artist" in the BCMA Radio Play Awards, 1991.

In 1992, Gerry released ***Can I Count on You*** and followed this with ***16 Country Favourites (Volume II)*** in 1994. The self-penned single, *Can I Count on You*, was No.1 on the Irish chart and it was nominated as "Country Single of the Year" by the BCMA in 1993. His latest single to date, *Memory Man*, written by Ted Harris, was released in Ireland to coincide with Gerry's tour. In 1994, Gerry's

The pride of Scotland, ***Gerry Ford***

album, ***Can I Count on You***, was named in the BCMA Radio Play Awards as "Best Album by a British Artist." JAB

RECOMMENDED ALBUMS:

(All U.K. releases)
"Some One to Give My Love To" (Emerald)(1978)
"With Love" (Emerald)(1979)
"On the Road" (Big R)(1981)
"Let's Hear It for the Working Man" (Big R)(1982)
"Memory Machine" (Trim Top)(1984)
"Thank God for the Radio" (Trim Top)(1986)
"All Over Again" (Trim Top)(1987)
"Stranger Things Have Happened" (Trim Top)(1989)
"16 Country Favourites, Vol. I" (Trim Top)(1990)
"Better Man" (Trim Top)(1991)
"Can I Count on You" (Trim Top)(1992)
"16 Country Favourites, Vol. II" (Trim Top)(1994)

Mary Ford refer LES PAUL and MARY FORD

TENNESSEE ERNIE FORD

(Singer, Songwriter, Guitar, Deejay)

Given Name: Ernest Jennings Ford
Date of Birth: February 13, 1919
Where Born: Fordtown, Tennessee
Married: 1. Betty Hemminger (dec'd.) 2. Beverly
Children: Buck, Brion
Date of Death: October 17, 1991

Ernie Ford, the "Old Pea Picker," is best remembered for his mammoth international hit, *Sixteen Tons*. However, his history shows he was a regular chart visitor many years before that hit.

Born in Fordtown, Tennessee, Ernie Ford was raised in Bristol, Tennessee. After graduating from high school, he began his radio career at Bristol's WOPI, then in 1939, he enrolled at the Cincinnati Conservatory of Music to study voice.

Ernie enlisted in the Army Air Corps and served as a bombardier instructor during WWII. After his discharge, he and his first wife settled on the West Coast, where Ford worked at KFXM in San Bernardino, California. During that time, he first adopted the nickname "Tennessee Ernie." While employed by KXLA in Pasadena, Ford was heard by entrepreneur Cliffie Stone, who recognized the announcer's potential as a vocalist and became his manager.

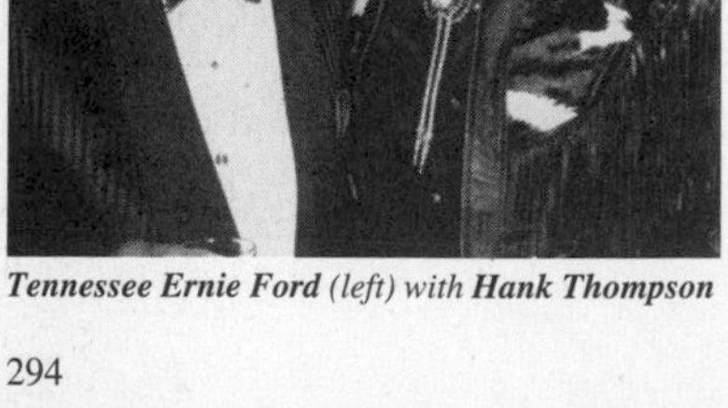

Tennessee Ernie Ford** (left) with **Hank Thompson

Ford became a featured performer on two of Stone's radio shows and in 1949, he was signed by Capitol Records. During that year, Ernie (credited as "Tennessee Ernie") had five sides on the Country chart: *Tennessee Border* (Top 10), *Country Junction* (Top 15), *Smokey Mountain Boogie* (Top 10), his first No.1, *Mule Train*, which stayed at the top for 4 weeks, crossing over to the Pop Top 10, and was backed by the Top 3 *Anticipation Blues*. In 1950, he made his debut on the *Grand Ole Opry*. He continued his chart success with *The Cry of the Wild Goose* (Top 3 Country/Top 15 Pop), *Ain't Nobody's Business But My Own* (Top 5) and the flip, *I'll Never Be Free* (Top 3 on both Country and Pop), both duets with Kay Starr. He rounded off the year with another No.1, *The Shot Gun Boogie*, which stayed at the top for 14 weeks.

The following year, Ernie played Las Vegas, and scored with *Tailor Made Woman* (Top 10, with Joe "Fingers" Carr), *Mr. and Mississippi* (Top 3 Country/Top 20 Pop) and the Top 10 *Strange Little Girl*. In 1952, Ernie's only hit was *Blackberry Boogie* (Top 10). In 1953, Ford became the first Country star to headline at the London Palladium. His solitary hit that year was the Top 10 *Hey, Mr. Cotton Picker*.

In 1954, he moved to network TV as the host of NBC's *College of Musical Knowledge* game show as well as his own weekday program. That year, Ernie charted with *River of No Return*, which went Top 10. The following year, he started with *Ballad of Davy Crockett* (Top 10 Country/Top 5 Pop). It was on his game show that he debuted *Sixteen Tons*, which sold 2 million copies in eight weeks.

Prime-time TV stardom followed on NBC's *The Ford Show* from 1956-1961, where Ernie's homespun expression "Bless your little pea-pickin' hearts" became a national catchphrase. He later had a daytime series on ABC and was a fixture of TV shows throughout the 1960's. ***Hymns***, his 1956 Gospel album, was the first Gospel record Certified Gold by RIAA in 1959.

In 1964, Ernie won a Grammy Award for "Best Gospel or Other Religious Recording (Musical)" for his album ***Great Gospel Songs***. Ernie had his last major hit in 1965 with the Top 10 *Hicktown*. He made several memorable appearances on *I Love Lucy*.

During his career, Ford recorded more than 100 albums of Country, Gospel and other types of music. The many honors bestowed on Ford during his illustrious career include the Medal of Freedom, America's civilian honor, which he received in 1984. Ernie was inducted to the Country Music Hall of Fame in 1990.

Ernie died from an advanced liver disease in HCA Reston Hospital, Reston, Virginia, following a visit to the White House.

RECOMMENDED ALBUMS:

"Hymns" (Capitol)(1956)
"Tennessee Ernie Ford Deluxe Set" (3 albums)(Capitol)(1968)
"Tennessee Ernie Ford Sings Civil War Songs of the South" (Capitol)(1975)
"Ernie Sings & Glen Picks" (Capitol)(1975) [With Glen Campbell]
"25th Anniversary (Yesterday)" (Capitol)(1980)
"25th Anniversary (Today)" (Capitol)(1980)
"Tennessee Ernie Ford—Spirituals" (Capitol)(1981)

Whitey Ford refer DUKE OF PADUCAH

FORESTER SISTERS

When Formed: 1982
KATHY FORESTER
Date of Birth: January 4, 1955
JUNE FORESTER
Date of Birth: September 22, 1956
KIM FORESTER
Date of Birth: November 4, 1960
CHRISTY FORESTER
Date of Birth: December 21, 1962
All Born: Lookout Mountain, Georgia

The Forester Sisters have established a reputation for sizzling sibling harmonies and for five years they were the foremost female vocal group on the Country chart.

The sisters were raised on a farm in New Salem, Georgia, and music soon began to play a major role. Kathy and June began singing harmonies in their local church, the New Salem United Methodist Church. Later Kim joined them but Christy was unable to find a part when she came along.

After gaining degrees, the two eldest girls began teaching but also started a group with some local male musicians, playing at local parties and clubs. Kim joined in 1978. The male members never stayed long, which led to the idea of forming an all-girl group. By now Kim and Christy had finished college. Kathy and June quit teaching and the Forester Sisters were born in 1982. As well as their precise harmonizing, the girls had between them mastered a considerable range of instruments, including piano, clarinet, flute, organ and guitar. They were influenced by other female groups, such as the Lennon Sisters, the McGuire Sisters, the Andrews Sisters and the Supremes. In 1988, the Foresters would score with a cover of the McGuire Sisters' *Sincerely*.

The Forester Sisters' break came when songwriters Bobby Keel and Billy Stone, having seen them perform at a local arts festival, gave them a song, *Yankee Go Home*, which was later featured on their debut album. Encouraged, the sisters did a demo session at the famous Muscle Shoals studio in Alabama in December 1983. Warner Brothers got hold of a copy of the ensuing tape and enthused. The label sent representatives to see them perform, which led to a formal audition, and they were signed by the label in summer of 1984. The Forester Sisters initially toured as opening act for Larry Gatlin and the Gatlin Brothers.

When their debut single, *(That's What You Do) When You're in Love,* reached the Top 10 in January 1985 and remained on the chart for over 5 months, the go-ahead was given for the recording of a debut album. Produced by Terry Skinner (Kathy's husband) and J.L. Wallace, ***The Forester Singers***, recorded at Muscle Shoals, was released that summer and yielded three successful chart toppers: *I Fell in Love Again Last Night, Just in Case* and *Mama's Never Seen Those Eyes.* This set a record, at the time, for a debut Country album.

Their success quickly spawned a follow-up album, ***Perfume, Ribbons & Pearls*** (1986). It was not as spontaneous and refreshing as its predecessor and the only hit single from it was *Lonely Again*, which just failed to make No.1, in July 1986.

At Fan Fair 1985, the Bellamy Brothers sought out the Foresters on account of their knowing the sisters' relatives in Florida and David Bellamy wrote *Too Much is Not Enough* and asked the Foresters to provide the fulsome vocal sound required. The combination was a winning one, with the single reaching the top spot in September 1986 and led to a "Brothers and Sisters" tour. The group won the ACM "Vocal Group of the Year" award in 1986.

No fewer than five producers were used for the next Foresters' album: Emory Gordy, Jr., James Stroud & Barry Beckett and J.L. Wallace & Terry Skinner. The extra effort paid off. A cover of Brenda Lee's 1965 hit *Too Many Rivers* made it to the Top 5. The title track of the third album, ***You Again***, written by Don Schlitz and Paul Overstreet, went to the top. The Foresters were then able to indulge in a long cherished project: they recorded a Christmas album, ***A Christmas Card***. Full of traditional favorites, the album included outstanding renditions of *An Old Christmas Card* and *White Christmas.*

During 1988, the Forester Sisters scored a Top 5 hit with *Lyin' in His Arms Again* and a Top 10 success with *Letter Home*. The next album, ***Sincerely***, was produced by Wendy Waldman, Jim Ed Norman and James Stroud & Barry Beckett.

In 1989, the Foresters' hits were *Sincerely, Love Will* and *Don't You*, all Top 10 entries. The following year, they had a Top 10 hit with *Leave It Alone*. Since this stellar period of chart success, the Foresters have found hit-making less easy. However, of interest, although only a Top 70 entry, was John Hiatt's *Drive South*, by the Foresters and the Bellamy Brothers from the Wendy Waldman-produced album, ***Come Hold Me***. This song went Top 3 in the hands of Suzy Bogguss in 1992. The Foresters' album was not successful, no doubt due in part to a very unremarkable sleeve design.

The highly ironic *Men*, from their last album on Warner Brothers, ***Talkin 'Bout Men***, which was produced by Robert Byrne and Alan Schulman, was the Forester Sisters' last Top 10 hit, in April 1991. The album sleeve was once again a good selling point. In 1992, the Forester Sisters released another Robert Byrne and Alan Schulman produced album, ***I Got a Date***, from which *What'll You Do About Me* made the Top 75 and the title track reached the Top 60.

As a live act the Foresters are outstanding and have appeared both in their own right and as support for such acts as Kenny Rogers and the Oak Ridge Boys. SM

RECOMMENDED ALBUMS:

"The Forester Sisters" (Warner Brothers)(1985)
"Perfume, Ribbons & Pearls" (Warner Brothers)(1986)
"You Again" (Warner Brothers)(1987)
"A Christmas Card" (Warner Brothers)(1987)
"Sincerely" (Warner Brothers)(1988)
"Greatest Hits" (Warner Brothers)(1989)
"Come Hold Me" (Warner Brothers)(1990)
"Talkin' 'Bout Men" (Warner Brothers)(1991)
"I Got a Date" (1992)

*The lively **Forester Sisters** in action*

PEGGY FORMAN

(Singer, Songwriter)

Where Born: **Centerville, Louisiana**
Married: **Wayne Forman**
Children: **Cindy Jo**

Peggy Forman came to national attention through the auspices of the late Conway Twitty. Peggy had recorded some material for Twitty band member Joe Lewis in Oklahoma City. Impressed with her writing style and vocal ability, Lewis introduced her to Twitty, who deemed her abilities worthy of his help and guidance.

Peggy comes from a tightly knit family with seven other siblings. Her father was an oil field worker and her mother a homemaker. To make extra money, Peggy and her brothers and sisters would pick cotton during the hot, muggy summers of the Louisiana flatlands. Peggy's first glimmer of interest in the music business occurred when she was age 7 and received a toy piano for Christmas. Her first performance happened when she was in the third grade and sang the Rockabilly classic *Blue Suede Shoes* for a school talent show. Peggy recalls her mother made her her first long gown, which she wore for the event, and thereafter she participated in every opportunity to sing at school.

It was during high school that Peggy met her husband, Wayne, while singing in a quartet. After they married, they joined a band together with Wayne playing lead guitar and Peggy singing harmonies. Soon Peggy was singing lead vocals, and her first solo was *If Teardrops Were Pennies and Heartaches Were*

Gold. The band was together four years, during which time Peggy and her husband did a couple of shows with former Louisiana Governor Jimmie Davis, who, along with his wife, encouraged her.

Six months after Joe Lewis had recorded Peggy's songs, Conway called her at home encouraging her as both a songwriter and a recording artist. Shortly afterward Loretta Lynn cut Peggy's *Out of My Head and Back in My Bed*, which was a No.1 hit, and that same year, Conway recorded the Forman-penned *Yours to Hurt Tomorrow* on his 1978 ***Georgia Keeps Pulling on My Ring*** album. With Conway's help Peggy landed a recording contract with MCA.

Under the production guidance of Twitty and producer Snuffy Miller, Peggy hit the charts with her MCA debut, *The Danger Zone*, in August 1977. It was on the charts for four weeks, squeaking in the Top 100. Other singles followed without chart action. In 1979, Margo Smith recorded Peggy's *Let's Build a Fire*, which appeared on Margo's ***Just Margo*** album.

Peggy signed with Dimension Records, an independent label, and returned to the charts in 1980 with *There Ain't Nothing Like a Rainy Night*, her debut single, which was followed by *Burning Up Your Memory* the same year. Other charting singles included 1981's *You're More to Me* and her most successful release, *I Wish You Could Have Turned My Head and Left My Heart Alone*, which went Top 60. Peggy's final chart entry was *That's What Your Lovin' Does to Me*, released in 1982.

If Peggy's career as a vocalist was unsuccessful, her credibility as a writer gained national attention early on. In 1977 SESAC named her "Most Promising Country Music Writer of the Year," and followed up the next year by naming her the SESAC "Country Music Writer of the Year." She also picked up the writer's award for SESAC "Single of the Year," for *Out of My Head and Back in My Bed.* This distinction garnered her the *Billboard* "Star Award" as well. Other artists that have recorded Peggy's songs include Bill Anderson, Kenny Dale, Jean Shepard, Mary Lou Turner, Connie Cato, and Randy Corners.

"I once worked in a hospital for 8 years with 25 other women," Peggy explained, when asked where her ideas for songs come from. "If you listened closely you could hear some pretty good stories for songs. Also, when you perform in clubs, you see quite a bit. I guess a lot of my songs come from other people's experiences I have observed." In 1983, George Strait recorded Peggy's song *Fifteen Years Going Up (and One Night Coming Down)* on his Gold album ***Right or Wrong***.

While her abilities as a vocalist may have been underrated, Peggy Forman will be remembered as one of the premier female Country songwriters. LAP

HOWDY FORRESTER

(Fiddle)
Given Name: Howard Wilson Forrester
Date of Birth: March 31, 1922
Where Born: Vernon, Hickman County, Tennessee
Married: Wilene "Sally Ann" Russell
Children: Robert Allen
Date of Death: August 1, 1987

One of Country music's great fiddlers, Big Howdy Forrester gained the most fame for the years he spent with Roy Acuff. Yet this work tended to obscure his earlier stints with bands such as those of Bill Monroe, Herald Goodman, Cowboy Copas and, most notably, Georgia Slim's Texas Roundup.

Howard Forrester grew up on a farm near Vernon, Tennessee, in a musical family. His father and uncle were both skilled fiddlers and during an eight-month period of recovery from rheumatic fever at age 11, the youthful Forrester developed his fiddling skills. In 1935, the family moved to Nashville and the following year Howard joined a band that included guitarist Billy Byrd and Hubert Gregory, who played at WSIX radio.

Two years later, Howard and his guitar-playing brother Joe joined Harold Goodman's Tennessee Valley Boys at the *Grand Ole Opry,* where the late and great Arthur Smith became his mentor. Howard also met another great fiddler, Robert "Georgia Slim" Rutland (1916-1969), and together they perfected the art of twin fiddling. The Tennessee Valley Boys moved to Texas later that year and they worked at various locations in the Lone Star State. He met Wilene "Billie"/"Sally Ann" Russell, an accordion player in Texas and they married in June 1940.

Not long afterward, Georgia Slim left to form his Texas Roundup and the Forresters joined them in Dallas. After U.S. involvement in WWII, the couple returned to Nashville, where "Big Howdy," as Howard had become known in Texas, worked primarily with Bill Monroe's Blue Grass Boys until he was drafted. Sally Ann remained with the Monroe unit in his absence.

Out of the service in 1946, Howdy, Joe and Wilene all returned to KRLD Dallas and Georgia Slim's *Texas Roundup,* where they remained until 1949, recording a session on Mercury in 1947. The couple returned to Nashville in 1949 where Howard worked for Cowboy Copas and in construction with another brother until 1951, when he joined Roy Acuff's Smoky Mountain Boys. Forrester remained with the Acuff organization for the rest of his working life. Although he did not travel the road all of that time, he did play with the band on the *Opry* consistently, except for three months in late 1967, until mid-1987. From 1964 to 1967, he worked primarily for Acuff-Rose Artists Corporation as a booking agent and thereafter in other capacities until 1983, when he retired from everything except the *Opry*. Howdy played with Mr. Roy until a few weeks before his death in 1987.

In addition to the many discs Forrester made with Roy Acuff's Smoky Mountain Boys on Capitol, MGM, Decca, and Hickory, the famed fiddler recorded a fair amount of solo fiddle tunes and twin fiddling numbers over the years. The latter included one twin fiddle album with Kenny Baker and two with Chubby Wise. In the late 60's, Kanawha released a limited edition of an album drawn from the radio transcriptions Howdy and Georgia Slim did with the *Texas Roundup.* IMT

RECOMMENDED ALBUMS:
"Fancy Fiddlin' Country Style" (MGM)(1962)
"Fiddlin' Country Style" (United Artists)(1963)
"Howdy's Fiddle and Howdy Too" (Stoneway)(1973)
"Big Howdy" (Stoneway)(1974)
"Leather Britches" (Stoneway)(1975)
"Stylish Fiddling" (Stoneway)(1976)
Howdy Forrester and Georgia Slim:
"Texas Roundup" (Kanawha)(1969)
Howdy Forrester and Chubby Wise:
"Sincerely Yours" (Stoneway)(1974)
"Fiddle Favorites" (Stoneway)(1975)
"Red Apple Rag" (County)(1983) [Note: Only two tunes feature twin fiddle; four are solos by Forrester, the remainder is Baker]
(See also Roy Acuff.)

FRED FOSTER

(Industry Executive, Record Producer)
Given Name: Fred Luther Foster
Where Born: North Carolina
Married: 1. Carol Jean "Billie" Wallace (m. 1955)(div.)
2. Lisa Lawalin (former Miss Georgia) (m. 1978)
Children: Vance, Michelle, Leah

Fred Foster is the stuff of which legends are made. His independent Monument Records was one of the most successful labels in Country music and could boast on its roster artists such as Dolly Parton, Kris Kristofferson, Roy Orbison, Larry Gatlin, Willie Nelson and Billy Swan.

Fred was the youngest of eight children and when Fred was just 15, he became the man of the house when his father died. He was at that time the only one of the children at home and he and his mother maintained the 3.5 acre farm. As a result, Fred left school at 10th grade. However, he gained his education through the pages of the books he read. He kept the farm going for two years and then had to give it up. At this time, he met Joe Volpe, who ran a home and auto supply store. Volpe gave Foster a part-time job and then advised him to leave his hometown and loaned him $20.

With $10, Fred secured a lift to Washington, D.C., where his sister lived and then got a job as a car hop at a Hot Shoppe restaurant. Soon, he was promoted to Curb Manager and then to Kitchen Manager at a salary of $70 per week. As the restaurant chain grew, Fred climbed up the managerial ladder and was soon moved into the commissary, where he worked with Chef Marquis Rinadout preparing meals for the other restaurants. It was while he was doing this that he met entertainer Billy Strickland. Strickland was a practical joker and one night introduced Foster as a famous songwriter who could create a song before the audience's eyes. The resulting poem was put to music by Strickland and became an instant favorite, being repeated 25 times that night, earning Strickland $1,000 in tips and Foster all the drinks he could handle.

The two of them started to write together and this resulted in a publishing deal for them both and a recording deal for Strickland. A little while later, Fred was in the Covered Wagon Club in D.C. when he heard Jimmy Dean. Fred decided to record a demo on Dean singing the song *Bumming Around*. Foster did a deal with 4 Star Records and the resulting record was a Top 5 hit for Dean in 1953.

In 1953, Foster tried to join the U.S. Air Force but was rejected for service because he had sustained an eye injury while working for Volpe. Fred started working for George Freedman at Irving Music before moving on to Mercury Records a year later, as field representative. While at Mercury, he met his first wife and married her in 1955. From Mercury, Fred moved to ABC-Paramount and then relocated to Baltimore, where he took over the distribution of Pop singles for J & F Company. In this job, he worked on a percentage basis and averaged $200 a week. While at J & F, he met Walt Maguire, a representative for London Records, which was then going through bad times. Foster told Maguire that London's output lacked something. Maguire challenged Foster to do better.

So in 1958 Fred created Monument Records, but was initially underfunded. The record from the first recording session was never released. By August, he had found *Gotta Travel On*, which was based on a 19th-century British song. He lined up Billy Grammer, then Jimmy Dean's guitarist, to cut it. However, before any recording could be done, Fred had to do a little dealing. He went to Nashville with $800 and met RCA's Chet Atkins. Atkins took him on honor for the studio rental and assisted in getting musicians and played on the session. Walt Maguire offered to take on distribution of the single, with Foster's proviso that the record be on the Monument label. The single reached the Top 5 on the Country chart and crossed over to the Top 5 on the Pop chart.

By 1960, thanks to Boudleaux Bryant's help, Fred and his family had moved to Nashville. During the first year of Monument's operation, Fred received free legal and financial guidance from Baltimore attorney Franklin Goldstein and accountant Gunther Borris. Fred brought into operation a second label, Sound Stage 7.

It was 1960 that saw Monument become a major force in Pop music when Roy Orbison began his first period with the label. *Only the Lonely (Know How I Feel)* went Top 3 on the Pop chart and this was followed by a string of major hits that included *Blue Angel*, *Running Scared* (No.1), *Crying*, *Dream Baby (How Long Must I Dream)*, *In Dreams*, *Mean Woman Blues*, *It's Over* and the million-selling No.1 *Oh, Pretty Woman*, all produced by Fred Foster. Not only were these records successful in the U.S., they were also international hits. *Only the Lonely*, *It's Over* and *Oh, Pretty Woman* went to No.1 in the U.K. Orbison decided to leave the label in 1965 when he received an attractive financial (but ultimately unproductive deal) from RCA.

Country music legend Grandpa Jones may have seemed a strange choice to come to Monument, but he had his only Top 5 record there with Jimmie Rodgers' *T for Texas* in 1962. The sax man Boots Randolph had four chart entries on the label, including the now classic *Yakety Sax* in 1963. By 1964, Foster had signed the newly arrived Dolly Parton to the label, but it was not until three years later that she had her first chart entry on Monument, *Dumb Blonde*.

Both Billy Walker and Jeannie Seely came to Monument in 1966, Walker with a chart record at Columbia and Seely new on the block. Billy stayed at the label until 1970, during which time he chalked up 5 Top 10 records, including *A Million and One*, *Bear with Me a Little Longer* and *Ramona*. Seely was on the label for two years and had two Top 10 singles, *Don't Touch Me* (1966) and *I'll Love You More (Than You Need)*, in 1967. That year, Henson Cargill provided the label with another No.1, *Skip a Rope*, and followed it up with several more hits, including the 1969 Top 10 record *None of My Business*.

Foster raved about Tony Joe White when he signed him up in 1969 and White repaid the confidence with the international hit *Polk Salad Annie*, following it up with the 1970 success *Groupie Girl*. During the end of 1969, Ray Stevens came on board and had a Top 60 success with Kristofferson's *Sunday Mornin' Comin' Down*.

Kris Kristofferson became one of the mainstays of the label when he signed in 1972. He had a No.1 hit the following year with the Gold single *Why Me*, which had back-up vocals from Rita Coolidge and Larry Gatlin. Gatlin became one of the label's foremost artists following his appearance in the charts in 1972. It was with Monument that he had his first No.1 single, *I Just Wish You Were Someone I Love*. He remained with Foster until 1978.

Monument had further chart action in the early 70's via Charlie McCoy, Billy Joe Shaver and Barefoot Jerry and in 1974, Billy Swan. Swan's *I Can Help* was a cross-over No.1 which went Gold, and was a Top 10 single in the U.K. During the 70's, CBS Records, who distributed the label, established a separate label identity for Monument in the U.K.

By 1979, the activity on the label was slowing down and in 1980, no singles were released at all. The final single was issued in 1982. This was the controversial record by United American, *Russian Bear*, which took a sideswipe at Moscow after the invasion of Afghanistan. There was a lot of interest in the 1983 double-album, ***The Winning Hand***, which starred Willie Nelson, Dolly Parton, Kris Kristofferson and Brenda Lee and featured duets by these artists. A single by Willie and Dolly, *Everything's Beautiful (In Its Own Way)*, had been pre-released from the project. In addition, Willie and Brenda charted with *You're Gonna Love Yourself (in the Morning)*.

Since 1983, Fred Foster has not been active, but one of his co-written songs, *Me and Bobby McGee*, remains one of the most popular and most recorded songs.

Monument may now be just another casualty of the well-entrenched trend of getting rid of independent labels, but the albums stand head and shoulders above most contemporary material. Fred Foster remains one of the finest producers in any musical discipline and his artist roster would still cause most label heads to go green with envy.

FOSTER AND LLOYD

When Formed: 1987
RADNEY FOSTER
(Singer, Songwriter, Guitar)
Date of Birth: July 20, 1959
Where Born: Del Rio, Texas
BILL LLOYD
(Singer, Songwriter, Guitar)
Date of Birth: December 6, 1955
Where Born: Bowling Green, Kentucky

Radney Foster and Bill Lloyd are two songwriters who as solo artists had their own bands and recording deals. They had teamed to write and, having made a demo tape of their songs to pitch to other artists, they were surprised to find they were being wooed by record companies to record and perform as a duo. Taking advantage of the situation, they went ahead with an offer from RCA.

Radney Foster is the son of a lawyer. He stepped outside of the family tradition when he left his roots, adventuring away from home to the University of the South in Sewanee, Tennessee. Playing a gig at a nightclub in Sewanee one night, a fan said he knew a producer in Nashville who really needed to hear his songs. Having heard this kind of talk before, he disregarded him, but it had given him an idea. So he went to Nashville and receiving encouraging signs, he took a year off from college and moved there. In the event, it turned out to be much longer than a year. He managed to get a songwriting deal with MTM Music Group, and later met and then teamed up with Bill Lloyd.

Bill Lloyd is the son of a military man, who played with a Swing band in his spare time. As a child, Bill spent his years on military bases around the world. As puberty approached, he began pouring his heart out into writing. He attended Western Kentucky University, where he was majoring in communications, but he quit college to pursue a musical career full time. Although he moved to Nashville in 1982, he spent a long time knocking on doors. Setting out to make a solo career, he recorded an album on the independent label Throbbing Lobster in 1987 called ***Feeling the Elephant***. He was writing and pitching his own songs and then he also got a songwriting deal with MTM Music and met Radney Foster.

They became a very successful writing team and in 1986 they wrote *Since I Found You*, which was recorded by Sweethearts of the Rodeo, went Top 10, and stayed in the charts for 22 weeks. The song was also included in the movie *Nadine*. Foster co-wrote *Love Someone Like Me* with Holly Dunn, which she recorded in 1987. Bill Lloyd played guitar on it and the single reached the Top 3 and stayed in the charts for 25 weeks.

After signing to RCA Victor, Foster & Lloyd began work on their album ***Foster and Lloyd*** in 1987 and were given complete creative and production control. The first single to be released was *Crazy Over You* and it went speedily up to the Top 5 and remained in the charts for 21 weeks. They appeared on the *Grand Ole Opry* in September and were introduced by Little Jimmy Dickens. In October they were guests of the CMA and performed on the awards show.

The second release, *Sure Thing,* went Top 10 in 1988. This was followed by *Texas in 1880*, which climbed to the Top 20 and was accompanied by a video (their first). *What Do You Want from Me This Time* did even better, reaching the Top 10 and staying in the charts for 23 weeks.

Faster and Llouder was the very original title of their second album in 1989. That year, they had a Top 5 single, *Fair Shake*, but both of their other chart entries, *Before the Heartache Rolls In* and *Suzette,* only made the Top 50. Their third and final album, ***Version of the Truth,*** was released in 1990. They had two singles that charted that year, *Is It Love* and *Can't Have Nothin'*, neither of which fared much better.

In 1992, Foster and Lloyd went their separate ways and Radney Foster carried on as a solo artist. On his first Arista album in 1992, called ***Del Rio, Tx—1959***, he wrote or co-wrote all of the 10 tracks, played acoustic guitar and co-produced it with Steve Fishell. The album had a more Country feel to it than the duo's work and the first single, *Just Call Me Lonesome*, which was accompanied by a good video, made the Top 10. It was followed by the Top 3 single *Nobody Wins* in 1993. Radney's other 1993 successes were *Easier Said Than Done* (Top 20) and *Hammer and Nails* (Top 40). In 1994, Radney reached the Top 60 with *Closing Time*. Bill Lloyd continues as a songwriter and session guitarist.

JAB

RECOMMENDED ALBUMS:
"Foster and Lloyd" (RCA Victor)(1987)
"Faster and Llouder" (RCA)(1989)
"Version of the Truth" (RCA)(1990)
Radney Foster:
"Del Rio, Tx—1959" (Arista)(1992)
Bill Lloyd:
"Feeling the Elephant" (Throbbing Lobster)(1987)

Bill Lloyd and Radney Foster, ***Foster and Lloyd***

JERRY FOSTER & BILL RICE

When Formed: 1960
JERRY FOSTER
(Songwriter, Singer, Guitar, Piano)
Given Name: Jerry Gaylon Foster
Date of Birth: November 19, 1935
Where Born: Tallapoosa, Missouri
BILL RICE
(Songwriter, Singer, Guitar, Piano)
Where Born: Datto, Arkansas
Married: Sharon Vaughn

For nearly a decade and a half, the songwriting team of Jerry Foster and Bill Rice was among the most successful in Country music. What was particularly of interest was that certain artists came back time and again for another Foster and Rice song, and they were rewarded for this loyalty by chalking up major hits. These artists included

Hit songwriter ***Jerry Foster***

Charley Pride (who recorded 19 Foster and Rice songs), Johnny Paycheck, Stan Hitchcock, Eddy Raven, Jerry Lee Lewis, Bob Luman, David Rogers, Patti Page, Narvel Felts and Nat Stuckey.

Jerry was born in a log house in a town with a population of 59. He was raised on music and hard work and from age 9 he travailed beside his father and their team of donkeys, raising cotton and corn. While at school, he earned extra cents by selling poems to his school seniors. His father had bought him a guitar at age 5 and taught him to play a few chords and soon Jerry was taking part in the family get-togethers. A natural performer, he eventually hit the road and earned money as a picker. Then he went to Parris Island and spent two months learning how to become a Marine. He formed a local group and played weekends. He began putting melodies to his poems and this led to a recording deal, in 1958, with the Houston-based Backbeat label. Foster's popularity began to grow, and he secured his first TV series on WSAF Savannah, Georgia. He then moved to KFVS-TV in Cape Girardeau, Missouri, with his own show and also as talent booker.

Bill was also raised on a farm, in a town with a population of 179, where he also worked on the land. By the time he reached his late teens, he was already a good guitarist, with a natural ability for songwriting. He traveled across the States, playing and writing as he went. It was at a show in Poplar Bluff, Missouri, that he met Jerry. There was an instant mutual respect and shortly after, Bill joined KFVS, as leader of the staff band.

They found themselves trading song ideas and soon guitarist Roland Janes entered the picture. He suggested that Jerry and Bill go to Memphis to demo some of their joint efforts. Through Janes' intervention, their material got to the legendary Jack Clement and Bill Hall, who were running Jack and Bill Music, out of Beaumont, Texas. Under Hall's direction, the twosome moved to Nashville. Initially, it seemed like a retrograde step, and they had to work as deejays on radio station WENO and take other odd jobs.

They had their first cut in 1968, when Charley Pride recorded *The Day the World Stood Still*, which reached the Top 5, and followed it up with the Top 3 hit, *The Easy Part's Over*, the latter earning the first of their two BMI awards. The following year, Jeannie C. Riley had a Top 40 success with *The Back Side of Dallas*. In 1970, Stan Hitchcock had back-to-back medium-sized hits with *Call Me Gone* and *Dixie Belle*. However, that same year, Mel Tillis had a Top 5 with *Heaven Everyday*. Charley Pride had a hit with *Wonder Could I Live There Anymore*, which Bill had written on his own. Jerry recorded on Mercury, as an artist with a pair of singles that failed to register.

In 1971, Foster and Rice racked up a slew of medium-sized hits that included *All I Want to Do Is Say I Love You* (Brian Collins), *At Least Part of the Way* (Stan Hitchcock), *Give Him Love* and *Think Again* (both Patti Page) and *Is It Any Wonder That I Love You* and *What About the Hurt* (both Bob Luman). In addition, as an artist, Bill Rice had two Country chart hits on Capitol, *Travelin' Minstrel Man* (Top 40) and *Honky-Tonk Stardust Cowboy* (which peaked in the Top 60). That year, they set the then ASCAP record, receiving 5 awards. The following year, the duo had a bumper crop of major hits that included *Somebody Loves Me*, *Someone to Give My Love To* and *Love Is a Good Thing* (all by Johnny Paycheck), *It Takes You* and *When You Say Love* (both by Bob Luman), *Is It Any Wonder That I Love You* (Nat Stuckey) and *Would You Take Another Chance on Me* (their first No.1, from Jerry Lee Lewis). Lewis also recorded *Think About It Darlin'* as the flip-side of his follow-up single, *Chantilly Lace*. During that year, Bill moved over to Epic Records and recorded a pair of hits around the 70s level, *A Girl Like Her Is Hard to Find* and *Something to Call Mine*. During the year, they broke their own ASCAP award record by receiving 10 awards.

In 1973, it was Jerry's turn to make his chart debut, when *Copperhead* scraped in and then *Looking Back* (a 1958 Pop hit for Nat "King" Cole) reached the Top 60, both on Cinnamon. That year, Foster and Rice had another generous helping of songs cut and made hits of by other artists, including *All in the Name of Love* (Narvel Felts), *Darling You Can Always Come Back Home* (Jody Miller), *I Hate Goodbyes* (Bobby Bare), *Something About You I Love* (Johnny Paycheck) and *Take Time to Love Her* (Nat Stuckey). Bill's song *You Lay So Easy on My Mind* became a Top 3 hit for Bobby G. Rice. The song would later be recorded by Narvel Felts (1984) and again by Bobby G. Rice in 1987.

During 1974, their run continued unabated with *Born to Love and Satisfy* (Karen Wheeler), *Loving You Has Changed My Life* and *Hey There Girl* (both David Rogers), *When Your Good Love Was Mine, Until the End of Time* and *I Want to Stay* (all by Narvel Felts, the second with Bill Rice's future wife, singer/songwriter Sharon Vaughn), *I'll Think of Something* (Hank Williams, Jr.), *Song and Dance Man* and *My Part of Forever* (both by Johnny Paycheck) and *Rosie Cries a Lot* (Ferlin Husky). Once again, they broke their own ASCAP record when they received 11 awards plus 4 production awards for their newly constituted production company, Farah. Their roster was Narvel Felts, Bobby Bare, Sharon Vaughn and Foster and Rice themselves.

During 1975, Eddy Raven had two moderate hits with Foster and Rice's *Ain't She Something Else* and *You're My Rainy Day Woman*. The following year, Paycheck scored with another of Jerry and Bill's songs, *I Can See Me Lovin' You Again*. In addition, they had hits from Jacky Ward with *I Never Said It Would Be Easy* and Jerry Lee Lewis with *Let's Put It Back Together Again*. Jerry returned to the Country charts with a low-level single, *I Knew You When*, on Motown's Hitsville label.

In 1977, Lois Johnson reprised *I Hate Goodbyes* and Marie Owens did the same with *When Your Good Love Was Mine*. This time, Bill returned to the basement area of the charts with *All the Love We Threw Away*, on which he duetted with Lois Johnson, on Polydor. He followed up the next year with another basement single, *Beggars and Choosers*. Jerry fared slightly better when, in tandem with Tennessee Tornado, he charted with *I Want to Love You*. That year, Mickey Gilley took their song *Here Comes the Hurt Again* into the Top 10. They were named *Cash Box*'s "Composers of the Year."

During the 80's, success was less frenetic, but they managed to rack up major cuts from Steve Wariner with a reprise of *The Easy Part's Over* (1980), Jerry Lee Lewis with the Top 5 single *Thirty Nine and Holding* (1981), Johnny Rodriguez with *First Time Burned*

(1984) and the No.1 hit from Conway Twitty, *Ain't She Something Else* (1985).

During 1988, Jerry acquired the Country Music Show Palace in Branson, Missouri, and renamed it Jerry Foster's Show Palace. By 1993, the duo was in receipt of over 60 ASCAP awards. Bill Rice and his wife, M. Sharon Rice (the former Sharon Vaughn), have gone on to become a successful writing duo. In 1994, Jerry Foster & Bill Rice were inducted into the Nashville Songwriters Hall of Fame.

RECOMMENDED ALBUM:

"Looking Back" (Cinnamon)(1974) [Jerry Foster solo album]

4 GUYS

When Formed: **Amateur Status: 1955**
Professional: January 1, 1967

Current Members:

Brent Burkett **Lead & Baritone (Original Member)**
Sam Wellington **Bass & Baritone (Original Member)**
Laddie Cain **Tenor & Lead (Joined March 1980)**
John Frost **Lead & Baritone (Joined May 1981)**

Former Members:

Armand Trasoline
Gary Cochran
Berl Lyons
George Wise
Richard Garrett
Dave Rowland
Gary Buck
Glen Bates
Dan Stephens
Gary Judkins
Gary Chadwick

For nearly 30 years, the 4 Guys have proven themselves as one of the most durable close harmony groups in Country music. They have not, however, received the record success that the Statler Brothers and the Oak Ridge Boys have achieved and that has resulted in the Guys being "best men" rather than "grooms."

*Laddie, Brent, John and Sam, the **4 Guys***

The group started back in the 50's while they were in high school, when Brent was in a group called the Four Guys in Steubenville, Ohio. Sam was in another group, the Jets, in a town close by. They competed in area talent shows. The two groups broke up and Brent and Sam got together with two others and named themselves the Four Guys. They went into the service and the group broke up. On returning to civilian life, they re-formed the group with Armand Trasoline and Gary Cochran. At that time Brent sang tenor and Sam sang the middle part with Armie singing lead and Gary singing bass.

They cut a tape in 1959 for some songwriters, who took it to New York and connected with Stan Cooper, a publisher. He invited them to New York and they cut some demos for him. They returned to Ohio to look for jobs while awaiting any action. In the interim, the Four Lads' contract with Columbia had expired and the label was looking for an act to replace them. The Four Guys reached the final two but were beaten out by the Brothers Four (this was the time of the self-contained Folk group). The group broke up and everyone got married.

Sam went to work for a newspaper and then a radio station. After some three years, Brent called Sam to inform him that he had put together a barber-shop group (also known as the Four Guys) and would he like to join singing bass. The other members were Berl Lyons and George Wise. This line-up lasted for three years, then George Wise left and Richard Garrett came in. At this time, they played their own instruments (not too well, according to Sam and Brent!). Brent played guitar and Sam played piano and drums.

Sam was broadcasting on WEIR Weirton, West Virginia, and Richard moved from that station to WWVA Wheeling. Toward the end of 1966, the Four Guys did backup vocals and despite requests from other artists, the group was not allowed by the station management to sing lead. After two weeks, Johnny Dollar got them to sing up front without permission. The audience reaction was great and they encored three times but they were fired by the station. Bill Brock, a successful songwriter, was in the audience and encouraged them to go to Nashville. This they did in November 1966, when they recorded some material, and they decided to turn professional. Brock lined them up some shows but met initial resistance from the *Opry*, who thought they were a Gospel group. They got onto Ralph Emery's afternoon show, where they were seen by Ott Devine, then General Manager of the *Grand Ole Opry*. They got a regular gig at Boots Randolph's Carousel Club. The manager encouraged the group to stop playing instruments.

They made their debut on the *Opry* on February 8, 1967, singing *Shenandoah*. They were invited back for 12 more weeks. On April 22, 1967, they were invited to become members. They became only the second act after Stonewall Jackson to get on the show without a major contract. They thought that wealth and success would come their way, but it didn't and it was only with the intervention of Pete Drake that they started doing regular sessions. Over the next three years, they were doing up to three sessions a day. They also cut some sides for Pete's Stop Records.

At the end of 1969, they got a call from Buddy Lee (Nashville's top booking agent), who invited them onto the Hank Williams, Jr., road show. They bought a motor home on time payments. The show included Merle Kilgore, the Duke of Paducah, Diana Trask and the Original Drifting Cowboys. They were with the show for two years. In 1969, they signed with Mercury Records through Faron Young's help and released one single, *When I Fall in Love*. They then joined Jimmy Dean at the Landmark in Las Vegas. They were with him for seven weeks and through Bill DiAngelis at the Landmark, they got lounge work and then backed Ferlin Husky, before continuing on their own. In 1972, they appeared in the Marty Robbins movie *Country Music* and in 1973, they appeared in the Goldie Hawn movie *Sugarland Express*.

In the spring of 1973, they became a part of Charley Pride's touring show. RCA had shown interest in them as far back as 1967 and in 1974, they joined the label and released *Too Late to Turn Back Now*, which became a Top 90 Country chart entry. At this time, Garrett left and Dave Rowland joined. However, this didn't work out and Rowland left and formed Dave & Sugar. The Four Guys were about to sign to MGM Records when Dick Glaser, who was to produce them, was fired. The replacement for Rowland, in 1971, was Gary Buck (not the Canadian singer). Brent's voice started lowering and Gary became the tenor.

On August 18, 1975, they opened their own Nashville restaurant/cabaret nightspot, the Harmony House. They stayed here for 10 years, utilizing the blossoming tourist industry to enhance their success. In 1979, they had a basement-level chart single, *Mama Rocked Us to Sleep (With Country Music)*, on the Collage label. In 1980, Laddie Cain replaced Buck and the following year, John Frost came on board. In 1982, the Four Guys again had a low-level entry on JNB, entitled *Made in the U.S.A.* The area around the Harmony House deteriorated, and they decided to close down at the end of 1984. They then moved to running the Stage Door lounge at the Opryland Hotel. They stayed here until the end of 1988. They then worked with Commodore Cruise Line on a nostalgia show, *Remember When.* They created a concept entitled *Those Golden Fours Forever*, featuring music by groups as diverse as the Mills Brothers, the Four Seasons, Alabama and the Oak Ridge Boys. This they did for 11 weeks of the year for the first year and then for 40 weeks the next year.

In 1992, they worked at the Ramada in Nashville and then Brent was taken ill with a serious heart problem. They eventually began their stint at the Celebrity Theater at the Ramada in 1993, but this ended later in the year. The Four Guys continue to entertain in three personas, as themselves, as the Golden Fours and as their rock'n'roll creations, "the Hot Rods." With a record contract, their music could be accessible to a much wider audience. They are still members of the *Opry*.

RECOMMENDED ALBUMS:

"Happy Days (& Nights) Live at the Harmony House" (1975)
"Those Golden Fours Forever" (1989)
"The 4 Guys Thru 25 Years on the Grand Ole Opry" (1992)

Tom C. Fouts refer CAPTAIN STUBBY

WALLY FOWLER

(Singer, Songwriter)

Given Name: John Wallace Fowler
Date of Birth: February 15, 1917
Where Born: Bartow County, Georgia
Married: 1. (div.)
2. Ann
Children: Sharon Kay, Hope

Wally Fowler's principal claim to fame is as the creator of the Oak Ridge Quartet, who would later evolve into the Oak Ridge Boys. He was also responsible for the all-night Gospel Sing which commenced at the Ryman Auditorium on August 11, 1948.

Wally began singing Gospel music at age 6 and was a student of "Professor" Lee Roy Abernathy, who was a great harmonizer of Gospel songs. By the time he was 15, Wally was leading a Gospel quartet in Rome, Georgia. He was spotted by John Daniel, another Gospel pioneer, while performing in Macon, Georgia, in 1935. Wally became a member of the John Daniel Quartet, singing baritone and handling comedy. In April 1940, they became the first Gospel quartet to become members of the *Grand Ole Opry*.

It was with Daniel that Wally learned what he was to put into force in the Oak Ridge Quartet. There was a contemporary feel about their music that had Gospel diehards angry. In 1943, Wally left the group and moved to Knoxville. He began to get a reputation as a good Country songwriter when Eddy Arnold recorded Wally's *Mommy Please Stay Home with Me Tonight* as his first solo single in 1944 and that same year, Jimmy Wakely had a Top 3 hit with Wally's *I'm Sending You Red Roses.*

Late in 1944, Wally began putting together a back-up group for personal appearances. In deference to the red hills of Georgia, where he had come from, he called the band the Georgia Clodhoppers. The initial line-up of the group was Wally (lead vocals), Curly Kinsey (bass vocals and guitar), Johnny New (tenor vocals and stand-up bass), Joe Carrol (fiddle and occasional vocals) and Zeb Turner (guitar). Kinsey and New had both been members of

The creator of the Oak Ridge Quartet, ***Wally Fowler***

the Gospel trio the North Georgia Boys, whom Wally had met in Rome. They had moved on to the Four Tones with Lee Roy Abernathy before joining Wally.

The Clodhoppers were often supported by Chet Atkins, who had moved to Knoxville in 1943 and played on WNOX's *Mid-Day Merry Go Round.* In 1945, the newly formed Capitol Records asked Wally and the band to record. They went to Atlanta and with Lee Gillette producing and with Atkins playing on his first session, they cut *Propaganda Papa* and *A Mother's Prayer* under the credit of Wallace Fowler and His Georgia Clodhoppers. Both songs were written by Wally and J. Graydon Hall, who would often write lyrics for Wally.

Oak Ridge had newly acquired its name, being the location for development of the atom bomb, known as the Manhattan Project. Wally started playing children's concerts at Oak Ridge during January 1945, which soon attracted adult audiences. The explosion of the first atomic bomb occurred on August 6, 1945, at Hiroshima and by the fall, the Gospel contingent within the group, which had been known as the Harmony Quartet, became known as the Oak Ridge Quartet.

On September 15, 1945, Wally returned to the *Opry* with his Clodhoppers and the Oak Ridge Quartet. For some months, they appeared on the *Crazy Water Crystals* segment. In 1946, the line-up of the Clodhoppers changed and Deacon Freeman, another ex-North Georgia Boy, joined as baritone, Zeke Turner replaced his brother Zeb and Charles Bares played steel guitar on occasions. Later in 1946, Red Bennett was added on accordion and Billy Byrd replaced Zeke Turner. By the spring/summer of 1946, Wally and the group had moved to the *Prince Albert* section of the *Opry.*

Even while recording for Capitol, Wally tried to become a partner in Bullet, the first independent label in Nashville, but he couldn't raise the money. He did, however, later become the area distributor for Mercury Records. In his advertisements in Minnie Pearl's newspaper, the *Grinder Switch Gazette*, Wally promoted "Fowler Publications, Platemaker-Publisher-Printer, Can Make Your Songbook with His Own Original Songs, or Will Print Your Songs." In addition, Wally promoted Wally Fowler's Mustard Seed as a way of bringing to the public's attention the Oak Ridge song *Faith As the Grain of a Mustard Seed.*

By 1948, Curly Blaylock had replaced Curly Kinsey as bass vocalist. In addition, Neal Matthews, Jr., another John Daniel alumnus, had joined on bass. He would later become a member of the Jordanaires. Joey Ross came in on accordion and first Bill Stepp and then Boyce Hawkins played piano. When Wally started the all-night Gospel sings at the Ryman, he helped spell the death-knell for the Clodhoppers, as Gospel at the time was preferred to secular music. Although WSM, the owners of the *Opry*, did not allow advertising of outside road shows, Wally found a way that was irresistible. He would offer a prayer to God to watch over the group as they travel to this or that town on their way to the local auditorium on such-and-such a night.

Wally had instilled into the Oak Ridge Quartet that they sing spirituals rather than Gospel, thus taking black music and getting white performers to sing it. In 1949, the quartet left Wally and became the Stone Mountain Quartet. Wally imported the Calvary Quartet of Bob Weber, Pat Patterson, Joe Allred and Bill Campbell. In 1952, Wally offered the group to Bob Weber for $10,000. Weber accepted but reported later that he never received the money back. By the end of 1956, the group had disbanded.

Later that year, Wally put together the Country Boys, but before it got under way, Wally heard of the demise of the Oak Ridge Quartet and formed a new Oak Ridge Quartet around his protégé Smitty Gatlin. Wally did another "loan" deal, this time for $3,000; Gatlin now owned the name. By 1964, the Oak Ridge Quartet was doing well and Wally started still another Oak Ridge Quartet; however, Smitty Gatlin of the now named Oak Ridge Boys sued to stop him, and the following year Wally was enjoined from using the name.

Wally continued to perform without the same visibility. During 1960, he recorded albums for Decca, King and Starday. In 1977, he recorded ***Wally Fowler Sings a Tribute to Elvis (Presley)*** on Dove Records. On this last named, he was supported by J.D. Sumner & the Stamps. Wally then moved to Branson, Missouri, where he entertained, singing Gospel and secular material.

RECOMMENDED ALBUMS:

"Call of the Cross" (Decca)(1960)
"Gospel Song Festival" (King)(1960) [With the Oak Ridge Quartet]
"Wally Fowler's All Nite Singing Gospel Concert (Featuring the Oak Ridge Quartet)" (Starday)(1960)
"More Wally Fowler All Nite Singing Concert" (Starday)(1964)
"Gospel Sing" (Vocalion)(1967)
"Wally Fowler Sings a Tribute to Elvis (Presley)"
(See also the Oak Ridge Boys.)

CURLY FOX AND TEXAS RUBY

When Formed: **1937**

CURLY FOX
(Singer, Fiddle, Guitar)

Given Name:	**Arnim LeRoy Fox**
Date of Birth:	**November 9, 1910**
Where Born:	**Graysville, Tennessee**
Married:	**1. (div.)**
	2. Ruby Agnes Owens
Children:	**two sons, two daughters**

TEXAS RUBY
(Singer)

Given Name:	**Ruby Agnes Owens**
Date of Birth:	**June 4, 1910**
Where Born:	**Wise County, Texas**
Married:	**Arnim LeRoy Fox**
Children:	**two sons**
Date of Death:	**March 29, 1963**

Curly Fox and Texas Ruby were one of Country music's great husband-wife teams of the 1940's and 1950's. Curly ranked as a premier hillbilly fiddler for some four decades while Ruby stood as one of the pioneer women in the trade.

Arnim Fox grew up in the East Tennessee community of Graysville learning to cut hair and play fiddle from his father, the town barber. He also learned some fiddle techniques from James McCarroll of the Roane County Ramblers, one of the truly great fiddlers of the roaring 20's. Fox served something of an apprenticeship with McCarroll's band. Curly also got an early taste of professionalism by joining an "Indian" medicine show run by a "Chief White Owl" with whom young Arnim journeyed as far north as Indiana.

According to one familiar story, the youth yearned for a professional career in music from the time Gid Tanner's Skillet Licket Lickers came through Graysville playing a show and stopped in the elder Fox's barbershop. Not long afterward, Curly set out for WSB Atlanta, where he joined Claude Davis and the Carolina Tar Heels (not the Victor recording act), acquired the nickname "Curly" and later started his own band called the Tennessee Firecrackers.

About 1934, the Shelton Brothers came to Atlanta and Curly joined forces with them, going to WWL New Orleans. He remained with the Sheltons long enough to do a pair of Decca sessions in 1935 and 1936, including six sides recorded under his own name. Leaving the Sheltons in 1936, Curly traveled for a while with promoter Larry Sunbrock, who staged a series of fiddling contests featuring Curly, Natchee the Indian (aka Lester Vernon Storer), and other noted fiddlers. At the Texas centennial celebration in 1937, Curly met the husky-voiced, cowgirl singer known as Miss Texas Ruby.

Ruby Owens entered radio a few years earlier as the younger sister of radio cowboy Tex Owens, who wrote and introduced the song *Cattle Call* to the commercial music world. Her niece was Laura Lee Owens McBride, who sang with Bob Wills. In 1930, Ruby had gone with her father and brothers to Fort Worth on a cattle drive. The younger Owenses began harmonizing and were heard by one of the cattle buyers who was also a stockholder of KMBC Kansas City. Ruby was offered a job at the station and over the next three years, she broadcast over stations in Detroit, Philadelphia and Cincinnati.

Curly Fox and Texas Ruby *(back)*

In 1933, Ruby joined up with Zeke Clements and His Bronco Busters. They soon began making appearances on the *Grand Ole Opry*. However, Ruby wanted to return to Texas and on their way, they heard about the barn dance on station WHO Des Moines, Iowa. Ruby and Zeke auditioned and ended up staying on the program for two years. Their announcer on the show was an aspiring actor named Ronald "Dutch" Reagan. However, Zeke and Ruby didn't get in and Ruby told Reagan exactly what she thought of him (using a few Anglo-Saxon words) and soon Zeke was told that he could stay at the station but Texas Ruby had to go. A few weeks earlier, Ruby had recorded her arrangement of *T for Texas* on the Decca label, backed by a duet with Zeke Clements entitled *Pride of the Prairie.*

Curly and Ruby soon married and worked extensively on major radio stations. They worked at WSM Nashville and the *Grand Ole Opry* from 1937 to 1939 and again from 1944 to 1948, and spent about three years at WLW Cincinnati and the *Boone County Jamboree*, from 1941. In between times, they had shorter stints at other major stations.

Curly and Ruby did some recordings, but not as much as might be expected. According to her husband, Ruby's deep contralto voice was difficult to capture on disc. They cut some MacGregor transcriptions in California in 1945 and 1946. Ruby recorded what may have been her best efforts for King in the fall of 1947, with the legendary Mose Rager—teacher of Merle Travis—playing lead guitar on his only commercial session. Curly also recorded a fine pair of fiddle tunes, *Black Mountain Rag* and *Come Here Son,* the latter more commonly known as *Fire on the Mountain.*

The couple went to Houston, Texas, in 1948, where they remained for a decade helping to pioneer Country music on local television. In 1956, they played a performance for the King and Queen of Greece, Paul and Fredrika, who made quite a hit with the American public that year when they toured the U.S. After traveling around the country for a time, Curly and Ruby returned to WSM in the early 60's, where Curly usually worked the *Opry* solo as Ruby's health was not good in this period, although they did cut an album for Starday in mid-March 1963. Several days later, while Curly was performing on the Friday Night *Opry*, Ruby died in a tragic mobile home fire; allegedly, she fell asleep while smoking a cigarette and it burned her bed.

After Ruby's death, Curly continued on the *Opry* by himself for a time, but eventually went to Chicago, where one of his daughters by his first marriage resided. In this period, he too had some health problems, but recorded a couple of albums for Rural Rhythm and made an appearance now and then. In 1976, Curly returned to his home town of Graysville. For a few years, he worked with Tom and Mary Morgan, who had a family type Bluegrass band that appeared throughout the region. According to the Morgans, Curly, now retired, has not played the fiddle for a couple of years. He shares a residence with an elderly sister and leads a quiet life, contented that he had made his mark in the show business and Country music world. Over the years, several of his and Ruby's recordings have appeared on various anthology albums, including a couple of the 1940 transcriptions in addition to the memorial Harmony and King albums listed below. IMT

RECOMMENDED ALBUMS:

"Traveling Blues: A Memorial Tribute to Texas Ruby" (Harmony)(1963)
"Texas Ruby Sings Her Favorite Songs" (King)(1963)
"Curly Fox and Texas Ruby" (Starday)(1963)
"Champion Fiddler Curly Fox, Volume One" (Rural Rhythm)(1972)
"Champion Fiddler Curly Fox, Volume Two" (Rural Rhythm)(1972)

GEORGE FOX

(Singer, Songwriter, Guitar, Harmonica)
Date of Birth: March 23, 1930
Where Born: Cochrane, Alberta, Canada

It was not until George Fox made a trip to Sweden when he was 21 that he became interested in Country music. His host family asked him to bring some Country albums with him and he took a selection of records by "names" that he had heard of but to whom he had never listened.

He was raised on a ranch and his family had a cattle ranching business. He started to play gigs on weekends, but it was still just a social/artistic outlet. However, he decided to take $30,000 that had been earmarked for a new tractor and make an album. Armed with six copies of the tape, he left one with WEA in Calgary. Back on the ranch, he was surprised by a call from the head of A & R at WEA Records in Toronto. Warner Brothers released the ***George Fox*** album in 1988 and George acquired the managerial services of Leonard Rambeau, who also manages Anne Murray, and who had not taken on a new act for 10 years.

George got his first Top 20 Canadian hit with his second release, *Long Distance,* in 1988. His three 1989 releases all reached the Top 20 on the Canadian Country charts and he picked up nominations for all the major Canadian awards. In 1989, he was named "Vista Rising Star" by the Canadian Country Music Association and he won an unprecedented four RPM Big Country awards: as "Composer of the Year" for his song *Angelina,* which also won the award as "Single of the Year." In addition, he garnered the RPM "Male Vocalist of the Year" and "Country Artist of the Year." George's second album, ***With All My Might*** (on which he wrote 11 of the 12 tracks), was issued in Canada in 1989. This album was released in the States with a different sleeve and different track listing. The singles *Angelina* and *No Trespassing* were released in the U.S. The album was Certified Gold in Canada before the year was out and George's growing popularity was indicated in the various awards ceremonies that year. In the Juno Awards, George was named "Country Male Vocalist of the Year," a feat he would repeat the next two years. He was also given the CCMA award as "Country Male Vocalist," which he again received in 1991. That year, he was named RPM's "Male Vocalist of the Year" again and made it 5 in a row with wins in 1992 and 1993. To date, he has also received 11 Calgary Country Music Association awards. In addition, he achieved his first Top 10 Canadian hit with *I Fell in Love & I Can't Get Out.*

During 1990, George starred in his own CBC special, *George Fox's New Country* and he has also appeared on the *Tommy Hunter Show*, *Nashville Now* and Anne Murray's *Family Christmas*. His third album, ***Spice of Life***, which was produced by Garth Fundis and contained four Fox songs, was released in the spring of 1991. It featured George's band the Enjoyers. There was a two year gap until his fourth album, ***Mustang Heart***, hit the streets. This album was produced by former Four Seasons member Bob Gaudio.

Canadian star ***George Fox***

Fox lists as his influences Ricky Nelson, Elvis, Hank Snow, Hank Williams, Charley Pride, Marty Robbins, Neil Young, Bob Dylan, Ricky Skaggs, George Strait and Buddy Holly. He also lists a nudist colony as the most unusual venue played by him: "I don't know who was entertaining who at those gigs."

At a time when Canadian Country performers are starting to surface in the broader Nashville scene, George Fox has the ability, both as a songwriter and a performer, to reach the upper rungs of stardom.

RECOMMENDED ALBUMS:

"George Fox" (Warner Brothers)(1988)
"With All My Might" (Warner Bros.)(1989)
"Spice of Life" (Warner Brothers)(1991)
"Mustang Heart" (Warner Brothers)(1993)

CLEVE FRANCIS

(Singer, Songwriter, Guitar, Cardiologist)
Given Name: Cleveland Francis, Jr.
Date of Birth: April 22, 1945
Where Born: Jennings, Louisiana

If the title "King of Hearts" belonged to anyone, then Cleve Francis would receive that sobriquet. Dr. Cleveland Francis, Jr., is president of a cardiology practice and director of the cardiac rehabilitation program at Mount Vernon Hospital in Alexandria, Virginia. He has also emerged as the black performer most likely to succeed in the 90's.

Cleve was born the eldest son of a janitor father and a maid/sharecropper mother. All of Cleve's five siblings are college graduates and professionals. He made his first guitar at the age of 8 from a cigar box and window screen wire. His mother saved up for a year and bought him a Sears Roebuck Silvertone guitar. Cleve's early influences came from Gospel music and he sang and played in the church. He attended Southern University at Baton Rouge, Louisiana, and went on to the College of William and Mary in Williamsburg, Virginia, where he obtained a master's degree in biology. In 1973, he earned his medical degree from the Medical College of Virginia in Richmond.

During the summer vacations, Cleve was playing gigs but after qualifying he got his medical career under way. What got his singing career going was the treatment of a heart-attack patient, Olaf Hall. Hall advised

The King of Hearts, ***Cleve Francis***

Cleve that he would be visited by his "big brother," Big John. Big John turned out to be John Garfield Hall, a member of the R & B group the Heartbeats. After talking with Cleve, John contacted Playback Records out of Miami. After hearing some of Cleve's material, he was signed to the label. He used his own money for promotion. He had already released three albums on his own Cleve Francis Productions label, but decided that he would spend a further $25,000 to get that elusive success. Although the Playback album died, the video for *Love Light*, his first single, caught a lot of attention when it was released in April 1990. It made the Top 10 on CMT and was named "Independent Country Video of The Year" in 1990 by the prestigious *Music Row* magazine.

The video was seen by Liberty (then Capitol Nashville) Records boss Jimmy Bowen. As a result, he signed Cleve to the label. Cleve's first album, ***Tourist in Paradise***, was released in 1991. A re-recorded version of *Love Light* became the debut single and a new video was made. The initial single peaked just below the Top 50 and was followed into the charts by *You Do My Heart Good* (Top 50) and *How Can I Hold You* (Top 75), two cuts from the album. In 1993, Cleve released his second album, ***Walkin'***, from which the title cut was the first picked up by the radio deejays and became a Top 70 chart entry.

Cleve names as his influences Sam Cooke, Hank Williams, Charley Pride, Kenny Rogers, Ray Charles, Glen Campbell, Bob Dylan, Harry Chapin and Brook Benton. However, Cleve could just be the performer with enough "heart" and soul to emerge as a major force in the 90's.

RECOMMENDED ALBUMS:

"Tourist in Paradise" (Capitol Nashville)(1991)
"Walkin'" (Liberty)(1993)

J.L. FRANK

(Manager, Agent, Promoter, Songwriter)

Given Name: **Joseph Lee Frank**
Date of Birth: **April 15, 1900**
Where Born: **Rossal, Limestone County, Alabama**
Married: **Marie (m. 1925)**
Children: **Lydia**
Date of Death: **May 4, 1952**

The words of Joe Frank's citation plaque on his induction to the Country Music Hall of Fame in 1967 say it all: "...this unselfish, compassionate man was one of the industry's most loved members."

J.L. Frank's parents were both dead by the time he was 7. He was reared in Pulaski, Tennessee. He tried several jobs while still in his youth, including steel worker in Birmingham, Alabama, coal miner in Illinois and hotel bellboy.

When he was 23, he moved to Chicago and worked at Edgewater Beach Hotel, where he met his future wife. She had already worked in artist management in the entertainment industry and persuaded J.L. to try it. They initially worked with vaudeville performers, including the radio stars Fibber McGee and Molly. J.L. produced the WLS *Roundup* from 1928, but he still had to drive a dry-cleaning truck to supplement their income. He worked on the show until 1935.

In the late 20's, J.L. took on the management of Gene Autry and Smiley Burnette. In 1935, he moved his operation to Louisville, Kentucky, and then in 1939, he relocated to Nashville. He realized that Nashville was fast becoming the capital of Country music.

He also realized that Country music should lose its hillbilly tag and would get quite angry at anyone who used the phrase. He started to promote Country music into auditoriums and put Country packages on the road, whereas before, the performers had only worked up to some 35 miles from their home base.

Frank, whose daughter was married to Pee Wee King, was instrumental in the careers of Roy Acuff, Eddy Arnold, Hank Williams, Hank Snow, Curly Fox & Texas Ruby, Minnie Pearl and Ernest Tubb. He also managed the Hoosier Hot Shots and Clayton McMichen and His Georgia Wildcats. It was through Frank's intervention that Roy Acuff came onto the *Grand Ole Opry*. During this time, the Franks would often house and feed these budding stars and J.L.'s interest in vegetable gardening came in useful.

Tubb felt that Frank had a feel for Country music talent and that he was largely instrumental in helping the *Grand Ole Opry* gain the reputation it now has. Because of his efforts, J.L. was known as the "Flo Ziegfeld of Country music show business." He worked closely with theater chain owner Tony Sudekum in booking acts into the Southeast. He occasionally wrote songs, although he couldn't play an instrument or read music. Among his successes were *Chapel on the Hill, My Main Trial Is Yet to Come* and *Sundown and Sorrow*. He died in 1952, of a strep throat infection, while promoting a show in Dallas, Texas.

DALLAS FRAZIER

(Songwriter, Singer, Guitar, Trumpet)

Date of Birth: **October 27, 1939**
Where Born: **Spiro, Oklahoma**

One of Country music's finest songwriters, Dallas Frazier was already an entertainment industry veteran when he had a hit with the Hollywood Argyles' recording of his song *Alley Oop* in 1957. Before he was into his teens, Dallas was a featured performer. His family moved to Bakersfield, California, and by the time he was 12 years old, he was adept at various instruments. By his mid-teens, he won first prize in a talent contest sponsored by Ferlin Husky and was offered a place on Husky's show.

Husky introduced Dallas to Capitol and by 1954, he was recording his first single, *Space Command/Ain't You Had No Bringin' Up at All*. The head of Capitol's Country operation, Cliffie Stone, made Dallas a regular member of his *Hometown Jamboree,* where Dallas became a favorite with Los Angeles audiences. He often teamed up with another teenage talent on the show, Molly Bee. By this time, he had started to write and then he had the hit with *Alley Oop*.

When the show folded at the end of the 50's, Frazier relocated to Nashville. He worked at his writing craft and carried on playing, then in 1964, he had a hit through Ferlin Husky with *Timber I'm Falling*. Then in 1966, he hit pay dirt. He had three major cuts that year, propelling him into the limelight. Jack Greene had a No.1 with *There Goes My Everything*, Connie Smith had a Top 3 with *Ain't Had No*

Lovin' and George Jones scored with the Top 10 *I'm a People*.

The following year, George Jones had a Top 5 hit with another Frazier song, *I Can't Get There from Here*, and of course, on the Pop charts Dallas' bankroll increased with the monster hit of *There Goes My Everything* by Engelbert Humperdinck. That year, Dallas was named "Songwriter of the Year" by NSAI and *There Goes My Everything* was made CMA and MCN "Song of the Year." 1968's Top 10 hits included *Say It's Not You* by George Jones and *Run Away Little Tears* from Connie Smith. He again struck the Pop charts via O.C. Smith with the Top 40 *The Son of Hickory Holler's Tramp*. This was also a Country hit by Johnny Darrell that year. Merle Haggard recorded a trio of Dallas' songs for his album ***The Legend of Bonnie and Clyde***. Willie Nelson had a hit with *Johnny One Time,* which Brenda Lee would reprise the next year.

Dallas has written a lot of hits on his own, but has also worked with two prime co-writers, A.L. "Doodle" Owens and Sanger D. "Whitey" Shafer, two of the best writers in the business. It was with Doodle that Dallas penned two Charley Pride hits in 1969, *All I Have to Offer You (Is Me)* and *I'm So Afraid of Losing You Again*. Among his other hits of the year was Jack Greene's rendition of *Back in the Arms of Love*.

Throughout the 70's, Dallas' list of cuts multiplied. Only a part of his recorded catalog can be listed here but it included: 1970: *I Can't Believe That You've Stopped Loving Me* (Charley Pride), *Lord Is that Me* (Jack Greene), *Beneath Still Waters* (Diana Trask); 1971: *There Goes My Everything* (Elvis Presley), 1972: *If It Ain't Love (Let's Leave It Alone)* (Connie Smith); 1974: *The Baptism of Jesse Taylor* (Johnny Russell), *Ain't Love a Good Thing* (Connie Smith), *Freckles and Polliwog Games* (Ferlin Husky), *Then Who Am I* (Charley Pride), *Sing for the Good Times* (Jack Greene); 1975: *The Way I Lose My Mind* (Carl Smith), *Give Me Liberty (Or Give Me Your Love)* (Moe Bandy), *Then Who Am I* (Charley Pride), *The Fiddlin' of Jacques Pierre Bordeaux* (Fiddlin' Frenchie Burke), *Big Mabel Murphy* (Sue Thompson), *Champagne Ladies and Blue Ribbon Babies* (Ferlin Husky); 1976: *The Door I Used to Close* (both Roy Head and Marilyn Sellars), *The Trouble with Hearts* (Leon Rausch); 1977: *The Son of Hickory Holler's Tramp* (Johnny Russell); 1978: *Elvira* (Rodney Crowell); and 1979: *Elvira* (Ronnie Hawkins). In 1976, Dallas was inducted into the Songwriters Hall of Fame.

Although his level of cuts decreased in the 80's, this was no reflection on the quality of the songs, just that there were more good writers chasing the elusive cuts. Throughout this decade, he had hits with *Beneath Still Waters*, a No.1 for Emmylou Harris, and in 1981 his evergreen *Elvira*, which became a No.1 (and a Top 5 Pop hit) for the Oak Ridge Boys, and *Fourteen Carat Mind,* which also topped the charts for Gene Watson. That year, new boy George Strait recorded *Honky Tonk Down Stairs*. 1982 brought *Trouble with Hearts* by Roy Head while would-be Country star Dean Martin cut *Shoulder to Shoulder* in 1983, on his Nashville recorded album. The CMA voted *Elvira* by the Oaks as its 1982 "Single of the Year."

The Whites picked up a song that had been good for Connie Smith in 1972 and turned it into a 1985 hit when they recorded *If It Ain't Love (Let's Leave It Alone)*. In 1988, Patty Loveless registered her first Top 10 hit with Dallas' *If My Heart Had Windows*. The song had been a major hit for George Jones back in 1967 and a minor one for Amy Wooley in 1982. In 1989, Randy Travis recorded *When Your World Was Turning for Me* on his ***No Holdin' Back*** album and Tammy Wynette cut *I'm So Afraid of Losing You*, which had been a No.1 for Charley Pride.

During the period 1967-72, Dallas had his share of medium-sized hits as an artist on Capitol and from 1969 on RCA Victor. His most successful single was the 1967 release *Everybody Oughta Sing a Song*, which went Top 30. His final hit, to date, was *North Carolina* in 1972.

In 1988, Dallas decided to call it a day with songwriting and performing and left Nashville to pursue a career as a minister of the cloth.

RECOMMENDED ALBUMS:

"Elvira" (Capitol)(1966)
"Tell It Like It Is" (Capitol)(1967)
"Singing My Songs" (RCA Victor)(1970)
"My Baby Packed Up My Mind and Left Me" (RCA Victor)(1971)
"If it Ain't Love (& Other Great Dallas Frazier Songs)" (RCA Victor)(1972) [This is a Connie Smith album of Frazier songs on which Dallas duets on three tracks]

JANIE FRICKE

(Singer, Songwriter, Guitar, Mandolin, Piano)

Given Name: Jane Marie Fricke
Date of Birth: December 19, 1947
Where Born: Fort Wayne, Indiana
Married: Randy Jackson (m. 1982) (div. 1993)

Janie Fricke was raised on a 400-acre farm near South Whitley. Her parents both played instruments and it wasn't long before Janie was singing, backed by her mother on the family organ. Although she took piano lessons, once Janie's father taught her guitar chords when she was 15, guitar became her favorite instrument. In the mid-60's Janie attended Indiana University. Influenced by Joan Baez, Judy Collins and Neil Diamond, she was able to ply her version of Folk music on campus in coffee houses, restaurants and bars.

During her sophomore year, Janie became increasingly convinced that her future lay with music rather than in teaching. That summer she secured a job in Memphis singing radio station call letters and jingles. After graduating in 1972 with a degree and teaching certificate, Janie traveled far and wide in pursuit of lucrative jingle work: Memphis, Dallas, Los Angeles, and Nashville, where she arrived in 1975. By then her ambitions had extended beyond jingles to include work as a session and back-up singer.

In Music City Janie marketed herself using some tapes and eventually landed a job with the Lea Jane Singers. For a while she also worked as a receptionist. Within two years, Janie had become the most sought after back-up/jingle singer in Nashville. Even after she landed a recording contract, Janie continued doing jingles when her schedule allowed.

As a back-up singer, Fricke's long credit list included work with Ronnie Milsap, England Dan and John Ford Coley, Charley Pride and Loretta Lynn. One of her proudest moments came when she was backstage at an Elvis Presley concert in Memphis and caught his eye. In summer 1977, she was engaged in overdubbing what proved to be his final concert recordings when he died. Janie was also involved in updating Jim Reeves' sound on the album ***Nashville 78***. It is estimated that Janie Fricke contributed to 1,200 albums in the 70's. Many hit singles featured her in the background, among them Crystal Gayle's *I'll Get Over You,* Tanya Tucker's *Here's Some*

From back-up singer to star, ***Janie Fricke***

Love and Conway Twitty's *I'd Love to Lay You Down.*

She might have continued in the same vein had not a track from a Johnny Duncan album come to the attention of producer Billy Sherrill. Duncan had been captivated by Janie's voice when she guested on his 1975 Top 30 single, *Jo and the Cowboy,* and asked her to take an uncredited part on his single of Kris Kristofferson's *Stranger* (which went Top 5 in 1976). More Duncan-Fricke singles followed: *Thinkin' of a Rainbow* (No.1) and *It Couldn't Have Been Better* (No.1, 1977).

Soon everyone was asking who possessed the mystery voice and the inevitable happened. Sherrill persuaded Janie to go solo and she signed with Columbia. Then with her name now known, her first single, *What're You Doin' Tonight* (1977), just failed to make the Top 20. Then her duet with Duncan, *Come a Little Bit Closer* went Top 5 in 1978. Sherrill produced Janie's first three albums, ***Singer of Songs*** (1978), ***Love Notes*** (1979) and ***From the Heart*** (1980). During this time, Janie was dubbed "the reluctant star." In fact, the tag was a press invention; Janie Fricke entered into her solo career wholeheartedly. During 1978, Janie's other hits were *Baby It's You* (Top 25), *Please Help Me, I'm Falling (In Love with You)* (Top 15) and the No.1 duet with Charlie Rich, *On My Knees.* Both *Billboard* and *Cash Box* agreed that year that Janie was "Top New Female Vocalist." In 1978 and 1979, she was nominated for the CMA "Female Vocalist of the Year" award.

In 1979, Janie's chart records were *Playin' Hard to Get* (Top 25), *I'll Love Away Your Troubles for a While* (Top 15) and *Let's Try Again* (Top 30). 1980 started with *But Love Me* (Top 30) and *Pass Me By (If You're Only Passing Through)* (Top 25). Then Janie linked up once more with Duncan, with whom she recorded the duet album ***Nice 'n' Easy***; it yielded a Country top 20 entry with *He's Out of My Life,* their version of Michael Jackson's *She's Out of My Life. Music City News* named her "Most Promising Female Artist."

Janie's first Country albums lacked cohesion. As Sherrill told her: "You can do so many styles, I'm getting confused." An identifiable sound was now provided by producer Jim Ed Norman with the albums ***I'll Need Someone to Hold Me (When I Cry)*** (1980) and ***Sleeping with Your Memory*** (1981), which took her in a more definite Country direction and moved her several notches up the singles chart. The former provided Janie with 1981 hits, *Down to My Last Broken Heart* (Top 3), *Pride* (Top 15) and the title song (Top 5). 1982 opened with the Top 5 hit *Do Me with Love* and Janie followed with the No.1 hit *Don't Worry 'Bout Me Baby* with Ricky Skaggs on harmony vocals.

Having now established herself as an outstanding ballad singer, Janie's next album, ***It Ain't Easy*** (1982), had high energy driving songs to prove her versatility and was produced by Bob Montgomery. *It Ain't Easy Bein' Easy* gave Janie her second-in-a-row No.1 single. The album also yielded, in 1983, *You Don't Know Love* (Top 5) and the No.1 hits *He's a Heartache (Looking for a Place to Happen)* and *Tell Me a Lie.* In 1982, Janie became "Top Female Artist" in *Billboard* and *Cash Box.* In 1982 and 1983, she was named by the CMA "Female Vocalist of the Year." In 1983, she received the same accolade from the ACM, while *Music City News* named her "Female Vocalist of the Year," that year.

Her first hit in 1984 was the No.1 *Let's Stop Talkin' About It.* This was followed by *If the Fall Don't Get You* (Top 10) and another No.1, *Your Heart's Not in It.* Her next hit, *A Place to Fall Apart,* was written by Merle Haggard, who shared the vocals with Janie and took it to No.1. It appeared on Merle's ***It's All in the Game*** album. Her fans included President Reagan, who asked her to make a special appearance at Camp David. In 1984 she won *Music City News*' "Female Vocalist of the Year."

In 1985, Janie had a Top 10 hit with the title track of her first album that year, ***The First Word in Memory Is Me***. It was followed by *She's Single Again* (Top 3), which came from ***The Very Best of Janie Fricke*** (1985). The year ended with the Top 5 title track of the album ***Somebody Else's Fire***. Janie was again named *Cash Box*'s "Female Vocalist of the Year." At the awards, Elvis Costello brought embarrassment to the proceedings when he mispronounced her surname as "Frick."

Janie opened up her chart account in 1986 with the Top 5 *Easy to Please.* As a result of Costello's faux pas, Janie changed the spelling to "Frickie" in 1986, although she later reverted to the original spelling. Her ***Black and White*** album, which was produced by Norro Wilson, yielded the No.1 hit, *Always Have Always Will.* Janie's remaining albums on Columbia were nothing as successful. ***After Midnight*** (1987) prompted Steve Buckingham to take Janie in a Western Swing direction, and ***Saddle the Wind*** (1988) was not a big seller. The next album, ***Labor of Love*** (1989), saw a return to more familiar territory, with some meaty ballads and top writers like Dave Loggins, Tom Russell and Jeff Tweel. It proved to be the last of Janie's 17 Columbia albums. During the period 1987-1989, Janie's most successful singles were *When a Woman Cries* (Top 20) and *From Time to Time (It Feels Like Love Again)* (Top 25). On the latter, Janie was accompanied by Larry Gatlin and the Gatlin Brothers.

As an established act, Janie suffered from Country radio playing her old hits rather than her new material. While she was without a label she continued to do many live performances with her "Heart City Band," including Nashville's *City Lights* in 1990. Finally, she secured a recording deal with the independent, Georgia-based Intersound. The result was an eponymous album, with a single, *You Never Crossed My Mind,* in 1991 and a return to form which proved to be popular in Europe. The penchant for major labels to ignore long established talent saw Janie Fricke move to the emerging Branson Entertainment label. Although totally uncommercial in terms of chart action, the resulting album, ***Crossroads: Hymns of Faith*** (1992), was much acclaimed. This was followed by the album ***Now & Then***, which consisted in the main of her re-recorded hits and was produced by Janie.

Home for Janie is a 19th century farmhouse south of Dallas. The two-story building was once home to Pat Garrett, the slayer of Billy the Kid. It has earned a historical marker from the Texas Historical Commission. Janie is also involved in selling clothes based on her stage wear. Janie is currently a regular performer on the *Statler Brothers* TV show on TNN. SM/BM

RECOMMENDED ALBUMS

"Greatest Hits" (Columbia)(1982)
"Black and White" (Columbia)(1986)
"After Midnight" (Columbia)(1987)
"Celebration" (double)(Columbia)(1987)
"Saddle the Wind" (Columbia)(1988)
"Labor of Love" (Columbia)(1989)
"Janie Fricke" (Intersound)(1991)
"Crossroads: Hymns of Faith" (Branson Entertainment)(1992) [Gospel]
"Now & Then" (Branson Entertainment)(1993)

KINKY FRIEDMAN

(Singer, Songwriter, Author, Guitar)

Given Name:	**Richard F. Friedman**
Date of Birth:	**October 31, 1944**
Where Born:	**Rio Duckworth, Palestine, Texas**

According to Kinky Friedman, he is the man who brought Frisbees to Borneo and he claimed the natives only used them to make their lips big. But then that is the sort of thought-provoking and provocative comment that should be expected from Kinky Friedman.

He was born the son of a professor at the

University of Texas at Austin, and showed that academia can settle even unto the second generation when he graduated from his father's seat of learning as a psychology major. While at college, he formed his first band, King Arthur and the Carrots, who cut a surfing single in 1966. He spent three years in Borneo as a member of the Peace Corps, employed as an agricultural extension worker distributing seeds. Kinky maintained that no seeds actually ever arrived while he was there, hence the preoccupation with Frisbees.

He returned to Rio Duckworth, the family ranch, where he and his brother, Roger, refer to themselves as "the Beauforts." In 1971, Kinky headed west for Los Angeles with his group, Kinky Friedman and His Texas Jewboys. He took great delight in being the Jew from Palestine. He established a reputation as being the Frank Zappa of Country music. The members of the band used appropriate sobriquets: Little Jewford, Big Nig, Panama Red, Rainbow Colors and Snakebite Jacobs.

Kinky bathed in the discomfort he created. He offended everyone who was an extremist. Yet within that mocking of the extreme, he retained a respect for tradition. A psychologist or rabbi would say that his inborn Jewish tradition overrode his reform tendency. However, Kinky and the band found themselves being canceled and kicked off stage for using language that is normally confined to the locker room. To Friedman, it was grist to the mill. It built up the band's reputation and in 1972, after getting total rejection from the record company chiefs in L.A., Kinky headed for Nashville at the suggestion of Chuck Glaser of the Glaser Brothers.

Commander Cody, another musical surrealist, got Vanguard Records interested in Kinky and in 1973, Friedman recorded ***Sold American*** at the Glaser Studio in Nashville. Featured on the album are John Hartford and Tompall Glaser. The title track hung around the bottom of the charts for a couple of months. However, it was the cut *Ride 'Em Jewboy* which eventually became a sort of anthem akin to *We Shall Overcome*. Eyebrows were raised when the band was invited onto the *Grand Ole Opry*, but Kinky's sense of Country music tradition prevailed and they made a lot of friends and got the Reverend Jimmie Rodgers Snow announcing that Kinky and his "mentshes" were the first "full-blooded" Jews to have appeared there.

The following year, Kinky recorded an eponymous album for ABC Records, which was produced by Willie Nelson and featured Willie and Waylon and Tompall Glaser and contained the classic putdown to anti-Semites, *They Ain't Making Jews Like Jesus Anymore*.

During the tail end of 1975 and beginning of 1976, Kinky and his band toured with Bob Dylan as part of Bob Dylan's Rolling Thunder Revue. By 1976, Friedman had moved to Epic Records, where he released ***Lasso from El Paso***, which features Bob Dylan and Eric Clapton.

In 1979, Kinky broke up the band and started a solo career. He moved to New York and started playing at the Lone Star Cafe. He didn't release another album until 1983, when he issued ***Under the Double Ego*** for Sunrise Records. Since then, Kinky Friedman, who is not the most enthusiastic performer, has concentrated on other facets of his life, including being an author. It started when he came to the rescue of a lady being mugged and he captured the assailant. The woman, it turned out, was Cathy Smith, who allegedly had given John Belushi his last cocaine injection. Kinky started writing mystery books in 1985 and they all feature "The Kinkster," a Greenwich Village Jewish P.I. and former Country singer (his alter ego?) and are *Greenwich Killing Time, A Case of Lone Star, When the Cat's Away* and *Frequent Flyer*. All the books are published by William Morrow & Company (17 publishers approached declined the debut novel). *Greenwich Killing Time* is now to be a TV movie with Ron Howard at the directorial helm. In 1986, Kinky ran for the office of Justice of the Peace in Kerr County, Texas, and lost. Kinky now lives in a trailer in Kerrville, Texas, and drives across the U.S. in his Cadillac, "Yom Kippur One, the Kippur Clipper."

RECOMMENDED ALBUMS:

"Sold American" (Vanguard)(1973)
"Kinky Friedman" (ABC)(1974)
"Lasso from El Paso" (Epic)(1976)
"Under the Double Ego" (Sunrise)(1983)

DAVID FRIZZELL

(Singer, Songwriter, Guitar)
Date of Birth: **September 26, 1941**
Where Born: **Texas**
Married: **Jo**

Being the young brother of a star can have its drawbacks, but David Frizzell stepped out from the shadow of Lefty to become a Country star himself.

He was still in his preteens and teens when Lefty stacked up his big successes, and in the early 50's hitched to be with his brother in California. He made his first appearance on stage at age 13 at a club in Bakersfield. He was brought on stage by Lefty to sing some rockabilly songs during his show. Lefty was still on Columbia at the time and under the tutelage of that label's Don Law. David started his recording career in 1958. However, success was not to be his, yet. He toured with Lefty and then joined the U.S. Air Force for four years.

He recorded for numerous small labels without success and then in 1970, he rejoined Columbia. He charted for the first time with *L.A. International Airport,* which peaked in the Top 70. He followed this with the Top 40 entry *I Just Can't Help Believing*. Then in 1971, he moved to Nashville and cut some sides for Ron Chancey's Cartwheel label. *Goodbye* gave him a low level chart record. In 1973, he became a regular on Buck Owens' *All American TV Show* and found himself signed to Capitol. He had two low level hits with *Words Don't Come Easy* and *Take Me One More Ride*.

In 1976, he scraped into the charts with his RSO recording of Joni Mitchell's *A Case of You*. He also cut what he felt was his best single, Janis Ian's *Jessie,* for MCA that year. By 1977, he was resident at a nightclub in Concord, California, when younger brother Allen arrived with his new bride, Shelly West, in tow. They became part of the house band until David organized a tour of Texas, Oklahoma, New Mexico and Southern California. When they returned to Concord after about six months, David set about getting a new record deal. He found interest with Snuff Garrett, who had produced Bobby Vee, Johnny Burnette and the Crickets in the early 60's.

One of the songs that Garrett had earmarked for David was *We're Lovin' on Borrowed Time*, which was a duet. David suggested that Shelly sing on the demo and Garrett was knocked out by the result. He fixed up a deal with Casablanca-West, the newly formed Country arm of the Disco label Casablanca. However, Polygram bought the

*Who Dat, dat's **David Frizzell***

company, axed the label and axed David and Shelly. Finding no interest in Nashville, Garrett resorted to using his connections. He had worked on Clint Eastwood's *Every Which Way But Loose* and knew that Eastwood had formed Viva Records. He slipped a cassette into the player in Eastwood's car and hoped to providence.

Eastwood didn't like the song, but did like *You're the Reason God Made Oklahoma*. He insisted that the song go into his new movie *Any Which Way You Can*. The soundtrack was licensed to Warner Brothers and the track started to pick up airplay on KDEN Tulare, California. Soon the couple found that with the advent of 1981, they had a No.1 hit on their hands. The awards flowed in. CMA made them "Duo of the Year"; *Billboard* made them "New Group/Duo-Singles," "New Group/Duo-Albums" and "New Artists-Singles"; *Cash Box* named them "New Duo-Singles" and "Duo of the Year"; *Record World* named them Vocal "Duo of the Year" and *Radio & Record* made them "Vocal Duo of the Year."

They followed this up with the Top 10 hit *A Texas State of Mind,* both of which could be found on the acclaimed *Carryin' on the Family Names*. David then released the solo single *Lefty,* which has vocal assistance from the legendary Merle Haggard and made the Top 50. This marvelous year was rounded off with another Top 20 duet, *Husbands and Wives,* from the pen of Roger Miller.

1982 was even better for David. He started off the year with the duet *Another Honky-Tonk Night on Broadway* ,which went Top 10, and followed this with the solo No.1 *I'm Gonna Hire a Wino to Decorate Our Home*. After this came another duet, *I Just Came Here to Dance,* which became a Top 5 record. Then there was another solo hit with the Top 5 single *Lost My Baby Blues*. The year was completed by *Please Surrender,* which only reached the mid 40s and came from the Eastwood movie *Honkytonk Man*, in which David and Shelly made a cameo appearance. They again scooped the pool with their awards that year. They were again CMA, *Billboard* and *Cash Box*'s "Duo of the Year." In addition, ACM weighed in with "Duo of the Year" and they also made *You're the Reason God Made Oklahoma* "Song of the Year." *Music City News* Cover Awards made them "Duo of the Year." They repeated ACM and MCN "Duo of the Year" the following year.

In 1983, the cracks started to appear. In the spring, David had a solo hit with *Where Are You Spending Your Nights These Days*, but then his chart levels fell away with the exception of the Top 40 single at the end of the year, *A Million Light Beers Ago*. On the duet level, they had to wait until 1984, when they had back-to-back Top 20 hits with *Silent Partners* and *It's a Be Together Night*. In 1985, they went their separate ways, mainly because they couldn't find good duet songs. They got back together in 1988 for some concert dates.

David and Allen got together on David's album *On My Own Again* in 1983, to record with the voice of Lefty for *We Won't Be Hearing "Always Late" Anymore* as the Frizzell Brothers.

At the end of 1984, he had a Top 50 hit with *No Way Jose* (since revived by Ray Kennedy). In 1986, he turned up on Nashville America with a low-level entry, *Celebrity*, and the following year on Charlie Fach's Compleat label, he repeated this with *Beautiful Body*. In 1992, David released his album ***My Life Is Just a Bridge*** on Fach's new label BFE and was back in the duet business with *The One That Got Away* with Ed Bruce, which had an accompanying video.

RECOMMENDED ALBUMS:

"Family's Fine, But This One's Mine" (Warner/Viva)(1982)
"On My Own Again" (Viva)(1983)
"My Life Is Just a Bridge" (BFE)(1993)
With Shelly West:
"Carryin' on the Family Name" (Warner Brothers)(1981)
"The David Frizzell & Shelly West Album" (Warner/Viva)(1982)
"Our Best To You" (Warner/Viva)(1982)
"In Session" (Viva)(1983)

LEFTY FRIZZELL

(Singer, Songwriter, Guitar)

Given Name:	**William Orville Frizzell**
Date of Birth:	**March 31, 1928**
Where Born:	**Corsicana, Texas**
Married:	**Alice**
Children:	**Marlon Jaray, Rick, Lois Aleta**
Date of Death:	**July 19, 1975**

In Country music, Lefty Frizzell was the quintessential singer's singer—someone whose influence on the music far outweighed his commercial success. In the early 1950's, Lefty and Hank Williams revolutionized the way Country music was sung; with Williams, his legacy was his songs; with Lefty, it was his style.

"I feel he was the most unique thing that ever happened to Country music," Merle Haggard, one of Lefty's followers, has said. George Jones was sent home from his first recording session because he sounded too much like Lefty. Willie Nelson has devoted an entire album to Lefty. Modern giants like Keith Whitley and Randy Travis have recalled how they sat in front of their record players and tried to emulate Lefty. In the 1990's, far more Country singers sounded like Lefty than Hank Williams and while Lefty's life was not as dramatic as Williams', Lefty's music was equally as potent. His 240 commercial recordings made between 1950 and his death in 1975 are amazingly consistent, with masterpieces sprinkled throughout and with moments of genius on even the most banal Nashville fodder.

Lefty's life began in the rough north Texas oil town of Corsicana, where he was one of eight children (three of whom, David, Billy and Allen, would also go into music). Known to his family as "Sonny," by the time he was 14 he was being called "Lefty" by others. Though popular legend has it that he won the nickname by being a Golden Gloves champ, his family says it came about as the result of a schoolyard brawl. As a boy growing up in El Dorado, Arkansas, where his family had moved shortly after Lefty's birth, Lefty was fascinated with

*The legendary **Lefty Frizzell***

the records of Jimmie Rodgers, and had perfected his famous "blue yodel." "I knew when I was 12 years old what I was gonna do," Lefty recalled; and, indeed, by then he was making his first radio appearances as a Country singer.

Throughout the 1940's, Lefty spent his teenage years playing local radio shows, talent contests and the honky tonk circuit as far west as Las Vegas. Early radio air checks from New Mexico in 1947 show him sounding a lot like Ernest Tubb and Ted Daffan. After a run-in with the law (which resulted in a jail term for statutory rape), Lefty temporarily quit music and went to work with his father in the oil fields.

By 1950, he was back at music, playing at the Ace of Clubs in Big Spring, Texas. There he caught the attention of Jim Beck, who ran a studio in Dallas and worked on the side for several major record companies, including Columbia. In April, Lefty drove over to Beck's studio, bringing several original songs, including one called *If You've Got the Money I've Got the Time*. Beck liked the song and had Lefty cut a demo—as a way to sell the song, not Lefty. Beck took the demo to Little Jimmy Dickens in Nashville, but found that Columbia producer Don Law was more interested in the singer he heard. Soon Lefty was being offered a contract with Columbia.

His first single in 1950 was *If You've Got the Money,* backed by a song he had written in the Roswell jail, *I Love You a Thousand Ways*. Released on September 4, it was an immediate success, with both sides going to No.1 for three weeks; eventually over 40 other artists would do cover versions of *Money*. Seventeen days after the release, Columbia was rushing Lefty back into the studio for more. Don Law was by now convinced he had stumbled onto a "Lefty sound," defined by the crack Dallas studio musicians who were at home with the new Honky-Tonk sound. Foremost among them was a young woman piano player named Madge Sutee from Wichita Falls, whose romping barrelhouse style was heard on almost all of Lefty's early Texas records.

In 1951, Lefty had another double-sided smash with *Look What Thoughts Will Do* (Top 5)/*Shine, Shave, Shower It's Saturday* (Top 10). He followed this with *I Want to Be with You Always* (written by Lefty and Jim Beck), which stayed at No.1 for 11 weeks and crossed to the Pop Top 30. After this came another No.1 smash, *Always Late (with Your Kisses)*, which stayed at the top for 12 weeks. The flip-side, *Mom and Dad's Waltz*, went Top 3. Lefty's other chart entries that year were *Travellin' Blues* (Top 10) and *Give Me More, More, More (of Your Kisses)*, which went No.1 in 1952. The flip-side, *How Long Will It Take (to Stop Loving You)* also went Top 10. His chart entries in 1952 were, *Don't Stay Away ('til Love Grows Cold)* (Top 3), *Forever (and Always)* (Top 10) and *I'm an Old, Old Man (Tryin' to Live While I Can)* (Top 3).

A series of bad management decisions almost derailed Lefty's early career. He left the *Opry* shortly after joining, tried to work by flying out of Beaumont, got rid of his original band (who knew his style), tried an abortive stint with Wayne Raney and finally left for California, where he found work on *Town Hall Party*. He continued to make good records, but the hits slowed down.

In 1953, he only had one record on the chart, *(Honey, Baby, Hurry!) Bring Your Sweet Self Back to Me*. The following year, he charted with *Run 'Em Off* (Top 10) and in 1955, he only had *I Love You Mostly*, which failed to make the Top 10. From 1955 to 1958 he was absent from the chart and the singer was now feeling burned out. In 1958, he returned to the lists with the Marty Robbins song *Cigarettes and Coffee Blues*, which went Top 15.

Then in 1959, Lefty began working with Jim Denny's Cedarwood publishing company in Nashville, and soon was offered a Marijohn Wilkin-Danny Dill song called *The Long Black Veil*. It became his biggest hit in years, and rejuvenated his career, although not his record career. In fact, he was so encouraged that in 1961 he relocated to Nashville and two years later had another massive hit with *Saginaw, Michigan*, which stayed at No.1 for 4 weeks.

Through the late 60's and early 70's, Lefty was getting used to being viewed as a "living legend" by younger Nashville singers and songwriters. However, he still managed the occasional big hit. He stayed at Columbia until 1972 and his biggest hit was *She's Gone Gone Gone* (Top 15, 1965). In 1973, Lefty moved to ABC Records, where his biggest hits were *I Never Go Around Mirrors* and *Lucky Arms*, both in 1974. Inarticulate and hesitant to open up in interviews in his early years, Lefty now began to sound more reflective and even eloquent about his famous style. "When I sing," he said, "to me every word has a feeling about it. I had to linger, had to hold it, I didn't want to let go of it. I want to hold one word through a whole line of melody, to linger with it all the way down. I didn't want to let go of that no more than I wanted to let go of the woman I loved."

Lefty died from a stroke in 1975, but his catalog continued being covered, most successfully by Willie Nelson (*If You've Got the Money I've Got the Time*, No.1, 1976) and Dwight Yoakam (*Always Late (with Your Kisses)*, Top 10, 1988). CKW

RECOMMENDED ALBUMS:

"Lefty Frizzell Sings the Songs of Jimmie Rodgers" (Columbia Historic Edition)(1973)
"The ABC Collection—Lefty Frizzell" (ABC)(1977)
"Treasures Untold: The Early Recordings of Lefty Frizzell" (Rounder)(1980)
"Lefty's 20 Golden Hits" (Columbia)(1980)
"The Legendary Lefty Frizzell—His Last Sessions" (double)(MCA)(1982)
"Lefty Frizzell" (Columbia Historic Edition)(1982)
"The Legend Lives On" (Columbia)(1983)

RAYMOND FROGGATT

(Singer, Songwriter)
Given Name: Raymond Froggatt
Date of Birth: 1941
Where Born: Birmingham, England

Raymond Froggatt has been a tenacious fighter for recognition on the British Country music scene. He is now one of the few who can truly call themselves Country stars in Europe but to the general public, he still is unknown; a fate that befalls most British Country music performers.

"Froggy" came from humble beginnings, one of four brothers and a sister. His father was killed in WWII, when Raymond's mother, Lucy, was just 23 years of age. She did her best to bring up her family while living in lodgings and working in a factory to feed them.

Before he was school age, Raymond developed tuberculosis and was taken to Yardley Sanatorium to recover. Here he learned what loneliness was like, with no one able to kiss or cuddle him, as it was considered too dangerous. This formed a pattern in his life. He grew up to remain lonely and still remains a solitary person, keeping his loves and losses to himself.

He made his singing debut at age 8 at a Dunlop factory party and was paid 10 cents. After leaving school in the 50's, he had a succession of jobs. He worked initially as a grocer's boy then as a scrap iron car breaker, a pipe lagger, sheet metal worker and a boiler insulator. He also did some boxing and a lot of drinking with his "mates," but all the time remaining "different."

When he was 18, tuberculosis struck again and this time it affected his kidneys and bladder. As Froggy put it, it is "not a very romantic illness." He eventually lost one of his kidneys. During this period of isolation, he wrote poetry and decided he wanted a band. An advertisement in the *Birmingham Evening Post* yielded three people, who were to become his close friends. They were Hartley Cain (known as H. Cain), a 17-year old guitarist, who was to become Raymond's greatest friend, his mechanic, driver and later agent, manager, arranger and advisor and remains that rare commodity, "a true friend"; Lou Clark on bass; and Len Ablethorpe on drums. They formed the band Monopoly.

They began their journey into the entertainment scene in Birmingham on the nightclub circuit. They soon played the prestigious Belfry, a large club run by John Parsons and John Sabel, who helped the band build a foundation and jumping-off point to their first venture abroad. They traveled to France, where on a skimpy budget, they survived the rip-off agents and sleazy hotels. The two-month experience proved to be the most valuable lesson in all the skills and sage presentation that an entertainer could need.

It was John Parsons who introduced the band to Polydor Records through Arthur Smith, the manager of another Birmingham band, the Applejacks, who had a hit record, *Tell Me When*, in 1964. Polydor signed Froggy and the band for a 5-year contract. It was a happy time during which Raymond met record producer Terry Kennedy and Stuart Reid, owner of E.H. Morrison Music Corp., a music publisher later bought by Chappell Music.

Raymond released his first successful single, the self-penned *Red Balloon,* and it was played on every radio show for two months, but through bad distribution, they failed to get the record into the shops. Fortunately for Raymond, it was recorded by the Dave Clark Five and reached the U.K. Top 10 in 1968. It also became a No.1 in France when recorded by Marie Laforet.

1972 brought changes with Froggy signing to Bell Records. His bass player, Lou Clark, left to take a four-year course at Leeds College of Music and was replaced by Mick Hucks. Ozzy Osbourne of Rock band Black Sabbath introduced Froggy to Roger Bain, who worked for Hummingbird Productions, and he produced Raymond's first album, ***Bleach***. The single *The Singer*, from the album, was released and was played at the wrong speed by the deejay Emperor Rosco on his *Roundtable* program, much to the hilarity of the panelists, and ruined any chart chances. The album, on the other hand, did very well.

At the end of the Bell contract, Raymond's next move was considered by him to be the most damaging of his career at the time, although he has subsequently had second thoughts. Roy Wood of Rock group the Move fame knew Froggy's contracts were about to expire and told him that music entrepreneur Don Arden had shown an interest in signing him for recording and publishing and Arden had a reputation for making people successful.

Stuart Reid offered Froggy a new 5-year worldwide publishing deal for a non-returnable advance of $60,000 but Raymond turned it down and Reid was professionally disappointed and personally hurt. According to Raymond he saw the Arden set-up as a chance to break into the U.S.; he took the chance and lost. He was signed to Arden's Darbilt company and as far as he could make out, his publishing was sold to a major publishing house for an advance of many thousands of dollars and Raymond became a writer for Robbins EMI Music Publishers and his future recordings were pre-sold to Warner Brothers. Froggy says that he received nothing because Arden had legally operated a Power of Attorney on Raymond's behalf through his company.

Raymond's first single for Warner Brothers was *French Painter*, which was released and forgotten. Then to his amazement, Warner Brothers suggested that he record an album at Richard Branson's new studio, The Manor, in Oxford. The studio was booked for a month, Froggy wrote all the songs and the 1974 Reprise album, ***Rogues and Thieves***, sold 8,000 copies the first week. This is usually enough to hit the album chart, but that week lots of name acts out-sold him.

Not knowing how to promote Raymond and his band, Arden decided to send them on tour with Roy Wood's new band, Wizzard, which was not the best of ideas, as the bands appealed to totally different audiences. Raymond's band began to lose its togetherness through discontent. Len Ablethorpe emigrated to Canada, H. Cain took his family on a tour of Africa for a year and Mick Hucks married and began his own business.

Froggy had been writing a musical based on the life of William Shakespeare over the previous two years as a form of relaxation and now showed the idea to Arden. He loved the idea. Lou Clark had graduated from his studies and now rejoined Raymond to orchestrate the musical. The Wembley Music Centre, an orchestra conducted by Lou Clark, and 40 singers were booked. During the recording, Jeff Lynne of the Electric Light Orchestra was in the next studio recording and decided to use Clark for his future work.

When the recording was finished, Arden took it to the U.S. and sold it to ATM Music in Los Angeles. It was then filmed for TV as a four-hour spectacular, but it is still waiting to be scheduled. Arden had by now formed Jet Records and moved to the U.S. Froggy asked Arden to release him from his contract, but he refused and soon, because of a dishonest business manager (not Arden), Raymond was in financial difficulties. He lost everything he had and was at rock bottom. He lost his home and a friend let him stay rent free in a run-down Victorian property. He didn't have any furniture and slept on the floor on a piece of foam.

H. Cain now returned from Africa but it took him six months to find Froggy and lift him out of his self-pity. Froggy rang Arden, who sent two air tickets for him and H. Cain to fly to the U.S. to record an album. They worked at the Midnight Hour studio in Memphis and recorded ***Memphis Moonshine***, but it was shelved.

Now Arden sent his son, David, to suggest that Raymond record a Country album with the Jordanaires and produced by Larry Butler in Jack Clements' studio in Nashville. $75,000 was to be paid to Britain's biggest Country music promoter to get Froggy launched onto the British Country music scene. Mervyn Conn booked Raymond onto the Tulsa Country Festival to try him out and the U.S. fans liked him. The new album, ***Southern Fried Frog,*** released on Jet in 1978 with all the songs written by Raymond, was marketed as if it was a Rock album and not sent to the Country music media and Mervyn's expertise was not utilized.

He was angry and disappointed as he had hoped that British Country music fans would know Raymond's name when the next Wembley Festival came around. Froggy had a 15-minute spot and was introduced as "Ladies and gentlemen, I have to introduce to you an artist who has told me that he has written a song for Shirley Bassey. Here is Raymond Froggatt." The audience was polite; they listened and the applause was polite. Controversy arose and the connection with Mervyn Conn was seen as an unfair privilege and that he had not paid his dues. He was an unknown and yet he was about to support Tammy Wynette on a national tour and represent Britain at Fan Fair.

Much to Conn's disappointment, Raymond refused to go to Fan Fair, but the damage had been done. It would take many years for Froggy to find the hearts of the British fans. Arden finally let him go after Froggy's 1979 album, ***Conversations***. Conn also separated from Arden but kept faith with Froggy. Raymond and his band supported the major U.S. Country artists in Britain. At first there was resentment and genuine hatred. Some people who didn't even know him tried, in Froggy's words to "kick me off the world," but as a fighter from the roughest areas of Birmingham, he says he has too many scars for dagger points to find space enough to pierce, "never mind, it's only my life, my dears."

It was a slow process trying to win over the Country fans, but everywhere he eventually felt a certain warmth breaking through. His loyal fans have turned him into a near icon. He has made many friends and toured with many Country stars like Hoyt Axton, Billie Jo Spears and Tammy Wynette. He has appeared at the Wembley Festival on five occasions and headlined at the Polish Music Festival in Mragowo. The show was televised in front of an audience of 50,000. He has toured extensively in the U.K. and also appeared in concert and on TV all over Europe and the U.S.

Raymond has won many awards and was voted "Best British Male Vocalist" in 1985, a title he held onto until 1992 and was "Ambassador for Birmingham" in 1990. He now arranges his own tours through his own company, Red Balloon Music. Froggy still writes his own songs and says that he will do so until his time is done.

His latest record was released on Red Balloon and was the cd ***Here's to Everybody***. His autobiography, *Raymond Who*, was published by Scala Music Ltd. in 1992, in which Froggy takes the reader on an odyssey of the success, failure, fans and loneliness of being a Country music star and reveals the above information. JAB

RECOMMENDED ALBUMS:

"Voice and Writing of Raymond Froggatt" (Polydor UK)(1969)
"Bleach" (Bell UK)(1972)
"Rogues and Thieves" (Reprise)(1974)
"Southern Fried Frog" (Jet)(1978)
"Conversations" (Jet)(1979)
"Here's to Everyone" (Red Balloon)(1993)

G

BOB GALLION

(Singer, Songwriter, Guitar)

Given Name: Robert H. Gallion
Date of Birth: April 22, 1929
Where Born: Ashland, Kentucky
Married: Betty June Dotson
Children: Melody Lynn

For most of his career, Bob Gallion followed in the path of the great Country Honky-Tonk singers. He found moderate success in the 1950's, 60's and 70's, spending two stints at the *Wheeling Jamboree* and another at the *Louisiana Hayride*.

Born in Ashland, Kentucky, Bob Gallion grew up in the same tri-state region that has produced such Country music notables as Hawkshaw Hawkins, Tom T. Hall, the Judds and Billy Ray Cyrus. Like Hawkins, he owed a debt of credit to the influence that Ernest Tubb provided for singers of the Honky-Tonk style. Bob first started to play guitar as a child and began working clubs as a musician at the age of 20, mostly in the tri-state towns of Ashland, Huntington, Ironton, Portsmouth and up to Columbus.

From there he became a featured vocalist for Wilma Lee and Stoney Cooper's Clinch Mountain Clan, which brought him to WWVA and the *Jamboree* where he soon went solo. By 1955, Bob had landed his own contract for MGM Records. While his first release, *Your Wild Life's Gonna Get You Down,* did not attain hit status, a subsequent cover by Kitty Wells scored high on the charts.

Although most of Gallion's early offerings favored a straight Honky-Tonk style, some had a Rockabilly flavor such as *My Square Dancin' Mama (She Done Learned to Rock and Roll), I Want Her Blues, This Should Go on Forever,* and *Baby, Love Me.* His real successes on the label, *That's What I Tell My Heart* and *You Take the Table (And I'll Take the Chairs)*, reached the Top 30 and Top 20 on the Country chart, respectively, while retaining a conventional Country sound. He also wrote a pair of numbers for the Osborne Brothers in this period, *Love Pains* and *Sweethearts Again.*

Meanwhile Bob had shifted his base from Wheeling to Shreveport and then to Nashville. Through the years, he had often combined artistry with deejay work at such locales as Newark, Ohio, and Mobile, Alabama. While in Music City, Gallion did guest spots on the *Grand Ole Opry* and toured with a variety of bigger name artists. He also went to work in sales promotion for the Acuff-Rose Artists Bureau when not on the road. In 1960, Bob signed with the Acuff-Rose record label, Hickory, where he enjoyed his biggest chart hits, *Loving You Was Worth This Broken Heart* (Top 10, 1960), *One Way Street* and *Sweethearts Again* (both Top 20, 1961), *Wall to Wall Love* (Top 5, 1962) and *Ain't Got Time for Nothin'* (Top 25, 1963).

During these years Bob continued with deejay work, spending six years at WGUN Atlanta (then known as the Big Gun) and a lesser period at East Point, Georgia. In 1968, Gallion contracted to United Artists, enjoying a minor hit with *Pick a Little Happy Song.* That same year, he returned to Wheeling, where for the next fifteen years he would rank among the more significant *Jamboree USA* regulars. By this time, Bob often toured with Patti Powell, a female vocalist he had met in Georgia and who recorded with both Hickory and Stop. Bob and Patti's duet single *Love By Appointment* on Metromedia Country became a minor hit in 1973 and marked the last time that a Gallion number would register in the charts.

When Gallion returned to Wheeling, he took over the Acuff-Rose Artists Bureau transforming it to Bob Gallion Productions. This company not only booked many *Jamboree* regulars but also many big-name Nashville acts at fairs and festivals through several states. As this business has grown, Bob has done much less as an artist in recent years. His last significant recordings apparently date from 1978 when he and Patti did a "greatest hits" album for Starday-Gusto, containing new recordings of eight of Bob's solo efforts and four of their duets. IMT

RECOMMENDED ALBUMS:

"Together and Alone (B &P)(1975) [As Bob Gallion and Patti Powell]
"Greatest Hits" (Starday-Gusto)(1978) [As Bob Gallion and Patti Powell]

Bob Gardner refer MAC AND BOB

HANK GARLAND

(Guitar, Mandolin, Singer)

Given Name: Walter Louis Garland
Date of Birth: November 11, 1930
Where Born: Cowpens, South Carolina

One of the original, and one of the best, Nashville session musicians, Hank Garland was one of the more innovative guitarists of his age, a splendid technician who was as much at home playing Jazz as he was Country. Though his discography as a soloist is somewhat slender, he was heard on dozens of hits by other artists, and only a tragic accident prevented him from becoming an influence as great as Chet Atkins or Merle Travis.

Hank was born and grew up in the Spartanburg area of South Carolina, the home turf of two other important guitar innovators, Arthur "Guitar Boogie" Smith and Zeke Turner. Smith, along with Maybelle Carter, was among the prime influences on Garland. As a teenager, Hank already had an enviable reputation locally, and in 1945 was asked to join the *Opry* band of Paul Howard (the Arkansas Cotton Pickers). He made a sensational debut on the *Opry*, whipping off a guitar boogie piece at a blistering pace. He soon learned, though, that union rules forbade anyone under 16 from working on the show. He went back home to wait things out, and then rejoined on his 16th birthday. With Howard, back then, were twin guitarists Cameron Hill and Jimmy Wyble, and they served as mentors as Hank developed his electric guitar technique. By 1947, Hank had moved to Cowboy Copas' band, recording lead guitar solos for pieces like *Honky Tonkin'* and *Down in Nashville, Tennessee*.

In 1949 Decca boss Paul Cohen signed Hank for a solo session, and was amazed at an original piece Garland had first worked up as a finger exercise, *Sugarfoot Boogie*. A few months later, Cohen had words put to the song, and Garland was back in the studio recording it with Red Foley. *Sugarfoot Rag* became one of the bigger hits of the year. It was so pervasive that record labels began to identify the young picker as Hank "Sugarfoot" Garland. None of the Decca solo efforts were really big hits, but they helped Hank gain entree to the emerging Nashville studio system. In the 50's, he was heard doing twin guitar leads (with Chet Atkins) on Don Gibson's *Sea of Heartbreak*, crafting the introduction to Patsy Cline's *I Fall to Pieces*, and backing Elvis on *Little Sister*.

In 1960, Hank and a group of Nashville pickers who were fond of playing Jazz in after-hours clubs went to the Newport Jazz Festival and cut an RCA lp, ***After the Riot at Newport***. Shortly after, he went into the studio with Nashville Jazz vibraphonist Gary Burton and did a well-received Jazz lp called ***Jazz Winds from a New Direction***. Hank hardly had time to reap the fame and rewards from these pioneering sets when, on September 8, 1961, he was severely injured in a car accident north of Nashville. He finally pulled through, but his abilities as a guitarist and creative musician were seriously compromised. He tried to make a comeback, but after the death of his wife in another car accident in 1963, he eventually moved back to South Carolina and retired.

CKW

RECOMMENDED ALBUMS:

"Jazz Winds from a New Direction" (Columbia)(1961) [Produced by Grady Martin]
"Guitar Genius" (Charly UK)(1985) [Also tracks by Grady Martin and Les Paul]

JIMMY GATELEY

(Singer, Fiddle, Guitar, Songwriter)
Given Name: James David Gateley
Date of Birth: May 1, 1931
Where Born: Greene County, Springfield, Missouri
Married: Esther May
Children: Robert James, Teresa Jane
Date of Death: March 17, 1985

Although Jimmy Gately was not able to boast of any hit records, as a writer he was responsible for penning such classics as *The Minute You've Gone* and *Bright Lights and Country Music*.

In 1951, Jimmy started his career playing fiddle with the Western Rhythm Kings on radio station KGBX Springfield, Missouri. He stayed with the band until 1953 and during this time, he also served in the Navy Reserve and did so until 1954. In 1953, Jimmy became a member of Virgil Cobia's Red River Rustlers on KSJB Jamestown, North Dakota. The following year, Jimmy joined WWVA *Wheeling Jamboree*, West Virginia, as a sideman with Dusty Owens' Rodeo Boys.

During 1954-63, Jimmy was part of Red Foley's troupe on KWTO and KYTV Springfield, Missouri, and as such was a founding cast member of the *Ozark Jubilee*. In 1959, he cut his first records for Cullman and stayed with the label until 1960. A year later, he signed with Starday's Nashville label. During 1963, Jimmy joined Bill Anderson's Po' Boys as fiddler, guitarist, singer and front man (and made his debut on the *Grand Ole Opry*) and also formed a double act with Harold Morrison. In addition that year, he signed to Decca Records and released *Dirt Under Her Feet/Gotta Lotta Blues to Love*. He continued recording for the label until 1967. Although Jimmy never had a chart hit on Decca, several of his numbers were very popular, including, *Melinda* (1964), *Why Don't They Go Home* (1965), *Sticks and Stones* (1966), *Cryin' Don't Pay* and *Don't Come Cryin' to Me* (1967). Jimmy also recorded sides for Columbia (1968), Chart (1970), Million (1976), Sapphire, Constoga (1979) and B.T. (1982).

Jimmy appeared in the movie *Forty Acre Feud*, during 1964, while a member of Po' Boys. He also appeared in the movies *The Road to Nashville* and *Las Vegas Hillbillies*.

Webb Pierce had a Top 5 hit with the 1962 recording of the Jimmy Gateley song *Alla My Love*, for which Jimmy received a BMI award. In 1963, Sonny James cut the Gateley composition *The Minute You're Gone* and had a Top 10 hit. Two years later, Jimmy's boss, Bill Anderson, co-wrote with Jimmy and recorded *Bright Lights and Country Music*. Johnny Wright had a 1966 hit with Jimmy's co-written song *Nickels, Quarters and Dimes*.

During the late 70's and up to his death, Jimmy operated the Jimmy Gateley Western Wear store on Gallatin Road, Madison, Tennessee. During this time, he turned more and more toward Gospel music. He was a former Deacon of Rivergate Calvary Church in Madison and he released the Gospel album ***Lookin' Up***. On September 7, 1973, he was honored with a "Jimmy Gateley Day" by Pleasant Hope, Missouri. A further album, ***My Kind of Country***, remained unreleased at his death.

RECOMMENDED ALBUMS:

"The Dreamer" (Sapphire)
"Jimmy Gateley" (Constoga)(1979)
"Lookin' Up" (B.T.)(1982)
"My Kind of Country" can be obtained from Rivergate Calvary Church, 2205 Gallatin Road, Madison, TN 37115.

LARRY GATLIN & THE GATLIN BROTHERS BAND

LARRY GATLIN
(Singer, Songwriter,Guitar)
Given Name: Larry Wayne Gatlin
Date of Birth: May 2, 1948
Where Born: Seminole, Texas
Married: Janis Moss (m. 1969)
Children: Kristin Kara, Joshua Cash

STEVE GATLIN
(Low Harmony Vocals, Bass Guitar)
Given Name: Steven Daryl Gatlin
Date of Birth: April 4,1951
Where Born: Olney, Texas
Married: Cynthia Guerra (m. 1974)
Children: Ashley Page, Allison Shea, Aubrie Laine

RUDY GATLIN
(High Harmony Vocals, Acoustic Guitar)
Given Name: Rudy Michael Gatlin
Date of Birth: August 20, 1952
Where Born: Olney, Texas

After over thirty-seven years of performing, touring and recording, the Gatlins, along with the Oak Ridge Boys and the Statlers, have become Country music's triumvirate of premier close harmony groups. However, one of their strengths lies in the ability of each brother to take lead vocals. Their music is built around the not inconsiderable songwriting skills of Larry Gatlin.

From their childhood, the Gatlin brothers were surrounded by music, in particular Gospel and harmony singing. They were influenced by Gospel groups like the Blackwood Brothers and the Statesmen Quartet. They were soon singing together and Larry, the eldest, always sang lead, while his younger brothers sang harmony, which they always seemed able to do from the very start. They made their first public performance when Larry, at age 6, sang in the Cavalcade of Talent at Hardin Simmons University of Abilene. At the insistence of their sister, La Donna, their mother was persuaded to allow the little ones to perform with him. Steve was age 4 and Rudy age 2, at the time. The following year they won first prize in this contest.

The brothers first paid job was singing on a local Abilene radio station's Sunday morning program for which the boys received 10 cents

Larry Gatlin & the Gatlin Brothers

per week. Larry had already started using his songwriting talents by making up new words to popular tunes. In addition, all three brothers were also very interested in sports and Larry won a football scholarship to the University of Houston, where he majored in English and studied law.

Larry also worked as a bricklayer, roofer and an oil field worker. His music career started in earnest when he started to sing with the Gospel group the Imperials, who had worked with Elvis Presley. While touring with the Imperials in Las Vegas, Larry met Dottie West, who befriended him. Later, he sent her eight of his original songs on a tape and he received from her, by return mail, an airline ticket to Nashville. Larry decided to move to Nashville after Dottie had recorded two of his songs, *Once You Are Mine* and *You're the Other Half of Me* (the latter, the first song he ever wrote, in 1971).

As a result of Dottie's help, and with her recording, he moved to Nashville. A few months later he had a songwriting contract with Dottie's newly formed First Generation Music Company. He was starting to get established as a well respected songwriter. At this time, his brothers were still at college, Steve earning a B.S. in elementary education from Texas Tech in Lubbock and Rudy, also at Texas Tech, majoring in finance and graduating with a B.A. in business administration.

Larry did some backup singing on some of Kris Kristofferson's early records and began getting his songs cut by Kris, Johnny Cash and many others. Then Fred Foster, President of Monument Records, offered Larry a recording contract. By the mid-70's, the younger boys and their sister, La Donna, along with her husband, Tim, had teamed up. Their group was called Young Country and they opened and sang back-up for Tammy Wynette, working with her for a year. Meanwhile, Larry had persuaded Steve and Rudy to come to Nashville to work on his debut Monument album, ***The Pilgrim***, released in January 1974. From this, *Sweet Becky Walker*, which was pre-released, went into the Top 40 in 1973 and *Bitter They Are the Harder They Fall* went Top 50 in 1974. *Delta Dirt* from the next album, ***Rainbow***, went Top 15 that same year. The next successful single came in 1976 and was *Broken Lady*, from the album, ***Larry Gatlin Family and Friends***. The single reached the Top 5 and was the recipient of a Grammy Award as "Best Country Song."

The following year, the album ***High Time*** yielded the hit single *Statues Without Hearts*, which also went Top 5. Larry followed up with *Anythin' But Leavin'* (Top 15), *I Don't Wanna Cry* (Top 3) and *Love Is Just a Game* (Top 3). In 1978, Larry enjoyed his first No.1, *I Just Wish You Were Someone I Love*. Larry's last album for Monument was ***Oh Brother***, which yielded *Night Time Magic* (Top 3), *Do It Again Tonight* (Top 15) and *I've Done Enough Dyin' Today* (Top 10, 1979).

In 1979, Larry and his brothers moved to Columbia Records and from here on, they were known as Larry Gatlin & the Gatlin Brothers Band. They immediately hit the No.1 spot with *All the Gold in California*, which became the ACM "Single of the Year" in 1979. As they got into the 80's, their chart success was somewhat erratic. *The Midnight Choir* only made it to the Top 50, *Taking Someone with Me When I Fall* reached the Top 15 and *We're Number One* made it to the Top 20. These four singles came from their 1979 ***Straight Ahead*** album, which was chosen as "Album of the Year" by the ACM. They ended 1980 with the Top 5 single *Take Me to Your Lovin' Place.*

1981's hits were *It Don't Get No Better Than This* (Top 25), *Wind Is Bound to Change* (Top 20) and *What Are We Doin' Lonesome* (Top 5). 1982 brought more major and minor chart hits with *In Like with Each Other* (Top 20), *She Used to Sing on Sunday* (Top 20) and the Top 5 single *Sure Feels Like Love*. The following year, the Gatlins totted up *Almost Called Her Baby By Mistake* (Top 20) and *Easy on the Eye* (Top 40). The No.1 hit *Houston (Means One Day Closer to You)* came from the 1984 album ***Houston to Denver***, which also produced two further Top 10 singles, *Denver* and *The Lady Takes the Cowboy Every Time.*

After a time, drug and alcohol abuse started to mess up their lives and in 1984-1985, they made a conscious decision to overcome their problems. Larry took a month-long rehabilitation program in California, to get him off cocaine and alcohol. Rudy, with some help from outpatient counseling, kicked his own habit. Steve, who was not so drug dependent, but was drinking more, took the oath to quit. After this traumatic time, Larry and his brothers re-started their career, trying to relax more and attempting to be more peaceful and laid back.

Smile, their 1985 album, yielded an interesting 1986 single, *Runaway, Go Home*. Although it only reached the Top 50, it was adopted as the national theme for the Runaway & Homeless Youth Bureau. The Gatlins are active in the national network of Runaway & Homeless Youth's public awareness campaign. Their second single from the album, *Nothing But Your Love Matters*, got to the Top 15. They wrapped up the year with the Top 5 hit *She Used to Be Somebody's Baby.* This single came from their Chip Young-produced album, ***Partners*** (which featured their road band), as did the Top 5 *Talkin' to the Moon*, in 1987. That year, Larry teamed up with Janie Fricke on the Top 30 single *From Time to Time(It Feels Like Love Again)* and the Gatlins had a Top 20 hit with *Changin' Partners.*

Their 1988 album, ***Alive and Well...Livin' in the Land of Dreams*** yielded the Top 5 *Love of a Lifetime* and the Top 40 hit *Alive and Well.* The Gatlins helped to introduce Jimmy Bowen's new Universal label with the 1989 album ***Pure and Simple***, from which came the three singles *When She Holds Me* (Top 60), *I Might Be What You're Looking for* (Top 40) and *#1 Heartache Place* (Top 60). When Bowen moved to Capitol in late 1989, the brothers went with him. *Boogie and Beethoven* (1990) was their first single from ***Cookin' Up a Storm***, but it was relatively unsuccessful. Larry Gatlin and the Gatlin Brothers announced their decision to stop touring at the end of 1992. They called their last tour the "Adios Tour" and brought out an album of the same name.

Now the Gatlin harmonies can be heard, not on the road, but at their entertainment complex at the tourist attraction of Branson, Missouri. This will have two theaters, two restaurants and a 240-suite hotel. So It was adios to the touring, but not goodbye to the Gatlins. In 1993, Larry took over the role of "Will Rogers" in the Broadway musical *Will Rogers Follies* and he and the Gatlin Brothers signed to the Branson Entertainment label. They released their debut album for the label, ***Moments to Remember***, which is a tribute to the Gatlins' vocal group heroes, the Ames Brothers, Four Aces, McGuire Sisters, Mills Brothers, Platters and the Sons of the Pioneers and features all three brothers taking lead vocals. JAB

RECOMMENDED ALBUMS:

"The Pilgrim" (Monument)(1974) [Re-issued on Columbia in 1980]
"Larry Gatlin (With Family and Friends)" (Monument)(1976) [Called "Broken Lady" in UK. Re-issued on Columbia in 1983 (with Steve, Rudy & La Donna)]
"Larry Gatlin Greatest Hits Vol. 1" (Monument)(1978)
"Greatest Hits" (Columbia)(1980)
"Greatest Hits Vol. 2" (Columbia)(1983)
"Gatlin Family Christmas" (Columbia)(1983)
"Houston to Denver" (Columbia)(1984)
"Partners" (Columbia)(1986)
"I Love Country" (CBS UK)(1986)
"Alive and Well...Livin' in the Land of Dreams" (Columbia)(1988)
"Cookin' Up a Storm" (Capitol)(1990)
"Adios" (Liberty)(1992)
"Moments to Remember" (Branson Entertainment)(1993)

CONNIE B. GAY

(Broadcasting Entrepreneur, Promoter)

Given Name:	**Connie Barriot Gay**
Date of Birth:	**August 22, 1914**
Where Born:	**Lizard Lick, North Carolina**
Married:	**1. Hazel (div.) 2. Katherine Comas**
Children:	**Jan, Cecilia, Caroline, Judy Ann**
Date of Death:	**December 4, 1989**

When Connie B. Gay was elected to the Country Music Hall of Fame in 1980, many would have thought that it was long overdue. His love for Country music and business acumen made him an important part of the industry. He was an advisor to five Presidents and pioneered the use of the term "Country music." That and his registered trademark of "Town and Country" were largely instrumental in changing the image to a more "uptown" one.

All dressed-up: Hall of Famer ***Connie B. Gay***

Named for a locally renowned preacher, Connie graduated from North Carolina State University in 1935 and worked as a street corner salesman, selling pocket knife sharpeners in Washington, D.C. He soon realized that inside the most sophisticated person, there is a bit of a hillbilly. He joined the U.S. Department of Agriculture that year and got into radio via USDA's radio show, *National Farm and Home Hour*, in the 40's. During his time with the government, Gay dreamed up various money-making schemes to supplement his income including his "Blistan" rug idea, whereby he advertised for rugs and then advertised rugs to sell, making a nice profit in one day. Another money-making scheme was his National Reading Scheme, which although profitable was a little reprehensible. When stories about soldiers stationed at local bases had warranted a write-up in the D.C. press, Gay wrote to their families and offered to send them a copy of the article, if they sent a dollar.

In 1946, Gay contacted Frank Blair, the Program Director of WARL Arlington, Virginia, and got a midday Country show. Connie took no salary, but took a percentage of the advertising revenue. He registered the name "Town and Country" and soon his one hour show, *Town and Country Time,* became a three hour one called *Gay Time* and WARL became the first urban radio station to have a full-time Country format.

On October 31, 1947, Gay booked the DAR's Constitution Hall for two Country shows headlined by Eddy Arnold. Both shows were sold out with thousands turned away. During this time, he started to work closely with Jim Denny (promoter, music publisher and General Manager of the *Grand Ole Opry*), probably the most important man in Country music. Through this connection, Gay was able to have the monopoly on *Opry* acts for the mid-Atlantic area. The following year, he promoted 26 straight sold-out shows at Constitution Hall. The shows were broadcast regionally by WNBW-TV and other NBC affiliates. The venue asked him to take his shows elsewhere, which he did. He now promoted in every conceivable venue, including amusement parks, the National Guard Armory and the Uline Arena. In 1949, the Watergate concert, held below the Lincoln Memorial, drew 15,000 fans. During that year, he promoted the Hillbilly Air Show at the Bailey's Crossroads' airport.

At this point, Gay started offering weekend train tours to Nashville to visit the *Grand Ole Opry*. In 1950, Gay teamed up with the Wilson Line and began "Hillbilly Moonlight Cruises," which operated on the Potomac. In September 1951, Gay staged a star-packed show at Griffith Stadium in Washington, D.C., that included Ernest Tubb, Lefty Frizzell, Carl Smith, Hank Snow and Flatt & Scruggs. The show drew a record 14,000 crowd. He then teamed up with Denny for a six-city promotion on New Year's Eve, 1951.

During 1952, Gay joined forces with the Department of Defense to organize Special Services Road Shows, which brought Country music to other parts of the world.

In 1954, Gay discovered Patsy Cline at the National Country Music Championships in Warrenton. During 1957, Gay had to face up to an increasing dependency on alcohol and it resulted in the break-up of his first marriage. He pulled out of Country music in 1959 and entered Alcoholics Anonymous. He remarried in 1961 and his new wife put his money into more cautious investments.

At his zenith, Gay's radio empire included *Town and Country Jamboree*, which came from the Capitol Arena, Washington, D.C., every week; *Town and Country Time*, which featured Roy Clark and was produced for RCA; and in 1975, he created *Country Style*, with Jimmy Dean, on WTOP-TV Washington, D.C. At one time, Gay owned nine radio stations.

He settled in St. Thomas, where he attempted to become the Governor of the Virgin Islands, in 1960, before moving to McLean, Virginia. He served as a founding President of the Country Music Association and was the impetus in creating the Country Music Foundation. He died in December 1989 from cancer.

CRYSTAL GAYLE

(Singer, Songwriter, Guitar)

Given Name:	**Brenda Gail Webb**
Date of Birth:	**January 9, 1951**
Where Born:	**Paintsville, Kentucky**
Married:	**Vassilios "Bill" Gatzimos**
Children:	**Catherine Claire, Christos James**

Crystal Gayle has become indelibly associated with two images: an alluring big ballad voice and an ankle-length mane of dark brown hair.

The sister of Loretta Lynn, Crystal's musical background was very different from her sister's. Although born in Kentucky, she was brought up in Wabash, Indiana, where her family had moved in 1955. Her father died in 1959 and her mother remarried. When Crystal was born, Loretta was already married and by the time Crystal had graduated from high school, Loretta's career was in full bloom. In Wabash, she was exposed to more urban musical influences than Loretta had been.

When Crystal was 16, she became a part of Loretta's road show. In 1970, she benefited from the family connection by being signed to Decca Records. At her first session, she was so nervous that she couldn't sing and had to add her vocal track later. Crystal's debut single that year was Loretta's song *I've Cried the Blue Right Out of My Eyes*, which gave Crystal a Top 30 chart entry. Moreover, it was Loretta who came up with a stage name for her sister, born out of a fondness for "Krystal" burgers. Loretta even gave Crystal her first manager, her husband Mooney.

However, while Loretta provided Crystal with her vital start, she also gave her a huge problem; that of establishing a separate identity. Not only was she recording several of her big sister's songs, but she also sounded like her. It was no wonder that Decca saw Crystal only in terms of Loretta's baby sister.

In 1972, after regular appearances on Jim Ed Brown's TV show, *The Country Place*, had given Crystal a higher profile, she signed with United Artists. This move marked the real start of her success. Here she teamed up with producer Allen Reynolds, who was hot through his work with Don Williams. It was Allen that forged a calculated softer voice approach matched with middle-of-the-road material. The first UA album, ***Crystal Gale***, in 1975, gave her three Country hits, the most successful being Reynolds' own *Wrong Road Again*, which went Top 10. She followed this up with a song that she had written with her husband, Bill Gatzimos, entitled *Beyond You* (Top 30) and the Top 25 success *This Is My Year for Mexico*. She ended the year with the title track from her second album, ***Somebody Loves You***, which was also written by Reynolds. That year, Crystal was named by *Music City News* as "Most Promising Female Artist." Allen gathered in material provided by an impressive array of songwriters including Bob McDill and Richard Leigh, and it was Leigh who provided Crystal with her first No.1 in 1976, *I'll Get Over You*, which also crossed over into the Pop charts. She finished off the year with another No.1, the McDill song *You Never Miss a Real Good Thing (Till He Says Goodbye)*. That year, she was named "Outstanding Female Vocalist" by the ACM.

If 1976 was good, then 1977 was even better. She started off the year with the Top 3 hit *I'll Do It All Over Again* and then came the career single that made her an international household name. *Don't It Make My Brown Eyes Blue* was written by Richard Leigh. Reynolds got Crystal to cut it to exploit the cross-over market. He persuaded the UA powers to release it and it gave Crystal a second No.1. It also rose to the Top 3 on the Pop chart and was No.5 on the U.K. Pop chart. The single was Certified Gold before the year finished. The album from which it came, ***We Must Believe in Magic***, also went Gold that year and the following year was Certified Platinum, thus making her the second female Country singer after Debby Boone to achieve this.

A clutch of awards followed and Crystal was given a Grammy for "Best Country Vocal Performance, Female," and *Don't It Make My Brown Eyes Blue* won a Grammy for Richard Leigh for "Best Country Song." In addition, Crystal was named ACM's "Top Female Vocalist" for a second year and the CMA named her "Female Vocalist of the Year," which they would repeat in 1978.

As 1978 got under way, the success rate accelerated. She had three-in-a-row No. 1's with *Ready for the Times to Get Better* and another international hit with the Roger Cook co-written *Talking in Your Sleep*. The latter crossed over to the Pop chart Top 20 and was a No.11 hit in the U.K. The third chart-topper of the year was *Why Have You Left the One You Left Me For*.

Crystal bathed in the international acclaim her cross-over hits had brought her. She had first appeared at the prestigious Wembley Country Music Festival in England with Loretta back in 1971. She returned in her own right in 1977 and 1979. She also became the first Country singer to visit China, which she did as part of Bob Hope's *Road to China* TV show in 1979. She also achieved a first, when she had her own TV special on CBS that same year. Also in 1979, she received another ACM "Top Female Vocalist" Award. 1979 was another good year for Crystal as she scored a Top 3 hit with the title track from her fifth album, ***When I Dream*** (the album went Platinum in 1982), and followed it with the Top 10 record *Your Kisses Will*. That same year, she moved to Columbia, taking Allen Reynolds with her as producer.

The debut album that followed, ***Miss the Mississippi***, quickly went Gold. It provided several 1980 single successes, including the passionate Top 3 Country hit *Half the Way*, which was also a Top 15 Pop hit; *Your Old Cold Shoulder* (Top 5); another No.1, *It's Like We Never Said Goodbye;* and the Top 10 hit, *The Blue Side*. She ended the year with another No. 1 in *If You Ever Change Your Mind*.

In 1981, Crystal worked with Tom Waits on the soundtrack for the Francis Ford Coppola movie *One from the Heart*, released in 1982. During 1981, she had three more major hits with *Take It Easy* (Top 20), *Too Many Lovers* (No. 1) and *The Woman in Me* (Top 3). The following year, she was named one of the ten most attractive women in the world. Most women who have "eye jobs" want their eyes to be like Crystal's.

She had two further hits for Columbia in 1982 before moving to Elektra. They were *You Never Gave Up on Me* (Top 5) and *Livin' in These Troubled Times* (Top 10). Her first success for her new label was *You and I*, a duet with Eddie Rabbitt. Rabbitt was convinced the song needed a second voice and he asked Crystal to join him. The single went to No.1 on the Country chart and crossed to the Pop Top 10. Crystal followed this with another No.1 with the Rodney Crowell song *'Til I Gain Control Again*. She then switched over to Elektra's parent, Warner Brothers and had three-in-a-row No.1's in 1983 with *Our Love Is on the Faultline, Baby; What About You*; and *The Sound of Goodbye*. 1984 arrived and the hits kept rolling in with *I Don't Wanna Lose Your Love* (Top 3), *Turning Away* (No.1) and *Me Against the Night* (Top 5).

During 1985, she continued her run of chart singles with *Nobody Wants to Be Alone* (Top 3) and *A Long and Lasting Love* (Top 5). She closed out the year with *Makin' Up for Lost Time (The Dallas Lovers Song)*, which was originally recorded for the *Dallas* TV series album. The single was a notable collaboration with Gary Morris, which led to a very forgettable album spin-off. The following year was to prove the last consistently successful one for Crystal's records. She had two No.1's that year with the remake of Johnny Ray's hit *Cry* and the Graham Lyle-Terry Brittain song *Straight to the Heart*.

She hit with another duet with Gary Morris in the spring of 1987 with *Another World*, which came from the daytime soap of the same name and then suddenly she was having problems. Although she was still charting, her records failed to make the Top 10. Her most successful singles were *Only Love Can Save Me Now* (Top 15) and *Nobody's Angel* (Top 25) (both 1988).

Crystal moved to Capitol (later called Liberty) and was reunited with Allen Reynolds. However, that didn't help and Buzz Stone became her producer. However, although the albums were still excellent, single success was elusive. In 1993, she moved to the new Branson Entertainment label and released ***Best Always***, a set of newly recorded favorites and standards.

As a live performer, Crystal is captivating, wringing every ounce of emotion from her hallmark ballads. She found favor in showrooms in Las Vegas and Atlantic City, and in September 1988 she appeared in concert with Loretta in Lake Tahoe. A 1982 video of her concert at Hamilton Place, Canada, captures Crystal at her peak. Her most prestigious assignment was singing *He Is Beautiful to Me* at President Reagan's inauguration. She also continued to tour in Europe, headlining at Wembley Festival in 1988 and touring Britain and Ireland in 1993. Crystal owns a store near her 9-acre ranch in Nashville, which specializes in Waterford Crystal and Swedish Crystal.

Crystal Gayle is still capable of producing yet another career single that will get the whole merry-go-round going again. SM

RECOMMENDED ALBUMS:

"We Must Believe in Magic" (United Artists)(1977)
"When I Dream" (United Artists)(1978)
"Miss the Mississippi" (Columbia)(1979) [Also available on Liberty]
"True Love" (Elektra)(1982)
"I Love Country" (CBS UK)(1987)
"The Best of Crystal Gayle" (Warner Bros.)(1987)
"Three Good Reasons" (Liberty)(1992)

GEEZINSLAW BROTHERS

When Formed: **1959**

SAM ALLRED

(Comedy, Singer, Mandolin)

Given Name: **Sam Norris Allred**
Date of Birth: **May 5, 1938**
Where Born: **Austin, Texas**
Married: **1. Margie (div.)**
2. Karen
Children: **Alison**

SON

(Comedy, Singer, Guitar)

Given Name: **Raymond DeWayne Smith**
Date of Birth: **September 17, 1946**
Where Born: **Austin, Texas**
Married: **Leslie**
Children: **Amy**

The Geezinslaws have been playing together over thirty-four years and still can't make up their minds whether they're a comedy team that sings Country music, or a Country music band that does comedy. Furthermore, they're not brothers and they are not named Geezinslaw.

The "brothers" met at high school in their hometown of Austin, Texas. Sam Allred and DeWayne Smith began picking and singing and decided on the name Geezinslaw because they thought it sounded funny. Sam played mandolin and "Son" played guitar and they began making appearances around their hometown. Their big break came in 1961, when Arthur Godfrey, who was in Houston, saw them and was so impressed that he invited them to New York to appear on his show. They stayed in the Big Apple until the 1970's.

During this time, they appeared on CBS-TV and at the Latin Quarter, Basin Street East and the Bitter End clubs. In 1963, they cut an album for Columbia Records entitled ***The Kooky World of the Geezinslaw Brothers*** and in 1966 through 1969, they recorded four albums for Capitol, ***Can You Believe***; ***My Dirty, Lowdown, Rotten, Cotton-Pickin', Little Darlin'; Chubby (Please Take Your Love to Town);*** and ***The Geezinslaws Are Alive (and Well)***. From these albums, they had three Country chart singles, *You Wouldn't Put the Shuck on Me* (Top 70, 1966), *Change of Wife* (Top 60) and *Chubby (Please Take Your Love to Town)* (Top 50) (both in 1967).

On their first out of town gig, they headlined a show at the Edgewater Beach Hotel in Chicago. They carried on from there, playing all over the U.S., and in California, they played at the Hollywood Bowl. They appeared on *The Tonight Show* five times and played the Hollywood Palace. In New York, they played at Carnegie Hall and on the *Ed Sullivan Show* and the *Jackie Gleason Show*. Other places played have been Las Vegas, Lake Tahoe, Reno and they have traveled abroad to Europe, Canada, Puerto Rico and Aruba. The Geezlinslaw Brothers have appeared with many famous stars, including Glen Campbell, Bobbie Gentry, Eddy Arnold, and Buck Owens, and they have have played on every Willie Nelson Picnic.

They returned to Austin in 1971 and Sam could be heard co-hosting the morning show on radio KVET. In Austin, they appeared at that city's honky tonk club, the Broken Spoke. In 1979, they turned up on Willie Nelson's Lone Star label with an album, ***If You Think I'm Crazy***. During the early 80's, the Geezinslaws opened Merle Haggard's shows at Hurrah's in Lake Tahoe and Reno.

When they came to Nashville to cut their albums for Capitol back in the late 60's, they met Ralph Emery and appeared on his all-night radio show on WSM. Ralph became a friend and a fan and had them on his *Pop Goes the Country* TV show. For seven years, the Geezinslaws disappeared from the Country music scene, re-emerging only once or twice a year for an appearance at a Willie Nelson Picnic or on *Pop Goes the Country*. They made their first appearance on Ralph Emery's TV show, *Nashville Now,* in February 1986.

In 1989, the Geezinslaws released their eponymous album for Step One. They followed this in 1990 with ***World Tour***. Both these albums were a mix of comedy and straight Country. In 1992, they released another album, ***Feelin' Good, Gittin' Up Gittin' Down***, which yielded *Help, I'm White and I Can't Get Down*, which gave them their first Country chart entry for twenty-five years, when it made the Top 60. They also released their version of Robert Earl Keen's song *Copenhagen*. With this renewed career, they started to be more visible. They were to be seen on *Austin City Limits* and the *Texas Connection*, both taped in Austin. They made further appearances in 1993 at the Broken Spoke in Austin, Texas, and on *Nashville Now*. That year they released a video of extracts from their appearances with Ralph Emery on *Nashville Now*, entitled *What a Crowd! What a Night*. In 1994, the "brothers" released the album ***I Wish I Had a Job to Shove***. Both these last two albums concentrated on the comedy aspect of their career.

They were nominated in the TNN/Music City News Comedy Award selection in both, 1992 and 1993 Awards. JAB

RECOMMENDED ALBUMS:

"The Kooky World of the Geezinslaw Brothers" (Columbia)(1963)
"Can You Believe" (Capitol)(1967)
"My Dirty, Lowdown, Rotten, Cotton-Pickin' Little Darlin'" (Capitol)(1967)
"Chubby (Please Take Your Love to Town)" (Capitol)(1968)
"The Geezinslaws Are Alive (And Well)" (Capitol)(1969)
"If You Think I'm Crazy Now" (Lone Star)(1979)
"The Geezinslaws" (Step One)(1989)
"World Tour" (Step One)(1990)
"Feelin' Good, Gittin' Up Gittin' Down" (Step One)(1992)
"I Wish I Had a Job to Shove" (Step One)(1994)
Video:
"What a Crowd! What a Night" (Step One)(1993) [With Ralph Emery]

BOBBIE GENTRY

(Singer, Songwriter, Guitar, Banjo, Bass, Piano, Vibes, Autoharp, Dancer)

Given Name: **Roberta Streeter**
Date of Birth: **July 27, 1944**
Where Born: **Chickasaw County, Mississippi**
Married: **1. William Harrah (div.)**
2. Jim Stafford (m. 1978)(div.)

With one record, beautiful and talented Bobbie Gentry leapt onto the international stage. *Ode to Billy Joe* was filled with such a three-dimensional feeling that it was difficult to follow.

From age 6, Bobbie, of Portuguese descent, was raised by her grandparents in a farmhouse in Chickasaw County, Mississippi. By the time she was 7, it was obvious to them that she had musical inclinations and they traded a cow for a piano. Bobbie taught herself to play by watching the local church pianist. The year she got her piano was also the year that she wrote her first song, *My Dog Sergeant Is a Good Dog*, which later became a part of her nightclub act.

When Bobbie was 13, the family moved to Palm Springs, California. It was there that she acquired her instrumental skills. Here also she started to perform in the neighborhood country club. After graduation she went to the University of California at Los Angeles (UCLA) and majored in philosophy. Bobbie played the occasional gig to help pay for her studies. She then transferred her seat of learning to Los Angeles Conservatory of Music, studying theory, composition and counterpoint.

After leaving college, Bobbie worked with various theater groups and then went to Las Vegas where she got work as a dancer. She took on her performing name after seeing the movie *Ruby Gentry*. In 1967, having gotten together a bunch of songs all with that swamp feel, she did the rounds of the West Coast labels.

That year, Capitol signed her and her first single was the self-penned *Ode to Billy Joe* and it became a monster. It topped the Pop charts for 4 weeks out of 14 on the charts and became a Top 20 Country hit. It was also very big in Europe and went to No.13 in the U.K. As would be expected, the awards flowed in. Both the single and the album of the same name were Certified Gold before the year was out and Bobbie won three Grammys for "Best Vocal Performance, Female," "Best New Artist" and "Best Contemporary Female Solo Performance." She was also named the year's "Most Promising Female Vocalist" by ACM.

The follow-up, *I Saw an Angel Die*, did die and it looked like Bobbie might become a one-hit wonder. *Okolona River Bottom Band* charted and peaked in the Top 60. Her first record for 1968, *Louisiana Man*, made it to the Top 100 on the Pop chart and instantly fell out and only did marginally better in the Country lists, with her next single totally bombing.

Then at the end of the year, Bobbie got together with Glen Campbell. Their single *Mornin' Glory* made the Pop Top 75 and the flip-side, *Less of Me*, became a Top 30 Country success. They followed this, the next year, with their version of the former Everly Brothers hit *Let It Be Me*. The single peaked in the Top 40 on the Pop list and in the Top 20 on the Country chart. In the U.K., Bobbie had a No.1 hit with *I'll Never Fall in Love Again*, which was not released in the U.S. In 1970, the duo released their rendition of another Everlys' past hit, *All I Have to Do Is Dream*. This made the Country Top 10 and crossed into the Pop Top 30. It had already made the No.3 position in the U.K. at the end of 1969. This would be Bobbie and Glen's last chart single. However, they had the satisfaction of knowing that their eponymous album had gone Gold in 1969.

Later in 1970, Bobbie had two more basement-level successes with *He Made a Woman Out of Me* and *Apartment 21*. She also had a Top 50 hit with *Raindrops Keep Fallin' on My Head*, in Britain. Her last recording for the label was in 1972, when she cut *Girl from Cincinnati/You and Me Together*. In 1976, a movie was made based on *Ode to Billy Joe*, and Bobbie had the record back in the Pop charts. In fact she had two versions, the original and the one re-recorded for the soundtrack.

As can be seen from the success of her records in Britain, and for that matter the rest of Europe, Bobbie was very popular there. This stemmed in part from her success at the *San Remo Song Festival* and the several TV series on BBC-TV from 1968 into the 70's where she was not afraid to appear in a bikini. Her weekly *Bobbie Gentry Show* occurred after she had created such a good impression on the *Tom Jones Show*. She went on to appear on Armed Forces Radio with her own show and was a much in demand emcee.

On October 15,1978, she married singer/songwriter Jim Stafford but that marriage eventually ended in divorce. In recent years, she has been involved in her own company in TV production.

RECOMMENDED ALBUMS:

"Ode to Billy Joe" (Capitol)(1968)
"Bobbie Gentry & Glen Campbell" (Capitol)(1968)
"Bobbie Gentry's Greatest" (Capitol)(1969)
"Sittin' Pretty"/"Tobacco Road" (double)(Capitol)(1971)
"Ode to Billy Joe" (soundtrack)(Warner Brothers)(1976)

GEORGIA CRACKERS, The (a.k.a. the Newman Brothers)

HANK NEWMAN
(Vocals, Guitar, String Bass)
Given Name: Henry J. Newman
Date of Birth: April 3, 1905
Date of Death: July 1978

SLIM NEWMAN
(Vocals, Guitar)
Given Name: Marion Alonzo Newman
Date of Birth: June 18, 1910
Date of Death: October 1, 1982

BOB NEWMAN
(Vocals, Songwriter, String Bass, Guitar)
Given Name: Robert Newman
Date of Birth: October 16, 1915
Date of Death: October 8, 1979

All Born: Cochran, Georgia

In more than a quarter century of performing, the Georgia Crackers evolved from sounding somewhat like a cross between a duet version of Jimmie Rodgers or Vernon Dalhart and Carson Robison to a smooth harmony trio that might be termed a midwestern version of the Sons of the Pioneers. Along the way, the Newmans expanded to a five-man group and became some of the first Deep South Country musicians to spend most of their careers in a northern locale.

*The Newman Brothers, aka the **Georgia Crackers***

Hank started in music first, working on radio at WCOC Meridian, Mississippi. Later, he went to KWKH Shreveport, where his brother Slim joined him. This duet soon went to WRDW Augusta, Georgia, and then to WTAM Cleveland, Ohio, where they worked with such musicians as Pie Plant Pete. After an extensive theater tour, the brothers wound up in 1931 in Columbus, Ohio, which they made their permanent home.

Hank and Slim got a daily radio program at WAIU and began building a following through the Midwest. Sponsored by such products as Georgie Porgie Breakfast Food and Texas Crystals, they would sometimes be sent for brief stints to stations in Atlanta, Wheeling, Charlotte, and both Lancaster and Reading in Pennsylvania. In 1934, they recorded eight songs under the direction of Art Satherley that were released on the Vocalion label as "Hank & Slim." Hank played guitar and both brothers contributed vocals in a variety of combinations.

In 1935, Bob Newman joined his older

brothers and began playing bass with them. By the end of the decade, they had added lead guitar and fiddle to their group, taking the name Georgia Crackers and developing more of a Sons of the Pioneers sound.

WWII broke up the group for a time, but they later reassembled their best-known band, which included Allan Myers on lead guitar and Johnnie Spies on accordion. In the later 40's, they divided their time between Hollywood and Columbus. In California, they made three Columbia pictures with Charles Starrett in the "Durango Kid" series (see Movie Section). The movies were *Fighting Frontiersman* (1946), *South of the Chisholm Trail* (1947) and *Desert Vigilante* (1949).

They also had a regular program on KXLA Pasadena and Slim Newman cut a pair of single discs on the Black and White label. The entire band contracted with RCA Victor and had sessions in Chicago in 1947 and January 1949, that resulted in a dozen released sides. While working out of Columbus, the Crackers had a daily radio program on WHKC which was carried by many stations on the Mutual Network. During this time, a girl vocalist named Janie Swetman often appeared with them. From 1950, they remained in the Ohio capital city year-round until 1958, when changing styles and Bob's ill-health forced the Newmans to disband. After their Victor contract expired, they had a final session with Robin Records.

In the early 50's, Bob Newman, who had written many of the Crackers' songs, also had a solo recording career on the King label. He waxed some 25 songs, including *Lonesome Truck Driver's Blues* and *Phfft, You Were Gone*, which Archie Campbell, Geordie Tapp, and various guests sang almost weekly on *Hee Haw* for many years. Bob also composed *The Leaf of Love,* which became a hit for Gene Autry and which others recorded as well.

In 1954, Hank Newman and his wife, Donna, opened a restaurant where Slim and his wife also worked. Bob Newman moved to Arizona, where he did deejay work at KHAT Phoenix for a time, and then he and his wife managed a trailer park. The Georgia Crackers reunited in the late 60's long enough to cut an album. After Hank's and Slim's deaths, their wives continued in the restaurant business, which is still operating in suburban Columbus.

IMT

RECOMMENDED ALBUMS

"The Georgia Crackers" (Jewel)(1972) [Taken from radio]
"Bob Newman: Hangover Boogie" (Bear Family Germany)(1984)[An expansion of the 1959 album on Audio Lab]

TERRI GIBBS

(Singer, Songwriter, Keyboards)
Given Name: **Teresa Fay Gibbs**
Date of Birth: **June 15, 1954**
Where Born: **Miami, Florida**
Married: **David Daughtry (m. 1988)**
Children: **David Wayne II**

Terri Gibbs came from a Gospel background and after a fair bit of success with Country music, returned to her roots. Possessing a voice rich with soul, not unlike a female Ronnie Milsap, she imbued her tracks with a quality only rarely heard among Country music divas.

Terri was born blind, and taught to play piano by her aunt when only 3. She showed immediately that she had a gift. From an early age, she had musical appreciation. This was almost certainly in the genes, for her great-grandfather had started all-day Gospel sings in Georgia. She started singing Gospel music in a church Bible school program.

She learned harmonies from listening to the Everly Brothers and Patti Page. She learned how to handle a Rock number by listening to Elvis, ballad singing from listening to Pat Boone and her great soul feel from the incomparable Ray Charles. She got her feel for a Country number by listening to the *Grand Ole Opry*. She had chosen well in her teachers.

By the time she was in high school, she was already winning talent contests and singing in local choruses. A meeting with Chet Atkins backstage at the Bell Auditorium in Augusta jump-started her career. Atkins asked her to send him a tape. She did so, and he called her back on her 18th birthday and encouraged her to go to Nashville. As she had just graduated from high school, she did, but without much success.

Terri returned home and joined Sound Dimension, playing keyboards and singing and stayed with the group until 1973. She then went to college for six months and then concentrated on her songwriting. In 1975, she got her own band together and they played the Steak and Ale Restaurant in Augusta until 1980.

*Augusta's pride, **Terri Gibbs***

Songwriter/producer Ed Penney heard a demo tape of Terri's in 1979, but unfortunately there was no address label on it. Shortly after, another cassette arrived and he scurried out to Augusta. Terri signed to MCA and in 1980, with Penney at the production helm, her debut album was released. ***Somebody's Knockin'*** was well received. During 1980, Terri won both ACM's and *Cash Box*'s "Best New Female Vocalist" awards and *Record World*'s accolade as "Most Promising Female Vocalist of Contemporary Music." The album's title track soared into the Top 10 in 1981, staying on the chart for five months. It also made the Pop chart, reaching the Top 15. Her follow-up single, *Rich Man,* made it into the Top 20 and also was a Top 90 Pop entry, while *I Wanna Be Around* only reached the Top 40. In September 1981, Terri made her debut on the *Grand Ole Opry*. Terri became the first recipient of CMA's "Horizon Award" and received a Grammy nomination for "Best Country Music Performance by a Female."

By 1982, Terri had two more albums in the racks, ***I'm a Lady*** (1981) and ***Some Days It Rains All Night***, both produced by Penney. During that year, she toured extensively with George Jones and duetted with him on stage. The 1982 release, *Mis'ry River* reached the Top 15 and *Ashes to Ashes* did well for Terri as did her 1983 Top 20 single, *Anybody Else's Heart But Mine,* which came from the Rick Hall produced album ***Over Easy***.

Then the hits started to dry up. In 1984, Terri released the album ***Hiding from Love*** on Phonorama. The following year, she signed to Warner Brothers and released the album ***Old Friends***, but the best she could achieve was a Top 50 entry with *A Few Good Men* in the spring of 1985.

Then in 1986, she made her return to Gospel music. She signed with Word Records and had two albums released, the title track of one, ***Turn Around*** (1987), becoming a low-level Country success when released on Horizon. Also, in 1987, her song *Before You,* which she had written with Chris Waters, was recorded by the Forester Sisters, and appeared on their ***You Again*** album.

In 1988, ***Comfort the People*** yielded three Top 5 Contemporary Christian hits with *Promise Land, Comfort the People* and *Unconditional Love*. It was a good year for Terri and on April 28, she got married.

One of Terri's greatest personal

achievements was having a new music building at her high school, Butler High, in Grovetown, Georgia, named the Terri Gibbs Music Building. While in New York, playing the Lone Star Cafe, she met romantic suspense novelist Phyllis Whitney and they became firm friends. As a trivia note, Terri used to keep pet chickens. She also has a wicked sense of humor. When writing with John Jarrard, who is also blind, she referred to their writing activities as "the blind leading the blind." She also suggested to John that they write a song called *I'm Blind in Love with You.*

In 1990, Terri signed to the new label Morning Gate and released ***What a Great Day***. Since then, she has concentrated on bringing up her young son, who was born on October 20, 1989. There is now talk about her moving into a more soulful vein and possibly a new album. We can but hope.

RECOMMENDED ALBUMS:

Country:
"Somebody's Knockin'" (MCA)(1981)
"I'm a Lady" (MCA)(1981)
"Some Days It Rains All Night Long" (MCA)(1982)
"Over Easy" (MCA)(1983)
"Hiding from Love" (Phonorama)(1984)
"The Best of Terri Gibbs" (MCA)(1985)
"Old Friends" (Warner Brothers)(1985)
Gospel:
"Turn Around" (Word)(1987)
"Comfort the People" (Word)(1988)
"What a Great Day" (Morning Gate)(1990)

DON GIBSON

(Singer, Songwriter, Guitar, Bass)

Given Name:	**Donald Eugene Gibson**
Date of Birth:	**April 3, 1928**
Where Born:	**Shelby, North Carolina**
Married:	**1. Bobbi (div.)**
	2. Barbara Patterson
Children:	**Autumn Scarlett**

Don Gibson, one of Country music's premier singer/songwriters, dominated the charts in the 50's and 60's. His songwriting genius has been recognized in every decade since then, as new artists continually take his songs to the top of the charts. As a staff writer for the legendary Acuff-Rose Music, Gibson's songs helped build the company into the giant it is today.

When he was 16 or 17 (he's not sure), he helped form the Sons of the Soil. Initially, in the absence of a bass player, Don took on this role. They played songs popularized by the Sons of the Pioneers. By 1948, they had their own show on WHOS Shelby, although they all still had day jobs. At the time, Don was working for J & K Music, moving and restocking jukeboxes. In 1949, Murray Nash, Mercury's A & R man, took them into the studio with a song that Claude Casey had been sent entitled *Cloudy Skies.* The group also cut *I Lost My Love (The Color Song), Why Am I So Lonely* and one Gibson song, *Automatic Mama.* By the time of the next session for RCA Victor in October 1950, Don had renamed the group Don Gibson and his King Cotton Kinfolks and he was more in evidence. Steve Sholes came down from New York to produce the session which included the Gibson co-written song *Roses Are Red.* The next session in October 1951 contained no Gibson originals and was again produced by Sholes and featured Chet Atkins.

At that time, Don moved from WHOS and became a featured performer on WNOX's *Tennessee Barn Dance* and *Mid-Day Merry Go Round* out of Knoxville. He also started to play at Esslinger's Club, where he stayed for four years. It was here that Wesley Rose spotted Don singing *Sweet Dreams.* Rose offered him a writing deal but Don said that although he appreciated the offer, he would only sign if Rose could promise him a recording contract as well. After the abortive efforts with RCA, Don had signed to Columbia, but again his recording efforts failed. Because of the Rose connection with MGM through Hank Williams, the label was interested in other artists Rose represented. Gibson signed to the label in 1955 and the following year, he reached the Top 10 with *Sweet Dreams.* A few months later, Faron Young's version of the song rose to the Top 3 and Don was under way.

However, his first taste of success didn't last long and in early 1957, Gibson was living just outside Knoxville in a trailer. He was struggling to make ends meet and one day his TV and radio were repossessed. That afternoon, Don wrote two songs at the Biltmore Courts Motel that would guarantee his financial future for life: *I Can't Stop Loving You* and *Oh, Lonesome Me.* (The latter was originally written as *Ole Lonesome Me*, but due to a typo at Acuff-Rose, it acquired its now famous title).

On the strength of these two songs, Chet Atkins signed Don to RCA Victor in 1958. Now, Don didn't much care for *Oh, Lonesome Me* for himself and felt it would be better for George Jones, however Atkins produced Don and released them as "A" and "B" sides of the same single. *Oh, Lonesome Me* quickly rose to No.1, where it remained for eight weeks out of a total of 34 weeks on the charts. It also crossed over to the Top 10 on the Pop charts. *I Can't Stop Loving You* made it to the Top 10 on the Country charts. In 1962, Ray Charles topped the Pop charts with *I Can't Stop Loving You.* The Gibson classic has been recorded more than 700 times and has received in excess of 4 million performances on the radio.

Blue Blue Day was Don's follow-up single in 1958 and it became a No.1 Country and Top 20 Pop hit, remaining on the charts for 24 weeks. Later that year, Gibson scored another double-sided hit with *Give Myself a Party* (Top 5) and *Look Who's Blue* (Top 10) and was invited to join the *Grand Ole Opry.*

Gibson's chart dominance continued in 1959 with the Top 5 hits *Who Cares* (the flip-

Don Gibson** (3rd left) with **Roy Acuff, Hank Williams, Jr.**, and **Carl Smith

side, *A Stranger to Me*, went Top 30) and *Don't Tell Me Your Troubles*. In between the two, he had a Top 15 hit with *Lonesome Old House*. He began the new decade with the double-sided hit *I'm Movin' On* (Top 15)/*Big Hearted Me* (Top 30). He followed up with the Top 3 hit (Top 30 Pop), *Just One Time, Far, Far Away* (Top 15) and hit the Top 10 again with a new version of *Sweet Dreams*. Three years later, Patsy Cline also had a big version of it and it became the title of the Cline biopic in 1985. The hits continued in 1961 with *What About Me* (Top 25) and then followed with a song not written by Gibson, *Sea of Heartache*, which went Top 3 and crossed to the Pop Top 25.

Don started 1962 with *Lonesome Number One*, which also went Top 3 and followed with the Top 5 *I Can Mend Your Broken Heart*. During the rest of 1962 through 1963, Don's chart success was less frenetic and he scored with *So How Come (No One Loves Me)* (Top 25, 1962), *Head Over Heels in Love with You* (Top 15) and *Anything New Gets Old (Except My Love for You)* (Top 25) (both 1963). Although he was out of the charts during 1964, Don was back on the charts in 1965 with *Cause I Believe in You* (Top 25), *Again* (Top 20) and the Top 10 hit *Watch Where You're Going*. The following year, he scored with *A Born Loser* (Top 15) and the Top 10 hit *(Yes) I'm Hurting*.

Over the next two years, Don's major hits were: 1967: *Funny, Familiar, Forgotten, Feelings* (Top 10) and *All My Love* (Top 25); 1968: *It's a Long, Long Way to Georgia* (Top 15). During 1969 and 1970, Don had some duet success with Dottie West. Two of their singles, *Rings of Gold* (1969) and *There's a Story (Goin' Round)* (1970) made the Top 10. Don's major successes during this time were; *Ever Changing Mind* (Top 30), *Solitary* (Top 30) and *I Will Always* (Top 25) (all 1969).

In 1970, Don signed with Hickory Records and scored with *Don't Take All Your Loving* and *A Perfect Mountain* (both Top 20). The following year, he had a Top 20 success with *Guess Away the Blues* and then he hit the Top 5 with Eddy Raven's *Country Green*.

In 1972, Don scored a Top 15 hit with a new recording of *Far, Far Away*. He then had his first and only No.1 with the Gary S. Paxton song *Woman (Sensuous Woman)*. His recording career was reactivated at Hickory and he had hits with *Is This the Best I'm Gonna Feel* (Top 15, 1972); *If You're Goin' Girl* (Top 30), Eddy Raven's *Touch the Morning* (Top 10) and *That's What I'll Do* (Top 30) (all 1973); *Snap Your Fingers* (Top 15), *One Day at a Time* (Top 10) and *Bring Back Your Love to Me* (Top 10) (all 1974); *I'll Sing for You* (Top 30) and *(There She Goes) I Wish Her Well* (Top 25) (both 1975). During his time at Hickory, Don also had some middle to low-level successes with Sue Thompson, of which the most successful was the 1974 record *Good Old Fashioned Country Love*.

In 1976, Hickory became ABC/Hickory and Don's major hits after this were: *I'm All Wrapped Up in You* (Top 25, 1976), *Fan the Flame, Feed the Fire* (Top 30) and *If You Ever Get to Houston (Look Me Down)* (Top 20) (both 1977), *Starting All Over Again* (Top 20) and *The Fool* (Top 25)(both 1978) and *Any Day Now* (Top 30, 1979).

In 1979, Don had a Top 40 success on MCA with *Forever One Day at a Time*, another Eddy Raven song. Don then moved over to Warner/Curb, where he had two chart singles, of which the more successful was the Top 50 *Sweet Sensuous Sensations*. Don Gibson's success as a recording artist ranks him among Country music's greatest achievers, placing more than eighty singles on the charts.

His greatest legacy is the songs he has written, providing enjoyment for millions of fans and launching the careers of many singers. Gibson's *(I'd Be) A Legend in My Time* helped consolidate the career of Ronnie Milsap when it became a No.1 hit for him in 1974. Emmylou Harris became the fourth artist to have a hit with *Sweet Dreams* when she took the song to No.1 in 1975 and it became fifth time lucky with Reba McEntire in 1979. Tompall and the Glaser Brothers scored a hit with *Just One Time*. The enduring quality of Don Gibson's songwriting was emphasized once again in 1990 when the Kentucky Headhunters scored a big hit with *Oh, Lonesome Me*.

Don Gibson was inducted into the Nashville Songwriters Hall of Fame in 1973 and in 1990, 1991 and 1993, he was nominated for the Country Music Hall of Fame. He was also given the keys to Knoxville in the mid-50's and in 1962, Ray Charles' version of *I Can't Stop Loving You* was awarded a Grammy for "Best R & B Recording." JIE

RECOMMENDED ALBUMS:

"The Best of Don Gibson" (RCA Victor)(1965)
"Dottie & Don" (RCA Victor)(1969) [With Dottie West]
"The Best of Don Gibson, Vol. 2" (RCA Victor)(1970)
"Hits—The Don Gibson Way" (Hickory)(1970)
"The 2 Of Us Together" (Hickory)(1973) [With Sue Thompson]
"If You Ever Get to Houston (Look Me Down)" (Hickory)(1977)
"20 of the Best" (RCA UK)(1981)
"Collector's Series" (RCA)(1985)
"The Don Gibson Collection" (double)(Castle UK)(1986)

GIBSON/MILLER BAND, The

Formed:	**1990**
Members:	
Dave Gibson	**Lead Vocals, Guitar**
Bill "Blue" Miller	**Lead Guitar, Lead Vocals**
Steve Grossman	**Drums, Percussion**
Bryan Grassmeyer	**Bass Guitar, Vocals**
Mike Daly	**Steel Guitar**

In the 90's, Country groups were on the ascendant. What Alabama had started a decade earlier was now being taken up by an ever increasing number of musicians who preferred to work within a band environment, rather than as solo performers. At the same time, a greater degree of rock'n'roll was coming into Country. Music that only a few years earlier would have been booted out because it was "too rocky," was now being hailed as being in the Honky-Tonk tradition. Such a band is the Gibson/Miller Band, a blending of North and South influences.

Dave Gibson hails from Arkansas, where he grew up on Eddy Arnold and Hank Williams right along with Elvis. During the 70's, he moved to Chicago and became a part of the Folk bloom and mixed with John Prine and Steve Goodman. He has emerged as a writer of note in Nashville, having major cuts with *Ships that Don't Come In*, recorded by Joe Diffie, *Jukebox in My Mind* by Alabama, Tanya Tucker's *If It Don't Come Easy* and two hits from Steve Wariner, *Midnight Fire* and *Heart*.

Blue Miller was born in Detroit and played on several albums by Bob Seger and the Silver Bullet Band. His style was then compared to Keith Richards from the Rolling Stones. His musical career was convoluted: singing jingles, winning an Emmy for a theme for an ABC-TV documentary, doing sessions and working in Isaac Hayes' road band. He moved about from Detroit to Florida to Georgia, finally settling in Nashville. He had never played Country music and thought that *Hee Haw* represented the gamut of Country music. When he played a honky tonk, he realized that there was more to it.

Doug Johnson, Vice President at Epic Records, suggested that Gibson and Miller get together to write. When he heard the demos, he realized that he had more than just a writing team. He signed the entire band that made the recordings.

The other members of the band had all paid their dues. Bryan Grassmeyer from Nebraska had played with Vince Gill, Suzy Bogguss and Sweethearts of the Rodeo. He had worked closely with Steve Grossman as one of the most in-demand rhythm sections in Country music. Grossman, from West Islip, New York, had also played with Sweethearts of the Rodeo and in every honky tonk in Dallas. Mike Daly, from Cleveland, Ohio, and Gibson had worked together for some years. He had played steel on all Dave's demos.

Their debut 1992 single, *Big Heart*, with attendant video, made a big impact, reaching the Top 40 in 1993. The follow-up, *High Rollin'*, reached the Top 20. Their final single of 1993, *Texas Tattoo*, had Epic Records mounting a full-blown promotion campaign around the band and the sassy young lady in the video. The band's first album, ***Where There's Smoke***, indicated that the Gibson/Miller Band is a force to be reckoned with. They have called their music "turbo-twang," but it's really just a blend of straight-ahead Country and good old rock'n'roll. In 1993, Epic released a five-track cd of dance mixes from their debut album. In 1994, the single *Stone Cold Country* reached the Top 40.

RECOMMENDED ALBUM:

"Where There's Smoke" (Epic)(1992)

VINCE GILL

(Singer, Songwriter, Guitar, Mandolin, Fiddle, Dobro)

Given Name:	**Vincent Grant Gill**
Date of Birth:	**April 12, 1957**
Where Born:	**Norman, Oklahoma**
Married:	**Janis Oliver (m. 1980)**
Children:	**Jenifer Jerene**

Vince Gill has many talents; he is versatile as a singer and songwriter and is also a golf fanatic. His ambition is to be respected in the business and he would like to feel that when he is older, young and up-and-coming artists will emulate him.

As a young lad, while playing his father's banjo, Vince broke a string. Eager to get it fixed before his father found out, he asked a mandolin-playing neighbor, Bobby Clark, for help. Clark introduced Vince to the acoustic guitar; he fell in love with it and never looked back. He began playing and singing with local Bluegrass musicians and joined a high school band, Mountain Smoke, which once opened for Prairie League.

When he was 18, Vince set off for Louisville, Kentucky, to play guitar with Bluegrass Alliance, which at that time included the now famous Sam Bush and Dan Crary. Vince stayed with them for a year, until Byron Berline called to invite him to join his group, Sundance, based in Los Angeles. He spent two satisfying years with Berline, before making another change. While accompanying a friend on his Prairie League audition (50 guitarists were auditioned), Vince wondered whether they would remember him from when Mountain Smoke opened for them. Not only did they remember him, but offered him a job on the spot. He became the lead singer in 1979 and stayed for three years. The group recorded six of Vince's songs on the album ***Firin' Up*** and also a single of his composition *I'm Almost Ready*. During that time, Rodney Crowell offered him a job with the Cherry Bombs, which he declined, but remained firm friends with Crowell.

Then he left Pure Prairie League to spend more time with his wife, Janis, who was pregnant. Janis was already an established act with her sister Kristine (Sweethearts of the Rodeo), on the West Coast Bluegrass circuit when Vince and she first met and it took three years for him to get his first date with her. However, they married in 1980. Vince contacted Rodney Crowell and offered his services if ever an opening should arise for a high harmony singer who plays guitar. He was taken up on the offer.

Tony Brown, who played keyboards for the Cherry Bombs and handled A & R for RCA, signed Vince to the label and in 1984, Vince and Janis moved to Nashville. That year, Vince cut his first record, a mini-album, ***Turn Me Loose***. He reached the Top 40 with the second single, *Victim of Life's Circumstances*. He was chosen ACM's "Top New Male Vocalist of the Year" that year. His next single that year was *Oh Carolina*, which also reached the Top 40.

In 1985 after a Top 40 hit, *True Love*, he went into the Top 10 with *If It Weren't for Him* (on which Rosanne Cash did harmonies) and *Oklahoma Borderline*. His only chart record in 1986 was one top 40 hit, *With You*. In 1987, Vince released his second album, ***The Things that Matter***. That year, *Cinderella* shot up to the Top 5, followed by a Top 20 hit, *Let's Do Something*. From his third album on RCA, ***The Way Back Home***, two songs telling of his own circumstances (with tongue in cheek), *Everybody's Sweetheart* and *The Radio*, made it to the Top 15 and Top 40 respectively. Janis was now away on the road a lot, with a revitalized Sweethearts of the Rodeo.

During these years, Vince was singing on records for more than 120 artists doing harmony vocals and playing guitar. He was concentrating on his songwriting and he co-wrote with Rosanne Cash, among others. He started playing with Emmylou Harris as guitarist and harmony singer on the road and he watched as his wife's career eclipsed his own.

A change was in the air and in 1989, Vince joined MCA. Here, he was reunited with Tony Brown, who had moved from RCA just after Vince had been signed by him. Vince was now able to open up and show what he could do. His first album for MCA, ***When I Call Your Name***, yielded *Never Alone*, which Vince co-wrote with Rosanne Cash and which reached the Top 25.

In 1990, *Oklahoma Swing*, a duet with Reba McEntire, made the Top 10 and the single, *When I Call Your Name*, went Top 3 and featured Patty Loveless singing harmonies. This song won the CMA "Single of the Year." He rounded off 1990 with the Top 3 hit *Never Knew Lonely*. The album went Gold in October

*One of Country music's finest talents, **Vince Gill***

and by October 1991, it was Certified Platinum. Vince received the 1990 Grammy Award for "Best Country Vocal Performance, Male" for the single *When I Call Your Name* and NSAI presented him with its "Songwriter/Artist of the Year" Award.

Vince continued in 1991 in similar vein with Top 10 hits via the title cut from his new album, ***Pocket Full of Gold***, *Liza Jane* and *Look at Us*. ***Pocket Full of Gold*** was Certified Gold in 1991 and Platinum in 1992. Many more honors followed, including CMA "Male Vocalist of the Year" and "Song of the Year" (for *When I Call Your Name*), TNN/*Music City News* Cover Awards' "Single of the Year" (for *When I Call Your Name*) and "Instrument Artist of the Year" and *Country Music People* magazine's "International Single of the Year." Vince also won the CMA "Vocal Event of the Year" and a Grammy Award for "Best Country Vocal Collaboration" for the single *Restless* (Warner Brothers) with Steve Wariner and Ricky Skaggs (from the ***Mark O'Connor & the Nashville Cats*** album). Also in 1991, after performing on the *Opry* stage for the CMA Awards, Vince was made a member of the *Grand Ole Opry* and to round off the honors he was asked to co-host the 1992 CMA Awards show with Reba McEntire.

By 1992, Vince had achieved superstar status and his singles that year reflect his following. *Take Your Memory with You* went Top 3; *I Still Believe in You* (the title track from his next album) and *Don't Let Our Love Start Slippin' Away* both reached No.1. The album, ***I Still Believe in You*** reached Platinum status within two months of release and in 1993 was Certified Double-Platinum. Also in 1992, the video of the album ***I Still Believe in You*** was Certified Gold, also going on to Platinum status in 1993. Once again, the CMA made him "Male Vocalist of the Year" and named *Look at Us* its "Song of the Year." TNN/*Music City News* also repeated itself by giving him the "Instrumentalist of the Year" Award. That year, the ACM made *I Still Believe in You* its "Song of the Year" and having been named "Top New Male Vocalist" in 1984, he finally reached the zenith in their eyes, by becoming "Top Male Vocalist." Vince also won two Grammy Awards for "Best Country Vocal Performance, Male" and "Best Country Song" for *I Still Believe in You*. Vince was also named BMI's "Songwriter of the Year."

In 1993, Vince's chart singles were *The Heart Won't Lie* (a No.1 duet with Reba McEntire), *No Future in the Past* (Top 3) and *One More Last Chance* (No.1). Vince was one of the performers on the Eagles' tribute, ***Common Thread: The Songs of the Eagles***, and his selection, *I Can't Tell You Why*, reached the Top 60. That year, Vince was named the CMA's "Entertainer of the Year" and also received the CMA awards for "Song of the Year" for *I Still Believe in You*, "Male Vocalist of the Year" and "Album of the Year" (***I Still Believe in You***). Vince was also a participant on George Jones' *I Don't Need Your Rockin' Chair*, which received the CMA's "Vocal Event of the Year." Vince was also named the ACM's "Male Vocalist of the Year."

During 1993, the RCA album ***Best of Vince Gill*** was Certified Gold, as was Vince's seasonal album, ***Let There Be Peace on Earth***. In 1994, Vince charted with *Tryin' to Get Over You* (No.1) and *Whenever You Come Round* (Top 3). Vince's 1994 album, ***When Love Finds You***, reached the Top 3 on the Country Albums chart and the Pop Albums Top 10.

Vince's other passion, apart from his music and his family, is his golf. He hosts the annual Pro-Am Golf Tournament that is played in Nashville.In 1994, Vince was named the CMA's "Entertainer of the Year" and "Male Vocalist of the Year," making him the biggest CMA award-winner of all time. JAB

RECOMMENDED ALBUMS:

"Best of Vince Gill" (RCA)(1989)
"When I Call Your Name" (MCA)(1989)
"Pocket Full of Gold" (MCA)(1991)
"I Still Believe in You" (MCA)(1992)
"When Love Finds You" (MCA)(1994)

MICKEY GILLEY

(Singer, Songwriter, Piano, Guitar, Actor)

Given Name:	**Mickey Leroy Gilley**
Date of Birth:	**March 9, 1936**
Where Born:	**Natchez, Mississippi**
Married:	**1. (div.)**
	2. Vivian
Children:	**Greg**

Mickey Gilley is quoted as saying that if his cousin Jerry Lee Lewis hadn't gotten into the music business, then he wouldn't have. However, Mickey has enough talent of his own and this has resulted in him being the star he is.

Mickey got a piano when he was 10 from money earned by his mother from waitressing. He grew up in Louisiana playing piano with Jerry Lee and his other famous first cousin, the Rev. Jimmy Swaggart. They performed Gospel music together in the Ferriday Assembly of God Church as well as boogie woogie in high school. Mickey had started to listen to boogie woogie at Haney's Big House in Ferriday.

He dropped out of college when 17 and moved to Houston. By 1954, he had married and was working as a mechanic and construction worker for between 75 cents and $1.25 an hour. After Jerry Lee scored with *Crazy Arms*, Mickey saw how much he was earning and decided to get into music.

Mickey Gilley *plays piano while cousin* ***Jerry Lee Lewis*** *fiddles*

He cut his first single at the Gold Star Studio in Houston but it would take until 1968 before he had a chart hit. In 1958, he cut a solitary single for Dot, *Call Me Shorty,* and then moved to New Orleans, where he did session work for Huey Meaux and cut some sides for Meaux's Crazy Cajun label. He moved on to Biloxi, Mississippi, before settling in Lake Charles, Louisiana, for two years, where he worked Ray's Lounge. When Mickey first moved back to Houston in 1961, he worked in construction again and contemplated leaving the business. He then got a regular gig at Houston's Nesadel Club, and spent most of the 60's there, building up a strong local following.

During this time, he recorded some sides for his own Astro label and for Paula Records, which were released without troubling the charts. These tracks were later released by Paula on two albums: ***Down the Line*** (1967); which was a re-issue of the Astro album ***Lonely Wine,*** and in 1974, ***Mickey Gilley at his Best***. From these came his first taste of chart success. *Now I Can Live Again*, which was out on Paula, made it into the Top 70 in 1968.

In 1970, Mickey was approached by Sherwood Cryer about re-opening Sherry's Club in Pasadena as Gilley's Club. He did, and it became "the world's biggest honky tonk."

In 1974, Mickey recorded *She Calls Me Baby* at the request of his ticket taker at Gilley's, as a jukebox single. The flip-side was *Room Full of Roses*, which had been a hit for George Morgan. Mickey felt that *Roses* had too much steel guitar, but since it was only going to be the flip-side, he didn't bother to do anything to correct it. The record was flipped, released on Astro and started to attract attention. Playboy Records picked it up and it went to No.1 and became a Top 50 success on the Pop chart. As a result, Mickey signed to Playboy Records, which was distributed by Epic.

He followed it up with two more chart toppers that year, *I Overlooked an Orchid* and Bill Anderson's *City Lights* (which peaked in 1975). In 1974, Mickey was named by the ACM as "Most Promising Male Vocalist" and by *Record World* as "Most Promising Male Artist." The following year, Mickey had his fourth straight No.1, with the remake of George Jones' *Window Up Above*. He had really established himself and Playboy. Although *Bouquet of Roses* reached the Top 15, *Roll You Like a Wheel*, a duet with Barbi Benton, only got to the Top 40. However, at the end of 1975, Mickey came back strongly with a Top 10 hit, *Overnight Sensation*. *Billboard* named him their 1975 "Top New Country Singles Artist."

1976 was another vintage year for Mickey. Baker Knight's chauvinistic honky tonker *Don't the Girls All Get Prettier at Closing Time* went to the top, as did the next release, Sam Cooke's *Bring It on Home to Me*. He ended the year with his version of the Lloyd Price rock'n'roll standard *Lawdy Miss Clawdy*, on which he sounds like Jerry Lee. The record peaked in the Top 3. The award givers went ecstatic over Mickey. *Music City News* named him "Most Promising Male" (after six No.1 records!). ACM voted him "Male Vocalist of the Year" and "Entertainer of the Year." *The Girls All Get Prettier...* was chosen as ACM's "Song of the Year" and *Bring It on Home* was their "Single of the Year." Mickey's album ***Gilley's Smokin'*** was ACM's "Album of the Year." In addition, he was awarded a spot on Hollywood's Walkway of the Stars.

In 1977-1978, Mickey continued to rack up major hits for Playboy: *She's Pulling Me Back Again* (No. 1), *Honky Tonk Memories* (Top 5) and *Chains of Love* (Top 10) in 1977 and *The Power of Positive Drinkin'* (Top 10) in 1978.

In 1978, Mickey signed directly to Epic, following the demise of Playboy and *Here Comes the Hurt Again* became his first Top 10 hit for his new label. The follow-up, *The Song We Made Love To*, only made it to the Top 15 but in 1979, Mickey was back in his winning ways. *Just Long Enough to Say Goodbye* and *My Silver Lining* went Top 10 and although *A Little Getting Used To* only just scraped into the Top 20, he was about to embark on the chart voyage of his lifetime. In 1979, Gilley's was ACM's "Nightclub of the Year." They were to repeat this honor in 1981, 1983 and 1984.

Between May 1980 and the end of 1986, Mickey had ten No. 1 hits and nine Top 10 placings, seven of them being Top 5 successes. This was due, in no small part, to the advent and success of the movie *Urban Cowboy*. It propelled Gilley, Johnny Lee and Gilley's to international acclaim. Mickey was named the *Billboard* "Country/Pop Breakthrough Artist" of 1980. His No.1 achievements in 1980 were *True Love Ways*, which had originally been a success for Buddy Holly, *Stand By Me*, which had been featured in *Urban Cowboy*, and was released from the Soundtrack album on Full Moon/Asylum and *That's All That Matters*. In 1981, he had Chick Rains' *A Headache Tomorrow (Or a Heartache Tonight)*, *You Don't Know Me*, which was a hit for Ray Charles the first time around, and the Keith Stegall-Stewart Harris song *Lonely Nights*, which completed an unbroken run of six chart toppers. That year, Mickey had a syndicated radio show *Live from Gilley's* which was carried by over 335 radio stations.

1982 got under way with the Top 3 single *Tears of the Lonely* and then he was back to his chart topping ways with *Put Your Dreams Away* and *Talk to Me*. He made it three in a row with *Fool for Your Love* in 1983 and added one more with his duet with Charly McClain, *Paradise Tonight*, from the highly successful album ***It Takes Believers***. Mickey and Charly won the *Cash Box* Award as 1983 "Best New Vocal Duo of the Year." *Paradise Tonight* represents Mickey's last No.1 to date.

However, the hits kept coming in: *Your Love Shines In* (Top 5, 1983), Smokey Robinson's *You've Really Got a Hold on Me* (Top 3), *Candy Man* (Top 5) and *The Right Stuff* (Top 15) (the last two with Charly McClain) and *Too Good to Stop Now* (Top 5) (all 1984). In 1984, *Cash Box* voted Mickey and Charly "Vocal Duet of the Year" and MCN made them "Duet of the Year." Mickey was also awarded the 1789th Star on Hollywood's Walk of Fame at 6930 Hollywood Boulevard, at Orange Drive. In 1985, he had hits with *I'm the One Mama Warned You About* (Top 10), *It Ain't Gonna Worry My Mind* (a duet with Ray Charles from Ray's ***Friendship*** album on Columbia), *You've Got Something on Your Mind* (Top 10) and at year end, *Your Memory Ain't What It Used to Be*, which reached the Top 5 in 1986.

1986 was Mickey's last year with Epic. *Doo-Wah Days* (Top 10) and *Full Grown Fool* (Top 20) came from his splendid album ***Back to Basics***. Then in 1987, he signed with the fledgling Airborne label and he found that *I'm Your Puppet* and *She Reminded Me of You* failed to ignite the radio stations. The former only just made the Top 50 and the latter reached the Top 25. The cover sleeve had Mickey looking like a cross between Robert Palmer and your friendly banker. Then Airborne went under. At the same time, he severed his connection with Gilley's Club. The club finally closed its doors amid some acrimony in 1989. There would be no more 4th of July Picnics, no more Country music spectaculars from Gilley's. In 1991, his 1980 Epic "greatest hits" album, ***Encore***, was Certified Gold.

He became one of the first Country music stars to open a theater in Branson. He had an album released through Heartland/Warner Brothers that was sold through direct response on television. He has appeared in several movies and TV drama series, including a cameo role in *Urban Cowboy, Murder She Wrote, Fantasy Island, The Fall Guy* and *The Dukes of Hazzard.*

Mickey's hobbies include golf, flying (he has his own jet), tennis and jogging. He is involved with the Association for Retarded Citizens and Hank Snow's annual Child Abuse Fund. He has also performed on USO tours. He is very involved in the Arthritis Foundation and in early 1986 was named Honorary Trustee.

Mickey Gilley is an artist who has had remarkable success in the singles charts and has turned out highly successful and consistently high quality albums. He is someone who could record another career single and be off on another run of chart success and perhaps, with his signing to Branson Entertainment in 1993, his record career will once more take off.

RECOMMENDED ALBUMS:

"Urban Cowboy" (Soundtrack album)(Full Moon/Asylum)(1980)
"Encore" (Epic)(1980)
"It Takes Believers" (Epic)(1984) [With Charly McClain]
"Live at Gilley's" (Epic)(1985)
"I Love Country" (Epic UK)(1986)
"Back to Basics" (Epic)(1987)
"Make It Like the First Time" (Brandon Entertainment)(1993) [Mainly re-recordings of his hits]

For his early material with Huey Meaux:
"Wild Side of Life" (Pickwick)(1975)
"The Hit-Kickers Volumes 2 & 3" (Festival)(1976) [A track on each]

JOHNNY GIMBLE

(Fiddle, Banjo, Mandolin and Occasional Singer)

Given Name:	**John Paul Gimble**
Date of Birth:	**May 30, 1926**
Where Born:	**Tyler, Texas**
Married:	**Barbara Kemp (m. 1949)**
Children:	**Dick, Cindy and Gay (twins)**

For most people four strings on a fiddle would be enough of a problem but Johnny Gimble decided to have a 5-string fiddle as well and adds a fifth more to the pleasure he gives his listeners. His fiddles, like B.B. King's guitar, have names. The 5-string is "Five" and the 4-string is called "Ole Red."

When Johnny was 12, he played with his brothers, Gene, Jerry, Jack and Bill, at local gigs. While still at high school, Johnny formed the Rose City Swingsters with Gene and Jerry and James Ivie and they played on radio station KGKB Tyler. Johnny left home in 1943 and played fiddle and banjo with Bob and Joe Shelton at KWKH Shreveport and also worked as part of the Jimmie Davis band.

From 1949 to 1951, Johnny played fiddle and electric mandolin with Bob Wills' Texas Playboys. For the next eighteen months, he had his own group that became the house band at Bob Wills' club. He rejoined the Playboys in 1953. He recorded with the group in 1964 and 1969.

When Western Swing went out of fashion, Johnny left the business and became a barber and then a hospital worker. He returned in 1968 and became one of the busiest session players in Country music.

In December 1973, Wills put the Playboys together for a new record project. He specifically asked for Johnny and for Keith Coleman. Partway through the sessions, Bob had a stroke and the musicians finished the project as ***The Last Time***. Bob Wills died in 1975 and Johnny played at the funeral.

Leon McAuliffe and Leon Rausch took over the group after Wills' death and Johnny continued with the band for their recordings with Capitol. He appeared on ***The Late Bob Wills' Texas Playboys Today***, which Capitol released in 1977.

In 1975, Johnny was named CMA "Instrumentalist of the Year." He would repeat this in 1986, 1987, 1989 and 1990. He has appeared at the prestigious Wembley Festival in England twice, in 1976 and 1977. At the 1976 Festival, he was with steelie Lloyd Green and stopped the show. He has been nominated twice for a Grammy as "Best Country Instrumental Performance," firstly as part of Chet Atkins' Superpickers and then for his 1988 album, ***Still Fiddlin' Around***. In 1978 through 1984 and again in 1987, he was named the "Best Fiddle" player by the ACM.

During 1979-81, he was a member of Willie Nelson's touring band. He continues to be very active. He is now based in Dripping Springs, near Austin, Texas, from where he still participates in *Austin City Limits*. He has also appeared on many of Garrison Keillor's TV shows.

In 1993, he became involved in a Mark O'Connor TV project about the fiddle and the ensuing Mark O'Connor album, ***Heroes***. Mark and Johnny's track, *Fiddlin' Around*, was nominated for a 1993 Grammy as "Best Country Instrumental Performance." Johnny also worked with Asleep at the Wheel and with some of the Texas Playboys. He runs his own band, Texas Swing, which includes his son Dick on bass. In addition, Johnny markets his own tutorial, ***Intro to Gimble Fiddlin'***.

On the recording front, Johnny Gimble has produced several albums over the years, all of which are consistently excellent and recommended below.

RECOMMENDED ALBUMS:

"Fiddlin' Around" (Capitol)(1974)
"Johnny Gimble, Texas Dance Party" (Lone Star)(1975)
"Johnny Gimble's Texas Dance Party" (Columbia)(1976)
"My Kind of Music" (Tejas)(1979)
"Still Swingin'—Johnny Gimble & the Texas Swing Pioneers" (double)(CMH)(1980)
"More Texas Dance Music" (Delta)
"Honky Tonk Hurtin' Songs" (Delta)(Early 80's)
"I Saw the Light" (Delta)
"Swingin' the Standards" (Delta) [As Johnny Gimble and Joe Bob Barnhill's Nashville Sound Company]
"Still Fiddlin' Around" (MCA)(1988) [Features Dick Gimble]

GIRLS NEXT DOOR

When Formed:	**1982 as "Belle"**
Members:	
Doris King	**First Alto**
Diane Williams	**First Soprano**
Cindy Nixon	**Second Alto**
Tammy Stephens	**Second Soprano**

When Girls Next Door burst on the scene, it had been some while since an all-female four-piece vocal group within Country music had been successful. The tradition of female quartets can be traced back to the Coon Creek Girls, but, although prevalent in Pop, Soul and Disco, Country music had ignored the format for some while.

The group got together in 1982 as a result of producer Tommy West approaching Doris King (b. February 13, 1957, Nashville, Tennessee). She rounded up three singers who, like herself, had all worked in different shows at Opryland and had also acted as backup singers. She contacted long-time friend Cindy (b. August 3, 1958, Nashville, Tennessee), who knew Diane (b. August 9, 1959, Hahn AFB, Germany). One more telephone call and her friend, Tammy (b. April 13, 1961, Arlington, Texas) was recruited, and Belle was born. When it was discovered that the name was in use, they switched to being called Wildflower for two weeks before discovering that *that* name was also in use, and then they became Girls Next Door (initially, the Girls Next Door).

Doris had started singing in church and had raised and exhibited Tennessee walking horses while a teenager. While attending Samford University, she was first runner-up in the Miss Birmingham Pageant. Tammy began singing Gospel music with her mother's family, the Wills Family, and their TV show, which was taped during the 60's, when Tammy was age 6, is still in syndication. While in high school, Tammy managed the boys' basketball team and ran track. After moving to Nashville in 1975, she continued to perform with her family in a Country-Bluegrass band. She is married to Jeff Smith of the *Hee Haw* TV series. Cindy started singing in church when age 6. Her father and uncle had their own Country music show on WSM radio as the Nixon Boys. Her uncle, Charlie Nixon, played Dobro with Lester Flatt and the Nashville Grass. Cindy was Belmont College Homecoming Queen in 1980. Diane spent six years at S.H.A.P.E. military headquarters in Belgium, where she created "backyard shows" with her sister.

The group signed to MTM, where Tommy West was acting as house producer. They spent two years on the road, and then in 1986 they released their debut album, ***The Girls Next Door,*** and had their first taste of Country chart singles success with *Love Will Get You Through Times with No Money*, which reached the Top 15 and stayed on the lists for over five months. This was followed by the Top 10 hit *Slow Boat to China*, which also stayed around for over five months. They wrapped up the year with the Top 30 success *Baby I Want It*. In 1987, they scored with *Walk Me in the Rain*, which also made the Top 30. They then released their second album, ***What a Girl Next Door Could Do***, the title track of which reached the Top 50. They followed up with *Easy to Find*, which only reached the Top 60. In 1988, they had their final single on the label, *Love and Other Fairy Tales*, which only climbed to the Top 75. By now, the label was on its way to closure and the group was suffering from the confusion at MTM.

They moved to Atlantic Records in 1989, and released their Atlantic debut album, ***How 'Bout Us***. The girls hit the Country charts again with the Top 60 single *He's Gotta Have Me*. They briefly hit the lists with the title track of the album in 1990. In 1991, Girls Next Door disbanded.

RECOMMENDED ALBUMS:
"The Girls Next Door" (MTM)(1986)
"What a Girl Next Door Could Do" (MTM)(1987)
"How 'Bout Us" (Atlantic)(1989)

GIRLS OF THE GOLDEN WEST, The

MILLIE GOOD
(Singer, Songwriter)

Given Name:	**Mildred Fern Goad**
Date of Birth:	**April 11, 1913**
Married:	**William ("Bill") Joseph McCluskey (m. 1934)**
Children:	**William J., Daniel E., Michael G., Patrick B., Kathy M.**
Date of Death:	**May 3, 1993**

DOLLY GOOD
(Singer, Songwriter)

Given Name:	**Dorothy Lavern Goad**
Date of Birth:	**December 11, 1915**
Married:	**1. Shelby ("Tex") David Atchison** **2. Raymond C. Motley**
Children:	**Biff Lawrence, Joy Anne**
Date of Death:	**November 12, 1967**
Both Born:	**Mt. Carmel, Illinois**

In an age of great duet singers—the 1930's—the Girls of the Golden West were recognized as the epitome of close-harmony female singing—easily an equivalent of the Blue Sky Boys. Historically, they were the precursors to the Judds, to the Davis Sisters, even to the Emmylou Harris-Linda Ronstadt-Dolly Parton "Trio" group. Throughout the 1930's, as they were heard over big stations and even network hookups from Chicago and Cincinnati, they made history as Country music's first successful female harmony duo. Their ultra-close harmony (stemming in part from the fact that they really were sisters), their well-chosen songs (many written or arranged from a woman's point of view), their high, keening, wordless passages that sounded like two Hawaiian guitars—all these gave them a distinctive style and sound that has yet to be matched in Country music.

The Good Sisters, the ***Girls of the Golden West***

Early in 1933, the Girls joined what was then about Country's biggest radio show, the *National Barn Dance*, over WLS in Chicago. Every year, the station produced, for its listeners, a well-printed, well-written yearbook called the "WLS Family Album" and in the 1933 edition, Millie and Dolly appeared for the first time. They wore knotted neckerchiefs and fringed shirts, with real six-shooters in their studded holsters. The copy insisted that they were two genuine cowgirls who had moseyed up from Texas—specifically, from the town of "Muleshoe, Texas." It was to be a "factoid" that would make its way into dozens of later history books. In fact, the Girls were both born in downstate Illinois in Mt. Carmel, on the banks of the Wabash, near the Indiana State line. Neither had ever set foot in Texas.

The Girls grew up in Mt. Vernon and later East St. Louis, where they listened to their mother singing old songs and learned from her the rudiments of harmony. When they entered their teens, Millie found she could sing a natural harmony to just about anything her sister sang. She later explained, "When I hear a note, I hear the harmony note to it." They were soon broadcasting over KIL and KMOX in St. Louis, quickly changing their family name of Goad to something easier on the listeners—Good. A friend of the family came up with the idea of using the name Girls of the Golden West, which was taken from an old cowboy story by Bret Harte and a subsequent opera by Puccini in 1910. After a short stay on the notorious "border station," XER and KFPI Milford, Kansas, they got a manager, returned to Illinois and got a job on WLS.

WLS not only had, at this time, major Country stars like Gene Autry, the Prairie Ramblers, Smiley Burnette, Bradley Kincaid and Lulu Belle and Scotty, they also had an enviable line-up of female stars, more so than any other station. There was Patsy Montana, Lily May Ledford, the Three Little Maids, Linda Parker, Grace Moore and others.

The Girls' earliest recordings for Bluebird were made in 1933 and featured older Western songs like *Old Chisholm Trail*, *My Love Is a Rider* and *Cowboy Jack*. They soon learned they needed to find new material and in a few months, they were writing their own custom-tailored songs like *Lonesome Cowgirl*, *Home Sweet Home in Texas* and, possibly their most famous, *There's a Silver Moon on the Golden Gate*. They also set about making their own costumes, which became more and more Western and more and more ornate. They used as their models the new crops of movie cowboys on the silver screen, since Millie recalled, "there were no cowgirls of the time that I knew of."

By the mid-1930's, both Girls had married men from WLS. Dolly married the Prairie Ramblers' fiddler Tex Atchison, and Millie wed the announcer and promoter Bill McCluskey. Towards the end of 1937, the team joined Red Foley and Lily May Ledford in a special program for Pinex Cough Syrup. This did so well that it eventually led both Girls to relocate to Cincinnati and station WLW, where they worked for a time on the *Boone County Jamboree*. In 1945, they were voted the most popular act on WLW. They remained more or less active until 1949, when they retired for a time. In 1963, they reunited for a series of albums for the Texas-based Bluebonnet label. CKW

RECOMMENDED ALBUM:
"The Girls of the Golden West" (Old Homestead) [Features Bradley Kincaid]

JIM GLASER

(Singer, Songwriter, Guitar)

Given Name:	**James William Glaser**
Date of Birth:	**December 16, 1937**
Where Born:	**Spalding, Nebraska**
Married:	**Jane**
Children:	**Jeffrey, James Williams II, Lynn, Connie**

For a lot of Jim Glaser's career, it is necessary to refer to Tompall & the Glaser Brothers, the family group that operated from the 1950's until 1973, and then from 1980 on an on-off basis.

Jim's initial solo project goes back to 1961 when he recorded for Starday. During 1966, he signed to RCA and over that year and the next, he had some medium sized hits, *God Help You Woman*, *Please Take Me Back*, *I'm Not Through Loving You* and *Molly*.

When the Glaser Brothers went their separate ways in 1973, Jim had already had several cuts as a songwriter. In 1965, Warner Mack recorded Jim's *Sittin' in an All Nite Cafe*, which became a Top 5 hit and in 1968, Gary Puckett and the Union Gap had a monster Pop hit with *Woman, Woman*, a song written by Jim and Jimmy Payne. Liz Anderson charted with Jim's *Thanks a Lot for Tryin' Anyway*. In 1973, Jim transferred to MGM, the label the group had been on. He racked up some medium to low-level entries. The most notable were *Forgettin' 'Bout You* in 1974 and his version of *Woman, Woman* the following year.

In 1982, Jim entered his most successful solo period. He signed with Noble Vision and reached the Top 20 with *When You're Not a Lady*. The follow-up, *You Got Me Running*, made the Top 30. *The Man in the Mirror*, which was the title of his highly successful debut album for the label, reached the Top 20 in 1983. The following year was a halcyon one for Jim. *If I Could Only Dance with You* received public favor and got to the Top 10 and that was followed by his first No.1, *You're Gettin' to Me Again*, which stayed on the charts for nearly six months. That was succeeded by *Lay Me Down Easy*, another Top 20 entry.

During 1985, Noble Vision merged their interests into MCA, and despite the release of two more albums, ***Past the Point of No Return*** and ***Everybody Knows I'm Yours***, the steam had gone out of Jim's success level. Only *In Another Minute* reached the Country Top 30. Then suddenly, after all the success, Jim was without a label.

He now concentrates on his stage show which includes a "Tribute to Marty Robbins." He had, after all, played on Marty's monster hit, *El Paso*.

RECOMMENDED ALBUMS:

"Just Looking for a Home" (Starday)(1961)
"The Man in the Mirror" (Noble Vision/MCA)(1983)
"Past the Point of No Return" (Noble Vision/MCA)(1984)
"Everybody Knows I'm Yours" (Noble Vision/MCA)(1984)
"The Very Best of Jim Glaser" (Country Store UK)(1985)

TOMPALL GLASER

(Lead Vocals, Songwriter, Guitar, Ukulele)

Given Name: Thomas Paul Glaser
Where Born: Spalding, Nebraska
Date of Birth: September 3, 1933
Married: 1. Rosemarie (div.)
2. Dorothy June

Of the three Glaser brothers, Tompall is probably the one with the highest public persona. In 1959, Jimmy Newman had a Top 10 hit with Tompall's song, *You're Makin' a Fool Out of Me*. In 1964, Flatt & Scruggs recorded Tompall's song *I Don't Care Anymore*. In 1966, Bobby Bare had a Top 5 hit with the Tompall Glaser-Harlan Howard song *The Streets of Baltimore* and Jimmy Dean had a Top 10 single with Tompall's *Stand Beside Me*.

Following the breakup of Tompall & the Glaser Brothers in 1973, Tompall very firmly nailed his colors to the "outlaw" movement mast. He continued with MGM, who had released the group's product and in 1972, Tompall released the album ***Tompall (Of Tompall & the Glaser Brothers)***. In 1973 Tompall's album ***Charlie*** appeared. His first three chart singles did not fare well, with the 1974 release *Musical Chairs* doing the best, going Top 70. This single came from the 1975 album ***Tompall (Sings the Songs of Shel Silverstein)***, which also yielded the 1975 single *Put Another Log on the Fire (Male Chauvinist National Anthem)*, which went Top 25. That year, Tompall also put together his Outlaw Band, made up of Fred Newell (electric guitar), Mel Brown (electric lead guitar), Ted Reynolds (bass guitar), Ben Keith (Dobro) and Charles Polk (drums), although Billy Williams (lead guitar) and "Big" Jim Webb (Dobro) played on record sessions.

In 1976, the album ***The Great Tompall and his Outlaw Band*** was released. It featured a mixture of old songs and new, and included a track with Tompall on ukulele (*Tompall in "D" on the Ukulele*). This track was featured in the 1977 movie *Thieves*. Musicians on the album as well as the band were Ralph Mooney, Johnny Gimble, Norman Blake, Willie Rainsford, Hargus "Pig" Robbins, Waylon Jennings, Troy Seals, Kyle Lehning and Bobby Thompson.

Tompall moved to Polydor, where his single *T for Texas* went Top 40. That year, Tompall got together with Waylon Jennings and Jessi Colter for the ground breaking ***Wanted! The Outlaws***, an album that, by 1985, had sold over 2 million copies. In 1977, ***Tompall and his Outlaw Band*** was released by ABC and yielded the Top 50 single *It'll Be Her*. Later that year, Tompall released another album on ABC, ***The Wonder of It All***, from which came two basement chart entries, *It Never Crossed My Mind* (1977) and *Drinking Them Beers* (1978).

Following the reunion of Tompall & the Glaser Brothers in 1979 and their final separation in 1983, Tompall returned to working in his recording studio in Nashville and encouraging new writers that included Gary Vincent. In 1986 Tompall released the ***Nights on the Borderline*** solo album on MCA Dot.

RECOMMENDED ALBUMS:

"Tompall (Of Tompall & the Glaser Brothers)" (MGM)(1972)
"Charlie" (MGM)(1973)
"Tompall (Sings the Songs of Shel Silverstein)" (MGM)(1975) [A complete album of Shel Silverstein songs]
"The Great Tompall and his Outlaw Band" (MGM)(1976)
"Wanted! The Outlaws" (RCA Victor)(1976) [With Waylon Jennings and Jessi Colter]
"Tompall and his Outlaw Band" (ABC)(1977)
"The Wonder of It All" (ABC)(1977)
"Nights on the Borderline" (MCA Dot)(1986)

LONNIE GLOSSON

(Harmonica, Guitar)

Given Name: Lonnie Glosson
Date of Birth: February 14, 1908
Where Born: Judsonia, Arkansas
Married: Ruth
Children: three sons, three daughters

Lonnie Glosson, along with Wayne Raney and Delford Bailey, ranks as one of the three most noted and legendary harmonica players in Country music history (other than the more contemporary Charlie McCoy and Terry McMillan), and the only one still living. Although he hasn't always been in the limelight, Lonnie has been around almost as long as Country music has been commercialized. From the early 30's into the mid-50's, Lonnie was a major figure playing his harmonica, singing his songs, and selling harmonicas and instruction books over such radio stations as WLS Chicago, WHAS Louisville, WCKY Cincinnati and various Mexican border stations.

A native of White County, Arkansas, Lonnie was taught to play harmonica by his mother in early childhood and he subsequently learned guitar as well. Cora Glosson supposedly wanted her son to pursue a stage career, but after 1920, the new medium of radio caught Lonnie's attention instead. In 1924, he caught a train to St. Louis to learn the bricklaying trade and also play his French harp over radio station KMOX. For the next six years, Lonnie allegedly wandered over the country playing and singing as an itinerant entertainer. At WLS Chicago, his career took a decided turn for the better as he began to receive a salary for his radio programs and appearances on the *National Barn Dance*.

Glosson continued his practice of moving from station to station every year or so. In the early 40's, he was closely associated with the *Renfro Valley Barn Dance* on Saturday nights and daily programs over WHAS Louisville. During this time he became acquainted with Lynn Davis and Molly O'Day, and taught Molly his composition about the Second Coming, *Matthew Twenty-four*. Lonnie remained with Lynn and Molly as they traveled to WJLS Beckley, West Virginia, and later rejoined them at WNOX Knoxville, Tennessee.

At times, his brother Buck and sister Esther also worked in radio, both with Lonnie and on their own. In 1948, Glosson began an association with the younger harmonica player Wayne Raney. In future years, both men played the harp on Raney's King recordings. They also had many transcribed radio programs selling harmonica and guitar lessons over the airwaves.

Lonnie Glosson seldom recorded on his own in his radio years. He had a session for the ARC group of labels in the mid-30's, on which he cut a Talking Blues-type recitation called *Arkansas Hard Luck* and the instrumental *Lonnie's Fox Chase*. In 1949-1950, he had sessions for Mercury and Decca respectively, recording songs and tunes like *Lost John, I've Got the Jitters Over You*, and *Del Rio Blues*. During the 50's, Glosson cut his best-known vocal number on the tiny Acme label, an inspirational song-recitation entitled *The Old Dutchman's Prayer* or *Gospel Snakes*. This recounts how a preacher used reverse psychology to win souls.

Since live radio as employment for traveling musicians had basically become a thing of the past (with a few exceptions), by the end of the 50's, Lonnie Glosson sought other outlets for his music. He found it, in giving matinee school assembly shows for children throughout the South and Midwest. This has been his mission in life for the better part of three decades, as he entertains while giving subtle warnings about the evils of alcohol and drugs. He has also made occasional visits to Bluegrass festivals, where he demonstrates the brand of entertainment that has made him a living legend.

Lonnie has also periodically recorded albums for Rimrock containing a variety of harmonica tunes, Country, and Gospel songs. In 1980, Lonnie and Wayne Raney got together for a reunion album. When not on the road, Glosson and his wife make their home in rural Arkansas. IMT

RECOMMENDED ALBUMS:

"All Harmonica" (Rimrock)
"The Living Legend" (Old Homestead)
"The Blues Harp Man" (Rimrock)
"Lonnie Glosson and Wayne Raney 'Collectors Item'" (Memory)(1981)

GOINS BROTHERS, The

When Formed: 1953

MELVIN GOINS
(Vocals, Guitar, Bass Fiddle, Comedy)
Given Name: Melvin Glen Goins
Date of Birth: December 30, 1933
Married: Willia
Children: Gregory

RAY GOINS
(Banjo)
Given Name: Ray Elwood Goins
Date of Birth: January 3, 1936
Married: Helen
Children: Arlene, Darlene, Timmy

Both Born: Bramwell, West Virginia

For a quarter of a century, the Goins Brothers have maintained a traditional Bluegrass band of high quality, keeping their base of operations in the heart of their native Appalachia.

Melvin and Ray grew up in a financially poor but musically rich part of southern West Virginia, as members of a large family of musicians. The early musicians to influence Melvin and Ray in the late 40's were Bill Monroe, Flatt & Scruggs and the Stanley Brothers as well as musicians who played the local station, WHIS Bluefield, West Virginia.

Both brothers spent an apprenticeship as key members of the Lonesome Pine Fiddlers, one of the pioneer bands of the Bluegrass genre. Melvin was already a member when Bob Osborne and Larry Richardson had left the group in 1951 and teenager Ray joined them as banjo player. Melvin and Ray recorded a pair of sessions with the band in 1952 for RCA Victor. When the Fiddlers left West Virginia for radio work in Detroit in 1953, Ray stayed behind and formed the first Goins Brothers group with Melvin on guitar and Ralph Meadows on fiddle.

Financial prosperity eluded the youthful pickers. When Ezra Cline brought the Lonesome Pine Fiddlers back to the mountains in November of that year, the brothers jumped at the opportunity to rejoin them. They had a daily program at WLSI Pikeville, Kentucky, and worked personal appearances. The Goins brothers remained with the Fiddlers until 1955, doing two more sessions for RCA Victor in 1954. They also worked with the band again from 1961 to 1964, helping on all their Starday recordings and working a show at WCYB-TV in Bristol, Virginia.

From 1964 to 1969, Ray was out of music while Melvin worked with Cecil Surratt and Hilo Brown. He also played with the Stanley Brothers as lead singer/guitarist and when Ralph Stanley took over the band in 1966, Melvin became "Big Wilbur," playing bass and handling the comedy, often appearing on stage attired in polka-dot suits.

In the spring of 1969, with the resurgence in popularity of Bluegrass, Melvin and Ray re-formed the Goins Brothers as a band, cutting an album, ***Bluegrass Hits: Old and New***, on the Rem label. Melvin has promoted a number of festivals in Kentucky, Ohio and West Virginia, and the band has remained quite active with Bluegrass festivals.

The band has had several splendid alumni and has featured the fine fiddling of Buddy Griffin, Joe Meadows and Art Stamper among others. Quality mandolin pickers have included Curley Lambert, Danny Jones and John Keith. Melvin and Ray's youngest brother, Conley, has periodically played bass in the band, vocalizing in a George Jones style. A women's Gospel quartet, the Woodettes, comprised of Melvin's wife, Willia, and her sisters, sometimes also appear with the band.

*Bluegrass stars the **Goins Brothers**, with younger brother, Conway*

They followed up their Rem album with ***Bluegrass Country*** in 1970 for Jalyn. They switched to Jessup the following year and recorded three of their best albums (see below). A fourth appeared some years later as a cassette on Plantation. In 1975, they signed to Dick Freeland's Rebel Records, where they released four albums (see below) featuring Buddy Griffin and Curley Lambert. Their two Old Homestead albums (see below) contain fiddling by Art Stamper and several vocals by mandolin player Danny Jones, which the brothers did not perform elsewhere.

In the later 80's, Melvin had a group within the group, nicknamed the Shedhouse Trio. It performed both comedy and Western songs. During the winter season, the Goins Brothers often supplement their work by doing shows in eastern Kentucky's elementary schools and since 1974, they have also appeared on a weekly program over WKYH-TV Hazard/Lexington, Kentucky.

In 1988, they signed with Vetco, where Lou Ukelson produced their best recording to date. Since then, they have brought out recordings on Riverside cassettes, including a fine live concert at the University of Chicago Folk Festival.

In the spring of 1991, the Goins Brothers contracted with Hay Holler Harvest of Blacksburg, Virginia, a firm dedicated to producing cds of quality traditional Bluegrass.

IMT

RECOMMENDED ALBUMS:

"Bluegrass Hits: Old and New" (Rem)(1969)
"In the Head of the Holler" (Jessup-Michigan Bluegrass)(1972)
"A Tribute to the Lonesome Pine Fiddlers" (Jessup-Michigan Bluegrass)(1973)
"God Bless Her, She's My Mother" (Jessup-Michigan Bluegrass)(1974)
"The Goins Brothers" (Rebel)(1975)
"On the Way Home" (Rebel)(1976)
"Take This Hammer" (Rebel)(1977)
"Wandering Soul" (Rebel)(1980)
"At Their Best" (Old Homestead)(1981)
"Sweet Sunny South" (Old Homestead)(1985)

BRIAN GOLBEY

(Fiddle, Singer, Songwriter, Harmonica, Guitar, Melodeon)

Given Name:	**Brian James Golbey**
Date of Birth:	**February 5, 1939**
Where Born:	**Pycombe, Sussex, England**
Married:	**1. Sandra Youngman (div.)** **2. Sandi Stubbs (m. 1980)**
Children:	**James, David, Daniel**

One of Brian Golbey's claims to fame is that he started the first Country music club in the U.K., together with friend Jim Marshall, who is a founding member and current President of the British Country Music Association. This was during the Folk revival of 1964-1965.

The son of a cowman, Brian inherited his father's love of early American Country music and sang along with the old records which were constantly playing in their home. Before the age of 11, Brian had already mastered the harmonica and the old-fashioned melodeon, which his father also played. For his eleventh birthday present, Brian was given a guitar and a chord chart and soon mastered both. Soon he was playing along with the Jimmie Rodgers and Carson J. Robison records. Guitars were not generally seen in the U.K. in 1950 except in Western movies and occasionally in a dance band.

At the Coronation of Queen Elizabeth II in 1953, Brian earned his first money playing, when he performed *Little Joe the Wrangler* and *When the Work's All Done This Fall*, at the local celebrations. Brian next started to learn to play the fiddle. His grandfather had brought back an old instrument from France during WWI.

While Brian was in the Army, he entertained at various military concerts. After he was discharged, Brian began playing on the emerging Folk club circuit and in 1966, he turned professional. He appeared principally at Folk clubs and then in September 1967, he teamed up with Pete Stanley, an excellent banjo player. They toured extensively and made regular radio and TV appearances. After a couple of years in Florence and Rome in Italy, Brian decided in 1970 that his future lay in the now emerging Country music scene in England and he embarked on a solo career. He made his first recordings in March and later that year, he made his first visit to the U.S.

Brian met many Old-Time stars during this trip including J.E. Mainer, Sam & Kirk McGee and Elton Britt. Brian kept up a correspondence with the McGees for the rest of the brothers' lives. While in Nashville, he met many stars of the day and represented Britain on Fan Fair's International concert. He was invited by Ernest Tubb to appear on the *Midnight Jamboree*. In the shop (from where the *Midnight Jamboree* is broadcast), Brian spotted Jimmie Rodgers' guitar (it was given to E.T. by Mrs. Rodgers) and E.T. let him handle it. During his visit, Brian went on to play the famed WWVA *Wheeling Jamboree* and John Lair's *Renfro Valley Barn Dance*, where he met Old-Time singers Cliff Carlisle and Buell Kazee.

British fiddle star ***Brian Golbey***

When Brian returned to the U.K., he formed a trio to tour with Patsy Montana and Mac Wiseman. Brian was honored in 1972 with two top awards: the *Billboard/Record Mirror* award for "Top U.K. Solo Performer" and the CMA (GB) "Male Vocalist of the Year." The following year, Brian again represented Britain at Fan Fair. He was kept busy for the next few years, touring, recording and making radio and TV appearances.

In 1975, Brian and an old friend, Allan Taylor, formed the Folk-oriented Cajun Moon. The band attracted a lot of attention, but owing to personnel disagreements and other difficulties, broke up after they had made one album, in 1976. That same year, Brian appeared on June Tabor and Maddy Prior's album ***Silly Sisters*** and Terry & Gay Woods' ***The Time Is Right***.

Once again, Brian joined forces with Pete Stanley and from 1977 until the mid-80's they toured Europe on a regular basis. Then Brian decided to cut down on the amount of touring and as a result, the duo only works together occasionally at festivals and clubs.

Brian collects the music he loves and has a sizable record collection from the golden age of Country music. He also writes articles on Country music and does voiceovers for commercials on radio and TV. In 1986, Brian appeared in the Dennis Hopper movie *The American Way*.

In 1993, Brian was honored by the BCMA with the "Committee Award" for his long and continuing service to Country music. JAB

RECOMMENDED ALBUMS:

Look out for Brian's name on U.K. Folk albums.

WILLIAM LEE GOLDEN

(Singer, Songwriter, Guitar, Actor)

Given Name:	**William Lee Golden**
Where Born:	**Brewton, Alabama**
Date of Birth:	**January 12, 1939**
Married:	**1. Forgene** **(m. 1957)(div. 1972)**

2. Luetta Callaway (div. 1987)
3. Brenda Kaye Hall
Children: Rusty, Craig, Chris

For 22 years, William Lee Golden rode the tide of success with one of Country's most well-known groups, the Oak Ridge Boys. Then, in 1987, the unbelievable happened: Golden was notified by letter from the other band members that his career as an Oak Ridge Boy was over. This low note in the baritone's career resulted in a 40 million dollar lawsuit being filed by the singer, but provided him with a golden opportunity, however, to launch a solo career and work with sons Rusty and Chris.

Before beginning school, William Lee was already singing in church. His sister taught him to sing and play guitar and they sang duets practicing at home, singing mainly spirituals and Gospel songs, and William Lee recalls being particularly influenced by Hank Williams' *I Saw the Light*. William Lee and his sister sang on their grandfather's show on radio station WEBJ in Brewton for several years from the age of 7.

He was raised in the rural countryside, the middle of three children: Ronnie, the youngest and his older sister, Lanette. His parents, Ruth and Luke Golden, farmed 40-acres with just a pair of mules, raising corn, cotton and soybeans. To say Golden's early years were spent in a primitive environment would be an understatement, for William Lee was raised without the benefit of electricity, running water, telephones or a car until he entered school. He joined a quartet in high school, and after graduating joined a trio while working at a local paper mill. Golden married his high school sweetheart, Forgene, in 1957, and sons Rusty, Craig, and Chris were born in 1959, 1960 and 1962. It was the early 60's, and Folk music was beginning to compete with the Nashville Sound and taking over the airways with a vengeance. The Oak Ridge Boys, looking for something different from Gospel, jumped on the newest sound and released their album ***Folk-Minded Spirituals for Spiritual-Minded Folks*** through Warner Brothers. Meanwhile down in southern Alabama, young William Lee "Bill" Golden, working with his group the Pilot's Trio, became hooked on the Oaks' music and even worked some shows with them. In 1964, Golden drove to Nashville and offered himself to the group as baritone singer, hoping to replace newly hired Jim Hammill, who he felt was detrimental to the Oaks' image.

The unique ***William Lee Golden***

It soon became apparent the group couldn't get along with Hammill anyway and in early 1965, Bill Golden landed the job and moved from Brewton, Alabama, to Nashville as the Oaks' new baritone singer. (For more information on Golden's career with the Oaks see the Oak Ridge Boys).

In 1972, William Lee and Forgene were divorced at a time when the Oaks were involved in a controversy with the Gospel purists due to their increasingly modern sound. In 1977, the Oak Ridge Boys made the transition from Gospel to Country with *Y'All Come Back Saloon* and eventually crossed into the Pop field with 1981's *Elvira*. During the early 80's, William Lee sang lead on three singles that were hits: *Trying to Love Two Women* (1980), *Thank God for Kids* (1982) and *Ozark Mountain Jubilee* (1983).

During the late 70's, William Lee began growing a beard and sporting long hair. He joined the American Mountain Man Association and lived an eccentric lifestyle as compared to the other members of the Oaks. Although he is generally credited with the Oak Ridge Boys multi-million dollar musical transformation from Gospel to Country, his lifestyle led to friction within the group, which eventually led to his dismissal from the group.

"We've still never had a meeting over that dismissal," Golden recalls. "They fought me over every issue, whether it was wanting to sing Country, or putting a big production on the road, and spending our money on the show itself, and giving the people their money's worth when they would come and see us. And also, passing the ball among ourselves, letting each guy take leads and making it a real group rather than a Gospel quartet. They threatened to kick me out several times before they actually did it. I was threatened with dismissal for things like wanting to record a Country record," he continued, "and not wanting to play on the PTL show and things like that. I was in it for the music business, not being a hypocrite. They also didn't like it because I took too much time with the fans, that was another thing they disapproved of." In 1986, a year before he split with the Oaks, Golden recorded a Pop-flavored solo lp, ***American Vagabond***. The album, produced by Booker T. Jones and featuring Joe Walsh on electric guitar, did disappointingly on the charts. According to Golden, the album evolved from his desire to sing a different type of music than what he was singing as an Oak Ridge Boy. *Love Is the Only Way Out* and *You Can't Take It with You* were the only two chart placements, reaching the Top 60 and Top 80, respectively.

The years following Bill's controversial 1987 split with the Oaks were stressful ones. He and second wife, Luetta, were divorced, he lost his record contract at MCA and sons Rusty and Chris lost theirs at CBS. His father died in 1989 and a lawsuit with the Oaks organization continued on. The 40 million dollar suit was finally settled in 1989 for what Golden says the group was worth 19 years ago as a struggling Gospel quartet before its transformation. In addition, he no longer receives Oaks' royalties.

In 1990, Mercury released the unapologetically Country *Louisiana Red Dirt Highway*, which failed to chart, although it became a CMT No.1 video in 1991. The video features the family farm near Brewton, Alabama, including the house in which William Lee was born. Standing in front of it is his mother, Ruth, waving goodbye as William Lee leaves the farm for the city.

During the years since, Golden has taken refuge in his 200-year-old Hendersonville plantation, Golden Era. The estate includes a slave house built in 1786, a historic 15 room home and a traditional Indian Ceremonial chamber known as a kiva, beside a creek, and acres of woodlands.

As part of a quest for inner fulfillment William Lee often participates in traditional Indian ceremonies. "I respect the ancient heritage of Native Americans," said Golden. "I've learned a lot from participating in and attending the ceremonies."

Sometimes Bill walks up to 10 miles a day. In January 1990, he married Brenda Kaye Hall, a former Miss Tennessee finalist, model and piano teacher. A new album is expected to be released during 1994 on North/South Records, distributed through Atlantic. Golden has also accepted a role in a comedy movie, *Poncho Stine*, to be filmed in 1994. The role will be his first as an actor. William Lee Golden is a man who marches to the beat of his own drummer. After several decades of success with one of Country's mega-groups, he is looking for his own place in life, and no doubt he'll eventually find it. LAP

RECOMMENDED ALBUM:
"American Vagabond" (MCA)(1986)

GOLDENS, The

RUSTY GOLDEN
(Singer, Songwriter, Keyboards, Drums)
Given Name: William Lee Golden, Jr.
Date of Birth: January 3, 1959
CHRIS GOLDEN
(Singer, Songwriter, Drums, Piano, Keyboards, Mandolin, Acoustic Guitar)
Given Name: Christopher Normand Golden
Date of Birth: October 17, 1962
Both Born: Brewton, Alabama

Chris Golden describes himself and his brother Rusty as "Backstage Babies." Born into a rich musical legacy, Rusty and Chris Golden, sons of ex-Oak Ridge Boy, William Lee Golden, began their musical career almost as soon as they could walk. "I was 2 1/2 years old when my father joined the Oak Ridge Boys," recalls Chris. "It was something I was surrounded by all my life and was something I thought I might want to do myself."

Chris and Rusty, until they reached their teens, only knew of Southern Gospel Music "with all the harmonies." Chris credits ex-Oaks sideman Don Breland; Greg Gorden, a former member of the Imperials Gospel group; and pedal steel player and ex-Tanya Tucker veteran John Rich as being his earliest musical influences. "That was all before I started getting into Dan Fogelberg, Jackson Browne, and Karla Bonoff, of course."

Chris never took any musical lessons and considers his ability to hear something a few times then play it a "gift from God." While growing up, both Chris and his brother Rusty spent summers on their grandparents' farm in Alabama, working in the fields and singing in church. During this time they developed an appreciation for family harmonies and a steadfast work ethic. At 15 Chris began playing piano for a group called the Telestials, touring the Southern Gospel circuit. At 18, he joined Cedar Creek, which had Top 10 chart action on the Canadian Country chart as well as the U.S. 1981 produced *Looks Like a Set-up to Me*, recorded on the now defunct Moonshine label, which peaked in the Top 80. This was followed by 1982's *Took It Like a Man, Cried Like a Baby*, which went Top 50. The following year produced two more singles which charted for the group: *Take a Ride on a River Boat* and *Lonely Heart*, both peaking in the Top 90. At 19 Chris stepped out from behind the drums and made his debut as lead vocalist on the *Hee Haw* TV show.

Rusty recalls mainstream Pop garnering his interest around 11 or 12, listening to artists like Glen Campbell, Kenny Rogers and the First Edition, and Three Dog Night. The turning point, according to Rusty, was when he saw Elton John perform when he was 12 years old. "I was a drummer up until then, but after I saw him I started trying to play piano, and that's how I learned, listening to his music, trying to play like him."

Rusty first played drums for the Oak Ridge Boys on weekends when he was 8 years old. At 12, he played Gospel music with the Rambos during the summer and weekends. By the time he was 15, Rusty was playing drums, keyboards and rhythm guitar on an on-and-off basis for the Oaks. At 18 he began performing with Larry Gatlin and continued for several years, both on tour and in the studio, playing piano on Gatlin's ***Love Is Just a Game*** album. In the early 80's, Rusty joined forces with two other young musicians, B. James Lowry and Greg Gorden, to form the Boys Band, a Pop group signed to Elektra/Asylum. The group charted with *Please Don't Stop Me Baby (I'm on Fire)*, which went Top 70 in 1982.

Chris Golden joined the trio the week he graduated from high school. Rusty also began to rack up credits as a songwriter. In 1982, he penned *Back in Your Arms* and *Until You*, recorded on the Oak Ridge Boys album ***Bobbie Sue***. Neither single charted but the album went Gold. He signed with EMI/Combine as a writer from 1987 to 1991. In 1986, Rusty co-wrote with Jimbeau Henson the title track of the Oaks ***Christmas Again*** album. In 1987, the two brothers began recording as the Goldens, charting with a couple of singles released on CBS/Epic and produced by James Stroud. *Put Us Together Again* went Top 60 in 1988, and *Sorry Girls*, penned by Rusty, went Top 70 the same year.

In 1991, on Capitol/SBK Records, the Goldens released the album ***Rush for Gold***. *Keep the Faith* was their one chart hit, reaching the Top 70 that year. The album also spawned a video the brothers wrote and produced themselves, which was filmed in their Alabama hometown utilizing the family farm, church, and cemetery, creating a musical tribute to their roots.

The Goldens currently consist of Chris, who sings leads, Rusty on keyboards, who also writes most of their material and is currently signed as a writer to Polygram, bassist Don Breland, guitarist Skip Mitchell, drummer Buster Phillips, and newest member Bobby Randall on fiddle and steel guitar. Don and Skip both played with the Oak Ridge Boys for many years, and Bobby Randall was formerly with Sawyer Brown.

The Goldens have played a number of venues including Jamboree in the Hills, KZLA's *Country Fest*, Charlie Daniels Volunteer Jam, West Fest, Canada's *Big Valley Jamboree* and Farm Aid II, III, IV and V. "We've always made music our own way," Rusty said. They prefer lyrically oriented songs, with a contemporary edge, Gospel heart, rural rootiness and a Pop edge.

As Chris sums it up, "Daddy always said, 'just take care of the music and it will take care of you.' That's all we've tried to do, and we'll keep on." LAP

RECOMMENDED ALBUM:
"Rush for Gold" (Capitol/SBK)(1991)

BOBBY GOLDSBORO

(Singer, Songwriter, Guitar, Ukulele)
Date of Birth: January 18, 1941
Where Born: Marianna, Florida
Married: Mary Alice Watson
Children: Terri, Danny, Brandy

Bobby has scored his greatest successes on the Pop charts and so, it may be difficult for many people to accept that he is a Country performer. However, his music is a mix of Rock, Country and ballads and this is the secret of his appeal.

While still in high school, Bobby was given a ukulele which he taught himself to play. In his mid-teens, his family moved to Dothan, Alabama. He got his first guitar when he was 15 and soon was singing his own songs at local gigs. After early Country influences, he soon came under the spell of Elvis Presley

*Pop and Country star **Bobby Goldsboro***

and Carl Perkins. Shortly after, he and some friends formed a band, the Webs.

Upon graduating, he enrolled at Auburn University, Alabama. The Webs were still going strong and during his second year at university, Bobby decided he wanted to make music his career. His father agreed, with the proviso that if he didn't make it, then it was back to college for his degree.

Bobby and the Webs auditioned for Roy Orbison, who took them on as his touring band. This association stretched into two years. Bobby and the Big O collaborated on several songs during their time together and after. During the time with Roy, the band opened for the Rolling Stones on their first U.S. tour and toured Britain with the Beatles. In 1962, Bobby went solo and signed to Laurie Records. His debut single, *Molly*, hovered around the lower level of the Pop charts. The following year, he moved over to United Artists Records.

His debut self-named album appeared in 1964, along with his first single for UA, *See the Funny Little Clown*, which became a Top 10 Pop hit. He followed this up with perfect Pop records in the shape of *Little Things* (Top 15, 1965), *Voodoo Woman* (Top 30, 1965) and *It's Too Late* (Top 25, 1966), among others. In 1968, he had a minor hit in the Country charts with *I Just Wanted the Rest*, a duet with Del Reeves.

Then later that year, his career took flight, thanks to the phenomenal success of his rendition of Bobby Russell's song *Honey*. The record sold 8 million copies worldwide and was the biggest selling single of the year. It charted internationally, stayed at No.1 on the Country chart for 3 weeks and was also a chart topper on the Pop list for 5 weeks and was Certified Gold. From now on, Bobby's singles made a dent in the Country chart as well as on the Pop list.

The follow-up single, *Autumn of My Life*, made the Top 20 in both charts. His next major Country hit was *Muddy Mississippi Line*, in 1969, taken from the 1970 album of the same name. During 1969, Vicki Carr cut his song *With Pen in Hand* and had a major success with it. In the fullness of time, some eighty versions of the song would be recorded. Bobby recorded another duet with Del Reeves, *Take a Little Good Will Home*, which stuck in the Top 40. In 1971, he had another career single with Mac Davis' *Watching Scotty Grow*. It made the Top 10 on the Country charts and climbed to the Pop Top 15.

For two years, 1972-1973, Bobby was missing from the Country charts and only had low-level Pop success; however, during this period, he had his own syndicated TV show, the *Bobby Goldsboro Show*. In 1973, he had a huge international hit with *Summer (The First Time)*. The song was the love theme for the movie *Summer of '42* and was instrumental in the record's success. It reached the Top 25 on the Pop chart and in the U.K., it reached No.9, even though its success on the U.S. Country chart was more muted, perhaps because of the movie's subject matter about a love affair between an older woman and a teenage boy.

The same happened with Bobby's 1974 release, *Hello Summertime*. The song, written by Roger Cook and Roger Greenaway, was a Top 20 hit in Britain but failed to make the Pop charts in the U.S. and only reached the Top 80 on the Country chart. Bobby was fading from the Pop charts and appearing with greater regularity in the Country listings. In 1976, Bobby registered a Top 25 Country hit with *A Butterfly for Bucky*.

In 1977, Bobby switched allegiance to Epic Records. In 1980, his song *The Cowboy and the Lady* was transformed into a Top 10 hit by Brenda Lee as *The Cowgirl and the Dandy*. Bobby's version hardly troubled the charts. However, that year, Bobby signed with Curb Records and had another success with the Top 20 *Goodbye Marie*, which made it to the Country Top 20 and was on the charts for nearly four months. He followed up with two more Top 20 hits, *Alice Doesn't Live Here Any More*, from the movie of the same name and the wonderfully ungrammatical *Love Ain't Never Hurt Nobody*.

During 1987, Bobby released ***Snuffy: The Elf Who Saved Christmas***, a book/cassette combination which he wrote. In 1990, he headlined *Jamboree USA* at Capitol Music Hall, Wheeling, West Virginia. He also headlined at the Nashville Gas Celebrity Kitchen at the Fifth Annual Southern Women's Show.

RECOMMENDED ALBUMS:

Bobby Goldsboro is one of the most attractive artists for compilation makers.
"Greatest Hits" (United Artists)(1970)
"10th Anniversary" (United Artists)(1976)
"Bobby Goldsboro" (CBS/Curb)(1980)

Dolly and Millie Good refer GIRLS OF THE GOLDEN WEST

HAPPY GOODMAN FAMILY, The

When Formed: 1940's
Members:
Howard Goodman
Gussie Mae Goodman
Stella Goodman
Eloise Goodman
Ruth Goodman
Sam Goodman
Rusty Goodman
Bob Goodman
Vestal Goodman
Tanya Goodman Sykes
Johnny Cook

This famous Gospel group began in Alabama in the 1940's as a duo featuring Howard and Gussie Mae Goodman, then expanded to a trio composed of Howard, Gussie Mae and Stella Goodman. It then became a family quartet consisting of Ruth, Sam, Rusty and Bob Goodman. Finally, Vestal Goodman (née Freeman) joined the group, which remained a quartet until 1973, when non-family member Johnny Cook joined as the group's tenor. Obviously, various family members have dropped out from time to time. For a period Sam, Rusty and Bob were in the armed forces, Howard served as the Pastor of Life Temple Church and Rusty was a member of the Martha Carson Show and for five years was bass singer with the Plainsmen Quartet.

The Happy Goodman Family's biggest successes came in the 1960's and 1970's. During these two decades they received a Grammy for "Best Gospel Album" (1968) for ***The Happy Gospel of the Happy Goodmans***. In 1969, Vestal Goodman won a Dove Award as "Female Vocalist of the Year." Sam (who became Choir Director of Life Temple Church) was selected the "Favorite Baritone" by *Singing News* in 1974 and Rusty was selected two years in a row as "Favorite Bass Singer" and "Best Male Vocalist." Rusty is also important for his songwriting, several of his efforts, such as *I Wouldn't Take Nothing for My Journey Now* and *Wait'll You See My Brand New Home*, are Gospel classics. In 1978, the family won a second Grammy Award for "Best Gospel Performance, Traditional" for their album ***Refreshing***.

The Happy Goodman Family were original members of the pioneering Gospel TV show *The Gospel Singing Jubilee*. This program won Dove Awards as "Television Program of the Year" in 1969, 1970, 1972-1975 and 1978. They also appeared on several other television shows, including *Weekend*, the *Dinah Shore Show*, and their own *Happy Goodman Family Hour*. Rusty died in 1990. His daughter, Tanya Goodman Sykes, who won a Grammy in 1989 for "Best Recording for Children" for ***The Rock-a-bye Collection, Vol.I*** with David Lehman and J. Aaron Brown, is now active as part of the group Heirloom, with Candy Hemphill and Barbara Fairchild. WKM

RECOMMENDED ALBUMS:

"The Best of the Happy Goodmans" (Canaan)
"The Happy Gospel of the Happy Goodmans" (Word)
"Good Times with the Happy Goodmans" (Canaan)
"Legendary" (Canaan)
"Happy Goodman Family Hour" (Canaan)
"Refreshing" (Canaan)(1978)

STEVE GOODMAN

(Singer, Songwriter, Guitar)
Date of Birth: July 25, 1948
Where Born: Chicago, Illinois
Married: Nancy
Children: Jessie, Sarah, Rosanne
Date of Death: September 20, 1984

Steve Goodman released ten albums between 1971 and 1984 but is best known for writing the Pop and Country hit *City of New Orleans*. Born and raised in Chicago, Steve was primarily a Folk singer.

By the time he was a teenager, Steve was an accomplished guitar player. When he was 14, he began performing at amateur nights in Chicago area Folk clubs. His early heroes were Bob Gibson, Pete Seeger and Woody Guthrie. He was also influenced by the Blues and Hank Williams. After spending some time performing on the streets of New York City, Steve returned to Chicago to attend Lake Forest University. He also began performing at the city's best known Folk club, The Earl of Old Town.

Steve developed a loyal following with his energetic and humorous stage presence. His acoustic guitar skill was impressive and his voice was well suited to his topical original songs. He mostly wrote about the world around him, and tales of Chicago's baseball team and famous Mayor Daly pleased the crowds.

Steve's big break came in 1971 when he opened a concert for Kris Kristofferson at the Quiet Knight Folk club in Chicago. Paul Anka was in the audience that night and after the show Kristofferson introduced him to Steve. Impressed with the writing skills of the young Folk singer, Anka offered Steve a plane ticket to New York and to pay for his demo recordings. Steve accepted the offer and also told Anka and Kristofferson about someone else they should hear. He took his two new friends to hear John Prine at the Earl of Old Town and they were equally impressed with him.

Steve's trip to New York proved successful and within weeks he signed with Buddah Records. His self-titled debut album was recorded in Nashville, with Kristofferson sharing producing chores with Norbert Putnam. The album, released in 1971, showcased Steve's excellent songwriting in *City of New Orleans, Would You Like to Learn to Dance* and *You Never Even Call Me By My Name* (written with John Prine).

Two of the songs from Steve's debut album became major hits for several other artists. In 1972, Arlo Guthrie reached the Top 20 on the Pop charts with *City of New Orleans*. The following year, Sammi Smith hit the Top 40 on the Country charts with her version. Willie Nelson scored the biggest hit when his rendition made No.1 in 1984. The song was also recorded by many other artists including Johnny Cash. In keeping with his philosophy of writing about real experiences, Steve composed the song in 1970 on a train. He and wife Nancy were traveling to see her grandmother in southern Illinois on the Illinois Central train. After his wife fell asleep, Steve began writing down everything he saw out the windows and in the car he was riding in. He then ventured to the club car and played cards with the old men he then wrote about. He chronicled everything that happened on the trip and the real-life tale has become a perennial favorite.

The other song from Steve's debut album that became a hit single for another artist was *You Never Even Call Me By My Name* in 1975. It was David Allen Coe's first Top 10 single, shortly after he signed with Columbia. Coe included a recitation in the song and discusses Steve composing the perfect Country and Western song, complete with mama, dogs, drinking and trains.

After releasing a second album on Buddah in 1972, ***Somebody Else's Trouble***, Steve had a dispute with the label, which kept him from recording for two years. He moved to Asylum Records in 1976. His first release on Asylum was titled ***Jessie's Jig and Other Favorites*** and teamed Steve for the first time with veteran mandolin player Jethro Burns, formerly a member of the hit comedy team Homer and Jethro. They became good friends and Burns played on several more of Steve's albums and often performed with him in concert and in particular on the 1977 "Say It in Private" tour.

Steve released four more albums on Asylum between 1976 and 1980. The year his association with the major label ended, Steve and his family moved from the Chicago suburb of Evanston to Southern California. Steve wanted to be closer to the record companies in hopes of securing another contract. When that failed to happen he started, with his manager, his own label called Red Pajamas. Most of his three albums for the label were from live concert recordings that best captured the heart of his music. Both the ***Artistic Hair*** (written about his own loss of hair due to illness and treatment) and ***Affordable Art*** albums were released in 1983.

In 1984, Steve lost his long battle with leukemia and died on September 20. He was first diagnosed with the disease in 1969 but maintained an active touring schedule until 1982, when his treatments became more frequent. Steve's final recording, ***Santa Ana Winds***, was released posthumously in October 1984. JIE

RECOMMENDED ALBUMS:

"Steve Goodman" (Buddah)(1971)
"Somebody Else's Troubles" (Buddah)(1972) [Features Jimmy Buffett, John Prine and Bob Dylan under name of Bob Landry]
"Jessie's Jigs and Other Favorites" (Asylum)(1975) [Features Jethro Burns]
"Words We Can Dance To" (Asylum)(1976) [Features Jethro Burns]
"Say It in Private" (Asylum)(1977) [Features Jethro Burns]
"High and Outside" (Asylum)(1979) [Features duet with Nicolette Larsen]
"Artistic Hair" (Red Pajamas)(1983)
"Affordable Art" (Red Pajamas)(1983)
"Santa Ana Winds" (Red Pajamas)(1984)

CHARLIE GORE

(Singer, Guitar, Fiddle)
Given Name: Charles Mansfield Gore
Date of Birth: October 4, 1940
Where Born: Chapmanville, West Virginia
Married: Gloria Ann Turner
Children: Jerry Lee
Date of Death: June 30, 1984

Charlie Gore starred on the *Midwestern Hayride* over WLW radio and television from Cincinnati in the early 50's. He achieved a wide following with his strong voice and good looks that led him to be known as "the tall handsome guy from West Virginia."

A native of Chapmanville, young Gore made his first radio appearance at WLOG Logan at the tender age of 12. After finishing high school, where he played basketball and married a cheerleader, Charlie moved on briefly to WSAZ Huntington until a job beckoned at WRFD Worthington, Ohio. This station had been opened by the Ohio Farm Bureau in 1947 with programming geared to a Midwestern rural audience. Despite these good intentions and moderate success, WRFD never proved quite as popular with the farm populace as long-time favorite WIW in Cincinnati, which had a quarter century start in gaining and holding their audience. So when opportunity knocked in 1951 for a position at WLW and the *Hayride*, Charlie took it and reigned for a few years as one of the program's premier performers.

As a summer replacement on the NBC-TV network, *Hayride* artists received some national prime-time exposure. When his son was born, the congenial Gore named him after two fellow stars on the program, steel guitarist Jerry Byrd and vocalist Ernie Lee. In the mid-1950's, Charlie moved over to Indianapolis, Indiana, where he worked on both radio and television until 1959.

In December 1952, Charlie Gore began recording on Syd Nathan's King label. His initial release, *If God Can Forgive You, So Can I*, did quite well, but since the Country charts listed only ten songs during this period, it never gained hit status (a fate that befell many high-selling discs in that era). Other Gore numbers also scored well with Country fans, including *I'm Gonna Lock You Up* and *It's a Long Walk Back to Town*. He also did some nice covers for King of hit songs from other labels including *This Orchid Means Goodbye, Dark as a Dungeon* and *Mexican Joe*. Charlie recorded thirty solo sides for King through 1956, as well as a pair of duets with WLW Pop songstress Ruby Wright and a pair with fellow *Hayride* star Louis Innis.

Charlie returned to West Virginia in 1959 working as a deejay at WVOW for a decade and also served a term in the West Virginia state legislature. In the 1960's, Charlie started his own label, Blank Records, and made a few additional sides. He eventually returned to the greater Cincinnati area where his name remained well-known in entertainment circles from his *Hayride* days. He resided in the Hamilton suburb of Fairfield for some years prior to his death. An album of some of his better King recordings has been periodically available in Germany. IMT

RECOMMENDED ALBUMS:

"The Country Gentleman" (Audio Lab)(1959)
"The Country Voice of West Virginia" (Cowgirlboy Germany)(1992) [Previously released on Danny and Castle]

VERN GOSDIN

(Singer, Songwriter, Guitar)

Given Name:	**Vernon Gosdin**
Date of Birth:	**August 5, 1934**
Where Born:	**Woodland, Alabama**
Married:	**1. Cathy (div. 1973)**
	2. Beverly (div. 1989)
Children:	**Steve, Marty**

After over 25 successful years in the music business, Vern Gosdin was rediscovered, when CBS, looking for a share in the so-called "New Country" market, gave the job of finding someone to producer Bob Montgomery. They were surprised that Bob chose Vern Gosdin, a seasoned performer whose pure emotional song delivery prompted his fans to lovingly call him "The Voice." Vern was soon topping the Country music charts.

Vern's early years were full of music through the church and listening to the *Grand Ole Opry* on the radio where his idols were the Louvin Brothers. Vern was the sixth in a family of nine children and he learned to play guitar with the help of his elder brother when he was 13. During the 1950's when the family moved to Birmingham, Alabama, they had their own *Gosdin Family Gospel Show* on KVOX radio.

In 1961, Vern and his brother Rex set off for California. He found himself a job in Long Beach as a welder. Rex and Vern also joined the Golden State Boys, a Bluegrass group with Don Parmley (later the founder of the Bluegrass Cardinals), which later included Chris Hillman. When Hillman joined the group, it became known as the Hillmen. When Chris went on to form the Byrds, Vern remained true to his Country roots and he and his brother Rex teamed up to form the Gosdin Brothers, opening shows for the Byrds. In late 1967, the Gosdin Brothers broke into the Country charts with their original version of *Hangin On*, which was released on a small independent label, Bakersfield International, and went Top 40. After some time together the pair became disillusioned and in 1968, the act was broken up. Vern returned to Atlanta, where he opened a glass and mirror business and, during the next six years, spent his time making the business successful and raising his family, although he still played small clubs locally.

In 1976, Vern decided to go to Nashville to do some recording. He re-cut *Hangin' On* and sold the master to Elektra Records. The song took off and became a Top 20 hit. The flip-side of the single, *Yesterday's Gone,* featured Emmylou Harris on harmony vocals and it became an even bigger hit, reaching the Top 10. He followed this with other hits on Elektra in 1977: *Till the End* (Top 10) and *Mother Country Music* (Top 20). In 1978, Vern scored with *It Started All Over Again* (Top 25); *Never My Love*, a Top 10 hit (featuring Janie Fricke on harmonies), and *Break My Mind* (Top 15). The following year, his hits were *You've Got Somebody, I've Got Somebody* (Top 20) and *All I Want and Need Forever* (Top 25).

"The Voice" . . . ***Vern Gosdin***

When Elektra's Country Division closed in 1980, Vern was forced to look for another recording deal. He signed with independent label Ovation and in 1981 had a Top 10 hit with *Dream of Me*. He moved over to AMI, another independent label, in 1982 and chalked up another Top 10 single, *Today My World Slipped Away*, in 1983. It was quite remarkable that even with the limitations of a small label, he still managed such success.

The following year, Vern signed with Charlie Fach's Polygram-distributed Compleat Records and started a most remarkable climb to stardom. It started with *If You're Gonna Do Me Wrong (Do It Right)* and *Way Down Deep*, which both went Top 5. 1983 ended with the Top 10 single *I Wonder Where We'd Be Tonight*. He continued his success rate in 1984 with the No.1, *I Can Tell By the Way You Dance (You're Gonna Love Me Tonight)*. This was followed by two Top 10 successes, *What Would Your Memories Do* and *Slow Burning Memory*. In 1985 and 1986, Vern's career seemed to be treading water and the only really successful record was the Top 20 hit *Dim Lights, Thick Smoke (And Loud, Loud Music)*, on which Lou Reed handled harmonies. As Compleat ran into problems, so Vern's career seemed to have the brakes applied.

However, in 1987, he signed to Columbia and Bob Montgomery. Vern's first single, *Do You Believe Me Now*, soon ran up the charts and reached the Top 5. In April 1988, this was followed by *Set 'Em Up Joe*, a No.1 Country hit. He wrapped up the year with *Chiseled in Stone* from the album of the same name. The title, which reached Top 10, was named by the CMA the following year as its "Song of the Year."

Alone (1989), the second album, focused on the aftermath of the singer's painful divorce from his second wife. The hits rolled in and were uniformly successful. There was the Top 3 record *Who You Gonna Blame It on This Time*, which was followed by another No.1, *I'm Still Crazy*. In 1990 Gosdin's hits from 1977 to 1986 were re-recorded by Bob Montgomery, and called ***10 Years of Greatest Hits—Newly Recorded***. That year saw a downswing in Vern's chart success. His first hit of the year was the Top 5 record *That Just About Does It*. The follow-up, *Right in the Wrong Direction,* made it to the Top 10, but the label attempted to promote the flip-side, *Tanqueray*, and it died (only reaching the Top 75). The follow-up single, *This Ain't My First Rodeo,* only got to the Top 15, however the last record of the year, *Is It Raining at Your House,* got to the Top 10 in 1991. In October 1990, Vern was hospitalized and underwent quintuple heart bypass surgery. The following year, Vern's singles showed up badly and not one of them made the Top 50. His album, ***Out of My Heart***, also failed to show up in the album charts. In 1993, Vern released a new album, ***Nickels and Dimes and Love***. This time, he was produced by Rick Hall.

As well as being an excellent singer, Vern Gosdin is also a very fine songwriter and one of the most significant meetings of his life was when he met Max D. Barnes. Max talked him into songwriting and the first song they wrote together was *If You're Gonna Do Me Wrong (Do It Right)*, in 1983. He has been writing ever since, not only with Max, but with Dean Dillon, Buddy Cannon and Hank Cochran. His song *Today My World Slipped Away*, which was co-written with Mark Wright, was a final nominee as CMA "Song of the Year" in 1983. Most of the songs on his albums are co-written by himself and his coterie of tried and trusted writers.

If you want to hear real Country music Vern Gosdin is about as Country as they come. Bob Oermann of the *Tennessean* newspaper wrote, "That's why they call Vern Gosdin 'The Voice.' He has the ability to hurt you, haunt you, and heal you. He has the rare gift of being able to make music sound like life itself. He has a talent that can stir your soul." JAB

RECOMMENDED ALBUMS

"Gene Clarke with the Gosdin Brothers" (Columbia) [Features Chris Hillman, Michael Clarke, Leon Russell, Doug Dillard and Glen Campbell]
"Sounds of Goodbye" (Capitol)(1968) [As the Gosdin Brothers]
"The Best of Vern Gosdin" (Elektra)(1979)
"Greatest Hits" (Compleat)(1986)
"Chiseled in Stone" (Columbia)(1987)
"Alone" (Columbia)(1989)
"10 Years of Greatest Hits—Newly Recorded" (Columbia)(1990)
"Out of My Heart" (Columbia)(1991)
"Nickels and Dimes and Love" (Columbia)(1993)

GOSPEL MUSIC ASSOCIATION

The Gospel Music Association was established in 1964 to bring unity to the fragmented music industry. The charter members were southern music leaders James Blackwood, J.D. Sumner, Cecil Blackwood, Torte Pate and Donald W. Butler, Sr. The purpose of the new organization was to promote music and serve as a central resource center where accurate information would be available about artists, record companies and music publishers. The GMA has grown from 41 members in 1964 to 3,000 members in 1994. Membership is available in two categories: professional, for those in the music industry, and associate, for those who want to support the industry but don't work in it. The categories of professional membership include artists and musicians, authors and composers, music publishers, record producers, managers and agents and radio and TV.

The GMA created the Dove Awards to honor the best achievements in Gospel music. The first awards were presented at the Peabody Hotel in Memphis in 1969 before a crowd of about 500. Winners of the first annual Dove Awards included Bill Gaither ("Songwriter"), James Blackwood ("Male Vocalist"), Vestal Goodman ("Female Vocalist"), Imperials ("Male Group"), Speer Family ("Mixed Group") and ***It's Happening*** (the Oak Ridge Boys) ("Album of the Year").

The Dove Awards were held at the Rivermont Hotel in Memphis in 1970 and videotaped for the *Gospel Singing Jubilee* syndicated TV show. Among the winners at the second annual Dove Awards were the Oak Ridge Boys for "Male Group of the Year." In 1971, the GMA moved the annual award ceremony to Nashville. The GMA held its first Gospel Music Week in 1978 at the Opryland Hotel. The following year, the GMA sponsored a Gospel music concert for President Carter on the White House lawn with artists Vestal Goodman, James Blackwood, Dave Boyer and Larry Norman. In 1982, the GMA helped take Gospel music to England, coordinating a concert during the annual Wembley Country Music Festival.

Over the years, the GMA has experienced many changes from its Southern Gospel roots as the music business has embraced a variety of musical genres. Contemporary Christian music emerged in the late 60's and black Gospel gained more exposure in the 70's. In the 80's, many Dove Award categories were added to reflect the expanding musical expression of the message, including Black Gospel, Rock, Country, Metal, Praise and Worship and Music Video. In the 90's, the GMA added a category for "Rap Recorded Song of the Year."

In 1984, the Dove Awards were seen live for the first time on the CBN Cable Network. Glen Campbell hosted the show and Sandi Patti was named "Artist of the Year." In 1990, the GMA moved the annual award show to the TNN cable network and to The Family Channel in 1993.

The GMA celebrated its 25th Anniversary on the 1994 Dove Awards at the Grand Ole *Opry* House, hosted by multiple Dove Award winner and million selling Christian artist Amy Grant. Industry veteran Bill Gaither paid tribute to the southern pioneers and reflected on the changes since he won his first Dove award in 1969. The growing popularity of Contemporary Christian music attracted a major retailer as a national sponsor for the two hour show on The Family Channel. Performing on the Silver Anniversary Dove Award show were Steven Curtis Chapman, Twila Paris, Wayne Watson, Michael W. English, 4 Him, DC Talk, Michael W. Smith and others.

From 1975 to 1986, the GMA gave a Dove Award to a secular artist who recorded a Gospel album. Winners over the years have included Charley Pride, Debby Boone, Bob Dylan, B.J. Thomas, Barbara Mandrell and Glen Campbell.

In 1991, Bruce Koblish took over leadership of the GMA from Donald W. Butler, Sr., who had served as Executive Director since 1976 (he is now the Curator of the Gospel Music Resource Center).

BILLY GRAMMER

(Singer, Songwriter, Guitar, Fiddle, Banjo, Mandolin, Guitar Designer)

Given Name:	**Billy Wayne Grammer**
Date of Birth:	**August 28, 1925**
Where Born:	**Benton, Franklin County, Illinois**
Married:	**Ruth (m. 1944)**
Children:	**Billy, Donna, Dianne**

Billy, a long-time star of the *Grand Ole Opry*, is one of the most proficient musicians in Country music. For many years, his musicianship has graced and enhanced other performers' records.

One of thirteen children, Billy was taught fiddle, at age 5, by his father, Billy, Sr., a coal miner. He soon moved on to guitar and mandolin and while still a youngster, performed at local events. During WWII, he was in the U.S. Army, but upon discharge from the service, he was bent on a music career. He worked for a while in a gun factory, but by 1947, he was a member of Connie Gay's *Radio Ranch* on WARL Arlington, Virginia. Billy first recorded for Plaza in 1949, but without any chart success.

Gay chose the gentle and slow path for Billy and it was not until 1955 that he suggested to Jimmy Dean that the Grammer talent would enhance the *Jimmy Dean* TV show. For three and a half years, Billy was on the show, which came out of Washington, D.C., and when Dean moved to a network show on CBS, Billy went with him.

Billy also played with other bands, including those of Clyde Moody, Pete Cassell, Grandpa Jones, T. Texas Tyler and Hawkshaw Hawkins. In 1958, Billy formed his own band. That year, Monument's boss, Fred Foster, gave Billy a solo record deal and the following year, they struck paydirt, when *Gotta Travel On*, which was based on a 19th century British Folk ballad, went to Top 5 on the Country and Pop charts. Billy followed up with *Bonaparte's Retreat*, but this didn't trouble the charts.

Billy moved over to Decca in 1962 and the following year charted Top 20 with *I Wanna Go Home*. In 1964, he attained a Top 50 entry with *I'll Leave the Porch Lights a-Burning*. By 1966, he was once again on the move, this time to Epic. Here, he had two Top 40 singles that year, *Bottles* and *The Real Thing*. The following year, he charted *Mabel (You Have Been a Friend to Me)*, which made the Top 50 on the Rice label.

Still not settling down, Billy moved to Mercury Records and, in 1968, got into the Top 70 with *The Ballad of John Dillinger*. He achieved his final chart entry in 1969,when his Stop recording, *Jesus Was a Soul Man*, reached the Top 70. Although he didn't hit the singles charts again, Billy continued to put out quality albums on Stoneway and Classic Christmas. Although no longer a session player or recording artist, Billy Grammer continues to delight audiences at the *Opry* with his instrumentals and vocals.

RECOMMENDED ALBUMS:

"Traveling On" (Monument)(1959) [Re-released in 1966]
"Gospel Guitar" (Decca)(1962)
"Country Guitar" (Decca)(1965)
"Sunday Guitar" (Epic)(1967)
"Billy Grammer Plays" (Stoneway)(1975)
"Christmas Guitars Featuring Guitar Chimes of Billy Grammer" (Classic Christmas)(1977)

GRAND OLE OPRY

(Radio show: WSM Nashville, Tennessee 1925 to present)

WSM's *Grand Ole Opry* is not only Country music's most famous musical radio show, but the longest running radio show in the United States. Its complete history can, and has, filled volumes, and its total cast over the years has included hundreds of musicians, major and minor. To a very large extent, its real history is found in the accounts of its individual stars, which range from early pioneers like Uncle Dave Macon to contemporary acts like Alison Krauss and Garth Brooks.

Though the show has gone through low points, such as the 1960's, when it seemed out of step with the cutting edge of the music, for a great many years the show has accurately reflected the trends and developments in Country music. By the 1990's the show had acquired a legendary status, where joining the show became something akin to be elected to the Hall of Fame or winning a Grammy. Veterans such as Little Jimmy Dickens, Bill Monroe, Porter Wagoner, Del Reeves, Jean Shepard, Jan Howard and Billy Walker shared the stage with the cream of the new generation, such as Clint Black, Vince Gill, Patty Loveless, Lorrie Morgan, Randy Travis, and Marty Stuart. And in the 1990's, the *Opry*, pretty much as it has always done, reflected a variety of the different styles of Country music.

The start of the *Opry* was almost synonymous with the start of radio station WSM in Nashville. Founded by the locally owned National Life and Accident Insurance Company (WSM stood for the company slogan, "We Shield Millions") and opened in September 1925, the following month, the station hired George D. Hay to be chief announcer and manager. It was Hay, who had been instrumental in starting the *National Barn Dance* at WLS Chicago in 1924, that got the idea of starting a regular barn dance type show at WSM. Artists like Uncle Dave Macon and Dr. Humphrey Bate, already established favorites in the area, had appeared on WSM informally even before Hay arrived, but in November 1925, when Hay casually invited a white-bearded fiddler named Uncle Jimmy Thompson to appear, cards and telegrams and phone calls poured in and Hay decided to start a regular program. This was listed in the radio logs simply as the *Barn Dance*, and the first regular program on December 28, 1925, featured Macon and Thompson.

Within a few months, Hay had gathered a cast of about twenty acts which rotated regularly on the program. Most were from the middle Tennessee area, and most were semi-professional musicians who held down day jobs during the week. To add color to the show, Hay invented colorful names for the bands: the Fruit Jar Drinkers, the Gully Jumpers, the Possum Hunters. His press releases emphasized the rustic nature of the music, and pioneered the "friends and neighbors" tone still common in Country shows today. Other stars from this first year included the Crook Brothers, who featured a twin harmonica string band, DeFord Bailey, a black harmonica player and Obed "Dad" Pickard, who was the first real vocal star of the show.

In May 1927, Hay found a better name for his new show; after ending a network feed from NBC that featured classical music, Hay quipped to his listeners, "Friends, for the past hour you've been listening to Grand Opera; but for the next hour we'll be listening to Grand Ole Opry!" The name stuck, and Hay continued to build his image around it.

Gradually, Hay and his staff realized the need to attract professional musicians who could work at the radio station full-time. The first professional group to hire on were the Vagabonds, a smooth-singing trio whose signature song was *When It's Lamp Lighting Time in the Valley*. Soon to follow were the Delmore Brothers, Zeke Clements, Asher and Jimmie Sizemore, vaudeville veteran Lasses White and others. By 1933, the station had created an Artists Service Bureau to help get concert and tour bookings for the artists, and a cadre of professional managers, headed by Harry Stone, began to slowly take control of the show from Hay.

By the later 1930's, Hay had several serious bouts with health problems and had to be absent from the station for months on end; this further eroded his power base, and when he really returned in 1938 he found the show was almost fully professionalized, and that his job was pretty much that of scriptwriter and announcer.

The late 1930's saw a number of significant acts on the show. For several years, the most popular were the Delmore Brothers and Arthur Smith. In 1938, Roy Acuff joined and a short time later one of the most "professional" of all bands, Pee Wee King and the Golden West Cowboys. 1939 saw the coming of Minnie Pearl and Bill Monroe. Also in 1939 the NBC network, through the sponsorship of Prince Albert Smoking Tobacco, added a thirty-minute segment of the *Opry* to its Saturday evening line-up, assuring the show a truly national audience. This audience was expanded even further in 1940 with the release of Republic Pictures' feature film *Grand Ole Opry*, featuring Roy Acuff and Uncle Dave Macon. By the time the war broke out, the *Opry* had emerged as the best known of all the various Country music radio shows.

During the war, portions of the *Opry* were transcribed for the Armed Forces Radio Network, and *Opry* stars like Pee Wee King toured military bases on the Camel Caravan. After the war, as Honky-Tonk music and amplified instruments came to dominate the music, it became harder for Hay to follow his famous dictum to "keep it down to earth, boys." Gradually men like Jack Stapp, Jim Denny and Ott Devine took over the actual running of the show. The *Opry*'s stubborn insistence that their artists had to be on hand for almost every Saturday night show meant that the more popular ones had to give up lucrative tour dates for *Opry* scale. This led to defections: Roy Acuff left temporarily in the late 1940's, and Lefty Frizzell left for the same reason in 1951.

In the early 1950's, the *Opry* was directly responsible for the rise of the recording industry in Nashville, yet the owners, National Life, refused to capitalize on this. They clung to their belief that they were an insurance company, and would stick to what they did best: sell insurance. Even the spectacular national success of Hank Williams on the show (1949-1952) failed to sway their course. A new generation of singers brought the show into the modern era: Hank Snow (joined 1950), Kitty Wells (1952), Webb Pierce and Marty Robbins (both 1953), Jim Reeves (1955). The ABC television series, *Stars of the Grand Ole Opry* brought the show into the national spotlight again in 1955. An ugly fight in 1956 caused a number of stars to be fired from the show because they went with an independent talent agency rather than stay with the *Opry* agency; the result was a relenting by the *Opry* management and the end of the Artists Service Bureau.

Other crises wracked the show in the 1960's. Patsy Cline, Hawkshaw Hawkins, Cowboy Copas, Jim Anglin, and Texas Ruby all died in an unbelievable string of accidents. In 1964 the show fired twelve of its biggest acts for failing to appear the required number of times, twenty-six per year. But by the mid-1960's newly named manager Bud Wendell was starting to bring things around, and by 1969 the roster included some fifty acts, ranging across the spectrum of Country music, from the barbershop harmony of the Four Guys to the Western Swing of Charlie Walker.

The show had moved into the Ryman Auditorium in downtown Nashville in 1943, but by the 1970's the area around the Ryman was becoming an urban slum. National Life decided to build a facility especially for the *Opry*, and in 1974 completed the new Grand Ole Opry House in a rural area some ten miles from downtown Nashville. A theme park, Opryland, as well as a huge hotel, soon followed. By the 1980's, the *Opry* and WSM had been bought by Gaylord Entertainment Corporation, and was part of a huge conglomerate that included a cable network (The Nashville Network). By 1994, the number of *Opry* cast members exceeded seventy, and the show is going as strong as ever. CKW

AMY GRANT

(Singer, Songwriter)

Given Name:	**Amy Lee Grant**
Date of Birth:	**November 25, 1960**
Where Born:	**Augusta, Georgia**
Married:	**Gary Chapman**
Children:	**Matthew Garrison, Gloria Millie (Millie), Sarah Cannon**

Amy Grant is known as the first lady of Contemporary Christian music and although she now has her feet firmly in Pop music as well, she is still one of the major selling Christian music artists.

She was born the youngest of four children and brought up in Nashville. Amy signed her first record deal at the age of 15 and released her debut eponymous album. In 1979, she signed with Myrrh/Word Records and began her ascendancy as one of the foremost Christian singers. In 1982, Amy married singer/songwriter Gary Chapman, who recorded for RCA in 1988 and became Amy's co-writer. It was Amy's 1982 album, ***Age to Age,*** that proved to be the breakthrough for her. It won for her a Grammy Award for "Best Gospel Performance, Female." By the following year, it was Certified Gold and the awards started to be heaped on her. She won three Dove Awards that year for "Artist of the Year," "Contemporary Album" and "Best Recorded Music Packaging." That year, she also won her second Grammy for the single *Ageless Medley*.

In 1984, Amy's seasonal ***A Christmas Album*** won a Dove Award for "Best Recorded Music Packaging." She also won another

Gospel and Pop star ***Amy Grant***

Grammy Award for "Best Gospel Performance, Female," this time for *Angels*, a track co-penned by Amy from her album that year, ***Straight Ahead***. This album netted for Amy a Dove Award as "Best Contemporary Album" in 1985. During 1985, ***Age to Age*** went Platinum, ***A Christmas Album*** and ***Straight Ahead*** went Gold, as did Amy's 1985 release, ***Unguarded***, which won Amy her fourth Grammy, this time for "Best Gospel Performance, Female."

During 1985, Amy signed with A&M Records for secular material and she found herself in the Pop chart with two singles, *Find a Way* (Top 30) and *Wise Up* (Top 70). In 1986, Amy was again a Dove Award winner as "Artist of the Year" and ***Unguarded***, which that year went Platinum, earned one for "Best Recorded Music Packaging," and Amy had a No.1 on the Pop chart with her duet with the former lead singer of Chicago, Peter Cetera, on *The Next Time I Fall*.

During 1987, Amy's 1979 album, ***Father's Eyes,*** was Certified Gold as was her 1986 compilation, ***The Collection***. In 1988, her A&M album, ***Lead Me On,*** went Gold the year of release and the title track scraped into the Pop chart. However, the album did win for Amy another Grammy for "Best Gospel Performance, Female," even though the album was largely secular. *Stay a While* won another Dove Award for Amy as "Best Short Form Video." The following year, Amy took home three Dove Awards for "Artist of the Year," "Best Short Form Video" for the single *Lead Me On,* while the album of the same name won "Best Contemporary Album." That year, both ***The Christmas Album*** and ***The Collection*** were Certified Gold. In addition, *Saved by Love* went Top 40 on the Adult Contemporary chart. Amy took one of the Dove Awards in 1990 for *'Tis So Sweet to Trust in Jesus*, which was named "Country Recorded Song of the Year."

In 1990, A&M got behind Amy and via music video projected her as a more contemporary artist with a sexier image. It worked and during 1991, she made a big impression on the Pop chart with *Baby Baby* (No.1), which was nominated for two Grammys, *Every Heartbeat* (Top 3) and *That's What Love Is For* (Top 10). The album from which they came, ***Heart in Motion***, went Double Platinum before year end and by 1993 had sold over 4 million copies. The video of the album had also gone Gold in 1992.

That year, Amy was still perceived as a Christian singer and won two Doves for "Artist of the Year" and "Song of the Year" for *Place in the World*, which she had written with

Michael W. Smith and Wayne Kirkpatrick. Amy's seasonal album ***Home for Christmas*** went Platinum before year end, as did the seasonal video ***Amy Grant's Old-Fashioned Christmas***. During the year, she had two Pop hits, *Good for Me* (Top 10) and *I Will Remember You* (Top 20).

Amy is very active in humanitarian efforts and was honored by the American Cancer Society with its prestigious "John C. Tune Award." In 1992, she was named "Young Tennessean of the Year" by the Nashville Chamber of Commerce and in 1994, she was honored at St. John's University by the Benedictine Order with the "Pax Christi Award" (The Peace of Christ).

RECOMMENDED ALBUMS:

"Father's Eyes" (Myrrh/Word)(1979)
"Amy Grant 'In Concert'" (Myrrh/Word)(1981)
"Amy Grant 'In Concert,' Vol. II" (Myrrh/Word)(1981)
"Age to Age" (Myrrh/Word)(1982)
"A Christmas Album" (Myrrh/Word)(1983)
"Straight Ahead" (Myrrh/Word)(1984)
"Unguarded" (Myrrh/Word)(1985)
"The Collection" (Myrrh/Word)(1986)
"Lead Me On" (A&M)(1988)
"Heart in Motion" (A&M)(1991)
"Home for Christmas" (A&M)(1992)
Videos:
"Heart in Motion" (A&M)(1992)
"Old-Fashioned Christmas" (A&M)(1992)

BILL GRANT AND DELIA BELL

When Formed: 1959

BILL GRANT
(Singer, Songwriter, Mandolin)
Given Name: Billy Joe Grant
Date of Birth: May 9
Where Born: Hugo, Oklahoma
Married: Juarez (dec'd.)

DELIA BELL
(Singer, Songwriter, Guitar)
Given Name: Delia Nowell
Date of Birth: April 16
Where Born: Bonham, Texas
Married: Bobby Bell
Children: Keith

If anyone in Bluegrass music can be said to have perfected the male-female duet, then that honor belongs to Bill Grant and Delia Bell. Bill's mandolin and both of their solo vocals, as well as duets, give them a distinctive sound, not imitative of anyone, yet still in the tradition of great duets of the past. Their piercing harmonies are reminiscent of the best moments of George Jones and Melba Montgomery or of Carl and Pearl Butler. Only Bill and Delia do it with Bluegrass instrumentation, which serves to make their sound all the more haunting and memorable. The duo also ranks as among the few Bluegrass folk from their region of America to have attained national prominence. Furthermore, Bill Grant has built his Hugo, Oklahoma, Bluegrass Festival into one of the nation's premier musical events and has won admiration for his songwriting skills. Delia Bell, on her part, has what is probably *the* outstanding female voice in Bluegrass and has charted Country with two singles, *Flame in My Heart* (a duet with John Anderson) and *Coyote Song* (both 1983).

Bill was born, reared and still resides on a ranch that has been owned by family members for more than a century. He grew up listening to the *Grand Ole Opry* and learning to work with cattle. He also recalls that during WWII he heard Hawkshaw Hawkins, who was stationed at an army base near Paris, Texas, singing *Sunny Side of the Mountain* over the local airwaves. Overall, however, Bill considers Bill Monroe and the Stanley Brothers to have been his major musical influences.

Delia moved from Texas to Oklahoma as a child and sang songs in church from age ten. Outside family influences, she also listened to the music of the Stanley Brothers along with Carl Story's Rambling Mountaineers and the Louvin Brothers. She met Bill, who was a longtime friend of her husband, about 1959, and they began singing as a duo shortly afterward.

For several years, Bill and Delia sang mostly for their own satisfaction and for local entertainment, but did include performing on the *Little Dixie Hayride* at KIHN Hugo and once a month on KTEN-TV in Ada, Oklahoma. After visiting Bill Monroe's Beanblossom Festival in 1969, where they were invited to share a spot with the great man, Bill and Delia formed the Kiamichi Mountain Boys. The group consisted of themselves and the Bonham Family. From 1969, they entertained at Grant's Salt Creek Park Bluegrass Festival as well as other venues in their region.

Delia Bell and Bill Grant

In 1971, Bill started his own Kiamichi label and over the course of the decade cut some three singles and nine albums on it. Bill's original songs and Delia's singing, as well as their vocal harmonies, began attracting increasing attention. During 1978, Delia cut what was essentially a solo album for Country (although it included three duets with Bill) and the following year, the duo toured the U.K., where they recorded a Country album on the Kama label. The song *Roses in the Snow* caught the attention of Country star Emmylou Harris, who made it the title cut for one of her best albums in 1980. Emmylou had first heard of Delia from the popular family group the Whites. Emmylou subsequently proclaimed Delia as her favorite female vocalist and helped her secure a Warner Brothers record contract, which yielded the self-titled album, which Emmylou produced. However, Warner Brothers were going through a difficult time and Delia was not well-treated by the label.

In the interim, Bill and Delia had cut two albums for Rebel and then went on to record a further three for Rounder, usually with instrumental support by the Johnson Mountain Boys. More recently, Bill Grant and Delia Bell have recorded for Old Homestead, a company that has also re-released some of their previously out-of-print Kiamichi albums.

Since the late 70's, Bill and Delia have been widely seen and heard on the Bluegrass festival circuit throughout the country. Since the Bonhams would not travel, the Kiamichi Mountain Boys were dissolved in 1980 and the duo generally worked with a pickup band.

Bill has proven himself a writer of quality, with such numbers as *Stairway to Heaven, Cheer of the Home Fires, A Few Dollars More, My Kiamichi Mountain Home, Dreaming of the Times* and *Rollin'*, which describes the traveling life of Bluegrass festival musicians as experienced by an Oklahoma "Country boy and a Kiamichi Mountain girl." Grant also has a manner of introducing an older song and giving it a near-epic quality, which can best be illustrated by his spoken beginning to the cowboy standard *Strawberry Roan*, or the Bluegrass oldie *Sunny Side of the Mountain*.

IMT

RECOMMENDED ALBUMS:

"My Kiamichi Mountain Home" (Kiamichi)(1972)
"Kiamichi Country" (Kiamichi)(1973) [Re-released on Old Homestead]
"There Is a Fountain" (Kiamichi)(1973)
"The Last Christmas Tree" (Kiamichi)(1976) [Re-released on Old Homestead]
"My Pathway Leads Me to Oklahoma" (Kiamichi)(1978)

"The Blues —Mountain Style" (Kiamichi)(1979) [Re-released on Old Homestead]
"The Man in the Middle" (Kiamichi)(1979) [Re-released on Old Homestead]
"Bill Grant and Delia Bell in England" (Kama UK)(1980)
"Rollin'" (Rebel)(1981)
"The Cheer of the Home Fires" (Rounder)(1984)
"A Few Dollars More" (Rounder)(1985)
"Following a Feeling" (Rounder)(1988)
"Dreaming of the Times" (Old Homestead)(1992)
Delia Bell:
"Bluer Than Midnight" (County)(1978)
"Delia Bell" (Warner Brothers)(1983)

JOSH GRAVES

(Dobro, Bass, Guitar, Vocals, Composer)

Given Name:	**Bucket K. Graves**
Where Born:	**Tellico Springs, Tennessee**
Married:	**Evelyn**
Children:	**Josh, Jr., plus three others**

Josh Graves has been called "the Dobro Virtuoso" and without doubt, he is one of the finest players of the instrument. He has the rare ability to emulate Blues phrasing and sweet sounds normally played on a Hawaiian guitar. He is also capable of playing lead lines played by fiddlers or mandolinists. Being a Blues fan, Josh utilized a lot of Blues licks used by such Blues players as Blind Boy Fuller.

Josh fell in love with the Dobro at age 9, when he saw the Carlisle Brothers and heard Cliff Carlisle's performance of Jimmie Rodgers' songs. Cliff became close to the young lad and they met many times afterward. Josh's first instrument was the bass, but times were hard and it would be a regular occurrence to pawn the instrument. He got his first break in 1942, when the Pierce Brothers hired him to play in Gatlinburg. The following year, Josh got a job playing with Esco Hankins on KNOX Knoxville. He then went on to play with Mac Wiseman and then he joined Wilma Lee and Stoney Cooper on the *Wheeling Jamboree*.

In 1957, Josh came with the Coopers to the *Grand Ole Opry*. At this time, Cliff Carlisle gave Josh one of his old Dobros. It was at the *Opry* that he was spotted by Flatt & Scruggs and he joined their Foggy Mountain Boys as a bass player, but, after a month, he was asked to switch to Dobro. Earl Scruggs taught Josh how to apply the Scruggs three-finger style to the Dobro; the result was dynamite and for the next 12 years, Josh was a mainstay of the band. While with them, Josh sessioned on the album ***Old Time Get-Together with Lew Childre*** in 1961.

When the band broke up in 1969, Josh joined Flatt in his new band, Nashville Grass. During his time with the band, he sessioned on Charlie McCoy's ***Harpin' the Blues***. Josh stayed with Flatt until 1971, when he became a member of Earl Scruggs Revue. While with Scruggs, Josh appeared on the band's ***Live at Kansas State*** (1972), ***The Earl Scruggs Revue*** (1973), ***Rocking Across the Country*** (1973) and ***Where the Lilies Bloom*** (soundtrack,1974) albums. During the time he was with Scruggs, Josh also appeared on several albums as a session man. These included J.J. Cale's ***Really*** and Steve Young's ***Seven Bridges Road*** (both 1972), Kris Kristofferson's ***Jesus Was a Capricorn*** and Kristofferson and Rita Coolidge's ***Full Moon*** (both 1973).

In 1974, Josh decided that he no longer wanted to be a sideman and quit the Scruggs band. That year, he appeared on Charlie McCoy's ***Nashville Hit Man*** and the Talbot Brothers' eponymous album. He also recorded his own "statement" album, ***Alone at Last,*** for Epic. From here on, Josh continued as a solo attraction and as a session man. In 1975, Josh released ***Just Joshing***, a duet album with Foggy Mountain Boy Jake Tullock, as Uncle Josh & Uncle Jake. Josh's sessions included Herb Pedersen's ***Southwest***, Charlie McCoy's ***Play It Again Charlie***, Boots Randolph's ***Country Boots*** and ***Jimmie Skinner Sings Bluegrass, Vol.2*** (all 1976), Charlie McCoy's ***Country Cookin'*** and James Talley's ***Blackjack Choir*** (both 1977).

In 1976, Josh and Bobby Smith recorded ***Sweet Sunny South,*** on which they were accompanied by the Boys from Shiloh and Benny Martin. The next year, Josh appeared on Joe Maphis' ***Grass 'n Jazz (Acoustic Bluegrass/Country Jazz)*** album on CMH, as one of Maphis Super Picker Pals. In 1978, Josh signed CMH himself and released ***Same Old Blues*** (1978), ***Sing Away the Pain*** (1979, with Vassar Clements) and ***King of the Dobro*** (1982).

Josh appeared on Bobby Smith and the Boys from Shiloh's 1978 album, ***Smokin' Bluegrass***. Cowboy Carl Records released the album ***Josh Graves and Friends*** in 1979, which comprised tracks recorded in 1962 and 1963. In 1985, he got together with Jerry Douglas and Mike Auldridge on a 30-minute video, ***Dobro Summit***. The back-up musicians included Vassar Clements and Marty Stuart.

In 1989, Josh joined forces with Eddie Adcock, Kenny Baker and Jesse McReynolds, in the supergroup the Masters and that year they released their self-titled album. Josh Graves still appears on such TNN shows as *American Music Shop*.

RECOMMENDED ALBUMS:
"Bobby Smith & Josh Graves" (Vetco)
"Uncle Josh & His Dobro" (Cottontown Jubilee)
"Just Joshing" (Cottontown Jubilee) [With Jake Tullock]
"Living Legends" (Old Homestead) [With Red Taylor]
"Alone at Last" (Epic)(1974)
"Sweet Sunny South" (CMH)(1976) [With Bobby Smith & the Boys from Shiloh and Benny Martin]
"Same Old Blues" (CMH)(1979)
"Josh Graves and Friends" (Cowboy Carl)(1979)
"King of the Dobro" (CMH)(1982)

BILLY GRAY

(Singer, Songwriter, Guitar)

Date of Birth:	**December 29, 1924**
Where Born:	**Paris, Texas**
Married:	**Billy Faye**
Children:	**Billy, Jr., Jack, Terry, Carolyn, Dottie**
Date of Death:	**March 27, 1975**

A classic example of his era, Billy Gray was a popular showman with his own Western Swing style band for many years, although he only had one chart hit.

Born near Paris, Texas, Billy picked cotton and did without candy and picture shows to accumulate enough money to buy his first second-hand guitar at age 15 from a pawn shop. In less than a year, he was playing and singing on a local radio station. His official debut, however, came in 1943, when at the age of 19 he organized his own band and his own show on Paris station KPLT, which lasted three years. During these years his show and following grew to become the envy of other performers.

Following this, Billy joined former Louisiana Governor James E. Knoe for a tour of Louisiana. He then toured several theater chains in Texas and the surrounding states with his band before moving to Dallas, where he worked for two years before joining Hank Thompson in 1950. In 1950, Billy became the bandleader of Hank Thompson's band, the Brazos Valley Boys. Several years later, they jointly formed the Texoma Music Publishing Company and the Brazos Valley Publishing Company.

Billy co-wrote with Hank many of his smash hits recorded on Capitol including *Waiting in the Lobby of Your Heart*, which went Top 3 on the Country charts for Hank, followed up by *The New Wears Off Too Fast*, which again charted in the Top 10. *Yesterday's Girl*, another joint effort for the two writers, charted in the Top 10 in 1953, followed by *Breaking the Rules*, which went Top 10 in 1954, and the flip-side, *A Fool, A Faker*, which also went Top 10.

Several years later, Billy left Thompson's group to go out on his own. He was instrumental in getting Wanda Jackson signed as a Country artist to Decca, and in 1954, the two recorded their Top 10 smash hit *You Can't Have My Love*, released on Decca. This was Billy's only charted record. In 1955, Billy recorded with his own band, the Western Oakies, and they released a 10" album on Decca, ***Dance-O-Rama***, which was also issued as two EPs. This failed to produce any hits and Billy eventually returned to his former position with Hank Thompson. In 1963, Billy attributed his failure as a solo artist to the fact that he hit the road with a much bigger band than was necessary, and while he had plenty of bookings, his travel expenses ate up the profits.

Other groups Billy worked with included the backing group the Nuggets and years later, the Cowtowners. He appeared in the syndicated television show *Music Country Style* and in later years appeared with the Ray Price Band as well. In 1962, Decca released the album ***Lovin' Country Style***, which features Gray with Wanda Jackson. In 1965, he released his debut eponymous album on Longhorn Records. Two singles, *Rotten Love* and *Blue for No Reason*, were also released which failed to chart. Hank Thompson and the Brazos Valley Boys were voted the Nation's Top Western Swing Band in 1954 by *Downbeat* and the Brazos Valley Boys played on both the Billy Gray and Hank Thompson recording sessions. Billy died in Dallas, Texas, on March 27, 1975, while undergoing heart surgery at the age of 50.

RECOMMENDED ALBUMS:

"Dance-O-Rama" (Decca)(1955) [10" album]
"Billy Gray" (Longhorn)(1965)

CLAUDE GRAY

(Singer, Songwriter, Guitar)
Given Name: **Claude N. Gray**
Date of Birth: **January 26, 1932**
Where Born: **Henderson, Texas**

Claude Gray, at 6'5", was described as the man "you have to look up to" and "the Tall Texan." He also showed some longevity in his career. He has charted records from 1960 through to 1986, and yet has never received the long-term acclaim due to him. Always smart on stage, Claude eschewed the wearing of gaudy clothes, but still managed to give a glittering performance.

Claude started out playing guitar while still at high school, and performed at local engagements. He was in the U.S. Navy from 1950 until 1954. He then worked as a salesman and then in the late 50's, he became an announcer on KOCA Kilgore, Texas. Claude then became a deejay on WDAL Meridian, Mississippi, while also playing the clubs.

His record career got under way in 1959, when he signed to Pappy Dailey's D Records and released *I'm Not Supposed*. He hit the chart the following year, with the Top 10 single *Family Bible*. This resulted in him getting signed to Mercury and he immediately struck for his new affiliation with the 1961 Top 5 single *I'll Just Have a Cup of Coffee (Then I'll Go)*, which crossed over to the Pop Top 90. The follow-up, *My Ears Should Burn (When Fools Are Talked About)*, fared even better, by reaching the Top 3 on the Country charts.

Claude's two chart entries for 1962 did not fare as well, with *Let's End It Before It Begins* (Top 30) and *Daddy Stopped In* (Top 20). He charted two times more for Mercury with *Knock Again, True Love* (Top 20, 1963) and *Eight Years (And Two Children Later)*, which reached the upper 40s the following year. He was named *Cash Box*'s "Most Promising Country and Western Singer." While with Mercury, Claude and Walt Breeland wrote *The Ballad of Jimmy Hoffa*, but the label wouldn't let him record it. Eventually, the song was released on Smokey Stover's Ol' Podner label, and was sold direct to the Teamsters' members.

For two years, Claude was absent from the charts and returned in 1966 with *Mean Old Woman*, on Columbia. At the end of the year, he moved to Decca and scored with the Top 10 hit *I Never Had the One I Wanted*. That year, he formed the Graymen, with Buck Evans on bass, Terry Bethal on steel guitar and Bob Taylor on drums. He maintained the band until 1968.

Over the next five years, he sold consistently and racked up another ten hits, starting with *Because of Him* (Top 50), backed by the Top 70 entry *If I Ever Need a Lady (I'll Call You)* and *How Fast Them Trucks Can Go*, which peaked in the Top 15 (all in 1967). The following year, Claude had *Night Life* (Top 40) and *The Love of a Woman* (Top 70). In 1969, he scored with *Don't Give Me a Chance* (Top 50) and *Take Off Time* (Top 40). He continued in 1970 with *The Cleanest Man in Cincinnati* (Top 60) and *Everything Will Be Alright* (Top 40). Claude's last hit for the label was the 1971 success *Angel*, which reached the Top 50.

This was the end of his major label connection. In 1972, Claude had a Top 70 single with *What Every Woman Wants to Hear*, on Million Records. He had a Top 60 release the following year on the same label, with *Woman Ease My Mind*. For three years, he was absent from the charts and then in 1976, he charted for the first time on the Granny label; however, none of the releases on this label got above the Top 70. One release worth mentioning was his 1982 duet with Norma Jean, *Let's Go All the Way*, which reached the Top 70. He made his final chart entry in 1986 with a cover of Neil Diamond's *Sweet Caroline*, on Country International.

Claude, who wrote most of his own songs, is still actively playing live engagements.

RECOMMENDED ALBUMS:

"Songs of Broken Love Affairs" (Mercury)(1962)
"Claude Gray Sings" (Decca)(1967)
"The Easy Way of Claude Gray" (Decca)(1968)
"Presenting Claude Gray" (Million)(1972)

MARK GRAY

(Singer, Songwriter, Piano)
Date of Birth: **October 24, 1953**
Where Born: **Vicksburg, Mississippi**
Married: **1. (Div.)**
2. Lori Keeton
Children: **LaToya**

From 1979 through 1985, Mark Gray was a much vaunted Pop-Country singer as a member of Exile and then as a solo artist. Familiar in his trademark gray fedora, Mark also made his mark as an oft-recorded songwriter.

Mark was born the youngest of seven children and by the time he was age 2, his mother died. He was raised on Lookout Mountain, Georgia, by his aunt and uncle. His aunt sang in a Gospel group and soon Mark joined her, singing Gospel solos. As he sometimes forgot the words, he began making them up. By the time he was 12, he began playing piano. When he was 15, he realized that he needed to get to know his brothers and moved back to his father's 250-acre farm in Mississippi. He worked with the tractor on the farm and then worked in a printing shop. He became a finalist on the *Ted Mack Amateur Hour*. Mark went on to sell used cars and then began recording advertising jingles at Malaco Recording Studios in Jackson.

However, the first important step on the success ladder was about to come. In 1972, Mark was working selling spots for an R & B radio station and had put together his own Gospel group, the Revelations, with a bass player and two girl singers, for playing on weekends. While playing in Meridian, Mississippi, the Oak Ridge Boys (then a Gospel group) asked him to go to Nashville to work with their publishing company and to appear with them on the road. By the following week, he had moved there, and in the process went from earning $175 a week to $76 a week. He stayed with the Oaks for nearly two years, during which time he nearly starved and it was only through the generosity of William Lee Golden that Mark didn't have his car repossessed.

After leaving the Oaks, Mark played piano and sang with another Gospel group, the Downings. However, after a month when it was discovered that audiences were applauding him, he was fired. He returned to his tractor at Vicksburg and then did lose his car. Over the next five years, Mark played in Jackson nightclubs. By 1979, he had accumulated about 40 of his own songs. Jeff Silbar, whose songwriting credits include *The Wind Beneath My Wings*, sent Mark's demo tape to record producer Mike Chapman, who signed Mark to join Exile.

While with the group, Mark wrote several songs with co-member J.P. Pennington, including two Alabama No.1s, *Take Me Down* (1982) and *The Closer You Get* (1983). The latter song was also a Top 30 single for Don King in 1981. He appeared on two albums while with Exile, ***Stage Pass*** (1979) and ***Don't Lead Me This Way*** (1981), on RCA and Warner Brothers respectively.

At the end of 1982, Mark left Exile to embark on a solo career. He pitched some songs including *Losing a Lover Ain't Nothing Like Losing a Friend* for Janie Fricke to her producer, Bob Montgomery (she recorded it), and this led to Mark being signed to Columbia Records and Janie recording *It Ain't Easy Being Easy* (a No.1 hit).

Mark's first solo Country chart entry, *If It Ain't Real (It Ain't You)*, went Top 30 in the spring of 1983 and was followed by the Top 20 single, *Wounded Hearts*, both co-written by Mark and coming from his debut album, ***Magic***, which was produced by Montgomery and Steve Buckingham. That year, Melissa Manchester recorded Mark's *Nice Girls*, which went Top 50 and Engelbert Humperdinck charted with Mark's *Til You and Your Lover Are Lovers Again*.

All three of Mark's 1984 singles went Top 10 and they were: *Left Side of the Bed* (written in his Exile days), *If All the Magic Is Gone* and *Diamond in the Dust*. The last track came from Mark's second album, ***This Ol' Piano***, as did Mark's opening single in 1985, a Top 10 duet with Tammy Wynette, Dan Hill-Barry Mann's *Sometimes When We Touch...* However, the follow-up, *Smooth Sailing (Rock in the Road)*, only reached the Top 50. The year ended with the Top 10 single *Please Be Love*. In 1986 he had his last chart single for Columbia, *Back When Love Was Enough* (Top 15).

Then Mark's career went off the rails as he asked for his release from Columbia due to not seeing "eye-to-eye with the president of the label." In 1988, he had two basement-level chart records with Bobbi Lace for the independent label, 615. Since then his career has been uneventful.

RECOMMENDED ALBUMS:

"Magic" (Columbia)(1984)
"This Ol' Piano" (Columbia)(1984)
"That Feeling Inside" (Columbia)(1986)

OTTO GRAY

(Band Leader, Emcee)
Date of Birth: **Ca. 1890**
Where Born: **Stillwater, Oklahoma**
Married: **Grace Means ("Mommie")**
Children: **Owen ("Zeb")**
Date of Death: **November 8, 1967**

Otto Gray became one of the most important people in the commercialization of Western music. He wasn't a musician of any note, or a singer, yet Otto Gray and his Oklahoma Cowboys became one of the best known acts during the 1920's and 1930's.

Otto and Mommie Gray married in 1905 and in 1907, they lost everything following a drought and a cholera epidemic. They moved from Oklahoma to Wyoming, where they lived in a tent on the prairie. They sang at fairs and circuses and formed their first band, Otto and his Rodeo Rubes, in 1918. Gray took over the leadership of the McGintey Cowboys in 1924. A string band comprised of genuine cowboys, it got its name from Oklahoman rodeo rider, Bill McGinty, who was one of Buffalo Bill's stars. They began appearing over radio station KFRU Bristow, Oklahoma. A few months later, the band was renamed Otto Gray and his Oklahoma Cowboys. They began playing over KVOO Tulsa, Oklahoma, and KFJF Oklahoma City. They then went to Kansas City to appear on a 15-minute spot on WHB, but ended up staying on air for two hours.

Gray started to advertise the band in *Billboard*, one of the few Country acts to get this sort of treatment. In their publicity piece on the band, *Billboard* said at the time, "They can broadcast for eighteen hours without repeating and without looking at a sheet of music or referring to memoranda for their radio program dialogue..."

From 1928 through 1932, the band played on the northeastern RKO and Orpheum vaudeville circuits and broadcast on radio stations around the country. They were particularly popular on KFRU Bristow, Oklahoma, WGY Schenectady, New York, and WLW Cincinnati, Ohio. They made broadcasts from some 146 radio stations, that included KMOX St. Louis, Missouri, WLS Chicago, WSYR Syracuse, New York, WHAM Rochester, New York, and KDKA Pittsburgh, Pennsylvania.

Gray had the band well organized. The band members were dressed in western style outfits and sported white ten-gallon hats. A publicity advance man ensured that they were well publicized before they hit a town where they were due to play. In addition, each band member traveled in a $20,000 customized Cadillac that boasted a two-way radio transmitter and was colorfully decorated. From the radiator of each vehicle extended a highly polished set of large longhorns. Their bookings were handled by two agencies: the Weber-Simon Agency in New York and the William Jacobs Agency based in Chicago.

The line-up of the Oklahoma Cowboys was: Otto Gray (emcee), Mommie Gray (vocals), Owen ("Zeb") Gray (banjo), Wade ("Hy") Allen (cello), Lee ("Zeke") Allen, Zeke Clements (vocals, guitar), Whitey Ford (The Duke of Paducah)(vocals, banjo) and Chief Sanders (fiddle). Mommie Gray was the featured singer and sang mainly sentimental songs. Other members of the band at varying times included Fred Wilson, Rube Tronson and Bill Crane.

Their most popular songs were *She'll Be Comin' Round the Mountain, Who Broke the Lock on the Henhouse Door?, The Song of the Dying Cowboy, Sucking Cider Through a Straw, The Cowboy's Lament, The Old Maid & the Burglar, Your Mother Still Prays for You, Where Is My Wandering Boy Tonight* and *I Had But 50 Cents.* They recorded for Gennett (Richmond, Indiana), General Phonograph (New York), Pathe, Paramount, Vocalion, OKeh, Columbia and Brunswick. In 1931, Otto and Mommie were signed by Film Exchange to film six shorts in New York. Gray disbanded the group in 1936. Mommie Gray died in 1946.

GRAYSON AND WHITTER

When Formed: **1927**

G.B. GRAYSON
(Singer, Songwriter, Fiddle)
Given Name: **Gilliam Banmon Grayson**
Date of Birth: **November 11, 1888**
Where Born: **Ashe County, North Carolina**
Date of Death: **August 16, 1930**

HENRY WHITTER
(Singer, Songwriter, Guitar)
Given Name: **Henry Whitter**
Date of Birth: **April 6, 1892**
Where Born: **Fries, Virginia**
Date of Death: **November 10, 1941**

Although their career together lasted only three years, G.B. Grayson and Henry Whitter were two of the most influential musicians to come out of the Appalachians. Their slender legacy of some forty recorded sides included some of the best and most emulated recordings in early Country music and their works were found in later repertoires of singers ranging from Doc Watson to Mick Jagger. To paraphrase Winston Churchill, never before have so many owed so much to so few recordings.

Among the Grayson-Whitter masterpieces were the original readings of fiddle standards like *Train 45* and *Lee Highway Blues* (*Going Down the Lee Highway*); famed murder ballads like *Tom Dooley* (the first recording of the song that became a million seller for the Kingston Trio during the later Folk revival) and *Banks of the Ohio* (which Grayson and Whitter called *I'll Never Be Yours*); *Handsome Molly*, which later entered the repertoires of Bob Dylan, Mike Seeger and Mick Jagger; *Little Maggie*, later associated with the Stanley Brothers; *Rose Conley*, later done by Charlie Monroe, Grandpa Jones and dozens of Bluegrass bands; *Nobody's Darling*, which J.E. Mainer redid; and a version of *Cluck Old Hen*, which became a favorite with younger musicians in the 70's and 80's.

Henry Whitter and G.B. Grayson were both experienced musicians when they first met at a fiddlers' convention in Mountain City, Tennessee, in the summer of 1927. Whitter had in fact recorded quite a bit. He was born in Fries, Virginia, and had become the area's first musician to record when he traveled to New York in 1923. There is some evidence that Whitter might have in fact been the first Country vocalist to actually record, but the OKeh Company hesitated to release his sides until the unexpected success of similar efforts by Fiddlin' John Carson. Whitter's singing and guitar playing were only adequate and Ernest Stoneman, reportedly, went up to Bristol, Tennessee, to record, in 1927, because he knew he could do better than Whitter. However, Whitter was an aggressive promoter of Old-Time music and managed to land numerous recording dates. He had hit recordings with *The Wreck on the Southern Old '97* and *Fox Chase*, a harmonica solo, which he recorded for Ralph Peer on August 2, 1927, during Peer's field trip to Bristol.

Grayson was born in Ashe County, North Carolina, and as a baby had suffered serious eye damage which left him almost blind. He soon found out he could make a living by busking through mountain towns and rural fairs and dances. He eventually settled down in Laurel Bloomery on the Tennessee-Virginia line. He knew other musicians including Clarence Tom Ashley and Doc Walsh and he often performed with them. He held his fiddle in the archaic manner of placing it not under the chin, but down on the shoulder, rocking the instrument back and forth to facilitate bowing. He was also a superb singer and many fans and scholars consider him the best to record, and note that he was one of the first to merge the old Appalachian ballad singing style with the newer forms of instrumentally accompanied vocalizing. To his credit, Henry Whitter sensed Grayson's superior singing abilities and often deferred to him on records, adding only guitar back-up and some occasional harmony.

By the fall of 1927, Whitter had managed to land not one but two record deals. In October, the pair cut eight songs for the Gennett label. Two weeks later, they recorded a half-dozen more for Victor. It was at this later session that they made what would be their career record, a double-sided hit of *Train 45* and *Handsome Molly*. It sold over 50,000 copies and stayed in print until 1934. It also guaranteed them a welcome at about any later Victor field sessions. None of their later Victor recordings sold as well, though, and the original *Lee Highway*, which they did not get around to recording until 1929, sold only about 1,300 copies, though every copy must have gone to an Old-Time fiddler, to judge from the title's impact.

On August 16, 1930, eleven months after their last recording session, Grayson was killed in an auto accident. Reportedly, he had been hitching a ride on the running board of a car, near Abingdon, Virginia, and was thrown from the car. He died about an hour later. Whitter never really got over the death of his partner, but continued to perform music, and even record a little. On November 10, 1941, he died of diabetes in Morganton, North Carolina.

CKW

RECOMMENDED ALBUMS:

"Grayson and Whitter, Complete Works" (double)(Old Homestead)

"Grayson and Whitter" (County)

GREAT PLAINS

When Formed:	**1991**
Members:	
Jack Sundrud	**Lead Vocals, Acoustic Guitar**
Denny Dadmun-Bixby	**Bass Guitar, Vocals**
Russ Pahl	**Lead Guitars, Pedal Steel Guitar (left)**
Michael Young	**Drums, Percussion (left)**

Before forming Great Plains, the individual members had all played on many records by other artists. They followed the tradition of their musical influences, the Eagles, by playing their own instruments on their album and not relying on studio musicians.

The original members of the group included Russ Pahl from Minnesota and Michael Young from Oregon. They left the band in 1993 to pursue other interests. Before becoming Great Plains, each of the members toured and recorded with a variety of artists. Paul played guitar with Dickey Betts, Cal Smith, Nicolette Larson and Don Williams. Sundrud toured with Poco, Gail Davies, Vince Gill, the O'Kanes and Kathy Mattea. Dadmun-Bixby provided back-up for Mary-Chapin Carpenter and Nanci Griffith and Young played drums for Gary Morris and Dire Strait's Mark Knopfler. At various times all members had performed with Michael Johnson and got the idea to form their own group while working with him.

Great Plains came to the attention of producer Brent Maher (Michael Johnson, the Judds) through Michael Young. However, it was not his musical skills that interested Maher. Young had built a reputation for himself restoring vintage automobiles. Maher had seen Young's work on cars owned by Mark Knopfler and Ricky Van Shelton. Michael pitched the idea of using the group to play on demos for Maher's publishing company. This association led to an interest in Sundrud's songwriting and the Country-Rock sound of Great Plains. The group cites a wide range of musical influences from the Everly Brothers to the Beatles to Creedence Clearwater Revival.

The band recorded their first self-titled album in 1991, under the production team of Brent Maher and Don Potter. All of the songs were written or co-written by Jack Sundrud and they hit the Country singles chart with *A Picture of You*. Although only a moderate success, the management team of Bob Doyle and Pam Lewis made Great Plains the opening act of another client, Garth Brooks. That major exposure helped the band gain significant airplay. In 1992, their single *Faster Gun* reached the Top 50 and was followed by the Top 70 single *Iola*.

Great Plains opened concerts for Ricky Van Shelton, but with the departure of Pahl and Young in 1993, there is a question mark over their future. However, Columbia is planning a second album for 1994 release.

JIE

RECOMMENDED ALBUM:

"Great Plains" (Columbia)(1991)

LLOYD GREEN

(Steel Guitar, Dobro, Vocals)
Given Name: **Lloyd Lamar Green**
Date of Birth: **October 4, 1937**
Where Born: **Mobile, Alabama**

Through the 60's and 70's, Lloyd Green was one of Country music's top and busiest sessionmen, appearing on numerous recordings made in Music City. He often played with Johnny Gimble, "Pig" Robbins and Charlie McCoy and was much lauded for his virtuoso work by British audiences, particularly those that experienced his work at Wembley Festival.

Lloyd started learning to play the Hawaiian guitar when he was 7 and by the time he was 10, he was playing professionally. His early influences were Little Roy Wiggins and Jerry Byrd. During his high school days, he spent his weekends playing rough and rowdy clubs and bars. In 1954, he enrolled at the University of Southern Mississippi as a psychology major, but quit in 1956 to move to Nashville. He intended to have a year off and return to get his degree. When he arrived, he shared a room with another great steelie, Jimmy Day, at Mama Upchurch's. On New Year's Night, 1957, Lloyd was hired by Faron Young and stayed with him for 18 months. During this time, he appeared on only one record session, that for George Jones on *Too Much Water Runs Under the Bridge* in 1957.

After leaving Faron Young, Lloyd returned to Mobile. He had already gotten married and the Greens were expecting their first child. Lloyd worked the clubs until he had saved some money and then nine months later he returned to Nashville. He did various tours, but sessions were few and far between because rock'n'roll had made the steel sound out of fashion. Lloyd worked for a month with Ferlin Husky and then decided never to tour again.

Lloyd "hung up" his steel and got a job selling shoes. While working in the shop, Mrs. Fred Rose, Wesley Rose's step-mother, found out about Lloyd wanting to get back into music and paid his Musicians' Union Dues. This meant that he could now play some *Opry* dates with Carl and Pearl Butler, Margie Bowes and Curly Fox. In 1964, Roy Drusky's wife, Bobbye, came into the shop and she mentioned that Roy was looking for an assistant at the SESAC office, which he was running. Drusky, after some while, employed Lloyd on a part-time basis at $50 per week but, more importantly, got him demo and recording sessions. He stayed at SESAC for over three years, by which time the $85 per week he was getting from the job paled into insignificance against the $50,000 he was earning for a year's sessions.

Lloyd's sessions started with Chart Records, for whom he first recorded in 1969 and included Lynn Anderson's *Ride, Ride, Ride*. However, over the years, his sessions have included *D.I.V.O.R.C.E.* for Tammy Wynette (1968), *Easy Loving* by Freddy Hart (1971), Mel Street's *Borrowed Angel* (1972) and *Farewell Party* for Gene Watson (1976).

He has also worked with several non-Country acts, including the U.K. "forces favorite" Dame Vera Lynn as well as Paul McCartney and Ringo Starr. In 1969, he played on most of the tracks of the Byrds' watershed album ***Sweetheart of the Rodeo*** (Jay Dee Maness played on the others).

Lloyd has been in the charts twice as a solo instrumentalist and once as a singer. The Johnny Nash Pop-Reggae song *I Can See Clearly Now* provided him with his first Top 40 hit in 1973 on Monument. This was followed by his rendition of Lennon-McCartney's *Here Comes the Sun*, also on Monument, which reached the Top 75. Three years later, he vocalized through *You and Me* on October Records, which just scraped into the Country chart. Lloyd's albums have been released widely in Europe and Australia, where he is a great favorite.

In the late 80's, Lloyd suffered from an inner ear infection and he had to cancel work because of it. He lost about $27,000 in an investment in Mercury Studio about this time. He recouped a lot of it, but this was at a time when new steelies like Paul Franklin and Sonny Garrish were starting to take the session work. However, with the renewed interest in the Dobro, Lloyd found himself back in demand on that instrument.

RECOMMENDED ALBUMS:

"Day for Decision" (Little Darlin')(1966)
"Mr. Nashville Sound" (Chart)(1968)
"Green Country" (Little Darlin')(1969)
"Lloyd Green and His Steel Guitar" (Prize)(1971)
"Shades of Steel" (Monument)(1973)
"Ten Shades of Green" (Mid-Land)(1976)
"Lloyd's of Nashville" (Mid-Land)(1980)
"California Dreamin'" (Flying Fish) [With Mike Auldridge on Dobro]

THE GREENBRIAR BOYS

When Formed: **1958**
Members:

John Herald	**Guitar, Lead Vocals**
Bob Yellin	**Banjo, Vocals**
Eric Weissberg	**Banjo, Vocals (left 1959)**
Ralph Rinzler	**Mandolin, Vocals (joined 1959/left 1964)**
Frank Wakefield	**Mandolin, Fiddle, Vocals (joined 1964)**
Jim Buchanan	**Fiddle (joined 1964)**

More popular with the urban Folk revival crowd than with rural audiences, the Greenbriar Boys nonetheless won top honors at the 1960 Union Grove Fiddlers' Convention. Moreover, they helped expand the audience for traditional Country music, so they are pioneers of a sort. The group was formed in 1958 and was originally made up of John Herald, Bob Yellin, and Eric Weissberg.

Herald, a native of Greenwich Village, became interested in music as a youngster when his father took him to Pete Seeger concerts. In high school he and several classmates formed an R & B band, but, after being exposed to the Folk revival music being performed in Washington Square in the summer of 1956, he became an enthusiastic fan of Bluegrass music.

Yellin, the son of professional musicians, came from a classical music background and had formal training in violin, voice, piano, and trumpet. In college, he heard his first record by Earl Scruggs and was inspired to teach himself banjo. Thereafter, he was a Bluegrass music enthusiast. Weissberg also came from a classical music background, studying at the Juilliard School of Music and performing with the Aspen Festival and Westchester Symphony Orchestras. The three joined forces as the Greenbriar Boys while at the University of Wisconsin, where they were all students.

In 1959, Weissberg left the group, and was replaced by Ralph Rinzler, a native of Passaic, New Jersey. As a child he had taken several years of piano lessons, but, after hearing some Library of Congress field recordings, he became a devoted fan of Folk music.

With Herald as guitarist and lead vocalist, Rinzler as mandolinist and baritone vocalist and Yellin as banjoist and tenor vocalist, the Greenbriar Boys became one of the favorite Bluegrass acts on the Folk festival circuit. Their repertoire was heavily slanted toward traditional material (*Stewball* being one of the songs most often associated with them), which they gathered not only from older commercial recordings but from field work in the rural South. Rinzler also helped establish the Friends of Old Time Music, an organization that brought artists such as Clarence Ashley and Arthel "Doc" Watson to New York and to other urban centers.

In 1964, Rinzler left the group to become the talent and folklore coordinator of the

Newport Folk Festival. He was replaced by mandolinist Frank Wakefield and fiddler Jim Buchanan was also added to the band. By this time, the heyday of the Greenbriar Boys was past and within a few years the group was defunct.

In 1972, Herald returned to performing as a solo act accompanied by a band featuring electric bass and cello, instruments that were taboo to most Folk revivalists in the 60's. That same year, Vanguard Records repackaged some of the Greenbriar Boys' recordings as ***The Best of John Herald and the Greenbriar Boys***. This offering, however, was neither satisfying nor very representative of the band's work.

In 1967, Rinzler became head of the Smithsonian Institution's Folklife Programs and in that capacity established the still ongoing Festival of American Folklife, a program that brings some of America's best traditional musicians and craftsmen to Washington, D.C., where they showcase their talents for a week. WKM

RECOMMENDED ALBUMS:

"The Greenbriar Boys" (Vanguard)(1963)
"Ragged But Right" (Vanguard)(1964)

Green Valley Quartet refer EASTER BROTHERS

JACK GREENE

(Singer, Songwriter, Guitar, Drums)

Given Name: Jack Henry Greene
Date of Birth: January 7, 1930
Where Born: Maryville, Tennessee
Married: Barbara Ann Stidham (div.)
Children: Jackie Wayne, Forest Anthony, Mark Allen, Barbara Lynn, Jan Thomas

Jack, known to his fans and friends as the "Jolly Green Giant," is one of the most enduring and affable people in Country music. He is a man who has retained his good singing voice and also puts entertaining at the top of his list.

He was raised in the Smoky Mountains and learned to play guitar when he was 8. His first appearance at junior high school led to his first radio show on WGAP Maryville and he stayed at the station from 1947 through 1948. From this, he got onto *Tennessee Barn Dance* on WNOX Knoxville, where he was a member of Clyde Grubb & the Tennessee Valley Boys. He moved to Atlanta, Georgia, where he joined the Cherokee Trio, with whom he played guitar and sang. In 1950, Jack became a member of the Rhythm Ranch Boys as drummer/guitarist. He also played with Cecil Griffith & the Young 'Uns. However, just as the band was starting to get a following, Uncle Sam beckoned and Jack was drafted into the U.S. Army. He spent the time in Alaska and Colorado, ending up as a member of the Special Drill Squad stationed at Camp Carson.

Following his discharge in 1952, Jack returned to Atlanta and joined the Peachtree Cowboys and for the next 10 years played with them around the South. Jack joined Ernest Tubb's Texas Troubadours in June 1962, principally as drummer. As a result, he started to appear at the *Grand Ole Opry*. Dottie West had recorded *Love Is No Excuse* with Jim Reeves and had a major hit with it in the spring of 1964. Following Jim's tragic death a few months later, Dottie chose Jack to sing the male part on the song at the *Opry*.

Ernest Tubb encouraged Jack to try playing on his own and his assertion was vindicated when the album ***Ernest Tubb Presents the Texas Troubadours*** was released in 1964 on Decca. Jack sang lead on *The Last Letter,* one of the tracks. The public responded favorably and as a result a single was released and picked up a lot of airplay. Jack decided that now was the time to go solo.

Jack's first release for Decca in 1965 was *Don't You Ever Get Tired of Hurting Me,* which was well received but with his follow-up, *Ever Since My Baby Went Away*, Jack made the Top 40. For nearly a year, he didn't have any releases, then in the fall of 1966, he shot to No.1 with Dallas Frazier's *There Goes My Everything*. It stayed at the top for 7 weeks and was on the chart for nearly six months and crossed over onto the Pop chart.

In 1967, Jack capitalized on this success by following up with another No.1, *All the Time*, which also crossed over. The record stayed at the top for five weeks and was on the list for five months. The flip-side, *Wanting You But Never Having You,* was also in demand. He ended the year with a Top 3 hit with *What Locks the Door*.

The Jolly Green Giant, ***Jack Greene***

The awards flowed in. *There Goes My Everything* was the newly constituted CMA's "Song of the Year" and "Single of the Year." The album with that title was made their "Album of the Year" and as well as these firsts, Jack was named the first recipient of their "Male Vocalist of the Year." To add to the excitement, he took part in Macy's Thanksgiving Parade on NBC-TV, became a member of the *Opry* and was introduced to the audience by Ernest Tubb. Jacksonville, Florida, declared August 26, 1967, as Jack Greene Day. With two No.1s behind him, *Cash Box* and *Record World* considered him to be the "Most Promising Male Vocalist" and, in addition, Jack received three Grammy nominations.

In 1968, *All the Time* became *Cash Box*'s "Most Programmed Song." That year, Jack scored more memorable and major hits with *You Are My Treasure* (No.1), *Love Takes Care of You* (Top 5) and another No.1, *Until My Dreams Come True*. During 1969, Jack divided his time between solo work and duetting with Jeannie Seely. He had another No.1 (making two in a row), with Jan Crutchfield's *Statue of a Fool*. This was followed by *Back in the Arms of Love*, a Top 5 entry. The flip-side, *The Key that Fits Her Door,* also charted at the lower end. Jack's duet with Jeannie Seely, *Wish I Didn't Have to Miss You,* got to the Top 3. That year, he and Jeannie appeared on the concert bill for "Nashville at the Garden" from Madison Square Garden, New York City.

Jack made a "command performance" at the 11th Annual United Nations in Washington, D.C., in 1970. As the 70's got under way, Jack's chart records were peaking at a lower level. His Top 20 hits to the end of 1971 were *Lord Is that Me* (Top 20), *The Whole World Comes to Me /If This Is Love* (Top 15—both 1970), *Something Unseen* (Top 15)/*What's the Use, There's a Whole Lot About a Woman (A Man Don't Know)* (Top 15)/*Makin' Up His Mind* (all 1971). In 1971, he had a Top 20 hit with Jeannie on *Much Oblige*. During the next year, he had but two Top 20 successes, one with Jeannie, *What in the World Has Gone Wrong with Our Love* and one on his own, *Satisfaction*.

In 1973, Jack and Jeannie appeared at and co-hosted the Wembley Festival in England. They were in the middle of their five CMA "Duo of the Year" nominations at this time. They would return again to Wembley in 1976.

At the end of 1973 and beginning of 1974, Jack had back-to-back Top 15 successes with *I Need Somebody Bad* and *It's Time to Cross that Bridge* on Decca's successor, MCA. Then the Decca/MCA party was over. Jack and Jeannie put together a more "outlaw" act and the Jolly Green Giants, who had been with Jack since 1965, became the Renegades. The band continued touring throughout the States and it was not until 1980 that Jack's name re-appeared on the Country charts. He had three chart singles on Frontline during that year, the most successful being the Top 30 *Yours for the Taking*. There was also an album of the same title that year.

By 1983, Jack had moved on to EMH and although he charted four times with them, all the singles were at the basement level. Jack was still actively making personal appearances and in 1989, he appeared at the ill-fated Grantham Festival in England, where he shrugged off the possibility of not getting paid with equanimity. He was just glad to be there to entertain.

RECOMMENDED ALBUMS:

"Jack Greene's Greatest Hits" (MCA)
"Jack Greene & Jeannie Seely (Live at the Grand Ole Opry)" (Pinnacle)(1979)
"Yours for the Taking" (Frontline)(1980)
"Jack Greene Sings His Best" (EMH Collector's Series)(1983)
"Time After Time" (51 West)(1984)

RICHARD GREENE

(Violin, Viola, Mandolin, Bass Guitar, Vocals, Composer)

Given Name: Richard S. Greene
Date of Birth: November 9, 1942
Where Born: Los Angeles, California
Married: Unknown
Children: Chelsey

Richard Greene has been long recognized as one of the finest fiddle players over the last thirty years. He started studying classical violin at the age of 5, becoming a member of his school's orchestra, and eventually, concertmaster of the Beverly Hills High School Orchestra. However as soon as he was "tall enough," he quit lessons and started to take an interest in Folk music.

When he entered the University of California at Berkeley in 1960, Richard became a member of a campus mountain music trio, the Coast Mountain Ramblers, along with Ken Frankel (guitar) and Dave Pollack (banjo). They tried to emulate the New Lost City Ramblers, who were their idols. The following year, Richard joined the Dry City Scat Band with Dave Lindley (guitar), Peter Madlem (banjo, guitar) and Chris Darrow (guitar, vocals). The group can be heard on the Elektra album ***String Band Project***.

After that band, Richard took a job selling real estate and then in 1963, he saw (and met) Scott Stoneman (of the Stoneman Family) perform and knew that he wanted to be a full-time musician. Stoneman and fiddler Dale Potter became the two biggest influences on Greene's style of playing.

Richard started playing with the Pine Valley Boys in the San Francisco/Palo Alto area and there he met mandolin wizard David Grisman and banjo supremo Herb Pederson. The three of them went across country to join other groups and while in New York, Richard met Bill Keith, who was playing with Bill Monroe. Richard was going east to join the Greenbriar Boys. He first met them in 1964, but they were not looking for a fiddle player, so he came on board playing bass.

In March 1966, Richard was given the opportunity to join Bill Monroe's (84th version of) Blue Grass Boys alongside Roland White, Peter Rowan, Lamar Grier and James Monroe. Richard was part of the group when they cut ***Bluegrass Time*** for Decca. He did a lot of twin fiddle work on the *Grand Ole Opry* while with Monroe, alongside Buddy Spicher.

Richard left Monroe in March 1967 and joined the fabled Jim Kweskin Jug Band, which at the time also boasted Geoff Muldaur, Maria D'Amato (later Muldaur) and Bill Keith. Richard played fiddle and viola in this outfit. He recorded the Reprise album ***Garden of Joy*** and then in April 1968, he moved to San Francisco and joined the Blues Project, which evolved into the first incarnation of Seatrain. He recorded two albums with this group, ***Planned Obsolescence*** (as the Blues Project, 1968) on Verve and ***Seatrain*** (1969) for A & M Records.

At the end of 1969, Richard got together with Eric Weissberg (a former Greenbriar Boy), Jim Rooney and Bill Keith in a recording studio project, the Blue Velvet Band. They recorded one album for Warner Brothers, ***Sweet Moments***. During the late 60's, Richard wrote the music for the highly acclaimed movie *Riverrun*.

Richard stayed with Seatrain (being reunited in 1969 with Peter Rowan) until August 1972, recording two albums for Capitol, under the production control of George Martin, entitled ***Seatrain*** (1971) and ***Marblehead Messenger*** (1972). Upon leaving the band, Richard decided to form his own band; however, as a stop-gap affair, he became a member of the initial line-up of Old and in the Way, with Jerry Garcia, David Grisman, John Khan and, once more, Peter Rowan. He didn't appear on the group's album, as by then he had left and Vassar Clements was in the fiddle seat.

In addition, Richard worked a little with Jane Getz and played on James Taylor's classic ***Mud Slide Slim*** album, before setting up Richard Greene & the Zone in October 1972. The line-up of the band was Larry Taylor (bass), Randy Resnick (guitar), Richard Martin (vocals) and Ken Collier (drums). They cut their debut self-titled album in 1974. In 1973, Greene was also playing with another "supergroup," Muleskinner, which included Clarence White, Bill Keith, David Grisman, Stuart Shulman and Peter Rowan. The band cut an eponymous album for Warner Brothers. That same year, Greene released ***Somebody's Gonna Love You***, a solo album for MCA.

Richard next moved on to another band, the Great American Music Band, with David Grisman and Taj Mahal (string bass), which was the first example of new acoustic music. The band played a fusion of Bluegrass and Jazz. Then in 1975, Richard was asked to join Loggins & Messina and this gave Richard the opportunity to play before very big audiences (up to 85,000). Although he left the group after the 1975 tour, Greene recorded three albums with Loggins & Messina, ***So Fine*** (1975), ***Native Sons*** (1976) and ***Finale*** (1978).

Richard decided that he wanted to produce at this time and during 1976 stopped playing fiddle. In 1977, he started to do movie sessions and TV and radio jingles and returned to taking violin lessons. He recorded two albums for Rounder, before and after these new lessons: ***Duets*** (1977), which featured Tony Trischka, J.D. Crowe and David Nichtern (before), and in 1979 ***Ramblin'*** with Maria Muldaur (after).

During the middle/late 70's, Richard was featured on various albums by other artists, including Emmylou Harris' ***Pieces of the Sky*** (1975), Rowan Brothers' ***Sibling Rivalry*** (1976), Rod Stewart's ***Footloose & Fancy Free*** (1977), Rodney Crowell's ***Ain't Living Long Like This*** (1978) and Melanie's ***Photograph*** (1979).

The Richard Greene Band recorded a demo tape at the Great American Music Hall and this was eventually released as the ***Blue Rondo*** album (on Sierra) that year. The line-up of the band was Bob Applebaum, John Kurnick and Tim Emmons. In the same year, just before the album was released, Richard toured Japan with Andy Statman, Tony Trischka and Peter Rowan. They recorded two albums in Japan: one as Rowan, Greene & the Red Hot Pickers (***Bluegrass Album***) and the other as Rowan, Greene, Trischka, Statman and Mason, entitled ***Hiroshima Mon-Amour***.

Richard's music has become more and more classically based and he has described it as "acoustic Country Classical music." He commissioned Frederic Myrow to write

Fantasy Rondo for Violin and Orchestra, which is based on *Amazing Grace*. This was featured on the album ***Buellgrass*** (named for Buell Neidlinger, a fellow pioneer in this field). In the early 80's, Richard played some dates with ex-Country Gentleman, Eddie Adcock. Greene continues to push back the musical barriers between Bluegrass, Jazz and the Classics.

RECOMMENDED ALBUMS:

"Marblehead Messenger" (Capitol)(1971) [As Seatrain]
"Muleskinner" (Warner Brothers)(1973) [As Muleskinner] [Also on Ridge Runner Records]
"Duets" (Rounder)(1977)
"Ramblin'" (Rounder)(1979)
"Blue Rondo" (Sierra)(1980)
"Bluegrass Album" (Nippon Columbia Japan)(1980) [As Rowan, Greene & the Red Hot Pickers]
"Hiroshima Mon-Amour" (Nippon Columbia Japan)(1980) [As Rowan, Greene, Trischka, Statman & Mason]

LEE GREENWOOD

(Singer, Songwriter, Woodwinds, Keyboards, Guitar, Banjo)

Given Name:	**Melvin Lee Greenwood**
Date of Birth:	**October 27, 1942**
Where Born:	**Los Angeles, California**
Married:	**1. Edna (div.)**
	2. Edna (remarried/div.)
	3. Roberta (div.)
	4. Melanie Cronk (div.)
	5. Kimberley Payne
Children:	**Marc, Kelly, Tedd, Laura**

It's not just President Clinton who hauls out a tenor sax. Lee Greenwood is also a reeds player who performs the old Champs' hit *Tequila* with the same amount of relish. However, it was as one of Country music's foremost singers during the 80's that Lee made his mark.

Lee, born of half-Cherokee parents who split up when he was one year old, was raised by his grandparents on a farm near Sacramento. When he was 9, he taught himself to play alto sax. Before he had reached his teens, he had appeared with My Moondreams, a Sacramento-based dance band. When his mother remarried, when he was 13, he moved to Anaheim, California, to be with her. She sent him back to Sacramento in 1958 as she felt that he would benefit from grandparental encouragement.

Lee joined Chester Smith's band and soon appeared on TV. He was hired by Del Reeves who taught him stage presence and showmanship. Lee formed Apollo and in 1962 went to Las Vegas with them. By 1967, the band was renamed the Lee Greenwood Affair and was playing Pop music. They moved to Los Angeles and recorded for Paramount, which tried to mold them into the Gary Puckett image but then the label folded and so did the band. Lee was approached by Dino Danelli and Felix Cavaliere to join a band called the Scotties. He declined the offer and saw the band develop into the Young Rascals.

Lee took jobs as music arranger, show tune writer, back-up singer and piano-bar performer. He joined a trio in Vegas, playing organ at the Palomino and providing the music for the strippers. In 1973, Lee came to a crossroads: he was offered two jobs, one as bass player and lead singer in a revue, *Bare Touch of Vegas,* and the other as a blackjack dealer at the Tropicana, and after the flip of a coin, he took on both gigs. He held down both jobs for four years. It was during this time that he met his third wife, dancer and choreographer Melanie (Greenwood).

By 1979, he was playing the lounges, this time in Reno, when he was spotted by Larry McFaden, who was band leader and bass player for Mel Tillis. McFaden talked to Lee about recording, but he was less than impressed. However, Lee bought himself a return ticket to Nashville and recorded four demos. McFaden became his manager and introduced him to Jerry Crutchfield at MCA Records, who became his producer. In June 1981, Lee signed as a recording artist to MCA/Panorama and staff writer to MCA Music.

Lee's first release, Jan Crutchfield's *It Turns Me Inside Out*, hit the charts in September and raced into the Top 20 staying around for over five months. The debut album, ***Inside Out,*** followed the next year and this yielded a further three hits, all Top 10: *Ring on Her Fingers, Time on Her Hands*; *She's Lying;* and *Ain't No Trick (It Takes Magic)*. The album went Gold in 1986. His initial Top 10 hit of 1983, *I.O.U.*, became the first of his sides to hit the Pop charts, by reaching the Top 60.

Lee Greenwood was now a star and the awards started to indicate this. In *Radio & Records* Readers Poll for 1983, he was named "Best New Artist" and the CMA voted him "Male Vocalist of the Year." He attained his first No.1 that year with the title track of his second Gold album, ***Somebody's Gonna Love You***. This single, like its predecessors, not only achieved high placing but also stayed on the charts for about five months. This has been a mark of Lee's singles: their chart longevity. Lee followed up with another No.1 with another Jan Crutchfield song, *Going, Going, Gone*.

1984 was a vintage year for Lee. His first hit single was *God Bless the U.S.A.* This song, written by Lee, has now achieved a status that could only have been guessed at. Its Top 10 chart position belied its eventual impact. Lee followed this with a Top 3 duet with Barbara Mandrell, *To Me*, which was taken from their album ***Meant for Each Other***. He wrapped up the year with two more Top 10 entries, *Fool's Gold* and *You've Got a Good Love Comin'*, both coming from his Gold album ***You've Got a Good Love Comin'***. His accolades for the year were quite staggering. He received a Grammy for "Best Country Vocal Performance, Male" for *I.O.U.* He was *Cash Box* Programmers' Choice Award pick as

Singer, Songwriter and Sax player ***Lee Greenwood***

"Male Vocalist of the Year." ACM and MCN named him as "Male Vocalist of the Year" and *Cash Box* made him "Male Vocalist of the Year—Albums" and the CMA made it two straight years as "Male Vocalist of the Year."

Lee got 1985 under way with another duet with Barbara Mandrell, *It Should Have Been Love By Now*, which went Top 20. He then had a run of four No.1s: *Dixie Road* from his Gold album ***Lee Greenwood's Greatest Hits***; *I Don't Mind the Thorns if You're the Rose*; *Don't Underestimate My Love for You* (all 1985); and *Hearts Aren't Made to Break (They're Made to Love)* (1986), all from ***Streamline***. During 1985, he received MCN Awards for "Single of the Year," *(God Bless the U.S.A.)* and "Male Vocalist of the Year." He also received the CMA's "Song of the Year" Award for *God Bless the U.S.A.* At the end of 1985, Lee released a seasonal album, ***Christmas to Christmas***.

The cover of ***Love Will Find Its Way to You*** (1986) shows Lee without his familiar beard. From this album, he charted with *Didn't We* (Top 10) and another No.1, the Steve Bogard-Jeff Tweel song *Mornin' Ride*. Lee continued into 1987 with three Top 10 hits, *Someone, If There's Any Justice* and *Touch and Go Crazy* all from his 1987 album, ***If There's***

Any Justice. Glen Campbell was featured on the track *Silver Dollar.* This was the first of Lee's albums to be produced by Jimmy Bowen.

In 1988, MCA released a second volume of ***Greatest Hits*** and then, the Bowen-Greenwood produced album, ***This Is My Country***, hit the streets. Lee had two single hits that were not quite as successful as his previous chart entries, *I Still Believe* (Top 15) and *You Can't Fall in Love When You're Cryin'* (Top 20). Lee's last major hit for MCA was the 1989 Top 20 single *I'll Be Lovin' You.*

In 1990, Lee moved over to Capitol Records and was reunited with producer Jerry Crutchfield. He released the album ***When You're in Love*** that year and returned to form with the Top 3 single *Holdin' a Good Hand.* He started 1991 with *We've Got It Made* going Top 15 and then he released the album ***A Perfect 10***. This was a duets album with top lady performers Carol Chase, Suzy Bogguss, Karen Staley, Tanya Tucker, Donna McElroy, Barbara Mandrell, Wild Rose, Lacy J. Dalton, Marie Osmond and Cee Cee Chapman. The track with Suzy Bogguss, *Hopelessly Yours*, a Top 15 hit, was nominated for a 1991 Grammy Award. Lee followed up with another album, ***You're in Love***.

When Lee's *American Patriot* (Liberty) was released in 1992, the title seemed most appropriate. The Gulf War had just finished and his *God Bless the U.S.A.* had been used widely to reflect the feelings of a nation. He had been awarded the "Congressional Medal of Honor Society's Patriot Award," the "Points of Light Foundation Award" for celebrity involvement, the "AMVET Silver Helmet Award," the American Legion National Commander's "Public Relations Award," the "VFW Americanism Gold Medal" and the Air Force "American Spirit Award." In addition, he is the mascot of the nuclear aircraft carrier USS *Theodore Roosevelt*, he is a Major General (Brevet) in the U.S. Air Force and he sits on the Board of Directors of the Challenger Center.

Later in 1992, Lee released his album ***Love's on the Way***. However, by now, his singles were only peaking in the lower regions of the chart. Although, Lee has chalked up many memorable hits, it is strange that one of his finest recordings was never released as a single. That track was Larry Henley and Jeff Silbar's classic *Wind Beneath My Wings.*

RECOMMENDED ALBUMS:

"Somebody's Gonna Love You" (MCA)(1983) [Just for Lee's version of "Wind Beneath My Wings"]
"Lee Greenwood's Greatest Hits" (MCA)(1985)
"Lee Greenwood's Greatest Hits—Volume Two" (MCA)(1988)
"A Perfect 10" (Capitol)(1991)
"American Patriot" (Liberty)(1992)
"Love's on the Way" (Liberty)(1992)

JIM GREER

(Singer, Banjo, Mandolin, 12-String Guitar)
Given Name: James Marvin Greer
Date of Birth: September 3, 1942
Where Born: West Liberty, Ohio
Married: Sharon

During the 1960's and into the early 70's, Jim Greer and the Mac-O-Chee Valley Folks constituted one of the more exciting Bluegrass bands in the Midwest. Their visits to fairs and local festivals won them a host of fans and friends over an area of several states who awaited their shows with considerable anticipation.

Jim Greer was born in central Ohio, where he has lived his entire life. He first gained an appreciation for Country music from his older sisters Bonnie and Valeda, who began singing on an early morning daily radio program in Bellefontaine, Ohio, about 1951. They also did weekend guest spots on other stations including WPFB in Middletown and even made a few appearances on the *Renfro Valley Barn Dance*. Jim learned to play mandolin to support their vocals. The Greer Sisters eventually disbanded, but Jim and Valeda brought in Bob McPherson on guitar and mandolin and then Dalton Burroughs on bass to form the Mac-O-Chee Valley Folks. They took their atypical name from Mac-O-Chee Creek, which flowed through their native Logan County. Valeda's husband John Wentz played Dobro and in 1965, Aaron Hicks, a transplanted Kentuckian, came in to play fiddle. At other times Herb "Sonny" Collins, formerly of the Kentucky Cutups, did the fiddling. Valeda played rhythm guitar and Jim now favored banjo over the mandolin. Jim points out that the band had a great deal of continuity for a semi-professional outfit and Valeda, Bob, Dalton, and himself were constant members.

Initially the band worked primarily on a local jamboree-type show but their musical quality soon led to a demand for making wider appearances. In 1965, they joined the cast of *Jamboree USA* at Wheeling and played there on alternate Saturdays for three and a half years. They traveled out on the other weekends, often to Lancaster, Pennsylvania, where they played frequently at the indoor *Shindig in the Barn* and the outdoor *Shindig at Cripple Creek*. In the summers they played at numerous fairs, festivals, and Country music parks, sometimes even on weeknights.

The Mac-O-Chee Valley Folks recorded four singles and five albums during their decade as an active group. Their first efforts dated from about 1963, for the Cincinnati-based custom label Rite, and consisted of two singles and the album entitled ***Bluegrass in Ohio***. The songs included several original compositions by McPherson, as well as several Old-Time songs such as *Banks of the Ohio* and *The Girl in Sunny Tennessee,* the currently popular *Ballad of Jed Clampett* and a couple of original instrumentals by Jim. They followed this with a session for Starday, which resulted in four sides on Starday's Nashville label.

Their most widely distributed records resulted from their WWVA affiliation when *Jamboree* announcer Lee Sutton produced three albums for Uncle Jim O'Neal's Rural Rhythm label. The songs and tunes nearly all came from Old-Time tradition and therefore no longer in copyright, which as Greer recalls enabled O'Neal to remain largely free of royalty payments. After the Mac-O-Chee Valley Folks left WWVA they cut another album for Rite, an all-Gospel effort which appeared on the Golden Shield label. It included some titles on which Greer played 12-string guitar.

In the early 70's, the band reached a point in their careers when they believed they could no longer maintain their current pace. Faced with a decision to go full-time or disband, they chose the latter. Jim had earlier opened a clothing store in West Liberty and the other members all held regular jobs. Constant

*Bluegrass star **Jim Greer***

traveling became increasingly trying, so they simply quit.

In May 1993, Jim Greer still operates his business and the band members still reside in the area, with the exception of Sonny Collins, who is deceased. Jim reports that only the re-opening of the historic opera house/theater in downtown West Liberty could induce him to reassemble the Mac-O-Chee Valley Folks for a concert. IMT

RECOMMENDED ALBUMS:

"Bluegrass in Ohio" (Rite)(1963)
"Log Cabin Songs" (Rural Rhythm)(1965)
"Memories in Song" (Rural Rhythm)(1966)
"Stars of the WWVA Jamboree" (Rural Rhythm)(1966)
"Gospel Singing Time" (Golden Shield)(1970)

CLINTON GREGORY

(Singer, Fiddle, Mandolin, Guitar, Banjo, String Bass, Drums)

Date of Birth: **March 1, 1966**
Where Born: **Martinsville, Virginia**
Married: **Mary**

Clinton Gregory has defied the odds and become a successful artist without the support of a major record company. His records on Step One Records made him the first independent artist to place a single in the Top 30 in trade magazines *Radio & Records, Billboard* and *Cash Box* since Alabama accomplished the feat in 1980.

Clinton is a fifth-generation fiddle player who first picked up the instrument when he was age 3. His father gave him a new fiddle when he was 4 and young Clinton performed for the first time on stage. Traveling to Bluegrass festivals with his father as a boy, Clinton had the opportunity to play with Bill Monroe and Ralph Stanley in informal jam sessions.

Clinton made his first trip to Nashville when he was 12. His father won a fiddle contest with the prize of performing on the *Grand Ole Opry*. Clinton met *Opry* stars Marty Robbins, Roy Acuff and Lester Flatt and decided, *that* night, that he wanted to spend his life making music. He became an accomplished fiddle player, winning over 70 championships and also learned to play the mandolin, guitar, banjo, upright bass and drums.

In 1987, Gregory moved to Nashville and took a job playing fiddle for Suzy Bogguss. After touring with her for a year and a half, Clinton joined the McCarters. While traveling with the sister trio he was featured as a vocalist on a few songs. When he left the McCarters, Clinton worked as a fiddler and vocalist in the house band of a popular Nashville nightclub.

Clinton recorded a demo of *Be Nobody's Darlin' But Mine* for $58 in 1989, in the hopes of securing a contract with a major record company. His demo generated interest from a few of the major labels but Gregory liked the offer from the independent Step One Records, with whom he signed in 1990 and released his debut album, ***Music 'N Me***. Although his debut release, *Music in Me*, failed to produce any major radio airplay, his first 1991 single, *Couldn't Love Have Picked a Better Place to Die*, did reach the Top 70. Gregory's second album produced his first Top 30 hit with the title track, *If It Weren't for Country Music (I'd Go Crazy)*, and two other mid-chart singles were *One Shot at a Time* and *Satisfy Me and I'll Satisfy You*.

In 1992, Gregory's ***Freeborn Man*** album yielded the hit singles *Play Ruby Play* (Top 25), *She Takes the Sad Out Of Saturday Night* (Top 50) and *Who Needs It* (Top 30). *Music Row* magazine named him the "Independent Artist of the Year" and gave him their "Best Independent Video award" in 1992 for *Play Ruby Play*. In 1993, Clinton's singles only fared moderately and the most successful was *Standing on the Edge of Love*. It was then Clinton decided to leave Step One Records and signed with Polydor Nashville in 1994. JIE

RECOMMENDED ALBUMS:

"Music 'N Me" (Step One)(1990)
"If It Weren't for Country Music (I'd Go Crazy)" (Step One)(1991)
"Freeborn Man" (Step One)(1992)
"Master of Illusion" (Step One)(1993)

Singer/Fiddle Player ***Clinton Gregory***

RAY GRIFF

(Singer, Songwriter, Guitar, Piano, Drums)

Given Name: **John Raymond David Griff**
Date of Birth: **April 22, 1940**
Where Born: **Vancouver, British Columbia, Canada**
Married: **1. Margaret (div.)**
2. Trudy

Lest we forget, Ray Griff is a very important person in the history of Country music. He could gain admission to this encyclopedia on the strength of his songwriting alone. He has composed some two thousand songs. Over a quarter of these have been recorded by other artists and have become major hits. Among these are *Baby* (Wilma Burgess, 1965), *Canadian Pacific* (George Hamilton IV, 1969), *Step Aside* (Faron Young, 1971), *Better Move It on Home* (Porter Wagoner and Dolly Parton, 1971), *Who's Gonna Play that Old Piano* (Jerry Lee Lewis, 1972), *Where Love Begins* (Gene Watson, 1975), *Her Body Couldn't Keep You Off My Mind* (Gene Watson, 1976) and *It Couldn't Have Been Any Better* (Johnny Duncan with Janie Fricke, 1977). In 1975 and 1976, Ray's songs earned him sixteen ASCAP Citations each year.

When he was 3, Ray's family moved to Winfield, Alberta. By that time, he was playing drums in a local band, the Winfield Amateurs, with his brother Ken on banjo, Jackie Brown, on clarinet, Robert Dolman on sax, Ruthie Brown on piano. Ray used to sing from behind his drums without the benefit of a microphone. His songwriting ability showed itself when at 7 he started writing songs. Just before he reached his teens, his family was on the move again, this time to Calgary, Alberta. Ray stuttered so badly that later, when he became a star, he rarely held interviews.

During his teens, Ray sang in choirs and barbershop quartets. While in high school, he formed his own band, the Blue Echoes, which played weekend gigs and on local TV. He played guitar and piano in the band. At this time, he started to submit his songs to publishers in Nashville. He started meeting with *Opry* performers when they came up to Canada and became a close friend of Johnny Horton. Horton recorded Griff's *Mr. Moonlight* during the late 50's. Jim Reeves, who in 1962 recorded Ray's *Where Do I Go from Here*, insisted that he would be better off in Nashville and in 1964, Ray made the move.

Ray was employed in a piano factory as a key repairer while hawking his songs around Music Row. He subsequently worked as a record presser. Then, his songs started getting recorded. Wilma Burgess' recording of *Baby* became a Top 10 hit, followed by the Marty Robbins cut *She Means Nothing to Me*.

Ray formed Blue Echo Music, his own publishing company. He was hired by Bob Ferguson who was then with RCA and owned the only sheet music publishing company in town. Ray recorded a single, *The Weeping Willow*, which was leased to RCA-Groove in 1965. Unfortunately, the label folded, and nothing much happened on the recording front until he released the single *Your Lily White Hands* on MGM two years later and this made the Top 50. He followed up with *The Sugar from My Candy* on Dot and this also peaked in the Top 50. During the next two years, he released a further four singles, including his version of *Baby*, but none of them troubled the charts.

In 1970, he signed to Royal American and although his first single didn't do anything, the follow-up, a reworking of Clarence Carter's Pop hit *Patches,* made the Top 30. However, Royal American failed to capitalize on this success, and the next two singles died. In 1971, *The Mornin' After Baby Let Me Down* reached the Top 15. Again the label failed to maximize on this success and Ray's next single didn't even chart. However, one of the tracks from this Royal American output, *Ray's Bar and Grill*, an instrumental, was very popular.

Ray was not pleased and proceeded to take legal action against the label. He subsequently won the suit, but the damage had been done. He moved back to Dot in 1972, but he could not regain the momentum. Fortunately, his songs were being covered in abundance and his name was being kept in the forefront. When Dot became ABC/Dot, Ray moved on. This time, with Capitol behind him, his records became successful. He released his fifth album, entitled ***Ray Griff***. The single *You Ring My Bell* was on the lists for some four months and narrowly missed the Top 10. During 1975 and 1976, Ray appeared on the *Global TV Show*, which ran weekly for 18 months and was the first live show on the Canadian Global Network. They shot the show in Ottawa, while the music was played in Toronto.

1976 and 1977 were vintage years for Ray. *If I Let You Come In* peaked in the Top 15, *I Love the Way You Love Me* (Top 40) and *That's What I Get (For Doin' My Own Thinkin')* (Top 25) (all 1976) and *The Last of the Winfield Amateurs/You Put the Bounce Back Into My Step* (Top 30) and *A Passing Thing* (Top 30) (all 1977) all consolidated his career.

In 1979, he was back in Canada with a series of half-hour shows for CBC-TV, Canada. While in Canada, he recorded four albums for Jury Krytiuk's Boot label: ***Canada***, ***Maple Leaf***, ***The Greatest Hits of Ray Griff,*** and ***Adam's Child***. The song *Canada* was originally meant for George Hamilton IV. On the first two albums, Ray used his own band on the recordings.

Ray had singles released in 1981-1982 on Vision and then he was back with RCA. Four singles on these two associations charted, but only at basement level. From 1986 to 1990, Ray was out of the business taking care of his ailing mother. From 1990 on, he was working on his TV advertised album, ***Through the Years,*** and playing dates in Branson, Missouri.

RECOMMENDED ALBUMS:

"Songs for Everyone" (Dot)(1973)
"The Last of the Winfield Amateurs" (Capitol)(1976)
"The Greatest Hits of Ray Griff" (Boot Canada)(1981)
"Adam's Child" (Boot Canada)(1981)
"Through the Years" (double)(1993)

REX GRIFFIN

(Singer, Songwriter, Guitar, Yodeler)
Given Name: **Alsie Griffin**
Date of Birth: **August 12, 1912**
Where Born: **Gasden, Alabama**
Married: **Margaret (div.)**
Date of Death: **October 11, 1959**

Too many Country fans remember Rex Griffin as the man from whom Hank Williams got *Lovesick Blues*. In truth, though, Griffin was a popular radio and record artist of the 1930's who helped bridge the gap between the older Jimmie Rodgers style songs of the 1920's and the newer Honky-Tonk songs of the 1940's. His singing style anticipated that of Williams; his songs (over 85 of them) lasted well into the modern era, and helped earn Griffin a place in the Nashville Songwriter's Hall of Fame. He was a close friend to Ernest Tubb, and as late as 1955 singers like Eddy Arnold and Jim Reeves were recording his *Just Call Me Lonesome*.

Griffin's professional career began about 1933, and his early radio experience included stints at Birmingham, Atlanta, Memphis, Chicago, Dallas, and Nashville. It was at WAPI Birmingham that he got the nickname "Rex." An announcer kept having trouble pronouncing the singer's given name, Alsie, and decided on Rex. The name stuck and Griffin finally had it legalized. He started off as a Rodgers clone, but soon evolved a "blue yodel" of his own. He often was booked out of Gasden (in later years with a young Hank Williams) and often worked with Johnny Barfield.

In March 1935, Rex signed a contract with the then-new Decca record company and journeyed to Chicago to make his first sides. He would eventually do some thirty-eight sides for the label between 1935 and 1939, using sidemen such as Johnny Motlow (banjo), Ted Brooks (guitar), and Smitty Smith (bass). Though none of his records were monstrous hits of the sort that Gene Autry and Bob Wills were producing, several did became favorites over the years. One was *Everybody's Trying to Be My Baby* (1936) and others included the haunting *Over the River* (1937) and *The Last Letter* (1937). The latter, which drew special praise from music historian Sigmund Spaeth as a near-perfect marriage of tune and words, was allegedly a "suicide note" Griffin wrote after his wife Margaret left him. (He did not, however, actually attempt to take his own life.)

At his last Decca session, in 1939, he remembered an old song he had seen blackface singer Emmett Miller do years before, *Lovesick Blues*. He recorded it, watched it become a minor hit, and taught it to Hank Williams. (Ten years later Williams recorded it, copying Griffin's arrangement note for note.)

Griffin continued to work on radio in the 1940's, but transcriptions made during this time show that he had pretty much lost his edge as a real Honky-Tonk singer. His health and personal life were also going downhill. He suffered from both alcoholism and diabetes. Plans by Ernest Tubb to cut an entire album of Griffin songs finally materialized, but too late. Rex Griffin died October 11, 1959. CKW

NANCI GRIFFITH

(Singer, Songwriter, Guitar)
Date of Birth: **July 16, 1954**
Where Born: **Seguin, Texas**
Married: **Eric Taylor (div.)**

Nanci Griffith crosses the divide between Folk and Country, occasionally infusing her music, which she calls "Folkabilly," with Pop influences.

Her mother, Ruelene, acted and her father, Marlin, was a barbershop quartet singer. They were never professional and for them it was more a major hobby. From the time she could walk, Nanci was involved in the theater and the arts in general. It was her interest in literature which drew her into songwriting. She saw songs in terms of "writing a little short story." Most of her album covers came to feature Nanci holding a novel that meant a lot to her.

Nanci's style owed much to her childhood idol, Folk singer Carolyn Hester, a native of Austin, where the Griffith family had moved. Nanci's writing style was heavily influenced by southern prose writers, especially Larry McMurtry, Eudora Welty, Carson McCullers and Thomas Wolfe. Her lyrics drew much from Loretta Lynn, who later formed the subject of a Griffith tribute song, *Listen to the Radio*.

At 14, Nanci began playing in local honky tonks with her supportive parents in attendance. Initially, she wanted to be a teacher, but after majoring in education at the University of Texas, Nanci kept her options open by teaching kindergarten by day and playing on the Austin music circuit by night. Austin's Hole in the Wall club gave her her first steady booking. Following her winning entry in the New Folk Contest at the 1976 Kerrville Folk Festival, Nanci finally decided to concentrate full-time on a musical career in 1977.

Her performance persuaded Mike Williams to give Nanci the chance to contribute three songs to a Folk sampler on his small, local label, BF Deal Records. In 1978, the same label released her debut album, ***There's a Light Beyond These Woods***. It was recorded live in an Austin studio and was comprised of mostly her own compositions and included a song written by her then husband, singer Eric Taylor, another Kerrville winner. The title cut, which referred to the childhood aspirations which Nanci shared with her friend Mary Margaret Graham, was later re-recorded. The album was used to promote Griffith at her shows and it was not until 1982 that she released her next album, ***Poet in My Window***, on another small label, Featherbed Records. All but one of the cuts were written by Nanci.

By now, Nanci had decided to pitch her talents beyond Texas. Her marriage had collapsed and she drove thousands of miles in her station wagon in search of success. Festival appearances across North America, plus radio and TV shows, enlarged her following, although substantial commercial success proved elusive. Her real breakthrough didn't happen until 1985, when producer, songwriter, guitarist Jim Rooney, whom she had met the previous year, produced the acclaimed ***Once in a Very Blue Moon***. The album, Nanci's first to be recorded in Nashville, featured Phillip Donnelly on lead guitar, Béla Fleck on banjo and Lloyd Green on steel. The title track provided the name for Nanci's backing band, the Blue Moon Orchestra, formed in 1986 when Philo Rounder re-released her first two albums. The title track single reached the Country Top 90.

In 1985, Nanci moved to Nashville to be at the heart of the Country scene, where she began playing local nightclubs for greater exposure. At parties and clubs, Griffith was pleased and surprised to find that most people already knew her music. She hadn't considered her material commercial enough to be accepted in Nashville, even though she'd always been rooted in Country. She would subsequently come to revise that opinion.

Philo released ***Last of the True Believers*** in 1986. Nanci's perplexing musical identity was underlined when the album secured a Grammy nomination for "Best Contemporary Folk Recording." Indeed, because there was resistance on American Country radio to Nanci's unusual voice, with its nasal twang and Texan drawl, it was left to others to fully exploit the commercial potential of the Griffith pen and song selections. Kathy Mattea scored her first Top 5 placing with Nanci's *Love at the Five and Dime* in 1986.

Nanci was pleased for Kathy, but at the same time confessed that it was a little bit heartbreaking that Country radio hadn't played her music that much. Nanci's growing disenchantment with Nashville's aversion to her singing saw her move to MCA, shifting her recordings temporarily to its Los Angeles base. The strong sales of her last two albums persuaded MCA producer/executive Tony Brown to fly to Boston to see Nanci play in a coffeehouse. He was blown away, overcoming any doubts about signing a singer with such Folk leanings.

In 1987, ***Lone Star State of Mind*** was produced by Brown. He didn't want to change anything other than to give the sound a little more electricity and power. Once more, it was not Nanci, but others, who benefited most from her song choices. In this case Julie Gold's *From a Distance* was to become a huge standard, attracting interest from a wide variety of musical fields. Kathy Mattea, Bette Midler and Cliff Richard, among others, cut it. It was fortunate indeed that Nanci published the song, which gave her her biggest royalty checks and allowed her to purchase a 100-year-old farmhouse in Franklin, Tennessee. However, the title track of the album, not written by Nanci, reached the Top 40. This was followed

Last of the True Believers . . . ***Nanci Griffith***

by her co-written *Trouble in the Fields*, which reached the Top 60. Her final single from the album was her *Cold Hearts/Closed Minds*, which reached the Top 70. That year, Nanci made her debut at England's Peterborough Festival with Danny Flowers and started a fan base in the U.K. that has remained loyal to her. She has made many subsequent visits to Britain.

Little Love Affairs, released in 1988, was a disappointment compared to what had gone before. Intended as a concept album, it was, in fact, a hodgepodge of material. What it did demonstrate was Nanci's increasing tendency to collaborate with others. Harlan Howard's *Never Mind* had been a Top 60 hit in 1987 and the other singles from the album to chart were *I Knew Love* (Top 40) and *Anyone Can Be Someone's Fool* (Top 70). Later in 1988, came ***One Fair Summer Evening***, a live album and video recorded at Houston's Anderson Fair Rental Restaurant which promoted ***Little Love Affairs*** and included a smattering of material not previously recorded.

Nanci Griffith's lack of recognition in the U.S. led her to seek ways to look beyond Nashville. ***Storms*** in 1989 was produced by Glyn Johns, who had worked with many Rock greats, and reflected this shift of emphasis. Former Eagle Bernie Leadon, Irish drummer Bran Breen (ex-Moving Hearts), guitarist Albert Lee and Phil Everly were all brought in. While the album was Nanci's best-seller to date, it did not find favor with Country audiences. Nanci continued her success overseas and the album made the Top 40 on the U.K. charts. Undoubtedly, though, her most receptive audience has been in Ireland, where she enjoys virtual superstar status. She has made several appearances with the Chieftains and was included on their album, ***The Bells of Dublin***, singing *The Wexford Carol*.

In 1990, Nanci guested in the Presley movie tribute *The Last Temptation of Elvis*, with an inspired version of *Wooden Heart*. Nanci's next album, ***Late Night Grande Hotel***, which was released in 1991, sought to emphasize her empathy with Pop audiences. It was co-produced by the British team of Rod Argent and Peter van Hook. British singer and songwriter Tinita Tikaram guested on *It's Too Late*, while Phil Everly re-appeared on *It's Just Another Morning Here*.

In 1992, Nanci signed with Elektra Records and at last came of musical age. Country traditionalists welcomed Griffith's return to form with ***Other Voices, Other Rooms***, in 1993. Taken from the title of Truman Capote's debut novel (1948), the album represented Nanci's tribute to her Folk-Country roots, of how earlier generations of singer-songwriters have passed on their expertise to later generations. Containing a generous seventeen songs, the album fully justified the view of Nanci's friend and confidant, fellow songwriter Harlan Howard, that "her love of music means that there isn't a Folk or Country songwriter, alive or dead, who she won't have listened to and have an opinion on."

This watershed album trawls through Nanci's many influences, from Bob Dylan to Tom Paxton, from Gordon Lightfoot to John Prine. Several of them, including Chet Atkins, Emmylou Harris and Prine, returned the compliment with guest appearances. To promote the album, Elektra released ***Present Echos***, an introduction to ***Other Voices, Other Rooms***, which featured tracks by Nanci, Woody Guthrie, Guy Clark, Bob Dylan, John Prine, Townes Van Zandt, Arlo Guthrie, Kate Wolf, Emmylou Harris, the Weavers, Indigo Girls, Leo Kottke and Odetta.

Critics may argue that Nanci falls between Country and Folk. A more positive view would be that she has made a unique contribution by bringing together both idioms. As she defines her music: "I'm a Country-Folk singer, I think the two have always complemented each other." SM/BM

RECOMMENDED ALBUMS:

"Once in a Very Blue Moon" (Philo)(1984)
"The Last of the True Believers" (Rounder)(1986)
"Lone Star State of Mind" (MCA)(1987)
"Other Voices, Other Rooms" (Elektra)(1993)

DAVID GRISMAN

(Mandolin, Guitar, Banjo, Saxophone, Piano, Singer, Composer)

Given Name:	**David Jay Grisman**
Date of Birth:	**March 17, 1945**
Where Born:	**Passaic, New Jersey**
Married:	**1. Jill (div.)**
	2. Pam
Children:	**Gillian, Monroe, Samson**

David Grisman was dubbed by *Newsweek* as "The Paganini of the mandolin," and certainly, he is one of the finest players in Country music. His skills have long been recognized by his peers and he was named as "Top Mandolin Player" by *Frets* magazine in 1981.

"Dawg," as he is nicknamed, was raised in Passaic, New Jersey, and while still in his teens, could play a number of stringed instruments as well as sax and piano. He was informed by his piano teacher that mandolin wasn't a real instrument. He wisely chose to ignore this uninformed remark and, with his mandolin in tow, enrolled at New York University.

He started to play in various Folk groups in New York, including the Even Dozen Jug Band. At this time, he met other folkies such as John Sebastian. After graduating in the mid-60's, David moved to San Francisco, where in 1964 he met and befriended Jerry Garcia, who would acquire international acclaim as the leader of the Grateful Dead.

David got a call from Peter Rowan to join Earth Opera. At this stage, Rowan was coming out of his Bluegrass phase and wanted to play rock'n'roll. David had first met him in 1963 in Union Grove, North Carolina. The band's debut album was released on Elektra in 1968; however, by the end of the year Earth Opera had reached its last act.

Over the next few years, David did session work and played with various bands. In 1973, he joined forces with Rowan and Garcia in Old and in the Way. The other members of the group were Vassar Clements on fiddle and bass player John Kahn. They played a few concerts including one in October 1973 at the Boarding House, San Francisco, where they recorded their self-named album released by Rounder in 1975.

During 1973, David and Rowan were also members of the Bluegrass band, Muleskinner, which also included Richard Greene, Bill Keith and Clarence White. They released an eponymous album on Warner Brothers. By 1974, Grisman had formed another band, the Great American Music Band and again Richard Greene was part of it. The band also included the legendary Taj Mahal on bass.

In 1976, David recorded ***The David Grisman Rounder Album***, which featured Tony Rice, Jerry Douglas, Bill Keith and Ricky Skaggs. Later in 1976, David formed the first incarnation of the David Grisman Quintet, which featured guitarist Tony Rice. The debut album on Kaleidoscope, ***The David Grisman Quintet***,was a fusion of various influences including a predominant Jazz feel. The line-up of string bass and violins plus Rice's guitar created, in Grisman's words "Dawg Music" and owed more than a nod at Django Reinhardt. The album sold some 80,000 copies and, as a result, when Grisman came to release the band's second album in 1979, ***Hot Dawg***, he had moved to the Warner Brothers' distributed Horizon Records.

David and his cohorts were appearing at a miscellany of venues ranging from Jazz clubs to opening for Rock acts at major auditoria. During that year, Stephane Grappelli visited the U.S. and played some dates with the band, emphasizing the Hot Club of France parallel. There were some changes to the line-up in 1980 when Tony Rice left and was replaced by soon-to-be sessionman extraordinaire Mark O'Connor, then already a veteran at 18, on guitar and fiddle. At the same time bass player Todd Phillips departed and was replaced by Rob Wasserman. The line-up was completed by existing players: Darol Anger on violin, violectra, cello and mandolin and Mike Marshall on mandolin. The first album with the new line-up was ***Quintet '80***, which was

Mandolin maestro ***David Grisman*** *(center)*

released on Warner Brothers. The record was voted "Album of the Year" by *Frets* magazine.

Buck White's 1980 album, ***There's More Pretty Girls than One*** (Sugar Hill), was just one release to feature Grisman's magic hand. That same year saw the release of some of David's early recordings, ***Early Dawg***, also on Sugar Hill, which included assistance from Del McCoury and Bill Keith.

In 1982, David was involved with Herb Pederson and Jim Buchanan on an album entitled ***Here Today***. This project was hailed as creating a form of Bluegrass called "supergrass." However, after the ***Here Today*** album on Rounder, they went their own ways. David appeared on a pair of albums made by Tony Rice on Rounder. He produced three more albums for Warner Brothers including one with Stephane Grappelli and Grisman's own ***Dawg Jazz/Dawg Grass*** in 1983. That same year, he released another album for Rounder, ***Acoustic Christmas***. Two years later, he brought out the album ***Acousticity*** for Zebra Acoustic.

From 1987 through 1990, David released several interesting albums: ***Svingin' with Svend***, featuring Svend Asmussen, on Zebra Acoustic (1987), ***Home Is Where the Heart Is***, on Rounder (1988) which was Grammy nominated, as was ***Dawg '90***, on Acoustic Disc (1990). In 1991, he recorded a duet album with Jerry Garcia entitled ***Garcia/Grisman*** on Acoustic Disc. The following year, he teamed up with Herb Pedersen, Jim Buchanan, Jim Kerwin, Red Allen and Jerry Garcia for the ***Bluegrass Reunion*** album. Two years later, the David Grisman Quintet brought out their latest "Dawg" album, ***Dawgwood***.

Over the years, David has played on albums by Judy Collins, John Sebastian, James Taylor, Linda Ronstadt, Jonathan Edwards, Mark O'Connor, Dolly Parton, Jethro Burns, Béla Fleck, Dan Fogelberg and Alison Brown.

RECOMMENDED ALBUMS:

"Old and in the Way" (Rounder)(1973) [As Old and in the Way]
"Muleskinner" (Warner Brothers)(1973) [As Muleskinner]
"David Grisman Rounder Album" (Rounder)(1976)
"Here Today" (Rounder)(1982)
"Mondo Mando" (Warner Brothers/Zebra Acoustic)(1982)
"Dawg Jazz/Dawg Grass" (Warner Brothers)(1983)
"Acousticity" (Zebra Acoustic)(1985)
"Home Is Where the Heart Is" (Rounder)(1988)
"Dawg '90" (Acoustic Disc)(1990)
"Garcia/Grisman" (Acoustic Disc)(1991)
"Bluegrass Reunion" (Acoustic Disc)(1992)
"Dawgwood" (Acoustic Disc)(1993)

BONNIE GUITAR

(Singer, Songwriter, Guitar, Record Producer, Record Company Executive)

Given Name:	**Bonnie Buckingham**
Date of Birth:	**March 25, 1923**
Where Born:	**Seattle, Washington**
Married:	**1. Paul Tutmarc (div.)**
	2. Mario Depiano (dec'd.)
Children:	**Paula, Tiffany**

Bonnie Guitar is one of the few women in the music industry to earn the sobriquet of renaissance woman. Her impact was not just on Country music, but on popular music generally.

From childhood, Bonnie was intensely interested in music and mastered a variety of stringed instruments, ultimately settling on the guitar as her favored instrument.

In her childhood years, Jimmie Rodgers was the only Country artist whom she liked. Influenced by her father, who eulogized Irish tenors, Bonnie preferred popular music. Doris Day, Perry Como and Frank Sinatra were among her favorites. Her early music reflected this eclectic background.

Before she had graduated, Bonnie began to write songs. Shortly after leaving school, she married and it was under her married name, Tutmarc, that she started working with bands in the Seattle area in a variety of styles including Western Swing and Jazz.

In the early 50's, a local female songwriter asked Bonnie to demo some of her compositions to help get them pitched. Through this route, Bonnie's pleasant on the ear and melodic singing voice came to the attention of Los Angeles-based, Fabor Robison, owner of Fabor, Abbott and Radio Records, who was known by the songwriter. He was sufficiently impressed to sign Bonnie to Fabor in 1956, both as a recording artist and a staff guitarist. In the latter capacity, she played on the early recording sessions of Jim Reeves and Ferlin Husky, and with such stalwart session musicians as Speedy West, James Burton and Jimmy Bryant. Robison suggested a name change to aid his protege's commercial acceptance. Her constant presence in the studio prompted someone to suggest "Bonnie Guitar," which she immediately adopted.

Three singles were released before Bonnie Guitar enjoyed the hit that made her reputation. She became aware of a demo from Ned Miller of a song called *Dark Moon*. Robison intended that Bonnie's labelmate Dorsey Burnette would record the title. Robison was excited by the song and Bonnie was due to play guitar on the session. Hearing the song beforehand, Bonnie was convinced that it could launch her solo career. Knowing Robison's renowned aversion to paying royalties, she cannily offered to waive these if her producer allowed her instead to put down *Dark Moon*.

Robison readily agreed and with Bonnie playing lead guitar to her own vocal, assisted by Miller pitching in with rhythm guitar, *Dark Moon* came out on the Fabor label (it was the final release on Fabor). It attracted the interest of a local radio show, *Lucky Logger Dance Time*. This provided Robison with sufficient ammunition, together with Ned Miller's equally promising *From a Jack to a King*, to secure a major outlet for his Fabor products on Dot Records in March 1957. Dot gained first refusal on all Fabor recordings. *From a Jack to a King* was to wait until 1963 before it became the hit it deserved to be. Bonnie's version of *Dark Moon* came out in 1957 on Dot, as did another by Pop singer Gale Storm. It was a common practice for Randy Wood, Dot's producer, to release slick cover versions of Country songs aimed at the Pop market.

Both versions made the chart listings in April 1957 with Bonnie's rendition ultimately peaking in the Top 10, just two places behind her rival's offering, but Bonnie enjoyed the bonus of a Top 15 placing on the Country chart. Although her career had only just begun, *Dark Moon* was to become the song with which Bonnie Guitar was forever associated. Randy Wood cemented Bonnie's identification with this song by producing her on an album of moon songs, ***Moonlight and Shadows*** (1957). Many artists would cover *Dark Moon*, including Jim Reeves and Elvis Presley (home recording).

Two further singles followed, but only the catchy *Mister Fire Eyes*, a half-finished Ned Miller song which Bonnie completed, had any real impact. Late in 1957, the song reached the Top 15 on the Country chart and crossed over to the Pop Top 75. It would prove to be Bonnie's last hit for nine barren years. Two further Dot singles died, one of which, *I Found Out/If You'll Be the Teacher*, recorded with Billy Vaughn and his Orchestra, provided early evidence of the emerging Nashville Sound.

Bonnie's career might have taken off in more dramatic fashion had she so desired, but she turned down the chance of a regular spot on the *Grand Ole Opry* because the commitment would interfere with her session work. This too received a blow when she and Robison had a parting of the ways, allegedly following his insistence that he enjoyed power of attorney over her career. Hollywood had pursued her to play Annie Oakley and to sing in the *Road* series of movies (with Bing Crosby and Bob Hope), but her first husband was not keen on the idea and she wasn't ready for it.

Bonnie returned to her native Seattle. Here she befriended Bob Reisdorf, a local part-time record promoter, when he came to repair her new refrigerator. Later, he asked her opinion on a local teenage doo-wop group called the Fleetwoods. Bonnie was very enthused and suggested they go to see a local record distributor, Lou Lavinthal. The outcome was the formation of the Dolphin label (later renamed Dolton), by Bonnie.

The Fleetwoods more than repaid Bonnie's faith in them. She produced their early hits in a small two-track Seattle studio. Bonnie played guitar as the Fleetwoods cut their composition *Come Softly to Me.* The single (which went Gold in 1959) topped the U.S. Pop charts and went Top 10 in Britain despite rival cover versions. Nor were the Fleetwoods one hit wonders, with their third single, *Mr. Blue*, also making No.1 in the U.S. Indeed, the group enjoyed eleven U.S. chart singles between 1959 and 1963.

In 1960 another local act, the Ventures, were signed to Dolton and brought further major success. An instrumental group, they transformed Arthur "Guitar Boogie" Smith's *Walk...Don't Run* into a Top 3 Pop hit. This, and the follow-up single, *Perfidia*, sold a million copies. They had twelve chart singles for Dolton between 1960 and 1966.

As well as producing and playing on Dolton sessions (contributing distinctive classical guitar patterns to the Fleetwoods' sound), Bonnie Guitar also recorded for the label, but individual success proved elusive, with only *Candy Apple Red* (1959) making any sort of impact. She came to see her involvement with other acts as a major hindrance to her own success and in the mid-60's sold Dolton.

In 1965, Bonnie re-signed to Dot, and for the rest of the 60's enjoyed major Country success. 1966 gave her three Top 20 hits, *I'm Living in Two Worlds* (Top 10), *Get Your Lie the Way You Want It* (Top 15) and *The Tallest Tree* (Top 25). The following year *A Woman's Love* reached the Top 5, her best ever effort. 1968 started off with the Top 15 single *Stop the Sun* and was followed by *I Believe in Love*, which went Top 10. The decade closed with Bonnie signed to Paramount and enjoying an unlikely duet success with future industry giant Buddy Killen on *A Truer Love You'll Never Find than Mine.* There was also a collaboration with Don Robertson on *Born to Be with You.* Dot continued to release singles and in 1969, Bonnie scored with the Top 40 *That See Me Later Look.* Her last hit for Paramount came in 1970 with the lowly *Allegheny*.

In the 1970's Bonnie Guitar recorded for a succession of labels as she struggled to repeat her earlier successes. The minor hit *Happy Everything* (1972) on Columbia wasn't sufficient to keep her on the label. The same pattern was repeated with MCA, with *From This Moment On* (1975) providing only a minor hit. Bonnie next moved to 4 Star with whom she had a basement chart entry in 1980 with *Honey on the Moon*, which only just broke the Top 100.

She settled down with her second husband on their 80-acre ranch near Orting, Washington, and when he fell ill, she nursed him until his death in 1983. She then discovered that her career had gone. That is until Marina Romary, a restaurateur and Mayor of Soap Lake, asked her to play in her reopened club. Bonnie was still there in 1989. In 1985, she signed to Tumbleweed Records out of Kirkland, Washington, and in 1988, she signed with Playback Records. In 1989, the label released, through their Capitol distribution, the album ***You're Still the Same*** and Bonnie returned to the Top 80 with the Bob Dylan song *Still the Same.* In 1990, Bonnie Guitar made some appearances on Country Music Television. SM

RECOMMENDED ALBUMS:

"Moonlight and Shadows" (Dot)(1957) [Re-released 1959]
"Two Worlds" (Dot)(1966)
"Miss Bonnie Guitar" (Dot)(1966)
"I Believe in Love" (Dot)(1968)
"Dark Moon" (Bear Family Germany)(1991)

GUITARS ON THE GRAND OLE OPRY

By Harold Bradley

Since I performed on the *Opry* at the Ryman Auditorium in 1943 with Ernest Tubb, I will try to use that as my starting date. When I worked in Ernest Tubb's Texas Troubadours, I played a Gibson E5150 electric guitar that I bought from Billy Byrd. The first electric guitarist allowed on the *Opry*, on a regular basis, was Jimmy Short, who played a Martin with a Di Armond pickup. I was the second, when I took Jimmy's place in the summer of 1943.

Previous to either of us, Bert Hutchinson played a Martin with a Di Armond and Cousin Jody (Clell Sumney) played an amplified steel guitar on the *Opry*, but were told not to do it again. Ernest Tubb played a Martin guitar given to him by Jimmie Rodgers' widow. Carl Smith, Hank Snow, George Morgan, Eddy Arnold and most of the artists played Martins. Little Jimmy Dickens played Gibsons, either a Jumbo or later a Super 400.

Two early guitar players, Zeke and Zeb Turner, played an Epiphone and a Gibson. Guy Willis of the Oklahoma Wranglers (later named the Willis Brothers) played a Gibson L5 and later a Stromberg. There were some arch top Gibson L7s and L5s.

In 1946, when I played behind Bradley Kincaid and Eddy Arnold, I used a blonde Gibson L7. Mother Maybelle Carter used her early Gibson and Chet Atkins used a Gibson, a Di Angelico and later a Gretch. Lew Childre played a Martin tuned open, neck up, like a Dobro, with a steel bar.

Also later on, Hank Garland, Billy Byrd and Grady Martin played Bigsby guitars. Hank Williams played a Martin and Sammy Pruitt played a Gibson 400, as did Don Gibson. At some point, the Fender Telecaster became popular. In present times, one of the most popular guitars favored by Country singers is the Takamine, although Martins and Gibsons are still much played and 6-string guitars are still preferred to the 12-string version. The Fender Stratocaster has become very much the standard electric guitar and effects pedals have broadened the guitarists' sound, as have advances in amplifiers. Of late, there has been a movement back to the use of tube amplifiers, as it is felt they give a cleaner sound to the solid state versions that had replaced them.

[For biographical information on Country music's major guitarists see: Chet Atkins, Harold Bradley, Jimmy Bryant, Billy Byrd, Hank Garland, Albert Lee, Joe Maphis, Grady Martin, Les Paul, Tony Rice, Arthur "Guitar Boogie" Smith, Merle Travis.]

GULLY JUMPERS

When Formed:	**1927**
Members:	
Paul Warmack	**Mandolin, Guitar, Vocals**
Charley Arrington	**Fiddle**
Roy Hardison	**Banjo**
Burt Hutcherson	**Guitar**

In many ways, Paul Warmack's band, the Gully Jumpers, was the real workhorse of the hoedown bands on the early *Grand Ole Opry*. In 1928, for instance, they appeared on fully half the year's shows, more than any of the other string bands. Individual members of the Gully Jumpers had their own individual shows or segments on WSM and the *Opry* in the 1920's and 1930's and this gave the band an "all star" cast. The band was a key participant in the 1928 Victor field sessions in Nashville, the first recordings done in that city, and recorded some 20 masters. The band survived the deaths of several members and remained an *Opry* fixture until the 1960's.

For most of the "golden days" of the 1920's and 1930's, the basic personnel of the Gully Jumpers included Warmack (b. 1890/d. 1954) (mandolin, guitar and vocals), Charley Arrington (fiddle), Roy Hardison (banjo) and Burt Hutcherson (guitar). Warmack, was a native of Goodlettsville, a small town just north of Nashville, and he spent most of his life in Davidson County. He married in 1913 and in 1921 opened up his own garage in downtown Nashville. In 1936, he went to work as a mechanic for the state highway garage and continued to work there until his death. His banjo player, Hardison, was also a mechanic and a garage foreman. Fiddler Charley Arrington, whom George Hay, the *Opry* founder, described as "an Irishman with quick wit," had a farm about 20 miles from Nashville in the Joelton community. Guitarist Hutcherson was a woodworker by trade and was later employed by the National Life Insurance Company, the owners of WSM and the *Opry*. All four men considered themselves only part-time musicians.

The band first began appearing on the *Opry* in July 1927, and caught on fast. Soon Warmack and Hutcherson were doing an additional early morning show on WSM, calling themselves the Early Birds. They would sing duets and Hutcherson would play some of the guitar solos (he was becoming famous for pieces, like *Dew Drop Waltz* and *House of David Blues*). Soon Hutcherson also had a solo spot on the *Opry*, probably the first guitarist to be featured as a soloist. In the 1930's, George Hay felt that the band had a good chance at becoming full-time professionals and he was able to charge $100 a week to sponsors wanting six ads on the Gully Jumpers' WSM spots, but it never really worked out, and the band continued their part-time status.

The best reflection of the band's working repertoire might be seen in their Victor 1928 recordings. There were parlor tunes like *Put My Little Shoes Away* and *The Little Red Caboose Behind the Train*. They did a version of the old *Tennessee Waltz* (not the Pee Wee King song, but an earlier one), and more up-tempo pieces like *Stone Rag* and *Robertson County*. Such an array of different types of songs reflected the band's versatility, as well as the diversity that helped make the *Opry* Country's most popular radio show. CKW

HARDROCK GUNTER

(Singer, Songwriter, Guitar)
Given Name: Sidney Louis Gunter, Jr.
Date of Birth: February 27, 1925
Where Born: Birmingham, Alabama
Married: E. Joanne Dunn
Children: Joandra Mae

A regional star who never really quite managed to grab the golden ring, Hardrock Gunter is remembered by fans today for his song *Birmingham Bounce* and his Rockabilly favorite *Jukebox Help Me Find My Baby.* His 25-year recording career included stints on several major labels and his radio vitae ranged from Birmingham to West Virginia, but seldom allowed him to rise beyond the level of an engaging novelty singer and songwriter. He got his sobriquet from the time that a car hood fell on his head and he felt nothing.

Growing up in Birmingham, a city that had more of a local Country radio and records scene than many give it credit for, Hardrock started off under the influence of Hank Penny, another Alabama native who won fame over Atlanta radio. Hardrock had his own band, the Hoot Owl Ramblers, by the time he was barely into his teens and shortly later was a member of Happy Wilson's Birmingham favorites, the Golden River Boys. (Wilson was a longtime WAPI Birmingham radio and early morning TV star who helped a number of singers get their start.) Gunter eventually became the band's manager, and then, in 1949, with the advent of local TV, had a children's show on WAFM-TV.

About 1949, he was invited to record for a local label, Bama, which was then best known for its records by the John Daniel Quartet. One of his early hits was a parody of a T. Texas Tyler recitation, *Dad Gave My Dog Away*, which Gunter changed to *Dad Gave My Hog Away.* Then he wrote a lightweight piece called *Birmingham Bounce,* a song that sought to capitalize on the current fad for "geographical songs." Bama's version sold well, but it was soon driven out of the market when Decca had Red Foley do a cover of it. In 1951, Gunter himself signed with Decca, doing several Country boogie types in the manner of Wayne Raney and Foley. (One unusual entry was *The Senator from Tennessee,* a topical song about Estes Kefauver.) His duet version of *Sixty Minute Man* (with Roberta Lee, 1951) made him one of the first Country artists to cover an R & B hit.

A tour of duty in the army interrupted his attempt to promote the Decca sides and short stays with MGM and Sam Phillips' Sun label were similarly unsuccessful.

From 1952 to 1953 and from 1954 (in 1953-1954, he was a deejay at WJLD Birmingham), Gunter spent his time at WWVA Wheeling, West Virginia, on the *Jamboree*. He recorded two sessions for King (one in 1954, the second in 1955) and cut his own version of *Jukebox Help Me Find My Baby* for the independent Cross Country label, which looked like it might be a hit, until Sam Phillips leased it for Sun. Phillips edited out the gimmicky Gunther overdubbed vocal bass line and as a result, it flopped. Other sides followed on the Emperor label (also based in Wheeling), and later Country efforts appeared on the Cullman, Starday, and other labels. By 1964, his recording career was pretty much over, though he did do an album of Hank Williams tunes in 1972. He went on to run Gunter Music and Insurance Agency. CKW

RECOMMENDED ALBUM:
"Boogie Woogie on a Saturday Night" (Charly UK)(1984)

JACK GUTHRIE

(Singer, Songwriter, Guitar, Fiddle, Bass)
Given Name: Leon Jerry Guthrie
Where Born: Olive, Oklahoma
Date of Birth: November 13, 1915
Married: Ruth Henderson
Date of Death: January 15, 1948

Though modern fans remember Jack Guthrie (if at all) as a cousin of Folk singer Woody Guthrie, in his day Jack was a much greater commercial success. Though his career was beset by bad timing and ill health, he was for a couple of years in the late 40's one of the most influential Country singers and his 1945 Capitol recording of *Oklahoma Hills* emerged as one of the top songs of the decade, and a Country standard that was still heard into the 90's.

Jack Guthrie's father was a rural Oklahoma blacksmith. Jack (called Leon by his family) grew up around horses, and early on learned to do trick roping and bullwhip tricks. As Jack grew up, the family often moved to various locations in Texas and Oklahoma. He listened to his father's fiddling, the records of Jimmie Rodgers and was reportedly taught some guitar chords by a young Gene Autry. During the lean years of the Dust Bowl era, Jack's family, like so many other "Okies," migrated to California, eventually settling in the Sacramento area. Here Jack worked in rodeos and in the forest service for the WPA (Works Progress Administration). He married Ruth Henderson in 1934 and invented a novelty act whereby he used a bullwhip to snap cigarettes out of her mouth.

In 1937 Jack's cousin, Woody, followed him to California, and the two worked up a duet act, *The Oklahoman and Woody Show*, and went on the air over KFVD Hollywood on July 17, 1937. After a couple of months, though, Jack had to quit radio to work at construction jobs to feed his growing family. He kept in touch, though, and was soon singing a new song Woody had written, *Oklahoma Hills*. When Woody left the coast to go to New York in 1939, Jack sort of took custody of the song, smoothing it out and making it a favorite at bars he played. In 1944, Jack made a demo and wangled a Capitol contract from Lee Gillette. On October 16, 1944, Jack took a pick-up band into a Hollywood studio for his first session (calling the band his Oklahomans). One side was *Oklahoma Hills*, and a follow-up session eleven days later yielded *When the Cactus Is in Bloom*.

Before the records were released, though, Jack was drafted and sent to the Pacific to serve at Iwo Jima. While there, he got word that his record was No.1 on the Country chart, where it stayed for 6 weeks (with the flip-side, *I'm a Brandin' My Darlin' with My Heart*, going Top 5). Frustrated that he was unable to capitalize on his hit status, Jack finally got back stateside in January, 1946, where he began playing with Buck Ritchey and his K-6 Wranglers out of Tacoma, Washington.

Jack got down to the Capitol studios for regular sessions (including *This Troubled Mind o' Mine* and *Oakie Boogie* (a Top 3 entry in 1947)), but his health began to bother him. He was eventually diagnosed with tuberculosis and discharged from the service. He managed to do a cameo in a film called *Hollywood Barn Dance* (1947), but soon his weight had dropped to 95 pounds. By July, 1947, he was in a veterans' hospital, being told that things looked grim. He continued to record, though, eventually amassing a discography of 33 songs, plus radio transcription. His final session, in October, 1947, resembled the last one of Jimmie Rodgers. The singer was so weak, he was driven to Los Angeles in an ambulance. During the day he rested and during the night did his last records. He died on January 15, 1948.

One of Guthrie's sidemen, Red Murrell, recalled that "he was so hot in those days that we could put almost any song with him and it could sell." Indeed, Jack's records did stay in print for many years, and Woody's son, Arlo Guthrie, kept the songs alive in many of his own best-selling albums in the 70's. CKW

RECOMMENDED ALBUM:

"Jack Guthrie and His Greatest Songs" (Capitol)(1966) [Re-released in the original sleeve by Stetson UK (1989)]

WOODY GUTHRIE

(Singer, Songwriter, Guitar)

Given Name:	**Woodrow Wilson Guthrie**
Date of Birth:	**July 14, 1912**
Where Born:	**Okemah, Oklahoma**
Married:	**1. Mary Jennings (div.)**
	2. Marjorie
Children:	**Arlo Guthrie**
Date of Death:	**October 3, 1967**

On October 7, 1967, Tom Paxton announced to a stunned audience, at London's Royal Albert Hall, that Woody Guthrie had died. He led the assembly, who sang as one *This Land Is Your Land*. Not with tears but with joy. This is the effect that Woody Guthrie had. He was considered by most as the first Country singer with a social conscience.

Woody was born of pioneering stock in an Oklahoma that was still considered American-Indian territory. His father came from Texas with a family tradition of prize fighting and guitar and banjo playing in cowboy bands. Charlie Guthrie settled down after marriage and ran a trading post and then a real estate office at the time of the first oil boom in Oklahoma. Woody started singing at age 4. Then while he was still at high school, Woody's father's business failed, his sister died in a coal oil stove explosion and his mother was committed to a state asylum. Woody learned to play harmonica and left home before he was 14 and his father moved back to Texas.

Woody traveled across America in the 20's and 30's looking for work. He arrived in Pampa, where his father's half brother, Jeff, taught him how to play guitar. He played with Jeff at various local gigs and later they had their own magic show.

After his first marriage, Woody set off for California, where he worked as a painter by day and a singer in the saloons at night. He often adapted existing Folk songs and put his own words to the tunes. Many years later, he would voice his objection to copyright laws. For most of his life, he wrote one or two songs a day.

In California, he teamed up with Maxine "Lefty Lou" Grissman as Woody and Lefty Lou. They got a regular spot on KFVD Los Angeles. However, the wanderlust got him, and after several years, he wandered down to Tijuana in Mexico and broadcast on XELO, but soon he was back at KFVD as a solo act.

When the Depression hit, Woody rode freight trains, slept in ditches and joined the Dust Bowl refugees on the trek to California. In the late 30's, he based himself in New York, where he met other Folk performers including Pete Seeger, who joined him in concerts. He wrote for the Communist paper *The Daily Worker* and played throughout the northeastern states.

Folk musicologist Alan Lomax invited Woody to Washington, D.C. There Guthrie recorded material for the Library of Congress Archive of Folk Song. The resultant recordings formed twelve albums entitled *Dust Bowl Ballads*. In addition, Lomax recorded conversations with Guthrie which ranged over various subjects including songwriting and collecting.

After New York, Woody moved out west to California, went to Bonneville Dam and then returned to New York. He formed the Almanac Singers in New York with Pete Seeger, Lee Hays and Millard Lampell. During the 40's, they covered the country doing tours and charity gigs, appearing at union and radical meetings and helping workers to form unions.

During WWII, Woody entered the Merchant Marines with Cisco Houston. He was twice torpedoed but still managed to continue collecting Folk songs when his vessel visited Britain and Russia. He also kept up his singing and writing. Just before the end of hostilities, he was drafted into the Army.

At the end of the war, Guthrie came back to New York, where he married for a second time. Marjorie had been a dancer with the Martha Graham troupe in Brooklyn. They had several children, including Arlo, who would go on to fame with his album/movie *Alice's Restaurant*. Woody started to appear with Pete Seeger and Huddie Ledbetter (Leadbelly) and also played solo gigs. During this time, he recorded material for that great man of Folk music, Moses Asch. For Asch's Folkways label, Woody recorded songs that would appear on various Folkways albums listed below, which included three volumes of children's songs. He wrote his autobiography, *Bound for Glory*, which was made into a superb movie in 1976, with David Carradine playing Guthrie.

Many of Woody's songs came into the repertoire of British Skiffle musicians in the late 50's. *Grand Coulie Dam* was cut in 1958 by Lonnie Donegan and became a Top 10 hit. In addition, Guthrie was the inspiration to the new generation of Folk singers that the 60's Folk boom generated, such as Tom Paxton, Phil Ochs and Bob Dylan. He also inspired his own generation, including fellow performers Cisco Houston, Burl Ives, Ramblin' Jack Elliott and Pete Seeger.

By the 60's, Woody was suffering from Huntington's chorea, a hereditary degenerative disease of the muscles which is carried through the female side of the family, and for which there is no known cure. Just before he died, Guthrie was visited at Greystone Park Hospital by Dylan and they became friends. In October, 1967, the guitar that wore with pride the slogan "this machine kills fascists" was silenced forever, yet the spirit and Guthrie's mantle were draped on other shoulders.

His relevance to Country audiences is that he created a template that took Folk music in a way that Jimmie Rodgers took Blues and molded it into something that Country writer/performers such as Hank Williams, Merle Haggard, Tom T. Hall and Waylon Jennings would later be able to build on. Music to touch the common man.

RECOMMENDED ALBUMS:

"Bound for Glory" (Folkways)(1961)
"Dust Bowl Ballads" (Folkways)(1961) & (1964)
"Ballads of Sacco and Vanzetti" (Folkways)(1961)
"Woody Guthrie Sings Folk Songs, Vol. 1" (Folkways)(1962) [With Cisco Houston]
"Woody Guthrie Sings Folk Songs, Vol. 2" (Folkways)(1964) [With Cisco Houston and Sonny Terry]
"Struggle" (Folkways)(1964)
"Woody Guthrie" (Library of Congress Recordings, 28 Folk Songs)(3 albums)(Elektra)(1964)
"Bed on the Floor" (Verve/Forecast)(1965)
"Bonneville" (Verve/Forecast)(1966)
"This Land Is Your Land" (Folkways)
"Immortal Woody Guthrie" (Olympic)(University of Washington)
"Songs to Grow On" Volumes 1-3 (children's songs)(Folkways)
"Cowboy Songs" (Stinson) [With Cisco Houston]
"Blind Sonny Terry & Woody Guthrie" (Archive of Folk)(1969)

H

HACKBERRY RAMBLERS, The

When Formed: 1933
Leader
Luderin Darbone Vocal, Fiddle
1936 Members:
Lennis Sonnier Vocals, Guitar
Edwin Duhon Vocals, Guitar, Accordion
Joe Werner Vocals, Harmonica, Guitar
Floyd Rainwater Vocals, Bass
Lonnie Rainwater Vocals, Guitar
Later Members:
Floyd Shreve Vocals, Guitar
Crawford Vincent Vocals, Drums, Multi-instrumentalist
Eddie Shuler Guitar, Vocals
Johnnie Parket Bass
Glen Croker Vocals, Steel Guitar
Other Members:
Boley Thibodeaux, L.D. Whitlow, Pierre Crader, Waverly Lejeune, Danny Shreve, Morris Broussard

The Hackberry Ramblers (also referred to as the Riverside Ramblers) were the best known and most recorded Cajun band in the half-dozen years prior to WWII, cutting many sides for the Bluebird label.

The son of a Cajun accordion player and oil field worker, Luderin Darbone (b. January 14, 1913, Evangeline, Louisiana) received his first fiddle as a gift from his parents at the age of 12. As his family spent some time in Texas, Luderin learned hillbilly tunes as well as those of French-Canadian origin. He attended Vincent Business College for two years, but as employment was scarce during the Depression, Darbone organized a band and got some time on a new radio station in Lake Charles, KFDM. This soon yielded work at Baker Andrus' Dance Hall in Basile, Louisiana.

By 1934, he also had a day job at a service station and the Hackberry Ramblers obtained a sound system; evidently, they were the first Cajun group to have one. As a result, their renown skyrocketed. In August 1935, the band started their recordings for Bluebird in sessions at New Orleans. Through 1939, they would have some 78 sides released on this RCA subsidiary.

When the Ramblers started a radio show sponsored by Montgomery Ward, in 1936, they began to use the name Riverside Ramblers, for Riverside Tires (Marshall Ward's tire brand). The show came from Marshall Ward's store in Lafayette and was broadcast over KVOL. Henceforth, their recordings in French continued to be released as the Hackberry Ramblers, while the sides cut in English used Riverside Ramblers.

Lennis Sonnier did most of the singing in Cajun, Luderin, Floyd Rainwater and Edwin Duhon also sang in that dialect, while Joe Werner usually sang on the English numbers. Werner's vocal on *Wondering* (1936) became something of a hit, enabling him to get his own contract with Decca. Later, however, he returned to the Ramblers and also led another Bluebird recording combo known as Joe's Acadians. One of the other Rambler vocalists, Floyd Shreve, also had a session for Decca.

In mid-1939, Luderin's father, Ed, died in an oil field accident. The incident gave Luderin such an emotional jolt, that he stopped playing for nearly a year. Thereafter, he played on weekends until WWII, when he went to work in a defense plant and the band became inactive.

They reorganized again in 1946 and began a ten-year Saturday night run at the Silver Star Club in Lake Charles. The following year, they went to New Orleans for another recording session, this time with the Deluxe label. Lennis Sonnier again handled most of the lead singing.

In 1963, the Ramblers were on the verge of disbanding when Chris Strachwitz, who wished to make Cajun music available to a national audience, induced them to record an album for Arhoolie. Later, they cut a pair of singles for Gold Band as well.

Since then, Darbone has maintained the band and they have periodically played at festivals and special events, including 1984's World Trade Fair in New Orleans and the 1988 New Orleans Jazz Festival. Like most Cajun groups, the Hackberry Ramblers were only a part-time operation, except for that brief period when no other work could be found. Nonetheless, over the years, Darbone managed to build a quality brick home from his "hobby" earnings and become one of the great legends of Cajun music. This was a band that played for fun and were very entertaining and made sure that they and their audiences had a good time.

As re-issue anthologies of Cajun pioneers began to appear on disc, several cuts by the Hackberry Ramblers were included. In 1988, Strachwitz devoted an entire album to them on Old Timey Records. IMT

RECOMMENDED ALBUMS:

"Louisiana Cajun Music" (Arhoolie)(1964)
"The Hackberry Ramblers: Early Recordings 1935-1948" (Old Timey)(1988)

DURWOOD HADDOCK

(Singer, Songwriter, Guitar, Fiddle)
Date of Birth: August 16, 1934
Where Born: Lamasco, Texas

Durwood Haddock developed an early interest in Country music and the radio business, spending his career weaving in and out of both.

Born in rural Fannin County, Texas, Durwood lived all over the state, either with his parents or an aunt, moving between farms and the city. He could play several instruments by the time he finished high school but didn't view Country music as a way to make a living, so he enrolled in radio school in Tyler, Texas, and took a year-long cram course.

Upon completion of his studies, Durwood rode a Greyhound bus to a job he had gotten at KSRY Seymour, Texas. The job lasted a week and he got fired for playing Bing Crosby's *White Christmas* in the middle of July. After that, he took off to play fiddle in southern Oklahoma honky tonks and beer joints. Later he went to West Texas and in 1954, landed his first professional gig at the Odessa Danceland. He worked for $60.00 a week, until three months later, the audience fell off and he got fired again. Then he moved 40 miles to Kermit, Texas, stayed another three months and did some recording for 4 Star.

During the same year, he met Eddie Miller and the two began writing together. They came up with the song *There She Goes*, inspired by the oil wells in operation in West Texas at that time. He cut the first recording of the song but it went nowhere. Then, in 1955, Carl Smith did a cover for Columbia, which went Top 3, and Jerry Wallace later recorded it in 1961 and it became a Pop Top 30 entry. In 1980, it was the lead song in the movie *Coal Miner's Daughter* and was featured on the soundtrack album as well.

About the same time as Durwood wrote the song, he went to Denison, Texas and started a 15-minute radio program and also did some club work. He began broadcasting on KFST in Ft. Stockton but was once again fired after three months because the station decided they couldn't afford to pay his $50.00 a week salary. He next worked for the news car in Odessa, but got tired of all the accidents and killings he saw on the beat.

From there, he moved to Monahans and worked at one station before moving over to KERV where he found a home from 1957 to 1962. He worked there as a deejay, salesman, and station manager, while working gigs at clubs during weekends and had some low level chart records. In 1962, he released the self-penned *Big Night in My House*, on United Artists. With the same general luck he had in the past, the label dropped him after this, so he formed his own label, Eagle International, and released two more singles, *How Are Things in Your City* (1963) and *Our Big House* (1964).

Durwood left KERV in 1962 and formed his own band, to tour and do personal appearances for the next 6 years. 1963-64 brought a contract with Monument, who released two singles over the next two years, *Wait'll I Get My Hands on You* and *Newest Thing in Night Life*. In 1968, Durwood made the move to Nashville, where he formed his own publishing company, and signed with Metromedia Records, where he cut a self-proclaimed "God awful record," *When the Swelling Goes Down* (1969), and Willie Nelson's *Gotta Get Drunk and I Sure Do Dread It* (1970). His final release with Metromedia was *East Bourbon Street* (1970).

During the early 70's, Durwood saw Country chart action. The most successful of his releases was *Angel in an Apron*, on Caprice, in 1974, which went Top 70. He then had five more chart singles between 1977 and 1980, on his own Eagle International and the independent Country International, with *The Perfect Love Song* being his most successful, in 1978, on the latter label.

All in all, Durwood has managed to overcome his many down times and periodic disenchantment with the industry to have the greatest success on his own label. In 1980, he was living on a farm in Lamasco, Texas.

LAP

HAGERS, The

JON HAGER
(Singer, Guitar, Harmonica, Percussion, Actor)

Date of Birth:	**August 30, 1946**
	(elder by 20 minutes)
Married:	**1. (Div.)**
	2. Catherine (div.)
Children:	**Mandy, Jessyca**

JIM HAGER
(Singer, Guitar, Drums, Actor)

Date of Birth:	**August 30, 1946**
Married:	**Betty**
Children:	**Ronnie**
Both Born:	**Chicago, Illinois**

The Hagers are the only set of twins to have made a major mark on Country music. They came to prominence as members of the long-running TV series *Hee Haw*, handling singing and playing as well as being participants in the cornball humor that flew about.

The identical twins were adopted by the Rev. John and Mrs. Fran Hager, who instilled in the boys a love of music. During high school days, Jon and Jim performed at various functions and appeared on a Saturday morning teen record TV show. After graduation from college, they were in the U.S. Army. The brothers were stationed in Germany and then Vietnam, where they performed for the troops in USO tours as well as in officer and NCO clubs. They returned to civilian life in Park Ridge, Illinois, and formed a three-piece group that debuted at the East Street club and played around lounges in the Chicago area for a year and a half.

They set out for California, where they were spotted by Randy Sparks of the New Christy Minstrels, who engaged them to appear at his Ledbetters club in Los Angeles. From there, they went on to appear regularly at Disneyland in Anaheim, where they were spotted by Buck Owens. He took on their management through his Omac Artists Corporation and they toured with the Buck Owens All-American Show for two years. In 1969, they signed to Capitol Records and hit the Country singles chart with *Gotta Get to Oklahoma ('Cause California's Gettin' to Me)* and the following year, they released their debut self-titled album.

That year, they joined *Hee Haw*, initially performing two songs and staying for 18 years. They had three minor hits during the year with *Loneliness Without You*, *Goin' Home to Your Mother* and *Silver Wings*. They had their final chart entry in 1971 with the Top 50 record *I'm Miles Away*. They changed record labels the following year, when they moved to Barnaby, and during 1974, they recorded for Elektra and both brothers could be discovered dating Karen Valentine!

The brothers have appeared quite a lot on television. Merv Griffin produced a TV pilot for network and in 1976, they could be seen in the ABC-TV movie *Twin Detectives* with Lillian Gish. They also made a guest appearance on *The Bionic Woman*, which starred Lindsay Wagner. They have made numerous commercials, including ones for J.C. Penney, What-A-Burger and Quaker Oats. They also co-hosted *Country Kitchen*, with Florence Henderson on TNN in 1987.

During 1977, they toured doing Country-Comedy and included impersonations and parodies which took a sideswipe at Richard Nixon. Shortly after leaving *Hee Haw* in 1987, there was talk of a sit-com/variety show that was tentatively called *Doubles*, but it didn't become a reality. They made their first video in 1990, which accompanied their Evergreen single, *I'm Wishin' I Could Go Fishin' Forever*, which ties in with their annual fishing tournament, the Hager Twins Musky Hunt, which is held at Lakewood, Wisconsin, and benefits several causes including Cerebral

Palsy and the Snowmobile Hall of Fame and the Cable Museum.

RECOMMENDED ALBUMS:

"The Hagers" (Capitol)(1970)
"Two Hagers Are Better than One" (Capitol)(1970)
"Motherhood, Apple Pie & the Flag" (Capitol)(1971)
"Countryside" (Barnaby)(1972)
"The Hagers" (Elektra)(1974)

MERLE HAGGARD

(Singer, Songwriter, Guitar, Fiddle, Kazoo)

Given Name:	**Merle Ronald Haggarerd**
Date of Birth:	**April 6, 1937**
Where Born:	**Bakersfield, California**
Married:	**1. Leona Hobbs (div.)** **2. Bonnie Owens (m. 1965)(div.)** **3. Leona Williams (m. 1978)(div.)** **4. Debora Parret (div.)** **5. Theresa Lane (m. 1993)**
Children:	**Dana, Marty Ronald, Kelli Marie, Noel Lee, Benny, Jenessa**

In Country music, there are stars, those who think they're stars, those who should be stars, and superstars. In the last category is, without doubt, Merle Haggard. If ever a performer was destined to be a superstar, then it is this man.

Merle's parents, James and Flossie Haggard, had migrated to California from the Dust Bowl of Oklahoma. James, who worked for the Santa Fe Railroad, was a competent fiddler, as was his father, but as Flossie was a strict Church of Christ member, she insisted that he stop playing in honky tonks after their marriage. When Merle was born, his family was living in a boxcar. When Merle was age 9, his father died from a brain tumor and young Haggard became restless and unruly. Flossie put him into a juvenile home to try and scare him into straightening out.

Influenced by the songs of Jimmie Rodgers and Lefty Frizzell, Merle ran away when he was 14 and worked in fruit orchards, oil fields, farms, drove a potato truck and was a short order cook and occasionally embarked on petty crimes. He began to listen more and more to Country music, especially Bob Wills, Rodgers, Frizzell and Stuart Hamblen. Merle made his professional debut at age 15, at a talent contest in Modesto, California, where he won $5.00. The following year, he sat in with Lefty Frizzell and Frizzell refused to go on stage, unless Merle played.

Then, in 1957, while drunk, Merle attempted to break into a bar that was still open. He was sent to San Quentin and became inmate #A-45200. He got into further trouble

*Country superstar **Merle Haggard***

(resulting in solitary confinement) by brewing beer in his cell. However, it was a conversation with a prisoner on death row, through the ventilation system, that turned his life around. The prisoner was the famed Caryl Chessman, known as the "Red Light Bandit."

Merle began to work in the prison's textile mill and took educational courses. He then became a member of the warden's Country band and started to think about a career as an entertainer. While Merle was in San Quentin, Johnny Cash played his famed concert there. Merle was paroled in 1960, after becoming a model prisoner. He returned to Bakersfield, where he worked for his older brother, Lowell, an electrical contractor, as a ditchdigger. He augmented his earnings by moonlighting as a guitar player in Bakersfield's infamous "beer can hill" area. He formed his own band, the High Pocket Band, and for a while played in Wynn Stewart's band.

Merle was initially helped by Buck and Bonnie Owens and then came to the attention of Charles "Fuzzy" Owen, an Arkansas musician, who became his manager. It was he who persuaded Merle to stop singing like Lefty Frizzell. Owen owned Tally Records, which he had purchased from his cousin, Lewis Talley. At the end of 1963, Merle hit the Country charts with his debut Tally single, *Sing a Sad Song*, which reached the Top 20. His follow-up single, in 1964, *Sam Hill*, did not fare as well, but then Merle teamed up with Bonnie Owens (who in 1966 would become the second Mrs. Haggard) and had a Top 30 success with *Just Between the Two of Us*. The big break-through came for Merle in 1965, when Liz Anderson's *(My Friends Are Gonna Be) Strangers* became Merle's first Top 10 hit.

Merle put together a backing band, the Strangers, and moved over to Capitol Records. His first single, *I'm Gonna Break Every Heart I Can*, only made it to the Top 50, but then the Merle Haggard career got under way with a flourish. In 1966, he had three major hits, *Swinging Doors* (Top 5), *The Bottle Let Me Down* (Top 3) and his first No.1, *The Fugitive* (later renamed *I'm a Lonesome Fugitive*). The flipside of the latter, *Someone Told My Story*, also reached the Top 40.

During the rest of the 60's, Merle could not go wrong. It was becoming very apparent that Merle was not only a first class singer, he was also a songwriter of the first order. In 1967, he reached the Top 3 with *I Threw Away the Roses* and then had a run of four No.1s, *Branded Man* and *Sing Me Back Home* (both 1967) and *The Legend of Bonnie and Clyde* and *Mama Tried* (both 1968). The flip-side of *Bonnie and Clyde* was a song that would eclipse all the others in becoming a classic and yet never became a hit, *I Started Loving You Again*. *Mama Tried* came from the movie *Killers Three*, in which Merle appeared. He wrapped up 1968 with *I Take a Lot of Pride in What I Am*, which reached the Top 3.

All three singles of 1969 went to No.1. They were *Hungry Eyes*, *Workin' Man Blues* and the now famous anti-liberal song, *Okie from Muskogee*, which also crossed over to the Top 50 on the Pop chart. Merle debuted the song before a crowd of NCOs at Fort Bragg, North Carolina. Following the public reaction to the song, he was asked to endorse George Wallace politically, but Haggard refused. He started off the new decade with another No.1, *The Fightin' Side of Me,* and then had a Top 10 hit with the instrumental *Street Singer*, followed by two Top 3 records, *Jesus Take Hold* and *I Can't Be Myself/Sidewalks of Chicago*.

Merle stayed with Capitol until 1976, during which time the hits just rolled in. In 1971, there were *Soldier's Last Letter* and *Someday We'll Look Back* (both Top 3), and two No.1s, *Daddy Frank (The Guitar Man)* and *Carolyn* (also a Top 60 Pop hit). In 1972, there were three No.1 singles, *Grandma's Harp/Turnin' Off a Memory*, *It's Not Love (But It's Not Bad)* and *I Wonder if They Ever Think of Me*. That year, Governor Ronald Reagan of California granted Merle a full pardon. The following year, Merle had *The Emptiest Arms in the World* (Top 3) and two No.1 records, *Everybody's Had the Blues* and *If We Make It Through December* (also a Top 30 Pop hit).

Merle then followed with a run of seven No.1 hits; 1974: *Things Aren't Funny Anymore*, *Old Man from the Mountain* and Dolly Parton's *Kentucky Gambler*; 1975: *Always Wanting You*, *Movin' On* (from the NBC-TV series of the same name) and *It's All in the Movies*. During 1976, his final year on Capitol, Merle had his seventh consecutive chart topper, *The Roots of My Raising*, which was followed by *Here Comes the Freedom Train* (Top 10) and *Cherokee Maiden/What Have You Got Planned Tonight Diana* (No.1). *Cherokee Maiden* was originally associated with its creator, Bob Wills.

Merle's connection with Wills was strengthened before the latter's death in 1975. In 1970, Merle recorded the album ***Tribute to the Best Damn Fiddle Player in the World (Or My Salute to Bob Wills)*** on which Wills and some of the Texas Playboys played. Merle reciprocated by playing on Wills' final album, ***For the Last Time***, in 1974. In Wills' will, his fiddle was bequeathed to Merle, and he still plays it on stage. While with Capitol, Merle tried to release the track *Irma Jackson*, a song about interracial love, but Capitol advised against it.

Merle moved over to MCA in 1977 and on the whole did not fare as well as his years on Capitol. That year, he had two Top 3 singles, *If We're Not in Love By Monday* and *Ramblin' Fever/When My Blue Moon Turns to Gold Again*. He followed up with the Top 20 record, *A Working Man Can't Get Nowhere Today* (on Capitol) and he wrapped up the year with *From Graceland to the Promised Land*, which went Top 5 Country and Top 60 Pop, from his tribute album to Elvis Presley, ***My Farewell to Elvis***.

1978 started out with a double-sided hit from Capitol, *Running Kind/Making Believe*, which reached the Top 15. This was followed by *I'm Always on a Mountain When I Fall* and *It's Been a Great Afternoon/Love Me When You Can*, both of which reached the Top 3. Capitol took its last chance at capitalizing on Merle's success, by releasing *The Way It Was in '51*, which had been the flip-side of *The Roots of My Raising*, but it flopped. Merle also got together with his third wife, Leona Williams, for a Top 10 single, *The Bull and the Beaver*. Merle would next have a hit with her, in 1983, when *We're Strangers Again*, from her album, reached the Top 50.

Merle stayed with MCA until 1981, during which time he racked up the 1979 hits *Red Bandana/I Must Have Done Something Bad* and *My Own Kind of Hat/Heaven Was a Drink of Wine*, both Top 5. That year, Merle appeared in several episodes of James Michener's *Centennial* on NBC-TV. In 1980, *The Way I Am* and *Misery and Gin* were both Top 3 hits and both from the Clint Eastwood movie *Bronco Billy*, in which Merle appeared. He wrapped up the year with another No.1, *I Think I'll Stay Here and Drink*. He also teamed up with Eastwood for *Bar Room Buddies*, which became a No.1 hit.

In 1981, Merle had two major hits, before moving to Epic Records, namely, *Leonard*, which was dedicated to his old drinking buddy, Tommy Collins, who was born Leonard Sipes. The single reached the Top 10 and was followed by the Top 5 release *Rainbow Stew*. He also made the Top 50 with *I Can't Hold Myself in Line*, in duet with Johnny Paycheck. That year, Merle wrote his autobiography, *Sing Me Back Home*, with help from Peggy Russell.

Whereas at MCA he had been produced by Fuzzy Owen and Hank Cochran, at Epic he took on the production chores himself, with the assistance of experienced producers such as Ray Baker and Bob Montgomery. The difference showed and his first two singles, *My Favorite Memory* (1981) and *Big City* (1982), went to No.1; the latter featuring harmonies from Leona Williams. MCA released *Dealing with the Devil*, which reached the Top 50, and then Merle had *Are the Good Times Really Over (I Wish a Buck Was Still Silver)* (Top 3) and another No.1, *Going Where the Lonely Go*. Merle also had two major hits with George Jones, taken from their duet album, ***A Taste of Yesterday's Wine***, the No.1 single *Yesterday's Wine* and the Top 10 release *C.C. Waterback*. He started off 1983 with yet one more No.1 with *You Take Me for Granted*, followed by the Top 3 hit, *What Am I Gonna Do (With the Rest of My Life)*. He also had a Top 10 duet with Willie Nelson, taken from their album ***Pancho and Lefty***. From the end of 1983 and into 1985, Merle had a run of five No.1 records, interspersed by a release from MCA, ***It's All in the Game***, which went Top 60. The five chart toppers were *Pancho and Lefty* (with Willie Nelson), *That's the Way Love Goes* (both 1983), *Someday When Things Are Good*, *Let's Chase Each Other Around the Room* and a duet with Janie Fricke, *A Place to Fall Apart* (all 1984), and *Natural High* (1985). With the arrival of the new bloods in Country music, Merle's chart success became more erratic and between 1985 and 1989, his only major hits were *Kern River* (Top 10, 1985), *I Had a Beautiful Time* (Top 5), *A Friend in California* (Top 10) and *Out Among the Stars* (Top 25) (all 1986), *Twinkle, Twinkle Lucky Star* (No.1, 1987), *Chill Factor* (Top 10), *We Never Touch at All* (Top 25) and *You Babe* (Top 25) (all 1988) and *5:01 Blues* (Top 20), *A Better Love Next Time* (Top 5) and *If You Want to Be My Woman* (Top 25) (all 1989).

In 1990, Merle signed with Curb Records, but by now success eluded him. In 1993, he was nominated for election to the Country Music Hall of Fame, but lost out to Willie Nelson. Merle Haggard is a unique performer with a mind of his own. He was once scheduled to appear in CBS-TV's version of *Oklahoma!*, with Jeannie C. Riley and Minnie Pearl, but he pulled out at the last minute, as, contrary to his wishes, he was expected to dance. However, he did appear in the movie version of *Huckleberry Finn*. In 1994, Merle released the album ***1994***, and from this he charted Top 60 with Max D. Barnes' song *In My Next Life*.

Merle's strengths lie in the fact that he writes most of his material, but is still adept at recording standards as well as contemporary material. He is also not afraid to use "non-Country" instruments such as horns, as perfectly exemplified on his version of *Pennies from Heaven*, from his 1986 album ***Out Among the Stars***.

He also has a keen sense of history and has all of his concerts filmed by his video company, to show his contribution to 20th century music. There is no doubt that he has left a legacy. His music was taken on the Apollo 16 mission to the Moon in a container and is also buried on Earth in a canister, which earned him a place in the *Guinness Book of Records*. That sense of history also manifests itself with relationships. His early experiences somewhat paralleled those of Biff Adam (the "General"), percussionist with the Strangers and VP of Merle's Silverthorn resort in California; the early loss of his father made Biff and Merle close friends.

Merle, who was the first major Country performer to be featured in the Jazz magazine *Downbeat*, wants the following epitaph: "He was the greatest Jazz guitar player, who loved to play Country Music." In 1994, Merle Haggard was inducted into the Country Music Hall of Fame.(For Merle's awards see Awards Section.)

RECOMMENDED ALBUMS:

In three words . . . all of them, but we have listed those essential ones to get.

"The Legend of Bonnie & Clyde" (Capitol)(1968) [Re-released by Stetson UK in the original sleeve (1989)]
"Same Train, Different Time" (Capitol)(1969)
"Okie from Muskogee" (Capitol)(1970)
"Land of Many Churches" (double)(Capitol)(1971) [Re-issued on Stetson UK in the original sleeve (1990)]
"Let Me Tell You About a Song" (Capitol)(1972)
"Ramblin' Fever" (MCA)(1977)
"My Farewell to Elvis" (MCA)(1977)
"I'm Always on a Mountain When I Fall" (MCA)(1978)
"Tribute to the Best Damn Fiddle Player in the World (Or My Salute to Bob Wills)" (Capitol)(1982)
"A Taste of Yesterday's Wine" (Epic)(1982) [With George Jones]
"The Epic Collection (Live)" (MCA)(1983)
"Pancho & Lefty" (Epic)(1984) [With Willie Nelson]
"It's All in the Game" (Epic)(1984)
"Amber Waves of Grain" (Epic)(1985)

"Out Among the Stars" (Epic)(1986)
"Merle Haggard Sings Country Favourites" (Capitol UK)(1987)
"Seashores of Old Mexico" (Epic)(1987) [With Willie Nelson]
"Chill Factor" (Epic)(1987)
"5:01 Blues" (Epic)(1989)
"1994" (Curb)(1994)

BJØRO HÅLAND

(Singer, Songwriter, Guitar)
Date of Birth: October 6, 1943
Where Born: Håland, Norway
Married: Liv
Children: Arne, Nina

It was while Bjøro Håland was working as a construction worker in New York for six years that he began to sing Country music. When he returned to Norway, he started his Country music career.

Bjøro is Norway's most successful Country star, by far. He has sold more records than any other Norwegian Country act and he was soon being invited to play in other countries, as well. In 1982, he was voted "Number One European Country Music Male Singer" at the Golden Star Awards in Holland. The following year, Bjøro was chosen to represent Scandinavia at the International Country Music Awards Gala in Fort Worth, Texas. When he appeared at the *Grand Ole Opry*, the audience was so enthused that they called him back for an encore.

His reputation gathered momentum and he guested four times at the Wembley Festival in England. He also appeared at England's other prestigious festival in Peterborough. He has also appeared on radio and TV in Europe and the U.S. In 1988, Bjøro was invited to the Praha International Country Festival in Czechoslovakia, where he appeared with Kathy Mattea and the Bellamy Brothers.

Bjøro's recordings have all been issued on Grappa Records and were made for the English and Norwegian speaking audience. Several of his albums were recorded at Pete Drake's Pete's Place Studio in Nashville, with Pete producing.

In 1994, Bjøro made his ninth visit to the four-day Minot Festival in North Dakota, where he is a very popular artist. JAB

RECOMMENDED ALBUMS:

(All Norwegian Releases)
"Bjøro Håland" (Grappa)
"I Love You Because" (Grappa)
"To My Friends" (Grappa)
"My Nashville Album" (Grappa)
"Adios Amigo" (Grappa)
"Min Stetson og Guitar" (Grappa)
"On Tour" (Grappa)
"Just for You" (Grappa)
"Bjøro's Best" (Grappa)
"Melody Man" (Grappa)
"Bjøro Håland '87" (Grappa)(1987)
"Mitt Jule Album" (Grappa)(1987)
"By Request" (Grappa)(1988)
Video:
"On Tour" (Grappa)

MONTE HALE

(Singer, Guitar, Actor)
Given Name: Monte Hale
Date of Birth: June 8, 1921
Where Born: San Angelo, Texas
Married: JoAnne

Monte Hale was a significant singing cowboy in the latter half of the 1940's, in a series of films for Republic Pictures. While it is true that he sang somewhat less than the others, he did sing as well and in a natural appealing down-home style rather than in the stilted trained voice personified by some of the lesser competitors. Also, unlike the other cowboy vocalists, Hale did not vigorously pursue a recording career, after his film career ended. As a result, his discs are scarce and no albums have ever been on the market.

According to the traditional account, Monte picked cotton for a month to earn sufficient funds to purchase an $8.50 guitar. He soon learned to play and from the age of 13, began earning his living working in clubs. In the early part of WWII, as bond drives began gathering steam, Monte made the acquaintance of character actor Chill Wills, who in turn introduced him to theater owner Phil Isley, the father of award-winning actress Jennifer Jones. Isley was the chairman of the Stars Over Texas Bond Drive. Monte joined the troupe as a singer and subsequently helped raise some $60 million in bonds.

Isley recommended Monte to Herbert Yates of Republic Pictures, who signed the young singer to a seven-year contract in 1944, after he had hitchhiked his way from Texas to Hollywood. Monte played small supporting roles in series westerns and serials such as *Stepping in Society* and *Big Bonanza* in the first year and a half. These early movies starred Richard Arlen, Sunset Carson, Bill Elliott and Rocky Lane. Beginning in the spring of 1946, Hale got his own series, which ran for five years. While he sang in most of his early films, Monte generally vocalized with less frequency than Gene Autry or Roy Rogers. His singing tended to fit into what could otherwise be termed an action Western, rather than the elaborate productions increasingly associated with Autry and Rogers. The Sons of the Pioneers provided vocal support in his first major film, *Home on the Range,* while Foy Willing and the Riders of the Purple Sage furnished musical backup in several others that included *Along the Oregon Trail.*

Singing cowboy ***Monte Hale***

Between April, 1946 and November, 1950, Monte starred in nineteen pictures for Republic, that also included *Out California Way*. Several of the movies were made in Trucolor and featured Adrian Booth as his leading lady, while others had Paul Hurst as a sidekick. Fawcett Publications printed a series of Monte Hale comic books, which fans generally cherished as among the best of their kind (See Movie Section). He was replaced at Republic by Rex Allen.

Although Monte's singing had originally brought him to Hollywood, he did not have a big recording career, as did other former screen cowboys such as Tex Ritter, Eddie Dean and Jimmy Wakely. He had record sessions with the smaller Bel-Tone label and the larger MGM. Some of his better-known songs included *In My Stable There's an Empty Stall* and *Statue in the Bay*, the latter being about the Statue of Liberty. In retrospect, it seems odd that no anthology of his collected recordings has appeared.

When Hale's series ended in 1950, he toured extensively for a time, often with Ray Whitley. Like many others of that era, Monte derived considerable satisfaction from his appearances in Shrine hospitals. In 1954, he co-starred with Kirby Grant in a Northwest Mounted Police film, *Yukon Vengeance,* and two years later, Monte had a small but significant role in the major film *Giant*. He also appeared in the 1966 movie *The Chase* and his last film role came in 1973 in *Guns of a Stranger*. He also appeared in such TV dramas as *Gunsmoke*, *Tales of Wells Fargo* and *Honey West*.

Although Monte has pretty much retired for several years, more recently, he has "retired from retirement" and made a variety of public appearances. Currently, Monte Hale resides in Santa Monica, California, and serves on the Board of the Gene Autry Museum, where his wife, JoAnne, is Director. IMT

THERON HALE AND DAUGHTERS

When Formed: **1926**

THERON HALE

(Vocals, Fiddle, Banjo)

Date of Birth: **ca. 1883**

Where Born: **Pikeville, Tennessee**

Married: **Laura Vaughn**

Children: **Mamie Ruth**
(Vocals, Mandolin, Fiddle)
Elizabeth
(Piano)

Date of Death: **January 29, 1954**

One of the pioneer *Opry* "hoedown bands" that George Hay helped to develop in the early days of the *Grand Ole Opry,* the band of Theron Hale was unusual in several respects. It had no colorful nickname like the Possum Hunters or Gully Jumpers; it was solely a family affair; and it had a more genteel sound, one more of the 19th-century parlor style than other *Opry* groups. This was in part due to the fact that Hale himself was in his 40's when he began broadcasting, making him a generation older than many of the other hoedown band players. It was also due to the fact that both the Hale daughters had received formal musical training; Mamie Ruth had studied violin at Vanderbilt University (she would later teach violin at Vanderbilt) and Elizabeth was a college graduate who taught in the Nashville city schools.

Hale was born in Pikeville, in the rugged Sequatchie Valley about 100 miles southeast of Nashville. His father and uncle were both Baptist church leaders who also taught shape-note singing schools in the area. His nephew was Homer Davenport, an influential banjo player who later recorded with Jess Young's band, and who pioneered a pre-Bluegrass three-finger banjo style. Hale, in fact, taught Davenport much of his style. As a young man Hale attended a church-supported college, Carson-Newman, near Bristol, in East Tennessee. In 1905, he married a Pikeville girl, Laura Vaughn, and soon started his family. After a try at homesteading in Altoona, Iowa, he returned to Nashville, where he ran a dairy farm and later sold sewing machines.

As his two daughters were growing up, Hale would make music with them around the house and they would occasionally play for square dances. Then, in 1926, someone told Judge Hay about them and he invited them to appear on the *Opry*. They began as regulars on the show in October, 1926, and continued until May, 1934. By then Mamie Ruth had married and moved away. This was a special problem since much of the band's sound came from the twin fiddles she played with her father (she played an alto second to her father's lead).

The signature number for the band, that one everybody remembered Hale for, was *Listen to the Mockingbird*. On this Theron would whistle on the fiddle with his finger. Other favorites included *Red Wing* and *Over the Waves*; in fact, much of the Hale music was characterized by slow waltzes featuring the two fiddles. In 1928 the Hales participated in the field session Victor held in Nashville, the first recording session there. They recorded some eight tunes on 21 masters, but only four of the tunes were issued. These included *Mockingbird* as well as *Turkey Gobbler*, a version of *Flop-Eared Mule* Hale called *The Jolly Blacksmith* and an old Kansas City rag called *Hale's Rag*.

The Hale Family did not play much in public except for their WSM show. They did not tour or do personal appearances and did not have any great desire to professionalize their music. While on the *Opry*, Hale's favorite fiddler was a young Howdy Forrester, who played with Roy Acuff.

Hale seemed content to retire and play only for local dances. In the 1940's, he did a series of square dance records for a local farm extension club, in which he added to his band the excellent guitar work of fellow *Opry* member Sam McGee and banjo player Fred Colby. Though extremely rare, these last records (on the Old-Time Play-Party label) show Hale still very much in command of his fiddling skills. He died on January 29, 1954.

CKW

RECOMMENDED ALBUMS:

"Nashville, the Early String Bands, Vol. 1" (County) [Various Artists]

"Nashville, the Early String Bands, Vol. 2" (County) [Various Artists]

BILL HALEY

(Singer, Songwriter, Guitar)

Given Name: **William John Clifton Haley, Jr.**

Date of Birth: **July 6, 1925**

Where Born: **Highland Park, Michigan**

Date of Death: **September 2, 1981**

Bill Haley was instantly identified by his "kiss curl" in the heady days of rock'n'roll in the early 50's. He was musically a direct descendant of the marriage of the Sons of the Pioneers and Bob Wills' Texas Playboys. Although he will always be remembered as being the pioneer of rock'n'roll, his musical career goes back much further.

While still a child, Bill's family moved to Chester, Pennsylvania, where he was exposed early on to the swing style that was prevalent in that area. He appeared as a soloist and as a member of Cousin Lee's band. Bill left home in 1945 and spent the next three years playing in Country bands, including the Down Homers (with whom he recorded) and the Range Drifters, performing alongside such worthies as Hank Williams and Red Foley. Bill returned to Chester at the behest of his parents, who got him a job on station WPWA. He put together a four-piece Country band, the Four Aces of Swing, which broadcast live twice a day on the station.

In 1949, they began recording for the Cowboy label out of Philadelphia, run by Jack Howard and Dave Myers. Among the three singles cut was a "hillbilly" version of *Candy Kisses*. Bill also cut sides for Center, Arcade, Keystone and Atlantic. In 1951, Dave Miller, who owned Essex Records, signed Bill to record *Rocket 88*. The song, when recorded by Jackie Brenston, had been called the first rock'n'roll record by Sam Phillips and it was released on Chess in 1951. Miller wanted to break the song into the white music area. The single was released on a non-union label, Holiday, as by Bill Haley and his Saddlemen. Bill had been forced to change the group's name because of the success of the close-harmony Pop group, the Four Aces. The record did moderately well, but four other singles didn't catch the world on fire. Miller switched Haley to Essex.

A booking agent took the band on for a two-week engagement at the Twin Bar, Gloucester, New Jersey. This booking eventually lasted for eighteen months. In 1952, the band recorded *Rock the Joint* as the flip-side of their initial single for the label. The band toured to support the single and found that the deejays were playing this flip-side. The record sold very well and persuaded Haley that he needed to record just uptempo songs.

WPWA deejay "Major" Jim Ferguson took over the band's management and convinced them to put away their cowboy outfits and replace them with tuxedos and suits. In 1953, with the addition of a session drummer, the group, now renamed Haley's Comets, cut the Haley song *Crazy Man Crazy*. However, Haley's career was getting bogged down, not helped by the feuding between Miller and Myers. In 1952, Myers had shown Haley *(We're Gonna) Rock Around the Clock* written by 63-year-old postal worker Max C. Freedman, but Miller was not so sure. The song was recorded by Sonny Dae on Jack Howard's Arcade label.

Knowing that the Essex deal was up for renewal, Myers went to New York and after some horse-trading, Bill was signed by Milt

Gabler to Decca on April 12, 1954 on a one-year contract. The line-up of the Comets at this point was Johnny Grande (piano), Billy Williamson (steel guitar) (each being a partner with Haley), Joey D'Ambrosia (tenor sax), Marshall Lytle (upright bass) and Danny Sedrone (lead guitar). Billy Gussack was added on drums for the session which yielded *(We're Gonna) Rock Around the Clock*. The record sold well, as did the follow-up, *Shake, Rattle and Roll*.

It was with the next single, *Dim, Dim the Lights (I Want Some Atmosphere)* that Haley had his first chart success. However, it was 1955 that would see Haley cracking open the world. It started with the double-sided hit, *Mambo Rock/Birth of the Boogie* and then *Rock Around the Clock* was re-released. Myers had arranged for the record to be used in the opening sequence of the MGM movie *The Blackboard Jungle*, which dealt with teenage delinquency. Then the roof came off. The song became the anthem of the blossoming youth culture. The record went to No.1 and was there for eight weeks. In the U.K., it made its second of a total of eight appearances and went to No.1. There, Haley had been taken to the bosom earlier, as *Shake, Rattle and Roll* had been a Top 5 hit. In Britain, Haley would become more successful chartwise than in the U.S. and *Rock Around the Clock* became the first million-selling single in Britain. It has been estimated that *Rock Around the Clock* has sold in excess of 20 million copies. In 1982, it was inducted into the Grammy Hall of Fame. It would have been nice if Bill could have received this award while he was still alive!

Because of Haley's touring schedule, recordings had to be made at New York's Pythian Temple. The Comets had undergone some line-up changes. Dick Richards had been playing drums but now Ralph Jones came in. The magical Rudy Pompelli came in on tenor sax, Frannie Beecher became lead guitarist and the gymnastic Al Rex became bassist. The three who left, D'Ambrosia, Lytle and Richards, formed the Jodimars. During the rest of 1955, Haley had major hits with *Razzle Dazzle/Two Hound Dogs* (Top 15) and *Burn that Candle/Rock-A-Beatin' Boogie* (Top 10).

In 1956, his popularity started to wane in the States. *See You Later, Alligator* made the Top 10 and *R-O-C-K*, which was featured in the Haley movie *Rock Around the Clock* and *The Saints Rock 'N Roll* both hit the Top 20, but after that only *Rip It Up* (1956) (a Top 20 hit for Little Richard) and *Skinny Minnie* (1958) were near the Top 20. However, in the U.K., he had five Top 10 singles. His appeal over there only faded after *Don't Knock the Rock*, from the other Haley movie of the same name. Bill had toured the U.K. and was greeted by a crowd of some 4,000 fans. By the time he left, there were only a handful of people to see him off, not helped by a live set of only twenty-five minutes. The advent of younger performers such as Elvis didn't help either.

In 1960, Bill moved over to Warner Brothers as one of the first artists to sign to the label, but by now the Haley comet had run its course. He went on to record for many labels such as Gone, Orfeon, Logo, Newtown, Apt, United Artists, Kama Sutra and Sonet without success. From the mid-60's, he lived with his family as a recluse in Mexico, recording for small local labels, and then moved to Harlingen, Texas. He was scheduled to visit England for a tour in January, 1981, but ill health prevented this, and he died in his sleep of a heart attack the following month at the age of 55. In 1987, Bill Haley was inducted into the Rock and Roll Hall of Fame.

RECOMMENDED ALBUMS:

"20 Golden Pieces of Bill Haley and the Comets" (Bulldog UK)(1978)
"Golden Country Origins" (Grass Roots)(1978)
"Armchair Rock'n'Roll" (MCA UK)(1978)
"Rock'n'Roll Revival" (Warner Brothers)(1981)
"Tribute to Bill" (MCA)(1981)
"Hillbilly Haley" (Rollercoaster UK)(1984)

CONNIE HALL

(Singer, Songwriter)
Date of Birth: **June 24, 1929**
Where Born: **Walden, Kentucky**
Married: **John**
Children: **Johnny, Jr.**

Pappy Dailey is often credited with bringing Connie Hall to national attention. Dailey was working as A & R man for Mercury Records when he heard Connie sing and signed her to a single artist contract.

Although she was born in Kentucky (in 1958, she became a Kentucky Colonel), Connie spent a good many of her growing-up years in Cincinnati, Ohio. While still in her teens she was already singing and performing at local events. For a time, after her schooling, she worked as a salesgirl at the Jimmie Skinner Music Center in Ohio. Then, she received an opportunity to sing regularly on radio station WZIP in Covington, Kentucky. She soon had a following that grew even larger after long-time friend and boss, Jimmie Skinner, gave her a chance to sing on his show on WNOP Newport, Kentucky, in 1954. For many years afterward, Connie was a regular on the show and guested on other shows in the area, as well as becoming a weather girl on a local TV station.

In 1957, she signed with Mercury Records. Her first recording was *We've Got Things in Common*, a duet with Jimmie Skinner, that year. Then Pappy Dailey recorded her as a solo and her first release was the 1958 single, *I'm the Girl in the U.S.A./Dixie Strut*. However, it was not until her 1959 year-end single, *The Bottle or Me*, that Connie saw chart action. The single, her last for Mercury, reached just below the Country Top 20 in 1960.

By the middle of the year, Connie was on the Decca label, where sessions produced by Harry Silverstein produced the Top 25 *Poison in Your Hand* and the flip-side, *It's Not Wrong* (an answer to Warner Mack's 1958 hit, *Is It Wrong (for Loving You)*), which went Top 20. Over the next three years, Connie had Decca hits with *Sleep, Baby, Sleep* (Top 20, 1961), *What a Pleasure* (Top 25, 1962) and her final chart entry, *Fool Me Once*, which went Top 15 in 1963. Other Decca sides that were popular, without charting, included *Don't Tempt Me* (1963), *Mark on My Finger* (1964), the self-penned *Daddy Doesn't Live Here Anymore* (1964) and *Back to Loneliness/Yellow Roses* (1965).

Connie re-joined Pappy Dailey on his new Musicor label in 1964, where her first release was *I Wish I Was the Bottle/Constantly*, at the end of the year. Other Musicor singles included *King and Queen of Fools* and *The Crowd* (both 1965) and *You Didn't Take Me* (1966).

During her career, Connie made guest appearances on the *Grand Ole Opry*, the *Louisiana Hayride* and the *Midwestern Hayride*. She toured all 50 states and all the provinces of Canada. Connie was, at one time, considered a rising star of Country music, but had a successful but altogether too brief career. She now lives in Fort Mitchell, Kentucky.

LAP

RECOMMENDED ALBUMS:

"Connie Hall" (Decca)(1962)
"Country Songs" (Vocalion)(1965)
"Country Style" (Vocalion)(1965)

ROY HALL

(Singer, Guitar)
Given Name: **Roy Davis Hall**
Date of Birth: **January 6, 1907**
Where Born: **Waynesville, North Carolina**
Married: **Mattie Hale Hall (dec'd.)**
Children: **Martha, Royce**
Date of Death: **May 16, 1943**

Roy Hall ranks as one of the major figures whose band played music that formed some of the key roots of Bluegrass. Several

Carolinians fell into a musical category that has been termed "pre-Bluegrass." Roy and his brothers Jay Hugh (1910-1972) and Rufus (b. 1921), along with the Mainers, Morris Brothers, and the Byron Parker group, all fit into this mold.

Roy, part of a family of twelve, grew up in rugged Haywood County, North Carolina, near the Great Smokies, in a musically rich mountain culture. As they reached adulthood, the Halls, like many of their generation, went to work in the textile mills, where Roy remained until he reached the age of 30. At that point he and Jay Hugh teamed up to form the Hall Brothers, broadcasting daily shows from WSPA Spartanburg, South Carolina. The Halls cut three sessions for Bluebird in 1937 and 1938, recording a total of twenty-four songs (eighteen of them being released). Jay then decided to rejoin Clyde Moody (with whom he had worked before) as the Happy-Go-Lucky Boys, within Wade Mainer's Sons of the Mountaineers. Roy then formed the Blue Ridge Entertainers with Tommy Magness on fiddle, Bill Brown on Dobro guitar, and Wayne Watson on bass.

The Blue Ridge Entertainers soon left Spartanburg for WAIR Winston-Salem, where they did a daily show sponsored by the soft drink firm Dr Pepper. In fact, Hall remained associated with Dr Pepper for the remainder of his career. In November 1938, the band traveled to Columbia, South Carolina, where they cut a session for the American Record Corporation under the direction of Art Satherley. The songs they waxed that day included *Wabash Cannonball, The Lonesome Dove,* and the first-ever recordings of *Come Back Little Pal* and *Orange Blossom Special*. Unfortunately, the latter was never released because of legal complications. In 1939, the Hall band added the duo of Clayton and Sandford, the Hall Twins (no kin to Roy), to their group and transferred their broadcast base to WDBJ Roanoke, Virginia. The Blue Ridge Entertainers attained a wide audience in the region, eventually forming two units and sometimes being booked a whole year in advance. Roy organized a Saturday night barn dance.

In 1940, Jay Hugh rejoined Roy at the *Virginia Jamboree* at Roanoke. Other musicians who gained some experience with the Hall band included Woody Mashburn, Clato Buchanan, Jim Eanes, and a very young Andy Griffith.

The Blue Ridge Entertainers had two sessions for Bluebird in October 1940 and 1941. The songs they recorded included several that went on to become Bluegrass standards such as *Don't Let Your Sweet Love Die, Loving You Too Well, Can You Forgive*, and *I Wonder Where You Are Tonight*. Two Magness fiddle tunes of significance from 1941 were *Polecat Blues* and *Natural Bridge Blues*.

Hall also had some appreciation for Western music, doing one of the first covers of *New San Antonio Rose* and often doing songs like *South of the Border* on radio. He had cowboy singers like Roy Rogers and Tex Ritter guest on the *Virginia Jamboree,* and in fact *I Wonder Where You Are Tonight* had actually been done by Hall as a cover of Jimmy Wakely's Decca disc. Although the Blue Ridge Entertainers recordings show more Appalachian influence than anything else, there are also hints that their tastes were suggestive of the musical style mergers that largely took place after Roy Hall's death.

In June, 1942, during WWII, the draft took some of the band members and the two bands merged into one. Most observers of Roy Hall's career believe that he stood at the edge of national stardom when the war broke up his band and a fatal auto crash took his life.

After the war, Jay Hugh and Rufus Hall reassembled some of the band and carried on in radio for a time, but things were not quite the same without Roy. Finally they dropped out of music (except for Eanes and Griffith), but nonetheless fans in Virginia and the Carolinas treasured Roy's memory and collectors everywhere sought his old records.

A few of his recordings appeared on anthologies and in 1979 an entire album preserved his most memorable numbers. Another one documenting Country music on Roanoke radio contained a complete show from WBDJ in 1942 including the Dr Pepper commercials. IMT

RECOMMENDED ALBUMS:

"Roy Hall and his Blue Ridge Entertainers, 1938-1941" (County)(1979)

"Virginia Traditions: Early Roanoke Country Radio" (Blue Ridge Institute)(1988)

ROY HALL (Rockabilly)

(Singer, Songwriter, Piano)

Given Name: James Faye Hall
Date of Birth: May 7, 1922
Where Born: Big Stone Gap, Virginia
Date of Death: March 3, 1984

Although Roy Hall never had a hit record, he managed to be an influential musician in the areas of Country-Boogie and Rockabilly. While he became a near legendary figure within a circle of insiders, Hall neither had the big number nor the long steady level of performing that won him wide acclaim among Country fans. His accomplishments included co-authorship and first recording of the Jerry Lee Lewis superhit *Whole Lotta Shakin' Goin' On* and also an early recording of another rock'n'roll standard, *See You Later Alligator*. Roy toured and did session work with many well known Country stars of the 50's.

James Hall hailed from that far western town in Virginia, the Appalachian mountain community of Big Stone Gap. He gained an early interest in the piano, learning the finer techniques on the instrument from a black musician named Smith Carson. Hall played and sang in local clubs throughout his region, where he not only pleased the customers, but also acquired a drinking habit which would plague him for some three decades. Meanwhile the Roanoke radio singer and Bluebird recording artist Roy Hall died in an auto crash in May 1943. About this time, James Hall began using "Roy" as a nickname. He also organized a Country band called the Cohutta Mountain Boys, and began playing music mostly in bars and clubs. By 1949, the group's headquarters was in Detroit, Michigan.

Hall and the band made their initial recordings for the Motor City-based Fortune label in 1949, with the somewhat off-color *Dirty Boogie* being the most memorable of several titles. The next year, Roy went to Nashville, where he cut singles for both Bullet and Tennessee and also opened his own club, the Music Box, on Commerce Street, where he sang and tickled the ivory keys. His music caught the attention of reigning hillbilly superstar Webb Pierce, who invited Hall to join his band. In this period Roy allegedly did sessions not only for Pierce, but also for Hawkshaw Hawkins and Marty Robbins. Meanwhile Hall hired both Elvis Presley and Jerry Lee Lewis to work in his club for brief stints, supposedly firing the former after one evening.

While on a fishing-drinking trip to the Florida Everglades, Roy and a black music friend named David Williams composed *Whole Lotta Shakin' Goin' On*. Webb Pierce helped his piano player get a contract with Decca and he recorded it in September, 1955, with a studio band called the Jumpin' Cats. *Billboard* gave it a favorable review, but it did little. Big Maybelle's R & B version went over better and the Jerry Lee Lewis rendition on Sun became a big hit. It yielded considerable royalties for Hall, but the Internal Revenue Service and an ex-wife got virtually all of the money. Roy's version of the swamp-Pop song *See You Later Alligator* didn't click either, but a few months later that of Bill Haley went to Top 10 on the Pop chart. Bill's last

Decca offering, *Diggin' the Boogie* and *Three Alley Cats*, probably captured Roy Hall at his best, but they too failed at the time.

After his Decca contract ended, Roy Hall continued playing for a time around Nashville, and also for a time at ABC-TV's *Ozark Jubilee*. He also recorded on smaller labels. From 1967 to 1973, he resided in Dallas, Texas, where he operated a booking agency. In 1972, Hall finally licked his drinking problem and a year later returned to Nashville. By the end of the decade, he had begun to attract some attention as a Rockabilly pioneer and recorded a Hank Williams tribute song entitled *Hunk and the Hound*, which showed he could still handle a mean piano. Some of Hall's earlier recordings also began to appear on various Rockabilly anthologies. In the year of his death, the British company Charly Records re-issued an entire album of his Decca sides. Roy Hall is considered important enough to be included in Nick Tosches' book *Unsung Heroes of Rock n'Roll.* IMT

RECOMMENDED ALBUM:

"Diggin' the Boogie" (Charly UK)(1984)

TOM T. HALL

(Singer, Singer, Guitar, Banjo, Author)

Given Name: Thomas Hall
Date of Birth: May 25, 1936
Where Born: Olive Hill, Kentucky
Married: Dixie Deen ("Miss Dixie") (m. 1964)

Known as "The Storyteller," Tom T. Hall has emerged as one of the most literate singer/songwriters within Folk-Country. With semi-singing, semi-talking vocal style, he sings his own songs better than anyone else has managed.

Born the son of a preacher, the Rev. Virgil L. Hall, Tom started playing guitar when he was age 4, on a Martin that his father repaired, and he wrote his first song when he was 9. He dropped out of school when he was 15 to work at a garment factory, after his father was accidentally shot by one of Tom's uncles. When he was 17, Tom formed his own Bluegrass band, the Kentucky Travelers, and they appeared on local radio station, WMOR Morehead, Kentucky, which was sponsored by a local flour company. After eighteen months, the band broke up and Tom stayed on at WMOR as a deejay for a further five years.

In 1957, Tom joined the U.S. Army and remained in the service for four years, being stationed part of the time in Germany. He finished his high school education while serving in the quartermaster corps. While in the service, he entertained the troops at night and also sang over AFN.

Tom returned stateside in 1961, rejoined WMOR and played with the Technicians, a local band. Moving on to Roanoke, Virginia, Tom studied writing at a local college as well as writing copy for a local radio station. He still retained the ambition of becoming a journalist and his favorite writers were (and still are) Mark Twain, Ernest Hemingway and Sinclair Lewis. While in Roanoke, Tom sent some songs to Jimmy Key at Newkeys Music in Nashville. As a result, Jimmy C. Newman recorded the Hall song *DJ for a Day* in 1963 and had a Top 10 hit with it.

Tom moved to Nashville on January 1, 1964 and embarked on a non-stop writing schedule at the pitiful amount of $50 per week. Among his songs recorded was *Mad*, which was a 1964 Top 10 single for Dave Dudley. He achieved his first No.1 record via Johnny Wright's 1965 recording of *Hello Vietnam*.

Because he had a surplus of songs, Tom started recording and in 1967 signed to Mercury and had his first chart entry, *I Washed My Face in the Morning Dew*, which reached the Top 30. His next two records, released in 1968, both peaked in the 60s, but in the summer of that year, Jeannie C. Riley took the Hall song *Harper Valley PTA* (based on a real event) to No.1 in both the Country and Pop charts and it was Certified Gold. It sold 1.75 million copies in two weeks and as a bonus was a big international hit. No doubt helped by the fame generated from this single, Tom found himself with a Top 5 record as an artist,

The Storyteller, ***Tom T. Hall***

with *Ballad of Forty Dollars*. The song would later be recorded by both Johnny Cash and Waylon Jennings.

During 1969, Tom's status as a performer was further enhanced with *Homecoming* (Top 5) and the No.1 hit *A Week in a County Jail.* That year, Bobby Bare took the Hall song *(Margie's At) The Lincoln Park Inn* and made it a major hit. Tom continued his success rate as an artist through the 70's with *Shoeshine Man* (Top 10), *Salute to a Switchblade* (Top 10), *Day Drinkin'* (a Top 25 duet with Dave Dudley) and *One Hundred Children* (Top 15) (all 1970). During 1971, Tom had a second No.1 with his recording of the classic song *The Day that Clayton Delaney Died.* The song crossed over to the Pop Top 50. He had a spring 1972 Top 10 record with *Me and Jesus*, on which he was accompanied by the Mt. Pisgah United Methodist Church Choir. He followed that with the wryly observed Top 15 hit *The Monkey That Became President*, and closed out the year with the beautiful *(Old Dogs, Children And) Watermelon Wine* which reached No.1, and a Top 15 duet with Patti Page, *Hello We're Lonely*. That year, Tom received a Grammy Award for "Best Album Notes" for his album ***Tom T. Hall's Greatest Hits***.

In 1973, Tom hit the Top 5 with *Ravishing Ruby* and followed up with the Top 20 political commentary *Watergate Blues*. Again he wrapped up the year with a No.1, *I Love*, which also reached the Top 15 on the Pop listing. 1974 was a memorable year for Tom, with the Top 3 hit *That Song Is Driving Me Crazy*, which was followed by back-to-back No.1 singles, *Country Is* and *I Care* (which peaked in 1975).

Through the rest of the 70's, Tom continued with *Deal* (Top 10), *I Like Beer* (Top 5) and the No.1 hit *Faster Horses (The Cowboy and the Poet)* (all 1975), *Negatory Romance* (Top 25) and *Fox on the Run* (Top 10, a song written by Manfred Mann) (both 1976), *Your Man Loves You Honey* (Top 5), *It's All in the Game* (Top 15, another non-Hall song) and *May the Force Be with You Always* (Top 15) (all 1977). The last named was Tom's first success for RCA Victor, to whom he signed that year.

In 1978, Tom scored with *I Wish I Loved Somebody Else* (Top 15, with harmonies from Maxine & Bonnie Brown) and *What Have I Got to Lose* (Top 10) (both 1978) and *Son of Clayton Delaney* (Top 15), *There Is a Miracle in You* (Top 20) and *You Show Me Your Heart (And I'll Show You Mine)* (Top 15) (all 1979).

In 1976, Tom recorded ***The Magnificent Music Machine*** with Bluegrass giants Bill

Monroe, Jimmy Martin, J.D. Crowe, Kenny Baker and Donna Stoneman, et al. Although Tom charted fifteen times during the 80's, only two singles reached the Top 10, *The Old Side of Town* (1980) and another non-Hall song, *P.S. I Love You* (1984).

In 1978, Tom was inducted into the Nashville Songwriters Hall of Fame. During 1980, Tom became the host of the syndicated TV show *Pop Goes Country*; the show lasted until 1983. In 1982, Tom teamed up with Earl Scruggs for the Columbia album ***The Storyteller & The Banjo Man***, from which a pair of singles, *There Ain't No Country Music on This Jukebox* and Bob McDill's *Song of the South*, made low level chart appearances. By 1983, Tom was back on Mercury, and released one of his finest (if not *the* finest) albums, ***From Jesus to Jack Daniel's***.

Tom has fulfilled his literary ambitions by writing three books, *The Storyteller's Nashville* (his autobiography), *The Laughing Man of Woodmont Coves* and *How I Write Songs—Why You Can*. In 1987, an instructional songwriting video, ***Tom T. Hall/Writing Songs***, was marketed by Opryland Video Productions. He has served as a Board member of the CMA and was also a member of the Board of Directors of a bank. He lists as his leisure activities golf, hunting, fishing, literary criticism, ornithology, photography, woodworking and politics. A confirmed Democrat (he once told the writer "I think we're the only two Democrats in Nashville"), he is a firm friend of former President Jimmy Carter and in 1982, Tom was persuaded to run for Governor of Tennessee.

Tom's wife, Dixie, was born in Birmingham, England. She was a trick rider for a Wild West Show in England and came to the U.S. in 1960 with the encouragement of Don Pierce of Starday Records. After her arrival in the U.S., she became a successful songwriter and columnist for *Music City News*, which was then owned by Faron Young.

Both of the Halls are environmentally aware, with Dixie operating an animal shelter and Tom raising thousands of dollars for humane causes and charities. Tom's brother Hillman, wrote the hit song, *Pass Me By* and in 1992, the Tom T. Hall catalog, Hallnote Music, was sold to Tom Collins Music.

RECOMMENDED ALBUMS:

"The Rhymer & Other Five and Dimers" (Mercury)(1973)
"Country Is" (Mercury)(1974)
"The Magnificent Music Machine" (Mercury)(1976) [Tom's Bluegrass album]
"Places I've Done Time" (RCA Victor)(1978)
"In Concert!" (RCA Victor)(1983)
"From Jesus to Jack Daniel's" (Mercury)(1983)
"Natural Dreams" (Mercury)(1984)
"Song in a Seashell" (Mercury)(1985)
"The Essential Tom T. Hall/Twentieth Anniversary Collection" (Mercury)(1988)
Children's Albums:
"Songs of Fox Hollow (For Children of All Ages)" (Mercury)(1974)
"Country Songs for Kids" (Mercury)(1988)

WENDELL HALL

(Singer, Songwriter,Ukulele)
Date of Birth: **August 23, 1886**
Where Born: **St. George, Kansas**
Date of Death: **1969**

Wendell Hall was partly instrumental in Victor Records going on its quest for "hillbilly" performers in the early 20's. In reality, he was not really a Country performer at all. However, his million-selling record, *It Ain't Gonna Rain No Mo'* on Victor, in 1923, was in the style of hillbilly music.

Hall had graduated from the University of Chicago and served in WWI. He was a vaudeville performer, being known as "The Red Headed Music Maker," singing and playing his ukulele.

He became a friend of Carson J. Robison and both went to New York to record for Victor in the early 20's. In 1929, Wendell was the director of the radio show *Majestic Theatre of the Air*. During the 30's, he directed many shows including *Fitch Band Wagon* (1932-1935) and *Gillette's Community Sing* with Milton Berle (1936-1937) and often guested on the WLS *National Barn Dance*. Wendell later became an advertising executive and was still involved in the music business up to his death in 1969, in Alabama.

JIM HALSEY

(Industry Executive, Entrepreneur)
Given Name: **James Albert Halsey**
Date of Birth: **October 7, 1930**
Where Born: **Independence, Kansas**
Married: **1. Joanne (div.)**
2. Minisa Crumbo
Children: **Sherman, Gina, Woody, Cris**

Jim Halsey began booking musical acts at Memorial Hall in Independence, Kansas, in 1949 while he was still a student at Independence Junior College, from which he graduated in 1950. In May of 1950, Jim promoted a show on Hank Thompson for the first time. In December, 1951, Hank, who was more than a little impressed with the energetic, young college student, asked Jim to represent and book him and his band. Thus was born the Jim Halsey Company which went on to become the largest Country music agency in the world, dealing in management, booking, video production, television packaging and production, packaging and production of festivals worldwide, motion picture packaging, music publishing, record production, advertising and broadcasting.

Jim pioneered many firsts for Country music. In 1952, he arranged for the first modern-style endorsement of a Country act when he teamed Hank Thompson with Falstaff Beer. Jim got Hank booked as the first Country casino headliner in Las Vegas in 1956. In 1976, he took Roy Clark and the Oak Ridge Boys into the Soviet Union for the first Country tour of Russia. In 1979, he introduced Country for the first time to Monte Carlo on the Riviera, the Montreux International Jazz Festival and the MIDEM Convention in France. In 1985, he became the first American to be named President of the International Federation of Festival Organizations (F.I.D.O.F.).

Besides Thompson, who's still with him today, Jim has guided the careers of such illustrious stars as Roy Clark, the Oak Ridge Boys, the Judds, Reba McEntire, Tammy Wynette, Dwight Yoakam, the Forester Sisters, Brenda Lee, Minnie Pearl, George "Goober" Lindsey, B.J. Thomas, Ronnie Milsap, Waylon Jennings, Pat Boone, Dottie West, Ray Price, Patty Loveless, Mary-Chapin Carpenter, Mel Tillis and dozens more. After headquartering for years in Tulsa, Oklahoma, Jim moved his corporate offices to Nashville, Tennessee, in 1987, where he maintains a staff of 30. He also has offices in Tulsa, Pacific Palisades, California, and London, England.

Jim has owned three radio stations, served on the Board of Directors for three banks, been involved in ranching, real estate and investing and TV special productions. His interest in the arts is shared by his wife, Minisa Crumbo, who is recognized as one of the leading American-Indian artists; she has exhibited her work on a worldwide basis. They have an extensive collection of American-Indian art. Jim has served as Director of the Thomas Gilcrease Museum, Director of the Tulsa Philharmonic Orchestra and as a Trustee of the Philbrook Art Museum. He has also held terms as either Director or Officer of both the Academy of Country Music and the Country Music Association.

Besides being listed in *Who's Who in America*, *Who's Who in the World*, *Who's Who in the Southwest* and *Who's Who in Industry and Finance*, Jim's long list of achievements and honors includes: "Jim Reeves Memorial" Award from ACM in 1977; *Cash Box* magazine's "Manager of the Year

Award" in 1978 and their "Outstanding Artistic Achievement in Booking Award" in 1980; the "International Ambassador of Country Music Award" from SESAC in 1980. He was the recipient of a citation at the Golden Orpheus Festival in Sunny Beach, Bulgaria, and named one of *Esquire* magazine's "Country Music Heavy 100" in 1982. Jim was cited with the "Founding President's Award" from the CMA in 1985 and received the "Frederic Chopin Music PAGART Award" from the Polish Artist Agency in 1987. He was presented with the "Distinguished Service Award" in 1988 from the International Theatrical Agents Association and served as the keynote speaker at the Canadian Country Music Association Annual Convention in 1988. He served as a Director and Officer of the Country Music Association from 1964 through 1984.

A low-keyed, quiet, persevering man, Jim Halsey owned 72 percent of his huge conglomerate until the company merged with the William Morris Organization at the beginning of the 90's. BB

STUART HAMBLEN

(Singer, Songwriter, Actor, Guitar)

Given Name:	**Carl Stuart Hamblen**
Date of Birth:	**October 20, 1908**
Where Born:	**Kellyville, Texas**
Married:	**Suzy (m. 1933)**
Children:	**Veeva, Obee**
Date of Death:	**March 8, 1989**

There cannot be anyone in the Western world who has not heard *This Ole House,* but how many people know about the man, or for that matter the story behind the song?

Stuart Hamblen was the writer and the story comes from a time when Stuart went on a hunting trip in the High Sierra mountains. He came upon an old dilapidated prospector cabin and found the body of a man inside who, it was found out later, had died of a heart attack. His old hound dog was lying outside near starvation. The episode fired Hamblen's imagination and writing on a brown paper bag, he wrote the song in about thirty minutes. From such tragic circumstances *This Ole House* was born. It became an up-tempo, million-selling Pop song, through a recording by Rosemary Clooney in 1954.

Stuart Hamblen was the son of an itinerant preacher from Texas. He traveled a good deal with his father when he was young and grew to love the rugged outdoor life, learning to ride and rope, a talent which he used later when he took part in rodeo events. He trained to be a teacher at McMurray College in Abilene and gained a degree in education. At this time he was learning and singing Western ballads; making music was his hobby. Later, he became more serious, considering music as a possible career. He appeared as "Cowboy Joe" on Dallas and Fort Worth radio stations around 1925.

In 1928, he went to Camden, New Jersey, and recorded some songs at the Victor Talking Machine Company. After he won a singing contest in Dallas, Texas, an opportunity arose to join a touring singing group. When the tour reached California, he decided to settle down there.

In the 30's, Stuart worked on the radio with great success, first with other groups, and then for a short time in 1930, with the Beverly Hill Billies, using the name "Dave Donner." He became a fixture as a radio cowboy right into the 40's, hosting such shows as his *Covered Wagon Jubilee* and his own radio group, the Lucky Stars. His work as a solo Western entertainer also paid off, and he was much sought after on the Pacific coast. Already writing songs such as *Texas Plains,* which was performed by almost every radio cowboy, he recorded this himself in 1934 on Decca and it became his theme song on radio. He had a giant hit with *My Mary,* recorded by the popular Jimmie Davis, and even let Davis cut himself in as half writer, but he never let that happen again. Other early Country songs written by him were *Little Old Rag Doll, Golden River* and *Brown Eyed Texas Rose.*

As a Western performer, Stuart was exactly the right material for the popular movies of the

The writer of "This Ole House," ***Stuart Hamblen***

time and soon found himself playing in many films usually as the "bad guy," being dispatched by heroes played by such greats as Roy Rogers and Gene Autry (see Movie Section). This bad guy often took his role into reality, drinking, getting into brawls and getting thrown into jail. His friends could not understand why he did such things. His love of horses and hunting led him into the horse racing life with all of its moral pitfalls. However, in spite of these downfalls, he had many friends.

In 1933, he married his beautiful wife, Suzy, who soon realized that Stuart was not content despite all of his success. Although Stuart was the son of a preacher, he had not followed his parents' faith and Suzy prayed long hours for him for many years. The songs that flowed from his pen showed the experiences of his life, and early hits on Columbia included *(I Won't Go Huntin', Jake) But I'll Go Chasin' Women* (Top 3, 1949) and *(Remember Me) I'm the One Who Loves You* (Top 3 and on the charts for 6 months). The latter was later recorded by Elvis Presley, Johnny Cash and Pat Boone.

In 1949, a turning point in Stuart's life came along in the form of evangelist Billy Graham. The famous preacher was conducting a campaign in Los Angeles, attracting huge crowds to a Canvas Cathedral set up there, and Stuart was one of those to make a commitment to Jesus Christ. That decision was to change his life. He stopped drinking, gave up his radio program and film career. People wondered how long it would last, but it did last. Soon after his conversion he met an old friend, movie star John Wayne, in the street and John inquired "What's this I hear about you, Stuart?" "Well, John," came the answer, "I guess it's no secret what God can do!" Wayne replied, "Sounds like a song." That remark started the creation of the beautiful song which became a Gospel standard, *It Is No Secret.* Stuart recorded it himself and it became a Country Top 3 and Pop Top 30 hit in 1951 on RCA.

After his success with *This Ole House*, in 1954, compositions like *Mainliner* hit the charts for Hank Snow in 1955. Hamblen has turned out other wonderful songs like *Open Up Your Heart and Let the Sun Shine In, The Lord Is Counting on You, Golden River* and *You Must Be Born Again.* Others are *His Hands,* recorded by Eddy Arnold, *Until Then* recorded by Jimmie Davis, and *Known Only to Him,* recorded by Don Gibson. In 1961, Stuart recorded an album for Coral Records of the poems of Robert Service entitled ***The Spell of the Yukon.***

For many years, Stuart had a popular radio program called *Cowboy Church of the Air,* which used to be broadcast every Sunday morning at 9:05. In 1952, Hamblen ran for the presidency of the U.S. on a prohibition ticket, but he didn't succeed. His success as a singer and songwriter in the religious field, however, helped him to make sacred ballad history. In 1970, Stuart was inducted as a charter member of the Nashville Songwriters Hall of Fame. The following year, the ACM awarded him with their "Pioneer Award." Stuart Hamblen has now gone to be with his Lord. He died in March, 1989, after surgery for a brain tumor. JAB

RECOMMENDED ALBUMS:

"It Is No Secret" (RCA Victor)(1956)
"The Spell of the Yukon" (Columbia)(1961)
"This Ole House Has Got to Go (There's a Freeway Comin' Thru)" (Kapp)(1966) [Re-issued by Stetson UK in the original sleeve (1992)]
"A Man & His Music" (Lamb & Lion)(1974)
"The Cowboy Church" (Word)
"A Visit with Stuart Hamblen" (Sacred-Stereo)

GEORGE HAMILTON IV

(Singer, Guitar)

Given Name: George Hamilton IV
Date of Birth: July 19, 1937
Where Born: Winston-Salem, North Carolina
Married: Adelaide Watson Peyton ("Tinky")
Children: Edwin Peton, George V ("Hege V"), Mary Dabney

Known as the "International Ambassador of Country Music," George Hamilton IV, with his brand of Folk-Country, has probably done more international tours than any other Country music artist in history. He has been successful from the beginning with his first million-seller in the Pop field and was the first Pop artist to switch to Country. Hamilton doesn't sport the usual cowboy gear most of his contemporaries wear, but appears in the Ivy League style which reflects his background and roots.

Hamilton first became interested in Country music after watching Gene Autry and Tex Ritter Westerns. He purchased his first guitar when he was 12 from the money earned delivering newspapers. While still in high school he formed his first band, a three-piece group. While attending the University of South Carolina, George IV met John D. Loudermilk, who was introduced to him by talent scout Orville Campbell, to whom he had sent a demo of *Out Behind the Barn*. It was during his freshman year that George's first Top 10 hit with Loudermilk's *A Rose and a Baby Ruth* was released. Originally recorded on Colonial Records, this single became a million-seller in 1956 and launched his career as a Pop star. Ironically, during that same period George appeared on the *Arthur Godfrey Talent Scouts* TV show and lost. He was, however, asked back numerous times by Godfrey. *A Rose and a Baby Ruth* was followed by several other Pop hits for George, the most successful being *Why Don't They Understand* (Top 10, 1957) and *Now and for Always* (Top 25, 1958).

Later, while attending American University in Washington, D.C., Hamilton would spend weekends and vacations touring the U.S. and Canada playing to sell-out audiences. Despite his tremendous success as a Pop star, George always considered himself a Country singer and was influenced by Country greats Carl Smith, Hank Williams, Eddy Arnold and Little Jimmy Dickens. He met his personal manager, Connie B. Gay, through Jimmy Dean and in 1957, became a regular cast member of the *Jimmy Dean Show*.

In 1959 George Hamilton IV turned his back on a brilliant Pop career to return to his first love, Country music. This was after the Top 30 spoken word single that year by Paul Anka, George and Johnny Nash, entitled *The Teen Commandment*. This was a radical move for an already established Pop singer, at a time when rock'n'roll was at its height and many Country stars were trying to "go Pop." George moved to Nashville and was given his first major break by Chet Atkins, who signed him to RCA Victor as a Country artist. This led to bookings on the Country package shows and he made his debut on the *Grand Ole Opry* in 1959. It was the realization of one of his dreams; he became a regular member of the *Opry*, where he remained until he resigned in 1971 and moved back to Matthews, North Carolina.

1960 marked the year for his first Country hit with the Top 5 *Before This Day Ends.* This was followed in 1961 with *Three Steps to the Phone (Millions of Miles)* (Top 10) and *To You and Yours (From Me and Mine)* (Top 15). The following year, George scored with *China Doll* (Top 25) and *If You Don't Know I Ain't Gonna Tell You* (Top 10).

In 1963, George started with the Top 25 single *In This Very Same Room,* and then he went to No.1 with another John D. Loudermilk song, *Abilene*, which went Top 15 on the Pop chart. During 1964, George's hits were: *There's More Pretty Girls Than One* (Top 25), the double-sided Top 30 hit *Linda with the Lonely Eyes/Fair and Tender Ladies* and *Fort Worth, Dallas, or Houston* (Top 10). He started off 1965 with the Top 20 hits *Truck Driving Man* (Top 15) and *Walking the Floor Over You.* He started 1966 with another Top 20 single, *Write Me a Picture.*

The International Ambassador of Country Music, ***George Hamilton IV***

In 1965, George heard a Gordon Lightfoot track at the Horseshoe Tavern in Toronto, Canada. He had already been turned on to Folk music after hearing Dylan and Peter, Paul & Mary, but later that year he met Lightfoot personally and now has the distinction of having recorded more of his songs than anyone else. George's rendition of Lightfoot's *Steel Rail Blues* reached the Top 15 and his *Early Morning Rain* reached the Top 10, in 1966. Hamilton has worked extensively in Canada and with many Canadian writers. *Urge for Going*, written by Joni Mitchell, reached the Top 10 in 1967 for George. He followed up with another Loudermilk song, *Break My Mind*, which also reached the Top 10.

George scored a Top 20 hit in 1968 with *Little World Girl* and the following year went Top 30 with *Back to Denver*. He followed this with *Canadian Pacific*, a song by another Canadian writer, Ray Griff. It was the title song of the album of the same name, which got to the Top 25. At one point, George was actually signed to RCA through the Canadian office. He also hosted a Canadian television series that ran for six years and recorded the first album of Canadian songs by a Country music singer.

George stayed with RCA until 1974 and his other most successful singles were: *Carolina in My Mind* (Top 30, 1969), *She's a Little Bit Country* (Top 3, 1970), *Back Where It's At* (Top 20, 1970), *Anyway* (Top 15, 1971), *West Texas Highway* (Top 25, 1971) and *Blue Train (of the Heartbreak Line)* (Top 25, 1972).

George Hamilton IV has to his credit eight nationwide tours of the U.K., nine BBC-TV series, including three in Northern Ireland, plus a BBC Radio series on the history of Country music. In 1973 he completed the longest international concert tour in Country music by performing seventy-three consecutive concerts in three months.

The following year, George became the first Country artist to perform on a concert tour behind the "Iron Curtain," before some 28,000 people in Prague, Czechoslovakia (accompanied by a Czech Country band), then Russia, which later opened the door for Ernie Ford and Roy Clark. On this tour, he lectured in Moscow, tracing the history of Country music.

In 1976, George signed with ABC/Dot (later ABC), where he was produced by Allen Reynolds, but failed to score with any major hits. By 1977, George had played the U.K., Ireland, New Zealand, South Africa, Hong Kong, as well as Australia in 1978. He has toured the Holy Land and videotaped two TV specials with Arthur Smith for nationwide syndication.

George has hosted the International Country Festival in England and the associated Gospel Celebration at the Wembley Conference Centre that is a part of the Festival. He has appeared at the Christian Artists Seminar in De Bron, Holland, and has appeared as a guest soloist with Dr. Billy Graham's Crusades in England, Alaska, Florida, Connecticut, and California.

He first visited Britain in 1967. He began playing Wembley on a regular basis in 1969, and appeared on stage there with his son, George V (also known as Hege V), in 1988. In 1979, George became the first American to get a summer season in the U.K. when he appeared at the Winter Gardens, Blackpool. In addition, George has sung in German and in Japanese.

George has at least 57 albums to his credit featuring his diverse styles of Pop, Country-Folk and religious music. While a Pop singer, George toured with Buddy Holly, Gene Vincent and the Everly Brothers. He has also recorded with Skeeter Davis and Arthur Smith.

Significant television appearances include the *Jimmy Dean Show* on CBS (1957-58), NBC's *Steve Allen Show*, and the *George Hamilton IV Show* on ABC (1959). George's other record label associations have been with Word, where he released Gospel material during 1961-1974, Lamb and Lion, where he did the same, and MRE, Colonial and Lamar.

With his upper class, urban background, George Hamilton IV was probably the least likely candidate for Country music stardom. Nevertheless, he has loved it since boyhood and has maintained a tremendous career that has spanned nearly four decades. In his own words, "You don't have to be poor, or live in the country to have sensitivity, to have a soul, to have a love for Country music." His sincere love and belief in this music continues to come across in his own great Country songs, putting him in the company of those other Country legends he has so long admired. LAP

RECOMMENDED ALBUMS:

"The Best of George Hamilton IV" (RCA Victor)(1970)
"International Ambassador of Country Music (RCA Victor)(1973)
"Bluegrass Gospel" (Lamb and Lion)(1974)
"George Hamilton IV's Greatest Hits" (RCA Victor)(1974)
"Back Home at the Opry" (RCA Victor)(1976)
"The ABC Collection:George Hamilton IV" (ABC)(1977)
"The Very Best of George Hamilton IV" (Country Store UK)(1986)
"American Country Gothic" (Lamon)(1989) [With the Moody Brothers]

HANK THE DRIFTER

(Singer, Songwriter, Guitar)
Given Name: Daniel Raye Andrade
Date of Birth: September 2, 1929
Where Born: Taunton, Massachusetts

When Daniel Andrade dreamed up his "Hank the Drifter" persona, he was tipping his hat at Hank Williams. He is similar in sound to the great man and has modeled himself after him.

Hank learned to play guitar while still in his teens. He joined a group called the Haymakers as lead singer. The group entered amateur competitions throughout New England and won fifteen times in a row.

As a result, he got a 15-minute show on WPEP Taunton. He got himself sponsored by the Bedford Times as "Hank the Drifter" on radio station WNBH and then decided to move to Texas. He appeared on *Corns a Poppin'* on KTRH, the *Big D Jamboree* out of Dallas and the *Cowtown Hoedown*, which emanated from Fort Worth. He appeared all over Texas at fairs and festivals and rodeos. His recordings appeared on New England Records as well as on two Canadian labels, Spartan and Quality.

ESCO HANKINS

(Singer, Guitar)
Date of Birth: Jan 1, 1924
Where Born: Union County, Tennessee
Married: Jackie Tincher
Date of Death: November 18, 1990

Esco Hankins became best known as a Roy Acuff sound-alike, although that characterization did not really do him justice. In many respects, the Hankins career was similar to, but yet both more and less than, that of the King of Country Music. Like his idol, Hankins was a native of Union County, Tennessee, took up music while convalescing from illness, began his radio career in Knoxville, and led a band called the Crazy Tennesseans. Unlike Acuff, Esco Hankins had much more modest success.

In his early years, young Esco had a long bout with ill health and took up the guitar during a period of gradual recovery. When he was 14, he secured a radio program at WROL Knoxville sponsored by the Hub Department Store. Later, he worked under the sponsorship of Cas Walker, the supermarket owner and politician. Roy Acuff's Uncle Charlie worked in the Hankins band during that period. In the latter part of WWII, Esco entered the Army, subsequently contending that he spent 22 of his 23 months in the service on K.P.

*Roy Acuff sound-alike **Esco Hankins***

After the war, Esco Hankins returned to his radio programs at WROL and also signed a contract with King Records in 1946, doing sixteen numbers in the spring of 1947, all covers of Roy Acuff's songs (as requested by King's Syd Nathan), featuring Monroe Queener on Dobro. According to Acuff biographer Elizabeth Schlappi, these numbers were done so effectively that they "even fooled Roy's mother." How much they did for Esco's career is difficult to assess. That December, Hankins did another session for King, doing six songs, none of which were previously recorded by Roy Acuff. These cuts had young Burkett ("Josh") Graves playing Dobro and are memorable as the initial recordings of that most renowned master of that instrument.

Esco also recorded his own best-known composition, *Mother Left Me Her Bible.* Ironically, he also waxed *Sweeter than the Flowers* that day. At that time, it was a hit for Moon Mullican, and would later be covered by Roy Acuff. Two of the songs from that session were later released on Federal Records.

By the end of the decade, Esco left Knoxville for Lexington, Kentucky, which would be home for the rest of his life. He worked on the *Kentucky Barn Dance* and also WKLS radio. Later, Hankins switched to WLAP radio and worked jamboree shows at Woodland Auditorium and at the *Happy Valley Barn Dance* in Brodhead, Kentucky. In 1951, he went to Nashville and cut four sides for Mercury. This may have been his best material in terms of quality, but unluckiest for artist credit. Mercury released one disc under the name "Roscoe Hankins" and totally omitted the artist credit on the other. The principal title was *I'm Praying for the Day That Peace Will Come*.

As the nature of live radio Country music began to change, Esco Hankins moved more and more into deejay work. Still he remained active as an artist and continued to record. In 1954, he married Jackie Tincher, who often sang harmony duets with him. Young banjo picker J.D. Crowe did some of his early professional work with Esco.

In the mid-60's, Esco signed with Columbia and cut several singles, the best-known title being a trucker song, *Johnny Overload*. Esco and Jackie also joined the WWVA *Jamboree* and sang there often. But by the end of the 60's, he began playing Gospel music almost exclusively. He and Jackie also had a record shop in Lexington. Esco recorded a sacred album for Rem in the early 60's and beginning with the latter part of that decade, he recorded several Gospel albums and EPs, for Rusty York's Jewel label. His earliest efforts on Jewel carried a more traditional instrumentation. As time went by, they tended increasingly toward Gospel sound.

During the 1980's, Esco's health went into decline again. He worked the 1982 World's Fair in Knoxville, but his strength slowly ebbed. Finally, he suffered a stroke then passed away in 1990, at the age of 66. Jackie survived him.

RECOMMENDED ALBUMS:
"Country Style (Audio Lab)(1960)
"Mother Left Me Her Bible" (Rem)(ca. 1965)
"Working God's Fields" (Jewel)(ca. 1970)

HARDEN TRIO/ARLEEN HARDEN/BOBBY HARDEN

Members:
Robbie Harden
Arleen Harden
Bobby Harden

All Born: **England, Arkansas**

Every so often Country music produces a family group that rises to the top in varying degrees, whether it be the Carter Family, the Stonemans, the Browns, the Whites or the Harden Trio. The success of the Hardens owes much to their harmonies and most certainly to the quality of Bobby Harden's songs.

The two sisters and a brother grew up with Country in this music-rich part of the Ozark Mountains. They started their entertainment career as teenagers, entertaining in their locale and gradually moved toward being professionals. They soon became members of *Barnyard Frolics* in Little Rock and as their popularity grew, they joined the *Ozark Mountain Jubilee* out of Springfield, Missouri, and also KWKH's *Louisiana Hayride*, Shreveport.

The Hayride lived up to its reputation as a training ground for the *Grand Ole Opry* and soon the trio was on its way to Nashville and appearances on WSM radio's *Opry Almanac*. They released their first single, *Poor Boy*, for Columbia in 1965 and while it gained interest, it didn't chart. The follow-up in 1966, Bobby's *Tippy Toeing*, was a whole different matter. It turned into a major cross-over hit, reached the Top 3 on the Country chart and stayed around for over five months, also hitting the Top 50 on the Pop chart. In addition, they became members of the Opry that year.

They never regained such giddy heights with their other singles. They had four more chart records, only one of which reached the Top 20. These were: *Seven Days of Crying (Makes One Weak)* (Top 30, 1966), *Sneaking 'Cross the Border* (Top 20, 1967), *He Looks a Lot Like You* (Top 60, 1968) and *Everybody Wants to Be Somebody Else* (Top 50, 1968).

Arleen and Robbie decided to leave in 1967 and Bobby soldiered on with Karen Wheeler and Shirley Michaels. However, in 1968, the trio decided to disband. Both Arleen and Bobby embarked on a solo career. For a while, they stayed with Columbia, but Arleen (or Arlene, as she now became) was the one to continue with chart success; yet Bobby is the one who has maintained longevity with his songwriting skills. During the next six years, Arleen had sixteen chart entries for Columbia, but only one made the Top 15, that being *Lovin' Man (Oh Pretty Woman)*, a female version of Roy Orbison's hit, in 1970. She and Bobby had a medium sized duet success with *Who Loves You* in 1968, but apart from that, her only Top 30 hits were *Lovin' Man (Oh Pretty Woman)* and *Crying* (both 1970) from her ***Arlene Harden Sings Roy Orbison*** album, *True Love is Greater Than Friendship* from the movie *Little Fauss and Big Halsy,* and *Married to a Memory* (both 1971), *A Special Day* (1972) and *Would You Walk with Me Jimmy* (1973).

In 1974, she signed with Capitol and reverted to being "Arleen" but apart from a low level entry with *Leave Me Alone (Ruby Red Dress)*, which had been a Pop hit for Helen Reddy the previous year on the same label, there was no further chart action. By 1977, Arleen had moved on to Elektra and had *A Place Where Love Has Been,* which just scraped in; *You're Not Free and I'm Not Easy* did only a little better.

Bobby had been beavering away at his writing and in 1975, he had a Top 50 record on United Artists with *One Step*.

RECOMMENDED ALBUMS:
"Great Country Hits" (Harmony)(1970)
Arleen Harden:
"What Can I Say" (Columbia)(1968)
"Arlene Harden Sings Roy Orbison" (Columbia)(1970)
"I Could Almost Say Goodbye" (Capitol)(1975)
Bobby Harden:
"Nashville Sensation" (Starday)(1969)

GUS HARDIN

(Singer)

Given Name: **Carolyn Ann Blankenship**
Date of Birth: **April 9, 1945**
Where Born: **Tulsa, Oklahoma**
Married: **1. (Div.)**
2. (Div.)
3. Steve Hardin (div.)
4. (Div.)
5. (Div.)
6. Unknown
Children: **Toni**

If the phrase "talent will out" is true then Gus Hardin should be at the very top. She has a voice that can be compared to Tanya Tucker or Lacy J. Dalton, and can be called "whiskey- soaked," or as Leon Russell put it, "She sounds like a combination of Tammy Wynette, Otis Redding and a truck driver." Gus at one time looked like she was going to be one of the princesses of Country music, but fate willed otherwise.

She was nicknamed "Gus" when she was a teenager, after having been called "Red" and "Cookie" on account of her red hair. She never knew her father, Irishman Mikey O'Malley, and she was raised by her Cherokee photographer mother, Hopie. Gus sang in church as a child and at a few talent contests while still at junior high school. She attended Will Rogers High School, which had already sent out into the world J.J. Cale, David Gates, Elvin Bishop, Gary Busey, Gailard Sartain and Leon Russell.

Gus was 23 when she made her first public appearance in third husband Steve's band. She sang Aretha Frankin's hit *(You Make Me Feel Like) A Natural Woman*. She played the nightclubs in Tulsa for 15 years, picking up six husbands on the way. She has been described as the "Elizabeth Taylor of Country music." She also picked up a lot of experience and a following. She cut three albums, two of which were shelved, including one for Leon Russell's Shelter label.

In 1974, Gus started to get side effects from taking steroids and cortisone derivatives. She had taken them to fight allergies and as a result cataracts formed on her eyes. From 1979 to 1984, she had to use atropine eyedrops to see anything. For five years, she was legally blind. In 1979, some oilmen from Giant Petroleum Company, Fred Williams, Rick Loewenherz and Mike Kimbrel, formed GPC Entertainment with the intention of making Gus Hardin a star. She spent three years preparing and during that time she opened for the likes of Johnny Paycheck and the Oak Ridge Boys and had sufficient following to sell out as a headliner in Tulsa at a 1,200-seater venue, within hours.

Tom Skeeter of Carmen Productions got a demo tape to Ralph Gordon, who passed it to Joe Galante at RCA. As a result Galante signed her in 1982 and she came under the production skills of Rick Hall at Fame Studios in Muscle Shoals, Alabama. The first eponymous album released the following year was actually a six selection mini-album. The single, *After the Last Goodbye,* made the Top 10 and she was under way. She followed up with *If I Didn't Love You* (Top 30) and *Loving You Hurts* (Top 40).

The following year, 1984, was a momentous one for her. She underwent two intraocular lens transplant operations in Tulsa and through the skills of Dr. Ned Reinstein, she was able to see her first audience, in Houghton, Michigan, in late June of that year. Gus released her next album, ***Fallen Angel***, this time a full album which yielded three chart singles, *Fallen Angel (Flyin' High Tonight)* (Top 50), *I Pass* (Top 50) and *How Are You Spending My Nights* (Top 60). Strangely, the Sam Lorber-Susan Longacre song, *Where's the Fire*, which became a hit for Susie Allanson in 1987, was not released as a single. Later in 1984, Gus' third album, ***Wall of Tears***, was released and from this came her biggest hit, a duet with Earl Thomas Conley, *All Tangled Up in Love*. For the first time she was produced by Mark Wright in Nashville at the Music Mill. The duet climbed to the Top 10 and stayed on the charts for some five months. However, she was not able to capitalize on this, and her follow-up in 1985, *My Mind Is on You*, just got into the Top 80. The next single, *Just as Long as I Have You*, a duet with Dave Loggins, fared little better, and her first single in 1986, *What We Gonna Do*, peaked at the same level and proved to be her last chart single. Known for her abrasive manner, Gus was then dropped by RCA and she returned to Tulsa, where she continued playing the clubs.

RECOMMENDED ALBUMS:

"Gus Hardin" (Mini-Album)(RCA)(1983)
"Fallen Angel" (RCA)(1984)
"Wall of Tears" (RCA)(1984)

LINDA HARGROVE

(Singer, Songwriter, Piano, French Horn, Organ, Guitar)

Given Name:	**Linda Ann Hargrove**
Date of Birth:	**February 3, 1949**
Where Born:	**Jacksonville, Florida**
Married:	**Charlie Bartholomew (m. 1980)**

Linda is one of those fortunate people whose lives were touched by the legendary Pete Drake. She is someone who can be described as a "renaissance woman." A rare talent that had disappeared from Country music, but is happily back in Nashville.

She took piano lessons from the age of 5, started playing guitar at 10 and played French horn in the school band. In her first year at Troy University, Troy, Alabama, she won a music scholarship to play French horn, but dropped out to play Pop music. At the end of the 60's, she was playing R & B and Blue-Eyed Soul in Florida. She was greatly influenced by Bob Dylan's foray into Country music, ***Nashville Skyline,*** and Pete Townshend.

A local band, After All, that had a record deal had chosen seven of her songs to record and she came along to Nashville with them, just in case work was needed on the songs. She made the move to Nashville in 1970 and had a hard time of it until Sandy Posey's husband, Billy Robinson, heard some of Linda's songs and got Sandy to cut *Saw Someone Else Before Me*, for Epic in 1971. Sandy introduced Linda to Billy Sherrill and Pete Drake.

Pete, who had played on Sandy's session, was instrumental in Linda getting work as a session guitarist. In addition, he signed her to a writing contract. She learned how to run Pete's 16-track recording console. In 1973, Leon Russell recorded two of Linda's songs as part of his Country project, ***Hank Wilson Is Back***. That same year, Linda met Michael Nesmith, and together with James Miner, they wrote *Winonah*, which appeared on Michael's ***Pretty Much Your Standard Ranch Stash*** album.

Nesmith introduced Linda to Russ Miller at Elektra and she signed with the label and was produced by Pete Drake. Two of her singles for the label squeaked into the Country chart, *Blue Jean Country Girl* (1974) and *I've Never Loved Anyone More* in 1975. In 1975, Linda moved over to Capitol and had a Top 40 hit with *Love Was (Once Around the Dance Floor)* in 1976. This remains her most successful single. In 1975, Linda had quite a few successful cuts including *Just Get Up and Close the Door* by Johnny Rodriguez and *I've Never Loved Anyone More*, which Linda wrote with Nesmith, from Lynn Anderson. In 1976, *Let it Shine* by Olivia Newton-John, became a Pop hit and in 1977 *Mem'ries*, which Linda wrote with her sister, Susan, was recorded by Johnny Rodriguez.

Linda sang back-up vocals on Nesmith's ***From a Radio Engine to the Photon Wing***, which appeared in 1976. By 1978, Linda had left Capitol and joined RCA but major chart success still eluded her. That year, she decided to change her direction and turned to inspirational music. She was approached in 1981 to join Calamity Jane with Pam Rose, Mary Ann Kennedy and Marshall Chapman, but she and Chapman declined. In 1981, Linda released the inspirational album ***A New Song*** under her married name of Linda Bartholomew and followed it six years later with ***Greater Works***.

It was then discovered that Linda had leukemia and for several years, she was out of the business. She underwent bone-marrow surgery (the graft being provided by her brother) and in 1992 she returned to Nashville to take up her rightful place as one of Country music's finest writers. She began appearing at gigs around Nashville and successfully underwent surgery in 1994 on her cataracts. Later that year, Linda signed with Great Cumberland Music.

RECOMMENDED ALBUMS:

"Music Is Your Mistress" (Elektra)(1973)
"Blue Jean Country Queen" (Elektra)(1974)
"Love, You're the Teacher" (Capitol)(1975)
"Just Like You" (Capitol)(1976)
"Impressions" (Capitol)(1977)
As Linda Bartholomew:
"A New Song" (Fig Tree)(1981)
"Greater Works" (Three Fold Productions)(1987)

BILL HARRELL

(Singer, Songwriter, Guitar, Mandolin)

Given Name:	**William Harrell**
Date of Birth:	**September 14, 1934**
Where Born:	**Marion, Virginia**
Married:	**Ellen (dec'd.)**
Children:	**two sons, one daughter**

Bill Harrell has been a major figure in Bluegrass for some three decades. Like the Country Gentlemen, Buzz Busby, the Bluegrass Champs and Benny & Vallie Cain, Bill contributed a lot to the growth of Bluegrass in the Washington, D.C., area. Bill is especially known for a pleasant and relaxed yet traditional approach that contrasts sharply with the hard-driving lonesome sounds and also with the more progressive and Newgrass styles as well.

A native of southwestern Virginia, Bill displayed some interest in music as a child and received his first guitar at the age of 9. Unlike most Country musicians, he took piano lessons and learned to read music. Harrell first took a serious interest in Bluegrass while attending the University of Maryland when he and two other students organized a band in which Bill played mandolin. He worked in several other bands around the Washington area, most notably the Rocky Mountain Boys, prior to entering the service in 1957. His musical associates in those years included Smiley Hobbs, Smitty Irvin, Eddie Adcock, Carl Nelson, Roy Self, and Donny Bryant.

While in the service, Bill was seriously injured in an auto crash and spent about a year in the hospital. After getting his release, Bill returned to the Washington area and had a band which cut three singles on the Starday label, accompanied by some of the aforementioned support musicians.

In 1960, Bill organized the Virginians, which included himself on guitar, Buck Ryan on fiddle, Smitty Irvin on banjo and Stoney Edwards on bass. Smiley Hobbs, by then a full-time policeman, also joined them on occasion, alternating between mandolin and 12-string guitar.

They did an album under their own name for United Artists and another one as Buck Ryan and Smitty Irvin for Monument. The band had a weekly television program on WSVA Harrisonburg, Virginia, guested several times on Jimmy Dean's network program, and worked clubs and parks throughout Virginia, Maryland, and adjacent states. Smitty Irvin left the band in 1965 and Don Stover took his place until Bill joined forces with Don Reno and the Tennessee Cut-Ups.

The Reno and Harrell partnership lasted just over ten years and coincided with the rise of Bluegrass festivals. Thus, this revamped version of the Tennessee Cut-Ups had ample opportunity to demonstrate their talents to live audiences and on record. Buck Ryan soon joined the group on fiddle and Ed Ferris, another long-time sideman of the Washington scene, played bass during the last four years of their work together, giving the band a line-up of experienced veterans. In addition, Red Smiley came out of retirement to work many shows with the band in 1970 and 1971 and the three cut two albums together in the studio, plus a third which was released from live festival appearances.

Reno and Harrell recorded albums for more established labels such as King, Starday, and Monument as well as lesser ones like Jalyn, Derbytown, and King Bluegrass. Toward the end of their association, they signed with the new CMH firm and cut both a double and a single album in Arthur Smith's Charlotte studio.

The Reno and Harrell partnership dissolved amicably in early 1977. Don wanted to boost his younger sons and Bill wanted to reorganize the Virginians. Ed Ferris went with Bill, who put a new band together with the aid of veteran fiddler Carl Nelson and youthful banjo picker Darrell Sanders. Bill said he wanted a group that would remain together for a while, and they did for a decade. In the meantime, mandolinist Larry Stephenson joined in 1979 and remained until 1983, when his own group began to gain a following. Paul Atkins also played mandolin through the mid-80's, until he left to form the Borderline Band. From 1988, only Nelson remained of the original Virginians of 1977. Ed Ferris and Darrell Sanders departed in the late 80's and new musicians, Billy Budd and Bob Lundy, took their respective places. After a beginning album on Adelphi and three for the now defunct Leather label, Bill Harrell and the Virginians joined Rebel Records and have consistently turned out a quality product associated with their relaxed, easy-going brand of Bluegrass.

Mike Auldridge on Dobro has been an added attraction on several albums and Bill's sons, Mitch and John, have added their vocal efforts to recent sessions IMT

***Bill Harrell** and the Virginians*

RECOMMENDED ALBUMS:

"The Wonderful World of Bluegrass Music" (UA)(1963)
"Bluegrass and Ballads" (Adelphi)(1978)
"Bluegrass Gospel, Pure and Simple" (Leather)(1980)
"I Can Hear Virginia Calling Me" (Rebel)(1980)
"The L&N Don't Stop Here Anymore" (Leather)(1981)
"Blue Ridge Mountain Boy" (Leather)(1981)
"Walking in the Early Morning Dew" (Rebel)(1983)
"Do You Remember?" (Rebel)(1985)
"Blue Virginia Blue" (Rebel)(1986)
"A Song for Everyone" (Rebel)(1987)
"After Sunrise" (Rebel)(1990)
"Classic Bluegrass" (Rebel)(1991) [Taken from earlier albums]

KELLY HARRELL

(Singer, Songwriter)

Given Name:	**Crockett Kelly Harrell**
Date of Birth:	**September 13, 1889**
Where Born:	**Draper's Valley, Wythe County, Virginia**
Married:	**Lula**
Children:	**E.K.**
Date of Death:	**1942**

Kelly Harrell ranks as one of the finest singers of traditional ballads to record in the 20's. A native of the musically rich highland region of western Virginia, he learned many old songs and ballads in his youth. When Harrell was about 14, the textile mills at Fries, Virginia, opened and he went to work there. At times, he worked at other mills in Virginia and briefly in Alabama. While laboring at Fries, he became acquainted with another musician, Henry Whitter. Like Ernest Stoneman, Harrell was inspired to make recordings because he believed he could do at least as well as Whitter.

Kelly Harrell journeyed to New York in January 1925 and cut four songs for Victor, with local studio musicians providing accompaniment, as the mountain vocalist played no instruments. His vocals included early versions of such Old-Time numbers as *New River Train* and *The Roving Gambler*. In August of that year, Harrell traveled to Asheville, North Carolina, and recorded eight songs for OKeh. Ironically, Henry Whitter provided instrumentation on harmonica and guitar. One of the titles they cut included Harrell's cover version of *The Wreck on the Southern Old 97*, which contained more verses than the Whitter rendition. It appeared on a 12" disc coupled with another traditional ballad, *Blue Eyed Ella*, usually known as *The Jealous Lover*.

The following June, Harrell returned to New York, recut the numbers from his first sessions using the newly instituted electrical process, and recorded six additional songs for Victor, the accompaniment remaining as it had been on his first efforts. Sometime in the latter half of 1926, Kelly Harrell moved to Fieldale, Virginia, a mill town near Martinsville, where he soon put together a string band consisting of Raymond Huntley on banjo, Alfred Steagall on guitar and Posy Rorer (of Charlie Poole's North Carolina Ramblers) on fiddle. In March 1927, this group went to Camden, New Jersey, where they recorded what undoubtedly constituted their masterpieces as Kelly Harrell and the Virginia String Band. The 1895 sentimental ballad *In The Shadow of the Pine*, the humorous *My Name is John Johanna* (usually known as *Misery in Arkansas*), *My Wife Has Gone and Left Me* and the two murder ballads *Charles Guiteau* and *Henry Clay Beattie* were all outstanding. Another session with this band in August yielded four more songs, including two duets with Henry Norton (who was a member of Red Patterson's Piedmont Log Rollers).

Somewhat earlier in 1927, two of Harrell's lyric compositions had been recorded by other Victor artists. Ernest Stoneman did *The Story of the Mighty Mississippi,* about the recent tragic flood, while Jimmie Rodgers waxed *Away Out on the Mountain*. The latter song yielded the Virginia mountaineer considerable writer royalties.

Kelly Harrell had a final session at Camden in February 1929, with Steagall on guitar and other musicians furnished by the studio. It proved to be his last record, because after the advent of the Great Depression, Victor officials refused to pay the costs of hiring musicians and Harrell refused to learn an instrument or pay for the band. With his recording career over, Harrell continued to work at the Fieldcrest Mill and sing at local events around Fieldale and Martinsville until he died of a heart attack at work in 1942. In the 60's, his ballads began to appear on various record anthologies, and in the 70's, County Records released an entire album of his best songs, while Bear Family of Germany re-issued his complete works on a three-album set. IMT

RECOMMENDED ALBUMS:

"Kelly Harrell and the Virginia String Band" (County)(1975)
"The Complete Kelly Harrell" (Bear Family Germany)(ca. 1974)

EMMYLOU HARRIS

(Singer, Songwriter, Guitar)

Given Name: Emmylou Harris
Date of Birth: April 2, 1947
Where Born: Birmingham, Alabama
Married: 1. Tom Slocum (div.)
2. Brian Ahern (div.)
3. Paul Kennerley (div.)
Children: Hallie, Meghann

Emmylou Harris' pure voice has not only graced her own successful albums, but she is increasingly in demand to add quality to others' releases both in duets and on harmonies.

Although Emmylou grew up in North Carolina, while she was in her teens the family moved to Quantico, Virginia. Her father was a career U.S. Marine who became a POW during the Korean War. Emmylou was an excellent student and played saxophone in the school marching band. Emmylou first heard Folk music on Dick Cerri's Washington, D.C., radio show and it became "the first passion" of her life. She bought a guitar and began listening to Bob Dylan while her elder brother listened to Loretta Lynn. When she was in high school, she wrote to the legendary Folk singer Pete Seeger informing him that she wanted to be a Folk singer, but didn't feel that she had suffered enough; he told her not to worry. In 1965, she was class valedictorian and also won the Miss Woodbridge beauty title (brains and beauty!).

Emmylou went to the University of North Carolina at Greensboro on a drama scholarship and she soon joined a Folk duo playing at an off-campus club. Unlike many Folk singers at that time, Emmylou's interest was in the music rather than in protest politics. She went on to Boston University and then dropped out of college after 18 months and went to New York, in 1967, where she worked as a waitress. In 1969, she released an album on Jubilee entitled ***Gliding Bird***, but the company went out of business. By now, she was married and pregnant, and she and her husband moved to Nashville in 1970. Her marriage started to break up and she bartended at the High Hat Restaurant. Things were so tough that she had to use food stamps to buy food for her baby.

She moved to Washington, D.C., where she took a typing course, at which she did disastrously. She then hostessed at a model home lot, thinking that music was now all behind her. In 1972, Bill Danoff and Taffy Nivert (half of Starland Vocal Band) got her a booking at the Cellar Door, a popular Georgetown nightclub. She also worked at the Red Fox in Bethesda, Maryland. During a show at Clyde's (another nightspot) in 1971, she was approached by Chris Hillman, then of the Flying Burrito Brothers, and through him, Gram Parsons invited her to sing on his album ***GP***. She waited a year and then an air ticket arrived and she went to Los Angeles. Parsons navigated her toward Country music, and during 1973, Emmylou toured with him. She began to get a following and duetted with Parsons on the ***Grievous Angel*** album. When Parsons suddenly died in September 1973, it was a severe blow to Emmylou. At the time, she was in Washington collecting her daughter to bring her to L.A. In the event, she stayed in D.C. and began to put a band together. The band evolved into her world-famous Hot Band.

Reprise Records, for whom Emmylou had been recording with Parsons, signed her. Her first album, ***Pieces of the Sky,*** was released in 1975 and revealed a style of music that would hereafter be a Harris trademark. Not for her the

*Emmylou Harris with **Roy Huskey, Jr.***

glitzy Country that was Pop dressed in other clothes. Emmylou's music hearkened back to the roots of Country: a blending of Country and Folk yet with a Rock back beat. Her first release, *Too Far Gone,* only made the Top 75, but in the summer, Emmylou released her version of the Louvins' *If I Could Only Win Your Love*, which reached the Country Top 5 and crossed to the Pop Top 60. The last single of the year, the seasonal, *Light of the Stable*, did not fare well, even though Dolly Parton, Neil Young and Linda Ronstadt did harmony vocals.

At the beginning of 1976, Emmylou was in the Top 15 with a duet with Linda Ronstadt, *The Sweetest Gift*, which appeared on Linda's ***Prisoner in Disguise*** album. Emmylou then had her first No.1, a remake of Buck Owens' hit *Together Again*. This was followed by the Top 3 hit *One of These Days*. At year end, Emmylou had her second No.1 with her version of *Sweet Dreams*. That year, Emmylou released her second album, ***Elite Hotel***, which earned her a Grammy Award for "Best Country Vocal Performance, Female."

At the end of 1976, Emmylou moved to Warner Brothers Records and at the beginning of 1977, she hit the Top 10 with Chuck Berry's *(You Never Can Tell) C'est la Vie* and Jimmy Work's *Making Believe*. At the end of the year, Emmylou hit the Top 3 with the Dolly Parton song *To Daddy*.

Emmylou was back at the No.1 spot at the beginning of 1978 with *Two More Bottles of Wine*. Then her next three singles, *Easy from Now On* (1978) and a re-recording of *Too Far Gone* and *Play Together Again Again* (both 1979), just failed to hit the Top 10. The last named was a Buck Owens' track on which Emmylou duetted. She came back strongly with her version of the Pomus-Shuman classic *Save the Last Dance for Me*, which went Top 5. She ended the year with a lowly placed duet with Charlie Louvin, *Love Don't Care,* and the title track of her ***Blue Kentucky Girl*** album, which went Top 10. That year, that album earned her another Grammy Award for "Best Country Vocal Performance, Female."

Emmylou started out 1980 with another No.1, *Beneath Still Waters,* and followed it with the Top 10 *Wayfaring Stranger*. That year, she released the Bluegrass album ***Roses in the Snow***. In the summer, Emmylou got together with Roy Orbison on *That Lovin' You Feelin' Again,* which featured in the movie *Roadie*. This release, which went Top 10, also crossed to the Pop Top 60 and earned them a Grammy Award for "Best Country Performance by a Duo or Group with Vocal." Emmylou finished the year with the Top 15 single *The Boxer*. The song, written by Paul Simon and synonymous with Simon & Garfunkel, did not sit well with a female vocal. Emmylou also appeared on Paul Kennerley's concept album ***The Legend of Jesse James***. That year, Emmylou was named CMA's "Female Vocalist of the Year."

In 1981, Emmylou had hits with *Mister Sandman* (Top 10 Country/Top 40 Pop) and *If I Needed You* (with Don Williams, Top 3). She also received 6 Gold Records that year in respect of past and present albums: ***Elite Hotel*** (1976), ***Luxury Liner*** (1977), ***Profile—Best of Emmylou Harris*** (1978), ***Blue Kentucky Girl*** (1979), ***Roses in the Snow*** (1980) and ***Evangeline*** (1981). During the rest of the first half of the 80's, Emmylou scored with 1982: *Tennessee Rose* (Top 10), *Born to Lose* (Top 3) and the No.1 *(Lost His Love) On our Last Date*, a vocal version of Floyd Cramer's 1960 instrumental; 1983: *I'm Movin' On* (Top 5). Emmylou's recording career then got bogged down, no doubt not helped by her disintegrating marriage. *So Sad (to Watch Good Love Go Bad)*, which had been a hit for the Everly Brothers, only reached the Top 30. Then Emmylou duetted with John Denver on *Wild Montana Skies*, which was on his ***It's About Time*** album, and it went Top 15.

With the release of her album ***White Shoes***, Emmylou had a resurgence in chart success. Although the final single of 1983, *Drivin' Wheel,* only reached the Top 30, the two opening singles of 1984, *In My Dreams* and *Pledging My Love*, both went Top 10. *In My Dreams* was written by British-born songwriter Paul Kennerley, whom she married in 1985. The single won for Emmylou another Grammy Award as "Best Country Vocal Performance, Female." Another interesting selection on the ***White Shoes*** album was Donna Summer's *On the Radio*.

From here on in, Emmylou's solo success became much more fragmented and her major hits through the rest of the early 80's were: *Someone Like You* (Top 30, 1984) and *White Line* (Top 15, 1985). The last named came from ***The Ballad of Sally Rose***, a critically acclaimed concept album written and produced by Emmylou and Kennerley. This is an album that will mature like good wine and will be hailed as a masterpiece in the future, much in the same way as Kennerley's early concept material. The musicians and support singers on the project include Albert Lee, Vince Gill, Waylon Jennings, Dolly Parton, Linda Ronstadt and Gail Davies. That year, 1985, Emmylou guested on Southern Pacific's *Thing About You*, which went Top 15.

Then in 1987, she joined forces with Dolly Parton and Linda Ronstadt for the watershed ***Trio*** project. It earned a Grammy Award for "Best Country Performance by a Duo or Group with Vocal." It also yielded a trio of major hits in 1987, namely, *To Know Him Is to Love Him* (No.1), *Telling Me Lies* (Top 3) and *Those Memories of You* (Top 5). The album also produced the 1988 Top 10 hit *Wildflowers*. It was named 1987 "Album of the Year" by the ACM, 1988 "Vocal Event of the Year" (a new category) by the CMA and "Vocal Collaboration of the Year" by *Music City News*.

In 1988, Emmylou returned to the top of the chart with a duet with Earl Thomas Conley, *We Believe in Happy Endings*, which appeared on his ***The Heart of It All*** album and then on Emmylou's 1990 ***Duets*** album. This was followed by Emmylou's return to Reprise and the release of her ***Bluebird*** album. From this came her last major hit, *Heartbreak Hill*, a song written by Emmylou and Paul. Emmylou appeared at the prestigious Wembley Festival in England in 1989 and 1990.

Emmylou released another classic album in 1992, when, backed by the Nash Ramblers, she recorded live in the spring of 1991 at the Ryman Auditorium. The material was a mixture of the old and the new and included Steve Earle's *Guitar Town*, Bruce Springsteen's *Mansion on the Hill* and Kieran Kane and Jamie O'Hara's *If I Could Be There* as well as Curley Williams' *Half as Much*, Tex Owens' *Cattle Call* and Bill Monroe's *Scotland*. The Nash Ramblers are comprised of Larry Atamanuik (drums), Roy Huskey, Jr. (upright bass), Sam Bush (mandolin, fiddle), Al Perkins (Dobro, banjo, guitar) and Jon Randall Stewart (guitar, mandolin). In 1992, Emmylou won the TNN/MCN prestigious "Minnie Pearl Award."

One of Emmylou's strengths has always been the quality of musicians who have backed her as part of the Hot Band. These have included Tony Brown (now President of MCA Nashville), legendary guitarists James Burton and Albert Lee, Rodney Crowell, steelie Hank De Vito, Emory Gordy, Jr. (now a noted Nashville producer and married to Patty Loveless), Steve Fishell (now a Nashville producer), legendary keyboardist Glen D. Hardin, Herb Pedersen (later in the Desert Rose Band), Country star Ricky Skaggs, Barry Tashian (now one half of the highly successful Barry & Holly Tashian) and slide-guitarist extraordinaire Philip Donnelly.

Emmylou moved labels to Asylum, newly established in Nashville in 1993, and released ***Cowgirl's Prayer***. She also divorced from Paul Kennerley and the album is noticeable for the absence of his fine songs. Again she was unable to get back to former record glory, although she is still greatly in demand on the concert scene.

RECOMMENDED ALBUMS:

"Pieces of the Sky" (Reprise)(1975)
"Elite Hotel" (Reprise)(1976)
"Luxury Liner" (Warner Brothers)(1977)
"Quarter Moon in a Ten Cent Town" (Warner Brothers)(1978)
"Blue Kentucky Girl" (Warner Brothers)(1979)
"Roses in the Snow" (Warner Brothers)(1980)
"Evangeline" (Warner Brothers)(1981)
"Cimarron" (Warner Brothers)(1981)
"Last Date" (Warner Brothers)(1982) [Live album]
"White Shoes" (Warner Brothers)(1983)
"The Ballad of Sally Rose" (Warner Brothers)(1983)
"Duets" (Reprise)(1984)
"Thirteen" (Warner Brothers)(1986)
"Bluebird" (Reprise)(1989)
"Brand New Dance" (Reprise)(1990)
"Emmylou Harris and the Nash Ramblers at the Ryman" (Reprise)(1992) [Live album]
"Cowgirl's Prayer" (Asylum)(1993)
With Gram Parsons:
"Grievous Angel" (Reprise)(1974)

TED HARRIS

(Singer, Guitar, Songwriter, Music Publisher)

Given Name:	**Theodore Clifford Harris**
Date of Birth:	**August 2, 1937**
Where Born:	**Lakeland, Florida**
Married:	**Jackie Ann Thompson (m. 1967)**
Children:	**Bradley Carlton, Joshua Chandler**

If you wander into Writer's Tape Copies on 19th Avenue in Nashville, chances are you will be greeted by a tall, slim, happy, mustachioed man. This unassuming person is, in fact, one of Country music's finest songwriters.

After graduating from high school, Ted Harris became District Circulation Manager of a local newspaper in Lakeland, Florida. Although he rapidly gained promotion at that time, he knew that he wanted to record. So, in 1958, armed with 17 songs, he headed for Nashville. The first publisher he met was the legendary songwriter/band leader Ted Daffan, who accepted seven of the songs. They were assigned to Silver Star Music and six weeks after arriving in town, Ted was signed by Chet Atkins to RCA Victor.

However, life isn't always like a fairy story and sales did no more than guarantee him that he was still interesting enough for Columbia to sign two years later. Despite Don Law's efforts, Ted earned most of his income from clerking in a grocery store and then from selling shoes. When Daffan returned to Texas and Joe Talbot, also with the company, went on the road, Harris decided to accept a shoe selling job in Memphis, which was then becoming a music hotbed.

Here, he got in with the Sun Records enclave, but nothing spectacular happened. When his father was taken ill, Ted returned to Florida. In 1965, he returned to Nashville and with Joe Talbot formed Harbot Music. His song *Crystal Chandelier* was cut by Carl Belew and quickly became a major success and would in time be recorded by some 40 artists. That year, he received a Grammy nomination. The following year, Roy Drusky had a hit with Ted's *Rainbows and Roses*. In 1967, Dottie West had a Top 10 with the Harris song *Paper Mansions*. This was followed by two Waylon Jennings cuts, *The Road* and *Dark Side of Fame*. Connie Smith followed on with *Don't Feel Sorry for Me*.

Within two years of its formation, Harbot had nearly 70 Harris songs on the market. Ted and Talbot decided to go their separate ways and Ted formed Contention Music. In 1968, Bobby Lord had a big hit with Ted's *Live Your Life Out Loud*. Lord recorded other Harris songs, including *The True and Lasting Time, Yesterday's Letters, Rainbow Girl, You and Me Against the World* and *Wake Me Up Early in the Morning*. In 1969, Wilma Burgess had a Top 50 success with the Harris songs *The Woman in Your Life* and *The Sun's Gonna Shine*. In 1971, Bobby Wright had a big hit with *Here I Go Again*. Charley Pride has recorded two Harris supersongs, *Crystal Chandelier* and *The Happiness of Having You*. In 1973, Marie Osmond had a No.1 Country hit with Ted's *Paper Roses*. The record crossed over to become a Top 5 Pop single and a No.2 Pop hit in the U.K.

Ted also helped other writers to get started. These included Betty Walker, Hugh King and Glen Ray. In 1972, he was asked to become a teacher for the songwriting course at the University of Tennessee. He was elected to a directorship in the Country Music Association and became the first Director to hold a special session for his fellow writers to try to improve their position under the auspices of the CMA. SESAC awarded him their "Songwriter of the Year" accolade in 1969, 1970, 1971 and 1972. He received the award again in 1976 and in 1987. In 1990, he was inducted into the NSAI Songwriters Hall of Fame. Among his more contemporary hits are *The Hand That Rocks the Cradle,* recorded by the Judds and Glenn Campbell/Steve Wariner. Unlike other Nashville scribes, Ted is a solo writer and never co-writes.

Ted lists his hobby as boating and has a houseboat. To understand the easy-goingness yet determination of Ted Harris, one need look no further than the day when, still a bachelor at 30, he looked out the window of a restaurant and saw a girl walking across the street and knew that he would marry her. He did!

FREDDIE HART

(Singer, Songwriter, Guitar)

Given Name:	**Frederick Segrest**
Date of Birth:	**December 21, 1926**
Where Born:	**Loachapoka, Alabama**
Married:	**Virginia Trendall**
Children:	**Freddie, Victor, Joe Andrew**

Long before Rambo, there was Freddie Hart. Long before Billy Ray Cyrus, Freddie Hart was the one Country performer who could be described as a "hunk." The one-time disruptive became one of the top performers of Country music during the 60's and 70's.

Freddie, who had 14 siblings, got his first "guitar" when he was 5. His Uncle Fletcher made one out of a cigar box and coil wire from an old Model T Ford. When Freddie was 7, he ran away from home and by the time he was 12, because he was so rebellious, his parents sent him to Civilian Conservation Corps camp. Four years later in 1942, he became a Marine, with his mother faking his age. He saw plenty of action and was present at Iwo Jima and Okinawa after being with the troops who retook Guam when just 17. He still found time to entertain in the NCO clubs.

After he left the forces, he had a variety of jobs including cotton picker, sawmill worker, pipeline layer in Texas and dishwasher in Hempstead, New York. He was a bouncer in Phoenix City, Alabama, but also did some band work with Bud Wilson in New York.

Freddie first came to Nashville in 1949, when he acted as a roadie for Hank Williams. It was with Williams that he started to learn about songwriting. Later that year, he had his first song cut, *Every Little Thing Rolled Into One,* by George Morgan. In 1950, Freddie moved on to Phoenix, Arizona, where he worked in a cotton-seed mill. That year, he met Lefty Frizzell in Phoenix when Freddie tried to pitch a song at him. When Lefty found out about the Morgan cut and the fact that Wayne Raney was thinking about recording another Hart song, he signed Hart to tour with him. At the same time, Freddie signed to Capitol for the first time, but apart from creating interest in his songs, none of the singles charted.

Freddie stayed with Lefty until 1953, when he became a regular on *Town Hall Party* in Compton, California, alongside Johnny Bond,

Johnny Cash and Tex Ritter. He stayed on the show until 1956. He was always a keen physical fitness expert and he became a black belt in karate and taught it at the Los Angeles Police Academy.

During 1955, another one of his songs, *Loose Talk*, was cut by Carl Smith. In time, the song would be recorded by over 50 artists, including Patsy Cline (it was the flip-side of *I Fall to Pieces*) and the duo of Buck Owens and Rose Maddox, both in 1961.

By 1959, Hart was signed to Columbia, where he started to experience chart success. *The Wall* went Top 25 and *Chain Gang* made the Top 20 mark that year. *The Key's in the Mailbox* (Top 20) and *Lying Again* (Top 30) both scored in 1960 and *What a Laugh!* made the Top 25 in 1961. Freddie started to appear at the *Opry* around this time and formed his group, the Heartbeats, but he was absent from the charts until 1965.

That year, he signed to Kapp, and both *Togetherness* and *Born a Fool* made the Top 25. By 1970, Freddie had returned to Capitol, where he scored a Top 30 hit with *The Whole World Holding Hands*. However, it was the following year that Freddie Hart became a major star. He started a run of five No.1's with *Easy Loving*. The single went Gold and was also a Top 20 Pop hit. It was the CMA's "Song of the Year" in 1971 and 1972. The ACM voted Freddie 1971 "Entertainer of the Year" and "Top Male Vocalist." They made *Easy Loving* the "Single of the Year" and "Song of the Year" and the album of the same title "Album of the Year." To top it off, both the single and album were Certified Gold, the single in 1971, the album the next year.

In 1972, every single Freddie released went to No.1. *My Hang-Up Is You* stayed on top for six weeks, *Bless Your Heart* was there for two weeks (from here until the end of 1976, Freddie was backed by the Heartbeats) and *Got the All Overs for You (All Over Me)* was on the peak for three weeks. He continued in this vein into 1973 with *Super Kind of Woman*. Then MCA stopped six No. 1's in a row by re-releasing *Born a Fool*. The public didn't respond and it sank in the Top 50. Quickly, *Trip to Heaven* was released by Capitol and redeemed the situation by going to No.1. Then from 1973 until the end of 1975, he couldn't miss. Every single targeted into the Top 10 of the charts: *If You Can't Feel It (It Ain't There)* (Top 3, 1973), *Hang in There Girl, The Want-To's* and *My Woman's Woman* (all Top 3, 1974), *I'd Like to Sleep Till I Get Over You* (Top 5), *The First Time* (Top 3) and the Top 10 *Warm Side of You* (all 1975).

Country strongman ***Freddie Hart***

By the following year, the public had started to find new heroes and Freddie's first three singles of the year, *Thank God She's Mine*, *She'll Throw Stones at You* and *That Look in Her Eyes*, all made the Top 15 and *Why Lovers Turn to Strangers* made the Top 10. However, the success level was definitely slowing and from here on, most of Freddie's singles peaked in the 30s and 40s. There were exceptions that peaked in the 20s and slightly higher. These were *Thank God She's Mine* and *The Pleasure's Been Mine/It's Heaven Loving You* (both Top 15, 1977) and *Toe to Toe* (Top 25, 1978).

Freddie moved from Capitol in 1980 to the independent Sunbird label. The most successful release during this association was *Sure Thing*, which peaked in the Top 15. The others leveled out in the 30s. By 1985, he was on El Dorado, where he registered a low-level entry with *I Don't Want to Lose You*, and in 1987, *Best Love I Never Had* was also at the lower level on Fifth Street Records.

Freddie has for some years been a prudent businessman and has interests outside the music industry. He and his partner, Buck Jones, own the trucking company Hartline. He also owns 40 acres of plum trees and over 200 breeding bulls. Freddie is also a man who is aware of those less fortunate and runs a school for handicapped children.

RECOMMENDED ALBUMS:

"The Best of Freddie Hart" (Harmony)(1967)
"Freddie Hart's Greatest Hits" (Kapp)(1969)
"Easy Loving" (Capitol)(1971)
"The Best of Freddie Hart" (double)(MCA)(1975)
"Freddie Hart Presents the Heartbeats" (Capitol)(1975)
"Freddie Hart's Greatest Hits" (Capitol)(1975)
"Sure Thing" (Sunbird)(1980)

JOHN HARTFORD

(Singer, Songwriter, Banjo, Guitar, Fiddle, Dobro, Womper-Stomper, Author, Riverboat Captain)

Given Name:	**John Harford**
Date of Birth:	**December 30, 1937**
Where Born:	**New York, New York**
Married:	**1. Marie (div.)**
	2. Betty
Children:	**Jamie**

To the casual observer, John Hartford is the writer of *Gentle on My Mind* and that is that. However, John is a very versatile man and *Gentle on My Mind* bears little resemblance to the other material that he has written. Sometimes he is quirky; sometimes deep; sometimes he is accompanied by other talented musicians and sometimes, his only accompaniment is his famed tap-dancing board, known as a womper-stomper. Certainly, John Hartford is unique.

Although born in New York, his family on both sides came from Missouri and when he was just two weeks old, his parents (his father, a new qualified doctor, and his mother, a painter) moved to St. Louis. From early on, John's influences were music and riverboats. His parents both loved square dancing and this has been passed on to John. By the age of 10, John had begun working on a steamboat. By the time he was 13, John had mastered the banjo and fiddle. He began with a 4-string banjo and adapted it to a 5-string version. His early influences were Earl Scruggs and Stringbean.

John's fiddle playing was helped by the instruction of Dr. James Gray, a state fiddling champion, and an old fiddle player named Goforth from St. Louis. While still in high school, John had his own Bluegrass band that played material by Reno & Smiley, Flatt & Scruggs and Bill Monroe. He then took up guitar and Dobro. In 1959, he attended Washington University at St. Louis, but dropped out in 1960. After leaving college, he had various jobs, including sign painter, deckhand on a Mississippi riverboat and deejay. Around this time, John cut some singles for Marlo and Shannon without success.

During the mid-60's, he moved to Nashville and he did some deejaying as well as session work. He got into the same "Bohemian movement" as Kris Kristofferson and Mickey Newbury. John also started pitching his songs. He came to the attention of the Glaser Brothers and was signed to their talent agency. They started pitching John to the record labels. It was now that "Harford" became "Hartford." John signed with RCA Victor and came under the production control of Chet Atkins. His first album, ***John Hartford Looks at Life***, in 1966, yielded several songs that were recorded by other performers.

However, it was John's second album, ***Earthwords & Music***, that yielded the famed *Gentle on My Mind*, which reached the Top 60 for John. It was to be Glen Campbell's version of the song that would lift John into the limelight. Strangely, Glen's version was never to be a major hit in the U.S., even though his album of the same name went Gold in 1968. It was just that everyone wanted to record the song, which was half Folk and half Pop. In 1969, Dean Martin had a Top 3 hit with it in the U.K. and it became the most recorded Country song, with versions by Patti Page, Floyd Cramer and Aretha Franklin. In 1967, John won two Grammy Awards for *Gentle on My Mind*: one for his version, as "Best Folk Performance" and the other for "Best Country & Western Song."

About this time, CBS-TV, spotting that John was "left field," offered him a detective series, but he declined the offer. By 1968,

Singer, Writer and Riverboat Pilot ***John Hartford***

John had enough income from *Gentle on My Mind* to turn his back on Pop music and concentrate on his own brand of Folk-Country. That year, he went to the West Coast and appeared on CBS-TV's *Smothers Brothers Comedy Hour,* and in 1969, he was featured on the *Glen Campbell Goodtime Hour*. During 1968, John guested on the Byrds' album ***Sweetheart of the Rodeo*** and the following year, he appeared on Doug Dillard's ***The Banjo Album***.

At the end of the 60's, John earned his riverboat pilot's license and became a frequent crew member aboard the steamboat *Julia Belle Swain*. He piloted the *JBS* in the annual Louisville Derby Days Steamboat Race. In 1970, he came to Nashville to appear on Johnny Cash's Bill Monroe tribute show and met guitarist Norman Blake.

By early 1971, John turned his back on California and put together a band with Blake, Tut Taylor (Dobro) and Vassar Clements (fiddle). The group played the Bluegrass festival circuit during 1971. That year, John appeared on Delaney & Bonnie Bramlett's ***Motel Shot*** album. John also changed labels and went to Warner Brothers for two albums, ***Aero Plain*** (1971) and ***Morning Bugle*** (1972). During the first half of the decade, John appeared on several albums, including James Taylor's ***Mud Slide Slim*** and Kate Taylor's ***Sister Kate*** (both 1971), Seals & Crofts' ***Summer Breeze*** and James Taylor's ***One Man Dog*** (both 1972), the Dillards' ***Tribute to the American Duck*** (1973) and Hoyt Axton's ***Southbound*** (1975).

In 1975, after a three year interval, John signed with Flying Fish Records. His debut album for the label later that year was a trio affair with Benny Martin and Lester Flatt, called ***Tennessee Jubilee***. The album also featured D.J. Fontana, Buddy Emmons, Charlie Collins and Curley Seckler. That same year, John started using his now famed womper-stomper board (an amplified piece of plywood) on which he danced in clogs (since then, he's turned to wearing sneakers) while he played and sang. It started out as a way for John to get exercise and it evolved from that.

The following year, John released his wonderful album ***Mark Twang***, which earned for him a Grammy Award as "Best Ethnic or Traditional Recording." In 1977, John appeared on Gene Clark's ***Two Sides to Every Story*** and teamed up with the Dillards as Dillard Hartford Dillard and recorded the album ***Glitter-Grass (From the Nashwood Hollyville Strings)***. John continued to release a series of solo and ensemble albums through the 70's, the solo ones being ***All in the Name of Love*** (1977) and ***Heading Down into the Mystery Below*** (1978). In 1979, John got together with Pat Burton and Benny Martin for ***Slumberin' on the Cumberland***, which also featured an all-star support group.

In 1980, John got back together with the Dillards for ***Permanent Wave***, which is a perfect example of how Bluegrass and rock'n'roll can work off of one another. John also appeared on the Dillards' ***Homecoming & Family Reunion*** album and the excellent Shel Silverstein album ***The Great Conch Train Robbery***.

During the rest of the 80's, John produced consistently fine albums. ***Catalogue*** has a cover which tells the booking agent what he will get with the John Hartford one man show. Of course, it didn't indicate the spontaneity of a Hartford performance or how he's likely to call a figure or two and get his audiences dancing.

John's 1984 album ***Gum Tree Canoe*** is a work of pure delight with Jack Clement, Mark O'Connor and Roy Huskey, Jr., as principal players and also featured Marty Stuart, Sam Bush and Jeannie Seely. One of the tracks, *Little Piece of My Heart* (in 1994 a hit for Faith Hill), was released with a surrealist video and made the basement area of the Country chart. The album also has a most distinctive version of the Rolling Stones' *No Expectations*. That same year, John was featured on the ***Bill Monroe & Friends*** album. In 1987, John wrote *Steamboat in a Cornfield* (Crown), which was turned into a comic strip in 1991 by Gasoline Alley. In 1987, John recorded an album for MCA/Dot supported by the Hartford String band, entitled ***Annual Waltz***.

Recently, John has written a special for TNN, *Banjos, Fiddles and Riverboats* and was one of the voices on Ken Burns' *Civil War* series on PBS.

RECOMMENDED ALBUMS:

All of John Hartford's have something to offer. Those listed below are a must.
"Earthwords & Music" (RCA Victor)(1967)
"Aero Plain" (Warner Brothers)(1971)
"Tennessee Jubilee" (Flying Fish)(1975) [With Benny Martin and Lester Flatt]
"Mark Twang" (Flying Fish)(1976)
"Glitter-Grass (From the Nashwood Hollyville Strings)" (Flying Fish)(1977) [As Dillard Hartford Dillard]
"Slumberin' on the Cumberland" (Flying Fish)(1979) [With Benny Martin and Pat Burton]
"Permanent Wave" (Flying Fish)(1980) [As Dillard Hartford Dillard]
"Gum Tree Canoe" (Flying Fish)(1984)
"Annual Waltz" (MCA/Dot)(1987)
"A John Hartford Collection" (Flying Fish)(1987)

ALEX HARVEY

(Singer, Songwriter, Guitar, Harmonica, Piano, Actor)

Given Name:	**Thomas Alexander Harvey**
Date of Birth:	**March 10, 1947**
Where Born:	**Dyersburg,Tennessee**
Married:	**1. Suzanne (div.)** **2. Barbra (div.)** **3. Ava**
Children:	**William Alexander,** **Brandon Alexander**

Alex Harvey has gained acclaim and respect as both a Hollywood actor and one of Nashville's most celebrated songwriters.

Hailing from Dyersburg, Tennessee, the son of a bootlegger father, Alex was raised in Haywood County, along with his brother, Legrande, and sister, Jean. Alex says his father was a traveling salesman who sold liquor out of a panel truck. He also owned a small country store in Haywood County. Alex's early musical influences were mostly black-oriented, since he spent a lot of time in the Delta region and in a predominantly black county. His father played harmonica with a black band that would often gather at the family store on Saturdays.

Alex sang in church when he was 6, winning a talent contest singing *Little Brown Jug*, with his father playing harmonica. Alex's mother was a die-hard Country fan who listened to the *Grand Ole Opry* every Saturday night. Alex says his style of music, a combination of black Rhythm and Blues and hillbilly, evolved from his southern black rooted background and his early musical idols, who included Ray Charles, Lefty Frizzell, Hank Williams, Muddy Waters, B.B. King, Jimmy Reed and Elvis.

In 1969, Alex graduated with a master's degree in music, and a minor in drama from Murray State University in Kentucky. It was that same year that he teamed up with songwriter Barry Etris, and the two went through 60 verses of *Ruben James* in a two-week time period before pitching the song to Kenny Rogers, who happened to be appearing on a TV show in Nashville at the time. According to the story, Alex and Etris hung around outside Rogers' dressing room door for three days before being acknowledged. Rogers listened, liked what he heard and cut the song and the rest, as they say, is history. Harvey has written 15 hits for Rogers to date, including *Someone Who Cares*, from the movie *Fools*, and *King of Oak Street*, *Making Music for Money* and *The Hoodooin' of Miss Fannie Deberry*, which were included on ***The Gambler*** album. After *Ruben James* was recorded, Rogers encouraged Alex to move from Nashville to Los Angeles, where his next major success was to co-write *Delta Dawn* with Larry Collins. This was his biggest song as it became Tanya Tucker's first hit in 1972 and was eventually recorded by Helen Reddy and more than 50 other artists. *Rings* was another hit written by Harvey, which has been recorded as both a Country and Pop hit by Cymarron (1971/Top 20), Lobo (1974/Top 50) and the Glaser Brothers (1971/Top 20). The song was Certified at BMI as having 1 million plays. *Hell and High Water*, written with and recorded by T. Graham Brown, went to No. 1 in 1986. Other hits Alex has written include *Dance in Circles*, recorded by Tim Ryan, which made the Top 50 (1990), Don Williams' *Catfish Bates* (1992) and Billy Ray Cyrus' Top 10 *Somebody New* (1993).

The Texas legislature voted Alex's song *No Place But Texas* the official song of the 1986 Texas sesquicentennial celebration. Other artists who have recorded Alex's songs include Bette Midler, Anne Murray, Waylon Jennings, Jerry Lee Lewis, Loretta Lynn, Peggy Lee, Andy Williams, Henry Mancini, Eydie Gorme and Willie Nelson.

"Nashville wouldn't have anything to do with me at first," Alex said in an interview. "Most of my success has been with people who think a bit broader. People were ready to listen in L.A."

Alex moved there in the early 70's and was encouraged by actor James Garner. He studied acting at the Beverly Hills Playhouse under Milton Katselas for four years and his first role was to guest star in a James Garner Movie of the Week titled *The Long Summer of George Adams* (1982). Since then his credits have included *The Dollmaker*, co-starring with Jane Fonda, *Country*, with Jessica Lange and Sam Shepard, *The Sky's No Limit*, *Adam*, *Houston Knights*, *Dallas*, *Days of Our Lives*, *Parent Trap 2*, *Shirley*, *The Dukes of Hazzard*, *Blind Vengeance* and *Gettysburg*.

In addition to writing and acting, Alex has pursued a singing career since shortly after Kenny Rogers recorded his first song. Through Rogers, he got a deal with Capitol Records. Although he has had no chart hits to date in the U.S. he recorded three albums at Capitol and had a Top 10 record in Europe. From Capitol he went to United Artists, where he recorded two more albums, and also has releases on Metromedia and Buddah.

Alex has performed on the road with artists like Willie Nelson, the Pointer Sisters, Bette Midler, Dolly Parton, Anne Murray, the Gatlin Brothers and others. In 1987 Harvey appeared on NPR's *Mountain Sage* with Larry Grose. The following year, he hosted a 2-hour TV special, *No Place But Texas*. In 1993, Harvey was nominated for the Nashville Songwriters Hall of Fame.

Because of the diversity of his interests, to some he may appear scattered. But according to Alex Harvey, "It's all the same thing if it comes from the fire. I love every moment of everything I do, and try to give with all my heart. I just appreciate so much the opportunities that have been afforded me, and I never want to let anyone down who's shown their faith in me and given me a chance."LAP

RECOMMENDED ALBUMS:

"Alex Harvey" (Capitol)(1971)
"Souvenirs" (Capitol)(1973)
"True Love" (Capitol)(1974)
"Alexander Harvey" (Buddah)(1974)
"Preshus Child" (Kama Sutra)(1976)
"Purple Crush" (Buddah)(1978)
"No Place But Texas" (Scarab)(1988)

ROY HARVEY

(Singer, Guitar)

Given Name:	**Roy Cecil Harvey**
Date of Birth:	**March 24, 1892**
Where Born:	**Monroe County, West Virginia**
Married:	**Mary Cleo Farley**
Children:	**seven**
Date of Death:	**July 11, 1958**

Roy Harvey played Old-Time music and recorded extensively between 1926 and 1931. Although perhaps best known as the guitarist with Charlie Poole and His North Carolina Ramblers, Harvey also made numerous sessions on his own with other musicians and got others into the studio and accompanied them even when they received primary label credit. Railroading seemed to be Roy's first love and his musical career flourished during a period when the Virginian rail strike curtailed his work opportunities. Eventually, he returned to the locomotives as an engineer on the Florida East Coast, remaining at that post until shortly before his death.

Born near the southeastern corner of West Virginia, Harvey moved to Princeton, Virginia, with his parents as a child. According to his widow, Roy could tune a guitar at the age of 6, which illustrates the keen ear he possessed for musical sound. In his mid-teens, the youth went to work for the Virginian Railway, becoming a fireman at 19 and an engineer by the time the Virginian trainmen went on strike in 1923. Out of his job as a result of the incident, Harvey first worked as a streetcar operator in Bluefield and then in Beckley at a music store. When he met Charlie Poole and Posey Rorer, who needed a replacement for Norm Wooleiff on guitar, Roy took the position. From then on, he alternated working in the store with recording and sometimes touring (or rambling) with Poole.

Roy appeared on all of Poole's Columbia sessions through 1930, but also recorded on his own and with other musicians. Some of the more interesting material lyrically are his duets (using the name Roy Harper) with Earle Shirkey that included such humorous views of prohibition as *Where the Roses Bloom for the*

Bootlegger, The Bootlegger's Dream of Home, We Have Moonshine in the West Virginia Hills, and the piece of labor controversy, *The Virginian Strike of '23*. Harvey's recorded repertoire also included such standard Victorian sentimental fare as *Poor Little Joe* and *I'll Be There, Mary Dear,* along with traditional ballads like *George Collins* and the newly composed *The Lilly Reunion.*

In addition to Shirkey, who was known primarily for his yodeling, Harvey also took on other duet partners, including Beckley resident Leonard Copeland, with whom he recorded six guitar duets, and fiddler Jess Johnson, playing guitar on the first version of Sylvester Weaver's *Guitar Rag* to be recorded by white musicians. Roy also took his own North Carolina Rambler group into the studios of both Brunswick and Paramount, using a somewhat different line-up than that used by Poole on his Columbia and Paramount discs.

In 1929, Roy accompanied brothers Vance and Wiley Weaver to Columbia Studios, where they cut a session. After Poole's death in May 1931, Harvey took Johnson and a duo living in Princeton, Ernest Branch and Bernice "Si" Coleman, to Richmond, Indiana, where they recorded 22 numbers as the West Virginia Ramblers, including the initial version of the now standard Bluegrass favorite *Footprints in the Snow,* and a fine original train wreck ballad, *The Wreck of the C & O Sportsman*. In October 1931, Harvey, Branch and Coleman did half a dozen sides for OKeh, which came out under the name of the latter two and included the ballad *The Telegraph Shack.* This proved to be Harvey's last session.

As the Great Depression deepened and recording opportunities lessened, Roy Harvey joined the Beckley police force (Leonard Copeland had already been on it) and later clerked in a furniture store. WWII gave him the opportunity to get back into railroading and he became an engineer on the Florida East Coast Railway. He retired a few months before his death and was buried in New Smyrna Beach. The North Carolina Rambler album on Biograph tends to focus more attention on Harvey's contributions to the band. A few of his numbers also appear on various anthologies. IMT

RECOMMENDED ALBUM:

"The North Carolina Ramblers, 1928-1930" (Biograph)(1972)
(See also Charlie Poole.)

HAWKSHAW HAWKINS

(Singer, Songwriter, Guitar, Mandolin)
Given Name: Harold Franklin Hawkins
Date of Birth: December 22, 1921
Where Born: Huntington, West Virginia
Married: 1. Reva Barbour (div.) 2. Jean Shepard
Children: Richard Hall, Harold Franklin II, Don Robin
Date of Death: March 5, 1963

With his rich and smooth voice, Hawkshaw Hawkins was and had long been classed as one of the best Honky-Tonk singers in Country music. He was tall, had a winning smile, dressed in decorated Western outfits and carried an Australian bullwhip which he used as part of his act.

Although superstardom had generally eluded him, the life of Hawkshaw Hawkins was successful. He married Country music star Jean Shepard and they lived on a beautiful ranch near Nashville, where they raised Tennessee walking horses. His latest recording, *Lonesome 7-7203*, had just charted, when he was killed in a plane crash on March 5, 1963. The crash, on a date forever etched in the minds of Country music fans, killed not only Hawkshaw Hawkins but Patsy Cline, Cowboy Copas, and Randy Hughes, who was the pilot, Cope's son-in-law and the personal manager of Patsy. They were all returning home to Nashville after playing at a benefit concert for the family of a deejay who had lost his life in a car crash. A blinding thunderstorm brought the plane down in the rugged wooded hills, near Camden, Tennessee. There were no survivors.

When he traded five trapped rabbits for his first guitar, Hawk had set his foot on the first rung of the entertainment ladder. At 15, he entered a talent show on radio WSAZ Huntington, West Virginia, and won $15. As a result of his win he began working there. He worked at WCHS Charleston and sometimes teamed up to sing with Clarence "Sherlock" Jack as a duo. During 1941, Hawkins joined a traveling show and ended up a few months later working on radio in Lawrence, Massachusetts. Just before WWII began, he worked in the shipyards in Baltimore. He spent his war years serving in the Pacific, performing from time to time on Manila's WTUM.

Hawkshaw Hawkins (right) holding back ***Little Jimmy Dickens***

In 1946, he returned to civilian life and joined WWVA Wheeling, West Virginia, where he stayed until 1954. During this time, he had colorful summer shows where he used trained horse acts and also did rope and whip tricks as part of the performance. He could be heard on CBS radio from 1946 to 1954 and was seen on ABC-TV's *Jubilee USA*. He was also a regular member of the *Grand Ole Opry* from 1955.

King Records' owner and founder, Sid Nathan, signed Hawkshaw and recorded him at the label's studios in Cincinnati, Ohio. Hawk hit the charts in 1948 with two Top 10 successes, *Pan American* and *Doghouse Boogie*. He followed the next year with *I Wasted a Nickel* (Top 15). In 1951, Hawk scored with two more Top 10 hits, *I Love You a Thousand Ways* and *I'm Waiting Just for You.* In 1952, Hawk had a Top 10 hit with his version of *Slow Poke* (also a Top 30 Pop hit).

The association with the King label lasted until 1953, when he joined RCA Victor, but he did not have hit record success with them. In 1959 he changed again, this time to Columbia, where he once more managed a Top 15 chart place with *Soldiers Joy,* a folkish pseudo Revolutionary War song which was set to the melody of an old fiddle tune. In September, 1962, Hawk returned to King Records and had just cut the Justin Tubb composition *Lonesome 7-7203*, but he did not live to see it reach No.1.

This Appalachian born and bred man was aptly called by his fans "eleven and a half yards of personality." His recordings with both RCA and Columbia were released in 1991 on the Bear Family label in the form of a cd box set. JAB

RECOMMENDED ALBUMS:

"Taken from Our Vaults, Volume 1" (King)(1963)
"Taken from Our Vaults, Volume 2" (King)(1963)
"Taken from Our Vaults, Volume 3" (King)(1964)
"Lonesome 7-7203" (King)(1969)
"Hawkshaw Hawkins Sings Hawkshaw Hawkins" (Camden)
[Re-issued by Stetson UK in the original sleeve (1992)]
"Hawk" (cd Box Set)(Bear Family Germany)(1991)

GEORGE D. HAY

(Industry Executive)
Given Name: George Dewey Hay
Date of Birth: November 9, 1895
Where Born: Attica, Indiana
Date of Death: May 8, 1968

Best known as the legendary founder of Nashville's *Grand Ole Opry*, George D. Hay was also a noted radio announcer, a skilled publicist, an astute historian, a popular newspaper writer, and an editor. It was his vision and dedication to what he routinely called "Folk music" that generated the ground rules for the nature of the *Grand Ole Opry*. His stubborn insistence that his musicians "keep it down to earth" gave the *Opry* much of its unique, conservative identity, and his image of the show as an informal, rustic collection of "friends and neighbors" prevailed for most of the program's first 25 years.

Hay was not a native southerner, but from the Midwest—a town called Attica, Indiana. He began his career as a print journalist, eventually working for the Memphis *Commercial Appeal* in 1919. For a time he was assigned the court beat, and this he converted to a series of humorous columns called *Howdy Judge,* a series that earned him the nickname "the Solemn Old Judge," though he was not yet 25 years old. The columns were popular enough so that he published a set of them in his first book, *Howdy Judge* (Nashville, 1926). In 1923, the Memphis newspaper started its own radio station, WMC, and Hay, somewhat against his will, was "elected" announcer. He took to this well, creating a series of popular audio gimmicks like chanting the station's call letters and blowing an imitation steamboat whistle to announce the start of WMC's "entertaining trip down the Mississippi."

Hay's popularity in Memphis grew to such an extent that in 1924 he was hired by Sears Roebuck, the giant catalog company, to be the announcer for their powerful new station, WLS in Chicago. By now, he was so popular with radio audiences that WLS artists were having him introduce them on phonograph records and *Radio Digest* was awarding him a gold cup for being the most popular announcer in the nation.

While he had been a cub reporter in Memphis, Hay attended the funeral of a hero in the hamlet of Mammoth Spring, Arkansas, and later attended a country dance; the spirit of the dance captivated him, and he began to wonder if there was some way to merchandise it. In Chicago, he now found himself assigned to be the announcer for a new show the station was trying, a show which became the *National Barn Dance*. Though he did not originate the show, he did help promote and design it, and was amazed at its popularity.

In September 1925, when Nashville's National Life Insurance Company started its new station, WSM, the management invited Hay to attend the opening broadcast as a special guest. Impressed, they invited him to come down and take over as Station Manager in October. Nothing was said at the time about Hay starting any kind of rival to the WLS *Barn Dance*, but when he arrived in Nashville he found that artists like Dr. Humphrey Bate and Uncle Dave Macon had been making occasional appearances on WSM, and had been well received. That November Hay invited the fiddler Uncle Jimmy Thompson to perform, and the overwhelming number of telegrams and phone calls convinced him that there was room in Nashville for an "authentic" *Barn Dance*, staffed by genuine traditional musicians from the hills around the town.

Hay carefully planted stories in the press. Taking advantage of the then-current interest in Henry Ford's attempts to revive Old-Time fiddling, Hay took bands with names like the Binkley Brothers String Orchestra and renamed them the Dixie Clodhoppers. In May 1927, he renamed the show the *Grand Ole Opry*. He helped organize a booking bureau for the performers, and staged publicity photos in which he took a group like Arthur Smith and the McGee Brothers and posed them in a pig pen with their instruments. The distinguished Dr. Humphrey Bate sat with his band in a corn field with a coon hound.

As the *Opry* and WSM grew through the 1930's, Hay became a victim of his own success. Soon professional managers like Harry Stone were brought in to do the actual day-to-day work at the station, and Hay found himself doing mostly announcing and publicity. A health crisis caused him to be on leave for over a year in the 1930's, but he returned to play a major role in brokering and appearing in the *Opry*'s first Hollywood film in 1940. In 1939, when part of the *Opry* went on the NBC network, Hay impressed everyone with his verve and smooth announcing.

Hay continued to be an announcer and figurehead through the 1940's, and routinely took to the road with the *Opry* tour troupes that were now traveling the country. Again, however, his health became a problem; in October 1947, at a special concert in Washington for senators and various politicians, Hay made one of his last appearances with a real *Opry* touring show.

He was still interested in writing, though, and in 1945 published an engaging memoir, *A Story of the Grand Ole Opry*, which he printed himself. This informal account became the source for much of the later *Opry* histories, and Hay revised and expanded it in the early 1950's. For a time in the early 1950's he edited a fan newspaper, *Pickin' and Singing News*, and appeared in cameo roles on the series of 1955-1956 films made by Ganaway of various *Opry* stars. There was a half-hearted attempt at a syndicated radio show, but nothing ever developed, and by the end of the 1950's the Judge had pretty much retired. He died in Virginia Beach, Virginia, on May 8, 1968.

CKW

Henry D. Haynes refer HOMER & JETHRO

ROY HEAD

(Singer, Rhythm Guitar)
Date of Birth: June 30, 1936
Where Born: Perkins, Oklahoma

Roy Head started out being successful in rock'n'roll and then came into Country music.

His family scratched a living doing farm work. When he was a youngster, he tended to be handy with his fists. By the time he was 9, he was farming with his older brother, Donald. When he reached his teens, Roy gravitated toward rock'n'roll and Rhythm and Blues.

After leaving school, he worked in a factory during the week and played in local bands at the weekend. He moved to Houston and initially sold cars and then became a door-to-door Bible salesman.

In 1958, he had a regional hit with *Baby Let Me Kiss You One More Time* and this led to his appearing on R & B and rock'n'roll shows by the end of the 50's and through the early 60's. Success came to him in 1965, when *Treat Her Right* became a Top 3 Pop smash on Back Beat. Only the Beatles prevented him from hitting the top slot. Yet strangely, it also became a Top 30 hit in Britain. With this success, he formed the Traits as his backing band. The record allegedly sold a million, but it never received a Gold Record, because it was never registered with BMI.

The Traits didn't want to go on the road and tour, so Roy went without them. They then sued him for six-sevenths of his earnings and the case took 18 months to settle. Then he ran into voice troubles. With a voice that at times took on a James Brown complexion, he developed nodes on his vocal cords and was ordered to rest. He didn't return to the business until the late 60's, by which time he meant nothing and went on the skids with drink.

Lee Savaggio, who operated the Club Savaggio in Houston, took over Roy's career. Roy worked at the club for 18 months. In 1974, Roy had a Top 70 Country success with his Mega recording of *Baby's Not Home*. Lee lined up a recording contract with Shannon. In the spring of 1975, Roy was again on the Country charts with *The Most Wanted Woman in Town.* The record peaked in the Top 20 and opened the door to a new phase of his career. His subsequent releases on Shannon hovered around the Top 50 mark. Then in 1976, ABC/Dot signed him and they licensed some of his Shannon material. For the next 18 months, he had middle-order successes and then at the end of 1977, *Come to Me* reached the Top 20. By 1978, ABC/Dot had become ABC and Roy celebrated the new label name with the Top 20 *Now You See 'Em, Now You Don't.* He followed this with his version of Rod Stewart's *Tonight's the Night (It's Gonna Be Alright).* This stuck in the Top 30 and represented the last major hit that he would have.

In 1979, Roy moved over to Elektra, without success. By 1981, he was on Jim Halsey's Churchill label and then through 1982-83 he saw low-level hits on Joe Gibson's NSD label. He moved on to Avion in 1983 and then to Texas Crude.

Roy Head would have felt more at ease with 1990's Country. His physical act would have had him acclaimed by the media as "a hunk." *Treat Her Right* was reactivated by the Commitments in the movie *The Commitments* in 1991.

RECOMMENDED ALBUMS:

"Treat Me Right" (Scepter)(1965)
"A-Head of His Time" (ABC/Dot)(1976) [Oh, how appropriate!]
"Tonight's the Night" (ABC)(1978)
"In Our Room" (Elektra)(1979)
"The Many Sides of Roy Head" (1980)

JIMMY HEAP

(Singer, Songwriter, Lead Guitar)

Given Name: James Arthur Heap
Date of Birth: March 3, 1922
Where Born: Taylor, Texas
Married: Jerry Joe
Children: Jimmy Joe, David Arthur
Date of Death: December 4, 1977

Outside of central Texas, Jimmy Heap and His Melody Masters are largely forgotten, although for some three decades this Western Swing Honky-Tonk Country band was very popular in that area. Like Bob Wills, another noted bandleader, Heap seldom sang on his records. Jimmy played lead guitar while his fiddler, Houston "Perk" Williams (b. 1926), handled most of the vocals.

Jimmy Heap started his musical career after serving in the Army Air Force during WWII when he organized the Melody Masters. Other early members of this group included Arlie Carter, Horace Barnett, Bill Glendining and Louis Renson. They had a daily radio show for a decade at KTAE Taylor, Texas, played a full schedule of clubs and in 1949 signed a contract with Imperial Records.

By the time the band began recording, Perk Williams had joined them. Somewhat ironically, Williams, who had earlier led his own band on radio in Bryan, never sang prior to joining the Melody Masters, but went over so well as the vocalist on their initial release of *Today, Tonight and Tomorrow*, that he did most of the singing from that point on, his vocal style having both distinction and originality. The Melody Masters remained with Imperial for nearly three years, but the company had not yet developed the effective nationwide distribution network that it would have a decade later.

Two of the many numbers that the band cut would have a major impact when recorded by others. *Haunted Hungry Heart*, co-written by Jimmy and piano player Arlie Carter, would later be successful for Slim Whitman, while *The Wild Side of Life*, also co-written by Carter, would become an all-time classic via the Capitol cover by Hank Thompson and the Brazos Valley Boys.

It was indeed through Thompson's influence that Ken Nelson signed Heap and the band to a contract with Capitol. They had their first session in Austin on November 17, 1951, and went on to have 32 sides released over the next five years. Their biggest number, *Release Me*, cut in February 1953, reached the Top 5 on the Country charts the following year. None of Heap's other Capitol discs charted, but some of their more outstanding numbers included the uniquely titled *Ethyl In My Tank*, a Country cover of Jaye P. Morgan's Pop hit *That's All I Want From You* and an original instrumental by steel guitarist Cecil "Butterball" Harris entitled *Butternut*.

After leaving Capitol, Jimmy started his own company, Fame Records, and the Melody Masters cut numerous sides for it over the next several years. With the advent of rock'n'roll, the group altered its style to keep up with the times and added a trumpet player. They were comfortable with Country, Pop and Rockabilly music, working from the dance halls of Texas to the nightclubs of Nevada.

In addition to Jimmy, two Melody Masters with long service included Cecil Harris and bass player Bill Glendining, who also helped with the singing. Heap disbanded the group in July 1977 for a well-earned rest. His own retirement proved to be of short duration because he drowned in a boating accident four months later. IMT

RECOMMENDED ALBUMS:

Some of Jimmy Heap's recordings have appeared on various anthologies.
"Jimmie Heap and the Melody Ranchers" (Bear Family Germany) (1992) [Contains nearly all his Capitol recordings]

HEE HAW

(TV Program)

This very popular TV program started on CBS-TV in the summer of 1968 and moved into syndication in 1971. The show was hosted by Buck Owens and Roy Clark and always boasted a balance of real Country music and cornball comedy. The program was similar to a Country version of *Rowan and Martin's Laugh In.* The show was created and founded by two Torontians, John Aylesworth and Frank Peppiatt, through their company Yonge Street Productions.

The original cast, as well as Owens and Clark, included Minnie Pearl, Archie Campbell, Don Harron, Gordie Tapp, Gunilla Hutton and Jack Burns. The show was directed by Bill Davis. Bob Boatman was in charge of sound and lighting and went on to become Executive Producer of TNN's *Nashville Now*, before his premature death. In charge of music was George Richey, who is now married to Tammy Wynette. The show was produced at WLAC-TV Nashville.

This became the first networked Country show of its kind that was actually produced in Nashville. Among the later comedy stars featured on the show were Kathy Baker, Junior Samples, Grandpa Jones, Stringbean, Kenny Price, Gailard Sartain, Lulu Roman and later, Grady Nutt.

In all, over 600 episodes of the show were made. During its 25th season, 1993-1994, it was decided not to produce new episodes and Gaylord Syndicom, who now own the show, decided to run a series entitled *Hee Haw Silver*, which was a collection of classic shows from previous years.

In addition, during 1994, a live stage show of *Hee Haw* was presented from the Acuff Theater in Opryland USA, entitled *Hee Haw Live*.

BOBBY HELMS

(Singer, Songwriter, Guitar)

Given Name: Bobby Lee Helms
Date of Birth: August 15, 1933
Where Born: Bloomington, Indiana
Married: 1. Esther Marie Hendrickson (div.) 2. Dori
Children: Bobby, Jr., Randy, Debbie, Tyanne, Rob, Angel,

When the Wilburn Brothers returned from a tour of Texas, they asked Decca Records, "Who is Bobby Helms?" Well may they have asked. Bobby's record for Decca,

"I'm the man," says ***Bobby Helms***

Fraulein, became such a success that it remained in the No.1 position for 11 weeks and remained in the charts for 52—yes, 52—weeks!

Bobby's father, Fred, managed the *Monroe County Jamboree*, and Bobby and his brother Freddie played together there for six years, Bobby singing and Freddie playing guitar. As they got older, chubby Bobby lost his billing as "the Bouncing" Bobby Helms. The brothers started to appear on radio and TV as the Helms Brothers and were a part of the Bob Hardy Country Show. They became popular and toured around doing personal appearances, fairs, etc. locally and were soon appearing further afield, gathering fans as they went.

After cutting a record, *Tennessee Rock and Roll*, Bobby began working on a local show in Bloomington, Indiana, called the *Hayloft Frolic Show*. The emcee, Bob Hardy, asked him to go to Nashville to sing on Ernest Tubb's *Midnight Jamboree*. Ernest asked for a tape, which he gave to Paul Cohen, who was then A & R Director for Decca Records. Bobby auditioned for him and very quickly afterward recorded *Fraulein,* written by Lawton Williams. Williams had been pitching it for six years to just about every Nashville recording artist. It was released on January 17, 1957, and for four months it didn't do much, then it took off in Texas. Bobby took a band of 11 musicians on the road and played around the country. He was also seen on such shows as the *Dick Clark Show, American Bandstand,* the *Patti Page Show* and the prestigious *Ed Sullivan Show*. In the fall of 1957, Bobby charted with *My Special Angel,* which reached the No.1 spot on the Country chart, where it stayed for 4 weeks, and stayed on the charts for 26 weeks. It also became a Top 10 Pop hit and also reached No. 22 in the U.K. charts. Bobby returned to the *Ed Sullivan Show* and was presented with a Gold Disc for the single. This was followed at year end by *Jingle Bell Rock*, which not only reached the Country Top 15, but also got into the Pop Top 10.

Bobby started off 1958 with another Country Top 10 release, *Just a Little Lonesome*. By now, Bobby was in demand everywhere and Hollywood beckoned, and he appeared in a film for Columbia Pictures, *The Case Against Brooklyn* (1958). One of the songs he sang in the movie was *Jacqueline*, on which he was backed by the Anita Kerr singers. The single of the song reached the Country Top 5 and crossed-over to the Pop Top 70 in 1958. This and *No Other Baby* were also in the Top 30 in the U.K. charts. Bobby sang *No Other Baby* on the syndicated *Ozark Jubilee*. At this time he also did a guest spot on the *Grand Ole Opry*. He soon found himself playing to more than Country audiences and was touring with the Four Preps, the Silhouettes and Fats Domino among others. He continued to record with Decca but although he had some chart success, his Country singles *New River Train* (Top 30, 1959) and *Lonely River Rhine* (Top 20, 1960) were his last successes for Decca. However, the label continued to re-release *Jingle Bell Rock*, in 1958, 1960, 1961 and 1962.

Over the years, Bobby has supported himself touring. First with the Bobby Helms Show, traveling the U.S. and Europe (especially Germany), then smaller clubs all across the U.S. Bobby has had albums released on various labels over the years, including ***The Best of Bobby Helms***, on Columbia (1963), ***I'm the Man*** and ***Sorry My Name Isn't Fred***, both on Kapp (1966), and ***All for You***, on Little Darlin' in 1968.

Returning to the charts in 1967, Bobby had four more singles on the Little Darlin' label, *He Thought He'd Die Laughing* (Top 50), and *The Day You Stopped Loving Me* (Top 60) (both 1967), *I Feel You, I Love You* (Top 60, 1968) and *So Long* (Top 50, 1969). His last single in the chart was the Top 50 success *Mary Goes 'Round*, on the Certron label.

In 1979, Bobby opened a club in Plainfield, Indiana, called the Special Angel Club, but this venture was not very successful and it ran aground in 1981. Another album was released by MCA in 1983, called ***Pop-a-Billy***. By now, Bobby was wearing a patch over his right eye. He lost the vision in it after working under harsh lights which aggravated a rare eye condition which his doctor had warned him about for years.

A movie on the life of Bobby Helms was planned to go ahead in 1989 and a contract with Capitol Records enabled him to re-cut many of his old hits for the soundtrack, but the film ran into contractual problems and was never made. JAB

RECOMMENDED ALBUMS:

"The Best of Bobby Helms" (Columbia)(1963)
"Bobby Helms Sings Fraulein" (Harmony)(1967) [Repack of "The Best"]
"All New Just for You" (Little Darlin')(1968)
"Greatest Performance" (Certron)(1970)
"Jingle Bell Rock" (Mistletoe)(1974)
"Bobby Helms Sings His Greatest Hits" (Power Pak)(1975)
"Pop-a-Billy" (MCA)(1983)

JOHN HERALD BAND

When Formed: 1976

Current Members:

John Herald	**Guitar, Vocals, Actor**
Bob Green	**Fiddle, Vocals**
George Quinn	**Bass Guitar, Vocals**
Vin Warner	**Stand-Up Bass, Vocals**
Bill Keith	**Banjo**
Orrin Starr	**Banjo, Vocals**

Former Members:

Carolyn Dutton (Fiddle, Vocals), Wanamaker Lewis (Banjo), Gordon Titcom (Mandolin), Aron Off (Bass), Jean-Marc Andres (Banjo, Vocals), Cyndi Cashdollar (Dobro, Vocals)

In the days of a rise in interest in Bluegrass, John Herald (b. John Whittier Sirabian, September 6, 1939, New York City) still remains largely unheralded. Yet, Herald has a pedigree in Urban Bluegrass as impeccable as any and a band that is one of the finest in the Northeast.

John's father was an Armenian poet in Greenwich Village, New York. After John's mother died when he was 3, his father, who had achieved fame through the literary magazines of the 1920's through 1940's, more or less stopped writing. John lived in a series of foster homes until he reached the age of 7, when he was reunited with his father, who was then working as a chef in the Bowery.

John was initially exposed to music when his father, who had union connections, took him to hear musicians such as Pete Seeger. During 1956 and 1957, he was a regular habitué of the Sunday afternoon picking sessions in Washington Square Park. In high school, he formed an R & B band, but on hearing Bluegrass, moved his musical inclinations in that direction. The summer before he started college, he was running a newspaper stand, but come Sunday afternoon, he was off to the park to hear Folk singers and Bluegrass musicians. While in his freshman year at the University of Wisconsin, John met Eric Weissberg and Marshall Brickman and he avidly devoured their music. He had learned a few guitar chords while at boarding school and his new friends taught him more.

During that first year, he visited Nashville and saw Bill Monroe and was totally hooked. His studies started to go downhill and when he bought his own Gibson guitar, he knew that there was no point in returning to college. He took a job selling dictionaries and continued doing this for two years. In the meanwhile, he had become a founding member of the Greenbriar Boys. The group got together in 1958, and John was still not adept as a guitarist, but he soon learned. His role in the trio was lead singer and lead guitar, while Bob Yellin played 5-string banjo and Paul Prestopino was on mandolin (Prestopino was replaced, initially by Eric Weissberg and then by Ralph Rinzler). In 1960, they won the Old-Time Band Competition at the Fiddlers' Convention in Union Grove, North Carolina. That year, the band was playing in Washington Square when they were heard by someone from Vanguard Records and signed to the label. Joan Baez heard their first release and took them on tour with her. They became possibly the first professional Bluegrass band in the Northeast.

In 1966, the band broke up and John retired to Woodstock, New York. He became a part of Mud Acres, with Bill Keith, Jim Rooney, Happy Traum, Lee Berg, Tony Brown, Eric Kaz, Maria Muldaur and Artie Traum and they released a self-titled album on Rounder in 1972. In 1969, John was in a group called the Flying Machine, with James Taylor and Danny Kortchmar. In 1972, John recorded a solo album for Paramount, part of which was recorded at Max's Kansas City in New York City (the first Bluegrass act to record there). John put together a new band, John Herald and the Honkies, in 1973, with Rob Stoner (bass), Al Stowell (fiddle) and Bob Danner (mandolin, fiddle).

Then in 1976, he put together the first incarnation of the John Herald Band with Wanamaker Lewis (banjo), Carolyn Dutton (fiddle), Gordon Titcom (mandolin) and Aron Off (bass). In addition, John has played on quite a few sessions for other artists, including David Bromberg's 1975 album ***Midnight on the Water*** and Bonnie Raitt's ***Home Plate*** in the same year. Bay Records released ***John Herald and the John Herald Band*** in the fall of 1978. Bay Records was also responsible for the Jody Stecher album ***Going Up the Mountain***, which featured John Herald, Fred Sokolow and Larry Hanks.

John's other talents lie in his songwriting skills. Among his songs, which have been recorded by Linda Ronstadt, Joan Baez, Maria Muldaur and Peter, Paul & Mary, are *Different Drum* (an adaptation of a Michael Nesmith number), *Stewball* and *Up to My Neck in High, Muddy Waters*. In addition, Herald has appeared and played in three movies, *Hi, Mom!*, *You Are What You Eat* and *White Line Fever*.

During 1984, he put together the longest running line-up of the band and they signed to Rooster Records and released the album ***The Real Thing***. Carolyn Dutton, from Indiana, was classically trained and has played fiddle with Herald in previous outfits. She has a broad background of working in theater and TV and played in and did vocal arrangements for the Meryl Streep 1982 NBC-TV presentation *Alice in Concert*. Cyndi Cashdollar, from New York City, is one of the world's finest Dobro players, and has an instructional video on the market. She has worked with John Sebastian, David Bromberg, Paul Butterfield, Rick Danko and Levon Helm. George Quinn has played with a selection of Jazz and R & B bands, while Jean-Marc, a friend and acolyte of Bill Keith, comes from France and was a former member of French Bluegrass band Transatlantic Bluegrass. Jean-Marc and Cyndi left the band in 1987, while Carolyn left in 1991.

The music of the band is eclectic, embracing Folk, Bluegrass, Old-Time Country, Honky-Tonk and Cajun. Unlike many traditionalists, John does not reject the use of electric instruments and in his own words, "I do like commercial stuff, not all of it, but I do like drumbeats and stuff like that."

RECOMMENDED ALBUMS:

"John Herald" (Paramount)(1972) [John Herald solo album]
"John Herald and the John Herald Band" (Bay)(1978)
"The Real Thing" (Rooster)(1984)

HIGHWAY 101

When Formed: 1986
Current Members:

Cactus Moser	**Vocals, Drums, Guitar**
Curtis Stone	**Vocals, Bass Guitar, Mandolin, Guitar**
Nikki Nelson	**Lead Vocals, Guitar**

Former Members:
Paulette Carlson (Lead Vocals, Guitar), Jack Daniels (Vocals, Guitar)

Highway 101 was the idea of Nitty Gritty Dirt Band manager Chuck Morris. He brought together three musicians he knew and a singer whose voice he discovered on some demo tapes. The four met for the first time in the fall of 1986 at a Los Angeles recording studio and in less than six months signed with Warner Brothers Records and scored a Top 5 hit with *The Bed You Made for Me*.

Paulette Carlson (b. October 11, 1953, Northfield, Minnesota) grew up in the farmlands of Minnesota and began performing with Country bar bands while still a teenager. In 1978, she moved to Nashville and landed a job as a staff writer for the Oak Ridge Boys publishing company. Paulette also spent some time singing back-up vocals for Gail Davies before signing her own record deal with RCA in 1983. Disappointed with her lack of success, Paulette turned home to Minnesota in 1985. She was invited to give the music business another try the following year and join the new group being formed in Los Angeles.

Guitarist Jack Daniels (b. October 27, 1949, Choctaw, Oklahoma) grew up in the San Francisco Bay Area and was playing in local dance halls by the time he was 16. Eventually he joined the band Silver Creek and signed with Tally Records. When the band broke up Daniels moved to Los Angeles, where he met Curtis Stone. In 1978 Daniels and Stone began touring with former Guess Who lead vocalist Burton Cummings. When not touring with Cummings, Daniels and Stone formed a band called the Lizards and often performed at the Palomino Club. Curtis Stone invited Jack to form the new band to be called Highway 101 as lead guitarist. Jack appeared in the movies *The Jazz Singer* (1980), *One from the Heart* (1982), and *Jimmy the Kid* (1983).

Curtis Stone (b. April 3. 1950, North Hollywood, California) grew up in the small California town of Stockton, the son of Country music great Cliffie Stone. In addition to having his own radio and TV shows, Stone owned Central Songs, the publishing company where Buck Owens and Harlan Howard got their starts. Curtis grew up around Country music stars and started playing guitar as a teenager. One day, his dad needed a bass player for a concert and Curtis moved to the instrument and stayed with it.

Stone's brother Steve, as a producer for Capitol, had hired him to play on records for a variety of artists, including Tennessee Ernie Ford, Brian Wilson, and Leon Russell. As a result of his studio work, Stone was named by the ACM "Bass Player of the Year" in 1976, 1980, 1981 and 1988. Stone spent two years touring with Rocky Burnette and then worked as a staff writer for MCA Music.

Drummer Cactus Moser (b. Scott Moser, May 3, 1957, Montrose, Colorado) grew up on a Colorado cattle and feed ranch. He started playing the drums when his family moved to Denver. After a short stint in college, Moser joined the Country-Rock group Firefall. Moser moved to Los Angeles and spent several years doing studio work and performing live with Johnny Rivers. He also worked on several movies, including Rodney Dangerfield's *Back to School.*

After meeting in the fall of 1986, the blend of talent and personalities seemed a perfect match for Highway 101. Paulette Carlson proved her songwriting skills by penning the group's debut single, *The Bed You Made for Me.* After recording part of their debut album in Los Angeles, the group moved to Nashville to finish the record with producer Paul Worley. Their self-titled album was released in the summer of 1987 and the group's second single, *Whiskey, If You Were a Woman,* shot to the Top 3. The third time was a charm for Highway 101 when *Somewhere Tonight* captured the No.1 spot on the Country chart.

In 1987, the ACM named Highway 101 "Vocal Group of the Year." A month after picking up the trophy, the group was back at No.1 with *Cry, Cry, Cry.* In the summer of 1988, the group's second album, ***Highway 101 2***, was released. In the fall, they scored their third successive No.1, *(Do You Love Me) Just Say Yes.* Their final chart entry that year was *All the Reasons Why*, which would reach the Top 5. To put the finishing touches to a great year, Highway 101 was named "Group of the Year" by the CMA and they retained their ACM "Vocal Group of the Year."

Highway 101 kicked off 1989 with the Mark Knopfler song *Setting Me Up*, which went Top 10. The hit singles continued with the Top 10 *Honky Tonk Heart* and the No.1 *Who's Lonely Now.* Their third album for Warner Brothers, ***Paint the Town***, was released in the fall of 1989. They retained their CMA crown as "Group of the Year."

As a new decade began, the group racked up their 10th hit single with a song written by Roger Miller and Justin Tubb, entitled *Walkin', Talkin', Cryin', Barely Beatin' Broken Heart.* Later in 1990, Highway 101 placed two more hit singles on the charts, *This Side of Goodbye* and *Someone Else's Trouble Now,* both of which reached the Top 15. That year, their debut album, ***Highway 101,*** was Certified Gold.

Paulette Carlson left the group in 1990 to pursue a solo career. The group that took its name from a California highway wasn't detoured by her exit and brought Nikki Nelson on board. Nikki (b. January 3, 1969, San Diego, California) grew up in California and started performing when she was 12 with her father's band. When she was 18, Nikki moved to Nashville and to make ends meet, worked at a photography studio. She came to the attention of Warner Brothers when a producer she was working with pitched her tape to label executive Martha Sharpe. She sent the tape to the members of Highway 101 and they called Nikki for an audition and offered her the job as lead vocalist. The first Highway 101 release with Nikki singing was *Bing Bang Boom* from the album of the same name in 1991, which went Top 15. However, the group had now ceased to reach the higher chart placings, and during 1991 and 1992 their chart singles were *The Blame* (Top 40, 1991), *Baby, I'm Missing You* (Top 25) and *Honky Tonk Baby* (Top 60 both 1992).

In 1993, Jack Daniels left the group and Highway 101 was reduced to a trio. They signed with Liberty Records and released the album ***The New Frontier***. As well as changing labels, the group changed producers. Gone were Paul Worley and Ed Seay and they were replaced by Chuck Howard, Cactus Moser and Curtis Stone. Their first release from the album, *You Baby You*, only went Top 70 and they must be wondering what the future holds.

JIE

RECOMMENDED ALBUMS:

"Highway 101" (Warner Brothers)(1987)
"Highway 101 2" (Warner Brothers)(1988)
"Paint the Town" (Warner Brothers)(1989)
"Bing Bang Boom" (Warner Brothers)(1991)
"The New Frontier" (Liberty)(1993)

Highway 101 *and friends*

FAITH HILL

(Singer)

Given Name: **Audrey Faith Perry**
Date of Birth: **September 21, 1967**
Where Born: **Jackson, Mississippi**
Married: **separated**

Born in Jackson, Mississippi, and adopted while less than a week old, Faith Hill was raised as Audrey Faith Perry in Star, Mississippi.

She grew up singing in church and anywhere else opportunity knocked. It didn't take her long to realize her goal in life was to pursue a singing career. She left her small town of approximately 1,500 people to move to Nashville at 19. Her first job in Music City was selling T-shirts at Fan Fair.

For several years she kept her true intentions to pursue singing a secret in order to get a job. "I would go places to try and get a job on Music Row," Faith recalled in an interview, "just anywhere trying to get in the door, and was turned away because I was a singer. They just weren't willing to hire a singer or a songwriter. They wanted somebody to sit behind the desk with that being their sole intention."

At this point, Hill decided that in her next job interview she would not point out her true dream to become an artist. She told the interviewer at the next job she sought out at Gary Morris' Nashville company that she was just in Nashville to go to school. The plan worked. Faith landed the job and worked there for a year before a songwriter heard her singing along with the radio. The song she was singing was *It Scares Me*, appropriately enough. The songwriter eventually asked her to sing on demo tapes and Faith was able to come out of the closet without losing her job.

Her first professional job after that was singing back-up for songwriter/musician Gary Burr, now her co-producer. She was signed to Warner Brothers Records and her debut

*A star in the ascendant, **Faith Hill***

release, *Wild One* (1993), zoomed straight up the charts to No.1. This was quite a feat for the torchy young singer because never before had a female newcomer garnered the No.1 slot for four consecutive weeks. The closest any other female singer has come to this was Jeannie C. Riley's debut, *Harper Valley PTA*, which held the top slot for three weeks, 25 years ago. The success of her first chart single soon landed her on *Late Night with David Letterman.* Her first album, ***Take Me as I Am*** (1993), made the Top 10 on the Country album chart and was Certified Gold in 1994.

Faith's next single, and last to date, *Piece of My Heart*, followed suit, once again hitting No.1. Her version of the song, written by Bert Berns and Jerry Ragavoy, is so far the most successful one, having been recorded earlier by Erma Franklin in 1967, Janis Joplin with Big Brother and the Holding Company in 1968 and John Hartford in 1984.

If her first two singles are any indication of what's to come, fans can expect to hear a lot more from Faith, who can now be "taken as she is." LAP

RECOMMENDED ALBUM:

"Take Me as I Am" (Warner Brothers)(1993)

GOLDIE HILL

(Singer)

Given Name: Angolda Voncile Hill
Date of Birth: January 11, 1933
Where Born: Karnes County, Texas
Married: Carl Smith (m. 1957)
Children: Carl, Jr., Larry Dean, Lori Lyn

If ever there was a case of an artist retiring too early, then it was that of Goldie Hill. "The Golden Hillbilly" started her career in the early 50's and had retired by 1957.

Goldie first appeared on KWKH's *Louisiana Hayride* from Shreveport in 1952, and by the end of that year, she was on Decca Records. Her initial single, *Don't Send Me No More Roses/Why Talk to My Heart*, didn't trouble the charts but it garnered some interest. The follow-up did the trick. *I Let the Stars Get in My Eyes* was the "answer" to *Don't Let the Stars Get in Your Eyes,* which was a No.1 for both Skeets McDonald and Slim Willet in the fall of 1952. By January 1953, Goldie's record was in the charts and went all the way to the top. It remained at No.1 for three weeks of a nine week chart stay. That year, she made her debut on the *Grand Ole Opry* and she was named *Country Song Roundup*'s "Best Female Artist."

It was another year before she returned to the charts, this time duetting with Justin Tubb on *Looking Back to See,* which made it to the Top 5 and was on the charts for over five months. She followed this with another duet with Tubb, *Sure Fire Kisses*, which reached the Top 15. In March of 1955, she teamed up with Red Sovine for *Are You Mine*, which also went Top 15.

In 1957, Goldie married one of Country music's giants, Carl Smith, and decided to retire. However, record labels have this habit of releasing records to maximize catalog on hand and in 1959, Decca issued *Yankee, Go Home,* which had a narration on it by Red Sovine, and it went into the Top 20.

During 1968, she returned to recording with Epic Records as Goldie Hill Smith and cut two albums. She had the basement hit *Lovable Fool* as the only single released from either album. She then returned to her homelife. It's a pity that Goldie and Carl never put together a duet album.

RECOMMENDED ALBUMS:

"Country Songs" (Vocalion)(1967)
"Goldie Sings Again" (Epic)(1968)
"Goldie Hill Sings Country" (Vocalion)(1969)
"The Country Gentleman's Lady Sings Her Favorites" (Epic)(1969)

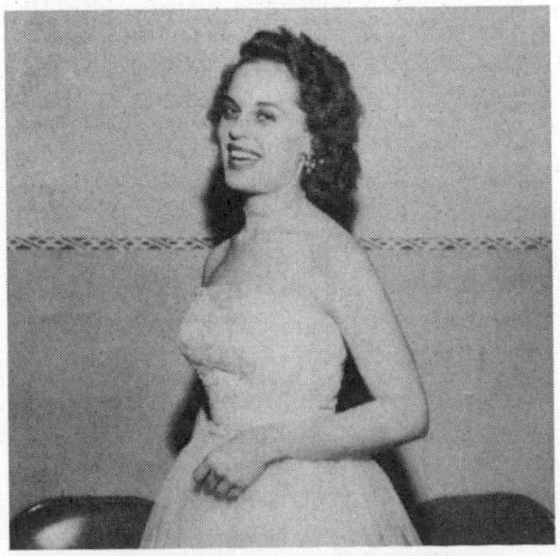

*The Golden Hillbilly, **Goldie Hill***

CHRIS HILLMAN

(Singer, Songwriter, Banjo, Guitar, Mandolin, Bass Guitar)

Date of Birth: December 4, 1944
Where Born: Los Angeles, California
Married: Connie
Children: Jesse, Catherine

Chris Hillman richly deserves the sobriquet of the "Godfather of Country-Rock." He was in at the beginning with bands like the Byrds and was still developing Country and Rock with the Desert Rose Band, thirty years later.

His early influences were Cliffie Stone and Spade Cooley. He learned to play by listening to records and having the occasional mandolin lesson. He began performing in high school with Larry Murray and Kenny Wertz in the Scottsville Squirrel Barkers in San Diego. In 1961, the group cut an album in just three hours and were paid $10 each. Chris can proudly say that he has supported himself and his family from music his entire life. In 1962, he joined the Bluegrass group the Golden Gate Boys, which comprised Vern and Rex Gosdin and Don Parmley. Chris was playing mandolin and vocals and as soon as he joined the group, it became the Hillmen. The group recorded one eponymous album for Together Records and broke up in 1963.

In 1964, Chris joined the first incarnation of the Byrds, playing bass. By the second version, in 1966, he was also handling vocal chores. He quit the group in 1968 after their return from South Africa and after the release of ***Sweetheart of the Rodeo***, by which time the band was on its fifth configuration.

In December of that year, Chris formed the first incarnation of the Flying Burrito Brothers, playing rhythm guitar and mandolin and handling vocals. However, he reverted to playing bass. In 1971, after the release of ***Last of the Red Hot Burritos***, he left the group to join Stephen Stills' Manassas.

Chris stayed with Stills until 1973, when he returned to the re-formed Byrds, but that was short-lived. In 1974, Chris formed the Souther, Hillman, Furay Band with John David Souther and Richie Furay. The group's debut eponymous album was released on Asylum, but after a second album, the members went their own way to solo careers. During 1976 and 1977, Chris recorded two solo albums for Asylum, ***Slippin' Away*** and ***Clear Sailin'***. On the 1976 album, Chris' wonderful song *(Take Me to Your) Lifeboat* can be found.

When Chris had reunited with the Byrds in 1973, it hadn't worked out; however, in 1978, he got back with Roger McGuinn and Gene

Clark. Their first eponymous album as McGuinn, Clark & Hillman was released on Capitol in 1979. A single, *Don't You Write Her Off*, made the Pop Top 40. This album was followed up by ***City***, with the three members described as Roger McGuinn & Chris Hillman, Featuring Gene Clark. The cover photos show Hillman and McGuinn with only one small shot of Clark. On both albums, Chris is handling the bass-playing chores.

With the arrival of 1982, Chris came to an interesting point in his career. His "Country-ness" surfaced more than it had done for some while. Sugar Hill had re-released ***The Hillmen*** album in 1981 (the Together label album plus other tracks) and now Chris cut a new album for the label, ***Morning Sky***. The musicians included Byron Berline on fiddle and steelie Al Perkins. Perkins had been a sideman on the Souther, Hillman, Furay Band project. Two years later, the album ***Desert Rose*** was released. This was the precursor to the Desert Rose Band and featured Herb Pedersen, James Burton, Bernie Leadon, Jay Dee Maness, Byron Berline, Al Perkins and Glen D. Hardin among others. It included the chart singles *Somebody's Back in Town* and *Running the Road Blocks*, both of which were in the bottom of the Country charts. Also on the album is Hillman's version of the Johnnie & Jack hit *Ashes of Love* which the Desert Rose Band would have a hit with three years later. The Desert Rose Band was formed by Hillman in 1986.

Chris Hillman's songwriting skills are often overlooked. However, in 1988, BMI recognized him for "21 Years of Hit Songwriting" for outstanding chart successes. His song, *Sin City*, which he co-wrote with Gram Parsons, was recorded by Emmylou Harris and the recording is in the Smithsonian Collection of Country Music. The song was also recorded by J.D. Crowe. Emmylou Harris recorded three other Hillman originals, *Juanita*, *Wheels* and *Christina's Tune*. The latter was also recorded by J.D. Crowe and Tony Rice. The Oak Ridge Boys cut his *Step on Out* in 1985 and made it the title of their album of that year. Rock performers have also been attracted to his songs. Punk poet Patti Smith recorded *So You Wanna Be a Rock n' Roll Star*, and Tom Petty and the Heartbreakers have also recorded it. Dan Fogelberg cut *It Doesn't Matter* and Dwight Yoakam and k.d. lang recorded *Sin City*.

His life's contribution was acknowledged in 1991, when he was inducted into the Rock and Roll Hall of Fame with the founding members of the Byrds. However, Chris Hillman is still making musical history.

RECOMMENDED ALBUMS:

"Slippin' Away" (Asylum)(1976)
"The Hillmen" (Sugar Hill)(1980) [With Vern and Rex Gosdin and Don Parmley]
"Morning Sky" (Sugar Hill)(1981)
"Desert Rose" (Sugar Hill)(1982)
(See also Byrds, Flying Burrito Brothers and Desert Rose Band)

HILLSIDERS, The

When Formed: **1964**

Original Members:

Joe Butler	**Bass Guitar, Vocals**
Brian Hilton	**Lead Guitar, Harmonica, Vocals**
Frankie Wan	**Steel Guitar**
"Noddy" Redman	**Drums**
Kenny Johnson	**Lead Vocals, Guitar**

Other Members:

Ronnie Bennett	**Steel Guitar**

Current Members:

Dave Rowlands	**Steel Guitar, Dobro**
Brian Hilton	**Lead Guitar, Harmonica, Vocals**
"Noddy" Redman	**Drums**
Kevin McGarry	**Lead Vocals, Guitar**
Mick Kinney	**Bass Guitar, Vocals**

The Hillsiders are Britain's most respected and longest-serving Country group. They are also one of the most successful and after nearly 30 years of being in existence, can still boast of having two of their original line-up on board.

In the beginning the band tried to emulate George Jones and Buck Owens' Buckaroos. Of the original line-up, only Joe Butler had played in a Country band (Sonny Webb and the Country Four). In 1964, Decca U.K. released their debut album, ***Hillsiders Play the Country Hits***. They toured Germany with Red Sovine and also toured with Molly Bee.

The following year, they signed with the short-lived but ambitious Lucky label. This was the first British Country label and it yielded their second album, ***It Takes a Lot of Money***. Following a German tour with Bobby Bare, they traveled to Nashville, in 1966, to record the Chet Atkins-produced ***The English Country Side (Bobby Bare from Nashville & the Hillsiders from Liverpool)*** which was released on RCA Victor in 1967. It climbed to the Country Album chart Top 20 and the Hillsiders became the first British band to appear on the *Grand Ole Opry*.

In 1968, the Hillies (as they are affectionately known) recorded the album ***The Leaving of Liverpool*** and appeared in a TV series with George Hamilton IV for BBC-TV, which was followed by a second series in 1969. The following year, they recorded the album, ***Heritage***, with George Hamilton IV. In 1971, the Hillsiders were part of RCA's Country Caravan tour of Scandinavia. It was also the year that they won their first "Group of the Year" award from the CMA (GB).

The Hillies changed labels in 1972 and released ***By Request*** on Polydor. The following year, they released *Our Country*, which contained 11 original songs. At the end of 1974, Kenny Johnson left and early in 1975 he was replaced by Kevin McGarry, who had formerly played with the Westerners. That year, the band released ***To Please You***, on Stile Records.

In 1976, the Hillies organized the ***Goodbye Scottie Road*** album with other northwest bands. During this period, the band lost some of its momentum and it took as its agents Live Promotions, to get them back on a positive tack. Their next album, ***On the Road***, was released on the LP label in 1978. That year, BBC-2 TV did an in-concert program on them, recorded from Snape Maltings, normally associated with classical music. The following year, Ronnie Bennett left to start a steel guitar business and Dave Rowland joined.

During 1981, the Hillies recorded a TV special with Billie Jo Spears for BBC-TV and another for Dutch TV. The following year, the group flew to the Falklands to entertain the troops. In 1984, the Hillsiders recorded their 13th album, ***Only One You***, on the Suitbag label. Two years later, they released their next album, ***If That's the Way You Feel,*** to support their tour with Slim Whitman.

The Hillies celebrated their 25th Anniversary in 1989 with the release of their ***15-25*** album, which also featured ex-Hillies Kenny Johnson and Ronnie Bennett. That year, they received the BCMA Committee Award. In 1993, founder member Joe Butler left to work with the band's booking agents, Ricky McCabe Entertainments, and was replaced by Mick Kinney. The band appeared on a live radio broadcast for the BBC that was transmitted live by satellite to over 200 million homes in the U.S. and Canada. JAB

RECOMMENDED ALBUMS:

"It Takes a Lot of Money" (Lucky UK)(1965)
"The English Country Side (Bobby Bare from Nashville & the Hillsiders from Liverpool)" (RCA Victor)(1967)
"The Leaving of Liverpool" (RCA Victor)(1968)
"Heritage" (RCA Victor)(1970) [With George Hamilton IV]
"By Request" (Polydor UK)(1972)
"Our Country" (Polydor UK)(1973)
"To Please You" (Stile UK)(1975)
"On the Road" (LP UK)(1978)
"Only One You" (Suitcase UK)(1984)
"If That's the Way You Feel" (Suitcase UK)(1986)
"15-25" (Suitcase UK)(1988)

TISH HINOJOSA

(Singer, Songwriter, Guitar)
Given Name: **Leticia Hinojosa**
Date of Birth: **December 6, 1955**
Where Born: **San Antonio Texas**
Married: **Craig Barker**

Tish Hinojosa was born to Mexican immigrant parents. As the 13th child of this Mexican-American family, she grew up speaking Spanish at home and English at parochial school. Tish also had multi-cultural musical influences growing up listening to the songs on Mexican radio along with the American Pop music of the 60's.

After she graduated from high school, Tish pursued her dream of making music. She landed a contract with Capitol Records' Lado A/Cara label and recorded several Top 10 hits for the Latino market. Tish also sang jingles for a variety of products and became a popular singer in southwest Texas clubs and coffee-houses.

In 1979, Tish won the "Best New Artist" award at the Kerrville Folk Festival and released an EP with three original songs. Also in 1979, Tish moved north to the mountains of New Mexico, living in the towns of Taos and Red River. There she befriended Michael Martin Murphey and did some vocal work with him. In hopes of signing with a major record company, Tish moved to Nashville in 1983. She quickly found work as a demo singer and signed a production deal with Mel Tillis. That led to a contract with Curb Records and the release of a duet with Craig Dillingham entitled *I'll Pull You Through,* which was chosen as the 1986 Red Cross national theme song and was a Top 80 Country hit that year.

Finding resistance from the Nashville labels to incorporating her ethnic heritage into her music, Tish returned to New Mexico in May 1987. She released an independent cassette, ***Taos to Tennessee***, that featured her first all-Spanish composition, *Amanecer (Daybreak)*. In 1992, the project was re-released on Watermelon Records.

After a year in New Mexico, Tish and her family returned to her home state, settling in the musically rich Austin. Tish became a favorite on the local music scene and gained the national attention of A & M Records, which offered her a recording contract. In 1989, she released ***Homeland,*** which presented her eclectic musical influences and contained the autobiographical *Border Trilogy*. The album was well received by critics in both the U.S. and Europe. Tish also won fans in Korea with Triple Platinum sales of the album. That success led to a tour of the country, and a song from ***Homeland*** became the theme for a South Korean soap opera. At the beginning of 1990, Tish had a Top 75 hit with *Till U Love Me Again*.

Tish recorded her second album for A & M in 1990 but the label decided not to release it. While pitching the project to other labels, Tish continued writing, performing and recording. In 1991, she recorded an all Spanish live album at the Waterloo Ice House in Austin entitled ***Aquella Noche (That Certain Night)***. The album was applauded by reviewers and made the Top 5 Folk Recordings list for 1991 in *Pulse* magazine. Also in 1991, Hinojosa released a Christmas EP entitled *Memorabilia Navidena*.

In 1992, Trish released her second studio album, ***Culture Swing***, upon signing with Rounder Records. Her self-produced effort was recorded in San Marcos, Texas, and featured the state's leading musicians including Flaco Jimenez. In addition to Hispanic themes on the album, Tish incorporated Folk, Pop and Western Swing. Hinojosa wrote all the songs but one (Chuck Pyle's *Drifter's Wind*) and explored a wide range of topics, from the light hearted *San Antonio Romeo* (an answer to Bob Wills' *San Antonio Rose*) to a call for global unity in *Bandera del Sol (Flag of the Sun)*.

Using her popularity to champion social causes, Tish has voiced her concern for the plight of immigrant workers. She filmed a video of her song *Something in the Rain*, that deals with the exposure of workers to hazardous pesticides. Her work on the behalf of migrant workers and other community issues earned Tish an invitation to perform at Texas Governor Ann Richards' inauguration in Austin in January 1991.

In 1993, Tish signed with Warner Brothers and released the album ***Destiny's Gate*** the following year. JIE

RECOMMENDED ALBUMS:
"Culture Swing" (Rounder)(1992)
"Destiny's Gate" (Warner Brothers)(1994)

STAN HITCHCOCK

(Singer,Songwriter, Industry Executive)
Given Name: **Stanley Edward Hitchcock**
Date of Birth: **March 21, 1936**
Where Born: **Kansas City, Missouri**
Married: **1. Jo Anne (div.)**
2. Denise
Children: **Marilyn, Jay, Lorrie, Jolie, Stan II, Scott Dennis (dec'd.)**

Discovered by Red Foley, Stan Hitchcock had an unexpected career in the music business and then went on to help form TV's premier music video channel.

Born in Kansas City, Hitchcock moved with his family to Springfield, Missouri, when he was 4 years old. Raised on a farm, he began singing and playing guitar in small country churches at the ripe old age of 10. His professional debut came when he was 12 in a Country talent show in Springfield. During his high school years, Stan was popular because of his appearances on local radio stations KWTO and WTTS. After graduation from high school he signed up for a four-year hitch in the Navy and it was during this time that he started his own Country band and entertained throughout the world. His travels eventually took him to Japan, Hawaii, the Phillippines, China, Germany, Canada and Mexico.

After his discharge he became interested in helping homeless boys, and along with a group of well-to-do businessmen in his area, purchased a 110-acre farm known as the Good Samaritan Boys Ranch. Over the next four years, Stan spent his time working with these homeless and neglected children. To raise funds he traveled around the country singing Gospel music. He also managed to find fourteen radio stations to help him promote his work with the boys.

"I was singing on radio mainly in the Midwest at that time," recalled Hitchcock, "Si Siman (founder of the *Ozark Jubilee/Red Foley Show*) sent a tape of me singing on the radio, without my knowledge, to Don Law at Columbia Records. Don called me at the Boys Ranch one day and said, 'I'd like for you to come to Nashville and talk.' I just thought he meant he wanted to talk about homeless boys and I saw an opportunity to get my first corporate sponsor. I didn't bring my guitar, but he had one sitting in the corner, and he asked me to sing. I sang, then went on back to the

Head of Americana, ***Stan Hitchcock***

story of homeless boys. About an hour later, he handed me a check for $500.00 as a donation to the homeless boys, and said, 'You'll be hearing from me.' I went back to the Boys Ranch, and thought I'd had a successful trip for those days in 1960. Toward the end of the year I got a big package in the mail and it was a long-term recording contract with Columbia Records. I recorded for the first time in 1961. I was later transferred to Epic and was the first Country music artist they ever had. It was very strange how it worked out because I was not actually seeking a career in the music business."

In 1962, Stan moved to Nashville and released a number of singles but his first chart hit wasn't until 1967 with *She's Looking Good*, which went Top 60. This was followed the same year by *Rings* (Top 70), *I'm Easy to Love* and *The Phoenix Flash* (all Top 60). 1969 produced *Honey, I'm Home*, which went Top 20 and was the highest charting record of his career. The follow-up, *Call Me Gone*, was another Top 60 and his final release with Epic. In 1970, he moved to GRT, where his most successful single was *Dixie Bell*, which went Top 60. By 1973, he was recording on Cinnamon, where he had 3 singles that went Top 100, the most successful of which was *The Same Old Way* (1973). In 1978, he was on MMI, and in keeping with the same pattern established over the past decade had a Top 80 with *Ramblin'*. In 1979 he released a duet with Sue Richards, *Finders Keepers, Losers Weepers*. In 1982, Stan released an eponymous album on Audiograph Alive.

If his recording career was slowing down, he was making up for it in his television and radio career. For a time, he hosted WLAC-TV's morning show in Nashville, and made guest appearances on *Hee Haw*, the *Porter Wagoner Show*, the *Bill Anderson Show*, *Del Reeves' Country Carnival*, *Jim Ed Brown's Country Place* and the *Hugh X. Lewis Show*. In 1964, he began his own series, the *Stan Hitchcock Show*, a variety show, which ran through 1970 and was syndicated in over 100 markets. *Stan Hitchcock from the Ozarks* was another brainchild of Hitchcock and appeared in some markets from 1979 to 1983.

In 1982, Stan became part of a team that founded Country Music Television. He ran the network under the title Senior Vice President in Charge of Nashville. During this time he created another show, *Heart to Heart*, which was aired on the network as well, and became popular among Country music fans.

In 1991, the network was sold to Gaylord Productions and Stan moved to Branson, Missouri, where he formed Americana Television Network. He currently lives there with his wife, Denise, and is CEO of Americana. LAP

RECOMMENDED ALBUMS:

"Just Call Me Lonesome" (Epic)(1965)
"Softly and Tenderly" (Epic)(1969)
"I'm Easy to Love" (Epic)(1968)
"Honey, I'm Home" (Epic)(1970)
"Dixie Bell" (GRT)(1970)
"Stan Hitchcock Country" (Cinnamon)(1970)
"Stan Hitchcock" (Audiograph Alive)(1982)
(See also Americana, Country Music Television)

BECKY HOBBS

(Singer, Songwriter, Piano, Accordion, Guitar)
Given Name: Rebecca Ann Hobbs
Date of Birth: January 24, 1950
Where Born: Bartlesville, Oklahoma

The "Beckaroo" is a bubbly energetic entertainer, a songwriter, singer and instrumentalist with a wide smile and a broad talent. An early entry in her childhood diary

The Beckaroo, ***Becky Hobbs***

states, "My name is Rebecca Ann Hobbs, I'm in the fifth grade and I am a songwriter."

Becky's father was a violinist. She started playing piano at age 9 and made up her own compositions. By the time she was 14, she got her first guitar and started writing protest songs, influenced by Bob Dylan. She was in a Folk duo with her friend Beth Morrison. At the age of 15, she had her first all-girl band, the Four Faces of Eve. That was superseded by Sir Prize Package while she attended Tulsa University. She moved to Baton Rouge and performed with Swampfox from 1971 through 1973. By now she was living in Los Angeles and had begun to get into Country music.

All the time, Becky was writing songs. In 1974, she recorded her first eponymous album for MCA. Helen Reddy heard the album and was impressed with the song *I'll Be Your Audience*. She recorded it and went on to cut three more of Becky's songs, *I Don't Know Why I Love that Guy*, *I Can't Say Goodbye to You* and *Long Distance Love*.

During 1976, Becky was managed by Alan Bernard at BNB Management. The company recorded two albums on her for their Tattoo label, ***From the Heartland*** in 1976 and ***Everyday*** the following year. At the end of 1978, Becky surfaced on Mercury with the single *The More I Get the More I Want* and it gave her the first taste of chart success, reaching the Top 100, the following year. She followed this with *I Can't Say Goodbye to You*, which reached the Top 50. Becky had three more chart entries on the label but they were all at the basement level.

During the 80's, Becky started to amass a healthy amount of cuts. *Feedin' the Fire* was recorded by both Lacy J. Dalton and Zella Lehr during 1981. John Anderson cut *Look What Followed Me Home* in 1983 and the Tennessee Valley Boys scored with *Lo and Behold*.

During that year, Becky had a Top 10 hit duet with Moe Bandy on Columbia entitled *Let's Get Over Them Together*. The following year and into 1985, she had four hit singles for Liberty/EMI-America of which the most successful were *Oklahoma Heart* (Top 50) and *Hottest "Ex" in Texas* (Top 40). During 1984, George Jones and Loretta Lynn recorded Becky's *We Sure Made Good Love*, which appeared on George's ***Ladies' Choice*** album.

1985 was a memorable year for Becky. Alabama recorded *I Want to Know You Before We Make Love* and it appeared on their Quadruple-Platinum album ***Forty Hour Week***. They also cut *Christmas Memories* for their ***Christmas*** album and that was Certified Double-Platinum. In addition, Becky had cuts by Moe Bandy & Joe Stampley (*Still on a Roll*) and Shelly West (*I'll Dance the Two Step* and *How It All Went Wrong*). Then, to top it all, she made her debut on the *Grand Ole Opry*.

If 1985 was memorable, then 1987 was vintage. Conway Twitty cut *I Want to Know You Before We Make Love* and took it into the Top 3 and Glen Campbell and Emmylou Harris duetted on *You Are* and it won a Grammy nomination. In addition, Moe Bandy cut Becky's *Rodeo Song*.

The following year, Becky was reunited

with Alan Bernard at the short-lived MTM Records. She released the superb album ***All Keyed Up***, on which every track is a winner. Three singles charted from it, of which the most successful was *Jones on the Jukebox*, which reached the Top 40. It seemed that MTM had their minds on other things and as a result, when the label closed down, Becky and stable-mate Judy Rodman were not supported.

Becky appeared at the ill-fated Grantham Festival in England in 1989 and tore the place apart with her stage act. RCA re-released the MTM album the same year and in 1990, she cut the old Ernest Ashworth hit, *Talk Back Tremblin' Lips*, for Curb. The video was successful but the single wasn't.

Becky has won several awards including first place in the American Song Festival for *I Can't Say Goodbye to You*, a BMI Performance Award for *I Want to Know You Before We Make Love* and a Gold Album for Helen Reddy's ***Live at the Palladium*** album. She was also named the "Most Promising Act of 1989" in the British Academy of Country Music's International Section.

Becky and her band, the Heartthrobs, toured Africa in 1992, as part of the U.S. Government agency Arts America, performing in nine countries. She has now signed to JRS, a new label set up by Artie Mogul and based in Los Angeles. It can only be hoped that at last a label will get behind Becky in a way that has been sadly lacking so far. This lady is one of the most talented in Country music. She continues to write with her long-time co-writer, Don Goodman.

RECOMMENDED ALBUMS:

"Becky Hobbs" (MCA)(1974)
"From the Heartland" (Tattoo)(1976)
"Everyday" (Tattoo)(1977)
"All Keyed Up" (MTM)(1988)

ADOLPH HOFNER

(Singer, Guitar)
Given Name: Adolph Hofner
Date of Birth: June 8, 1916
Where Born: Moulton, Texas
Married: Unknown
Children: Kathy, Darlene

Adolph Hofner has been one of the most long-lived figures in Western Swing music, having a career that has spanned more than half a century. Coming from a German-Czech background, Hofner also incorporated some European-style Bohemian music into his sound, which enabled him to make records for a select ethnic market as well, while Adolph himself has primarily been a lead vocalist in the tradition of Milton Brown.

Adolph Hofner grew up on a farm in Lavaca County, Texas, along with his brother Emil (b. 1918), who would become his steel player. Czech was the language spoken in the household. In 1928, the Hofners moved to San Antonio and about 1932, the sons began to play music in the local clubs. Adolph had been attracted to the singing of Bing Crosby, but after hearing Milton Brown and Bob Wills, became a convert to Western Swing.

The boys worked in various bands around San Antonio, where Adolph also labored during the day as a mechanic. He recorded extensively as guitarist/vocalist on Bluebird with Jimmie Revard's Oklahoma Playboys and somewhat less under his own name and with Tom Dickey's Showboys. His vocal with the latter group on the Floyd Tillman song *It Makes No Difference Now* attracted considerable attention and inspired him to start his own band, beginning in May 1939. His earlier waxings on Bluebird had been credited to Adolph Hofner and his Texans, but after moving over to OKeh and Columbia, in 1941, they became known as the San Antonians. Some of their best known recordings included *Maria Elena*, which featured Adolph's Pop-influenced vocal and hot instrumentals like *South Texas Swing* and *Alamo Rag*, highlighted by the fine fiddle work of J.R. Chatwell and Emil ("Bash") Hofner's steel.

During WWII, the San Antonians went West and worked out of southern California for a time, chiefly under the auspices of Foreman Phillips. In this era, the leader discreetly took the nickname "Dub" Hofner, given the unpopularity of "Adolf" at the time. Later in the decade, Hofner returned to south Texas, where he was already established under his old name. Hofner also began to record some of the Czech and German polka music with which he had grown up, as well as continuing with material in the Country-Western Swing vein. In 1949, he began a long period of sponsorship by Pearl Beer and the band changed its name to the Pearl Wranglers.

However, the name San Antonians continued to be used on major record labels. They did sessions for Imperial and Decca, and in 1955, had a 10" album release for Decca's famed "Dance-O-Rama" series. Hofner and the Pearl Wranglers later recorded for small local labels such as Sarg. They continued as an active group in the San Antonio area and south Texas well into the 80's, often playing shows four and five nights a week.

In 1980, Arhoolie released an album of Hofner's early recordings while several other numbers appeared on a variety of Western Swing anthologies, chiefly on Old-Timey, Rambler, and String. Folk-Lyric's ethnic music series contained another cut by Hofner on their Texas Czech-Bohemian album. IMT

RECOMMENDED ALBUMS:

"Dance-O-Rama" (Decca)(1955)
"South Texas Swing" (Arhoolie)(1980)

GERRY HOGAN

(Steel Guitar, Dobro, Guitar, Piano)
Date of Birth: October 3, 1943
Where Born: Calcutta, India
Married: Barbara Jeffries (m. 1965)
Children: Patrick, Sian

Gerry Hogan is an excellent and much in demand session musician, performer, magazine contributor and festival organizer. He is a dedicated pedal steel guitarist who does everything that he can to promote the instrument. He demonstrates it at trade shows, where he also gives clinics.

Gerry began playing music as a child, starting piano when he was age 4, and played until he was age 13. In the meanwhile, he acquired a guitar, which he soon mastered, and played in Jon Derek's group from 1958. In 1966, Gerry started to play pedal steel and Dobro, playing initially with Jon Derek's successor group, Country Fever.

He became continually in demand as a session musician and the list of stars he has worked with or recorded with reads like a "Who's Who" of Country and Pop music. It includes Ricky Skaggs, Emmylou Harris, Sonny Curtis, Don Gibson, Connie Smith, the Everly Brothers, Albert Lee, Charley Pride, Nanci Griffith, Lefty Frizzell, Lonnie Donegan, Mott the Hoople and Dave Edmunds. Gerry also played on the London Cast Recording of the musical *Grease*.

He has made countless TV/radio and cinematographic advertising jingles. He has also performed on TV studio sessions, not only in the U.K. but also all over Europe, and appeared on radio. Among the many BBC programs that he has been heard on are *Country Club*, on which he has made studio and concert appearances, and *Kaleidoscope*, which did a featured interview with him. He has broadcast all over Europe and has toured in Europe and the U.S. In addition, Gerry has been featured in two movies: *Bloomfield* with Richard Harris (1971) and *The American Way* with Dennis Hopper (1980).

In 1986, Gerry was awarded the "British Steelies Society Scroll of Honour" and at the International Steel Guitar Convention, St.

Louis, Missouri, he received an "Appreciation Award." That year, Gerry produced an album for Yugoslavian band Plava Trava Zaborava. The following year, *Guitarist* magazine featured Gerry's work, and from 1989, he has written a regular monthly column for them called "Rockabilly and Country Licks," which is a guitarist tutorial giving guitar tablature and comment on recorded pieces of music.

In 1990, Gerry received another "Appreciation Award" from the Pedal Steel Guitar Association, Inc. The following year, Gerry produced five tracks on Sonny Curtis' album. He is currently recording material for the BBC-TV murder mystery series *The Brighton Boy*. He continues session work and has been doing concert tours with Albert Lee and Hogan's Heroes (Gerry's band), following the release of ***Albert Lee and Hogan's Heroes in Flight—Live at Montreux***.

Gerry is also the organizer of the British Steel Guitar Festival, which started in 1983. In 1994, it will feature U.S. steel guitar giants Buddy Emmons and Lloyd Green. Gerry also runs a music shop in Newbury in Berkshire, in the southwest of England. JAB

WENDY HOLCOMBE

(Singer, Songwriter, Banjo, Fiddle, Guitar, Mandolin, Dobro, Bass, Trumpet, Ukulele, Drums, Actress)

Given Name: Wendy Lou Holcombe
Date of Birth: April 19, 1963
Where Born: Alabaster, Alabama ("somewhere between Dogwood and Fungo Holler")
Married: Thomas Blossor
Date of Death: February 14, 1987

The story of Wendy Holcombe is probably the most tragic in Country music. A lady of inestimable talent, she succumbed to an enlarged heart at the age of 23. She was an 11-year-old with straw-colored pigtails when she picked up her father Billy Jack's banjo. He had spent some six months trying to learn to play it unsuccessfully. However, Wendy took to it immediately and played *Morning Dew*. Billy Jack gave her the instrument.

Seven months later, Wendy persuaded her father to take her to the *Grand Ole Opry* for her 12th birthday. They couldn't get tickets and so went along to a music shop in Nashville, intent on trying out a banjo in the window. Wendy played *Foggy Mountain Breakdown* and was heard by Roni Stoneman's bass player. He introduced the Holcombes to some friends who got them backstage. There, she met Roy Acuff and played banjo in his dressing room with Grandpa Jones and the Smoky Mountain Boys. Mr. Roy was so impressed that he had her play the next night on Ernest Tubb's *Midnight Jamboree*. A month later (December 1975), she played on the *Grand Ole Opry*, as the guest of Jim Ed Brown. This led to her appearing on Porter Wagoner's show and *Pop Goes the Country*. She also appeared on an early morning TV show out of Birmingham, Alabama, the *Country Eddie Show*. She often appeared at bookings backed by her father on guitar and her brother, Billy Jack, Jr. ("Muley"), on bass. Her sister, Cindy, was also a musician, playing church organ.

Wendy's favorite banjo player was Buck Trent, who had played with Porter Wagoner and Roy Clark. Wendy had the opportunity to play with Buck, on TV, playing *Dueling Banjos*, unrehearsed. By the time she was 13, Wendy was appearing in Nashville on the Road alongside Jim Ed Brown and Jerry Clower. It was Clower who saved the life of Wendy's mother by suggesting she have a physical. It was discovered she had cancer, but action could be taken. Clower also convinced Wendy to wear braces on her teeth.

In 1978, Wendy was signed by ABC-TV, but they failed to materialize with a suitable vehicle and so in 1981, NBC-TV signed her to a development contract. They made a pilot film, *At Ease*. The project was later renamed *Wendy Hooper, U.S. Army*. In 1980, she appeared with Dennis Weaver in *The Big Show* (NBC). She went on to regularly appear on *Nashville Swing* with Thom Bresh and acted on the TV series *Lewis and Clark* with Gabe Kaplan. She performed in all states of the U.S. with the exception of Alaska and Hawaii and also played at Britain's Wembley Silk Cut Festival.

In 1981, Wendy collapsed during a performance in Fort Wayne, Indiana, and it was discovered that she had an enlarged heart. This forced her to retire from the music business, and although there was talk of a heart transplant, she was not on a donor list. She became a housewife, but in February, 1987, her brief life came to an end.

RECOMMENDED ALBUMS:
Contact Adonda Records

BUDDY HOLLY

(Singer, Songwriter, Guitar)

Given Name: Charles Hardin Holley
Date of Birth: September 7, 1936
Where Born: Lubbock, Texas
Married: Maria Elena Santiago
Date of Death: February 3, 1959

The impact of Buddy Holly upon popular music, both as a songwriter and performer, is incalculable. Without his presence on the music stage, many of the developments that have been experienced since his death might not have taken place. Whether his impact would have been quite as great had he lived longer is difficult to ascertain. As someone who experimented with the boundaries of rock'n'roll, it is impossible to know where he would have been today. However, the basic concept of a three-piece Rock band, with the leader not only being the main songwriter, but also the singer and lead guitarist, which has become the norm even in Heavy Metal, can be traced back to probably two rock'n'roll heroes—Buddy Holly and Carl Perkins.

*The legendary **Buddy Holly***

Buddy (he got his nickname from his mother) and his brothers Larry and Travis came under the spell of Hank Williams and Jimmie Rodgers as well as the Louvin Brothers and Bill Monroe. Buddy started to play guitar while still at school and was soon appearing at school dances, accompanied on occasions by school friends who would later become musicians on his sessions. By the time he was 15, he could play most Country songs and soon decided that he wanted to be an entertainer.

Forming "Buddy and Bob, Western Bop" with Bob Montgomery (now a famed Nashville record producer), Buddy showed a style that was somewhere between Rockabilly and Country. The duo (really a trio, as Larry Welborn played string bass) tried to get a record deal without success. However, they did land their own radio show on KDAV

Lubbock and played local concerts. They acquired their first manager, "Hi-Pockets" Duncan, a local deejay, who booked acts in the Lubbock area. A major influence on the duo at this time was Elvis Presley. They had appeared with him when he opened a Lubbock Pontiac dealership.

Buddy and Bob opened for Bill Haley and the Comets and Marty Robbins and attracted the attention of Nashville-based booking agent Eddie Crandall. Crandall played some of Buddy and Bob's demos (cut on KDAV's *Sunday Party* and at Nesman Recording Studios, Wichita Falls) to publisher/industry executive Jim Denny, who signed Buddy to Decca Records. Bob was not included in the deal, but he persuaded Buddy to accept the contract.

On January 26, 1956, Buddy recorded four sides under the production eye of Owen Bradley: *Love Me*, *Don't Come Back a Knockin'*, *Midnight Shift* and *Blue Days, Black Nights*. Holly didn't play on any of the tracks, his place being taken by the legendary Grady Martin. However Sonny Curtis, who had played fiddle on Buddy and Bob's demos, put down the lead guitar parts and Don Guess played bass. Welborn and Buddy's normal drummer, Jerry Allison, were not allowed to travel to Nashville, as they were still at school. The initial single, *Blue Days, Black Nights/Love Me*, was released in the States and the U.K. and was well received.

Holly returned to Nashville on July 22, 1956, and recorded *Rock Around with Ollie Vee*, *Ting-A-Ling*, *Changing All These Changes*, *Girl on My Mind* and the original version of *That'll Be the Day*. The line-up was Buddy, Sonny Curtis, Don Guess and Jerry Allison (the three musicians being known as the Three Tunes). Again Owen Bradley was the producer. However, Decca, in the shape of A & R Director Paul Cohen, was not pro-Buddy and described him as "the biggest no talent I have ever worked with." Buddy returned to Nashville on November 15, 1956 and recorded a second version of *Rock Around with Ollie Vee* as well as *You Are My One Desire* and *Modern Don Juan*. He was accompanied on these tracks by Grady Martin, Boots Randolph, Faris Coursey (drums) and Owen Bradley on piano. A second single, *Modern Don Juan/You Are My One Desire*, was released at Christmas, but failed to do anything.

After this, Buddy (with the help of Buddy Knox) went to Norman Petty's studios in Clovis, New Mexico, and recorded *Brown-Eyed Handsome Man* and *Bo Diddley*, but Decca was not interested and released him from his contract. With Petty, Buddy found the artistic freedom he had sought with Decca. With Allison, Niki Sullivan (guitar) and Welborn (later replaced by Joe B. Mauldin), Buddy started to put down songs for a possible deal with Roulette Records that included a new version of *That'll Be the Day*. However, the label turned him down, as did Columbia, but Bob Thiele at the newly reactivated Brunswick gave him the nod in 1957. However, Brunswick was a subsidiary of Decca and to avoid contractual difficulties over *That'll Be the Day*, the single was put out under the group name of the Crickets.

Despite a slow start, *That'll Be the Day* hit the Pop chart and climbed to No.1. It was released in the U.K. and did the same. Decca released the original version as by Buddy Holly and the Three Tunes, but it failed to register. Holly by now had signed, as a solo, to Coral and the single *Words of Love* was released without charting (the song would later be the title of a BBC-TV play (U.K., 1991) about a young boy who is a fan of Holly's and how he copes with Holly's death).

In November, 1957, Buddy had a major solo hit with *Peggy Sue* (the song referred to Jerry Allison's girl friend), which rose to the Top 3 on the Pop chart and No.6 in the U.K. While their initial single was still on the charts, the Crickets had a Top 10 hit with *Oh Boy*, which also went Top 3 in Britain. In 1958, Buddy and the Crickets continued their hit run with *Maybe Baby* (Top 20) and *Fool's Paradise* (Top 60), while in the U.K. they were equally successful, with *Maybe Baby* and *Think It Over* being big hits. Buddy's solo successes were the Top 40 hits *Rave On* and *Early in the Morning*. Both fared better in Britain, where additionally, he scored with *Listen to Me*.

During 1958, Buddy and the Crickets, which now comprised Allison and Mauldin, toured the U.K. and Australia. Holly's bespectacled look was a definite influence on guitarist Hank B. Marvin (of Cliff Richard's Shadows), who, in turn, influenced generations of guitarists. Buddy's influence would later carry on to Elton John and more especially Elvis Costello.

By October 1958 Holly had decided to split from Petty and the Crickets. It is certain that his career at this time was starting to look shaky and his records were not faring well, with *Heartbeat* only reaching the Top 90. Also, his marriage to Maria Elena (who worked at Southern Music, Buddy's publishers) seemed to make him more serious. He began recording with Dick Jacobs at the Pythian Temple in New York. This took Holly into a new realm of rock'n'roll with the introduction of strings on his recordings. During the October 21 session, Buddy recorded *True Love Ways* (Maria Elena's favorite track), *Moonbeams*, the Bryants' *Raining in My Heart* and Paul Anka's *It Doesn't Matter Anymore*. These were Holly's first stereo recordings.

In December of that year, Buddy called Waylon Jennings to New York and arranged for and produced Waylon's first recording, *Jole Blon*. Waylon, who was a deejay at KLLL Lubbock, joined Buddy on bass guitar, and along with Tommy Allsup on guitar and drummer Charlie Burch they began rehearsing for the upcoming Winter Dance Party. In addition, Buddy and Phil Everly produced and played on a couple of sides for singer Lou Giordano. Buddy had discussed his future with Coral Records and all was fine. Maria Elena was now pregnant (she lost the baby after Holly's death) and so didn't accompany Buddy on what would be a grueling tour.

Part of the reason for Holly undertaking this tour was that his earnings were caught up in a law settlement and so he was near to penniless. However, the rigors of traveling in an unheated bus and the slowness of getting laundry done made him decide to charter a plane to get to the next city. Originally, Allsup and Jennings were going to travel with him, but Allsup gave up his seat to Ritchie Valens, and Jennings and the Big Bopper flipped a coin, and the latter got the seat. The costs were shared and just before 1:00 am on February 3, 1959, the plane took off. Shortly after takeoff, the craft got into difficulties and crashed in Clear Lake, Iowa, killing the three stars and the pilot.

The world was shocked and responded. Buddy's current single, *It Doesn't Matter Anymore*, went to No.1 in the U.K. and so began the creation of the on-going Buddy Holly "legend." In the U.S., the single rose to the Top 15 and was followed by the low-entry *Raining in My Heart*. Coral dug into Buddy's supply of demo tapes and turned them into finished masters. Special Musicians' Union permission had to be sought to achieve this. This overdubbing continued until 1965, when the supply of tapes dried up, and the last releases came out in 1969. The tracks that were so doctored included *Peggy Sue Got Married*, *Crying, Waiting, Hoping* and *What to Do* (overdubbed by Jack Hansen in New York), and many of the same tracks were redone in 1962 by Norman Petty in Clovis, using the Fireballs on instrumental and vocal backup.

In Britain, Buddy's singles continued to chart, and between 1959 and 1968 he had 16 chart entries, including the 1963 back-to-back Top 10 hits *Brown-Eyed Handsome Man*

(No.3), *Bo Diddley* (No.4) and *Wishing* (No.10). Hollywood decided to get into the act when they cast Gary Busey in the appalling 1978 biopic, *The Buddy Holly Story*, which has to rate as one of the most inaccurate movies of its genre. It resulted in Sonny Curtis writing and recording the song *The Real Buddy Holly Story* in 1980. Also inaccurate but greater fun was the 1988 stage musical *Buddy*, which has been a smash hit.

The Crickets have continued to function with varying members and although Buddy never charted Country, his songs continue to be recorded by Country artists including Linda Ronstadt, Mickey Gilley and Tanya Tucker, as well as by Rock acts Blondie, Santana and the 70's group Raw Holly, and of course, Buddy Holly's name lives on in the group the Hollies. In addition, the Beatles chose their own name as a tribute to the Crickets. In 1986, MCA, the inheritors of the Holly catalog, released a 50th Birthday 4-track EP in celebration, and every year Paul McCartney, who now owns Buddy's publishing catalog, holds a Buddy Holly celebration. In 1994, Buddy Holly was inducted into the Nashville Songwriters Hall of Fame.

RECOMMENDED ALBUMS:

"The Complete Buddy Holly" (6 album box set)(MCA)(1979) [includes interviews]; but if you can't afford that, then any Buddy Holly album will demonstrate the great man's ability.

DOYLE HOLLY

(Singer, Songwriter, Bass Guitar, Comedy)

Given Name: Doyle Floyd Hendricks
Date of Birth: June 30, 1936
Where Born: Perkins, Oklahoma
Married: 1. (Div.)
2. Unknown

Doyle is a protégé of Buck Owens and a former member of the Buckaroos, who for a couple of years looked like he might emerge as a major solo star.

He started out playing bass guitar while still young and formed a band with his older brothers, playing venues including rodeos. By the time he was 13, he worked in the oilfields in Oklahoma, Kansas and California. In 1953, he left to join the U.S. Army and was stationed in Okinawa and Korea. He was discharged in 1957 and returned to the oilfields in Bakersfield, California. For a while, he played on a part-time basis in Johnny Burnette's band alongside Fuzzy Owen and Merle Haggard. However, work was not plentiful, and some of the time, the going was tough.

Doyle joined the Buckaroos in August 1963 and stayed with the group until late 1970, often being the comedian of the band. In 1970,

Former Buckaroo ***Doyle Holly***

he organized his own band, the Vanishing Breed, and two years later, signed with Barnaby Records. That same year, he was named ACM's "Bass Player of the Year."

He hit the Country charts at the end of 1972 with his version of *My Heart Cries for You*, peaking in the Top 70. The following year was his most successful, with the Top 30 single *Queen of the Silver Dollar* (a popular turntable hit) and the Top 20 hit *Lila*. Doyle had four more chart entries in 1974, but none of them achieved the same heights. They were *Lord How Long Has This Been Going On* (Top 60), *A Rainbow in My Hand* (Top 75), *Just Another Cowboy Song* (Top 70) and *Richard and the Cadillac Kings*, which peaked in the Top 60.

Doyle never again achieved this sort of success, and in the early 90's, he left performing Country music.

RECOMMENDED ALBUMS:

"Doyle Holly" (Barnaby)(1973)
"Just Another Cowboy Song" (Barnaby)(1973)

Salty Holmes refer PRAIRIE RAMBLERS

DAVID HOLT

(Singer, Songwriter, Banjo, Autoharp, Guitar, Slide Guitar, Ukulele, Harmonica, Accordion, Fiddle, Jews Harp, Hambone, Spoons, Washboard, Mouth Bow, Paper Sack)

Given name: David Lowrey Holt
Date of Birth: October 15, 1946
Where Born: Gatesville, Texas
Married: Virginia Callaway
Children: Zeb, Sara Jane (dec'd.)

Best known for hosting TNN's *Fire on the Mountain* and appearances on TNN's *American Music Shop*, David Holt emerged in the 1980's as one of the most popular exemplars of Old-Time and Folk music. His engaging personality, sense of tradition, immense talent and innovative promotional techniques won him a unique place in the modern Country scene. He is at once a musician, a storyteller, an educator, an historian, a television personality, and an important musical ambassador.

David's family had been in Texas for five generations when he came along, and when he was 10 years old his father taught him a distinctive musical tradition of the family, playing the spoons and bones. When the family moved to California, when David was a teenager, he began taking drum lessons and played drums for a time in various rock'n'roll and Jazz bands.

He also began to get interested in traditional music, and after hearing a 78 by Carl T. Sprague, sought out in Bryan, Texas, the veteran cowboy singer, who taught David to play the harmonica and encouraged him to learn the old songs. Another move to Folk music came in 1969, when David and a college friend named Steve Keith (a banjo player) traveled to the southern Appalachians and found what Holt called "a world of living traditional music." He began learning the Old-Time clawhammer banjo from some of its last original masters, in particular Obray Ramsey.

David graduated from the University of California with degrees in biology and art and got teaching credentials. In 1973, David moved to western North Carolina, near Asheville, with the express purpose of collecting and learning more mountain music. In 1975, he founded and directed the Appalachian Music program at Warren Wilson College in

The multi-talented ***David Holt***

Swannanoa, North Carolina, near Asheville. During these years he was active in taping and interviewing many veteran musicians, and getting them work at local festivals (his recordings and research are in the collection of the Library of Congress). An especially fruitful association was with Asheville fiddler Luke Smathers, and with the Smathers String Band,

David made some of his first recordings for the June Appal label. David has also taken State Department tours to Nepal, Thailand and South America. By 1980 David decided to begin performing full-time.

Working primarily as a soloist, David, complete with his trademark fedora, soon became a three time winner of the annual *Frets* magazine poll for "Best Old-Time Banjoist" and had a string of albums to his credit, some through his own label, High Windy. In addition to concerts, he developed shows like *Banjo Reb and the Blue Ghost*, which also starred William Mooney. David made frequent appearances on *Hee Haw*, *Nashville Now* and the *Grand Ole Opry*—where he became the first performer to perform on a paper sack. Later he was host of TNN's *Fire on the Mountain*, in which he performed with numerous Old-Time and Bluegrass acts and spotlighted segments filmed in the homes of many of the traditional Folk artists from whom David had learned.

Later jobs included working on *Celebration Express*, *American Music Shop* and the PBS 7-part series *Folkways*. Later he became host and featured singer for American Public Radio's *Riverwalk: Live from the Landing*, which originated live from San Antonio and featured David with the Jim Cullum Jazz Band. David's 1992 album ***Grandfather's Greatest Hits*** featured Chet Atkins and Duane Eddy (the first time they had played together on record) and was nominated for a Grammy Award.

His interest in using music for education (he later received a degree in education) led David to do albums and tapes of storytelling, as well as a cd set called *I Got a Bullfrog: Folksongs for the Fun of It* in 1994. These and other activities won him a place in *Esquire* magazine's first annual "Register of Men and Women Who Are Changing America."CKW

RECOMMENDED ALBUMS:

"The Hairyman & Other Wild Tales" (High Windy)(1981) [American Library Association "Notable Record"]

"Tailybone & Other Strange Stories" (High Windy)(1986)

"Reel & Rock" (Flying Fish)(1986) [Features Doc Watson, Merle Watson and Jerry Douglas] [Re-released on High Windy (1991)]

"Grandfather's Greatest Hits" (High Windy)(1992)

"I Got a Bullfrog: Folksongs for the Fun of It" (High Windy)(1994)

HOMER AND JETHRO

When Formed: **1932**

HOMER

(Singer, Guitar, Comedy (Parody))

Given Name: **Henry D. Haynes**
Date of Birth: **July 27, 1920**
Where Born: **Knoxville, Tennessee**
Date of Death: **August 7, 1971**

JETHRO

(Singer, Mandolin, Banjo, Guitar, Comedy (Parody))

Given Name: **Kenneth C. Burns**
Date of Birth: **March 10, 1920**
Where Born: **Conasuga, Tennessee**
Married: **Louise**
Children: **John, Terry (daughter)**
Date of Death: **February 4, 1989**

Known for their madcap humor, Homer and Jethro were two of the funniest men to hit Country music, producing gales of laughter from their audiences, as they parodied the popular songs of the day. They were, however, very fine musicians—Homer a fine guitarist and Jethro a virtuoso on mandolin.

Their career together began when they were both 12 years old. They met at a local talent contest (which neither of them won), at WNOX Knoxville. Jethro had entered with his older brother Aychie, and Henry had entered with two friends as a trio. The station manager wanted a studio band for WNOX's *Mid-day Merry-Go-Round* and formed a group from their combined talents, called the String Dusters. They stayed with WNOX for five years and during that time the two boys, who were used to fooling around off stage, were given the names "Homer" and "Jethro." They worked some of their antics into their act and became stage hillbillies, wearing ill-fitting hayseed costumes and "put over" a droll backwoods humor on *Mid-day Merry-Go-Round* with great success, and so the comedy duo was born.

In 1939, they auditioned successfully for the *Renfro Valley Barn Dance*, in Renfro Valley, Kentucky. Their parodies of songs were extremely popular and they were soon appearing on both NBC and CBS network shows. Then in 1941, both were drafted into the services during WWII; Homer serving in the Pacific and Jethro in Europe.

After the war, Homer and Jethro re-formed their act and were soon employed on WLW Cincinnati's *Plantation Party*, where they stayed for two and a half years, gaining in popularity. Sid Nathan signed them to his King Records and their first single was *Five Minutes More/Rye Whiskey*, followed by *Over the Rainbow*. They stayed with King from 1946 to 1948 and made five albums in that time. Leaving King, they were signed by producer Steve Sholes to RCA Victor. They had a Top 15 hit in 1949 with their King recording *I Feel that Old Age Coming On*. That same year, they had a Top 10 hit with their RCA single *Baby It's Cold Outside*, with June Carter. To get permission to do the parody, they had written to the composer, Frank Loesser. He agreed to it, but with the proviso that the label must read, "With Apologies to Frank Loesser." During this time, Homer and Jethro earned themselves the title "The Song Butchers." Also in 1949, they hit the Top 15 with *Tennessee Border No.2*.

For six months they had toured the U.S. with their own tented show. On their return, they went on to join KWTO Springfield, Missouri, which had a brand new Red Foley show. Also in 1949, Homer and Jethro joined a management company run by the late Spike Jones and went out on the road touring with him. When they had the opportunity to join WLS *National Barn Dance*, Chicago, Spike graciously let them out of their contract with him. The duo was on the *Barn Dance* every Saturday night and stayed until 1958. During the week, they worked on Don McNeil's *Breakfast Club*.

During the 50's, Homer and Jethro abandoned the hillbilly image they had previously used in favor of business suits or casual attire. When they took their act into night clubs around the country, although the song parodies continued, their dialogue tended to be considerably more sophisticated. Their musicianship was appreciated by all types of audiences, not only the Country ones. Las Vegas loved them and although they were initially booked as a supporting act, by the second night, they had become the headliners. They returned to Vegas many times and appeared on TV shows like *The Tonight Show*, which had them back repeatedly. They appeared on the *Johnny Cash Show* eight times and also performed on *Jubilee USA* (ABC-TV) and WSM's *Grand Ole Opry*.

The next hit record for RCA came in 1953 and was the hilarious *(How Much Is) That Hound Dog in the Window* (Top 3). They had another chart success, the following year, with *Hernando's Hideaway* (Top 15). 1959 brought the famous *The Battle of Kookamonga* (Top 30), which received a Grammy for the "Best Humorous Record of 1959," and the last chart entry for the pair was in 1964 with Lennon and McCartney's *I Want to Hold Your Hand* (Top 50).

For four years during the mid-60's, Kellogg's Corn Flakes featured the duo in their

"Ooh! That's Corny!" commercials on both TV and radio, and these advertisements created a whole new interest in Homer and Jethro, as viewers followed their crazy antics.

Together with Chet Atkins in 1970, the pair formed the Nashville String Band (Jethro was Chet's brother-in-law) and recorded for RCA Victor the albums ***Down Home*** (1970), ***Identified*** (1971), ***Strung Up*** (1971), ***The Bandit*** (released 1972) and ***The World's Greatest Melodies*** (released 1972).

When Homer died of a heart attack in 1971, it took Jethro quite a time to get over it. They had been such close friends for so many years and had enjoyed such a wonderful partnership. It would be virtually impossible to match their musical ability combined with their Country humor again. As they wrote on one of their albums, "Today we feel we have a great future behind us, and we have never let failure go to our heads." Jethro died after a long struggle with cancer on February 4, 1989, in Evanston, Illinois. JAB

RECOMMENDED ALBUMS:

"Barefoot Ballads" (RCA Victor)(1957) [Re-issued by Stetson UK in the original sleeve (1988)]
"Homer & Jethro at the Country Club" (RCA Victor)(1960)
"The Best of Homer & Jethro" (RCA Victor)(1966)
"Nashville Cats" (RCA Victor)(1967)
"24 Great Songs in the Homer and Jethro Style" (King)(1967)
The Best of Homer & Jethro" (Nashville)(1969)
There are many more albums we could recommend, so if you see a Homer and Jethro album we say buy it. Also the Nashville String Band albums mentioned above.
[See also Jethro Burns]

HOOSIER HOT SHOTS, The

When Formed: Early 1930's
Members:
"Gabe" Ward Clarinet, Saxophone, Fife, Leader
"Hezzie" Triesch Song Whistle, Washboard, Drums, Alto Horn
"Rudy" Triesch Banjo, Tenor Guitar, Bass Horn
Frank Kettering Banjo, Guitar, Flute, Piccolo, Bass Fiddle, Piano
Other Members:
Nathan Harrison, Keith Milheim

If one thinks of the zany cornball humor of Spike Jones & the City Slickers, then one has an idea of what the Hoosier Hot Shots were about, even though they predated Jones and his madcap crew.

The group, formed in Fort Wayne, Indiana, was led by derby-hatted Gabe Ward (b. Charles Otto Ward), who bore a likeness to Lou Costello of Abbott and Costello, and included the Triesch brothers, Paul ("Hezzie") and Kenneth ("Rudy"). They started out as a dance band, but their predilection for comedy and strange instruments had them joining the WLS *National Barn Dance* in 1933 (and remaining until 1942) as a novelty group. Their arrival on stage was always heralded by the cry, "Are you ready, Hezzie?" They appeared in several movies, including *Mountain Rhythm* with Gene Autry (1939), *Sing Me a Song of Texas* with Tom Tyler (1945) and several with Ken Curtis. (See Movie Section.)

The Hot Shots recorded for several labels including the ARC group, but it was their recordings for Decca during and after WWII that gained them even more fame. In 1944, they reached the Top 3 on the Country chart with *She Broke My Heart in Three Places* and crossed-over to the Pop Top 25. In 1946, with Sally Foster and Gil Taylor guesting on vocals, they again reached the Top 3 Country and Top 15 Pop with *Someday (You'll Want Me to Want You)*. At the end of the year, they teamed up with Two Ton Baker for the Top 3 Country hit *Sioux City Sue*.

The Hoosier Hot Shots moved to California and retired in the mid-50's, although the occasional album was still released into the mid-70's.

RECOMMENDED ALBUMS:

"The Original Hoosier Hot Shots" (Dot)(1964)
"It's the Hoosier Hot Shots (National Barn Dance)" (Sunbeam)(1975)

*The zany antics of the **Hoosier Hot Shots***

DOC HOPKINS

(Singer, Banjo, Guitar)
Given Name: Doctor Howard Hopkins
Date of Birth: January 26, 1900
Where Born: Wallins Creek (Harlan County), Kentucky
Married: Mary Lock
Children: Howard
Date of Death: January, 1988

Doc Hopkins (yes, his name really was "Doctor") sang simple unadorned songs on radio for some two decades. Like Frank Dudgeon, Hopkins cast himself in a similar mold to Bradley Kincaid. Doc spent the greater part of his career in Chicago and although he recorded only occasionally, he managed to put a sizable portion of broad repertoire on M. M. Cole transcriptions which were played on a variety of radio stations during the 40's.

Born in mountainous Harlan County, Doc moved with his family to a farm in the Appalachian foothills of Rockcastle County (site of John Lair's future Renfro Valley) when he was about 5. As Doc grew up, he had a stuttering problem that made it difficult for him to talk, but which vanished when he sang (like Mel Tillis). He learned and thrived on singing by the time he reached age 9, providing his own accompaniment on either fretless banjo or guitar.

Doc joined the Army during WWI, and eventually served in France. Back home in Kentucky, he joined a medicine show for a time and enlisted in the Marine Corps for three years. He then followed a variety of jobs until 1929, when John Lair brought him to radio at WLS Chicago, where they all became part of the Cumberland Ridge Runners. Doc subsequently spent about twenty years in radio, mostly in Chicago at either WLS or WJJD, although he did spend some time in both Detroit and Kansas City.

Although Hopkins moved into Chicago after Bradley Kincaid departed the Windy City, it is said that their styles developed independently. Be that as it may, Doc soon earned the sobriquet "America's Favorite Folk Singer" on his radio programs. He must have been the recipient of one of the most unusual listener requests in radio history when the man who killed J.B. Marcum asked Doc to sing *The Murder of J. B. Marcum* on the air.

In 1931 and 1932, Hopkins cut a half dozen sides for the Paramount label, and five years later for the ARC group of labels, both with the Cumberland Runners and by himself. In 1941, he did his last work on a major label when he recorded six songs for Decca Records. In later years, he recorded four songs for a small Renfro Valley-based firm and a couple of EP Gospel discs. In addition, he recorded for his own DH label. However, the M. M. Cole Transcription Library provided the best showcase for Doc's vocal work when he made a series of electrical transcriptions in 1944 for radio use. These contained more than 160 older, newer, secular, and sacred numbers.

Doc Hopkins left radio in 1949 when changing times in the industry became increasingly apparent. He went to work as a machinist, first in Chicago, and then from 1956 in Los Angeles for a dozen years. After retirement, the Hopkins family returned to Chicago. Meanwhile in 1956, Doc appeared at the UCLA Folk Festival, where Dr. D.K. Wilgus and other scholars taped many of his songs. After coming back to Chicago, he performed at a Renfro Valley reunion show. Some years later, Birch Records released an album of material from the UCLA tapes and in 1986, the German firm Cattle issued an album of 16 songs from the Cole Transcriptions.

IMT

RECOMMENDED ALBUMS:

"Doc Hopkins" (Birch) (1945)
"Memories of the WLS Barn Dance Days" (Cattle Germany)(1986)

JOHNNY HORTON

(Singer, Songwriter, Guitar)

Give Name:	**John Gale Horton**
Date of Birth:	**April 3, 1925**
Where Born:	**Los Angeles, California**
Married:	**Billie Jean Williams (m. September 1953)**
Date of Death:	**November 5, 1960**

Johnny Horton, despite being a reluctant star, has become a Country music legend. The songs he wrote and the recordings he made during his brief career have left a lasting imprint.

Born into a sharecropping family, Johnny soon found himself in Tyler, Texas, where work could be found. His mother taught him to play guitar when he was 11. Johnny attended college in Jacksonville and Kilgore, Texas, and he subsequently won basketball scholarships to Baylor University at Waco, Texas, and then Seattle University, Washington.

The singing fisherman, ***Johnny Horton***

He then moved up to Alaska before completing his degree and worked in the fishing industry. In 1950, he moved to Los Angeles, where he continued in fishing. Some friends persuaded him to enter a talent contest at Harmony Park Corral in Anaheim, which he won. He came to the attention of Cliffie Stone and Tennessee Ernie Ford and he soon got a spot on KXLA Pasadena. He quickly acquired the sobriquet of "the Singing Fisherman." In addition to his Pasadena show, Johnny also appeared on Cliffie Stone's *Hometown Jamboree* on KLAC.

In 1951, Fabor Robison became Johnny's manager and got Johnny onto Cormac Records but the label folded and as a result Robison formed his own Abbott label, specifically to record Horton. Again, success proved elusive, so Horton went on to cut sides for Dot and Mercury without any chart action.

During 1953, Johnny married Hank Williams' widow, the vivacious singer Billie Jean. She had received a lump-sum from Audrey Williams, Hank's first wife, in return for which she agreed to stop performing as "Mrs. Hank Williams." This money helped bail Johnny out of his not inconsiderable debts. According to Billie Jean, Johnny was more interested in fishing and hunting than going on the road. It was only the thought of her leaving that stopped him quitting music. Outside of Shreveport, he could only count on Johnny Cash as a friend in the music business.

However, Johnny's name was getting around and in 1955 he joined the *Louisiana Hayride* out of KWKH Shreveport. The following year, now managed by Tillman Franks, Johnny moved to Columbia. The day after Elvis cut *Heartbreak Hotel*, Horton cut *Honky Tonk Man*, which he had written with Franks and Howard Hausey. The bass player on the session was Bill Black. The single climbed into the Top 10 in 1956 and was quickly followed into the Top 10 by *I'm a One Woman Man*. He now started to appear on the *Grand Ole Opry* and had his own show on KLTV Tyler, Texas.

During 1957, Johnny chalked up further hits with *I'm Coming Home* (Top 15), *The Woman I Need* (Top 10) and in 1958, *All Grown Up* (Top 10). Still Johnny was looking for that elusive No.1 and an identifiable sound. In 1959 came the change of direction which was to make his name. The previous year, the Kingston Trio had hit with *Tom Dooley*, which started a trend toward Country-Folk. At Franks' suggestion Johnny started to record "saga" songs and enjoyed his first chart-topper with the Franks song, *When It's Springtime in Alaska (It's Forty Below)*. However, it was the next single that guaranteed Johnny lasting fame. He put out a version of Jimmie Driftwood's *The Battle of New Orleans*. It topped the Country chart for 10 weeks and crossed over to top the Pop chart for 6 weeks. The record sold over 2 million copies (being Certified Gold) and was the biggest selling Pop and Country single of 1959. However, in the U.K., the record was banned as being offensive because of the "bloody British" line and so it was Britain's Skiffle King, Lonnie Donegan, who had the successful version there. Johnny followed up with the Top 10 single, *Johnny Reb*, which also made it into the Pop chart. The flip-side, *Sal's Got a Sugar Lip*, also reached the Country Top 20.

During 1960, Johnny had a major crossover hit with *Sink the Bismarck,* which was inspired by the movie of the same name. However, this taste of fame didn't change Johnny one iota. He spent his money on a bait factory in Natchitoches, Louisiana. Billie Jean had to make him close it down and, to make ends meet, opened a bar and restaurant. Like other ill-fated entertainers, notably Eddie Cochran, something told Johnny that he was going to die violently and prematurely. Soon after recording *North to Alaska*, which was the theme song from the soundtrack of the John Wayne movie of the same name, Horton told his family and close friends of his premonitions.

What was destined to be his last stage performance took place at Austin's Skyline Club, ironically, the setting for Hank Williams' final appearance. Johnny informed Merle Kilgore that he was destined to die at the hands of a drunk. In a morose mood, Horton stayed backstage as much as possible. After playing two sets, Johnny drove his car the 220 miles back to Shreveport, accompanied by Franks and his bass player and guitarist, Tommy Tomlinson, who had driven them to the club. Suddenly, in the early hours of November 5, 1960, a drunk driver hit Horton's car head on and Johnny was killed.

The funeral was a bizarre affair, with Horton's psychic counselor, Bernard Ricks, handing out fish drawings which intimated that the singer was in heaven. Standing before the casket, Johnny's brother, Frank, a professional gambler, found Jesus and vowed to change his ways.

North to Alaska hit the Country chart a week after Johnny's death and reached No.1, where it stayed for 5 weeks out of a 22 week stay. It also made the Top 5 on the Pop chart. This was followed by the Top 10 Country hit *Sleepy Eyed John* and a re-issue of *Honky Tonk Man*, in 1962. Johnny's final chart entry came in 1963 with a re-issue of *All Grown Up*.

Horton's music has been influential, with Dwight Yoakam reviving *Honky Tonk Man* in 1986. The title *Honkytonk Man* was also that of the Clancy Carlisle novel which was made into a movie by Clint Eastwood in 1982. In 1989, George Jones put out his version of *I'm a One Woman Man*. Johnny's versatility was underlined by the unissued material that appeared after his death. The Columbia Records 1961 compilation *Johnny Horton's Greatest Hits* was Certified Platinum in November 1986. As the album had gone Gold in 1964, it meant that in the intervening 20 years, 500,000 copies had been sold. SM

RECOMMENDED ALBUMS:

"The Fantastic Johnny Horton" (Mercury)(1959)
"America's Most Creative Folk Singer" (Columbia)(1960) [Re-issued by Stetson UK in the original sleeve (1988)]
"Johnny Horton's Greatest Hits"(Columbia) (1961)
"Johnny Horton" (Dot)(1966) [Material recorded on Abbott]
"Johnny Horton on the Louisiana Hayride" (Columbia)(1966)
"The World of Johnny Horton" (double) (Columbia)(1971)
"Rockin' Rollin' Johnny Horton" (Bear Family Germany)(1983)
"Johnny Horton 1956-60" (Bear Family Germany) (1991)
"Done Rovin'" (Briar International) [Material recorded on Abbott]

VAUGHN HORTON

(Singer, Songwriter, Steel Guitar)
Date of Birth: June 6, 1911
Where Born: Broad Top, Pennsylvania
Date of Death: March 1, 1988

Vaughn Horton, the brother of Hall of Famer Roy Horton, made his name as the writer of some of popular music's most enduring songs, like *Choo Choo Ch'Boogie* (a 1975 hit for Asleep at the Wheel), *Mockin' Bird Hill* (a 1951 hit for Les Paul and Mary Ford and a 1977 success for Donna Fargo), *Hillbilly Fever* (a 1950 hit for Little Jimmy Dickens and Ernest Tubb & Red Foley), *Till the End of the World, An Old Christmas Card, Dixie Cannonball, Teardrops in My Heart, Address Unknown, Jolly Old St. Nicholas, Come What May* and *Sugarfoot Rag* (a 1950 success for Red Foley).

At Pennsylvania State College, Horton began playing in college dance bands. During the 30's, he played in big bands and in the 40's, he was with Country groups and was considered a superb steel guitar player. He started singing on the radio and then after moving to Nashville, he promoted records and then produced sides for RCA, Columbia and Decca, including a revival of Elton Britt's *There's a Star-Spangled Banner Waving Somewhere*.

Vaughn and Roy formed a group and moved to New York City, in 1935. They had their own show on NBC and CBS radio. They added Ray Smith, Rusty Keefer and Johnny Browers, and became the Pinetoppers. The featured vocalists of the group were Trudy and Gloria Marlin, known as the Beaver Valley Sweethearts. In 1950, they had a Top 3 Country hit and Top 10 Pop single with *Mockin' Bird Hill*, on Coral Records. Becoming a member of ASCAP in 1945, Vaughn Horton was elected to the Nashville Songwriters Hall of Fame, in 1971. He died at his home in Florida, on March 1, 1988.

HOTMUD FAMILY

When Formed: 1970
Members:

Suzanne Edmundson	**Vocals, Guitar, Banjo, Fiddle, Mandolin, Autoharp, Piano**
Dave Edmundson	**Vocals, Mandolin, Fiddle**
Rick Good	**Vocals, Banjo, Guitar**
Tom Harley Campbell	**Stand-Up Bass**
Tom McCreesh	**Fiddle**
Jerry Ray Weinert	**Stand-Up Bass**
Gary Hopkins	**Stand-Up Bass**
T.J. Lundy	**Fiddle**
Greg Dearth	**Fiddle**

The Hotmud Family was built around the considerable talents of Suzanne Edmundson (now Thomas). The group started informally when she and former husband, Dave, and Rick Good sat around playing Carter Family songs. They realized that musically they gelled and how like a family they seemed. They compared astrological signs and discovered that they represented earth, fire and water and thought of what would happen if those elements were blended; the answer was "hot mud."

Based in Yellow Springs near Dayton, Ohio, the trio soon found a local following. Initially, they played in elementary schools demonstrating the roots of musical history in America. They had their own local radio show and were soon becoming popular on the Bluegrass festival circuit. Blessed with a powerful alto voice and the ability to play many instruments, Suzanne demonstrated her skills at performing a wide range of songs. In 1974, Tom Harley Campbell joined on bass.

That year, the group began recording for the Vetco label out of Cincinnati. In all, they recorded four albums for the label, ***'Til We Meet Again***, ***Stone Mountain Wobble***, ***Buckeyes in the Briar Patch*** and ***Years in the Making***. In 1975, Tom McCreesh joined on fiddle and they then worked as a quintet. For their albums, the Hotmud Family utilized outside guest musicians including Fiddlin' Van Kidwell and Joseph Jones. In 1976, Jerry Ray Weinert replaced Campbell on bass.

In 1978, the group moved to the prestigious Flying Fish label, opting for a more Bluegrass sound. Their first album, ***Live, As We Know It***, was recorded that year at the Towne Crier Cafe in Hopewell Junction, New York, and the following year at the Down Home Pickin' Parlor, Johnson City, Tennessee, and was completed at WUHY-FM Studios in Philadelphia. In 1979, Gary Hopkins replaced Jerry Ray on bass and the following year, T.J. Lundy came in on fiddle.

Their next album, ***Meat & Potatoes & Stuff Like That*** was released in 1981. In 1982, the Hotmud Family had their final line-up change when Lundy left and Greg Dearth became the group's fiddle player.

However, years on the road without the remunerative benefits that should have come their way led to the group becoming disenchanted. Then Suzanne and Dave divorced and in 1983, the group disbanded. Following the group break-up, both Dave and Suzanne joined the Dry Branch Fire Squad, of which Suzanne is still a member.

RECOMMENDED ALBUMS:
"'Til We Meet Again" (Vetco)(1974)
"Stone Mountain Wobble" (Vetco)(1975)
"Buckeyes in the Briar Patch" (Vetco)(1976)
"Years in the Making" (Vetco)(1977)
"Live, As We Know It" (Flying Fish)(1979)
"Meat & Potatoes & Stuff Like That" (Flying Fish)(1982)

HOT RIZE

When Formed: 1976
Members:
Tim O'Brien Lead and Harmony Vocals, Mandolin, Fiddle
Pete Wernick Banjo, Harmony Vocals
Charles Sawtelle Bass Guitar, Guitar, Harmony and Lead Vocals
(Switched to Guitar on departure of Mike Scap and Nick Forster joining)
Nick Forster Lead and Harmony Vocals, Bass Guitar, Emcee (joined May 1978)
Former Member:
Mike Scap Guitar, Harmony Vocals (left May 1978)

Hot Rize have managed to cross the road between Bluegrass and Folk-Country with consummate ease. As a result, Tim O'Brien has established himself as a Country performer and songwriter of note, and the group became in their own words "the Greatest Show in Bluegrass." They became the first Bluegrass band to be featured on TNN's *New Country* album spotlight show.

The name of the band emanates from the secret ingredient of Martha White Self-Rising Flour, a product that Flatt & Scruggs helped to promote during the years that they were sponsored by the company. Pete, Tim and Charles were/are great fans of Lester and Earl and the name of the band was a compliment to them.

After Mike Scap left in 1976, and Nick Forster came on board, the line-up stayed static until the group folded in 1992, an almost unprecedented occurrence for a Bluegrass band. Before joining Hot Rize, Tim O'Brien (from West Virginia) had played with Ophelia Swing Band. Pete Wernick (from New York City) is known as "Dr. Banjo" and is an honest to goodness Doctor, having earned a Ph.D. He is one of the leading banjo teachers, with a book, *Bluegrass Banjo*, videos and "banjo-camps." He was formerly with Country Cooking. Charles Sawtelle is sometimes referred to as "the Bluegrass Mystery" and comes from Austin, Texas. He started out playing steel guitar. He played in the Drifting Ramblers in early 1976, with Pete Wernick and Tim O'Brien. His other claim to fame is that he talks to dogs! Nick Forster comes from Red Hook, New York, and has a remarkable harmony range that goes from tenor to bass. He is also a multi-instrumentalist, playing guitar and lap steel, a square dance caller and is fluent in French. Pete, Tim and Charles had recorded together on Tim's album ***Guess Who's in Town*** on Biscuit City.

In 1977, Pete Wernick recorded a solo album for Flying Fish and Hot Rize's debut eponymous album came two years later for the same label. It contains a mix of traditional, cover and original material.Their second album, ***Radio Boogie***, was unveiled in 1981 and has more of the same and further underlined their star quality.

By 1982, their alter ego, Red Knuckles & the Trailblazers ("those guys that ride in the back of the Hot Rize bus") had taken on a Mr. Hyde quality, with "Red" himself (O'Brien) on vocals and acoustic guitar, "Wendell Mercantile" (Forester) on electric guitar, "Waldo Otto" (Wernick) on steel guitar and "Slade" (Sawtelle) on bass guitar. Their debut live album was entitled ***Hot Rize Presents Red Knuckles & the Trailblazers***. Their music is straight-ahead Honky-Tonk with a generous helping of humor. They occupied a segment in the middle of the Hot Rize stage show. Any similarity between the two groups is probably intentional.

One of Hot Rize's finest live Bluegrass albums, ***Hot Rize in Concert***, appeared in 1984 and featured two tracks from the Red Knuckles "geezers." There is only one original song, but the Bluegrass classics include ones by Ralph Stanley, Cousin Emmy and Grandpa Jones. Shortly after this, Tim O'Brien released his second solo album, ***Hard Year Blues***.

The following year, Hot Rize moved over to another superb indie label, Sugar Hill. Their debut album on the label, ***Traditional Ties***, is excellent and features Tim O'Brien's *Walk the Way the Wind Blows* (which became a Top 10 single for Kathy Mattea, the following year), *Frank's Blues,* written by Pete Wernick and Frank Edmonson (the band's right-hand man and technical assistant), and Keith Whitley's *You Don't Have to Move the Mountain.*

Their follow-up album, ***Untold Stories*** in 1987, continued their journey with just a shade less traditional material and more original songs, including two from Nick Forster. In 1991, Red Knuckles released another album, ***Shades of the Past.*** Hot Rize recorded their final album, ***Take It Home***, in 1992 and ended over fifteen years of splendid music. Tim O'Brien (with his sister, Molly) and Pete Wernick have continued with solo careers.

RECOMMENDED ALBUMS:
"Hot Rize" (Flying Fish)(1979)
"Radio Boogie" (Flying Fish)(1981)
"Hot Rize in Concert" (1984)
"Traditional Ties" (Sugar Hill)(1985)
"Untold Stories" (Sugar Hill)(1987)
"Take It Home" (Sugar Hill)(1992)
Red Knuckles & the Trailblazers:
"Hot Rize Presents Red Knuckles & the Trailblazers" (Flying Fish)(1982)
"Shades of the Past" (Sugar Hill)(1991)

CISCO HOUSTON

(Singer, Songwriter, Guitar)
Given Name: Gilbert Houston
Date of Birth: August 18, 1918
Where Born: Wilmington, Delaware
Date of Death: April 29, 1961

Cisco Houston represents that part of Folk music that is at the root of all real Country music. His music is as vibrant and meaningful over the thirty years since his death, as when he first recorded it.

His family originally came from the Carolinas and Virginia. When he was still a small boy, he heard his grandmother sing Folk melodies and this made an impression on him. He was approaching school age when his family moved to Los Angeles. He learned to play guitar before graduating and then as the Depression started biting, he began to wander around the U.S.

First, he worked in California and then in Colorado. During most of the 30s, he was a cowboy and learned cowboy songs firsthand. He started to sing in local clubs and on the radio. Toward the end of the 30's, he met Woody Guthrie, Leadbelly and John Jacob Niles and in the late 30's and early 40's, Cisco and Woody toured together. They played union meetings and small clubs.

Although Cisco suffered from bad eyesight, he managed to enlist in the Merchant Marines in WWII. Wherever he made port, he learned local Folk songs and added them to his collection. He was on three ships that got torpedoed and lived to tell the tale. At the end of hostilities, he returned to New York, where he renewed his acquaintance with Moses Asch. Asch would soon have Folkways Records in operation; a label that would be one of the most influential in Folk music.

Soon Cisco was on the move again. He returned to California and started working with Leadbelly as well as resuming his collaboration with Guthrie. He also played with Lee Hays—who would form the Weavers in 1948—John Jacob Niles and Burl Ives. In 1948, he recorded three 10" albums for Folkways, among the first to be released by the label. ***900 Miles & Other Railroad Songs***, ***Cowboy Songs*** and ***Hard Travelin'*** have all stood the test of time.

His popularity continued into the 1950's, when he achieved a following on the campus circuit and also appeared at major venues such as Madison Square Garden. He could also be heard on radio and seen on TV. Among these broadcasts were the *American Inventory* and Folk programs broadcast by Mutual Broadcasting System. In 1958, Folkways released ***Cisco Sings***. A year later, Cisco Houston, the inveterate traveler, toured India under the sponsorship of the State Department and the American National Theatre and Academy.

1960 was to be a momentous year for Cisco Houston. His album ***Cisco Special*** was released on Vanguard. He had recorded material for several labels besides Folkways. These included Decca, Coral and Disc. Cisco also cut an album with Woody Guthrie for Stinson, ***Cowboy Songs***. In June, he had emcee'd the CBS program *Folk Music U.S.A.* and then came the thunderbolt. It was discovered that he had cancer. His friend Woody Guthrie was also dying. The two traveling men would soon exchange one voyage of discovery for another.

Cisco Houston died in a hospital in April 1961. It is ironic that at the time of his death, Folk music was beginning to enjoy a new revival. All who followed, and became major stars, owe a debt to Cisco Houston. Yet, not one of them experienced life at the sharp end like he did. There are several songs dedicated to his memory that have been written by his musical descendants. Tom Paxton, who at one time seemed to be the nearest in spirit to Woody Guthrie, wrote *Fare Thee Well, Cisco*, which appeared on his ***Ramblin' Boy*** album. Peter LaFarge, a poet among Folk songwriters who wrote the evocative *The Ballad of Ira Hayes*, was an acolyte of Houston's and he wrote *Cisco Houston Passed this Way* in tribute.

In 1965, a songbook, *900 Miles, The Ballads, Blues and Folksongs of Cisco Houston*, was published by Oak Publications. It included some of his memorable compositions and adaptations, including, *The Ramblin' Gamblin' Man*. Since his death, there have been numerous albums released primarily on Folkways, but also on Stinson and Vanguard.

RECOMMENDED ALBUMS:

"900 Miles & Other Railroad Songs" (Folkways)
"Cowboy Songs" (Folkways)
"Hard Travelin'" (Folkways)
"Cisco Sings" (Folkways)(1958)
"Cisco Houston Sings American Folk Songs" (Folkways)
"Cisco Special" (Vanguard)(1960)
"I Ain't Got No Home" (Vanguard)(1962)
"Legacy of Cisco Houston" (Disc)(1964)
"Songs of the Open Road" (Folkways)(1964)
"Cowboy Songs" (Stinson) [With Woody Guthrie]
"Lonesome Valley Railroad Songs" (Folkways)
"Cisco Houston" (Evergreen)

DAVID HOUSTON

(Singer, Songwriter, Guitar, Piano, Actor)

Date of Birth:	**December 9, 1938**
Where Born:	**Shreveport, Louisiana**
Married:	**1. Linda (div.)**
	2. Kathy Raye
Children:	**David Louis**
Date of Death:	**November 25, 1993**

David Houston is a singer with genealogical pedigree. Not for him is a background of being brought up in one room with 10 brothers and picking cotton to make ends meet. He could boast of ancestors that included General Robert E. Lee and Sam Houston. His father and brother built houses in the Bossier City area of Louisiana where he was raised. He is also a cousin of another famous Country singer, Tommy Overstreet.

He started singing lessons when he was age 4 and was given a guitar by an aunt who taught him to play. His godfather was Gene Austin, who had been one of the great popular singers of the 20's with such successes as *My Blue Heaven* and *Ramona*. He greatly encouraged David as he could see potential in him even as a child. By the time he was 12, David could also play piano.

He made his first appearance on KWKH's *Louisiana Hayride* when he was 12 and became a member while still at high school. It was here that he met the soon-to-be-legendary Tillman Franks, who was the talent manager for the *Hayride*. Franks would soon become very involved in the career of Johnny Horton and would be a co-writer of *Honky Tonk Man.*

David attended Centenary College in Shreveport but left before graduating to join his father and brother in their construction work. He also sold insurance and sang around the clubs in the area. In 1963, Franks called him and told him that he had a song that would be ideal for him. They traveled to Tyler in Texas and cut Harold Dorman's *Mountain of Love.* Tillman took the tapes to Epic in Nashville, where David was signed and came under Billy Sherrill's production guidance. The result was that the single went Top 3 and David Houston was on his way to stardom. The next four singles all peaked in the teens: *Chickashay, One If for Him, Two If for Me, Love Looks Good on You* and *Sweet, Sweet Judy.*

Then in 1965, he came back strongly with *Livin' in a House Full of Love,* which was a Top 5 hit. Two records later, in the summer of 1966, he hit the No.1 spot with *Almost Persuaded.* It stayed at the top for 9 weeks and was on the charts for almost six months and it crossed to the Pop Top 25. As a result, David won two Grammy Awards for the song as

Country stylist ***David Houston***

"Best Country & Western Recording" and "Best Country & Western Vocal Performance, Male." The song also won for its writers, Billy Sherrill and Glenn Sutton, the Grammy for "Best Country & Western Song"; all in 1966. It also gave him the name of his band, the Persuaders. In addition, David was named "Most Promising Male Artist" by *Billboard.* The flip-side of his next single did the trick and *A Loser's Cathedral* was up in the Top 3.

From now on, he was as hot as they come. He made his movie debut in 1967 in *Cottonpickin' Chicken-Pluckers* (he also made *Horse Soldiers* and *Carnival Rock* and provided the title song for the NBC movie *Kansas City, I Love You*) and had a run of three straight No.1s: *With One Exception*, followed by a duet with Tammy Wynette, *My Elusive Dreams* and the solo *You Mean the World to Me*. He continued the following year with another successful hit with Tammy, *It's All Over* (Top 15), and then had back-to-back chart toppers with *Have a Little Faith* and *Already in Heaven,* wrapping up the year with a Top 3 success, *Where Love Used to Live*.

So it continued unabated for the next two years. His 1969 hits were *My Woman's Good to Me* (Top 5), *I'm Down to My Last I Love You* (Top 3) and the No.1 *Baby Baby (I Know That You're a Lady)*. During 1970, he scored with *I Do My Swinging at Home* (Top 3) and *Wonders of the Wine* (Top 10). He teamed up with newcomer Barbara Mandrell at the end of the year and had the first of their six hits, *After Closing Time* (Top 10).

During 1971, David hit with *A Woman Always Knows* (Top 3), *Nashville* (Top 10), *A Maiden's Prayer/Home Sweet Home* (Top 10) and the duet with Barbara Mandrell, *We've Got Everything But Love* (Top 20). In 1972, David charted with *The Day that Love Walked In* (Top 20), *Soft, Sweet and Warm* (Top 10), *A Perfect Match* (with Barbara Mandrell, Top 25) and the seasonal single *I Wonder How John Felt (When He Baptized Jesus)*, which peaked in the Top 50. *Good Things* (Top 3) redeemed the situation. That year, David became a member of the *Grand Ole Opry*.

David's only major hits in 1973 were *She's All Woman* (Top 3) and *The Lady of the Night* (Top 25). David started 1974 with the Top 10 *I Love You, I Love You* and *Ten Commandments of Love* (Top 15), both with Barbara Mandrell. He wrapped the year with his last Top 10 record, *Can You Feel It* .

His last major hit, *Come on Down (to Our Favorite Forget-About-Her Place)*, in 1976, went Top 25. By the end of 1976, David was off of Epic and on Gusto/Starday, but that didn't help. Two years later, he moved on to Colonial and then immediately to Elektra, but he still couldn't get those hits to rise above the middle to low area of the charts. By 1977, he was with the Derrick label. In 1980, he surfaced on Country International and finally, he had a small hit on Excelsior in the spring of 1981. The ascent to the top and the descent were as swift. The sad thing is that the records he was producing on the way down were not bad ones. As with all forms of music, new heroes come along.

Since 1989, David had been doing laudable work, performing for residents of nursing homes and senior citizens' centers throughout the Country. He joined the Senior Citizens Appreciation Day organization, which has presented some 3,000 shows for confined elderly people since 1979. David died from a ruptured brain aneurysm in 1993.

RECOMMENDED ALBUMS:

"My Elusive Dreams" (Epic)(1967) [With Tammy Wynette]
"Greatest Hits" (Epic)(1969)
"A Perfect Match" (Epic)(1972) [With Barbara Mandrell]
"David Houston's Greatest Hits Vol. 2" (Epic)(1972) [Limited Edition]
"Old Time Religion" (Harmony)(1973)
"David Houston's Greatest Hits/Best of David Houston and Barbara Mandrell" (double)(Epic)(1975)
"David Houston" (Starday)(1977)
"The Best of David Houston" (Gusto)(1978) [With Sherri Jerrico]
"From the Heart of Houston" (Derrick)(1979)
"From Houston to You" (Excelsior)(1981)
"David Houston Sings Texas Honky Tonk" (Delta)(1982)

COUNTRY PAUL HOWARD

(Singer, Guitar, Violin, Banjo)

Given Name:	**Paul Jack Howard**
Date of Birth:	**July, 10, 1913**
Where Born:	**Midland, Arkansas**
Married:	**1. Rosella (dec'd.) 2. Nell Rose Harper**
Children:	**Melissa Elizabeth, Paul Jason, Miranda Kathleen, Keith (stepson)**
Date of Death:	**June 18, 1984**

Paul Howard claimed to be the first performer to ever play an electric guitar or use two and three-part fiddle harmonies on the *Grand Ole Opry*. He also claims to have "brought" comedian Rod Brasfield, Rollin Sullivan of Lonzo & Oscar, and guitarist Hank "Sugarfoot" Garland to the *Grand Ole Opry*.

Born in Midland, Arkansas, the heart of Folk music country, Paul came from a heritage of English, Irish, and Cherokee Indian descent, the son of John and Melissa Howard. He learned to play guitar in his teens, and began his career on radio station KOY Phoenix, Arizona, in 1931. He made his first personal appearance in Fort Smith, Arkansas, in 1933. Initially, Paul also worked in farming, mining and as a salesman. After that he appeared on the *Barn Dance*, in Paducah, Kentucky, from 1935 to 1936, WSM's *Grand Ole Opry* from 1940 to 1949 and NBC's *Shower of Stars* (1945).

He began writing songs in 1940, being influenced by Fred Rose of Acuff-Rose Publishing, who handled his material. Paul penned *With Tears in My Eyes*, *Texas Boogie*, *Torn Between True Love and Desire*, *Drinking All My Troubles Away*, *The Fiddler with the Patch on His Pants*, *You Couldn't See the Trees for the Forest*, *Rock Candy Heart*, *I'm Sending You Red Roses*, and co-wrote *Mother's Prayer*.

Star of the Grand Ole Opry ***Country Paul Howard***

That first year on the *Opry*, Paul played with the John Daniels Quartet, as well as his band, the Arkansas Cotton Pickers. According to Howard, Judge D. Hay tagged him "the Arkansas Cottonpicker" the first night he ever performed on the *Opry*. He became a member in April, 1942.

Paul's instrumental group, the Cotton Pickers, was made up of eight competent musicians and singers of bright Western Swing songs and sweet folksy ballads, with a distinctive fiddle section. Among the line-up were Roy Wiggins, Leroy Walters, J.B. Thomas, Roddy Bristol, Slim Idaho, Jack Brown, Billy Bowman and Harold Hensley

Paul's courtship and subsequent marriage to his first wife, Rosella, is said to have happened like a storybook romance. Rosella was President of the "Paul Howard Fan Club." This led to their introduction which culminated in matrimony. Rosella later sang with his band and wrote some of their material. Between 1944 and 1948, Paul recorded on Liberty (1944), Columbia (1945-1947) and King (1948) Records. Rosella composed Paul's first release on King Records in 1949, *Torn Between True Love and Desire* backed by *Texas Boogie*.

Paul's most popular singles included: *Oklahoma City*, *I've Been Lonesome Since You Went Away*, *You Left a Red Cross on My Heart*, *Hora Sta Cotton Picker*, *The Boogie's Fine Tonight*, *Rock Candy Heart*, *I'm Sending My Heart for Repairs*, *Lazy Morning*, *Rootie Tootie*, *You're Never Satisfied*, *Somebody Else's Trouble*, *Honest as the Day Is Long* (Columbia), *12 O'clock Waltz* (King) (1948), *You Couldn't See the Trees for the Forest* (King) (1949), *Texas Boogie* and *Torn Between True Love and Desire* (King) (1949).

Howard played the *Opry* for nine years, leaving due to the lack of attention Western Swing was receiving at that time. He then went on to KPRC in Houston from 1949 to 1950, KTBS Shreveport (1950-1951), KCIG Shreveport (1951-1952) and then KAPK, in Minden, Louisiana (1952-1953), where he became Program Director and Commercial Manager as well as deejay.

In subsequent years he also pursued farming, mining and selling. In 1955, Paul left Nashville for Shreveport, Louisiana, to host the *Louisiana Hayride* radio show. In subsequent years, he formed a group known as

Paul Howard and Band and toured throughout Arkansas. He returned to Nashville every year except one until his death to perform at the *Oldtimers Show*, which served as a homecoming for former *Opry* members. Paul was a member of the Country Music Association. In 1989, he donated a Martin guitar to the Country Music Foundation. Howard spent the last several years of his life performing with the Cotton Pickers in Louisiana, Arkansas and Southern Texas, before succumbing to congestive heart failure at the age of 75. LAP

RECOMMENDED ALBUM:

"Faded Picture Blues" (King)(1970) [With Ralph Willis]

HARLAN HOWARD

(Songwriter, Singer, Guitar, Music Publisher)

Given Name:	**Harlan Perry Howard**
Date of Birth:	**September 8, 1929**
Where Born:	**Lexington, Kentucky**
Married:	**1. Jan Howard (div.)**
	2. (Div.)
	3. (Div.)
	4. (Div.)
	5. Melanie
Children:	**Kenneth, Harlan, Jr., Donna Gail**

If one had to name Nashville's most enduring songwriter, then Harlan Howard would qualify. He has written over 4,000 songs and can boast a plethora of hit credits in every decade from the 50's to the 90's.

Harlan spent only two years in his native Kentucky before his family moved north to Detroit, Michigan, where Harlan's father got a job with Ford. His parents separated and it was against this sad personal background that Harlan listened intently to the *Grand Ole Opry* on WSM. Ernest Tubb's line, "I wonder why you said goodbye," struck a chord and E.T. became Harlan's idol. As Harlan listened to the broadcasts, he would try to write down Tubb's lyrics, retaining the melodies in his head. Inevitably, there were gaps, which prompted Harlan to invent lines and verses.

It was a natural progression from this to composing complete songs based on the 3 and 4 chord structures of Tubb and Harlan's other heroes, Floyd Tillman, Fred Rose and Rex Griffin. In learning his craft, he read voraciously, allegedly devouring four to five books a day. Songwriting also proved to be an escape from his early shyness with women, which derived from what the young Howard considered to be his limitations; "I was lonely, ugly, rejected, big nose, two teeth knocked out in front, but I could write."

After graduation, Harlan spent four years with the paratroopers at Fort Benning, Georgia. Here he learned how to play guitar and on Friday nights, he would hitchhike with a friend to Nashville, where he spent his weekends. Following his army tour, Harlan had a spell of job-hopping, taking him to Michigan, Tucson and Los Angeles, working in gas stations, paper mills and at truck driving and cab driving.

In California in the late 50's, several Country acts were touring, including Wynn Stewart, Skeets McDonald, Buck Owens and Bobby Bare. In this environment, Harlan's luck came good. His talents were recognized by Tex Ritter and Johnny Bond and they published his early material. Harlan also met Lula Grace "Jan" Johnson, whom he would later marry and who would become Country star Jan Howard. Then Wynn Stewart cut Harlan's *You Took Her Off My Hands*.

All of a sudden, Harlan's songs were in demand. In 1958, Charlie Walker had a major hit with *Pick Me Up on Your Way Down* and the same year Jimmie Skinner had a hit with *What Makes a Man Wander?* With Jan making his demos, Harlan's success started to come in a big way the next year. *Mommy for a Day* provided Kitty Wells with a hit and then Harlan scored his first cross-over success. *Heartaches by the Number* was a Country success for Ray Price and a No.1 Pop hit for Guy Mitchell.

With the royalties coming in, Howard decided to move to Nashville and arrived in June 1960. The Howard pen soon provided hits for a slew of major artists. During 1960, he had hits with *I Wish I Could Fall in Love Today* (Ray Price), *Excuse Me (I Think I've Got a Heartache)* and *Above and Beyond* (both Buck Owens). The following year, he wrote *I Fall to Pieces* with Hank Cochran. Although Jan Howard wanted to record it, Harlan saved it for Patsy Cline and in her hands it was another cross-over smash. Harlan wrote *Three Steps to the Phone (Millions of Miles)* for Jim Reeves, as the follow-up to *He'll Have to Go*, but Reeves rejected it and George Hamilton IV cut it and turned it into a Top 10 hit. Reeves did, however, record Howard's *The Blizzard* and it became a Top 5 hit. Harlan called this "about my favorite song." Other hits that year included *Heartbreak USA* for Kitty Wells and *Foolin' Around* and *Under the Influence of Love*, both for Buck Owens. During 1961, Harlan had at one time 15 of his songs on the Country charts.

Country music's premier songwriter, ***Harlan Howard***

This was a period where Harlan Howard was writing two and three songs a day and as many as eight to twelve songs a week would be recorded. In 1961, he picked up 10 BMI Awards and the following two years, he was named *Billboard* "Songwriter of the Year." During 1962 and 1963, Harlan had major hits with *You Took Her Off My Hands* (Ray Price), *Busted* (Johnny Cash), *You Comb Her Hair* (George Jones) and *Second Hand Rose* (Roy Drusky). In 1964, Harlan started his own publishing firm, Wilderness Music Publishing Company.

During 1961, Harlan recorded his first album for Capitol and in 1965 moved over to Monument for two albums, before joining RCA in 1968. He had a medium sized hit, in 1971, with *Sunday Morning Christian*, on Nugget, but he never considered a recording career seriously. His love for fishing influenced his dislike of touring.

As the 60's progressed, so his credits resembled the "Who's Who" of Country. *Don't Call Me from a Honky Tonk* gave Johnny & Jonie Mosby a 1963 hit and the same year Ray Charles had a Top 5 Pop hit with *Busted*. The following year, George Jones had a major success with *Your Heart Turned Left (And I Was on the Right)*. In 1965, Harlan co-penned with Buck Owens Buck's No. 1, *I've Got a Tiger By the Tail*.

Other hits during the rest of the 60's included the 1966 *Streets of Baltimore* for Bobby Bare (he co-wrote it with Tompall Glaser), *Evil on Your Mind* (Jan Howard) and then in 1967, the biggest compliment that could be paid to him, a complete album of his songs recorded by another artist. The artist was Waylon Jennings and the album was ***Waylon Jennings Sings Ol' Harlan***. That same year, Mel Tillis cut one of Harlan's finest songs, *Life Turned Her that Way*, which would be reprised in 1988 by Ricky Van Shelton. In 1968, Hank Williams, Jr. had a Top 5 hit with *It's All Over (But the Crying)*.

Melba Montgomery had her one and only No.1 with Harlan's classic song *No Charge* in

1974 and this song would become a No.1 in the U.K. Pop charts via J.J. Barrie two years later. Other versions included one by Tammy Wynette, as well as parody versions by Billy Connelly and Bob Williamson.

At this point, Harlan suffered a bout of writer's block produced by a combination of pressure to continue turning out top notch material and the trauma of a painful divorce. It was fortunate that Charlie Rich took another Howard song, *He Called Me Baby*, changed the "he" to "she" and had a No.1 hit with it.

Major success returned in the 80's, when Harlan demonstrated his ability to work with upcoming writers at Tree Publishing. He also proved how universal his songs were for any generation. In 1982, John Conlee had a Top 10 with the Howard chestnut *Busted*. 1984 yielded *I Don't Know a Thing About Love (The Moon Song),* which was a No.1 for Conway Twitty, and *Why Not Me* (co-written with Sonny Throckmorton and Brent Maher), which was also a chart-topper for the Judds. *Someone Should Leave*, which Harlan wrote with Chick Rains, provided Reba McEntire with a No.1 during 1985, and in 1987, Highway 101 topped the Country lists with *Somewhere Tonight,* which Howard wrote with Rodney Crowell. k.d. lang took a song that Harlan had written with Billy Walker, *I'm Down to My Last Cigarette,* and it provided her with her second hit in 1988.

During 1984, Harlan instituted (with the NSAI) the Harlan Howard Birthday Bash, which takes place in the parking lot of BMI on Music Row in Nashville. It is a wonderful opportunity to see Country music's brightest songwriting talents perform in honor of the great man and the enthusiastic industry crowd.

Where in the past quality and quantity came hand-in-hand, these days Harlan Howard doesn't write anything like as much, but when he does, the material has class stamped all over it. Some titles are written on bar napkins at his favored haunts. Five times married, he has plenty of personal experience to call on while the stories of waitresses and bartenders add outside ingredients. Some writers boast of having written major hits in 15 minutes. Not Harlan. "I say 'My life plus 15 minutes.'"

SM/BM

RECOMMENDED ALBUMS:

"Harlan Howard Sings Harlan Howard" (Capitol)(1961) [Re-issued by Stetson UK in the original sleeve (1992)]
"All-Time Favorite Country Songwriter (Billboard Award)" (Monument)(1965)
"Mr. Songwriter" (RCA Victor)(1967)
"To the Silent Majority with Love" (Nugget)(1971)

JAN HOWARD

(Singer, Songwriter, Author, Actress)

Given Name:	**Lula Grace Johnson**
Date of Birth:	**March 13, 1930**
Where Born:	**West Plains, Missouri**
Married:	**1. Mearle Wood (div.) 2. Lowell Alexander "Smitty" Smith (div.) 3. Harlan Howard (div.) 4. Dr. Maurice M. Acree, Jr.**
Children:	**Jimmy (dec'd.), Carter ("Corky"), David (dec'd.)**

To anyone who knows her, Jan Howard is one of the gutsiest as well as talented ladies in Country music. Her life was graphically described in her frank bestselling autobiography, *Sunshine and Shadow*. She has suffered personal tragedy that included the death of her eldest son, Jimmy, in the Vietnam War and the suicide of her youngest son, David.

Born of an Irish father and Cherokee mother, Jan was married by the time she was 16, the mother of three by the time she was 21, and divorced at age 24. After her divorce, she became a waitress and then met and married Smitty Smith. She moved to Los Angeles in 1953 and after their divorce, met, through Wynn Stewart, who was dating a friend of hers, songwriter Harlan Howard. Just 30 days after meeting, they married.

After hearing Jan sing, Harlan got her to demo some of his songs. She came to the attention of Tex Ritter and Johnny Bond, who also used her in a demo situation. She recorded *Yankee Go Home* with Wynn Stewart for Challenge in 1959 as Jan Howard (Jan being short for January!). Jan, Harlan and family moved to Nashville in 1960, following the success of Harlan's *Heartaches by the Number*. Just before they actually moved, Jan went with Harlan to receive a BMI award for the song in

*The sunshine that is **Jan Howard***

Nashville. While there, she guested on the *Prince Albert Show* sector of the *Grand Ole Opry*, where she was introduced by Ray Price.

Her success with the Stewart duet led to Challenge recording a solo single, *The One You Slip Around With*. It entered the charts and rose to the Top 15. She followed up with another duet with Wynn Stewart, *Wrong Company*, which made the Top 30. That year, Jan was named "Most Promising Country/Western Vocalist" by the Juke Box Operators and *Billboard* magazine. The following year, *Cash Box* did the same.

Then further record success eluded her and, in 1962, her contract was sold to Capitol Records. This was not a happy time for her and only one single, *I Wish I Was a Single Girl Again*, made the charts, peaking in the Top 30. She had one self-titled album released in 1962 on the Wrangler label. Although her recording career was not setting the world alight, she was busy touring through booking agent Hubert Long. The turning point in her career came when she signed to Decca Records in late 1964, where she was produced by Owen Bradley.

She returned to the singles charts with the 1965 Top 30 hit, *What Makes a Man Wander?* which was somewhat appropriate considering her troubled marriage to Harlan. That year, Jan joined the Bill Anderson touring show and TV show.

The following year, Jan had a double-sided hit with Anderson, *I Know You're Married (But I Love You Still)* (Top 30)/*Time Out* (Top 50). She then had her first solo Top 5 single, *Evil on Your Mind*. She followed this with the Top 10 release *Bad Seed*. That same month (October), she had a No.1 hit with Anderson, *For Loving You*, which stayed at the top for 4 weeks. Although she would never again reach those heady heights as a solo, she continued to achieve a good level of success. In 1967, she had *Any Old Way You Do* (Top 40) and *Roll Over and Play Dead* (Top 30), and the following year, *Count Your Blessings, Woman* (Top 20) and *I Still Believe in Love* (Top 30).

In October, 1968, Jan's eldest son, Jimmy, was killed in Vietnam; Jan, who is psychic, dreamed of the tragic event. Just after Jimmy's death, Decca released her single *My Son*, which climbed to the Top 15. She became a member of the *Grand Ole Opry* on March 27, 1971. She continued with Decca until 1973, and racked up further hits. In 1969, there were *When We Tried* (Top 25) and the Top 20 *We Had All the Good Things Going*, as well as the Top 3 Anderson duet, *If It's All the Same to You*.

In 1970, Jan had *Rock Me Back to Little*

Rock (Top 30), a duet with Bill Anderson, *Someday We'll Be Together*, which reached the Top 5 (the song had been a No.1 for Diana Ross and the Supremes). Then the chart levels started tapering off, *The Soul You Never Had* only reaching the Top 70. She had two medium-sized hits in *Love Is Like a Spinning Wheel* (1971) and *Let Him Have It* (1972), which were split by the final chart duet with Anderson, *Dis-Satisfied*, which reached the Top 5 in 1971. Following the death of her youngest son, David, Jan contemplated leaving the business but financial considerations forced her to continue. She left Decca, as she knew that the label was supporting her, and at the same time, she stopped working with Bill Anderson. During 1974, she had a basement-level chart entry with *Seein' Is Believin'* on GRT. In 1975, she joined the *Johnny Cash Show*. Johnny and June Carter had been very supportive of Jan's early career and helped her tour with Johnny Horton and Archie Campbell. During 1977, Jan signed with Con Brio and had three mid- to low-level chart records, *I'll Hold You in My Heart (Till I Can Hold You in My Arms), Better Off Alone* and *To Love a Rolling Stone*. She left Cash in July 1979 and joined up with long-time friend Tammy Wynette to tour the States and U.K.

Although she didn't have any further record hits, Jan continued recording. In 1981, Pete Drake produced an album on her in the *Stars of the Grand Ole Opry* series, and in 1984 she released an album, ***Tainted Love***, on AVI. She recorded for Phonorama the album ***Life of a Country Girl Singer***, before turning up on MCA/Dot with the 1987 self-titled album.

That year, she produced her autobiography, *Sunshine and Shadow*, which became a best-seller. At the time, she also held a realtor's license, but has subsequently let that go. She still appears on the *Grand Ole Opry* and in 1990, Jan remarried.

RECOMMENDED ALBUMS:

"Sweethearts of Country Music" (Challenge)(1961) [With Wynn Stewart]
"Sweet and Sentimental" (Capitol)(1962)
"Jan Howard Sings Evil on Your Mind" (Decca)(1966)
"For Loving You" (Decca)(1968) [With Bill Anderson]
"Wynn Stewart & Jan Howard Sing Their Hits" (Starday)(1968)
"Rock Me Back to Little Rock" (Decca)(1970) [Re-released on MCA]
"Singing His Praise" (Decca)(1972) [With Bill Anderson]
"Stars of the Grand Ole Opry" (First Generation)(1981)
"Jan Howard" (MCA/Dot)(1987)

RAY WYLIE HUBBARD

(Singer, Songwriter, Guitar)

Given Name: **Ray Wylie Hubbard**
Date of Birth: **November 13, 1946**
Where Born: **Soper, Oklahoma**
Married: **Deann (div.)**
Children: **Cory**

When Jerry Jeff Walker recorded Ray Wylie Hubbard's song *Up Against the Wall, Redneck Mother*, he helped turn Hubbard into an underground hero.

Ray Wylie grew up in the small town of Soper until he was 9 and then the family moved to Oak Cliff near Dallas, Texas, where his father continued his career as a high school principal. Ray Wylie went to Adamson High School, the same high school as future stars Larry Gross, B.W. Stephenson, Steve Fromholz and Michael Martin Murphey. Hubbard learned to play guitar at school and got into a Folk group with Murphey. He played a coffee house called the Rubaiyat and visitors included Jerry Jeff Walker and Ramblin' Jack Elliott. At this time he was getting into the Kingston Trio and Woodie Guthrie material.

After graduating, he formed a three piece band, the Coachmen, with Wayne Kidd and Rick Fowler. After attending the University of Texas at Arlington, where he majored in English, and North Texas State University, they moved to Red River, New Mexico and for many years they played their own club, the Outpost. After the band split up, Ray set out on the coffee house circuit playing Houston, Austin and Dallas.

Ray next formed Texas Fever with Rick Fowler, Michael McGary and Bob Livingston and this band lasted for about a year, at which point Livingston left to join Michael Martin Murphey. Ray Wylie returned to Red River, where he and musician Terry Ware joined up with Jim Herpst and Clovis Roblain (also known as Dennis Meehan) and formed Ray Wylie Hubbard and the Cowboy Twinkies and they continued playing at the Outpost.

Once again, Jerry Jeff Walker crossed Hubbard's path. They became close friends and Walker sold him a 1938 Roy Smeck Stage Deluxe guitar complete with an angel painted on it. Walker's only condition of the sale was that Hubbard didn't sell what became known as "That Old Beat-up Guitar" to anyone else. Ray Wylie moved back to Dallas and was mainly writing and playing with Jerry Jeff. In 1973, Walker recorded *Up Against the Wall, Redneck Mother* on his ***Viva Terlingua*** album.

Ray's audiences were not good and he became disillusioned as his band's music was too Rock for Country and too Country for Rock. Ray decided to cut a demo album and he booked a studio in Austin. The album landed the band a deal with Atlantic, but nothing happened. And then in 1975, Warner Brothers signed the band. They left for Nashville and recorded ***Ray Wylie Hubbard & the Cowboy Twinkies***, which came out on Reprise. However, there was no market for Hubbard's type of music and the band fell apart.

In 1978, Hubbard recorded the ***Off the Wall*** album for Willie Nelson's Lone Star label. This contained his version of *Redneck Mother* as well as material from other writers such as Tony Joe White. The following year, Ray Wylie Hubbard picked up the Lost Gonzo Band, who had backed Jerry Jeff Walker, as his backing band and they became the Ray Wylie Hubbard Band. This comprised John Inmon on guitar, Bob Livingston on bass guitar and Paul Pearcy on drums.

The next album recorded was a live affair, ***Caught in the Act***, which was recorded at Soap Creek Saloon in Texas and released on Waterloo Records. He followed this with ***Something About the Night*** for Renegade Records, and this album featured Jerry Jeff Walker. In 1984, Ray acquired a new backing group in the Bugs Henderson Trio (also known as Bugs Henderson and the Stratocasters). The group featured Henderson on guitar, Bobby Chitwood on bass guitar and Ron Thompson on drums.

Hubbard made the news in 1987, when his $2,000 1954 Martin guitar was stolen from a pawn shop in Dallas, where it had been temporarily residing. Ray released his first album in 8 years in 1992, ***Lost Train of Thought***. This album, released on the Misery Loves Company label, was described as what film director Martin Scorsese might sound like if he turned to Country-Rock.

Ray Wylie is a great supporter of charities. He held a concert at Cedar Creek and donated the proceedings to the Vietnam Veterans and then he started a Birthday Bash at the Bronco Bowland. Recipients of his generosity have included the Clown Ministry, an organization that provides clowns to terminally ill children. Quite a guy is Ray Wylie Hubbard!

RECOMMENDED ALBUMS:

"Ray Wylie Hubbard and the Cowboy Twinkies" (Reprise)(1975)
"Off the Wall" (Lone Star)(1978)
"Caught In the Act" (Waterloo)
"Something About the Night" (Renegade)
"Lost Train of Thought" (Misery Loves Company)(1992)

GEORGE HUG

(Singer, Songwriter, Guitar)

Given Name: **George Hug**
Date of Birth: **October 27, 1952**
Where Born: **Weesen, Switzerland**

George Hug became hooked on Country music listening to the radio, at a young age, and he remains a traditional Country artist perpetuating the Old West image of ranches and cattle drives. He also has a taste for Cajun and Tex-Mex music. George sums up the problems of a European act playing Country music in his song *Old Continent*: "The Swiss hillbilly in old Switzerland, hope there's a future for a Country band. Here Country music is rather rare. Can gold be made in our mountain air?"

George formed his band, Steak and Beans, in 1981 with his brother Pepi, who plays bass and does back-up vocals. By 1987, the band became a six-piece with Nik Ronner on drums, Roland Jud on steel guitar and lead guitar, Martin Gugger on fiddle and Marc Welti on piano.

That year, George signed with K-Tel International (Switzerland) and recorded his debut album, ***Go to Nashville***, which was produced by Swiss Country star John Brack. John and Austrian Country singer Jeff Turner guested on the album. Five of the songs on the album were co-written by George.

The following year, George went to Nashville and recorded ***Back from Nashville*** at Hilltop Recording Studio and used session players Sonny Garrish (steel guitar, Dobro), Willie Rainsford (piano), Sandy Posey and Bobby Harden (backup vocals). George was featured in *Cash Box*'s "Rising Stars" column and appeared on the *Grand Ole Opry*, *Nashville Now* and *Midnight Jamboree*. George has the distinction of being the first Swiss Country singer to have his records released in the U.S., when Ace-Hi Records picked up his albums.

George appeared at the Wembley Festival in 1988 and received such a good reception that he was invited back the following year, when he received a standing ovation. At a competition held by the Country Music Federation of Switzerland, George and his band were chosen by the public to represent Switzerland at the Euro Country Music Masters in Holland with 10 times more votes than the second place act. Two of George's songs, *Friendship* and *If I Ever Need a Lady*, did well. The band placed 6th in the overall ratings, but George was awarded 1st place in the "Singing Songwriter" category.

Swiss Country star ***George Hug***

In 1989, George released ***George Hug with Friends***, which was again recorded in Nashville. He followed this with a duet album with Ursula Hotz, ***In Love*** (1990), and ***10 Years*** (1991). In 1992, George issued his first compilation, ***Best of George Hug***, which was released on Rising AG.

George with his winning smile is one of the most likable characters in Country music and he is especially popular in Germany.

RECOMMENDED ALBUMS:

(All Swiss releases; released in U.S. on Ace-Hi)
"Go to Nashville" (K-Tel International)(Switzerland)(1987)
"Back from Nashville" (K-Tel International) (Switzerland)(1988)
"George Hug and Friends" (K-Tel International) (Switzerland)(1989)
"In Love" (K-Tel International)(Switzerland)(1990) [With Ursula Hotz]
"10 Years" (K-Tel International)(Switzerland)(1991)
"Best of George Hug" (Rising AG)(1992)

CON HUNLEY

(Singer, Songwriter, Piano)
Given Name: **Conrad Logan Hunley**
Date of Birth: **April 9, 1945**
Where Born: **Fountain City, Tennessee**

Con Hunley considers himself a balladeer, describes his voice as "Country with a little gray around the edges, Country with Soul." He has earned his own place in the arena of Country music.

Con was raised near the foothills of the Smoky Mountains in East Tennessee, the oldest of a family of six children—four boys and two girls. He grew up in a religious environment and his earliest musical training was singing Gospel music in church. His family made their living farming, and his father, Kenneth, worked as a textile worker, as well. His mother, Clodell, was the daughter of a Church of God preacher.

Con's first idol was Chet Atkins, but he soon realized his own limitations on guitar and switched to piano. He taught himself to play by ear on a piano bought for his sister, and soon learned the Ray Charles hit *What'd I Say*. It is Ray Charles whom he credits with influencing his career and style the most. "That record was like a monster that just gobbled me up," Con said, and it kept alive his motivation to play.

He soon began to study the techniques of Charlie Rich and Jerry Lee Lewis, as well as Ray Charles, and he began playing in local groups while still in high school. 1963 found Hunley working as a bundle boy at a mill in Knoxville, but the same year marked his professional debut playing in a local nightspot, the Eagles Club, for $12.00 a night. At one point Hunley played in a band with his two brothers, Tim and Kenny, calling themselves "the Hunley Brothers Band." Their performances featured acoustic sets, middle-of-the-road Rock, and Top 40 material.

In 1965, Con began a four year stint in the Air Force, teaching aircraft maintenance. He continued to play music, however, and sat in with local musicians wherever he could. After being discharged in 1969 he accepted a job singing at a lounge in Los Angeles, but soon returned to Knoxville, where he went back to work at Standard Knitting Mills, as well as singing at the Corner Lounge. Around this time he also took up golf as a hobby, which would later play a role in his first major label record contract.

Con's first singles were released in 1977 on Prairie Dust Records, a label founded by Sam Kirkpatrick, a Knoxville stockbroker. Kirkpatrick spotted Hunley, who was by then a top draw locally, at the Village Barn, and wanted to do something with him. Con became the label's first recording artist. Kirkpatrick took Con to Nashville and arranged for Larry Morton (guitarist with Danny Davis) to produce a session. Five singles were released, and Con briefly entered the Country chart with *Pick Up the Pieces* at the beginning of 1977, but the fourth one, *I'll Always Remember That Song*, written by Charlie Daniels, became a Top 75 hit. He followed this with the Top 70

Singer/Pianist ***Con Hunley***

single *Breaking Up Is Hard to Do* in the summer of 1977.

In the meantime, Con was turned down by RCA, but it was at the Acuff-Rose Golf Tournament in Nashville that a Warner Brothers executive met Con and, following a showcase, offered him a deal, and a four album association followed.

Con's first Warner Brothers single, *Cry Cry Darling*, went Top 40 in 1978. Then, in the spring of that year, Con, at last, came good, when *Week-End Friend* reached the Top 15 and it was followed by *You've Still Got a Place in My Heart*. In 1979, all three of Con's singles went Top 20: *I've Been Waiting for You All of My Life*, *Since I Fell for You* and *I Don't Want to Lose You*.

The following year, Con started off with back-to-back Top 20 singles, *You Lay a Whole Lot of Love on Me* and *They Never Lost You*. Then he released what was to become his biggest hit, *What's New with You*, which reached just below the Top 10 in 1981. He ended 1981 with *She's Steppin' Out*, which peaked in the Top 20. He opened his account in 1982 with *Oh Girl*, which became his second biggest hit. The song was an old Chi-Lites hit recommended by songwriter/arranger Steve Dorff, who also produced Con's album of the same name. With Dorff's guidance the album turned out to be the perfect vehicle for the R & B edge Con was noted for, but in keeping with his Country roots, backup singers on the album included the Oak Ridge Boys, with whom Con had toured.

In 1982, Con moved over to MCA and in 1983 released the album ***Once You Get the Feel for It,*** which was previewed by its title single, his second collaboration with Dorff, but it only went Top 50. *Satisfied Mind,* another single on the album, was released in the same year, and featured Porter Wagoner, but only reached the lower rungs of the chart. Con returned to Prairie Dust for one Top 75 single, *Deep in the Arms of Texas*.

In 1984 music executive Jim Fogelsong took Hunley to Capitol Records, but failed to get Con back to the higher rungs of the charts and, although he was produced by Kyle Lehning, Con's highest placed single was *What Am I Gonna Do About You*,which went Top 50.

Con has been nominated 5 times as CMA "Vocalist of the Year." In 1979, Hunley played at the wedding of President Carter's daughter, Amy. During the same year, he sang before the WBA Heavyweight Championship fight in Pretoria, South Africa, between Knoxville based fighter John Tate and South African champ Gerry Coetzee. In 1986, Hunley performed with the Knoxville Symphony Orchestra accompanied by a 70-piece orchestra and his 5-piece band, a Knoxville first.

Hunley currently resides in Knoxville, where he has organized charity golf tournaments. He likes to unwind by restoring antique cars. The mill worker's son whose voice has charted fresh musical groundwork has traveled a long way but still carries Smoky Mountain soul every time he performs. LAS

RECOMMENDED ALBUMS:

"Con Hunley" (Warner Brothers)(1979)
"I Don't Want to Lose You" (Warner Brothers)(1980)
"Don't It Break Your Heart" (Warner Brothers)(1980)
"Oh Girl" (Warner Brothers)(1982)
"Once You Get the Feel for It" (MCA)(1983)

Canadian star ***Tommy Hunter***

TOMMY HUNTER

(Singer, Songwriter, Guitar, Fiddle)

Given Name:	**Thomas James Hunter**
Date of Birth:	**March 20, 1937**
Where Born:	**London, Ontario, Canada**
Married:	**Shirley**
Children:	**Jeffrey, Gregory, Mark**

For 27 years, Tommy Hunter hosted the *Tommy Hunter Show* on CBC in Canada, which became the longest running network Country music show in the world.

Tommy became interested in Country music at age 9 when Roy Acuff and his Smoky Mountain Boys appeared in London, Ontario. By the time he was age 12, Tommy had made his professional appearance at a theater in Woodstock, Pennsylvania, and started to play guitar at local dances when he was 14. He made his radio debut in 1952 on CBC radio.

He left home when he was 16 and played in a variety of honky tonks in Canada and the U.S. In 1956, Tommy appeared with the Sons of the West and they auditioned for a new CBC-TV show called *Country Hoedown*. The show ran until 1965 with Tommy as a featured singer. He also hosted a daily noontime network radio show, the *Tommy Hunter Show,* and this led to his 1962 TV show. In 1958, Tommy appeared for 8 weeks on *Arthur Godfrey's Talent Scouts* on CBS.

In 1965, Tommy made his debut on the *Grand Ole Opry*, where he was introduced by Stoney & Wilma Lee Cooper. The *Tommy Hunter Show* (TV version) was also syndicated on TNN from 1983 to 1989.

Tommy started his recording career in 1956 for RCA Victor, but although he has put out many albums, he still does not consider recording as his most important area of achievement. The other labels he has recorded for are Capitol (1962), Columbia (1964-1970), Columbia Canada (1970-1972), RCA (1972-1990) and his own Edith label (1990 to date).

During his long career, Tommy has been the recipient of numerous awards. In 1985, Tommy received the C.F. Martin Award from the CCMA. In 1986 he received Canada's highest honor to a civilian, the Order of Canada. In 1987, Tommy was made a Citizen of Tennessee and also a Kentucky Colonel.

The *Tommy Hunter Show* ended in 1989 and Tommy continues to perform with his group, the Travlin Men, and record. In 1990, Tommy's name was added to the Walkway of the Stars in Nashville. Tommy's autobiography, *My Story*, was published in 1985. Although Tommy only writes songs occasionally, his principal copyrights are *Stampede (*which appeared in the movie *Golden Rod*), *Canada—No Place Like Home* and *Tommy Hunter Breakdown*. Tommy Hunter and his wife, Shirley, reside in Penetanguishene, Ontario (summer) and Stuart, Florida (winter).

RECOMMENDED ALBUMS:

"Anniversary Sessions" (RCA)
"Tommy Hunter Readings" (Edith Canada)
"Songs of Inspiration" (Edith Canada)
"Tommy Hunter Sings for You" (Edith Canada)

FERLIN HUSKY

(Singer, Songwriter, Guitar, Bass, Actor, Comedy)

Date of Birth:	**December 3, 1927**
Where Born:	**Hickory Grove, Flat River, Missouri**
Married:	**1. Marvis Thompson (div.)** **2. Betty (div.)** **3. (Div.)** **4. (Div.)** **5. Eileen Patricia McGladery (m. 1964) (div. 1965)** **6. Marvis**
Children:	**David, Kelly, Terry Preston, Donna, Dana, Denise, Danny (dec'd.)**

Ferlin Husky went through several name changes until he settled upon his own name. He also lighted up "Simon Crum," his comedy alter ago. For over 20 years, Ferlin's name was on the Country charts, and he still continues to entertain into the 90's.

He was raised on a farm, 75 miles outside of St. Louis. His father tried to trade a chicken for a guitar, but the hen failed to lay and the guitar had to go back. However, Ferlin did learn to play and he started singing at church and entered amateur contests. During WWII, he was in the U.S. Merchant Marine with the army transport and ended up at the invasion of France on D-Day. While on board ship, he entertained the troops. He also received a citation as "Volunteer Gunner." He left the service in 1947, and began playing honky-tonks in St. Louis and worked as a deejay in Bakersfield. He played bass with Big Jim De Noone and a fiddler named Fred McMurray and when, after getting a record deal with 4 Star Records, they decided to move to Salinas, California, Ferlin went with them.

It was there that Ferlin met up with Smiley Burnette and Gene Autry. Burnette hired Ferlin to open the show for him on tour. Initially Smiley had a full group, but after a while, he let them go and continued with Ferlin on guitar. Ferlin appeared with Burnette on KXLW St. Louis for a year-and-a-half.

With Big Jim De Noone and the Melody Rangers, Ferlin released five instrumental singles on 4 Star in 1949. At the same time, Ferlin, as "Terry Preston" released his first solo single on the same label, *Remembrance of Franklin D/Ozark Waltz*. Initially, Ferlin called himself "Tex Terry" but after finding out that there was an actor in the movies with the same name (he did a bullwhip act), he changed it to "Terry Preston." It was Burnette's suggestion, that the name "Terry Preston" be used. As well as recording sides with Big Bill, Ferlin had another eight singles released on 4 Star, stretching into 1951.

That year, he signed to Capitol Records, thanks to the assistance of Cliffie Stone, who was then Tennessee Ernie Ford's manager. Ferlin had replaced Ford on Stone's *Hometown Jamboree* when Ford returned to the *Grand Ole Opry*. Although his initial single, *China Doll/Tennessee Central #9,* was put out by "Ferlin Husky," all subsequent singles bore the name "Terry Preston." One of these was *Gone*, which was written by Smokey Rogers. Rogers was so convinced that the song should be a hit, that he didn't write another song until it was a hit in 1957. In 1953, following the death of Hank Williams, Ferlin, who also did impersonations of Hank and other Country performers, was asked to release a tribute single to Hank. He and Tommy Collins wrote *Hank's Song*, and as he was starting to get a following as "Terry Preston," it was decided to use the name "Ferlin Husky." Although the record was not a chart single, it did garner a lot of interest. As a result, he became Ferlin Husky.

By any other name, it's ***Ferlin Husky***

Ferlin had his first chart hit in 1953, when he teamed up with Jean Shepard (as Ferlin Huskey) on the No.1 record *Dear John Letter*. The single stayed at No.1 for 6 weeks, was on the charts for over 5 months and crossed-over to peak in the Top 5 on the Pop chart. The duo followed this up in 1953 with *Forgive Me John*, which, although not quite as successful, reached the Top 5 Country and Top 25 Pop.

Ferlin had to wait until 1955 before he had his next hit and this time he came up with the double-sided smash *I Feel Better All Over (More Than Anywhere's Else)/Little Tom*, both of which made the Top 10. He followed this up with a hit from his alter ego, "Simon Crum." Simon is a comic philosopher, the epitome of the Country bumpkin. In that guise, Ferlin struck pay dirt with the 1955 single *Cuzz You're So Sweet*, which reached the Top 5. His final hit of the year was *I'll Baby Sit with You*. This represented the last time that he spelled his name "Huskey." During this time, Ferlin instituted his talent contests, one of the winners of which was songwriter/singer Dallas Frazier.

Ferlin didn't have another hit until early 1957, when he released a re-recorded version of *Gone* and took it to No.1. It stayed in that position for 10 weeks out of over six months on the chart. In addition, it crossed-over to the Top 5 in the Pop list. He followed this up with *A Fallen Star,* which made the Top 10; the flip-side, *I Will*, made the Top 25.

In 1957, Ferlin appeared on the *Kraft Television Theatre* show playing a dramatic role. He was also CBS' choice for Arthur Godfrey's TV and radio show. He also made his movie debut in *Mr. Rock and Roll*, for Paramount. He followed this up the next year with *Country Music Holiday* with Zsa Zsa Gabor and Faron Young. That year, he had a major "Simon Crum" hit with *Country Music Is Here to Stay*, which reached the Top 3 in 1959.

The Husky career has been marked by hills and troughs as regards chart records. In all, including the "Simon Crum" singles, he has 51 entries, although only 22 have been in the Top 20, of which 11 have been Top 10 hits. This may in part have been due to Ferlin's diversity of talents. Most "entertainers" in Country music have suffered with the same situation. However, Ferlin with his band, the Hush Puppies, has been a tireless tourer.

In 1959, Ferlin charted with *My Reason for Living* and *Draggin' the River* (both Top 15) and *Black Sheep* (Top 25). He had his next major hit in 1960, with a song that will always be associated with him, *Wings of a Dove*. The single was at No.1 for 10 weeks of a remarkable 36 weeks on the chart. In addition, it crossed over to the Top 15 on the Pop list. Throughout most of the 60's, Ferlin had medium to minor hits, the most successful being *Willow Tree* (Top 25, 1961), *The Waltz You Saved for Me* (Top 15), *Somebody Save Me* (Top 20), *Stand Up* (Top 30) and *It Was You* (Top 25 all 1962), *Timber I'm Falling* (Top 15, 1964), *I Could Sing All Night* (Top 30) and *I Hear a Little Rock Calling* (Top 20, both 1966).

Then in 1967, Ferlin hit the Top 5 with *Once* and followed with the Simon Crum release *You Pushed Me Too Far*, which went Top 15. The following year, Ferlin was again in the Top 5 with *Just for You*. This would be his last major hit, and his only important successes between 1967 and 1972, when he left Capitol, were *That's Why I Love You So Much* (Top 20, 1969), *Heavenly Sunshine* and *Sweet Misery* (both Top 15, 1970).

Ferlin made two more movies, both with funny man Don Bowman. They were *Las Vegas Hillbillies* (Warner Brothers, 1966) with Jayne Mansfield and *Hillbillies in a Haunted House* (Warner Brothers, 1967) with Basil Rathbone. He would go on to make another 14 movies (see Movie Section).

During 1970, Ferlin's life took a tumble when his 17-year old son Danny, who had been his drummer, was killed in an auto crash. In 1973, Ferlin signed with ABC Records, but was unable to relight the chart success that he had known. Between 1973 and 1975, his only significant hits were *Rosie Cries a Lot*

(Top 20, 1973), *Freckles and Polliwog Days* (1974), *Champagne Ladies and Blue Ribbon Babies* (Top 30, 1974) and *Burning* (Top 40, 1975). He then went on to Cachet Records, but the label folded. He made one self-titled album for the equally short-lived Audiograph Live in 1982. Then in 1984, Ferlin signed to MCA and released a video of *Truck Drivin' Son of a Gun*.

In 1977, Ferlin had to undergo heart by-pass surgery. Around 1984, he started work on his Wings of a Dove Museum in Hendersonville, Tennessee, which was later incorporated as part of Twitty City. At that time, he was hospitalized with further heart problems. During 1988, Ferlin turned toward inspirational music, having given up drinking. In 1989, he created the Ferlin Husky Jubilee and Wings of a Dove Museum at Grand Strand, Myrtle Beach, South Carolina, but the venture was a financial disaster and by April 1990 the project was wrapped up, among a lot of acrimony. At the end of the year, Ferlin underwent a triple by-pass operation but returned to playing at the *Opry*. He still performs and in 1993, appeared at Christy Lane's Theater in Branson, Missouri.

Ferlin's achievements during his long career are interesting. He was the first performer on the *Grand Ole Opry* to be accompanied by drums and the first to use a modern vocal backing group. He was the first Country performer to be awarded a "star" on Hollywood Boulevard. He is a member of the Fraternal Order of Police and the National Sheriffs Association.

RECOMMENDED ALBUMS:

"Walkin' and Hummin'" (Capitol)(1961) [Re-released by Stetson UK in original sleeve (1987)]
"Songs of the Home & the Heart" (Capitol)(1956) [Re-released by Stetson UK in original sleeve (1990)]
"Ferlin's Favorites" (Capitol)(1960)
"The Hits of Ferlin Husky" (Capitol)(1975)
"The Foster and Rice Songbook" (ABC)(1975) [An album of songs written by Jerry Foster & Bill Rice]

FRANK HUTCHISON

(Guitar, Slide Guitar, Harmonica)

Date of Birth: March 20, 1897
Where Born: Raleigh County, West Virginia
Married: Minnie Garrett
Children: two daughters
Date of Death: November 9, 1945

Known as "the Pride of West Virginia," Frank Hutchison was born in the mountains of Raleigh County, but moved to Logan County with his family in early childhood.

By the time he reached age 8, he could play harmonica and became infatuated with the guitar after hearing one played by a black railroad worker. His later guitar stylings displayed a considerable black Blues influence. In 1917, he married and he and his wife, Minnie, subsequently reared a pair of daughters. Sometimes, Frank worked in the coal mines of Logan County or at other labor above ground.

For a decade from the mid-20's, Hutchison earned his living as a musician and also showed motion pictures in small theaters and schools through western and eastern Kentucky. Between October 1926 and July 1929, Frank made some 32 recordings for the OKeh label and also appeared on an additional six sides in their Medicine Show series of skits. On his last session, he was accompanied by a Logan County fiddler named Sherman Lawson (b. 1894). Frank's recordings display his Blues influenced guitar stylings, some of which made use of a pocket knife for fretting purposes.

Several of his songs have had a lasting influence, especially *Worried Blues*, *The Train that Carried My Girl from Town* and *Coney Isle*. The latter, which referred to an amusement park near Cincinnati, Ohio, was rewritten slightly as *Alabam* and became a top Country hit for Cowboy Copas in 1960.

As for many early Country musicians, the Great Depression curtailed Hutchison's performing career and ended his recording. In 1934, he moved briefly to Chesapeake, Ohio, and then to Lake, West Virginia, where he operated a grocery store. In April 1942, fire destroyed both his home and business. The Hutchisons then moved to Ohio, where Frank died from cancer of the liver, in Dayton, three and one-half years later. In 1974, an album containing 16 of his best recordings was issued, while others have appeared on anthologies released on County, Folkways and Old Homestead IMT

RECOMMENDED ALBUM:

"The Train that Carried My Girl from Town" (Rounder)(1974)

GUNILLA HUTTON

(Singer, Actress)

Given Name: Gunilla Birgitta Hutton
Date of Birth: May 15, 1946
Where Born: Goteborg, Sweden
Children: Amber (adopted)

Gunilla Hutton is best known to Country music fans for her longtime membership on the cast of the long running television show *Hee Haw*. While filling a variety of roles on the program, she is undoubtedly best remembered for the skits in which she took the part of "Doc" Archie Campbell's aide, "Nurse Goodbody." The beautiful, slender blonde had earlier worked for a season in the CBS comedy *Petticoat Junction* and has proven herself a capable Country vocalist.

Gunilla immigrated from Sweden to the U.S. at the age of 6, settling with her family in Fort Worth, Texas. She took the surname Hutton from her step-father, William F. Hutton. After graduating from Arlington Heights High School, the Swedish-Danish young woman went to the University of California at Los Angeles for two years, where she studied singing and dancing. This resulted in jobs in Las Vegas shows with both Nat "King" Cole and Jack Benny. Producer Paul Henning spotted her there and suggested that she try out for the part of "Billie Jo Bradley" on *Petticoat Junction*, as a replacement for the departing Jeannine Riley, which she did. Later, she had a part in a stage version of *That Certain Girl*. In 1969, Gunilla learned about the possibility of a part in the new CBS Country music-comedy-variety show, *Hee Haw*, from her agent. Having been attracted to Country sounds from her growing-up days in Fort Worth, she felt delighted to get the position, beginning that December.

On *Hee Haw*, Gunilla not only perfected the "Nurse Goodbody" role, but did parts in numerous other skits and sang two or three times each season as well. Her single recordings appeared on such labels as Dial and Dot, where her recording of *You're Gonna Get Loved* received considerable airplay. From time to time, Gunilla guested on a variety of TV shows and made personal appearances as a vocalist in clubs and at fairs. Her connections with *Hee Haw* extended over a period of 22 years and the 5'6", 113 pound "sunshine blonde" ranked among the show's most popular regulars. Long-time fans of the program, as well as Gunilla and several other cast members, experienced considerable shock when they were suddenly dropped from the cast in September, 1991. IMT

Nurse Goodbody, aka ***Gunilla Hutton***

I

FRANK IFIELD

(Singer, Songwriter, Guitar, Yodeler, Actor)
Date of Birth: **November 30, 1937**
Where Born: **Coventry, England**
Married: **Gillian**

Frank Ifield is often thought of as the Australian who came to England and became a star. In fact, he was born in England, and was early on exposed to Country music via the radio in Coventry. His parents were Australian and his father was an engineer-inventor who created the Ifield pump which is used in the fuel systems of jet planes.

In 1948, the family moved to Dural in New South Wales, Australia. It was here that Frank was further exposed to Country music and soon was an adept yodeler. Soon after, his grandmother bought him a ukulele (she meant to buy a guitar!).

In 1950, they moved to Beecroft and Frank began to hang round the Tim McNamara Shows, when they started in 1951. Frank appeared on *Australia's Amateur Hour* and on hearing that one of the artists had not turned up for the *Hornsby McNamara Show*, the 15-year old Frank went backstage and asked Tim for the gig. He was given a short audition and appeared on the show, impressing audience and performers alike with his ability.

Shortly after, Frank left school and never worked at anything but being a performer. He became a regular member of *Bonnington's Bunkhouse* radio show before leaving school and he soon augmented this with other radio work. He joined the Ted Quigg Show circuit and was associated with Quigg even after he had become a star.

In August 1953, Frank signed with EMI Australia and his first singles, *Did You See My Daddy Over There* and *There's a Loveknot in My Lariat*, were highly successful. He appeared on the weekly radio shows *Sundown Sing Song* and *The Youth Parade*. When TV came to Sydney in 1956, Frank was the second singer and the first Country performer to appear on the screen (on the second night). He soon had his own weekly TV show, *Campfire Favourites*, which ran for over a year. By 1959, he was appearing on all three Sydney channels.

At the end of that year, Frank left on the inaugural flight from Australia to London. He gave himself four months to make it in the U.K. By 1960, he had gotten a modest hit with *Lucky Devil* on EMI's Columbia label and decided to stay in the U.K. However, it was in 1962 that Frank emerged as a major international star. His recording of *I Remember You* was a yodeling stunner. The song was originally a hit for Jimmy Dorsey in 1942. It hit the No.1 spot on the U.K. charts and stayed in that spot for 7 weeks out of 28 weeks on the charts. In the U.S., it was released on the Vee-Jay label, and reached the Top 5 on the Pop charts. He followed this with a remake of Hank Williams' hit *Lovesick Blues*, which stayed at No.1 in the U.K. for 5 weeks. This also got into the U.S. Pop charts, and peaked in the Top 50, also on Vee-Jay.

If 1962 was good, 1963 was better. He started off the year with another reworking; this time *The Wayward Wind*. This made it the third No.1 in a row in the U.K. The next single was another Country classic, *Nobody's Darlin' But Mine*, which rose to No.4. He then weighed in with another No.1, *Confessin'*. The song had been a hit for both Guy Lombardo and Rudy Vallee in 1930 and provided Frank with his third U.S. Pop hit, reaching the Top 60 on Capitol. He wrapped up the year with a low level success, *Mule Train*. In the U.S., he reached the Pop charts with the low level single on Capitol *Please*, which had been a No.1 for Bing Crosby in 1932. In 1964, Frank had his final Top 10 hit in the U.K. with the old big band hit *Don't Blame Me*. From here on until 1966, the steam went out of his recording career and all of his chart entries only got as far as the Top 30.

In 1966, his career in Britain was waning, so he started to get in the Country charts in the U.S. Frank came to Nashville in 1966 and was made an Honorary Tennessean by Governor Frank Clement. While in Nashville, he recorded the album ***Frank Ifield's Tale of Two Cities*** for Hickory Records, where he was produced by Wesley Rose. In addition, Frank appeared to rapturous applause on the *Grand Ole Opry*.

From 1966 through 1968, he charted four times on Hickory, with *No One Will Ever Know* (Top 50) and *Call Her Your Sweetheart* (Top 30) (both 1966), *Oh, Such a Stranger* (Top 70, 1967) and *Good Morning Dear* (Top 70, 1968).

During the 70's, Frank became extremely popular in Europe, in particular the Benelux countries (Belgium, Holland and Luxembourg), where he had hits with *Joanne*, *California Cotton Fields* and *Silver Wings*. In 1979, he signed to Warner Brothers, where he was again produced by the legendary Wesley Rose. However, despite those credentials, a single, *Crystal,* written by Dennis Morgan and Bobby Barker, coupled with Eddy Raven's *Touch the Morning,* failed to ignite the charts.

Frank continues to appear at Country music festivals and in cabaret and has even appeared in pantomime in the U.K. He remains one of the finest original talents to emerge out of non-North American territories.

RECOMMENDED ALBUMS:
"I'll Remember You" (Columbia UK)(1962)
"The Best of Frank Ifield" (Columbia UK)(1966) [Released in the U.S. on Hickory]
"Frank Ifield's Tale of Two Cities" (Hickory)(1966)
"Portrait of Frank Ifield" (PRT UK)(1983)

AUTRY INMAN

(Singer, Songwriter, Guitar, String Bass, Comedy)
Given Name: **Robert Autry Inman**
Date of Birth: **January 6, 1929**
Where Born: **Florence, Alabama**
Married: **Mary Nell**
Children: **Terry Ray, Mark Westley, Mary Angelic, Brenda Lynn**
Date of Death: **September 6, 1988**

When Decca signed Autry Inman to its roster in February, 1952, it looked like a major star was entering the firmament, however his chart placings never kept abreast of his actual popularity.

Inman started to play guitar at age 5. By the age of 12, he had formed his first band, the Alabama Blue Boys. He made his radio debut on station WLAY Muscle Shoals. However, he was not earning enough to keep him in music full-time, and so he took a job in a cotton mill. At this time, he was also working at WJOI and WMFT. Shortly afterward, he took on another job as court reporter in the Law & Equity Court in Atlanta.

He started appearing on WWVA *Wheeling Jamboree* and this led to him being asked onto the *Grand Ole Opry* in 1947. In 1949 and 1950, he was the bass player in Cowboy Copas' Oklahoma Cowboys and then he joined George Morgan's Candy Kids, where he stayed until 1952. At this point, he signed to Decca and his first single, *Let's Take the Long Way Home*, although it didn't chart, garnered a lot of attention. The following year, he was the darling of the jukeboxes, when *That's All Right* zoomed into the Top 5. However, although he continued to release singles through to 1955 with Decca, none of them made any major impact.

In 1958, he surfaced on RCA Victor with one single, *Mary Nell/The Hard Way*, that also failed to ignite the charts. He moved on to United Artists in 1960 and released *Farther to Go Than I've Been/That's All Right* but that went the way of its predecessor. The following year, he released the live album ***Autry Inman at the Frontier Club*** on his own Lakeside Records. He moved to Mercury in 1962 with the solitary single *I Guess I'm Crazy/Living with One and Loving Two*. Autry returned to the Top 25 with his Sims single *The Volunteer*, but again, although he released further singles into 1964, he was unable to capitalize on them.

During 1964, Inman released two "risqué" live albums on Jubilee, ***Riscoteque—Saturday Night*** and ***Riscoteque Adult Comedy, Volume 2 (New Year's Eve with Autry Inman)*** and a pair of singles. In 1968, he signed to Epic and once more returned to the charts with the cross-over hit *Ballad of Two Brothers*, which

From court reporter to star, ***Autry Inman***

reached the Top 15 on the Country charts and also climbed into the Top 50 of the Pop chart. This was his third single for the label and was to be his last. Various albums have been released by Autry Inman on Alshire and Guest Star, including **Country Gospel** on the latter label. In addition, Autry appeared in two movies, *A Face in the Crowd* for United Artists and *Music City USA* for Gemini.

RECOMMENDED ALBUMS:

"Autry Inman at the Frontier Club" (Lakeside)(1961) [Re-released on Sims in 1964]
"Ballad of Two Brothers" (Epic)(1968)
"12 Country Hits from Autry Inman" (Alshire)(1969)
"Country Gospel" (Guest Star)

INTERNATIONAL BLUEGRASS MUSIC ASSOCIATION

The International Bluegrass Music Association (IBMA), headquartered in Owensboro, Kentucky, since March of 1986, has grown with a speed virtually unparalleled by any music industry group. In the eight years since the first exploratory meeting leading to its creation, IBMA has grown to include some 2,000 members in forty-nine U.S. states and twenty-seven foreign countries on five continents. More than 14,000 people go to Owensboro each September for the annual IBMA "World of Bluegrass" Trade Show and Fan Fest and its International Bluegrass Music Awards, which air live to a worldwide radio audience. In 1995, the International Bluegrass Music Museum will open on a permanent basis as a joint project of IBMA and Owensboro's RiverPark Center arts complex. The success of IBMA results from a remarkable marriage of a community, a music, and a non-profit trade organization.

IBMA grew out of a meeting of two dozen industry representatives called together at Nashville's BMI building in June of 1985 by talent representative Lance LeRoy. The group agreed to proceed with the careful establishment of an organization to promote the Bluegrass industry and unity within it. A second small meeting two months later produced a set of by-laws and a temporary Board of Directors, chaired by Peter V. Kuykendall of *Bluegrass Unlimited* magazine. Other original directors included Sugar Hill Records' President Barry Poss, artists Doyle Lawson, Sonny Osborne and Allen Mills, and Larry Jones of the Minnesota Bluegrass & Old Time Music Association. Composer Randall Hylton and author Art Menius assumed the positions of Treasurer and Secretary respectively. This body organized the first public IBMA meeting at Nashville's Vanderbilt University on October 16, 1985. There fifty-seven people and organizations contributed $100 each to become founding members of the new society.

A few weeks later, the board hired Art Menius as its acting Executive Director on a part-time basis, which became a full-time position the following August, with him serving as IBMA's chief staff person through March 1990. In December 1985 he produced the first edition of IBMA's bimonthly newsletter, *International Bluegrass*.

At the same time as the formation of IBMA, the Owensboro-Daviess County Tourist Commission, under the leadership of then-Chair Terry Woodward of WaxWorks, developed a bold plan to capitalize on Kentucky's Bluegrass heritage. The Tourist Commission produced a free Bluegrass festival, Bluegrass with Class, at English Park in 1985, featuring the Osborne Brothers with the Owensboro Symphony. Woodward envisioned the creation of a Bluegrass organization, industry trade show, and a museum before he learned of IBMA through Barry Poss. Shortly after discussions and presentations to the newly formed IBMA Board, Woodward, Menius, and Tourist Commission Executive Director Burley Phelan announced IBMA would establish its worldwide headquarters in Owensboro in March of 1986. The Commission extended a $20,000 start-up grant to the new Bluegrass trade group, in addition to extensive administrative support services. In conjunction with the Tourist Commission's Bluegrass with Class festival, IBMA presented its first trade show with 36 exhibits at English Park that August.

Fueled by the Tourist Commission's support, IBMA grew rapidly. *International Bluegrass* soon grew to a sixteen page trade publication. The IBMA "World of Bluegrass" Trade Show, with 250 attendees, adopted its current format in September 1987, while the Bluegrass Fan Fest merged with and ultimately replaced Bluegrass with Class. The Fan Fest became the primary fund-raiser for the Bluegrass Trust Fund, an independent agency created to assist Bluegrass professionals in times of dire need. (Since its creation, the Bluegrass Trust Fund has granted more than $30,000 of such assistance.)

With Woodward chairing the IBMA Board from 1986 through 1989, IBMA's staff expanded while the movement to create the International Bluegrass Music Museum gained momentum. The museum became a chief component and catalyst in the development of RiverPark Center, a dynamic $16 million performing arts complex on the riverfront in downtown Owensboro.

Rodney Berry became IBMA's second employee in 1987, serving as both IBMA's Executive Director for Projects and as RiverPark Center's Executive Director. The organizations also shared administrative support staff. Art Menius remained busy with IBMA aggressively expanding member services, which by 1988 included extensive computer database information on presenters, media contacts, broadcasting outlets, and organizations in Bluegrass, an event liability insurance plan, general consultation, and publicity and media relations services for the entire industry. IBMA also proved effective during this time in convincing NARAS to include Bluegrass as a category for its annual Grammy Awards program.

When Dan Hays assumed the position of Executive Director of IBMA in August of

1990, it marked a major point of maturation for the business league. With Milton Harkey elected as the new Chair of the Board of Directors, IBMA moved beyond the foundation building stage. IBMA presented its first International Bluegrass Music Awards Show, hosted by Vince Gill and John McEuen, that September, while Trade Show registration exceeded 800 attendees. Bluegrass Fan Fest developed into a major event and a place to see the superstars of yesterday, today, and tomorrow. In 1991, Hays pulled off the live radio syndication broadcast of the awards show and initiated several sponsorship relationships with major corporations for the industry and for IBMA's events. Also, during his first year as Executive Director, IBMA's membership grew by more than 50% to 1,800 artists, composers, agents, record companies, merchandisers, broadcasters, educators, journalists, talent buyers, fans, and member supported associations.

In September 1992, IBMA celebrated the completion of RiverPark Center's initial phase of construction by coordinating "Preview '92," the International Bluegrass Music Museum's opening exhibits. The critically acclaimed movie *High Lonesome*, produced by Rachel Leibling and Andrew Serwer, saw its premiere before the music industry during IBMA's annual events. RiverPark also offered IBMA the chance to enhance its awards show in the center's new 1500 seat theater and broadcast production facilities.

By 1993, the awards show was syndicated to more than 160 U.S. radio markets and around the world via the Voice of America, Armed Forces Radio, the BBC and several other international networks, thanks to sponsorship by Owensboro's world famous Moonlite Bar-B-Q Inn. Hays also coordinated a unique alliance between BMG Video, TNN and Bluegrass artists and record companies for the film production and television broadcast of *Gather at the River—A Bluegrass Celebration*, which focused attention on IBMA, its award-winning artists, and the unique alliance created by uniting the various facets of the Bluegrass family.

The annual "World of Bluegrass" Trade Show now boasts more than 1,500 attendees, 100 exhibitors, twenty-four artists' showcases, more than a dozen educational seminars, a golf tournament, and songwriter spotlights. IBMA has also initiated its second publication, *Bluegrass Signal*, focusing attention on Bluegrass in broadcasting, while RiverPark Center serves as the production facility for Americana Television's CableAce-nominated show, *Reno's Old Time Music Festival*. The finals of Pizza Hut's Bluegrass talent search, the Bluegrass Showdown, are also hosted in Owensboro just prior to IBMA's September events.

Under the new chairmanship of Mary Tyler Doub, IBMA has planned the Bluegrass industry's first major nationwide market research project during 1994 and 1995, expanding its international perspective with plans for wide-ranging programs and services and the addition of regional conferences to its busy agenda. Now operating on an annual budget in excess of a quarter of a million dollars, IBMA's future continues to be as bright as that of the music its members work feverishly to support.

JERRY IRBY

(Singer, Songwriter, Guitar)
Given Name: Jerry Irby
Date of Birth: 1917
Where Born: Pineland, Texas
Married: Betty
Children: Unknown

Jerry Irby made a mild impact on the Country scene in the late 40's. With his band the Texas Ranchers, he achieved considerable popularity and authored a Country standard with the Honky-Tonk hit *Driving Nails in My Coffin*.

A native of the piney woods section of East Texas, Jerry grew up in several towns in the region as his mother and stepfather moved with frequent shifts of oil boom activity. At 14, he sold "Grit" and the "San Antonio Light" (types of oil) to earn money to buy a guitar. Three years later, the aspiring youth moved to Houston and worked in a service station while hoping to land a musical job, but with little success.

He finally began singing in clubs for tips and gained some good experience. He journeyed to California for a while but Jerry ultimately returned to Houston, where he started a club. He ultimately joined an established Western Swing band, the Bar X Cowboys, and cut some records with them on both Decca and Bluebird. Around 1945, after five years, he went on his own and started the Texas Ranchers.

The Texas Ranchers worked regularly on Houston radio and at a club called the Texas Corral. Jerry introduced *Driving Nails in My Coffin* on a program at KTHT and later recorded it and other songs on the small Globe label. Ernest Tubb's cover on Decca became a national hit and its author landed his own contract on MGM in 1947. He cut several sides for them including *Roses Have Thorns*, *Cryin' in My Beer* and *Great Long Pistol*; the latter two reaching respectively the Country Top 15 and Top 10 in 1948.

In the 50's, Irby recorded for Mercury, Imperial, and 4 Star. He worked with Ted Daffan for a time in the early 50's and continued playing clubs in the Houston area except for a six month period when he went to Midland and starred on his own TV show. Back in Houston in the later 50's, Jerry cut some Rockabilly sides, a couple on Ted Daffan's Daffana label.

Jerry Irby dropped out of music for a decade, but in 1971, came back and opened Jerry's Country Club in San Leon, Texas, playing both there and a few club dates elsewhere. Then on July 8, 1973, both he and his wife had a conversion experience and thereafter the one-time Honky-Tonk vocalist turned to sacred music. He had three albums of Gospel songs—mostly of his own composition—in the mid-70's and a thrice-weekly TV program in Houston during 1977. After that, he went into full-time evangelical work in a twelve state area. As of 1988, he remained engaged in this endeavor.

The only material re-issued from his early days are two numbers by the Bar X Cowboys, plus one of his own, on Western Swing anthologies on MCA Japan, Old Timey and String. IMT

RECOMMENDED ALBUMS:
"Hot Line to Heaven" (Bagatelle)(1975)
"Are You Ready" (World Witness)(1976)

BUD ISAACS

(Steel Guitar, Guitar, Composer)
Date of Birth: March 26, 1928
Where Born: Bedford Indiana
Married: Geri Mapes

Bud Isaacs goes into the history books as the man who added pedals to the steel guitar. He started his career at the age of 16 initially playing lead guitar. He switched to steel guitar after taking preliminary instruction at music school. He got his first job at WIBC Indianapolis working with Asher Sizemore and from there he went to WOAI in San Antonio, Texas, and then on to Arkansas.

In 1951, Bud joined Eddie Hill's band and started to appear on the *Grand Ole Opry*. During the early 50's, he also played with Jimmy Dickens. In 1953, he had hit upon the idea of putting pedals onto the steel guitar in order to change the pitch of the strings. The first record to feature this new device was Webb Pierce's No.1 hit *Slowly* in 1954. Soon Bud was in great demand as a session player in Nashville and was instrumental in changing the sound of Country music records. He signed to RCA Victor in 1954, and his first single for the label was *Hot Mockingbird/Waltz You Saved for Me*. That year, Bud released three more solo singles, *Steelin' Away/Indian Love Call*, *Skokiaan/Yesterday's Waltz* and *Panhandle Rag/Beautiful Kahama*.

By 1955, he was a featured member of the *Ozark Jubilee* on ABC-TV and radio and appeared with Red Foley on Foley's daily radio program. During that year, he played on the top eleven Country hits of the year. During 1955, Isaacs released a single that will always be identified with him, *Bud's Bounce*. He had three more singles for the label, *Steel Guitar Breakdown/Waltz of the Ozarks* (1955), *Boing!/Westphalia Waltz* and *Bud's Waltz/Bohemian Polka* (1956).

In 1978, Bud and his wife, singer/yodeler/bass player Geri Mapes (she recorded for Midland Records), were inducted into the Colorado Country Music Hall of Fame, and in 1984, Bud Isaacs was inducted into the Steel Guitar Hall of Fame. Bud and Geri put together an act known as the Golden West Singers. The Isaacses have for some years lived in Yuma, Arizona.

RECOMMENDED ALBUMS:

"The Legendary Bud Isaacs" (Midland)
"The Best of Bud Isaacs" (Jabs)
"Steel Guitar on Radio/Mid 50's" (Danny Germany)
"More Steel Guitar Transcriptions" (Danny Germany)
EP worth looking for:
"Bud Isaacs and his Cryin' Steel Guitar" (RCA Victor)(1955)

JOE ISAACS

(Singer, Songwriter, Banjo, Guitar, Mandolin)
Given Name: Joe Isaacs
Date of Birth: January 24, 1947
Where Born: Jackson County, Kentucky
Married: Lily Fishman
Children: Benjamin, Sonya, Rebecca

Joe Isaacs began his career as a Bluegrass banjo picker and lonesome-voiced lead singer in the tradition of Carter Stanley. After 1971, he and his wife became one of the best family Gospel groups on the contemporary scene with the emphasis on good solo singing, fine harmony and quality acoustical instrumentation.

A native of mountainous Jackson County in eastern Kentucky, Joe was the youngest of seventeen children of a struggling preacher and his wife. The youth had some appreciation for music as a child, but did not really begin to play seriously until he finished high school and moved to Lebanon, Ohio.

At that time, he began developing a deep love for the music of his heritage. In company with other products of Appalachian migrant culture such as Lee Centers, Larry Sparks, and Fred Spencer, Joe later explained, "I learned real quick and I kept going on deeper into the music." At age 20, Joe went to New York with Frank Wakefield and became one of the Greenbriar Boys. Friends described his New York experience as a lonely one far from his family and friends in Kentucky and Ohio. Nonetheless, Joe gained some valuable experience in New York and met his future wife, Lily Fishman. At the time, Lily, German-born of Jewish holocaust survivors, worked as half of a Folk-oriented duet, Lily and Marie, who recorded for Columbia. In 1969, they married and returned to Ohio, where Joe played banjo for Larry Sparks and his Lonesome Ramblers, recording a pair of albums for Pine Tree Records and a single under his own name.

On December 22, 1970, Joe's brother Delmer died in a tragic auto accident and the incident changed the Isaacses' lives. Shortly afterward, both Joe and Lily had born-again experiences and since that time, they have played only Gospel music. They called their first band the Calvary Mountain Boys, but then began using the name Sacred Bluegrass. They had a regular TV show on a station in Hamilton, Ohio, for four years. Joe and Lily also assisted Tommy Crank on some recordings. As the three Isaacs children grew older, they took an increasingly larger role in the music. Benjamin took over playing bass fiddle, Sonya developed into a fine mandolin picker and Rebecca plays guitar. Like their parents, the children have all proved to be excellent singers. They cut albums for both Old Homestead and Sacred Sounds Records. Joe continued to favor banjo and occasionally guitar.

In 1988, the group changed its name to the Isaacs, which not only reflected the group's all-family composition, but also the broadening of their musical horizons somewhat beyond the confining perimeters of Bluegrass. Although their instrumentation remains primarily acoustical, they sing in a variety of stylings and their recordings, since 1988, produced by Eddie Crook on Harvest and Morning Star, received much wider airplay on the contemporary, southern Gospel stations.

One of Joe's songs, *Press Through the Crowd*, has been recorded by numerous Gospel groups. The band has also co-hosted four tours of the Holy Land. In mid-1992, the Isaacs shifted from their long-time home in Morrow, Ohio, to La Follette, Tennessee, a more central locale for their touring schedule. IMT

RECOMMENDED ALBUMS:

"Live It Everyday" (Pine Tree)(1971)
"Dreams of Home" (Old Homestead)(1975)
"Family Circle" (Old Homestead)(1975)
"Lord Light My Way" (Old Homestead)(1981)
"Joe Isaacs: The Greenbriar Years" (Old Homestead)(1981) [Recorded 1968]
"Fond Memories" (Old Homestead)(1984)
"Live at Hominy Valley" (Morning Star)(1990)
"20th Anniversary" (Morning Star)(1991)
"Live in Atlanta" (Morning Star)(1992)

J

ALAN JACKSON

(Singer, Songwriter, Guitar,)
Given Name: Alan Eugene Jackson
Date of Birth: October 17, 1958
Where Born: Newman, Georgia
Married : Denise
Children: Mattie Denise

There have been many claimants for the mantle of Hank Williams' songwriting legacy. Alan Jackson has proven himself to be supreme amongst those claimants. His songs are straight ahead with a simplicity that makes you greet them as welcome friends. He writes songs, sings songs and is Country through and through. However, Alan Jackson didn't start in the time-honored way, struggling up the ladder. He was 20 before he even thought of music as a career and began writing songs after that.

Alan came from a loving, close knit family, with four older sisters, and lived a normal family life. Alan's early preoccupation was with cars. His father, Eugene, is a mechanic and when Alan was 15, the two of them spent a year rebuilding a 1955 Thunderbird, which became Alan's first car. The family loved Gospel songs and they all sang at church, but Alan never had any driving ambition to be anything. He left school and went into the used car business and also built some houses. He met his wife when he was 17 and she got used to him buying and selling cars, boats and motorcycles. He even once bought her a car part as a present. They married when he was 20 and as he became increasingly bored with his life, he began sitting in with local Country bands playing cover tunes.

He began to write some songs of his own,

learning as he went along, and in 1985, although he had never thought seriously of pursuing a music career, he decided to sell his house and move to Nashville. Three people started a chain of events toward this decision. The first was a school friend with ambition, who used to fly small planes and realized his dreams to become an airline pilot. The second was his wife Denise. She was a flight attendant and one day while waiting for a flight at Atlanta Airport, she spotted Glen Campbell. She approached him and said, "Excuse me, my husband's about to move to Nashville to be a singer/songwriter, what does he need to do?" Glen gave her a card with his office address in Nashville. Thus, Glen became the third person.

After moving to Nashville in 1985, Glen Campbell's office gave him advice and Alan found a job in the mail room at TNN. Gradually he began to support himself by singing song demos, his Country voice being an asset. He eventually got a songwriting deal and became a staff writer with Glen Campbell Music. He started to learn how the business worked and put a band together and played some one nighters. He then acquired Barry Coburn as his manager and he and producer Keith Stegall demoed some of Alan's own songs. This led to Alan being the first act signed to the new-to-Nashville Arista label.

Alan's first album, ***Here in the Real World***, was released in March, 1990, and it went Gold by September and Platinum by March, 1991. Although his first single, *Blue-Blooded Woman*, only reached the Top 50 in 1989, there were then three consecutive Top 3 singles in 1990, namely *Here in the Real World*, *Wanted* and *Chasin' That Neon Rainbow*. Some of Alan's awards for 1990 were: "Top New Male Vocalist," from the ACM, *Music City News* Country Songwriters Award, "Song of the Year" for *Here in the Real World* (co-written with Mark Irwin), TNN Music City News Country Awards "Album of the Year for ***Here in the Real World*** and "Star of Tomorrow" Award, and *Radio and Records*' Country Radio Readers Poll "Best New Male Artist," and Airplay Awards "Best New Male Artist." The video released in November entitled ***Here in the Reel World*** was Certified Gold in March, 1991, and Platinum in 1992.

What a beginning to his recording career! He toured extensively and even visited England and Germany and had his picture on the *USA Weekend* cover and best of all, his daughter Mattie Denise was born.

Alan continued his winning ways as 1991 unfolded. He again reeled off three No.1's with *I'd Love You All Over Again, Don't Rock the Jukebox* and *Someday*. He ended up the year with a Christmas record, *I Only Want You for Christmas*, which made the Top 50. The album ***Don't Rock the Jukebox*** was released in May, 1991, and it had gone Double-Platinum by August, 1992. The honors once more poured in that year. The ACM made *Don't Rock the Jukebox* their "Single Record of the Year" and the album, its "Album of the Year." Billboard No.1 Awards made the single its "Top Country Single" and TNN Music City News Country Awards named the album its "Album of the Year," and the single its "Single of the Year." They also named Alan as "Male Artist of the Year." *Country Gazette* in Holland named him "Most Promising Act" while the NSAI made him "Songwriter/Artist of the Year." He also won the CMA's Entertainment Expo SRO Award for "New Touring Artist of the Year." During 1991, Alan was made a member of the *Grand Ole Opry*.

It would have seemed difficult to top 1991, but come 1992 and Alan did just that. He started off with another No.1, *Dallas*, and then had the momentous tribute to Hank Williams *Midnight in Montgomery*, which reached the Top 3. This was followed by another No.1, *Love's Got a Hold on You*. He wrapped up the year with yet another No.1, the highly infectious *She's Got the Rhythm (And I Got the Blues)* which had a most delicious video that found favor on CMT. The song was written by Alan and Randy Travis, who proved to be a revelation with their co-writing skills. The 1992 album, ***A Lot About Livin' (And a Little 'Bout Love)*** was released in October and went Gold on December 1, Platinum by December 3, Double-Platinum in 1993 and Triple-Platinum in 1994. Alan's awards in 1992 included ASCAP making *Don't Rock the Jukebox* its "Country Song of the Year" and the CMA making the wonderfully moody video for *Midnight in Montgomery* its "Music Video of the Year."

In 1993, Alan started off the year with the Top 5 release *Tonight I Climbed the Wall* and then followed it with what has been his biggest hit to date, *Chattahoochie*. The single stayed at No.1 for 4 weeks, crossed to the Pop Top 50 and was Certified Gold. Alan's other chart records that year were: *Tropical Depression* (a cut from the album, which only lasted in the Top 75 for 1 week), *Mercury Blues* (Top 3) and *Tequila Sunrise* (Alan's track from the Giant Records album ***Common Thread: The Songs of the Eagles***). At year end, Alan reached the Top 60 with the title track of his seasonal album ***Honky Tonk Christmas***. The album was Certified Gold in 1994.

Alan's awards in 1993 included: CMA "Single of the Year" and "Music Video of the Year" (*Chattahoochie*); ACM "Song of the Year" and "Single Record of the Year" (*Chattahoochie*) and "Album of the Year" (*A Lot About Livin' (And a Little 'Bout Love)*). In 1994, Alan charted with *(Who Says) We Can't Have It All*, which reached the Top 5.

Alan tours with six band members, the Strayhorns, and a crew of twenty-three, traveling in three buses with three tractor trailers hauling 35 tons of lighting, equipment, video and a stage set. In an era when new artists come and go with alarming speed, Alan Jackson is certain to be around as long as he wants to be. JAB

***Alan Jackson** (left) with **Buddy Killen** at the Easter Seals Auction at the Stockyard in Nashville*

RECOMMENDED ALBUMS:
"Here in the Real World" (Arista)(1989)
"Don't Rock the Jukebox" (Arista)(1991)
"A Lot About Livin' (And a Little 'Bout Love)" (Arista)(1992)

AUNT MOLLY JACKSON

(Singer, Songwriter, Political Activist)
Given Name: Mary Magdalene Garland
Date of Birth: 1880
Where Born: Clay County, Kentucky
Married: 1. (Dec'd.)
2. (Div.)
Children: one son (dec'd.)
Date of Death: September 1, 1960

Though her association with Country music was only peripheral, Aunt Molly Jackson won fame both as a singer of traditional Kentucky mountain songs and as a creator of powerful protest songs. One of her admirers, Woody Guthrie, once referred to her as a "female Leadbelly," in regard not only to her singing but to her long and hard life.

Molly came from a family active in trying to organize the miners in rural Kentucky, and along with her brothers and sisters, Molly was walking the picket line when just a child of 5. When she was 6 she saw her mother die of starvation. Molly married when she was 14 and mining accidents later took the lives of her brother, husband, and son.

As a young girl, she began to chronicle some of these tragedies in songs, such as *Poor Miner's Farewell, Hard Times in Coleman's Mines* and *Dishonest Miller.* She continued to work for the union causes through the 20's, going to New York in 1931 to record her only commercial sides for Columbia: *Kentucky Miner's Wife*, a two-sided song, and two other pieces that were never released. These as well as her flair for publicity managed to help bring national attention to the plight of miners—though the unions forced her to leave Kentucky and relocate her base of operations to New York City.

There she worked with other relatives from eastern Kentucky, like Jim Garland and Sara Ogan Gunning, preserving Folk songs and speaking out for union causes. She remarried to a chef in a New York restaurant (who later divorced her for fear of reprisals from Molly's opponents), and got to know most of the New York Folk song community.

Between 1935 and 1939, through the efforts of folklorists like Mary Barnicle and Alan Lomax, Aunt Molly recorded some 150 of her songs for the Library of Congress, some of which were issued in the 70's on a Rounder lp. In 1940, she appeared with Leadbelly and Josh White in the stage show *Cavalcade of American Song.* Molly claimed to be the inspiration for Al Dexter's hit *Pistol Packin' Mama.* According to her her cousin had written *Pistol-Packin' Woman*, which is very similar. Eventually settling in California, Aunt Molly Jackson lived to see her work appreciated by folklorists and music historians. She even wrote letters to *Sing Out* magazine, including one that said: "I have never received one cent from anyone out of all the protest songs I have composed." She was working on an autobiographical lp with John Greenway when she died in 1960 in relative obscurity and in abject poverty. CKW

RECOMMENDED ALBUM:
"Library of Congress Recordings" (Rounder)

CARL JACKSON

(Singer, Songwriter, Banjo, Guitar, Mandolin, Dobro, Fiddle)
Date of Birth: September 18, 1953
Where Born: Louisville, Mississippi

Carl Jackson fell in love with Bluegrass music as a young boy growing up in the small town of Louisville, Mississippi. He displayed a natural ability for music and became accomplished on both guitar and banjo. He learned to play the 5-string banjo primarily by imitating Earl Scruggs licks from Flatt & Scruggs records.

By the time he was 13, Carl was playing banjo in his father and uncle's Bluegrass band. When he was 14, his talent was discovered by Bluegrass greats Jim & Jesse. They heard young Jackson playing backstage and offered him a job with their band, the Virginia Boys. He spent the next five years playing banjo for various *Grand Ole Opry* stars. Jackson then left the Virginia Boys to play for the Sullivan Family Gospel group. During the 60's, Carl recorded the album ***Bluegrass Festival*** for the independent Prize label.

After performing with the Sullivan Family for less than a year, Carl traveled to Columbus, Ohio, in 1972, to form his own group, called the Country Store, with friends including Bluegrass veterans Keith Whitley and Jimmy Gaudreau. Carl left the group shortly after its formation when he was invited to join the band of Country star Glen Campbell.

Carl was a big fan of Glen, so when he performed at the Ohio State Fair, Carl attended the show. Following the show, Carl visited with Campbell's banjo player, Larry McNeely, who invited Carl to come back the next day for a jam session. McNeely was impressed with Carl's mastery of the 5-string banjo and told him he had been looking for someone to take his place in Glen's band. Carl auditioned for Campbell and was hired on the spot He spent the next twelve years as a member of Glen Campbell's touring band.

During his tenure with Campbell, Jackson launched his own recording career in 1973. He recorded two albums for Capitol, ***Banjo Player*** and ***Old Friend***. Carl also recorded a trio of albums for the independent label Sugar Hill, ***Banjo Man (A Tribute to Earl Scruggs)*** (1981) featuring Jerry Douglas, Marty Stuart and Vassar Clements; ***Song of the South*** (1982) with Emmylou Harris, Marty Stuart, Jerry Douglas, Jesse McReynolds and Blaine Sprouse; and ***Banjo Hits*** (1983) with Jim & Jesse. Carl's pairing with Columbia Records produced the Country chart hits *She's Gone, Gone, Gone* (Top 50, 1984), *All That's Left for Me* (Top 70) and *Dixie Train* (Top 50) (both 1985) and *You Are the Rock (And I'm a Rolling Stone)* (1986).

Carl left the Glen Campbell show in the mid-80's to pursue his solo career full-time. In addition to continuing his own recording, Jackson was in great demand to sing harmony vocals for other artists. He recorded with Emmylou Harris, Ricky Skaggs, Vince Gill, Alabama, Sweethearts of the Rodeo, Steve Wariner, Dolly Parton, Roger Miller, Pam Tillis, John Anderson, Dwight Yoakam and Garth Brooks.

Carl Jackson has also enjoyed great success as a songwriter. In 1985, Glen Campbell charted Carl's *(Love Always) Letter to Home* and in 1989, Carl scored the Top 15 hit *Breaking New Ground* for the all-girl group Wild Rose.

Pam Tillis collaborated with Carl for her 1992 hit *Put Yourself in My Place*. Other notable 1992 recordings include Garth Brooks with *Against the Grain*, Trisha Yearwood's *Lonesome Dove* and Diamond Rio's *Close to the Edge*. In 1993, Carl celebrated a Top 3 hit with Vince Gill on their co-written *No Future in the Past*. Other artists who have recorded Carl's songs include Ricky Skaggs, Patty Loveless, Mel Tillis, Charly McClain, the Nitty Gritty Dirt Band, Doyle Lawson & Quicksilver and the Whites.

Carl's awards include the 1990 International Bluegrass Association "Song of the Year" for *Little Mountain Church House*. The song was on the album ***Will the Circle Be Unbroken, Volume II*** by the Nitty Gritty Dirt Band and featured lead vocals by Ricky Skaggs. In 1991, Jackson earned a Grammy Award for "Best Bluegrass Album" with John Starling and the Nash Ramblers for the Sugar Hill album entitled ***Spring Training***. Also in 1992, Carl earned a Dove Award from the Gospel Music Association for "Southern

Gospel Record Song of the Year" for Glen Campbell's *Where Shadows Never Fall*, which Carl wrote with another song craftsman, Jim Weatherly.

RECOMMENDED ALBUMS:

"Bluegrass Festival" (Prize)
"Banjo Player" (Capitol)(1973)
"Banjo Man (A Tribute to Earl Scruggs)" (Sugar Hill)(1981)
"Song of the South" (Sugar Hill)(1982)
"Banjo Hits" (Sugar Hill)(1983)
"Spring Training" (Sugar Hill)(1991)

SHOT JACKSON

(Steel Guitar, Dobro)

Given Name: Harold B. Jackson
Date of Birth: September 4, 1920
Where Born: Wilmington, North Carolina
Married: Donna Darlene
Children: Shotsy
Date of Death: January 24, 1991

Shot Jackson ranks as one of the better-known steel guitar and Dobro players of the generation following WWII. Mechanically inclined, he and Buddy Emmons together designed an electric pedal steel guitar in the late 50's and manufactured it under the brand name Sho-Bud until they sold out in 1980. Over a long career, Jackson worked as a sideman with many Country acts, sometimes recording under his own name and with his singing wife, Donna Darlene, as well. As he restricted his activities with advancing age, Shot maintained a reputation as an instrument craftsman and repairman until he retired in 1983.

Born in North Carolina, Jackson moved as an infant to a farm near Brashear, Georgia, with his parents. He received the nickname "buckshot" as a child, which was eventually shortened to "Shot." As a youth, he listened regularly to the *Grand Ole Opry*, being especially infatuated with the Dobro as played by Bashful Brother Oswald in Roy Acuff's Smoky Mountain Boys. In 1941, he joined a Country band on a Jacksonville radio station and in 1944, he came to Nashville and the *Opry* as a sideman with Cousin Wilbur Westbrooks.

Shot spent a year in the U.S. Navy and when he came out joined the Bailes Brothers, playing primarily electric steel guitar. He recorded with them on King in November, 1946, and twice for Columbia in 1947. When they went to KWKH Shreveport, Shot went along and remained with them until they left the *Louisiana Hayride*.

Remaining at KWKH, he worked and recorded with various groups, including Jimmie Osborne, Webb Pierce, Red Sovine and Johnnie & Jack until the summer of 1951, when he joined Johnnie & Jack's Tennessee Mountain Boys as a regular. For the next six years, Jackson worked on the road and on virtually all sessions with Johnnie & Jack (playing Dobro) and Kitty Wells (on electric steel), who became the first female Country superstar in that period. Shot also made a few recordings under his own name, on Pacemaker, in Shreveport, and on Specialty in Nashville. Shot then spent the next five years with Roy Acuff's Smoky Mountain Boys playing electric steel.

During his years with Roy Acuff, Shot Jackson and Buddy Emmons developed their now famous Sho-Bud pedal steel guitar. From an operation that started in a garage, they built Sho-Bud into a successful business. Remaining active as a musician, Jackson managed and played steel for Melba Montgomery, who had left Acuff to go on her own. He did the steel work on many of her United Artists recordings as well as on her duets with George Jones. Shot also did session work for various other artists in those years, in addition to recording albums on his own, with both Starday and Cumberland.

In 1964, Jackson rejoined Roy Acuff's band, but his second sojourn ended suddenly on July 10, 1965, when he, Roy, and June Stearns survived a near fatal auto crash in East Tennessee. After his slow and painful recovery, he began touring and working with his wife, former WWVA *Jamboree* songstress Donna Darlene.

Meanwhile Jackson developed a seven string resonator guitar which he marketed under the name Sho-Bro. Through the years he kept up his contacts with the Bailes Brothers, helping out on several of their reunion concerts and recordings. He also loaned his professionalism to the Roy Clark Family Band when they guested on *Hee Haw* and did a pair of albums with them for Dot.

Shot Jackson sold Sho-Bud to Baldwin-Gretsch in 1980 and his instrument repair business in 1983. Unfortunately, a happy retirement was cut short when he suffered a serious stroke two months later. Although he recovered to some extent, he neither regained his speech nor the ability to play. Shot was inducted into the Steel Guitar Hall of Fame in 1986. Jackson suffered another stroke in June, 1990, and declined rapidly thereafter. He passed away seven months later. Walter Bailes, long-time friend and musical associate, preached at his funeral. IMT

RECOMMENDED ALBUMS:

"Singing Strings of Steel Guitar and Dobro" (Starday)(1962)
"Bluegrass Dobro" (Cumberland)(1965)
[See also Bailes Brothers, the, Johnnie & Jack, Kitty Wells]

STONEWALL JACKSON

(Singer, Songwriter, Guitar)

Given Name: Stonewall Jackson
Date of Birth: November 6, 1932
Where Born: Emerson, near Tabor City, North Carolina
Married: Juanita Carmene Wair
Children: Stonewall Jr. ("Turp")

Stonewall Jackson has gone down in history as the first performer to be signed to the *Grand Ole Opry* roster who was not already signed to a record company.

Jackson can trace his lineage back to the celebrated Confederate general, Thomas Jonathan "Stonewall" Jackson. His father, Waymon David Jackson, was a railroad engineer on a logging train and had died of complications from a hernia, just before Stonewall was born. "Stone's" mother, Lulu Loraine Turner Jackson, was half Seminole and she had a rough time bringing up her three children until she married James Leviner. However, Leviner had a nasty temper and was violent. His mistreatment of Stonewall led directly to Lulu leaving with the boys and hitching down to south Georgia in 1936 to stay with Waymon's brother, Monroe, near Meggs. However, Leviner and his brother came after them, with the result that Leviner and Stonewall's mother decided to get back together.

Stonewall began working as a waterboy and then later, he worked in the tobacco and cotton fields. He was continually being beaten by his stepfather; on one occasion, he was left for dead. When he was 10, Stonewall traded in a bicycle without any tires for a guitar, and a year later, started to write songs. When he was 14, Stonewall left home and hitched his way to his grandmother in North Carolina. He then went back on the road and wound up in Jacksonville, Florida, where he was propositioned by a pedophile; Jackson knocked him out with a brick.

Stonewall then headed to Atlanta, where he was arrested and then rescued by the Red Cross. He was returned to his grandparents in North Carolina. He returned to his mother in 1948, but again it didn't work out and so at the age of 16, Stonewall joined the U.S. Army by falsifying his birth certificate. When the falsification was discovered, he was tossed out of the forces and set off for Tabor City. There, he teamed up with another youngster, James Nealy, and did a Louvin Brothers type of act singing Gospel. When he was 17, Jackson joined the U.S. Navy and served on submarines. While in the service, he bought his first good guitar in Norfolk, Virginia, and learned to play properly.

While stationed on the *USS Kittywake*, a submarine rescue ship, he discovered that the Captain was a Country music fan and owned a Chet Atkins guitar. The captain let Stonewall borrow his guitar and rigged up a sound system so that Jackson could play before the movies. In 1952, Stonewall got his discharge from the Navy. From 1952 until 1954, he farmed around Greenville, North Carolina, and played in his brother Wade's band. At the time, his big influences were Hank Williams, Eddy Arnold and Ernest Tubb.

In 1954, "Stone" returned to Georgia, where he worked on his performing and songwriting while he still farmed. He decided to try his luck in Nashville and in 1956, in his 1955 Chevrolet pick-up truck, he arrived via the Franklin Road. He stayed at the York Motel, which was across the street from Acuff-Rose Music Publishing. He went to Acuff-Rose, where he was asked to demo a couple of songs (imagine that happening now!) and he put down *Getting Older*, a song he had written with brother Wade entitled *Don't Be Angry,* and *Knock Off Your Nagging*. Wesley Rose called him straight back and arranged for him to audition with George D. Hay at the *Opry*. The "Judge" called in Dee Kilpatrick, the station manager. As a result, Stonewall was signed to a five-year contract to appear on the *Opry*.

His first broadcast was on the *Friday Night Frolic* show, the following day, where he was backed by Ernest Tubb's Texas Troubadours. He sang *Don't Be Angry*, and initially was snickered at because, with his patched clothes, he looked like he was a comedian. However, they soon realized how good he was, and he was called back for four encores. Ernest Tubb took Stonewall under his wing and bought him a couple of Western outfits. Stonewall was now ready to make his first appearance on the *Opry* and it was the second week of November, 1956.

It was at this time that Stonewall met his wife, and some two years later they married. Ernest Tubb took Jackson on tour with him and E.T. was also responsible for helping set up a record deal for "Stone." Among the labels interested was Columbia, and it was E.T. who suggested to Jackson that he sign with them and also told him to try and sound less like Hank Williams. Stonewall remained on the label for 18 years. His first overseas trip was to Hawaii, where he stood in for George Jones, who became an early friend.

However, Jackson still did not have sufficient money to live on and the *Opry* management got him a job packing books. In January, 1957, Stonewall made his first recording in Columbia's Studio B. From that first session came *Don't Be Angry*. However, it was not until 1958 that he had his first taste of chart success with his version of the George Jones song *Life to Go*, which climbed to the Top 3 on the Country charts. In June, 1959, Stonewall had a No.1 hit with a song that will forever be associated with him, *Waterloo*. It was at No.1 for 5 weeks and crossed-over to peak in the Top 5 on the Pop chart. It even traveled over the Atlantic to reach the Top 30 in the U.K. The flip-side, *Smoke Along the Track*, made the Top 25. By now, the famed Jim Denny had taken over Stonewall's managerial reins, and backed by the Minutemen, Jackson toured the country. Stonewall completed the year with the Top 30 hit *Igmoo (The Pride of South Central High)*, which also reached the Pop Top 100.

During 1960, "Stone" chalked up hits with *Mary Don't You Weep* (Top 15 Country/Top 50 Pop) and the Top 10 hit *Why I'm Walkin'*, the flip-side of which, *Life of a Poor Boy*, went Top 15. He completed the year with the Top 15 *A Little Guy Called Joe*. During 1961, both Stonewall's chart records only reached the Top 30. They were *Greener Pastures* and *Hungry for Love*. He scored in 1962 with *A Wound Time Can't Erase* (Top 3), of which the flip-side, *Second Choice*, went Top 10. He followed this with *One Look at Heaven* (Top 15)/*Leona* (Top 10).

The following year, Stonewall succeeded with *Can't Hang Up the Phone* (Top 15), *Old Showboat* (Top 10) and *Wild Wild Wind* (Top 15). Stonewall started 1964 with the No.1 record *B.J. the D.J.* He followed with the re-issue of *Don't Be Angry*, which this time around went Top 5. He followed this up in February, 1965, with his version of the Johnny Rivers hit *I Washed My Hands in Muddy Water*. That year, Stonewall appeared in the movie *Country Music on Broadway*.

His other major hits in the second half of the 60's were *Trouble and Me/Lost in the Shuffle* (both sides Top 30, 1965), *If This House Could Talk* (Top 25), *The Minute Men (Are Turning in Their Graves)* (Top 25) and *Blues Plus Booze (Means I Lose)* (Top 15) (all 1966), *Stamp Out Loneliness* (Top 5), *Promises and Hearts (Were Made to Break)* (Top 15) and *This World Holds Nothing (Since You're Gone)* (Top 30) (all 1967), *Angry Words* (Top 20, 1968) and *"Never More" Quote the Raven* (Top 25) and *Ship in the Bottle* (Top 20) (both 1969).

Just when it looked like Stonewall's career was starting to peter out, he had a Top 10 hit in 1971, with his rendition of the Lobo song *Me and You and a Dog Named Boo*. He was now starting to have angry words with Columbia, which he considers, in retrospect, that he may have precipitated.

"Stone" moved to MGM Records and in 1973, he had his final chart success with the Top 50 single *Herman Schwartz*. For a while after leaving MGM, Stonewall was in semi-retirement. He recorded an Inspirational album for Myrrh, ***Make Me Like a Child Again***, in 1976 and then he moved to Little Darlin' Records, where he cut ***Stonewall (Platinum***

Grand Ole Opry star ***Stonewall Jackson***

Country). Gene Watson had a 1979 hit with Stonewall's song *Should I Come Home (Or Should I Go Crazy)*.

Pete Drake took "Stone" into the studio as part of his First Generation series of recordings by *Opry* performers and as a result, the album ***Stonewall Jackson*** hit the streets in 1981. The short-lived Audiograph Alive put out the 1982 album ***Stonewall Jackson***, while Phonorama issued ***Stonewall,*** and Allegiance Records released the ***Up Against the Wall*** album in 1983, which was mainly re-recordings of Jackson's hits, but also included a good version of *I'm an Old Lump of Coal*. Stonewall then moved over to MSR Records in the late 80's, but failed to ignite the charts, although he still remained very popular in the U.S. and in Europe. In 1980 and 1988, he appeared at the famed Wembley Festival in England to rapturous applause.

In 1991, Stonewall issued privately his autobiography, *From the Bottom Up*. During 1992, Stonewall went into the studio to cut a "greatest hits" album for MSR. The word went around, and suddenly contemporary performers such as Garth Brooks, Dolly Parton, George Jones and Lorrie Morgan wanted to guest on the album. It grew into a double package and then just as it was completed, Stonewall and his producer got into a legal confrontation. It has now been settled, but it has not yet been decided on which label the project will be released.

RECOMMENDED ALBUMS:

"A Tribute to Hank Williams" (Columbia)(1969)
"Stonewall Jackson Recorded Live at the Grand Ole Opry" (Columbia)(1971)
"The World of Stonewall Jackson" (double)(Columbia)(1972)
"Make Me Like a Child Again" (Myrrh)(1976)
"Stonewall Jackson" (First Generation)(1981)

TOMMY JACKSON

(Fiddle, Mandolin, Guitar, Vocals)

Given Name: **Thomas Lee Jackson, Jr.**
Date of Birth: **March 31, 1926**
Where Born: **Birmingham, Alabama**
Date of Death: **December 9, 1979**

The first great Nashville session fiddler, Tommy Jackson has probably been heard on more Country records than any other musician. Throughout the 50's and 60's, he dominated the field, appearing on records by every major star of the era, from Hank Williams to Bill Monroe, from Ray Price to George Jones. He virtually invented the standard Country fiddle back-up style and in the early 1950's had a string of hit albums of his own that both reflected and stimulated the square dance craze.

Though Tommy was born in Birmingham, he and his family moved to Nashville when he was barely one, and he grew up listening to the *Grand Ole Opry* and Nashville radio. He remembered being especially impressed with two of the fiddlers on the early *Opry*, George Wilkerson (of the Fruit Jar Drinkers) and Arthur Smith (of the Dixieliners). Even though there was not much music in his immediate family, Tommy's father (a barber) encouraged him, and Tommy became a child prodigy of sorts. When he was age 7, he went into Nashville bars and sawed out fiddle tunes for nickels and dimes. By the time he was 12, he went on tour with Johnny Wright and Kitty Wells. With a neighbor, he formed a group called the Tennessee Mountaineers and soon began to play over Nashville station WSIX. By the time he was 17, Tommy was playing regularly on the *Opry* with Curly Williams and his Georgia Peach Pickers, and later with Paul Howard. But on April 17, 1944, he enlisted in the Army Air Corps, and spent the rest of the war as a tail gunner on a B-29. (He eventually won four Bronze Stars and an Air Medal for his work.)

Discharged in April, 1946, Tommy returned to Nashville and did road tours with various *Opry* stars, including Whitey Ford and Jimmy Selph. He didn't like the road grind, though, and he hooked up with Milton Estes, then starting a radio show on WSM. This led to a similar job with Red Foley, who had just come to town as a replacement for Roy Acuff on the *Opry*. Foley's band, the Cumberland Valley Boys, also included guitarist Zeke Turner, steel player Jerry Byrd, and rhythm guitarist Louis Innis. They constituted the first Nashville "A-team," and soon they were doing all manner of studio work, for all manner of labels. Tommy's first commercial record was a Sterling session for young Hank Williams in 1947. Two months later, another Williams session followed, and Jackson created the famous fiddle intro for *I Saw the Light*. In 1948, Tommy backed Williams on *Lovesick Blues* and later backed Red Foley on pieces like *Satisfied Mind*.

In November, 1948, the band moved en masse to Cincinnati and struck out on its own as the Pleasant Valley Boys. They continued to do session work, now for King as well as others, and recorded with Cowboy Copas, Hawkshaw Hawkins, Grandpa Jones and the York Brothers. It was in Cincinnati that Tommy cut his first solo sides under his own name for Mercury. They sold well and in 1953, he signed a contract with the newly-formed Dot Records, in Gallatin, Tennessee. Square dancing was becoming a big fad then and Tommy began doing a series of albums and EPs of fiddle music for dancing. Before the fad was over, Tommy had amassed eleven lps for Dot, and around 30 singles. These albums were among the few solo fiddle records on the market then and they were grabbed up by younger fiddlers. Soon Tommy was the most imitated fiddler of his generation.

Breaking with Foley in 1954, Jackson also found that he could make a living by doing nothing but studio work and soon found himself with all the dates he could handle. Among his favorite session cuts were ones with Faron Young, on whose sides Tommy popularized a double-stop back-up technique, and Ray Price, with whom he pioneered what Bob Wills later called a "walking fiddle" style.

In the 70's, the vocation Tommy invented became filled with so many other fiddlers, that he had a hard time getting work. Health problems began to develop. There was an interesting experimental, free-form fiddle album he had always wanted to do, but it never materialized. Tommy died on December 9, 1979, but only the sharp-eyed reader looking through the death notices in the Nashville papers would have learned about it. CKW

RECOMMENDED ALBUMS:

"Square Dance Fiddle Favorites" (Mercury)(1958)
"Greatest Bluegrass Hits" (Dot)(1962)
"Square Dance Jamboree" (Hamilton)(1964)
"Guitar and Fiddle Country Style" (Mercury/Wing)(1965) [With Lloyd Ellis]

WANDA JACKSON

(Singer, Songwriter, Guitar, Piano)

Given Name: **Wanda Lavonne Jackson**
Date of Birth: **October 20, 1937**
Where Born: **Maud, Oklahoma**
Married: **Wendell Goodman (m. 1961)**
Children: **Gregory Jackson, Gina Gail**

At one time, Wanda seemed to be the female answer to Elvis. She was hailed by many as "The Queen of Rock'n'Roll.". Yet her career before rock'n'roll and after is pure Country.

Her father, Tom, had played in bands in Oklahoma. In 1941, he moved the family to California. In Los Angeles he learned to become a barber and three months later, the family moved to Bakersfield. In 1943, he saved enough money to buy a guitar for Wanda and proceeded to teach her. When she was 9, she was encouraged when she asked to play piano. She also started to write at this time.

When she was 12, the family moved on to Oklahoma City, where Tom got a job selling used cars. In 1952, Wanda tried out for station KLPR and was given a 15-minute show. The program was so successful that it was upped to a 30-minute show. The following year, Wanda joined the Merle Lindsay Band. Hank Thompson heard her radio show and asked her to join the Brazos Valley Boys on tour. At the time, she was still in high school. She joined Thompson in 1954 and stayed with him until late 1955.

Thompson tried to persuade Capitol to sign Wanda, but they declined because of her age. Along came Billy Gray, who had been a sideman for Hank Thompson and had now been signed as a solo performer to Decca. Through Gray's attempts, Wanda was signed to Decca in March, 1954. She cut fifteen sides for the label, but only one single, *You Can't Have My Love* (1954), a duet with Billy Gray, made it to the charts, peaking in the Top 10.

After graduating from high school, in 1954, she joined the *Ozark Jubilee*.

During October 1955, Wanda toured with Elvis (she also toured with him the next year) and it was he who encouraged her to sing rock'n'roll. However, she was unsure and continued to cut pure Country. In April, 1956, she signed with Jim Halsey for management. Halsey already represented Hank Thompson and had Wanda signed to Capitol.

Her second record, *I Gotta Know*, which is half Country/half Rockabilly became a Top 20 Country entry in 1956. Playing on the record were Joe Maphis, Buck Owens, Skeets McDonald and Speedy West. *Cash Box* magazine voted her "Most Promising Female Vocalist."

In 1957, she recorded some sides with Merle Travis and Billy Strange on guitars. At this point, Halsey had found the Poe Cats, which included Big Al Downing on piano, and the group was signed to back Wanda. In

Fujiyama Mama, ***Wanda Jackson***

April, 1958, Wanda cut a song that would become a major career single for her. *Fujiyama Mama* sizzled and became a monster success in Japan. A day after the session that created that track, she did it all over again with *Let's Have a Party*, her version of the Presley smash hit, which became a Top 40 Pop hit for her in 1960.

During the 50's and 60's, Wanda became a big attraction in Las Vegas. In 1958, she was named "Best Country & Western Female Vocalist" by *Trail* magazine and "Best New Female Singer" by *Disc Jockey* magazine. With the success of her rock'n'roll hits, in 1960, she renamed her band the Party Timers; among the members was Roy Clark on lead guitar.

By the end of 1960, Wanda had started to record Country music again. Among the tracks recorded was the self-penned *Right or Wrong*. It crashed into the Country charts in 1961and rose to the Top 10 and crossed to the Pop Top 30. She allegedly wrote the song while in a daydream. She followed this with another Top 10 entry, *In the Middle of a Heartache*, which was also a Top 30 Pop hit. That same year, she married IBM programmer Wendell Goodman, who took over her management. He also packaged her highly successful syndicated *Music Village* TV show.

Wanda's next major successes were the 1966 Top 20 singles *The Box It Came In* and *Tears Will Be the Chaser for the Wine*. She also had enormous success in Germany with *Santo Domingo*, which was sung in Dutch and made No.1, edging out the Beatles. Over the next few years, Wanda racked up a series of middle order hits. She was not back in the Top 20 again until 1969. In that year, she scored with *My Big Skillet*. She followed in 1970 with *A Woman Loves for Love* and in 1971 with *Fancy Satin Pillows*, both Top 20 successes.

In 1971, Wanda announced that she had become a born-again Christian and was not going to record any more secular material. During that year and the following, she was voted "The Favorite Female Country Music Singer" of Scandinavia.

In 1972, she released the first of her Gospel albums, ***Praise the Lord***, on Capitol. In 1973, Wanda moved on to the religious label Myrrh Records. For them she recorded ***When It's Time to Fall in Love*** (1973), ***Now I Have Everything*** (1974) and ***Make Me a Child Again*** (1975). During 1977, Wanda recorded ***Country Gospel*** and ***Closer to Jesus*** for Word Records.

Wanda has now returned to recording and performing secular material. In 1980 and 1981, she toured Europe and recorded an album in Sweden which brought her back into the rock'n'roll arena. She is a true ambassador of popular music and has toured Japan, where she was lauded, and she played Country music to fans in the Philippines, Korea and the Middle East. She was chosen as one of the Country music stars to make the first U.N./CMA-sponsored tour of Australia, New Zealand and Japan. She has recorded in German, Japanese and Dutch. At one time, she was Capitol Records' best selling female vocalist in the German language. She has twice been nominated for a Grammy Award for "Best Country Vocal Performance, Female" and sang on the first live Grammy Award TV show.

RECOMMENDED ALBUMS:

Her Country tracks:

"Lovin' Country Style" (Capitol)(1962) [With Billy Gray] [Re-issued by Stetson Records UK in the original sleeve (1987)]

"Wanda Jackson in Person (Live)" (Capitol)(1969) [Recorded at Mr. Lucky's, Phoenix, Arizona]

"Wanda Jackson Country!" (Capitol)(1970)

Her rock'n'roll tracks:

"Let's Have a Party" (double)(Charly UK)(1986)

Her Gospel tracks:

"Now I Have Everything" (Myrrh)(1974)

"Closer to Jesus" (Word)(1977

The lady with the blue fiddle, ***Jana Jae***

JANA JAE

(Violin, Fiddle, Piano, Guitar, Bass, Singer)

Given Name:	**Jana Margaret Meyer**
Date of Birth:	**August 30, 1942**
Where Born:	**Great Falls, Montana**
Married:	**1. Sydney Greif (dec'd.)**
	2. Buck Owens (div. twice)
Children:	**Matt, Sydni**

Jana Jae, of French, Pennsylvania Dutch and English heritage, is often described as either the "First Lady of Country Fiddle" or the "Fiddling Femme Fatale." She holds the distinction of being the first female member of Buck Owens' Buckaroos.

Both Jana's parents had studied at the famed Juilliard School of Music in New York and it seemed that her future lay in classical music. However, her mother's father was an accomplished Country fiddler. She started to learn classical violin at the age of two and a half while her parents were studying violin at Juilliard. That year, they visited her grandfather in Colorado and he taught her how to play by ear.

When her parents divorced, Jana went to live with her mother in Colorado. This brought her into contact with even more Country music. Her mother re-married and the family moved to Fruitland, Idaho. There, Jana played in the high school orchestras. She also entered the National Oldtime Fiddlers' Contest in Weiser, Idaho. She won a scholarship to the Interlochen Music Camp in Michigan and the International String Congress in Puerto Rico. She majored in classical music at a woman's college in Denver, also on a scholarship, and then spent a year at the Vienna Academy of Music in Austria. She had intended to become a music teacher but shortly after finishing her studies, she married another student and they relocated to Redding, California.

Although she got into teaching violin and fiddle, she was soon on maternity leave and between 1967 and 1970 she gave birth to her two children. Shortly after the birth of their youngest, the couple divorced. Her thoughts moved to performing and she joined a Bluegrass band. She traveled up to the National Fiddling Championships in Weiser, Idaho, in 1973 and won the women's division. The following year, she repeated this feat.

Buck Owens had heard her play and in 1974, when Buck and the Buckaroos were playing Redding, Jana was invited to join them on stage. She duetted with Don Rich on *Orange Blossom Special.* Shortly afterward, Don was killed in a motorcycle accident and in 1975, Jana was invited to join the band and her blue fiddle became known on *Hee Haw* and wherever Buck and the Buckaroos played throughout the world.

However, things went sour in 1977. She recorded an instrumental album of Buck Owens' songs and found herself in trouble with the Owens organization. She hadn't asked them to organize the record contract. She found herself fired when she had the temerity to question this. She was still under contract, and with two children to support, found that she was not allowed to work.

In desperation, she tried to get Buck to resolve the problem. They solved that problem but created others when they got married. Buck annulled the marriage, they were reconciled, and then Jana annulled it. Buck launched a nationwide advertising campaign to try and win her back.

However, professionally, she was soon appearing with Owens again, on the TV show *Hee Haw.* At the end of the 70's, she went solo and in 1979 she signed with Lark Records. She has been able to divide her talents between Country and Jazz with appearances at the Montreux Jazz Festival in Switzerland and the Country Music Festival at Wembley, England.

Since 1983, Jana has worked closely with the Wal-Mart Stores chain and has appeared on TV commercials for the company, playing with her band, Hotwire. Jana is listed in *Who's Who in the World, Who's Who in Entertainment, Who's Who in the Southwest* and *Who's Who in American Women.*

RECOMMENDED ALBUMS:

"I Love Fiddlin'" (American Heritage)
"Don't Rock the Bow" (Lark)
"The Devil You Say!" (Lark)
"Jana Jae 'Live'" (Lark)
"Symphony Pops" (Lark)
"By Request" (Lark)

JAMBOREE U.S.A. (a.k.a. The World's Original Jamboree)

(Radio Show, WWVA Wheeling, West Virginia)

Next to the *Grand Ole Opry*, the program from WWVA Wheeling has been the longest-running live-audience radio program in Country music history.The initial broadcast of the program commonly known as the WWVA *Jamboree* or the *Wheeling Jamboree* took place at the Capitol Theater on January 7, 1933. Although the *Jamboree* had neither as much prestige nor quite the audience of the *Opry*, it has certainly played a significant role. In the northeastern states and adjoining portions, it has a distinct image and identity of its own.

In earlier years, the *Jamboree* had its own stable of established performers, but from the late 60's as a more complex star system evolved in the genre, the program placed increasing emphasis on the special guests and relegated their own artists to a secondary position.

Radio station WWVA originated in 1926. By the end of the next year the management had begun programming which could be classed as Country music, featuring, from neighboring communities, local musicians like Fred Craddock, Elmer Crowe and Bill Jones, who developed into a quality yodeler. Program Director George Smith saw the potential that the musical culture of common folk had for commercial development and encouraged more of it. As a result, additional musicians came to WWVA, including the trio of Cap, Andy and Flip, Cowboy Loye Pack and a fiddle band, the Tweedy Brothers. Beginning on January 7, 1933, the *Jamboree* moved from the studio to a live show at the Capitol Theater at midnight. A little later it was moved to the Wheeling Market Auditorium and to an earlier hour. Other acts came to WWVA, including Hugh and Shug's Radio Pals, Murrell Poore and Curley Miller. In May, 1937, Doc Williams and his Border Riders and that December, Big Slim, the Lone Cowboy, joined the *Jamboree* cast and remained there for a long time. Others spent less time there in their quest for stardom, including Floyd Tillman, Grandpa Jones, Blaine Smith and Lew Childre.

In October, 1942, WWVA became a

*Wheeling and **Jamboree U.S.A.***

50,000-watt station, thus increasing the size of the already substantial WWVA audience. Beginning in January, 1943, however, the management decided to discontinue the live shows until the war ended. Meanwhile, daily broadcasts and a studio-based *Jamboree* continued for the duration of the armed conflict. Since many male singers had entered military service, women came on the scene a bit stronger in the persons of Bonnie Baldwin, Shirley Barker, Mary "Sunflower" Calvas and Millie Wayne, among others. Songs designed to boost morale, comfort loved ones and strengthen patriotic feelings took up a large part of musical repertoires in those years.

In mid-1946, the *Jamboree* resumed its live show status and crowds flocked into the Virginia Theater to see the program for the next decade. In addition to old favorites like Doc Williams and Big Slim, younger and newer stars, such as Pete Cassell, Wilma Lee and Stoney Cooper, the Lilly Brothers and Hawkshaw Hawkins, soon added to the *Jamboree's* luster. People who would later hit it big in Nashville, who had briefer associations with Wheeling radio, included George Morgan and Hank Snow.

By February 8, 1947, a million people had paid admission to see the *Jamboree*. Other artists who made their mark on the program's history in this era included the Bailey Brothers, Bob Gallion, Hardrock Gunter, Lee and Juanita Moore, Jimmy Walker and Lone Pine & Betty Cody.

Beginning in the mid-50's, the CBS Network carried a portion of the *Jamboree* nationwide every third week, but it came too late in the age of radio to give the *Jamboree* as wide a listening audience as the *Opry* and the *National Barn Dance* once enjoyed. However, it may have been a factor in the program's survival as the other big live audience radio broadcasts pretty much died in the late 50's and early 60's.

The Virginia Theater came down in 1962 and for the next four years, the Rex Theater, with less than a thousand seats, served as home for the *Jamboree*. Doc and Chickie Williams remained, but the Coopers and Hawkins had gone to Nashville. Lee and Juanita split, with Lee remaining at the station. Big Slim stuck with the *Jamboree* until ill health and then death overtook him.The *Jamboree* moved to Wheeling Island and its exhibition center in 1966. Folks like Red Smiley and the Bluegrass Cut-Ups, Jim Eanes, Jimmie Stephens, Dick Curless and Esco Hankins entertained *Jamboree* audiences who came from locales extending from Ohio to Nova Scotia and Virginia to Ontario.

In 1969, the program, now called *Jamboree U.S.A.*, moved to its original and hopefully permanent home at the Capitol Theater on Main Street in downtown Wheeling. By then an increasing emphasis on guest stars had become a trend that steadily escalated through the decade. *Jamboree* regulars include artists like Bob Gallion and Patti Powell, Johnnie Russell, Junio Norman, and the ageless Doc and Chickie. Yet the evolving guest star system saw them appear with ever decreasing frequency. Major Country stars based in Bakersfield, Austin and Nashville received top billing while folks like Leon Douglas and Darnell Miller served as "warm up" acts. In 1983, *Jamboree U.S.A.* celebrated its Golden Anniversary, which included a visit by fiddler Senator Robert Byrd, and unveiled their own "Walkway of the Stars" with such luminaries present as Charley Pride, Billy Craddock, Dusty Owens, Betty Cody and Doc Williams.

So even if the *Jamboree's* format of recent years has resulted in the program's turning itself into a Nashville outpost instead of an alternative center, at least the show survives. There are also acts making it in Nashville who got their starts at WWVA, including the *Opry*'s popular Four Guys and relative newcomer Lionel Cartwright. *Jamboree U.S.A.* does have a tradition of its own and it is now moving into its seventh decade. IMT

Jesseca James refer CONWAY TWITTY

MARK JAMES

(Singer, Songwriter, Guitar, Violin, Keyboards)

Given Name:	**Francis Zambon**
Date of Birth:	**1940**
Where Born:	**Houston, Texas**
Married:	**Karen**

Mark James has become a major songwriter, mainly through the fact that Elvis Presley covered five of his songs. His fame became assured when he wrote the two classics *Suspicious Minds* and *Always on My Mind*.

His Italian father bought him a violin when Mark was age 4 and by the time he was 12 Mark also played electric guitar and keyboards. Mark formed a band while in high school and built up a reputation throughout Texas and Louisiana. He cut his first single, *Jive Note*, under the name of "Francis Zambon and the Naturals" and it became a regional hit in 1959. However, he was having trouble with people mispronouncing his name, and so "Mark James" was born. He formed the Mark James Trio and recorded *Running Back* and *She's Gone Away*, which were both regional hits and started Mark's career as a writer, artist and record producer.

In 1964, Mark was drafted and served two years in the armed forces, including a tour of duty in Vietnam. After his discharge, he was asked by producer Chips Moman to come to Memphis to produce and record. Mark enjoyed his first big success as a songwriter in 1968, when B.J. Thomas recorded *Eyes of a New York Woman*. The following year, Thomas cut another James song, *Hooked on a Feeling*, which went Top 5 and was Certified Gold. The song would also be recorded by Jonathan King (a U.K. Pop hit in 1971) and become a No.1 hit in 1974, when Swedish group Blue Swede cut it. Other versions have included those by Lloyd Price and the Twinkle Brothers. Also in 1969, B.J. recorded another Mark James song, *It's Only Love*, which was cut by Elvis Presley and most importantly, that year, Elvis recorded *Suspicious Minds*. The record went to No.1 and was Certified Gold. Mark commented that Elvis had utilized the exact arrangements that Mark had used on his own original version, which often happens. A year later, Waylon Jennings and Jessi Colter would release it and have a Top 25 Country hit. They re-released it in 1976 and had a Top 3 Country hit. In 1971, Dee Dee Warwick charted with her version. The song has also been recorded by Cleo Laine and Disco divas Merry Clayton and Candi Staton.

In 1972, Brenda Lee had a hit with *Always on My Mind* (written with Johnny Christopher and Wayne Carson) and a year later, Elvis recorded the song as the flip-side of *Separate Ways*. That same year, Elvis released another James song, *Raised on Rock*, which was also recorded by legendary albino Bluesman Johnny Winter. Also in 1973, Brenda Lee cut another James song, *Sunday Sunrise*, which would be recorded two years later by Anne Murray. In 1974, songwriter Mac Davis delved into the James' writing pad and recorded *One Hell of a Woman*. A year later, he chose *I Still Love You (You Still Love Me)* and charted with both.

During 1974, Mark moved to New York and signed with Screen Gems-EMI Music and also sang on nationally broadcast commercials. He wrote the song *Disco Ryder* with Wayne Carson (on the telephone) around this time, which Mark released as a single. His version was eventually part of the soundtrack of the 1979 movie *Kramer vs. Kramer*.

Just before Elvis died in 1977, he recorded Mark's song *Moody Blue*, which was a Top 10 hit in the U.K. The following year, B.J. Thomas converted another Mark James song, *Everybody Loves a Rain Song*, into a Top 50 hit. In 1979,

Mark was approached by the producers of the projected movie *The King of Rock and Roll* to write a song for the project. After some soul-searching, he wrote *Blue Suede Heaven*. The movie was never made, but Mark sang the song during the 1984 and 1985 celebration of Elvis Presley Week in Memphis. That year, John Wesley Ryles had a Top 20 Country hit with *Always on My Mind*, but three years down the road, Willie Nelson recorded what has to be the definitive version of the song. The record reached No.1 on the Country chart and Top 5 on the Pop list. When asked, at the 1988 Wembley Festival in England, what he thought of the Pet Shop Boys' U.K. chart topping Pop version, Willie's only comment (with a smile) was "Fast, wasn't it!"

Mark has been the recipient of numerous awards over the years including Memphis Music Association's "Outstanding Songwriter" in 1971. He won this award again in 1977 and 1982. *Always on My Mind* was named BMI's "Most Performed Song" (1982), NSAI's "Song of the Year" (1982) and National Music Publishers Association "Song of the Year" and "Country Song of the Year (1982). In addition, the song won two Grammy Awards in 1982 as "Song of the Year" and "Best Country Song" and it won for Willie Nelson the Grammy that year for "Best Country Vocal Performance, Male." In 1982 and 1983, it achieved a rarity by being named "Song of the Year" by the CMA. Mark has also won the International Music Exposition "World Music Award of Merit." Mark is still active in Nashville as a songwriter.

SONNY JAMES

(Singer, Songwriter, Guitar, Fiddle)
Given Name: James Loden
Date of Birth: May 1, 1929
Where Born: Hackleburg, Alabama
Married: Doris

The Southern Gentleman, ***Sonny James***

Known as "the Southern Gentleman," because of his good looks, respectable appearance and elegant manners, Sonny James has enjoyed 72 Country hits, including 23 chart-toppers and 18 Pop hits, making him one of the most successful acts of all time.

He enjoyed the advantage of being born into a show business family and he got his first guitar, which was made by his father, when he was age 3. That guitar is now in the Country Music Hall of Fame. The next year, Sonny, with his parents and sister Thelma, won a Folk contest in Birmingham, Alabama. There, legend has it, singer Kate Smith predicted a golden future for the young boy.

By the time he was in his teens, Sonny (his teenage nickname) had clocked up innumerable hours performing with the Loden Family group (he and his four sisters), was proficient on both guitar and fiddle and had appeared on several regional Country shows like the *Big D Jamboree*, *Louisiana Hayride* and *Saturday Night Shindig*. Even when the Korean War took 15 months of his time, he honed his performing skills by entertaining fellow servicemen and Korean orphans, and he wrote songs. The guitar his father sent to him when he went to Korea was used as the unit guitar and is stamped "252 Truck Company" on its back. It must have brought them luck, as only one member of the unit was killed in combat.

Upon his discharge in 1952, Sonny played gigs and became friends with Chet Atkins. Looking for a recording contract, he visited Chet in Nashville, who introduced him to Capitol Records producer Ken Nelson. Nelson liked Sonny's singing style and his compositions, leading to a fruitful and long-standing recording contract. Sonny released his first single, *That's Me Without You*, that year, and it reached the Top 10 on the Country charts the following year. It was not until the end of 1954 that he achieved any further chart success, when *She Done Give Her Heart to Me* got into the Top 15. Sonny established a pattern of playing guitar on all his records.

Come 1956 and Sonny started to chart with some regularity. *For Rent* reached the Top 10 and was followed by two Top 15 successes, *Twenty Feet of Muddy Water* and *The Cat Came Back* (the latter went Top 30 in the U.K.). He ended the year with a song that became his first career single. *Young Love* topped the Country charts for 9 weeks out of a total 24 weeks and crossed over to top the Pop charts. Although he came a poor second to Tab Hunter's version in the U.K., he did reach No.11 there. The flip-side, *You're the Reason I'm in Love*, was also a Country Top 10 hit in 1957. Sonny followed-up with another Top 10 record, *First Date, First Kiss, First Love*, which was also a Top 30 Pop hit. He wrapped up the year with his version of *Lovesick Blues*. In 1958, he had a further Top 10 single with *Uh-Huh—Mm* which also scraped into the Pop Top 100.

For a time, Sonny was more often at Pop and rock'n'roll concerts than at Country venues. Then suddenly, Sonny hit a barren patch. Sonny left Capitol for a while and tried his luck with NRC Records in 1960 and RCA Victor in 1961. Between 1958 and 1963, he only had one Top 30 entry, *Jenny Lou*, in 1960, on NRC and his Pop successes were all at the basement level and included his solitary RCA Pop entry, *Apache*.

Then in 1963, he returned to Capitol wearing a clearly defined Country hat. He immediately hit the Country Top 10 with *The Minute You're Gone* (this was a No.1 Pop hit in the U.K. for superstar Cliff Richard). The following year, Sonny again made the Top 10 with *Baltimore,* and then later that year he had his second No.1 with *You're the Only World I Know*, which stayed at the top for 4 weeks out of 25 weeks on the charts.

He consolidated his career in 1965 with *I'll Keep Holding On (Just to Your Love)*, which went Top 3, *Behind the Tear*, another No.1, and *True Love's a Blessing*, which peaked in the Top 3. If 1965 was good, then 1966 was equal to it. He started off the year with a remake of the Adam Wade hit *Take Good Care of Her*, which went to No.1, and followed it with the Top 3 success *Room in Your Heart*.

Then, in 1967, Sonny started a run of No.1 successes that continued until 1971. In all, he had 16 consecutive chart-toppers during this period. They were, 1967: *Need You*, *I'll Never Find Another You* (a Pop hit for the Seekers) and *It's the Little Things*; 1968: *A World of Our Own* (also a Pop hit for the Seekers), *Heaven Says Hello* and *Born to Be with You* (a Pop success for the Chordettes); 1969: Roy Orbison's *Only the Lonely*, *Running Bear* (a No.1 for Johnny Preston) and Ivory Joe Hunter's classic *Since I Met You Baby*; 1970: Brook Benton's *It's Just a Matter of Time*, *My Love* (a No.1 Pop hit for Petula Clark), *Don't Keep Me Hangin' On* and another Brook Benton classic, *Endlessly*; 1971: *Empty Arms*, *Bright Lights* as well as *Big City* and *Here Comes Honey Again*.

As the hit singles tumbled out, so did the albums, which were also immensely successful. There were tours, too, both in the U.S. and abroad, where Sonny was backed by his band, the Southern Gentlemen. TV appearances included the *Jimmy Dean Show*, the *Bob Hope Show*, the *Ed Sullivan Show* and *Hee Haw*. He also appeared in several movies, namely *Las Vegas Hillbillies* with Jayne Mansfield (1966), *Hillbillies in a Haunted House* with Lon Chaney, Jr., and Basil Rathbone (1967), *Second Fiddle to a Steel Guitar* (1967) and *Nashville Rebel* (1967).

As 1972 got under way, Sonny had a Top 3 hit with *Only Love Can Break a Heart*, which had been a Pop hit for Gene Pitney a decade earlier. Sonny followed this up with his final No.1 for Capitol, *That's Why I Love You Like I Do*. He then moved over to Columbia and immediately scored with another No.1, *When the Snow Is on the Roses*, which was his last cross-over single. Capitol was still releasing singles, but it was with his Columbia releases that Sonny continued to make his mark. He wrapped up 1972 with the Top 5 hit *White Silver Sands*. As 1973 got under way, Sonny racked up another Top 5 hit with his remake of the Al Martino hit *I Love You More and More Every Day*. Then he had his first single that failed to make the Top 10, *If She Just Helps Me Get Over You*. In 1974, Sonny came back in sparkling form with what would be his last No.1, *Is It Wrong (For Loving You)*. He followed this with *A Mi Esposa con Amor (To My Wife with Love)* (Top 5).

In this period, Sonny diversified. He produced material for several artists, most notably three albums for Marie Osmond, including the transatlantic hit revival single *Paper Roses* in 1973. He also extended his activities to music publishing.

During 1975 until he left Columbia in 1978, Sonny continued to chart with regularity. The hits weren't quite as big, but he still hit the Top 10 on six more occasions with *A Little Bit South of Saskatoon*, *Little Band of Gold* and *What in the World Came Over You* (all 1975), *When Something Is Wrong with My Baby* and *Come on In* (both 1976) and *You're Free to Go* (1977). Sonny also hit the Top 15 in 1976 with the interesting coupling *The Prisoner's Song/Back in the Saddle Again*. In 1977, he cut the album ***Sonny James in Prison, in Person***, in Tennessee State Prison.

He moved from Columbia and surfaced on Monument in 1979. He had a couple of medium level singles, and by 1981, he had moved to Dimension Records. He came back into the Top 20 with *Innocent Lies* that year and continued charting. From 1982, he was backed by a new group, Silver. He released his final album on Dot in 1986, without success.

He now raises Black Angus cattle on his farms in Hackleburg. He also likes bass fishing, sailing and keeping to himself. His peak years are littered with awards, including *Record World*'s "Record of the Year" award in 1965, *Billboard*'s "No.1 Artist" (1969) and *Record World*'s "Country Music's Male Artist of the Decade" (1977). SM

RECOMMENDED ALBUMS:

"Sonny" (Capitol)(1957) [Re-issued by Stetson UK in the original sleeve (1988)]
"The Best of Sonny James" (Capitol)(1966)
"The Best of Sonny James, Vol. 2" (Capitol)(1969)
"The Astrodome Presents the Southern Gentleman" (Capitol)(1969)
"The Best of Sonny James, Vol. 3" (Capitol)(1972)
"200 Years of Country Music" (Columbia)(1976)
"Sonny James in Prison, in Person" (Columbia)(1977)
"Greatest Hits—Sonny James" (Columbia)(1978)
"I'm Looking Over the Rainbow" (Dimension)(1982) [With Ricky Skaggs, the Whites, Anthony Crawford & Silver]

J.D. JARVIS

(Singer, Songwriter, Guitar, Most String Instruments)
Given Name: **John Dill Jarvis**
Date of Birth: **April 21, 1924**
Where Born: **Manchester, Kentucky**
Married: **Rosie Owens**
Children: **Lucky**

J.D. Jarvis has been one of the most active Bluegrass-Gospel singers of the past three decades. Although he has appeared in person most often in churches within a 100-mile radius of his adopted home city of Hamilton, Ohio, his recordings have found their way to Europe and other parts of the world. In addition to cutting many albums, Jarvis has been a prolific writer. Two of his compositions, *Take Your Shoes Off, Moses* and *Six Hours on the Cross*, have become Bluegrass Gospel standards.

He was born in the mountainous Clay County, Kentucky, and absorbed the music of his Appalachian culture, both sacred and secular, from early childhood. He began playing guitar at age 7 and eventually learned the rudiments of most string instruments as well. Like many other mountain families, J.D.'s shifted back and forth between their preferred life in the Cumberland Mountains and the more prosperous economic opportunity found in southwestern Ohio.

A few weeks prior to his eighteenth birthday, young Jarvis, then residing in Hamilton, enlisted in the U.S. Army, serving most of WWII and the early phases of the Cold War. During WWII, he suffered serious combat wounds and believes that only a Divine Miracle enabled him to survive. In early 1948, after six years, he received his discharge.

For approximately a decade after this, J.D. rotated between living in Kentucky and Ohio, finally locating permanently in Hamilton in 1959. Always interested in music, he sometimes assisted a singing preacher friend named Brother Claude Ely from Big Stone Gap, Virginia, who pastored a church in Cumberland, Kentucky. J.D. was playing tambourine the night in 1953 when King Records taped Ely singing his classic composition *There Ain't No Grave Gonna Hold My Body Down* and other numbers during a service.

After Jarvis settled in Hamilton, he started a paint contracting business which he operated successfully until his retirement. Interested in both Country and Gospel music, J.D. wrote songs and sang them for years before he began to get seriously involved in recording them. His able but somewhat raw primitive vocals could often be heard on local radio and TV and in numerous churches.

Beginning in the early 60's, Jarvis took to recording his songs and music with considerable gusto. He usually used Bluegrass accompaniment, although electrical instruments and piano could sometimes be heard. Since he did not employ a band to travel with him, he generally recruited able musicians from the local migrant community such as banjoist Noah Crase, fiddler Paul Munnins, Dobroist Harley Gabbard and Joe and Lily Isaacson for his sessions. Sometimes he used Burkett "Uncle Josh" Graves or Ralph Stanley's Clinch Mountain Boys for recordings. Many of these sessions were held in Rusty York's Jewel Recording Studio in Mount Healthy, Ohio. Several of Jarvis' albums appeared on York's Jewel label and some on J.D.'s own Down Home or Log Cabin label. However, those with the widest distribution were on Uncle Jim O'Neal's Rural Rhythm Records.

The Jarvis repertoire consisted of a variety of Old-Time Gospel songs, numbers from the more recent hillbilly sacred tradition and a scattering of his own originals. Through recordings by the Lewis Family, Ralph Stanley and the Isaacs among others, the songs of J.D. Jarvis have been heard by people who were probably unaware of Jarvis' original versions. Some of his other outstanding originals include, *My Lord Will Send a Moses, Life of Ransom,* his topical *The Hyden Miner's Tragedy* and the patriotic *Thank God for Old Glory*.

On the personal side, J.D. and his wife, Rosie, still reside in their long-time home on Flamingo Drive in Hamilton. Their son, Lucky, who has taken over the paint contracting business, lives nearby and J.D. remains active on the local Gospel music scene. IMT

RECOMMENDED ALBUM:

"Bluegrass Hymn Time" (Jewel)(1967)

JENKINS & SHERRILL (a.k.a. the Hired Hands)

SNUFFY JENKINS
(Singer, Banjo, Washboard, Guitar)

Given Name: DeWitt Jenkins
Date of Birth: October 27, 1908
Where Born: Harris, North Carolina
Married: Margaret Cannon
Children: Toby DeWitt
Date of Death: April 30, 1990

PAPPY SHERRILL
(Singer, Fiddle)

Given Name: Homer Lee Sherrill
Date of Birth: March 23, 1915
Where Born: Sherrill's Ford, North Carolina
Married: Doris Lyle
Children: Wayne, Carol, Gerald

Snuffy Jenkins and Pappy Sherrill rank as key transitional figures in the evolution of Old-Time music as it moved toward Bluegrass. Jenkins pioneered in the use of three-finger banjo on radio and record, which protégés such as Earl Scruggs and Don Reno further developed.

Jenkins was born in Rutherford County, North Carolina. Both Snuffy and a brother, Verl, took to music early in life with the former eventually settling on banjo. According to his own recollection, Snuffy started playing in the three-finger style about 1927, the same year that he and Verl began competing in fiddling contests.

In 1934, they added a guitar-picking cousin and another picker to their entourage and became the Jenkins String Band at WBT Charlotte. In 1936, this band dissolved and Snuffy joined J.E. Mainer's Mountaineers, first at WSPA Spartanburg and then at WIS Columbia, both in South Carolina. Jenkins recorded several numbers on Bluebird with the Mountaineers, being especially prominent on the song *Kiss Me Cindy* from a 1938 session.

When Mainer left to go elsewhere, the band members remained at WIS and Verl Jenkins first filled in on fiddle and then Homer Sherrill on a permanent basis in October, 1939. Announcer Byron Parker took leadership of what now had become the WIS Hillbillies on radio and Byron Parker's Mountaineers on record.

Homer Sherrill was born near Hickory, North Carolina, and took to the fiddle at age 7, making his radio debut at 13 in Gastonia. His first real professional experience of note came at WBT with his East Hickory String Band, also known as the Crazy Hickory Nuts. He also gained some brief experience with the Blue Sky Boys, Mack and Shorty, Mainer's Mountaineers, with the Morris Brothers and Wiley, Zeke and Homer. Sherrill managed to get in some sessions with the latter three groups, all on the Bluebird label.

The Parker-led group also included two guitar pickers, Leonard Stokes and Clyde Robbins, among their members when they recorded twice in 1940 (February 9 and October 10) in Atlanta for Bluebird. The band cut eight sides each time and featured a variety of numbers that included vocal solos, duets and quartets, as well as instrumentals. Jenkins and Sherrill served as the instrumental stars, while Stokes and Robbins divided the vocal chores. Parker confined his role to singing bass in the quartets. The band did not make records again until 1946, when they did four sides on the DeLuxe label, by which time Floyd Lacewell and Gene Ray had joined the WIS Hillbillies.

After Byron Parker died in October 1948, Snuffy and Pappy took over the band, changing their name to the Hired Hands (Parker referred to himself as "the Old Hired Hand"). By this time, Snuffy had added a great deal of comedy to his act and the group worked up some elaborate skits, several of which also involved Julian "Greasy" Medlin, a former medicine and minstrel showman, who joined them in 1941.

When WIS added TV in 1953, the Hired Hands added television to their résumé. The band got another recording opportunity in 1962, making an album on the Folk-Lyric label. With the growth of Bluegrass festivals, Jenkins & Sherrill, by then legendary figures, received opportunities to be heard by audiences outside their native Carolinas who appreciated their blend of Old-Time and Bluegrass music mixed with comedy, which they also had ample opportunity to display on a pair of Rounder albums, featuring some of Medlin's varied show-business background.

With the passage of time, advancing age began to take some toll on the group. Medlin died and ill health increasingly plagued Snuffy. Harold Lucas, who handled rhythm guitar and most of the vocals after 1971, took on a bigger role and his son Randy showed promise as an up and coming banjo and lead guitar picker. By the time of the group's last album, in 1989, Snuffy picked banjo on only two numbers and washboard on a few others. When the venerable musician passed away the following year, he was buried with Masonic honors. Homer Sherrill continues as one of the true living masters of the Old-Time fiddle. IMT

*The Hired Hands, **Jenkins & Sherrill***

RECOMMENDED ALBUMS:

"Carolina Bluegrass" (Folk-Lyric)(1962) [Re-issued on Arhoolie]
"33 Years of Pickin' and Pluckin'" (Rounder)(1972)
"Crazy Water Barn Dance" (Rounder)(1976)
"Something Special" (Old Homestead)(1989)

ANDREW JENKINS

(Singer, Songwriter, Guitar, French Harp, Mandolin)

Given Name: Andrew Jenkins
Date of Birth: November 26, 1885
Where Born: Jenkinsburg, Georgia
Married: 1. Mattie Chandler; 2. Frances Jane Walden Eskew
Children: Irene, Mary Lee, T.P. (adopted)
Date of Death: 1956

Andrew Jenkins was one of the more important Country composers of the 1920's with numerous songs to his credit.

Born on the outskirts of Atlanta, Andrew was made virtually sightless by a faulty medication prescribed for him as an infant. In 1939, he lost even this limited vision. During his early adulthood, Jenkins made his living selling newspapers, but at age 21 he became a preacher and thereafter, was addressed as the Reverend Jenkins. This move surprised no one who knew him well.

At age 9, he converted to Methodism and frequently preached to playmates from tree stumps and porches. The other thing the child was noted for was being able to play almost any instrument placed in his hands. During his youth, Andrew also began to write songs, an activity at which he excelled. Still, it was only after he married his second wife, in 1919, that Jenkins' abilities gained a wide audience. With his wife's three children, Irene, Mary Lee, and T.P., he formed the Jenkins Family, a group that debuted on Atlanta's radio WSB.

They soon became very popular and during the 20's the family received fan mail from throughout the U.S. as well as Canada and Mexico. This popularity led to their initial recording session, in 1924, when they recorded *Church in the Wildwood* and *If I Could Hear My Mother Pray Again.* They were probably Country music's first family group, preceding the now better remembered Carter Family into the studio by three years. In subsequent years members of the Jenkins Family recorded in various combinations and under several names: Jenkins Sacred Singers, the Irene Spain Family, Blind Andy, Gooby Jenkins and Andrew Jenkins & Carson Robison.

Despite his extensive recording career, it is as a songwriter that Jenkins is best remembered today, his output consisting mainly of religious songs, tragedy and disaster ballads, and outlaw songs. Of Jenkins' numerous religious songs, only *God Put a Rainbow in the Clouds* is well known today. His several tragedy and disaster songs include *Little Marian Parker*, *Ben Dewberry's Final Run*, *Wreck of the Royal Palm* and *The Death of Floyd Collins*. Of his several outlaw ballads, the two best known are *Kinnie Wagner* and *Billy the Kid*. Over his career Jenkins produced approximately 800 songs, but despite his prolific output and the popularity of many of his songs, he made little money from his compositions. His work as an evangelist was his prime source of income until his death in 1956.

WKM

WAYLON JENNINGS

(Singer, Songwriter, Guitar, Bass Guitar, Actor)

Date of Birth:	**June 15, 1937**
Where Born:	**Littlefield, Texas**
Married:	**1. Maxine (div.)**
	2. Lynne (div.)
	3. Barbara (div.)
	4. Jessi Colter (m. 1969)
Children:	**Terry, Julie, Buddy, Deanna, Jennifer (stepdaughter), Tammy Lynn (adopted), Shooter**

There is no doubt that when it comes to listing the superstars of Country music, that Waylon (and yes, only the first name is necessary), is among the megastars. For over 40 years, "Hoss" has been involved in music, and since 1965, he has consistently charted. As one of the leaders of the "outlaw" movement, he helped turn Country music around from the Pop direction that it was heading toward, and in the process, he has written songs that are part of the backbone of the harder edge of Country music.

Waylon learned his first guitar chords from his mother when he was about 8, and by the time he was 12 he was a deejay on his local radio station. He soon put together his first band, using Hank Williams and Ernest Tubb material. He left school at age 14, and picked cotton until he was 16. He moved to Lubbock, Texas, in 1954, and the following year while working on KILL's *Sunday Dance Party* he met Buddy Holly. Buddy, although only slightly older, greatly influenced him and taught Waylon different guitar rhythm patterns.

Waylon Jennings** with his wife, **Jessi Colter

From 1958 through February 1959, Waylon played bass in Holly's band. In 1958, Buddy financed and produced Waylon's first single, *Jole Blon*, which was released on Brunswick. Waylon was scheduled to fly with Buddy on the ill-fated flight; instead, he gave up his seat to The Big Bopper, who was suffering with a bad cold. Greatly affected by Holly's death, Waylon moved back to Lubbock, to mull over the future. He worked as a deejay, and then in 1960 moved to Phoenix and formed his own band, the Waylors.

He started to get a following at JD's, a venue in Phoenix, and released *My Baby Walks All Over Me* on Trend in 1961. He went on to work for Audio Recorders in Phoenix, as a producer, and three masters recorded for Trend were leased to Ramco, who released two singles, *Never Again* and *My World,* and then in 1963 Herb Alpert produced the single *Sing the Girl a Song, Bill*, which was released on A & M and a subsequent, unsuccessful album. With the help of Bobby Bare, Waylon was signed by Chet Atkins to RCA and in 1965, he moved to Nashville.

When he first arrived in Nashville, Waylon lived with Johnny Cash, with Cash doing the cooking, and the two of them commenced an enduring friendship. Waylon hit the charts with his first single, *That's the Chance I'll Have to Take*, which reached the Top 50, and followed it with the Top 20 hit *Stop the World (And Let Me Off)*.

From then until the end of 1969, Waylon chalked up a series of major hits that turned him into an internationally acknowledged leader of the Folk-Country style. In 1966, he had *Anita, You're Dreaming* (Top 20), *Time to Bum Again* (Top 20), Gordon Lightfoot's *(That's What You Get) For Lovin' Me* (Top 10) and *Green River* (Top 15). The last named was from the movie *Nashville Rebel*, in which Waylon appeared. It was written by Harlan Howard and was one of the tracks on the album ***Waylon Jennings Sings Ol' Harlan***. Waylon's 1967 hits were *Mental Revenge* (Top 15) and *The Chokin' Kind* (Top 10). In addition, the flip-side of the latter, *Love of the Common People*, also went Top 70. Interestingly, on Waylon's February 14 and April 27, 1967, sessions, the piano player was Ray Stevens. Waylon's three hits in 1968 all went Top 5, and were *Walk on Out of My Mind*, *Only Daddy That'll Walk the Line* (Top 3) and *Yours Love*. In addition, he had a Top 5 duet with Anita Carter entitled *I Got You*. He underwent a slight dip in 1969, with hits with *Something Wrong in California, The Days of Sand and Shovels/Delia's Gone, MacArthur Park* (with the Kimberleys, earning a Grammy Award for "Best Country Performance by a Duo or Group") and then an upswing with Chuck Berry's *Brown Eyed Handsome Man*, which had once been recorded by Buddy Holly, and now became a Top 3 hit for Waylon.

The 70's are split into two distinct portions, as Waylon became disillusioned with the Nashville bureaucracy and the outlaw movement started to take root. In 1970, his hits were *Singer of Sad Songs* (Top 15), Kristofferson's *The Taker* (Top 5) and *(Don't Let the Sun Set on You) Tulsa* (Top 20). He also had a Top 25 duet with Jessi Colter, *Suspicious Minds*.

Waylon had two Top 15 hits in 1971, namely *Mississippi Woman* and *Cedartown, Georgia*, as well as another duet with Jessi, *Under Your Spell Again* (Top 40). Because of his lack of production control, Waylon was considering quitting the business and was talked around by drummer Richie Albright, who introduced him to Neil Reshen, who took both Waylon and Willie Nelson under his wing.

From 1972, Waylon took over his own production chores and on one occasion, took a gun into the studio, threatening to shoot the fingers off any musicians who looked at their charts rather than played by feeling. Shortly after, he decided to use his road band in the studio rather than session players. His hits in 1972 show an upswing in audience and radio acceptance. All three singles that year made the Top 10; they were *Good-Hearted Woman* (Top 3), *Sweet Dream Woman* and *Pretend I Never Happened*. This also marked the arrival of Waylon Jennings, songwriter and collaborator with Willie Nelson.

In 1973, he had a Top 10 hit with *You Can Have Her* and then dipped for *We Had It All*, which only reached the Top 30, but he closed out the year with the Top 10 single *You Ask Me To*. With the advent of 1974, his public acceptance soared, and he had back-to-back No.1 hits with *This Time* and *I'm a Ramblin' Man*, the latter becoming a Top 75 Pop success. He wrapped up the year with the Top 3 hit *Rainy Day Woman/Let's All Help the Cowboys (Sing the Blues)*. That year, he was featured on the soundtrack album of *Ned Kelly* alongside Mick Jagger and Kristofferson.

Waylon continued on his Top 10 way in 1975 and had hits with *Dreaming My Dreams with You, Are You Sure Hank Done It This Way/Bob Wills Is Still King* (No.1) and the re-recorded *Good-Hearted Woman*, a duet from Waylon and Willie (No.1 and Top 25 Pop hit, which also became CMA's "Single of the Year"). That year, Waylon was named CMA's "Male Vocalist of the Year." He got 1976 under way with the re-release of *Suspicious Minds* with Jessi. This time around it went Top 3. His other hits for the year were *Can't You See/I'll Go Back to Her* (Top 5) and *Are You Ready for the Country* (Top 10). That year, he appeared in the movie *Mackintosh and TJ*. The other memorable event of the year for Waylon was the album ***Wanted! The Outluws***, with Jessi, Willie and Tompall Glaser. The album would go Double Platinum in 1985. In addition, it was named CMA's "Album of the Year" and Waylon and Willie became CMA's "Duo of the Year."

From 1977 through 1983, such was his success that his singles and albums only bore the name "Waylon." Both his solo hits in 1977 went to No.1. The first was *Luckenbach, Texas (Back to the Basics of Life)*, which stayed at the top for 6 weeks, featured an end vocal from Willie and became a Top 25 Pop hit. The other chart-topper was *The Wurlitzer Prize (I Don't Want to Get Over You)/Lookin' for a Feeling*. He followed up with more major hits in 1978. The Waylon and Willie classic duet of Ed Bruce's *Mammas Don't Let Your Babies Grow Up to Be Cowboys/I Can Get Off on You* made it three No.1s in a row and earned the twosome a Grammy for "Best Country Performance by a Duo or Group." His duet with Johnny Cash, *There Ain't No Good Chain Gang*, went Top 3. He had another solo No.1 record, *I've Always Been Crazy*, which stayed at the top for three weeks. He closed out the year with the Top 5 single that was almost a calling card for his future work, *Don't You Think This Outlaw Bit's Done Got Out of Hand/Girl I Can Tell (You're Trying to Work It Out)*. That year, he was featured on Paul Kennerley's wonderful concept album ***White Mansions***. In 1977, Waylon's albums ***Dreaming My Dreams*** and ***Are You Ready for the Country*** went Gold, and ***Ol' Waylon*** went Platinum. The following year, ***Waylon Live*** and ***I've Always Been Crazy*** were Certified Gold and ***Waylon and Willie*** went Platinum; by 1985 it had sold over 2 million copies.

Waylon ended the decade with two No.1 solo hits, Bob McDill's *Amanda*, which also reached the Top 60 on the Pop list, and *Come with Me*. In addition, *I Wish I Was Crazy Again*, the flip-side of *There Ain't No Good Chain Gang*, reached the Top 25 for Waylon and Cash. In addition, Waylon's ***Greatest Hits*** package was Certified Platinum and by 1985 had sold in excess of 3 million copies.

As 1980 got under way, Waylon had another No.1 with *I Ain't Living Long Like This*, a Top 10 success with *Clyde* and the No.1 smash *Theme from The Dukes of Hazzard (Good Ol' Boys)*, which also reached the Top 25 on the Pop list and was Certified Gold. Waylon appeared as "the Balladeer" in the TV series *The Dukes of Hazzard*. That year, he had two albums Certified Gold, ***What Goes Around*** and ***Music Man***. During the year, he appeared in the hit movie *Urban Cowboy*.

He started out 1981 with a pair of hits with Jessi, *Storms Never Last* (Top 20) and the Top 10 single medley *Wild Side of Life—It Wasn't God Who Made Honky Tonk Angels*. He had the Top 5 solo single *Shine* to close out the year. Waylon and Jessi's album ***Leather and Lace*** went Gold before the fall. He and Willie started off 1982 with a splash, when *Just to Satisfy You* went to No.1. He followed with the solo Top 5 single *Women Do Know How to Carry On* and ended the year with another duet with Willie, a remake of *(Sittin' on) The Dock of the Bay*. In 1983, he released one of his finest albums, ***Waylon and Company***, which featured duets with Jerry Reed, Hank Williams, Jr., Ernest Tubb, Emmylou Harris, Willie, Tony Joe White, Jessi, James Garner, and Mel Tillis. Three of the tracks, *Just to Satisfy You, Hold On, I'm Comin'* (with Jerry Reed) and *The Conversation* (with Hank Williams, Jr.) were Top 20 entries. The latter had originally been released on Hank, Jr.'s 1979 album ***Family Tradition***. Waylon had two solo hits that year, the No.1 *Lucille (You Don't Do Your Daddy's Will)* and *Breakin' Down*, both from the album ***It's Only Rock'n'Roll***. He finished the year with a duet with Willie, *Take It to the Limit*, from their duet album of the same title. The Waylon and Willie album ***WWII*** earned a Gold Disc in 1983.

Waylon stayed with RCA until 1985 and chalked up the following hits: 1984: *I May Be Used (But Baby I Ain't Used Up)* (Top 5), *Never Could Toe the Mark* (Top 10) and *America* (Top 10); 1985: *Waltz Me to Heaven* (Top 10, written by Dolly Parton), *Drinkin' and Dreamin'* (Top 3) and *The Devil's on the Loose* (Top 15). Waylon teamed up with Willie, Cash and Kristofferson for the project called ***Highwayman***. The title track of the album became a No.1 hit (earning ACM's nod as "Single Record of the Year") and was followed by a Top 20 single, Guy Clark's *Desperados Waiting for a Train*. The ***Highwayman*** album was Certified Gold in 1986.

Waylon signed with MCA in 1986 and came under the production control of Jimmy Bowen, for whom Waylon has total respect. Waylon had three solo hits that year, all making the Top 10, and they were *Working Without a Net, Will the Wolf Survive* and *What You'll Do When I'm Gone*. In addition, he teamed up with Johnny Cash for the Top 40 success *Even Cowgirls Get the Blues*. He started off 1987 with another No.1, *Rose in Paradise,* and followed it with two Top 10 singles, *Fallin' Out* and *My Rough and Rowdy Days*. The last named came from an autobiographical project that Waylon wrote with top Nashville songwriter Roger Murrah, entitled ***A Man Called Hoss***. The project, "the story of my life...before somebody gets it wrong," was originally planned as a book. On the album, Waylon talked frankly of his 21-year drug problem, and how he kicked the habit. As a result of this collaboration with Murrah and his new-found vigor, Waylon found his songs being cut by others, including *Angels Love Bad Men* by Barbara Mandrell and *Somewhere Between Ragged and Right*, on which John Anderson duetted with Waylon.

A second single from the album, *If Ole Hank Could Only See Us Now (Chapter Five...Nashville),* reached the Top 20, and then suddenly, his singles were not as successful. The follow-up, *How Much Is It Worth to Live in L.A.*, only reached the Top 40 and then he had to undergo a heart by-pass operation, which, as he told the writer, only left him with the vice of "chasing Jessi."

Although his record success was at a lower level, he still managed to chart through 1989 with *Which Way Do I Go (Now That I'm Gone)* (Top 30), *Trouble Man* (Top 70) and *You Put the Soul in the Song* (Top 60). During 1990, he moved to Epic Records and charted with *Wrong* (Top 5) and *Where Corn Don't Grow* (Top 70), both coming from his Top 10 album ***The Eagle***. He also hit the charts with *Silver Stallion*, taken from the ***Highwayman 2*** album and again featuring Cash, Kristofferson and Nelson. The following year, he had two solo hits, also from ***The Eagle*** album, *What Bothers Me Most* (Top 70) and *The Eagle* (Top 30), as well as a duet with Willie, *If I Can Find a Clean Shirt*, which peaked in the Top 60. That year, Prism Leisure Video issued the video ***Waylon—Renegade, Outlaw, Legend***.

In 1992, Waylon released the album ***Too Dumb for New York, Too Ugly for L.A.***, which did not fare well on the Country Album chart, and no singles charted. The following year, Waylon released ***Cowboys, Sisters, Rascals & Dirt***, a children's album, on Ode 2 Kids label. In 1994, Waylon re-signed to RCA.

RECOMMENDED ALBUMS:

"Waylon Jennings Sings Ol' Harlan" (RCA Victor)(1967)
"Just to Satisfy You" (RCA Victor)(1969) [Features Anita Carter]
"Ladies Love Outlaws" (RCA Victor)(1972)
"Wanted! The Outlaws" (RCA Victor)(1976) [With Willie Nelson, Jessi Colter and Tompall Glaser]
"Ol' Waylon" (RCA Victor)(1977)
"Waylon & Willie" (RCA Victor)(1978)
"I've Always Been Crazy" (RCA Victor)(1978) [Re-released 1981][With the Crickets]
"Greatest Hits" (RCA Victor)(1979)
"What Goes Around" (RCA Victor)(1979)
"Music Man" (RCA Victor)(1980) [Re-released 1982] [With Jerry Reed, Johnny Rodriguez and Gary Scruggs]
"Leather and Lace" (RCA Victor)(1981) [With Jessi Colter]
"Dreaming My Dreams" (RCA Victor)(1981)
"Waylon Live" (RCA Victor)(1981)
"WWII" (RCA Victor)(1982) [With Willie Nelson]
"It's Only Rock'n'Roll" (RCA Victor)(1983)
"Take It to the Limit" (Columbia)(1983) [With Willie Nelson]
"Waylon & Company" (RCA Victor)(1983)
"Highwayman" (Columbia)(1986)
"Will the Wolf Survive" (MCA)(1986)
"A Man Called Hoss" (MCA)(1987)
"Highwayman 2" (Columbia)(1990)
"The Eagle" (Epic)(1990)
"Clean Shirt" (Epic)(1991) [With Willie Nelson]

Jet Set refer BYRDS

JIM & JESSE

JIM McREYNOLDS
(Vocals, Guitar, Mandolin)

Given Name:	**James Monroe McReynolds**
Date of Birth:	**February 13, 1927**
Married:	**Arretta June McCoy**
Children:	**Janeen**

JESSE McREYNOLDS
(Vocals, Fiddle, Guitar, Mandolin)

Given Name:	**Jesse Lester McReynolds**
Date of Birth:	**July 9, 1929**
Married:	**Constance Darlene McCoy**
Children:	**Gwen, Keith, Michael, Randy**
Both Born:	**Coeburn, Virginia**

Jim & Jesse, above all else, illustrate how the harmony duet translation of the 30's has survived into another generation of Bluegrass. Natives of mountainous western Virginia, the McReynolds brothers started their careers as a mandolin-guitar duet. However, they quickly acquired a full Bluegrass band, the Virginia Boys, which they have maintained for some decades, with occasional forays into a more modern Country sound.

Family musicians helped provide early inspiration for Jim & Jesse, as their grandfather Charles McReynolds was a locally renowned fiddler who recorded a session for Victor in 1927 with a band known as the Bull Mountain Moonshiners. Their father worked in the coal mines but also fiddled. Duet acts in the 30's, such as the Monroe Brothers, also influenced them somewhat later.

Jim McReynolds got out of the Army, in 1947, after a two-year hitch and the brothers began their first regular professional work that year with a 15-minute daily program at WNVA Norton, Virginia, where the Stanley Brothers had initiated their careers several months earlier. They earned little cash on this initial effort, a situation that would characterize many of their early years in radio. The brothers toiled for a few months each on stations that included WJHL Johnson City, Tennessee, WCHS Charleston, West Virginia, and WFHG Bristol, West Virginia. In 1949, they went to WGAC Augusta, Georgia, for a year. They then went on to KXEL Waterloo, Iowa, WMY Cedar Rapids and KFBI Wichita, Kansas, with minimal success.

While at WPFB Middletown, Ohio, in 1951, they cut ten Gospel songs with a third vocalist, Larry Roll, as the Virginian Trio. Jim & Jesse left KFBI and moved to WWNC Asheville, North Carolina, and then joined the *Kentucky Barn Dance* on WVLK Versailles, Kentucky. In 1952, Jim & Jesse got a contract with Capitol Records, recording eight sides at a Nashville session on June 13 that year, with the help of band members Hoke Jenkins on banjo, Curly Sechler on second guitar, and studio musician Bob Moore on bass. James Loden, soon to be famous as Sonny James, helped out on fiddle. The session included one of their trademark songs, *Are You Missing Me*, which featured some of Jesse's unique mandolin picking and established them as performers of near-perfect pure Bluegrass.

While performing on WCYB Bristol's *Farm and Fun Time*, Jesse received his draft notice and entered the Army. Their second Capitol session was made on March 16, 1953, while Jesse was home on leave and included

*Bluegrass legends **Jim & Jesse***

Air Mail Special and *A Memory of You.* A third trip to the Capitol studio in January 1955 yielded *I'll Wear the Banner* and *Tears of Regret*. In 1955, Jim & Jesse joined the WWVA *Wheeling Jamboree.*

After several years of little more than bare subsistence radio and personal appearance work, Jim & Jesse finally began to prosper in music, when they located at WNER Live Oak, Florida, and the *Suwanee River Jamboree*. They remained there for three years and built up a large following in north Florida and adjacent parts of Alabama and Georgia. At one time or another they also had TV programs on WCTV Tallahassee, Florida, WALB-TV Albany, Georgia, WEAR-TV Pensacola, Florida (all 1956), WTVY-TV Dothan, Alabama (1958), WSFA-TV Montgomery, Alabama (1961), and WJTV-TV Jackson, Mississippi (1961). Some of those broadcasts were sponsored by Martha White Mills.

Jim & Jesse's only recordings in the late 50's came with two Starday sessions in 1958, which resulted in a total of fourteen songs. However, in 1960, they signed with Columbia and after two single discs their recordings were released on Epic. They remained with Epic throughout the 60's, having a total of seventeen singles and ten albums. Some of the more noted members of the Virginia Boys on these waxings included Bobby Thompson and Allen Shelton on banjo, Jim Brock, Jim Buchanan and Vasser Clements on fiddle, and Don McHan.

On the strength of their regional popularity and their Epic contract, Jim & Jesse first guested on the *Grand Ole Opry* in 1961 and became regular members in 1964. Buying a farm near Nashville, the duo came to be ranked as a top-notch Bluegrass group and as solid performers, although never quite in the echelons of major stardom.

They had their first charted single, *Cotton Mill Man,* in 1964, reaching the Top 50, which they followed with the Top 40 success *Better Times A-Coming* in 1965. That year, Jim & Jesse released their ground-breaking album ***Berry Pickin' in the Country***. On this they took Chuck Berry's rock'n'roll classics and played them Bluegrass-style. Between 1967 and 1972, their recordings took more of a Country than a Bluegrass flavor, but the quality of their duets never wavered. In 1967, they had a Top 20 hit with *Diesel on My Tail* and a Top 50 success with *Ballad of Thunder Road.* In 1970, the duo returned to Capitol, but before they had their first release for the new label, Epic had scored a Top 40 hit with *The Golden Rocket.* At Capitol they had a Top 50 hit with Elizabeth Cotton's *Freight Train* the following spring.

With the growing popularity of Bluegrass festivals in the 70's, Jim & Jesse returned to a straight Bluegrass sound in 1972 and have pretty much retained it ever since, except for a session with Opryland in 1973. They cut many of their Bluegrass sessions on their own Old Dominion or Double J labels with the help of band members like Vic Jordan and Joe Meadows, on respective banjo and fiddle. During the course of the decade the McReynolds brothers released six albums on this label plus a double album of live performances from a 1975 tour of Japan and another double set taken from a series of radio transcriptions made for Martha White Mills in 1962. They also did some recordings for CMH.

Moving into the 80's, the McReynolds brothers continued to exemplify the brothers duet and Bluegrass traditions both on the *Grand Ole Opry* and the festival circuit. They cut a pair of albums with Charlie Louvin in 1982, which yielded the Top 60 single *Northwind,* and another album for MSR in 1986, which resulted in their last charted single, *Oh Louisiana*, which went Top 80.

As trends in the market have moved away from vinyl albums, some of their recent Double J releases have been on cassette only. In 1989, Jesse got together with Eddie Adcock, Kenny Baker and Josh Graves as "The Masters" and released an album of that name for CMH and also undertook concerts together under that banner. Throughout the more than forty years that Jim & Jesse have worked as a team in music, whether in hard times or the more prosperous, the McReynolds brothers have always exemplified a high standard of professionalism and displayed personal character that illustrates the strength of Appalachian Mountain people at its best. IMT

RECOMMENDED ALBUMS:

"The Old Country Church" (Epic)(1964)
"Berry Pickin' in the Country" (Epic)(1965)
"Jim & Jesse—Twenty Great Songs" (Capitol)(1969)
"The Jim & Jesse Show" (Old Dominion)(1972)
"The Jim & Jesse Show: Alive in Japan" (Old Dominion)(1976)
"The Jim & Jesse Story" (CMH)(1980)
"Jim & Jesse & Charlie Louvin" (Soundwaves)(1982)
"The Epic Bluegrass Hits" (Rounder)(1985)
"Some Old, Some New, Some Borrowed, Some True" (MSR)(1986)

JOHNNIE & JACK

JOHNNIE WRIGHT
(Singer, Songwriter, Guitar)

Given Name:	**Johnnie Robert Wright**
Date of Birth:	**May 13, 1914**
Where Born:	**Mount Juliet, Tennessee**
Married:	**Ellen Muriel Deason (a.k.a. Kitty Wells)**
Children:	**Ruby, Bobby, Carol Sue**

JACK ANGLIN
(Singer, Songwriter, Guitar)

Given Name:	**Jack Anglin**
Date of Birth:	**May 13, 1916**
Where Born:	**Franklin, Tennessee**
Married:	**Louise Wright**
Children:	**Terry Wayne**
Date of Death:	**March 7, 1963**

Johnnie & Jack ranked as one of the great Country duets of the 40's and 50's. They had a unique sound which was often augmented by a third voice on their recordings (usually Eddie Hill). Their style generally held to a traditional instrumentation although a Latin beat was infused into their music.

Both Johnnie and Jack were natives of middle Tennessee although Jack spent part of his growing-up years in northern Alabama. The pair met in 1936 and became brothers-in-law the following year when Anglin married Wright's sister, Louise. Even though the two worked some together musically, Jack spent more of his early professional years on various radio stations with his brothers Jim and Van ("Red").

When the Anglin Brothers broke up, Jack joined a part-time group Johnnie had formed that had a radio program at Nashville's WSIX; they eventually took the name Tennessee Hillbillies. In January, 1941, they embarked on a full-time career that took them to such radio station locales as Raleigh, Charleston and Bluefield in West Virginia, and by late 1942, to WNOX Knoxville's *Mid-Day Merry-Go-Round.* Their entourage included such notable musicians as fiddler Paul Warren, mandolinist Ernest Ferguson, Kitty Wells, and one-armed banjo player Emory Martin.

Unfortunately, the WWII draft depleted the band. Johnnie worked in a defense plant for a time and then teamed up with Eddie Hill. In 1945, they left Knoxville for WPTF Raleigh where Jack rejoined them in January, 1946. A year later they came to Nashville and the *Grand Ole Opry*, where they renamed their group the Tennessee Mountain Boys. During this year at WSM, they did a session for Apollo Records in New York and another for Syd Nathan at King in Cincinnati, the latter as the King Sacred Quartet (with Clyde Moody and Ray Atkins). In February, 1948, Wright and Anglin took their group to KWKH Shreveport and the soon-to-be formed *Louisiana Hayride.* In 1949 they signed with RCA Victor and in 1951, they had the Top 5 hit song *Poison Love*

***Johnnie & Jack** and the Tennessee Mountain Boys*

that elevated them from entertainers to stars. They followed this with another Top 5 hit, *Cryin' Heart Blues*.

In early 1952, Johnnie & Jack returned to the *Opry* to stay and had a Top 10 hit with *Three Ways of Knowing*. When Kitty Wells also had a hit that year with *It Wasn't God Who Made Honky Tonk Angels*, their road show contained what one might term double-barreled appeal. Eventually their band went through some changes, as Shot Jackson replaced Atkins while Benny Martin and then Ray Crisp took Warren's old spot on fiddle.

In 1954, their sound changed somewhat as they added songs like *Oh Baby (I Get So Lonely)* (No.1), *Goodnight Sweetheart Goodnight* (Top 5) and the double-sided Top 10 hit, *Beware of "It"/Kiss-Crazy Baby*. The addition of Jordanaire bass singer Culley Holt on their sessions provided a principal reason for the shift, as well as the type of song. Johnnie & Jack's other hits on RCA were: *No One Dear But You* and *S.O.S.* (both Top 15, 1955), *I Want to Be Loved* (Top 15, 1956, with Johnnie's daughter, Ruby Wright), *Stop the World (And Let Me Off)* (Top 10), *Lonely Island Pearl* (Top 20) (both 1958) and *Sailor Man* (Top 20, 1959).

In 1961, Johnnie & Jack switched to Decca Records after nearly a dozen years with RCA Victor. Only one of their eighteen numbers produced by Owen Bradley, *Slow Poison* (Top 20), made the charts. However, the duo continued as popular as before, touring heavily with Kitty Wells as they had done for a decade until Jack died in an auto crash, allegedly en route to a memorial service for Patsy Cline.

Johnnie and Kitty have remained active in music with Johnnie and son Bobby often performing medleys of Johnnie & Jack songs in their stage shows. Bear Family Records recently reissued their entire output in a cd box set. Nashville journalist Walt Trott is writing a biography of this memorable team.

IMT

RECOMMENDED ALBUMS:

"Johnnie and Jack and the Tennessee Mountain Boys" (RCA Victor)(1957)
"Hits by Johnnie & Jack" (RCA Victor)(1959)
"Smiles and Tears" (Decca)(1962)
"Poison Love" (RCA Victor)(1963)
"Sincerely" (RCA Victor)(1964)
"All the Best of Johnnie & Jack" (RCA Victor)(1970)
"Carry On" (CMH)(1973)
"Johnnie & Jack (with Kitty Wells)" (ACM)(1980)
"Johnnie & Jack" (Bear Family Germany)(1992)
"Apollo Days and Others" (Country Classics)
"Johnnie & Jack featuring Kitty Wells" (Golden Country)
"Johnnie & Jack" (Golden Country)
(See also Anglin Brothers, the, Johnny Wright*)*

JOHNSON MOUNTAIN BOYS, The

When Formed: **1978**

Current Members:

Dudley Connell	**Lead, Tenor and High Baritone Vocals, Guitar, Banjo**
David McLaughlin	**Lead, Tenor and Baritone Vocals, Mandolin, Fiddle, Lead Guitar**
Tom Adams	**Baritone Vocals, Banjo, Mandolin**
Eddie Stubbs	**Bass Vocals, Fiddle**

Former Members:
Larry Robbins (Banjo), Ed D'Zmura (Mandolin), Marshall Willborn (Bass Fiddle), Richard Underwood (Bass Fiddle), Earl "the Pearl" Yager (Bass Fiddle)

For traditional Bluegrass fans, the 80's might well be remembered as the decade of the Johnson Mountain Boys. Until the arrival of this group of youngsters, no "new" Bluegrass band had ever quite achieved the stature associated with the founding fathers of the genre. Newer bands that gained acclaim such as the Country Gentlemen and the Seldom Scene had been associated with more progressive or "Newgrass" sounds. That changed with the Johnson Mountain Boys, a group of young men from the Maryland suburbs of Washington, D.C. who put together a traditional sound that could hold its own with the originals and yet be new and creative, not imitative.

The roots of the band date back to 1975 when Dudley Connell (b. Dudley Dale Connell, February 18, 1956, Scherr, West Virginia) and Ron Welch formed a duet favoring traditional Bluegrass material. In those days, Connell played banjo and Welch the guitar. By early 1978, Connell had formed the Johnson Mountain Boys, which consisted of Richard Underwood (b. July 14, 1956, Seabrook, Maryland) on banjo (Connell switched to guitar), David McLaughlin (b. David Wallace McLaughlin, February 13, 1958, Washington, D.C.) on mandolin, Eddie Stubbs (b. November 25, 1961, Gaithersburg, Maryland) on fiddle and the somewhat older Larry Robbins (b. April 25, 1945, Montgomery County, Maryland) on bass. McLaughlin dropped out in the fall of 1978, but returned in May 1981. Ed D'Zmura played mandolin during the interim, including their early recordings. The band made its initial recordings, a single for Copper Creek in October 1978 (followed by an EP) and acquired a following in the Bluegrass clubs of the Washington area. However, they did not begin to hit big on the festival circuit until the early 80's, particularly after the release of their eponymous album for Rounder, in the spring of 1981.

From then onward, the band's reputation grew rapidly. By the time of their second album, ***Walls of Time***, McLaughlin had returned and this five-man combination might be termed the "classic" Johnson Mountain Boys. They remained together until 1986 and cut four Rounder albums. The only personnel changes came in June 1986, when Marshall Willborn replaced Robbins and Tom Adams

Bluegrass favorites the ***Johnson Mountain Boys***

(b. Gettysburg, Pennsylvania) took over for Underwood that October.

Whether performing old, forgotten songs from the past or newly composed (often by Connell) numbers in a traditional vein, the band always had outstanding arrangements and gave superb performances. In this era, they played in thirty-six states, toured England and Canada, and brought their music to such locales as the 1982 Knoxville World's Fair, the White House, and the *Grand Ole Opry*.

If one song made a deeper impression than any other in the Johnson Mountain Boys band repertoire, it was *Let the Whole World Talk*, in 1987, a number that Jimmy Newman cut on Dot some three decades earlier. It attracted wide attention, but still neither made the Country charts nor got them regular spots on the TV networks. With much fan regret, the band pre-announced their retirement for February 1988 following a concert in Lucketts, Virginia (subsequently released by Rounder on a two-album set). Adams and Willborn then went into the Lynn Morris Band (with Willborn marrying Ms. Morris as well), while the others occupied themselves in various projects both inside and outside of music.

They played a couple of festivals in 1989, fifteen dates in 1990, and twenty-five in 1991. This part-time approach proved satisfying to the group. Again they had but slight shifts in personnel. Earl Yager (b. Charlottesville, Virginia), formerly of Whetstone Run and the Jimmy Martin band, played bass. Richard Underwood came back on banjo in 1989 and 1990, and Tom Adams thereafter.

In 1993, they had a new cd released by Rounder, with selected cuts quickly going to the top of the Bluegrass charts. As Charles Wolfe wrote about their return, "still the same band . . still the same combination we've come to expect." As of 1994, the band is without a bass player and according to Dudley Connell, they are using freelance players, until one is settled on. IMT

RECOMMENDED ALBUMS:

"The Johnson Mountain Boys" (Copper Creek)(1984) [Note: a 12" 45 rpm EP originally released in 1980 in a 7" format]
"The Johnson Mountain Boys" (Rounder)(1981)
"Walls of Time" (Rounder)(1982)
"Working Close" (Rounder)(1983)
"Live at the Birchmere" (Rounder)(1984)
"We'll Still Sing On" (Rounder)(1985)
"Let the Whole World Talk" (Rounder)(1987)
"Requests" (Rounder)(1988)
"Favorites" (Rounder)(ca. 1988) [Compiled from material on earlier Rounder albums)
"At the Old Schoolhouse" (Rounder)(1989)
"Blue Diamond" (Rounder)(1993)

MICHAEL JOHNSON

(Singer, Songwriter, Guitar, Actor)
Date of Birth: August 8, 1944
Where Born: Alamosa, Colorado
Married: Sally

Michael is one of the finest guitar players currently working in Country music. He is not a three chord strummer, but is a classically trained musician, who brings to his playing and singing a dimension of Folk and Country that has brought him success in the U.S. as well as throughout Europe.

He was raised in Denver, Colorado, and when he was age 13, he and his older brother, Paul, taught themselves to play guitar. At 19, he was studying at Colorado State College, majoring in music education. He won a national talent contest sponsored by Columbia Records and Chicago radio station WHN (home of the *Barn Dance*), the prize being a recording contract with Epic Records. He began playing the coffeehouse and campus circuit. In 1966, he traveled to Spain to expand his guitar technique. He studied under maestros Graciano and Renata Tarrango at a conservatory in Barcelona.

On returning to the U.S., Michael played for a short while with the Back Porch Majority, who sprung out of the New Christy Minstrels. In 1967 and 1968, he toured with the Chad Mitchell Trio, alongside another newcomer, John Denver. Michael and John wrote the song *Circus* together, which was recorded by both Denver and Mary Travis, from Peter, Paul and Mary. Michael and John also formed two-thirds of the short-lived successor group to the Chad Mitchell Trio, Denver, Boise and Johnson. Michael then appeared for a year in the stage production of *Jacques Brel Is Alive and Well and Living in Paris* in Chicago, Los Angeles and New York. He then moved to Minnesota and, in 1971, Michael signed to Atlantic Records. He released the album ***There Is a Breeze***, which was produced by Peter Yarrow (ex-Peter, Paul & Mary) and Phil Ramone (who would later produce Billy Joel), to a largely unresponsive audience.

Michael's next two albums, ***For All You Mad Musicians*** (1975) and ***Ain't Dis Da Life*** (1977), were both self-produced and helped to create greater interest in his live work. In 1978, Michael came to Nashville and teamed up with producers Brent Maher (notable for his work with the Judds) and Steve Gibson, to record *Bluer Than Blue* and *Almost Like Being in Love*, which they intended to use to get a record deal for Michael. As a result, he signed with EMI America, and both songs were released as singles, *Bluer Than Blue* reaching the Top 15 on the Pop chart and *Almost Like Being in Love* peaking in the Top 40 on the Pop chart. He followed these with the 1979 Top 20 Pop hit *This Night Won't Last Forever*. This song was found on his next album, ***Dialogue***. The following year, Michael had his last Pop chart hit with the low-level single *You Can Call Me Blue*.

In 1985, Michael recorded a duet with Sylvia entitled *I Love You By Heart* and it reached the Country chart Top 10. As a result, Joe Galante signed Michael to a deal with RCA. Michael's debut album, ***Wings*** (1986), was marked by the twin acoustic guitars of Michael and Don Potter. His first solo single, *Gotta Learn to Love Without You*, was written by Michael and Kent Robbins, and reached the Top 15 on the Country list. Michael wrapped up the year with his first No.1, *Give Me Wings*, which stayed on the Country chart for over five months.

As 1987 dawned, Michael followed up with another No.1 single, *The Moon Is Still Over Her Shoulder*. The track was found on both the ***Wings*** album and also the new album ***That's That***, released in 1988. This was followed by *Ponies*, which only reached the Top 30. He finished off 1987 with the Top 5 single *Crying Shame*. He started off 1988 with *I Will Whisper Your Name* and the title track, *That's That*, both of which went Top 10. However, Michael recognized that he was still a performer who was not always acceptable to Country audiences, especially when he got away from his trademark ballads. This became apparent when, after this success, *Roller Coaster Run (Up Too Slow, Down Too Fast)*, only reached the Top 60.

Michael came to Britain as part of the CMA's Route '88 with K.T. Oslin. This led to the release of the 1989 16-track cd ***Life's a Bitch***, which was geared towards the European market and was a combination of his two albums on RCA plus three additional tracks, including *Jacques Cousteau*, which was released in Britain as a single. Since the days of heady heights, Michael continues to play solo gigs. Michael's former session band went on to chart action as Great Plains.

RECOMMENDED ALBUMS:

"Dialogue" (EMI America)(1979)
"Wings" (RCA Victor)(1986)
"That's That" (RCA Victor)(1988)
"Life's a Bitch" (RCA)(1989) [Combination of two RCA Victor albums]

ANTHONY ARMSTRONG JONES

(Singer, Guitar)
Given Name: Ronnie Jones
Date of Birth: June 2, 1949
Where Born: Ada, Oklahoma

Ronnie Jones took his stage name from the then husband of Princess Margaret, photographer Anthony Armstrong-Jones, later the Earl of Snowden.

Ronnie was originally a professional golfer who also played the clubs. He was spotted by Conway Twitty in 1962 and worked with Twitty's band. He signed with Chart Records in 1969 and over the next two years, chalked up a series of major successes, most of which were covers of Pop hits. In 1969, he had *Proud Mary* (Top 25) and *New Orleans* (Top 30) and then he opened his account in 1970 with the Top 10 single *Take a Letter Maria*. From then on, his success was at a lower level and his most successful singles on Chart were *Sugar in the Flowers* and *Sweet Caroline*, both which went Top 40, in 1970.

In 1973, Jones moved to Epic and had a Top 40 hit with *Bad, Bad Leroy Brown*. He was absent from the chart for 13 years, but returned in 1986 for the Top 75 single *Those Eyes* on AIR.

RECOMMENDED ALBUM:

"Greatest Hits, Vol. 1" (Chart)(1971)

DAVID LYNN JONES

(Singer, Songwriter, Bass Guitar, Guitar, Keyboards, Drums)
Given Name: David Lynn Jones
Date of Birth: January 15, 1950
Where Born: Bexar, Arkansas

When David Lynn Jones first hit upon the Country scene in 1987, Waylon Jennings hailed him as the leader of the new generation in Nashville.

David had been playing the clubs, including the Blue Moon in Bexar, since he was a youngster. His telephone calls trying to reassure his mother were captured in his song *The Rogue*. He began to write seriously in his late teens. Until 1970, he made a living selling cars in Fayetteville, Arkansas, and then he quit his day job to play bass for Freddy Morrison and the Bandana Blues Band.

On the road, David honed his songs. A lot of his early material had a humor about it. When he was 19, he came to Nashville and started pitching songs. Curly Putman heard them and gave David encouragement. During 1975, David moved to Houston. He hocked his stereo to buy food and rent a room. He worked as a session musician. He played bass on some Kenny Dale sessions including *Bluest Heartache of the Year* and worked with Fiddlin' Frenchie Burke and Randy Corner. In 1976, he wrote Corner's Top 40 hit *Heart Don't Fail Me Now*.

David and producer Richie Albright put together a tape which was presented to Mercury Records. On it, David played all instruments except saxophone. He moved back to Arkansas and then a copy of the tape reached Willie Nelson and, as a result, Nelson cut *Living in the Promiseland* and had a No.1 with it in 1986.

David's first album, ***Hard Times on Easy Street***, was released in 1987 on Mercury. There were shades of Springsteen and Mellencamp about his recordings, with the depth of a latter-day Kristofferson. His first single release, *Bonnie Jean (Little Sister)*, was written about his elder sibling and reached the Top 10 and hung around for five months on the charts. Waylon Jennings joined him on *High Ridin' Heroes*, which became a Top 15 success the following year. His next two singles, *The Rogue* and *Tonight in America*, did not fare as well.

He followed up with a new album, ***Wood, Wind and Stone***. In 1992, David signed with Liberty Records and released ***Mixed Emotions***. He recorded the album in his home studio in Bexar using musicians he had worked with over the last decade. Like his other projects, it was co-produced by Richie Albright. David Lynn Jones remains on the cutting edge of Country-Rock and need not worry about single success as long as he continues to release quality albums.

RECOMMENDED ALBUMS:

"Hard Time on Easy Street" (Mercury)(1987)
"Wood, Wind and Stone" (Mercury)(1989)
"Mixed Emotions" (Liberty)(1992)

GEORGE JONES

(Singer, Songwriter, Guitar)
Given Name: George Glenn Jones
Date of Birth: September 12, 1931
Where Born: Saratoga, Texas
Married: 1. Dorothy (m. 1950)(div.)
2. Shirley (m. 1954)(div.)
3. Tammy Wynette (m. 1968)(div.)
4. Nancy Sepulvada (m. 1983)
Children: Susan, Jeffrey, Bryan, Tamela Georgette

George Jones, universally known as "the Rolls-Royce" of Country singers, has the style that all genuine Country male singers aspire to. Although known in the late 70's and 80's as "No Show Jones," he has now become one of the most admired "fathers" of modern Country, due in no small way to the support of his wife, Nancy.

He was raised in the "Big Thicket" area of East Texas by a piano playing mother (Clara) and a guitar playing father (George Washington) and it was his father who bought him his first guitar at age 9. By the time he was 12, George was earning money playing on the streets of Beaumont. He appeared on the afternoon show on station KTXJ Jasper while still in his teens. When he was 17, he began appearing with Eddie and Pearl in Beaumont's Playground and appeared with them on KRIC Beaumont. In 1950, George married for the first time, but the marriage soon ran into problems, when his wife Dorothy became pregnant, and so in November that year he enlisted in the U.S. Marines, serving in Korea.

After leaving the service in late 1952, he returned to Texas and became a house painter. By now George was a great admirer of Hank Williams and his death made a great impression on George. In 1953, he was spotted in Beaumont by Pappy Dailey, who was co-owner of Starday Records, and was signed to the label. At the time, George sounded like Roy Acuff, Lefty Frizzell and Hank Williams, and had not straightened out his own style. The following year, George released his debut single, *No Money in This Deal*, but nothing much happened. That year, while George was playing in Houston, he met his future second wife and married. He also appeared on KNUZ's *Houston Jamboree* and became a deejay on KTRM Beaumont.

George made his breakthrough in 1955, with *Why, Baby, Why*, which went Top 5. Immediately he was revealed as a songwriter to be contended with. The following year, he had Top 10 hits with *What Am I Worth* and *You Gotta Be My Baby* and the Top 3 success *Just One More/Gonna Come Get You*. During the year, George recorded some Rockabilly material as "Thumper Jones," releasing the single *Rock It/How Come It* (he also cut Rockabilly sides as "Hank Smith"). He also began appearing on the *Louisiana Hayride* in February that year, and then in August he made his debut on the *Grand Ole Opry*.

In 1956, his duet with Jeanette Hicks, *Yearning*, became a Top 10 hit. When Mercury approached Don Pierce and Pappy Dailey to

The Possum, ***George Jones***

take over their Country office and form Mercury-Starday, George came under the Mercury banner. His hits for the new affiliation were the Top 10 *Don't Stop the Music/Uh, Oh, No* and the Top 15 *Too Much Water*.

George started off 1958 with consecutive Top 10 hits, *Color of the Blues* and *Treasure of Love/If I Don't Love You*. That year, Starday split from Mercury amid much acrimony, resulting in the split-up of the assets of Starday between Pierce, Dailey and Jack Starns. However, George stayed at Mercury with Dailey.

The following year, George started out with the No.1 smash *White Lightning*, which not only stayed at the top of the Country charts for five weeks, but also crossed over to the Pop Top 75. He followed up with the Top 10 single *Who Shot Sam*, which also made the Pop Top 100. Then George hit a bad patch, and the last single of the year, a double-entry affair, *Money to Burn/Big Harlan Taylor*, only made the Top 20.

He started out 1960 with the Top 20 *Accidentally on Purpose/Sparkling Blue Eyes* (the flip-side going Top 30) and followed with the Top 25 release *Out of Control*. George ended the year with one of his finest songs, *The Window Up Above*, which went Top 3. The following year, *Family Bible* went Top 20 and was followed by George's second No.1, *Tender Years*. This single stayed at the top for 7 weeks and crossed-over to the Pop Top 80. He closed out the year with the Top 15 *Did I Ever Tell You*, a duet with Margie Singleton.

He started out 1962 with a Top 5 single with a somewhat familiar title, *Aching, Breaking Heart*. It was followed by *That's All It Took*, another duet with Margie, which just failed to make the Top 10. This was George's last release for Mercury and now he moved to United Artists, where Art Talmadge, the record company executive who had been at Mercury, now resided. George was still managed and produced by Dailey.

The first release for George at UA, in 1962, was his version of a song that became a classic, *She Thinks I Still Care*, which stayed at the top of the Country charts for six weeks. The flip-side, *Sometimes You Just Can't Win*, went Top 20. This was followed by *Open Pit Mine*, which peaked in the Top 15, and the Mercury release *You're Still on My Mind*, which went Top 30. George closed out the year with the Top 3 *A Girl I Used to Know/Big Fool of the Year* (the flip-side going Top 15).

George stayed with UA until the end of 1964 and his hits were *Not What I Had in Mind* (Top 3)/*I Saw Me and You Comb Her Hair* (Top 5) (both 1963) and in 1964 *Your Heart Turned Left (And I Was on the Right)* (Top 5)/*My Tears Are Overdue* (Top 15). Then Mercury released *The Last Town I Painted*, which went Top 40. In June, George had a double-sided hit, *Something I Dreamed/ Where Does a Little Tear Come From*, and this was a case where the flip-side becomes the major side; and in this case, it reached the Top 10. George closed out the year with a record that would instantly become a classic, *The Race Is On*. It went Top 3 on the Country chart and crossed-over to the Top 100 on the Pop chart.

During 1963 and 1964, George teamed up with Melba Montgomery for a series of hit duets that started with the Top 3 *We Must Have Been Out of Our Minds*, which was written by Melba. They finished 1963 with the Top 20 double-sided hit *What's in Our Heart/Let's Invite Them Over*. Their hits in 1964 were *Please Be My Love*, which peaked just shy of the Top 30, and *Multiply the Heartaches*, which made the Top 25.

When Art Talmadge created Musicor Records in 1964, George moved to the label, where Dailey continued to produce him. That year, his back-up group, the Jones Boys, released their debut album, ***The Jones Boys (Country & Western Songbook)***. United Artists started out 1965 with *Least of All*, which went Top 15, and then George had his first Musicor release, *Things Have Gone to Pieces*, which went Top 10. This was followed by another UA release, *Wrong Number*, which also went Top 15. He had two more major hits that year with *Love Bug* and *Take Me*, both going Top 10.

One of the most unlikely pairings occurred in 1965, when George duetted with Gene Pitney on the Top 20 hit *I've Got Five Dollars and It's Saturday Night* and the Top 25 *Louisiana Man*. They had two further chart entries, but they were low level.

George had two more Top 10 releases the following year, *I'm a People* and *Four-O-Thirty Three*. George started out 1967 with his first No.1 for nearly five years, *Walk Through This World With Me,* and followed it with the Top 5 record *I Can't Get There From Here* and the Top 10 *If My Heart Had Windows*. During the year, he also had a Top 25 hit with Melba Montgomery (who had moved to Musicor) on the Alex Zanetis song *Party Pickin'*.

In 1968, George met Tammy Wynette, and the following year they were married. Up to now, George had insisted on living in Texas, but now he moved to Nashville. He continued to record for Musicor, even though he and Tammy wanted to duet. He was unhappy with the way he was recorded and in particular, the way his tapes were mixed at Musicor by Dailey. Despite this, he continued to turn out a string of major hits. These were *Say It's Not You* (Top 10), *As Long as I Live* and *When the Grass Grows Over Me* (Top 3) (all 1968), *I'll Share My World with You* (Top 3), *If Not for You* (Top 10) and *She's Mine/No Blues Is Good News* (Top 10) (all 1969). He also had a major hit with Brenda Carter on *Milwaukee, Here I Come*, which reached the Top 15 in 1968. The following year, George was made a member of the *Grand Ole Opry*.

George's most successful single of 1970 was to become another classic and was the Top 3 *A Good Year for the Roses*, written by Jerry Chesnut. As his opening release of 1971, George re-recorded his 1962 hit *Sometimes You Just Can't Win*, which this time around went Top 10. This was followed by his last Top 10 entry for Musicor, *Right Won't Touch a Hand*. George was now anxious to move to Epic, where Tammy recorded. His departure from Musicor was acrimonious and severed his connection with Pappy Dailey after twenty-eight years. Allegedly, George handed over his royalties in order to get out of the contract.

His move to Epic partnered him with the production skills of Billy Sherrill, and at the end of the year George and Tammy got together for *Take Me*, which went Top 10. George then had his debut solo single, *We*

Can Make It, during the beginning of 1972. On the same day that it charted, RCA entered the lists with a Musicor master, *A Day in the Life of a Fool*, which reached the Top 30. His next Epic release, *Loving You Could Never Be Better*, was highly successful and reached the Top 3. He and Tammy got together for another Top 10 single, *The Ceremony*, and then George soloed on Norro Wilson-George Richey's *A Picture of Me (Without You)*, which went Top 5. However, the final single of the year, the duet *Old Fashioned Singing*, only made the Top 40.

In 1973, all of George's solo singles went Top 10: *What My Woman Can't Do*, *Nothing Ever Hurt Me (Half as Bad)* and the Top 3 *Once You've Had the Best*. However, his duets with Tammy had mixed fortune. *Let's Build a World Together* just failed to make the Top 30, but *We're Gonna Hold On* climbed to No.1. Both of his solo efforts during 1974, *The Grand Tour* and *The Door*, were chart toppers. However, he and Tammy again were not as consistent with *(We're Not) The Jet Set* going Top 15 and *We Love It Away* being a Top 10 record. George did have one other singing partner that year; his young step-daughter, Tina, who helped him have a Top 25 hit, *The Telephone Call*, which was billed as "Tina & Daddy." George and Tammy went to England to appear at the Wembley Festival but were called home by the death of George's mother.

By now George and Tammy's marriage was shaky and in 1975 they divorced amid much shock and consternation from their fans. Following the divorce, George filed for bankruptcy. However, the hits kept coming, and that year he had a Top 10 hit with *These Days I Barely Get By*. Then his solo consistency fell away and his only major hits between 1976 and the end of 1979 were *The Battle* (Top 20), *Her Name Is* (Top 10) and *Bartender's Blues* (Top 10, with James Taylor) and *I'll Just Take It Out in Love*, which just fell below the Top 10.

His residual duets with Tammy were more successful and in 1976 they had back-to-back No.1s with *Golden Ring* and *Near You*, and in 1977 they made the Top 5. During 1978 through 1980, George had a quartet of hits with former Jones Boy Johnny Paycheck, and these were: *Maybellene* (Top 10, 1978), *You Can Have Her* (Top 15, 1979), *When You're Ugly Like Us (You Just Naturally Got to Be Cool)* (Top 40, 1980) and *You Better Move on* (Top 20, 1980).

During 1979, George was warned by his doctors to quit drinking and he checked into an Alabama clinic for a month for an alcoholism cure. That year, he acquired the nickname of "No Show Jones" due to the fact that he missed some fifty-four concert dates. In time he would turn what was a negative comment into a positive one, when he recorded the song of the same name. In addition, George dropped from 150 pounds to 100 pounds.

In 1980, George enjoyed a resurgence of his fortunes and it started with the modern classic *He Stopped Loving Her Today*. Written by Bobby Braddock and Curly Putman, it became a No.1 record during the spring. That year, George and Tammy got back together under more congenial conditions and they returned to the Top 3 with *Two Story House*. George then followed up with the Top 3 single *I'm Not Ready Yet* and closed out the year with the Top 20 duet *A Pair of Old Sneakers*. George released the album ***I Am What I Am***, which went Gold the following year.

Through the rest of the first half of the decade, George racked up a series of major hits. These were: 1981: *If Drinkin' Don't Kill Me (Her Memory Will)* (Top 10) and *Still Doin' Time* (No.1); 1982: *Same Ole Me* (Top 5, with backing vocals from the Oak Ridge Boys); 1983: *Shine On (Shine All Your Sweet Love on Me)*, *I Always Get Lucky with You* (No.1) and the Top 3 *Tennessee Whiskey*; 1984: *You've Still Got a Place in My Heart* and *She's My Heart* (both Top 3); 1985: *Who's Gonna Fill Their Shoes* and *The One I Loved Back Then (The Corvette Song)* (both Top 3). However, George was suffering greatly with an ever-increasing dependency on alcohol and cocaine and it was the strength of his new wife, Nancy, that at last gave George the courage to kick these habits. He had now found the right woman to thankfully turn him around.

George had a fruitful period of duetting, including the much lauded album with Merle Haggard, ***A Taste of Yesterday's Wine***, in 1982. This yielded the No.1 *Yesterday's Wine* and the Top 10 *C.C. Waterback*. The following year, George teamed up with Ray Charles on the Top 10 hit *We Didn't See a Thing*, with Chet Atkins guesting on guitar. In 1984, George released the ***Ladies' Choice*** album, which featured him duetting with Brenda Lee, Janie Fricke, Loretta Lynn, Barbara Mandrell, Emmylou Harris, Lacy J. Dalton, Deborah Allen, Terri Gibbs and Leona Williams. This spawned the Top 20 releases *Hallelujah, I Love You So* with Brenda and *Size Seven Round (Made of Gold)* with Lacy J.

On Labor Day, 1983, George realized a dream by opening the 65-acre Jones Country Music Park in southeast Texas, just 45 miles from Saratoga. He had anticipated a crowd of 5,000 but more than 10,000 fans were there for the opening.

George stayed with Epic through 1988, although from 1987, his success level waned. His major hits were *Somebody Wants Me Out of the Way* and *Wine Colored Roses* (both Top 10, 1986), *The Right Left Hand* (Top 10, 1987). In 1988, George duetted with newcomer Shelby Lynne on the Dean Dillon-Paul Overstreet song *If I Could Bottle It Up*. However, it only reached the Top 50 and would reappear on his 1991 album ***Friends in High Places***. Also in 1988, *I'm a One Woman Man* went Top 5 and George's album of the same title reached the Top 15 on the Country Album chart during 1989. Although not a major success, his record *The King Is Gone (So Are You)*, which was originally titled *Ya Ba Da Ba Do (So Are You)*, and was based on the well-known phrase of the cartoon character Fred Flintstone, was certainly one of the most novel songs recorded by George. During 1989, George's 1982 double album ***Anniversary (Ten Years of Hits)*** was Certified Gold.

In 1990, he had a Top 10 entry in tandem with Randy Travis entitled *A Few Ole Country Boys* (produced by Kyle Lehning), which appeared on Randy's Certified Gold Album ***Heroes and Friends*** and on George's own duet album ***Friends in High Places***. During 1991, George moved labels and had a Top 40 single, *You Couldn't Get the Picture*, which came from his MCA debut album ***And Along Came Jones***, also produced by Lehning, which was well received by the fans and made the Top 25 on the Country Album chart.

George's most successful single of 1992 was the Top 40 release *I Don't Need No Rocking Chair*, which also featured Vince Gill, Mark Chesnutt, Garth Brooks, Travis Tritt, Joe Diffie, Pam Tillis, T. Graham Brown, Patty Loveless and Clint Black. The very popular video of the song also featured former World Heavyweight Boxing Champion George Foreman. The track came from George's album ***Walls Can Fall***, which was produced by Emory Gordy, Jr., and was a Top 25 Country Album chart success. That year, his 1987 album ***Super Hits*** was Certified Gold. During 1992, George received the ultimate accolade when he was inducted into the Country Music Hall of Fame.

In 1993, George was inducted into the Cool Hall of Fame by *Entertainment Today*. The readers of *Country America* magazine voted *He Stopped Loving Her Today* "The No.1 Country Song of All Time." He received the same honor from European Country fans in a poll held by the BBC. George changed producers again when Buddy Cannon and Norro Wilson held the reins on ***High-Tech Redneck***. In 1994, George duetted with B.B. King on a reprise of the old Clarence Carter hit *Patches*, which was one track on the multi-artist concept album ***Rhythm, Country and Blues***.

Songwriter Tom T. Hall once said of George, who is known to his friends as "Possum," "I've never talked to a Country music performer who didn't say his or her favorite singer was George Jones." He could have added that the public felt the same way. (For George's awards see Award Section).

RECOMMENDED ALBUMS:

"Bluegrass Hootenanny" (United Artists)(1964) [With Melba Montgomery] [Re-released by Stetson UK in the original sleeve (1987)]
"My Country" (double)(Mercury)(1969)
"George Jones & Gene Pitney (Recorded in Nashville!)" (Musicor)(1965)
"George Jones Sings the Great Songs of Leon Payne" (Musicor)(1971) [Re-released by Gusto (1984)]
"George Jones Superpak" (United Artists)(1971)
"We Go Together"/"Me and the First Lady" (double)(Epic)(1975) [With Tammy Wynette]
"16 Greatest Hits" (Starday)(1977)
"My Very Special Guests" (Epic)(1979) [With Waylon Jennings, James Taylor, Emmylou Harris, Linda Ronstadt, Tammy Wynette, Willie Nelson, Johnny Paycheck, Elvis Costello, Dennis Locorriere and Ray Sawyer and Pop and Mavis Staples]
"George Jones & Tammy Wynette Together Again" (Epic)(1980)
"I Am What I Am" (Epic)(1980)
"Anniversary (Ten Years of Hits)" (double)(Epic)(1982)
"A Taste of Yesterday's Wine" (Epic)(1982) [With Merle Haggard]
"Party Pickin'" (Musicor)(1984) [With Melba Montgomery] [Re-pack of "Let's Get Together (Boy Meets Girl)" (1967)]
"The King of Country Music" (Liberty)(1984)
"Ladies' Choice" (Epic)(1984) [See text for duet partners]
"Super Hits" (Epic)(1987)
"Friends in High Places" (Epic)(1991) [With Randy Travis, Emmylou Harris, Charlie Daniels, Vern Gosdin, Buck Owens, Shelby Lynne, Tim Mensy, Ricky Skaggs, Ricky Van Shelton and Sweethearts of the Rodeo.]
"And Along Came Jones" (MCA)(1991)
"Walls Can Fall" (MCA)(1992)
"George Jones Salutes Hank Williams and Bob Wills" (Liberty)(1992) [Originally released as "George Jones Salutes Hank Williams" and "My Favorites of Hank Williams" on Mercury (1960) and United Artists (1962) respectively. The former was also re-released by Stetson UK in the original sleeve (1988)]
"Super Hits Vol.2" (Epic)(1993)
"High-Tech Redneck" (MCA)(1993)

GRANDPA JONES

(Singer, Guitar, Banjo, Cowbells, Yodeler)
Given Name: **Louis Marshall Jones**
Date of Birth: **October 20, 1913**
Where Born: **Niagra, Kentucky**
Married: **Ramona Riggins**
Children: **Mark Alan, Eloise, Alise June, Marsha**

During the 30's and 40's, when the banjo virtually disappeared from Country music, it was Grandpa Jones who kept the instrument alive with his classic hits like *Rattler* and *Mountain Dew*. His forceful singing and boisterous performing style have emerged as one of the most distinctive in music, and his comedy has graced places like the *Grand Ole Opry* and *Hee Haw* for some 40 years. In the later part of his long career, he has also become one of the leading advocates for traditional Country music and Old-Time Gospel singing.

Grandpa's birthplace, Niagra, Kentucky, is on the southern banks of the Ohio River, and his formative years were spent not in the mountains or rural plains, but in the industrial cities of Ohio and Kentucky, where a sizable population of "briars" (transplanted southerners) had migrated in the 1930's. Grandpa's mother sang old ballads and his father was an Old-Time fiddler, and as a boy he listened on the radio to barn dances in Missouri and Chicago (the *National Barn Dance*). By 1929, he was himself on the radio in Akron, Ohio (WJW, WADC and WFJC between 1929 and 1934), billing himself as "The Young Singer of Old Songs," and doing songs inspired by Jimmie Rodgers (including the famous "blue yodels," which Grandpa became adept at imitating). He later spent time on WTAM Cleveland with Joe Tryoan ("Bashful Harmonica Joe") and as a musician on the popular *Lum and Abner* show.

Next, Grandpa began working with ballad singer Bradley Kincaid, who became his most important mentor. By 1935, Grandpa was performing with Kincaid over WBZ Boston, where they found that rural New Englanders liked their ballads and old songs as well as southerners. It was Kincaid who dubbed Jones "Grandpa." Though he was only 22, his grouchiness during early morning radio shows reminded Kincaid of an old man. The familiar Grandpa Jones costume, high-topped boots, fake mustache and bright suspenders, was created about this time with help from vaudeville comic Bert Swor.

In 1937, Grandpa struck out on his own, going first to WWVA in Wheeling, West Virginia, and then in 1939 to WTIC Hartford, Connecticut, in 1940 to WMNN Fairmont, West Virginia, and from 1941 on, to the even

Grand Ole Opry star ***Grandpa Jones***

stronger station WLW in Cincinnati, Ohio. Following Kincaid's lead, Grandpa began issuing his own songbooks (while in West Virginia) and started developing a large repertoire of traditional Folk ballads, Old-Time songs, current Country favorites, Gospel songs and even recitations. In his spare time, he learned to play the banjo from Cousin Emmy (Cynthia May Carver), then a popular radio star from south-central Kentucky.

At WLW, Grandpa met three of the most influential musicians in Country music history, Alton and Rabon Delmore and Merle Travis. Though their tenure at Cincinnati was constantly being interrupted by the draft and wartime restrictions, the four influenced each other in countless ways. One of their projects was a Gospel quartet called the Brown's Ferry Four, which helped popularize (on radio and records) some of the dynamic new Gospel songs by writers like Albert Brumley and Cleavant Derrick.

Another was their work for the newly-founded King Records, which would emerge after the war as the nation's leading independent company and the one most devoted to vernacular music. Grandpa's own first records were done here in the mid-40's: *It's Raining Here this Morning*, *Eight More Miles to Louisville*, *Rattler*, and *Mountain Dew*. It was these King sides that won him his national reputation.

After marrying Ramona Riggins, a talented fiddler, singer, and mandolin player, Grandpa moved to Nashville and began working on the *Opry* in 1946 (originally with Kincaid). In 1949, Grandpa moved to WARL Arlington, Virginia. From 1951, Grandpa was at the Richmond, Virginia, *Old Dominion Barn Dance*, but he returned to Nashville in 1952 and stayed on the *Opry* until 1956. He then spent time in Washington, D.C., working for Connie B. Gay on his TV show. In 1959,

Grandpa returned to Nashville and became a regular on the *Opry* (he is still a member).

In 1959, Grandpa had a Top 25 hit with his version of Bobby Bare's (then known as Bill Parsons) *The All American Boy* on Decca. In 1963, Grandpa had a Top 5 hit with his rendition of Jimmie Rodgers' *T for Texas* on Monument. Tours of Korea, Hollywood films and, after 1969, a regular slot on the CBS television show *Hee Haw* helped make Grandpa's image one of the best-known in Country music.

His election in 1978 to the Hall of Fame was one of the institution's most popular selections. In 1984, he wrote (with Charles Wolfe) his autobiography, *Everybody's Grandpa* (University of Tennessee Press). Monument Records' Fred Foster once told Barry McCloud that Grandpa Jones was the only Country music performer ever to age into his act. CKW

RECOMMENDED ALBUMS:

"Grandpa Jones Makes the Rafters Ring" (Monument)(1962)
"Grandpa Jones' Yodeling Hits" (Monument)(1963)
"Hall of Fame Series" (MCA) [His mid-1950's Decca recordings, generally mediocre]
"16 Greatest Hits" (Hollywood) [Best collection of the original King sides]
"The Grandpa Jones Story" (double)(CMH)(1976)
"Old Time Country Music Collection" (double)(CMH)(1978) [With Ramona Jones]
"Grandpa Jones' Family Album" (double)(CMH)(1979) [With Ramona Jones and their children]
"Family Gathering" (double)(CMH)(1981)

JORDANAIRES, The

When Formed: 1948
Members (at height of fame):

(Hugh) Gordon Stoker	**Lead Tenor Vocals (only original member)**
Neal Matthews, Jr.	**Second Tenor Vocals**
Hoyt H. Hawkins	**Baritone Vocals**
Ray C. Walker	**Bass Vocals**

Other Members:
Bob Hubbard, Bill Matthews, Monty Matthews, Hugh Jarrett, Louis Nunley, Culley Holt, Duane West

At their peak, the Jordanaires were heard on more hit records than any other vocal group. Among the artists they have backed up are Elvis Presley, Patsy Cline, Jim Reeves, George Jones and Gene Pitney.

The group got together singing barber shop and spiritual songs in Springfield, Missouri, in 1949 and that year they debuted on the *Grand Ole Opry*. The original line-up was Bob Hubbard, Bill Matthews, Monty Matthews (baritone) and Culley Holt (bass). Hubbard

The legendary ***Jordanaires***

was drafted, Bill Matthews became seriously ill and in 1950, Gordon Stoker (b. Hugh Gordon Stoker, August 3, 1924, Gleason, Tennessee) and Hoyt Hawkins (b. March 31, Paducah, Kentucky/d. 1982) joined.

Stoker was also a pianist and had played in the John Daniels Quartet on WSM radio. He spent three years of WWII in the Air Force and then attended Oklahoma Baptist College in Shawnee, Oklahoma, afterward majoring in psychology and music at George Peabody College, Nashville. Hawkins had sung in a family quartet back in the 30's over WPAD Paducah. He was in the Army for two years and then also went to Peabody College.

When Monty Matthews left the Jordanaires for family reasons in 1953, Neal Matthews (b. October 26, Nashville, Tennessee) joined. Both Stoker and Hawkins had worked with Matthews in an earlier group. Matthews had attended Belmont College in Nashville as a psychology major and then between 1948 and 1949 had played lead guitar with Wally Fowler's Georgia Clodhoppers and had gone on to sing with the Stone Mountain Quartet. He had served with the Army in Korea prior to joining the Jordanaires.

In 1954, the line-up of Stoker, Matthews, Hawkins and Holt was soon providing vocal back-up to Elton Britt, Red Foley, Jimmy Wakely and Hank Snow. In 1954, the Jordanaires appeared with Eddy Arnold on his TV series *Eddy Arnold Time*. Their big breakthrough occurred when they appeared with Arnold in Memphis. Elvis Presley, a big fan of theirs, sought them out backstage and promised that if he landed a major recording contract, they would back him. Elvis was true to his word. After he was signed by RCA Victor, the Jordanaires recorded with him in New York. Presley further promised that if any of the cuts were hits, then he wanted them to work with him all the time.

The million-selling *Heartbreak Hotel* was among the cuts and the Jordanaires went on to work with the King until 1970. Their liaison included extensive film work that took in *Loving You, Jailhouse Rock, King Creole* and *G.I. Blues* and Gospel recordings.

When Culley Holt left the Jordanaires in 1958 due to ill health, Hugh Jarrett replaced him. However, Jarrett had outside interests and later that year Ray Walker joined. Walker (b. March 16, 1934, Centerville, Mississippi) had a background in radio announcing and solo and quartet singing. He attended David Lipscomb College, Nashville (with Pat Boone), where he gained a B.A. degree.

The group was an integral part of the Nashville Sound. It was Neal Matthews who did the arrangement on Jim Reeves' *Four Walls* (1957). Their other successful association was with Patsy Cline beginning in January, 1959. At first, she resisted their presence, but soon came to see them as friends. On occasions, she asked them the meaning of certain words, helping her to project a song's meaning so much better. In their busiest period, it was the Jordanaires who originated the famous Nashville number system of chords that is now standard use in recording studios and on live work.

The Jordanaires came to be a familiar sight on national TV. In 1956, they had won *Arthur Godfrey's Talent Scouts* program and the same year were seen backing Elvis as he shot to national fame on the Ed Sullivan and Steve Allen shows. Other TV appearances included the *Tennessee Ernie Ford Show, The Tonight Show,* the *Frank Sinatra Show* (1960), the *Milton Berle Show* and *American Bandstand*. By 1974, it was estimated that each member was earning $65,000 per year. At that point, they could be heard on millions of records and could boast involvement in over 30 movies. Most of these were Presley vehicles, but they also appeared in films with Ferlin Husky and Zsa Zsa Gabor. In 1980, they appeared in *Coal Miner's Daughter* and in 1985 in *Sweet Dreams*.

The Jordanaires have put out a number of albums in their own right, the majority being Gospel. In 1964, they picked up a Grammy for "Best Religious Album" for ***Great Gospel Songs*** with Tennessee Ernie Ford. They were the driving force behind the establishment of the American Federation of Television/Radio Artists-Screen Actors' Guild in Nashville (AFTRA/SAG). They were also important in establishing the lucrative jingle market in Nashville which has provided entrees into Country music for such singers as Janie Fricke and Judy Rodman.

During their career, the Jordanaires have carried off numerous awards. Perhaps the most important came in 1979, when they picked up the NARAS Award for having sung on more Top 10 records than any other vocal group. In 1976, 1977 and 1979, they carried off the "Superpicker Award" from NARAS and in 1984 they received a "Masters Award" from the Nashville Entertainment Association.

Other pieces of information about the Jordanaires include the fact that they had two lady singers who came in for supporting work. These were Millie Kirkham and Dolores Dinning Edgin, the latter being one of the Dinning Sisters. Since 1965, the members of the Jordanaires are Honorary Kentucky Colonels, and from 1960-1970 they were members of the Tennessee Governor's Staff. In 1984, they received the "Tennessee Outstanding Achievement Award." They played for President Gerald Ford at the White House in 1976 and appeared in the Broadway play *Elvis: The Legend Lives On*, three years later. From 1980 on, they appeared with Don McLean at the Annual Thanksgiving concert at Carnegie Hall. In 1982, Hoyt Hawkins died and was replaced by Duane West, who along with long-time associate Louis Nunley, had subbed with the Jordanaires.

During the 50's, their solo recordings appeared on RCA Victor, Decca and Capitol. In the 60's, they were on Capitol, Columbia and Stop. In 1987, they signed with Step One for the album ***A Tribute to Elvis' Favorite Spirituals***. In 1994, they were planning the release of another Gospel album and an Elvis package where each member was singing Elvis' lead parts. SM/BM

RECOMMENDED ALBUMS:

"Big Country Hits" (Columbia)(1966)
"Great Gospel Songs" (Capitol)(1975) [With Tennessee Ernie Ford]
"Christmas to Elvis from the Jordanaires" (Classic)(1978) [Features Scotty Moore and D.J. Fontana]
"A Tribute to Elvis' Favorite Spirituals" (Step One)(1987)
(For their harmony work listen to records by Elvis, Tennessee Ernie Ford, Don Gibson, Patsy Cline and Red Foley.)

SARAH JORY

(Steel Guitar, Singer, Songwriter)
Given Name: Sarah Jory
Date of Birth: November 20, 1969
Where Born: Reading, Berkshire, England

*Steel guitar princess **Sarah Jory***

Sarah Jory is known as "The Princess of the Pedal Steel." To date, although only 25 years old, she has already amassed some 4,000 public performances.

When she was age 5, Sarah received a lap steel from her parents and by the time she was age 9, she was playing pedal steel and joined her first band, Colorado Country, earning $1.50 a night, playing in social clubs, hotels and barn dances. Although good enough to perform at the famed Wembley Festival in England, which was at the time sponsored by Silk Cut, a brand of cigarette, she was prevented from appearing by the authorities, who felt that an artist under age of 18 should not be seen to promote tobacco.

Sarah was invited to play in the U.S. when she was only 13 and has since returned many times, recording several albums in Nashville. In 1987, Sarah was made a "Lifetime Honorary Member" of the Texas Steel Guitar Association, and the following year she fulfilled her ambition to play at the Wembley Festival.

In 1991 through 1993, Sarah was voted "Best Female Entertainer" by the BCMA. Sarah Jory and the Sarah Jory Band were special guests, touring with such stars as Eric Clapton (1990), Glen Campbell (1991) and Charley Pride (1992). Encouraged by Ritz Records, Sarah released a video of a 1992 live performance recorded in Aberdeen as ***An Evening with Sarah Jory***, released in June, 1993. That same year, her debut album for Ritz, ***New Horizons***, was voted "Album of the Year" by the Country Music Press Association. That year, Sarah headlined a European tour for Ritz to support the album. She is currently at work writing new material for her second Ritz album.

RECOMMENDED ALBUMS:

(All U.K. releases)
"Sarah's Steel Line" (Crow)
"Sarah on Steel" (Sarah Records) [Re-released on Point]
"New Horizons" (Ritz)(1993)
Video:
"An Evening with Sarah Jory" (Ritz)(1993)

JUDDS, The

NAOMI JUDD
(Singer, Songwriter, Author, Actress)
Given Name: Diana Ellen Judd
Date of Birth: January 11, 1946
Where Born: Ashland, Kentucky
Married: 1. Michael Ciminella (div. 1972)
2. Larry Strickland (m. 1989)
Children: Christina (Wynonna), Ashley

WYNONNA
(Singer, Songwriter, Guitar)
Given Name: Christina Claire Ciminella
Date of Birth: May 30, 1964
Where Born: Ashland, Kentucky
Children: Elijah

It's just not the thing to do in Music City; you can't just walk into a record company, sing to the boss and get a record deal, especially if you have no experience behind you. However, that is just about what happened to the mother and daughter duo, the Judds, Naomi and Wynonna.

When Naomi was 18 she gave birth to Wynonna and because of this event, she missed her graduation ceremony. After a few years she and her two children (by now she had Ashley too) set off for Hollywood, where they stayed for seven years and experienced the glamour of the area, as well as the pitfalls. While there, Naomi worked as a partner in a video production company, was a girl Friday to a millionaire and also spent time as a professional model.

Returning to Kentucky in 1976, they lived in a house on a hill with no TV and no telephone and settled down to enjoy a family atmosphere. The two girls continued their education and Naomi enrolled in nursing school. The family listened to the *Grand Ole Opry* on Saturday nights and did the family wash in their old Maytag wringer washing machine. They grew together and had freedom to develop their imaginations. When Wynonna was 12 it was evident that she had been blessed with a wonderful voice. She got her first guitar and taught herself to play, and began to sing around the house with her mother.

The family headed back to the West Coast, where they spent the next two years, and Naomi finished her nursing degree. A vintage Chevrolet owned by Naomi was spotted at an intersection by an employee of the Lucasfilm Company, and her 1957 car was rented for use in the film *More American Graffiti*. Naomi and Wynonna landed jobs as extras, with

Naomi also getting secretarial work on the movie set. The money they earned set them up for their move to Nashville in 1979.

After they found a place to live, Naomi found work as a country nurse, while Wynonna completed high school, and they began to find their way around the music business. They would often rise at 3:30 a.m. to make frequent early morning appearances on the *Ralph Emery Show*. The Judds didn't have demo tapes, so they would just go and sing to anyone they thought could help them. This is how they made their rapid ascent up the hierarchy of the musical ranks. They managed to get an audition with Woody Bowles, a publicist/manager, and his partner Ken Stilts and they set up a live audition with producer Brent Maher and another with Dick Whitehouse of Curb Records. A crude demo tape had been made and Whitehouse took this to a meeting in L.A. with RCA's Joe Galante, who listened on his Walkman and wanted to hear more. So another live audition took place in the boardroom with only the accompaniment of Wynonna's acoustic guitar. Within 30 minutes RCA had made a commitment and signed the Judds (Wynonna & Naomi) to the label.

Their first single, *Had a Dream (For the Heart)*, was released in December, 1983, and went Top 20. They released a mini-album, ***The Judds: Wynonna and Naomi*** in 1984. Now the Judds were to go out to perform at the AK-SAR-BEN Festival in Omaha, Nebraska, with the Statler Brothers, but they had no show, no band and no bus. The musicians used for their recordings were hired and after several days of rehearsals, they went out in front of 10,000 people for their first performance. Their next two singles in 1984, *Mama He's Crazy* and *Why Not Me*, both went to No.1.

In 1984, the Judds won a Grammy Award for "Best Country Performance by a Duo or Group with Vocal," for *Mama He's Crazy*, CMA's "Horizon Award" and ACM Awards or "Top Vocal Duet" (they retained the title every year from 1985 through 1990 and 1992) and "Song of the Year" (*Why Not Me*).

In 1985, all three of their singles went to No.1 and they were: *Girls Night Out, Love Is Alive* and *Have Mercy*. That year, *Why Not Me* was named the CMA's "Single of the Year." The Judds were named the CMA "Vocal Group of the Year" (a title they retained in 1986 and 1987). In addition, they won a Grammy Award for "Best Country Performance by a Duo or Group with Vocal," for *Why Not Me*. *Music City News* Cover Awards named the Judds "Stars of Tomorrow"!! and "Duet of the Year." The Judds held on to the title every year up to and including 1992. In 1985, their album ***Why Not Me*** was Certified Gold and by 1992 it would reach Double-Platinum status.

All three of their 1986 singles went to No.1: *Grandpa (Tell Me 'Bout the Good Old Days), Rockin' with the Rhythm of the Rain* and *Cry Myself to Sleep*. That year, the Judds won a third Grammy Award for "Best Country Performance by a Duo or Group with Vocal," for *Grandpa (Tell Me 'Bout the Good Old Days)*. Their album ***Rockin' with the Rhythm*** was Certified Gold and Platinum. In 1987, the Judds had a Top 10 hit with *Don't Be Cruel* and two No. 1 hits, *I Know Where I'm Going* and *Maybe Your Baby's Got the Blues*. In the American Music Awards *Grandpa (Tell Me 'Bout the Good Old Days)* was named "Favorite Single" and "Favorite Video Single" in the Country Category. Their album ***Heartland*** was Certified Gold and by 1989 it had reached Platinum status.

In 1988, the Judds had *Turn It Loose* (No.1), *Give a Little Love* (Top 3) and *Change of Heart* (No.1). The last named was the first single to drop "Wynonna & Naomi." That year, the CMA named them "Vocal Group of the Year," a title they held until 1991. They also won a Grammy Award for "Best Country Performance by a Duo or Group with Vocal," for *Give a Little Love*. Their album ***The Judds' Greatest Hits*** went Gold that year and by 1992, it had sold over 2 million copies.

The Judds chalked up further No.1 hits in 1989 with *Young Love* and *Let Me Tell You About Love* and then had a Top 10 hit with *One-Man Woman*. Their album ***Rivers of Time*** was Certified Gold that year, as was ***Christmas Time with the Judds***, which went on to Platinum status in 1993. Their opening single of 1990, *Guardian Angels,* only reached the Top 20. Both their other singles that year, *Born to Be Blue* and *Love Can Build a Bridge*, went Top 5. That year, *Billboard* named the Judds as "No. 5 Top Artist of the Decade." The Judds' ***Greatest Video Hits*** was Certified Gold.

In 1991, *Love Can Build a Bridge* won two Grammy Awards as "Best Country Performance by a Duo or Group with Vocal" and "Best Country Song." Because of Naomi's chronic active hepatitis, she decided to retire. In December 1991, after a 124-date farewell tour, the curtain was brought down on the Judds. So, sadly, it was goodbye to the Judds, but, happily it was hello Wynonna, as she embarked on a successful solo career. During 1991, the album ***Love Can Build a Bridge*** was certified Gold and by 1993 had reached Platinum status, ***Greatest Hits Volume 2*** had gone Gold, and the video of ***Love Can Build a Bridge*** had gone Platinum. The following year, the video *The Final Concert* went Platinum. Two of their albums, ***Collector's Series*** and ***Wynonna & Naomi,*** were both Certified Gold.

In 1993, Naomi's autobiography, *Love Can Build a Bridge*, was published. Naomi's other daughter, Ashley, is starting to cause a stir in Hollywood with her acting. JAB

RECOMMENDED ALBUMS:

"Why Not Me" (RCA/Curb)(1984)
"Rockin' with the Rhythm" (RCA/Curb)(1985)
"Heartland" (RCA/Curb)(1987)
"Greatest Hits" (RCA/Curb)(1988)
"River of Time" (RCA/Curb)(1989)
"Love Can Build a Bridge" (RCA/Curb)(1990)

Naomi and Wynonna, the ***Judds***

K

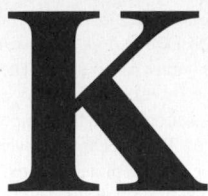

Kierna Kane refer O'KANES

KARL AND HARTY

When Formed: 1930
KARL
(Singer, Songwriter, Mandolin)
Given Name: Karl Victor Davis
Date of Birth: December 17, 1905
Date of Death: May 29, 1979
HARTY
(Singer, Guitar)
Given Name: Hartford Connecticut Taylor
Date of Birth: April 11, 1905
Date of Death: October 1963
Both Born: Mount Vernon, Kentucky

Although they are often overlooked by devotees of 30's duet singing (who prefer to think of the Blue Sky Boys or the Monroe Brothers), Karl and Harty were actually more influential during the 30's than any other group. They worked out of a powerful radio base in Chicago and recorded extensively for one of the country's largest labels, the ARC group. They were responsible for some of the most enduring of all the duet songs, and influenced many later musicians, including a young Bill Monroe.

Karl and Harty grew up in their eastern Kentucky homes at Mount Vernon (just a few miles from Renfro Valley), listening to the mountain musicians who would come into town on Saturdays to play on the courthouse lawn. They also got a taste of Pop music from an old man who played "mood music" on an old piano for the local silent movie house. By the time the two had graduated high school, they had "catalog" instruments and decided to form a string band, the Kentucky Krazy Kats, with Doc Hopkins, another local boy, who would later become a major player on the Chicago Country music scene. For a time they played over WHAS in Louisville, and toured as part of a semi-pro basketball team (playing music for the crowd at intermission).

In 1930 Bradley Kincaid got the boys jobs at WLS Chicago, where they became members of John Lair's Cumberland Ridge Runners. Since they soon began to specialize in duet singing with the band, they became desperate to get "new" old songs for their daily grind of radio shows. Karl wrote his mother, asking her to hunt up some of the older people in the hills and get songs from them. Old Carter Family records were another fertile source. Yet another was old Gospel songbooks, such as put out by the Vaughan or Stamps-Baxter companies; two of their biggest hits came from these: *I Dreamed I Searched Heaven for You* (1934) and *I Need the Prayers of Those I Love* (1936). But their best song was one Karl worked up after driving the WLS minister up to Madison, *I'm Here to Get My Baby Out of Jail*. After the duo's recording of it (with the Cumberland Ridge Runners) in 1934, it became the most popular duet song in Country music, imitated and covered by almost every duet act on radio.

The earliest recordings by the group were released in January 1932, on the Paramount label, as the Renfro Valley Boys. In the depths of the Depression, however, and on a minor label, the records sank into obscurity, almost at once. Their more productive session occurred in March 1934, when they recorded *I'm Here to Get My Baby Out of Jail* for the ARC group. For the next five years, they were regular visitors to the ARC studios, scoring with *The Prisoner's Dream* (1936), *I'm Going Home This Evening* (1936), *I'm S-A-V-E-D* (1936), *Seven Beers with the Wrong Woman* (1940), and their biggest of all, *Kentucky* (1941). The latter Karl wrote during the early days of the war and their Columbia record became especially popular with lonely servicemen. The Blue Sky Boys also recorded it, giving it another lease on life and making it into a Bluegrass and Country standard.

Hart's tenor and Karl's lead singing graced the duo's radio shows on the WLS *Barn Dance* until 1937, when they switched to rival Chicago station WJJD, with its *Suppertime Frolic*. Their appeal was not only to southerners, but to rural mid-westerners, Finns from Wisconsin, Indians from Michigan's Upper Peninsula, and Pennsylvania Dutch. After the war, though, with the decline in sentimental songs and rise of Honky-Tonk, Karl and Harty gradually saw their appeal decline.

By the early 50's, they had retired from performing. Karl continued to be a successful songwriter who saw his works recorded by singers like Emmylou Harris and Linda Ronstadt, but he worked in radio only as a "record runner" for WLS. Harty spent his last years as a toll-gate collector in Chicago. Harty died in October 1963 from a stroke and Karl of cancer on May 29, 1979. CKW

RECOMMENDED ALBUM:
"Early Recordings" (Old Homestead)

BUELL KAZEE

(Singer, Banjo, Guitar)
Given Name: Buell Kazee
Date of Birth: August 29, 1900
Where Born: Burton Fork, Magoffin County, Kentucky
Married: Unknown
Children: Phil
Date of Death: August 1976

Though historians have called him the greatest white male Folk singer in the U.S., friends and family remember Buell Kazee as an affable minister who liked to play the banjo and sing old songs. To a casual fan listening to his old 1920's records, Kazee sounds like the epitome of a Kentucky mountain songster; he uses a high, tight, lonesome voice, accompanied by a banjo set in unusual tunings; many of his best-known songs, like *Lady Gay* or *The Butcher's Boy*, are ancient ballads he learned as a boy. No wonder that when he was rediscovered by the Folk revival enthusiasts in the 1960's, he seemed to be the real thing: a genuine mountain balladeer, as opposed to the smoother, more commercial singers like Bradley Kincaid. But the fans who looked more closely at Kazee's career saw a more complex story, a conflict between an articulate and creative musician and the image the world tried to thrust on him.

Kazee came from a genuine rural background. Born in the foothills about 60 miles east of Richmond, he learned old songs and hymns from his parents and family. "Everybody sang and nobody thought there was anything unusual about it," he recalled. By the time he was 5, young Buell had also gotten a little banjo and was whacking away at it. He grew up attending the mountain "frolics," brush arbor meetings, bean stringings, and the like.

As a teenager, Buell began to prepare for the ministry. He completed high school and enrolled in Georgetown College in central Kentucky. There he studied English, Greek and Latin, and began to understand the cultural importance of the old ballads and songs he had learned. He also began to study voice and music, and to replace his natural mountain voice with a more formal, cultured singing style. He soon began to combine his two musical worlds.

In 1925, after he had graduated from Georgetown, Buell presented a concert of "Folk music" at the University of Kentucky. In tie and tails, young Buell played the banjo, sang to piano accompaniment and even lectured on the history of old ballads. This was successful, and he repeated the show several times over the next few years. In April 1927 Buell was invited to come to New York to make records for Brunswick and he assumed the sophisticated record producers wanted the same thing.

He was wrong. They listened politely when he sang some parlor songs and religious songs in his "formal" voice, but none of them really perked up until he took out his banjo and began to sing in the old mountain style. Years later he recalled: "I had to make a record seven or eight times to get it bad enough to sell. They said, 'If you want to sound Country, you sing with a tight throat.'" He finally got a good enough mountain sound to satisfy the Brunswick people, and during the next two years he recorded over 50 songs for them. About a fifth of them were Gospel or religious numbers, reflecting Buell's career in the ministry; others were Pop tunes or sentimental laments on which he was backed by New York studio musicians. However, well over half were wonderful versions of some of the best traditional ballads, including what many consider the finest recorded versions of the old Scottish ballad *Lady Gay,* as well as *East Virginia, The Sporting Bachelors, The Wagoner's Lad* and *The Orphan Girl*. His best seller turned out to be *Little Mohee* (a version of *On Top of Old Smokey*) backed with *Roving Cowboy*, a release that sold over 15,000 copies (good for the time) and sold best, surprisingly, in Texas. His singing style won acclaim from the national press. A *Billboard* writer in 1933 saw Buell as a good bet for radio, "an honest-to-goodness sample of soul-tearing keoboy [sic] lamentation." Kazee, who had recently married, was not really interested in furthering his career, and although his records were sold as far away as Australia and Japan, he stayed at home.

He in fact became a minister, serving one church at Morehead, Kentucky, for some 22 years and singing at revival meetings. In later years, he composed a number of formal pieces of music using Folk themes, including a cantata based on the old Sacred Harp piece *The White Pilgrim*. He lived into the age of Folk festivals and was one of the first to appear at the Newport festivals in the 1960's. He also wrote three books about religion, a book on banjo techniques, and an unpublished autobiography. When he died he left behind all this, some fine recordings (including some newer ones), and a son (Phil), who had the skill and interest to keep his father's music alive.

CKW

RECOMMENDED ALBUM:

"Buell Kazee" (June Appal) [With large illustrated book]

BILL KEITH

(Banjo, Pedal Steel Guitar, Composer)

Given Name: **William Bradford Keith**
Date of Birth: **December 20, 1939**
Where Born: **Boston, Massachusetts**
Married: **Claire**
Children: **Charles Patrick, Martin Eldon**

In banjo players' parlance, there are three styles of playing: Scruggs, Reno and Melodic. The latter is often also referred to as the "Keith" style. Bill Keith decided that he could play fiddle melodies on banjo, note by note. This is also known as chromatic banjo playing. His playing in the late 50's and 60's greatly influenced the generation of banjo pickers that followed into "Newgrass" and "Jazzgrass."

Bill grew up in Brockton, Massachusetts, near Boston. He started playing ukulele while still a child and then took piano lessons. However, his interest in banjo surfaced when he was about 12. He rented a tenor banjo and had lessons with a guitar teacher, Phil Cooper. Bill started to play in a school Dixieland group in junior high school and then, when he was at prep school, he played in various Dixieland bands. By 1957, he had begun to come under the spell of Folk music. He was early on impressed with the styles of Pete Seeger and Earl Scruggs. In 1957, Bill attended Amherst College in Massachusetts and started to master these styles. He bought a $15 banjo and Pete Seeger's manual *How to Play the Five-String Banjo* (the yellow copy) that year. Having got to grips with the two ways of playing, he began experimenting and perfecting his own style.

In 1958, Bill met Jim Rooney at Amherst and they started to jam together. They formed a duo and played the coffee houses and on campus. They also did some TV out of Springfield, Massachusetts. They met promoter Manny Greenhill and he helped them form the Connecticut Folklore Society. This led to a series of concerts around the campus circuit of New England.

Bill graduated in 1961 and served for eight months in the U.S. Air Force Reserve. After this, he moved to Washington, D.C., to learn banjo-making techniques under Tom Morgan. Rooney moved there and through Morgan, they met mandolin player Frank Wakefield and guitarist Red Allen. Together, they formed the Kentuckians.

Earl Scruggs wanted someone to lay out the tablature for a new book on the 5-string banjo. He knew of Bill through Greenhill and in 1963, he invited Bill to Nashville; the result was the Peer Publications book *Earl Scruggs and the 5-String Banjo*. That same year, Bill worked with Dan Bump, also at Amherst, in developing a new banjo tuner. They both had an interest in rebuilding old cars. They designed a tuner peg which incorporated a pitch changer. This was an improvement on the Scruggs peg, as it replaced the existing pegs, rather than having a hole drilled and cams inserted. Earl Scruggs lent his name to the venture and became a director of the company that was set up in 1964, in Putney, Vermont, to produce them.

Bill Monroe heard Bill playing *Devil's Dream* backstage at the *Opry*. He brought Bill into the Blue Grass Boys, giving him the name "Brad" so as not to confuse him with any other Bill. Monroe considered Bill to be the best banjo player in the country. Bill stayed with Bill Monroe for eight months, during which time he had a great impact on the upswing in renewed attention for Monroe. During his time with the Blue Grass Boys, Bill made his first appearance at the Newport Folk Festival. On leaving the band, he turned his attention to session work.

In 1964, Bill joined the legendary Jim Kweskin's Jug Band. He remained with them for four years and made two appearances at Newport. After leaving the Jug Band, Bill, Jim Rooney, Eric Weissberg and Richard Greene put together the Blue Velvet Band. Then in 1968, he stopped playing banjo and switched over to pedal steel guitar. This was partly occasioned by his appearances with Ian and Sylvia, where steel was more in demand.

Bill moved to Woodstock, New York, in 1970 and that year joined Jonathan Edwards. He stayed with him for about a year and then spent some time with Judy Collins. Throughout the 70's and 80's, Bill continued to play with Jim Rooney and they toured all over North America. They toured throughout Europe together and as solos and Bill became very popular in France.

A community of musicians had started to play together in Woodstock, on an ad hoc basis, and Bill became the banjo player for what loosely evolved into the Woodstock Mountain Review. They reunited every so often, the last time being for Happy Traum's 50th birthday. A double album of this concert was released on the Japanese label Pony Canyon.

During 1977, Bill became a charter columnist for *Frets* magazine, writing on music theory, but he soon realized that he preferred to play music rather than write about it. He, Rooney and Weissberg resurrected the Blue Velvet Band in 1989 as the New Blue Velvet

Band and added Kenny Kosek. The group continues into the 90's. As of 1994, Bill was occasionally playing with the John Herald Band.

Bill Keith's contribution to music, in general, is immeasurable. Probably, more than any other instrumentalist, he not only turned banjo playing on its head, but opened the door for the development of Bluegrass music and, by inference, Bluegrass-Country, into how it is perceived in the 80's and 90's.

RECOMMENDED ALBUMS:

"Livin' on the Mountain" (Prestige Folklore)(1963) [With Jim Rooney]
"Something Auld, Something Newgrass, Something Borrowed, Something Bluegrass (Strictly Clean and Decent)" (Rounder)
"Fiddle Tunes for the Banjo" (Rounder) [As Tony Trischka, Bela Fleck and Bill Keith]
"Banjoland and Mud Acres— Music Among Friends" (Rounder) [Features Bill Keith]
"Banjo Paris Sessions" (Musigrass-Diffusion) [Features Bill Keith]
"Bluegrass Time" (MCA) [Features Bill Keith]

TOBY KEITH

(Singer, Songwriter, Guitar)
Where Born: Oklahoma City, Oklahoma
Married: Tricia
Children: Shelley, Krystal

Toby Keith is among the third wave of new traditionists to help turn around radio playlists to a purer Country sound.

As a child, he was interested in the musicians who played at his grandmother's supper club. However, as he grew, his part-time and summer work with a rodeo company and his passionate pursuit of football left little time for music. After graduation from high school he worked in the oil fields. Initially he was a roughneck and then worked his way up to become operational manager. Then the oil boom slumped and Toby began playing Country-Rock with garage bands, basically copying Alabama. Some of the members of that band are still in Toby's Easy Money Band.

New traditionalist ***Toby Keith***

They began playing gigs in South Oklahoma City and Norman, Oklahoma. These were beer and blood joints, but Toby was pleased to be playing. The band took runner-up place for Oklahoma in the Wrangler-Dodge band competition. For the next few years, Toby worked the oil fields, played music and played semi-pro football for the USFL system.

By 1988, he was recording for independent labels and was soon visiting Nashville. On one such trip, he met Harold Shedd of Mercury Records, who had been Alabama's producer. Shedd heard a tape and then flew to Oklahoma City to see Toby and the band live. The next day, Toby was offered a record deal with Shedd and Nelson Larkin to produce.

The result was his debut 1992 album, ***Toby Keith***. The following year, Toby's single *Should've Been a Cowboy* went to No.1 and crossed to the Pop 100 and was followed by *He Ain't Worth Missing*, which went Top 5. At year end, Toby released *A Little Less Talk and a Lot More Action*, which had been recorded by Hank Williams, Jr., two years earlier. Toby's version made it to the Top 3. To make a year's dream come true, Toby's debut album was Certified Gold in 1994. In 1994, Toby moved with Shedd to the newly opened Polydor label.

RECOMMENDED ALBUM:

"Toby Keith" (Mercury)(1993)

KENDALLS, The

When Formed: 1969
ROYCE KENDALL
(Singer, Guitar)
Given Name: Royce Kykendall
Date of Birth: September 25, 1934
Where Born: St. Louis, Missouri
Married: Melba
Children: Jeannie
JEANNIE KENDALL
(Singer, Guitar)
Date of Birth: November 30, 1954
Where Born: St. Louis, Missouri
Married: Mack Watkins (m. 1978)

The Kendalls are without doubt one of the most successful father-daughter vocal acts in Country music. Royce had started to play a little while in the U.S. merchant marine and in the late 50's, he and his brother Floyce were a mandolin-guitar duo known as the Austin Brothers. They left their home in Arkansas and went to play on *Town Hall Party* on TV in Los Angeles alongside Cal Smith and Hank Cochran for some two years.

Royce returned to St. Louis and settled down with his wife. He went to barber school and in the fullness of time, the couple owned a barber shop/beauty salon.

Their daughter, Jeannie, was starting to grow and inherited a liking for music. Her preference was Folk and Country. When she was 15, she and her father started to sing and play together but the turning point was a visit to the *Grand Ole Opry*. Royce and Melba decided to use their own money to finance a recording session. They set up a mail-order business and started to sell the record. Royce and Jeannie also did some live work around St. Louis.

A St. Louis deejay brought the tracks to the attention of Pete Drake. He recorded them for Stop Records and their first release in 1970, John Denver's *Leavin' on a Jet Plane*, narrowly missed the Top 50. They had two further singles, including *You've Lost That Lovin' Feelin'*, which made no impression on the charts. In 1972, they signed to Dot Records, but were immediately disillusioned with their treatment. The company wanted to exclude Royce and turn Jeannie into something she didn't want to be. Only two singles made the charts but only at the lower end and both of these were really Pop songs.

They left the label and bided their time. They played live dates until 1976, when they met Brien Fisher, who signed them to Ovation Records. They recorded the ***Making Believe*** album and released the title track, which didn't fare well because of the success of the Emmylou Harris version. In August, they issued the second single, *Live and Let Live*. But it was the flip-side that caught the attention of the deejays. The record was flipped and *Heaven's Just a Sin Away* became a No.1

Royce and Jeannie, the ***Kendalls***

Country hit as well as a minor Pop success. The record was on the chart for five months. It earned a Grammy Award as "Best Country Vocal Performance by a Duo or Group," in 1977 and was the CMA's "Single of the Year" in 1978. It is also one of George Jones' Top 10 favorite songs of all time.

In 1978, they continued their winning ways with *It Don't Feel Like Sinnin' to Me* (Top 3), *Pittsburgh Stealers* (Top 10) and their second No.1, *Sweet Desire/Old Fashioned Love*. If 1979 was a good year with the Top 5 hit *I Had a Lovely Time* and Top 20 successes *Just Like Real People* and *I Don't Like That No More/Never My Love,* then 1980 was even better. They had three Top 10 hits that year with *You'd Make an Angel Wanna Cheat, I'm Already Blue* and Dolly Parton's *Put It Off Until Tomorrow*.

However, the writing was on the wall for Ovation. The Kendalls had a middling hit in 1981 with *Heart of the Matter* from their 1979 album of the same title. Then Ovation was bankrupt.

The Kendalls moved to Mercury and continued their hit run that year with yet another "cheating" song, *Teach Me to Cheat* and then *If You're Waiting on Me (You're Backing Up)*, both of which made the Top 10.

Their luck eluded them in 1982, with two records only making the middle order. The 1983 single *Precious Love,* with harmony vocals from Emmylou Harris, regrouped their position slightly; it made the Top 20. The same happened to *Movin' Train* and then they were back on top with their 1984 release of the title tracks from ***Thank God for the Radio...and All the Hits***. *Thank God for the Radio* was on the lists for nearly six months. However, Mercury failed to capitalize on its success. *My Baby's Gone* and *I'd Dance Every Dance with You* only made it into the Top 20, even though they were both on the charts for over four months each.

Then success eluded them again. The rest of their output only made the middle order and in 1986, they again moved labels, this time to MCA/Curb. It didn't help. Neither did their move to Step One in 1987. In 1989, Epic released a cd entitled ***20 Favorites***. However, Country music had moved on and the pleasant records of the Kendalls had ceased to be in favor. As they say, everything comes in cycles.

RECOMMENDED ALBUMS:

"Leavin' on a Jet Plane" (Power Pak)(1974)

"1978 Grammy Award Winners—Best Country Duo" (Gusto)(1978)

"Best of the Kendalls" (Ovation)(1980)

"Movin' Train" (Mercury)(1983)

"Thank God for the Radio...and All the Hits" (Mercury)(1985)

"Fire at First Sight" (MCA/Curb)(1986)

"Break the Routine" (Step One)(1987

Mary Ann Kennedy refer CALAMITY JANE

RAY KENNEDY

(Singer, Songwriter, Guitar, National Steel Guitar, Drums, Bass Guitar, Keyboards, Sitar, Record Producer, Engineer, Arranger)

Given Name:	**Raymond Kennedy, Jr.**
Date of Birth:	**May 13, 1954**
Where Born:	**Buffalo, New York**
Married:	**Ann**
Children:	**Phineas**

One thing that impresses folks about Ray Kennedy is his versatility. The other thing is that clad in black leather jacket, black pants, T-shirt and boots, he looks the part of a guitar hero. Standing just under 6 feet tall, Ray is just sufficiently left-field to make him a publicists' dream.

Born the son of Ray Kennedy, Sr., the National Credit Manager for Sears who created the concept of the Discover credit card and eventually became a Vice-President of the company, Ray considered no place home because, as a child, he was always on the move due to his father's work. When he was 15, Ray built his own guitar because his parents wouldn't get him one. Ray, Jr., attended college in Iowa with the intent of studying business, but found his apprenticeship better served in the Iowa clubs.

He moved on to Oregon, before arriving in Nashville in 1980. He built himself a studio to demo his songs and got so adept at engineering that he was producing most of Tree Publishing's Pop demos. One of his tracks was used for Stevie Nicks' *Battle of the Dragon*. He became a staff writer at Tree, but although he had cuts by John Anderson, Charley Pride, David Allan Coe and T. Graham Brown, there wasn't a rush to record Kennedy's songs. He therefore decided he had to pursue a recording career of his own.

He signed with Atlantic Records in 1990 and his first album was ***What a Way to Go***. What was of note with this release was that Ray produced it (in his own Skyline studio) and played everything but steel guitar, Dobro and Weissenborn on it (played by Bruce Bouton). He also featured many of his collection of vintage instruments on it, including guitars, National steel and bass guitars. In addition, he played drums and keyboards. He also wrote or co-wrote all of the songs, and mixed the album as well. The result was an album that shone head and

*Master talent **Ray Kennedy***

shoulders above the normal run of conveyor belt releases that sometimes emanate from Nashville.

That year, Ray hit the Country singles chart with the title track of the album, which reached the Top 10. The album itself climbed to the Top 60 on the Country album charts. In 1991, his two singles didn't fare as well, and the excellent *Scars* only reached the Top 60 and *I Like the Way It Feels* only got to the Top 75, and flipped out of the charts after only one week. During 1991, Ray engineered and co-produced fellow songwriter Don Henry's solo album ***Wild in the Backyard***.

He also got together with producer/songwriter Monty Powell to start work on his new album, ***Guitar Man***, which was released in 1992. Powell had up to then been associated with Diamond Rio, as co-producer. Preceding the album came the 1991 single, *No Way Jose*, which deserved to be more successful than the Top 70 peak that it attained. The album was not nearly as satisfactory as its predecessor, due to several facts. First, Ray was less involved with the project, bringing in a whole parcel of pickers, only playing guitar (billed on the cd as "Art Deco"). Second, only 6 of the 10 tracks were written by Ray. Third, too many hands were on the recording and mixing console.

Ray Kennedy is a star in the making, and is probably one of those that can truly be described as unique. However, his ideas are his, and when he works on his own, he has the ability to translate them into reality. It can only be hoped that, if Atlantic keeps faith with him—and the label's main man, Rick Blackburn, is not known for giving up at the first hurdle—then Ray could become the first Country performer to find acceptability among Rock audiences, who delight in originality.

RECOMMENDED ALBUMS:

"What a Way to Go" (Atlantic)(1990)

"Guitar Man" (Atlantic)(1992)

KENTUCKY COLONELS, The

(Originally the Three Little Country Boys; then known as the Country Boys)

When Formed: 1958 (as the Country Boys), 1963 (as the Kentucky Colonels)

Members:

Roland White	Mandolin, Banjo, Vocals
Clarence White	Lead Guitar, Vocals
Eric White	String Bass, Vocals (left 1961)
Billy Ray Lathum	Banjo (joined 1958)
LeRoy Mack	Dobro (joined 1959)
Roger Bush	String Bass, Vocals (joined 1961)
Bobby Sloane	Fiddle (joined 1963)

The group originally started out as a family affair back in 1952. Although the Whites were born in Lewiston, Maine (of Canadian parents, being originally LeBlancs from New Brunswick), by 1951, they were living in Los Angeles, California. The family band was originally made up of Roland, Clarence, Eric and sister Joann. Their sound was initially in the Louvin Brothers vein, but in 1954, they switched to Bluegrass.

The three brothers began appearing on L.A. TV shows as the Three Little Country Boys. This came about after they had won first prize in a talent contest—a TV appearance. In 1958, they added Billy Ray Lathum from Cave City, Arkansas, as banjo player and a year later, they enlisted LeRoy Mack on Dobro. Until Billy Ray's appearance, Roland had been playing banjo for the preceding year but now he could revert to mandolin. That year, as the Country Boys, they recorded their first single for Sundown, *I'm Head Over Heels in Love with You/Kentucky Hills*.

The group, then averaging only 18 years of age, became resident on *Town Hall Party* and *Hometown Jamboree*. They recorded some sides for Gene Autry's label at this time. In 1961, Roger Bush came in on bass and second banjo to replace Eric, who had left after getting married. That same year, four of their tracks appeared on the *Andy Griffith Show* album, released on Capitol, ***Songs, Themes & Laughs from the Andy Griffith Show***. As the year came to a close, Roland was drafted into the Army, where he stayed for two years.

For a while, they operated without a mandolin player and brought in a rhythm guitarist, but then Clarence heard Doc Watson and he started to utilize Doc's style, by playing lead guitar using mandolin-type breaks. During Roland's absence, the group made their first album, using the services of Joe Maphis. The album was on Briar, a label owned by Paul Cohen. Briar did not want the album released under the name of the Country Boys and phoned the group with a list of alternative names. "Kentucky Colonels" was the best of a bad lot and was adopted.

Bobby Sloane was added to the line-up, on fiddle, in 1963. Bobby was different; he played left-handed on a standard right-hand-strung fiddle. Shortly after, Roland White returned to civilian life. The group now became more active and they toured New York, Washington, Detroit, the Dakotas and Canada. In 1964, they appeared at the UCLA and Newport Folk Festivals.

They now increased their recorded output. Thanks to Ed Pearl, who ran the Ash Grove in Hollywood, the Colonels became session musicians on Dick Bock's World Pacific label. The label, due to the success of Glen Campbell's 12-string guitar albums, had become active in West Coast Bluegrass material. They made one album, ***Appalachian Swing***. Roland and Clarence backed Dobroist Tut Taylor on his ***12 String Dobro*** album and Roland, Clarence and Billy Ray supported him on the Taylor album ***Dobro Country***. They also appeared in the movie *The Farmer's Other Daughter*.

When Bobby Sloane left the group, Scott Stoneman from the Stonemans joined, playing fiddle. Scott's addition acted like an explosion. Each member seemed to feed off one another with magnificent results. The group disbanded in 1965, with Clarence going on to stardom with, among others, the Byrds and then premature death. Roland went on to join Bill Monroe and the Blue Grass Boys, Country Gazette and the Nashville Bluegrass Band. Billy Ray returned to Arkansas and worked as a comedian and banjo player on the *Ozark Opry*. Bobby Sloane went on to play with J.D. Crowe and the Kentucky Mountain Boys while Roger Bush left the business for a while and went into engineering before joining Country Gazette in 1971.

RECOMMENDED ALBUMS:

"The Kentucky Colonels 1965-1967" (Rounder)
"The White Brothers (The New Kentucky Colonels) Live in Sweden, 1973" (Rounder)
"Clarence White and the Kentucky Colonels" (Rounder)(1980)

KENTUCKY HEADHUNTERS, The

When Formed: 1986

Members:

Richard Young	Rhythm Guitar
Fred Young	Drums
Greg Martin	Lead Guitar
Anthony Kenney	Bass Guitar (joined 1992)
Doug Phelps	Bass Guitar (left 1992)
Ricky Lee Phelps	Lead Singer (left 1992)
Mark Orr	Lead Singer (joined 1992)

When the Kentucky Headhunters won the CMA "Vocal Group of the Year" award in 1990, they opened up a floodgate for other rockier bands. What Alabama had started in the early 1980's was now set into full flow. When Mercury Nashville executive Harold Shed

***The Kentucky Headhunters**, who rocked the Country establishment*

signed them to the label, an important decision was made not to alter or commercialize them; instead the high spirited Country-Blues-Rockers were allowed to be themselves and stretch their creative wings, causing Country music to widen its boundaries. Their debut album, ***Pickin' on Nashville***, was Certified Platinum in only 7 months. The first Country group lp to do this, it also became CMA Album of the Year 1990. Some will ask themselves "Is this Country?" Some think the beat is too driving, the sound too earpiercing, but these five rednecks from backwoods Arkansas and the remote hills of Kentucky prove they can still sell records and pack in the crowds on the merit of the music alone.

In 1968, brothers Fred and Richard Young, Greg Martin and another cousin, Anthony Kenney, and later Mark Orr, used the Youngs' grandmother's place called "the practice house" to set up a group called the Ichy Brothers.They played together for 13 years and never disbanded but kind of ran out of steam. Next Richard joined Acuff-Rose as a songwriter, Fred toured with Sylvia and appeared in the movie *Sweet Dreams* as Patsy Cline's drummer, and Greg joined Ronnie McDowell's band where he met Doug Phelps; they played together until 1985. Doug and his brother Ricky Lee are sons of a rural preacher and were raised in the delta region of Arkansas and Missouri. Doug, Fred and Greg started to put the Ichy Brothers together again but Anthony Kenny decided not to continue. They got Doug Phelps to join them and changed the name to the Kentucky Headhunters. They worked for six months but felt something was missing; they just couldn't get what they wanted. Then Ricky Phelps came to jam with them and suddenly the magic was there.

Over WLOC Munfordville, Kentucky, the band launched a 90-minute live unrehearsed show twice a month called *The Chitlin' Show*. This show helped to build the Headhunters' local reputation. After borrowing $4,500, they recorded over a three-day period an 8-song demo which they pitched to Mercury Records. This demo, with a little remixing, became their first album, ***Pickin' on Nashville*** (1989) which sold nearly two million copies worldwide. Popular singles from the album included *Walk Softly on This Heart of Mine,* a Top 25 chart hit. In 1990, *Dumas Walker* reached the Top 15, *Oh, Lonesome Me* went Top 10 and *Rock 'N Roll Angel* reached the Top 25.

The industry loaded them with awards. The ACM named them "Best Group of the Year," the CMA awarded them "Vocal Group of the Year," "Album of the Year" and "Producers of the Year." They also received the *Billboard* Music Video Award for "Best Group" and "Best New Artist." AMOA Jukebox Awards named them "Best New Group." National Association of Record Merchandisers (NARM) awarded them for "Best Selling Country Album," American Music Awards named them "Best New Artists, Country Category" and they received a Grammy Award for "Best Country Performance by a Duo or Group with Vocal."

After two years of relentless touring throughout the U.S., the group's second album, ***Electric Barnyard***, was released just after the Grammy Award show in 1991. It included the songs *The Ballad of Davy Crockett, With Body and Soul, It's Chitlin' Time*, and *Only Daddy That'll Walk the Line,* none of which were Top 60 or worse. With the release of this album, the group hit the road again. In 1991, the group was again named the CMA's "Vocal Group of the Year." In June 1992 Ricky Lee and Doug Phelps left to form the more Country-oriented Brother Phelps. Reinforcements were called in in the guise of old Ichy Brother band members Anthony Kenney and Mark Orr. Then it was on the road again to prove the new line-up. The band then returned to Nashville to record a new album, ***Rave On***. However, the new album had too little Country content and was far too much like a Heavy Rock album and was largely unsuccessful. Product after this date has taken the band completely out of the Country fold. JAB

RECOMMENDED ALBUMS:

"Pickin' on Nashville" (Mercury)(1989)
"Electric Barnyard" (Mercury)(1991)

Kentucky Ramblers refer PRAIRIE RAMBLERS

ANITA KERR

(Singer, Piano, Arranger, Leader of Anita Kerr Singers)

Given Name:	**Anita Jean Grilli**
Date of Birth:	**October 31, 1927**
Where Born:	**Memphis, Tennessee**
Married:	**1. (Div.)**
	2. Alex Grob

Together with the Jordanaires, the Anita Kerr Singers handled the majority of vocal backings involved in the Nashville Sound. Their leader was a prolific talent.

Born into a musical family, Anita began taking piano lessons from age 4, at the behest of her mother, who had a musical show in Memphis. Anita's aptitude for musical arrangements first surfaced publicly when she arranged songs for a church group while attending elementary school. Even before reaching high school, Anita had formed her own girl trio, the Grilli Sisters. They were regulars on her mother's radio program on WREC Memphis. When Anita was 14, she applied for the post of staff pianist at the station and held down the job until her graduation, undertaking vocal arrangements for church music in this formative period.

In 1948, she left for Memphis in search of a musical career. She survived by playing piano at local night spots. The following year, Anita formed her first professional vocal group made up of Anita on lead vocals, Dottie Dillard (alto) (featured singer on WSM for several years), Gil Wright (tenor) and Louis Nunley (baritone), whose first recording session was with Red Foley.

After making some waves on WSM radio, Anita was then asked to provide an eight-voice choir for the NBC regional show *Sunday Down South*. As Chorus Director, Anita was responsible for all the choral arrangements. Her endeavors brought bids from artists and record companies to work for them.

During 1956, the Anita Kerr Singers auditioned for the New York–based *Arthur Godfrey Talent Scouts* show. Godfrey felt that 8 voices were too many and so the Anita Kerr Quartet (later known as the Anita Kerr Singers) emerged (with the line-up of Dillard, Wright and Nunley). First appearing in June, they became semi-regulars, working four to five months a year on TV and the rest of the time on Nashville recording sessions.

In their heyday in the 50's and 60's, the Anita Kerr Singers were one of the most widely heard groups in the Country field. Indeed, by the early 60's, it is estimated that they were appearing on a quarter of all Nashville's recorded output. They were in at the start of the Nashville Sound, when in 1957, they backed Ray Price on a religious album which featured 17 violins! They were especially important in the later career of Jim Reeves, who greatly respected Anita Kerr for her arranging abilities. Among Anita's arrangements (either vocal or instrumental) are those on Bobby Helms' *My Special Angel* (1957), Jim Reeves' *He'll Have to Go* and the Browns' *Three Bells* (both 1959), Floyd Cramer's *Last Date*, Roy Orbison's *Only the Lonely* (1960) and *Running Scared* (1961), Skeeter Davis' *The End of the World* (1962), Bobby Bare's *Detroit City* (1963) and Dottie West's *Here Comes My Baby*.

Anita joined the A & R staff of RCA Victor in 1961 and she stayed there until 1965. During this stellar period, the Anita Kerr Singers backed a host of Country talent that included Chet Atkins, Floyd Cramer, Hank Snow, Skeeter Davis, Eddy Arnold, Webb

Pierce and Lorne Greene. Their work was also in demand from non-Country artists like Brook Benton and Perry Como.

Under the name of Anita and th' So-and-So's, the group had a Top 100 Country hit with the 1962 single *Joey Baby*. The Anita Kerr Singers toured the U.S. extensively and found themselves in demand to perform on network TV and at clubs and hotels. In spring 1964, they were part of the ground-breaking RCA package tour of Europe featuring Jim Reeves, Chet Atkins and Bobby Bare.

In 1965, having remarried, Anita moved to California, where she engaged in freelance production and writing. That year, the Anita Kerr Singers won a Grammy Award for their RCA album ***We Dig Mancini*** as "Best Performance by a Vocal Group." They also won the "Best Gospel or Other Religious Recording (Musical)" Grammy that year for their collaboration with George Beverly Shea, entitled ***Southland Favorites***. The following year, the Anita Kerr Singers won the Grammy Award for "Best Performance by a Vocal Group" for the album ***A Man and a Woman***, on Warner Brothers. Somewhat disenchanted with the Country scene, Anita pursued "mood-music" projects with Rod McKuen in 1967-1968. These were titled ***The Sea***, ***The Earth*** and ***The Sky***. The Anita Kerr Singers appeared on his poetry albums as the San Sebastian Strings and Singers. In the 70's, Anita produced records for the easy listening market and moved to Switzerland, her husband's native country, to write film music, but later returned to Memphis.

The Anita Kerr Singers continued for a time and had two further lead singers after Anita's departure. First was Chrissy Hubbard, Jerry Reed's wife, and then Genene Walker, wife of arranger Bill Walker. Of the initial group, only Louis Nunley continues to be active, often as a part of the Jordanaires. SM

RECOMMENDED ALBUMS:
"It's Anita Kerr Country" (Dot)(1976)
"I Sang with Jim Reeves" (Phillips UK)

DOUG KERSHAW

(Singer, Songwriter, Fiddle)

Given Name:	**Douglas James Kershaw**
Date of Birth:	**January 24, 1936**
Where Born:	**Tiel Ridge, Cameron Parish, Louisiana**
Married:	**1. Elsie Carol Griffin (m. 1968) (div. 1975) 2. Pam**
Children:	**1. Doug James, Jr., Victor Conrad; 2. Zachary, Tyler, Eli**

Doug Kershaw will go down into immortality as the writer of *Louisiana Man*, a song that is tantamount to the modern Cajun's anthem. It has now been recorded over 850 times. He is also one of the most versatile musicians, playing some 29 instruments.

He was born on a houseboat on a little island on the Gulf Coast, to Jackson Kershaw (a fisherman and trapper and accordionist) and Mama Rita Broussard Kershaw (a singer, guitarist, accordionist and fiddler). The Kershaws trace their ancestry back to an English doctor, John Nedham Kershaw, who came to Louisiana in 1817. The Broussards are also a famous family of Cajun musicians.

Doug had three older brothers, Edward (known as Big Brother Ed), Nelson (Pee Wee) and Russell Lee (Rusty, b. February 2, 1938). Jack Kershaw committed suicide when Doug was just 7 years old and the family moved to Lake Arthur, Louisiana. At the time, Doug only spoke French and didn't come to grips with English until he was 8. Doug started to shine shoes to supplement the family income, but kept getting chased out until one day, he took his fiddle with him and found a crowd around him. They wanted him to keep on playing but he told them, "The only way I'd play is if y'all let me shine your shoes." He ended up with $10.20.

Along with his mother, Doug started to play at a club in Lake Arthur called the Bucket of Blood. The club lived up to its name. When he was 9 years old, he joined his first band, Zenis Le Comp and the White Shirt Band. By the time he was 11, the family moved to Jennings, Louisiana, where he finished high school. It was now that he decided to change his life-style. He worked out that if he slept for eight hours a day and lived to be 60, then he would have slept for 20 years. So he decided to sleep less!

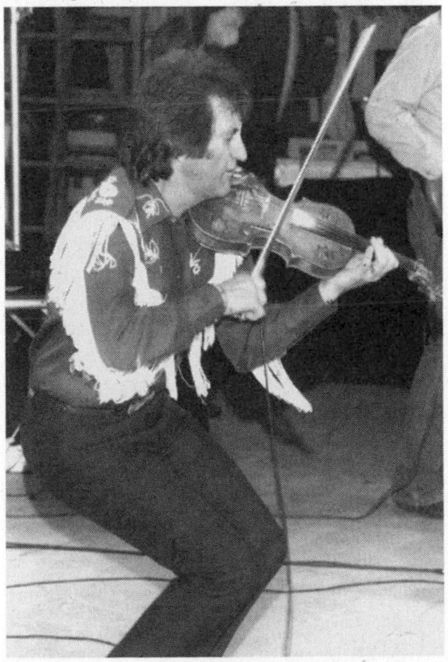

The Crazy Cajun, ***Doug Kershaw***

When Pee Wee quit the band he was playing in during 1948, he and Doug decided to form a band. They needed a guitar player and Doug suggested Rusty (complete with Captain Marvel T-shirt) play guitar. Rusty had never played guitar before, but he said that he could, and he did. So was born Pee Wee Kershaw & the Continental Playboys, a Cajun French group. By 1953, they started broadcasting over KPLC-TV in Lake Charles. They continued on this station until 1955. During that time, Doug attended McNeese State College in Lake Charles.

Doug then decided to record in English and then he met J.D. "Jay" Miller in Crowley, Louisiana. Miller owned a recording studio and a record label (Feature Records) and was a songwriter (he co-wrote Cajun classic *Diggy Liggy Lo*). He made a record of Doug's song *When Will I Learn* as Douglas Kershaw and the Bewley Gang and released it over the counter. Then a year later, Doug was recording another self-penned song, *No, No It's Not So*, when Rusty entered the recording studio and started harmonizing on it. Doug persuaded Miller to go to Nashville to get it released. Miller not only agreed to this but also recorded some other tracks of Doug and Rusty. This led to a record deal with Hickory Records and a publishing deal with Acuff-Rose. Rusty & Doug's first record was released in 1955 and was another Doug original, *So Lovely Baby*. The single reached the Top 15 on the Country chart. On their early material for the label, they were supported by pianist Wiley Barkdull and guitarist Hank Garland.

That year, Rusty & Doug's Music Makers joined the *Louisiana Hayride* and they remained on the show until the following year. In May 1956, they became members of WWVA's *Wheeling Jamboree* and stayed on the show until 1957. During 1956, they were named *Cash Box*'s "No.1 Duet." In November 1957, they joined the *Grand Ole Opry*. During that year, their single *Love Me to Pieces* reached the Top 15. This was followed in 1958 by the Top 25 single *Hey, Sheriff*.

Doug now received the call from "Uncle Sam" and joined the Army and Rusty decided to do the same. They got out in 1960, and it was then that Doug wrote *Louisiana Man*. During an October 1960 recording session, the brothers recorded that song plus *(Our Own) Jole Blon* and *Diggy Liggy Lo*. *Louisiana Man* gave the brothers their first Top 10 hit and also crossed over to the lower regions of the Pop chart. This was followed into the Country chart by *Diggy Liggy Lo*, which reached the Top 15.

In 1963, the brothers moved over to RCA Victor, where they recorded another Doug Kershaw classic song, *Cajun Stripper*. Then, the following year, Doug and Rusty decided to go their separate ways. Rusty went on to become an electrician with a national pipeline company. After the split, Doug moved on to Mercury Records and MGM. In 1968, Doug signed to Tree Publishing and Warner Brothers Records and the following year, he appeared on the *Johnny Cash Show* alongside Bob Dylan. That year, Doug had a solo hit with *Diggy Liggy Lo*, which reached the lower levels of the Country charts. He stayed with Warners until 1978, producing 11 albums along the way. "The Ragin' Cajun," as he is called, managed to chart three more singles in the basement level for the label.

For some while, his backing band had been the Louisiana Men, and then in 1976 he put together Slidin' Jake, which comprised Max Schwennsen (lead singer and guitar), Al Kaatz (vocals and guitar), Rose DeArmas (vocals and back-up guitar and percussion), Marty Vadalbene (drums) and Brian Smith (bass guitar). Doug has appeared in several movies: *Zachariah* with Bob Dylan (1971), *Medicine Ball Caravan* (1971) and the 1978 production *Days of Heaven* with Richard Gere. He also appeared in the 1977 special for CBS-TV *Mary Tyler Moore's Incredible Dream*. Doug was very much in the public eye when *Louisiana Man* was played during the Apollo 12 moon shot.

In 1981, Doug signed to Scotti Bros. Records and returned to the Country charts with *Hello Woman*, which made it into the Top 30. For the next few years, Doug plied his trade around the U.S. and eventually, in 1984, got himself clear of a twin dependency on alcohol and cocaine (which also afflicted brother Rusty). He teamed up with Hank Williams, Jr., in 1988 on the Hank Williams/Hank Williams, Jr., song *Cajun Baby*, for BGM Records out of San Antonio, Texas. This and the duet with Fats Domino on *Toot Toot* were the 2 decent tracks on an otherwise unremarkable 1989 album, ***Hot Diggidy Doug***.

In the spring of 1989, Doug proved that he is still the consummate live showman when he appeared at the Wembley Festival in England. Always flamboyant in his velvet suits and with a demonic look and a still angular frame, Doug Kershaw grabbed the audience like a Cajun Paganini and defied them not to like him. They loved him!

Doug now lives on a ranch near Greeley, Colorado, where he indulges his pastime—golf. Big brother Pee Wee lives in Galveston and does a guitar and magic fiddle act, Rusty still plays with bands in the New Orleans area and Big Ed died in 1979.

Doug is a man who still holds on to his Cajun roots. When asked what was the difference between Cajun and Country, he averred unequivocally, "The difference between Cajun and Country is that Cajun was around before Country was."

RECOMMENDED ALBUMS:

"Louisiana Man" (Hickory)(1961)
"The Cajun Way" (Warner Brothers)(1969)
"Spanish Moss" (Warner Brothers)(1970)
"Doug Kershaw" (Warner Brothers)(1971)
"Swamp Grass" (Warner Brothers)(1972)
"Devil's Elbow" (Warner Brothers)(1972)
"Douglas James Kershaw" (Warner Brothers)(1973)
"Mama Kershaw's Boy" (Warner Brothers)(1974)
"Louisiana Man" (DJM UK)(1974) [As Rusty & Doug Kershaw] [Hickory material]
"Alive and Pickin'" (Warner Brothers)(1975)
"Ragin' Cajun" (Warner Brothers)(1976)
"Flip, Flop & Fly" (Warner Brothers)(1977)
"Louisiana Man" (Warner Brothers)(1978)
"Instant Hero" (Scotti Bros.)(1981)
"Cajun Country Rockers" (Bear Family Germany)
also Rusty Kershaw:
"Rusty...Cajun in the Blues Country" (Cotillion)(1970) [Produced by Doug Kershaw]

SAMMY KERSHAW

(Singer, Songwriter, Guitar)

Date of Birth:	**1959**
Where Born:	**Kaplan, Louisiana**
Married:	**1. (Div.)**
	2. Kim
Children:	**Brandon, Sammie, Emily Kristina**

Sammy is one of the new generation of performers who hail from Louisiana. He is also a third cousin to the legendary Cajun fiddler, Doug Kershaw.

Sammy's hometown of Kaplan is about 25 miles south of Lafayette and 40 miles north of the Gulf of Mexico. While still a baby, his mama rocked him to sleep singing Hank Williams songs. Sammy was exposed to Country music from an early age with the family collection of Hank, Conway Twitty, George Jones and Buck Owens. When he was 11, his father died of lung cancer and his mother worked full-time as a waitress to support her four children, Sammy being the eldest.

Around the time his father died, his grandfather bought him a Western Auto Tel Star electric guitar. Sammy made his debut while in fourth grade, at a Christmas play at school. When he was 12, his mother arranged for him to work for an accomplished and popular local musician, J.B. Perry. For the next eight years, he came under Perry's tutelage. Sammy was responsible for setting up the equipment wherever they played and he also sang on the shows with Perry. This was excellent experience for the young Kershaw and he got to open for a lot of major Country stars. Sammy was broadening his repertoire and now included material by Charlie Rich, Ray Charles and the Allman Brothers. While with Perry, he got to duet with Lorrie Morgan, who was then a part of George Jones' band.

Sammy started to be influenced by some of the performers that he played alongside including Cal Smith and most especially Mel Street. Even today, he still plays a couple of Mel Street's songs, *Borrowed Angel* and *Lovin' on Back Streets*.

Throughout his 20's, Sammy found himself at times in financial problems and had to resort to regular jobs, including shoveling rice in a rice mill, welding, carpentry, running a dry cleaning business and deejaying. He tried his hand at baseball and almost became a professional. However, it was still music that called him and eventually, he joined a band, Blackwater, playing clubs in south Louisiana, Texas, Wyoming, New Mexico and South Dakota. He cut occasional singles for local independent labels and a couple of them got "recommended" mentions in *Billboard*.

***Sammy Kershaw**, one of Country's new stars*

By the end of the 80's, Sammy had felt that he and the music business should go separate ways. He was now on his second marriage and playing clubs was starting to wreck that. So he took work as a remodeling supervisor for the Wal-Mart corporation. For the next two years, he traveled across the country remodeling Wal-Mart stores. During the first year, he was only at home for 20 days, but he built up his finances. It was while he was working on a store in Texas and having thoughts about starting his own remodeling business, that he got a call from a friend in Nashville suggesting that he come to Nashville and try and get a record deal.

In 1991, Sammy did a live showcase audition for Mercury's Harold Shedd and Buddy Cannon and as a result, he got signed to the label. Sammy's debut album, ***Don't Go Near the Water***, was produced by Norro Wilson. Sammy hit the Country charts with *Cadillac Style* and it reached the Top 3 and stayed on the lists for five months. Because of the single, Sammy was chosen to be the spokesman for the Gold Key Cadillac Dealers Association. He appeared in both TV and radio spots and this helped the sales of the vehicle. The album reached the Top 25 on the Country albums chart and was Certified Gold in August 1992. During that year, he hit the Top 20 with the title track of the album and *Yard Sale* and ended the year with *Anywhere But Here*, which reached the Top 10.

In 1993, Sammy released a new album, ***Haunted Heart***, which went Gold that year. From this album came *She Don't Know She's Beautiful*, which went to No.1. Sammy's other 1993 hits were *Haunted Heart* and *Queen of My Double Wide Trailer*, both of which went Top 10. In 1994, Sammy had a Top 3 hit with *I Can't Reach Her Anymore*. That year, he released his third album, ***Feelin' Good Train***. During the summer of 1994, *National Working Woman's Holiday* reached the Top 15 and was still climbing.

Sammy Kershaw, complete with his trademark saddle-bags that he carries on his shoulders onto the stage, has proved to be a very adept performer and seems certain to be around for many years. Although he comes from a Cajun background, his voice and styling are smack-dab in the middle of straight ahead Country. He has also shown himself to have a great sense of fun and a warm personality. He is also an excellent self-taught Cajun chef.

RECOMMENDED ALBUMS:

"Don't Go Near the Water" (Mercury Nashville)(1991)
"Haunted Heart" (Mercury Nashville)(1993)
"Feelin' Good Train" (Mercury Nashville)(1994)

KESSINGER BROTHERS, The

CLARK KESSINGER
(Fiddle)

Given Name: Clark W. Kessinger
Date of Birth: July 27, 1896
Married: Rosie
Children: six
Date of Death: June 4, 1975

LUKE KESSINGER
(Guitar)

Given Name: Luke (or Luches) W. Kessinger
Date of Birth: August 21, 1906
Date of Death: May 6, 1944

Both Born: Kanawha County, West Virginia

Clark Kessinger is considered one of the greatest Old-Time fiddlers. With guitar backing from his nephew, Luke, and recording as the Kessinger Brothers, he made some 70 sides on the Brunswick and Vocalion labels between 1928 and 1930.

Born across the Kanawha River from Charleston, Clark came from a family of fiddlers and was reared there and in rural Lincoln County. According to the best available information, he became interested in the fiddle and by age 5 had sufficiently mastered the instrument to make several dollars nightly in tips at a local saloon. At 10, Clark played regularly for local dances. He learned tunes from older area fiddlers such as George Dillon, Bob and Abe Glen, and the legendary Blind Ed Haley.

After serving in the Army during WWI, Clark commenced playing with guitar backup furnished by his nephew Luke, son of Clark's older brother, Charlie Kessinger. They were an early act on WOBU radio in Charleston (as was Billy Cox) and through a local violin teacher named Richmond Huston they received an opportunity to record with Brunswick.

The Kessingers did 14 numbers at the first session for Brunswick at Ashland, Kentucky, in February 1928. James O'Keefe, the company talent scout, named them the Kessinger Brothers for the artist credit on the labels. Several of their tunes, such as *Turkey in the Straw*, *Wednesday Night Waltz* and *Kanawha March,* rank among the better-selling items in the Brunswick "Songs from Dixie" series.

Over the next two years, the Kessinger Brothers made trips to New York, playing both well-known and obscure tunes on disc. Clark meanwhile continued to fiddle on local radio and in contests, sometimes competing with other nationally known fiddlers, including Eck Robertson, Bert Layne, Clayton McMichen and Natchee the Indian (Lester Vernon Storer). During much of this time, Clark earned his principal livelihood as a caretaker and chauffeur for an affluent Charlestonian named Harrison Smith, who helped introduce him to such classical violinists as Fritz Kreisler, who once gave a concert in Charleston.

The Great Depression ended Clark's recording career for a third of a century, and after his nephew's death, he worked less often, but continued to sometimes work at a dance or a club in the vicinity of Charleston. He earned his primary living at a variety of jobs, but mostly as an interior house painter. In 1964, Ken Davidson, an Old-Time music fan and aspiring record company owner, found the 68-year-old Kessinger fiddling at a club in Hurricane, Virginia, and induced him to get back into music in a serious way. Clark soon won a fiddling contest in Pulaski, Virginia, and followed it up with other impressive showings at Galax, Virginia; Union Grove, North Carolina; Weiser, Idaho; and Pomeroy, Ohio, among other places. Davidson collected enough material for four albums on his Kanawha label and Rounder recorded a fifth. Clark encored on his *Grand Ole Opry* guest spot, backed by Lester Flatt and Earl Scruggs. Always a congenial showman, the aging fiddler enjoyed his revived career until suffering a stroke in July 1971 which effectively ended his comeback. He recovered somewhat, but never sufficiently to fiddle again. After Kanawha closed up shop, Folkways kept one of Clark's Kanawha albums in print for some years and County did the same with two others. Both Kanawha and County re-issued albums each of which contain a dozen numbers from Kessinger Brothers originals. In recent years, a young kinsman of Clark, Ronin Kessinger of Mason County, West Virginia, has emerged as a widely respected flat-top guitar picker. IMT

RECOMMENDED ALBUMS:

"Original Fiddle Classics, 1928-1930" (Kanawha)(1970)
"The Kessinger Brothers, 1928-1930" (County)(1974)
Clark Kessinger:
"The Legend of Clark Kessinger" (Folk Promotion)(1964) [Later released on Kanawha & County]
"Sweet Bunch of Daisies" (Kanawha)(1966) [Later released on County]
"Live at Union Grove" (Kanawha)(1968) [Later released on Folkways]
"Clark Kessinger" (Rounder)(1972)
"Clark Kessinger Memorial Album" (Kanawha)(1976)

HAL KETCHUM

(Singer, Songwriter, Guitar, Drums)

Given Name: Hal Michael Ketchum
Date of Birth: April 9, 1953
Where Born: Greenwich, New York
Married: Terrell Tye

This is a man who ploughs his own furrow and has more than a share of the New York Folk singer about his style. He writes with a plain simple approach and he calls his collection of songs American music.

From a Scottish and Irish background, Hal had a grandfather, a concert violinist, who later went on to play at square dances and then had a swing band. Hal's father played the banjo, so he was no stranger to music. He was brought up in the Adirondack Mountains, near the Vermont border. He was influenced by Buck Owens and was once a member of Owens' fan club. At the age of 15, Hal started playing drums, and when he played with a local R & B trio, he had to get his dad to sign a permission slip, because he was under age.

When he was 17, Hal moved to Florida and continued to play drums and also worked as a carpenter's helper. (As a result of this training, he was able to build a lot of his own furniture for his house, in the 80's.) Hal next moved to Texas, and the night he moved into his house, he heard music in the distance. On investigating, he found a local dance hall with live music. He began to go there to play and used the experience as a proving ground for his music and songwriting.

In 1986, Hal came to Nashville, where he focused on his songwriting and then decided to record 10 of his original songs. He did this, using an independent label, Watermelon Records. The album was called ***Threadbare Alibis*** (1989), and it was released by Line Records in Europe. With this album as ammunition, Hal eventually signed with a publisher, Forerunner Music, and with their guidance and demos managed to get a record deal. Hal had attracted the attention of Dick Whitehouse of Curb Records and was signed to a recording contract.

*Singer/Songwriter **Hal Ketchum***

His debut album, ***Past the Point of Rescue*** (1991), offered a selection of Ketchum's original songs among others and went Gold in February1992. His debut single, *Small Town Saturday Night,* became 1991's "No.1 Single of the Year Nationwide" in *Radio & Records* and made the Top 3 on the charts. The video of this single did well on CMT, Nashville Network and on VH-1 Country. *I Know Where Love Lies*, the second single and video, managed a Top 20 placing on the Country music charts in 1992 and it also earned a BMI award for Hal.

Hal appeared at Fan Fair in 1991 representing Curb Records, and also performed at the CMA, SRO Talent Buyers showcase. Two other singles hit the charts in 1992, *Past the Point of Rescue* (with a popular video), which reached the Top 3, and *Five O'Clock World*, with a Top 20 placing. September 1992 brought another album release, ***Sure Love***. The title track was released as a single and went Top 5. During 1993, Hal charted with *Hearts Are Gonna Roll* (Top 3), *Mama Knows the Highway* (Top 10) and *Someplace Far Away (Careful What You're Dreamin')* (Top 20).

In 1994, Hal was made a member of the *Grand Ole Opry* and his single, *(Tonight We Just Might) Fall in Love Again*, reached the Top 25. Hal also appeared as part of the Maverick Choir singing *Amazing Grace*, on the soundtrack album of the movie *Maverick*. JAB

RECOMMENDED ALBUMS:

"Past the Point of Rescue" (Curb)(1991)
"Sure Love" (Curb)(1992)

MERLE KILGORE

(Singer, Songwriter, Guitar, Deejay, Actor)

Given Name:	**Wyatt Merle Kilgore**
Date of Birth:	**September 9, 1934**
Where Born:	**Chickasha, Oklahoma**
Married:	**Dorothy Lee Salley**
Children:	**Pamela Ann, Stephen Merle, Kimberly Lynn, Johnny Gale (dec'd.)**

Big Merle—he's 6'4"—has in recent times been the managerial force behind Hank Williams, Jr., and the man who gets Hank Jr.'s shows under way. However, he is also a multitalented man who has written many memorable hits, had a recording career that has spanned 25 years and been a movie actor and a deejay.

While he was still young, his family moved to Shreveport, Louisiana. He learned how to play guitar while still a lad and got a job as a deejay/musician at KENT Shreveport, when he was 16. During the following year, Merle deejayed and played on various stations in Louisiana including KZEA Springhill. At the end of the year, he joined KWKH's *Louisiana Hayride* as principal guitar accompanist and stayed with them throughout the 50's. 1952 was an interesting year for Merle. He started a two-year stint on KFAZ-TV in West Monroe on *Ouachita Valley Jamboree*, made his debut playing on the *Grand Ole Opry*, played the *Big D Jamboree* out of Dallas and attended Louisiana Tech to complete his education.

During 1953, he worked at the American Optical Company by day, continued his TV work in Monroe and performed at night. The next year, his career started to take off and he was signed to Imperial Records and had his first song recorded. *More and More* was co-written with Webb Pierce, who took it to No.1 for 10 weeks. It was later recorded by Guy Lombardo, Johnny Duncan and in 1983 it again became a hit in the hands of Charley Pride. Merle received a BMI award for the song.

Merle's recordings for Imperial did nothing more than enhance his reputation. However, this did not deter him from helping others. One of these was Joe Stampley, then 15, whom Merle wrote with and assisted to get his first record deal with Imperial. By 1959, he had moved to D Records. That year, Johnny Horton recorded the Kilgore composition *Johnny Reb,*

*Big **Merle Kilgore***

which provided Horton with a Top 10 hit and earned Merle another BMI award.

1960 became a vintage year. Merle signed to Starday and at last, the hits started rolling for him as an artist. *Dear Mama* rose to the Top 15 at the beginning of the year and racked up his BMI awards to three. This was followed by his first Top 10 hit, *Love Has Made You Beautiful*. The flipside, *Gettin' Old Before My Time*, also made the Top 30. That year, Frankie Miller recorded Merle's *Baby Rocked Her Dolly* and had a major hit. Merle started playing the *Grand Ole Opry* and was featured on KTVE-TV's *Big 10 Jamboree* out of Eldorado, Arkansas, and on the *Riley Springs Jamboree* from Riley Springs, Texas.

Wolverton Mountain was written by Merle and Claude King. It provided King with his first No.1 and stayed in that position for 9 weeks and was on the charts for 6 months. It also became a Top 10 Pop hit (Clifton Clowers, who is barrier to the lady he loves in the song, was actually Merle's uncle). The following year, Kilgore came up with another classic. *Ring of Fire* had been written with June Carter and provided Johnny Cash with a monster hit. The song has since been recorded by many artists in Country and Rock.

Starday continued to release albums, including ***There's Gold in Them There Hills*** (1963) and ***Merle Kilgore*** (1964). Merle headlined in Las Vegas and Reno and played Carnegie Hall and the Hollywood Bowl. In 1966, he surfaced on Mercury with ***Merle Kilgore, The Tall Texan***. That year, he played the title song (released on Epic) for the Steve McQueen movie *Nevada Smith* and also appeared in it. This was an acting role as opposed to the cameo appearance in *Country Music on Broadway*.

By 1967, Merle was with Columbia and returned to the charts with *Fast Talkin' Louisiana Man,* which peaked in the Top 75. The following year, he appeared in the movie *Five Card Stud* with Debbie Reynolds. He cut an album for Leon Ashley's Ashley label, entitled ***Ring of Fire***, in 1969, and Starday released ***Big Merle Kilgore*** in 1973.

Merle had another minor hit in 1974 for Warner Brothers with *Montgomery Mable*. He charted three times more with *Mr. Garfield* on Elektra in 1982, *Just Out of Reach* (1984) and *Guilty* (1985), both on Warner. On *Mr. Garfield*, he was assisted by Hank, Jr., and Johnny Cash. Well, it's credited as being Cash, but as Merle does the most marvelous Cash impression, who knows!

Merle Kilgore is still out there, still giving the audiences a lot of pleasure. Now he is much more of an industry executive, with interests in publishing and of course management.

RECOMMENDED ALBUMS:

"There's Gold in Them There Hills" (Starday)(1963)
"Ring of Fire" (Ashley)(1969)

BUDDY KILLEN

(Bass Player, Music Publisher, Record Producer, Singer, Actor, Industry Executive, Restaurateur)

Given Name:	**William D. Killen**
Date of Birth:	**November 13, 1932**
Where Born:	**Florence, Alabama**
Married:	**1. June (div.)**
	2. Sue (div.)
	3. Carolyn
Children:	**Linda Richardson, Robin Smith**

Born and raised in Florence, Alabama, Buddy Killen has run the gamut from performer to publishing company executive, to songwriter to successful restaurateur, and that only covers a few of the hats he has worn along the way.

One of eight children, he recalls singing in his mother's lap when he was 3 years old, growing up in the rural South. Friends and neighbors gave him pennies for his performances. He recalls that he and his sister, Joyce, once "canned" 200 of the family's live chicks. Along with the rest of his family, he chopped and picked cotton, listening to tales of ghosts and his great-grandmother's sightings of the James Gang, years before.

Killen grew up in the shadow of abject poverty in a one-room shack. The family was so poor, one sister died of what he calls "economic malnutrition." His father, Willie Killen, was a preacher who later owned a cafe. Killen recalls his only escape from the grinding poverty and hard times was music.

His first band, during his childhood years, was called the Hillbilly Pals and featured Nashville producer Kelso Herston. Over the next few years, he formed another band called the Dixie Ramblers and they began singing and playing on local radio stations. He wrote: "Before the advent of television, people in the rural South seemingly retained their innocence. 'Their senses' and their imagination remained active." Twenty-four hours after graduation from high school Buddy was offered a job playing bass for two blackface comedians called Jam Up & Honey on the *Grand Ole Opry*. Buddy grabbed the job, moved to Nashville and went to work as a musician traveling and performing with acts including Jim Reeves, Ray Price, Moon Mullican, George Morgan, Cowboy Copas and Hank Williams. Success, however, eluded him, particularly on the financial end of things. Then, while pickin' as a sideman on the *Wheeling Jamboree*, a traumatic event occurred that Buddy says changed his life: His car was repossessed by GMAC. He recalls, "I made up my mind to never let that happen again. I've never been without work even for a day since that terrifying time." Aided by his southern charm, and being on the *Opry*'s payroll, Buddy became acquainted with the stars and well- known personalities of the day.

One of those was Jack Stapp, who had recently formed Tree International in Nashville, at that time a one-man publishing company. "I was doing demos for Tree at $10.00 a session," Buddy recounted in an interview, "and Jack would come into the studio and ask me to get together with this singer or that writer. It went well and Jack asked me if I would come to work for him. The job would pay $35.00 a week and I said yes. I began picking up songs and getting them recorded. We didn't have an office. I would carry a tape recorder around, begging for songs. It was a sheer case of determination." Unbeknownst to Buddy at the time, this relationship, which began in 1953, would blossom into one of the most successful relationships in Country music history.

In 1957, Jack made Buddy a partner and he began his meteoric rise from songplugger to President of one of the world's most flourishing music publishing companies. The road was a long one but Buddy ended up with the pot of gold when he eventually sold the company to CBS/Sony. Prior to Buddy becoming Jack's partner, Tree had already gained recognition in the industry after Elvis Presley's hit *Heartbreak Hotel*, written by Tree writers Mae Boren Axton and Tommy Durden (plus Elvis Presley). The song laid the foundation for what was to come. In 1958, Buddy signed then-struggling songwriter Roger Miller to the fold. Two years later, he managed to sign 14-year-old Dolly Parton. The same year (1960) Buddy's group of Music City session players, the Little Dippers, scored a Pop hit with *Forever* (on University Records), one of a number of songs written by Buddy; the song went Top 10 on the Pop charts. The group included Dolores Denning, Emily Gilmore, Darrell McCall and Hurshel Wiginton.

Buddy's next big accomplishment came when in 1963 he signed Soul star Joe Tex to Tree. That same year Tree Publishing saw its first million-dollar year. The following year Jack Stapp moved to Tree full-time. Prior to this he had also worked as General Manager of radio station WKDA. After his move, he named

Buddy Executive Vice President and the company moved its headquarters to 905 16th Avenue South. In 1965, Tex launched his streak of Soul hits with *Hold What You've Got*, produced by Buddy and marketed on Tree's Dial Record label. Three years later, Tree went international with 13 overseas offices.

A year later, in 1969, Tree acquired Pamper Music, which included a number of Willie Nelson songs and doubled the size of the company. This was the first in a long series of catalog acquisitions. In 1972, Tree was named "No.1 Publisher of the Year" by *Billboard* magazine. Three years later, in 1975, Buddy Killen was promoted to the presidency of Tree, as Stapp became Board Chairman and CEO. The same year, "Buddy Killen Day" was declared in the publisher's hometown of Florence, Alabama. On December 20, 1980, Jack Stapp died and Buddy became the sole owner of the giant publishing company. During the first half of the 80's, Tree blossomed, acquiring additional catalogs such as Buck Owens' Blue Book Song Catalog. By now, they had 130 staff writers. Buddy produced Exile, which began its hit streak of Country-Pop songs.

In 1985 Buddy made his acting debut with a part in the Louis Malle film *Alamo Bay* and was inducted into the Alabama Music Hall of Fame and given Nashville's Metronome Award. He also paid an estimated $1.6 million for full ownership of the Stockyard Restaurant, a business he had partially owned since 1980.

Throughout the latter part of the 80's, Tree and Buddy continued on the same roll, acquiring more catalogs, reentering the record business and announcing an arrangement with Columbia Pictures in Hollywood to get its songs in movies and TV. In 1988 Tree was named Country publisher of the year for the 16th consecutive year and amidst rumors to the contrary began negotiations with prospective buyers. Finally, in 1989 Buddy sold Tree to CBS Records/Sony for an estimated $50 million, the largest transaction in Music Row history at the time.

In Buddy's *By the Seat of My Pants* (Simon & Schuster), he offers readers a behind-the-scenes look at stars ranging from his early years with Hank Williams to celebrities such as Burt Reynolds. Buddy's credits as a record producer include Exile, T.G. Sheppard, Bill Anderson, Doug Kershaw, Dinah Shore, Burt Reynolds, Jack Palance, Diana Trask, Louise Mandrell, Ronnie Robbins, Paul Kelly, Clarence "Frogman" Henry, Bonnie Guitar, Jimmy Holiday, Joe Tex, Dottie West, Gunilla Hutton, Dolly Parton, Donna Meade and Ronnie McDowell.

After the sale of Tree, Buddy was to remain at the helm for five years. The plan, however, didn't work out and Buddy didn't like corporate life. So, he negotiated his way out of the contract, said goodbye to a lot of friends and began Buddy Killen Enterprises in 1991. Since then, BKE has grown fast enough to claim the No. 59 spot in the Greater Nashville 100. Under the BKE umbrella are music publishing companies Killen Songs, Killen Music and Killen Productions, who produce Ronnie McDowell and Six Shooter. He also owns Killen Entertainment Booking Agency, Sound Shop recording studio, Meadowgreen Music and the Stockyard Restaurant, currently ranked as the No. 21 restaurant in the United States, according to *Restaurant Hospitality* magazine. He is majority stockholder in Praise Hymn/Tape Factory, working with his daughter Robin Smith. He raises Arabian horses and is pursuing a career in television and movies. Buddy also spends time working with Nashville's Chamber of Commerce, city officials, financial institutions, charities, the arts, state government and the Easter Seal Society. Since 1991 Buddy has held an annual auction at the Stockyard Restaurant, which has raised an estimated $500,000 for charity. Today, he lives in the Nashville area with his wife Carolyn and still works 14-hour days. Buddy Killen is an example for all who believe in their dreams. As a tribute to his work, Tree is, in 1994, still the No. 1 music publishing company. LAP

BRADLEY KINCAID

(Singer, Guitar)

Given Name: Bradley Kincaid
Date of Birth: July 13, 1895
Where Born: Garrard County, Kentucky
Married: Irma Forman
Children: Barbara, Allyne, Billy Jimmy
Date of Death: September 23, 1989

Bradley Kincaid, nicknamed the "Kentucky Mountain Boy," became the first major Country music star created by the medium of radio. He was also known as the "Man Who First Brought Kentucky Mountain Songs and Ballads to Radio," "America's Foremost Folk Singer" and the "Dean of the Folk Singers." From 1926 to 1930, Kincaid became a Country singer whose popularity with fans rivaled that of Jimmie Rodgers. Unlike the Blue Yodeler, Kincaid lived a long life and sustained popularity for a generation through regular programs on a series of major radio stations. Although he was essentially a radio star, the Kentucky Mountain Boy also experienced a recording career that extended to 1973.

A native of Garrard County, Kentucky, in the Cumberland foothills, Kincaid obtained his first instrument as a child when his father traded a fox hound for it (hence the term "hound dog" guitar). After Kincaid's mother died, the guitar proved to be one of his few consolations as the youngster found himself largely on his own with very limited schooling. He worked as a farm laborer until the age of 19, when he went to Berea College to further his education in their ungraded academy section. After three years, Kincaid enlisted in the Army during WWI, served in France and then returned to Berea, completing his high school work in 1921.

Three years later, Kincaid moved to Chicago with his wife to attend the WMCA College. He first played on newly opened WLS radio in 1926, with a quartet, but found that the station wanted an Old-Time ballad singer for their new *National Barn Dance* program. Bradley filled the role and his rise to the top was a little short of phenomenal.

As he explained, he went to Chicago with $412 and four years later, graduated from college after paying his way through, had $10,000 or $15,000 in the bank and drove the biggest car in Chicago. Songbook sales and personal appearances through Illinois and adjacent states yielded handsome profits. Kincaid sang his songs in a simple, unadorned style, but listeners loved his renditions of old ballads like *Barbara Allen* and Victorian numbers like *Two Little Girls in Blue* and *The Letter Edged in Black.*

In 1930, Kincaid moved to WLW Cincinnati for a year. He spent the next decade at various eastern stations: WGY Pittsburgh, Schenectady, New York, WBZ Boston, Massachusetts, KDKH Pittsburgh, Pennsylvania, WTIC Hartford, Connecticut and WHAM Rochester, New York. Kincaid remained popular wherever he went and added

The Kentucky Mountain Boy, ***Bradley Kincaid***

Louis Marshall "Grandpa" Jones and Harmonica wizard Bashful Joe Troyan to his entourage for a time in the mid-30's. In 1941, Bradley returned to WLW for three years and then spent 1944 to 1949 at WSM and the *Grand Ole Opry* (his only venture into the South), where he shared the limelight with a wide panorama of stars. In 1949, Kincaid bought radio station WWSO Springfield, Ohio, and gradually wound down his musical career, operating a music store in that midwestern city for many years.

Kincaid's recording career began in December 1927, with Gennett, whose masters also appeared on such Sears Roebuck-owned labels as Silvertone and Supertone. (Sears Roebuck and WLS radio were a part of the same corporate conglomerate so they pushed not only Kincaid's records but also a Kincaid model of guitar.) After several sessions extending through October 1929, Kincaid switched to Brunswick in November 1929, to Bluebird in 1933, and Decca in 1934. Bradley did not record again until he went to Nashville in 1944, when he did sessions for Bullett and Majestic. He closed out active recording in 1950, when he cut four sides for Capitol, which he recorded at his radio station in Springfield. Only on his later waxings did he make any accommodation to modernization and that was somewhat minimal.

In part-retirement, he went to Fort Worth, Texas, in August 1963 and recorded some 162 songs over a four-day period, from which at least seven albums were released on the Bluebonnet label. In 1973, he made two more albums for a company called McMonigle. The Kentucky Mountain Boy rarely emerged from retirement, but did appear several times at the Berea College Celebrations of Traditional Music. He always retained a soft spot for the educational opportunity he received there. Kincaid also appeared one time at Mac Wiseman's Renfro Valley Festival. Through the 60's and 70's various anthologies and entire album reissues made many of his early recordings available again. IMT

RECOMMENDED ALBUMS:

"Mountain Ballads and Old Time Songs" (Bluebonnet)(1963)
"Mountain Ballads and Old Time Songs, Album Number Two" (Bluebonnet)(1964)
"Mountain Ballads and Old Time Songs, Album Number Three" (Bluebonnet)(1965)
"Mountain Ballads and Old Time Songs, Album Number Four" (Bluebonnet) (1966)
[All above also released on Old Homestead]
"Mountain Ballads and Old Time Songs, Album Number Five" (Bluebonnet)(1967)
"Mountain Ballads and Old Time Songs, Album Number Six" (Bluebonnet)(1968)
"Mountain Ballads and Old Time Songs, Album Number Seven" (Bluebonnet)(1987)
"Favorite Old-Time Songs" (Old Homestead)(1984) [1927-1934 material]

CLAUDE KING

(Singer, Songwriter, Guitar, Actor)
Date of Birth: February 5, 1933
Where Born: Shreveport, Louisiana
Married: Barbara Jean Coco
Children: Duane Coco, Bradley Thomas, Jerome Jay
Date of Death: 1983

It was with one song, *Wolverton Mountain*, that big Claude King became a major star. The song, co-written by Claude and Merle Kilgore, became an international best-seller and paved the way to an illustrious career.

Like many other Country singers, his first love was sport and it was not until he was 12 that he started playing guitar, having bought one from a farmer for 50 cents. Growing up, he was exposed to the Country sounds on the *Grand Ole Opry* and Shreveport's own *Louisiana Hayride*.

At school, he entertained his classmates, but also showed prowess as a baseball and football player. He got a baseball scholarship to the University of Idaho at Moscow. After graduation, Claude returned to Shreveport, where he attended Meadows Draughan Business College. During the 50's, while working as a construction engineer, he also performed in clubs and on radio and TV. He began playing on the *Hayride* from 1952 and that year recorded his first sides for the Gotham label, although no singles were released.

Claude's big break came in 1961, when he signed with Columbia. His debut single, *Big River, Big Man*, not only reached the Country Top 10, but also crossed over to the bottom regions of the Pop charts. The follow-up, *The Comancheros*, inspired by the movie of the same name, also went Top 10 in 1962 and fared slightly better on the Pop chart, reaching the Top 75. However, it was *Wolverton Mountain* that went to No.1, where it stayed for 9 weeks, and reached the Top 10 on the Pop list, in 1962. Claude wrapped up the year with two more successful singles, *The Burning of Atlanta*, which went Top 10 Country and reached the Top 60 on the Pop charts, and *I've Got the World by the Tail*, which reached the Top 15. Backed by the Nashville Knights, he became a major Country draw.

Claude King, the Wolverton Mountain man

Over the next two years, Claude chalked up six more chart hits: *Sheepskin Valley, Building a Bridge* and *Hey Lucille!* (all Top 15, 1963) and *That's What Makes the World Go Around* (Top 40), *Sam Hill* (Top 15) and *Whirlpool (of Your Love)* (Top 50)(all1964).

In 1965, Claude came back strongly with another song co-written with Merle Kilgore, *Tiger Woman*, which reached the Top 10 on the Country charts and won a BMI award. Claude started 1966 with the Top 20 hit *Little Buddy*. During the rest of 1966 through 1968, Claude failed to register at quite the same level and his principal hits for that period were *Catch a Little Raindrop* (Top 15, 1966) and *The Watchman* (Top 40, 1967). In 1969, he had another Top 10 hit with *All for the Love of a Girl*. From then until the end of 1972, when he left the label, his main hits were *Friend, Lover, Woman, Wife* (Top 20, 1969), Bob Dylan's *I'll Be Your Baby Tonight* (Top 40), *Mary's Vineyard* (Top 20, both 1970) and *Chip 'n' Dale's Place* (Top 25, 1971).

Between the end of 1972 and the middle of 1977, Claude was absent from the charts, and then on the independent label, True, he had a basement-level entry, *Cotton Dan*. That was to mark the end of Claude's chart history.

Arkansas Governor Frank White declared August 7, 1981, as Wolverton Mountain Day. The following year, Claude appeared in the TV mini-series *The Blue and the Gray*. This was not his first screen appearance. He had already performed in the movies *Swamp Girl* and *Year of the Wahoo*. Sadly, Claude King passed away in 1983.

RECOMMENDED ALBUMS:

"Meet Claude King" (Columbia)(1962)
"Tiger Woman" (Columbia)(1965)
"I Remember Johnny Horton" (Columbia)(1968)
"Chip 'n' Dale's Place" (Columbia)(1971)
"Claude King's Greatest Hits" (True)(1977)
"Claude King's Best" (Gusto)(1980)

DON KING

(Singer, Songwriter, Guitar, Trumpet)
Given Name: Donald Alan King
Date of Birth: May 1, 1954
Where Born: Freemont, Nebraska
Married: Peggy
Children: Katie

Don King grew up in Nebraska and got his first taste of music playing the trumpet in the school band. A few years later he traded in the trumpet for an electric guitar and learned to play by ear. When he was 14, he exchanged the electric for an acoustic classical guitar and studied classical and flamenco-style music with a teacher in Omaha.

Don began performing in various clubs in Omaha and developed a good following. He decided that he wanted to take his music to a wider audience and felt Nashville was the place to go. Don's family decided to make the move with him and his father left the accounting firm he had been with for 20 years. Don's father, mother and sister packed up and made the move to Nashville in the summer of 1974.

When Don arrived in Nashville he landed a job performing at the Quality Inn Hotel. During the two-year period he played at the hotel club he met many people in the music business who helped him land a contract with Con Brio Records. He debuted on the Country chart in the late summer of 1976 with *Cabin High (in the Blue Ridge Mountains)*. In early 1977, Don scored a Top 20 hit with *I've Got You to Come Home To*. Later in the year he had another Top 20 hit with *She's the Girl of My Dreams*. Don closed the year with the Top 50 *I Must Be Dreaming*.

Don continued to find success on the chart in 1978 with four Top 30 hits: *Music Is My Woman, Don't Make No Promises (You Can't Keep), The Feelings So Right Tonight* and *You Were Worth Waiting For*. The following year, Don had a Top 40 hit with *Live Entertainment* and also cut the lowly *I've Got Country Music in My Soul*. Don recorded two albums while with Con Brio, ***Dreams & Things*** (1977) and ***Feelings So Right*** (1978).

Don's consistent singles success attracted the attention of Rick Blackburn of CBS Records, who signed Don to Epic at the end of 1979. His first release on the major label was the Top 40 *Lonely Hotel*, the title track of his debut album on the label. Don scored two more hit singles in 1980 with *Here Comes That Feeling Again* and *Take This Heart*. The ACM nominated Don in the "New Male Artist" category that year. Don toured heavily, opening shows for Alabama, Reba McEntire, John Anderson, the Oak Ridge Boys, Conway Twitty, Tammy Wynette and others. Don's touring band later renamed itself Sawyer Brown and went on to stardom.

In 1981, Don had a Top 40 hit with his version of Johnny Cash's *I Still Miss Someone*, on which Rosanne Cash appears, and a Top 30 hit with *The Closer You Get*. Don released a second album on Epic, ***Whirlwind***, and in 1982 had a Top 40 hit with *Running on Love*. Don's final chart entry on Epic was the lowly *Maximum Security (to Maximum Wage)*. When his association with Epic Records ended later that year he started the Don King Music Group with his father, Don Sr. Don had two more chart entries, both at the lower levels: *All We Had Was One Another*, on Bench Mark in 1986, and *Can't Stop the Music*, on 615 in 1988.

Father and son built a 24-track studio called the Cypress Room in 1985 to record the company's demos. In 1992, they added a music video production company to the operation.

Don King's songwriting credits include *Only the Lonely Know* by Charly McClain in 1980, *You Don't Know Love* (co-written by Beckie Foster) by Janie Fricke (1983), *Why Do We Want What We Know We Can't Have* (1983) and *I'm in Love All Over* (1985), both by Reba McEntire, *Past the Point of No Return* by Jim Glaser (1984), *Stayin' Afloat* by both the Oak Ridge Boys and Sawyer Brown in 1985, *Party Line* (1986) and *Call Before Midnight* (1987), both by the Kendalls, and *Words* by Jeannie C. Riley (1990).

RECOMMENDED ALBUMS:
"Dreams & Things" (Con Brio)(1977)
"Feelings So Right" (Con Brio)(1978)
"Lonely Hotel" (Epic)(1990)
"Whirlwind" (Epic)(1991)

PEE WEE KING

(Singer, Songwriter, Accordion, Harmonica, Fiddle)
Given Name: Julius Frank Kuczynski
Date of Birth: February 14, 1914
Where Born: Abrams, Wisconsin
Married: Lydia H. Frank
Children: Gene, Larry, Frank, Jr., Marietta Jo

A member of the Country Music Hall of Fame and long-time sponsor of the Country Music Association, Pee Wee King is best known to Country fans as the man who brought the accordion into the music, and the man who co-wrote *The Tennessee Waltz*. Historians credit him as being one of the first true professionals in Country music, one of the people who brought a new level of style and organization to the stage of the *Opry* and one who pioneered the expansion of Country music to a national base.

*The legendary **Pee Wee King***

To begin with, Pee Wee was also one of the first big Country stars who was not from the South or Southwest. He was from the rich dairy country in Wisconsin, where his Polish-American father led a local polka band. Soon young Frank had his first accordion and was expanding his repertoire into cowboy and Pop songs on local radio stations. One day cowboy star Gene Autry heard him and hired his band to back him over station WLS; it was Autry who came up with the name "Pee Wee," since his new accordion player was, at 5'7", the smallest member of the band. The "King" part Pee Wee borrowed from Wayne King, a popular Pop band leader of the day.

In 1934 Autry and Pee Wee moved to WHAS Louisville, but after eight months Autry set forth for Hollywood, leaving Pee Wee to take a job with a local band, Frankie More's Log Cabin Boys (1935-1936). Sponsored by the popular laxative Crazy Water Crystals, the band, accompanied by Bob Atcher and the Callahan Brothers, toured widely throughout Kentucky. When it became obvious that Gene Autry was in Hollywood to stay, Pee Wee formed his own band, the Golden West Cowboys, in 1936 (the name taken from a WLS act, the Girls of the Golden West). Original members included fiddler Abner Sims, singer Texas Daisy, and guitarist Curly Rhodes. Inspired by the slick, more sophisticated sound of Clayton McMichen's Georgia Wildcats and Louise Massey and the Westerners, Pee Wee worked out intricate arrangements and choreographed stage shows —as well as finding new Pop and cowboy songs. He also got the services of J.L. Frank, one of the great innovators in promotion and marketing and, incidentally, King's father-in-law. By the time the band joined the *Grand Ole Opry*, for the first time, in 1937, Pee Wee was able to bring "organization" to the show, as well as union musicians and one of the first electric steel guitars.

Pee Wee was more of a bandleader and an organizer than a singer, and he discovered a parade of important singers during the 1940's. The band soon became a major training ground for vocalists. One of the first was young Eddy Arnold, whom Pee Wee found at a gig in St. Louis and featured as his lead singer from 1940 to 1943. Later came the versatile Tommy Sosebee, who was their singer when the band began to record, as well as Milton Estes, who soon carved out his own career. In 1944 the leading girl singer was 16-year-old Becky Barfield, the amazing yodeler, and in 1945 Pee Wee hired Lloyd "Cowboy" Copas. Many of these singers worked with the band on a series of tours to military bases during WWII, a tour called the Camel Caravan.

In 1937, another important figure had joined the band: pianist, fiddler, guitarist, singer, and songwriter Redd Stewart. Pee Wee and Redd hit it off especially well, and began to do some writing together. In 1946, inspired by Bill Monroe's hit *Kentucky Waltz*, the pair took an old waltz that Redd had written which the band had been using as a theme song and came up with *Tennessee Waltz*. In December 1947 the band recorded the new song in Chicago for RCA Victor, with Redd singing and playing twin fiddles with James Boyd. It became Pee Wee's first really giant hit, in 1948 reaching the Top 3 and staying on the Country chart for nearly 9 months. It became a Pop hit in 1950, when Patti Page recorded it. Over the next 30 years, *Tennessee Waltz* would be recorded over 300 times and sell over 40 million records.

Pee Wee had moderate success with *Tennessee Tears* but *Tennessee Polka* went Top 3, both in 1949. In 1950, the King-Stewart song *Bonaparte's Retreat* went Top 10, as did the reissue of *Tennessee Waltz*, that year. Pee Wee really struck pay dirt with *Slow Poke* in the fall of 1950, which stayed at the top of the Country chart for 15 weeks and also topped the Pop chart. This became his personal biggest seller, but later songs that were done by other artists included *You Belong to Me*. Pee Wee eventually tallied up some 400 songs listing himself as composer or co-composer. His other major hits were *Silver and Gold* (Top 5) and *Busybody* (Top 10, both in 1952) and *Changing Partners* (Top 5) and the flip-side, *Bimbo* (Top 10), in 1954. That year, Pee Wee had his final chart entry with *Backward, Turn Backward*.

At the height of the popularity of *Tennessee Waltz*, Pee Wee left Nashville to return to Louisville. "The main reason I left the *Opry* was that I wanted television," he recalled. As a result, he got in on the ground floor with TV, and soon had his own show over WAVE in Louisville. Within a few months, he had similar shows on WBBM Chicago, WLW Cincinnati, and in Cleveland, at the same time. This pace, which soon also included a network radio show, continued through much of the 1950's, and by the end of the decade, Pee Wee was also a major force in music promotion and tour packaging. On February 17, 1965, *Tennessee Waltz* was officially proclaimed by Governor Frank Clement as the Tennessee state song.

In 1970, Pee Wee King was inducted to the Nashville Songwriters Hall of Fame. In October 1971, the Governor of Kentucky proclaimed "Pee Wee King Day" and dozens of luminaries celebrated Pee Wee's achievements. In 1974, he was elected to the Country Music Hall of Fame. Pee Wee, who has one of the most remarkable memories and can remember minutiae of his career, retired to Louisville during the 1990's. CKW

RECOMMENDED ALBUMS:

"The Best of Pee Wee King and Redd Stewart" (Starday)(1975)
"Rompin', Stompin', Singin', Swingin'" (Bear Family Germany)(1983) [Released on Rollercoaster in the U.K.]

FRED KIRBY

(Singer, Songwriter, Guitar)

Given Name:	**Fred Kirby**
Date of Birth:	**July 19, 1910**
Where Born:	**Charlotte, North Carolina**
Married:	**1. Mildred (dec'd.)**
	2. Mary
Children:	**Patricia, Dianne, Yvonne, Nanette**

Fred Kirby has spent nearly his entire musical career in the Carolinas. Favoring a Western style of music, Fred has acquired such nicknames as "the Carolina Cowboy."

Although a native of Charlotte, Fred Kirby spent his childhood in various communities where his father's job as a minister took him. He began his radio career at WIS Columbia, South Carolina, in 1927. By that time, he had learned to play the guitar and sang a pretty decent song. After a year at WIS, Fred came to WBT Charlotte, which became his permanent home (except from 1939 to 1943).

Fred made his first recordings in Charlotte for Bluebird in February 1936, subsequently cutting masters with Cliff Carlisle, Bob Phillips, and Don White, as well as several solo numbers. In 1938, he switched to Decca and recorded, as Fred Kirby's Carolina Boys, some 16 sides (14 released), mostly with fiddle played by Tiny Dodson and steel guitar support. Dodson's group, the Circle B Boys, which probably included Kirby, cut six more numbers at the same session.

In 1939, Fred, along with Don White, left Charlotte for WLM Cincinnati, where they worked for a year or so. The duo worked briefly at WLS Chicago until Kirby went to St. Louis. In more than two years there, Fred earned the sobriquet "Victory Cowboy" for his helping the treasury Department in War Bond sales.

In 1943, Fred returned to Charlotte to stay, working with the Briarhoppers and then on his own. Following the dropping of the bombs on Hiroshima and Nagasaki, Fred composed the song *Atomic Power*, which he subsequently recorded for Sonora Records and saw half a dozen other artists do cover versions of on other labels. Another Sonora waxing, *Reveille Time in Heaven*, a sacred tribute to fallen soldiers, went on to become a Bluegrass standard after Mac Wiseman cut it for Dot in 1953.

Fred Kirby's discs also appeared on the Gotham label, among them his rendition of that railroad standard *Wreck of the Old 97*. In 1950, he had a final session for a major label when he cut four songs for Columbia, including *The Old Country Preacher* and a lyric dealing with the newly tested hydrogen bomb entitled *When That Hell Bomb Falls*. In 1951, Fred was one of several Country musicians who appeared in the Lippert motion picture *Kentucky Jubilee*.

Although Fred Kirby's career as an adult entertainer began to wane in the 50's, his star still shone brightly in youth entertainment, thanks to his cowboy image. His earliest experiences with children occurred in St. Louis, when he sang for kids in the Shrine Hospital, and he subsequently did a Saturday morning radio show at WBT called *Cowboy Roundup Time*. When WBTV went on the air, Fred soon had a program there entitled *Fred Kirby's Junior Rancho*. He continued as a host of Saturday kiddie programs until he finally retired in 1991, after some 40 years.

Through much of the 70's and 80's, Kirby entertained during the summer weekdays at the Tweetsie Railroad, one of the top tourist attractions in the mountain region of western North Carolina. As of the spring of 1993, the octogenarian entertainer resides in a retirement center, having been diagnosed with Parkinson's disease. Unfortunately little of Kirby's original material has been on the re-issue market, with the only items being one of his Decca sides on a Japanese MCA anthology and a historical collection containing two of his cowboy songs. IMT

Pete Kirby refer BASHFUL BROTHER OSWALD

EDDIE KIRK

(Singer, Yodeler, Songwriter, Guitar)
Given Name: Edward Merle Kirk
Date of Birth: March 21, 1919
Where Born: Greeley, Colorado
Married: Barby
Children: Diane

During the 40's, Eddie Kirk was one of the band of musicians who fought to have the term "hillbilly" replaced by the less offensive phrase "Country music."

Raised on a cattle ranch, Eddie learned to play guitar at a young age. In his early days, he was also adept with his fists and boxed as an amateur in the flyweight division, finally quitting in 1937. He worked in the shipyards and then spent two years in college.

His musical career got under way in earnest with a stint as a singer-guitarist with the Beverly Hill Billies. In 1935, he joined Larry Sunbrock's band and traveled throughout the U.S. That year, Eddie won the National Yodeling Championship and repeated this the following year. He served in the Navy during WWII and on his return to civilian life, settled in Hollywood. During the 40's, Eddie was resident on two major California Country shows, KXLA *Hometown Jamboree,* which at the time came from Pasadena, and KFI/KTTV-TV's *Town Hall Party* from Compton. He also appeared on the *Gene Autry Show* and appeared in various movies. (See Movie Section)

Possessing a smooth voice in the Eddy Arnold mold, Kirk was signed to Capitol Records in 1947 and released a single with Merle Travis and Tennessee Ernie Ford which was the Delmore Brothers-Wayne Raney-Henry Grover song *Blues Stay Away from Me*. He hit the Top 10 in 1948 with *The Gods Were Angry with Me*, with his backing group, the String Band; the single contained a recitation by Tex Ritter. His next two singles missed the mark, but in 1949, Eddie made the charts with his version of George Morgan's *Candy Kisses*. He was overshadowed by Morgan's chart-topping original, but still managed to peak in the Top 10. Through 1951, Eddie Kirk produced a string of singles, none of which troubled the charts.

In 1953, he turned up on RCA, which also housed Eddy Arnold and Elton Britt. After two singles, he was off the label. From then on, he faded into the background.

KLAUDT INDIAN FAMILY, The

When Formed: 1930's
Members:
Ronald H. Klaudt
Lillian Klaudt
Vernon Klaudt
Ken Klaudt
Ray Klaudt
Melvin Klaudt
Betty Klaudt
Mel Stewart — Piano
Ralph Seibel — Piano

The Klaudts, who first started singing professionally in the 1930's, are the best known American Indian Gospel group. They are Arikara Indians, who originally came from Fort Berthold Indian Reservation in North Dakota and then later moved to Norcross, Georgia.

Musically their trademarks are close vocal harmony, solos and proficiency on organ, tenor and baritone saxophones, slide trombone, violin, bass, guitar and piano. Their other distinction is that they wear authentic Indian costumes in their shows. With the exception of pianists Mel Stewart and Ralph Seibel this group is composed of family members.

Originally, their father, Ronald, sang with the group, but he later withdrew to serve as manager. Their mother, Lillian, remained as a singer and Betty, Vernon's wife, later joined the group.

The Klaudts put on Gospel concerts throughout the nation in a variety of venues ranging from churches to concert halls, radio and television. They appeared regularly on Wally Fowler and Bob Poole's syndicated TV shows. On these and other programs, they showed their versatility by performing in a variety of arrangements, from solos to quartets and in several different vocal stylings. In addition to their regular shows they also appeared in the musical movie *Sing Me a Song for Heaven's Sake*. In recent years, their albums have appeared on their own Klaudt Family label.

RECOMMENDED ALBUMS:
"Gospel Favorites" (Klaudt Family)
"The Klaudt Indian Family" (Klaudt Family)
"Gospel War Whoops" (Klaudt Family)

SNEAKY PETE KLEINOW

(Steel Guitar, Songwriter, Special Effects Producer)
Given Name: Peter Kleinow
Date of Birth: August 20, 1934
Where Born: South Bend, Indiana
Married: 1. Ernesteen (div.)
2. Connie Williams
Children: Anita, Martin, Aaron, Tammy, Cosmo

For many years, Sneaky Pete has been the backbone of Country-Rock, both as a band member and as one of the busiest of session players. Although he doesn't consider himself a Country musician, one listen to his playing and one discovers someone whose non-Country music is more Country than some contemporary outpourings.

Pete grew up in Indiana but longed to be in the Los Angeles he saw portrayed in the movies. In 1951, he heard steel player Jerry Byrd, who became the motivation for Pete to learn to play the steel guitar. When he left school, he became a road maintenance worker for the Michigan State Highway Department. In 1963, Pete moved to Los Angeles, where he played around the clubs in L.A. and San Diego. He also earned money writing jingles, including the theme for the animated character "Gumby." From the start, Pete had twin occupations: being a musician and being involved in movie special effects.

Pete's first recording session came about in 1965, when he played on the Ventures track *Blue Star*. Gram Parsons and Chris Hillman hung out at one of the clubs Pete played in and liking his playing, approached him about joining a band they were planning as a spin-off from the Byrds, of which they were members. In 1968, Pete played at Derek Taylor's "leaving Hollywood party" and then became an "auxiliary" Byrd for a few gigs before becoming a member of the new group, the Flying Burrito Brothers.

Sneaky Pete stayed with the Burritos until April 1971, during which time he recorded the albums ***Gilded Palace of Sin*** (1969), ***Burrito Deluxe*** (1970) and ***The Flying Burrito Brothers*** (1971). During this time, Pete played on various album projects including Joe Cocker's eponymous album (1969) and Delaney & Bonnie Bramlett's ***To Bonnie from Delaney*** (1970). In 1971, Pete became a very active sessionman and appeared on the Byrds' ***Byrdmaniax***, the Flying Burrito Brothers' ***Last of the Red Hot Burritos***, Mimi Farina & Tom Jans' self-titled album and Little Feat's self-named album.

In 1972, Pete played on Jackson Browne's eponymous album, Rita Coolidge's ***Lady's Not for Sale***, Linda Ronstadt's self-titled album, Little Feat's ***Sailin' Shoes*** and Frank Zappa's ***Waka Jawaka***. In 1973, Pete appeared on Eric Kaz's ***Cul De Sac***, Jackson Browne's ***For Everyone***, John Lennon's ***Mind Games***, Little Feat's ***Dixie Chicken*** and the Steve Miller Band's ***The Joker***.

During 1974 and 1975, Sneaky Pete continued being in demand with sessions for Doug Dillard (***Douglas Flint Dillard***), the Hagers (***The Hagers***), Linda Ronstadt (***Heart Like a Wheel***), Stevie Wonder (***Fulfillingness'***

First Finale) and Fleetwood Mac's ***Heroes Are Hard to Find*** (all 1974) and Dillard & Clark (***Gene Clark & Doug Dillard***) and Brian Cadd (***White on White***) (both 1975). In 1974, Pete was part of the band Cold Steel, whose other members included Richard and Mike Bowden and Gib Gilbeau. The following year, Pete joined the re-formed Flying Burrito Brothers and recorded the album ***Flying Again***.

In 1976, the Burritos recorded ***Airborne*** and Pete continued to appear on other albums, including Ringo Starr's ***Rotogravure*** and Stevie Wonder's ***Songs in the Key of Life*** (both 1976) and Olivia Newton-John's ***Making a Good Thing Better*** (1977). Pete was still with the Burritos in 1978, when the band traveled to Japan to record the in-concert album ***Live from Tokyo***. The following year, Pete released his debut solo album, ***Sneaky Pete,*** on Shiloh, supported by, among others, Gib Gilbeau, Gene Parsons and Mrs. Sneaky Pete, Connie Williams. During 1980, he played on the Burritos' ***Hearts on the Line*** and sessioned on Johnny Lee's ***Lookin' for Love***.

By now, Pete was starting to ease down his playing as he became more celebrated for his movie special effects work. His movie tasks have included model and puppet making, miniature effects and stop-motion sequences. Among the movies he has worked on are *The Wonderful World of the Brothers Grimm* (1962), *Seven Faces of Dr. Lao* (1964), *Black Sunday* (1977), *Meteor* (1979), *The Empire Strikes Back* and *The Power* (both 1980), *Caveman* (1981), *The Right Stuff* (1983) and *Gremlins* and *Terminator* (both 1984), *Flight of the Navigator* (1986) and *Terminator 2: Judgment Day* (1991). Recent movies have included *Robocop II, Under Siege* and *Joyride*. Pete has also worked on the music videos *Give It Up* by Z.Z. Top and *Extreme (Rest in Peace)* by Faith No More.

Recently Pete has been working alongside West Coast band the Lemonheads and in 1994, Sneaky Pete, the lone original member of the Flying Burrito Brothers, was preparing to go on a European tour with the band. He is still actively recording and in 1994, Shiloh released ***The Legend and the Legacy***, which was picked up by Rhino Records. He currently has two albums in the works, to be released in 1995.

RECOMMENDED ALBUMS:

"Gilded Palace of Sin" (A & M)(1969) [As Flying Burrito Brothers]
"Burrito Deluxe" (A & M)(1970) [As Flying Burrito Brothers]
"Cold Steel" (Ariola)(1974) [As Cold Steel]
"Live from Tokyo" (Regency)(1978) [As Flying Burrito Brothers]
"Sneaky Pete" (Shiloh)(1979)
"The Legend and the Legacy" (Shiloh and Rhino)(1994)

Fred Knobloch refer SKO/SKB

ALISON KRAUSS

(Singer, Fiddle, Mandolin)
Date of Birth: **July 23, 1971**
Where Born: **Champaign, Illinois**

When Alison Krauss was inducted in the *Grand Ole Opry* on June 26, 1993, it was Garth Brooks who did the honors. Such is the esteem in which she is held by her fellow professionals in all branches of Country music.

Alison's father, Fred, plays guitar and her mother, Louise, plays guitar and banjo. When she was 5 years old, Alison started violin lessons, playing classical music, but soon she started on fiddle "workouts." By the time she was 8, Alison had begun entering contests, taking fourth place at a county fair in Champaign and two years later, she had her first band. In 1983, Alison won her first State Fiddle Championship and was named "Most Promising Fiddler in the Midwest" by the Society for Preservation of Bluegrass in America. The next year, she won the $200 first prize in the Heartland Junction Fiddling Contest and was the youngest contestant in the event. Interestingly, another star in the making, Rhonda Vincent, came in third. Alison's early influences were Kenny Baker (formerly with Bill Monroe) and Stuart Duncan.

She was named the winner of the Winfield (Kansas) Championship ("National Flatpicking" award) in 1985. That same year, she appeared on an album with her brother Viktor (he plays Jazz bass, cornet, tuba and piano), Jim Hoiles and Bruce Weiss, entitled ***Different Strokes***, on the Fiddle Tunes label. The following year, still only age 14, she signed to Rounder Records. In 1986, she starred at the famed Newport Folk Festival and the Kentucky Fried Chicken Bluegrass Championship.

In 1987, Alison released ***Too Late to Cry***, her first solo album, for Rounder, to universal acclaim. The following year, Alison and her band, Union Station, won the Society for Preservation of Bluegrass in America's "National Band Championship." Also in 1988, Alison was named "Best New Talent" in *Frets* magazine's Readers' Poll and at the tender age of 17, she was included in the Country Music Foundation's book, *Country: The Music and the Musicians*.

Union Station (the band was still being billed as that) released ***Two Highways*** for Rounder in 1989 and the album was nominated for "Best Bluegrass Recording." Although the Nitty Gritty Dirt Band with Bruce Hornsby won, NGDB's Jimmy Ibbotson said at the awards, "It's an honor being nominated in the same category as someone who sings and plays with as much fire as Alison. She's very simply one of the best singers on the planet." Since the legendary William Warfield is her vocal coach, that comment is not misplaced. That year, as Alison Krauss & Union Station, the group launched a performing and educational tour of the Near East, visiting Pakistan, Syria, Jordan, Israel and Tunisia.

1990 also found her traveling abroad, when she and the band were one of five groups representing American folk culture at the International Folklore Festival in Kiev. Alison released a new album that year, ***I've Got That Old Feeling***. The album won the Grammy for "Best Bluegrass Recording" that year. In addition, Alison was named "Female Vocalist of the Year" at the International Bluegrass Awards. The video of *I've Got That Old Feeling* (the song was written by Sidney Cox), which was her first, went to No.1 on CMT and won on *Video Challenge* for several weeks. The album cut *Steel Rails* reached the Country Top 75.

The following year found Alison and Union Station achieving a status within Country music circles that was unheard of in recent times for a Bluegrass act and Alison herself was invited onto popular Country music shows. The group's 1992 album ***Every Time You Say Goodbye*** was produced by Alison and the group. Alison has always been eclectic and she has shunned the standards like *Orange Blossom Special* in favor of covers such as Lennon and McCartney's *I Will* and Gregg Allman's *Midnight Rider*. This album was no different and featured stand-out tracks including Karla Bonoff's *Lose Again*, Sidney Cox's *Last Love Letter* and Shawn Colvin's *I Don't Know Why*. Also heavily featured were the vocals of guitarist Tim Stafford. The album made a brief appearance in the Country charts, but more importantly, videos of the band were shown on CMT. The line-up of Union Station on that album was Barry Bales (string bass, vocals), Adam Steffey (mandolin), Ron Block (banjo, guitar, vocals) and Tim Stafford (guitar, vocals). Past members of the group have been Jeff White (guitar), super talented Alison Brown (banjo, guitar), brother Viktor Krauss (string bass) and John Pennell (string bass). Pennell, Sidney Cox (of the Cox Family) and Nelson Mandrell have contributed many of the songs for the group.

Alison, who at one time nearly opted for a career as a roller-skater, has shown a maturity that is almost unbelievable. Not only has she produced such wonderful albums in company with Union Station, but she has now been asked to appear with her peers on programs like TNN's *American Music Shop* and also on their albums. Most important among these have been her harmony vocals on *More Where That Came From* on Dolly Parton's 1993 ***Slow Dancing with the Moon***. In her own words, "Nothing will top getting to sing with Dolly Parton. Now I can die."

RECOMMENDED ALBUMS:

"Different Strikes" (Fiddle Tunes)(1985)
"Too Late to Cry" (Rounder)(1987)
"Two Highways" (Rounder)(1989)
"I've Got That Old Feeling" (Rounder)(1990)
"Every Time You Say Goodbye" (Rounder)(1992).

KRIS KRISTOFFERSON

(Singer, Songwriter, Guitar, Actor)

Given Name:	**Kristoffer Kristofferson**
Date of Birth:	**June 22, 1936**
Where Born:	**Brownsville, Texas**
Married:	**1. Fran Blair (div.)** **2. Rita Coolidge (div.)** **3. Lisa**
Children:	**Tracy, Kris, Jr., Casey, Jesse, Jody, John Robert, Kelly, Blake**

A talent like Kris Kristofferson emerges only very occasionally. As a songwriter, he has become the benchmark that all other contemporary writers have to aspire to. As a singer, his "no voice" has breathed life into his songs and made them the version to try and better, and as an actor, he has appeared in a number of movies over the last twenty years. Kris is a thinker and to get him onto the poems of William Blake or other metaphysical poets is a soul-searching experience

Kris is the son of a U.S. Air Force Major General who became Head of Air Operations for Aramco in Saudi Arabia. Kris majored in creative writing at Pomona College, California. He excelled in boxing and football and boxed for the Golden Gloves. He won First Prize in an *Atlantic Monthly* short story contest and also won third place and two honorable mentions. In 1958, he won a Rhodes Scholarship to Merton College, Oxford (England), where he gained a Master's Degree in English. While at university, he began writing songs for Larry Parnes, one of the major rock'n'roll impresarios in Britain. He also wrote two novels, which were both rejected by publishers.

In 1959, after college, he got married and joined the U.S. Army. He went to jump school, ranger school and flight school and became a pilot. He was stationed in Germany as a helicopter pilot. During a two-week furlough, in 1965, when he returned to the U.S., he visited Nashville and met Johnny Cash. That year, he became English Literature instructor at West Point Academy. Kris resumed his writing and an army friend suggested that Kris send some of his songs to a relative of his, songwriter Marijohn Wilkin.

Kris left the army that year and moved to Nashville and became a janitor at Columbia Records, as well as working as a bartender at the Tally-Ho Tavern. He initially performed as "Kris Carson," without much success. He moved on to flying men and equipment to oil rigs in the Gulf of Mexico. He got his first major cut in 1968, when Roy Drusky recorded *Jody and the Kid*. In 1969, he was about to take a job in construction, when Roger Miller asked him to come to California, as he was going to record Kris' *Me and Bobby McGee*, which was based on a song idea from Monument Records boss Fred Foster. Roger went on to cut *Darby's Castle* and *Casey's Last Ride*. Ray Stevens also had a mid-level crossover chart single with *Sunday Morning Coming Down*.

That year, Johnny Cash pushed Kris on stage at the Newport Folk Festival and Fred Foster signed him to Monument Records. In 1970, Johnny Cash had a No.1 Country hit with Kris' *Sunday Morning Coming Down*, which crossed over to the Pop charts Top 50. Kris also had a major hit through Waylon Jennings with *The Taker* and Ray Price via the No.1 Country hit (Top 15 Pop) *For the Good Times*. The latter was named both CMA's and ACM's "Song of the Year," for 1970. The following year, Kris debuted on the Pop charts with *Loving Her Was Easier (Than Anything I'll Ever Do Again)*, which reached the Top 30. Janis Joplin had a No.1 Pop hit with her version of *Me and Bobby McGee*, while Sammi Smith had a No.1 Country hit with *Help Me Make It Through the Night*. Her version also crossed over to the Pop Top 10 and the CMA named it "Single of the Year." There were also Pop charted versions by Joe Simon and O.C. Smith. Bobby Bare weighed in with the Top 10 version of Kris' *Please Don't Tell Me How the Story Ends*. Kristofferson won his first Grammy Award, in 1971, for "Best Country Song," for *Help Me Make It Through the Night*.

In 1972, Kris as an artist had two Pop chart entries with *Josie* and *Jesus Was a Capricorn*. *Josie* also marked his debut on the Country chart. He also had Pop hits through Jerry Lee Lewis' version of *Me and Bobby McGee* and Gladys Knight & the Pips' version of *Help Me Make It Through the Night*, which also registered major success in the U.K. During 1973, Kris married songstress Rita Coolidge and they recorded their first duet album, ***Full Moon***, for A & M. Kris had his first No.1 Country hit with *Why Me*, which has harmony vocals from Rita and Larry Gatlin. The single also went Top 20 on the Pop chart and was Certified Gold. He and Rita then had a duet single, *A Song I'd Like to Sing*, which went Top 50 on the Pop chart. Another track from the duet album, *From the Bottle to the Bottom*, won a Grammy for "Best Country Vocal Performance by a Duo or Group."

During 1973, the 1971 album ***The Silver Tongued Devil and I*** and the 1972 album

Kris Kristofferson *(right) with fellow Highwayman* ***Willie Nelson***

Jesus Was a Capricorn were both Certified Gold. That same year, Ronnie Milsap had a No.1 Country hit with *Please Don't Tell Me How the Story Ends*. Over in the U.K., Reggae star John Holt had a Top 10 hit with his version of *Help Me Make It Through the Night*. Kristofferson, a committed Christian, wrote with Marijohn Wilkin the classic *One Day at a Time*, which became a 1974 hit for Don Gibson and a cross-over success for Marilyn Sellars. The song became a No.1 Pop hit for Lena Martell in the U.K. and a Country No.1, a year later, for Cristy Lane. Kris' 1971 album ***Me and Bobby McGee*** went Gold during 1974.

In 1975, the debut Kris-Rita album, ***Full Moon***, was Certified Gold. That year, he and Rita won a Grammy Award for the single *Lover Please*, as "Best Country Vocal Performance by a Duo or Group." Kris registered his final Pop chart hit in 1977, with *Watch Closely Now*, which came from the movie *A Star Is Born*. The soundtrack album was Certified Gold in 1976, Platinum in 1977 and by 1984, had sold over 4 million copies.

In 1978, the compilation album ***Songs of Kristofferson*** went Gold. During 1979, Willie Nelson recorded an album of Kristofferson songs, ***Willie Nelson Sings Kristofferson***, on which Kris sang backup. From this album came the 1980 Top 5 hit, *Help Me Make It Through the Night*. Kris had a basement-level chart entry through *Prove It to You One More Time*. During that year, Kris and Rita Coolidge decided to go their separate ways. The following year, Kris had a Top 70 hit with *Nobody Loves Anybody Anymore*. He didn't return to the Country singles chart again until 1984, when *How Do You Feel About Foolin' Around*, a duet with Willie Nelson, taken from their album ***Music from "Songwriter,"*** made the Top 50.

During 1985, Kris joined forces with Willie Nelson, Johnny Cash and Waylon Jennings, for ***Highwayman***. The title song went to No.1 on the Country chart and was named the CMA's "Single of the Year" for the year. The foursome followed-up with Guy Clark's *Desperados Waiting for a Train*, which reached the Top 15. The ***Highwayman*** album went Gold in 1986. Just when it seemed that Kristofferson's film career had taken over, he came up with the memorable album ***Repossessed***, which featured another hit-maker, Billy Swan. From this album came the amazing song *They Killed Him*, which had previously been recorded by Bob Dylan in 1986. Kris' version made the Top 70.

Kris made his acting debut in Dennis Hopper's *The Last Movie* (1971). He has subsequently appeared in *Cisco Pike* (1971), *Blume in Love* and *Pat Garrett and Billy the Kid* (both 1973), *Alice Doesn't Live Here Anymore* and *Bring Me the Head of Alfredo Garcia* (both 1974), *The Sailor Who Fell from Grace with the Sea* and *Vigilante Force* (both 1975), *A Star Is Born* (with Barbra Streisand, 1976), *Semi-Tough* (1977), *Convoy* (1978), *Heaven's Gate* (1980), *Rollover* (1981), *Flashpoint* and *Songwriter* (both 1984), *Trouble in Mind* (1985), *Big Top Pee-Wee* (1988), *Millennium* and *Welcome Home* (both 1989) and *Perfume of the Cyclone* (1990).

In addition, Kristofferson's songs and music have graced several movies: *The Last Movie* and *Cisco Pike* (both 1971), *Fat City* and *The Gospel Road* (both 1972), *Blume in Love* (1973), *Janis* (1974), *The Sailor Who Fell from Grace with the Sea* (1975), *Sailor Jack* (1979), *Beyond Reasonable Doubt* and *One-Trick Pony* (both 1980), *Maeve, Rollover* and *Traveller* (all 1981), *Songwriter* (the title song was nominated for an Oscar, 1984), *Trouble in Mind* (1985), *Something Wild* (1986), *Mascara* (1987), *Walking After Midnight* (1988) and *Tennessee Nights* (1989).

In 1990, a track from ***Highwayman 2***, *Silver Stallion*, reached the Top 25 on the Country charts, again in company with Messrs. Nelson, Cash and Jennings. In 1994, Kris was preparing to record ***Highwayman 3*** and also to go out on the road. That year, his wife (also a Blake admirer) gave birth to another son, Blake.

RECOMMENDED ALBUMS:

"Me and Bobby McGee" (Monument)(1971)
"The Silver Tongued Devil and I" (Monument)(1971)
"Border Lord" (Monument)(1972)
"Jesus Was a Capricorn" (Monument)(1972)
"Full Moon" (A & M)(1973) [With Rita Coolidge]
"Spooky Lady's Sideshow" (Monument)(1974)
"Breakaway" (Monument)(1974) [With Rita Coolidge]
"Who's to Bless and Who's to Blame" (Monument)(1975)
"Surreal Thing" (Monument)(1976)
"Songs of Kristofferson" (double)(Monument)(1977)
"Easter Island" (Monument)(1978)
"Natural Act" (A & M)(1978) [With Rita Coolidge]
"Shake Hands with the Devil" (Monument)(1979)
"To the Bone" (Monument)(1980)
"Kris, Willie, Dolly & Brenda...The Winning Hand" (double)(Monument)(1983) [With Willie Nelson, Brenda Lee and Dolly Parton]
"Music from 'Songwriter'" (Monument)(1984) [With Willie Nelson]
"Highwayman" (Columbia)(1985) [With Johnny Cash, Waylon Jennings and Willie Nelson]
"Repossessed" (Mercury)(1986) [As Kris Kristofferson and the Borderlords]
"Highwayman 2" (Columbia)(1987) [With Johnny Cash, Waylon Jennings and Willie Nelson]

L

SLEEPY LaBEEF

(Singer, Songwriter, Guitar)
Given Name: **Thomas Paulsley LaBeff**
Date of Birth: **July 20, 1935**
Where Born: **Smackover, Arkansas**

It is just possible that the 6'7" Sleepy LaBeef is one of the last of the Rockabilly greats. He was certainly the last of the major acts to record for Sun Records. With a voice that booms, he is capable of lightening his tonal quality until it sounds very similar to Elvis Presley.

Called Sleepy because his eyes look half-closed, he early on helped his father to sell melons that they grew on their struggling farm. His father taught him to play guitar by the time he was 15, and his early musical influences were both Country and Blues.

When he was 18, Sleepy moved to Houston. His early jobs included being a land surveyor, wrestler and deejay. He began singing Gospel on various radio shows and then he started his own band performing

*Rockabilly singer **Sleepy LaBeef***

Rockabilly and rock'n'roll. In 1957, he began recording for Starday Records and cut his first single, *All Alone/I'm Through*. He recorded for various labels, including Mercury, Dixie, Gulf, Picture, Crescent and Wayside, either under his own name or as Tommy LaBeff, quite often cutting covers.

In 1964, Sleepy moved to Nashville. The following year, he signed to Columbia Records and his first release was *Everybody's Got to Have Somebody (to Love)/You Can't Catch Me*. However, it was not until his sixth release, *Every Day* in 1968, that he had his first Country chart entry. The record reached the Top 75.

In 1969, he signed with Shelby Singleton's Plantation label and here produced some of his most memorable sides, starting out with *Too Much Monkey Business*. It was his third release, Frankie Miller's *Blackland Farmer*, that did the trick. The single hit the Country Top 70, but has since become a career single for Sleepy. In 1974, he moved over to Singleton's incarnation of Sun Records and recorded some classic Rockabilly and Country material that included *Thunder Road, Ghost Riders in the Sky, There Ain't Much After Taxes, Good Rockin' Boogie* and *Boogie Woogie Country Girl/Flying Saucer Rock & Roll*.

He appeared at the prestigious Wembley Festival in 1979 and 1987 and has remained very popular in Europe. In 1981, Sleepy moved to Rounder Records, who issued the album ***It Ain't What You Eat (It's the Way You Chew It)***. The album was released in Europe via Rounder-Europa (Demon in the U.K.). It is estimated that Sleepy knows 6,000 songs and has never forgotten the words to one of them.

RECOMMENDED ALBUMS:

"The Bull's Night Out" (Sun)(1974)
"Western Gold" (Sun)(1976)
"1977 Rockabilly" (Sun)(1978)
"Downhome Rockabilly" (Sun)(1979) [Charly in the UK]
"Early, Rare & Rockin'" (Baron)(1979)
"It Ain't What You Eat (It's the Way You Chew It)" (Rounder)(1981)
"Ain't Got No Home" (Rockhouse UK)(1983)
"Beefy Rockabilly" (Charly UK)

LA COSTA

(Singer)

Given Name:	**La Costa Tucker**
Date of Birth:	**December 12, 1951**
Where Born:	**Seminole, Texas**
Married:	**Darrell Sorenson**
Children:	**one son, one daughter**

La Costa was the oldest of the Tucker children and it was she who wanted a career in music. She and her younger sister, Tanya (Tanya Tucker), used to sing together, performing in local shows, and they dreamed of being a famous sisters act. At one time in Arizona, La Costa and Tanya worked with a band called the Country Westerners.

In her mid-teens, La Costa took part, as a solo act, in many talent shows and also entered beauty contests. Her early musical influence was Jimmie Rodgers. She was a conscientious student and in high school received a scholarship for music from the Fine Arts Department of the University of Arizona. Later she changed to Cochise College in Douglas, Arizona, and received an associate degree.

The first work she undertook was as a medical records technician, located in Phoenix. At this time, she entered more contests and became Miss Country Music, Phoenix. She also began singing in local clubs, with her back-up group, the Stone Bridge Band, and La Costa began to build her career in music. At this time Tanya had made an impact on the Country music scene and was having hit records.

La Costa got married and her husband, along with her father, Beau Tucker, who acted as her manager, secured in 1974, a recording contract with Capitol Records. Her first chart record was *I Wanna Get to You*, which reached the Top 25. La Costa very quickly became a success when her next single, *Get on My Love Train*, reached the Top 3. In 1975, she charted with the Top 10 *He Took Me for a Ride*. The remaining singles that year were *This House Runs on Sunshine* and *Western Man*, which both peaked in the Top 20. The next year's hits were *I Just Got a Feeling* (Top 30), *Lovin' Somebody on a Rainy Night* (Top 25) and *What'll I Do* (Top 40). She continued to have singles on the chart, usually at the lower end of the scale, until the beginning of the 80's. La Costa left Capitol in 1980. In 1982, she signed with Elektra as La Costa Tucker, but she had only one charted single, *Love Take It Easy on Me*, which reached the Top 50 and was her final single to appear on the Country list.

La Costa has appeared on many TV shows including those hosted by Bob Hope and Hoyt Axton. In 1979 a personal tragedy halted her career when her husband, Darrell, was involved in a motorcycle accident and required her full attention. La Costa staged a come-back in 1989 and toured with Tanya. She was gratified that people still remembered her. She and Tanya were part of a lineup in a Memorial Festival for Jimmie Rodgers. However, as of 1993, La Costa was running Tanya Tucker's fan club.

JAB

RECOMMENDED ALBUMS:

"With All My Love" (Capitol)(1975)
"Get on My Love Train" (Capitol)(1976)
"Lovin' Somebody" (Capitol)(1977)

JOHN LAIR

(Songwriter, Musical Director, Impresario, Talent Scout, Music Archivist, Folksong Collector)

Given Name:	**John Lee Lair**
Date of Birth:	**July 1, 1894**
Where Born:	**Livingston, Kentucky**
Married:	**Virginia Frances Crawford**
Children:	**Ann Crawford, Virginia Lee, Nancy Carolyn, Barbara Burks**
Date of Death:	**November 11, 1985**

John Lair goes down in Country music history as the founder of the *Renfro Valley Barn Dance*, which was one of the most successful radio jamboree programs from 1937.

Lair attended high school in Mt. Vernon, Kentucky, and moved to Battle Creek, Michigan, where between 1916 and 1917, he attended the Art Institute. Between 1917 and 1928, he worked on a newspaper, in insurance, as a teacher and as a farmer. In 1927, Lair moved to WLS Chicago, where he worked on the *National Barn Dance*; the following year, he became Musical Director at WLS.

In 1934 through 1936, Lair worked on NBC's *Front Porch Serenade* and then moved on to NBC's *Olsen Review*. In 1937, John Lair inaugurated the *Renfro Valley Barn Dance* from WLW Cincinnati. Two years later, he took his show to WHAS Louisville, Kentucky. By 1940, Lair's partners, the Duke of Paducah, Red Foley and Cotton Foley, had sold their shares to him.

Lair introduced other programs: *Aladdin Play Party* on CBS (1942-1960) and *Sunday Morning Gatherin'* (1943 on). In 1966, Lair appeared in the movie *Renfro Valley Barn Dance* (Seven Arts). Lair's other business interests included the Pioneer Museum and the *Renfro Valley Bugle*, both in Renfro Valley, Kentucky.

In 1968, Lair sold his operation to Hall Smith, a former fiddler and Nashville businessman. However, some years later, when Smith could not get sufficient investment finance, Lair purchased back the company. John Lair died in 1985 with the *Renfro Valley Barn Dance* still in operation. (See also Renfro Valley Barn Dance)

JAKE LANDERS

(Singer, Songwriter, Guitar)

Given Name:	**Jacob Landers**
Date of Birth:	**August 14, 1938**
Where Born:	**Lawrence County, Alabama**
Married:	**JoAnn**
Children:	**Phyllis, Wanda, Karen, Allen**

In more than three decades in Country music, Jake Landers has achieved distinction both as a Bluegrass vocalist and songwriter. During the early 60's, Jake sang lead with the Dixie Gentlemen and a decade later filled a similar role with the Dixiemen. As a composer Landers not only wrote many of the songs associated with the aforementioned groups, but also the 1969 Bill Monroe song *Walk Softly on My Heart*, which became a major Country-Rock hit for the Kentucky Headhunters, in 1989.

A native of northern Alabama, Jake grew up with Country and Bluegrass and his professional career in music tended to be closely interwoven with that of his friends Herschel Sizemore and Rual Yarbrough, who formed the nucleus of the Dixie Gentlemen. After Sizemore relocated in Virginia, Jake and Rual continued with the Dixiemen for a time. Of five albums recorded by the former group, three consisted of standard Bluegrass songs while two contained largely originals, fifteen numbers of which had been written or co-written by Jake Landers. Such songs included *Soldiers Return, I Will Follow Jesus* and *Your Heart Tells the Truth.* After Herschel and Rual left to become sidemen first for Bobby Smith and then Jimmy Martin (Herschel) and Bill Monroe (Rual), Jake was left by himself for a time. Nonetheless, he continued to pen songs including *Walk Softly on My Heart* and *Beyond the Gate*, both recorded by Bill Monroe for Decca in 1969.

Jake remained active in music on a part-time basis. He shared an album with banjo picker Tom McKinney, released on Yarbrough's Tune label, on which he sang six originals, one of which, *This Last Request*, had been recorded earlier by Mac Martin and the Dixie Travelers. When Rual Yarbrough left Bill Monroe, he and Jake formed the Dixiemen, a band which cut four albums during its flourishing in the early 70's, including several Landers compositions. The title cut of their second album, ***Down by the Waterfall***, became something of a Bluegrass standard with a version by the Country Gentlemen gaining even greater popularity than their own. After the Dixiemen disbanded, Jake cut an album of his own for Old Homestead in 1976, which contained ten of his originals and another in 1981, an all-sacred effort which included five of his contributions. Jake's old pal, Rual Yarbrough, played banjo on both albums and two of Landers' daughters, Wanda and Phyllis, helped on vocals.

Having recently retired from his regular job, Jake had more time to devote to music in the 90's. The Dixie Gentlemen recently released a reunion album on Rutabaga and the newly organized Jake Landers Band had another one on Old Homestead. The respective title-cut originals on each, *Take Me Back to Dixie* and *I'd Like to Ride That Big Train Again*, offer fresh looks at the time-honored subjects of nostalgia for the South and the railroad. Furthermore, the Kentucky Headhunters' recent big success with *Walk Softly on My Heart* has refocused attention on Jake Landers' writing skills. IMT

RECOMMENDED ALBUMS:

"Jake Landers and Tom McKinney Present Original Songs and New Banjo Sounds" (Tune)(1970) [One side each]
"Singer/Writer" (Old Homestead)(1970)
"The Old Folks Don't Live Here" (Old Homestead)(1981)
"I'd Like to Ride That Big Train Again" (Old Homestead) (1992)
(See also Dixie Gentlemen)

CHARLIE LANDSBOROUGH

(Singer, Songwriter, Guitar)
Date of Birth: October 26, 1941
Where Born: Wrexham, North Wales
Married: Thelma
Children: Charlie, Jr., Allan, Jamie

Charlie Landsborough is fast becoming one of the most important Country songwriters to emerge from Europe.

As the youngest of nine children, he was raised in Birkenhead, near Liverpool, in the north of England. His musical interests came from his father, who was known as a silver-voiced tenor, his mother, who loved all kinds of music, and most especially Hank Williams. Charlie's brothers, when they returned from their seafaring travels, brought him home presents of records and then a guitar.

The guitar meant more to him than his studies and after leaving school, Charlie played lead guitar with a local band. He then studied music theory at college while working as a telephone engineer. Unfortunately, all this work meant that Charlie often missed bookings playing with a band named the Top Spots. One of these dates was at the Grosvenor Ballroom, Wallasey, where the band was to support the Silver Beatles (later re-named the Beatles!).

Then Charlie went and joined the Army, while the Top Spots became the Undertakers and enjoyed a successful career during the "Mersey Sound" boom. While serving in Germany, Charlie entertained the troops while in various bands as well as performing solo. On leaving the service, he worked in various short-lived jobs during the day, while pursuing a musical career at night. He played as a solo performer, playing Country music around the clubs and pubs.

Bad luck pursued Charlie when he began playing with a band in Germany called Chicago Set. After staying with them for nine months, he returned to the U.K. to get married and missed out on a recording deal with Ariola in Cologne. Charlie's big break came in 1968, when Roy Orbison, who was still very popular in Britain, came to the U.K. to tour. After the tour, Roy decided to set up a recording studio and began casting around for talent. A tape of original material by Charlie was given to Roy and he was interested. An appointment was arranged and on September 14, on his way to the meeting, Charlie heard that Roy's house had caught fire in Nashville and that two of Roy's children had been killed in the blaze. Roy returned to the U.S. and the project was folded.

Now married with two children, Charlie pushed music into the background and after qualifying as a teacher, he started teaching under-11-year-olds at a school in Birkenhead. However, in true artist style, Charlie continued to write songs in his attic. Some musician friends pursuaded him to make an album and so on a shoestring budget, a studio was booked in Bolton, Lancashire, and the debut album, ***Heaven Knows***, was cut. All eleven tracks were written by Charlie and one of the songs, *No Time at All*, was later recorded by British Country star Little Ginny on her U.S. album ***I Will Love You All My Life***. The song was later recorded by Foster and Allan and became a Top 50 hit on the U.K. Pop chart. The recording also became a big success in Australasia, South Africa and Canada.

George Hamilton IV, who like Charlie is a deeply religious man, recorded Charlie's *Heaven Knows* on his ***American Country Gothic*** album, along with other Landsborough songs, *I Will Love You All My Life* and *No Time at All*. Charlie's single *How Do You Do These Things/Heaven Knows* won the *International Country Music News* and the BCMA's "Single of the Year Award" in 1990.

Other artists to have recorded Charlie's songs are Foster and Allan (*Jamie's Song, No Time at All, Lily of the Valley, Fireside Dreams* and *Love You Every Second*) and Daniel O'Donnell (*Lovers Chain, Part of Me* and *I Will Love You All My Life*).

Charlie is of the old-fashioned school of writing, in that he writes from the heart. He describes his work as warm and sincere and probably too folky for British Country music clubs. He is a gentle and sensitive artist and will compromise his music just to please an audience.

In 1990, Charlie appeared at the Royal Albert Hall in London at the Promenade of British Country and then undertook a major tour of British theaters. After signing to Ritz Records, Charlie won the BCMA's "Best British Solo Performer" Award in 1992. The same year, his song *I Wish It Was Me* won the Southern Country Radio Awards "Song of the Year" title. In 1994, his *What Colour Is the Wind* won the British North Country Awards' "Song of the Year" title. JAB

CRISTY LANE

(Singer, Songwriter, Author)
Given Name: Eleanor Johnston
Date of Birth: January 8, 1940
Where Born: Peoria, Illinois
Married: Lee Stoller
Children: Tammy Lee, Cindy, Kevin Leland

Although the Gospel song *One Day at a Time*, written by Marijohn Wilkin and Kris Kristofferson, had been recorded many times before, it was the song that made Cristy Lane famous.

Cristy (or Eleanor, as she still was) came from a family of 12 children and although they were poor they were very happy. Cristy

*The very talented **Cristy Lane***

was a shy child who loved singing but was too timid to perform in public. She met Lee Stoller when she was 17 and they were soon married and had three children. Lee was a go-getter, and when he found out that she could sing, he made a demo tape and carried it everywhere he went. He soon interested Bobby Mac, a singer in a night club called Waynes Club in Peoria. Wayne said to bring Cristy to the club, and see what the public thought. After much persuasion because of her shyness, she sang *Paper Roses* and because the crowd liked her, she followed up with *Crazy Arms*. To get experience she performed at dance halls and Lee pushed her to write songs too.

Lee paid for a demo tape to be made of four songs and he sent them to radio stations and vocal stars. One of the tapes went to the *National Barn Dance*. They wrote and invited her onto the show. She was soon in Chicago shaking hands with the *National Barn Dance*'s Dolph Hewitt, and Eleanor made her first live professional performance and was paid $87. Now Eleanor changed her name to Cristy Lane, from a flyer which had the name of a deejay, "Chris Lane," on it. Lee went to see the real Chris Lane, taking with him Cristy's tape. After hearing it, Chris was impressed and said Eleanor could use his name with his blessing. Lane also said that he emceed a TV show called *Swing Around*, which had 8 million viewers. After seeing her performance at the Rivoli Club in Chicago, which was a great success, Chris Lane invited her onto his show.

Now Lee wanted the "Nashville Sound" and look for Cristy, so he changed her image by persuading her to go blonde and in 1966, he took her to Nashville. Lee paid to have a professional tape made of two of Cristy's self-penned songs, *Stop Fooling with Me* and *Heart in the Sand* and two covers, *Janie Took My Place* and *I'm Saving My Kisses*. When the tape was finished Cristy waited in the hotel room, while Lee pounded on the record company doors without success.

After this Lee decided to market Cristy himself, so he paid K-Ark record distributors for promotion and to manufacture 800 records. They mailed out 300 to the Country music stations, but the record never got national sales. Cristy continued to perform in the night club she and Lee ran.

Then in 1969, Lee arranged for her to undertake a tour of Vietnam. They went for three months and it was an experience that Christy would never forget: the squalor of the war-ridden country, the dangerous journeys to the camps, the 110-degree heat, poor food, the horror of being under attack and actually seeing men killed and, for Lee and Cristy, a couple bouts of sickness brought about by a virus. By the time they returned home, Cristy had performed 120 shows for more than 350,000 servicemen. Then she did another round of the clubs and was now in demand at military bases as well.

In 1972, Cristy, Lee and the children moved to Nashville to the suburb of Madison, aiming to launch Cristy's career from there, but after further disappointments, Lee formed LS Records in 1976 to release Cristy's music and his action was vindicated. Her first record to reach the Country charts in 1977 was *Tryin' to Forget About You*, followed by *Sweet Deceiver*, both of which were in the Top 60. Cristy then had her first Top 10 hit, *Let Me Down Easy*, which was followed by a Top 20 hit, *Shake Me I Rattle*. In 1978, Cristy had further successes with *I'm Gonna Love You Anyway* (Top 10), *Penny Arcade* (Top 10) and her most successful release, *I Just Can't Stay Married to You*, which reached the Top 5.

Cristy received the ACM Award for "New Vocalist of the Year" in 1979. At the awards show Cristy sang her single *Simple Little Words*, which became a Top 10 hit that year. While in Hollywood she appeared on the *Merv Griffin Show* and *Dinah!* Later in the year, Cristy signed to United Artists Records and UA picked up *Simple Little Words* as her debut major release. Cristy followed with two Top 20 records, *Slippin' Up, Slippin' Around* (1979) and *Come to My Love* (1980). *One Day at a Time* had been recorded by other artists before but UA reluctantly let Cristy release it as a single. It was an instant success, reaching No.1 on the Country chart. Her next 1980 single was *Sweet Sexy Eyes*, which was also her last Top 10 entry.

In 1981, Cristy signed with Liberty Records, with whom she stayed until 1983. Her most successful releases were *I Have a Dream* (Top 20), *Love to Love You* (Top 25) (both 1981) and *Lies on Your Lips* (Top 25, 1982). In 1987, Cristy had her last chart entry, *He's Got the Whole World In His Hands*, on LS, but it only reached the Top 90.

Christy's 1986 album ***One Day at a Time*** was marketed through TV and has become one of the biggest-selling albums in the world. It is the only Gospel album ever honored with an "Ampex Golden Reel Award." Her biography, *One Day at a Time*, by Lee Stoller with Pete Chaney, was published by St. Martin's Press in 1993.

Christy Lane owns her own theater in Branson, Missouri, where she now regularly appears. JAB

RECOMMENDED ALBUMS:
"One Day at a Time" (LS Records)(1986)
"Country Classics Vol. 1" (LS Records)(1989)
"Top 10 Songs of All Time Plus Star Spangled Banner" (LS Records)(1991)

RED LANE

(Singer, Songwriter, Guitar, Keyboards, Lap Steel Guitar)
Given Name: Hollis Rudolph DeLaughter
Date of Birth: February 9, 1939
Where Born: Bogalusa, Louisiana
Married: Penni (m. 1969)

In Nashville, a town full of songwriters, Red Lane stands as one of the finest. Unlike some of the "johnny-come-latelies," Red is capable of writing words that are not full of clichés and melodies that can still be remembered five minutes after they're heard.

Red and his family wandered all over the U.S. during his early childhood, traveling in a caravan of cars. In one year, he attended four different schools. Red worked at sharecropping, migrant farming and as an auto mechanic. He and his father played music together, with Red on lap steel and his father playing guitar. After high school, Red joined the U.S. Air Force as an aircraft and engine mechanic. For a year and a half of his service time, he was based in Hawaii and had plenty of time off. During this leisure period, he learned to play guitar well, becoming a Chet Atkins expert. He also listened to Merle Travis and Jazz guitarist Johnny Smith. At the time, he didn't own a guitar, but had one on permanent loan from the service club.

He was talked into joining the Air Force Tops in Blue talent shows and entered all the solo guitar contests in the semi-classical and Pop fields. He won through to the "All Pacific" contest, but got drunk and came in second. Before leaving the service, he was transferred to Omaha, Nebraska, where he began working with a Country band. Thinking they were going to make it, the group moved to Dallas, but after nearly starving for two months, Red rejoined his family in Indiana and played there. He started writing songs after asking himself, as a guitarist, what would he do if anything happened to his hands and he couldn't play.

Soon the family was off to California, but Red returned to Indiana and then played with a group in Phoenix, Arizona. A friend took him to Kentucky to meet Justin Tubb and Red began working with Tubb, arriving in Nashville in 1964. Red soon signed with Tree Publishing and debuted with Justin on the *Grand Ole Opry* in November 1964. That year, Faron Young had a Top 15 hit with Red's *My Friend on the Right*, which won a BMI Award. Red stayed with Justin for three years and then joined Dottie West, as front man of her band, the Heartaches, and emcee for six months. In 1967, Claude King had a low-level entry with Red's *Yellow Haired Woman*. With Dottie, Red wrote *Country Girl*, which in 1968 became a Top 20 record for Dottie.

Red now decided to give up playing on the road to concentrate on his songwriting. As well as *Country Girl*, Red chalked up other good cuts in 1968 with *Raggedy Ann (You've Been Quite a Doll)* by Charlie Rich (Little Jimmy Dickens would have a hit with it in 1970), *Three Six Packs, Two Arms and a Juke Box* by Johnny Seay and *Walk Out on My Mind* by Waylon Jennings. The following year was even more successful, with *Darlin' You Know I Wouldn't Lie* (Conway Twitty) (written with Wayne Kemp), *Clinging to My Baby's Hand* (Dottie West), *I'm a Good Man (In a Bad Frame of Mind)* (Jack Reno), *Love Is Just a State of Mind* (Roy Clark), *The Pathway of My Life* (Hank Thompson), *They Don't Make Love Like They Used To* (Eddy Arnold) and *A Truer Love You'll Never Find (Than Mine)* (Bonnie Guitar and Buddy Killen). At the end of the 60's, Red was involved with Merle Travis in writing the "Ride This Train" segment on the *Johnny Cash Show*. It was here that Red met his wife, Penni, who was on the production staff of the show.

During 1970, Jerry Reed went to see Chet Atkins at RCA, with the result that Red was signed to the label that year. He released his first single in 1970, *It Always Rains on Tuesday*, which he co-wrote with Hank Cochran. Boating buddies, Lane and Cochran have written many songs together and Cochran remains Red's favorite co-writer, when he doesn't do it all himself. His principal cuts in 1970 were *Brother River* (Johnny Darrell), *But That's All Right* (Hank Thompson) and *Country Girl* (Jeannie C. Riley).

Red hit the Country singles chart during 1971 with the title track from his debut album, ***The World Needs a Melody*** (also written with Cochran), which peaked in the Top 40. During that year, he had cuts with *Hanging Over Me* (Jack Greene), *The Hunter* (Alice Creech) and *Mississippi Woman* (Jerry Inman, also recorded by Waylon Jennings). At the end of the year, Red charted in the Top 70 with *Set the World on Fire (With Love)*. He started off 1972 with another Top 70 entry, *Throw a Rope Around the Wind*. This song was featured in the movie *Goin' Home* and was written with Larry Henley. Red wrote three other songs for the movie, including *Silver Bird* and *Singeree Singaroe* (the latter also with Henley). Red's principal cut for the year was the Carter Family and Johnny Cash's version of *The World Needs a Melody* (Bill Anderson used the song at one time to close his concerts). Red wrapped up the year with his last chart single, *It Was Love While It Lasted*.

Red's other cuts in the 70's included *Between the King and I* (Jeannie Seely), *Satisfaction* (Jack Greene), both 1973, *Country Girl* (Jody Miller, 1975) and *An Ordinary Man* (Dale McBride, 1977). Other Red Lane songs have included *Black Jack County Chains* by Willie Nelson, *Courtroom* (Clarence Carter), *The Day I Jumped from Uncle Harvey's Plane* (Roger Miller), *Everything Is Leaving* (Wanda Jackson), *Ode to a Critter* (Billy Edd Wheeler), *Poor Town USA* (Jack Barlow), *Walk Out of My Mind* (Frankie Laine), *What I'd Give to Be the Wind* (Roger Miller) and *When a Man Becomes a Man* (Ed Bruce).

In 1981, John Conlee had a major success with the left-field song *Miss Emily's Picture*. Red has continued writing and if his songs have been covered a little less, it's partly due to the competition and also to Nashville having a little less good taste than before.

RECOMMENDED ALBUM:
"The World Needs a Melody" (RCA Victor)(1971)

k.d. lang

(Singer, Songwriter, Guitar, Fiddle)
Given Name: **Kathryn Dawn Lang**
Date of Birth: **November 2, 1961**
Where Born: **Consort, Alberta, Canada**

Whether k.d. lang still regards herself as a Country performer is uncertain. However, she has played a major part in linking Rock and Country, in a way that has made Country music far more accessible to a wider public, without watering it down either.

k.d. and her band, the reclines (named after k.d.'s heroine, Patsy Cline), first came to public attention in Canada, and in 1985, she won a Juno Award as "Most Promising Female Vocalist of the Year." However, it was her signing to the non-Country label, Sire, that opened up her career internationally.

Her first album, ***Angel with a Lariat***, was produced in England by British rocker Dave Edmunds and contained material written by k.d. and guitarist Ben Mink. The album was Certified Gold in Canada, and led to a slew of awards there. The CCMA gave her the 1987 "Vista (Rising Star)" award, and also named her "Entertainer of the Year," an honor she would repeat in 1988 and 1989. In 1987, the Juno Awards named her "Country Female Vocalist of the Year," a title which she was to receive again in 1988 and 1990. She was also named "Best New Female Vocalist" by *Rolling Stone* magazine. At the end of 1987, she made her debut on the Country charts with the Top 50 single *Crying*, on which she duetted with Roy Orbison. It was taken from the movie *Hiding Out*, and won a Grammy Award for "Best Country Vocal Performance, Female" in 1988, one of three Grammy nominations she received that year.

Among a lot of media coverage, k.d. recorded ***Shadowland***, which was produced by the legendary Owen Bradley. This was originally to be a 6-track EP, featuring Loretta Lynn, Kitty Wells and Brenda Lee, but the project got expanded. The video of the *Honky Tonk Angels' Medley* also had Minnie Pearl guesting. This was k.d. with a deep respect for Country music, with songs by Roger Miller, Cindy Walker, Don Goodman, Billy Walker, Harlan Howard, Ernest Tubb and the Delmore Brothers. The album was named CCMA's "Album of the Year" in both 1988 and 1989. k.d. was named CCMA's "Vocalist of the Year (Female)" in both 1988 and 1989. She also won the 1988 Juno Award for "Female Vocalist of the Year." In addition, the reclines were named "Backing Band of the Year" in 1988, 1989 and 1990. In Canada, ***Shadowland*** went Gold in 1988 and Platinum in 1989, and in 1992 went Gold in the U.S.

In 1988, k.d. was chosen to close the Winter Olympics in Calgary, when she sang *Turn Me Round.* In May of that year, she made her fourth appearance within a year on *The Tonight Show* with Johnny Carson. She also appeared in Europe as part of CMA's Route 88, and repeated this in 1990. She had two U.S. Country chart entries in 1988, with *I'm Down to My Last Cigarette* (Top 25) and *Lock, Stock and Teardrops* (Top 60). In 1989, k.d. released the album ***Absolute Torch and Twang***, which was mainly made up of songs written by k.d. and Ben Mink. The following year, the album had gone Platinum in Canada, and in 1992, it went Gold in the U.S. It was named the CCMA's "Album of the Year" and won their "Graphics of the Year" award in 1990. It was also responsible for k.d. winning a Grammy Award for "Best Country Vocal Performance, Female." k.d.'s U.S. Country hits in 1989 were *Full Moon Full of Love* (Top 25) and *Three Days* (Top 60).

In 1990, k.d. become the first recipient of the CCMA "Bud Country Fan Choice Entertainer of the Year" Award. During 1990, she worked on the *Riding the Rails* melody for the soundtrack of the movie *Dick Tracy*. Ben Mink was named as one of the CCMA's "All Star Band of the Year" in 1990 and 1991. With the release of her 1992 album ***Ingenue***, k.d. seemed to turn her back on Country music. However, her fans stuck, and in Canada, it went Platinum the same year and Gold in the U.S. before year end. During 1994, she co-wrote (with Ben Mink) and sang the Soundtrack music for the movie *Even Cowgirls Get the Blues*.

Although k.d. is one of the most talented of Country singers, when she is inclined, her lack of acceptance by the conservative Nashville Country establishment may have more to do with her declared lesbianism than with her musical ability. Sex and Nashville have often been uncomfortable companions.

RECOMMENDED ALBUMS:
"Angel with a Lariat" (Sire)(1987)
"Hiding Out" (soundtrack)(Virgin)(1988)
"Shadowland" (Sire)(1988)
"Absolute Torch and Twang" (Sire)(1989)
"Even Cowgirls Get the Blues" (soundtrack)(Sire)(1994)

From session singer to star, ***Nicolette Larson***

NICOLETTE LARSON

(Singer, Songwriter, Guitar, Actress)
Date of Birth: July 17, 1952
Where Born: Helena, Montana
Married: Russ Kunkel
Children: Elsie May

Emerging from being a backup singer, Nicolette Larson looked at some time in the middle/end of the 80's that she would emerge as a contender in the female diva stakes.

Nicolette was born in Montana of a father who worked with the Treasury Department and was constantly on the move around the Midwest. By the time she was of high school age, the family settled in Kansas City. Although her mother had aspirations of becoming a professional singer, Nicolette was not that way inclined. After finishing school, Nicolette moved to San Francisco, where she got a job as production secretary with the Golden Gate Country/Bluegrass Festival. She met a lot of Bluegrass and Rock musicians, who on hearing her sing, encouraged her to do it professionally.

During 1975, Nicolette was playing the Bay Area bars, as part of David Nichtern and the Nocturnes. David wrote *Midnight at the Oasis*, which Maria Muldaur had made into an international hit the preceding year. Nicolette moved on to Los Angeles, where she began working with Hoyt Axton, and appeared on his 1977 album ***Roadsongs***. She then became a vocalist with Commander Cody and the Lost Planet Airmen and toured the U.S. with them, appearing on three albums, ***Tales from the Ozone*** (1975), ***Rock'n'Roll Again*** (1977) and ***Flying Dreams*** (1978). She was getting attention from industry people and sang on recording sessions for Guy Clark (***Texas Cookin'***, 1976), Norton Buffalo (***Loving in the Valley of the Moon***, 1977), Jesse Winchester (***Nothing But a Breeze***, 1977), Jesse Colin Young (***Love on a Wing***, 1977), Emmylou Harris (***Luxury Liner***, 1977 and ***1/4 Moon in a Ten Cent Town***, 1978), Neil Young (***American Stars & Bars***, 1977, where she and Linda Ronstadt were billed as the Bullets, ***Comes a Time***, 1978, recorded in Nashville, and ***Rust Never Sleeps***, 1979), Rodney Crowell (***Ain't Livin' Long Like This***, 1978), the Doobie Brothers (***Minute by Minute***, 1979 and ***One Step Closer***, 1980), Graham Nash (***Earth & Sky***, 1980), Linda Ronstadt (***Mad Love***, 1980) and John Stewart (***Dream Babies Go Hollywood***, 1980).

Becoming friends with Emmylou, Linda Ronstadt and Mary Kay Place stoked Nicolette's interest in Country music. She was approached by Warner Brothers Records and signed with the label. She hit the Pop charts with the Neil Young song *Lotta Love*, which made the Top 10, in 1978. She then released her first album, ***Nicolette***, in 1979, which was Certified Gold later the same year. That year, she again hit the Pop singles charts with the Top 50 record *Rhumba Girl* and released a second album, ***In the Nick of Time***. In 1980, she reached the Top 40 with a duet with former Steely Dan keyboardist and upcoming star Michael McDonald, entitled *Let Me Go, Love*. She also put out her third album, ***Radioland***. She next hit the charts in 1982, with *I Only Want to Be with You*, which reached the Top 60. That same year, she released her fourth album, ***All Dressed Up and No Place to Go***.

In 1983, Nicolette toured with the hit musical *Pump Boys and Dinettes* and wound up in Nashville, where she was offered a record deal by MCA. Without any Country hits, she was named by the ACM as "Best New Female Vocalist" in 1984. The following year, she hit the Country charts with *Only Love Will Make It Right*, which made the Top 50. She followed up with two further successes that year, *When You Get a Little Lonely* (Top 50) and *Building Bridges* (Top 75). She also released her debut album for the label, ***...Say When***, and was named "Best New Female Vocalist" by *Cash Box* magazine.

Nicolette started off 1986 with *Let Me Be the First*, which reached the Top 70, but it was the next single, *That's How You Know When Love's Right*, a duet with Steve Wariner, that took the charts by storm. It reached the Top 10 and stayed around for over five months. Both CMA and ACM nominated the couple for "Vocal Duet of the Year." Both songs, and the follow-up solo, *That's More About Love (Than I Wanted to Know)* (Top 50), came from the excellent album ***Rose of My Heart***.

During 1987, Nicolette spent some time in Italy, recorded an album, ***Shadows of Love,*** and taped a soundtrack for the movie *Renegades*. The following year, Nicolette appeared on a black Gospel music show, *Family Reunion*, and took on the role of racing driver in the Long Beach Grand Prix. She also appeared in 1988 singing in the Danny DeVito/Arnold Schwarzenegger movie *Twins* and in an episode of the Diana Canova TV series *Throb*. She began to do some bookings with singers Valerie Carter and Lauren Wood, and this led to a USO tour that year.

RECOMMENDED ALBUMS:

"Nicolette" (Warner Brothers)(1979)
"In the Nick of Time" (Warner Brothers)(1979)
"Radioland" (Warner Brothers)(1980)
"All Dressed Up and No Place to Go" (Warner Brothers)(1982)
"...Say When" (MCA)(1985)
"Rose of My Heart" (MCA)(1986)

TRACY LAWRENCE

(Singer, Songwriter, Guitar)

Given Name:	**Tracy Lawrence**
Date of Birth:	**January 27, 1968**
Where Born :	**Atlanta, Texas**
Married:	**Frances Weatherford**

Shortly after signing to Atlantic Records and with his debut album, ***Sticks and Stones***, just completed, Tracy Lawrence was shot four times in a holdup. He remembers thinking,"Why has all this happened to me? My whole life is just starting, and I'm fixing to die." Tracy was dropping off a friend from his hometown in Arkansas at her hotel, when they were confronted by three muggers. They took their money and credit cards and then were intent on taking them to the woman's room. Tracy, fearing they were about to rape her, very courageously tried to wrestle the gun from one of the men, which enabled his friend to escape, but in the scuffle Tracy was shot. Providentially the wounds were not fatal and after only three days in hospital and a short convalescence, he was back at work. The experience however has changed the way he looks at things, opening his eyes to what is really important in life.

*New traditionalist **Tracy Lawrence***

Tracy's childhood with three brothers and two sisters was a happy one. It seems that Tracy's mind had always been on show business and he wrote his first song at age 4, although his mother had plans for him to be a Methodist minister. At the age of 16, he began working with a band and in 1986, he set off for college at Southern Arkansas University, to study mass communications. After two years, he dropped out of college, to accept a lead singing offer from a band in Louisiana.

When that band broke up in 1990, Tracy went to Nashville to try his luck. To keep the wolf from the door, he worked as a telemarketer, an ironworker and also went in for talent contests around town. He managed to come in first or second at $100 or $75 every time and lived off his winnings. After one of the contests, he was offered a spot on a WBVR Daysville, Kentucky, show called *Live at Libby's* for $25 per night, which involved a long drive there and back. At a showcase at the Bluebird Cafe on January 22, 1991, he met his future manager, Wayne Edwards. He was offered a contract and by May 21 the same year, he signed with Atlantic Records.

It was May 31, 1991, when Tracy was shot and between June and August, he played night club benefit shows for his medical expenses and went through physical therapy, but he was soon feeling well and surprised his doctors with his quick recovery. On October 15, his debut single, *Sticks and Stones*, was released, and had more airplay than any other new act before that time. It quickly hit the charts and went to No.1. Tracy had the distinction of being the first artist on the Atlantic Country roster to get a No.1 hit. The second single, *Today's Lonely Fool* (1992), also hit the charts and climbed to the Top 3. The next cut, *Runnin' Behind*, went Top 5. Tracy's final single of 1992, *Somebody Paints the Wall*, reached the Top 10 in 1993.

1992 found Tracy touring the country extensively, so much so that he felt he couldn't sleep in a bed that wasn't moving. He toured with such greats as George Jones and John Anderson. He was honored by *Billboard* in 1992 as the "Best New Male Artist," and the ACM named him "Top New Male Vocalist" in 1993. His second album, ***Alibis,*** was Certified Gold just 17 days after it was released and shortly after went Platinum. Tracy's singles in 1993 all went to No.1. They were *Alibis*, *Can't Break It to My Heart* and *My Second Home*. In 1994, Tracy's single *If the Good Die Young* also reached the No.1 spot. JAB

RECOMMENDED ALBUMS:

"Sticks and Stones" (Atlantic)(1991)
"Alibis" (Atlantic)(1993)

DOYLE LAWSON

(Singer, Songwriter, Mandolin, Guitar)

Given Name:	**Doyle Wayne Lawson**
Date of Birth:	**April 20, 1944**
Where Born:	**Kingsport, Tennessee**
Married:	**1. Christine (div.)**
	2. Suzanne
Children:	**Robert Doyle, Suzi, Kristi**

Doyle Lawson is one of Bluegrass music's most respected mandolin players. The band he leads, Quicksilver, is considered one of the premier Gospel-Bluegrass bands.

Doyle became interested in Bluegrass when he was age 5 and listened to the music of the Stanley Brothers, Flatt & Scruggs and Bill Monroe. It was Monroe's mandolin playing that convinced Doyle that he wanted to play the mandolin. The family moved to Sneedville, Tennessee, in 1954 and Doyle got his first mandolin at age 11, when a member of his father's Gospel quartet loaned him one and he taught himself to play. He also quickly learned to play 5-string banjo and guitar.

One of Doyle's neighbors was Jimmy Martin, who was helpful to him and a great musical influence. Doyle's other influences were Red Rector, Paul Williams, Frank Wakefield and Bobby Osborne. In 1963, Martin invited Doyle to join his Sunny Mountain Boys as banjo player. He only stayed with Jimmy Martin for seven months and then he moved to Louisville, Kentucky, where he played in various groups and also worked with Lonnie Preece. In 1966, he played guitar on a part-time basis with J.D. Crowe. When Crowe moved to Lexington, Kentucky, Doyle joined Crowe's Kentucky Mountain Boys on a full-time basis as mandolin player.

In 1968, Doyle, Red Allen and bassist

Bobby Slone recorded ***Bluegrass Holiday*** for Rebel, Doyle's first recording experience. Doyle recorded two albums while with Crowe, ***Model Church*** and ***Rambling Boy*** (later renamed ***Blackjack***). Doyle left Crowe in 1971, when he joined the Country Gentlemen. In 1972, he traveled with them to Japan and that same year, the group was named "Best Band" in the *Muleskinner News* poll. While with the band, Doyle recorded ten albums including ***The Award Winning Country Gentlemen*** (1972) and ***The Country Gentlemen*** (1973). In 1977, Doyle recorded ***Tennessee Dream***, an album of mandolin instrumentals with musical support from, among others, Jerry Douglas, J.D. Crowe and Kenny Baker.

Doyle left the Country Gentlemen in 1979 and formed Doyle Lawson & Quicksilver with three musicians who had played in the group Southbound. They were Terry Baucom (banjo), Jimmy Haley (guitar) and Lou Reid (electric bass). The band signed with Sugar Hill Records and in 1980 released their eponymous album. Later that year, the band released the album that would help launch them. It was ***Rock My Soul*** and from here on in, they alternately released a Bluegrass and a Gospel album and surprisingly, their Gospel releases outsold the Bluegrass ones by two to one.

In 1981, they released ***Quicksilver Rides Again***, which featured Jerry Douglas, Mike Auldridge and Sam Bush, while their Gospel album of the year was ***Heavenly Treasures***. By the time the last album was recorded, Lou Reid had left and was replaced by former Bluegrass Cardinal Terry Baucum. They didn't release another album until 1985, when ***Once and for Always*** was issued. This marked a change, in that as well as Bluegrass numbers, Doyle also included Gospel material. It also marked a new line-up for Quicksilver. All the previous band members had gone and Doyle again found three musicians playing in one band, Southern Connection. The new line-up was Scott Vestal (banjo), Curtis Vestal (Scott's brother) (electric bass) and Russell Moore (guitar). This group recorded the 1986 album ***Beyond the Shadows***. Shortly after the album was recorded Curtis Vestal left and was replaced by Ray Deaton, who had played in Clearwater.

In 1987, Doyle released the most adventurous album yet in ***Heaven's Joy Awaits***. On his previous Gospel albums, there were always at least two a cappella songs, but this album consisted entirely of unaccompanied material, with Doyle and Russell sharing lead and alternate tenor parts, Scott singing baritone and Ray singing bass.

Later that year, the group released the imaginative album ***The News Is Out!*** on which Glen Duncan (fiddle, piano) and Jerry Douglas (Dobro) guested. By the time that Quicksilver released ***Hymn Time in the Country***, in 1988, the band had totally changed. Now the line-up was John Bowman (lead singer, guitar), Jim Mills (banjo, vocals) and Shelton Feazell (bass). Between 1988 and 1990, Doyle Lawson and Quicksilver released ***I'll Wander Back Someday***, ***I Heard the Angels Singing*** and ***My Heart is Yours***.

In 1990, Doyle was approached by Brentwood Music and signed with them. The debut album of this label was ***Treasures***, another all-Gospel album. This was followed by ***Pressing on Regardless***, his latest Bluegrass offering. As of writing, the current line-up of Quicksilver is: Jimmy Stewart (Dobro), John Berry (bass guitar), Shawn Lane (guitar) and Brad Campbell (banjo).

Doyle Lawson *(second left) and Quicksilver*

RECOMMENDED ALBUMS:

"Tennessee Dream" (County)(1977)
"Doyle Lawson & Quicksilver" (Sugar Hill)(1980)
"Rock My Soul" (Sugar Hill)(1980)
"Quicksilver Rides Again" (Sugar Hill)(1981)
"Heavenly Treasures" (Sugar Hill)(1981)
"Once and for Always" (Sugar Hill)(1985)
"Beyond the Shadows" (Sugar Hill)(1986)
"The News Is Out!" (Sugar Hill)(1987)
"Heaven's Joy Awaits" (Sugar Hill)(1988)
"Hymn Time in the Country" (Sugar Hill)(1988)
"I'll Wander Back Someday" (Sugar Hill)(1989)
"I Heard the Angels Singing" (Sugar Hill)(1989)
"My Heart Is Yours" (Sugar Hill)(1990)
"Treasures Money Can't Buy" (Brentwood Music)(1990)
"Pressing on Regardless" (Brentwood Music)(1991)

RODNEY LAY

(Singer, Songwriter, Guitar, Actor)

Given Name:	**Rodney Paul Lay**
Date of Birth:	**February 13, 1940**
Where Born:	**Coffeyville, Kansas**
Married:	**Karen**
Children:	**Rodney, Jr., John**

Rodney Lay may not have made it to the highest echelons of Country music, but for many years, he has been representative of the performers who have provided the backbone that keeps Country music alive.

Both Rodney's grandfather and father were part-time musicians, his dad playing guitar at square dances. Rodney played from an early age and debuted publicly at his school at age 9. He and his sister Sue formed a double act, performing at talent shows. When he was 15, Rodney joined Tommy Joe Ryan and the Country Rhythm Boys, getting $4.00 a night. In 1957, he formed his own band, Rodney Lay and the Off Beats, which by 1960 had become the rock'n'roll band the Blazers. He took the band to Kansas City, cut a master tape, printing up thousands of copies of a record on their own Kampus label, for rock radio stations, and selling them at a profit of 35 cents a copy. A copy was bought by Johnny Tillotson's manager, who wanted the song *Teen-age Cinderella*, for his star. However, Rodney's version was heard by a record executive at Dore in Hollywood, who occupied the office next to the manager, and the record was leased by the label as by Rodney and the Blazers. Rodney went on to record *Snow White/Tell Me Baby*, for Dore, in 1961.

At the suggestion of Joey Dee (and the Starliters), the band moved to New York in 1962, where they played the Peppermint

Lounge. During the 60's, the Blazers toured with Jerry Lee Lewis and then from 1964 through 1966, Wanda Jackson.

However, the big turning point for Lay was in 1962. It was that year that he met and played with Roy Clark (also managed by Jim Halsey) in Las Vegas. Clark would later play a major part in the Lay career. By 1965, Rodney had turned his back on Rock music. Gone were the silver hair, silver shirts and wraparound sunglasses and in were the denims and boots. In 1966, Rodney became a deejay on station KGGF Coffeyville (he stayed with the station until 1972), the following year putting together his band, Rodney Lay and the Wild West.

However, he was also starting to get his own songs recorded. In 1967, Hank Thompson had a Top 20 hit with Rodney's *He's Got a Way with Women*, which Bob Luman would record a decade later. In 1969, Waylon Jennings hit the Top 20 with *Something's Wrong in California,* and the same year, the Hagers scored with *Gotta Get to Oklahoma*. During 1970, an interview with Buck Owens on Rodney's radio show led to Owens arranging a record deal for Rodney, initially with his Blue Book label and then with Capitol. He released two singles for the label, *Georgia Boy/I Don't Wanna Make It* and *Tennessee Woman/I Don't Know Enough*.

Rodney made his screen debut in 1973, when he appeared in the Sam Peckinpah movie *Pat Garrett and Billy the Kid*. For eighteen months between 1975 and 1976, the band backed Freddy Fender during his halcyon days. Then, in October 1976 Rodney was reunited with Roy Clark, as Clark's band leader. With Clark, Rodney became exposed to a wider international audience.

By 1979, Rodney had signed to Sun Records, and his 1980 album ***Rockabilly Nuggets*** was critically acclaimed. He hit the Country charts for the first time in 1981 with the Top 90 single *Seven Days Come Sunday*. By the end of that year, Rodney had moved to Halsey's Churchill label, as Rodney Lay & the Wild West, and in 1982, they had a Top 75 hit with *Happy Country Birthday Darling*. He followed it up with the much acclaimed single *I Wish I Had a Job to Shove*, which gave him his first Top 50 hit. In 1983, he racked up two more middle entry successes for the label, *You Could've Heard a Heart Break* (a No.1 song for Johnny Lee, the next year) and *Mary Lee*.

He next hit the charts with the Evergreen single *Walk Softly on the Bridges*, in 1986. His version of *Rock Around the Clock*, which came from the album ***Rockabilly Nuggets***, was featured in the Tom Cruise movie *Born on the Fourth of July*, which was released in 1989. Rodney currently still manages Roy Clark's band and jointly owns with Roy the Roy Clark Celebrity Theater in Branson, Missouri.

Through the years, Rodney's second love has been horses and he and his family currently live on a ranch in Oklahoma, where he raises racehorses. His other interest is politics and he once ran for Montgomery County commissioner. In his own words, "I'm a big fan of America."

RECOMMENDED ALBUMS:
"Rockabilly Nuggets" (Sun)(1980)
"Silent Partners" (Sun)(1981)
"Heartbreak" (Churchill)(1982)

LEAKE COUNTY REVELERS, The

When Formed: **1926**
Members:

Will Gilmer	**Fiddle**
Oscar Mosley	**Mandolin**
Jim Wolverton	**Banjo**
Dallas Jones	**Guitar**

Most fans think of classic Old-Time string bands as coming from either north Georgia or southwest Virginia, but one of the most successful (in terms of record sales) came from central Mississippi, a few miles northeast of Jackson. This was the Leake County Revelers, described in a Columbia catalog as "the finest interpreters of old waltz melodies in the Southland."

Best known for their original recording of *Wednesday Night Waltz* (one of the best-selling of all Old-Time records), the band had one of the most distinctive ensemble sounds in early Country music—a sound defined largely through the smooth, gliding fiddle style of Will Gilmer (b. William Bryant Gilmer, February 27, 1897, Leake County, Mississippi/d. December 28, 1960). The Revelers seldom played at breakneck speeds but preferred waltzes and easy-going tempos that probably better reflected the rural string bands of an earlier age.

The band came together in 1926, when the four members got together after work around the town of Sebastopol (actually in Scott County, not Leake County). Apart from Gilmer, they were R.O. Mosley (b. R. Oscar Mosley, 1885, Sebastopol, Mississippi/d. early 1930's), Jim Wolverton (b. 1895, Leake County, Mississippi/d. 1950's) and Dallas Jones (b. December 17, 1889, Sebastopol, Mississippi).

A Columbia talent scout in Jackson, H.C. Spier, heard them and got them an audition with Frank Walker, the A & R chief of Columbia. At the time, the quartet had no formal name, and it was Spier who came up with the name Leake County Revelers. In April 1927 the four traveled to New Orleans, where they cut four sides for Columbia, including what would be their most famous song, *Wednesday Night Waltz*, in an arrangement that started as a waltz but then broke into a double-time tempo at intervals.

The success of these first records meant that the band would get to record on a regular basis, twice a year. They did so throughout 1930, eventually releasing 22 records. They never found another *Wednesday Night Waltz,* but they did produce favorites like *Monkey in a Dog Cart* (1927), *Crow Black Chicken* (1928), *Make Me a Bed on the Floor* (1928), and *Birds in the Brook* (1928). Buoyed by the success of their records, the band toured widely and had its own radio show on Jackson station WJDX. There is a persistent story that they played for Louisiana Governor Huey Long in one of his campaigns.

The band broke up in the early 1930's, about the time that R.O. Mosley, the senior member of the group, died. Gilmer continued to travel around the state, playing with other groups and, for a time, working in a medicine show. Dallas Jones continued to perform on local radio for some years. Jim Wolverton died in the 50's, and fiddler Will Gilmer died on December 28, 1960. CKW

RECOMMENDED ALBUM:
"The Leake County Revelers (1927-30)" (County)

Lily May Ledford refer COON CREEK GIRLS

STEVE LEDFORD
(a.k.a. LEDFORD STRING BAND)

(Fiddle)

Given Name:	**Steven Walter Ledford**
Date of Birth:	**June 2, 1906**
Where Born:	**Bakersville, North Carolina**
Married:	**Stella Mae Edwards (dec'd.)**
Children:	**Janet, Joe, Paul (stepchildren)**
Date of Death:	**September 19, 1980**

Steve Ledford served as one of the major fiddlers in string bands of the 30's.

Born into a family of twelve children in mountainous Mitchell County, North Carolina, Steve Ledford began to learn fiddle at age 7. He picked up the rudiments of music from neighbor Mark Edwards and from his father, A.W. Ledford. He won a local fiddling contest in Bakersville at age 9. As Steve grew older, he and other family members began to delve into a primitive professionalism, playing shows in one-room schoolhouses in Mitchell and adjacent counties of the Roan Mountain region. This group evolved into the Carolina Ramblers Stringband, whose membership at various times included Steve along with his brothers George and Taft Ledford, Audie Rodgers, and Dan Nicholson.

About 1931, the boys all went to New York and secured a regular radio program which lasted about six months. While there, they cut twenty masters for the American Record Corporation in February 1932, of which eight sides were released on such labels as Conqueror, Perfect, and Romeo. Later that year, Steve returned to Mitchell County, married Stella Edwards and settled down to farming.

Within a few years, Steve got back into music when he joined forces with Wade Mainer and Zeke Morris. When Zeke left to work with his brother Wiley, Taft Ledford joined them for a short time and Jay Hugh Hall and Clyde Moody for a longer period. He recorded several numbers with Mainer's Sons of the Mountaineers, including *Little Maggie*, which became his virtual trademark number. They worked on radio at such locales as Asheville, Raleigh, and Columbia. He also recorded a session with Jay Hugh Hall and Clyde Moody as the Happy-Go-Lucky Boys. In the early 40's, Ledford worked in Roanoke radio with Jay Hall and his brother Roy. Then about 1942, Steve went back to farming again.

In his later years, Steve Ledford became musically active once more. He reorganized the Carolina Ramblers with his younger brother, Wayne, and another kinsman, James Gardner. For some time they worked at the Ghost Town Park in Maggie Valley. As the Ledford String Band they recorded a fine album on Rounder in 1971 and Steve also had a pair of singles on the Roan Mountain label. The old fiddler also worked some with a youthful banjo picker named Phil Potter. In later years Ledford printed a short booklet containing his life story. Steve's wife, Stella, died several years before him. IMT

RECOMMENDED ALBUM:

"Ledford String Band" (Rounder) (1972)

(See also Wade Mainer)

CHRIS LeDOUX

(Singer, Songwriter, Guitar)

Date of Birth: October 2, 1948
Where Born: Biloxi, Mississippi
Married: Peggy
Children: Clay, Ned, Will, Cindi, Beau

What an exciting life Chris LeDoux has had. So far, he has found fame not only on the rodeo circuit, but as a successful recording artist, entertainer and songwriter. In addition, he is a first-class sculptor and house builder.

When Chris was 12, his family moved to Austin, Texas, and his riding dreams began soon after. Getting his own horse, Chris was taught to ride by a retired cavalry sergeant. When he was 14, Chris entered the national finals of the Little Britches Rodeo. He won the

Rodeo and Country star ***Chris LeDoux***

bareback riding championship and was runner-up in the bull riding competition.

By the time he was 16, Chris was serious about training to be a professional. In the summer vacation, he worked on a ranch by day and competed against professionals at night at the Cody Rodeo. In his senior year of high school, Chris rode for his school rodeo team. He went on to win the Wyoming State Championship. A rodeo scholarship was offered to him at Casper College, Wyoming. Spending another summer of Cody night rodeo, he joined the college rodeo circuit for three years. From Casper, Chris went on to Sheridan College, where he won the Intercollegiate National Bareback Riding Championship. In his third year at Eastern New Mexico State College, Midway, Chris turned professional and joined the Professional Rodeo Championship Association (PRCA) in 1970.

At college, Chris majored in commercial art and while there he made a bronze of a bucking bronco and rider, which was favorably acclaimed by the art world. The very first year as a rodeo professional, he made the National Finals Rodeo. He reached the height of his career in 1976, when he won the World Championship Bareback Rider buckle. Chris continued in rodeo until 1980, when he hung up his spurs and began concentrating on the musical side of his career.

During his college years, Chris had always written authentic rodeo songs and had played guitar and sung such songs as *Rodeo Life, Bareback Jack, Copenhagen* and *Bull Rider*. His first recordings were made in a basement studio in Sheridan. Then his father arranged a recording session in Nashville with the best musicians available. These first sides constituted Chris' first album, released on Lucky Man, a label which is part of American Cowboy Songs, the family music business. During a period of over 20 years Chris recorded twenty-two albums as an independent artist. He recorded all the old cowboy songs he could get hold of and also over a hundred songs he had written himself. He built up a loyal fan following and his tapes were sold year after year on the rodeo circuit. His company also sells song books that include words, music and guitar chords, and there are three volumes covering all of the songs on his albums. Chris actually had some basement chart action in 1979 and 1980, with three singles, *Lean, Mean and Hungry, Caballo Diablo or "Devil Horse"* and *Ten Seconds in the Saddle*, all on Lucky Man.

After 20 years of successful touring, building a tremendous fan following and also successfully distributing his own records with no major backing, at last, in 1990, Chris signed a recording and marketing contract, with Capitol Records (now Liberty Records). Liberty thought so much of the quality of Chris' previous albums that they re-released all twenty-two, on cd and cassettes.

Chris' debut album on the new label, ***Western Underground***, was released in 1991 and the first single, *This Cowboy Hat*, went into the Country charts and reached the Top 70. This was followed by *Working Man's Dollar*, which also went Top 70, and *Riding for a Fall* (Top 75). In 1992, Chris got together with his friend Garth Brooks for the title cut and first single of the album ***Watcha Gonna Do with a Cowboy***, and it went into the Top 10. The two artists toured together and Garth Brooks fans were delighted to meet the Chris LeDoux whose name was eulogized in Garth's song *Much Too Young (To Feel This Damn Old)*.

The last of Chris' 1992 singles that charted was *Cadillac Ranch*, which reached the Top 20, the following year. This single came from his next album, ***Under This Old Hat.*** In 1993, Chris' singles only achieved moderate success and were *Look at You Girl, Under This Old Hat* (both Top 60) and *Every Time I Roll the Dice*. In 1994, the single *For Your Love* reached the Top 50.

Chris LeDoux is a prime example of "talent will out" and if you wait long enough the record industry will realize what everyone else knew a decade before. He is a happily married family man, who is totally in love with his wife and family. He once built his own log house single-handedly, taking five years on the job. He now lives on a 500-acre spread called Haywire Ranch in Wyoming. JAB

RECOMMENDED ALBUMS:

All 22 original Chris LeDoux albums are available in KMarts, Wal-Marts, and from his own American Cowboy Songs, Inc., and are all on Liberty.
"Western Underground" (Capitol)(1991)
"Watcha Gonna Do with a Cowboy" (Liberty)(1992)
"Under This Old Hat" (Liberty)(1993)

ALBERT LEE

(Guitar, Singer, Songwriter, Composer, Piano, Mandolin, Hambone)
Date of Birth: December 21, 1953
Where Born: Herefordshire, England

Over the last thirty years, Albert Lee has emerged as the superior Country guitarist. Although not born in the U.S., his early love for American and particularly Country music has made him the player that all others try to emulate.

Albert was born into a musical family; his father played piano and accordion in the local pubs. At the age of 7, Albert started piano lessons and formally studied for two years, mixing the classics with rock'n'roll, and developing a love for the music of Jerry Lee Lewis. In 1958, he got his first guitar, a Hofner President acoustic arch-top. His liking for Buddy Holly and the Crickets resulted in his learning all of their material from their records. Soon he acquired the nearest thing to a Fender Stratocaster that he could afford, a Czechoslovakian copy called a Grazioso.

Albert assiduously listened to the recordings of Jimmy Bryant, Cliff Gallup (Gene Vincent and the Blue Caps' lead guitarist), the Louvin Brothers, James Burton (then Ricky Nelson's lead player) and most especially the Everly Brothers. However, it was listening to Hank Garland's groundbreaking album ***Jazz Winds from a New Direction***, in 1960, that really turned his head around.

Albert played in various local groups and first appeared on a recording in 1963, playing on the Bo Diddley EP, *Hey Bo Diddley*. In 1964, he joined the seminal R & B/Rock group Chris Farlowe and the Thunderbirds. He stayed with the group for four years, touring and recording two albums, ***Chris Farlowe & the Thunderbirds*** (Columbia, 1966) and ***Stormy Monday*** (CBS, 1966). Albert's influence was felt on up-and-coming players like Jimmy Page, who would go on to lead Led Zeppelin, and Steve Howe, who would go on and play with Yes and Asia.

During 1968 through 1970, Albert played with various bands including formative British Country group Country Fever, who supported various U.S. Country artists on tour in the U.K., Neil Christian's Crusaders and the Flintlocks. He also recorded with Joe Cocker on *With a Little Help from My Friends*, in 1968, with Green Bullfrog, which would later become Deep Purple, and with Poet & the One Man Band, in 1969, a band that included Tony Colton on vocals. Colton would eventually move to Nashville and become an established Country songwriter.

Albert then went on to help form Heads Hands & Feet, a U.K. band that blended Rock and Country. Among the members were Colton, Pete Gavin (drums), Chas Hodges (bass, guitar, fiddle), and Ray Smith (guitar, bass). Hodges would go on to become the "Chas" of Chas & Dave, who would have a lot of success in the late 70's and early 80's. The band's self-titled debut album was released in 1971 and included the original recording of the Lee-Colton-Smith Country classic *Country Boy*, which would be a No.1 hit for Ricky Skaggs in 1985. However, the group was light years ahead of its time and after the 1972 album ***Tracks*** and the 1973 offering ***Old Soldiers Never Die***, the band folded. The ***Tracks*** album featured U.K. steelie guru Gerry Hogan.

During his time with Heads Hands & Feet, Albert also played on other albums. These included Jon Lord's ***Gemini Suite*** (1971) and Jackson Browne's eponymous album (1972). Just after HH&F's end, the rhythm section was retained to back Jerry Lee Lewis on his ***The Session*** album, in 1973. That year, Albert began touring and recording with his old idols, the Crickets. He can be heard on their ***Remnants*** album (1973) and ***Long Way From Lubbock*** (1974).

In 1974, Albert Lee moved to Los Angeles and tried unsuccessfully to tour. He found that he received his rewards when he got into the L.A. session world. Through his work with the Crickets, he met his other idol, Don Everly, and they became and remain firm friends. At that time, Everly was playing at the Sundance Saloon in Calabasas, near L.A. Albert was invited by Don to join him and master steelie Buddy Emmons. The playing of the three proved to be very popular and resulted in the Don Everly album ***Sunset Towers***, in 1974. During that year, Albert played guitar on Jazz flautist Herbie Mann's ***London Underground*** album, proving his diversity of style. In addition, he toured with Joe Cocker in Australasia and as a direct result of that connection with Cocker, Albert was signed as a solo artist to A & M.

However, before Albert could finish his debut album, keyboardist Glen D. Hardin, with whom he had worked in the Crickets, asked him to join Emmylou Harris' Hot Band as a replacement for yet another hero, James Burton. The position was at first temporary, but in 1976, Albert became permanent, playing both guitar and mandolin. During that "temporary" period, Albert played on albums

Super guitarist ***Albert Lee***

by Lindisfarne's Alan Hull (***Squire***, 1975), Jackson Browne (***The Pretender***, 1976) and Joe Cocker (***Stingray***, 1976).

Even while playing with Emmylou, Albert was still guesting on other artists' albums. He turned up as one of the superpickers on the King of Skiffle, Lonnie Donegan's marvelous ***Puttin' on the Style*** album (1977) and Jonathan Edwards' ***Sailboat***, the same year. In 1977, Albert recorded his first album with Emmylou, ***Luxury Liner***. During 1978, he appeared on Guy Clark's self-titled album, fellow Hot Bander Rodney Crowell's debut album, ***Ain't Living Long Like This,*** and Nicolette Larsen's ***Nicolette*** album. Albert made a second album with Emmylou entitled ***1/4 Moon in a Ten Cent Town***. By the end of 1978, Albert left the Hot Band for a solo career.

In 1979, with the assistance of Emmylou's then husband, Brian Ahern, Albert finished and released his debut album, ***Holding***, which featured a new recording of *Country Boy*. Although Albert had left the Hot Band, he continued to contribute to Emmylou's albums including ***Blue Kentucky Girl*** (1979), ***Evangeline*** and ***Cimarron*** (both 1981) and ***The Ballad of Sally Rose*** (1985). Albert continued to play on other albums and these included Marc Benno's ***Lost in Austin***, Chas & Dave's ***Don't Give a Monkeys***, Juice Newton's ***Take Heart***, Dave Edmunds & Rockpile's ***Repeat When Necessary*** and Ricky Skaggs' ***Sweet Temptation***, all in 1979.

Albert was placed No. 3 in the "Best Country Guitarist" category in *Guitar Player's* Readers' Poll in 1980. During that year, he went on the road with the legendary Eric Clapton and recorded the live album ***Just One Night*** with Clapton. He also appeared on Rodney Crowell's second album, ***But What Will the Neighbors Think***. He was still with Clapton in 1981 and recorded a second album with him, ***Another Ticket***. He also appeared on Rodney Crowell's self-titled album and *This Old House* by Britain's Rockabilly King, Shakin' Stevens.

Every year between 1982 and 1986, *Guitar Player*'s Readers Poll voted Albert "Best Country Guitarist" and he was permanently inducted into the magazine's "Gallery of the Greats." During 1982, Albert released his self-titled album for Polydor as well as appearing on an album by Gary Brooker (ex Procol Harum)(***Lead Me to the Water***) and Dave Edmunds & Rockpile's ***DE7***. When the Everly Brothers reunited in 1983, Albert Lee was the centerpiece of the new band. In addition, he cut another album with Eric Clapton, ***Money & Cigarettes,*** and played on Leo Kottke's ***Time Step***.

In 1985, Albert left Clapton and a year later released the instrumental album ***Speechless*** as part of the MCA Master Series. The album was nominated for a Grammy Award as the "Best Country Instrumental Performance." That year, his playing graced the million-selling album ***Trio***, which featured Dolly Parton, Linda Ronstadt and Emmylou Harris. In 1987, Albert released his second album for MCA, the delicious ***Gagged But Not Bound***.

Nowadays, Albert continues to be as busy as ever. He has appeared in his own right at the prestigious Wembley Festival in England, he plays with a group of friends as Biff Baby's All Stars and he continues to add magic to other artists' albums.

He is renowned for his speed playing but unlike some Rock guitarists who are all technique, Albert adds substance and feeling to his playing and he is adept at all of his instruments and no mean singer.

RECOMMENDED ALBUMS:

"Hiding" (A & M)(1979)
"Albert Lee" (Polydor)(1982)
"Speechless" (MCA Master Series)(1986)
"Gagged But Not Bound" (MCA Master Series)(1987)
Also listen to:
Heads Hands & Feet albums mentioned above
Emmylou Harris albums mentioned above
Plus any cd cover that says Albert was here!

BRENDA LEE

(Singer)

Given Name:	**Brenda Mae Tarpley**
Date of Birth:	**December 11, 1944**
Where Born:	**Lithonia, Augusta, Georgia**
Married:	**Charles R. ("Ronnie") Shacklett**
Children:	**Julie Leanne, Jolie Lenee**

Little Miss Dynamite, ***Brenda Lee***

If you have had the opportunity to see Brenda Lee perform you will be in no doubt why she became known as "Little Miss Dynamite." She may be small (4'11") and although she has now outgrown the teen queen image of the 50's and the 60's, she is a sophisticated, respected international star, and is still on the road touring and traveling the world to entertain her army of fans. Brenda also influenced many future stars, including Barbara Mandrell, who used to practice before a mirror, singing to Brenda Lee records.

By the time she was age 3, Brenda could sing a song after hearing it only twice. At the age of 5, Brenda won a trophy for singing *Take Me Out to the Ball Game* and her singing ability was then recognized. She was taken by her mother to auditions for shows and when she was 7, Brenda had a regular spot on the Atlanta radio show *Starmaker's Review*, and had become "Brenda Lee." From her exposure there, she was offered some guest spots on WAGA-TV Atlanta's program *TV Ranch*. She was "discovered" by Red Foley in 1955 and *his* manager, Dub Albritten, became *her* manager. She began by sharing bills with Red Foley on the *Ozark Jubilee* TV Show and soon she was booked to appear on national TV on the *Ed Sullivan*, *Red Skelton* and *Steve Allen* shows.

Brenda's father was killed in a freak accident at work, in 1953, leaving her mother to try to support her four children by working in a cotton mill and so Brenda's salary helped them to survive. It also helped to put her brother and two sisters through college, and Brenda, who would have loved to have been a doctor, found herself taken out of her Nashville high school in 11th grade and put into a private school in Los Angeles, nearer to the hub of her business. Her only regret in that exciting time was the fact she was unable to make friends and close relationships. She does treasure the friendships she did develop. At Nashville Maplewood Senior High, Rita Coolidge and Brenda were close friends and remain so today. Brenda also became a friend of Patsy Cline on the Country concert circuit, when Brenda was only 12. Later, Brenda's daughter Julie was named after Patsy's daughter.

The record companies were soon interested in her and on July 30, 1956, she signed to Decca Records and began to record in Nashville with Owen Bradley. Her first cut was *Rockin' Around the Christmas Tree*. Her first chart entry was *One Step at a Time*, which went into the Pop charts Top 50 and later into the Country lists Top 15. In 1959, she had *Sweet Nothin's* in the Top 5. At this time, Brenda was considered to be in the mainstream of rock'n'roll. In 1960, at the age of 16 she had her first No.1 with the ballad *I'm Sorry*. The flip-side, *That's All You Gotta Do*, also went Top 10. She followed up with another No.1, *I Want to Be Wanted*, and at the end of the year, *Rockin' Around the Christmas Tree* went into the Top 15.

Brenda went to the U.K. for the first time as a Rock artist and during this tour, the Beatles were an opening act for her. Between 1961 and 1963 Brenda had 25 Pop chart hits, including *You Can Depend on Me* (Top 10), *Dum Dum* (Top 5), *Fool #1* (Top 3)(all 1961), *Break It to Me Gently* (Top 5), *Everybody Loves Me But You* (Top 10), *All Alone Am I* (Top 3)(all 1962) and *Losing You* (Top 10)(1963). The Top 20 hits up to 1966 were *Heart in Hand* (1962), *The Grass Is Greener*, *As Usual* (both 1963), *Too Many Rivers* (1965) and *Coming on Strong* (1966).

Brenda Lee was now classed as a Pop superstar. She performed at all the major auditoriums, the top nightclubs and played concerts all over the United States. She traveled abroad extensively and had concerts in Europe. She even played a Royal Command Performance before Queen Elizabeth II in England in 1964. On April 24, 1963, Brenda, then aged 18, married Ronald Shacklett.

After her Pop success during the 50's and 60's Brenda's singles were not hitting the top spots and she changed direction toward Country and reappeared on the Country chart from 1969, *Johnny One Time* being her first Country single placing in twelve years. Brenda had a great run of Top 10 hits between 1973 and 1975 when Decca changed to MCA, with *Nobody Wins* (Top 5), *Sunday Sunrise* (Top 10) (both 1973), *Wrong Ideas* (Top 10), *Big Four Poster Bed* (Top 5), *Rock on Baby* (Top 10) (all 1974) and *He's My Rock* (Top 10, with the Holladays, 1975). Other mid chart placings followed but she was up there again in the Top 10 in 1979 and 1980 with *Tell Me What It's Like* (Top 10, 1979), *The Cowboy and the Dandy* and *Broken Trust* (with the Oak Ridge Boys) (both Top 10, 1980).

In 1983 she performed a duet with Willie Nelson called *You're Gonna Love Yourself (In the Morning)* on Monument and in 1984 she had a Top 15 hit with George Jones, *Hallelujah, I Love You So*, on Epic. Her last chart place to date was in 1985 with *Why Have You Been Gone So Long*.

Brenda Lee sued MCA Records in 1988 for $20 million, claiming unpaid royalties during her 30-year career with the label. She said MCA failed to account to her for more than 180 records released outside the United States. MCA's attorneys claimed that the statute of limitations ran out on her claims years ago. In 1989, they reached an out-of-court settlement. The details of the agreement have been sealed at the request of both parties.

A Broadway-sized production called *Music! Music! Music!* was headlined by Brenda Lee from 1988 to 1990, at the Acuff Theater at Opryland USA. She played 260 performances each year, which enabled her to go home every night. Brenda has always kept up a punishing schedule of working days. For instance in 1987 she was on the road for 225 days, including a three-week tour of Japan, which was sold out. *Music! Music! Music!* was not her only stage experience. She had previously performed in *Bye, Bye Birdie* and *The Wizard of Oz*. Her film credit was in a small acting role in *Smokey and the Bandit*. In addition, she has appeared in such TV shows as *Hollywood Palace*, *Barbara Mandrell and the Mandrell Sisters*, *Nashville Alive*, *The Winning Hand*, *The Dolly Show* and of course her own syndicated radio show *Brenda Lee's Country Profile*. Internationally Brenda has appeared on the *Tommy Hunter Show* in Canada, Brenda Lee Japanese Specials, *Des O'Connor Show* (BBC-TV, U.K.), *Brenda Rocks from Rio* (Brazil), Barcelona International Festival (Spain), Belfast Special Telecast (Northern Ireland) and the Frankfurt International Festival (Germany) among others.

During her long career Brenda has been awarded a number of honors, among which are a special Grammy Award from NARAS, the "Governors Award" in 1984 (which is one of only four ever presented), Georgia Music Hall of Fame in 1983 and several *Cash Box* and *Billboard* awards and also a NARM Award. She has also received four Gold Discs and one Silver Disc from the U.K. for sales in that market, including ***The Very Best of Brenda Lee***, a double-album package which achieved Gold status in less than 6 weeks.

In 1991, Brenda signed with Warner Brothers Records. In 1993, Brenda Lee spent time touring in the U.K. and Japan and at the end of that year was on the road with the Oak Ridge Boys. JAB

RECOMMENDED ALBUMS:

"Brenda Lee Sings Songs Everybody Knows" (Decca)(1964) [A re-pack of "Grandma, What Great Songs You Sang" (Decca) (1959)]

"Brenda Lee Story—Her Greatest Hits" (double)(MCA)(1973)

"L.A. Sessions" (MCA)(1976)

"Kris, Willie, Dolly & Brenda/The Winning Hand" (Monument) (1983) [With Kris Kristofferson, Willie Nelson and Dolly Parton]

"Brenda Lee" (Warner Bros.)(1991)

DICKEY LEE

(Singer, Songwriter, Guitar)

Given Name: **Royden Dickey Lipscombe**
Date of Birth: **September 21, 1941**
Where Born: **Memphis, Tennessee**
Married: **1. Linda (div.)**
2. Katie Brooks
Children: **Danna, Amanda**

Dickey Lee's career to date has stretched over a period of over 35 years, and yet he still retains a boyish charm. He has emerged as a successful recording artist and songwriter, and although he is now no longer on a label, he is still writing hit songs into the 90's.

Dickey first played professionally with a three-piece Country band while in high school. They won several talent shows and during one summer vacation, they got a 15-minute daily spot on a radio show in Santa Barbara, California. In 1957, Dickey was spotted by noted Memphis deejay Dewey Phillips, who produced Dickey's first single, *Dream Boy*. Phillips introduced him to Jack Clement and persuaded him to sign Dickey to Sun Records, where he recorded in a hard rocky style. His first single for Sun, *Good Lovin'*, was produced by Clement, and outsold Presley's first single for the label! On the single he was billed as Dickey Lee and the Collegiates. He released one further single for Sun, *Fool, Fool, Fool*. While with Sun, he played as a backing musician on Edwin Bruce's *Sweet Woman/Part of My Life*.

One of his major loves was boxing and he became welter-weight champion in Memphis, getting into Memphis State University (where he majored in art) partly on a boxing scholarship. He remains an Unofficial Goodwill and Recruiting Ambassador for the university's football program.

When Jack Clement moved to Beaumont, Texas, Dickey and the then unknown Allen Reynolds (a former Collegiate) started making records together, at Hallway Records, each taking on the nickname of "Cowboy." In 1962, they came up with a major Pop hit when Dickey had his first Top 10 record with *Patches*, on Smash Records. He followed it up at the end of the year with *I Saw Linda Yesterday*, which reached the Top 15. He had one more hit for Smash, the following year, with *Don't Wanna Think About Paula*, which reached the Top 70.

During 1962, Dickey wrote his classic *She Thinks I Still Care*, which has since been recorded by, among others, George Jones (No.1, 1962), Connie Francis (also 1962), Elvis Presley and as *He Thinks I Still Care*, by Anne Murray, who had a No.1 in 1974.

Dickey next had a hit, in 1965, with the "sickie" *Laurie (Strange Things Happen)*, which reached the Pop Top 15 on TCF Hall

Dickey Lee (right) with ***Bob McDill***

Records. This was followed by the low-level single *The Girl from Peyton Place*. Dickey got somewhat disappointed with the recording side and decided to concentrate on record production, songwriting and publishing.

Jack Clement contacted Dickey in 1969 and urged him to return to record again in Nashville. Dickey's next recording, *Charlie (My Whole World)*, was leased to RCA and this led to his being signed by the label in 1971. He hit the Country charts with the Top 60 single *The Mahogany Pulpit*. This was followed by his Country Top 10 version of *Never Ending Song of Love*. He continued in 1962 with *I Saw My Lady, Ashes of Love* (Top 15) and *Baby, Bye, Bye* (Top 40). His successes through 1973 and 1974 hovered mainly around the Top 50 with the most successful being *Put Me Down Softly*, a Top 30 hit in 1972, and *The Busiest Memory in Town*, which reached the Top 25, in 1974.

In 1975, Dickey had his first No.1 with *Rocky* (a Pop hit for Austin Roberts). He followed it up with the 1976 Top 10 single *Angels, Roses and Rain*. Although the next single, *Makin' Love Don't Always Make Love Grow*, only reached the Top 40, the final single of the year, *9,999,999 Tears*, a Razzy Bailey song, made it to the Top 3 and crossed over to the Top 60 on the Pop chart.

Dickey stayed with RCA until the end of 1978 and chalked up further major hits, the most successful of which were *If You Gotta Make a Fool of Somebody* (Top 20), *Virginia How Far Will You Go* (Top 25) and *Peanut Butter* (Top 25) (all 1977) and *Love Is a Word* (Top 30,1978). He signed with Mercury in 1979, and his most successful singles with that label were *Workin' My Way to Your Heart* (Top 30) and *Lost in Love* (Top 30, with Kathy Burdick)(both 1980) and *Honky Tonk Hearts* (Top 40, 1981).

Dickey signed to the Welk Music Group as a writer and continues to write for the successor, Polygram Music. He continues to perform on 60's revival package shows.

RECOMMENDED ALBUMS:

"The Tale of Patches Sung by Dickey Lee (& 11 Other Songs That Tell a Story)" (Smash)(1962)
"Dickey Lee Sings Laurie & The Girl from Peyton Place" (TCF Hall)(1965)
"Never Ending Song of Love" (RCA Victor)(1972)
"Rocky" (RCA Victor)(1975)
"Everybody Loves a Winner" (Mercury)(1981)

ERNIE LEE

(Singer, Guitar, Emcee)

Given Name: Ernest Eli Cornelison
Date of Birth: April 12, 1916
Where Born: Berea, Kentucky
Married: Jean Ethel Moore
Children: Gordon, Sam, Stephen
Date of Death: May 23, 1991

Ernie Lee warmed the hearts of Country fans for a half-century with his friendly, down-home style. He had a type of appeal that went over especially well with radio and television audiences. Unlike Red Foley, who also came from Berea, Ernie never got the big hit records that would propel him to national stardom, but he also avoided the personal problems that plagued the "old redhead" and outlived him by nearly a generation.

Ernie grew up in an area that would produce a large contingent of Country music notables as divergent as Fiddlin' Doc Roberts and J.P. Pennington of Exile. Ernie's father served for some years as jailer of Madison County and the youth learned to play guitar from one of the inmates. He soon began picking evenings and weekends with local musicians. After finishing high school in 1934, Ernie worked a variety of day jobs while playing music part-time. In 1940, when Red Foley missed a show at the *Renfro Valley Barn Dance*, owner-producer John Lair, who had some prior knowledge of Ernie's ability, virtually plucked him out of the audience as a temporary replacement. Lair then made him a regular on the program, shortening his name to "Ernie Lee" and teaming him with young steel guitarist Jerry Byrd. Under the name of the Happy Valley Boys, Jerry and Ernie cut eight sides for Bluebird during their first year in show business. These included such numbers as *My Renfro Valley Home*, *Weeping Willow Valley*, *Home Coming Time in Happy Valley* and a pair of Hawaiian steel numbers.

Ernie and Jerry remained at Renfro Valley for four years before they moved on to Detroit and powerful WJR radio, spending exactly two years from October 1, 1944, with the Goodwill Frolic Gang, which also included their Renfro Valley associate Barefoot Brownie Reynolds, Smiling Red Maxedon, and fiddler Casey Clark. In 1947, Ernie joined the entertainers at another major outlet, WLW Cincinnati, where he appeared on and hosted the *Midwestern Hayride* and a variety of daytime programs as well. For a time, he, along with vocalist Judy Perkins, Louis Innis, and the Turner Brothers, had a network radio program for the Mutual Broadcasting System.

In 1953 Ernie moved to Dayton for a year, appearing on WHIO while retaining his following in nearby Cincinnati. Meanwhile, Lee revived his recording career in 1947 doing sessions for RCA Victor as Ernie Lee and His Midwesterners both before and after the Petrillo ban kept the studios closed through most of 1948. None of his discs became major hits although *Hominy Grits* (a song also associated with Smiley Burnette) and *Heading Home to Old Kentucky* probably had the most impact. In 1950 he went to Mercury, where his cover of Stuart Hamblen's *It Is No Secret* did well. His final effort for a major label was in 1951, when he had a session with MGM.

During 1950 through 1952, he appeared on the *Midwestern Hayride* when NBC took the show. Despite his popularity in the Midwest,

Singer/Guitarist ***Ernie Lee***

Ernie always aspired to reside in Florida where he could enjoy the warm climate and indulge in fishing during his leisure moments. In 1954, his ambition became reality when he secured a daily program at WSUN radio and TV in St. Petersburg. After four years Ernie switched over to WTVT Tampa.

For the next thirty-five years, Ernie reigned as a major figure on the Florida Country music scene. He made personal appearances throughout the Bay area and became a fixture at the Florida State Fair each year. Former associates from his *Midwestern Hayride* days came down and worked the program with him, including Herb and Kay Adams and Brownie Reynolds. His only recordings from that era were on an album, in 1961, for sale through his programs and a live cut of *Hominy Grits* on a Fan Fair Reunion album from 1975.

Ernie had occasional health problems in 1965 and 1979, but bounced back each time. However, a third stroke in 1991 ended both the career and life of a musician and personality much loved in Florida and much of the Midwest. IMT

RECOMMENDED ALBUM:

"Ernie Lee's Big Thirteen" (Ernie Lee)(1961)

JOHNNY LEE

(Singer, Songwriter, Guitar, Trumpet, Actor)

Given Name:	**John Lee Ham**
Date of Birth:	**July 3, 1946**
Where Born:	**Texas City, Texas**
Married:	**1. (Div.)**
	2. Charlene Tilton (m. 1982)(div. 1984)
	3. Debbie (m. 1986)
Children:	**Cherish Lee**

Johnny Lee came to fame on the wave of Country music interest occasioned by the movie *Urban Cowboy*. The movie that made a star out of Gilley's did the same for Johnny. His fame was further enforced by his marriage to *Dallas* star Charlene Tilton, and their subsequent divorce.

Shortly after Johnny was born, his father deserted the family and his mother drifted into two unhappy marriages before getting it right with husband No.4. Johnny was raised on a dairy farm in Alta Loma, Texas. While in high school, he formed Johnny Lee and the Roadrunners, and as such won several prizes. He was initially a rock'n'roll fan and thought that Country music was too twangy. He finally got to meet his father when he was 19, when a complete stranger walked up to him and said, "Hi, I'm your dad and I want to be your friend." His father would later sue him for $2 million, citing embarrassment and grief.

Johnny enlisted in the U.S. Navy and served aboard a guided missile cruiser in Southeast Asia, including Vietnamese waters. After four years in the service, he briefly moved to California, where he was married for a short while. He returned to Texas, where he talked his way into a job with Mickey Gilley by saying that they had met on TV's *Larry Kane Show* in Galveston (they hadn't!). He joined Gilley's band as singer/trumpet player and debuted at the Nestadel Club in Houston.

In 1971, when Gilley's Club was opened, Johnny was fronting the band and headlining when Mickey was on tour. He left Gilley's for a while in 1973 to try for a solo career, but returned again in the mid-70's. Johnny's initial recordings were on Astro and then in 1975, he hit the Country Top 60 with *Sometimes*, on ABC/Dot. The following year, Johnny signed to GRT and scored with *Red Sails in the Sunset*, which went Top 25. He closed out the year with the Top 40 hit *Ramblin' Rose*. In 1977, Johnny reached the Top 20 with a Country version of Rick Nelson's *Garden Party* entitled *Country Party* and followed it up with *Dear Alice* (Top 60) and the 1978 Top 50 single *This Time*.

During 1979, Johnny had his first screen role in a TV movie, *The Girls in the Office*, in which John Conlee also appeared. The following year, he landed a bit part in *Urban Cowboy*, which was to transform his career. The first soundtrack album went Triple Platinum (***Urban Cowboy II*** also fared well). Johnny's single release, *Lookin' for Love*, went to No.1 in the Country charts and crossed over to the Pop Top 5. In addition, it was Certified Gold. The album of the same title, on Full Moon Records, followed and also went Gold and yielded *One in a Million*, which also became a Country No.1. The follow-up, in 1981, *Pickin' Up Strangers,* reached the Top 3. From the ***Urban Cowboy*** album came another

Urban cowboy ***Johnny Lee***

track, *Rode Hard and Put Up Wet*, which reached the Top 60. Johnny closed out the year with *Prisoner of Hope*, which reached the Top 3. From his second album, ***Bet Your Heart on Me***, the title track went No.1 and crossed to the Pop Top 60.

In 1981, Johnny left Gilley's band and formed his own group, the Western Union Band, and opened his own club, Johnny Lee's, just down the road from Gilley's in Pasadena. He was named ACM's "Best New Artist." *Ampersand* magazine named *Lookin' for Love* its "Favorite Country Single of 1981." In 1982, Johnny lost some chart impetus and his successes were *Be There for Me Baby* (No.10), *When You Fall in Love* (Top 15) and *Cherokee Fiddle* (Top 10). On the latter, Michael Martin Murphey and Charlie Daniels were featured.

Then, in 1983, Johnny was back to his winning ways with *Sounds Like Love* (Top 10) and *Hey Bartender* (Top 3). He finished the year on a down note, when *My Baby Don't Slow Dance* only reached the Top 25. That year, Johnny played at the Wembley Festival in England and found that the audience did not take to his "Pop" stylings. He also set up the Johnny Lee Pro-Am Golf Tournament in aid of the Home of Guiding Hands, a charity for the mentally handicapped.

In 1984, Johnny hit the No.1 spot with a duet with Lane Brody, entitled *The Yellow Rose*, from the short-lived TV series of the same name. The follow-up, *One More Shot*, only reached the Top 50, but in August that year, Johnny bounced back with *You Could've Heard a Heart Break*, which went to No.1.

He started off 1985 with the Top 10 hit *Rollin' Lonely* but then *Save the Last Chance* only reached the Top 15 and *They Never Had to Get Over You* just made the Top 20.

Come 1986, and Johnny was in trouble as David Allan Coe's "Dallas-esque" *The Loneliness in Lucy's Eyes (The Life Sue Ellen Is Living)* only reached the Top 60 and Johnny's duet with Lane Brody, *I Could Get Used to This*, only made the Top 50.

For three years, Johnny was without a record deal and found himself playing small clubs and in financial straits. In his own words, "I lost everything but my talent." There was the occasional "one off" release, including a single and three EPs on his own Lee label and an album on JMS. Then in 1989, he signed to Curb Records and released the album ***New Directions***. However, the album was not up to the standard of its predecessors, and the four singles released all peaked around the Top 60 mark. That same year, he brought out his autobiography, *Lookin' for Love*, which was co-written with Randy Wiles and was published by Diamond Books, a part of Ekan Publishing. In addition, he issued a TV-marketed album, ***Woods & Water***.

Johnny and Mickey Gilley were estranged after the legal battles with Sherwood Cryer over Gilley's Club and now Johnny Lee, the man with 100 cowboy hats, continues to play around the clubs.

RECOMMENDED ALBUMS:

"Lookin' for Love" (Full Moon/Asylum)(1980)
"Hey Bartender" (Full Moon/Warner Brothers)(1983)
"Greatest Hits" (Full Moon/Warner Brothers)(1983)
"'Til the Bars Burn Down" (Full Moon/Warner Brothers) (1984)
"Floyd Tillman & Friends" (Gilleys) [Features Johnny Lee, Ernest Tubb, Merle Haggard and Willie Nelson]

ROBIN LEE

(Singer, Songwriter, Piano)

Given Name: Robin Lee Irwin
Date of Birth: November 7, 1953
Where Born: Nashville, Tennessee

Robin Lee is one of the very few Country music singers to have been born in Nashville. She began in music while still at Overton High School, performing with the Practical Stylists at school dances and talent shows. After graduation, she began doing demo recordings for publishing companies in Nashville and this led to her being picked up by the independent Evergreen label, at the end of 1982.

Robin's first two chart singles, in 1983, *Turning Back the Covers* and *Heart for a Heart*, only reached the Top 90, but in 1984, her chart placings improved with *Angel in Your Arms* (Top 60), *Want Ads* (Top 70), *Cold in July* (Top 70) and *I Heard It on the Radio* (Top 75). In 1985, she teamed up with Lobo for the Top 50 single *Paint the Town Blue*, and then had another Top 50 solo hit with *Safe in the Arms of Love*.

Nashville's own ***Robin Lee***

The following year was Robin's final one with Evergreen. She charted with *I'll Take Your Love Anytime* (Top 40) and *If You're Anything Like Your Eyes* (Top 50). That year, she was among the final five nominees for the ACM's "Best New Female Vocalist."

In 1987, Robin signed with the major label Atlantic America, and during 1988 had three singles that peaked in the 50s, *This Old Flame, Shine a Light on a Lie* and *Before You Cheat Me Once (You Better Think Twice)*. Although she didn't chart during 1989, she came back with a major hit in 1990, with the title track of her ***Black Velvet*** album, which reached the Top 15. The album itself reached the Top 25 on the Country album chart. Two other singles, *How About Goodbye* and *Love Letter*, only reached the Top 70.

In 1991, she had only one hit with *Nothin' But You*, which just failed to make the Top 50. Since then, her recording career has hit a roadblock, but no doubt Robin Lee still has more to offer.

RECOMMENDED ALBUMS:

"Robin Lee" (Evergreen)
"This Old Flame" (Atlantic America)(1988)
"Black Velvet" (Atlantic)(1990)
"Heart on a Chain" (Atlantic)(1991)

LeGARDE TWINS, The

TOM LeGARDE

(Singer, Songwriter, Guitar, Yodeler, Rodeo Rider)

Given Name: Thomas LeGarde
Date of Birth: March 15, 1931
Married: 1. (Div.) 2. (Div.) 3. Diane
Children: Faron, Damon, Todd, Mike

TED LeGARDE

(Singer, Songwriter, Guitar, Harmonica, Yodeler, Rodeo Rider)

Given Name: Edward LeGarde
Date of Birth: March 15, 1931
Married: Sharon
Children: Lisa

Both Born: Mackay, Queensland, Australia

The LeGarde Twins or Australia, as they are sometimes known, are one of the antipodes' most successful Country music exports to Nashville. Their brand of Australian Bush music blended with no-nonsense American Country music has endeared them to audiences throughout the world.

Tom (the elder by 30 minutes) and Ted were born of a French father (Edward) and English mother (Ada). Their father was a dairy and sugar cane farmer while their mother had been a nurse. Growing up on the farm, they soon became adept horsemen and later won many prizes riding broncos. When they were age 9, their elder brother, George, bought a portable gramophone and some records and they were immediately turned on to the singing and yodeling of Canadian Wilf Carter (Montana Slim). They both decided that they wanted to become cowboy stars. That same brother (who would later die in an accident) bought them a guitar.

When they were age 13, the twins saw a Hopalong Cassidy movie and they were totally hooked. They left school and home at age 15 and with one guitar and less than $10 between them, they headed northwest. They got jobs on Queensland's biggest cattle station, Rocky Ponds, where they worked for almost a year. While on a cattle drive to the Merinda Meat Works, they learned of a rodeo in Bowen and entered every event without winning, but they also sang to the crowd and got a very positive response.

In the audience was the ringmaster of Buddy Williams' Circus and Rodeo, and Tom and Ted were engaged as rough riders for a tour of Northern Queensland. By the time they were 17, they were the youngest professional riders in rodeos and began developing their interest in showmanship that included whip-cracking, rifle-shooting and card tricks. They then decided to go to Brisbane to see what a big city was like. It was also an education for Brisbane, as the two young boys arrived wearing flycatcher hats and hobnailed boots. At the time, the Brisbane Exhibition was taking place and Tom and Ted got to meet the legendary Tex Morton. Morton hired the twins to sing and ride during the Exhibition week.

In 1949, they went to Melbourne to work again with Buddy Williams as advance agents and entertainers. They arrived back in Brisbane in 1950 and decided to go to Sydney, which was starting to boom as an entertainment center. They were signed to the fledgling Rodeo label. They released five singles on the label, *One Little Letter/The Sunset Yodel*, *Echo Yodel/Pony Boy*, *Before the Dawn/There's a Bridle Hanging on the Wall*, *They Cut Down the Old Pine Tree/Gallop Along* and *The Sinner's Prayer/Ting a Ling a Jingle*, all of which did well. As their appeal widened, the LeGardes were billed as "Australia's Yodelling Stockmen."

During 1951, the twins spent 10 months studying dramatic art. In 1952, they signed with the prestigious Regal-Zonophone label and released a string of singles through 1957, including *Nobody's Darlin' But Mine*, *There Stands the Glass*, *I Don't Hurt Anymore*, *In the Jailhouse Now*, *Release Me* and *The Waltz You Saved for Me*. They started to work a lot with disabled children and have helped the Crippled Children's Appeal. In 1954, the twins appeared with Hopalong Cassidy (William Boyd) when he toured Australia.

In 1957, they decided to try their luck in the U.S. and after a period of time in Canada went to Hollywood, where they worked on Doye O'Dell's *Western Varieties* TV shows and hosted their own TV series on KTLA TV Los Angeles. By 1958, they were settled in Nashville and they released *Freight Train Yodel* on Dot. In 1960, Joe Allison produced them on their single *Baby Sitter*, which was released on Liberty. The following year, Earl Palmer produced them on *Roll Rock and Roll That Hula Hoop*, which was released on Bel Canto Records. While in Nashville, they appeared on the *Grand Ole Opry*, singing their self-penned song *Cooee Call*.

The LeGardes returned to Australia in 1963 with the intention of opening the equivalent of the *Opry* in Sydney. They acquired an old theater in Paddington, Sydney, called Wests and began shows there. They brought in Marty Robbins, Speedy West and Lorne Green. The twins began recording for Columbia and cut three albums, ***Ballads of the Bushland***, ***Twincerely Yours*** and ***Songs of Slim and Dusty*** as well as a quartet of singles, *I'm Moving On*, *Don't Let Me Cross Over* (with another Australian star, Reg Lindsay), *Faded Love* and *Trouble's Back in Town*. They also began emceeing two Country music shows, *Studio A*, which was built around them, and *Country Style*, which they took over.

By 1965, their business interests had come to an end and they returned to the U.S. For a while, they were managed by Colonel Tom Parker and appeared in Las Vegas. They also appeared in *Star Trek* as androids. Over the next few years, the LeGarde Twins recorded singles for Era (1968), Entity (1968), Dot (1972), American Heritage (1972) and Edge (1974). In 1975, they recorded *True Love* with Gary Paxton producing, which was released on Raindrop Records. In 1978, this single became a Top 90 Country hit. In the meanwhile, the twins had recorded for Koala in 1976, and then in 1979, again with Gary Paxton producing, they had another Top 90 single, *I Can Almost Touch the Feelin'* on 4 Star.

The following year, the LeGardes scraped into the charts with *Daddy's Making Records in Nashville*, which was released on Invitation. On January 27, 1987, they imprinted their hands in Tamworth's Hands of Fame, being recognized as significant contributors to the history of Australian Country music. During the 80's, the LeGarde Twins became very popular in Britain, appearing at the Wembley Festival and in 1988, hosting one of the concerts. That year, they made another basement entry on the Country chart with *Crocodile Man from Walk-About Creek* on the Bear label.

In recent years, the LeGarde Twins have operated their own LeGarde Twins Country Music Theatre out of Twitty City in Hendersonville, Tennessee. With the death of Conway Twitty and the sale of Twitty City, the LeGardes relocated their theater to the Quality Inn Hall of Fame Hotel close to Nashville's Music Row.

RECOMMENDED ALBUMS:

"Australia—Down Under Country Vol. 1" (Boomerang)(1983) [Their own label]

"Australia—Down Under Country Vol. 2" (Boomerang)(1984)

"Songs of Slim and Buddy" (Columbia Australia)(1987)

ZELLA LEHR (a.k.a. ZELLA)

(Singer, Juggler, Unicycle Rider, Dancer)

Given Name: Zella Lehr
Date of Birth: March 14, 1951
Where Born: Burbank, California
Married: Al Bello

When Zella Lehr did her audition for *Hee Haw,* she entered on a six-foot unicycle in front of producer Sam Lovullo. Needless to say she was hired. Zella had been riding this form of conveyance since she was 6 years of age!

Zella's ancestors can be traced back to 17th-century England where they were part of that entertainment scene. Her father ran a West Coast talent agency which he sold, as it was not very successful, and he set up a vaudeville/circus act, the Lehr Family, also known as the Crazy Lehrs from Hollywood, California. By the time she was age 6, Zella was adept as a juggler as well as on the unicycle. She traveled with her family for 12 years through Europe and the Far East. In the act, she sang the song *I Can't Get Off My Horse, 'Cuz Some Dirty Dog Put Glue on My Saddle*.

When her parents retired, she carried on the act with her two brothers and sister-in-law as the Young Lehrs. Her father became homesick for America and managed to get return passages on condition that the family entertained the passengers. During the voyage, her father became ill, fell into a coma and died. Zella and her mother stayed in New York while the rest of the troupe returned to Europe. Zella was so shattered with grief that it took two years for her to recover. During that time, she took singing and dancing lessons and began doing TV commercials, all of which helped the mourning process.

It was then that she did her famed *Hee Haw* audition. During her second season on the show, she started to get booked onto the Lake Tahoe-Las Vegas cabaret circuit, and while appearing at the Flamingo Hotel in Las Vegas, she put together her own group. She came to Nashville in 1977 and was spotted by Jerry Bradley and Pat Carter (then at RCA), while performing at the Captain's Table. Two weeks later, after an audition, she was signed to RCA.

Between 1977 and 1980, Zella chalked up nine hits for the label. Her most successful offering was her first chart entry, Dolly Parton's *Two Doors Down*, which reached the Top 10. The rest of her successes peaked around the Top 20 through Top 60 level with most being at the Top 30 level. The most successful were *When the Fire Gets Hot* (Top 40) and *Danger, Heartbreak Ahead* (Top 20) (both 1978), *Play Me a Memory* (Top 25), *Once in a Blue Moon* (Top 40) and *Love Has Taken Its Time* (Top 30) (all 1979) and *Rodeo Eyes* (Top 25) and *Love Crazy Love* (Top 40) (both 1980).

Zella moved labels in 1981 and chalked up four more chart successes of which the most successful by far was the 1981 single *Feedin' the Fire*, which went Top 20. In 1984, she moved to Charlie Fach's Compleat label. Here she had two more low level singles, *All Heaven Is About to Break Loose* (1984) and *You Bring Out the Lover in Me*.

Although Zella had no further chart success, she and her group, the Gypsy Riders, continued to be in demand at cabaret centers such as Reno, Nevada. She was also popular in Australia and toured there in 1988 and 1989.

RECOMMENDED ALBUM:

"Feedin' the Fire" (Columbia)(1982)

LEWIS FAMILY, The

(Vocals, Bass, Guitar, Fiddle, Mandolin, Piano, Banjo)
When Formed: 1951
Members:
Roy Lewis, Sr. ("Pop")
(b. September 22, 1905)
Nannie Omega Lewis
(b. May 22, 1926)
Wallace Lewis
(b. July 6, 1928)
Talmadge Lewis
(b. December 31, 1934)
Polly Lewis
(b. January 23, 1937)
Janis Lewis
(b. February 13, 1939)
Roy Lewis, Jr. ("Little Roy")
(b. February 24, 1942)
Travis Lewis
(b. December 26, 1958)
Lewis Phillips
(b. April 5, 1972)
All Born: Lincolnton, Georgia

The Lewis Family of Lincoln County, Georgia, has gained wide renown as the first family of Bluegrass-Gospel music. They have found acceptance in both of these fields, an achievement few groups have made. Their musical skills compounded with equal strength as entertainers, particularly that of Little Roy Lewis, have made them favorites of a national audience for at least a quarter century in a career that spans more than four decades.

The family's appreciation for quality Country music dates back more than 50 years. Pop Lewis recalls the Monroe Brothers giving a performance in their home community and the family's having Charlie and Bill at their house for supper. A decade or so later, Wallace, Esley, and Talmadge Lewis got together and began to perform for neighborhood events as the Lewis Brothers. When Esley entered military service in 1951, 9-year-old Little Roy became their banjo picker. In the meantime, Pop and the girls began doing songs with them, and the Lewis Family as a singing group came into being. Their professionalism took a major leap forward in the spring of 1954 when they started a weekly program over WJBF-TV Augusta, Georgia. This program ran for some 38 years (although they were mostly reruns in the final two). Since then, the family has done three specials yearly for WJBF. At times during the 60's and 70's, as many as nine stations carried their show extending from Arkansas to North Dakota. Until the 60's, most family members held "day jobs" at McCormick Mills in McCormick, South Carolina. As Polly recalls, between 1963 and 1967, they began to make music their full-time occupation.

Even for family groups, the Lewis Family has had few changes in personnel. Esley dropped out fairly early after his return from the service and Talmadge stopped playing in 1972 to concentrate on his retail auto business. The only significant additions have been Wallace's son Travis, who took over Pop's bass fiddle chores in 1974, and Janis's son, Lewis Phillips, who traveled with the family from early childhood. Sheri and Jeff Easter worked with them for a time in the mid-80's before striking out on their own. The Lewis group played mostly Gospel concerts prior to August 1970, when they made their first Bluegrass festival date at Hugo, Oklahoma. Since then, their brand of entertainment mixed with good sacred singing has made them perhaps the leading crowd pleasers in the history of Bluegrass festivals.

The dynamism of the Lewis Family show has been nearly impossible to capture on record, but their albums have had a history of steady and consistent sales. Their earliest efforts from about 1954, on Sullivan and Hollywood, were limited pressings with only local distribution, but some of them later appeared on Starday and Nashville. In the later 50's, they did several 45 rpm EPs for Starday. Throughout the 60's, they turned out a steady string of albums on Starday until 1968, when the label had one of its periodic upheavals.

After a single custom album on Solid Rock, they entered into another long-term contractual arrangement in 1969, with Canaan, which resulted in some of their best efforts. In 1986 they began a new association with Benson-Riversong and continue to turn out quality recordings at a steady pace. Overall, their total recorded output among Bluegrass groups is surpassed only by that of the Stanley Brothers and Ralph Stanley, whose earlier discs appeared some seven or eight years prior to the first Lewis sessions. The Lewis Family continues as active as ever on concert and festival tours as Pop Lewis goes into his 89th year.

IMT

Gospel greats the ***Lewis Family***

RECOMMENDED ALBUMS:
"Singing Time Down South" (Starday)(1960)
"Anniversary Celebration" (Starday)(1961)
"Gospel Special" (Starday)(1962)
"The First Family of Gospel Song" (Starday)(1965)
"The Lewis Family Album" (Starday)(1965)
"Shall We Gather at the River" (Starday)(1966)
"Lewis Country" (Canaan)(1970)
"Country Sunday in Georgia" (Canaan)(1973)
"Absolutely Lewis" (Canaan)(1975)
"Alive and Pickin'" (Canaan)(1976)
"The Lewis Family in Concert" (Canaan)(1983)
"Best of the Lewis Family" (Canaan)(1985)
"The Lewis Family" (Riversong)(1986)
"Live in Georgia" (Riversong)(1993)
(See also Little Roy Lewis)

BOBBY LEWIS

(Singer, Songwriter, Lute, Guitar)
Date of Birth: May 9
Where Born: Hodgenville, Kentucky
Married: Patricia Ann Blayton (Patty) (m. 1962)
Children: (Robert) Lyric

Billed as "the artist who plays the lute," Bobby Lewis has his slight stature to thank for taking up this unusual instrument. Standing at 5'4", Bobby had trouble with his Gibson J-200, which was too heavy for him. He was in Louisville, Kentucky, when he saw a "funny" guitar in a music show window. He tried the lute and found its lightness suited him. He re-strung it with steel strings and adapted it, and it became his trademark. The original lute is now in the Country Music Hall of Fame.

Born in Abraham Lincoln's hometown, Bobby was taught a few chords by his brother Jack on his guitar, at age 9. Soon after, his father bought him his own guitar. Bobby, whose biggest influence is Ernest Tubb, started entering and winning amateur contests and became one of the best musicians in the area. At age 13, he auditioned for WHAS-TV's teenage show *Hi Varieties* and promptly became a regular. Soon after, he joined the *Old Kentucky Barn Dance* on WHAS radio (he stayed on the show for over 10 years) and CBS *Saturday Night Country Style* (remaining there for 4 years). He also appeared on radio stations WTCO Campbellsville, Kentucky, and WIEL Elizabethtown, Kentucky.

In 1963, Bobby signed with Saber Records and released his first single, *Sandra Kay/I Miss All of You*, both sides being written by Bobby. He followed this with *Forty Dollars a Week/I'm Nervous*, the following year. In 1964, he moved to Fraternity Records and released the single *Crying in Public/The Local Memory*. By this time, Bobby was working on the *Grand Ole Opry* as a guest and was headlining Ernest Tubb's *Midnight Jamboree* quite often. He had by now written over 200 songs.

Bobby stepped up into the big time, in 1966, when he signed with United Artists Records. He hit the Top 10 that year with *How Long Has It Been*, and although he charted 11 times while with UA, his success level was inconsistent. His major hits in the five-year period were *Love Me Make It All Better* (Top 15) and *I Doubt It* (Top 30, both 1967), *Ordinary Miracle* (Top 30), *From Heaven to Heartache* (Top 10) and *Each and Every Part of Me* (Top 30) (all 1968), *Things for You and I* (Top 25, 1969) and *Hello Mary Lou* (Top 15, 1970).

In 1969, Bobby was nominated for a Grammy Award for "Best Country Vocal Performance, Male" for *From Heaven to Heartache*. For some while from 1971, Bobby traveled to bookings in a motor home with his family, in order to be close to them.

Bobby then moved on to Ace of Hearts Records and had two more sizable hits, *Too Many Memories* (Top 25, 1973) and *I Never Get Through Missing You* (Top 40, 1974). He then moved to GRT and had the 1974 Top 50 single, *Ladylover*. By 1976, Bobby had moved on to RPA, for which the most successful single was *For Your Love*, which reached the Top 60. He had one more meaningful hit, the Top 40 *She's Been Keepin' Me Up Nights*, on Capricorn. His last chart record, *Love Is an Overload*, came in 1985, on HME, but only reached the Top 100.

During his career, Lewis appeared on many major shows such as the TV shows *Hayloft Hoedown*, the *Bobby Lord Show*, the *Wilburn Brothers Show*, the *Shultz Show* and *Louisiana Hayride*. A lot of Bobby's recordings are marked by the use of a full orchestra. He has toured all over the world including Canada, the Caribbean, Europe and the Far East. In addition, he has received 16 ASCAP awards for his songs.

RECOMMENDED ALBUMS:

"The Best of Bobby Lewis" (United Artists)(1970)
"Too Many Memories" (Ace of Hearts)(1973)
"Portrait in Love" (RPA)(1977)
"Soul Full of Music" (RPA)(1977)

HUGH X. LEWIS

(Singer, Songwriter, Guitar)

Given Name:	**Hubert Brad Lewis**
Date of Birth:	**December 7, 1932**
Where Born:	**Yeaddiss, Kentucky**
Married:	**Anna**
Children:	**Lance, Lamont, Sandra**

For some while, Hugh X. Lewis carried on the dual careers of performer and working in the mines. Originally this happened because his parents could not afford to pay his way while he tried for success in music. He started out by playing weekends and on days off, and his first paying engagement was at a club in Cumberland, Kentucky. During the mid and late 50's, Hugh became a regular member of a weekly TV show in Johnson City, Tennessee, and on Saturday nights, he went to Knoxville to appear on *Tennessee Barn Dance*. Then in 1959, he became foreman at the U.S. Steel mine in Lynch, Kentucky.

By the 1960's, Hugh was getting quite a reputation with his fellow artists because of his 1963 performances on WSAZ's *Saturday Night Jamboree* from Huntingdon and the *Ernest Tubb Show* from Nashville. He had already started writing and now he quit his day job and moved to Nashville. He did the rounds and was picked up by publisher Jim Denny, who died shortly after. Hugh got his first major cut in 1963, when Stonewall Jackson recorded the Lewis song *B.J. the D.J.* and took it to No.1. This song was later recorded by both Kitty Wells and Carl Smith.

By 1964, Lewis was signed to Kapp Records and he hit the Country charts with *What I Need Most*, which peaked in the Top 25. He stayed with the label until 1969, during which time he chalked up 11 hits of which the most successful were *Out Where the Oceans Meet the Sky* (Top 40), *I'd Better Call the Law on Me* (Top 30, both 1965), *You're So Cold (I'm Turning Blue)* (Top 40, 1967) and *Evolution and the Bible* (Top 40, 1968).

This success had a knock-on effect. He made his debut on the *Grand Ole Opry* in 1964 and that same year, Stonewall Jackson had a hit with another Lewis song, *Not My Kind of People*. Jackson would go on and record a third Lewis composition, *Picket Sign*. During the year, Carl Smith recorded Hugh's *Take My Ring Off Your Finger*. The following year, Carl and Pearl Butler had a hit with Hugh's *Just Thought I'd Let You Know*, which was also recorded by Leon McAuliffe. During 1966, Hugh made his movie debut in Atlantic's *Forty Acre Feud*. The following year, he made appearances in a further two movies, *Gold Guitar* (Airlon) and *Cotton-Pickin' Chicken-Pickers* (South Eastern).

At the end of 1969, Hugh moved over to Columbia Records, but only managed one Top 60 single, *Everything I Love*, in 1970. By the end of 1970, Hugh was on the move again, this time to GRT, where he had one Top 70 record, *Blues Sell a Lot of Booze*. Nothing much happened on the recording front until 1978, when he signed to Little Darlin'. There he had two basement-level entries, *Love Don't Hide from Me* (1978) and *What Can I Do (to Make You Love Me)* (1979).

RECOMMENDED ALBUMS:

"The Hugh X. Lewis Album" (Kapp)(1966)
"Just Before the Dawn" (Kapp)(1966)
"My Kind of Country" (Kapp)(1967)
"Just a Prayer Away" (Kapp)(1968)
"Country Fever" (Kapp)(1968)

JERRY LEE LEWIS

(Singer, Songwriter, Piano, Guitar, Actor)

Given Name:	**Jerry Lee Lewis**
Date of Birth:	**September 29, 1935**
Where Born:	**Ferriday, Louisiana**
Married:	**1. Dorothy Barton (div.)** **2. Jane Mitcham (div.)** **3. Myra Gail Brown (m. 1958)(div. 1971)** **4. Jaren Pate (m. 1971)(div. 1981)(d. 1982)** **5. Shawn Stephens (m. 1983)(d. 1983)** **6. Kerry McCarver (m. 1984)**
Children:	**Jerry Lee, Jr. (dec'd.),** **Ronnie Guy,** **Stevie Allen (dec'd.),** **Phoebe Allen**

Jerry Lee refers to himself as "The Killer," but perhaps a better name would be "The Survivor." He has seen most of his contemporaries go to their graves, and he, who suffers personal tragedies and illnesses, just keeps on going, and pumping his legendary piano. His brand of raw Rockabilly and Countrybilly has ensured that he is still the performer that everyone wants to see and hear.

Jerry Lee was the son of a carpenter, Elmo (who was also a bootlegger and spent some time in Angola, Louisiana, prison) and a doting mother, Mamie. When Jerry Lee was age 3, his 8-year-old brother, Elmo, Jr., was killed when the tailgate of a truck, driven by a drunken driver, hit him on the back of the head. This left a mark on Jerry Lee, and he got closer to his mother. During WWII, Jerry Lee spent a lot of time with his cousins, Jimmy Lee Swaggart and Mickey Gilley, and like all kids they watched the westerns of Gene Autry, Hopalong Cassidy and Johnny Mack Brown. On Sundays, they would go to church. An evangelical calling came upon Mamie, and she soon converted the rest of the family. Jerry Lee was not initially filled with the Holy Spirit, but he enjoyed the music. His father taught him to play guitar, but by the time he was age 9, Jerry Lee became attracted to his Aunt Stella's spinet, and knew he wanted to play piano. He started to play like his preacher and then started to emulate "Big Sam," who played at Haney's Big House in Ferriday.

Then Elmo started to give Jerry Lee lessons and took out a mortgage to buy his son a piano. Jerry Lee's two biggest idols at this time were Al Jolson and Jimmie Rodgers. Jerry Lee was asked to play at the Texas Street Assembly of God, but the 12-year-old's boogie style did not endear him with the traditional church members, although he caused a sensation when he played at tent revivals. He was asked to appear on WNAT in Natchez.

By the time he was 13, he was running wild, but it was his music, and the fact that he could earn money from it, that led him to wander off, some two years later, and run afoul of the police in New Orleans, where he was trying to get work as a musician. He made his professional debut in 1948, at a Ford car agency in Ferriday, playing *Drinkin' Wine Spo Dee O Dee*.

Jerry Lee won $10 on a *Ted Mack Amateur Show* and got a thirty-minute spot on WNAT, where he started to build up a following. It was at this time that he met Cecil J. Harrelson, who would be a long-time friend of Jerry Lee's. By the time he was 16, Jerry Lee had

*"The Killer," **Jerry Lee Lewis***

married and he studied at the Southwestern Bible Institute in Waxahachie, Texas, near Dallas, and became a very successful preacher, where he was billed as "Jerry Lee Lewis and His Pumping Piano."

By the time he was 18, Jerry Lee had remarried (initially bigamously), but that marriage soon ran into trouble. Jerry Lee tried to get on KWKH's *Louisiana Hayride*, without success. He did, however, record two demo songs, *If I Ever Needed You* and *I Don't Hurt Anymore*. He had been advised by Henry Logan at KWKH to try Nashville. He did, without success, although he did get support from pianist Del Wood, and advice ("learn guitar") from Chet Atkins.

In 1956, using the money obtained from selling eggs, Jerry and Elmo went to Memphis and Sun Records. He arrived before 7:00 am, and waited until he got to see Jack Clement, who asked him to play. Clement recorded the Country song *Seasons of My Heart* for Sam Phillips to hear, but Jerry Lee did not hear from Phillips. While trying to get his music career going, Jerry Lee had jobs that included selling sewing machines.

Jerry Lee returned to Memphis with his cousin Jay. Sam Phillips decided to have Jerry Lee record various songs, including *Crazy Arms* and the Lewis original *End of the Road*. To get his career going, Jerry Lee put a group together comprising Roland Janes (guitar), Jimmy Van Eaton (drums) and Jay Brown (bass). He also got Bob Neal as a manager. Neal had previously managed Elvis before being cut out by Colonel Parker.

During 1957, Jerry Lee played on Carl Perkins' *Matchbox* and also on a pair of Billy Lee Riley singles. He also took part in what became known as the Million Dollar Quartet, with Elvis, Carl Perkins and allegedly Johnny Cash. Then in 1957, he hit the big time with his second single, *Whole Lotta Shakin' Goin' On*, which went to No.1 on the Country charts and Top 3 on the Pop lists. It also turned Jerry Lee into an international star, when it reached the U.K. Pop Top 10. This was partly due to the efforts of publicist Jud Phillips, who had spotted Jerry Lee on a Johnny Cash/Webb Pierce tour. When Carl Perkins was injured during the year, he advised that Sun put all their efforts behind Lewis. The single went on to sell over 6 million copies. When Lewis appeared on the *Steve Allen Show* on CBS-TV and threw furniture around the stage, Allen did likewise.

He wrapped up the year with another Country No.1, *Great Balls of Fire*. The single also reached the Top 3 on the Pop lists and became a No.1 hit in the U.K. He performed the song in the all-star movie *Jamboree* (called *Disc Jockey Jamboree* in Britain). The flip-side, Hank Williams' *You Win Again*, reached the Top 3 and crossed over to the Pop 100. In 1958, Jerry Lee's single *Breathless* made the Country Top 5 and the Pop Top 10. Consolidating his success in Britain, the single reached the Top 10. However, the storm clouds were gathering. He went on a tour of the U.K., but almost immediately, the press discovered that Jerry's new wife, his cousin Myra, was only 13, and that yet again, Jerry Lee was a bigamist. Soon, he was on his way back, his career in tatters.

His record *High School Confidential*, from the movie of the same name, in which Lewis appeared, reached the Top 10 and crossed over to Pop Top 25. Jerry Lee had enough fan base in Britain to ensure that the single got to No.12. Back in the U.S., the backlash started when *I'll Make It Up to You* only reached the Top 10. He then found that his records were being blacklisted. Strangely enough, in the U.K. he had two further chart entries with *Lovin' Up a Storm* (Top 30, 1959) and *Baby Baby Bye Bye* (Top 50, 1960). In the U.S., his only chart entries for the end of 1959 and in 1960 were low level ones.

Then in 1961, his career began to take on some shape again, when his version of Ray Charles' *What'd I Say* reached both the Pop and Country Top 30 and was a Top 10 hit in Britain, where it would appear that Jerry Lee was now forgiven. He had one more hit that year, with another Hank Williams song, *Cold, Cold Heart* (Top 25 Country). On the strength of his U.K. success, a tour was lined up, but the Home Office refused him a work permit. Fan and media intervention, however, made the authorities change their mind and a tour was lined up. Cruel fate then intervened, when Stevie, Jerry Lee's son, died in a swimming accident at age 2. Stevie already showed prodigious talent as a singer and piano player. There was some adverse press at Lewis' decision to go ahead with the tour, which in the event turned out successfully. Jerry Lee's boat kept afloat in Britain with *Sweet Little Sixteen* (Top 40, 1962) and *Good Golly Miss Molly* (Top 40, 1963). However, in the U.S. he didn't chart again (except for a basement level Pop entry) until 1964. He even recorded as "The Hawk," without success.

By then, Jerry Lee had moved on to Smash Records, where he was produced by Kerry Kennedy, and embarked on a new career as a Country singer. His first success came with the Country Top 40 single *Pen and Paper*. Then, in 1968, he got into gear, with *Another Place Another Time* (Top 5), Glenn Sutton's *What Made Milwaukee Famous (Has Made a Loser Out of Me)* and *She Still Comes Around (to Love What's Left of Me)* (both Top 3).

During the year, he appeared as Iago in Jack Good's rock musical, *Catch My Soul*, which was based on Shakespeare's *Othello*. The year ended with *To Make Love Sweeter for You*, which would go to No.1, in 1969. The year continued with a Top 10 duet with his sister, Linda Gail Lewis, *Don't Let Me Cross Over*. His four other solo hits that year were *One Has My Name (the Other Has My Heart)* (Top 3), a release from Sun, *Invitation to Your Party* (Top 10), *She Even Woke Me Up to Say Goodbye* (Top 3) and a further Sun single, *One Minute Past Eternity* (Top 3).

As the new decade arrived, Jerry Lee continued his success. The first single was another duet with Linda Gail, on a remake of Chuck Berry's *Roll Over Beethoven*. There is an interesting story that once, when Berry was due to follow him in concert, Jerry Lee set fire to the piano and snarled, "Let's see any son-of-a-bitch follow that!"

Jerry Lee followed up with three more major successes, *Once More with Feeling* (Top 3), *I Can't Seem to Say Goodbye* (Top 10) and *There Must Be More to Love Than This* (No.1), the latter being his first release on Mercury, which took over Smash's catalog. He ended the year with the Sun release *Waiting for a Train (All Around the Watertank)*, which reached the Top 15.

He decided that he wanted to give up Rock for Gospel, and he canceled all his shows, vowing never to set foot in a nightclub again. At the time, he and Myra had split up and it looked like it was an attempt to get her back. However, his desires soon changed and just 10 days after his decision, he tried to kick in Myra's front door. Then Jerry Lee's mother, Mamie, died and then Myra divorced him. Shortly after, he married Jaren, but it only lasted a couple of weeks (it took a decade for the divorce to go through).

Jerry Lee stayed with Mercury until 1978, and although his hits were more sporadic, he still racked up some memorable successes: 1971: *Touching Home* (Top 3), *When He Walks on You (Like You Have Walked on Me)* (Top 15) and *Would You Take Another Chance on Me/Me and Bobby McGee* (No.1/Top 40 Pop); 1972: *Chantilly Lace/Think About It Darlin'* (No.1/Top 50 Pop and U.K. No.33), *Lonely Weekends* (Top 15) and *Who's Gonna Play This Old Piano* (Top 15); 1973: *No More Hanging On* (Top 20), *Drinking Wine Spo-Dee O Dee* (Country Top 20/Pop Top 50) and *Sometimes a Memory Ain't Enough* (Top 10); 1974: *I'm Left, You're Right, She's Gone* (Top 25), *Tell Tale Signs* (Top 20) and *He Can't Fill My Shoes* (Top 10); 1975: *I Can Still Hear the Music in the Restroom* (Top 15) and *Boogie Woogie Country Man* (Top 25); 1976: *Let's Put It Back Together Again* (Top 10) and *The Closest Thing to You* (Top 30); 1977: *Middle Age Crazy* (Top 5); 1978: *Come On In* and *I'll Find It Where I Can* (both Top 10) and *Save the Last Dance for Me* (Top 30). When he played Britain in 1972, the result was near disaster, as he failed to satisfy the two factions of his followers. To the Country fans, it was a case of too much rock'n'roll and to the rockers, too much Country.

In 1973, Jerry Lee's life received another blow when his son Jerry Lee, Jr., was killed in an auto accident. He returned to the U.K. in 1978 and played a first-rate series of concerts. That same year, Jerry Lee appeared as himself in the biopic *Hot Wax*, based on the life of Alan Freed.

In 1979, he moved over to Elektra and had major hits that year with *Rockin' My Life Away/I Wish I Was Eighteen Again* (Top 20) and *Who Will the Next Fool Be* (Top 20). The following year, he charted with *When Two Worlds Collide* (Top 15), *Honky Tonk Stuff* (Top 30) and the Top 10 record *Over the Rainbow*. In 1981, Jerry Lee had his last major hit with *Thirty Nine and Holding*, which went Top 5.

Then in June of that year, Jerry Lee was hospitalized and almost died from a two-inch stomach tear. The following year, he moved to MCA, with the most successful single being *My Fingers Do the Talkin'*, which went Top 50. That same year, he got together with Johnny Cash and Carl Perkins for the ***Survivors*** album. It came about after Lewis and Perkins had unexpectedly joined Cash on stage in Stuttgart, Germany, the previous year, and their collective efforts were recorded by Lou Robin, and later remixed by Rodney Crowell. The album features Marty Stuart on guitar and mandolin.

In 1982, Lewis' fourth wife, Jaren, was found dead in her pool. During the Grammy Awards that year, he came on stage to play a duet with his cousin, Mickey Gilley. The following year, Jerry Lee married for the fifth time, but just two months after the wedding, his wife, Shawn, was found dead, in their home in Memphis, due to an overdose of methadone. Myra Lewis with Murray Silver wrote the 1982 book *Great Balls of Fire, The True Story of Jerry Lee Lewis*.

Jerry Lee got together with Cash, Perkins and Roy Orbison for the remarkable album ***Class of '55***, which was released on America Smash, in 1986. From it came the low level Lewis hit *Sixteen Candles*. Also featured on the album were Ace Cannon, Jack Clement, Dave Edmunds, John Fogerty, the Judds, Rick Nelson, June Carter, Marty Stuart and Sam Phillips. That year, Jerry Lee Lewis was inducted into the Rock and Roll Hall of Fame.

He returned to Britain in 1987, to re-appear at the Wembley Festival (he had played there in 1981), but his performance was lackluster, and he played electric piano, which didn't really work to accentuate his famed thumb runs. The most dramatic event of the evening was when someone jumped on stage, in an attempt to kiss his daughter, who was among the back-up singers. In 1988, Hallway Production released the video *I Am What I Am,* a 90-minute docudrama. Some years earlier, there had been an Arena Special documentary on BBC-TV, in Britain, covering the same area. The following year, Jason D. Williams played and sang for Dennis Quaid's portrayal of Jerry Lee, in the biopic *Great Balls of Fire*.

In 1993, Jerry Lee ran afoul of the IRS, which contended he owed $3 million in taxes. They had been chasing him since the 70's, but now they tried to auction off his be-longings. By now, he was living in Ireland with his sixth wife and latest son, unable to actively pursue his career.

The stories about the volatile Mr. Lewis are apocryphal. They include the time, in 1976, he was invited by Elvis to Graceland and was stopped by the guards because he was toting a gun, in a very drunk state. There was the time, also in 1976, that he shot his bass player, Butch Owens, with a .57 magnum, while they were horsing around in the office. Personal traumas aside, there is no doubt that Jerry Lee

Lewis is among the greatest performers ever to have graced a record or stage.

RECOMMENDED ALBUMS:

Charly Records in the U.K. have released and re-released all of the Sun Records masters on many albums. Below are just some worth listening to. Dates are original release dates by Sun.

Rockabilly period:

"Jerry Lee's Greatest!—Jerry Lee Lewis" (Sun)(1961)

"Johnny Cash & Jerry Lee Lewis Sing Hank Williams" (Sun)(1971) [Not duets]

"The Original Jerry Lee Lewis" (Sun)(1978)

"Duets" (Sun)(1978) [With Charlie Rich and Jimmy Ellis (Orion, the Elvis impersonator)]

"The Greatest Show on Earth" (Smash)(1964)

Country/Gospel period:

"Jerry Lee Lewis & Linda Gail Lewis Together" (Smash)(1969) [Re-released on Mercury]

"In Loving Memory—The Jerry Lee Lewis Gospel Album" (Smash)(1971)

"The Killer Rocks On" (Mercury)(1972)

"The Session" (double)(Mercury)(1973)

"When Two Worlds Collide" (Elektra)(1980)

"The Best of Jerry Lee Lewis" (Elektra)(1982)

"The Survivors" (Columbia)(1982) [With Johnny Cash and Carl Perkins]

"My Fingers Do the Talkin'" (MCA)(1982)

"Class of '55" (America/Smash)(1986)

LINDA GAIL LEWIS

(Singer, Songwriter)

Given Name:	**Linda Gail Lewis**
Date of Birth:	**July 18, 1947**
Where Born:	**Ferriday, Louisiana**
Married:	**1. Mr. Goza (div.)**
	2. Jim Bushlen (div.)
	3. Cecil Harrelson (div.)
	4. Ken Lovelace

There is no doubt that without the help of her elder brother, Jerry Lee, Linda Gail would not have made it into the music business, or for that matter, had the inclination to be a singer. However, although there may have been doubts about her early ability, her performance at the 1987 Wembley Festival in England showed her to have a good voice.

Linda was married for a second time, before her 16th birthday, to Jim Bushlen, a sailor on leave, whom she met and married within three days. He went back to sea and she never heard from him again. Still only 16, she then went on to marry Jerry Lee's best friend, Cecil, who had always been the love of her life. Jerry Lee's mother put pressure on him to put Linda Gail into his show. In 1960, Jerry Lee was coerced by his mother to take Linda Gail and their other sister, Frankie Jean, into the Sun studio, where they cut a less than satisfactory version of *Good Golly Miss Molly*, which was then hidden away in the vaults. Linda Gail's next recording attempt occurred in 1963, when Jerry Lee took her again to Sun to record a duet on the old George Jones hit, *Seasons of My Heart*, but Jerry Lee's harmonies and Linda Gail's voice, which was flat, didn't make it a memorable event.

However, she joined Jerry Lee's bill from April 1963. When English rock'n'roll guru Jack Good, who would go on to create *Catch My Soul*, produced *Shindig* on ABC-TV, in 1964, he was prevailed upon to put Linda Gail on the show, and ultimately in the touring version. This led to Linda Gail's record deal with ABC-Paramount. Her only single for the label was *Break Up the Party/Small Red Diary*, that same year.

Linda Gail followed Jerry Lee to Smash Records, and in 1968, released *Turn Back the Hands of Time/Good*. It was the following year that she hit the big time, with a duet with Jerry Lee entitled *Don't Let Me Cross Over*, which made the Top 10. It was followed the next year with a low-level entry of their remake of Chuck Berry's *Roll Over Beethoven*. She had one further solo hit, in 1972, with her Mercury recording of *Smile, Somebody Loves You*, which reached the Top 40.

Linda Gail retired in 1977, and apart from the occasional appearances, such as Wembley, her career has gotten no further.

RECOMMENDED ALBUMS:

"Two Sides of Linda Gail Lewis" (Smash)(1969) [Features Jerry Lee Lewis]

"Jerry Lee Lewis & Linda Gail Lewis Together" (Smash)(1969) [Re-issued on Mercury]

LITTLE ROY LEWIS

(Singer, Comedy, Banjo, Guitar, Autoharp, Bass Fiddle, Mandolin)

Given Name:	**Roy M. Lewis, Jr.**
Date of Birth:	**February 24, 1942**
Where Born:	**Lincolnton, Georgia**
Married:	**Bonnie Reeves**

Although Little Roy Lewis has spent his entire musical career with his father and siblings as a member of the Lewis Family—often termed the first family of Bluegrass-Gospel music—his individual accomplishments and comedy talents merit special attention.

The youngest member of a large family, Little Roy earned his nickname from the mere fact that his father had the same first name, rather than from any lack of size. When he first demonstrated his skills on the banjo, however, he was indeed quite "little." Taking up the instrument at the age of 6, mastering the techniques of banjo great Earl Scruggs, he won his first prize in a local contest at 8. The next year, Roy started playing banjo with the family group when older brother Esley entered the Army. When Esley returned, Roy's expertise was such that Esley went to bass fiddle before dropping out entirely. In the spring of 1954, the Lewis Family began their long-running program at WJBF-TV Augusta and the rest is history.

From the Lewis Family, ***Little Roy Lewis***

In addition to playing on all Lewis Family recordings from their first efforts on Hollywood and Sullivan, in 1954, right up through a long string of albums on Starday, Canaan, and Riversong, Little Roy has cut a number of banjo records. His initial offering consisted of an EP on Starday, in the early 60's, followed by the album ***Golden Gospel Banjo***, in 1968.

After the family went to the Canaan label in 1969, Roy had four more banjo albums as well as a Best Of album containing highlight numbers from his earlier releases. Some of these include specialty items with his protégé-nephew Lewis Phillips. In addition to sometimes singing solo and banjo picking, Little Roy has shown himself equally adept on lead guitar and autoharp on certain arrangements.

The Little Roy Lewis comedy has a great deal to do with his enduring popularity. His constant banter and sound effects on songs like *Honey in the Rock* contribute a great deal to the entire group's success as entertainers. His good-natured harassment of other family members gives the entire band an on-stage charisma that is virtually unique in any form of Country music today.

A bachelor until the age of 44, Little Roy married a Louisiana gal in 1986 and built a home in Lincolnton near those of the others in the Lewis clan. The Little Roy Lewis touch, while difficult to capture on disc, manages to shine through on several banjo albums and on Lewis Family live show recordings. IMT

RECOMMENDED ALBUMS:
"Golden Gospel Banjo" (Starday)(1968)
"Gospel Banjo" (Canaan)(1972)
"The Entertainer" (Canaan)(1977)
"Super Pickin'" (Canaan)(1981)
"In the Heart of Dixie" (Canaan)(1984)
"The Best of Little Roy Lewis" (Canaan)(1985)

TEXAS JIM LEWIS

(Guitar, Bass, "Hootenanny")

Given Name:	**James Lewis, Jr.**
Date of Birth:	**October 15, 1909**
Where Born:	**Meigs, Georgia**
Married:	**1. (Div.)**
	2. Pattie
Children:	**six**
Date of Death:	**January 23, 1990**

Texas Jim Lewis led a small Western Swing band called the Lone Star Cowboys. During the late 30's and 40's, it was based, at different times, in New York and in California. Lewis ended his professional career in Seattle, Washington, where he had a long-running children's TV show during the 50's.

Lewis was born in Meigs, Georgia, into a musical family. His mother died about 1915. Later, his father remarried and had two additional children, one named Rivers Lewis (aka Jack Rivers), who would be associated with Jim off and on for much of his career.

The family settled in Fort Myers, Florida, in 1919. Jim remained at home until 1928, when he went to Texas, where he acquired his nickname. He tried his hand at farming and also worked in an ice plant, but mostly dabbled in entertainment. In the early 30's, Jim went to Detroit, where his family had relocated. He and his half-brother, Jack (then 14), played music in speakeasies for a time, but then he went to Houston in 1932 and joined the Swift Jewel Cowboys. He remained with this band until 1934 when he went to Detroit again and worked in a band, Jack West and His Circle Star Cowboys, at WJR radio and in clubs.

Eventually, Jim formed his own Lone Star Cowboys, which included some former members of the West group such as Eugene "Smoky" Rogers, Andrew "Cactus" Soldi, and half-brother Jack. In October, Texas Jim and the group moved to New York, where they soon found a variety of club jobs in spots like the Village Barn.

The band worked out of New York for five years and stayed busy with radio, theater, and club work. They had a record session for Vocalion and cut numerous transcriptions. Appearances on the Mutual Network helped popularize Western Swing in the eastern half of the U.S. In August 1940, the band signed with Decca. That same year, they went on an extensive tour and wound up in California. By this time, Ginger Snow had joined the band as girl vocalist and Pedro DePaul played accordion. The Lone Star Cowboys played conventional Western Swing along with novelty material. By this time, Jim Lewis had built his trademark musical instrument, the hootenanny, a contraption that included two washboards, a variety of horns, siren, bell, and even a gun that fired blanks! The group also appeared in a few films in this period, most notably *Pardon My Gun*, with Charles Starrett (see Movie Section). In late 1942, it all came to an end when Uncle Sam called Lewis into military service. Spade Cooley took over Lewis' band.

In 1944, Jim Lewis got out of the Army and resumed his career. He organized a new band and opened the 97th Street Corral, a popular club, and later switched to the Redondo Beach Barn. That year he recorded one of his biggest numbers, *'Leven Miles from Leavenworth* and a year or so later *Squaws Along the Yukon,* which was revived a decade later with great success by Hank Thompson and the Brazos Valley Boys.

In 1947, Lewis appeared in two "Durango Kid" movies and then toured until 1950, when he settled in Seattle, where he initially had radio programs on KIRO. Later, Lewis started *Rainier Ranch*, a popular show on KING-TV.

His greatest television success came with *Sheriff Tex's Safety Junction*, a children's program on the same station. It made Lewis a hero with local youth. Jim Lewis spent seven years as "Sheriff Tex" at King Records. His recordings such as *Ophelia the Cow* and *Safety Songs* increasingly reflected his new orientation toward the children's market. Later, he took the program to Vancouver, British Columbia, for a time.

Back in Seattle, Lewis played several more years in the clubs, most notably the Golden Apple. In the mid-80's, he began to get some recognition as a Western Swing pioneer. Cattle Germany Records in Germany re-issued five albums of his early transcriptions and recordings and another one which spotlighted the talents of Jack Rivers. IMT

RECOMMENDED ALBUMS:
"Texas Jim Lewis and His Lone Star Cowboys, Vol. 1" (Cattle Germany)(1981)
"Texas Jim Lewis and His Lone Star Cowboys, Vol. 2" (Cattle Germany)(1981)
"Squaws Along the Yukon" (Cattle Germany)(1985)
"Rootin, Tootin, Hootenanny" (Cattle Germany)(1985)
"The King of North Western Swing" (Cattle Germany)(1985)
Jack Rivers:
"Just Plain Old Ordinary Me" (Cattle Germany)(1985)

LIGHT CRUST DOUGHBOYS

When Formed:	**1932**
Members:	
W. Lee O'Daniel	**Leader, Emcee**
Bob Wills	**Fiddle**
Herman Arnspiger	**Guitar**
Milton Brown	**Lead Vocals**
"Sleepy" Johnson	**Guitar, Fiddle, Tenor Guitar, Tenor Banjo**
Durwood Brown	**Guitar**
Tommy Duncan	**Lead Vocals**
Clifford Gross	**Fiddle**
Leon McAuliffe	**Steel Guitar**
"Zeke" Campbell	**Electric Guitar**
"Knocky" Parker	**Piano**
Marvin Montgomery	**Tenor Banjo**
Eddie Dunn	**Emcee**
Dick Reinhart	**Bass, Vocals**
Cousin Cecil Brower	**Fiddle**
Jack Perry	**Emcee**

Other Members:
Jim Boyd, Pat O'Daniel, Mike O'Daniel, Bert Dodson

The Light Crust Doughboys provide the important stepping stone in the development of Western Swing that would come to full bloom with Bob Wills and His Texas Playboys and Milton Brown's Musical Brownies, among others.

The start of the Light Crust Doughboys goes back to 1929 when Bob Wills and Herman Arnspiger got together and formed the Wills Fiddle Band. Then, at the end of the year, Milton Brown was added and in 1930, they began broadcasting on WBAP Fort Worth, Texas. When their show became sponsored by the Aladdin Mantle Lamp Company, the group was renamed the Aladdin Laddies.

In 1931, the threesome began working for Burrus Mill and Elevator Company advertising Light Crust Flour on KFJZ Fort Worth with two shows, at 7:00 am and noon. The General Manager of Burrus Mills was Wilbert Lee "Pappy" O'Daniel, who engaged them and acted as emcee on their shows. Wills, Arnspiger and Brown worked in other non-musical capacities for the company when not playing. Brown was a salesman while the other two were dock loaders and truck drivers. They also played some evenings at the Crystal Springs Ballroom in Fort Worth. The trio became known initially as the Forth Worth Doughboys and then assumed the name of the Light Crust Doughboys.

By January 1931, with W. Lee promoting the band, their show on KFJZ was also broadcast on WBAP at the prime 12:30 pm slot (they moved to the latter in 1933). By 1931 year's end, they were also broadcasting over

WOAI San Antonio and KPRC Houston. Later, the Southwest Quality Network, including KTAT Fort Worth and KOMA Oklahoma City, was added.

In 1932, Arnspiger left the group and was replaced by "Sleepy" Johnson, who played tenor banjo, rhythm style. The group became a quartet with the addition, that year, of Milton Brown's brother, Durwood Brown. On February 9 that year, they recorded two sides for Victor Records in Dallas, *Nancy Jane* and *Sunbonnet Sue*. However, the records lacked the group's broadcast vitality and did not fare well.

Gray clouds were on the horizon. O'Daniel told the group to cease playing dances. This was the start of bad feeling between Wills and his leader. As a result of O'Daniel's edict, Milton Brown left and formed his Musical Brownies. He died in 1936, as a result of an auto crash. Had he lived, he would no doubt have rivaled and possibly surpassed Wills in achievement. Tommy Duncan was hired as Milton's replacement after 67 vocalists had been auditioned.

During 1933 through 1935, the Light Crust Doughboys made many recordings for Vocalion, including *I'll Keep on Loving You*, *Little Rubber Dolly*, *Have I Lost Your Love Forever*, *Why Did You Lie to Me*, *Knocky Knocky*, *Gin Mill Blues*, *Blue Guitars*, *Beautiful Texas*, *On to Victory, Mr. Roosevelt*, *Gangster's Moll*, *Alamo Waltz*, *Kelly Waltz* and *Old Sweetheart of Mine*.

However, the end of the first phase of the Doughboys was looming. Arguments between O'Daniel and Wills occurred over the hiring and firing of band members and Wills' drinking. Wills was missing broadcasts and in August 1933, after several mornings, O'Daniel fired Wills, although another story says that it was over a pay dispute. Wills moved to Waco and most of the Doughboys followed. Later that year, they would become Bob Wills and His Texas Playboys.

However, for a while the name of the Light Crust Doughboys continued with Burrus. With Wills gone, O'Daniel brought in fiddler Clifford Gross from Kentucky. That same year, Leon McAuliffe, then 16, joined, but he left in 1934 to join Wills. The following year, Zeke Campbell joined, to be followed by Knocky Parker. In addition, W. Lee used his sons in the band.

Although O'Daniel left Burrus in 1935, he occasionally used the Doughboys to assist his political aspirations. Eddie Dunn joined the group as emcee and he brought with him Marvin Montgomery, Dick Reinhart, Zeke Campbell and Bert Dodson.

The following year, fiddler Cousin Cecil Brower became leader. In 1942, Burrus stopped sponsoring the group and they changed names to the Coffee Grinders, when Duncan Coffee Co. took over. However, after WWII, they reverted to the Light Crust Doughboys, with Jack Perry becoming emcee. They continued under his leadership into the 70's.

RECOMMENDED ALBUMS:

"The Light Crust Doughboys" (Audio Lab)(1959)
"String Band Swing" (Longhorn)(1981)
"The Light Crust Doughboys—1934-37" (Texas Rose)(1983)
"The Light Crust Doughboys Original Hit Songs" (Aolt)
"We're the Light Crust Doughboys from Burrus Mills" (Doughboy)
[See also W. Lee O'Daniel, Bob Wills and Milton Brown]

LILLY BROTHERS

EVERETT LILLY
(Singer, Mandolin, Banjo, Fiddle)

Given Name: Charles Everett Lilly
Date of Birth: July 1, 1924
Married: Joann
Children: Everett Alan, Tennis, Diana, La Verne, Jiles (dec'd.), Charles, Karen, Mark, Daniel

B. LILLY
(Singer, Guitar)

Given Name: Michell Burt Lilly
Date of Birth: December 15, 1921
Married: Joan
Children: Floragale, Mitchell, Monty, Daphene, Joey, Shelly, Cindy, Michael, Jody

Both Born: Clear Creek, Raleigh County, West Virginia

The Lilly Brothers began their career as an Old-Time duet on radio stations in their native West Virginia. However, with the addition of a finger-picked banjo they graduated toward a Bluegrass sound. In a musical career that spanned three active decades the Lilly Brothers played on a variety of radio stations extending from Knoxville to Wheeling. Their best known contribution to the genre, however, derived from lengthy stints at a Boston, Massachusetts, night club, the Hillbilly Ranch, where they helped to popularize Bluegrass not only in New England and the Boston area, but also among followers in the academic and intellectual world.

Natives of the remote mountain community of Clear Creek in south central West Virginia, Everett and B. Lilly grew up in a traditional mountain culture that took the commercial harmony duets of the mid-30's to their hearts. Learning the songs of the Callahan, Delmore, and Monroe Brothers, the Lilly Brothers did their first radio guest spot on the *Old Farm Hour* at WCHS Charleston about 1938 under the sobriquet Lonesome Holler Boys.

When WKLS Beckley opened in 1939, they worked for several years both as a duet and with other musicians like Dobro picker George "Speedy" Krise. In the summer of 1945, they moved to WNOX Knoxville, where they were a featured act with Lynn Davis and Molly O'Day for a while and then as half of the Smiling Mountain Boys with fiddler Burk Barbour and a banjo picking buddy from back home named Paul Taylor.

In 1948, the Lilly Brothers moved to the WWVA *Wheeling Jamboree*, where they served as the major talent in Red Belcher's Kentucky Ridge Runners unit. Soon they also made the

The Lilly Brothers *with Tex Logan (fiddle) and Don Stove (banjo) in the Confederate Mountaineers*

friendship of Benjamin "Tex" Logan, a skilled fiddler from Texas, who worked in the band and later again with the Lilly Brothers, in Boston.

The brothers cut a single for Page Records during their WWVA days and B. and Tex helped Belcher cut a pair of singles on the same label. They also cut four songs on the Cozy label of Davis, West Virginia, which were never released. After two years with Belcher, the Lilly Brothers had a financial dispute with Red and departed for WMMN Fairmont. Their sojourn there was a brief one and the boys returned to Clear Creek.

Everett soon joined Lester Flatt and Earl Scruggs, playing mandolin and singing tenor. He participated in two Columbia recording sessions in 1951, cutting a total of 14 songs with the Foggy Mountain Boys. Early in 1952, Tex Logan persuaded both Everett and B. to join him in Boston, where with the addition of Don Stover on banjo, they took Bluegrass sounds to New England.

Initially they worked at WCOP Boston on the *Hayloft Jamboree* and then at various clubs, mostly notably a long stint at the Hillbilly Ranch. They recorded some material for Event Records in 1956 and 1957 (later released on County) and albums for Folkways and Prestige International, the latter being cut and marketed in the era of the urban Folk revival. An album of live recordings from 1960 was also released in Japan, being some of the first Bluegrass to be sold in that country.

With the exception of a few brief periods such as when Everett left for a second stint with Flatt and Scruggs in 1958-59 and Don Stover toured with some other bands, the Lilly Brothers and Stover worked constantly in the Boston area from 1952 until January 1970. In the 60's, they also worked concerts at several major colleges and Folk festivals helping to disseminate Bluegrass to urban audiences.

The death of Everett Lilly's son Jiles in an auto crash on January 17, 1970, ended the Lilly career in Boston. Everett and Joann decided to get out of the city and go back to West Virginia. For a time in the fall of 1970, B. Lilly returned and the brothers had a TV show at WOAY Oak Hill, West Virginia, but B. became restless and returned to Boston.

For several years from 1971, Everett, B., Don Stover and Tex Logan made a few festival appearances each summer and the brothers cut a Gospel album for County. In September 1973, the brothers with Don Stover and Everett Alan Lilly toured Japan, where they were well received and had three albums of their appearances released. From the later 70's, they appeared together once or twice a year.

Everett worked as a school bus driver and played music on a part-time basis with his younger son, Mark. In 1979, a documentary film recounted the Lilly career; *True Facts in a Country Song* premiered at the West Virginia State Culture Center, followed by a Lilly Brothers concert. Through the 80's and up to the present, Everett and son Mark worked as part of a band called Clear Creek Crossin'. Rounder Records re-issued the Prestige International albums as well as their Page material on the initial volume of their *Early Days of Bluegrass* anthology. Rebel released a cd of their masters made for Event, which ranks among the all-time classics of traditional Bluegrass. Everett says another album recorded in the later 70's should be released soon. IMT

RECOMMENDED ALBUMS:

"Folk Songs from Southern Mountains" (Folkways)(1961)
"Bluegrass Breakdown" (Prestige International) (Rounder) (1964)
"Country Songs" (Prestige International) (Rounder)(1964)
"Live at Hillbilly Ranch" (Globe Japan)(1965)
"Early Recordings" (County)(1970)
"What Will I Leave Behind" (County)(1973)
"Holiday in Japan" (Towa)(1974)

LaWANDA LINDSEY

(Singer, Songwriter)
Date of Birth: January 12, 1953
Where Born: Tampa, Florida
Married: Bill Smith, Jr.

LaWanda is another example of a performer who became a star at a very young age. Her father, N.H. "Lefty" Lindsey, was the manager of Country radio station WEAS Savannah, Georgia, and also ran his own band, the Dixie Showboys.

LaWanda became interested in Country music when she was 5 and made her stage debut at that tender age. She was swarmed by autograph hunters, but she could not yet write her name!

She made her radio debut four years later. Shortly afterward, her father gave up the band. By 1964, she was an avid fan of Connie Smith and LaWanda's father decided to re-form the band as LaWanda Lindsey and the Dixie Show Boys.

LaWanda's talents were brought to the attention of Conway Twitty by his business manager and as a result she moved to Nashville, where she stayed with booking agent Joe Taylor and his family and played with Conway's band for two years. She signed to Chart Records in 1967 at age 14. Her first single, *Beggars Can't Be Choosers*, was released in January 1968 and did well, but didn't chart. Neither did her next four releases. She first appeared in the lists with a duet with Kenny Vernon, *Eye to Eye*, which made the Top 60 at the start of 1969. Her first solo hit was *Partly Bill*, which made the Top 50, later that year. Her most successful single was another duet with Vernon, *Pickin' Wild Mountain Berries*, in 1970. She was named "Teen Country Queen" by a group of Country deejays.

During 1972, LaWanda's career was taken over by the Buck Owens Organization. While a regular on the *Wheeling Jamboree*, she became friends with Susan Raye, who was singing with Owens, and in November 1972, he contacted LaWanda and she signed with Owens' Omac Artist Corporation. At the same time, she signed to Capitol Records and began appearing on *Hee Haw*. Her most successful single on the label was the 1974 Top 30 record *Hello Out There*. During the mid-70's, LaWanda and her family moved from Nashville to Bakersfield in California, the center of the Owens empire.

By 1977, LaWanda had left Capitol and was on Mercury. She had two further chart records, *Walk Right Back* (1977) and *I'm a Woman in Love* (1978), both of which only reached the basement level. She left the business when she married club owner Bill Smith, Jr., and they now operate several clubs in the Albuquerque area.

RECOMMENDED ALBUMS:

"Pickin' Wild Mountain Berries" (Chart)(1970) [With Kenny Vernon]
"LaWanda Lindsey's Greatest Hits, Vol. 1" (Chart)(1971)
"This Is LaWanda Lindsey" (Capitol)(1974)

LINE DANCING TO COUNTRY MUSIC

By Virginia Rainey

Line dancing is a form of dancing where an individual can get on the dance floor even if they do not have a partner. This allows many singles to dance that ordinarily might not get the opportunity.

It would seem that Line dancing started with the Twist in the 1960's. This individual style of dancing grew out of the "break-away" part of rock'n'roll, becoming Disco dancing as we know it today. Line dancing is enormously popular in some parts of the U.S. and the U.K.

One of the earliest Line dances, the "Four Corner," was probably borrowed from the Rock world. The "Texas Freeze," another very early Line dance, is done wherever one might travel, sometimes with a little variation in step and maybe called something else, but usually with the same beat. "Slappin' Leather" or the "Louie" are very similar to the "Texas Freeze," with just added steps.

The "Texas Freeze" is also sometimes referred to as the "Freeze" or the old "Bus Stop." The "Electric Slide," which is danced in every type of club, is a spin-off of the "Texas Freeze," but has two added steps and counts when the dancer moves forward. Dancers do not always start these dances in the same place.

The "Tush Push" and the "County Line" come from the ballroom with some cha-cha steps. Probably one of the most widely recognized Line dances is the "Achy Breaky," which was choreographed by Melanie Greenwood for Billy Ray Cyrus' "Achy Breaky Heart." For more information contact: PO Box 62, Sanger, Texas 76266; telephone (817) 458-7276. For Line dancing videos contact: Reel Productions, Inc., PO Box 41115, Nashville, Tennessee 37204; telephone: (615) 297-5036.

GLOSSARY:

Emphasis: Accent or added force; can be through larger amount of space covered.

Fan (C.E.J.): Can be performed with two or more people. Right hand over left. On the moving part of the C.E.J. (the polka steps), the person on the right (outside) rotates to the other side on one set of polka steps. It is important that the next person waits until the next set of polka steps starts to begin their rotation to the inside.

Grapevine: (Right or left) Example: Right Grapevine:

1. Right foot step to the right side
2. Left foot step behind the right foot
3. Right foot to the right side
4. Bring left foot even, kick or stomp with the left foot on the 4th beat.

Grapevine (Turning) (Right or left): In the three steps that form the grapevine, turn 360°, then on the 4th beat, kick, stomp or bring the foot over.

Hip Bump: Right hip pump—push hip to the right, with weight on the right foot.

Hold: A pause, no beat or accent (requires a specific count or amount of time).

Home: Normally the starting position used in Line dances and mixers.

Jazz Step: Right Jazz step—cross right over left, step back slightly with left, bring right foot even, transfer weight to left foot.

Kick-Ball-Change: Right kick-ball-change—kick out with the right foot, bring even with left and put weight on right, then quickly transfer weight to the left foot. This is three steps, but you use two beats of music.

Landmark: When everyone does the same thing at the same time. That is, clap their hands or stomp their feet at the same time.

Lend: The indication of intent to move in a direction just prior to actual movement.

Line of Dance: The counterclockwise direction in a circle formation. Most dances travel in this direction.

Lunge: Right lunge—lean upper body to the right, shifting weight to the right foot and return.

Measure: A grouping of beats. Sometimes referred to as a bar or a set.

Meter: The grouping of beats and accents in music.

Off Beat: Anything that falls in between the beat of the music.

On Beat: Anything that falls directly on the actual beat of the music.

LITTLE GINNY (a.k.a. GINNY BROWN)

(Singer, Songwriter, Guitar, Actress)

Given Name: Ginnette Patricia Brown
Date of Birth: March 15, 1953
Where Born: Kingston-upon-Thames, Surrey, England
Married: Paul Kirkby

Ginny Brown started her career as featured vocalist with the world-famous Ivy Benson All-Girls Band as Little Ginny at the tender age of 15.

She embarked upon a solo career as a Country singer and was soon a regular performer on BBC radio and TV, including Christmas shows and an appearance on *In Concert* on BBC2-TV. She recorded with the BBC Orchestra, as well as with her own musicians. She was twice named "Top Female Country Singer" at the Wembley Festival in England.

In 1986, Ginny joined forces with Tammy Cline to form Two Hearts. In short time, they were named "Top European Duo" in the Country Music Round Up National Poll. As a result, they represented Britain at Fan Fair in Nashville. They both toured the U.K. with the hit production of the musical *Pump Boys and Dinettes.*

In 1989, Two Hearts released their eponymous album. In 1992, the duo broke up when Tammy announced her retirement. Ginny has gone on and expanded her scope by appearing in pantomime in Britain, starring in *Jack and the Beanstalk* and *Cinderella.* In 1994, Ginny toured the U.K. with her Best of British Country show. JAB

RECOMMENDED ALBUM:

"Two Hearts" (PCM)(1989) [With Tammy Cline]

LITTLE TEXAS

When Formed: 1988
Members:

Tim Rushlow	**Lead Vocals**
Dwayne O'Brien	**Acoustic Guitar, Vocals**
Porter Howell	**Lead Guitar, Vocals**
Duane Propes	**Bass Guitar, Vocals**
Brady Seals	**Keyboards, Vocals**
Del Gray	**Drums**

Little Texas is a Country-Rock band that follows in the tradition of Poco and Pure Prairie League. Their looks may not fit in with the accepted image of a Country act—they look more like a Heavy Metal band—but long hair and flashy stage apparel should not detract from the fact that they play solid Country-Rock.

The nucleus of the band dates back to 1984, when Tim Rushlow and Dwayne O'Brien met in Arlington, Texas. Tim's father was Tom Rushlow, who was the lead singer of 60's group Moby Dick and the Whalers. Tim and Dwayne worked together until Tim moved to Nashville in 1986. Dwayne finished getting his degree in chemistry at East Central State University in Oklahoma and then moved to Nashville in 1987. The two started playing again and then joined up with Texans Porter Howell and Duane Propes, who were at the time students at Nashville's Belmont University. The band hit the road, and at a fair in Massachusetts, they shared a stage with Brady Seals (a nephew of legendary songwriter Troy Seals, and cousin to Country star Dan Seals) and Del Gray, who were then touring with Country performers Sandi Powell and Josh Logan. Shortly after, the two joined the band.

By the fall of 1988, the band's future manager, Christy DiNapoli, was showing interest and got Warner Brothers' Doug Grau to see the group live in Birmingham. Grau signed the group to a development deal with the label. It was at this stage that they settled on the name "Little Texas," after the name of the road leading to the Graus' farm, Little Texas Lane. They then scraped up enough money to buy a $300 1972 Chevy van and a home-made trailer, and set off on a series of cross-country club dates, getting together material for their debut album.

At the end of 1990, Little Texas began to work in the studio and an initial single, *Some Guys Have All the Love*, was released in July 1991. By September it was on the charts and rose to the Top 10, staying around the lists for 5 months. The video went to No.1 on TNN. They then released their first album, ***First Time for Everything***, which hit the Country album chart in March 1992 and reached the Top 20. Their three singles in 1992 all fared well, with the album title track reaching the Top 15, followed by *You and Forever and Me* peaking at No.5 and *What Were You Thinkin'* reaching the Top 20 in 1993. *I'd Rather Miss You* (Top 20) was the last single to chart from the first album.

Little Texas then released its second album, ***Big Time***. This was to be the turning point in the band's career. *What Might Have Been* reached the Top 3 and crossed over to the Pop Top 80 and was followed by *God Bless Texas,* which went Top 5 Country and crossed to the Pop Top 60. The band then charted Top 75 with *Peaceful Easy Feeling*, a track from ***Common Thread: The Songs of the Eagles***. In 1994, Little Texas went to No.1 with *My Love,* and the album ***Big Time***, in quick succession, went Gold and then Platinum. At the ACM awards, Little Texas was named "Vocal Group of the Year."

RECOMMENDED ALBUMS:
"First Time for Everything" (Warner Brothers)(1991)
"Big Time" (Warner Brothers)(1994)

Bill Lloyd refer FOSTER & LLOYD

HANK LOCKLIN

(Singer, Songwriter, Guitar)

Given Name:	**Lawrence Hankins Locklin**
Date of Birth:	**February 15, 1918**
Where Born:	**McClellan, Florida**
Married:	**Willa Jean Murphy**
Children:	**Margaret, Maurice, Beth**

Hank Locklin had one of the more pleasing and popular Country voices of the 60's. His numbers were often quite popular in Britain and Ireland, some being the kind of "sing along" lyrics that found favor there.

A native of the Florida Panhandle, Hank grew up and attended school in Munson and won his first amateur contest in nearby Milton at age 10. As a young man, Hank worked on the WPA and on various other laboring jobs. Hank took his initial radio position at WCOA in nearby Pensacola in 1942. He also made appearances on the airwaves in Panama City and Mobile, Alabama.

Military service soon intervened and after the war, Hank's career took him westward to Louisiana and Texas, where he further developed his musical talents in association with such veteran Country vocalists as Harmie Smith (1908-1973). At various times, Hank was heard on Shreveport's *Louisiana Hayride* over KWKH, Dallas' *Big D Jamboree* over KRLD, and on KLIT Houston as well as at smaller radio outlets.

The legendary ***Hank Locklin***

Other than a few releases on Decca, most of Locklin's early recordings appeared on Bill McCall's 4 Star label. His first hit came in 1949 with a song titled *The Same Sweet Girl*, a Top 10 Country hit. Four years later *Let Me Be the One* reached No.1, staying there for 3 weeks out of a total stay on the charts of 8 months, giving Locklin national recognition as a Country vocalist. It also helped land him a contract with RCA Victor.

Although his first appearance on the charts for the label was a cover of the gigantic Webb Pierce-Red Sovine hit *Why Baby, Why*, Hank came into his own in 1957 with the Top 5 hit (it stayed on the Country charts for nearly 10 months and also went Top 70 Pop) *Geisha Girl*, a song which along with Bobby Helms' *Fraulein* inaugurated a brief fad for songs featuring foreign love themes. RCA Victor quickly got on the bandwagon by recording an entire thematic Locklin album dealing with the subject, entitled ***Foreign Love***. From then on for the next dozen years, Locklin appeared regularly on the charts.

Hank had two major hits in succession in 1958, his own song *Send Me the Pillow That You Dream On* (Top 5 Country/Top 80 Pop) and the Country Top 3 success *It's a Little More Like Heaven/Blue Grass Skirt*. However, his biggest winner, *Please Help Me, I'm Falling*, in 1960, spent 14 weeks at No.1 and remained on the charts for 8 months. Furthermore, it reached the Pop Top 10 in both the U.S. and the U.K. In November 1960, he became a *Grand Ole Opry* member (at writing, he is still a member).

Hank followed up with *One Step Ahead of My Time* (1960) and *From Here to There to You* (1961), both of which reached the Top 15, but *Happy Birthday to Me*, the flip-side of *You're the Reason* (Top 15), and *Happy Journey* both made the Top 10 in 1961 and 1962 respectively.

Hank had made his first European tour in 1957 and quickly became a favorite in Ireland. He responded with an album of Irish songs in 1964. Three more of his songs made the British charts during the 60's, one of the stronger ones being *We're Gonna Go Fishin'* in 1962, which was also a Country Top 15 hit. Over the years Hank made more trips to Great Britain and Ireland. He also did more theme albums, including tributes to such major musical figures as Roy Acuff, Eddy Arnold, and Hank Williams.

Hank's major successes between 1963 and 1970 were *Flyin' South* (Top 25, 1963), *Followed Closely By My Teardrops* (Top 15, 1964) and in 1967, the Top 10 hit *The Country Hall of Fame*. His chart ratings began slipping by 1970 and RCA reacted by combining him with Danny Davis and the Nashville Brass. This resulted in a brace of minor hits, including a revival of *Please Help Me, I'm Falling*.

After 1972, however, he left RCA and went over to MGM, releasing an album in 1975. He then moved on to Plantation, which released three albums over the next six years. During his peak time in the 60's, many of Hank's earlier 4 Star efforts remained in print via album releases on King and Pickwick/ Hilltop.

While retaining his *Opry* membership throughout his career, Hank Locklin managed to keep a certain degree of independence from Nashville, preferring to reside on his farm near Milton, Florida, when not touring, recording, or appearing on the *Opry* stage. Raising beef cattle on his farm, he took the unofficial subtitle "Mayor of McClellan, Florida," although the community is so small that it doesn't appear on many maps. Unlike many aging Country singers, Hank retains the strong, clear voice that has been his musical distinction. IMT

RECOMMENDED ALBUMS:
"The Best of Hank Locklin" (King)(1961)
"Foreign Love" (RCA Victor)(1958)
"Please Help Me, I'm Falling" (RCA)(1960)
"A Tribute to Roy Acuff" (RCA Victor)(1962)
"Irish Songs, Country Style" (RCA Victor)(1964)
"Hank Locklin Sings Hank Williams" (RCA)(1964)
"Hank Locklin Sings Eddy Arnold" (RCA)(1965)
"The Best of Hank Locklin" (RCA Victor)(1966)
"Send Me the Pillow You Dream On" (RCA Victor)(1967)
"Country Hall of Fame" (RCA Victor)(1968)
"My Love Song for You" (RCA Victor)(1968)
"Softly" (RCA Victor)(1969)
"With Danny Davis & the Nashville Brass" (RCA Victor)(1970)
"Mayor of McClellan, Florida" (RCA Victor)(1972)
"Hank Locklin" (MGM)(1975)
"Golden Hits" (Plantation)(1977)
"There Never Was a Time" (Plantation)(1977)
"Greatest Hits" (Plantation)(1981)

Bud Logan refer BLUE BOYS

JIMMIE LOGSDON

(Singer, Deejay, Songwriter, Guitar)

Given Name:	**James Lloyd Logsdon**
Date of Birth:	**April 1, 1922**
Where Born:	**Panther, Kentucky**
Married:	**1. Evelyn (div.)**
	2. Mary Gertrude (div.)
	3. Mary Gertrude (remarried)
Children:	**James Richard, Mary Lee**

Although Jimmie Logsdon never had any of his singles appear in the Country charts, he became a very popular singer during the 50's and more importantly, one of the top Country deejays.

Jimmie was born the son of a Methodist minister and started his singing career at the age of 12, when he and his sister, Martha Jean, sang in the choir at their father's church. He had clarinet lessons at an early age and played in the Fleetwoods High School band, then started playing guitar (he borrowed his neighbor's instrument). He married, for the first time, in 1940 and four years later, during WWII, he enlisted in the U.S. Air Force. He spent two years in the service, where he learned electronics and radio technology. While in the military, he entertained his buddies and wrote songs. Upon returning to civilian life, in 1946, he opened a record and radio shop in LeGrange, Kentucky. Buying his first guitar in 1948, Jimmie continued to entertain professionally and in 1950 got his first big break with the help of his friend Cliff Mercer, who worked on radio station WGN in Chicago. Logsdon started his own 15-minute Country show on radio station WLOU Louisville, Kentucky. Later that year, he moved to another Louisville station, WINN.

Jimmie's show, on which he played and sang, caught the attention of Decca Records, which signed him to the label in October 1952. Jimmie was also helped by his close friends Hank Williams, whom he had met at the Memorial Auditorium, Louisville, and toured with during 1952, and songwriter Vic McAlpin. Logsdon's first release was *I Want to Be Moma'd/That's When I'll Love You the Best*. In January of the following year, Jimmie released a double-sided Hank Williams tribute entitled *The Death of Hank Williams* and *Hank Williams Sings the Blues No More*.

In the spring of 1953, he got a weekly sponsored TV show on WHAS-TV, then the world's most powerful TV station, in addition to his radio show on WKLO. His *Country & Western Music Show* on WHAS-TV went out live and featured Jimmie's backing group, the Golden Harvest Boys. The members were Clyde Coffey (steel guitar), Howard Whited (electric guitar) and Lonnie Pierce (fiddle).

Jimmie released three more singles for Decca in 1953, the final outing being *Papaya Mama/In the Mission of Saint Augustine*, but not one made the lists.

By the beginning of 1956, he had one release for Dot, *Cold Cold Rain/Midnight Blues* and by the following year, Jimmie surfaced on Starday with *Can't Make Up My Mind/No Longer Do I Cry*. That same year, he recorded a pair of singles for Roulette under the name of Jimmie Lloyd. These recordings, *Beginning of the End/Where the Rio Rosa Flows* and *I Got a Rocket in My Pocket/You're Gone Baby*, are now collector's items. In June 1962, Jimmie joined the highly prestigious WCKY Cincinnati, taking over the night-time spot from Wayne Raney. Soon Jimmie's "Howdy, neighbors" became a familiar greeting.

Jimmie was also an adept songwriter, and both Johnny Horton and Jazz great Woody Herman recorded the Logsdon song *No True Love*, while *Where the Rio Rosa Flows* was cut by Carl Perkins.

Jimmie signed to King Records in 1962, and the following year, he released the album ***Howdy Neighbors***. After WCKY changed their format in 1964, Jimmie relocated to WTVF in Mobile, Alabama. In October 1965, Logsdon became WCLU Louisville's first deejay. He left the station to work in his brother-in-law's swimming pool business and do some commercials, nightclub singing, and deejaying on WGEE and WZIP. In 1976, he went to work for the Commonwealth of Kentucky's Labor Department. Nick Tosches included a chapter on Jimmie in his *Unsung Heroes of Rock'n'Roll* (1984). BM/IMT

RECOMMENDED ALBUMS:

"Howdy Neighbors" (King)(1963)
"Doing It Hank's Way" (Castle Germany)(1980)
"I Got a Rocket in My Pocket" (Bear Family Germany)(1993)

LARRIE LONDIN

(Drums)
Date of Birth: **October 15, 1943**
Where Born: **Norfolk, Virginia**
Married: **Debbie**
Date of Death: **August 24, 1992**

Larrie Londin was one of Nashville's premier studio musicians. His forceful and creative drumming technique made him a favorite of many producers and artists. Londin played on thousands of recording sessions for such artists as Merle Haggard, Dolly Parton, Charley Pride, Barbara Mandrell, Hank Williams, Jr., Jerry Reed, Crystal Gayle, Charlie Rich, K.T. Oslin, Vince Gill, Rosanne Cash, Ricky Skaggs, Brenda Lee, Chet Atkins, the Judds, Ronnie Milsap and Reba McEntire.

Larrie developed his interest in playing the drums when he was 8 years old, growing up in Miami. He was on the boxing team at school and to help with the family finances, took a job as a bodyguard for an older student who played drums in local night clubs. The crowds were often unruly and picked on the young drummer, who was small in stature and of Cuban descent. With Larrie by his side, no one bothered him.

By the time he was 15, Larrie was playing drums in a band called the Tornadoes. A few years later, the band changed its name to the Headliners and moved to Detroit from Miami. The band was hired as studio staff musicians for Motown Records and worked for 9 years backing up artists such as the Temptations, Marvin Gaye and the Supremes. The Headliners had their most successful single with *We Call It Fun*.

Chet Atkins encouraged Larrie to move to Nashville when the two met at a Texas golf tournament, in 1963. Six years later, when studio work was slowing down in Detroit, Larrie made the trip south to Music City.

Larrie discovered that the recording scene in Nashville was very different from Detroit. Although drums were included on most records, they were not played with the force and energy for which Larrie was noted. Larrie's philosophy was that drums were more than just a necessary evil on a record, they were an integral part of the musical expression. His exciting performance on records made waves in the Nashville recording industry. Larrie was the first to use electronic synthesized drums in a Nashville studio.

A highlight of Larrie's career was performing with Elvis Presley, who was so impressed with his drumming on his studio records that he invited Larrie to tour with him in 1976-1977. In later years, Larrie occasionally took a break from studio work to tour with other artists including the Everly Brothers and Rosanne Cash.

In the 80's, Larrie divided his time between Nashville and Los Angeles. One of his finest moments was playing on the 1980 Merle Haggard No.1, *I Think I'll Just Sit Here and Drink*. He was often called on to play on the records of major Rock artists such as Journey and Steve Perry. Larrie was a major supporter of new talent and conducted drum clinics around the country. While conducting a clinic in Denton, Texas, on April 24, 1992, Larrie suffered a cardiac arrest. He was returned to a Nashville hospital, but lapsed into a coma and died on August 24. JIE

RECOMMENDED ALBUMS:

For Larrie Londin's body of work, just check out the musicians on Country albums from 1970 on, as well as albums by Rock acts such as Journey and Steve Perry.

LONE PINE AND BETTY CODY

LONE PINE
(Vocals, Guitar)
Given Name: **Harold John Breau**

Date of Birth: June 5, 1916
Where Born: Pea Cove, Maine
Married: 1. Rita M. Coté (Betty Cody)
2. Bernice
Date of Death: March 26, 1977

BETTY CODY
(Vocals, Guitar)
Given Name: Rita M. Coté
Date of Birth: August 17, 1921
Where Born: Sherbrooke, Quebec, Canada
Married: 1. Harold John Breau (Lone Pine)
2. George Binette
Children: Leonard (Lenny Breau) (dec'd.), Dickie, Dennie, Bobby

The team of Lone Pine and Betty Cody, who worked both together and separately, was one of the more notable husband-wife Country teams of the 40's and 50's. They were also representative of, and perhaps the most successful of, a brand of traditional Country music that took root and flourished in rural New England and the adjacent Maritime Provinces of Canada.

Harold Breau grew up near Old Town, Maine, and according to one story received his atypical nickname from the Penobscot Indians. He initiated his radio career at WABI in Bangor in the mid-30's and soon came to lead a group known as the Lone Pine Mountaineers. Meanwhile, young Rita Coté had moved to Auburn, Maine, with her parents. She took an interest in singing at an early age.

About 1936, her brother brought home a Patsy Montana record and the "little French girl," as Rita was known, determined to perfect the technique. The following year, Rita started to sing on radio at WCOU in nearby Lewiston with a group called Curly and the Country Boys. In 1938, she met Lone Pine in the radio studio and the two married on June 29, 1940. Rita began using the stage name "Betty Lou," later changing to Betty Cody, which was an Anglicized form of her maiden name.

The Lone Pine Mountaineers continued on radio in Maine through the 40's and into the 50's. In 1952, they signed with RCA Victor and each had several solo and duet releases over the next three or four years. Ray Couture, an excellent lead guitar picker, worked in their band and later came to Wheeling where he took the stage name "Abner Doolittle." The latter taught the fundamentals of guitar to the Breaus' older son Lenny, who went on to eventual world renown as Jazz guitarist Lenny Breau (he was murdered in 1984).

Meanwhile, Lone Pine and Betty Cody waxed such memorable duets as *Trail of the Lonesome Pine* and *It's Goodbye and So Long to You*, a cover of which by Mac Wiseman became a Bluegrass classic. Betty's record of *Tom Tom Yodel* became a major hit in Canada and her *I Found Out More Than You Ever Knew* made the Country Top 10 in December 1953. This was an answer song to the Davis Sisters' No.1 that year, *I Forgot More (Than You'll Ever Know)*. From 1953, Lone Pine and Betty Cody worked as regulars on the *World's Original Jamboree* at WWVA Wheeling, West Virginia.

Sometime later in the 50's, the Breaus went to Winnipeg, Manitoba, where they subsequently split. Hal "Lone Pine," as he generally became known in this later period, remained based in Winnipeg, where he cut albums for the Canadian label Arc, some with a girl vocalist named Jean Ward. Later, he returned to Maine and remarried, working at some of his old haunts in New England and the Maritimes until his death. By then, several of his songs such as *When It's Apple Blossom Time in Annapolis Valley* and *Prince Edward Island Is Heaven to Me* had become Canadian standards.

Betty Cody remained out of music for some years until her children had grown older. In the early 70's, she toured some with Dick Curless and played one night a week for ten years (1972-1982) at the Poland Springs Inn. She remarried in 1979, the same year that she cut a new record album.

Today Betty makes her home near Lisbon Falls, Maine. The petite lady still makes an occasional appearance with her third son, Dennis. Betty's younger sister Flo and her husband Gene Hooper (b. 1924) had a somewhat less spectacular although more durable Country music career that continues to the present. They all sometimes do shows with Allen McHale's Old-Time Radio Gang. Both Lone Pine and Betty Cody have had albums of their recordings from the 50's reissued in Germany. IMT

Lone Pine and Betty Cody

RECOMMENDED ALBUMS:
"Lone Pine & His Mountaineers" (RCA Camden)
"Hal 'Lone Pine'" (Arc)(ca. 1960)
"More Show Stoppers" (Arc)(ca. 1961)
"Songs Everyone Remembers" (Arc)(ca. 1962)
"Coast of Maine" (Arc)(ca. 1963)
"Betty Cody Singing Again" (1979)
"Hal Lone Pine and His Mountaineers" (Castle Germany)(ca. 1979)
"Betty Cody's Country Souvenir Album" (Cattle Germany)(1985)
"Duets & Memories" (Elmwood Station)(1992) (cassette)

LONESOME PINE FIDDLERS, The

When Formed: 1938

EZRA CLINE
(Leader, Bass Fiddle)
Date of Birth: January 13, 1907
Where Born: Baisden, West Virginia
Married: Margaret Cline
Children: Patsy, Ireland ("Scotty")
Date of Death: July 11, 1984
Other significant Lonesome Pine Fiddler members include:
Charlie Cline, Curly Ray Cline, Lee Cline, Ireland "Ned" Cline, Billy Edwards, Melvin Goins, Ray Goins, Walter Hensley, Gordon Jennings, Udell McPeak, Landon Messer, Ray Morgan, Bob Osborne, Larry Richardson, Lowell Varney, Jimmy Williams, Paul Williams (Paul Humphries) (Recording sessions only: Timmy Cline, Charles "Rex" Parker, Albert Puntari, James Carson)

The Lonesome Pine Fiddlers constituted an Appalachian Country music group that in some three decades of existence helped pioneer Bluegrass music, although the band's style varied somewhat with its personnel at any given time. In the beginning, the Fiddlers were a mountain string band and for a while in the later 50's played contemporary Country.

The Lonesome Pine Fiddlers originated with Ezra Cline of Baisden, West Virginia, who formed a band about 1938 consisting of himself and his teenage cousins (and brothers-in-law) Ray and Ned Cline. When they started a radio program at WHIS Bluefield, they added an aspiring singer-guitarist named Gordon Jennings to their group.

WWII curtailed their activity for a time and Ned and Jennings went to St. Louis to play prior to Ned's being shipped to Europe as an army private, where he died in the Normandy invasion. When the band regrouped after the war and recommenced their radio work at WHIS, young Charlie Cline joined the group. He and Curly featured a Delmore Southern-styled duet as the band's most distinguished feature. Late in

1949 the Cline Brothers dropped out and Ezra hired a fiddler named Ray Morgan and the duo of Bob Osborne and Larry Richardson to replace them. This combination gave them a full Bluegrass sound, which was excellently displayed in the four sides they waxed for Cozy in March 1950, especially the original song *Pain in My Heart*, which was leased to Coral and also quickly covered by Flatt and Scruggs on Mercury.

After Bob and Larry left the Fiddlers in mid-1951, Ezra got Curly Ray back, along with a pair of talented teenagers—Jimmy Williams on mandolin and Paul Williams on guitar. When the former left to go with Mac Wiseman, Ezra secured another banjo picker, 16-year-old Ray Goins. This foursome, with borrowed mandolinist Rex Parker, recorded four sides for RCA Victor in May 1952 and another four that October. That fall the band moved to WOAY Oak Hill and in January 1953 to WJR Detroit.

Charlie Cline had returned to pick banjo during the Fiddlers' sojourn in Detroit. The group cut six more numbers for Victor at a session in Chicago, including their best-known song, *Dirty Dishes Blues,* and a pair of banjo originals by Charlie Cline. In mid-November Charlie went back to Bill Monroe and Paul Williams went off to military service. Ezra and Curly Ray got Ray Goins and his brother Melvin to replace them and relocated at WLSI Pikeville, Kentucky.

The Lonesome Pine Fiddlers remained based at Pikeville for the remainder of their existence. They had a daily radio show at WLSI for several years. In 1954 they had two more four-song sessions for RCA Victor in February and September, respectively. In addition to Melvin, Ray, Curly Ray, and Ezra, they got James Carson, then at WNOX, to play mandolin, and Charlie Cline also came over and did the February session. Their final RCA outing produced *Windy Mountain* and *No Curb Service,* which also became Bluegrass classics.

In 1955, first Ray and then Melvin Goins departed from the band to be replaced by a pair of young Virginians, Billy Edwards on banjo and Udell McPeak, who developed a fine harmony duet. According to Melvin Goins, the Fiddlers had been offered the sponsored program by Martha White at WSM that Flatt and Scruggs subsequently accepted. He believes that Ezra's rejection of this opportunity prevented their gaining major Bluegrass immortality.

Be that as it may, the band continued to flourish in Appalachia. When Billy and Udell departed in 1957, Charlie Cline and his wife Lee joined Curly and Ezra and the band went modern for a couple of years with Charlie switching to electric lead guitar, and the group worked a live television show at WSAZ Huntington.

In 1961, the Lonesome Pine Fiddlers obtained a weekly TV program at WCYB Bristol, Virginia. Ezra went back to Bluegrass and got Melvin and Ray Goins working again with him and Curly Ray. The band also became active in recording, cutting three albums for Starday and backing Hylo Brown on another.

From 1964, the Fiddlers became part-time, doing shows from time to time with Ezra and Curly, using Lowell Varney and Landon Messer on respective banjo and guitar. When Curly Ray Cline joined the Stanley Brothers in 1966, they became even less active. Ezra and his wife, Margaret, had been operating a restaurant in Pikeville for some years and the others had moved on to other positions. Nonetheless, they are fondly remembered as a pioneer group in the field and their early recordings have all been reissued on both album and cd. Their Starday efforts are treasured by collectors. Anecdotal tales about their activities as a struggling mountain band with their "candy shows" in coal camps and hill country communities show signs of entering regional folklore.

In later years Ezra Cline moved back to Gilbert, West Virginia, and remained active in community action and senior citizens programs for some years prior to his death. In November 1988, the Cline and Goins brothers cut a Lonesome Pine Fiddlers' reunion album which contained both songs and reminiscences, with Curly Ray's son Timmy filling in on bass. It was released on cassette only. Charlie Cline has kept their name alive for his own band, but the Goins Brothers come closer to replicating the Lonesome Pine Fiddlers' Bluegrass sound. IMT

RECOMMENDED ALBUMS:

"The Lonesome Pine Fiddlers" (Starday)(1961) [Largely reissued as "Kentucky Bluegrass" (Nashville)]
"Bluegrass!" (Starday)(1962)
"Hylo Brown Meets the Lonesome Pine Fiddlers" (Starday)(1963)
"More Bluegrass!" (Starday)(1963)
"The Lonesome Pine Fiddlers" (Collector's Classics)(ca. 1974)
"Early Bluegrass, Volume I" (Old Homestead)(1979)
"Early Bluegrass, Volume II" (Old Homestead)(1983)
"Windy Mountain" (Bear Family Germany)(1992) [Complete Cozy and Victor masters]
"Lonesome Pine Fiddlers Reunion" (Riverside cassette)
(See also Charlie Cline, Curly Ray Cline, Goins Brothers, Osborne Brothers, Lowell Varney.)

***The Lonesome Pine Fiddlers** led by Ezra Cline*

HUBERT LONG

(Industry Executive)

Given Name: Hubert Long
Date of Birth: December 3, 1923
Where Born: Poteet, Texas
Date of Death: September 7, 1982

Although Hubert Long died at the young age of 58, he had by then made himself one of the most influential people in Country music. His election to the Country Music Hall of Fame just seven years later attested to that.

Long was raised in Freer, Texas, and played the trumpet and drums in the high school band. Upon graduation, he served three years in the South Pacific in the U.S. Navy. Upon his return to civilian life, he returned to Texas and served in the record department of a dime store in Corpus Christi. In just a few weeks, he had upped their weekly sales fivefold.

However, in 1946, Long left Corpus Christi for a job with Decca Records in San Antonio. Hubert's immediate boss, at Decca, left to join RCA Victor and took Hubert with him. This meant a move to Houston, where he met the legendary Colonel Tom Parker, who was then managing Eddy Arnold. Parker hired Hubert as a publicity advance man for the Eddy Arnold Show, with the result that Long moved to Nashville, and Parker became Long's mentor.

During the early 50's, Long moved to Shreveport to became Manager of the *Louisiana Hayride*. While there, he signed Faron Young and Webb Pierce. He began to book, advise and manage several Country acts, including Johnnie and Jack, Kitty Wells, Hank Snow, Roy Drusky, Ferlin Husky and Skeeter Davis, setting up the Hubert Long Agency in 1952. In 1955, he set up the first Country music management company in Nashville, called the Stable of Stars, which represented Bill Anderson, David Houston, George Jones, Tammy Wynette, Leroy Van Dyke, Charlie Walker, Jan Howard, Faron Young, Mel Tillis, Ray Price, Del Reeves, Jim Ed Brown and Ferlin Husky. Four years later, he opened his first music publishing company, Moss Rose, named after the street he lived on. That same year, he built the SESAC Building in Nashville. The building included Long's lavishly decorated apartment.

By 1959, his business interests included the Hubert Long Agency, Music City Advertising, Moss Rose Publications, Inc. (BMI), Stallion Music, Inc. (BMI), Husky Music, Inc. (BMI), Buckhorn Music, Inc. (BMI), Woodshed Music, Inc. (BMI), Pawnee Rose Publications, Inc. (SESAC), Ramblin' Rose Publications, Inc. (ASCAP). He had publishing offices in England, Belgium, Luxembourg, France, Italy, Germany, Australia, Japan and South Africa.

Hubert Long had a reputation for feeling the market and he was a shrewd businessman, owning a lot of property on Music Row in Nashville, including the (then) Capitol Records building.

Hubert was among the instigators of the Country Music Association and the Country Music Foundation. He was the first person to serve as both President and Chairman of the CMA. He was a life member of NARAS and First President and member of the Nashville Association of Talent Directors. He was a member of the Country and Western Academy (ACM). He was an Honorary Colonel of the Governor's Staff of Tennessee, an Honorary Admiral of the Texas Navy (his favorite diversion was boating) and Honorary Colonel on the Governor's Staff of Oklahoma.

On March 29, 1982, Hubert underwent surgery for a brain tumor, but died on September 7 that year, at Baptist Hospital, Nashville.

LONZO & OSCAR

When Formed: 1944

LONZO
(Guitar, Mandolin, Banjo)
Given Name: John Y. Sullivan
Date of Birth: January 19, 1919
Married: Mildred Perry
Children: Danny, Donny, Perry
Date of Death: June 5, 1967

OSCAR
Given Name: Rollin Sullivan
Date of Birth: July 7, 1917
Married: 1. Helen (dec'd.)
2. Geneva Busby
Children: Linda Kay

Both Born: Edmonton, Kentucky
LONZO MARK I: Lloyd L. George (better known as Ken Marvin) (1944-1950)
LONZO MARK III: David Hooten (1967-)

The duo of Lonzo & Oscar ranked as the *Grand Ole Opry*'s premier musical comedy team for a quarter century, performing both original humorous songs and parodies of current hits. Actually there were three "Lonzos" during the team's four-plus decades of existence, with John Sullivan being the most significant; the original was Lloyd George (better known as Ken Marvin) and the third was David Hooten. Toward their last decade as an act, Lonzo & Oscar abandoned much of their zany comedy, becoming a nearly straight Country Bluegrass duet, placing a serious song on the *Billboard* charts and working numerous Bluegrass festivals.

The Sullivans grew up in a family of 10, not far from the cave country of south central Kentucky. Rollin and Johnny began playing square dances at a fairly early age and also played in a local group called the Kentucky Ramblers. About 1939, Rollin went to WTJS Jackson, Tennessee, and began playing in a band led by Cousin Wilbur Webrooks (later a comedian with Bill Monroe on the *Opry*) where he received the nickname "Oscar." Later Oscar went to Louisville for a while, but in 1942 journeyed to Nashville's WSM and the *Opry*, finding a job picking mandolin with Paul Howard's Arkansas Cotton Pickers. Two years later, he became a sideman for the show's new superstar, Eddy Arnold, as did his brother John and an Alabama boy named Lloyd L. George (1924-1991). Oscar and Lloyd became a comedy team and Eddy finally

*Comedy antics from **Lonzo & Oscar***

hit upon the name "Lonzo" for Lloyd. Thus was born the team of Lonzo & Oscar.

The Tennessee Plowboy also helped the duo land a contract with his own label, RCA Victor. Their initial release, *You Blacked My Blue Eyes Once Too Often, and* then *I Am My Own Grandpa* became mild hits. Soon the duo went on their own, subtitling themselves the Winston County Pea Pickers (from a locale in the Alabama hill country) and became *Opry* regulars in 1947. George left the act in 1950 to embark on a solo career as "Ken Marvin."

Johnny Sullivan stepped into the Lonzo role, holding it until his death some 17 years later. Their parodies of hits like Hank Snow's *I'm Movin' On* and other comedy numbers like *Onions, Onions* found favor with *Opry* fans, as did the antics of Clell "Cousin Jody" Summey, who contributed his own brand of humor to their act. The rival team of Homer and Jethro generally had more chartmakers, but the two continued to record, placing singles on such labels as Capitol, Starday, Columbia, Nugget, and Decca as well as album releases. In 1948, Lonzo & Oscar hit the Country singles chart with *I'm My Own Grandpa*, which reached the Top 5 and on which they were backed by Winston County Pea Pickers. They did not return to the chart until 1961, when *Country Music Time* made the Top 30.

In 1959, Oscar's wife, Helen, was killed in a car crash. John Sullivan died in mid 1967, but Oscar found a new Lonzo in David Hooten and continued the act. Hooten tended to dress in the conventional style of a Country singer of the time, but Oscar still favored the old rube comedian appearance. While they still did humorous songs, they also began to experiment with more serious material. They had a Top 30 hit in 1974 with *Traces of Life* on the GRC label. By this time Oscar had abandoned much of his hillbilly costume and the duo had moved toward a more contemporary Country sound.

In the later 70's, they shifted toward Bluegrass, hiring a banjo picker named Grady Eldridge, and included their bass player in a trio sound influenced by the success of the Osborne Brothers. They worked often on the Bluegrass festivals circuit and for a time also operated their Ranch House, a night club in Nashville. By the time they announced their retirement from the *Opry,* Hooten had played the Lonzo role longer than Johnny Sullivan. Afterward they worked part time at a jamboree show in Kentucky.

Many of their recordings have long been out of print, but Stetson re-issued their Decca album and Cowgirlboy released a collector's edition containing several of their early singles.

IMT

RECOMMENDED ALBUMS:

"America's Greatest Country Comedians" (Starday)(1960)
"Country Music Time" (Starday)(1963)
"Country Comedy Time" (Decca)(1963) [Re-released by Stetson UK in original sleeve (1989)]
"Hole in the Bottom of the Sea" (Nugget)(1965)
"Mountain Dew" (Columbia)(1968)
"Take Your Pick" (Chalet)(1972)
"Traces of Life" (GRC)(1975)
"Old & New Songs" (Brylen)(1982)
"Live at the Opry" (LOS)(1984)
"Honky Tonk Sweetheart" (Cowgirlboy Germany)(1992)

BOBBY LORD

(Singer, Songwriter, Guitar)

Date of Birth:	**January 6, 1934**
Where Born:	**Sanford, Florida**
Married:	**Violet Mozelle**
Children:	**Robert, Jr., Cabot Wesley**

Bobby Lord's recording career was somewhat fragmented, but his TV show was one of the most important Country music shows of the mid-60's.

Bobby started his career as a teenage Jazz singer on Paul Whiteman's TV show in New York City. He returned to Florida, where he studied at the University of Tampa. During his first year, he had his own TV show, *Bobby Lord Homefolks Show*. During the late 50's, he became a cast member of *Jubilee USA* out of Springfield, Missouri.

Bobby had his first chart success with Columbia Records in 1956, when *Without Your Love* made the Country Top 10. By 1960, he had joined the *Grand Ole Opry* and also appeared on most of the major TV Country shows including those of Porter Wagoner and the Wilburn Brothers. In 1961, he joined Hickory Records but it was not until 1963 that he returned to the chart with the Top 25 hit *Life Can Have Meaning*. He stayed on the label until 1966 without further chart action.

In 1965, he began his own syndicated TV show, the *Bobby Lord Show*, which featured Jerry Byrd's band, the Marijohn Wilkin Singers and most of the big names in Country music as guests. Having moved to Decca Records and with wider exposure via his TV show, Bobby began to enjoy greater continuity with chart success.

During 1968, Bobby had two Top 50 singles, *Live Your Life Out Loud* and *The True and Lasting Kind*. His other hits on the label were: *Yesterday's Letters* (Top 40) and *Rainbow Girl* (Top 30)(both 1969), *You and Me Against the World* (Top 15) and *Wake Me Up Early in the Morning* (Top 25)(both 1970) and *Goodbye Jukebox* (Top 75) (1971).

Bobby is a practicing Christian and in 1969 wrote a book on Christianity and Country music entitled *Hit the Glory Road*. He was also a Kentucky Colonel. He moved back to Florida where he is involved in real estate and insurance. He still performs, making occasional visits to Nashville for appearances on the *Grand Ole Opry* and TNN's *Music City Tonight*.

RECOMMENDED ALBUMS:

"Bobby Lord's Best" (Harmony)(1964)
"The Bobby Lord Show" (Hickory)(1965)
"Bobby Lord" (Decca)(1970)

LOST AND FOUND, The

When Formed:	**1973**
Members:	
Allen Mills	**Bass Fiddle, Guitar, Vocals, Emcee**
Dempsey Young	**Mandolin, Most String Instruments, Vocals**
Ray Berrier	**Guitar, Vocals**
Lynwood Lunsford	**Banjo, Guitar, Vocals**

Former Members:

Roger Handy (Guitar, Vocals), Bubba Chandler (Guitar, Vocals), Steve Wilson (Guitar, Vocals), Ronnie Bowman (Guitar, Vocals), Gene Parker (Banjo, Guitar, Vocals—Co-Founder—Member 1973-1987), Jody King (Banjo, Vocals)

The Lost and Found is a southwestern Virginia Bluegrass band that has made a name on the basis of original songs, quality musicianship and the inspired emcee work of Allen Mills (b. Allen Herman Mills, November 4, 1937, Danville, Virginia). Founded in 1973 by Mills, banjo picker Gene Parker (b. April 28, 1942), mandolinist Dempsey Young (b. Dempsey Edwin Young, Jr., July 1, 1954, Richmond, Virginia) and guitarist Roger Handy, the group rose to prominence within a few years, becoming favorites on the festival circuit. Parker, who conceived the original idea of their formation, remained a key band member for 14 years, with Mills and Young continuing from the original 4 to maintain the sound for which the Lost and Found has become known.

The founding members of Lost and Found all came of age in a region immersed in traditional music, and all had amassed some seasoned experience prior to their formation. Roger Handy had been a member of the New Grass Express, Parker had learned his trade from banjo master Allen Shelton, Mills had played bass since his teens, recording on King with the much-respected Easter Brothers, and Young, while still a teenager, had twice taken first prize in mandolin at the prestigious Galax convention. After a year and a half together, the four cut their initial album for Outlet Records, which contained a mixture of older and newer numbers, including Allen's original composition *Love of the Mountains*, a nostalgic parents and homeplace song. It quickly became a standard in the field, taking its place beside *I'm on My Way Back to the Old Home* and *Blue Ridge Cabin Home*.

In the years to come, Mills would contribute other lyrics that gained considerable popularity, including *Sweet Rosie By the River, Wild Mountain Flowers for Mary* and *Papa Wants to Go Back*. The band also cut other new songs and revived nearly forgotten oldies such as *Left Over Biscuits*, the one-time Phil Harris Pop favorite *My Window Faces the South*, the humorous look at matrimony *The Man Who Wrote Home Sweet Home Never Was a Married Man* and Charlie Poole's one-time signature piece, *Don't Let Your Deal Go Down.* While neither the originals nor the revivals quite attained the impact of *Love of the Mountains,* they managed to give the Lost and Found a distinct repertoire which in turn provided them with musical identity.

As the band grew in reputation, after three albums for Outlet, they switched over to David Freeman's Rebel Records, in 1980. In the next dozen years, they cut several more albums, generally continuing their pattern of mixing tasteful new songs with revived oldies. Eventually the group underwent personnel changes with only Mills and Young remaining from the founders, although Parker stayed until 1987. Earlier Bubba Chandler had replaced Handy; he in turn gave way to Steve Wilson, and then to Ronnie Bowman. Jody King initially took over for Parker on banjo. In 1991, current members Barry Berrier (b. Barry Ray Berrier, October 10, 1960, Mount Airy, North Carolina) and Lynwood Lunsford (b. Lynwood Lee Lunsford, January 31, 1962, Roxboro, North Carolina) took their respective positions on guitar and banjo beside the veterans Mills and Young. Dempsey Young, over the years, has attained a name as a top-flight mandolinist with his own particular touch. As the Bluegrass world moves toward the mid-90's, the Lost and Found has attained a status as a quality band ready to carry the most traditional form of commercial Country music into the new century. IMT

RECOMMENDED ALBUMS:

"The Best of Lost & Found" (Rebel)(1984)
"Hymn Time" (Rebel)(1988)
"January Rain" (Rebel)(1993)
"Bluegrass Classics" (Rebel)(1991)

JOHN D. LOUDERMILK

(Singer, Songwriter, Trumpet, Saxophone, Trombone, Bass Drum, Ukulele, Guitar, Harmonica, Stand-up Bass, Banjo, Mandolin, Cornet, Organ)

Given Name: John D. Loudermilk
Date of Birth: March 31, 1934
Where Born: Durham, North Carolina
Married: Gwen Cooke (m. 1959)
Children: John, Ricky, Michael Phillip

The son of a carpenter who helped build the chapel at Duke University, John has constructed some of Country and Pop's finest songs. In fact, John D. is one of the master craftsmen of songwriters. He is also a consummate performer and musician and first cousin to those Country giants, the Louvin Brothers (real name Loudermilk).

John's father couldn't read or write and so he got John to go to the local grocery store and endorse his paychecks. Although remaining within the same area, John's family was often on the move. In all, the family moved 19 times before he had finished high school. John's first public appearance was with his mother, singing and playing *Life's Railway to Heaven* in church. John gained his early experience as a musician as a member of the Salvation Army Band. When he was 12, he won a place on the Capitol Records Talent Contest in Charlotte, North Carolina, which was hosted by Tex Ritter. Shortly after, John learned to play a homemade ukulele.

By the time he was 13, he had his own radio show on WTIK Durham, as "Johnny Dee." His initial influences were Eddy Arnold, Jazz organist Jimmy Reed, classical guitarist Andres Segovia, songwriter Ivory Joe Hunter, Fats Domino and Lloyd Price. In addition, he was influenced by philosopher-poet Kahlil Gibran, and this led to John writing his own poetry. John was employed by WTVD-TV, where he painted sets and played stand-up bass in the *Noon Show* band. In 1955, he came to the show with a piece of poetry that he'd set to music and played it on the program. The song was *A Rose and a Baby Ruth*. The audience reaction was very favorable and Orville Campbell of Colonial Records wanted his artist George Hamilton IV to record it. The ensuing record was picked up by ABC-Paramount and in 1956, it went to the Top 10 on the Pop charts and sold some 4 million copies worldwide. As John had no intention of a career in music, he left the TV station to return to his studies at Campbell University in Buies Creek. It was here that he wrote *Sittin' in the Balcony*. Colonial released John's version, under the name of "Johnny Dee," and it went Top 30 on the Pop charts in 1957. The song was then recorded by Eddie Cochran and it became his first chart entry, going Top 20. In addition to his Johnny Dee pseudonym, John also recorded for Colonial as "Ebe Sneezer."

While at university, he met fellow student Gwen Cooke and in 1959, they married in the chapel that John's father had built. That year, John wrote one of the big cross-over hits, Stonewall Jackson's *Waterloo*. He was now courted by music publishers in New York but initially he signed with Jim Denny at Cedarwood Music and moved to Nashville. He had a Pop hit with *Angela Jones,* which went Top 30 in the U.S. by Johnny Ferguson and Top 10 in the U.K. by Michael Cox. Then in 1961, John moved his allegiance to Acuff-Rose Music. This move led to his meeting Chet Atkins and signing to RCA Victor the same year.

In 1961, John had a Top 40 Pop hit with the self-penned *Language of Love* (it was a No.13 hit in the U.K.). He would not have another sizable hit until 1963, when *Bad News* made the Top 30 on the Country charts. However, it was not as a recording artist that he was making his name. His songwriting skills were producing hit after hit for other artists. In 1961, the Everly Brothers recorded John's "tragedy" song *Ebony Eyes* and took it into the Pop Top 10 and the Country Top 30. Sue Thompson had a Top 5 Pop hit with *Sad Movies (Make Me Cry)* that year and went on to have a Top 3 Pop hit with the novelty number *Norman*, in 1962. That year, Kris Jensen had his sole chart hit with another Loudermilk song, *Torture*.

1963 produced two big Loudermilk successes. George Hamilton IV recorded a song that will always be associated with him, *Abilene*. He took it all the way to No.1 on the Country charts and into the Pop Top 20. This was followed into the No.1 slot by another John D. song, *Talk Back Trembling Lips*, by Ernest Ashworth. U.K. Pop group Nashville Teens provided John with a pair of Top 10 hits in Britain, during 1964, *Tobacco Road* and *Google Eye*. The group took the former into the U.S. Pop charts Top 20. In addition, Johnny Cash recorded his classic version of *Bad News* and made it a Top 10 Country hit.

During 1965, Loudermilk had three charted songs, with Sue Thompson having a Top 30 hit with *Paper Tiger*, Marianne Faithfull going Top 40 with *This Little Bird* (a Top 10 hit in the U.K.) and Dick & DeeDee having a Top 20 hit with *Thou Shalt Not Steal*. George Hamilton IV recorded another career single in 1967, when he had a Top 10 success with John's *Break My Mind*. That same year, the Casinos had a big Pop hit with the now much recorded *Then You Can Tell Me Goodbye*.

The following year, Eddy Arnold had a No.1 Country hit with the song and in 1976, Glen Campbell merged it into a medley and had a major cross-over hit with the song as *Don't Pull Your Love—Then You Can Tell Me Goodbye*. In 1967, John's album ***Suburban Attitudes in Country Verse*** received a Grammy Award for "Best Album Notes."

1968 produced some other Loudermilk classics that included *Big Daddy* by the Browns, *I Wanna Live*, a No.1 Country hit for Glen Campbell, *It's My Time* from George Hamilton IV and the marvelous *Indian Reservation (The Lament of the Cherokee Reservation Indian)*, recorded by England's Don Fardon. This became a Top 20 Pop hit in the U.S. but was also a No.3 hit in the U.K. The song was recorded in 1971 by the Raiders, and went to No.1 on the Pop chart.

George Hamilton IV gave John another Top 30 Country hit when he recorded *Blue Train (of the Heartbreak Line)* in 1973 and four years later, Sonny James took an earlier Hamilton hit, *Abilene*, and had Country Top 30 success with it. The following year, 1978, gave Vern Gosdin a Country Top 20 hit with another former Hamilton hit, *Break My Mind*. In 1982, Boxcar Willie cut his version of *Bad News* and took it into the Country Top 40.

John D. has remained popular in the U.K. and toured with Pete Sayers there and has appeared on several TV shows. In addition, he has appeared at the Wembley Festival in London. However, he is a reluctant tourer and prefers to stay at home with his family. Loudermilk is a writer who has chosen not to co-write, and obviously his success level has proven him to be correct.

In 1971, John moved from RCA Victor to Warner Brothers and released the album ***Elloree Vol. 1***. During the 70's, he became interested in ethnomusicology and its relationship to modern record production. He lectured a lot at folklore societies and colleges on, inter alia, Pete Seeger's and Jimmie Driftwood's contributions. By 1978, John had once again changed labels and was with Mim, where he recorded ***Just Passing Through***.

He received a Manny from the NSAI and in 1976, John was inducted into the NSAI Songwriters Hall of Fame. In addition, he has received a number of BMI awards for his songs and was a two-time Director of the CMA. He also served as a member of the Board of Directors of the National Academy of Recording Arts & Sciences (NARAS). John's name was back on the Country and Pop charts in 1994 when Tim McGraw's *Indian Outlaw* became a monster hit. The song included phrases from *Indian Reservation*. John now lives with his wife just outside of Murfreesboro, Tennessee.

RECOMMENDED ALBUMS:

"12 Sides of John D. Loudermilk" (RCA Victor)(1962)
"Suburban Attitudes in Country Verse" (RCA Victor)(1967)
"Elloree Vol. 1" (Warner Brothers)(1971)
"Just Passing Through" (Mim)(1978)

LOUISIANA HAYRIDE

(Radio Show, KWKH Shreveport, Louisiana)

From its inception on April 3, 1948, at the Municipal Auditorium, the *Louisiana Hayride* was the one show that got nearer than any other to the *Grand Ole Opry* in popularity. It never proved to be a real challenge to the *Opry,* because as soon as performers became popular on the *Hayride*, they moved over to the *Opry* .

The show, which was aired on KWKH Shreveport, Louisiana, was the brainchild of Station Manager Henry Clay, announcer and Program Director Horace Logan and Commercial Manager Dean Upson. Upson had formerly been a member of the Vagabonds.

KWKH, a 50,000-watt station, was not new to Country music. As far back as 1936, the station had a Sunday afternoon talent show hosted by the Shelton Brothers and from 1940, the Rice Brothers Gang among others was featured on *Saturday Night Roundup*. The first *Louisiana Hayride*'s cast was the Bailes Brothers, Johnnie and Jack and the Tennessee Mountain Boys, Kitty Wells, Harmie Smith, Pappy Covington and Tex Grimley.

The show, which went out weekly, was intended to reach Louisiana, Texas and Arkansas, but in reality reached further. However, the acts on the show tended to work only so far from Shreveport, so as to be able to return at the weekend. In August 1948, the show's ratings were boosted by the addition to the membership of Hank Williams. Along with him came Curley Williams, Wayne Rainey, Zeke Clements, the Mercer Brothers, Red Sovine and Patsy Montana.

A year after its commencement, the Wilburn Brothers joined the show. This was followed by Hank Williams returning to the *Opry* in June 1949. That same month Red Sovine became the main artist and he was joined by Leon Payne, T. Texas Tyler, Slim Whitman and Webb Pierce. As the show developed, it gained the name of "the cradle of the stars," and certainly many performers made their name while on the *Hayride*. It was also known as "Heaven's Gate."

In 1952, Hank Williams returned to the show and he was joined by Floyd Cramer, Jimmy Day, Johnny Horton, Sonny James and Billy Walker. Webb Pierce left to join the *Opry* and Jim Reeves came on board as the announcer, and later in the year, he performed as Gentleman Jim Reeves. The following year, CBS radio network made the *Hayride* part of *Saturday Night—Country Style*. The Hayride also joined the Far East Network of the Armed Forces Radio Service.

Among the stars that graced the *Hayride* through to 1955 were the Duke of Paducah, Ernest Tubb, Minnie Pearl, Loretta Lynn and George Jones. On October 6, 1954, a 19-year-old Elvis Presley, then a budding star, joined the *Hayride* and stayed on it for 18 months, making his final appearance on December 15, 1956. When Elvis left, a lot of his audience went as well. During the 60's, the main performers included Nat Stuckey, David Houston and Hank Williams, Jr. About this time, the *Hayride* started to suffer a decline and both KWKH and the *Shreveport Times* decided they wanted out. Soon after Johnny Horton's death, the show became biweekly, then monthly and then quarterly. Local business-man David Kent bought it and moved it to an auditorium on Benton Road, Bossier Parish, in 1973.

The star quality from now on didn't equal its illustrious past, but it still could boast quality. In 1974, Micki Fuhrman joined the show and other performers in the late 70's included songwriters Michael Garvin and Keith Stegall. In 1979, British Rockabilly act Levi and the Rockats recorded a live album from the *Hayride*. During the 80's, Fuhrman was joined by Craig Dillingham, Perry LaPointe, Linda Davis and Dennis Bottoms. In 1984, Rick Smith produced a documentary on the *Hayride* for Louisiana Public Broadcasting.

In February 1987, David Kent and Texas TV producer Bill Starnes (the son of Starday Records' Jack Starnes) expanded the *Hayride* as a TV show. This was an interesting collaboration, as Starday had recorded many of the early *Hayride* performers. On March 11, 1987, Starnes announced that the show was returning to the Municipal Auditorium and on June 12-14 that year, the revamped *Louisiana Hayride* gave its first performances. The line-up included Slim Whitman, Johnny Wright, Bobby Wright, Micki Fuhrman and the singing pharmacist Bubba Talbert. The Sunday Gospel line-up included Fuhrman, the Florida Boys and the Rex Nelon Singers. Although the halcyon days of 3,300 people in the un-air-conditioned auditorium was not achieved in the now air-conditioned one, the *Louisiana Hayride* was back where it belongs.

Songwriter/Manager Tillman Franks called Shreveport "the Country soul of the whole wide world" and there is no doubt that it could have rivaled Nashville to a greater degree. One of the reasons that Shreveport never became the music capital of the world was that with all the advantages of having the Hayride, KWKH never allowed Horace Logan to set up a talent agency, as the management of the *Grand Ole Opry* had done. Logan often referred to the *Grand Ole Opry* as "the Tennessee branch of the *Louisiana Hayride*."

LOUVIN BROTHERS, The

When Formed: 1944
IRA LOUVIN
(Vocals, Songwriter, Mandolin, Banjo)
Given Name: Ira Lonnie Loudermilk
Date of Birth: April 21, 1924
Married: 1. Annie Lou Roberts (div.)
2. Bobbie Lowery (div.)
3. Faye Cunningham (div.)
4. Anne Young (dec'd.)
Children: Gail, Terry, Kathy
Date of Death: June 20, 1965
CHARLIE LOUVIN
(Vocals, Songwriter, Guitar)
Given Name: Charlie Elzer Loudermilk
Date of Birth: July 7, 1927
Married: Betty Harrison
Children: Charlie, Jr. ("Sonny"), Ken, Glenn
Both Born: Section, Alabama

The Louvin Brothers probably rank as the all-time favorite among brother/harmony duets.

Ira and Charlie Loudermilk grew up in the Sand Mountain country of Appalachian Alabama in an era when brother duets constituted the dominant Country music form. The Delmores, Monroes, Callahans and the Blue Sky Boys (Bolicks) were at their popularity peaks when the Loudermilk boys came into adolescence. Needless to say, they all had some influence on the Louvin style, especially the high tenor harmonies of the Monroe Brothers and the smoothness of Bill and Earl Bolick, which Ira and Charlie managed to combine. The Louvins began their professional careers at a small radio station in Chattanooga, WDEF, with a modest quarter-hour early morning program.

Charlie and Ira, the ***Louvin Brothers***

Charlie had a hitch in the Army during which time Ira worked for Charlie Monroe and then the brothers went to Knoxville, working first at WROL and then at WNOX. By this time, they had shortened their last name to Louvin, which seemed better for professional purposes, although their first cousin, songwriter John D. Loudermilk, retained the family name. After a couple of years on WMPS Memphis with Eddie Hill's group and doing a single for Apollo Records, the Louvins returned to Knoxville and worked again at WNOX.

They cut a single for Decca in 1949 and then signed with MGM, recording a dozen songs in 1951 and 1952. They went back to Memphis, where they secured postal clerk jobs, did a daily radio show and played selective personal appearances. Acuff-Rose was publishing their songs and Fred Rose helped them get a contract with Capitol, where their first release, *The Family Who Prays*, went on to become a Gospel standard. However, Charlie's recall to military service in the Korean conflict halted their promising career.

When Charlie got out of the Army, the Louvins selected Birmingham and station WOVK as a spot to relaunch their musical lives, but their stylistic similarity to the already-established Rebe (Gosdin) and Rabe (Perkins), who ironically sang a lot of Louvin compositions, made the going tough. They had reached a near state of desperation when Ken Nelson of Capitol talked the *Grand Ole Opry* management into hiring them.

Their early Capitol waxings had been all sacred material, but when they went to the *Opry* they branched over into secular songs as well, having a major hit with *When I Stop Dreaming,* which was on the charts for 13 weeks in 1955, peaking in the Top 10. In 1956, a tough year for many hard-Country acts, the Louvins started off with the No.1 *I Don't Believe You've Met My Baby* and then had three Top 10 hits, *Hoping That You're Hoping* and *You're Running Wild/Cash on the Barrel Head.* At the same time Ira and Charlie had a fine theme album, ***Tragic Songs of Life,*** and a quality sacred effort in ***Nearer My God to Thee***, which reflected well on their original roots.

The late 50's saw the Louvins continue with somewhat more modest success as *Don't Laugh* and *Plenty of Everything But You* both reached the Top 20 in 1957 and *My Baby's Gone* went Top 10, late in 1958. *Knoxville Girl*, a traditional ballad which reached the Top 20 in early 1959, was their last hit in the 50's.

They made the charts three times in the early 60's with *I Love You Best of All* (Top 15) and *How's the World Treating You* (Top 30)(both 1961) and *Must You Throw Dirt in My Face* (Top 25, 1962). The brothers also continued turning out some memorable albums, including one of war songs and fine tributes to both Roy Acuff and the Delmores.

Meanwhile, their career went through a series of ups and downs. They left the *Opry* for the WWVA *Wheeling Jamboree* in 1957, returning to WSM after about a year and a half. Ira had a temper which, combined with periodic drinking binges, could create some serious problems, such as a bitter fight with his third wife, Faye, that culminated in a shooting scrape in 1961 and nearly cost Ira his life.

Although Ira's creative genius had produced a disproportionate share of their success, Charlie had borne an unequal share of the burden. Finally, they split in August 1963, although they subsequently did a final album that September. Ira returned to Alabama, where he lived quietly with his fourth wife, Anne Young.

Both Ira and Charlie recorded separately for Capitol and Ira eventually began to make some appearances. In June 1965, Ira and Anne worked a week-long engagement in Kansas City and were both killed in an auto crash near Williamsburg, Missouri, on the road home. He had one posthumous chart single, *Yodel Sweet Molly*, later that summer. Charlie Louvin's solo career continues to the present.

Interest in the Louvins as a duet persists and several albums of their music were reissued, culminating with a Bear Family cd box set of their entire recorded output. Ira's daughter, Kathy, is now an established songwriter in Nashville. IMT

RECOMMENDED ALBUMS:
"Tragic Songs of Life" (Capitol)(1956)
"The Louvin Brothers" (MGM)(1957) [Re-issued on Rounder]
"Nearer My God to Thee" (Capitol)(1957) [Re-issued on Country Classics]
"Ira and Charlie" (Capitol)(1958) [Re-issued on Stetson UK (1988)]
"The Family Who Prays" (Capitol)(1959)
"Country Love Ballads" (Capitol)(1959)
"Satan Is Real" (Capitol)(1960) [Re-issued on Stetson UK (1990)]

"My Baby's Gone" (Capitol)(1960) [Re-issued on Stetson UK (1987)]
"A Tribute to the Delmore Brothers" (Capitol)(1960) [Re-issued on Golden Country]
"Encore" (Capitol)(1961)
"Country Christmas" (Capitol)(1961)
"Their Current Hits" (Capitol)(1964)
"Thank God for My Christian Home" (Capitol)(1965)
"The Great Roy Acuff Songs" (Capitol)(1967)
"The Great Gospel Singing by the Louvin Brothers" (Capitol) (1973)
"Early Rare Recordings" (Anthology of Country Music)(ca. 1979) [Note: Capitol Masters]
"The Best of the Early Louvin Brothers" (Rebel)(1986) [Note: Capitol Masters]
"Sing Their Hearts Out" (See for Miles)(1989)[Note: Capitol masters]
"The Louvin Brothers: Close Harmony" (box set)(Bear Family Germany) (1992)
"Songs That Tell a Story" (Rounder)(1978) [Note: from radio transcriptions]
"Live at New River Ranch" (Copper Creek)(1988)
Ira Louvin:
"The Unforgettable Ira Louvin" (Capitol)(1965)

CHARLIE LOUVIN

(Singer, Songwriter, Guitar)
Given Name: Charlie Elzer Loudermilk
Date of Birth: July 7, 1927
Where Born: Section, Alabama
Married: Betty Harrison
Children: Charlie, Jr. ("Sonny"), Ken, Glenn

After the Louvin Brothers split in 1963, Charlie Louvin went on to enjoy a lengthy career as a solo performer. In fact, Charlie actually had more hit singles on his own than the brothers had as a team.

Until 1963, Charlie and Ira established themselves as perhaps the greatest brother team in Country music history and after their dissolution, Charlie continued as a solo performer for Capitol and at the *Grand Ole Opry*. He had his greatest success rather quickly in 1964 with *I Don't Love You Anymore*, which peaked in the Top 5 and was followed by the Top 30 *Less and Less*. *See the Big Man Cry* did well in 1965, reaching the Top 10. Through 1972, Louvin had seventeen other chartmakers for Capitol of which the most successful solo efforts were: *Think I'll Go Somewhere and Cry Myself to Sleep* (Top 30, 1965), *You Finally Said Something Good (When You Said Goodbye)* (Top 15, 1966), *Will You Visit Me on Sunday?* and *Hey Daddy* (both Top 20, 1968) and *What Are Those Things (with Big Black Wings)* (Top 20), *Let's Put Our World Back Together* and *Little Reasons* (both Top 30) (all 1969).

Charlie has also done well in recordings with various duet partners, especially Melba Montgomery. The two had three successful songs together in 1970 and 1971 with *Something to Brag About*, *Did You Ever* and *Baby, You've Got What It Takes*. Three other numbers by this twosome hit the lower echelons of the charts through 1973. Charlie then moved on to United Artists, where he had a couple of modest charted hits in the mid-70's, the most successful being the 1974 Top 40 single *You're My Wife, She's My Woman*. A duet with Emmylou Harris, *Love Don't Care*, charted briefly in 1979 and *North Wind* with the Bluegrass duo of Jim & Jesse did somewhat better in 1982, on Soundwaves. Charlie's last solo appearance on the charts took place in 1989 when he had a minor hit with a revival of Roy Acuff's 1940 classic *The Precious Jewel*, in duet with Mr. Roy on Hal Kat Records.

Charlie Louvin, like many Country artists of his era, has found getting hit records and airplay something of a challenge in recent years. Among other things, he has toured and made some effort to re-create the original Louvin sound with the help of Charles Whitstein. In 1992, the two did an album together, toured Europe, and played some Bluegrass festivals (their fans have always had great respect for the Louvin Brothers' harmony). As of May 1994, Charlie continues his affiliation with the *Grand Ole Opry*, a show on which he has performed for over three decades. IMT

RECOMMENDED ALBUMS:
"Less & Less/I Don't Love You Anymore" (Capitol)(1965)
"The Many Moods of Charlie Louvin" (Capitol)(1966)
"Lonesome Is Me" (Capitol)(1966)
"I'll Remember Always" (Capitol)(1967)
"I Forgot to Cry" (Capitol)(1967) [Re-issued on Stetson UK in the original sleeve (1989)]
"Will You Visit Me on Sundays" (Capitol)(1968)
"Hey Daddy" (Capitol)(1969)
"The Kind of a Man I Am" (Capitol)(1969)
"Here's a Toast to Mama" (Capitol)(1969)
"Ten Times Charlie" (Capitol)(1970)
"The Best of Charlie Louvin" (Capitol)(1972)
"It Almost Felt Like Love" (United Artists)(1974)
"Country Souvenirs" (Accord)(1981)
"Charlie Louvin" (Audiogragh Alive)(1982)
Charlie Louvin and Melba Montgomery:
"Something to Brag About" (Capitol)(1971)
"Baby, You've Got What It Takes" (Capitol)(1971)
Charlie Louvin and Jim & Jesse:
"Jim & Jesse and Charlie Louvin" (Soundwaves)(1982)
(See also Louvin Brothers)

Lost Planet Airmen refer COMMANDER CODY AND HIS LOST PLANET AIRMEN

PATTY LOVELESS

(Singer, Songwriter, Guitar)
Given Name: Patricia Ramey
Date of Birth: January 4, 1958

Another coal miner's daughter, ***Patty Loveless***

Where Born: Pikeville, Kentucky
Married: 1.Terry Loveless (div.)
2. Emory Gordy, Jr.

Patty Loveless emerged in the middle of the 80's as one of the major female singers in Country music. Her career has gone from strength to strength during the 80's and 90's.

Patty was one of a large family and started to write songs and sing duets with her elder brother, Roger, before she was 12 years old. He brought her to Nashville when she was 14, armed with her catalog of 30 songs. She met Porter Wagoner, who became a friend and advisor, meeting also his singing partner, Dolly Parton, who encouraged her. Soon she had a meeting with Doyle and Teddy Wilburn, who were impressed with her singing. They were looking for a vocalist to replace Lorretta Lynn, another coal miner's daughter (and a distant cousin). For three years, while she finished high school, Patty was the featured singer with the Wilburn Brothers. She was also signed to their publishing company, Surefire Music, as a songwriter.

Marrying Terry Loveless, a former Wilburn Brothers drummer, shortly after graduating from high school, she moved to North Carolina to her husband's home at Kings Mountain near Charlotte. They spent the next eight years working with a series of bands.

In 1983, Patty returned to songwriting and for the next two years she continued to sing in clubs, fairs and hotels. She returned to Nashville in 1985, to record a five-song demo tape. Roger circulated this tape to recording companies and several showed interest. MCA's Tony Brown played the tape to other MCA executives and within two months of making the demo, Patty was signed to MCA. She was also divorced from Terry Loveless.

Her initial singles, *Lonely Days, Lonely Nights* (1985) and *Wicked Ways* (1986), both hit the Top 50 on the Country chart. She followed with two further singles, *I Did* and *After All*,which also charted in 1987. These four singles were included on her eponymous debut album, which was also released in 1987.

The single *You Saved Me* (1987) made the Top 50. However the next two releases, *If My Heart Had Windows* (Top 10) and *A Little Bit of Love* (Top 3) in 1988, opened up the Loveless career. This last single bore the name of her second album. These first two albums were produced by Emory Gordy, Jr., and Tony Brown. With commercial endorsements becoming more and more important in Country music, Patty began promoting ladies' boots for Justin Western Footwear. 1987 and 1988 were busy years. Patty appeared at Wembley Festival in England both years. She did 29 straight one-nighters on the U.S. West Coast and in June, 1988, she joined the *Grand Ole Opry* and also toured with Kenny Rogers.

From her album ***Honky Tonk Angels*** came five hit singles, *Blue Side of Town* (Top 5), *Don't Toss Us Away* (Top 5), *Timber I'm Falling in Love* (No.1), *Lonely Side of Life* (No.6), all in 1989, and another No.1, *Chains*, in 1990.

Patty has been nominated for a number of awards and won the MCN "Star of Tomorrow" award in 1989, and the MCN "Best Female Artist" award in 1990. Also in 1989 she went on a sponsored tour for the USO to Japan, Korea and Alaska with Randy Travis. This tour was filmed by Nashville Network for a special show.

The album ***On Down the Line*** (1990) again produced more hit singles, the title track (Top 5) and *The Night's Too Long* (Top 20), both in 1990, and in 1991 the hits were *I'm That Kind of Girl* (Top 5) and *Blue Memories* (Top 25). ***Up Against My Heart***, in 1991, was her last album released on MCA. The singles from it were *Hurt Me Bad (in a Real Good Way)* (Top 3), *Jealous Bone* (Top 15) and *Can't Stop Myself from Loving You* (Top 30), all released in 1992. MCA released a ***Greatest Hits*** album, in 1993. That year, Patty sang a duet, *Send a Message to My Heart*, with Dwight Yoakam, which was a Top 50 hit and which was on Dwight's ***If There Was a Way*** album.

Having just signed a lucrative contract with Sony Music/Epic, Patty was just half through recording her first album for them and was due to start her road tour the very next day when she had a leaky blood vessel in one of her vocal cords and an operation was necessary. She was afraid and wondering what was going to happen to her. She was greatly encouraged by Kathy Mattea, who had been through the same thing and talked her through it.

After Patty's emergency laser surgery, she was given a two-month "gag" order. After extensive vocal therapy she was back in the studio finishing her album on Epic, which was released in 1993, entitled ***Only What I Feel***. On the liner notes is a thank-you to the doctors and staff of the Vanderbilt Voice Centre. From this album, Patty had another No.1, *Blame It on Your Heart* and followed it with the Top 20 hit *Nothin' but the Wheel*. In 1994, Patty had a Top 10 hit with *You Will* and followed with the Top 3 success *How Can I Help You Say Goodbye*. The album ***Only What I Feel*** was Certified Gold.

RECOMMENDED ALBUMS:

"Patty Loveless" (MCA)(1987)
"If My Heart Had Windows" (MCA)(1988)
"Honky Tonk Angel" (MCA)(1988)
"On Down the Line" (MCA)(1990)
"Up Against My Heart" (MCA)(1991)
"Greatest Hits" (MCA)(1993)
"Only What I Feel" (Epic)(1993)

LYLE LOVETT

(Singer, Songwriter, Guitar)
Date of Birth: **November 1, 1957**
Where Born: **Klein, Texas**
Married: **Julia Roberts**

Lyle Lovett has become one of the most innovative writer/performers to tread the boards. Lyle has created albums that are brimful with good songs, without putting himself into any musical bag. His music is a blend of Country, Blues, Folk, Jazz and Swing. Lyle is easily identifiable with his giant-sized coif ("tall hair"), and his looks are less than "hunky."

He grew up just north of Houston, in Klein, which was named for his German great-great-grandfather, one of the area's original settlers in the late 1840's. Lyle listened to the radio, watched TV and was influenced by fellow Texan songwriter/performers Guy Clark, Willie Nelson and Townes Van Zandt. At Texas A & M University, Lyle studied journalism and German. He got degrees in both subjects in 1980 and 1981 respectively.

*Troubadour from Texas **Lyle Lovett***

By 1979, he was already playing clubs around Houston, Dallas, Austin and San Antonio and had started writing songs. In 1983, he was playing all over the country and that same year appeared in the CBS-TV movie *Bill on His Own*, starring Mickey Rooney. He also wrote a song for the movie. At the end of the year, he appeared at the Schueberfouer Fair in Luxembourg and while there, he met J. David Sloan and his band, from Phoenix. They worked together at the fair and Sloan encouraged Lyle to come to Phoenix and record with them.

In the summer of 1984, helped by Billy Williams from the band, Lyle put down four songs. Lyle came to Nashville and, through a friend, got a meeting with ASCAP's Merlin Littlefield, who enthused over the demoed material. Producer/musician Jim Rooney sent a copy of the tape to Criterion Music, which gave Lyle a writer's deal, and Guy Clark got a copy to MCA's Tony Brown. The result was that in 1986, Lyle signed with MCA/Curb. His first, self-titled album was released that year, with all songs written by Lyle (except *This Old Porch*, which he wrote with Robert Earl Keen) and he immediately hit the Country charts with his initial single, *Farther Down the Line*, which reached the Top 25. He followed up, that year, with the Top 10 single *Cowboy Man*. During 1987, two more singles from the album reached the Top 20: *God Will* and *Why I Don't Know*.

In 1987, he released another much acclaimed album, ***Pontiac***, on which Lyle wrote all the songs. This album introduced John Hagen, on cello, who would soon become a regular member of Lyle's musical entourage and who was, in fact at one point, Lyle's sole "backing band." Lyle ended the year with the first title track from the new album, ***Give Me Back My Heart***, which also reached the Top 15. Lyle had four hits in 1988, with varying results. He started off with the humorous *She's No Lady*, which made the Top 20, and followed up with *I Loved You Yesterday* (Top 30), *If I Had a Boat* (in which we learned that the Lone Ranger's sidekick Tonto's "kemo sabe" did not mean "my friend"), which only reached the Top 70, and, from his 1988 album ***Lyle Lovett and His Large Band***, *I Married Her Because She Looks Like You*, which reached the Top 50.

The new album reached the Top 10 on the

Country album charts, but the singles did not fare well. Lyle's version of *Stand by Your Man* and *Nobody Knows Me* only reached the Top 90. MCA dug back into his debut album for *If I Were the Man You Wanted*, which made the Top 50.

By now, Lyle had been superseded by other heroes and he did not release another album until 1992, when he issued ***Joshua Judges Ruth***. This was a strange affair and showed that, although Lyle continued to experiment, the album lacked musical direction. During the year, Lyle worked on the movie *The Player* and it was at this time that he met actress Julia Roberts. On June 27, 1993, Lyle and Julia married.

Lyle Lovett will continue to have a fan base, but like other experimental artists, he will either become an alternative performer or suddenly get back into the limelight with another career single.

RECOMMENDED ALBUMS:

"Lyle Lovett" (MCA/Curb)(1986)
"Pontiac" (MCA/Curb)(1987)
"Lyle Lovett and His Large Band" (MCA/Curb)(1988)
"Joshua Judges Ruth" (Curb/MCA)(1992)

LULU BELLE AND SCOTTY

When Formed: **1934**

LULU BELLE
(Singer, Guitar)
Given Name: **Myrtle Eleanor Cooper**
Date of Birth: **December 24, 1913**
Where Born: **Boone, North Carolina**
Married: **1. Scotty Wiseman (dec'd.)**
2. Ernest Stamey

Lulu Belle and Scotty

SCOTTY
(Singer, Songwriter, Banjo, Guitar)
Given Name: **Scott Greene Wiseman**
Date of Birth: **November 8, 1909**
Where Born: **Ingalls, North Carolina**
Married: **Lulu Belle**
Date of Death: **January 31, 1981**
Children: **Linda Lou, Steven Scott**

For a generation from 1934, Lulu Belle and Scotty were the nation's leading Country husband-wife team. They starred on the *National Barn Dance* from WLS Chicago for some twenty years and spent a shorter period at the *Boone County Jamboree* over WLW Cincinnati. They also graced several motion pictures with their charm, music, and personalities.

Scotty was born in the mountain country of far western North Carolina, where his family had lived for generations and where he learned to pick the banjo and sing the old ballads. Scott had his heart set on a college education and worked his way through a year at Duke University in Durham, North Carolina. Bradley Kincaid visited him that summer collecting ballads and told him that he could make it on radio, but Scotty was determined to finish college.

Scotty obtained a part-time job at the YMCA in Fairmont, West Virginia, and attended nearby Fairmont State. He soon also began announcing at WMMN radio, where he took the nickname "Skyland Scotty." After graduation, Wiseman successfully auditioned for a spot at WLS Chicago. Meanwhile young Myrtle Cooper, also a native of the Carolina mountain country, had moved with her parents to Evanston, Illinois, at age 16 and in 1932, had also gotten a job at WLS, where John Lair had teamed her up with Red Foley as the song-comedy duo of Lulu Belle and Burrhead. However, this team seemed destined for oblivion as Foley's wife, Eva, preferred that the pair not work together.

The WLS management decided to team Lulu Belle and Skyland Scotty. Their act proved not only a commercial hit on the *National Barn Dance* but a romantic one as well and the pair married on December 13, 1934. In 1936, Lulu Belle won the title "Radio Queen" in a popularity poll sponsored by *Radio Guide* magazine, surprisingly defeating a host of Hollywood and New York-based luminaries.

They remained top stars on the program until 1958 when they retired from active performing except for two years (1938-1940) when they were at WLW Cincinnati. Also beginning in 1938, they periodically journeyed to Hollywood, where they made a total of seven motion pictures beginning with *Shine on, Harvest Moon* for Republic and continuing through *National Barn Dance*. One of their most popular film efforts, *Swing Your Partner*, cast them as betrothed lovers working in a cheese processing factory, with Dale Evans as the likable niece of a crotchety old lady who owns the plant.

As recording artists, the duo never made as much of an impact as they did on radio or on the screen, but they still chalked up some impressive discs. Scotty cut four solo efforts for Bluebird, in 1933, and Lulu Belle and Burrhead made four for Conqueror, in 1934. In 1935, they began recording together for the American Record Corporation, for whom they cut a variety of Old-Time and novelty songs, including Scotty's partly recomposed version of Bascom Lamar Lunsford's *Good Old Mountain Dew*, which became the adaptation used by all later singers of the number. They also contributed some original love songs such as *Remember Me* and *Have I Told You Lately That I Love You*, for Vocalion in 1939 and Vogue in 1945, respectively, which became Country standards.

In the post-war years they recorded for such labels as Emerald, London, Ka-Hill, Trutone, and eventually for Mercury. In the early 50's, while still at Chicago, Lulu Belle and Scotty made a widely heard series of radio transcriptions titled *Breakfast in the Blue Ridge*.

In 1958, the Hayloft Sweethearts retired from the *National Barn Dance* and went back to their mountain home in Spruce Pine, North Carolina. Scott, who had obtained a Master's degree at Northwestern, taught school, farmed, and served as a bank director. Lulu Belle participated in community activities and in the mid-70's, served two terms in the North Carolina legislature representing Avery, Burke, and Mitchell counties (as Democrat in a normally GOP district). They recorded periodically, cutting three albums for Starday, in the 60's and a final one for Old Homestead, in 1974. Other recorded material appeared on such labels as Birch and Super. They also made a few rare concert appearances in the 70's.

Scotty died in 1981 while returning from a Florida vacation. He left an unfinished autobiography which was subsequently published as *Wiseman's View* by the North Carolina Folklore Society in 1986. Lulu Belle married a retired lawyer and long-time family friend in 1983. She did a solo album for Old Homestead in 1986. Surprisingly, little of Lulu Belle and Scotty's original recordings has been reissued. One album of 1930's material appeared in the Old Homestead collector series and another on the German label Castle from later material. Beginning in 1989, Mar-Lu began releasing radio transcription material in a collector's edition of which three had come out by 1993. IMT

RECOMMENDED ALBUMS:

"The Sweethearts of Country Music" (Starday)(1963)
"Down Memory Lane" (Starday)(1964)
"Sweethearts Still" (Starday)(1965)
"Just a Closer Walk with Thee" (Birch)(1974)
"Have I Told You Lately That I Love You" (Old Homestead)(1974)
"Lulu Belle & Scotty" (Castle Germany)(1980)
"Early and Great" (Old Homestead)(1985)
"Tender Memories Recalled" (Mar-Lu)(1989)
"Lulabelle & Scotty" (Super)
Lulu Belle:
"Snickers and Tender Memories" (Old Homestead)(1986)

BOB LUMAN

(Singer, Songwriter, Guitar)

Given Name:	**Bobby Glynn Luman**
Date of Birth:	**April 15, 1937**
Where Born:	**Nacogdoches, Texas**
Married:	**Barbara**
Children:	**Melissa**
Date of Death:	**December 27, 1978**

Bob Luman was ready to trade in his guitar for a baseball bat in 1959. Although a major label recording artist, Luman had failed to score a hit record. One night, he announced from the stage his retirement from Country music to accept an offer to play professional baseball for the Pittsburgh Pirates. As fate would have it, Don and Phil Everly were in the audience that night. The famous brothers were impressed with Luman's performance and spoke with him after the show. The Everly Brothers persuaded him to give Country music one more shot with the Boudleaux Bryant song *Let's Think About Living.* The song went Top 10 on both the Country and Pop charts and eventually sold a million copies. His breakthrough record even went to No.3 on the R & B chart and No.6 on the U.K. chart.

Country-Pop star ***Bob Luman***

Growing up in Nacogdoches, Texas, Bobby Glynn Luman's two favorite things were music and sports. He listened to the *Grand Ole Opry* on Saturday nights and never missed the Friday night fights on his battery-powered radio. Luman's father was an accomplished musician and taught him to play the guitar and other stringed instruments.

When his family moved to Kilgore, Texas, Bob excelled in sports and became the star of his high school baseball team. His skill on the playing field was noted by several major league scouts. When he wasn't playing sports Luman was working on his music. A key event in Luman's musical development was attending a Country package show in Kilgore when he was seventeen. He witnessed a young Elvis Presley create a frenzy and recalling the impressionable show said, "That was the last time I ever tried to sing like Lefty Frizzell." He was hooked on the Rockabilly sound and blended the new music's energy with his smooth Country voice. Luman formed his own band and performed at school activities and in local clubs. Following high school graduation he won a talent contest that paved the way for an appearance on Shreveport's *Louisiana Hayride* radio show. His performance was so popular that he was invited to be a member of the important show in the mid-50's. Luman's strong voice and handsome looks made him a natural for television appearances. This exciting young talent also caught the attention of Hollywood and a spot in the 1957 film *Carnival Rock.* Luman also shared the stage at the Showboat Hotel in Las Vegas with Johnny Cash and Tex Ritter.

Luman followed his 1960 million-selling *Let's Think About Living* with another hit record, *The Great Snowman.* Before Bob could tour to support the record, he received notice from Selective Service that it was his time to serve his country. Military service put Luman's career in a two-year holding pattern. He found his fans waiting when he returned and recorded new material for Hickory Records. His principal hit on Hickory was the 1964 Top 25 single *The File.* Although his records were not attracting much attention on radio, Luman's career got a boost when he joined the *Grand Ole Opry*, in 1965. A few years later he signed with Epic Records and scored a Top 20 hit with *Ain't Got Time to Be Happy.* Over the next ten years Luman produced a string of hits for the label including *Come on Home and Sing the Blues to Daddy* and *Every Day I Have to Cry Some* (both Top 25, 1969), *Honky Tonk Man* (Top 25, 1970), *When You Say Love* (Top 10), *It Takes You* (Top 25) and *Lonely Women Make Good Lovers* (Top 5) (all 1972), *Neither One of Us* (*Wants to Be the First to Say Goodbye)* (Top 10) and *A Good Love Is Like a Good Song* (Top 25) (both 1973), *Still Loving You* (Top 10, originally released in 1970, when it only made the Top 60), *Just Enough to Make Me Stay* (Top 25), *Let Me Make the Bright Lights Shine for You* (Top 25) (all 1974), and *Proud of You Baby* (Top 25, 1975).

Luman maintained a heavy touring schedule in both the U.S. and around the world. In addition to many tours in Europe, Luman made history as the first Country artist to perform at the San Jeronimo Hilton in San Juan, Puerto Rico. He also took Country music to new audiences in Japan and Germany. Luman had many fans in Canada via his television appearances on the *Ian Tyson Show* and *Nashville North.* He also performed on all the major music programs of the day in the U.S., including the *Johnny Cash Show, American Bandstand, Hee Haw*, the *Bill Anderson Show, That Good Old Nashville Music*, the *Del Reeves Show* and *Dean Martin's Music Country.*

While Luman was popular with most fans of the *Grand Ole Opry*, some of the patriarchs thought he often leaned too far to the Rock side of music. In addition to performing his many hits, Luman often stirred up the *Opry* with songs like Chuck Berry's *Johnny B. Goode* backed by drums, electric bass, electric guitar, piano, and harmonica.

In 1975, Luman suffered a major heart attack in Texas and was rushed to Parkland Hospital in Dallas. Nine days later he was transferred to Nashville, where he spent nearly five months in the hospital. Luman turned thirty-eight while bedridden and joked about his ordeal when he returned to the *Opry* stage, telling the audience of his $39,000 medical bill. In 1976, Luman signed with Polydor Records and had a Top 15 success with *The Pay Phone*, in 1977. In 1978, Bob was back in the hospital suffering from pneumonia. Bob Luman died on December 27, 1978, at the age of 41. JIE

RECOMMENDED ALBUMS:

"Let's Think About Living" (Warner Brothers)(1960)
"Greatest Hits" (Hickory)(1964)
"When You Say Love"/"Lonely Women Make Good Lovers" (double)(Epic)(1975)
"Bob Luman (The Pay Phone)" (Polydor)(1978)
"The Rocker—Bob Luman" (Bear Family Germany)
"More of That Rocker" (Bear Family Germany)

TED LUNDY

(Banjo, Guitar)
Given Name: Teddy Joe Lundy
Date of Birth: January 26, 1937
Where Born: Galax, Virginia
Married: Joyce
Children: T.J., Cathy, Bobby
Date of Death: June 23, 1980

Like the Stoneman and Ward families, the Lundys constituted one of the major musical clans of the Carroll-Grayson portion of the Blue Ridge Mountains. Emmett Lundy, the legendary Old-Time fiddler, was Ted's great-uncle, and his own parents had musical interests too.

Ted started picking guitar at 8 and took up the banjo at 14, favoring the newer Scruggs style over the clawhammer playing that his father used. Within a year, he had become part of a local group airing on Galax radio WBOB. Two years later, Lundy opted for a higher degree of professionalism when he went to WHIS Bluefield, West Virginia, with Udell McPeak and became banjoist for Jimmy Williams and the Shady Valley Boys. Later they moved to WCYB Bristol, Tennessee. Ted remained with them for about a year, averaging about $40 in weekly earnings.

In 1956, Lundy moved to Wilmington, Delaware, where an older brother had preceded him. He found not only a day job, but a variety of part-time musical endeavors as well. His first experience occurred with Roma Jackson and the Tennessee Pals. The best-known group in which he played was Alex Campbell and Ola Belle and the New River Boys, with whom he recorded a pair of albums on Starday in the early 60's. Ted also put his own Southern Mountain Boys together, which included Fred Hannah on mandolin, Bob Paisley on guitar, and his second cousin Jerry Lundy, grandson of Emmett, on fiddle. The Southern Mountain Boys worked together for quite a number of years with some changes in personnel as time went by. They worked locally and also went back to Galax, where they proved strong competitors both as a band and as individual instrumentalists.

The Southern Mountain Boys made their first four recordings about 1962 on Alex Campbell's New River label at a time when they were also working as a band for Campbell. They did not do another session for nearly a decade, when they cut an album for Gerd Hadeler's German firm, the GHP Recording Company. Thereafter, they went to Rounder, recording three albums in succession. By the time of their second Rounder release, Paisley had attained co-leader status. Fred Hannah left the band after the GHP album, and John Haftl, Don Eldreth and Ted's older son, T.J., later occupied this position. Wes Rineer, Don Baer, and Bill Graybeal played bass with the Southern Mountain Boys at various times. Paisley left to start his own band in 1979, and after Ted's tragic suicide, the entire group stopped performing. IMT

RECOMMENDED ALBUMS:
"Ted Lundy & the Southern Mountain Boys" (HP)(1972)
"The Old Swinging Ridge" (Rounder)(1973)
"Slipping Away" (Rounder)(1976)
"Lovesick and Sorrow" (Rounder)(1978)

ROBERT LUNN

(Singer, Guitar, Impressionist, Ventriloquist)
Given Name: Robert Rainey Lunn
Date of Birth: 1912
Where Born: Franklin, Tennessee

Billed throughout most of his career as "The Talking Blues Man," Robert Lunn was a veteran *Grand Ole Opry* star whose main claim to fame is that he took the Talking Blues genre to a national audience. He was born and grew up in Franklin, Tennessee (about 20 miles south of Nashville), where he was a friend and contemporary of the McGee Brothers, Sam and Kirk. Lunn spent his youth in vaudeville, where he used his odd left-handed guitar playing style and indifferent singing voice to develop a superb sense of showmanship and timing, and to become an expert imitator and ventriloquist.

In the 1930's, he, like many ex-vaudevillians, moved to radio — first to WCHS (West Virginia) and KWTO (Missouri) and then finally to Nashville in 1935. By that time he had picked up *The Talking Blues,* a piece that had been originated in 1926, when a South Carolina singer and comedian named Chris Bouchillon made it into a nationwide hit on Columbia Records. The popularity of Bouchillon's original recording, as well as the many follow-ups he made in the same mode, carried across the country and was imitated by dozens of Country and Blues performers. When Lunn arrived in Nashville, he was only 23 and he took a job as a bellboy at the plush Hermitage Hotel. The hotel had a mini-radio station that piped music into all the guest rooms, and Lunn began entertaining over it, featuring the *Talking Blues.*

Soon an official of the *Grand Ole Opry* heard him and invited him to perform on the show Saturday nights. In 1935 WSM was broadcasting at 50,000 watts with a clear channel, and was heard in 32 states: an impressive forum for any entertainer. Lunn was soon billed, by Judge Hay, as "The Talking Blues Man" and almost immediately found a sponsored niche on the show — the segment sponsored by Clark's Teaberry Chewing Gum. For the next several years, Lunn featured his *Talking Blues* almost every Saturday night. Building on Bouchillon's original verses, Lunn began adding new ones — including topical ones — until he soon had over 100 verses in his repertory. The fans loved it. In 1936 Lunn was voted the most popular star on the *Opry,* and seven extra staff people had to be hired to take care of the mail he was receiving. (One letter was from a very young Roy Acuff, asking for a job with Lunn.)

Lunn also toured widely with the tent shows the *Opry* began sending out in 1940, where his experience in vaudeville made him invaluable. Like many vaudeville and radio veterans, he was not especially anxious to record and did not get around to recording his *Talking Blues* until the 1950's, when he cut it for Mercury. He did publish the song in a collection issued by M.M. Cole in 1942, and he copyrighted the song the same year. (Among the younger radio entertainers who were by now using the *Talking Blues* was Woody Guthrie.) In 1943, while in the service, Lunn composed a popular sequel, *Military Talking Blues.*

After the war, Lunn returned to the *Opry,* eventually taking a job with the state of Tennessee and entertaining part-time. He did comedy for live shows like Acuff's, and watched his son get into the business, recording and performing with Bill Carlisle. Toward the end of his career, Lunn did a fine, informal album for Starday, even though he had retired from the *Opry* in 1958. CKW

RECOMMENDED ALBUM:
"The Original Talking Blues Man" (Starday)(1962)

FRANK LUTHER

(Singer, Songwriter, Piano)
Given Name: Frank Luther Crow
Date of Birth: August 5, 1905
Where Born: Kansas City, Missouri
Married: Zora Layman

Frank Luther's principal claim to fame is as the writer of the musical hall standard *Barnacle Bill the Sailor,* which he wrote with Carson J. Robison. Although born in Missouri, Luther was raised in Bakersfield, California. His earliest experiences were as singer/pianist with Gospel quartets.

In the late 20's, Frank moved to New York City. In 1928, Carson J. Robison and his partner Vernon Dalhart went their own ways, and Robison joined forces with Frank and Phil Crow, the Luther Brothers, and became generally known as the Carson Robison Trio. Frank's singing sounded so remarkably like

Dalhart's that listeners didn't notice the change of personnel.

After Phil had gone his own way, Frank and Carson, performing as a duo, were often billed as Bud and Joe Billings. Throughout the late 20's and early 30's, the duo cut sides for Victor, Conqueror and Decca Records. During 1933 through 1935, Frank was a regular guest on Ethel Park Richardson's dramatizations on WOR and the NBC network, which helped teach New Yorkers of the wonders of folk culture. During this time, he made some early Country music movies.

Frank moved into children's records during the 30's and 40's and made recordings of stories, ballads and cowboy songs, primarily for Decca. He later lectured on American music and wrote the book *Americans and Their Songs*. Frank also recorded with his wife and with singing cowboy Ray Whitley. In the 50's, he became an executive in the music industry.

RECOMMENDED ALBUMS:

"Just a Melody" (Old Homestead) [Frank Luther is featured on this Carson J. Robison album]

"Those Authentic Beverly Hill Billies" (RCA Victor) [Various artists, features Carson J. Robison and Frank Luther playing "The Little Cabin in Cascade Mountains"]

RAY LYNAM

(Singer, Songwriter, Guitar)

Where Born: Moate, County Westmeath, Ireland
Married: Unknown
Children: two

When Ray Lynam first began performing, he sang cover versions of Rolling Stones songs. That all changed when he fell in love with Bluegrass, after being introduced to the genre by Kevin Sherin, the leader of the group the Hillbillies, in 1970.

Ray soon became a very popular Country singer, being greatly influenced by Buck Owens and George Jones. Ray was hailed as "the Great Irish Hope of Country Music." His first hit singles on the Irish chart were *Sweet Rosie Jones* and *Gypsy, Jo and Me* and his first release in the U.S.was *There Ought to Be a Law*. In 1980, with his band, the Hillbillies, Ray recorded the album ***Music Man***.

He first saw Philomena Begley on TV in 1971 and considered her to be a great Country singer. They teamed up in 1974 and performed as a duo, appearing at Wembley Festival in London, and were named "Top European Duo" by the CMA (GB). While together, they recorded the albums ***We Go Together*** and ***The Two of Us***.

Although Ray and Philo rarely work together nowadays, both having such busy solo careers, they do occasionally return to perform their duo act. They released a reunion album, ***Simply Divine***, on Ritz Records. One of Ray's most popular singles was *Mona Lisa Lost Her Smile*.

Ray spent a lot of time seeking out material for his latest album, ***Back in Love by Monday***. He is still performing around the Dublin area and as of 1994, he continues to have a strong fan base. JAB

RECOMMENDED ALBUMS:

(All U.K. Releases)

"Simply Divine" (Ritz)

"Back in Love by Monday" (Ritz)

JUDY LYNN

(Singer, Songwriter, Yodeler)

Given Name: Judy Voiten
Date of Birth: April 12, 1936
Where Born: Boise, Idaho
Married: Jack Kelly

Judy Lynn, the daughter of bandleader Joe Voiten, was one of Country music's first stars to appear regularly in Las Vegas. Although she made her first public appearance when she was only 10, her route to stardom was somewhat circuitous.

Learning to rope and ride while still a youngster, Judy, who was quite a beauty, became "Queen of the Snake River Jamboree" in 1952 and "Miss Idaho" in 1955. The latter title led to her taking part in the "Miss America" contest and emerging as the runner-up. In 1953, she had been named America's "Champion Yodeler," and in 1955, *Pioneer* magazine made her their "Best Dressed Female Vocalist." The following year, she signed with ABC-Paramount and although she had no chart success, *Billboard* made her their "Most Promising Female Vocalist" in 1957.

Soon, Judy was touring with the likes of Red Foley, Elvis, Eddy Arnold and Rex Allen. She was renowned for her flamboyant western wear and traveled with an 8-piece band. In 1956, she replaced Jean Shepard (who was ill) in the *Opry* touring show. She co-hosted the first coast-to-coast *Grand Ole Opry* telecast, with Ernest Tubb, in 1957. By the early 60's, she had her own television show, the *Judy Lynn Show*, which was shown in many parts of the country. She made USO trips to the troops overseas and in 1962, signed with United Artists.

She hit the Top 10 with her single *Footsteps of a Fool,* and that remained her most successful single. She followed it up with the Top 30 record ***My Secret*** and the Top 20 single *My Father's Voice* (a self-penned song), in 1963. She stayed with United Artists until 1965, without any further chart action, and then in 1966, she moved to Pappy Dailey's Musicor label, again without any further notable success. By the end of 1967, she had once again moved, this time to Musart. Here she cut the album ***Judy Lynn in Las Vegas***.

By 1969, Judy had label hopped again and turned up on Columbia, where she recorded another live album, ***Judy Lynn Sings at Caesar's Palace***. She returned to the Country charts in 1971 with her Amaret recording *Married to a Memory*, which although it only reached the Top 75, also crossed over to just under the 100 mark on the Pop charts. In 1975, she made a further move to Warner Brothers, and had her final chart single, *Padre*.

She made a move in 1980 that seems contrary to the flamboyant character she had created. Judy Lynn decided to give up all the trappings of fame and success and became an ordained minister.

RECOMMENDED ALBUMS:

"Judy Lynn Sings at the Golden Nugget" (United Artists)(1962) [With the Sunshine Boys]

"The Judy Lynn Show" (United Artists)(1964)

"The Judy Lynn Show, Act 2" (United Artists)(1965)

"Judy Lynn—Honey Stuff" (Musicor)(1966) [With the Jordanaires]

"Judy Lynn in Las Vegas" (Unart)(1967)

"Judy Lynn Sings at Caesar's Palace" (Columbia)(1969)

"Parts of Love" (Amaret)(1971)

LORETTA LYNN

(Singer, Songwriter, Guitar)

Given Name: Loretta Webb
Date of Birth: April 14, 1935
Where Born: Johnson County, Kentucky
Married: Oliver V. "Mooney" Lynn
Children: Betty Sue, Jack Benny (dec'd.), Ernest Ray, Clara Marie ("Cissy"), Patsy Eileen, Peggy Jean

Loretta Lynn ranks as one of the few real giants of Country music and has become a household name throughout America. From humble Appalachian Kentucky beginnings, Loretta's star rose throughout the 60's to reigning status as a superstar of the 70's. Since then she has continued as a virtual living legend with a host of enduring fans, having amassed some 59 charted numbers through 1994 as a soloist and 18 more with duet partners the late Ernest Tubb and Conway Twitty.

Born and reared in Butcher "Holler" near the company town of Van Lear, Kentucky, Loretta Webb knew tough times from early childhood as an older member of a poor but proud mountain family. Music played an important role in the regional culture and Loretta remembered the girl singers she heard as a child. In 1949, she married Oliver Lynn (nicknamed "Doolittle" and "Mooney") and a year later, moved to the distant Pacific Northwest and within four years became mother to four children. Her fondness for Country music helped sustain the relative isolation she felt from being so far from home.

A decade later she began singing at local functions and in February 1960 cut some sides for the small Zero record label. Through her own and Mooney's hard efforts at self-promotion, one side of her first release, *I'm a Honky-Tonk Girl,* rose to the Top 15 on the Country charts, brought her to Nashville, and helped secure a contract with Decca in 1961.

She cut her first session that September. One of her early releases, *Success,* made the Top 10 in the summer of 1962 and led to her joining the *Grand Old Opry* that September. She became a regular on the Wilburn Brothers syndicated television show, which helped further increase her popularity. Loretta had a Top 15 single, *The Other Woman*, the following year. However, it was her Top 5 single at the end of the year, *Before I'm Over You,* that finally launched the Lynn career. She had two Top 3 singles, in 1964, *Wine, Women and Song* and *Happy Birthday.* By the end of 1965 she had added another two, the classic *Blue Kentucky Girl* and *The Home You're Tearin' Down.*

In 1966, Lynn left the Wilburns and went on her own, adding the Top 5 single *Dear Uncle Sam* plus two classic songs of female assertiveness that year, *You Ain't Woman Enough* and *Don't Come Home a Drinkin' (with Lovin' on Your Mind)*, the latter becoming her first No.1 hit. She continued in 1967 with *If You're Not Gone Too Long* and *What Kind of a Girl (Do You Think I Am). First City* (No.1), *You've Just Stepped In (from Stepping Out on Me)* (Top 3) and *Your Squaw Is on the Warpath* (Top 3) all followed in 1968. With the advent of 1969, Loretta had her third No.1 single, *Woman of the World (Leave My Man Alone).* She followed this with the Top 3 hit *To Make a Man (Feel Like a Man).* She closed out the year with *Wings Upon Your Horns* (Top 15), which was her first non-Top 10 record in seven years.

With the arrival of a new decade, Loretta moved up a gear. *I Know How* reached the Top 5 and *You Wanna Give Me a Lift* made it to the Top 10. In October 1969, she recorded her all-time favorite, *Coal Miner's Daughter,* a song which combined pride in her mountain heritage, parental affection, and glorification of working folk. This later became the title of a best-selling autobiography and award-winning motion picture. The single entered the charts at the end of October, 1970, and became a No.1,

The one and only ***Loretta Lynn***

also crossing over to the Pop Top 90. In 1980, the song again became a Country hit for Oscar-winning actress Sissy Spacek, who played Loretta in the film. Perhaps more than anything except her songs, the book and film helped make her a virtual cultural icon. In 1970, Loretta's 1967 album ***Don't Come Home a Drinkin'*** was Certified Gold.

Loretta continued to turn out hits through the 70's with *I Wanna Be Free* (Top 3), *You're Looking at Country* (Top 5) and the No.1 hit *One's on the Way* (all 1971), *Here I Am Again* (Top 3) and the No.1 *Rated "X"* (both 1972). In 1972, Loretta became the first female recipient of the CMA's "Entertertainer of the Year" award. That year, Loretta's 1968 album ***Loretta Lynn's Greatest Hits*** was Certified Gold. In 1973, with Decca becoming MCA, she followed with another No.1, *Love Is the Foundation,* and the Top 3 single *Hey Loretta.* The following year, she had the Top 5 release *They Don't Make 'Em Like My Daddy* and another No.1, *Trouble in Paradise.* During the rest of the 70's, she maintained this level of success with songs that often were contentious in subject matter, but written by Loretta with a sincerity and concern that made them readily acceptable. In 1975, she hit the Top 5 with *The Pill*, following with *Home* and the Top 3 single *When the Tingle Becomes a Chill.* Her opening release of 1976, *Red, White and Blue,* only made it to the Top 20 but in the late summer, she went to No.1 with *Somebody Somewhere (Don't Know What He's Missin' Tonight).* In 1975, Loretta became the first female recipient of the ACM's "Entertainer of the Year" award.

In 1977, she started off with another No.1, *She's Got You*, which was followed by the Top 10 record *Why Can't He Be You.* The year ended with one more No.1, *Out of My Head and Back in My Bed.* During the end of the decade, her chart success showed signs of tapering off, and of her two singles in 1978, *Spring Fever* reached the Top 15 and *We've Come a Long Way Baby* got to the Top 10. She enjoyed a revival in 1979, with *I Can't Feel You Anymore* and *I've Got a Picture of Us on My Mind*, which both made the Top 5.

With the arrival of the 80's, she only reached the Top 10, as a solo, on one occasion, with the 1982 single *I Lie.* However, she did release memorable singles that did well, including *Pregnant Again, Naked in the Rain* and *Cheatin' on a Cheater* (Top 20, all 1980), *Somebody Led Me Away* (1981), *Making Love from Memory* (Top 20, 1982) and *Heart Don't Do This to Me* (Top 20, 1985). In 1981, two of Loretta's albums went Gold: ***Greatest Hits Vol. II*** (1974) and ***Lead Me On*** (1971). In 1983, Loretta was inducted into the Nashville Songwriters Hall of Fame. In 1986, Loretta was the recipient of *Music City News* Cover Awards' "Living Legend Award." Two years later, she received the ultimate accolade, when she was inducted into the Country Music Hall of Fame. Also in 1988, two of Loretta's albums were Certified Gold. They were ***The Very Best of Conway Twitty & Loretta Lynn*** (1984) and ***We Only Make Believe*** (1971, with Conway Twitty).

As well as an illustrious solo career, Loretta also enjoyed much success as one half of two memorable duos. In the 60's, Decca teamed Loretta with Ernest Tubb, forming a duet that produced some strong chartmakers like *Mr. and Mrs. Used to Be* (Top 15, 1964), *Our Hearts Are Holding Hands* (Top 25, 1965) and *Who's Gonna Take the Garbage Out* (Top 20, 1969). That combination seemed almost trivial when compared to Lynn and Conway Twitty, who chalked up five consecutive No.1 hits beginning with *After the Fire Is Gone* (also a Top 60 Pop hit) and continuing with *Lead Me On* (both in 1971). Two years later, they followed up with *Louisiana Woman, Mississippi Man.* Their final No.1 successes were *As Soon as I Hang Up the Phone* (1974) and *Feelin's* (1975). Their other hits were all Top 10 entries: *The Letter* (Top 3, 1976), *I Can't Love You Enough* (1977), *From Seven Till Ten/You're the Reason Our Kids Are Ugly* (1978), *You Know Just What I'd Do/The Sadness of It All* (1979), *It's True Love* (Top 5, 1980) and *Lovin' What Your Lovin' Does to Me* and *I Still Believe in Waltzes* (Top 3, both, 1981).

Over the years, several of Loretta's kin have also worked in Country music, including sisters Peggy Sue and Crystal Gayle, brother Jay Lee Webb, brother-in-law Sonny Wright, daughter Cissy, and son Ernest Ray.

In the last 10 years, Loretta Lynn has persisted as an active performer, although most of her recent singles have been nearer the bottom than the top of the charts. She often appears at Lowes Theater in Branson, Missouri, when not touring elsewhere or playing at the *Opry* . In the latter part of 1993, she curtailed her musical activity because of Mooney Lynn's declining health, and of course, she was greatly affected by the sudden deaths of both her brother and her great friend, Conway Twitty. Her place, along with that of Dolly Parton, as one of the preeminent females in Country music, appears at this time to be secure. It was with Dolly and that other female stalwart of Country music,Tammy Wynette, that Loretta re-emerged into the limelight with the highly successful chart album ***Honky Tonk Angels*** at the end of 1993, which went Gold in 1994 and yielded the Top 70 single *Silver Threads and Golden Needles.*

The honors and awards (for full details see Awards Section) bestowed upon her by fans, the music industry, and former President George Bush may be unprecedented in the annals of the genre. Loretta's unabashed and unapologetic Country ways have also played a key role in her gaining an enduring popularity.

IMT

RECOMMENDED ALBUMS:

"Greatest Hits" (Decca)(1968)
"Greatest Hits, Volume II" (MCA)(1974)
"I Remember Patsy" (MCA)(1977)
"Out of My Head and Back in My Bed" (MCA)(1978)
"Lyin' Cheatin', Woman Chasin', Honky Tonkin', Whiskey Drinkin' You" (MCA)(1983) [Features cover of Mooney Lynn, doing just that!]
With Ernest Tubb:
"The Ernest Tubb/Loretta Lynn Story" (double)(MCA)(1973)
With Conway Twitty:
"The Very Best of Conway Twitty and Loretta Lynn" (MCA)(1979)
"Two's a Party" (MCA)(1981)
With Dolly Parton and Tammy Wynette:
"Honky Tonk Angels" (Columbia)(1993)

SHELBY LYNNE

(Singer)

Given Name:	**Shelby Lynn Moorer**
Date of Birth:	**October 22, 1968**
Where Born:	**Quantico, Virginia**
Married:	**Unknown**

Whether Shelby Lynne will "make it" in Country Music is a matter of conjecture, but there is no doubt she will become a major force in popular music, possessing a voice that has already garnered tributes from her peers within the industry. Shelby's style is best described as Country with a touch of the Blues. She has a powerful emotion-filled voice which comes through loud and clear.

Shelby was raised in Jackson, Alabama, and it was her mother who early on wanted her to be a star. She taught Shelby and her sister, Allison, harmony on their long journey to and from school. Their father, an ex-Marine, was a vocational school instructor and a local Country singer. Shelby and her mom had planned to become a singing duo. They were becoming serious about it, but it was not meant to be. Her father's drinking and violence, which was often aimed at Shelby when she took her mother's side, broke up the family and they fled to a new home. Late one night, her father called. Not wanting him to come into the house, her mother went out into the driveway, and her father shot her mother and then turned the gun on himself. Shelby was 17 and Allison 13. After the tragedy the girls had to get on with their lives, and although Shelby married, it didn't last.

In 1990, Shelby and her sister moved to Nashville and were sharing a house and looking out for one another. When not at college, Allison sang back-up for her sister. Shelby has always been a fan of Country and big band music and in recent years has discovered Jazz. After leaving high school, Shelby toured all the clubs in the Mobile area trying to sing with the house bands. She also entered every talent show and singing contest in southern Alabama, which she usually won.

Following an unsuccessful Opryland audition, she was asked to demo some songs by a local songwriter. One of the demos was heard by Bob Tubert, who had done some work for the Nashville Network, and he was impressed by Shelby's sound. He got her onto *Nashville Now*. The day after the show, four major labels contacted her, including producer Billy Sherrill. Later that day, she was in Sherrill's office when a call came through from George Jones, who had also seen her performance on *Nashville Now*. George was considering recording a song on his new album with her. The phone was handed to Shelby and a voice said, "This is George Jones. Let's get together and sing." That call resulted in the single *If I Could Bottle This Up* (1988), which went Top 50 and in 1991, found its way onto George's ***Friends in High Places*** album.

Needless to say, Shelby chose to put her career in the hands of Billy Sherrill, Bob Montgomery and Epic Records. The first three singles on Epic, in 1989, entered the Country charts: *Under Your Spell Again* (Top 100), *The Hurtin' Side* (Top 40) and *Little Bits and Pieces* (Top 70). Shelby's debut album, ***Sunrise***, was critically acclaimed.

Two Top 30 singles followed in 1990, *I'll Lie Myself to Sleep* and *Things Are Tough All Over,* and a second album, ***Tough All Over***, came out in the same year. That year, Shelby opened for Randy Travis, but still the radio stations failed to play her records to any great degree. Her 1991 single *What About the Love We Made* only reached the Top 50, as did the duet with Les Taylor *The Very First Lasting Love*, while her last charted single for Epic, *Don't Cross Your Heart*, only made it to the Top 60. Her album for that year was ***Soft Talk***, but no singles from the album reached the charts in 1992 and so that year she left Epic.

In 1993, Morgan Creek Entertainment, the company that produced the film *Dances with Wolves*, released Shelby Lynne's new album, ***Temptation***, on their new label. This album reflects Shelby's love of big band music and although it was critically acclaimed, only the single *Feelin' Kind of Lonely Tonight* reached the chart. It only made the Top 70 in spite of heavy promotion via the music video on CMT. The cd sleeve revealed Shelby with a new waif-like image, but she must now be wondering what else she has to change to get radio acceptance of her singles.

JAB

RECOMMENDED ALBUMS:

"Sunrise" (Epic)(1989)
"Tough All Over" (Epic)(1990)
"Soft Talk" (Epic)(1991)
"Temptation" (Morgan Creek)(1993)

M

MAC AND BOB

(McFARLAND AND GARDNER)

When Formed: **1922**

MAC

(Vocals, Songwriter, Harmonica, Mandolin, Fiddle)

Given Name:	**Lester McFarland**
Date of Birth:	**February 2, 1902**
Where Born:	**Gray, Kentucky**

Married: Ruby Weems
Children: Kenneth, Larry, Carol
Date of Death: July 24, 1984

BOB
(Vocals, Songwriter, Guitar)
Given Name: Robert Alexander Gardner
Date of Birth: December 16, 1897
Where Born: Oliver Springs, Tennessee
Married: Francis Blatt
Date of Death: September 30, 1978

Mac and Bob, as they were known during their peak years of radio fame in the 1930's, were the first really popular close harmony duet in Country singing. Though most of their music sounds too restrained and polite to modern ears, they were intensely popular on records, on radio, and even through songbooks during the first decade of Country music. Their huge popularity with numbers like *When the Roses Bloom Again* and *Twenty-One Years* helped make those numbers Country standards.

Both Mac and Bob grew up in areas rich in traditional and Old-Time music—north-central Tennessee and southern Kentucky respectively. They met in 1915, when both were students at the Kentucky School for the Blind in Louisville; here they were given some formal musical training to augment their natural singing abilities, and by 1922 they had decided to embark on a career of full-time singing.

By 1925 they were among the first and best-received acts on the new radio station WNOX at Knoxville, and through the efforts of a local promoter named Gus Fannensteil were given an audition with the Vocalion Record Company. Unlike other companies of the time, Vocalion was not yet into the practice of field recordings, and was trying to bring its prospective stars into its New York studios. In October 1926 they brought McFarland and Gardner (as they were still known) to New York for a marathon session that yielded some 24 titles. These included their biggest hit, *When the Roses Bloom Again*, a 1901 Pop song by the composer of *School Days*, as well as *Bully of the Town*, *Hand Me Down My Walking Cane*, *There's No Disappointment in Heaven*, *You're as Welcome as the Flowers in May* and *Are You Tired of Me My Darling*— all of which would be covered again and again by later artists.

So spectacular was the success of *When the Roses Bloom Again*, that the labels had the pair back in the New York studios barely two months later, on December 10. Here they cut another of their anthems, *Knoxville Girl*, a song that would be covered by everybody from the Blue Sky Boys to the Louvin Brothers, as well as a number of Gospel favorites as part of a studio quartet called the Old Southern Singers. By this time Vocalion (and its sister company Brunswick) was convinced that they had something special with the duo, and began to record them on a regular basis twice a year. Except for various studio "citybillies" like Vernon Dalhart and Carson Robison, McFarland and Gardner became about the most heavily recorded Old-Time music act of the day. While they sounded best on old sentimental songs and pious Gospel offerings, they showed a surprising Blues feel when they did *Chattanooga Blues* (1926), an Irish touch with their success with *Three Leaves of Shamrock* (1927) and even a talent for topical songs like *Woman Sufferage* (1928). In 1927, their record company sent them on a tour of the Southwest, making them one of the first Country acts to go on such a tour.

In April 1931, the team moved to Chicago, where they became regulars on the WLS *National Barn Dance*. Here they became Mac and Bob and expanded their fame considerably through the power and publicity resources of the huge Sears company, sponsors of the show. By 1933, Mac and Bob had switched over to the American Record Company and were seeing their records issued on dozens of labels, including Banner, Oriole, Melotone, Conqueror, Perfect, Romeo, and Decca, and under a battery of different names, such as the Perry Brothers, Kentucky Mountain Boys, Parsons & Kent, Miller Brothers, Bob Lester & Bud Green, Harper Brothers, Radio Duo, and others.

For a time in the 1930's, the duo worked at KDKA Pittsburgh and other stations, but returned to WLS in 1939, where they stayed until 1950. At that time, Bob Gardner retired to devote his efforts to evangelism. (Folklorist Harlan Daniel, who extensively interviewed both men in later life, noted that the two were quite opposite temperamentally: Gardner was reserved, serious, pious, and very much the minister; McFarland was lively, liked his bottle, and was a lively joker.)

Both men made a handful of later records, none of which were especially interesting, and Mac eventually began working for the Chicago State Hospital, from where he retired in 1970. In later years, both men moved back to the hills north of Knoxville, Tennessee, living near the town of Oliver Springs, both somewhat bitter about their musical days. There Bob died on September 30, 1978, and Mac on July 24, 1984. CKW

RECOMMENDED ALBUMS:
"Mac & Bob" (Birch)
"Precious Memories" (Birch) [This is a Patsy Montana album that features Mac]

WARNER MACK

(Singer, Songwriter, Guitar)
Given Name: Warner MacPherson
Date of Birth: April 2, 1938
Where Born: Nashville, Tennessee
Married: Peggy Sue
Children: Melodie, Sherry, Marty

For a couple of decades, Warner Mack was present on the Country music charts, and for at least ten years, he was one of Decca Records' brightest stars.

Warner Mack was born in Nashville, the son of a Presbyterian minister, and raised in Vicksburg, Mississippi, where he developed an interest in music at an early age. He learned to play guitar by impersonating his favorite Country singers on the radio. During his time at Jett High School, Warner received offers to play baseball and football from several universities in Mississippi and Louisiana. The most tempting offer came from the St. Louis Cardinals but Warner's love of music was stronger than his love of baseball and soon the invitation came to join the KWKH *Louisiana Hayride*.

He became a popular performer in and around Louisiana and gained more fans when he appeared on Red Foley's *Ozark Jamboree*. However, he still worked full-time for a tire company and was a radio announcer on WVIM Vicksburg. In the late 50's, Warner moved back to Nashville and signed with Decca in 1957, where due to a secretarial error, he was signed as "Mack" rather than MacPherson. His first hit, the self-penned *Is It Wrong (For Loving You)*, reached the Top 10, stayed on the Country charts for 9 months, and crossed over to the Pop Chart Top 70, and then there was no further immediate chart action, although, in 1960, Webb Pierce had a No.1 with this Mack song.

Warner joined Kapp Records in 1961, where the tracks he recorded included one single, *Tears for Two/Forever We'll Walk Hand in Hand,* He released several albums on Kapp that sold well and his popularity was mounting steadily in the 60's. Mack was invited to perform on the *Grand Ole Opry* and then he was offered a new contract by Decca Records. His first release for the label, *Surely*, made the Top 30 and his second, *Sittin' in an All Nite Cafe*, hit the Top 5. Warner suffered a major setback in 1964 when a serious auto accident curtailed his performing for several months.

Warner Mack returned to Country music stronger than ever in 1965 and scored the biggest hit of his career, his self-penned *The*

Bridge Washed Out, which reached No.1 and stayed on the chart for nearly six months. Later in the year, Mack had a Top 3 with his co-written *Sittin' on a Rock (Crying in a Creek)*. In 1966, Warner had two back-to-back Top 5 hits with *Talkin' to the Wall* and *It Takes a Lot of Money*. The following year, the hits continued with the Top 10 *Driftin' Apart*, the Top 5 *How Long Will It Take* and *I'd Give the World (To Be Back Loving You)*, which just failed to make the Top 10. In 1968 Mack was back in the Top 10 with *I'm Gonna Move On*.

Warner closed out the 60's with two more Top 10 hits, *Leave My Dreams Alone* and *I'll Still Be Missing You*. As the 70's began Warner continued to record for Decca and hit the Top 20 with *Love Hungry* and *Live for the Good Times*. These were to be Warner's major successes, and even though he had seven more chart entries, the Top 40 *You Make Me Feel Like a Man*, in 1971, was his most successful release. Warner left the label at the end of 1973. The following year, Sonny James had a No.1 with *Is It Wrong (For Loving You)*. In 1977, Warner surfaced on Pageboy Records, where he had one basement-level chart entry, *These Crazy Thoughts (Run Through My Mind)*. By 1984, Warner was recording for Sapphire Records.

Warner Mack's songwriting skills were tapped by many other Country singers. In addition to writing songs for himself, Mack composed material that was recorded by Bill Anderson, Kitty Wells, Loretta Lynn, Charlie Louvin and Brenda Lee. Warner for a while operated the Warner Mack Country Store in Madison, Tennessee. JIE

RECOMMENDED ALBUMS:

"The Best of Warner Mack" (Kapp)(1965)
"Songs We Sang in Church & Home" (Decca)(1967) [With Sister Dean]
"The Many Moods of Warner Mack" (Decca)(1968)
"Great Country" (Coral)(1973)
"The Best of the Best of Warner Mack" (Gusto)(1978)
"At Your Service" (Sapphire)(1984)

UNCLE DAVE MACON

(Banjo, Guitar, Vocals)

Given Name:	**David Harrison Macon**
Date of Birth:	**October 7, 1870**
Where Born:	**Smart Station (Warren County), Tennessee**
Married:	**Matilda**
Children:	**Archie, Dorris, Harry, Eston, Glenn, plus two who died young**
Date of Death:	**March 22, 1952**

According to fellow *Opry* pioneer Kirk McGee, "Uncle Dave Macon may not have been the best banjo player and maybe not the best singer, but he sure was the best something." Others have noted that, if Jimmie Rodgers was the father of Country music, then Uncle Dave was certainly the grandfather.

Folklorists have noted that he was a crucial link between the southern Folk music of the 19th century and the modern age of radio, records, and commercial Country music. What is undeniable is that Uncle Dave Macon, with his gold teeth, chin whiskers and gates-ajar collar, was one of the first-generation pioneers who helped define Country music and establish the *Grand Ole Opry*. Uncle Dave himself described himself merely as a "banjoist songster," but his exuberant banjo playing, boisterous singing, and ornate jokes and one-liners made him a legend.

Casual observers and listeners sometimes describe Macon's banjo playing as "frailing," to distinguish it from modern Bluegrass playing; he could play that way, but more serious banjo students have isolated some sixteen different styles on his records, including a variety of up-picking and two-finger methods. His repertoire included well over 200 songs, ranging from old ballads to 19th-century Tin Pan Alley fare and from Gospel tunes to ancient minstrel show walkabouts. Recent research has shown that many of his comic lyrics came from black Folk music of the upland South.

Macon's father was a Confederate captain who turned to distilling after the war. The family lived near Smart Station, in Warren County, Tennessee, about 60 miles southeast of Nashville. As a boy, Macon absorbed some of the Folk songs in the region, but his real musical awakening came in 1884 when the family moved to Nashville. There they ran a hotel that was a headquarters for many of the circus and vaudeville acts that came to town. Macon watched many rehearse in the basement of the hotel and was fascinated by the vaudeville banjo players he saw. By the time he was 14, his mother had bought him his first banjo. His interest in vaudeville, however, was cut short when his father was murdered on the streets on Nashville, and the family was forced to return to rural Cannon County.

Grand Ole Opry pioneer ***Uncle Dave Macon***

For the next 35 years, Macon worked a large farm, raised a family, and ran a mule-drawn freight line. He continued to learn songs from all sorts of sources and adapt them to his banjo style. Then, about 1923, his freight line was rendered obsolete by Henry Ford's new trucks and he signed a contract to try his luck on stage at Loew's theaters. Starting in Birmingham, he was a spectacular success. He was soon touring everywhere from Boston to Florida. His comic songs, like *Chewing Gum*, *Keep My Skillet Good and Greasy*, and *Hill Billie Blues*, endeared him to audiences and in the fall of 1925, when Nashville's radio station WSM opened, Uncle Dave became one of its first regulars. Soon, he was appearing on the Saturday night *Barn Dance*, which, in 1927, was renamed the *Grand Ole Opry*.

Though he was over 50 when he began performing professionally, Macon often worked with younger musicians who were able to match his own skills: fiddler Sid Harkreader, instrumentalists Sam and Kirk McGee, singers Alton and Rabon Delmore. From 1924 until 1938, Macon recorded over 180 songs for every major record label. Hits included topical songs like *The Bible's True* (about the Scopes trial), *Rockabout My Saro Jane* (learned from black roustabouts on the Cumberland River), *Buddy Won't You Roll Down the Line* (an early labor song re-popularized during the 1960's), *Late Last Night When Willie Came Home*, and *The Death of John Henry*. About a third of the Macon repertoire was Gospel music, as exemplified by his unofficial theme song, *How Beautiful Heaven Must Be*.

In his later years, Macon traveled to Hollywood to make a film (*Grand Ole Opry*, 1940), appeared on the network radio portion of the *Opry*, toured with Roy Acuff, Bill Monroe, Curly Fox, and others and even did local television. He continued to appear on the *Opry* until days before his death. He left no real protégé to carry on his music, though David "Stringbean" Akeman inherited his banjo, many of his songs, and some of his jokes. Macon's old records have remained in print on lp and cd, and festivals like the Uncle

Dave Macon Days Celebration in Murfreesboro, Tennessee, have become forums for younger musicians who want to keep alive his music. Uncle Dave Macon died in 1952, and in 1966, he was inducted into the Country Music Hall of Fame. CKW

RECOMMENDED ALBUMS:

"Original Recordings 1925-1935" (County Records)
"Country Music Hall of Fame" (MCA)

MADDOX BROTHERS AND ROSE, The

CLIFF MADDOX
(Vocals, Guitar, Mandolin)
Given Name: Clifton R.E. Maddox
Date of Birth: ca. 1912
Date of Death: 1949
CAL MADDOX
(Vocals, Guitar, Harmonica)
Given Name: John Calvin Maddox
Date of Birth: November 3, 1915
Date of Death: 1968
FRED MADDOX
(Vocals, Bass)
Given Name: Fred Roscoe Maddox
Date of Birth: July 3, 1919
Date of Death: October 29, 1992
DON MADDOX
(Vocals, Fiddle)
Given Name: Kenneth Chalmer Maddox
Date of Birth: December 7, 1922
HENRY MADDOX
(Vocals, Mandolin, Lead Guitar)
Given Name: Henry Ford Maddox
Date of Birth: March 19, 1928
Date of Death: 1974
ROSE MADDOX
(Vocals, Bass, Snare Drum)
Given Name: Roselea Arbana Maddox
Date of Birth: August 15, 1925

All Born: Boaz, Alabama
Support Musicians included:
Bud Duncan (Steel Guitar), Jimmy Winkle (Lead Guitar), Roy Nichols (Lead Guitar), Gene Breeden (Lead Guitar)

The Maddox Brothers and Rose advertised themselves as "the most colorful hillbilly band in America" during their prime years, which extended from the mid-40's through the mid-50's. They lived up to their publicity, which not only featured colorful costumes but loads of talent and humor in various vocal and instrumental combinations. The Maddox Family offered West Coast Country fans an exciting alternative to Western Swing and Cowboy music.

The Maddox family hailed from the Sand Mountain country of Appalachian Alabama where Charlie and Lula Maddox struggled to earn a living as sharecroppers during the 20's. By the end of that decade, they had a family of seven children.

With the onset of the Great Depression and a drop in cotton prices, Mom Maddox determined to better the family's condition and decided to fulfill her lifelong dream of taking them to California. Selling their few possessions gained the parents $30 in cash. Cliff and Alta, the two elder children who were grown and married, remained in Alabama for the time being. Initially the rest of the family walked and hitchhiked to Meridian, Mississippi. From there freight trains provided their means of transportation. Miraculously, they survived and arrived in Oakland, California, where they found temporary refuge in "Pipe City," an informal community of homeless folk. Following a not very successful effort to pan gold in the mountains near Tuolumne, the family settled in Modesto, where they became "fruit tramps," or farm laborers traveling up and down the great interior valley. Cliff, Alta and their spouses soon joined the rest of the family. Although the family remained poor, their condition apparently did improve.

The Maddox family brought their musical culture with them, and in 1937, Fred finally talked the management at KTRB Modesto into giving them a time slot, which they did on condition that they include a girl vocalist among their numbers. Thus Rose, not quite 12, began her radio career with a repertoire of three songs. At night, they played in bars and clubs, initially for tips. In 1939, they won a competition at the California State Fair. In early 1940, they secured two years at KFBK in Sacramento, and several other stations in the West Coast states also carried the program. All through the early years of the group's work, Mom Maddox kept a firm grip on their management.

The WWII draft broke up the band as Cal, Fred and later Don all spent some years in the service. Cliff's life-long health problems kept him out and Henry was too young. Cliff at times had his own band, the Rhythm Ramblers. Rose worked with such bands as those of Arky Stark and Dave Stogner, trying unsuccessfully to join Bob Wills' Texas Playboys as a vocalist. Also during the war years, Rose married and had a child, but the union soon dissolved.

The Maddox Brothers** with sister **Rose Maddox

After the war, the Maddox Brothers and Rose regrouped, working initially at KGDM Stockton. As many of their fellow Dust Bowl-Depression refugees had achieved a new level of prosperity, so, too, did their entertainers. For the next decade, the family did quite well with their unique blend of humor, showmanship, old-fashioned hillbilly, new Country, Western, Gospel and even some Pop musical influences. They recorded extensively on the 4 Star label through 1954, when they switched to Columbia and cut another forty-four sides. Like their shows, the Maddox Brothers and Rose waxed a wide variety of material. However, the numbers that featured Rose on vocals such as Woody Guthrie's *Philadelphia Lawyer* and Billy Cox's raucous *Sally, Let Your Bangs Hang Down* probably had the biggest impact. Many keen-eared listeners have also noticed roots of rock'n'roll in their Country boogie numbers and Fred's slapping-bass style.

In March, 1949, the Maddoxes traveled to Nashville for a guest spot on the *Opry,* and in the early 50's, they spent four months of each year at the *Louisiana Hayride*, but otherwise based their main operations on the West Coast, where their biggest audience was concentrated and made occasional guest spots on the *Town Hall Party* and *Hometown Jamboree*. From time to time, the Maddoxes had some non-family members in their group, too. These included Bud Duncan on steel guitar and Jimmy Winkle, Roy Nichols, and Gene Breeden on lead guitar.

Toward the end of their Columbia years, Rose began to record solo and also cut a few duets with Henry's wife, Loretta, as Rose and Retta. The Maddox Brothers and Rose had their last sessions together on August 30, 1957, although they had separated into two groups the previous year. Fred, Don, Henry, and Loretta worked in one unit while Rose went solo assisted by Cal as band member. The first group had a relatively short career. Fred later operated the Fred Maddox Playhouse, a notable night club, for some years. Henry and Cal later worked on some of Rose's Capitol recordings.

Heart disease plagued the Maddox family as they grew older and one by one the brothers died until today only Don, who lives near Ashland, Oregon, survives. Rose continues to be an active performer as her health permits. King Records released some of the Maddox 4 Star material in the early 60's and later Arhoolie did the same. Bear Family released two albums from Columbia material and Arhoolie took two albums from radio transcriptions. Since their music represents a compendium of so many traditions and trends, it has continued to appeal to a wide variety of listeners. IMT

RECOMMENDED ALBUMS:

"A Collection of Standard Sacred Songs" (King)(1960)
"The Maddox Brothers & Rose" (King)(1961)
"I'll Still Write Your Name in the Sand" (King)(1961)
"The Maddox Brothers & Rose" (Wrangler and Forum)(1962) [4 Star masters]
"Go Honky-Tonkin'" (Pickwick/Hilltop and Sears) (1965) [4 Star masters]
"The Maddox Brothers & Rose, 1946-1951, Vol. 1 & Vol. 2" (Arhoolie)(1976)
"Rockin' Rollin' Maddox Bros. & Rose" (Bear Family Germany)(1981)
"Family Folks" (Bear Family Germany)(1981)
"On the Air, Vol. 1 & Vol. 2" (Arhoolie)(1983-1984)
"Columbia Historic Edition" (Columbia)(1985)

ROSE MADDOX

(Singer, Songwriter, Bass Fiddle, Snare Drum)

Given Name:	**Roselea Arbana Maddox**
Date of Birth:	**August 15, 1925**
Where Born:	**Boaz, Alabama**
Married:	**1. Enoch Byford Hale (div.)** **2. Jimmy Clarence Brogdan (div.)**
Children:	**Donald Douglas Hale (dec'd.)**

The singing career of Rose Maddox extends over a period of fifty-five years. One of Country music's great survivors, she has fought her way back from three heart attacks to gain recognition as a pioneering female artist in her profession while continuing to perform as health and circumstances permit.

Rose Maddox at age 7 had taken the difficult trek from Alabama to California with her parents and four brothers in the spring of 1933. Her career as the Maddox Brothers and Rose began in 1937 at KTRB Modesto and lasted until 1956 with time out for her brothers' military service. During that time Rose worked in some other bands, married, had a child and divorced. After WWII, the group reorganized and worked together for more than a decade. Although the Maddoxes constituted a highly talented unit, Rose's lead and solo vocals were a major contribution to their appeal and commercial success.

In May 1953, Rose began to record for Columbia as a solo artist. Over the next four years, she had thirty-six sides released, in addition to those made with her brothers. After the dissolution of the entire unit, Rose cut a fine Gospel album in February 1958, which marked the first appearance of a Maddox as soloist on an album. Later, a collection of her Columbia singles appeared on the firm's budget label, Harmony.

In January 1959, Ken Nelson and Cliffie Stone signed Rose to a five-year Capitol contract. Her first session in February resulted in *Gambler's Love*, which became her first charted hit (Top 25) that spring. Her years with Nelson produced nine more chartmakers, *Kissing My Pillow/I Want to Live Again* and *Conscience, I'm Guilty* (all Top 15, 1961), *Sing a Little Song of Heartache* (Top 3, 1962), *Lonely Teardrops, Down to the River, Somebody Told Somebody* (all Top 20, 1963), *Alone with You* (Top 50) and *Blue Bird Let Me Tag Along* (Top 30) (both 1964). Rose also cut six duets with Buck Owens, four of which were hits: *Loose Talk* (Top 5)/*Mental Cruelty* (Top 10) (1961) and *We're the Talk of the Town* (Top 15)/*Sweethearts in Heaven* (Top 20) (1963).

Simultaneous to Rose's Capitol singles, all aimed at the charts, Nelson produced five albums. These are probably the most treasured of her solo recordings today among collectors. Her album ***Rose Maddox Sings Bluegrass*** was the first all-Bluegrass album by a female performer and ranks as a true classic. Ironically, this album, cut in March 1962, was her only one recorded in Nashville. It featured instrumental support from such greats in their own right as Tommy Jackson, Bill Monroe, John Palmer, Don Reno, Red Smiley and Donna Stoneman.

Following the last Capitol session in March 1965, she recorded for some smaller labels such as Portland and an album for Starday in 1970. All during the 60's, Rose toured extensively with brothers Cal and Henry. Later her son, Donnie, worked a great deal with her until his untimely death in 1982. Rose also went on some tours with Buck Owens, who admired her music a great deal.

By the mid-70's, Rose, who had continued working whenever and wherever she could, began to gain some respect as a pioneer female in Country music. She ranks alongside Wilma Lee Cooper and Molly O'Day as one of a triumvirate of strong-voiced women of Appalachian origin who paved the way for the likes of Kitty Wells, Wanda Jackson, and Jean Shepard, who carried the tradition a bit further.

Arhoolie and Bear Family reissued some of the Maddox Brothers and Rose recordings of a generation earlier, and her new albums on Varrick, Takoma, and another Bluegrass effort for Arhoolie showed that the venerable lady still had plenty of the old fire left. She played at major Folk and Bluegrass festivals throughout the country.

During the 80's, Rose Maddox survived three heart attacks, one of which left her in a coma for three months, and the death of her only child, son Donnie, from a stroke. Still, even after her last recovery, the trouper and survivor went back to work as soon as she could. She plans another album for Chris Strachwitz's Arhoolie Records. As of late April 1994, Rose still resides in her long-time Ashland, Oregon, home.

Bear Family Records has recently reissued her entire Capitol collection of 111 songs, including the six with Buck Owens, in a compact disc set with an authoritative booklet by Charlie Seemann. Meanwhile, the completed manuscript biography *Queen of the West: The Manifest Destiny of Rose Maddox* by Johnny Whiteside awaits publication. IMT

RECOMMENDED ALBUMS:

"Precious Memories" (Columbia)(1958)
"The One Rose" (Capitol)(1960)
"Glorybound Train" (Capitol)(1960) [Re-released by Stetson UK in the original sleeve (1987)]
"A Big Bouquet of Rose's" (Capitol)(1961)
"Rose Maddox Sings Bluegrass" (Capitol)(1962) [Re-released by Stetson UK in the original sleeve (1987)]
"Alone with You" (Capitol)(1963)
"Rose Maddox's Best" (Harmony)(1964)
"Rosie" (Starday)(1970)
"California Rose" (See for Miles UK) (1989) [Capitol masters]
"The One Rose, The Capitol Years" (Box Set)(Bear Family Germany)(1993)
"Queen of the West" (Varrick)
"Reckless Love and Bold Adventure" (Takoma)(1977)
"This Is Rose Maddox" (Arhoolie)(1982)
"A Beautiful Bouquet" (Arhoolie)(1983) [with Vern Williams]

J.E. MAINER

(Singer, Fiddle, Clawhammer Banjo, Jew's Harp)

Given Name:	**Joseph Emmett Mainer**
Dare of Birth:	**July 20, 1898**
Where Born:	**Buncombe County, North Carolina**
Married:	**Sadie Gertrude Mainer**
Children:	**J.E., Jr., Glen, Earl, Charlie, Carolyn, Mary**
Date of Death:	**June 12, 1971**

J.E. Mainer's Mountaineers were a mountain string band in the early 1930's that achieved considerable popularity. J.E. maintained a musical group with various personnel changes for nearly forty years. Although the Mainer band moved in the direction of Bluegrass, most observers have placed them in a category that technically falls a bit short of that definition, at least in the pre-WWII period. J.E. Mainer played a respectable, albeit somewhat rough, Old-Time fiddle and many of the musicians who worked with him, including Snuffy Jenkins, George Morris, Leonard Stokes and younger brother Wade Mainer, all played key roles in the transition of Old-Time string music toward the Bluegrass sound.

The Mainers came from a Carolina mountain family that resided several miles from Asheville, eventually settling near the community of Weaverville. J.E. left home at age 12 and spent the next dozen years working in cotton mills in various locales. In 1922, he came to Concord in the Piedmont region, got married and settled down on a more or less permanent basis.

J.E. had already learned to play a bit of banjo so he could accompany his fiddling brother-in-law Roscoe Banks at dances, and he went to work at mastering the fiddle as well. When his younger brother, Wade, came to Concord, the two finally got to know each other and to play music together.

With the addition of guitarist-vocalist "Daddy" John Love along with Lester and Howard Lay, the Mainer's Mountaineers began winning local fiddling and other talent contests. They also began to appear on radio at WSOC Gastonia and from 1934, on the *Crazy Barn Dance* at powerful WBT Charlotte. Later, Hubert Fincher of Crazy Water Crystals (a laxative and mineral water product) sent them to WWL New Orleans for three months and to WWNC Asheville for a briefer period. They then returned to WBT. Meanwhile, the Lays departed and Claude ("Zeke") Morris, then 18 years old, took their place.

The two Mainers, Love and Morris constituted the Mountaineers at the time of their first Bluebird session at Atlanta in

***J.E.** and **Wade Mainer** and the Mountaineers*

August 1935. These recordings resulted in 14 fine numbers, but by far the hit of the day was the Mainer rendition of *Maple on the Hill*, a Victorian sentimental song to which they put a new tune. J.E. fiddled prominently on that particular piece while Wade and Zeke sang a duet. By the time of their next session, in February 1936, Wade and Zeke recorded by themselves while J.E. used Clarence Todd, Ollie Bunn and Howard Bumgardner as a band. That June, J.E., Wade and Zeke with some additional musicians worked together again. Soon afterward, they parted company as J.E. remained with Crazy Water Crystals at WPTF Raleigh, and Wade and Zeke went on their own as Sons of the Mountaineers.

J.E. put together a new band composed of Snuffy Jenkins, George Morris and Leonard Stokes. They worked for a time on radio at WSPA Spartanburg and for a longer stint at WIS Columbia. While there, the band had two additional sessions for Bluebird. When J.E. eventually left, Byron Parker took over the band. In 1939, after his split from the band, J.E. had another session for Bluebird, at which time he borrowed Clyde Moody and Jay Hugh Hall from Wade's entourage to help him record. In 1940 J.E. got still another band together that included Price Saunders, Mitchell Parker and Gurney Thomas. This group worked on radio in Greensboro and Birmingham and, with slight personnel change, on the Mexican border stations and at KMOX St. Louis.

During WWII, J.E. returned to Concord and for the better part of the next two decades, he confined most of his playing to the Carolinas, Tennessee and Virginia. He recorded again for King in 1946, with a band whose most prominent members were his sons J.E., Jr. (usually known as "Curly") and Glenn, who developed into a quality Bluegrass banjo picker. Fifteen years later, J.E. Mainer's Mountaineers cut two singles and an album for King.

In 1962, Chris Strachwitz of the El Cerrito, California-based Arhoolie label visited J.E. in Concord and subsequently cut a new album, ***The Legendary Family from the Blue Ridge Mountains***. This led to the rediscovery of Mainer's Mountaineers by a new generation of fans across the U.S. Beginning in 1967, J.E. cut a series of albums for Uncle Jim O'Neal's Rural Rhythm label, guested on the WWVA *Jamboree* and played numerous festivals while continuing to live modestly in his country home, on the outskirts of town. Two re-issues on Strachwitz's Old Timey label of early material, along with J.E.'s King album from 1946 and a pair of albums that J.E. himself put out, helped keep his earlier material in print.

In his later years, a banjo picker named Morris Herbert became the main vocalist in J.E.'s band. J.E. Mainer stayed active in music until his death in 1971, as he prepared to leave home for a festival appearance in Culpepper, Virginia. IMT

RECOMMENDED ALBUMS:

Pre-1950 Records:

"J. E. Mainer's Crazy Mountaineers" (Old Timey)(1967)[Vol. 2 (1968)] [Both also released on Ball Mountain (1969 and 1970)]

"Good Ole Mountain Music" (King)(1960) [First recorded in 1946]

Post-1960 Recordings:

"A Variety Album" (King)(1961)

"The Legendary Family from the Blue Ridge Mountains" (Arhoolie)(1963)

"Old Time Mountain Music" (Rural Rhythm)(1967)

"More Old Time Mountain Music" (Rural Rhythm)(1967)

"The Legendary J.E. Mainer with Red Smiley's Blue Grass Cut-Ups" (Rural Rhythm)(1968)

"The Legendary J.E. Mainer, Vol. 4" (Rural Rhythm) and "Vol. 5" (1968)

"70th Happy Birthday Album" (BlueJay)(1968)

"Fiddling with His Girl Susan, Vol. 6" (Rural Rhythm)(1969)

"The Legendary J.E. Mainer, Vol. 8" (Rural Rhythm) and "Vol. 9" (both 1970)

(There are further volumes up to Vol. 20 available, but quality decreases steadily from Vol. 9; the last five of six albums are re-packaged from earlier releases)

WADE MAINER

(Singer, Banjo, Harmonica, Guitar)

Given name:	**Wade E. Mainer**
Date of Birth:	**April 21, 1907**
Where Born:	**Buncombe County, North Carolina**
Married:	**Julia Brown**
Children:	**Frank, Kelly, Leon (dec'd.), Polly, Randy**

Of the various Old-Time musicians who sang and played string music on radio and recorded in the 30's, Wade Mainer perhaps came closer to what would be termed Bluegrass than anyone else except for Bill Monroe himself. Wade's two-finger banjo style is generally considered a cross between the older clawhammer form and the later three-finger approach of Snuffy Jenkins and Earl Scruggs.

Wade grew up on his father's little mountain farm near Weaverville, North Carolina. His principal musical influence was fiddle-playing brother-in-law Roscoe Banks, for whom young Wade toiled in a sawmill job at 50 cents a day. Later, Wade moved to Concord, where he worked in a cotton mill and became part of the Mainer Mountaineer group led by brother J.E. Their radio programs, sponsored by Crazy Water Crystals, made them a household name throughout the Carolina Piedmont, and their Bluebird disc of *Maple on the Hill*, cut in August 1935, spread their fame even wider.

In 1936, Wade and Zeke Morris went on their own, and when Zeke joined his younger brother Wiley to form the Morris Brothers, Wade organized his own band. Initial members included his youthful nephews Buck and Buddy Banks. Wade played around with names for the band, considering the Little Smiling Rangers but eventually settling on Sons of the Mountaineers. Key band members included Jay Hugh Hall and Clyde Moody on guitars and Steve Ledford on fiddle. They did radio work at Raleigh, Charlotte, and Asheville, continuing to cut numerous sides for Bluebird. A later line-up of the band included Jack and Curly Shelton on guitars augmented by Walter "Tiny" Dodson on fiddle and Howard Dixon on acoustic steel guitar. The Sheltons accompanied Wade on his final Bluebird session in 1941, by which time he had moved his radio locale across the mountains to Knoxville's WROL. With gasoline hard to obtain in wartime, Wade dropped out of radio (which used up a lot of gas to get to and from) and farmed, although he did get Dodson and Jack Shelton to accompany him on a concert at the White House in 1942. In another instance, he took brothers J.E. and teenagers Red Rector and Fred Smith to New York, where they appeared in a BBC (U.K.) production of *The Chisholm Trail*.

After the war, Wade reorganized the Sons of the Mountaineers, and they appeared at North Carolina radio stations in Forest City, Mount Airy, and Asheville. He had sessions for King in 1947, and two in 1951. Although his music from this period actually was quite good, it no longer seemed on the cutting edge of innovation, as it had been a decade earlier. Furthermore, he could not get back on at WBT Charlotte, the major station in the region. In 1953, he professed religion and quit entertainment, although he did accompany an evangelist to Flint, Michigan, to help with singing at revivals. Obtaining regular employment at the local General Motors plant, Wade brought his wife and children to Flint in December 1953. He sang in religious services locally for the next several years, but he totally gave up banjo picking for a time, until Molly O'Day convinced him that the banjo and Gospel music were not incompatible.

On April 7, 1961, Wade had another session for King. His wife, Julia, who had once had her own radio show in Winston-Salem and vocalized on one of Wade's Bluebird sides, did a number of songs on these mostly mountain sacred music recordings. Later in the decade, he cut an album for Tommy Crank's I.R.M.A. label and a single on Knob records. In addition to local churches, Wade and Julia made occasional appearances on the Gospel sing at a Bluegrass festival.

In 1973, Wade retired from General Motors. John Morris of Old Homestead Records had persuaded him and Julia to cut some new material, including an occasional foray back into secular song. Although he hardly resumed a heavy touring schedule, he found enough demand for his music to keep him relatively active for a retired person. In the meantime, Wade began to receive some recognition for his contributions to traditional Country music including a "National Heritage Award" from President Reagan in 1987. A string of albums and tapes from Old Homestead as well as a cd on the June Appal label reveal that the octogenarian musician still retains most of his vigor and musical talent. The summer of 1993 found Wade and Julia still active at festivals with their exciting brand of mountain sacred (and sometimes secular) picking and singing. IMT

RECOMMENDED ALBUMS:

Re-issues from 1935-1941:

"Sacred Songs of Mother and Home" (Old Homestead)(1971)
"The Songs of Wade Mainer" (County)(1973)
"Early Radio" (1941) (Old Homestead)(1979)
"Early and Great, Vol. 1" (Old Homestead), also "Volume 2" (1983), and "Volume 3" (1993)

Later Recordings:

"Soulful Sacred Songs" (King)(1961)
"From the Maple to the Hill" (double)(Old Homestead)(1976)
"Old Time Songs" (Old Homestead)(1980)
"Old Time Banjo Tunes" (Old Homestead)(1984)
"How Sweet to Walk" (Old Homestead)(1989)
"String Band Music" (Old Homestead)(1990)
"Carolina Mule" (Old Homestead)(1993)
"Old Time Gospel Favorites" (Old Homestead)(1993)

MAINES BROTHERS BAND, The

When Formed:	**1976**
Members:	
Steve Maines	**Acoustic Guitar, Vocals**
Lloyd Maines	**Steel Guitar, Lead Guitar, Dobro, Hawaiian Guitar**
Kenny Maines	**Guitar, Harmonica**
Donnie Maines	**Drums, Percussion (1977-1987)**
Richard Bowden	**Fiddle, Mandolin, Trumpet**
Jerry Brownlow	**Bass Guitar, Vocals**
Gary Banks	**Keyboards, Guitar**
Mark Gillespie	**Drums (from 1987)**

The Maines Brothers carry on a tradition of family acts that goes back to the beginning of Country music. In the early to mid-80's, they reeled off half-a-dozen chart singles and the same amount of very worthy spirited Country albums.

The brothers' father and uncles had a band in West Texas, the Maines Brothers Band, and the boys were surrounded by music at an early age. They first played together as the "Little Maines Brothers Band." Lloyd (b. June 28, 1951) went on to play with the Joe Ely Band and stayed with them for six years and five albums. His brothers are Steve (b. November 24, 1952), Kenny (b. July 26, 1954) and Donnie (b. August 2, 1958). Kenny played with his brothers at age 11, and after the band broke up, he joined an outfit in Las Vegas and then joined the re-formed Maines in 1977. Donnie first played with a local group, the Tommy Lee Show, and left them when the Maines Brothers re-formed.

The other members of the group had also some musical pedigree. Richard Bowden (b. April 18, 1952), now one-half of comedy act Pinkard and Bowden, had played with Joe Ely and Ronnie Sessions. He became the Maines' fiddle player in 1978. Jerry Brownlow (b. August 18, 1952) was in the Brownlow Family Band and then on the road with Robby Allbright and the Boothill Express. He joined the band in 1976. Gary Banks (b. January 24, 1950) joined the band in 1983. He had played with the group on and off since 1978 and also written regional jingles; he was finalist in the

The Maines Brothers Band from Texas

American Songwriting Festival in 1977, 1978 and 1980 through 1983. He had also received Honorable Mention in the Music City Song Festival in 1983.

On their own Texas Soul label, the band released four albums and picked up a big following in Texas and beyond. They had been chased by several Nashville-based labels, who all wanted them to record in Nashville. They never approached the labels themselves. Having come to the attention of Rick Peoples at Mercury in May 1983, they were signed to the label, and this was on reflection a retrograde move. They were signed to an 8-year contract under the aegis of Jerry Kennedy and Peoples; however shortly after, Kennedy left to become an independent producer. The band insisted that they still wanted to work with Kennedy (and Peoples) and they did, recording their albums in Lubbock. The powers that be at the label had their feathers ruffled, and despite the band wanting to get out of their contract, after not getting a video financed by the company, this was not achieved until November 26, 1986. While at the label, most of their chart singles were Top 60 and below, with the exception of the 1985 release *Everybody Needs Love on Saturday Night*, which peaked in the Top 25.

In 1987, Donnie Maines decided to leave to work with his father-in-law in his farming and cotton gin mill operation, and he was replaced by Mark Gillespie from Louisiana. Gillespie had played with Country band Crystal Creek. The Maines Brothers, with a sense of relief, went back to making their own records on their own label.

RECOMMENDED ALBUMS:

"Maines Brothers and Friends" (Texas Soul)
"Rt. 1 Acuff" (Texas Soul)
"Hub City Moan" (Texas Soul)
"Panhandle Dancer" (Texas Soul)(1983)
"High Rollin'" (Mercury)(1984)
"The Boys Are Back in Town" (Mercury)(1986)
"Red, Hot and Blue" (Texas Soul)(1987)

TIM MALCHAK

(Singer, Songwriter, Guitar)

Date of Birth:	**June 25, 1957**
Where Born:	**Binghamton, New York**
Married:	**1. Diane DeYulio (div.)**
	2. Judy Ann Del Muro
Children:	**Travis Ryan**

It was Tim Malchak's fate that when he signed to a major label, his weight caused a problem because of the fact that all artists are now required to appear in videos, and despite having an excellent voice, he didn't fit the bill physically. When Tim Malchak initially charted with his partner, Dwight Rucker, they became the only charted Country white/black duo.

Tim Malchak has played guitar since age 9, and he joined his first band, the Hardware Company, while in the fifth grade. However, the burly Mr. Malchak had his eyes on a football career. While still in high school, he was tackled, ripped up a shoulder and finished his senior year playing in a brace. He was told he would lose the use of his right arm if he played college football.

After a year at college, he hit the road as a Folk singer. By 1978, he was in Southern California, opening for Commander Cody and Spyro Gyra. He was in New York, in 1982, when he and Dwight Rucker met. At the time, Tim was working part-time with computers and Dwight owned a health food restaurant.

Rucker (b. March 21, 1952, in Oxford, New York) was a fine arts major at New Paltz State. From 1971 to 1976, he was a member of Jazz-Fusion group Dry Jack, which opened for Jazz greats such as Freddie Hubbard, McCoy Tyner and Dizzy Gillespie. Then, Rucker became a Pop singer. Malchak and Rucker landed the opening spot for Michael Martin Murphey. They moved to Nashville in 1983 and played at the 1984 Fan Fair. That year, the duo signed with Revolver Records and scraped into the Top 100 with *Just Like That*. They started out 1985 with *Why Didn't I Think of That*, which fared even better, reaching the Top 70. Later that year, Johnny Rutenschroer, their coproducer, set up Alpine Records, and their debut single on the label, *I Could Love You in a Heartbeat*, also reached the Top 70. The video of this last track garnered a lot of interest. 1986 was to be their last year together, and they had two further Top 70 entries, *Let Me Down Easy* and *Slow Motion*.

After the breakup of the duo, Tim continued recording for Alpine. His first single, the self-penned *Easy Does It*, also reached the Top 70, but he was starting to gain attention and his first release of 1987, *Colorado Moon*, again self-penned, made it to the Top 40, as did *Restless Angel*. That year saw the release of his debut album, ***Colorado Moon***, which contained five of Malchak's songs. That year, too, he was named "Most Promising Star of Tomorrow (Male)" by the Independent Country Music Awards and "Top Indie Act" by *Indie Bullet*. The Nashville Music Fest named him "Male Artist of the Year" and *Colorado Moon* as "Song of the Year." He was also named one of *Billboard*'s "Top Ten New Country Artists."

In 1988, he hit the Top 40 with *It Goes Without Saying* and the Top 50 with *Not a Night Goes By*. He was invited to perform on the New Faces Show at the Country Radio Seminar in Nashville. He was awarded "Vocalist of the Year" honors from the Independent Record Industry, which chose his record *It Goes Without Saying* as "Single of the Year." He was also chosen as "Top Male Vocalist" by the *Music Review* Readers' Poll.

He was just about to ship a second album, ***American Man***, when he signed to Universal Records. Here he released the album ***Different Circles*** in 1989, which was more or less the same album. However, he didn't fare well on the label and his releases that year, *Not Like This* and *If You Had a Heart*, did not achieve the same chart success as his earlier Alpine releases. This has spelled the end of Tim's chart career to date. He is now on Full House Records.

RECOMMENDED ALBUMS:

"Colorado Moon" (Alpine)(1987)
"Different Circles" (Universal)(1989)

MANDOLIN

By Frank Wakefield

The two main types of mandolin are the regular A model (developed from the Tater Bug) and the F model. While growing up, I was influenced by the styles of Bill Monroe, Jesse McReynolds (of Jim & Jesse) and the Blue Sky Boys. The mandolin started to become popular during the 30's and led to the mandolin orchestras that still exist.

There are many different styles of playing and as I grew up, I imitated the masters, but I was told by Bill Monroe to develop my own style. This I have done. Other styles, however, are important to know about. There is ragtime, in which the mandolin is played like a tenor banjo, with definite strokes across the strings. The McReynolds style again emulates a banjo but instead of strokes, there is cross-picking. Monroe's style is really what Bluegrass is based on and is very distinctive.

My style of playing creates a duo sound, whereby it sounds like there are two mandolins being heard. This is done by using a pick while at the same time finger-picking. In this way, I can play lead and rhythm at the same time.

(For biographies on mandolin players, see entries for Blue Sky Boys, Jim & Jesse, Bill Monroe, New Grass Revival, Frank Wakefield, etc.)

BARBARA MANDRELL

(Singer, Bass Guitar, Banjo, Guitar, Mandolin, Pedal Steel, Dobro, Saxophone, Accordion)

Given Name: Barbara Ann Mandrell
Date of Birth: December 25, 1948
Where Born: Houston, Texas
Married: Ken Dudley (m. 1967)
Children: Matthew, Jaimie, Nathaniel

Barbara Mandrell is a very talented and glamorous star who has been in show business for most of her life. She is a multi-instrumentalist who has demonstrated her ability on her stage shows and also on her highly praised *Barbara Mandrell and the Mandrell Sisters* TV show. She was the first artist ever to win the CMA "Entertainer of the Year" Award for two consecutive years. Barbara is the eldest daughter of Irby and Mary Ellen Mandrell, who were musically talented themselves and passed on their precious gift to their children. Both Louise and Irlene, Barbara's younger sisters, pursued musical careers in their own right. Barbara learned to read music and play accordion by the age of 5, when she played to her first audience in her uncle's church. She so much enjoyed playing a Gospel tune she had learned, that she played it twice.

Leaving Texas, the family set up home in Oceanside, California. At school Barbara excelled not only in class work, but also in sports. She became the captain of the basketball and baseball teams and has continued her interest in sports throughout her life. She continued to master many instruments. When she was 11, her pedal steel playing was so good that her father took her to a music trade convention in Chicago, where she demonstrated the instrument. Guitarists Joe Maphis and Chet Atkins saw her there, and she was invited to join the Joe Maphis Show at the Showboat club in Las Vegas.

Multi-talented ***Barbara Mandrell***

At the grand old age of 12, she made her debut nationwide TV appearance on the ABC Country program *Five Star Jubilee*, and she was soon touring with stars like Red Foley, Tex Ritter and Johnny Cash. The Mandrells family band was formed when Barbara was 14, in which Irby played guitar and sang, Mary Ellen played electric bass and Barbara was featured on pedal steel and saxophone. The other member of the ensemble was a drummer, Ken Dudley, who was seven years older than Barbara. She fell madly in love with him and although it was said that it was "puppy love," Ken and Barbara married in 1967, just before her high school graduation, and have been living happily ever after.

Soon the group began touring the U.S. and appeared on *Town Hall Party*. They played military bases and hospitals abroad, touring in Japan, Thailand, Vietnam and the Philippines. Barbara first recorded for the Mosrite label in 1963. During the early 60's, there were appearances on both the Johnny Cash and Red Foley TV shows. At 16, Barbara won the "Miss Oceanside" beauty contest. Ken was drafted shortly after and became a U.S. Navy pilot and was sent overseas. The group then broke up and Barbara became a housewife. That did not last for long, and during a trip with her father to the *Grand Ole Opry*, at the Ryman Auditorium in Nashville, she told him she felt she wasn't cut out to be in the audience and would like to be back behind the microphone. Irby became her manager and soon, Barbara was working again. It was not long before recording offers came her way. She signed with Columbia in 1969. Her first hit on the Country chart, *I've Been Loving You Too Long*, peaked in the Top 60. In 1970, Barbara hit the Top 20 with *Playin' Around with Love*. That year, Barbara teamed up with David Houston for the Top 10 single *After Closing Time*. Barbara stayed with Columbia until the end of 1975, during which time her major hits were *Do Right Woman, Do Right Man* (Top 20, after which her group, the Do-Rites, was named), *Treat Him Right* (Top 15) and *We've Got Everything But Love* (Top 20, with David Houston) (all 1971), *Tonight My Baby's Coming Home* (Top 10), *Show Me* (Top 15) and *A Perfect Match* (Top 25, with David Houston) (all 1972), *Give a Little, Take a Little* (Top 25) and *The Midnight Oil* (Top 10) (both 1973), *I Love You, I Love You* (Top 10, with David Houston) and *This Time I Almost Made It* (Top 15) (both 1974) and *Ten Commandments of Love* (Top 15, with David Houston, 1975).

In 1976, Barbara signed with ABC/Dot (which later became MCA Records) and came under the production skills of Tom Collins. Her first single with them, *Standing Room Only*, peaked in the Top 5 in 1976. This was followed by *That's What Friends Are For* (Top 20) and *Love Is Thin Ice* (Top 25).

Barbara opened her 1977 account with *Midnight Angel* (Top 20) and then reached the Top 3 with *Married But Not to Each Other*. She closed the year with *Hold Me* (Top 15) and then had the Top 5 single *Woman to Woman*, which was followed by another Top 5 single, *Tonight*. In the fall of 1978, Barbara had her first No.1 hit, *Sleeping Single in a Double Bed*.

This was followed in 1978 by another No.1, *(If Loving You Is Wrong) I Don't Want to Be Right*, which crossed over to the Top 40 on the Pop chart, and a Top 5 hit, *Fooled By a Feeling*. Between 1980 and 1984, Barbara's chart singles were *Years* (No.1), *Crackers* (Top 3), *The Best of Strangers* (Top 10) (all 1980), *I Was Country When Country Wasn't Cool* (No.1, with George Jones), *Love Is Fair* (Top 15), *Wish You Were Here* (Top 3) (all 1981), *Till You're Gone* (No.1) and *Operator, Long Distance Please* (Top 10) (both 1982), *In Times Like These* (Top 5) and *One Of a Kind Pair of Fools* (No.1) (both 1983), *Happy Birthday Dear Heartache, Only a Lonely Heart Knows, To Me* (Top 3, with Lee Greenwood, from their album ***Clean Cut***) and *Crossword Puzzle* (all 1984).

During these years of rising stardom, Barbara was described by certain sections of the media as "Nashville's Snow White." She banned alcohol, drugs and groupies from her tour bus. Although she had been nominated for the CMA "Female Vocalist of the Year" Award on three occasions, she didn't win it until 1979. She was also honored with awards from *Music City News* and *Cash Box*. In 1980, she became both the CMA and ACM's "Entertainer of the Year." In 1981, Barbara was named "Female Vocalist of the Year" by the CMA, ACM and *Music City News*. MCN also named her "Musician of the Year" and with her sisters, "Best Comedy Act" and "Best TV Series." *Music City News* continued to honor her in 1982, as "Female Vocalist of the Year," "Best TV Series" and "Musician of the Year." In 1982, Barbara won two Grammy Awards for "Best Inspirational Performance" for her ***He Set My Life to Music*** album and "Best Gospel Performance by a Duo or Group" for *I'm So Glad I'm Standing Here Today*, which she won with her duet partner, Bobby Jones. In addition, both ***The Best of Barbara Mandrell*** (1980) and ***Live*** (1981) were Certified Gold, in 1981 and 1982, respectively.

In 1983, the TV show *Barbara Mandrell and the Mandrell Sisters* debuted in November. The half-hour show featured guest performers and always closed with a Gospel number. Due to strain, Barbara began having vocal problems, and on doctor's orders she ended the series. It was re-aired from January 1990 to 1991 every Saturday night on TNN and was the channel's highest rated show; it was also sold overseas.

Barbara then resumed her busy touring schedule and in 1983, was a hit in Las Vegas with her stage show *The Lady Is a Champ* at the MGM Grand Hotel. The show was performed at the Tennessee Performing Arts Center and was taped for an HBO cable TV special. Barbara released two albums on Hallmark, ***Black and White*** and a Gospel one entitled ***He Set My Life to Music***.

In 1984, Barbara was involved in a horrific auto accident. The head-on collision killed the young driver of the other car and left Barbara with severe head and leg injuries. She had her two children (Matthew, then 14, and his sister Jaimie, 8) in the car with her. Both were injured, but fortunately not seriously; all were wearing their seat belts. The wearing of seat belts became a cause célèbre for Barbara and due to her intervention, seat belt wearing has become mandatory in Tennessee. Barbara was in intensive care for a while, and her recovery took time and meant a break in her touring and other engagements. She also became pregnant with her third child, and the baby was born in 1985.

In 1985, Barbara had a successful year with all three of her singles, *It Should Have Been Love By Now* (Top 20, with Lee Greenwood), *There's No Love in Tennessee* (Top 10) and *Angel in Your Arms* (Top 10). The following year was her final one with MCA, and she chalked up a Top 10 hit with *Fast Lanes and Country Roads*, a Top 20 hit with *When You Get to the Heart* with the Oak Ridge Boys, and the solo Top 10 success, *No One Mends a Broken Heart Like You*.

Barbara moved over to EMI America (later Capitol) and success somewhat deserted her. Her three major entries on the label were *Child Support* (Top 15, 1987), *I Wish I Could Fall in Love Today* (Top 5, 1988) and *My Train of Thought* (Top 20, 1989). In 1987, Barbara appeared in the TV movie *Burning Rage* with Tom Wopat.

Although not now visible on the recording scene, Barbara still remains very much in demand as a live performer. She has an entire museum in Nashville called Mandrell Country, where her life is on show. Her autobiography, *Get to the Heart: My Story*, co-written with George Vecsey, was released in September 1990 (Bantam Books; the paperback version was released in September 1991).

Barbara feels that her strong faith in God helps her with her positive outlook on life. She puts all decisions into His hands, then things just fall into place. JAB

RECOMMENDED ALBUMS:

"The Best of David Houston & Barbara Mandrell" (Epic)(1974)
"The Best of Barbara Mandrell" (Columbia)(1977)
"Barbara Mandrell—Her Greatest Recordings" (ABC)(1978)
"The Best of Barbara Mandrell" (ABC)(1979)
"The Best of Barbara Mandrell" (MCA)(1980)
"Barbara Mandrell 'Live'" (MCA)(1981) [Features George Jones]
"He Set My Life to Music" (Songbird/MCA)(1982) [Gospel, also released on Word in 1983]
"Spun Gold" (MCA)(1983)
"Clean Cut" (MCA)(1984) [With Lee Greenwood]
"Greatest Hits" (MCA)(1985)
"Sure Feels Good" (EMI America)(1987)
"I'll Be Your Jukebox Tonight" (Capitol)(1988)

LOUISE MANDRELL

(Singer, Banjo, Guitar, Fiddle, Upright Bass, Accordion, Drums, Mandolin, Clarinet, Autoharp, Bass Guitar, Synthesizer, Author, Actress)

Given Name:	**Louise Mandrell**
Date of Birth:	**July 13, 1954**
Where Born:	**Corpus Christi, Texas**
Married:	**1. Ronny (div.)**
	2. Gary Buck (div.)
	3. R.C. Bannon (div.)
	4. John Haywood
Children:	**Meegan Nicole (adopted)**

Louise Mandrell is an extremely talented lady who has not been overwhelmed by the stardom of her sister, Barbara. Louise has emerged as a great entertainer, writer and actress.

She began her show business career while still at junior high school, performing for her sister Barbara as bass guitarist with Barbara's back-up band, the Do-Rites, and as such worked all over the U.S. and in Europe. Her first TV appearance was on the *Ralph Emery Show,* and while she was still in her teens, Louise appeared on the *Stu Phillips Show* and on the *Grand Ole Opry*. She also toured with Merle Haggard. When the NBC-TV series *Barbara Mandrell and the Mandrell Sisters* was screened, Louise found herself in the spotlight. She soon became a respected instrumentalist in Nashville, and in 1978, Louise signed with Epic Records.

Between 1978 and 1980, Louise charted as a solo six times; the most successful was *Love Insurance*, which peaked in the Top 70. While on the label, she also recorded with her then-husband, R.C. Bannon, and of their three charted singles, the Top 15 release *Reunited* was the most successful.

In 1982, Louise signed with RCA, where she fared better. Her major hits on the label were *(You Sure Know Your Way) Around My Heart* (Top 40) and *Some of My Best Friends Are Old Songs* (Top 20) (both 1982), *Romance* (Top 25), *Save Me* (Top 10), and *Too Hot to Sleep* (all 1983), *Runaway Heart* (Top 15), *I'm Not Through Loving You Yet* (Top 10) and *Goodbye Heartache* (Top 25) (all 1984), *Maybe My Baby* (Top 10) and I *Wanna Say Yes* (Top 5) (both 1985). From here on, Louise's most successful singles were *Some Girls Have All the Luck* (Top 25) and *I Wanna Hear It from Your Lips* (Top 40) (both 1986) and *Do I Have to Say Goodbye* (Top 30, 1987). Louise also had three hits with R.C. Bannon, but only *Where There's Smoke There's Fire* and *Christmas Is Just a Song for Us This Year* got as high as the Top 40. In 1988, Louise got together with Eric Carmen for the Top 60 release *As Long as We Got Each Other*.

Louise has performed on every major Country music show including her own two-

Beautiful and talented ***Louise Mandrell***

hour star-studded special, *Louise Mandrell—Diamonds, Gold and Platinum.* She also appeared in the daytime soap *Another World, The Tonight Show, Austin City Limits, Solid Gold* and *Hee Haw*. She has been seen on several CBS series shows, *Crazy Like a Fox, The New Mike Hammer*, and also on the *Home Show*. The highlight of her career was when she co-hosted the *Battle of the Bands* with the late Sammy Davis, Jr., on a syndicated TV special.

In 1991, Louise had an overwhelming success with her show *Love My Country* and also her dynamic road show. After this success the Grand Palace Theater in Branson, Missouri, booked Glen Campbell and Louise Mandrell to alternately host their shows at the 4,000-seat venue. In the show, Louise combines Bluegrass traditions with pure Country harmonies; she plays with wonderful versatility a number of musical instruments and she dances. The talented singers and dancers who accompany her are called Spellbound, and the emphasis is on entertainment. Louise is usually touring and also spends time working at Walt Disney World and Opryland.

Her first book, which emphasized her writing skills, was the autobiographical *The Mandrell Family Album*, which was published in 1983 and came out in paperback in 1984. She is also writing a series of children's books. Her hobbies are shooting, interior decorating, skiing and playing cards (she always plays to win). JAB

RECOMMENDED ALBUMS:

"Louise Mandrell" (Epic)(1979) [Features R.C. Bannon]
"Me and My R.C." (RCA Victor)(1982) [With R.C. Bannon]
"The Best of Louise Mandrell & R.C. Bannon" (RCA Victor)(1983)
"The Best of Louise Mandrell" (RCA Victor)(1988)

ZEKE MANNERS

(Singer, Songwriter, Accordion, Piano, Fiddle, Banjo, Deejay)

Given Name:	**Leo Manness**
Date of Birth:	**October 10, 1911**
Where Born:	**San Francisco, California**
Married:	**Beatrice Einstein**
Children:	**one son and one daughter**

If someone hadn't stolen Zeke's banjo, he might never have taken up the piano and then the accordion, and perhaps his career might have taken a different direction. As it was, Zeke became the centerpiece of the Beverly Hill Billies during the 30's.

He took up the violin as a youngster, and his parents had designs on his becoming a classical violinist, but he leaned toward a more Swing style of fiddle playing. When he was 10, his family moved to Hollywood. It was during high school that the banjo event occurred and Zeke started playing keyboards. After high school, Zeke joined a traveling tent show and eventually became leader of the group. He then became a member of Ben Nash's Hillbilly Orchestra. From there, he joined Bill Sharpel's *Breakfast Club* radio show, in 1930.

However, it was the intervention of Glen Rice that turned Zeke into a famed full-time performer. Rice had dreamed up the idea of the Beverly Hill Billies along with KMPC Los Angeles owner Raymond S. MacMilland and station staff announcer John McIntire. Zeke was playing children's parts on a show on KMPC and had stopped by the station on the way back from the beach. Rice decided that Zeke would be an excellent focal point of the group. Within the Hill Billies, he took on the persona of "Craddock." They recorded for Brunswick and made several movies starring Jackie Oakie, Charles Starrett, Ray Whitley, Gene Autry, Tex Ritter and Smith Ballew (see Movie Section).

Following the group's split from KMPC, Manners found himself in the Salvation Army band, until KMPC executives asked him to form Zeke and his City Fellows.

In 1933, Zeke headed east, where he began appearing on the *Rudy Vallee Show*. He and his band played theaters in the U.S. and then successfully played in London, England. In 1935, he and former Hill Billy Elton Britt moved to New York, where they worked solo and together. It was while in New York that Zeke enlarged his band and staged the world's largest barn dance at the Manhattan Center.

He joined the U.S. Army Air Force in 1942 and stayed in the service for 3 years. On discharge, he moved back to California, where he turned to songwriting and got the first coast-to-coast deejay show over the ABC network.

During 1946, Zeke signed with RCA Victor and that year had the double-sided Top 5 Country hit *Sioux City Sue/Inflation*. In 1951, he moved his *Milkman's Melchoir* ABC radio show from Hollywood to New York, where he broadcast Folk music early in the mornings on weekdays. That year, he signed to Capitol and released a pair of singles, *Satins and Lace* and *Piano Players*, without any chart action.

RECOMMENDED ALBUMS:

"The Wandering Cowboy" (ABC-Paramount)(1959) [Elton Britt album featuring Zeke Manners' Band]
"Those Fabulous Beverly Hill Billies" (Rar-Arts)(1961) [Features, Zeke Manners as guest]

JOE AND ROSE LEE MAPHIS

When Formed: 1952

JOE MAPHIS

(Vocals, Electric Lead Guitar, Fiddle, Mandolin, Banjo, Bass)

Given Name:	**Otis Wilson Maphis**
Date of Birth:	**May 12, 1921**
Where Born:	**Suffolk, Virginia**
Date of Death:	**June 27, 1986**

ROSE LEE MAPHIS

(Vocals, Guitar)

Given Name:	**Rose Lee Schetrompf**
Date of Birth:	**December 29, 1922**
Where Born:	**Baltimore, Maryland**
Children:	**Jody, Lori, Dale (dec'd.)**

Joe and Rose Maphis made up one of Country music's major husband-wife teams of the 50's and 60's. Their career activity wound down somewhat in later years although they remained a working team until Joe's death in 1986. Joe's varied instrumental talents also made him an outstanding session musician. His electric lead guitar stylings over the years made him a virtual legend in that field.

Joe Maphis was reared near Harpers Ferry on the Maryland-West Virginia border where he grew up helping his father and brothers furnish music for square dances in that area. About 1938 he went full-time with a band in Fredericksburg, Virginia, and some months later joined Sunshine Sue (Workman) and her Rangers, coming to WLW Cincinnati. He went to WLS Chicago before entering the service in WWII.

Meanwhile, Rose Lee Schetrompf had been growing up near Hagerstown, Maryland. At 15, she put her musical talents to work on local station WJEJ, where she joined three other girls to form the Saddle Sweethearts. They moved to a station in Norristown, Pennsylvania, and then to Baltimore before landing a program at powerful KMOX, the "Voice of St. Louis." Eventually, two girls

Joe and Rose Lee Maphis

left and the Saddle Sweethearts became a duet consisting of Rose Lee and Mary Klick. They worked for one winter at KLCN in Blytheville, Arkansas, and then landed a spot at WRVA Richmond, Virginia, another 50,000-watt station, where Joe's former employer, Sunshine Sue, had been organizing the *Old Dominion Barn Dance*. When Joe got out of the service, he, too, joined the big new radio jamboree after briefly going back to WLS.

Not yet a team, both Joe Maphis and Rose Lee worked as part of the show from Richmond, on the road and over the air until 1951. Joe had known both Grandpa Jones and Merle Travis from his Cincinnati radio days, and the latter persuaded him to come to California and work television for Foreman Phillips. Rose soon came to California and the pair married in February 1952. The following year, they signed with Columbia, recording their initial session on April 27, 1953. The first release consisted of the Honky-Tonk classic *Dim Lights, Thick Smoke (and Loud, Loud Music)* and a jazzed-up (with added lyrics) version of the fiddle tune *Black Mountain Rag*. Their first dozen sides came out on the OKeh subsidiary, but from 1955 they were released on Columbia. The Maphises were regulars on the West Coast Country scene. Joe's hot guitar work kept him busy in the studios when not on the road. Rose gave birth to three children during the later 50's.

As a lead guitarist, Maphis came out with such instrumental classics as *Fire on the Strings*, *Flying Fingers* and *Guitar Rock and Roll* on the electric double-neck Mos-Rite Special guitar he helped design. In addition to sessioning for most of the West Coast Country and Western artists, Joe did session work for rock'n'roll heroes like Ricky Nelson and Pop vocal groups like the Four Preps, as well as most of the California-based Country stars. He earned the nickname "King of the Strings." Some of his most exciting instrumental work occurred in September 1957 when he cut four tunes with his adolescent protege Larry Collins (of the Collins Kids). Joe also did a tenor banjo album for Columbia in 1958, and Rose Lee did one of Country standards in 1960.

In 1961, Rose and Joe switched to Capitol, where the following year they cut a fine duet album with Bluegrass accompaniment. In 1964 Joe and Merle Travis did a fine twin-guitar effort. That same year, Joe and Rose Lee went with Starday, their first album release bearing the title for which they had become known over the past dozen years, "Mr. and Mrs. Country Music." Joe also recorded guitar albums for Starday and others for Kapp, Sacred and Mosrite. Joe also composed the background for TV series such as *The FBI*, *Thunder Road*, *God's Little Acre*, *Riverboat Deputy*, *The Virginian* and *The Richard Boone Show*.

In 1968, the Maphis family moved to Nashville, which remained their home for the remainder of their careers. Initially, they didn't record a great deal although Joe and oldest son Jody did an album for Chart. Beginning in 1977, Joe and sometimes Rose as well began an association with Martin Haerle's CMH Records, which resulted in several albums spotlighting the versatile Maphis talents. These included some new recordings with Merle Travis and also with Grandpa and Ramona Jones. After Joe passed away in 1986, Rose Lee gave up performing and went to work in the costume-making department at Opryland.

IMT

RECOMMENDED ALBUMS:

Joe Maphis:
"Fire on the Strings" (Columbia)(1957)
"Hi-Fi Holiday for Banjo" (Harmony)(1959)
"Hootenanny Star" (Kapp)(1964)
"King of the Strings" (Starday)(1965)
"Golden Gospel Guitar" (Starday)(1965)
"The New Sound of Joe Maphis" (Mosrite)(1967)
"Gospel Guitar" (Sacred)(ca. 1968)
"Gospel Guitar, Vol. 2" (Sacred)(1970)
"Grass 'n' Jazz" (CMH)(1977)
Rose Lee and Joe Maphis:
"Rose Lee Maphis (with Joe Maphis)" (Columbia)(1961)
"Rose Lee & Joe Maphis with the Blue Ridge Mountain Boys" (Capitol)(1962) [Re-issued by Stetson UK in the original sleeve (1987)]
"Mr. & Mrs. Country Music" (Starday)(1964)
"Dim Lights, Thick Smoke" (CMH)(1978)
"Boogie Woogie Flattop Guitar Pickin' Man" (CMH)(1979)
"Honky Tonk Cowboy" (CMH)(1980)
Joe and Jody Maphis:
"Guitaration Gap" (Chart)(1971)
Merle Travis and Joe Maphis:
"Country Music's Two Guitar Greats" (Capitol)(1964)
Larry Collins and Joe Maphis:
"Rockin' Rollin'" (Bear Family Germany)(1983) [Includes solo and duet cuts]

MARSHALL TUCKER BAND, The

When Formed:	**1970**
Original Members:	
Toy Caldwell	**Lead Guitar, Steel Guitar, Vocals**
Tommy Caldwell	**Bass Guitar, Vocals**
Doug Gray	**Lead Vocals, Percussion**
George McCorkle	**Guitars**
Jerry Eubanks	**Saxophone, Flute, Vocals**
Paul T. Riddle	**Drums**
Later Members:	
Franklin Wilkie	**Horns**
Rusty Milner	**Lead Guitar**
Bobby Ogdin	**Keyboards**

Other Members:
Stuart Swanlund, Tim Lawter, Frank Toler, Ronald Radford, Mark Petty, Don Cameron

The Marshall Tucker Band helped pioneer and popularize southern Rock music. Blending elements of Rock, Rhythm and Blues, Jazz, Gospel, and Country to create their own sound, the South Carolina-based band came to national attention in 1973, with their self-titled debut album on Capricorn Records.

Brothers Toy and Tommy Caldwell formed the band in 1970 with Doug Gray and Jerry Eubanks. The high school friends named the band after their Spartanburg, South Carolina, hometown piano tuner, Marshall Tucker. After developing a regional following, the group came to the attention of Macon, Georgia-based Capricorn Records. This label that found success with The Allman Brothers and Wet Willie signed the Marshall Tucker Band to a recording contract.

To support the release of their 1973 debut album, the band opened concerts for the Allman Brothers. Within a year Marshall Tucker was headlining their own concerts and maintained a grueling tour schedule of 300 shows per year. Their debut album sold more than 500,000 copies and went Gold in 1975. Later in 1973 the band released their second album, ***A New Life***, that also earned Gold status, in 1977.

Where We All Belong was the third Marshall Tucker Band release, in 1975, and it earned a Gold Record the same year. In addition, they debuted on the Pop chart with the single *This Ol' Cowboy*, a minor success, and followed it with the Top 40 *Fire on the Mountain*. The 1975 album ***Searching for A Rainbow*** went Gold in 1976, and the 1977 ***Carolina Dreams*** albums was Certified Platinum, by 1978. In 1976, the band released the album ***Long Hard Ride***. The popularity of the group continued in 1978 when the album ***Together Forever*** went Gold the year of release. In addition, the band's ***Greatest Hits*** (1978) also went Gold that year. In 1979, ***Running Like the Wind*** was their first album on Warner Brothers. From this album came the Top 50 single *Last of the Singing Cowboys*.

The driving force of the Marshall Tucker Band from 1970 to 1985 was lead singer and guitar player Toy Caldwell. He was also the group's main songwriter, penning the band's biggest hit, *Heard It in A Love Song*, which rose to the Top 15 on the Pop chart and just missed the Top 50 on the Country chart in 1977. Caldwell also wrote another of Marshall Tucker's signature songs, *Can't You See*,

Marshall Tucker Band*'s Toy Caldwell on guitar with* ***Charlie Daniels*** *on fiddle*

another 1977 chart entry albeit a low level one.

Tragedy struck the band in 1980 when Toy's brother, Tommy, was killed in an auto accident. He was replaced by Franklin Wilkie, and Marshall Tucker released their ***Tenth*** album. Their other Warner Brothers albums were ***Dedicated*** (1981), ***Tuckerized*** (1982) and ***Just Us*** (1983).

In 1985 Toy Caldwell left the band to spend time with his family. Three years later he formed the Toy Caldwell Band and toured with Lynyrd Skynyrd and the Allman Brothers. In 1991 he released a solo album entitled ***Toy Caldwell*** and in 1992 performed at Charlie Daniels' Volunteer Jam. He also performed at Willie Nelson's Farm Aid concert in Dallas, where the crowd of 50,000 cheered his rendition of the Marshall Tucker Band classic, *Can't You See*. On February 5, 1993, Toy Caldwell died of respiratory failure at his home in Spartanburg, South Carolina.

The Marshall Tucker Band continued to record and tour following Toy Caldwell's departure from the band. In 1987, they signed with Mercury Records and had a Top 40 Country hit with *Hangin' Out in Smoky Places*. After releasing albums in 1988 (***Still Holdin' On***) and 1990 (***Southern Spirit***), the group took a two-year break from the studio. In 1992 they signed with the Cabin Fever label and released ***Still Smokin'***, from which *Driving You Out of Your Mind* became a Top 70 Country success.

Twenty years after their debut album, the Marshall Tucker Band continued their southern rock legacy with ***Walk Outside the Lines***, from which came the 1993 Top 75 title track, which was written by Garth Brooks and Charley Stefl. A big fan of the group, Brooks called their recording of his song "a milestone in my career."

The Marshall Tucker Band provided inspiration to many other artists. In the early days, they developed lasting friendships with Charlie Daniels. When Hank Williams, Jr., wanted to find his own sound he drew heavily from Marshall Tucker and recorded his own version of *Can't You See*. The influence of the Marshall Tucker Band has often been cited by many other stars including the Kentucky Headhunters and Travis Tritt. JIE

RECOMMENDED ALBUMS:

"Marshall Tucker Band" (Capricorn)(1973)
"A New Life" (Capricorn)(1974)
"Where We All Belong" (Capricorn)(1975)
"Searchin' for a Rainbow" (Capricorn)(1975)
"Long Hard Ride" (Capricorn)(1976)
"Carolina Dreams" (Capricorn)(1977)
"Together Forever" (Capricorn)(1978)
"Greatest Hits" (Capricorn)(1978)
"Running Like the Wind" (Warner Brothers)(1979)
"Tenth" (Warner Brothers)(1980)
"Dedicated" (Warner Brothers)(1981)
"Tuckerized" (Warner Brothers)(1982)
"Just Us" (Warner Brothers)(1983)
"Still Holdin' On" (Mercury)(1988)
"Southern Spirit" (Mercury)(1990)
"Still Smokin'" (Cabin Fever)(1992)
"Walk Outside the Lines" (Cabin Fever)(1993)

LINDA MARTELL

(Singer)

Where Born: **Leesville, South Carolina**

There have been very few black performers to have made it in Country music. Of the male singers, only Charley Pride, Stoney Edwards and O.B. McClinton have had major success. Of the female singers, although the Pointer Sisters and Anita Pointer have had some success with one-off projects, only Linda Martell and Ruby Falls have had any modicum of solo success.

Unlike Ruby Falls, Linda Martell did not cut her teeth on Country music. Linda started out playing the R & B clubs in Columbia, South Carolina. However, at the end of the 60's, she signed with Shelby Singleton's Plantation label. In the summer of 1969, Linda hit the Country chart with the Top 25 *Color Him Father*. This led to her becoming the first black female Country singer to appear on the *Grand Ole Opry*, that year.

Linda followed up in 1970 with two more chart records, *Before the Next Teardrop Falls* (Top 40) and *Bad Case of the Blues* (Top 60). That marked the end of Linda's Country music chart career, and after this success she has disappeared from the scene.

RECOMMENDED ALBUM:

"Color Me Country" (Plantation)(1970)

ASA MARTIN

(Singer, Guitar, Musical Saw)

Given Name:	**Asa Martin**
Date of Birth:	**June 28, 1900**
Where Born:	**Winchester, Clark County, Kentucky**
Married:	**1. Eliza (div.) 2. Geneva**
Children:	**Walter, J. William, Henry A.**
Date of Death:	**August 15, 1979**

A widely recorded Kentucky Old-Time singer of the 20's and 30's, Asa Martin's musical career was closely tied to that of the celebrated fiddler Doc Roberts. Asa provided guitar rhythm for Doc's fiddle numbers, and Doc in turn played mandolin for both Asa's solo vocals and the duet of Martin and Roberts, on which Doc's adolescent son James sang the tenor part. In the 70's, Old-Time music scholars found an eager source of information in Asa, who loved to reminisce and impart lore about the early days of records and radio and his role in them.

According to his recollections, Asa Martin developed an early fondness for music, both the traditional sound of rural Kentucky and what he heard on the minstrel and vaudeville stage, despite his father's hopes that he enter the higher professions. Martin had some traveling show experience and had developed considerable dexterity as a rhythm guitarist when Doc Roberts recruited him for a record session at the Gennett studios in Richmond, Indiana. Asa also sang creditable vocals on Old-Time songs. As a soloist he did a variety of numbers, but parodies seem to have been his special forte as illustrated by such songs as *The Virginia Bootlegger, The Little Old Jailhouse,* and *There's No Place Like Home (For a Married Man).*

Toward the end of the 20's Asa began singing duets with young James Roberts and tended to move toward traditional ballads like *Knoxville Girl,* and Victorian sentimental fare such as *Lilly Dale, The East Bound Train* and *Give My Love to Nell.* They also cut some new songs that sounded old, such as *The Little Box of Pine on the 7:29.* Asa also had sessions in 1932 and 1933 with mandolinist Roy "Shorty" Hobbs that produced the first recording of *Hot Corn Cold Corn,* a memorable song that would later be revived by a Martin protege, David "Stringbean" Akeman.

After Martin and Roberts made their last recordings in 1934, Asa went into radio, where he had a group of musicians on the *Morning Roundup* at WLAP Lexington. He provided early experience on this show for lanky banjoist-comedian Stringbean, and the Amburgey Sisters, one of whom would attain greater prominence as Martha Carson. He had a final session in 1938, recording largely comedy material for Vocalion, but the numbers also included the fine ballad *Harlan Town Tragedy.* About 1940 he moved to WCMI Ashland, where his group included younger Elmer Bird, a native of Hurricane, West Virginia, who would attain renown as a clawhammer banjo picker on festival circuits in the 80's and 90's. At the advent of WWII, Asa went to work for the Armco Corporation, eventually moving to Middletown, Ohio.

After Asa retired about 1965, he came back to Kentucky, residing near Irvine. He gathered together several musicians known as the Cumberland Rangers, who entertained in the locality. About 1968, scholars like Archie Green and Norm Cohen rediscovered him. Along with Doc and James Roberts, he participated in a 1971 reunion concert at Berea College. He also made occasional appearances with the McLain Family. The highlight of his later career came when Asa and the Cumberland Rangers recorded a fine album of Old-Time music for Rounder in 1974.

Scholars generally found Asa's stories and lore from the early days a delight to their ears, and he in turn enjoyed the attention he received from them. Considerable discussion of re-issue albums of his vocals (both solo and with James Roberts) has taken place, but to date only a few of his sides have appeared on scattered anthologies. Doc Roberts has fared better, having a pair of albums released, on most cuts of which Asa played rhythm guitar. One of his associates in the Cumberland Rangers, Jim Gaskin, has emceed the *Renfro Valley Morning Gatherin'* in recent years. IMT

RECOMMENDED ALBUM:

"Dr. Ginger Blue" (Rounder)(1974)

BENNY MARTIN

(Fiddle, Guitar, Bass, Mandolin)

Given Name:	**Benny Martin**
Date of Birth:	**May 8, 1928**
Where Born:	**Sparta, Tennessee**
Married:	**1. Espey Fykes (div.)**
	2. Regina (div.)
	3. Thelma
Children:	**Benny, Jr., Belinda, Karen**

Benny Martin is well known in Bluegrass circles as one of the genre's great fiddlers. As a musical innovator, he invented and perfected the 8-string fiddle. Benny has also, from time to time, worked as a vocalist and leader of his own band, recording on a variety of labels, and authoring such songs as *Me and My Fiddle* and *Ice Cold Love.*

A native of Sparta, Tennessee, the same town where Lester Flatt spent his formative years, Benny grew up in a musical family. He learned to play several instruments, but favored the fiddle, making his radio debut at age 8, on a local station in nearby Cookeville. Later Martin also played in a family band headed by some folks named Randolph. At age 13, he came to Nashville, where he worked as part of Big Jeff and the Radio Playboys at WLAC. The young fiddler remained with Big Jeff off and on for a decade, during which time he made his first recordings as a sideman on Dot and also a solo single on his own for a small label called Pioneer. One side of the latter contained the original waxing of his signature song, *Me and My Fiddle,* which he would subsequently recut several times. From about 1947, the youthful fiddler also did periodic sideman work for other bands, including those of Bill Monroe, Roy Acuff, Johnnie and Jack, Kitty Wells, and especially, Lester Flatt and Earl Scruggs. The fifteen sides he recorded with Flatt & Scruggs in 1952 and 1953 are often cited as the near ultimate in Bluegrass fiddle work.

In 1954, Benny Martin went on his own as leader of his group, recording several sides for Mercury and enjoying *Grand Ole Opry* member status for a while. Colonel Tom Parker managed his career at one point, including a thirty-five-concert tour as an opening act for the Colonel's most famous client, Elvis Presley. The rise of rock'n'roll took a heavy toll on traditional Country acts like Martin's, but he struggled on by working as a single along with occasional sideman and session work. Moving to Starday in 1961, he had his only chartmaker, *Rosebuds and You,* in the spring of 1963. In the fall of 1962 he rejoined Roy Acuff for a seven-week military base tour of the Mediterranean region. Invited to Carlton Haney's first Bluegrass festival at Fincastle, Virginia, in 1965, Benny formed a brief partnership with Don Reno that resulted in a Gospel album on Cabin Creek and an early 1966 minor hit titled *Soldier's Prayer in Viet Nam,* for Monument.

Since the 60's, Martin has periodically worked both Country shows and Bluegrass festivals. He also recorded fairly extensively, which included a pair of two-album sets for CMH as well as one for Lamb and Lion, the Canadian label Condor, and perhaps his best effort for Flying Fish. The latter included a few fiddle tunes along with vocals on old and new songs, including *One Drink Is Too Many,* a refreshingly frank look at his own problems with alcohol.

During the 80's Benny began experiencing serious health problems, which took a heavy toll on his throat and ability to speak, but he still did some session work like a 1986 Bluegrass-Gospel album with the Stoneman Family. Benny also had a brother, Gene Martin (d. 1985), who sometimes worked with him as a sideman for Roy Acuff and as a soloist on Starday. IMT

RECOMMENDED ALBUMS:

"Country Music's Sensational Entertainer" (Starday)(1961)
"Old Time Fiddlin' & Singing" (Mercury/Wing)(1964)
"The Greatest Hits of Benny Martin" (Power Pak)(1973)
"Tennessee Jubilee" (Flying Fish)(1975)
"Rollin'" (Lamb and Lion)(1975)
"The Fiddle Collection" (CMH)(1977)
"Turkey in the Grass" (CMH)(1977)
"Big Daddy of the Fiddle & Bow" (CMH)(1979)
"Southern Bluegrass Fiddle" (Condor)

GRADY MARTIN

(Guitar, Fiddle, Vibraphone, Composer)

Given Name:	**Thomas Grady Martin**
Date of Birth:	**January 17, 1929**
Where Born:	**Chapel Hill, Tennessee**

One of the unsung heroes of Country music is guitarist Grady Martin. He has been content to remain in the background, even though his licks have graced countless recording sessions from the late 40's on.

Grady knew that he wanted to move from his farming background, and while still a boy, he listened on the home radio to DeFord Bailey and Roy Acuff on the *Grand Ole Opry.* His mother, a piano player, encouraged him and soon he was playing piano and using his older brother's guitar. However, the first instrument he mastered was a fiddle, and in 1944, Big Jeff Bess, the star of WLAC Nashville, heard Grady playing on a local show and asked Grady's parents to let him come to Nashville, to join his band. Although Grady's mother was reluctant, his father agreed and at the age of 15, Grady joined the band.

After two years of playing with Big Jeff, on the road and on air, Grady wanted a change. He approached Jim Denny, who was then the *Opry* 's booking manager, who helped Martin become a member of the Bailes Brothers' backing band, on guitar and fiddle, in 1946.

Still only 17, Grady played on his first recording session, on February 15, 1946, under the direction of Art Satherley. The session, in Chicago, was for Curly Fox and Texas Ruby, and also playing was fellow guitarist Jabbo Arrington. Grady and Jabbo had become friends when Grady had first arrived in town, and began to develop a twin-guitar style. In September of that year, they returned for a second session, and the Martin-Arrington pairing was heard to good effect.

Grady continued playing on sessions, and as a member of the Paul Howard Band he played on the *Opry*. In 1949, when Howard left Nashville, Grady and Jabbo joined Little Jimmy Dickens' Country Boys. When Jabbo left the band (he died a few years later from a heart ailment), he was replaced by steelie Thumbs Carlille, and a new Martin-Carlille sound emerged. It was in 1950 that more folks started to notice the 21-year-old Grady Martin. This was mainly due to his guitar work on Red Foley's *Chattanoogie Shoe Shine Boy*. As a result, Foley invited Grady to lead his band. However, before he joined, Grady appeared on two Dickens hit singles, *A-Sleeping at the Foot of the Bed* and *Hillbilly Fever*. By now, Grady was playing his famed twin-neck guitar.

Guitar maestro ***Grady Martin***

For most of the 50's, Martin played with Foley on the *Ozark Jubilee*, on tour and on a series of hit singles and albums. In addition, he was still playing on other artists' recording sessions. He was, by now, almost exclusively playing guitar, and the last time Grady played fiddle live was behind Hank Williams on Kate Smith's TV Show, in 1952. He continued playing it on record until 1955, when he recorded some instrumentals at the Ryman Auditorium, as part of Decca's Country and Western Dance-O-Rama series. On these, Grady played twin fiddles and guitar, Tommy Jackson played guitar and fiddle, Hank Garland played guitar, Bud Isaacs played steel and Bob Moore, bass.

In 1951, Martin put together a band known as Grady Martin and the Slew Foot Five. In 1952, they backed Burl Ives for the Top 10 Country hit *Wild Side of Life* and then went on, the same year, to rack up a cross-over hit with Bing Crosby, *Till the End of the World*. The group released a slew of recordings from 1951 that included *San Antonio Rose, Stardust, Slewfoot Rag, Get Up and Go, The Little Green Valley, Diesel Smoke Dangerous Curve* and a bunch of standards such as *Alexander's Ragtime Band* and *Sioux City Sue*, but none of them achieved chart status. Of interest is the fact that the very prominent piano on all the tracks is played by Owen Bradley.

With the advent of rock'n'roll, Grady, a member of the "A-team" of Nashville session players, found himself in great demand, along with fellow guitarists Hank Garland and Harold Bradley. When the developing Buddy Holly came to Nashville in 1956 to record, Grady was on hand to give musical support. He also appeared on Johnny Horton's *Honky Tonk Man* and Ronnie Self's *Big Fool*, also in 1956.

In 1959, Grady played on one of his finest sessions when he assisted on Marty Robbins' record, *El Paso*, playing nylon-string guitar. While recording Robbins' classy *Don't Worry*, Grady was playing a 6-string bass guitar. In the middle of his solo, the studio desk's pre-amp went on the blink, and the resultant playback revealed a raspy distortion that was left in. This is the first occasion when what is now known as "fuzz" was heard on record. In 1960, Grady played vibes on Floyd Cramer's hit record *Last Date*.

Following Hank Garland's horrible auto accident in 1961, Grady found himself even more in demand for sessions. The triumvirate of Martin, Garland and Harold Bradley was no more, and guitarist Ray Edenton became an "A-team" player. That year, Grady tried his hand at recording a rock'n'roll instrumental, *The Fuzz/Tippin' In*, and the following year, he did it again with *Big Bad Guitar*.

Among the hits that he played on were Lefty Frizzell's *Saginaw Michigan* and the No.1 smash hit *Oh, Pretty Woman*, by Roy Orbison (both in 1964). He played on Jimmy Dickens' *May the Bird of Paradise Fly Up Your Nose*, which went to No.1. He stayed with Decca as a solo artist until 1966, by which time he had recorded over 170 tracks.

In 1969, Grady appeared on Ray Price's *For the Good Times*, but as the 70's unrolled, he felt that recording methods were not to his liking and that his creativity was being stifled. He continued to play on most of Conway Twitty and Loretta Lynn's records and in 1973 appeared on Kris Kristofferson's *Why Me* and Jeanne Pruett's *Satin Sheets*.

In the mid and late 70's, Grady led the TV band on the *T. Tommy Cutrer Show*. He began producing for Monument Records and worked with Brush Arbor, before joining Jerry Reed's band in 1978 and returning to live gigs. While in Austin, Texas, he met up again with Willie Nelson, and played on the 1979 soundtrack of *Honeysuckle Rose*. Martin and Nelson had met back in the mid-60's, and it is likely that Grady's nylon-string playing had influenced Willie. Grady then joined Willie's band and has remained with him since.

In 1983, the Nashville Music Association hosted a gala tribute to Grady, but he refused to play with the all-star band, preferring, as always, to be in the background.

RECOMMENDED ALBUMS:

"Country & Western Dance" (Decca)(1954)
"Powerhouse Dance Party" (Decca)(1955)
"The Roaring Twenties" (Decca)(1957)
"Instrumentally Yours" (Decca)(1965)
"Cowboy Classics" (Monument)(1977)
"Willie Nelson Sings Kristofferson" (Columbia)(1979) [Features Grady Martin]
"Little Jimmy Dickens" (Columbia Historic Edition)(1984) [Features Grady Martin]

JIMMY MARTIN

(Singer, Guitar, Mandolin)

Given Name:	**James Henry Martin**
Date of Birth:	**August 10, 1927**
Where Born:	**Sneedville, Tennessee**
Married:	**1. Barbara Gibson (div.)**
	2. Teresa Sutherland
Children:	**James H., Jr., Ray Willard, Lisa Sarah, Buddy Lee**

A native of the Cumberland Mountain area of East Tennessee, Jimmy Martin was once described by author Bob Artis as "the king of the Bluegrass lead singers." The name is appropriate since Martin's voice has been virtually unsurpassed in the ideal qualities desired for a traditional Bluegrass vocal solo.

Alternately loved and hated by many for his brashness on stage, Martin served an apprenticeship with Bill Monroe, working briefly in partnership with the Osborne Brothers, and since 1955 has led his own Sunny Mountain Boys, racking up five Country chart hits and numerous other Bluegrass standards in an eighteen-year career with Decca Records.

Growing up poor in the mountain country, Martin played and sang traditional music from childhood, but became especially attracted to the sound of Bill Monroe's Blue Grass Boys as a teenager. He gained some early professional experience on radio around Morristown and Knoxville, but worked as a housepainter until age 22, when he rode a bus to Nashville and successfully auditioned with the Monroe band as a replacement for the departing Mac Wiseman. Jimmy worked for Bill off and on for some four years, during which time he cut some forty-six numbers as a Blue Grass Boy on Decca, including several Bluegrass standards. Martin also had a brief partnership with Bob Osborne in 1951, recording four sides for King. As a member of the Monroe "sub-group" the Shenandoah Valley Trio, Martin recorded four songs on Columbia, harmonizing with Joel Price and Merle "Red" Taylor.

In 1954, Martin formed a partnership with the Osborne Brothers, going to WJR Detroit, where they sang on the *Big Barn Frolic* program. In one memorable session for RCA Victor, this threesome recorded six classic Bluegrass numbers, including *20/20 Vision* and *That's How I Can Count on You*. In 1955, they went their separate ways, with Martin taking the band name Sunny Mountain Boys, which had hitherto been more associated with the Osbornes. In May 1956, Jimmy cut his first solo songs with Decca, using a band that included Sam "Porky" Hutchins on banjo and Earl Taylor on mandolin as its nucleus. One of their first recordings, *Hit Parade of Love*, is considered as a Martin classic, although it did not reach the charts. Other songs from the early years closely associated with Jimmy included *Ocean of Diamonds*, *Sophronie* and *Rock Hearts* (all from 1958), the latter song being his first to chart, reaching the Top 15 followed in 1959 with the Top 30 *Night*. By then Martin had achieved his ideal sound, characterized by a hard-driving banjo in the capable hands of a young J.D. Crowe, the tenor vocal and mandolin of Paul Williams and Martin's own flawless guitar rhythm, perfect timing and crisp lead singing.

Jimmy Martin and His Sunny Mountain Boys

Through the 60's, the Sunny Mountain Boys encountered unusual personnel changes with some of the more noted sidemen being Bill Emerson and Meredith "Mike" Miller on banjo, Clarence "Tater" Tate on fiddle, Herschel Sizemore on mandolin, Vernon Derrick, adept on both fiddle and mandolin, and Gloria Belle (Flickinger), who often played bass while working as a featured vocalist. Jimmy also continued turning out chartmakers such as the trucker's hit *Widow Maker* (Top 20, 1964), *I Can't Quit Cigarettes* (Top 50, 1966) and *Tennessee* (Top 75, 1968), as well as such favorites with his own fans as the old Big Slim-Hawkshaw Hawkins' favorite *Sunny Side of the Mountain*, *Free Born Man* and his particular arrangement of several Jimmie Skinner compositions. Martin served stints as a regular performer on both the *Louisiana Hayride* and the *Wheeling Jamboree,* and as Bluegrass festivals gained popularity, he quickly became a favorite on the circuit.

Shortly after release of his ***Fly Me to Frisco*** album in 1974, Jimmy Martin severed his long-time association with Decca/MCA. Following a brief interlude, he signed with Starday/Gusto, then being revitalized by producer Moe Lytle. Through the early 80's, Jimmy cut six new albums, including one with fellow Bluegrass legend Ralph Stanley. All the while, he continued as a favorite on the Bluegrass festival circuit. Based in Nashville, he guested on the *Opry* periodically, but membership on the venerable show eluded him. When Gusto went into another eclipse in the 80's, Martin, left without a label, started his own, King of Bluegrass, repackaging many of his old Decca masters.

Known for his ability to sing with conviction in a variety of styles ranging from comic novelty numbers to Gospel, Martin's status as a revered figure in his field remains undaunted as he nears ending his fourth decade on his own. In addition to the many early recordings with his Sunny Mountain Boys, Martin's guest vocals on numbers with the Nitty Gritty Dirt Band such as the chartmaking *Grand Ole Opry Song* (1973) (from their watershed album, ***Will the Circle Be Unbroken***) rank as outstanding traditional Bluegrass. IMT

RECOMMENDED ALBUMS:

"Widow Maker" (Decca)(1964)
"Sunny Side of the Mountain" (Decca)(1965)
"Big & Country Instrumentals" (Decca)(1967)
"Tennessee" (Decca)(1966)
"Me 'n' Ole Pete" (Gusto)(1977)
"Greatest Bluegrass Hits" (Gusto)(1977)
"Will the Circle Be Unbroken" (Gusto)(1978)
"First Time Together" (Gusto)(1980)
"You Don't Know My Mind" (Rounder)(1990)

JUDY MARTIN

(Singer, Guitar)

Given Name:	**Eva Alaine Overstake**
Date of Birth:	**July 16, 1918**
Where Born:	**Decatur, Illinois**
Married:	**Clyde "Red" Foley**
Children:	**Shirley, Julia Ann, Jenny Lou**
Date of Death:	**November 1951**

Judy as Eva Overstake was a part of the sister act the Three Maids, with her sisters Evelyn (b. 1913) and Lucille (1915-1978). They had their beginnings with the Salvation Army, and one of their most popular pieces was *I Ain't Gonna Study War No More*.

They became regulars on WLS Chicago in 1931, but when Judy married Red Foley in 1934, it broke up the act and also the duet of Red Foley and Lulu Belle. Both the other sisters went on to solo careers, with Lucille becoming Jenny Lou Carson, the noted Country songwriter.

Judy raised not only her own children but also Betty Foley, Red's daughter from his first marriage. Betty's mother had died while giving birth to her. From 1933 through 1947, Judy was a resident member on the WLS *Barn Dance*. When her children had grown, she returned to performing as Judy Martin. However, her career was cut short in 1951 when she committed suicide by taking an overdose of sleeping tablets, allegedly after finding out that Foley had been having an affair with Sally Sweet (whom he later married).

Judy/Eva's daughters included Shirley, who married Pat Boone, and among their children is award-winning singer Debby Boone.

MAC MARTIN

(Singer, Guitar)

Given Name:	**William Colleran**
Date of Birth:	**April 26, 1925**

Where Born: Pittsburgh, Pennsylvania
Married: Jean
Children: five

For some forty years Mac Martin has led a high-quality Bluegrass band in the Pittsburgh area. Although Mac and his Dixie Travelers have not made a large number of personal appearances outside of the region of western Pennsylvania, their quality recordings have won them a dedicated audience among fans of traditional Bluegrass throughout the world. Martin has shown an especially able knack for taking good-quality songs from the near-forgotten past and developing excellent arrangements of them that fit the style of the Dixie Travelers.

A lifelong resident of Pittsburgh, William Colleran, whose parents come from Ireland, listened both to the *Grand Ole Opry* and *Wheeling Jamboree* since childhood. In his teens, he and a friend named Ed Brozi formed a duet, developing a rich repertoire of Country and hillbilly songs learned from the radio, records and songbooks. During the latter part of WWII, young Colleran served as a Navy Seabee in the Pacific theater and on the island of Okinawa. All this time, he continued to learn songs and add them to his repertoire. After the war, Bill Colleran returned to Pennsylvania.

Mac formed a Country band, in 1948, called the Pike County Boys, which he described as akin to Bluegrass but initially without a banjo. They worked clubs in the Pittsburgh area and did weekly radio programs, first at WHJB Greensburg, then at WHOD Homestead. Various musicians worked in his group, including Brozi, Bill Higgins, Bill Wagner and Earl Banner. With so many people named Bill in his group, Colleran then took the name Mac Martin for stage purposes.

In the mid-50's, Mac took on as band members fiddler Mike Carson (b. 1937) and Billy Bryant (b. 1938), which gave him a full Bluegrass sound, augmented by the continuing presence of Banner on mandolin and a bass player named Slim Jones. Taking the name Dixie Travelers, they did irregular club work for a couple of years until 1957, when they began appearing at Walsh's Lounge. They played one and sometimes two nights a week at Walsh's for some nineteen years. They also made occasional appearances elsewhere and in 1963 made their initial album and a single, both for Gateway Records. Jones left the band in 1965 and Banner in 1967, to be respectively replaced by Frank Basista and after a brief interim, Bob Artis.

Just before Artis joined the Dixie Travelers, Mac contracted with Rural Rhythm Records. Their first album consisted entirely of instrumentals, but the next three contained both vocal and musical numbers and showcased the talents of the band quite well. So too did the ***Dixie Bound*** album that the Dixie Travelers cut for County in 1972. Many critics would consider these five albums among the best, albeit underrated, traditional Bluegrass produced in the late 60's and early 70's.

While the Dixie Travelers continued to work through the 70's, Mac took a leave from September 1972 until 1977, during which time Artis initially and then Bryant led the group. In 1974, they cut an album for Revonah Records. In 1977, Mac returned to his old spot, just prior to the band ending its long tenure at Walsh's. The Dixie Travelers then went to work at Gustines, a club owned by former Pittsburgh baseball hero Frank Gustine, where they made regular appearances for 6 years. Cutting another album for Revonah, the band now also boasted the talents of Edgar "Bud" Smith on mandolin and Norm Azinger on bass.

In 1984, they began another lengthy association, this time with the Elizabeth Moose Lodge, where they appeared every other Saturday night for several years. In 1987 and 1989 they did a pair of albums for Old Homestead. That year Buzz Matherson replaced Smith on mandolin. In the 80's, the band guested several times on WWVA's *Jamboree USA*.

Throughout their careers, Mac Martin and the Dixie Travelers have displayed a consistent quality of straight traditional Bluegrass that is virtually unsurpassed by a semiprofessional band. (Mac worked a day job as an accountant.)

While their form may be more limited than some, their standard of musicianship, which has always put distinctiveness ahead of commercial expediency, is indeed admirable. A host of loyal fans and a handful of superior recordings rank among their legacy to date. IMT

RECOMMENDED ALBUMS:
"Traveling Blues" (Rural Rhythm)(1968)
"Back Trackin'" (Rural Rhythm)(1971)
"Dixie Bound" (County)(1974)
"Travelin' On" (Revonah)(1978)
"Basic Bluegrass" (Old Homestead)(1987)
"Traveler's Portrait" (Old Homestead)(1989)
"Free Wheeling" (Revonah)(1974) [Dixie Travelers only]

*Bluegrass great **Mac Martin** flanked by his worthy Dixie Travelers*

TROY MARTIN

(Industry Executive, Singer, Comedian)
Given Name: Troy Lee Martin
Date of Birth: May 16, 1911
Where Born: Danville, Virginia
Married: Barbara Ann (div.)
Date of Death: February 20, 1977

Although now almost forgotten, Troy Martin contributed an enormous amount to the fledgling Country music industry from the late 40's. As a "picker" of songs he was probably second only to Fred Rose, and as a "picker" of talent he probably had no peers. Yet, strangely, his death was not even recorded in the *Journal of Country Music*.

Troy Martin suffered with polio as a child and this left him with a slight disability on his left side. During his early teens, he became a comedian with the medicine shows of Doc Marshall and Doctor Butler. He then went into vaudeville with Gene Vaughn, Sweet Papa Bozo, Emmett Miller and Skinny Chandler, and worked the carnivals and walkathons. For a while, he managed the Old Miller Brothers 101 Ranch Wild West Show.

During the early 30's, he did some recordings for the ARC group of labels and opened up some of the initial commercial radio stations in the South. During WWII, he volunteered his services to the USO and appeared with Donald O'Connor, the Mills Brothers and others. In 1949, he moved to Nashville to open the local office for music publishers Peer International. He based himself in the James Robertson Hotel, where he kept an office for some years. He maintained that "all a man needs for an office is a place big enough to hold his brains."

His big break came that year when the head of A & R at Columbia, Art Satherley, announced his retirement. His replacement was a fellow Englishman, Don Law, and Troy saw his opportunity to make inroads into the music business. Martin acted as a talent scout for the label and helped on production while he got the publishing rights of the songs the acts recorded. Over the next few years, he spent his time equally between Knoxville and Dallas. He made his first discovery in 1950, when he found Carl Smith. Shortly after, he discovered Lefty Frizzell. The following year, it was Ray Price and Marty Robbins.

Both Martin and Law had a reputation as heavy drinkers, but they had an unwritten agreement that they would not drink in the studio until they were ready to record the third song. This often resulted in them recording the third song first. At this time, Martin only signed writers on a song-by-song basis, and these writers included J.D. Miller, Jack Toombs and Onie Wheeler. In addition, Peer published the only Hank Williams song not with Acuff-Rose, *Lonesome Whistle*. Troy could also see the Pop potential of a Country song, and it was he who passed *Don't Let the Stars Get in Your Eyes* to Perry Como, who then sold over 2 million copies.

Martin was increasingly unhappy with what he was earning, but Ralph Peer disagreed, and so to supplement his earnings, Martin resorted to the odious practice of "cutting himself in" on a song's copyright under a miscellany of aliases, such as Jerry Organ, George Sherry, Toni Lee and Shirley Lynn, among others. It didn't last for long, but certain songs, especially those written by Arthur Q. Smith, bear these names. Smith was an alcoholic hotel bellhop who sold almost all his outpourings.

In addition, while still being paid by Peer, Martin began placing songs with Cedarwood, a new publishing company of which he was a partner, along with Jim Denny, Webb Pierce and Carl Smith. Peer soon got an inkling something was wrong and sent Roy Horton to Nashville to investigate. The truth came out and Martin was fired. However, he was immediately engaged to head Gene Autry's Golden West Music. While with this company, he had a 3-million Pop seller via Johnny Ray's version of *Just Walkin' in the Rain*, in 1956. In 1958, Troy returned to Peer, but the chemistry had gone. He was still working with Don Law and supplying him songs from the Cedarwood writers such as Mel Tillis, Wayne Walker and John D. Loudermilk, as well as getting artists signed to Columbia. Later that year, Troy produced Billy Brown on the original version of *He'll Have to Go*. It was also rumored that Troy produced Johnny Horton, another one of his finds, for his monster hit *The Battle of New Orleans*, in Don Law's absence. He would later hold that Law prevented him from heading up another record company.

He returned to Autry's companies after leaving Peer, and among the songs picked up was *You're the Only Good Thing*; however, he did pass on Willie Nelson as an artist. In 1962, he returned to Nashville, on the sickness of his mother, and sold his interest in Cedarwood and teamed up with Cohen Williams of Martha White Flour and formed Troy Martin Music. In their initial year, they garnered BMI awards for *Don't Let Me Cross Over* and *Widow Maker*, both written by Penny Jay, whom Troy managed. However, disagreement between Martin and Williams soon resulted in the company being folded.

Martin moved on to Hank Snow's Silver Star Music, where his lucrative copyrights included Yvonne Devaney's *A Million and One*, which was a Country hit for another Martin discoveree, Billy Walker, and a Pop hit for Dean Martin. He then started another publishing house in 1963, and in 1967 the company scored with Jim & Jesse's hit *Diesel on My Tail*. During the early 70's, he had a brief stay with the Wilburn Brothers' Sure-Fire Music and he also undertook independent production. However, he was very set in his ways and was more than a little bitter about life.

His reputation as a "storyteller" and admirer of the ladies was equaled by his ability as a song picker, and some of his signings only became hits years after he signed them. These included *I Overlooked an Orchid* (a No.1 for Mickey Gilley in 1974) and *Crying My Heart Out Over You* (a No.1 in 1982 for Ricky Skaggs). Skaggs also had a No.1 with a song that Martin had signed to Peer in the early 50's, *I Wouldn't Change You If I Could*. Even *Don't Let Me Cross Over* was pitched to 20 artists before Carl Butler, and then it was a "B" side, until it was flipped and became *Cash Box*'s "Song of the Year." However, it was Mel Tillis who gave Troy Martin a posthumous present, when *Steppin' Out* became a Top 10 single in 1980. Troy had been saying since the mid-50's that it was a hit song.

Over the years, Martin had brought many songs to the public's notice, and these included *If You've Got the Money, I Love You a Thousand Ways, Mocking Bird Hill, Kentucky Waltz, If Teardrops Were Pennies, It Wasn't God Who Made Honky Tonk Angels* and *One Woman Man*. He also discovered Freddie Hart and Carl and Pearl Butler, among many others. In his final years, his protege became Billy Joe Burnette, whom he saw as a younger version of himself. He was made an Honorary Member of the Senate of Louisiana and a Deputy Sheriff of Harris County, Texas. He died of a stroke on February 20, 1977.

FRANKIE MARVIN

(Singer, Songwriter, Steel Guitar, Guitar, Actor)

Given Name:	**Frank James Marvin**
Date of Birth:	**January 27, 1904**
Where Born:	**Butler, Indian Territory (now Oklahoma)**
Date of Death:	**ca. 1988**

Frankie Marvin is best remembered today for his long association with Gene Autry.

Born near Butler in what became Oklahoma, Frankie's older brother had been in show business almost as long as the younger sibling could remember. By the time Frankie reached adulthood, Johnny was a radio and recording star, and the younger Marvin learned all of his songs. In 1929, Frankie also went to New York and soon had his own record contract doing numbers like *Oh for the Wild and Wooly West, The Gangster's Warning* and *Oklahoma, Land of the Sunny West*, on labels such as Cameo and Melotone.

He also did some of the first covers of Jimmie Rodgers songs and originals in the same vein, some under the pseudonym "Frankie Wallace." His style tended to be more Country than that of his brother or the so-called citybilly artists like Vernon Dalhart, Carson J. Robison and Frank Luther, but less so than the hard-core Country practitioners. He also worked up a comedy act with Ben "Whitey" Ford (later known as the Duke of

Paducah), calling themselves Ralph and Elmer. Frank's steel guitar also provided instrumental support to other recording stars.

In 1934, when Gene Autry went to Hollywood, both Marvins soon joined him. Johnny wrote songs for his and other singing cowboy films, while Frankie backed Gene and had small parts in virtually all his films (see Movie Section) and radio programs. As cowboy song historian Jim Bob Tinsley states, Marvin's steel guitar style was a distinctive part of the Gene Autry sound. Frank also wrote several songs for Gene, most notably *Cowboy's Heaven.*

As the years went by, Frankie's contributions to the Autry organization receded into the background as the star made accommodations to modernization, although Marvin remained with him until 1955. After retiring, Frankie moved to Frazier Park, California. He either remained there or moved to Florida shortly before his death. A few of his recordings have appeared on anthologies, most notably *Oh for the Wild and Wooly West* and *Barber's Blues.* His steel guitar, however, can be heard on many of the re-issues of early Autry material. IMT

RECOMMENDED ALBUMS:

(See Gene Autry)

JOHNNY MARVIN

(Songwriter, Guitar, Ukulele, Steel Guitar)

Given Name:	**John Senator Marvin**
Date of Birth:	**July 11, 1897**
Where Born:	**Butler, Oklahoma**
Married:	**Gloria Price**
Date of Death:	**December 20, 1944**

Although Johnny Marvin spent his own career as a musician and songwriter in the field of mainstream popular sounds during the 20's and 30's, his brother Frankie's musical activity remained solidly in the Western field.

When Johnny Marvin's mother gave birth to her older of two musician sons in a covered wagon in Curtis County, Oklahoma Territory, the family was only a few miles from the ranch where they would soon settle. Johnny displayed more interest in the show business than cowpunching in his childhood. By age 12 he was providing guitar rhythm for his square-dance fiddling father. At that time, Johnny ran away to join the circus. He returned to Butler at age 14 and eventually learned the barbering trade, but later hit the entertainment trail again with the Royal Hawaiians. After U.S. Navy service in WWI, Johnny went on the vaudeville circuit billed as "Honey Duke and His Uke."

In New York from the mid-20's, Johnny had an early network radio show and recorded for such labels as Columbia, Edison, OKeh and especially Victor. His more notable hits included *Breezin' Along with the Breeze, Half a Moon, The Little White House (At the End of Honeymoon Lane)*, and numbers that became standards like *Ain't She Sweet* and *Side by Side,* the latter a duet with Aileen Stanley. Later Frankie Marvin came to New York and initiated his own recording work. Johnny and Frankie's friendship and help to a young Gene Autry when he first came to the big city would later prove beneficial to both Marvins when their individual careers began to wane.

In spite of his own place in the popular mainstream, Johnny apparently never totally abandoned his affinity for the West, as a photo of one of his touring groups in the early 30's shows him and his wife, Gloria, in stage cowboy costumes. When Gene Autry hit the top in Hollywood as the original singing cowboy star in 1935, Johnny soon joined the Autry entourage as a songwriter. Over the next eight years, he wrote or co-wrote some 80 songs, largely for Autry films. Ironically, his most acclaimed composition, *Dust,* nominated for an Oscar as "Best Song" in 1938, had been done by Roy Rogers in his initial starring role, *Under Western Stars.*

Johnny Marvin's demise could be described as an unfortunate tragedy. While on a tour entertaining military forces in the South Pacific in 1943, he contracted a tropical disease known as dengue fever in the jungles of New Guinea. He never regained his health and succumbed to a heart attack the following year. IMT

MASON DIXON

When Formed:	**1975**
Members:	
Frank Gilligan	**Lead Vocals, Bass Guitar**
Jerry Dengler	**High Harmony Vocals, Lead Guitar, Banjo**
Rick Henderson	**Low Harmony Vocals, Acoustic Guitar**
Terry "Caz" Casburn	**Vocals, Bass Guitar**

As its name suggests, the group is a mix of members from north and south of the Mason Dixon Line. One of the strengths of Mason Dixon had been its vocal harmonies.

The group started as an acoustic duo when Frank (b. November 2, 1955, Queens, New York) and Rick (b. March 29, 1953, Beaumont, Texas) met while students at Lamar University in Beaumont and played around southern Texas. In 1979, Jerry Dengler (b. May 29, 1955, Colorado Springs, Colorado) joined. Jerry had been playing as a solo around the Odessa, Texas, area. The trio hired a drummer and hit the road. For a while the band expanded to a seven-piece, but they couldn't get enough bookings to support that number of players and so settled on being a five-piece.

The group released the single *Armadillo Country* on its own label, and it caught the attention of NBC's *Real Country* program, which featured it on one of their weekly segments, about armadillo racing. The band reached the ears of the Texas promoter, producer and manager Don Schafer and performed on Schafer's annual Texas Music Talent Showcase, and Shafer signed them to Texas Records. The group's initial single, *Mason Dixon Lines*, did well without charting

***Mason Dixon** in action*

and opened up the airwaves for what was to follow. The band's next single, *Every Breath You Take*, hit the charts at the end of 1983. The song, a Country version of the No.1 by Rock group the Police, reached the Top 70 on the Country list. Mason Dixon had two hits in 1984 with *I Never Had a Chance with You* (Top 60) and *Gettin' Over You* (Top 50).

The band continued its association with Texas Records through 1985 and the beginning of 1986. The group hit the charts again with *Only a Dream Away* and *Houston Heartache* (1985) and *Got My Heart Set on You* (1986). In December 1985, Mason Dixon released an album celebrating the Texas Sesquicentennial entitled ***The Spirit of Texas***, on NLT Records. The proceeds of the record were donated by WFAA-TV, KPLX-FM and Tom Thumb/Page stores to the Salesmanship Club's Youth Camps. By the middle of 1986, the group moved over to Dan Mitchell's Premier One Records, and under Mitchell's production control, Mason Dixon started to make even bigger inroads. The band charted with *Home Grown* (Top 60, 1986), *3935 West End Avenue* (Top 40) and *Don't Say No Tonight* (Top 60) (both 1987).

In January 1988, Mason Dixon signed for the first time with a major label, Capitol, and released the album ***Exception to the Rule***, which was produced by Bud Logan. From the album, the group had two chart singles, *Dangerous Road*, which peaked in the Top 70, and *When Karen Comes Around*, which made the Top 50. That year, the band appeared at Charlie Daniels' Chili Cook-Out in Nashville. The following year, two more singles from the album charted, the title track, which was a Top 40 entry, and *A Mountain Ago*, which reached the Top 60.

Founding member Henderson decided to leave the group, and he was replaced by Texan Terry "Caz" Casburn, who also became bass player, while Gilligan moved over to playing guitar. During April 1990, the group continued its tradition of good works by taking part in the Cowboy Crisis Relief Fund Drive. The following month, they were involved in a wreck on I-55 near Kentwood, Louisiana, in which, thankfully, no one was fatally injured. During 1990, Capitol released Mason Dixon's second album, ***Reach for It***, but by now Mason Dixon's chart success had dried up.

RECOMMENDED ALBUMS:

"The Spirit of Texas" (NLT)(1986)
"Homegrown" (Premier One)(1987)
"Exception to the Rule" (Capitol)(1988)
"Reach for It" (Capitol)(1990)

LOUISE MASSEY (a.k.a. LOUISE MASSEY & THE WESTERNERS)

(Singer, Songwriter, Piano [not often played on stage shows])

Given Name: Victoria Louise Massey
Date of Birth: August 10, 1902
Where Born: Hart County, Texas
Married: Milton James Mabie (dec'd.)
Children: Joy
Date of Death: June 22 , 1983

Louise Massey ranks with Patsy Montana and the Girls of the Golden West as a popularizer of Cowgirl and Western songs. Unlike the others, Louise came to the forefront as the major vocalist in a family group that included her father, two brothers, and a husband. She also had a somewhat more sophisticated style than some of her contemporaries and projected an image of glamor. Her greatest claim to fame is as composer of the Western standard *My Adobe Hacienda*, named for a place in New Mexico that she and her husband planned as a retirement residence.

Louise was one of eight children of Henry "Dad" Massey, an Old-Time fiddler and cattleman from Hart County, Texas, who eventually settled in the Capitan ranges of Lincoln County, New Mexico. There he ran the K Bar Ranch and taught music fundamentals to his children, three of whom—Louise, Allen (b.1907), and Curt (b. 1910)—pursued it as a career. When Louise married Milt Mabie (1900-1973) in 1919, the band gained another significant member. Much later, they added accordion player Larry Wellington to their entourage when Dad Massey decided to retire from active touring and go back to his ranch.

The Massey Family played primarily for their own and local entertainment until about 1928, when a representative of the Chautaqua

***Louise Massey** without the Westerners*

circuit in Roswell, New Mexico, heard and subsequently placed them on tour for two seasons. They then came to Kansas City, where they worked regularly on KMBC radio and Curt studied at the Horner Conservatory of Music. It was after they started their routine radio work that Dad returned to the K Bar, and Wellington and they became known as the Westerners. Various members exhibited a wide range of vocal and instrumental talents on both horns and string instruments although Curt favored the fiddle, Allen the tenor banjo or guitar, and Milt the bass. Since the Masseys had fluency in Spanish they also added a Latin or Mexican touch to several of their songs, which included their own originals, traditional cowboy ballads and instrumental tunes.

In 1933, the Westerners came to WLS Chicago, where they worked the *National Barn Dance* for the next two years. With Louise's increasing popularity, her name began appearing in front of the group. They also began a ten-year association with the American Record Corporation during which time Dad Massey even came out of retirement to fiddle a few of his Old-Time numbers. Most of their 100-plus sides featured either Curt (e.g. *The Honey Song*) or Louise on vocals, although they also did quite a few instrumentals such as *Beer and Skittles* and the Mexican-flavored *Quiera Mi Jesusita*. Three of Louise's best-known numbers were *When the White Azaleas Start Blooming*, *I Only Want a Buddy Not a Sweetheart*, and her own 1941 composition *My Adobe Hacienda*, which was covered during the decade by several other Western and Pop artists as well. *Ridin' Down That Old Texas Trail* was another Massey original (Curt and Milt) which gained standard status.

In 1936, the Westerners moved on to New York, where they appeared on a pair of NBC network variety programs over the next couple of seasons. In the summer of 1938, they journeyed to California, where they made a Monogram film with Tex Ritter, *Where the Buffalo Roam,* and also appeared in some shorts. The next year they returned to Chicago, where WLS and the *National Barn Dance* along with a daytime program, *Plantation Party*, became their major outlet for media exposure.

After some twenty years in show business, the Westerners disbanded with only Curt remaining in music. The younger brother went to Los Angeles, where he had a quarter-hour network radio program and later composed the theme song and background music for both *The Beverly Hillbillies* and *Petticoat Junction* CBS-TV comedy shows.

Milt and Louise retired to their Adobe

Hacienda in New Mexico, where they ranched until Milt passed away. In this period Louise gave but two performances yearly at a local function in Roswell and a few interviews. The onetime "Sweetheart of the West" outlived her husband by a decade and died as an octogenarian in San Angelo, Texas. Although Columbia released a 10" album of Louise Massey and the Westerners more than four decades ago, the only items recently available have been a re-issue of *My Adobe Hacienda* on the Time/Life anthology ***The Women*** and two others in the Columbia Special Products collection ***Legendary Songs of the Old West***. IMT

RECOMMENDED ALBUM:
"Louise Massey & the Westerners" (Columbia)(1952)

MASTERS FAMILY, The

When Formed: 1946
JOHNNIE MASTERS
(Vocals, Songwriter, Guitar, 12-String Guitar, Mandolin)
Given Name: John Mace Purdom
Date of Birth: May 27, 1913
Where Born: Jacksonville, Florida
Married: Lucille Ferdon
Date of Death: January 21, 1980
LUCILLE MASTERS
(Vocals, Songwriter)
Given Name: Lucille Ferdon
Date of Birth: September 13, 1917
Where Born: Homerville, Georgia
Married: John Purdom
Children: Johnnie Owen, Evelyn, Deanna
OWEN MASTERS
(Vocals, Songwriter, Guitar)
Given Name: Johnnie Owen Masters
Date of Birth: February 3, 1935
Where Born: Jacksonville, Florida

The Masters Family ranked as a highly significant Country-Gospel group of the 40's and 50's. One of their principal innovations came when they became the first sacred music act to add standard Country and Western instrumentation to their vocals. Earlier efforts usually just had either piano or guitar accompaniment. Some used just guitar and mandolin, which is what the Masters used on their early recordings.

Born near Jacksonville, Florida, John Purdom later changed his name to Masters when his widowed mother married P.S. Masters. At age 12, the youth got a guitar and soon learned to play it, picking up songs from hearing records of Country pioneers like Riley Puckett and Jimmie Rodgers.

In 1932, he began to play with some other musicians at WJAX radio in Jacksonville. The following year, he met and soon married Lucille Ferdon, a south Georgia girl. The couple had three children by 1941, which was the year before Lucille began doing duets with Johnnie at WPDQ radio. Oddly enough many of their stylings were borrowed from the younger but dynamic new duet of James and Martha Carson at WSB Atlanta.

Calling themselves the Dixie Sweethearts, they soon moved over to Jacksonville's top station, WJHP, and the *Dixie Jamboree*, which had a thrice-weekly afternoon show carried by the Mutual Network. When their son Owen and (sometimes) their daughter Deanna joined in, they became the Masters Family.

Johnnie and Lucille cut their first single disc on Rich-R-Tone in 1946 as the Dixie Sweethearts. Shortly afterward they signed with Mercury and subsequently cut eight songs in two sessions with Owen on lead guitar and Johnnie playing mandolin. Their best numbers included *I Found It in Mother's Bible*, *It's All Coming True* and *That Little Old Country Church House*.

On the strength of their Mercury recordings, the Masters Family moved to Knoxville, where they usually worked on shows sponsored by supermarket tycoon Cas Walker at WROL. In 1950, they signed with Columbia and cut some thirty-four songs over the next six years under the direction of Art Satherley and Don Law. *Glory Land March* and *Cry from the Cross* were their biggest numbers, although they had many fine songs, including *Happiness Comes on Spiritual Wings*, *This Old World Is Rockin' in Sin*, *Noah and the Mighty Ark* and *They Made a New Bible*.

From 1952, they used standard Country instrumentation on their discs. On their last three sessions, James Carson worked with them and sang lead on some of his own compositions like *Everlasting Joy* and *I Wasn't There But I Wish I Could Have Been*. Johnnie Masters composed a number of standard Country hymns such as *Glory Land March*, *Cry from the Cross* and *That Little Old Country Church House*. He also composed a few Country hits of the 50's including *Honeymoon on a Rocket Ship* (Hank Snow, 1953), *Sixteen Chickens and a Tambourine* and the all-time nostalgia classic *When the Wagon Was New*.

Owen Masters suffered serious injuries in an auto crash on April 1, 1955, and took several months to recover. Many believe that things were never quite the same for the family after that. They moved back to Jacksonville and periodically made personal appearances—mostly churches and Gospel sings.

On October 12, 1961, they cut an album for Decca, which was partly remakes of their older standards, but also some new songs like *Medals for Mothers* and *Walk Around Heaven*. They did a final album for Starday in 1963. By this time, Owen had grown up and much of their old fervency had eroded.

Johnnie and Lucille went their separate ways for several years but later reunited and remarried. Johnnie had hopes of a Masters Family comeback in the late 70's, but his heart ailments had advanced too far and he died early in 1980 with his dream unfulfilled. Lucille and her two grown daughters continued to make their homes in Florida, while Owen settled in Mt. Juliet, Tennessee. They occasionally turned out quality sacred songs that major label Gospel singers recorded. IMT

RECOMMENDED ALBUMS:
"Sacred Songs by the Masters Family" (Harmony)(1959)
"Everlasting Joy" (Harmony)(1962)
"Gospel Sing" (Decca)(1962)
"Spiritual Wings" (Harmony)(1963)
"The Gloryland March" (Starday)(1963)

*Texas star **"Country" Johnny Mathis***

"COUNTRY" JOHNNY MATHIS

(Singer, Songwriter, Guitar)
Given Name: John Wesley Mathis
Date of Birth: September 28, 1933
Where Born: Maude, Texas

Not to be confused with a certain Pop singer, this Johnny Mathis, although not as successful as Mr. Twelfth of Never, made his presence felt in the Country charts. Johnny added the "Country" prefix to his name following the success of the other Mr. Mathis.

When Johnny was born, his daddy wanted him to follow in his footsteps as a Church of Christ minister. Johnny learned to play guitar while still a youngster, and played and sang at his daddy's church. However, Johnny wanted to be a professional boxer and was on course for this during high school in Dallas when he was laid low with the bone disease osteomyelitis. He spent three years in a Dallas hospital, where he took up songwriting to pass the time.

His career got under way as a member of the *Big D Jamboree* out of Dallas. From there, he moved on to the *Louisiana Hayride*, where he stayed until 1960. Although he recorded for several labels, his first hit was in 1954 with the self-penned *If You Don't Somebody Else Will*, on which he teamed up with Jimmy Lee Fautheree as Jimmy & Johnny. The single, on Chess, reached the Top 3 on the Country charts.

Johnny moved around the record labels, including Talent and Decca, and in 1957 duetted with Johnny Horton on the Columbia flip-side *You're My Baby*. After recording for Mercury, Mathis moved on to D Records in 1958, where his most successful record was *I've Been Known to Cry/Lonely Night*. Another favored single was *Carl Chessman*, in 1960. The following year, he moved on to Republic for another duet with Fautheree, *Let Me Be the One*.

Johnny had a solo hit for United Artists in 1963, *Please Talk to My Heart*. The single reached the Top 15 on the Country charts. In 1965, Johnny moved toward Gospel material and recorded, for Hilltop Gospel, the album ***Country Johnny Mathis***. He signed with Little Darlin' Records in 1967 and recorded a pair of inspirational albums for the label.

RECOMMENDED ALBUMS:

"Country Johnny Mathis" (Hilltop Gospel)(1965)
"He Keeps Me Singing" (Little Darlin')(1967)
"Come Home to My Heart" (Little Darlin')(1970)
"In the House of the Lord" (Pickwick)

TOKYO MATSU

(Singer, Fiddle, Yodeler)
Where Born: Tokyo, Japan
Married: Unknown
Children: Unknown

As her first name implies, Tokyo was born and brought up in that city in Japan. She became a student at the Kunitachi School of Music and was taught classical violin; she also had voice training. After hearing Country music on the American Forces Network, she soon decided that rather than being a violinist, she would be a "fiddler."

In 1968, Tokyo toured the Far East and performed for U.S. troops in Vietnam. She was booked for personal appearances at major fairs, clubs and concerts and has been on TV shows such as Bill Anderson, Arthur Smith and the WWVA *Jamboree*, West Virginia. As a successful performer, she has opened for such greats as George Jones, Faron Young, Little Jimmy Dickens,Tammy Wynette, Dolly Parton, Billy Walker, Charlie Pride, Barbara Mandrell and many others. When she appeared on the *Grand Ole Opry*, she received a standing ovation.

Her repertoire ranges from Country classics such as *Orange Blossom Special* to a delightful rendering of *Rocky Top*. She also is an excellent yodeler.

In 1987, on one of her European tours, she appeared at the Wembley International Festival of Country Music in London. She was a finalist in the "Best Fiddle" category at the Academy of Country and Western Music Awards.

Matsu is an exciting and dynamic entertainer. She lives in Nashville with her husband and children. JAB

KATHY MATTEA

(Singer, Songwriter, Guitar)
Date of Birth: June 21, 1959
Where Born: Cross Lanes, West Virginia
Married: Jon Vezner

As a teenager growing up in tiny Cross Lanes, West Virginia, Kathy Mattea soaked up the sounds of Folk-Pop stars Joni Mitchell, James Taylor and Buffy Sainte-Marie. The daughter of a chemical plant worker, she began playing guitar in junior high school, learning the songs of her favorite singers. Kathy learned traditional Folk songs at Girl Scout Camp and played guitar and sang at Folk masses on a regular basis. She developed her vocal skills in her high school choir singing classical music.

When Kathy entered West Virginia University in 1976 she turned her attention to Bluegrass, joining the group Pennsboro. When the group leader graduated two years later and moved to Nashville, Kathy quit college to give Music City a try. Before long Kathy was left alone in the city as her former bandmate abandoned Nashville to attend medical school. To make ends meet Kathy worked as a tour guide at the Country Music Hall of Fame, where she acquired a good knowledge and appreciation of Country music pioneers. She was also employed as a waitress and an insurance secretary. After a few years in Nashville, Kathy began to get some calls to sing demos for publishers and songwriters on Music Row. Her vocal work came to the attention of Mercury Records, which offered her a contract in 1983, with Allen Reynolds as her producer.

The following year her debut album, ***Kathy Mattea***, was released and produced the hit singles *Street Talk* (Top 25) and *Someone Is Falling in Love*. Mercury also experimented with the new Country music video field with *You've Got a Soft Place to Fall* (Top 50). Kathy closed the year with *That's Easy for You to Say* (Top 50). Based on the success of the album, *Billboard* named Kathy "Top New Country Artist of the Year."

Kathy's 1985 ***From My Heart*** album helped gain her a nomination for the CMA's "Horizon Award" with the radio favorite *It's Your Reputation Talkin'* (Top 40) and *He Won't Give In* (Top 25). Kathy closed out the year with the Top 50 single *Heart of the Country*.

Kathy's biggest radio success to date came with her folksy acoustic album ***Walk the Way the Wind Blows***, in 1986. She scored her first major hit with Nanci Griffith's *Love at the Five and Dime*, which went Top 3. The album also contained the autobiographical *Leaving West Virginia*, a song Kathy wrote upon arriving in Nashville. She helped out her home state by appearing in a major tourism campaign and spent most of the year opening concerts for George Strait. She followed up with the album's title track, which went Top 10.

1987 proved to be a breakthrough year for Kathy. *You're the Power* reached the Top 5 and *Train of Memories* peaked in the Top 10. ***Untasted Honey*** was a pivotal album for the young singer, providing her with her first No.1 hit, *Goin' Gone*. She followed that success in 1988, with another No.1, *Eighteen Wheels and a Dozen Roses*. The song won "Single of the Year" honors from both the CMA and the ACM in 1988. It was also named "Song of the Year" by the ACM. Kathy also took "Top Female Vocalist" honors from the CMA and the ACM. Her two other singles of the year, *Untold Stories* and *Life As We Knew It*, both went Top 5.

On Valentine's Day 1988, Kathy married songwriter Jon Vezner, who would provide several hit songs for his new wife and had established himself with recordings by Reba McEntire, Mel McDaniel and Dave and Sugar.

Kathy's reign at the top of the charts continued in 1989 with the release of her fifth album, ***Willow in the Wind***. *Come from the Heart* shot to No.1, accompanied by a hit music video. She followed up with another No.1, *Burnin' Old Memories*. Late in the year, Kathy released a single that was to become one of the most important—although, only reaching the Top 10, not the biggest—of her career. The touching tale of a married couple's lifelong devotion that ends in a nursing home was co-written by husband Jon Vezner. The inspiration for *Where've You Been* came from Vezner's own grandparents. The song was a

Kathy Mattea with her husband, Jon Vezner

Country radio hit and crossed over to the Adult Contemporary chart. Mattea was invited to perform the song on NBC's *The Tonight Show*. *Where've You Been* was named "Song of the Year" by both the CMA and the ACM.

In 1990 Kathy was named "Female Vocalist of the Year" by the CMA and earned a Grammy Award for "Best Country Vocal Performance, Female," for *Where've You Been*. Also in 1990, Kathy received a Gold Disc for ***Willow in the Wind***, marking sales in excess of 500,000. That year, she had the Top 3 hit *She Came from Fort Worth* and two singles that peaked in the Top 10, *The Battle Hymn of Love* (with Tim O'Brien) and *A Few Good Things Remain*. Mercury also released ***A Collection of Hits***, which went Gold in 1991.

With a desire to explore her Celtic music influences, Kathy traveled to Scotland to record with longtime friend Dougie McLean. They collaborated on the plea for peace and understanding *From a Distance*. The song was included on her ***Time Passes By*** album, in 1991. However, her other singles of the year did not fare so well, with *Whole Lotta Holes* going Top 20 and *Asking Us to Dance* only reaching the Top 30.

Lonesome Standard Time was released in the fall of 1992, and the driving title track was supported by a poignant music video but only reached the Top 15. Other hits from the album were *Standing Knee Deep in a River* (*Dying of Thirst*) (Top 20), and *Seeds* (Top 50, 1993). Shortly after completing work on the album, Kathy entered Vanderbilt University Hospital and underwent vocal cord surgery. The delicate procedure to repair a blood blister on her vocal cords was a success and after extensive vocal therapy, she returned to performing.

In 1992, Kathy made headlines as the first Nashville star to speak openly about the AIDS issue. After losing several friends to the disease she decided to get involved. One of her boldest moves was to break ranks with the CMA during the 1992 television awards show. The CMA officials had distributed green lapel ribbons for participants to signify environmental awareness, opting not to use red for AIDS awareness as other awards shows had been doing. Mattea chose to wear a red ribbon in memory of the three friends she had lost to AIDS. When she asked permission to explain why she was wearing a red ribbon on camera, officials declined. The two-time CMA award winner followed her convictions and gave a brief, heartfelt explanation on the nationally televised show. She received tremendous support from industry friends, and her example encouraged other Country artists to get involved. In 1993, Mattea spearheaded an effort for the American Federation for Aids Research (AmFAR) called ***Red, Hot & Country***. The album project featured many of her fellow stars, with profits going for AIDS research.

In addition, as Honorary Chairperson, she led the second "From All Walks of Life" pledge walk in Nashville. In 1993, Kathy came back in favor with her spiritual album ***Good News***. She followed this in 1994 with ***Walking Away a Winner***, which climbed into the Country Albums Top 15, and the title track reached the Top 3. She told Barry McCloud in 1993 that if her career ended, she would spend her time researching Scottish Folk music. JIE

RECOMMENDED ALBUMS:

"Kathy Mattea" (Mercury)(1984)
"From My Heart" (Mercury)(1985)
"Walk the Way the Wind Blows" (Mercury)(1986)
"Untasted Honey" (Mercury)(1987)
"Willow in the Wind" (Mercury)(1989)
"A Collection of Hits" (Mercury)(1990)
"Time Passes By" (Mercury)(1991)
"Lonesome Standard Time" (Mercury)(1992)
"Good News" (Mercury)(1993)
"Walking Away a Winner" (Mercury)(1994)

MATTHEWS, WRIGHT & KING

When Formed: 1991
Members:
Raymond Matthews — Guitar, Vocals
Woody Wright — Bass Guitar, Vocals
Tony King — Guitar, Vocals

Although Matthews, Wright & King promised much as an early 90's vocal group, they failed to achieve a sufficient level of radio acceptance and after three years disbanded.

Initially Columbia Records had planned to record a solo album on Raymond Matthews. Nashville producer Larry Strickland suggested Raymond (b. October 13, 1956, Centre, Alabama) get together with Woody Wright (b. October 10, 1957, East Tennessee) and Tony King (b. June 27, 1957, North Carolina), and their voices blended so well that the group was born. Raymond grew up singing in various groups in Alabama. He operated his own carpentry business until he made the move to Nashville with the group Southern Gray. When the group disbanded Matthews pursued a solo career.

Woody Wright cut his musical teeth on Bluegrass and Gospel music. His father was a Bluegrass musician and Woody learned to sing harmony listening to Gospel quartets. In high school, he formed his own Gospel music group. When he graduated from high school, Wright moved to Nashville to play bass and sing with the Tennesseans, a Gospel group headed by former Oak Ridge Boy Willie Wynn. Wright also performed with a group called Memphis and did studio vocal work with the Judds and the Bellamy Brothers.

Tony King spent three years touring and recording with award-winning Bluegrass group J.D. Crowe & the New South. The North Carolina native sang lead vocals and played rhythm guitar. King later traveled with Holly Dunn and spent several years in Vince Gill's band. Tony also found success as a songwriter with *I've Cried My Last Tear for You*, recorded by Ricky Van Shelton.

The trio first hit the chart in 1992 with the Top 50 single *The Power of Love*, which remained their most successful. Other chart singles that year were *Mother's Eyes* (Top 60) and *House Huntin'* (Top 70). In 1993 Matthews, Wright & King joined forces with producer Randy Scruggs to record their second album, ***Dream Seekers***. Matthews penned the title song and three others on the album. The trio scored a radio Top 50 hit with the harmony-heavy *I Got a Love* and completed 1993 with the Top 75 *One of These Days*. Matthews, Wright & King received nominations for best new group by the Academy of Country Music and best vocal group by the TNN/*Music City News* Country Awards. In 1994, without further success coming their way, Matthews, Wright & King decided to go their separate ways. JIE

RECOMMENDED ALBUMS:

"Power of Love" (Columbia)(1992)
"Dream Seekers" (Columbia)(1993)

MAVERICKS, The

When Formed: 1990
Members:
Raul Malo Lead Vocals, Guitar, Piano
Robert Reynolds Bass Guitar, Guitar
Paul Deakin Drums
Nick Kane Lead Guitar (also plays Drums)
Former Member:
David Lee Holt Lead Guitar

The brand of Country-Rock purveyed by the Mavericks is the nearest to the true blending of traditional Country music and 50's rock'n'roll. However, unlike most Country-Rock musicians, who hail from California or Texas, three-quarters of the band come from Miami, Florida.

Lead singer and songwriter Raul Malo (b. August 7, 1965, Miami, Florida) was born of Cuban parents who relocated to Miami in 1959. Raul grew up listening to their collection of 50's records by Bill Haley, Elvis Presley, Hank Williams and Johnny Cash. When he was age 8, Raul began collecting Presley records and at age 11, he first saw Elvis in concert. Raul found that although he played in bands at school, his love of 50's music was not shared by his band-mates.

Then he met Robert Reynolds (b. Robert Earl Reynolds, April 30, 1962, Kansas City Missouri), who was also a record collector and had started to play guitar before he was 16. Robert's first band played covers of Buddy Holly, Elvis and Hank Williams. Everyone in the band was at least 10 years older than him. It was with this band that he first heard Buck Owens' music. Paul Deakin (b. Paul Wylie Deakin, September 2, 1959, Miami, Florida) was Robert's best friend, although they had never played in bands together. Paul earned a BA in music at the University of Miami. He played in a series of bands and then for the next six years, Paul did studio work playing progressive Rock, Punk and Funk. However, he wanted to play more acoustic music, and it was Robert who introduced him to the music of Patsy Cline, Johnny Cash and Hank Williams.

Because Raul, who had been playing bass guitar, wanted to play rhythm guitar, Robert took over the bass-playing role. They began playing around Miami and building up a following around the Rock clubs. In October 1990, they got together enough money to record a 13-track album. KISS-FM, with one of the tightest playlists, aired several tracks and a copy of their tape got to Joe Deters, a regional promotion man for MCA, who passed it to MCA Nashville's President, Bruce Hinton.

The band came to Nashville in May 1991 for a showcase, which was attended by A & R scouts from all the labels, but MCA won out. It was decided to record their debut album in Miami rather than in Nashville. Steve Fishell, who had produced McBride & the Ride, was brought in to produce with Raul, with the exception of *This Broken Heart*, which was produced by Fishell and Richard Bennett.

David Lee Holt was brought in on lead guitar. Brought up in Lubbock, Texas, he had played with Joe Ely and had been playing around Austin, playing with the house band at Antone's club. He had played in Rosie Flores's band and when the rest of the Mavericks first saw him on TNN's *Nashville Now*, he was playing in Carlene Carter's band.

The initial album, ***From Hell to Paradise***, consisting mainly of Raul Malo songs, was released in 1992. However, it did not fare well and only their reprise of Hank Williams' *Hey Good Lookin'* made the singles chart, reaching the Top 75 and then falling out after one week. By the time of their second album, ***What a Crying Shame***, Raul had been writing with master songsmith Kostas, and four of their joint efforts were on the album. Don Cook replaced Steve Fishell as producer and David Lee Holt had left, to be replaced by Nick Kane (b. Nicholas James Kane, August 21, 1954, Jerusalem, Georgia), although he didn't play on the album. The album was recorded in Nashville and is infinitely better than its predecessor. Don Cook manages to control Raul's voice, which with its dramatic tonal quality (like Patsy Cline meets Roy Orbison meets Dwight Yoakam) can become histrionic. The result of this album was that the Mavericks found themselves in both the Album and Singles charts. The title track reached the Top 30 in 1994, while the album was still on the chart, having peaked in the Top 40. Trisha Yearwood, who is married to Robert Reynolds, lends a hand with backup vocals. Nick is the son of Jim Kane, a former opera singer, and Maria, a former professor. He was formerly a cabinet maker and is married to Kim; they have three children, Ruby, Fae and Oskar. Paul is now divorced and has one son, Harrison Dean, while Raul has yet to take the matrimonial plunge.

On the basis of this second album, Raul Malo as a songwriter and the Mavericks as a group should be around for some while.

RECOMMENDED ALBUM:
"What a Crying Shame" (MCA)(1994)

KEN MAYNARD

(Singer, Fiddle, Harmonica, Guitar, Actor)
Given Name: Kenneth Maynard
Date of Birth: July 21, 1895
Where Born: Vevay, Indiana
Married: 1. or 2. Mary (div.)
3. Bertha Rowland (dec'd.)
Date of Death: March 1973

Although Ken Maynard is remembered primarily today as a Hollywood action cowboy in the tradition of Tom Mix, he also deserves credit for being the pioneer singing cowboy on the silver screen. True, Maynard's musical interludes in the films seem relatively minor compared to the later Gene Autry and Roy Rogers offerings, but they started the trend.

While born and bred as a Hoosier, Kenneth Maynard, in keeping with the cowboy image, often gave Mission, Texas, as his birthplace. Possessed with wanderlust and an adventurous spirit in his youth, Ken ran away at 12 and joined a Wild West show. However, his father soon located the youngster near Cincinnati and brought him home. At 16, he left again and worked as a ranch hand and then for various circus units. Maynard served in the U.S. Army Engineering Corps during WWI, after which time he returned to the circus and to rodeo riding. By 1922, when he came to Hollywood, his annual income from salary and prize money hovered in the $40,000 range, a phenomenal sum for that era.

By 1927, after a slow start, Maynard along with his white palomino, Tarzan, became one of the five top cowboys in silent pictures (the others being Tom Mix, Buck Jones, Hoot Gibson and Fred Thomson; William S. Hart had retired by this time). Of these only Jones and Maynard really hit big in sound films as well. For music fans, the first significant move for Ken came in September 1929, when he made the movies *The Wagon Master* (which included his fiddling and singing two songs), *The Cowboy's Lament* and *The Lone Star Trail*. The following April, Maynard recorded

*Singing cowboy **Ken Maynard***

these last two songs for Columbia along with six others that were unissued (*Home on the Range* did appear on an anthology of cowboy songs from Columbia Special Products in 1981). Ken sang a song or two in several other pictures, most notably *Strawberry Roan* (1933). His style, while adequate in terms of voice, tended toward the rough and unpolished, but was certainly authentic. In essence, Maynard more nearly resembled Jules Allen or Carl Sprague than Jimmy Wakely or Gene Autry.

In 1934, Ken introduced Autry to motion picture viewers as a supporting performer in the serial *Mystery Mountain* and in the feature *In Old Santa Fe*. Within a year, Gene emerged as the full-fledged singing cowboy star that would send many older performers, such as his mentor Maynard, into eclipse, and inaugurate a new type of Western hero.

In the later 30's, Ken's star began to fade as younger screen cowpokes, not all of them singers, increasingly moved to the forefront. His last appearance as a solo star came in 1940 with *Lightning Strikes West*. Maynard co-starred with other veterans Hoot Gibson and Bob Steele in the Trail Blazer series in 1943-1944 and with singing cowboy Eddie Dean in *Harmony Trail* in 1944. Thereafter he toured in the circus and appeared at rodeos until retiring.

A cantankerous and sometimes offensive personality compounded with his drinking problems did not make him a particularly endearing individual. Researcher Ken Griffis found him quite congenial early in 1968, when he did an interview and accepted a set of Maynard's Columbia test pressings on behalf of the John Edwards Memorial Foundation. Later that year Ken's wife of twenty-nine years, former high-wire artist Bertha Rowland, passed away, after which his health and condition deteriorated.

He spent his last years in a mobile home in the San Fernando Valley, moving to a nursing home two months before his death. An entire album of his Columbia waxings and some cuts from motion picture soundtracks would make a welcome compilation, but to date, no company has seen fit to undertake such a product. As a matter of interest, Ken's brother, Kermit Maynard, was also a star of the Western "B" movies. IMT

MAC McANALLY

(Singer, Songwriter, Producer)
Given Name: Lyman McAnally, Jr.
Date of Birth: 1957
Where Born: Red Bay, Alabama
Married: Vicki

Mac McAnally is a critically acclaimed singer, songwriter, recording artist, producer and studio musician who is best known to Country music fans for the hit songs he's written for other artists. Mac's songwriting credits include *Old Flame* for Alabama (1981), *Crime of Passion* for Ricky Van Shelton (1987), *Two Dozen Roses* by Shenandoah (1989), *Precious Thing* by Steve Wariner (1990) and *Cafe on the Corner* for Sawyer Brown (1992). Other artists who have recorded his songs include Randy Travis, Dan Seals, John Anderson, Hank Williams, Jr., Gary Morris and Ricky Skaggs. Mac's expert acoustic guitar playing can be heard on recordings by many of these artists and also on albums by Dolly Parton, Lyle Lovett, Patty Loveless, Keith Whitley and Nanci Griffith.

Mac began his musical journey in the small town of Belmont, Mississippi. He soaked up the rich southern heritage and was an avid reader of William Faulkner and Ernest Hemingway. Through their writings he traveled, in his imagination, far beyond the little town where he lived. His musical roots came in church where his mother was the pianist. Mac learned to play the piano easily and was often called upon to play for the Gospel singing at church.

Mac got his first job in the music business when he was only 13, playing the piano in a small night club north of the Tennessee-Mississippi border. Mac lived in a dry county where no alcohol sales were allowed, so people had to go north for a taste of liquor. Recalling the experience, Mac relates, "I had never been to a bar, had heard nothing but horror stories, many of which turned out to be true, so I was scared to death at first. When the band took a break, I would lie down on stage behind the piano until time to play again. I had only played in church before and when I recognized so many of the church folks in the night clubs, it made me a little leery of going to either place."

Mac dedicated much of his time as a high school student to playing the guitar. He also began writing songs, drawing inspiration from the great American authors he was reading and from observing life in his small town. Mac took his skills as a guitarist to the recording studios of Muscle Shoals, Alabama. The producers there were impressed with his mastery of the finger-picking guitar style and used him often on recording sessions. Before long Mac had the opportunity to record some of his own songs that resulted in a recording contract with Ariola Records when he was 18 years old. His debut album was titled ***Mac McAnally*** and produced a No.2 Adult Contemporary radio hit, *It's a Crazy World*. The song also became a Top 40 Pop hit, and critics compared him with his literary heroes William Faulkner and Flannery O'Connor and musical influences James Taylor and Jimmy Buffet. Mac's second album for Ariola, ***No Problem Here***, was released in 1978.

In 1980, Mac moved to RCA Records and produced ***Cuttin' Corners***. While the album was praised by critics it was not a commercial success. Music business power broker David Geffen heard the album and wanted to sign Mac to a new label he was starting. He bought McAnally's contract from RCA and made him the first artist on Geffen Records. Mac continued his literary approach to songwriting on his Geffen recordings and called his songs "collaborations between the heart and mind." He produced the lps ***Nothin' But the Truth*** (1983), ***Finish Lines*** (1989) and ***Simple Life***, in 1990. His ***Simple Life*** album, on Warner Brothers, produced the Top 15 Country hit *Back Where I Come From*, that told the story of his childhood in Belmont, Mississippi.

McAnally took a break from his own recording in 1991 to co-produce Ricky Skaggs' album ***My Father's Son*** with Skaggs. In addition to his production assistance, Mac played guitar and sang on Skaggs' version of his song *Simple Life*. In 1992, McAnally was persuaded by long-time friend and label executive Tony Brown to record an album for MCA Records. The result was ***Live and Learn***, and McAnally paid tribute to Brown in the liner notes, giving him special thanks for "having the attention span of at least 15 years while the ducks lined up to make this record." ***Live and Learn*** served to display Mac's masterful songwriting with *Only Passing Through, The Trouble with Diamonds*, and *Still Life*. Also included on the album was the touching ballad *All These Years*, which became a big hit for Sawyer Brown. Mac was called on by the group to co-produce albums in 1992 and 1993. He teamed up with Sawyer Brown lead singer Mark Miller to write their 1993 hit single *Thank God for You*.

Mac was back in the studio in the fall of 1993 working on his sophomore release for MCA Records. He also continued his studio and songwriting work with Sawyer Brown. In early 1994, Mac co-produced a Gospel album with Ricky Skaggs. JIE

RECOMMENDED ALBUMS:
"Nothin' But the Truth" (Geffen)(1983)
"Finish Lines" (Geffen)(1989)
"Simple Life" (Warner Brothers)(1990)
"Live and Learn" (MCA)(1992)

LEON McAULIFFE

(Steel Guitar, Singer)

Given Name:	**William Leon McAuliffe**
Date of Birth:	**January 3, 1917**
Where Born:	**Houston, Texas**
Married:	**Eleanor Ann Murphy**
Children:	**Roger, Leon, Lucy Ellen**
Date of Death:	**August 20, 1988**

The phrase "Take it away, Leon" spoken by Bob Wills on many of his recordings, radio programs and concert shows helped make Leon McAuliffe the most famous and acclaimed steel guitarist in the history of Western Swing music.

Leon McAuliffe obtained his first guitar at age 14, when a man named Ladis Marek taught him the fundamentals of both standard and Hawaiian styles. Before 1931 ended, Leon and some friends had obtained a show at KTLC radio as the Waikiki Strummers, later moving over to KPRC. In the early fall of 1933, Leon auditioned for a position with W. Lee O'Daniel's Light Crust Doughboys and after only a few days with them participated in an American Record Company session in Chicago. He went back to Houston in November but returned to Fort Worth in January as a full-time member. He also met Bob Dunn of the Milton Brown's Brownies, who taught him how to electrify his National resonator guitar.

In March 1935, Jesse Ashlock recruited Leon to join Bob Wills' Texas Playboys, and the 18-year-old steel guitarist moved to Tulsa and "Take it away, Leon" soon became so popular that it eventually entered the vernacular. McAuliffe's tenure with the Wills band lasted through a move to California, many record sessions and motion pictures with Tex Ritter and Russell Hayden (see Movie Section). *Steel Guitar Rag*, a number adapted from a Blues tune by Sylvester Weaver, became Leon's trademark.

Steel guitar wizard ***Leon McAuliffe***

McAuliffe served as a flight instructor during WWII. He was stationed with Glenn Miller tenor sax player/singer Tex Beneke, and they traded music ideas. Leon decided to start his own group after the war. Initially, he gravitated toward a big band sound, but the fans demanded Western Swing, so Leon combined the two, building a style around his own steel, clarinet, saxophone, trumpet, guitar and twin fiddles. The band worked on KVOO radio in Tulsa and recorded first for Majestic and then Columbia Records from 1949 to 1955. *Panhandle Rag* resulted from Leon's desire to create a new steel guitar instrumental classic, and it reached the Top 10 in the summer of 1949. Other efforts, while of high quality, did not fare quite so well. Leon and his Cimarron Boys continued to work out of Tulsa alternating work at the Cimarron Ballroom with tours. He initiated his own record label, Cimarron, and had a pair of mid-level hits with *Cozy Inn* (Top 20) and *Faded Love* (Top 25) in 1961 and 1962. As Western Swing influences waned in the 60's, he found himself more of a regional performer.

Starday re-released some of his Cimarron material and he recorded a new album for them, two for Dot and one for Capitol. From the mid-60's, Mr. Steel Guitar went into the radio station business as the owner of KAMO Rogers, Arkansas.

As interest in Western Swing music revived in the 70's, McAuliffe's significance gained more recognition. He participated in a Bob Wills recording session in 1971 and Wills' final work for United Artists, two years later. After Bob's death, Leon took part in a Fan Fair Wills tribute in June 1975. Leon also played a prominent role in the Texas Playboy reunions, tours and recording efforts for Delta and Capitol in the late 70's. He also did Stoneway and Delta albums on his own. Four years before his death, Columbia re-issued an album of McAuliffe's own work in their Historic Edition Series. In addition, many of the classic Wills recordings on which he played so prominent a role became available again.

IMT

RECOMMENDED ALBUMS:

"Take Off" (Dot)(1958)
"Mister Western Swing" (Cimarron, Starday and Pine Mountain)(1960)
"Swinging West" (Starday)(1964)
"Swingin' Western Strings" (Cimarron, Starday)(1964)
"The Dancin'est Band Around" (Capitol)(1964)
"Golden Country Hits" (Dot)(1966)
"Take It Away Leon" (Stoneway)(1974)
"Steel Guitar Rag" (Delta)(1982)
"Columbia Historic Edition" (Columbia)(1984)
(See also Bob Wills, Light Crust Doughboys, Texas Playboys)

MARTINA McBRIDE

(Singer)

Given Name:	**Martina Mariea Schiff**
Date of Birth:	**July 29, 1966**
Where Born:	**Sharon, Kansas**
Married:	**John McBride**

There are many people within the media who are hailing Martina as in the same league as Linda Ronstadt, Reba McEntire and Emmylou Harris. It was her opening for Garth Brooks in 1991 that first brought her to public attention.

She grew up listening to Country music, and definitely leans toward the more traditional side of Country. Although she now listens to other types of music, she still tries to retain that traditional edge. Her maxim is, If her father likes it, it's Country. She has been lucky in her marriage, in that her husband, John, is a Garth Brooks sound engineer, and so Martina and John have managed to spend time together.

Martina signed with RCA at the end of 1991, and the following year, her debut album, ***The Time Has Come***, was released and reached the Country Album Top 50 and hung around for nearly 6 months. She debuted on the singles chart with the title track, a Lonnie Wilson-Susan Longacre song, which reached the Top 25 but was on the charts for 5 months. It was followed by *That's Me* and *Cheap Whiskey*, which both reached the Top 50.

By the time of her second album, ***The Way That I Am***, in 1993, Martina was sporting a shorter haircut. This album, like its predecessor, was produced by Paul Worley and Ed Seay (plus on this one, Martina herself). It was as good as, if not better than, the debut album. During the year, *My Baby Loves Me* reached the Top 3. In 1994, *Life #9* reached the Top 10 and *Independence Day* was following it up the chart. In 1994, Martina's video for *Independence Day* was named the CMA's "Music Video of the year."

RECOMMENDED ALBUMS:

"The Time Has Come" (RCA)(1992)
"The Way That I Am" (RCA)(1993)

McBRIDE & THE RIDE/TERRY McBRIDE & THE RIDE

Formed:	**1989**
Members:	
Terry McBride	**Singer, Songwriter, Guitar, Bass Guitar**
Kenny Vaughn	**Guitar, Vocals**
Randy Frazier	**Bass**
Keith Edwards	**Drums, Vocals**
Former Members:	
Ray Herndon	**Guitar, Vocals**
Billy Thomas	**Drums, Vocals**

The group was formed when Tony Brown, Nashville Executive Vice President of MCA, took three complete strangers to meet one another. Songwriter Terry McBride and two studio musicians, Ray Herndon and Billy Thomas, thus became McBride & the Ride. The combination of musicianship and harmony vocals was magical. They realized after the first rehearsal that their voices blended perfectly.

Terry McBride (b. September 16, 1958), the son of singer Dale McBride, was born in Bell County, Texas, but raised in Lampasas, Texas. Dale played guitar from the age of 13 and soon became a member of the Down Beats with Jimmy Heap. In the 1970's, he had 13 minor chart hits, with the highest, *Ordinary Man*, in 1977, peaking in the Country chart Top 30. All but one of his hits were on the independent label Con Brio (one being on Thunderbird).

Terry got his first guitar from his father when he was 9 years old and was shown three chords and left to see how he got on. At school, Terry was into traditional and Texas music. After he had completed high school, he had to audition for a place in his dad's band, with whom he worked for the next three years. Then after a short break "doing his own thing," Terry joined Delbert McClinton for two years and part of that time toured with John Fogerty. Then Terry began to concentrate on his songwriting and moved to Nashville to pitch his work. He has written with such names as Kostas, Skip Ewing, John Scott Sherrill, Curtis Wright and Walt Aldridge. Two years before the Ride was formed Terry decided to quit drinking. He is married to Cathy and has a daughter, Beth Ann

Ray Herndon comes from a musical family. He and his two brothers were child stars on the *Lew King Rangers* TV show in Phoenix, singing, tap dancing, playing the accordion and playing guitar. Tanya Tucker and Wayne Newton also performed on the show. Although he started singing when he was only 3, Ray's recording debut was made at the age of 4, when he cut a song in Hollywood, called *Christmas Eve*. During his teens he worked in his father's band and performed at the family-owned bar and restaurant called the Handlebar J., in Scottsdale, Arizona. Next, he and his brothers joined David Sloan and the Rogues, the house band at Mr. Luckies Club, also in Scottsdale. After meeting the then unknown Lyle Lovett while on a European tour, the band recorded a demo with him including songs that became part of his debut album on MCA, like *Cowboy Man* and *Further Down the Line*. The band became the core of the ensemble of Lyle Lovett's Large Band. Ray still records with Lovett. Ray is married to Karri and has a daughter, Jessica.

Billy Thomas began playing a set of hand-me-down drums when he was in the sixth grade. He later joined the Rock music scene, around the Fort Myers Gulf Coast of Florida. He moved to Los Angeles in 1973 and worked with Rick Nelson, Mac Davis, and the Hudson Brothers. In 1975, he moved to Music City to do recording session work. While working on a session for Sonny Burgess, he met Vince Gill. He played on Emmylou Harris' ***Bluebird*** album and when her drummer left, Billy joined and played on gigs. His recording credits also include Dan Seals, Steve Wariner, Marty Stewart, Gail Davis, Earl Thomas Conley and Jann Brown. He is married to Mickie and has two sons, Chris and Matt.

McBride and the Ride's debut appearance was in Detroit, and then they went on tour of the U.S. After a heavy schedule, where they monitored the response of their audiences, the group felt they were well received, but in that first year the hits did not come. The Ride's debut album, ***Burnin' Up the Road***, contained nine songs written or co-written by Terry McBride. The group's first two singles, *Every Step of the Way* and *Felicia*, died. As an opening act for the Judds, they were gaining experience. Then, at a Country Radio Seminar, in mid-song, there was a power cut; the instruments went dead but the group continued to harmonize, proving that they really could sing.

In 1991, the group was in danger of losing its recording contract with MCA when the video of the single *Can I Count on You* caught on with viewers of CMT, and became the video that was most watched in 1991. Consequently, the single peaked in the Top 15 on the Country charts. It was followed by *Same Old Star*, which reached the Top 30. *Cash Box* named the Ride "Top New Group" in 1991, and the group was also nominated by the ACM as "New Vocal Duet or Group," and by the CMA as "Vocal Group of the Year."

In 1992, the single *Sacred Ground*, written by Kix Brooks and Vernon Rust, became a Top 3 hit for the group and was followed by two more Top 10 hits, *Going Out of My Mind* and *Just One Night*, all coming from the album ***Sacred Ground***. In 1993, the group had a new album out called ***Hurry Sundown***, which was dedicated to Terry's father, Dale McBride, who had died of a brain tumor on November 30, 1992. The album yielded the 1993 singles *Love on the Loose, Heart on the Run* (Top 3) and *Hurry Sundown* (Top 20). At year-end, the group had a Top 30 single, *No More Cryin'*, which came from the Soundtrack of *8 Seconds*. Following the release of ***Hurry Sundown***, Herndon and Thomas left and in January 1994, Vaughn, Frazier and Edwards joined Terry McBride. The new group now calls itself Terry McBride & the Ride. JAB

RECOMMENDED ALBUMS:

"Burnin' Up the Road" (MCA)(1991)
"Sacred Ground" (MCA)(1992)
"Hurry Sundown" (MCA)(1993)

C.W. McCALL

(Singer, Songwriter, Clarinet, Advertising Executive, Politician)

Given Name:	**William Fries**
Date of Birth:	**November 15, 1928**
Where Born:	**Audubon, Iowa**
Married:	**Rena**
Children:	**Bill, Jr., Mark, Nancy**

It was with the success of the song *Convoy* that the name of C.W. McCall became known worldwide. The song spawned copies and also the 1978 motion picture *Convoy*, starring Kris Kristofferson. Yet, in effect, C.W. McCall didn't really exist, other than in the mind of his creator, advertising executive Bill Fries.

Both of Bill's parents were musicians who played piano and fiddle for silent movies and local dances. While in grade school, Bill sang, played clarinet and also showed promise with his ability to draw. He helped pay his way through school by painting signs on trucks and store fronts in his home area. Bill was drum major in his high school marching band and when he went to the University of Iowa, he became a member of the concert band and studied music. However, his artistic skills also surfaced and he majored in fine arts.

With the advent of TV in the Midwest, Fries walked into an Omaha, Nebraska, TV station and offered his services as a set designer or anything else of an artistic nature, for free. He was taken on at $35 a week. At the end of five years, he had his own TV show, on which he drew caricatures of famous people. In the early 60's, he joined the B & J Agency in Omaha as Art Director and soon his songwriting ability surfaced. He worked his way up the company ladder and in 1968 became Creative Director.

It was his campaign for the Metz Baking Company of Sioux City, Iowa, that paved the way to a new career. Asked by the client to come up with a new way to sell bread, he created "C.W. McCall," a trucker for Old Home Bread, "Mavis," a gum-chewing waitress, and a truckstop, "The Old Home

Filler-Up-an'-Keep-on-a-Truckin' Cafe." The setup was used in three TV commercials and had an enormous viewer response and sold millions of loaves of bread. It also won for Bill the most important award in advertising, the Clio Award, for "Best Television Campaign in the U.S." He also wrote *Great Big, Rollin' Railroad*, which was used by the Union Pacific for its national advertising.

Fries couldn't find an actor to "talk" his songs and so he did his own voice-overs. A friend suggested that Bill do a recording as "C.W. McCall," and so in 1974, he recorded for American Gramophone the single *Old Home Filler-Up an' Keep on-a-Truckin' Cafe*, which was, like Bill, picked up by MGM Records. He recorded in what he describes as a "walkin', talkin', singin' style." The record reached the Top 60 on the Pop chart and crossed over to the Top 20 on the Country lists. The follow-up single, *Wolf Creek Pass*, did even better, reaching the Pop Top 40 and getting to the Country Top 15.

In 1975, Bill, or as he was now legally known, C.W. McCall, reached the Top 15 on the Country charts with *Classified*, and was followed by the Top 25 Country success *Black Bear Road*. At the end of the year, he struck with *Convoy*, which reached No.1 on both Country and Pop charts and stayed atop the Country lists for 6 weeks. By 1975, the single had been Certified Gold, and the album from which it came, ***Black Bear Road***, went Gold in 1976. In the U.K., the single reached No.2 and spawned a local parody, *Convoy UK*, by Larry Lingo and the Dipsticks (in actuality, Radio 1 deejays Dave Lee Travis and Paul Burnette), which reached No.4 on the U.K. charts in 1976. *Convoy* eventually sold over 6 million copies worldwide.

From 1976, C.W.'s records were released on Polydor, and he opened his account for the year with his last meaningful cross-over single, *There Won't Be No Country Music (There Won't Be No Rock 'N' Roll)*, which reached the Country Top 20 and the Pop Top 75. He had three more moderate successes that year, *Crispy Critters* (Top 40), *Four Wheel Cowboy* (Top 90) and *'Round the World with the Rubber Duck* (Top 40). In 1977, just when it looked like his career was drawing to a close, with *Audubon* only reaching the Top 60, he came back strongly with *Roses for Mama*, a spoken record, which reached the Top 3. He had his last Country chart single in 1979, with the basement-level single *Outlaws and Lone Star Beer*.

In 1977, C.W. made plans to leave the business. He got onto an ecology kick, as he felt a great need to protect the environment. Bill (he had reverted to his real name, again) had wanted to move to Ouray in Colorado, during the 60's, and in 1983, he did just that. He put together a 40-minute flash-photo program in Ouray's old Opera House every summer called *San Juan Odyssey*, using 15 slide projectors, a motion picture projector, five screens, and music by the London Symphony Orchestra. Shortly after the initial performance, Bill was elected Mayor of Ouray.

RECOMMENDED ALBUMS:

"Black Bear Road" (MGM)(1975)
"Wolf Creek Pass" (MGM)(1975)
"Roses for Mama" (Polydor)(1977)
"C.W. McCall's Greatest Hits" (Polydor)(1978)
"C.W. McCall & Co." (Polydor)(1979)

DARRELL McCALL

(Singer, Songwriter, Guitar, Bass Guitar, Actor)

Date of Birth:	**April 30, 1940**
Where Born:	**New Jasper, Greene County, Ohio**
Married:	**Mona Vary**
Children:	**Gyane, Cody**

Say the name Darrell McCall in Texas, and the folks there know you are talking about a real Country singer who sings and writes real Country songs. In fact, the sign on his mailbox reads, "Darrell, the Real McCall."

Darrell began in the music business when he was 15 and had a Saturday morning Country deejay show on WSRW Hillsboro, Ohio. He also played local dances as a musician. On finishing high school, he joined the U.S. Army Reserves, where he served in the Heavy Weapons and Anti-Tank Division in Kentucky.

Darrell then moved to Nashville with boyhood friend Johnny Paycheck in 1958. They wanted to make it as a duo, but Darrell wound up as a harmony singer, working on sessions for George Jones, Faron Young and Ray Price. He also went on the road as a band member for Faron Young, Ray Price and Hank Williams, Jr., as his ability to play bass and yet sing high harmonies made him somewhat unusual. It was during a recording session, in 1959, that Darrell was spotted by the legendary producer-publisher Buddy Killen. Killen put Darrell (lead tenor) with Delores Dinning, Emily Gilmore and Hurshel Wigintin as the Little Dippers. They racked up the 1960 Top 10 Pop hit *Forever*. As a result, Darrell appeared on Pop shows like *American Bandstand*.

Darrell signed as a solo act to Capitol in 1961 and two singles that year, *My Kind of Lovin'* and *Call the Zoo*, served to get his name around the Pop scene. By 1962, he was on the Phillips label, and the following January, he chalked up his first Country hit, the Top 20 single *A Stranger Was Here*. In 1963, he sang the theme song for the movie *Hud*, which starred Paul Newman. Shortly after, Darrell made his acting debut in *Nashville Rebel* (1965) and went on to appear in *Road to Nashville* (1966) and *What Am I Bid*. He studied acting under Gene Nash in Hollywood. During this time, Darrell also became a cowboy working in the Southwest and took part in some smaller rodeos.

In 1968, Darrell signed with Wayside Records and during the period with the label, charted four times, of which the most successful was the 1969 single *Hurry Up*, which peaked in the Top 60. His debut album for Wayside, ***Meet Darrell McCall***, was licensed to Mercury. During 1971, Darrell decided to move to San Antonio, Texas, and stayed there until 1975, before moving back to Nashville. He had a No.1 hit in 1972, via Hank Williams, Jr.'s recording of the Darrell McCall/Lamar Morris song *Eleven Roses*. This led to him signing with Tree International as a writer. In 1974, Darrell had a chart single with his Atlantic recording of *There's Still a Lot of Love in San Antone*, which made the Country Top 50.

The following year, Darrell signed with Columbia Records and reached the Top 60 with the self-penned song *Pins and Needles (In My Heart)* in the spring of 1976. The record won a Producer's Award. A year later, he teamed up with Willie Nelson for the Top 40 single *Lily Dale*. The single had been the title of an album that McCall cut for Nelson's Lone Star label, and the single received *Cash Box*'s "Best Duet" Award. He followed up with the solo Top 40 record *Dreams of a Dreamer*. In 1978, Darrell made the Top 60 with *Down the Road of Daddy's Dreams* and then just scraped in with the *Weeds Outlived the Roses*. He moved to Hillside Records and had a 1980 low-level duet with Curtis Potter, *San Antonio Medley*.

Later that year, his friend Ronnie Milsap and Rob Galbraith produced him on the single *Long Line of Empties*, and, released on RCA, it made the Top 50. However, the new breed of Country radio deejay that was emerging at that time considered the single "TOO COUNTRY." Darrell returned to the lower levels of the charts with the 1984 Indigo recording of *Memphis in May*. That year, Darrell decided to return to San Antonio. In 1982, Darrell appeared as "Friend" on Connie Hanson and Friend's Top 70 single, *There's Still a Lot of Love in San Antone*, on Soundwaves.

Darrell and his band the Tennessee

Volunteers—Will Roberts (drums), Larry Patton (bass guitar), Dickie Overby (steel guitar), Will Cason (lead guitar) and Slim Roberts (fiddle)—cut an album for BGM Records in 1986, entitled ***Reunion***. That same year, Darrell teamed up with another Honky-Tonk great, Johnny Bush, for the excellent Step One album ***Hot Texas Country***.

Darrell has a great sense of humor and is known as "the Joker." He is a tireless worker for charity and his favorite charitable organization is the Muscular Dystrophy Association. As an interesting point, Darrell's wife, Mona, used to play with Audrey Williams' all-girl band. Furthermore, whenever a fan of Darrell's requests a photograph, he requests one of the fan for his photo album.

RECOMMENDED ALBUMS:

"Meet Darrell McCall" (Wayside)(1970)
"Lily Dale" (Columbia)(1977)
"Texas Dance Hall Music" (Hillside)(1980) [Also Curtis Potter and Ray Sanders]
"Reunion" (BGM)(1986) [With the Tennessee Volunteers]
"Hot Texas Country" (Step One)(1986) [With Johnny Bush]

SUSAN McCANN

(Singer)

Given Name: Patricia Susan McCann
Date of Birth: February 2, 1949
Where Born: Fork Hill, County Armagh, Northern Ireland
Married: Dennis Heaney
Children: Brendan, Linda

When in the U.S. in 1994 to make her third appearance at the Strawberry Festival in Plant City, Florida, Susan McCann and her band were invited by General H. Norman Schwarzkopf ("Stormin' Norman") to perform at a high-profile charity concert in Saddlebrook, Florida. The affair was a western-style evening which was part of the Schwarzkopf Cup weekend event.

Susan had come a long way from her roots in Northern Ireland, where she was one of eight children born into a musical family. She began performing at concerts from the age of 8 and as a teenager, sang with a local band. Soon she was dating one of the band members, Dennis Heaney, and although they wanted to marry immediately, they both decided to qualify first; Susan became a hairdresser and Dennis an accountant. During this time, they formed a trio called the Fairylanders, with another local musician. They played locally and later became the Storytellers.

Susan's big break came when she performed at a carnival which was owned by Irish Country music legend Philomena Begley's manager, Tony Loughman. Under his guidance, Susan very quickly became a much-sought-after performer, and even though she had decided not to travel more than 60 miles from her home for bookings, she was soon in demand farther afield.

In 1976, Susan made her first single, *Santa and the Kids*, but it was her second, *Big Tom Is Still King*, that launched her to stardom. The song was a tribute to Big Tom McBride, one of Ireland's best-known Country entertainers. As a result of the success of the record, she toured the U.K. and Europe and went to Nashville in 1977 as part of her first U.S. tour. On her return to Ireland, Susan released her first album, ***Papa's Wagon***.

Susan was injured in a car crash in 1978 and fought back after suffering serious injuries. She made a short-lived return and then was back in hospital with throat problems. By Christmas 1978, she was back performing and recording, releasing two albums, ***Santa and the Kids*** and ***Down River Road***.

In 1979, Susan made her debut at England's prestigious Royal Festival Hall. On October 8, 1979, Susan was introduced on the stage of the *Grand Ole Opry* by Porter Wagoner, and she was invited back the following Saturday to perform again.

1980 found her touring Europe with Charley Pride, Emmylou Harris and the Kendalls as part of the International Music Carnival. She also appeared at the International Country Music Festival at Wembley, England, and returned there in 1981, when she met one of her early influences, Tammy Wynette.

In 1982, Susan won the Gold Star "Top Female Country Artist," which is given to Europe's Top Country performers. She held on to this title for five consecutive years. In 1982 and 1983, she picked up the "Top International Female Award" at Fort Worth, Texas. Over the next few years, Susan continued recording, touring at home and overseas and appearing at both the *Opry* and Carnegie Hall in 1983. Susan represented Ireland at Fan Fair in Nashville in 1987 and then, in 1988, became the first non-American to appear at Dollywood. She also appeared at the Wembley Festival in 1985 and 1990. In 1990, Susan recorded the Gospel collection ***You Gave Me Love*** for the Word label.

In June 1993, she performed in Russia at the multi-cultural festival White Nights in St. Petersburg, where she received a special "Diploma for Country Songs."

Most of Susan's albums have been recorded at Merit Studios in Nashville, under the production direction of Tom Pick and Bobby Dyson. As a Country singer, Susan blends in a mix of Irish, Folk and Pop music. In her words, her program is "50% Country and 50% Irish." Susan is also a rarity for a non-American Country singer in having a U.S. fan club, which operates out of Auburndale, Florida. JAB

RECOMMENDED ALBUMS:

"Down River Road" (Top Spin)(1978)
"Tribute to Buck Owens" (Outlet)(1985)
"Twenty Country Classics" (Harmac)(1987)
"Give Me More Time" (Music Box)(1988)
"You Gave Me Love" (Word)(1989)
"Country Love Affair" (Prism)(1991)
"Diamonds and Dreams" (Prism)(1992)
"Memories" (Prism)(1993)
Videos:
"Ireland's First Lady" (Prism)(1990)
"Country Love Affair" (Prism)(1991)
"Memories" (Prism)(1993)

DAVE McCARN

(Singer, Songwriter, Guitar, Harmonica)

Given Name: David McCarn
Date of Birth: 1905
Where Born: Gaston County, North Carolina
Date of Death: November 7, 1964

Best known for his vivid protest songs and strong singing, Dave McCarn was one of the early recording artists whose reputation today is probably higher than it was during his active career. He came from the Piedmont region of North Carolina, a region that produced singers like Henry Whitter, Dock Walsh, Gwen Foster (of the Carolina Tar Heels), Charlie Poole, and the Dixon Brothers. Like most of these other singers, McCarn knew and worked in the textile mills in the area, and was one of the first Country singers to deal with the effects of industrialization firsthand.

McCarn began working in the mills at an early age, but also got interested in playing the guitar and singing. Though details of his influences are sparse, he soon developed a "hot" guitar style that resembles the picking of other Carolina players like Blind Boy Fuller and the Rev. Gary Davis. By the time he was 20, McCarn was good enough to be playing with a local string band, and to start writing original songs. One of these was *Cotton Mill Colic*, which would become his best known: "I'm a gonna starve, and everybody will,/ Cause you can't make a living at a cotton mill." After McCarn recorded the song in 1930, it was recorded later by both Lester Pete Bivins and the Blue Sky Boys, and was being sung by striking textile workers in the Piedmont area. Folk song collector Alan Lomax encountered the song in 1939 and included it in his book *Folksongs of North America*.

Through much of this time, though,

McCarn never thought seriously about his music except as a hobby. But in 1929, Gastonia, where McCarn worked, was rocked by the murder of union organizer Ella May Wiggins, and McCarn, with his brother, left to start rambling around the country. In May 1930, in the midst of the Depression, they found themselves stranded in Memphis, and heard about a field recording team from Victor in town. Desperate for money, McCarn auditioned for Ralph Peer and got to record his first sides, *Cotton Mill Colic* and *Everyday Dirt*, a version of the ancient ballad *Will the Weaver*. This sold well enough to garner McCarn a second Victor session, on November 19-20, 1930, again in Memphis. Here he did six more original songs, including a follow-up to *Colic, Poor Man Rich Man*, a song about Fords called *Take Them for a Ride*, and a raggy guitar piece called *Gastonia Gallop*. Yet a third session six months later, in Charlotte, produced the third of his cotton mill protest songs, *Serves 'Em Fine*. The results of this last session were released under the credit Dave and Howard.

After these sessions, McCarn dropped back into obscurity and resumed his work in the mills. Though he was rediscovered and interviewed by Mike Seeger during the Folk revival in 1961, he never sought to try for a comeback or make it to many festivals. He died in Stanley, North Carolina, on November 7, 1964. CKW

RECOMMENDED ALBUM:
"Dave McCarn and Gwen Foster—Singers of the Piedmont" (Bear Family Germany)

McCARTERS

When Formed: **Mid-1980's**
JENNIFER
Given Name: **Jennifer Lorene McCarter**
Date of Birth: **March 7, 1964**
TERESA
Given Name: **Teresa Faye McCarter**
Date of Birth: **November 21, 1966**
LISA
Given name: **Lisa Kaye McCarter**
Date of Birth: **November 21, 1966**

All Born: **Knoxville, Tennessee**

For a while at the end of the 80's, Warner Brothers Records had two successful sister vocal acts with the McCarters and the Forester Sisters. However, both groups failed to sustain their level of success into the 90's, and, especially in the case of the McCarters, they have become almost forgotten in the rush of new talent. Their main problem, which is one that will appear more and more, was that they were too Country for contemporary Country radio programmers.

Raised in Sevierville, Tennessee, famed as being Dolly Parton's birthplace, Jennifer was just age 7 when she started clogging after watching Ralph Sloan and the Tennessee Travelers on *That Good Ole Nashville Music*, and the twins, Lisa and Teresa, joined in. Clogging at the county's bicentennial led to them dancing on a TV show out of Knoxville, for the next four years. When their dad said that any of the girls who learned to play could have his 1969 Martin guitar, eldest sister Jennifer took up the challenge. She was just 14 when she started playing and singing, with the twins joining in on high harmonies. Later, Archie Campbell taught Teresa to sing low harmony. The "McCarter harmony" now became known around Pigeon Forge, where the girls sang for tips on the county courthouse steps.

Coming to Nashville in 1987, they landed a record deal with Warner Brothers, who were looking for another Foresters. At the end of the year, they toured Europe with Randy Travis, on a USO tour. Their *Timeless and True Love* single charted in January 1988, while they were still overseas, and reached the Top 5. They were invited by Dolly Parton to appear on her nationally syndicated *Dolly Show*, which was filmed in Los Angeles. Their second single, the title track of their debut album, ***The Gift***, did even better and reached higher in the Top 5. Their next single, *I Give You Music*, didn't find favor, and only reached the Top 30.

1989 saw an upswing in fortunes with the single *Up and Gone*, which went Top 10. However, their fall/winter chart entry, *Quit While I'm Behind*, a fine song from Bill Caswell and Verlon Thompson, only reached the Top 30. This last single was credited to Jennifer McCarter and the McCarters, as was the 1990 album ***Better Be Home Soon***. The title track provided them with a Top 75 record during 1990, having done better for Pop-Rock group Crowded House, in 1988 (Neil Finn, the writer of the song, was a member of Crowded House). The McCarters followed up with another Top 75 single, their version of Bob McDill's modern classic *Shot Full of Love*. That year, the sisters were inducted into the East Tennessee Hall of Fame.

That single represented the end of their recording career with Warner Brothers, and although they maintain a busy live schedule (they're a great live act), and have extended their career into modeling and product endorsement, they are still trying to get back onto a major label.

RECOMMENDED ALBUMS:
"The Gift" (Warner Brothers)(1988)
"Better Be Home Soon" (Warner Brothers)(1990)

MARY McCASLIN

(Singer, Songwriter, Guitar, Banjo)
Given Name: **Mary Noel McCaslin**
Date of Birth: **December 22, 1946**
Where Born: **Indianapolis, Indiana**
Married: **Jim Ringer (dec'd.)**

Mary McCaslin is a performer who deserves to be in the same peer group as Emmylou Harris and Dolly Parton. However, to date Mary has not received the acclaim that she richly deserves. Performing as a solo and duetting with her late husband, Jim Ringer, Mary has added a richness to Country-Folk that is precious in days of Country dilution. If one can coin a phrase, her music is Folk-Western.

Her family moved to the Los Angeles suburbs when she was age 6 and by the time she was age 15, she was playing Country music on the guitar. Her father once told her that if she ever cracked her head open, little guitars, musical notes, records and banjos would come flying out. She became eclectic in her musical taste and from early on featured Beatles songs. She started songwriting but admits to not being a prolific writer. She sang in high school and in church and had her first professional booking at age 18. However, it was some while until she could rely on music as a full-time career.

She started her career with Capitol in 1967 with the single *Rain/This All Happened Once Before*. In 1969, she cut the album ***Goodnight Everybody*** for Barnaby Records, which is still in demand into the 90's, although long since out of print. During 1972, Mary met singer Jim Ringer at Sweet's Mill Folk music camp-out in California. She stayed on and when she did return to L.A., Jim came after her, fetched her and they continued living together, and were rarely apart.

In 1973, she was described by *Rolling Stone* as "one of the best of the singer/songwriters (who are) still being overlooked." Later it would describe her as "a prairie songstress" who creates "musical moments of crystalized romance."

In 1973 she went with Jim to Philo Records, as they were interested in recording him. She wound up doing a demo for them and that led to her 1974 album ***Way Out West***. The following year, she brought a new album, ***Prairie in the Sky***, which, like the debut album, honed in on life in the West. In November 1976, she was spotted by Folklore Productions out of Santa Monica, California, who had represented Joan Baez and still look after Doc Watson. She signed with them and as a result, her career stepped up a gear. The following year, she released her third Philo album, ***Old Friends***, which contained a collection of her favorite songs by writers such as Cole Porter, Lennon and McCartney, the Everly Brothers, Dozier and Holland as well as the title cut, which was written by Mary herself. She recorded her first duet album with Jim Ringer in 1978, also on Philo, entitled ***The Bramble and the Rose***. That same year (on July 22), Mary and Jim got married. The manager of the shop that Mary bought her dress at, Old Mexico, was another famed Folk singer, Hazel Dickens.

The following year, Philo licensed Mary's album ***Sunny California*** to Mercury Records. In addition, she had the two tracks from her debut album released as a single. They were Lennon and McCartney's *Things We Said Today*/Mary's own *Young Westley*. In 1981, Mary moved over to Flying Fish for the splendid album ***A Life and Time***. With the wrapping up of Philo Records, all of her releases for that label were picked up by Rounder Records, although Philo retained its label identity. That year, Mary's music could be heard on the soundtrack of the Burt Lancaster movie *Cattle Annie and Little Britches*. Mary's music was also heard on the Oscar-nominated documentary *With Babies and Banners*.

The duo continued to play at festivals across the U.S. and Canada until 1989, when Mary and Jim separated and subsequently divorced. Jim was to die two years later. Mary has continued to be active as a performing artist and in 1993, a new album was to be recorded for Philo.

RECOMMENDED ALBUMS:

"Way Out West" (Philo/Rounder)(1975)
"Prairie in the Sky" (Philo/Rounder)(1975)
"Old Friends" (Philo/Rounder)(1977)
"The Bramble and the Rose" (Philo/Rounder)(1978) [With Jim Ringer]
"Sunny California" (Mercury/Philo)(1979)
"A Life and Time" (Flying Fish)(1981)

CHARLY McCLAIN

(Singer, Songwriter, Actress)

Given Name:	**Charlotte Denise McClain**
Date of Birth:	**March 26, 1956**
Where Born:	**Memphis, Tennessee**
Married:	**Wayne Massey (m. 1984)**

Although Charly McClain is no longer featured in the Country charts, during the early 80's, she was one of the princesses of Country music.

She began her interest in music when she was 9 and "recorded" songs from school for her father, who was in the hospital with tuberculosis. Later, she sang in a band formed by her brother. By the time she was 17, she had won a chance to appear as a regular singer on the *Mid South Jamboree*, a Country music showcase in Memphis. It became a regular weekend gig for her and she was soon asked to perform at other venues in the town.

In 1977, she began recording for Epic Records. Her first hit single was *Lay Down*, which peaked in the Top 70. The next four singles went into the charts but it wasn't until *That's What You Do to Me*, in 1978, that she first hit the Top 10. In 1979, Charly had two Top 20 singles, *When a Love Ain't Right* and *I Hate the Way I Love You*, the latter being a duet with Johnny Rodriguez. In 1980, she achieved another Top 10 placing with the song *Men*, and wrapped up the year with the Top 20 success *Women Get Lonely*.

Her first No.1 came in 1981 with *Who's Cheatin' Who*. This was followed by the Top 5 hits, *Surround Me with Love, Sleepin' with the Radio On* and *The Very Best Is You*. The next year, *Dancing Your Memory Away* went Top 3 and she then had the Top 10 release *With You*. Charly's next major hits came in 1983, when she had a No.1, *Paradise Tonight*, in tandem with Mickey Gilley and then reached the Top 3 with *Sentimental Ol' You*. She and Mickey also had a 1984 Top 5 hit with *Candy Man* (which had been a hit for Roy Orbison on the Pop chart) and a Top 15 duet, *The Right Stuff*.

Charly's live shows were popular and she toured with such great name acts as Willie Nelson, Larry Gatlin and the Gatlin Brothers Band, Mel Tillis, Kenny Rogers, Ronnie Milsap, Eddie Rabbitt and Don Williams. Her TV appearances included *Austin City Limits, Solid Gold, Dance Fever, Country's Top 20* and the HBO special *So You Want to Be a Star*, showing her lonely life on the road. In 1981, Charly made her debut appearance as an actress when she featured in the ABC-TV series *Hart to Hart*. She later appeared in NBC's *CHiPs* and ABC's *Fantasy Island*.

Wayne Massey, who was a TV soap opera star playing a successful Country music star called "Johnny Drummond" on the show *One Life to Live*, met Charly McClain, they fell in love and married in July 1984. The next year Charly had her final No.1 with *Radio Heart* and then teamed up with Wayne for the Top 5 hit *With Just One Look in Your Eyes* and the Top 10 record ***You Are My Music, You Are My Song***.

By this time, Wayne was very involved in producing and looking after Charly's career. After this time, although she was still producing chart singles, there were no high-placed positions except the 1987 single *Don't Touch Me There*, which made the Top 20. She moved to Mercury in 1988, but she fared no better and after this she disappeared from the charts.

Charly had many albums, and her fourth, ***Women Get Lonely***, was an album that appealed to female fans. Charly and Wayne bought 15 acres of land in Memphis when they married and planned to build a new home there. JAB

RECOMMENDED ALBUMS:

"Greatest Hits—Charly McClain" (Epic)(1982)
"It Takes Believers" (Epic)(1984) [With Mickey Gilley]
"Ten-Year Anniversary: Then and Now" (Epic)(1987)
"Charlie McClain" (Mercury)(1988)

HARRY McCLINTOCK (a.k.a. HAYWIRE MAC)

(Singer, Songwriter, Guitar, Actor)

Given Name:	**Harry Kirby McClintock**
Date of Birth:	**October 8, 1882**
Where Born:	**Knoxville, Tennessee**
Married:	**Bessie Katherine Johnson**
Children:	**Joan Virginia**
Date of Death:	**April 24, 1957**

Harry "Mac" McClintock was one of the colorful characters in early-day Country music who had a wide range of backgrounds and life experiences. Mac, more than anyone else, made the hobo song a part of the genre with his original compositions. He also had a good repertoire of cowboy, railroad and comedy songs which sustained him through several Victor sessions and a lengthy career on radio in the San Francisco Bay Area.

The two most distinguishing characteristics of Mac's childhood were his love for singing in a local church and an infatuation for railroading, from various uncles who had experience with the long-steel rails. In the winter of 1896, he ran away to Anniston, Alabama, to hop another freight later to New Orleans. Rather quickly, the youth learned that he could nearly always avoid hunger and total destitution by singing for tips in saloons.

For the next several years, McClintock led an adventurous life as a wandering muleskinner, seaman, railroader and occasional hobo. His travels took him to the Philippines in the Spanish-American War, to China in the Boxer Rebellion, to South Africa in the Boer Wars, to England for the coronation of King Edward VII and to Australia and Argentina in between.

Back in the U.S. by 1903, he more or less settled down to railroading, mostly as a brakeman, but he continued wandering increasingly into the Far West. For a time Mac belonged to the Industrial Workers of the World (the "Wobblies"), a radical but musically oriented labor union. He married a locomotive engineer's daughter in 1914 and from 1917 made his home in San Francisco. His longest stint of employment came with three steady years as a switchman in the yards for the Southern Pacific.

In 1925, Mac switched careers again, becoming a radio entertainer at KFRC San Francisco. He remained there for 13 years and became quite popular in the Bay Area. Sometimes Mac performed solo and sometimes with a group called the Haywire Orchestra. He also cut 37 songs for Victor from 1928 to 1931, including several authentic cowboy songs. However, his original of *The Big Rock Candy Mountain, Hallelujah! I'm a Bum* and the two renditions of *The Bum Song* were the titles that provided him with a major niche in the history books.

In 1938, Mac moved to Los Angeles, where he had bit parts in a few films and made new recordings of his four best-known songs for Decca. However, the following year, he dropped out of entertainment, taking a position as a guard in San Pedro. He soon gave up to become a switchman again for the Outer Harbor Terminal Railway, remaining until 1942, by which time he had accumulated sufficient service to qualify for a railroad pension.

He spent the last 10 years of work in a guard position for the Los Angeles Harbor Department. McClintock continued semiactive in entertainment by performing for servicemen at a USO center and on a weekly radio program. Mac also wrote articles for railroad men. About the time of his retirement, Folk singer Sam Eskin recorded him for Folkways Records.

In 1953, Haywire Mac and his wife returned to San Francisco to be nearer their married daughter and three grandchildren. In retirement, McClintock took up painting and made occasional appearances on a *Breakfast Gang* radio program and even guested on TV a few times before his health failed. At his death, he had a Masonic funeral and his remains were cremated. In addition to the 10" Folkways album and several items on various anthologies, Rounder released an entire lp of his Victor material from 1928 to 1929. IMT

RECOMMENDED ALBUMS:

"Haywire Mac" (Folkways)(1952)
"Hallelujah! I'm a Bum" (Rounder)(1980)

O.B. McCLINTON

(Singer, Songwriter, Guitar)

Given Name:	**Obie Burnett McClinton**
Date of Birth:	**April 25, 1940**
Where Born:	**Senatobia, Mississippi**
Married:	**Jo Ann**
Children:	**Drexel**
Date of Death:	**September 23, 1987**

When black Country star O.B. McClinton was sick with abdominal cancer, the Country music community rallied around and put on a star-studded benefit concert to help to defray his medical expenses. "The Chocolate Cowboy," as he styled himself, was on an upward swing and he had just released a new TV-marketed album called ***The Only One***, which O.B considered his best album yet.

His father, Rev. G.A. McClinton, had three sons and four daughters and the family grew up on his 700-acre ranch near Memphis. O.B., the second youngest, was around the age of 9 or 10 when he began to dream of being in show business while doing his mundane chores around the farm. Listening to Hank Williams sparked his initial interest in Country music and subconsciously shaped his singing style. After high school, he ran away from home and headed for San Francisco. However, he only reached Memphis and there, in a Beale Street shop, he bought his first guitar.

With his travel money gone, O.B. returned home. He won a choir scholarship to Rust College in Holly Springs, Mississippi, where he sang in the a cappella choir. He graduated in 1966, after four years' study. Soon, he was drafted into the Army, but as this didn't please him, he volunteered for the Air Force, during December 1966. While in the Armed Forces, he began winning service talent shows, and as a result, he spent a lot of time entertaining and writing R & B songs. This led to a writing contract from Fame Publishing Company in Muscle Shoals, Alabama. He remained in the services for four years and after discharge, his original R & B songs became popular. James Carr recorded *Baby You Got Your Mind Messed Up* and *A Man Needs a Woman,* Clarence Carter released *Why You Can't Measure* and the great Otis Redding cut *Keep Your Arms Around Me.* Although O.B. tried to be an R & B singer, he was not successful.

When he was in the Air Force, a friend had introduced him to a Charley Pride album and this encouraged him to further his career. He wrote some Country songs and then made a demo tape. One day in a hotel, he met an ex-deejay friend of his named Al Bell, who had since become a top executive for Stax Records, and O.B. played him his Country demo tape. Bell was impressed and asked who the singer was. When McClinton told him who it was, Al refused to believe him and the only way he could convince him was to sing along with the tapes. The result of this chance meeting was a recording contract signed on January 12, 1971, and O.B. became the first Country artist on Stax's Country label, Enterprise.

In all, he had seven chart hits on the label from 1972 to 1975, of which the most successful were *Don't Let the Green Grass Fool You* (Top 40, 1972) and *My Whole World Is Falling Down* (Top 40, 1973). After Stax went out of business in 1975, O.B. moved over to Mercury the following year and had a basement-level chart single, *It's So Good Lovin' You.*

For a couple of years, O.B. relied on his live work and then, in 1978, Epic signed him and released *Hello, This Is Anna,* which featured Peggy Jo Adams and *Natural Love,* both of which charted at the lower levels. The following year, *Soap* reached the Top 60. In 1980, he moved to Sunbird and had a moderate hit with *Not Exactly Free*, on which he was credited as "The Chocolate Cowboy." This was his last chart record until 1984, when he had a Top 70 single on the Moon Shine label titled *Honky Tonk Tan*, which seemed almost autobiographical.

In 1987, O.B. was once more back on Epic Records, with a hit single, *Turn the Music On*, when he succumbed to cancer after a year-long battle. His death was announced on TNN's *Nashville Now* by Ralph Emery. JAB

RECOMMENDED ALBUMS:

"Country" (Enterprise)(1972)
"Obie from Senatobie" (Enterprise)(1973)
"Live at Randy's Rodeo" (Enterprise)(1973)
"If You Love Her That Way" (Enterprise)(1974)
"The Only One" (Epic)(1987)

DEL McCOURY

(Guitar, Banjo, Bass, Singer)

Given Name:	**Delano Floyd McCoury**
Date of Birth:	**February 1, 1930**
Where Born:	**Bakersville, North Carolina**
Married:	**Jean**
Children:	**Rhonda, Ronnie, Robbie**

After some 20 years of leading his own band, the Dixie Pals, Bluegrass singer Del McCoury finally began to gain some of the fan recognition that many insiders had long thought he deserved. He favored a traditional band of Bluegrass, singing a variety of new songs, old standards, and Country numbers from the 50's.

McCoury hailed from the same mountain community that produced famed Old-Time fiddler Steve Ledford, a generation earlier.

Del's family migrated northward to Glen Rock, Pennsylvania, in 1941, although he unconsciously managed to take much of his Appalachian culture with him. Del's earliest musical interest, however, centered on the 5-string banjo, first with Keith Daniels and the Blue Ridge Ramblers and then with Jack Cooke's Virginia Mountain Boys. The latter played in the Baltimore area.

Early in 1963, Bill Monroe borrowed the band to play some dates in New York. This led to Monroe's offering McCoury a job with the Blue Grass Boys. A month later, Del joined the band, switching to lead vocal and rhythm guitar, as Monroe now had Bill Keith as a banjoist. Del worked with the band for a year, doing one session with Monroe on Decca in January 1964. In February 1964, Del left the Blue Grass Boys, went home and married and then went to California with fiddler Billy Baker to work with the Golden State Boys for three months.

Back home by June 1964, McCoury joined the Shady Valley Boys, a new band led by Baker, and cut some material on Rebel. Then he organized his own band in 1967. That December, the Dixie Pals cut their first album (subsequently released on the Arhoolie label), with the help of Bill Emerson, Wayne Yates and Billy Baker.

Del's "high lonesome" lead voice augmented by capable sidemen has long made him a favorite among Bluegrass purists, and he has appeared often at Bluegrass festivals. In addition to Billy Baker, fiddlers who have worked for McCoury include Bill Poffinberger and, later, Sonny Miller while Bill Rumble, Dick Smith and John Farmer have handled the banjo chores. Dick Staber, Herschel Sizemore and Don Eldreth have been among the more talented mandolin pickers who have loaned their talents to the Dixie Pals. Dewey Renfro played bass for a long time and so did brother Jerry McCoury (b. 1948). Over the years, the band cut albums for Rounder, Revonah, Grassound, Leather and three for Rebel.

In 1987, the leader dropped the name Dixie Pals and restyled his group as the Del McCoury Band. That same year, Lester Flatt's former manager, Lance LeRoy, took over management efforts and their bookings began to increase a good deal. Del relied more on sons Ronnie and Robbie, who played fine mandolin and banjo respectively, as mainstays of the band, aided by such musicians as fiddler Tad Marks and bassist Mike Brantley. Bluegrass purists and insiders had long realized McCoury's skill, but the wider audience began taking more notice from 1989, when he began to win honors like IBMA's "Vocalist of the Year" award. In recent years, in addition to their own recordings for Rebel and Rounder, Del and his sons also cut a well-received disc with Don and Dave Parmley of the Bluegrass Cardinals. Somewhat earlier, he and his bass-playing brother Jerry cut a fine harmony duet album for Rounder. IMT

RECOMMENDED ALBUMS:

"Del McCoury Sings Bluegrass" (Arhoolie)(1968)
"Collector's Special" (Grassound)(1971)
"High on a Mountain" (Rounder)(1972)
"Del McCoury and the Dixie Pals" (Revonah)(1975)
"Del McCoury" (Rebel)(1975)
"Our Kind of Grass" (Rebel)(1978)
"The Best of Del McCoury" (Rebel)(1980)
"Take Me to the Mountains" (Leather and Rebel)(1981)
"Sawmill" (Rebel)(1985)
"Classic Bluegrass" (Rebel)(1991)
"Don't Stop the Music" (Rounder)(1988)
"The Blue Side of Town" (Rounder)(1992)
"A Deeper Shade of Blue" (Rounder)(1993)

Bluegrass great ***Del McCoury*** *and his band*

CHARLIE McCOY

(Harmonica, Guitar, Drums, Vibes, Keyboards, Bass, Trumpet, Saxophone, Tuba, Singer, Songwriter)

Given Name:	**Charles Ray McCoy**
Date of Birth:	**March 28, 1941**
Where Born:	**Oak Hill, West Virginia**
Married:	**1. Susan (div.)**
	2. Pat
Children:	**Charlie, Jr., Ginger**

In Charlie's words, there are four stages of being a session player: "Who's Charlie McCoy, We must have Charlie McCoy, We need someone younger who plays like Charlie McCoy and Who's Charlie McCoy." In Charlie's case, no one is ever going to ask the first and fourth questions. Since 1961, he has been one of Nashville's elite studio superpickers.

Growing up in Miami, Florida, Charlie began playing harmonica at age 8 and started his musical career there at age 15, playing harmonica and guitar in a rock'n'roll band. For some while, he played Country and Rock, and while playing on the Old South Jamboree, he was heard by Mel Tillis, who suggested he move to Nashville, where he could work as a session player while furthering his own solo career.

Charlie arrived in Nashville in 1959 and auditioned for various producers without success. He returned to Florida and studied music theory, arranging, conducting and took singing lessons. When deejay and singer Johnny Ferguson was looking for a guitarist, Charlie went to audition, only to find that the slot had been filled. However, Ferguson was still looking for a drummer, so Charlie, who up to then didn't play, went out and bought a kit and was hired. Tillis introduced him to agent-publisher-*Opry* executive Jim Denny, who helped smooth Charlie's path as a session player in Nashville.

Charlie's first session was Roy Orbison's *Candy Man* in 1961, and this led to his being one of the busiest session players in Country music. During the early 60's, he toured with Stonewall Jackson, as his drummer. Charlie signed with Monument Records and released his first single for the label, *My Babe/Will*

Harmonica wizard ***Charlie McCoy***

You Love Me Tomorrow, in 1964, on which he was supported by the Escorts.

In 1965, Charlie's harmonica could be heard to great effect on the classic Erwin Rouse song *Orange Blossom Special*. Charlie was also working outside of Country and he became a mainstay on Elvis Presley's recording sessions in Nashville and Los Angeles. During 1965, Charlie began his connection with Bob Dylan by playing on ***Highway 61 Revisited***. Blues-Rock giant Al Kooper described a typical Charlie McCoy incident in his book *Backstage Pass*. While recording the ***Blonde on Blonde*** album in 1966, one track called for a trumpet part, which could easily be overdubbed. However, Dylan was averse to overdubs, so while Charlie was playing bass guitar with his left hand, he played trumpet with his right, without missing a beat. The only person who stopped was Dylan, who was totally amazed. Charlie also appeared on Dylan's albums ***John Wesley Harding*** (1968), ***Nashville Skyline*** (1969) and ***Self Portrait*** (1970).

Charlie became a member of Country-Rock group Area Code 615 in 1969 and stayed with them during their life, appearing on their eponymous album (1969) and ***A Trip in the Country*** (1970). Charlie's tour de force track *Stone Fox Chase* became the theme for Britain's BBC-TV music series *The Old Grey Whistle Test*. Charlie appeared on several important albums including Gordon Lightfoot's ***Way I Feel*** (1967), Al Kooper's ***I Stand Alone***, John Stewart's ***California Bloodlines*** and Mickey Newbury's ***Looks Like Rain*** (all 1969), Al Kooper's ***Kooper Sessions***, Ringo Starr's ***Beaucoup of Blues*** and John Stewart's ***Willard*** (all 1970).

In 1969, Charlie recorded the album ***Charlie McCoy/The Real McCoy***. Two years later, a deejay in Florida "discovered" *I Started Loving Her Again* on the album and started playing it on the air. The response was phenomenal with the station's switchboard getting jammed, but the callers were informed that the record had been deleted. Monument quickly released a single of the track and at the beginning of 1972, it charted and became a Top 20 hit. Charlie followed up with *I'm So Lonesome I Could Cry*, which went Top 25 and *I Really Don't Want to Know*, which went Top 20. That year, Charlie won a Grammy Award for "Best Country Instrumental Performance" for the 1969 album and his first CMA "Musician of the Year." He held on to this crown in 1973.

During 1971 through 1973, Charlie appeared on Steve Goodman's eponymous album, Kris Kristofferson's ***The Silver Tongued Devil & I***, Gordon Lightfoot's ***Summerside of Love*** and Mickey Newbury's ***Frisco Mabel Joy*** (all 1971); Joan Baez's ***Come from the Shadows***, Doug Kershaw's ***Devil's Elbow***, Kris Kristofferson's ***Border Lord***, Dave Loggins' ***Personal Belongings***, Paul Simon's self-titled album and Steve Young's ***Seven Bridges Road*** (all 1972); Leon Russell's ***Hank Wilson's Back***, John Stewart's ***Cannons in the Rain***, and Mickey Newbury's ***Heaven Help the Child*** (all 1973).

In 1973, Charlie had three singles on the Country chart, *Orange Blossom Special* (which also crossed to the lower rungs of the Pop chart), which went Top 30 and *Shenandoah* and *Release Me*, which both went Top 40. That year, MCN named him "Instrumentalist of the Year." The following year, he recorded with some of his old friends from Area Code 615 who had re-formed as Barefoot Jerry. He appeared on three of the group's albums, ***You Can't Get off with Your Shoes On*** (1975), ***Keys to the Country*** (1976) and ***Barefootin'*** (1977). From the first album came the 1974 Top 25 single *Boogie Woogie (A/K/A T.D.'s Boogie Woogie)*, which was credited to Charlie McCoy & Barefoot Jerry. Also in 1974, MCN named Charlie "Instrumental Entertainer of the Year."

During the rest of the 70's, Charlie's sessions included Waylon Jennings' ***Dreaming My Dreams*** (1975), Wanda Jackson's ***I'll Still Love You*** and Tanya Tucker's ***Lovin' & Learnin'*** (both 1976) and Steve Young's ***No Place to Fall*** (1978). In 1977, the ACM presented Charlie with the first of his seven "Specialty Instrument" awards. He went on to win the award in 1978 through 1981, 1983 and 1988. In 1978, Charlie returned to the Top 30 with *Fair and Tender Ladies*, which was to be his last major hit. That year, he played Wembley Festival in England with Lloyd Green, and this started Charlie's great popularity in Europe that has led to his touring there regularly.

When Monument folded in 1982, Charlie was without a record label for five years, although they did cut a road album, ***One for the Road***, in 1986. The following year, Charlie recorded two albums in Denmark for World Wide Music. These were released in the U.S. by Step One Records: ***Charley McCoy's 13th*** (1988) and ***Beam Me Up Charlie*** (1989). In 1989, Charlie recorded another album for World Wide, ***Candlelight, Wine and Charlie***.

In 1991, Step One released the album ***Out on a Limb***, which was recorded partly in Holland and partly in Nashville. Some of the tracks were recorded at Cinderella Studio, where Charlie was reunited with his friend Wayne Moss (ex-Area Code 615 and Barefoot Jerry). The following year, Charlie with Euro group the United (who had played on ***Out on a Limb***) recorded a live album at the Utopia Club in Paris, ***Live in Paris***.

Although Charlie no longer works the 400 sessions a year that he did back in the 60's and 70's, he is still very much in demand. His popularity in Europe has him touring there 3 or 4 times a year. He still holds a 4th of July concert in Fayetteville, Virginia, in aid of the city's athletic program. Charlie, an avid sports fan, has held this concert for over 20 years.

Charlie, who wanted to be a singer in his younger days, has been able to incorporate all of his musical talents in his stage and recording act. He has for some while been the Musical Director for the long-running syndicated TV show *Hee Haw*, and he was a member of the Hee Haw Quartet.

For the technical, Charlie plays a Hohner harmonica (which he endorses). When asked by the writer how he manages to play melody so well on a diatonic harmonica rather than a chromatic, Charlie responded, "I practiced a lot." Seems like practice makes perfect, because without fear of contradiction, Charlie McCoy is the finest Country harmonica player. In 1994, Charlie made two harmonica instructional videos, which will shortly be followed by an instructional book.

RECOMMENDED ALBUMS:

"Charlie McCoy/The Real McCoy" (Monument)(1969) [Re-released in 1972]
"Charlie McCoy—Good Time Charlies/Fastest Harp in the South" (double)(Monument)(1975)
"The Greatest Hits of Charlie McCoy" (Monument)(1982)
"Harmonica Jones" (World Wide Denmark)(1987)
"Charlie McCoy's 13th" (Step One)(1988)
"Beam Me Up Charlie" (Step One)(1989)
"Out on a Limb" (Step One)(1991)
"Live in Paris" (PSB Disques France)(1992)

One of the best live acts around, ***Neal McCoy***

NEAL McCOY

(Singer)

Given Name: **Hubert Neal McGauhey, Jr.**
Date of Birth: **1959**
Where Born: **Jacksonville, Texas**
Married: **Melinda**
Children: **Miki**

Neal McCoy rates himself more of an entertainer than a singer. On stage, he has a very lively act and he just can't stand still. He has the ability to generate excitement and is a true crowd pleaser.

Coming from an Irish-Filipino family, he is often mistaken for an American Indian when he wears his cowboy hat. Throughout his childhood, he assimilated music from his family's eclectic tastes, which included Country, Gospel, Jazz and Rock. At school, he sang in musicals, Gospel quartets, choirs, in fact anywhere they would let him sing. He joined the Texas honky-tonk circuit, where he won a nightclub contest.

Neal turned professional when he was 20, and began to play club shows. Janie Fricke had seen him on the finals of the nightclub contest and arranged for him to meet Charley Pride's agent. Janie was Charley's opening act at that time. Later, when Janie moved on, Neal took over her place on Charley's tour and stayed with him for seven years. Continually gaining experience, Neal toured in almost every state in the U.S., as well as in England, Australia, New Zealand and Canada.

In 1988, he had his first chart entry, *That's How Much I Love You*, on the now defunct 16th Avenue label, under the name of "Neal McGoy." In 1991, Neal signed with Atlantic Records and released his debut album, ***At this Moment***, and his first single, *If I Built a Fire*, reached the Top 50. His second hit, *This Time I Hurt Her More (Than She Loves Me)*, also reached the Top 50 and had a companion video that was very well received on CMT.

Opening for Dolly Parton at Ponderosa Park in July 1992, Neal provided a fun-filled opening set, with his dynamic presence and his six-piece band, entertaining the audience during the long wait for Dolly, with a diverse selection of Country music.

The album ***Where Forever Begins*** in 1992 was well received and the title cut provided Neal with a Top 40 placing. This was followed by another cut, *There Ain't Nothin' I Don't Like About You*, which climbed into the Top 60 and the Top 30 cut *Now I Pray for Rain*. Neal appeared at the IFCO concert at 1993's Fan Fair, in Nashville, and won himself a lot of new friends and fans.

In 1994, Neal became a star when his single *No Doubt About It*, the title track of his third album, went to No.1. It was followed by a second No.1, *Wink*. JAB

RECOMMENDED ALBUMS:

"At This Moment" (Atlantic)(1991)
"Where Forever Begins" (Atlantic)(1992)
"No Doubt About It" (Atlantic)(1994)

MEL McDANIEL

(Singer, Songwriter, Guitar)

Date of Birth: **September 9, 1942**
Where Born: **Checotah, Oklahoma**
Married: **Mary Pitchford**
Children: **Danielle ("Dee")**

Mel McDaniel always appears to be smiling, but one wonders if he looked as happy when, after not being able to survive his first encounter with Nashville, he headed for the frozen climate of Alaska.

When Mel was a small boy his parents divorced and Mel felt the separation from his father deeply. His early memories were of his dad chopping wood or working on his truck or car. After the separation, because his father was a truck driver and moved around a lot and his mother worked in various places, Mel never really settled down. It made him withdraw into himself. After seeing Elvis Presley on a TV in a store and watching the onlookers' reaction, Mel decided to be a singer.

When he was 15, he made his professional debut at a talent contest at his school in Okmulgee, Oklahoma. Upon graduation from high school, Mel married Mary, his childhood sweetheart.

In the early 60's, he formed a group, wrote songs and worked when he could around Tulsa. Nashville called, but Mary and Mel found the timing wasn't right and after getting disillusioned, packed up and moved to Alaska. Here, he discovered that the crowds loved Country music. He also had the opportunity to make an adult relationship with his father. Mel spent the next two years polishing up his act. His first full-time musical job was at a club in Alaska called King X.

In 1973, Nashville beckoned again and now Mel felt he had to give it another try. Mel landed a job as a demo singer and signed a publishing contract with Combine Music. He also entertained for nine months at the Holiday Inn lounge. However, it was the

Mel McDaniel *at the Wembley Festival in England*

Wilburn Brothers who are given the credit by Mel for bringing him to the attention of recording executives, leading to his joining Capitol in 1976.

Mel's debut single in 1976, *Have a Dream on Me,* and the follow-up, *I Thank God She Isn't Mine,* on which he was credited as "Mel McDaniels," were low-level chart successes. In 1977, another single, *All the Sweet*, reached the Top 40 and then came the Top 20 single *Gentle to Your Senses*, the title track of his first album. *Soul of a Honky Tonk Woman* followed and went Top 30.

In 1978, Mel reached the Top 15 with *God Made Love* and during the rest of that year and 1979, Mel had singles in the Country charts in the Top 30 positions, including *Bordertown Woman* (1978), *Play Her Back to Yesterday* and *Lovin' Starts Where Friendship Ends* (both 1979). His second album, ***Mello,*** was released in 1978 and things now began to heat up for Mel. In 1980, he had *Hello Daddy, Good Morning Darling* (Top 40) and the title track from his new album, ***Countryfied***, which went Top 30. 1981 brought *Louisiana Saturday Night*, his most successful release thus far, which peaked in the Top 10, and *Right in the Palm of Your Hand* also went Top 10. Mel closed out the year with a Top 20 single, *Preaching Up a Storm.*

Take Me to the Country, the album and the single, were released in 1982, with the single in the Top 10. Mel had a huge success with *Big Ole Brew,* which reached the Top 5 and was followed by a Top 20 entry, *I Wish I Was in Nashville*. The following year, he opened his account with *Old Man River (I've Come to Talk Again)*. However, it was the third single of the year, *I Call It Love*, that got to the Top 10 in 1984.

The first three chart singles in 1984 came from his album ***Mel McDaniel with Oklahoma Wind*** and seemed to herald a low point for Mel. However, with his year-end *Baby's Got Her Blue Jeans On*, from his ***Let It Roll*** album, Mel at last achieved his first No.1 hit. The song, written by Bob McDill, stayed in the charts for 28 weeks.

Now came the time for honors. Mel was nominated for the CMA "Horizon Award" and "Single of the Year" for *Baby's Got Her Blue Jeans On* and received a Grammy nomination for "Best Country Vocal Performance, Male." The 1985 singles *Let It Roll (Let It Rock)* and *Stand Up* were both Top 10 placings. Both ***Let It Roll*** and his other 1985 album, ***Stand Up,*** were highly placed on the Country album chart.

During the period 1986 through 1988, Mel's record success faltered and his only major hits were *Shoe String* (Top 25) and Bruce Springsteen's *Stand on It* (Top 15), both in 1986, and *Real Good Feel Good Song* (Top 10), in 1988. Although Mel was represented in the charts in 1989, the most successful was *Walk That Way*, which only reached the Top 60.

Mel McDaniel's songwriting career has also been successful. Hoyt Axton was the first to record one of his songs with *Roll Your Own*, which was also recorded by both Commander Cody and the Poodles. Conway Twitty recorded *Grandest Lady of Them All*, in 1978. This song, co-written with Bob Morrison, was used for the Grand Finale on the *Opry* 's nationally televised 60th anniversary special. He also co-wrote with Dennis Linde a song called *Goodbye Marie*, which was included in the highly successful Kenny Rogers album ***Kenny***. The original version of the song was recorded by Bobby Goldsboro and became a 1981 hit for him. It was also cut by Johnny Rodriguez. Other McDaniel songs include *I Could Sure Use This Feeling* (Earl Scruggs Revue), *I Just Want to Feel the Magic* (both Doug Kershaw and Ronnie Prophet) and *Never Say Never* (Dickey Lee).

Mel was inducted as the 62nd member of the *Grand Ole Opry*, in early 1986. He has toured extensively in the U.S. and in 1987, he appeared at the Wembley Festival in London, England.

After his break with Capitol Records, in 1990, Mel continued to tour, doing about 200 dates a year, traveling with his six-piece band, Oklahoma Wind. In 1993, Mel signed with Intersound's new label, Branson Entertainment, and released his debut album with them, ***Baby's Got Her Blue Jeans On***.

Mel McDaniel has dedicated the past 20 years to Country music and is still going strong. His favorite hobby is fishing, when he gets the chance, and he has a BassCat boat. As he says, "Although there's nothing like making a living doing what you love, there's not a thing that can top being out on that lake!" JAB

RECOMMENDED ALBUMS:

"Mello" (Capitol)(1978)
"Naturally Country"(Capitol)(1983)
"Mel McDaniel with Oklahoma Wind" (Capitol)(1984)
"Stand Up" (Capitol)(1985)
"Greatest Hits" (Capitol)(1987)
"Now You're Talkin' "(Capitol)(1988)
"Baby's Got Her Blue Jeans On" (Branson Entertainment)(1993)

BOB McDILL

(Songwriter, Singer, Guitar)

Given Name:	**Robert Lee McDill**
Date of Birth:	**April 4, 1944**
Where Born:	**Walden, Texas**
Married:	**Nancy ("Nan")**
Children:	**Becky, Gavin, Katy**

In an age when every Country singer imagines he's a songwriter, and when a youngster will opt for songwriting instead of being a veterinarian because it pays better, and when a bored housewife will make believe she can write, gets a cut, but can't write a tune to save her life, Bob McDill stands solidly as the real thing.

Bob was born in what is now a suburb of Beaumont,Texas. In Bob's words, he was "a weird little kid who used to sit in class, stare out the window and write poems about butterflies." His early musical influences came from his mother, who played piano, and Bob and his brother sat around singing Gospel songs. Bob got his first guitar at age 14 and played in bands and Folk groups. He studied English at Lamar University and while there played in a Folk group, the Newcomers.

It was at this time that he became friends with Allen Reynolds, who operated Gulf Coast Recording Studios with Dickey Lee, Jack Clement and Bill Hall, in Beaumont. Bob then got drafted into the U.S. Navy and was shipped to Vietnam, as a boatswain's mate. While he was away, Reynolds continued pitching the fledgling McDill songs. Bob's first hits were not Country and he initially scored with *Black Sheep* (Sam the Sham, 1967) and *The Happy Man* (Perry Como).

After his hitch in the service, Bob moved to Memphis to write. However, some two years later, Jack Clement bought out the publishing company Bob was with and moved the operation to Nashville, with the result that in 1969, Bob also moved to Nashville. He was still not into Country music, but it was hearing George Jones singing *A Good Year for the Roses* the following year, that turned him around.

Bob had his first Country hit in 1972 with *Catfish Jones* (co-written with Allen Reynolds), which provided Johnny Russell with a hit. However, it was the following year that Bob came good. It started with Russell's Top 5 recording of *Rednecks, White Socks and Blue Ribbon Beer* and continued through Don Williams' version of *Amanda* and Tommy Cash's rendition of *I Recall a Gypsy Woman*. McDill's songs would play a major part in Don Williams' career. Russell had a further hit in 1974 with McDill's song *She's in Love with a Rodeo Man*, which would later be recorded by Williams. In 1975, Williams had a No.1 hit (McDill's first) with *(Turn Out the Light) And Love Me Tonight*, while Jo-El Sonnier scored his first chart success with the McDill-Dickey Lee song *I've Been Around Enough to Know*.

With the arrival of 1976, McDill found his songs in great demand and he had two No.1 hits via Dave & Sugar's *The Door is Always Open* and Don Williams' *Say It Again*. His other hits that year included *I Met a Friend of Yours Today* (Mel Street), *Overnight Sensation* (Mickey Gilley) and *Put a Little Lovin' on Me* (Bobby Bare). In addition, Don Williams had hits with the McDill-Wayland Holyfield song *She Never Knew Me* and in the U.K. *I Recall a Gypsy Woman*, which McDill wrote with Allen Reynolds.

In 1977, Crystal Gayle had back-to-back hits with Bob's *You Never Miss a Good Thing (Until He Says Goodbye)* (No.1) and *I'll Do It All Over Again* (Top 3). In addition, he had successful cuts from Bobby Bare with the double-sided *Look Who I'm Cheating on Tonight* and *If You Think I'm Crazy Now (Shoulda' Seen Me When I Was a Kid)*. These tracks were on the Bare album that totally comprised McDill songs, entitled ***Me and McDill***. Tommy Overstreet weighed in, that year, with his cover of *This Time I'm in It for the Love* and Jerry Lee Lewis charted with *Closest Thing to You*. As the 70's rolled over, Bob continued his merry way with *No No No (I'd Rather Be Free)* (Rex Allen, Jr.) and *Rake and Ramblin' Man* (Don Williams), both 1978, and three No.1 hits in 1979, *Amanda* (Waylon Jennings), *It Must Be Love* (Don Williams) and *Nobody Likes Sad Songs* (Ronnie Milsap).

Through the 80's, Bob racked up further No.1 successes: *Why Don't You Spend the Night* (Ronnie Milsap, 1980), *If Hollywood Don't Need You* (Don Williams, 1983), *I've Been Around Enough to Know* (John Schneider, 1984), *Baby's Got Her Blue Jeans On* (Mel McDaniel, 1985), *Everything That Glitters (Is Not Gold)* (Dan Seals, 1986), *Fallin' Again* (Alabama, 1986), *Don't Close Your Eyes* (Keith Whitley, 1988, Bob's 20th No.1), *We Believe in Happy Endings* (Earl Thomas Conley and Emmylou Harris, 1988), *Big Wheels in the Moonlight* (Dan Seals, 1989) and *Song of the South* (Alabama, 1989).

Other memorable hits chalked up in the 80's were: 1980: *I Wish I Was Crazy Again* (Johnny Cash & Waylon Jennings), *I've Never Seen the Likes of You* (Conway Twitty), *Save Your Heart for Me* (Jacky Ward), *Starting Over* (Tammy Wynette), *Good Ol' Boys Like Me* (Don Williams); 1981: *Fallin' Again* (Don Williams), *I Recall a Gypsy Woman* (B.J. Thomas), *I'll Need Someone to Hold Me (When I Cry)* (Janie Fricke), *Right in the Palm of Your Hand* (Mel McDaniel), *Song of the South* (Johnny Russell) and *They Could Put Me in Jail for What I've Been Thinkin' About You)* (the Bellamy Brothers); 1982: *Song of the South* (Tom T. Hall & Earl Scruggs); 1983: *Somebody's Always Saying Goodbye* (Anne Murray); 1984: *I Call It Love* (Mel McDaniel), *I May Be Used (but Baby I Ain't Used Up)* (Waylon Jennings), *Too Good to Stop Now* (Mickey Gilley); 1985: *All Tangled Up in Love* (Gus Hardin with Earl Thomas Conley), *I Never Made Love (till I Made Love with You)* (Mac Davis), *It's Time for Love* (Don Williams), *My Baby's Got a Good Timing* (Dan Seals), *Nothing Can Hurt Me Now* (Gail Davies), *Only Love Will Make It Right* (Nicolette Larson), *Someone Like You* (Emmylou Harris) and *You Turn Me On (Like a Radio)* (Ed Bruce); 1989: *They Rage On* (Dan Seals).

Like all the great songwriters, Bob McDill is very well read, which adds a literacy to his lyrics that lesser mortals fail to provide. Among his favorites are the writers of the American South, including William Faulkner, James Dickey, Thomas Wolfe, Robert Penn Warren, William Prince Fox, Eudora Welty, Carson McCullers, Will Campbell and Thomas Connelly. Historian Thomas Connelly dedicated his book *The Civil War in Tennessee* to Bob and his wife, Nan. Bob has spoken on the writing of Robert Penn Warren at the University of South Carolina and taken part in a symposium on the South with Connelly and the Reverend Will Campbell. Bob's musical influences, as regards songwriters, are Paul Simon ("he's the best, my hero") and Robbie Robertson.

In 1976 and 1985, Bob was named the NSAI "Songwriter of the Year" and in 1985, he was inducted into the Nashville Songwriters Hall of Fame. Bob has recorded very little. In the 70's, he cut an album, ***Short Stories,*** and in 1988, he sang *Song of the South* and *Still Got You Baby* on the first issue of RCA's songwriters albums, ***Signatures***. He recalls the words of Bobby Bare about recording, as being the highest level of aggravation. Bob is also one of the rare breed who are quite capable of writing on their own, and he's very choosy about his co-writers, who for the main part have been Wayland Holyfield, Dickey Lee and Allen Reynolds.

RECOMMENDED ALBUM:

"Signatures" (RCA Victor)(1988) [With tracks by Don Schlitz, Mark Wright, Rhonda Fleming and Mike Reid]

SKEETS McDONALD

(Singer, Songwriter, Guitar)

Given Name: **Enos William McDonald**
Date of Birth: **October 1, 1915**
Where Born: **Greenway, Arkansas**
Married: **Josephine**
Children: **Robert**
Date of Death: **March 31, 1968**

One of the better Honky-Tonk stylists to emerge in the 1950's, Skeets McDonald is best remembered today for his 1952 hit *Don't Let the Stars Get in Your Eyes* as well as his long tenure on the West Coast and on the long-running *Town Hall Party*. Better than Lefty Frizzell or Buck Owens, Skeets managed to move his hard-driving Country sound toward rock'n'roll, and like them he became a "musician's musician," a singer whose influence was far greater than a view of his chart hits might indicate.

Skeets (the name came from a childhood incident involving mosquitoes, which young McDonald called "skeets") was born in Greenway, Arkansas, about 80 miles northwest of Memphis. His family picked cotton and Skeets was the baby in a family of seven. Though none of his immediate family was musical, he learned music at Ozark "music parties," and was soon adept at calling sets for square dances in the area. The Victrola brought him Jimmie Rodgers, and by the time he was 12, according to family legend, he had traded a red hound dog for a guitar and $6.00.

"A farm boy became a musician," recalls his brother Lynn. A few years later he followed an older brother north to work in Michigan, where an entire "cracker culture" had developed from all the transplanted southerners.

By 1935, Skeets was working full-time in a Detroit band led by the Buffington Brothers and called the Lonesome Cowboys over station WEXL in Royal Oak. Skeets' singing proved so popular that he soon sent for some more of his buddies from Arkansas and organized his own band. He worked with the band on radio on WFDF Flint and WCAR Pontiac and

*Honky-Tonk singer **Skeets McDonald***

played at a club on Seven Mile Road in Detroit.

The war intervened, and after service in North Africa, India, and Okinawa, Skeets returned to Michigan and a TV show over WKHH in Dearborn. With a fiddler named Johnnie White and a band called the Rhythm Riders, Skeets made his first records, for the Fortune label in 1950. These included two Skeets originals, *The Tattoed Lady* and *Mean and Evil Blues,* which were locally popular. This success encouraged him to make a serious run at the record business and within months he had done sessions for London (four sides) and Mercury (two sides, under the name Skeets Saunders). In February 1951 he decided to move his family to California. (See Movie Section.)

Almost at once, Cliffie Stone signed him to the TV show *Hometown Jamboree* and then got him a contract with Capitol's Ken Nelson, who saw him as Capitol's answer to Lefty Frizzell. On April 5, 1951, he was in the studios doing his first record, *Scoot, Git, and Begone*, which would be the first of some 85 recordings he would do for Capitol, in a stint that would extend to the end of 1958.

Though only *Don't Let the Stars* went to No.1 on the Country chart in 1953, several others sold well or were especially influential: *I'm Hurting* (also recorded by Nat "King" Cole), *Baby Brown Eyes* (written for his wife, Jo), *Wheel of Fortune*, and *I've Got to Win Your Love Again.* Though on early Capitol releases Skeets sounded like Lefty or Hank Williams, he found his own style with the up-tempo songs set off by a romping piano, a Cajun-style fiddle and Skeets' own long melodic lines. By 1956, this style allowed him to start moving toward straight-out Rockabilly with cuts like *Heart Breakin' Mama* and *You Ought to See Grandma Rock*. Songwriter Harlan Howard, who grew up in Detroit listening to Skeets when he was big up there, sent some of his earliest songs to Skeets, titles like *You Better Not Go* and *The All-American Boy*.

Skeets' career did not end when his Capitol contract lapsed in 1959. He soon won a new contract with Columbia and for them he continued to record regularly from 1959 to 1966. He first hit the chart with the Top 25 *This Old Heart*. Skeets' 1963 hit *Call Me Mr. Brown*, which went Top 10, was the biggest since *Don't Let the Stars*. In later years, he began to break away somewhat from the West Coast scene, traveling to Nashville to record and to appear on the *Opry* and to Dallas to guest on the *Big D Jamboree*. He resisted efforts to modernize his sound, and in the 1960's reviewers were saying, "He belongs in another age. Listening to him sing is like playing a record you liked 20 years ago. It's the plaintive sound from a thousand beer joints along the highways from Altoona to Albuquerque." Such was hardly criticism for Skeets, though; he continued to sing those plaintive songs until he was felled by a massive heart attack on March 31, 1968. CKW

RECOMMENDED ALBUMS:

"The Country's Best" (Capitol)(1959)
"Call Me Skeets!" (Columbia)(1964)
"Tattoed Lady Plus Other Songs" (Fortune)(1969)
"Rockin' Rollin'" (Bear Family Germany)(1986)

RONNIE McDOWELL

(Singer, Songwriter, Guitar)

Given Name:	**Ronald Dean McDowell**
Date of Birth:	**March 26, 1950**
Where Born:	**Fountain Head, Tennessee**
Married:	**Karan**
Children:	**Kara, Athena, Ronnie Dean, Tyler Dean**

It was through his (when he wants to) uncanny vocal resemblance to Elvis Presley that Ronnie McDowell came to public prominence. The song *The King Is Gone* was written by Ronnie and Lee Morgan within hours of Presley's death in 1977, and was the most heard tribute song to Elvis, reaching No.13 in both the Pop and Country charts, earning Ronnie a Gold Record. He became the only Elvis "voice" with whom Priscilla Presley would work, and during the filming of the TV movie *Elvis*, she actually thought she was listening to the King singing *Baby, Let's Play House*, when in actuality it was Ronnie.

Ronnie was raised on Highland Rim of Portland, Tennessee, which is the strawberry capital of the world. He started his singing career while in the U.S. Navy, and during 1968, he could be found entertaining his shipmates on the USS *Hancock*. After leaving the service, he worked as a commercial sign painter and painter in oils of Tennessee landmarks and landscapes. He has retained an interest in painting and architecture, as well as being a collector of Clark Gable memorabilia, and has an avid interest in the history of the Civil War.

Following the success of *The King is Gone*, Ronnie followed up with the Top 5 Country success *I Love You, I Love You, I Love You*, which crossed over to the lower regions of the Pop charts. He stayed with Scorpion until the end of 1978, and had five more chart records, of which the most successful were *Here Comes the Reason I Live* (Top 15) and *This Is a Holdup* (Top 40).

In 1979, Ronnie signed with Epic Records, where he was produced by Buddy Killen, and had the Top 20 single *World's Most Perfect Woman*. He followed this with a double-sided Top 30 hit, *Love Me Now/Never Seen a Mountain So High*. During that year, Ronnie was selected by Dick Clark to sing on the soundtrack of the TV movie *Elvis*. He started out 1980 with *Lovin' a Livin' Dream*, and then his next single was a relative flop. He came back with *Gone* and then, at the end of the year, he charted with *Wandering Eyes*, which climbed to the Top 3. He had his first No.1 the following year, with *Older Women*, and followed this, at year end, with the Top 5 hit *Watchin' Girls Go By*.

Personally it's ***Ronnie McDowell***

Ronnie stayed with Epic until the end of 1985, and continued to release singles that were major hits: *I Just Cut Myself* and *Step Back* (Top 10)(both 1982); *Personally* (Top 10), *You're Gonna Ruin My Bad Reputation* (No.1) and *You Made a Wanted Man of Me* (Top 3)(all 1983); *I Dream of a Woman Like You* and *I Got a Million of 'Em* (both Top 10, 1984) and *In a New York Minute* (Top 5) and *Love Talks* (Top 10) (both 1985).

In 1986, Ronnie signed with Curb Records and began to produce his own records, which came out on MCA/Curb. He had a Top 10 hit with *All Tied Up*, but then his singles success started to fall away. His other two singles of the year, *When You Hurt, I Hurt* and *Lovin' That Crazy Feelin'*, only reached the Top 40 and Top 30 respectively. His opening single for 1987, *Make Me Late for Work Today*, fared worse, only reaching the Top 60. At the end of that year, he teamed up with Conway Twitty for a remake of Conway's *It's Only Make Believe*, and this reached the Top 10, on Curb. However, in 1988, his two singles, *I'm Still Missing You* and *Suspicion*, only reached Top 40 and Top 30 respectively. During that year, he again vocally portrayed

Elvis, this time in the TV mini-series *Elvis and Me*.

In 1989, Ronnie teamed up with Jerry Lee Lewis for the McDowell song *Never Too Old to Rock 'n' Roll*, which reached the Top 50. Interestingly, among the members of his backing band, the Rhythm Kings, at this time were Doug Phelps and Greg Martin, soon to become members of the Kentucky Headhunters, and in Doug's case, also, Brother Phelps. Ronnie followed up with his remake of *Sea of Heartache*, which made the Top 40. His other singles of the year were *Who'll Turn Out the Lights* (Top 70) and *She's a Little Past Forty* (Top 50). During 1990, Ronnie registered just one Top 30 hit, a remake of the evergreen *Unchained Melody*.

This was to prove Ronnie's chart swan song, and although he still releases good-quality albums, he is content to leave the limelight to his son, Ronnie Dean McDowell, who is a member of the teen group Six Shooter. Ronnie has produced through his career a lot of good self-written recordings. His main co-writer is Joe Meador, and since joining Curb, he and Joe, often in a threesome with Richard O. Young (another future Headhunter) or Bill Conn, have written more and more of the McDowell recorded material.

RECOMMENDED ALBUMS:

"A Tribute to the King (Elvis) in Memory" (Scorpion)(1979) [With the Jordanaires]
"Elvis" (Dick Clark)(1979)
"Greatest Hits" (Epic)(1982)
"Personally" (Epic)(1983)
"The Best of Ronnie McDowell" (Curb)(1990)
"When a Man Loves a Woman" (Curb)(1992)

RED RIVER DAVE McENERY

(Vocals, Guitar, Banjo, Yodeler)

Given name: David McEnery
Date of Birth: December 15, 1914
Where Born: San Antonio, Texas
Married: Alberta Hayes

One of numerous strong-voiced singing cowboys who worked in films and radio as well as records, Red River Dave is distinguished by his uncanny ability to create topical songs and modern-day "event" songs. Though he has a number of impressive firsts to his credit, modern fans probably remember him best for songs like *Amelia Earhart's Last Flight* and *The Ballad of Patty Hearst*.

Dave began his career in Texas during the Depression, singing over local San Antonio stations as well as the notorious "border" stations along the Mexican border. Unlike a lot of silver screen cowboys, Dave had a real cowboy background and learned many of his stories and tales directly from the old trail

Singing cowboy ***Red River Dave***

drivers and cowboys around the ranches near his home.

As a teenager, he became adept at doing rope tricks, similar to Will Rogers, and was winning Texas state championships in yodeling. By 1938, he was in New York, doing his own network radio show for Mutual and later for NBC. Along with Texas Jim Robertson, Wilf Carter, and Elton Britt, Red River Dave popularized cowboy songs for a generation of middle-class Americans.

In 1939 Dave took his band to the New York World's Fair and participated in an experiment called television—thereby becoming the first singing television star. By now he was also recording for Decca, initiating a discography that would eventually total over 200 sides—not including radio transcriptions. His warm baritone delighted thousands of fans when his theme song wafted out of radio speakers: *Is the Range Still the Same?* After a stint in the service in WWII, he relocated to Hollywood, where he appeared in films with the likes of Jimmy Wakely, Rosalie Allen, and the Hoosier Hot Shots (see Movie Section). In 1948, Universal Films featured Dave in a series of featurettes, but he was camera shy and after three of these "movies," he was replaced by Tex Williams. Returning to Texas in the 1950's, he enjoyed a long-running TV show and then retired for a time to sell real estate. The 1970's, though, saw him making a comeback in Nashville, where he taught many of his yodeling tricks to a young protege, Doug Green, of Riders in the Sky.

In Texas in the 1960's Dave found out he could record and release on his own 45 rpm labels a variety of topical songs and proceeded to do so. He did songs about WWII (*I Want to Give My Dog to Uncle Sam*) and about Vietnam (*Viet Nam Guitar*); he did songs about James Dean, Billy Graham, the Kennedy years, Emmet Till, the Bay of Pigs, the Manson murders, Watergate, Don Larson (he of the perfect game) and the deaths of Bing Crosby and Bob Wills. Some of his more bizarre songs dealt with an eccentric Texas woman who wanted to be buried in her blue Ferrari, and a Kenyan witch doctor who managed to glue together two adulterous lovers (*The Clinging Lovers of Kenya*). Eventually he returned to California, where he appeared at Knott's Berry Farm and continued to write—one effort chronicling the events of the Gulf War.

Sadly, none of these topical efforts on independent labels have ever been collected or offered to a general audience, but they remain Red River Dave's most interesting contribution to the Country genre. CKW

RECOMMENDED ALBUMS:

"Red River Dave Sings" (Continental)(1962)
"Red River Dave, Vol. 1" (Bluebonnet)(1968)
"Red River Dave, Vol. 2" (Bluebonnet)(1968)
"Songs of the Rodeo" (Place) [With the Texas]
"Saddle Songs of the West" (Varsity) [With Jesse Rogers]

PAKE McENTIRE

(Singer, Guitar)

Given Name: Dale Stanley McEntire
Date of Birth: June 23, 1953
Where Born: Chockie, Oklahoma
Married: Katy
Children: Autumn, Calamity, Chisom

At one time in the middle 80's, Pake McEntire looked like he was going to be the second McEntire to make it in a big way, but after two albums, the fates decreed otherwise.

Pake was born the son of Clark (a champion rodeo rider) and Jacqueline (a gifted singer). He had an elder sister, Alice, and would later be joined by two talented siblings, Reba and Susie. The twin talents of rodeo and music were in the blood, as their grandfather was also a rodeo rider. Dale Stanley was nicknamed "Pecos," which was quickly shortened to "Pake."

As a child, he traveled with his father and sisters to rodeo competitions. The children sang in the hotel lobbies for change. While Pake sang *Jesus Loves Me*, Reba sang *Hound Dog*. With Pake, Reba and Susie under the name of the Singing McEntires, their mother booked them into rodeos, clubs and community centers. They recorded for the Boss label in 1972 and continued as a group until Reba signed to a solo contract with Mercury.

Pake became a member of the Professional Rodeo Cowboys Association in 1971 and continued to compete in the "Single Steer Roping" category. His biggest musical influence was Merle Haggard, and after the family group folded, Pake put together a band, Limestone Gap, and landed a once-a-week job at the Corral Club in Sulphur, Texas, a club which had played host to Willie Nelson and Ray Price. He continued at the venue for two years.

Rodeo rider and Country singer ***Pake McEntire***

Pake set up his own label, Old Cross, and issued two albums and a handful of singles, but his dream was to be on RCA, the label that boasted Elvis. Pake sang back-up vocals on several of Reba's albums and thanks to the help of Reba's manager, Bill Carter, Pake landed a recording deal with RCA, where he was produced by Mark Wright.

His first album, ***Too Old to Grow Up Now***, released in 1986, was a revelation. Parts of it, especially the track *Savin' My Love for You*, gave an indication of what Buddy Holly might have done, had he lived. The album was very well received, and the debut single, *Every Night*, reached the Top 20 on the Country charts. The second single, *Savin' My Love for You*, climbed all the way to the Top 3 and it looked like Pake was a star in the making. The final single of the year, the infectious *Bad Love* peaked in the Top 15. However, the first single of 1987, *Heart vs. Heart*, a sort of *Kramer vs. Kramer* song, deserved to do better than it did. With harmonies from Reba, it only reached the Top 5, and the follow-up, which was the title track of the album, just made the Top 50.

The second album, ***My Whole World***, had as a 1987 pre-release *Thank God, I Had It Good*, which showed some improvement by peaking in the Top 30. Pake had given up his 1,000-acre Kiowa, Oklahoma, cattle ranch in 1985, and he must have been wondering whether that was a good idea, especially when the second single from the new album, *Life in the City,* dipped in the Top 70. This was primarily due to the fact that as good as the debut album had been, the new one just did not live up to it. With just two albums behind him, Pake's major recording career came to an end and he returned to rodeo riding and ranching.

RECOMMENDED ALBUM:

"Too Old to Grow Up" (RCA Victor)(1986)

REBA McENTIRE

(Singer, Songwriter, Guitar, Piano, Fiddle, Drums)

Given Name:	**Reba Nell McEntire**
Date of Birth:	**March 28, 1954**
Where Born:	**Chockie, Oklahoma**
Married:	**1. Charlie Battles (div.)**
	2. Narvel Blackstock
Children:	**Shelby**

Reba has emerged as the foremost female singer of the 80's and 90's. Her success on video owes a lot to the fact that she is a very talented actress, who brings a dramatic quality to videos that is unique. She is also a very capable businesswoman who has made her Starstruck company one of the most successful in Country music.

As a child, Reba was raised in a household that boasted a champion rodeo cowboy father (Clark) and a gifted singer/teacher mother (Jacqueline), and both influences rubbed off on Reba and her siblings. She used to go with her father to rodeo competitions and sang, with brother Pake and sister Suzy, in hotel foyers, for change. The trio was booked into rodeos, clubs and community centers by their mother, as the Singing McEntires. Reba also took part in rodeos as a horseback barrel rider. The group recorded on the Boss label back in 1972 and remained together until Reba was discovered by Red Steagall, in 1974, when she sang the national anthem at the National Rodeo Finals in Oklahoma City.

She signed with Mercury Records in 1975, and her first Country chart entry, in 1976, was *I Don't Want to Be a One Night Stand*, which just got into the Top 90. It was with her fourth chart entry, *Last Night, Ev'ry Night*, that she started making her mark. The single reached the Top 30, in 1978. That year, she had a double-sided duet with Jacky Ward entitled *Three Sheets in the Wind/I'd Really Love to See You Tonight*, which reached the Top 20. In 1979, *Runaway Heart* reached the Top 40 and *Sweet Dreams* climbed to the Top 20. She also had another duet with Jacky, *That Makes Two of Us*, which reached the Top 30.

In 1980, Reba hit initially with the Top 40 record *(I Still Long to Hold You) Now and Then* and then she had her first Top 10 single, *(You Lift Me) Up to Heaven*. She wrapped up the year with the Top 20 hit *I Can See Forever in Your Eyes*. By 1981, Reba was starting to establish a pattern of hits: *I Don't Think Love Ought to Be That Way* (Top 15), *Today All Over Again* (Top 5) and *Only You (and You Again)* (Top 15).

Reba stayed with Mercury until the end of 1983, and racked up a string of major hits. In 1982, she had the Top 3 single *I'm Not That Lonely Yet* and then she had her first No.1, *Can't Even Get the Blues*. She followed this, in 1983, with another No.1, *You're the First Time I've Thought About Leaving*, and then had the Top 10 hit *Why Do We Want (What We Know We Can't Have)* and wrapped up the year with *There Ain't No Future in This*, which reached the Top 15.

Country superstar ***Reba McEntire***

Reba moved to MCA in 1984 and commenced a remarkable run of hit singles. *Just a Little Love* went Top 5, *He Broke Your Mem'ry Last Night*, Top 15 and then she had another No.1 with *How Blue*. That year, Reba was named ACM's "Female Vocalist of the Year" and she was the recipient of the title in 1985, 1986, 1987, 1990 and 1991. Reba received the same accolade from the CMA in 1984 through 1987.

She followed with another No.1 in 1985, with *Somebody Should Leave*. Her two other singles that year were *Have I Got a Deal for You* and *Only in My Mind*, both of which went Top 10. She was named "Female Vocalist of the Year" by *Music City News* and she repeated the title (MCN awards became

TNN/MCN awards) in 1986 through 1989, 1991 and 1992. She also received RS's Critics Choice Poll: "Top Five Country Artists."

All three of her 1986 singles went to No.1, and were *Whoever's in New England, Little Rock* and *What Am I Gonna Do About You.* That year, *Whoever's in New England* received the ACM's "Video of the Year" award and Reba received a Grammy Award for "Best Country Vocal Performance, Female" for the same song. Reba was named the CMA's "Entertainer of the Year."

Her first single of 1987, *Let the Music Lift You Up,* went Top 5 and then the next three releases went to No.1 and they were *One Promise Too Late* and *The Last One to Know* (both 1987) and *Love Will Find Its Way to You* (1988). During 1987, at the American Music Awards Reba was named "Favorite Female Video Artist—Country Category," NARM cited her for "Best-Selling Country Album by a Female Artist" and MCN awarded *Whoever's in New England* with the "Country Music Video" award. The 1986 album of the same title was Certified Gold in 1987, as was ***What Am I Gonna Do About You***. Her ***Greatest Hits*** album went Gold in 1987 and had gone Platinum by 1989. The next single, *Sunday Kind of Love*, went Top 5 and it was followed by three further No.1's, *I Know How He Feels* and *New Fool at an Old Game* (both 1988) and *Cathy's Clown* (1989). The other singles, in 1989, were *'Til Love Comes Again* (Top 5) and *Little Girl* (Top 10). In addition, her 16th album, ***Sweet Sixteen***, went to the top of the Country album chart, where it stayed for 13 weeks. Reba released the double album, ***Live***, which was recorded at the McCallum Theatre in Palm Desert, California, and it went Gold in 1990. In 1988, the 1987 album ***The Last One to Know*** was Certified Gold, as was the 1988 album ***Reba***.

Reba teamed up with label-mate Vince Gill for the Top 15 single *Oklahoma Swing*. Her three other singles during 1990, *Walk On, You Lie* and *Rumor Has It*, all made the Top 3, with *You Lie* going to No.1. Reba maintained her success level into 1991, when *Fancy* made the Top 10, *Fallin' in Love* went Top 3 and *For My Broken Heart* gave her another No.1. That year, the 1990 album ***Rumor Has It*** went Gold, as did the 1984 album ***My Kind of Country***, and ***For My Broken Heart*** had shipped over 1 million copies. In addition, the video *Reba* also achieved Gold status.

She followed up with another No.1 in 1992, when *Is There Life Out There* hit the top. She followed this with what was a comparative failure, when *The Night the Lights Went Out in Georgia* only reached the Top 15. The year was wrapped up with *The Greatest Man I Never Knew* (Top 3) and *Take It Back* (with its fun video) (Top 5). Reba had the pleasure of seeing ***For My Broken Heart*** reach sales figures of over 2 million and the video of the same name going Platinum. Her other video, *Reba in Concert,* attained Gold Certification.

In 1993, Reba's chart successes were *The Heart Won't Lie* (No.1 with Vince Gill), *It's Your Call* (Top 5) and *Does He Love You* (No.1 with Linda Davis). The last-named single earned Reba and Linda a Grammy Award in 1993 for "Best Country Vocal Collaboration." That year, Reba's ***Greatest Hits Volume Two***, ***It's Your Call*** and ***Rumor Has It*** all reached Double-Platinum status, ***Reba***, ***Sweet Sixteen*** and ***Whoever's in New England*** all went Platinum and ***Merry Christmas to You*** went Gold.

In 1994, Reba went Top 10 with *They Asked About You,* and then the radio stations started playing *If I Had Only Known* but soon lost interest, and it only reached the Top 75. Reba then reached the Top 5 with *Why Haven't I Heard from You,* which also had a fun video that found favor on CMT. Her album ***Read My Mind*** reached the Country album chart Top 3.

Reba made her movie debut in the 1990 movie *Tremors* with Kevin Bacon, appeared in Kenny Rogers' TV movie *Luck of the Draw: The Gambler Returns*, and in 1993, was in the Rob Reiner movie *North.* Reba McEntire's autobiography, *Reba*, was published in 1994 by Bantam and quickly entered the best-seller list.

RECOMMENDED ALBUMS:

"Out of a Dream" (Mercury)(1979)
"Feel the Fire" (Mercury)(1980)
"Heart to Heart" (Mercury)(1981)
"Unlimited" (Mercury)(1982)
"Behind the Scene" (Mercury)(1983)
"Whoever's in New England" (MCA)(1986)
"What Am I Gonna Do About You" (MCA)(1986)
"Greatest Hits" (MCA)(1987)
"Reba" (MCA)(1988)
"Sweet Sixteen" (MCA)(1989)
"Live" (double)(MCA)(1989)
"Rumor Has It" (MCA)(1990)
"For My Broken Heart" (MCA)(1991)
"Greatest Hits Volume Two" (MCA)(1993)

JOHN McEUEN

(Singer, Songwriter, Composer, 5-String Banjo, Fiddle, Guitar, Mandolin, Accordion, Piano, Dulcimer, Lap Steel)

Date of Birth:	**December 19, 1945**
Where Born:	**Garden Grove, California**
Married:	**Unknown**
Children:	**Jonathan and 5 others**

John could go down in history as the man who taught comedian Steve Martin how to play the banjo. He could be remembered as a founding member of the Nitty Gritty Dirt Band. However, it is more likely that he is still writing history as one of the finest multi-instrumentalists in any form of music.

When he was 18, John got his first 5-string banjo. At the time, he was living in Southern California, where he worked as a magician in Disneyland and attended college. It was after watching the Dillards, in 1964, that he got turned on to performing. His influences at this time were Flatt & Scruggs, Merle Travis, Lightnin' Hopkins and his brother Bill. He started playing with various Folk groups as well as with Bill and Alice McEuen, Jose Feliciano and Steve Martin (he had been at high school and at Disneyland with Steve). In 1965, he teamed up with Michael Martin Murphey (then without the "Martin"). Over the years, John has appeared on five of Murphey's albums.

They played together for about a year and then Murphey returned to Texas. In August 1966, John was in McCabe's Guitar Shop, a musicians' hangout in Long Beach, when he overheard four guys talking about forming a group. John joined them, and so the Nitty Gritty Dirt Band was born.

John stayed with the NGDB until 1987, when, for some reason, they felt they could do without him (for his work with NGDB, see Nitty Gritty Dirt Band). From 1972, he had always had a solo spot within the Dirt Band's act, and from 1976, he even did solo bookings. Now he was on his own, he could fully develop his versatility. While with the Dirt Band, John also guested on other artists' albums. These included Bill Wyman's ***Monkey Grip*** (1974), the Marshall Tucker Band's ***Long Hard Ride*** (1976), Hoyt Axton's ***Rusty Old Halo*** (1979) and David Allan Coe's ***Just Divorced*** (1984). He also played on the soundtrack of the 1969 musical *Paint Your Wagon.*

*String wizard **John McEuen***

John has written extensively for TV and the movies, and his scores include *Paint Your Wagon* (1969), *For Singles Only*, *Wild and Crazy Guy*, *Comedy Is Not Pretty*, *Badrock*, *Take It to the Limit* and *The Man Outside*. John has also been a guest host on TNN's *Nashville Now*.

Despite not being a member of the Dirt Band, John was still invited to take part in the recording of ***Will the Circle Be Unbroken II***, released in 1989. The following year, John produced and directed the live video/album ***The Dillards—A Night in the Ozarks***.

In 1991, he cut the solo album ***String Wizards***, which was released on Vanguard. This was the first time that John was featured solely on banjo. The guests on the album were Earl Scruggs, Vassar Clements & Bobby Hicks, Josh Graves and Byron Berline. He had his first video with *Return to Dismal Swamp*. This was followed by a video on *Miner's Night Out*, in 1992. That year, John and synthesizer player David Hoffner scored the *National Geographic* PBS special *Braving Alaska*. The recording featured guest musicians Kenny Malone, Josh Graves, David Grier, Craig Nelson and Bill Miller. The music manages to give the ethnic sound of Alaska, due in part to Miller's courting flute. In 1994, John released ***String Wizards II***.

RECOMMENDED ALBUMS:

See Nitty Gritty Dirt Band albums to 1987, plus "Will the Circle Be Unbroken II"
"String Wizards" (Vanguard)(1991)
"String Wizards II" (Vanguard)(1994)

Lester McFarland refer MAC AND BOB

SAM AND KIRK McGEE

SAM McGEE
(Vocals, Guitar, Banjo, Tiple, Steel Guitar)
Given Name: **Sam Fleming McGee**
Date of Birth: **May 1, 1894**
Date of Death: **August 21, 1975**
KIRK McGEE
(Vocals, Guitar, Fiddle, Mandolin)
Given Name: **Kirk McGee**
Date of Birth: **November 4, 1899**
Date of Death: **October 24, 1983**
Both Born: **Williamson County, Tennessee**

One of Country's earliest and most distinctive brother groups, Sam and Kirk McGee for years held forth on Nashville's *Grand Ole Opry*, bringing to the show an amazing instrumental dexterity and strong links to the pre-commercial world of Folk music and medicine shows. Though often viewed as sidemen for legends like Uncle Dave Macon and Fiddling Arthur Smith, the McGees set the instrumental standards for music from their professional start in the mid-1920's. Sam's virtuoso "flat-top" guitar style influenced generations of pickers, and Kirk's odd, acerbic fiddling and warm vocals were among the most recognizable in the South.

Sam and Kirk were both born in rural Williamson County, south of Nashville, in the rolling hills of middle Tennessee. Their father was an accomplished Old-Time fiddler who competed in local contests against such players as Uncle Jimmy Thompson and Uncle Bunt Stephens and who played in events sponsored by Henry Ford. The McGee family was full of other pickers and singers. One cousin would later perform with Roy Acuff under the name Rachel Veach, and another, Theron Hale, would become leader of a pioneer *Opry* string band. It was natural that the McGee boys should take up music.

Sam played his first square dance as early as 1906 for the sum of $1.50—big money at the time. Like many early instrumentalists, Sam played the banjo before the guitar, as guitars didn't appear in rural middle Tennessee until about 1910. Sam's father had at that time a rural country store, where local black railroad hands and day workers gathered for lunch and made music on their guitars. Sam listened with interest and picked up a lot of guitar and Blues technique: sliding notes, odd tunings, strange time signatures.

Kirk, on the other hand, took up the fiddle and began learning his father's repertoire. He also developed a love of singing, and as a child attended the rural singing schools conducted by publishers like the James D. Vaughan company in nearby Lawrenceburg. Kirk developed a fondness for the older, more sentimental songs, while Sam liked the comic and novelty pieces. Kirk, however, also came to love the Blues, and was more inclined to learn them from records, especially those of Papa Charlie Jackson and Kokomo Arnold, from whom he would learn one of his best-remembered songs, *Milk Cow Blues*.

In 1925 Sam met Uncle Dave Macon, who was to have a dominant influence on his career. For several years, Sam toured and recorded with Macon, occasionally incurring the older man's jealousy when he bested him at fiddling or picking contests. Sam's first records were made at Macon sessions, and included such 1926 guitar solos as *Buck Dancer's Choice*, *Franklin Blues* and *Knoxville Blues*.

By 1927, Kirk joined in the tours with Macon and became a member of the band Macon took to New York to record as Uncle Dave Macon and His Fruit Jar Drinkers and as the Dixie Sacred Singers. At this time, the brothers recorded several Vocalion sides on their own. The following year, 1928, Kirk recorded a popular series of records with his cousin Blythe Poteet for Gennett, including *Kicking Mule*. In the meantime, both brothers continued to work with Macon on the early *Grand Ole Opry*.

In 1931, Sam broke off with Macon and the two brothers began to play with the fiddler Arthur Smith. They formed the Dixieliners, one of the most popular string bands of the 1930's and one of the *Opry*'s most popular acts. Though the McGees never recorded with Smith on his long string of Bluebird hits (that job usually fell to the Delmore Brothers), they routinely toured with him, and composed songs with him. It was Kirk who came up with *Chittlin' Cooking Time in Cheatham County*. Sam's biggest hit of this time was *Railroad Blues*, which he recorded for Champion/Decca in 1934.

The 1940's were rough times for the brothers, and for a while both dropped out of music. For a time, too, they moved to Knoxville, where they worked on WNOX with Johnnie & Jack. Kirk began to tour with Bill Monroe, and did this intermittently for some 10 years or so. In 1955, the *Opry* threatened to fire the brothers unless they toured more, but Kirk backed the management down. The next year, the brothers began a comeback by appearing at the New River Ranch, and by being discovered by a new Folk revival audience.

In 1957, the McGees reunited with Fiddlin' Arthur Smith, recorded the first of two lps for Folkways, and began a tour of the North, sponsored by the Newport Folk Foundation.

Throughout the 1960's the brothers continued to specialize in Old-Time music for the Folk revival audience, as well as newly appreciative *Opry* fans. Kirk occasionally recorded singles for labels like Tennessee and both did an lp for Starday. Sam recorded his first solo record, for Arhoolie, in 1970, and in 1971 he formed his own record company, MBA, with Kirk and a couple of friends. This company saw the release of three more lps, all recorded in a studio in Franklin, Tennessee. Kirk cut the solo single *Pig Ankle Rag* in 1971 for the Jo-Mar label.

In 1974, the McGees played their last date at the old Ryman Auditorium, inspiring a visiting journalist named Garrison Keillor to write, "It was the acoustic moment of the show....Stunning and simple." As the oldest members of the *Opry*, the McGees were allowed to perform first in the new *Opry* House. Respect for their work had never been higher. But a little over a year later, Sam was killed in a farming accident near Franklin. Kirk continued on as a soloist, and as fiddler for the Fruit Jar Drinkers, until his death in 1983. CKW

RECOMMENDED ALBUMS:

"Sam & Kirk McGee & the Crook Brothers" (Starday)(1962) [Tracks by both groups]
"The Grand Dad of the Country Guitar Pickers" (Arhoolie)(1963) [Sam McGee solo]

John McGhee refer FRANK WELLING & JOHN McGHEE

TIM McGRAW

(Singer, Songwriter, Guitar)
Date of Birth: May 1, 1967
Where Born: Delhi, Louisiana

Raised in the small town of Start, Louisiana, Tim McGraw is the son of well-known baseball player Tug McGraw, who played baseball on championship teams for the New York Mets and the Philadelphia Phillies during a distinguished 20-year career (1964-1984).

Tim, however, was raised by his mother, (who divorced Tug when Tim was an infant) and his stepfather, and he didn't even know about his father's illustrious career until he was 11 years old. Tim recalls listening to all kinds of music while growing up but mainly Country, Motown, rock'n'roll and Elvis. Tim attended Northeast Louisiana University on several sports scholarships. Years later, he and his real father began the business of catching up and have been close ever since.

Tim's earliest goal was to be a lawyer, but his first job was working in a plant nursery and he studied public relations in college. He dabbled as a rodeo competitor for a few years and didn't really become serious about music until a pawn-shop guitar sparked his interest. Then, in 1989, he made the move to Nashville after becoming enthralled with gigging around northeastern Louisiana and Jacksonville, Florida.

Tim describes his music as "turbo-tonk." His favorite music is "heartbreak ballads in the Honky-Tonk tradition." While performing in clubs around Nashville, one of Tim's demos led to a deal with Curb Records, in 1990. His debut single, *Welcome to the Club*, released at the end of 1992, went Top 50. His next chart hit, *Memory Lane*, from his self-titled album, went Top 60 (1993) and was followed by *Two Steppin' Mind*, which made the Top 75, the same year.

1994 brought him recognition with the Top 10 hit *Indian Outlaw*, which crossed over to the Pop chart, making it into the Top 20. The single was soon Certified Gold. The single didn't make it, however, without a certain amount of controversy concerning some of the lyrics. Written by Tommy Barnes, Gene Simmons and John D. Loudermilk, it contains lines such as "pull out the peace pipe and smoke some and pass it around," and "sitting in my wigwam beating on my tom-tom." Detractors say the song promotes images Native Americans have been fighting for years and some radio stations pulled it from their playlists. In response, McGraw, Curb and Image Management announced plans for a concert and clothing drive that will benefit the Native American community.

Following *Outlaw*, McGraw released the1994 album ***Not a Moment Too Soon***, which entered at No.1 on the Country album chart and No.2 on the Pop Album chart (reaching No.1 on the latter). Within 4 months of release, the album had been Certified Double Platinum. This was followed by his latest single to date, *Don't Take the Girl*, which went Top 10. Tim is produced by James Stroud and Byron Gilmore. Tim may be a newcomer to Country Music but his Honky-Tonk style has found favor with radio and fans alike. LAP

RECOMMENDED ALBUMS:

"Tim McGraw" (Curb)(1993)
"Not a Moment Too Soon" (Curb)(1994)

McGUFFEY LANE

Formed:	**1972**
Members:	
Terry Efaw	**Steel Guitar, Guitar (Original Member)**
Steve Reis	**Bass Guitar, Vocals (Original Member)**
Dave Rangeler	**Drums (Final Member)**
Bobby Gene McNelley	**Lead Vocals, Acoustic Guitar (1974-1984)**
John Schwab	**Lead Guitar,Vocals (Joined 1977)**
"Tebes" Douglass	**Keyboards, Harmonica (died 1984)**
Dick Smith	**Drums (Original Member)**
John Campigotto	**Drums (Joined 1980)**
Tom Ingham	**Harmonica (1990)**
Casey McKeown	**Keyboards**

The story of McGuffey Lane is one strewn with tragedies, and yet for a while in the early 80's, this Country-Rock sextet threatened to break through in a big way, among the groups following in the wake of Alabama.

They started out as Scotch and Soda, a duo comprising Terry Efaw and Steve Reis (b. Stephen George Reis). When he was 19, Efaw won a Chet Atkins Guitar Competition. With the addition of Bobby Gene McNelly, the trio became very successful playing Folk music. The new name of the outfit came from the name of the road that Reis lived on in Athens, Ohio, McGuffey Lane. Soon Tebes Douglass and Dick Smith were added to make the group a five-piece. They became the house band at Zachariah's in Columbus. In 1977, the band became a six-piece with the addition of guitarist John Schwab, who had been opening for them as a solo. They began to build up a tremendous following in Ohio.

Although they tried to get a record deal, it was only when Alabama unlocked doors in Nashville that McGuffey Lane found themselves on a major label. They had already put together an album at their own expense, which had sold 40,000, with just independent distribution on their own Paradise Island label. In their area, they were outselling the Rolling Stones' ***Emotional Rescue*** album. Atco released this album as the band's first self-titled product for the label in 1980, and soon McGuffey Lane began touring as opening act for southern Rock bands Charlie Daniels and the Allman Brothers. Their first chart success was on the Pop lists with *Long Time Lovin' You*. Later that year, Atco released McGuffey Lane's second album, ***Aqua Dream***, which features Charlie Daniels. The following year, they scraped into the Pop Top 100 with *Start It All Over* and then they made their first appearance in the Country singles chart with *Making a Living's Been Killing Me*, which reached the Top 50. They followed it up in 1983 with *Doing It Right*, which reached the Top 70. That year, they released their third album, ***Let the Hard Times Roll***, which was produced by Paul Worley (later to produce Highway 101) and Eagles engineer Marshall Morgan.

In 1984, McGuffey Lane moved to Atlantic American, because Atco was still not equipped to handle a Country act. Before they had finished their fourth album, ***Day By Day***, Douglass was killed in an automobile accident while returning home from a gig.

From this album, dedicated to Douglass, the group had two more hits, *Day By Day* (Top 50) and *The First Time* (Top 70). The album was compared favorably with the work of the Eagles. In December that year, McNelley decided to leave the group to concentrate on a songwriting career in Nashville.

With the advent of the mid-80's, the interest in Country-Rock faded, and the band was dropped from Atlantic and reverted to just being a live band. They released a Christmas album in 1986 to benefit the Central Ohio Lung Association, which quickly sold over 10,000 copies. At that time, they had become resident at Bogart's in Columbus,

Ohio. They also secured sponsorship from Miller Beer that year. On January 5, 1987, former member Bobby Gene McNelley committed suicide after fatally shooting his fiancee, Linda Sue Green. Later that year, McGuffey Lane returned to the recording studio, but nothing happened with any further releases.

The group decided to call it a day in 1990, with Efaw, Reis and Schwab still present. The final concert on July 23 featured Bobby Gene's son Rob on guitar and reunited many of the former members. In the final years, the band had moved into more of a "party band," but with the addition of harmonica player Tom Ingham, they returned to Country-Rock. Just prior to their demise, they recorded the album ***Live on High Street***. There would probably have been a lot of room for McGuffey Lane in the 1990's.

RECOMMENDED ALBUMS:

"McGuffey Lane" (Atco)(1980)
"Aqua Dream" (Atco)(1981)
"Let the Hard Times Roll" (Atco)(1983)
"Day By Day" (Atlantic America)(1984)

McLAIN FAMILY BAND, The

When Formed: 1970

RAYMOND K. McLAIN
(Vocals, Guitar)
Given Name: Raymond K. McLain
Date of Birth: Ca. 1930
Where Born: Unknown
Married: Unknown
Children: Raymond W., Alice, Ruth, Nancy, Michael

RAYMOND W. McLAIN
(Vocals, All String Instruments)
Given Name: Raymond W. McLain
Date of Birth: December 18, 1953
Where Born: Unknown
Married: Beverly Buchanan (div.)

ALICE McLAIN
(Vocals, Mandolin)
Given Name: Alice McLain
Date of Birth: Ca. 1957
Where Born: Hindman, Kentucky
Married: Al White

RUTH McLAIN
(Vocals, Mandolin, Bass)
Date of Birth: Ca. 1958
Where Born: Hindman, Kentucky
Married: Michael Riopel

Other members of the McLain Family Band at various times included: Beverly Buchanan, Nancy McLain, Michael McLain, Michael Riopel, Al White

The McLain Family Band constituted one of the more unusual family Bluegrass bands of the 70's and 80's for a variety of reasons.

The origins of the band were rooted in the musical evolution of Raymond K. McLain, a graduate of Denison University, who majored in music theory and who spent 17 years from 1954 at the Hindman Settlement School in the heart of the Kentucky Mountains. He began teaching his son Raymond W. the banjo, then daughter Alice learned mandolin and her younger sister Ruth the bass. Since Raymond K. already played guitar, the McLains were a band by 1970.

Raymond K. also joined the faculty at Berea College, where he taught one semester and then traveled with the band during the other. Initially known as the Bluegrass State, they soon abandoned that name for their family name (which is what the public insisted on calling them anyway). They played for local entertainments at first, but by 1971 they were hitting the festival trail heavily, entering band contests initially and by the next year, they had begun to get bookings.

Almost from the beginning they became known for their broad eclectic repertoire, drawing their songs and tunes from a wide variety of sources, some rather atypical for Bluegrass. The McLains not only gained a wide following on the festival circuit but also played numerous colleges and concert halls (including working with symphony orchestras) along with extensive foreign tours. The family took their music not only to western Europe and Japan, but to unusual third world countries such as Bolivia, Kenya, Nepal, and Zambia.

During their active years, various children and sometimes in-laws entered and left the band, although the principal members remained—Raymond K. McLain, eldest son Raymond W., and older daughters Alice and Ruth. For a steady 18 years the McLains stayed quite busy. The band also waxed a string of albums on their own Country Life Records.

When daughter Alice married Al White in 1977, the latter joined the group and remained until both moved to Alaska, although they returned some years later. During Raymond W. McLain's brief marriage to Beverly Buchanan, she played banjo in the band. Ruth's marriage to Mike Riopel brought him into the entourage, and the departure of the Whites for Alaska made an opening for the younger children Michael and Nancy. As one wit at the Charlotte, Michigan, festival described with only slight exaggeration, the McLains—who played that locale every year but one during their working days—practically grew up, married, had children and sometimes even divorced right there on the stage.

The McLains also developed their own festival at a place called Big Hill near Irvine, Kentucky, which featured only family bands. It did quite well during the 80's. Once the McLains had gotten older, working as a family unit became increasingly more of a challenge, and the group dissolved after the 1989 festival season. In their final year, Raymond K. made a career switch, moved to Lexington, and no longer traveled. The others kept the group together for one more season. Today the only McLain active in music is Raymond W., who has been banjo player with Jim & Jesse's Virginia Boys since 1989. IMT

RECOMMENDED ALBUMS:

"The McLain Family Band" (Country Life)(1973)
"Country Ham" (Country Life)(1974)
"Country Life" (Country Life)(1975)
"On the Road" (Country Life)(1976)
"Kentucky Wind" (Country Life)(1977)
"Family Album" (Country Life)(1978)
"7th Album" (Country Life)(1979)
"Big Hill" (Country Life)(1980)
"The McLain Family Band and the Carleton Orchestra" (Country Life)(1981)
"In Concert at Carnegie Hall" (Country Life)(1982)
"All Natural Ingredients" (Country Life)(1983)
"Sunday Singing" (Country Life)(1984)

DON McLEAN

(Singer, Songwriter, Guitar, Banjo, Poet)
Date of Birth: October 2, 1945
Where Born: New Rochelle, New York
Married: 1. (Div.)
2. Patricia Schnier

There is something almost quixotic about Don McLean and his work. Like Halley's comet, he has struck infrequently, but when he does, it is with a major hit. It was with the enormous hit *American Pie* that he was catapulted from apparent obscurity into an international star. However, this in itself, added to his inherent shyness, has meant that Don has not had the sustained career that his obvious talent has warranted.

From an early age, Don's idol was Buddy

Folk-Country star ***Don McLean***

Holly, but because he was such a loner, he found that playing in bands while in high school was not for him and he became a solo performer. After studying at Iona Prep School, a Catholic school, he enrolled at Villanova University. However, after six months he left to start a career as a Folk performer. He began playing the coffee houses and small clubs in upstate New York. He then moved on to New York City and played the Bitter End and the Gaslight. He also played dates in Philadelphia, Baltimore and north of the border, in Canada.

It was at this time that he was befriended by Lee Hays, one of the guiding lights of the burgeoning Folk movement. He also met and was influenced by black Folk and Blues artists such as Josh White and Sonny Terry and Brownie McGhee. Although he attended Iona College, studying philosophy and theology, it was music that had taken him over. His influences began changing with the advent of the British invasion of the Beatles and the Rolling Stones; he even began to admire the work of "the Godfather of Soul," James Brown.

It was in 1966 that he began entertaining during the summer at Lena Spencer's Cafe Lena in Saratoga Springs, New York. It was this connection that proved a turning point for McLean. When asked by the New York State Council of the Arts, Ms. Spencer recommended Don for a series of free concerts on behalf of the ecology of the Hudson River. For over a month, as the "Hudson River Troubadour," he played to some 50 river communities. Through this, he was contacted by Pete Seeger, in 1969, to join the sloop *Clearwater* for a cruise from South Bristol, Maine, to New York City, as an attempt by some Folk singers to get public support against industrial river pollution. The project was the subject of a National Education Television special, *The Sloop at Nyack*. Don also edited a book of the voyage, *Songs and Sketches of the First Clearwater Crew*.

Seeger became a flag-waver on behalf of Don and referred to him as the "finest singer and songwriter I have met since Bob Dylan"; praise indeed. Soon Don was not only appearing alongside the glitterati of Folk music but also opening for Rock and Country acts such as Blood Sweat & Tears and the Nitty Gritty Dirt Band. However, it was not until 1970, after approaching 27 record companies, that he secured a record deal with Mediarts. The debut album ***Tapestry*** was released and Don toured in support of the product. By 1971, he had written the nine-minute saga *American Pie* and now United Artists signed him. They re-released ***Tapestry*** and issued ***American Pie***, both the single and album. The single went to No.1 on the Pop chart and was Certified Gold, as was the album, by 1972. In the U.K., the single went to No.2 on the Pop chart.

On the heels of this came a song inspired by Vincent Van Gogh's painting *Starry Night*, entitled *Vincent*. The song achieved such fame that it is still played daily at the Van Gogh Museum in Amsterdam, Holland. The single reached the Top 15 on the Pop charts, where it was coupled with *Castles in the Air*. In the U.K., it fared even better, reaching No.1. However, all this success with the attendant acclamation proved too much for Don, and for a while he refused to play *American Pie*. His unhappiness manifested itself on the next album, ***Don McLean***, from which came the uptempo *Dreidel*, which made it to just under the Top 20 on the Pop chart. However, the follow-up, *If We Try*, only made the Top 60. In 1972, Roberta Flack recorded *Killing Me Softly with His Song*, a song written by Norman Gimble and Charles Fox and inspired by Don McLean's rendition of *Vincent*.

Through 1973, Don hit a dry spell, but with the help of mandolinist Frank Wakefield, a friend from his days at the Cafe Lena, he recorded ***Playin' Favorites***, which was the most Country-flavored album he had recorded. It was a mix of Bluegrass and Country with a pair of Buddy Holly songs. It also highlighted McLean as a pretty fair banjo player. On the back of it, he toured Europe and Australia, to an excellent reception. That year, Perry Como had a major hit with Don's poetic song *And I Love You So*.

In 1974, Don released his album ***Homeless Brother***, which extols the hobo and was dedicated to Pete Seeger. He hit the Top 100 on the Pop singles chart, in 1975, with *Wonderful Baby*, a song dedicated to Fred Astaire. The following year, he released his live double album ***Solo*** and then, the same year, he signed with Arista. He made some concert appearances before the release of his debut album for the label, ***Prime Time***. The album was released the next year. Don had a fractious time with his label and refused to play an encore during a concert, because some record company executives were talking while he played.

For three years, Don trod water career-wise and then in 1980, he signed with Millennium Records and the following year, he released the album ***Chain Lightning***, from which came another career single, Roy Orbison's *Crying*. The single reached the Top 5 on the Pop chart, and he made his debut on the Country chart when the single reached the Top 10. In addition, it went to No.1 in the U.K. He followed up with his version of *Since I Don't Have You*, which reached the Top 25 Pop and Top 70 Country. Don had two more Pop entries in 1981, *It's Just the Sun* (Top 90) and a re-recorded version of *Castles in the Air*.

While performing with the Nashville Symphony, in 1985, Don was spotted by Jim Fogelsong and signed to EMI America, the following year. The first album under this deal was the 1987 release ***Don McLean's Greatest Hits—Then & Now***. From this came the low-level Country chart entry, Hank Cochran's *He's Got You*. Later that year, Dave Burgess produced Don's new album, ***Love Tracks***, from which came *You Can't Blame the Train* (Country Top 50) and *Love in the Heart* (Country Top 60). Since then, his recording career has ground to a halt and he contents himself with his live appearances.

RECOMMENDED ALBUMS:

"Tapestry" (United Artists)(1972)
"American Pie" (United Artists)(1972)
"Playin' Favorites" (United Artists)(1973)
"Homeless Brother" (United Artists)(1974)
"Solo" (double)(United Artists)(1976)
"Chain Lightning" (Millennium/Casablanca)(1978)
"Don McLean's Greatest Hits—Then & Now" (EMI America)(1987)
"Love Tracks" (Capitol)(1988)

CLAYTON McMICHEN

(Fiddle)

Date of Birth: **January 26, 1900**
Where Born: **Allatoona, Georgia**
Date of Death: **1970**

In late 1929, when Clayton McMichen was advertising a concert in Chattanooga featuring blues yodeler Jimmie Rodgers, he carefully listed all the musicians on the program, along with a short blurb about each. When he got to himself, at the end of the playbill, he added simply, "Everybody knows McMichen."

In truth, he was not being immodest; through the late 1920's into the late 1940's, the name of Clayton McMichen was almost synonymous with fiddling. Eighteen times he was declared National Fiddling Champion, and his many records made him the most influential fiddler player of two generations of instrumentalists.

Fiddling historians give him (along with *Grand Ole Opry* star Arthur Smith) credit for popularizing the "long bow" style which dominates contest fiddling today. Yet McMichen has far more claim to fame than this. He was a gifted songwriter (Rodgers' *Peach Picking Time in Georgia*), a best-selling vocalist (often under the pseudonym "Bob Nichols"), a founding member of the most famous Old-Time string band, the Skillet Lickers, an influential bandleader who sought to merge Western Swing and Jazz with string band music, a pioneer studio musician, an important accompanist for Jimmie Rodgers and a tireless promoter who gave people like Merle Travis, Slim Bryant, Carl Cotner, and Red Foley their important first breaks.

For much of his life, McMichen sought to better the musicianship and professionalism of Country music; in his own words, he wanted to "take Country music uptown," even if it didn't want to go.

Born in Allatoona, a small town northwest of Atlanta, McMichen had training as a fiddler, which was unusual from the start. He learned much from his father and uncles, Old-Time fiddlers who were also trained violinists, who could play a Viennese waltz as readily as a breakdown. As a boy, he also hung out at an instrument repair shop that was frequented by members of the Atlanta Metropolitan Opera, and they also taught him the fine points of violin technique. Another teacher was the brilliant young fiddler Lowe Stokes, the Mark O'Connor of his day, who taught McMichen much of the long bow style (which emphasized fingering over fast, choppy bow strokes) which he had learned from north Georgia fiddler Joe Lee.

By 1914, Atlanta had become the center of southern fiddling contests, and young McMichen was soon attracted to them. He moved there when he was about 14, working for a time as an auto mechanic and then for a while as a railroad fireman. In his spare time, he played (and learned) music, winning his first local contest in 1914. For several years, he traveled with "physic operas," or rural medicine shows, doing blackface routines and learning how to add Blues, Jazz, Ragtime, Hokum, and Pop music to his repertoire. He soon made friends with a circle of young musicians around Atlanta, including the strange and innovative mandolin player Ted Hawkins, the blind guitarist and singer Riley Puckett, and the stately and reserved violinist who became his brother-in-law, Bert Layne. By 1922, Atlanta's radio station, WSB ("We cover Dixie like the dew") took to the air, and Mac formed his first band, the Home Town Boys, in part to play on it. This first band recorded the first fiddle version of *Down Yonder,* in 1925.

One of Mac's pals was a short, wise-cracking man named Bill Brown, who was a local A & R man for Frank Walker of Columbia Records. In 1926, Columbia decided to make Atlanta their recording headquarters for Old-Time music, doing long sessions there each spring and fall. Walker came up with the idea of pairing Mac with two established Columbia stars, Riley Puckett and an older fiddler named Gid Tanner, known primarily for his comedy. The band, which was at first mainly a studio group, was called the Skillet Lickers, and from the first their records were a spectacular success. Pieces like *Bully of the Town, Pass Around the Bottle,* and *Watermelon on the Vine,* sold upwards of a quarter million copies each. A contrived skit, in which the musicians pretended to be drunken moonshiners, was called *A Corn Licker Still in Georgia,* and became the best-selling record in the Columbia catalog, to McMichen's embarrassment. Between 1926 and 1931, the Skillet Lickers did almost 100 sides for Columbia, and donned tuxedos to tour the South; they were the most famous string band of the age, and for generations later.

McMichen, though, did not like the band or his role in it, feeling it was demeaning and too "old-time" sounding; "the band stunk," he wrote later. To pacify him, Frank Walter let him do dozens of recordings on the side, including some with a group called McMichen's Melody Men, who had a hit with *Sweet Bunch of Daisies*, and with Riley Puckett as a vocalist dubbed "Bob Nichols." (Their duet of *My Carolina Home* became one of the biggest hits of the late 1920's.) McMichen also did a lot of studio work, appearing with many other acts, usually uncredited, and was paid a retainer by Columbia. In 1932, he recorded a number of sides with Jimmie Rodgers.

By 1931, McMichen had finally split from the Skillet Lickers, and had organized a new band, the Georgia Wildcats, built around the hot, Jazz-like guitar work of Hoyt "Slim" Bryant. By this time, McMichen had determined to forge a new string band music that borrowed heavily from Big-Band Swing, a kind of southeastern brand of the kind of material Bob Wills and Milton Brown were doing in Texas and Oklahoma.

Throughout the 30's, his band worked steadily, appearing on WLS Chicago, WMCA New York City, KDKA Pittsburgh, WLW Cincinnati, WTAM Cleveland and WGY Schenectady. Between 1937 and 1939, they made a series of Decca records that featured hot take-off solos, intricate twin fiddling, and smooth vocals. Yet the really big breakthrough never came, and McMichen became increasingly frustrated at people who only saw him as a fiddler and the man that wrote *Bile'm Cabbage Down.* By 1944, he had given up his string band format, and was leading a Dixieland band over WAVE-TV in Louisville.

McMichen thought he had retired in the late 1950's, but he was rediscovered in a few years by the young Folk music fans of the Folk revival. He did a number of comeback concerts (including an appearance at the Newport Folk Festival), but still found it hard to shake off the Skillet Licker image. He died in 1970 at Battlesboro, Kentucky. CKW

RECOMMENDED ALBUMS:

"The Traditional Years" (Davis Unlimited)

[There are no current cds featuring McMichen's work. However, refer to Recommended Albums for the Skillet Lickers (on County and Rounder) which feature him. He is also heard live at Newport on Vanguard's cd "Bluegrass Breakdown" and as a singer on Legacy's cd set "White Country Blues."]

TERRY McMILLAN

(Harmonica, Vocals, Songwriter, Drums, Percussion, Flute, Piano)

Given Name:	**Terry Lee McMillan**
Date of Birth:	**October 12, 1953**
Where Born:	**Lexington, North Carolina**
Married:	**Peggy**
Children:	**Sarah Laine, Adam Taylor, Lucas Andrew**

Terry McMillan is different from any other session harmonica player in that his style is rooted in Blues rather than what is known as the "Nashville" style.

Terry went to 13 different schools while his alcoholic parents moved from town to town. He started playing drums at age 7 as a means of escape from an unhappy home life. In 1973, Terry went out on the road with a band which broke up while in Nashville. The following day, he gained a place in Eddy Raven's band, playing nights at the King of the Road. It was Jimmy Dean who provided the breakthrough for Terry, 18 months later, by introducing him to Chet Atkins. Terry played for Chet, and a month later, Chet hired him to play harmonica on the road with him. Terry at the time didn't play melodies, but Chet obviously saw that he had promise and helped him to learn the "Nashville" style.

From Chet, Terry went on to work for Jeannie C. Riley and Jerry Reed. In 1976, Terry married and came off the road and started receiving calls to do sessions. One of his first sessions was Steve Young's ***Renegade Picker***. During the late 70's, Terry worked with Mickey Newbury on three of his albums, ***Rusty Tracks*** (1977), ***His Eye on the Sparrow*** (1978) and ***The Sailor*** (1979). In 1979, he also appeared on Marshall Chapman's ***Marshall*** album and Gary Stewart's ***Gary***.

Terry signed to RCA Victor as a solo performer in the early 80's, and anyone who saw him live echoed the comments made by the *Tennessean* newspaper, "a charismatic human motion machine." Although a good singer, Terry's deal with RCA didn't work out and he reverted to his session work. As well as his harmonica work, it was discovered that Terry was an excellent percussionist, and many of his sessions have him playing percussion rather than harmonica.

Over the years, he has worked with Ray Charles, Elvis Presley, J.J. Cale and virtually every recording artist in Nashville. He has also appeared on numerous TV specials, including *Live Aid* (with Neil Young), *The Chet Atkins Special* (Cinemax), *The Randy Travis/George Jones Special* (Showtime), *The Tonight Show* (with Garth Brooks), *The Garth Brooks Special* from Texas Stadium and numerous shows on the religious cable channel, Trinity Broadcast Network. He has also toured with Amy Grant, Michael McDonald, Michael W. Smith and Larry Carlton. During the 80's, he made his debut at the Wembley Festival in England.

Among his recent sessions are *Boot Scootin' Boogie (Dance Remix)* by Brooks & Dunn and Dolly Parton's *Romeo*. When he played on Garth Brooks' *Ain't Goin' Down ('Til the Sun Comes Up)*, producer Allen Reynolds told Terry to really "go for" the end tag. Terry did and both Allen and Garth were thunderstruck. "That's not humanly possible" was Allen's comment on Terry's playing.

In 1993, Terry was chosen by David Pack of Ambrosia to be a member of Packman's Dream Team Band, which performed at President Clinton's Arkansas inaugural ball. The rest of the band was Michael McDonald, Bruce Hornsby, Kenny Loggins, Carole King and Judy Collins. Terry played a stand-out version of *Amazing Grace* on harmonica.

In recent years, Terry has backed off his wild man image (although he still has a shaggy mop of red hair) and has found a closeness with God. This conversion came about at the end of 1992, when his house caught fire and his wife and children "barely got out alive." All of the Nashville music community waded in to help the McMillan family. "Dolly Parton gave us a place to stay over the Christmas holidays with a tree and everything. That's when you realize what counts," Terry recalled. "We lost all our 'stuff,' but what remains is love, hope, faith and friends."

In 1993, Terry released his first solo album, ***I've Got a Feeling,*** for Step One. This inspirational set has the famed Christchurch Choir from Nashville giving vocal support. He also appears as a duet artist on Larry Carlton's album ***Renegade Gentleman***. In 1994, Terry was the recipient of the ACM award in the "Specialty Instrument" category.

RECOMMENDED ALBUM:

"I've Got a Feeling" (Step One)(1993)

LARRY McNEELY

(Singer, Songwriter, Banjo, Guitar, Harmonica, Piano)

Given Name: Larry Paul McNeely
Date of Birth: January 3, 1948
Where Born: Lafayette, Indiana
Married: Elizabeth ("Bethe") M. Harris
Children: J.P., Martha

Larry McNeely may not have the high profile of the banjo greats, but for many years, he played with two of the legends of popular music, Roy Acuff and Glen Campbell.

Larry came from a musical family and he got his first piano lesson from his mother at age 13, but he maintained he wanted a guitar, which he got at age 14. A year later, however, as soon as he heard a 5-string banjo for the first time, he traded in his guitar and bought a "no name" instrument for $4.00. He would have paid $5.00, but the octave peg was missing for the fifth string.

Larry played around Lafayette and when he was 17, he joined the Pinnacle Mountain Boys and then in 1964, he left for Tennessee. He settled in La Follette for nine months and then in 1965, he relocated to Nashville. He started working for the Sho-Bud Guitar Company, where he met Roy Acuff. He joined Roy Acuff's Smoky Mountain Boys and stayed with him until 1969. Larry then moved to the West Coast, where he became a member of Glen Campbell's band, replacing John Hartford. The following year, he got married to Bethe.

Larry soon proved that he was not just a fine banjo player, but was also adept at harmonica. In 1971, he made his solo debut on Capitol with ***Glen Campbell Presents Larry McNeely***. Larry remained with Glen until 1974, but he wanted to cut back on road work. He recommended that Carl Jackson take his place in the band. Soon he was busy with studio work, including the 1977 Carpenters' album ***Passage***. He played on movie soundtracks, commercials and live dates. He also released ***Live at McCabe's*** on Takoma and ***Rhapsody for Banjo*** on Flying Fish, that year. On the latter album, he was supported by Charlie Collins (a fellow Smoky Mountain Boy and longtime associate of Larry's), Jethro Burns and Junior Husky. The following year, Larry got together with Geoff Levin and Jack Skinner for the Sheffield Lab direct-to-disc recording ***Confederation***.

Then in 1984, Larry decided to return to Nashville, where he spent a "non-profitable nine months in Bluegrass, where I was making a hundred dollars a week or less." He then rejoined Roy Acuff, staying with him until Mr. Roy's death in November 1992. Since then, Larry has played full-time with Russ and Becky Jeffers and Smoky Mountain Sunshine.

RECOMMENDED ALBUMS:

"Glen Campbell Presents Larry McNeely" (Capitol)(1971)
"Live at McCabe's" (Takoma)(1977)
"Rhapsody for Banjo" (Flying Fish)(1977)
"Confederation" (Sheffield Lab)(1978) [With Geoff Levin and Jack Skinner]

McPEAK BROTHERS, The

DEWEY McPEAK
(Vocals, Banjo, Guitar)
Given Name: Dewey McPeak
Date of Birth: August 12, 1941
Married: (Div.)
Children: Steve

LARRY McPEAK
(Vocals, Bass, Guitar)
Given Name: Larry James McPeak
Date of Birth: July 13, 1947
Married: Judy

MIKE McPEAK
(Lead Vocals, Guitar)
Given Name: Michael Eugene McPeak
Date of Birth: May 4, 1949
Married: Debbie
Children: Sammi

All Born: Wytheville, Virginia

For a quarter of a century, the McPeak Brothers have been a fine Bluegrass band from Wytheville, Virginia. They tended to be much influenced by the strong trio sound and mainstream Country-flavored brand of Bluegrass of the Osborne Brothers, who were a hot act in the later 60's. Still, they maintained a sufficient level of individuality in their style and were well received in the decade from about 1973 onward.

The McPeaks were all born and reared in the valley town of Wytheville, Virginia, where older brother Udell entered music in the mid-50's, working for a time with the Lonesome Pine Fiddlers in Pikeville, Kentucky, and then with Jimmy Williams at WCYB Bristol, Virginia. He, Dewey and Larry formed the first McPeak Brothers unit in 1963. However, Udell subsequently left them, later to go with Red Smiley and then with the Shenandoah Cut-Ups. Youngest brother Mike took his place on guitar and vocal lead.

By 1969, the McPeaks had a weekly program on the local WYVE radio with a couple of additional band members, fiddler

Ernest Atkins and mandolinist Gus Ingo, to fill out their ranks. They also played for various local functions, the numerous fiddlers' conventions in the region, and guested on TV in Bluefield and Roanoke. In 1970, they recorded a single and in 1972, they cut their first album for Dominion. The next year, they did a second album for Major and won first prize in the East Coast Bluegrass Championship competition. By that time, Mickey Connor had replaced Ingo on mandolin.

Through Ernest Atkins' friendship with Mel Tillis, the McPeaks secured both a guest spot on his syndicated TV show and a contract for an album with RCA Victor in 1974. While their major label affiliation tended to be brief, the brothers went on to cut three more albums for David Freeman, two on County and one on Rebel. Some of their solid trios were instrumentally supplemented by noteworthy studio musicians, including Ricky Skaggs, Jerry Douglas, Ricky Simpkins, and Jim Buchanan. Over the years the boys built a repertoire of songs that show signs of becoming standards among newer grass groups including *Somebody Socked It to Mine*, *The Last Time*, *Simon Crutchfield's Grave*, *Preachin' Up a Storm*, *Bend in the River* and *Bobbi*. Young bands such as Ohio's Rarely Herd, in particular, show a strong McPeak influence.

In the mid and late 80's, the McPeaks, who had never been full-time musicians, became more or less inactive, playing only locally. However, they have recently started to work more often and cut a new cd in 1992 for Commonwealth. In addition, Rebel released a cd containing a compendium of their best numbers for County and Rebel. IMT

RECOMMENDED ALBUMS:

"Virginia, Where It All Began" (Dominion)(1972)
"Bluegrass at Its Peak" (Major)(1973)
"Bluegrass at Its Peak" (RCA Victor)(1974) [Different album from the Major release]
"The McPeak Brothers" (County)(1977)
"Bend in the River" (County)(1978)
"Makin' Tracks" (Rebel)(1983)
"Classic Bluegrass" (Rebel)(1992)
"You Won't Ever Forget Me" (Commonwealth)(1992)

JOE MEADOWS

(Fiddle, Guitar)

Given Name: **Ralph Meadows**
Date of Birth: **December 31, 1934**
Where Born: **Basin, West Virginia**

In the 50's and early 60's, Joe Meadows earned respect as one of the finest traditional fiddlers in Country music. Then he dropped out of music for a decade but returned in 1973, having lost none of his youthful magic. Over the years, Joe served notable stints with such Bluegrass groups as the Stanley Brothers, Jim & Jesse, the Goins Brothers and Larry Sparks, as well as the Country vocalist Buddy Starcher.

A native of southern West Virginia, Meadows grew up listening to local fiddle players in the community as well as Curly Ray Cline of the Lonesome Pine Fiddlers on Bluefield radio, Leslie Keith with the Stanley Brothers at Bristol, and performers at the *Opry* such as Howdy Forrester, Benny Martin and Chubby Wise. Joe little knew that some day he would be ranked in the same quality with them.

From the age of 14, he started serious efforts to master the instrument. About 1950, he began his professional career with the Whispering Strings, a Western Swing radio band at nearby Princeton that worked a lot of square dances. After about six months, he moved to WHIS Bluefield, fiddling in the band of Rex and Eleanor Parker.

In August 1953, Ralph began playing fiddle for the equally youthful Melvin and Ray Goins, who were trying to make it on their own in Bluegrass. The boys struggled for four months trying to establish a name, but dissolved when Cousin Ezra Cline invited Melvin and Ray to join the Lonesome Pine Fiddlers. Ray Cline recommended Meadows to the Stanley Brothers at WCYB Bristol. At that time he became known as "Joe," since the Stanleys already had a Ralph in their group. During some two years as a Clinch Mountain Boy, Meadows played fiddle on several of their Mercury recordings, including such classic instrumentals as *Hard Times* and *Orange Blossom Special*, as well as vocal numbers like *Nobody's Love Is Like Mine*. Following this time with the Stanleys, Joe journeyed around a bit working for several months each with the Lilly Brothers, Bill Monroe, Jim & Jesse, Bill and Mary Reid and Buddy Starcher. He fiddled on some Starday recordings with both the Reids and Starcher.

For a decade from the early 60's, Joe dropped out of music almost completely except for an occasional contest or local appearance. In 1972, he played with the Goins Brothers at their Lake Stephens festival and the following February joined them on a regular basis. In the meantime he had already recorded a fiddle album with some local musicians, did another one for Jessup and subsequently, three as a sideman for the Goins Brothers (he later helped on a fourth).

Early in 1974, Joe moved to Larry Sparks' Lonesome Ramblers, doing several sessions with his band and cutting his third fiddle album (on Old Homestead), in a two-year period. However, Joe spent less than six months with Sparks. In all, 1973 and 1974 proved busy years for a fiddler who had spent the prior decade in relative musical obscurity.

In mid-1974, Joe Meadows rejoined Jim & Jesse's Virginia Boys, remaining with them for about four and a half years. During this time, he not only worked extensively with them on the *Grand Ole Opry* and the Bluegrass festival circuit, but did four albums with them in the studio and also their two-album set ***Live in Japan***, cut in 1975.

In that period, Joe recorded two more fiddle albums, a second effort for Old Homestead and another for Jim & Jesse's Old Dominion label. On a 1977 album, Meadows and a musical protege from Nicholas County, West Virginia, named Buddy Griffin did some twin-fiddling and also some lead guitar picking. Joe also promoted his own fiddlers' contest for three years, holding it twice in Princeton and once in Point Pleasant, West Virginia.

Weary of constant traveling, Joe Meadows left the Virginia Boys at the end of the 70's. In 1981 he cut two albums with an Illinois-based Bluegrass group, the Lost Kentuckians. For the better part of the 80's, Meadows lived and worked in the Washington, D.C., area holding a day job as a mail clerk. Content to fiddle part-time, he often got together with another famous West Virginia fiddler, Senator Robert C. Byrd and according to numerous reports, these two Mountain State fellows can really fiddle up a storm. IMT

RECOMMENDED ALBUMS:

"Ralph Meadows and His Blue Grass Fiddle" (Bluegrass)(1973)
"Ralph 'Joe' Meadows Rejoins Bluegrass" (Jessup)(1973)
"Portrait of a Fiddler" (Old Homestead)(1974)
"West Virginia Fiddler" (Old Homestead)(1977)
"Two O'Clock in the Morning" (Old Homestead)(1977) [Joe Meadows and Buddy Griffin]
"Super Fiddle" (Old Dominion)(1978)
"The Lost Kentuckians with Joe Meadows" (Old Homestead)(1981)
"No One to Welcome Me Home" (Old Homestead)(1981) [With the Lost Kentuckians]

Men of Kent refer J.T. ADAMS

MIDWESTERN HAYRIDE, The (a.k.a. BOONE COUNTY JAMBOREE and COUNTRY HAYRIDE)

(Radio/TV show, WLW Cincinnati, Ohio)

Cincinnati had a major radio/TV jamboree-type program from powerful WLW. Initially known as the *Boone County Jamboree* when it premiered in 1939 (following the departure of John Lair's *Renfro Valley Barn*

Dance for the hills of Kentucky), the program gained its most familiar name—*Midwestern Hayride*—in 1945. It continued on radio for several more years and also began on television on WLWT in 1948.

At times it had prime-time network TV exposure, primarily as a summer replacement, and under the name *Country Hayride* it continued locally and in syndication until 1974. Over the years the program had a hand in the development of those who gained national stardom, ranging from Merle Travis to Kenny Price. Other performers had a long association with the Queen City such as Bonnie Lou, the Luck Penny Trio, and Charlie Gore.

Powell Crosley's broadcasting empire, which dated from 1922, had some Country programming in the early days, including Bradley Kincaid, who first came there in 1930, but when John Lair brought several acts from WLS Chicago as the initial step in his *Renfro Valley Barn Dance* project in 1937, the station really went in for the format in a big way.

When Lair prepared to move his operation to his "Big Barn" near Mount Vernon, Kentucky (and WHAS Louisville became his "flagship" station), WLW management decided to enlarge their own talent roster, hiring George Biggar in September 1938 from WLS. They named their show the *Boone County Jamboree* and built their original talent roster around Millie and Dolly Good—the Girls of the Golden West (who had come to Cincinnati with Lair, but remained at WLW)—the Drifting Pioneers (which included a young Merle Travis), long-time stalwarts Ma and Pa McCormick, singing news comic Lazy Jim Day, and Hugh Cross, among others. Named for a just-across-the-river county in Kentucky, the *Boone County Jamboree* originally broadcast on Friday nights, but it soon moved to Saturday. Most of their stars also had daily shows as well.

During WWII some other name acts came to WLW, which proudly called itself "the Nation's Station," including Curly Fox and Texas Ruby, Hank Penny, Grandpa Jones and the Delmore Brothers. Lulu Belle and Scotty came over from Chicago for a time and Kincaid came back for three more years.

Biggar grouped Jones, Travis, and the Delmores together as the Brown's Ferry Four. When George became station Program Director, Bill McCluskey took over the show's direction. Other important performing figures included Roy Lanham and Bonnie Lou, a cowgirl singer who became a longtime favorite.

From 1948, the show was in part simulcast on both WLW radio and WLWT television. Periodically (1951-1959), the program was used as a summer replacement on the NBC and the ABC networks. In 1955-56, NBC ran a half-hour during their regular season when it moved to Wednesday, and Hugh Cherry served as emcee, an unpopular move as far as many cast members were concerned.

By then, a new wave of popular figures had joined the cast such as Ernie Lee, Kenny Roberts, Lee Jones, Charlie Gore, and duos such as the Turner Brothers, Helen and Billy Scott, and Herb and Kay Adams. The Lucky Penny Trio, composed in part of Dean and Penny Maxedon, was another popular group, and later well-liked performers included Neal Burris, Billy Holmes, Bobby Bobo and Clay Eager. Willie Thall, a one-time Prairie Rambler/Sweet Violet Boy, spent several years as an emcee. His removal in 1955 initiated a controversy of sorts. Later emcees included Paul Dixon, a daytime variety show host, and Dean Richards.

By the 60's, the program was carried only on TV. In 1969, the show became known as *Country Hayride* and Henson Cargill became the principal performer, then known for his hit *Skip a Rope*. After a season, Kenny Price took over and became the program's last star. Price had an earlier association with the show, several chart hits on Boone and RCA in this period, and an identity as "the round mound of sound."

As *Country Hayride*, the program was syndicated and remained until phased out in 1974. During much of its existence, the Hayride, like the *National Barn Dance*, featured more of a Midwestern soft Country sound, eschewing the harder hillbilly style associated with Appalachia. Bluegrass musicians and performers like Jimmie Skinner were generally kept at a distance by the WLW crowd although they sometimes mixed and mingled in certain circumstances. On the whole, however, through name changes and a thirty-five-year history, the *Midwestern Hayride* contributed a great deal to the Country scene in its day. IMT

MIKI & GRIFF

When Formed: 1950's

MIKI

(Singer, Songwriter, Poet, Keyboards)

Given Name: Barbara McDonald

Date of Birth: June 20

Where Born: Ayrshire, Scotland

Date of Death: April 1989

GRIFF

(Singer)

Given Name: Emyr Morus Griffith

Date of Birth: May 9, 1923

Where Born: Holywell, Wales

To the average Country music fan in the U.S., the names of the husband-and-wife team of Miki and Griff would bring a perplexed look. However, the importance of this couple from Britain is impossible to overstate. It is unlikely that the doors to Country music in Britain would have been opened without them. Their 1959 recording of *Hold Back Tomorrow* is widely considered to be the first real Country recording to hit the U.K. charts. Until 1989, when Miki died, the duo continued to be revered wherever they played; revered and truly loved.

Miki and Griff first met when they were both singers with the highly successful George Mitchell Choir. Miki had spent most of her early years on the beautiful Isle of Bute, while Griff was raised in the Welsh seaside town of Llandudno. They married in the early 50's and then joined Tom Arnold's Ice Spectacular at Wembley, England, as backing singers. They specialized in comedy vocals and in 1955, they went out on their own, playing with Johnny Dennis and His Ranchers, where Miki discovered her marvelous harmony skills.

They began experimenting with early Country material released by the Everly Brothers, and developing their own style. When they became a part of Skiffle King Lonnie Donegan's touring and TV show, Miki & Griff became very well known nationally. They also played overseas and on the way back from a tour of Australia, they stopped off in Nashville, where they picked up some locally written songs.

There then followed the success of *Hold Back Tomorrow* (one of the songs found in Nashville), which reached No.26 on the U.K. Pop chart. Initially there was a problem over their names (who was who), and to solve the public dilemma, Pye Records released the 4-track EP ***This Is Miki—This Is Griff***. The record contained *Rockin' Alone (In an Old Rocking Chair), I'm Here to Get My Baby Out of Jail, I Heard the Bluebirds Sing* and *A New Love*. The first-named track reached No.44 on the U.K. Pop chart and this led to the EP, after a slow start, to selling over a quarter of a million copies.

They released their first album for Pye in 1961 entitled ***Miki & Griff***, which contained the show-stopper *These Hands* and had musical backing from the Lonnie Donegan Group. In 1962, they reached No.16 with *A Little Bitty Tear*, which was overshadowed by Burl Ives' Top 10 version. The following year, they had another Top 30 hit with *I Wanna Stay Here*.

During the advent of Beatlemania, their popularity on TV and in concerts continued unabated and reached places as far afield as France, Cyprus, Australia, India, Africa, New Zealand, the West Indies, Malta, Germany and the U.S. Their success in the U.S. can be dated to their appearance on the *Grand Ole Opry* in 1965, at the Ryman Auditorium. Their appearance was arranged by their publishers, Acuff-Rose. Introduced by Roy Acuff (who had fun with their accents), the duo was tremendously well received and earned a standing ovation for their rendition of *My Baby's Gone*.

In 1974, Miki & Griff were named "Best Group" at the CMA (U.K.) Awards. For most of their career, they recorded for the Pye label (and its successor PRT), although during the late 60's they recorded two albums for Major-Minor Records, and in the late 80's, for the Scottish company BGS, on their Scotdisc label.

Miki, as well as enjoying gardening (in Twickenham, Middlesex), was also an adept writer of whimsical poetry, while Griff is an avid golfer. Her death brought to a close an important chapter in not only British Country music but Country music worldwide. If the Hall of Fame broadened its net to include important contributors to Country music from outside the U.S., then Miki & Griff would become charter members.

RECOMMENDED ALBUMS:

All U.K. releases, but worth getting a flight to London!
"Miki & Griff" (Pye)(1961)
"Two's Company" (Pye)
"Country Is Miki & Griff" (Pye)
"The Country Side of Miki & Griff" (Pye)
"Let the Rest of the World Go By" (Pye)
"This Is Miki—This Is Griff" (Pye)
"Golden Hour Presents Miki & Griff Rockin' Alone (In an Old Rocking Chair)" (Golden Hour)
"At Home with Miki & Griff" (Scotdisc)(1988)

DAVID MILLER

(Singer, Guitar)

Given Name:	**David Owen Miller**
Date of Birth:	**March 17, 1883**
Where Born:	**Nr. Ohio River, Ohio**
Married:	**1. Izora Estep (dec'd.)**
	2. (Dec'd.)
Children:	**David Jr., Vivian, William Callaway, Harold, Robert**

A street singer from Huntington, West Virginia, Davy Miller, known as the "Blind Soldier," ranked among the earliest Country vocalists on record. He also had a unique finger-picking guitar style. Miller also pioneered radio in the Mid-Ohio Valley and influenced a generation of later and better-known musicians from the Tri-state area who achieved national stardom.

Miller possessed normal eyesight as a child. Orphaned at an early age, he moved across the Ohio River to the Huntington suburb of Guyandotte in his teens. During WWI, he joined the West Virginia National Guard, but was discharged after a few months when doctors found his eyesight was rapidly failing. Becoming totally blind within a couple of years, the one-time laborer soon learned to play guitar and sing on the streets for his livelihood.

Miller made his first recording in Cincinnati for Gennett in December 1924, when with the aid of a local banjo picker named Cecil "Cobb" Adkins, he cut two sides, the only one released being a cover of Fiddlin' John Carson's *Little Old Log Cabin in the Lane*. He did not make discs again until 1927, by which time he had come under the management of William Callaway, an early A & R man who would also direct early recordings for the Huntington team of Frank Welling and John McGhee, Cliff Carlisle, and Gene Autry.

Miller later recorded for Paramount in 1929 and the ARC group of labels in 1931. Welling and McGee accompanied him on his Paramount sides and an unreleased Gennett session in April 1930. Some of the more significant numbers among his two dozen released sides included *It's Hard to Be Shut Up in Prison*, *My Little Indian Napanee*, *Sweet Floetta* (a variant of *The Jealous Lover*), *The Faded Coat of Blue* and a pair of fine guitar instrumentals.

The Blind Soldier was not only the first Country vocalist from the Mountain State but also the first radio singer. From 1926 to 1933, he sang with some regularity on station WSAZ and on a few occasions thereafter, often with a local string band called the Guyandotte Mockingbirds. He also sang regularly on the streets of Huntington and influenced some of the folks who worked on the station in the late 30's, including Cowboy Copas, Hawkshaw Hawkins and T. Texas Tyler. Miller's wife died in 1935 leaving him with five children, age 4 through 14. Dave spent his last years in Guyandotte in relative poverty although he managed to outlive a second wife. In recent years, four of his numbers have been reissued on various anthologies. IMT

FRANKIE MILLER

(Singer, Songwriter, Guitar)

Given Name:	**Frank Miller**
Date of Birth:	**December 17, 1931**
Where Born:	**Victoria, Texas**

Frankie Miller recorded some fine Texas Honky-Tonk music in the 50's and early 60's. Miller eventually faded into relative obscurity, perhaps because of his reported shyness concerning performing in public.

A native of south Texas, Frankie Miller had both the appearance and characteristics of the quintessential all-American boy. He did well in sports, especially basketball, boxing and football. The latter won him an athletic scholarship at Victoria Junior College. He also took an interest in Country music, organizing a band called the Drifting Texans, and began making regular visits to local radio station KNAL. He also did some guest spots at KLEE Houston, where he met Hank Locklin, who helped him get a contract with Guilt Edge Records, a subsidiary of 4 Star.

Frankie had five singles released from a session made in 1951 and then military service halted his musical career for two years. Frankie served with distinction in the Korean conflict, receiving the Bronze Star and attaining the rank of sergeant. He also got to do some entertaining while in the Army and wrote some songs.

Back from the war, Frankie Miller renewed his career by signing with Columbia. Between July 1954 and November 1955 he cut a dozen numbers in Jim Beck's Dallas studio, a locale which had been the scene of some of Columbia's best sessions for Lefty Frizzell. Although musically quite successful, none of Miller's five singles proved to be hits or strong sellers and Columbia failed to renew his contract for a third year. Frankie continued to appear on the *Cowtown Hoedown* on Fort Worth radio and played shows in Texas, recording one single each for the Cowtown Hoedown and Manco labels.

In 1959, Miller signed with Starday Records. The label's owner, Don Pierce, had admired his early efforts for Guilt Edge. Frankie's first cut, *Blackland Farmer,* a song with a rural values theme, became one of Starday's biggest sellers and won the writer considerable acclaim. It appeared on the Country charts initially in April 1959, went to Top 5 and subsequently came back in 1961 to peak in the Top 20 and cracked the lower echelons of the Pop listings as well. In 1971, Sleepy LaBeef had a Top 70 chart entry with the song. A second single, *Family Man*, also made the Top 10. Two other releases, *Baby Rocked Her Dolly* (Top 15, 1960) and *A Little South of Memphis* (Top 40, 1964), also made the Country chart.

Over a period of seven years, Miller had nearly 50 songs released on Starday. *Cash Box* selected him as "Most Promising Country Artist" in 1960 and for a time he appeared as a regular on the *Louisiana Hayride* and guested on both the *Grand Ole Opry* and the *Ozark Jubilee*.

By 1965, Frankie had cut a pair of singles for United Artists, but had apparently become disenchanted with Nashville and returned to the Dallas-Arlington-Ft. Worth area. In 1968, he had a single on the Stop label. Material from a session in 1979 was never released.

In 1992, Graham and Pauline Fincher reported that Frankie had spent the last two decades in the employ of Mid-City Chrysler of Arlington, Texas, presumably as Service Manager. Interest in his music continues high, however, particularly in Germany, where three albums of his work from Guilt Edge, Columbia and Starday have been reissued in recent years.

IMT

RECOMMENDED ALBUMS:

"Country Music's New Star" (Starday)(1961)
"The True Country Style of Frankie Miller" (Starday)(1962)
"Blackland Farmer" (Starday)(1965)
"Frankie Miller Sings" (Audio Lab)(1965) [Re-issued on Cowgirlboy Germany]
"Hey! Where Ya Goin?" (Bear Family Germany)(1981)
"Rockin' Rollin' Frankie Miller" (Bear Family Germany)(1983)

JODY MILLER

(Singer, Songwriter, Guitar)

Given Name: Myrna Joy Miller
Date of Birth: November 29, 1941
Where Born: Phoenix, Arizona
Married: Monty Brooks
Children: Robin

When Jody Miller made her recording debut in 1963, she was pioneering the merging of Folk and Pop music with Country. She became the first female star to successfully combine the contemporary musical stylings, with her Folk-influenced *Wednesday's Child Is Full of Woe*, for Capitol Records. Such groundbreaking recordings paved the way for artists like Linda Ronstadt and Nicolette Larson.

When Jody heard Joan Baez sing and play guitar, she knew that's what she wanted to do. At 14, she got a guitar and began learning her favorite Folk songs. Jody learned to sing from her mother and five older sisters, while her father played the fiddle for family sing-a-longs. Jody formed a Folk trio while a high school student in Blanchard, Oklahoma.

Jody's first professional performance was at Norman, Oklahoma's, Jester Coffee House on the campus of Oklahoma State University. She was discovered there by Lou Gotlieb of the popular Limelighters Folk group. Gotlieb was so impressed with her voice he offered to help her get a recording contract, if she would move to Los Angeles. However, Jody had recently married her high school sweetheart, Monty Brooks, and decided to stay in Oklahoma.

Eventually the urge to record prompted Jody and Monty to take a two-week vacation in California. The two weeks turned into a seven-year stay on the West Coast. It was actor Dale Robertson, a friend of Monty's, who got Jody an audition with Capitol Records. They offered her a contract and changed her name from Myrna Brooks to Jody Miller, suggesting that "Jody" fit the Folk music image they wanted for her. Her debut album for Capitol in 1963 was entitled ***Wednesday's Child Is Full of Woe***. The album was well received and earned Jody a regular spot on a TV show hosted by Folk music star Tom Paxton. Jody's first major success for Capitol was on the Pop chart with *He Walks Like a Man*, in 1964.

Jody Miller made the switch to Country music with an "answer" to Roger Miller's *King of the Road*, entitled *Queen of the House*. Jody was eight months pregnant with daughter Robin when she recorded the song. It became the biggest hit of her career, receiving heavy airplay on both Country and Pop radio in 1965 and that year, she received the coveted Grammy Award for "Best Country Vocal Performance, Female." Her follow-up release was *Silver Threads and Golden Needles*, which would later become a hit for Linda Ronstadt and become a Country standard. Jody's version of the song didn't catch on with radio, but the next release fared better. *Home of the Brave* reached the Top 20 late in 1965, in spite of its uptempo protest message. Jody followed her self-titled debut album with 1966's ***Great Hits of Buck Owens***. To support her recordings, Jody maintained a heavy performance schedule on stage and television, and she was a major attraction at the Riviera and Frontier nightspots in Las Vegas.

With dwindling success on record and wanting to spend more time with her family, Jody retired to her Oklahoma ranch in the late 60's. A few years later, she got the urge to record again and contacted Billy Sherrill at Epic Records in Nashville. Jody was a fan of the records he had produced for Tammy Wynette and wanted him to produce her. Their collaboration produced the Epic lp ***Look at Mine***, in 1971. Rather than recording strictly Country songs, Sherrill experimented with cutting some Pop songs with Jody backed with traditional Country instruments. The combination worked and Jody scored a Top 25 hit with *Look at Mine* in 1970. In 1971, Jody reached the Top 15 with *If You Think I Love You Now (I've Just Started)* and went Top 5 with *He's So Fine* (also going Pop Top 60 and earning Jody a Grammy nomination for her vocal performance) and *Baby I'm Yours* (Top 5, 1971), *Be My Baby* (Top 15) and *Let's All Go Down to the River* (with Johnny Paycheck, Top 15) (both 1972).

Jody continued her chart success in 1972 with the Top 5 single *There's a Party Goin' On* and the Top 20 reprise of *To Know Him Is to Love Him*. In 1972, Jody won *Billboard* magazine's "Artist Resurgence of the Year" Award.

Her other major hits on Epic were *Good News* (Top 10) and *Darling, You Can Always Come Back Home* (Top 5) (both 1973). Jody continued to record for Epic with producers Larry Butler and later Glenn Sutton. She stayed with the label until 1979 and her only other big hit was *When the New Wears Off the Old* (Top 25, 1977).

By the end of the 70's, Jody was disillusioned with her career and frustrated with the lack of radio success. Her concert appearances were falling off, so she decided to retire a second time from Country music to help her husband raise quarter horses and spend time with her teenage daughter. With no major plans to re-enter the business, Jody recorded an album of patriotic songs in 1987 on a local record label. Her ***My Country*** album found its way to presidential hopeful George Bush. When he was elected President, he invited Jody to perform at his 1988 Inaugural Ball.

When Jody's daughter, Robin, graduated from Oklahoma City University with a degree in music/theater, she encouraged her mother to consider returning to Country music with her as a duo. They began rehearsing and performed together at the 1989 State Fair in Oklahoma. Robin appeared in numerous musicals in college and also performed in the Opryland theme park and on the *General Jackson* Showboat. Jody came to Nashville in 1990 seeking a recording contract for the duo. She didn't secure a major label deal, but while in Nashville, co-hosted five shows of The Nashville Network's retrospective video show, *Country Standard Time* with Bill Anderson.

JIE

RECOMMENDED ALBUMS:

"Jody Miller Sings the Great Hits of Buck Owens" (Capitol)(1966)
"The Best of Jody Miller" (Capitol)(1973)
"House of the Rising Sun" (Epic)(1974)
"Will You Love Me Tomorrow" (Epic)(1976)

NED MILLER

(Singer, Songwriter, Guitar)

Given Name: Henry Ned Miller
Date of Birth: April 12, 1925
Where Born: Raines, Utah
Married: Sue
Children: Jack Henry, Lynda Sue, Karen Gean, Rhonda Louise, Lezlie Gwen

With just one song, *From a Jack to a King*, Ned Miller leapt into the international arena in 1962. From then until 1970, he had a total of 11 chart hits, including 3 crossover successes.

He was born in a little coal mining town in Utah and attended school in Murray and West Jordan, just outside Salt Lake City. He bought his first guitar at age 9, with money he earned cutting and selling firewood. He wrote his first songs when he was 16 and in his early years, sang at local parties and on local radio stations. After high school, he served three years in the U.S. Marines in the Pacific theater. After returning home, he studied air conditioning and refrigeration under the G.I. Bill at the Salt Lake City Vocational School, and worked as a journeyman fitter.

Ned became the manager of a taxicab company in Vernal, Utah, where he stayed for three years and at the same time, he and a friend had a 15-minute daily radio show on the local radio station. In 1956, he decided to fulfill his dream of being a songwriter, so he moved his family to California.

In the spring of 1957, Gale Storm took Ned's song *Dark Moon* to the Top 5 on the Pop charts, and Bonnie Guitar followed up with her version of the song and took it to the Top 15 on the Country charts. Both Bonnie and Gale recorded further Miller material, Bonnie following up her version of *Dark Moon* with *Mister Fire Eyes*.

Ned first started recording in 1957, when he released two singles for Dot. His initial release was the original version of *From a Jack to a King*. That year, Ned signed with Fabor Records and released his first single, *Roll O Rollin' Stone/Old Mother Nature*. However, it was not until 1962 that he achieved the chart break-through he had been seeking. The self-penned song *From a Jack to a King*, this time around, reached the Top 3 on the Country chart and crossed over to the Top 10 on the Pop lists. In addition, it attained a No.2 spot on the U.K. Pop charts. In 1963, he had two further Country hits, *One Among the Many* and *Another Fool Like Me*, which both reached the Top 30. That year, Ned won the Music Vendor Hit Award.

In 1964, Ned reached the Top 15 with *Invisible Tears*, which stayed around for over 5 months. The song was also a Pop hit for the Ray Conniff Singers, that year. As 1965 got under way, Miller had another career single with his self-penned *Do What You Do Do Well*, which was also recorded by Ernest Tubb. Ned's version reached the Top 10 and crossed over to peak in the Top 60 on the Pop chart. It also was a minor hit in the U.K. This was his last success on Fabor and later in the year, he signed with Capitol. His first success for the new affiliation was the Top 30 record *Whistle Walkin'*. He could, however, further rejoice that year with the success of Sonny James' version of Ned's *Behind the Tear*, which reached No.1.

Ned stayed with the label until 1968, during which time he had four further chart singles, *Summer Roses* (Top 40) and *Teardrop Lane* (Top 50), both in 1966, *Hobo* (Top 60, 1967) and *Only a Fool* (Top 60, 1967). He returned in 1970 with *The Lover's Song*, on Republic. In 1971, Hank Thompson recorded the Miller song *Next Time I Fall in Love (I Won't)*.

As a songwriter, Ned has often co-written with his wife, Sue, and cuts have included: *Just Before Dawn* (Johnny & Jonie Mosby), *Love By the Juke Box Light* (Gale Storm), *Have I Grown Used to Missing You* (Wanda Jackson), *Safely in Love Again* (Faron Young), *Next Time I Fall in Love (I Won't)* (Leon McAuliff), *Two Voices, Two Shadows, Two Faces* (Jean Shepard), *When Love Forgets to Die* (Ray Sanders), *Your Kind of People* (Porter Wagoner) and *The Change of the Tide* and *The Man Behind the Gun* (both Hank Snow). His name came back into the limelight in 1989, when Ricky Van Shelton resurrected *From a Jack to a King* and took it to No.1 on the Country charts.

RECOMMENDED ALBUMS:

"From a Jack to a King" (Fabor)(1963)
"The Best of Ned Miller" (Capitol)(1966)
"Ned Miller's Back" (Republic)(1970)
"From a Jack to a King" (Plantation)(1981)

ROGER MILLER

(Singer, Songwriter, Composer, Guitar, Fiddle, Drums, Humorist)

Given Name: Roger Dean Miller
Date of Birth: January 2, 1936
Where Born: Fort Worth, Texas
Married: 1. Barbara (div. 1966)
2. Leah Kendrick (div. 1974)
3. Mary Arnold
Children: Alan Douglas, Rhonda Darlene, Shari Dell, Roger Dean, Jr., Margaret (Taylor), Shannon Elizabeth, Adam Gray
Date of Death: October 25, 1992

There is no doubt that Roger Miller was unique. As a songwriter, he wrote cleverly, humorously and with a skill unsurpassed. As a singer, he had a voice that could immediately be identified. He was not a clone of anyone and that was one of his strengths. Roy Clark said of him, "When they made him, they threw away the gyroscope," while Miller said of himself, "When they made me, they smoked the mold." Although a consummate songwriter, Roger was never afraid of recording material by other great writers.

When Roger was 13 months old his father died, and his mother struggled to bring up Roger and his two brothers. Eventually, it proved too much and her husband's three brothers took a son each, with Roger going to his uncle Elmer on their two-mule cotton farm in Erick, Oklahoma, when he was age 3. Shortly after, Elmer's daughter married singer and actor Sheb Wooley, who became a great influence on Roger. When he was 5, Roger sang for the first time in public at Erick's one-room schoolhouse. He picked cotton to get enough money to buy a guitar, and when he was 11, he was given a fiddle by Wooley. The family was so poor that Roger didn't use a telephone until he was 17.

His first appearance outside of Erick was for Bill Mack in Delhi, Oklahoma, during the early 50's; however, Mack soon realized that Roger's skills on fiddle only reached to playing *Bile Dem Cabbage Down*. In 1956, Roger joined the U.S. Army and was shipped to Korea, and then he was assigned to a hillbilly band at Fort McPherson, Atlanta, through a Special Services officer. While in the Army, he met Jethro Burns' brother, Happy, who was a sergeant, who suggested that Roger should go to Nashville after leaving the Army. He also began a lifelong friendship with Bill Anderson, whom he'd met at Atlanta's Tower Theater. He left the service in 1956 and played in various Western Swing bands and the following year headed for Nashville.

On arriving in Music City, Roger became a bellhop at the Andrew Jackson Hotel (having allegedly stayed as a hotel guest the previous day). He began his songwriting career here and shortly after hitting town, he auditioned for Chet Atkins. He met George Jones and Pappy Dailey, who introduced him to Don Pierce of Mercury/Starday Records. Through him, Roger got his first cut when Jimmy Dean recorded *Happy Child*. By the fall of that year, Roger recorded his first single, *Poor Little John/My Pillow*, which sank without trace. His second single, on Starday, *You're Forgetting Me/Can't Stop Loving You*, was equally unsuccessful.

Shortly after arriving in Nashville, Roger

The King of the Road, **Roger Miller**

joined Judy Lynn's band as fiddler and the band backed Minnie Pearl on tour. While touring, he became friends with Mel Tillis. He also met Buddy Killen, who was instrumental in Miller's signing to Tree Publishing, where he stayed all his life. However, soon Roger left Nashville for Amarillo, Texas, where he worked as a fireman but got fired after two months because he fell asleep on the job and missed two fires.

While in Amarillo, Roger joined Ray Price's Cherokee Cowboys. In 1958, Price recorded the Miller song *Invitation to the Blues* (the top side was Bill Anderson's *City Lights*). This led to Ernest Tubb recording *Half a Mind,* Faron Young cutting *That's the Way I Feel* and Porter Wagoner recording *Dear Lonesome.* Buddy Killen got Roger onto Decca, where he duetted with both Donny Young (Johnny Paycheck) and Justin Tubb.

In 1959, Roger had hits through *Big Harlan Taylor* (George Jones), *Billy Bayou* and *Home* (both Jim Reeves) and *Last Night at a Party* (Faron Young). Johnny Paycheck, then known as Donny Young, had his first mini-hit with Miller's *Old Man and the River.* Roger also recorded a pair of singles for Decca, without success. The following year, Ray Sanders had a hit with *World So Full of Love,* which was a hit again in 1961 for Faron Young. Roger had his first Country chart single, in 1960, with *You Don't Want My Love,* which was released on RCA. This was the first Miller track to feature the trademark "scat" singing. The flipside, *Footprints in the Snow,* had long been associated with Bill Monroe, and this was the start of Roger's experimentation with Bluegrass-to-Country. *You Don't Want My Love* was also a Pop hit for Andy Williams. Both Jan Howard and Jaye P. Morgan recorded *A World I Can't Live In,* without success.

In 1961, Roger had a Top 10 hit with *When Two Worlds Collide,* which he had written with Bill Anderson. Miller also had a hit through Claude Gray's recording of *My Ears Should Burn (When Fools Are Talked About).* In 1962, Roger moved over to join Faron Young's band. Miller had his final hit for RCA, in 1963, with *Lock, Stock and Teardrops.*

The following year, Roger decided to move to Hollywood, to study acting. At the same time, he signed to Smash Records, and there his recording career took off and forced him to abandon any ideas of being an actor. From the album ***Roger and Out*** (which was later renamed ***Roger Miller Featuring Dang Me (& The New Hit Chug-a-Lug)***, came the monster hit *Dang Me,* which went to No.1 on the Country chart and Top 10 on the Pop list. It was followed by *Chug-a-Lug,* which went Top 3 on the Country list and Top 10 Pop.

At the 1964 Grammy Awards, Roger won five awards for "Best Country & Western Single" (*Dang Me*), "Best Country & Western Album" (***Roger Miller***), "Best Country & Western Vocal Performance, Male," "Best Country & Western Song" (*Dang Me*) and "Best New Country & Western Artist." He closed out the year with *Do-Wacka-Do,* which went Top 15 Country and Top 40 Pop. His songs continued to be recorded by other artists and that year Johnny Wright charted with *Walkin', Talkin', Cryin', Barely Beatin' Broken Heart,* which Highway 101 reprised in 1990, and which gave them a Top 5 hit.

It was with the first single of 1965 that Roger firmly established himself as an international star, when he created a song that became a classic. *King of the Road* went to the top of the Country charts and made the Top 5 on the Pop list and went Gold. It also topped the National charts in the U.K. That year, he couldn't do wrong; he had *Engine Engine #9* (Top 3 Country/Top 10 Pop), *One Dyin' and a Buryin'* (Top 10 Country/Top 40 Pop), *Kansas City Star* (Top 10 Country/Top 40 Pop) and *England Swings* (Top 3 Country/Top 10 Pop). At the 1965 Grammy Awards, Roger won an unprecedented six awards. For *King of the Road,* he won "Best Contemporary (R & R) Single," "Best Country & Western Single," "Best Country & Western Performance, Male," "Best Country & Western Song" and "Best Contemporary (R & R) Vocal Performance, Male." His album ***The Return of Roger Miller*** was named "Best Country & Western Album." In addition, Jody Miller's "answer" song, *Queen of the House,* netted her the Grammy for "Best Country & Western Vocal Performance, Female."

With the arrival of 1966, Roger had a Top 5 success (Top 30 Pop) with *Husbands and Wives* (the flip-side, *I've Been a Long Time Leavin' (But I'll Be a Long Time Gone),* going Top 15). Then suddenly, he wasn't hitting so high, and *You Can't Roller Skate in a Buffalo Herd* only reached the Top 40, although it crossed over to the Pop Top 40, as well. His other hits of the year were *My Uncle Used to Love Me But He Died* (Top 40 Country/Top 60 Pop) and *Heartbreak Hotel* (Top 60 Country/Top 90 Pop). During the year, he had his own *Roger Miller Show* on NBC-TV, but it was canceled before the end of the season, as his performance was being swamped by dancers and other things that the directors felt he needed to project him, and also by Roger's own drug problems.

His recording career enjoyed a resurgence in 1967, with the Top 10 Country hit *Walkin' in the Sunshine* (it also went Top 40 Pop) and the Top 30 single the *Ballad of Waterhole #3 (Code of the West),* which came from the movie *Waterhole #3.* The following year, Roger had his last Top 10 single, Bobby Russell's *Little Green Apples,* which also made the Top 40 on the Pop list (his last major Pop hit). His other hit of the year was *Vance,* which went Top 15. That year, Diana Trask reprised Roger's *Lock, Stock and Teardrop* and had a Top 70 hit.

In 1969, RCA released Jim Reeves' version of Roger's *When Two Worlds Collide,* and had a Top 10 hit with it. Roger had two Top 20 singles, *Me and Bobby McGee* and *Where Have All the Average People Gone.* From then on, his major hits were 1970: *The Tom Green County Fair, South/Don't We All Have the Right*; 1971: *Tomorrow Night in Baltimore, Loving Her Was Easier (Than Anything I'll Ever Do Again)*; 1972: *We Found It in Each Other's Arms.*

He had been switched from Smash to the parent Mercury label in 1970, and in 1973, he moved over to Columbia and had the Top 15 hit *Open Up Your Heart,* that year. His other big hit for the label, also in 1974, was entitled *I Believe in the Sunshine.* That year, he narrated the voice of the Rooster in the Disney animated version of *Robin Hood,* and the song *Whistle Stop* from the movie made the Top 90. (Roger strongly felt that his music should reach children as well as adults.) Around the time of his second divorce, in 1974, his "Kings of the Road" motor inns failed.

Loretta Lynn released her version of *Home* in 1975 and had a Top 10 hit with it. Roger moved over to Windsong Records, in 1977, without major success and then two years later, he signed with 20th Century, with the same result. Jerry Lee Lewis had a major hit, in 1980, with his version of *When Two Worlds Collide*, and the following year, David Frizzell and Shelly West had a Top 20 hit with *Husbands and Wives*. That year, Roger had a Top 40 single on Elektra, entitled *Everyone Gets Crazy Now and Then*. This was a most appropriate title, as Roger (like all geniuses), who was totally lovable, could also be more than a little unpredictable, earning the sobriquet "the Wild Child" and being referred to as "one of the great iconoclasts and eccentrics in Country music—indeed, in any form of music."

Roger teamed up with Willie Nelson and Ray Price, in 1982, and hit the Top 20 with *Old Friends*. When he wrote the Broadway musical *Big River*, based on Huckleberry Finn, Roger had not written for 5 years. He created the musical in eighteen months, and the result was a show that netted 7 Tony Awards. From this musical, Roger had the Top 40 single *River in the Rain*, on MCA. When the show played Nashville's Tennessee Performing Arts Center (built on the old Andrew Jackson Hotel site), in 1988, Roger played the role of Pap. His final chart entry was in 1986, entitled *Some Hearts Get All the Breaks*.

His songs continued to be recorded in the late 80's, and Ricky Van Shelton had a No.1 with *Don't We All Have the Right* and k.d. lang scored with *Lock, Stock and Teardrop*, both in 1988. The following year, Andy Lee Smith took *Invitation to the Blues* back into the lists.

In 1991, Roger was diagnosed with cancer in his throat, and on October 25, 1992, he succumbed. Merle Travis once stated that he rated Roger Miller above Hank Williams. That has to be the highest praise.

RECOMMENDED ALBUMS:

"Roger Miller Featuring Dang Me (& The New Hit Chug-a-Lug)" (Smash)(1964)
"The Return of Roger Miller" (Smash)(1965)
"Roger Miller—The Third Time Around" (Smash)(1965)
"Roger Miller 1970" (Smash)(1970)
"Dear Folks, Sorry I Haven't Written Lately" (Columbia)(1973)
"Off the Wall" (Windsong)(1977)
"Painted Poetry" (Starday)(1977)
"Making a Name for Myself" (20th Century)(1979)
"Old Friends" (Columbia)(1982) [With Willie Nelson and Ray Price]

RONNIE MILSAP

(Singer, Songwriter, Keyboards, Violin, Guitar, Woodwinds)

Where Born:	**Robbinsville, North Carolina**
Married:	**Joyce (m. 1965)**
Children:	**Todd**

Over the last twenty-five years, Ronnie Milsap has proved to be one of the most enduring performers in Pop-Country. His musical style has been one of constant experiment between Country-Rock, Blues and even Soul.

Coming from a family of Baptists and authentic hillbillies, Ronnie grew up with his father and grandparents, following his parents' marriage break-up. Ronnie was born blind with congenital glaucoma and from the age of 5, he attended Governor Moorhead School for the Blind. At this time, he discovered an aptitude for music and from age 7, he studied music while at school. He was grounded in the classics and his favorite composers were Mozart and Bach. He considers that his early influence was Wallace Greaves, his first violin teacher, who opened up the world of music for Ronnie and who worked with him for eight years. Up to then, Ronnie had listened to Country and Bluegrass music (he would later be influenced by rockers such as Little Richard). Before he was 8, Ronnie had become a violin virtuoso and by the time he was 8, he had also mastered the piano. He added guitar to his instrumental arsenal. He later went on to play all keyboards, string instruments, percussion and woodwinds.

Ronnie started his own 4-piece Rock group, the Apparitions, while at school. He studied pre-law at Young Harris Junior College in Atlanta, Georgia. Ronnie won a full scholarship to Emory University, but he opted for music. He became a sideman for J.J. Cale and in 1965, formed his own band. During this time, he made his first records for Scepter. His first single for the label was *Never Had It So Good*, which became an R & B hit in 1965. He moved to Memphis in late 1969 and played keyboards on several records, especially for producer Chips Moman, including Elvis Presley's recording of *Kentucky Rain*, and sang harmony on Elvis' recording of *Don't Cry Daddy*. He also played on sessions for Petula Clark and Dionne Warwick. In addition, he and his band were resident at TJ's Club in Memphis.

Ronnie stayed with Scepter until 1970, at which point he moved to Moman's Chips label and had his first Pop entry with *Loving You Is a Natural Thing*. The following year, he turned up on Warner Brothers Records and recorded his first self-titled album for the label in 1971. By 1973, Ronnie felt that he was treading water career-wise and moved to Nashville. He became resident at Roger Miller's King of the Road motel and signed a management deal with Jack D. Johnson, who also looked after Charley Pride. Ronnie also made contact with Tom Collins, who was, at the time, Vice President at Pi-Gem Music and Gemini Productions. Tom would play a major part in Ronnie's career, as producer and provider of hit material. That year, Ronnie signed to RCA Victor Records and embarked on one of the major careers of Country music.

His first single, *I Hate You*, reached the Top 10 on the Country chart, and the follow-up, *That Girl Who Waits on Tables*, peaked in the Top 15. In 1974, Ronnie became a major act when all three of his hits of the year reached No.1, starting with Eddie Rabbitt's *Pure Love*, continuing with *Please Don't Tell Me How the Story Ends* and closing out with Don Gibson's *(I'd Be) A Legend in My Time*. In 1975, Ronnie continued his winning ways with the Top 10 record *Too Late to Worry, Too Blue to Cry* and followed up with another No.1, *Daydreams About Night Things*. Warner Brothers released *She Even Woke Me Up to Say Goodbye*, and such was the Milsap appeal by this time that this single reached the Top 15. A month later, RCA released the next "official" single, *Just in Case*, and that made it to the Top 5.

Ronnie then embarked on a No.1 spree that carried him from 1976 into 1978. He had seven consecutive chart toppers, which were also supplemented by a pair of Warner Brothers low level entries. In 1976, he had *What Goes on When the Sun Goes Down*, *(I'm A) Stand By My Woman Man* and *Let My Love Be Your Pillow*. The following year, there was *It Was Almost Like a Song* (which crossed over to the Pop chart's Top 20) and *What a Difference You've Made in My Life*. For three weeks, *Only One Love in My Life* topped the charts in 1978 and was followed by *Let's Take the Long Way Around The World*. The third single of the year, *Back on My Mind Again*, reached the the Top 3 position. In 1979, Ronnie hit the top of the charts with *Nobody Likes Sad Songs* and he followed this with the Top 10 hit *In No Time at All*, which was also a Top 50 Pop hit. During this year, Ronnie appeared at the Wembley Festival in England.

As the 80's arrived, so Ronnie had another remarkable run of No.1 records from 1980 through 1982. He had 10 consecutive chart toppers starting with *Why Don't You Spend the Night* and racked up three more No.1s in 1980, *My Heart*, *Cowboys and Clowns* and *Smoky Mountain Rain* (a Top 30 Pop hit). In 1981, he had *Am I Losing You*, *(There's) No Gettin' Over Me* (a Pop Top 5 hit) and *I Wouldn't Have Missed It for the World*. In 1982, Ronnie continued with *Any Day Now* (a Pop Top 15 entry), *He Got You* and *Inside*. Ronnie's first single of 1983, the title track from his ***Stranger***

in My House album, went Top 5 and he followed up with two more No.1s that year, *Don't You Know How Much I Love You* and *Show Her* and one in 1984, *Still Losing You*. He wrapped up 1984 with the Top 10 record *Prisoner of the Highway*. That year, Ronnie received an Honorary Doctorate of Laws degree from Adrian College, Adrian, Michigan.

With *She Keeps the Home Fires Burning*, he began another chart-topping run. This time, he reeled off eight consecutive No.1s taking him to the end of 1987. His other No.1 in 1985 was *Lost in the Fifties Tonight (In the Still of the Night)*. This was followed by *Happy, Happy Birthday Darling*, *In Love* and *How Do I Turn You On* during 1986. His first No.1 in 1987 was *Snap Your Fingers* and he followed this with a duet with Kenny Rogers, *Make No Mistake, She's Mine*, which had been a "female" hit for Barbra Streisand and Kim Carnes, two years earlier. Ronnie wrapped up the year with his 50th Country hit and his 33rd No.1, *Where Do the Nights Go*.

By the middle of the 80's, Ronnie was working less and less with Tom Collins and more and more with Ron Galbraith, and by the end of the decade, the Milsap-Galbraith production team was at the helm of Ronnie's Groundstar Laboratories recording studio and was heading toward a full partnership.

Ronnie teamed up with Mike Reid in 1988, for the Top 3 hit *Old Folks* and Ronnie followed it with the Top 5 single *Button Off My Shirt*. He closed the year with another No.1, *Don't You Ever Get Tired (Of Hurting Me)*. During the year, Ronnie had vocal gland problems and was forced to pull out of the Peterborough Festival in England at the insistence of Dr. Richard Quisling, who had Ronnie undergo surgery to save his vocal glands. He got things under way in 1989 with the Top 5 hit *Houston Solution* and followed up with his 35th No.1, *A Woman in Love*.

During 1990, he only had one chart entry, *Stranger Things Have Happened*, from the album of the same name. The single reached the Top 3 and stayed on the charts for 6 months. Ronnie weathered the new influx of artists in 1991 and still had a good year with *Are You Lovin' Me Like I'm Lovin' You* (Top 3), *Since I Don't Have You* (Top 10) and *Turn That Radio On* (Top 5). The three singles came from the album ***Back to the Grindstone***, which also featured a duet with Patti Labelle, *Love Certified* (a very "non-Country" track).

However, 1992 indicated some falling off, when *All Is Fair in Love and War* only reached the Top 15 and *L.A. to the Moon* just made the Top 50. The following year, Ronnie ended his long association with RCA and moved to Liberty Records. ***True Believer*** was the first album under this new association and is a most delicious release, with *Better Off with the Blues*, the title track, and the standard *These Foolish Things (Remind Me of You)* being standout tracks. The title track reached the Top 30.

Ronnie Milsap is a much awarded performer and he is the recipient of six Grammy Awards for "Best Country Vocal Performance, Male" for *Please Don't Tell Me How the Story Ends* (1974), *(I'm A) Stand By My Woman Man* (1976), *(There's) No Gettin' Over Me* (1981), *Lost in the Fifties Tonight (In the Still of the Night)* (1985), the album ***Lost in the Fifties Tonight*** (1986) and *Make No Mistake, She's Mine* (1987). In 1975, *Music City News* Cover Awards made him their "Most Promising Male Artist." The CMA has made Ronnie its "Male Vocalist of the Year" on three occasions, 1974, 1976 and 1977. He was named their "Entertainer of the Year" in 1977. He has also won the Award for "Best Album of the Year" on four occasions, for ***A Legend in My Time*** (1975), ***Ronnie Milsap Live*** (1977), ***It Was Almost Like a Song*** (1978) and ***Lost in the Fifties Tonight*** (1986). He has also received the 1982 "Top Male Vocalist" Award from the ACM and his recording of *Lost in the Fifties Tonight (In the Still of the Night)* helped writers Mike Reid-Troy Seals/Fred Paris to the ACM "Song of the Year" Award in 1985.

In addition, five of Ronnie's albums have been Certified Gold: ***It Was Almost Like a Song*** (1978), ***Only One Love in My Life*** (1978), ***Ronnie Milsap Live*** (1979), ***There's No Gettin' Over Me*** (1981) and ***Lost in the Fifties Tonight*** (1990). His ***Greatest Hits*** album was Certified Double Platinum in 1989, while ***Greatest Hits, Volume 2*** went Platinum in 1990 and his video collection ***Great Video Hits*** was Certified Gold in 1990. Ronnie appeared in the NBC-TV Movie of the Week *Murder in Music City*.

Ronnie has said that "in some ways it's a blessing that I was born blind...if I had been born sighted in western North Carolina...I certainly wouldn't be doing what I'm doing now." In 1980, Ronnie had his right eye removed by surgeons at Duke University Medical Center. He was awake and joking during the 105-minute operation. Ronnie has given back for those early years of guidance. In 1986, the Ronnie Milsap Cottage was dedicated at his former alma mater. In addition, the Ronnie Milsap Foundation was created to aid the blind and visually impaired. The foreword of *The Texbook of Glaucoma* by Dr. Bruce Shields is dedicated to Ronnie.

RECOMMENDED ALBUMS:

"It Was Almost Like a Song" (RCA Victor)(1977)
"Only One Love in My Life" (RCA Victor)(1978)
"There's No Gettin' Over Me" (RCA Victor)(1981)
"Ronnie Milsap Live" (RCA Victor)(1982)
"Greatest Hits" (RCA Victor)(1984)
"Greatest Hits, Volume 2" (RCA Victor)(1985)
"Lost in the Fifties Tonight" (RCA Victor)(1986)
"Stranger Things Have Happened" (RCA)(1989)
"Greatest Hits, Volume 3" (RCA)(1992)
"True Believers" (Liberty)(1993)
For very early Ronnie Milsap tracks, listen to the Hit-Kickers Series on Festival Records, which was released in 1976. He is featured on several tracks that come from Gold Records, Platinum Voices, Dade Records, Goldcoast Associates, Northern Voices & Lighthouse Investments and Andasol Records & Cinema Finance Associates.

Ronnie Milsap** (left) with **Kenny Rogers

MINNIE PEARL

(Comedy, Piano)
Given Name: Sarah Ophelia Colley
Date of Birth: October 25, 1912
Where Born: Centerville, Tennessee
Married: Henry Cannon

Minnie Pearl has been the premier comedienne on the *Grand Old Opry* and in all of Country music. For half a century, "Miss Minnie," the man-hungry old maid from Grinder's Switch, has delighted both rural and urban audiences with her brand of down-home humor. Throughout her entire career, the character known as "Minnie Pearl" lived her private life as the epitome of middle-class southern womanhood who eventually resided next door to the Governor of Tennessee.

Howdy, it's Miss ***Minnie Pearl***

Born in Centerville, Tennessee, the daughter of a prosperous sawmill owner and lumber dealer, Sarah Colley grew up as a town girl. Her father's business encountered tough times in the Great Depression, but she managed to get in two years of education at Ward-Belmont Finishing School.

For most of the next eight years, she toured the South, organizing amateur musicals and dramatic productions for the Sewell Company. During this experience she began to develop her "Minnie Pearl" routine. The job for Sewell Productions terminated in the spring of 1940 and Sarah returned to Centerville broke and unemployed. That fall, she successfully auditioned "Minnie" for the *Opry* . Minnie's stature as an *Opry* performer increased steadily through the 40's, especially after she became a regular feature on the network portion of the program.

Perhaps because of her education and middle-class background, Minnie Pearl gained a degree of acceptance and respectability from the establishment that most people connected with Country music lacked. At the same time, the under-schooled musicians with whom she traveled and worked gained considerable respect for her as well. Veteran tent-show comic Rod Brasfield appeared with Minnie for a decade or so on the *Prince Albert* portion of the *Opry* and later on the syndicated Gannaway Productions television programs in the mid-50's, where their contrasting portrayals of differing bucolic types found wide favor with Country fans.

Minnie Pearl also made periodic guest appearances on network television, and in the mid-50's became one of the only people in Country music honored as a subject on the NBC network's popular *This Is Your Life* program hosted by Ralph Edwards.

Unlike Brasfield, Minnie also enjoyed a singing career of sorts, albeit mostly in a comic vein. She played piano and either sang outlandishly off-key renditions of Country standards like *Jealous Hearted Me* or songs designed to reinforce her image such as *How to Catch a Man (On the Minnie Pearl Plan)*, which she recorded for RCA Victor. Minnie also did five duet numbers with Grandpa Jones in 1954 and 1955, typified by such fare as *Kissin' Games*. Later, she recorded comedy albums for Starday and had a Top 10 hit with her *Giddy-up Go Answer*, in 1966. But mostly Minnie delighted *Opry* and road-show audiences with gossip about mythical characters at Grinder's Switch: "Brother," "Uncle Nabob" and "Aunt Ambrosia," her "feller" "Hezzie," and others. Minnie's not-quite-successful encounters with strange men and various Country music personalities also became parts of her routines.

In addition to her *Opry* work, Minnie also appeared as a *Hee Haw* regular for several seasons in a variety of skits including "Grandpa and Minnie's Kitchen." In 1975, she became the first person elected to the Country Music Hall of Fame for comedy work. In 1980, Minnie authored a successful autobiography. In the early days of TNN, she often appeared on talk shows. Her ability to reminisce with authority about the classic years of the *Opry* in the 40's and 50's could usually hold audience interest both there and in a variety of documentaries.

From the mid-80's, however, she was dogged with bouts of ill health. She survived a cancer operation in 1985, a bad fall in 1989 and heart surgery in 1990, only to suffer a stroke the following year. As of November 1993, she resides in a nursing home, but Minnie Pearl's position as the all-time Queen of Hillbilly Comedy remains secure. IMT

RECOMMENDED ALBUMS:
"Howdee: The Gal from Grinder's Switch at the Party" (Starday)(1963)
"America's Beloved Minnie Pearl" (Starday)(1965)
"The Country Music Story" (Starday)(1966)
"Howdy!" (Sunset)(1967)
"Lookin' for a Feller" (Nashville)(1969)
Grandpa Jones & Minnie Pearl:
"Grand Ole Opry Stars" (RCA)(1974)

JOEY MISKULIN

(Singer, Songwriter, Accordion, Record Producer)
Given Name: Joseph Michael Miskulin
Date of Birth: January 6, 1949
Where Born: Chicago, Illinois
Married: Pat
Children: Joey, John, Michael, Katherine

Joey Miskulin started playing the accordion when he was 4 years old. He began by playing the simple melodies he heard on his grandfather's Polka records. His parents were so impressed with his natural ability that they enrolled him in formal musical training when he was 5. Joey excelled at his accordion playing and within a few years he was performing at picnics and social functions. When he was 11, Joey joined the Ronnie Lee Band and the following year made his first record with Chicago favorite Roman Possedi. Although he mostly played Polka music in his early years, Joey's musical influences included the big band sounds of Benny Goodman and Artie Shaw. He also enjoyed Rhythm and Blues and the Country music he heard on the WLS *National Barn Dance*.

Crown Prince of the accordion ***Joey Miskulin***

In 1962, Joey came to the attention of "America's Polka King," Frank Yankovic. The Polka star invited 13-year-old Joey to join his popular touring band and Joey spent the next 13 years on the road with Yankovic. Yankovic convinced the executives at Columbia Records to let Joey record with him. Working in the studio with Yankovic convinced Joey of his life's mission: "I think it was the first recording session with Frank that helped make up my mind. I wanted to make music my career."

Joey left Yankovic briefly when he was 19 to tour with the Hawaii International Revue. After performing in Hong Kong, Japan, Thailand, Vietnam and Okinawa, Joey rejoined Yankovic. Over the next several years, Joey played on five more albums with him. Some of the recording was done in Nashville at the famed RCA studio, and that was Joey's introduction to the city.

When he was not touring or recording with Yankovic, Joey made his home in Cleveland, Ohio. His expert skill on the accordion brought him studio work with many other artists, including Andy Williams, Doc Severinsen and Charlie Daniels. For six years Joey owned and operated his own nightclub that featured a variety of musical styles from Polka to Jazz to Country. He also hosted his own weekly TV show on the CBS affiliate, WCLQ.

In the 1980's Miskulin was producing records as well as playing on them. His longtime friend Frank Yankovic enlisted his talents for his 1985 ***70 Years of Hits*** album. It became the first Polka recording to be awarded a Grammy by NARAS.

Miskulin was encouraged to move to Nashville in 1987 by record executive Steve Popovich. The two had been friends for many years and Popovich had moved from Cleveland to head up Polygram Records in Nashville. Popovich introduced Joey to legendary Nashville producer Jack "Cowboy" Clement, who hired him to play on some Johnny Cash sessions.

The Western music trio Riders in the Sky invited Joey to record with them and liked the sound so well they asked him to join them on stage. When they launched their weekly show for National Public Radio, the Riders dubbed Joey the "Cow-Polka King" on their *Riders Radio Theater*. Miskulin's work with the Riders in the Sky brought him in contact with other Western artists including Don Edwards, the Sons of the San Joaquin and Waddie Mitchell.

In the 90's, Joey's role as a producer expanded when he teamed up with Michael Martin Murphey to produce a series of albums for the Warner Western label. Joey also produced Murphey's 1993 release ***Cowboy Songs III/ Rhymes of the Renegades***. In addition to producing Murphey, Joey played on his recordings and did some limited touring with him. Other artists who have called on Joey to play on their records include Crystal Gayle, Emmylou Harris, Sammy Kershaw, Brenda Lee, Loretta Lynn, Tammy Wynette, Ricky Skaggs, Marty Stuart and Hank Williams, Jr.

Miskulin has been awarded Platinum Albums for his work with Garth Brooks, Dolly Parton, Ricky Van Shelton and Andrej Sifer. Joey appeared in the motion picture *Rattle and Hum*, performing with U2, and has performed on a variety of TV shows including *The Tonight Show* and the *Phil Donahue Show*.

JIE

RECOMMENDED ALBUMS:

(See Frank Yankovic and albums on the Warner Western label.)

WADDIE MITCHELL

(Poet)

Given Name:	**Bruce Douglas Mitchell**
Date of Birth:	**1950**
Where Born:	**Elko, Nevada**
Married:	**Tudi Martin (div.)**
Children:	**Chaz, Sage, Cy, Seth, Shade**

From the vast cattle ranches of the Wild West to Johnny Carson's *Tonight Show*, Waddie Mitchell brought the age-old art of cowboy poetry to millions. Without guitars, banjos, or fiddles, he tells the tales of the cowboy with humor, nostalgia, and keen insight.

Born Bruce Douglas Mitchell, his father named him "Waddie," which is slang for cowboy. He grew up on the Horseshoe Ranch, thirty-six miles south of Elko, Nevada. The massive cattle ranch was fourteen miles from the nearest neighbor and thirty miles to a paved road. As a child he was fascinated by the tales the cowboys told and by age 10, he could recite a dozen poems. When he was 16, he quit school to be a full-time cowboy. He ranched and roped and pulled a chuck wagon (traveling meals) until he was drafted into the Army. Even his service for Uncle Sam was in the cowboy business. Waddie was stationed at Fort Carson, Colorado, on the Army's 24,000-acre ranch where he broke horses and trained them for the U.S. Cavalry. He was also a member of the Cavalry team that traveled to rodeos and rode out on drill teams.

Waddie Mitchell's first national exposure came in the early 80's with the PBS television documentary *The Vanishing Breed*. The program chronicled the last of the real cowboys in America. The television crew traveled to the ranch where Waddie was a foreman, located a hundred miles from the nearest town. According to Waddie in a personal interview in June 1993, "There was no electricity, TVs, or telephones and we'd do the strangest thing at night....we'd sit around and talk to each other. When you're living like that, and all the rest of the cowboys that were working for me there, we'd sit around and have bull sessions and that's really your entertainment, your socializing for the night." Some of Waddie's poetry was in the TV documentary, and that led to an invitation from Johnny Carson to appear on his late-night network talk show. Waddie had never seen *The Tonight Show* and didn't know who Johnny Carson was but accepted the invitation. Carson fell in love with his wry sense of humor and authentic cowboy manner. Mitchell performed Wallace McCray's poem *Reincarnation* and was invited back several times to the show. Waddie was also a guest on the *Larry King Radio Show* and featured in *Time*, *Life*, *People*, *USA Today* and *National Geographic*.

In 1984 Mitchell teamed up with friend Hal Cannon to organize the first Elko Cowboy Poetry Gathering that drew 2,000 people. The 10th annual gathering in 1994 drew nearly 14,000. The growing interest in his poetry led Waddie to record his first album in 1984. "I drove up to Hal Cannon's house in Idaho, sat down and said my poetry, never even listened to it, and drove home." The tape was released on his own label and sold about 5,000 copies. Waddie traveled to Dallas to record his second album, his first for GM Records. Former Bob Wills band member Tommy Allsup produced the background for Waddie's poetry, and the album sold over 10,000 copies.

When Warner Brothers created the Warner Western label in 1992, Mitchell was one of the debut artists signed to the label. With the release of ***Lone Driftin' Rider***, Mitchell embarked on a major promotional tour with label-mate Don Edwards. In addition to festivals and concert halls the Western artists were often invited to perform at schools and universities, where they combined entertainment with education. One of the hardest parts of his major label touring schedule was performing for a month in New York City. Mitchell teamed up with Michael Martin Murphey at the Rainbow Room on the 63rd floor of the Rockefeller Center.

"For a guy who used to go to town four times a year and that was to Elko, Nevada, New York was a pretty big change and it was a little hard for me to get used to," he recalled in a personal interview in 1993. The tickets for the dinner shows were in the $200 range and were constant sellouts.

In 1993, Mitchell released his second collection of poetry on Warner Western called ***Buckaroo Poet*** and went international by performing at a music festival in Switzerland. He also guest-hosted cable's VH1's *Country Country* and was praised by the *New York Times*. Waddie Mitchell's honors include the Governor's Art Award for Literature in

Nevada, and induction into the Cowboy Poets and Singers Hall of Fame. JIE

RECOMMENDED ALBUMS:

"Lone Driftin' Rider" (Warner Western)(1992)
"Buckaroo Poet" (Warner Western)(1993)

BILLY MIZE

(Singer, Songwriter, Steel Guitar, Guitar, Deejay, TV Producer, Actor)

Given Name:	**William Robert Mize**
Date of Birth:	**April 29, 1935**
Where Born:	**Kansas City, Kansas**
Married:	**Martha**
Children:	**Karen, Carrie, Billy, Jr., Margi, Robbie (dec'd.)**

Billy Mize is one of Country music's multi-talented performers, who is an able singer and songwriter as well as a talented steel player. Although born in Kansas, he was raised in rural California and while still a youngster, he started to play guitar. When he was 18, he went to an auction with his father and bought a steel guitar. He quickly learned to play the instrument and soon made his professional debut on radio station KUZZ Bakersfield with deejay Bill Woods.

In September 1953, Billy and Woods became members of *The Trading Post Show* on KERO-TV Bakersfield. During this time, Billy also traveled to and from Los Angeles to play on the *Hank Penny Show*. In 1957, he moved to L.A. for concert bookings and performed regularly on *Town Hall Party* (where he did solos and duetted with Cliff Crofford), the *Cal Worthington Show* and *Country Music Time*. Billy stayed on *The Trading Post Show* until 1968. During 1957, he released two singles for Decca.

In 1964, Johnny Sea had a crossover hit with the Mize song *My Baby Walks All Over Me*. Two years later, Billy became the host of Gene Autry's *Melody Ranch* TV show on KTLA Hollywood, where he stayed until 1967.

Steel guitarist ***Billy Mize***

He also appeared for some while at Bonnie Price's Foothill Club in Long Beach.

During 1965, Billy signed to Columbia Records and released his first single, *Terrible Tangled Web/You Don't Have Very Far to Go*. However, it was with his third single, *You Can't Stop Me,* in 1966, on which he was backed by the Jordanaires, that he had his first chart entry on Columbia, reaching the Top 60. He didn't return to the charts again until 1968, when he had another Top 60 single, *Walking Through the Memories of My Mind.* He was the recipient of the "Top TV Personality" award from the Country and Western Music Academy (ACM). He also received from them the "Most Promising Male Singer" award for 1966.

During 1968, he was sent with Dorothy Collins to Caracas, Venezuela, to represent the six U.S. Time-Life TV stations at the inauguration of Colteve television in Venezuela. At the end of 1968, Billy signed to Imperial Records and in the spring of the next year, he had a Top 40 entry with *Make It Rain.* He followed up with the Top 50 *While I'm Thinkin' About It.*

During 1969, Billy served on the Board of Directors of the Country and Western Music Academy (later renamed the ACM). He had one more chart record, in 1970, with *If This Was the Last Song* (Top 75), and this was Billy's last hit on Imperial. He then moved to United Artists Records, and had a Top 50 single, *Beer Drinking, Honky Tonkin' Blues.* It would be another two years before he returned to the charts, when *Take It Easy* reached the Top 70. He had two further chart entries in 1973 and 1974, but neither rose above the Top 80.

By 1976, Billy had moved to Zodiac Records, and had the Top 40 record *It Hurts to Know the Feeling's Gone*. In 1977, he had his final chart entry with *Livin' Her Life in a Song*, but it only reached the Top 70. Billy went on to become a TV producer for his own television production company. Billy's songs have been recorded by Dean Martin, Merle Haggard, Ray Price, Jerry Lee Lewis, Mickey Gilley, Ernest Tubb, Hank Snow, Glen Campbell, Bobbie Gentry, Vicki Carr and Pat Boone. Billy also appeared as an actor in various TV shows, including *The Virginian.*

During 1986, he cut a new album, ***Billy Mize's Tribute to Swing***, and released a new single, *Baby You've Got a Good Livin' Coming*, on G & M Records. At that time, he was also working on a movie about Bob Wills, which was to star Willie Nelson and Merle Haggard.

RECOMMENDED ALBUMS:

"This Time and Place" (Imperial)(1969)
"You're Alright with Me" (United Artists)(1971)
"Love 'N' Stuff" (Zodiac)(1976)

HUGH MOFFATT

(Singer, Songwriter, Guitar, Trumpet)

Date of Birth:	**November 10, 1948**
Where Born:	**Fort Worth, Texas**
Married:	**1. Pebe Sebert (div.) 2. Mary Vaughan**
Children:	**Lagan, Corianna**

Hugh Moffatt is, like his sister Katy, one of those singer/songwriters to have come out of Texas who have been kept out of stardom by the mediocrity of others. His acceptance as a songwriter has been to a large degree due to the fact that songs written by Hugh are of such high quality that they could not be ignored.

His first recollection of music was hearing the Sons of the Pioneers on the radio. He started piano lessons, but switched to trumpet. In high school, he played this latter instrument in the school big band, playing swing music. At the time, Hugh, who is now gaunt and very hairy, was somewhat overweight.

After school, he attended Rice University, Houston, where he majored in physics but gained a degree in English. He moved to Houston in the late 60's and learned guitar. He started to listen to Blues and then was re-introduced to Country music. While in Houston, he played with a Top 40 band called Rollin' Wood. He moved to Austin in 1971 and played Folk-Country, doing two venues a night, the Saxon Pub (6:30-8:30) and Ferrari's 21 Club (9:00-1:00), the latter playing for strippers.

In 1973, Hugh decided to move to Washington, D.C. However, en route, he stopped off in Nashville, saw Stringbean and Marty Robbins at the *Grand Ole Opry* and stayed. His biggest influence as he started writing was Kris Kristofferson, and then Ed Penney, the writer and producer, became his guiding light. Hugh got his first cut in 1974, when Ronnie Milsap recorded his *Just in Case*, which became a Top 5 single the following year. It was two years before he had another song recorded, during which time he signed with Chappell Music.

He signed as an artist with Mercury Records in 1977 and had a minor chart success with his initial release, Don Schlitz's *The Gambler*, the following year. He followed it with his own *Love and Only Love*, which did nothing, and he was dropped from the label. In 1978, Joe Sun recorded the song that remains

*Singer/Songwriter **Hugh Moffatt** takes the stage*

Hugh's best known, *Old Flames (Can't Hold a Candle to You)*, which was written with his first wife, L.A. songwriter, Pebe Sebert. The song was revived in 1980 by Dolly Parton, who took it to No.1. The following year, he had the successful cut of *Wild Turkey*, which was recorded by Lacy J. Dalton. In 1982, Alabama put *Words at Twenty Paces* on their multimillion-selling album ***Mountain Music***, and Bobby Bare had a minor hit with *Praise the Lord and Send Me the Money*. Johnny Rodriguez went Top 10 with his version of the Moffatt song *How Could I Love Her So Much*, in 1983.

During the early 80's Hugh put together Ratz, a four-piece band. The other members were Wade McCurdy (bass guitar), John Dietrich (drums), who now plays as part of Restless Heart and Michael Bonagura (now half of Baillie and the Boys). Other occasional singers with the group were Kathie Baillie and Hugh's first wife, Pebe. During 1984, the group recorded a 5-song EP, *Puttin' on the Ratz*. With help from his parents, Hugh could afford to press 1,000 copies.

At the end of 1985, a friend of Hugh's inherited a lot of money and offered to finance the recording of a solo album. At the beginning of the next year, Hugh had recorded some tracks and then Philo/Rounder approached him to record. By the end of January 1987, using some of his 1986 tracks, he had completed the album ***Loving You***, which comprised ten penned or part-penned Moffatt songs, the odd man out being Dylan's *Tomorrow Is a Long Time*. Hugh followed this with the aptly named 1989 album ***Troubadour*** and a year later, Hugh got together with his sister, Kate, for the splendid ***Dance Me Outside***.

Hugh's songs have now been recorded by Earl Scruggs, Tammy Wynette, Jerry Lee Lewis, Bill Anderson, Dottie West, Barbara Mandrell, Conway Twitty, Nitty Gritty Dirt Band, Merle Haggard and Rex Allen, Jr. Hugh lived for a while with his second wife in Virginia Beach, Virginia, but now he lives once again in Nashville.

RECOMMENDED ALBUMS:

"Loving You" (Philo/Rounder)(1987)
"Troubadour" (Philo/Rounder)(1989)
"Dance Me Outside" (Philo/Rounder)(1991)

KATY MOFFATT

(Singer, Guitar)

Given Name:	**Katherine Louella Moffatt**
Date of Birth:	**1950**
Where Born:	**Fort Worth, Texas**

There are certain performers who never chart but have a loyal fan following and receive the approbation of their peers. Such a performer is Katy Moffatt. She is the sister of songwriter/singer Hugh Moffatt, and with a grandmother who was a concert pianist, she is proof positive that talent is in the genes.

Katy made her professional debut in 1966 at Fort Worth's Patriot Coffeehouse, singing Leonard Cohen's *Dress Rehearsal Rag*. Inherently a shy person, Katy found herself in a singing role in the 1969 movie *Black Jack*. At the time, she was a student at St. John's College, Santa Fe, New Mexico. She left college and went to Corpus Christi, Texas, where she got a production job with a local TV station and also sang with a local Blues band. Things came to a halt when Hurricane Celia destroyed the station's broadcast tower.

She moved on to Austin, where she stayed awhile before moving on to Colorado. She intended to go to Boulder but took a wrong road and ended up in Denver. In 1973, she made her radio debut on Denver's KFML-FM station. She started to get a following in the area and in 1975, Don Ellis of Columbia Records flew out to see her perform and signed her to the label, with Billy Sherrill producing. However, as often happens, this was not a smart move. The label recorded her debut album, ***Katy***, which was released in 1976, and promoted it as Country, while she had been playing Rock venues. However, one single, *I Can Almost See Houston from Here*, did make the Top 90 on the Country charts. By now, Columbia had changed tack and decided that Katy was a Pop artist and so the 1977 album ***Kissin' in the California Sun*** was promoted that way. However, by now, she was opening for Charlie Daniels, Warren Zevon, Muddy Waters, Kenny Rankin and Steve Martin. During that year, she toured Europe with Leo Kottke and the following year, she toured with Willie Nelson and Andrew Gold, as well as being featured on Michael Martin Murphey's album ***Peaks & Valleys, Honky Tonks & Alleys***.

In 1979, Katy was special guest for Poco at L.A.'s Roxy and for John Prine at the Palomino. She toured California with Jerry Jeff Walker and Texas with John David Souther. The following year, she toured with the Allman Brothers. In 1981, she was a featured singer with Tanya Tucker, Lynn Anderson and Hoyt Axton. She was also featured on the ***Hard Country*** soundtrack album as well appearing in the movie. *Take It as It Comes*, a duet with Michael Martin Murphey from that album, also made the Top 90.

Katy's most positive move came in 1983, when she signed with Permian Records. The label's president, Chuck Robinson, recognized Katy's ability to blend Country, Rock, Blues and Folk and brought her into the studio under the direction of Jerry Crutchfield. While with the label, she had three chart records, *Under Loved and Over Lonely* (1983), *Reynosa* and *This Ain't Tennessee and He Ain't You* (1984). However, only the former got as high as the Top 70. In 1985, Katy was nominated as ACM's "Female Vocalist of the Year."

With the collapse of Permian, Katy at last found the perfect label in Philo/Rounder. She signed with them in 1987 and has since produced a series of excellent albums. In addition, she found that her product was being released overseas via Red Moon (Switzerland), Heartland (U.K.), Round Tower Music (Ireland) and Centerfire (Canada). Brother Hugh duetted with her on the 1991 release ***Dance Me Outside***, and she has recorded with excellent singer and songwriter Tom Russell (he wrote *Navajo Rug*) and worked with Mary Flower and Rosie Flores. In 1990, Katy appeared at the Wembley Festival in London, England. In 1992, she appeared in two movies, *Honeymoon in Vegas* and *The Thing Called Love*. She now lives in Los Angeles.

Legendary Nashville writer Robert K. Oermann once described Katy as having "a voice as big and pure and clean as her native Texas. And a heart to match. It's the blend of Folk and Country that is the wellspring of so much great music from the American heartland, the kind of stuff they used to call 'troubadour' or 'song poet' music." That just about says it.

RECOMMENDED ALBUMS:
"Katy" (Columbia)(1976)
"Kissin' in the California Sun" (Columbia)(1977)
"Walking on the Moon" (Philo/Rounder)(1987) [Recorded in Switzerland/re-released 1989]
"Child Bride" (Philo/Rounder)(1989)
"Dance Me Outside" (Philo/Rounder)(1991) [With Hugh Moffatt]
"Indoor Fireworks" (Red Moon Switzerland)(1992)
"The Greatest Show on Earth" (Philo/Rounder)(1993) [Re-titled "The Evangeline Hotel"]

BILL MONROE

(Singer, Songwriter, Mandolin, Guitar)
Given Name: **William Smith Monroe**
Date of Birth: **September 13, 1911**
Where Born: **Rosine, Kentucky**
Married: **Caroline Brown**
Children: **Melissa, James**

Bill Monroe, deservedly known as the "Father of Bluegrass," is widely recognized as a rare American original genius, on a par with Louis Armstrong, Duke Ellington or Charles Ives. People who know virtually nothing about other Country stars recognize Monroe's name. He has been given a wide variety of honors, from election into the Country Music Hall of Fame to canonization in the pages of *Rolling Stone*. Yet he is one of the most enigmatic and complex artists in the modern Country pantheon. Many of his songs have become standards, performed and known throughout the nation, yet Monroe's own recordings of these same songs have rarely made the hit charts. His festivals, such as the annual one at Beanblossom, Indiana, are known worldwide, yet Monroe has no palatial estate in Nashville, nor any private Lear jet. He has always been his own man, forging his own music with a fierce determination and singularity of purpose, withstanding musical trends, changes of personnel and personal problems to maintain the integrity of his music.

For a private man, Monroe has been surprisingly autobiographical in his music. He was indeed from "the hills of old Kentucky," from the rolling hills of the northwestern part of the state; he did indeed learn to play from his "Uncle Pen," the colorful Pendleton Vandiver who is still remembered today in the region as a fine fiddler. His father was J.B. or "Buck" Monroe, his mother Melissa Vandiver Monroe, and these two had already had seven children when Bill came along in 1911. Bill's older brothers were already playing music when he was born, and he learned from them, as well as from a local singing school teacher. He learned the mandolin because no other member of his family played it.

Bill's mother died when he was 10 and not long after, his father passed away and Bill went to live with his Uncle Pen, riding with him on horseback to play remote square dances. Like many Kentucky boys, Bill's brothers Charlie and Birch moved north to Chicago to find work in the 1920's, and when Bill was 18, in 1929, he joined them in Whiting, Indiana. The trio soon had a job playing regularly on a Gary, Indiana, radio station, and when Birch dropped out, Bill and Charlie continued on as the Monroe Brothers. From 1934 until 1938 the pair worked radio stations throughout the South and Midwest and recorded some 60 titles for Victor's Bluebird label. Among these was a significant hit, *What Would You Give in Exchange for Your Soul?*

The break-up came in 1938: Bill formed a band called the Kentuckians and headed for Arkansas. Next he tried Atlanta, where he reorganized the group, calling it the Blue Grass Boys. It was with this band that he made an audition for Harry Stone and the *Grand Ole Opry* in October 1939. Much of the Monroe sound was in place by now: breathtaking tempos, a featuring of the fiddle, songs pitched in unusually high keys with Monroe's tenor going sky-high. *Mule Skinner Blues*, the first song he did on the *Opry,* was also one of the first Victor records done under his own name (in 1940). His sidemen included vocalist Clyde Moody, the gifted Georgia fiddler Tommy Magness, and, for a time, the banjoist Stringbean.

During the war years, Monroe emerged as an *Opry* favorite—though he still saw himself as a Country musician, not especially a Bluegrass one. He took out *Opry* tent shows and traveled the South giving musical shows and, when possible, having his band play for local baseball teams. As the war years wound down, he signed with Columbia and began to reorganize his band. He added vocalist Lester

The Father of Bluegrass, ***Bill Monroe***

Flatt, three-finger banjo specialist Earl Scruggs and Florida fiddler Chubby Wise. These revolutionary young players helped form what many have called "the World's Greatest Bluegrass Band," and with them Monroe's music really took off. New hot songs included such now classic tunes as *Blue Moon of Kentucky*, *Will You Be Loving Another Man*, *Molly and Ten Brooks (The Racehorse Song)*, *Sweetheart You Done Me Wrong* and *I'm Going Back to Old Kentucky*. On the charts his best-selling numbers were *Kentucky Waltz* and *Footprints in the Snow*. This band, sparked by Scruggs, stayed pretty much intact until 1948.

Other Monroe chart entries were *Sweetheart You Done Me Wrong*, *Wicked Path of Sin* and *Little Community Church* (all 1948) and *Toy Heart* and *When You Are Lonely* (both 1949). With the "defection" of Flatt and Scruggs and their decision to start their own band, Monroe went through a period of indecision. He left Columbia Records because he was angry over their signing the Stanley Brothers, a band that Monroe felt was copying his new Bluegrass style.

When he joined his new company, Decca, he found the producers wanted him to try mainstream Country, and actually produced a couple of sessions with electric guitar backup. Monroe fought these attempts off, though, and soon found a new singing partner in Jimmy Martin. Together they did a series of masterworks, including *Memories of You*, *Memories of Mother and Dad* and *When the Golden Leaves Begin to Fall*.

The 1950's also saw Monroe cut his first version of *Uncle Pen*, as well as such "true" (i.e., autobiographical) pieces as *My Little Georgia Rose*, *I'm on My Way to the Old Home*, *Letter from My Darling* and *In Despair*. His fame was great enough that when young Elvis Presley tried out on the *Opry* in 1954 and sang *Blue Moon of Kentucky* (his first Sun single), he came to Monroe and apologized for changing the arrangement of his song. Monroe subsequently used that arrangement as an alternative way of playing the song.

Bill had his two final chart entries with the classic instrumental *Scotland* (1958) and *Gotta Travel On* (1959). Toward the end of the decade, Monroe began to expand his audience to include many of the young northerners involved in the Folk revival movement. In 1963, Monroe made his first Folk festival appearance, at the University of Chicago Folk Festival, and his first New York appearance a few weeks later. Under the management of Ralph Rinzler, this venue expanded, and Monroe began to sense that he was reaching a new audience—one that did not necessarily have a southern background.

Throughout the 1960's festivals proliferated and became a main way for Monroe to get to his fans. In 1970, Bill Monroe was elected to the Country Music Hall of Fame, and the following year, he was inducted into the Nashville Songwriters Hall of Fame. Bill received a Grammy Award in 1988 for "Best Bluegrass Recording (Vocal or Instrumental)" for the album ***Southern Flavor***. In 1993, Bill was the charter inductee into the Bluegrass Hall of Fame and that same year, he was presented with the Grammy's "Lifetime Achievement Award."

Throughout the years, Monroe's band served as a school for dozens of talented musicians who later went on to make a name for themselves in Bluegrass and Country, and Monroe continued to serve as his own talent scout in finding young replacements. He survived a cancer scare in the early 1980's, and a broken hip in 1994, but generally maintained his band and continued to play on the *Opry* and at shows. A constant succession of albums for Decca (then MCA) allowed him to keep writing and rearranging songs and instrumentals, and to keep pushing the envelope to challenge the hundreds of young musicians who looked to him as both a patriarch and a challenge.

Among former members of the Blue Grass Boys are Bill Keith, Howdy Forrester, Clyde Moody, Jimmy Martin, Red Smiley, Don Reno, Carter Stanley, Vassar Clements, Chubby Wise, Cedric Rainwater, Mac Wiseman, Gordon Terry, Sonny Osborne and Byron Berline. CKW

RECOMMENDED ALBUMS:

"Knee Deep in Blue Grass" (Decca)(1958) [Re-released on Stetson UK in the original sleeve (1987)]
"Bluegrass Ramble" (Decca)(1962) [Re-released on MCA and Stetson UK in the original sleeve (1987)]
"The High Lonesome Sound of Bill Monroe" (Decca)(1966) [Re-issued on MCA]
"Bill Monroe & His Bluegrass Boys (16 Hits)" (Columbia)(1970)
"Bill Monroe's Country Music Hall of Fame" (Decca)(1971) [Re-released on MCA]
"Uncle Pen" (Decca)(1972) [Re-released on MCA]
"Bean Blossom" (double)(MCA)(1973)
"Best of Bill Monroe" (double)(MCA)(1975)
"Weary Traveler" (MCA)(1976)
"Bean Blossom '79" (MCA)(1980)
"Bill Monroe and Friends" (MCA)(1983) [With the Oak Ridge Boys, Willie Nelson, Ricky Skaggs, Johnny Cash, Emmylou Harris, Barbara Mandrell, the Gatlins, Waylon Jennings, John Hartford and Mel Tillis]
"Bluegrass '87" (MCA)(1987)
"Southern Flavor" (MCA)(1988)
"Mule Skinner Blues" (RCA)(1991) [Bluebird Masters]

CHARLIE MONROE

(Singer, Guitar, Old-Time Banjo)

Given Name:	**Charles Pendleton Monroe**
Date of Birth:	**July 4, 1903**
Where Born:	**Ohio County, Kentucky**
Married:	**1. Betty Miller (dec'd.)**
	2. Martha
Date of Death:	**September 27, 1975**

Charlie Monroe began his professional career as the lead-singing older half of the Monroe Brothers, the dynamic-sounding harmony duet of the mid-30's. After splitting with brother Bill in 1938, Charlie formed his own group and for the next 20 years made a success with a band sound that could best be described as suspended somewhere between Old-Time and Bluegrass with a touch of newer Country thrown in for good measure. Charlie also possessed a jovial, extroverted personality that added to his appeal.

Born in the Pennyroyal region of Western Kentucky, Charlie Monroe was raised on traditional music, being exposed to his musical mother and her fiddling brother "Uncle Pen" at an early age. He attended elementary school and worked on the farm and his dad's sawmill, but after his parents had died, Charlie went to Detroit with his brother, Birch, and worked in a factory. Later, he came back to Kentucky and then journeyed to Hammond, Indiana, where he worked at Sinclair Oil first, then for Standard Oil. He and younger brother Bill attended local square dances and through a chance meeting with Tom Owens of WLS Chicago, they became part of a unit that danced on the *National Barn Dance* and went on some of its tours as well.

When Charlie and Bill formed a duet, they performed some numbers on WLS, which led to the Texas Crystal Company hiring the Monroe Brothers in 1933 to go to KFNF Shenandoah, Iowa, for three months. From there, they went to WAAW Omaha, Nebraska, where they hooked up with ace announcer Byron Parker. In 1933, this threesome went to the Carolinas, where the Monroe Brothers worked at a variety of stations for the next three years, most notably WBT Charlotte, WFBC Greenville and WPTF Raleigh. In February 1936 they began their recording career with Bluebird, waxing some 60 sides through the spring of 1938.

In mid-1938, the brothers quarreled at WPTF Raleigh and went their own ways. Charlie went to WNOX Knoxville, where he added a pair of musicians to his entourage. These were Bill Calhoun, and then Zeke Morris, a veteran of both Mainer's Mountaineers and the Morris Brothers. Later they switched to WDBJ

Roanoke, Virginia. In the fall of 1939, Charlie added more musicians to his group, including Tommy Scott and Curly Sechler. Other noted musicians who worked with Charlie's Kentucky Pardners group included Lester Flatt, David "Stringbean" Akeman, Larry "Tex" Isley, Ira Loudermilk (Louvin), Red Rector, the Spencer Brothers, and the husband-wife team of Slim and Wilma Martin.

Charlie moved his radio base periodically, serving stints at such locales as WWVA *Wheeling Jamboree* (1939-1940), WHAS Louisville, Kentucky (1940-1941), KWKH Shreveport, Louisiana, and another sojourn in Knoxville, but he always felt most comfortable in the Carolinas working out of such spots as Charlotte, Greensboro, Raleigh and Winston-Salem.

Charlie started recording with RCA Victor again in 1946, remaining on that label until 1951 and cutting some forty-four songs. Among his best-known numbers were *Who's Calling You Sweetheart?, Down in the Willow Garden, The End of Memory Lane, Rosa Lee McFall* and the classic train songs *Bringing in the Georgia Mail* and *That Wild Black Engine.* In 1952, Charlie switched over to Decca, recording four songs there and an additional four in 1956. *Find 'Em, Fool 'Em and Leave 'Em Alone* and *I'm Old Kentucky Bound* are his best-known numbers from those sessions, the latter of which has become an oft-covered minor Bluegrass classic.

In March 1957, with Country styles changing, Charlie decided to retire to his farm near Beaver Dam, Kentucky. With the exception of a few public appearances and cutting a pair of albums for Rem Records in 1962 and 1964, he generally remained musically inactive for some 15 years. In the meantime, his wife, Betty, went through a terminal bout with cancer that drained most of his savings.

Charlie later remarried and settled in Cross Plains, Tennessee. In 1972 Jimmy Martin and Bluegrass festival promoter Carlton Haney talked Charlie into appearing at the Gettysburg and Camp Springs Bluegrass Festivals. His enthusiastic reception encouraged Charlie to get back into the business. He moved back to North Carolina, got some old and new band members together and remained quite active until early 1975 when he, too, began a losing battle with cancer.

Late in 1972, Charlie made an album for Starday with the help of Jimmy Martin's Sunny Mountain Boys and cut a live album for Pine Tree in December 1974. Some of his late 40's Victor sides came out on a Camden album in 1969 and three more appeared on a collector label. County did a pair of releases from 1944 radio transcriptions, which included some cuts featuring the equally legendary Lester Flatt.

IMT

RECOMMENDED ALBUMS:

"Charlie Monroe Sings Again" (Rem)(1965) [Also re-released on Starday, Pine Mountain and Old Homestead]
"Charlie Monroe on the Noonday Jamboree—1944" (County)(1974)
"Charlie Monroe and his Kentucky Partners" (Golden Country)(1974)
"Charlie Monroe Live" (Pine Tree)(1975)
"Feast Here Tonight" (double)(Bluebird)(1975)
"Charlie Monroe's Boys: The Early Years, 1938-1939" (Old Homestead)(1981)

MONTANA SLIM

(Singer, Yodeler, Guitar)
Given Name: **Wilf Carter**
Date of Birth: **December 18,1904**
Where Born: **Port Hilford, Nova Scotia, Canada**
Married: **Bobbie (dec'd.)**
Children: **Sheila Rose, Carol Joyce**

One of Country music's longest careers has been enjoyed by Canadian artist Wilf Carter, whose American name, Montana Slim, is almost as well known. Unlike some musicians whose style has changed with the times, Wilf Carter has more or less kept to the same simple format featuring unadorned singing and yodeling, largely of cowboy material, and had relatively simple instrumentation supplementing his own guitar chords.

Wilf grew up as the son of a Baptist minister in the Annapolis Valley region of Nova Scotia. As a youth he heard a concert by a traveling musician known as the Yodeling Fool that inspired him to develop yodeling skills. Moving away from home, Wilf tried carpentry work in Boston, but didn't like it. Riding a freight train westward to Calgary, Alberta, he worked for several years in various aspects of cowboy work. During his Alberta days he became friends with several rodeo riders including the legendary Pete Knight of whom he would later sing.

Wilf Carter, aka ***Montana Slim***

About 1930, Wilf began singing at CFCN radio in Calgary. He also entertained for trail rides in the Rockies sponsored by the Canadian Pacific Railway. Later in 1933, C.P.R. hired him to sing on the maiden voyage of their cruise ship, *Empress of Britain*, to the West Indies. The company provided him with a rail pass eastward. Stopping over in Montreal, he cut two sides for Canadian Bluebird, *My Swiss Moonlight Lullaby* and *Capture of Albert Johnson* on December 20. It proved to be the start of a long career.

Carter soon got a job on CBS network radio in New York, where he received the name "Montana Slim." As Victor began to release his records on their American Bluebird label they used the nickname, but "Wilf Carter" continued as the credit in their Canadian series. Quite active in the studio, the tall ex-cowpoke from Nova Scotia had some 190 sides released through 1941, when recording activity slowed down because of WWII. Thereafter, he had only two sessions of 6 and 15 songs each in 1944. During the war years, he also experienced some physical problems in recuperating from an auto accident in Montana.

In 1947, he resumed a more active recording role again for Victor, who had discontinued their Bluebird series in the U.S. That same year Carter began using a fuller band on his sessions which usually included a bass, additional guitars and sometimes fiddle, piano and steel guitar. Some of his better known songs date from this period, including *There's a Love Knot in My Lariat* and *I'm Gonna Tear Down the Mailbox.*

In 1954, he began a four-year affiliation with Decca, which resulted in sessions in Nashville arranged by Owen Bradley, featuring a more contemporary Country sound. Some of these sides, plus additional ones, appeared in Canada on the Apex label.

Since Victor wanted him back, Wilf returned to the company he termed home, recording many numbers primarily for Canadian releases although some also came out in the U.S. Except for a pair of albums made for Starday in the mid-60's, Carter remained with Victor, with a new album being released as recently as 1988, when the venerable vocalist neared 84. By that time his total of recorded masters had gone well beyond the 500 mark and he had spent some fifty-five years on the label.

Although his star always shone more brightly in Canada than anywhere else, Montana Slim increasingly made the U.S. his prime residence. Following his CBS radio work in New York, Carter resided on a New Jersey farm for a time with his wife and two daughters, but from the late 50's made his home in Winter Park, Florida, where he also owned and—for a time—operated a motel. In 1971, Wilf Carter was inducted into the Nashville Songwriters Hall of Fame and a decade later, he received the "C.F. Martin" Award from the CCMA.

More recently, the respected cowboy singer has resided in Sun City, Arizona. A widower since 1989, Wilf Carter at 86 continued his annual Canadian touring schedule in the summer of 1990, as he had customarily done for decades. Meanwhile reissues of his earlier recordings continue being marketed for collectors in locales as distant as Germany and Australia as well as the U.S. and Canada.

IMT

RECOMMENDED ALBUMS:

"Reminiscin' with Montana Slim" (RCA Camden)(1962) [Re-issued by Stetson UK in the original sleeve (1988)]
"God Bless Our Canada" (RCA Camden) [Canada only]
"Wilf Carter Sings Songs of Australia" (RCA Camden) [Canada only]
"Montana Slim's Greatest Hits" (RCA Camden)(1974)
"Have a Nice Day" (RCA US) and (RCA Canada)(1977)
"Wilf Carter (Montana Slim)" (Cowgirlboy Germany)(1988 & 1989)
"The Dynamite Trail" (Bear Family Germany)(1990) [The complete Decca sessions]
"The Legendary Yodeling Cowboy" (Cowgirlboy Germany)(1991)
"Brown-Eyed Prairie Rose" (Cowgirlboy Germany)(1991)
"Dawn on the Prairie" (Cowgirlboy Germany)(1991)
"My Oklahoma Rose" (Cowgirlboy Germany)(1992)
"In the Begining" (Cowgirlboy Germany)(1993)
"Returning to My Old Prairie Home" (Cowgirlboy Germany)(1993)
"The Calgary Roundup" (Cowgirlboy Germany)(1993)

PATSY MONTANA

(Singer, Yodeler, Guitar, Violin)

Given Name:	**Ruby Blevins**
Date of Birth:	**October 30, 1914**
Where Born:	**Hot Springs, Arkansas**
Married:	**Paul Rose**
Children:	**Beverly, Judy Rose**

Although Patsy Montana is usually remembered for her famous hit recording of *I Want to Be a Cowboy's Sweetheart*, that achievement tends to obscure a long list of her accomplishments as a female pioneer in Country music. Not only did she do this major song but indeed with a whole host of other numbers focusing on Western themes, she helped create the yodeling cowgirl image that helped elevate women to prominent if not quite equal position among Country and Western vocalists. Through some six decades in the business, Patsy has also had a continuing presence. She has made herself readily accessible to later generations of Country fans for whom most pioneer figures in the trade are either long gone or totally retired.

Raised in Hope, Arkansas, Ruby Blevins had some exposure to Jimmie Rodgers' records as well as church and violin music in her youth. In 1930, she moved to California with an older brother and sister-in-law where she soon won a talent contest and got a program on a local radio station. This led to a radio job with Stuart Hamblen, an established Country-Western singer and Victor recording artist. In 1932, she went back to Arkansas to visit relatives and guested on KWKH Shreveport for a week. Jimmie Davis then took her to a Victor session where she not only assisted him but cut four numbers on her own as "Patsy Montana," a name she had used in California. Her trademark song in the early days was *Montana Plains*, a re-composition of Hamblen's *Texas Plains*.

In 1933, Patsy went to Chicago and took a job at WLS as vocalist with the Prairie Ramblers. Over the next several years she worked as a regular at the *National Barn Dance* and waxed numerous songs for the American Record Corporation, usually backed by the Ramblers. *I Want to Be a Cowboy's Sweetheart* from 1935 was her big hit, but there were others too. These included *Rodeo Sweetheart, Shy Anne from Old Cheyenne, I Wanna Be a Western Cowgirl, The She Buckaroo* and *I Want to Be a Cowboy's Dream Girl*. Such lyrics all helped Patsy to create and reinforce the yodeling cowgirl image, with some support from the Girls of the Golden West and Louise Massey. Patsy left Chicago for brief periods such as a short sojourn at WOR New York in 1935-1936, and a few trips west to make film shorts and the feature *Colorado Sunset* with Gene Autry in 1939.

In 1941, Patsy Montana switched to Decca

The legendary ***Patsy Montana***

Records, for whom she had only 12 sides released in the next four years. Undoubtedly wartime shortages held the numbers down as additional masters had been cut. After the war she signed with RCA Victor and had several new releases on the label where her first recordings had appeared. While these later efforts had less impact than those of the 30's, one must remember that the styles of Country music had begun to move away from yodeling cowboys and cowgirls toward the Honky-Tonk sounds.

Patsy left WLS and the *Barn Dance* for an extended leave about 1941, working for a time on Mexican border stations. She went back to Arkansas in 1948 and lived on a farm with her husband and two children. During this time, Patsy worked daily radio at KTHS Hot Springs and often appeared on Saturday nights at the *Louisiana Hayride* in Shreveport. When her husband, Paul Rose, took a job transfer to California, the Rose family relocated on the West Coast, where they have made their home ever since.

Patsy's career slowed down somewhat, but she has remained semi-active. Among other things, the "cowgirl sweetheart" guested on the *Ozark Jubilee* on ABC-TV and appeared several times on the *National Barn Dance* in its fading years. In 1964, she recorded an album at the Matador Room in Safford, Arizona, with a band that included a then unknown Waylon Jennings on lead guitar; it initially appeared on the Sims label.

In recent years, Patsy Montana continues to make herself available as one of Country music's most visible pioneers. She has done albums for such specialty labels as Birch, Old Homestead and most recently Flying Fish. With some frequency Patsy has been seen at a variety of film fairs, old-timer reunions and even academic conferences, always winning admirers with her spunkiness and cheerfulness. A recent example occurred at the 1993 Country Music Conference at Mississippi State University, Meridian, held in conjunction with the annual Jimmie Rodgers Festival.

Thanks to the Columbia Historic Edition series and several reissue albums on Cattle Records of Germany, a sizable portion of her vintage material has become available to album collectors in recent years.

IMT

RECOMMENDED ALBUMS:

Vintage recordings:
."Original Hits from the West" (Cattle Germany)(1980)
"The Very Early Patsy Montana and the Prairie Ramblers" (Cattle Germany)(1981)
"The Cowboy's Sweetheart" (Cattle Germany)(1981)
"The Yodeling Cowgirl" (Cattle Germany)(1983))
"Columbia Historic Edition" (Columbia)(1984) [Some of the cuts are the Prairie Ramblers only]

"Out in the Western Country" (Cattle Germany)(1984)
"I Wanna Be a Western Cowgirl" (Cattle Germany)(1985)
"The She Buckaroo" (Cattle Germany)(1987)
Later recordings:
"Cowboy's Sweetheart" (Sims)[Re-issued on Starday and Old Homestead in 1964]
"Precious Memories" (Birch)(1971)
"I Want to Be a Cowboy's Sweetheart" (Birch)(1978)
"Cowboy Songs & Ballads" (Old Homestead)(1985)
"The Cowboy's Sweetheart" (Flying Fish)(1988)

BOB MONTGOMERY

(Singer, Songwriter, Guitar, Record Producer, Industry Executive, Music Publisher)

Given Name: Bobby LaRoy Montgomery
Date of Birth: May 12, 1937
Where Born: Lampasas, Texas
Married: 1. Carol (div.) 2. Cathy
Children: Echo Annette, Dee Dee Dawn, Kevin Lee

Coming into the music business as one half of "Buddy and Bob, Western and Bop," with Buddy Holly, Bob Montgomery has emerged as one of the major industry figures in Country music, and one of the most respected. To have your album produced by Bob Montgomery is to ensure that you have quality.

Bob got to know Buddy while they were both in their early teens. They started to make demos together in 1954 and most of the songs that they cut were Montgomery compositions. They started recording at Nesman Recording Studios in Wichita, Kansas, and also at the Jim Beck Studios, Dallas, Texas. When Buddy was offered a solo deal by Decca, Bob accepted this with equanimity. When Buddy went to Norman Petty's studio in Clovis, New Mexico, to record, Bob became the studio engineer. He continued to write songs for Holly, including *Heartbeat* and *Love's Made a Fool of You* (which Holly co-wrote).

When Bob first came to Nashville, in 1960, the year after Buddy's death, he knew he wanted to stay. He became a staff writer with Acuff-Rose and in 1962, Sue Thompson had a Top 50 hit with Bob's *Two of a Kind.* Later that year, Patsy Cline recorded Bob's song *Back in Baby's Arms* and it would also be covered by Stan Hitchcock and Connie Smith. Sissy Spacek and Beverly D'Angelo duetted on the song in the movie *Coal Miner's Daughter*. In 1988, Emmylou Harris recorded it on her album ***Planes, Trains and Automobiles***.

Bob performed as a duo with his first wife and they cut several records, without success. In 1963, he formed Talmont Music, with John Talley. However, it was Bob's song *Misty Blue* that became an even greater success. The song was initially a Top 5 Country hit for Wilma Burgess in 1966 and then, the following year, Eddy Arnold had a Top 3 Country hit and a Top 60 Pop success with it. The song became a hit all over again in 1976, when Billie Jo Spears took it to No.5 on the Country chart and Dorothy Moore made it a Pop Top 3 hit. In 1977, the song won for Bob the 8th annual Robert J. Burton Award for writing the most-performed BMI Country song. In 1967, Bob sold the Talmont catalog and in the late 80's proceeded to buy it back.

In 1967, he became the head of United Artists Records' Nashville office and went into record production with Bobby Goldsboro. Their early successes included Goldsboro's *Honey* and *Watching Scotty Grow.* In 1969, the two of them formed the publishing firm House of Gold. This company ended up owning *Behind Closed Doors* (Kenny O'Dell was one of their writers), *Til I Get It Right, Rose Colored Glasses, Love in the First Degree* and *Bobby Sue.* It became the No.1 Pop music publisher on Music Row and had songs recorded by Dr. Hook, Juice Newton, Sheena Easton, Kenny Rogers, Gladys Knight, the Pointer Sisters, Lobo and Millie Jackson, among others.

During 1975, Bob set up his own production company and produced Austin Roberts' hit *Rocky.* He followed this with hits by Razzy Bailey, Merle Haggard, Jim Stafford, Dobie Gray, Engelbert Humperdinck, Slim Whitman, Johnny Rodriguez and B.J. Thomas. Bob was also the producer of Marty Robbins' 1982 hit *Some Memories Just Won't Die* and several tracks for Janie Fricke, including *It Ain't Easy Bein' Easy*, also in 1982.

In 1981, Bob took to the stage again at a Buddy Holly tribute concert, alongside Paul McCartney, the Everly Brothers and the Crickets. This was the first time he'd been on stage in 20 years. At the end of 1982, House of Gold was sold to Warner Brothers Music and Bob joined Warner Brothers as an administrator. He moved over to Tree International as Director of Creative Services. While in this position, he helped consolidate Tree's preeminent position and took on the production reins for Vern Gosdin. He continued to write sporadically with Tree staff superwriter Red Lane.

By 1988, with Sony's purchase of CBS and Tree, Bob moved over to CBS as Vice President. Here he continued producing Gosdin through his own company. In 1991, Bob moved from CBS and began working solely through his own production company, where he has been responsible for, among others, Joe Diffie, Vern Gosdin and Tammy Wynette. In 1993, he reactivated his publishing interests.

JOHN MICHAEL MONTGOMERY

(Singer, Songwriter, Guitar)

Given Name: John Michael Montgomery
Date of Birth: January 20, 1965
Where Born: Danville, Kentucky

The meteoric rise to stardom of black-hatted John Michael Montgomery has heralded the return to traditional Country music in 1992, even more strongly than Alan Jackson's debut three years earlier. Almost without exception, radio stations are now playing straight-ahead Country, where six months earlier they were

One of the hottest singers around, ***John Michael Montgomery***

playing a form of Country that was Pop music dressed up.

John began performing at the age of 5, when his parents, who were also musicians, brought him on stage to sing Country classics. He spent most weekends listening and learning the music that his singer/guitarist father and his drummer mother played. When he was 15, John bought his first guitar and soon he was playing in local bands. His parents divorced when he was age 17 and he played music for a while with his father, Harold, and brother, Eddie. The divorces of his dad and brother dissuaded him from getting married. John was also an anti-mornings person and this led to him failing his high school diploma, but he later went back to school to get his general equivalency diploma (GED). He also did some promotional spots for Kentucky Public Broadcasting to help others in the same situation.

While playing in Lexington, Kentucky, John met the owner of the Austin City Saloon and began to get a following. Estil Sowards became his manager (later to be joined by John Dorris). John Michael soon came to the attention of Atlantic Records. Songwriter Steve Clark also became a champion of the Montgomery cause and introduced John to the "right" people in Nashville.

The release of his first album, ***Life's a Dance***, was universally greeted with critical plaudits. It reached the Top 5 on the Country album chart, Top 30 on the Pop album chart and was Certified Platinum in 1993. The title track reached the Top 5 at the end of 1992. The follow-up single, *I Love the Way You Love Me*, soon went to No.1 in the spring of 1993 and stayed there for 3 weeks, crossing over to the Pop Top 60. However, *Beer and Bones* did not fare that well and peaked below the Top 20. This was redeemed by the first single from his second album, *I Swear*, which went to No.1 and stayed there for 4 weeks. The new album, ***Kickin' It Up***, produced by Scott Hendricks, was released in 1994, shipped 800,000 copies, went straight to No.1 on the Country album chart and was shortly Certified Platinum. It also debuted at No.3 on the Pop album chart and went to No.1. During 1994, John charted with *Rope the Moon* (Top 5), *Kick-in' It Up* (Top 75 album cuts) and *Be My Baby Tonight* (Top 30). That year, he was named "Favorite Newcomer" in the AMA Country Category. In addition, the ACM named him "New Male Vocalist of the Year" and *I Love the Way You Love Me* (written by Victoria Shaw and Chuck Cannon) was named "Song of the Year." In 1994, John Michael's hit *I Swear* was named the CMA's "Single of the Year" and he won the prestigious CMA "Horizon Award."

RECOMMENDED ALBUMS:
"Life's a Dance" (Atlantic)(1992)
"Kickin' It Up" (Atlantic)(1994)

MELBA MONTGOMERY

(Singer, Songwriter, Guitar, Fiddle)
Given Name: **Melba Joyce Montgomery**
Date of Birth: **October 14, 1938**
Where Born: **Iron City, Tennessee**
Married: **Jack L. Soloman**
Children: **Jackie, Missy**

Melba Montgomery described her life as an entertainer as "a rewarding and good career." She is what traditional Country music is all about: a genuine, likable star with a ready smile and a bluesy southern, Country voice. When this redhead talks, she is the South.

Melba was raised on a farm in rural Tennessee. She spent her first 14 years there, with her five brothers and sister, Ruth. Her mother and father were both musical. Her father played fiddle and guitar and taught singing at the local Methodist church, where Melba was in the choir. She and her siblings soon started singing around the town at cakewalks and talent shows. Melba remembers Ruth singing lead and herself singing harmonies, while swinging on the porch swing.

When she was 10, Melba received her first guitar. The family moved to Florence in Alabama, and in 1958, Melba and her brother entered the Pet Milk talent contest and became one of the six finalists. They came to Nashville for the final at WSM's Studio C, then home of the *Grand Ole Opry,* and won. Melba was seen by *Opry* star Roy Acuff. As luck would have it, his lead vocalist, June Webb, was just about to quit and Melba took her place. She worked with Acuff for four years, touring the U.S. and Europe, North Africa, Australia and Canada and visiting almost every military base as well as appearing on the *Grand Ole Opry*, as part of Roy Acuff's troupe.

She also worked with the comedy team Lonzo & Oscar, who encouraged her to record. Her first two singles were released on their Nugget label and were *Just Another Fool Along the Way* and *Your Picture Keeps Smiling Back at Me*.

In 1962, Melba left Roy Acuff and was signed to United Artists Records. Pappy Daily, then head of UA, liked her work and she soon released her first album, ***Melba Montgomery***, which included some of her own compositions. Melba and George Jones were teamed together, and so began a duet partnership that delighted fans all over the world. Melba had written a song, on both sides of a postcard, in the back of a van while traveling to a gig with Lonzo & Oscar, entitled *We Must Have Been Out of Our Minds*. This song was released as a duet single in 1963 and took Melba and George into the Top 3. Melba then had two solo Top 30 hits that year, *Hall of Shame* and *The Greatest One of All*.

Melba and George finished off the year with a double-sided Top 20 hit, *What's in Our Heart* and *Let's Invite Them Over*. Melba was also voted "Most Promising Female Vocalist" by *Cash Box*. George and Melba did a lot of shows together, and in 1964 had two more hits, *Please Be My Love* (Top 40) and at year end, *Multiply the Heartaches* (Top 25).

Pappy Daily set up his own label, Musicor, in 1965 and George and Melba were among the artists who went with him. Another Musicor artist was Gene Pitney, and Melba was teamed with him for an album of duets, ***Being Together*** (1966). Their most successful single was the Top 15 chart hit *Baby Ain't That Fine*. Among the albums Melba released in 1966 was one with George Jones called ***Close Together***, which gave them another chart hit, *Close Together (As You and Me)* (Top 70) and a Starday album that included her as one of the ***Queens of Country Music***. Her last chart single with George Jones was in 1967, entitled *Party Pickin'* (Top 25), which came from their last album together, ***Let's Get Together (Boy Meets Girl)***. That year, Melba had her last solo chart placing with Musicor, *What Can I Tell the Folks Back Home*, which went Top 70.

Jack Soloman was a musician for George Jones when Melba met him and they fell in love and married in 1968. Later he became a studio picker and production manager. Melba moved to Capitol Records in 1969, where she teamed up with Charlie Louvin. Between 1970 and 1973, they racked up six chart hits, the most successful being *Something to Brag About* (Top 20, 1970), *Did You Ever* and *Baby, You've Got What It Takes* (both Top 30, 1971). She also continued releasing solo singles, without major success.

However, in 1974 she had her smash hit *No Charge* for her new label, Elektra. Written by Harlan Howard, it not only reached No.1 on the Country chart but also crossed over onto the Pop Top 40. Melba continued to appear on the charts until 1977, with her most successful singles being *Don't Let the Good Times Fool You* (Top 15, 1975) and *Angel of the Morning* (Top 25, 1977), the latter on United Artists. In 1980 and 1986, Melba re-appeared on the chart with a couple of indie labels, Kari and Compass, at the lower level of the charts.

She continued to tour and in 1975, she appeared at the Wembley Festival of Country Music in England. Once more, she joined George Jones on stage to sing some of their hits to the delight of the fans. Among the TV shows she has appeared on are *Musical Chairs*, *Pop Goes Country*, the *Porter Wagoner Show* and TNN's *Nashville Now*.

In 1988, she was still touring, doing 70 to 90 dates a year at festivals, concerts and fairs. Melba turned to writing when she published a cookbook of her family recipes. She continues to write songs, and enjoys home life with her family on their 25-acre estate, west of Nashville. JAB

RECOMMENDED ALBUMS:

"America's Number One Country & Western Girl Singer" (United Artists)(1964)
"Blue Grass Hootenanny" (United Artists)(1964) [Re-issued by Stetson UK in the original sleeve (1989)]
"Being Together" (Musicor)(1966) [With Gene Pitney]
"Something to Brag About" (Capitol)(1971) [With Charlie Louvin]
"Melba Montgomery—No Charge" (Elektra)(1973)
"Don't Let the Good Times Fool You" (Elektra)(1975)
"Aching Breaking Heart" (Capitol)(1975)
"What's in Our Hearts" (Liberty)(1982)

MOODY BROTHERS

CARLTON MOODY

(Vocals, Guitar, Banjo, Dobro, Mandolin, Fiddle, Piano)

Given Name: Carlton Laymond Moody
Date of Birth: September 20, 1955
Where Born: Durham, North Carolina
Married: Margaret (Margie) Schuld (m. 1988)

DAVID MOODY

(Vocals, Drums, Guitar, Percussion, Mandolin, Keyboards, Harmonica, Autoharp)

Given Name: David Byron Moody
Date of Birth: May 24, 1962
Where Born: Fayetteville, North Carolina
Married: Susan Davis (m. 1984)
Children: Joshua Davis

TRENT MOODY

(Vocals, Bass Guitar, Guitar, Fiddle, Piano, Drums)

Given Name: Trent Jackson Moody
Date of Birth: November 29, 1966
Where Born: Charlotte, North Carolina

Most artists on major labels would be jealous of the achievements of the Moody Brothers. Recording for their own independent Lamon label out of North Carolina, they have been nominated for a Grammy Award on two occasions. At times known as Carlton Moody and the Moody Brothers, they are one group that most critics agree produce quality recordings and live performances.

The brothers began singing with their parents, Dwight and Cathy, on the family's weekly TV show on WTVI-TV Charlotte between 1968 and 1971, playing Country Gospel music. Carlton went on to gain a B.A. degree at the University of North Carolina, Charlotte, in history. David attended the same college and gained the same degree, plus a State Teaching Certificate in social studies. Trent studied at Central Piedmont Community College.

Dwight J. Moody, Jr., had been a traveling musician and Methodist minister, playing fiddle, and he and the family played Gospel music at church revivals and services all over the Carolinas. He set up the Lamon label back in 1962, and this has acted as a springboard for the European market, which favors independent labels. As a result, the Moody Brothers have established a strong base in both England and what was Czechoslovakia.

They first came to Europe as George Hamilton IV's backup band and in 1985 appeared in their own right. The year before, they had been nominated as "Record Producers of the Year" by the Beach Music Awards. However, it was in 1985 that the world knew a little more about the brothers. They were nominated by the WSOC Bluegrass Awards as "Best Brothers Band" and February 26, 1985, was made Moody Brothers Day by Charlotte and Mecklenburg County, North Carolina. That year, their rendition of *Cotton-Eyed Joe* was nominated for a 1984 Grammy for "Best Country Instrumental Performance." This was a strange nomination for a group that prides itself on its vocal harmonies.

In 1986, they were named "Independent Vocal Group of the Year" in the *Cash Box* Year-End Awards. They were also nominated as "Most Promising International Act" in the International Country Music Awards. That year, they appeared at the Intercountry Festival in Prague, and four of the songs recorded at the concert were included in a venue live album. Because of this, a deal was established with the Czech label Supraphon. In 1988, they recorded an album, ***Friends***, with Jiri Brabec and Country Beat, at Mozarteum Recording Studio near Prague. The album was released in the U.S. and the Eastern Bloc, as well as other parts of Europe. Lamon became the first Country label to have such an arrangement. One of their shows in Prague was recorded for a national broadcast on the *Television Club* show in Czechoslovakia.

In 1987, they appeared at the Peterborough Country Music Festival and were very well received. In addition, they were named "Most Popular International Trio" at the International Country Music Awards. They repeated the award the following year. In 1988, they received a Gold Record for 500,000 accumulative records sold worldwide. The following year was a momentous one for the brothers. They received a second Grammy nomination (for 1988), again in the "Best Country Instrumental Performance" category for *The Great Train Song Medley*. They also received a Silver Disc for their ***Friends*** album for 60,000 units sold. In 1990, this was elevated to Gold level, when the album had sold in excess of 100,000 units. That year, the University of North Carolina, Charlotte, honored the Moody Brothers with a "Distinguished Alumni" Award.

Their band comprises Craig Wright (drums), Nelson McSwain (drums), Myron Hill (keyboards) and their dad, Dwight, on fiddle. During 1990, Trent took leave of absence from the band to complete his education. To date, despite all of this success, the Moody Brothers have never charted in the U.S., indicative of the fact that singles charts are airplay-oriented rather than based on actual sales.

RECOMMENDED ALBUMS:

"No Hard Feelings" (Lamon)
"Gimme a Smile" (Lamon)
"We've Got It All in North Carolina" (Lamon)
"Cotton Eyed Joe" (Lamon)
"Do the Sugar Foot Rag" (Lamon)
"Start with the Talking" (Lamon)
"Carlton Moody & the Moody Brothers" (Lamon)
"Christmas with the Moody Brothers" (Lamon)
"Friends" (Lamon)(1988)

CLYDE MOODY

(Singer, Songwriter, Guitar, Mandolin)

Given Name: Clyde Leonard Moody
Date of Birth: September 19, 1915
Where Born: Cherokee, North Carolina
Married: Frances, Eletha
Children: Susan Lynne, Debra Jo
Date of Death: April 7, 1989

Clyde Moody, in a musical career that spanned more than a half century, managed to adapt himself well to several different forms of the genre, including Old-Time duets and string bands, Bluegrass and the modern form of Country crooning as it emerged in the mid 40's. Clyde never became a superstar although he did spend some time as a star at the *Grand Ole Opry* and wrote the lyrics to the classic *Shenandoah Waltz* and had some other popular numbers on King Records in the late 40's.

Clyde sprang from Cherokee and Scots-Irish stock and grew up as a product of the traditional mountain culture. When Country duets became popular in the mid-30's, he teamed up with Roy Hall's brother Jay Hugh to form the Happy-Go-Lucky Boys on WSPA Spartanburg, North Carolina. Their limited success took a turn for the better when they joined forces with Wade Mainer and became

Country music legend ***Clyde Moody***

part of the Sons of the Mountaineers along with fiddler Steve Ledford. During this time, they worked regularly on WPTF Raleigh, North Carolina, and also made several recordings on Bluebird with Wade's group. The Happy-Go-Lucky Boys also had a session of their own on that label and assisted Wade's older brother, J.E. Mainer, on his last work for Bluebird. The Happy-Go-Lucky Boys then had a short stint on their own in 1940, but things went awry and Clyde was on the verge of dropping out of music altogether when he received an offer to join Bill Monroe and his Blue Grass Boys at WSM and the *Grand Ole Opry* in Nashville that September.

The Monroe band was in the process of evolving from an Old-Time to a Bluegrass group in this period, as can be demonstrated by their recordings for Bluebird in October 1940, which included Clyde's solo of *Six White Horses* and Bill's *Mule Skinner Blues*, on which Bill played guitar and Clyde the mandolin.

Early in 1941, Moody went to Burlington, North Carolina, for several months where he and Lester Flatt had a duet act on WBBB radio and missed the October 1941 session. Rejoining the Blue Grass Boys early in 1942, Clyde remained with them until the beginning of 1945, when he again resolved to try it as a solo performer.

Moody signed on as an *Opry* artist and played some dates as a featured artist with Roy Acuff for a few weeks. In February 1945, he did a session with Columbia, from which a single was released and another for the independent Nashville-based Bullett label. Then in 1947, Clyde signed with King, the new fast-rising Cincinnati firm headed by Syd Nathan. His initial release, *Shenandoah Waltz*, co-written with fiddler Chubby Wise, became an instant favorite and started a pattern for waltz-type lyrics which gained the vocalist a name as the "Hillbilly Waltz King." *Cherokee Waltz, West Virginia Waltz, Waltz of the Wind* and *I Waltz Alone* augmented this image. He also did well with *Where the Old Red River Flows* and *Next Sunday Darling Is My Birthday*.

Carolina Waltz (Top 15) and its Top 10 flip-side, *Red Roses Tied in Blue,* made the charts in 1948, as did the top 10 cover of Leon Payne's *I Love You Because*, in 1950. In all, Clyde had more than 50 sides released on King and Federal through 1952. Like Eddy Arnold and Red Foley, Moody helped popularize the crooning style of Country singing in the 40's which gave it a more modern sound while still retaining its down-home flavor.

Clyde left the *Opry* at the end of the 40's to work for Connie B. Gay in the Washington, D.C., area. He then traveled around a bit, headlining the *Carolina Barn Dance* in Danville, Virginia, for a while and then the *Old* and *New Dominion Barn Dance* in Richmond, Virginia. Clyde left King in 1952, to sign with Decca, but they released only a few singles through the mid-50's. In 1957, Moody encountered health problems and dropped out of music for a time to enter the mobile home business.

In 1962, Clyde came back, cutting both a solo album for Wango Records with guitar backing only and a more contemporary Country effort for Starday. He had a daily TV show in Raleigh for a time and cut a few singles for Aubrey Mayhew's Little Darlin' label. In the later 60's, Clyde began working an occasional Bluegrass festival and in 1972 moved back to Nashville. From then until his death, Clyde worked sporadically in both Country and Bluegrass. For a couple of years in the mid 70's, he toured extensively with Tommy Scott's Country Caravan and Last Real Medicine Show, recording with him on both Starday and Old Homestead.

In the early 70's, Moody cut his only real Bluegrass album for Old Homestead with the backing of the Detroit-based Sunnysiders. Later he did both a Country-oriented tribute album to Fred Rose, for Old Homestead, and one of mostly new waltz songs for Longhorn. His last effort, a Gospel album for Old Homestead, saw a return to a more traditional sound.

IMT

RECOMMENDED ALBUMS:

"White House Blues" (Wango)(1962) [Re-released on Rebel in 1989]
"The Genial Gentleman of Country Songs" (Audio Lab)(1963)
"Songs That Made Him Famous" (Starday)(1963)
"The Best of Clyde Moody" (King)(1964)
"Moody Blues" (Old Homestead)(1973)
"Early Country Favorites" (Old Homestead)(1977)
"We've Played Every Place (More Than Once)" (Starday)(1978)
"Country Waltz King" (Longhorn)(1985)
Clyde Moody & Tommy Scott:
"A Country Tribute to Fred Rose" (Old Homestead)(1989)
"A Sacred Collection" (Old Homestead)(1989)

RALPH MOONEY

(Steel Guitar, Guitar, Fiddle, Mandolin, Songwriter)

Given Name:	**Ralph Mooney**
Date of Birth:	**September 1928**
Where Born:	**Duncan, Oklahoma**
Married:	**Wanda (Miss Moon)**
Children:	**Ricky, Linda**

The distinctive sound of Ralph Mooney's steel guitar has spanned four decades and has helped to define many of the classic recordings of Wynn Stewart, Buck Owens, Merle Haggard and Waylon Jennings. Ralph has also written a number of songs as well, most notably the Country standards *Crazy Arms* and *Falling For You*.

Ralph became interested in music as a very young child and was taught how to play the guitar, mandolin and fiddle by a brother-in-law. He listened to Bob Wills' steel player Leon McAuliffe and learned to play McAuliffe's *Steel Guitar Rag* using an old knife to fret his flat-top guitar. He didn't see his first steel guitar until 1941, however, when he followed his older sisters to the Los Angeles area, working for a while as a machinist at Douglas Aircraft and Alcoa Aluminum before turning his attention to music full-time.

In a little town called Bell Gardens, filled with other Oklahomans, or Okies, Ralph lived across the street from bandleader Merle Lindsey, who gave him his first professional gig in 1942, a one-nighter with Lindsey's 10-piece band, the Oklahoma Nightriders. After that Ralph started getting weekend jobs and then began doing session work with Skeets McDonald and others. He had come to California playing straight steel guitar, but in the mid-40's learned how to play around the melody from another Bob Wills band member, fiddler Jesse Ashlock. For much of his early career, he played a steel guitar he fashioned himself using birch slabs for the body, coat hangers for pullers and thick steel rods for legs.

Around 1950, Ralph was a regular performer on Squeakin' Deacon's radio show when he met the teenage Wynn Stewart, who started winning all of Squeakin' Deacon's weekly talent contests. Ralph lived and worked in Las Vegas for a while after that, and when he returned to the Los Angeles area, he began to play regularly with Stewart, whom he calls "about the greatest singer I ever worked with."

Ralph played lead guitar on Wynn's first Capitol sessions. By the late 50's, after recording with Stewart, McDonald, Buck Owens and other Capitol artists, Mooney had forged out his trademark rolling chord steel guitar sound, establishing his reputation as the West Coast's foremost steel guitar player.

Ralph was writing a lot of songs too, and cutting instrumentals for Joe Johnson's Challenge Records (like *Moonshine* and *Release Me)*. In 1956, Ray Price had his first No.1 hit record with *Crazy Arms,* which Mooney had written with Chuck Seals a number of years earlier in Las Vegas when his wife had temporarily left him because he had been drinking too much. Other hit versions were by Marion Worth (1963) and Willie Nelson (1979).

In 1961, Mooney moved to Las Vegas with Wynn to open the Nashville Nevada Club. Merle Haggard came to play bass and sing with Wynn's band a year or so later, and when Merle recorded his first sessions, for Talley Records in 1963, Ralph was there to play steel guitar. Ralph recorded with Merle (and played the road with him occasionally) and continued to work off and on with Wynn, finally following Stewart to Texas in the late 60's. When personal problems sidelined Stewart, Ralph was offered a job in Waylon Jennings' band, which he accepted.

Ralph Mooney has also played on record sessions with Donna Fargo, Rose Maddox, Bobby Austin, Bonnie Owens, Wanda Jackson, George Hamilton IV, and Hoyt Axton. In 1967, Ralph and guitarist James Burton collaborated on an album for Capitol called ***Corn Pickin' and Slick Slidin'***. Another of his songs, *Foolin',* was a Top 5 hit on the Country charts for Johnny Rodriguez in 1983.

Ralph toured and recorded with Waylon Jennings for 20 years and then retired, now limiting his appearances to guitar shows and conventions, where he talks about his long career in Country music, plays a few tunes, and demonstrates the latest in steel guitar technologies. DV

RECOMMENDED ALBUM:

"Corn Pickin' and Slick Slidin'" (Capitol)(1967)

CHARLIE MOORE

(Singer, Guitar)

Given Name:	**Charlie B. Moore, Jr.**
Date of Birth:	**February 13, 1935**
Where Born:	**Piedmont, South Carolina**
Married:	**1. Nancy Patterson (div.)**
	2. Lois Constable (div.)
Children:	**Lisa Ann, Patricia Leigh**

Charlie Moore had one of the great lead singing voices in Bluegrass Music. Although he never quite got the recognition his talents deserved, he amply displayed them on a series of albums on King Records in partnership with Bill Napier and later as leader of his own group on various labels.

Charlie grew up in western South Carolina, where his musical roots were much influenced by the many Country radio performers who broadcast programs from Charlotte, Greenville, Spartanburg and other cities in the Piedmont region, where thousands of country folks worked in the textile mills and tobacco farms that dominated the local economy.

As his voice matured he developed a smoother, Country type of singing more like that of Red Smiley, Jim Eanes or Clyde Moody than that of Bill Monroe or "the high lonesome" types of mountain Bluegrass vocalists. Charlie worked on various radio and TV programs in the western Carolinas during the mid-50's, including a stint with former Blue Grass Boy Cousin Wilbur Westbrooks on daily TV in Asheville. Always favoring acoustic instrumentation, Charlie made his first single recordings for Starday and the small American label in 1958 and 1960, respectively.

Charlie's career took a jump forward in 1960, when he teamed up with the ex-Stanley Brothers sideman Bill Napier, who had diverse skills on such instruments as mandolin, banjo and lead guitar. With their band, the Dixie Partners, Moore and Napier began recording for King on December 28, 1962, when they cut the first of what would be nine albums. During their association, which lasted until 1967 (their final album in 1968 was not released until after their partnership had dissolved), Charlie and Bill usually worked on daily TV in such locales as Spartanburg, South Carolina, and Panama City, Florida, and did personal appearances in those areas and sometimes nationally.

Although they had some well-known sidemen in their band over the years including Chubby Anthony Henry Dockery, Curly Lambert and Jimmy Williams, some critics viewed the group as somewhat lacking in depth, but none ever faulted either Charlie's singing or Bill's picking. Overall the duo recorded some 108 numbers together on King with their best-known song being *Truck Driver's Queen*, which better-known artists such as Jimmy Martin and the Willis Brothers subsequently covered on other labels.

After a couple of years of doing deejay work in the late 60's, Charlie Moore re-emerged in 1970 as sole leader of a new version of the Dixie Partners. His initial album appeared on the tiny Country Jubilee label. In the next two years, he also did two albums for Vetco and one each for Wango and Starday, although only a single was ever released for the latter firm. Meanwhile Moore joined the cast of Wheeling's *Jamboree USA.* and became increasingly active on the festival circuit, working club dates in the colder season.

From 1973, Charlie began recording on a more or less regular basis for the Old Homestead label, whose owner, John Morris, appreciated Charlie's feel for traditional Bluegrass as well as his fine vocal style. His fourth album, ***The Fiddle***, contained *The Legend of the Rebel Soldier*, a re-composition of an older song that Charlie had cut in 1971 as a single for Wango. Both the album and *The Rebel Soldier* became one of the Bluegrass hits of the decade, not only for Charlie, but also for the Country Gentlemen among others.

Meanwhile Charlie Moore continued to be beset by personal problems. Support of children from a failed first marriage took much of his earnings. Furthermore, a second marriage did not work out satisfactorily, and recurring drinking problems led to deteriorating health and periodic liver problems.

Charlie experienced the usual difficulties in holding a band together, although some top sidemen passed through the ranks of the Dixie Partners, including Terry Baucom, Johnny Dacus, Larry Jefferson and Curly Lambert. Bill Napier rejoined him on one record session but their reunion was brief. Still Charlie continued to work as conditions permitted, including two trips to Europe, during which time he cut an album each in the Netherlands and Belgium.

In late November 1979, following a date at the Mountaineer Opry House in Milton, West Virginia, the Dixie Partners headed to Maryland for another show date. When they arrived Charlie was so ill that he was taken to Johns Hopkins Medical Center, where he subsequently fell into a coma. He expired on Christmas Eve. After nearly 15 years, many of his recordings remain in print and his version of *The Rebel Soldier* is on the Smithsonian Collection of Classic Country Music. IMT

RECOMMENDED ALBUMS:

Charlie Moore and Bill Napier:

"The Best of Moore & Napier" (King)(1963)

"For All Lonesome Truck Drivers" (King)(1965)

"Gospel and Sacred Songs" (King)(1967)

"Charlie Moore and Bill Napier and the Dixie Partners (With Al Elliott)" (Old Homestead)(1978) and (1983)

Charlie Moore:

"Charlie Moore Sings Good Bluegrass" (Vetco)(1970)

"Gospel Time with Charlie Moore" (Vetco)(1973)

"The Traditional Sound of Charlie Moore" (Old Homestead)(1975)
"The Original Rebel Soldier" (Wango)(1976) [Also released on Rebel]
"A Tribute to Clyde Moody" (Old Homestead)(1976)
"The Legendary Charlie Moore and the Dixie Partners" (Leather Germany)(1980)
"Country Music Memories, I" (Old Homestead)(1980)
"Country Music Memories, II" (Old Homestead)(1981)

Singer and Deejay **Lee Moore**

LEE MOORE

(Singer, Guitar, Dobro, Deejay)
Given Name: Walter LeRoy Moore
Date of Birth: September 24, 1914
Where Born: Circleville, Ohio
Married: 1. Juanita (div.)
2. Ersi (div.)
3. Thelma
Children: Roger Lee Moore

A traditionally oriented Country vocalist, Lee Moore attained a considerable following via radio from 1935. He often sang duets with his wife Juanita in the 40's and 50's. For some two decades from 1953, Lee also achieved fame as one of the pioneer all-night deejays from WWVA Wheeling. Moreover, Lee's origins, while rural, reflected neither a Southern nor a mountain heritage.

As a youth in south-central Ohio, Lee first gained an interest in music through hearing Hawaiian steel guitarists on network radio and early hillbilly broadcasts from WAIU, in nearby Columbus. He later made his first radio broadcast from that Ohio city. After completing high school in 1932, Lee joined a traveling show group known as Doc Schneider's Yodeling Texas Cowboys, journeying at least as far as Texas with them. After returning home, Lee landed a radio program at WPAY in the Ohio River city of Portsmouth. Later, he moved upstream to WCMI Ashland, Kentucky, where he served as a featured vocalist with a group known as the Mountain Melody Boys. In 1937, he went to WRHS Charleston, where he served in a similar capacity with Buddy Starcher's Mountaineers. Lee also met a girl from Jackson County, Kentucky, who sang at the station, Juanita Picklesimer (b. 1917), known as the "Gal from the Hills." Lee and Juanita married on November 15, 1938, and formed a duet act.

Lee and Juanita worked together as a radio team for some 20 years and won wide acceptance with their down-home-style harmonies, which included numerous older ballads and sacred songs. Lee continued to project a cowboy image on stage, even wearing two holstered pistols, while Juanita contributed some fine original sacred songs such as *The Legend of the Dogwood Tree* and *When Angels Rolled the Stone Away* (popularized on record by Wilma Lee Cooper and Molly O'Day respectively).

For a dozen years, they followed the traditional lifestyle of Country radio entertainers of the time, moving to a new place every year or two. During this era they did daily broadcasts from such locales as WHIS Bluefield, West Virginia; WMMN Fairmont, West Virginia; WSVA Harrisonburg, Virginia; KFNF Shenandoah, Iowa; WROL Knoxville, Tennessee; WPAQ Mt. Airy, North Carolina, and finally at the end of 1949, WWVA Wheeling, West Virginia. On May 1, 1940, the couple had a son, Roger Lee Moore, who became part of their act, even as a small child.

The Moores found a more or less permanent home at the *World's Original Jamboree*, where they did both daily broadcasts and Saturday night shows as well. In 1953, Lee also took a late-night deejay position with the station, gaining a near legendary status as the "Coffee Drinking Night Hawk," a job he filled with only a brief break until 1969.

The duo never recorded until 1953, when they began making discs for the small New Jersey-based Cross Country label. These consisted of some twenty sides nearly evenly divided between duets and solo vocals by Lee. Some of these numbers later appeared in Canada on an album released by Point Records. The best-known title, an old comic song from 1893, *The Cat Came Back*, has virtually become Moore's trademark.

Lee and Juanita split in 1960, after which Lee continued as a solo performer, remaining with the *Jamboree* through 1974. In the early 60's Lee did some additional recording, primarily for such smaller companies as Wheeling, Mark, Essgee and Emperor. Somewhat later he did two albums each for the ARC label in Canada and Rural Rhythm in the U.S. The latter release had full Bluegrass band accompaniment furnished by Red Smiley's Bluegrass Cut-Ups. An unreleased album for the Texas-based Bluebonnet label eventually came to Germany on Cattle Records.

In 1974, having remarried and settled in the Troy, New York, suburb of Wynantskill, Moore left the *Jamboree* after a quarter century. He continued working as a musician primarily in the Northeastern states. He made additional single recordings for such labels as Fontone, Tenn-Cann, and Revonah, as well as another album for Cattle. Today, Lee is semiretired but does play a show or Bluegrass festival from time to time. As a recording artist one might conclude that his influence has been minimal, but as a radio performer and deejay Lee Moore has been quite a significant figure in the development of Country music.

Recently, Lee was presented with both a U.S. flag and a New York state flag that had been flown over their capitals in his honor. For more than half a century, he has entertained audiences with his tasteful, straight-forward approach to traditional Country songs to the simple accompaniment of either his own guitar or Dobro. IMT

RECOMMENDED ALBUMS:
"Lee and Juanita Moore" (Point)(1962)
"The Coffee Drinking Night Hawk" (ARC)(1965)
"More Coffee Drinking Night Hawk" (ARC)(1965)
"Radio Favorites of Country Music" (Rural Rhythm)(1967)
"Everybody's Favorite" (Rural Rhythms)(1967)
"Wheeling's Coffee Drinking Night Hawk" (Cattle Germany)(1983)
"A Living Legend in Country Music" (Cattle Germany)(1984)

MERRILL E. MOORE

(Singer, Songwriter, Piano, Guitar)
Given Name: Merrill Everett Moore
Date of Birth: September 26, 1923
Where Born: Algona, Iowa
Married: Doris
Children: one daughter

Merrill E. Moore is a Country-Boogie piano player and vocalist who has spent most of his adult life as a nightclub and hotel lounge entertainer. Moore himself considered his music to be a mixture of Western Swing, Boogie-Woogie and Rhythm and Blues, expressing considerable admiration for Bob Wills, Moon Mullican, and most especially Boogie pianist Freddie Slack.

Merrill grew up on a livestock farm in Algona, Iowa. His mother played piano and he began taking formal lessons at age 6. At age 12, he guested on radio station WHO in nearby

Des Moines. In high school he learned more about music and met his future wife, Doris. After WWII service in the U.S. Navy, Merrill and Doris married and moved west, living briefly in Tucson and Denver, before settling permanently in San Diego. He did some piano work in clubs in all these locales while also retaining a day job. After several months in Southern California, tickling the ivories became his full-time work.

In 1950, Merrill put together his own band consisting of Monty Gibson (bass), John Stokes (drums) and Dave Carpenter (steel guitar). In mid-June, they began a six-night-a-week stint for nightclub owner Jimmy Kennedy, who owned eleven establishments around the city. Merrill and his Saddle Rhythm Boys worked mostly at the Buckaroo Club.

Kennedy helped the group land a contract with Capitol, and Merrill and his boys had their initial session in May with their first release being *Big Bug Boogie* and *Corrine, Corrina*. Unfortunately, the San Diego club owner insisted that Merrill maintain his six-night-a-week schedule at the Buckaroo, so he missed out on opportunities to tour and promote his records when they were hot items. His best-known number, *House of Blue Lights* (July 1953), was a cover of an original Freddie Slack classic from 1946. In addition to his piano, Merrill had a pleasant and appealing vocal style which also went over well, but his piano stylings tended to have the longest-lasting appeal.

Merrill finally left San Diego for Los Angeles in March 1955, when he joined Cliffie Stone and the *Hometown Jamboree*. Doing session work for Capitol in the later 50's, his piano was heard on such Rockabilly classics as Wanda Jackson's *Let's Have a Party* and such Pop hits as *Teen Age Crush* by Tommy Sands.

Merrill also appeared on many Country sessions of the later 50's, ranging from those of Sonny James to Faron Young. He did his last solo work for Capitol in the fall of 1958, recording material for an instrumental album, but it remained unreleased until 1990.

After being dropped by Capitol, Merrill returned to San Diego, where his work has continued up to the present. Moore has also made forays into Las Vegas, Reno, Phoenix and elsewhere, including cruise ships. When he toured Europe in 1970, he somewhat surprisingly found himself regarded as a Rockabilly pioneer.

Merrill made some more recordings in 1969 for a British firm, but none were released; however, Capitol efforts reappeared in Britain on such labels as Ember and Bulldog. Nick Tosches included a chapter on Merrill in *Unsung Heroes of Rock'n'Roll* (1984). Bear Family released all of his sides from the 50's on cd in 1990. In the accompanying booklet, Western Swing researcher Cary Ginnell suggested that while Moore's style is not easy to categorize, it is perhaps closest to the music offerings associated with Bob Wills. IMT

RECOMMENDED ALBUMS:

"20 Golden Pieces of Merrill E. Moore" (Bulldog UK)(1979)
"Boogie My Blues Away" (Bear Family Germany)(1990)

TINY MOORE

(Fiddle, Electric Mandolin, Guitar)

Given Name:	**Billie Moore**
Date of Birth:	**May 12, 1920**
Where Born:	**Energy, Hamilton County, Texas**
Married:	**Dean (one half of the McKinney Sisters)**
Children:	**Kim, Debbie, Richard**
Date of Death:	**December 15, 1987**

Tiny Moore has been described as Western Swing's great mandolinist and he was mostly known for popularizing the electric mandolin while playing with Bob Wills and His Texas Playboys in the 40's. He became one of Country music's most respected and beloved pickers, influencing a whole generation of string musicians.

While still a baby, Tiny went around in a buggy, as his mother, a piano teacher, went visiting. On his father's side, his grandfather was a fiddle player. Just after starting school, Tiny's family moved to Port Arthur, Texas, where he had his first violin lessons, but before he finished high school, his brother Dee's asthma forced them to Dallas and then back to Energy. There, Tiny played with his uncle, a fiddler and guitarist, his mother and a couple of cousins, at country dances, earning 75 cents.

Tiny was in the school orchestra and played fiddle and guitar with a group of fellow students known as the Clod Hoppers. He stayed with them until 1937, when he graduated. The family joined Tiny's father in Port Arthur, where Tiny worked in a grocery store. He soon met banjo player Woody Edmunston and through him, guitarist Jimmy Wyble. They began playing popular music together, and as Tiny was not a fan of the *Grand Ole Opry* in those days, he found himself copying Benny Goodman's music.

It was during this time that he got his nickname, because he *wasn't* tiny. He then weighed in at 267 pounds and would always have a weight problem. In 1940, he began working in a trio with jazz guitarist Lloyd Ellis. They put together a band and moved to Mobile, Alabama, where Tiny got his first taste of broadcasting, but it didn't pan out, and he returned to Port Arthur. He then moved to Rayne, Louisiana, with Happy Fats and His Rainbow Ramblers, a Cajun band, playing on KVOL Lafayette. He then moved back to Port Arthur to play in the Jubileers, who were formed to advertise Sears Roebuck. He took the band over and they cut some sides for Bluebird.

Tiny then moved to Houston, working with the Crustene Ranch Gang, who had a weekly radio show on Texas Quality Network and also in Little Rock. He stayed with them (and also worked in the shipyards) until he got drafted in 1943. Tiny spent two years in the U.S. Air Force, as a radio operator and teacher in Sioux Falls, South Dakota. It was just prior to his service that Tiny started to play mandolin, and he watched various people and developed his style. Among those was electric mandolinist Leo Raley out of Houston, Jazz guitarist Charlie Christian, Jazz sax player Coleman Hawkins and steelie Bob Dunn.

After leaving the service, Tiny returned to Port Arthur, where in the summer of 1946, he came to the attention of Bob Wills, who was playing at the Pleasure Pier. It was a chance meeting that got him into the band. Tiny had intended to go up to Oklahoma with a drummer friend, Richard Prine, in search of bookings, when they passed a sandwich stand. They decided to go back and get some food, and to their surprise, eating there were Wills, brother Billy Jack and Tommy Duncan. Wills got Tiny to play mandolin, there and then. As a result, Tiny worked with Bob Wills for four years.

In early 1950, he was still with the band but was also managing the Wills Point Ballroom in Sacramento and was getting tired of traveling. He started playing with Billy Jack Wills and they got on KFBK in Sacramento; as the Billy Jack Wills Band, they were successful locally. During a visit to Los Angeles, he met famed instrument builder Paul Bigsby and got Bigsby to build him a 5-string electric mandolin (tuned C-G-D-A-E), which arrived in 1952.

Tiny played with Wills briefly in 1955 but again refused to go back on the road. He then worked on a local TV station, as "Ranger Roy," for the youngsters, as well as playing music at weekends. In 1961, he lost his job at the station due to a strike and so, in the cause of financial stability, he opened the Tiny Moore Music Center in Sacramento, where he taught guitar, fiddle and mandolin.

In 1970, Merle Haggard got together some of the original Texas Playboys, including Tiny, to record a tribute album to Bob Wills, *A*

Tribute to the Best Damn Fiddle Player in the World (Or My Salute to Bob Wills). In 1973, Tiny appeared on the last album that Wills played on, ***The Last Time***, and then became a member of Merle Haggard's Strangers from 1973 through 1976. He became an active member of the California Old Time Fiddlers Association and frequently participated in their contests. He also played quite a lot at this stage with his friend, former Texas Playboy rhythm guitarist Eldon Shamblin.

During 1979, Tiny was invited to record an album on Kaleidoscope entitled ***Back to Back***, with another mandolin star, Jethro Burns, which was produced by a third wizard of the instrument, David Grisman, who also played on a couple of cuts. Tiny also went on to record a solo album, ***Tiny Moore Music***, for the label in 1980. In December 1987, while playing at Cactus Pete's in Jackpot, Nevada, with the Cadillac Band, Tiny Moore suffered a heart attack and died.

RECOMMENDED ALBUMS:

"Back to Back" (Kaleidoscope)(1980) [With Jethro Burns]
"Tiny Moore Music" (Kaleidoscope)(1980)
"Bob Wills and his Texas Playboys—The Tiffany Transcriptions 1946-47, Volume 1 through 6" (6 albums)(Kaleidoscope)(1983)
"Crazy Man Crazy" (Western) [Billy Jack Wills album features Tiny Moore]
"Western Swing Band (Sacramento 1952-1954)" (Western) [Billy Jack Wills album features Tiny Moore]

GEORGE MORGAN

(Singer, Songwriter, Guitar)

Given Name:	**George Thomas Morgan**
Date of Birth:	**June 28, 1924**
Where Born:	**Waverly, Tennessee**
Married:	**Anastasia "Anna" Paridon**
Children:	**Candy Kay, Bethany Belle, Liana Lee, Matthew Martin, Loretta Lynn (Lorrie Morgan)**
Date of Death:	**July 7, 1975**

George Morgan catapulted to Country music stardom on the strength of a super hit, *Candy Kisses*, in 1949.

Born in Waverly, Tennessee, George Morgan moved to Barberton, Ohio, in early childhood after his father lost his leg in a lumbering accident and subsequently found employment at the Sieberling Rubber Company. George grew up listening to the *Grand Ole Opry* and after WWII put together a little Country band.

He did some spots at local WAKR and a regular slot at newly opened WWST Wooster. His career seemed stalled, however, until writing *Candy Kisses*. He had previously tried to get on at WWVA to no avail, but after *Candy Kisses*, they welcomed "Tennessee George," as he was then known. Columbia contracted him in September 1948, but could not record him until the following January 16 after the Petrillo ban had ended. *Candy Kisses* shot quickly to the top of the Country charts by early April and would likely have remained longer had not Hank Williams' *Lovesick Blues* displaced it. The flip-side of the single, *Please Don't Let Me Love You*, also reached the Top 5.

The Candy Kid, ***George Morgan***

Morgan had six more chartmakers that year: *Rainbow in My Heart* (Top 10) and the flipside, *All I Need Is Some More Lovin'* (Top 15), *Room Full of Roses* (Top 5) (which even hit the Pop chart Top 25) and the double-sided Top 5 hit *Cry-Baby Heart/I Love Everything About You* closed out the year.

Since George, a Country crooner in the Eddy Arnold style, seemed a likely successor to the Tennessee Plowboy, the *Grand Old Opry* hired the "Candy Kid," as he became known, as Arnold's replacement. While Morgan never quite became a second Eddy Arnold, he did become a mainstay at the *Opry* and a solid, dependable performer.

Despite his early successes, there was a three-year gap until his next chart run. In 1952, *Almost* reached the Top 3, where it stayed for 6 weeks. The following year, *(I Just Had a Date) A Lover's Quarrel* became a Top 10 record. George also became one of the few Country singers of his era to be recorded in duets with Pop vocalists, namely Dinah Shore and Rosemary Clooney, although he had less success than Ernest Tubb and Jimmy Wakely did in these endeavors. George did leave WSM in 1956 for a television program at WLAC, but by 1959, he again became an *Opry* regular.

George briefly returned to the charts, in 1957, with *There Goes My Love* (Top 15). Two years later, the Candy Kid returned to WSM, and also scored his biggest hit since *Almost* with *I'm in Love Again*, which made it to the Top 3. He followed up with *Little Dutch Girl* (Top 20)/*The Last Thing I Want to Know* (Top 30).

In 1960, George had a Top 5 success with *You're the Only Good Thing (That's Happened to Me)*. It was not until 1964 that George returned to the chart with *One Dozen Roses (And Our Love)* (Top 25)/*All Right (I'll Sign the Papers)* (Top 50). Later that year, George and Marion Worth had a Top 25 duet success with a revival of the old Floyd Tillman favorite, *Slipping Around*. George closed out the year with the Top 40 hit *Tears and Roses*. George had one more chart entry for Columbia, the Top 30 success *A Picture That's New* in 1966.

In the last decade of his life, Morgan recorded for Starday, Stop, MCA, and 4 Star, making the charts fifteen more times, the most successful being *I Couldn't See* (Top 40, Starday, 1967), *Sounds of Goodbye* (Top 40, Starday, 1968), *Like a Bird* (Top 30, Stop, 1969), *Lilacs and Fire* (Top 20, Stop, 1970) and *Red Rose from the Blue Side of Town* (Top 25, MCA, 1974).

In that time, George's youngest daughter, Lorrie, began to sing, singing *Paper Roses* on her *Opry* debut, and she sometimes went out on the road with her dad. Morgan experienced a heart attack in May 1975 while repairing a TV antenna on the roof of his home. He returned to the *Opry* in late June and celebrated his fifty-first birthday but then passed away several days afterward.

His last appearance on the charts took place in 1979, in the form of a duet with Lorrie titled *I'm Completely Satisfied with You*. Given Lorrie Morgan's later musical achievements, her father undoubtedly would have thought the title more than apt. IMT

RECOMMENDED ALBUMS:

"Morgan, By George" (Columbia)(1957)
"Golden Memories" (Columbia)(1961)
"Tender Lovin' Care" (Columbia)(1964)
"Red Roses for a Blue Lady" (Columbia)(1965)
"Room Full of Roses" (Harmony)(1967)
"Candy Kisses" (Starday)(1967)
"Barbara" (Starday)(1968)
"Sounds of Goodbye" (Starday)(1969)
"Misty Blue" (Nashville)(1969)
"George Morgan Sings Like a Bird" (Stop)(1969)
"Candy Kisses" (Harmony)(1969)
"The Best of George Morgan" (Starday)(1970)
"The Real George" (Stop)(1970)
"Red Roses from the Blue Side of Town" (MCA)(1974)
"A Candy Mountain Melody" (MCA)(1974)
"From This Moment On" (4 Star)(1975)
"Remembering the Greatest Hits of George Morgan" (Columbia)(1975)

LORRIE MORGAN

(Singer, Songwriter, Guitar, Piano, Actress)
Given Name: Loretta Lynn Morgan
Date of Birth: June 27, 1960
Married: 1. Ron Gaddis (div.)
2. Keith Whitley (dec'd.)
3. Brad Thompson (separated)
Children: (Anastasia) Morgan, Jesse Keith

There was never any doubt that Lorrie Morgan would become a star. What is surprising is that it took so long for the industry and the buying public to wake up to her.

Lorrie, the daughter of Country music star George Morgan, began her career at the age of 13, when she sang *Paper Roses* on the *Grand Ole Opry*, at the Ryman Auditorium, to a standing ovation, the first there in 12 years. While at St. Bernard Academy, Nashville, she put together her own band. In 1977, she was named first runner-up in the Miss Nashville Beauty Pageant. For a while, she played in the Little Roy Wiggins band. Roy had been George Morgan's steelie.

Lorrie initially worked for Acuff-Rose as a receptionist and part-time demo singer, and she also signed to the company as a songwriter. She first appeared on record in 1978, when she did an unnamed appearance on Freddy Weller's hit *Love Got in the Way*. She had her first chart entry the following year, when her Hickory single *Two People in Love* reached the Top 75. She moved over to MCA that same year, and had a Top 90 single, *Tell Me I'm Only Dreaming*. Thanks to electronic wizardry, her voice was dubbed onto a recording by her father. The resulting duet, *I'm Completely Satisfied with You*, on 4 Star, scraped into the Top 100.

*Watch her! It's **Lorrie Morgan***

Having toured around the Nashville night spots, she then became the opening act for Billy Thunderkloud, Jack Greene and Jeannie Seely. In 1981, she joined George Jones as opening act and stage duet partner. She became a featured act in Opryland's *Country Bluegrass Show* and was a regular featured singer on TNN's *Nashville Now*.

She again got into the charts in 1984, when her MCA recording *Don't Go Changing* got into the Top 70. That year, she joined the cast of the *Grand Ole Opry*, just over ten years after her debut. In 1986, Lorrie married singer Keith Whitley and in 1988, she joined him as an artist on RCA. At the end of the year, she had a Top 20 hit with the Jon Vezner-Alan Rhody song *Trainwreck of Emotion*.

It was in 1989 that her career took off, and tragedy struck. Her single *Dear Me* reached the Top 10 and then on May 9, Keith Whitley died. With grit and determination, Lorrie appeared at the *Grand Ole Opry*, the Saturday after Whitley's death. With equal fortitude, she pulled her career together and became a major star. Her single *Out of Your Shoes* reached the Top 3 and stayed on the charts for 6 months. Her album ***Leave the Light On*** spent a total of 84 weeks on the Country Album charts and was Certified Gold.

With *Five Minutes*, she achieved her first No.1 single, in 1990. It was followed by *He Talks to Me*, which reached the Top 5, and she wrapped up the year with *'Til a Tear Becomes a Rose*, a Top 15 duet with Keith. All of her three chart singles in 1991 were major hits: *We Both Walk* reached the Top 3, *A Picture of Me (With You)*, a former hit for George Jones, peaked in the Top 10 and *Except for Monday* climbed to the Top 5. Her album ***Something in Red*** reached No.10 on the Country Album chart and was around for 46 weeks; by 1992, it had been Certified Platinum.

During the spring of 1992, her single of Angela Kasset's *Something in Red* reached the Top 15, which is disappointing since it's such a fine record. However, the follow-up, *Watch Me*, the title track of her next album, on her new label, BNA, reached the Top 3 and like all her hits was accompanied by a snappy video. At the end of the year, Lorrie charted *What Part of No*, which reached No.1, where it stayed for 3 weeks. Like its predecessors, the ***Watch Me*** album was also Certified Gold.

Lorrie made her TV movie debut in 1993, in *Proudheart* for TNN. The same year, she was named Female Stylemaster by the National Cosmetology Association, and became NCA Spokesperson for "Look Good...Feel Better Program." At the end of 1993, Lorrie released ***Merry Christmas from London***, which featured the New World Philharmonic Orchestra and duets with Andy Williams, Johnny Mathis and Tammy Wynette. Lorrie's chart singles in 1993 were *I Guess You Had to Be There* (Top 15) and *Half Enough* (Top 10). Her other chart single that year was her Top 60 version of *Crying Time*, which came from the Soundtrack of *The Beverly Hillbillies*. In 1994, Lorrie had a lowly seasonal chart single with *My Favorite Things* and followed it with *My Night to Howl* (Top 40) and *If You Come Back from Heaven* (Top 60). Both these singles came from the album ***War Paint***, which was produced by Lorrie with her longtime producer Richard Landis. In the summer of 1994, Lorrie announced that she was returning to RCA and breaking from Landis.

RECOMMENDED ALBUMS:
"Leave the Light On" (RCA)(1989)
"Something in Red" (RCA)(1991)
"Watch Me" (BNA)(1992)
"War Paint" (BNA)(1994)

MORRIS BROTHERS, The

When Formed: 1938

ZEKE MORRIS
(Singer, Mandolin)
Given Name: Zeke Edward Morris
Date of Birth: May 9, 1916
Married: Frances
Children: Carolyn, Linda, Patricia, Barbara, John, Camille

WILEY MORRIS
(Singer, Guitar)
Given Name: Wiley Andrew Morris
Date of Birth: February 1, 1919
Where Born: Old Fort, North Carolina
Married: Evelyn (dec'd.)
Children: Ronald, Sharon, Ralph, Donna, Dale
Date of Death: September 22, 1990

The Morris Brothers constituted one of the major duets in pre-WWII Country music. Their best known song, *Let Me Be Your Salty Dog*, went on to become a staple in the Bluegrass field as *Salty Dog Blues*.

Natives of Old Fort, North Carolina, Wiley and Zeke grew up in a musical family of six boys, with older brother George (1912-1978) first becoming a proficient guitarist. Three of the boys seemingly inherited their talents from a fiddler mother, who died when Wiley was an infant. George worked with J.E. Mainer along with brother Wade, and when John Love came to Old Fort to recruit George into their band, he wound up taking 17-year-old Zeke instead. Zeke stayed with the band for three years, appearing on WBT radio and on their first Bluebird session of 1935, which included the Mainers' major hit *Maple on the Hill* featuring Wade and Zeke's duet. Not long afterward, this pair separated from the Mountaineers and formed their own group, recording more for Bluebird and working on radio at WPTF Raleigh. Homer Sherrill also joined them. Later, Wade left to go elsewhere and the others remained together, going on to do radio work in Danville and cutting eight numbers for Bluebird in January 1938 as Wiley, Zeke, and Homer. Nine months later they did another session simply as the Morris Brothers, doing nine songs, including their first rendition of *Salty Dog Blues.* Zeke also helped Charlie Monroe on a session.

Meanwhile, the Morris Brothers continued sporadic radio work. Their most active broadcasts stemmed from the near-to-home station of WWNC Asheville, North Carolina, where they appeared regularly on the *Western Carolina Farm Hour*. Sometimes brother George worked with them after his stint with Mainer's Mountaineers. Zeke described his older brother as a fine musician although his voice did not blend well in harmony with his or Wiley's. Although remembered primarily as a duet, they did carry a band from time to time, which included not only veterans like fiddler Tiny Dodson, but youngsters who went on to major achievements in Bluegrass such as Earl Scruggs, Hoke Jenkins, Don Reno, Red Rector, Red Smiley and Fred Smith. At times the brothers led groups separately. Both worked at Knoxville for a while, in the early 40's, but then Zeke departed and Wiley remained in a band called the Dixie Pardners that included Ray Atkins and Buster Moore at WROL, while Zeke had a band at Johnson City radio. In November 1945, the Morris Brothers had a final session for RCA Victor which included a new recording of *Salty Dog Blues*, *Tragic Romance, Grave on the Green Hillside*, and *Somebody Loves You Darling*.

Following that session, the boys virtually retired from active performing. Wiley helped Wade Mainer on one of his postwar King sessions. Wiley and Zeke settled in Black Mountain, North Carolina, where they ran an automobile body shop. They did make a few festival appearances in the 60's and 70's and with Homer Sherrill on fiddle cut a fine album for Rounder in 1972. They also appeared on a PBS-TV special with Earl Scruggs and recorded a new arrangement of *Salty Dog Blues*, which showed up on one of his Columbia albums. They made their last public concert at a Charlotte radio old-timers reunion in October 1985. Since Wiley's death, Zeke continues to operate his body shop business and picks a bit for friends and neighbors, but reports he has no interest to perform in public, despite offers. He still receives two royalty checks a year for *Salty Dog Blues*. Although they have appeared on a couple of RCA anthologies, oddly enough no extensive re-issues of Morris Brothers originals have been done even though adequate material exists for a couple of excellent albums. IMT

RECOMMENDED ALBUM:

"Wiley, Zeke and Homer" (Rounder) (1973)

(See also J.E. Mainer, Wade Mainer, Charlie Monroe, Earl Scruggs.)

GARY MORRIS

(Singer, Songwriter, Guitar, Actor)

Given Name: Gary Gwyn Morris
Date of Birth: December 7, 1948
Where Born: Fort Worth, Texas
Married: (Div.)
Children: Samuel, Matthew, Hunter

Gary Morris is one of the select few artists who have been able to transcend musical boundaries and create their own brand of music: in Gary's case, a unique hybrid of Country, Folk and Pop that suits his own style.

Born and raised in Fort Worth, Texas, Gary had a paternal grandfather who could supposedly play just about any string instrument. His grandfather on his mother's side was a vocal teacher who wrote songs in the Baptist hymnal. Also, his mother was a singer herself; thus, Gary's musical roots run deep. When he was in the third grade he sang in a duo with his twin sister, Carrie. Like many other singers, Gary began his musical career in his church choir. He became quite an athlete during his school years, playing football, basketball and being adept on the running track. Later, he attended junior college in Cisco, Texas, on a football scholarship. He played strong safety and his freshman team made top ten ranking in the nation.

Gary Morris with ***Crystal Gayle***

While still in high school, however, it became apparent that music would become the main thrust in his life as he began playing guitar, writing songs and performing professionally around the Fort Worth area in small groups and as a solo artist. While a sophomore in high school he appeared on *Ted Mack's Amateur Hour*.

The die was soon cast and in 1969, Gary became a full-time musician. He performed initially in a trio called Taylor's Cowboys, based in Denver. Later, he traveled the country in a duo for two years, then returned to Denver and formed his own seven-piece band, Breakaway, which featured original material written almost exclusively by Gary. During these years, he also did studio work, sang regularly at a Denver nightspot and wrote and sang jingles for accounts like Coors and Frontier Airlines.

In 1976, he was part of a whistle-stop campaign tour with Jimmy Carter, and recalled they visited seventeen cities in two days. He was asked to perform at one of the Carter inaugural balls and *People* magazine reported that Gary Morris was President and Mrs. Carter's favorite singer. Gary was later asked to represent his native Texas at a command performance for Queen Elizabeth II and was invited by former President and Mrs. George Bush to be their Goodwill Ambassador on a trip to the Soviet Union.

While performing at President Carter's Inauguration, Gary was spotted by Nashville producer/A&R man Norro Wilson. Through Wilson, Gary got his first recording contract with Warner Brothers, as well as a publishing contract, and released his first single, *Sweet Red Wine*, in 1980. The song made Top 40 in the charts and was followed up the next year with *Fire in Your Eyes*, which also went Top 40. Gary's third single in 1981, *Headed for a Heartache*, hit the Top 10 and moved into the hot radio recurrent category. He followed these first three singles with the self-penned *Don't*

Look Back, which made the Top 15 in 1982. *Dreams Die Hard*, another Top 15, and his Top 10 *Velvet Chains* completed his 1982 hit list.

In 1983, Gary released the popular *The Love She Found in Me*, which became his signature song, peaking in the Top 5. This was, however, only a prelude to his next hit in August of that year, the modern classic *The Wind Beneath My Wings*, which went Top 5, in 1983. The self-penned *Why Lady Why* was to become his next hit, also going Top 5. Gary completed the year with a duet with Lynn Anderson, *You're Welcome to the Night*, which went Top 10.

1984 got off to a good start with back-to-back Top 10 hits, *Between Two Fires* and *Second Hand Heart*. His next hit, *Baby, Bye, Bye*, became his first No.1 single. Gary started off 1985 in much the same way as the past four years, with *Lasso the Moon* reaching the Top 10. What followed next proved to be a peak in his musical career with three back-to-back No.1 hits, *I'll Never Stop Loving You, 100% Chance of Rain*, and his duet with Crystal Gayle, *Makin' Up for Lost Time (The Dallas Lovers' Song)*. The following year brought fans the Top 30 *Anything Goes*, followed by *Honeycomb*, which was originally a No.1 Pop hit for Jimmie Rodgers (not the Singing Brakeman!), in 1957. Gary finished out the year with another No.1, *Leave Me Lonely*.

During 1987, he went Top 10 with *Plain Brown Wrapper*, the title track of his 1986 album, and Top 5 with *Another World*, the theme song from the daytime TV series of the same title, on which he duetted with Crystal Gayle. He closed out 1987 with *Finishing Touches*, which only reached the Top 70. In 1988, he had his final Warner Brothers release, *All of This and More*, another duet with Crystal, which went Top 30.

In 1989, Gary had a short-lived career with Universal Records, which produced the Top 50 *Never Had a Love Song*, then *The Jaws of Modern Romance*, which proved to be one of his lowest-charting records. In 1991, he moved to Capitol and released his final single to date, the Top 50 *Miles Across the Bedroom*, from his last album, ***These Days***.

Gary recorded two children's songs for the soundtrack to the film *The Giant of Mountain*. During the 80's Gary was nominated for a number of awards: "New Male Artist of the Year," by the ACM (1983), the CMA "Horizon Award," "Single of the Year" and "Song of the Year" for *The Love She Found in Me* (1983), and *The Wind Beneath My Wings* was nominated as "Song of the Year" by both *Music City News* and the ACM (1983), winning the latter; the album containing his performance in *Les Misérables* (1987) won a Grammy Award for "Best Musical Cast Show Album."

Gary's songwriting career received a lot of acclaim during the 80's as well. A rodeo song, *Playin' Cowboy*, was featured on ABC's *Wide World of Sports Cheyenne Frontier Days* soundtrack. Additionally, he wrote several of his own songs including *Don't Look Back* and *Why Lady Why*. Reba McEntire recorded *Whoever's Watchin'*, a song written by Gary and Kevin Welch, in 1982.

In 1984, Gary turned his talents toward acting, making his debut in Joseph Papp's New York Shakespeare Festival production of *La Bohème*, playing the role of Rodolfo, opposite Linda Ronstadt. This represented the first time a Country music singer had performed in a legitimate stage production in New York. He also appeared in Broadway's *Les Misérables*, in 1988. These roles led to guest appearances in *Dynasty 2* and *The Colbys*, playing a blind Country singer, "Wayne Masterson," in the latter. Other television credits include: the *Merv Griffin Show*, *Austin City Limits*, *That's Country*, *Fantasy*, *The Music City News' Songwriters Award Show*, *Nashville Now*, *Inside Country Cookin'*, the *Bob Braun Show*, *Nashville Alive* and *NBC's Academy of Country Music Special*. Radio appearances include *Live from Gilley's*, *The Silver Eagle*, *America's Country Countdown* and *Country Crossroads*. As a producer, Gary's credits include producing an album for the Hungarian Rock Band MHV.

For more than a decade Gary Morris had one of the most incredible careers in show business. Where his musical path takes him over the next decade will no doubt keep his fans guessing. LAP

RECOMMENDED ALBUMS:

"Gary Morris" (Warner Brothers)(1982)
"Why Lady Why" (Warner Brothers) 1983)
"Hits" (Warner Brothers)(1983) [Re-issued in 1987]
"Faded Blues" (Warner Brothers)(1984)
"Second Hand Heart" (Warner Brothers)(1986)
"Plain Brown Wrapper" (Warner Brothers)(1986)
"What If We Fall in Love" (Warner Brothers)(1987) [With Crystal Gayle]
"Stones" (Universal)(1989)
"These Days" (Capitol)(1991)

MORRISON TWIN BROTHERS STRING BAND, The

ABBIE MORRISON
(Fiddle)

Given Name:	**Abbie Sherman Morrison**
Date of Birth:	**November 11, 1876**
Date of Death:	**July 4, 1965**

APSIE MORRISON
(Fiddle)

Given Name:	**Apsie Sherdon Morrison**
Date of Birth:	**November 11, 1876**
Date of Death:	**1964**
Both Born:	**Searcy County, Arkansas**
Other Members	**(Both Abbie's sons):**

Claude Morrison Guitar
Lawson Morrison Guitar

One of the most unusual Old-Time string bands made only one recording session, in 1930, for Victor. Twins Abbie and Apsie Morrison's father, uncle, and grandfather were all well-known local fiddlers, so it was hardly surprising that the twins also became fiddlers. While they never thought of themselves as professional performers, for several years they were active playing in informal bands with several members of their own family and other local musicians. They attended such events as the Ozark Fiddle Contest held annually in Joplin, Missouri, for several years.

Possibly their appearances at such events led to their June 3, 1930, recording session in Memphis. On this occasion they recorded two traditional fiddle tunes, *Dry and Dusty* and *Ozark Waltz*. The band that recorded that day included two of Abbie's sons, Claude and Lawson. A third son was scheduled to play banjo on that session but had to drop out because he broke a string and had no spare.

The Morrisons had the misfortune to make their sole recordings when America was mired in the Great Depression, and luxury items, such as records, didn't sell very well. As it turned out they probably would not have recorded again anyway because, as a result of the death of a family member, the brothers became estranged. They never performed together after the 1930's, and Apsie moved more than 100 miles away from his brother, to Jonesboro, Arkansas. The two never gave up their music and in later years were revered as elder statesmen of Ozark fiddle music. Apsie died in 1964; his brother Abbie followed on July 4, 1965. Their two 1930 sides remain as fine examples of string band music from the Arkansas Ozarks. WKM

RECOMMENDED ALBUM:

"Echoes of the Ozarks, Volume l" (County)

HAROLD MORRISON

(Banjo, Guitar, Dobro, Steel Guitar, Comedy)

Given Name:	**Harold Ralph Morrison**
Date of Birth:	**January 30, 1931**
Where Born:	**Highlonesome, Missouri**
Married:	**Eva Lou**

Children: Georgia Lynn, Karla Jo, Gina Lou
Date of Death: December 21, 1993

Harold Morrison experienced a long career as a Country entertainer. He distinguished himself as both a musician and a comedian.

A native of the Ozark highlands of southwestern Missouri, Harold attended high school in the regional metropolis of Springfield, where he had his first radio experience at local station KGBX in 1950. The next year he moved over to KWTO, a more Country music-oriented outlet. There he met fiddler/guitarist Jimmy Gatley and the two formed a duo, going first to KJSB Jamestown, North Dakota, with the Red River Rustlers. Then they traveled to WWVA Wheeling, where they worked as a duet and as band members for Dusty Owens, with whom they recorded a session on Columbia in 1954. When the *Ozark Jubilee* started in 1955, Harold and Jimmy returned to Springfield, where they became cast members and worked many personal appearances with Red Foley. Harold also did sessions with the Browns in 1956 and Porter Wagoner in 1955, both for RCA Victor.

Harold moved to Nashville in February 1957 to replace Shot Jackson as steel guitarist/Dobroist with the Kitty Wells-Johnny & Jack Show. He participated in several recording sessions with each, on Decca and RCA Victor respectively. From there, Morrison went with the Wilburn Brothers, gaining a wide audience via their syndicated television program as well as personal appearances.

In 1959, Harold had cut an album for Reader's Digest with a group of studio musicians, which reappeared on Old Homestead in 1984. His best-circulated recordings, however, were his Decca efforts of the mid-60's, which included an album that featured both comedy songs and instrumental tunes as well as a spot on the Wilburns Show album. When George Jones and Tammy Wynette combined in 1969, Harold joined their entourage, remaining with them for the duration of their marriage and with Tammy for about a year after their split.

In 1975, Harold organized the Smoking Bluegrass Band with Benny Williams and daughter Karla Morrison, which worked the festival circuit for some years. From 1985 until 1987, Harold had a band at Silver Dollar City in Branson, Missouri. He then joined Ferlin Husky in Myrtle Beach, South Carolina, until Hurricane Hugo wiped out Ferlin's show site in September 1989.

Morrison then worked in Mountain View, Arkansas, at the Grandpa and Ramona Jones Dinner Theater for a few months and then took a group to Myrtle Beach again. In 1992, Harold returned to Branson, working in various entertainment endeavors until felled by two strokes about ten days apart. His demise followed the second one, late in 1993. Harold's widow felt much comforted by the outpouring of sympathy she received from fans and former employers, including both George Jones and Tammy Wynette. IMT

RECOMMENDED ALBUMS:

"Hoss, He's the Boss" (Decca)(1965)

"Harold Morrison & the Smoking Bluegrass" (Autumn)(ca 1979)

"Blue Grass Classics" (Old Homestead)(1984) [Originally recorded in 1959 and released on Reader's Digest, credited to Harold Morrison and the Maple Hill Boys]

TEX MORTON

(Guitar, Harmonica)
Given Name: Robert William Lane
Date of Birth: August 30, 1916
Where Born: Nelson, New Zealand
Married: Marjorie Frederica Brisbane (div.)
Children: Robert, Bernard (dec'd.) (twins)
Date of Death: July 23, 1983

Known as the "Yodeling Boundary Rider," Tex Morton was Australia's original Country music recording artist and star. A native of New Zealand, he migrated to Australia in his later teens, and from shortly after his first record releases in 1936 until his death, enjoyed a celebrity status "Down Under." Morton's life and rise to prominence bear a considerable resemblance, in many respects, to some of the better known American performers of the same era.

Born as Robert William Lane, this pioneer-to-be benefited from a relatively normal youth except that he showed an unusual interest in plays and entertaining in school. At the age of 14, he ran away from home in pursuit of a show business career. After returning several times he went to Australia about 1934, where he "busked" around for a time in a variety of entertaining jobs. In later years, he credited such American performers as Jimmie Rodgers, Carson Robinson, and the Carter Family as being major influences on him. In February 1936, using the name "Tex Morton," he recorded four sides in Sydney for the Regal Zonophone label, and four more a week later. Most of these early cuts were lyrics of American origin, such as *Texas in the Spring, Going Back to Texas,* and *You're Going to Leave the Old Home, Jim.* His yodeling style owed a considerable debt to Goebel Reeves. Later in 1936, Morton began adding originals and songs of Aussie origin to his recorded repertoire, such as *The Yodeling Bagman, Wrap Me Up with My Stockwhip and Blanket,* and *On the Gundagi Line.* From then on his recordings generally reflected a mixture of local and American material.

Although Morton continued to live an itinerant life for several weeks after these initial sessions, the release of his discs soon made him well-known in both Australia and New Zealand. For the next several years, he toured extensively, often as part of his own circus and rodeo. In addition to singing he also exhibited his trick-shooting skills. Through 1943, Tex recorded ninety-three songs for Regal Zonophone. One of his early posters boasted that his discs sold at an average of 10,000 per month, a sizable total when one realizes that Australia and New Zealand combined had a smaller population than the state of New York in 1940.

After several years out of the studio, Morton cut some two dozen masters for the new Rodeo label in 1949. This time most of the songs were of American origin, but included a mixture of oldies associated with singers like Jimmie Rodgers and new hits such as Eddie Dean's *One Has My Name* and Floyd Tillman's *This Cold War with You.* Shortly afterward Tex came to North America, spending most of the decade in Canada after touring with one Dixie Bill Hilton. He had one recording venture in Nashville (1953), which resulted in a couple of singles released back in Australia. Apparently Morton spent most of his Canadian and American years touring as a hypnotist. According to one of his P. R. advertisements, he spent some six months in Montreal alone, and another four in Toronto, billing himself as "the Greatest Morton."

Back in Australia in 1959, Tex cut some numbers for Festival Records in the early 60's, but did not really get his career into high gear again until mid-decade. Then he spent 1968-1970 in his native New Zealand headlining a popular television program, *Country Touch.* In 1972 he cut a duet single with his onetime archrival Buddy Williams, and the following year a new recording about a horse, *The Goondiwindi Grey,* hit the top of the charts. His album consisting largely of recitations—***Tex Morton's Australia***—won him wide respect. Three years later he became the first inductee to the Australian Country Music Roll of Renown.

In his last years Tex Morton played a variety of dramatic roles in various Aussie television programs and motion pictures. Some of his older singles came back into print via album reissues, including a box set containing all of his old Regal Zonophone sides (more recently on compact disc as well). Like American Country musicians, those in Australia have often had to combat being ignored and snubbed by the media mainstream. However, by the time of his death Morton had begun to gain some recognition for his achievements, as the "Down Under" Country music pioneer who exercised a wide influence on many of those who followed. Aussie researchers Andrew Smith, Hedley Charles, and Peter Burgis are currently at work on a detailed Morton biography, which should separate fact from legend concerning this important figure. IMT

RECOMMENDED ALBUMS:

(All Australian releases)
"Tex Morton Today" (Columbia)(1970)
"Tex Morton's Goondiwindi Grey" (Festival)(1977)
"You and My Old Guitar" (Festival)(1981)
"The Man from Snowy River and Other Poems" (Festival)(1982)
"The Tex Morton Collection" (Regal Zonophone)(1987)

JOHNNY & JONIE MOSBY

JOHNNY MOSBY
(Singer, Songwriter, Band Leader)
Given Name: John R. Mosby
Date of Birth: April 26, 1933
Where Born: Fort Smith, Arkansas
Married: Janice Irene Shields (Jonie) (m. 1958)(div.)
Children: Tammy, Tracy, Lindy Rae, one son

JONIE MOSBY
(Singer, Songwriter)
Given Name: Janice Irene Shields
Date of Birth: August 10, 1940
Where Born: Van Nuys, California
Married: 1. John R. Mosby (m. 1958)(div.)
2. Donnie Mitchell (m. 1977)
Children: Tammy, Tracy, Lindy Rae, Morgan Bradford, Sydney (adopted)

This husband-and-wife team was known as "Mr. & Mrs. Country Music" during the late 50's through to the mid-70's. They met in early 1958, when Jonie auditioned to sing with Johnny's popular West Coast orchestra. She got the job and later that year, they married.

That same year, they signed with Challenge Records as Johnny and Jonie, and released their first single, *Just Before Dawn.* They released three more singles, and then left the label in 1960. Although none of the records charted, they did herald their arrival. In 1961, they signed to Toppa Records, but without any success. They appeared on numerous TV shows and in 1962, *Cash Box* voted them "Most Promising Vocal Group."

That year, Johnny & Jonie signed with Columbia and by the following spring, they had entered the Country charts with the Top 15 hit *Don't Call Me from a Honky Tonk.* They followed up with the double-sided hit *Trouble in My Arms* (Top 15)/*Who's Been Cheatin' Who* (Top 30). They continued on their winning ways in 1964, with *Keep Those Cards and Letters Coming In* (Top 20) and *How the Other Half Lives* (Top 25). During 1964, 1965 and 1966, they were voted in the Top 5 in the *Billboard*, *Cash Box* and *Record World* popularity polls. During 1966 and 1967, they appeared five times on Gene Autry's *Melody Ranch.* They also appeared on the *Big D Jamboree*, *Louisiana Hayride* and the *Grand Ole Opry.* In addition, they made one appearance a month at the Palomino in Hollywood, during 1967 and 1968.

During 1965 and 1966, they had no single successes, although they released two albums during this time, ***Mr. & Mrs. Country Music***, for Columbia, and ***Johnny & Jonie Mosby—The New Sweethearts of Country Music***, for Starday, both in 1965. During this time, Johnny and Jonie were starting their family.

In 1967, they signed with Capitol and began recording more of their own material. *Make a Left and Then a Right* (Top 40) became their first self-penned hit and was followed by two medium-level records, in 1968 (also written by the Mosbys), *Mr. & Mrs. John Smith* and *Our Golden Wedding Day* (both Top 60). During 1969, Johnny & Jonie had three major successes, *Just Hold My Hand* (Top 15), *Hold Me, Thrill Me, Kiss Me* (Top 40) and *I'll Never Be Free* (Top 30). That year, they were named the Academy of Country & Western Music's (ACM) "Top Vocal Group." Again in 1970, they racked up three more hits of varying sizes, *Third World* (Top 40), *I'm Leaving It Up to You* (Top 20) and *My Happiness* (Top 50).

However, 1971 was to be their final year of success, with the Top 50 single *Oh, Love of Mine* and the low-level chart record *Just One More Time.* At this time, the couple operated the popular West Coast nightclub The Ban Dar in Ventura, California. Both were very much involved with the Board of the ACM, Johnny being a past Director.

Shortly after, the couple split and in 1973, Jonie had the solo Top 75 chart record *I've Been There.* She came back into the public limelight in 1992, when, at age 52, she became the oldest woman in the U.S. known to have given birth to an in vitro fertilized baby.

RECOMMENDED ALBUMS:

"Mr. & Mrs. Country Music" (Columbia)(1965)
"Johnny & Jonie Mosby—The New Sweethearts of Country Music" (Starday)(1965)
"Make a Left & Then a Right" (Capitol)(1968)
"Just Hold My Hand" (Capitol)(1969)
"I'll Never Be Free" (Capitol)(1969)
"My Happiness" (Capitol)(1970)

MOON MULLICAN

(Piano, Guitar, Organ)
Given Name: Aubrey Wilson Mullican
Date of Birth: March 29, 1909
Where Born: Corrigan, Texas
Married: Eunice
Date of Death: January 1, 1967

Moon Mullican gained the sobriquet "King of the Hillbilly Piano Players," a title he well deserved. His earlier professionalism came in Western Swing bands of the 30's, but he is virtually unique for being the only pianist of that idiom to emerge as a major vocalist in later decades. In addition to being a major artist in the 40's and 50's with several well-known songs, Moon had a wide influence on later Country pianist/singers including Merrill Moore and Jerry Lee Lewis.

Born of a religious farm family in the "piney woods" country of Polk County, Texas, Aubrey Mullican's musical interests began when his father bought an organ for the older sisters to practice for church services. The youngster, however, soon showed an attraction to more worldly tunes like *St. Louis Blues*, which more than aroused his daddy's ire, and about 1925, Aubrey left the farm for Houston, where he received the nickname Moon. He tickled the ivories in clubs for several years and perhaps brothels as well. As Western Swing bands began to emerge in the mid-30's, Mullican became a member of Leon "Pappy"

The great ***Moon Mullican***

Selph's Blue Ridge Playboys for a time. He really came into his own as pianist for Cliff Bruner's Texas Wanderers, a band with whom he played for several years, waxing many numbers with them on Decca, including the first recording of his long-time favorite, *Pipe Liner's Blues*. The Bruner band also provided backup at record sessions for other Decca artists, including Jimmie Davis, Buddy Jones, Bob Dunn, and the Shelton Brothers, while helping the Modern Mountaineers and Sunshine Boys on other labels.

Much to Cliff Bruner's chagrin, Moon left him late in 1943 to work in the Jimmie Davis band during the gubernatorial race in Louisiana. Mullican's hard work not only helped Davis succeed, but also netted him $10,000 in savings. According to one story, Moon invested it all in slot machines, which soon vanished, but Joe Duhon, a Bruner sideman, got Moon and Cliff back together in time for a November 7, 1944, Decca session in New York. For two more years Bruner and Mullican co-led a band called the Showboys in the Beaumont/Houston area, working also at KPBX Beaumont. In late 1946 Moon went on his own and began recording for King. His earliest release didn't do all that much, but beginning with his parody of the Harry Choates hit *New Jole Blon*, they began to find public favor. That number went to Top 3 and *Jole Blon's Sister* made a brief appearance in the Top 10.

In 1948, a sentimental mother song, *Sweeter Than the Flowers,* went Top 3 and remained on the charts for six months. However, the biggest hit, *I'll Sail My Ship Along*, stayed at the top for four weeks and charted for thirty-six. Both of these numbers were somewhat atypical for Moon, whose style ran more to Country boogies like *Cherokee Boogie* and the aforementioned *Pipeliner's Blues*, which he recorded again in 1952. His covers of songs like *Jambalaya, Good Deal Lucille*, and the Pop hit *Mona Lisa* also displayed his style quite well. Moon joined the *Grand Ole Opry* for a time and toured often with folks like Hank Williams in the early 50's. By mid-decade he delved into Rockabilly with numbers like *Seven Nights to Rock* and *Honolulu Rock-a-Roll-a*, but was somewhat old to compete in a youth market with stars like Elvis Presley and Jerry Lee Lewis. In ten years with King, the colorful musician cut about a hundred sides for the company.

In 1958, Mullican signed with Decca, where he had several fine releases, but no real hits, although one album released on Coral, ***Moon Over Mullican***, has become a high-demand item on the collector market. Moon later recorded for labels like Kapp and Starday, making the charts a final time in 1961 with his version of the old favorite *Ragged But Right*. The aging piano player/vocalist had recurring health problems from 1962, when he suffered a heart attack on stage in Kansas City. He bounced back the following year, but began to lose much of the old zip that he had displayed when he was quoted as saying, "You got to make those bottles bounce on the table."

Trying to stay contemporary, one of his last recordings, for Spar, bore the title *I Ain't No Beatle (But I Want to Hold Your Hand)*. He succumbed to another heart attack on New Year's morning 1967. His old musical compatriot Jimmie Davis delivered the eulogy and sang at his funeral in Beaumont. Interest in the roots of rock'n'roll as displayed in Mullican's music has helped keep several of his key waxings available. IMT

RECOMMENDED ALBUMS:

"All Time Greatest Hits" (King)(1958)
"Moon Over Mullican" (Coral)(1958)
"Moon Mullican Sings and Plays" (King)(1959)
"Many Moods of Moon Mullican" (King)(1960)
"Moon Mullican Instrumentals" (Audio Lab)(1962)
"Mister Piano Man" (Starday)(1964)
"Mister Honky Tonk Piano Man" (Spar)(1968)
"The Moon Mullican Showcase" (Kapp)(1969)
"Seven Nights to Rock" (Western)(1981)
"Sweet Rockin' Music" (Charly UK)(1984)
"Moonshine Jamboree" (Ace)(1993)
"The Unforgettable Moon Mullican" (Starday)
(See also Cliff Bruner)

PAUL "MOON" MULLINS

(Fiddle, Guitar, Mandolin, Bass, Deejay)

Given Name:	**Paul Mullins**
Date of Birth:	**September 24, 1936**
Where Born:	**Frenchburg, Kentucky**
Married:	**Prudence**
Children:	**William Joseph, Christy**

Paul "Moon" Mullins has been a notable deejay and Bluegrass sideman and in the last decade has led a fine acoustic band, the Traditional Grass.

A native of Menifee County in eastern Kentucky, Mullins originally was drawn to the guitar. He joined the Army in 1954, spending two years of his service hitch in Alaska testing and installing signal equipment. Having spare time, he began learning the fiddle, mandolin and bass and worked in a little Country band that played in NCO clubs. When he got out of the service in 1958, Moon began playing with a band from Mt. Sterling called the Skidmore Brothers.

This soon led to his joining the Stanley Brothers that September, in Bristol on the Tennessee-Virginia border. He stayed until January 1959. Paul describes his initial work with the Stanleys as less than successful because of stage fright. He says that he began deejay and radio work to conquer this nervousness, and it worked! When he completed a third stint with Ralph and Carter, his problems had ended. Having begun his record spinning at WGOH in Grayson, Kentucky, he later went to such neighboring locales as Mt. Sterling and Ashland.

He also played fiddle in a band called the Bluegrass Playboys, who had a program on WHTN-TV Huntington, West Virginia, and secured a recording contract with Briar, subsequently recording two albums. In the summer of 1963, they went on a national Folk music package tour that lasted three months. Mullins then returned to Grayson as a deejay, during which time he also worked in a band called the Log Cabin Boys.

In October 1964, Moon went to Middletown and WPFB, where he worked for most of the next twenty-five years, becoming a virtual institution among his large audience, which consisted primarily of Appalachian migrants. His independent spirit did not always sit well with his employers, and he sometimes left the station for brief periods, going to such locales as Jellico, Tennessee, to spin the discs.

Paul also fiddles in a variety of local bands and did some session work at King Records in Cincinnati. He also cut his first album under his own name on the Vetco label. Bands in which he played included those of Jim McCall and Benny Birchfield, the Valley Ramblers and Nu-Grass Pickers, all of whom recorded either singles or albums. Banjo picker Noah Crase also worked in some of these groups.

In 1974, Mullins and Crase became fiddler and banjoist respectively with the Boys from Indiana, built around the trio vocals of the Holt Brothers and Harley Gabbard, remaining with them until 1979 and recording seven albums chiefly for King Bluegrass. As the group gained increasing popularity, however, their travel became something of a strain on one who also held a day job.

Paul continued playing fiddle with bands that had less rigorous schedules and in 1983, he put together the Traditional Grass. The band consisted of himself, son Joe on banjo, Mark Rader on guitar and Bill Adams on bass. Later, Glen Inman played bass and more recently Mike Clevinger has filled this role. In 1990, Gerald Evans, a veteran of the Goins Brothers, joined on mandolin. The group worked mostly on a regional basis for the first several years, but when they joined Rebel Records in 1991, they became a full-time band and a major force in traditional Bluegrass. Their three album releases in the past two years display their musical skill and integrity quite well, and they seem likely to do for traditional Bluegrass in the 90's what the Johnson Mountain Boys did in the 80's. IMT

RECOMMENDED ALBUMS:
"Paul 'Moon' Mullins" (Vetco)(1969)
The Traditional Grass:
"A Touch of the Fifties" (cassette)(1987)
"Traditional Favorites" (cassette)(1989)
"A Lonesome Road to Travel" (Riverside)(1990)
"Howdy Neighbor Howdy" (Rebel)(1992)
"I Believe in the Old Time Way" (Rebel)(1993)
"10th Anniversary Collection" (Rebel)(1993)
(See also Boys from Indiana)

MICHAEL MARTIN MURPHEY

(Singer, Songwriter, Guitar, Actor)
Given Name: Michael Martin Murphey
Date of Birth: March 13, 1945
Where Born: Dallas, Texas
Married: 1. Caroline (div.)
2. Mary Maciukas
Children: Ryan, Brennan, Laura Lynn

In his thirty-year career as a songwriter and recording artist, Michael Martin Murphey has embraced many musical styles. Drawing on the heritage of Bob Wills and Hank Williams, Michael was also influenced by the social conscience of Woody Guthrie and Pete Seeger. As a young man, Michael was an avid reader of great American writers, including William Faulkner and Mark Twain. Winning both Pop and Country music fans with love songs, Michael also addressed a variety of issues in his songwriting, from Indian rights to the plight of migrant farm workers and the environment.

Sharing a love of reading and music, Michael started playing the ukulele and writing poetry as a young boy. He loved cowboy stories and one of his first public performances was singing cowboy songs for a gathering around a campfire at the Sky Ranch in Lewisville, Texas. By the time he was in high school, Michael was experimenting with combining Country, Folk and Rock music in the coffee houses and clubs around Texas, playing in the Texas Twosome. He formed a band and gained a loyal following in the Dallas/Denton area.

After a few years of performing in Texas, and a brief stint at North Texas State College, Michael moved to California to study poetry and writing at the University of California at Los Angeles. Six months after his arrival he was offered a songwriting contract with Sparrow Music. Michael became a regular performer at the popular Folk music club Ledbetters, which was owned by Randy Sparks (of New Christy Minstrel fame). In 1964, while still a student, he got together with Michael Nesmith, John London and John Raines as the Trinity River Boys. They recorded an eponymous album for Prospector Records, but it was not released. While at North Texas State, studying classics with the intention of becoming a Baptist minister, Michael joined with Steve Fromholz in the Dallas County Jug Band.

In 1967, Michael, with Owen "Boomer" Castleman, put together a band named after western pioneer trailblazers Lewis and Clark. Michael (as Travis Lewis) called the group the Lewis and Clark Expedition and recorded an album for Colgems called ***I Feel Good, I Feel Bad***. Although the title track became a Top 40 Pop hit, Michael wanted a change of direction and retreated from Los Angeles to the nearby San Gabriel Mountains and the Mohave Desert.

The move away from the city resulted in a burst of creative output for Michael. Eventually he signed with major music publisher Screen Gems and his songs were recorded by Roger Miller, Bobbie Gentry, and Flatt & Scruggs. Michael wrote more than 400 songs for Screen Gems before he left to start his own publishing company.

Creating one of the first concept albums, Michael wrote 22 songs about a Mohave ghost town called ***The Ballad of Calico*** that was recorded by Kenny Rogers. Another group that took advantage of Michael's songwriting skills were the Monkees, who recorded his *What Am I Doing Hangin' Around.*

After six years in the Los Angeles area Murphey returned to Texas in the early 70's, and in 1971 settled in Austin. He became a fixture in the city's songwriter clubs and developed friendships with fellow Austin transplants Willie Nelson, Jerry Jeff Walker, and B.W. Stevenson. Michael put together a band with local favorite Gary P. Nunn and performed their mixture of Country, Folk and Rock at the popular Armadillo World Headquarters club.

Michael's original music attracted the attention of Nashville producer Bob Johnston. His production credits included Bob Dylan, Leonard Cohen, Simon and Garfunkel and Johnny Cash. Johnston persuaded Michael to put some of his new songs on tape. Those recording sessions led to a contract with A & M Records as Michael Murphey in 1971 and the album ***Geronimo's Cadillac*** in 1972. The title song, a Top 40 Pop success, was embraced by the Indian rights movement and became the anthem of the Indian activists' confrontation with the Federal Marshal at Wounded Knee. The song was also recorded by several other artists including Hoyt Axton and Cher.

Geronimo's Cadillac was critically acclaimed and *Cosmic Cowboy* from his follow-up album, ***Cosmic Cowboy Souvenir***, yielded the unofficial theme song of the Austin music scene and led to Michael's early sobriquet of the "Cosmic Cowboy." He wrote the song when he learned that Jerry Jeff Walker was to attend one of Michael's concerts in New York City and he wondered how that city would cope with Walker. After two albums for A & M, Michael signed with Epic and in 1974 released his ***Michael Murphey*** album.

That year, Michael moved to Colorado and worked on his next album at the Caribou Ranch Recording Studio. The result was his 1975 album for Epic, entitled ***Blue Sky—Night Thunder***, which went Gold the same year. It was the album that launched his career to new heights with *Wildfire,* which was a Top 3 Pop hit and was Certified Gold, and *Carolina in the Pines*, which just missed the Pop Top 20.

Wildfire, with its haunting melody and mythical midwestern tale, came to Murphey in a dream, and waking up at 3:00 a.m., he composed the song in 30 minutes. When Michael was a child, his grandfather had told him of a legendary ghost horse that saved people in danger.

Michael followed his highly successful album with ***Swans Against the Sun*** and made his first appearance on the Country chart with *A Mansion on the Hill* in 1976, on which fellow Pop star John Denver harmonized. The flip-side of the single was the more Rock-oriented *Renegade* and it became a Top 40 Pop hit.

Cherokee Fiddle from Michael's ***Flowing Free Forever*** album marked his second entry on the Country charts. The single reached the Top 60 in 1977, but in 1982, it became a Top 10 for Johnny Lee (the single featured Michael and Charlie Daniels) and was featured in the movie *Urban Cowboy*. Michael released two more albums for Epic, ***Lone Wolf*** (1978) and ***Peaks, Valleys, Honky Tonks and Alleys*** (1979). Although Michael had three more Country chart singles that year, they were all at the basement level.

Michael took a break from recording, and in 1979, he married former fashion model Mary Maciukas and moved to Taos, New Mexico, to focus on his writing and to study the Native American culture. He also delved into the history of the West and the cowboy lifestyle. Mary became Michael's right hand, video project partner and photographer. Michael developed his musical style to what he describes as "Americana."

In 1982, Michael signed with Liberty Records in Nashville and released the album ***Michael Martin Murphey***. Michael began using his middle name to distinguish himself from the actor Michael Murphy. The issue came about when Murphey appeared in the 1981 films *Take This Job and Shove It* and *Hard Country* that starred Jan-Michael Vincent and Kim Bassinger. The latter was based on Michael's screenplay and co-written by him.

Michael's first chart single for Liberty was the Top 50 *The Two-Step Is Easy*, in 1982. He then scored his first No.1 Country hit with *What's Forever For,* which also reached the Pop Top 20. His year-end single *Still Taking Chances* went Top 3 on the Country chart and crossed to the Pop Top 80. The ACM named Michael "Best New Male Vocalist" that year. His string of hits continued in 1983-84 with *Love Affairs* and the Top 10 *Don't Count the Rainy Days* (both 1983) and *Will It Be Love by Morning* (Top 10), *Disenchanted* and *Radio Land* (all 1984). At the end of 1984, Liberty became EMI America and Michael saw out the year with the Top 10 *What She Wants*.

Michael included his Pop hits of the 70's with the Country radio hits of the early 80's on his ***The Best of Michael Martin Murphey*** album in 1985. His updated version of the 1975 Pop hit *Carolina in the Pines* featured Ricky Skaggs on mandolin and became a 1985 Top 10 Country hit. That year, Michael moved to Warner Brothers Records and his success dipped initially with *Tonight We Ride*, which only went Top 30, and the celebration of hobo rail riders, *Rollin' Nowhere*. The year ended with the Top 40 *Fiddlin' Man*.

In 1987, Michael teamed up with Holly Dunn for the Top 5 hit *A Face in the Crowd*. He then returned to No.1 with *A Long Line of Love*. Michael filmed the video for the song in Palo Duro Canyon in Texas. He included his wife, children, and parents in the video to portray the different generations described in the song. A highlight of the video was a 30-acre earth sculpture of a double wedding ring created by Kansas artist Stan Herd.

Michael began 1988 with the Top 5 hit *I'm Gonna Miss You Girl*, a song written by Jesse Winchester. He teamed up with his son Ryan for a light-hearted look at a father's advice to his son on love (and vice versa), *Talkin' to the Wrong Man,* and it reached the Top 5. His last two singles of the year were the Top 30 *Pilgrims on the Way (Matthew's Song)* and *From the Word Go*, from the album ***River of Time***. In 1989, Michael had his last Top 10 entry to date, with *Never Givin' Up on Love* from the Clint Eastwood movie *Pink Cadillac.*

Michael now turned his attention to the roots of Western music and the songs of the cowboy in the 90's. However, radio play on his future singles became selective and none of his releases got above Top 50. On his ***Cowboy Songs*** collection most of the songs were traditional cowboy songs, and the album was well received by Country fans, outselling his previous seven Warner Brothers albums. The recording was honored with the "Heritage Award" from the Cowboy Hall of Fame. The success of the album encouraged Warner Brothers to launch a new label devoted to Western music called Warner Western, with Michael and long-time Frank Yankovic associate Joey Miskulin as producers. Joining Michael on the roster were traditional Western singers Don Edwards, Sons of the San Joaquin and cowboy poet Waddie Mitchell.

Michael continued his successful treatment of Western music with ***Cowboy Christmas, Cowboy Songs Volume II***, in 1991 and 1993's ***Cowboy Songs III***. The seventeen-song collection included several American Folk music standards including *Streets of Laredo, Birmingham Jail* and *Ghost Riders*. Michael also recorded several outlaw classics composed in the late 1800's such as *The Ballad of Jesse James* and *The Ballad of Billy the Kid*. A special highlight of the project for Michael was recording a duet with his Western music hero Marty Robbins. Michael transferred Marty's voice from his 1960 gunfighter ballad *Big Iron* to a new recording of the classic. The music video for the song mixed old performance footage of Marty intercut with Michael singing. The album also featured duets with Hal Ketchum and Michael's son Ryan.

Inspired by Buffalo Bill Cody's Wild West events in the late 1880's, Michael launched his "West Fest" in the late 1980's. The three-day festivals of Western Americana spotlighted major Country stars along with American Indian weavers, dancers, and singers. Michael staged the annual festivals in various locations in New Mexico, Colorado, and Texas. JIE

RECOMMENDED ALBUMS:

"Geronimo's Cadillac" (A & M)(1972)
"Cosmic Cowboy Souvenir" (A & M)(1973)
"Michael Murphey" (Epic)(1974)
"Blue Sky—Night Thunder" (Epic)(1975)
"Swans Against the Sun" (Epic)(1975)
"Flowing Free Forever" (Epic)(1976)
"Lone Wolf" (Epic)(1978)
"Peaks, Valleys, Honky Tonks & Alleys" (Epic)(1979)
"Michael Martin Murphey" (Liberty)(1982)
"The Heart Never Lies" (Liberty)(1983)
"The Best of Michael Martin Murphey" (Liberty)(1985)
"Tonight We Ride" (Warner Brothers)(1986)
"Americana" (Warner Brothers)(1987)
"River of Time" (Warner Brothers)(1988)
"Land of Enchantment" (Warner Brothers)(1989)
"Cowboy Songs" (Warner Western)(1990)
"Cowboy Christmas, Cowboy Songs II" (Warner Western)(1991)
"Cowboy Songs III" (Warner Western)(1993)

JIMMY MURPHY

(Singer, Songwriter, Guitar)

Given Name:	**James Murphy**
Date of Birth:	**October 11, 1925**
Where Born:	**Republic, Alabama**
Married:	**Flo**
Children:	**six**
Date of Death:	**June 1, 1981**

Jimmy Murphy recorded some of the most creative and original traditional Country music made in the 50's. He never became a star but the limited audiences who heard his music gained an unforgettable appreciation for it. Most of his material was self-composed and contained touches of tongue-in-cheek humor. An eccentric personality, Jimmy seems to have placed limitations on his commercial success.

Born in the Alabama coal region, Jimmy was early on exposed to the Blues. His father had a great admiration for Blues guitarists and bought their records. As a result young Jimmy picked up a great deal of black Blues stylings in his own guitar work. Both Jimmy and his father went into construction work and Jimmy learned the bricklaying trade. For much of his adult life, Jimmy alternated between an entertainment career and brickmasonry.

He gained some of his early professional music experience at WBRC Birmingham in the mid and late 40's with irregular appearances on the *Happy Hal Burns Show*. About 1950, Murphy came to Knoxville and worked first on WROL and then at WNOX. A friendship with Chet Atkins resulted in a contract with RCA Victor and Jimmy cut his first session on January 19, 1951. It included his two best-known numbers, *Electricity* and *Mother, Where Is Your Daughter Tonight,* songs that dealt with the unseen hand of God and touched on the delicate subject of female juvenile delinquency, respectively. Only an unobtrusive bass fiddle by Anita Carter and Murphy's own fancy guitar work provided instrumentation on the session. While critics considered the sound both fantastic and wonderful they did not sell well, and after another four-song-session, Victor dropped him from its roster.

Jimmy continued on radio in Knoxville, and then in 1955, he signed with Columbia and had two more sessions of eight songs each. These numbers had more of a Rockabilly—or perhaps a parody of Rockabilly—flavor. The best-known number was a recomposition of Tennessee Ernie Ford's current hit *Sixteen Tons* as *Sixteen Tons Rock and Roll.*

Others had such wild titles as *Baboon Boogie* and *Looking for a Mustard Patch.* Although the music was fine and the lyrics cleverly written, they also failed to rack up sales figures of any note and Columbia did not renew his contract. In 1962, Murphy cut four sides for K-Ark including a fine Hank Williams tribute titled *I Get a Longing to Hear Hank Sing the Blues*.

Later in the decade, Jimmy cut singles for Rem and Loyal. In 1978, Jimmy emerged from several years of relative obscurity, during which time the Library of Congress re-issued *Electricity*, and recorded an excellent album for Sugar Hill of the same name, with studio back-up that included Ricky Skaggs and Jerry Douglas.

Back in circulation again, Murphy had arranged for a European tour when his untimely death ended his comeback. In the meantime some of his Columbia material had reappeared on Rockabilly anthologies. Tales of his eccentricities continue to circulate among his musical associates, contributing to his status as a minor legend. In 1990, Bear Family Records of Germany released a cd containing his entire Victor and Columbia output. IMT

RECOMMENDED ALBUMS:

"Electricity" (Sugar Hill)(1978)

"Sixteen Tons Rock 'n' Roll" (Bear Family Germany)(1990)

ANNE MURRAY

(Singer, Guitar, Piano, Ukulele)

Given Name:	**Morna Anne Murray**
Date of Birth:	**June 20, 1945**
Where Born:	**Springhill, Nova Scotia, Canada**
Married:	**William Stewart ("Bill") Langstroth**
Children:	**William Stewart, Jr., Dawn Joann**

Anne Murray is unquestionably the most successful female cross-over artist of all time. For over 20 years, from 1970, she has chalked up more than 50 Country chart entries and nearly 30 Pop successes, as well as having many of her albums listed on both the Country and Pop Album charts. Yet despite this success, her music defies categorization; suffice it to say she is an entertainer.

Born and raised in the coal mining area of Nova Scotia, this bluenose pursued music as a hobby while graduating from the University of New Brunswick with a degree in physical education. While still in college, she was auditioned for the chorus by Bill Langstroth, the producer of the CBC's weekly Halifax-based TV series *Singalong Jubilee*, but she didn't get the job because they already had an alto singer. Two years later, Bill contacted her with a job offer, but by then she was teaching high school and wasn't interested. However, after a lot of coaxing, she joined the show (while still teaching) and remained on it for four years and began working with its musical director, Brian Ahern, who later married Emmylou Harris.

In 1968, Anne was still teaching school and Brian called her to Toronto. He produced Anne's first album, ***What About Me***, for the local Arc label. That led to Anne signing with Capitol Records of Canada and the recording of Gene McLelland's *Snowbird.* The single went Top 10 on the Country and Pop charts in the U.S., going Gold the same year, and was a Top 30 single in Britain. From nowhere, Anne had become an international star. The album ***Snowbird***, released that year, went Gold in 1973.

For a short while, she became a semi-regular on Glen Campbell's *Goodtime Hour* TV series, but Los Angeles did not suit her. However, for some while it looked like further major success was going to elude her. Apart from a Top 30 Country placing with Kenny Rogers' *A Stranger in My Place* and a Top 40 duet with Glen Campbell on *I Say a Little Prayer/By the Time I Get to Phoenix*, in 1971, Anne had to wait until the beginning of 1972 for her next major success, *Cotton Jenny*, a Gordon Lightfoot song, which peaked just below the Country Top 10. Then at the end of the year, she released *Danny's Song*, written by Kenny Loggins. It went Top 10 on both the Country and Pop charts. The 1973 album of the same name went Gold in Canada in 1991.

Canada's finest asset, ***Anne Murray***

During 1973, *What About Me* went Top 20 on the Country chart. At the end of the year, Anne consolidated her career with *Love Song*, which went Top 5 on the Country chart and reached the Pop Top 15. The album of the same name earned Anne her first Grammy Award for "Best Country Vocal Performance, Female" in 1974. That year, she had her first Country No.1 with *He Thinks I Still Care*. The flip-side, Lennon and McCartney's *You Won't See Me*, reached the Top 10 on the Pop chart. Anne ended 1974 with the Top 5 hit *Son of a Rotten Gambler*. Anne's 1974 album ***Country*** was Certified Gold in 1987.

In 1975, Anne married Bill Langstroth and a year later (August 1976) came their first-born, William, Jr. During 1975 through 1977, Anne's record career took a temporary slide with *Uproar* (Country Top 30, 1975) and *The Call* (Top 20) and *Things* (Top 25) (both 1976) as her only major successes, mainly because Anne had more important things to consider: her family.

At the beginning of 1978, Anne came back strongly with the Top 5 reprise of the Everly Brothers' *Walk Right Back*, with Jim Ed Norman producing. She followed this with her first No.1 Pop hit, *You Needed Me*, which went Top 5 on the Country chart and went Gold in 1979. It also went Gold in Canada in 1979 and Platinum in 1984. The single earned Anne a second Grammy Award for "Best Pop Vocal Performance, Female." She was also nominated for "Record of the Year" and "Best Country Vocal Performance, Female." Her 1978 album ***Let's Keep It That Way*** went Gold and Platinum the same year and by 1980 had achieved Double Platinum sales in Canada. She also released a children's album, ***Hippo in My Tub***, which was released by Sesame Street Records in the U.S., and it went Platinum in Canada in 1979.

At the beginning of 1979, she had another monster hit, *I Just Fall in Love Again*, which went to No.1 on the Country chart for 3 weeks and reached the Pop Top 15. Anne then had two more back-to-back Country No.1 hits with *Shadows in the Moonlight* (also Pop Top 25) and *Broken Hearted Me* (also Pop Top 15). Her albums in 1979 were also highly successful. ***New Kind of Feeling*** went Gold the same year and Platinum in 1987 and had reached Platinum status in Canada during the year of release. ***I'll Always Love You*** went Gold in the U.S. and Platinum in Canada in 1980. She also gave birth to her second child in April of that year. During the year, Anne served as Chairperson of the Canada Save the Children Fund and fostered three children.

With the advent of the new decade, Anne

continued her run of success with *Daydream Believer* (Top 3 Country/Top 15 Pop) and *Lucky Me* (Top 10 Country). Her next single, *I'm Happy Just to Dance with Me*, only reached the Country Top 25, but her year-end single, *Could I Have This Dance* (from the movie *Urban Cowboy*), went to No.1 on the Country chart and Top 40 on the Pop lists. It also earned Anne her third Grammy Award as "Best Country Vocal Performance, Female." Because Anne had by this time won so many Canadian Juno Awards, a journalist writing in the *Toronto Sun* suggested that the award should be retitled the "Annies." Her 1980 album ***Somebody's Waiting*** went Gold in Canada during the year of release. However, Anne's ***Anne Murray's Greatest Hits*** became a phenomenal seller. During the year of release, it went Platinum and by 1991, it had sold over 4 million copies in the U.S. In Canada, it had sold over 600,000 copies by 1984.

Anne started 1981 with the No.1 Country hit *Blessed are the Believers*, which was also a Top 40 Pop hit. Her other hits that year were *We Don't Have to Hold Out* (Country Top 20) and *It's All I Can Do* (Country Top 10). Anne's album ***Where Do You Go When You Dream*** went Gold and in Canada had gone Platinum, that same year. That Christmas, Anne had her first TV special for CBS, which co-starred Kris Kristofferson and was filmed in Nova Scotia. Anne's seasonal album ***Christmas Wishes*** had sold 2 million copies in the U.S. by 1991 and reached Triple Platinum by 1994.

All three of her hits in 1982 went Top 10 on the Country chart and were *Another Sleepless Night* (Top 5), the reprise of Bruce Channel's *Hey! Baby!* and *Somebody's Always Saying Goodbye*. During the spring of that year, Anne toured Australia and New Zealand. Anne's album that year, ***Hottest Night of the Year***, went Gold in Canada before the year was out.

During 1983, Anne had only one Country chart entry but that entry was *A Little Good News*, which went to No.1 and became the CMA's "Single of the Year" and earned Anne her fourth Grammy Award for "Best Country Vocal Performance, Female." The album of the same name went Gold in Canada the same year and in the U.S. in 1985. Anne's follow-up single at the beginning of 1984, *That's Not the Way (It's S'posed to Be)* only reached the Top 50.

Anne's prolific period of chart hits lasted until 1986. In 1985 she had back-to-back No.1 singles, *Just Another Woman in Love* and the duet with Dave Loggins *Nobody Loves Me Like You Do*. Anne's album ***Heart Over Mind*** went Gold that same year in Canada, and in the U.S. the following year. During 1985, Anne had a Top 3 single with *Time Don't Run Out on Me* and the Top 10 release *I Don't Think I'm Ready for You*, the latter coming from Burt Reynolds' movie *Stick*.

She started 1986 with the No.1 hit *Now and Forever (You and Me)*, and then the radio stations suddenly stopped playing Anne's records. She stayed on Capitol until 1992, but her only major hits were *My Life's a Dance* and *On and On* (both Top 30 in 1986), *Are You Still in Love with Me* (Top 20) and *Anyone Can Do the Heartbreak* (Top 30) (both 1987). In 1989, Anne got together with Kenny Rogers for *If I Ever Fall in Love Again*, which went Top 30. Then the radio deejays selected *Feed the Fire*, a cut from her ***You Will*** album, and it went Top 5. During this period several of Anne's albums achieved heavy sales. ***Something to Talk About*** and ***Harmony*** (1986) both went Gold in Canada the same year and the former went Gold in the U.S. in 1987. Anne's 1988 seasonal album ***Christmas*** went Gold in Canada in 1989, as did her ***Greatest Hits, Volume II***. In 1992, the Capitol box set ***Her Greatest Hits & Finest Performances*** went Platinum in Canada during the year of release.

In 1992, Anne was beginning to feel that Capitol, which was shortly to become Liberty Records, was trying to turn her into a Country singer rather than just a singer and so she decided to leave the label. Back in 1973, Anne had concurred with producer Tommy West that one day she would like to record an album as a tribute to her heroines of the 50's. In 1993, Anne signed with EMI Canada/SBK Records and released this long-awaited album, ***Croonin'***. Although not well promoted, the album made the Country Album chart Top 60.

Anne is sure to continue a successful career, as she has a loyal and constant fan base. Anne still puts her family first and mainly tours on three-day weekends. Elton John once said, "There are only two things I know about Canada: hockey and Anne Murray." (For the full list of Anne Murray's awards, see Awards Section.)

RECOMMENDED ALBUMS:

"Snowbird" (Capitol)(1970)
"Let's Keep It That Way" (Capitol)(1978)
"New Kind of Feeling" (Capitol)(1979)
"Anne Murray's Greatest Hits" (Capitol)(1980)
"Christmas Wishes" (Capitol)(1981)
"Something to Talk About" (Capitol)(1986)
"Greatest Hits, Volume II" (Capitol)(1989)
"You Will" (Capitol)(1992)
"Her Greatest Hits & Finest Performances" (box set)(Capitol)(1992)

N

BILL NAPIER

(Singer, Mandolin, Lead Guitar, Banjo)
Given Name: **William Napier**
Date of Birth: **December 17, 1935**
Where Born: **Wize County, Virginia**

From 1957, Bill Napier gained a reputation as one of the more creative instrumentalists in Bluegrass music, primarily from his work as a sideman with the Stanley Brothers' Clinch Mountain Boys. In the 60's he and Charlie Moore formed the Dixie Partners, recording over a hundred numbers for King. Since then Bill has been semi-active from time to time, primarily in the Detroit area, where he had first moved in his late teens.

A native of the Grundy, Virginia, region of the Appalachians, Bill Napier's early interest in music stemmed largely from listening to various groups on radio at WCYB Bristol, particularly to the Stanley Brothers. Their original mandolinist, Pee Wee Lambert, made a special impression upon Napier, as well as Bill Monroe to a lesser degree.

Moving to Detroit to find work in the factories about 1954, Napier obtained a good mandolin and began playing on a part-time basis with Curly Dan and Wilma Ann's Danville Mountain Boys. Later Bill met veteran sideman Jimmy Williams, who suggested that the young migrant apply for a job with the Stanleys. Although his initial audition did not succeed, Napier went back to Detroit, practiced some more and about four months later joined their band. He remained with them for some three years, doing comedy and recording several numbers on Mercury, Starday and King. Highlights of Napier's work with the Clinch Mountain Boys included waxing his original instrumental *Daybreak in Dixie* and his introduction of acoustical lead guitar picking to Stanley record sessions (which subsequently became standard for their sound).

In 1960, Bill left the Stanleys to form a

partnership with Charlie Moore. He usually sang baritone and divided his instrumental talents between lead guitar and banjo. Ironically, he had not played a banjo before and seldom touched mandolin during this period. In their seven years together, the Moore and Napier team recorded nine albums for King and over one hundred numbers. While *Truck Driver's Queen* became their best-known song, the highlight for Napier probably came in 1966 when the pair cut their ***Spectacular Instrumentals*** album, of which one critic remarked that its main weakness stemmed from Napier not being able to play all the instruments at once (this was done in the days that preceded overdubbing).

In the past quarter century, Bill's musical activity has generally manifested itself in spurts. In the 70's, he played and recorded a bit with old friends Curly Dan and Wilma Ann and in 1978 had a brief reunion with Charlie Moore, cutting seven songs with him. In 1984, Napier cut his only solo album for Old Homestead, with a short-lived band he named the Mountain Music Clan. Later in the decade he joined forces with Larry Taylor and the Waterloo Bluegrass Boys, remaining in the partnership long enough to cut a pair of albums, one of which was a tribute to his old mentors, the Stanley Brothers. IMT

RECOMMENDED ALBUMS:

Bill Napier:
"Hillbilly Fever" (Old Homestead)(1984)
Bill Napier & Larry Taylor:
"We Salute the Stanley Brothers" (Old Homestead)(1986)
"Country Boy's Life" (Old Homestead)(1986)
Charlie Moore & Bill Napier:
"The Best of Charlie Moore & Bill Napier" (King)(1963) [Re-released on Starday in 1975]
"Songs by Moore & Napier for the Lonesome Truck Drivers" (King)(1967)
"Spectacular Instrumentals" (King)(1967)
"Collector's Classics" (Old Homestead)
(See also Charlie Moore)

NASHVILLE BLUEGRASS BAND, The

When Formed: 1984

Current Members:

Alan O'Bryant	**Banjo, Vocals**
Pat Enright	**Guitar, Vocals**
Stuart Duncan	**Fiddle, Mandolin**
Roland White	**Mandolin, Vocals**
Gene Libbea	**Acoustic Bass, Ukulele, Vocals**

Former Members:

Mike Compton	**Mandolin, Vocals**
Mark Hembree	**Acoustic Bass, Vocals**

The first thing that is apparent about the Nashville Bluegrass Band is that they are first and foremost a band. Although each of the individual members is of star quality, that individuality is forgotten when they play together.

Their music is rooted in the tradition of Bluegrass and the Old-Time string bands with a Blues vocal feel, but yet it is not backward-looking; they experiment and make the music modern without losing the essence of Bluegrass. They formed originally as a quartet with O'Bryant, Enright, Compton and Hembree.

Alan O'Bryant was born in North Carolina and moved to Nashville in 1974. He had played Bluegrass since his teenage years. He has recorded and performed with Bill and James Monroe, Doc Watson, Peter Rowan and John Starling. His songs have been recorded by the Monroes, John Starling and Vern Gosdin. In 1987, his song *Those Memories of You* was a Top 5 hit for Emmylou Harris, Linda Ronstadt and Dolly Parton (the Trio).

Pat Enright was raised in Indiana and began playing Bluegrass in the early 70's in San Francisco. His band, the Phantoms of the *Opry*, became a favorite on the West Coast. He moved to Nashville in 1974 and met Alan, and the two began playing the clubs together. Pat moved to Boston in 1978 to play with Tasty Licks, a band that also included Bela Fleck. Pat recorded the album ***Anchored to the Shore*** with them, for Rounder. He returned to Nashville in 1979 and recorded with the Dreadful Snakes and Fleck.

Mike Compton was born in Meridian, Mississippi, the birthplace of Jimmie Rodgers. He went to Nashville in 1976 and began playing with banjo player Hubert Davis, recording three albums with him. Mike's influences are Bill Monroe and Delta Bluesman Robert Johnson. He met Alan and Pat and played clubs with them.

Mark Hembree was raised in Appleton, Wisconsin, and left home in 1977 to join Monroe Doctrine, a group that included Tony Trischka, Danny Weiss (both of whom would go on to Skyline) and Charles Sawtelle (who would help form Hot Rize). Two years later, Mark moved to Nashville to work with Bill Monroe. He stayed with Monroe for five years and recorded the ***Bill Monroe and Friends*** and ***Master of Bluegrass*** albums while with the Blue Grass Boys. He met Pat while recording with the Dreadful Snakes on ***Snakes Alive***.

In 1985, the NBB released their debut album, ***My Native Home***, on Rounder, which was produced by Bela Fleck and featured Blaine Sprouse on fiddle. Later than year, they added Stuart Duncan to the line-up. Stuart became a professional in 1973 in Southern California. He toured and recorded with Alison Brown, California's Lost Highway and Larry Sparks. Stuart moved to Nashville in 1985 and soon became a much-in-demand session musician, recording with Nanci Griffith, John Prine, Jerry Jeff Walker, Dolly Parton and Ricky Skaggs.

NBB became the first Bluegrass band to appear in China, which they did in 1986. In 1987, the band released their second album for Rounder, entitled ***Idle Time***; it was also produced by Bela Fleck. They followed that year with their last album for Rounder, the Bluegrass-Gospel lp ***To Be His Child***. They also played on Doc Watson's 1987 Sugar Hill album, called ***Portrait***.

The NBB toured Bahrain, Qatar, Bangladesh, Iraq, Egypt and Israel in 1988 for the Arts America program. On July 21, 1988, the band was involved in a serious accident outside of Roanoke, Virginia, in which their bus was totally wrecked. Mark Hembree was seriously injured and as a result had to leave the band. Shortly after, Mike Compton, whose mandolin was broken in the accident, also left the group. For a while, the band was down to a four-piece, using Nick Haney as bassist. However, Nick was not well and later in 1988, Gene Libbea became the group's bass player. At the same time, Country Gazette was winding down and the legendary Roland White joined the NBB. They supported Peter Rowan on the Grammy-nominated album ***New Moon Rising***, for Sugar Hill.

Gene, born and raised in southern California, began playing bass in 1969 with his brother, the late Steve Libbea. Together the brothers played with Byron Berline, Pat Cloud, John Hickman and Vince Gill. The Libbea brothers formed Truckee and were based in West Germany, touring Europe for three years.

In 1990, the NBB toured in Holland, France, Germany, England and Switzerland. That year, they released their Sugar Hill album ***The Boys Are Back in Town***, which was produced by Jerry Douglas. They followed this with ***Home of the Blues*** (1991) and ***Waitin' for the Hard Times to Go*** (1993). This last named album won the band their first Grammy Award for "Best Bluegrass Album," the group having been nominated every year since they started.

In 1992, Stuart Duncan released his solo eponymous album, which was produced by Bela Fleck. This album was named the IBMA's "Instrumental Recording of the Year." Stuart has also captured the IBMA's "Fiddle" category every year since its inception in 1990. The Nashville Bluegrass Band have become firm crowd pleasers when they play the *Grand Ole Opry*.

RECOMMENDED ALBUMS:
"My Native Home" (Rounder)(1985)
"Idle Home" (Rounder)(1987)
"To Be His Child" (Rounder)(1987)
"New Moon Rising" (Sugar Hill)(1988) [With Peter Rowan]
"The Boys Are Back in Town" (Sugar Hill)(1990)
"Home of the Blues" (Sugar Hill)(1991)
"Waitin' for the Hard Times to Go" (Sugar Hill)(1993)
Stuart Duncan:
"Stuart Duncan" (Rounder)(1992)

NASHVILLE SONGWRITERS ASSOCIATION INTERNATIONAL (NSAI)

The beginnings of NSAI go back to 1967, when the few songwriters there were in Nashville received little respect and were given hardly any credit for their work. Although ASCAP, BMI and SESAC had annual songwriters awards, the writers received small compensation financially. In November of that year, songwriter Eddie Miller (*Release Me*) started to develop an idea that would improve the songwriters' lot.

He had been involved with the ACM and he discussed the idea with fellow songwriters Buddy Mize and Bill Brock over lunch at Ireland's. They were excited about the idea, and over the next few weeks they discussed the concept with every writer they met. On December 6, the Nashville Songwriters Association's first organizational meeting was held at the Old Professional's Club on 16th Avenue South, and among the 40 that were present that night were Marijohn Wilkin, Kris Kristofferson, Clarence Selman, Johnny Scoggins, Rusty Adams, Felice and Boudleaux Bryant, Liz and Casey Anderson and Eddie Miller. These 40 (more than half the writers in town) became the founding membership of NSA.

Interim officers were chosen until a formal constitution could be approved. They were Buddy Mize (President), Eddie Miller (Vice President), Marijohn Wilkin (Secretary), Johnny Scoggins (Treasurer) and Clarence Selman (Sergeant-at-Arms). The constitution committee comprised the Bryants, the Andersons, Kris Kristofferson, Marijohn Wilkin, Eddie Miller, Clarence Selman, Buddy Mize, Ted Harris and Eddie Noack.

In February 1968, NSA held its first Songwriter Achievement Awards Ceremony at the Biltmore Hotel. Based on the criterion "Songs I Wish I Had Written," writers were honored for the previous year. The ceremony was emceed by Biff Collie, and those honored were Gene Chrysler, Bill Anderson, Autry Inman, John D. Loudermilk, Darrell Statler, Dolly Parton, Bill Owens, Marty Robbins, Darrell Glen, Jim Glaser, Leon Ashley, Margie Singleton, Jack Clement, Harlan Howard, Curly Putman, Loretta Lynn, Tom T. Hall, Mel Tillis, Wayne Walker and Vic McAlpin. The first NSA "Songwriter of the Year" was Dallas Frazier. His song, *There Goes My Everything*, was named "Song of the Year."

However, there was a down side. Initially, music publishers viewed NSA as a union and feared that writers would strike and they tried to dissuade their writers from joining. Many writers were threatened with blackballing, but ASCAP, BMI and SESAC intervened and gave the fledgling organization credibility. In October 1968, the constitution was ratified and chartered by the State of Tennessee as a non-profit organization. By 1969, their first headquarters were established at Buddy Mize's office at Central Songs. By the end of the year, NSA had 100 members.

In 1970, Eddie Noack became the first Lifetime Member and BMI's Frances Preston became the first non-writer Lifetime Member. NSA President Eddie Miller and Frances Preston worked to make record companies print the writers' names on their record labels. This was followed by getting writer credits on record sleeves. Later that year, NSA established the Nashville Songwriters Hall of Fame, electing its first 21 inductees. During May, NSA began its newsletter to its members. In October, the first Hall of Fame Banquet was held at the Holiday Inn-Vanderbilt. At the end of the year, plans were made to persuade Congress to take action on a new copyright law. This would take a further six years.

NSA started its initial course in songwriting in 1971 at the University of Tennessee at Nashville, which three years later became a full credit-earning course. Maggie Cavender became Executive Director in 1972 and the organization moved to her office at 811 18th Avenue South. During 1974, sculptor Bud Mayes was commissioned to create the "Manny," which from 1975 on was presented to all Hall of Fame inductees. NSA moved again, this time to 903 16th Avenue South. That year, the President's Award was introduced "to be given to a person inside or outside the industry who the President believes had done the most for the benefit of songwriters in that year." The first recipient was Frances Preston. By the end of that year, the membership numbered 500.

In 1977, NSA became NSAI, denoting its desire to be international. The new Copyright Law came into effect on January 1, 1978. During the year, NSAI sponsored the songwriting seminar outside of Nashville. It was held in Kansas City and 100 writers attended. This led to its first workshop and the following year, they held their first Spring Symposium. By the end of the decade, NSAI had 1,000 members.

NSAI began another annual event when it held the first Harlan Howard Birthday Bash on September 7, 1984. By early 1985, membership had increased to 2,500 members. In May 1989, Maggie Cavender became Director Emerita and Pat Rogers became Executive Director. The Maggie Cavender Award of Service was established to be given annually "to an individual who has worked hard for the interests of songwriters," with Bobby Bare becoming the first recipient.

In 1991, NSAI joined the National Academy of Songwriters and the Songwriters Guild of America to form the Songwriter Alliance. In December that year, NSAI moved to its current offices at 15 Music Square West. From the initial 40 members, as of 1994, NSAI has a membership of 2,600.

NATIONAL BARN DANCE, The
(Radio show, WLS Chicago)

During the early years of Country music commercialization on radio, the *National Barn Dance* out of Chicago reigned as the most significant of the live-audience broadcast, jamboree-type programs.

The WLS *Barn Dance* originated in April 1924, when station officials put together a program designed to appeal to rural folk with square dance-type fiddle music and vocals. A Vice President of Sears Roebuck who owned the station found the initial April 19 broadcast offensive to his sophisticated ears, but dropped his objections when he realized how much listeners liked the program. George D. Hay was the first announcer and he later went on to initiate the *Grand Ole Opry*.

Early performers on the program included folks like Grace Wilson, Chubby Parker, Walter Peterson, and Tommy Dandur, but the first real star was the Kentucky ballad singer Bradley Kincaid, who began with the show in 1926. Stars of lesser stature included Pie Plant Pete (Claud Moye), Arkie the Arkansas Woodchopper (Luther Ossenbrink), and the blind duo of Mac and Bob (Lester McFarland and Robert Gardner).

Early programs were performed in front of a live audience of about one hundred from a small theater in the Sherman Hotel, although shows held elsewhere drew crowds of 10,000 and 20,000. Beginning in March 1932, the

National Barn Dance played to two sell-out crowds of 1,200 each Saturday night for the next twenty-five years, at the TV studio built for this purpose at the Eighth Street Theater.

By then star performers included Gene Autry, who subsequently became Hollywood's premier singing cowboy, his later comic sidekick, Smiley Burnette, Red Foley and the Cumberland Ridge Runners with Karl and Harty, George Gobel, Patsy Montana, the Prairie Ramblers, Louise Massey, and somewhat later Country radio's all-time favorite couple, Lulu Belle and Scotty. From May 1932, the NBC network carried a half hour of the program.

By the late 40's, the *National Barn Dance* had lost some prestige due to the increasing concentration of the Country music industry in Nashville and at the *Grand Ole Opry*, but could still make its share of waves. Folks like Bob Atcher, Dolph Hewitt, the DeZurick Sisters, and the comic duo of Homer and Jethro had star stature and the station that gave America its first singing cowboy star in Autry also provided its last in Rex Allen.

The ABC-TV network carried a half hour of the show for thirty-nine weeks in 1949, and by the time the Eighth Street Theater closed at the end of August 1957, some 2,617,000 paid customers had seen the program live. The *Barn Dance* continued until March 1960 when WLS changed formats and terminated the program.

However, the show did not die. With Hewitt providing the leadership, the *Barn Dance* moved over to WGN radio and initiated a syndicated version for television as well. Atcher, Hewitt, Arkie the Arkansas Woodchopper, and comedian Don "Red" Blanchard from the older days became mainstays of the rejuvenated program, assisted by such newer artists as Ruth and Edith Johnson, instrumentalists Bob and Bobbie Thomas, Holly "Cousin Tilford" Swanson, and the Sage Riders band. Kapp Records released a good sampler album of *Barn Dance* performers from this period. Under this format the show continued until 1969.

During its period of existence, only the slightly younger *Grand Ole Opry* rivaled the *National Barn Dance* in significance and overall only the *Opry* and the *Wheeling Jamboree* survived longer on a major station. In a sense, virtually all the great radio barn dances emulated the one in Chicago and the *Renfro Valley Barn Dance* and the *Boone County Jamboree/Midwestern Hayride* could be characterized as direct spin-offs since John Lair started the former when he left Chicago for Cincinnati. The WLW management initiated the *Hayride* when Lair moved his operation to its permanent home in Renfro Valley, Kentucky. Overall, it is quite difficult to overestimate the importance that the *National Barn Dance* played in the growth of Country music on radio in the second quarter of the 20th century. Sadly, no anthologies of the music of performers from that era have ever been released. IMT

RECOMMENDED ALBUM:

"Saturday Night at the Old Barn Dance" (Kapp)(ca. 1965)

JERRY NAYLOR

(Singer, Songwriter, Bass Guitar)

Date of Birth: **March 6, 1939**

Where Born: **Stephensville, Texas**

Jerry Naylor formed his first band when he was only 14. They worked on the *Louisiana Hayride* and toured with Elvis Presley, Johnny Cash and Johnny Horton. During his high school days, he was a deejay in San Angelo, Texas. He later enrolled at the Elkins Electronics Institute. He utilized his radio knowledge when he joined the American Forces Radio Service (AFRS) in Germany, during 1957, but he was discharged following a spinal injury. Jerry recorded two singles for Skyla Records, *You're 13/Stop Your Crying* (1961) and *Judee Malone/I'm Tired* (1962). Shortly after, he befriended Glen Campbell and then moved with Campbell to Los Angeles.

Jerry worked for a while at KRLA and KDAY and then in 1961 he became a member of the Crickets, replacing Joe B. Maudlin on bass. However, Jerry was suffering from ill health and in 1964, he had a heart attack and left the group. He fully recovered and found himself drifting more toward Country music.

Jerry signed to Columbia in 1969 and released the single *Posters on the Wall*. He first charted for that label in 1970, when *But for Love* made the Pop Top 70. During 1973 and 1974, he hosted *Continental Country*, which was voted by *Billboard* the "Best Syndicated Country Radio Show" of 1973 and 1974. He got into the Country Top 30, with *Is This All There Is to a Honky Tonk?* on Motown's Melodyland label. When the label became Hitsville, Naylor continued with them and had the basement-level *The Bad Part of Me* and the Top 50 *The Last Time You Love Me*, both in 1976.

In 1978, Jerry moved over to MCA/Curb Records and had the Top 40 hit *If You Don't Want to Love Her* and the lower level *Rave On* (the former Buddy Holly hit)/*Lady, Would You Like to Dance*. The following year, he emerged on Warner/Curb with a remake of his 1970 Pop hit *But for Love* (Top 60) and his version of Rod Stewart's *She Wears it Well* (Top 75). Later that year, Jerry charted Top 70 on Jeremiah Records with *Don't Touch Me*, on which he was joined by Kelli Warren.

Jerry had a one-off single on Oak during 1980 entitled *Cheating Eyes*, which made the Top 70, and then there was no further chart action until 1986, when his West Records single *For Old Time Sake* reached the Top 75.

FRANK NECESSARY

(Banjo, Guitar)

Date of Birth: **December 20, 1935**

Where Born: **Boone's Camp, Kentucky**

Frank Necessary and Al Jones

Frank Necessary has been leader or co-leader of some fine Bluegrass bands over the years. In the late 60's, he led the Stone Mountain Boys, which worked out of Ashland, Ohio, at the *Wheeling Jamboree* and appeared at festivals throughout the Midwest.

A native of the same portion of Appalachian Kentucky that produced superstar songstress Loretta Lynn, Frank grew up as the youngest member of a large family with musical interests. He learned his first guitar chords at the age of 7. However, Frank never really got serious about music until he was doing Air Force duty in Germany in the late 50's. A friend named Fred Smith urged him to learn banjo and they organized a Bluegrass band called the Dixie Ramblers that worked NCO service clubs and had a program on the local AFR station.

After returning to the U.S., Frank worked with a Country band or two, getting back to Bluegrass with a band called the Wichita Mountain Boys. By the mid-60's, he found himself in the Baltimore/Washington area working in a variety of bands including those of Buzz Busby and Patsy Stoneman. From 1966 to 1968, Necessary played mostly with a band called the Spruce Mountain Boys led by the high lonesome vocalist from White Top, Virginia named Al Jones (b. 1932). This group cut a pair of singles on Rebel.

In 1968, Frank moved to Ashland, Ohio where he joined forces with the Stone Mountain Boys. For a half-dozen years this band worked at the WWVA *Jamboree* and played Bluegrass festivals throughout the Midwest. The Stone Mountain Boys built their sound largely around Frank's varied talent, but also boasted the skills of Donald Highman (b. 1933), a lead singing guitarist, and Bill Highman (b. 1935), a tenor vocalist and mandolin picker. Leslie Fieber (b. 1946) on electric bass rounded out the group. Their style could best be described as somewhat reminiscent of the Osborne Brothers whose membership also included Troy Bailey and Larry Fowler. During their years together, Frank and the boys recorded respective albums for Cabut, Arby, and Old Homestead. They had an additional single on Cabut and reportedly cut sufficient material for an album on Jalyn, although some singles were never released.

In 1974, Frank Necessary returned to the Baltimore/Washington area, where he and Al Jones became co-leaders of the Spruce Mountain Boys. They played clubs and some festivals in the region and made a well-produced album for Rounder. Later Buzz Busby came into their group for a while, during which time they cut an album for Old Homestead. In recent years, they have continued to work in the D.C. and surrounding areas. Frank currently makes his home in Mechanicsville, Maryland. IMT

RECOMMENDED ALBUMS:

Frank Necessary and the Stone Mountain Boys:
"No More Tomorrows" (Cabut)(1970)
"The Ballad of Penny Dollar" (Arby)(1972)
"Cimarron Bluegrass" (Old Homestead)(1973)
The Spruce Mountain Boys:
"Al Jones, Frank Necessary & the Spruce Mountain Boys" (Rounder)(1976)
"Frank Necessary, Al Jones and Buzz Busby" (Old Homestead)(1987)

SAM NEELY

(Singer, Songwriter, Guitar)

Date of Birth: **August 22, 1948**
Where Born: **Cuero, Texas**
Married: **Unknown**
Children: **Jason**

Sam Neely is an example of a performer that should have had more acclaim than he actually received. At a time when his brand of Country-Rock is acceptable with Country radio, it seems hard to understand why some enterprising record label doesn't now make a star out of him.

Sam fell in love with the guitar when he was age 10. He'd spend every Sunday at his aunt's house and his mother told him not to touch the guitar that stood in the corner. One Sunday, his aunt caught him staring at the instrument and told him to pick it up. He began playing professionally by the time he was 11. His family moved to Corpus Christi, Texas, and by the time he was 15, he was playing guitar in local bands.

In 1966, he joined a local Rock band called Buckle, whose principal venue was the Rogue, and recorded for the first time. Three years later, Sam was on the *Merv Griffin* TV show when he met a movie producer who requested songs for a soundtrack that he was working on. Sam submitted material that in 1978 emerged in the movie *Tilt*, which starred Brooke Shields. With the help of a movie producer, Sam signed to Capitol in 1971. That year, he released his first single for the label Change, *A Sad to a Happy Song/Long Road to Texas*. It was with his third single, *Loving You Just Crossed My Mind*, in 1972, that Sam hit the Pop chart for the first time. The record peaked in the Top 30 and the follow-up, *Rosalie*, made it to the Top 50 the following year.

Texan Country and Pop singer ***Sam Neely***

In 1974, Sam signed to A & M Records and had the cross-over hit *You Can Have Her*. It reached the Pop Top 40 and the Country Top 50. The following year, his follow-up, *I Fought the Law*, was a Top 60 Pop and Country success. By now, Sam was supporting name acts, but major chart success still eluded him. He stayed with A & M until 1976 and then moved to Elektra. For his new label, Sam had a basement cross-over single in *Sail Away*, but although he was with Elektra until 1978, he had no further success. Around this time, he started what would be a long-term residency at the Electric Eel in Corpus Christi.

Sam had two songs in movies; *Blue Time* in *Bonnie's Kids* and *Long Road to Texas* in *Tilt*. He then turned his energy to running a nightclub in Corpus Christi called Neely's. He was spotted by Roger Ramsey, an MCA regional employee, who brought Sam's talents to the attention of producer Ron Chancey. As a result, Sam was signed to MCA in 1983. Sam had three more Country chart records during 1983 and 1984, *The Party's Over (Everybody's Gone), When You Leave That Way You Can Never Go Back* and *Old Photographs*. Since then, Sam Neely has not had any further chart action.

KEN NELSON

(Industry Executive)

During the 60's and 70's, Capitol Records and Ken Nelson were inseparable. As head of the Country Music Department, he was responsible for producing many of the hit records that emanated from the West Coast.

Ken made his first radio broadcast at the age of 14 as a singer. In 1935, he became a radio announcer at WAAF Chicago and later became Music Director. In 1939, he became Musical Director at WJJD and WIND in Chicago, where he began *The Suppertime Frolic*, which became a major music program.

In 1946, Ken Nelson began working for Capitol Records and two years later he was sent to California as head of the label's Transcription Department. Six years later, he became the Head of the Country Music Department. While with the label, he produced Merle Haggard, Jean Shepard, Jan Howard, Roy Clark, Buck Owens, Hank Thompson and Freddie Hart.

Ken was also a leading light in the expansion of Country music. He was a founding Director and President of the CMA, a Trustee and Chairman of the Country Music Foundation and was instrumental in persuading NARAS to establish a chapter and open an office in Nashville in 1964.

Ken is now retired in Southern California. In 1989, he was a nominee for induction to the Country Music Hall of Fame.

RICK NELSON

(Singer, Songwriter, Guitar, Piano, Drums, Actor)

Given Name:	**Eric Hilliard Nelson**
Date of Birth:	**May 8, 1940**
Where Born:	**Teaneck, New Jersey**
Married:	**Kristin Harmon (div.)**
Children:	**Twins: Matthew, Gunnar; Tracy**
Date of Death:	**December 31, 1985**

Ricky Nelson became one of the "founding fathers" of rock'n'roll with his special variety of teen music; and that is how he will always be remembered. However, as Rick Nelson, he emerged as one of the finest and most creative Country-Rock performers during the late 60's and early 70's.

From March, 1949, Ricky Nelson and his brother, David, grew up playing themselves on their parents' radio show (1949-52) and TV show (1952-66), *The Adventures of Ozzie and Harriet*. Ozzie was a bandleader and Harriet a singer. When he was 16, Ricky appeared in an episode playing drums and singing *I'm Walkin'*. The reaction from the viewing public was phenomenal. In 1957, he signed with Verve Records. His first single was *I'm Walkin'/Teenager's Romance*. Allegedly, this recording was made so that Ricky could impress a girlfriend who preferred Elvis. The "A" side reached the Top 5 on the Pop chart, while the flip-side climbed to the Top 3. The follow-up, *You're My One and Only Love/Honey Rock*, was not quite so successful and only reached the Top 15 on the Pop chart. On the flip-side, famed guitarist Barney Kessel conducted the orchestra.

At the end of 1957, Ricky signed with Imperial Records and would there enjoy a run of Pop hits that would continue until 1963.

The immortal ***Rick Nelson***

He was backed by Bob Luman's band, which included the incomparable James Burton on lead guitar. The Imperial hits started in 1957 with *Be-Bop Baby*, which climbed to the Top 3 and was backed by the Top 30 hit *Have I Told You Lately That I Love You*. He wrapped up the year with the double-sided hit *Stood Up/Waitin' in School*. The top-side reached the Top 3 on the Pop chart and the following January, both sides crossed over into the Country charts, with the top-side reaching the Top 10 and the flip-side, Top 15.

In 1958, Ricky started a loose association with Johnny and Dorsey Burnette, who, together and individually, provided him with some outstanding songs. The first to be recorded was *Believe What You Say*, which reached the Top 10 on both the Pop and Country lists. The flip-side, *My Bucket's Got a Hole in It*, also reached the Top 10 on the Country charts and No.12 on the Pop charts. He followed this up with what would become his first No.1, *Poor Little Fool*. This also reached the Top 3 on the Country charts and would be his last Country hit for nine years. He closed out the year with the double-sided Top 10 hit *Lonesome Town/I Got a Feeling*.

He got 1959 under way with another double-sided Top 10 single, *Never Be Anyone Else But You/It's Late*. This was followed by yet one more double-sider, *Just a Little Too Much/Sweeter Than You*. Then suddenly, Ricky's success level dropped. The last single of the year, *I Wanna Be Loved/Mighty Good,* only reached the Top 20. That year, he made his movie debut as "Colorado Ryan" in the John Wayne film *Rio Bravo*. Ricky would go on to appear in two other films, *The Wackiest Ship in the Army* and *Love and Kisses*, but acting was not really his forte.

As 1960 got under way, Ricky's singles still failed to reach their previously heady heights. *Young Emotions/Right By My Side* fell short of the Top 10 and *I'm Not Afraid/Yes Sir, That's My Baby* only made the Top 30. The year ended with *You Are the Only One/Milk Cow Blues,* which peaked in the Top 25. Just as suddenly as his success level fell, so, as 1961 started, he had a monster hit with the Gold single *Travelin' Man*, which reached No.1. The flip-side, *Hello Mary Lou*, written by Gene Pitney, also made the Top 10. For his final hit of the year, Ricky became Rick, as he felt he was too old for the "Ricky" tag. That hit was *A Wonder Like You/ Everlovin'*.

In 1962, he made the Top 5 with *Young World*, while the "B" side, *Summertime*, reached the Top 90. He followed this with *Teen Age Idol* and *It's Up to You*, both Top 10 records. The following year, Rick moved to Decca and signed a 20-year contract, while Imperial still continued releasing singles, the most successful being *You Don't Love Me Anymore (And I Can Tell)/I Got a Woman*, which only reached the Top 50 in 1963. During this period with Decca, his material was not as appreciated as it should have been. Rick's most successful singles for Decca that year were *Fools Rush In* (Top 15) and *For You* (Top 10). With the advent of Beatlemania, Rick's star started to wane, and in 1964 his highest entry was *The Very Thought of You*, which climbed to the Top 30. During the year, Rick married Kristin Harmon, the sister of actor Mark Harmon. Rick released two albums, ***Bright Lights and Country Music*** (1966) and ***Country Fever*** (1967), the latter containing a sensational version of *Mystery Train*, which indicated what was about to come musically.

He made an appearance in the Country charts during 1967 with Gib Gilbeau's *Take a City Bride*, which came from the ***Country Fever*** album, but it was with the formation of the Stone Canyon Band that Rick Nelson came of age and Rock credibility. The original line-up was former Buckaroo Tom Brumley on steel guitar, Jim Cetera on bass and vocals, Allen Kemp on lead guitar and vocals, Patrick Shanahan on drums, while Rick weighed in on lead vocals, rhythm guitar and piano. The band hit the Pop charts with Dylan's *She Belongs to Me* in 1969 and followed it up the following March with *Easy to Be Free*.

In 1971, the band released its debut album, ***Rick Sings Nelson***, on which all the songs were penned by Nelson, who also produced it. Later that year, the magnificent album ***Rudy the Fifth*** made its appearance. By now, Cetera had left and Eagles member-to-be Randy Meisner came in on bass and vocals. Every track is a standout one, with *Honky Tonk*

Women and Nelson's own psychedelic *Gypsy Pilot* being worthy of note.

The following year marked a watershed in Rick's career with the appearance of his autobiographical *Garden Party*, from the album of the same name. The single went Top 10 on the Pop charts and Top 50 on the Country charts. The follow-up, *Palace Guard*, did not fare nearly as well, only reaching the Top 70 on the Pop charts, and this would be Rick's final Pop placing. Once again, the Stone Canyon Band bass player had changed. Now Stephen A. Love was in the bassist hot seat.

The 1974 album ***Windfall*** yielded the minor Country chart success *One Night Stand*. By now, the line-up only had Nelson and Brumley as the constant factor. Dennis Larden was now in on lead guitar and vocals, J. DeWitt White was on bass and vocals and Ty Grimes played drums. The band moved to Epic in 1977 and released the album ***Intakes***. For this, their last album, Steve Duncan came in on drums and vocals and Roger Bush of Country Gazette fame played bass. The single *Dream Lover* made the Country Top 60 and then the "Garden Party" was over. The band continued to play but without any further albums or hits.

On December 31, 1985, Rick and most of the members of the Stone Canyon Band were killed in a charter aircraft crash. The single *Dream Lover* was re-released and made the Country charts, yet it seems strange that in light of his stature, his record label didn't achieve a major posthumous hit. In 1987, Rick(y) Nelson was inducted into the Rock and Roll Hall of Fame.

Rick Nelson's sons, Matthew (vocals, bass) and Gunnar (vocals, rhythm guitar), with long blond hair, their crowning glory, have continued the family musical heritage as the Rock act Nelson. They achieved a No.1 hit with *(Can't Live Without Your) Love and Affection*, which went Gold in 1990. Their album, ***After the Rain***, had gone Platinum by the following year. Rick's daughter, Tracy, is a film and TV actress, who appears as "Sister Steve" in the mystery series *Father Dowling*.

During his career, Rick maintained a popularity overseas as well as in the U.S. In the U.K., four of his singles made the Top 10, *Poor Little Fool*, *Someday*, *It's Late* and *Hello Mary Lou/Travellin' Man*. In all, he had twenty-one hits in Britain and maintained an active fan club there.

RECOMMENDED ALBUMS:

Imperial recordings:
"The Ricky Nelson Singles Album" (United Artists)(1979)
Decca/MCA recordings:
"Country" (double)(MCA)(1973)
"The Rick Nelson Singles Album 1963-1976" (MCA Coral)(1977) [Compilation and sleeve notes by Tim Rice]
"String Along with Rick" (Charly UK)(1984)
Rick Nelson & the Stone Canyon Band:
"Rick Sings Nelson" (MCA)(1971)
"Rudy the Fifth" (MCA)(1971)
"Garden Party" (MCA)(1972)
"Windfall" (MCA)(1974)
"Intakes" (Epic)(1977)

WILLIE NELSON

(Singer, Guitar, Songwriter, Actor)

Given Name:	**Willie Hugh Nelson**
Date of Birth:	**April 30, 1933**
Where Born:	**Fort Worth, Texas**
Married:	**1. Martha Matthews (div.)**
	2. Shirley Collie (div.)
	3. Connie (div.)
	4. Annie D'Angelo
Children:	**Billy (dec'd.), Shirley, Paula Carlene, Lana, Amy**

Notwithstanding a series of calamities, Willie Nelson has proved to be one of Country's most enduring stars. The first tragedy to hit Willie occurred when his parents split up and he and sister Bobbie were raised by their grandparents in the small farming town of Abbott, Texas. Willie found solace in songwriting and by the age of 7 was penning heartbreak songs. Three years earlier he had made his singing debut at a Gospel picnic. Nelson's unique style partly derived from his cosmopolitan influences—Blues and Jazz, *Hayride* and *Opry* broadcasts, cowboy stars like the Sons of the Pioneers and Gene Autry, honky-tonker Ernest Tubb, the Western swing of Bob Wills, the singing styles of Floyd Tillman and Lefty Frizzell, even crooners like Frank Sinatra.

Both Willie's grandparents played guitar and he began to develop a style of picking all his own. Barely 9, he joined the Raychecks' Polka Band, soon learning how to drink, and in his teens fronted Bobbie's husband's band, Bud Fletcher and the Texans. Upon leaving high school, Willie spent a short spell in the Air Force, subsequently enrolling part-time at Baylor University with a farming career in mind. Having gotten married, he soon found he had three children to support, which forced him to take a succession of part-time jobs and abandon his course.

Finally he found a job he could hold down for a time: deejay. On Fort Worth's KCNC in 1954, Nelson was no ordinary deejay. "This is your ol' cotton pickin', snuff dippin', tobacco chewin', coffee pot dodgin', dumplin' eatin', frog giggin' hillbilly from Hill Country" was his opening line. At the end of the 50's, Willie decided to go for the big time. "Giving away" the rights to a song called *Family Bible* for $50 (it subsequently went Top 10 for Claude Gray), the Nelson family headed for Nashville in their clapped out 1941 Buick.

Willie soon learned how to ply his trade: spend as much time as possible drinking in Tootsie's Orchid Lounge and pitching songs. He was soon befriended by Hank Cochran, who helped secure Willie a songwriting contract with Pamper Music. Then part-owner Ray Price gave Willie a place in his band as bass player. Price would eventually take a

*On the left, **Willie Nelson** and on the right, **Charlie Daniels***

Nelson composition, *Night Life*, which became his theme song.

1961 was a seminal year for Willie Nelson, songwriter. First, Faron Young took *Hello Walls* to the top for a nine week run. Next Billy Walker took *Funny How Time Slips Away* to the Top 25 in October. Finally, Patsy Cline's husband Charlie Dick happened to hear Willie's recording of *Crazy* on Tootsie's jukebox, loved it, and with her producer and manager persuaded his reluctant wife to record it, a decision vindicated by it just missing the top spot. Further, all three songs crossed over into the Pop charts.

Two years later, *Pretty Paper* was a Christmas hit for Roy Orbison. But if Willie Nelson had arrived as a songwriter, he still encountered resistance to his behind-the-beat semi-narrative singing style. He claimed to have developed his idiosyncratic technique from singing countless times in small clubs where he became bored with performing the set list the same way. Critics suggested he talked rather than sang.

Industry reservations didn't stop him being signed by Liberty Records, with whom he enjoyed two Top 10 hits in 1962, *Willingly* (a duet with his then wife, Shirley Collie) and *Touch Me*. Willie had two other hits on the label, *Half a Man* (Top 25, 1963) and *You Took My Happy Away* (Top 40, 1964).

In 1965, after Liberty closed their Country division, Nelson joined RCA and became a regular cast member of the *Opry*. During the seven years at RCA, Willie's major hits were: *One in a Row* (Top 20, 1966), *The Party's Over* and *Blackjack County Chain* (both Top 25, in 1967), *Little Things* (Top 25, 1968), *Bring Me Sunshine* (Top 15, 1969) and *I'm a Memory* (Top 30, 1971). However, Willie didn't have a career-making single. His approach simply didn't fit the Nashville Sound. He later confessed to being unable to capture the feel he wanted in a three hour session. The nadir of his career was reached when his two final RCA singles, *Yesterday's Wine* and *The Words Don't Fit the Picture*, reached the Top 70 and Top 75 respectively in 1971 and 1972.

With his second marriage failing and his musical career seemingly over, Willie got drunk and he lay down in the middle of Music Row waiting for a vehicle to run him over. Fortunately, as it was in the small hours, nothing came. Disenchanted with Nashville, for a time he tried pig farming in Tennessee — which ended when his property burned down —then moved to Austin with retirement on his mind.

Willie noticed that long-haired college students and hippies at the Armadillo World Headquarters Rock venue were getting into Country music. Add to these farm boys and crew-cut rednecks and a vast audience beckoned for a left field singer. So Willie cannily elected to emphasize the connection by ditching his clean-cut Nashville Sound-derived image and re-created himself as one of their number. He grew his hair long, sported a bandanna and adopted the attire of T-shirt, ragged jeans and jaded tennis shoes. He also started reading books on positive thinking, karma and reincarnation.

Willie had moved to Atlantic Records and though major success was still elusive, two singles broke the Top 20, *Bloody Monday Morning* and the duet with Tracy Nelson (no relation) entitled *After the Fire Is Gone*, in 1974. In this period he began to make adjustments to his style. Moving to Columbia, Willie crucially gained control of the production of his recordings. Unfettered, he cut songs he wanted to, often in stripped down form and containing tinges of all his varied influences. Industry people who heard his pre-release cuts of the debut Columbia album, ***Red Headed Stranger***, couldn't believe it was the finished product. But Willie was vindicated when his cover of *Blue Eyes Crying in the Rain* went to No.1 in 1975 and the album achieved Platinum status. Willie was now at the forefront of a new musical movement which was variously called Progressive Country, Redneck Rock or, more usually, Outlaw music. His old label, RCA, capitalized by bringing out an album, ***Wanted: The Outlaws***, which also featured Waylon Jennings, Jessi Colter and Tompall Glaser. A nationwide tour helped to make it a chart topper. In 1975 came another roaring success, ***Waylon and Willie***, which was again promoted by a tour. From this Nelson and Jennings had the No.1 hit *Good Hearted Woman*, which was named the CMA's "Single of the Year" and became a Top 25 Pop hit.

During 1976, Willie had major hits with *Remember Me* (Top 3) and *If You've Got the Money I've Got the Time* (No.1). The following year, he went Top 5 with *Uncloudy Day* and top 10 with *I Love You a Thousand Ways*. He started out 1978 with the Top 10 duet *Something to Brag About* with Mary Kay Place. This was followed by the No.1 duet with Waylon of Ed Bruce's *Mammas Don't Let Your Babies Grow Up to Be Cowboys*. The single stayed on top of the Country chart for 4 weeks and crossed to the Pop Top 50. After this, Willie went Top 5 with *If You Can Touch Her at All*.

Willie gambled that there would be a market for a 1978 album of old standards. Not only was ***Stardust*** a mega-selling album (eventually selling 4 million units), it also gave Nelson two consecutive No.1s, *Georgia on My Mind* and *Blue Skies*. He closed out 1978 with another track, *All of Me*, which went Top 3.

Willie's other major successes during the late 70's and early 80's were: *Whiskey River* (Top 15), *Sweet Memories* (Top 5), *Heartbreak Hotel* (No.1, with Leon Russell), *Crazy Arms* (Top 20) (all 1979), *Help Me Make it Through the Night* (Top 5), *My Heroes Have Always Been Cowboys* (No.1), *Night Life* (Top 20, with Danny Davis), *Faded Love* (Top 3, with Ray Price) and *On the Road Again* (No.1) (all 1980), *Don't You Ever Get Tired (Of Hurting Me)* (Top 15, with Ray Price), *Angel Flying Too Close to the Ground* (No.1) and *Mona Lisa* (Top 15) (all 1981).

Film parts began with the role of Robert Redford's manager in *The Electric Horseman* (1979) in which Willie famously ad-libbed one line: "I'm gonna get me a bottle of tequila, and one of those girls who can suck the chrome off a trailer hitch." Later films included *Honeysuckle Rose* (1980), *The Songwriter* with Kris Kristofferson (1984) and *Red Headed Stranger* (1987).

Yet if he acquired the trappings of fame, not least a Lear jet—Air Willie—he was much more generous with others. Friends received houses and cars and Willie provided for his increasing Family band which traveled around in five tour buses. Indeed, such was Willie's generosity that he literally gave away millions. After concerts fans would besiege his bus not seeking his autograph but signed checks readily elicited by hard luck stories.

By the early 80's, Nelson's career had moved into even higher gear. Platinum albums were now the norm, as well as his own No.1 hits, like his superlative cover of *Always on My Mind* in 1982. This single crossed to the Pop Top 5 and was Certified Platinum.

He began to be the performer with whom everyone wanted to record. His partners included Waylon Jennings, Roger Miller, Webb Pierce, Merle Haggard, Julio Iglesias and Ray Charles. From 1982 through 1983, Willie's major hits were: *Just to Satisfy You* (No.1, with Waylon), *Old Friends* (Top 20, with Roger Miller and Ray Price), *Let It Be Me* (Top 3 Country/Top 40 Pop) and *(Sittin' On) The Dock of the Bay* (Top 15, with Waylon) (all 1982), *Last Thing I Needed First Thing This Morning* (Top 3), *Everything's Beautiful (In Its Own Way)* (Top 10, with Dolly Parton), *Reasons to Quit* (Top 10, with Merle Haggard), *Little Old Fashioned Karma* (Top 10), *Pancho and*

Lefty (No.1, with Merle Haggard) and *Take It to the Limit* (Top 10, with Waylon) (all 1983).

In 1984, Willie got together with Julio Iglesias for the international hit *To All the Girls I've Loved Before*. The single reached No.1 on the Country chart and Top 10 on the Pop chart and became a big European hit. Willie followed up with another No.1 hit, *City of New Orleans*. He started off 1985 with *Seven Spanish Angels,* a No.1 duet with Ray Charles. With Kenny Rogers, Willie represented Country on the No.1 single *We Are the World* as part of USA (United Support of Artists) for Africa. In addition, Willie's 4th of July Picnic, started in 1973, evolved into the annual Farm Aid music festivals, which raise millions to help U.S. farmers.

In 1985, Willie went to No.1 with *Forgiving You Was Easy*. He then got together with Waylon Jennings, Johnny Cash and Kris Kristofferson for the ***Highwayman*** album. From this, the title track went to No.1. During the rest of the decade, Willie's major successes were: *Me and Paul* (Top 15), *Desperados Waiting for a Train* (Top 15, with Jennings, Cash and Kristofferson) (both 1985), *Living in the Promiseland* (No.1, 1986), *Spanish Eyes* (Top 10, with Julio Iglesias, 1988), *Nothing I Can Do About It Now* (No.1, 1989), *There You Are* (Top 10), and *Ain't Necessarily So* (Top 20) (both 1990).

Then in November, 1990, Willie was hit with a tax bill for $16.7 million. The singer was typically philosophical about it all—"If I say it fast it don't seem so bad"—but the IRS wasn't. Unable to pay in full, Willie was stripped of his assets—several houses and farms, a motel, apartment block, his private jet and golf course, recording studios, even the replica western town built for the movie *Red Headed Stranger*. He was most concerned to save his trademark guitar, "Trigger," with its distinctive gut-strung sound. To help meet his liabilities, Nelson put out a double album poignantly titled ***The IRS Tapes: Who'll Buy My Memories,*** on which he restricted the accompaniment to his precious guitar.

His friends also staged "Willie Aid" and fans sent him money. By 1993, Willie had reached a compromise agreement with the IRS. That year he turned sixty and was fittingly elected to the Country Music Hall of Fame as well as being named "Native American of the Year" and proclaimed a "Living Texas Legend" by the state governor. A CBS television tribute, "The Big Six-O," featured some big stars playing tribute, including Bob Dylan, B.B. King, Neil Young and Paul Simon.

1993 was also memorable for Nelson's best album in years, ***Across the Borderline***, which was littered with star guests from different musical fields. Indeed, by that year no fewer than 75 artists had dueted with Nelson. Appropriately some of them were stars who had helped him on his way up and he was returning the favor when they were in decline. The awards have been many. Among the accolades were lifetime achievement awards from the National Academy of Popular Music and the Songwriters Hall of Fame and CMA's 1979 "Entertainer of the Year." *Always on My Mind*, Willie's biggest crossover hit, won a Grammy (one of several) and was voted *Billboard*'s "Single of the Decade." In 1994, Willie signed with Justice Records to release another MOR-type album, ***Moonlight Becomes You***, which reached the Country Albums Top 40.

Willie Nelson has nothing left to prove but it is thankfully not in his nature to quit. Above his bed is a plaque which reads: "He who lives by the road shall die by the road." A restless nature and abundant talent could well provide further career highs to an already more than memorable career.

SM/BM

RECOMMENDED ALBUMS:

"The Complete Liberty Recordings 1962-1964" (EMI Country Masters)(1993)
"Phases and Stages" (Columbia)(1974)
"Red Headed Stranger" (Columbia)(1975)
"Waylon and Willie" (Columbia)(1978)
"Stardust" (Columbia)(1978)
"Pancho and Lefty" (Columbia)(1982) [With Merle Haggard]
"City of New Orleans" (Columbia)(1984)
"Island in the Sea" (Columbia)(1987)
"What a Wonderful World" (Columbia)(1987)
"Across the Borderline" (Columbia)(1993)
"Moonlight Becomes You" (Justice)(1994)

JIM NESBITT

(Singer, Comedy, Deejay)

Given Name:	**James Nesbitt**
Date of Birth:	**December 1, 1931**
Where Born:	**Bishopville, South Carolina**
Married:	**Unknown**
Children:	**Unknown**

Jim Nesbitt was a South Carolina deejay who had a flair for tongue-in-cheek humor. This talent put his name on the Country charts thirteen times between 1964 and 1970. Many of his "songs" tended toward Talking Blues and recitations, but most displayed a clever wit—often directed to political satire—which delighted numerous radio audiences and those who attended many of the package shows in that era.

Little detail is available on Nesbitt's life, but during his years on the charts, he worked as a deejay at WAGS radio in his hometown of Bishopville, which was some twenty-five miles west of the larger city of Florence. There he made TV appearances with Slim Mims and his Dream Ranch Boys. Jim recorded initially for Dot and then for Chart, the same company that would later elevate Junior Samples to his first taste of fame. While Jim never got the national TV exposure that raised Samples to star status, he did do much better on the record charts.

His initial appearance in front of a national audience came in the spring of 1961 with *Please Mr. Kennedy*, which reached the Top 15. The song, based on *The Ballad of Davy Crockett*, was initially released on Country Jubilee and Ace, becoming a hit on Dot. Two years later *Livin' Offa Credit* made a brief appearance; however, his biggest number came in 1964 on Chart, with *Looking for More in '64*, which remained on the charts for nearly 6 months and reached the Top 10. Done in a Talking Blues style, the single satirized the level of rising expectations that resulted from the current presidential election. A North Carolina gubernatorial hopeful, Dan K. Moore, used it successfully for a campaign theme. It inspired a series of sequels: *Still Alive in '65*, *Heck of a Fix in '66*, *Clear the State in '68* and *Having Fun in '71*, the first two of which also charted in the Top 40.

In between these singles, Jim had other humorous ditties like *Mother-in-Law* (Top 20, 1964), *A Tiger in My Tank* (Top 15) and *The Friendly Undertaker* (Top 25) (both 1965), *You Better Watch Your Friends* (Top 50, 1966) and *Runnin' Bare* (Top 20, 1970). Other songs by Jim poked gentle fun at the problem of [Air] *Pollution*, *Spiro* [Agnew] and *Social Security*. His name vanished from the charts after 1970, but he came back with an album titled ***Phone Call from the Devil*** in 1976 (undoubtedly a reaction to Jerry Jordan's *Phone Call from God*). After that, Nesbitt seemingly dropped from the national scene. Bruce Jones of the Jones Brothers, a popular Carolina Bluegrass band, reports that a few years ago Nesbitt was located in Florence, South Carolina, engaged in the mobile home business.

IMT

RECOMMENDED ALBUMS:

"Your Favorite Comedy & Heart Songs" (Chart)(1964)
"Truck Drivin' Cat with Nine Wives" (Chart)(1968)
"Runnin' Bare" (Chart)(1970)
"The Best of Jim Nesbitt" (Chart)(1971)
"Phone Call from the Devil" (Scorpion)(1976)

MICHAEL NESMITH

(Singer, Songwriter, Guitar, Saxophone, Actor, Video Maker, Movie Maker)
Date of Birth: December 30, 1942
Where Born: Houston, Texas

The general public could be excused if they thought of Michael Nesmith as one quarter of that zany foursome, the Monkees (the one with the woolly hat). However, Mike is a multi-talented individual, who has had a major impact on the development of music video and has also created some of the most interesting Country-Rock songs and recordings.

Mike grew up in Farmer's Branch near Dallas (his mother invented Tippex white-out), where his first love was the Blues. Although he played saxophone in high school, he didn't consider it as a career until after he had left the U.S. Air Force in 1962 after a two-year stint. At that time, the Folk boom was happening and Mike got caught up in it. He learned to play guitar and after a year, started playing rhythm in local groups. He traveled around playing various groups and did some session work. He arrived in Memphis and did back-up work with Stax-Volt Records.

Arriving in Los Angeles, Michael played the local Folk clubs. In the fall of 1965, Michael attended an audition for a new TV show that would become the Monkees. Other auditioners included Stephen Stills and Charles Manson (!). The foursome making up the group, intended as a U.S. response to the Beatles, was Mike, Peter Tork, Mickey Dolenz and Davy Jones. Mike led a revolt against the fact that, initially, the group didn't play on their early recordings; they did later. The TV series lasted for 56 episodes over three years. In 1968, Mike wrote the title song for the highly praiseworthy but oft ignored Monkees movie, *Head.* During 1969, Mike's song *Listen to the Band* became a minor hit for the Monkees.

The multi-talented ***Michael Nesmith***

The group folded in 1969 and Michael decided to develop his musicianship and songwriting. He had already tried solo recording in 1968 when he recorded ***Wichita Train Whistle Sings*** for Dot Records. At the end of 1969, he put together the First National Band and signed with RCA. The line-up comprised steel guitarist and Dobroist Red Rhodes, drummer John Ware, and bassist John London. Rhodes had been named the ACM's "Steel Guitarist of the Year" in 1965 through 1968 (he would later win it again in 1973).

In 1970, they released two albums, ***Magnetic South*** and ***Loose Salute***. That year, they had the Top 25 Pop hit *Joanne*, which was followed up at year end by the Top 50 *Silver Moon.* In 1971, the line-up of the group started evolving and although the original members played on ***Nevada Fighter***, other players were also featured. Mike changed the name of the group to the Second National Band. The title track of the album became a Top 70 Pop chart entry and their last single hit. That year, Mike's song *Some of Shelly's Blues* became a hit for the Nitty Gritty Dirt Band.

In 1972, ***Tantamount to Treason*** was released but by the time he released ***And the Hits Just Keep on Comin'***, Michael had dropped the band format, although Red Rhodes continued to play with him. The album contained Mike's version of his song *Different Drum*, which had been Linda Ronstadt and the Stone Poney's first hit in 1967. The following year, Michael released ***Pretty Much Your Standard Stash***, which featured versions of *Some of Shelly's Blues*, Cindy Walker's *Born to Love You* and Bill Monroe's *Uncle Pen.*

Michael established his own communications company, Pacific Arts Corporation, in 1974. ***The Prison***, a multi-media book/record combination, was the company's first release in 1975. That year, Olivia Newton-John had a Top 30 hit with *Let it Shine*, which was written by Michael and Linda Hargrove. This was followed by the 1976 album ***From a Radio Engine to a Photon Wing***, from which came the U.K. Pop hit, *Rio.* Mike produced its filmed accompaniment and along with the Rock group Queen (see their ground-breaking *Bohemian Rhapsody* from 1975) helped develop the music video. While touring Australia, Michael noted that Top 40 TV shows played video clips. Back in the U.S., Michael created a 30 minute Top 40 show called *Popclips.* The show and the concept were sold to Warner AMEX and *Popclips* became MTV. Michael produced over 50 of the early episodes.

During 1978, Michael released the album ***Live at the Palais*** on Pacific Arts, and the following year Pacific Arts acquired several of Michael's albums. During that year, he released ***Infinite Rider on the Big Dogma***. This was to be his last album for almost 10 years as he concentrated on film production. He produced shorts for *Saturday Night Live* and *Fridays.* In 1981, Michael won the first Video Grammy Award for the original home video *Elephant Parts.* In 1984, he produced eight episodes of *Michael Nesmith in Television Parts*, the TV equivalent to the video. In the interim, Michael had commenced his film production career.

In 1982, he produced, co-wrote and performed the music for *Timerider: The Adventures of Lyle Swann.* In 1984, he was the Executive Producer of *Repo Man.* Three years later, Michael appeared in *Burglar* and the same year was Executive Producer of *Square Dance* (Winona Ryder's starring debut). In 1988, Michael appeared in and was Executive Producer of *Tapeheads*, which starred John Cusack and Tim Robbins.

In 1989, Michael returned to music and licensed his material and distributed unreleased tracks and tracks from later albums through the U.K. label Awareness as ***The Newer Stuff***. In late 1991, Rhino Records released a cd of Michael's earlier material, as ***The Older Stuff: The Best of Michael Nesmith (1970-73)***.

Meanwhile, Pacific Arts increased in size and in 1990 PBS Home Video was created. By 1992, Pacific Arts had tripled in size and is now the most important video publisher in the U.S., and Michael is still the owner and CEO. In 1992, Michael released the video ***Nesmith Live***, which was recorded at the Britt Festival in Jacksonville, Oregon, and also a new album, ***...Tropical Campfire's...***. Michael, now looking more and more like John Entwistle from the Who, has continuously produced quality material that *Rolling Stone* once called "...the greatest music never heard."

RECOMMENDED ALBUMS:

"Wichita Train Whistle Sings" (Dot)(1968) [Re-released on Pacific Arts in 1978]
"Magnetic South" (RCA Victor)(1970)
"Loose Salute" (RCA Victor)(1970)
"Nevada Fighter" (RCA Victor)(1971)
"Tantamount to Treason" (RCA Victor)(1972)
"And the Hits Keep on Coming" (RCA Victor)(1972) [Re-released on Pacific Arts in 1979]
"Pretty Much Your Standard Stash" (RCA Victor)(1973) [Re-released on Pacific Arts in 1979]
"The Prison" (Pacific Arts)(1975)
"From a Radio Engine to a Photon Wing" (Pacific Arts)(1977)
"Live at the Palais" (Pacific Arts)(1978)
"Infinite Rider on the Big Dogma" (Pacific Arts)(1979)
"The Newer Stuff" (Awareness UK)(1989)

"The Older Stuff: The Best of Michael Nesmith (1970-73)" (Rhino)(1991)
"...Tropical Campfire's...." (Pacific Arts)(1992)
Video:
"Nesmith Live" (Pacific Arts Video)(1992)

NEVADA SLIM
(a.k.a. Yodelin' Slim Dallas)
(Singer, Songwriter, Yodeler, Guitar)

Given Name:	**Dallas Turner**
Date of Birth:	**November 27, 1927**
Where Born:	**Walla Walla, Washington**
Married:	**Unknown**
Children:	**Nolen**

Dallas Turner, who usually used the name "Nevada Slim," was one of the last notable cowboy singers on the powerful "Mexican Border Stations" that once beamed across to listeners in the American Southwest.

As an infant, Dallas Turner found himself given away twice—first by his birth mother and then by an eccentric nurse named Lizzie Brown. However, his life stabilized when a ranch couple, Jim and Liz Turner, who lived near Elko, Nevada, adopted the hitherto unwanted baby. From then onward he had a fairly typical boyhood on the ranch.

At a rodeo once he saw the aging performers Powder River Jack and Kitty Lee, but his greatest inspirations came from those he heard on the border radio stations. As a youth, Dallas came under the influence of Cowboy Slim Rinehart (1911-1948), the "King of the Border Radio" Western singers, and about 1945 the young man aspired to follow his hero on the border stations. As soon as Rinehart induced him to be more original and less imitative, Cowboy Dallas Turner did quite well performing under such pseudonyms as "Nevada Slim" and "Yodeling Slim Dallas" in addition to his real name.

He also learned how to be a good "pitchman" or produce salesman, which comprised the economic life blood of the border stations like XERF, XELO, XEG and others that broadcast from powerful transmitters located across the border in Mexico. Singers such as Roy Faulkner and the aforementioned Rinehart had pioneered this market, and sometimes established artists like the Carter Family and Mainer's Mountaineers also did programs. The programs were nearly always transcribed and later taped. Nevada Slim followed this occupation for the better part of the next thirty years.

Turner also did some programs in the U.S. For a time, he was based in Portland, Oregon, but quickly grew unhappy. In the later 50's and early 60's, Nevada Slim had transcribed programs on U.S. stations like WCKY Cincinnati, WWVA Wheeling, and KXEL Waterloo, where he sold songbooks via mail order, but the border stations remained his best area.

In the early years, Turner recorded sparingly, if at all, but in the mid-60's he cut a series of albums for Uncle Jim O'Neal's Rural Rhythm label which he sold via radio and mail order. After he had conquered a drinking problem some years earlier, Turner entered the ministry and had some religious programs on the border stations as well as a Gospel album on Rural Rhythm under his own name.

In more recent years, Nevada Slim has appeared on some live programs in the West whenever an authentic cowboy singer is needed. He has been a valuable source of information for both cowboy-song scholars such as Guy Logsdon and border radio historians like Gene Fowler and Bill Crawford. Professor Logsdon reports that Dallas Turner resides in Reno and appeared at the 1993 Cowboy Poetry Gathering near his old hometown of Elko, Nevada. IMT

RECOMMENDED ALBUMS:
"Songs of the Wild West, Vols. 1-4" (Rural Rhythm)(ca. 1965)
"Nevada Slim Sings Heart Songs" (Rural Rhythm)(ca. 1965)
"Reverend Dallas Turner Sings Pentecostal Revival Songs" (Rural Rhythm)(ca. 1966)
"Old Time Country Favorites" (Rural Rhythm)(ca. 1966)

NEW GRASS REVIVAL
When Formed: **1972**
Members:

Sam Bush	**Vocals, Fiddle, Mandolin, Guitar (Founding Member)**
Béla Fleck	**Vocals, Banjo**
John Cowan	**Vocals, Bass Guitar**
Pat Flynn	**Vocals, Guitar, Mandolin, Banjo**
Other Founding Members:	
Courtney Johnson	**Vocals, Banjo**
Curtis Burch	**Vocals, Guitar, Dobro**
Ebo Walker	**Vocals, Bass Guitar**
Other Former Members:	
Butch Robbins	**Vocals, Bass Guitar**

For a while, in the late 80's, New Grass Revival took their brand of Bluegrass into chart areas undreamed of before. However, the fine musicianship of the quartet was not matched by their material, which was quite often esoteric and also not that musical.

New Grass Revival was formed in 1972 by Sam Bush (b. April 15, 1952, Bowling Green, Kentucky), Courtney Johnson (b. December 20, 1939, Barren County, Kentucky), Curtis Burch (b. January 24, 1945, Montgomery, Alabama) and Ebo Walker. Bush bought his first mandolin when age 11 and then took up the fiddle. At his first try, he was placed 5th at the National Old Time Fiddle Contest in Weiser, Idaho. For the next three years, he won. He joined forces with Wayne Stewart and Alan Munde to form Poor Richard's Almanac and they cut a self-named album for American Heritage.

When Munde left, he was replaced by Courtney Johnson. Courtney had started to play guitar at age 7. However, he didn't start

John Cowan, Béla Fleck, Pat Flynn and Sam Bush, ***New Grass Revival***

on banjo until he was 25, and he names as his major influence the legendary Ralph Stanley. In 1970, Johnson and Bush became members of Bluegrass Alliance, with Lonnie Peerce on fiddle and Ebo Walker on bass. The following year, while playing in Savannah, Georgia, they met Curtis Burch. Curtis had been listening to Bluegrass from early on from his father, who played guitar and sang. However, it was hearing Jim & Jesse that made Curtis head toward a career in music, and he joined the Bluegrass Alliance in November, 1971.

In 1972, Peerce left the group and they renamed themselves New Grass Revival. That year, they cut their first album, ***Arrival of the New Grass Revival***, on Starday. The following year, Walker left and Butch Robbins came on board. However, he was a talented banjo player and balked at playing bass, and so he left and was replaced by John Cowan (b. August 24, 1952, Evansville, Indiana) later that year. John was not a Bluegrass player. His background was Rock and he had started out playing trumpet, then went on to bass fiddle and then at 13 learned guitar. He played in various teen Rock bands while at high school. He was not only a good musician but also a fine singer. Throughout the 70's, they cut a string of albums for Flying Fish. In 1979, they became backup group and opening act for Leon Russell and this further alienated them from the mainstream Bluegrass community.

In 1981, they recorded the ***Live Album***, with Russell, which appeared on his Paradise label. That same year, Johnson and Burch decided that they had tired of touring and allowed Bush and Cowan to continue using the band name. The following year, they met Pat Flynn at a Colorado Bluegrass festival and then the amazing Béla Fleck was added. This resulted in the group becoming more acceptable to traditional Bluegrass fans. Pat began doing studio work in L.A., while still in high school. He recorded and played with Phil Everly, Dorsey Burnette, Andy Williams, Cher, Delaney Bramlett and Larry McNeely. In 1975, he recorded an album with his own group, Fresh Air, on Columbia. In 1982, he co-wrote, with Denny Gore, the soundtrack for the movie *Shannon County Home* on PBS. He later played on several Kathy Mattea tracks including *Love at the Five and Dime* in 1986. Béla got his first banjo when he was 15, and just five years later his debut solo album, ***Crossing the Tracks***, was named "Best Overall Album" in the 1981 *Frets* magazine Readers' Poll. He claims Tony Trischka as his major banjo influence. He had already released two albums with the New England–based group Tasty Licks, which he joined straight from high school and with whom he stayed until their disbandment in 1979. He then became a member of Spectrum, and stayed with them until he joined NGR.

During 1982, NGR signed with Jim Halsey's agency and in 1984 moved from Flying Fish to Sugar Hill, where they released ***On the Boardwalk***, which was co-produced by Garth Fundis and was voted "Acoustic Album of the Year" in *Frets*' poll. That year, they toured extensively in Japan, France, Spain, Turkey and Greece. With Fundis' help, the group secured a record deal with EMI America in 1986, and Fundis continued his production role. NGR had two chart entries that year: *What You Do to Me*, which reached the Top 80, and their version of Marvin Gaye's hit *Ain't That Peculiar*, which peaked in the Top 60. Béla's *Seven by Seven* was nominated for a Grammy Award as "Best Country Instrumental" in 1987. With EMI becoming Capitol that year, NGR released their second album, ***Hold to a Dream***.

They made their debut at England's Wembley Festival, but their music was only warmly received, Bluegrass being still very traditional on those shores. They again toured extensively and visited Morocco, Egypt, India, Bangladesh and Nepal. They also appeared on the nationally syndicated radio show *Prairie Home Companion*, hosted by Garrison Keillor, which was created to show off "Newgrass."

From the second album, *Unconditional Love* became a Top 50 success, and the following year *Can't Stop Now* did the same. During 1988, they performed *Can't Stop Now* and *Metric Lips* in *Tanner '88*, a satire on presidential campaigns written by Garry Trudeau and shown on HBO.

They released their third album, ***Friday Night in America***, in 1989 and two singles charted that year, *Callin' Baton Rouge* (Top 40) and *You Plant Your Fields* (Top 60). However, that was to be the end of the road for New Grass Revival. Sam Bush has now become a much-in-demand session man and Béla Fleck has gone on to the Flecktones.

RECOMMENDED ALBUMS:

"Arrival of the New Grass Revival" (Starday)(1972)
"Fly Through the Country" (Flying Fish)(1975)
"Live Album" (Paradise)(1981) [With Leon Russell]
"On the Boulevard" (Sugar Hill)(1984)
"New Grass Revival" (EMI America)(1986)
"Hold to a Dream" (Capitol)(1987)
"Friday Night in America" (Capitol)(1989)
(See also Béla Fleck.)

NEW LOST CITY RAMBLERS, The

When Formed: **1958**

Members:

John Cohen	**Vocals, Guitar, Banjo, Mandolin**
Mike Seeger	**Vocals, All String Instruments, Harmonica**
Tom Paley	**Vocals, Banjo, Guitar (left 1962)**
Tracy Schwarz	**Vocals, Fiddle, Guitar, Banjo, Mandolin, Accordion (joined 1962)**

The New Lost City Ramblers are a Folk group who specialize in playing Old-Time string band music common on recordings from the 1920's and 1930's. The Ramblers had considerable impact in the rekindling of interest among both urban audiences and younger rural folk who had forgotten their own musical roots.

The original members of the New Lost City Ramblers were Mike Seeger (b. August 15, 1933, New York City), John Cohen (b. August 2, 1932, New York City) and Tom Paley (b. March 19, 1928, New York City). They all hailed from urban backgrounds, outside the culture which normally nurtured hillbilly musical traditions.

Mike gained something of a childhood background for the sounds as the son of ethnomusicologist and Folksong scholar Charles Seeger. The others gained an appreciation for Old-Time sounds through an interest in urban Folk music. The Ramblers learned most of their music from pre-WWII phonograph records and Library of Congress field recordings in the beginning, although eventually they began to get material directly from such authentic folk as Roscoe Holcomb and others.

While many of their concerts were in Folk clubs and on college campuses, they did succeed in reacquainting some students with the music of their rural heritage and stimulated interest in what might be described as a relatively dynamic area of Folk music, or as John Pankake rather bluntly expressed in 1978, "they brought a fresh, aggressively vernacular rural repertoire of spunky songs...to audiences politely bored with bland croonings of *I Gave My Love a Cherry* and such ilk."

In August, 1962, Tom Paley, who had attained a graduate degree in mathematics, decided to devote himself full-time to academics, ultimately moving to England. Tracy Schwarz (b. November 13, 1938, New York City), who played several instruments but was especially adept on fiddle, replaced him. The Ramblers continued their pattern of concerts and recordings, eventually switching to the somewhat more commercial Verve label.

Seeger and Cohen also edited one of the first and best collections of Old-Time music in *The New Lost City Ramblers Song Book* (1964). Seeger, the brother of Pete and Peggy Seeger, also did some solo recording, initially for Folkways, but later for Mercury and eventually for Rounder. Also, unlike many groups that strived to re-create Old-Time music, the New Lost City Ramblers always treated the idiom with respect and decorum. The group worked at initiating Folk festivals, some of which are still going strong today, such as that at the University of Chicago.

By the 70's, with Bluegrass and Old-Time music having boomed somewhat in comparison to a few years earlier, the Ramblers seemed less in demand, having successfully re-ignited the flame of interest in the music they had once sought to preserve. They still gave concerts from time to time, but much less frequently than before. In 1979, Flying Fish issued a two album set from live appearances to commemorate twenty years of the Ramblers' work. Tracy Schwarz reports that in the last decade they have given from one to ten concerts per year depending on demand.

Nonetheless, each member continues to contribute to the music they helped revive. Mike Seeger conducts many workshops and performs at many events each year. John Cohen is on the photography faculty at SUNY Purchase and still produces films dealing with Folk music, often on an international scale. Reflecting back in May, 1994, he takes a just pride in the records and films he has produced. He especially deserves credit for coining the phrase "high lonesome," originally in reference to Roscoe Holcomb, but later aptly extended by others to such Bluegrass vocalists as Bill Monroe, Del McCoury, Harold Austin, and Ralph Stanley.

Schwarz has also been involved in a variety of Old-Time music endeavors ranging from the Strange Creek Singers to the West Virginia duet of Ginny Hawker and Kay Justice. Richard Straw of Radford University has been engaged in a study that promises to look not only at the New Lost City Ramblers as part of the "Folk revival," but also to help revive tradition among the folk themselves.

IMT

RECOMMENDED ALBUMS:

"The New Lost City Ramblers, Vol. 1" (Folkways)(1958)
"The New Lost City Ramblers, Vol. 2" (Folkways)(1960)
"The New Lost City Ramblers, Vol. 3" (Folkways)(1961)
"The New Lost City Ramblers, Vol. 4" (Folkways)(1962)
"The New Lost City Ramblers, Vol. 5" (Folkways)(1962)
"Old Timey Songs for Children" (Folkways)(1959)
"Songs of the Depression" (Folkways)(1959)
"American Moonshine & Prohibition" (Folkways)(1962)
"Gone to the Country" (Folkways)(1963)
"Songs of the New Lost City Ramblers" (Aravel)(1963) [Folkways masters]
"String Band Instrumentals" (Folkways)(1964)
"Rural Delivery No. 1" (Folkways/Verve-Folkways)(1965)
"Modern Times" (Folkways)(1966)
"Remembrance of Things to Come" (Folkways/Verve-Folkways)(1966)
"The Great Divide" (Folkways)(1967)
"Twenty Years of Concert Performances" (Flying Fish)(1979)
Mike Seeger:
"Old Time Country Music" (Folkways)(1962)
"Sings and Plays Autoharp" (Folkways)(ca. 1963)
"Hello Stranger" (Vanguard)(1964)
"Tipple, Loom & Rail" (Folkways)(1966)
"Music from the True Vine" (Mercury)(ca. 1967)
"Fresh Oldtime String Band Music" (Rounder)(1988)
[See also Tracy Schwarz]

NEW RIDERS OF THE PURPLE SAGE

Formed:	**1969**
Current Members:	
John Dawson	**Vocals, Rhythm Guitar, Songwriter**
Gary Vogenson	**Guitar, Vocals**
Rusty Gauthier	**Vocals, Fiddle, Guitar, Mandolin, Banjo, Songwriter**
Michael White	**Bass**
Greg Legardo	**Drums**
Former Members:	
David Nelson	**Vocals, Lead Guitar**
Spencer Dryden	**Drums**
Buddy Cage	**Pedal Steel Guitar**
Stephen Love	**Bass Guitar, Vocals**
Jerry Garcia	**Pedal Steel**
Mickey Hart	**Drums, Pedal Steel**
Phil Lesh	**Bass**
Dave Torbert	**Bass (d.1982)**
Skip Battin	**Bass**
Allen Kemp	**Vocals, Songwriter, Guitar**
Val Fuentes	**Drums**
Bill Wolf	**Bass**

The band got together in the first place for an informal jam session, when Jerry Garcia, mastermind behind the Grateful Dead, obtained a steel guitar. John "Marmaduke" Dawson, who would become NRPS's principal songwriter, suggested they form a Country band as a splinter group. The name, New Riders of the Purple Sage, was chosen because they were a bunch of cowboys, and came from a novel written in 1912 by Zane Grey called *Riders of the Purple Sage.*

The band signed with Columbia and in 1971 released its debut eponymous album. By this time, Mickey Hart, the original drummer, had been replaced by Canadian Spencer Dryden, formerly with Jefferson Airplane, and original bassist Phil Lesh had been replaced by Dave Torbert. As the band developed its own image, Jerry Garcia found it impossible to cope with the Dead and New Riders' gigs, and was replaced by Buddy Cage, formerly with Ian and Sylvia and Anne Murray.

Their second album, ***Powerglide***, was released in 1972, and had Nicky Hopkins on keyboards and Jerry Garcia guesting on guitar. One of the tracks, *I Don't Need No Doctor*, made a month-long visit to the lower reaches of the Pop chart. By 1973, the band had settled down to a line-up of Dawson, Dryden, Nelson, Torbert and Cage. For their album of that year, the band released ***Gypsy Cowboy***, which featured the fiddle playing of Richard Greene. Later that year, they released the watershed album ***Adventures of Panama Red***, which featured as guests the Memphis Horns and Buffy Sainte-Marie. The album was Certified Gold in 1979.

The 1974 album ***Home Home on the Road*** was the last one for bass player Dave Torbert. That year, he left the band to be replaced by a former member of the Byrds, Skip Battin. The album featured the sax playing of Andy Stein and the guitar work of Jerry Garcia. Battin's debut album, ***Brujo***, was released at the end of 1974, and was followed by ***Oh What a Mighty Time*** the following year. The album featured six back-up singers, plus Sly Stone on keyboards and vocals. It marked the end of the NRPS's time with Columbia, and their move to MCA indicated a lack of drive in their output. Although still produced by legendary producer Bob Johnston, their lack of good material now became evident.

Their debut album for the label, ***New Riders***, would herald the end of the road for Skip Battin, who left and was replaced by Stephen A. Love. He was present for their 1977 album, ***Who Are These Guys?*** The following year, ***Marin County Line*** was the band's offering, and then the rot set in, and members came and went, with Dawson being the one constant.

In 1981, they turned up on A & M Records, with the less than average ***Feelin' All Right.*** By 1983, the line-up was Dawson, Allen Kemp, Val Fuentes, Bill Wolf and Rusty Gauthier. Gauthier's other claim to fame is as the composer of the music for the Joffrey Ballet's *Light Rain*. By 1990, only Dawson and Gauthier remained, and they had been joined for the new album, ***Keep on Keepin' On***, by Gary Vogenson, Michael White and Greg Legardo. Vogenson and White had both previously played with Commander Cody and Norton Buffalo, while Legardo had toured with Elmo n' Patsy. The band continues to tour into the 90's.

RECOMMENDED ALBUMS:

"New Riders of the Purple Sage" (Columbia)(1971)
"Powerglide" (Columbia)(1972)

"Adventures of Panama Red" (Columbia)(1973)
"Best of New Riders of the Purple Sage" (Columbia)(1976)

MICKEY NEWBURY

(Singer, Songwriter, Guitar)
Given Name: **Milton S. Newbury, Jr.**
Date of Birth: **May 19, 1940**
Where Born: **Houston, Texas**
Married: **Susan**
Children: **four**

Mickey Newbury made his mark in Nashville as a songwriter with haunting melodies and lyrics crafted like a poet laureate. Newbury's signature style on songwriting provided hits for dozens of artists from Eddy Arnold to Kenny Rogers. Perhaps his best known work is not a song he wrote, but adapted. His arrangement of three songs, *Dixie*, *Battle Hymn of the Republic* and *All My Trials*, as the compilation *American Trilogy*, became one of Elvis Presley's signature songs.

Mickey grew up in the musically rich metropolitan area of Houston. As a child, he soaked up the Blues, R & B, Mexican music, Jazz, Folk and Country music. He started singing while in grammar school and his first creative output was writing poetry. He recited his poems in local coffee houses and eventually added melodies to compose his first song. By the time he was 15, Mickey was playing in a band and performing at Texas Army bases.

When he joined the U.S. Air Force in 1959, Mickey took a break from music for a while, but by the time he left the service, he was writing songs again. In 1963, on leaving the Air Force, he moved to Nashville and hit the streets with his songs. He befriended other recent arrivals including Willie Nelson and Kris Kristofferson and they all held court at Tootsie's Orchid Lounge.

Mickey's skill as a songwriter was recognized by Acuff-Rose Music, who offered him a contract. At the end of 1966, he had his first Top 10 Country hit when Don Gibson recorded *Funny, Familiar, Forgotten Feelings*. The song became a Pop hit in 1967 for Tom Jones. Childhood friend Kenny Rogers (with the First Edition) recorded Mickey's *Just Dropped In (To See What Condition My Condition was In)* and it became a Top 5 single in 1968. Also in 1968, Eddy Arnold had a Top 5 single with Mickey's *Here Comes the Rain, Baby*. Other hits followed on the Pop chart with *Sweet Memories* by Andy Williams (1968), and Dottie West & Don Gibson placed the song on Country chart in 1969. That year, Jerry Lee Lewis recorded a

Master songwriter ***Mickey Newbury***

song co-written by Mickey, *She Even Wrote Me Up to Say Goodbye*.

Mickey's songwriting success led to his own recording contract in 1968 with RCA Victor, where he released the album ***Harlequin Memories***. The following year, he moved to Mercury and recorded the album ***Looks Like Rain***. In 1970, Mickey relocated to Elektra, where he released: ***'Frisco Mabel Joy*** (1971), ***Heaven Help the Child*** (1973) and ***Live at Montezuma Hall/Looks Like Rain*** (1973), ***I Came to Hear the Music*** (1974) and ***Lovers*** (1975). While with the label, he made his Pop chart debut with *An America Trilogy*, which reached the Top 30, at the beginning of 1972. In 1973, he charted with *Sunshine*, which reached the Country Top 60 and the Pop Top 90.

In 1977, Mickey signed with ABC/Hickory, and although he had three Country chart singles during 1977-1979, they were at the basement level, as were subsequent releases on MCA and Hickory. While most of his recordings went mostly unnoticed by the masses, they were embraced and studied by other singers and songwriters. Waylon Jennings recorded Mickey's *Frisco Mabel Joy* and *33rd of August*, as did Joan Baez. Willie Nelson, Jerry Lee Lewis, Ray Charles and the Everly Brothers also recorded Mickey's songs.

In 1980, Mickey was elected to the Nashville Songwriters Hall of Fame. During the 80's, Mickey recorded ***After All These Years*** for Mercury and ***In a New Age*** for the independent Airborne label. The highly acclaimed songwriter moved to Eugene, Oregon and continued to write and perform occasionally.

In 1994, Mickey recorded an album of material that other artists had previously recorded. JIE

RECOMMENDED ALBUMS:
"Harlequin Memories" (RCA Victor)(1968)
"Frisco Mabel Joy" (Elektra)(1971)
"Mickey Newbury Sings his Own" (RCA Victor)(1972)
"Heaven Help the Child" (Elektra)(1973)
"Live at Montezuma Hall/Looks Like Rain" (double)(1973)
"I Came to Hear the Music" (Elektra)(1974)
"Lovers" (Elektra)(1975)
"Rusty Tracks" (ABC/Hickory)(1977)
"His Eye on the Sparrow" (ABC/Hickory)(1978) [Re-released on MCA]
"The Sailor" (ABC/Hickory)(1979) [Re-released on MCA]
"Sweet Memories" (MCA)(1985)
"In a New Age" (Airborne)(1988)

Newman Brothers refer GEORGIA CRACKERS

JIMMY C. NEWMAN

(Singer, Songwriter, Guitar)
Given Name: **Jimmy Yves Newman**
Date of Birth: **August 27, 1927**
Where Born: **High Point, Louisiana**
Married: **(Edna) May Daire**
Children: **Gary**

Jimmy C. Newman has for the last three decades become perhaps best known for being a major exponent of Cajun and Country fusion in music. Jimmy's Cajun-Country has kept him a popular figure even though he hasn't had a chart record since 1970.

Born near the community of Big Mamou in southern Louisiana, Jimmy grew up in a bilingual family more interested in the music of Gene Autry than the sounds of the swamp. He got in six years of schooling before his farmer father passed away and Jimmy had to work hard to support the family. His older brother Walter had a guitar and Jimmy learned to play it, developing a new-found fondness for Ernest Tubb, whose star had risen during the war years.

During the latter part of WWII, Newman worked as a welder's helper in a defense plant and met music store owner J.D. Miller, who also worked there. Later he purchased a guitar from Miller and joined Chuck Guillory's Rhythm Boys, where he sang mostly in English, but also did a few Cajun numbers. He recorded a few songs while with the Guillory band for the Modern label in New Orleans and when its leader dropped out about 1950, Jimmy took over.

Jimmy made a solo single for J.D. Miller's Feature Records in 1949 and subsequently cut two or three more for Khoury including one called *Darling*, but they had limited distribution and little success.

He had a TV show in Lake Charles and a strong local following, but hoped to find a wider market. Miller then talked Nashville writer/producer Fred Rose into doing sessions for both Newman and Al Terry in Music City.

Jimmy made four numbers in Fred's garage studio in late 1953 and sold them to Randy Wood at Dot. His earlier song, *Cry*, revised as *Cry Cry Darling*, became a hit, reaching the Top 5 in 1954 and landed Jimmy a regular spot on the *Louisiana Hayride* in Shreveport that year. He followed with four more Top 10 successes, *Daydreamin'*, *Blue Darlin'* and *God Was So Good*, in 1955, and another, *Seasons of My Heart*, in 1956. He joined the *Grand Ole Opry* that August. In 1957, he had his biggest success with *A Fallen Star*, which went Top 3 Country and Top 25 in Pop, remaining on the former listing for five months.

By mid-1958, Jimmy believed his career was in decline with Dot and signed with MGM. The switch in labels provided the necessary jolt for rejuvenation of his career and by the end of the year *You're Making a Fool Out of Me* was on its way to the Top 10. Through 1959 and 1960, Jimmy had seven more singles on the charts, of which *Grin and Bear It* (1959) and *A Lovely Work of Art* (1960) were the most successful and went Top 10, while the 1960 single *Wanting You with Me Tonight* went Top 15.

Jimmy joined Decca Records early in 1961 and over the next decade placed another eighteen songs on the charts, the most successful being: *Everybody's Dying for Love* (Top 15, 1961), *D.J. for a Day* (Top 10, 1964), *Back in Circulation* (Top 15), *Artificial Rose* (Top 10) (both 1965), *Back Pocket Money* (1966), *Blue Lonely Night* (Top 15) and *Born to Love You* (Top 20) (both 1968).

Cajun King ***Jimmy C. Newman***

Few of his Dot and MGM offerings had displayed much Cajun influence, but beginning with *Alligator Man* (Top 25, 1962) and *Bayou Talk* (Top 15, 1963), the French Arcadian sound began intruding into Jimmy's sound. His made-up middle initial of "C" (for Cajun) began appearing on some of his label credits about this time and in 1963 he recorded an album, ***Folk Songs of the Bayou Country***, which featured part of the lyrics in Cajun. Fiddler Rufus Thibodeaux (who had periodically worked with Jimmy since the early 50's) and accordionist Shorty LeBlanc added much to the authentic sound of this effort. With the exception of *Louisiana Saturday Night* in 1967, most of his late 60's offerings veered back more toward Nashville-Sound Country, although Cajun-flavored items such as *Tibby Dough and his Cajun Band* and Rusty and Doug Kershaw's *Louisiana Man* still appeared on his albums.

Jimmy's last appearance on the charts occurred in late 1970 when *I'm Holding Your Memory* peaked in the Top 70. However, his career continued to thrive largely on the strength of his Cajun-Country fusion which found favor with fans.

He kept such southern Louisianians in his band as accordionist Bessyl Duhon and fiddler Wade Landry and recorded albums for Cajun labels like La Louisianne and Swallow as well as the Boston-based Rounder, which specializes in Bluegrass and a variety of ethnic music. Songs like *Lach Pas La Patate (Don't Drop the Potato)* found favor among French-Canadians and a revival of Bill Nettle's *Hadacol Boogie* became popular in Louisiana as it revived memories of this once-famous patent remedy.

Jimmy took some foreign tours as well, being especially well received at Britain's famed Wembley Festival. Back in Nashville, Jimmy signed with Shelby Singleton's Plantation Records and did new versions of his older hits in addition to Cajun-type numbers. Some four decades after his first hit appeared, Jimmy C. Newman and Cajun Country still bring down the house at the *Grand Ole Opry* with their spirited versions of numbers like *Louisiana Saturday Night* and *Alligator Man*. Interest in his earlier music remains high in Europe as companies such as Bear Family, Charly, and Stetson have released several of his vintage items on vinyl album and compact disc. IMT

RECOMMENDED ALBUMS:

"This is Jimmy Newman" (MGM)(1959)
"Songs by Jimmy Newman" (MGM)(1962)
"Jimmy Newman" (Decca)(1962) [Re-released by Stetson UK in the original sleeve)(1987)]
"Folk Songs of the Bayou Country" (Decca)(1963)
"Artificial Rose" (Decca)(1966)
"Jimmy Newman Sings Country Songs" (Decca)(1966)
"A Fallen Star" (Dot)(1966)
"Country Crossroads" (Dot)(1966)
"The World of Country Music" (Decca)(1967)
"The Jimmy Newman Way" (Decca)(1968)
"Born to Love You" (Decca)(1968)
"The Jimmy Newman Style" (Decca)(1969)
"Country Time" (Decca)(1970)
"Las Pas La Patate" (La Louisianne)(1974)
"Jimmy C. Newman's Greatest Hits" (Plantation)(1977)
"Progressive C.C. [Cajun Country]" (Plantation)(1977)
"The Cajun Cowboy" (Plantation)(1978)
"The Happy Cajun" (Plantation and Charly UK)(1979)
"Cajun Country" (Delta)(1982)
"Cajun and Country Too" (Swallow)(1983)
"Alligator Man" (Charly UK)(1985) [Decca masters]
"16 Best of Jimmy C. Newman" (Plantation)(1987) [Cassette only]
"Bop a Hula" (Bear Family Germany)(1990) [Contains all Dot masters]
"Cajun & Country Too" (Swallow)

ROY NEWMAN

(Piano, Guitar, Accordion)

Given Name:	**Roy Newman**
Date of Birth:	**ca. 1900**
Where Born:	**Dallas, Texas**
Married:	**Unknown**
Children:	**Unknown**
Date of Death:	**February 23, 1981**

Roy Newman and his Boys were a pioneering Western Swing band in the Dallas-Fort Worth area who recorded extensively between 1934 and 1939. The Newman aggregation, which sometimes numbered as many as ten members, displayed a higher degree of Jazz and Blues influence than many of their contemporary rivals.

Little is known of Roy Newman's early life but by the mid-20's he had become a staff musician at WRR in the Texas metropolis. In 1926, he and another station employee, John Thorvald, had a piano-guitar act known as the Mystery Duo. In 1931, he formed a three-piece combo known as the Wanderers with Dick Reinhart and Bert Dodson on, respectively, mandolin and bass. Roy played guitar in this unit, which soon added a fourth member in Alfredo Casares on fiddle. Jim Boyd replaced Reinhart, and after a dispute with management the group defected to rival station WFAA. Later in 1933, Newman returned to WRR with a new group that included Jim Boyd on guitar, Art Davis and Thurman Neal on fiddles, clarinetist Holly Horton and banjoist Walter Kirkes.

Roy Newman and his Boys shared billing on the Dallas station with Bill "Cowboy

Rambler" Boyd who did not really carry a band except on his Bluebird and RCA Victor recording sessions. Therefore many of these staff musicians from WRR who helped him on record were part of Newman's band on American Record Corporation discs and part of the Cowboy Ramblers on Bluebird waxings. Shared band personnel included Jim Boyd, Art Davis, and Walter Kirkes, but each group had its own distinct style, as Western Swing historian Cary Ginnell points out. Newman's Boys and Boyd both had high rank on WRR's popular *Noon Hour Varieties* program. The Boys apparently also worked dances in the Dallas area. Between September, 1934 and June, 1939, Newman's group recorded seventy-two sides, released primarily on Vocalion and other ARC labels. Helping to add distinctiveness to the Newman sound were "hot" fiddler Thurman Neal, clarinet man Holly Horton, and vocalist Earl Brown. On his last sessions Gene Sullivan, of the later team of Wiley and Gene, took over the vocal chores.

Roy Newman and his Boys disbanded in 1940. Roy continued work as a staff musician at WRR and later was again associated with WFAA. He died in Dallas at age 81, visited before his death by long-time friends Jim Boyd and Art Davis, having some satisfaction that people were once again showing interest in his music; the Western Swing revival had started. A reissue album on the Origin Jazz Library label was in the works and other numbers appeared on various anthologies.

IMT

RECOMMENDED ALBUM:

"Roy Newman and his Boys 1934-1938" (Origin Jazz Library)(1981)

JUICE NEWTON

(Singer, Songwriter, Guitar)

Given Name: **Judy Kay Newton**

Singer, Songwriter and horse rider ***Juice Newton***

Date of Birth: **February 18, 1952**
Where Born: **Virginia Beach, Virginia**
Married: **1. John (div.)**
2. Tom Goodspeed
Children: **Jessica, Tyler**

If you pick up a piece of Juice Newton's stationery, you will be struck by the black horse logo that proudly stands atop it. This is no mere embellishment. Juice is an accomplished equestrian, and through this talent she met her husband, Tom, who is a professional polo player. However, it is her ability as a singer/songwriter that has made her one of the most durable Country-Rock performers over the last two decades.

Juice's father was a navy man and is her greatest fan. Juice (a family nickname) got her first guitar when she was 13 and was early on influenced by the Supremes, Otis Redding and especially by Rhythm and Blues. Her passion for horses and riding began during her teenage years, but music was starting to run parallel to it. She attended college in Northern California during the Folk music boom of the 60's and got turned on to Joan Baez, Bob Dylan, Peter, Paul & Mary and Phil Ochs. To this day, she is still more influenced by female artists such as Bonnie Raitt, Joni Mitchell and Judy Collins.

During the late 60's, Juice was playing in the coffee houses in Los Gatos, California, when she met singer/songwriter/guitarist Otha Young. They began fronting a Rock band called Dixie Peach, which became popular locally and lasted for about a year. She and Otha have remained playing partners to date. In 1973, they formed Juice Newton & Silver Spur. They were very involved in the beginnings of Country-Rock that came out of California, and later that year they moved to Los Angeles and began playing original material there.

They signed to RCA in 1975 and released the ***Juice Newton & Silver Spur*** album, which yielded the single *Love Is a Word* the following February, which reached the lower levels of the Country charts. Later in 1976, they released the album ***After the Dust Settles***. The following year, the group moved to Capitol and released ***Come to Me***. Silver Spur was disbanded in 1978 and all future albums were released under Juice's name.

Juice first hit the lower levels of the Pop charts with *It's a Heartache*, which was also a monster Pop hit for Bonnie Tyler. That year she released the album ***Well Kept Secret***, and in 1979, ***Take Heart***. During that year, Juice had four singles in the Country charts, of which the most successful were *Let's Keep It That Way* and *Until Tonight*. In 1980, she had two moderate hits with *Sunshine* and *You Fill My Life*.

During 1981, she met Richard Landis, a staff producer at Capitol in Los Angeles. At last, under his production guidance, Juice's career took off. She released the album ***Juice*** (which went Platinum in 1982) and the single *Angel of the Morning*, which had been a big hit for Merilee Rush in 1968, went Gold for Juice, reaching the Top 5 in the Pop charts and Top 25 on the Country lists. She followed up with an even bigger hit, *Queen of Hearts*. This also went Gold and reached the Top 3 on the Pop charts and Top 15 on the Country charts. She wrapped up the year with *The Sweetest Thing (I've Ever Known)*, which was a Top 10 Pop single and went to No.1 on the Country charts. She was given the 1981 People's Choice Award as "Best Female Vocalist" and the ACM's "New Female Vocalist of the Year."

As 1982 unfurled, Juice had the Top 10 Pop hit *Love's Been a Little Bit Hard on Me*, which was also a Top 30 Country record. It came from her album of the year, ***Quiet Lies***. The album was Certified Gold in 1982. Also from the album was *Break It to Me Gently*, which only reached the Top 15 but made it to the Top 3 in the Country lists. She received a Grammy Award for the single as "Best Country Vocal Performance, Female" (she would later receive a further four Grammy nominations). Also in 1982, she was named *Billboard*'s "Album Artist of the Year," a feat she was to repeat in 1983. This was very much a pivotal single. From here on, her Pop positions fared badly, while her Country placings also went downhill during 1983 and 1984, and then dramatically improved.

During 1984, she moved from Capitol back to RCA. That year, she performed before President and Mrs. Reagan at the White House and took her father along to see his Commander-in-Chief. *You Make Me Want to Make You Mine* was from the 1985 album ***Old Flame***. It went to No.1 on the Country charts, as did the next single, *Hurt*, which had been a big hit for Timi Yuro back in 1961. The title track from the album reached the Top 5 in 1986, and then Juice got together with Eddie Rabbitt for *Both to Each Other (Friends & Lovers)*, from the TV soap *Days of Our Lives*. The record went to No.1 and as a result, RCA re-issued the album, replacing *Let Your Woman Take Care of You* with the duet. The album yielded two more Top 10 Country singles, Del Shannon's *Cheap Love* and Otha Young's *What Can I Do With My Heart*.

Her first single of 1987 came from the album of that year, ***Emotion***. It only made the Top 25, while the follow-up, *Tell Me True,* reached the Top 10. During 1989, Juice and Otha decided to form Trio with bass player Jay Cawley, in an attempt to return to the performing feel that had permeated Silver Spur. From her 1989 album ***Ain't Gonna Cry***, Juice had a Top 40 hit with *When Love Comes Around the Bend*. Since then, she has made no further appearances in the charts and the only album product made available was the ***Greatest Hits*** package on Curb in 1990, which went Gold in 1991.

Juice is getting a new album deal together and in the meanwhile tours and plays arena polo at Rancho Santa Fe Polo Club, watches the news and weather and enjoys being a wife and mother. Juice once had the reputation of being difficult and a feminist, quite often being misrepresented about her views and comments. However, what cannot be open to misrepresentation is her record sales both in the U.S. and overseas. In Canada, ***Juice*** has now reached Triple Platinum status, while the single *Queen of Hearts* went Platinum and both *Quiet Lies* and *Dirty Looks* went Gold.

RECOMMENDED ALBUMS:

"Juice Newton & Silver Spur" (RCA)(1975)
"After the Dust Settles" (RCA)(1976)
"Juice" (Capitol)(1981)
"Quiet Lies" (Capitol)(1982)
"Dirty Looks" (Capitol)(1983)
"Can't Wait All Night" (RCA Victor)(1984)
"Old Flames" (RCA Victor)(1987) [Two versions]
"Ain't Gonna Cry" (RCA)(1989)

OLIVIA NEWTON-JOHN

(Singer, Songwriter, Actress, Designer)
Given Name: **Olivia Newton-John**
Date of Birth: **September 26, 1948**
Where Born: **Cambridge, England**
Married: **Matt Lattanzi**

Most of Olivia Newton-John's career falls outside the parameters of this work. Unlike Anne Murray or most of the early rock'n'roll and Rockabilly acts, her music before 1973 and post-1977 makes no pretense at being even vaguely Country. Perhaps in the 90's climate of "if it's from Nashville, it must be Country," even Olivia's Pop work would be acceptable.

Although she was exposed early to Folk music in Australia, where her family moved in 1953, by the 60's she was totally immersed in Pop music. The granddaughter of Nobel Prize-winning physicist Max Born, Olivia soon made a successful career in Britain from 1971, thanks to superstar Cliff Richard. Although she had started to hit the U.S. Pop charts in 1971, it was *Let Me Be There*, in 1973, that broke her into the U.S. Pop and Country charts, reaching Top 10 on both and going Gold. This was followed in 1974 by *If You Love Me (Let Me Know)*, which went Top 3 on the Country chart, Top 5 on the Pop chart and also went Gold. In the summer, *I Honestly Love You* went Top 10 on the Country chart, No.1 on the Pop chart and made it three-in-a-row Gold Certification.

That year, in what at the time and on reflection still seems an act of folly, the CMA membership named Olivia "Female Vocalist of the Year." Folly, because the 1973 winner was Loretta Lynn and the 1975 winner was Dolly Parton and either Dolly, Tammy Wynette, Tanya Tucker, Melba Montgomery or Donna Fargo, all with No.1 hits, should have taken the title. In fact Dolly had topped the charts that year with *Jolene* and *I Will Always Love You.*

The backlash from Country music purists was immediate. Olivia's case was not helped by the fact that she had wanted to meet Hank Williams....he had been dead for over 20 years! As a result the Association of Country Entertainers (ACE) was set up "to preserve Country music as a separate and distinct form of entertainment." Billy Walker's words at the time would become so prophetic: "....efforts to take Country music to a wider audience would dilute it to the point where it no longer exists as an art form." However, ACE fell apart and at the end of the day, Olivia was not the one to blame. After all, she didn't see herself as a Country performer and that same year, she represented Great Britain in the Eurovision Song Contest singing the very Pop *Long Live Love* (and came in 3rd).

In 1975, she again reached the Country Top 3 with *Have You Never Been Mellow*, which reached No.1 on the Pop chart and again went Gold. This was followed by *Please Mr. Please*, which went Top 5 Country, Top 3 Pop and also went Gold. Of her last two singles in 1975, *Something Better to Do* went Top 20 on both Country and Pop and *Let it Shine* (written by Nashville writer Linda Hargrove) went Top 5 Country and Top 30 Pop.

Olivia's other Country hits were *Come on Over* (Top 5 Country/Top 25 Pop), *Don't Stop Believin'* (Top 15 Country/Top 40 Pop) and *Every Face Tells a Story* (Top 25 Country/Top 60 Pop) (all 1976). In 1977 she had the solitary Top 40 Country entry, *Sam*, which also went Top 20 Pop. In 1978, she appeared in the movie *Grease* and one of the singles from the soundtrack, *Hopelessly Devoted to You*, became a Top 20 Country hit, a Top 3 Pop hit and went Gold.

In 1979, *A Little More Love* just scraped into the Country chart, although it was a Pop hit. The same applied to *Deeper Than the Night.* Olivia's final Country entrant was *Dancin' 'Round and 'Round* from the totally Disco-oriented ***Totally Hot*** album. That same year, she was honored with the Order of the British Empire (as an O.B.E.) by Queen Elizabeth II.

Although frowned on as a Country singer, there can be no doubt that for many years, Olivia was able to sell records in large numbers. As well as having Gold singles, she racked up several Gold albums. ***Let Me Be There*** and ***If You Love Me (Let Me Know)*** both went Gold in 1974, ***Clearly Love*** and ***Have You Never Been Mellow*** in 1975, and ***Come on Over*** and ***Don't Stop Believing*** in 1976. Her ***Greatest Hits*** album went Platinum in 1977 and Double-Platinum in 1984. Olivia married actor Matt Lattanzi in 1984, the same year she opened her clothing boutique chain, Koala Blue. Sadly, in 1992, she was diagnosed as having breast cancer, but has battled it successfully. (For her awards, see Awards Section).

RECOMMENDED ALBUM:

"Greatest Hits" (MCA)(1977)

SAM NICHOLS

(Singer, Songwriter, Guitar, Actor)
Given Names: **Sam Nichols**
Date of Birth: **August 31, 1918**
Where Born: **Eula, Texas**

Cowboy Sam Nichols, a Texas Honky-Tonk singer, plied his trade at various locales extending from Mexican border stations to the California nightclub scene. In the later 40's, he recorded several sides for MGM and might be considered that firm's response to the popularity of Ernest Tubb. In fact, the Texas Troubadour's cover of a Nichols song, *That Wild and Wicked Look in Your Eye*, has become something of a classic in the field and may well stand as Sam's most lasting achievement in Country music.

A native of south Texas, Sam Nichols grew up in San Angelo, where he first aspired to sing cowboy and hillbilly songs at the age of 10. His grandfather taught him a few chords and as the youth grew older he began to display his skills in local cafes and clubs.

Soon Sam had a regular radio program at KGKL, which brought him an $8.00 weekly salary. After six months, he moved to KNEL in Brady, which had newly opened in December, 1935. By 1937, Nichols had a daily program at the border station XEPN, across from Eagle Pass, Texas, where he became known as "The Roaming Cowboy." In essence, Sam followed a path taken earlier by Cowboy Slim Rinehart (1911-1948) who also went from Brady to XEPN.

Nichols had his first songbook published while at Eagle Pass and remained with the station until he entered the U.S. Navy at the beginning of WWII. After the war, Sam joined the booming West Coast Country music scene where the new-found prosperity of former Dust Bowl refugees made central and southern California something of a Mecca for rural culture. The Texan toured frequently with such better known luminaries as Gene Autry and Spade Cooley. In between tours, Sam played clubs on his own through western states and worked as an extra in motion pictures.

His earliest recordings appeared on the Memo label in 1946, but he soon went over to MGM, probably on the strength of *That Wild and Wicked Look in Your Eye*, which he cut for both firms. Among his more significant other waxings, *I'm Telling You* later became even more widely heard through Audrey Williams singing it on one of husband Hank's albums. A Nichols original about an unfortunate swinger heading back to the farm, entitled *Sows, Cows and Plows*, is also noteworthy. A studio band named the Melody Rangers, headed by lead guitarist Porky Freeman, enhanced the sound of Cowboy Sam's recordings. In 1972, Nichols retired from music. He returned to south Texas, where he settled on a little farm-ranch near Sonora. In 1987, Reimar Binge's Cattle Records released an album containing some of the best material from this forgotten Country hero of the 40's. IMT

RECOMMENDED ALBUM:

"Sam Nichols with the Melody Rangers" (Cattle Germany)(1987)

NITTY GRITTY DIRT BAND

When Formed:	**1966**
Current Members:	
Jeff Hanna	**Vocals, Guitar**
Jimmie Fadden	**Vocals, Drums, Harmonica**
Jimmy Ibbotson	**Vocals, Bass Guitar, Mandolin, Guitar**
Bob Carpenter	**Vocals, Keyboards**
Former Members:	
Ralph Barr	**Vocals, Guitar**
Leslie Thompson	**Vocals, Bass Guitar, Guitar**
John McEuen	**Banjo, Fiddle, Mandolin**
Bruce Kunkel	**Drums**
Chris Darrow	**Vocals, Guitar, Violin**
Bernie Leadon	**Vocals, Guitar, Banjo, Mandolin**
Jackson Browne	**Vocals, Guitar**
Jackie Clark	**Bass Guitar**
John Cable	**Guitar, Vocal**
Al Garth	**Violin, Vocals, Saxophone**
Richard Hathaway	**Bass Guitar**
Merle Brigante	**Drums, Vocals**
Vic Mastriani	**Drums**
Michael Gardner	**Drums**

From its inauspicious days as the Illegitimate Jug Band back in 1966, the Nitty Gritty Dirt Band has proven to be one of the most enduring Country-Rock bands. From its early Folk-Country leanings, the group has moved more toward a Pop-Rock edge over the years. The band assumed a high level of respect via its ***Will the Circle Be Unbroken*** album in 1971. Drummer Jimmie Fadden told the writer back in 1987 that the band played "American music."

With its original line-up of Hanna, Fadden, Thompson, Kunkel, Barr and Browne, the group hung around McCabe's Guitar Shop in Long Beach, California as the Illegitimate Jug Band. The band played around the L.A./Orange County area wearing 20's pinstriped suits and cowboy boots. In the fall of 1966, Browne left and the multi-talented John McEuen joined.

The band recorded its first self-titled album in 1967 for Liberty and followed it later that year with the album ***Ricochet***. From this latter album came *Buy for Me the Rain*, which gave the band its first Pop chart single when it reached the Top 50. The band shared the "Dirt House" in the Hollywood Hills with Duane and Greg Allman, Steve Martin, the Sunshine Company and their joint manager, Bill McEuen.

By the fall of 1968, Kunkel had left and Chris Darrow had joined. That year, the group recorded the ***Rare Junk*** and ***Alive*** albums. The band took time out in Walt Whitman National Forest in Oregon, appearing in the musical movie *Paint Your Wagon*, with Clint Eastwood and Lee Marvin. The group played Carnegie Hall, where it jammed with Dizzy Gillespie, as opening act for Bill Cosby.

By the end of 1968, Barr and Darrow had left and the band decided to move to Colorado. Jim Ibbotson, formerly with the Hagers, joined on bass guitar. Bookings for the group were dropping off and by February, 1969, the members of the band went their separate ways; they got back together six months later. The NGDB toured Japan and, by the end of the year, had recorded a new album, ***Uncle Charlie & His Dog Teddy***, from which came the Top 10 Pop hit *Mr. Bojangles*.

In 1971, the group released the new album ***All the Good Times***, from which came *House at Pooh Corner* and *Some of Shelly's Blues*, both of which peaked in the middle of the Pop charts. The NGDB duetted with Roy Acuff on *I Saw the Light* and made it to the Top 60 in the Country charts.The following year, they had a low-level success with *Jambalaya (On the Bayou)* and in August, 1972, the band returned to Nashville ("four guys with long hair") and recorded the three-record set ***Will the Circle Be Unbroken*** with Roy Acuff, Mother Maybelle Carter, Junior Huskey, Doc Watson, Vassar Clements, etc. This became a watershed album for Country music and helped legitimize the band in a lot of purists' eyes, as well as helping to re-establish older performers with a younger audience. However, this was not translated into singles sales and in 1973, the band had a poor showing on the Country chart with *Grand Ole Opry Song*.

By 1974, Thompson had left, and the band was now a quartet. That year, the group released the double album ***Stars and Stripes Forever*** and, that same year, had a low-level Pop success with *The Battle of New Orleans*.

During the mid-70's, comedian/banjo player Steve Martin acted as opening act for the band and even after he achieved stardom, often made guest appearances, playing banjo duets with McEuen. At the beginning of 1975, the band released the album ***Dream*** and had a Country and Pop middle-chart success with *(All I Have to Do Is) Dream*. By the end of 1975, Ibbotson had left the group and was replaced by Cable and Clark. With the departure of Ibbotson, the band shortened its name to "the Dirt Band" and recorded the 1976, triple album ***Dirt, Silver and Gold***.

1977 was a momentous year, as the group became the first American group to tour the USSR. The tour was fairly laid-back until the group played to nearly 6,000 people in Armenia. NGDB released the 1978 album ***Wild Nights***, which marked the debut of Al Garth, Richard Hathaway and Merle Brigante. The band had another low level Pop hit that year, with *In for the Night*. That year, it backed Steve Martin on his hit single *King Tut*. The NGDB's 1979 album ***An American Dream*** yielded the title track as a cross-over hit and featured Linda Ronstadt on harmony vocals. The group followed this up with another cross-over single, *Make a Little Magic*, featuring Nicolette Larson, the following year.

The line-up changed again with Brigante

leaving and Mastriani and Gardner coming in. The group recorded the 1980 album ***Make a Little Magic*** and followed it up with ***Jealousy*** in 1981, from which was culled the low-level Pop single *Fire in the Sky*, its last Pop success. However, major single success eluded the group until Ibbotson returned and the quartet of Hanna, Fadden, McEuen and Ibbotson was in place and recorded its last album for Liberty, ***Let's Go***, in Nashville (1983). Chuck Morris came in as manager, and a new phase of the band's career got underway. From this album, the group had the Top 20 Country hit, Bob McDill's *Shot Full of Love,* and the Top 10 Country hit *Dance Little Jean.*

In 1984, NGDB signed with Warner Brothers Records and acquired Bob Carpenter on keyboards. That year, the band chalked up its first No.1 hit, *Long Hard Road (The Sharecropper's Dream)* and wrapped up the year with the Top 3 single *I Love Only You.* The band's success in 1985 consolidated its new career. NGDB scored with *High Horse* (No.2), *Modern Day Romance* (No.1) and *Home Again in My Heart* (Top 3). The next year was more of the same with *Partners, Brothers and Friends, Stand a Little Rain* and *Fire in the Sky*, all Top 10 successes. That year, the album ***Twenty Years of Dirt*** was released, to celebrate the band's 20th anniversary. It celebrated with a sell-out concert in Denver with Ricky Skaggs, Emmylou Harris, Michael Martin Murphey, Doc Watson, John Prine and Rodney Crowell. On New Year's Eve, John McEuen departed the group, with mixed explanations being offered. He was replaced by ex-Eagle Bernie Leadon.

In 1987 through 1988, the NGDB continued with further major hits, *Baby's Got a Hold on Me* (Top 3), *Fishin' in the Dark* (No.1) and *Oh What a Love* (Top 5) (all 1987) and *Workin' Man (Nowhere to Go)*(Top 5), *I've Been Lookin*' (Top 3) and *Down That Road Tonight* (Top 10)(all 1988).

The group released the double album ***Will the Circle Be Unbroken, Volume Two*** on Universal, which won for NGDB two 1989 Grammy Awards for "Best Country Performance by a Duo or Group with Vocal" and "Best Bluegrass Recording." The latter was for the track *The Valley Road*, on which the group is joined by Bruce Hornsby. However, this success was repeated in the charts in varying degrees. *Turn of the Century* went Top 30, *And So it Goes* (with John Denver) reached the Top 15 and *When It's Gone* made it to the Top 10. However, the album reached the Top 5 on the Country Album chart. The album is packed with a host of guests including Roy Acuff, the Carter Family, Roy Huskey, Jr., Earl Scruggs, Chris Hillman and Ricky Skaggs. Also guesting was Bernie Leadon, who had now left the group.

The group signed with MCA in 1990, but the success level had fallen away. All three singles that charted peaked in the Top 70 and the album ***The Rest of the Dream*** also only fared moderately. The following year, their album ***In Concert—Live Two Five***, celebrating their 25th anniversary at a concert in Canada, reached the Top 50, but they had no single success. Things got no better in 1992 and both chart singles were at a low level. It would now appear that newer and younger but not necessarily as talented groups will take the NGDB's place in the charts, but it still remains a much-in-demand live band. In 1994, the NGDB returned to their roots by releasing the album ***Acoustic***. As a footnote, Jimmy Ibbotson got together with Jim Ratts and Jim Salestrom as the Wild Jimbos, releasing an eponymous album in 1991 on MCA.

RECOMMENDED ALBUMS:

"Will the Circle Be Unbroken" (triple album)(United Artists)(1972)
"Partners, Brothers and Friends" (Warner Brothers)(1985)
"The Nitty Gritty Dirt Band: Early Dirt 1967-1970" (Decal UK)(1986)
"Will the Circle Be Unbroken, Volume Two" (double album)(Universal)(1988)
"Not Fade Away" (Liberty)(1992)
"Acoustic" (Liberty)(1994)
"The Wild Jimbos" (MCA)(1991) [Jimmy Ibbotson external project]

EDDIE NOACK

(Singer, Songwriter, Guitar)

Given Name:	**Armona A. Noack, Jr.**
Where Born:	**Houston, Texas**
Date of Birth:	**April 29, 1930**
Married:	**Unknown**
Children:	**Terry Lynn**
Date of Death:	**February 6, 1978**

Although Eddie Noack was not phenomenally successful as a recording artist, he did claim some fame as a songwriter, primarily being recorded by George Jones.

He made his radio debut in Bayton, Texas, in 1947, after winning an amateur talent contest, and recorded for Gold Star Records in 1949, and released the single *Gentlemen Prefer Blondes*. He graduated from the University of Houston in journalism and English. The following year, he recorded for 4 Star, and by 1952 he was with Allstar, cutting *Too Hot to Handle*. In 1954, he signed with Starday and came under the production control of Pappy Dailey. He put out singles between 1954 and 1957, but none of them achieved chart success.

In 1956, Hank Snow recorded Eddie's song *These Hands*, which reached the Top 5 in the Country charts. During 1968, Noack signed to Dailey's D label and issued a Rockabilly single, *Can't Play Hooky/My Steady Dream*, under the name of "Tommy Wood." He also recorded Country singles and his first release, *Have Blues Will Travel*, reached the Top 15 on the Country chart. He continued releasing singles into 1960. In 1969, George Jones recorded *No Blues is Good News*, which was a low level hit. Jones also recorded *Barbara Jay, For Mama, The Poor Chinee* and *For Better or for Worse.*

Noack also recorded sides for K-Ark, Ram and World Wide. Eddie Noack died in 1978.

RECOMMENDED ALBUMS:

"Remembering Jimmie Rodgers" (Wide World)
"Eddie Noack" (Look)

NORMA JEAN

(Singer, Guitar)

Given Name:	**Norma Jean Beasler**
Date of Birth:	**January 30, 1938**
Where Born:	**Wellston, Oklahoma**
Married:	**1. (Div.)**
	2. Harold "Jody" Taylor (div.)
	3. George Riddle
Children:	**Roma**

When the Nashville Sound achieved prominence in the 60's, several girl Country singers carved out successful careers for themselves, among them the strong-voiced and beautiful "Miss Norma Jean."

Born to a poor farm family near Wellston, Oklahoma, Norma Jean debuted on KLPR radio in Oklahoma City at age 12 singing *If Teardrops Were Pennies*. With the commercial success of Kitty Wells as a model, the young lady became increasingly determined to carve out a career in Country music. While still in high school, she toured with some Western Swing bands led by Billy Gray, Leon McDuffey and Merle Lindsay.

The beautiful Miss ***Norma Jean***

With several years of local radio and television experience behind her, Norma Beasler made her initial plunge into the big time in 1958 when she joined the cast of ABC-TV's *Ozark Jubilee* in Springfield, Missouri, where, at the request of Red Foley, she shortened her name to "Norma Jean."

By March 1960, Norma Jean had arrived in Nashville and took a job as girl vocalist with Porter Wagoner's touring group. Her earliest recordings for Columbia in 1959 gained little attention, but with exposure on Wagoner's syndicated TV show she was signed to RCA Victor and her discs started to enjoy success. After an initial appearance on the *Porter Wagoner Show* her single *Let's Go All the Way* hit the charts the first week of January, 1964 and ultimately peaked in the Top 15. She followed with *I'm a Walkin' Advertisement (For the Blues)* (Top 40)/*Put Your Arms Around Her* (Top 25). That fall, *Go Cat Go* made the Top 10, remaining on the charts for four months, and crossed to the lower rungs of the Pop chart.

In 1965, Norma Jean followed with *I Cried All the Way to the Bank* (Top 25) and *I Wouldn't Buy a Used Car from Him* (Top 10). During 1966, Norma Jean's most successful singles were *The Shirt* (Top 30), *Pursuing Happiness* (Top 30) and then *The Game of Triangles*, a single with Bobby Bare and Liz Anderson which went Top 5 and became her biggest record.

Meanwhile, her albums also revealed Norma Jean as a strong-voiced singer with deep Country roots, as amply illustrated on such efforts as a tribute to Kitty Wells. Many of her own best numbers concentrated on complex male-female romantic entanglements which contrasted sharply with the wholesomeness Norma Jean projected on the TV program. Norma Jean herself bore considerable resemblance to her TV image, but did become romantically involved with Wagoner, who at the time was separated from his wife.

The situation eventually resulted in her departure from Wagoner's organization, although she continued to work the *Grand Ole Opry* and record with RCA. In 1967, she had a Top 25 hit with *Don't Let that Doorknob Hit You*. Her song from late 1967 titled *Heaven Help the Working Girl* made the Top 20 and became something of a statement for the emerging feminist movement.

Norma Jean moved back to Oklahoma when she married Jody Taylor, and although she commuted back to the *Opry* for a time and remained with RCA until 1973, her last chartmaker with the label had come with *The Kind of Needin' I Need* in early 1971, which peaked in the Top 50 and was her strongest showing since the summer of 1968.

Although less than active during her years back in Oklahoma, Norma Jean was never totally away from music. She recorded an album for Bearsville in 1978 and had a minor hit with a Claude Gray duet in a revival of *Let's Go All the Way*, in 1982, on Granny White. In 1984, Norma Jean returned to Nashville and subsequently did a come-back album on Roma, a label named for her daughter. In recent years, she has played shows from time to time and has been active in the R.O.P.E. (Reunion of Professional Entertainers) organization.

In 1990, she married George Riddle, a long-time front man for many bigger name Nashville acts, especially George Jones and Tammy Wynette. Her RCA albums from the 60's are increasingly looked upon as classic Country from that era and widely sought by many collectors. IMT

RECOMMENDED ALBUMS:

"Let's Go All the Way" (RCA Victor)(1964)
"Pretty Miss Norma Jean" (RCA Victor)(1965)
"The Country Favorite" (Harmony)(1966)
"Please Don't Hurt Me" (RCA Victor)(1966)
"A Tribute to Kitty Wells" (RCA Victor)(1966)
"Norma Jean Sings with Porter Wagoner" (RCA Victor)(1967)
"Heaven's Just a Step Away" (RCA Victor)(1968)
"Heaven Help the Working Girl" (RCA Victor)(1968)
"The Best of Norma Jean" (RCA Victor)(1969)
"Norma Jean" (Bearsville, Germany)(1978)
"Pretty Miss Norma Jean" (Roma)(1985)

NOTTING HILLBILLIES

Formed: 1990
Members:

Mark Knopfler	**Vocals, Guitar**
Brendan Croker	**Vocals, Guitar**
Guy Fletcher	**Vocals, Keyboards**
Steve Phillips	**Vocals, Guitars**
Paul Franklin	**Steel Guitar**

This was a group that happened by accident. In 1988, Knopfler and Fletcher were producing an album for Croker and Phillips at Knopfler's home studio in Notting Hill in West London, England, when the project started to assume greater proportions. Guitar guru Knopfler, of Dire Straits fame, had first met Phillips when they were both students at Leeds University some 20 years earlier. They played National steel guitars together and called themselves the Duolian String Pickers. Croker, also from Leeds, was one of the featured vocalists on the Johnny Cash tribute album ***Till Things Are Brighter***. He also played on Tanita Tikaram's debut album and wrote and recorded with Guy Fletcher the theme music for the television series *On the Big Hill*. He also has his own group, Brendan Croker & the Five O'Clock Shadows, who record for Silvertone.

Fletcher is also a prolific writer. He joined Dire Straits in 1983 for the ***Brothers in Arms*** album, and has written with Knopfler on the 1983 soundtrack of *Cal*. They also collaborated for the soundtracks of *Comfort and Joy*, *The Princess Bride* and *Last Exit to Brooklyn*. They also worked on the Randy Newman album ***Land of Dreams***. Guy was also on the duet album of Chet Atkins and Knopfler, ***Neck and Neck***. Phillips is one of the best Bluesmen in Britain and learned his skills from old Rockabilly records.

Knopfler has become one of the guitar maestros of all time. His fluent style of playing has made him much in demand to lift a good album into the realms of the exquisite. His songs transcend all areas of music. Like Karla Bonoff, he finds his material recorded by Rock and Country performers. He is also greatly in demand as the writer of movie soundtracks that have included *Local Hero* and *Cal*, and as a record producer. He is a three-time Grammy winner. In 1985, he and Chet Atkins won "Best Country Instrumental Performance" for *Cosmic Square Dance* from Atkins' ***Stay Tuned*** album. In 1990, the two of them won two Grammy Awards for "Best Country Vocal Performance" for *Poor Boy Blues* and "Best Country Instrumental Performance" for *So Soft, Your Goodbye*, both from ***Neck and Neck***. Mark has also won two further Grammy Awards as a member of Dire Straits.

The Notting Hillbillies sole album, ***Missing . . . Presumed Having a Good Time***, was released in 1990. Although the majority of the album was recorded in England, Paul Franklin's pedal steel overdubs were recorded in Nashville. Although not officially a member at the beginning, Franklin toured with the Hillbillies after the release of the album, and went on to play with Dire Straits.

One of the tracks, a Knopfler original, *Your Own Sweet Way*, reached No.20 on the singles chart and the album reached the Top 60 on the Pop Albums chart. To date, no follow-up album has been mooted.

RECOMMENDED ALBUM:

"Missing...Presumed Having a Good Time" (Warner Brothers/Vertigo UK)(1990)

CECIL NULL

(Autoharp, Songwriter, Guitar, Musaharp, Instrument Designer)

Date of Birth:	**April 26, 1927**
Where Born:	**War, West Virginia**
Married:	**(Doris) Annette**

Big Cecil Null (he's 6'4") has probably done more than anyone, except Mother Maybelle, to popularize the autoharp. He also created, from birds-eye maple, a variant of the autoharp called the Musaharp.

He began writing poetry at age 9 and by the time he was 15 he was playing guitar. While in the U.S. Navy, in 1944, he started to write songs and entertained his shipmates. Upon leaving the service, Cecil and his sister Freda commenced studying American Folk music.

In 1947, Cecil appeared on WOPI Bristol, Tennessee, as a member of the Pioneer Pals, staying until the following year. While in Bristol, Cecil taught the "ear" method of playing guitar and became interested in the autoharp. He counts among his pleasures visiting Mother Maybelle Carter, to service her autoharp. He would write a song dedicated to her in 1964, called *Mother Maybelle*. Also in 1947, he wrote *I Forgot More Than You'll Ever Know*, which became a No.1 Country hit for the Davis Sisters in 1953 and a Top 60 success for Jeanne Pruett in 1972. In all, it would be recorded over 30 times.

In 1948, Cecil moved to station WCYB, also in Bristol, where he stayed until the following year, as a member of Cousin Zeke's Band. While with the band, he recorded for Twin City-Rich-R-Tone. He became a teacher of the autoharp and with the interest he created in the instrument, he was responsible for sales of the instrument increasing. The company making them asked him to demonstrate it at the National Music Merchants Trade Show in Chicago. He became a consultant at the factory. He discovered that if he held the autoharp like a guitar, it could be plucked, and he soon developed a much more melodic style than previously utilized. He soon put his method into print, and the book that evolved, *Pickin' Style Auto-Harp* [sic], became very popular. In 1950, he left Cousin Zeke's band, and a year later he became a member of the Tennessee Serenaders. He began recording for Revolvo in 1952 and stayed with the label until 1958. In 1964, Cecil joined up with his wife, Annette, as Cecil Null and Annette.

Annette (b. September 30, 1939, Oklahoma) is a fine autoharp and guitar player and also yodels. In 1964, they recorded an album for Paul Cohen at Briar, entitled ***New Sounds in Folk Music***. During 1965 through 1967, they appeared on the syndicated *Bobby Lord TV Show*. They recorded sides for Epic in 1965. In 1966, they started a stint on the *Ralph Emery Show* on WSM, staying with Ralph until 1968.

During 1967, they began appearing on the *Grand Ole Opry* and on WALC-TV Nashville. That year, they recorded the ***Folk Instrumentals*** album for Jed, and in 1968, they moved to Decca, where they cut ***Instrumental Country Hymns***. In 1970, Bill Phillips had a Top 50 single with Cecil's song *Hungry Again*. In 1990, *I Forgot More Than You'll Ever Know* was reprised by the very talented Jann Browne.

RECOMMENDED ALBUMS:
"New Sounds in Folk Music" (Briar)(1964)
"Folk Instrumentals" (Jed)(1967)
"Instrumental Country Hymns" (Decca)(1968)

MAYF NUTTER

(Singer, Guitar, Narrator, Actor)
Given Name: **Mayfred Nutter Adamson**
Date of Birth: **October 19, 1941**
Where Born: **Jane Lew, West Virginia**

Mayf Nutter came out of a northern West Virginia background to enjoy a varied career as a musician and actor.

Born in West Virginia to a family of local Country performers headed by father Lawrence "Peanut" Nutter, Mayf made his first radio appearance at age 12 on WPDX with local favorites Cherokee Sue and Little John Graham. Later, while in high school, he had a part-time job at WBOY-TV, which had a program called the Big Boy Frolics. At 18 he went off to college in Michigan, but soon embarked on a series of radio and TV work which eventually led him to Atlanta, where he cut his initial record on Vault in 1966.

In the late 60's, Mayf cut a few sides for Starday and MGM and then went to California where he first hit the charts in February, 1970 with the Top 70 *Hey There Johnny*, on Reprise, a lyric about current favorite Johnny Cash. This landed him on Capitol, where he had four chartmaking singles over a three-year period, *Never Ending Song of Love* (Top 70) and *Never Had a Doubt* (Top 60) (both 1971), *The Sing-Along Song* (Top 60, 1972) and *Green Door* (Top 80, 1973).

During this time, Mayf taped 56 syndicated *TV Ranch* shows with Buck Owens. He worked in TV production and as an actor appeared on *The Waltons*, *Falcon Crest*, *The Fall Guy* and *Charlie's Angels*. Mayf also did some film narrations for Walt Disney Studios.

In 1976, Nutter signed with GNP Crescendo Records and turned out two basement hits, *Sweet Southern Lovin'* and *Goin' Skinny Dippin'*. Having once been a regular on the *Wheeling Jamboree*, he returned eastward to perform on several occasions at their outdoor festival *Jamboree in the Hills* and in 1978 recorded an official theme song of the same title released on the D Mand label. Mayf toured the People's Republic of China in March 1982 and became the first American Country singer to appear on Chinese TV. Thereafter, his performing career began to recede into the background as other aspects of the entertainment business occupied most of his time. IMT

RECOMMENDED ALBUMS:
"The First Batch" (Capitol)(1973)
"Goin' Skinny Dippin'" (GNP Crescendo)(1976)

O

MARK O'CONNOR

(Fiddle, Guitar, Dobro, Banjo, Mandolin, Steel Guitar, Bass, Synthesizer, Mandola)
Date of Birth: **1962**
Where Born: **Seattle, Washington**
Married: **Unknown**
Children: **Forrest**

Mark O'Connor is a master of the fiddle, a musical genius and is still a young man who has almost 30 years' experience behind him. This gentle man has a humble and modest attitude and has the ability to encourage other musicians to higher and greater things.

Mark was a child prodigy, who at age 3 had the ability to identify specific classics recordings and composers. He began taking guitar lessons at age 6 and learning was never a problem for Mark. When he was 11, his teacher was John Burke, an Old-Time banjo and fiddle player, who in the 70's played with the Old Hat Band. When Benny Thomasson, the legendary Texas fiddler, moved to Washington, it was not long before Mark was introduced to him. Benny became Mark's role model and mentor and gave Mark a white violin.

Only seven months after picking up the violin, Mark entered the National Old Time Fiddle Championships. His mother, Marty, and his younger sister, who is also a fine fiddle player, were always with him. His mother guided him and acted as a facilitator, although she was never known as a "stage mother." Mark had the honor of appearing on the *Grand*

Fiddle maestro ***Mark O'Connor***

Ole Opry and also made his debut album, ***Mark O'Connor***, on the Rounder label, when he was 12. Between the ages of 11 and 13, Mark learned over 200 fiddle tunes. He won the Classical/Flamenco contest at the University of Washington, the National Guitar Flat Picking Championship and within two years had won two National Junior Fiddle Championships and the Grand Masters Fiddle Championship at Fan Fair in Nashville in 1975. Mark then recorded the albums ***Markology***, ***On the Rampage***, ***Pickin' in the Wind*** and ***Soppin' Up the Gravy***, all before he reached his fourteenth birthday.

In 1980, he began touring with Dave Grisman for eighteen months and played with Jazzman Stephane Grappelli. Mark was violinist and guitarist for the Dixie Dregs, again for eighteen months. During this time, Mark began listening to Indian music, modern Fusion music, Japanese Kabuki music and Gamelan music from Indonesia, all of which had an effect on his future compositions.

In the early 80's, Mark and Fred Carpenter recorded the album ***Cuttin' Loose***. Around this time, Mark toured with Doc and Merle Watson, John McEuen, Chris Hillman and Peter Rowan and in 1983 he moved to Nashville, where he became a much sought-after session musician. He played on recordings by nearly every major Country music star, including artists such as Johnny Cash, Ricky Skaggs, the Judds, Dolly Parton, James Taylor and Amy Grant. Mark's fiddle and mandolin can be heard on over 450 albums, often in company with another prodigy, Dobroist Jerry Douglas, who have formed a sort of "Sly and Robbie" playing combination within Country music, becoming in Jerry's words "the sweeteners."

In 1986, Mark was named ACM's "Fiddler of the Year" for the first time. Mark signed to Warner Brothers Records and released the 1988 solo album ***Elysian Forest***, which, although released from Nashville, was not a Country album. A year later, he released ***On the Mark***, which again, while being technically brilliant, owed more to Jazz violinist Travis Biggs, than to Gimble, Wills or Clements.

As a sessionman, he became so popular that he was eventually able to command $150,000 a year, and after six years, he decided to quit session playing to concentrate on his own album projects and his solo career. In that final year, 1991, he gathered fifty-three top musicians in Nashville and put together an album called ***New Nashville Cats***. These included Eddie Bayers, Sam Bush, Jerry Douglas, Béla Fleck, Paul Franklin, Carl Jackson, Terry McMillan, David Schnaufer, Gove Scrivenor, Lisa Silver and Billy Joe Walker. In addition, the talents of Ricky Skaggs, Vince Gill, Marty Stuart and Steve Wariner were utilized. This was altogether a much more Country album that featured much more "musical soul." The first single from the album was Carl Perkins' *Restless*, and featured Wariner, Gill and Skaggs playing and singing. This went to the Top 25 on the Country charts and made the Top 10 on the CMT top listings for the video. The single won the 1991 Grammy Award for "Best Country Vocal Collaboration" and it was also named, in 1992, as "Vocal Event of the Year" by the CMA and "Vocal Collaboration of the Year" by the TNN/ *Music City News* Awards. The second single was *Now it Belongs to You*, which featured Steve Wariner on vocals, and also had an accompanying video. By 1991, the album had sold 65,000 copies and one of the tunes from it, *Bowtie*, was adopted as the theme tune for the TNN series *American Music Shop*, on which Mark leads the house band. In 1991, Mark was awarded the ACM's "Fiddler of the Year." In 1992, he was again named CMA's "Musician of the Year" and for a fourth time, he won the ACM's "Fiddler of the Year" Award. He went on to win the title again in 1993.

Mark has played at Carnegie Hall with Stephane Grappelli and David Grisman and has appeared as a guest soloist with the Boston Pops Orchestra and at Montreux Jazz Festival. He has been playing solo concerts, in which he alternates between violin, guitar and mandolin and takes audiences on a journey through all American styles of music, from Bluegrass to Classics to Texas Swing.

During 1993, Mark put together a group of his violin peers, under the title of "Heroes," and an album of that name was released on Warner Brothers. In Chet Atkins' words, Mark and "Itzhak Perlman are two of the greatest musicians on the planet today." In 1994, Mark was named the CMA's "Musician of the Year." JAB

RECOMMENDED ALBUMS:

"Mark O'Connor" (Rounder)(1978)
"Markology" (Rounder)
"On the Rampage" (Rounder)
"Pickin' in the Wind" (Rounder)
"Soppin' the Gravy" (Rounder)
"New Nashville Cats" (Warner Brothers)(1991)
"Heroes" (Warner Brothers)(1993)

W. LEE "PAPPY" O'DANIEL

(Emcee, Songwriter, Industry Executive, Politician)

Given Name:	**Wilbert Lee O'Daniel**
Date of Birth:	**March 11, 1890**
Where Born:	**Malta, Ohio**
Married:	**Merle Estella Butcher**
Children:	**Pat, Mike, Molly**
Date of Death:	**May 11, 1969**

Perhaps W. Lee O' Daniel's greatest accomplishment came in displaying the appeal that Country music could bring to the political arena. As a statesman, "Pappy" O'Daniel may have left a lot to be desired, but as a show business personality who entered politics, he could be said to have blazed a trail that persons ranging from Jimmie Davis to Ronald Reagan would later follow.

A native of the southeast Ohio hill country, O'Daniel moved to Kansas at the age of 5 with his widowed mother and stepfather, where he grew up on a wheat farm/cattle ranch near Arlington. After attending a business school in Hutchinson, the youth went to work in the office of a flour milling company. In 1925, he became Sales Manager for Burrus Mill and Elevator of Fort Worth, Texas, manufacturers of Light Crust Flour. He hired Bob Wills, Milton Brown, and Herman Armspiger to do a musical program for the mill in 1930. As the Light Crust Doughboys, this group gained considerable popularity although Wills and Brown soon left to form their own bands.

O'Daniel hired more musicians and the Light Crust Doughboys continued on for several more decades. O'Daniel, while not a musician himself, did their announcing on radio and wrote a few of their songs, most notably *Beautiful Texas*. Wills and Brown had recorded one single for Victor (as the Fort Worth Doughboys in 1932), but the new band, whose members included a teenage Leon McAuliffe, began a long association in 1933 with the American Record Corporation.

In 1935, O'Daniel, frequently known by now as "Pappy," left Burrus Mills and started his own company, which began producing Hillbilly Flour. The Hillbilly Boys, O'Daniel's new group, also secured an American Record Corporation contract and recorded sixty-six numbers over the next three years, all in Western Swing style. *Please, Pass the Biscuits Pappy* was likely their best-known song and key musicians in the group included vocalist Leon Huff, fiddler Carroll Hubbard, and Pat and Mike O'Daniel (Pappy's sons). Kitty "Texas Rose" Williamson, who sang on a few songs, had the honor of being the first female vocalist on a Western Swing recording.

In May 1938, O'Daniel announced his candidacy for Governor and won an easy victory in the July 23, 1938 Democratic primary with no prior political experience. Two years later, Pappy won a second term in spite of a break with Leon Huff, who had departed from the band because O'Daniel had failed to deliver on his promise of a salary increase. This situation pretty much ended the Hillbilly Boys as a quality musical entity.

Even with a mixed record as Governor, Texas Democrats sent Pappy to the U.S. Senate in preference to future President Lyndon Johnson at a special election in 1941 and to a full six-year term in 1942. By this time, his earlier "populist" approach to politics had evolved into membership in the anti-New Deal wing of the Democratic party. He chose to retire in 1948. Afterward, O'Daniel operated an insurance firm in Dallas and made two weak and unsuccessful tries for the Texas statehouse in 1956 and 1958. More than a decade after his death, a resurgence of interest in the roots of Western Swing led to re-issue albums of both the Hillbilly Boys and the Light Crust Doughboys. IMT

RECOMMENDED ALBUMS:

"W. Lee O'Daniel and his Hillbilly Boys, 1935-1938" (Texas Rose)(1982)
"The Light Crust Doughboys" (AOLT)(1982) [Actually two-thirds of this album is the Hillbilly Boys]

MOLLY O'DAY

(Singer, Guitar, Old-Time Banjo)
Given Name: Lois LaVerne Williamson
Date of Birth: July 9, 1923
Where Born: McVeigh, Pike County, Kentucky
Married: Leonard "Lynn" Davis
Date of Death: December 5, 1987

Molly O'Day pioneered the position of solo female Country vocalist during a Country music career that lasted little more than a decade. Molly's recorded repertoire consisted largely of sentimental tear-jerkers and Gospel songs, but she possessed such a powerful and sincere voice that no one ever projected more conviction. Even then, every one of her 36 solo and duet numbers recorded for Columbia is now considered a classic and her few songs recovered from radio transcriptions and later Gospel sessions only slightly less so.

Molly hailed from one of the more remote parts of Appalachian eastern Kentucky, where she and her two brothers listened to local musicians as well as recordings by such traditionalists as Burnett and Rutherford. Later Molly received inspiration from hillbilly radio females like Lulu Belle Wiseman, Patsy Montana, Lily May Ledford and Texas Ruby Owens. With Molly playing guitar and singing, brother Cecil ("Skeets") on fiddle, and Joe ("Duke") on banjo, the youngsters had the makings of a pretty good Old-Time string band. In 1939, Skeets went to SCHS radio in Charleston to play music and Molly soon followed, where she took the name "Mountain Fern." That fall, they came back to the nearest station to home, WBTH Williamson, West Virginia, where Duke joined them. In the spring of 1940, they went to newly-opened WJLS Beckley, where they worked in a group that also included such aspirants as Johnnie Bailes and Little Jimmy Dickens.

Molly O'Day and husband, Lynn Davis

When they moved to WHIS Bluefield, Molly met Leonard "Lynn" Davis (b. 1914), an announcer, lead guitar picker and leader of a band called the Forty-Niners. By now the young lady had changed her name again to "Dixie Lee Williamson." In April 1941, she married Lynn Davis.

The Davis group, following the common practice of changing locations frequently in order to play live shows for fresh audiences, worked out of such locales as WAPI Birmingham, WHAS Louisville, the *Renfro Valley Barn Dance*, KRLD Dallas and finally WNOX Knoxville over the next five years. They attracted a large following of fans wherever they went. Only when they went to WHAS Louisville did the name Molly O'Day come into use. Lynn and Molly had a high quality duet, but her inspiring solo numbers had the biggest impact. The souls of listeners were in particular deeply moved by her rendition of numbers with religious content such as *Tramp on the Street* and *Matthew Twenty-Four*.

When writer-publisher Fred Rose, an old friend of Lynn's, heard Molly at WNOX in the summer of 1946, he knew that he had to get her on Columbia Records. He also saw her as a vehicle for the material being composed by a lanky songwriter from Alabama named Hank Williams. Ironically, Lynn and Molly knew Hank from their Alabama radio days as she had learned *Tramp on the Street* from him (a song Williams had apparently taken from its Georgia-based composers, Grady and Hazel Cole, who waxed it on Bluebird in 1939).

Molly cut *Tramp on the Street* and seven other songs for Columbia (including two Williams numbers) in December, 1946. The Davis band, bearing a strong albeit unintentional resemblance to the Acuff sound of the time, included Skeets Williamson on fiddle, George "Speedy" Krise on Dobro and Mac Wiseman on bass. The recordings helped increase O'Day's popularity, which in turn intensified her own nervous and stress levels rather than raised her self-confidence.

For a time, Molly and Lynn got out of radio and off the road although she cut more songs for Columbia (two by Williams) in December, 1947, including *Matthew Twenty-Four*. She and Lynn later went back to radio, spending several months each at WBIG Greensboro, WROL Knoxville and WVLK Versailles, Kentucky. An April, 1949 session resulted in such classics as *Teardrops Falling in the Snow*, her banjo picking version of *Poor Ellen Smith* and the Williams-composed tear-jerker, *On the Evening Train*.

However, by the early weeks of 1950, Molly and Lynn decided to be with the Lord and give up show business. She later realized that she could not find release from her mental tension until she had found salvation. Thereafter, she sang only in churches and Lynn entered the ministry. Recurring battles with ill-health notwithstanding, Molly remained at peace for the remainder of her life, most of which was spent in the Huntington, West Virginia area.

After her conversion, Molly did two more sessions with Columbia in 1950 and 1951. In 1961 and 1968, she recorded albums for REM and GBS. Beginning in 1973, Molly and Lynn initiated a daily Gospel record program at WMMN-FM Huntington, which Lynn continued after his wife's death from cancer in 1987.

One recent article used the descriptive phrase "On the Threshold of Greatness" to describe Molly's career. Interest in Molly's music and singing has remained high and most of her recordings have continued to be in print on both album and cd. Since much of her song repertoire consists of newly composed material with Victorian sentimental overtones, such as *At the First Fall of Snow, I Heard My Mother Weeping, Why Do You Weep Dear Willow* and *Don't Sell Daddy Anymore Whiskey*, it remains a matter of conjecture whether she could have successfully performed songs of the style that took Kitty Wells to stardom. However, her renditions of numbers like *Mule Skinner Blues* and *Too Late to Worry, Too Blue to Cry* suggest that she might have done it. IMT

RECOMMENDED ALBUMS:

"The Unforgettable Molly O'Day" (Harmony)(1963)
"The Living Legend" (REM)(1962) [Also released on Starday, Pine Mountain and Old Homestead]
"The Heart and Soul of Molly O'Day" (GRS)(1968) [Also released on QCA and Old Homestead as "The Soul of Molly O'Day"]
"A Sacred Collection" (Old Homestead)(1975)
"Radio Favorites" (Old Homestead)(1990)
"In Memory" (Old Homestead)(1990)
"Molly O'Day and the Cumberland Mountain Folks" (Bear Family Germany)(1992)

DANIEL O'DONNELL

(Singer, Guitar)
Date of Birth: December 12, 1961
Where Born: Kincasslagh, County Donegal, Ireland

This very personable young man has shot to stardom and remains popular with fans of all ages. He performs an easy-listening style of Country music and his tour dates are sold out immediately once they are announced.

Daniel is the younger brother of one of Ireland's most successful Country singers, Margo. He initially studied commerce at Galway College, but then joined Margo's band as rhythm guitarist. Although on his own admission, "I was the best actor in Ireland. I couldn't play a note but it was better than sticking at a career my heart wasn't in."

In 1983, Daniel sang a couple of songs with Margo and this gave him the courage to start on his own as a singer. However, although he worked with local musicians, life was a struggle and Daniel was on the verge of emigrating when his first recording, *My Donegal Shore*, which had been getting airplay in Ireland, started to take off in the U.K.

Ritz Records signed him in 1985 and released his debut album, ***Two Sides of Daniel O'Donnell***. This contained one side of Irish songs and the other Country material. Daniel's second album, ***I Need You***, was released in 1987 and made the U.K. Country Music chart. Seven months later, Daniel released his third album ***Don't Forget to Remember***, and it went straight into the U.K. Country Music chart at No.1. This was the first time that a domestic artist had done this.

Daniel then went from strength to strength, touring extensively and appearing at all the major festivals including Wembley and Peterborough. His video, ***Daniel O'Donnell—Live in Concert***, was released to coincide with his fall 1988 tour and was so successful that it appeared on the Top 20 Video chart.

His fourth album, ***From the Heart***, was released on Telstar and also topped the U.K. Country chart and had a 12 week run on the National Pop Album chart. It was named "Country Album of the Year" in the *Music Week* Awards in 1989. In Ireland, Daniel taped his first TV Special, *Country Comes Home*, where he introduced U.S. guests the Judds and Charley Pride. This led to a series of ten one-hour shows, *The Daniel O'Donnell Show*, which featured national and international guests including Loretta Lynn, Lorrie Morgan, Ed Bruce, the Forrester Sisters and Stella Parton as well as many stars of Irish music including the Dubliners, Foster & Allen and Philomena Begley.

As Daniel grew more popular in the British Isles, he also started to develop a following in the U.S. He began by representing Ireland at Fan Fair in Nashville in 1988, appearing on the International Show. He appeared on the *Grand Ole Opry*, at the Summer Lights Festival and at the Stockyard. He also guested three times on *Nashville Now* as well as on *Crook and Chase* and *Video Country*, all on TNN.

In 1989, Daniel recorded the single *My Shoes Keep Walking Back to You* which topped the Irish chart. That year, he came to Nashville to record the album ***The Last Waltz***, which was produced by the famed Allen Reynolds (Garth Brooks and Kathy Mattea) and released in 1990. That year, Daniel undertook his first concert dates in Chicago, Philadelphia, Boston and a sell-out performance at the Town Hall, New York. He returned to the U.S. in 1991 for a second tour, which finished with the sell-out appearance at New York's Carnegie Hall. That year, Daniel's awards included "Top Male Artist" and "Top Album" (***The Last Waltz***) from *Country Music People* magazine and "Most Popular Male Vocalist" from *Country Music Round Up* newspaper. He was also nominated in the BCMA Awards for the "International Act" category alongside Garth Brooks, Alan Jackson and George Strait.

Daniel had two U.K. singles chart successes, *I Just Want to Dance with You* and *Whatever Happened to Old Fashioned Love*, in 1992. He then toured Australia where his video *The Very Best of Daniel O'Donnell* topped the Country music chart and in October 1993, ***A Date with Daniel Live*** was released by Ritz at the start of a major three-month U.K. tour.

Daniel has a tremendous fan following and Daniel O'Donnell Appreciation Societies regularly meet to exchange photographs and snippets of information. They also travel miles to see him in concert. JAB

RECOMMENDED ALBUMS:

"Two Sides of Daniel O'Donnell" (Ritz)(1985)
"I Need You" (Ritz)(1987)
"Don't Forget to Remember" (Ritz)(1987)
"From the Heart" (Telstar)(1988)
"Favorites" (Ritz)(1990)
"The Last Waltz" (Ritz)(1990)
"Follow Your Dream" (Ritz)(1992)
"A Date with Daniel Live" (Ritz)(1993)
Video:
"The Very Best of Daniel O'Donnell" (Ritz)(1992)

JAMES O'GWYNN

(Singer, Songwriter)
Given Name: James Leroy O'Gwynn
Date of Birth: January 26, 1928
Where Born: Winchester, Mississippi
Married: Mary Almedia
Children: Robert James, Brenda Gail, Carolyn Ann

James O'Gwynn was known as "the Smilin' Irishman of Country music" and for some five years during the late 50's and early 60's, he was a successful chartmaker.

He was raised on a farm in Hattiesburg, Mississippi, of an auto mechanic father and a mother who was a versatile musician. It was she who taught James how to play guitar, while the lad was age 8. He was early influenced by Jimmie Rodgers and Hank Williams. He left school in the sixth grade to help his father in the mechanic business and then left to join the U.S. Marine Corps, where he remained for four years. It was at this time that he decided he wanted to make singing his profession.

On leaving the service, he made his first appearance before an audience during a political function for a candidate for Governor of Mississippi. The candidate advised James to contact Hal Harris, a deejay in Houston who passed him to Biff Collie, who was the producer and emcee of *Houston Jamboree*, and James joined the show in 1954, alongside George Jones. It was through this connection that James met famed producer Pappy Dailey, who took up the reins of his recording career.

James cut his first single, *Losing Game*, which was released on Starday, in 1956. That year, he left *Houston Jamboree* and moved on to KWKH's *Louisiana Hayride*. The following year, he also began a two-year stint on KSLA-TV Shreveport, Louisiana. In 1957, he released *I Cry/Do You Miss Me* and *Two Little Hearts* on Mercury-Starday. The following year, he moved to Dailey's D label, and started to rack up a series of Country chart hits. It started with *Talk to Me Lonesome Heart*, which reached the Top 10. He followed this with *Blue Memories*, which made the Top 30. During 1958, *Cash Box* voted him "Most Promising Country Artist," an honor *Billboard* followed up a year later.

James joined Mercury in 1959, where he was produced by Shelby Singleton (whom he had met on the Hayride), and had two more hit singles that year with *How Can I Think of Tomorrow*, which reached the Top 15, and *Easy Money*, a Top 30 hit. James started to make appearances on the *Grand Ole Opry*, thanks to the assistance of Jim Reeves. He left the *Louisiana Hayride* and moved to Nashville in 1961, and for two years he appeared on the *Opry*. He had two further chart successes that year, *House of Blue Lovers* and the Top 10 hit *My Name is Mud*.

When Singleton left Mercury, in 1963, James signed with United Artists, where Pappy Dailey was producing George Jones. None of his four singles made the charts, and when Dailey left the label in 1964, James also departed and, in 1965, signed with Hickory, where he again failed to chart. In 1969, James signed a two-year contract with Pete Drake's Stop Records, where his two releases also failed to register.

It became clear that his recording career was coming to an end, and so James moved to Darnelle, Arkansas and semi-retired from the recording scene. In 1971, he signed with Shelby Singleton's Plantation Records. Although his records were well received, he again failed to have any chart entries.

RECOMMENDED ALBUMS:

"The Best of James O'Gwynn" (Mercury)(1962)
"Heartaches & Memories" (Mercury/Wing)(1964)
"James O'Gwynn's Greatest Hits" (Plantation)(1976)
"Country Dance Time" (Plantation)(1978)

The Smilin' Irishman, ***James O'Gwynn***

O'KANES, The/ KIERAN KANE/JAMIE O'HARA

When Formed: 1986
KIERAN KANE
(Singer, Songwriter, Mandolin, Guitar, Drums)
Date of Birth: October 7, 1949
Where Born: Queens, New York
JAMIE O'HARA
(Singer, Songwriter, Guitar)
Date of Birth: August 8, 1950
Where Born: Toledo, Ohio

In the O'Kanes, there were all the harmonic sounds that one identifies with brother acts such as the Louvin Brothers, the Everly Brothers and the Delmore Brothers. Yet there was a distinctive "Bluegrass" sound that was driven by Kieran Kane's mandolin and by the fine songs that come from the pens of both writers. They were also helped by the talents of Kieran's brother, Richard, on fiddle, guitar and banjo and Jay Spell on accordion and by good looks that ensured that even those unappreciative of their music would still ogle. In fact, perhaps they were the start of "hunks" in Country music.

Kieran was the son of an Irish-American sausage manufacturer. He began playing drums in his brother's rock'n'roll band when he was age 9. He was soon playing Bluegrass and Folk music around the Northeast, from his base in Boston. As his reputation grew, he began opening for the Steve Miller Band and Country Joe and the Fish. He moved to Los Angeles in 1970 and worked as a lead guitarist and songwriter, and in 1978 he moved to Nashville, through his connections to Rafe Van Hoy and Deborah Allen, who originally had talked Kieran into coming to Music City for a week.

Kieran came to the attention of Jimmy Bowen at Warner Brothers Records while playing mandolin on a Hank Williams, Jr. album and was signed to Elektra (Warner Brothers' sister label) in 1980. He first hit the Country charts in 1981 with the low-level success *The Baby*. He followed up with *You're the Best*, which reached the Top 15. He wrapped up the year with *It's Who You Love*, which made it to the Top 20. He had three more chart entries the following year with two Top 30 singles, *I Feel It With You* and *I'll Be Your Man Around the House* and the Top 50 record *Gonna Have a Party*. Keiran moved to Warner Brothers in 1983 and scored a Top 30 hit with *It's You*. The following year, he had another Top 30 single, *Dedicate*. He co-wrote *Gonna Have a Party*, which appeared on Alabama's album ***Mountain Music***. In 1984, John Conlee had a No.1 with Kieran's *As Long as I'm Rockin' with You*.

Jamie was a high school All-American halfback, who was intent on becoming a professional player until, at age 22, while at the University of Indiana, a knee injury changed his direction. After getting a guitar from his father, he began to play and write songs. He began working clubs and honky tonks across the Midwest, while still doing other jobs. He painted houses, hauled railroad ties and worked as a substitute teacher. He came to Nashville in 1975 and took his songs to Tree Publishing, whose Bob Montgomery encouraged him and signed him as a writer to the company. Jamie started getting major cuts in 1981, when Ronnie McDowell had a Top 3 hit with *Wandering Eyes* and its follow-up No.1, *Older Women*. One of Jamie's earliest collaborations with Kieran, at Tree, came in 1985, when

Southern Pacific recorded the Kane-O'Hara song *Bluegrass Blues*, which would later be recorded by the Judds. Also, in 1985, John Conlee recorded the O'Hara song *The Day He Turned Sixty-Five*. In 1986, Jamie had a No.1 hit via the Judds' recording of *Grandpa (Tell Me 'Bout the Good Old Days)*, which won a Grammy Award for Jamie for "Best Country Song." In 1988, Tammy Wynette had a Top 20 hit with Jamie's *Talkin' to Myself Again*.

The two started to record demos together in an attic studio and in 1986 decided to become a duo. They played their tapes to Bob Montgomery, who played them to producer Steve Buckingham, who in turn brought them to the attention of Columbia Nashville's head, Rick Blackburn. The O'Kanes first self-named album was their studio work tapes in their entirety. They hit the Country charts with the Top 10 single *Oh Darlin'*. The debut album reached the Country Albums Top 10. In 1987, they had three Top 10 hits, *Can't Stop My Heart from Loving You* (a No.1), *Daddies Need to Grow Up Too* and *Just Lovin' You.* The following year, the duo released their second album, ***Tired of the Runnin'***. That year, they had two Top 10 hits with *One True Love* and *Blue Love*. Their final single, *Rocky Road*, did not ignite the charts and peaked in the Top 75. In 1988, the duo appeared at the prestigious Wembley Festival in England. The duo decided to split up in 1989, but Columbia still released their third (1990) album, entitled ***Imagine That***, which was largely produced by Allen Reynolds. However, none of the singles released scored on the chart.

Kieran and Jamie have continued writing, but in 1992, Kieran approached Tree for enough money to make some "really expensive demos" and he and drummer Harry Stinson came in as co-producer with Kane. The resultant tape was taken to Rick Blackburn, now head of Atlantic's Nashville office. He signed Kieran and in 1993, the self-titled album hit the streets. In 1994, Jamie released his debut solo album, ***Rise Above It***, on RCA.

RECOMMENDED ALBUMS:

"The O'Kanes" (Columbia)(1986)
"Tired of the Runnin'" (Columbia)(1988)
"Imagine That" (Columbia)(1990)
Kieran Kane:
"Kieran Kane" (Atlantic)(1993)
Jamie O'Hara:
"Rise Above It" (RCA)(1994)

OAK RIDGE BOYS/ OAK RIDGE QUARTET

Formed: 1945 as the Oak Ridge Quartet and then re-formed 1956 and became the Oak Ridge Boys in 1961

Oak Ridge Quartet (1945-49):

Original Members:

Wally Fowler	Lead Singer
Curly Kinsey	Bass Singer, Guitarist
Johnny New	Tenor Singer, Stand-Up Bass
Lon "Deacon" Freeman	Baritone Singer

Other Members:

Neal Matthews	Baritone Singer, Electric Guitar

Oak Ridge Quartet (1949-56):

Bob Weber	Bass Singer
Joe Alfred	Tenor Singer
Bill Campbell	Guitar
Johnny New	Tenor Singer
Pat Patterson	Baritone Singer
Bobby Whitfield	Piano
Livy Freeman	Piano
Glenn Allred	Baritone Singer, Guitar
Bob Prather	Baritone Singer
Walt Cornell	Baritone Singer, Lead Singer
Carlos Cook	Baritone Singer, Lead Singer
A.D. Soward	Bass Singer
"Sister" Cat Freeman	Tenor Singer
Calvin Newton	Lead Singer
Les Roberson	Baritone Singer
Ron Page	Bass Singer

Oak Ridge Quartet (1956-61)/Oak Ridge Boys (1961-1972)

Smitty Gatlin	Lead Singer
Ron Page	Baritone Singer
Hobart Evans	Tenor Singer
Bill Smith	Bass Singer
Powell Hassell	Piano
Herman Harper	Bass Singer
Bobby Clark	Tenor Singer
Tommy Fairchild	Piano
"Little" Willie Wynn	Tenor Singer
Gary Trusler	Piano
James Goss	Piano
Gary McSpadden	Baritone Singer
Jim Hammill	Baritone Singer
Noel Fox	Bass Singer

Plus Messrs. Golden, Allen, Sterban, Bonsall below

Oak Ridge Boys:

Current Members:

Joe Bonsall	Tenor Singer, Piano
Duane Allen	Lead Tenor Singer, Guitar, Piano
Richard Sterban	Bass Singer, Trumpet, Baritone Horn, French Horn, E-Flat Tuba, Sousaphone
Steve Sanders	Baritone Singer

Former Member:

William Lee Golden	Baritone Singer, Guitar

The Oak Ridge Boys and the Statler Brothers stand as Country music's two most enduring and best loved harmony vocal groups. Although they did not achieve their aim of becoming the first group to become CMA's "Entertainer of the Year," most Country fans would point that out as an error by the CMA and not as any reflection on the group, who are far greater entertainers than most of the recipients.

The Oaks were originally formed in 1945, in Knoxville, by Gospel guru Wally Fowler as a quartet called the Harmony Quartet, during WWII. Fowler had utilized the three members of a group known as the North Georgia Boys, who had sung around Rome, Georgia, between 1936 and 1941. They entertained the employees in an atomic energy plant in Oak Ridge. As the workers had to live inside the plant, all entertainment had to be imported. The group soon began to be known as the Oak Ridge Quartet. Their material at the time was primarily inspirational. In 1949, the Calvary Quartet became the Oak Ridge Quartet when Bob Weber bought the name from Wally Fowler. They became members of the *Grand Ole Opry*'s *Prince Albert Show* at the end of that year.

The group disbanded in the mid-50's, having been featured on the cover of *Time* magazine as one of the top drawing Gospel groups. They were re-formed, in 1956, by Smitty Gatlin and the name was sold to him in return for debts owed by Weber, in the early 60's. They worked on a part-time basis until April, 1961, when they went professional and became the Oak Ridge Boys in 1963. They appeared on Cadence Records during 1959 and then in 1963 signed with Warner Brothers. William Lee Golden (b. January 12, 1939, Brewton, Alabama) had seen the original group in Brewton while still at high school and vowed that one day he would join them. He did so in 1964. He had started out playing guitar and singing with his sister on WEBJ radio in Brewton, when he was age 7. He formed the Pilot Trio and played locally and also worked on the family farm, as well as working for a container manufacturer in a pulp mill.

The group recorded for Skylite and Starday during 1965, before moving on to United Artists the following year. In 1966, Duane Allen (b. April 29, 1943, Taylortown, Texas) joined the group from the Prophets. He began his singing career at age 4 in church and then went on to sing baritone with the Southernaires Quartet in Paris, Texas. He attended East Texas

Steve Sanders, Duane Allen, Richard Sterban and Joe Bonsall, the ***Oak Ridge Boys***

University and gained a B.S. degree in music. He once raised a prize hog, but his main work included being a shoe salesman and deejay/Music Director and ad salesman for KPLT radio in Paris.

During the late 60's they recorded for Skyline and Canaan before moving on to Nashville Records in 1970 and Heartwarming in 1970 through 1973. In 1972, Joe Bonsall (b. May 18, 1948, Philadelphia, Pennsylvania) and Richard Sterban (b. April 24, 1943, Camden, New Jersey) joined the group. Joe debuted at age 6 on the *Horn & Hardart* TV program. He worked as an assistant to a veterinarian, as well as having jobs as a salesman in a sugar refinery and short-order cook for Betty Angelino's Luncheonette. He became a member of the Faith Four in Philadelphia. Richard performed a soprano solo in Sunday school when age 7. He went on to attend Trenton State College, studying music education. He became a member of the Keystone Quartet in Bristol, Pennsylvania, and then J.D. Sumner & the Stamps. His other jobs included selling men's clothes and running a printing press.

During the 60's and early 70's, they projected a more flamboyant image, mixing in secular material, adding a drummer, choreographing their act and having long hair. The Gospel establishment was affronted and there was some opposition to the group. As a result, they decided to move away from Gospel material. This did not stop them from being the recipient of the 1970 Grammy for "Best Gospel Performance (Other Than Soul Gospel)" for their Heartwarming single *Talk About the Good Times,* and the 1972 Dove Awards for "Best Male Group," "Best Instrumentalist" (backup pianist, Tony Brown, now head of MCA Nashville), "Best Album" (***Light***), "Best Photo or Cover Art" (***Street Gospel***) and "Best Backliner Notes" (by Johnny Cash for ***Light***).

They made their chart debut in 1973, on the Johnny Cash single *Praise the Lord and Pass the Soup*, along with the Carter Family. In 1974, they signed with Columbia Records, but their material was still Country and Gospel and the group nearly went under financially, although they did win a Grammy for "Best Gospel Performance" for their single *The Baptism of Jesse Taylor*. They appeared on the Country charts, in 1976, with *Family Reunion* and also won a Grammy for "Best Gospel Performance" for their single *Where the Heart Never Dies*. The following year, they received their fourth Grammy for the track *Just a Little Talk with Jesus*, from their ***Rockland Road*** album. However, it was their signing to ABC/Dot and their decision to record only secular material, in 1977, that made them into stars. Their first hit came that year, with *Y'All Come Back Saloon*, which went Top 3. They closed out the year with another Top 3 single, *You're the One*. They also appeared (without credit) on Paul Simon's Pop hit *Slip Slidin' Away*. The Oaks had a sensational 1978, starting with *I'll Be True to You*, which went to No.1 and crossed over into the Pop charts, as did the follow-up, *Cryin' Again*, which made the Top 3. *Come on In* completed the year and reached No.3. That year, they were named both ACM and CMA "Vocal Group of the Year." Their album ***Y'All Come Back Saloon*** became the ACM's "Album of the Year" and the Oak Ridge Boys Band was named "Instrumental Group of the Year." The following year was equally rewarding, as ABC became MCA and the Oaks chalked up further major hits. It started with *Sail Away*, which reached the Top 3, was followed by an old track, *Rhythm Guitar*, on Columbia, then they had *Dream On* (Top 10) and ended with the No.1 single *Leaving Louisiana in the Broad Daylight*. *Music City News* named them "Band of the Year."

As 1980 got under way, the Oaks chalked up another No.1, *Trying to Love Two Women*. This was followed by two singles that peaked at No.3, *Heart of Mine* and *Beautiful You*. They also duetted with Brenda Lee on *Broken Trust* on her ***Take Me Back*** album. Then, in 1981, they hit the jackpot with the Dallas Frazier effervescent song *Elvira*, which went to No.1 and crossed over to the Top 5 on the Pop lists. It went Platinum and won a 1981 Grammy for "Best Country Performance by a Duo or Group with Vocal" and was made both the ACM's and CMA's "Single of the Year," with *Music City News* doing the same the following year. They followed-up with two more No.1s, *Fancy Free* and *Bobby Sue*. The latter, charting in 1982, crossed over to the Top 15 on the Pop list. They also duetted with George Jones on the title track of Jones' ***Still the Same Ole Me*** album (1981). Their next release, *So Fine*, was a relative failure in the Country charts, even though it reached the Pop Top 80. As a result, MCA quickly released *I Wish You Could Have Turned My Head (And Left My Heart Alone)*, which made it to the Top 3. The year was completed by the Top 3 single *Thank God for Kids*.

They started off 1983 with back-to-back No.1 records, *American Made* and *Love Song*. The year was completed by the Top 5 record *Ozark Mountain Jubilee*. They then had a run of five consecutive No.1s that went from 1984 through 1985, starting with *I Guess It Never Hurts to Hurt Sometimes* and running on to *Everyday*, then *Make My Life with You* and in 1985, *Little Things* and *Touch a Hand, Make a Friend*. They finished 1985 with the Top 3 record *Come on In (You Did the Best You Could Do)*. During 1984, they duetted with Bill Monroe on ***Bill Monroe and Friends***.

Their first single of 1986, *Juliet*, only reached the Top 15 and their duet with Barbara Mandrell, *When You Get to the Heart*, only got to the Top 20. Their last single of the year, *You Made a Rock of a Rolling Stone*, was the worst of the three, only getting to the Top 25. That same year, the Oak Ridge Boys Band was voted the CMA's "Instrumental Group of the Year."

It was apparent that there was something wrong and it manifested itself the following year, when Bill Golden was ousted from the group. Since the late 70's, he had started growing a beard, which had now assumed monstrous proportions and in addition to which he was acting somewhat "different." There had allegedly been an agreement that he would retire when he was age 50, but this sacking came two years early. He was replaced by the Oak Ridge Boys band's rhythm guitarist and backup singer, Steve Sanders (b. September 17, 1952, Richland, Georgia).

In 1987, the Oaks had back-to-back No.1 singles entitled *It Takes a Little Rain (To Make*

Love Grow) and *This Crazy Love*. They closed out the year with the Top 20 record *Time In*. They continued in 1988 with *True Heart* (Top 5), *Gonna Take a Lot of River* (No.1) and *Bridges and Walls* (Top 10). In 1989, they had further Top 10 hits with *Beyond Those Years, An American Family* (Top 5) and *No Matter How High* (No.1). In the *Music City News*' Readers Poll, the Oaks were voted "Favorite Group" in both 1988 and 1989.

1990 was not a good year for the Oaks, with *Baby, You'll Be My Baby* only reaching the Top 75 and their debut single for RCA, *(You're My) Soul and Inspiration*, which came from the soundtrack of *My Heroes Have Always Been Cowboys*, just failing to make the Top 30. The following year, *Lucky Moon* reached the Top 10, but the two other chart entries were not successful, with *Change My Mind* only getting to the Top 70 and *Baby on Board* going Top 50. Only one 1992 single, *Fall*, reached the lists and then only got as far as the Top 70.

Although all of their albums have been good sellers, the ones that have done particularly well are ***Fancy Free*** (1981), ***Bobbie Sue*** and ***Oak Ridge Boys—Christmas*** (both 1982), ***American Made*** and ***Deliver*** (both 1983), all of which went Gold.

The Oaks are very active in the national prevention of child abuse campaign and they were selected as the 1985 Honorary Chairmen of the National Committee for Prevention of Child Abuse. Richard Sterban, who has business interests in five minor league baseball teams, was the founder of the annual Music City All-Star Fantasy Baseball Camp.

Although they are a vocal group, they all play instruments, but only Duane plays guitar on stage. Their television credits are long and include an appearance on *Country Rock '82* (an HBO Special that they hosted), *The Dukes of Hazzard* and *Johnny Cash Cowboy Heroes*. They have also made appearances before King Gustaf of Sweden, Princess Caroline of Monaco and HRH Princess Anne (the Princess Royal) of Great Britain, as well as before Presidents Carter and Reagan.

RECOMMENDED ALBUMS:

"Greatest Hits" (MCA)(1980)
"Greatest Hits 2" (MCA)(1984)
"Monongahela" (MCA)(1988)
"Greatest Hits Volume Three" (MCA)(1989)
"Long Haul" (RCA)(1992)
Gospel Material:
"The Light" (Heartwarming)(1972)
"The Sensational Oak Ridge Boys (From Nashville, Tennessee)" (Starday)(1975)
"Old Fashioned, Down Home, Hand Clappin', Foot Stompin', Southern Style Gospel Quartet Music" (Columbia)(1976)
"20 Country Gospel Classics" (Astan Germany)(1984)

Lucky Oceans refer ASLEEP AT THE WHEEL

MAC ODELL

(Singer, Songwriter, Guitar, Harmonica, Mandolin)

Given Name:	**Odell McLeod**
Date of Birth:	**May 31, 1916**
Where Born:	**Roanoke, Alabama**
Married:	**Adeline Wood ("Little Addie")**
Children:	**Bonnie, Barbara, Billy**

Mac Odell is often cited as a prime example of a once flourishing—but now vanished—breed of Country musician known as the "studio star." Mac and his wife, "Little Addie," had a well-known presence for a dozen years via their daily radio programs on Nashville's other 50,000 watt station, WLAC, but made relatively few personal appearances. Mac also published several fine song books and made some memorable recordings for Mercury and King. Under his real name, Odell authored numerous songs, primarily sacred, that have reached standard and classic status.

Born in Alabama, the son of a railroader, McLeod grew up in the Georgia communities of LaGrange and Hogansville playing the harmonica and listening to recordings by the Skillet Lickers, Riley Puckett and Jimmie Rodgers. On WSM Nashville, he loved to hear DeFord Bailey, who became his own musical favorite. Mac and a friend named John "Slim" Bassett formed a duet and wandered around the country in search of a musical job. They worked for a time in a club in Benton Harbor, Michigan, a town where they met their future wives. Later, they found radio work at a major station, WWL New Orleans, where as the duet of Mac and Slim they did quite well. However, they got lonesome for their lady friends in Michigan and returned to Benton Harbor, where Mac married Adeline Wood on August 22, 1936.

Mac and Addie formed a duet and won a local talent contest which landed them a guest appearance on WLS Chicago. This led to a regular spot on nearby WJJD and its famous *Supper Time Frolic*. They worked there for some time and then went to KBTM Jonesboro, Arkansas, where they did some personal appearances with the emerging "King of Country Music" Roy Acuff. When the attack on Pearl Harbor came, Mac went to work in a Michigan defense plant, remaining there throughout the war. He did some songwriting, however, and with Acuff in mind sent five to him. Since Acuff-Rose was then in its early stages as a publishing business, Mac became one of their first contracted writers with such numbers as *The Battle of Armageddon, Radio Station S-A-V-E-D*, and *That Glory Bound Train*. The latter became a minor hit for Roy Acuff.

After the war, Mac wanted back into music as a performer and Fred Rose helped him secure the spot at WLAC, where he did two or sometimes three daily shows for several years. As Mac Odell and Little Addie, Mac and his wife became quite popular as a duet and Mac did solo numbers too. In 1949, he began recording for Mercury, eventually cutting some eight numbers including *Red Ball Rocket Train*, with Speedy Krise on Dobro, *Thirty Pieces of Silver* and *From the Manger to the Cross*. Although Mac's renditions of the latter two songs did not become hits, cover versions by Wilma Lee and Stoney Cooper, Cowboy Copas, Johnnie & Jack and Carl Story helped them to become Country-Gospel standards. Songs Mac wrote but never recorded also became classics such as *Cora is Gone* by Flatt & Scruggs and *Purple Robe* by Cowboy Copas and others.

In 1952, Mac signed with King, recording some sixteen songs at four sessions over three years. As with Mercury, the numbers were largely his own compositions. Mac's writing skills showed special strength in two areas. He could infuse religious themes into songs dealing with technology: trains, radios and elevators. His other strong area was composing lyrics about the life of Christ, dressed in the style of Country songs about topics and events so current in his own formative years. Rural people took them to heart, so that they now started to be collected as Folk songs.

With musical styles changing from the mid-50's and the old days of radio rapidly coming to an end, Mac took leave of WLAC in 1957, sold his Nashville home and returned to Benton Harbor, Michigan. For some years he prospered in the sign painting business until he retired. After 1976, he began to get back into music on a limited basis.

The German firm Folk Variety reissued his original recordings in two albums and released two more made at new sessions held in Nashville and Austin. Old Homestead put together an album from his old radio shows and in 1985 he and Addie toured the Netherlands with the Dutch duo A.G. and Kate.

In 1986, Mac and Addie celebrated their Golden Wedding anniversary. In recent years, Mac has worked with a trio of senior musicians in the Benton Harbor-Kalamazoo area known as the Silver Threads. As Mac told a friend in 1989, they don't make much money, but they have a lot of fun entertaining their neighbors.

IMT

RECOMMENDED ALBUMS:

"Hymns for the Country Folk" (Audio Lab)(1961)
"Be on Time" (Folk Variety)(1977)

"Wild Rose of the Mountain" (Folk Variety)(1978)
"Seven Seven Nashville Session" (Folk Variety)(1978)
"Austin, Texas Git Together" (Folk Variety)(1981)
"Early Radio" (Old Homestead)(1981)

Old and in the Way refer PETER ROWAN, DAVID GRISMAN

Old Country Boy refer MAC ODELL

ROY ORBISON

(Singer, Songwriter, Guitar)

Given Name: Roy Kelton Orbison
Date of Birth: April 23, 1936
Where Born: Vernon, Texas
Married: 1. Claudette Frady
2. Barbara Jakobs
Children: Roy DeWayne (dec'd.), Tony (dec'd.), Wesley, Roy Kelton, Jr.
Date of Death: December 7, 1988

Roy Orbison was a Pop-Country balladeer whose soaring voice gave him many majestic hits. Elvis Presley referred to him as "the greatest singer in the world."

Roy's early influences were Country-tinged and later the writing of Don Gibson had a great impact on him. Having mastered the guitar at high school, he formed, in 1952, his own Country group, the Wink Westerners, and enjoyed his own radio spot on KVWC in his home town. That year, he represented Texas at the International Lions Convention in Chicago. At North Texas State University, Roy met Pat Boone, who encouraged him, and in 1955, with a new band, the Teen Kings, Roy was doing television work out of Midland, Texas, and playing small venues. As the Teen Kings, Roy recorded his own song, *Ooby Dooby*, at Norman Petty's Clovis studio and it was released on Je-Wel Records.

Roy encountered several upcoming artists, including Jerry Lee Lewis and Johnny Cash, who suggested he make a demo tape for Sam Phillips. Roy sent Phillips *Ooby Dooby*, but when Phillips found that Cash had recommended Roy, his immediate response was "Johnny Cash doesn't run my business." But sense prevailed and he signed Roy. *Ooby Dooby* became a Top 60 Pop hit and Roy was into a Rockabilly phase when he really wanted to do big ballads. He got the Everly Brothers to cut another of his compositions, *Claudette*, which related to his wife. There was a dispute over the publishing rights, which led Roy to depart Sun to become a staff writer for Acuff-Rose. *Claudette* was the flip-side of *All I Have to Do Is Dream*, the success of which enabled Roy to buy a new Cadillac.

In 1958, Roy was offered a record deal at RCA Victor, but this didn't prove fruitful. Roy was in Texas when Wesley Rose, who was also his manager, called him and arranged for him to sign to Monument Records. Fred Foster, who owned Monument, and Roy, who was not overly enthused about another deal, met for the first time when Roy was cutting *Paper Boy*. There was instant chemistry between the two. The second single, *Up Town*, reached the Pop Top 75 in 1960. Roy showed Foster two songs that he and Joe Melson had written. Fred suggested that Roy merge them; the result was *Only the Lonely (Know How I Feel)*. Roy recorded it, with strings provided by Bob Moore's Orchestra and Chorus, and Roy's operatic tenor gave him a worldwide hit, with the single going Top 3 on the Pop chart and making it to No.1 in Britain and Australia. Critics called him "the Caruso of Rock" and enthused about his three octave range.

Roy Orbison** on the right with **Carl Perkins, Johnny Cash** and **Jerry Lee Lewis

Roy's success prompted a move to Nashville. He followed up in 1960 with another Orbison-Melson song, *Blue Angel*, which went Top 10 and peaked at No.11 in the U.K. Although *I'm Hurtin'* just missed the Pop Top 20, Roy had his first U.S. No.1, in 1961, with the dramatic Orbison-Melson song *Running Scared*, which also went Top 10 in the U.K. He followed up with *Crying*, also written with Joe Melson. The flip-side, *Candy Man*, which was not an Orbison song, also reached the Top 25. Roy named his backing group the Candy Men after this hit.

In 1962, Roy reached the Top 5 with the Cindy Walker song *Dream Baby (How Long Must I Dream)*, which went to No.2 in the U.K. Roy's next two singles, *The Crowd* and *Leah/Workin' for the Man*, did not fare well and reached the Top 25 and Top 40 respectively. However, he started off 1963 with the Top 10 release *In Dreams*, which did the same in the U.K. That year, Roy toured England with the Beatles. On his way to England, he realized that he had left his spectacles behind and wore his prescription sunglasses instead. The effect of his dark hair, dark glasses and black suits was dramatic and became his trademark image. This trip and subsequent visits to the U.K. touring with, among others, the Rolling Stones, cemented a relationship with the British fans that has remained undiminished.

Roy's other hits in 1963 were *Falling* (Top 25 U.S./Top 10 U.K.) and *Mean Woman Blues* (Top 5)/*Blue Bayou* (Top 30). In Britain the last coupling was reversed and produced a Top 3 hit. Roy's last hit of the year was Willie Nelson's *Pretty Paper*, which went Top 15 (Top 10 in Britain). Roy's 1964 account was opened with the Top 10 *It's Over* (a No.1 in the U.K.) and was followed by the Orbison-Bill Dees song *Oh, Pretty Woman*, which went to No.1 on both sides of the Atlantic and earned Roy a Gold Record. There then followed a dry spell in the U.S. with two Monument singles, *Goodnight* and *(Say) You're My Girl*, only reaching the Top 30 and Top 40 respectively, in 1965.

That year, Roy switched labels to MGM, whom the singer considered the top record company with the best facilities, producers and arrangers, for an alleged $1 million. The lure of money proved irresistible as did the promise of movie and television work; the move proved a mistake. During his period with the label, although he charted, only a handful of singles were hits: *Ride Away* (Top 25, 1965), *Breakin' Up is Breakin' My Heart* and *Twinkle Toes* (both Top 40, 1966). Roy still scored in the U.K. with *Goodnight* and *(Say) You're My Girl* (both 1965), *Crawlin' Back* and *Breakin' Up Is Breakin' My Heart*, *Lana*, *Too Soon to Know* (Top 3) and *There Won't Be Many Coming Home* (all 1966). That year, Roy's ***Greatest Hits*** album was Certified Gold.

As proved by his first and only film, the Civil War story *The Fastest Guitar Alive* (1966), Roy was no John Wayne and it was less than successful. His creativity dried up not least because of personal tragedy. First his wife Claudette was killed in a motorcycle accident, and he worked even harder on the road; then, just as he was starting to write again, two of his sons died when his Nashville home caught fire. Wesley Rose felt that Orbison's songs, reflecting his circumstances, became "sick kind of things," and after Roy's death, Fred Foster criticized the decision to record tribute albums to Hank Williams and Don Gibson. Roy himself was to bemoan: "It was just frustrating to record for a company who didn't know you were recording for them!"

For much of the 1970's, Roy toured abroad, where he remained popular and his live act relived his old hits. Gradually, U.S. acts began to pay homage, which led to a rekindling of interest in his work in his home country. In 1977, Roy happily returned to Monument and recorded the critically acclaimed ***Regeneration*** album. That year, Linda Ronstadt scored with a revival of *Blue Bayou*, leading Roy to tour California, after which he was signed by Elektra in 1979. His debut album, ***Laminar Flow***, proved a disappointment but Orbison's fortunes improved in 1980, when a duet with Emmylou Harris, *That Lovin' You Feelin' Again*, from the film *Roadie*, was a Top 10 Country hit and won a Grammy Award as "Best Country Performance by a Duo or Group with Vocal." The following year, Don McLean had a worldwide hit with his version of Roy's *Crying*.

In 1986, movie producer David Lynch used *In Dreams* as the focal musical piece in the runaway success *Blue Velvet* and the single became a 1987 Top 75 Country success. Also in 1986, Roy joined his old Sun colleagues, Jerry Lee Lewis, Johnny Cash and Carl Perkins to cut the album ***Class of '55***, the interviews from which earned Roy a second Grammy for "Best Spoken Word or Non-Musical Recording."

In 1987, Orbison was inducted into the Rock and Roll Hall of Fame and at the induction ceremony, he sang with Bruce Springsteen. That year, Virgin Records signed Roy to a new recording deal, which began with him re-recording his old hits. He considered the results to be better than the originals. A full-length video, *A Black and White Night*, was shot with Orbison singing his old classics with admirers like Springsteen, Elvis Costello and Tom Waits. The revival continued with Orbison playing a stellar role in the Traveling Wilburys (as Lefty Wilbury), whose other members were George Harrison, Bob Dylan, Tom Petty and Jeff Lynne. Their debut album, ***The Traveling Wilburys/Volume One***, in 1988, was greatly acclaimed and more were set to follow. It earned a 1989 Grammy Award as "Best Rock Performance by a Duo or Group with Vocal." k.d. lang duetted with Orbison on *Crying* (from the movie *Hidin' Out*) and although the result didn't repeat its 1961 chart success (being a Top 50 Country hit), it was another sign of the reverence in which Orbison was held. It also earned for Roy another 1988 Grammy for "Best Country Vocal Collaboration."

Jeff Lynne produced what was to be Roy's last album, ***Mystery Girl***. The album went Platinum in 1989. One of the cuts, *She's a Mystery to Me*, was written for Roy by Bono and the Edge, of Rock group U2. Roy had a Top 10 Country hit from the album, *You Got It*, which was written by Roy, Jeff Lynne and Tom Petty, who also contributed the brilliant *California Blue*, which peaked just under the Country Top 50. However, Roy was not to live to see the release of his most successful album. After playing what was to be his last date in Ohio, Roy returned home, looking forward to promoting his upcoming album in 1989. Instead, he died of a massive heart attack in his bathroom.

In 1989, *Oh, Pretty Woman*, from his 1987 ***A Black and White Night Live***, appeared as a Top 90 Country chart record a year after Roy's death and the following year earned a Grammy as "Best Pop Vocal Performance, Male." In 1989, ***In Dreams: Greatest Hits*** went Gold and the following year, ***All-Time Greatest Hits of Roy Orbison, Volume 1*** did the same. In 1991, ***The Greatest Hits of Roy Orbison, Volume 2*** was also Certified Gold.

Like other great singers before him, death was not to kill Orbison commercially and in 1992, his widow, Barbara, put together a fitting album, ***King of Hearts***, culled mainly from demos and vocal tracks from his last sessions. On the soaring ballad *We'll Take the Night*, Clarence Clemons, from Springsteen's famous E-Street Band, contributed a saxophone solo while k.d. lang added backing vocals on *You're the One*. Considering the circumstances, it was a remarkably good album.

Roy Orbison's songs have continued to feature in films, notably *Pretty Woman* (1990), and in 1993, *I Drove All Night*, a posthumous U.K. hit, was used in a car commercial and re-released as a result. As long as great singing is in vogue, there will always be a place for "the Big O." SM/BM

RECOMMENDED ALBUMS:

"Orbisongs" (Monument)(1965)
"Roy Orbison Sings Don Gibson" (Monument)(1967)
"Hank Williams Songs (Hank Williams, the Roy Orbison Way)" (MGM)(1970)
"Milestones" (MGM)(1973)
"Regeneration" (Monument)(1977)
"Laminar Flow" (Elektra)(1979)
"At the Rockhouse" (Charly UK)(1980) [Sun Masters]
"The All-Time Greatest Hits of Roy Orbison" (double)(Monument)(1982)
"The Sun Years" (double)(Charly UK)(1984)
"In Dreams: The Greatest Hits" (Virgin) (1987)
"Mystery Girl" (Virgin)(1989)
"A Black and White Night Live" (Virgin) (1989)
"King of Hearts" (Virgin)(1992)

ORION

(Singer)
Given Name: **Jimmy Ellis**
Date of Birth: **1945**
Where Born: **Orrville, Alabama**

A singer whose natural speaking and singing voice bears a startling resemblance to Elvis Presley's, Orion has one of the most bizarre stories in the history of popular music. The name Orion was taken from a novel about a singing superstar who faked his own death in his Tennessee mansion to escape the "fishbowl existence" his fame had perpetuated. Author Gail Brewer-Giorgio had begun writing the novel upon hearing of the death of Elvis Presley in August of 1977, basing her plot on the "purely intuitive feeling" that Elvis' death might possibly have been a hoax.

In early 1979, she received a mysterious phone call from a man who sounded exactly like Elvis and who introduced himself as "Orion." When she protested that Orion was only the product of her imagination, the caller responded, "I know. I am Orion, and I was born today!"

Jimmy Ellis began recording in 1964 for the Dradco label. He first recorded for Shelby Singleton and Sun Records in Nashville in 1972, cutting Elvis' original two sides, *That's All Right* and *Blue Moon of Kentucky*. (Presley's versions of the songs were also recorded for Sun, in Memphis, with legendary producer and Sun founder Sam Phillips, from whom Singleton purchased the label in 1969.) Ellis' single was released without artist credits, and he went on to record for various other minor labels before finally signing with Sun in November of 1978.

In early 1979, Sun released *Save the Last Dance for Me* (from the Sun archives), featuring Ellis' voice overdubbed onto a Jerry Lee Lewis record. The duet was credited to Jerry Lee Lewis and Friend and entered the Top 20 on the Pop chart, causing wild speculation about the identity of Lewis' mystery partner. An album entitled ***Duets***, with the same artist credits, followed. At the height of the controversy, the TV show *Good Morning America* actually conducted a "scientific voice scan" of the unidentified singer and concluded that it *was indeed Elvis.* It was about this time that Brewer-Giorgio's book appeared, and Shelby Singleton conceived the plan to transform his mystery singer into the mythic Orion.

Sun Records launched a massive promotional campaign on Orion, using a fictional biography derived from the novel: Orion Eckley Darnell was born in 1936 in Ribbonsville, Tennessee, to Jess and Dixie Darnell, had attended high school in Nashville and had a wife named Danielle and a 10-year-old daughter named Mele Leilani. To complete his image, Orion's hair and long sideburns were dyed jet black and he dressed in sequined, elaborate stage costumes. A mask was added, as well, purportedly to protect him from "overzealous fans" in the event that he became a superstar.

Orion's first single, *Ebony Eyes,* was released by Sun in 1979, followed by an album, ***Reborn***, picturing a ghostly singer wearing a mask emerging from a coffin. (Considered by some to be in poor taste, the album cover was revised for a later reissue.) In 1980, *Cash Box* magazine included Orion's next two albums, ***Sunrise*** and ***Trio Plus*** (where his voice was overdubbed on old Jerry Lee Lewis, Carl Perkins, and Charlie Rich cuts), in their list of Top 75 albums. The following year, the magazine rated him one of the three most promising male Country artists.

Orion continued to put singles on the Country chart, *A Stranger in My Place*, *Texas Tea* and *Am I That Easy to Forget* all reaching the Top 70, in 1980. The following year, he had a quartet of chart records, none of which fared any better, although of interest are his versions of U.K. Rockabilly band Matchbox's hit *Rockabilly Rebel* and Queen's *Crazy Little Thing Called Love*, both of which, although contemporary, bore a Rockabilly sound. His final Country chart single was the Top 70 double-sided entrant, *Morning, Noon and Night/Honky Tonk Heaven.*

By 1983, however, the charade had definitely lost its charm for Ellis/Orion. His desire to be taken seriously by the music industry as an artist in his own right caused him to sever his connections with Sun and strip off the mask before a capacity crowd at the Eastern States Exposition, vowing never to wear it again. (When his career subsequently waned, he re-donned the mask in 1987.)

Not a true Elvis impersonator in the sense that he did not make a career of recording and performing Elvis' material, Orion has always been confronted with the irony that unless he altered his natural vocal intonations, he could not avoid sounding incredibly like the *real* Elvis Presley. His recording of *I'm Trying Not to Sound Like Elvis* seems like a cri de coeur.

Since his debut as a Sun recording artist in 1979, Orion has recorded 11 albums and has appeared on shows with the Oak Ridge Boys, Jerry Lee Lewis, Reba McEntire, Ricky Skaggs, Lee Greenwood, Ronnie Milsap and Dionne Warwick. His latest album, ***New Beginnings***, on Aron International Records of Canada, was released in 1987. He continues to perform throughout the U.S. and Canada. DV

RECOMMENDED ALBUMS:

"By Request: Ellis Sings Elvis [Presley]" (Boblo)(1978) [By Jimmy Ellis]
"Orion Reborn" (Sun)(1978) [On Gold Vinyl]
"Sunrise" (Sun)(1979) [On Gold Vinyl]
"Orion Country" (Sun)(1980) [Gold Vinyl]
"Fresh-Orion" (Sun)(1981) [Gold Vinyl]
"New Beginnings" (Aron International Canada)(1987)

OSBORNE BROTHERS

When Formed: **1956**

BOBBY OSBORNE
(Singer, Songwriter, Mandolin, Guitar, Banjo)

Given Name:	**Robert Van Osborne, Jr.**
Date of Birth:	**December 7, 1931**
Where Born:	**Hyden, Kentucky**
Married:	**1. Patsy Cline (div.)**
	2. Unknown
Children:	**Robby, Wynn, Tina Renea**

SONNY OSBORNE
(Singer, Songwriter, Banjo, Guitar)

Given Name:	**Sonny Roland Osborne**
Date of Birth:	**October 29, 1937**
Where Born:	**Hyden, Kentucky**
Married:	**Judy Rose**
Children:	**Steve Russell, Karen Deanna**

One of the pioneer Bluegrass bands, the Osborne Brothers, with the help of Red Allen and several successors, developed a unique trio sound which distinguished them from other groups in the genre. For a decade from the mid-60's they had experimented with incorporating some Country instruments into their work without abandoning Bluegrass. By the late 70's they veered back toward a more traditional approach. Through some four decades of work the Osbornes have displayed considerable flair for creation and innovation within the somewhat narrow constraints of Bluegrass tradition.

Natives of the mountainous region near Hyden, Kentucky, the Osborne family settled in Dayton, Ohio, after a brief wartime stay in Radford, Virginia. The elder Osborne worked at the National Cash Register Company and knew something about the fundamentals of traditional music, which he taught his children. Bobby became involved in music first, playing electric guitar in a band around Dayton and Middletown known as the Miami Valley Play Boys. They did some club dates and appeared on WWFB radio.

When Bob met banjo picker Larry Richardson from the Galax/Mount Airy Blue Ridge section, the two teamed up in the summer of 1949 and soon sought radio work elsewhere, eventually finding it at WBRW Welch, West Virginia. They soon moved to WHIS Bluefield, initially in a band with Rex and Eleanor Parker, but settled with Ezra Cline's Lonesome Pine Fiddlers. They remained with this band for a year, converting the band to a Bluegrass sound and cutting four sides on Cozy Records, including the now standard *Pain in My Heart.*

In the summer of 1951, Bob formed a short-lived band with Jimmy Martin, doing a session for King Records. He also helped his sister, Louise, and younger brother, Sonny, on a single recording of Louise's composition *New Freedom Bell.* Bob then worked briefly with the Stanley Brothers before being called to military service. Meanwhile, Sonny, who had been perfecting his banjo skills, worked

Country music greats the ***Osborne Brothers***

two stints with Bill Monroe, cutting two sessions with the Blue Grass Boys for Decca.

Sonny did some recording with the Cincinnati-based Gateway label, doing budget covers of Bill Monroe and Flatt & Scruggs discs. Local musicians such as Carlos Brock, Enos Johnson, Billy Thomas, Smoky Ward, and Bobby, after returning home, helped on these sessions, including a few originals such as *A Brother in Korea* and *Sunny Mountain Chimes*.

With Bobby out of the service, the Osbornes formed a team, working for a time at Knoxville with Jimmy Martin on RCA Victor and at WJR Detroit and then with Charlie Bailey at WWVA Wheeling. Early in 1956, Bob and Sonny were working clubs around Dayton, as was Red Allen, who joined forces with them in March. That July they had their first session for MGM which included the now-standard *Ruby*. By the time of their third session in July 1957 they had perfected their trio sound, as best exemplified on the Dusty Owens composition *Once More*, which became their first charted hit early in 1958, going Top 15. Allen left the trio in April and was replaced by a succession of singer-musicians: Johnny Dacus, Ray Anderson, Jimmy Brown and Benny Birchfield. The group continued as a regular on the *Wheeling Jamboree* and on MGM Records for some seven years. A few personal appearances did not provide them with adequate income so the Osbornes drove taxis in Dayton to supplement their earnings. In 1960 they appeared at Antioch College, making them the first Bluegrass band to do a college concert.

By 1963, Bob and Sonny believed they needed to change both labels and home base to give their career a needed shot in the arm. Through friendship with Doyle Wilburn, they got a contract with Decca and began making guest appearances on the *Grand Ole Opry*. *Up This Hill and Down* made the charts in 1966 and several others followed, most notably *Rocky Top* (Top 40, 1967) and *Georgia Pinewoods* (Top 40, 1971). In fact, through the later 60's and early 70's, the Osborne Brothers constituted the only Bluegrass group consistently on the Country charts, although pure traditionalists complained that they compromised their music by adding more contemporary instrumentation on their sessions. While none of their numbers became major hits, Bob and Sonny placed more songs on the charts than any Bluegrass act other than Flatt & Scruggs. They also became perhaps the first Bluegrass band to play the White House, in 1974, as part of a package show that included Merle Haggard.

After 1975, the Osbornes left Decca/MCA but continued as a popular act on the *Grand Ole Opry* and the Bluegrass festival circuit. They reverted toward an older Bluegrass sound, recording successively for CMH, RCA Victor and Sugar Hill, including a double album with Mac Wiseman for CMH.

In September 1993 they announced a new recording pact with Pinecastle. Through the years several noted musicians have worked in their band as guitarists and third member of the trio such as Dale Sledd, Paul Brewster, and Robby Osborne. Their quality fiddlers included Blaine Sprouse and Glen Duncan. With more than 40 years of professionalism under their belt, Bobby and Sonny seem assured of a significant and pivotal role in the history of Bluegrass music. IMT

RECOMMENDED ALBUMS:

"The Early Recordings of Sonny Osborne (Vol.1-3)" (Gateway)(1973)
"Country Pickin' and Hillside Singin'" (MGM)(1959) [With Red Allen] [Re-issued by Collectors Classics, Rounder and also by Stetson UK in the original sleeve (1989)]
"Modern Sounds of Bluegrass Music" (Decca/MCA)(1967) [Partly re-issued on Pickwick] [Re-issued by Stetson UK in the original sleeve (1988)]
"Bluegrass Express" (Coral)(1973)
"Bobby and His Mandolin" (CMH)(1981)
"The Essential Bluegrass Album" (CMH)(1979)
"Some Things I Want to Sing About" (Sugar Hill)(1984)
"Once More" (Sugar Hill)(1986)
"Singing Shouting Praises" (Sugar Hill)(1988)
"Hillbilly Fever" (CMH)(1991)

JIMMIE OSBORNE

(Singer, Songwriter, Guitar, Deejay)

Given Name:	**James Osborne, Jr.**
Date of Birth:	**April 8, 1923**
Where Born:	**Winchester, Kentucky**
Married:	**1. Margaret Catherine Lacy (div.)**
	2. Leona May Patterson
Children:	**Gerald Douglas Osborne, one daughter**
Date of Death:	**December 26, 1957**

Jimmie Osborne, who billed himself as the "Kentucky Folk Singer," ranked as one of the more traditional Country singers who achieved popularity in the decade following WWII. More than any other vocalist of his time, Osborne (and perhaps Red River Dave McEnery) took the topical ballad into the modern era with his hit *The Death of Little Kathy Fiscus* and several moderate successes about the Korean War.

A native of Winchester in the bluegrass country of Kentucky, Osborne came from a farm background. When he received a guitar as a gift, the youngster became determined to carve out a musical career. About 1939 he began to appear on WLAP radio in nearby Lexington. During the war, Jimmie worked in defense plants but still played music on weekends.

About 1945, he went back to WLAP and later sang at stations in Asheville and Texarkana. He came to KWKH Shreveport in 1947 and was a featured vocalist with the Bailes Brothers. He became quite popular and signed with King Records. His initial release, a Bailes song titled *My Heart Echoes*, made the Top 10 and helped land him a position back in his home state as performer and deejay at WLEX Lexington.

In April, 1949, Jimmie wrote and recorded *The Death of Little Kathy Fiscus* about the tragic accidental death of a child in San Marino, California. It shot up to the Top 10 and became his biggest seller. In June, 1950, the outbreak of the Korean conflict provided another opportunity for Osborne's zest for topical material: *God Please Protect America*, *The Voice of Free America*, *Thank God for Victory in Korea*, *The Korean Story*, *My Prodigal Song*, and *A Tribute to Robert A. Taft*. Some Osborne songs, like *A Million People Have Died* which expresses sorrow and warning about increasing numbers of fatal highway accidents, dealt with contemporary society while others concerned traditional, romantic themes.

Osborne moved to Louisville in 1952, where he opened a record shop and had a popular deejay show at WKLO. Jimmie Logsdon, a contemporary, describes him as extremely popular and well liked by fans in addition to being an excellent salesman. He went over to smaller station WGRC for a time, but had an agreement to return to WKLO when he evidently made the decision to end his life. He had a despondent side, which apparently contributed to his fateful suicide late in 1957.

The Kentucky Folk Singer, ***Jimmie Osborne***

He had continued recording with King through May, 1955, leaving a legacy of 66 songs. Many of his recordings appeared on albums released by King in the 60's and the Dutch firm, Strictly Country, re-issued 15 of his other singles on an album in 1988. IMT

RECOMMENDED ALBUMS:

"Jimmie Osborne Singing Songs He Wrote" (Audio Lab)(1959)
"The Legendary Jimmie Osborne" (King)(1961)
"Golden Harvest" (King)(1963)
"The Very Best of Jimmie Osborne" (King and Pine Mountain)(1964)
"The Voice of Free America" (Strictly Country Holland)(1988)

K.T. OSLIN

(Singer, Songwriter, Piano)
Given Name: Kay Toinette Oslin
Date of Birth: May 15, 1941
Where Born: Crossett, Arkansas

K.T. Oslin disproved the maxim that you have to be 21 and cute. By the time she made it in 1987, she had paid her dues and, as they say in the music business, "been there and back again."

K.T. spent her early years in Mobile, Alabama, but when she was age 5, her father, a paper-mill foreman, died from leukemia at the age of 38. Her mother, who had sung briefly with Les Brown's Orchestra and had her own radio show, had to quit the business and became a medical laboratory technician. The family lived in various southern towns, until it settled in Houston. K.T. took lessons in acrobatics and ballet when she was 11. She majored in drama at Jacksonville, Texas, Junior College.

She formed a Folk group with Guy Clark and radio producer David Jones in the 60's, and shortly after she teamed up with Frank Davis, a Texas singer, and traveled to Los Angeles. She returned to Houston on her own and began appearing in several shows there, including a part in the chorus in Carol Channing's National Touring Company's *Hello, Dolly!* After a year, she was invited to New York to be in the Betty Grable Broadway Company of the musical. She then appeared in the Lincoln Center revival of *West Side Story* and in the Bacharach-David musical *Promises, Promises*.

K.T. started to do back-up singing and jingles in New York and then she began touring as a college attraction. She sang back-up vocals on Guy Clark's 1978 eponymous album. While in Due West, North Carolina, she saw graffiti in the ladies' rest room, and that turned her into a songwriter. She sent some songs to Dianne Petty at SESAC, who helped her to a deal with Elektra Records. She first hit the Country charts in 1981, as Kay T. Oslin, with *Clean Your Own Tables,* which reached the Top 80. The following year, Gail Davis (no mean slouch as a songwriter) recorded the Oslin song *Round the Clock Lovin'*.

During 1984, Dottie West recorded *Where Is a Woman to Go* and Gail Davis cut the song the following year. During 1984, K.T. appeared in a Pacifica Radio special with Guy Clark, Rodney Crowell, Jerry Jeff Walker, Townes Van Zandt and Mickey Newbury. Judy Rodman recorded K.T.'s song *Come Next Monday* in 1985.

In 1986, K.T. decided that she had gotten some credibility in Nashville via her Davis and West cuts and decided to put together a band, borrowed $7,000 and promoted herself in a showcase in Nashville. In the audience was producer Harold Shedd (who at the time produced Alabama). He was impressed enough with her rendition of *Two Hearts* that he took her into the recording studio. RCA's President, Joe Galante, was so impressed with the results that K.T. was signed to the label.

Her 1987 debut album, ***80's Ladies***, made chart history when it entered the album charts at 15 with a bullet. This was the highest debut position for a female Country artist, beating Loretta Lynn's previous 1964 record. K.T. had recorded an earlier live album on Whirly Bird in Los Angeles. The album was recorded at a club called the Ice House, but it had never been released. In 1987, she hit the Country charts with *Wall of Tears*, which peaked in the Top 40. She followed this with the title track of the album and made the long-awaited breakthrough when it reached the Top 10. She finished the year with her first No.1, *Do Ya'*, which hung around the charts for nearly 6 months, and she made the move to Nashville, where she had lived for some 20 years. Just to add value to the year, the Judds recorded K.T.'s *Old Pictures*.

1988 opened up with another No.1, *I'll Always Come Back*, which also came from the debut album. That year, she released her second album, ***This Woman,*** and the initial single, *Money*, only reached the Top 15, but the next single, *Hold Me,* got all the way to No.1. She continued her winning ways in 1989 when *Hey Bobby* climbed to the Top 3 and *This Woman* reached the Top 5. The final single of the year, *Didn't Expect It to Go Down this Way,* only got to the Top 25. 1990 brought the release of a new album, ***Love in a Small Town***. The first single, *Two Hearts*, only got to the Top 75, but the follow-up, *Come Next Monday,* made it all the way to No.1. With the advent of 1991, K.T.'s singles failed to achieve a high level of success. *Mary and Willie* got to the Top 30, while *You Call Everybody Darling* and *Cornell Crawford* only reached the Top 70. In 1993, K.T. Oslin played the part of Amy Kurland, the owner of Nashville's premier writers' club, the Bluebird Cafe, in Peter Bogdanovich's movie *The Thing Called Love*. That year, K.T. returned to the chart with the Top 70 *New Way Home* and she released the album ***Songs from an Aging Sex Bomb***.

During what has been a short recording career, K.T. won many prestigious awards, including, in 1987, ACM's "Video of the

*80's lady **K.T. Oslin**, still a star in the 90's*

Year" for *80's Ladies* and a Grammy Award as "Best Country Vocal Performance, Female" for the same song. In 1988, she won the following awards: CMA "Female Vocalist of the Year" and "Song of the Year" for *80's Ladies*, ACM award for "Album of the Year" for ***This Woman*** and "Female Vocalist of the Year" and a Grammy Award for "Best Country Vocal Performance, Female" for *Hold Me*, which also won a Grammy for "Best Country Song." In addition, both ***80's Ladies*** and ***This Woman*** have been Certified Platinum, while both the cd and video of ***Love in a Small Town*** have been Certified Gold. The K.T. Oslin recording career may now appear to be at an end but during 1987 through 1989, she was most certainly the 80's lady, with a style of sophisticated and thematic Pop-Country that harkened back to Carole King and Janis Ian. K.T. continues to play live dates and write wonderfully expressive songs.

RECOMMENDED ALBUMS:

"80's Ladies" (RCA Victor)(1987)
"This Woman" (RCA Victor)(1988)
"Love in a Small Town" (RCA)(1990)
"Songs from an Aging Sex Bomb" (RCA)(1993)

MARIE OSMOND

(Singer, Actress, Author)

Given Name:	**Olive Marie Osmond**
Date of Birth:	**October 13, 1959**
Where Born:	**Ogden, Utah**
Married:	**1. Steve Craig (m. 1983)(div. 1985)** **2. Brian Blosil (m. 1986)**
Children:	**Stephen James**

For part of the 70's and 80's, Marie Osmond straddled that fine line between Country and Pop, ultimately scoring more Country chart hits than Pop.

Growing up as the only girl among eight brothers in a strictly Mormon household, Marie saw her brothers, Alan (b. June 22, 1949), Wayne (b. August 28, 1951) and Merrill (b. April 30, 1953) begin a career as a quartet singing religious and barbershop music, appearing at Disneyland in 1962. That year, the brothers joined the *Andy Williams Show* on television and were joined by brother Donny (b. December 9, 1957). Marie made her debut on the show that year, although she was just 3 years of age.

Marie signed with MGM Records and hit the Pop and Country charts in 1973, when not yet 14, with *Paper Roses*. The single was arranged and produced by Sonny James and topped the Country chart, crossed over to the Top 5 on the Pop chart, went Gold and, for good measure, went to No.2 on the U.K. Pop chart. By then, her youngest brother, Jimmy (b. April 16, 1963), had already had a U.K. No.1 hit with *Long Haired Lover from Liverpool*. Marie's single earned her two Grammy nominations.

Marie began to appear in concert with her brothers and she continued to have further Country chart entries. These were *I'm Leaving it (All) up to You*, a duet with Donny that reached the Country Top 20, the Pop Top 5, went Gold and went Top 3 in Britain, and the solo *In My Little Corner of the World*, which went Top 40 Country (both 1974), *Who's Sorry Now* (Top 30 Country/Top 40 Pop,1975) and the 1975 Top 80 Country/Top 40 Pop duet with Donny, *Make the World Go Away*, which was a Top 20 hit in the U.K.

In 1975, Donny and Marie began their own TV series, which ran for four seasons and won People's Choice Awards two years in a row for "Best TV Variety Show." The following year, Marie was voted by the public one of the "Top Three Favorite Female Performers of the Year." Her hairstyle was copied by teenagers across the country and the famous "Marie Cut" won her "the Best Coiffured Woman in the United States" award for 5 consecutive years.

In 1978, Marie appeared with Donny in the movie *Goin' Coconuts* and in 1979 and on her own in *The Gift of Love*. She began to study acting in New York with Lee Strasberg, then in 1980, she authored *Marie Osmond's Guide to Beauty, Health and Style* (Simon & Schuster). In 1981, she signed with long-time mentor Mike Curb's label and was licensed to Elektra. However, her most successful single, *Back to Believing Again*, only reached the Top 60 in 1982.

By 1984, she was with RCA/Curb without any success. However, when Curb linked her with Capitol, success came in abundance. Her 1985 duet with Dan Seals, *Meet Me in Montana,* became a No.1 Country hit and was followed by another solo No.1, *There's No Stopping Your Heart*. Her duet with Seals earned the CMA "Vocal Duo of the Year" award in 1986. That year, *Read My Lips* went Top 5 and was followed by yet another No.1 duet, this time *You're Still New to Me*, with Paul Davis. She ended the year with the Top 15 release *I Only Wanted You*.

From then on, her singles fared less well and between 1987 and 1989, her most successful releases were *Everybody's Crazy 'bout My Baby* (Top 25), *Cry Just a Little* (Top 50)(both 1987), *Without a Trace* (Top 50) and *Sweet Life* (both 1988). The latter, a duet with Paul Davis, was a Top 50 reprise of Paul's 1978 Pop hit. In 1990, Marie had her last chart single, *Like a Hurricane*, on which she was billed as "Marie" and which went Top 60.

Marie's other projects have included the Marie Osmond Signature Series of young girls' clothes, an exercise video for expectant mothers and being National Chairperson of the Osmond Foundation, for which she hosts the Children's Miracle Network Telethon, which raises millions of dollars for medical research and assistance benefiting children.

RECOMMENDED ALBUM:

"The Best of Marie Osmond" (Curb)(1990

Luther Ossenbrink refer ARKIE THE ARKANSAS WOODCHOPPER

OUTLAWS, The

When Formed:	**1974/Re-formed 1987**
Members:	
Billy Jones	**Guitar, Vocals**
Frank O'Keefe	**Bass Guitar (left 1977)**
Hughie Thomasson	**Guitar, Vocals**
Monte Yoho	**Drums (left 1980)**
Henry Paul	**Guitar, Vocals (left 1977)(rejoined 1987-1988, then left again)**
Harvey Dalton Arnold	**Vocals, Bass Guitar (joined 1977/left 1980)**
Freddie Salem	**Guitar,Vocals (joined 1977)**
David Dix	**Drums, Percussion (joined 1978)**
Rick Cua	**Bass Guitar, Vocals (joined 1980)**
David Lane	**Guitar, Fiddle (joined 1982)**
Chris Anderson	**Guitar,Vocals (1987-8)**
B.B. Bordon	**Drums (1989-)**
Billy Yates	**Guitar, Vocals (1989-1990)**
Anthony Catanzaro	**Bass Guitar, Vocals (1989-1990)**
Billy Greer	**Bass Guitar, Vocals (1990-)**
Chris Hicks	**Lead Vocals, Guitar (1990-)**

At one time, the inclusion of the Outlaws in an encyclopedia of Country music would have caused eyebrows to be raised, but since the advent of the group concept in Country music, in the wake of Alabama and most especially with the arrival of more Rock-oriented bands such as Restless Heart, the Outlaws' brand of southern boogie /Country-Rock fits more into the contemporary pocket of Country. This is especially true because of their "today" sound of four-part harmonies.

The band was originally formed in Tampa, Florida, by Hank Paul and Hughie Thomasson, and for a while the band played under various names and worked bars, dances and participated in "battles of the bands." Their turning point occurred in Columbus, Georgia, where the Outlaws appeared with Lynyrd Skynyrd. Skynyrd's leader, Ronnie Van Zandt, recommended the Outlaws to Clive Davis, President of Arista Records, who signed them as the first act to the label. They may well have been signed to Phil Walden's Capricorn label, had they not been managed by Alan Walden, Phil's brother, who saw no benefit in the arrangement.

The band's debut self-titled album in 1975 spawned *There Goes Another Love Song*, which reached the Top 40 on the Pop charts. The album became a big seller and by 1977 had been Certified Gold. In 1976, they released their second album, ***Lady in Waiting***, from which came *Breaker-Breaker*, which just flirted with the basement level of the Pop charts. Their third single hit came in 1977, the title track of their third album, ***Hurry Sundown,*** and reached the Top 60 on the Pop charts.

This was the first album with bass player Harvey Dalton Arnold, who had replaced Frank O'Keefe, and soon founder Henry Paul was on his way and Freddie Salem had joined. Salem had, by the time he was 19, played with the Chambers Brothers band on their first album.The Outlaws' fourth album, ***Bring it Back Alive,*** was released in 1978 and was Certified Gold by 1979. This album also marked the debut of drummer David Dix. The next album to hit the street was ***In the Eye of the Storm***, at the end of 1978. This was the last album to feature the double-drumming of Yoho and Dix, as Yoho was on his way in 1980, as was bass player Arnold.

For their 1981 album ***Ghost Riders***, the band was joined by Rick Cua, on bass guitar. The album spawned the classic *(Ghost) Riders in the Sky*, which reached the Top 40 on the Pop chart. As a result the album went Gold during the year of release. With the departure of Billy Jones, the Outlaws' three-guitar line-up was no more, and for their 1982 album ***Les Hombres Malo***, Thomasson and Salem did the guitar honors; however, the release did mark the debut of electric fiddler Dave Lane.

For a while, the band's fortunes were at a low ebb, then in 1986, they released the ***Soldiers of Fortune*** album and then Thomasson got together with Paul, Dix, Salem and Chris Anderson. Since then, the line-up has consistently changed, with Thomasson being the only constant player, and still the principal proponent of throwing guitar picks to the audience.

RECOMMENDED ALBUMS:

"The Outlaws" (Arista)(1975)
"Lady in Waiting" (Arista)(1976)
"Hurry Sundown" (Arista)(1977)
"Bring it Back Alive" (Arista)(1978)
"Playing to Win" (Arista)(1978)
"In the Eye of the Storm" (Arista)(1979)
"Ghost Riders" (Arista)(1981)
"Los Hombres Malo" (Arista)(1982)
"Soldiers of Fortune" (Pasha/CBS)(1986)

Eva Overstake refer JUDY MARTIN

Lucille Overstake refer JENNY LOU CARSON

PAUL OVERSTREET

(Singer, Songwriter, Guitar)

Date of Birth: **March 17, 1955**
Where Born: **Newton, Mississippi**
Married: **1. Freida Parton**
2. Julie Miller
Children: **Nash, Summer, Chord, Harmony**

There is no doubt that Paul Overstreet is one of the most important songwriters to emerge in Country music in the last decade. A man driven by his Christian beliefs, Paul is one of the old style of songwriter, capable of writing meaningful lyrics and strong melodies, sometimes in tandem, but also on his own.

Paul left his Mississippi home, in 1973, straight from high school and headed for Nashville, with the proverbial fist full of dollars. As the money ran out, he became a welder and carpenter and then played with various groups, normally under the influence of drink or drugs. At last fed up with his way of life, he arrived at a pact with God, in which Paul promised to give up drinking if God would take him off of the lounge circuit.

*Super songwriter and singer **Paul Overstreet***

God delivered, with George Jones cutting Paul's *Same Ole Me*, in 1982. That year, Paul charted for the first time with *Beautiful Baby*, which reached the Top 80. However, Paul wasted his earnings and came close to financial ruin. In 1984, he met his second wife and when he saw the effect his habits were having on her, he straightened himself out. This marked the turning point in his career.

In 1985, the Forester Sisters presented Paul with his first No.1 hit with *I Fell in Love Again Last Night*, which he wrote with Thom Schuyler. That same year, *On the Other Hand*, which he wrote with Don Schlitz, was released by the newcomer Randy Travis, and peaked in the Top 70. The following year, the Travis bandwagon was rolling and the song provided Randy with his first No.1, to be followed up by the Overstreet-Gore song *Diggin' Up Bones*, which also went to No.1. During the year, Tanya Tucker had a Top 3 success with Paul's *One Love at a Time* and Marie Osmond with Paul Davis topped the charts with the Overstreet-Davis song *You're Still New to Me*.

During 1986, Paul entered another phase of his career, as recording artist. He got together with Thom Schuyler and J. Fred Knobloch, as Schuyler, Knobloch and Overstreet (SKO), and signed to MTM Records. They hit the Top 10 with *You Can't Stop Love* and then followed up with the No.1 single *Baby's Got a New Baby*. That year, Paul received his first awards when both the ACM and CMA named *On the Other Hand* as "Song of the Year," and the CMA made it their 1986 "Single of the Year."

The following year, his career reached even higher levels. He had No.1 hits with *Forever and Ever, Amen* (Randy Travis), *A Long Line of Love* (Michael Martin Murphey) and *You Again* (Forester Sisters). He also had another major hit with *No Place Like Home* from Randy Travis. Paul had one further chart entry with SKO, *American Me*, before leaving the group. He was again the recipient of a slew of awards. Both the ACM and the CMA named *Forever and Ever, Amen* as "Song of the Year." ACM also named the song as "Single of the Year." It also won a Grammy for "Best Country Song" and was CMA's "Single of the Year." *On the Other Hand* became *Music City News*' "Single of the Year." He also became NSAI "Songwriter of the Year."

In 1988, Paul had three No.1 hits in *I*

Won't Take Less than Your Love (Tanya Tucker and Paul Davis), *Strong Enough to Bend* (Tanya Tucker) and *When You Say Nothing at All* (Keith Whitley). His other success was the George Jones and Shelby Lynne *If I Could Bottle This Up*. He also had a Top 3 single himself, *Love Helps Those*, on MTM. *Forever and Ever, Amen* was named *Music City News*' "Single of the Year."

The following year, Randy Travis presented Paul with another No.1, *Deeper Than the Holler*. Paul's other Top 10 covers were *Houston Solution* (Ronnie Milsap) and *My Arms Stay Open All Night* (Tanya Tucker). His own recording career now took full flight with the release of his debut album for RCA, ***Sowin' Love***. From this, the title track reached the Top 10 and the follow-up, *All the Fun*, reached the Top 5. The album itself reached the Top 40 and stayed on the Country Album chart for about 8 months. That year, Paul appeared at the ill-fated Grantham Festival, in England.

In 1990, his two prime cuts were the Top 10 singles *Battle Hymn of Love* (Kathy Mattea and Tim O'Brien) and *Love Can Build a Bridge* (the Judds). The latter track collected a pair of Grammy Awards in 1991, for "Best Country Performance by a Duo or Group, with Vocals" and "Best Country Song." During 1990, Paul racked up three major hits: *Seein' My Father in Me* (Top 3), *Richest Man on Earth* (Top 3) and the No.1 hit *Daddy's Come Around*.

Overstreet released his second album, ***Heroes***, during 1991, and it made the Top 20 of the Country Album chart, staying around for over a year. His single hits for the year were the Top 5 hits *Heroes* and *Ball and Chain*. He wrapped up the year with his version of *If I Could Bottle This Up*. He also had major cuts from Pam Tillis with *One of These Things* and a further posthumous Keith Whitley success, *Somebody's Doing Me Right*.

However, it was another track on the ***Heroes*** album that caused a lot of interest. The song *Billy Can't Read* was performed before the 1990 Convention of the Literary Volunteers of America, "Blazing New Trails...Reaching New Heights." He had already sung the song in New York at Stars for Literacy.

He released his third album, ***Love is Strong***, in 1992, but it was by no means as successful as its predecessors. This also befell his single chart entries. *Billy Can't Read* only reached the Top 60, while *Me and My Baby* peaked in the Top 30 and *Still Out There Swinging* also only reached the Top 60.

Paul has been putting more emphasis of late in writing inspirational material and recording with Reba McEntire's sister, Susie Luchsinger.

RECOMMENDED ALBUMS:
"Sowin' Love" (RCA)(1989)
"Heroes" (RCA)(1990)
"Love is Strong" (RCA)(1992)

International favorite ***Tommy Overstreet***

TOMMY OVERSTREET

(Singer, Songwriter, Guitar)

Given Name:	**Thomas Cary Overstreet II**
Date of Birth:	**September 10, 1937**
Where Born:	**Oklahoma City, Oklahoma**
Married:	**1. Nancy (div.)**
	2. Diane
Children:	**Thomas Cary III (dec'd.), Elizabeth Nan (Lisa)**

Tommy has emerged as one of the most popular Country performers, not only in the U.S. but internationally.

As a lad, Tommy was encouraged by Gene Austin, a cousin, who taught him the business. Austin had come to fame with his hit records *My Blue Heaven* and *Ramona*. Tommy got his first guitar as a present from his parents when he was 13. He appeared on *Kitchen Canteen* on KTHT Houston for four months and then he joined a musical called *Hit the Road*, in Houston, replacing the Pop vocalist Tommy Sands, who had been a high school friend of his.

When he finished high school, the family moved to Abeline, where Tommy attended the University of Texas, studying radio and TV production. While in college, he worked on local radio and TV stations as a host/singer and was known as "Tommy Dean from Abilene." He also spent his summers on the road with Gene Austin. After graduation, he toured for a while and then served in the Army for two years.

In the early 60's, he moved to Los Angeles, and worked for Pat Boone, as a writer, and then signed with Dunhill Records as a Pop singer, although no records were ever released. After moving back to Texas, in the mid-60's, Tommy appeared on TV on the *Slim Willet Show*. He then formed his own band playing at local air bases and clubs.

Tommy moved to Nashville, in 1967, and soon found a position with Dot Records as their Professional Manager. To supplement his income, he played local clubs and was signed to Dot as an artist. His debut single in 1969, *Rocking a Memory (That Won't Go to Sleep)*, went into the lower end of the charts, as did his next chart entry, *If You're Looking for a Fool*, in 1971. He had his first majot hit, in 1971, with *Gwen (Congratulations)*, which went Top 5. He repeated this with *I Don't Know You (Anymore)*, and in the same year, Tommy released his debut album also called ***Gwen (Congratulations)***.

In 1972, Tommy had three more singles charted, *Ann (Don't Go Runnin')* (Top 3), *A Seed Before the Rose* (Top 20) and *Heaven Is My Woman's Love* (Top 3), the latter being his second album's title. A run of Top 10 singles followed in 1973 and 1974, namely, *Send Me No Roses* and *I'll Never Break These Chains* (both 1973), *(Jeannie Marie) You Were a Lady* (Top 3), *If I Miss You Again Tonight* and *I'm a Believer* (all 1974).

Tommy's chart singles during the second half of the 70's were *That's When My Woman Begins* (Top 10), *From Woman to Woman* (Top 20)(both 1975) and *Here Comes that Girl Again* (Top 15) and *Young Girl* (Top 30) (both 1976), *If Love Was a Bottle of Wine* (Top 15), *Don't Go City Girl on Me* (Top 5), *This Time I'm in it for the Love* (Top 20)(all 1977) and *Yes Ma'am* (Top 15), *Better Me* (Top 20) and *Fadin' in, Fadin' Out* (Top 15)(all 1978).

In 1979, Tommy had a low-level chart record on Tina Records, and then moved to Elektra, where his most successful records were *I'll Never Let You Down* (Top 30), *What More Could a Man Need* (Top 25) and *Fadin' Renegade* (Top 40)(all 1979) and *Down in the Quarter* and *Sue* (both Top 50, 1980).

Tommy had further chart success through the 80's on AMI, Gervasi and Silver Dollar. He continued to tour with his five-piece band, the Nashville Express, and the International Rodeo Association named him "Entertainer of the Year," in 1979, 1980, and 1982. Tommy appeared on many TV shows such as *Hee Haw*, *Nashville Alive* and the *Tonight Show*, among many others.

In 1985, Tommy married Diane and moved to Branson, Missouri. The following year, his son, Thomas, who was his road manager, was tragically killed in an accident. This, of course, hit Tommy hard, but he began rebuilding his life. He opened a restaurant and also signed to a new record label, Silver Dollar Records. He appeared at the Peterborough Country Festival in England during 1988, and the following year, he appeared in Branson. He still tours on a regular basis. JAB

RECOMMENDED ALBUMS:

"Gwen (Congratulations)" (Dot)(1971)
"Tommy Overstreet Show, Live From The Silver Slipper" (ABC/Dot)(1975)
"A Better Me (Tenth Anniversary Album)" (ABC/Dot)(1978)
"The Best of Tommy Overstreet" (Electra)(1980)
"I Can Hear Kentucky Calling Me" (CMH)(1980)
"A Better Me (Tenth Anniversary Album)" (MCA)(1981)
"Dream Maker" (Intercord Germany)(1983)

JIM OWEN

(Singer, Songwriter, Guitar, Actor)
Date of Birth: April 21, 1941
Where Born: Robards, Kentucky
Married: Yvette Robards

It is easy to dismiss Jim Owen as a man who does a one-man show imitating Hank Williams, but that would be to undervalue Jim as a performer and songwriter. His show is rightly hailed as being superb and he manages to get not only the sound but also the essence of Hank Williams, but he has also written some fine songs that Hank would have been proud to write.

Jim's earliest remembrance of Hank was in 1949, when he saw the great man at the Hi-Y-Drive-In in Henderson, Tennessee, and even at 8 years of age, he was touched by the man. When Hank's death was announced on the radio, Jim cried. He began to research Williams' life and found that what was a hobby soon became an obsession.

He attended Murray State University and worked as a sports editor for the *Princeton, Indiana Clarion*. He also had a job working at the Singer Company, Breckinridge Job Corps Center and was a golf coach. He started writing songs, and with help from Mel Tillis, Jim moved to Nashville in 1969. Tillis recorded two of Owen's songs, *Too Lonely Too Long*, in 1970, and *One More Drink*, in 1971. Porter Wagoner had a Top 50 hit with Jim's song *Little Boy's Prayer,* and the following year, June Stearns charted with *Sweet Baby on My Mind*. Both of these songs would be recorded by other artists, in the first case by Hank Williams, Jr. and in the latter, Crystal Gayle.

Soon after coming to Nashville, Owen put together a club act and played Las Vegas, among other locations. In 1973, Jim had a bumper crop of chart hits when Conway Twitty and Loretta Lynn took *Louisiana Woman, Mississippi Man* to the No.1 position and Jim Ed Brown scored heavily with *Southern Loving* and *Broad-Minded Man*.

Jerry Reed provided Jim with another minor hit with the Owen song *The Telephone*. It was in 1976 that Jim put into reality an idea that had first come in a dream. Jim's wife, Yvette, had dreamed, some six years earlier, that Jim was playing on the *Grand Ole Opry*, but that Hank Williams' voice was coming from his mouth. For four years, he talked with Williams' relatives, so that he could get Hank's mannerisms correct. He practiced Hank's way of yodeling and walking and even perfected how Williams leaned into the microphone, and how Hank played guitar.

So he wrote and starred in, first, *Hank*, a one hour PBS special, via WDCN Nashville, which won an Emmy Award for "Best Show of the Year on Public TV." He then went on to present the 90-minute *An Evening with Hank Williams*, which debuted at the Fourth Annual Southeastern Commodity Producers Conference and Trade Show. The taped background music for the show was played by the Drifting Cowboys. Jim proved that he could alter his own vocal tones so as to sound like Hank.

In 1978, Jim in company with the Drifting Cowboys had a low-level chart entry with *Lovesick Blues*. By 1980, Owen had a solo record deal with Sun Records, and had another basement level recitation single called *Ten Anniversary Presents*. As a result of his PBS special, he played the lead in the movie *Hank Williams: The Man & His Music*, for which he was nominated for an Emmy. It would be another two years before he hit the charts again, with the low-level *Hell Yes, I Cheated*.

During 1985, Jim wrote and produced a 10-hour Hank Williams radio special which was broadcast on New Year's Day. Jim also re-created Hank for *Legends in Concert* at the Imperial Palace in Las Vegas.

By 1990, he had returned to Henderson County and his garage of classic cars. He learned to become an auctioneer, while still maintaining a grueling schedule with his *Evening with Hank Williams*. He has appeared frequently on the *Opry*, doing exactly what his wife foretold. At the anniversary show for Hank Williams, on January 2, 1993, marking the 40th anniversary of the great man's death, Jim got as big a reception as Hank himself would have gotten. In Owen's own words, "I'm taking Hank to the people." However, Jim Owen is still enough of a songwriter to have his songs recorded by Roy Clark, Faron Young, Charley Pride, Eddy Arnold, Waylon Jennings, Jimmy Dean, Dottie West, Don Gibson and Nat Stuckey.

RECOMMENDED ALBUM:

"Hank" (Sun)(1982)

BONNIE OWENS

(Singer, Songwriter, Yodeler, Guitar)
Given Name: Bonnie Campbell
Date of Birth: October 1, 1932
Where Born: Blanchard, Oklahoma
Married: 1. Buck Owens (m. 1946)(div.)
2. Merle Haggard (m.1965)(div.1978)
Children: Alvis Alan (Buddy Alan), Mike

It would be simple to think of Bonnie Owens as the wife of Buck Owens and Merle Haggard. However, she had several Country chart hits in the 1960's and was also a good songwriter.

As a child, her family moved from Oklahoma to Arizona and she began her show business career while still a teenager, as a yodeler, being acclaimed as the best yodeler in the state. She worked various clubs in Arizona and then teamed up with Buck Owens on the *Buck and Britt Show* on station KTYL Mesa, Arizona.

Soon after, they became part of a band known as Mac's Skillet Lickers and they toured extensively throughout the western U.S. Bonnie and Buck married and had two boys, and then moved to Bakersfield, California. Bonnie decided to split with Buck as she wanted to try a solo career. She began by recording for the Marvel and Tally labels and soon began to work on local radio. Three of her records with Tally went into the Top 30, namely, *Why Don't Daddy Live Here Anymore* (1963), *Don't Take Advantage of Me* (1964) and a duet made with Merle Haggard, *Just Between the Two of Us* (1964).

In 1965, Bonnie married Haggard and the pair moved to the major Capitol label. Bonnie released three more hit records that produced mid-chart placings. They were *Number One Heel* (1965), *Consider the Children* (1966) and *Lead Me On* (1969).

She now looked set for stardom, being an acclaimed performer on the *Merle Haggard Show*. In addition, Merle began to sell and was up in the No.1 spot regularly. He became a star and Bonnie continued to tour with him, rather than pursue her own solo career. In 1966, Bonnie and Merle were named "Best Vocal Group" by the ACWM (later the ACM) and Bonnie was selected as "Top Female Vocalist."

Eventually, she grew tired of touring and in

1975, she announced she would concentrate on running Haggard's business affairs. Also that year, she filed for legal separation from Haggard and they divorced in 1978. In spite of this, Bonnie and Merle remain good friends and she even appeared as part of the *Merle Haggard Show* quite a few times in the late 70's. She also traveled with Haggard to London, to appear on the 1978 Wembley Festival of Country Music, and was still with the show, in 1988, when Haggard returned to Wembley. JAB

RECOMMENDED ALBUMS:

"Lead Me On" (Capitol)(1969) [With the Strangers]
"The Land of Many Churches" (Capitol)(1971)(double) [Merle Haggard album features Bonnie Owens and the Carter Family] [Re-issued on Stetson UK in the original sleeve (1989)]
"Just Between the Two of Us" (Capitol)(1966) [With Merle Haggard and the Strangers] [Re-issued on Stetson UK in the original sleeve (1989)]

BUCK OWENS

(Singer, Songwriter, Guitar, Steel Guitar, Bass, Saxophone, Trumpet)

Given Name:	**Alvin Edgar Owens, Jr.**
Date of Birth:	**August 12, 1929**
Where Born:	**Sherman, Texas**
Married:	**1. Bonnie Campbell (Bonnie Owens)(div.)**
	2. Phyllis (div.)
	3. Jana Grief (Jana Jae)(div.)
	4. Jennifer Smith
Children:	**Alan Edgar (Buddy Alan), Michael L., Johnnie D.**

The decade of American history that spans the years of the Lyndon Johnson-Richard Nixon presidencies might also be termed the Age of Buck Owens because he dominated the Country music scene in those years. Owens also brought the Bakersfield Sound to prominence in this era with his long string of hard Country, Honky-Tonk hits. His connection with Bakersfield became so prominent that it was amusingly known as "Buckersfield."

The King of Bakersfield, ***Buck Owens***

Buck Owens came from a poor but honest family of Texas sharecroppers who migrated to Mesa, Arizona, during the darker days of the Great Depression. Known as "Buck" since early childhood, he grew up with a love for Country music and a fierce yearning to better his station in life. Education didn't constitute his vehicle for advancement as he became a ninth-grade dropout, but he persisted in his musical endeavors, working a little on the KTYL Mesa radio station on the *Buck & Britt Show* and in honky tonks and bars in the Phoenix area.

At 19, he married another aspiring singer named Bonnie Campbell, and by 1950, they had two sons. Buck supplemented his income by driving a truck. In May, 1951, the Owens family moved to Bakersfield, California, where Buck found steady work in the clubs. Soon he became leader of the house band, the Schoolhouse Playboys, at a popular night spot called the Blackboard, playing saxophone and trumpet. He also worked in other bands, such as that of Bill Woods.

After a couple of years, Buck got an opportunity to do some session work for Capitol, initially playing lead guitar for Tommy Collins on his hit recording of *You Better Not Do That*, in 1954. Over the next four years, Buck picked lead guitar on many Capitol waxings produced by Ken Nelson, including those of Faron Young, Wanda Jackson, and Tommy Sands. He also did some work at Lewis Talley's studio in Bakersfield, including Terry Fell's *Don't Drop It* and *Truck Driving Man* for the RCA subsidiary "X," also in 1954.

Buck cut 10 sides at Talley's for the Pep label, two of which came out under the name Corky Jones. The numbers included two of his early classics, *Sweethearts in Heaven* and *Down on the Corner of Love*. After fearing that Columbia might be about to sign him, Ken Nelson of Capitol contracted Buck in February, 1957, while he was working a session with the Farmer Boys (Bobby Adamson and Woody Murray).

His first Capitol sides cut that August produced nothing of consequence, but his fourth release, *Second Fiddle*, made the Top 5, as did the next four, *Under Your Spell Again* (1959), *Above and Beyond, Excuse Me (I Think I've Got a Heartache)* (all 1960) and *Foolin' Around* (1961).

For a brief period at the beginning of the 60's, Buck moved his base of operations to Tacoma, Washington, where he did local TV and met Don Rich (Donald Eugene Ulrich), who would become a close friend and key member of his band, the Buckaroos. This group would also come to include Tom Brumley on steel, Doyle Holly on bass and Willie Cantu on drums. Capitol teamed Buck briefly with songstress Rose Maddox in 1961 and they turned out a double-sided hit with *Mental Cruelty* (Top 10) and *Loose Talk* (Top 5).

Meanwhile, Buck returned to Bakersfield and continued to turn out the hits. *Under the Influence of Love* made the Top 3 late in 1961, and in 1962, *Nobody's Fool but Yours* and *Save the Last Dance for Me* just failed to make the Top 10, but *Kickin' Our Hearts Around* crashed the Top 10, with the flip-side, *I Can't Stop (My Lovin' You)*, going Top 20. Buck wrapped up the year with the Top 10 *You're for Me*.

Then in June 1963 one of the few songs that Buck didn't write, *Act Naturally* (by Johnny Russell and Voni Morrison), hit the top of the Country chart and remained there for a month. He closed out the year with another duet with Rose Maddox, *We're the Talk of the Town/Sweethearts in Heaven*, which went Top 20. His solo hit *Love's Gonna Live Here* did even better, remaining No.1 from October into the following February.

A string of No.1 hits through 1964 and 1965 kept Owens constantly in the Country music limelight: *My Heart Skips a Beat* (7 weeks at the top), *Together Again* and *I Don't Care (Just as Long as You Love Me)* (at the top for 6 weeks)(all 1964) and *I've Got a Tiger by the Tail* (also a Pop Top 25 hit), *Before You Go, Only You (Can Break My Heart)*(all 1965). The flip-side of the last, *Gonna Have Love*, also made the Top 10. From *Buckaroo* in 1965 until *Ain't it Amazing, Gracie*, all Buck's solo hits were credited to "Buck Owens & the Buckaroos." *Buckaroo*, an instrumental, also went to No.1. In 1965, the ACM named Buck "Male Vocalist of the Year." In addition, the Buckaroos became "Touring Band of the Year," an honor they were to receive from 1965 to 1968.

By the mid-60's, Buck had already reached a level of Country music success matched by very few. Through 1966 and 1967, he continued a string of No.1 singles. It started with *Waitin' in Your Welfare Line* (7 weeks at No.1) and was followed by *Think of Me* (6 weeks at No.1) and *Open up Your Heart* (4 weeks at the top)(all 1966) and *Where Does the Good Times Go* (4 weeks at No.1), *Sam's Place* (3 weeks at the top) and *Your Tender Loving Care* (all 1967). He shut out the year with the Top 3 *It Takes People Like You (to Make People Like Me)*.

On March 25, 1966, Buck played to a sell-out crowd at New York City's Carnegie Hall (recorded on a live album for Capitol). By that time, according to the *Saturday Evening Post*, he commanded a nightly fee of $2,500, an amount equaled only by Johnny Cash and Roger Miller at that time. He also appeared in a couple of films, *Country Music on Broadway* (1962) and *Buck Owens on Tour* (1967). The same year of his Carnegie Hall concert, Buck also started his syndicated *Buck Owens Ranch TV Show*. In addition to himself and the Buckaroos, his older son appeared regularly as Buddy Alan along with the Hager Twins and such girl vocalists as Cheryl Poole, Kenni Huskey and especially Susan Raye. West Virginia vocalist Mayf Nutter and Floridian Tony Booth also worked as regulars for a time. Buck kept the show in production until 1973, eventually turning out 400 half-hour programs. In 1967 and 1968, the Buckaroos were named the CMA's "Instrumental Group of the Year." Also in 1967, MCN named them "Band of the Year" and repeated the award in 1968, 1969 and 1970 and then again in 1974.

In the meantime, Ken Nelson continued to churn out Owens' hits at the Capitol Tower. In 1968, Buck opened his account with the No.1 *How Long Will My Baby Be Gone* and followed with the Top 3 *Sweet Rosie Jones*. He then had a Top 10 duet with his son, Buddy Alan, titled *Let the World Keep on a Turnin'*. Buck finished the year with the Top 5 *I've Got You on My Mind Again*. In addition, the Buckaroos chalked up two hits of their own, *I'm Coming Back Home to Stay* (Top 40) and *I'm Goin' Back Home Where I Belong* (Top 50).

Buck's first three singles of the last year of the decade, *Who's Gonna Mow Your Grass*, Chuck Berry's *Johnny B. Goode* and *Tall Dark Stranger*, went to No.1. Buck closed out the year with the Top 5 *Big in Vegas*. In addition, the Buckaroos had a Top 50 hit in *Nobody but You*, credited to Don Rich and the Buckaroos.

By the time of *Big in Vegas*, Buck Owens had also become big at CBS television as the co-star of *Hee Haw*. This program made the Bakersfield King an even bigger star although it eventually sapped his capacity to turn out top quality Honky-Tonk hits. Buck started out 1970 with two Top 15 duets with Susan Raye, *We're Gonna Get Together* and *Togetherness*. Buck then continued with the Top 3 *The Kansas City Song*. This was followed by another Owens-Raye duet, the Top 10 *The Great White Horse*. Buck wrapped up the year with the Top 10 *I Wouldn't Live in New York City (If They Gave Me the Whole Dang Town)*.

During 1971, Buck's hits were *Bridge Over Troubled Water* (Top 10) and his two Bluegrass hits, *Ruby (Are You Mad)* and *Rollin' in My Sweet Baby's Arms*. He ended the year with another duet with his son, *Too Old to Cut the Mustard*, as Buck & Buddy, which went Top 30. The following year, he scored with *I'll Still Be Waiting for You* (Top 10), *Made in Japan* (No.1) and another Top 15 duet with Susan Raye, *Looking Back to See*. He followed up with the Top 15 *You Ain't Gonna Have Ol' Buck to Kick Around No More*.

Over the next two years, Buck's principal hits were *Ain't It Amazing, Gracie* (Top 15) and *Big Game Hunter* (Top 10)(both 1973) and a spoof of the Dr. Hook hit, *Cover of "Rolling Stone"* entitled *On the Cover of the Music City News* (Top 10), the children's Halloween favorite *Monsters' Holiday* (Top 10) and *Great Expectations* (Top 10)(all 1974). 1975 was Buck's last year with Capitol and he had Top 20 hits with *41st Street Lonely Hearts' Club* and a final duet with Susan Raye, *Love Is Strange*.

The success and exposure of *Hee Haw*, first on the network and then in syndication, meant that Buck didn't have to concentrate on turning out hit records. He had invested his money wisely and didn't really have to struggle for success at all, having a management company with his manager, Jack McFadden, and music publishing interests. Furthermore, the death of Don Rich in a July 1974 motorcycle accident also took a lot of the fire out of Buck. As he later said, "From the day of Don's death, I went through the paces...things were over at that time for me."

From 1976, Buck recorded for Warner Brothers; his first sessions were in Nashville. Most were modest mid and lower level chart entries that were not especially memorable. His most successful efforts were *Nights Are Forever Without You* (1978), *Play Together Again Again* (1979, with Emmylou Harris) and *Let Jesse Rob the Train* (1979).

After 1981, Buck's name disappeared from the charts for seven years. He remained with *Hee Haw* for five more years, but even before then Owens devoted more time to his business affairs and enjoying life. His only recordings in that era came in the series of albums he recorded as part of the Hee Haw Gospel Quartet. He had remarried in 1979 and longed for a more quiet existence. As he told Country music scholar Rich Kienzle, "I spent a lot of...time...doin' things that I wanted to do." In 1980, *Music City News* presented Buck with the "Founders Award."

In 1988, the man who had referred to himself in one of his songs as "Ol' Buck" resurfaced in duet with neo-traditional Honky-Tonk acolyte Dwight Yoakam. Their *Streets of Bakersfield* reached No.1 in October 1988 and was named MCN's 1989 "Vocal Collaboration of the Year." In 1988, Buck had been presented with the ACM's "Pioneer Award." In the meantime, he re-signed with Capitol and cut a new album of which the title song, *Hot Dog*, had been one of his Rockabilly Pop singles as Corky Jones in 1956. Although it only peaked in the Top 50, it showed that Owens could still cut the mustard, as did his duet with former Beatle Ringo Starr on *Act Naturally* in 1989, which went Top 30. That same year, Buck appeared on a *Hee Haw* 20th anniversary special, and made a welcome return to England, where he appeared at the Wembley Festival. As Buck approaches the retirement age for normal folks, he can sing when he wants. His small business empire includes four radio stations, KUZZ-TV in Bakersfield, and two community newspapers. He can also look back on a career that shows what one can accomplish with talent and determination. His position as a major factor upon the music of his generation is assured. IMT

RECOMMENDED ALBUMS:

"Buck Owens" (LaBrea)(1961) [Pep masters][Much of this material was also released in various forms on Starday albums]
"Buck Owens Sings Harlan Howard" (Capitol)(1961)
"Buck Owens Sings Tommy Collins" (Capitol)(1963)
"The Best of Buck Owens" (Capitol)(1964)
"I've Got a Tiger By the Tail" (Capitol)(1965)
"The Instrumental Hits" (Capitol)(1965)
"Dust on Mother's Bible" (Capitol ST)(1966)
"Carnegie Hall Concert" (Capitol)(1966) [Re-issued with additional tracks in 1988 as "Live at Carnegie Hall" (Country Music Foundation)]
"Buck Owens...In Japan" (Capitol)(1967)
"The Best of Buck Owens, Vol. 2" (Capitol)(1968)
"Buck Owens, the Guitar Player" (Capitol)(1968)
"Best of Buck Owens, Vol. 3" (Capitol)(1969)
"Buck Owens in London" (Capitol)(1969)
"Best of Buck Owens, Vol. 4" (Capitol)(1971)
"Too Old to Cut the Mustard" (Capitol)(1972) [With Buddy Alan]
"Buck Owens Live at the Nugget" (Capitol)(1972)
"Best of Buck Owens and Susan Raye" (Capitol)(1972)
"Buck Owens Live at the White House" (Capitol)(1972)
"Best of Buck Owens, Vol. 5" (Capitol)(1974)
"(It's a) Monster's Holiday" (Capitol)(1974)
"Best of Buck Owens, Vol. 6" (Capitol)(1976)
"Buck 'Em" (Warner Brothers)(1976)
"Our Old Mansion" (Warner Brothers)(1977)
"Hot Dog" (Capitol)(1988)
"Act Naturally" (Capitol)(1989)
"The Buck Owens Collection, 1959-1990" (Rhino)(1993) [Three cd box set, mostly from Capitol masters]
"Buck Owens Live in Scandinavia" (Capitol 1970)
"Buck Owens Show in Japan" (Capitol)(1974)

"Buck Owens Live in New Zealand" (Capitol)(1974)
"Buck Owens Live at the Sydney Opera House" (Capitol)(1974)
[The four above albums not released in U.S.A.]
(See also Hee Haw Gospel Quartet, Buddy Alan)

Jim Owens & Associates refer CROOK AND CHASE

TEX OWENS

(Singer, Songwriter, Guitar)

Given Name:	**Doye Owens**
Date of Birth:	**June 15, 1892**
Where Born:	**Killeen, Texas**
Married:	**Maude J.**
Children:	**Laura Lee (dec'd.), Dolpha Jane**
Date of Death:	**September 9, 1962**

Tex Owens, the Original Texas Ranger, came to fame as the writer of Eddy Arnold's No.1 hit, *The Cattle Call.* It was a song that he wrote from experience. He was a former cowboy who was at home on the ranch and had worked for the King Ranch. He wrote the song, in 1934, while in the Pickwick Hotel in Kansas City, Missouri, just prior to broadcasting on KMBC. As it started to snow it made Tex recall the days that he had fed cattle while still a young man, and within 30 minutes, he had written the song.

Like his father, Tex, the youngest of 12, had led a nomadic existence. Before becoming a performer, Tex worked as a Deputy Sheriff in Lamar, Colorado, and an automobile mechanic. During his long career, Tex was featured on *Red Horse Ranch*, on the CBS radio affiliate KMBC out of Kansas City, Missouri. Tex was backed by a quartet called the Texas Rangers. During the 30's, he made some appearances with the Beverly Hill Billies.

Tex was a great lover of the outdoors and indulged in fishing, hunting and traveling whenever he had the opportunity. While filming *Red River* with John Wayne in 1948, Tex, who was leading the posse, had his horse fall and he broke his shoulder. He never fully recovered from this.

Among Tex Owens' other more memorable songs were *Pride of the Prairie* and *Prairie Dream Boat.* He died from a heart attack, in 1962. A year later, his sister, Texas Ruby, was killed in a trailer home fire.

Tex's daughters, Laura Lee McBride (1920-1989) and Dolpha Jane, sang as a duo on Tex's KMBC show. Laura Lee then went on to form her own group, Laura Lee and her Ranger Buddies. In 1943, she joined Bob Wills' Texas Playboys for a short while.

RECOMMENDED ALBUMS:

None of his exist, but he can be heard, with his Texas Ramblers, on:
"The 50-Year History of Country Music" (MCA) [Various artists; Tex sings "Pride of the Prairie"]
"Cowboy Image" (MCA) [Various Artists, Tex sings "Cattle Call"]
"Those Authentic 'Beverly Hillbillies' Starring Ezra Paulette" (Rambler) [Tex sings "Prairie Dream Boat"]
"Those Authentic Beverly Hillbillies" (Rambler) [Tex sings "Cattle Call," just with guitar]

VERNON OXFORD

(Singer, Songwriter, Guitar, Fiddle)

Given Name:	**Vernon Paul Oxford**
Date of Birth:	**June 8, 1941**
Where Born:	**Larue, Arkansas**
Married:	**Loretta Robertson**
Children:	**Michael, David**

Vernon Oxford burst upon the Country scene in the mid-60's as the epitome of hard Country tradition at a time when the Nashville Sound approached its heyday.

Born near Rogers, Arkansas, Vernon Oxford's entire family took an interest in Country music and sang or played some type of instrument, especially his father, who had some reputation as an Old-Time fiddler. In the early 50's, the Oxfords relocated to Wichita, Kansas, where Vernon learned fiddle, guitar and Honky-Tonk style Country singing. About 1960, he landed a six month club engagement in Utah, and upon returning to Kansas continued working at night clubs and for square dances. In March, 1962, Oxford married Loretta Robertson, an Oklahoma girl he had met the previous year.

In May 1964, Vernon came to Nashville in hopes of pursuing a full-time Country career. Initially the young Arkansan found Music City more interested in folks whose vocals seemed more in tune with the Nashville Sound rather than his unabashed Country approach. However, with some help from songwriter Harlan Howard, he finally landed a contract with RCA Victor, holding his first session on December 17, 1965. Over the next couple of years, seven singles and an album came off the presses, all praised by traditionalists, but none registering as hits. RCA dropped him and after a pair of singles on Stop his career seemed headed downhill, but then the British fans discovered Vernon. They soon persuaded RCA to release a double album in the United Kingdom and fans arranged a tour in 1974.

Shortly afterward, RCA Victor signed Oxford to a new contract. This time, he enjoyed some chart success in the U.S. *Shadows of My Mind* went Top 60 in the winter of 1975-1976 and it had a 12 week stay. In 1976, Vernon followed with the basement chart entry *Your Wanting Me Is Gone,* and then *Redneck (the Redneck National Anthem)* became a genuine hit, reaching the Top 20. He ended the year with the Top 60 *Clean Your Own Tables.* During 1977, Vernon had three chart entries, with the Top 60 *A Good Old Fashioned Saturday Night Honky Tonk Barroom Brawl* being the most successful.

In Britain, fans really appreciated his down home touch on songs like *I've Got to Get Peter off Your Mind* and *Field of Flowers.* After 1977, Vernon no longer made the charts and RCA released him again. Rounder Records picked him up and cut four albums in the next five years. Rich-R-Tone did another one consisting primarily of songs composed by one-time *Music City News* editor Everett Corbin.

About 1981, Vernon Oxford had a conversion experience, reflected in his third Rounder album ***A Better Way of Life.*** Thereafter, he did a fair amount of Gospel singing and even preached a bit from time to time. Still quite popular in Europe, Vernon appeared at the 1987 Wembley Festival in England. He reports that in recent years, he has made several junkets abroad and last guested on the *Opry* in 1993. He has material from recent record sessions which he hopes will soon appear on the American market. Meanwhile, his latest release in Europe, a 1992 cd on the Swiss label Montana Country, is reportedly doing well on the Continent.IMT

RECOMMENDED ALBUMS:

"Woman, Let Me Sing You a Song" (RCA Victor)(1967)
"If I Had My Wife to Love Over" (Rounder)(1979)
"His and Hers" (Rounder)(1980)
"A Better Way of Life" (Rounder)(1981)
"America's Unknown Super Star" (Rich-R-Tone)(ca. 1981)
"Keepin' it Country" (Rounder)(1982)
"20 of the Best" (RCA UK)(1984)
"100% Country" (Montana Country Switzerland)(1992)

OZARK JUBILEE, The (a.k.a. JUBILEE USA and COUNTRY MUSIC JUBILEE)

(TV show, ABC-TV)

Although it had a shorter history than some other significant jamboree-type shows, the *Ozark Jubilee* was the first to make it in prime-time TV. Former *Grand Ole Opry* favorite Red Foley held center stage at the Springfield, Missouri-based show which provided a springboard for such future Country stars as Brenda Lee and Porter Wagoner. The show also boasted groups like the Foggy River Boys and comedy by the likes of Uncle Cyp and Aunt Sap Brasfield (actually Mr. and Mrs. Lawrence L. "Boob" Brasfield).

The *Ozark Jubilee* was the brainchild of

Ely E. "Si" Siman (b. 1921), a promoter associated with KWTO radio in Springfield. He started it as a local TV show at KYTV in December 1953 and got the Jubilee on ABC network radio on July 17, 1954. Siman's goal was to sell the program to ABC-TV and he managed to do so by luring Red Foley away from Nashville. The logistics of transmitting a network television program from the somewhat remote Springfield proved something of a problem, but eventually the show debuted at 9:00 pm EST on January 12, 1955.

Although the Jubilee never became a high-rated hit show, it did attract a wide audience and cost less than most. In addition to the aforementioned acts, those who gained prominence on the program for more than one season included Bobby Lord, Slim Wilson's band, Wanda Jackson, and the Tall Timber Trio. Those with shorter tenures included comedian Pete Stamper, Marvin Rainwater, Norma Jean (Beasler), Billy Walker, Suzi Arden, Leroy Van Dyke, Jean Shepard, Hawkshaw Hawkins and Lew Childre.

Usually ABC carried an hour of the show, which originated in Springfield's Jewell Theater, although from July 1955 to September 1956, it ran for 90 minutes, and in the summer of 1957, only a half-hour was seen and heard. The hour varied during the nearly six years that the program flourished. It ended somewhat abruptly in September 1960 as a result of star Red Foley's problems with the IRS. After his acquittal in a second trial for tax fraud, the "Old Redhead" resurfaced in a character role in a shortlived situation comedy, *Mr. Smith Goes to Washington*. In retrospect, while the *Ozark Jubilee* hardly compares with the major radio jamboree in terms of longevity, the show stands as the first major Country music television program. Also, rightly or wrongly, some have seen in the Jubilee the roots of the recent Country music tourist boom in Branson, Missouri. IMT

OZARK MOUNTAIN DAREDEVILS

When Formed:	**1971**
Original Members:	
Steve Cash	**Harmonica, Vocals**
John Dillon	**Guitar, Vocal, Keyboards**
Larry Lee	**Guitar, Drums, Keyboards**
Mike "Supe" Granda	**Bass Guitar, Vocals**
Later Members:	
Randle Chowning	**Vocals, Guitar, Harmonica (left 1976)**
Buddy Brayfield	**Keyboards, Oboe, Vocals (left 1976)**
Steve Canady	**Drums, Guitar, Vocals (joined 1975)**
Rune Walle	**Guitar, Vocals, Banjo (joined 1976)**
Russell Chappell	**Keyboards, Vocals (joined 1978)**
Jerry Mills	**Mandolin (joined 1978)**
D. Clinton Thompson	**Guitar**

In the mid and late 70's, the Ozark Mountain Daredevils attracted a lot of attention as one of the foremost Country-Rock bands around. Based in Springfield, Missouri, they always homed back to nearby Arkansas. Unlike other Country-Rock bands based on the West Coast, the Daredevils never used the talents of fellow "stars" in the genre, but have a steady flow of musicians to boost the nucleus of Cash, Dillon, Lee and Granda.

Steve Cash was raised in Springfield and his early interests were baseball and writing poetry and short stories. He began songwriting and played in local bands until he met John Dillon and Larry Lee. Dillon was brought up on a farm in Stuttgart, Arkansas. His mother, who played harmonica, instilled in him a love for Country music and Delta Blues. She then bought him a guitar. He started listening to Country-Rock and in particular, Ronnie Hawkins. In 1965, he enrolled in Drury College in Springfield, where he majored in philosophy and theater. During his second year, he started writing songs and after graduation, moved to Nashville. He got signed to a management deal and then got ripped off by his manager and moved back to Springfield, where he worked as a session musician.

Larry Lee also grew up in Springfield, and then attended Southwest Missouri State University. In 1965, he enlisted in the U.S. Navy. He trained as a postal clerk at Bainbridge, Maryland and then was stationed in Puerto Rico, where he formed a band named Trilogy that played on the base. He began to write songs and after his discharge from the service, he played with a band called Granny's Bathwater, until he joined the Daredevils in 1971.

It was while Steve was sessioning that he met Larry and Steve and they formed a band, the Emergency Band, with John's wife. The group went under various names including Buffalo Chips, Burlap Socks and Family Tree, before settling on Ozark Mountain Daredevils. Supe Granda now joined the band full-time, after being in and out of the group for some time. He was born in St. Louis and educated at Southwest Missouri State. He learned to play guitar while still young and also played with various local bands.

The band originally approached Columbia and the legendary John Hammond, Sr., was getting ready to sign them, when it was discovered that they had no management, legal representative or agent, and so matters did not proceed. The Daredevils' newly acquired manager, Steve Plesser, sent a demo tape to famed Rock producer/engineer Glyn Johns, who was sufficiently interested to take the tape to David Anderle at A & M Records. Anderle signed the group and Johns and Anderle acted as producers. By now, Randle Chowning had joined on vocals, guitar and harmonica and Buddy Brayfield had come in on keyboards. They traveled to Olympic Studios in London, England and recorded their debut eponymous album which was released in 1973. From this album came the 1974 Top 30 Pop hit *If You Wanna Get to Heaven*. That year, the Daredevils released their second album, ***It'll Shine When It Shines***. This album yielded their 1975 Top 3 Pop hit, *Jackie Blue*, which was written by Larry and Steve.

Their third album, ***The Car Over the Lake Album,*** was released in 1975 and yielded the Top 70 single *If I Only Knew*, in 1976. The guest players on the album included Weldon Myrick and Nancy Blake. In 1975, Steve Canady joined the band on drums, guitar and vocals. Canady had received a drum kit from his father when still a boy. His hero was Elvis Presley and by 1958, he was playing in his first Rock band. He played in various bands until he started playing at the New Bijou Theatre in Springfield. Larry had been a bartender there, and Steve, Supe and John had all played in a band at the venue. The club eventually burned down. Canaby had helped the others initially by playing on their demo for A & M.

In 1976, Buddy Brayfield left and Jerry Mills came on board. He had worked as a deejay on KFML-FM in Denver and had played with the Nitty Gritty Dirt Band, Michael (Martin) Murphey and Mason Williams. That year, the band released a new album, ***Men from Earth,*** and this yielded the Country minor hit *You Made It Right*. When Randle Chowning left the group during the recording of the album, Rune Walle came in on guitar. He had played in the Flying Norwegians, who had opened for the Daredevils during their European tour.

During 1977, the band released their album ***Don't Look Now***, and Cash and Dillon were featured artists on the Paul Kennerley record concept project ***White Mansions***. The Daredevils also had a Top 75 Pop hit with *You Know Like I Know*.

The following year, OMD released their

last album for A & M, a live double-album project, ***It's Alive***. This album introduced a new keyboard player, Russell Chapman. As the Daredevils got ready to leave A & M and join Columbia, Larry Lee left to start a solo career. Now OMD released the 1980 self-titled album for the label. The album produced a Top 70 Pop hit, *Take You Tonight*. Larry Lee, who now also signed to Columbia, as a solo act, had a minor hit in 1982, with *Don't Talk*. He subsequently became a record producer in Nashville, as Larry Michael Lee.

After nearly a decade of recording silence, the Daredevils emerged with the 1989 album ***Modern History***, which was produced by Wendy Waldman. The group continues as a five-piece band with Canady, Granda, Cash, Dillon and Thompson. Their blend of Country, rock'n'roll and Appalachia sounds better in the 90's than it has done for some while.

RECOMMENDED ALBUMS:
"Ozark Mountain Daredevils" (A & M)(1973)
"It'll Shine When it Shines" (A & M)(1974)
"The Car Over the Lake Album" (A & M)(1975)
"Man from Earth" (A & M)(1976)
"Don't Look Down" (A & M)(1977)
"It's Alive" (double) (A & M)(1978)
"Ozark Mountain Daredevils" (Columbia)(1980)
"Modern History" (Conifer Request)(1989)

P

PATTI PAGE

(Singer, Actress)

Given Name:	**Clara Ann Fowler**
Date of Birth:	**November 8, 1927**
Where Born:	**Muskogee, Oklahoma**
Married:	**1. Charles O'Curran (div.)**
	2. Jerry Filiciotto
Children:	**two**

For nearly 30 years, from the late 40's through the early 80's, Patti Page's name appeared on the Country and/or the Pop charts. Known as the "singing rage," Patti will forever be associated with her cross-over version of *The Tennessee Waltz*.

Patti was raised in Tulsa, Oklahoma, one of 11 children. She first sang in church with her seven sisters. Following WWII, she and her sisters Ruby and Rema formed the Fowler Sisters. However, Patti really wanted to be a painter. She was adept enough to win an art scholarship, during the mid-40's, but as Ann Fowler, she was also offered a singing job with Al Klauser & his Oklahomans on KTUL Tulsa; she opted for the latter. The station had scheduled a program that was sponsored by the Page Milk Company called *Meet Patti Page*. However, the selected singer decided not to continue with the show and so Ann Fowler became Patti Page and her music career got under way.

In 1947, band leader Jack Rael persuaded her to leave the station, where she was earning $125 a week, to join the Jimmy Joy Band in Chicago at $75 a week. Although the job only lasted for six weeks, Rael helped her get a recording contract with Mercury that year. In 1948, Patti had a Top 15 hit with *Confess*, which was notable for its double-tracking and which was credited to "Patti Page and Patti Page." She followed that with a duet with Vic Damone entitled *Say Something Sweet to Your Sweetheart*. During the year, Patti appeared with Jack Rael's cousin, Benny Goodman. She then became a regular on Don McNeill's *Breakfast Club* on ABC network radio from Chicago.

In 1949, she charted with *So in Love*, *Money, Marbles and Chalk* (Top 30 and also Top 15 on the Country chart) and *I'll Keep the Lovelight Burning*. The following year, Patti had her first million-selling single, *With My Eyes Wide Open* (which was credited to "The Patti Page Quintet") which was followed by the Top 10 *I Don't Care if the Sun Don't Shine*. She then had her first No.1 Pop hit, *All My Love*.

Then in 1951 came *The Tennessee Waltz*. Patti's multi-tracked version actually predated that of Les Paul & Mary Ford. Patti's single went to No.1 on the Pop chart, where it stayed for 13 weeks. It also crossed to the Country Top 3 and was Certified Gold. This was followed by *Mockin' Bird Hill*.

Patti continued with *Down the Trail of Achin' Hearts* and *I Went to Your Wedding*, and in 1953, she had a No.1 with the novelty song *How Much is that Doggie in the Window*. In 1954, she had a big hit with *Let Me Go Lover!* Patti's other major Pop hits during the 50's were: *Croce Di Oro (Cross of Gold)* (Top 20, 1955), *Go on with the Wedding* (Top 15), *Allegheny Moon* (Top 3) and *Mama from the Train* (Top 15) (all 1956), *A Poor Man's Roses (Or a Rich Man's Gold)* (Top 15), *Old Cape Cod* (Top 3)/*Wondering* (Top 15) and *I'll Remember Today* (Top 25) (all 1957), *Belonging to Someone* (Top 15), *Another Time, Another Place* (Top 20) and *Left Right Out of Your Heart (Hi Lee Hi Lo Hi Lup Up Up)* (Top 10) (all 1958).

In 1955 through 1958, Patti, who is naturally a shy person, came over very well on TV and had her own TV series, the *Patti Page Show*, and from 1957 to 1958, she hosted the TV series *The Big Record*. In 1960, Patti appeared in the award-winning movie *Elmer Gantry* as a psalm singer.

Mercury remained Patti's label until 1962, during which time her most successful singles were on the Country charts and were *Mom and Dad's Waltz* (Top 25, 1961) and *Go on Home* (Top 15, 1962). Patti also had a Top 30 Pop hit, *More People Get Married*, in 1962. At the end of that year, Patti moved to Columbia Records, but she didn't have a sizable hit until 1965, when *Hush, Hush Sweet Charlotte*, from the movie of the same name (although not sung by her in the movie), became a Pop Top 10 hit.

By 1969, Patti had ceased to chart on the Pop lists and her next success was the Country Top 25 record *I Wish I Had a Mommy Like You*. At the end of 1970, Patti returned to Mercury, where she stayed until 1972. Her major hits there were: *Give Him Love* (Top 25) and *Make Me Your Kind of Woman* and *Think Again/A Woman Left Lonely* (all Top 40, 1971) and *Hello We're Lonely*, a duet with Tom T. Hall, which went Top 15 in 1973.

Patti moved on to Epic in 1973, where she had three hits, the most successful being the Top 30 *You're Gonna Hurt Me (One More Time)*. At the end of 1974, Patti moved to Avco, but her two chart successes were only minor ones. In 1979, Patti was presented with a "Pioneer Award" by the ACM. Then in 1981, Patti joined Plantation Records, and that year, she had her last major success with the Top 40 *No Aces*. That year, Patti was given an

Meet ***Patti Page***

Honorary Degree in Art from the University of Oklahoma, just prior to her mother's death, thus ensuring that her mom had one child that finished college.

In 1983, Patti co-hosted the opening of TNN, with Roy Acuff. Patti has written her autobiography, *Once Upon a Time*, which is now out of print. Patti Page has been inducted into the Oklahoma Hall of Fame. She is known for her loyalty to those she works with and her management agreement with Jack Rael was still in operation after 46 years. Patti still plays the music rooms in Reno and Atlantic City and she was still recording for Plantation into the 90's.

RECOMMENDED ALBUMS:

"Indiscretion" (Mercury)
"Three Little Words" (Mercury)
"Just a Closer Walk with Thee" (Mercury)(1956)
"What a Dream" (Heritage Sound)(1983)

STU PAGE

(Singer, Songwriter, Guitar, Fiddle)

Given Name: Stuart Page
Date of Birth: May 12, 1954
Where Born: Leeds, England
Married: Janet Smith
Children: Andrew, Thomas

Stu Page is an Englishman who has had to fight a long hard battle to get the British Country music fans to accept his songs. Stu has a clear, melodic voice and is a gifted musician on acoustic and electric guitars and fiddle.

He was 10 years old when he got his first guitar and soon music became an important part of his life. He formed bands while in school, playing rock'n'roll. After leaving school, Stu became apprenticed to a printing firm and played music in his spare time. Stu initially played all types of music at clubs and Rock venues in the North of England and in Scotland.

Stu began to get a reputation as a good guitarist and was soon in demand as a session player. One of these sessions led to a job with a visiting U.S. group, Cheshire Country Crossroads Band, that invited him to join it in the U.S., which he did in 1973, spending a year working the North American circuit. He then joined a Soul-Pop band, the New Division, but he soon returned to the U.K., a little disillusioned.

After trying various jobs, Stu found the pull of show business drawing him back and he began playing with various semi-professional bands as a guitarist and back-up singer. With his friend Terry Clayton (bass), Stu formed a duo in 1984. Their first bookings were for seven weeks in Switzerland. Stu then decided that a band format would be better and he formed Stu Page and Remuda. Soon they became successful through Europe and the band was renamed the Stu Page Band.

Past members of the band have been Terry Clayton (bass), Pat McPartling (drums) and Tim Howard (steel guitar, mandolin and banjo). The present line-up is Andy Whelan on guitar, Bob Price on bass guitar and South African George Voros on drums. The band was voted BCMA's "Band of the Year" in 1990, 1991, 1992 and 1993.

In 1988, Stu signed to Barge and released the debut album ***Are You in Love with Me***, and the following year, he released ***Stu Page Band***. In 1990 came ***Front Page News***. All were well received. Stu recorded a single, *Everyday*, in Nashville on which Buddy Emmons played. That year, Stu appeared at Fan Fair in Nashville.

Stu toured Switzerland in 1993 and did a U.K. tour with visiting MCA recording artist James House. Stu has been working with Brendan Croker of the Notting Hillbillies doing session work and as a result Croker is to produce Stu's next album in 1994. Stu wrote all the music for a TV series on art called *Brush with Ashley* and got a deal with EMI just for these programs. JAB

RECOMMENDED ALBUMS:

(All U.K. releases)
"Are You in Love with Me" (Barge)(1988)
"Stu Page Band" (Barge)(1989)
"Front Page News" (Barge)(1990)

BOB PAISLEY

(Guitar, Mandolin, Clawhammer Banjo, Harmonica)

Given Name: James Robert Paisley
Date of Birth: March 14, 1931
Where Born: Ashe County, North Carolina
Married: Vivian O'Connor
Children: James, Jr., Michael, Daniel, Donna, Kay

Bob Paisley has led a traditional Bluegrass band since 1979 that has earned distinction for both musical quality and good taste.

A native of mountainous Ashe County, North Carolina, Bob Paisley migrated northward to southeast Pennsylvania when he was an infant, settling near the town of Landenberg. His parents played Old-Time music for their own amusement and Paisley took up harmonica and guitar while still a child. He also was influenced by various radio acts such as those heard on the *Grand Ole Opry* and recording artists like the Monroe Brothers and Blue Sky Boys. A Country group, Shorty Woods and his North Carolina Ridge Runners, also played Old-Time music in the region.

When Bob entered military service, he played music with other country boys in Georgia and Alabama. After he left the service, Bob returned to Pennsylvania and settled back near Landenberg, where he married, raised a family and found employment as a chemist. After some years, Paisley renewed his musical interests and joined a part-time Country band based in nearby Wilmington, Delaware.

When Bob met Ted Lundy, a banjo picker transplanted from Galax, Virginia, and a veteran of Alex Campbell and Ole Belle's New River Boys, the two soon joined with others about 1964 to form the Southern Mountain Boys. Between 1973 and 1978, the Southern Mountain Boys cut four albums, the latter three for Rounder. On the last two, Bob received credit as co-leader.

Bob played with this band for about fifteen years, and then in 1979 he had a series of hip ailments which sidelined him for a time and left him walking with a cane after recovery. Rebounding from his temporary infirmity, Bob reorganized the old group as the Southern Grass, with his son Dan and Jerry Lundy, who had been in the old band and started anew. They gained a following fairly quickly on the festival circuit and recorded an album for Rounder with new band members LeRoy Mumma, Dick Staber, Randy Steward, and Earl Yager.

In October 1981 they cut a second album with slight changes in personnel. The following spring the Southern Grass made their first European tour, which included six countries and a live album for Strictly Country Records, cut in the Netherlands on March 31, 1982. Over the next decade, Paisley took a band to Europe four more times and in 1986 to Japan as well.

Meanwhile, Bob Paisley and the Southern Grass continued as a popular band at Bluegrass festivals. The group went through some personnel changes which included Randall Boring, Steve Huber and Richard Underwood on banjo, Joe Allison on mandolin and Jack Leiderman on mandolin and fiddle and Mike Paisley on bass fiddle. The band recorded albums for Mountain Laurel in 1985 and 1988 and a cd for Brandywine in 1992.

Southern Grass' current line-up consists of sons Dan and Mike, Leiderman and Underwood. IMT

RECOMMENDED ALBUMS:

"Bob Paisley and Southern Grass" (Rounder)(1981)
"An Old Love Affair" (Brandywine)(1982)
"Pickin' in Holland" (Strictly Country)(1983)
"I Still Love You Yet" (Mountain Laurel)(1985)
"Home of Light and Love" (Mountain Laurel)(1988)
"No Vacancy" (Brandywine)(1992)
(See also Ted Lundy)

PARKER FAMILY, The
(a.k.a. REX AND ELEANOR PARKER)

When Formed: 1941

REX PARKER

(Vocals, Mandolin, Guitar, Other String Instruments)

Given Name: Charles Parker
Date of Birth: September 21, 1921
Where Born: Maplewood, West Virginia

ELEANOR PARKER

(Vocals, Guitar)

Given Name: Eleanora D. Niera
Date of Birth: February 28, 1922
Where Born: Beard's Fork, West Virginia
Children: Conizene ("Goff"), Charles Clarence, Rexana Delleen ("Champ"), Ola Marcina (dec'd.)

The husband-wife team of Rex and Eleanor Parker has spent virtually their entire professional career based in their native southern West Virginia playing their traditional brand of Country and Gospel music. By 1992, the Parkers had been regularly appearing on the airwaves of southern West Virginia for more than a half century.

Both Parkers hailed from the coal camps of southern West Virginia. Rex came from traditional Appalachian stock while Eleanor's parents were recent immigrants from Barcelona, Spain. The two met at elementary school in Layland, West Virginia and fell in love before they completed grade school. However, Eleanor went to New York City and lived with an older sister. After graduating from William Cullen Bryant High School in 1941, she returned to West Virginia, where she and Rex were reunited and married in Beckley on August 31, 1941, as part of a stage show put together by Lynn Davis.

Rex, who had learned guitar at the age of 10, went on to master other stringed instruments, especially mandolin. He had worked with a variety of Country radio groups at both WCHS Charleston and WJLS Beckley while Eleanor had been in New York. Originally nicknamed "Curley" Parker, he took the name "Rex" while in a duo with a musician known as Tex McGuire. This also prevented any confusion with a noted fiddler known as Curley Parker.

On September 1, 1941, Rex and Eleanor began their career as a team with a daily program at WHIS Bluefield, where they replaced the popular duo of Lee and Juanita Moore. The Parkers retained an affiliation with WHIS on either radio and/or television (beginning in 1955) for eighteen years although they sometimes had programs on other area stations as well, including those at Princeton, Welch and Oak Hill.

During WWII, when military service interrupted the careers of many musical acts, the duo played as many as five shows daily. While Rex provided the team with instrumental virtuosity, they sometimes carried other band members, with the entire aggregate known as the Merrymakers. Sometimes they shared musicians like Curly Ray Cline with the Lonesome Pine Fiddlers. Bobby Osborne and Larry Richardson also spent a brief stint with the Parkers.

As the Parker children, especially Conizene and Rexana, became old enough, they joined their parents, singing on stage. From 1959, the Parkers, who had recently had religious conversion experiences, now played sacred music almost exclusively.

Neither Rex and Eleanor nor the extended Parker Family were ever adequately captured on record to best advantage. Their earliest discs were on the Cozy label in the late 40's, but they lacked adequate distribution. However, they did include their best original numbers, *Build Your Treasures in Heaven* and *Moonlight on West Virginia*, both published by Cozy owner John Bava. They also furnished back-up for Rev. Freddie Steele on a session.

In 1952, they cut four sides for the major label Coral, but only one single, which contained a pair of Korean War songs, was ever released. The Dobro of Shot Jackson and fiddle of Curly Ray Cline augmented their own instrumentation.

In 1959, the Parker Family began recording sacred songs in Cincinnati for King Records, turning out three albums, two of them on the firm's budget label, Audio Lab. The best cut from these later recordings was probably a fine mandolin-guitar duet rendition of *Build Your Treasures in Heaven*. Later the Parkers recorded two singles for Country Sun and a Gospel album for Joyful Sound.

Through the 60's and 70's, Rex and Eleanor had a weekly TV program at WOAY in Oak Hill, West Virginia. Daughter Conizene married, settled in Indiana and became a nurse, but Rexana continued to work often with her parents. They played some Bluegrass festivals in the mid-70's, including one appearance on Bill Monroe's Bean Blossom extravaganza, a visit to Fan Fair in 1975, and the Vandalia old-time radio reunion at Charleston in 1979. However, by the 80's, their appearances were almost all in church services and their media work a Sunday morning Gospel radio program, *Songs for Salvation* at WAEY Princeton.

The Parkers reside at their long-time home in Lerona, West Virginia. Howard Dorgan of Appalachian State University, a scholar of mountain religious practices, included a chapter on Rex and Eleanor Parker in his recent book *Airwaves of Zion*. IMT

RECOMMENDED ALBUMS:

"Songs for Salvation, Volume One" (Audio Lab)(1961)
"Songs for Salvation, Volume Two" (Audio Lab)(ca.1963)
"Just a Real Nice Family" (King)(1965)
"Songs of Salvation" (Joyful Sound)(1971)

ANDY PARKER

(Singer, Songwriter, Guitar)

Date of Birth: March 17, 1913
Where Born: Mangum, Oklahoma

Andy Parker made his radio debut at age 16, on KGMP Elk City, Oklahoma. He moved to San Francisco, where he became the singing cowboy on NBC radio's *Death Valley Days*, from 1937 to 1941. During WWII, Andy worked for a time in a defense plant, and then in 1944, he moved to Los Angeles.

By 1946, he had formed Andy Parker and the Plainsmen with Charlie Morgan (of the Morgan Family) on lead guitar, Clem Smith on standup bass, George Bamby (who had worked with Spade Cooley and went on to work with the Sons of the Pioneers) on accordion and doubling as arranger, and one of the finest steel guitar players ever, Joaquin Murphy.

They worked primarily at station KNX Hollywood. The group appeared in eight movies with Eddie Dean for PRC (see Movie Section). In 1947, the group signed to Capitol Records, but never achieved the fame of other Western harmony groups such as the Sons of the Pioneers.

In later years, Parker was plagued by a heart condition which prevented him from working and touring and he retired to San Francisco.

RECOMMENDED ALBUMS:

There is a fine set of transcriptions on Capitol Records.

BILLY PARKER

(Singer, Songwriter, Deejay, Guitar)

Given Name: Billy Joe Parker
Date of Birth: July 19, 1937
Where Born: Okemah, Oklahoma
Married: Jerri
Children: Kris, Billy Joe

Singer and Deejay ***Billy Parker***

Although Billy Parker has spent a lot of his life spinning records, he is very adept at recording his own. Although he has never charted on a major label, he has charted 21 times on independent labels, no mean feat.

Billy received his first guitar when he was 11, and within three years, he had made his professional debut on the *Big Red Jamboree* out of Tulsa. He soon became popular on the club circuit and also played other venues. He then went on to play on the *Ozark Jubilee*. In 1959, he started deejaying on KFMJ Tulsa.

By 1963, he was the regular daytime deejay on KFDI Wichita, Kansas and also did a TV show from Tulsa. Billy's principal influences are George Jones, Hank Williams, Lefty Frizzell and Ernest Tubb and this shows in his own music, which is pretty-much straight-ahead Country. During 1963, Billy released a single on Sims, entitled *The Line Between Love and Hate/I Hurt Me Instead of You*. That same year, he was named "Mr. DJ USA" and was given the honor of playing records on Nashville's WSM. While in Music City, he also appeared on Ernest Tubb's *Midnight Jamboree*, singing the Sims single.

He first recorded for a major label, in 1966, when he released *I'm Drinking All the Time/She's Just Getting Back at Me*, for Decca. Billy's first big break came in 1968, when he began playing with Ernest Tubb's Texas Troubadours, with whom he stayed for three years. His time with E.T. was remembered in 1979 and 1988, when he twice recorded *Thanks E.T., Thanks a Lot*. Decca released another single on Billy in 1969, *I'll Drink to That/The Pillow* and *Only a Woman Like You/Room Full of Fools*, and then in 1970, *I Get a Happy Feeling/If These Tears Could Talk*. Neither of these singles troubled the charts.

In 1971, Billy joined KVOO Tulsa and became Program Director in 1973. He started to collect awards in 1975, when the ACM (then the Academy of Country & Western Music) named Billy "Disc Jockey of the Year." He would collect this award again in 1977, 1978 and 1984. In addition, KVOO Tulsa was named "Radio Station of the Year" by the ACM in 1978 and 1984. He first hit the Country charts in 1976, with the Top 80 single *It's Bad When You're Caught (With the Goods)*, on Sunshine County Records. During 1977 through 1979, he charted 10 more times for the label, with the most successful singles being *You Read Between the Lines* (Top 70, 1978) and *Until the Next Time* (Top 50, 1978).

In 1981, Billy had a solitary Top 75 on the Oak label, entitled *Better Side of Thirty*, before he moved over to Soundwaves, with whom he had a further seven hits. They were *I'll Drink to That* (Top 60, 1981), *I See an Angel Every Day* (Top 60), *(Who's Gonna Sing) The Last Country Song* (Top 50), *If I Ever Need a Woman* (with harmony vocals from Darrell McCall, Top 60) (all 1982), *Who Said Love Was Fair* (Top 70) and *Love Don't Know a Lady (From a Honky Tonk Girl)* (Top 60) (both 1983). He also had a middle-placed duet with Cal Smith entitled *Too Many Irons in the Fire*, also on Soundwaves, in 1982.

He was absent from the charts from 1982 until 1988, as he concentrated on his job as Program Director at KVOO. Then he signed with Canyon Creek and had two low-placed singles, *You Are My Angel* and *She's Sittin' Pretty*. Worth noting is the 1988 single he had with label mate Rosemary Sharp, *Who You're Gonna Turn To*, which came from his Canyon Creek/RCA album, as did the solo single *You Are My Angel*, which was a Top 10 chart entry in Canada. He had his final entry, to date, in 1989, with *It's Time for Your Dreams to Come True*. In 1990, he released ***I'll Speak Out for You, Jesus***, a Gospel album on Canyon Creek. He was inducted into the Country Music Disc Jockey Hall of Fame, in 1992. Billy is now Executive Director at KVOO, assisting General Manager Mike DeMarco.

RECOMMENDED ALBUMS:

"Average Man" (Sunshine County)(1976)
"Billy Parker" (Sunshine County) (1977)
"(Who's Gonna Sing) The Last Country Song" (Soundwaves)(1982) [As by Billy Parker and Friends, features Dave Kirby, Hoot Hester, Vassar Clements, Doyle Grisham, the Cates Sisters, Karen Taylor (later Taylor-Good) and Darrell McCall]
"Something Old, Something New" (Soundwaves)(1983) [Features duets with Jack Greene, Webb Pierce, Cal Smith, Bill Carlisle, Johnny Lee Wills, Ernest Tubb and Darrell McCall, and harmonies from Jimmy Payne and Darrell McCall]
"Always Country" (Canyon Creek)(1988)
"I'll Speak Out for You, Jesus" (Canyon Creek)(1990)

BYRON PARKER

(Singer, Guitar)

Given Name:	**Byron Harry Parker**
Date of Birth:	**September 6, 1911**
Where Born:	**Hastings, Iowa**
Married:	**Ruth**
Children:	**Jimmy**
Date of Death:	**October 6, 1948**

Although Byron Parker made minimal contributions as a musician, he is fondly remembered as leader of a group known at various times as the Mountaineers and the WIS Hillbillies. As an announcer called the "Old Hired Hand," Parker had become a virtual legend as a radio salesman in the Carolinas and Georgia by the time of his early death at age 37. Musicians closely associated with Byron at one time or another included the Monroe Brothers, J.E. Mainer and the duo of Snuffy Jenkins and Homer Sherrill.

Despite his later association with mountain-style musicians, Byron Parker hailed from the broad and flat Mississippi Valley. He entered radio at KFNF Shenandoah, Iowa, as half of a sacred singing duet known as the Gospel Twins in the early 30's. In the latter part of 1934, he became an announcer at WAAW in Omaha, Nebraska, where he met the Monroe Brothers. He announced on all their programs and moved with them to the Carolinas in 1935. In addition to the emcee chores, he also began singing the bass part in their Gospel harmonies. In April, 1937, Parker left the Monroes and started his own group.

Parker's principal talent was his superb announcing and skill as pitchman or salesman. One friend contended that if Byron tried, he could have sold struck matches! He did a little performing, but mostly emceed his group and sang bass in quartets. His initial Hillbillies at WIS Columbia included J.E. Mainer, George Morris, Leonard Stokes, and Snuffy Jenkins. Eventually Mainer and Morris, and temporarily Stokes, left the band and fiddler Homer Sherrill and guitarist Clyde Robbins joined. At two separate sessions for Bluebird in 1940, the band cut a total of sixteen songs as Byron Parker's Mountaineers. Later other musicians worked in the band including Greasy Medlin, Ira Dimmery, Floyd Lacewell and Tommy Faile, but Jenkins and Sherrill always remained as the nucleus. In 1946 they recorded four more sides for DeLuxe.

Parker remained as leader of the group until 1947 when he began experiencing heart problems and his physician ordered him to stop traveling. He then worked solely as a radio announcer at WFIX Columbia until his death the following year. Snuffy Jenkins and Homer Sherrill renamed their band the Hired Hands in his honor and continued performing into the 80's. The Mountaineers' recordings from 1940, fine examples of "pre-Bluegrass," were all reissued in 1985. A song from the DeLuxe session appeared on a Rounder anthology. Furthermore, later-day Country star Bill Anderson credited the Old Hired Hand with being the major inspiration in his childhood who led "Whispering Bill" to a successful career in Country music. IMT

RECOMMENDED ALBUM:

"Bluegrass Roots" (Old Homestead) (1985)
(See also Jenkins and Sherrill)

LEE ROY PARNELL

(Singer, Songwriter, Guitar, Slide Guitar)

Given Name:	**Lee Roy Parnell**
Date of Birth:	**December 21, 1956**

Where Born: Stephenville, Texas
Married: Kim
Children: Blake, Allison

Lee Roy Parnell is a master of the slide guitar who plays and sings Country music with a touch of the Blues. He has always been intrigued with roots music and is a fan of Merle Haggard, whom he considers to be different from anyone else he has ever heard.

Lee Roy grew up on his parents' ranch listening to Bob Wills (a friend of his father, who was a blackface comedian and traveled with a medicine show). At age 6, Lee Roy sang *San Antonio Rose* with Bob Wills on WBAP radio in Fort Worth and knew that he wanted a career in music. Lee Roy was exposed to music at an early age and his mother, Anna Belle, majored in voice at Texas Tech. He remembers the time when his dad bought him a $17 guitar and stopped by Bob Wills' house on the way back, to show off his new acquisition to Bob, who felt the neck and gave an approving nod. Even now, Bob is still one of Lee Roy's heroes.

He began playing drums in a band, but they really needed a guitar player, so Lee Roy soon mastered the instrument. He went with his dad to the honky tonks in Fort Worth. After high school, Lee Roy based himself in Austin and went on the road. For twelve years, he played the honky tonks and bars. After he married, he did a stint of selling ads on a radio station, because money was tight.

In the early 1970's, Lee Roy had made an unsuccessful trip to Nashville and returned to Austin, but in 1987, he returned determined to succeed. After an introduction to Welk Music (now Polygram Music) by a friend, he soon got a publishing contract, and this gave him enough to form a band. Performing at the Bluebird Cafe one night, he was heard by Tim Dubois, the head of Arista Records, which led to him, eventually, signing a recording contract with the label. The next step was to write some songs and Lee Roy found this a difficult process.

On his debut album, ***Lee Roy Parnell*** (1990), he co-wrote 7 of the 10 songs. He had three mid-placed singles in the Country charts in 1990, *Crocodile Tears, Oughta Be a Law* and *Family Tree.* He was missing from the lists during 1991, but came back strongly in 1992. His album ***Love Without Mercy*** was released and the lead-off single, *The Rock* (which also had a video that Lee Roy really enjoyed doing), reached the Top 50. However, it was the next single, *What Kind of Fool Do You Think I Am*, which propelled his career. It reached the Top 3 and stayed around for five months. This was followed by the Top 10 hit *Love Without Mercy*. In 1993, Lee Roy returned to the Top 3 with *Tender Moment* and then hit the Top 10 with the title track of his third album, ***On the Road***. In 1994, *I'm Holding My Own* reached the Top 3.

As a songwriter, Lee Roy has had cuts by other artists, including Sweethearts of the Rodeo, Jo-El Sonnier, Pirates of the Mississippi, David Wills and Johnny Lee. In addition, Lee Roy has worked quite a lote of late with Bluesman Delbert McClinton. JAB

RECOMMENDED ALBUMS:
"Lee Roy Parnell" (Arista)(1990)
"Love Without Mercy" (Arista)(1992)
"On the Road" (Arista)(1993)

Country-Blues star ***Lee Roy Parnell***

GENE PARSONS

(Singer, Songwriter, Drums, Guitar, Banjo, Pedal Steel, Bass Guitar, Harmonica, Mandolin, String Bender Designer)

Given Name: Gene Victor Parsons
Date of Birth: September 4, 1944
Where Born: Los Angeles
Married: 1. JoEllen (div.)
2. Camille (div.)
3. Meridian Green
Children: Jaimi Susan, Jodee, Lily Raintree

Gene Parsons came to fame as the drummer with the legendary Folk-Rock band the Byrds. His musical partnership with Clarence White helped lift the group into one of the finest in Country-Rock. He is one of the few drummers who is also a multi-instrumentalist, having started out as a string player.

Gene started with the Castaways (a group that included Gib Gilbeau) in 1963, and then in 1967 joined up with Gilbeau, as Cajun Gib & Gene. This duo continued until the spring of 1968, when Gene joined Nashville West, alongside Gilbeau, Wayne Moore and Clarence White. This began a musical and personal friendship with White that would last until the latter's death in July 1973. The group produced a self-titled album for Sierra in 1968.

In November 1968, Gene followed Clarence White into the Byrds. He was with the group while they recorded ***Dr. Byrd & Mr. Hyde*** (1969), ***Ballad of Easy Rider*** (1970), ***Untitled*** (1970), ***Byrdmaniax*** (1971) and ***Farther Along*** (1972). He also appeared on their low-level Pop chart singles *Ballad of Easy Rider* (1969), which came from the movie *Easy Rider*, and *Jesus Is Just Alright* (1970). During the end of his tenure with the Byrds, Gene injured his wrist, and against medical advice continued drumming.

In 1970, he appeared on Randy Newman's ***12 Songs*** and two years later was on Newman's ***Sail Away***. In August 1972, Gene left the Byrds for a solo career, having signed with Warner Brothers Records, and recorded ***Kindling*** in 1973. He went on tour, that year, with Clarence White, Emmylou Harris and Gram Parsons, among others, as a Superstar Reunion Tour. He soon teamed up again with Gilbeau and then turned up on Arlo Guthrie's ***Last of the Brooklyn Cowboys*** (1973). The following year, he played on Elliott Murphy's ***Aquashow***.

Gene, Chris Etheridge, Joel Scott-Hill and Tommy Kendall became the Docker Hill Boys, and were joined by Booker T. on occasions. (Kendall was replaced by Johnny Barbado).

Gene joined forces with the Flying Burrito Brothers, in 1974, and recorded two albums with them: ***Flying Again*** (1975) and ***Airborne*** (1976). His wrist injury flared up in 1976 and he had an operation that was not totally successful, and as a result, ceased playing drums on live appearances. In 1979, he appeared on ex-Burrito Sneaky Pete Kleinow's ***Sneaky Pete*** album. Gene started a relationship with Sierra Records, in 1980, that included some time in an A & R position. He released his debut album on the label that year, entitled ***Melodies***. Following this, he put together the Gene Parsons Trio with Peter Oliba on bass and Richie Rosenbaum on drums.

1985 was a memorable year for Gene, as he went into partnership with singer/guitarist Meridian Green (daughter of celebrated Folk singer Bob Gibson) and a year later, they were married. During the spring of 1991, Parsons Green was put together as a group with Gene, Meridian, Mona Gnader (bass guitar, upright bass and 8-string bass), John Bush (sax, keyboards and bass) and Vic Carberry (drums). They recorded the album ***Birds of a Feather***, which was eventually released at the end of 1992. At the same time, Sierra released ***The Kindling Collection***, which is Gene's Warner Brothers' album plus 11 tracks recorded while Gene was with the Byrds and the Flying Burrito Brothers.

By the end of 1993, Bush and Carberry had left the group and Tommy Kendall (drums) and Michael Hubbard (sax, flute, clarinet, penny whistle, bagpipes, fiddle and mandolin) had joined. Tommy had played with Gene in the Docker Hill Boys and also the Platters, while Michael is a builder of hurdy gurdies and flutes.

Gene has one other claim to fame. In 1967, he had invented the *String Bender* to facilitate the unusual pedal steel-like bends that Clarence White played on his Telecaster guitar. On a guitar with a *Parsons/White String Bender*, pushing down on the guitar neck activates a linkage system inside the guitar body that connects to the B string and raises the pitch, one full step. Between 1970 and 1987, Gene hand-made and installed over a thousand *String Benders* for guitarists such as Albert Lee, Pete Townsend and Ronnie Wood. By 1988, the demand for the Bender had outgrown Gene's production capacity, and he modernized the device. Meridian became his partner in the business and they went into mass production, wrote an installation manual and set up authorized dealers around the world. In 1993, they created a *String Bender* for the acoustic guitar. More information can be obtained from 44201 Caspar Orchard Road, Box 76, Caspar, California 95420 (Telephone: (707) 964-9538/Fax: (707) 961-1187). In 1994, Gene embarked on a reunion tour with the Byrds.

RECOMMENDED ALBUMS:

"Kindling" (Warner Brothers)(1973)
"Melodies" (Sierra)(1980)
"The Kindling Collection" (Sierra)(1992)
"Birds of a Feather" (Sierra)(1992) [Parsons Green]
(See also albums by the Byrds and the Flying Burrito Brothers, as named above)

GRAM PARSONS

(Singer, Songwriter, Guitar, Keyboards)

Given Name: **Cecil Ingram Connor**
Date of Birth: **November 5, 1946**
Where Born: **Winter Haven, Florida**
Married: **Unknown**
Date of Death: **September 19, 1973**

Gram Parsons has become the ultimate cult figure in popular music. He is considered to be the creator of Country-Rock. His life was a confusion mixed with genius and his death and subsequent body-snatching have now entered the world of the twilight zone. Gram was not born into poverty; he was not one of sixteen children; he was born into wealth and perhaps his subsequent life-style could only have generated from early security.

His grandfather, John Snively, owned one-third of the citrus fields in Florida, plus other holdings worth $28 million. Gram's father, "Coon Dog" Connor, owned a packing plant in Waycross, Georgia, but shot himself when Gram was age 13. Gram's mother re-married, this time to a rich New Orleans businessman, Robert Parsons, who formally adopted Gram and changed his last name.

Parsons came from a family of heavy drinkers and Gram ran away when he was 14. By the time he was 16, he had arrived in New York's Greenwich Village and got caught up in the burgeoning Folk boom and began singing protest songs. At one time he formed a Folk group with Jim Stafford and also belonged to the Folk group Shiloh. In 1965, he studied theology at Harvard University and then formed the International Submarine Band. After dropping out of college in 1967, he re-formed the band in New York. In 1968, the International Submarine Band recorded the ***Safe at Home*** album for Lee Hazelwood's LHI label. Among the sessionmen on the album were Glen Campbell, pianist Earl Ball and steelie Jay Dee Maness.

By the time the album came out, Parsons had joined the fifth incarnation of the Byrds. From the time of his joining, Parsons was a disruptive force in the group. He persuaded them to move away from Folk toward a more Country sound. He found that he had a willing disciple in Chris Hillman, a roots Bluegrass musician. However, the result of Parsons' influence was the Byrds' album ***Sweetheart of the Rodeo***, which is considered the first Country-Rock album. Gram's voice was removed from the recording, as he was still under contract with LHI. The Byrds appeared on the *Grand Ole Opry* and sang Parsons' *Hickory Wind*.

His attempts to marry Country and Rock led to a connection with the Rolling Stones. He left the Byrds on the eve of a tour of South Africa in July, 1968, due to his anti-apartheid views, creating a lot of bad feeling. He reunited with Chris Hillman in December, 1968, when they formed the Flying Burrito Brothers. The following year they released their debut album, ***Gilded Palace of Sin***.

Gram was getting into the West Coast drug life-style helped by his trust fund. During the year, he had a motorcycle accident and while recovering, he seemed to change his musical ideas. Parsons decided to go solo in April, 1970, due to "personality conflict," but before he departed, he recorded ***Burrito Deluxe*** with the band. By the time of this album he was more interested in hanging around with Messrs. Jagger and Richards, and fantasizing that he was a Rock superstar.

At one point, it looked like he was going to record for the Stones' own label and he traveled to France to be with them, but that came to naught. In 1971, Gram toured with the Stones in the U.K. and then returned to Los Angeles. He spent most of the rest of the year and 1972 writing material for a solo album. He also guested on Jesse Ed Davis' self-titled album. 1973 saw the release of his solo effort, ***Gram Parsons*** (also known as ***GP***), on Reprise. Originally Merle Haggard was to produce the album but after the two met in Bakersfield, Haggard changed his mind. The sessions went ahead with Merle's engineer, Hugh Davis. On the sessions were Glen D. Hardin, James Burton, Buddy Emmons, Alan Munde, Barry Tashian, Byron Berline and new singer Emmylou Harris. Emmylou was very much a Parsons protégée, and she held Gram's music in high esteem, so much so that when she started her own recording career, she cut several of his songs, giving him an acceptance that he could never achieve during his lifetime.

Gram recorded a second album, ***Grievous Angel***, with Emmylou, Burton, Berline, Hardin, Bernie Leadon, Herb Pedersen, Linda Ronstadt and Emory Gordy, Jr. Parsons was allegedly so drunk during the sessions that he was on the point of falling down. A tour with Emmylou and the Fallen Angel Band followed. The album was released after Parsons' death, and only years later was the importance of the project recognized.

On September 19, 1973, Parsons was found unconscious on the floor of his room at the Joshua Tree Inn. Even though he was rushed to Yucca Valley High Desert Hospital, he died shortly after arrival. It was stated that he had a heart attack following a heavy mix of drugs and drink and allegedly a lovemaking bout with his wife.

At L.A. International Airport, his body was snatched and instead of being buried in the family plot in New Orleans, it was cremated in the desert in Joshua Tree. Apparently, he and his friend and manager, Phil Kaufman, had made a pact that whoever died first would be taken to the desert and cremated. So in death, he achieved heroic proportions, like his hero—Hank Williams.

RECOMMENDED ALBUMS:

"Safe at Home" (LHI)(1968) [As the International Submarine Band]
"The Gilded Palace of Sin" (A & M)(1969) [As Flying Burrito Brothers]
"Burrito Deluxe" (A & M)(1970) [As Flying Burrito Brothers]
"Gram Parsons (or GP)" (Reprise)(1973)
"Grievous Angel" (Reprise)(1974)
"Doin' All Right" (Excitable)(1978) [As Byrds]
(See also Byrds and Flying Burrito Brothers]

Terry Parsons refer FERLIN HUSKY

DOLLY PARTON

(Singer, Songwriter, Guitar, Actress)
Given Name: **Dolly Rebecca Parton**
Date of Birth: **January 19, 1946**
Where Born: **Sevier County, Tennessee**
Married: **Carl Thomas Dean**

Dolly Parton is Country music's most successful female entertainer—and probably the best known Country music singer in the world. Her visual impact of wigs and famous physique have detracted somewhat from her own personal first preference of songwriting. She is one of the most prolific female singer-songwriters in American recording history (having cut approximately 300 of her own songs).

Dolly was born on the edge of the Smoky Mountains National Forest, in a modern-day log cabin on Andy Manier Mountain, just off the Pittman Center road, near the Little Pigeon River, a few miles north of Gatlinburg. She was the fourth of twelve children. Her father, Robert Lee Parton, was of Scots-Irish stock; her mother, Avie Lee Owens Parton, was part Cherokee. Her grandfather, Rev. Jake Owens, was a fiddler who wrote *Singing His Praise,* recorded by Kitty Wells. Dolly's mother sang and played guitar (releasing two albums herself in 1990, styled as the "Smoky Mountain Mama"), and her sisters Willadeene, Stella, Cassie and later Rachel, plus brothers Randy and Floyd, all sang and occasionally wrote songs together, as did her uncles Bill, Louis and Robert Owens and aunt Dorothy Jo Hope.

Robert Lee Parton was a struggling tobacco farmer and his wife, Avie Lee, was often incapacitated with illness. The impoverished Parton children withstood considerable derision from their classmates and neighbors. When Dolly was 9 years old, her fellow students at Caton's Chapel School ridiculed her patchwork coat of many colors, inspiring her most famous song. Music helped relieve the pangs of Smoky Mountain poverty and the showcase for the Partons' singing was the Rev. Owens' house.

Uncle Bill Owens became Dolly's musical mentor, buying her a Martin acoustic guitar when she was only 7 and getting her on the *Cas Walker Farm and Home Hour* radio show on station WIVK Knoxville. She began appearing regularly at age 10, often staying in Knoxville at the home of *Opry* stars Carl and Pearl Butler. She made her *Grand Ole Opry* debut in 1959 and cut her first record, *Puppy Love*, in 1960 at Lake Charles, Louisiana, for Eddie Shuler's Goldband Records. Its "B" side, *Girl Left Alone*, was written by Dolly with Bill and Louis Owens.

By 1961, Dorothy Gable, Vice President of the CMA, brought Dolly to Tree Music, where Buddy Killen signed her, getting her onto Mercury Records. However, her next single, *It's Sure Gonna Hurt*, in 1962, failed to sell—and there was no follow-up. Dolly made other trips to Nashville and recorded songs (probably in 1963) which have turned up on budget albums over the years, ultimately from Alshire International.

As a teenager in the mountains, trying to uplift her spirits, Dolly listened to her share of radio rock'n'roll. She attended Sevier County High School, playing snare-drum in the marching band, while stealing time to write songs. She was graduated in 1964 (the first in her family to matriculate) and the following day rode a bus to Nashville with a suitcase full of dirty laundry and songs, following her uncle Bill Owens, who had recently moved there, and in the subsequent months they pitched their songs in vain.

Dolly did demo singing for Moss-Rose Music, while holding mundane jobs (receptionist, waitress) and living in mean straits (garret apartment and a trailer park). In early 1965, Dolly and Bill Owens signed with Fred Foster's Combine Music and Foster signed Dolly to his Monument Records. Ray Stevens often produced her records.

Fred Foster was a Pop and Country visionary who had begun using Sam Phillips' latter-day studio in the Cumberland Lodge building at 319 7th Avenue North. Roy Orbison had recorded there for Monument—and now, so would Dolly Parton. Foster kept a Los Angeles office and prophetically (because of her later Pop success), Dolly's second Monument release, *Happy, Happy Birthday Baby* (1965) went to No.108 on the Pop chart. Dolly and Bill Owens wrote a future Country standard, *Put It Off Until Tomorrow*, which went Top 10 for Bill Phillips (1966)—with Dolly singing uncredited back-up harmony,

***Dolly Parton** (right) with **Linda Ronstadt** and **Emmylou Harris**, the Trio*

marking her radio airplay debut. Phillips followed up with their *The Company You Keep* (Top 10) and in 1967, Skeeter Davis took their song *Fuel to the Flame* to the Top 15. That same year, Hank Williams, Jr. charted Dolly's *I'm in No Condition*.

Foster himself began producing Dolly in a more Country vein—her song *Dumb Blonde* was placed in the Top 25 in 1967, followed by *Something Fishy* (by Curly Putman) in the Top 20. Dolly finally married asphalt contractor Carl Thomas Dean (whom she had met on her very first day in Nashville). Dolly and Carl lived in a one-bedroom apartment and Ralph Emery chauffeured her to his morning WSM-TV show since she didn't own a car.

One day in August, 1967, Porter Wagoner's office telephoned. Dolly was invited for an interview—and Wagoner recruited her for his syndicated TV program, which reached over three million viewers. Dolly replaced Norma Jean. Her appearance, her unusual voice and especially her songwriting, distinguished her from the typical girl singers of that period. Her first TV performance for the *Porter Wagoner Show* was September 5, 1967. (Over the years, Dolly would convincingly advertise *Cardui*, the quaint women's menstrual tonic, produced by the show's sponsor, the folksy Chattanooga Medicine Company.)

Her first live show with Wagoner was September 14, in Lebanon, Virginia. The audience somewhat resented her, chanting, "We want Norma Jean." Such adverse reactions persisted for at least a year—but that very night, Wagoner desperately devised the strategy of singing duets.

Dolly's contracts with Monument Records and Combine Music were expiring, so Wagoner persuaded RCA to sign her. Girl singers were not in demand, so he wagered his own RCA royalties to offset any losses. As a safeguard, the first RCA Dolly release (1967) was a Porter-Dolly duet, *The Last Thing on My Mind* (by Tom Paxton). It went Top 10 and her next release was also a duet, *Holding on to Nothin'*, which also went Top 10, in 1968. In October, 1967, occurred one of the most important events of her career, the founding of her own publishing company, Owepar.

Finally, she scored her first single RCA hit, *Just Because I'm a Woman*, in June, 1968 (Top 20). Dolly joined the *Grand Ole Opry* on February 4, 1969. But industry competition from other Country women singers was considerable. Her single records did not chart high at first, including songs she wrote, like *In the Good Old Days When Times Were Bad*, *Daddy*, *My Blue Ridge Mountain Boy* and *Daddy, Come and Get Me*. Her cover of Elvis' hit *In the Ghetto* (1969) only went Top 50.

Porter Wagoner felt she needed something exciting, almost outrageous, to grab attention. Perhaps a *woman* could sing the Jimmie Rodgers classic about a mule team driver! So he had Dolly sing *Mule Skinner Blues (Blue Yodel No. 8)* and his whip-cracking production of the song—lightened by Dolly's yodeling—went Top 3 in 1970. Progressive Rock stations played the record and it earned a Grammy nomination.

In 1971, Dolly evoked her rich Gospel music heritage with the album ***Golden Streets of Glory,*** with *Comin' for to Carry Me Home* going Top 25. Meanwhile, the duet act outpaced Dolly the solo artist, getting into the Top 10 five times from 1968-1970 with *We'll Get Ahead Someday* (Top 5, 1968), *Yours Love* and *Just Someone I Used to Know* (both 1969) and *Tomorrow Is Forever* and *Daddy Was an Old Time Preacher Man* (1970). One that Dolly wrote, *Jeannie's Afraid of the Dark*, only went Top 60 in 1968, but it was a "B" side hit and became the most requested Porter-Dolly duet of all. It's the most famous of Dolly's many songs about aggrieved and usually dying children, evoking another childhood trauma, when her schoolmates at Caton's Chapel School had locked her in the coat closet. (Ever since, she has slept with the lights on).

The duet act won the CMA's "Vocal Group of the Year" Award in 1968 and "Vocal Duo of the Year" in 1970 and 1971, as well as MCN's "Vocal Duo of the Year" award for 1968, 1969, 1970 (and Grammy nominations in 1969, 1970, 1971 and 1973). The funny "fight" numbers that Dolly and Porter specialized in, usually written by Dolly, were comical verbal spats worthy of Lucille Ball and Desi Arnaz (such as *Fight and Scratch*, *Run That By Me One More Time* and *Two Sides to Every Story)*.

In 1969, RCA gave Wagoner co-producer control (with Bob Ferguson, who usually yielded to Wagoner out of expedience). Porter's producer instincts led him to keep Dolly's voice as pure and natural as possible. The songs were polished and perfected onstage, on the bus and (starting in 1972) at Fireside Studio, built by Wagoner and co-owned with Dolly.

When they went into the RCA studio, they were relaxed and ready. The result is audible in all the permanent-quality Dolly material from this period. Wagoner did not need to tamper with Dolly's singing, however—a surviving Owepar demo, recorded without amplification or equipment, shows that she sings on key, with versatility and plays hard-driving rhythm guitar and can finger-pick as well. She often played her guitar on the *Porter Wagoner Show* on TV and in the summer of 1976 finger-picked (and sang) her song *Do I Ever Cross Your Mind?* with Chet Atkins, preserved on ***Chet Atkins: The RCA Years*** (1992).

Dolly achieved her first No.1 single with *Joshua* in 1971 and the song got a Grammy nomination. It was one of her countless songs written out of personal experience or observation—the most famous of which was *Coat of Many Colors* (Top 5 in 1971). "That is my favorite song and I think people relate to that one more than any other of the songs I've written. I love that Joseph's coat or that raggedy coat..." (interview with Steve Eng, July 3, 1990). *Touch Your Woman* went Top 10 in 1972—but not till late 1973 would Dolly make it back into the Top 10. Dolly's other hits at this time were: *Washday Blues* (Top 20, 1972), *My Tennessee Mountain Home* and *Traveling Man* (both Top 20, 1973).

Wagoner was as frustrated by the lack of promotion given Dolly as anyone, since he had a special contract with Dolly to compensate him after she left his show. So for years he tussled with RCA over their lackadaisical marketing of her. The Wagoner-Parton business partnership was incredibly enmeshed. Wagoner had received 49% of her Owepar publishing in 1969.

Finally, in 1973, Dolly had another No.1 song with *Jolene*. It crossed to the Pop Top 60. *Jolene* was Dolly's passport for leaving the Porter Wagoner road show, in early 1974, but she continued to make appearances on his TV show and he continued to produce her records, including more duets, well into 1976. Between 1971 and 1976, they chalked up further top duet hits with *Better Move It on Home* (Top 10, 1971), *The Right Combination* (Top 15, 1971), *Burning the Midnight Oil* (Top 15, 1972), *Lost Forever in Your Kiss* (Top 10, 1972), *Together Always* (Top 15, 1972), *If Teardrops Were Pennies* (Top 3, 1973), *Please Don't Stop Loving Me* (No.1, 1974), *Say Forever You'll Be Mine* (Top 3, 1975) and *Is Forever Longer Than Always* (Top 10, 1976). Dolly had received further Grammy nominations (*Touch Your Woman*, 1972, *Jolene*, 1974) without success.

After *Jolene* came three more No.1s in a row, which she wrote: *I Will Always Love You* (1974), her legendary farewell to Wagoner; *Love Is Like a Butterfly* (1974) and *The Bargain Store* (1975). These were followed by the Top 3 placed *The Seeker*, in 1975. Dolly had finally won the CMA "Female Vocalist of the Year" Award (twice: 1975 and 1976) and had made it to England for the annual Wembley Festival in 1975.

There were three more hits in 1975-76, *We Used To* (Top 10, 1975), *Hey, Lucky Lady* (Top 20, 1976) and *All I Can Do* (Top 3, 1976), all produced by Porter Wagoner. Dolly put together the Travelling Family Band, a clannish crew of siblings, uncles and cousins (including brother Randy Parton, who later recorded for RCA), but before long, they were replaced by the Gypsy Fever Band.

In late 1976, she also launched the syndicated *Dolly* show, produced by Wagoner's old TV guru, Bill Graham. Its half-hour format was successful, but she chose not to renew it. By 1977 she gained production control of her next album, ***New Harvest, First Gathering***, and its chart single *Light of a Clear Blue Morning* went Top 15. The album also featured a Country tribute, *Apple-Jack*, crammed full of back-up singers ranging from Roy Acuff, Kitty Wells, Ernest Tubb and Minnie Pearl, to her own mother and father. The myth that only Dolly can sing Dolly songs was already being refuted by other artists' cuts: Kitty Wells (*J. J. Sneed*), Emmylou Harris (*Coat of Many Colors*), Olivia Newton-John (*Jolene*), Maria Muldaur, as well as Rose Maddox (*My Tennessee Mountain Home*) and Linda Ronstadt (*I Will Always Love You*), to mention a few. Emmylou would score a hit with *To Daddy* (Top 3 in 1977) and Stella Parton with *Steady as the Rain* (Top 30, in 1979).

Dolly's big crossover hit, produced by Gary Klein, was *Here You Come Again*, written by pop writers Barry Mann and Cynthia Weil. Despite its totally Tin Pan Alley quality, it went to No.1 Country in 1977 and Top 3 Pop and went Gold. Finally, the first female superstar in Country music had been created. That year, Dolly was named CMA's "Entertainer of the Year." The album ***Here You Come Again*** went Platinum in 1978 and the title song won her her first Grammy for "Best Country Vocal Performance, Female" in 1978. The album also contained the No.1 self-penned hit *It's All Wrong, But It's All Right*.

In 1978, the 1976 album ***The Best of Dolly Parton*** went Gold as did her ***Heartbreaker*** album. Dolly now became a cover girl (*Rolling Stone, People, Playboy*)—and probably was the most often photographed American female. The tabloids made her a staple subject of mostly humorous notoriety, since show business publicity is where you find it, especially at the grocery store check-out line. (She once purchased a tabloid with a "Dolly Parton diet" inside—tried it out herself—but it didn't help her lose weight!)

Her contract with Porter Wagoner exploded in a lawsuit in 1979 and their business marriage finally ended in financial divorce. Dolly retrieved her copyrights, while Porter received a financial settlement and their recording studio. A delayed ***Porter & Dolly*** album appeared and the fittingly-sad *Making Plans* went Top 3 in 1980.

From 1978 through 1980, Dolly charted six No.1 hits: *It's All Wrong, But It's All Right* and *Heartbreaker* (both 1978), *I Really Got the Feeling* and *You're the Only One* (1979), *Starting Over Again* and *Old Flames Can't Hold a Candle to You* (both 1980). She also had a Top 10 single in 1979 entitled *Sweet Summer Love*. In 1979, Dolly's album ***Great Balls of Fire*** was Certified Gold. Most successful of all was her own *9 to 5* (1980), which was also a No.1 Pop hit and was Certified Gold. It also won two 1981 Grammy Awards for "Best Country Vocal Performance" and "Best Country Song." It was the title-tune of her major film debut. The album ***9 to 5 and Odd Jobs*** was also Certified Gold.

In 1981, Dolly had another No.1, *But You Know I Love You*, which also crossed to the Pop Top 50. She followed this with the Top 15 version of *House of the Rising Sun*. She started 1982 with *Single Woman* and followed with *Heartbreak Express*, both Top 10 hits. Her next No.1 was another soundtrack song, a remake of *I Will Always Love You* (1982), from *The Best Little Whorehouse in Texas*, in which Dolly co-starred with Burt Reynolds. The movie also yielded the seasonal hit *Hard Candy Christmas* (Top 10). The year closed with a track from Monument's double-album ***The Winning Hand***, which paired Dolly with Willie Nelson for the Top 10 *Everything Is Beautiful*.

A forlorn-faced Dolly adorns the cover of the 1982 ***Heartbreak Express*** album (in this period, she had been tormented by weight loss attempts, a hysterectomy, a death threat and the brief contemplation of suicide).

Dolly started 1983 with the Top 20 single *Potential New Boyfriend* and then teamed up with Kenny Rogers for the Bee Gees' song (and Barry Gibbs-produced) *Islands in the Stream*, which went to No.1 on both Country and Pop charts and was Certified Platinum the same year. She closed the year with her Top 3 rendition of *Save the Last Dance for Me*. In 1983, Dolly's ***Greatest Hits*** package was also Certified Gold.

Dolly started 1984 with Tony Hatch's *Downtown*, which had been a big Pop hit for Petula Clark, but Dolly's version only went Top 40 Country and Top 80 Pop. The movie *Rhinestone* (1984) was not well received. Dolly tried and failed to make a singer out of co-star Sylvester Stallone. Dolly still escaped with a No.1 hit, *Tennessee Homesick Blues*, which she wrote. Also from the movie was the Top 10 *God Won't Get You*. Dolly's duet album with Kenny Rogers, ***Once Upon a Christmas***, was Certified Platinum and in 1989 reached Double-Platinum status.

In 1985, Dolly's first chart record was *Don't Call it Love* (Top 3). She followed with the title song of her ***Real Love*** album, another Kenny Rogers duet, which went to No.1. She finished the year with another No.1, *Think About Love*. During 1986, her most successful single was the Top 40 *Tie Our Love (in a Double Knot)*.

Her best album in years, ***Trio*** (1987), with Linda Ronstadt and Emmylou Harris, charted four hits, *To Know Him Is to Love Him* (No.1), *Telling Me Lies* (Top 3), *Those Memories of You* (Top 5)(all 1987) and *Wildflowers* (Top 10, 1988). The album was the recipient of a Grammy for "Best Country Performance by a Duo or Group with Vocal," in 1987. It reached Platinum status during the year of release.

However, the more-or-less weekly ABC-TV *Dolly* show (1987-88) lasted but a season. The February 20, 1988 program brought Dolly back to Nashville (The Ryman and Tootsie's), reunited with Porter Wagoner. And each show carried a vignette where Dolly played a waitress—landing her a part in the major film *Steel Magnolias* (1990). Her most challenging film role was in the TV film *Wild Texas Wind* (1991).

In 1985, Dolly opened the Dollywood theme park in Pigeon Forge, Tennessee, near her birthplace and her Dollywood Foundation cut the Sevier County High School dropout rate in half, thanks to her practical "buddies" program. In 1986, Dolly was inducted to the Nashville Songwriters Hall of Fame. Dolly was herself dropped out of her RCA contract in 1986, but was signed in 1987 by Columbia (today's Sony). Critics grumbled at her Pop ***Rainbow*** album (1987). She swung back to Country with the Ricky Skaggs–produced ***White Limozeen*** (1989), scoring two No.1s: *Why'd You Come in Here Lookin' Like That* and *Yellow Roses*. It was Certified Gold in 1991. A song written by her brother Floyd, *Rockin' Years*, was a No.1 duet for Dolly and Ricky Van Shelton, appearing on the ***Eagle When She Flies*** album (1991), which went Platinum in 1992. Her film *Straight Talk* (1992) was laden with nine of her songs.

In late 1992, *I Will Always Love You* went to No.1 on the Pop charts thanks to the

Bodyguard film version sung by Whitney Houston, which sold more than any single record ever had, and in 1994, Dolly presented Whitney with her Grammy award on TV. Her 1993 album ***Slow Dancing with the Moon*** included the novelty hit *Romeo,* which had a music video that helped it become a Country Top 30 and Pop Top 50 and featured Billy Ray Cyrus, Mary-Chapin Carpenter, Kathy Mattea, Pam Tillis and Tanya Tucker. The album had gone Platinum before year end.

In 1993, Dolly teamed up with Loretta Lynn and Tammy Wynette for the ***Honky Tonk Angels*** trio-album which was Certified Gold. In 1994, Dolly announced that she was founding her own record label, to be managed by parent-company Sony, and released her autobiography, *My Life and Other Unfinished Business* (Harper Collins). (For full list of awards, see Awards Section). SE

RECOMMENDED ALBUMS:

"In the Good Old Days (When Times Were Bad)" (RCA Victor)(1969)
"My Blue Ridge Mountain Boy" (RCA Victor)(1969)
"Golden Streets of Glory" (RCA Victor)(1971)
"The Best of Porter Wagoner and Dolly Parton" (RCA Victor)(1971)
"Joshua" (RCA Victor)(1971)
"Coat of Many Colors" (RCA Victor)(1971)
"The World of Dolly Parton" (double)(Monument)(1972)
"My Tennessee Mountain Home" (RCA Victor)(1973)
"Bubbling Over" (RCA Victor)(1973)
"Jolene" (RCA Victor)(1974)
"Love is Like a Butterfly" (RCA Victor)(1974)
"The Bargain Store" (RCA Victor)(1975)
"Best of Dolly Parton" (RCA Victor)(1975)
"Dolly—The Seeker, We Used To" (RCA Victor)(1975)
"Here You Come Again" (RCA Victor)(1977)
"9 to 5 and Odd Jobs" (RCA Victor)(1980)
"The Best Little Whorehouse in Texas" (RCA Victor)(1982) [With Burt Reynolds]
"Sweet Harmony—Porter Wagoner and Dolly Parton" (double)(RCA Victor)(1982)
"Heartbreak Express" (RCA Victor)(1982)
"Kris, Willie, Dolly & Brenda...The Winning Hand" (Monument)(1982) [With Kris Kristofferson, Willie Nelson, Brenda Lee]
"Burlap and Satin" (RCA Victor)(1983)
"Trio" (Warner Brothers)(1987) [With Linda Ronstadt and Emmylou Harris]
"White Limozeen" (Columbia)(1989)
"Eagle When She Flies" (Columbia)(1991)
"Slow Dancing with the Moon" (Columbia)(1993)
"Dolly Parton: The RCA Years 1967-1986" [Double cd Box Set] (RCA)(1993) [With Booklet by Mary A. Bufwak and Robert K. Oermann]
"Honky Tonk Angels" (Columbia)(1994) [With Loretta Lynn and Tammy Wynette]

STELLA PARTON

(Singer, Songwriter, Guitar, Autoharp, Actress)

Given Name:	**Stella Parton**
Date of Birth:	**May 4, 1949**
Where Born:	**Locust Ridge, Sevier County, Tennessee**
Married:	**1. Mr. Rauhuff (div.) 2. Jim Molloy (div.) 3. Steve Messer (div.)**
Children:	**Tim**

On stage, Stella is an exciting performer, whether as a Country music singer, as a musical comedy star or a talk-show guest, and she has never lived in the shadow of her famous sister Dolly; Stella Parton has always been her own person.

As a child, she considered herself to be a loner and a maverick, which is not surprising when you have to compete with eleven brothers and sisters. Early on, she began singing and performing with her sisters, brothers, uncles and aunts. By the age of 7, she was a TV performer in Knoxville. She sang *You Are My Sunshine*, with Dolly, on radio in Tennessee when she was 9. Later, Stella and two of her sisters found work on dozens of radio station shows and did commercial jingles in east Tennessee. Stella played autoharp and guitar and performed and sang her own songs. She was in high school when she married for the first time, but continued to perform and tour. Stella was initially very interested in recording Gospel material and she recorded as the Stella Parton Singers and as Stella and the Gospel Carrolls for Inspiration Records.

In 1975, after setting up her own record label, Country Soul, she released an album from which the title single, *I Wanna Hold You in My Dreams*, attracted national attention when it went into the Top 10 on the Country chart. Her second single in 1975, on the Soul, Country & Blues label, *It's Not Funny Anymore*, was less of a success. That year, she recorded *Ode to Olivia*, as a defense of Olivia Newton-John's success at the CMA Awards. Stella's two chart singles led to a record deal with Elektra, in 1976.

Stella's first chart entry for Elektra was *Neon Women* (1977), a duet with Carmol Taylor. However, major success had to wait for the middle of 1977, when she hit the Top 15 with two successive releases, *The Danger of a Stranger* and *Standard Lie Number One*. The former was also a U.K. Top 40 Pop success. Her three 1978 singles, *Four Little Letters* (Top 20), *Undercover Lovers* (Top 30) and *Stormy Weather* (Top 25), continued her success. Stella's final year with the label was 1979 and she chalked up *Steady As the Rain* (Top 30) and *The Room at the Top of the Stairs* (Top 40). Stella had four albums released on Elektra and seemed to be building up a steady career, but following her departure from the label, she was missing from the charts until 1982, when her sixth album, ***So Far So Good***, was released on Town House/Accord and the two chart singles from it were *I'll Miss You* and *Young Love*. In 1987 and 1989 she had two further low level chart hits, *Cross My Heart*, on the Luv label, and *I Don't Miss You Like I Used To,* on the Airborne label. However, Airborne folded and no chart hits followed.

Her TV appearances have been on such shows as *The Today Show, Nashville Now, Hee Haw,* the *Mike Douglas Show* and her own pilot, *Under Stella's Hat*. She also appeared in the 1982 movie *Country Gold*. She has also had great success in Broadway musicals, appearing in *The Best Little Whorehouse in Texas* (playing the same role that Dolly played in the film version), *Seven Brides for Seven Brothers* and *Pump Boys and Dinettes*. She was commended by the press for her performances in all of these shows. Stella wrote and choreographed the main musical show for the theme park Dollywood.

As a writer, her cook book, *Really Cookin'*, a guide to healthy eating Southern style, containing 200 recipes, with pictures of the Parton family, was released and a portion of each sale goes to the Nashville Coalition for the Homeless. A second volume was published in 1993. Stella is currently promoting a line of natural foods on TV. Stella appeared in a 16-week run of *Gentlemen Prefer Blondes* at the end of 1993. She is still very busy touring, especially in Europe. Stella is very active in children's charities and keeps herself very busy all the time. She is also an avid collector of dolls and can be seen at the Flea Market at Tennessee State Fair Grounds, looking for a bargain. JAB

RECOMMENDED ALBUMS:

"Country Sweet" (Elektra)(1977)
"Stella Parton" (Elektra)(1978)
"The Best of Stella Parton" (Elektra)(1979)

*Beautiful and talented **Stella Parton***

RAY AND INA PATTERSON

When Formed: 1947

RAY PATTERSON

(Singer, Songwriter, Mandolin, Other Stringed Instruments)

Given Name: Ora Ray Patterson
Date of Birth: April 17, 1926
Where Born: Clayton, New Mexico

INA PATTERSON

(Singer, Songwriter, Guitar)

Given Name: Ina Lee Phelps
Date of Birth: March 13, 1929
Where Born: Dexter, Texas

Ray and Ina Patterson persisted in the classic duet styles of the 30's for a generation after they virtually vanished as a mainstream entity in Country music. They possessed some of the finest harmony in the history of the genre although they arrived on the scene a little too late to have the impact of the Blue Sky Boys or the Monroe Brothers and never landed a major label record contract. Nonetheless, the Pattersons worked as a husband-wife team in radio—largely in the West.

Born near Clayton, New Mexico, Ray listened to Old-Time records from early childhood, and radio from 1934, when his parents settled on a farm near Roswell. They endeavored to steer him toward classical violin, but Ray showed more interest in Country sounds, taking up first the guitar and then, at the age of 16, the mandolin. In WWII, Ray received serious arm injuries while serving in the European Theater and while recovering in a Colorado hospital, he met Ina Phelps whom he married on October 12, 1945. The pair went back to Ray's hometown of Roswell where they perfected their Country harmony singing style.

Ray and Ina began their radio career in 1947 at KGFL on Roswell's *Saturday Night Jamboree*. They soon had a regular daily program there and another at KSWS as well. From then until 1960, they worked radio at a variety of locations which extended east and west from North Carolina to Colorado and from WCKY in Cincinnati to Alabama and Texas in the South. As Ina recalls, they managed to get into some of the best days of the last years of the golden age of live radio. They also transcribed programs for use on Mexican border stations and cut single records for such small companies as Gold Star, Cozy, and Glenmar. Their released numbers included songs like *Those Brown Eyes*, *You Branded Your Name on My Heart*, *Welcome to New Mexico*, and *Beautiful Lost River Valley*. In 1949, they published a fine song book titled *Ray and Ina's Favorite Folk Songs and Hymns*. Their last regular daily radio work took place at KPIK Colorado Springs in the late 50's. They also appeared often on KK-TV Colorado Springs.

In 1962, the Pattersons moved to Woodland Park, Colorado, where they made their home until 1985. Ray worked as a photographer and telephone operator and the duo continued to play Old-Time music at home, eschewing the modern trends in the industry. In 1966, they recorded an album of Old-Time duets for County and by 1973 had done two more for the same firm. All the albums were well received by those in the specialized but dedicated market for traditional sounds. The Pattersons also played a number of festivals primarily on the West Coast.

In 1981, when Ina developed some hearing problems, they curtailed their music activities. Ray and Ina moved back to Colorado Springs in 1985, where they still play for their own amusement and continue to be crusaders for traditional music in the Great Plains and Rocky Mountain region. IMT

RECOMMENDED ALBUMS:

"Old Time Ballads & Hymns" (County)(1967)
"Old-Time Songs" (County)(1969)
"Songs of Home and Childhood" (County)(1973)

LES PAUL AND MARY FORD

When Formed: 1947

LES PAUL

(Guitar, Recording Genius, Electronics Wizard, Guitar Designer, Harmonica, Banjo)

Given Name: Lester Williams Polfus
Date of Birth: June 9, 1916
Where Born: Waukeska, Wisconsin
Married: Iris Colleen Summers (Mary Ford) (m. 1949)(div. 1962)

MARY FORD

(Guitar, Singer)

Given Name: Iris Colleen Summers
Date of Birth: July 7, 1928
Where Born: Pasadena, California
Married: Lester Williams Polfus (Les Paul) (m. 1949)(div. 1962)
Date of Death: September 30, 1977

Les Paul's position as one of the greatest guitarists in any form of music was assured many years ago. Not just a picker, he is a man who has advanced the electric instrument itself to a point unrecognizable to early players. In addition, his recording techniques with multi-tracking have certainly laid the foundation for the current recording industry. The latter was never more in evidence than when he cut with his then wife, Mary Ford, some memorable multi-track recordings in the late 40's and early 50's.

Les started out programming pianola rolls in his house, while still quite young. He built himself a crystal radio in 1927 and then learned harmonica, before progressing to banjo and a Sears Roebuck acoustic guitar. He designed a harmonica holder and was one of the first musicians to play guitar and harmonica at the same time. He began playing professionally when just age 13, at a local drive-in restaurant. He started his career in Country music as a musician/comedian, "Hot Rod Red," and then changed his name to "Rhubarb Red." For a while, he toured with a popular Chicago group, Rube Tronson and his Texas Cowboys, but he was starting to get interested in playing Jazz.

From 1934 through 1935, Les had a Country show as Rhubarb Red on WJJD Chicago and an afternoon Jazz show as Les Paul on Chicago's WIND. In 1936, he put together the Les Paul Trio with Chet Atkins' half-brother Jim Atkins and bass player Ernie Newton. They successfully auditioned for Fred Waring (of Pennsylvanians fame), and stayed with him for five years. The trio played alongside some of the greats of Jazz, including Louis Armstrong.

In the mid-30's, Les became an unpaid consultant for the Gibson Guitar Company and tried out all their new models of guitar. It was back then that he started to develop the idea of a solid bodied guitar.

In 1941, Les disbanded the group and went to Hollywood to try and persuade Bing Crosby to hire him, which after two years he did. Crosby also arranged for a recording contract for Les with Decca and they had a hit together with *It's Been a Long, Long Time*. During WWII, Les served for a year in the Armed Forces Radio Service, under Meredith Wilson, in Hollywood, and played for Kate Smith, Rudy Vallee and Crosby.

At the end of the war, Les toured with the Andrews Sisters and then with "Jazz at the Philharmonic." He then formed Mark II of the Les Paul Trio. While playing at the London Palladium, he flew to Paris and met with his idol, Django Reinhardt. After Django's death in 1953, his widow gave Les his guitar, which Les still owns and keeps in his house in New Jersey.

While in Hollywood, Les built a recording studio in his garage and introduced the concept of multiple recording and overdubbing. He built a recording machine from the flywheel of a Cadillac, which had been dynamically balanced to act as a turntable, a jukebox motor and a linking belt provided by a dental house. He also used glass-based acetate recordings, which was old-fashioned even then. He also broke the taboo about standing two feet from the microphone, by introducing close mic technique, which is still utilized. He also brought in delay echo by putting a playback pickup behind the recording head of a wire recorder. As a result, his studio became in demand and stars such as Kay Starr, Jo Stafford and the Andrews Sisters recorded there.

Although the tape recorder had been invented in Germany before WWII, it was only when one had been confiscated and got back to the U.S. that Paul and Crosby could see the benefits of tape at first hand. As machines from Ampex and Westrex started to appear, Les introduced innovations into his own studio, which was upgraded to 8-track. Remarkably, he stacked his machines and synchronized them. Unfortunately, Les never patented any of his ideas, but Ampex did buy up the 8-track design, in 1954, after Westrex had turned it down.

The first Les Paul instrumental records using this multi-tracking technique were released in 1948 on Capitol, and entitled *Lover* and *Brazil*. Other hits followed, including *Nola, Josephine, Tiger Rag* and *Meet Mr. Callaghan*. In 1948, he smashed his arm in an auto accident and had it reset crooked in a guitar player's position.

In 1947, he teamed up with Colleen Summers, who had played with Gene Autry and was such a fine guitarist that she played lead guitar with Jimmy Wakely's band and sang harmony on his 1948 No.1 hit, *One Has My Name (The Other Has My Heart)*. Les suggested she change her name to Mary Ford, and in 1949 they married.

The result of their collaboration was a series of recordings cut in the garage studio that started with the No.1 Pop hit *The Tennessee Waltz* in 1950. They followed this with the Certified Gold single *Mockin' Bird Hill*, which went Top 10 on the Country charts and Top 3 on the Pop lists. They followed up with *The World is Waiting for the Sunrise, How High the Moon, Vaya Con Dios, I'm Sitting on Top of the World* and the Top 10 Pop charted single *Hummingbird*, in 1955. In 1956, they had their last major hit together, *Amukiriki (The Lord Willing)*, which was a Top 40 Pop hit.

Initially, Gibson was not interested when Les developed the electric solid body guitar in 1941, but in 1952, the Gibson Les Paul was issued, and with modifications has been the guitar that all solid electrics have tried to emulate. Les' own guitar, known as the "Les Pulverizer," was utilized for the duo's stage work and was able to copy perfectly the sound that they achieved on record.

Les had two instrumental solo hits at the end of the 50's, entitled *Cinco Robles (Five Oaks)* (Capitol, 1957) and *Put a Ring on My Finger* (Columbia, 1958). However, as the 60's got under way, Les began to have health problems and he had to have a bone graft operation and treatment for an inner ear problem. He had a 1961 Top 40 instrumental Pop hit with *Jura (I Swear I Love You)* on Columbia. Then in 1962, Les and Mary divorced, and Les semi-retired to concentrate on his electronics work.

He reduced the size of the Pulverizer and in 1967, Les turned in the design of the Les Paul Recording Guitar, which Gibson put on the market in 1971. In 1976, Les received a Grammy Award for "Best Country Instrumental Performance" for ***Chester and Lester***, with Chet Atkins. They recorded the album ***Guitar Monsters***, in 1978.

In 1983, Les received the NARAS "Trustees Award" and was the subject of a 1988 Arena Special on British BBC-2 TV. He was inducted into the Rock and Roll Hall of Fame in 1988.

Although now afflicted with arthritis, which makes two of his fingers largely unworkable, he, like his hero, Django (who had two fingers burned in a mobile home fire), has adjusted his playing. He is still a hero to all guitar pickers, for his playing and for the simple fact that if he hadn't invented the electric solid body guitar, there would probably have been no Rock industry, and Country would not have developed to where it is now.

RECOMMENDED ALBUMS:

"The World is Waiting for the Sunrise" (Capitol)(1974) [With Mary Ford]
"Chester and Lester" (RCA Victor)(1976) [With Chet Atkins]
"Guitar Monsters" (RCA Victor)(1978) [With Chet Atkins]
"Guitar Tapestry" (Project 3)
"All Time Greatest Hits" (EMI Holland)(1983)
"The Very Best of Les Paul & Mary Ford" (Music for Pleasure UK)(1983)

JOHNNY PAYCHECK

(Singer, Songwriter, Guitar, Steel Guitar, Bass Guitar)

Given Name:	**Donald Eugene Lytle**
Date of Birth:	**May 31, 1938**
Where Born:	**Greenfield, Ohio**
Married:	**1. (Div.)**
	2. (Div.)
	3. Sharon
Children:	**Jonathan, two Daughters**

During the 1970s, Johnny Paycheck had some genuine moments of glory in the annals of Country music, but he has perhaps become best known for his "outlaw" image. However, the image got out of hand and Johnny's career was interrupted by several years in prison.

Born and raised in the sedate southern Ohio town of Greenfield, Johnny played guitar from age 6 and exhibited wanderlust as a child, in addition to an interest in Country music. From the age of 15, as "the Ohio Kid," he hitchhiked around the country, sometimes singing in bars and clubs with a borrowed guitar. A little later, he joined the U.S. Navy, but soon got into a serious fight with a superior officer which resulted in a court martial followed by a time in the brig. Not long after his release, Johnny went to Nashville, where he was heard by Buddy Killen, who landed Johnny a contract with Decca, which produced four singles (under the name of Donny Young) and then two more for Mercury.

In the meantime, other musicians recognized his talents and he worked in Porter Wagoner's Wagonmasters, Faron Young's Country Deputies and Ray Price's Cherokee Cowboys and fronted George Jones' Jones Boys (1962-1966). Frequent shifts from one band to another reflected his erratic temperament and lifestyle along with career frustrations.

In 1965, he restyled himself Johnny Paycheck (from John Austin Paycheck, a Chicago prize fighter) and legally assumed the name in 1966 after he met producer Aubrey Mayhew, who got him a pair of minor-charted singles, *A-11* (which was nominated for a Grammy in every category available) and *Heartbreak Tennessee* on Hilltop, a company that generally released only budget-price albums with material leased from major labels. Johnny was being heralded as the new George Jones.

Mayhew and Paycheck formed Little

From sideman to star, ***Johnny Paycheck***

Darlin' Records in 1966 largely as a vehicle for Paycheck, but also signed Lloyd Green, Jeannie C. Riley and Bobby Helms. *The Lovin' Machine* became Johnny's first major hit in the summer of 1966, reaching the Top 10. He followed up with the Top 15 placed *Motel Time Again* (1966) and *Juke Box Charlie* (1967). In 1966, Johnny's co-written song *Apartment #9* was Tammy Wynette's first chart single and the song won the ACM's "Song of the Year" Award that year, which he shared with co-writers Bobby Austin and Fuzzy Owen. That same year, Ray Price cut Johnny's *Touch My Heart* and had a Top 3 hit with it. Johnny had seven other releases on Little Darlin' and made the charts with *Wherever You Are*, which peaked just below the Top 30 in 1969, ranking highest, and the most interestingly titled being the 1967 *Don't Monkey with Another Monkey's Monkey*. The label went bankrupt, because of several reasons, but not helped by Johnny's heavy drinking.

Heavily in debt and with no other label willing to record him, Johnny then went to California where he hit the skids, living on drink and drugs, until drying out in 1970. Another producer, Billy Sherrill, rescued him with an Epic contract in 1971 (having been tracked down by CBS executive Nick Hunter). *She's All I Got* became Top 3 hit in the winter of 1971-72, crossing over to the lower rungs of the Pop charts, and Paycheck was back on the road to stardom. Johnny had sung the song at the D.J. Convention in Nashville, in 1971, in front of 10,000 people, to a standing ovation. In 1972, Johnny was convicted of check forgery and given a suspended sentence.

In the early 70's, Sherrill crafted Johnny's image as a singer of Nashville Sound love songs with follow-up hits such as *Someone to Give My Love To* (Top 5, 1972). Johnny's other hits that year were *Let's All Go Down to the River* (a Gospel-flavored duet with Jody Miller), *Love is a Good Thing* (both Top 15) and *Somebody Loves Me*. Johnny had a highly successful year in 1973 with *Something About You I Love* (Top 10), *Mr. Lovemaker* (Top 3) and the lighthearted Top 10 hit *Song and Dance Man*. His major successes during the next two years were *My Part of Forever* and *For a Minute There* (both 1974).

By 1976, Johnny was being recast in the new Willie Nelson-Waylon Jennings "outlaw" mold on ***11 Months and 29 Days*** which has an album cover photo from a jail cell. His brushes with the law and financial problems which led to bankruptcy and tax difficulties contributed to his image. After a couple of years with only moderate success, Johnny started 1977 with the two Top 10 hits *Slide Off of Your Satin Sheets* and *I'm the Only Hell (Mama Raised)*. Paycheck had his biggest hit in the form of *Take this Job and Shove It*, a song written by David Allan Coe, about a relationship gone sour that somehow became misconstrued as an anthem of workplace dissatisfaction. A movie of the same title was made in 1981 starring Robert Hays.

In 1978, Johnny had a Top 20 hit with *Georgia in a Jug*, which had on the flip the Top 40 *Me and the I.R.S.* He then had back-to-back Top 10 singles, *Friend, Lover, Wife* and the first of four charted singles with George Jones, *Maybellene*. The others were *You Can Have Her* (1979), *When You're Ugly Like Us (You Just Naturally Got to Be Cool)* and *You Better Move On* (both 1980). In 1979, he and his ex-manager, Glenn Ferguson, started on a legal battle.

Two years later, a Frontier Airlines female flight attendant sued Johnny for slander after his unruly behavior on a flight. From 1981 through 1983, Johnny toured with Merle Haggard and in 1981 recorded the album ***Mr. Hag Told My Story***. Battles with drugs and alcohol took some toll on the singer, and Johnny continued to have only modest success on the charts through 1982, but in 1983 Epic removed him from their roster.

Paycheck signed with AMI in 1984 and had three charted singles, of which *I Never Got Over You* did best, going Top 30. Then on December 19, 1985, he stopped at the North High Lounge in Hillsboro, Ohio, on a trip to visit family in Greenfield, and shot a man with whom he had a bar-room brawl. Found guilty of aggravated assault, he received a prison sentence which he began serving on February 7, 1989 after exhausting the appeal process.

During this four-year period, he signed with Mercury Records and scored with *Old Violin*, which just failed to make the Top 20. However, by 1988, he was off the label on to Desperado Records and thence, having got religion, recorded for Damascus.

He entered the Chillicothe Correctional Institute, where he served nearly two years. During his tenure behind bars, Johnny participated in a live concert with Merle Haggard that has yet to be released on disc. Governor Richard Celeste freed the Greenfield native on January 10, 1991, on the condition that he stay straight and perform 200 hours of community service. Since then Johnny has maintained himself in stable fashion, having a small role in the film *Paradise Park*, working showdates in Branson, Missouri, and elsewhere while giving anti-drug talks to youngsters. To date, Paycheck's main post-penitentiary recording has been a live concert in Branson and recordings for Playback Records. IMT

RECOMMENDED ALBUMS:

"Johnny Paycheck at Carnegie Hall" (Little Darlin')(1966)
"Gospeltime in My Fashion" (Little Darlin')(1967)
"Johnny Paycheck's Greatest Hits" (Little Darlin')(1969)
"Johnny Paycheck's Greatest Hits" (Epic)(1974)
"11 Months and 29 Days" (Epic)(1976)
"Slide Off of Your Satin Sheets" (Epic)(1977)
"Take this Job and Shove It" (Epic)(1977)
"Johnny Paycheck's Greatest Hits, Vol. 2" (Epic)(1978)
"Mr. Hag Told My Story" (Epic)(1981) [Features Merle Haggard]
"Biggest Hits" (Epic)(1982)
"Hell Raisers" (CBS UK)(1986) [One side Johnny Paycheck, the other Billy Joe Shaver]
"Modern Times" (Mercury)(1987)
With George Jones:
"George Jones & Johnny Paycheck/Double Trouble" (Epic)(1980) [Features Janie Fricke]

LEON PAYNE

(Singer, Songwriter, Guitar, Piano, Organ, Drums, Trombone)

Given Name:	**Leon Roger Payne**
Date of Birth:	**June 15, 1917**
Where Born:	**Alba, Texas**
Married:	**Myrtie Velma Cormier**
Children:	**Leon Roger, Jr., Rene Agee, Patricia Lee, Myrtie Lee**
Date of Death:	**September 11, 1969**

Leon Payne was responsible for writing two of the finest songs to grace Country music, *Lost Highway* and *I Love You Because*. However, he was not just a fine songwriter, he was also a very fine singer and talented musician.

Leon was blind from childhood and between 1924 and 1935 he attended the Texas School for the Blind in Austin. While there, he displayed an aptitude for music and mastered a whole array of instruments before he was out of his teens. He learned Country material by listening to records and the radio and by the

Legendary singer and songwriter ***Leon Payne***

mid 30's, he had started to play with various Texas bands.

He began appearing on the radio in 1935, when he debuted on KWET Palestine, Texas, as a virtual one-man band. He soon found himself in demand and in 1938, he started an association with Bob Wills and his Texas Playboys that would run through much of his career. From now on, Leon became a songwriter. How many songs he actually wrote is not known, but it is estimated that during his life, he was responsible for several thousand.

Leon began his recording career in 1939, cutting sides for Decca, TNT, Starday, Dee, MGM, Bullet and Capitol. Among his most popular early recordings were *You Don't Love Me But I'll Always Care* (1939), *Ten Thousand Tomorrows* and *Down Where the Violets Grow* (both 1940). For many years, he hitchhiked around Texas, playing with various groups, and was introduced as the "Texas Blind Hitchhiker."

In 1948, Leon became a member of Jack Rhodes & the Rhythm Boys and stayed with them until 1949. During the same period, he was also a member of Wills' Texas Playboys. He decided to strike out on his own in 1949 and formed the Lone Star Buddies. He played with them on the *Grand Ole Opry*, *Big D Jamboree* and the *Louisiana Hayride*. That year, two of his songs were converted into major hits; there was *Cry-Baby Heart* (written in 1944), a Top 5 hit for George Morgan and *Lost Highway* (written that year) which Hank Williams had as the flip-side of *You're Gonna Change*, but also reached the Top 15 in its own right. In addition, Leon also signed as an artist with Capitol Records.

1950 was a memorable year for Leon. His song *I Love You Because*, which he had written for his wife in 1949, gave him a No.1 hit as an artist. During that year, the song was also a hit for Ernest Tubb who took it to the Top 3 and Clyde Moody who reached Top 10 with it. In addition, Hank Williams had a Top 5 hit with Leon's *They'll Never Take Her Love from Me*.

During the 50's, Leon and the Lone Star Buddies, although regular guests on the *Opry*, were never members, as for some strange reason the management felt he would have trouble going on road tours. In view of his life of hitchhiking, this seems a nonsense. In fact, the group appeared at various stations around the country including WOAI and WOAI-TV in San Antonio, KGRO Dallas, KMJ Fresno, California, KLEE Houston, and KTEM-TV Temple, Texas. In addition, Leon turned out several singles for Capitol until 1953, but none of them had the success of *I Love You Because*. Leon moved on to Starday in 1955 and continued to put out singles up to 1964. He also cut a Rockabilly single *That Ain't It/Little Rock*, under the name "Rock Rogers," for the label.

Leon's early songs were published by Fred Rose Music, but during the 50's and 60's, he signed with Hill and Range, but returned to Acuff-Rose on a 10-year contract. During the 50's, Leon's songs racked up many major cuts including *For Now and Always* by Hank Snow (1953), *More Than Anything Else in the World* by Carl Smith (1954) and *Doorstep to Heaven*, also by Carl Smith in 1956. *More Than Anything Else in the World* earned for Leon a Citation of Achievement from ASCAP in 1955.

Throughout the 60's, Leon Payne's songs remained in demand and he chalked up many major hits. In 1960, Ernest Ashworth had *You Can't Pick a Rose in December* and Johnny Cash resurrected *I Love You Because*, while Al Martino did the same with it three years later and took it to the Pop Top 3. In 1964, the song was converted into a major hit through Jim Reeves. Reeves had recorded other Payne songs which would become posthumous hits; they include *Blue Side of Lonesome* (1966) and *I Heard a Heart Break Last Night* (1968). Reeves' version of *I Love You Because* would again be a hit in 1971 and 1976 and the song would be charted by Carl Smith (1969), Don Gibson (1978) and Roger Whittaker (1983).

In 1965, Payne was sidelined by a heart attack, which curtailed his performing activities. That year, George Jones had a major hit with Leon's *Things Have Gone To Pieces*. Two years later, Don Gibson, no slouch as a songwriter himself, put *Lost Highway* on the flipside of *Funny, Familiar, Forgotten Feelings*. The following year, Johnny Darrell hit the charts with his version of *They'll Never Take Her Love from Me*.

Leon Payne died on September 11, 1969, and left behind a treasury of wonderful songs that still find favor today.

RECOMMENDED ALBUMS:
"Leon Payne - A Living Legend of Country Music" (Starday)(1963)
"Americana" (Starday)(1963)

Pearl, Minnie refer MINNIE PEARL

HERB PEDERSEN

(Singer, Songwriter, 5-String Banjo, Guitar)
Date of Birth: April 27, 1944
Where Born: Berkeley, California

It took the supergroup Desert Rose Band to project long-time Bluegrass musician Herb Pedersen into the limelight. He had, however, been a musician's musician for many years.

Herb, the son of a policeman, first listened seriously to Country music at the Bay Area Folk festivals. Along with other hopefuls like David Nelson (New Riders of the Purple Sage) and Jerry Garcia, they wallowed in the delights of Flatt & Scruggs and the Stanley Brothers. While other musicians got into Rock music, Herb plowed his furrow deep in Country, forming the Pine Valley Boys, a Bluegrass group, and meeting another youngster who would come in and out of his career, Chris Hillman. Herb moved to Nashville in 1961, where he reckoned that only he and Archie Campbell had a mustache (!).

After only six months in town, he was playing on *Carl Tipton's Bluegrass TV Show*. In 1963, Herb joined David Grisman in the Smokey Grass Boys. The following year, he joined Bluegrass veterans Vern and Ray, singing and playing 5-string banjo, and it was here that he was spotted by Lester Flatt. Flatt chose Herb to replace Earl Scruggs during his absence from the band for a hip operation in 1967. The following year, he replaced Doug Dillard in the Dillards and his songwriting and tenor vocals altered the overall sound of the group. With the Dillards, Herb recorded ***Wheatsheaf Suite*** (1968) and ***Copperfields*** (1970).

Herb became one of the most sought-after session musicians in Los Angeles. Either on banjo or guitar or singing harmonics, he appeared on numerous albums. Among the albums that he played on were ***Evangeline*** (1971) and ***Pieces of the Sky*** (1975) (both Emmylou Harris), ***Traitor in Our Midst*** and ***Don't Give Up Your Day Job*** (Country Gazette, 1972 and 1973), Linda Ronstadt's self-titled album (1972), her ***Heart Like a Wheel*** (1974) and ***Prisoner in Disguise*** (1975), ***LA Reggae***, ***Blue Suede Shoes*** (both 1973), ***Last Boogie in Paris*** (1974), ***Help Me Rhonda*** (1975) and ***New Loves and Old Friends*** (1975) (all Johnny Rivers), ***Fall into Spring*** (Rita Coolidge, 1974), ***Douglas Flint Dillard*** (Doug Dillard, 1974), ***Close Up the Honky Tonks*** (Flying Burrito Brothers, 1974), ***Spooky Lady's Sideshow*** (1974), ***Who's to Bless & Who's to Blame*** (1975)(both Kris Kristofferson), ***Grievous Angel*** (Gram Parsons, 1974), ***Common Sense*** (John Prine, 1975), ***Change*** (Spanky & Our Gang, 1975) and ***Stoned Slow Rugged*** (Rusty Weir, 1975).

During 1975, Herb toured with Jackson Browne, and the following year, he recorded his first solo album, ***Southwest***, for Epic. That year, Herb was featured on several important albums that included ***Sleepless Nights*** (Gram Parsons/Flying Burrito Brothers), ***Elite Hotel*** (Emmylou Harris), ***Slippin' Away*** (Chris

Hillman), ***Surreal Thing*** (Kris Kristofferson), ***Hasten Down the Wind*** (Linda Ronstadt), and ***In the Pocket*** (James Taylor).

In 1977, Herb released his second solo album, ***Sandman***, and the single *Our Baby's Gone* reached the Top 60 on the Country charts. From 1977 to 1980, Herb was a member of John Denver's touring band and appeared on Denver's albums during this period. He continued to appear on other albums including, in 1977, ***Luxury Liner*** (Emmylou Harris), ***Simple Dream*** (Linda Ronstadt), ***Fire in the Wind*** (John Stewart), Jennifer Warnes' self-titled album and ***Nothing But the Breeze*** (Jesse Winchester); and in 1978, ***I Wasn't Born Yesterday*** (Allan Clarke), ***Nicolette*** (Nicolette Larson) and ***Outside Help*** (Johnny Rivers); in 1979, ***Decade Waltz*** (the Dillards), ***Minute by Minute*** (Doobie Brothers) and ***Thanks I'll Eat Here*** (Lowell George); in 1980, ***Romance Dance*** (Kim Carnes), ***Mountain Rock*** and ***Homecoming & Family Reunion*** (both the Dillards) and ***Dream Street Rose*** (Gordon Lightfoot).

Herb continued sessioning during 1981 through 1984 and appeared on Emmylou Harris' ***Cimarron*** and Tanya Tucker's ***Should I Do It***, both in 1981. During 1984, he recorded the solo album ***Lonesome Feeling*** for Sugar Hill. That same year, he appeared on Chris Hillman's ***Desert Rose*** album and this led directly to Herb and Chris backing Dan Fogelberg on his 1985 Bluegrass project, ***High Country Snows***. This in turn led to Herb becoming a founding member of the Desert Rose Band, the following year. While with the band, he also did outside projects. In 1988, he arranged the vocals on several cuts for the ***Trio*** album. The following year, he produced the Dillards for Vanguard Records and the Vega Brothers for Curb.

In addition to the above named projects, Herb has played on sessions for Diana Ross, Stephen Stills, Anne Murray, Kenny Rogers, Buck Owens and Earl Scruggs. He has written the music for various TV series, including all the episodes of *The Rockford Files, Kojak, The A-Team* and *The Dukes of Hazzard*. He also wrote music for the movies *Heroes* (1972) and *Smokey and the Bandit* (1977). Herb continued as one of the triumvirate running Desert Rose Band until their cessation in 1993. He continues as a session musician, singer and producer.

RECOMMENDED ALBUMS:

"Southwest" (Epic)(1976)
"Sandman" (Epic)(1977)
"Lonesome Feeling" (Sugar Hill)(1984)
(Also listen to Desert Rose Band albums)

"HAP" PEEBLES

(Music Promoter, Booking Agent)

Given Name: Harry Alexander Peebles
Date of Birth: January 4, 1913
Where Born: Anthony, Kansas
Married: Unknown
Children: Carol, Linda
Date of Death: January 8, 1993

Known as the "Dean of Country Music Bookers," "Hap" Peebles worked as a promoter and booking agent for 62 years. He founded the Harry Peebles Agency and in his familiar broad-brimmed white cowboy hat, this tall, stocky man became a legend. He got into promoting after working for the *Anthony Republican* newspaper. When a new auditorium was built in the town, Peebles saw the opportunity to bring shows and sporting events into the venue.

From 1931, he booked Country acts such as Bob Wills & the Texas Playboys (whom he later managed), Roy Acuff, Ernest Tubb, Minnie Pearl and the Duke of Paducah and went on to represent Dolly Parton. He was also a rodeo promoter for over 25 years. In partnership with rancher Harry Shepler, Hap formed the Kansas Horse Racing Association, which led to them promoting rodeos. He was also active in other sporting events, and served as the Executive Secretary of the Southern Kansas-Northern Oklahoma baseball and basketball leagues. He was also President of a semi-professional ice hockey association and was Missouri's first state baseball commissioner.

He became the first promoter to provide Country music talent to fairs throughout the Midwest in any sort of systematic way. In his words, "I think fairs are the last form of family entertainment in this country." He was a member of the Halls of Fame of the state fair associations of Kansas, Iowa, South Dakota, North Dakota, Oklahoma, Arkansas and Louisiana.

During the 40's, Hap booked 247 big band tours, including those by Guy Lombardo and Louis Armstrong. He also arranged for touring versions of *My Fair Lady, No Time for Sergeants* and *Hair*. However, his first love was always Country music.

He helped in the formation of the International Entertainment Buyers Association, in 1971, and he was elected Chairman of the Board and then President Emeritus. It was Hap who introduced the concept of a seminar for Country music buyers, which from its start in 1972 eventually led to SRO. He was also life-time Director of the Louisiana Association of Fairs & Festivals. He lived in Wichita, Kansas, until 1972 and then moved to Kansas City.

He was a life-time member of the Country Music Association, and served on the Board of Directors for 16 years, and was nominated for the Country Music Hall of Fame. He was also the CMA's first recipient of its "Talent Buyer & Promoter of the Year" Award.

In addition, Hap had a student scholarship named after him at Nashville's Belmont University. His proudest feat was booking three generations of the Foley family, Red, daughter Betty and grandson Clyde Foley Cummins. He died at St. Luke's Hospital in Kansas City, and was survived by his daughters, and his partner and longtime companion, Evelyn Zerr.

RALPH PEER

(Industry Executive)

Given Name: Ralph Sylvester Peer
Date of Birth: May 22, 1892
Where Born: Kansas City, Missouri
Married: Monique I. (dec'd.)
Children: Ralph II
Date of Death: January 19, 1960

Ralph Peer was one of the pioneering A & R men who helped create the Country music record and publishing industry in the 1920's. He is perhaps best known as the Victor talent scout who discovered Jimmie Rodgers and the Carter Family during the famed "Bristol Sessions," but he was also a giant in the field of publishing, creating and managing the Peer-Southern company. He was also important as an early advocate and producer of Blues recordings and *he* was the one who recorded what many consider the very first Country recording, by Fiddlin' John Carson, in 1923.

Though Peer by nature was cynical and businesslike in his dealings with artists, he had an incredible feel for the music, and though he would have laughed at the idea of seeing himself as a preserver of culture, he in fact was. His field recordings of Country, Blues, Gospel, Cajun, Mexican and cowboy music in the 1920's and 1930's rival the early work of the Library of Congress, and survive as an exemplary body of what his company liked to advertise as "Native American Melodies."

Born the son of a phonograph dealer, Peer grew up listening to all sorts of music in his father's store and after high school he went to work for Columbia. He worked at all kinds of jobs in the company and by 1915 had transferred to the Chicago office. WWI brought service in the Navy and by 1920 he was working for the General Phonograph Company, which produced OKeh records. In 1920 Peer was attracted to Mamie Smith's *Crazy Blues*—by some standards the first Blues recording—and invented the term "race" to describe it.

Three years later came his initial recording with Fiddlin' John Carson—at his first southern field session. He left OKeh in 1925 and went to work for Victor, under a special agreement in which Peer was allowed to solicit the publishing rights for any song he recorded. This also resulted in the formation of Southern Music, as a company in which to house the copyrights.

With this arrangement, Peer naturally sought out "original" material by his artists —as opposed to remakes of current hits or versions of older Tin Pan Alley songs. This turned out to be good both for him and the music and it encouraged the new Country performers to come up with their own songs, or at least do new arrangements of older ones.

Starting in March, 1927, he began the first of a regular series of field trips around the South, going to Atlanta, Memphis, and New Orleans. Later that summer, Peer made his famous trip to Bristol, as well as ones to Charlotte and Atlanta. His finds ranged from the Carolina Tar Heels to the Georgia Yellow Hammers, from Ernest Stoneman to Jimmie Davis.

By 1932, Peer was eased out of his job with Victor by his protégé, Eli Oberstein, and he turned his full attention to publishing and to promoting his Country music catalog. (He also continued to serve as the manager for the Carter Family.) By the late 1950's, he had opened up overseas branches of his company and was one of the first to see the benefits of becoming international. His Southern Music joined ASCAP in 1940, but Peer knew that many of his Country songwriters could not join ASCAP and could join BMI, its rival organization. To that end he created another firm, Peer International, to work with BMI. Soon his catalog became one of the largest with BMI and included songs like *You Are My Sunshine*, *Born to Lose*, *Blue Moon of Kentucky*, *Wabash Cannon Ball*, *Muleskinner Blues* and most of the Carter and Rodgers songs.

Peer died in 1960, and his wife Monique continued to run his company until her death on August 30, 1987. Their son, Ralph Peer II, a longtime Board member of the CMA, now runs the company. CKW

PEGGY SUE

(Singer, Songwriter)

Given Name: Peggy Sue Webb
Date of Birth: March 24,1947
Where Born: Butchers Hollow, Kentucky
Married: 1. Douglas Wells
2. Sonny Wright
Children: Doletta Gail (dec'd.)

Peggy Sue is the sister of Loretta Lynn and Crystal Gayle, and in the late 60's and early 70's she performed as a member of the Webb family with her father and mother, Melvin and Clara, and brothers Jay Lee Webb and Herbert.

When she was 12, her father was forced by ill health to retire from his job as a coal miner. The family was a large one, and, virtually starving, they all moved to Indiana. There Peggy Sue finished her education at the Wabash High School, and Loretta, Crystal and Peggy Sue sang together as the Loretta Lynn Sisters.

Peggy Sue toured with Loretta Lynn's road show as a featured act and the two sisters wrote songs together. One of Loretta's biggest hits, in 1966, was a co-written effort of theirs, called *Don't Come Home A-Drinkin' (With Lovin' on Your Mind)*. Loretta wrote Peggy Sue's debut single on Decca, in 1969, called *I'm Dynamite*. It peaked on the Country charts in the Top 30. The flip-side was a Peggy Sue and Loretta composition, *Love Whatcha Got at Home*. Peggy Sue followed, that year, with another Top 30 release, *I'm Gettin' Tired of Babyin' You*.

She remained with Decca until the end of 1971 and her most successful single in that period was, *All American Husband* (Top 40, 1970).

During 1970, Peggy Sue appeared in England, with Loretta Lynn, at the Second International Festival of Country Music at

Peggy Sue and Sonny Wright

Wembley. Peggy Sue was absent from the charts between 1971 and 1977 and then she signed with her second husband, Sonny Wright, to the independent Door Knob label.

She stayed with Door Knob until 1980, and racked up some moderately successful singles, including *Every Beat of My Heart* (Top 40, 1977), *How I Love You in the Morning* (Top 40, 1979) and *I Want to See Me in Your Eyes* (Top 30, 1979). She had two low level duets with Sonny Wright, namely, *If This is What Love's All About* (1977) and *Gently Hold Me* (1979). Peggy Sue's final solo success was the basement level single *Why Don't You Go to Dallas*, in 1980. In 1983, she signed with Country International.

Peggy Sue's daughter, Doletta (a name created from the first names of close friend Doyle Wilburn and Loretta Lynn), was murdered by her husband, a Mr. McCannless. Peggy Sue currently sings backup for Crystal Gayle and also makes stage costumes. JAB

RECOMMENDED ALBUMS:

"Peggy Sue—Dynamite" (Decca)(1969) [Re-released on MCA (1970)]
"All American Husband" (Decca)(1970)
"I Just Came in Here (To Let a Little Hurt Out)" (Door Knob)(1977) [Shown as Peggy Sue Wells]
"One Side of Peggy Sue/One Side of Sonny Wright" (Country International)(1983) [Solos]
"Gently Hold Me" (Big R UK) [With Sonny Wright]

RAY PENNINGTON

(Singer, Songwriter, Guitar, Industry Executive)

Given Name: Ramon Daniel Pennington
Date of Birth: 1933
Where Born: Clay County, Kentucky
Married: Charlotte
Children: Lynn, Sharon, Julie

It was as a songwriter that Ray Pennington made his mark, with songs such as *Three Hearts in a Tangle, Walking on New Grass* and *Ramblin' Man*. In recent years, he has been involved as the main man at the excellent independent label Step One and as co-leader with Buddy Emmons of the wonderful Swing Shift Band.

Ray began singing at age 6, under the tutelage of his father, Alva, who was the church choral director in Clay County. He acquired his first guitar at age 15, by trading a bicycle. By the time he was 16, Ray was singing on TV in Cincinnati and he formed his own Western Swing band, the Mid-West Rhythm Boys, at age 19 and they toured the Ohio Valley, Kentucky and Indiana. By 1957, with Country music undergoing a decline in their area, the band switched to playing Rhythm and Blues. However, they later returned to playing Country.

He began his industry career as an A & R man, in 1959, when he joined King Records in Cincinnati. He had his first major cut as a songwriter in 1961, when Roy Drusky had a Top 3 hit with Ray's *Three Hearts in a Tangle*. In 1962, Roy released an R & B single, *I Have to Laugh to Keep from Crying/In the Middle of Two Hearts*, for King, under the name of "Ray Starr." In 1963, Ray signed to Pamper Music and became not just a writer, but also production coordinator–arranger and A & R man. He also released his first Country single for King that year, *The First Step Down Is the Longest*. The following year, Bob Jennings had a medium sized hit with the same song.

In 1966, Ray started to produce for Boone Records and the label's artist Kenny Price had a Top 10 single with the Pennington song *Walking on New Grass*. That same year, Ray signed to Capitol Records and had a Top 50 hit with *Who's Been Mowing the Lawn*. The following year, Kenny Price had a follow-up Top 10 single, *Happy Feet*, another Pennington song. Ray had two chart entries himself with the Top 30 entry *Ramblin' Man* and the Top 70 *Who's Gonna Walk the Dog (And Put Out the Cat)*.

During 1968 Ray moved to Monument Records, and up to 1971 he racked up six more chart entries, none of which reached higher than the Top 70 *You Don't Know Me*. In 1973, both Gary Stewart and Jimmy Payne had low level successes with *Happy Feet*. By 1978, Ray had moved to MRC Records, where he had one chart entry, *She Wanted a Little Bit More*.

In 1980, Ray teamed up with Jerry McBee, as Bluestone, and charted *Haven't I Loved You Somewhere Before*, on Dimension. He moved over to EMH in 1984, and recorded *Nothing's Changed, Nothing's New*.

With the emergence of Step One Records in 1984, Ray took over the reins as the head man in Nashville and also the label's producer. He teamed up with steel guitar maestro Buddy Emmons for an on-going series of Swing-orientated albums under the name of the Swing Shift Band, starting with ***Swingin' from the 40's Thru the 80's***.

RECOMMENDED ALBUMS:

"Ray Pennington Sings for the Other Woman" (Monument)(1970)
"Memories" (Dimension)(1983)
"Dear Lord, I've Changed Since I've Been Unchained" (Step One)(1987)
Swing Shift Band:
"Swingin' from the 40's Thru the 80's" (Step One)(1984)
"In the Mood for Swinging" (Step One)(1986)
"Swingin' Our Way" (Step One)(1990)
"Swingin' By Request" (Step One)(1992)

HANK PENNY

(Singer, Songwriter, Comedian, Deejay, Bandleader, Banjo, Guitar)

Given Name: Herbert Clayton Penny
Date of Birth: August 18, 1918
Where Born: Birmingham, Alabama
Married: 3. Sue Thompson (m.1953)(div. 1963)
5. Shari Bayne (m. 1967)
Date of Death: April 17, 1992

During the late 40's and early 50's, Hank Penny and his Radio Cowboys were up there with the best in Western Swing, without getting the true acclaim deserved. He was probably better known for his open criticism of Country music, other performers, deejays and industry executives.

Hank was one of eight children born to a disabled coal miner and his wife. Spending his early years in abject poverty, he found inspiration in the talents of his father, an amateur guitarist, poet and magician, who died in 1928. Penny became a performer at age 15, when he joined WAPI as a banjo player. WAPI's Hal Burns needed a banjo player, but at the time Hank only played guitar. So he traded his new Epiphone guitar for a banjo, tuned it to guitar tuning and got the job. He stayed with Burns for three years, learning valuable lessons about playing and the music business, and how to handle comedy.

In 1936, he joined WWL New Orleans as a soloist and started to get turned on to the Western Swing stylings of Bob Wills and Milton Brown. Staying with famed steel player Noel Boggs only got him more enthusiastic for the music. After a couple of stints at the station, Hank returned to Birmingham, where he set up his first band, the Radio Cowboys, which comprised Julian Akins (guitar), Sammy Forsmark (steel guitar), Louis Damont (tenor banjo), Carl Stewart (bass) and Sheldon Bennett (fiddle, guitar, vocals).

*Bandleader and comedy star **Hank Penny***

The band first broadcast on WKBC Birmingham and moved shortly after to WAPI. In 1937, they (without Akins) joined the WDOD *Chattanooga Playhouse*. At this time, the 19-year old Penny started to promote local concerts which local companies sponsored. He soon fell foul of the booking offices of WSM, who tried to undercut him and adopted spoiling tactics, although they probably considered it to be "just business."

In 1938, the band was signed to ARC and they cut their first record in Columbia, South Carolina, with Art Satherley producing. The first session yielded *Hesitation Blues, When I Take My Sugar to Tea* (both Milton Brown staples) and the Penny original, *Flamin' Mamie*, which sold the best. On November 18 that year, the band joined the cast of WSB Atlanta's *Crossroad Follies*. Early the next year, Forsmark left the band and was replaced by the infinitely better Noel Boggs and a new fiddle player came on board by the name of Boudleaux Bryant.

Penny's acclaim reached the ears of impresario J.L. Frank, who offered him the vocal position with Pee Wee King's Golden West Cowboys, when Eddy Arnold left for a while. He also received an offer to join the Light Crust Doughboys, but declined both. Later in 1939, the band moved to Nashville, where they auditioned for the *Grand Ole Opry*. WSM's Charlie Reel offered them a spot on the show if they had Boggs play Hawaiian guitar, instead of steel; they declined. In July, they had a second record session with Satherley and then shortly after, Boggs left the group to join Jimmy Wakely. Eddie Duncan, formerly with the Tune Wranglers, joined the band at $15 per week.

In June 1940, the band went to Chicago for their third record session and among the tracks recorded were *Peach Tree Shuffle* and *Tobacco State Swing*. However, WWII was looming and by the fall of that year, the band was no more, as the draft bit. WSB offered Hank a job as morning deejay, for which he received the princely sum of $35 a week.

In June 1941, Hank put together a band made up of Carl Stewart (fiddle and bass), Jimmy Colvard (steel guitar), Kelland Clark (accordion) and Eddie Smith (piano and harmonica) to made his last recording session for ARC in Charlotte, North Carolina. From that session, *Why Did I Cry* and *Lonesome Train Blues* were issued on OKeh and Columbia. He soon moved to what sounded a great gig as a back-up musician at KXEL Waterloo, Iowa, but it was just slave labor and Hank was soon on his way back to Atlanta.

He left without notice and ended up being fined by the Musicians' Union.

After eight months at WSB, Hank moved on to WLW Cincinnati, where he joined the cast of the *Boone County Jamboree* and the *Midwestern Hayride*. Here Hank led a new band, the Plantation Boys, which comprised Carl Stewart (fiddle), Louis Innis (bass and guitar), Zed Tennis (fiddle) and Roy Lanham (electric lead guitar). He also worked with the Delmore Brothers, Merle Travis, Bradley Kincaid and Grandpa Jones. He also backed-up the station's Pop singer, Doris Day, and worked as announcer on a shopper's program.

In 1944, Hank and the Plantation Boys (except Langham) went on a USO tour through the South. The organizers were so pleased that Hank was offered the rank of Captain and the band was offered a tour of European bases. However, the Atlantic was still full of U-Boats, and Hank declined and at the end of the tour returned to Cincinnati. He was urged to come to California by Merle Travis. Here he fell under the spell of band leader Spade Cooley. Through Travis, Penny met Cooley's former manager, Foreman Phillips, who was running the County Barn Dance organization. Phillips offered Penny a band leader's job.

Returning to Cincinnati to tidy his affairs in 1945, he was approached by Syd Nathan, the owner of the new King label, to record for him. He did so, and fell foul of the WLW hierarchy, who didn't like their staff members to record. Four indifferent sides were recorded for the label and then Hank headed back to L.A. Here he put together a new band with Harold Hensley (fiddle), Noel Boggs, Jimmy Dyble (lead guitar), plus a bass player, drummer and accordion player. However, trouble was soon coming and when Phillips tried to tell Hank how to play, the band quit and then split up.

Hank was forced to pawn most of his belongings including his Martin guitar. Then he fronted an all-girl band at the Silver Spur in L.A. A month later, Hank was approached by Spade Cooley's manager, Bobbie Bennett, who asked him to put together a band for a Charles Starrett movie and to front a band to handle bookings that Cooley was too busy to do. Tex Ritter led one band and Merle Travis led another.

She (Bobbie) booked Penny into Hoot Gibson's Painted Post, where he played with a band which became known as the Painted Post Rangers. Early in 1946, they recorded some sides for King and suddenly found themselves with a chart hit when *Steel Guitar Stomp* and *Get Yourself a Redhead* both made the Top 5. When the Painted Post folded, Penny moved over to the Riverside Rancho, where he took over a large band, which Penny didn't consider played well.

By the end of 1946, Hank had joined Slim Duncan on ABC radio's *Roundup Time* as a comedian, leaving Western Swing behind. He moved back to WLW and then moved on to Connie B. Gay's WARl in Arlington, Virginia. However, after another dispute, Hank returned to California.

With the dance hall scene down, Hank returned to being a deejay, on the *Penny Serenade* on KGIL Sherman Oaks. When Decca refused to service his show, Hank organized a boycott of the label...which worked! Hank put together a new band, the Penny Serenaders, which included Speedy West, Bud Sievert (accordion), Slim Duncan, Billy Hill (fiddle) and Hank Caldwell (bass). Bemoaning the lack of venues, he got talking to Amand Gautier, who owned Pop's Willow Lake. As a result, they built a 600-capacity dance hall and presented Bob Wills on the opening night.

Hank now got involved in TV and in June 1948, appeared on Spade Cooley's show on KTLA-TV, as a comedian, and soon became a regular cast member, dressed in baggy coat, beaten-up hat, vest and pants and billed as "That Plain Ol' Country Boy," telling jokes about his "hometown" of Rimlap, Alabama. In 1949, Hank recorded again and among the sides cut was *Hillbilly Bebop*, the first time a Country performer had recorded this form of Jazz. He also cut *Bloodshot Eyes*, which was a Top 5 hit in 1950.

Later that year, Penny and partner Gautier discovered another possible venue site and that soon became the famed Palomino. Hank put together a new incarnation of the Penny Serenaders that included Herb Remington, Benny Garcia (lead guitar), Billy Hill, Stan Ellison (accordion), Pee Wee Adams (drums) and singer Mary Morgan (who became Jaye P. Morgan). He was now very popular indeed and had his own fan club, the Penny Pushers. In March, 1950, the band recorded the excellent *Remington Ride* and *Wham Bam! Thank You, Ma'am*. However, shortly after, the group folded and Hank concentrated on his radio work on KWIK Burbank.

Later in the year, Hank put together a new smaller unit with Remington, Garcia, Caldwell, fiddler Max Fidler and drummer Warren Pennington. They signed to Victor Records and, augmented by guitarist Billy Strange and steelie Joaquin Murphy, began cutting sides. However, Hank soon came to "blows" with RCA's Steve Sholes and Henry Rene, because of the inferior material he was being offered. He cut some transcriptions for Standard Music and then, in 1952, he was approached by the singer Dude Martin to appear on his upcoming TV show for Sears Roebuck. Hank left Cooley and joined Martin. However, one result of the move was that Hank met Dude's wife, singer Sue Thompson, eventually marrying her. Leaving Martin's show, Hank was given his own TV show, the *Hank Penny Show* on KHJ-TV. After seven weeks of the proposed 13 week run, the sponsor, Bill Murphy Buick, canceled and a legal battle ensued.

In 1954, Hank signed with Decca but without any meaningful recordings being released. That year he and Sue moved to Las Vegas and he was booked into the Golden Nugget, where he stayed for seven years. He cut various sides in 1957 for Decca and in 1961 he cut a Jazz album for Atlanta's NRC label. During 1961 and 1962, his band moved back to a more Country feel and included in the line-up Curly Chalker and Roy Clark. Clark was an avid student of Penny's comedy style.

Following his divorce, Hank moved to Carson City, Nevada, where he remained until 1970. He worked at Harrah's with Merle Travis's son, Thom Bresh, who became his protégé. Hank recorded comedy material for the Wasp label and in 1969, gave the band to Bresh. Returning to Nashville, Hank was considered for a part on *Hee Haw*, and his claim was pushed by Archie Campbell, but Roy Clark was preferred. He stayed in Nashville until 1972 and then became a deejay on KFRM Wichita, Kansas. In 1975, with his new wife, Shari, Hank moved back to the San Fernando Valley. After that, he and Shari played together with Hank using a drum machine and he appeared in Norman Lear's *America 2-Nite* program. Hank died from a heart attack on April 17, 1992.

RECOMMENDED ALBUMS:

"Rompin' Stompin' Singin' Swingin' (Bear Family Germany/Rollercoaster UK)(1982)

"Tobacco State Swing" (Rambler)

CARL PERKINS

(Singer, Songwriter, Guitar)

Given Name:	**Carl Lee Perkins**
Date of Birth:	**April 9, 1932**
Where Born:	**Near Tiptonville, Tennessee**
Married:	**Valda de Vese**
Children:	**Steve, Stan, Greg, Debra**

To everyone in Rockabilly and rock'n'roll, Carl Perkins is the "guv'nor." It's not as if he gyrates on stage, but when he is up there in front of an audience, he is in charge and his audience delightedly responds to any movement and joins in on *Blue Suede Shoes* at his bidding.

Carl was raised in a poor farming community, where his parents, Forrie Arber and Mary Louise, eked out a living on a cotton plantation, and the first guitar he got was made out of a cigar box, broom handle, and baling wire for strings. Carl was given the nickname "one string Perkins" because of his guitar style, which had a lot to do with the fact that in those early days if he broke a string, he had to tie a knot in it. He was taught Blues licks by a black cotton worker, Uncle John Westbrooks. Eventually, Carl's father bought Uncle John's guitar from him for $3.50. In 1945, Carl won a talent contest in Bemis and as a result performed *Home on the Range* on WTJS in Jackson. When Carl was 15, the family moved to Jackson, Tennessee.

He started playing at local country dances and honky tonks with his brothers, calling themselves the Perkins Brothers; Jay playing rhythm guitar and Clayton string bass. They performed on WTJS and were retained for 5 nights a week at a honky tonk called the El Rancho Club. Carl married when he was 21 and decided to make his career in music full-time. He then bought his first quality guitar, a Les Paul. Later that year, W.S. "Fluke" Holland was added to the group on drums. Carl was encouraged to write by his wife and Curley Griffin, a blind singer/songwriter, who also collaborated with Perkins.

Carl approached Sam Phillips, who signed him to a two-year contract on January 25, 1955. The first single, *Movie Magg/Just Turn Around,* was released on Flip, a month later. There was a lot of deejay approval and later that month Carl and the band were back in the studio. They then went on tour with Elvis Presley and newcomer Johnny Cash. The next single, *Let the Jukebox Keep on Playing/Gone, Gone, Gone*, was released in September on Sun.

By November that year, Presley had gone to RCA Victor, and Carl became the performer likely to be heavily promoted. Carl and the band appeared on the *Grand Ole Opry*, but were not allowed to use a full drum kit. Carl persuaded Phillips to let him record his own song, *Blue Suede Shoes*, which he had written in December, 1955. This marked a distinct change of musical policy at Sun. The Country-influenced songs that Carl had cut were largely gone and a more Rockabilly style came into play. He was not now in competition with Elvis. The single was released on January 1, 1956 and became the first record to top the Pop (*Cash Box*), Country and R & B charts. It was also a Top 10 hit in Britain. The song had

The King of Rockabilly, ***Carl Perkins***

been originally written on a brown paper potato bag.

As a result of the success of the single the Perkins band was being booked onto major TV shows. They were on their way to New York to appear on the Perry Como and Ed Sullivan shows, when the car they were traveling in was involved in an accident in Delaware. Jay was seriously injured and died from these injuries in 1958. Carl had a fractured skull and a broken neck. He had the awful experience of watching the *Ed Sullivan Show* and seeing Elvis sing *Blue Suede Shoes* in his stead.

Sun continued releasing Carl's singles and the 1956 follow-up, *Boppin' the Blues*, went Top 10 on the Country chart and also crossed over into the Pop Top 70. He finished up the year with another Top 10 Country hit, *Dixie Fried/I'm Sorry I'm Not Sorry*, which failed to find favor with the urban rock'n'rollers. Then Carl's career nose-dived, and he had now taken second position behind Johnny Cash. His medical bills nearly bankrupted him and Clayton had started to drink heavily. Only *Your True Love* made any sort of showing, in 1957, peaking in the Top 15 on the Country chart. In December of that year, Sun released the wonderful rocker *Glad All Over*, which was featured in the Warner Brothers movie *Jamboree* (called *Disc Jockey Jamboree* in Europe).

During 1958, Carl was now surpassed in the Sun roster, not only by Cash, but also Jerry Lee Lewis. During the year, Carl, billed as "the Rockin' Guitar Man," appeared in the movie *Hawaiian Boy* (United Artists). His contract with Sun came to an end and he and Cash signed with Columbia. His only notable success on the label was *Pink Pedal Pushers*, which was a Top 20 Country success. He stayed with the label until 1960 and then moved to Decca, but further success still eluded him. He was now playing dates in Las Vegas and Reno and thinking about giving up show business. It was only a tour of U.S. forces' bases in Europe that stopped him. During 1962, Patsy Cline had a hit with Carl's song *So Wrong*.

In 1964, after five years of bad gigs and too much drink, he re-emerged for a tour of the U.K. with Chuck Berry (newly released from prison). Carl was greeted in England by an enthusiastic crowd. He was lauded by the Beatles, who had learned their craft from Carl's ***Dance Album*** and they jammed with Carl, but the result was never released. The Beatles had recorded three Perkins songs, *Matchbox, Honey Don't* and *Everybody's Trying to Be My Baby*.

Carl moved over to Dollie Records in 1966 and had two Country hits, *Country Boy's Dream* (Top 25, 1966) and *Shine, Shine* (Top 40, 1967). He decided to join Johnny Cash's show and beat his drinking problem. With Cash, Carl toured the world and started to get back the kudos he deserved. He moved back to Columbia Records and had a Top 20 Country hit with *Restless*. The following year, Cash recorded the Perkins classic *Daddy Sang Bass*, and took it to No.1. During 1971, Cash and Perkins wrote the music for the movie

Little Fauss and Big Halsy. He hung around the label until 1973, but the highest placed single was *Cotton Top*, which peaked in the Top 60. That year, he moved to Mercury Records and was reunited with Jerry Lee Lewis. He had a minor hit with *(Let's Get) Dixiefried*, a re-recording of his 1956 hit, featuring Jerry Lee.

In 1975, Carl left the Cash troupe and started his own band, which featured his sons Stan and Greg on drums and bass respectively. He and the band appeared at the Wembley Festival in England in 1976, 1977 and 1978. Carl left Mercury in 1976, and formed his own label, Suede. He still recorded for other labels and turned up on Music Mill and MMI, before the major re-launch of his career by the English label, Jet. The resultant album, ***Ol' Blue Suede's Back***, was successful in Britain but got lost in the U.S.

During 1985, Delilah Films presented a TV Special, *Blue Suede Shoes*, that featured Carl with Dave Edmunds, George Harrison, Eric Clapton, Ringo Starr, the Stray Cats and Rosanne Cash. Billy Strange produced a series of albums for MCA/Dot in 1985, one of which was ***Carl Perkins***, but it was the 1986 "alma mater" album ***The Class of '55***, with Cash, Lewis and Roy Orbison, that caught the public imagination. From this came Carl's hits *Birth of Rock and Roll* (Top 40, 1986) and *Class of '55* (1987). When Jimmy Bowen opened his short-lived Universal Records, Carl's ***Born to Rock*** (1989) was the first release. In 1992, Carl Perkins suffered heart problems, but is now fully recovered.

It seems strange that when Carl's early output is examined, little of it found public favor, yet now, nearly forty years later, his work is considered to be of such great importance and without Carl Perkins, would there have been a James Burton, Shakin' Stevens, Stray Cats, Dave Edmunds or for that matter...a Billy Ray Cyrus!

RECOMMENDED ALBUMS

Really just about all of them, but below is a list of "must gets."
"Dance Album" (Sun)(1957)
"Country Boy's Dream" (Dollie)(1966)
"Blue Suede Shoes" (Sun)(1969)
"Carl Perkins' Greatest Hits" (Columbia)(1969)
"Boppin' the Blues" (Columbia)(1970) [With NRBQ]
"Ol' Blue Suede's Back" (Jet)(1978)
"Carl Perkins & the C.P. Express (Live at Austin City Limits)" (Suede)(1981)
"The Survivors" (Columbia)(1982) [With Johnny Cash and Jerry Lee Lewis]
"Carl Perkins" (MCA/Dot)(1985)
"Class of '55" (America/Smash)(1986) [With Johnny Cash, Roy Orbison and Jerry Lee Lewis]
"Dixie Fried" (Sun/Charly UK)(1988)
"Born to Rock" (Universal)(1989)

BILL PHILLIPS

(Singer, Songwriter, Guitar, Actor)

Given Name:	**William Clarence Phillips**
Date of Birth:	**January 28, 1938**
Where Born:	**Canton, North Carolina**
Married:	**1. Juanita June Rich ("Nita") (div.)** **2. Ann**
Children:	**William George ("Chip"), Lawrence Raymond ("Rayme")**

For two decades, "Tater" Phillips was a regular visitor to the Country charts and for a while looked like he was going to emerge as a major player in the Country music hierarchy.

Bill's interest in music came from his mother, Charlotte, who played her brother's guitar as a youngster. It was she who gave Bill his nickname of "Tater," because when he tried to sing *Old Faithful* as a child, it came out as "Old Tater." Two of Bill's brothers played music, an elder one who had a band on a radio station in Waynesville and a younger brother, Herman, who sometimes sang with Bill.

While still at high school, Bill played guitar, but he initially worked as an upholsterer. His career started to take off in 1955, when he joined the cast of the *Old Southern Jamboree* on WHIL Miami and got a residency at The Granada Club, Miami.

He moved to Nashville in 1957 and with Mel Tillis' help he signed a writer's deal with Cedarwood Music. In 1958, Bill wrote *Falling Back to You*, which became a Country hit for Webb Pierce. That same year, Bill signed with Columbia Records and released his first single, *Lying Lips*, and then, in 1959, Bill had a Top 30 duet single entitled *Sawmill* with Mel Tillis. In 1960, he followed up with another duet with Mel, entitled *Georgia Town Blues*, which also went Top 30. During this time, he became a regular on the *Grand Ole Opry*.

Although he continued to release singles on Columbia until 1962, he had no further chart action. He moved to a 10-year contract with Decca, in 1963, and the following year, had two Top 30 chart singles, *I Can Stand It (As Long as She Can)* and *Stop Me*. Then for the next year, his singles failed to make the lists, but Bill had the consolation of Kitty Wells taking his *I'll Repossess Your Heart* into the Top 10. Kitty would go on to record several of Bill's songs. As a recording artist, Bill came back strongly in 1966, with two songs written by Dolly Parton, *Put It Off Until Tomorrow*, on which Dolly did harmony vocals, and *The Company You Keep*. Both the singles made the Top 10, as did the the first single of 1967, *The Words I'm Gonna Have to Eat*. His other singles of the year fared less successfully, with *I Learn Something New Everyday* going Top 40 and *Love's Dead End* peaking in the Top 25.

Bill didn't chart at all in 1968, but Kitty and Johnny Wright charted with the Phillips song *We'll Stick Together*. In 1969, Bill became a regular on the *Kitty Wells, Johnny Wright, Bobby Wright, Family Show* and also became a major part of their roadshow. That year, he charted with *I Only Regret*, which went Top 60, and then came back with his version of the Johnny Burnette hit, *Little Boy Sad*, which made the Top 10. This was to be Bill's last major hit, but he continued to chart for Decca with *She's Hungry Again* and *Same Old Story, Same Old Lie* in 1970 and *Big Rock Candy Mountain* in 1971. At the end of 1971, Bill moved to United Artists and had a 1972 low-level hit with his version of Neil Diamond's *I Am, I Said*. The following year, he had the basement hit *It's Only Over Now and Then*.

In 1974, Bill appeared in the movie *The Sugarland Express*, which starred Goldie Hawn. He had already appeared in music roles in *Road to Nashville* and *Second Fiddle to a Steel Guitar* in the 60's. Bill returned to the charts in 1978 with *Divorce Suit (You Were Named Co-Respondent)*, on Soundwaves, and the following year, he had two further basement entries with *You're Gonna Make a Cheater Out of Me* and *At the Moonlite*. He has also recorded for Tanglewood without further success. He left the Wells-Wright show in 1984, and in 1988, he appeared on the ABC variety show, *Dolly*. He still continues to travel around the country, where his brand of straight-ahead Country is again acceptable.

RECOMMENDED ALBUMS:

"Put it Off Until Tomorrow" (Decca)(1966) [Features Dolly Parton]
"Country Action" (Decca)(1968) [Re-released on MCA]
"Little Boy Sad" (Decca)(1970)

STU PHILLIPS

(Singer, Songwriter, Guitar)

Given Name:	**Stuart John Tristram Phillips**
Date of Birth:	**January 19, 1933**
Where Born:	**Montreal, Canada**
Married:	**Aldona**
Children:	**Leagh, Joel, Jasson**

Throughout the short history of Country music, there have been several eminent Canadians to have made it in Nashville. Among those is Montreal-born Stu Phillips, known as the "Western Gentleman," who first came to star prominence in the mid-60's and is still creating fine music.

Although self-taught, by the time he was 13, a friend's guitar teacher entered Stu in a guitar contest and he won first prize of $200, playing *Back in the Saddle Again*. He had his own Country band while still in school. Stu's early influences were Don Gibson, George Jones, Hank Williams and Chet Atkins. He moved to Calgary, Alberta, in the foothills of the Canadian Rockies.

He got his career under way by becoming an announcer for radio station CFRN. This led to him occupying nearly every job in broadcasting, including producer, engineer and deejay. He started out with an early-morning live Country show, *Stu for Breakfast*, sponsored by Ace Hardware Store, then he did an all-Saturday afternoon live show, *Town and Country,* and then he did a Friday show called *Cowtown Jamboree*. He then moved to network TV with a 15-minute show, *The Outrider*. After this, Stu became the star of *Red River Jamboree*, a major Saturday p.m. show sponsored by Kraft Foods. Stu stayed with CBC for some four and a half years.

Among his early record successes, on Rodeo Records, London Records and Columbia Records in Canada was *Squaws Along the Yukon,* and he also had the successful album ***Echoes of the Canadian Foothills***. On moving to Nashville, Stu worked initially for the ABC affiliate WSIX, where he had his own morning TV show. In 1965, he was signed by RCA Victor, where he was produced by one of his idols, Chet Atkins. He hit the Country singles chart with *Bracero*, in 1966, which reached the Top 40. The follow-up, *The Great El Tigre (The Tiger),* also reached the Top 40 and won an ASCAP Award. In 1967, Stu had three successes with *Vin Rose* (Top 25), *Juanita Jones* (Top 15), which was an ASCAP Award winner, and *Note in Box #9* (Top 70). On June 1, 1967, after some twenty appearances on the *Grand Ole Opry*, he was added to its membership.

The following year, Stu had two more medium sized hits with *The Top of the World* and *Bring Love Back into Our World*. He moved to Capitol Records, but no further singles were released. Stu had his own TV series, *Music Place*, which he taped out of Louisville, Kentucky on WAVE-TV. He has traveled throughout the Far East, the Middle East, Africa and Europe and he has recorded in German and Afrikaans. In the early 80's, Stu became a minister of the Episcopalian Church.

Stu Phillips, who lives in Nashville, has continued to entertain and has released albums into the 90's, including the 1993 album ***Don't Give Up on Me***, on Broadland International.

RECOMMENDED ALBUMS:

"Singing Stu Phillips" (RCA Victor)(1966)
"Grass Roots Country" (RCA Victor)(1966)
"Our Last Rendezvous" (RCA Victor)(1968)
"Don't Give Up on Me" (Broadland International)(1993)

PHIPPS FAMILY, The

When Formed: 1943

A.L. PHIPPS
(Vocals, Lead Guitar)
Given Name: Arthur Leroy Phipps
Date of Birth: August 12, 1916
Where Born: Knox County, Kentucky

KATHLEEN PHIPPS
(Vocals, Autoharp, Guitar)
Given Name: Kathleen Norris Helton
Date of Birth: April 22, 1924
Where Born: Knox County, Kentucky
Date of Death: November 4, 1992
Children: Arthur Codell, Mary Mae (dec'd.), James Minor, Leeman, Ray, Trueleen Helen, Bowlin, Roamin, John Wayne, Louella, William Roger, Donna Ann, Melinda

Other Members of the Group have included: Hester Anderson, Trueleen Helen Phipps (Guitar, Autoharp), Leeman Phipps (Guitar), Bowlin Phipps (Guitar), Luella Phipps, Donna Phipps

The Phipps Family of Knox County, Kentucky has carried on the Carter Family tradition of Old-Time trio singing. Although the Phipps clan never quite equaled the Carters in fame or influence, they certainly exemplified a fine brand of mountain vocal styling on a wide variety of hymns and ballads.

Both Arthur Phipps and Kathleen Helton hailed from rural Knox County, Kentucky, in the Cumberland Mountain country and they learned to love and sing the old hymns and ballads of their native region. In fact, their singing attracted them to one another and after a courtship of a few months, they married on September 6, 1937. They raised a large family, all of whom displayed some musical skills and five of whom helped the Phipps Family on record at one time or another. A.L. and Kathleen began singing together for local entertainment and in church about 1943.

In the earlier years, A.L.'s niece Hester Anderson sang the third part in trio numbers, although as the years went by, various Phipps children sang in the group, especially the oldest surviving daughter, Trueleen Helen, who appeared on most of their records. The family began to work on radio regularly at WCTT Corbin, Kentucky, in 1950. Later, they also had programs at WYWY Barbourville. For a time, they appeared with some regularity on the *Mid-Day Merry-Go-Round* at WNOX Knoxville. At times, the family also guested at more distant stations such as WWVA, but since they never moved from their eastern Kentucky homeland, most of their broad media exposure came through recordings and taped radio programs. A.L. recalls that they first sang secular songs on radio in more of a Western style, but got so many requests for Carter Family songs that they increasingly adopted the Carter manner.

A.P. Carter lived over the mountains in Hiltons, Virginia, where he ran a country store, and since he liked the way A.L. Phipps played lead guitar, he did several live shows in the area with the Carter Family (including a couple that subsequently appeared on album).

The Phipps family cut some of their first recordings in the mid-50's on the same local Acme label that the A.P. Carter Family made their last waxings on in 1956. In 1960, the Phipps Family made the first of three albums for Starday. The first and last Starday effort consisted of Carter Family songs while the second contained some less common Old-Time numbers, including a few Phipps originals such as *The Yellow Tomb*, a topical number about the 1957 Floyd County school bus wreck that inspired several songs.

In 1962, the Phipps Family began taping quarter-hour radio programs for broadcast on various stations including WCKY Cincinnati, KXEL Waterloo, Iowa, and XEG Monterrey, Mexico, on which they sold their records via mail order. They continued this format for a decade and reached a wide audience with their brand of Old-Time music. A.L. recalls that their version of *Little Poplar Log House* had really gone over well at WCKY, which encouraged them to initiate these broadcasts. Meanwhile, they did an album for Folkways in 1964, following an appearance at the Newport Folk Festival. A little later, A.L. started his own Pine Mountain Records. He also issued Phipps recordings on Mountain Eagle.

The family made contact with urban Folk audiences through people like Ralph Rinzler and Mike Seeger, ultimately taking their music to thirty-two states. While their records were never big sellers in a commercial sense, the Phipps Family found a world-wide audience for their music. In addition to A.L., Kathleen, and Helen, sons Leeman and Bowlin along with daughters Louella and Donna appeared on several of their many albums. Besides numerous recordings of Carter songs and Old-Time ballads, the Family has cut thematic albums of Christmas and Easter season numbers, another of a cappella mountain hymns and one with Helen Carter.

In 1991, doctors diagnosed Kathleen Phipps as having cancer and she subsequently spent seven months in a coma before her death. Since then, the Phipps Family has not recorded or worked showdates, but A.L. Phipps looks forward to getting together with some of the children and making more recordings and delighting audiences with their quality music.

IMT

RECOMMENDED ALBUMS:

"Most Requested Songs of the Carter Family" (Starday)(1960)
"Old Time Mountain Pickin' & Singin'" (Starday)(1962)
"Echoes of the Carter Family" (Starday)(1963)
"The Phipps Family" (Folkways)(1965)
"Greatest Old Time Gospel Hymns" (Pine Mountain)(1966)
"Suffering, Crucifixion, and Resurrection of Christ" (Pine Mountain)
"Christmas with the Phipps Family" (Pine Mountain)
"The Phipps Family" (Pine Mountain)
"In the Sweet Bye and Bye" (Pine Mountain)
"Sings 'Em Mountain Style" (Pine Mountain)
"Just a Few More Days" (Pine Mountain)
"Hills of Home" (Mountain Eagle)(ca. 1977) [With Helen Carter]
"A. P. Carter and the Phipps Family" (Mountain Eagle)

PIE PLANT PETE

(Singer, Guitar, Harmonica)
Given Name: Claud J. Moye
Date of Birth: July 9, 1906
Where Born: Shawneetown, Illinois
Date of Death: February 7, 1988

Pie Plant Pete was an Old-Time musician who spent virtually his entire career in the Midwest and East.

Born and reared near Shawneetown, Illinois, Claud Moye began to play chords on the guitar about as soon as his fingers could reach the proper strings. By the time of his 16th birthday, the farm youth could also play harmonica. Like one of the first traditional musicians to work at WLS Chicago, Walter Peterson, "the Kentucky Wonder Bean," young Moye played both instruments simultaneously with his harmonica held on a rack. Several weeks before his twenty-first birthday he auditioned at WLS and went to work there beginning on May 5, 1927. He took the nickname "Pie Plant Pete" because he thought it would be difficult to pronounce, yet easy to remember. He also attracted attention by referring to his self-provided accompaniment as a "two-cylinder cob-crusher." After a couple of years in Chicago, the management of WTAM radio in Cleveland, Ohio, hired him to do a daily radio program. Pete remained in Cleveland for five years. It was during this stay that he met Bashful Harmonica Joe (b. Joseph Troyan, March 25, 1913, Pleasant City, Ohio), who had moved to the Forest City from tiny Pleasant City, Ohio, with his family in 1929. However, the two would not become a team until about 1936.

Pie Plant Pete began his recording career while still based in Chicago for Gennett in January 1929. He subsequently had two more sessions for that firm in March and August, 1930 with twenty-one sides released out of twenty-six cut in a two-year period. The Champion releases used the pseudonym "Asparagus Joe" and those on Superior, "Jerry Wallace." In 1934, Pete made five songs for Decca, one of which was not released.

In 1935 and 1936, Pete had sessions for the American Record Corporation in Chicago. In addition to traditional ballads like *Boston Burglar* and *When the Work's All Done This Fall*, several of his songs like *Farming By the Fire*, *Stay on the Farm*, *The Potato Song*, and *The Farmer* reflected the agricultural interests of his Midwestern audience.

About 1936, Joe Troyan left Bradley Kincaid and he and Pete became a regular team from then onward, having done some work together in 1935. They started with a ten-month stint at WBZ Boston, where Joe had earlier gained some experience with Kincaid and Grandpa Jones. Later they also had programs at WHAM Rochester, New York and then came back to Cleveland in 1939. WWII played havoc with their careers for a time. Pete served in the Army Quartermaster Corps, but since he was somewhat old for military service, he received an early discharge. Joe went into the Army Air Corps, but managed to get into Special Services and spent much of his time entertaining troops.

After the war, they resumed their radio careers again, working radio in Cleveland, Rochester, Toledo and especially at WJR in Detroit. Their only post-war recording came in the form of twenty sides cut at two sessions in Buffalo, New York, in April and December, 1947 for Norman Kelly's Franklin, Pennsylvania-based Process company. Pete worked in children's television for a time in the later 50's.

Later in semi-retirement, Pete ran a custom jingle (or radio advertising) business in Ridgway, Illinois. Joe Troyan eventually returned to Cleveland, where he still lived in 1989. In that year, Cattle Records re-issued an album containing the entire Process collection. None of his earlier material has been reissued.

IMT

RECOMMENDED ALBUM:

"The Oldtime Country Music Collection" (Cattle Germany)(1989)

DON PIERCE

(Producer, Record Company Executive)
Given Name: Don Pierce
Date of Birth: October 10, 1915
Where Born: Ballard, Washington

Although Pierce had little exposure to Country music before entering the field, he became one of the most successful independent record impresarios of the post-WWII years.

During his school days in Washington Pierce's primary interests were in sports; he was a member of his high school tennis and golf teams. Later, he earned a degree in business administration from the University of Washington, helping pay for his education by part-time work as a caddy and other odd jobs.

After being discharged from the military at the end of WWII, Pierce happened to play golf with popular composer Hoagy Carmichael, an encounter that turned Don's interests toward music. Soon after this meeting, Pierce saw a notice in a Los Angeles paper advertising for investors in a record company. Unaware of the company's financial condition, Don used some money he'd saved during the war to take advantage of the offer and was immediately sent on the road as a record salesman for the firm, 4 Star Records.

He soon realized that most dealers were primarily interested in records by Country singer T. Texas Tyler and as a result Pierce became more involved in this kind of music and started working with Tyler on new records. Several of their collaborative efforts were very successful, including *Deck of Cards* (a WWII version of a medieval tale), *Dad Gave My Dog Away*, *Remember Me*, *Filipino Baby*, *Divorce Me C. O. D.*, and *Bummin' Around.*

In October, 1953, Pierce sold his share of 4 Star at a handsome profit and bought a one-third interest in Starday, a new company based in Houston. The label had been started earlier in 1953 by Jack and Neva Starnes of Beaumont, Texas, and Harold W. "Pappy" Dailey of Houston. The owners combined their last names to come up with the company name. Pierce became President of the new company and in 1955, when Jack and Neva left, he became co-owner with Dailey. During his early years with the company, Don continued the original emphasis on Texas Country music. The company's first hit, *Y'all Come*, was by Texas schoolteacher Arlie Duff. Later they acquired George Jones, a Texas singer who was gaining a national reputation and his hits, such as *Why Baby Why*, were covered by other Country singers. These, and other hits, brought Starday to the attention of Nashville and also led to the company expanding its area of emphasis.

Pierce was skillful not only at signing promising artists who could sell well regionally and occasionally nationally, but was also very adept at marketing and at making money for Starday. Starrite, Starday's publishing company, maintained the rights to songs such as *Y'All Come* and *Why Baby Why* and Pierce often placed this material with other artists, thereby bringing considerable income to Starday. Pierce's development of mail order sales for Starday proved very lucrative, particularly ***Hillbilly Hit Parade*** and Gospel music packages sold over the radio. Of course, some luck was involved in these ventures, notably the decision by the Country music industry to release singles on plastic discs rather than shellac discs, thereby making records easier to mail, but Pierce's ability to take advantage of such fortuitous circumstances must be acknowledged.

Impressed with Pierce's innovative marketing ideas, Mercury Records signed a five-year contract with Starday. At the time, this was announced as a merger of the two companies, but it was really an arrangement by which Pierce and Dailey would concentrate on producing Country records for Mercury. Initially this seemed like a great opportunity for Starday, but because of the rock'n'roll onslaught that caused a temporary depression in Country music's sales it soon was viewed in a different light. In 1958, the agreement was dissolved and Pierce and Dailey went their separate ways, dividing their copyrights between them.

As a result of the Mercury arrangement, Pierce relocated to Nashville and, after Dailey's departure, reactivated the Starday label. This proved to be a very successful decision, resulting in numerous hit recordings by Cowboy Copas, Johnny Cash, Merle Kilgore, Red Sovine, Johnny Bond and Minnie Pearl, among others.

During the 60's, the label entered the Bluegrass field in a big way, recording such artists as Bill Clifton, Jim Eanes, the Stanley Brothers, Flatt & Scruggs, Carl Story and others. For a time, Pierce even referred to Starday as "the Bluegrass label," but after the mid-1960s, the company started divesting itself of the Bluegrass portion of its catalog.

In a controversial move, Starday reissued masters of songs by such artists as Dottie West, Roger Miller, and Buck Owens. Country music collectors loved these re-issues because they made long unavailable material accessible, but some performers felt that older recordings were either not representative of their best work or of their current styles, or both.

Don Pierce left Starday in 1970, two years before the company went bankrupt, and since then, has been inactive in the music business.

WKM

WEBB PIERCE

(Singer, Songwriter, Guitar)

Date of Birth:	**August 8, 1926**
Where Born:	**West Monroe, Louisiana**
Married:	**Audrey**
Children:	**Debbie, Webb, Jr.**
Date of Death:	**February 24, 1991**

Webb Pierce was one of the most successful Country singers ever to emerge. Like Carl Smith, he was a consummate Honky-Tonk singer. In a period from 1952 through 1982, he chalked up ninety-seven chart records of which eight crossed over into the Pop listings. Not always popular with his fellow professionals, Pierce nonetheless built up a loyal fan following that ensured that he had thirteen No.1 hits during his career and a remarkable total of fifty-five Top 10 records.

Webb was raised in Louisiana and learned to play guitar at age 12, and by the time he was 16 he had his own show, *Songs by Webb Pierce*, on KMLB Monroe. He did a three-year stint in the U.S. Army. He moved to Shreveport and had to be content to play his music while also working as a Sears Roebuck shoes salesman. In 1950, he came to the notice of Horace Logan, then the Program Director at KWKH, and that year, Webb joined KWKH's *Louisiana Hayride*. Early on he recorded for Pacemaker and then in 1950 for 4 Star without chart success. In 1951, Webb signed to Decca. His first single that year was *If Crying Would Make You Care/Drifting Texas Sand*, but it only acted to get his name around. It was his third release that did the trick. *Wondering*, which had first been recorded by another Louisiana favorite, Joe Wener and the Riverside Ramblers, back in 1936, gave Webb not only his first chart entry, but also his first No.1. Entering the charts in 1952, it stayed there for over six months and thereafter, Pierce had a penchant for digging out older songs and making hits from them.

The consummate Honky-Tonk singer ***Webb Pierce***

His next two singles, *That Heart Belongs to Me* and *Back Street Affair*, both went to No. 1, each being on the charts for over five months. He was voted "No.1 Folk Singer" by *Farm and Ranch* magazine, an honor he received again the next year. He started off 1953 with a double-sided Top 5 record, *I'll Go on Alone/That's Me Without You*. He followed up with another double-sided Top 5 single, *The Last Waltz/I Haven't Got the Heart*. After this came another two-sided smash, *It's Been So Long/Don't Throw Your Life Away*. The top-side reached No.1 and stayed there for 8 weeks, while the flip-side reached the Top 10. He ended the year with a song that will always be associated with Webb, *There Stands the Glass*. The single went to No.1 and stayed there for 12 weeks out of a 6 month stay in the charts. The flip-side, *I'm Walking the Dog*, went Top 3. During the year, he was named the "No.1 Singer" by the American Juke Box Operators.

His first two singles of 1954, *Slowly* and *Even Tho*, both went No.1. The former stayed at No.1 for 17 weeks out of a 36 week stay on the charts. The flip-side of *Even Tho*, *Sparkling Brown Eyes*, reached the Top 5. He followed up with yet another double-sided hit, *More and More/You're Not Mine Anymore*. The top-side went to No.1 and stayed there for 10 weeks and the single went Top 25 on the Pop charts, while the flip-side reached the Top 5. He received the *Billboard* Award for "Outstanding Achievement in Country Western Music," that year.

He got 1955 underway with the Jimmie Rodgers classic *In the Jailhouse Now*, which reached No.1 and stayed there for 21 weeks (!) out of 37 on the charts, with the "B"side, *I'm Gonna Fall Out of Love with You*, reaching the Top 10. He followed this with a 12-week stay at the top with *I Don't Care*. He then had the double-sided smash, *Love, Love, Love/If You Were Me*. The "A" side was a 13 week No.1, while the "B" side went Top 10. He wrapped up the year with the George Jones-Darrell Edwards' song *Why Baby Why*, which he took to No.1 in tandem with Red Sovine. During 1955, Pierce left the *Louisiana Hayride* and moved to Nashville, where he joined the *Grand Ole Opry*.

By Webb's standard, 1956 was not as successful. *Yes I Know Why* and the flip-side, *'Cause I Love You*, both went Top 3. The follow-ups, *Any Old Time* and *Teenage Boogie*, reached the Top 10, but only stayed on the charts for about two months. He also had a Top 5 double-sided hit with Red Sovine with *Little Rosa/Hold Everything*.

His first single of 1957, *I'm Tired*, reached the Top 3 and he was back to his chart-topping form with the next release, *Honky Tonk Song*. His other hits of the year were *Bye, Bye Love* coupled with *Missing You* and *Holiday for Love*; all were Top 10 hits. He also had a Top 10 hit with Kitty Wells on *Oh, So Many Years*. During 1958, Webb had two double-sided Top 10 hits, *Cryin' Over You/You'll Come Back* and *Falling Back to You/Tupelo County Jail*. He also had a lesser success with Kitty Wells on *One Week Later*.

He started off 1959 with his first relative failure, *I'm Letting You Go*, which only reached the Top 25 and was on the charts for a mere 3 weeks. However, he soon came back stronger than ever with the Top 10 *A Thousand Miles Ago* and the Top 3 hit (and Top 30 Pop hit) *I Ain't Never*. The latter was another song that would always be associated with Webb and was written by him and Mel Tillis. Webb closed the year with another Top 5 single (and Top 60 Pop hit), *No Love Have I*. His 1960 *(Doin' the) Lovers' Leap/Is It Wrong (For Loving You)* and *Drifting Texas Sand* only reached the Top 20, but by the end of the year, he was back in favor with the Top 5 hit *Fallen Angel*.

Webb continued to rack up a series of major chart hits. There were the 1961 hits *Let Forgiveness In* (Top 5), *Sweet Lips* (Top 3), *Walking the Streets* (Top 5)/*How Do You Talk To a Baby* (Top 10), and in 1962, he succeeded with *Alla My Love* (Top 5), *Crazy Wild Desire/Take Time* (both Top 10) and *Cow Town* (Top 5). Webb teamed up with Mel Tillis for the 1963 Top 30 single *How Come Your Dog Don't Bite Nobody But Me*. Webb followed this with the solo hits *Sawmill* (Top 20), *Sands of Gold* (Top 10) and *These Wonderful Years* (Top 10).

1964 marked a turning point in Webb's chart success level. That year, his only meaningful singles were the Top 3 *Memory #1* and the Top 10 duet with Kitty Wells, *Finally*. Between 1965 and 1972 when he left Decca, Webb only had major success with *Who Do I Think I Am* (Top 20, 1965), *Where'd Ya Stay Last Night* (Top 20, 1966), *Fool Fool Fool* (Top 10, 1967) and *This Thing* (Top 20, 1969).

Webb moved to Plantation, but could only manage a couple of low level chart placings. It was only in 1982 that he managed a return to the charts via a Top 75 duet with Willie Nelson, with the title track of their album ***In the Jailhouse Now***.

Webb had wide business interests that included part ownership of Cedarwood Publishing, one of Nashville's major music publishing houses. He owned three radio stations in Georgia: WJAT Swainsboro, WBRO Waynesboro and WSNT Sandersville. He had at one time tried to run his own record label, but that failed. He did, however, achieve many notable "firsts." His 1954 hit *Slowly* was the first recording to feature a pedal steel, which was played by Bud Isaacs. His band, the Wandering Boys, which at times included Bill Phillips, Jimmy Day, Floyd Cramer, the Wilburn Brothers and Faron Young, was one of the first non-Western groups to feature twin fiddles and one of the first to wear rhinestone suits.

As well as his music, Webb was famous for his guitar-shaped swimming pool, a copy of which can be seen at Spence Manor on Music Square West in Nashville. Webb underwent heart surgery in 1987, but succumbed to pancreatic cancer after a long battle. To date, his achievements have not been recognized by the Country Music Hall of Fame, although election may come in the near future.

RECOMMENDED ALBUMS:

"The Wondering Boy" (Decca)(1956) [Re-released by Stetson UK in the original sleeve (1987)]
"Bugle Call from Heaven" (Vocalion)(1966)
"The Best of Webb Pierce" (double)(MCA)(1975)
"Carol Channing & Webb Pierce—Country & Western" (Plantation)(1976)
"Faith, Hope & Love" (Skylite)(1977)
"In the Jailhouse Now" (Columbia)(1982) [With Willie Nelson]
"I Ain't Never" (Charly UK)(1984)

RAY PILLOW

(Singer, Songwriter, Guitar, Industry Executive)
Date of Birth: July 4, 1937
Where Born: Lynchburg, Virginia
Married: Jo Ann
Children: Dale, Selena, Daryl Ray

Ray Pillow's importance in Country music far outstrips his record success. In recent years, he has emerged as a major publisher with Sycamore Music, a company owned jointly with Larry McFaden, which handled all of Lee Greenwood's self-penned songs. Ray is someone who can spot a good song and new artists often use his skills to select the right material for them to record.

He first became interested in music when he was confined to bed for two weeks with water on the knee, following a fall. His father bought him a guitar and a cousin taught him some chords. He was a reluctant public performer until a school teacher made him play at a school show. In 1954, just a year from graduation, he left school and joined the U.S. Navy. Two years later, he and Jo Ann married. He left the Navy in 1958 and attended Lynchburg College, while still working for a gas company. He graduated, within three years, with a bachelor's degree in business. While in college, an uncle asked him to sing with his band in Appomattox, which was the first time he had sung in public. Ray took over the band (the Stardusters) and worked with it all through his college years.

He first came to Nashville in 1961 as a regional winner in the National Pet Milk talent contest and came in second. He returned to Lynchburg to finish his degree. However, he was invited to appear on the *Grand Ole Opry* by General Manager Ott Devine and did on August 26, 1961. He returned to Lynchburg and became an assistant manager for a truck sales company. Ray was playing for dances, but desperately wanted to go to Nashville. With Jo Ann's support, they sold all their belongings and Jo Ann and the children stayed with her mother while Ray tried for success.

Ray had met Joe Taylor, then handling promotion with the Martha White Company, at one of their concerts in Roanoke. He promised to help Ray when he came to Nashville. He was true to his word and introduced him to the directors of Martha White. Within a few weeks, Ray had been signed to a personal management contract with the company.

Soon Ray's family was with him in Nashville and in 1963, with Taylor as his Personal Manager, Ray signed a record deal with Capitol Records. It took six months for Ray to release his initial single, *Left Out*, but it was the follow-up, *Take Your Hands Off My*

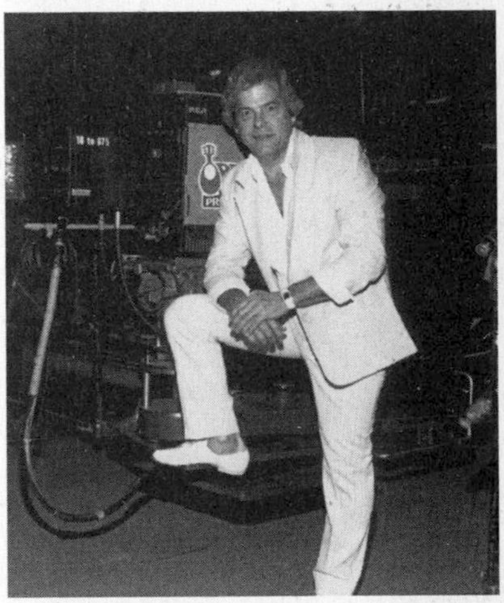

*Singer and industry executive **Ray Pillow***

Heart, in 1965, that broke into the Country charts Top 50. At the end of that year, he reached the Top 20 with *Thank You Ma'am*. He had two hits around the Top 40, during 1966, entitled *Common Colds and Broken Hearts* and *Volkswagen* and a Top 10 duet with Jean Shepard, *I'll Take the Dog*. He wrapped up the year with another Shepard duet, *Mr. Do-It-Yourself*, which made the Top 30. He was honored by his hometown, Lynchburg, which proclaimed April 15, 1966 as Ray Pillow Day. On April 30 that year, Ray was introduced by Ernest Tubb and made a member of the *Grand Ole Opry* and has continued as such to date. He received several awards in 1966, when the national D.J. Poll voted him "Most Programmed New Artist," *Billboard* named him "Most Promising Male Artist" and *Cash Box* named him "Most Promising New Artist."

He and Jean started off 1967 with a Top 15 single, *Heart, We Did All We Could*. He had two solo chart entries, *I Just Want to Be Alone* (Top 60) and *Gone with the Wine*, which reached the Top 70. He moved to ABC Records in 1968, but only *Wonderful Day* made it to the Top 60. The following year, he was on Plantation and his *Reconsider Me* reached the Top 40.

Ray was absent from the charts in 1970 and 1971 and then emerged on Mega in 1972 with two Top 70 releases, *Since Then* and *She's Doing it to Me Again*. He had six further chart entries in 1974 through 1981, on Mega, ABC/Dot, Hilltop, MCA and First Generation, but none of them got up to the Top 80.

On the industry business side, Ray went into partnership, in the mid-60's, with Joe Taylor in Joe Taylor Artist Management, Shoji Music Publications and Ming Music, Inc. At the beginning of the 80's, Ray started his partnership with Larry McFaden, then the bass player with Mel Tillis, and this led to the Lee Greenwood connection. In the late 80's, Ray was approached to be in the A & R team at Capitol Records, which he did. Following a shake-up at Capitol's successor, Liberty Records, Ray moved into independent record consultancy.

As a matter of interest, whenever Ray played the clubs in Alabama his back-up group on some gigs was Wildcountry, who went on to become Alabama.

RECOMMENDED ALBUMS:

"I'll Take the Dog" (Capitol)(1966) [With Jean Shepard]
"Even When It's Bad, It's Good" (Capitol)(1967)
"Ray Pillow Sings" (ABC)(1969)
"People Music" (Plantation)(1970)
"Slippin' Around with Ray Pillow" (Mega)(1972)
"One Too Many Memories" (Allegiance)(1984)

PINKARD & BOWDEN

When Formed: 1983

SANDY PINKARD
(Singer, Songwriter, Guitar)

Given Name: James Sanford Pinkard, Jr.
Date of Birth: January 16, 1947
Where Born: Abbeville, Louisiana
Married: 1. (Div.)
2. Amanda

RICHARD BOWDEN
(Singer, Songwriter, Guitar)

Given Name: Richard Bowden
Date of Birth: September 30, 1945
Where Born: Linden, Texas
Married: Karen

Pinkard & Bowden have kept alive the dying art of Country music comedy in the 80's. In the tradition of Homer & Jethro, they write and perform parodies of Country music hits. One of their first recordings was a take-off of the Judds, *Mama He's Crazy*. The duo's version, *Mama He's Lazy*, became a Top 40 hit in 1984. To promote the release they dressed in drag, adopting the names Wyoming and Nairobi (a la Wynona & Naomi).

Prior to teaming up to make people laugh, Pinkard and Bowden had successful careers as songwriters and musicians. Sandy Pinkard's first entry into the music business was working with Ramblin' Jack Elliott in California. After an unsuccessful attempt to break into Nashville's music scene, Sandy settled in Fort Worth, Texas, working at a professional rodeo in 1973. Two years later, he met John Anderson when the Country star was performing in Fort Worth. Anderson had heard some demo recordings of Pinkard's songs and encouraged him to give it another try in Nashville. John was so convinced Sandy should go to Nashville that he bought him a round-trip ticket to Music City. It proved to be a good move for Pinkard, who soon began to see his songs recorded by Tanya Tucker, Ray Charles, and Brenda Lee. He also penned four No.1 songs: *Coca Cola Cowboy* by Mel Tillis (1979); *You're the Reason God Made Oklahoma* by David Frizzell and Shelly West (1981); *Blessed Are the Believers* by Anne Murray (1981); and *I Can Tell By the Way You Dance* by Vern Gosdin (1984).

While his future partner was learning to write songs, Richard Bowden formed a group called Shiloh with fellow Texan Don Henley. Following the demise of their group, the long-time friends joined Linda Ronstadt's band whose other members included Detroit-transplant Glen Frey. Henley and Frey left Ronstadt to form the Eagles and Bowden teamed up with another bandmate, pedal steel guitarist Sneaky Pete (of Flying Burrito Brothers fame) to create a band called Cold Steel. Bowden's group was short lived and he went on the road playing guitar for Dan Fogelberg and later Roger McGuinn. Blue Steel was another band Bowden formed that was the opening act for 1980's "Long Run" tour by the Eagles.

Record producer and label executive Jim Ed Norman, a mutual friend, arranged a meeting for Pinkard and Bowden to get together and write songs. They never got down to serious business because everything they

Writers in disguise ***Sandy Pinkard and Richard Bowden***

wrote made them laugh. The duo decided to work up an act and began building a following at top comedy clubs including The Punch Line in San Francisco and Catch A Rising Star in New York. Pinkard and Bowden also landed a recording contract with the label run by Jim Ed Norman, Warner Brothers.

The duo's 1984 debut album, ***Writers in Disguise***, included satires *Blue Hairs Drivin' in My Lane* (*Blue Eyes Crying in the Rain*) and *Somebody Done Somebody's Song Wrong* (originally *Hey, Won't You Play Another Somebody Done Somebody Wrong Song*). Chicago native Rob Strandlund joined Pinkard and Bowden as guitarist and vocalist in 1983. Formerly a member of the Burrito Brothers, Strandlund also found success as a songwriter of the Eagles' *Already Gone* and Mickey Gilley's *I've Given Up Getting Over You*. After working on their first album and touring to promote it, Strandlund left the duo to pursue other interests.

They hit the singles charts with *Adventures in Parodies*, a montage of song clips. Later in the 80's, Pinkard & Bowden released *PG-13* and continued the humorous offerings with *Elvis Was a Narc* and *Don't Pet the Dog*. They again hit the charts in 1986 with the low entry *She Thinks I Steal Cars*, a parody of *She Thinks I Still Care*. In 1988, they played Wembley Festival in England, and charted with *Arab, Alabama*.

In 1992 the duo released ***Cousins, Cattle, and Other Love Stories*** with the distinction of being the first Nashville-based album to carry a "Parental Advisory" sticker. It captured segments of their off-color live show along with parodies of Tom Petty's *Freefalling* (*Freeloading*) and Eric Clapton's *Cocaine* (*Propane*). Drummer Randy Pander joined Pinkard & Bowden in recording the album and became a member of the comedians' live show. He previously played drums for Ernest Tubb, Gatemouth Brown, and the Platters.

In the early 90's Pinkard & Bowden began to distance themselves from the Country music audience, performing primarily in comedy clubs. They often appeared on Rock radio station morning shows to promote their evening appearances. Some music critics questioned Pinkard & Bowden's parodies of *Wind Beneath My Sheets* (*Wind Beneath My Wings*) and serial killer Jeffrey Dahmer–inspired *Friends in Crawl Spaces* (*Friends in Low Places*). In a review of a comedy club appearance entitled *It's Perfect for Bathroom Joke Fans*, John Austin of the *Fort Worth Star Telegram* called Pinkard & Bowden an "X-rated Homer and Jethro."

Richard Bowden moonlighted in 1993, and became part of the comedic Austin Lounge Lizards, recording the album ***Paint Me on Velvet***, released on Flying Fish. JIE

RECOMMENDED ALBUMS:

"Writers in Disguise" (Warner Brothers)(1984)
"Cousins, Cattle and Other Love Stories" (Warner Brothers)(1992)
"Paint Me on Velvet" (Flying Fish)(1993) [As the Austin Lounge Lizards]

PIRATES OF THE MISSISSIPPI

When Formed: 1987

Members:

"Wild" Bill McCorvey	Guitar, Lead Vocals
Rich "Dude" Alves	Guitar
Dean Townson	Bass Guitar
Greg Trostle	Steel Guitar (joined 1994)
Jimmy Lowe	Drums

Former Member:

Pat Severs	Steel Guitar (left 1994)

Unlike the groups that have proliferated since Alabama arrived in the early 80's, Pirates of the Mississippi was not on the search for a record deal. They got together as five Nashville musicians who worked during the day and wanted an outlet to "blow off steam," and were originally known as the Cloggers.

Bill McCorvey came from Montgomery, Alabama, Rich Alves from Pleasanton, California, Dean Townson from Battle Creek, Mississippi, Pat Severs from Camden, South Carolina, and Jimmy Lowe from Atlanta, Georgia. They found that people, especially at the VFW outside Nashville, liked what they played and in 1989, they were spotted by James Stroud, who got them signed to Capitol Records. The group's brand of Country-Rock, which has been described as "a rocketship built in a basement," is reminiscent of those great jamming garage bands. Its name came from a song that Alves and McCorvey had written about the band's drummer, in which the lyrics appeared, "if this guy was a modern-day pirate, he'd probably be out on the Mississippi River."

The group released its first album in the summer of 1990 and the single, Hank Williams' *Honky Tonk Blues*, made the Top 30. The follow-up single *Rollin' Home* only reached the Top 50, and the album peaked in the Top 40 on the Country Album chart.

In 1991, the band released one of its career singles, *Feed Jake*, which went Top 15. The video of the song was named "Best Video By a Group" by *Music Row* magazine and *Nashville Scene* newspaper's readers voted it "Top Overall Video." That year, the band was named "Top New Group" by *Radio & Records* and the ACM voted the band "Top New Vocal Group." The Pirates' other chart singles of 1991 were *Speak of the Devil* (Top 30) and *Fighting for You*, which reached the Top 50. The band's second album, ***Walk the Plank***, which contained nine songs co-written by Alves and McCorvey, peaked in the Top 40 on the Country album charts.

The following year, the Pirates had three more chart entries, *'Til I'm Holding You Again* (Top 30), Guy Clark-Lee Roy Parnell's *Too Much* (Top 40) and *A Street Man Named Desire* (Top 60). The band's third album, ***A Street Man Named Desire***, failed to ignite and only reached the Top 75 on the Country Album chart. In 1993, *Dream You*, the title track of the band's album of that year, reached the Top 70.

To date, the Pirates of the Mississippi is like a bridesmaid, waiting for the big day to happen. As yet, the band hasn't had the really big single or album that would launch it into the superstar status. The one strength that the group has that could put it at the top is the writing skills of Rich Alves and Bill McCorvey. In 1994, Pat Severs left the group following an accident onstage, and was replaced by Knoxville, Tennessee, steelie Greg Trostle. That year, they left Liberty and joined Giant.

RECOMMENDED ALBUMS:

"Pirates of the Mississippi" (Capitol)(1990)
"Walk the Plank" (Capitol)(1991)
"A Street Man Named Desire" (Liberty)(1992)
"Dream You" (Liberty)(1993

POCO

When Formed: 1968

Original Members:

Jim Messina	Guitar, Vocals
Richie Furay	Guitar, Vocals
George Grantham	Drums
Rusty Young	Fiddle, Steel Guitar
Randy Meisner	Bass Guitar, Guitar, Vocals

Later Members:

Timothy B. Schmit (Bass Guitar, Vocals), Paul Cotton (Guitar, Vocals), Steve Chapman (Drums), Charlie Harrison (Bass Guitar, Vocals)

Poco was one of the first groups to pioneer Country-Rock music. The harmonies and instruments of Country mixed with rock'n'roll rhythms paved the way for supergroups like the Eagles, and while hits for Poco were few, their influence runs deep in both Country and Pop music.

Richie Furay (b. May 9, 1944, Yellow Springs, Ohio) and Jim Messina (b. December 5, 1947, Maywood, California) formed Poco after Buffalo Springfield broke up in 1968 when Stephen Stills and Neil Young left the group to form Crosby, Stills, Nash and Young. Rusty Young (b. February 23, 1946, Long Beach, California) had come from Colorado to play pedal steel guitar on the last Buffalo Springfield album. Furay loved what Rusty played on his song *Kind Woman* and invited Young to join Poco. Auditions were held for the other band members and among the hopeful was Gram Parsons. He played with Poco for a few weeks but things didn't work out and he left the band. Eventually Rusty Young suggested bringing two of his friends from Colorado to join the band. Drummer George Grantham (b. November 20, 1947, Cordell, Oklahoma) and bass player Randy Meisner (b. March 8, 1947, Scottsbluff, Nebraska) moved to California and signed on as Poco's rhythm section.

Poco began performing in Hollywood at clubs like The Troubadour and gained the attention of several record companies. They signed with Epic in the fall of 1968 and released their debut album, ***Pickin' Up the Pieces***, in 1969. Poco originally called themselves Pogo but changed their name when cartoonist Walt Kelly, creator of the "Pogo" syndicated strip, instigated legal proceedings to prevent the use of the name.

Randy Meisner left the band after the first album to play with Rick Nelson & the Stone Canyon Band. A few years later, he became a founding member of the Eagles and wrote and sang lead on their hit *Take it to the Limit*. Jim Messina moved to bass to cover the spot Meisner left in Poco, until Timothy B. Schmit joined the band. Following their second album, ***Poco***, in 1970, the band recorded a live album called ***Deliverin'*** (released in 1971). The singles *You Better Think Twice* (1970) and *C'mon* (1971) made a brief appearance on the Pop singles chart.

In the fall of 1970, Jim Messina decided to leave Poco to spend more time with his new wife and work as a staff producer for Columbia Records. He was assigned to work with a new artist named Kenny Loggins and the two worked together so well in the studio that they decided to form a band together. Loggins and Messina went on to record nine albums and several hit singles, including *Your Mama Don't Dance*.

Singer, songwriter, and guitarist Paul Cotton joined Poco in 1970 after leading the popular Chicago-based band Illinois Speed Press. Cotton contributed *Bad Weather* and *Railroad Days* on the album ***From the Inside***, produced by Steve Cropper and recorded in Memphis. Richie Furay began to share more of the songwriting and lead vocals and Tim Schmit also sang two songs on the album.

Poco recorded their next album, ***Good Feelin' to Know***, in Chicago and returned to Los Angeles for the making of their ***Crazy Eyes*** album. Richie Furay left Poco in 1973 to form the attempted supergroup, the Souther, Hillman, Furay Band. Richie recorded two albums with J.D. Souther and Chris Hillman but commercial success eluded the group.

From 1973 to 1977, Poco toured and recorded as a four-piece with Paul Cotton and Timothy Schmit sharing songwriting and lead vocals. Rusty Young began to contribute as a writer and vocalist on Poco's first album for ABC, ***Seven*** (1974), with *Rocky Mountain Breakdown*. Over the next four years Poco released the albums ***Cantamos*** (1975), ***The Very Best of*** (1975), ***Live*** (1975), ***Head Over Heels*** (1975) (that produced the Top 50 Pop hit, *Keep on Trying*), ***Rose of Cimarron*** (1976) and ***Indian Summer*** (1977). The title tracks of both the last two albums were Pop chart singles with *Rose of Cimarron* going Top 100 (1976) and *Indian Summer* going Top 50 (1977).

More personnel changes came in 1977 when George Grantham moved to Nashville to play drums for Ricky Skaggs and then Steve Wariner. Timothy Schmit also made his exit from Poco to replace Randy Meisner in the Eagles. He recorded ***The Long Run*** and ***Live*** albums with the supergroup and wrote and sang the hit *I Can't Tell You Why*.

Rusty and Paul again held auditions in Los Angeles to find a new rhythm section. They hired Englishmen Steve Chapman (drums) and Charlie Harrison (bass, vocals) who had been members of Al Stewart's band. This sixth re-formation of Poco proved to be the magical one. They released the ***Legend*** album for ABC in 1978. *Crazy Love*, written and sung by Rusty Young, became Poco's biggest hit, reaching the Top 20 on the Pop singles chart and crossing to the Country Top 100 the following year. Paul Cotton's *Heart Of The Night* also became a Top 20 Pop hit and helped propel sales past the 500,000 unit mark. Poco earned their first Gold Disc and the ***Legend*** album eventually passed the one million sales mark to be Certified Platinum.

The title track of Poco's 1980 album, ***Under the Gun***, reached the 40s on the Pop chart and *Midnight Rain* went Top 75. The band recorded the Civil War theme album ***Blue and Grey*** (1981) and ***Cowboys and Englishmen*** (1982) for MCA before moving to Atlantic Records in 1982. ***The Ghost Town*** album provided the Top 50 hit *Shoot for the Moon*. Their second Atlantic album was titled ***Inamorata*** and featured a reunion of sorts when Furay, Grantham, Meisner, and Schmit joined Poco in the studio to sing on a few tracks.

In 1984, Poco decided to take a break from recording and touring. Chapman took over management of his former employer Al Stewart. Bassist Charlie Harrison stayed in L.A. and formed a new group. Paul Cotton and Rusty Young relocated to Nashville to focus on songwriting and session work. Later in the 80's, Rusty and Paul occasionally performed as Poco with various Nashville studio musicians providing the rhythm section. Rusty Young played steel guitar on albums for many Country artists and performed live for a while with Vince Gill.

In 1989 Rusty Young and Richie Furay thought it would be fun to get the original Poco back together to record an album. Grantham, Meisner, and Messina agreed and they began writing and rehearsing at Messina's Santa Barbara, California, studio. Poco signed a new record deal with RCA and released ***Legacy*** in 1990. The reunion album produced the pre-released 1989 Top 20 Pop hit and video *Call It Love* and Poco embarked on a worldwide tour to support the album. They had a 1990 Top 40 Pop hit with *Nothin' to Hide*, which was co-written and produced by Richard Marx. Poco has continued to tour in the 90's.

RECOMMENDED ALBUMS:

"Pickin' up the Pieces" (Epic)(1969)
"Poco" (Epic)(1970)
"Deliverin'" (Epic)(1971)
"From the Inside" (Epic)(1971)
"Good Feelin' to Know" (Epic)(1972)
"Crazy Eyes" (Epic)(1973)
"Seven" (Epic)(1974)
"Cantamos" (Epic)(1974)
"The Very Best of Poco" (Epic)(1975)
"Head Over Heels" (ABC)(1975)
"Live" (Epic)(1976)
"Rose of Cimarron" (ABC)(1976)
"Indian Summer" (ABC)(1977)
"Legend" (ABC)(1978)
"Under the Gun" (MCA)(1980)
"Blue and Grey" (MCA)(1981)
"Cowboys and Englishmen" (MCA)(1982)
"Ghost Town" (Atlantic)(1982)
"Inamorata" (Atlantic)(1984)
"Legacy" (RCA)(1990))

CHARLIE POOLE

(Singer, Banjo)

Given Name:	**Charles Cleveland Poole**
Date of Birth:	**March 22, 1892**
Where Born:	**Randolph County, North Carolina**
Married:	**1. Maude Gibson (div.) 2. Lou Emma Rorer**
Children:	**James Clay Poole**
Date of Death:	**May, 1931**

Banjo giant ***Charlie Poole***

Charlie Poole's North Carolina Ramblers, along with Gid Tanner's Skillet Lickers and Ernest Stoneman's Dixie Mountaineers/ Blue Ridge Corn Shuckers, rank as one of the giants of Old-Time string band music. More than anyone else, Poole made the banjo an instrument of distinction in the string band, creating a tradition on the instrument that would be carried into the next decade by Snuffy Jenkins and Wade Mainer. They in turn would pave the way for that first generation of Bluegrass pickers typified by Earl Scruggs and Don Reno, who, like Poole, hailed from the Carolina Piedmont. Also like another type of Old-Time banjo picker, Uncle Dave Macon, Poole helped enrich the repertoire of early Country music with a heritage of minstrel songs, Victorian sentimental ballads and vaudeville ditties from an earlier generation. Unfortunately, Poole lived a reckless life, not unlike several others in the trade, which contributed to a relatively early death.

Charlie Poole, as well as many other Country music pioneers, came from the textile mill culture that brought many southern poor whites of tenant farmer and sharecropper backgrounds into an industrial society. While these folk remained poor, their living standard was probably an improvement over the less visible rural poverty they had earlier endured. Poole's parents had toiled in the Piedmont mill for some years prior to his birth and Charlie himself went to work at the looms at an early age. Mill management encouraged music and other social activity to help keep the work force content and Charlie took to the banjo before his parents moved to Haw River in Alamance County, just after the turn of the century.

The youthful textile worker played baseball, picked the banjo and often rambled from the mill villages to more distant locales as far from the Piedmont as Missoula, Montana. He also became known as something of a rowdy and a rounder. About 1918, he settled in Spray, North Carolina, where in 1920, he married Lou Emma Rorer, whose brother Posey would become fiddler with the North Carolina Ramblers. Charlie and Posey played music together with other local pickers and from these folk the North Carolina Ramblers emerged.

In 1925, Charlie Poole, Posey Rorer and guitarist Norm Woodlief went to New York, where they cut four numbers for Columbia including *Don't Let Your Deal Go Down* and *Can I Sleep in Your Barn Tonight, Mister*, which went on to sell some 102,000 copies and established the North Carolina Ramblers as the premier Old-Time string band. Roy Harvey replaced Woodlief on guitar at subsequent trips to the studio and in 1928 and 1929, Lonnie Austin took over for Rorer on fiddle. Odell Smith fiddled on a session for Paramount in 1929 as the Highlanders and on the recordings made in 1930.

Through some fifty-eight released sides on Columbia, the band maintained a high musical standard on all of their recording sessions, producing what has been termed a chamber music form of Old-Time string sound in comparison to the wilder, less disciplined style associated with the Georgia-based Skillet Lickers.

Poole continued his erratic lifestyle, surviving several narrow escapes from death. The economic downswing of 1930 shook his self-confidence and his record sales dropped sharply. In May, 1931, an offer to play in a Hollywood motion picture revived his spirits and he went on a prolonged drinking spree which ended with his death. He had been a much admired musical figure in the Carolina Piedmont and northward to West Virginia, where his band sound was much copied. In addition, his son James (1912-1968), who often used the name Charlie, Jr., led a band called the Swingbillies.

Even during Poole's lifetime, Harvey and Rorer led North Carolina Rambler bands that made recordings without Poole. A minor renaissance of interest in Poole's music began in the mid-60's and most of his recordings appeared on long-play albums in the next few years, chiefly on County Records. Kenny Rorer, a kinsman of Poole's first fiddler, wrote a fine biographical study. A cd of some of Charlie Poole's best sides came out in 1993.

IMT

RECOMMENDED ALBUMS:

"Charlie Poole and the North Carolina Ramblers" (County)(1965) "Vol.2" (1966) "Vol. 3" (1968) and "Vol. 4" (1975)
"Charlie Poole and the Highlanders" (Arbor)(1970)
"Charlie Poole, 1926-1930" (Historical)(1975)
"Charlie Poole and the North Carolina Ramblers" (County)(1993)

SANDY POSEY

(Singer)
Given Name: **Sandra Lou Posey**
Date of Birth: **June 18, 1947**
Where Born: **Jasper, Alabama**
Married: **Wade Cummins**
Children: **Amy**

Sandy Posey had several successful songs in both the Pop and Country fields, but ironically none that could be called cross-over hits.

Born in Alabama, Sandra Lou Posey moved to Memphis as a teenager, where she soon went to work as a background vocalist in recording studios, both locally and in Nashville. This was at a time when numerous Pop stars were doing Nashville Sound material in the studios, and MGM producer Chips Moman signed her to a solo contract for the Pop market.

In 1966, when barely 19, Sandy scored with two major Pop hits, *Born a Woman* and *Single Girl*, both peaking in the Top 15 and both written by Martha Sharp, who subsequently became a Vice President of Warner Brothers Records. The following year, Sandy's rendition of a John D. Loudermilk song, *What a Woman in Love Won't Do*, just fell short of the Pop Top 30. That summer, *I Take it Back* reached the Top 15. Her last Pop entry was at the end of 1967, and was *Are You Never Coming Home*, which only reached the Top 60.

Sandy dropped out of the musical scene in 1968, but resurfaced two years later. Signed to Columbia, she scored a Top 20 Country hit in 1971 with *Bring Him Home Safely to Me*. She stayed with Columbia until 1973, and her most successful singles were Top 40 revivals of *Happy, Happy Birthday Baby* (1972), previously a Pop hit for the Tune Weavers, and *Don't* (1973), a 1958 No.1 for Elvis Presley.

After a brief affiliation with Monument, the talented songstress went to Warner Brothers in 1976, where in 1978 she had a Top 25 success with the revival of *Born to Be with You*, which had previously been hits for the Chordettes in 1956 and Sonny James in 1968, *Love, Love, Love/Chapel of Love* (Top 30, 1978) and *Love Is Sometimes Easy* (Top 30, 1979). Her last chart appearance in 1983 was a basement entry for Audiograph with *Can't Get Used to*

Sleeping Without You. Her final solo album came out on 51 West that same year.

Background vocals had always been Sandy's bread and butter as she had always done a great deal of studio session work, even when recording under her own name, and for several years from the mid-80's, her harmonies supported other performers on TNN. In 1991 she remarried Wade Cummins, who has been a long-time re-creator of Elvis Presley as "Elvis Wade," in a stage presentation. Sandy had done back-up work on several Presley sessions from the mid-60's and fits well into the program. The Elvis Wade and the Jordanaires Featuring Sandy Posey Show has toured in both the domestic and foreign markets with Sandy as the opener.

She now mostly performs her Pop hits of the later 60's. She still does session work and in the spring of 1994, Sandy, who is a committed Christian, was in the process of cutting both a secular and a Gospel album as a featured vocalist. IMT

RECOMMENDED ALBUMS:

"The Best of Sandy Posey" (MGM)(1967)
"Looking at You" (MGM)(1968)
"Sandy Posey" (MGM)(1970)
"Why Don't We Go Somewhere & Love" (Columbia)(1972)
"Tennessee Rose" (51 West)(1983)

Possum Hunters refer DR. HUMPHREY BATE

PRAIRIE OYSTER

When Formed: 1975

Original Members:

Russell de Carle	**Lead Vocals, Bass Guitar**
Keith Glass	**Guitars, Vocals**
Denis Delorme	**Steel Guitar**

Members added:

John P. Allen	**Fiddle, Mandolin, Guitar, Vocals (joined 1983)**
Joan Besen	**Keyboards, Vocals (joined 1983)**
Bruce Moffet	**Drums, Percussion (joined 1986)**

When the Canadian group Prairie Oyster hit the U.S. Country charts in 1989, it appeared to the public that here was yet another new group. However, in this case, nothing could be further from the truth. The band came together as a trio made up of Russell de Carle, Keith Glass and Denis Delorme back in 1975. Playing basically Western Swing, the threesome toured a lot and appeared on TV, but did not record. They broke up in 1978, but decided to re-group for some reunion gigs, in 1982. They added John P. Allen, a fine musician and licensed auctioneer, and talented keyboardist and songwriter Joan Besen. John had played with Russell in Bluegrass groups back in the 70's and Joan had been with Sylvia Tyson's band and was official limerick writer for CBC radio's *Morningside* program. Bruce joined the band in 1986.

That year, they recorded their first album, ***Oyster Tracks***. They released six singles from it and, as a result of the ensuing chart success in Canada, won the prestigious Juno Award for "Country Group or Duo of the Year" in both 1986 and 1987. They cut four demo tracks with Steve Berlin of Los Lobos, which reached Joe Galante at RCA in Nashville. He flew up to see the band, and signed them. They recorded ***Different Kind of Fire*** with Berlin, up in Hamilton, Ontario. The cd was released in a tin box with a "pearl" sitting in the center of the record. The first single, *Goodbye, So Long, Hello* (written by de Carle and Toronto-based singer Willie P. Bennett) reached the Top 70 on the Country chart in 1990 and the same year, was named Canadian Country Music Association's "Song of the Year." At the CCMA Awards that year, the group won several other awards. It was named "Group of the Year" (only the second band to unseat the Family Brown since 1982) and Joan Besen was named Keyboard player in the "All Star Band of the Year." In the middle of the year, they had a Top 70 single with Hank Snow's old hit *I Don't Hurt Anymore*.

In 1991, they reached the Top 60 with Joan Besen's *One Precious Love*, which came from their new album, ***Everybody Knows***, which they recorded in Nashville. That year, the group won a further slew of awards. They became CCMA's "Group of the Year" and Joan Besen's *Lonely You, Lonely Me* was named CCMA's "Song of the Year" and the quartet of Besen, Alan, de Carle and Delorme was named to the CCMA's "All Star Band of the Year." They also took the Juno Award for "Country Group or Duo of the Year" for a third time. By February, 1992, ***Everybody Knows*** had been Certified Gold in Canada and by December, it had turned Platinum. It became the CCMA's 1992 "Album of the Year" and *Did You Fall in Love with Me* (another Besen composition) was named "Song of the Year." The Besen, Alan, de Carle and Delorme names again appeared in the "All Star Band of the Year," and for a fourth time, they scooped up the Juno for "Country Group or Duo of the Year."

Since 1991, their name has been missing from the U.S. Country charts and no further albums have been released. In 1993, Besen, Alan, de Carle and Delorme were again in the CCMA "All Star Band of the Year."

RECOMMENDED ALBUMS:

"Different Kind of Fire" (RCA)(1990)
"Everybody Knows" (RCA)(1991)

PRAIRIE RAMBLERS, The

When Formed: 1930's

Original Members:

"Chick" Hurt	**Mandolin, Mandola, Tenor Banjo**
Jack Taylor	**Guitar**
"Tex" Atchison	**Fiddle, Vocals**
"Salty" Holmes	**Guitar, Harmonica, Jug**

Other Members:

Willie Thawl	**Clarinet**
Alan Crockett	**Fiddle**
Patsy Montana	**Guitar, Vocals**
Ken Houchens	**Guitar**
Bob Long	**Guitar**
Rusty Gill	**Guitar**
George Barnes	**Guitar**
Wade Ray	**Fiddle**
Wally Moore	**Fiddle**

The most commercially successful of the Kentucky bands who made it onto records and radio in the 1930's, the Prairie Ramblers were a fixture on WLS for some 20 years. They made dozens of successful records for the old American Recording Company, served as Gene Autry's original back-up band, broke new ground with their work with Country's first female singing star, Patsy Montana, made Hollywood films, and toured widely with the cast from the popular WLS *National Barn Dance*.

Their vocals eventually tended to become slick and smooth, sounding a lot like the Sons of the Pioneers, and their hit records included such Pop pieces as *Isle of Capri* and *Goofus*. Their musicianship, however, was always superb, and was a major influence on younger musicians who were interested in seeing how they could adapt older folk styles to the new age of radio and records.

The two members who formed the keystone for the group were Chick Hurt (b. Charles Hurt, 1901, Summer Shade, Kentucky/d. 1967) and Jack Taylor (b. ca. 1900, Western, Kentucky/d. 1962); boyhood friends who originally formed a band called the Kentucky Ramblers. They made their radio debut on WOC Davenport, Iowa. Augmented by the driving fiddle and vocals of Tex Atchison (b. Shelby David Atchison) and harmonica and jug of Salty Holmes (b. Floyd Holmes, 1910, Glasgow, Kentucky), this band made a series of exciting records for Victor in December 1933, including seminal versions of *Shady Grove*, *Blue River* and *D Blues*. By this time, the band had met and joined forces with a young singer from Arkansas, Rubye Blevins, who eventually changed her name to Patsy Montana and joined the Ramblers to record an early favorite called *Montana Plains*.

In 1934, after two years, the Ramblers took a leave of absence from WLS and moved to New York, where they appeared for six months over WOR. This was a crucial stay. Atchison recalled, "We left Chicago as an Old-Time string band and we came back from New York as a cowboy band." The New York stay exposed the band to Cowboy and Swing music, and the group learned how to sell its music. While there, they began recording for the ARC group of labels, which distributed records through Sears mail order sales. They had their biggest hit with sweet numbers like *Nobody's Darling But Mine* and *When I Grow Too Old to Dream*. They also were the back-up band for Gene Autry when he recorded such classics as *Tumbling Tumbleweeds* and *Old Faithful*.

By the end of 1936, the group had recorded almost 100 songs, and their repertoire was gradually shifting away from the tough instrumental Blues and fiddle breakdowns to smoother songs. *Riding Down the Canyon* became their theme song, and publicity poses after their return from New York showed them on horses and in western garb.

They then returned to WLS and the *National Barn Dance* (staying until 1956). They still used some of their old Kentucky tunes, such as *Beaver Creek* and *Sugar Hill*, but added to their smooth vocal harmonies Jazz-like clarinet (Willie Thawl) and piano solos. Sacred songs became a part of their repertoire, but so did off-color songs like *Sweet Violets* and *There's a Man Who Comes to Our House*—songs which were recorded under the pseudonym the Sweet Violet Boys. They also recorded as the Blue Ridge Ramblers.

In 1937, Atchison left the band to go to California, where he worked with Jimmy Wakely, Merle Travis, Ray Whitley and others. Salty Holmes also left, returned later and then teamed up with his wife, Maddie (the sister of Martha Carson), as Salty and Maddie, and for many years appeared on the *Grand Ole Opry*. Hurt found replacements in guitarist Ken Houchens and fiddler Alan Crockett, formerly a member of the string band Crockett's Kentucky Mountaineers.

The 1940's saw the band modernize even more with the addition of accordion player Augie Kline and electric guitarist George Barnes. Rusty Gill also joined in 1941, about the time Patsy Montana left to go out on her own. By the end of WWII, the group was reduced to doing novelty songs like *Have a Heart, Taft Hartley*. In 1947 Alan Crockett shot himself and Wade Ray took his place in the group. Chick and Taylor eventually broke up the band, in 1956, and with later member fiddler Wally Moore, worked for some ten years as members of Stan Wallowick and his Polka Chips. CKW

RECOMMENDED ALBUMS:

"Tex's Dance" (Cattle Germany)(1983)
"Rolling Along: An Anthology of Western Swing" (Tishomingo) [Various Artists]
"Texas Sand: Anthology of Western Swing" (Rambler) [Various Artists]
"Patsy Montana & the Prairie Ramblers" (Columbia Historic Edition)(1984)

ELVIS PRESLEY

(Singer, Songwriter, Guitar, Piano, Actor)

Given Name:	**Elvis Aaron Presley**
Date of Birth:	**January 8, 1935**
Where Born:	**Tupelo, Mississippi**
Married:	**Priscilla Beaulieu (m. 1967)(div. 1973)**
Children:	**Lisa Marie**
Date of Death:	**August 16, 1977**

Although Elvis was the "King of Rock'n'Roll," as a Country singer, Elvis was no George Jones. However, as rock'n'roll is re-absorbed into the fabric of contemporary Country, Elvis has increasingly become more important to Country music and material recorded by him is now being covered by even traditional-based performers. This was never more evident than on the soundtrack of the 1992 movie *Honeymoon in Vegas*, which featured a selection of songs associated with Elvis performed by Country, Rock and Pop performers. The Country performers included Ricky Van Shelton (*Wear My Ring Around Your Neck*), Travis Tritt (*Burning Love*), Dwight Yoakam (*Suspicious Minds*), Trisha Yearwood (*You're the) Devil in Disguise*, Vince Gill (*That's All Right*) and Willie Nelson (*Blue Hawaii*).

The King of Rock'n'Roll, ***Elvis Presley***

Elvis was born a twin, but his brother, Jesse Garon, died at birth. From early on, Elvis was exposed to church music through the Pentecostal Assembly of God, borrowing a black style of psalm singing. He came second in his first talent show at the Mississippi-Alabama Fair and Dairy Show, at age 8, singing the Red Foley favorite *Old Shep*. He began playing guitar at age 11, after his father gave up smoking to save the money for one. Two years later, the family moved to Memphis. He sang in high school shows and listened to the music of Roy Acuff, Ernest Tubb and Jimmie Rodgers, as well as non-Country artists such as Sister Rosetta Tharpe, John Lee Hooker, Howlin' Wolf and B.B. King.

Shy by nature, Elvis was initially selective about whom he sang to, and he took jobs as a theater usher and nightworker at a metal products company. When he left school in 1953, he joined the Precision Tool Company and then drove trucks for Crown Electric. At this stage, Elvis' favorite singer was Dean Martin. Stopping by the Memphis Recording Service studio (an offshoot of Sun Records, which made custom recordings), Elvis cut *My Happiness* and *That's When Your Heartaches Begin*. It was here that Elvis was heard by Marion Keisker and she told her boss, Sam Phillips, about "sideburns," as Phillips referred to Elvis.

In 1954, Elvis signed with Sun Records, and although he soon came up with the style of music that would lead him very quickly to stardom, Sam Phillips, his deejay associate, Dewey Phillips and then Bob Neal, who became his first real manager (guitarist Scotty Moore acted in this capacity initially), had problems where to pitch Elvis. For all intents and purposes, he was a Country act, but then yet again, he wasn't. The flip-side of Elvis' first single, *That's All Right*, was a speeded-up version of Bill Monroe's *Blue Moon of Kentucky* (Monroe would later play the song in Elvis' style) and on October 6, 1954, Elvis debuted on the *Louisiana Hayride*. He stayed on the show for eighteen months. During 1955, he appeared on other Country shows including the *Big D Jamboree* (Dallas), *Grand Prize Saturday Night Jamboree* (Houston) and *Hank Snow's All-Star Jamboree* (a three-week tour) as well as the *Grand Ole Opry*, on which he was introduced by Hank Snow.

It was while Elvis was appearing on the *Louisiana Hayride* that he came to the attention of Colonel Tom Parker, who was at the time managing Eddy Arnold and Hank Snow. Parker worked his way into Elvis' career and became his manager, much to the chagrin of Snow, who had signed papers with an underaged Elvis. In 1955, Elvis made his debut on the Country charts with *Baby Let's Play House/I'm Left, You're Right, She's Gone*, which reached the Top 5. This was followed by the No.1 *I Forget to Remember to Forget/Mystery Train*, which stayed at the top for 5 weeks out of 39 on the charts.

With Parker in the saddle as manager, Elvis was soon signed to RCA Victor and Sun Records received the then enormous amount of $35,000 for his contract, of which Elvis received $5,000. When *Heartbreak Hotel* went to No.1 in the spring of 1956 and stayed there for 17 weeks, the Country music establishment shook its head. To them, it looked like the death knell for Country music was in sight.

From then until the end of 1958, Elvis racked up a series of major hits on the Country charts (as well as many more on the Pop charts). They were, 1956: *I Was the One* (Top 10, the flip of *Heartbreak Hotel), I Want You, I Need You, I Love You/My Baby Left Me* (No.1), *Don't Be Cruel/Hound Dog* (both sides No.1), *Love Me Tender* (Top 3)/*Love Me* (Top 10); 1957: *Too Much* (Top 3)/*Playing For Keeps* (Top 10), *All Shook Up* (No.1), *(Let Me Be Your) Teddy Bear* (No.1), *Jailhouse Rock* (No.1); 1958: *Don't* (Top 3)/*I Beg of You* (Top 5), *Wear My Ring Around Your Neck* (Top 3) and *Hard Headed Woman* (Top 3).

During this period, Elvis commenced his movie career. Most of the movies were just vehicles for the songs, mainly written by Jerry Leiber and Mike Stoller and Doc Pomus and Mort Shuman. Some were better, in particular the early ones, *Love Me Tender* (1956), *Loving You* and *Jailhouse Rock* (1957) and *King Creole* (1958, based on Harold Robbins' novel *A Stone for Danny Fisher*).

In 1958, Elvis was drafted into the U.S. Army and served for a while in Germany. This served as the basis for his first post-Army movie, *G.I. Blues*, in 1960. From this time on, Elvis recorded more and more Country material. Among these songs were Jerry Reed's *Guitar Man* and *U.S. Male* (1968), Mac Davis' *In the Ghetto* and *Don't Cry Daddy* (both 1969), Mark James' *Suspicious Minds* (1969) and *Moody Blue* (1976), Eddie Rabbitt's *Kentucky Rain* (1970), Dallas Frazier's *There Goes My Everything*, Mickey Newbury's arrangement called *An American Trilogy*, Dennis Linde's *Burning Love*, Mark James/Wayne Carson/Johnny Christopher's *Always on My Mind* (1972), Jerry Chesnut's *T-R-O-U-B-L-E* (1975, a hit for Travis Tritt in 1993) and Dickeys Lee's *She Thinks I Still Care* (1976).

Following Elvis' return from the Army, he recorded his excellent inspirational album ***His Hand in Mine*** and seven years later, recorded ***How Great Thou Art***, with the Jordanaires and the Imperials Quartet. ***How Great Thou Art*** won a 1967 Grammy for Elvis as "Best Sacred Performance." This album featured his 1965 Top 3 single *Crying in the Chapel*.

In 1969, Elvis recorded the highly lauded album ***From Elvis in Memphis***, which was re-released in 1987 as ***The Memphis Record***. This was recorded at Chip Moman's American Studios and contained several non-charting Country songs: Vern Stovall's *Long Black Limousine*, Dallas Frazier and "Doodle" Owens' *Wearin' that Loved on Look* and *True Love Travels on a Gravel Road*, Eddie Rabbitt's *Inherit the Wind*, John Hartford's *Gentle on My Mind*, Hank Snow's *I'm Movin' On*, Eddy Arnold's *I'll Hold You in My Heart (Till I Can Hold You in My Arms)* and Johnny Christopher's *Mama Liked the Roses*. Among the back-up vocalists were Ronnie Milsap, who also played piano on *Gentle on My Mind*, and Sandy Posey.

That same year, Elvis appeared in one of his more critically acclaimed movies, *The Trouble with Girls (And How to Get Into It)*, which also featured Vincent Price and Joyce Van Patten. In 1971, Elvis released ***Elvis Country***, which was, to be generous, a strange album. It did contain a good mix of Country material, but selections were interwoven with segments of the song *I Was Born About Ten Thousand Years Ago*. The album revealed Elvis' lack of real Country feel, with him using his "operatic" voice and even *Whole Lot-ta* [sic] *Shakin' Goin' On* has Elvis handling badly a rock'n'roll classic.

That year, Elvis was presented with the NARAS "Lifetime Award" "in recognition of his artistic creativity and his influence in the field of recorded music upon a generation of performers and listeners whose lives and musical horizons have been enriched and expanded by his unique contributions." His album ***He Touched Me*** won the 1972 Grammy for "Best Inspirational Performance." In 1974, Elvis received another Grammy for the track *How Great Thou Art*, as "Best Inspirational Performance."

When Elvis died in 1977 following years of abuse of prescribed drugs, the world was shattered. Just prior to his death, he had enjoyed a Top 20 hit with *Way Down*, which also became a No.1 Country success. Posthumously, Elvis had several more Country chart hits, of which the most successful were the live recording *My Way* (Top 3) and the Top 10 success *Unchained Melody* (both 1978) and *There's a Honky Tonk Angel (Who Will Take Me Back In)*, a Top 10 hit in 1979, which had been a No. 1 for Conway Twitty in 1974.

In 1981, the Presley name was back at the top of the Country chart with Felton Jarvis' remix of *Guitar Man*, which also made the Pop Top 30. Elvis' last major hit was later that year when Tom Jans' *Lovin' Arms* reached the Country Top 10. The following year *The Elvis Medley*, a collage of eight Elvis hits, made the Pop Top 75.

Elvis' recording of *Hound Dog* was inducted into the NARAS Hall of Fame in 1988. On March 27, 1992, the RIAA awarded Gold, Platinum and Multi-Platinum Discs to nearly 90 of Elvis' singles and albums, in an unprecedented catch-up (see RIAA Awards in Awards Section). There is no doubt that Elvis Presley record and video sales will continue.

RECOMMENDED ALBUMS:

Most Elvis albums have something for everyone, with the possible exception of some of the movie soundtracks. Below are some that emphasize the Country and Gospel side of "the King of Rock and Roll."

"Elvis' 40 Greatest" (RCA)(1978) [On Pink Vinyl]
"The Sun Collection" (RCA)(1979)
"The Memphis Record" (RCA)(1987)
"The All-Time Greatest Hits" (RCA)(1987)
Gospel:
"His Hand in Mine" (RCA)(1960)
"How Great Thou Art" (RCA)(1967)
"He Touched Me" (RCA)(1972)

FRANCES PRESTON

(Industry Executive)

Given Name:	**Frances Loree Williams**
Date of Birth:	**August 27, 1934**
Where Born:	**Nashville, Tennessee**
Married:	**Ernest Jerome Preston (E.J.)**
Children:	**David, Donald, Kirk (E.J.'s children adopted by Frances)**

In 1990, *Ladies' Home Journal* listed Frances Preston as one of the "50 Most Powerful Women in America," and two years later, *Entertainment Weekly* placed her second in the Top 10 listing of "The Powers of Country Music." In a *Savvy* magazine feature, in 1989, her magic was described as "coming as much from her empathy as from her business power. She has a gift, the ability to make everyone she touches feel special, golden." This is how the world sees Frances Preston, President and CEO of Broadcast Music, International (BMI).

Frances sang in church choirs and glee

clubs, but had no aspirations of becoming a performer. After graduating from Peabody College, she worked for WSM radio and television. She also moonlighted handling the fan club letters for Hank Williams, Hank Snow and Cowboy Copas, among others. Each year, she worked on the Disc Jockey Festival. At the time, BMI awards to songwriters were given at the same time as record company awards to artists, but as soon as the record company awards were given, the audience left. In 1957, Frances went to Robert J. Burton, the then Executive VP of BMI, and suggested a special event to award the writers. He asked her to help plan it, and so the writers were honored at a 7:00 am breakfast at the Maxwell House hotel.

She had, at the time, good political connections, and knew all the performers, and in 1958, she was asked by BMI to open up its first regional office in Nashville, becoming Southern Regional Office Manager. When she asked what her job was, Bob Burton told her "whatever you make of it." The office grew to include Memphis, Georgia and Alabama, and finally enveloped sixteen states. She signed writers such as Jimmie Davies, Floyd Tillman, Eddy Arnold and Albert Brumley.

She rose in importance in the BMI hierarchy and in 1964, became a Vice-President, in 1985, became Senior VP, Performing Rights and in 1986, President and Chief Executive Officer. She is also a member of BMI's Board of Directors.

She is a life-time member of the Board of Directors of the CMA, being only one of five individuals so honored. She has also acted as its President and Chairperson of the CMA. She is also a life-time member of the NSAI and is a Board member and Executive VP of the Nashville Chapter of NARAS. She is also a member of the Board of Advisers for the Steinway Foundation.

She also serves as a Board Member of the Rock and Roll Hall of Fame and the Rhythm & Blues Foundation. She is a member of the Administrative Council of CISAC (the International Confederation of Societies of Authors and Composers). She is Vice President of the National Music Council and Honorary Trustee of the National Academy of Popular Music. She is a member of the National Advisory Board of the George Foster Peabody Awards. She is also a member of the Film, Entertainment and Music Commission Advisory Council of the State of Tennessee.

She is a member of the Recording Industry Advisory Board of Middle Tennessee State University College of Mass Communication. She is a member of the Board of Directors for the Foundation for a Creative America. She served on President Carter's President's Panama Canal Study Committee and was a member of the Commission for the White House Record Library. She is a member of the Rotary Club, the first woman to join the Nashville arm of the Club. She was also one of the first four women to be invited to join New York's Friars Club. She also serves on NARAS's President's Advisory Council and on the Board of Directors for the NARAS Foundation.

She has been recognized by all facets of American society. She was one of the recipients of an award from the Women's Equity Action League. In 1982, she was singled out by *Esquire* magazine as "the most influential and powerful person in the Country music business." She was profiled by *Fortune* magazine, in January, 1987, in the year's "Most Fascinating Business People." That same year, she was the winner of the "Irving Waugh Award of Excellence," presented for only the second time by the CMA.

In 1988, she received the American Women in Radio and Television "Outstanding Achievement Award." She received Honorary Degrees from the Berklee School of Music, Boston, and Lincoln College, Lincoln, Illinois. She received the 1992 "Humanitarian Award" from the T.J. Martell Foundation for Leukemia, Cancer and AIDS Research. She serves on the Foundation's Board of Directors and the Frances Williams Preston Laboratory at Vanderbilt Hospital was named in her honor. In 1992, she received the highest accolade in Country music when she was inducted into the Country Music Hall of Fame.

Frances Preston is without doubt one of the world's workaholics. If she has quality time, it is spent skiing or organizing skiing charity events. She still has the same drive that brought her to BMI, and she's even more ornery (even more so, according to her). She is a fighter for copyright protection, and played a key role in protecting older compositions through the Copyright Amendments Act, 1992. With the break-up of the old Soviet bloc, Frances has gotten involved with copyrighting in the constituent countries and also China.

KENNY PRICE

(Singer, Songwriter, Drums, Guitar, Banjo, Stand-up Bass)

Date of Birth: May 27, 1931
Where Born: Florence, Kentucky
Date of Death: August 4, 1987

Although Kenny Price never achieved the lasting fame that he deserved, for some 15 years he was a consistent presence in the Country charts. Known as the "Round Mound of Sound," the bulky stature of Kenny Price (he weighed in at 300 pounds and stood over 6 feet tall) was a popular figure on TV's *Hee Haw*. His rich voice, not unlike Red Foley's, ensured that he racked up 34 chart singles.

He was raised on a Boone County, Kentucky, ranch and learned to play on a Sears Roebuck catalog guitar when age 5. Although he played at local gigs and at age 14 debuted on WZIP Cincinnati, it was still his intention to become a farmer. In 1952, Kenny was drafted into the U.S. Army and from then until 1954, he spent most of the time stationed in Korea. He successfully auditioned for Horace Heldt's USO Show in Korea and on discharge from the service decided to pursue a career in music.

He enrolled at the Cincinnati Conservatory of Music and in 1954 joined WLW Cincinnati's *Midwestern Hayride* and in 1957 WLW-TV's Buddy Ross's *Hometowners*. He started on the Hayride as lead singer of the Hometowners and then spent two years as emcee.

Among the cast members of the *Hayride* was Bobby Bobo who, in the early 60's, put together the Boone label. Bobo's other acts included Tex Williams, Lamar Morris and the Acorn Sisters. Kenny's first single was *Somebody Told Mary/White Silver Sands*, but it was with Kenny's third release, Ray Pennington's *Walking on New Grass*, that he broke into the Country chart, reaching the Top 10 in the summer of 1966. His next single, *Happy Tracks*, entered the charts on Christmas Eve that year and also went into the Top 10. The first two singles of 1967, *Pretty Girl, Pretty Clothes, Pretty Sad* and *Grass Won't Grow on a Busy Street* reached the Top 20, but his final release of the year, *My Goal for Today*, reached the Top 15.

During 1968 and 1969, his singles hovered around the middle of the charts and then in 1969 he signed with RCA Victor. On moving labels, many of his earlier singles were re-released by Boone. His first sizable hit for RCA was in 1970 with the Top 20 *Northeast Arkansas Mississippi County Bootlegger*, but later that year he had two Top 10 hits with *Biloxi* and *The Sheriff of Boone County*; the latter creeping into the bottom of the Pop charts.

Kenny didn't again reach those heady heights with his releases and between 1971 and 1976 when he left the label, his biggest hits were *Sea of Heartbreak* (1972) and *Turn on Your Light (And Let it Shine)* (1973). In 1976, he joined the cast of *Hee Haw* and a year later, left RCA for the independent label MRC.

Although five of his singles charted, none of them climbed higher than *Afraid You'd Come Back*, which went to No.50. In 1980, he moved on to Dimension Records, but again the two singles that charted were at the middle to lower levels.

He moved to Phonorama Records and released the album ***A Pocket Full of Tunes***. As a part of the Hee Haw Gospel Quartet, with Roy Clark, Grandpa Jones and Buck Owens, he could be heard on the ***Hee Haw Gospel Quartet*** album on the Hee Haw label in 1984. That same year, he also released the single *If I Just Had You*, on the Jewel label. Kenny Price died from a heart attack in 1987.

RECOMMENDED ALBUMS:

"One Hit Follows Another" (Boone)(1967)
"A Red Foley Songbook" (RCA Victor)(1971)
"Kenny Price (The Sheriff of Boone County)" (RCA Victor)(1971)
"Sea of Heartbreak (& Other Don Gibson Hits)" (RCA Victor)(1973)
"The Best of Both" (Dimension)(1980)
"A Pocket Full of Tunes" (Phonorama)(1982)
"The Hee Haw Gospel Quartet" (Hee Haw)(1984)

RAY PRICE

(Singer, Songwriter, Guitar)

Given Name:	**Ray Noble Price**
Date of Birth:	**January 12, 1926**
Where Born:	**Perryville,Upshur County, Texas**
Married:	**1. Betty B. Greg (Linda Powers) (div.)** **2. Janie**
Children:	**Clifton Ray**

Ray Price, known as the "Cherokee Cowboy," is one of the most successful singers in Country music. For nearly 50 years, his name graced the Country charts and although his style has moved from Honky-Tonk to smooth ballads, he has retained a singing voice that is still pleasant on the ear and his albums still contain musical adventure.

*The Cherokee Cowboy, **Ray Price***

Ray enlisted for active service with the U.S. Marines during WWII and spent the period 1944 through 1946 in uniform, serving in the Pacific. After leaving the service, Ray attended North Texas Agricultural College near Dallas with the intention of becoming a veterinarian. While studying, he started to play and sing at local gigs and college dates. In 1948, he made his radio debut on KRBC Abilene's *Hillbilly Jamboree*, as the Cherokee Cowboy, and a year later, joined the *Big D Jamboree* in Dallas, where he stayed until 1950. As the show was shown on the CBS network, Ray soon got national attention. Ray recorded his first single, *Your Wedding Corsage/Jealous Lies*, for the Dallas-based Bullet label, in 1949.

Ray was greatly influenced by Hank Williams and in 1951, when he joined Columbia, Ray became great friends with his idol. Ray's signing to Columbia occurred after his champion, the legendary Troy Martin, told the label's Don Law that Paul Cohen at Decca was going to record him. Law had turned Ray down 20 times and he had threatened Martin that he would throw him out his window if Ray's name was mentioned again. As a result of his signing to Columbia, Paul Cohen signed seventeen singers from Dallas just so Don Law wouldn't get them.

For many years, Ray was stylistically very close to Hank. Williams even wrote a song for Ray to sing, entitled *Weary Blues*. This connection with Williams led to Ray being signed to the *Grand Ole Opry* in January 1952. Ray's first chart entry came later that year when *Talk to Your Heart* reached the Top 3. Six months later, Ray was back in the Top 5 with *Don't Let the Stars Get in Your Eyes*, which became a No.1 Pop hit for Perry Como the following year. During 1952, Ray wrote *Give Me More, More, More (of Your Kisses)* at Lefty Frizzell's request. The song took 15 minutes to write and went to No.1 for Lefty.

After Hank Williams' death in 1953, the Drifting Cowboys became Ray's backing band on tour and on recordings. Ray was absent from the chart during 1953 but returned to the Top 3 in 1954 with *I'll Be There (If You Ever Want Me)*. The flip-side, *Release Me*, also made the Top 10. He completed the year with *Much Too Young to Die*, which went Top 15, and *If You Don't, Somebody Else Will*. That year, Ray formed the Cherokee Cowboys as his backing band. This came about because by then Ray realized that the Drifting Cowboys made him sound like Hank Williams and so he engaged Lefty Frizzell's band, the Western Cherokees. The Cherokee Cowboys became one of the major back-up bands in Country music and members of the band over the years included Roger Miller, Buddy Emmons, Jimmy Day, Johnny Bush and Johnny Paycheck (then known as Donny Young). Its most famous alumnus was Willie Nelson, who took some of the Cowboys with him when he formed the Record Men.

Ray was absent from the chart in 1955, but in 1956 he firmly established himself as one of the major Country music performers. At the beginning of the year, he had the Top 5 single *Run Boy*. This was followed by a single that has become a classic. The song was Chuck Seals/Ralph Mooney's *Crazy Arms*, which went to No.1 and remained there for 20 weeks out of 45 weeks on the charts!! It also crossed over to the Pop Top 70. The flip-side, *You Done Me Wrong*, also went Top 10. At year end, Ray had a Top 3 single with *I've Got a New Heartache*, backed with the Top 5 *Wasted Words*.

The following year, his opening single *I'll Be There (When You Get Lonely)* only reached the Top 15 and Columbia immediately followed-up with *My Shoes Keep Walking Back to You*, which went to No.1 for 4 weeks out of over 9 months on the charts. The single also crossed to the Pop Top 70. In 1958, Ray started with the Top 3 *Curtain in the Window/It's All Your Fault*. In the summer, Ray charted with Bill Anderson's *City Lights*. Ray had been driving with Ernest Tubb when they heard Bill's version on the radio and E.T. told Ray that he had to record the song. The single went to No.1 for 13 weeks out of over 8 months on the Country charts, and the flip-side, *Invitation to the Blues*, also reached the Top 3. Both sides crossed to the lower regions of the Pop chart. Ray finished the 50's with a string of hits: *That's What It's Like to Be Lonesome* (Top 10), Harlan Howard's *Heartaches By the Number* (Top 3) and *The Same Ole Me* (No.1)/*Under Your Spell Again* (Top 5).

During the 60's, Ray didn't have a No.1, but he still racked up 33 chart entries, 16 of them going Top 10. These early 60's entries were: 1960: *One More Time* (Top 3) and *I Wish I Could Fall in Love Again* (Top 5); 1961: *Heart Over Mind* (Top 5)/*The Twenty-Fourth Hour* (Top 15) and *Soft Rain* (Top 3); 1962: *I've Just Destroyed the World (I'm Living In)* (Top 15) and *Pride* (Top 5); 1963: *Walk Me to the Door* (Top 10)/*You Took Her Off My Hands (Now Please Take Her Off My Mind)* (Top 15) and *Make the World Go Away* (Top 3). The flip-side of the last named was

Ray's fine version of Willie Nelson's *Night Life*, which also went Top 30.

By now, Ray's style had changed to a more Pop-Country one and Ray incorporated a 20-piece orchestra in his act. His other hits during the 60's were: 1964: *Burning Memories* (Top 3) and *Please Talk to My Heart* (Top 10); 1965: *The Other Woman* (Top 3) and *Don't You Ever Get Tired of Hurting Me* (Top 15); 1966: *A Way to Survive* (Top 10) and *Touch My Heart* (Top 3); 1967: *Danny Boy* (Top 10), *I'm Still Not Over You* (Top 10 and also a Pop Top 60 entry) and *Take Me as I Am (Or Let Me Go)* (all Top 10); 1968: *I've Been There Before* (Top 15) and *She Wears My Ring* (Top 10). In 1969, all three of Ray's singles went Top 15 and they were *Sweetheart of the Year*, *Raining in My Heart* and *April's Fool*. During 1969, Ray left Nashville to return to Texas when his father was diagnosed with cancer.

The new decade started with an upswing when *You Wouldn't Know Love* went Top 10. He followed this with his chart-topping version of Kristofferson's *For the Good Times*, which also crossed over to the Pop Top 15. He followed up in 1971 with another No.1, *I Won't Mention it Again*, which stayed at the top for 3 weeks and became a Pop Top 50 success. Ray ended the year with *I'd Rather Be Lonely*, which went Top 3. The following year, he went Top 3 with *The Lonesomest Lonesome* and went to the top again with *She's Got to Be a Saint*. Ray had one chart entry in 1973 when *You're the Best Thing that Ever Happened to Me* went to No.1. The following year, Gladys Knight & the Pips took the song to the Pop chart Top 3. 1974 was Ray's last year with Columbia and he charted with *Storms of Troubled Times* (Top 25) and *Like a First Time Thing* (Top 15).

At the end of 1974, Ray had a Top 5 hit with *Like Old Times Again* on Myrrh. The following year, he had a Top 3 single on the same label, *Roses and Love Songs*. That year, Ray signed to ABC/Dot, but he did again reach the same high chart placings. His major hits were: *A Mansion on the Hill* (1976) and *Different Kind of Flower* (Top 30) and *Born to Love Me* (Top 25) (both 1977). The last named was also released on Columbia.

In 1978, Ray moved to Fred Foster's Monument label, where he had two Top 20 singles, *Feet* (1978) and *That's the Only Way to Say Good Morning* (1979). By 1980, Willie Nelson was getting a reputation for recording with all the major names in Country music. Ray approached Willie and as a result they recorded the album ***San Antonio Rose***. The album was a great success and from it, two singles, *Faded Love* (Top 3) and *Don't You Ever Get Tired (of Hurting Me)* (Top 15), charted.

At the end of 1980, Ray signed to Dimension Records, where he was produced by Ray Pennington and where the following year he chalked up two Top 10 singles, *It Don't Hurt Me Half As Bad* and *Diamonds in the Stars*. The following year, Ray headlined a talent search operation called Ray Price's Country Starsearch 1981. He appeared at the finals in all 50 states and starred in the winners TV show.

On August 26 that year, he was recognized by the State of Mississippi, by their Senate Concurrent Resolution No. 505, which stated "A Concurrent Resolution recognizing the Outstanding Musical career of Ray Price, expressing appreciation to him for his efforts to raise funds for the construction of a chapel at the Mississippi State Penitentiary and proclaiming 'Ray Price Week.'"

In 1982, Ray had his last two Top 20 hits, *Forty and Fadin'* on Dimension and *Old Friends*. The last named came from the Willie Nelson and Roger Miller album of the same name, on which Ray guested. That year, Ray appeared in the Clint Eastwood movie *Honkytonk Man*, from which came the Top 70 single *One Fiddle, Two Fiddle/San Antonio Rose*, on which he was backed by Johnny Gimble & the Texas Swing Band.

In 1983, Ray went to Warner Brothers and Clint Eastwood's Viva Records, without major success. Two years later, Ray moved to Step One Records where he was reunited with producer Ray Pennington. His most successful singles were *When You Gave Your Love to Me* (1986) and *Just Enough Love* (1987), which both went Top 60. By 1989, Ray operated his own theater in Branson, Missouri. Ray returned to Columbia to record the Norro Wilson-produced album, ***Sometimes a Rose***. In 1993, Ray was nominated for the Country Music Hall of Fame but lost out to Willie Nelson. However, in his acceptance speech, Willie said of the other nominees, "....We've got to remember Harlan [Howard], Merle [Haggard], Ray [Price] and Don [Gibson] next year." (For Ray's awards, see Awards Section.)

RECOMMENDED ALBUMS:

"Ray Price's Greatest Hits" (Columbia)(1961)
"Ray Price's Greatest Hits Vol. II" (Columbia)(1967)
"The World of Ray Price" (double)(Columbia)(1970)
"Ray Price's All-Time Greatest Hits" (double)(Columbia)(1972)
"Ray Price Sings San Antonio Rose (A Tribute to the Great Bob Wills)" (Columbia)(1973)
"Like Old Times Again" (ABC/Myrrh)(1974)
"Hank (Williams) 'n' Me" (ABC/Dot)(1976)
"Reunited—Ray Price & the Cherokee Cowboys" (ABC/Dot)(1977) [Re-released on MCA in 1983]
"San Antonio Rose" (Columbia)(1980) [With Willie Nelson]
"Tribute to Willie & Kris (Nelson & Kristofferson)" (Columbia)(1981)
"Ray Price's Greatest Hits" (Dimension)(1981)
"Master of the Art" (Warner/Viva)(1983)
"Portrait of a Singer" (double)(Step One)(1985)
"Greatest Hits, Volume 1" (Step One)(1986)
"Greatest Hits, Volume 2" (Step One)(1986)
"Greatest Hits, Volume 3" (Step One)(1986)
"The Heart of Country Music" (double)(Step One)(1987)
"Just Enough Love" (Step One)(1988)
"Sometimes a Rose" (Columbia)(1992)

CHARLEY PRIDE

(Singer, Songwriter, Guitar)

Given Name: **Charley Frank Pride**
Date of Birth: **March 18, 1938**
Where Born: **Sledge, Mississippi**
Married: **Rozene**
Children: **Kraig, Dion, Angela**

It is often stated that Charley Pride is by far the most successful black Country singer of all time. In fact, Charley is just about one of the most successful Country singers—period. His resonant baritone voice and straight-ahead style have put him in direct lineage of the greats of Country music, such as Ernest Tubb and Hank Williams.

Charley was born on a 40-acre cotton farm where his daddy, Mack, was a sharecropper. He purchased his first guitar, a $10 model from Sears Roebuck, when he was age 14. Up to the age of 16, Charley picked cotton and then in 1954, he played baseball for the Negro American League with, initially, the Detroit Eagles and then Memphis Red Sox as a pitcher and outfielder. He stayed with them until 1956, when he joined the U.S. Army. While in the service, he married Rozene, whom he had met in Memphis.

He left the service in 1958 and although he returned to baseball, he quit after injuries affected his arm. Charley became a

Superstar ***Charley Pride***

construction worker in Helena, Montana, working at the Anaconda Mining zinc smelting plant, while still playing semi-pro ball in the Pioneer League. In 1961, he reached the Major League where he pitched and played outfield with the California Angels, in training camp. However, the Angels turned him down, as did the New York Mets, the following year.

In 1963, Charley met Red Foley and Red Sovine at the Helena Civic Center and wound up singing *Lovesick Blues* backstage for them. They encouraged him to try his luck in Nashville. He did just that the following year, initially without success. However, at the urging of the two Reds and with help from Webb Pierce, Charley tried his luck again. It was Pierce who introduced him to Jack Johnson, who became Charley's manager.

Johnson introduced Charley to "Cowboy" Jack Clement, who cut some sides on him and got a tape to Chet Atkins at RCA. Jack wanted to rename Charley, "George Washington III," but fortunately, this didn't happen. Atkins signed Charley and in 1966, billed as "Country Charley Pride," RCA released his debut single *The Snakes Crawl at Night*. So as not to have radio station resistance because of his color, RCA released the single and failed to enclose a photograph. The single started picking up interest, as did the follow-up, *Before I Met You*, but it was the third release, *Just Between You and Me*, that did the trick. It reached the Top 10 and the Pride career was underway. Charley's debut album ***(Country) Charley Pride*** was Certified Gold in 1975.

In 1967, Charley made his debut on the *Grand Ole Opry*, where he was introduced by Ernest Tubb. Charley scored with the Top 10 *I Know One* and the Top 5 *Does My Ring Hurt Your Finger*. Charley's third album, ***The Country Way,*** was Certified Gold in 1973. That year, *Country Song Roundup* named Charley "Most Promising Male Artist." With the advent of 1968, RCA dropped the "Country" prefix to Charley's name and that year his record successes were: *The Day the World Stood Still* (Top 5), *The Easy Part's Over* (Top 3) and *Let the Chips Fall* (Top 5).

1969 marked the start of Charley's crossover appeal when his reprise of Hank Williams' *Kaw-Liga* went Top 3 and also reached the lower rungs of the Pop chart. He then had a string of six back-to-back No.1 hits starting with *All I Have to Offer You (Is Me)* and continuing with *(I'm So) Afraid of Losing You Again* and in 1970, *Is Anyone Goin' to San Antone*, which gave his highest placing on the Pop chart, Top 70. The year continued with *Wonder Could I Live There Anymore* and *I Can't Believe that You've Stopped Loving Me*. Charley's albums in 1969 and 1970 were all highly successful. ***Charley Pride....In Person (Live at Panther Hall)*** was released in 1969 and went Gold that same year; ***The Sensational Charley Pride,*** also released that year, was Certified Gold in 1973; the last album of 1969, ***The Best of Charley Pride***, went Gold in 1970. The following year, Charley released ***Just Plain Charley*** and ***Charley Pride's 10th Album*** and they were both Certified Gold in 1971. In 1969, *Music City News* Cover Awards named Charley "Male Vocalist of the Year." He retained the title in 1970, 1971, 1972 and 1973.

Charley started 1971 with *I'd Rather Love You*, which stayed at the top for 3 weeks. Although *Let Me Live* from the inspirational album ***Did You Think to Pray?*** failed to make the Top 20, it did win for Charley a 1971 Grammy Award as "Best Gospel Performance (Other Than Soul Gospel)." The album also won a Grammy Award that year as "Best Sacred Performance." Next came *I'm Just Me*, which went to No.1 and stayed there for 4 weeks and was followed by his most successful career single, *Kiss an Angel Good Mornin'*, which stayed at No.1 for 5 weeks, crossed-over to the Top 25 on the Pop chart and earned a Gold Record the following year.

Charley's 1971 albums were also highly successful; ***From Me to You (To All My Wonderful Fans)*** went Gold in 1973, ***Did You Think to Pray?*** achieved Gold status in 1975 and ***Charlie Pride Sings Heart Songs*** was Certified Gold in 1972 and that same year earned Charley a Grammy Award for "Best Country Vocal Performance, Male." In 1971, Charley received the CMA's top prize when he was named "Entertainer of the Year." The CMA also named him "Male Vocalist of the Year," an honor they repeated in 1972.

Charley opened his 1972 account with the Top 3 release *All His Children*, which paired him with Henry Mancini and was featured in the Paul Newman movie *Sometimes a Great Notion*. Charley then had five back-to-back No. 1 records: *It's Gonna Take a Little Time* and *She's Too Good to be True* (both at the top for 3 weeks, both 1972), *A Shoulder to Cry On* (written by Merle Haggard), *Don't Fight the Feelings of Love* and *Amazing Love* (all 1973). Charley's 1972 compilation, ***The Best of Charley Pride, Volume II***, went Gold that year.

From 1974 to 1976, Charley continued to chalk up major successes. In 1974 he had *We Could* and *Mississippi Cotton Picking Delta Town* (both Top 3), and the No.1 *Then Who Am I*. In 1975 there were *I Ain't All Bad* (Top 10), *Hope You're Feelin' Me (Like I'm Feelin' You)* (No.1) and the Top 3 *The Happiness of Having You*. His two successes in 1976 were the No.1 *My Eyes Can Only See as Far as You* and the Top 3 *A Whole Lotta Things to Sing About*. In 1975, Charley received a Dove Award from the Gospel Music Association for "Best Album by a Secular Recording Artist" for ***Sunday Morning with Charley Pride***. Around this time, Dave and Sugar became Charley's backing vocal group.

Charley started a run of four straight No.1 hits in 1977 with *She's Just an Old Love Turned Memory* and continued with *I'll Be Leaving Alone* and *More to Me* (both 1977) and *Someone Loves You Honey* (1978). His other hits during the decade were all Top 3 singles, with the exception of *Dallas Cowboys* (1979), a special tribute to the NFL team. The hits were: *When I Stop Leaving (I'll be Gone)* and *Burgers and Fries* (both 1978), *Where Do I Put Her Money* and *You're My Jamaica* (both No.1) and *Missin' You* (all 1979).

He started off the new decade with two No.1 hits, Hank Williams' *Honky Tonk Blues* and *You Win Again*. He closed out 1980 with the Top 5 *You Almost Slipped My Mind*. Between 1981 and 1983, Charley's successes were: 1981: *Roll on Mississippi* (Top 10) and successive No.1s, *Never Been So Loved (In All My Life)* and *Mountain of Love*; 1982: *I Don't Think She's in Love Anymore* (Top 3) and back-to back No.1s, *You're So Good When You're Bad* and Webb Pierce's standard, *Why Baby Why*; 1983: *More and More* (Top 10), *Night Games* (No.1) and *Every Heart Should Have One* (Top 3).

In 1984, following the Top 10 hit *The Power of Love*, the title track of his 1984 album, his singles found less favor with the radio stations, and none of them during 1984 through 1986 rose above the Top 25. In 1986, Charley moved to Opryland's new 16th Avenue label, which was being masterminded by his earlier producer, Jerry Bradley. By early 1987, Charley was back in the Top 15 with *Have I Got Some Blues for You* from his debut album ***After All This Time***, and by year end, he had the Top 5 hit *Shouldn't it Be Easier Than This* from his second album for the label, ***I'm Gonna Love Her on the Radio***. The title track provided Charley with his last Top 15 single in the spring of 1988. His last major hit, *Amy's Eyes*, made the Top 30, in 1989.

With the demise of 16th Avenue, Charley moved to Honest Entertainment, who released the much praised ***My 6 Latest & 6 Greatest***, a blend of old and new material, on which he was joined by Travis Tritt, Marty Stuart, Hal Ketchum and Joe Diffie. Although absent from the charts, Charley Pride still continues to be a major concert draw. He is now joined on stage by his lead guitarist/singer son, Dion. In 1994, the ACM honored Charley and his body of work with its "Pioneer Award."

Charley's motto that gets him through life is "Get it Done." He certainly has done that business-wise. He is a majority stockholder in the First Texas Bank in Dallas and now owns the 199-acre farm where his father was once a sharecropper.

RECOMMENDED ALBUMS:

"(Country) Charley Pride" (RCA Victor)(1966)
"The Country Way" (RCA Victor)(1967)
"Charley Pride...In Person (At Panther Hall)" (RCA Victor)(1969)
"The Sensational Charley Pride" (RCA Victor)(1969)
"Just Plain Charley" (RCA Victor)(1970)
"Charley Pride's 10th Album" (RCA Victor)(1970)
"From Me to You (To My Wonderful Fans)" (RCA Victor)(1970)
"Did You Think to Pray?" (RCA Victor)(1971)
"Charley Pride Sings Heart Songs" (RCA Victor)(1971)
"Sunday Morning with Charley Pride" (RCA Victor)(1976)
"There's a Little Bit of Hank (Williams) in Me" (RCA Victor)(1980)
"Charley Pride Live" (RCA Victor)(1982) [With Dion Pride]
"Country Classics" (RCA Victor)(1983)
"Night Games" (RCA Victor)(1983)
"Power of Love" (RCA Victor)(1984)
"20 of the Best" (RCA UK)(1986)
"Back to the Country" (RCA Victor)(1986)
"After All This Time" (16th Avenue)(1987)
"I'm Gonna Love Her on the Radio" (16th Avenue)(1988)
"My 6 Latest & 6 Greatest" (Honest Entertainment)(1994)

JOHN PRINE

(Singer, Songwriter, Guitar, Actor)

Date of Birth:	**October 10, 1946**
Where Born:	**Maywood, Illinois**
Married:	**1. (Div.)**
	2. (Div.)

John Prine has been a cult hero with a loyal following for more years than most superstars could ever hope for a career. His music, which walks the tightrope between Folk, Country and Soft-Rock, is a mixture of the acerbic, the witty, the poignant and the amusing, but is always thought-provoking.

John started writing songs while still a teenager in the suburbs of Chicago. He served in the U.S. Army and on leaving the service became a mailman. He soon left that job, when he found he could earn more money playing in local Folk clubs at the weekends. His big break came when Paul Anka and Kristofferson saw Kris' opening act, Steve Goodman, play in concert. Goodman, who was Prine's best friend, told them that if they felt *he* was good, they should check out Prine. Later that night, John played a set for Kristofferson, Anka and Goodman.

A few weeks later, Anka sent Prine and Goodman airline tickets and told them to come to New York. John was somewhat reluctant, but he went. From the airport, they went straight to a Kristofferson show at The Bitter End. Kris got both Prine and Goodman on stage to perform. In the audience was Jerry Wexler from Atlantic Records, who told John to be in his office the next morning. By midday, John had been offered a $25,000 record contract.

His first self-titled album came out in 1971, and spawned the classic songs *Hello in There, Sam Stone, Angel from Montgomery, Donald and Lydia* and the wonderful *Spanish Pipedream* (with the line "I knew that topless waitress had something up her sleeve"). After its release, John was hailed as "the new Dylan." He stayed with Atlantic until 1975, releasing ***Diamonds in the Rough*** (1972), ***Sweet Revenge*** (1973) and ***Common Sense*** (1975). In 1972, John was nominated for a Grammy for "Best New Artist" and subsequently was nominated three more times. In 1976, Atlantic issued a compilation of John's work, under the title of ***Prime Prine***.

After his five-year stay at Atlantic, John moved over to Asylum Records and in 1978, released his ***Bruised Orange*** album (produced by Steve Goodman). He followed up with two more albums while with the label, ***Pink Cadillac*** (1979) and ***Storm Windows*** (1980). In 1980, John left Asylum and set up his own label, Oh Boy, along with his longtime manager, Al Bunetta. The first album release for the label was ***Aimless Love*** in 1984. This became Bob Dylan's favorite record during the 1986 tour with Tom Petty in Australia. In 1986, John released another album which was to be his last studio record for nearly 6 years, ***German Afternoons*** (Grammy-nominated). He followed it up two years later with the splendid ***John Prine Live*** (also Grammy-nominated).

At this point in time, Prine contemplated leaving the business and going back to school. He was going through a divorce and he felt that he "didn't want to write more songs just so there would be more songs on the planet." He was approached by a major label to sell Oh Boy to the major and record for it. The papers were signed and then John went to a Grammy party and met the label executives. One slapped him on the back and said "Welcome aboard." It was then that he "realized the last place on earth" he "wanted to be was on a boat with this guy."

John and Bunetta realized that they were at a crossroads and that the next album had to be something special. With that in mind, they called in Howie Epstein, the bass player with Tom Petty and the Heartbreakers, who had just produced Carlene Carter's album ***I Fell in Love***. Howie put together a set of musicians that included fellow Heartbreakers Mike Campbell and Benmont Tench, as well as Dave Lindley and Albert Lee. In addition, on harmony vocals he got some well-known Prine fans, Bonnie Raitt, Tom Petty, Phil Everly and Bruce Springsteen. The result was the 1991 album ***The Missing Years***. That year, John received a Grammy Award for the album as "Best Contemporary Folk Album." In addition, whereas John's albums at best sold 60,000 copies, this album sold nearly a quarter of a million. In addition, John opened for Bonnie Raitt on her 1991 tour. He was backed by his band, the Sins of Mephisto (multi-instrumentalists Phil Parlapiano and Bill Bonk and bassist Rolley Salley). He even found time to get involved in a new career, when he acted in the John Mellencamp movie *Falling from Grace*. He also made his first video, *Picture Show*, in which Tom Petty also appeared, and duetted with Margo Timmons on *If You Were the Woman and I Were the Man* on the Cowboy Junkies' album ***Black Eyed Man***. He traveled to Ireland to host the splendid Country/Folk music series *Town and Country*, which was the follow-up to the equally splendid *Sessions*, made by the same Irish team, the previous year, in which John also appeared.

John has to date not made the singles charts, but that hasn't stopped his songs being recorded by others, including *Spanish Pipedream* (John Denver), *Hello in There* (Bette Midler), *Angel from Montgomery* (Bonnie Raitt) and *Unwed Fathers* (Gail Davies, Tammy Wynette and Johnny Cash).

John continues to plow his own furrow, even if it is at a slightly more visible level. He has proven that you do not have to be on a major label to sell records and most certainly, if you avoid the majors, you can end up with your artistic integrity intact.

RECOMMENDED ALBUMS:

"John Prine" (Atlantic)(1971)
"Diamonds in the Rough" (Atlantic)(1972)
"Sweet Revenge" (Atlantic)(1973)
"Common Sense" (Atlantic)(1975)
"Prime Prine" (Atlantic)(1976)
"Bruised Orange" (Asylum)(1978) [Now on Oh Boy]
"Pink Cadillac" (Asylum)(1979) [Now on Oh Boy]
"Storm Windows" (Asylum)(1980) [Now on Oh Boy]
"Aimless Love" (Oh Boy)(1984)
"German Afternoons" (Oh Boy)(1986)
"John Prine Live" (Oh Boy)(1988)
"The Missing Years" (Oh Boy)(1991)

RONNIE PROPHET

(Singer, Songwriter, Guitar, Impressionist Entertainer, Showman, Raconteur)

Given Name:	**Ronald Lawrence Victor Prophet**
Date of Birth:	**December 26, 1938**
Where Born:	**Calmut, Quebec, Canada**
Married:	**1. Jeanne (div.) 2. Glory-Anne Carriere**
Children:	**Ron Anthony (Tony), James Charles**

One of the few all-round entertainers in Country music, Ronnie Prophet not only sings when he performs, he moves from songs to stories, does comic impersonations and has special sound pedals to enhance his guitar. His rendition of *Phantom of the Opry* is still a stand-out blend of musicianship and technology. He has become a sought-after host and emcee all over the U.S., Canada and Europe.

Ronnie, the youngest of three children, comes from a farming family. His father died in 1945, and Ronnie, then age 7, helped on the farm. At school, Ronnie was the school clown and that is where his comedy started. From when he was 17, Ronnie played at square dances around his home and then around Montreal and areas out as far as Toronto.

He then went to work in upstate New York, at Rhone Brook Dude Ranch. He worked there in the summers of 1962 through 1964 and in the summer and winter of 1966. Ronnie was booked by Dick Hoekstra of an agency called Florida Tractions and found that he made more money than all the summer work. In 1966, he took out U.S. Immigration papers and moved to Florida. He then gave up his rented house there, and went to the Bahamas for the winters, performing at the Jack Tar Hotel. He contracted to build a house in Fort Lauderdale, Florida, and employed a gardener and pool man for his Roman Pool, but he never lived there. After working in Nashville, he sold the house, and never went back.

Canadian-born Country star ***Ronnie Prophet***

In Nashville, he played at what was Boots Randolph's Carousel Club and did so well that the owners changed the name to Ronnie Prophet's Carousel Club. At this time, Ronnie was also spending three months of the year with Danny Thomas and Perry Como in Las Vegas. Ronnie made his TV debut on the *Tommy Hunter Show* in the early 70's, on CBC-TV. When this show was replaced, CBC-TV started the *Ronnie Prophet Show,* which began with six one-hour shows. During 1973 and 1974, Ronnie made eleven episodes and this show ran until 1981.

He then moved to CTV Network and did *Grand Old Country,* which he hosted for six years. Then he did twenty-six shows of *Rocky Mountain Inn* on CTV. In England, he was the host and main performer on the show *Ronnie Prophet Entertains*, on BBC-TV.

Ronnie's recording career began when he was signed to RCA in 1975. He first entered the Country chart in 1975, with *Sanctuary*, which went Top 30. This was followed by *Shine On* (Top 40), *It's Enough* (Top 50) and the minor hits *Big Big World*, in 1976, and *It Ain't Easy Lovin' Me*, in 1977.

Ronnie's desire to meet his fans put him back on the road and he began doing fairs, festivals, conventions and clubs throughout the U.S., Canada and Europe. He has appeared at such venues as the World's Fair Expo in Vancouver in 1986 and the Wembley and Peterborough Country Music Festivals in England. In addition, Ronnie has done Armed Forces tours in England, Germany, Holland and the Arctic Circle. He met his second wife, Glory-Anne, when she was appearing on a tour with him. They were both invited to a get-together at the home of one of Ronnie's friends. They began to talk and have talked ever since and were married in April 1986.

Ronnie has appeared on TV shows such as *That's Country* in New Zealand, *Nashville Now*, *Mike Douglas Show*, the *Family Brown Show,* and *Hee Haw*. His charity work involves shows for the disabled and handicapped, including the Jerry Lewis Telethon; Variety Club 47, British Columbia, Canada; ACT Telethon, Edmonton, Alberta, and St. Jude's Hospital, Memphis, Tennessee.

Ronnie has won many awards including the Juno Award for "Country Male Vocalist of the Year" in both 1977 and 1978 and "Entertainer of the Year" and "Duo of the Year," with Glory-Anne, both from the CCMA in 1984. The CCMA presented Ronnie with the "C.F. Martin Award" in 1988. He also received an "Angel Award" from St. Jude's Children's Hospital. JAB

RECOMMENDED ALBUMS

"Ronnie Prophet" (RCA Victor)(1976)
"Ronnie Prophet" (Audiograph Alive)(1982)
"I'm Gonna Love Him Out of You" (Audiograph)(1983)
"Sure Thing" (Bookshop)(1987) [With Glory-Anne]

JEANNE PRUETT

(Singer, Songwriter, Guitar)

Given Name:	**Norma Jean Bowman**
Date of Birth:	**January 30, 1937**
Where Born:	**Pell City, Alabama**
Married:	**Jack Pruett**
Children:	**Jack, Jael**

Jeanne Pruett is almost as famous as a cook as she is a *Grand Ole Opry* star. In recent years, she has appeared on TV shows equally as much to promote her Jeanne Pruett's *Feedin' Friends Cookbook* as to enchant her audiences with her superb voice.

Jeanne was raised in Alabama with her nine brothers and sisters. Her father was a full-time farmer and Jeanne enjoyed the rural life. After Saturdays spent selling home-grown goods in town, the family, who were Country music fans, would settle down to listen to the *Grand Ole Opry*. Other nights would be taken up with pickin' and singin' on their front porch. While at school, Jeanne took every opportunity to sing and was soon determined to make music her career.

In 1956, she came to Nashville and married Jack Pruett, who was the guitar player for Marty Robbins. She started to raise a family and write songs. In the mid 60's, she worked as a songwriter for Marty Robbins Enterprises and stayed with the company for seven years. Among her songs that were recorded by Marty Robbins were: *Count Me Out, Waiting in Reno, Lily of the Valley* and *Christmas is for the Kids*. When her children began growing up, she started doing some session work, played some nightclubs and fairs and also made demo tapes of her own songs to pitch. An executive of Decca Records heard one and as a result, Jeanne signed with the label in 1970.

Jeanne's debut chart single in 1971 was *Hold On to My Unchanging Love*, which peaked in the Top 70. Her first release in 1972, *Love Me*, reached the Top 40, but major success came in 1973 (by which time Decca had become MCA). She hit the No.1 position with *Satin Sheets*, which also crossed over to the Pop chart Top 30. This was followed by the

Top 10 hit *I'm Your Woman.* During 1973, *The Grand Ole Opry* made her their 63rd member, and she became a featured guest on nationally syndicated TV shows. She has also toured Europe several times. Jeanne stayed with MCA until 1977, during which time her most successful records were: *You Don't Need to Move a Mountain* (Top 15), *Welcome to the Sunshine (Sweet Baby Jane)* (Top 25) (both 1974), *Just Like Your Daddy* and *A Poor Man's Woman* (both Top 25, 1975) and *I'm Living A Lie* (Top 30, 1977).

Jeanne moved over to Mercury in 1978 without major success. Signing with the IBC label, in 1979, proved to be beneficial. Her debut chart single, *Please Sing Satin Sheets for Me*, returned her to the Top 60 and then, in 1980, she had three Top 10 hits with *Back to Back*, *Temporarily Yours* and *It's Too Late*. She moved on again, this time to Paid, but all she could manage were two low placed chart entries in 1981.

In 1983, Jeanne had a Top 60 record with a duet with Marty Robbins, entitled *Love Me*, on the Audiograph label. Marty had recently died, and the song had been a hit for him in 1973, and for Jeanne a year earlier. She had one more basement success for Audiograph and then moved on to MSR, where she was again unable to recapture her earlier success.

Jeanne was named "Female Vocalist of the Year" in England, and in 1973 she received nominations from the CMA for "Female Artist of the Year," "Song of the Year" (for *Satin Sheets*) and "Album of the Year." *Billboard* magazine also awarded her with "Female Singer," and "Best Album of the Year," in 1974.

Singer, Songwriter and Cook ***Jeanne Pruett***

Fan Fair in Nashville became synonymous with Jeanne's fish fry. She is a great worker on behalf of charities and has been honored by them many times. As Jeanne says, she just tries to put something back into the business for all the great things it's given to her. JAB

RECOMMENDED ALBUMS:

"Satin Sheets" (MCA)(1973)
"Encore" (IBC)(1979)
"Star Studded Nights" (Audiograph)(1982)
"Jeanne Pruett" (MCA/Dot)(1985)

HOLLAND PUCKETT (a.k.a. SI PUCKETT)

(Singer, Guitar, Harmonica, Banjo)

Given Name: Holland Puckett
Date of Birth: July 15, 1899
Where Born: The Hollow, Patrick County, Virginia
Date of Death: July 28, 1934

Holland "Si" Puckett recorded many Old-Time numbers for Gennett in 1927-1928. A Virginian by birth, Puckett spent much of his adult life in the vicinity of Mount Airy, North Carolina, where he worked as a bookkeeper at a tobacco warehouse. He often picked and sang with the numerous musicians in Patrick and Surry counties. Along with the Texas music pioneer Prince Albert Hunt, Puckett was one of the first recording artists to become a homicide victim.

As various Old-Time musicians from southwestern Virginia and North Carolina such as Al Hopkins, Charlie Poole, and Ernest Stoneman began to journey to recording studios, others became inspired to emulate them. Among them were Puckett and the string band known as DaCosta Woltz's Southern Broadcasters, who journeyed together to Richmond, Indiana, for their first session. He cut seven numbers including what became his most popular song, *The Dying Cowboy*.

A month later, he returned to Indiana to cut seven more songs for Gennett. Some of his recordings came out under the name "Si Puckett" and others used the pseudonym "Harvey Watson." Holland returned for his third and last recording session in May, 1928. Like many other pioneers, his recording career ended with the Great Depression.

Five years later, Puckett died from a knife wound, apparently inflicted in a fight over a card game. Although a fine Old-Time vocalist who recorded more than enough material to fill an album, somewhat surprisingly none of it has been re-issued. IMT

RILEY PUCKETT

(Singer, Guitar, 5-String Banjo, Dobro, Fiddle, Piano, Mandolin)

Given Name: George Riley Puckett
Date of Birth: May 7, 1894
Where Born: Alpharetta, Georgia
Married: 1. (Div.) 2. Unknown
Children: one daughter
Date of Death: July 14, 1946

Riley Puckett remains one of the most important singer/musicians to emerge in the period just after WWI. His high, forceful tenor voice and his ability on guitar have stood the test of time and sound as fresh in the 90's as they did when first recorded.

Shortly after he was born, Riley Puckett had sore eyes and when they were treated with sugar and lead, the medication blinded him. By 1901, he attended a school for the blind in Macon, where he learned to read Braille and started to get musical training. In 1912, Riley learned to play 5-string banjo at dances and on street corners. As the guitar became the instrument to use, Riley switched to that and soon gained a reputation at regional fiddling contests (which included other categories) for his singing and playing. However, life was a struggle for him as he tried to earn a living as a troubadour around Atlanta.

On September 28, 1922, Riley made his radio debut on WSB Atlanta playing in Clayton McMichen's Hometown Band. This station could be received throughout the U.S. and reached an enormous audience. Soon he was considered by the station to be a star and made many broadcasts, often as a soloist. The following year, Riley joined with Ted Hawkins (mandolin) and Lowe Stokes (fiddle) to form the Hometown Boys. It was with this band that Riley gained even further national recognition.

During the summer of 1923, the group broadcast regularly on Saturday nights over WSB. Audiences delighted in Puckett's voice, which was especially suited to ballads, and his delightful yodeling. Among his most popular numbers were *Thompson's Old Gray Mule*, *My Buddy* and *You've Got to See Mama*. Soon Riley's fans referred to him as "the Ball Mountain Caruso."

When Gid Tanner was approached by Columbia to record in 1924, he took Riley to New York with him, where they both recorded, supporting each other. Riley's first record release was *The Little Old Log Cabin in the Lake*, a cover of Fiddlin' John Carson's hit. The flip-side, *Rock All Our Babies to Sleep*, featured Riley's yodeling. Puckett also recorded versions of *Casey Jones*, *Steamboat Bill* and *Sleep Baby Sleep*.

The records did so well, being promoted in Columbia's Popular series, that in the late summer of 1924, Riley and Gid returned to New York and for the first time Riley recorded with his banjo. These sides included *Oh Susanah*, *When You and I Were Young Maggie* and *You'll Never Miss Your Mother Till She's Gone*.

When Columbia introduced their 15000-D Hillbilly Series, Riley became the second most recorded Southern artist after John Carson. With Frank Walker in charge of the series, the label, in 1925, started to record in Atlanta. Between 1925 and 1931, Riley recorded 14 sides for the label out of a total of 24 hillbilly recordings. Soon, only Vernon Dalhart was selling more records than Riley. When Riley married in 1925, Columbia paid for the honeymoon (his wife would later leave him and he remarried).

In 1926, Riley joined the "supergroup" the Skillet Lickers, which included Clayton McMichen and Gid Tanner. Between 1926 and 1931, Riley played on every Skillet Lickers recording, including the famed comedy skit *Corn Licker Still in Georgia*. Riley had to memorize his part in these skits by listening to Frank Walker read them.

Despite his reputation as a good guitarist, his playing caused problems for musicians who played with him, in much the same way that Willie Nelson did 40 years later. His complex bass ran through the timing of the fiddler, Lowe Stokes. So Stokes chose to ignore what Riley was playing so as to keep his own timing.

Riley joined up with high tenor Hugh Cross on the original 1927 record of *Red River Valley* (the first recording of the cowboy classic, which featured Clayton McMichen on fiddle) for Columbia. Puckett and Cross cut a further seven sides together in two sessions in April and October, 1928, including *Gonna Raise Ruckus Tonight*, which was later released on Regal as by the Alabama Barn Stormers, *My Wild Irish Rose* and *Call Me Back Pal o' Mine*.

From the mid-30's, Riley began playing Dobro, although he never recorded using it. As the Depression bit, Riley recorded fewer sides; however, since he was on a monthly salary, he was not adversely affected. Riley recorded several sides under different group names and one of the most popular records of the time, *My Carolina Home*, as by McMichen's Melody Men. When the Skillet Lickers broke up in 1931, Puckett played with Tanner and McMichen's Georgia Wildcats and then he began broadcasting over radio stations in Columbus and Cleveland, Ohio.

By 1932, the Skillet Lickers had been revived and by the end of the year, Riley was playing with both this band and Bert Layne's Mountaineers. Two years later, Victor's new Bluebird label asked Tanner to record again with the Skillet Lickers and Riley was present on the session. Later that year, with his duet partner, Red Jones, Riley cut six sides for Bluebird, including *I Only Want a Buddy Not a Sweetheart*, *Puckett Blues* and *St. Louis Blues*. Riley recorded more sides during 1935 and 1936 for Bluebird, and then in 1936, he began touring with "Daddy" John Love. Love had been a member of Mainer's Mountaineers. Then Riley played for a while with Bert Layne's Fiddling Mountaineers and also broadcast on WSAZ Huntington, West Virginia, as well as in Memphis and Cincinnati.

Riley then organized his own tent show which traveled through the South and especially the Texan and Oklahoman oil-fields. Having been dropped by Bluebird in 1936, Riley went to New York to record for Decca with Red Jones and recorded *Alttoona Train Wreck*, *Take Me Back to My Carolina Home*, *Gulf Coast Blues*, *The Longest Train* and *The Broken Engagement*. By 1940, he was back in Atlanta playing over WSB. When Columbia executive Frank Walker moved to Bluebird, he went to Atlanta and recorded some sides on Riley, which were of a more Pop variety and included *Oh, Johnny, Oh*, *South of the Border* and *Little Sir Echo*.

In 1941, Riley's last Bluebird session produced *The New Giving Everything Away*, *How Come You Do Me Like You Do*, *Peach Picking Time in Georgia* and *Railroad Blues*. Riley continued playing on the radio during WWII. In 1946, he was playing over WACA Atlanta with the Stone Mountain Boys.

In July that year, Riley developed blood poisoning from a boil on his neck and on July 14 died from this. With proper medical attention, his death could have been avoided.

Riley Puckett could have been remembered in the same breath as Jimmie Rodgers, but unlike Rodgers, Riley did not have a Ralph Peer to look after his interests. Also, his blindness, in days when transport was difficult, was frustrating, but he was philosophical when he said, "Seeing is believing. Feeling is natural." Riley Puckett was a natural.

BM/CKW

RECOMMENDED ALBUMS:

"Early Country" (Old Homestead)
"Riley Puckett" (County)
"Riley Puckett—Old Time Greats, Vol.1" (GHP Germany)
"The Riley Puckett Story" (Roots Australia)

PURE PRAIRIE LEAGUE

When Formed:	**1970**
Members:	
Craig Fuller	**Guitar, Lead Vocals**
Jim Lanham	**Bass Guitar, Vocals**
Jim "Koffe" Caughlan	**Drums**
George Powell	**Guitar, Vocals**
John David Call	**Steel Guitar, Banjo, Dobro**
Billy Hinds	**Drums**
Larry Goshorn	**Lead Guitar**
Michael O'Connor	**Keyboards**
Mike Reilly	**Bass Guitar**
Tim Goshorn	**Guitar, Vocals**
Vince Gill	**Guitar, Vocals, Fiddle, Banjo**
Patrick Bolin	**Saxophones, Clarinet**
Gary Meilke	**Synthesizer**
Jeff Wilson	**Guitar, Vocals**

Pure Prairie League, formed in Columbus, Ohio, emerged as one of the most popular Country-Rock bands. They also marketed their albums well with each one identified by an illustration of a grizzled character named "Luke," a cowpoke who resembled a later famous glove puppet named "Shotgun Red" who became a star on TNN's Nashville Now. The sleeve illustrations were the work of *Saturday Evening Post*'s Norman Rockwell.

The group's original line-up was George Powell (b. George Edward Powell, Winston-Salem, North Carolina) and Craig Fuller (b. Craig Lee Fuller, Cincinnati, Ohio), Jim "Koffe" Caughlan (b. Cincinnati, Ohio) and Jim Lanham (b. Los Angeles, California). Formed in 1970, they took their name from a women's temperance union in one of Errol Flynn's movies. They played around the Cincinnati area for just over a year at Billy's club and then signed to RCA Victor.

For their debut eponymous album in 1972, the group added steel guitarist John David Call (b. Waverly, Ohio). The album revealed a selection of good material primarily written by Powell and Fuller. Billy Hinds (b. William Frank Hinds, Covington, Kentucky) had played drums during their prerecording days for some months but then left. He returned, replacing Caughlan, in time for their second album, ***Bustin' Out***. Call was replaced by Al Briscoe and James Rolleston played bass and Michael Connor (b. Covington, Kentucky) played piano on the session. Also featured on the album was David Bowie associate Mick Ronson on guitar.

Immediately after the release of the album O'Connor and Mike Reilly (b. Fort Thomas, Kentucky), both of whom had played with Hinds, joined the group for the subsequent tour. However, as neither of the albums was overly successful, RCA dropped the group. Then in 1975, a track from ***Bustin' Out*** entitled *Amie*, a Craig Fuller song, was picked up by some deejays and three years after the album's release, *Amie* reached the Pop Top 30.

RCA immediately re-signed the group and *Two Lane Highway*, the title track of their new album, scraped into the Pop Top 100. By this time, Fuller had left to be replaced by Larry Goshorn (b. Cincinnati, Ohio) and John Call rejoined. John Boylan replaced producer Bob Ringe and among the guests on the album were Chet Atkins, Emmylou Harris, Don Felder (of the Eagles) and master fiddler Johnny Gimble.

The group was now in great demand and toured continuously, taking time out to record the 1976 albums ***If the Shoe Fits*** and ***Dance***, both of which retained the same line-up as ***Two Lane Highway***, without the guests. From ***If the Shoe Fits*** came the group's version of *That'll Be the Day*, which scraped into the Country Top 100. In 1977, Pure Prairie League recorded the live set ***Live Takin' the Stage***. Following this album Call left and was replaced by Larry Goshorn's brother, Tim Goshorn (b. Cincinnati, Ohio), and this revised line-up played on the 1978 album ***Just Fly***.

Following this album Larry and Tim quit the band to form the Goshorn Brothers, with a younger brother. Founder member George Powell now left the group and came off the road, to concentrate on songwriting and to be with his family.

The group was now based in Los Angeles and after auditioning a lot of musicians, in September 1978, Pure Prairie League opted for Vince Gill, who brought his considerable talent to the group, including his songwriting skills. In 1979, Patrick Bolin (b. Los Angeles, California) joined the band in time for their final album for RCA, ***Can't Hold Back***, but left before their next album.

In 1980, Pure Prairie League moved to Casablanca Records, a label whose music was far removed from Country-Rock, having established itself with such artists as Disco diva Donna Summer. However, Casablanca's singles marketing skills came into play and that year, the group had three singles on the Pop chart: *Let Me Love You Tonight* (Top 10), *I'm Almost Ready* (Top 40) and *I Can't Stop the Feelin'* (Top 80). The singles came from the album ***Firin' Up***, which introduced synthesizer player Gary Meilke, and guitarist Jeff Wilson (b. Los Angeles, California), and featured two ladies who would soon be making the Country charts, Janis Gill and Kristine Arnold, who became Sweethearts of the Rodeo.

The same line-up was featured on their second and final album for Casablanca, ***Something in the Night***. This time, two singles made the Pop charts: *Still Right Here in My Heart* (Top 30) and *You're Mine Tonight* (Top 70). However, the group was now starting to run out of steam and in 1983, Vince Gill left the group and two years later was on his way to stardom.

Pure Prairie League's records still sound good today, which is primarily due to the quality of production and the high level of songs.

RECOMMENDED ALBUMS:

"Pure Prairie League" (RCA Victor)(1972)
"Bustin' Out" (RCA Victor)(1972)
"Two Lane Highway" (RCA Victor)(1975)
"If the Shoe Fits" (RCA Victor)(1976)
"Dance" (RCA Victor)(1976)
"Live Takin' the Stage" (RCA Victor)(1977)
"Just Fly" (RCA Victor)(1978)
"Can't Hold Back" (RCA Victor)(1979)
"Firin' Up" (Casablanca)(1980)
"Something in the Night" (Casablanca)(1981)

CURLY PUTMAN

(Songwriter, Singer, Guitar, Steel Guitar)

Given Name:	**Claude Putman, Jr.**
Date of Birth:	**November 20, 1930**
Where Born:	**Princeton, Alabama**
Married:	**Bernice**
Children:	**Gregory, Troy**

Curly Putman ranks as one of the finest songwriters of Country and Pop-Country to have emerged since the 60's. His songs have been covered by the top names in Country music as well as the superstars of adult Pop.

He was raised in northeast Alabama, the son of a sawmill worker, and the mountain he lived on was named for his family. Curly briefly attended Southern Union College in Wadley, Alabama, and then spent four years in the U.S. Navy. After leaving the service, he worked in a sawmill, attended trade school and sold shoes. He aso played steel guitar in several bands, and was actively writing and singing. He had his first Country chart entry in 1960, on Cherokee, when *The Prison Song* reached the Top 30.

In late 1963, he left his shoe sales job to join Tree Publishing as a staff writer. For the first two years that he lived in Nashville, he worked for a clothing company. In 1965, he had his first major Country hit with a song that would become one of his biggest, *Green, Green Grass of Home*. The first hit version by Porter Wagoner reached the Top 5. The following year, Curly had hits with *As Long as the Wind Blows* (Johnny Darrell) and *The Last Laugh* (Jim Ed Brown).

1967 was a prime year for Curly and he had a multitude of hit recordings. Among those were the four chart recordings of *My Elusive Dreams* (which Curly wrote with Billy Sherrill) by David Houston & Tammy Wynette (No.1), Rusty Draper (Top 70), Johnny Darrell (Top 75) and Curly's own version on ABC Records, which reached the Top 50. Curly followed up his version with the Top 70 single *Set Me Free*.

His other major hit in 1967 (1966/UK), was Tom Jones' version of *Green Green Grass of Home*. The single reached the Top 15 on the Pop charts, but went to No.1 on the UK Pop charts, where it remained for 7 weeks. It became the first single in Britain that sold over a million copies. Curly's other hits of the year included *Dumb Blonde* (Dolly Parton), *The Private* (Del Reeves), *You Can't Have Your Kate & Edith Too* (Statler Brothers) and *That See Me Later Look* (Bobby Wright). The following year, Tammy Wynette gave Curly another big record with *D.I.V.O.R.C.E.*, which Putman had written with Bobby Braddock. The record would be released again in the UK in 1975, and would become a No.12 Pop hit; however, a parody version by Scottish actor/comedian Billy Connelly went to No.1. In 1968, Curly also had a major hit with *Just for You*, which Ferlin Husky took to the Top 5. That same year, Charlie Rich had a Top 50 success with *Set Me Free*, which the following year Ray Price took to the Top 60 and which would later be recorded by Merle Haggard. Also in 1969, Bonnie Guitar had a Top 40 hit with *That See Me Later Look*.

Curly's next big single occurred in 1973, when Tanya Tucker went to No.1 with *Blood Red and Goin' Down*. *My Elusive Dreams* became a Top 30 hit for Bobby Vinton in 1970, but Charlie Rich's version in 1975 went far better, by reaching the Top 3. As the 70's continued, so Curly's successes continued. He was inducted into the Nashville Songwriters' Hall of Fame in 1976. In 1978, Joe Sun went Top 20 with *High and Dry* and the Kendalls reached the Top 3 with *It Don't Feel Like Sinnin' to Me*. The following year, Moe Bandy reached the Top 3 with a classic Putman-Sonny Throckmorton song, *It's a Cheating Situation*. This was made the ACM's 1979 "Song of the Year."

As 1980 got under way, Curly and Bobby Braddock had another No.1 hit via George Jones' rendition of *He Stopped Loving Her Today*. This had the effect of propelling Jones back to the very top again. He was named CMA's 1980 (and 1981) "Male Vocalist of the Year," and the song was made "Song of the Year" by the CMA in 1980 and 1981 and "Single of the Year" in 1980. In addition, the ACM named it 1980 "Single of the Year" and "Song of the Year." During the rest of the 80's, Curly's songs were less in demand, but he came back strongly in 1992 with *Cafe on the Corner*, a Top 5 hit for Sawyer Brown, as well as *I Was Born with a Broken Heart* (Aaron Tippin), *She Likes to Dance* (Michael White) and *A Street Man Named Desire* (Pirates of the Mississippi).

R

EDDIE RABBITT

(Singer, Songwriter, Guitar)

Given Name: Edward Thomas Rabbitt
Date of Birth: November 27, 1941
Where Born: Brooklyn, New York
Married: Janine
Children: Demelza, Tommy

Eddie is 100% Irish and his father, Thomas, emigrated from County Galway to the U.S. in 1924, while his mother, Mae, came from County Mayo. The name "Rabbitt" is Gaelic for "counselor to chiefs." Although born in Brooklyn, Eddie was raised in Orange County, New Jersey. He was exposed to music from an early age listening to his father playing Irish jigs and reels on the fiddle and accordion. Eddie started to play guitar at age 12 (being taught by his scoutmaster, Tony Schwickrath, who performed as "Texas Bob Randall") and began entering talent contests. That year, Eddie wrote his first song, *Susie*. (His early life was told in his 1990 autobiographical song, *Jersey Boy*.)

Jersey Boy **Eddie Rabbitt**

Eddie's parents divorced while he was at high school, with the result that his grades dropped and he dropped out (he later got his high school diploma at night school) and hit the road. He had various jobs including driving a truck, working as an attendant in a mental hospital, working in an electronics plant and scooping ice cream at a Howard Johnson's. In 1964, he got a job singing in the Six Steps Down club in East Orange, New Jersey. That same year, Eddie made his recording debut on 20th Century Records with *Next to the Note/Six Nights & Seven Days*.

During the next four years, Eddie played with various bands around the New Jersey-New York area and then in 1968, he arrived in Nashville aboard a Greyhound bus with $1,000 as his seed money. The first night in town, while soaking in the tub at the James Robertson Hotel, depressed with his surroundings, he wrote *Working My Way up to the Bottom*. The song was soon recorded by Roy Drusky but then Eddie realized that such luck didn't happen every day. He concentrated on songwriting, spending up to 18 hours a day writing. After pounding the streets, he became a staff writer with Hill & Range Publishing Company, earning $37.50 a week. Here he met Billy Swan, Chris Gantry and Kris Kristofferson.

Eddie's big break came in 1970, when Elvis Presley recorded his song *Kentucky Rain*. This single earned Elvis his 50th Gold Single and he went on to record two other Rabbitt songs, *Inherit the Wind* and *Patch it Up*. In the spring of 1974, Ronnie Milsap had his first No.1 with Eddie's *Pure Love*. Later that year, Eddie signed with Elektra Records and entered the Country chart with the Top 40 *You Get to Me*. In 1975, he twice hit the Country chart with singles that just failed to make the Top 10: *Forgive and Forget* and *I Should Have Married You*.

At the beginning of 1976, Eddie got his first No.1 with *Drinkin' My Baby (off My Mind)* and followed with the Top 5 *Rocky Mountain Music*, which also crossed-over to the Pop Top 80. He ended the year with the Top 3 Country hit, *Two Dollars in the Jukebox*. He started 1977 with the Top 3 release *I Can't Help Myself*, which also went into the Pop Top 80. He followed this with *We Can't Go on Living Like This*, which went Top 10. That year, Eddie was named "Best New Artist of the Year" by *Country Music* magazine.

1978 was a memorable year for Eddie. He started out with the Top 3 single *Hearts on Fire* and then had three back-to-back No.1 hits: *You Don't Love Me Anymore* (also Pop Top 60), *I Just Want to Love You* and *Every Which Way but Loose*. The latter was the title song for the Clint Eastwood movie of the same name, in which Eddie had a cameo appearance. The single stayed at No.1 for 3 weeks and crossed-over to the Pop Top 30. The single also was a No.41 single in Britain. That year, Eddie was named ACM's "New Male Vocalist of the Year."

Eddie opened his 1979 account with another No.1, *Suspicions*, which crossed to the Pop Top 15 and earned for him the 1980 BMI Robert J. Burton Award as the "Most Performed Song of the Year." Eddie's other 1979 single was the Top 5 *Pour Me a Tequila*. That year, he was named "Songwriter of the Year" in the *Music City News* Cover Awards. His 1979 album ***The Best of Eddie Rabbitt*** was Certified Gold in 1980. During 1979, Dr. Hook recorded Eddie's *What Do You Want?* They also cut *Do You Right Tonight* and *In Over My Head*. Stella Parton also recorded Eddie's *Room at the Top of the Stairs*. Other Rabbitt songs recorded by other artists were *Who Put My Xs in Texas* by Jim Ed Brown & Helen Cornelius, *The Bed* by Tom Jones, and in the 80's, the Chipmunks recorded *I Love a Rainy Night*.

Eddie then had an unbroken run of five straight No.1 hits, three of which were: in1980: *Gone Too Far*, *Drivin' My Life Away* (which was from the Meat Loaf movie, *Roadie*, and which became a Top 5 Pop hit and was Certified Gold in 1981) and *I Love a Rainy Night*. The latter went to No.1 Country and Pop and earned Eddie another Gold Record in 1981. That year, *Performance* magazine's Readers' Poll named him "Best Country Music Act." Eddie's 1980 album ***Horizon*** was Certified Gold the same year and went Platinum in 1981.

In 1981, Eddie's No.1 hits were *Step by Step* (Top 5 Pop), which was the title track of his 1981 album (which went Gold the same year) and *Someone Could Lose a Heart Tonight* (Top 20 Pop). That year Eddie was named *Cash Box*'s "Top Country Crossover, Male (Pop Albums)" and "Top Country Crossover, Male (Pop Singles)." He also received two Grammy nominations for "Best Country Song" and "Best Country Vocal

Performance, Male" for *Drivin' My Life Away*. *Record World,* in what must have been one of the most confused awards selections, named Eddie "Most Promising Male Vocalist (Pop Singles)" (he'd already had 8 No.1 records!), "Top New Male Vocalist," "Top Crossover Artist (Pop)" and "Top Male Country Crossover Artist (Pop)." Eddie also received a nomination for "Best Pop Male Vocalist" by the American Music Awards.

Eddie had his last year with Elektra in 1982 and scored with the Top 3 Country hit, *I Don't Know Where to Start*, which also went Top 40 on the Pop chart and *You and I*, a No.1 duet with Crystal Gayle, which also reached the Pop Top 10. That year *Record World* named Eddie "Top Crossover Male Artist (Pop Singles)" and "Top Male Country Crossover Artist (Pop Singles)." *Cash Box* named him "#1 Country Male Artist (Pop Singles)," "#1 Adult Contemporary Male Artist (Pop Singles)" and "#1 Country Male Artist (Pop Albums)." Eddie was also nominated for a Grammy Award as "Best Country Performance, Male" for the single *Step by Step* and was named WHN "Male Artist of the Year."

Eddie moved to Warner Brothers at the end of 1982 and stayed with them for three years, during which time his hits were: 1983: *You Can't Run from Love* (No.1 Country/Top 60 Pop), *You Can't Put the Beat in My Heart* (Top 10 and Eddie's last Pop chart entry at Top 90) and *Nothing Like Falling in Love* (Top 10); 1984: *B B-B-Burnin' up with Love* (Top 3) and *The Best Year of My Life* (No.1); 1985: *Warning Sign* (Top 5) and *She's Comin' Back to Say Goodbye* (Top 10).

At the end of 1985, Eddie moved to RCA and long-time producer (and co-writer) David Malloy was replaced by Richard Landis. Eddie completed 1985 with the Top 10 *A World Without Love*. He stayed with RCA until 1989 and he continued to rack up a stream of major hits. In 1986, he had *Repetitive Regret* (Top 5), *Both to Each Other (Friends and Lovers)*, a No.1 duet with Juice Newton and *Gotta Have You* (Top 10). In 1987, Eddie did not release any singles, but worked on his album ***I Wanna Dance with You***, which was released in 1988. During that year, Eddie had back-to-back No.1 hits with the title track and a reprise of *The Wanderer*, the Ernie Maresca song that had been a monster hit for Dion in 1961. Eddie ended the year with the Top 10 *We Must be Doin' Somethin' Right*.

Although his opening single in 1989, *That's Why I Fell in Love with You*, only reached the Top 70, Eddie was already on his way to Jimmy Bowen's short-lived Universal label, where he charted at year end with *On Second Thought*, which went to No.1 in 1990. When Bowen went to Capitol Records, Eddie signed to the label and immediately gave his new label a Top 10 hit with *Runnin' with the Wind*. His other hits on Capitol were not singles, but deejay selected cuts from his ***Jersey Boy*** and ***Ten Rounds*** albums. These were *It's Lonely Out Tonite* (Top 40) and *American Boy* (Top 15)(both 1990) and *Tennessee Born and Bred* (Top 60) and *Hang up the Phone* (Top 50)(both 1991).

Since 1992, Eddie has been without a label; however, he and his band, Hare Trigger, are still popular at live dates. Eddie can feel gratified that in 1990, six of his songs were given BMI "Million-Air" awards in recognition for national popularity as measured by over 1 million performances. They were *I Love a Rainy Night, Step by Step, Suspicions, Someone Could Lose a Heart Tonight, Drivin' My Life Away* and *Kentucky Rain*. In 1993, Janine Rabbitt, Eddie's wife, released the exercise video *Belly Dancing for Fun and Fitness*.

RECOMMENDED ALBUMS:

"The Best of Eddie Rabbitt" (Elektra)(1979)
"Horizon" (Elektra)(1980)
"Step by Step" (Elektra)(1981)
"Radio Romance" (Elektra)(1982)
"Eddie Rabbitt's Greatest Hits" (Warner Brothers)(1983)
"Rabbitt Trax" (RCA Victor)(1986)
"I Wanna Dance with You" (RCA Victor)(1988)
"Greatest Hits of Eddie Rabbitt" (RCA)(1989)
"Jersey Boy" (Capitol)(1990)
"Ten Rounds" (Capitol)(1991)

MARVIN RAINWATER

(Singer, Songwriter, Guitar, Piano)
Given Name: Marvin Karlton Percy
Date of Birth: July 2, 1925
Where Born: Wichita, Kansas

When Marvin Rainwater hit the big-time, there was great emphasis made that he was a full-blooded Cherokee. He is in fact one quarter Cherokee. He took his mother's maiden name, "Rainwater," as his stage name.

Marvin played classical piano as a child and began writing songs at age 8. He majored in mathematics at Washington State University at Walla Falls and began a pre-veterinary course. WWII ended his studies and he found himself in the U.S. Navy as a pharmacist's mate. He entertained his fellow shipmates and the idea that he might become a performer crossed his mind.

On leaving the service after two years, he initially became a tree surgeon in the logging camps in Oregon. He then played in small clubs and fairs around the South and Southwest. In 1946, he cut some 50 songs in a local studio, some of which were heard by the legendary Red Foley, who invited Marvin onto the *Ozark Mountain Jubilee*. Marvin recorded sides for 4 Star and in 1955 he cut a single, *I Gotta Go Get My Baby/Daddy's Glad You Came Home*, for Coral, without much success.

That same year, Marvin appeared on Arthur Godfrey's *Talent Scout* TV Show singing *Gonna Find Me a Bluebird,* and was brought back for four straight weeks. As a result, he appeared on Godfrey's morning radio show. This led to a successful residency at the Shamrock Club in Washington, D.C. and to cast membership on the WWVA *Wheeling Jamboree* and Foley's *Jubilee USA*. In 1955, Marvin signed with MGM Records and his first single was *Sticks & Stones/Albino Stallion*. Marvin had some luck now with his song *I Gotta Go Get My Baby*, which Justin Tubb made a Top 10 hit. The song was also recorded by Teresa Brewer, in 1955, and was a minor Pop hit.

However, it was not until 1957 that Marvin hit the big time as an artist. *Gonna Find Me a Bluebird* reached the Top 3 on the Country chart and the Top 20 in the Pop chart. A year later, he became an international star when *Whole Lotta Woman* reached No.1 in the U.K. and stayed there for 3 weeks. The British audiences were mesmerized by this young man wearing full American Indian headdress. In the U.S., the record was not nearly as successful. It reached the Top 15 in the Country charts and only the Top 60 in the Pop listings. This was partly due to the fact that some U.S. radio stations found the song too suggestive and banned it. By June of that year, Marvin was back in the U.K. charts with *I Dig You Baby*, and that was his last British success. In September, Marvin had another success with *Nothin' Needs Nothin'*, which just failed to reach the Country Top 10. During

A whole lotta ***Marvin Rainwater***

the year, Marvin appeared at the London Palladium in support of his success. His song *I Miss You Already (and You're Not Even Gone)*, which he wrote with Faron Young, was recorded by Faron that year. The song would later be a hit, as well, for Jimmy C. Newman in 1960 and Billy Joe Royal in 1986.

In 1959, Marvin had his final chart success with the Country Top 20 single *Half Breed.* Carl Smith recorded the Rainwater song *Be Good to Her*. In the 60's, he had calluses on his vocal cords, which led to an operation, and he was not able to record for 4 years. He also had problems with the IRS over royalties from his records. With his brother (and manager) Ray, Marvin set up the ill-fated Country magazine *Trail*, which almost bankrupted him. Rainwater returned to the U.K. in 1971 on tour and recorded an album with local group Country Fever. He was a regular visitor to Britain and appeared at the Wembley Festival in London in 1979.

Over the years, Marvin has recorded for Warner Brothers, United Artists and his own Brave label. In 1988, he released *I'm Gonna Go Where the Livin' and Lovin' is Good*, on his own Okie label.

RECOMMENDED ALBUMS:

"Songs by Marvin Rainwater" (MGM)(1957)
"Gonna Find Me a Bluebird" (MGM)(1962)
"Some Old, Some New, Especially for You" (Westwood UK)

BOOTS RANDOLPH

(Saxophone, Composer)

Given Name: Homer Louis Randolph III
Date of Birth: June 3, 1926

*Yakety sax man **Boots Randolph***

Where Born: Paducah, Kentucky
Married: Dee
Children: Randy, Linda

If Chet Atkins was the commanding general of the "Nashville Sound" emanating from RCA Victor in the 60's, then Boots Randolph and Floyd Cramer were his two principal lieutenants. Like Cramer, Boots enjoyed a career as both a session musician and a successful soloist. His *Yakety Sax* later became the theme for the TV shows of British comic genius Benny Hill.

He began playing ukulele when about age 10. His family moved to Cadiz, Kentucky, and then to Evansville, Indiana. He played trombone while in elementary school in Cadiz. While a member of Central High School Band in Evansville, he switched to sax because it was easier to play when marching. He and his brother Bob put together a six-piece group and played army bases.

At the end of WWII, in 1945, Boots was drafted into the services. After his discharge in 1948, he worked for the American Fork and Hoe Company, driving wedges into hammer heads, but he quit after four weeks. He played in various bands throughout the Midwest, and was spotted by Homer and Jethro, who saw him at a Decatur, Illinois, club, where he had worked since 1954. He stayed at the club for four years, during which time he wrote the tune that would become his signature song, *Yakety Sax*, with James "Spider" Rich. Homer and Jethro told Chet Atkins about him, who listened to a tape of Boots playing *Chicken Reel*. Atkins enthused about him to his friends, and a few days later, Owen Bradley hired Randolph for a Brenda Lee session. He soon became one of the most sought-after sessionmen in Nashville.

Boots released his first single under the name of Randy Randolph, but he failed to register any personal singles success while at RCA, and he left the label in 1961. He moved over to Monument, and it would be his 1963 recording of *Yakety Sax*, which he recorded three years earlier at RCA, that broke into the singles chart. It reached the Top 40 on the Pop chart. He had three further chart entries, *Hey, Mr. Sax Man* (1964), *The Shadow of Your Smile* (1966) and *Temptation* (1967), but none of them rose above the Top 80 mark.

He continued releasing a stream of albums on Monument through the 60's and 70's, which sold well. He went into the nightclub business when he opened the popular Boots Randolph Club in Printers Alley, Nashville. In 1983, he moved over to the small independent Palo Alto label, where he released *Yakety Madness* with Richie Cole. However, it was all pretty much formula stuff, and Boots' finest can either be heard on *Yakety Sax*, which set a style, on his session work, or his group work with Chet Atkins and Floyd Cramer.

RECOMMENDED ALBUMS:

"Yakety Sax" (Monument)(1963)
"The Five String Banjo" (Capitol)(1964) [Walter Hensley album featuring Boots]
"Boots & Stockings" (Monument)(1969) [Re-released in1976 and 1982]
"Chet, Floyd & Boots" (Camden)(1971) [With Chet Atkins and Floyd Cramer]
"Country Boots" (Monument)(1974) [With Mother Maybelle Carter, Chet Atkins and Uncle Josh Graves]
"Greatest Hits of Boots Randolph" (Monument)(1982)

WAYNE RANEY

(Harmonica, Singer)

Given Name: Wayne T. Raney
Date of Birth: August 17, 1921
Where Born: Wolf Bayou, Arkansas
Married: Loys J. Sutherland
Children: Zydall, Norma, Wanda
Date of Death: January 23, 1993

Wayne Raney gained a degree of immortality in Country music as a harmonica wizard. His hard Country voice also turned out some good vocal work in the late 40's and early 50's, particularly his biggest hit, *Why Don't You Haul Off and Love Me*.

Born in rural Arkansas to a farm family, Wayne had a crippled foot from early childhood which prevented him from doing heavy work so he began hanging around town, where he heard a street musician "choke" a harmonica and became determined to learn it. About 1932, Wayne also came under the influence of Lonnie Glosson, then working at KMOX radio in St. Louis.

Hitchhiking to various radio stations, Wayne and Lonnie eventually met and the two became lifelong friends. In 1938, they teamed up to form a twin harmonica act on Little Rock radio for a year. Periodically they would work together again. After some radio work on various Mexican border stations, Wayne came to station WCKY Cincinnati, where he remained for several years in various capacities, eventually gaining fame for his mail-order harmonica sales. He also taped shows for other stations and for the five years from 1945 is alleged to have average sales of a million harmonicas annually.

He also helped the Delmore Brothers on recording sessions in the King studios, which led to Raney's securing his own contract with Syd Nathan's company. Two of his hillbilly boogie numbers, *Lost John Boogie* and *Jack and Jill Boogie*, became Top 15 hits in 1948.

On May 6, 1949, with Lonnie Glosson playing a second French harp, Wayne Raney recorded his own *Why Don't You Haul Off and Love Me,* which spent three weeks at No.1 and five months on the chart. It even went to the Top 25 on the Pop listings, which could be considered something of a surprise considering that Wayne's unabashed Country style and Arkansas twang seemed unlikely to hit in the cross-over market. Raney remained with King until 1955, but never had another song that could match his big hit. There were some fine novelty and boogie numbers among them such as *Pardon My Whiskers*, *I Love My Little Yo Yo*, *Catfish Baby*, and *Undertakin' Daddy.* He also spent a year at the *Grand Ole Opry* and in 1953 toured for several months with Lefty Frizzell, but eventually returned to WCKY, where he did deejay work and his transcribed harmonica sales programs until 1960, when he returned permanently to Arkansas.

He had recorded a few sides for Decca in the late 50's, but they had limited success in spite of their high quality (*40th and Plum* is a Country humor classic). Although harmonica sales during the 50's had dropped, it remained a significant sideline until 1960, when Wayne could no longer buy them in the quantity and at a price low enough to turn a profit.

From Arkansas, Raney recorded initially for Starday, turning out a family Gospel album that contained *We Need a Whole Lot More of Jesus (and a Lot Less Rock and Roll)*, as well as a later Country effort, ***Don't Try to Be What You Ain't***. He operated a chicken farm near Concord and also started Rimrock Records, which included not only a studio but also a pressing plant. Rimrock not only recorded material themselves but also did custom pressings. Artists on Rimrock included Red Smiley, the Stanley Brothers, Carl Story, Lonnie Glosson, and of course the Raneys. As he grew older and his health declined, Raney sold his operations and moved to Drasco. He was living there when he and Glosson cut an album together. Not long afterward his health took another downturn with the resulting loss of his voice box. In 1990, he published an autobiographical booklet, *Life Has Not Been a Bed of Roses.*

IMT

Harmonica wizard ***Wayne Raney***

RECOMMENDED ALBUMS:

"Songs of the Hills" (King)(1958)
"Wayne Raney and the Raney Family" (Starday)(1960)
"Don't Try to Be What You Ain't" (Starday)(1964)
"Pardon My Whiskers" (Rimrock)(1970)
"Tear Down the Mountains" (Rimrock)(1970)
"Gathering in the Sky" (Rimrock)(1970)
Lonnie Glosson & Wayne Raney:
"The Living Legends" (Memory)

RATTLESNAKE ANNIE

(Singer, Songwriter, Guitar)

Given Name:	**Rosan Gallimore**
Date of Birth:	**December 26, 1941**
Where Born:	**Puryear, Tennessee**
Married:	**Max McGowan**
Children:	**two sons**

In many ways, Rattlesnake Annie is unique in that she straddles traditional and contemporary musical values. She has not been content to stay in the U.S., but has become a "missionary" of Country music throughout Europe and the world.

Born of Scots-Irish and Cherokee heritage, Annie was raised on her parents' cotton and tobacco farm. She was carried to the fields in a washtub while still an infant and heard the field calls as a young child, working the fields alongside the hands. Her father was a well-known Blues and Country singer and by the time she was 10 she was writing poems and playing guitar. She formed a group, the Gallimore Sisters, with her two cousins and by the time she was 12 they were performing for money at local churches, funerals and political rallies.

They appeared on their own radio show over station WTPR Paris, Tennessee, and around 1953 they won a stateside contest, the first prize being an appearance on the *Grand Ole Opry* at the Ryman Auditorium. The trio split up on leaving high school. When she was 16, she left home and traveled alone to Memphis and sat in with Ma Rainey, Lightning Hopkins and Furry Lewis. She then moved to Huntsville, Alabama, and for two years she was the featured entertainer at the Carriage House, an up-market nightclub catering mostly to well-paid space industry employees like Dr. Wernher von Braun and James Lovell.

Late in the 60's, Annie moved to Texas, where she married Max McGowan, who became her manager. They settled on a 200-acre ranch on the Brazos River near Fort Worth. In 1969, she met Willie Nelson in a bar in Grand Prairie and they became firm friends and exchanged songs. Her nickname, "Rattlesnake," came from a group of people called "cedar hackers," because she had learned to live in harmony with the rattlesnakes on her farm and wouldn't allow people to kill them, as the rattlesnake is the healing sign of the Cherokee. She performed several benefits for the cedar hackers when she found out that one of their children had multiple sclerosis. Their sobriquet for her was "the rattlesnake woman."

In 1974, Annie released a single, *Texas Lullabye*, on her own Rattlesnake label. The song was later covered by David Allen Coe, with whom she had written it. In 1975, she began an album project for RCA, but nothing came of it. She was named "Most Original Performer" at the 1977 Jimmie Rodgers Festival in Meridian, Mississippi. In 1980, she released her widely praised album ***Rattlesnakes & Rusty Water***, on Rattlesnake, which garnered a lot of interest in Europe and began her relationship with the Continent.

During 1982, she worked with Willie Nelson in the studio and toured with Floyd Tillman. She made her first visit to England that year and was planning to stay for four weeks but ended up staying in Europe for four and a half years. She returned to the U.S. to complete work on her second album, ***Country Livin'***, which was released in 1986, again on her own label. Both albums benefited from the co-production talents of songwriter/banjoist Buddy Blackmon (he wrote *1982* for Randy Travis). Returning to Europe, Annie became the first female Country artist to appear in person in East Germany, Poland and Czechoslovakia. She appeared on East German TV, toured Poland for two weeks and recorded an album, ***Rattlesnake Annie & the Last Cowboy, in Czechoslovakia***, with Czech Country star Michael Tucny. The album has sold over 600,000 copies, of which 100,000 were sold in the former USSR. In 1984, she appeared in Leipzig, then East Germany, in the Country musical *The Man from Colorado*.

She was at last recognized by the mainstream Country industry when Rick Blackburn, then at Columbia, signed her to the label. Her 1987 album, ***Rattlesnake Annie***, again produced by Annie and Buddy Blackmon, included four tracks from the ***Country Livin'*** album. Among the featured players were Willie Nelson, Lonnie Mack, Charlie McCoy, Johnny Gimble, Sam Bush,

Jerry Douglas, Buddy Spicher, Vassar Clements and David Schnaufer. One of the tracks, *Goodbye to a River*, was adopted by the West German chapter of Greenpeace as its unofficial anthem. Two of the tracks, *Callin' Your Bluff* (1987) and *Somewhere South of Macon* (1988), reached the Top 80 on the Country chart.

During 1990, Annie secured a distribution deal for her label from Montana Records in Switzerland and she undertook production work for them, including Swiss Country acts H.R. Krush and J.G. Duke and the Children of Grindewald. During that year, she played Wembley Festival in England and recorded a new album, ***Indian Dreams***, in Cologne, West Germany. She also spent some time in 1990 studying flamenco guitar in Provincia de Granada, Spain.

Annie was named "No.1 Female Artist" by the British Country magazine *Country Music People*. She recorded a single in Northern Ireland, where she was backed by Van Morrison's former group, Them. She was featured in the Swiss/French production of the *Other Side of Nashville*, a full-length video documentary. Patsy Montana recorded Annie's *Good Old Country Music* and duetted with Annie on her classic *I Wanna Be a Cowboy's Sweetheart*.

Although she had the experience of recording for a major label, her heart and mentality are more content with plowing her own furrow, successfully. However, in May, 1991, Sony Music Japan signed Annie, as the first American Country artist to be signed directly by Tokyo. Here she has produced a consistently high quality product, which Nashville could well learn from. These albums were ***Crossroads***, ***Rattlesnake Annie Sings Hank Williams*** (both 1992) and ***Painted Bird*** (1993).

RECOMMENDED ALBUMS:

"Rattlesnakes & Rusty Water" (Rattlesnake)(1980)
"Country Livin'" (Rattlesnake)(1986)
"Rattlesnake Annie & the Last Cowboy" (Supraphone)(1987) [With Michael Tucny]
"Rattlesnake Annie" (Columbia)(1987)
"Indian Dreams" (Sony)(1991)
"Crossroads" (Sony)(1992)
"Rattlesnake Annie Sings Hank Williams" (Sony)(1992)
"Painted Bird" (Sony)(1993)

LEON RAUSCH

(Singer, Songwriter, Guitar)

Given Name: Edgar Leon Rausch
Date of Birth: October 2, 1927
Where Born: Springfield, Missouri
Married: Vonda Lee
Children: William Lawrence, Michael Dean

When Bob Wills uttered his famed "Take it away, Leon" to Leon McAuliff, it could be excused if folks thought that Bob was referring to Leon Rausch. For three years, from 1958-1961, Rausch was a member of the Texas Playboys alongside McAuliff.

Leon was raised in Billings, Missouri, of a family steeped in Country music. He learned to play several instruments while still a youngster. By the time he was age 11, he played in a band with his father at local dances. After leaving school, Leon spent three years in the U.S. Navy during WWII. He was intent on a career in music, but on his way there he worked at various jobs, including truck driver, farm worker, typewriter mechanic and glass worker.

He also played in various bands in Springfield. In 1955, he moved to Tulsa, Oklahoma, and then in 1956, he worked on the *Louisiana Hayride*. That year, he cut his first recordings for the Central label. Two years later, he joined Bob Wills' Texas Playboys, as vocal replacement for Tommy Duncan's brother, Glynn. As the band's commitments in Las Vegas increased, a decision was made to move there. It was while Leon was with Wills that the three reunion albums with Tommy Duncan were made in 1960-1961.

After leaving Wills, Leon joined Johnnie Lee Wills' group and stayed with the junior Wills until 1964, appearing on two of Wills' albums. After leaving, he formed his own band, the New Texas Playboys. Based in Fort Worth, the new band appeared on *Cowtown Jamboree* until 1968, and from 1965, KTVT out of Fort Worth. Leon recorded for Ric in 1965, cutting the popular *Someday I'll Sober Up*. The following year, the band recorded for Kapp and then signed to Longhorn Records. For this label, they released several singles, including *Painted Angels*, *The Brand New World* (both 1967) and *The Winner Gets the Dime* (1968).

Bob Wills, then suffering ill health, approached Leon in 1973 to join the Texas Playboys as bass player and singer for a final album. However, Wills had a stroke before the project was finished, and the band completed what became ***For the Last Time***. After Wills' death in 1975, the Original Texas Playboys, with Rausch, enjoyed a renewed lease of life, with appearances on *Austin City Limits* (an album of the appearance was released on Delta) and with Asleep at the Wheel. That same year, Rausch signed with the Derrick label and in 1976 through 1979 he enjoyed six minor Country hits, of which the most successful was the Top 90 *Palimony*, in 1979.

In 1977, the Original Texas Playboys signed with Capitol Records and released three albums for this association from 1977 through 1979. When the Texas Playboys re-formed in 1983 as Playboys II, Leon was a member of the group with Herb Remington, Eldon Shamblin and Johnny Gimble. In 1989, Leon appeared with Boxcar Willie at the Wembley Festival in England, playing bass guitar and singing, to the audience's delight. Leon appeared on ***Asleep at the Wheel's Tribute to the Music of Bob Wills***, released in 1993. Leon continues to perform around the Fort Worth, Texas, area.

RECOMMENDED ALBUMS:

"From the Heart of Texas" (Kapp)(1966)
"She's the Trip That I've Been On" (Derrick)(1967)
"For the Last Time" (double)(United Artists)(1974)
"Bob Wills' Original Texas Playboys Live! from Austin City Limits" (double)(Delta)
"Bob Wills Day (Live From Turkey, Texas)(Delta)
"The Late Bob Wills' Original Texas Playboys" (Capitol)(1977)
"Live & Kickin'" (Capitol)(1978)

EDDY RAVEN

(Singer, Songwriter, Guitar)

Given Name: Edward Garvin Futch
Date of Birth: August 19, 1944
Where Born: Lafayette, Louisiana
Married: (Div.)
Children: Ryan, Coby

If one had to look for a performer that represented the melting pot that is truly the generic Country music, then there is no need to look further than Eddy Raven. His blend of Cajun, Rock, R & B and straight-ahead Country has not only created a unique performer, but also the writer of fine across-the-board songs.

Eddy was born the eldest of 10 children. His father, Levy Garvin Futch, a Country Blues singer and guitarist/trucker/baseball pitcher, traveled all over the South. Eddy got his first guitar when he was age 7 and by the time he was 13, he had his first band. As a youngster, he did everything from selling newspapers to running moonshine. He enrolled at the University of Southwestern Louisiana at Lafayette on a baseball scholarship (his early ambition was to play for the Boston Red Sox), but a broken ankle forced him to abandon any aspirations in that quarter.

For a while, his family lived in Georgia and Eddy had his own radio slot on WHAB. In 1962, he cut his first single, a self-penned song, *Once a Fool*, for the Cosmos label, based

***Eddy Raven** entertaining his fans*

in Brunswick, Georgia. He was somewhat surprised to note that the label had renamed him "Raven." However, the record fared well locally and the name stuck.

Eddy moved back to Lafayette and worked at La Louisianne record store. He got himself involved with the store's record label of the same name and played alongside Dale and Grace, John Fred and the Playboy Band, Professor Longhair, Dr. John, Bud Fletcher and Bobby Charles. Charles, who was an early mentor of Eddy's, had written such classics as *Walking to New Orleans* and *See You Later, Alligator* and under his tutelage, Eddy's songs were getting recorded. During the 60's, Eddy played with groups like the Swing Kings and the Boogie Kings along the Gulf Coast.

During the summer of 1969, La Louisianne released the Raven album ***The Cajun Country Sound***. As a result, Jimmy C. Newman invited Eddy to Nashville and in 1970, thanks to Newman's help, Eddy signed as a writer to Acuff-Rose. Eddy returned to Lafayette, where he wrote *Country Green* and *Touch the Morning* (recorded in 1971 and 1973 respectively by master songwriter Don Gibson and converted into Top 10 hits) and *Good Morning Country Rain* (recorded by Jeannie C. Riley). During 1970 and 1971, Eddy toured as lead singer with the Jimmie Davis Band and traveled extensively with Davis during his gubernatorial campaign.

At the insistence of Don Gant at Acuff-Rose, Eddy moved to Nashville in 1972. It became apparent that Eddy's brand of Country was not, as he puts it, "the bless-your-heart kind of Country." Wesley Rose approached Eddy in 1974, and asked him to write a song that might get Roy Acuff back in the charts again after nine years (he had actually appeared in the lists in 1971, but that was in a supporting role with the Nitty Gritty Dirt Band on *I Saw the Light*). Eddy did the trick with the song *Back in the Country*. Acuff turned down another Raven song, *Thank God for Kids*. However, in 1982, the Oak Ridge Boys had a Top 3 single with it and *Music City News* named it one of the top 10 Country songs of the year.

When Gant moved to ABC Records, Eddy signed with the label and during the period 1974-1976, Eddy charted eight singles on the ABC and ABC/Dot labels, the most successful of which were *Good News Bad News* and *Free to Be* (Top 40, 1976). That year, he released another album, ***This is Eddy Raven***, on ABC/Dot. He moved over to Monument in 1978, but only had one low level chart entry, *You're a Dancer*. The following year, he had a happier time when he signed to Dimension. It was here that he started to make a serious impression on the charts. His first single, *Sweet Mother Texas*, made the Top 50 and then in 1980, all three singles, *Dealin' with the Devil, You've Got Those Eyes* and *Another Texas Song*, reached the Top 30. Then with his final Dimension single, in 1981, *Peace of Mind*, he got to the Top 25.

Later that year, he signed with Elektra, then being run by Jimmy Bowen, and again he climbed another rung up the success ladder. *I Should've Called* (Top 15) provided him with his highest entry to date and was then surpassed by the follow-up, *Who Do You Know in California*. In 1982, Eddy started off with the Top 15 hit *A Little Bit Crazy* and then he had his first Top 10 success, *She's Playing Hard to Forget*. The final single of the year, and his last chart entry for Elektra, *San Antonio Nights*, only reached the Top 30.

When Eddy moved to RCA at the end of 1983, he was reunited with his old mentor, Don Gant, and at last Eddy came good. He struck with the No.1 hit *I Got Mexico*. He followed-up with two Top 10 singles, *I Could Use Another You* and *She's Gonna Win Your Heart*. From 1985 through 1986, Eddy continued to rack up further major singles with *Operator, Operator, I Wanna Hear It From You* and the Top 3 single *You Should Have Gone by Now* in 1985, and in 1986, he had two singles that both peaked in the Top 3, *Sometimes a Lady* and *Right Hand Man*.

With the arrival of 1987, Eddy cranked up a gear. His first single of the year, *You're Never Too Old for Young Love,* also reached the Top 3, but the follow-up, *Shine, Shine, Shine*, provided Eddy with his second No.1. His next two releases in 1988, *I'm Gonna Get You* and *Joe Knows How to Live*, both went to No.1. His last single of the year, *'Til You Cry*, made it to the Top 5. His 1987 album, ***Right Hand Man***, was the last album produced by Don Gant, who died shortly afterward.

In 1989, Eddy was reunited with Jimmy Bowen at Universal. Here he reeled off two more No.1 singles, *In a Letter to You* and *Bayou Boys*. With the demise of the label, Eddy moved with Bowen to Capitol. His final single of 1988 was *Sooner or Later*, which had originally been issued on Universal, but was re-released on Capitol, and provided him with a Top 10 single that, like *Bayou Boys*, stayed on the charts for 6 months.

With the arrival of 1990, Eddy's fortunes started to falter. His first release, *Island*, made the Top 10, but the follow-up, *Zydeco Lady,* only reached the Top 60, and matters did not improve in 1991, when both *Rock Me in the Rhythm of Your Love* and *Too Much Candy for a Dime* struggled in the Top 60 area. Although Eddy is now without a label, it seems only a matter of time before that is remedied.

RECOMMENDED ALBUMS:

"This is Cajun Country Sound" (La Louisianne)(1969)
"This is Eddy Raven" (ABC/Dot)(1975) [Re-released on MCA]
"Eyes" (Dimension) (1980)
"Desperate Dreams" (Elektra)(1981)
"I Could Use Another You" (RCA Victor)(1984)
"Right Hand Man" (RCA Victor)(1987)
"Temporary Insanity" (Universal)(1989)
"Greatest Country Hits" (Curb)(1990)
"Greatest Hits" (Warner Brothers)(1990)
"Right for the Flight" (Capitol)(1991)
"Best of Eddy Raven" (Liberty)(1992)

WADE RAY

(Singer, Fiddle, Guitar, Tenor Banjo, Actor)

Given Name:	**Lyman Wade Ray**
Date of Birth:	**April 6, 1916**
Where Born:	**Evansville, Indiana**
Married:	**Grace Young**

Wade Ray is another example of someone who performed almost as soon as he could go to school. He was raised in Boynton, Arkansas, and showed early indications of his interest in music. His parents fashioned a violin for him out of a cigar box when he was age 4. He soon progressed to the real thing and by the time he was 5, he made his stage debut as "the Youngest Violin Player in the World." He added the tenor banjo to his arsenal and his family found that crowds would come on a Sunday to hear young Wade play.

Soon Wade was on the Orpheum Vaudeville Circuit, which toured around the Indiana area. By the time he was 10, it was estimated that he had been given some 200 violins by his fans. He toured around until 1931, when he was 18, when he joined Pappy Cheshire's National Champion Hillbillies on KMOX St. Louis. He stayed with the show as singer/fiddler/musical director until 1943, when he was drafted into the U.S. Army. He only remained in the service until 1944, when he moved to Chicago and became a member of the Prairie Ramblers on the WLS *National Barn Dance*. While with the group, he appeared and recorded with Patsy Montana. He stayed on the *Barn Dance* until 1949. That year, he signed with Capitol, where he was backed by the Ozark Mountain Boys. He released three singles for the label during the year, but none of them did more than put his name around.

He moved to Los Angeles and appeared on the *Rex Allen Show* on CBS (KLAC-TV) that year and then appeared in the movie *Hollywood*. In the early 50's, Wade undertook a two-week engagement at the Cowtown. This booking turned into a 10-year stay. During the 50's and 60's, Wade appeared at major showrooms in Las Vegas, Reno and Lake Tahoe. He also appeared in the 60's on the *Grand Ole Opry* and the *Ernest Tubb Show* (NBC-TV) and was a regular cast member of the *Roy Rogers Show* on ABC-TV.

Wade signed with RCA Victor in 1951 and released 23 singles, none of which troubled the charts. He left the label in 1957. This draws an interesting comparison with the present recording artist situation. It would now be inconceivable for an artist to still be on a label after that many uncharted records. In 1966, Wade signed with ABC-Paramount and released the album ***A Ray of Country Sun***.

From 1964 to 1979, Wade was a member of the A-team of musicians in Nashville. In 1967, Wade recorded the album ***Down Yonder—the Country Fiddlers*** with, among others, Homer & Jethro, Sonny Osborne and Pig Robbins. The album was produced by Chet Atkins. In 1979, Wade moved to Illinois, where he played in KSD-AM St. Louis' roadshow. Wade, suffering from ill health, retired to Florida, Illinois.

The smiling face of the talented ***Wade Ray***

RECOMMENDED ALBUMS:

"A Ray of Country Sun" (ABC-Paramount)(1966)
"Walk Softly (& Other Country Songs)" (RCA Victor)(1966)
"Down Yonder—the Country Fiddlers" (RCA Victor)(1967) [As the Country Fiddlers]

COLLIN RAYE

(Singer, Songwriter, Guitar)

Given Name: **Floyd Collin Wray**
Date of Birth: **August 22, 1960**
Where Born: **DeQueen, Arkansas**
Married: **Connie Parker (div.)**
Children: **Jacob, Brittany**

Collin Raye, looking like he could be a boxing champion, got his first taste of performing as a child growing up in Texas and Arkansas. His mother, Lois, was a regional star who opened shows for Johnny Cash, Carl Perkins and Elvis Presley. She occasionally brought Collin and his brother Scott on stage to sing harmony. Collin grew up on the music of Bob Wills, Waylon Jennings and Buddy Holly. He was also a big fan of Johnny Horton and often memorized the words to his hit songs.

As a teenager Collin and his brother formed a Country-Rock band, the Wray Brothers Band. In 1980, they moved to Oregon and then on to Reno, Nevada, where they performed in casinos. Other members of the group included, at various times, Jim Covert, Lynn Phillips and Joe Dale Cleghorn. At the time Collin was known as Bubba Wray. In 1983, their recording of *Reason to Believe* became a low-level Country success on the CIS label. Two years later, they had another basement chart record with *Until We Meet Again* on Sasparilla. As the Wrays, they signed to Mercury in 1986 and had a low-level single, *I Don't Want to Know Your Name,* and then, in 1987, they had the Top 50 success, *You Lay a Lotta Love on Me*.

Scott was in and out of the group, but when it folded, Collin pursued a solo career as a regular in the Nevada nightclubs. He honed his performance skills and amassed a vast repertoire of nearly 4,000 songs.

Epic Records signed Collin in 1991 and his first album, ***All I Can Be***, was recorded in Los Angeles and Nashville. The first single was Harlan Howard's *All I Can Be (Is a Sweet Memory)*. Vince Gill added high harmonies and the song became a Top 30 hit. The album's second single, *Love Me*, quickly moved to No.1 for a three week stay at the top and established Collin as a powerful ballad singer (he is also a very good uptempo singer as well). The success of the song generated significant media coverage with a feature story in *People* magazine and an appearance on NBC's *Today Show*. *USA Today* named Collin's ***All I Can Be*** on their list of the Top Country albums of 1991.

His opening single of 1992, *Every Second,*

Singing from the heart, ***Collin Raye***

went Top 3, but the radio deejays ruined his average by picking *I Could've Been So Good*, which only made the Top 75. Collin then returned to the top of the charts for 2 weeks with the title track of his second album, ***In This Life***. *I Want You Bad (and That Ain't Good)* followed and became a Top 10 hit. The album was Certified Gold and, in 1993, produced two more Top 5 hits, *Somebody Else's Moon* and *That Was a River*.

In 1993, Raye released his third album, ***Extremes***. The first hit single from the album was *That's My Story,* co-written by LeRoy Parnell, which went Top 10. Collin Raye addressed the problem of alcohol with his 1994 hit Tom Douglas' *Little Rock.* He portrayed a man struggling to overcome addiction in the music video that included a phone number for people to call for help with overcoming alcoholism. ***Extremes*** also included a re-make of the 1975 Waylon Jennings hit *Dreaming My Dreams*. JIE

RECOMMENDED ALBUMS:

"All I Can Be" (Epic)(1991)
"In this Life" (Epic)(1992)
"Extremes" (Epic)(1993)

SUSAN RAYE

(Singer)

Date of Birth: **October 18, 1944**
Where Born: **Eugene, Oregon**

Married: 1. Jerry Wiggins
2. James
Children: Steven and five others

Susan Raye was discovered in a Portland, Oregon, nightclub by Buck Owens' manager, Jack McFadden. McFadden's enthusiasm persuaded Buck to fly Susan to Bakersfield, California, for an audition. Owens liked her voice and invited her to join him on a Northwest tour.

Growing up in the small Portland suburb of Forest Grove, Susan had little interest in singing or Country music. When she first gave music a try it was singing Rock music with some fellow high school students. Shortly after the Rock group disbanded, Susan auditioned for local radio station KWAY, which was looking for a singer to perform on a live Country music program. Susan got the job and also worked as a deejay at the station in the afternoon. Susan also became a favorite in local nightclubs and eventually was invited to join the cast of a Portland TV show called *Hoedown*.

In 1968, Buck Owens offered Susan a management contract that required her to move to Bakersfield. By 1969, she signed with Capitol Records and released her debut single, *Maybe If I Close My Eyes (It'll Go Away)*. Susan scored her first Top 30 hit with a reprise of the Jackie DeShannon Pop hit, *Put a Little Love in Your Heart*.

Susan Raye was introduced to millions of fans in the late 60's and 70's as a featured performer on the *Hee Haw* TV series, and she was a regular guest on the syndicated program for nine years. In 1969, Susan appeared in the movie *From Nashville with Music*.

In 1970, Susan released her first solo album, ***One Night Stand***. The title song became a Top 30 hit and the album also produced her first Top 10 solo hit, *Willy Jones*. Susan had started to record with Buck Owens, and in 1970, they charted with *We're Gonna Get Together* and *Togetherness* (both Top 15). The duo scored their biggest hit in the summer of that year, with the Top 10 hit *The Great White Horse*.

Susan's next solo single, the up-tempo *L.A. International Airport*, also went Top 10, in 1971, and became a signature song for her. It also crossed over to the Top 60 Pop chart. Her string of hits continued, in 1971, with the Top 5 *Pitty, Pitty, Patter* and the Top 3 *(I've Got a) Happy Heart*. In 1972, Susan hit the Top 10 with *My Heart Has a Mind of its Own* and then she teamed up with Buck for the Top 15 success *Looking Back to See*.

Other notable hits from the 70's were

Former Buck Owens singing partner ***Susan Raye***

Wheel of Fortune and *Love Sure Feels Good in My Heart* (both Top 20, 1972), *Cheating Game* (Top 20) and *Plastic Trains, Paper Plains* (both 1973), *Stop the World (and Let Me Off)* (Top 20) and *Whatcha Gonna Do With a Dog Like That* (Top 10)(both 1974) and the Top 20 duet with Buck, *Love is Strange* (1975).

By 1976, Susan had left Buck Owens and Capitol and moved to United Artists Records, but she failed to have any further major successes.

After scoring more than 20 hits and recording an equal number of albums, Susan Raye retired in 1978 to raise her six children. She also went back to college earning a degree in psychology, taught weekly Bible classes, and became an active PTA member. Susan Raye revived her career in the mid-80's, recording for the Westexas America label. In 1985, she released the album ***Susan Raye: There and Back***, which produced the single and video *Just Can't Take the Leaving Anymore*. JIE

RECOMMENDED ALBUMS:

"Willy Jones" (Capitol)(1971)
"Pitty, Pitty, Patter" (Capitol)(1971)
"(I've Got a) Happy Heart" (Capitol)(1972)
"My Heart Has a Mind of its Own" (Capitol)(1972)
"Wheel of Fortune"/"L.A. International Airport" (Capitol)(1972)
"Hymns by Susan Raye" (Capitol)(1973)
"The Best of Susan Raye" (Capitol)(1974)
"Whatcha Gonna Do with a Dog Like That" (Capitol)(1975)
"Honey, Toast and Sunshine" (Capitol)(1976)
"Susan Raye" (United Artists)(1977)
With Buck Owens:
"We're Gonna Get Together" (Capitol)(1970)
"The Great White Horse" (Capitol)(1970)
"The Best of Buck Owens and Susan Raye" (Capitol)(1972)
"The Good Ole Days (Are Here Again)" (Capitol) 1973)

RED RECTOR

(Singer, Mandolin, Guitar)
Given Name: William Eugene Rector
Date of Birth: December 15, 1929
Where Born: Marshall, North Carolina
Married: Ernestine Parker
Children: Ronald Lee, William E., Jr., James Larry, Anita Marie
Date of Death: May 31, 1990

Red Rector was one of Country and Bluegrass music's real wizards of the mandolin. Red started his musical career as a sideman in his mid-teens and was a seasoned veteran of radio, recording, and personals by the time he reached voting age.

Possessing a congenial personality and a good singing voice, Rector worked for many years in his adopted city of Knoxville as a mainstay talent on the early morning daily TV program, the *Cas Walker Farm and Home Show*.

Born in the Appalachian region of North Carolina, Red grew up in the mountain city of Asheville, where he listened to radio musicians like the Morris Brothers and Wade Mainer over local station WWNC. By the time he reached his teens, Red and a group of other young pickers had a program on the smaller local WISE station. In 1943, Wade Mainer took him to New York to appear in a BBC production, *The Chisholm Trail*. Red played around Asheville with various local acts on both WISE and WWNC and also at WJHL Johnson City, Tennessee. In 1946, he got a chance to go with a name act, Johnnie & Jack and the Tennessee Mountain Boys at WPTF Raleigh, North Carolina. After 10 months with this group, he joined Charlie Monroe's Kentucky Pardners at WNOX Knoxville. Red subsequently did two RCA Victor recording sessions with Monroe. When Charlie took his band south to open a new station, WBOK Birmingham, Red went along, but after a few months returned to Knoxville, where he joined Carl Story's Rambling Mountaineers. During this time, Red helped Carl on several record sessions with both Mercury and Columbia, singing solo leads on some songs like *Love and Wealth* and playing fast and flawless on his mandolin. Unlike most mandolin pickers, Red tended to favor a Gibson A-12 model over the more popular F5 and played it without using a cord around his neck to support the instrument. In 1953, he helped Don Reno and Red Smiley cut their second session for King Records. The Rambling Mountaineers remained in Knoxville for a time, but ultimately spent three popular years at WAYS in Charlotte.

In 1955 Red teamed up with another former Rambling Mountaineer, Fred Smith, to form the duet and comedy team Red and

Fred. They worked daily on the *Mid-Day Merry-Go-Round* on WNOX until the show ended early in 1958. At that point, Red joined Hylo Brown's Timberliners, one of the greatest albeit short-lived Bluegrass combinations of all time. They worked TV shows in a variety of locales and in August 1958 recorded 20 memorable songs for Capitol. After a year or so with Hylo, Red returned to Knoxville, where he went to work on daily TV shows for the Cas Walker supermarkets, a job that would last until 1983. Again he often worked in partnership with Fred Smith.

After the use of video-taped shows freed him to travel a bit, he worked on some Nashville recording sessions with artists as diverse as Grandpa Jones and Tommy Jackson. He also appeared on many Bluegrass festivals both as a solo act and with a variety of other individuals, including not only Fred Smith but also Bill Clifton and Don Stover. In 1975, Red spent a month in England and in the summer of 1982 appeared often at the Knoxville World's Fair. He recorded on his own for such labels as Old Homestead and Revonah and on Country with Fred Smith, and Norman Blake, each individually. On a foreign tour with Bill Clifton, in 1976, they made another album subsequently released in Germany and Japan, but not the U.S. Red also assisted other artists on a variety of recordings. His last album, a twin mandolin effort, was made with Jethro Burns who along with Red had pioneered the so-called Knoxville sound for Mandolin. After the Cas Walker program ended, Rector continued to be active in a variety of musical ventures until his sudden death from a heart attack at his Knoxville home. IMT

RECOMMENDED ALBUMS:

"Songs from the Heart" (Old Homestead)(1973)
"Appaloosa" (Old Homestead)(1975)
"Norman Blake and Red Rector" (County)(1976)
"Red Rector and Friends" (Revonah)(1978)
"Back Home in Madison County" (County)(1981)
"Old Friends" (Rebel)(1983) [With Jethro Burns]

RED FOX CHASERS, The (a.k.a. CRANFORD AND THOMPSON)

When Formed: 1927

Members:

A.P. Thompson	**Vocals, Guitar**
Bob Cranford	**Vocals, Harmonica**
Paul Miles	**Vocals, Banjo**
Guy Brooks	**Fiddle**

One of the more popular mountain string bands of the 1920's, the Red Fox Chasers were formed at the 1927 Union Grove Fiddling Convention in western North Carolina. A.P. "Fonzie" Thompson and Bob Cranford had already been singing partners since they were children growing up in Surry County. Both had learned rudiments of harmony by attending church singing schools in the area, where they learned to sing from seven-shape note songbooks, and to join in local Gospel quartets. In their spare time, they also adapted old traditional songs like *Katy Cline* to their duet style. Paul Miles and Guy Brooks also grew up together, playing for square dances in nearby Alleghany County, North Carolina; Miles learned to play banjo when he was age 5 on a homemade instrument crafted from a meal sifter and a groundhog hide.

When the band formed in Union Grove, the real leader was Paul Miles. It was he who named the group and it was he who arranged for their first recordings, for the Gennett Company, in April 1928. The success of records like *Did You Ever See a Devil, Uncle Joe?* got them called back to the studios several times in the next few years, and they eventually amassed a total of 48 sides. These included several hits that were to remain influential for years: *Stolen Love*, *Goodbye Little Bonnie*, *Little Darling Pal of Mine*, *Honeysuckle Time*, *Sweet Fern* and *Pretty Polly*. One of their original songs, *Wreck on the Mountain Road*, based on a true incident, was one of the first "wreck on the highway" type songs in Country music.

Cranford and Thompson also recorded a number of mountain Gospel favorites for the same company. Since Gennett routinely leased many of its sides to specialty labels like those run by Sears Roebuck and Montgomery Ward, some of the Red Fox Chasers' biggest sellers came out under other names, such as the Virginia Possum Tamers and the Black Mountain Gang.

After the band broke up in the 1930's, all the members stayed active in music. Paul Miles recorded for the Library of Congress in the late 1930's, and A.P. Thompson continued to teach singing schools and to sing with local quartets. In 1967 County records issued an LP retrospective of the band's best work. CKW

RECOMMENDED ALBUM:

"The Red Fox Chasers (1928-1930)" (County)(1967)

Red Knuckles & the Trailblazers refer HOT RIZE

Red River Dave refer RED RIVER DAVE McENERY

RED, WHITE & BLUE(GRASS)

When Formed 1969

Original Members:

Grant Boatwright	**Lead and Rhythm Guitars, Vocals**
Ginger Boatwright	**Lead Vocals, Rhythm Guitar**
Dale Whitcomb	**5-String Banjo, Fiddle, Vocals**

Later Members:

Dave Sebolt	**Lead Vocals, Bass**
Norman Blake	**Mandolin, Dobro, Fiddle**
Dave Hall	**Vocals, Bass**
Michael Barnett	**Drums, Percussion**
Ed Barnett	**Vocals, Bass**

The start of this group occurred in 1966, when Ginger Boatwright was in the audience at the Lowenbrau House in Birmingham, Alabama (their home state), where Grant Boatwright was performing. He asked her to join him on stage and this resulted in their performing as Grant and Ginger. The duo persuaded Ginger's cousin Dale Whitcomb to join them and so Grant, Dale and Ginger came into being. For two years, they appeared on the *Sunday Show* on Channel 6 in Birmingham as well as playing parties and colleges.

It was then discovered that Ginger had a rare form of cancer. As a result, she had to leave college six hours short of a degree and had to give up her aspirations of becoming a juvenile probation officer. However, the Sunday she was released from hospital, the trio were performing on their radio show, with Ginger propped up on a stool.

By 1969, Grant and Ginger had married and the threesome headed for Chicago. Ray Tate, who was with the Old Town School of Folk Music, had asked Ginger on the telephone what the group was called and she told him "Grant, Dale and Ginger," but Tate said that there was already "Peter, Paul and Mary." Ginger then suggested the name of a 20's band from Sand Mountain, Alabama, the Red, White and Bluegrass Band Old Time Banjo Pickers and Hoss Hair Pullers Without Portfolio, and by the time they arrived at the venue, they were billed as "Red, White & Blue(grass)." In Ginger's words, "I used to say the band's name stood for redneck, white trash and old blue. 'Cause I was the only dog in the group."

Over the next year, the trio played Folk clubs and coffee houses, and the voluptuous Mrs. Boatwright was a surprise to traditional Bluegrass audiences, as it was not the norm for a woman to be the lead singer in a Bluegrass group. Come 1971 they played regularly at Mulenbrinks in Underground Atlanta. By 1973, Dave Sebolt had joined them on male lead vocals and bass. That year, the group signed with the General Recording Company (GRC), and had a Top 70 Country hit with

John Stewart's *July You're a Woman,* and released its eponymous album. Ginger also signed with the label and had a success with *The Lovin's Over.* The following year, the group released the album ***Pickin' Up***, which earned them a lot of accolades. This album featured Norman Blake and the Atlanta Symphony Orchestra.

In 1975, their third album, ***Red, White and Blue(grass) Collector's Album,*** was released. That same year, Grant and Ginger did the soundtrack music for the unsuccessful Shelley Winters movie *Poor Pretty Eddie* and Grant appeared playing guitar behind Karen Black in the Robert Altman movie *Nashville*. In 1976, the Barnett brothers joined the group. Ed had been playing in a Latin American band in Bogota, Colombia, prior to joining the group. Red, White & Blue(grass) moved over to Mercury Records in 1977 and released ***Red, White & Blue(grass) & Co.***, but by now their music had moved from its "Newgrass" beginnings. In addition, Ginger got a solo deal with the label. However, neither she nor the group had any success with Mercury.

Red, White & Blue(grass) split up in 1979. (For the early part and the rest of the Ginger Boatwright story, refer to her entry.)

RECOMMENDED ALBUMS:

"Red, White & Blue(grass)" (GRC)(1974)
"Pickin' Up" (GRC)(1974)
"Red, White & Blue(grass) Collector's Album" (GRC)(1975)
"Red, White & Blue(grass) & Co." (Mercury)(1977)

BLIND ALFRED REED

(Singer, Songwriter, Fiddle, Guitar, Banjo, Mandolin)

Given Name:	**Alfred Reed**
Date of Birth:	**June 15, 1880**
Where Born:	**Floyd, Virginia**
Married:	**Nettie**
Children:	**six**
Date of Death:	**January 17, 1956**

Blind Alfred Reed had a rich baritone voice and accompanied himself on fiddle, performing in an archaic style. Like many blind musicians in the pre-welfare state era, Reed earned his living through his music by necessity. Alfred also had a knack for composing and authored most of the numbers he recorded for Victor. His lyrics not only contain a great deal of social commentary, but also reveal considerable humor, irony and satire.

Reed lived most of his life near Princeton, West Virginia, where he and his wife reared six children including son Arville, who helped his dad make records (incorrectly identified on the labels as Orville). Blind from birth, Reed learned to play a fine fiddle and other instruments as well to accompany his rich singing voice. He played for dances and various entertainment functions in the Princeton vicinity. He also fiddled on the streets of Princeton, Hinton and Bluefield. When a train wreck took place at Ingleside, West Virginia, on May 24, 1927, ending the life of P.C Aldrich, a renowned local engineer, Reed composed a ballad about the incident. He contacted the Victor Talking Machine Company, who scheduled a session for him at Bristol, Tennessee, on July 28. He recorded *Wreck of the Virginian* and three additional numbers of a sacred nature. Alfred, who was deeply religious, composed lyrics that were often quite critical of what he viewed as excessive materialism, hypocrisy and modern lifestyles among women.

The success of his early self-accompanied sides led to a second session in New York City in December, 1927. Reed took fiddler Fred Pendleton and guitar playing son Arville with him. The latter two recorded as the West Virginian Night Owls. Arville played rhythm guitar behind his father's fiddle and vocal and did a solo on one song, *The Telephone Girl*. The songs cut included *The Fate of Chris Lively and Wife*, about an elderly couple killed by a train at Pax, West Virginia, and *Why Do You Bob Your Hair Girls?*, a critique of flapper hair styles. Nearly two years later, Alfred and Arville had their final Victor date in New York, which yielded 10 released sides, including *There'll Be No Distinction There, Beware* and a lighter-veined version than the original, *Why Do You Bob Your Hair Girls, #2.* The Great Depression ended Reed's recording career (as fewer records were sold), but he continued to play in the Princeton area, by himself, with the West Virginia Night Owls and with another locally known blind musician, Richard Harold (1884-1947), who had himself cut four numbers for Columbia in 1928. In later years, Reed played less frequently in public as local laws concerning street musicians greatly restricted his freedom to earn an independent income.

Arville Reed and Fred Pendleton both survived into the early 70's when researchers interviewed them. Rounder Records released an entire album of Blind Alfred Reed songs about a quarter-century after his death. Most of his other recordings appeared on various anthology albums. So too did masters cut by his associates, Harold Pendleton and the West Virginia Night Owls. IMT

RECOMMENDED ALBUM:

"How Can a Poor Man Stand Such Times and Live" (Rounder)(1972)

JERRY REED

(Singer, Songwriter, Guitar, Actor)

Given Name:	**Jerry Reed Hubbard**
Date of Birth:	**March 20, 1937**
Where Born:	**Atlanta, Georgia**
Married:	**1. Priscilla Mitchell (div.) 2. Chrissie**
Children:	**Seidina, Charlotte Louise (Lottie)**

Jerry is one of the few multi-talented performers in Country music who have actually been recognized for their all-around ability. To top all of that, he is one of the entertainment industry's supreme characters.

Known as "the Guitar Man," his career began in Atlanta, where he worked in cotton mills during the day and played the clubs at night. When he was 16, a policeman friend introduced him to Bill Lowery, the publisher and producer, who took on Jerry's management and obtained a record deal with Capitol for him in 1955. His first single for the label was *If the Good Lord's Willing & the Creeks Don't Rise.* He cut a mixture of Country and Rockabilly tracks for Capitol, without much success, until 1958. One of his major cuts occurred in 1958, when legendary rock'n'roller Gene Vincent cut the "Hubbard" song (his credits always stated "Hubbard"), *Crazy Legs.*

From 1959 until 1961, Jerry served in the Armed Forces and then moved to Nashville, to further his songwriting career. During the time he was in the service, Brenda Lee had a 1960 Pop hit with Jerry's song *That's All You Got to Do.* He found that he could also supplement his earnings with session work and became a much-in-demand session guitarist, as well as an on-tour player.

He had his first taste of chart success in 1962, while with Columbia. Two of his singles, *Goodnight Irene* and *Hully Gully Guitar*, made it to the lower level of the Pop 100. It was Chet Atkins at RCA who took a particular interest in Jerry's work and gave him a lot of guidance. He signed Jerry to the label in 1965, and released his debut single, *If I Don't Live Up to It/I Feel a Sin Coming On*, that year. However, it was not until 1967 that Jerry had his first Country chart success, when *Guitar Man* got into the Top 60. The following year, Elvis Presley had back-to-back chart success with two of Jerry's songs, *Guitar Man* and *U.S. Male.* Jerry had his first Top 20 hit at the end of 1967 with a sort of "thanks, Elvis" song, *Tupelo Mississippi Flash.*

He got 1968 under way with another Top 20 hit, *Remembering*, which was followed by a song that gave him one of his nicknames,

"Alabama Wild Man." In 1969, Jerry started to gain a level of consistency when he had a Top 15 hit with *Are You from Dixie (Cause I'm from Dixie Too)*, which was followed by *Talk About the Good Times* and *Georgia Sunshine* (both Top 20, 1970). Then at the end of 1970, he achieved his first Gold level single with *Amos Moses*, for which he received a Grammy nomination. The record reached the Pop Top 10 and Country Top 20. That year, he recorded a duet album with Chet Atkins, ***Me and Jerry***, for which they received the Grammy Award for "Best Country Instrumental Performance." Jerry got a regular spot on the *Glen Campbell Goodtime Hour* on CBS-TV during 1970-71 and went on to tour with Campbell during 1971.

In 1971, Jerry had the career single *When You're Hot, You're Hot*, a half-spoken, half-sung song in the Phil Harris vein, which went to No.1 on the Country chart, staying there for 5 weeks and being a Top 10 Pop hit. He won his second Grammy Award for the song as "Best Country Vocal Performance, Male." He wrapped up the year with a single that peaked just below the Top 10, *Ko-Ko Joe*.

The first three singles of 1972, *Another Puff, Smell the Flowers* and a re-issue of *Alabama Wild Man*, all went Top 30. The final release of the year, *You Took All the Ramblin' Out of Me,* fared slightly better and made the Top 20. That year, Jerry recorded a second album with Chet Atkins, ***Me and Chet***. He came back strongly in 1973, with the No.1 record *Lord Mr. Ford*. However, the follow-up, a remake of Phil Harris' *The Uptown Poker Club*, only got to the Top 25. Jerry also hosted *Music Country USA* on several occasions during 1973.

For the rest of the 70's, Jerry's fortunes were mixed, as he got more involved in making movies, mainly with his good buddy Burt Reynolds. He says of Reynolds that "I had to have a co-star." His first movie with Reynolds was in 1974, entitled *W.W. and the Dixie Dance Kings*. He followed up in 1976 with *Gator* and then appeared in *Smokey and the Bandit* (1977), *High Ballin'* (1978), *Hot Stuff* (with Dom DeLuise)(1979), *Smokey and the Bandit II* (1980), *Bat 21* and *Smokey and the Bandit III* (1983).

From 1974 through 1979, Jerry's only major hits were *The Crude Oil Blues* (Top 15), *A Good Woman's Love* (Top 15) and *Let's Sing Our Song* (Top 20)(all 1974), *Semolita* (Top 20), *East Bound and Down* (Top 3 both 1977), *You Know What* (a Top 20 duet by Jerry and his daughter Seidina), *(I Love You) What Can I Say* (Top 10)(both 1978) and *Gimme Back My Blues* (Top 15) and *Second-Hand Satin Lady (and a Bargain Basement Boy)* (Top 20)(both 1979).

In 1979, Jerry recorded the half vocal/half instrumental album, ***Half & Half***. In 1980, Jerry had a Top 15 hit with *Sugar Foot Rag*. 1981 was marked by the interesting project ***Jerry Reed Sings Jim Croce***. In 1982, Jerry enjoyed a renewed interest in his recordings, prompted by a No.1 single that had all the hallmarks of *When You're Hot, You're Hot*, entitled *She Got the Goldmine (I Got the Shaft)*, which also crossed to the Pop Top 90. He followed this with *The Bird*, a Top 3 single that contained his impressions of Willie Nelson singing *Whiskey River* and George Jones singing *He Stopped Loving Her Today*. The following year, he hit the Top 15 with his re-working of Creedence Clearwater Revival's *Down on the Corner* and then had two further Top 20 entries with *Good Ole Boys* and a duet with Waylon Jennings (from the album ***Waylon & Company***), *Hold on, I'm Comin'*.

Jerry moved from RCA in 1986 and signed with Capitol Records, but this proved to be a largely unproductive move. The album ***Lookin' at You*** was not marked by any stand-out tracks and no singles released charted. In 1992, Jerry got back together with his old mentor Chet Atkins for the well-received album ***Sneakin' Around***.

Jerry Reed, who likes golf, fishing and philosophizing, is unique within popular music. His frenetic songs often make it hard to believe that he could write and record gentle ballads.

RECOMMENDED ALBUMS:

"Me & Jerry" (RCA Victor)(1970) [With Chet Atkins]
"When You're Hot, You're Hot" (RCA Victor)(1971)
"Me & Chet" (RCA Victor)(1972) [With Chet Atkins]
"The Best of Jerry Reed" (RCA Victor)(1972)
"The Uptown Poker Club" (RCA Victor)(1973)
"Half & Half" (RCA Victor)(1979)
"Jerry Reed Sings Jim Croce" (RCA Victor)(1980)
"The Best of Jerry Reed"(RCA Victor)(1981)
"The Bird" (RCA Victor)(1982)
"Jerry Reed's Greatest Hits" (RCA Victor)(1984)
"Sneakin' Around" (Columbia)(1992) [With Chet Atkins]

DEL REEVES

(Singer, Songwriter, Guitar, Fiddle, Piano, Banjo, Bass)

Given Name:	**Franklin Delano Reeves**
Date of Birth:	**July 14, 1933**
Where Born:	**Sparta, North Carolina**
Married:	**Ellen Schiell**
Children:	**Anne Delana, Kari Elizabeth, Bethany**

For over 30 years, Del Reeves has been a favorite of Country audiences throughout the world. From the early 60's through the mid-70's, he had major chart hits and still continues to be one of the mainstays of the *Grand Ole Opry*.

When his four elder brothers were away in the service during WWII, they left their guitars around the family home and Del started to play, with his mother initially having to tune the instrument for him. He appeared on his own radio show by the time he was age 12. He attended Appalachia State College in Boone, North Carolina, and then joined the U.S. Air Force for four years, being stationed at Travis Air Force Base in California. While in California, he appeared on television on the *Chester Smith Show*, and it was with Chester that Del made his initial recording for Capitol in 1958, *Love Love Love/You're Not the Changing Kind*. He released two more singles for the label, but nothing came of them.

After he left the service, Del stayed on in California and got his own TV show, the *Del Reeves Country Carnival*, which stayed on the air for four years. He had by now married, and he and Ellen started to write songs together and he started to get cuts by artists such as Roy Drusky, Carl Smith, Rose Maddox and Sheb Wooley. Del signed to Decca in 1961 and had a hit with his initial single, *Be Quiet Mind*, which reached the Country Top 10. He didn't have another hit until a year later, when *He Stands Real Tall* reached the Top 15. During 1962, at the urging of songwriter Hank Cochran, Del moved to Nashville. By 1963, he was on Reprise, and had the solitary success *The Only Girl I Can't Forget* (Top 15). The following year, he was again label hopping, this time to Columbia, where he again had only one hit, the mid-level *Talking to the Night Lights*.

In 1965, Del at last settled at United Artists Records and had his first No.1 hit, *Girl on the Billboard,* a song allegedly written about Dolly Parton. He followed this with the Top 5 success *The Belles of Southern Bell*. The following year, Del had the Top 10 single *Women Do Funny Things to Me*. He then slipped from record favor and his next single in 1966, *One Bum Town*, only made it to the Top 50. His other singles that year, *Gettin' Any Feed for Your Chickens* (Top 40) and *This Must Be the Bottom* (Top 30), were only enhanced by the fact that Del became a member of the *Grand Ole Opry* in October.

His next major hit occurred in 1967, when he had *A Dime at a Time*, which went Top 15. Del followed this with a minor duet success with Bobby Goldsboro. Del completed the year with the Top 20 record *Wild Blood* and the Top 5 successes *Looking at the World Through a Windshield* and *Good Time Charlies*. From this last hit, he got the name for his backing band, the Good Time Charlies. This sums up Del and his band, who adopt a light-hearted image for their stage appearances. This is why he is also known as "the Dean Martin of Country Music."

He started off 1969 with another Top 5 hit, *Be Glad*. The follow-up, *There Wouldn't Be a Lonely Heart in Town*, reached No.12 and the final chart entry of the year, *Take a Little Good Will Home*, on which he was again paired with Bobby Goldsboro, just fell short of the Top 30.

During the 60's, Del appeared in 6 movies: *Second Fiddle to a Steel Guitar*, *Forty Acre Feud*, *Gold Guitar*, *Cotton-Pickin' Chickenpickers*, *Whiskey's Renegades* and in 1969, *Sam Whiskey*, which starred Angie Dickinson, Clint Walker and Burt Reynolds. During the 70's, he had some major successes, but most of his chart records peaked in the middle to low levels. Those successes he did have included *A Lover's Question* (Top 15, a major Pop hit for Clyde McPhatter back in 1959), *Land Mark Tavern* (Top 20, on which he was joined by Penny DeHaven) and *Right Back Loving You Again* (Top 25)(all 1970), *Bar Room Talk* (Top 30),*The Philadelphia Fillies* (Top 10)(both 1971), *The Best is Yet to Come* (Top 30, 1972), *Lay a Little Lovin' on Me* (Top 25, 1973), and *On the Rebound* (Top 30, 1976, a duet with Billie Joe Spears). In 1973, Del was thrown from a horse and as a result, his leg was in a cast, but he didn't miss a booking.

Del moved to the independent label Koala in 1980, but although he had five chart records, the most successful, *Slow Hand,* only reached the Top 60. He had his last chart record in 1986, when his Playback single *The Second Time Around* scraped into the Top 100.

RECOMMENDED ALBUMS:

"Del Reeves Sings Jim Reeves" (United Artists)(1966)
"The Little Church in the Dell" (United Artists)(1967)
"The Best of Del Reeves" (United Artists)(1967)
"The Best of Del Reeves, Volume 2" (United Artists)(1969)
"The Very Best of Del Reeves" (United Artists)(1971)
"10th Anniversary" (United Artists)(1976)
"By Request: Del & Billie Jo" (United Artists)(1976) [With Billie Jo Spears]
"Del Reeves' Greatest Hits" (Gusto/Starday)(1978)
"Let's Go to Heaven Tonight" (Koala)(1980) [With Liz Tyndell]

Star of the Grand Ole Opry ***Del Reeves***

GOEBEL REEVES

(Singer, Songwriter, Guitar)

Given Name: Goebel Leon Reeves
Date of Birth: October 9, 1899
Where Born: Sherman, Texas
Married: Unknown (div.)
Date of Death: January 26, 1959

Goebel Reeves, as a pioneer Country singer and poet, had a life and career which in many respects parallels that of his somewhat older contemporary, Harry McClintock. Both led exciting lives and had a special feel for hobo and cowboy songs, many of which were self composed. Known usually on radio and record by such nicknames as "the Texas Drifter," Reeves spent fewer years as an itinerant entertainer and remained somewhat more obscure than McClintock although he actually recorded more.

Born in the Red River Valley of north Texas, Reeves had a fairly normal childhood until 1917, when he entered the U.S. Army. He received a bullet wound while on the front lines and spent some months recuperating prior to his discharge in 1921. Goebel then made a conscious decision to lead an itinerant life, hoboing his way around the country, working at times or earning a few dollars with his guitar and singing a few songs. Sometimes he traveled with a fellow named Lucius Parks. At one time Reeves enlisted in the merchant marine. After allegedly returning from a voyage to Italy, he heard a Jimmie Rodgers record and decided to emulate him. His initial sessions were for OKeh in June, 1929 at San Antonio and he had another studio trip to New York the following January.

He seems to have first used the pseudonyms "Texas Drifter" and also "George Riley, the Yodeling Rustler" beginning in July, 1930. Over the next five years, he cut several more sides, chiefly for Gennett and the American Record Corporation for release on such labels as Banner, Melotone, and Perfect. He made his last recordings in Los Angeles about 1938, for C.P. MacGregor Transcriptions of Hollywood, a rather lengthy series which included numerous recitations and poems.

From time to time, the Texas Drifter also appeared on radio. Since he wandered about a great deal, his broadcasts over the airwaves were sporadic, but are said to have extended from Chattanooga to Halifax and westward to Los Angeles. He claimed to have appeared briefly on both WSM Nashville and WLS Chicago. He returned to the merchant marine in the 30's and spent enough time in Japan to learn a bit of the language.

After some early work at entertaining servicemen at the beginning of WWII, Reeves returned to the merchant marine again where he spent most of the war years. Later, he also did some work for the government in connection with Japanese-American relocation camps, as he had numerous friends among the Japanese-American community in California. Record collector Fred Hoeptner also became a friend of Reeves' and gathered biographical data from him in the later 50's.

The Texas Drifter died in a Long Beach Veterans Administration Hospital eight months prior to his 60th birthday. Overall, he probably had more impact in some of the foreign markets where his discs were released. For instance, many Australians appear to emulate parts of his yodeling style. Two of his songs with a lasting impact have been *The Hobo's Last Long Ride,* renamed *The Last Ride* by Hank Snow, and *The Hobo's Lullaby*, which several Folk revival groups have recorded. Interest in his music remained sufficiently high for four albums of his music to be reissued, two in Europe and two in the U.S. Three of the albums took material from the MacGregor transcriptions with some duplication of sides. IMT

RECOMMENDED ALBUMS:

"The Legendary Texas Drifter, Volume 1" (CMH) (1972)
"The Legendary Texas Drifter, Volume 2" (CMH) (1973)
"The Texas Drifter" (Glendale) (1978)
"The Texas Drifter in Story and Song" (Glendale) (1979)

JIM REEVES

(Singer, Songwriter, Guitar, Actor)

Given Name: James Travis Reeves
Date of Birth: August 20, 1924
Where Born: Galloway, Panola County, Texas
Married: Mary Elizabeth White (m. 1947)
Date of Death: July 31, 1964

Jim Reeves is still one of the most important cross-over Country singers of all time and most certainly the most important international Country performer. Twenty years after his death, "Gentleman" Jim's records were still appearing on the U.S. Country charts, and in the U.K. Reeves' singles were still charting on the Pop lists. In addition, his albums are still in demand worldwide. His style started out as almost "hillbilly" but by 1957, Jim's "touch of velvet" style had surfaced.

Jim, one of nine children, was raised in a working class family. When he was 10 months old, his father, Tom, died and his mother, Beaulah, was forced to work in the fields to feed and clothe her children. When he was 5 years old, Jim received a broken guitar, which was repaired by an oil construction worker who taught him a few chords. His early influence was Jimmie Rodgers and when he was age 9, Jim made his radio debut.

However, Jim's sights were not set on a career in music; instead he was hoping for a career in baseball. After attending Carthage High School, Jim went on to the University of Texas in Austin, where he majored in speech and drama. Here he showed his prowess as a star athlete, but after 6 weeks, Jim dropped out and went to work for Brown and Root in the Houston shipyards, helping to build Liberty ships.

In 1944, after playing semi-professional baseball, Jim signed with the St. Louis Cardinals, initially playing in the Evangeline League as a pitcher. He then went on to play for Marshall and Henderson in the East Texas League. In 1947, Jim injured his ankle while sliding into second base on a wet pitch and it didn't heal properly and spelled the end of his baseball aspirations.

*Gentleman **Jim Reeves***

Now married to Mary, a former schoolteacher, Jim had to decide on a career. He tried his hand as an insurance salesman, boxer, truck driver and shipping clerk. He also began singing around the East Texas area and for a short while was a sideman with Moon Mullican's band in Beaumont and led a band at the Reo Palm Isle Ballroom in Longview. Jim recorded his first sides for the Macy label in Houston in 1949.

However, because he had such a fine speaking voice, he opted for a full-time career as a broadcaster. In 1952, Jim worked for KSIG Gladewater, Texas, but later that year joined KGRI Henderson, Texas, as a deejay and a newscaster, later becoming Program Director and Assistant Manager. In time, Jim would jointly own the station with deejay Tom Perryman.

Jim reached a crossroad time later that year and flipped a coin to decide whether to go to Dallas or Shreveport. Shreveport won and Jim joined KWKH as announcer and singer. At the end of the year, Hank Williams failed to appear on the *Louisiana Hayride*, also out of KWKH, and Jim was asked to deputize. Fabor Robinson, the head of Abbott and Fabor Records, was in the audience and was so impressed with Jim's singing that he immediately signed him.

Jim's debut single on Abbott, Mitchell Torok's *Mexican Joe*, on which he was backed by the Circle O Ranch Boys, became a No.1 hit, staying atop the Country charts for 9 weeks. This led to Jim's becoming a member of the *Louisiana Hayride*, where he stayed until 1963. The year ended with the charting of *Bimbo*, which topped the charts for 3 weeks.

Jim opened his 1954 account with a duet with Georgia-born Ginny Wright, entitled *I Love You*. The single, released on Fabor, reached the Top 3 and was followed by *Then I'll Stop Loving You*, which only reached the Top 15. However, in the fall, Jim charted Top 5 with *Penny Candy* on which he was backed by the Louisiana Hayride Band. Later Jim would have his own band, the Wagonmasters, who were renamed the Blue Boys. The original name was then adopted by Porter Wagoner for his band. During 1954, Jim toured Europe as part of a USO tour.

Drinking Tequila, in 1955, was Jim's last chart record on Abbott. It reached the Top 10, but by now, Jim had moved to the more prestigious RCA Victor. While with Abbott, Jim recorded 36 sides, which would later surface on Abbott and RCA. His first release for RCA was the Top 5 *Yonder Comes a Sucker/I'm Hurtin' Inside*. On October 19 that year, Jim became a member of the *Grand Ole Opry*.

During 1956, Jim chalked up *My Lips are Sealed* (Top 10) and *According to My Heart* (Top 5). The following year was to become a memorable one on many levels. He started off the year with the self-penned *Am I Losing You*, which reached the Top 3. This was followed by the chart-topping *Four Walls*. The single stayed at No.1 on the Country chart for 8 weeks and crossed-over to the Pop Top 15. His other hits that year were *Two Shadows on the Wall* (Top 10)/*Young Hearts* (Top 15) and *Anna Marie* (Top 3). That year, Jim toured Europe again, this time with the Browns, Del Wood and Hank Locklin, as part of a USO tour. However, they never played the U.K. due to labor problems. That same year, Jim had his own ABC-TV show and his own ABC radio series.

During 1958 and 1959, Jim racked up further major hits starting with the double-sided Top 10 success *Overnight/I Love You More* and continuing with the Top 3 *Blue Boy* (which also crossed to the Pop Top 50). At the end of 1958, Jim charted with the Roger Miller song *Billy Bayou*, which went to No.1 for 5 weeks. The flip-side, *I'd Like to Be*, also reached the Top 20. He started 1959 with the Top 5 *Partners* and the flip-side *I'm Beginning to Forget You* (Top 20). Then came his momentous career single, *He'll Have to Go*. Written by Joe and Audrey Allison, the record opened up the world to Jim. It stayed at No.1 on the Country chart for 14 weeks, went Top 3 on the

Pop chart, opened his U.K. account by reaching No.12 on the Pop chart and was Certified Gold.

During 1960, Jim's song *I'm Gettin' Better* provided him with his first hit of the year, going Top 3 and crossing-over to the Pop Top 40. The flip, *I Know One*, also went Top 10. He completed the year with *I Missed Me*, which went Top 3 Country and Top 50 Pop. The flip-side was a re-release of *Am I Losing You*, which this time around went Top 10 Country and Top 40 Pop. The following year, Harlan Howard's *The Blizzard* gave Jim a Top 5 hit, but his next release, *What Would You Do?/Stand at Your Window*, only went Top 20. The final single of the year made up for this with *Losing Your Love*, which went Top 3, and the flip-side, *(How Can I Write on Paper) What I Feel in My Heart*, which reached the Top 10.

In the spring of 1962, RCA released *A Letter to My Heart*, which only went Top 20; however, the public and radio decided that the flip-side, *Adios Amigo,* would be the hit. It reached the Top 3, being kept from the top for over 2 months by George Jones' *She Thinks I Still Care* and Claude King's *Wolverton Mountain*. At the end of the summer, Jim went Top 3 with *I'm Gonna Change Everything* and took the flip-side, *Pride Goes Before a Fall,* into the Top 20. During the year, Jim toured South Africa with Chet Atkins and Floyd Cramer and broke all box office records.

The following year, Jim had a Top 3 hit with Dottie West's *Is This Me?* He then went to South Africa, where he filmed the movie *Kimberley Jim*. Jim built up an enormous reputation in South Africa and recorded some tracks in Afrikaans, including *Verreland* and *Net'N Stille Uurtjie*. In the late summer of 1963, Jim had a Top 3 hit with Alex Zanetis' *Guilty*. The flip-side, *Little Ole Me*, just failed to make the Top 10.

Jim's opening hit of 1964, *Welcome to My World*, had already been a Top 10 single in the U.K. in 1963. This was Jim's seventh U.K. hit and in 1962, he had hit the Top 20 there with *You're the Only Good Thing*. In 1964, Jim toured the U.K. to promote *I Love You Because*, written by Leon Payne, and sang the song on British TV and radio. It became a Top 5 hit in the U.K. but was not a hit in the U.S. until 1976. In the spring of 1964, Jim got together with Dottie West for the Top 10 *Love is No Excuse*.

On November 7, Jim charted with *I Guess I'm Crazy*. Sadly, 24 days later, Jim Reeves was killed when his private plane crashed during a storm in Nashville. At his funeral, the honorary pall bearers included Chet Atkins and Steve Sholes, who had signed Jim to RCA. Jim was buried in Carthage, Texas. *I Guess I'm Crazy* presented Jim with his first posthumous hit, going to No.1 for 7 weeks. His success after his death almost made it seem like his fans refused to believe he had died. Thanks to endeavors of Jim's widow, his success continued unabated. The year was completed by the Top 3 *I Won't Forget You*, which like all his singles since *He'll Have to Go*, crossed to the Pop chart. It also went to No.3 in Britain. In the U.K., *There's a Heartache Following Me* went Top 3, but did not chart in the U.S.

Jim's success in 1965 through 1967 was unprecedented for a deceased artist. He started out with back-to-back No.1 hits, *This Is It* and *Is it Really Over?*, both of which stayed at the top for 3 weeks and crossed to the Pop chart. In the U.K., Jim had a Top 10 hit with *It Hurts So Much* and reached No.13 with *Not Until the Next Time* and No.17 with *Is it Really Over?* In 1966, *Snow Flake* went Top 3 on the Country chart and was followed by three successive No.1 singles. The first was Cindy Walker's *Distant Drums*, which stayed at the top for 4 weeks and became a Top 50 Pop hit. This was followed by *Blue Side of Lonesome* (1966) and *I Won't Come in While He's There*, the last named being Jim's final cross-over single. *Distant Drums* also gave Jim his first U.K. No.1, staying at the top of the chart for 5 weeks. Although he charted in Britain 10 more times, his most successful records there were *I Won't Come in While He's There* (1967), *When Two Words Collide* (1969) and *But You Love Me Daddy* (1969), all of which went Top 20. In 1966, Jim's British fan club was formed in Britain.

Throughout the 60's and 70's, further Jim Reeves records hit the Country chart, the most successful being: 1967: *The Storm* (Top 20) and *I Heard a Heart Break Last Night* (Top 10); 1968: *That's When I See the Blues (in Your Pretty Brown Eyes)* and *When You Are Gone* (both Top 10); 1969: *When Two Words Collide* and *Nobody's Fool* (both Top 10). In 1969, five of the Top 10 in Sweden were Jim Reeves singles. Two of Jim's albums, ***The Best of Jim Reeves*** (1964) and ***Distant Drums*** (1966), went Gold in 1966 and 1968 respectively.

During the 70's, Jim's singles on the Country charts were: 1970: *Angels Don't Lie* (Top 5); 1971: *Gypsy Feet* (Top 20); 1972: *The Writing's on the Wall* (Top 20) and *Missing You* (Top 10); 1973: *Am I That Easy to Forget* (Top 20); 1974: *I'd Fight the World* (Top 20); 1977: *It's Nothin' to Me* (Top 20).

In 1979, through electronic ingenuity, rising Country star Deborah Allen was overdubbed with Jim's vocal tracks and the songs so "doctored" were released on the album ***Don't Let Me Cross Over***. From this album, three singles hit the Top 10: the title track, *Oh, How I Miss You Tonight* (both 1979) and *Take Me in Your Arms and Hold Me* (1980).

In 1981, electronic wizardry did it again by pairing Jim with another deceased star, Patsy Cline. Their "duet" track, *Have You Ever Been Lonely (Have You Ever Been Blue)* reached the Top 5. They had one more hit "together," *I Fall to Pieces*, but it only reached the Top 60.

In 1967, Jim Reeves was inducted to the Country Music Hall of Fame. Two years later, the ACM created the "Jim Reeves Memorial Award," the first recipient being Joe Allison, the writer of *He'll Have to Go*. Mary Reeves operates the Jim Reeves Museum in Nashville and is instrumental in keeping alive the flame of Jim's memory and music.

RECOMMENDED ALBUMS:

"(Music from the Movie) Kimberley Jim" (RCA Victor)(1964)
"The Best of Jim Reeves" (RCA Victor)(1964)
"The Best of Jim Reeves, Vol. 2" (RCA Victor)(1966)
"The Best of Jim Reeves, Vol. 3" (RCA Victor)(1969)
"The Best of Jim Reeves' Sacred Songs" (RCA Victor)(1974) [Re-released in 1980]
"Forever" (double)(RCA International UK)(1975)
"The Unforgettable Jim Reeves" (6-album Box Set)(RCA Victor)(1976) [Available through Reader's Digest]
"The Best of Jim Reeves, Vol. 4" (RCA Victor)(1979)
"Let Me Cross Over" (RCA Victor)(1979) [With Deborah Allen]
"Greatest Hits—Jim Reeves & Patsy Cline" (RCA Victor)(1981)
"The Abbott Recordings, Volume 1" (RCA International UK)(1982)
"The Abbott Recordings, Volume 2" (RCA International UK)(1982)
"Special Collection" (RCA Victor)(1983)
"50 All-Time Worldwide Favorites" (4-album box set)(RCA Victor)

RONNA REEVES

(Singer, Songwriter, Tap-Dancer)

Given Name: Ronna Renee Reeves
Date of Birth: September 21, 1966
Where Born: Big Spring, Texas
Married: Pete (div.)

Of the new breed of female singers to emerge in the 90's, Ronna Reeves is one who is likely to have a long career. However, in Ronna's case there is an added plus, in that she has probably the most dedicated managers in the business in Ronald and Joy Cotton.

Ronna's career started when she was age 8, when she won the Little Miss Big Spring competition. For her talent presentation, she tap-danced while she sang. Her singing got one of the judges excited and this led to her parents taking her to a local guitar/fiddle instructor to see if she had talent. As a result, he put Ronna on stage with his band. By the time she was 11, she had her own band, whose oldest member was 16. While she was playing clubs like Billy Bob's in Forth Worth, she met Ron and Joy Cotton, who were promoting in Waco, Texas.

When Ronna was nearly 17, Ron called her and advised her that he was doing shows with George Strait and invited her to open for George. This she did for a year and a half. She also opened for Randy Travis, Ronnie Milsap, Reba McEntire, Garth Brooks, Lee Greenwood, the Judds and Steve Wariner. She made occasional trips to Nashville and there producer Clyde Brooks helped her get a record deal with Mercury, where he and Mercury Vice President Harold Shedd produced her.

Her first album, ***Only the Heart*** (1991), failed to produce any hit singles. She first hit the Country singles charts, in 1992, with *The More I Learn (the Less I Understand About Love)*, which reached the Top 50. Her two follow-up singles, *What If You're Wrong* and *We Can Hold Our Own*, fared less well, and only reached the Top 80. These all came from the second album, ***The More I Learn***. The album also had a duet with Sammy Kershaw, *There's Love on the Line*, which was not released as a single. During 1993, she released her third album, ***What Comes Naturally***, to critical acclaim. Her double-sided single that year, *Never Let Him See Me Cry/He's My Weakness*, reached the Top 75. Ronna has now left Mercury and her management is label shopping.

RECOMMENDED ALBUMS:

"Only the Heart" (Mercury)(1991)
"The More I Learn" (Mercury)(1992)
"What Comes Naturally" (Mercury)(1993)

MIKE REID

(Singer, Songwriter, Keyboards)
Date of Birth: May 24, 1947
Where Born: Altoona, Pennsylvania

It was not an injury that persuaded Mike Reid to switch from playing football to becoming one of Country music's top songwriters. However, it must have dawned on Mike that it made more sense to beat your brains out over a song than to have some jock beating them.

Mike grew up with a love for sports and he got a scholarship to Penn State University. He became All-American, Outland Trophy Winner in 1969. While at university, his other love, music, came to the fore.

In 1970, he left college with a music degree, and was offered a professional contract with the Cincinnati Bengals. He became first-round draft pick and was AFC/NFL Defensive Rookie of the Year. While playing football, Mike also played with local bands. It was during 1970, when Mike was laid up with an injury, that he met Larry Gatlin, who was visiting his roommate, and Larry encouraged Mike and admired the first song that Mike had written, entitled *Time Runs Away*. As he continued with football, Mike gained much acclaim, being named All-Pro in 1972 and 1973. He also made off-season appearances with the symphony orchestras in Cincinnati, Dallas, San Antonio, Texas, and Utah as a classical pianist.

Mike quit the Bengals in 1975 to tour with the Apple Butter Band. He soon put together his own band and tried to emulate Leonard Cohen and Randy Newman. He split from the band after a year on the road and continued as a solo artist. Back in those days, he was billed as a former NFL All-Pro, which made him somewhat of a novelty.

He moved to Nashville in 1980 and was signed to ATV Publishing. He stayed with them for 18 months and then met Rob Galbraith, who runs Milsap Music. Mike joined the company in August, 1981 and his first cuts appeared on the Ronnie Milsap 1982 album ***Inside***, the title track of which was a No.1 hit. He also followed up with Milsap's next cut, *Stranger in My House*, which won a Grammy Award for "Best New Country Song" in the year of release (1983). That same year, Sylvia had a Top 3 hit with *I Never Quite Got Back (from Losing You)*.

In 1984, Mike continued his connection with Milsap and, by inference, producer Tom Collins, by writing Ronnie's No.1 hit *Still Losing You* and his Top 10 single *Prisoner of the Highway*. He also wrote the Top 3 hit for Barbara Mandrell and Lee Greenwood *To Me*. The following year, Mike had back-to-back No.1 singles by Ronnie Milsap with *She Keeps the Home Fires Burning* and *Lost in the Fifties Tonight* (which was made into a medley with *In the Still of the Night*), the latter winning a Grammy Award for Milsap. That year, Mike was named ASCAP "Writer of the Year."

He continued his winning ways in 1986 with hits for Mark Gray (*Back When Love Was Enough*), Marie Osmond (*Everybody's Crazy 'bout My Baby*) and a Top 10 success for Tanya Tucker (*It's Only Over for You*). He chalked up a Top 3 hit with Conway Twitty on *Fallin' for You for Years*, and had two-in-a-row No.1 singles from Ronnie Milsap, *In Love* and *How Do I Turn You On*. He had two memorable hits during 1987, *I Wouldn't Be a Man* (Don Williams) and yet another Milsap No.1 (*Where Do the Nights Go*).

Mike teamed up with Ronnie for the memorable Top 3 hit *Old Folks*, which charted in 1988, and marked Mike's chart debut. It first appeared on ***Signatures: A Songwriter's Album***. The following year, Mike had four further major cuts by other artists, *One Good Well* (Don Williams), *He Talks to Me* (Lorrie Morgan), *Born to Be Blue* (the Judds) and *There You Are* (Willie Nelson). In addition, Gene Watson had a Top 20 hit with *Back in the Fire* and newcomer Shelby Lynne reached the Top 40 with *The Hurtin' Side*.

He signed to Columbia in 1990, and released his debut album, ***Turning for Home***, which yielded his first No.1 hit as an artist, *Walk on Faith*. During 1991, he hit the charts three times, with *Till You Were Gone* and *As Simple as That* (Top 20) and *I'll Stop Loving You* (Top 25). He also had a major success via Bonnie Raitt's classy recording of *I Can't Make You Love Me* (from her ***Luck of the Draw*** album), which although not a monster chart record, has already been acclaimed as a classic. Bonnie had already recorded Mike's *Too Soon to Tell* on her ***Nick of Time*** album.

Mike celebrated a memorable year in 1992, with major successes from Collin Raye with the No.1 hit *In this Life*, Top 5 hits from Wynonna (*My Strongest Weakness*) and Tanya Tucker (*Some Kind of Trouble*) and a Top 10 single by Lee Roy Parnell, *Love without Mercy*. That same year, Mike released his much acclaimed second album, ***Twilight Town***. However, his own singles only fared moderately with *I Got a Life* going Top 60 and both *Keep on Walkin'* and *Call Home* peaking in the Top 50. This probably comprised the most straight-ahead Country material that he has written.

There is no denying Mike Reid's success as a songwriter of the highest worth. He is probably one of the finest Pop/Blue Collar songwriters of all time and this is why his songs appeal to the same audience that acclaim Jimmy Webb and Bruce Springsteen. His melodies may not always be "true" Country, but his lyrics are, in the main, about the man in the street or on the farm.

RECOMMENDED ALBUMS:

"Turning for Home" (Columbia)(1990)
"Twilight Town" (Columbia)(1992)

HERB REMINGTON

(Steel Guitar (Pedal and Non-Pedal), Guitar, Ukulele, Bass, Composer)

Given Name: Herbert Leroy Remington
Date of Birth: June 9, 1926
Where Born: Meshawaka, Indiana
Married: Melba ("Mel")
Children: Mark, Steve

Herb Remington, who at times recorded as Johnny Lee, has brought to steel guitar playing the stylings normally associated with the Hawaiian guitar. Sometimes known as Herbie, he was influenced by Dick McIntire, Andy Iona and Sol Hoopii, and is recognized as one of the finest players of his chosen instrument.

When he was around age 6, he was taught piano by his mother and when he was 12, he took Spanish guitar lessons. He teamed up with a neighborhood boy who played guitar and they won third prize in a local talent contest, playing *Home on the Range*. They practiced hard and from then on won first prize every week. When Herb saw the movie *Hawaii*, starring Bing Crosby, he was hooked on the Hawaiian guitar. Fate was soon at his door, as a salesman showed him how to raise the action on his guitar and he enrolled for a course of lessons through Oahu Publishing Company.

After a while, he was a member of the company's Professional Club and joined the largest steel guitar band, totaling some 225 pickers, all playing Oahu guitars. In 1942, he formed the Honolulu Serenaders and graduated in 1944. As the interest in Hawaiian music was on the wane, Herb decided to move to California. Here, against all the odds, he was hired as Ray Whitley's steelie in his new Western Swing band, a band that included Merle Travis. So he began playing at the Riverside Rancho Ballroom. However, the Musicians' Union caught up with him, and he had to wait for three months after joining before he could take a booking.

Although Ray promised to rehire him, Herb was drafted into the U.S. Army and was sent to Camp Roberts in California, where he was instructed to rehearse with some Polynesian recruits to entertain the troops. After basic training, he was stationed at Fort Bragg, North Carolina, where he formed a trio to play the NCO clubs. About a week after his discharge, in 1946, he heard that Bob Wills was auditioning for a steel player for his brother Luke's band. As a result, Bob's regular player was seconded to Luke Wills' band, and Herb joined Bob Wills. His first engagement with Wills was a "battle" dance with Spade Cooley's band in the Santa Monica Ballroom. However, Herb dropped his steel bar just as he was going to play his solo in *San Antonio Rose*, and Noel Boggs, the steelie with Cooley, played the part.

Herb stayed with Wills for 4 years, and composed several tunes that became Wills' staples, such as *Boot Heel Drag*, which was released as the flipside of *Faded Love*. After leaving Wills, Herb joined Hank Penny's band, where he recorded his now classic tune *Remington Ride*. He went on to play with T. Texas Tyler and Slim Whitman.

He moved to Houston in 1950, and during 1952 through 1956 he played in a "commonwealth" band, the Ranch Hands. In 1956, he started a four year stint with the Laura Lee and Dickie McBride band (Laura Lee and Dickie had played in the Ranch Hands). He also played, occasionally, with the Sundowners during 1957 and 1958. He had his own band, in 1958, called Herbie's Hawaiians. In 1960, he returned to his first love, Hawaiian music, and formed the Herb Remington Combo, with his talented wife, Mel, Dean Reynolds and Paul Buskirk. In 1961, he cut a single for D Records, *Fiddlesteel/Soft Shoe Slide*. From 1960 through 1963, the combo worked the Las Vegas area. After that until 1971, they played luau parties. In 1971, Herb and Mel played pizza parlors as a duo, having decided to stop playing on the road.

In 1973, Herb set up a store in Houston selling steel guitars, and then in 1978, he became a Peavey dealer. When the Texas Playboys re-formed in 1983 as Playboys II, Herb played steel alongside Leon Rausch, Eldon Shamblin and Johnny Gimble. In 1989, he formed his own steel guitar manufacturing company, Remington Steel (he agreed not to try and emulate the TV show of the same name!).

Herb has been recognized by his peers and in 1978, he was inducted into the Nebraska Country Music Hall of Fame; in 1979, the International Steel Guitar Hall of Fame; in 1988, the Western Swing Association Hall of Fame (California); in 1990, the Texas Steel Guitar Hall of Fame, and in 1991, the Texas Western Swing Association Hall of Fame. An interesting note is that Herb and that other maestro of the steel guitar, Buddy Emmons, were both born in St. Joseph's Hospital in Meshawaka. Herb is still active in his store and playing with Playboys II.

RECOMMENDED ALBUMS:

"Steel Guitar Holiday" (United Artists)(1961) [Also released on Vintage Classics/Point (Canada)]
"Remington Rides Again" (Vintage Classics) [Also on Pickwick/Hilltop (1965)]
"Pure Remington Steel" (Stoneway) [Released on Boot (Canada)]
"Boot Heel Drag" (Stoneway)(1977)
"Jean Street Swing" (Steel Guitar Record Club)
"Aloha Hawaii" (Vintage Classics) [Originally released on D Records]
Also check out Bob Wills' recordings.

RENFRO VALLEY BARN DANCE, The

(Radio show, WHAS Louisville, Kentucky)

The *Renfro Valley Barn Dance* was one of the most unusual live audience radio jamboree programs. The most atypical feature of this show was its actual location in a rural community rather than in a studio or theater of a southern or midwestern city.

Renfro Valley originally had been a rural community north of Mount Vernon, Kentucky, and south of Berea. John Lair (1895-1985) had gone to Chicago in the wake of Bradley Kincaid's success at WLS radio. Lair brought other local musicians from the *National Barn Dance* such as Karl Davis, Harty Taylor, Doc Hopkins, and Red Foley, combining them to form the Cumberland Ridge Runners. Later Lair brought Lily May Ledford to Chicago.

By the mid-30's, Lair conceived the notion of a barn dance in a rural area such as back home in Rockcastle County. Initially, however, he inaugurated his *Renfro Valley Barn Dance* from the Music Hall in Cincinnati and over radio WLW in the fall of 1937. He raided a fair segment of the talent from WLS to accompany him, including Red Foley, the Girls of the Golden West and Lily May. The facilities in Renfro Valley including the "Big Barn" went under construction.

After a year in Cincinnati, the show moved to Dayton. Lair had three original partners, Benny "Duke of Paducah" Ford, Red Foley, and the latter's brother Clarence (Cotton). By the fall of 1939, the Renfro Valley complex had been sufficiently completed and the first broadcast came from the Barn on November 4, via WHAS Louisville.

Some of his original recruits such as the Girls of the Golden West chose to remain at WLW. By 1940, all the original partners had sold out to Lair, as the first winter had not seen a boom in ticket sales. Lair's faith in his project paid off, however, as the arrival of warmer temperatures brought scads of paying customers and for the next dozen years or so, Renfro Valley became the Country music fan's dream come true. Lair inaugurated his *Sunday Morning Gatherin'* in 1943 and had a quarter hour daily *Country Store* program for several years following WWII. All these programs were heard over all or parts of the major networks.

Lair always pushed *Renfro Valley* as an entity rather than individual acts. The Coon Creek Girls were probably his most significant act, originally consisting of Lily May, sister Rosie, Violet Koehler, and Daisy Lange (later Lily May, Rosie and Minnie or Black-Eyed Susan), along with such groups as the Red Bud trio and the Mountain Rangers (Guy Blakeman, Roland Gaines, and Jerry Behrens). A few performers who actually gained a fair degree of fame passed through the Valley as regulars, but got no more or less special treatment than any others, including Jimmy Dickens, Molly O'Day and Lynn Davis and Ernie Lee. Comedy teams such as Aunt Ida, Uncle Junie and Little Clifford, as well as Shorty Hobbs and Little Eller Long, and later Manuel "Old Joe" Clark, always attracted fans.

Popular individuals who spent significant stints on the *Barn Dance* at one time or another included Fairly Holden, Roy Davidson, Slim Miller, Howard "Nick" Foley, the Farmer Sisters, the Baker Brothers, and former *Ozark Jubilee* comic Pete Stamper. Lair himself won many fans with his sentimental readings and poems. When he took the show on the road to fairs and auditoriums, they were invariably advertised as the *Renfro Valley Gang* or *Renfro Valley Barn Dance*, never as individuals.

Lair and *Renfro Valley* never really adjusted to the demise of network radio, although being adjacent to a major north-south highway (U.S. 25 and Interstate 75) helped the show to survive, along with syndication of the *Sunday Morning Gatherin'*. Some major stations such as WJR Detroit carried the program from the very beginning and in 1958, the *Valley* got their own local WRVK. For *Renfro Valley* to thrive, it needed an infusion of capital that an aging John Lair simply lacked. In August, 1968, he sold the operation to former fiddler and Nashville businessman Hal Smith. However, Smith could not corral the investment cash either and some years later Lair bought it back. Finally, another corporation took over the property, built another barn, made other improvements, and today *Renfro Valley* flourishes, albeit not quite to the degree that it did before television came along and "the valley where time stands still" (except for inflation!) was a place made legendary in the annals of Country music.

IMT

RECOMMENDED ALBUMS:

"The Renfro Valley Gatherin'" (Renfro Valley)(ca. 1965)
"The Renfro Valley Barn Dance" (Renfro Valley)(ca. 1966)
"Renfro Valley" (Renfro Valley)(ca. 1969)
"Down Memory Lane #1" (Renfro Valley)(1990) [Two Renfro Valley Country Store shows from 1951; cassette only]
"Down Memory Lane #2" (Renfro Valley)(1990) [The radio portion of the June 29, 1946, Barn Dance; cassette only].

RENO AND SMILEY

When Formed: 1951

DON RENO
(Banjo, Guitar, Other String Instruments)

Given Name:	**Donald Wesley Reno**
Date of Birth:	**February 21, 1926**
Where Born:	**Spartanburg, South Carolina**
Married:	**1. Chloe (div.)** **2. Betty**
Children:	**Ronnie, Jean, Donna, Dale, Don Wayne**
Date of Death:	**October 16, 1984**

RED SMILEY
(Guitar)

Given Name:	**Arthur Lee Smiley, Jr.**
Date of Birth:	**May 17, 1925**
Where Born:	**Asheville, North Carolina**
Married:	**Gladys**
Children:	**Kenneth (adopted)**
Date of Death:	**January 2, 1972**

Don Reno and Red Smiley together with their band the Tennessee Cut-Ups are usually ranked as one of the four most significant Bluegrass bands from the genre's first generation (the others being Bill Monroe, Flatt & Scruggs, and the Stanley Brothers). As critic Bill Vernon once wrote, the essence of their music resulted from their "ability to add just enough musical garnish to the Reno and Smiley sound to keep it compatible with changing tastes in Country music without ever diminishing its appeal to followers of the more traditional." Although both Reno and Smiley had been born in cities, each spent much of their childhood in rural areas, Don on a farm in Haywood County, North Carolina, and Red in Bushville, North Carolina. Both also spent early musical apprenticeships with the Morris Brothers although not at the same time or place: Don at WSPA Spartanburg and Red at WWNC Asheville and also at WJHL Johnson City, Tennessee. Don worked for a time at WSPA with Arthur Smith and His Crackerjacks before entering the Army, where he had combat experience in Burma with the unit that became famous as Merrill's Marauders. Red served in the Army, too, and sustained a serious wound in Sicily, losing a lung and spending two years in an army hospital. After the war, both men worked in Country music groups in various locales, including Don's spending a year with Bill Monroe in 1948-49 as a replacement for Earl Scruggs.

Don and Red first met in December 1949 at WDBJ Roanoke, where they had both been recruited by fiddler Tommy Magness for his band the Tennessee Buddies. They did not immediately begin performing duets together until the following summer. In March, 1951, as part of the Magness group, they cut four sides for King in Cincinnati that were released on the Federal label. Not long afterward, they left Roanoke and worked as a duet with Toby Stroud's Blue Mountain Boys until that fall when they left to form their own band in South

***Reno and Smiley** and the Tennessee Cut-Ups*

Carolina—the Tennessee Cut-Ups—a name Don had used before. They worked radio programs in Union and Spartanburg, South Carolina, but found it difficult obtaining show dates.

They went to Cincinnati in January, 1952 and cut 16 numbers for King including *I'm Using My Bible for a Roadmap*. However, the going continued to be rough back in Spartanburg and the Tennessee Cut-Ups dissolved before the first record release in April. Ironically, those discs sold relatively well and Syd Nathan periodically recalled the group to cut more sides even though they were not an active performing team until 1955.

During the three year interim, Don Reno worked out of Charlotte with Arthur "Guitar Boogie" Smith. He helped out on Smith's recording of *Feuding Banjos* for MGM in April 1955 as well as on other Smith sessions. Red lived in Asheville, working primarily as a mechanic, but occasionally played a bit of music with Cousin Wilbur. Don and Red had sessions for King in the WBT studios in January 1953 and April 1954, cutting 12 sides each time with the help of musicians like Tommy Faile, Jimmy Lunsford, and Red Rector. In November 1954, they journeyed back to Cincinnati and waxed 20 songs. These were the first recordings to utilize the services of their long-time fiddler Mack Magaha and bass player John Palmer. The early Reno and Smiley repertoire consisted of a mixture of sacred numbers, heart songs, and instrumentals nearly all composed by Don. Highlights included such fare as *I'm the Talk of the Town,* the first recitation in Bluegrass *Someone Will Love Me in Heaven,* snappy songs *Barefoot Nellie* and *Tally Ho,* and original tunes like *Banjo Signal* and *Choking the Strings*.

Don and Red got back together as a performing group in the spring of 1955 and remained together this time for nearly a decade. They became regulars on the *Old Dominion Barn Dance* at WRVA and from December 1956 they had a popular morning daily TV show at WDBJ Roanoke. After a while they dropped the trips to Richmond and did another *Barn Dance* in Danville, Virginia. For seven years, they also did television programs at WSVA Harrisonburg, Virginia. Except for a year in 1957, when they recorded a dozen numbers for Dot, they remained with King through June, 1964, cutting enough material to fill some 20 albums. In addition they made another album in 1961 that John Palmer released some years later on his own Grassound Records. Don's adolescent son Ronnie and lead guitarist Steve Chapman also became regulars with the Tennessee Cut-Ups in the early 60's.

Red Smiley's declining health (diabetes) and Don Reno's desire for greener pastures led to the dissolution of the team at the end of 1964. Red remained in Roanoke with the morning TV show, cutting back on travel except for some periodic trips to the WWVA *Jamboree*. Palmer remained with him and he had first Dave Deese and then Billy Edwards on banjo. Clarence "Tater" Tate eventually settled in as regular fiddler and Gene Burrows and then Udell McPeak played mandolin and rhythm guitar. The band known as the Bluegrass Cut-Ups cut one sacred album for Rimrock, three secular ones for Rural Rhythm and had another released from live shows on the Japanese label Seven Seas. The Bluegrass Cut-Ups also furnished a band for several other Rural Rhythm artists, including Tate, Lee Moore, Jim Eanes, and J.E. Mainer. WDBJ changed owners in March, 1968 and abruptly canceled the TV show. Smiley retired rather than face extensive traveling. His band continued as the Shenandoah Cut-Ups.

Don Reno bounced around a bit before settling into a new partnership with Bill Harrell in December 1966. He cut an album for Dot with a new band and had a brief partnership with Benny Martin that yielded a sacred album on Cabin Creek and another one for Monument. Reno had a Top 50 Country hit with *Soldier's Prayer in Viet Nam*, for Monument, on which he was partnered by Benny Martin. However, the partnership with Harrell endured for a decade and produced numerous recordings on a wide variety of labels, including King, Jalyn, Starday, King Bluegrass, CMH and Monument. They also became favorites on the Bluegrass festival circuit which began to boom just as their partnership blossomed. They acquired a top notch fiddler in 1968 with Buck Ryan and a superb bass player in 1973 with Ed Ferris. Red Smiley came back and worked several dates in 1970 and some in 1971 prior to his death the following January.

In 1973, following the success of *Dueling Banjos*, which was featured in the movie *Deliverance*, Don Reno and Arthur "Guitar Boogie" Smith successfully sued for infringement of their copyrighted *Feudin' Banjos*. When Don and Bill dissolved their partnership in the fall of 1976, Don moved to Lynchburg, Virginia, which became his base for the rest of his life. Younger sons Dale and Don Wayne became key band members in those years as well as Bonny Beverley, a fiddler who had once worked briefly with Red Smiley. Ronnie Reno, who had left Don in 1968 to work in Nashville with various groups, sometimes returned. Don kept as active as his declining health permitted until his death. Ronnie and his younger half-brothers kept the family musical tradition going. IMT

RECOMMENDED ALBUMS:

Reno and Smiley:
"Together Again" (Rome)(1971)
"Live at the Lone Star Bluegrass Festival" (Atteiram)(1977)
"Don Reno & Red Smiley, 1951-1959" (King)(1993)
Don Reno:
"Don Reno on Stage" (Viechi)(1973)
"Live" (Seven Seas Japan)(1974)
"The Don Reno Story" (CMH)(1976)
"30th Anniversary Album" (CMH)(1979)
"Feudin' Again" (CMH)(1979)
"Family & Friends" (Kaleidoscope)(1988)
"Letter Edged in Black" (Wango)(1988)
Don Reno & Bill Harrell:
"Bi-Centennial Bluegrass" (Monument)(1975)
Don Reno & Eddie Adcock:
"Sensational Twin Banjos" (Rebel)(1968 & 1992)

RENO BROTHERS, The

When Formed: 1984
RONNIE RENO
(Vocals, Guitar, Mandolin, Electric Bass)
Date of Birth: September 28, 1947
Where Born: Buffalo, South Carolina
Married: Debbie Smink
DALE RENO
(Vocals, Mandolin)
Date of Birth: February 6, 1961
Where Born: Roanoke, Virginia
DON WAYNE RENO
(Vocals, Banjo, Bass)
Date of Birth: February 8, 1963
Where Born: Roanoke, Virginia

The Reno Brothers are a Country-Bluegrass-picking trio comprised of the three sons of the late banjo great Don Reno.

Ronnie Reno first began to play with his father and Red Smiley's daily *Top o' the Mornin'* show on WDBJ TV in Roanoke, Virginia, about 1956. In those days he picked mandolin and did covers of numbers like the early George Jones favorite *You Gotta Be My Baby,* which he also cut on a King album. When Don and Red went their own ways, Ronnie remained with his dad, working and recording briefly with Reno and Harrell before becoming the bass man with the Osborne Brothers in 1968. During his years with the Osbornes, Ronnie worked on many of their Decca albums. In January 1971, Reno moved into the guitar picker-third voice in the trio position, where he remained until joining the Haggard organization as front man.

During the seven years that Ronnie Reno fronted for Merle Haggard's Strangers, he had

The talented sons of Don Reno, the ***Reno Brothers***

the opportunity to cut some material on MCA Records. However, his first appearance on the charts came in 1983, on EMH Records, when *Homemade Love* became a basement entry, and later in the year, *The Letter* did the same. In addition to music, Ronnie gained a great deal of valued experience in varied aspects of the Country music industry and in 1980 appeared in the Clint Eastwood movie *Bronco Billy*.

Meanwhile, Dale and Don Wayne Reno moved into more or less regular spots with the Tennessee Cut-Ups after Don Reno and Bill Harrell split in 1976. Like Ronnie before them, the brothers became skilled musicians. The older son sometimes returned to help out on shows and do record sessions. After Don's passing in 1984, the brothers drew closer together. Their music included elements of both Country and Bluegrass. They recorded for Step One and their version of *Yonder Comes a Freight Train* made the Top 80 and the following year, they had a basement level entry with *Love Will Never Be the Same*.

In the spring of 1993, the Reno Brothers initiated a regular TV program on the Branson, Missouri-based Americana TV cable network. As of a year after its beginning, it is the only regular TV venue for Bluegrass music available to a national audience. Other name Bluegrass acts appear often as guests and Dan Hayes of the IBMA views the program as a fine vehicle for broadening the Bluegrass audience. IMT

RECOMMENDED ALBUMS:

"For the First Time" (MCA)(1975) [Ronnie only]
"Reno Brothers" (Step One)(1988)

JACK RENO

(Singer, Songwriter, Guitar, Deejay)
Date of Birth: **November 30, 1935**
Where Born: **Bloomfield, Iowa**

Although Jack Reno has spent much of his adult life as a deejay, for a decade from the mid-60's through the mid-70's, he charted 12 singles. It all started when he was 16 and began playing records on KCOG Centerville, Iowa. As a result of his popularity, the station gave him his own program. From there, he moved to WNAX Yankton, South Dakota. He began touring with the WNAX Band.

In 1955, Jack became a regular on the *Ozark Jubilee*. However, just as his career started to take flight, he was drafted into the U.S. Army. Two years later, he was discharged from the service and continued his broadcasting career. He played in KWNT Davenport, Iowa, KCKN Kansas City, Kansas, KLLL Lubbock, Texas, and WXCL Peoria, Illinois.

He had his first taste of success, in 1963, when *Blue* was an airplay hit. In the latter half of 1968, Jack was signed to JAB Records. JAB was a label issued by Tree Publishing and Jack's recordings were produced by Tree's Buddy Killen. *Repeat After Me*, which charted at the end of 1967, reached the Country Top 10 during 1968. It was followed in the spring of 1968 by *How Sweet It Is (To Be in Love with You)*, which made the Top 50. That year, Jack signed with Dot and at the end of the year, he reached the Top 20 with *I Want One*.

He had two hits in 1969 with *I'm a Good Man (in a Bad Frame of Mind)* (Top 40) and *We All Go Crazy* (Top 25). His final chart record, for Dot, came in 1970, when *That's the Way I See It* reached the Top 70. In 1971, he moved to Target Records, and had three chart records in 1971 and 1972, *Hitchin' a Ride* (Top 15, 1971), *Heartaches by the Number* (Top 30, 1972) and *Do You Want to Dance* (Top 40, 1972).

In 1973, he signed with United Artists, where his most successful record for the label was *Let the Four Winds Blow*, which went Top 60, in 1974. By 1978, Jack had moved to Derbytown Records, where he cut the album ***Interstate 7***.

RECOMMENDED ALBUMS:

"Meet Jack Reno" (Atco)(1968)
"I Want One" (Dot)(1968)
"I'm a Good Man in a Bad Frame of Mind" (Dot)(1968)
"Hitchin' a Ride" (Target)(1972)
"Interstate 7" (Derbytown)(1978)

RESTLESS HEART

When Formed: **1984**
Current Members:

John Dittrich	**Drums, Vocals**
Paul Gregg	**Bass Guitar, Vocals**
Greg Jennings	**Guitar, Vocals**

Former Members:

Larry Stewart	**Lead Vocals, Guitar, Keyboards (left 1993)**
Dave Innis	**Keyboards, Guitar, Vocals (left 1993)**

Restless Heart held sway in Country music in the middle to late 80's . Their brand of Country-Pop-Rock found favor with the radio stations, and resulted in a stream of No.1 singles, but the record-buying public and Country music industry have not reinforced this support.

Put together by Tim Dubois and produced by Tim and Scott Hendricks, Restless Heart charted in 1985 with *Let the Heartache Ride*, which reached the Top 25. They followed-up with two Top 10 singles that year, *I Want Everyone to Cry* and *(Back to the) Heartbreak Kid*. They again reached the No.10 slot with their first 1986 single, *Till I Loved You*. Then it was No.1's all the way with *That Rock Won't Roll, I'll Still be Loving You* (also Pop No.33) (both 1986), *Why Does it Have to Be (Wrong or Right)* and *Wheels* (both 1987), *Bluest Eyes in Texas* and *A Tender Lie* (both 1988).

In 1989, their three singles, *Big Dreams in a Small Town, Say What's in Your Heart* and *Fast Movin' Train*, all reached the Top 5, but by the next year, their charm had palled with the radio stations and this was reflected in

Country-Rock-Pop group ***Restless Heart***

their chart placings. *Dancy's Dream* reached the Top 5, but *When Somebody Loves You* only reached the Top 25 and *Long Lost Friend* peaked in the Top 20. In 1991, they had only one single on the charts, the successful *You Can Depend on Me*, which reached the Top 5 and which was on their ***Best of Restless Heart*** album.

The group's success level was not predictable by 1992 and *Familiar Pain* only reached the Top 40, although *When She Cries* peaked in the Top 10 and also crossed to the Pop Top 15. In 1992 lead singer Larry Stewart left the group to commence a solo career and the group soldiered on as a four-piece. However, the following year, Dave Innis also departed and Restless Heart became a trio. The group's 1993 chart records were *Mending Fences* (Top 15), *We Got the Love* (Top 15) and the title track of their 1993 album ***Big Iron Horses*** (Top 75). In 1994, *Baby Needs New Shoes* only reached the Top 70.

Of their six albums, only three have attained Gold status, those being ***Wheels*** (1988), ***Big Dreams in a Small Town*** (1990) and ***Fast Movin' Train*** (1991). Their moment of glory came in 1989 when the Academy of Country Music named them "Vocal Group of the Year." They have received four Grammy nominations and a slew of CMA nominations, without success. Although they have produced some of the most impeccable harmonies on record, they have never risen above being easy listening, and at times, their sound is more Bee Gees than Country.

RECOMMENDED ALBUMS:

"Restless Heart" (RCA Victor)(1985)
"Wheels" (RCA Victor)(1986)
"Big Dreams in a Small Town" (RCA Victor)(1988)
"Fast Movin' Train" (RCA)(1990)
"The Best of Restless Heart" (RCA)(1991)
"Big Iron Horses" (RCA)(1993)

JIMMIE REVARD

(Singer, Bass Fiddle, Clarinet)

Given Name: **James Revard**
Date of Birth: **November 26, 1909**
Where Born: **Pawhuska, Oklahoma**

When Western Swing sprouted up in the mid-30's, in the wake of those bands led by Milton Brown and Bob Wills, one of the more successful combos was that of the Oklahoma Playboys, which was based in San Antonio and led by Jimmie Revard.

Jimmie Revard moved from his native Oklahoma to the San Antonio suburbs with his family at age 9. From about 1928, he worked with small dance bands in various clubs and dance halls in south Texas. In the mid-30's, he began to put a larger swing band together. Adolph Hofner (b. 1916) and Emil "Bash" Hofner (b. 1918)—of Texas German and Czech descent—were early recruits to a group that typically numbered about 8 to 10 members. Other Oklahoma Playboy mainstays included fiddler Ben McKay, pianist Eddie Whitley, and guitarist Curly Williams, all of whom also spent time with Buster Coward's fine group the Tune Wranglers.

Overall, the band did quite well in the San Antonio area, starting at smaller stations KMAC and KONO and moving up to larger ones like KTSA and WOAI. They cut their first Bluebird session at San Antonio in October, 1936 and eventually went on to record more than 75 masters over the next four years. They shared honors with the Tune Wranglers as being the top group in south Texas at the time (Adolph Hofner's Texans later came in for a share of the honors) and second only to Bill Boyd's Cowboy Ramblers among Western Swing groups on the Victor roster.

Early in 1938, Revard decided to move the band to KOAM Pittsburg, Kansas, where they served as staff musicians and played dances, too. Six members of the band went to Kansas, but found things difficult as the economy suffered a decline that year and there were few dance opportunities. With the going tough, the band pretty much dissolved after their record session of October 25, 1938. Adolph Hofner picked up the pieces and continued as The Texans. Jimmie had a final record session in February 1940 with a pick-up band. He had already dropped out of music to become a San Antonio policeman.

Jimmie Revard worked in and later led other local bands in the San Antonio area and remained musically active into his 70's. Meanwhile Western Swing enthusiasts retained an interest in the Oklahoma Playboys and a few of their numbers appeared on various anthology albums. In 1982, Rambler Records of San Francisco devoted an entire album to their Bluebird originals. IMT

RECOMMENDED ALBUM:

"Oh! Swing It" (Rambler)(1982)

ALLEN REYNOLDS

(Songwriter, Guitar, Record Producer, Music Publisher)

Given Name: **Lee Allen Reynolds**
Date of Birth: **August 18, 1938**
Where Born: **North Little Rock, Arkansas**
Married: **(Div.)**
Children: **David, Molly**

Allen Reynolds has made a significant contribution to Country music as an award-winning producer and songwriter.

Born in Arkansas and raised in Memphis, Allen bought his first guitar when he was in high school. He began writing songs while pursuing a degree in English at Rhodes College. During his college years, Allen became friends and wrote songs with Dickey Lee. They became friends with Jack Clement, who was an engineer/producer at Sun Records.

After a stint as a high school English teacher, Reynolds moved to Beaumont, Texas, where Jack Clement had opened a recording studio. Dickey Lee also made the move and he and Allen wrote *I Saw Linda Yesterday*, which became a Top 15 Pop hit for Dickey. According to Cowboy Jack Clement, at this time they all received the sobriquet of "Cowboy."

In 1964, Allen and Dickey returned to Memphis and signed with Screen Gems Publishing Company in Nashville. The writing team made frequent trips to Nashville to record demos. Later they started their own Memphis production/publishing company in partnership with Stan Kessler, who was producing Pop artist Sam the Sham. The company's writing staff included future hit composers Bob McDill and Paul Craft.

To support his family Reynolds worked at a bank. In the evenings he wrote songs and produced artists for several record companies. Writing about his job at the bank, Reynolds composed *Five O'Clock World*, which became a Top 5 Pop single for the Vogues in 1965.

In 1970, Allen left his position as bank branch manager to move to Nashville. Jack Clement hired him to produce and manage his new JMI Records and Allen produced Don Williams' first two albums for the label. When Clement closed the label in 1975, Allen became an independent producer. The following year Reynolds purchased Jack's Tracks Recording Studio and set up operations. One of the first artists he made records with was Crystal Gayle. Of the ten albums he produced for Crystal, five earned Gold awards (500,000 sales) and two passed the one million mark, to be Certified Platinum. Their pairing also produced a string of No.1 singles.

Allen Reynolds wrote many of Crystal's hits, including *Wrong Road Again*, *Somebody Loves You*, *Ready for the Times to Get Better* and *We Must Believe in Magic*. Other artists who have had success with Allen's compositions included Don Williams, who recorded his *We Should Be Together* and *I Recall a Gypsy Woman,* and Johnny Russell, who hit the upper regions of the chart with *Catfish John*. Waylon Jennings had a hit with *Dreaming My Dreams with You*. The song was also covered by the Cowboy Junkies and Collin Raye.

In the mid-80's, Allen began producing Kathy Mattea. The five albums he produced for her generated many hits, including the CMA's "Single" and "Song of the Year" awards for *Eighteen Wheels and a Dozen Roses*. The crossover hit *Where've You Been* was a Grammy winner and Kathy was named "Female Vocalist of the Year" by the CMA.

Allen made Country music history in the 90's producing Garth Brooks, who generated combined sales of six albums exceeding 30 million units. He also contributed several of Garth's hits as a music publisher. Allen's Forerunner Music (co-owned with Jim Rooney and Terrell Ketchum) provided *The Thunder Rolls*, *Unanswered Prayer*, *What She's Doing Now* and *That Summer*.

Allen has also produced albums for Bobby Bare, the Cactus Brothers, George Hamilton IV, the O'Kanes, Dickey Lee, Richard Leigh, Johnny Rodriguez and Randy VanWarmer. He has also co-produced albums for Hall Ketchum (with Jim Rooney) and Emmylou Harris (with Richard Bennett).

Two of Allen's compositions, *Ready for the Times to Get Better*, recorded by Crystal Gayle, and *Five O'Clock World*, recorded by the Vogues, have received more than one million performances, earning him the "Millionair" award from BMI. JIE

RED RHODES

(Steel Guitar, Dobro, Lap Steel, Composer)
Given Name: **Orville J. Rhodes**
Date of Birth: **December 30, 1930**
Where Born: **East Alston, Illinois**

Over the last twenty years, the steel guitar has broken out of being heard only in Country music. Red Rhodes' playing has graced a wider range of music than probably any other steel player.

He began playing Dobro when he was only 5, when his mother taught him A Major tuning. He became proficient on the instrument, and by the time he was 15, he switched to lap steel, which he fitted to a stand. His first paid booking was at the Bill Jones Bar in Illinois along with his step-father, who played rhythm guitar and sang. In 1960, he moved to Los Angeles and became a session musician. One of his early sessions was for Curt Boetcher's ***The Goldbriars*** album in 1963. From 1968, he became a very in-demand sessionman and among his projects that year was Millenium's ***Begin***, Michael Nesmith's ***Wichita Train Whistle Blues*** and the Byrds' ***Sweetheart of the Rodeo***.

For some while, Red led his own band, the Roadrunners, at the Palamino in Los Angeles and his performance was captured on the Happy Feet album ***Live at the Palamino***. He worked on various sessions for the Monkees and this led to him becoming the steel player for Michael Nesmith's First National Band in 1969. He subsequently stayed with Nesmith, when the band became the Second National Band. During 1969, Red appeared on sessions for Bamboo's self-titled album, Bluesman Mike Broomfield's ***It's Not Killing Me***, Brewer & Shipley's ***Weeds***, Danny Cox's ***Birth Announcement*** and rock'n'roll legend Gene Vincent's ***I'm Back and I'm Proud***.

With the arrival of 1970, Red found himself appearing on some of the most prestigious albums of the decade. There were two Michael Nesmith albums that year, ***Magnetic South*** and ***Loose Salute***; John Phillips (ex-Mamas and Papas) recorded ***Wolfking of L.A.***, Tom Rush released his eponymous album and James Taylor recorded ***Sweet Baby James***. In 1971, Red could be heard on another Michael Nesmith album, ***Nevada Fighter***. From 1972, Red found himself in great demand with A & M Records, and appeared on many of their releases. These included the Carpenters' ***A Song for You*** and songwriter Willis Alan Ramsey's self-titled album. His other projects that year included Kim Fowley's ***I'm Bad***, Carole King's ***Rhymes & Reasons***, Michael Nesmith's ***Tantamount to Treason*** and ***And the Hits Keep on Coming***, Seals & Croft's ***Summer Breeze***, B.W. Stevenson's ***Lead Free***, James Taylor's ***One Man Dog*** and Domenic Troiano's self-titled album.

His notable assignments in 1973 were David Accles' ***Five & Dime***, Ian Matthews & Southern Comfort's ***Valley Hi***, Michael Nesmith's ***Pretty Much Your Standard Stash*** and Rock band Redbone's ***Already Here***. That year, Red also appeared on the Anglo-American project, Free Creek's ***Music from Free Creek***. The album also featured Delaney Bramlett, Dr. John, Eric Clapton, Keith Emerson, Linda Ronstadt, Todd Rundgren and Bernie Leadon. This was ample proof that Red was at home in basically a Rock/R & B environment. During 1973, Red released his solo album, ***Velvet Hammer in a Cowboy Band***, on Countryside.

Red played on two interesting British albums during 1974. Bert Jansch had for many years been a stalwart of British Folk music and as part of the group Pentangle had achieved almost revered status. His album ***L.A. Turnaround*** remains one of the finest modern Folk albums and benefits from the Rhodes touch. Red also played on Chilli Willi & the Red Hot Peppers' ***Bongos Over Balham***. This group featured some of the finest of British Blues singers, including Jo Ann Kelly and Carole Grimes, as well as Nick Lowe and former Pentangle member Jacqui McShee. Red's other projects that year included Hoyt Axton's ***Life Machine*** and B.W. Stevenson's ***Calabasas***. Joan Baez's ***Diamonds & Rust***, David Bromberg's ***Midnight on the Water*** and Michael Nesmith's ***The Prison*** were among the albums that Red's steel playing could be heard during 1975. The following year, he was among the session players on Steve Fromholz's ***A Rumor in My Time*** and British rocker Steve Marriott's ***Marriott*** album. Red worked again with Hoyt Axton, this time on the Axton album ***Road-songs*** and he was also reunited with Steve Fromholz on the album ***Frolicking in the Myth***.

Two solo albums of Red's work were released in 1979 and 1980, ***Red Rhodes' Steel Guitar*** on Alshire and ***Fantastic Steel Guitar*** on Exact. In recent years, Red has run his own guitar workshop.

RECOMMENDED ALBUMS:

"Live at The Palamino" (Happy Feet)
"Velvet Hammer in a Cowboy Band" (Countryside)(1973)
[Also available on Steel Guitar Record Club]
"Red Rhodes' Steel Guitar" (Alshire)(1979)
"Fantastic Steel Guitar" (Exact)(1980)
*"Once a Day" (Crown)**
*"Blue Blue Day" (Crown)**
*"Steel Guitar Rag" (Crown)**
"Guitars Go Country" (Crown)
*"Famous Country & Western Favorites Featuring Steel Guitar" (Vogue) [Box set includes *]*

AL RICE

(Singer, Writer, Actor, Producer)
Given Name: Alan Richard Rice
Date of Birth: January, 1904
Where Born: New Jersey
Married: Marian

During the 1920's, Al Rice led the Canary Cottage Players, who toured Canada with the Prince of Wales, who later became King Edward VIII (the Duke of Windsor). Rice became a member of the Maple City Four in 1928 on WLS *National Barn Dance* out of Chicago and he stayed with them until 1953. The quartet was originally organized at La Porte, Indiana in 1926. The other members of the group were Bob Bender (second tenor, 1926-8, d.1928), Fritz Meissner (first tenor, 1926-53), Art James (baritone, 1926-40, d. 1942), Leroy Pat Paterson (bass, 1926-53), Chuck Kerner (second tenor, 1940-53, d. 1953) and Arwin Schweig (bass on only Maple City Four recording after Patterson's death).

Al created the "Professor Dunck" character on the *Barn Dance* during the 30's. In the 30's and 40's, the group appeared on the *Alka-Seltzer National Barn Dance* on NBC. After the Maple City Four left WLS, Al wrote scripts and continuity for the *National Barn Dance*. In 1961, he became the producer of the WGN *Barn Dance*.

The group first recorded for Vocalion in 1928 where they released the single *Tiger Rag*. By 1930, they were on Perfect Records and released *Will the Angels Play their Harps for Me* and *Tell Mother I'm in Heaven with the Angels*. By 1947, the group was on Mercury and released four singles, *Heart of My Heart, Shine on Harvest Moon, I'd Love to Live in England* and *Stephen Foster Medley*. In 1959, Al released the album ***Dr. Lou Klatt and his Musical Interns*** on Coast Records. Among other labels that Al Rice could be found on were Gennett, Silvertone-Silvertime and Conqueror. He appeared in three movies for Republic, *Under Western Stars*, *Get Along Little Dogies* and *Old Barn Dance*.

RECOMMENDED ALBUM:
"Dr. Lou Klatt and his Musical Interns" (Coast)(1959)

BOBBY G. RICE

(Singer, Songwriter, Guitar, Banjo, Bass, Steel Guitar)
Given Name: Robert Gene Rice
Date of Birth: July 11, 1944
Where Born: Boscobel, Wisconsin
Married: Alice Kay Briskey
Children: Tammy, Connie, Michelle

As a popular Country music singer, his fame time came in the 1970's. He has always been in show business and his early career was in rock'n'roll.

At the age of 3, Bobby made his debut with the Rice Family Band. His father, Neil, opened a Country dance hall called the Circle D Ballroom and later had a show on WROC Richland Center, Wisconsin, called *The Ridge Ramblers*, which lasted for seven years. All the family performed and Bobby, by then 11, played piano and bass. The family band broke up in 1964 and Bobby formed a duo with his sister, Lorraine, performing on local TV, that year. Later, Bobby formed his own group, the Bobby Rice Band, which came to Nashville to record some demos. In 1970, Bobby managed to get a recording deal with the Royal American label.

He made his Country chart debut that year with *Sugar Shack (*Top 40) and followed with his Top 40 version of Bruce Channel's *Hey Baby*. In 1971, *Lover Please* reached the Top 50 and *Mountain of Love* got to the Top 20. The following year, Bobby had a Top 40 success with another cover, *Suspicion.* That was the year that Royal American collapsed and Bobby moved on to Metromedia. He began to achieve major success with the Top 3 hit *You Lay So Easy on My Mind.* The song, which he had co-written, was later recorded by Loretta Lynn, Conway Twitty and Narvel Felts. Two other hits followed in 1973: a Top 10 single, You *Give Me You,* and a Top 20 record, *The Whole World's Making Love Again Tonight.*

He changed labels once more and moved to GRT, in 1974. His major successes on the label were *Make it Feel Like Love Again* (Top 30, 1974), two 1975 Top 10 hits, *Write Me a Letter* and *Freda Comes, Freda Goes* and the 1976 Top 40 hit, *Pick Me Up on Your Way Down.* Bobby left GRT in 1977 and went on to Republic, Sunbird, Charta and Door Knob. He had chart records on all of them and the most successful were *The Softest Touch in Town* (Top 30, Republic, 1978) and *Oh Baby Mine (I Get So Lonely) (*Top 50, Republic, 1979). He also chalked up two minor duet hits, with Wayne Kemp, *Red Neck* and *Over Thirty* (Door Knob, 1986), and Perry LaPointe, *Clean Livin' Folk* (Door Knob, 1988).

Bobby was nominated as the CMA "Male Vocalist of the Year," in 1973. Although he was popular in the U.S, he never got the opportunity to go abroad. He continues with his songwriting and although he is not at present signed to a label, he is still singing and touring as much as possible, and when he's not, he's off playing golf and bowling.

JAB

RECOMMENDED ALBUMS:
"Bobby G Rice—Hit After Hit" (Royal America)(1972)
"You Lay So Easy on My Mind" (Metromedia)(1973)
"Instant Rice (The Best of Bobby G Rice)" (GRT)(1976)
"Silk on Silk" (Audiograph)(1982)

Bill Rice refer JERRY FOSTER AND BILL RICE

TONY RICE

(Guitar, Singer, Songwriter)
Given Name: David Anthony Rice
Date of Birth: June 8, 1951
Where Born: Danville, Virginia
Married: 1. (Div.)
2. Pamela

By combining Jazz and classical music with traditional Bluegrass, Tony Rice distinguished himself as one of acoustic music's most innovative guitar players. A master of the acoustic flat-picking guitar style, Tony expanded the Bluegrass genre as a member of several progressive Bluegrass groups, including J.D. Crowe and the New South and the Bluegrass Alliance.

Born in Virginia and raised in California, Tony and his brothers, Larry and Wayne, first played Bluegrass with their father. Tony was influenced in the early days by West Coast musicians like Roland and Clarence White of the Kentucky Colonels. Tony also learned from veteran musicians Herb Pedersen, Ry Cooder and Chris Hillman.

Tony moved to Kentucky in 1970 to play in the Bluegrass Alliance and then with Crowe's New South, whose progressive group included drums and electric instruments. In the early 70's, the group members, in addition to Tony, were Ricky Skaggs on fiddle and mandolin, Jerry Douglas on Dobro, Bobby Slone on bass and Crowe on banjo and vocals.

*Guitar wizard **Tony Rice***

Tony left New South in the mid-70's to join the ground-breaking David Grisman Quintet. The experimental group led by the master mandolinist blended Jazz and classical treatments with Bluegrass instruments.

In 1977, Tony Rice embarked on a solo career with a self-titled debut album. He was hailed as "quite probably the most important living Bluegrass guitarist" by music historian Jack Tottle. Tony also displayed a unique vocal approach that blended Folk and Pop inflections with the traditional singing style. He followed his first solo album with ***Acoustics*** and ***Manzanita***. In addition to his solo recordings, Rice teamed up with Bobby Hicks, Doyle Lawson and Todd Phillips in 1980 to record the first of a series of five albums as the Bluegrass Album Band.

Forming the Tony Rice Unit in 1980, he expanded his music even further to create the Jazz-laced "spacegrass" on the albums ***Mar West*** (1980), ***Still Inside*** (1981) and ***Backwaters*** (1982). Tony continued a successful solo career in the 80's with the albums ***Church Street Blues*** (1983) on Sugar Hill and the Rounder albums ***Cold on the Shoulder*** (1984), ***Native American*** (1985) and ***Me & My Guitar*** (1986). The albums were critically acclaimed as the Bluegrass innovator interpreted the songs of Folk artists Ian Tyson, Joni Mitchell, Phil Ochs and Gordon Lightfoot. Tony teamed up with Norman Blake for two albums and also recorded a reunion album with his brothers as the Rice Brothers. In 1990 and 1991, Tony won the IBMA's "Instrumental Performance of the Year—Guitar" and in 1991, the Tony Rice Unit was named IBMA's "Instrumental Group of the Year."

Tony Rice returned to traditional Bluegrass as a recording artist in 1993 with his Rounder album ***Tony Rice Plays and Sings Bluegrass***. Rice included Bill Monroe standards *On and On* and *Will You Be Loving Another Man*, as well as songs popularized by Flatt & Scruggs, *I'll Stay Around,* and the Stanley Brothers, *How Mountain Girls Can Love*. He also included Bob Dylan's *Girl from the North Country* and the classic *I Wonder Where You Are Tonight*. This album was nominated in the "Best Bluegrass Album" category for the 36th annual Grammy Awards.

RECOMMENDED ALBUMS:

"Acoustics" (Kaleidoscope)
"Tony Rice" (Rounder)(1978)
"Manzanita" (Rounder)(1979)
"Mar West" (Rounder)(1980)
"Still Inside" (Rounder)(1981)
"Backwaters" (Rounder)(1982)
"Church Street Blues" (Sugar Hill)(1983)
"Cold on My Shoulder" (Rounder)(1984)
"Native American" (Rounder)(1985)
"Me & My Guitar" (Rounder)(1986)
"Tony Rice Plays and Sings Bluegrass" (Rounder)(1993)
The Bluegrass Album Band:
"The Bluegrass Album" (Rounder)(1981)
"The Bluegrass Album, Volume II" (Rounder)
"The Bluegrass Album, Volume III, California Connection" (Rounder)
"The Bluegrass Album, Volume IV" (Rounder)
"The Bluegrass Album, Volume V, Sweet Sunny South" (Rounder)(1989)

CHARLIE RICH

(Singer, Songwriter, Piano, Tenor Saxophone)
Date of Birth: **December 14, 1932**
Where Born: **Colt, Arkansas**
Married: **Margaret Ann**
Children: **Renee, Laurie, Allen, Jack**

There must be times in Charlie Rich's life when he asks himself whether he is a star or a forgotten man. With a career spanning over 35 years and with 13 Pop hits and 45 Country hits, Charlie's major successes occurred during 1972 through 1979. Yet, he is a performer that has shown his ability across a wide range of musical styles, and perhaps that in itself has proven the reason for inconsistent showing in the charts. As has often been shown, the media never knows how to handle and program an entertainer and that is definitely what Charlie Rich is.

Charlie was born into a family of missionaries, but while at high school and at the University of Arkansas at Fayetteville, he was influenced by Jazz and Blues, in particular the works of Stan Kenton and Oscar Peterson. He had lessons on both piano and tenor saxophone and studied musical theory at university, and joined the university marching band. He enlisted in the U.S. Air Force in 1953. While posted to Enid, Oklahoma, he was piano player and skat singer in one of his early groups. He formed the Velvetones, playing Jazz and Blues. They had their own weekly TV program, and featured Charlie's fiancée Margaret Ann on lead vocals.

On leaving the service, in 1956, Charlie moved to West Memphis, Arkansas, to work on his father's cotton farm. In his spare time, he played Jazz and non-Jazz bookings and did sessions for Judd Records, owned by Judd Phillips, brother of Sam Phillips. About this time, he started to write his own material and did arrangements for saxophone player/producer Bill Justis, who had discovered Charlie at the Sharecropper Club. One night while sitting in with Justis' band, he was invited to go to Memphis to put down some demo recordings. However, he was then told that he was too jazzy, and was handed a pile of Jerry Lee Lewis records and told to come back when he "got that bad." In 1958, Charlie started to play some sessions for Sun, including ones for Warren Smith, Ray Smith and Billy Lee Riley. His first single for Phillips International, in 1958, was *Whirlwind/ Philadelphia.* He also released an instrumental, on Sun, in 1959 as "Bobby Sheridan." It was his third Phillips release, *Lonely Weekends*, in 1960, that did the trick. It reached the Top 30 on the Pop chart, however, all of his seven follow-up singles on the label failed to register. Some of his releases on Phillips were produced by Billy Sherrill.

For a while, he toured with a road band, but gave it up in favor of a smaller unit. In 1964, he moved to RCA's Groove label, where Bill Justis had recently transferred, and *Big Boss Man* became an underground hit for Charlie. After this single, Chet Atkins took over the production reins, but the first album he produced, ***That's Rich***,was not well received and showed direction confusion. This was not a happy time for Charlie, and it was further exacerbated by Groove folding.

Shelby Singleton, who would later own Sun Records, was at this time at Smash Records and he encouraged Charlie to direct himself toward Country and Rock. At Smash, he was produced by Jerry Kennedy and once again Charlie found himself in the Pop charts with *Mohair Sam*, which reached the Top 3, in 1965. He moved to the Memphis-based Hi Records, where he recorded several Country weepies without success.

It was his move to Epic Records in 1967 that proved a turning point. Here he was reunited with Billy Sherrill. Epic Records was undertaking a contemporary Country push and Sherrill was the main producer. Epic had problems in selling Charlie's music, but gradually, under Sherrill's direction, Charlie broke into the Country charts. He chalked up two Top 50 Country hits in 1970 with *Set Me Free* and *Raggedy Ann*. He followed up with *Life's Little Ups and Downs* which also reached the Top 50. Then Sun released a track previously on Phillips, *Who Will the Next Fool Be*, which went Top 70. This was to be a pattern in Charlie's career; his old labels releasing material to capitalize on his new-found fortune. The other successes in 1970 were *July 12, 1939*, which went Top 50 Country and Top 90 Pop, and *Nice'N' Easy*, a Top 40 Country success. His next medium success occurred at the end of 1971, when *Part of Your Life* reached the Top 40.

Then in 1972, he had his first Top 10 Country hit with *I Take It on Home*. It was

1973 that elevated Charlie into international stardom. It started with *Behind Closed Doors*, which went to No.1 Country and Top 15 on the Pop list, being Certified Gold. In addition, it reached No.16 on the U.K. Pop chart. He followed this with a track recorded for RCA, *Tomorrow Night*, which made the Country Top 30. He closed out the year with *The Most Beautiful Girl*, which topped both the Pop and Country charts and was Certified Gold. It went to No.2 in the U.K., actually pre-dating *Behind Closed Doors*. (Both the U.K. chart entries were in 1974). Charlie received a 1973 Grammy for *Behind Closed Doors*, as "Best Country Vocal Performance, Male." That year he also was named the CMA's and the ACM's "Male Vocalist of the Year" and *Behind Closed Doors* was named CMA's "Single of the Year" and "Album of the Year" and ACM's "Song of the Year," "Single Record of the Year" and "Album of the Year." In addition, the album ***Behind Closed Doors*** was also Certified Gold.

If anything, 1974 was even more successful a year. *There Won't Be Anymore* had entered the Country charts at the end of 1973 and became a No.1 Country hit and a Top 20 Pop success. He then had a phenomenal run with *A Very Special Love Song* (No.1 Country/Top 15 Pop), *I Don't See Me in Your Eyes Anymore* (an RCA single, No.1 Country/Top 50 Pop), *A Field of Yellow Dreams* (written by Charlie's wife, Margaret Ann, a very gifted songwriter), a Mercury single (Top 25 Country), *I Love My Friend* (No.1 Country/Top 25 Pop), *She Called Me Baby* (an RCA single, No.1 Country/Top 50 Pop) and *Something Just Came Over Me* (a Mercury single, No.71). In all, he spent 8 weeks at No.1 during the year. The awards kept flowing in. He was named by *Billboard* as their "Pop Singles Male Vocalist," *There Won't Be Anymore* was named "Top Country Single" and ***Behind Closed Doors*** was named "Country Album." The CMA voted him their "Entertainer of the Year" and ***A Very Special Love Song*** won out as "Album of the Year." At the American Music Awards, he was named "Favorite Male Vocalist—Country Category" and ***Behind Closed Doors*** was voted "Favorite Album-Pop Category" and *The Most Beautiful Girl* received the accolade as "Favorite Single—Country Category." During the year, two albums were Certified Gold, namely ***Very Special Love Songs*** and ***There Won't Be Anymore***.

In 1975, Charlie's successes were *My Elusive Dreams* (Top 3 Country/Top 50 Pop), *It's All Over Now* (RCA, Top 25 Country), *Every Time You Touch Me (I Get High)* (Top 3 Country/Top 20 Pop), *Now Everybody Knows* (RCA, Top 60) and *Since I Fell for You* (Top 10 Country/Top 80 Pop). The last named was his last Pop chart success. In the U.K., Charlie had a further Top 20 with *We Love Each Other*. Through 1976 and the beginning of 1977, Charlie's singles only reached the Top 30, and they were *America, the Beautiful* (1976), *Road Song* and *My Mountain Dew*. Then *Easy Look* reached the Top 15 and suddenly, he was back at No.1 with *Rollin' with the Flow*.

Around this time, Charlie wrote the score for the movie *Benji* and its sequel, *For the Love of Benji*. During the end of 1977, he moved to United Artists Records and struck with *Puttin' in Overtime at Home* and *Beautiful Woman*, which both went Top 10. Then *I Still Believe in Love* only reached the Top 50. He closed out the year with another No.1, *On My Knees*, on which he was joined by Janie Fricke. This was followed up by *I'll Wake You Up When I Go Home*, which came from the movie *Every Which Way But Loose*, and this reached the Top 3.

Between 1979 and 1980, he failed to hit the heady heights and the only major hits were *I Lost My Head* (Top 30), *Spanish Eyes* (Top 20) (both 1979) and *You're Gonna Love Yourself in the Morning* (Top 25, 1980). In 1980, Charlie moved to Elektra, and he scored that year with *A Man Just Don't Know What a Woman Goes Through*, which peaked in the Top 15, and then the following year, he had a Top 30 hit with *Are We Dreamin' the Same Dream*.

In 1990, he came out of semi-retirement following the success of the Notting Hillbillies with Charlie's *Feel Like Goin' Home*. In addition, that year, Ricky Van Shelton had a major hit with Margaret Ann Rich's song *Life's Little Ups and Downs*, which has also been recorded by Shelby Lynne.

Charlie is known as "The Silver Fox" and like a fox, he comes a-sneakin' up on you. This he did again in 1992, when he signed with Sire Records and released the album ***Pictures and Paintings***, on their Blue Horizon Heritage label. Apart from his version of the Eddy Arnold and Mickey Gilley hit *You Don't Know Me*, a bossa nova version of his own hit *Every Time You Touch Me (I Get High)*, and a couple of Margaret Ann songs, this album was a collage of all of Charlie's influences, including Blues and Jazz.

RECOMMENDED ALBUMS:

"20 Golden Hits" (Sun)(1970)
"Behind Closed Doors" (Epic)(1973)
"Very Special Love Songs" (Epic)(1974)
"There Won't Be Anymore" (RCA Victor)(1974) [Re-pack of tracks recorded on Groove]
"Greatest Hits—Charlie Rich" (RCA Victor)(1975)
"The Greatest Hits of Charlie Rich" (Epic)(1976)
"Take Me" (Epic)(1977)
"She Called Me Baby" (RCA Victor)(1977)
"I Still Believe in Love" (United Artists)(1978)
"The Fool Strikes Again" (United Artists)(1979)
"Original Hits and Midnight Demos" (double)(Charly UK)(1985)
"Pictures and Paintings" (Blue Horizon Heritage)(1992)

DON RICH

(Fiddle, Guitar, Singer, Songwriter)

Given Name:	**Donald Ulrich**
Date of Birth:	**August 15, 1941**
Where Born:	**Olympia, Washington**
Married:	**Marline**
Children:	**Vance Owen, Victor William (Vic)**
Date of Death:	**July 17, 1974**

For 14 years, Don Rich played fiddle and guitar in the Buckaroos, becoming leader of the band. His boss, Buck Owens, regarded "Dangerous" Don (so named because he wouldn't hurt a fly) as his "right-hand man." He began his interest in Country music at age three-and-a-half, when he started singing and playing guitar. By the time he was 5, he was appearing on the radio and a year later, he started violin lessons. He began appearing with dance bands on local radio and by the time he was age 8 he had started to learn lead guitar. When age 11, Don won a two-week trip to Hollywood in a talent contest. At age 15, he was playing lead guitar with Tex Mitchell and then a year later, he joined Buck Owens on a part-time basis.

He began playing fiddle for Owens on a TV show in Tacoma, Washington. For two years he worked at Steve's Gay 90's in Tacoma, while majoring in music at college. He was intent on becoming a music teacher, but after eighteen months moved to Califonia, in 1960, and began working for Owens full-time, as tenor singer, fiddler and lead guitarist.

Don had several songs recorded by Owens, of which the most successful was *Before You Go*, which stayed at the No.1 spot of the Country chart for 6 weeks in 1965. The following year, he penned another No.1 for Buck, *Waiting in Your Welfare Line*. Don made his only solo album, ***That Fiddlin' Man***, in 1971, on which he was backed by the Buckaroos. That same year, he teamed up with Buck's son, Buddy Alan, for the superb ***Cowboy Convention*** album. The title track had entered the Country singles chart the preceding November, and became a Top 20 hit. In 1971, they followed up with the Top 60 single *I'm on the Road to Memphis*.

During Don's time with the Buckaroos, they won several prestigious awards. The ACM named them "Touring Band of the Year" in 1965 through 1968, the CMA voted them "Instrumental Group of the Year" for 1967 and 1968 and *Music City News* named them "Band of the Year" in 1967 through 1970 and 1974. Don himself was named CMA's "Musician of the Year" in 1974.

As well as playing on over 50 Buck Owens chart singles, Don also appeared on 7 chart records of the Buckaroos. These were the instrumentals *Buckaroo*, which was a No.1 and a Top 60 Pop hit in 1965, and two years later, a Top 70 single, *Chicken Pickin'*. During 1968, with Don at the helm, the Buckaroos had *I'm Coming Home to Stay* (Top 40) and *I'm Goin' Back Home Where I Belong*. In 1969, they charted with *Anywhere USA* (Top 70) and *Nobody But You* (Top 50). The following year, Don and the Buckaroos took Robbie Robertson's *The Night They Drove Old Dixie Down* into the Top 75.

When Don Rich was killed in a motorcycle accident, in July 1974, Country music lost one of its most talented sidemen (Buck Owens was shattered by it), and in all probability, had he lived, Don would have gone on to become a star in his own right.

RECOMMENDED ALBUMS:

"Buck Owens & his Buckaroos in Japan (Recorded at Kosei Nenkin Hall, Tokyo)" (Capitol)(1967)
"America's Most Wanted Band" (Capitol)(1967) [As the Buckaroos]
"Buck Owens' Buckaroos Strike Again" (Capitol)(1967) [As the Buckaroos]
"Meanwhile Back at the Ranch" (Capitol)(1968) [As the Buckaroos]
"Anywhere USA" (Capitol)(1969) [As the Buckaroos]
"Roll Your Own with Buck Owens' Buckaroos" (Capitol)(1969) [As the Buckaroos]
"Rompin' & Stompin'" (Capitol)(1970) [As the Buckaroos]
"Boot Hill" (Capitol)(1970) [As the Buckaroos]
"The Buckaroos Play the Hits" (Capitol)(1971) [As the Buckaroos]
"That Fiddlin' Man" (Capitol)(1971) [As Don Rich & the Buckaroos]
"Cowboy Convention" (Capitol)(1971) [Buddy Alan & Don Rich]

JIMMIE RIDDLE

(Singer, Harmonica, Piano, Guitar, Bass, Accordion)

Given Name:	**James Riddle**
Date of Birth:	**September 3, 1918**
Where Born:	**Dyersburg, Tennessee**
Married:	**Susie Guster**
Children:	**Susan, Steve**
Date of Death:	**December 10, 1982**

Country music fans remember Jimmie Riddle as one of the genre's great harmonica players. Although he spent most of his career as a sideman with Roy Acuff's Smoky Mountain Boys he had several other accomplishments to his credit. He made some records on his own, did some notable session work at various times, and appeared—often with Jackie Phelps—as a regular on *Hee Haw* for several years, which gave him an audience to display his talent for "eeephin'" (hiccuping noise made with one's throat and mouth to a musical tune).

A native of West Tennessee, Riddle grew up in Memphis playing a harmonica which his granddad had given him at the age of 4. He gave his first public performance as a first grader. As Riddle grew older he learned other instruments too, including piano, accordion and guitar. From his mid-teens, he worked with various musical groups including the Pea Ridge Ramblers at WMC radio. His most notable early work was at WREC with a Western Swing Group, the Swift Jewel Cowboys, with whom he recorded in 1939, being featured on three harmonica tunes. The recordings appeared primarily on the Vocalion label. Later that year he moved to Houston, where he worked in a band alternately known as the Crustens Ranch Gang and the Texans. When the war came along he remained with this group but also took a defense-related job in the shipyard. Roy Acuff offered him a position with the Smoky Mountain Boys in March, 1943, but he did not join them until September.

After completing the Republic film *Sing Neighbor Sing* in April 1944, Jimmie Riddle entered the Army. He spent the early part of his service career guarding prisoners and later in Special Services entertaining other soldiers. He rejoined the Acuff band in July 1946 and maintained this job for the rest of his life except for a few months in 1973-1974. In addition to tours and *Opry* appearances with Roy, Jimmie appeared in six of his films and cut a single for Decca in the late 40's. He also gained a reputation as the band's intellectual. Riddle also earned something of a reputation as a big game hunter in the early 50's by bagging a bear when some of the Smoky Mountain Boys went on a hunt. A feature article on their adventure appeared in a national hunting magazine.

When Roy became less active in the later years, Jimmie did some session work with other artists, cut harmonica albums for Briar and Cumberland, and appeared on *Hee Haw* with Jackie Phelps. They engaged in the old folk-talent of "eeephin'," which Riddle had learned as a child from his uncle, Ralph. He also made a single disc for Decca, *Wildwood Eeeph/Yokety Eeeph*. As his health declined in his last year Riddle became less active, but his long career of nearly four decades as a Smoky Mountain Boy—along with Pete "Brother Oswald" Kirby and Howdy Forrester—made him one of the few sidemen to achieve a legendary status along with Roy Acuff himself. IMT

RECOMMENDED ALBUMS:

"Country Harmonica" (Cumberland)(1964)
"Country Music Cannonball with the Smoky Mountain Boys" (Starday)(1964)
"Let's Go" (Briar)(1967)
Swift Jewel Cowboys:
"Chuck Wagon Swing" (String)((1980)

RIDERS IN THE SKY

When Formed:	**1977**
Members:	
Ranger Doug	**Lead & Baritone Vocals, Guitar, Yodeler**
Woody Paul	**Lead & Tenor Vocals, Fiddle, Guitar, Accordion, Harmonica, Mandolin**
Too Slim	**Melody Vocals, Stand-up Bass, Guitar, Accordion**

The phrase "It's the Cowboy Way" is associated with Riders in the Sky. In an attempt to re-create the cowboy style epitomized in the B Westerns, this trio has created a style all its own, musically true to the original, but evolved for a contemporary audience, that just fights shy of being a pastiche.

Ranger Doug, "Idol of American Youth," is the mouthpiece of the group, the singer of romantic Western ballads and a yodeler extraordinaire. Replete in big white hat and wearing the biggest grin imaginable, Doug was once known as Douglas B. Green, musician and Country music historian. Coming from Michigan, he was at one time a member of Bill Monroe's Blue Grass Boys and editor of the *Country Music Foundation Press* and the *Journal of Country Music*. He headed up the Oral History Project at the Country Music Foundation. He also answers to "Sgt. Dudley, RCMP" and "Trader Doug."

Woody Paul, better known as King of the Cowboy Fiddlers, was once simply known as Dr. Paul Chrisman and then the rot set in. Gaining his Ph.D. in theoretical plasma physics from Massachusetts Institute of Technology, he once worked at the Atomic Energy Commission in Oak Ridge, Tennessee. He became fiddle player for Loggins and Messina, before donning the white hat and fringed shirt. He also responds to being called "Drywall Paul."

Too Slim follows in the grand tradition of Gabby Hayes and Smiley Burnette, as one of the world's perfect side-kicks. Born Fred LaBour, he also portrays "Too Jaws" (he's the voice of the world-famous talking horse skull), "Side Meat" (the old camp cook) and "Freddy La" (the Surfin' Cowboy). He is an established songwriter, who was formerly a member of Dickey Lee's band. He is also an adept "varmint" dancer, specializing in the jack rabbit, armadillo and most especially, the draped sloth!

They started out playing once a week at the Wind in the Willows, a now defunct Bluegrass club in Nashville. They quickly achieved near legendary status in Country music and wound up hosting TNN's *Tumbleweed Theater*, which was aired daily from 1983 through 1986. They signed to Rounder and released five albums during the early and mid-80's, including the 1984 ***Live*** album. Their debut on film occurred in 1985, when they appeared in the Patsy Cline biopic *Sweet Dreams* with Jessica Lange. That year, they also appeared in the CBS Movie of the Week *Wild Horses* with Kenny Rogers. Their album ***Saddle Pals*** was voted "Independent Children's Album of the Year." However, it was their signing to MCA in 1987 that marked the establishment of the trio on the international scene. That year, they emceed the Wembley Festival in England and made a lot of friends.

They released their debut album for MCA, ***The Cowboy Way***, the recording of which was attended by their friends, who enjoyed an evening of tacos, free beer and of course great fun and yes, cardboard cactus and an electric campfire! The album began, as do all their shows, with the greeting "Mighty fine and a great big Western 'Howdy,' all you buckaroos and buckarettes." The album was the first Western album to be recorded on MCA in 20 years and the first to be recorded digitally. Like its successor, ***Riders Radio Theater***, it was a mixture of existing Western material and original songs. This 1988 album was their way of creating a radio program and featured *Trail Traffic Report* and *Triple X Stock Report*. It only had two external songs. That year, they began the popular weekend radio show *Riders Radio Theater* on National Public Radio, which is still running.

In 1989, they continued this theme with ***Riders Go Commercial***. Their final album for MCA was in 1990, entitled ***Horse Opera***. They moved over to Columbia records in 1991 and released ***Harmony Ranch***. This coincided with a new CBS-TV series, *Riders in the Sky*, on Saturday mornings, which was aired from 1991 through 1992. *Harmony Ranch* was a children's album, which was also accessible to adults. In 1992, they came up with ***Merry Christmas from Harmony Ranch***.

This emphasizes the fact that the music and humor of Riders in the Sky crosses age barriers and to a large degree also international barriers, as, unlike other humor-based groups, their style, which hangs on the well-loved B movies, is globally acceptable.

Ranger Doug was the recipient of two Wrangler Awards issued by the Cowboy Hall of Fame for Western songs. In 1991 he received it for the 1990 song *The Line Rider* and in 1993 for the 1992 song *The First Cowboy Song*, which he wrote with Gary McMann.

RECOMMENDED ALBUMS:
"Three on the Trail" (Rounder)(1979)
"Cowboy Jubilee" (Rounder)(1981)
"Prairie Serenade" (Rounder)(1982)
"Weeds and Water" (Rounder)(1983)
"Live" (Rounder)(1984)
"Saddle Pals" (Rounder)(1985)
"New Trails" (Rounder)(1986)
"The Cowboy Way" (MCA)(1987)
"Riders Radio Theater" (MCA)(1988)
"Riders Go Commercial" (MCA)(1989)
"Horse Opera" (MCA)(1990)
"Harmony Ranch" (Columbia)(1991)
"Merry Christmas from Harmony Ranch" (Columbia)(1992)

Riders of the Purple Sage refer FOY WILLING

Ranger Doug, Too Slim and Woody Paul, ***Riders in the Sky***

JEANNIE C. RILEY

(Singer, Songwriter, Guitar)

Given Name:	**Jeanne Carolyn Stephenson**
Date of Birth:	**October 19, 1945**
Where Born:	**Anson, Texas**
Married:	**Mitchell ("Mickey") Riley**
Children:	**Kim Michelle**

Jeannie C. Riley shot to sudden fame in 1968 on the strength of the super-hit *Harper Valley P.T.A.*

A native of Anson in Jones County, Texas, Jeannie grew up in a working class family listening to, singing, and enjoying Country music. She was a majorette in her high school band and learned shorthand so that she could copy song lyrics rapidly. She appeared on her uncle's jamboree show in Anson, but did not have a lot of experience in the music business. After high school, Jeannie married Mickey Riley and went to Nashville to pursue a musical career.

Jeannie worked as a secretary at Passkey Music and made some demos. She initially recorded for Little Darlin' Records as Jean Riley and released the single *What About Them/You Write the Music*. However, nothing much happened, and then like a fairy story, she was offered Tom T. Hall's *Harper Valley P.T.A.* to record, after Jeannie's then manager, Paul Perry, had approached Shelby Singleton. The song has lyrics about a brash young widow standing up to small-town hypocrites and had already been recorded by Singleton's ex-wife, Margie Singleton. Singleton launched Plantation Records and Jeannie with her single of the song. Her version went to No.1 on the Country chart a month after release, staying at the top for three weeks. It also crossed over to No.1 on the Pop chart, and became a multi-million seller around the world.

At the behest of Shelby Singleton, Jeannie somewhat reluctantly tried to fit her public image to match the girl in the song. In 1968, Jeannie received a Grammy Award for "Best Country Vocal Performance, Female." Just as Jeannie was about to go onstage to receive her award, Singleton cut off Jeannie's full-length skirt to mini length, much to her chagrin. A decade later, *Harper Valley P.T.A.* inspired a feature-length motion picture, which cast glamorous Barbara Eden in the role of the sexy widow Johnson and led to a spin-off TV series. In 1968, Jeannie made her debut on the *Grand Ole Opry*.

Jeannie followed up with *The Girl Most Likely*, in which she was cast in a similar mold to *Harper Valley P.T.A.* This release went Top 10 on the Country chart and Top 60 on the Pop chart. The album of *Harper Valley P.T.A.* went Gold and Jeannie was the first recipient of a Gold Cartridge (8-Track).

Her third and fourth major hits, *There Never Was a Time* (1969) and *Country Girl* (1970), were more indicative of Jeannie's real style. She followed up with *Oh, Singer* and *Good Enough to Be Your Wife* and both made the Top 10 in 1971. Jeannie's last success for Plantation was *After Roses and Thorns*, which went Top 20 in 1971. She moved over to MGM Records later in 1971 and had seven more charted singles over the next two years, of which *Give Myself a Party* and *Good Morning Country Rain* (both 1972) were her most successful. She transferred to Mercury, in 1974, without success.

Although commercially successful, Jeannie was not especially happy with either herself or her career. She went through a divorce, and had some other personal problems. Jeannie subsequently rejected her swinging, mini-skirted, go-go boots image, had a conversion experience, and remarried Mickey Riley in 1975. Her mid-70's touring band, the Red River Symphony, included sidemen with Bluegrass experience such as fiddler Mike Hartgrove and banjoist Ray Edwards, and presented an excellent stage show although their only two numbers to make the charts in that era, *Plain Vanilla* and *The Best I've Ever Had*, both on Warner Brothers, only reached the basement of the Country chart.

Country and Gospel star ***Jeannie C. Riley***

In 1975, Jeannie recorded Gospel for her own label, God's Country. In 1979, she cut another Gospel album, ***Wings to Fly***, for Cross Country Records and then in 1981, she released the Gospel album ***From Harper Valley to the Mountain Top*** on MCA/Songbird. Her rendition of the song of the same name can be a moving experience as can the swinging Gospel-flavored *Lemonade* (both her own compositions). Both the last two albums were nominated for a Dove Award. The MCA/Songbird album was the same title as her inspirational autobiography, which had been published in 1981. She went on to release Country albums on Sapphire Records (***Total Woman***) in 1984 and MCA/Dot (***Jeannie C. Riley***) in 1986.

Even without hit records, Jeannie continued to work regularly on the road. She had one of her most active seasons in 1987, and in 1993 continued to present a dynamic stage show that even included a song or two with her grandchild. In 1992 and 1993, Jeannie has recorded on the Playback label, cutting a variety of songs ranging from Bill Monroe's *Blue Moon of Kentucky* to Huey "Piano" Smith's *Rockin' Pneumonia and the Boogie Woogie Flu*. She is currently working on a new Gospel album. IMT

RECOMMENDED ALBUMS:

"Harper Valley P.T.A." (Plantation)(1968)
"The Songs of Jeannie C. Riley" (Capitol)(1969)
"Greatest Hits" (Plantation)(1971)
"Greatest Hits, Vol. 2" (Plantation)(1981)
"Give Myself a Party" (MGM) (1972)
"Down to Earth" (MGM)(1973)
"Just Jeannie" (MGM)(1974)
"Wings to Fly" (Heartwarming and Cross Country)(1979)
"From Harper Valley to the Mountain Top" (MCA/Songbird)(1981)
"Jeannie C. Riley" (MCA/Dot)(1986)
"Here's Jeannie C." (Playback)(1992)

JIM RINGER

(Singer, Songwriter, Guitar)

Given Name: James Westley Ringer
Date of Birth: February 29, 1936
Where Born: Yell County, Arkansas
Married: 1. Ann (div.)
2. Mary McCaslin (div.)
Children: Jeffrey, Rebecca, Gregory, Kimberley
Date of Death: March 17, 1992

Jim Ringer was a talented singer/songwriter who, if the fates had been kind, should have been a major star, but like performers such as Richard Dobson, he remained a cult figure on the performing circuit. In tandem with his wife, singer/songwriter Mary McCaslin, he toured the U.S. and Canada. He also produced meaningful songs and worthy product and still never received the acclaim he deserved.

Waylon Jennings once said that to be a good Country writer, "you have to be over 40, been divorced at least once, been drunk at least once and been in prison at least once." What he meant was that you had to have lived life, and if that is the truth, then Jim Ringer epitomized the perfect songwriter and performer. He was born in the Ozark Mountains and when he was 11, his family moved to California's Central Valley to escape the Dust Bowl. All of his family, with the exception of his mother, played musical instruments. At 18, he found himself in prison and stayed there for the next three years. He worked in construction and logging camps until 1969, hopping freight trains along the way, through Oregon and California.

In 1969, he started his professional music career. He got involved with the Berkeley hippie crowd and in 1971 toured the country with a dozen other musicians in a 1948 Chevy school bus, as the Portable Folk Festival. On and off during the end of 1971 and into 1972, he played with Kenny Hall and the Sweet's Mill String Band and they cut an album for Bay Records in 1972. That same year, he cut his first solo album for Folk-Legacy Records, entitled ***Waitin' for the Hard Times to Go***. In 1993, the Nashville Bluegrass Band would release this Ringer original title song as a single. During 1972, Jim met Mary McCaslin at Sweet's Mill Folk music camp-out and formed a double act that still incorporated solo performances. Jim recorded his first album, ***Good to Get Home***, for Philo in 1973 and it was released the following year. He released two further albums for the label, ***Any Old Wind That Blows*** (1975) and ***Tramps and Hawks*** (1976). Jim and Mary married in 1978, a year in which they recorded ***The Bramble and the Rose***, a duet album for Philo.

Jim moved to Flying Fish and in 1981 released the excellent album ***Endangered Species***. Featured on the album is the memorable self-penned song *Whiskey and*

Cocaine. Among the "good friends and neighbors" on the album were the Dillards, the Burrito Brothers and the Hot Band.

In 1989, Jim and Mary decided to separate. Jim died on St. Patrick's Day, 1992. He maintained that he wasn't a good singer or guitar player, considering that he played as well at 50 as he did when he was 10. However, he could sing and could surprise with his playing, and perhaps one day someone will discover the talent that was Jim Ringer.

RECOMMENDED ALBUMS:

"Waiting for the Hard Times" (Folk-Legacy)(1972)
"Good to Get Home" (Philo/Rounder)(1974)
"Any Old Wind That Blows" (Philo/Rounder)(1975)
"Tramps and Hawkers" (Philo/Rounder)(1976)
"The Bramble and the Rose" (Philo/Rounder)(1978) [With Mary McCaslin]
"Endangered Species" (Flying Fish)(1981)

TEX RITTER

(Singer, Guitar, Actor)

Given Name: Maurice Woodward Ritter
Date of Birth: January 12, 1907
Where Born: Murvaul, Texas
Married: Dorothy Fay Southworth
Children: Thomas Matthew, Jonathan Southworth (John Ritter)
Date of Death: January 2, 1974

Tex Ritter began his musical career in New York, but attained most of his fame as a Hollywood singing cowboy in the decade from 1936. When his film work as an actor fell sharply in the mid-40's, he continued to pursue a singing career with success. After serving two years as President of the Country Music Association, Tex moved to Nashville and spent the last years of his life as a *Grand Ole Opry* star. Throughout his labors as a musician, Ritter helped to give Country and Western sounds a degree of dignity that they had not always possessed.

Singing cowboy ***Tex Ritter***

Born in rural East Texas, the Ritters moved to Beaumont, where youngest son Maurice finished high school, graduating at the head of his class. He then went to the University of Texas as a pre-law student. At the Austin institution, however, his interests turned toward acting, folklore, and music and in 1928 he left Texas for New York with a theater company. He found the route to stardom difficult and after a year or two he returned to college, this time at Northwestern, but again show business beckoned and he never returned to law school. For the next six years, Ritter alternated between radio and stage. His role in the Broadway play *Green Grow the Lilacs* as a singer of cowboy songs drew considerable attention while programs on the airwaves such as *Tex Ritter's Campfire* and *Cowboy Tom's Roundup* won him a following. Art Satherly of the American Record Corporation made four cuts of his deep-voiced, rough but authentic singing on March 15, 1933, including his classic rendition of *Rye Whiskey*. Two years later, Tex began doing sessions for the newly opened Decca label, a company for which he would make 29 sides over the next four years.

In the meantime, Hollywood producer Edward Finney, looking for a singing cowboy to emulate the success of Gene Autry, selected Ritter and brought him to California to star in his new B Western, *Song of the Gringo*, in November 1936 for Grand National Pictures. Unfortunately, the company had financial problems and went bankrupt after a dozen films although the Ritter oaters always turned a profit. Probably his most memorable early effort was *Trouble in Texas*, which co-starred the not yet (but soon to be) international sex symbol Rita Hayworth.

In 1938, Finney moved to Monogram for his next 20 films, of which *Take Me Back to Oklahoma* with Bob Wills ranks as among the best. Tex then became something of a journeyman doing 8 pictures at Columbia with Wild Bill Elliott and 11 at Universal (8 of them with Johnny Mack Brown). Many critics consider his three starring roles at Universal in 1944 as his strongest. Ritter closed out his motion picture series work at PRC with Dave O'Brien and Guy Wilkerson in *The Texas Rangers*. While the Tex Ritter pictures (see Movie Section) had neither the popularity nor the quality of those of Roy Rogers and Gene Autry, they did do well and made his name a household word. After his acting career ended, his distinctive voice contributed much to the soundtracks of such major westerns as *High Noon* (1952) and *Wichita* (1955).

While Tex's acting career went into eclipse after 1945, his recording work continued without interruption. In 1942, he signed with the new Capitol label and remained with that firm for the rest of his life, doing at least one session yearly for thirty-two years. He had some fairly big numbers in the 40's. In 1944, Tex Ritter and His Texans scored a No.1 with *I'm Wasting My Tears on You*, which stayed at the top for 6 weeks and crossed to the Pop chart Top 15. The flip-side, *There's a New Moon Over My Shoulder*, also reached the Top 3 and crossed to the Pop Top 25. In 1945, Tex had another Top 3 single with *Jealous Heart* and followed up with *You Two-Timed Me Once Too Often*, which stayed at No.1 for 11 weeks. During 1946, Tex's hits were *You Will Have to Pay* (3 weeks at No.1)/*Christmas Carols by the Old Corral* (Top 3), *Long Time Gone* (Top 5), *When You Leave Don't Slam the Door/Have I Told You Lately That I Love You* (both sides Top 3). Tex's hits during the rest of the 40's were: *Rye Whiskey*, *Deck of Cards* (both Top 10), *Pecos Bill* (Top 15) and *Rock and Rye* (Top 5)(all 1948). *Pecos Bill* came from the Walt Disney movie *Melody Time* and Tex was backed by Andy Parker and the Plainsmen.

In 1950, Tex had a Top 10 hit with the narration *Daddy's Last Letter (Private First Class, John H. McCormick)*, which was based on an actual letter from a soldier killed in the Korean War. *High Noon* scored high on the Pop charts but Ritter's songs from the 50's by and large were not big sellers although he did have a fine album of cowboy songs in 1959. From 1953 to 1960, he headlined and emceed the *Town Hall Party* in Compton, California. He bounced back in 1961 with his Top 5 revival of Eddie Dean's *I Dreamed of a Hillbilly Heaven*. After his two-year service as CMA President in 1963 and 1964 and elevation to the Country Music Hall of Fame (before Gene Autry!), Tex moved to Nashville in 1965 and joined the *Grand Ole Opry*.

From the time of his *Opry* membership, Tex Ritter made the charts consistently although none of his songs could be termed major hits. *Just Beyond the Moon* (Top 15, 1967) and his rendition of Gordon Sinclair's patriotic recitation *The Americans (A Canadian's Opinion)* (Top 40, 1974) probably had the most impact. Ritter made a brief foray into politics in 1970 as a Republican hopeful for the U.S. Senate, but failed to gain the party's nomination in a race against the experienced Congressman William Brock. He died from a heart attack while helping a band member get out of jail. Ironically, Tex's earlier recordings, particularly those from Decca, have been more readily available thanks to a pair of Bear Family picture discs and a cd in the MCA Hall of Fame series.

In recent years, his younger son, John, has become known for his comedy roles with Suzanne Somers and Joyce DeWitt in *Three's Company*, and with Markie Post in *Hearts Afire*. IMT

RECOMMENDED ALBUMS:

"Songs from the Western Screen" (Capitol)(1958)
"Psalms" (Capitol)(1959)
"Hillbilly Heaven" (Capitol)(1961)
"The Friendly Voice of Tex Ritter" (Capitol)(1966)
"Bump Tiddil de Bum Bum" (Capitol)(1968)
"Tex Ritter's Wild West" (Capitol)(1968)
"Chuck Wagon Days" (Capitol)(1969)
"High Noon" (Pickwick)(1970)
"Tex" (Pickwick)(1971)
"Green, Green Valley" (Capitol)(1971)
"An American Legend" (Capitol)(1973)
"High Noon" (Bear Family Germany)(1983)
"Lady Killin' Cowboy" (Bear Family Germany)(1985)
"Singin' in the Saddle" (Bear Family Germany)(1986)
"Hall of Fame" (MCA)(1992)

ROANE COUNTY RAMBLERS, The

When Formed: Late 1920's
Members:
Jimmy McCarroll Leader, Fiddle
Luke Brandon Guitar
John Kelly Mandolin
Howard Wyatt Banjo

The Roane County Ramblers were a popular recording band of the late 1920's who left a legacy of a dozen or so sides on Columbia records. These sides, though, were potent far beyond their numbers, and included such favorites as *Callahan Rag*, *Johnson City Rag*, *Free a Little Bird*, *Green River March* and *Southern Train No. 111*— all of which became popular with later string bands.

Roane County, located some thirty miles west of Knoxville, Tennessee, is the head of the long Sequatchie Valley, and much of the distinctive music played by McCarroll came from the fiddling traditions of this area—a tradition that included the music of Curly Fox, Jess Young, Bob Douglas, John Lusk, Sawmill Tom Smith and many others. McCarroll, who played with a driving abandon and exuberance, also bragged that he had learned some of his fiddle tunes and much of his style from his Cherokee relatives. The handful of recordings the band made were done in nearby Johnson City in 1928 and 1929—in part because the band members all worked at day jobs in the area and had little real ambition to go to New York or to seek out radio work.

In later years, after the original members of the Ramblers drifted away, McCarroll continued to play local square dances, often calling his assembly simply the Roane County Band. He enjoyed his reputation as a local eccentric, and farmed for years on Buttermilk Road near Oak Ridge. Luke Brandon's son, Luke Junior, followed in his father's footsteps as a guitarist, eventually winning fame on WNOX's *Mid-Day Merry-Go-Round* and other Knoxville venues. Wyatt and Brandon also recorded a handful of duet sides for Columbia.

In the 1970's, County Records issued an album containing most of the Roane County Ramblers' recordings. CKW

RECOMMENDED ALBUM:

"The Roane County Ramblers (Complete Recordings 1928-1929)" (County)

DENNIS ROBBINS

(Singer, Songwriter, Guitar, Slide Guitar)
Where Born: Hazelwood, North Carolina

Dennis Robbins grew up in North Carolina drawing his musical influences from the Bluegrass sounds around him and the rock'n'roll he heard on the radio. By the time he was a teenager, Dennis was playing guitar, experimenting with Country, Rock, and the Blues. After high school graduation, Dennis served in the Marine Corps and then settled in Detroit on the advice of his older brother. He joined his brother in several club bands before landing a job with the popular regional Rock band the Rockets. Dennis recorded four albums and toured with the band during the next six years as slide guitar player. The Michigan-based band shared the bill with the likes of ZZ Top, Kiss and Bob Seeger. Eventually, Dennis grew tired of life on the road and returned home briefly to North Carolina before moving to Nashville.

Country-Rock singer/songwriter ***Dennis Robbins***

In 1986, Dennis landed a deal with MCA Records and released an album, ***The First of Me,*** and the singles *Two of a Kind (Working on a Full House)* and *Church on Cumberland Road.* His co-written songs got no attention on radio. A few years later both songs were big hits, respectively, for Garth Brooks and Shenandoah. When his solo efforts didn't work, Dennis decided to form a new band, Billy Hill, alongside his co-writers, John Scott Sherrill and Bob DiPiero, signing with Warner Brothers. He joined the group as one of the lead vocalists and guitarists, co-writing the debut single, *Too Much Month at the End of the Money.* After two years, one album, and a tour, Billy Hill disbanded in 1990.

Dennis became the first artist signed to Giant Records' venture into Country music. He made a fair showing on the charts with his rollicking *Home Sweet Home* debut single. Music critic John Wooley of the *Tulsa World* described Dennis' vocal performance on the single as "Lefty Frizzell singing lead for the Yardbirds." The song was included on his debut album, ***Man with a Plan***, released in early 1992. Dennis re-recorded the title cut from the Billy Hill album, *I Am Just a Rebel*, because he identified strongly with the song, growing up with rebels, serving with them in the military and finding rebels when he came back home. Dennis' Giant album also contained *Paris, Tennessee*, which was covered by Tracy Lawrence. Other artists who have recorded Robbins compositions include Earl Thomas Conley (*Finally Friday*) and Highway 101 (*Just Say Yes*). JIE

RECOMMENDED ALBUMS:

"The First of Me" (MCA)(1986)
"I Am Just a Rebel" (Warner Brothers)(1989)
"Man with a Plan" (Giant)(1992)

HARGUS "PIG" ROBBINS

(Keyboards, Composer, Vocals)
Given Name: Hargus Melvin Robbins
Date of Birth: January 18, 1938
Where Born: Spring City, Tennessee
Married: Vicki
Children: David

Hargus "Pig" Robbins is one of Country music's top sessionmen, and his piano playing has graced many chart records. Like Nashville's other legendary piano player, Floyd Cramer, Robbins has a distinctive style that has been rewarded by accolades from his peers. Like Cramer, Pig was influenced by the early stylings of Don Robertson, the writer of *Please Help Me I'm Falling*.

He was raised in a house without electricity and one day, when aged about two and a half, the young Robbins got a knife out of his father's pocket. He climbed on a chair while the knife was half-open and drove the point into an eye. His parents took him to a local doctor and eventually he was taken to specialists in Chattanooga; however, the medical advice was confusing and although eventually the damaged eye was removed, it had already affected the other and by the time he was age 4, he had gone blind. The only color that he remembers is green, as it was the color of the family '37 Chevrolet.

His early favorite was Tex Ritter and he took piano lessons at age 7 at the Tennessee School for the Blind in Nashville. It was here that he acquired the nickname of Pig from a teacher who kept telling him he looked like a little pig. His early piano training was classical and so Robbins developed his own style by listening to the radio and records. By the time he was 15, he had quit lessons. Having graduated from high school, Pig played in clubs around Nashville. As a result of playing on a friend's demo recording, he joined the American Federation of Musicians (Musicians Union) and began getting session work.

Pig's first major break came in 1959, when he appeared on George Jones' *White Lightning*. This led to him appearing on many of the records to emerge from Nashville. However, he also made his presence felt in non-Country releases. He released his first solo album, ***A Bit of Country Piano***, in 1963, on the Time label. In 1966, Pig appeared on Bob Dylan's ***Blonde on Blonde*** album and from then on, to date, he has been in great demand. His prime contributions, during the late 60's,

*Master session musician **Hargus "Pig" Robbins***

included: 1968: ***Any Day Now*** (Joan Baez) and ***Cristo Redenter*** (Harvey Mandel); 1969: ***David's Album*** (Joan Baez), ***Thinking of Woody Guthrie*** (Country Joe McDonald and the Fish) and ***California Bloodlines*** (John Stewart). In 1969, Pig released his ***One More Time*** album, for Chart Records.

During the early 70's, Robbins appeared on numerous albums, including: 1970: ***Harpin' the Blues*** (Charlie McCoy) and ***Tonight I'm Singing for You*** (Country Joe and the Fish); 1971: ***Ladies Love Outlaws*** (Waylon Jennings), ***Summerside of Life*** (Gordon Lightfoot) and ***In Search of a Song*** (Tom T. Hall); 1972: ***Okie*** (J.J. Cale); 1973: ***Pass the Chicken*** (the Everly Brothers), ***Music is Your Mistress*** (Linda Hargrove), ***My Head, My Bed & My Red Guitar*** (Tommy James & the Shondells), ***Hank Wilson's Back*** (Leon Russell) and ***Cannons in the Rain*** (John Stewart); 1974: ***Blue Jean Country Queen*** (Linda Hargrove), ***Nashville Hit Man*** (Charlie McCoy), ***My Kind of Country*** (Carl Perkins) and ***Country Is*** (Tom T. Hall); 1975: ***Blanket on the Ground*** (Billie Jo Spears) and ***I Wrote a Song About It*** (Tom T. Hall).

In 1976, Pig was named ACM's "Keyboardist of the Year." He went on to be the recipient in 1977, 1979-82 and 1984. Also in 1976, Pig was chosen as "Musician of the Year." In addition that year, he appeared on the album of Charlie McCoy (***Play It Again Sam***), Eddie Rabbitt (***Rocky Mountain Music***), Tanya Tucker (***Lovin' and Learnin'***) and Conway Twitty (***Now and Then***).

During 1977, Robbins received a Grammy Award for "Best Country Instrumental Performance" for his Elektra album ***Country Instrumentalist of the Year***, which was released that year, and was named by NARAS as "Superpicker of the Year," having appeared on many of the fifty-seven nominees for a Grammy. His sessions that year included Marshall Chapman's ***Me I'm Feelin' Free***, Dillard Hartford Dillard's self-titled album, Don Everly's ***Brother Juke Box***, John Hartford's ***All in the Name of Love***, Charlie McCoy's ***Country Cookin'***, Eddie Rabbitt's ***Rabbitt*** and Johnny Rodriguez's ***Just for You***. He also appeared on Joe Maphis' ***Grass 'n' Jazz*** album, as one of Maphis' Super Picker Pals. One of the biggest singles to benefit from his playing was Crystal Gayle's *Don't It Make Your Brown Eyes Blue*.

Pig released his second album for Elektra, entitled ***A Pig in a Poke***, during 1978. This was the year that he appeared at the prestigious Wembley Festival in England, alongside Charlie McCoy and Lloyd Green. He appeared on several major singles that year, including Jacky Ward's *A Lover's Question*, Eddie Rabbitt's *Hearts on Fire*, Kenny Rogers & Dottie West's *Everytime Two Fools Collide*, Crystal Gayle's *Ready for the Time to Get Better* and Johnny Duncan's *She Can Put Her Shoes Under My Bed (Anytime)*. He also appeared on Kenny Rogers' album ***The Gambler*** and Conway Twitty's ***Conway***. He wrapped up the decade by playing on Don McLean's ***Chain Lightning***, Gary Stewart's ***Gary***, Johnny Rodriguez's ***Rodriguez Was Here*** and ***Rodriguez*** and George Jones' ***My Very Special Friends***. Also in 1979, Pig had his third (and final) album for Elektra, entitled ***Unbreakable Hearts***, on which he sang. He also appeared on ***Live from Austin City Limits*** as part of the Nashville Superpickers Band, on Flying Fish Records.

During the 80's, although other keyboard players were emerging onto the Nashville session scene, Pig was still very much in demand. He played on these albums, among others: 1980: ***Kenny*** (Kenny Rogers), ***Great Conch Train Robbery*** (Shel Silverstein) and ***Lookin' Good*** (Loretta Lynn); 1981: ***Dream Lovers*** (Tanya Tucker) and ***Out Where The Bright Lights Are Glowing*** (Ronnie Milsap); 1982: ***Going Where the Lonely Go*** (Merle Haggard); 1983: ***Lyin', Cheatin', Woman Chasin', Honky Tonkin', Whiskey Drinkin' You*** (Loretta Lynn), ***Everything from Jesus to Jack Daniels*** (Tom T. Hall) and ***Memory Lane*** (Joe Stampley); 1984: ***Friendship*** (Ray Charles) and ***Natural Dreams*** (Tom T. Hall); 1985: ***I'll Still Be Loving You*** (Joe Stampley); 1987: ***Heart and Soul*** (Ronnie Milsap) and ***Too Wild Too Long*** (George Jones); 1988: ***Gracias*** (Johnny Rodriguez); 1989: ***Stranger Things Have Happened*** (Ronnie Milsap) and ***Here in the Real World*** (Alan Jackson). In 1982, as part of the Nashville Superpickers, he cut ***The Nashville Superpickers***, for Audiograph Alive.

As the new generation of traditionalists arrived in the spotlight, Pig's piano sound was heard by millions rather than thousands of young record buyers, as Country music record sales and radio stations escalated. In 1990, he could be heard on Mark Chesnutt's ***Too Cold at Home*** and Randy Travis' ***Heroes and Friends***. The following year, George Jones used Pig's skills for his MCA debut album, ***And Along Came Jones***. Robbins also appeared on the ***Don't Rock the Jukebox*** album from Alan Jackson and Randy Travis' ***High Lonesome*** album. He was featured on another George Jones album in 1992, ***Walls Can Fall***. He also played on Mark Chesnutt's ***Longnecks and Short Stories***, Alan Jackson's ***A Lot About Livin' and a Little 'Bout Love*** and Travis Tritt's ***T-R-O-U-B-L-E***.

When Steve Buckingham took Dolly Parton, Tammy Wynette and Loretta Lynn into the studio to record ***Honky Tonk Angels*** in 1993, he brought in the redoubtable Pig Robbins to give the authentic Country styling that he wanted.

Hargus is a man not only respected for his playing, but also admired by others whose paths he crosses. As producer Jerry Kennedy put it, "I'm lucky—I know him and I work with him; although I don't feel like I've ever worked a day in my life with Pig...Work couldn't be that much fun."

RECOMMENDED ALBUMS:

"A Bit of Country Piano" (Time)(1963)
"One More Time" (Chart)(1969)
"Country Instrumentalist of the Year" (Elektra)(1977)
"A Pig in a Poke" (Elektra)(1978)
"Unbreakable Hearts" (Elektra)(1979)
"Alive from Austin City Limits" (Flying Fish)(1979) [As the Nashville Superpickers]

MARTY ROBBINS

(Singer, Songwriter, Guitar, Piano, Actor, Race Driver)

Given Name: Martin David Robertson
Date of Birth: September 26, 1925
Where Born: Glendale, Arizona
Married: Marizona
Children: Ronald Carson (Ronnie Robbins)
Date of Death: December 8, 1982

There will never be another Marty Robbins or anyone to compare with him. In everything he undertook, he gave 150% and was one of the most beloved of performers in Country music. He was the consummate entertainer and showman; he was a singer who could really sing with his distinctive tenor; he could handle a ballad as ably as he could a gunfighter ballad or an up-tempo number; he was one of the finest songwriters in popular music; he was a highly praised race driver; he was a demon card player and no one who ever knew him had a bad word for him. Who could forget that smile as he held his three-quarter-sized guitar and played with his songs and with his audience in that self-mocking style, all the time with that wonderful smile on his face.

Marty grew up in the desert north of Glendale. His father was a harmonica player, but it was his grandfather, "Texas" Bob Heckle, who had the greatest effect on the young Marty. Texas Bob was a traveling medicine man and from age 6, Marty spent hours listening to his grandfather's stories. Marty was also influenced by the movies of Gene Autry and early on he wanted to be a singing cowboy. He picked cotton to get money to watch Autry's latest Western.

In 1937, Marty's family moved to Phoenix. Seven years later, Marty enlisted in the U.S. Navy, serving in the Pacific and learning to play guitar so as to write songs. Three years later, he left the service and joined a band run by a friend of his in Phoenix. In 1948, he appeared on KTYL Mesa, Arizona. He also worked in construction to earn additional money. Marty decided to change his last name so as to hide from his parents his musical ambitions.

While driving a brick truck, Marty tuned in to station KPHO and after hearing the cowboy singer on a Country show, contacted the station Program Director, told him he could do better and got a spot on the show. This led to his being taken onto the *Lew King Show* on KPHO-TV (which also featured Wayne Newton) when a guest failed to arrive. After favorable audience response, he was given his own show, *Western Caravan*, in 1951. On the show, his backing group was called the K-Bar Boys. One day, Little Jimmy Dickens guested on the show and was so impressed with Marty that he spoke to the Columbia Records office in California suggesting that the label should sign Marty. As a result, a representative flew out to Phoenix and signed him.

Marty's first two singles in 1952, *Love Me or Leave Me Alone* and *Crying 'Cause I Love You*, didn't chart, but they opened up the door to Marty's amazing talent, and at year end, he released *I'll Go on Alone*, which within the first month of 1953 soared to No.1, being a favorite of the radio deejays. Fred Rose of Acuff-Rose flew from Nashville to Phoenix and signed Marty to a songwriting contract. Marty had debuted on the *Grand Ole Opry* in 1952, and in 1953 he was made a member and he moved to Nashville (he eventually moved to Franklin, where he had a 250-acre farm and raised Angus cattle). He stayed a loyal supporter of the *Opry* till he died. He also had an early morning show on Nashville's WSM. Marty's other 1953 hit was *I Couldn't Keep from Crying*, which went Top 5.

At this point in time, Marty didn't chart with all his releases and through 1954 and 1955, Marty only appeared on the Country charts with *Pretty Words* and *Call Me Up* (both Top 15, 1954) and two rock'n'roll songs, *That's All Right* and *Maybelline* (both Top 10, 1955). He was still releasing records that missed the charts, including a 1956 duet with Lee Emerson, *I'll Know You're Gone*. Then in the fall of 1956, Marty had what was to be his biggest chart single, Melvin Endsley's *Singing the Blues*. The record went to No.1, where it stayed for 13 weeks out of over 7 months on the charts. It also crossed to the Pop Top 20. The flip-side, *I Can't Quit (I've Gone Too Far)*, was also a Country Top 10 hit.

Once again, his next two records didn't chart. One of these was his version of *Long*

The one and only ***Marty Robbins***

Tall Sally, which appeared on his 10" album, ***Rock'n'Roll'n Robbins***, which subsequently became a collector's item being worth around $500, and the song would resurface in 1987 on the Columbia compilation album ***Rockabilly Hot***. He also released *Mr. Teardrop*, which although it didn't chart, gave Marty his early sobriquet.

In 1957, Marty charted with another Endsley song, *Knee Deep in the Blues*, which went Top 3, with the flip, *The Same Two Lips*, reaching the Top 15. This was followed quickly with a monster hit from the Robbins' pen, *A White Sport Coat (and a Pink Carnation)*. The single stayed at No.1 on the Country chart for 5 weeks, Top 3 on the Pop chart and was Certified Gold. The title obviously helped Jimmy Buffett select his 1973 album's title, ***A White Sport Coat and a Pink Crustation***. Marty had a double-sided hit in the fall with *Please Don't Blame Me/Teenage Dream*, which reached the Top 15. In December, Marty released his Hawaiian album, ***Song of the Islands***, which failed to yield any hit songs. He rounded off the year with *The Story of My Life*, which charted in 1957 and went to No.1 during January 1958. It stayed atop the Country chart for 4 weeks and crossed over to the Top 15 on the Pop lists. During 1957, Marty appeared in the Western *Raiders of Old California* as Voyle, a gunman. That year, Marty started his own Robbins label, among whose artists were Tompall & the Glaser Brothers.

He followed up, in 1958, with another No.1, *Just Married*, which also crossed over to the Pop Top 30. The flip-side, *Stairway of Love*, also reached the Country Top 3. That year, Marty appeared in the Western *Badge of Marshal Brennan* playing Felipe, a Mexican. In the summer of 1958, Marty scored a Top 5 hit with *She Was Only Seventeen*. He closed out the year with the Top 25 *Ain't I the Lucky One*. Marty also sang in the movie *Country Music Holiday*, but was not given credits.

1959 and 1960 was to be a period of change for Marty. ***Marty's Greatest Hits*** album, in 1959, contained his own song, *The Hangin' Tree*, which was featured in the movie of the same name starring Gary Cooper. This revealed Marty's original ambitions of being a singing cowboy. Toward the end of the year, this became even more evident with the release of his memorable Mexican-flavored classic *El Paso*, which just a few weeks later soared to No.1, where it stayed for 7 weeks out of 6 months on the Country chart. It also became a No.1 Pop hit and became a 1960 Top 20 Pop hit in the U.K. It became the first recipient of a Grammy Award for "Best Country and Western Performance." The single could be found on the 1959 watershed ***Gunfighter Ballads and Trail Songs*** album. By 1965, the album was Certified Gold and by 1966, it had gone Platinum. In 1959, Marty appeared in the movie *Buffalo Gun* with Webb Pierce and Carl Smith. That year, Marty began his love affair with motor racing when he started driving Micro Midgets.

Marty's next single, another Robbins classic, *Big Iron*, went Top 5 and crossed to the Pop Top 30, in the spring of 1960. Marty's final single, Tompall Glaser's *Five Brothers*, reached the Top 30 and came from Marty's album ***More Gunfighter Ballads and Trail Songs***. At the time, Tompall & the Glaser Brothers formed part of Marty's backup entourage. Marty appeared in the movie *Country Music Jubilee* with Ernest Tubb, Faron Young and others.

Marty's ***More Greatest Hits*** (1961) yielded his next No.1, *Don't Worry*, which stayed atop the Country chart for 10 out of 19 weeks on the chart and crossed over to the Pop Top 3. *Jimmy Martinez*, a Top 25 single, and *It's Your World*, a Top 3 release during the summer of 1961, did not initially appear on an album. The same was true of Marty's first two 1962 releases, *Sometimes I'm Tempted* and *Love Can't Wait*, which both reached the Top 15. That year, Marty released an album of popular standards, ***Marty After Midnight***, thus predating Willie Nelson's ***Stardust*** by some 16 years.

Marty then had two back-to-back No.1 records. The self-penned *Devil Woman* stayed at the top for 8 weeks and became a Top 20 Pop hit. It also gave Marty his biggest success in the U.K. when it reached the Pop Top 5 and led to a life-long love of Marty by British Country music fans. The other No.1 was *Ruby Ann*, which also made the Pop Top 20. In 1962, Marty began dirt track racing in Nashville, much to his family's concern. He went on to drive in the NASCAR, Grand National Division. 1963 did not start out too well for Marty with both *Cigarettes and Coffee Blues* and *Not So Long Ago* failing to reach the Top 10. However, the year-end *Begging to You* went to No.1 for 3 weeks and crossed to the Pop Top 75. That year, Marty appeared in the movie *Ballad of a Gunfighter*, which was based on the songs *San Angelo* and *El Paso* and had Marty atop the "world's most magnificent white horse," Traveler. After Hawkshaw Hawkins was killed in a plane crash, Marty wrote *Two Little Boys* for Hawkshaw's widow, Jean Shepard, and put the copyright in the names of the two little Hawkins boys so that they could earn royalties from it.

Marty started off 1964 with the Top 15 *Girl from Spanish Town* and then he had *The Cowboy in the Continental Suit* (Top 3) and *One of These Days* (Top 10). He also appeared with Jim Reeves, Ernest Tubb and others in the movie *Country Music Caravan* and with Jim Reeves and Webb Pierce in *Tennessee Jamboree*. With the advent of 1965, Marty's recording career started to get somewhat patchy. Although his initial single, Gordon Lightfoot's *Ribbon of Darkness*, went to No.1, his follow-up single, *Old Red*, only went to No.50 and *While You're Dancing* failed to make the Top 20. Marty appeared in the 13-part TV series *The Drifter*, built around a character created by him. The following year, the double-sided single *Count Me Out/Private Wilson White* also failed to make the Top 10, although the follow-up, *The Shoe Goes on the Other Foot Tonight,* went Top 3. The year ended with the Top 20 *Mr. Shorty*. That year, Marty appeared in the movie *Road to Nashville*.

He started out 1967 with the double-sided *No Tears Milady/Fly Butterfly Fly*, which made the Top 20 and Top 40 respectively. Then Marty's career enjoyed a resurgence. *Tonight Carmen* from the album of the same name became a No.1. The year was completed by the Top 10 hit *Gardenias in Her Hair*. During the year, Marty starred in *Hell on Wheels*, a movie about stock cars. 1968 started with *Love Is in the Air*, which went Top 10 and was followed by the No.1 *I Walk Alone*, which went Top 70 Pop. In October 1968, Marty was felled by a heart attack caused by a cholesterol problem. All three of Marty's 1969 singles went Top 10: *It's a Sin* (Top 5), *I Can't Say Goodbye* and *Camelia*. That year, Marty could be seen in the movie *From Nashville with Music*. Marty hosted his *Marty Robbins Show*, which lasted for 26 weeks. He also suffered his second heart attack and this time, he had to undergo surgery.

Marty started the new decade with the title track of his 1970 album, ***My Woman, My Woman, My Wife***, which went to No.1

and crossed to the Pop Top 50 and earned for him a Grammy Award that year as "Best Country Song." He followed up with two tracks from his ***Greatest Hits, Vol. III***, *Jolie Girl* (Top 10) and *Padre* (Top 5). When Marty returned to the *Opry* after his surgery, he was forced to remain onstage for 45 minutes by his adoring fans.The following year, Marty had Top 10 hits with both his releases, *The Chair/Seventeen Years* and *Early Morning Sunshine*. 1972 was Marty's final year with Columbia. He opened his account with the Top 10 *Early Morning Sunshine*, but by the time Columbia released *I've Got a Woman's Love* from the album of the same name, Marty was with Decca (soon to be MCA). That year, he released the double-album ***All-Time Greatest Hits***, which went Gold in 1982. During 1972, Marty starred in the movie *Country Music*, which was partly filmed at Ontario Speedway.

Marty's time with MCA was not to be a particularly successful period. His debut single for his new label, *This Much a Man*, came from the album of the same name, which just failed to make the Top 10. He started off 1973 with *Walking Piece of Heaven*, a Top 10 single. *A Man and a Train*, which came from the Lee Marvin movie *Emperor of the North Pole*, only reached the Top 40. He completed the year with Jeanne Pruett's *Love Me,* which went Top 10. Marty stayed with the label until 1975 and his principal successes were *Twentieth Century Drifter* (Top 10) and *Don't You Think* (both 1974) and *Life* (1975). During 1973, Marty starred in the Western *Guns of a Stranger*. This was his first starring role as a straight actor. The character he played was an ex-sheriff named Matthew Roberts. Originally the character was named John Trenton, but as Marty had just received a Colt .45 with "M.R." in silver on it, he wanted to use the gun in the movie. Marty was the last performer to grace the stage of the Ryman Auditorium when the *Grand Ole Opry* left that venue on March 9, 1974, and the first to appear on the stage of the new Grand Ole Opry House on March 16 that year. He was also roasted at Nashville Speedway's Marty Robbins Appreciation Night, in July. However in October, he was injured in the National 500 in Charlotte, North Carolina, and had two broken ribs and a broken tailbone and had to have 37 stitches in his face. At the time of his crash, he was traveling at 160 mph, hitting a wall to avoid stalled cars.

In 1975, Marty was inducted to the Nashville Songwriters Hall of Fame. He was also involved in another racing accident, this time in the Winston 500. At the end of 1975, Marty rejoined Columbia and immediately his level of success re-emerged. From the 1976 album ***El Paso City***, the title track went to No.1. It was followed to the top by *Among My Souvenirs*. During the spring of that year, Marty appeared at the Wembley Festival in England, where he was reminded by some of the audience of the impact his rock'n'roll releases had in Europe. The following year, *Adios Amigo* from the album of the same name went Top 5 and was followed into the Top 10 by *I Don't Know Why (I Just Do)* and *Don't Let Me Touch You*. That year, Marty starred in the TV series *Marty Robbins' Spotlight*, which ran for 48 shows.

1978 started out with the Top 10 single *Return to Me*. From here to Marty's death in 1982, his singles failed to be as successful and his principal successes were: *Please Don't Play a Love Song* (Top 20, 1978), *Touch Me with Magic* and *All Around Cowboy* (both Top 20, 1979), *Buenos Dias Argentina* (1979), *An Occasional Rose* (1980), *Some Memories Just Won't Die* (Top 10, 1982), *Tie Your Dreams to Mine* and the 1982 Top 10 entry *Honkytonk Man*, from the Clint Eastwood movie of the same name, in which Marty played a highly praised role. Three years earlier, Marty had started filming the movie *Atoka*, but it was never released.

Marty was felled by a third heart attack on New Year's Day, 1982, but by July, he was racing cars. His last race was on November 7, 1982, and was the Atlanta Journal 500 in Hampton, Georgia, in which he drove a Buick Regal and finished 33rd. Following open-heart surgery, Marty Robbins died on December 8, 1982, much missed by his fans and friends around the world. He had three posthumous chart entries, all in 1983: *Change of Heart, Love Me* (with Jeanne Pruett, who was one of Marty's protégées) and *What If I Said I Love You*. Just prior to his death, Marty was elected to the Country Music Hall of Fame.

During the period 1955 through 1974, he had at least one Top 10 single every year. His musicians also showed their loyalty to Marty by being with him for many years; these included Jack Pruett (Jeanne's husband), who then went on to play with Marty's son, Ronnie, Don Winters and Bobby Sykes. Other members had included Floyd Cramer, R.C. Bannon and Jim Farmer. Marty's son, Ronnie, has continued the family tradition, albeit with low-level chart singles. During his life, Marty's talents ran in other directions and he had many business interests, including his own TV production company, real estate and music publishing, but he was also a genius with a pack of cards and it was a brave man who sat down to play with him.

In 1993, Michael Martin Murphey transferred Marty's voice from *Big Iron* to his own recording and mixed old film footage of Marty singing the song onto his own video, and the music video found great favor on CMT. (For Marty's full list of awards, see Awards section.) (Also see Movie section.)

RECOMMENDED ALBUMS:

Marty Robbins never produced a bad album, therefore our recommendations are just pointers toward the great body of work that can be heard in compilations and re-issues.

"Gunfighter Ballads and Trail Songs" (Columbia)(1959)
"More Gunfighter Ballads and Trail Songs" (Columbia)(1960)
"Marty After Midnight" (Columbia)(1962)
"Devil Woman" (Columbia)(1962)
"Return of the Gunfighter" (Columbia)(1963)
"The Drifter" (Columbia)(1966)
"Marty's Country" (Columbia)(1969)
"Marty!" (5 albums)(Columbia Musical Treasury)(1972)
"Marty Robbins" (MCA)(1973)
"Good 'n Country" (MCA)(1974)
"El Paso City" (Columbia)(1976)
"All Around Cowboy" (Columbia)(1979)
"The Legend" (Columbia)(1981)
"Come Back to Me" (Columbia)(1982)
"Some Memories Just Won't Die" (Columbia)(1983)
"A Lifetime of Song 1951-1982" (double)(Columbia)(1983)
"Country & Western Classics" (3 albums)(Time-Life)(1983)
"Marty Robbins—His Greatest Hits and Finest Performances" (5 albums)(Reader's Digest)(1983)
"Rock'n'Roll'n Robbins" (Bear Family Germany)(1982)
"Rock'n'Roll'n Robbins Vol. 2" (Bear Family Germany)(1982)
"Rock'n'Roll'n Robbins Vol. 3" (Bear Family Germany)(1985)
"Marty Robbins Files, Vol. 1" (Bear Family Germany)(1983)
"Marty Robbins Files, Vol. 2" (Bear Family Germany)(1983)
"Marty Robbins Files, Vol. 3" (Bear Family Germany)(1984)
"Marty Robbins Files, Vol. 4" (Bear Family Germany)(1984)
"Marty Robbins Files, Vol. 5" (Bear Family Germany)(1984)
"In the Wild West, Part 1" (Bear Family Germany)(1985)
"In the Wild West, Part 2" (Bear Family Germany)(1985)
"In the Wild West, Part 3" (Bear Family Germany)(1985)
"In the Wild West, Part 4" (Bear Family Germany)(1985)
"In the Wild West, Part 5" (Bear Family Germany)(1985)
"Just Me and My Guitar" (Bear Family Germany)(1983)
"Hawaii's Calling Me" (Bear Family Germany)(1983)
"Song of the Islands" (Bear Family Germany)(1983)
"Pieces of Your Heart" (Bear Family Germany)(1985)

FIDDLING DOC ROBERTS

(Fiddle, Mandolin)

Given Name:	**Phillip Roberts**
Date of Birth:	**April 26, 1897**
Where Born:	**Richmond, Kentucky**
Married:	**Anna Frances Risk**

Children: Rosella, Curaleen, James (James Carson), Anna Mae, Tom, Doris, Cleva, Donald, Kenneth, Phillip, Jr. (dec'd.), Margaret (dec'd.)
Date of Death: August 4, 1978

One of the best Old-Time fiddlers from Country Music's first commercial decade, Phil ("Doc") Roberts spent most of his adult life as a farmer in Madison County, Kentucky. Two or three times a year Roberts would journey to the recording studios and make discs for such companies as Gennett, Paramount and the ARC group, logging a total of more than 80 tunes. At the same time, he would support other neighboring musicians who had accompanied him, most notably his son James and Asa Martin. In this latter role he contributed at least 80 more, sometimes picking mandolin. Long, flowing, smooth bow strokes generally characterized his fiddle style.

Growing up near Richmond, Kentucky, Doc first learned to play fiddle at the age of 7. He spent the next twenty-five years perfecting his style and absorbing a wide variety of tunes from both black and white traditions. His sources for music included local skilled black fiddlers such as Owen Walker, Jim Booker, and John Booker.

About 1924, a local man named Dennis Taylor began rounding up local talent for trips to the Gennett studio in Richmond, Indiana, or the Paramount studios near Chicago. Among his early discoveries were Roberts, a guitarist, Edgar Boas, and a ballad singer, Welby Toomey. Doc soon found out that he could arrange his own visits and avoid sharing the profits with Taylor. The other musicians Roberts took to Indiana included Ted Chestnut and Dick Parman, who played and sang in a variety of arrangements. Green Bailey, a fine Old-Time singer, also accompanied them. From August 1927 onward, Asa Martin and James Roberts tended to be Doc's preferred associates. When they went to work for the American Record Corporation in 1931, the threesome began using the name Fiddling Doc Roberts Trio on their fiddle band numbers and the credit Martin and Roberts for the vocals. Doc usually played mandolin on the latter.

By all accounts, Doc Roberts did not like cities and preferred farm life, fiddling at local dances and performances in rural schoolhouses, to a full-time career in music. According to his son James, his dad played once for a week at WLS radio but left because he found it impossible to get any rest in Chicago. For several months in 1932 and 1933, Doc and James traveled to Council Bluffs, Iowa, where they were heard on a three-station hookup in Davenport, Des Moines, and Omaha, Nebraska, for Georgie Porgie breakfast foods. Beyond that, occasional guest appearances on Lexington and Louisville radio as well as recording satisfied his demands to fiddle for the masses. After his recording career ended, he continued farming in Madison County, and also worked as keeper at the Madison County Home for the infirmed until retirement. Rediscovered in the late 60's, he gave a concert at Berea College in 1971, accompanied by Asa Martin and James (who used the stage name James Carson in later years). Declining health limited Doc's playing. A scattering of his fiddle work appeared on various anthologies as well as a pair of albums devoted to his repertoire of both common and atypical tunes. IMT

RECOMMENDED ALBUMS:

"Fiddling Doc Roberts: 1927-1933" (Davis Unlimited)(1975)
"Old Time Tunes" (County)(1983)

KENNY ROBERTS

(Singer, Songwriter, Guitar, Bass, Harmonica)

Given Name: George Kingsbury
Date of Birth: October 14, 1926
Where Born: Lenoir City, Tennessee
Married: 1. Freda (div.) 2. Bettyanne
Children: eight

Yodelin' Kenny Roberts became a popular radio vocalist in the 40's working initially with a group called the Down Homers but soon going on his own. He specialized in songs that featured considerable yodeling and lyrics that won favor with children.

Born in Lenoir City, Tennessee, Kenny Roberts was raised on a farm near Greenfield, Massachusetts, where one suspects he came under the influence of Yodelin' Slim Clark. He made his radio debut at 15, over WHAI Greenfield. His first regular work with the Down Homers came at WKNE Keene, New Hampshire, the station which had provided Clark with an early boost. From there the outfit went to the large midwestern outlet KXEL Waterloo, Iowa, followed by WOWO Fort Wayne, Indiana, which then had a major radio jamboree known as the *Hoosier Hop*.

Yodelin' ***Kenny Roberts***

By that time, Roberts had attained some renown as a yodeler and vocalist. He recorded with the Down Homers on a Vogue Picture disc. Other band members included Shorty Cook, Guy Campbell, Lloyd Cornell, and Bob Mason. The war also caught up with Kenny about this time and on January 30, 1945, he entered the U.S. Navy. A few days earlier, he married his sweetheart, Freda, a Brattleboro, Vermont, girl whom he had met during his sojourn at Keene.

Shortly after the war ended, Kenny returned to Fort Wayne and the *Hoosier Hop* where he now became a solo star. In the spring of 1948 he moved on to KMOX, "The Voice of St. Louis." He appeared on daily shows there and on a Saturday morning CBS program called *Barnyard Frolics*. After having another single on Vitacoustic, he signed with Coral and had his most noted recordings on that label. Kenny's biggest hit, *I Never See Maggie Alone*, waxed in May 1949, made it to the Country Top 5 and peaked on the Pop Top 10. The flip-side, *Wedding Bells*, reached the Top 15. He finished 1949 with the Top 15 *Jealous Heart*. He made the Top 10 again in the spring of 1950 with a kids' favorite, *Choc'late Ice Cream Cone*. Another children's favorite, *Billy and Nanny Goat*, from 1950, constituted a modernized version of the old story about the shirt-eating goat who coughed one up and flagged a train, a story that dates back at least to the early efforts of Fiddlin' John Carson.

In the meantime, Kenny moved to daily shows at WLW Cincinnati and the *Midwestern Hayride*, where he achieved great popularity in the early 50's. About 1952, he moved to nearby Dayton, where he went into TV, and while he continued to attract fans locally, Roberts increasingly became a regional figure from this point. Through the next several years, the Yodeler worked out of various TV markets, including Indianapolis and Saginaw, Michigan.

About 1962, he started working on a regular basis over the *Wheeling Jamboree* from WWVA, but continued in daily TV for a time, too. Lee Sutton and Hardrock Gunter started Essgee Records and Kenny waxed an extended play record on the label. By 1973, he had settled back in Dayton working personal appearances throughout the midwest, eastern states, and Canada, where he cut a pair of albums on the Point label. In the U.S., Kenny recorded on Starday in the later 60's.

By the later 70's, Kenny had moved back to Massachusetts, as his show dates were mainly in the Northeast. He recorded an album for Don Cleary's Palomino label, and in 1981, Longhorn released an album which included a variety of old and new material ranging from his two Vogue sides with the Down Homers and the Essgee cuts of 1964 to four brand-new items from a session in Nashville. At last report, Kenny Roberts made his home in Athol, Massachusetts, not far from his boyhood residence of Greenfield, and remains active on the Country scene in that region. IMT

RECOMMENDED ALBUMS:

"Yodelin' Kenny Roberts Sings Country Songs" (Vocalion, MCA and Point)(1966) [Coral Masters]
"Yodelin' with Kenny Roberts" (Point)
"Indian Love Call" (Starday)(1965)
"The Incredible Kenny Roberts" (Starday)(1967)
"Country Music Singing Sensation" (Starday)(1969)
"Jealous Heart" (Starday)(1970)
"I Never See Maggie Alone" (Nashville)(1971)
"Kenny Roberts" (Palomino)
"Then and Now" (Longhorn)(1981)

ECK ROBERTSON

(Fiddle, Guitar)

Given Name:	**Alexander Campbell Robertson**
Date of Birth:	**November 20, 1887**
Where Born:	**Delaney, Madison County, Arkansas**
Married:	**Jeanetta ("Nettie") Belle Levy**
Children:	**Daphne, Dueron ("Eck Junior"), Marguerite, plus seven**
Date of Death:	**February 17, 1975**

Most historians credit Eck Robertson with being the first southern Country artist to make records, when he traveled to New York in June 1922 to record a series of sides for the Victor Talking Machine Company. Unfortunately, too often that is all he is given credit for. In truth, Robertson was a powerful and influential fiddler whose importance extended far beyond the "first" Country records. Though he recorded only a few other times after that historic 1922 session, he continued to be a major force on the Texas music scene well into the 1960's.

Modern fiddlers such as Mark O'Connor and Texas Shorty acknowledge Robertson as the father of the so-called Texas style or contest style of playing, whereby fiddlers use a long bow stroke to create a series of subtle variations on the basic fiddle tune. Robertson's 1922 solo version of *Sallie Gooden* (Victor VI8956) is now hailed as the definitive reading of that piece, and one of the most important instrumental recordings of the 20th century.

Though he was born in Arkansas, Eck and his family moved to the hamlet of Hamlin, in the Texas Panhandle, in 1890, when he was only 3. There, his father, Joseph, farmed and served as a preacher in the Church of Christ; Joseph had himself been a serious fiddler until he took up his calling, so young Eck learned his music from an uncle and an older brother named Quince. His first instrument, at age 5, was made from a long-necked gourd and a tanned cat hide. Soon he had a real fiddle, and was learning tunes from Civil War veterans like Polk Harris and from fiddlers like Matt Brown, a local legend who is generally credited with composing *Ragtime Annie* and *Done Gone*, both of which Eck would make definitive recordings of.

When he was 16, Eck joined a traveling medicine show, and for the next few years did the circuits, gaining professional experience. In 1906 he married Jeanetta Belle Levy (Nettie), a childhood sweetheart who was also a skilled musician and together the two did "magic lantern" shows, to the accompaniment of their own music. For a time, Eck also worked as a piano tuner, in towns like Big Spring and Clarendon, Texas. The pair started their family, which would eventually number two sons and eight daughters. Later some of these would perform with Eck and Nettie as a family band: Daphne, Dueron (always billed as "Eck Junior"), and Marguerite.

By the end of WWI, Eck had become a well-known area fiddler, and a fixture at the many fiddling contests held in the state. By now he was living at Vernon, often performing with two senior musicians (Lewis Franklin and A.P. Howard). In early 1922 the three were featured in a Fox Movietone newsreel, and even though the film was silent, it impressed Eck and probably gave him the idea to explore other forms of mass media. His chance came in June 1922, when he and a friend, a Civil War veteran named Henry Galliland, attended an Old Confederate Soldiers Reunion in Richmond, Virginia. Galliland had a friend in New York who did legal work for the Victor company, and with this in mind the two men decided to take the train on up and try to make some records.

Here the Eck Robertson saga becomes entwined with legend. The standard story has always been that Eck and Galliland, dressed in Confederate uniforms, appeared at the door to Victor begging for a try-out, and that the Victor officials finally cut a couple of tunes to placate them, grudgingly releasing them at a later date. In fact, Robertson was wearing what one witness called "the garb of a western plainsman," and the Victor A & R men were quite impressed: so much so that they actually recorded 12 sides over the two-day span of June 30 and July 1. All but 4 sides were issued, and stayed in print for a number of years. Technically, four unaccompanied fiddle duets between Eck and Galliland were the first sides committed to wax: *Arkansas Traveller*, *Apple Blossom* (not released), *Forked Deer* (not released), and *Turkey in the Straw*.

By 1924, Victor was impressed enough with their work to issue what was probably the first special Country catalog, *Old Time Fiddlin' Tunes*.

Unlike Fiddlin' John Carson, Eck Robertson seemed unable or unwilling to really capitalize on his fame from records. He did not record again until 1929, when he and his family string band returned to the studios to do a session in August and another in October, amassing eight more released sides, some of which were only a cut or two above average string band sides of the time. Eck tried to get Victor to record him again during the height of the Western Swing craze in the 1930's, but they felt his music—ironically a major influence on Bob Wills—was too old-fashioned.

Recent research has confirmed that Eck recorded some 100 sides for the Sellers Transcription service in the late 1930's, but none of these have been traced. Fortunately, in 1963, members of the New Lost City Ramblers visited Eck and made new field tapes of some of his best material, which were issued in 1991 as ***Eck Robertson: Famous Cowboy Fiddler*** (County).

In the 1960's Eck continued to appear at Texas contests, and even traveled to Folk festivals at UCLA and Newport. He was interviewed on numerous occasions by folklorists and fiddle students, as well as countless newspaper feature writers. His last years were spent in a rest home, and he died on

February 17, 1975; he was buried in Fritch, Texas. CKW

RECOMMENDED ALBUM:

"Eck Robertson: Famous Cowboy Fiddler" (County)(1991)

CARSON J. ROBISON

(Guitar, Singer, Songwriter)

Given Name: Carson Jay Robison
Date of Birth: August 9, 1890
Where Born: Oswego, Kansas
Married: Catherine
Children: Donald, Patricia, Robert, Ken
Date of Death: March 24, 1957

Although a native of rural Kansas, Carson Robison's career is often grouped with the "citybilly" musicians who moved into Country music from the New York recording studios rather than being discovered in some southern textile mill or backwoods square dance in the manner of a Henry Whitter, Ernest Stoneman, or John Carson. However one classifies Robison, he made a major impact on the development of the Country scene in the thirty-three years he spent in the business as a performing artist and songwriter.

Born in Oswego and reared in Chetopa, Kansas, to a fiddler father and a singing pianist mother, Carson absorbed music as a child, becoming especially adept on guitar and at whistling. The growing metropolis of Kansas City offered opportunities for a career and Robison moved there about 1920 after having worked at a variety of farm, ranch, and oil field chores. He soon acquired work with the Coon-Sanders Orchestra and performed on the pioneer radio station WDAF. In 1924, Carson came to New York at the urging of Wendell Hall, who had just had a major hit record, *It Ain't Gonna Rain No Mo.* Carson soon joined forces with Vernon Dalhart, who was in the process of adapting to Country sounds. The two formed a virtual partnership that produced a wide variety of recorded duets as well as Robison's writing a number of Dalhart's more significant songs, some under the pseudonym of Maggie Andrews. Robison's compositions included *My Blue Ridge Mountain Home, The Wreck of Number Nine, The Santa Barbara Earthquake, Zeb Turney's Gal* and *Naomi Wise. Collier's* magazine featured a story on Robison's writing of formula-pattern topical songs in 1929.

Meanwhile Dalhart and Robison split in 1928 and the latter took Frank Luther for a partner. The general opinion is that Carson did much better on his own and with his new co-worker than did Dalhart, who rather quickly faded from the forefront. Robison and Luther had several good songs, most notably *Barnacle Bill the Sailor*, which was recorded for Victor under the names Bub and Joe Billings. Several of their numbers came out under the name Carson Robison Trio (which included Frank Luther and his brother Phil Crow, and perhaps sometimes Frank's wife, Zora Layman). About 1931, he formed a band alternately known as the Buckaroos and the Pioneers that became popular on radio and toured widely, including the British Isles in 1932. The band included Bill and John Mitchell and Bill's wife, Pearl Pickens. During their British tour, they even cut some sessions on the Zonophone label in England. Later in 1936 and 1939, they returned to the United Kingdom.

The WWII era stirred Robison's creative urges again. He came up with a variety of new songs directed against the Axis Powers, often through ridicule, such as *1942 Turkey in the Straw, Hirohito's Letter to Hitler, Hitler's Last Reply to Hirohito, 1945 Mother Goose Rhymes*, and a shrewd comment on gasoline rationing titled *The Old Gray Mare Is Back Where She Used to Be,* all recorded for Bluebird or RCA Victor. In the post-war years, he became one of the first artists to sign with MGM. One of his best-known numbers, the humorous *Life Gets Teejus Don't It,* came from 1947, climbing to the Top 3 by 1948.

A follow-up, *More and More Teejus*, continued in the same vein, but was less of a commercial success. In 1952 Carson delved into topical material again with songs like *Ike's Letter to Harry* and the oft-recorded *I'm No Communist.* Active until near the end of his life, one of his last efforts, *Rockin' and Rollin' with Grandma*, was labeled by one wit as "geriatric Rockabilly."

In those last years, Robison resided on a farm near Poughkeepsie, New York, and did some programs at WKIP radio. Like many of the citybilly performers, initial re-issues tended to ignore Robison, but eventually four albums reached the market, one of them of Australian origin and another, German. IMT

RECOMMENDED ALBUMS:

"The Immortal Carson Robison" (Glendale)(1978)
"Just a Melody" (Old Homestead)(1981)
"The Kansas Jayhawk" (Cattle Germany)(1987)
"A Hillbilly Mixture" (Axis)(1988)
Vernon Dalhart and Carson Robison:
"That Good Old Country Town" (Old Homestead)(1990)
(See also Vernon Dalhart.)

JIMMIE RODGERS

(Singer, Songwriter, Yodeler, Guitar, Ukulele, Banjo, Mandolin)

Given Name: James Charles Rodgers
Date of Birth: September 8, 1897
Where Born: Nr. Meridian, Mississippi
Married: 1. (Div.)
2. Carrie
Children: Anita, June
Date of Death: May 26, 1933

Whether he is referred to as "America's Blue Yodeler," "the Singing Brakeman," "the Father of Country Music," or the simple name that his original 78s bore, "Jimmie Rodgers," James Charles Rodgers was the preeminent star of early Country music. During the height of his career, in the late 1920's, nobody could even approach him in terms of national appeal and media success. His record sales were five or seven times that of his nearest competitor. His picture graced the covers of a dozen pieces of sheet music; major vaudeville companies dangled fat contracts before him; Hollywood called; songwriters vied to get songs to him, in the manner of modern Nashville. His imitators were legion, even before he died and rival record companies began to add the phrase "singing with yodel" to their records in hopes of capitalizing on his vocal style.

Lefty Frizzell learned to sing by sticking his head in a Victrola speaker when Rodgers songs were playing; Hank Snow named his son after Rodgers and cut dozens of Rodgers songs; Ernest Tubb began his career by

Jimmie Rodgers (left) with ***Will Rogers***

reverently playing Rodgers' guitar. For eight decades, Jimmie Rodgers' name has been the best known in Country music and his influence, like that of the Roman Empire, extends to all corners of the realm.

Rodgers was born in southern Mississippi. His father was a railroad worker and part-time farmer, his mother the genteel daughter of a local landowner who died when Rodgers was only 6. Young Rodgers grew up shuttling back and forth between relatives and absorbing the vaudeville and dance hall music of Meridian. Though the area he lived in was in fact a center for traditional Blues and though later biographers made much of the Blues influence in Rodgers' singing, there is little evidence that he had any direct contact with black performers. One of his first performances was at age 12, when he entered a local talent contest singing a popular song, *Steamboat Bill*. His father didn't think much of a show business career, though, and eventually persuaded Jimmie to take a job on the railroad. For a dozen or so years starting in the late 1910's, Rodgers traveled around the country, working on the railroad. For a time he was briefly married and even had a daughter, who died in 1938.

In 1920, he remarried, this time to a local minister's daughter, Carrie, who would play an important role in his life and later legend. His railroading came to an end in 1924, when he was diagnosed with tuberculosis. Not heeding his doctor's advice to take life easy, Rodgers redoubled his efforts to carve out a musical career. By 1927, he had settled in Asheville (where he thought the mountain air might help his health), working on local radio WWNC, at carnivals as the Jimmie Rodgers Entertainers and at whatever jobs he could pick up.

That summer, he and his band heard about Ralph Peer, the Victor talent scout who was recording in Bristol, and they made the trip over the mountains and wangled an audition. The night before, however, he and the band (a quartet led by two local boys, the Grant brothers) got into a dispute over how the billing on the records would be and split.

The next day the band recorded as the Tenneva Ramblers, while Rodgers auditioned solo. Peer rejected Rodgers' signature song, *T for Texas*, with its interesting yodel and instead settled on an old war ballad, *The Soldier's Sweetheart*, and an old lullaby, *Sleep, Baby, Sleep*, that had been earlier popularized by Riley Puckett.

The record, released in October, was not a spectacular success, but Rodgers himself contacted the company and they agreed to a second session. This one did include *T for Texas*, officially listed on the Victor label as *Blue Yodel*, and this record did take off. It eventually became one of the very few early Country discs to sell a million copies. With it, Rodgers' career was launched.

Over the next six years, Rodgers would record some 110 songs for Victor and their influence was so pervasive and their reissuing so frequent that it is sometimes hard to tell just which of his records were big hits during his own life. Recently discovered sales figures, though, reveal that in addition to *Blue Yodel*, his biggest sellers were *Way Out on the Mountain* (1927), *Blue Yodel No.4* (1928), *Waiting for a Train* (1928) and *A Drunkard's Child* (1929). Lesser sellers were novelty items like *Everybody Does It in Hawaii*, *Brakeman's Blues*, *I'm Lonely and Blue*, *Little Old Home Down in New Orleans*, *My Old Pal*, *Never No Mo' Blues* and *The Sailor's Plea*. Many of his best songs were co-written by his sister-in-law Elsie McWilliams.

Ralph Peer consistently experimented with Jimmie's back-up arrangements; sometimes he used a Hawaiian string band, at others a Jazz band (once including Louis Armstrong), at others a Victor studio orchestra, at others just Jimmie's guitar and on one forgettable session, a musical saw. Though Jimmie seldom used radio to good advantage, he did tour widely on the vaudeville circuit and in 1929 journeyed to Hollywood to shoot a 15-minute film short called *The Singing Brakeman*. His royalties allowed him to build a huge home in Kerrville, Texas which he named Blue Yodeler's Paradise. By 1930, he had a national reputation and made appearances with film stars like Will Rogers.

However, by 1933, his tuberculosis was catching up with him and plans for more Hollywood films had to be postponed. The Depression was impacting even Jimmie's record sales. His 1933 release *Mississippi Delta Blues* only managed to sell about 1,700 copies. Still, he refused the rest that might have given him a few more years; "I want to die with my boots on," he told his wife. In May, he did one last marathon session for Victor, trying to get some money to provide for his family. Twelve titles resulted, including some of his more impressive performances. Two days later, though, he was dead from a lung hemorrhage.

In 1955, *In the Jailhouse Now No.2*, with overdubbed backing that included Chet Atkins and Hank Snow, became a Top 10 hit on the Country chart. Jimmie Rodgers was a charter inductee to the Country Music Hall of Fame in 1961, and in 1986, in a move that showed that his influence was far beyond Country music, he was inducted into the Rock and Roll Hall of Fame. In 1985, *Blue Yodel (T for Texas)* was inducted into the Grammy Hall of Fame.

CKW

RECOMMENDED ALBUMS:

"Never No Mo' Blues" (Jimmie Rodgers Memorial Album)(RCA Victor)(1955)
"My Rough and Rowdy Ways" (RCA Victor)(1960) [Re-issued in 1975 and by Stetson UK in original packaging (1988)]
"Jimmie the Kid (The Legendary Jimmie Rodgers)" (RCA Victor)(1961)
"My Time Ain't Long" (RCA Victor)(1964)
"Unissued Jimmie Rodgers" (Anthology of Country Music)(1983)
"This Is Jimmie Rodgers" (double)(RCA Victor)(1983)
"20 of the Best" (RCA UK)(1984)
"You & My Old Guitar" (Request UK)(1989)
Jimmie Rodgers' songs done by other artists:
"The Superstars Salute Jimmie Rodgers" (Jimmie Rodgers Foundation) [Artists are: Willie Nelson, Merle Haggard, Dolly Parton, Crystal Gayle, Waylon Jennings, Conway Twitty, Ernest Tubb, Tanya Tucker, Merle Travis, Hank Thompson, Lefty Frizzell, Slim Whitman, Red Foley, Grandpa Jones, Jim Reeves, Webb Pierce, Bill Monroe, Hank Snow, Gene Autry, Boxcar Willie, Jimmie Dale Court and Jack Greene]

JUDY RODMAN

(Singer, Songwriter, Piano, Guitar)

Given Name:	**Judy Mae Robbins**
Date of Birth:	**May 23, 1951**
Where Born:	**Riverside, California**
Married:	**John A. Rodman**
Children:	**Peter**

When MTM Records decided to end operations in 1988, there were several talented performers who were hit hard; these included Judy Rodman, who had started to

*Singer/Songwriter **Judy Rodman***

emerge as a name to be reckoned with, winning *Music City News*' 1985 title of "New Female Vocalist of the Year."

Judy is the daughter of an air-traffic controller who also played in Bluegrass bands. When she was six months old, the family moved to London, England, where she "learned to talk." Two years later, they moved to Memphis and then on to Mississippi, Alaska and Florida. Judy started singing harmony when she was age 4, and started playing breakdowns on guitar when she was around 6. She earned her first money as a musician at age 8, performing in her father's band on a cruise ship party. She started to get interested in Calypso and Cajun music while she lived in Miami, and Rock and Classical music while she was in Jacksonville.

Judy began doing jingles when she was 17, her first one being a nationally aired commercial for Jeno's Pizza. She then attended Jacksonville University, where she studied music. She moved with her family to Memphis and became a jingle singer at the Tanner Agency. She also started playing with a local nightclub group, Phase II, alongside Karen Taylor (later Taylor-Good). Judy befriended another jingle singer, Janie Fricke, and they became roommates.

During the mid-70's, Judy started to do back-up singing on recording sessions and worked with O.B. McClinton, Mel McDaniel and Charly McClain, as well as soul singers Ann Peebles and O.V. Wright. In 1975, Judy married drummer and professional bass fisherman John Rodman. They moved to Nashville in 1980, and continued doing jingle work for companies such as Miller Beer, Kellogg, Opryland, South Central Bell, Budweiser, Schlitz, McDonald's, Coors, Piedmont and Chevrolet. She also did back-up for, among others, Johnny Cash, Tammy Wynette, Jerry Lee Lewis, Merle Haggard, Ray Charles, Janie Fricke (now on her way to stardom), T.G. Sheppard, Tom Jones, Brenda Lee, Crystal Gayle, George Jones and Dolly Parton.

Judy was introduced to Tommy West by Karen Taylor-Good. West had been one-half of recording act Cashman & West, and was now a respected Pop producer. He had been working with Country singers Ed Bruce and Ronnie Rogers and when he became Senior Vice President at MTM, he made Judy his first signee. She hit the Country charts with her debut 1985 release, *I've Been Had by Love Before*, which went Top 40. Her follow-up, *You're Gonna Miss Me When I'm Gone*, fared slightly better, and her year-end release, her own self-written song *I Sure Need Your Lovin'*, got into the Top 30.

Her first release of 1986, *Until I Met You*, presented MTM with their first No.1, and it stayed on the Country chart for nearly six months. This led to her making her debut on the *Grand Ole Opry*. The follow-up, another Rodman co-written title, *She Thinks That She'll Marry*, went Top 10. All of the above singles came from her debut album, ***Judy***.

In 1987, Judy released her second album, ***A Place Called Love***, and the initial single, *Girls Ride Horses Too*, also made the Top 10. This was followed by Bob Dylan's *I'll Be Your Baby Tonight*, which Dylan had sent to her. This release reached No.5, and was her last (to date) Top 10 release. The year ended with *I Want a Love Like That*, which went Top 20. Her last two singles for the label, *Goin' to Work* and *I Can Love You*, which would have been on a third album, only reached the Top 50, but by now MTM was about to become history.

With the fall of MTM, Judy found herself without a label, and she reverted to singing backup and becoming a songwriter. In 1993, her song *Demons and Angels* was recorded by Diamond Rio. Judy now writes for Warner-Chappell Music, and is now busy making another attack on a recording and performing career, with material that she describes as being "on the cutting edge." Judy is a fine angler, and her determined attitude is sure to land her another crack at stardom.

Gracias, ***Johnny Rodriguez***

RECOMMENDED ALBUMS:
"Judy" (MTM)(1985)
"A Place Called Love" (MTM)(1987)

JOHNNY RODRIGUEZ

(Singer, Songwriter, Guitar)
Given Name: **Juan Raoul Davis Rodriguez**
Date of Birth: **December 10, 1951**
Where Born: **Sabinal, Texas**

Without doubt, Johnny Rodriguez is the first and most successful Chicano Country singer of all time.

Johnny lived in a four-room house about 90 miles north of the Mexican border. He learned a love of Country music from his elder brother, Andres, who bought Johnny his first guitar when his younger brother was age 7. Their father died of cancer when Johnny was just 16 and a year later, Andres died in an auto crash. Johnny was captain of his high school football team, a high school letterman and an altar boy. However, by the time he was 18, Johnny had been in jail four times.

However, he had already got the music bug, and when he was 16 he had already formed a rock'n'roll band, in which he played lead guitar and sang. There has always been a story that he and some friends were caught after stealing and barbecuing a goat and took the rap. However, it would appear that this was a publicist's made-up yarn and there is doubt whether the event even happened. The tale is that Johnny's singing in the jailhouse caught the attention of Texas Ranger Joaquin Jackson, who told Happy Shahan, a promoter, about Johnny. When he was 19, he played the Alamo Village Amusement Park in Brackettville under the guidance of Happy Shahan, who became his co-manager. He spent the summers of 1970 and 1971 driving stagecoaches, riding horses and singing.

In 1971, Johnny was heard by Tom T. Hall and Bobby Bare, who were on tour. Johnny left for Nashville with his guitar and $14 that year. Tom's office had been trying to contact Johnny and so he became lead guitarist in Tom's band, the Storytellers, as well as having his own spot. Tom took Johnny to Ron Dea at Mercury, who signed him and had him produced by Jerry Kennedy.

Johnny immediately struck with his first single, *Pass Me By*, which peaked in the Top 10 in the winter of 1972. That year, the ACM named him their "Most Promising Male Vocalist." All three of his 1973 releases went to No.1. They were *You Always Come Back (To Hurting Me)*, *Ridin' My Thumb to Mexico* (also Pop Top 70) and *That's the Way Love Goes*. As a result, he was nominated for the CMA's "Male Vocalist of the Year." Although he didn't win that, he did collect a number of awards that year, including *Cash Box*'s "New Male Vocalist—Singles" and "New Male Vocalist—Albums" and *Music City News*' "Most Promising Male Vocalist." In addition, he won the *Billboard* "Trendsetter" Award, *Cash Box*'s "Upcoming Male" Award and *Record Review*'s "Most Promising Male Vocalist—Album Charts" and "Most Promising Male Vocalist—Singles Charts."

In 1974, Johnny hit the Top 10 with his re-working of the Beatles' hit *Something*. This was followed by *Dance with Me (Just One More Time)* and *We're Over* (both Top 3). For some peculiar reason, *Music City News* named Johnny as their "Most Promising Male Vocalist" a second time, after having three No.1's plus 4 Top 10 hits! It seems especially strange considering that Johnny's name was added to the Walkway of the Stars in the Country Music Hall of Fame. During the year, he made his TV debut as an actor, appearing in *Adam-12*. This led to his appearance in the Western movie *Rio Diablo*. The following year, all three of Johnny's releases again went to No.1. These were *I Just Can't Get Her Out of My Mind, Just Get Up and Close the Door* and *Love Put a Song in My Heart*.

In 1976, he had two Top 3 singles, *I Couldn't Be Me Without You* and *I Wonder If I Ever Said Goodbye* and the Top 5 release, *Hillbilly Heart*. The following year, he continued with two Top 5 singles, the Eagles' *Desperado* and *If Practice Makes Perfect*. His next two singles didn't fare quite as well, with *Eres Tu* going Top 30 and *Savin' This Love Song for You* reaching the Top 20. His first two singles of 1978, *We Believe in Happy Endings* and *Love Me With All of Your Heart (Cuando Calienta el Sol)*, went Top 10. He wrapped up the year with the Top 20 hit *Alibis*.

As 1979 came around, Johnny moved labels to Epic, and had a Top 10 hit with *Down on the Rio Grande*, followed by three Top 20 successes, *Fools for Each Other, I Hate the Way I Love It* (a duet with Charly McClain) and *What'll I Tell Virginia*.

Johnny broke his sternum and collarbones while doing a karate backflip. Then he developed troubles with his vocal cords and his marriage broke up. With the arrival of the 80's, Johnny's success rate slowed down and his 1980 hits were *Love, Look at Us Now* (Top 30) and *North of the Border* (Top 20). From 1981 through 1985, when Johnny left Epic, his major successes were *I Want You Tonight* and *Trying Not to Love You* (1980, Top 30), *Foolin'* and *How Could I Love Her So Much* (1983, Top 10), *Too Late to Go Home* (1984). In 1987, Johnny moved again, this time to Capitol. He immediately saw some upsurge in his career with *I Didn't (Every Chance I Had)*, which made it to the Top 15. He stayed with Capitol until the end of 1989. In 1993, Branson Entertainment, Intersound's new label, released the Rodriguez album ***Run for the Border***, from which the title track was released as a single and video.

One of the charms of Johnny's recordings is his ability to break into Spanish, especially during his rendition of Country standards. He is a tireless charity worker and organizes all-star concerts through the Johnny Rodriguez Life Enrichment Center.

RECOMMENDED ALBUMS:

"The Greatest Hits of Johnny Rodriguez" (Mercury)(1976)
"The Best of Johnny Rodriguez (20 Original Hits)" (K-Tel)(1977)
"Biggest Hits—Johnny Rodriguez" (Epic)(1982) [Features Charly McClain]
"Gracias" (Capitol)(1988)
"Run for the Border" (Branson Entertainment)(1993)

DAVID ROGERS

(Singer, Songwriter, Guitar)

Given Name: David Pierce Rogers
Date of Birth: March 27, 1936
Where Born: Atlanta, Georgia
Married: Barbara Ann
Children: Anthony Kyle (Tony), Tonya Lynn
Date of Death: August 10, 1993

For a while during the early 70's, David Rogers' name appeared with regularity on the Country chart. During a period of 16 years, he chalked up thirty-seven Country chart singles, with two of them being Top 10 hits.

As a boy he listened to the *Grand Ole Opry* and got his first guitar when 11. He began playing the clubs around Atlanta and in 1956 auditioned for Roger Miller for the U.S. Army's Special Services Division, but was drafted instead. He left the service and initially worked as a structural draftsman, electrician's assistant and a door-to-door salesman. He then started working the clubs in Atlanta with the David Rogers Band.

He met a former employer, Kathleen Jackson and her husband, who had owned the Longhorn and now opened The Egyptian Ballroom in Atlanta. Pete Drake had worked there initially, and persuaded Kathleen to buy the venue. In 1962, Kathleen booked David on a regular basis and eventually became his manager. In 1966, Kathleen took a tape of David's to Pete Drake and he made a demo of David, which Kathleen paid for, with a backup group that included Larry Butler, Sandy Posey, Herschel Wiggins and Pete Drake. The tape came to the ears of Columbia's A & R Manager, Frank Jones, and led to a five-year contract with the label.

David's first single was *Forgiven Fruit/ You Can't Sell Me That Song & Dance*, in 1967. In June of that year, he debuted on the *Grand Ole Opry* and in October, he began making regular monthly appearances on WWVA *Wheeling Jamboree*. With his second single, *I'd Be Your Fool Again* (1968), he made his first appearance in the Country charts, reaching the Top 70. The next single, *I'm in Love with My Wife*, reached the Top 40, as did the last single of the year, *You Touched My Heart*. That year, David left The Egyptian Room and moved to Nashville and appeared on most of the popular TV shows, including the *Bobby Lord Show*, the *Bill Anderson Show*, the *Eddie Hill Show* on WLAC-TV and the *Ralph Emery Show* on WSM-TV.

During 1969, he had two chart entries with *Dearly Beloved* (Top 60) and the Top 30 *A World Called You*. David's 1970 hits were *So Much Love* (Top 50) and *I Wake Up in Heaven* (Top 30). In 1971, he had a Top 20 hit with *She Makes Me Cry* and the Top 25 success *Ruby You're Warm*. The following year, David had his first Top 10 record, *Need You*, but his last two hits that year did not build on this success and both *Goodbye* and *All Heaven Breaks Loose* only made the Top 40.

David now became the first Country act to sign to Atlantic Records. He immediately hit the Top 20 in 1973 with *Just Thank Me* and followed up with *It'll Be Her*, which peaked in the Top 25. He started 1974 with another Top 10 entry, *Loving You Has Changed My Life*. He had two further successes that year with *Hey There Girl* (Top 25) and the Top 60 single *I Just Can't Help Believin'*. That year, his son Tony, then 13, formed his own band. David wanted him to be a doctor, as David's father had wanted him to be.

In 1975, David moved labels again, this time to United Artists. However, his time with UA only yielded one single, the title track from the album ***It Takes a Whole Lotta Livin' in a House***, which reached the Top 60. David moved to Republic Records in 1976, where he stayed until 1979. His most successful records with this affiliation were *I'm Gonna Love You Right Out of This World* and *You and Me Alone* (both Top 25 in 1977), *I'll Be There (When You Get Lonely)* (Top 25), *Let's Try to Remember* (Top 40) and *When a Woman Cries* (Top 40) (all 1978), *Darlin'* (Top 20), *You Are My Rainbow* (Top 40) and *You're Amazing* (Top 40) (all 1979).

David turned up on the Kari label in 1981, with the low-level entry *Houston Blue*. He next charted on Music Masters with *Crown Prince of the Barroom* (1982) and *Hold Me* (1983), both of which only made the lower levels. He had three further chart entries in 1983 and 1984, *You Still Got Me* and *The Devil Is a Woman* (Mr. Music in 1983) and *I'm a Country Song* (Hall Katt Country in 1984). David continued to make live appearances and in 1992, he made a tour of Britain. David Rogers died in 1993.

RECOMMENDED ALBUMS:

"She Don't Make Me Cry" (Columbia)(1971)
"Farewell to the Ryman" (Atlantic)(1973)
"Whole Lotta Livin' in a House" (United Artists)(1975)
"I'm Gonna Love You Right Out of This World" (Republic)
"The Best of David Rogers" (Music Masters)(1983)
"Country" (Hall Katt Country)(1984)

ERNEST ROGERS

(Singer, Songwriter, Guitar)

Given Name:	**Ernest Rogers**
Date of Birth:	**October 27, 1897**
Where Born:	**Atlanta, Georgia**
Married:	**Bertha Turnipseed**
Children:	**Wallace Rogers II**
Date of Death:	**October 9, 1967**

Because of his association with Atlanta's radio station WSB from 1922 to 1940, an era when the station featured numerous Country music programs, Ernest Rogers deserves inclusion in an encyclopedia of Country music personalities. It is equally certain that Rogers would have considered the honor a dubious one at best for, despite his own involvement in the art form, he was no admirer of traditional Country music. His attitude is evident in his comments about Fiddlin' John Carson which appeared in the 1956 memoir *Peachtree Parade*: "Credit—if such it may be called—goes to WSB for having introduced hillbilly music to radio, or vice versa. It arrived in the person of Fiddlin' John Carson, an itinerant musician who enjoyed a reputation of sorts in the back country." Clearly Rogers would prefer being remembered as a journalist rather than for his connections with Country music.

Rogers was the son of Dr. Wallace Rogers, a minister for more than sixty-five years in the North Georgia Methodist Conference. As a 2-year-old, Ernest was afflicted with polio but he never let his handicap interfere with his activities. He attended his hometown Emory University, where he proved a very popular student. A member of the school's glee club, Ernest also founded the *Emory Wheel* in 1919 and edited the student weekly his senior year. He capped off his college career by being elected president of the student body. After graduating with honors in 1920, he worked three months on a Dublin, Georgia, newspaper, then returned to Atlanta intending to enter the insurance business but instead he became a copy editor for the *Atlanta Journal*. Eventually, he worked his way up to columnist and from 1943 to 1967 penned the *Peachtree Parade* column.

His connection with the *Journal*, which owned WSB, led to his entry into radio work. In 1922, Rogers originated a music show on which he played guitar, cracked jokes, and sang songs such as *Willie the Weeper* and *Mythological Blues* and even some songs that he wrote. Rogers later got a recording contract with the Victor label and cut at least ten sides, which were almost equally divided between traditional songs and older Pop numbers like *Steamboat Bill* and *Waitin' for the Robert E. Lee*. Considering his general attitude toward Country music it seems likely that if he were forced to label his style he would have called it Folk rather than Country or Hillbilly. It is also entirely possible that his approach to the music was not entirely serious.

For the last five years of his WSB tenure Rogers did newscasting, working the program *The Birthday Table of the Air* into his 7:15 a.m. newscast. He also helped organize the Unorganized Cheerful Givers, who between 1930 and 1940 raised large sums of money for the needy at Christmas. During his eighteen years at WSB Rogers also continued his duties on the *Journal*. Because of the title of his column, he became known as the Mayor of Peachtree. A frequent fictional personality appearing in his column was a character called Percentage Sam.

In 1956, Rogers was the subject of "The Most Unforgettable Character I Ever Met" column in the *Reader's Digest*. The story emphasized how Rogers overcame polio and related an incident where he wore out a thick set of crutch tips climbing Stone Mountain unassisted. Four years later, in 1960, Rogers appeared on the cover of the *Saturday Evening Post*.

Rogers published two books based on his columns. *The Old Hokum Bucket* appeared in 1949 and *The Peachtree Parade* in 1956. In 1962, Rogers officially retired, but continued to contribute three columns a week until shortly before his death. For the last several weeks prior to his death, Rogers was confined to a hospital. He died less than three weeks before his 70th birthday. WKM

KENNY ROGERS

(Singer, Songwriter, Guitar, Bass Guitar, Piano, Actor, TV Program Host, Photographer)

Given Name:	**Kenneth Donald Rogers**
Date of Birth:	**August 21, 1938**
Where Born:	**Houston, Texas**
Married:	**1. (Div.)**
	2. (Div.)
	3. Margo Gladys Anderson (div.)
	4. Marianne Gordon (m. 1977)
Children:	**Carole, Kenny, Jr.**

While the media likes to pigeonhole performers, superstar Kenny Rogers defies categorization. His records have run the gamut from Pop-Country to Soul. He is also an adept actor and TV presenter.

Kenny's family was very poor, but closely knit. His uncles used to visit his home and play guitar and fiddle. Kenny started to sing at church and in 1956, while still a senior at Jefferson Davis High School, Kenny formed his first band, the Scholars, playing Rockabilly. As "Kenneth Rogers" he signed to Carlton Records in 1958 and released two singles that year, *We'll Always Fall in Love Again/That Crazy Feeling* and *For You Alone/I've Got a Lot to Learn*. The local success of *That Crazy Feeling* led to an appearance on *American Bandstand*.

In 1959, Kenny enrolled at the University of Texas at Houston, but soon left to play stand-up bass in Jazz group the Bobby Doyle Trio, with whom he recorded an album for Columbia. From this group, Kenny joined the Kirby Stone Four and then in 1966, he became a member of the New Christy Minstrels. Kenny stayed with them until the following year, when he formed the First Edition with Mike Settle, Thelma Lou Camacho, Terry Williams and Mickey Jones. All but Jones had been members of the Minstrels. Jones had formerly played drums with Bob Dylan, Trini Lopez and Johnny Rivers.

At the end of 1967, as the First Edition, they signed with Reprise Records and at the beginning of 1968, they scored their first Pop hit, Mickey Newbury's *Just Dropped In (to See What Condition My Condition Was In)*, which went Top 5. It took another year for the group to chart again when they had a Top 20 Pop hit with *But You Know I Love You*. By the time of their next hit, the group had become known as Kenny Rogers and the First Edition. The hit that would start Kenny's Country chart success was Mel Tillis' *Ruby, Don't Take Your Love to Town*. The single went Top 10 on the Pop chart and reached the Country Top 40. It also reached No.2 on the U.K. Pop chart. They rounded off 1969 with *Ruben James*, which went Top 30 on the Pop chart and Top 50 on the Country lists.

The group stayed on Reprise until 1972 and their principal Pop hits were *Something's Burning* and *Tell It All Brother* (both 1970). *Something's Burning* also became a Top 10 Pop hit in the U.K. Their 1971 ***Greatest Hits*** album was Certified Gold in 1973. During 1972, they hosted their own syndicated TV variety series, *Rollin' on the River,* and toured the world. In 1973, Kenny and the group switched to the Jolly Rogers label, but only chalked up a Top 70 version of the Merle Haggard-Bonnie Owens song *Today I Started Loving You Again*. That year, Kenny left the group and in 1975, they went their separate ways.

During 1975, Kenny signed with United Artists, with Larry Butler as his producer, and his first solo chart effort was *Love Lifted Me*, which was a Top 20 Country hit. He had two Country chart singles during 1976, *While the Feeling's Good* (Top 50) and *Laura (What's He Got That I Ain't Got)* (Top 20). However, it was the follow-up single, Roger Bowling and Hal Bynum's *Lucille*, that launched Kenny into the superstar realm. The record went to the top of the Country chart, crossed to the Pop Top 5 and became a No.1 Pop hit in the U.K. The record became the CMA's "Single of the Year" and was Certified Gold in 1977. Kenny's ***Kenny Rogers*** album was released in 1976 and was Certified Gold the following year. Kenny followed up with another No.1, *Daytime Friends*, which also became a Pop hit, reaching the Top 30. He ended the year with his own song, *Sweet Music Man*, which went Top 10 Country and Top 50 Pop. The song would be covered by a wide range of performers, including Dolly Parton, Millie Jackson, Anne Murray, Tammy Wynette, Dottie West, Lynda Carter and Waylon Jennings, and became a No.1 hit in France for French idol Johnny Halliday. During 1977, Kenny married *Hee Haw* regular Marianne Gordon. Kenny released two albums that year, ***Daytime Friends*** and ***Ten Years of Gold***, both of which went Gold in 1977 and 1978 respectively, with ***Ten Years of Gold*** also going Platinum in 1978.

Superstar ***Kenny Rogers***

Kenny then commenced a run of five successive No.1 solo singles. It started with *Love or Something Like It* (Pop Top 40) and continued in 1978 with the classic Don Schlitz epic *The Gambler* (Pop Top 20). In addition, that year, he had a No.1 Country hit with his duet with Dottie West, *Every Time Two Fools Collide,* and a Top 3 with Dottie on *Anyone Who Isn't Me Tonight*. Kenny's two albums that year, ***Love or Something Like It*** and ***The Gambler***, were both Certified Gold during the same year and ***The Gambler*** was Certified Platinum in 1979.

In 1979, the No.1's were *She Believes in Me*, which crossed to the Pop Top 5 and was Certified Gold the same year, *You Decorated My Life* (Pop Top 10) and the awesome Roger Bowling-Billy Edd Wheeler saga, *Coward of the County*, which also was a Pop Top 3 hit, topped the British charts and was Certified Gold the following year. Kenny also had a No.1 with Dottie on *All I Ever Need Is You* and a Top 3 duet, *'Til I Can Make It on My Own*. That year, Kenny appeared in two specials for CBS-TV, *A Special Kenny Rogers* and *Kenny Rogers and the American Cowboy*. During 1979, Kenny released the albums ***Classics*** (with Dottie West) and ***Kenny***. The former went Gold the same year and the latter went Gold in 1980.

The new decade started with another duet, this time the husky voice of Kim Carnes. Their single *Don't Fall in Love with a Dreamer* reached the Country Top 3 and the Pop Top 5. This was followed by the Top 5 Country hit *Love the World Away*, which was featured in the movie *Urban Cowboy*. It also became a Top 15 Pop hit. During this time, United Artists became Liberty Records and Kenny completed 1980 with the exquisite Lionel Richie ballad *Lady* (it was also produced by Richie). It reached No.1 on the Country chart, but stayed in that position atop the Pop chart for 6 weeks, went Gold the same year and became a major hit in Britain. That year Kenny made his acting debut as Brady Hawkes in the made-for-TV mini-series *Kenny Rogers as the Gambler*, in which he starred with Bruce Boxleitner and which received the highest rating for the year for any TV movie. Kenny also starred in the CBS-TV special *Kenny Rogers' American*. Kenny's two albums that year, ***Greatest Hits*** and ***Gideon***, were both

Certified Gold and then Platinum in 1980. His Christmas album was Certified Platinum in 1982.

Kenny remained with Liberty until 1983 and continued to rack up a continuous stream of major hits. They were *What Are You Doin' in Love* (a No.1 duet with Dottie West), *I Don't Need You* (No.1 Country/Top 3 Pop), *Share Your Love with Me* (Top 5 Country/Top 15 Pop) and *Blaze of Glory* (Top 10 Country) (all in 1981). That year, Kenny starred in the TV movie *Coward of the County*. The album ***Share Your Love***, which was produced by Lionel Richie and featured Richie, Michael Jackson and Gladys Knight & the Pips, was Certified Gold and Platinum that same year.

His hits in 1982 were *Through the Years* (Top 5 Country/Top 15 Pop), *Love Will Turn You Around*, from Kenny's debut motion picture *Six Pack* (No.1 Country/Top 15 Pop), and *A Love Song* (Top 3 Country/Top 50 Pop). That year, Kenny and Marianne established the World Hunger Media Awards, which presents $100,000 each year to members of the media who have made significant impact with their coverage of the hunger issue. The first ceremony was held at the United Nations. ***Love Will Turn You Around,*** the soundtrack album for the movie *Six Pack*, went Gold the same year.

In 1983, Kenny scored with Bob Seger's *We've Got Tonight*, a No.1 Country and Top 10 Pop success on which Kenny was joined by Scottish singer Sheena Easton, *All My Life* (Top 15 Country/Top 40 Pop) and the Top 5 Country hit *Scarlet Fever*. During 1983, Kenny starred with Linda Evans and Bruce Boxleitner in the mini-series *Kenny Rogers as the Gambler II: The Adventure Continues*. At the American Music Awards, Kenny was given the "Special Award of Merit." The album ***We've Got Tonight*** was Certified Gold during its year of release.

Kenny moved to RCA in 1983 and debuted with the ***Eyes That See in the Dark*** album, which was co-produced by Barry Gibb of Bees Gees fame. The first single, *Islands in the Stream*, written by the Bees Gees, was a tour-de-force duet with Dolly Parton and marked the beginning of an ongoing professional relationship between Kenny and Dolly. The single went to No.1 on both Country and Pop charts and was Certified Platinum that year and was named the AMA's "Best Country Single." The year ended with the Liberty release *You Were a Good Friend*, which went Top 20. Kenny's ***20 Greatest Hits*** was Certified Gold in 1983, the year of release.

Kenny's five-year period with RCA was continuously interspersed with Liberty products being released. Not all of his RCA releases were major successes and because of his choice of material certain singles did well on the Country chart and failed on the Pop chart and vice versa. His major hits in 1984 were *Buried Treasure* (Top 3 Country), *Together Again* (a Top 20 duet with Dottie West on Liberty), *Evening Star/Midsummer Nights* (which peaked just shy of the Country Top 10), *What About Me* (Pop Top 20) with Kim Carnes and James Ingram and *Crazy* (which went to No.1 Country in 1985).

During 1984, Kenny toured Australia and New Zealand as well as touring in the U.S. with Dolly Parton. His 1983 album ***Eyes That See in the Dark*** was the "Best Selling Country Album by a Male Artist" at the 1984 National Association of Recording Merchandisers Convention, having gone Platinum in 1983. Kenny's 1984 U.S. Food Drive raised in excess of 1 million pounds of canned goods from concert goers and by the time of his concert at Nassau Coliseum, New York, it reached 2,017,080 pounds. The special *Kenny and Dolly: A Christmas to Remember* on CBS-TV was the top-rated TV program of the week. Kenny released two albums in 1984, ***What About Me*** and ***Once Upon a Christmas***. They both went Platinum the same year, with the latter going Double-Platinum in 1989.

In 1985, Kenny's hits were *Real Love* (No.1 Country) with Dolly Parton and *Morning Desire* (which went to No.1 Country in 1986). During 1985, Kenny received three awards from the AMA, "Best Country Single" for *Islands in the Stream*, "Best Country Album" for ***Eyes That See in the Dark*** and as "Best Male Vocalist." That year, Kenny was a part of USA for Africa which had the No.1 Platinum Certified single *We Are the World,* and appeared at Farm Aid. He also toured Japan and with Dolly starred in the in-concert HBO TV special *Kenny & Dolly: Real Love*. Kenny and Marianne received the "High Hopes Award" at the Carousel Ball in Denver in aid of the Children's Diabetes Foundation. Kenny also appeared in the CBS-TV Movie of the Week *Wild Horses*. Kenny's 1985 album ***The Heart of the Matter*** was produced by George Martin, best known for his production skills on the Beatles' records, and went Gold the same year.

By 1986, Kenny's Pop chart success had evaporated. That year, *Tomb of the Unknown Love* became a No.1 Country hit and at the end of the year, *Twenty Years Ago* charted and, in 1987, went Top 3. His other hits in 1987 were *Make No Mistake, She's Mine*, a duet with Ronnie Milsap and the Top 3 *I Prefer the Moonlight*. During 1986, in a national poll conducted by *PM Magazine* and *U.S. Today*, Kenny was voted "Favorite Singer of All Time" and in the same poll, in response to the question "If you could get free tickets to any concert, who would you most like to see?" the majority response was Kenny Rogers. In the 1986 People's Choice Awards, Kenny was named "Favorite Country Music Performer." That year, he became Co-Chair of the charitable organization Hands Across America, which was set up by Kenny's long-term manager, Ken Kragen. Kenny also appeared in the CBS-TV Special *Kenny Rogers' Working America* and *Kenny Rogers as the Gambler III: The Legend Continues*, both in 1987.

Kenny's last major success for RCA was *The Factory*, which went Top 10. His move to Reprise came about the time that his record career took a decided nose-dive. His successes between 1988 and 1991, when he had his last chart single, primarily peaked at a lower level and were *When You Put Your Heart in It* (Top 30) (1988), the magnificent sci-fi Western saga *Planet Texas* (Top 30), *The Vows Go Unbroken* (Top 10) and the duet with Anne Murray *If I Ever Fall in Love Again* (Top 30) (all 1989), *Maybe* with Holly Dunn and *Love Is Strange* with Dolly Parton (both Top 30, 1990). Kenny's 1989 album ***Something Inside So Strong*** went Gold in 1990. During 1990, his video *Great Video Hits* was also Certified Gold.

Through this period, Kenny's specials on TV were *The Kenny Rogers Classic Weekend* (Sports and Entertainment Special on ABC-TV, 1988), *Kenny Rogers in Concert: A Holiday Special for Public Television* (PBS), *The Second Annual Kenny Rogers/J.C. Penney Classic Weekend* (Sports and Entertainment Special, NBC-TV), *Kenny, Dolly & Willie: Something Inside So Strong* (NBC-TV) and *Christmas in America: A Love Story* (which also starred his son, Kenny Rogers, Jr.) (all 1989). During 1990, Kenny was a recipient (the only Country one) of the Horatio Alger Award for people who have distinguished themselves though coming from humble beginnings. His special that year was *The Third Annual Kenny Rogers/J.C. Penney*

Classic Weekend (Sports and Entertainment Special, NBC-TV).

In 1991, Kenny teamed up with Linda Davis, and their duet *If You Want to Find Love* peaked just below the Top 10. Kenny also starred in the mini-series *The Luck of the Draw: The Gambler Returns*, which also featured Reba McEntire in her acting debut. During 1992, Kenny made *Kenny Rogers: Keep Christmas with You*. In 1993, he starred in a Movie of the Week, *El Diablo*, which also featured Naomi Judd and Travis Tritt. During the year, ***Christmas in America*** was Certified Gold. Kenny's projects during 1994 were *MacShayne: Winner Takes All*, *MacShayne: Final Roll of the Dice* and *Gambler V*.

As well as being a singer, songwriter and actor, Kenny is also a fine photographer. An exhibition of his work was staged at the Country Music Hall of Fame in Nashville and he has published two books of photographs, *Kenny Rogers' America* and *Kenny Rogers: Your Friends and Mine*. One of his photographs graced the cover of Glen Campbell's 1977 album ***Southern Nights***. In 1988, Kenny took the official team photograph of the Olympic U.S. gymnastics team (he also sang their theme song, *When You Put Your Heart in It*). Kenny's TV Special *A Day in the Life of Country Music* included some footage of him taking the photograph of Hillary Rodham Clinton.

During 1993, Kenny could be seen each week on the Arts & Entertainment channel hosting *The Real West*. His autobiography, *Making It with Music* (written with Len Epand), was published by Harper & Row.

RECOMMENDED ALBUMS:

"Kenny Rogers & the First Edition Greatest Hits" (Reprise)(1971)
"Ten Years of Gold" (United Artists)(1977)
"The Gambler" (United Artists)(1978)
"Classics" (United Artists)(1979) [With Dottie West]
"Share Your Love" (Liberty)(1981)
"We've Got Tonight" (Liberty)(1983)
"Twenty Greatest Hits" (Liberty)(1983)
"Eyes That See in the Dark" (RCA Victor)(1984)
"What About Me?" (RCA Victor)(1984)
"The Heart of the Matter" (RCA Victor)(1985)
"I Prefer the Moonlight" (Reprise)(1987)
"Greatest Hits" (RCA Victor)(1989)
"Something Inside So Strong" (Reprise)(1989)
"Back Home Again" (Reprise)(1991)

ROY ROGERS

(Singer, Songwriter, Guitar, Mandolin, Fiddle, Actor)

Given Name: Leonard Franklin Slye
Date of Birth: November 5, 1911
Where Born: Cincinnati, Ohio
Married: 1. Arlene Williams (dec'd.) 2. Dale Evans (m. 1947)
Children: Roy Jr. ("Dusty"), John (dec'd.), Robin Elizabeth (dec'd.), Cheryl Darlene, Linda Lu, Marion, Mary, Little Doe, Deborah Lee (dec'd.) [all except Roy, Jr., and Robin adopted]

For most kids who went to watch the Westerns, you were either a Gene Autry or a Roy Rogers fan. To a Rogers follower, he always was and always will be the "King of the Cowboys." With his beloved palomino, Trigger (now stuffed and mounted at the Rogers ranch in California), and his dog, Bullit (also stuffed), Roy was the personification of the hero in the white hat who rid the West of the bad guy in the black hat. He found it somewhat ironic to be working in the late 80's with Clint Black, a good guy in a black hat.

Roy was born into a musical family on a farm near Duck Run, Ohio. He was influenced by his father and performed locally, while also having several jobs, including working in a shoe factory in Cincinnati. In the late 20's, he appeared with his cousin, Stanley Slye, as the Slye Brothers. In 1929, the family moved to California and Roy worked as a peach picker and truck driver. However, he was determined to make it as a performer.

In 1931, he and Stan got on KMCS Inglewood, without much success. Roy was offered a job as singer with the Rocky Mountaineers on KGFJ. Because he lacked confidence as a solo singer, Roy suggested they add another singer, and Bob Nolan answered his advertisement. Shortly after, "Slumber" Nichols joined them, and soon after, Bob left and Tim Spencer joined. In 1932, Roy, Slumber and Tim joined the International Cowboys, led by Benny Nawahi. However, this didn't work out, and they formed the trio O-Bar-O Cowboys and they toured without success. However, Roy did meet his first wife on the tour.

Roy Rogers and Dale Evans

He joined the International Cowboys while rehearsing with Nolan and Spencer, and then Bob and Tim also joined the group. In 1933, they formed the Pioneer Trio. Spencer was working at the time as a manager in a Safeway food store, and hadn't wanted to leave and Nolan had been discouraged by the earlier attempts to make it in the music business, and had not been in a hurry to return. However, along with Hugh Farr and then his brother Karl, the group Sons of the Pioneers was formed in 1934.

They made their movie debut in 1935 in *The Old Homestead* and then went on to appear in the Gene Autry movie *Tumbling Tumbleweeds* and the "Three Mesquiteers" series. They then appeared in *Rhythm on the Range* and another Gene Autry movie, *The Big Show*, the following year. In 1937, they were signed to appear in a series of Columbia Westerns starring Charles Starrett and the Gene Autry film *The Old Corral*. Roy left the group to spend a year on a ranch in Montana to learn to shoot and ride. He had brief parts in the movie *Wild Horse Rodeo* as Dick Weston.

The following year, Roy, finding out that Republic Pictures was looking for a new singing cowboy to act as a threat to Gene Autry, got a screen test, singing *Tumbling Tumbleweeds*, and on October 13 was signed to the company. Roy made one final movie with Autry, the 1938 picture *The Old Barn Dance*, playing a not so bad "baddie" who has to fight Autry. He now became Roy Rogers.

His first movie, *Under Western Skies*, had originally been planned as a Gene Autry vehicle entitled *Washington Cowboy*, but when Autry had his showdown with Republic, he was out and Roy was in. When Autry returned from suspension, Roy found that he was relegated to second place. During the rest of 1938 and 1939, Roy appeared in *Billy the Kid Returns* (1938), *Frontier Pony Express*, *The Arizona Kid* and *Days of Jesse James* (1939).

From 1939, he acquired George ("Gabby")

Hayes as a humorous sidekick. Many people were surprised by Roy's ability to act and his appearance in John Wayne's *Dark Command* in 1940 was a revelation. During that year, Roy also made the movies *Carson City Kid, The Trail from Music Mountain* and *Young Buffalo Bill*. In 1941, Roy made the movie *Red River Valley*.

In 1942, when Autry entered the armed forces, Roy was promoted into big-budget movies and given the sobriquet "King of the Cowboys." This led to the start of the famed fancy outfits and silver-plated guns. During 1942, Roy made the movie *Robin Hood of the Pecos*. Roy teamed up with Dale Evans, as his leading lady, and in 1944 and they appeared in *The Cowboy and the Senorita, Yellow Rose of Texas, The Man from Music Mountain* and *San Fernando Valley* (all 1944) and *Along the Navajo Trail* (1945), *Night Time in Nevada* (1946) and *My Pal Trigger* (1946). All of Roy and Dale's movies were notable for their strong music content, provided by the Sons of the Pioneers, Spade Cooley or Foy Willing and the Riders of the Purple Sage. In all Roy and Dale made twenty-five movies together in seven years. As the interest in musical Westerns diminished in the late 40's, so the plots of his movies seemed to get darker. The fist fights got more brutal and the harmless plots of earlier movies were replaced by more meaningful ones.

In the 50's, Roy made the movies *Pals of the Golden West* and *South of Caliente* (1951) and appeared in features such as *Son of Paleface*, which starred Bob Hope and Jane Russell. At this point, Roy decided to quit making movies. He had now made 91 of them. He and Dale now moved on to hosting an NBC radio series, the *Roy Rogers Show,* and then the nationwide *Roy Rogers Show* on NBC-TV (1952-54) and the *Chevy Show*, with the Sons of the Pioneers. He appeared in just one more movie in 1975, *Mackintosh and T.J.* In the late 80's Roy and Dale hosted *The Roy Rogers and Dale Evans Theater* on TNN and Roy appeared with Gene Autry as joint hosts for several Western movie introductions.

Unlike Gene Autry and Tex Ritter, Roy never had a major recording career. As a member of the Sons of the Pioneers, he first recorded for Decca in 1934. His first solo hit was *Hi-Yo Silver*, in 1938. During the 40's, Roy recorded for Victor, and he chalked up hits at the end of the decade with *A Little White Cross on the Hill* (1946), *My Chickashay Gal* (1947) and *Blue Shadows on the Trail/Pecos Bill* (1948, featuring the Sons of the Pioneers). In 1950, again supported by the Pioneers, he had a major hit with *Stampede*.

During the mid and late 50's, Roy and Dale recorded religious material for RCA Victor and RCA-Bluebird and in the 60's and 70's, they did the same for Capitol, and in addition, Roy recorded solo albums for both Capitol and Golden. This was quite a velvet patch for Roy as regards chart singles. He chalked up four hits between 1970 and 1972, *Money Can't Buy Love* (Top 40, 1970), *Lovenworth* (Top 15, 1971), *Happy Anniversary* (Top 50, 1971) and *These Are the Good Old Days* (Top 75, 1972).

By 1974, he was with 20th Century Records and had a major cross-over hit with *Hoppy, Gene and Me*, which charted Top 20 Country and reached the Top 70 on the Pop list. He appeared in the Country charts in 1980, with *Ride Concrete Cowboy, Ride*, which was taken from the movie *Smokey and the Bandit II*. Roy made a guest appearance along with Rex Allen on Rex Allen, Jr.'s 1982 album ***The Singing Cowboy***. RCA released the album ***Roy Rogers' Tribute***, which featured Dusty Rogers, the Kentucky Headhunters, Randy Travis, Clint Black, K.T. Oslin, Restless Heart, Emmylou Harris, Ricky Van Shelton, Kathy Mattea, Lorrie Morgan, the Oak Ridge Boys, Willie Nelson and Dale Evans. A single from the project, *Hold on Partner*, with Clint Black, gave Roy a 1991 Country Top 50 single.

As a member of the Sons of the Pioneers, Roy was inducted in the Country Music Hall of Fame in 1980 and as an individual, he gained that honor in 1989. He was honored by the Cowboy Hall of Fame in a special ceremony at the Gene Autry Museum in 1993.

As a matter of trivia, Trigger appeared in 87 films and 101 TV shows. It was said that he knew 100 tricks and at one time received 1,000 fan letters per week. His saddle and bridle were decorated with 130 ounces of gold, 1,400 ounces of silver and 1,500 rubies and was insured for $50,000. Roy bought Trigger for $80 and refused offers of $150,000 for him. At his most popular, Roy was earning more than $1 million per year.

Roy launched the Roy Rogers chain of fast-food eateries, and now spends his time making personal appearances and looking after his business interests that include the Roy Rogers Western Museum in Apple Valley, California. IMT/BM

RECOMMENDED ALBUMS:

"Sweet Hour of Prayer" (Capitol)(1957) [Re-released by Stetson UK in the original sleeve (1988)] [With Dale Evans]
"The Country Side of Roy Rogers" (Word)(1970) [Re-released by Stetson UK in the original sleeve (1989)]
"Happy Trails to You" (20th Century-Fox)(1975)
"King of the Cowboys" (Bear Family Germany)(1983) [With the Sons of the Pioneers]
"Roy Rogers (Columbia Historic Edition)" (Columbia)(1984)
"Roy Rogers Tribute" (RCA)(1991)
"Sons of the Pioneers with Leonard Slye" (Vim Japan)

LINDA RONSTADT

(Singer, Songwriter, Guitar, Actress)
Date of Birth: July 15, 1946
Where Born: Tucson, Arizona

Linda Ronstadt has become one of the most versatile performers, not just in Country music, but in the entire musical spectrum. She has tackled most areas of music including Country, Folk, Country-Rock, Swing, light Opera and R & B and has slipped from one to the other with consummate ease. Not only has she made many fine albums, but she has also graced and enriched those of other performers. Her early heroes were Hank Williams and Elvis Presley and they have obviously influenced her.

Linda comes from a musical family, steeped in cowboy songs and ballads of Mexico. Her grandfather was a multi-instrumentalist and arranger who led a band back in the 1880's, and she learned to play on her grandfather's guitar. She formed a Folk trio with her brother and sister, the Three Ronstadts, while still in high school. The group was also known as the New Union Ramblers and they played Folk, Country and Mexican songs.

After a year at the University of Arizona, in 1964, she moved to Los Angeles and teamed up with the Kimmel Brothers (Bobby Kimmel on guitar and Kenny Edwards on bass). This evolved into the Stone Poneys. They cut their first sides for Sidewalk, *So Fine/Everybody Has Their Own Ideas*, the following year, but they were not released until 1968.

They signed to Capitol in 1967 and that year had their first chart success with the Top 15 Pop hit *Different Drum*. Their next single, *Up to My Neck in High Muddy Water*, didn't capitalize on this success and in 1968, the trio broke up and Linda went solo, staying with Capitol.

Her first album, in 1969, was ***Hand Sown, Home Grown***, which was critically acclaimed, but yielded no hit singles. She followed this with ***Silk Purse*** the following year and this time, she reached the Top 30 with *Long Long*

Time, which was Grammy-nominated. She followed up in 1972 with her self-titled album, but without much success. On that album, she put together a band that included Glenn Frey, Don Henley, Randy Meisner and Bernie Leadon. They would go on to form the Eagles and then Frey and Henley would go on to illustrious solo careers.

In 1973, Linda signed with Asylum Records and also signed to Peter Asher for management and production. However, Linda owed Capitol an album. The album, ***Heart Like a Wheel***, was a major success and by 1975 had been Certified Gold and would by 1991 reach Double-Platinum status. In March 1974, Linda debuted on the Country chart with *Silver Threads and Golden Needles*, which went Top 20 Country and Top 70 Pop. At the end of the year, Linda's Capitol recording of *I Can't Help It (If I'm Still in Love with You)* entered the Country chart and in 1975 went Top 3 and earned for her the Grammy Award for "Best Country Vocal Performance, Female." The flip-side, *You're No Good*, became a No.1 pop hit. This was followed into the Pop chart by *When Will I Be Loved*, which went Top 3. The flip-side, a re-make of *It Doesn't Matter Any More*, reached the Pop Top 50. As a result of all this action, Linda's 1973 debut album for Asylum, ***Don't Cry Now***, also went Gold in 1975.

Linda's next album for Asylum, ***Prisoner in Disguise*** (1975), was a marvelous piece of work and went Gold shortly after release; it would go Platinum in 1989. From this album, Linda had the Pop Top 5 hit *Heatwave* (the old Motown hit), but the Country audience flipped the record and made the Neil Young song *Love Is a Rose* a Top 5 Country hit. Other releases from the album fared less well, *Tracks of My Tears* (1976) being a Top 25 Pop and Top 15 Country hit, with the flip-side, *The Sweetest Gift*, a duet with Emmylou Harris, reaching the Country Top 15.

That year, Linda released the excellent ***Hasten Down the Wind***. The album was Certified Platinum almost immediately and won for Linda a Grammy Award for "Best Pop Vocal Performance, Female." The first release from the album was a remake of *That'll Be the Day*, which went Top 30 in the Country charts and Top 15 on the Pop chart. At the end of the year, Linda had a Top 10 single with Willie Nelson's *Crazy*. The flip-side, Karla Bonoff's *Someone to Lay Down Beside Me*, made the Pop Top 50. She followed up with another Karla Bonoff song, *Lose Again*, but this time it only made the Pop Top 80, at the beginning of 1977. Among the tracks on the album was Linda's first self-penned recorded tracks, *Try Me Again* (written with Andrew Gold) and *Lo Siento Mi Vida* (written with Kenny Edwards and Linda's father, Gilbert). At the end of 1976, Linda had her first album of ***Greatest Hits***, which went Gold that year and Platinum in 1977 and by 1989 had sold over 4 million copies. She was named "Top Female Singer" in both Pop and Country categories of the *Playboy* Poll.

Simple Dreams, which was released in 1977, was also a major success. It quickly went Platinum and by 1990, it had sold over 3 million copies. The album package received a Grammy Award for "Best Album Package" (Art Director: Kosh). The first single, Roy Orbison's *Blue Bayou*, became a monster hit. It reached the Top 3 on the Country and Pop charts. By 1978, the single was Certified Gold and by 1990, it had reached Platinum status. Linda made a Spanish version of the song and it became a mammoth hit in Mexico and Latin America. She followed up with a remake of yet another Buddy Holly song, *It's So Easy*, which rose to the Top 5 on the Pop charts. The album also yielded the Top 10 Country success *I Never Will Marry*. In 1978, the 1977 Capitol album ***A Retrospective*** was Certified Gold. Linda repeated her double wins in the *Playboy* Poll in 1978.

Linda released her next album, ***Back in the USA***, in 1978. Shortly after, it went Platinum. Two singles from this album, the title track and *Ooh Baby Baby*, were both successful. 1979 did not yield very much in the way of chart success, but with the advent of 1980, Linda was back strong. Both *How Do I Make You* and *Hurt So Bad* were Pop Top 10 hits. They both came from the album ***Mad Love***, which, like its predecessors, found a loyal purchasing public and by the end of the year, had gone Platinum. That year, a second volume of ***Greatest Hits*** was released and that went Gold the same year and would go Platinum in 1989. During 1980, Linda appeared in the New York presentation of the Gilbert and Sullivan light opera *Pirates of Penzance* and in 1983, she made her big screen debut in the film version.

Linda's 1982 album ***Get Closer*** went Gold that year, however, the only successful single was the duet with John David Souther, *Sometimes You Just Can't Win*. The 1983 album ***What's New*** was Certified as Double-Platinum, the following year. This was an interesting album that paired Linda with the Nelson Riddle Orchestra. Her two 1984 albums, ***Lush Life*** and ***For Sentimental Reasons***, were both successful, but did not yield any chart singles.

In 1986, Linda teamed up with soul singer James Ingram for the single *Somewhere Out There* (MCA), which came from the animated movie *An American Tail*. In 1992, the single had been Certified Platinum. It was 1987 that proved a pivotal year for Linda. That year, she teamed up with her longtime friends Dolly Parton and Emmylou Harris for the ***Trio*** album. It won a Grammy Award for "Best Country Performance by a Duo or Group with Vocal Trio" and soon had sold over 1 million copies. The first single from the project, a remake of the Teddy Bears' *To Know Him Is to Love Him*, reached No.1 on the Country chart. Two more singles from the album went Top 5 on the Country charts; they were *Telling Me Lies* and *These Memories of You*.

Linda released a very interesting album that year in ***Canciones de Mi Padre***. The project comprised a selection of Mexican Folk songs derived from the mariachi and ranchera traditions of the 30's and 40's. The album went Gold in 1988 and by 1991, it was Certified Platinum. It was also the recipient of a 1988 Grammy Award for "Best Mexican-American Performance." That year, *Wildflowers* (from ***Trio***) made the Country Top 10. From here on, Linda moved away from Country toward a more Soul feel. The 1989 album ***Cry Like a Rainstorm Howl Like the Wind*** included four duets with super Soul singer Aaron Neville. The album had sold over 2 million copies by 1990. *Don't Know Much*, one of the duets, reached the Top 3 on the Pop chart and went Gold. It also won the 1989 Grammy Award for "Best Pop Performance by a Duo or Group with Vocal." The following year, Linda and Neville repeated this feat for the single *All My Life*, which went to No.1 on the Adult chart. They followed up in the Top 5 Adult Contemporary chart with *When Something Is Wrong with My Baby* and the Top 10 solo hit *Adios*.

Linda's 1991 album, ***Mas Canciones***, was not nearly as successful as its predecessors. She did however have a Top 20 hit on the Adult Contemporary chart with *Dreams to Dream*, from the movie *An American Tail—Fievel Goes West*. The 1992 album ***Frenesi***, which also features Ray Santos and his Orchestra, was very unsuccessful. During the year, Linda and Aaron returned to the Adult Contemporary chart Top 40 with *Close Your Eyes* from his ***Warm Your Heart*** album. In 1993, Linda released ***Winter Light*** on Elektra.

RECOMMENDED ALBUMS:

"Don't Cry Now" (Capitol)(1973)
"Heart Like a Wheel" (Capitol)(1974)
"Prisoner in Disguise" (Asylum)(1975)
"Hasten Down the Wind" (Asylum)(1976)
"Greatest Hits" (Asylum)(1976)
"Simple Dreams" (Asylum)(1977)
"Living in the USA" (Asylum)(1978)
"Greatest Hits Volume 2" (Asylum)(1980)
"Mad Love" (Asylum)(1980)
"Get Closer" (Asylum)(1982)
"What's New" (Asylum)(1983)
"Lush Life" (Asylum)(1984)
"For Sentimental Reasons" (Asylum)(1984)
"Trio" (Warner Brothers)(1987) [With Dolly Parton and Emmylou Harris]
"Canciones de Mi Padre" (Asylum)(1987)
"Cry Like a Rainstorm Howl Like the Wind" (Elektra)(1989)
"Mas Canciones" (Elektra)(1991)
"Frenesi" (Elektra)(1992)
"Winter Light" (Elektra)(1993)

FRED ROSE

(Songwriter, Singer, Piano, Industry Executive)

Date of Birth: **August 24, 1897**
Where Born: **Evansville, Indiana**
Married: **Unknown**
Children: **Wesley**
Date of Death: **December 1, 1954**

It is possible that Fred Rose was the single most important person within Country music. As one-half of Acuff-Rose, the first music publisher dedicated to Country music and based in Nashville, as mentor to the legendary Hank Williams, as a songwriter in both Country and Pop music and as a discoverer of talent, Rose had no equal.

By the time he was age 7, Fred had, without lessons, become a proficient pianist, and by the time he was 10, he was playing professionally. At age 15, he took a freight train to Chicago to develop his singing (allegedly his first love) and played the honky-tonks and restaurants. He progressed to up-market night clubs and landed a recording contract with Brunswick.

There were dozens of applicants to cut player piano rolls for the QRS Company, but Fred and future Jazz great Fats Waller were chosen. Around this time, at the still tender age of 17, Rose began his career as a songwriter. During the 20's, he had major success with songs such as *Deed I Do, Honest and Truly*, and a song that would always be associated with chanteuse Sophie Tucker, *Red Hot Mama*. Then Fred auditioned with at least another fifty hopefuls for the piano slot with the great Paul Whiteman's band. He landed the job and in tandem with Roy Bargy played the famed white grand pianos, on opposite sides of the stage, being billed as "Whiteman's Twin Pianos."

Fred then returned to Chicago, where he and singer/whistler Elmo Tanner formed a double act, the Tune Peddlers. They performed on KYW Chicago, until Tanner left and Rose began his own program, *Fred Rose's Song Shop*, which broadcast five times a week for more than a year. On the show, he wrote songs spontaneously based on titles suggested by listeners. This resulted in his being offered a show on Chicago's WBBM, which was networked by CBS. In 1933, he moved to Nashville, where the *Song Shop* ran on WSM until midway through the next year.

At this time, he returned to Chicago during the final year of the Windy City's Century of Progress World's Fair, and had a featured spot on NBC. From there he returned to Nashville and then journeyed to New York, where he became a Christian Scientist, and polarized his ambitions within the music business. He then went to Hollywood, where he wrote a number of songs for Gene Autry, including the Academy Award-nominated *Be Honest with Me* (1940) and *Tears on My Pillow* (1940). In all, Fred wrote sixteen songs for Autry movies.

During late 1942, Rose returned to Nashville, where he became the staff pianist for WSM. He still did not really understand the meaning of Country music. However, it was hearing Roy Acuff tearfully sing, on the *Grand Ole Opry, Don't Make Me Go to Bed and I'll Be Good*, a song about infant mortality, that opened his eyes. With Acuff, Acuff-Rose Publications was formed in October 1942 and Fred began writing in the Country vein, under his own name and as Floyd Jenkins and Bart Dawson.

However, by 1945, Rose found that being a business executive was getting in the way of his songwriting and talent discovery. As a result, his son, Wesley, an accountant, was brought in to handle the day-to-day running of the company. The Country songs to flow from Rose's pen included such classics as *Low and Lonely, Pins and Needles (In My Heart), Fire Ball Mail, No One Will Ever Know, Blue Eyes Cryin' in the Rain, Roly Poly* (a 1946 Top 3 hit for Bob Wills), *It's a Sin* (a 1947 No.1 for Eddy Arnold), *Texarkana Baby* (a 1948 No.1 for Eddy Arnold and a Top 20 hit for Bob Wills the same year), *Waltz of the Wind* (a 1948 Top 10 single for Roy Acuff), *Deep Water, Foggy River, Faded Love and Winter Roses, No One Will Ever Know* and *We Live in Two Different Worlds*. In 1945, Fred Rose recorded and charted the single *Tender-Hearted Sue* for OKeh Records, under the name of Rambling Rogue.

It was in 1946 that Hank and Audrey Williams entered the Acuff-Rose office. At the time, the Roses, father and son, were playing their daily Ping-Pong match. They stopped to listen to Hank play some of his songs, signed him on the spot and took on board six of his songs. Williams was still thought of as more of a writer than performer by Rose. Acuff-Rose's other writers at the time were Pee Wee King, Redd Stewart, Jenny Lou Carson, Paul Howard, Clyde Moody and Mel Foree.

When Sterling Records wanted a Country singer, Rose put Hank forward, at Wesley's suggestion. At both sessions Hank sang well and the subsequent releases sold well, so Rose contacted Frank Walker, who had just started the MGM label, and as a result Williams joined the label. Fred guided Hank's recording career and any song recorded by him was with Fred's approval and either he or Wesley was present at all recording sessions. Fred also got involved with Hank on his songs and often polished up Hank's raw material. Sometimes he took credit, other times he didn't bother. Those songs that he took credit for were *A Mansion on the Hill, Kaw-Liga* and *I'll Never Get Out of This World Alive*.

Fred also worked with Molly O'Day, Leon Payne and Marty Robbins and with a selection of co-writers that included Ed G. Nelson, Hy Heath, Mel Foree, Zeb Turner, Ray Whitley and Cottonseed Clark. From 1949 to 1954, Rose wrote more memorable songs, including *Afraid* (a Top 15 hit for Rex Allen in 1949), *Crazy Heart* (a Top 5 single for Hank Williams, 1951), *Settin' the Woods on Fire* (a Top 3 record for Hank Williams, 1952) and *Take These Chains from My Heart* (a posthumous 1953 No.1 for Hank Williams). Fred Rose wrote his final song, *I Wonder When We'll Ever Know*, just before his death in 1954.

He died of a heart attack, at the young age of 57, and among those at his funeral were Pee Wee King, Chet Atkins and Redd Stewart.

In June 1955, Wesley Rose accepted the 1954 *Billboard* Award for "C & W Man of the Year," on behalf of his father, who was named the man who had contributed most to C & W music. In 1961 Fred Rose was one of the first three inductees into the Country Music Hall of Fame, along with his acolyte, Hank Williams (who had predeceased Fred) and Jimmie Rodgers.

It is a mark of the quality of Fred Rose's compositions that some of the biggest recordings of his songs occurred after his death. These included *No One Will Ever Know* (Jimmie Rodgers, the Folk-Pop singer, 1962, and Gene Watson, 1980), *Take These Chains from My Heart* (Ray Charles, 1963), *Deep Water, Foggy River* and *Faded Love and Winter Roses* (all Carl Smith, 1967-1968), *It's a Sin* (Marty Robbins, 1969), *Kaw-Liga* (Charley Pride, 1969, and Hank Williams, Jr., 1980), *Blue Eyes Crying in the Rain* (a Willie Nelson 1975 No.1), *Mansion on the Hill* (Michael Murphey, 1976, and Ray Price the following year).

Fred used his power only to benefit and this helped Broadcast Music, Inc. (BMI) break the hold of ASCAP, even though he was a member of ASCAP. This has been of major assistance to songwriters to this day. Like all Renaissance men, Fred Rose lived up to his own motto, "Why Limit Yourself."

WESLEY ROSE

(Industry Executive, Music Publisher, Producer)

Date of Birth:	**February 11, 1918**
Where Born:	**Chicago, Illinois**
Married:	**Margaret**
Children:	**Scarlett**
Date of Death:	**April 26, 1990**

Both Fred Rose and his son Wesley made a powerful contribution to the songwriter, in Nashville in particular and Country music in general. Wesley obtained a B.S. degree in accounting at Chicago's Walton School of Commerce and initially worked in the Accounting Department of Standard Oil. In 1942, Fred Rose and Roy Acuff set up Acuff-Rose Music and a year later, Milene Music as the first music publishing operation in Nashville. However, neither Fred Rose nor Acuff had the time or inclination to run the company and so, in 1945, Fred persuaded Wesley to move to Nashville and become Acuff-Rose's General Manager. Wesley envisaged staying with the company for three months.

It was a meeting with band leader and Columbia A & R man Mitch Mitchell that helped take Country songs into the world of Pop. Wesley went to see him and Mitchell decided to take *Cold, Cold Heart* and record Tony Bennett with it. It became a smash hit. As a result of this, other non-Country performers also recorded Country material.

Following his father's death in 1954, Wesley took over the reins of the company. He also moved more into record production, initially for RCA, Mercury, MGM and Columbia. In 1954, Wesley set up Hickory Records as part of the empire and artists signed to the label included Sue Thompson, the Kershaws, Don Gibson, the Newbeats, Carl Smith, Mickey Newbury, Frank Ifield and Roy Acuff. Wesley was the guiding hand behind the career of the Everly Brothers, when they emerged in 1957. He was also responsible for discovering Stonewall Jackson and Ernie Ashworth.

Wesley was one of the major forces behind the creation of the Country Music Association and three times served as its Chairman. He was also a former National President of the National Academy of Recording Arts and Sciences (NARAS). Under Wesley's hand, Acuff-Rose became one of the major publishing houses with an office in London, England, and the first with a promotion team. He remained the head of Acuff-Rose until the company was sold to Opryland USA in 1985. In 1986, he was elected to the Country Music Hall of Fame. He battled with illness for some while and died in 1990.

PETER ROWAN

(Singer, Songwriter, Yodeler, Guitar, Mandolin, Mandola, Saxophone)

Date of Birth:	**July 4, 1942**
Where Born:	**Boston, Massachusetts**

Several singer/songwriters have become cult heroes rather than stars in the conventional sense. Most of these performers have more talent in one finger than most stars have in all their rhinestone-covered bodies. Most of these cult figures record for labels such as Flying Fish, Sugar Hill, Rounder, Rebel and CMH. Among these talented performers is Peter Rowan.

Peter was born into a musical family, with both parents playing piano and being singers. He learned guitar from an uncle and a grandfather. He studied Thoreau and Transcendentalists in Concord and Wayland, Massachusetts. He eventually became, in his own words, a Pentecostal Buddhist.

In 1956, while still at high school, he formed the Cupids, who performed original Tex-Mex material in the New England area. They released a single on their own label, which got heavy airplay around Boston. From early on, he was into Blues and Folk music. He used to go to the Hillbilly Ranch in Cambridge to watch the Lilly Brothers, Tex Logan and Don Stover. He attended Colgate University from 1961 until 1963 and left to pursue a career in music. That same year, he became lead singer and mandolinist in Mother Bay State Entertainers, out of Cambridge, Massachusetts, and recorded one album, ***The String Band Project***, for Elektra.

The following year, he was playing mandolin with Jim Rooney and Bill Keith. Bill Monroe turned up for a festival in Vermont without a band and because Keith had played with him, Monroe invited Peter to join Bill Monroe and the Blue Grass Boys, with whom he stayed as rhythm guitarist and lead singer until 1967. While with the group, he made his debut on the *Grand Ole Opry* and recorded the ***Bluegrass Time*** album, on Decca, and wrote *Walls of Time* with Monroe, which the band recorded. On leaving the traditional Bluegrass sounds of Monroe, he moved into the Folk-Rock band Earth Opera, along with that wizard of the mandolin, David Grisman. They released two albums, ***Earth Opera*** (1968) and ***The Great American Eagle Tragedy*** (1969). In 1969, they made a one-week appearance in the Top 100 in the Pop charts with *Home to You*. Among the songs they recorded was *It's Love*, which Peter had written with Bill

Folk-Country star ***Peter Rowan***

Monroe. The band supported the Doors on many dates.

He joined the Rock-Fusion band SeaTrain, whose members included Richard Greene, and they recorded in London, under the production guidance of the legendary George Martin. Peter recorded two albums while with the band, namely ***SeaTrain*** (1971) and ***Marblehead Messenger*** (1972). Peter joined forces with his younger brothers Chris (piano, guitar) and Lorin (guitar, mandolin), as the Rowan Brothers. They recorded the self-titled Columbia album.

On leaving them, he got together with Jerry Garcia of Grateful Dead, David Grisman, Vassar Clements and John Kahn, as Old & in the Way. They recorded one self-titled album, live at The Boarding House, in San Francisco, on Round Records, which was released in 1973 and then, in 1975, on Sugar Hill.

Peter's songwriting prowess again surfaced with the New Riders of the Purple Sage's version of Rowan's *Panama Red*, in 1973. The following year, he and Grisman, Clarence White and Richard Greene formed the Bluegrass group Muleskinner, which released an eponymous album for Warner Brothers. During 1975, he rejoined his brothers for three albums on Asylum, ***The Rowans*** (1975), ***Sibling Rivalry*** (1976) and ***Jubilation*** (1978). They later (1982) had an album released on Teentees, entitled ***Hot Love in the City***.

Around 1979, Peter put together the Free Mexican Airforce, which was a mix of Rock and Bluegrass and recorded an eponymous album of original material for Flying Fish, with the support of accordion ace Flaco Jiminez, that included the song *The Free Mexican Airforce*. The following year, the album ***Medicine Trail*** was released.

After visiting Ireland, Peter recorded a Celtic-tinged Bluegrass album, ***The Walls of Time*** (released 1982), in Nashville, for Sugar Hill Records. During that year, Peter appeared on Ricky Skaggs' album ***Family and Friends***. In 1982, Peter got together with Flaco Jiminez and recorded, in London, ***Flaco Jiminez and Peter Rowan Live Rockin' Tex-Mex***, on the U.K. Waterfront label, which also issued Peter's 1984 album ***Revelry***. In 1983, Peter moved to Nashville and put together the Wild Stallions and released the Rockabilly album ***Peter Rowan and the Wild Stallions***, which was released on the Appaloosa label.

Several of Peter's compositions were recorded during this time, including *You Make Me Feel Like a Man* and *Rendezvous* (Ricky Skaggs, 1985), *Dance Time in Texas* (George Strait, 1986), *Where Does Love Go (When It's Gone)* (Janie Frickie, 1988) and *In the Land of the Navajo* (Michael Martin Murphey).

During 1985, Peter undertook a State Department-sponsored concert tour of Ecuador. The following year, he released the Sugar Hill album ***The First Whippoorwill***, a tribute to Bill Monroe, which became WAMU (PBS station) Washington, D.C.'s, "Album of the Year."

In 1987, Peter appeared at the Wembley Festival in England, accompanied by Mark O'Connor and Jerry Douglas. He got together with noted Bluegrass group the Nashville Bluegrass Band and released the 1988 album ***New Moon Rising***, which was a finalist for a Grammy Award for "Best Bluegrass Album." Peter's song *Meadow Green*, a duet with Maura O'Connell, from that album, was included on the soundtrack for the movie *Steel Magnolias*. Peter also appeared on the Flaco Jiminez Arhoolie album ***Flaco's Friends***, along with Ry Cooder. The album was nominated for a Grammy for "Best Mexican-American Album."

Peter released a memorable album, in 1989, on Sugar Hill Records, entitled ***Dust Bowl Children***. On this release he accompanied himself on guitar and mandola. He continues to provide a wide variety of music at both concert and album level.

RECOMMENDED ALBUMS:

"Peter Rowan" (Flying Fish)(1979)
"Medicine Trail" (Flying Fish)(1980)
"The Walls of Time" (Sugar Hill)(1982)
"Peter Rowan and the Wild Stallions" (Appaloosa)(1983)
"Peter Rowan & the Red Hot Pickers" (Sugar Hill) [Features Richard Greene and Tony Trischka. First recorded in 2 volumes for Nippon Columbia for release in Japan. These are the best cuts.]
"The First Whippoorwill" (Sugar Hill)(1986)
"New Moon Rising" (Sugar Hill)(1988)
"Dust Bowl Children" (Sugar Hill)(1989)
U.K. releases:
"Revelry" (Waterfront)(1984)
"Hot Bluegrass" (Waterfront)
"San Antonio Sound" (Waterfront)

DAVE ROWLAND/DAVE & SUGAR

When Formed: 1975
DAVE ROWLAND
(Singer, Songwriter, Trumpet, Piano, Drums, Guitar, Bass Guitar, Actor)
Date of Birth: January 26, 1942
Where Born: Sanger, California
Married: Terri
SUGAR
Original Members:
Vicki Hackeman (also known as Vicki Baker), Jackie Frantz
Newer Members: Sue Powell, Melissa Dean (also known as Melissa Pruett), Patti Cainco, Jamie Kaye, Velvet Williams, Regina Leigh, Cindy Smith, Lisa Alvey, Tina Pappas, Penny Cardin
Final Line-up: Regina Leigh, Lori Mason

During the middle 70's and through the early 80's, Dave & Sugar were among

Dave Rowland and Sugar**, also known as **Dave & Sugar

the most successful vocal groups in Country music. Dave Rowland and an assortment of lovely and talented ladies (in twos) purveyed what has been described as "Tuxedo Country."

The son of a Gospel minister, Dave started out as a dance band vocalist and then, after being drafted, in 1965, he became a trumpeter with the 75th Army Band and while at Fort Belvoir, Virginia, he formed his own group. During his army period, he became the only serviceman to receive a theatrical scholarship from the Entertainment Division of the Army. He also studied acting under Estelle Harmon. He graduated from the Stamps School of Music in Texas and moving to Nashville, became a member of the Stamps Quartet, in 1970. He also qualified for a real estate license. For a year and a half, he toured, as a member of the Stamps, with Elvis Presley. He and Presley became friends because of their common interests in karate and Gospel music.

Dave left the Stamps to get into Country music, and joined the Four Guys, replacing Richard Garrett, in 1974. During his nine-month stay with the group, they played the *Grand Ole Opry* and more importantly, they supported Charley Pride. When he left the Guys, Dave acted as a singing waiter at Papa Leone's in Nashville and had a Country-Rock group, Wild Oates, until he heard that Pride and Tammy Wynette were both looking for a harmony backing group. He held auditions and recruited Jackie Frantz and Vicki Hackeman, and signed on with Pride and Chardon, the company managing Pride.

Vicki (b. Louisville, Kentucky) moved to West Palm Beach, Florida, at an early age. She was active in church choirs and school chorus and sang in a local group while in high school. She was part of a trio that won a statewide contest. She worked with the group the Dallas Star and worked in Nashville as a back-up singer.

Jackie (b. Sydney, Ohio) made her musical debut, winning on the *Ted Mack's Original Amateur Hour*, at age 15 with a trumpet solo. While at Western Kentucky University, she sang and played trumpet with an all-girl group that played USO tours in the Caribbean and Europe. After graduation, she moved to Nashville, to develop as a singer and songwriter. She worked as a soloist and did a lot of studio work. She became lead singer of Friction and toured with the Buck Findley Show.

On September 18, 1975, Dave & Sugar signed to RCA Records, with a little help from Charley Pride. They hit the Country charts at the end of the year, with Shel Silverstein's *Queen of the Silver Dollar*, which reached the Top 25. They followed up with the No.1 hit *The Door Is Always Open*. This opened up a door to a string of major hits from 1976 through 1979. They closed out 1976 with the Top 3 single *I'm Gonna Love You*. In 1977, they had three major hits with *Don't Throw It All Away* (Top 5), *That's the Way Love Should Be* (Top 10) and *I'm Knee Deep in Loving You* (Top 3).

That same year, Jackie Frantz decided that she had had enough of being on the road and Sue Powell joined. Sue (b. Gallatin, Tennessee) was raised in Sellersburg, Indiana. Her mother was a singer, and her father built his own recording studio in their home. Sue began singing in shows around Louisville at age 7. A year later, her father recorded her first single. During her teen years, she was spotted by Brenda Lee's stepfather, Jay Rainwater, who signed her to a management contract when she was 13. As a result, she had a local hit with *Little People*.

The group had two further hits in 1978, *Gotta Quit Lookin' at You Baby* (Top 5) and the No.1 hit *Tear Time*. That year, Vicki left the group and was replaced by Melissa Dean. Melissa had built up a following in Kentucky. During the spring of 1978, the group appeared at the Wembley Festival in London, England. Dave & Sugar hit 1979 with another No.1, *Golden Tears*, the Top 10 single *Stay with Me* and the Top 5 double-sided hit *My World Begins and Ends with You/Why Did You Have to Be So Good*. Toward the end of the year, Sue left the group to go solo, having signed a record deal with RCA. She went on to have a pair of mid-level hits in 1981, *Midnite Flyer* and *(There's No Me) Without You*, and then in 1982, she co-hosted the *Nashville on the Road* TV series.

She was replaced by Jamie Kaye (from Lexington, Kentucky), who had been a back-up singer and had landed a record deal with Mercury Records, while still in high school. In 1980, the group had a Top 20 entry, *New York Wine and Tennessee Shine*, and a Top 40 single, *A Love Song*. During 1980, the group toured with Kenny Rogers, and gained even more public attention. Rogers was one of Dave's tennis opponents, Dave being a highly proficient tennis player. That year, Jamie left and was replaced by a former member of *Jamboree USA*, Patti Caines. Dave, Melissa and Patti remained together as Dave Rowland and Sugar, until 1982 (Melissa, having got a divorce, reverted to her maiden name of Dean). Their final chart records occurred in 1981, when they had *It's a Heartache* (Top 40), the Top 10 single *Fool By Your Side* and *The Pleasure's All Mine* (Top 40), the last two records being on their new label, Elektra.

Elektra persuaded Dave to record a solo album, ***Sugar Free***, but two singles that charted for him during that year failed to make much impact. They were *Natalie/Why Didn't I Think of That* and *Lovin' Our Lives Away*. Dave now got together with Sue and Melissa for a re-formed Dave & Sugar, but that was short-lived and that year, he enlisted Cindy Smith and Lisa Alvey.

Cindy competed in Miss Georgia World and sang and danced on the *Country Music USA* show, while Lisa recorded Gospel music with her parents and won 1st place in the Wrangler Country Starsearch for Kentucky. In 1984, Dave was asked by Helen Cornelius to play Frank Butler in Irving Berlin's *Annie Get Your Gun*.

By the time Dave & Sugar cut their 1986 album, which was produced by Nelson Larkin, Tina Pappas was the voice of Sugar, due to the fact that the other new member, Penny Cardin, was in the hospital. Penny was a former Miss Nashville and was an award-winning pianist. Upon Tina's departure, another former Miss Nashville, Velvet Williams (from Jacksonville, Florida), came on board. Velvet played piano, organ, guitar and banjo, as well as being an adept singer. By 1988, Penny had departed and was replaced by Regina Leigh (from Marshville, North Carolina). A former Miss Union County, she played bass guitar, piano and drums. The current Sugars are Regina Leigh and Lori Mason.

Although Dave & Sugar were one of the top vocal groups in Country, and although they were nominated for several awards, including ACM's "Vocal Group of the Year," they did not receive the acknowledgment they deserved.

RECOMMENDED ALBUMS:

"Pleasure" (Elektra)(1981)
"Greatest Hits—Dave & Sugar" (RCA)(1982)
"Sugar Free" (Elektra)(1982)
"Dave & Sugar" (MCA/Dot)(1986)

BILLY JOE ROYAL

(Singer, Songwriter, Guitar, Piano, Drums)

Date of Birth: **April 3, 1942**
Where Born: **Valdosta, Georgia**
Married: **(div. 1983)**

From making his professional debut at Knotty Pines in Georgia, as opening act for Gladys Knight & the Pips for $5.00, to being a Country music star some thirty years later, Billy Joe Royal has charted a music course that has garnered some twenty-plus hits in both the Pop and Country charts. He has had his ups and downs, but has made a comeback that proves he is still a potent force.

Billy Joe grew up among a family of entertainers and appeared on his uncle's radio show in Valdosta, when only 11. By the time he was 12, he had started to play steel guitar, as his ambition was to play in his uncle's band as a steelie. The family moved to Marietta near Atlanta and at age 14, Billy Joe auditioned for WTJH's *Atlanta Jubilee* (*East Point Jubilee*) and got a spot alongside Joe South, Jerry Reed, Ray Stevens and Freddy Weller. While still at high school, Billy Joe had his own rock'n'roll band, the Corvettes. Their first public appearance was for the PTA at Valdosta's Remerton Grammar School.

By the time he was 16, Billy Joe was the featured singer in an Atlanta strip club. His recording career started in 1962, when he cut sides for local labels, and then the following year, he headed for Cincinnati, where he attended acting school. In 1965, Joe South called Billy Joe, telling him he had written a song that would be ideal for Gene Pitney; however, at the time, Pitney was a major star,

***Billy Joe Royal** at Nashville's Fan Fair*

and so Billy Joe flew down to Atlanta to demo *Down in the Boondocks*. Publisher Bill Lowery took the demo to Columbia Records, which signed Billy Joe to a six-year deal. The single went Top 10 on the Pop chart and he was on his way.

For the next six years, Billy Joe toured constantly and at one time performed seventy-two consecutive one-nighters. He appeared on Dick Clark's *Cavalcade of Stars*, which became *Where the Action Is*. He then toured with Paul Revere and the Raiders. On the record front, Billy Joe followed-up *Boondocks* with *I Knew You When* (Top 15, 1965) and *I've Got to Be Somebody* (Top 40, 1966). He then had two 1966 low-level entries, *Heart's Desire* and *Camp Girls*. Up to and including *Heart's Desire*, the songs were written by Joe South, who was also responsible for the 1967 hit *Hush*, which reached the Top 60. During 1968, Billy Joe was absent from the charts, but he returned to the Pop list in 1969, with the Top 15 hit *Cherry Hill Park*. It was another 16 months before he had another chart entry, when *Tulsa* reached the Top 90.

By now the bubble had burst and although he continued recording, the hits didn't come. He became a regular performer at Las Vegas and Lake Tahoe. He did TV, movie and commercial work, and in 1978, he had a low-level single for Private Stock Records, with his version of *Under the Boardwalk*. He recorded an album for Mercury, which was produced by Atlanta Rhythm Section's drummer, Robert Nix. In 1980, he moved back to Georgia.

By 1984, he was determined to revitalize his recording career, and came across a song that he felt would be a smash, Gary Burr's *Burned Like a Rocket*. He came to Nashville and found that none of the record companies shared his enthusiasm. He returned to Atlanta and the song was released on Southern Tracks. It was picked up by Atlantic America Records, which was returning to Country music, and Billy Joe was signed to the label. Billy Joe was proven right as the record went to No.10 on the Country chart. It would probably have done better, but airplay was killed off by the *Challenger* disaster.

In 1986, Billy Joe had *Boardwalk Angel*, which reached the Top 50, and *I Miss You Already* reached the Top 15. This last single, written by Marvin Rainwater and Faron Young, acted as a trigger to his career and in 1987, he had the Top 15 single *Old Bridges Burn Slow*, the Top 30 record *Members Only* (which was a duet with Donna Fargo) and the Top 5 solo hit *I'll Pin a Note on Your Pillow*. He continued with his success in 1988, with *Out of Sight and Out of Mind* (Top 10) (which had a very popular video) and his version of *It Keeps Right on Hurtin'*, which went Top 20.

His career leapt forward in 1989, when the title track of his album ***Tell It Like It Is*** reached the Top 3 and was followed by *Love Has No Right* (Top 5) and *Till I Can't Take It Anymore*, which reached the Top 3 and stayed on the Country charts for 6 months. The album ***Tell It Like It Is*** reached the Country Album chart Top 15 and was on the chart for 63 weeks. That year, Billy Joe was inducted into the Georgia Music Hall of Fame. He lost some steam in 1990, as Country tastes changed, and *Searchin' for Some Kind of Clue* reached the Top 20 and *Ring Where a Ring Used to Be* only made the Top 40. The album ***Out of the Shadows*** reached the Top 25 on the Country album chart.

During 1991, Billy Joe only had one chart record, the Top 30 entry *If the Jukebox Took Teardrops*. His **Greatest Hits** album reached the Top 40, but only stayed around for 9 weeks. By the following year, his star had waned and his one chart entry, *I'm Okay (and Gettin' Better)*, just failed to make the Top 50.

Billy Joe does not have a "Country" voice. Having an amazing top register, his vocal tones are something like a melting pot of Sam Cooke, B.J. Thomas and Jackie Wilson, and every so often, his style of bluesy-poppy Country comes into vogue. In the 90's, it is out, but that's not to say that Billy Joe, whose pastime is tennis, may not serve up another ace.

RECOMMENDED ALBUMS:

"The Royal Treatment" (Atlantic America)(1987)
"Billy Joe Royal" (Mercury)(1987) [Re-issue]
"Looking Ahead" (Atlantic America)(1989)
"Tell It Like It Is" (Atlantic America)(1989)
"Greatest Hits" (Columbia)(1989)
"Greatest Hits" (Atlantic)(1991)
"Billy Joe Royal" (Atlantic)(1992)

BOBBY RUSSELL

(Singer, Songwriter)

Date of Birth:	**April 19, 1941**
Where Born:	**Nashville, Tennessee**
Married:	**1. Vicki Lawrence (div.)**
	2. Cynthia
Date of Death:	**November 19, 1992**

It was for his superb songwriting skills that Bobby Russell will always be remembered. He is the man who wrote, among others, *Honey* and *Little Green Apples*. However,

Bobby Russell was also a successful recording artist for Elf, United Artists and Columbia.

Bobby first came to public notice as a songwriter in 1966 with Brian Hyland's Top 20 Pop hit *The Joker Went Wild.* Then in 1968, he specifically wrote *Little Green Apples* for Roger Miller. The song became a Top 10 Country and Top 40 Pop hit for Miller. It earned two Grammy Awards that year for Bobby, as "Song of the Year" and "Best Country Song." The same month it charted (March 1968), Bobby Goldsboro took the Russell song *Honey* to No.1 on both the Country and Pop charts and earned a Gold Record. The same year, *Little Green Apples* became a summer Top 3 Pop hit for O.C. Smith, which earned him a Gold Record, and in addition, Patti Page charted with the song. That year, on Elf Records, Bobby made his debut on the Country chart with the Top 70 *1432 Franklin Pike Circle Hero,* which did become a Top 40 Pop hit.

In 1969, Bobby had two Country chart entries with *Carlie* (Top 70) and *Better Homes and Gardens*. In addition, O.C. Smith charted Pop Top 50 with *Honey*. In 1971, Bobby had a major chart success as a United Artists recording artist with *Saturday Morning Confusion*, which went Top 25 Country and Top 30 Pop. Bobby had more success in 1973, when his then wife, Vicki Lawrence, had a No.1 Pop hit with *The Night the Lights Went Out on Georgia*, which was Certified Gold. That year, Bobby had his final chart single as an artist with his Columbia release *Mid American Manufacturing Tycoon*, which just scraped into the Country chart.

In 1992, Reba McEntire took *The Night the Lights Went Out on Georgia* into the Country Top 15. For some while, Bobby had suffered with coronary artery disease and in November 1992, Bobby Russell died. In 1994 Bobby Russell was inducted into the Nashville Songwriters Hall of Fame.

RECOMMENDED ALBUMS:

"Words, Music, Laughter & Tears" (Elf)(1968)
"Dial-a-Hit" (Bell)(1969)
"Saturday Morning Confusion" (United Artists)(1971)

The fun-loving ***Johnny Russell***

JOHNNY RUSSELL

(Singer, Songwriter, Guitar)

Given Name: **John Bright Russell**
Date of Birth: **January 23, 1940**
Where Born: **Sunflower County, Mississippi**
Married: **Beverley Heckel (div.)**

The quip that he carries a lot of weight in Nashville perhaps describes Johnny Russell in more ways than one. As a successful songwriter, his songs have been recorded by such names as Jim Reeves, Buck Owens, Loretta Lynn, the Beatles, the Statler Brothers and Dolly Parton. As a Country singer whose recordings have delighted his fans for many years and as a great storyteller with the catch phrase "Can you all see me?" Johnny has been billed as "the Biggest Act in Country Music."

Johnny's rural upbringing in Roundway, Mississippi, exposed him to the delicious food of the area and he has always been partial to fried okra, butterbeans, fried chicken and cornbread. His early musical influences were Ernest Tubb, Lefty Frizzell and Roy Acuff and listening to the *Grand Ole Opry*. Around the age of 11, his family moved to Fresno, California, and throughout his school years, Johnny was into music. He entered and won talent contests and later acted in character parts on TV shows. At one time, he worked as a deejay on station KEAP and then began performing in bars and clubs. He had always written songs and in 1958 decided to record one, *In a Mansion Stands My Love*.

This recording led to an airing on WSM Nashville's *Ralph Emery's Late Night Show.* As a result of this airplay, Johnny met Chet Atkins, Eddy Arnold, Hank Locklin and Archie Campbell (on the same day) and all of these entertainers became long-lasting friends of Johnny's. He moved to Nashville for a while in 1958. Then Chet Atkins chose *In a Mansion Stands My Love* to be recorded by the great Jim Reeves as the flip-side of *He'll Have to Go*, which became a million seller. Now Johnny developed further songwriting and recording deals. He was not successful at this time as a recording artist and so he returned to California and was soon working hard at his songwriting. Buck Owens recorded Johnny's song *Act Naturally* (1963) and the single went to No.1 on the Country chart. This song was also recorded by the Beatles in 1965 and became a hit in the Pop charts. It became a hit again in 1989 when Buck Owens teamed up with former Beatle Ringo Starr.

Wanting to renew his recording career, Johnny decided to move back to Nashville in 1971. Chet Atkins signed Johnny to RCA Records, with Jerry Bradley producing. Johnny's first chart entry was *Mr. and Mrs. Untrue*, which was followed by *What a Price*, both being medium-sized successes. In 1972, Johnny had chart success with *Mr. Fiddle Man* (Top 60) and *Rain Falling on Me* (Top 40). In 1973, Johnny had his first Top 20 hit with *Catfish John.* He followed up with *Chained* (Top 40) and then he had the career single *Rednecks, White Socks and Blue Ribbon Beer*, which went Top 5.

In 1974, Johnny opened his account with *The Baptism of Jesse Taylor*, which reached the Top 15. Although he never reached the same level of record success, Johnny continued to appear on the Country chart. *She's in Love with a Rodeo Man* and *She Burn't the Little Roadside Tavern Down* both went Top 40, in 1974. In 1975, he had *That's How My Baby Builds a Fire* (Top 25), *Hello I Love You* (Top 15) and *Our Marriage Was a Failure* (Top 50).

Johnny stayed with RCA until 1977, during which time his other hits were *I'm a Trucker* (Top 60), *This Man and Woman Thing* (Top 50) (both 1976) and *The Son of Hickory Holler's Tramp* (Top 40), *Obscene Phone Call* (Top 100, with his former wife, Beverley Heckel) and *Leona* (Top 70) (all 1977). In 1978, after changing labels to Polydor, Johnny made the Top 25 with *You'll Be Back (Every Night in My Dreams)*. The next Top 30 hit, *How Deep in Love Am I?* was on Mercury. He continued having chart placings on Mercury until 1981. Of the six singles to chart, the most successful was *Here's to the Horses*, which went Top 50.

Songwriting is a major part of Johnny's career and he has many successes including *You'll Be Back (Every Night in My Dreams)* (Statler Brothers, 1982), *Let's Fall to Pieces Together* (George Strait, 1984), *Got No Reason Now for Goin' Home* (Gene Watson, 1985). Dolly Parton, Emmylou Harris and Linda Ronstadt included *Makin' Plans* on their ***Trio*** album (1988).

One of Johnny's first experiences with comedy was on the *Grand Ole Opry*, as part of Archie Campbell's act. Archie thinks that Johnny has perfect timing and that his delivery of punch lines is flawless. When Russell joined the *Grand Ole Opry* in 1985, it fulfilled one of his lifetime ambitions and he has contributed handsomely. He always delights his audiences with his comedy and his singing, and has appeared on many TV shows such as *Country Music U.S.A.* and *Nashville Now.* Johnny was a regular performer on *Hee Haw,* and has been a popular guest on many TV talk shows. His ability as a raconteur also enhances his performance.

In 1987, Johnny teamed up with Little David Wilkins for the Top 75 single *Butterbeans*, on 16th Avenue Records. When Johnny toured Europe, he was very surprised that he had so many fans there. In 1987, Johnny suffered a mild stroke, and once again in 1988, he was taken to hospital with chest pains and underwent an operation for a blockage, which was successful. He told Barry McCloud that he had formed a new group with Johnny Cash and Waylon Jennings, called By-Pass 101 (a pun on Highway 101).

Although his girth has diminished slightly, he is still broadly amusing and his many fans still enjoy his songs, quick wit and flair. When Johnny comes on stage, be prepared to stay all night. JAB

RECOMMENDED ALBUMS:

"Mr & Mrs. Untrue" (RCA Victor)(1971)
"Rednecks, White Socks & Blue Ribbon Beer" (RCA Victor)(1973 & 1977)
"Here Comes Johnny Russell" (RCA Victor)(1975)
"The Country Store Collection" (Country Store UK)(1988)

BUCK RYAN

(Fiddle)

Given Name: Arnold Walter Ryan
Date of Birth: May 9, 1925
Where Born: Mt. Jackson, Virginia
Married: Mary ("Chick")
Children: Sonny, Sandra, Steve, Sherry
Date of Death: January 7, 1982

Buck Ryan toiled as a Country and Bluegrass fiddler for some forty years, beginning his career at the age of 14. The high spots of his career are probably his tenure with Jimmy Dean's Texas Wildcats in the 50's and the dozen years spent with the Tennessee Cut-Ups, led by Don Reno and Bill Harrell. In addition to his many recordings with these groups, Buck managed to make a moderate number of instrumental discs under his own name.

A native of Mt. Jackson, Virginia, near the northern end of the Shenandoah Valley, young Arnold took up the fiddle at the age of 9 at the urging of his father, a local square dance fiddler. He soon mastered *Turkey in the Straw,* and as he told a *Toledo Blade* journalist in 1973, "from then on everything came almost automatically." In 1939, Ryan journeyed down the valley to Harrisonburg and WSVA radio, where he joined the band of the onetime vaudeville stars turned Country sweethearts Salt and Peanuts (Frank Kurtz and Margaret McConnell). Over the next several years, Buck played for several different Country radio acts, including Lee Moore, Toby Stroud and Little Robert at Harrisonburg, Charlotte, Wheeling, Knoxville and other stations, and on the *Old Dominion Barn Dance* at WRVA Richmond.

In 1956, Buck joined Jimmy Dean's Texas Wildcats, who were then gaining national renown via CBS television and Connie B. Gay's *Town and Country Time* radio programs. During the 50's, Ryan was one of the few fiddlers to have a major label recording contract, cutting several sides on Mercury. Tunes on which Ryan fiddled included *Uncle Herm's Hornpipe*, *Nervous Breakdown* and *Cincinnati Rag.* He also established himself as a contest fiddler of note. As early as 1946, he had won a $500.00 prize, which paid his wife's hospital bill. In 1952, he finished first at the Warrentown, Virginia, contests and in 1965 and 1968 took top honors at Berryville.

In the early 60's, Buck moved into the Washington-area Bluegrass scene working with such bands as Bill Harrell and the Virginians. Essentially this same group, under the name Buck Ryan and Smitty Irvin, also cut an album on Monument of which half consisted of Buck's lead fiddle work, including another one of his specialties, *Kansas City Railroad Blues.* Through his acquaintance with Bill Harrell, he joined the Tennessee Cut-Ups in 1968, remaining a key band member until Don and Bill split in 1976, and Buck then played with Reno until illness began to slow him down in 1980. In addition to his many recordings with the Tennessee Cut-Ups, Ryan recorded three fine fiddle albums in the 70's, one for Rural Rhythm and two for Rebel. IMT

RECOMMENDED ALBUMS:

"Buck Ryan with Don Reno and Red Smiley" (Rural Rhythm) (1971)
"Fiddler on the Rock" (Rebel)(1976)
"Dream Train Engineer" (Rebel)(1980)
Buck Ryan and Smitty Irvin:
"Ballads & Bluegrass" (Monument)(1965)
(See also Bill Harrell, Don Reno and Red Smiley.)

JOHN WESLEY RYLES

(Singer, Songwriter, Guitar)

Given Name: John Wesley Ryles
Date of Birth: December 2, 1950
Where Born: Bastrop, Louisiana

John Wesley Ryles placed nearly thirty singles on the Country charts between 1968 and 1988. His future looked bright when his debut single, *Kay*, reached the Top 10, but most subsequent releases didn't fare as well and major stardom eluded John Wesley.

Singing was the only entertainment John Wesley knew as a young boy, growing up in Louisiana and Texas. His first musical memories were not from radio or records (there was no electricity in his home), but from the family singing together. Music proved to be a way to better things for the family. John Wesley had learned to play guitar at age 6 and was performing on KTRY Bastrop by the time he was 7. Performing on local Texas radio stations earned the Ryles Family Singers an invitation to join the cast of the *Cowtown Hoedown* in Fort Worth. Eventually, the family group reached a national radio and television audience when they joined the *Big D Jamboree* in Dallas.

After four years in Dallas, the Ryles family moved to Nashville in 1965, where John planned to pursue a solo career. John teamed up with the Hubert Long Agency and found work in Nashville singing song demos for music publishers and working closely with Audie Ashworth of Moss Rose Publications. He also worked as a studio engineer and performed with various club bands in town.

John Wesley signed with Columbia Records in 1968 and the label teamed him with producer George Richey. John Wesley found the song *Kay* (written by Hank Mills) and convinced Richey to let him record it. The story of a man who financed his wife's rise to stardom by driving a cab in Music City only to be dumped when she "made it" connected with Country music fans. At age 18, John Wesley I (as he then styled himself) scored his first hit when *Kay* reached the Country Top 10 and crossed to the Pop Top 90.

His follow-up singles, *Heaven Below* and *The Weakest Kind of Man*, only made the Top 60, in 1969. Then in 1970, he returned to the Top 20 with *I've Just Been Wasting My Time*. That year, he was booked to appear at the prestigious Wembley Festival in England, but he failed to show and the reason given was that his extreme youth was having trouble coping with stardom. However, due to a management change at the label, he was dropped from Columbia. In 1971, John charted Top 40 with his Plantation single *Reconsider Me*.

John left Nashville heartbroken and spent the next several years performing in clubs wondering if he would get another chance at stardom. In 1976, he was back on the chart with two lowly entries, *Tell It Like It Is* and *When a Man Loves a Woman*, on the independent Music Mill label. Both these songs had been hits for R & B artists Aaron Neville and Percy Sledge respectively.

In 1977, John got another chance on a major label when ABC/Dot offered him a contract. His debut single, *Fool*, made a poor initial showing, falling off the chart after only two weeks. In a strange turn of events, some deejays in Houston began playing the song again four months later and that led to a national revival that took *Fool* to the Top 20. John then scored the highest single of his career when his follow-up release, *Once in a Lifetime Thing*, became a Top 5 hit. He finished the year by entering the chart with *Shine on Me (The Sun Still Shines When It Rains)*, which went Top 15 in 1978.

By 1978, ABC/Dot had become ABC and a year later, the label was taken over by MCA. John stayed with the label until 1981 with his major hits being *Liberated Woman* (Top 15) and *You Are Always on My Mind* (Top 20) (both 1969) and *Perfect Strangers* (Top 25, 1970).

In 1982, John signed with the independent Primero label but only achieved a pair of low-charted singles. In 1984, he moved on to Opryland's 16th Avenue, but again he only achieved a lowly entry. In 1987, he was once again on a major label, Warner Brothers, and scored a Top 40 hit with *Midnight Blue* and a Top 30 hit with *Louisiana Man*. In 1988, John Wesley had his last chart entry, the Top 60 *Nobody Knows*.

Although no longer recording as an artist in the 90's, John Wesley Ryles worked steadily in Nashville recording studios. In addition to adding harmony vocals to many hit records, John has sung hundreds of song demos for dozens of music publishers.

RECOMMENDED ALBUMS:

"Kay" (Columbia)(1969)
"Reconsider Me" (Plantation)(1977)
"John Wesley Ryles" (ABC/Dot)(1977)
"Shine on Me" (MCA)(1978)
"Let the Night Begin" (MCA)(1979)

S

DOUG SAHM

(Singer, Songwriter, Guitar, Slide Guitar, Steel Guitar, Piano, Requinto, Vihuela)

Given Name:	**Douglas Saldana**
Date of Birth:	**November 6, 1941**
Where Born:	**San Antonio, Texas**
Married:	**Unknown**
Children:	**Shawn, Shandon**

Doug Sahm is one of the leading lights of Tex-Mex music. From his early hits as leader of Sir Douglas Quintet through to his membership in the Texas Tornados, he has emerged as a major influence on Country and Rock, without ever having achieved the stardom that his talent warrants.

Born and raised in San Antonio, Doug could play steel guitar by age 6, as "Little Doug," and often sat in with visiting bands. He was asked to play on the *Grand Ole Opry*, but his mother insisted that he complete his education. However, he did appear on the *Louisiana Hayride* by the time he was 9. As he grew into his teens, Doug was influenced by the growing rock'n'roll movement as well as by Blues and Country. Before the end of the 50's, he had recorded for several local labels.

It was the British invasion that proved the turning point for Doug. He formed the Sir Douglas Quintet in an attempt to seem to be part of this invasion. It worked to a degree, as their Tribe label release *She's About a Mover* (featuring the Farfisa organ of Augie Meyers) reached the Pop chart and became a Top 15 success in the U.K. The following year, the group just missed the Pop Top 30 with *The Rains Came*. The band toured with stars like the Rolling Stones and Bob Dylan.

During the late 60's, the quintet moved to San Francisco and, in 1968, signed to Smash Records, releasing the album ***Honkey Blues*** that same year. The following year, they released ***Mendocino***, considered by most as their best album. The title track reached the Pop Top 30, while *Dynamite Woman*, another track from the album, just crawled into the Top 90. In 1970, they released the albums ***1+1+1=4*** and ***Together After Five***. For Philips, Doug recorded the album ***The Return of Doug Saldana***, which has him returning to his Texas roots, with songs such as *Wasted Days and Wasted Nights*. Although the band was greatly admired by its followers and its peers, in 1972 it quickly disbanded, having not made that major breakthrough.

Following the break-up of the quintet, Doug played on a pair of sessions for the Grateful Dead, namely ***Wake of the Flood*** (1973) and ***From Mars Hotel*** (1974). He signed with Atlantic Records, and in 1973, released his album ***Doug Sahm & the Band***. It was an album that tried to please on too many musical fronts and as a result, pleased no one. Among the guest musicians were Bob Dylan, Dr. John, David Bromberg, Flaco Jimenez and mandolinist Andy Statman. The following year, Doug released a second album for Atlantic, entitled ***Texas Tornado***, but again, it didn't fare well.

In 1974, Doug got together with the rhythm section of Creedence Clearwater Revival, Stu Cook and Doug Clifford and they became Doug Sahm & the Texas Tornados. Their first album, for Warner Brothers Records, was ***Groovers Paradise***. The album featured the keyboards and fiddle of Link Davis and the steel playing of Gary Potterton. They cut their next album, ***Texas Rock for Country Rollers***, for ABC/Dot, in 1976. From this album came the track *Cowboy Peyton Place*, which appeared on the Country charts for 1 week at position 100. During 1977, Doug appeared on Rick Danko's self-titled album, which also features Eric Clapton. Doug released ***Live Love*** on the Texas label.

By 1979, the band had changed labels and released ***Hell of a Spell*** on Takoma. This was an attempt to get airplay, but it didn't lead to any hits. With the follow-up, ***Border Wave***, the following year, Doug attempted to take the band back to Sir Douglas days in their sound.

During the 80's, Doug produced a series of albums for a variety of labels and there were also several compilations issued. These included the Varrick release ***Quintessence*** (1983) and the Sonet album ***Rio Medina*** (1984). He continued playing live dates until, in 1990, he joined Texas Tornados. (For the rest of the story, see Texas Tornados.)

RECOMMENDED ALBUMS:

"Best of Sir Douglas Quintet" (Tribe)(1965) [Re-released on Crazy Cajun (1976)]
"Honkey Blues" (Smash)(1968)
"Mendocino" (Smash)(1969) [Re-released by Mercury (1975)]
"Texas Tornado" (Atlantic)(1974)
"Groovers Paradise" (Warner Brothers)(1974)

"Texas Rock for Country Rollers" (Dot)(1976)
"Live Love" (Texas)(1977)
"Hell of a Spell" (Takoma)(1980)
"Border Wave" (Takoma)(1981)

JUNIOR SAMPLES

(Comedy, Singer, Harmonica)
Given Name: Alvin Samples
Date of Birth: August 10, 1926
Where Born: Cumming, Georgia
Married: Grace
Children: six
Date of Death: November 13, 1983

Junior Samples gained considerable fame as a Country comedian, primarily on the television program *Hee Haw*. Although he had only a sixth-grade education and no show business experience until past age 40, Junior proved himself a fine natural humorist. In essence, he had a natural flair for telling a good story and when coupled with his heavy Georgia mountain accent, archaic rural mannerisms and word usage, it made him a star.

For the first forty years of his life, Junior labored as a sawmill hand and carpenter. He liked to drink, fish, and tell yarns. One day, one of his sons found a big fish head and Junior bragged that he had caught a 22-pound 9-ounce bass. When the Georgia Fish and Game Commission sent Jim Morrison to interview him, his story was broadcast over the radio in the spring of 1966. A year later, Chart Records added a little background music and released it as a single under the title *World's Biggest Whopper*, which reached No.52 on the Country charts. Junior also made guest appearances on radio and TV in Nashville, where his humorous remarks quickly made him a favorite interviewee with such hosts as Ralph Emery and the late Smilin' Eddie Hill. In a relatively short time, he went from authentic country bumpkin to popular comedian.

Meanwhile, CBS initiated their Country variety show *Hee Haw*, which premiered on June 15, 1969. Junior signed on as a regular and quickly became a favorite. Even his ineptness at reading cue cards worked to his advantage on the program and he remained until his death some fourteen years later.

In addition to the many skits from the cornfield and haystack, he appeared on the Culhanes segments and in the used-car commercial with glamorous blonde Misty Rowe as his mechanic. Junior's closing phrase announcing the phone number "BR 5-4-9" even entered the language.

Continuing to record for Chart Records, Samples had both single and album releases, some material being taken from the interviews on talk shows. He even sang credibly on a few numbers such as *The Rabbit Song* and *Daddy and the Wine* and entertained audiences on the road as well. Junior also cut an album with fellow *Hee Haw* cast member Archie Campbell as straight man, in 1968.

While none of his records achieved the success of *World's Biggest Whopper*, they remain quite revealing of Junior's humor and rural life style of pre-1965 southern Appalachia. A few of his stories such as those about the bird-hunting mule and how to cook carp have been current in oral tradition for decades. The greater number, however, were drawn from his own experiences or embellishments thereof. Junior Samples died of a heart attack in 1983. IMT

RECOMMENDED ALBUMS:
"The World of Junior Samples" (Chart)(1967)
"Bull Session at Bull's Gap" (Chart)(1968) [With Archie Campbell]
"That's a Hee Haw" (Chart)(1970)

JIM SANDERS

(Comedy, Writer)
Given Name: James M. Sanders
Date of Birth: 1896
Where Born: South Alabama
Married: Frances
Children: Paul, Julia
Date of Death: June 6, 1968

Jim Sanders is someone who is often forgotten when Country comedians are discussed. Yet he was responsible for creating more characters than probably any other funnyman.

During WWI, Jim served as a captain in the military and this leadership stood him in good stead when he became the Manager of radio station WDOA Pensacola, Florida. He spent several years as a vaudevillian, and in 1942, he went to WSM in Nashville. By 1947, he was resident on the *Crustene Ranch Party* on the Texas Quality Network.

He became a writer for other funny folk like Minnie Pearl and Rod Brasfield and from 1950 through 1955, he was a regular on the WSM as Ruffin Ready. He also appeared on the *Eddy Arnold Show* as Calamity Cal.

In 1955, Jim was made an Honorary Marshal of Tombstone, Arizona. Among his other famed persona were Lige, Lothar Potts, Uncle Amby, Cap'n Jim and Ben Franklin. In 1966, he became the winner of one of the "World's Best Broadcast Advertisements." Jim Sanders died in 1968 and is buried in Harpeth Hills Memory Gardens in Nashville.

RAY SANDERS

(Singer, Songwriter, Guitar, Actor)
Given Name: Raymon Sanders
Date of Birth: October 1, 1935
Where Born: St. John, Kentucky

For two decades from 1960 through 1980, Ray Sanders chalked up 14 chart hits of which three went Top 20. Although not up in the high echelons of Country music, Ray was nonetheless very popular on the club circuit. A big man, standing 6'2" and weighing 200 pounds, Ray possessed a powerful voice. This combination and his curly hair (he was nicknamed Curly) particularly appealed to the ladies in the audiences.

Ray started out his entertainment career in 1950 when he became a deejay on WIFL Elizabethtown, Kentucky. He stayed at the station until 1957, and also appeared during this sojourn as a deejay and performer at other stations. In 1952, Ray began a two-year stay on the *Lincoln Jamboree* out of Hodgenville, Kentucky, and then joined Kentucky's *Renfro Valley Barn Dance* and WLEX-TV Lexington, Kentucky, staying at both until 1956. In 1955, he began broadcasting on WBRT Bardstown, Kentucky, also leaving there in 1956.

Ray attended Texas Western University in El Paso and graduated in 1957. He stayed on in El Paso, where he joined station KHEY for a 12-month stay. During 1957, Ray made his first recordings for the San label, without success, and between 1958 and 1960, he released singles on Cullman, Concept and Logan. During this time, he appeared on the Hal Smith shows (1958) and then in 1959, he debuted on the *Grand Ole Opry*. That same year, Ray Price chose Ray Sanders to be his opening act on the road.

Ray hit the big time in 1960 when, as a result of his appearance on the *Opry*, he signed with Liberty Records and at the end of the year scored his debut Country chart hit with *World So Full of Love*, which went Top 20. That same year, he appeared in the movie *Drummer Boy of Shiloh*. He followed up in the spring of 1961 with another Top 20 single, *Lonelyville*. That same year, Ray appeared as the Prince in an El Paso production of *Sleeping Beauty*. His next three record releases failed to score, and in 1962, he was without a major label. He cut some sides for Stadium Records, but without success.

In 1968, without any current chart action, Ray was named the ACM's "New Vocalist of the Year." The following year saw him back on the Country charts with *Beer Drinkin' Music*, on Imperial. In 1970, he chalked up two Top 40 singles for United Artists, entitled *Blame It on Rosey* and *Judy*. The following year, Ray returned to the Top 20 with *All I Ever Need Is You*.

He stayed with United Artists until 1973, without racking up any major hits. He moved to Republic Records in 1977, where his most successful chart record was the Top 60 release *I Don't Want to Be Alone Tonight*. The following year, Ray and his band began a residency at the White Sands, a nightclub and dinner house in Riverside, California. In 1980, he appeared on the Hillside album ***Texas Dance Hall Music*** with Curtis Potter and Darrell McCall.

RECOMMENDED ALBUMS:

"Feeling Good Is Easy" (Imperial)(1969)
"Ray Sanders" (United Artists)(1972)
"Texas Dance Hall Music" (Hillside)(1980) [With Curtis Potter and Darrell McCall]

"UNCLE" ART SATHERLEY

(Industry Executive)

Given Name: Arthur Edward Satherley
Date of Birth: October 17, 1889
Where Born: Bristol, England
Date of Death: February 10, 1986

Art Satherley has the distinction of being the only British-born inductee to the Country Music Hall of Fame. As a pioneer of Country music record production, "Uncle" Art ranks as one of the most important people in the history of Country music.

The son of a clergyman, Art worked as a boy on a farm in Somerset, in the English West Country. After attending private school, Art joined the British Army. After leaving the service, he worked for the Triumph Motor Cycle Company. Art was fascinated by the stories of the American Wild West and he traveled to Wisconsin in 1913. He got a job grading timber for the Wisconsin Chair Company which made the cabinets to house Thomas Edison's phonographs.

This connection to Edison eventually led to Art's getting involved in the fledgling record industry. He began to work for Paramount Records, helping to promote the "race" records of Blues artists such as Blind Lemon Jefferson and Ma Rainey. However, by 1925, Paramount was not keeping up with the development of the new electrical recording process and in 1928, Art moved on to QS Records as Recording Manager.

The following year, Art moved on to the American Record Corporation (ARC), which was an umbrella for labels such as Banner, Oriole, Perfect, Melotone and Romeo. That year, he signed Gene Autry, because he had similarities to Jimmie Rodgers. Art produced him for ARC and Sears' Conqueror label. This directly led to Autry appearing on his own radio show, *Conqueror Record Time*, and WLS's *Barn Dance*.

Art's boss at ARC was Herbert J. Yates, who was also in charge of Consolidated Film Industries and funded smaller film companies. These included Mascot, and Art lobbied on Autry's behalf. In 1934, Gene was given a supporting role in Ken Maynard's *In Old Santa Fe* and as a result became a star. In 1938, ARC was taken over by the Columbia Broadcasting System and Art became A & R man for Columbia, replacing William R. Calaway. He became involved in recording Roy Acuff and Hank Penny for Columbia's OKeh label. He remained in this position until 1952, when he retired.

During this time, he was responsible for signing Lefty Frizzell, Little Jimmy Dickens, Marty Robbins and Carl Smith. Art also helped the careers of Bob Wills, Red Foley, Molly O'Day, Al Dexter and Tex Ritter. In 1968, the ACM awarded Art with the first "Pioneer Award." In 1971, Art Satherley was inducted into the Country Music Hall of Fame for his work as a record pioneer. He was a man that was not averse to change but his musical preferences would have him described as a traditionalist. Uncle Art died in 1986.

CARL SAUCEMAN

(Singer, Guitar, Bass)

Given Name: James Carl Sauceman
Date of Birth: March 6, 1922
Where Born: Green County, Tennessee
Married: Mary Louise Ketner
Children: Ted, Linda (dec'd.), James C., Jr., Terry, Jerry D. (dec'd.)

Carl Sauceman, together with his brother John Paul "J.P." (1926-84), was among the early pioneers of Bluegrass music. During the 70's, Carl worked a few Bluegrass festivals and cut a couple of albums proving that he still has a fine touch for Bluegrass.

He grew up in the Bride Hope community near Greenville, Tennessee, where his father was a noted sacred singer in all the revivals in his area. Carl's mother knew a lot of old ballads and songs, and in the late 30's, he listened to Mainer's Mountaineers on record. With this musical background, Carl began to sing and play guitar as well. In 1941, he teamed up with Dudley Watson and Curley Shelton and they began working on radio at WISE in Asheville and then at WHKY Hickory, both in North Carolina.

Wartime rationing hampered both their own and the fans' ability to get to their shows so they finally got on at WNOX Knoxville briefly and for a longer stretch at WWNC Asheville. Early in 1945 Carl went into the U.S. Navy, getting out near the end of 1946. He returned to Asheville briefly and then went to a new hometown station, WGRV in Greenville, Tennessee. By this time, Carl had a band called the Hillbilly Ramblers.

The Saucemans cut their first records for Rich-R-Tone. The Sauceman Brothers cut four sides and J.P. did a Country single. In between the two Rich-R-Tone sessions, they did one as the Hillbilly Ramblers for Mercury. One of their Rich-R-Tone efforts included among the sidemen such notables as Carl Butler, Joe Stuart, and Tater Tate.

The Sauceman Brothers left Greenville for WROL Knoxville in 1948, where they spent a year working for supermarket tycoon Cas Walker. They then went to Detroit briefly before going to Bristol's WCYB, where they remained for a couple of years laboring on the *Farm and Fun Time* program, where they shared the limelight with such luminaries as the Stanley Brothers and Curly King. At the beginning of 1952, Carl took his Green Valley Boys south to WRAG Carrollton, Alabama, where he spent ten years and signed a contract with Capitol. The boys in his band at various times included Tater Tate, Joe Stuart, Curly Sechler, Don McHan, Fred Richardson, Buddy Rose, and Monroe Fields.

In 1954, they switched over to Republic, where their recordings of *A White Cross Marks the Grave* and *I'll Be an Angel Too* constitute a pair of McHan originals and all-time Bluegrass classics. The Green Valley Boys pioneered Bluegrass in that portion of the country and once it caught on they did quite well with three weekly TV shows, regular radio, and Carl's doing a deejay show at WRAG in Carrollton. J.P. eventually went back to Greenville and went into radio management.

Carl's group worked out of Carrollton until the end of 1962. In the latter period he cut a few sides for N Records, a local label in

Alabama, and a few more for Pappy Dailey's D Records. Their best song for Dailey—*Please Be My Love*, a Monroe Fields original—later became a minor classic by George Jones and Melba Montgomery. At the time Sauceman quit show business, he had become part owner of the station, but his youngest son, Terry, had a terminal illness and Carl felt he needed to devote full attention to him. After 1964, friends urged him to become musically active again, but he resisted the temptation.

Carl Sauceman came to Gonzales, Louisiana, in 1969 as owner and General Manager of WLSG radio. The business prospered and he sold the station and retired in 1985. Carl returned to Carrollton for a once-a-year get-together, did three or four shows annually, and cut a new album for Rich-R-Tone in 1976 and a reunion effort for Atteiram in 1977 with onetime sideman Joe Stuart. Rebel released a few transcription cuts from WCYB on a *Farm and Fun Time* anthology album and Rounder did a collection of most of his pioneering Bluegrass efforts. Carl has generally enjoyed his retirement and in April 1994 reflected positively on his role as a Bluegrass pioneer, but has no regrets about leaving it either. IMT

RECOMMENDED ALBUMS:

"Tribute to the King" (Rich-R-Tone)(1976)
"The Sauceman Brothers" (Rounder)(ca. 1977)
"Together Again" (Atteiram)(1977)

SAWYER BROWN

When Formed: 1981

Current Members:

Mark Miller	**Lead Vocals, Rhythm Guitar**
Gregg Hubbard	**Keyboards, Vocals**
Jim Scholten	**Bass Guitar**
Joe Smyth	**Drums, Percussion**
Duncan Cameron	**Guitars, Dobro, Mandolin, Vocals (joined 1992)**

Former Member:

Bobby Randall	**Lead Guitar, Vocals (left 1992)**

From its arrival in the Country star firmament, Sawyer Brown, under the leadership of Mark Miller, has established itself as a group that goes for a colorful "electric" image with a very visual stage act and good songs, increasingly self-written (mainly by Mark Miller). For Sawyer Brown, there was no "Country" image, but instead the group went for clothes that would normally be associated with Funk groups.

It was 1979 and Bobby Randall hit Nashville with the intention of forming a band. He joined Don King's back-up band, where he met Joe Smyth. The following year, Jim, Mark and Hobie joined the band, and by 1981, when King decided to stop touring, the band went its own way. It initially called itself Savanna, but obviously this was too close to the Mercury Records group, Savannah. So the name Sawyer Brown was arrived at from a street name in Nashville.

Sawyer Brown led by Mark Miller (center)

Of the founding members of Sawyer Brown, Mark Miller was born on October 25, 1958, just outside Dayton, Ohio, where he lived until he was age 9. His family moved to Apopka, Florida, where he met Hobie Hubbard at high school. Hobie began playing piano at the local church. Mark played football, while Hobie majored in English. When Hobie heard a tape of Mark singing his own songs, they began working together. Mark's influences were the Jackson 5, Marvin Gaye and James Brown, as well as Elvis Presley, Charley Pride and Conway Twitty, but most especially, Chuck Berry. Possessing natural rhythm, Mark was always dancing, which has transferred itself into his vigorous stage act. When he arrived in Nashville, he tried to write traditional Country material without success, and realized that he wasn't being true to himself and concentrated on writing more contemporary material.

Bobby ("Rockin") Randall was raised in Midland, Michigan, where his father was a Country singer. Bobby was very much into the Blues greats such as B.B. King and Eric Clapton. He met Jim ("Starbuck") Scholten, who had played in a Rock band and performed at the Montreux Jazz Festival. "Curly" Joe Smyth had played with both the Maine and Miami Symphony Orchestras as a percussionist and is able to play some 300 percussion instruments.

They paid their dues and toured around the U.S. and then, in 1983, their agent asked that they come to Nashville to make a video. As it turned out, it was for the TV talent show, *Star Search*. They traveled to Los Angeles and won the contest and a cool $100,000 in prize money. They signed to Capitol/Curb in 1984, and released their debut eponymous album that same year. It sold 150,000 copies within the first two weeks. Their debut single, *Leona*, reached the Top 20, but it was in 1985, with their second release, *Step That Step*, a Mark A. Miller original, that Sawyer Brown hit No.1. That year, they followed up with the Top 3 single *Used to Blue* and the Top 5 *Betty's Bein' Bad*. That year, they became the first group to receive the CMA's "Horizon Award."

They then began to suffer from something that would hurt them until 1991. They were being ignored by the radio stations, with the accusation that they played "teeny-bop" and "bubblegum" Country. This resulted in a poor showing for a lot of their singles, whereas many mediocre records by other acts have found favor with the deejays, and in the days of singles charts being based solely on airplay, have been made to look better than they should. As a result, Sawyer Brown's 1986 singles *Hearts Don't Fall Now, Shakin'* and

Out Goin' Cattin' (with "Cat" Joe Bonsall of the Oak Ridge Boys) only reached the Top 20.

By 1987, their singles' success was getting to rock bottom, with *Gypsies on Parade* getting to No.25, *Savin' the Honey for the Honeymoon* only making the Top 60 and *Somewhere in the Night* Top 30. Then, out of nowhere, their single *This Missin' You Heart of Mine* climbed to the Top 3. However, 1988 was back to as they were, when *Old Photographs* went Top 30, *My Baby's Gone* managed to get to the Top 15 and the exquisite *It Wasn't His Child* got no higher than the Top 60. In 1989, it looked like the troubles were still there and their opening single *Old Pair of Shoes* also only made the Top 50. Then their re-working of the George Jones hit *The Race Is On* went Top 5 and their album ***The Boys Are Back*** did the same on the Country Album chart.

This was only a temporary thing, as all three of their 1990 releases, *Did It for Love, Puttin' the Dark Back into the Night* and *When Love Comes Callin'*, went Top 40. By the time of their third album, Curb had established itself as a separate label and the band moved to that label. Their ***Greatest Hits*** compilation reached the Top 30 on the Country Album charts, confirming that the public still wanted Sawyer Brown. During the first quarter of 1991, things looked lower than a gravedigger's well, with *One Less Pony* and *Mama's Little Baby Loves Me* only making the Top 70. Then at the end of the year, they released the album ***The Dirt Road*** and, suddenly, they became the darlings of the radio stations. Their next single, *The Walk*, reached the Top 3 and the follow-up, the album title track (which features Earl Scruggs), went Top 5. A lot of the success should also be credited to Duncan Cameron, who has brought to the band a much broader style of lead guitar playing, as well as bringing a wider range of instrumentation, including Dobro and mandolin. Duncan had played with the Amazing Rhythm Aces and Glenn Frey. Bobby Randall left to pursue TV work and in 1993, he joined the Killen Organization as Head of Publishing and then joined the Goldens band.

With the arrival of 1992, Sawyer Brown couldn't do wrong. *Some Girls Do* went to No.1, *Cafe on the Corner* (from the album of the same name) reached the Top 5 and *All These Years* became a Top 3 single. In addition, the album ***The Dirt Road*** reached the Top 15 on the Country Album chart. Their 1993 album ***Outskirts of Town*** reaffirmed their popularity by reaching the Top 15 on the Country album chart. During the year, they continued their single success with *Trouble on the Line* (Top 5), *Thank God for You* (No.1) and *The Boys and Me* (Top 5). In 1994, their single *Outskirts of Town* went Top 40.

RECOMMENDED ALBUMS:

"Sawyer Brown" (Capitol/Curb)(1984)
"Shakin'" (Capitol/Curb)(1985)
"Out Goin' Cattin'" (Capitol/Curb)(1986)
"Somewhere in the Night" (Capitol/Curb)(1987)
"Wide Open" (Capitol/Curb)(1988)
"The Boys Are Back" (Capitol/Curb)(1989)
"Buick" (Capitol/Curb)(1991)
"The Dirt Road" (Capitol/Curb)(1992)
"Cafe on the Corner" (Curb)(1992)
"Outskirts of Town" (Curb)(1993)

PETE SAYERS

(Singer, Songwriter, Guitar, Banjo, Dobro, Autoharp, Ukulele, One-Man Band, Actor)

Given Name: Peter Esmond Bernard Sayers
Date of Birth: November 6, 1942
Where Born: Bath, Somerset, England
Married: Elizabeth Twynam
Children: John, Dinah

Pete Sayers is the only English performer to have been a regular on the *Grand Ole Opry*. Pete achieved what many Europeans have tried to do—make it big in Nashville.

He was born in the beautiful City of Bath and by the time Pete was age 18, he had begun playing in the clubs and pubs. He played "Travis-style" guitar and worked with U.S. singer Johnny Duncan and his Blue Grass Boys. Duncan had scored in Britain with his 1957 hit *Last Train to San Fernando* and had followed with a pair of minor chart singles. Pete also recorded and made a TV special with Peter, Paul & Mary. Pete formed the first Bluegrass band in Britain and was in a TV series on Tyne Tees Television, in the north of England.

Multi-talented British Country star ***Pete Sayers***

In 1966, Pete went to Nashville for a vacation and stayed five years. In August, within six weeks of arriving, he made his debut on the *Grand Ole Opry* and soon became a regular member. During his time in the U.S., Pete co-hosted a daily breakfast TV show for four years. He won the "National Broadcasting" award and worked with Kris Kristofferson and John D. Loudermilk. He also appeared on the *Porter Wagoner Show, Pop 'n' Country* and with Flatt & Scruggs and the *Kitty Wells Show*, among others.

Pete returned to Britain in 1971 and three nationwide tours with George Hamilton IV followed. Pete was invited to perform and emcee at the Wembley Festival on three occasions, 1973, 1976 and 1980. He has also appeared in concert at the Royal Festival Hall, the Royal Albert Hall and the London Palladium as well as performing throughout Europe and the Middle East.

He turned to acting when he appeared in the U.K. as the narrator in *Joseph and His Technicolor Dreamcoat* and starred in the first Country music summer season at Blackpool Winter Gardens at the famous seaside resort in the north of England. In addition, Pete was chosen to appear at two Royal Charity Gala Shows. Through his TV series *Country Hoedown* and BBC-TV Specials with Crystal Gayle, Billie Joe Spears, Roy Clark and George Hamilton IV, Pete went on to host three major BBC-TV series, *Pete Sayers Entertains*, *Electric Music Show* and *Pete Sayers Sings Country*.

In 1973, Pete released the album ***Bye Bye Tennessee*** on Pye Nashville International. He followed with a pair of albums on Transatlantic, ***Grand Ole Opry Road Show*** (1975) and ***Watermelon Summer*** (1976). In 1979, he journeyed to Bogalusa, Louisiana, where John D. Loudermilk produced Pete's ***Bogalusa Gumbo***, which was released on Response Records. His other albums are ***Cyclone*** (1983) on Country Roads Records and ***Midnight Special*** (1988) on Pinorrekk Records, on which he was joined by the legendary Monty Sunshine's Jazz Band. These albums include many of Pete's original songs.

Pete currently performs with his band, the Dixie Bluebirds and he has evolved a show combining Country Blues with a dash of rock'n'roll. He also incorporates his comedy characters (making for lightning costume changes) such as Dennis, a Suffolk yokel; Ricky Storme, Superstar and rock'n'roller; LaWanda Davis, Sweetheart of North America, a star who rose to fame from a humble background; and the Phoenix Phantom, an Elvis type. Pete finds these comedy characters have a universal appeal whether in Europe or the U.S.

He also works as a session musician and has recently worked with legendary Skiffle musician Lonnie Donegan. Pete also does gigs as a one-man band and has been recognized in the U.K. for his ability. He was, to the delight of his many admirers, named "Best Singer" and "Best Songwriter" by the Country Music Association (GB). JAB

RECOMMENDED ALBUMS:

(All U.K. releases)
"Bye Bye Tennessee" (Pye Nashville International)(1973)
"Grand Ole Opry Road Show" (Transatlantic)(1975)
"Watermelon Summer" (Transatlantic)(1976)
"Bogalusa Gumbo" (Response)(1979)
"Cy-clone" (Country Roads)(1983)
"Midnight Special" (Pinorrekk)(1988)

DON SCHLITZ

(Songwriter, Singer, Guitar)
Date of Birth: **August 29, 1952**
Where Born: **Durham, North Carolina**

Don Schlitz established himself as one of Nashville's most successful songwriters, placing more than 50 songs on the charts between 1978 and 1994, including 20 No.1 hits.

Born and raised in Durham, North Carolina, Don briefly attended Duke University. He had his sights set on Nashville and made the move in 1973. For the next five years he worked the night shift as a computer operator at Vanderbilt University.

Master songwriter ***Don Schlitz***

During the day, Don worked at his songwriting and pitched his songs to publishers.

Don got his big break when Kenny Rogers recorded *The Gambler* in 1978. The song spent three weeks at No.1 on the Country singles chart and became one of Rogers' signature songs. *The Gambler* was also developed into a series of made-for-TV movies starring Kenny Rogers that was based on the character in the song. That year, Don won a Grammy Award for the song as "Best Country Song" and the following year, Kenny's single won the MCN's "Single of the Year." Don's own version of the song reached the Top 70 in 1978 and came from his Capitol album ***Dreamers Matinee***, as did the Top 100 single *You're the One Who Rewrote My Life Story*, in 1979.

In 1984, *I Love Only You* became a hit for the Nitty Gritty Dirt Band. The following year, Don composed hit singles for John Conlee (*Old School*) and Alabama (*Forty Hour Week*). Also in 1985, a new artist named Randy Travis recorded the Don Schlitz-Paul Overstreet composition *On the Other Hand*, but it only made it to the Top 70. Randy's record company, Warner Brothers, was so convinced the song was a hit they re-issued it in early 1986 and it shot to No.1 and earned the CMA, ACM and NSAI "Song of the Year" awards. Don racked up two more No.1 singles in 1986 with *Rockin' with the Rhythm of the Rain* for the Judds and Michael Johnson's *Give Me Wings*. Also in 1986, Don provided Top 5 hits for the Nitty Gritty Dirt Band (*Stand a Little Rain*) and Sweethearts of the Rodeo (*Midnight Girl/Sunset Town*).

Don added five more No.1 singles to his credit in 1987 with *One Promise Too Late* (Reba McEntire), *I Know Where I'm Going* (the Judds), *You Again* (the Forester Sisters), *I Won't Take Less than Your Love* (Tanya Tucker, Paul Overstreet and Paul Davis) and *Forever and Ever, Amen* (Randy Travis). The Travis hit brought Don and co-writer Paul Overstreet a Grammy as "Best Country Song" and CMA, ACM and NSAI "Song of the Year" awards and *On the Other Hand* was named MCN's "Single of the Year." Don was named NSAI's "Songwriter of the Year." Other hits in 1987 included *No Easy Horses* (SKB), *Crying Shame* (Michael Johnson) and *Crazy from the Heart* (the Bellamy Brothers).

1988 proved to be another stellar year for Don with seven more hit singles to his credit, including the No.1's *Turn It Loose* (the Judds), *Strong Enough to Bend* (Tanya Tucker), *When You Say Nothing at All* (Keith Whitley) and *Deeper than the Holler* (Randy Travis). That year, *Forever and Ever, Amen* was named MCN's "Single of the Year" and Don was named ASCAP "Writer of the Year," a title he again held in 1989, 1990 and 1991. In 1988, Don was one of five premier songwriters included on RCA's ***Signatures*** album, on which he recorded *Life's Too Short* and *Letter in the Fire*.

Don placed 10 more singles on the Country chart in 1989. The Top 5 hits included Restless Heart's *Say What's in Your Heart* and Ronnie Milsap's *Houston Solution*. Artists scoring Top 10 hits with Don's songs were Baillie and the Boys (*She Deserves You*), the Bellamy Brothers' *You'll Never Be Sorry*, the Nitty Gritty Dirt Band's *When It's Gone* and his frequent co-writer Paul Overstreet with Paul's hit *Sowin' Love*.

Six of Don's songs hit the chart in 1990, including Paul Overstreet's Top 3 *Richest Man on Earth* and No.1 *Daddy's Come Around*. The Judds recorded *Guardian Angels* and Lionel Cartwright hit the Top 10 with *I Watched It All on My Radio*. The duet team of Kathy Mattea and Tim O'Brien had a hit with *Battle Hymn of Love* and the Bellamy Brothers with *I Could Be Persuaded*.

In 1991, Don wrote two more hits for Randy Travis, *Heroes and Friends* and *Point of Light*, a song commissioned by President George Bush for the theme of his Points of Light campaign recognizing outstanding community service. Paul Overstreet teamed up once again with Don for the Top 5 hit *Ball and Chain*.

Garth Brooks recorded *Learning to Live Again*, early in 1992, and later in the year Mary-Chapin Carpenter hit the Top 5 with a song that she had written with Don, *I Feel Lucky*. She also teamed up with label-mate Joe Diffie to record *Not Too Much to Ask*. The following year Mark Chesnutt hit the No.1 spot with *Almost Goodbye* and Mary-Chapin Carpenter had a hit with another song written with Don, *He Thinks He'll Keep Her*. In 1994, she once again had a hit with one more Carpenter-Schlitz song, *I Take My Chances*.

In 1993, Don was inducted into the Nashville Songwriters Hall of Fame. JIE

RECOMMENDED ALBUMS:

"Dreamers Matinee" (Capitol)(1978)
"Signatures" (RCA Victor)(1988) [Also Bob McDill, Mark Wright, Rhonda Fleming and Mike Reid]

JOHN SCHNEIDER

(Singer, Songwriter, Guitar, Piano, Actor)

Given Name:	**John Richard Schneider**
Date of Birth:	**April 8, 1960**
Where Born:	**Mount Kisco, Kentucky**
Married:	**Tawny (div. 1985)**
Children:	**Leaha, Cason (stepchildren)**

John Schneider is one of those rare talents who has had two successful careers, both as singer and actor. During his recording career with MCA, John had the best material written by the best writers in Country music, such as Dickey Lee, Bob McDill, Dennis Linde, Troy Seals, Max D. Barnes, Sonny Curtis, Tom Shapiro, Don Goodman and Don Schlitz. His decision to cut back on his recording work came as a serious blow to his many fans.

When John was age 2, his parents divorced and by the time he was 12, he had moved with his mother to Atlanta, Georgia. He began acting when age 8, joining a local community theater group and while he was in grammar school, he appeared in Gilbert and Sullivan's *Mikado*. John's principal diversion, as a boy, was magic and he became accomplished, performing magic shows at children's birthday parties. He acted in high school plays and began to get experience onstage and behind the scenes and became very adept at makeup. He also started to learn to play guitar.

John began doing shows for sick and handicapped children in the local hospital. He extended his appearances to summer stock and did bit parts in movies and on TV. Following graduation, he worked in a dinner theater group, wrote and staged plays for the Academy Children's Theater and acted in commercials and played local clubs.

He recorded his first album, ***Small One***, for Hope Records, in 1975. However, 1977 was the year in which he became a household name. He was cast as Bo Duke in CBS-TV's *The Dukes of Hazzard*, which ran from 1978 to 1985. When he arrived for his audition, he had grown a disheveled beard, hired a pickup truck and arrived with a beer can in his hand. The show became an international blockbuster and John and fellow star Tom Wopat became feted. However, John wanted to extend his vistas and was allowed to direct one of the episodes of the *Dukes* series, entitled "Opening Night at the Boar's Nest."

In 1981, John signed to Scotti Brothers Records and that year, he had a major hit with *It's Now or Never*, which went Top 5 on the Country charts and Top 15 on the Pop lists. He followed up with *Them Good Ol' Boys Are Bad*, which made it to the Top 15 on the Country chart. That same year, he appeared in *Dream House* and *Happy Endings*, both CBS movies for TV and the CBS-TV special *John Schneider Back Home*. The following year, John had a Top 40 Country hit, *Dreamin'*, which also went Top 50 on the Pop chart and *In the Driver's Seat* went Top 60 (Country) and Top 80 (Pop).

During 1983, John appeared in his first feature film, the Universal movie *Eddie Macon's Run* with Kirk Douglas. His two records didn't fare too well and they were *Are You Lonesome Tonight*, a duet with Jill Michaels, and *If You Believe*, which only reached the basement level. John now moved to MCA Records, where he made a transition that only an actor could manage: he consciously lowered his voice and concentrated on being "Country." His first single, in 1984, *I've Been Around Enough to Know*, was issued with a blank label and got the deejays excited. The record gave John his first No.1 Country record, and remained on the charts for over 6 months. After his initial album for MCA, ***Too Good to Stop Now***, John co-produced all his albums with Jimmy Bowen.

John's first single of 1985, *Country Girls*, also went to No.1 and was followed by two Top 10 records, *It's a Short Walk from Heaven to Hell* and *I'm Going to Leave You Tomorrow*, which all remained on the charts for over 5 months. He wrapped up the year with yet another No.1, *What's a Memory Like You (Doing in a Love Like This)*. During the year, he appeared in *Gus Brown and Midnight Brewster*, an NBC movie for TV, and the feature film *Cocaine Wars*. On the negative side, John's workaholic life-style caused his marriage to his wife, a former Miss America, to come to an end, although they remained friends.

John's success continued in 1986, and his opening single *You're the Last Thing I Needed Tonight*, gave him his fourth No.1. This was followed by the Top 5 record *At the Sound of the Tone* and the Top 10 release *Take the Long Way Home*, a song co-written by Doug Crider. The last two songs came from the album ***Take the Long Way Home***, which also featured *Better Class of Losers*, written by Ron Peterson and Harlan Howard, and featured vocals by Waylon Jennings and Johnny Cash. John appeared with Waylon, Johnny, Willie Nelson and Kris Kristofferson in the CBS movie for TV, the remake of *Stagecoach*. That year, he won the People's Choice award for "Star of Tomorrow."

John was co-founder (in 1982) and co-Chairman of the Children's Miracle Network Telethon (televised live from Disneyland), which in 1986 was broadcast to 140 markets across the U.S., Mexico, Australia and Canada and brought in $30 million for children's hospitals throughout the U.S. He also became involved as a spokesman for the John Wayne Cancer Clinic at the University of California at Los Angeles.

John released the album ***You Ain't Seen the Last of Me*** in 1987, and it yielded *Love, You Ain't Seen the Last of Me*, which went Top 10, and then *When the Right One Comes Along*, which only made it to the Top 40, and *If It Was Anyone But You*, a disappointing Top 60. The album also included *The Gunfighter*, an outstanding song written by John.

John now concentrated on his acting, and recording went on the back burner. He appeared in the feature film *The Curse* and the CBS movie for TV *Christmas Comes to Willow Creek*, both in 1987. The following year, he appeared in another CBS-TV movie, *Outback Bound*. His other screen credits, to date, are *Wild Jack*, a 1989 Disney/NBC *Wonderful World of Disney*, *Grand Slam*, a TV movie in 1990, and Roger Gorman's *Ministry of Vengeance*, a 1990 feature film. In 1991, John played the part of the Baron for his Broadway stage debut in the revival of *Grand Hotel*, a musical that was a Tony winner. John has formed a production company, Priority Entertainment, with his partner Lee Mimms. John appeared in *Highway Heartbreaker*, a 1992 CBS movie.

John has high moral values and the seeds that he has sown have been repaid in abundance. He has now decided to return to recording, and a new album is about to be shopped. His admirers look forward to his return.

RECOMMENDED ALBUMS:

"Now or Never" (Scotti Brothers)(1981)
"If You Believe" (Scotti Brothers)(1983)
"Too Good to Stop Now" (MCA)(1984)
"Tryin' to Outrun the Wind" (MCA)(1985)
"A Memory Like You" (MCA)(1986)
"Take the Long Way Home" (MCA)(1986)
"You Ain't Seen the Last of Me" (MCA)(1987)

SCHUYLER, KNOBLOCH & OVERSTREET/SCHUYLER, KNOBLOCH & BICKHARDT

When Formed: 1986

Members:

Thom Schuyler	**Vocals, Rhythm Guitar**
J. Fred Knobloch	**Vocals, Rhythm Guitar**
Paul Overstreet	**Vocals, Rhythm Guitar (left 1987)**
Craig Bickhardt	**Vocals, Rhythm Guitar (joined 1987)**

S-K-O/S-K-B was a short-lived aggregation of some of the most successful songwriters in Nashville. Their music was difficult to categorize, but fell into the area sometimes called contemporary Country, which is a mix of Country, Folk and Pop.

Thom Schuyler (b. 1952, Bethlehem, Pennsylvania) had come to fame as the writer of *16th Avenue*, a 1982 Top 10 hit for Lacy J. Dalton. Fred Knobloch (b. Jackson, Mississippi) had played with the rock band Let's Eat, during the late 70's. He had signed to Scotti Brothers Records in 1980, and had racked up five chart entries as Fred Knoblock. These were *Why Not Me* (also a Top 20 Pop hit), *Let Me Love You* and the Top 10 duet with Susan Anton *Killin' Time* (also a Top 30 Pop hit)(all in 1980), *Memphis* (Top 10) in 1981 and *I Had It All* (1982). Paul Overstreet (b. March 17, 1956, Newton, Mississippi) was fast becoming one of Country music's most prolific songwriters, having written such songs as *Same Ole Me* for George Jones, and going on to write, inter alia, *On the Other Hand* and *Diggin' Up Bones* for Randy Travis.

Schuyler, Knobloch & Overstreet signed with MTM Records, in 1986, and opened their account later that year with the Top 10 Country hit *You Can't Stop Love*, which stayed on the charts for nearly seven months. By the end of the year, they had abbreviated their name to S-K-O, and they scored their first No.1 with *Baby's Got a New Baby*. In the spring of 1987, they had a Top 20 single, *American Me*. All of these tracks came from their album ***S-K-O***.

In 1987, Paul decided to leave the trio to concentrate on his solo career. He was replaced by Craig Bickhardt. Craig had played the clubs in the Philadelphia area with his band, Wire and Wood. His single *You Are What Love Means to Me*, which was featured in the movie *Tender Mercies*, was a Top 90 success, on Liberty, in 1984. The new trio released the album ***No Easy Horses*** and the title track became a Top 20 hit, during the summer of 1987, and the year was completed by the Schuyler-Bickhardt song *This Old House*, which went Top 25. They opened their 1988 account with *Givers and Takers*, which went Top 10. Their final chart entry, *Rigamarole*, only got into the Top 50, but by now, the MTM label was drawing a close to their activities, and artists such as S-K-B, Holly Dunn and Judy Rodman found themselves without a label.

From left to right, ***Schuyler, Knobloch & Bickhardt***

Thom went on to become RCA's Country Vice President, while Fred and Craig continue as successful songwriters, occasionally performing in the round at venues such as Nashville's famed Bluebird Cafe.

RECOMMENDED ALBUMS:

"S-K-O" (MTM)(1987)
"No Easy Horses" (MTM)(1988)

TRACY SCHWARZ

(Singer, Songwriter, Fiddle, Banjo, Guitar, Mandolin, Bass, Triangle, Accordion, Spoons)

Given Name:	**Daniel Tracy Schwarz**
Date of Birth:	**November 13, 1938**
Where Born:	**New York, New York**
Married:	**1. Eloise (div.)**
	2. Virginia Magnolia Hawker
Children:	**Sallyann, Peter, Robert**

Tracy Schwarz, while perhaps best known as one of the New Lost City Ramblers, has also been involved in a variety of other Bluegrass, Country and Folk music activity.

Born in New York City, Tracy Schwarz gained his first knowledge of Country music as a child in New Jersey by listening to the radio in the late 40's. He soon became an avid listener and also began to master instruments, beginning with guitar and banjo. By the time Tracy reached college, his interests broadened to bass fiddle and mandolin and he began playing with various Bluegrass bands in the Washington, D.C., area.

He spent the years 1960 to 1962 in the U.S. Army and by the time of his discharge, he had mastered the fiddle. In August 1962, Tracy started his work, as a replacement for Tom Paley, in the New Lost City Ramblers.

The Ramblers were fairly active during Tracy's first decade with them, playing numerous concerts and recording some seven albums, although with the passing of time he spent more time farming in Pennsylvania. By the end of the 70's, he and other group members involved themselves in other musical groups, too. These included the Strange Creek Singers, whose personnel consisted of Tracy, Mike and Alice Seeger, LaMar Greer and Hazel Dickens. Tracy also did a couple of fiddle instruction albums for Folkways and a pair of duet efforts with wife Eloise, one for Old Homestead and another on the German label Folk Variety. He developed a serious interest in Cajun music in this era and learned to play additional instruments, including the accordion.

In 1990, Schwarz moved to Cox's Mills, West Virginia. He has worked as a musician with Kay Justice and Ginny Hawker, including two albums with them for June Appal. Tracy and Ginny also work together. IMT

RECOMMENDED ALBUMS:

"Learn to Fiddle Country Style" (Folkways)(ca. 1965)
"Tracy Schwarz's Fiddler's Companion" (Folkways)(ca. 1965)
Tracy & Eloise Schwarz:
"Our Kind of Music" (Old Homestead)(1978)
"Home Among the Hills" (Folk Variety Germany)(ca. 1980)
(See also New Lost City Ramblers.)

ROY SCOTT

(Singer, Guitar, Fiddle, Banjo, Steel Guitar)

Given Name:	**Roy Scott**
Date of Birth:	**April 11, 1926**
Where Born:	**Washington, Pennsylvania**
Married:	**(Div.)**
Children:	**Lois, Janice, Lori**

Roy Scott has been a long-time Country music favorite in the Northeast. For more than twenty years on the *Wheeling Jamboree*, Roy earned a reputation as a durable Honky Tonk singer and versatile musician as well.

A native of Washington, Pennsylvania, Roy grew up in an area not far from Wheeling, West Virginia, and station WWVA and in the same community as future Jamboree songstress Chickie Williams (Jessie Wanda Crupe). He learned his music fundamentals as an adolescent and obtained his first radio job at local station WJPA. Two years later he took a jump upward and fronted the band of Hank Snow, a position which provided him with ample touring experience.

After a year, he came to "the World's Original Jamboree," remaining at WWVA Wheeling for twenty-one years except for a short stint at WMMN in Fairmont, West Virginia, where he worked in a trio with Eddie Miller and Jackie Starr, led by pitchman and banjo picker Red Belcher. They cut a single

Wheeling Jamboree favorite ***Roy Scott***

together for Cozy Records of Davis, West Virginia, one side a cover of Snow's then current hit, *I'm Movin' On*.

This led to Scott's signing with MGM. Unfortunately, his one release, *Lucky from Kentucky*, never got much attention because the company was pushing Hank Williams so heavily, much to the detriment of their other artists. Nonetheless, Roy continued as an ever-popular *Jamboree* star, heading the staff band, the Country Harmony Boys. At its peak, this group included accordion virtuoso Monte Blake, lead guitarist Gene Jenkins, onetime Clinch Mountain Clan fiddler Bill Carver, and for a time, mandolinist James Carson.

Roy continued as a *Jamboree* regular for some time, being quite popular throughout Pennsylvania and other northeastern states. He recorded for several small labels in the 50's and 60's, including some releases on Pennant, Buddy Durham's Emperor label, and a fine EP for Lee Sutton and Hardrock Gunter's Essgee Records. However, as Roy himself once said jokingly, most of his records could best be described as having "escaped" rather than being "released." From 1964 to 1968 Roy did deejay work at WPIT in Pittsburgh. In 1968, he left the *Jamboree* as a regular, but returned periodically on special occasions.

In recent years, Roy Scott has continued to be musically active, largely in western Pennsylvania, which includes Pittsburgh. In the fall of 1993, he reported that he generally performed on an average four to five nights weekly. His only recent recording, a single on the Jeree label, came out about 1982: *Honest to God Cowboy/Lonely Together*. He also works on occasion with long-time friends Doc and Chickie Williams and his daughters, Lois, Janice, and Lori. In the mid-80's, he helped daughter Lois record an album on the Green Dolphin label. Roy resides in Washington, Pennsylvania. IMT

RECOMMENDED ALBUM:

"Great Songs of Yesterday" (Essgee)(ca. 1963) [Six-song 7" record]

TOMMY SCOTT

(Singer, Songwriter, Guitar, Piano, Ventriloquist)

Given Name:	**Tommy Lee Scott**
Date of Birth:	**June 24, 1917**
Where Born:	**Stephens County, Georgia**
Married:	**Mary Frank "Frankie" Thomas**
Children:	**Sandra Yvette**

Tommy Scott, also known as Doc Tommy Scott and Ramblin' Tommy Scott, has been in Country music for some six decades. As a medicine show performer in his early show business days, Tommy has in recent years revived this motif to advertise his stage act as "America's Last Real Medicine Show." Through the decades Scott has exemplified a wide range of talent that includes not only picking and singing but also ventriloquism.

A native of Stephens County in the Blue Ridge foothills, Tommy Scott learned to play guitar from a neighbor and got his first job in a medicine show about 1936. By that time he had already played on radio at WAIM in nearby Anderson, South Carolina. Tommy worked with various medicine shows and at radio stations in Greensboro, Greenville, and Raleigh, all in the Carolinas, when he went to WWVA Wheeling in 1939 as a member of Charlie Monroe's Kentucky Pardners. Another band member, John R. ("Curly") Sechler, would become Tommy's lifelong friend and after a time they formed a partnership which had programs at WRDW Augusta, Georgia, and WSPA Spartanburg, South Carolina, sponsored by Vim-Herb Tonic, where they were known as Ramblin' Scotty and Smilin' Bill. After a freak snowstorm destroyed their tent show, however, the pair split, although they would later reunite for recording. Tommy went back to playing medicine shows and later spent a year at WSM Nashville and the *Grand Ole Opry*. The Georgian also developed a

Just the medicine, Doc ***Tommy Scott***

ventriloquist dummy named Luke McLuke which he incorporated into his work along with some blackface comedy, as was then the custom.

For the next decade Tommy Scott worked the road heavily, usually based at various radio stations. His wife, Frankie, often worked with him and he acquired a long-time band member in Gaines Blevins, known as Old Bleb. Tommy's daughter, Sandra, worked in the act as a child, and later Blevins' son, Scotty Lee, was with the group for many years.

In 1946, Tommy filmed some fifty-two quarter-hour television shows for syndication, putting him somewhat ahead of his time in this respect. The shows were later combined to make twenty-six half-hour programs. Over the years, Tommy recorded for several labels including Bullet, 4 Star, Macy's, and especially King. While none of his discs became hits, they stand as fine examples of mainstream Country music of the late 40's and early 50's. Tommy also appeared in a western film, *Trail of the Hawk*, and made some movie "shorts." As a composer, he wrote *You Are the Rainbow of My Dreams*, which became a minor Bluegrass classic via recordings by Charlie Bailey and Lester Flatt.

As live radio work vanished from all but a few stations, Ramblin' Tommy took to the road with his show at an even heavier pace. To broaden its appeal, he added such old-time movie heroes as Tim McCoy, Johnnie Mack Brown, and Sunset Carson to his entourage at various times. In some years Scott's caravan stayed out as many as 352 days traveling all over the U.S. and Canada. A variety of musicians entered and left his group at times, including the youthful duo of Bill and Wilma Millsaps. Clyde Moody, another friend from the early days, worked with Tommy for a few years in the late 70's. By that time Scott had begun to emphasize the medicine show angle and to gain some recognition as a cultural preservator. Actually the medicine show aspect was more of a parody of the original than the real thing, but it did contain many elements of the vanished tradition right down to the bottled "snake oil," which many folks bought simply as a souvenir.

In more recent years, Scott has continued with his medicine show, although he has cut back somewhat (from 300 to 150 days, he reported in March 1994). Tommy also continued to make records and cut reunion albums with both Clyde Moody and Curly Sechler. Interest in his early work prompted Cattle Records to re-issue three albums of his older material and Old Homestead released one featuring his radio shows with Curly from 1941. When not on the road, "Doc" Tommy Scott and his wife of fifty-five years reside in their house in Tommy's hometown of Toccoa, Georgia, which is notable for its Chinese architecture. IMT

RECOMMENDED ALBUMS:

"Original Country Oldies" (Cattle Germany)(1983)
"Original Old Hillbilly Music" (Cattle Germany)(1984)
"Hillbilly and Rockabilly Rarities" (Cattle Germany)(1989)
"Tommy Scott's Country Caravan" (Request)
"The Best of Tommy Scott's Blue Grass" (Request)
"Songs of the Road" (Request)
"At the Medicine Show" (Concorde)(1977)
"Real Medicine Show Songs" (Katona)(1984)
"Greatest Songs" (Katona)(1988)
Tommy Scott & Clyde Moody:
"We've Played Every Place More Than Once" (Starday)(1978)
[Contains older King masters plus newly cut masters]
"Early Country Favorites" (Old Homestead)(1979)
Tommy Scott & Curly Sechler:
"Blue Grass Gospel" (Family)
"Early Radio, 1941" (Old Homestead)(1980)
"Now & Then" (Folkways)(1980)

SCRATCH BAND, The

When Formed: 1980 (with this membership)
Members:
Danny Flowers Lead Guitar, Harmonica
Biff Watson Keyboards, Guitar
Dave Pomeroy Bass Guitar
Pat McInerney Drums, Percussion

For many years, the Scratch Band was Don Williams' backing group on tour. However, the members of the group were a cut above the average band of musicians, and in 1982, they stepped out front for an album, ***The Scratch Band Featuring Danny Flowers***, on MCA, which was produced by Williams and Garth Fundis.

Danny Flowers was raised in North Carolina and came to Nashville as a session musician in 1971. He met Don Williams when he was booked to play harmonica on the session that produced, among other tracks, *I Recall a Gypsy Woman*. In 1973, Emmylou Harris recorded Danny's song *Before Believing*, and one of the lines in the song led to her naming the album ***Pieces of the Sky***. Danny joined Don's group in 1974, and in 1978, while in Tulsa, snowed in, he wrote (but never finished) *Tulsa Time*, which Don made a No.1 hit that year, and Eric Clapton converted into a Top 30 Pop hit two years later. (According to Danny, Don took the song and over Danny's protestations, said he wanted to record it. One look at the song chart shows that it only has two chords.)

Biff Watson arrived in Nashville from Chatham, Virginia, in 1971, straight from high school. Soon after arriving in town, he joined the Country-Rock band Tennessee Pulleybone. He then worked with Tracy Nelson and Crystal Gayle. He stayed with Crystal's band, Peace and Quiet, for two years, and then, in 1979, joined Don Williams.

Dave Pomeroy was born on an Air Force base in Naples, Italy. His family settled in Alexandria, Virginia, and at age 10, he started to play string bass. He majored in history, but decided that music was for him. He played in various bands on the East Coast, and worked on the road with Sleepy LaBeef. After spending time in London, England, he moved to Nashville, in 1978, where he worked with Guy Clark and Billy Joe Shaver. He joined Don Williams in 1980.

Pat McInerney was born in London, England, and raised in Hemel Hempstead, just north of London. He began playing drums at age 11, and after he gained a degree in sociology, he became a professional musician in 1974. He played with the popular Soul group Jimmy James and the Vagabonds. In 1976, he was a member of Pop-Rock group Limey (as Mac McInerney), and recorded two albums with them, ***Limey*** (1976) and ***Silver Eagle*** (1977), for RCA. He subbed for Barbara Fairchild's drummer when Barbara toured Europe with Don in 1977 and this led to his being invited to join Don's band. Pat relocated to Nashville the following year.

Although the MCA album was well received, the band did not release another and continued to play behind Williams as long as he toured. Danny has subsequently toured with Nancy Griffith, both Biff and Dave are in-demand session players and Pat has backed performers such as the McCarters and Linda Hargrove.

RECOMMENDED ALBUM:

"The Scratch Band Featuring Danny Flowers" (MCA)(1982)

EARL SCRUGGS

(Banjo, Guitar)
Given Name: Earl Eugene Scruggs
Date of Birth: January 6, 1924
Where Born: Cleveland County, North Carolina
Married: Ann Louise Cirtain
Children: Gary Eugene, Randy Lynn, Steven Earl (dec'd.)

One of the most influential banjo players in Country music history, Earl Scruggs provided one of the distinctive features of Bluegrass music—the three-finger method of playing banjo. He did not, however, invent the style, as is sometimes claimed. Musicians in his home area of North Carolina, regional artists, such as his distant cousin Smith Hammett (whom Earl saw play at age 5), Dewitt "Snuffy" Jenkins (whom Scruggs saw perform) and Charlie Poole and several other recording artists all played a three-finger style of banjo prior to Earl. Scruggs' contribution was that he brought the style to a wider audience by blending it with Bluegrass. Simultaneously he gave Bluegrass a sound that at the time seemed fresh, thereby greatly increasing the form's appeal.

Earl started performing in public at the age of 6 as part of a band made up of his brothers. By 1939, he was appearing on radio with a group called the Carolina Wildcats as well as with Wiley and Zeke, the Morris Brothers. Even so, he didn't immediately embark on a career in music after graduating from high school, but worked on a farm and in a textile mill to support his widowed mother. Soon, however, he began performing with "Lost" John Miller and the Allied Kentuckians, a band that played on WNOX Knoxville and WSM Nashville.

Shortly afterward, Miller stopped touring, leaving Scruggs out of work. Jim Shumate, a fiddler Earl knew from North Carolina, was a member of Bill Monroe's band at the time and recommended Earl to replace Stringbean, who had recently left the Blue Grass Boys. Earl was hired and in a very short time became a star instrumentalist. Monroe gave Scruggs a free hand to develop his banjo technique and Earl helped popularize a number of tunes, such as *Blue Grass Breakdown*, that were associated with him even after he left Monroe. That departure came in 1948 when Earl and guitarist-singer Lester Flatt both resigned, ostensibly to escape Monroe's heavy traveling schedule but, according to one biographer, because they realized that it was more financially remunerative to be band leader,

Earl Scruggs** (right) with **Randy Scruggs** and **Josh Graves

rather than sideman. (See Flatt & Scruggs' entry.)

In 1951 Flatt and Scruggs' recording of *Earl's Breakdown* is significant because it was the first recording on which Earl used the "Scruggs peg," a device that made it possible to change the tuning of banjo strings while playing. This invention has continued to appeal to 5-string banjo players. Scruggs pushed Flatt to experiment with modern "Folk songs," drums and Gospel-style harmonies. However, these innovations mostly produced some unsatisfying music and marked the beginning of the end for Flatt and Scruggs and the Foggy Mountain Boys.

In 1969, the pair went their separate ways, with Flatt pursuing a more traditional sound with the Nashville Grass and Scruggs going off in new directions with the Earl Scruggs Revue, featuring his own songs and a more Rock-oriented sound. The group signed with Columbia Records and released a series of albums. These included ***Earl Scruggs—His Family & Friends***, in 1971, which featured Bob Dylan, Doc Watson, Joan Baez and the Byrds.

Earl played a major part in assembling the older musicians for the Nitty Gritty Dirt Band project, ***Will the Circle Be Unbroken***, which was released in 1972. In 1974, the Earl Scruggs Revue plus Dobroist Josh Graves and guitarist Jody Maphis recorded the soundtrack music for the movie *Where the Lilacs Bloom*. They also had three Country chart entries during 1979 and 1980, of which the most successful was the Top 30 *I Could Sure Use the Feeling*. In 1982, Earl got together with Tom T. Hall for the album ***The Storyteller & The Banjo Man***, from which came two low-level Country chart entries, *There Ain't No Country Music on This Jukebox* and *Song of the South*. The following year, Earl released the album ***Top of the World***, on which he was joined by Ricky Skaggs, Lacy J. Dalton, Rodney Dillard and the Burrito Brothers. Earl was present to lend his skills when the Nitty Gritty Dirt Band put together ***Will the Circle Be Unbroken, Volume II***, in 1989.

Due to health problems, Earl Scruggs has now retired. In September 1992, his life was touched with tragedy when his youngest son, Steve, committed suicide after murdering his wife. WKM

RECOMMENDED ALBUMS:

"Earl Scruggs—His Family & Friends" (Columbia)(1971)
"Top of the World" (Columbia)(1983)
Earl Scruggs Revue:
"Earl Scruggs & the Earl Scruggs Revue Live at Kansas State" (Columbia)(1972)
"Rockin' 'Cross the Country—The Earl Scruggs Revue" (Columbia)(1974)
"Live from Austin City Limits" (Columbia)(1977)
Tom T. Hall & Earl Scruggs:
"The Storyteller & The Banjo Man" (Columbia)(1982

JOHNNY SEA

(Singer, Songwriter, 12-String Guitar, Actor, Artist)
Given Name: John Allan Seay, Jr.
Date of Birth: July 15, 1940
Where Born: Gulfport, Mississippi
Married: Conneigh
Children: Shannon, John Allan III

Although born in Mississippi, Johnny, known as "the Singing Sea," was raised in Atlanta, Georgia, where he appeared on the *Georgia Jubilee*.

When he was age 17, he won a state-wide talent competition. A record company executive heard Johnny at the finals, and signed him to a record contract. Another record executive arranged for Johnny to join the *Louisiana Hayride*, where he stayed for two years. Shortly after, he made his debut on the *Grand Ole Opry*.

In 1959, Johnny made his Country chart debut with his NRC release *Frankie's Man Johnny*, which reached the Top 15. The following year, *Nobody's Darling but Mine* did exactly the same. He studied acting at Strasberg's Actors' Studio in New York and then appeared in the play *The Biggest Circus*.

However, now his career started treading water, and so Johnny moved to St. Petersburg, Florida, and then out west, becoming a cowboy. He lived in Los Angeles, Pawhuska, Oklahoma, and Carlsbad, New Mexico. He stayed away for two years and then returned to a ranch in Big East Fork in Franklin, Tennessee, where he raised Black Angus cattle and trained quarter horses. He also took time out to ride in rodeos and collect guns.

Johnny returned to the Country charts in 1964 with the Top 30 single *My Baby Walks All Over Me* on the Philips label. He followed this a year later with the Top 20 record *My Old Faded Love*. He was then signed to a major label for the first time, and in 1966, scored a monster hit for Warner Brothers with *Day for Decision*. The record reached the Top 15 and crossed over to the Pop Top 40. It was Johnny's patriotic spoken response to Barry McGuire's *Eve of Destruction*. Although he had a minor success in 1967, with *Nothin's Bad As Bein' Lonely*, Johnny soon moved to Columbia Records, as Johnny Seay, where he had a Top 70 record in 1968 with *Going to Tulsa* and he had his final chart entry, that year, with *Three Six Packs, Two Arms and a Juke Box*.

In 1968, Johnny was getting itchy feet and was intent on leaving Tennessee for the Texas Panhandle. However, just before he left he passed by the house belonging to his neighbors, Willie and Nellie York. Willie York had served 10 years in prison for the killing of a Franklin law officer in 1944. Johnny heard that Willie was drunk and that

Nellie was in a Nashville hospital undergoing her fourth cancer operation. Johnny went home and wrote *Willie's Drunk and Nellie's Dyin'* and it was released as a single. As a result, David Snell, a former Executive Editor of *Life* magazine, heard the single on KIKK Houston, and bought two copies of the record. He and photographer Arthur Shatz came to Tennessee and did a piece on Willie York.

In 1969, Johnny moved to Justiceburg, Texas, gave up playing music and became a cowboy.

RECOMMENDED ALBUMS:

"Johnny Sea, Live at the Bitter End" (Philips)(1965)
"Day for Decision—Johnny Sea" (Warner Brothers)(1966)

DAN SEALS

(Singer, Songwriter, 9-String Guitar, Guitar, Alto and Soprano Saxophone)

Date of Birth:	**February 8, 1948**
Where Born:	**McCamey, Texas**
Married:	**1. (Div.)**
	2. Andrea (Andi)
Children:	**Holly, Jeremy, Jimmy, Jesse**

The Seals family is probably the most successful in the history of popular music. As well as Dan, celebrated members have included brother Jim (one-half of Seals & Crofts), brother Eddie (one-half of Eddie & Joe), Chuck (who wrote *Crazy Arms*), Troy (who is one of Country music's premier songwriters), Brady (a member of Little Texas) and cousin Johnny Duncan.

Dan learned to play at the feet of his father, E.W. "Waylon" Seals, who worked by day as a pipe fitter and repair specialist for Shell Oil and also played guitar. He formed the Seals Family band and Dan played a stand-up bass, when he was age 4, standing on an apple crate. In that same band was his brother Jim, who became State Fiddle Champion at age 9. Shortly after the family band, Dan's parents split up, with him going with his mother, moving to Iraan and then back to McCamey, on to Sweetwater and Abilene, before arriving in Dallas in 1958.

One friend, one ***Dan Seals***

While in high school, he played garage bands, such as the Playboys Five and These Few. In 1965, Dan came to Nashville to record with John Ford Coley and Shane Keister. They cut some sides at RCA's studio, with the intention of becoming known as the Shimmerers, but their producer died from a heart attack and nothing happened. They changed their name to Southwest F.O.B. in 1967.

The group released their first single, *The Smell of Incense*, the following year, on the local label GPC, and once it started to happen, it was licensed to Stax's Hip label. The single reached the Top 60 on the Pop chart. The band released an album of the same name plus three more singles, with only *Feelin' Groovy* getting as high as the Top 120. They were in the midst of making a new album in Memphis when Stax let them go, because they were too rowdy for the label's liking.

Dan and John Ford Coley split from the band in 1969, and went to California to try and get a record deal. However, they were unsuccessful and returned home, where they met Louis Shelton, a friend of Seals & Crofts, and he persuaded Herb Alpert at A & M to sign the duo "England Dan & John Ford Coley," and said that he would like to produce them.

Only one single, *New Jersey*, achieved Pop chart status, in 1971, but even then just fell short of the Top 100. However, *Simone* from their second album, ***Fables***, became a No.1 in Japan. By 1973, they were off the label and returned to playing clubs and writing songs.

The turning point came in Los Angeles, in 1976, when Dan met producer Kyle Lehning. He had with him Parker McGee, who had written a song called *I'd Really Love to See You Tonight.* With Kyle's help, they recorded a demo and played it to Atlantic Records, who turned it down. However, the next-door office to Atlantic belonged to Big Tree Records and Doug Morris from that label rushed in and signed the duo and the song. In the end it reached the Top 3 and sold over 2 million copies. Strangely enough, it was released in the U.K. through Atlantic, and went Top 30.

The duo followed up with the Top 10 hit *Nights Are Forever Without You* and the album of the same title reached the Pop albums Top 20 and was Certified Gold that year. Dan wrote the theme song for the movie *Joe Panther*, starring Brian Keith and Ricardo Montalban. England Dan & John Ford Coley's two hits in 1977 were *It's Sad to Belong* (which went to No.1 on the Adult Contemporary chart) and *Gone Too Far*, which both reached the Top 30. The following year, they had another Top 10 success with *We'll Never Have to Say Goodbye Again* (No.1 on the Adult Contemporary chart), and followed with the Top 50 *You Can't Dance*.

During 1979, their last year together, the duo started with a Top 10 hit, *Love Is the Answer* (another Adult Contemporary No.1), and followed with the Top 50 *What Can I Do with This Broken Heart.*

The following year, Dan was signed as a solo act (England Dan) to Atlantic Records (who had acquired Big Tree), with Kyle Lehning staying as producer (which he has continued to do). Dan hit the Pop charts with the Top 60 record *Late at Night*, and then in 1981, he moved to MCA, where he had a Top 50 Adult Contemporary hit, *Part of Me, Part of You*. That year, he sang the theme song for the George Segal movie *Carbon Copy*.

At this time, Dan was experiencing a lot of financial problems, due to bad management, among other things, and was now down to sleeping under a piano. The IRS took everything, but still he kept on and in 1983, signed with Liberty Records, and this was to be the rebirth of Dan Seals. That rebirth was helped by his adoption of the Persian-originated Baha'i religion, having tried to "rescue" brother Jim and his mother from what he thought was a cult. That year, he struck three times on the Country charts with *Everybody's Dream Girl* (Top 20), *After You* (Top 30) and *You Really Go for the Heart* (Top 40).

However, now Dan's songwriting prowess came into its own, when *God Must Be a Cowboy* (released in India as *God Must Be a Cow, Boy*!)went Top 10, in 1984. He followed up with his own *(You Bring Out) The Wild Side of Me*, which reached No.9. He wrapped up the year with the Top 3 single *My Baby's Got Good Timing*. 1985 was to be a watershed year for Dan. It started out with the Top 10 single Thom Schuyler's *My Old Yellow Car*, and was followed by the No.1 hit duo with Marie Osmond, *Meet Me in Montana*. Dan also went to No.1 with his highly lauded album ***Won't Be Blue Anymore***, which went Gold in 1987. He finished off 1986 with the marvelous *Bop*, which also went to No.1 and crossed over to the Pop Top 50, and became the biggest cross-over from Country to Pop in three years.

The following year, two of these songs featured in the CMA awards. *Bop* was named "Single of the Year" and *Meet Me in Montana* won "Duet of the Year." He also received a nomination for the CMA Horizon Award. He then had seven consecutive No.1 records, namely, *Everything That Glitters (Is Not Gold)* and *You Still Move Me* (both 1986), *I Will Be There*, *Three Time Loser* and *One Friend* (all 1987), Cheryl Wheeler's *Addicted* (a Grammy nominee) and *Big Wheels in the Moonlight* (both 1988). In 1987, he appeared at England's Peterborough Country Festival.

In 1989, Dan racked up one chart hit, the Top 5 single *They Rage On*. Come 1990, and he had back-to-back No.1 hits with *Love on Arrival* (three weeks at the top) and *Good Times* (two weeks at the top). His album ***On Arrival*** made the Top 15 of the Country Album chart. He ended the year with the Top 50 single *Bordertown*.

His last chart single for Capitol only reached the Top 60 in 1991 and was *Water Under the Bridge*. Dan moved to Warner Brothers that year, but his initial chart entry for the label, *Sweet Little Shoe*, only reached the Top 70. He was not able to regain his chart popularity as 1992 arrived and *Mason Dixon Line* only got the Top 50, while *Where Love Comes Around the Bend* peaked in the Top 60. The album ***Walking the Wire*** deserved to have done better than it did.

When Dan is not writing his memorable songs or touring, he can be found fly fishing on Hendersonville Lake in Nashville. Dan's children are following in his musical footsteps.

RECOMMENDED ALBUMS:

"Smell of Incense" (Hip)(1968) [As Southwest F.O.B.]
"Best of England Dan & John Ford Coley" (Big Tree)(1980)
"Stones" (Atlantic)(1980)
"Harbinger" (Atlantic)(1981)
"Just Tell Me That You Love Me" (MCA)(1981)
"Rebel Heart" (Liberty)(1983)
"San Antone" (EMI America)(1984)
"Won't Be Blue Anymore" (EMI America)(1985)
"On the Front Line" (EMI America)(1986)
"The Best" (Capitol)(1987)
"Rage On" (Capitol)(1988)
"Greatest Hits" (Capitol)(1991)
"Walking the Wire" (Warner Brothers)(1992)

CURLY SECHLER

(Singer, Songwriter, Guitar, Mandolin, Tenor Banjo)

Given Name:	**John Ray Sechler**
Date of Birth:	**December 25, 1919**
Where Born:	**China Grove, North Carolina**
Married:	**1. Juanita (div.)**
	2. Mabel (dec'd.)
Children:	**two sons**

Curly Sechler is one of Bluegrass music's great tenor singers, being especially known for the harmonies he provided with Lester Flatt. Over a musical career that stretched back over a half century, Curly worked as a sideman in many pioneer Country and Bluegrass bands.

Curly hailed from the North Carolina Piedmont and came by his vocal talents through his father, a locally renowned tenor who died about 1929. His mother taught him a couple of guitar chords and he later learned the fundamentals of tenor banjo and mandolin. About 1935, he and his brothers formed a string band called the Yodeling Rangers, which had a show on a local station in nearby Salisbury.

The Sechlers maintained this program until 1939, when Charlie Monroe talked Curly into joining his Kentucky Pardners, a unit that also included Tommy Edwards and Tommy Scott. They went to WWVA Wheeling, West Virginia, and then to WHAS Louisville, Kentucky. In 1941, Curly, then known as Smiling Bill, and Scott decided to form a duet and go to Georgia and South Carolina, where they worked radio and tent shows until a freak snowstorm destroyed their tent and Curly returned to Charlie Monroe. In September 1946, he cut his first commercial session for RCA Victor, doing four songs with Monroe, including *Who's Calling You Sweetheart* and the original recording of *Mother's Not Dead, She's Only Sleeping*.

Curly worked in an early version of Jim & Jesse's Virginia Boys, but left to join Lester Flatt and Earl Scruggs' Foggy Mountain Boys, in March 1949, at Bristol and later Knoxville (both Tennessee). He subsequently recorded three sessions with them on Mercury and eventually many on Columbia. In 1951 and part of 1952, Sechler left the Foggy Mountain Boys and worked brief stints with Carl Sauceman, the Stanley Brothers, and Jim and Jesse, helping the latter on their initial Capitol session in June 1952, at which time they recorded his classic Korean War song *Purple Heart*.

Soon afterward, he rejoined Flatt and Scruggs, remaining with them until 1962 (except for several months in 1958-1959). During this period, Lester and Earl moved to WSM Nashville and the *Opry* and began their long association with Martha White Flour. They also worked a series of live television shows in a variety of Appalachian cities. Curly's tenor work on numerous vocals with Lester endeared him to a whole generation of Bluegrass fans, and he contributed some notable vocal leads as well, such as *That Old Book of Mine*.

In March 1962, Sechler left the Foggy Mountain Boys and spent a decade in the trucking business. In 1971, he made an album for County backed by the Shenandoah Cut-Ups and made a few festival appearances. This led to his being reunited with Lester as a member of the Nashville Grass in 1973. This last sojourn with Flatt lasted for six years and resulted in Curly's work on albums with RCA Victor, Flying Fish, Canaan, and CMH, as well as many festival and *Opry* appearances.

In the meantime, Curly cut another solo album in 1978, for Revonah, and became leader of Nashville Grass when Lester died the following spring. Honoring Lester's request that he keep the band together, Curly has continued on for some fifteen years now, with several changes in personnel. In addition to cutting new albums for CMH, Folkways, Rich-R-Tone, and Rebel, Curly also made an album with his one-time partner Tommy Scott on Folkways. In keeping the Flatt tradition alive at festivals, Curly has been much helped with the addition of Willis Spears (b. 1940), a vocalist steeped in Lester's style. In recent years, Curly and Willis have co-led the Nashville Grass into the 90's. IMT

RECOMMENDED ALBUMS:

"Curly Seckler[sic] Sings Again" (County)(1972)
"No Doubt About It" (Revonah)(1979) [Includes Marty Stuart]
"Take a Little Time" (CMH)(1980) [Includes Johnny Cash]
"There's Gonna Be a Singing" (CMH)(1981)
"Nashville" (Folkways)(1982)
"Bluegrass Gospel" (Rich-R-Tone)(ca. 1985)
"A Tribute to Lester Flatt" (Rebel)(1990) [Cassette]
Curly Sechler and Tommy Scott:
"Early Radio" (Old Homestead)(1980)
"Now & Then" (Folkways)(1980)
[See also Lester Flatt, Flatt & Scruggs.]

II GENERATION

When Formed:	**1971**
Members:	
Eddie Adcock	**Vocals, Banjo**
Wendy Thatcher	**Vocals, Guitar**

Jimmy Gaudreau	**Vocals, Mandolin**
Bob White (Quail)	**Bass Guitar**
Randy Stockwell	**Bass Guitar**
Eddie Adcock	**Vocals, Banjo**
Martha Hearon	**Vocals, Guitar**
Jeff Wisor	**Vocals, Fiddle**
Gene Johnson	**Vocals, Mandolin**
Johnny Castle	**Vocals, Bass Guitar**
Tommy Lee Brooks	**Vocals, Bass Guitar**

After leaving the Country Gentlemen in 1970, Eddie Adcock went to California and started a Country-Rock band under the alias of Clinton Kodack, and became quite successful. Adcock played lead guitar, as he put it, "loud and fuzzy." This lasted for about a year and then he returned to playing Bluegrass as a single. He then met up again with Wendy Thatcher and Jimmy Gaudreau. He had played with Gaudreau in the Country Gentlemen and his connections with Wendy Thatcher went back to the days when she had been Adcock's partner during his Folk and Folk-Rock days in California. At first, Adcock and Gaudreau wanted Tony Rice to play guitar, but when he couldn't join them, they approached A.L. Wood. With just two days before their first gig, Adcock called Wendy to advise her she was in the new group, II Generation. Making up the line-up on that first booking was "Quail," who had played string bass with the New Deal String Band. However, after a short while, Randy Stockwell replaced him on bass.

The group underwent many changes and in 1974, the line-up behind Adcock was Martha Hearon, who later became Mrs. Adcock. She played guitar in the group and was responsible for much of the material. She got into Bluegrass via Folk music. After hearing Bill Monroe, she got a job at C.E. Ward's shop, working and repairing instruments. She moved on to Randy Wood's Pickin' Parlor, where she met Adcock. Gene Johnson was formerly a member of Cliff Waldron's New Shades of Grass and various groups around his home area of New York. He had worked with Jeff Wisor and recorded an album with Jeff and others as General Store. Johnny Castle had been a member of the Washington, D.C., Rock band Crank. He was capable of playing both bass guitar and upright bass, but due to shortage of space in their band truck, Johnny only played bass guitar in II Generation.

Vocally, the group had a mixture of trios and solos, with each member being able to take lead. Adcock was adamant about the quality of their sound system and spent some $10,000 on sound equipment to achieve that end. This meant that they did not have to play their brand of Bluegrass-Rock with any sound distortion or too loud. By 1980, Eddie and Martha had decided to break up the group and they went on to form Talk of the Town.

RECOMMENDED ALBUMS:

"Introducing the II Generation" (Rome)
"Head Cleaner" (Rebel)
"The II Generation" (CMH)
"We Call It Grass" (Rebel)(1975)
"Second Impression" (Rebel)(1976)
"State of Mind" (CMH)

JEANNIE SEELY

(Singer, Songwriter, Guitar, Actress, Author)

Given Name:	**Marilyn Jean Seely**
Date of Birth:	**July 6, 1940**
Where Born:	**Titusville, Pennsylvania**
Married:	**Hank Cochran (div.)**

It was Jeannie Seely who was largely responsible for updating the image of female Country singers, and caused more than a few eyebrows to be raised by appearing wearing miniskirts and wigs on stage.

When she was age 11, she began singing on a weekly radio program in Meadville, Pennsylvania. During 1954 through 1958, while attending Townville High School, she appeared on WLW *Midwest Hayride*, Cincinnati, and on radio, TV and amusement parks, including two years on Armed Forces Radio. In 1959 through 1961, Jeannie studied banking at the American Institute of Banking, Oil City, Pennsylvania.

She moved to Los Angeles in 1962 and, into 1963, she worked as an Executive Secretary at Imperial Records. She started making contacts, one of whom was songwriter Hank Cochran, whom she would marry in 1969. She met him in 1963 when she was on the *Country Music Time* TV show in LA and he was guesting. Hank gave her encouragement and tried to get her to move to Nashville. However, she didn't make the move...yet.

She went to see Joe Johnson, who then owned Challenge Records and 4 Star Music, and he signed her to both companies. While with 4 Star, she had songs recorded by Tex Williams, Connie Smith (*Senses*), Dottie West (*It Just Takes Practice*), Norma Jean (*Leavin' and Sayin' Goodbye*) and Ray Price (*Enough to Lie*). The first song she had recorded, *Anyone Who Knows What Love Is (Will Understand)*, was charted, in 1964, by R & B singer Irma Thomas. The following year, Jeannie recorded two singles for Challenge, *Bring It on Back/World Without You* and *Today Is Not the Day/Please Release Me*.

Jeannie moved to Nashville in October 1965, and was signed by Fred Foster to Monument Records. She also signed to Tree Publishing as a songwriter. She hit the Country charts in the spring of 1966, with the Cochran song *Don't Touch Me*, which reached the Top 3 and also crossed over to the Pop chart Top 90. She followed up with two Top 20 records, Cochran's *It's Only Love* and *A Wanderin' Man*. That year, she was named "Most Promising Female Artist" by *Billboard*, *Country Song Roundup* and *Cash Box*, and "Fastest Rising Female Star" by *Record World*. She also won a Grammy Award for "Best Country & Western Vocal Performance, Female." During the year, Norma Jean decided to spend more time with her daughter and so a vacancy occurred with the Porter Wagoner Show on the road. At the time, Jeannie roomed with Porter's secretary and Jeannie applied and got the job. That year, she also debuted on the *Grand Ole Opry* and appeared on NBC-TV's *Swingin' Country* and the *Lloyd Thaxton TV Show*.

In 1967, her first two singles didn't fare too well, with *When It's Over* going Top 40 and *These Memories* reaching the Top 50. However, her third single, *I'll Love You More (Than You Need)*, became a Top 10 hit. That year, she became a member of the *Grand Ole Opry* and joined Ernest Tubb's syndicated TV show. She also made appearances on the Wilburn Brothers syndicated TV show. She had two more chart entries for Monument in 1968, both of which made the Top 25, and they were *Welcome Home to Nothing* and *How Is He?*

Jeannie moved to Decca Records in 1969, where she was produced by Owen Bradley and Walter Haynes. She became a part of the Jack Greene Show that year, and they began recording together. Jeannie's fortunes with Decca and its successor, MCA, were mixed. In all, she had nineteen chart entries, but very few were major hits. In 1969, she and Jack had a Top 3 single, Dave Kirby and Hank Cochran's *Wish I Didn't Have to Miss You*. That year, they toured U.S. military bases in Southeast Asia, Europe and Hawaii.

Two years later, they returned to the charts with the Top 20 record *Much Oblige*. The same year, Faron Young had a Top 10 hit with Jeannie's *Leavin' and Sayin' Goodbye*. In 1972, Jeannie and Jack had their last chart entry, a Top 20 single, *What in the World Has Gone Wrong with our Love*. The following year, Jeannie had a Top 10 solo hit with another Hank Cochran song, *Can I Sleep in Your Arms*. She closed out the year with yet one more Cochran song, *Lucky Ladies*, which reached the Top 15. During that year, she and Jack appeared at the Wembley Festival in England (they would return in 1976).

She continued to have success in 1974, with *I Miss You* (Top 40) and *He Can Be Mine* (Top 30). She and Jack adopted a more "outlaw" stance and changed the name of the Jolly Green Giants to the Renegades. She stayed with MCA until 1976, without having any major successes. She then moved to Columbia, in 1977, with the same result. That same year, she was in a serious auto accident. In 1980, she appeared on the soundtrack album of Willie Nelson's *Honeysuckle Rose*. In 1983, she was featured on Kat Family's ***All American Cowboys***, where she sang a duet with Willie Nelson, *You've Been Leaving Me for Years*, and a solo, her own song, *When Will I See You Again*.

Jeannie opened a nightclub in Nashville in 1985, but it folded after a year. In 1986, she got together with Jean Shepard and Lorrie Morgan in the Country musical *Takin' It Home*. Two years later, she portrayed Miss Mona in a Nashville production of *The Best Little Whorehouse in Texas*. That same year she published *Pieces of a Puzzled Mind*, a book of witty remarks. In 1989, she was one of the stars at the unveiling of the statue of Athena in the Parthenon in Nashville. She also appeared in a non-singing role, as the bag-lady in *Everybody Loves Opal*.

In recent years, she has continued to appear around the country and on the *Opry*. She has also written two books on backstage anecdotes at the *Opry*.

RECOMMENDED ALBUMS:

"Thanks Hank [Cochran]" (Monument)(1967)
"Jeannie Seely's Greatest Hits" (Monument)(1972)
"Can I Sleep in Your Arms"/"Lucky Ladies" (MCA)(1973)
"Live at the Grand Ole Opry" (double)(Pinnacle)(1978) [With Jack Greene]
"Greatest Hits" (Gusto)(1982) [With Jack Greene]
"All-American Cowboys" (Kat Family)(1983) [Also features Merle Haggard, Moe Bandy, Willie Nelson and David Allan Coe]

SELDOM SCENE, The

When Formed: 1971
Members:

Mike Auldridge	**Vocals, Dobro, Guitar**
John Duffey	**Vocals, Mandolin, Dobro, Guitar**
Ben Eldridge	**Vocals, Banjo, Guitar**
Tom Gray	**Vocals, Bass**
John Starling	**Vocals, Guitar**

Other significant members have included:
T. Michael Coleman, Lou Reid, Phil Rosenthal

From the time of their founding on November 1, 1971, the Seldom Scene has been a major force in new or progressive Bluegrass. All but one of the original members had been previously associated with either the Country Gentlemen or the New Shades of Grass and wanted to work as a part-time band. For a semi-professional group, however, the Scene found itself in considerable demand. They had relatively few changes in personnel.

John Duffey (b. March 4, 1934, Washington, D.C.), the best-known member of the Seldom Scene, whose father sang with the Metropolitan Opera, had been a twelve year veteran of the Country Gentlemen when he assembled the Seldom Scene. The group included Tom Gray (b. February 1, 1941, Chicago, Illinois), another former Gentleman from the early 60's, Ben Eldridge (b. August 15, 1938, Richmond, Virginia) and Mike Auldridge (b. December 30, 1938, Washington, D.C.), who were both alumni of Cliff Waldron-led bands. Lead singer-guitarist John Starling (b. March 26, 1940, Durham, North Carolina), an army surgeon at Walter Reed Hospital, rounded out the quintet and although he was the only member not previously associated with a name act, he could certainly be termed a well-seasoned amateur. The Scene appeared one night a week at the Red Fox Inn in Bethesda, Maryland, and later at the Birchmere in Alexandria, Virginia.

In summer, the Seldom Scene quickly became favorites on the festival circuit, particularly those in the eastern seaboard states. Their albums generally contained a few numbers long associated with traditional Bluegrass, but also had several songs or tunes new to the genre such as the old Ricky Nelson hit *Hello Mary Lou* and the Blues-flavored *Rider*. For D.C.-area football fans they produced a fine instrumental version of *Hail to the Redskins* and once provided halftime entertainment at one of their games. Traditionalists could appreciate their rendition of early Bluegrass like *Hit Parade of Love*, even if their arrangement added a touch of parody to the original. Through their initial seven years, the Scene cut seven albums for Dick Freeland's Rebel label, including a double effort taped live at a club called the Cellar Door.

Since none of the musicians in the Seldom Scene totally depended on music for a livelihood, commercial pressures did not drive their music to the degree that it did some bands. Thus the Scene could be innovative within the format they chose for themselves. Starling eventually left the Washington area and departed the group following the 1977 festival season. Phil Rosenthal (b. 1948) took his place and sang lead on their early albums for Sugar Hill. A second round of changes took place when Lou Reid (b. 1954) took over for the lead vocal/guitar slot in 1986 and T. Michael Coleman (b. 1951), formerly with Doc Watson, replaced Tom Gray. Coleman favored the electric bass over Tom's familiar upright, but there was little change in their basic sound, which showed a strong Duffey influence throughout with his strong tenor vocal and innovative mandolin. In 1993, John Starling returned to the Scene and took over his old spot. A photo of the band on their latest album shows the Seldom Scene looking some twenty years older and sounding a bit more traditional than they did in 1971, but still producing the quality brand of music that made their reputation. IMT

RECOMMENDED ALBUMS:

"Act 1" (Rebel)(1972)
"Act 2" (Rebel)(1973)
"Act 3" (Rebel)(1973)
"The Old Train" (Rebel)(1974)
"Live at the Cellar Door" (Rebel)(1975)
"The New Seldom Scene Album" (Rebel)(1976)
"Baptizing" (Rebel)(1977)
"Act Four" (Sugar Hill)(1979)
"After Midnight" (Sugar Hill)(1981)
"At the Scene" (Sugar Hill)(1983)
"Blue Ridge" (Sugar Hill)(1985) [With Jonathan Edwards]
"15th Anniversary Celebration" (double)(Sugar Hill)(1987)
"A Change of Scenery" (Sugar Hill)(1988)
"Scenic Roots" (Sugar Hill)(1990)
"The Best of the Seldom Scene" (Rebel)(1990)
"Like We Used to Be" (Sugar Hill)(1994)
[See also Mike Auldridge, Country Gentlemen, John Starling, Cliff Waldron]

SESAC
(Society of European Stage Authors and Composers)

SESAC is one of three performing rights organizations in the United States representing songwriters and music publishers by licensing their songs for public performance. Radio stations, television stations, concert halls, nightclubs, restaurants, etc., are required by the United States Copyright Law to pay a royalty for the public performance of music protected under the law.

SESAC is the second oldest and the smallest performing rights organization in the U.S. Paul Heinicke established the Society of European Stage Authors and Composers in 1930 to help foreign composers collect performance royalties for the use of their songs in the U.S. SESAC historically has licensed the music not given attention by the larger performing rights organizations, ASCAP (American Society of Composers, Authors and Publishers, established 1914) and BMI (Broadcast Music, Incorporated, established 1939). The SESAC repertoire includes a large body of Gospel and Jazz copyrights. Over the past two decades, SESAC has represented some major Country music, including the songs written by K.T. Oslin. Susan Longacre was named SESAC "Songwriter of the Year" in 1992 and 1993 for writing such hits as Reba McEntire's *Is There Life Out There*, Steve Wariner's *Leave Him Out of This*, Ricky Van Shelton's *Wild Man* and Collin Raye's *That Was a River*.

In 1992, SESAC was purchased by entrepreneurs Ira Smith, Stephen Swid and Freddie Gershon. Smith and Gershon are also principals in the grand rights licensing organization, Music Theater International. Swid is also a music businessman as the "S" in the major music publishing and record company SBK.

Historically, SESAC paid songwriters and publishers based on the chart success achieved in trade magazines, including *Billboard*, *Radio and Records* and *Gavin*. SESAC is the only performing rights organization that provides a guaranteed royalty payment amount to their affiliates. In 1991, a No.1 Country song earned $87,000 over a four-year period (first year, $60,000; second year, $15,000; third year, $9,000; and fourth year, $3,000). Both the songwriter and song publisher would earn $87,000 each.

In 1993, SESAC introduced a revolutionary new method to track the broadcast of the songs they represent. Joining forces with the Broadcast Data Systems Company, a computer system was programmed to recognize the "thumbprint" of each song within 54 seconds of airplay. The information is gathered on sophisticated monitors placed around the country, equipped to pick up the radio signal and register the thumbprints. SESAC plans to have the new system operational in all the major Country music radio markets by 1995. The new system is designed to give an accurate account of each performance, unlike the random sampling method utilized by ASCAP, BMI and PRS (the Performing Rights Society, the U.K. performing rights organization).

In 1994, SESAC was under the direction of 24-year veteran Vincent Candilora, President and Chief Executive Officer. Former Nashville record executive Dianne Petty continued her long-standing position of Vice President. It was Dianne who was instrumental in bringing K.T. Oslin to SESAC. JIE

RONNIE SESSIONS

(Singer, Songwriter, Guitar)

Date of Birth: December 7, 1948
Where Born: Henrietta, Oklahoma
Married: Patty Tierney
Children: Shauna, Mandy

Ronnie Sessions is an example of a child prodigy who looks like he is certain to make it in a big way as a recording artist, but somehow doesn't. It wasn't that Ronnie lacked talent and his self-titled MCA album remains one of the most solid Country-Rock albums, with songs by Tony Joe White, Delbert McClinton and Bob McDill and featuring harmony vocals from Janie Fricke and musicians such as Joe South and Reggie Young. Ronnie's problems partly stemmed from the fact that Ronnie spent too much time honky tonkin'.

When he was age 6, Ronnie's family moved to Bakersfield, California. By the time he was 8, he became a regular on the *Herb Henson Trading Post* TV show and this led to his being signed to Pike Records, where for his first single, *Bunny Rabbit (Without Any Tail)/Mommy's Japanese*, he was billed as "Little Ronnie Sessions." On his second single, *Keep a Knockin'*, he was backed by Little Richard's original band.

By the time he was 10, Ronnie appeared in Las Vegas nightclubs, including the Golden Nugget. Having left high school, he studied veterinary science at Bakersfield Junior College. He recorded for the independent labels Starview and Moserite and then, in 1969, he signed with the re-activated Republic label and released the singles *My Daddy Was a Guitar Man* (1969) and *More Than Satisfied* (1970). Ronnie toured for four years with Buck Owens and then with Merle Haggard and Glen Campbell, for a year each.

In 1971, Ronnie moved to Nashville, where he lived with Hank Cochran and Jeannie Seely. Ronnie signed to Tree Publishing as a writer and shopped around for a record label. In 1972, he signed to MGM, where he was produced by Chip Young, and his version of Hoyt Axton's *Never Been to Spain* reached the Top 40. He closed out the year with *Tossin' and Turnin'* (which had been a big Pop hit for Bobby Lewis, a decade earlier), which went Top 60. He had two further chart entries for the label, during 1973, *I Just Can't Put Her Down* and *If That Back Door Could Talk*.

Come 1975, and Ronnie released a pair of singles for the Moserite label, *Scaredy Cat* and *Queen of Snob Hill,* and then he had a low-level hit, *Makin' Love*, for his new label, MCA, where he was again produced by Chip Young. The following year, Ronnie had another basement entry, *Support Your Local Honky Tonks*, which was more than a little appropriate to Ronnie's way of life. However, at the end of the year, he had a Top 20 success with *Wiggle Wiggle*. He followed this with another Top 20 record, *Me and Millie (Stompin' Grapes and Gettin' Silly)* and the Top 30 record *Ambush* (after which he named his band, Ambush). However, by the end of the year, *I Like to Be with You* only reached the Top 60.

Ronnie had only one more major hit on MCA, when *Juliet and Romeo* reached the Top 25, in 1978. He and his band continued to be an in-demand act on the live circuit, and in 1986, he signed with Compleat, but only achieved one lowly entry, *I Bought the Shoes That Just Walked Out on Me*.

RECOMMENDED ALBUM:

"Ronnie Sessions" (MCA)(1977)

BILLY JOE SHAVER

(Singer, Songwriter, Poet, Guitar)

Given Name: Billy Joe Shaver
Date of Birth: 1941
Where Born: Corsicana, Texas
Married: Married and divorced same lady three times!
Children: Eddy

When Billy Joe released his album ***Salt of the Earth***, he could have been referring to himself. His songs have become classics when recorded by members of the "outlaw" movement, such as Waylon Jennings and Kris

Kristofferson. In fact, Jennings was so impressed with Billy Joe's songs that in 1973, he recorded an entire album of his songs (except one), entitled ***Honky Tonk Heroes***. His lived-in face and denims betray the soul of a man who has lived in his songs and is not afraid to be controversial with songs like *Black Rose*.

He was born into a family background that was song material in itself. His parents separated before he was born, and his mother worked in a honky-tonk. He was raised by his grandmother, and moved to Waco at age 12. He was encouraged to write poetry by his English teacher, Miss Leff, and dedicated many of his early poems to her.

He left school in the eighth grade, to work on his uncles' farms, and then he joined the U.S. Navy. On release from the service, he moved to Houston, where he worked as a bull rider, bronco buster, gas station attendant, car salesman and sawmill worker. It was in the last named that Billy Joe came to grief. He lost part of four fingers on his right hand, in an accident.

He began writing songs after hearing Waylon Jennings, and around 1965, he started traveling between Texas and Nashville trying to get his songs heard. However, Billy Joe is quite a shy person, and had problems getting heard. Then one day, in 1968, he stopped by Bobby Bare's Return Music. Bare told him that he wasn't looking to sign any new writers, but more in pity, listened to Billy Joe's songs and was so impressed that he signed him to a $50-a-week draw deal. However, this still meant that it was a difficult time financially for Billy Joe and he resorted to sleeping on the floor of Bare's office.

He began his own recording career in 1970, thanks to Bare's help. However, his Mercury single *Chicken on the Ground* failed to score. The following year, Bare recorded the Shaver song *Short and Sweet*, but unfortunately, it was one of Bare's rare flops. Kristofferson recorded *Good Christian Soldier*, which Billy Joe had co-written with Bare, and included it on his ***Silver Tongued Devil*** album.

The following year, the Shaver song *Music City USA* was the flip-side of Bare's version of *Sylvia's Mother*. In 1973, Tom T. Hall, with whom Billy Joe had been touring, recorded two of his songs, *Willie the Wandering Gypsy and Me* (which later became a theme for the Austin outlaw movement) and *Old Five and Dimers Like Me*. Bare had a major hit with the Shaver song *Ride Me Down Easy*. During the recording of Waylon's album ***Honky Tonk Heroes***, Billy Joe and Waylon nearly came to blows, as Billy Joe was angered by Waylon "messing with the melodies." However, the resulting album, which was probably the first outlaw release, was one of Waylon's finest.

In 1973, Kristofferson produced Billy Joe's first album, ***Old Five and Dimers Like Me***, for Monument, and Tom T. Hall wrote the liner notes. It includes Billy Joe's classic song of dedication to Willie Nelson, *Willy the Wandering Gypsy and Me*. The songs were fresh and represented the Shaver principle of writing about real life. From this album, Monument released *I Been to Georgia on a Fast Train* and it reached the basement level of the Country charts.

By the end of 1974, Billy Joe had signed to MGM Records for an album, with Willie Nelson and Bobby Bare as producers, but nothing came of this. At the time, he was suffering with the effects of excessive drinking and for the next two years, dropped out of sight. Billy Joe was lured back by Dickie Betts of the Allman Brothers Band. As a result, Billy Joe signed with Capricorn Records and released two albums, ***When I Get to You*** (1976) and ***Gypsy Boy*** (1977). The latter was produced by Brian Ahern and featured Emmylou Harris, Ricky Skaggs, Rodney Crowell and Willie Nelson. From this came his only other chart single, *You Asked Me To*, which reached the Top 80.

Around this time, Billy Joe's songs were recorded by other artists, including *You Asked Me To* (Elvis Presley), *Sweet Pea* (Allman Brothers Band), *I Could Be Me Without You* (both Johnny Rodriguez and Bobby Bare), *Jesus Was Our Savior (Cotton Was Our King)* and *I'm Just an Old Lump of Coal (But I'm Gonna Be a Diamond Some Day)* (both Johnny Cash). The latter song proved to be a pivotal song for Billy Joe. Just before he wrote it, he decided to give up drink and drugs and asked God to direct his life; the result was the song. Just after Cash recorded it, in 1978, he signed Billy Joe to a writer's deal at House of Cash.

As Capricorn had closed its doors, in 1980, Billy Joe got a deal with Columbia Records and, the following year, released ***I'm Just an Old Lump of Coal...But I'm Gonna Be a Diamond Some Day***, which was very well received. That year, John Anderson recorded the song and took it to the Top 5 on the Country chart, resulting in its being nominated for the CMA "Song of the Year." The following year. Billy Joe released his self-titled album for Columbia. This album included re-recordings of many of his classics including *Ride Me Down Easy*, *Lowdown Freedom*, *Old Five and Dimers* and *I Been to Georgia on a Fast Train*.

His next album release was five years later, when Columbia issued ***Salt of the Earth***. Although not praised in all quarters, it is in fact a kaleidoscope of different styles and was produced by Billy Joe and his extremely

Billy Joe Shaver *(right) with his talented son, Eddy*

talented guitarist son, Eddy, and reveals the path that Billy Joe walks between religion and street mentality, with songs such as *You Can't Beat Jesus* and *The Devil Made Me Do It the First Time* and the wonderfully evocative *Fun While It Lasted.*

Billy Joe's career then trod water until he appeared at the International Festival of Country Music at Wembley, England, in 1989. Under the group name of Shaver, Billy Joe released the 1993 album ***Tramp on Your Street***, which featured Eddy Shaver and keyboardist Al Kooper. There is also vocal support from Merle Haggard and Brother Phelps. As this has video support, which CMT aired, it is to be hoped that Billy Joe Shaver will at long last break through as he deserves.

RECOMMENDED ALBUMS:

"Old Five and Dimers Like Me" (Monument)(1973)
"When I Get My Wings" (Capricorn)(1976)
"Gypsy Boy" (Capricorn)(1977)
"I'm Just an Old Lump of Coal...But I'm Gonna Be a Diamond Some Day" (Columbia)(1981)
"Billy Joe Shaver" (Columbia)(1982)
"Salt of the Earth" (Columbia)(1987)
"Tramp on Your Street" (Praxis)(1993)

DOROTHY SHAY

(Singer, Actress)

Given Name:	**Dorothy Nell Sims**
Date of Birth:	**1921**
Where Born:	**Jacksonville, Florida**
Married:	**Dick Looman (div.)**
Date of Death:	**October 22, 1978**

Imagine if you will a dark-haired lady robed in exquisite gowns, looking every bit like a pinup. Imagine that same lady singing in a broad southern accent songs such as *Sagebrush Sadie, Makin' Love, Mountain Style* and *Feudin' and Fightin'*, and you have Dorothy Shay, the star known as "the Park Avenue Hillbillie."

Dorothy spent her early career trying to get rid of her southern drawl, taking acting lessons, so that when she auditioned to become a vocalist with a band in Pittsburgh, she wouldn't appear to be a hick. After the start of WWII, she moved to New York to become a part of the USO circuit. After the end of hostilities, she became the singer with the Morton Gould Orchestra and became a major attraction in New York City. The turning point came one evening when she encored with the rube song *Uncle Fud*. The audience showed their appreciation, and Dorothy's career took off. She was given her sobriquet by the agent Merrill Jacobs, in 1945. She is said to have actually sparked a fire at Ciro's in Hollywood. In 1947, for Columbia Records, she released the single *Feudin' and Fightin'*, which came from the Broadway musical *Laffing Room Only*. The single became a monster cross-over hit, reaching the Top 5 on both Country and Pop charts. From that year, she made regular appearances on the Spike Jones radio show.

From 1948 through 1950, Dorothy released a stream of singles for Columbia, including *I'm in Love with a Married Man, Two Gun Harry from Tucumcari* and *Joan of Arkansas* (all 1948), *Another Notch on Father's Shotgun* (1949) and *What fer Didja* and *Diamonds Are a Girl's Best Friend* (both 1950). None of these or her other singles charted, but formed a part of her very popular live act.

In 1951, she appeared in the movie *Comin' Round the Mountain* with Abbott and Costello. At this time, she was receiving $5,000 a performance. Two years later, she was asked to perform at Dwight D. Eisenhower's 1953 Inaugural Ball; he was a great fan of hers. She also appeared at a royal command performance before Queen Elizabeth II. Dorothy married Dick Loorman, a Los Angeles publicist, in 1958, but by the following year, that marriage had ended in divorce.

From the end of the 50's through the 60's little was heard of Dorothy. During the 70's, she made regular appearances on the CBS-TV series *The Waltons*. She died in 1978, following complications from a stroke.

GEORGE BEVERLY SHEA

(Gospel Singer, Songwriter)

Given Name:	**George Beverly Shea**
Date of Birth:	**February 1, 1909**
Where Born:	**Winchester, Ontario, Canada**
Married:	**Erma L. Scharfe**
Children:	**Ronnie, Elaine**

George Beverly Shea is best known for his long association with the Billy Graham Evangelistic Association, being the featured soloist on Graham's crusades since 1947. He is largely responsible for the current popularity of *How Great Thou Art*. Still, his accomplishments are even greater because he is a talented songwriter who has produced a number of classic hymns, including *The Wonder of It All, I Will Praise Him in the Morning* and *I'd Rather Have Jesus*. In the late 1920's, however, Shea would have thought the musical acclaim he later reached was an impossibility.

Gospel great ***George Beverly Shea***

The son of a Wesleyan Methodist minister, George grew up in parsonages in New York and New Jersey. Both parents encouraged their son's musical interests and as a youth, he frequently sang in his father's church and other local churches. After high school, he attended Houghton College in New York, but family financial problems made it impossible for him to continue his college education. Therefore, he dropped out and spent the next several years working as a clerk in the New York City offices of the Mutual of New York Life Insurance Company.

During these years, George continued his vocal training and singing in churches and for local religious broadcasts. One day a network radio director heard him sing and was sufficiently impressed that he arranged an audition for a national program with the Lynn Murray Singers. George passed the audition and was offered a job, but reluctantly turned the position down because he didn't feel right about performing secular music.

In 1934, Shea married his childhood sweetheart and a short time later the couple moved to Chicago. There George became a member of the staff at radio station WMBI. In June 1944, the thirty-five-year-old singer realized his ambition to sing Gospel music on a nationally aired radio program. Herbert J. Taylor, a Christian businessman who headed an aluminum firm, sponsored *Club Time* for the next eight years. This show brought George national recognition, as did his participation in large Youth for Christ rallies throughout the United States and Canada during the 40's and 50's. In 1947, he became a soloist with Graham's team. In fulfilling his duties, he has had the opportunity to introduce a number of songs to Graham's audiences. The best known of these is *How Great Thou Art*, which was written by the Rev. Stuart K. Hine in the 20's and was based on an 1886 Swedish poem by the Rev. Carl Boberg, *O Stor Gud*. It was introduced into the U.S. by Dr. J. Edwin Orr in 1954. That year, a leaflet containing the song was given to George, who then sang it at the Toronto, Canada Crusade of 1955. Since then, the song has generally been cited as the most recorded Gospel song. In 1974, *Christian Herald* magazine conducted a poll in which they decided it was the No.1 hymn in America.

In 1951, George signed with RCA Victor and his 1965 album ***Southland Favorites***, on which he was supported by the Anita Kerr Singers, earned him a Grammy Award for "Best Gospel or Other Religious Recording (Musical)." To honor George Beverly Shea's many years of effective Christian ministry, Houghton College, which he attended in 1928-1929, awarded him an honorary doctorate in 1956. In 1978, George was inducted into the Gospel Music Association Hall of Fame.

WKM

RECOMMENDED ALBUMS:

"Day Is Dying in the West" (RCA Victor)(1963)
"Southland Favorites" (RCA Victor)(1965)
"The Greatest Hits of George Beverly Shea" (RCA Victor)(1965)
"There's More to Life" (RCA Victor)(1970)

SHELTON BROTHERS, The

BOB SHELTON
(Vocals, Guitar, Fiddle)
Given Name: **Robert Attlesey**
Date of Birth: **July 4, 1909**
Date of Death: **1983**
JOE SHELTON
(Vocals, Guitar, Mandolin)
Given Name: **Joseph Attlesey**
Date of Birth: **January 27, 1911**
Date of Death: **December 26, 1980**

Both Born: **Reilly Springs, Texas**

While less remembered today than some of the other brother duets of the 30's—primarily because few roots of Bluegrass can be found in their sound—Bob and Joe Shelton ranked as perhaps the most recorded brother team of the late 30's. While such brother teams as the Blue Sky Boys (Bolicks), Callahans and Monroes, with their high harmonies and lead mandolin, paved the way for later generations of Bluegrass musicians, the music of Bob and Joe moved toward Honky-Tonk sounds and the Country mainstream where duets had less impact.

Bob and Joe sprang from a farm family in Hopkins County, Texas. In their early teens, they listened to a Dallas radio singer, "Peg" Moreland, who did a lot of Old-Time numbers and also recorded for Victor. Then from 1927, Jimmie Rodgers also became an inspiration to them. They began to furnish local entertainment for the community. During the late 20's, the boys went to Longview, which was then in the midst of an oil boom, where they performed in cafes for meals and tips, and a little later to KGKB radio in Tyler, Texas, where they met Leon Chappelear, another aspiring singer. About 1930, all three went to KWKH in Shreveport, Louisiana.

In August 1933, Bob, Joe and Leon journeyed to Chicago, did a session for Bluebird as the Lone Star Cowboys and provided instrumental support for Jimmie Davis, who would become a longtime friend. Afterward, Bob and Joe toured with Lew Childre, and during a brief stop in Atlanta at WSB radio, Curly Fox joined their entourage and they went to WWL New Orleans. They did their first of many sessions for Decca in February 1935. Producer Dave Kapp suggested that they needed a shorter, more commercial-sounding name than Attlesey so they took their mother's maiden name, Shelton, and used it thereafter. Some of their earliest and best known numbers were covers of songs they had done as the Lone Star Cowboys, including *Just Because*, *Deep Elm Blues* and *Hang Out the Front Door Key* (which had been in the repertoire of both Peg Moreland and Lew Childre). Their later sessions in 1935 and 1936 included fiddler Curly Fox, which gave them an updated Old-Time string band sound. After leaving New Orleans, the Sheltons generally based their radio work at either KWKH Shreveport or stations in the Dallas-Fort Worth area such as KRLD, WBAP, and especially WFAA. Through 1941, they ranked with Jimmie Davis as among the most heavily recorded Country artists on the Decca label. They had nearly 150 sides including a few solo numbers.

In the later 30's, the Sheltons began adding band members and moved increasingly toward a more modern sound. A younger brother, Merle (b. 1917), joined for a time as did Gene Sullivan, who later formed a partnership with Wiley Walker. In 1944, Bob and Joe campaigned for Jimmie Davis in his successful quest for the Louisiana governorship. In 1947, they made their last recordings on Syd Nathan's King label. By the end of the decade, their musical careers were about over although Bob worked as a Country comedian in the Dallas-Fort Worth area into the 1970's. Joe died in 1980 and Bob is believed to have expired about three years later. At that time, the only notable Shelton re-issue had been one side of a Japanese MCA album. In 1993, two collector reissues of sixteen songs each appeared—one in the U.S. and the other in Germany. Remarkably, only three numbers were duplicated on these albums. A second Shelton Brothers act (Jack and Curly) played music in Tennessee and North Carolina, but are unrelated.

IMT

RECOMMENDED ALBUMS:

"The Shelton Brothers/The Carlisle Brothers" (MCA)(1976) [Side A]
"The Shelton Brothers: Bob & Joe" (Old Homestead)(1993)
"Just Because" (Cowgirlboy Germany)(1993)

RICKY VAN SHELTON

(Singer, Songwriter, Guitar, Artist, Author)
Given Name: **Ricky Van Shelton**
Date of Birth: **January 12, 1952**
Where Born: **Grit, Virginia**
Married: **Bettye**

Along with George Strait and Randy Travis, Ricky Van Shelton became a leader of the revival of straight-ahead Country, known as new traditional. However, unlike Strait and Travis, Ricky Van brought another dimension that would directly lead to the "hunks" of the 90's. The cover of his debut album, ***Wild-Eyed Dream***, reveals him in a white T-shirt, looking every bit the muscle man.

Ricky Van's father, Jenks, was a part-time Gospel musician and he took his family whenever he played out-of-town revivals. Ricky took to Gospel straight away and was singing hymns by the time he was age 3 in his local church. It was around this time that he developed a fascination for star shapes, which continue to adorn his attire. When a friend of his mother's asked what Ricky wanted to be when he grew up, he is alleged to have said that he wasn't going to work for a living, he was going to sing.

When he reached his early teens, Ricky learned to play guitar and became a fan of the Beatles and the Rolling Stones and he avers that Paul McCartney is his favorite songwriter and *Yesterday* one of his favorite songs. When he was age 13, he wrote his first song, a slow rocker entitled *My Conscience Is Bothering Me*. Ricky's older brother, Ronnie, is an able mandolin player and was in a band, playing Country music, at the Little Red Barn. At the time, Ricky couldn't stand the music. However, the band needed a baritone singer and Ricky, then age 14, was coerced with the promise of driving Ronnie's 1964 Ford Fairlane. From then, he was turned on to the music. In particular he listened to the music of Hank Williams and the Osborne Brothers. At high school, he excelled at art, and graduated (just) from high school and worked in construction, laid bricks, fitted pipes, managed an appliance store and sold cars, but music was always a burning ambition within him.

Luck was on his side. His then girlfriend (now his wife) was offered a job in Nashville. This ensured that Ricky could concentrate full-time on his music. Bettye worked with and befriended Linda, the wife of *The Tennesseean* newspaper journalist Jerry Thompson. The Sheltons were invited to the Thompsons for a barbecue and Ricky Van played some of his songs. Jerry was very impressed and made a tape of Ricky and took it to then CBS Nashville chief Rick Blackburn. He wasn't overly impressed, but Jerry persuaded him to set up a showcase at Nashville's Stockyard restaurant, in June 1986. Blackburn took with him a reluctant producer, Steve Buckingham. By the end of the evening, Ricky Van was signed to Columbia Records and Jerry became his manager.

Within two weeks, Ricky was in the studio with "Buck" producing. They were in such a hurry to get product released, that none of Ricky's songs were yet published and so were omitted from the debut album. Ricky went on to sign as a writer with Welk (now Polygram) Music. As time showed, Ricky has not recorded very many of his own songs. His first single, *Wild-Eyed Dream*, reached the Top 25, but it was the following year that saw the meteoric rise to fame for Ricky. The opening single, *Crime of Passion*, went Top 10 and was followed by a run of five No.1 singles. In 1987, he had *Somebody Lied* and followed in 1988 with Harlan Howard's *Life Turned Her That Way*, Roger Miller's *Don't We All Have the Right* and Wayne Kemp's *I'll Leave This World Loving You*, the first single from ***Loving Proof***, his second album. The fifth No.1 was his first release of 1989, a reprise of Ned Miller's hit *From a Jack to a King*.

The man with wild-eyed dreams, ***Ricky Van Shelton***

Ricky's debut album, ***Wild-Eyed Dream,*** was Certified Gold in 1988 and Platinum in 1989, as was the second album, ***Loving Proof***. He became the recipient of a slew of award nominations and won a truckload. In 1987, the ACM voted him "New Male Vocalist of the Year" and the following year, he won the highly prestigious CMA "Horizon Award." He was named by TNN/*Music City News* as "Star of Tomorrow" and "Favorite Newcomer." During 1988, he made his debut on the *Grand Ole Opry*.

His second single of 1989, *Hole in My Pocket*, from the prolific pen of Boudleaux and Felice Bryant, reached No.4. He followed up with yet another No.1, *Loving Proof,* and the No.2 single, *Statue of a Fool*, which had been a No.1 for Jack Greene in 1969. Ricky's Christmas album ***Ricky Van Shelton Sings Christmas*** made a major impression on the Country album charts. During the year, Ricky collected another handful of awards. He won both the CMA and TNN/MCN titles of "Male Vocalist of the Year." The video of *I'll Leave This World Loving You* was named TNN/MCN's "Video of the Year," ***Loving Proof*** was their "Album of the Year" and *I'll Leave This Night Loving You* became their "Single of the Year."

Ricky continued his successful way in 1990 and his new album, ***RVS III***, reached No.1 on the Country Album chart, where it stayed for 9 weeks and it also reached the Pop Albums chart Top 60. It went Gold the same year and Platinum in 1991. His opening single, *I've Cried My Last Tear for You*, went to No.1, the followup, *I Meant Every Word He Said*, got to the Top 3 and *Life's Little Ups and Downs* got to the Top 5. On the album was Mickey Newbury's *Sweet Memories*, on which Ricky duetted with Brenda Lee. He was named TNN/MCN "Entertainer of the Year" and "Male Vocalist of the Year."

In 1991, Ricky had three No.1s in a row and they were *Rockin' Years* (a duet with Dolly Parton), *I Am a Simple Man* and *Keep it Between the Lines*. However, his final single of the year, the old Warner Mack song *After the Lights Go Out*, only got to the Top 15. That year, he released his ***Backroads*** album, which reached the Top 3 on the Country Album chart and Top 25 on the Pop Album chart and went Gold and Platinum, in 1991. Ricky's video ***To Be Continued***, which had been released in 1990, was Certified Gold in 1991, having sold over 50,000 units. He held on to his TNN/MCN "Entertainer of the Year" and "Male Vocalist of the Year" titles.

Ricky started 1992 with Canadian singer/songwriter Charlie Majors' *Backroads* and took it to the Top 3. He followed this with his version of the old Elvis Presley hit *Wear My Ring Around Your Neck*, a track from the movie *Honeymoon in Vegas*, but this only reached the Top 30. Columbia released ***Greatest Hits Plus***, which almost immediately went Gold. One of the "plus" tracks was *Wild Man*, which reached the Top 5. The video of *Rockin' Years* was named TNN/MCN's "Video of the Year."

Ricky released a second album in 1992, this time a Gospel one, ***Don't Overlook Salvation***, as a tribute to his parents. On the cover of this album is a photograph of Ricky in front of one of his paintings. That year, he wrote his first children's book, *Tales from a Duck Named Quacker* (RVS Books), which was illustrated by Shan Williams and which sold some 60,000 copies.

The following year, he released the album ***A Bridge I Didn't Burn***. However, this was not nearly as successful as its predecessors. He became the center of controversy when he correctly refused to appear at the CMA's 35th Anniversary show, when a song's key change would have been unsatisfactory for him. He announced that he had stopped drinking and the result was an RVS who enjoyed life more. During the year, he wrote another children's book, *Quacker Meets Mrs. Moo*. Ricky has said that he plans to record an album of original material, as well as a big band one, a Bluegrass one, a rock'n'roll one and even a Pop one. Both his chart singles in 1993 showed a tapering off in deejay appeal, with *Just As I Am* going Top 30 and *A Couple of Good Years Left* only making the Top 50. In 1994, Ricky's single *Where Was I* went Top 20.

RECOMMENDED ALBUMS:

"Wild-Eyed Dreams" (Columbia)(1987)
"Loving Proof" (Columbia)(1988)
"RVS III" (Columbia)(1990)
"Backroads" (Columbia)(1991)
"Don't Overlook Salvation" (Columbia)(1992)
"Greatest Hits Plus" (Columbia)(1992)
"A Bridge I Didn't Burn" (Columbia)(1993)

*Just goofing around, **Shenandoah**, with Cowboys' quarterback Troy Aikman*

SHENANDOAH

When Formed: **1985**
Members:

Marty Raybon	**Lead Vocals**
Jimmy Seales	**Lead Guitar, Vocals**
Ralph Ezell	**Bass Guitar, Vocals**
Stan Thorn	**Keyboards, Vocals**
Mike McGuire	**Drums, Vocals**

Of all the groups that have followed in the wake of Alabama, Shenandoah seems to be the one assured to have longevity.

Seales, Thorn and McGuire were playing together as the house band at the MGM Club in Muscle Shoals, Alabama. They were joined by Ezell and Raybon, in 1985. Mike had invited super songwriter Robert Byrne to the club, more as a friend, and more to see Marty, for whom the group was trying to get greater exposure as a soloist. Robert was very closely associated with Rick Hall and his Fame Studios set up in Muscle Shoals. When he heard the band, then known as the MGM Band, he was impressed. He and Hall took the band into the studio and recorded seven sides and then took the resulting tape to CBS, with whom Hall had a production deal. They were so impressed that they signed the band to the Columbia label.

The members of Shenandoah have all paid their dues. Marty Raybon was born in Greenville, Alabama, and raised in Sanford, Florida. He started out being a bricklayer, like his father, but then joined American Bluegrass Express, where he remained for nine years. He then joined Heartbreak Mountain, with whom he stayed for eighteen months. He had been a songwriter for Larry Butler Music and a session player in Nashville, and had cuts by Johnny Duncan and George Jones.

Jim Seales came from a musical family, however, he wanted to be an English teacher. However, the lure of music soon made itself manifest and he moved to Muscle Shoals where he became a session player/songwriter. Ralph Ezell began playing while in junior high school in his hometown of Jackson, Mississippi. He came to Muscle Shoals during the 70's, and became a session musician at Fame Studios. He has played on albums by Jimmy C. Newman, David Allan Coe and Mac Davis and he was on Bill Haley's final studio album.

Stan Thorn began singing in a family Gospel group while still young. He got to college on a music scholarship then dropped out to concentrate on playing music. He was a member of the outrageous George Clinton group, Funkadelic. Mike McGuire has played drums since second grade, and came to Muscle Shoals after attending the University of Alabama, where he was a football team manager under Coach "Bear" Bryant. After Bryant's death, Mike moved to Muscle Shoals, and joined his brother. In 1987, he co-wrote T. Graham Brown's Top 5 hit *She Couldn't Love Me Anymore*.

The group's debut eponymous album was released in 1987, and contained the seven tracks originally recorded. It hit the Country charts with *They Don't Make Love Like We Used To*, which reached the Top 60. The next single, *Stop the Rain*, reached the Top 30. In 1988, the group started out with a Top 10 single, *She Doesn't Cry Anymore*. This was followed by the Top 5 single *Mama Knows*, which came from the band's second album, ***The Road Not Taken***, which was released in 1989. That year, it had all three singles go to No.1. They were *The Church on Cumberland Road*, *Sunday in the South* and *Two Dozen Roses*. The album was also a major success, peaking in the Top 10 and going Gold in 1991. Shenandoah received the "Favorite Newcomer" award from *Music City News* that year.

Their success continued in 1990, with *See If I Care* (Top 10), the highly infectious *Next to You, Next to Me* (No.1) and the Top 5 *Ghost in This House*. Again every single stayed on the charts for over five months, the last two being from their third album, ***Extra Mile***, which also did very well in the Country charts. The ACM named them 1990 "Group of the Year." In 1991, they had two Top 10 records with *I Got You* and *The Moon Over Georgia*. Their third single, *When You Were Mine*, only made the Top 40, but by then, Shenandoah were on their way from Columbia to RCA. In 1991, ***The Road Not Taken*** was Certified Gold.

Their debut album on RCA was ***Long Time Comin'***, from which came *Rock My Baby*, which reached the Top 3. They followed up with *Hey Mister (I Need This Job)*, which made the Top 30, and *Leavin's Been a Long Time Comin'* (Top 15). They released a second album for RCA, ***Under the Kudzu***, in 1993, produced by Don Cook. From this album, they charted with *Janie Baker's Love Slave* (Top 15) and the Top 3 *I Want to Be Loved Like That*. In 1994, Shenandoah had the No.1 hit *If Bubba Can Dance (I Can Too)*, and *I'll Go Down Loving You* was climbing the chart.

RECOMMENDED ALBUMS:

"Shenandoah" (Columbia)(1987)
"The Road Not Taken" (Columbia)(1989)
"Extra Mile" (Columbia)(1990)
"Long Time Comin'" (RCA)(1992)
"Greatest Hits" (Columbia)(1992)
"Under the Kudzu" (RCA)(1993)

SHENANDOAH CUT-UPS, The

When Formed:	**1969**
Members:	
Billy Edwards	**Banjo, Bass, Vocals**
John Palmer	**Bass, Guitar**
Herschel Sizemore	**Mandolin, Guitar**
"Tater" Tate	**Fiddle, All Other Bluegrass Instruments**
Jim Eanes	**Vocals, Guitar**
Cliff Waldron	**Vocals, Guitar**
Wesley Golding	**Guitar**
Gene Burrows	**Guitar, Mandolin**
Tom McKinney	**Banjo, Vocals**
Udell McPeak	**Guitar**
Larry Hall	**Banjo**
Bobby Hicks	**Fiddle**
Other Members:	
Earl Link, J. P. Pulliem	

The Shenandoah Cut-Ups ranked as one of the best traditional Bluegrass bands of the 70's, although they never quite received the recognition that their talents merited. Through eighteen years of their existence, veteran fiddler Clarence E. "Tater" Tate acted as spokesman for the group, although bass player John Palmer was actually the only constant member of the band during its entire existence. Nonetheless, the band left a legacy of several fine albums during their most active decade.

The Cut-Ups came into being when WDBJ-TV in Roanoke, Virginia, terminated the Bluegrass Cut-Ups' long-running *Top o' the Morning Show* in the spring of 1969. Red Smiley chose to retire rather than face heavy traveling, but the longtime band members—Tater Tate, Billy Edwards (b. William Gene Edwards, September 26, 1936, Tazewell County, Virginia) and John Palmer (b. John David Palmer, May 28, 1927, Union, South Carolina/d. December 26, 1993)—decided to remain together and imported Herschel Sizemore (b. Herschel Lee Sizemore, August 6, 1935, Sheffield, Alabama) on mandolin to complete their foursome. Brief liaisons with veteran vocalist Jim Eanes and the younger Cliff Waldron did not work out, but musically it seemed not to matter as banjo picker Billy Edwards could hold his own with any lead singer in the business and could even pick lead melodies at the same time. As long as the group had only four members, Tater Tate had to play rhythm guitar so they usually tried to have a fifth member so that Tater could stay on fiddle. The band stayed active on the festival circuit during summers and often appeared in clubs or at WWVA's *Jamboree USA* in winter. They were a virtual fixture on Carlton Haney festivals and many others as well.

They cut their first album for David Freeman's County Records in New York City during March 1970, as the Shenandoah Valley Quartet. Jim Eanes sang on four numbers and Billy Edwards on the remaining ten. The band took their name from a merger of the old Eanes group the Shenandoah Valley Boys and the Bluegrass Cut-Ups. Smilin' Jim soon left to go solo again but the name remained. Cliff Waldron joined the group for a few weeks, but he, too, soon went back to Washington and reorganized the New Shades of Grass.

Bluegrass greats the ***Shenandoah Cut-Ups***

The Cut-Ups worked as a four-man group for a time and recorded an album of largely new songs for Major Records of Waynesboro, Virginia. Highlights included Billy Edwards' lead vocal on the novelty *Harold's Super Service* and a new prison song by Pete Gobel, *I Won't Need Your Nine Pound Hammer*. In 1972, they found a sympathetic record producer in Paul Gerry, who cut the band on three excellent albums for his Revonah label. Teenager Wesley Golding, an able guitar picker, joined the group about this time.

After the 1972 season, Billy Edwards decided to hang it up for a while and Tom McKinney took his place. McKinney and Golding, while excellent musicians, moved the band toward a more progressive sound that Tate and Palmer found somewhat uncomfortable and after one album for Rebel in 1973, the band went through a major shake-up. Golding, McKinney and Sizemore left to organize the Country Grass while John and Tater persuaded Billy Edwards to return and recruited two more Smiley alumni, Gene Burrows (b. September 12, 1928, Bedford County, Virginia/d. September 14, 1992) and Udell McPeak (b. Udell Marion McPeak, June 12, 1935, Wytheville, Virginia), who played mandolin and guitar respectively. Edwards and McPeak had earlier experience as a twosome with the Lonesome Pine Fiddlers while Gene also had a high-quality vocal. This group remained intact until 1977, cutting another pair of excellent albums on Revonah and assisting Mac Wiseman on several sessions and backing him on some festival shows. However, Lester Flatt tapped Tate as a replacement for the ailing Paul Warren, at which time John Palmer assumed leadership and secured Bobby Hicks to play fiddle for the Cut-Ups. When Edwards left a second time, Larry Hall, a veteran of Clinton King's Virginia Mountaineers, came into the band. Herschel Sizemore also rejoined from time to time, but from 1982, the band increasingly played only locally. They did their final recording on John Palmer's Grassound label.

By the late 80's, the band had pretty much become a memory. Burrows and Palmer resided in the Roanoke area until their deaths. The fine fiddlers Tate and Hicks both remained in Nashville as sidemen for Bill Monroe and

Ricky Skaggs respectively. Herschel Sizemore, after some years of relative inactivity, joined the Bluegrass Cardinals and in 1993 recorded a new mandolin album for Hay Holler Harvest (having made an earlier one for County). He remained a close friend of Palmer, who suffered through a terminal bout with cancer in 1993. Edwards worked for a time with a Gospel group called the Spirits of Bluegrass, but is currently inactive, while McPeak plays with a part-time band, the Big Country Bluegrass. In retrospect, the Shenandoah Cut-Ups both as a band and individually as sidemen in other groups were a fine bunch of pickers who also rated as excellent human beings. They did Bluegrass music proud and Bluegrass can feel proud of them. IMT

RECOMMENDED ALBUMS:

"The Shenandoah Valley Quartet" (County)(1970)
"The Shenandoah Cut-Ups Plant Grass in Your Ear" (Major)(1971)
"Bluegrass Autumn" (Revonah)(1972)
"The Shenandoah Cut-Ups Sing Gospel" (Revonah)(1973)
"Traditional Bluegrass" (Revonah)(1973)
"Shenandoah Cut-Ups" (Rebel)(1973)
"A Tribute to the Louvin Brothers" (Revonah)(1975)
"Bluegrass Spring" (Revonah)(1976)
"Keep It Bluegrass" (Grassound)(1979)
"Bluegrass Blaze of Glory" (Grassound)(ca.1983) [Half of album by Shenandoah Cut-Ups and half by Stonyridge]
(See also Tater Tate, Mac Wiseman.)

JEAN SHEPARD

(Singer, Songwriter, Bass)

Given Name:	**Ollie Imogene Shepard**
Date of Birth:	**November 21, 1933**
Where Born:	**Paul's Valley, Oklahoma**
Married:	**1. Hawkshaw Hawkins (d. 1963) 2. Benny Birchfield**
Children:	**1. Don Robin, Harold Franklin II; 2. Corey**

Just watch Jean's hand, behind her back, during a live performance and you will see it keeping strict time with the music and dictating the tempo to her musicians. This is just one indication of the perfection that she brings to her performances. Jean reigned as one of the Queens of Country music and was one of the principal advocates of keeping Country music uncontaminated by Pop influences.

Jean learned to sing by listening to Jimmie Rodgers records on a wind-up Victrola. Her family moved to Visalia, California, where she went to high school. During 1947, she formed the all-girl group the Melody Ranch Girls and a year later, they recorded Hank Thompson's song *Help*. She was discovered when the group played a booking with Hank Thompson and the Brazos Valley Boys. Thompson was impressed and introduced Jean to Capitol Records.

Her first solo recording came in 1953 and was *Crying Steel Guitar Waltz/Twice the Lovin'*. However, it was with her second release, a duet with Ferlin Husky, that she charted and in a big way. *A Dear John Letter* reached No.1 and stayed at the top for 6 weeks and crossed over to the Top 5 on the Pop charts. The follow-up at the end of 1953, *Forgive Me John*, also with Husky, made it to No.4 and also crossed over to the Top 25 on the Pop lists.

Although she released several singles during 1954 and early 1955, she was absent from the charts until *A Satisfied Mind* reached the Top 5, during the early summer. The flip-side, *Take Possession*, also reached the Top 15. That year, Jean became a member of the *Grand Ole Opry* (she is still a member) and moved to Nashville. She also joined Red Foley's *Ozark Jubilee*, where she stayed until 1957. During the fall of 1955, Jean racked up another double-sided Top 10 hit, *Beautiful Lies/I Thought of You*.

Again, Jean was absent from the charts, this time until the Top 20 success *I Want to Go Where No One Knows Me*, at the end of 1958. She followed up with the Top 30 single *Have Heart, Will Love*, during the spring of the following year. During 1959, she was named "Top Female Singer" by *Cash Box*. Although Jean continued to release singles into 1963, she failed to chart. Then, in 1963, her husband Hawkshaw Hawkins was killed in a plane crash in Camden, Tennessee, which also killed Patsy Cline, Cowboy Copas and Roger Hughes.

*The backbone of Country music, **Jean Shepard***

In 1964, Jean began charting with regularity. Her first hit of this run was *Second Fiddle (To a Steel Guitar)*, which reached the Top 5 and became a song forever associated with her. The flip-side, *Two Little Boys*, was written by Marty Robbins, who as a generous gesture gave the writer credits to Jean and Hawk's two young sons. She now put together a full-time band, the Second Fiddles.

Although she rarely had Top 10 hits, she had a stream of medium-sized successes. Her biggest hits were, in 1966, *Many Happy Hangovers to You* (Top 15), *If Teardrops Were Silver* (Top 10), *I'll Take the Dog* (Top 10) and *Mr. Do-It-Yourself* (Top 25), the last two being duets with Ray Pillow. She started off 1967 with another big hit, with Pillow, *Heart, We Did All We Could* (Top 15). Her other memorable hits of the 60's were *Your Forevers (Don't Last Very Long)* (Top 20, 1967) and *Seven Lonely Days* (Top 20, 1969).

Jean stayed with Capitol until the end of 1972 and her principal successes were *Then He Touched Me* (Top 10), *A Woman's Hand* (Top 25), *I Want You Free* (Top 25) and *Another Lonely Night* (Top 15) (all 1970) and *With His Hand in Mine* (Top 25, 1971).

In 1973, she moved to United Artists Records and had a Top 5 single, during the summer. *Slippin' Away* reached the Top 5 on the Country chart and crossed over to the Top 90 on the Pop list. Jean remained on UA until 1977 and her biggest hits were *At the Time* (Top 15), *I'll Do Anything It Takes (To Stay With You)* (Top 20) and *Poor Sweet Baby* (Top 15) (all 1974) and *The Tips of My Fingers* (Top 20, 1975).

In 1977, at the Wembley Festival in England, Jean stated to the audience, "John Denver, Glen Campbell and Mac Davis are not Country." This re-affirmed Jean's deep feeling for the retention of certain pure values in Country music.

Jean's final chart record occurred in 1988, when *The Real Thing* reached the Top 90, on Scorpion Records. In 1987, she initiated the annual Veterans Appreciation Show. For many years, she has been very popular in the U.K. and she continues to tour there. She is still a favorite of the *Opry* audiences.

RECOMMENDED ALBUMS:
"Songs of a Love Affair" (Capitol)(1956) [Re-released by Stetson UK in the original sleeve (1987)]
"Lonesome Love" (Capitol)(1959) [Re-released by Stetson UK in the original sleeve (1988)]
"This Is Jean Shepard" (Capitol)(1959) [Re-released by Stetson UK in the original sleeve (1990)]
"The Best of Jean Shepard" (Capitol)(1963)
"I'll Take the Dog" (Capitol)(1966) [With Ray Pillow]
"Declassified Jean Shepard" (Mercury)(1971)
"Jean Shepard's Greatest Hits" (United Artists)(1976)
"The Best of Jean Shepard" (Capitol)(1979) [Includes duets with Ferlin Husky]

T.G. SHEPPARD

(Singer, Songwriter, Guitar, Saxophone, Piano)

Given Name:	**William Browder**
Date of Birth:	**July 20, 1944**
Where Born:	**Humboldt, Tennessee**
Married:	**1. Diana (m. 1965)(div.)**
	2. Leah (m. 1992)
Children:	**Jason**

During the late 70's and most of the 80's, T.G. Sheppard ruled supreme as one of the kings of Pop-Country music, just before and in the wake of the *Urban Cowboy* movie. T.G.'s recordings helped launch the career of many budding songwriters in Nashville.

Bill Browder came from a musical background, and among his relations was *Grand Ole Opry* comedy star Rod Brasfield, who was his uncle. Bill's mother gave him piano lessons every Sunday afternoon. When Bill was 16, he ran away from home, and in 1960, settled in Memphis, where he joined the Travis Wammack Band as singer/guitarist. At this time, he called himself Brian Stacy. He originally signed with Sonic Records without success and then, in 1966, moved to Atco Records, where he released *High School Days*, which caused ripples in the lower levels of the regional Pop charts. As a result, he opened for the Animals, Jan and Dean and the Beach Boys. While in Memphis, he befriended Elvis Presley, who later bought him a tour bus.

In 1965, he had gotten married and decided, after the Atco single, to settle down and quit performing. He got into record promotion with the local Hot Line Distributors, looking after Stax Records' product. Shortly after, he worked as the Southern Regional Promoter for RCA, in Memphis. He then set up his own production and promotion company, Umbrella Productions.

In 1972, he found a song by the then unknown songwriter Bobby David, entitled *Devil in a Bottle*. Bill tried to pitch the song, but eight major record companies turned it

That great singer ***T.G. Sheppard***

down and eighteen months later, it was still unrecorded. He decided to cut a demo on the song, with himself singing. He was advised to go to Nashville to record a master. This he did and licensed it to Motown, who was trying to get into Country music.

At this time, Bill Browder song plugger, became T.G. Sheppard recording artist. The name, according to his own account, was created after seeing some German shepherd dogs from his office window. Someone suggested that he call himself the German Shepherd. Later, he said "T.G." stood for The Good and still later, he said that it means whatever you want it to mean.

At the end of 1974, *Devil in the Bottle* became the second release on Motown's new Melodyland label (the first being Pat Boone's *Candy Lips/Young Girl*). The single reached No.1 the following February and crossed over to the Pop Top 60. He followed up with another No.1, *Tryin' to Beat the Morning Home*. His other hits in 1975 were *Another Woman* (Top 15) and *Motel and Memories* (Top 10). Motown was forced to drop the Melodyland name for the label when a Los Angeles church of the same name took Motown to court and won. Motown had a public vote and the label was renamed Hitsville. T.G. stayed with the label until 1977 and racked up hits with Neil Diamond's *Solitary Man* (Top 15), *Show Me a Man* (Top 10) and the Top 40 single *May I Spend Every New Year's Eve With You* (all in 1976). In 1976, T.G. was named the "Best New Male Artist" by *Cash Box*. He had his final hit with Hitsville, *Lovin' On*, in 1977. By now, the powers at Motown had grown tired of Country music and the label shut up shop two releases later (Pat Boone's *Colorado Country Morning* and Wendel Adkins' *Laid Back Country Picker*).

That same year, T.G. signed with Warner/Curb and started his phenomenal chart run. His first hit was at the end of 1977, and was the Top 15 *Mister D.J.* The following year, all three of his singles made the Top 10, and were *When Can We Do This Again, Daylight* and his version of the Turtles' hit *Happy Together*. His first release of 1979, *You Feel Good All Over*, reached the Top 5, then he had back-to-back No.1 hits with *Last Cheater's Waltz* and *I'll Be Comin' Back for More*.

T.G. opened up the 80's with the Top 10 single *Smooth Sailin'*, the title track of his 1980 album, and then had a run of eight No.1 hits that stretched into the end of 1982. They were *Do You Wanna Go to Heaven* and *I Feel Like Loving You Again* (both 1980), *I Loved 'Em Every One* (also a Pop Top 40 hit), *Party Time* and *Only One You* (a Top 70 Pop hit) (all 1981) and *Finally* (also Pop Top 60 single), *War Is Hell (On the Homefront Too)* and a duet with talented newcomer Karen Brooks, *Faking Love* (all 1982). That year, *Music City News* made what has to be the most tardy award ever given, when T.G. was named "Most Promising Male Vocalist" after 12 No.1 hits, and having had over 20 hits going back eight years!

In 1983, T.G. reprised Nilsson's 1972 hit *Without You* and took it to the Top 15. He closed out the year with the title track of his album of that year, *Slow Burn*, which became his 13th No.1 hit. His opening single of 1984 was a duet with Clint Eastwood, *Make My Day*, which came from the Eastwood movie *Sudden Impact* and also crossed over to the Pop charts, reaching the Top 70. T.G.'s other hits of the year were the Top 3 single *Somewhere Down the Line*, followed by a duet with Judy Collins, *Home Again* (Top 60), and a Top 5 release, *One Owner Heart*. His final hit for Warner/Curb came in the spring of 1985, and was the Top 10 single *You're Going Out of My Mind*.

During 1985, he changed labels and moved to Columbia, where he was produced by Rick Hall at Fame's Muscle Shoals studio. His first chart record, Elvin Bishop's *Fooled Around and Fell in Love*, came from the ***Livin' on the Edge*** album. It reached a moderately low Top 25, but it was followed by two Top 10 singles, *Doncha?* and *In Over My Heart*, both written entirely or in part by Walt Aldridge. T.G. returned to the top of the chart with the 1986 single *Strong Heart*, and wrapped up the year with the Top 3 release *Half Past Forever (Till I'm Blue in the Heart)*.

In 1987, T.G. had back-to-back Top 3 singles, *You're My First Lady* and *One for the Money*, the latter being the title track of his 1987 album. By 1988, a new breed of more traditional performer was emerging and T.G.'s fortunes started to wane. His opening single of the year, *Don't Say It with Diamonds (Say It with Love)* only reached the Top 50, while *You Still Do* peaked in the Top 15 and both were from the Bob Montgomery-produced album ***Crossroads***.

The following year, T.G. was absent from the charts, as he was in 1990. He returned to the lists, in 1991, when his Curb/Capitol recording of *Born in a High Wind* climbed to the Top 70. However, that was the last chart single that he had. Currently, T.G. is without a label. He still tours with his band, Slow Burn. In a way T.G. Sheppard's Pop-Country songs act as role models to the current songs that are in the charts.

RECOMMENDED ALBUMS:

"Solitary Man" (Hitsville)(1977) [Named "Nashville Hitmaker" in the U.K.]
"T.G. Sheppard's Greatest Hits" (Warner/Curb)(1983)
"Biggest Hits" (Columbia)(1988)
"Crossroads" (Columbia)(1988)

BILLY SHERRILL

(Industry Executive, Record Producer, Songwriter, Saxophone, Piano, Guitar)

Given Name:	**Billy Norris Sherrill**
Date of Birth:	**November 5, 1936**
Where Born:	**Phil Campbell, Alabama**
Married:	**Charlene**
Children:	**Catherine**

For over two decades, Billy Sherrill held sway as one of the premier producers of Country records, as well as being one of the most successful songwriters. It was Billy's recording techniques that turned Country music on its head during the 60's and 70's with the use of strings, overdubbing to create a greater level of cross-over Country than ever before experienced. This made him a hero or a villain, depending on whether the listener wanted honest-to-goodness Country or a more Pop-orientated version.

Billy, the son of a Baptist evangelical preacher, played piano and sang publicly from age 5. He toured the South with his parents, playing tent meetings where his father preached. At age 10, he played piano at a funeral and earned his first money as a musician, the princely sum of $10. By his teens he could play six instruments, but he majored on piano and saxophone. After he left high school, he played in various Rock and R & B bands in Tennessee and Alabama.

Billy decided to come off the road in 1960 and, along with two friends, he opened a small recording studio in Nashville. He even released a single by himself, on which he played all the instruments. He then worked as a producer for Sam Philips in Philips' Nashville studio. Here he worked with Charlie Rich who would later play a major part in Billy's life. In 1964, Billy joined CBS and began a career that would make him as legendary as the artists he produced. Billy also got into trouble with the Musicians' Union because his recording techniques using over-dubbing reduced the amount earned by musicians.

David Houston had scored a major hit in 1963 with *Mountain of Love*, but since then his recording career had trodden water. This would change in 1965 when Billy took over the reins. The Sherrill song *Livin' in a House Full of Love* put David back into the Top 3, but better things were to come. The following year, David recorded the Sherrill-Glenn Sutton song *Almost Persuaded* (originally the flip-side) which went to No.1, where it stayed for 9 weeks. That year, it won the writers a Grammy Award for "Best Country & Western Song," and *Billboard* named *Almost Persuaded* as its 1966 "Favorite Country Song." That year, Ben Colder (aka Sheb Wooley) took a parody version of the song and reached the Top 10. In time, it would become one of the most recorded songs with versions by such diverse performers as virtually every major Country performer to Etta James, Louis Prima, Ray Anthony and Louis Armstrong.

In 1966, he signed Tammy Wynette, after other labels had turned her down. Her launch-pad song, *Your Good Girl's Gonna Go Bad*, also a Sherrill-Sutton song, was a Top 3 single in 1967. She and David Houston then followed up with another classic song, *My Elusive Dreams*, which Billy had written with Curly Putman. Billy's other co-written No.1s that year were *I Don't Wanna Play House* (Tammy Wynette), *With One Exception* and *You Mean All the World to Me* (David Houston). In addition, David Houston's recording of *A Loser's Cathedral* reached the Top 3. Billy went into the recording studio in 1967 and released the album ***Classical Country*** as the Billy Sherrill Quintet.

In 1968, Billy continued to produce and write a string of hits that included *Have a Little Faith, Already It's Heaven* and *Where Love Used to Live* (David Houston) and *Take Me to Your World* (Tammy Wynette). That year, Billy and Tammy wrote what is probably one of the best known and successful Country songs, *Stand By Your Man*, which not only topped the Country charts but also became a Top 20 Pop hit. That year, Billy received 5 BMI citations as a writer.

The following year, David Houston presented Billy with even more successes, namely *My Woman's Good to Me* and *I'm Down to My Last "I Love You"* while Tammy scored back-to-back No.1s with *Singing My Song* and *The Ways to Love a Man*. With the advent of a new decade, Billy continued his success as a producer and writer unabated. His hits in 1970 with Tammy were *I'll See Him Through* and *He Loves Me All the Way*, and with David *I Do My Swinging at Home*. Billy had another new signer that year, Barbara Mandrell, and she had her first Top 20 entry with a Sherrill song, *Playin' Around With Love*. That year, Billy received 7 citations from BMI for his songwriting.

Tammy started off her account in 1971 with a Top 3 written by her and Billy, *We Sure Can Love Each Other*, and followed up with the Sherrill song *Good Lovin' (Makes It Right)*, which went to No.1. David's successes on Sherrill songs were *A Woman Always Knows* and the double-sided hit *A Maiden's Prayer/Home Sweet Home*. Billy's other successes that year included Jody Miller's rendition of *If You Think I Love You (I've Just Started)*.

1972 was to be a very busy year for Billy. All three of Tammy's singles were co-written by Billy and were *Bedtime Story*, *Reach Out Your Hand* and *My Man*. George Jones had now moved to Epic and Billy became his producer. George's duet with Tammy, *The Ceremony*, written by Billy, went Top 10. In addition, George's solo hit *We Can Make It* also went Top 10. Other major songwriter/producer credits for Billy that year were *The Day That Love Walked In* (David Houston), *There's a Party Goin' On* (Jody Miller), *Bring Him Safely Home to Me* (Sandy Posey), *Tonight My Baby's Coming Home* (Barbara

Mandrell) and *Ballad of a Hillbilly Singer* (Freddy Weller). That year, Billy signed the fledgling Tanya Tucker. It is rumored that when he recorded her on David Allan Coe's *Will You Lay With Me (In a Field of Stone)*, he was in a beery state, and on a whim, wanted to see if the song would damage her career.

Billy's principle hits in 1973 were *Kids Say the Darndest Things* and *Another Lonely Song* (Tammy Wynette), *What My Woman Can't Do* (George Jones), *Good News* (Jody Miller) and *Good Things* (David Houston). In addition, Billy wrote *Soul Song* and *Too Far Gone*, both hits for Joe Stampley, who would move to Epic in 1975. Billy helped launch Charlie Rich into international stardom during 1973. Charlie had been on Epic since 1968, but didn't start scoring heavily on the Country chart until 1972. Billy had produced Charlie on his 1973 mega hit *Behind Closed Doors*, which had been written by Alan O'Day. That year, Billy received a Producer Award from the ACM and CMA for the "Single Record of the Year" for *Behind Closed Doors* and for the "Album of the Year" of the same name. However it would be the Sherrill-Norro Wilson-Rory Michael Bourke song *The Most Beautiful Girl* that would prove to be the monster hit Charlie had been waiting for. It topped both the Country and Pop charts and also the U.K. charts and was Certified Gold. That year, *Billboard* named *The Most Beautiful Girl* as "Top Country Song of the Year" and the CMA gave him a Producer's Award for the "Album of the Year" (***A Very Special Love Song***).

In 1974, Billy helped consolidate Charlie's success with the No.1 *A Very Special Love Song*, which netted Billy and co-writer Norro Wilson a Grammy Award for "Best Country Song." Other Rich chart toppers that year were *I Love My Friend* and *She Called Me Baby*. Billy's other production/writer successes that year included *The Telephone Call* by Tina & Daddy ("Daddy" being George Jones), *This Time I Almost Made It* (Barbara Mandrell) and *Woman to Woman* (Tammy Wynette).

During the remainder of the decade, Billy continued to be successful as a songwriter, but he had also become like an icon within Country music circles, and the ultimate accolade was to be produced by Billy Sherrill. His major songwriter/producer credits during this period were *(You Make Me Want to Be) a Mother* (Tammy Wynette), *The Door* (George Jones), *My Elusive Dreams* and *Everytime You Touch Me (I Get High)* (Charlie Rich), *Proud of You Baby* (Bob Luman), *There's a Song on the Jukebox* (David Wills) (all 1975), *'Til I Can Make It on My Own* and *You Me* (Tammy Wynette). He also wrote *(I'm a) Stand By My Woman Man* (Ronnie Milsap) (all 1976); *(Let's Get Together) One Last Time* and *One of a Kind* (Tammy Wynette), and *Southern California* (George Jones & Tammy Wynette). He also wrote *Don't Let Me Touch You* (Marty Robbins) (all 1977); *Beautiful Woman* (Charlie Rich), *Friend, Lover, Wife* (Johnny Paycheck), *Hello Mexico (And Adios Baby to You)* (Johnny Duncan), *Red Wine and Blue Memories* (Joe Stampley), *Woman to Woman* and *Tonight* (Barbara Mandrell), *Please Don't Play a Love Song* (Marty Robbins) (all 1978); *No One Else in the World* (Tammy Wynette), *Outlaw's Prayer* (Johnny Paycheck), and *Put Your Clothes Back On* (Joe Stampley) (all 1979). In addition, Kenny Rogers & Dottie West had a 1979 Top 3 single with Billy's song *'Til I Can Make It on My Own*. Among other hits produced by Billy during 1978 was Johnny Paycheck's *Take This Job and Shove It*.

With the arrival of the 1980's, Billy's songwriting success took a tumble, as Tom Collins' team of Dennis Morgan and Kye Rhonda Fleming became the Pop-Country songwriters in vogue. In addition, Collins himself assumed the mantle of the Country-Pop producer that new acts wanted to be produced by. However, Billy still chalked up some memorable songwriting hits that included *North of the Border* (Johnny Rodriguez) and *One of a Kind* (Moe Bandy) (both 1980); *The Baron* (Johnny Cash) and *Takin' It Easy* (Lacy J. Dalton) (both 1981); *Everybody Makes Mistakes* and *Slow Down* (Lacy J. Dalton) (both 1982). In 1980, Billy received a Producer Award from the ACM and CMA for "Single Record of the Year" (*He Stopped Loving Her Today*). During 1981, Billy produced Elvis Costello's album ***Almost Blue***.

Billy had been Vice President/A & R of CBS in Nashville and then, in 1980, he became Vice President/Executive Producer. In 1984, Billy was inducted into the Nashville Songwriters Hall of Fame. The following year, he received the Musical Creator's Award from the Alabama Music Hall of Fame. That year, Billy produced Ray Charles' ***Friendship*** album, which was a collection of duets with Country stars. He then decided to become an independent producer but shortly after, in 1986, returned to CBS with an exclusive long-term production agreement. In 1986, the Nashville Entertainment Association honored Billy with the 3rd Master Award. In addition, Billy has received nearly 90 Writer Performance Awards from BMI, making him the most awarded songwriter. He has also received nearly 40 ASCAP Producers Awards. Among the other acts produced by Billy are Gene Austin, Barbara Fairchild, Janie Fricke, Andy Griffith, Stan Hitchcock, Lois Johnson, Debbie Lori Kaye, Merle Kilgore, Kris Kristofferson, Major Lance, Jim & Jesse, Jim Nabors, Patti Page, Jimmy Payne, Peaches & Herb, Pozo Seco Singers, Troy Seals, Shel Silverstein, the Staple Singers, Jerry Vale, Bobby Vinton, Charlie Walker and Andy Williams.

In 1988, Billy was at long last forced to give up smoking following triple heart bypass surgery. Billy has never tried to achieve popularity and is in fact a quiet man, who has a grasp on what sells to Country music buyers. He has been described as aloof and inaccessible and eschews awards dinners and has been known to stub out his cigarettes on the shoes of CBS executives, yet still remains a private person. Let it suffice to say that Billy Sherrill is the collective entity of his songs and his production, and most of all he is one of the chief architects of modern Country music.

RECOMMENDED ALBUM:

"Classical Country" (Epic)(1967) [as the Billy Sherrill Quintet]

STEVE SHOLES

(Industry Executive)

Given Name:	**Stephen H. Sholes**
Date of Birth:	**February 12, 1911**
Where Born:	**Washington, D.C.**
Date of Death:	**April 22, 1968**

Steve Sholes is either a hero or a villain, depending on your viewpoint of the development of the Country music sound, and the principal architect of the Nashville Sound of the late 50's and most of the 60's, with his acolyte Chet Atkins. Certainly, he is responsible, more than any other record company executive, for the spread of Country music, and was instrumental in the success of a whole host of Country stars at RCA Victor.

During the 20's, Sholes moved with his family to New Jersey, and in 1929, while still at high school, he got a part-time job with RCA. He remained with the company all his working life, except for the periods he was at Rutgers University and in the armed forces during WWII. He left college in 1935 and returned to the company. Two years later, he joined the Artists and Repertoire Department working with Jazz artists.

In 1943, he joined the U.S. Army and he assisted in the production of V-Discs that were sent out to Army Special Services. He worked with Fats Waller on his final recordings. In 1945, Steve returned to RCA and became Studio and Custom Manager. Later that year, he became Manager of Country and Western and Rhythm and Blues A & R. During 1949, having "discovered" Chet Atkins, whom he saw as RCA's answer to Merle Travis, he began using him as a studio guitarist in Nashville. Among the Country acts that Sholes signed to RCA were Elton Britt, Eddy Arnold, the Browns, Homer & Jethro, Hank Snow, Hank Locklin, Jim Reeves, the Sons of the Pioneers, Roy Rogers, Pee Wee King and Elvis Presley.

Sholes made Atkins a part-time producer in 1957. When he was promoted to Manager of Pop Singles later that year and moved to New York, he made Atkins full-time Manager, in Nashville. The following year, Steve became Manager for Pop Albums. He moved to Los Angeles in 1961 when he was promoted to Manager of West Coast Operations. During the late 60's, Sholes was one of those devoted Country supporters who helped conduct a fund-raising campaign to build the Country Music Hall of Fame, in Nashville, which was inaugurated in 1967. That year, Steve, now Division Vice President, Popular Artists and Repertoire, in New York, was himself elected to the Country Music Hall of Fame.

The following year, while driving to Nashville Metro Airport from the recording studios, Steve Sholes suffered a heart attack and died. That same year, Chet Atkins was promoted to Vice President of RCA's Country Division.

SHEL SILVERSTEIN

(Singer, Songwriter, Artist, Author)
Given Name: **Shelby Silverstein**
Date of Birth: **1932**
Where Born: **Chicago, Illionois**

Shel Silverstein grew up in Chicago listening to the *Grand Ole Opry* with his mother. He soaked in the Country sounds and, even as a young child, took special interest in the lyrics. When he was age 3, he began drawing cartoons and performed the art as he grew older.

While in the U.S. Army, Shel became a staff artist for *Stars and Stripes*, the service magazine. After leaving the service, he became associated with *Playboy* magazine, where he was a contributor of satirical cartoons into the 70's. He also drew for other magazines, including *Time*, who carried, from 1967, his series *Now Here's My Plan*.

Shel turned his attention to songwriting in the early 60's and released his first album, ***Hairy Jazz***, in 1961, for Elektra. The following year, he released ***Inside Folk Song*** for Atlantic, which included his original version of *The Unicorn Song*, which became a Top 10 Pop hit for the Irish Rovers in 1968. Shel released a series of albums for Atlantic and Cadet, which contained humorous and adult-orientated compositions. He also appeared on the book best-seller lists with his collection of cartoons, *Grab My Box,* and an illustrated children's book, *Uncle Shelby's ABC*.

In 1968, Shel released the album ***A Boy Named Sue*** for RCA, and the following year the title song, when recorded by Johnny Cash, became a No.1 hit, a million seller and earned a Grammy Award for "Best Country Song." Soon other artists were recording Shel's songs, including Faron Young (*Your Time's Comin'*, 1969), Jerry Lee Lewis (*Once More with Feeling*, 1970), Waylon Jennings (*The Taker*, 1970, written with Kris Kristofferson), Loretta Lynn (*Hey Loretta*, 1974), Brenda Lee (*Wrong Ideas*, 1974).

During 1970, Shel was busy scoring the music for the movie *Ned Kelly* and in 1971, the shaven-headed Shel was scoring the movie *Who Is Harry Kellerman and Why Is He Saying All Those Terrible Things About Me?* when he teamed up with the left field Dr. Hook and the Medicine Show and proceeded to write for them a series of major hits that included *Sylvia's Mother* and *Carry Me, Carrie* (1972) and *The Cover of "Rolling Stone"* (1973). In 1973, Shel released the album ***Freakin' at the Freakers Ball*** on Columbia.

When Bobby Bare's favorite Nashville songwriters, Tom T. Hall and Kris Kristofferson, couldn't provide him with songs (because they were recording their own albums), he turned to Shel. The result was the 14 song album ***Lullabies, Legends and Lies*** (1973), which produced the 1974 hit *Daddy What If.* All of the selections were written or co-written by Silverstein. Shel and Bare have occasionally worked together on record projects, the most notable being ***Drinkin' from the Bottle, Singin' from the Heart***, in 1983.

During the 70's, Shel continued his literary output with the children's book *The Giving Tree*, plus *Lafcadio, The Lion Who Shot Back, Uncle Shelby's Zoo, Don't Bump the Glump* and *Where the Sidewalk Ends*. In 1976, Dave & Sugar had a hit with a Silverstein song that has gone to classic proportions, *Queen of the Silver Dollar*. In 1980, Shel released what is probably his classic album, ***The Great Conch Train Robbery***, for Flying Fish. The following year, Shel had a new children's book, *A Light in the Attic*.

In 1994, Shel teamed up with 60's Folk star Bob Gibson on the album ***Making a Mess of Commercial Success***, which was released on Asylum, with all songs written by Shel.

RECOMMENDED ALBUMS:
"Freakin' at the Freakers Ball" (Columbia)(1973)
"The Great Conch Train Robbery" (Flying Fish)(1980)
"Making a Mess of Commercial Success" (Asylum)(1994) [With Bob Gibson]

RED SIMPSON

(Singer, Songwriter, Guitar, Fiddle, Piano)
Given Name: **Joseph Simpson**
Date of Birth: **March 6, 1934**
Where Born: **Higley, Arizona**

Red Simpson will be forever associated with the hit song *I'm a Truck* and it is with the trucking genre that Red has carved out a living for some 30 years.

Born in Arizona, Red was raised in Bakersfield, California, the youngest of 12 children. He was age 14 when he wrote his first song, *Chicken House Boogie*, which he sang to the chickens in their coops. His father played banjo and his brother was bass player in a Country band and Red wanted to get in the business. During the Korean War, Red was stationed on the USS *Repose*, a Navy hospital ship that was constantly under attack. He formed a Country band called the Repose Ramblers and practiced on whatever instrument he could find and when in Japan bought some instruments and perfected his future craft.

On returning to the U.S., Red got his first professional music job at the Wagon Wheel in Lamont, California. Fuzzy Owens (later Merle Haggard's manager), who worked the Clover Club, arranged for Red to play piano at the club. Red later went on to play the Blackboard Club, where he relieved Buck Owens on weekends. The rest of the week was spent by Red driving an ice cream truck.

Red started playing with various local bands. At this stage, his influences were Owens, Merle Haggard and Country entertainer Bill Woods. Woods asked Red to write him a truck-driving song; Red wrote four. However, Woods then stopped recording. In 1962, Red signed as a writer with Cliffie Stone and then began writing songs with Buck Owens. *Someone to Love* became a local hit for the Farmer Boys and then, in 1965, Buck had a Top 10 hit with a song they had written, *Gonna Have Love*, which was the flip-side of the No.1 *Only You (Can Break My Heart)*.

Capitol Records' head of A&R, Ken Nelson, wanted to record some trucking songs and approached his artist, Merle Haggard, but Haggard was not enthusiastic. Nelson then spoke to Red, who jumped at the idea, and so in 1966, Red recorded Tommy Collins' *Roll, Truck, Roll*. The single sailed into the Country chart and became a Top 40 hit. Red followed up with an album of the same name. He had two further chart entries that year in *The Highway Patrol* (Top 40) and *Diesel, Smoke, Dangerous Curves* (Top 50).

In 1967, Buck Owens had a No.1 with a song written with Red, *Sam's Place*. The following year, Red decided to quit recording to concentrate on writing, and in 1970, *The Kansas City Song* became a Top 3 single for Owens. That year, a friend mentioned a song that mailman Bob Staunton had written. In 1971, Red was back recording when Ken Nelson also mentioned the song; it was *I'm a Truck*. Red recorded it and it went Top 5, in 1972, and made him known to every truck driver in the U.S.

Cash Box named Red "Top New Male Artist" and *Record World* made him their "Most Promising Album Artist, No. 1." He was also named "Most Promising Male Vocalist" by *Record World*. That year, Red's song *Bill Woods of Bakersfield* appeared on Merle Haggard's highly successful album ***Let Me Tell You About a Song***. Red began appearing on the *Grand Ole Opry* and during 1972 and 1973, he had two final hits for Capitol, *Country Western Truck Drivin' Singer* (1972) and *Awful Lot to Learn About Truck Drivin'* (1973), both Top 70 singles.

By 1976, Red had moved to Warner Brothers Records and had a Top 100 single with his version of *Hillbilly Heaven*, called *Truck Driver's Heaven*. During 1977, he began recording duets with Lorraine Walden and their single *Truck Driver Man and Wife* proved popular without charting. Red had his last chart entry in 1979 when *The Flying Saucer Man and the Truck Driver* reached the Top 100 on the K.E.Y. label. He continued performing and writing through the 80's.

1988 was a good and bad year for Red. Merle Haggard recorded Red's *Lucky Old Colorado*, which had previously been cut by Annette Funicello. However, during the year, he was twice hospitalized, first for the removal of a malignant mole from his back and then he received surgery for cancer of the nose. Red, known as Suitcase Red because of the suitcase full of songs that he carries with him, is continually adding to his thousands of songs. He still performs and writes and has the enthusiasm to hope for another big hit.

RECOMMENDED ALBUMS:

"Roll Truck Roll" (Capitol)(1966) [Re-issued by Stetson UK in the original sleeve (1988)]
"The Man Behind the Badge" (Capitol)(1966)
"Truck Drivin' Fool" (Capitol)(1967)
"Red Simpson Sings a Bakersfield Dozen" (Capitol)(1967)
"I'm a Truck" (Capitol)(1971)
"The Very Real Red Simpson" (Capitol)(1972)
"Trucker's Christmas" (Capitol)(1973)

MARGIE SINGLETON

(Singer, Songwriter, Guitar)

Given Name:	**Margaret Louise Ebey**
Date of Birth:	**October 5, 1935**
Where Born:	**Coushatta, Louisiana**
Married:	**1. Shelby Singleton (div.)**
	2. Leon Ashley (m. 1965)
Children:	**Steve Shelby Singleton,**
	Sidney Sheldon Singleton

Although Margie never reached superstar status, for a few years in the mid-60's she had several major hits, as a solo artist and in tandem with George Jones and Faron Young. Her style was influenced by Blues and Southern Gospel.

Margie signed with Starday Records in 1957, and her debut single, *One Step Near to You* and the flip-side *Not What He's Got* were self-penned. She made her radio and professional debut, in 1958, on KWKH's *Louisiana Hayride*. Her third single, *Nothing but True Love*, also self-penned, reached the Top 25.

Margie stayed with the *Hayride* until 1959 and then, in 1960, she joined *Jubilee USA*. That year, she had *Eyes of Love* (also written by Margie), which reached the Top 15. She moved over to Mercury, in 1961, where her husband, Shelby Singleton, was running record production. That year, she teamed up with George Jones on the Top 20 hit *Did I Ever Tell You*.

The following year, they repeated the experience and reached the Top 15 with *Waltz of the Angels*. That same year, Brook Benton, who was produced by Shelby Singleton, had a major Pop hit with Margie's song *Lie to Me*. In 1963, he had a Pop success with another of her songs, *My True Confession*. That was the year that Margie made her debut on the *Grand Ole Opry*. She also had the solo single *Old Records*, which reached the Top 15.

During the 60's, Margie sang back-up to many major Country performers as part of the Merry Melody Singers and with the Jordanaires. In addition, several performers recorded her songs, including Teresa Brewer, Tammy Wynette, Charley Pride and Marty Robbins.

In 1964, Margie teamed up with Faron Young for the Top 5 duet *Keeping Up With the Joneses*. The flip-side, *No Thanks, I Just Had One*, also made the Top 40. At the end of the year, they reached the Top 40 with the duet *Another Woman's Man Another Man's Woman*. The following year, Margie married Leon Ashley and moved to United Artist Records, where she recorded without success.

From 1967, all her records came out on the Ashley label. She re-appeared on the charts that year with her version of Bobbie Gentry's *Ode to Billy Joe*, which peaked in the Top 40. She closed out the year with a Top 60 duet with Leon, *Hangin' On*. That year, Margie appeared in the movie *Road to Nashville*, with Marty Robbins. She had two Top 60 entries during 1968, a solo, *Wandering Mind,* and a duet with Leon, *You'll Never Be Lonely Again*. During the year, she made the original recording of Tom T. Hall's *Harper Valley P.T.A.* Margie's ex-husband, Shelby, now running Plantation Records, later in the year recorded Jeannie C. Riley, who had a No.1 cross-over hit with it.

Although Margie continued recording for the Ashley label, she didn't have any further chart entries. She and Leon have since toured with the Country Music Spectacular, backed by their group, the Strings of Nashville.

RECOMMENDED ALBUMS:

"Duets Country Style" (Mercury)(1962) [With George Jones]
"Crying Time" (United Artists)(1965)
"Margie Singleton Sings Country Music with Soul" (Ashley)(1967)
"A New Brand of Country" (Ashley)(1969) [With Leon Ashley]

SHELBY SINGLETON

(Industry Executive, Record Producer)

Given Name: Shelby Singleton, Jr.
Date of Birth: December 16, 1931
Where Born: Waskom, Texas
Married: 1. Margie Singleton (div.)
2. Sandy (div.)
Children: Stephen Shelby, Sidney Sheldon, Shana

Nowadays, it is virtually impossible for an independent label to get a No.1 record on the singles charts. This is mainly due to the fact that charts are now based on air-play, rather than sales, and radio stations rarely play singles released on indie labels. On that basis, Jeannie C. Riley's *Harper Valley P.T.A.*, released on Shelby Singleton's Plantation label, would never have gone to No.1 and certainly would not have gone Gold and sold over 4 million copies. However, back in the late 60's, things were different, and for record company bosses with the wealth of experience that Shelby Singleton has, it was always possible.

He served in the Marine Corps in Korea, and was injured in combat, and still has a metal plate in his head. He moved to Shreveport, Louisiana, at the end of the Korean War and, in 1959, he became the local promotion man for Mercury Records. It was here that Shelby met his future wife, Margie, who was appearing on the *Louisiana Hayride*. A year after joining Mercury, he had made sufficient headway to be promoted to Southern Regional Sales Manager. A year after that, he became Product Manager and then a record producer for the label. Although he spent some of his time in Nashville, he chose to base himself in New York.

He had the knack of taking Country songs and having them recorded by non-Country acts. This started with Brook Benton's recording of *The Boll Weevil Song*, in 1960, which became a Top 3 record the following year. He also kept his ears to the ground, and when he heard that a record was doing well on an independent label, he would try and pick it up for Mercury. He was put in charge of Smash Records and eventually became VP of Mercury. Among the hits during Shelby's nine year period with Mercury and its sister label, Smash, were *Walk on By* by Leroy Van Dyke (1961), *Wooden Heart* by Joe Dowell (1961), *Hey Baby* by Bruce Channel (1962) and *Ahab the Arab* by Ray Stevens (1962). In addition, he was involved with Jerry Lee Lewis, Roger Miller, Charlie Rich, Dave Dudley and Brook Benton's other hits.

Shelby resigned from Mercury in 1966, and set up his own production company. He launched SSS International Records and shortly after, Shelby set up his Plantation label, and in 1968 had his No.1 hit with *Harper Valley P.T.A.* The following year, he purchased Sun Records from Sam Phillips, which contained all the classic rock'n'roll records by Elvis, Johnny Cash, Carl Perkins and Jerry Lee Lewis. He licensed the catalog to Charly Records for Europe, and this has proven to be a big money earner, as rock'n'roll and Rockabilly are still popular there. Shelby also operated the Silver Fox label and Shelby Singleton Music. Although he has never had another hit of the magnitude of *Harper Valley P.T.A.*, Plantation racked up another thirty-six chart entries since the label was established. One single released in 1980 on Sun was not a big hit, but has since become a trucker's classic. It was Dave Dudley's *Rolaids, Doan's Pills and Preparation H.* In 1993, Jason D. Williams became the first artist to sign to a renovated Sun Records.

ASHER SIZEMORE AND LITTLE JIMMY

ASHER SIZEMORE

(Guitar, Singer)

Date of Birth: June 6, 1906
Where Born: Manchester, Kentucky
Married: Odessa Foley
Children: Jimmy, Charles Edward ("Buddy"), Nancy Louise
Date of Death: 1973

LITTLE JIMMY

(Singer)

Date of Birth: January 29, 1928
Where Born: Paintsville, Kentucky
Date of Death: 1985

Asher and Little Jimmy Sizemore

Country music's major child star of the 30's was Jimmy Sizemore, a member of the cast of the *Grand Ole Opry* by the time he was 5 years old. His success was largely due to the efforts of his father, Asher Sizemore, a singer who was more important as one of the great innovators in Country music promotion.

Born June 6, 1906, in Manchester, Kentucky, Asher worked for a time as a bookkeeper for a coal mining company in Pike County, Kentucky. After his marriage to Odessa Foley, he decided to try his hand as a singer. He succeeded in getting a show on a station in Huntington, West Virginia, where he sang Old-Time songs and cowboy ballads. Eventually, he moved to WCKY Cincinnati and WHAS Louisville. By this time Jimmy was performing with his father. By 1933, they were splitting their time between WSM's *Grand Ole Opry* and WHAS, where Little Jimmy sang songs such as *The Booger Bear, Has Anybody Seen My Kitty* and *Little Feat.* In 1934, he recorded *Little Jimmy's Goodbye to Jimmie Rodgers*, which proved to be his best-selling record.

The act was very popular in the 30's, acclaim that was as much due to Asher's promotional abilities as to Little Jimmy's talent. He missed few opportunities to promote his son's musical abilities. In 1933, Asher boasted that the then 5-year-old Jimmy could sing over 200 songs from memory. In addition to appearances on WHAS and WSM, the duo cut 15-minute transcriptions that were syndicated throughout the Midwest. The profitability of these shows was increased by the use of paperback songbooks that Asher hawked on each program, he being one of the first Country performers to use this method of raising additional income. Asher also explored other means of making show business profitable; for example, he worked hard placing songs he owned or published with other acts.

In the late 30's, Jimmy's younger brother, Charles Edward, who was called Buddy Boy, was brought into the family act. Later, sister Nancy Louise was also added to the show, but neither was as popular as Little Jimmy. In 1942 the Sizemores left the *Opry* and later appeared on KXEL Waterloo, Iowa, WHO Des Moines, KMOX St. Louis, and WSB Atlanta. On November 2, 1950, Buddy Boy was lost in action during the Korean War. Both Asher and Jimmy later moved to Arkansas, Asher to De Queen, where he died in 1973. Until his death in 1985, Jimmy was an executive with KGMR Jacksonville, Arkansas. WKM

RECOMMENDED ALBUMS:

"Mountain Ballads & Old Hymns" (Decca)(1966)
"Songs of the Soil" (Old Homestead)(1984)

RICKY SKAGGS

(Singer, Songwriter, Guitar, Mandolin, Fiddle)

Given Name:	**Ricky Lee Skaggs**
Date of Birth:	**July 18, 1954**
Where Born:	**Cordell, Kentucky**
Married:	**Sharon White**
Children:	**Mandy, Andrew, Molly Kate, Lucas**

There are few Country music stars who have had a life filled with more music than Ricky Skaggs. Hobert and Dorothy Skaggs knew their new son was a prodigy when he was singing solos in the Free Will Baptist Church.

Ricky's dad bought him a pawnshop mandolin when he was 5 and taught Ricky the basic three chords. Hobert Skaggs lost a brother in WWII who had played the mandolin, and he made a vow that if he ever had a son who was interested in music, he would teach him to play the mandolin. Every weekend, Ricky and his dad would gather with other musicians at the local grocery store to play. Hobert would help Ricky get on top of the soda pop case and he'd sit there for hours and play along on the mandolin.

When Bill Monroe came to perform at the high school in Martha, Kentucky, Ricky attended the show with his parents. Repeated requests came from the crowd for Monroe to call up little Ricky Skaggs to play and sing. Eventually, the Bluegrass legend called little Ricky to the stage. Monroe took off his mandolin and adjusted the strap to fit Ricky and he performed the Osborne Brothers' hit *Ruby Are You Mad at Your Man*. The crowd erupted into applause for their local child prodigy. More than twenty years later, Ricky took Bill Monroe's *Uncle Pen* to the top of the Country chart.

Ricky traveled with his parents around Kentucky performing at churches and little theaters as the Skaggs Family. When he was 7, the family moved to Nashville in hopes of getting Ricky a spot on the *Grand Ole Opry*, but the management said he was too young. His parents were able to get him on the popular Flatt & Scruggs TV show. Ricky performed *Ruby Are You Mad at Your Man* and *Honky Tonk Swing* and earned $52.50.

The Skaggs family moved back to Kentucky after two years and Ricky continued to sharpen his musical skills. He would slow down the old 78 recordings of Bill Monroe, Flatt & Scruggs and the Stanley Brothers to learn the mandolin parts and then transpose the music to play the notes faster. Ricky also spent many hours listening to the powerful AM radio station from Cincinnati, Ohio, and the music of Buck Owens, George Jones and Ray Price.

By the time he was 8, Ricky was amazing his friends and family with his crystal-clear flat-picking on his dad's Martin D-28 guitar. As a teenager Ricky added the fiddle and electric guitar to his list of instruments. He also discovered the music of the Beatles, Rolling Stones and the Hollies and for a short time played in some local rock'n'roll bands. However, he never strayed far from his roots and would soon land his first professional job as a musician.

One of Country music's greatest assets, ***Ricky Skaggs***

Ricky was playing fiddle with his dad at a talent show in Estill, Kentucky, when he met Keith Whitley, who was also performing, hoping to win first prize. Neither won, but they became fast friends and started performing together. When the two buddies went to see their idol, Ralph Stanley, perform at a local club, they wound up onstage performing because Stanley's bus had broken down and the band was late for the show. Stanley came in while Whitley and Skaggs were performing flawless renditions of the Stanley Brothers' songs. Ralph was so impressed at Keith and Ricky duplicating the sound he made famous with his late brother, Carter, that he invited them to join him onstage. Ralph Stanley asked Ricky to join his Clinch Mountain Boys in 1970 when he was 15.

Over the next few years, Ricky recorded six albums with the Bluegrass pioneer. Ricky also recorded two albums with Keith Whitley, ***2nd Generation Bluegrass*** (1972) and ***That's It*** (1975) on the Rebel label. When he was 19, Ricky grew tired of the constant travel and low pay of a Bluegrass musician. He moved to Washington, D.C., where he worked as a boiler operator for the Virginia Electric Power Company. Ricky was glad to quit the job when he was invited to play fiddle with the progressive Bluegrass group the Country Gentlemen. To expand his skill on the fiddle, Ricky immersed himself in the Swing recordings of Stephane Grappelli and the Jazz recordings of guitarist Django Reinhardt.

After stints with the innovative J.D. Crowe and the New South and the Seldom Scene, Ricky formed his own Bluegrass group, Boone Creek. Ricky laid the groundwork for his breakthrough success in the 80's working with Boone Creek by adding the elements of drums, electric guitar and piano to the traditional Bluegrass instruments. He recorded two albums with the band, ***Boone Creek*** (1977) and ***One Way Track*** (1978), before joining Emmylou Harris' Hot Band. In addition to touring, Ricky appeared on the Emmylou albums ***Blue Kentucky Girl***, ***Evangeline*** and ***Cimarron***. He also played a pivotal role in her 1980 all-acoustic ***Roses in the Snow***, by serving as arranger, musician and singer.

While working with Emmylou Harris, Ricky recorded a solo album for Sugar Hill called ***Sweet Temptation***, on which he broke new ground by mixing Bluegrass and Country music together. His adaptation of the Stanley Brothers ballad *I'll Take the Blame* was No.1 at KIKK radio in Houston and Ricky knew he was onto something. The success of the 1980 single, which scraped into the Country chart, encouraged Ricky to seek a contract with a major label.

After being turned down by every label in Nashville for being "too Country," Ricky was given a shot by the CBS label Epic, in 1981. He convinced label head Rick Blackburn to let him produce his own album, something almost unheard-of for a new artist. Ricky proved the fans were ready to return to the roots of Country and Bluegrass music with his ***Waitin' for the Sun to Shine*** debut LP. He put a driving beat behind the Flatt and Scruggs classic *Don't Get Above Your Raisin'* and it became a Top 20 hit. His second single, *You May See Me Walkin'*, made the Top 10 and the third time was a charm as the 1982 single *Crying My Heart Out Over You* shot to No.1. His first major label album also provided a second No.1 single, *I Don't Care*, in mid-1982. ***Waitin' for the Sun to Shine*** rose to the top of the Country Album chart and earned a Gold Album for sales of 500,000, an accomplishment achieved by few in Country music in the early 80's.

1982 was a stellar year for Ricky, as he picked up the "Male Vocalist of the Year" and the Horizon Award from the CMA. The ACM named him "New Male Vocalist." Ricky fulfilled a lifelong dream when he was invited to become the 61st member of the *Grand Ole Opry*. Ricky racked up two more No.1's, *Heartbroke* (1982) and *I Wouldn't Change You If I Could* (1983), and released his second album, ***Highways and Heartaches***. His sophomore release also went Gold and in 1992 passed the one million sales mark to be Certified Platinum.

Ricky was hailed as the leader of the "New Traditionalist" movement that gave rise to the careers of George Strait, Reba McEntire and Randy Travis. He also set new standards for live performances, assembling an impressive group of musicians, and picked up "Instrumental Group of the Year" honors from the CMA and "Touring Band of the Year" from the ACM in both 1983 and 1984. Ricky also broke with Nashville tradition and recorded many of his albums with his band rather than studio musicians.

The No.1 hits continued with *Highway 40 Blues* and then he had the Top 3 *You've Got a Lover* (both 1983) and returned to his No.1's with *Don't Cheat in Our Hometown* and *Honey (Open that Door)* (both 1984). Ricky continued to fulfill his mission to bring Bluegrass to a new generation when he took Bill Monroe's *Uncle Pen* to No.1, in 1984. He also invited the Father of Bluegrass to New York City to appear in his *Country Boy* music video. *Something in My Heart* went Top 3 in 1985, then *Country Boy* became a No.1 hit and the album of the same name was Certified Gold. 1983's ***Don't Cheat in Our Hometown*** was also a Gold-selling album and was the only Country album listed in *People* magazine's list of the Top 10 albums of the 80's. The honor put Ricky alongside albums by Michael Jackson, Prince and Bruce Springsteen.

Ricky earned the prestigious "Entertainer of the Year" award in 1985 from the CMA. He was also honored as "Instrumentalist of the Year" by the CMA. The ACM gave him awards for "Touring Band of the Year" and in the "Instrumentalist" category for his mandolin playing. Ricky also picked up a Grammy Award in 1985 for "Best Country Instrumental Performance" for *Wheel Hoss*. Ricky took his traditional brand of Country music to Europe in 1985, performing in England, Ireland, Germany and Sweden, and recorded the ***Live in London*** album that yielded the No.1 hit *Cajun Moon* and the Top 10 *I've Got a New Heartache*.

In 1986, Ricky was back in the Top 5 with the title track from ***Love's Gonna Get Ya***. The album also contained the duet of *New Star Shining* with James Taylor. The following year, Ricky scored a Top 10 hit duet with wife Sharon White on *Love Can't Ever Get Better Than This* that earned a CMA award for "Vocal Duo" in 1987. Ricky received multiple awards for his musicianship from *Playboy*, *Guitar Player* and *Frets* magazines in the 80's. Other hits in the 80's were *I'm Tired*, *(Angel on My Mind) That's Why I'm Walkin'*, *Thanks Again* and *Old Kind of Love*, all in 1988. In 1989, Ricky was back at No.1 with *Lovin' Only Me* from his ***Kentucky Thunder*** album. Ricky took time off in 1989 to produce Dolly Parton's Country comeback album, ***White Limozeen***, that put her back at No.1 with *Why'd You Come in Here Lookin' Like That?*

In 1990, Ricky was named "Artist of the Decade" in the BBC Radio 2 Listeners Poll. As a member of Mark O'Connor's New Nashville Cats, Skaggs joined friends Vince Gill and Steve Wariner to record the hit single *Restless*. The collaborative effort was honored with CMA and Grammy awards.

On his 1991 ***My Father's Son*** album, Ricky included a mixture of Country and Gospel songs. It produced the Top 15 Country hit *Same Ol' Love* and the No.1 Gospel hit *Somebody's Praying*. His twelfth album for Epic was also released on the Word Records Gospel label.

Skaggs launched his own syndicated radio show in 1993 called *Simple Life*. The one-hour weekly show features interviews with fellow Country stars about their music, families and the positive things they do for the community. By 1994, the program was heard on more than 400 Country radio stations in the U.S. and Canada and in Europe on the BBC and CMR. JIE

RECOMMENDED ALBUMS:

"Sweet Temptation" (Sugar Hill)(1979)
"Waitin' for the Sun to Shine" (Epic)(1981)
"Family & Friends" (Rounder)(1982)
"Highways & Heartaches" (Epic)(1982)
"Don't Cheat in Our Hometown" (Epic)(1983)
"Country Boy" (Epic)(1984)
"Live in London" (Epic)(1985)
"Love's Gonna Get Ya!" (Epic)(1986)
"Comin' Home to Stay" (Epic)(1988)
"Kentucky Thunder" (Epic)(1989)
"My Father's Son" (Epic)(1991)

Skillet Lickers refer GID TANNER

JIMMIE SKINNER

(Singer, Songwriter, Guitar, Clawhammer Banjo, Fiddle)

Given Name: James Skinner
Date of Birth: April 27, 1909
Where Born: Berea, Kentucky
Married: Betty
Children: James, Jr.
Date of Death: October 27, 1979

Jimmie Skinner, known as the Kentucky Colonel, was one of those Country singers

The Kentucky Colonel, ***Jimmie Skinner***

whose unique style sets them apart. His main appeal came from a love for traditional-sounding material, often of his own composition, coupled with Honky-Tonk instrumentation often featuring an electric mandolin. In addition to singing and writing, Skinner endeared himself to a generation of Country fans for his large record store, where during the 50's and 60's, one could often find favorite discs that might be otherwise almost unobtainable.

Jimmie spent his early years near Berea, Kentucky, which even at that early date boasted some outstanding traditional musicians such as banjoist Marion Underwood with his unique tunes like Coal Creek March. About 1925, the Skinners moved to Hamilton, Ohio, where young Jimmie went to work in a factory, but he and his brother Esmer would pick up a few extra dollars with their musical instruments. An early recording effort for Gennett in 1933 never got out of the studio and an offer from Bluebird in 1942 became a casualty of wartime shortages. Jimmie guested on local radio stations now and then, but his career in music made little headway until he had passed 35.

About 1945, Skinner made his initial six recordings on the Red Barn label. While none of them became hits, one received sufficient attention in Knoxville for Jimmie to be offered a regular job at WROL radio. Although he didn't stay all that long it provided enough incentive (along with Ernest Tubb's 1948 hit recording of Skinner's *Let's Say Goodbye Like We Said Hello*) to launch a full-time venture into music. Back in Cincinnati, he cut several sides for Radio Artists Records. By now, Jimmie had already recorded his most famous originals on disc: *Don't Give Your Heart to a Rambler*, *You Don't Know My Mind*, *Will You Be Satisfied That Way* and *Doin' My Time*.

In 1949, Jimmie had his first Country chart entry, *Tennessee Border* (Top 15), on Radio Artists. The following year, he signed with Capitol and subsequently turned out some thirteen singles over the next three years, but no real hits. *Send Me a Penny Postcard*, *Holy Life Insurance*, *There's Nothing About You Special* and the Hank Williams tribute *Singing Teacher in Heaven* probably rank among the more memorable.

He followed this with three more years on Decca beginning in 1953, with *John Henry and the Water Boy* and *Too Hot to Handle* getting considerable airplay but failing to register on the charts. For a man with no major hits, Jimmie still managed to be quite popular as a performer, landing in fifth place among vocalists in a *Country Song Roundup* poll in 1951. Only Snow, Arnold, Williams and Tubb, all Hall of Famers today, came in ahead of him in the first poll. He took ninth and seventeenth places, respectively, in 1952 and 1953. In the meantime, Skinner toured extensively, did daily programs at WNOP Newport, Kentucky, and opened a record shop in downtown Cincinnati.

In 1956, Jimmie signed with Mercury and began to turn out some major hits. *I Found My Girl in the U.S.A.* (an answer song to *Fraulein* and *Geisha Girl*) went Top 5 on the Country chart in 1957. Eight more chartmakers followed in the next three years, including *What Makes a Man Wander* (Top 10, 1958), *Dark Hollow* (Top 10), the flip-side of *Walkin' My Blues Away* (Top 25), *John Wesley Hardin* (Top 20) (all 1959), *Riverboat Gambler* (Top 20), *Lonesome Road Blues* (Top 25), *Reasons to Live* (Top 15) and *Careless Love* (Top 30) (all 1960).

Ray Lunsford's mandolin, a longtime standard feature on Jimmie's recordings, was heard somewhat less on the Mercury sides and Rusty York's lead and steel guitar work became more prominent, being especially notable on the 1962 Jimmie Rodgers tribute album. Following his Mercury years, Skinner went to Starday, where he cut a pair of albums for Don Pierce. Ironically, despite their short-term popularity, none of his hits from this period endured in the manner of his early standards.

For another decade, Jimmie worked out of the Cincinnati area and recorded for local firms such as Jewel, Queen City, and Vetco, the latter being associated with the Jimmie Skinner Music Center (the original manager, Lou Epstein, had died in 1963, and Lou Ukelson took over the business).

In 1974, Jimmie moved to Nashville, cutting discs for Starday again and Jim Stanton's Rich-R-Tone label as well as further releases on Vetco. His instrumental sound moved closer to Bluegrass and the Monroe Talent Agency handled his bookings. Jimmie made the move largely to better plug his songs in the Nashville market. Ohio and Kentucky continued to be the areas where he played most often until felled by a heart attack in the fall of 1979. Rich-R-Tone, Barnyard, Stetson, and Bear Family have re-issued some of his vintage recordings from Radio Artists, Capitol and Mercury over the past fifteen years. IMT

RECOMMENDED ALBUMS:

"Songs That Make the Juke Box Play" (Mercury)(1957) [Re-issued on Stetson UK in the original sleeve (1988)]
"Country Singer" (Decca)(1961)
"Jimmie Skinner Sings Jimmie Rodgers" (Mercury)(1962)
"The Kentucky Colonel" (Starday)(1963)
"Let's Say Goodbye Like We Said Hello" (Starday)(1964)
"Country Blues" (Mercury Wing)(1964)
"Jimmie Skinner Sings Bluegrass" (Vetco)(ca. 1967)
"Jimmie Skinner Sings the Blues" (Vetco)(1969)
"Requestfully Yours" (Q. C. A.)(1973)
"Jimmie Skinner Sings Bluegrass, II" (Vetco)(1976)
"Jimmie Skinner's #1 Bluegrass" (Starday)(1977)
"The Golden Hits of Jimmie Skinner" (Rich-R-Tone)(1978) [From Radio Artists masters]
"Have You Said Hello to Jesus Today" (Rich-R-Tone)(1980)
"Hillbilly Memories" (Barnyard)(ca. 1980) [From Capitol]
"Another Saturday Night" (Bear Family Germany)(1988) [From Mercury]
"Jimmie Skinner & His Country Music Friends" (Jewel)

PATSY SLEDD

(Singer, Songwriter, Piano, Guitar, Dobro, Autoharp)

Given Name:	**Patricia Randolph**
Date of Birth:	**January 29, 1944**
Where Born:	**Falcon, Missouri**
Married:	**1. Dale Sledd (div.)**
	2. William D. Langfelt (div.)
	3. Van Barker
Children:	**Jeb**

Like many other Country artists, Patsy Sledd grew up in a musical family and her brother Jack gave her her first guitar at age 10. She got her first performing experience with a family group; under the name of the Randolph Sisters, Patsy and her sisters sang in local churches and similar venues. In 1965, at age 21, she moved to Nashville with her husband Dale Sledd, longtime guitarist with the Osborne Brothers, and soon impressed Roy Acuff, who invited her to work on his 1967 Caribbean tour. She later became part of Acuff's touring show, appearing with them on many U.S. tours and on a trip to Vietnam.

In 1968, Patsy signed a contract with United Artists Records but had no real success until she signed on with Mega in 1972. Her first release for this company, *Nothing Can Stop My Love*, gave her a Top 70 Country hit. It was eighteen months until she had another chart entry and this time, she had her biggest hit, the Top 40 *Chip Chip*. She followed up with *See Saw*, but it only reached the Top 75.

During the 1970's, Patsy was quite busy, appearing on the *Hee Haw* and *Midwestern Hayride* TV shows, backing up Tammy Wynette on recordings and working shows headlined by George Jones and Tammy Wynette, Del Reeves, Billy Walker and the Wilburn Brothers.

In 1974, Patsy accompanied George and Tammy to England for the Wembley Festival and when they had to return to the U.S. when George's mother died, Patsy took over their spot and greatly impressed the audience. In 1976, she had a Top 90 single with *The Cowboy and the Lady*.

Following the birth of her son in 1977, she dropped out of performing for a while. During this period, she spent most of her time making and designing costumes for Barbara and Louise Mandrell, Dottie West, Helen Cornelius and Tammy Wynette. By the late 1980's, she was performing once again but her only chart single has been the Top 80 *Don't Stay If You Don't Love Me*, in 1987 for Showtime Records. WKM

RECOMMENDED ALBUMS:

"Yours Sincerely" (Mega)(1973)
"Chip, Chip" (Mega)(1974)

Len Slye refer ROY ROGERS

BOB SMALLWOOD

(Deejay, Singer, Banjo, Saxophone, Other String Instruments)

Given Name:	**Robert Smallwood**
Date of Birth:	**October 23, 1940**
Where Born:	**Bradshaw, West Virginia**
Married:	**Rita Jo Laws**
Children:	**Robin Lee**

Bob Smallwood is one of a now diminishing breed of deejays who also had secondary careers as musicians. During a deejay career spent in West Virginia, Ohio, Michigan and Virginia, Bob often worked as a member of a local band or organized his own.

Born to a family of coal miners and railroaders, Bob was taught to play clawhammer banjo by his father and he learned to play saxophone for the high school band. At age 16, Bob had his own radio show at WNRG Grundy, Virginia, and guested on a Country TV show at WHIS Bluefield, West Virginia. Two years later, he went off to college at West Virginia Tech., where he sometimes made guest spots on Buddy Starcher's TV show in Charleston. Later Smallwood moved his family to Cleveland, Ohio, where he worked on the railroad, did a radio deejay show, and played Country music four nights a week, usually at the Dewey Road Inn. Finally, he went into radio full-time, first at WELW Cleveland and then at WEXL Detroit, where he also served as Program Director.

Although Bob had recorded a few scattered singles through the 60's, his interest turned to albums when in Michigan. He cut two albums for Old Homestead with Bluegrass accompaniment, one furnished by Roy McGinnis' Sunnysiders and the other by Charlie Moore's Dixie Partners. In 1975, Bob moved back to his own town of Bradshaw and took a job at WRIC Richland, Virginia. He cut a Gospel album with more help from the Dixie Partners.

Some years later Bob purchased radio station WYVE Wytheville, where he still holds forth as a small but significant force for tradition in Country music. According to John Morris, who produced his Old Homestead albums, Bob recently cut material for a compact disc with instrumental support from Ralph Stanley's Clinch Mountain Boys. IMT

RECOMMENDED ALBUMS:

"Have You Seen Papa's Coal Loadin' Hands" (Old Homestead)(1973)
"Rebel Soldier (Your Memory Will Never Die)" (Old Homestead)(1975) [With Charlie Moore & the Dixie Partners]
"Let Me Tell You about a Preacher" (Old Homestead)(1976)

BEN SMATHERS

(Clogger, Actor)

Given Name:	**Ben Ray Smathers**
Date of Birth:	**May 17, 1928**
Where Born:	**Hendersonville, North Carolina**
Married:	**Margaret**
Children:	**Hal, Mickey, Candy, Debbie, Sally**
Date of Death:	**September 13, 1990**

For many years, Ben Smathers and his troupe, the Stoney Mountain Cloggers, delighted *Grand Ole Opry* audiences with their impeccable and colorful routines. Ben utilized the high-stepping clogging style that can be traced back to German, Irish and Dutch immigrants that located themselves in western North Carolina.

Ben began dancing at the age of 14 and formed the Stoney Mountain Cloggers four years later (1946). The group became regulars on *Promenade Party* from Greenville,South Carolina, from 1956 to 1958 and then on September 13, 1958, they became members of the *Opry*. They had appeared on the show before this, and during the 50's, Ben commuted to Nashville from North Carolina, where he worked as a railroad switchman. He actually worked for the railroad until 1966.

During 1960 to 1964, they toured with Red Foley. In 1961, Ben and his Cloggers appeared at the *Opry* with Jim Reeves and Patsy Cline and they became the first square dancers to appear at Carnegie Hall in 1962 with Roy Acuff and other *Opry* stars. During 1967 through 1969, they toured with Roy Rogers and Dale Evans as well as the Charlie Daniels Band. In 1981, they appeared at New York's Carnegie Hall with Tammy Wynette and Merle Haggard. They also appeared on the *Ed Sullivan Show*, the *Hollywood Palace*, the *Lennon Sisters Show*, the *Dinah Shore Show*, the *Kraft Music Hall*, the *Steve Lawrence Show*, the *Jimmy Dean Show*, the *Mike Douglas Show* and for a year, they were regulars on the *Carl Smith Show*. They also appeared several times on *Hee Haw*.

Meredith Wilson wrote *The Unsinkable Molly Brown* with the Cloggers in mind, but the New York producers would not spend the money to fly them to Broadway. However, the Cloggers appeared on the TV special from Hollywood. Ben and the Cloggers appeared in several movies, including *Tennessee Beat* and *Country Music on Broadway*, and Ben also had a secondary career as an actor and appeared in several movies and TV series, including *America's Most Wanted*, and did a video for the IRS! He died in Nashville in 1990, following complications from open-heart surgery, on the 32nd anniversary of his membership in the *Opry*. After Ben's death, his widow, Margaret, kept the Cloggers going until September 11, 1993, their 35th anniversary.

SMITH BROTHERS, The

TENNESSEE SMITH
(Vocals, Mandolin, Fiddle)

Given Name:	**John Onvia Smith**
Date of Birth:	**August 15, 1918**
Married:	**Carolyn**
Children:	**Billy Lee**

SMITTY SMITH
(Vocals, Guitar)

Given Name:	**Aubrey Lee Smith**
Date of Birth:	**March 13, 1916**
Married:	**Eleanor**
Children:	**Shirley**
Date of Death:	**August 27, 1916**
Both Born:	**Oneida, Tennessee**

The Smith Brothers spent more than a quarter century in a career that encompassed both Country and Gospel music. The brothers headquartered at a number of locales during their musical years—including Hollywood, where they worked in several Western films.

Natives of Oneida in mountainous East Tennessee, the Smiths formed a string band while still youngsters and dreamed of a Country music career when they reached adulthood. That moment arrived in 1938 when they journeyed to Cincinnati and landed a spot on WCPO radio. While there, they met another aspiring musician in Milton "Ace" Richman. The three went to WKRC Columbus, Ohio, where they worked with Hank Newman's

Georgia Crackers, an experience which broadened their musical diversity.

In 1940, the three moved to WCHS Charleston, South Carolina, where they styled themselves into a Western trio, the Red River Rangers, until a coal strike ruined the local economy and drove them to seek the warmer climes of south Georgia. After brief stints in Macon and Albany, they settled, more or less permanently, in Atlanta.

By that time Eddie Wallace had joined them and they had formed the Sunshine Boys Quartet. However, their broad talent and skills had them doing Western Swing, Gospel, Country, and even barbershop material on varying programs at WSB and other Atlanta stations. Between 1945 and 1948, they spent part of each year in Hollywood, where they made movies with Lash LaRue, Charles Starrett, and especially Eddie Dean. As a quartet, the Sunshine Boys also did a session for Decca, which included their most popular song, *Lead Me to That Rock*.

From 1948, the Smiths increasingly worked on their own as a duet or with steel guitarist Boots Woodall. For nine years they had a daily 75-minute program on WAGA Atlanta, called the *TV Ranch*, whose cast also included Pat Patterson, Cotton Carrier, Paul Rice, and Woodall. For most of those years, they also had a separate 15-minute Gospel program titled *Camp Meeting*. Tennessee and Smitty did their first record session on their own for Mercury in 1951, with their most noted effort being a lyric in the "dying child" genre titled *Happy Birthday in Heaven*. They also contributed the vocals on Woodall's Mercury waxings, including one of the earliest renditions of the Cold War classic *They Locked God Outside the Iron Curtain*. The Smiths signed with Capitol in 1953, by which time they did virtually all Gospel. Their best number, *I Have But One Goal*, featured Bill Lowery assisting on a commercialized form of the old Baptist tradition of lining out hymns. Other Smith favorites included *Working in God's Factory*, *I'm Gonna Shout*, *Child of the King* and *God's Rocket Ship*. Although they never recorded it, Tennessee and Smitty composed a popular secular song, *Pitfalls*, which did quite well when recorded by the Louvin Brothers.

In 1960, the Smith Brothers departed from Atlanta and went to Pittsburgh's KDKA-TV, where they worked as a featured act with Slim Bryant's Wildcats by day and on the *Wheeling Jamboree* at WWVA on Saturday nights. Two years later, they went to Macon, Georgia, and spent three years at WMAZ-TV. The boys made their only lp during that time on the LeFevres' Sing label.

After 1965, they left the music business behind. Tennessee worked as a draftsman until retirement while Smitty took charge of rental properties in Atlanta until his death. Tennessee still lives in the Atlanta suburbs and reportedly fiddled up a storm at a recent reunion of WSB *Barn Dance* performers. IMT

RECOMMENDED ALBUM:

"That's My Jesus" (Sing)(ca. 1964)

(See Sunshine Boys, the)

Country and Gospel group the ***Smith Brothers***

Arthur "Guitar Boogie" Smith *also played fiddle*

ARTHUR "GUITAR BOOGIE" SMITH

(Songwriter, Guitar, Tenor Banjo, Fiddle, Others)

Given Name: **Arthur Smith**
Date of Birth: **April 1, 1921**
Where Born: **Clinton, South Carolina**
Married: **Dorothy Byars**
Children: **Arthur Reginald, Robert Clayton, Constance Adele**

Arthur Smith became one of the best known Country guitarists on the strength of his big instrumental hit *Guitar Boogie*.

Like many other Piedmont-area Country musicians, Arthur Smith came out of the textile mill culture where his father worked as a loom fixer and musical director in Kershaw, South Carolina. The son's original attraction tended to horn music, but he soon learned string instruments as well. Like others of his generation Arthur went to work in the mills, but also started a Dixieland Jazz band which played at WSPA in nearby Spartanburg. They had little fan response, however, until switching to Country sounds and becoming Smith's Carolina Crackerjacks. This group also had a session for Bluebird Records in the fall of 1938 in Rock Hill, South Carolina, where they waxed at least four titles, including *Going Back to Old Carolina*.

Meanwhile, Arthur had been experimenting with electric guitar and became one of the first musicians in his locality to abandon acoustical instrumentation. Ironically, his conversion to Country music became a success largely because of the Jazz influences he incorporated into his guitar style.

Smith first came to WBT Charlotte about 1943 and, with pickers in short supply, band members sometimes doubled and so Arthur filled in at times with both the Briarhoppers and the Tennessee Ramblers. It was with the latter group that he cut the original version of the Jazz-influenced *Guitar Boogie* about 1945 on Super Disc. Later he signed with MGM. Arthur Smith and His Crackerjacks worked with WBT radio and TV for many years, recording periodically for MGM and later Starday and Dot.

In 1948, he had a Top 10 Country hit with *Banjo Boogie*. He followed up at year's end with the double-sided Top 10 hit *Guitar Boogie* and *Boomerang*. During most of the 50's and 60's, Smith had both a daily and a weekly show on WBTV, with the weekly program being syndicated on numerous other stations. In addition to his own guitar expertise, the program featured a wide variety of talent, including his own brothers Ralph and Sonny Smith, banjoists Don Reno and David Deese, Ray and Lois Atkins, and for an eighteen-year stretch (1951-1969), singer-guitarist Tommy Faile. One of the most popular portions of his shows always featured some fine Gospel numbers by the Crossroads Quartet. Smith always presented his entourage in a respectable setting, which helped broaden his appeal among the growing southern middle class.

Guitar Boogie was reprised during the rock'n'roll era as *Guitar Boogie Shuffle* and became a U.S. Top 5 Pop hit for the Virtues in 1959, and it was also recorded by the Ventures. In the U.K., it became a Top 10 by local guitarist Bert Weedon, and among other versions was one by the John Barry 7 (John Barry would later go on to became a composer of such movie themes as that for the James Bond movies). In 1962, the Virtues once again dusted off the tune and had a basement Pop success with *Guitar Boogie Shuffle Twist*.

Arthur's presentations lacked not for humor either and his last appearance on the *Billboard* charts came in 1963 with *Tie My Hunting Dog Down, Jed*, a parody of the Australian Rolf Harris' novelty hit *Tie Me Kangaroo Down, Sport*. Various other aspiring musicians worked in Arthur's show from time to time, including blind pianist Ronnie Millsap, who went on to become a Nashville superstar.

In the 70's, Smith recorded for Monument Records and also for CMH, in which he had a financial interest for a time. In fact, many of that label's albums were cut in his Charlotte studio. That same decade his and Don Reno's instrumental from 1955 called *Feudin' Banjos* appeared in the popular film *Deliverance* as *Dueling Banjos* in a new recording by Eric Weisberg and Steve Mandel. Smith had cut the original on MGM with himself on tenor banjo and Don Reno on 5-string. They successfully contested the case and received back royalties. Arthur had also made many commercials in his Charlotte studio and engaged in other business ventures which enabled him to largely retire from active performing in relative comfort. As one historian wrote in 1985, "he remains a leading citizen of the Charlotte community." A re-issue of radio transcription cuts from 1945 displays his pioneering Jazz-influenced skills on electric lead guitar. IMT

RECOMMENDED ALBUMS:

"Mister Guitar" (Starday)(1962)
"Arthur Smith & the Crossroads Quartet" (Starday)(1962)
"Goes to Town" (Starday)(1963)
"In Person" (Starday)(1963)
"Arthur Smith & Voices" (ABC/Paramount)(1963)
"Down Home" (Starday)(1964)
"Original Guitar Boogie" (Dot)(1964)
"The Arthur Smith Show" (Hamilton)(1964)
"Great Country & Western Hits" (Dot)(1965)
"Singing on the Mountain" (Dot)(1965)
"A Tribute to Jim Reeves" (Dot)(1966)
"The Guitars of Arthur Smith" (Starday)(1968)
"Guitar Boogie" (Nashville)(1968)
"Arthur Smith" (Monument)(1970)
"Battling Banjos" (Monument)(1973)
"Guitars Galore" (Monument)(1975)
"Jumpin' Guitar" (Relaxed Rabbitt)(1985) [From 1945 radio transcriptions]
Arthur Smith & Don Reno:
"Feudin' Again" (CMH)(1979)

BLAINE SMITH

(Singer, Songwriter, Guitar)

Given Name:	**Blaine Smith**
Date of Birth:	**September 2, 1915**
Where Born:	**Dickens, Iowa**
Married:	**Lillian**
Children:	**Blaine H., Lee B., Lorelei L., Heather A.**

Blaine Smith parlayed a smooth singing voice and rugged handsome looks into a musical career that spanned some three decades. Sometimes by himself and other times in duet with his brother Cal (b. 1912), Blaine had a voice that could best be described as "early day uptown Country," but his large repertoire of Old-Time songs and championing of traditional values nonetheless kept him in good standing with rural folk. He never had the hit record to catapult him into national stardom, but he managed to acquire and retain a broad regional audience.

The Virginia Folk Singer ***Blaine Smith***

Born in rural Iowa of parents native to West Virginia, Blaine returned eastward to Virginia and then to Macedonia in northeast Ohio, where his father operated a large farm. He attended high school in Macedonia and in 1933 won a talent contest in Jefferson, Ohio, which landed him a radio show at WTAM and then WGAR in Cleveland. From there, he went to Wheeling, Pittsburgh and Fairmont where he spent lengthy stints at each locale. In February 1939, he and Cal recorded a half-dozen duets for Vocalion at Chicago in a style more reminiscent of Mac and Bob than of the hard Country harmony duos of the time. Henry Burr, a ballad singer from the WWI era, who later sang at the *National Barn Dance*, also influenced Smith's vocal approach.

Blaine and Cal then spent a year at WLS, where they called themselves the Boys from Virginia. Ironically, when working radio further east they became the Boys from Iowa (faraway places always seem more exotic!). After a year at Chicago, they returned to West Virginia and WMMN.

After WWII, Blaine worked at WWVA again and at various stations in Ohio and Pennsylvania. Over the next several years, he recorded several more sides for various firms, including Bullet, Essex, and Dome. Among his Dome efforts was the initial waxing of *There Stands the Glass*, as originally written by Mary Jean Shurtz, an Ohio housewife. With a few word changes, this would later become a major Country classic when recorded by Webb Pierce.

In 1953, Blaine matriculated to WSVA Harrisonburg, Virginia, which would become his permanent base. For the next decade, he worked initially on radio and then moved into TV. For part of that time, he also sang as a regular at the *Old Dominion Barn Dance*. Although Smith had recorded but sparingly in his career, he had issued several songbooks, some of them filled with the Old-Time songs—many of Victorian origins—that comprised much of his extensive repertoire.

From about 1963, Blaine gave up his TV

program and earned his living primarily in the aluminum siding business. However, he never got totally out of music, as he went to Fort Worth, Texas, and recorded extensively for Bluebonnet, although the company released only a single album from the sessions. Some years later he cut a single on Stop. He also made a few appearances from time to time and talked of rejuvenating his career. However, it never happened and Blaine lives in retirement near Harrisonburg. A photo of Blaine and his band from Fairmont about 1938 adorned the cover of *Mountaineer Jamboree: Country Music in West Virginia* (1984) and one of his duets with Cal appeared on an Old Homestead anthology of Old-Time artists from West Virginia. IMT

RECOMMENDED ALBUM:

"Virginia Folk Singer" (Bluebonnet)(1967)

CAL SMITH

(Singer, Guitar)

Given Name:	**Calvin Grant Shofner**
Date of Birth:	**April 7, 1932**
Where Born:	**Gans, Oklahoma**
Married:	**1. (Div.)**
	2. Darlene Renee
Children:	**Calvin Arthur, Jimmy Todd**

Ernest Tubb once predicted that Cal Smith would take a long while to get to the top, but would most certainly do so. In fact, it took 18 years from his debut on the *California Hayride* until his first Top 10 record. Part of the reason may have been that Cal was not a songwriter, and therefore, he had to wait for the right song to be handed to him.

Cal (not to be confused with Carl) Smith was raised in Oakland, California. He learned guitar while in his pre-high school years, and began entertaining at talent contests. He began playing local clubs and started playing professionally, when he was 15, at a beer joint, named The Remember Me Cafe, in San Jose. However, he took on several other jobs to supplement his meager music income during the 50's, including truck driver, steel mill worker and horse breaker. His first wife tried to get him to quit the business, and although she gave him an ultimatum, he soldiered on and lost a wife!

In 1954, he could be seen and his dark brown voice heard on the *California Hayride* out of Stockton. He stayed on the show until 1956, when he went off to serve in the military. Returning to civilian life, he became a deejay on radio station KEEN, San Jose. At the same time, he was playing in a group in San Jose, alongside Bill White, whose brother, Jack, played in the Texas Troubadours. As luck would have it, Ernest Tubb was playing San Jose and Cal auditioned for him, and in 1961, he became a Texas Troubadour. He stayed with E.T., as emcee and vocalist, touring and appearing on the *Grand Ole Opry*, remaining with the band until 1967.

It was with E.T.'s help that Cal was signed to Kapp Records, in 1966, and his first single was *I'll Just Go on Home/Silver Dew on the Blue Grass Tonight*. That year, his band, the Nite Hawks, were name K-Bar-T "Band of the Year." With his second release, *The Only Thing I Want*, Cal debuted on the Country chart, reaching the Top 60. He remained with Kapp until midway through 1970, and although he charted eight more times, his most successful titles were Warner Mack's *Drinking Champagne*, a Top 40 record in 1968, and *Heaven Is Just a Touch Away*, which went Top 50, the following year.

He signed with Decca (later MCA) in 1970. He had recorded for the label as part of the Texas Troubadours, but now he would emerge as a star in his own right. However, again he had to wait, and it was not until the spring of 1972 that he had his first major hit, when *I've Found Someone of My Own* reached the Top 5. He was not able to sustain his chart success, and his next single, *For My Baby*, only got into the Top 60. However, at year end, he charted with *The Lord Knows I'm Drinking*, which took three months to surface to the top. It not only became a Country No.1, it also crossed over to the Pop Top 70.

Again, consistency eluded Cal, and his next release, *I Can Feel the Leavin' Comin' On/I Loved You All Over the World*, only reached the Top 25, while *Bleep You/An Hour and a Six Pack* just failed to make the Top 60. However, 1974 was to be Cal's year. His opening single was one that would forever be associated with him, Don Wayne's *Country Bumpkin*. It reached No.1. It also became the recipient of a slew of awards. That year it became both ACM's and CMA's "Song of the Year," CMA's "Single of the Year" and ACM's "Single Record of the Year." The following year, *Music City News* named it "Song of the Year" and Cal was named "Most Promising Male Artist." The latter award was due not only to *Country Bumpkin* but also to Cal's other hits of 1974, *Between Lust and Watching TV*, which reached the Top 15, and his third No.1, *It's Time to Pay the Fiddler*.

No Country Bumpkin is ***Cal Smith***

He stayed with MCA until 1979, but he would not enjoy the same level of success again. His principal hits while on the label were *She Talked a Lot About Texas* and *Jason's Farm* (both Top 20 hits, 1975), *Thunderclouds*, *McArthur's Hand* and *Woman Don't Try to Sing My Song* (all 1976) and *I Just Came Home to Count the Memories* (Top 20) and *Come See About Me* (both 1977).

Cal reappeared on the charts in 1982, when his duet with Billy Parker, *Too Many Irons in the Fire*, made the Top 70. The track came from Billy's ***Something Old, Something New*** album (1983), which also contained another duet with Cal, *Honky Tonk Girl*. Ray Pennington produced Cal on his 1986 Step One album, ***Stories of Life by Cal Smith***. Cal returned to the lower level of the singles chart with a track from this album, *King Lear*.

Although he has not returned to the singles chart, Cal still appears around the country and as a guest on TV shows such as *The Statler Brothers* on TNN.

RECOMMENDED ALBUMS:

"The Best of Cal Smith" (Kapp)(1971)
"The Best of Cal Smith" (MCA)(1973)
"It's Time to Pay the Fiddler" (MCA)(1975)
"Cal's Country" (MCA UK)(1975) [UK compilation]
"Jason's Farm" (MCA)(1976)
"I Just Came Home to Count the Memories" (MCA)(1977)
"Something Old, Something New" (Soundwaves)(1983) [Billy Parker album features two duets with Cal Smith]
"Stories of Life by Cal Smith" (Step One)(1986)

CARL SMITH

(Singer, Songwriter, Guitar, Bass)

Date of Birth:	**March 15, 1927**
Where Born:	**Maynardsville, Tennessee**
Married:	**1. June Carter (div.)**
	2. Goldie Hill (m. 1957)
Children:	**1. Rebecca Carlene (Carlene Carter);**
	2. Lorri Lynn, Carl, Jr., Larry Dean

When Carl Smith, known as the Country Gentleman, retired in 1977, he was one of the most successful Country singers around. For over twenty-five years, he was just about the best Honky-Tonk singer around, and he probably could have continued for many more years. In addition, he had the looks and build that, in the 90's, would have qualified him for the description of being a "hunk." However, none of the hunks of today have the voice of Carl Smith.

Carl was exposed to Country from a very early age, and sold flower seeds to get enough money to buy his first guitar and cut grass to pay for the lessons. He entered his first talent contest by the time he was age 13 and in 1944, while still at high school, he gained his first radio experience courtesy of Cas Walker at WROL in Knoxville. After graduation, he enlisted in the U.S. Navy and over an eighteen month period, had four tours in the Philippines, including time served aboard the U.S.S. *Admiral Sims*. After he left the service in August 1946, he returned to WROL and for a while played guitar in the Brewster Brothers Band.

In June 1947, Carl and banjo player Hoke Jenkins moved to Asheville, North Carolina, where they played for nothing on WWNC. They survived by playing local live bookings. Carl moved to WGAC Augusta, Georgia, in February 1948, but the financial shortcomings forced him to return to Knoxville. The following year, Carl became bass player in Skeets Williamson's band. He also occasionally sang, but the star of the show was Skeets' sister, Molly O'Day. However, the band soon moved on to Greensboro, North Carolina, and Carl was out of work. Lady luck stepped in and Carl was hired as Archie Campbell's bass player (and occasional singer) on his WROL shows, *Country Playhouse* and *The Dinner Bell*.

While with Archie, Carl was demo-recorded by Speedy Krise, and the result was sent to Troy Martin, who was at the time music publisher Peer International's man in Nashville. Martin, a man who could spot talent a mile away, recognized it in Carl's singing, and arranged for Carl to audition for Jack Stapp, General Manager of the *Grand Ole Opry*. Carl first appeared on the *Opry*, in March 1950, as a guest of Hank Williams on the *Duck Head Work Clothes Show*, singing Jimmie Davis' *I Just Dropped in to Say Goodbye*.

Then Carl hit a brick wall. Stapp said he would only sign Carl as a member of the *Opry* if Don Law, head of Columbia Records' Country Division, would sign him to a record deal. Then Law said he would sign Carl if Stapp hired him and so it went on until Stapp broke the impasse in May. He offered Carl a six-day-a-week morning show and an appearance on the *Opry* about every third Saturday. Immediately, Law signed Carl to Columbia and took him into the recording studio.

However, success didn't come immediately and both Stapp and Law took time to develop what they both considered a very fine talent. It was from his second recording session that Carl hit the jackpot. *Let's Live a Little* was released in 1951, and reached the Top 3 on the Country charts and stayed around for five months. He followed it up with a double-sided smash, *Mr. Moon* (a song co-written by Carl) and *If Teardrops Were Pennies*, both of which made the Top 10. Carl was befriended by both Hank Williams and Ernest Tubb, and toured with E.T. and the Texas Troubadours. E.T. also assisted in finding material for Smith to record, while Hank became a very close friend.

Shortly after, Carl put together his own backing band, the Tunesmiths, whose line-up, by 1952, was Grady Martin (lead guitar), Sammy Pruett (guitar), Johnny Sibert (steel guitar), Junior Huskey (bass) and Jimmy Smith (rhythm guitar). With his original hits, Carl Smith trademarked his highly emotional style, which was characterized by Sibert's wailing steel guitar. Carl wrapped up 1951 with his first No.1 record, *Let Old Mother Nature Have Her Way*. The single stayed at the top for 8 weeks out of a chart stay of 33 weeks, and sold over 900,000 copies.

He started 1952 with back-to-back No.1's, *(When You Feel Like You're in Love) Don't Just Stand There* and the Louvin Brothers' song *Are You Teasing Me*. The former stayed at the top for 8 weeks. The flip-side of the latter, *It's a Lovely, Lovely World*, also became a Top 5 chart entry. During April that year, he recorded some Gospel material on which he was supported by Mother Maybelle Carter and the Carter Sisters. Three months after the session, Carl married June Carter. He closed out 1952 with a most appropriately titled *Our Honeymoon*.

The following year was also highly successful. Carl started off with *That's the Kind of Love I'm Looking For*, which found brief favor on the jukeboxes and had a 1-week stay in the Top 10. He followed with another double-sided Top 10 hit, *Just Wait Till I Get You Alone* and *This Orchid Means Goodbye*. This was followed by more of the same when the coupling *Trademark/Do I Like It?* went Top 10, with the A-side reaching the Top 3. He then had another No.1, *Hey Joe*. This single, which stayed at the top for 8 weeks out of a 6-month chart residency, was written by Boudleaux Bryant, and marked the continuation of an association between Carl and the Bryants that started with *Just Wait 'Til I Get You Alone*. Carl finished the year with the Top 10 single *Satisfaction Guaranteed*.

Carl continued with his chart success throughout 1954 with *Dog-Gone It, Baby I'm in Love*, which reached the Top 10. His other hits of the year were *Back Up Buddy* (Top 3), *Go, Boy, Go* and his fifth No.1, *Loose Talk*. The flip-side of the latter, *More Than Anything Else in the World*, reached the Top 5. That year, he added Buddy Harmon on drums to the Tunesmiths and Carl set up his own Driftwood Music publishing company.

His hits during 1955 were *Kisses Don't Lie* (Top 5)/*No I Don't Believe I Will, Wait a Little Longer, Please, Jesus* (Top 15), *There She Goes* (Top 3)/*Old Lonesome Times, Don't Tease Me* (Top 15), *You're Free to Go/I Feel Like Cryin'* (both sides Top 10).

In 1956, Carl Smith decided to leave the *Opry*, so as to allow time for movie work and additional bookings on Saturday nights, and indeed, he did appear in two movies, *The Badge of Marshal Brennan* and *Buffalo Guns*. During the year, he had *I've Changed*, which just failed to make the Top 10, followed by *You Are the One/Doorstep to Heaven*, a Top 5 coupling, and *Before I Met You/Wicked Lies*, a Top 10 pairing.

During 1957, Carl commenced an eighteen-month connection with the *Philip Morris Country Music Show*, which toured around most of the U.S. Rock'n'roll had started to make an impact on the success of Country performers, but in Carl's case, this took longer than others. Although his first record of the year, *You Can't Hurt Me Anymore*, only reached the Top 15, the follow-up, *Why, Why*, climbed to the Top 3. By 1957, Carl and June had divorced and now he married a lady who could have been one of the major female stars of Country music, Goldie Hill.

Your Name Is Beautiful, Carl's first release of 1958, not only reached the Top 10 on the Country charts, it also got to the Top 80 on the Pop charts. However, the next single, *Walking the Slow Walk*, only got to the Top 30. After the *Philip Morris Show* ended, in 1959, Carl became a member of the *Ozark Jubilee* TV show out of Springfield, Missouri.

From here on, only two singles reached the Top 10, *Ten Thousand Drums* (1959), which also reached the Top 50 on the Pop charts, and the 1967 record *Deep Water*. His other hits were *The Best Years of Your Life, It's All My Heartache* and *Tomorrow Night* (1959), *Make the Watermill Roll* and *Cut Across Shorty* (both 1960) and *You Make Me Live Again* and *Kisses Never Lie* (both 1961). In 1961, he became one of the hosts on ABC-TV's *Four Star Jubilee*.

Carl's hits between 1962 and 1964 were *Air Mail to Heaven* (Top 15)/*Things That Mean the Most* and *The Best Dressed Beggar (In Town)* (Top 20) (both 1962), *Live for Tomorrow, In the Back Room Tonight* (Top 20) and *I Almost Forgot Her Today/Triangle* (Top 20) (all 1963) and *The Pillow That Whispers* (Top 20), *Take My Ring Off Your Finger* (Top 20) and *Lonely Girl* (Top 20)/*When It's Over* (all 1964). Carl was invited by Canadian Television Network (CTV) to host the first three episodes of their 1964 Country music series. It proved so popular that it went on to run, as *Carl Smith's Country Music Hall*, for 190 weekly episodes, over a five-year period. The show was syndicated across Canada and to several U.S. TV stations. Carl was voted the No.1 Country star in Canada.

Carl stayed with Columbia twenty-three years, and between 1965 and 1973, he racked up another 20 chart entries, the most successful being *She Called Me Baby, Be Good to Her* and *Let's Walk Away Strangers* (all 1965), *Deep Water* (1967), *Foggy River* (Top 20, 1968), *Faded Love and Winter Roses, Good Deal, Lucille* (Top 20), *I Love You Because* (Top 15) and *Heartbreak Avenue* (all 1969), *Pull My String and Wind Me Up* (Top 20) and *How I Love Those Love Songs* (both 1970), *Red Door* and *Don't Say You're Mine* (both 1971). While with Columbia, Carl sold around 15 million records.

In 1974, Carl semiretired from performing and recording, but by 1975, he had signed with Hickory Records, with whom his most successful single was the Top 70 *The Way I Lose My Mind*, in 1975. Carl decided to retire in 1977 (Goldie had done so back in 1957 and 1969). He settled down on the 500-acre ranch, in Franklin, Tennessee (just south of Nashville), that he had bought back in 1957. Here he raises and trains award-winning quarter horses.

Carl came out of retirement on three occasions. First, in 1978, to appear at Wembley Festival in England; second, in 1980, to record an album for Gusto; and finally, in 1983, for a benefit concert, as a favor to Billy Grammer. He has left a legacy of recorded jewels that would only have been enhanced by a duet album with Goldie Hill. He has also passed on his genes to his very talented daughter Carlene Carter.

RECOMMENDED ALBUMS:

"Sunday Down South" (Columbia)(1957)
"Carl Smith—Anniversary Album (20 Years of Hits)" (double)(Columbia)(1970)
"Carl Smith Sings Bluegrass" (Columbia)(1971)
"The Way I Lose My Mind" (Hickory)(1975)
"Greatest Hits Volume One" (Gusto)(1980)
"Carl Smith (Columbia Historic Edition)" (Columbia)(1984) [Contains unreleased material]

CONNIE SMITH

(Singer, Songwriter, Guitar, Piano)

Given Name:	**Constance June Meador**
Date of Birth:	**August 14, 1941**
Where Born:	**Elkhart, Indiana**
Married:	**1. Jerry Smith (div.)**
	2. Jack Watkins (div.)
	3. Marshall Haynes (div.)
Children:	**Darren, Kerry, Julie Ray, Jeanne Lynn, Jodi Leigh**

Connie Smith was a housewife who burst onto the Country scene with *Once a Day* and continued to have hits for nearly two decades. Connie continues to delight *Opry* audiences and to work some dates on the road while serving as an inspirational role model to thousands of committed Christian women.

Born in Indiana, Constance Meador spent most of her childhood in Hinton, West Virginia, and then Warner, Ohio, near Marietta, where she married Jerry Smith and became a housewife and mother. She sang featured numbers with a local square dance band as a teenager and appeared with some frequency on weekly local Country TV shows such as the *Saturday Night Jamboree* and the *Big Red Jubilee*, in Huntington and Parkersburg, respectively.

***Connie Smith** at the Wembley Festival in England*

However, her big break came when Bill Anderson heard her sing at Frontier Ranch, a park near Columbus, Ohio, in August 1963. Bill offered to help her if she should choose to attempt a career in the music business. After a few months she decided to do so and with Anderson's help (he actually contemplated managing her), she signed to RCA Victor and cut *Once a Day* and three other songs on July 16, 1964. Three months later *Once a Day* was climbing the charts and hit the top in late November, where it stayed for 8 weeks out of a 7-month stay on the Country chart, and even crossed over to the lower rungs of the Pop chart.

In 1965, the follow-up, *Then and Only Then*, went Top 5 and also crossed over to the Pop chart, with the flip-side, *Tiny Blue Transistor Radio*, going Top 25, and it became obvious that the petite housewife was not a one-hit wonder. Connie finished off 1965 with *I Can't Remember* (Top 10) and *If I Talk to Him* (Top 5). The following year, Connie continued with *Nobody But a Fool (Would Love You)* (Top 5) and back-to-back Top 3 releases, *Ain't Had No Lovin'* and *The Hurtin's All Over*.

During 1967 and 1968, Connie continued to be a hit machine with *I'll Come Runnin'* (Top 10) and consecutive Top 5 successes, *Cincinnati, Ohio* and *Burning a Hole in My Mind* (all 1967), and the Top 10 hits *Baby's Back Again* and *Run Away Little Tears* (both 1968).

Once she started, it seemed that stardom came so easy that it nearly overwhelmed the young woman. In constant demand for personal appearances, she toured heavily, appeared in Country music motion pictures such as *Las Vegas Hillbillies* (1966) and *The Road to Nashville* (1967) and guested so much on Lawrence Welk's TV show that they offered her a regular spot on the program.

By 1968, Connie felt so pressured by stardom and fed up with the phoniness of the music industry that she began contemplating ending it all and sought psychiatric assistance, but ultimately found solace in Christianity. She reduced her touring schedule, married again and began devoting more time to church and family. Ultimately, she paid something of a price in a reduced level of career achievement, but the satisfaction apparently meant more to her and she had no regrets.

Connie stayed with RCA until 1972 and chalked up more hits. They were *Cry, Cry, Cry* (Top 20, 1968), *Ribbon of Darkness* and *Young Love* (a duet with Nat Stuckey) (both Top 20) and the Top 10 hit *You and Your Sweet Love* (all 1969). In 1970, she made the Top 5 with *I Never Once Stopped Loving You* and followed with a revival of Rusty and Doug Kershaw's *Louisiana Man*. She started 1971 with *Where Is My Castle*, which just missed the Top 10, and followed with *Just One Time*, which went Top 3 (and crossed over to the lower rungs of the Pop chart) and closed out the year with the Top 15 *I'm Sorry If My Love Got in the Way*. All three of her 1972 singles went Top 10, with the opener, *Just for What I Am*, reaching the Top 5. The other two were *If It Ain't Love (Let's Leave It Alone)* and *Love Is the Love You're Looking For*.

In 1973, Connie joined Columbia because they permitted her to record more Gospel music. Her major successes on the label were *Ain't Love a Good Thing* (Top 10, 1973), *I Never Knew (What That Song Meant Before)* and *I've Got My Baby on My Mind* (both Top 15, 1974), *Why Don't You Love Me* (Top 15, 1975) and *('Til) I Kissed You* (Top 10) and *I Don't Want to Talk It Over Anymore* (Top 15) (both 1976). Connie's 1975 album of Hank Williams Gospel songs ranks among the best of Country sacred collections.

She signed with Monument in 1977 and placed seven more songs on the charts in three years, but except for *I Just Want to Be Your Everything*, which went Top 15 that year, the others were modest hits. Her last appearance on the charts took place in 1985, when her Epic single, *A Far Cry from You*, peaked in the Top 75.

Connie joined the *Grand Ole Opry* in 1971 and retained this connection even during times when she spent little time on the road and has been one of the institution's more popular stalwarts in the past quarter century. She continues as an appealing performer and a real trouper. As an example, in January 1994, Connie suffered a serious ankle injury during a show in Georgia with Marty Stuart, but bounced back to play the *Opry* within a week and sang at the Winter Olympics in Norway the following month. IMT

RECOMMENDED ALBUMS:

"Sings Great Sacred Songs" (RCA Victor)(1966)
"Connie Smith Sings Bill Anderson" (RCA Victor)(1967)
"The Best of Connie Smith" (RCA Victor)(1967)
"Soul of Country Music" (RCA Victor)(1968)
"I Love Charley Brown" (RCA Victor)(1968)
"Back in Baby's Arms" (RCA Victor)(1969)
"Sunday Morning" (RCA Victor)(1970)
"The Best of Connie Smith, Vol. 2" (RCA Victor)(1970)
"Dream Painter" (RCA Victor)(1973)
"A Lady Named Smith" (Columbia)(1973)
"God Is Abundant" (Columbia KC 32494)(1973)
"Connie Smith Now" (RCA Victor)(1974)
"Connie Smith's Greatest Hits" (RCA Victor)(1975)
"Connie Smith Sings Hank Williams Gospel" (Columbia)(1975)
"Joy to the World" (Columbia)(1975)
"The Song We Fell in Love To" (Columbia)(1976)
"I Don't Want to Talk It Over Anymore" (Columbia)(1976)
"The Best of Connie Smith" (Columbia)(1977)
"Pure Connie Smith" (Monument)(1977)
"New Horizons" (Monument)(1978)
"Live in Branson Mo., U.S.A." (LLT cd)(ca. 1991)
"Clinging to a Saving Hand" (CS) [Cassette]
"Connie Smith by Request" (CS) [Cassette]

EMMA SMITH

(Singer, Songwriter, Guitar)

Given Name:	**Emma Lee Maggard**
Date of Birth:	**February 25, 1945**
Where Born:	**Hindman, Kentucky**
Married:	**1. Marvin Smith (dec'd.)** **2. Robert Adkins**
Children:	**Marvis Lee ("Marty") Smith, Joseph Wayne Smith, Angela Adkins (dec'd.)**

Emma Smith became one of the new and most refreshing voices and pens in traditional Bluegrass during the 80's. Her original lyrics and strong mountain vocal style won her a small but dedicated legion of fans that admired her approach to old musical forms. While Emma has yet to achieve major commercial success, one can nonetheless applaud the level of artistic accomplishment she has reached.

Born and reared near Hindman, Kentucky, Emma grew up experiencing the typical mountain girl's life of her generation. When her older brother went into the service about 1950, she began to "plunk" on his guitar and eventually learned some chords to accompany her own singing. Perhaps the most unusual characteristic Emma manifested in this era was the ability to observe life and human experience in a manner that she would later incorporate into her song lyrics. Emma married in her late teens and began rearing a family in Hazard, Kentucky.

Traditional Bluegrass singer ***Emma Smith***

The mountain town of Hazard had a local UHF TV station and their *Saturday Night Jamboree* provided an outlet for Emma's creative and artistic expressions. She did some of her songs on the program and one of the local artists recorded one of them about 1970. Two years later, Emma ventured into the studio for her own first recording experience, a custom album for the Memphis-based Majestic label with Country backing. Her title song, *Angel Mother*, had been written shortly after Emma's own mother had passed away in 1962. The limited pressing sold out on the basis of local sales. Emma worked for local entertainments and the local TV program. She gained some popularity in her immediate area, but remained little known to the potentially broader audience for her music.

Meanwhile, Emma left Kentucky and settled in Portsmouth, Ohio, in 1981. Having known the wife of the legendary musician Larry Sparks from some years earlier when both worked in the same clothing store, Emma did some of her songs for Larry and they subsequently recorded ten numbers together, originally on an 8-track tape, which Larry released on his Lesco label (later released as an Old Homestead album). It contained *Don't Neglect the Rose*, a song that went on to become one of Larry's all-time most popular numbers.

This led to Emma contracting with Old Homestead as a solo artist. Her initial album, ***Hazard***, in the spring of 1982 was followed by a sacred offering, ***Ship from King's Harbor Shore***, later that same year. Both title cuts constituted outstanding originals. Old Homestead then released her duets with Sparks on album (with two additional songs) and an album with hard-core Bluegrass traditionalist Dave Evans on their Rutabaga subsidiary.

Besides festival appearances on her own or with a band, Emma also worked many shows with super instrumentalists Kenny Baker and Josh Graves. Although she cut one album with them, it has not been released. Over the years, her songs won two SPGMA awards and two Midwest Bluegrass Association awards.

Even though her musical efforts remain somewhat under-recognized, Emma has continued to make visits on the festival circuits and elsewhere. During the Persian Gulf War she recorded a patriotic tribute to the troops that the Portsmouth American Legion promoted with some fanfare. Larry Sparks has recorded eight of her songs, Ralph Stanley three and the Lonesome River Band, the Isaacs, and Wild and Blue, one each. In the past five years, Emma has had three more Old Homestead albums to her credit and is readying material for another.

April 1994 found Emma residing in Flatwoods, Kentucky, and looking forward to meeting her old fans and friends on the summer festival circuit and making new ones as well. No better tribute to this fine lady and her music has been made than that of Country music authority Charles K. Wolfe, who wrote in 1989, "There are few singers today who can interpret Old-Time Country or traditional Gospel songs with the sincerity and honesty of Emma Smith." IMT

RECOMMENDED ALBUMS:

"Angel Mother" (Majestic)(1972)
"Hazard" (Old Homestead)(1982)
"Ship from Kings Harbor Shore" (Old Homestead)(1982)
"We Are One" (Old Homestead)(1984) [Originally recorded for Lesco in 1981][With Larry Sparks]
"Don't Let Me Cross Over" (Rutabaga)(1984) [With Dave Evans]
"I Will Sing of My Redeemer" (Old Homestead)(1989)
"Memories" (Old Homestead)(1991)
"Back to the Basics" (Old Homestead)(1993) [Cassette]

FIDDLIN' ARTHUR SMITH

(Singer, Fiddle, Banjo)

Given Name:	**Arthur Q. Smith**
Date of Birth:	**April 10, 1898**
Where Born:	**Humphreys County, Tennessee**
Married:	**Unknown**
Children:	**Unknown**
Date of Death:	**February 28, 1971**

Not to be confused with Arthur "Guitar Boogie" Smith the guitarist, nor Arthur Q. Smith the songwriter, Fiddlin' Arthur Smith was one of the premier instrumentalists in Country music history. Along with Clayton McMichen, he helped popularize the "long bow" technique among southern fiddlers. He and McMichen were by far the most influential fiddlers of their era—the period from 1930 to 1950.

Smith's style and many tunes, such as *Blackberry Blossom, Florida Blues, Pig at Home in the Pen, More Pretty Girls Than One* and *Red Apple Rag,* made him the most famous "radio fiddler" of all time. "He was the King of the fiddlers," recalled Roy Acuff. Even modern Bluegrass fiddlers agree that Smith's style paved the way for Bluegrass fiddling styles. Kenny Baker, who listened to Smith on the radio as a child, recalls: "Arthur was one of the greatest fiddlers of all time."

Smith's distinctive bowing style, smooth and rolling with a lot of clean, clear noting on the E string, was partly the product of his own genius, but was also part of a well-defined West Tennessee Folk fiddling tradition. The region around Dickson, Cheatham, and Humphreys counties was a hilly, rather remote area due west of Nashville, and produced a number of other fine fiddlers, like Howdy Forrester, Paul Warren, Jim and Grady Stringer and others. Smith's father was a fiddler, but he died when the lad was only 5 and the Stringer Brothers became his mentors.

Young Smith grew up fiddling for local dances, and eventually married (September 17, 1914) a young lady who played guitar for him. By 1921 he had started working for the North Carolina and St. Louis (N.C. and St. L.) railroad, known locally as the Dixie Line. It was another Dixie Line employee, Harry Stone, who invited Smith to begin playing on the new Nashville radio station where Stone went to work, WSM. In December 1927, Smith made his debut on the show that had just recently been renamed the *Grand Ole Opry*.

Thus began a tenure that lasted some twelve years, and that would propel Smith to nationwide fame. At first, he performed with his cousin Homer and then, about 1930, he started working with the McGee Brothers, forming the Dixieliners. In January, 1935, another *Opry* act, the Delmore Brothers, invited Arthur to go with them to record for the new Bluebird label and through this, Arthur made the first in a long series of Bluebird records. (He would not get to record with the McGees until the 50's.) He eventually did some 52 sides with the Delmores, most of them issued under the name Arthur Smith Trio; he also backed the Delmores on a number of their records. All were not fiddle tunes: the biggest Bluebird hits were vocals like *More Pretty Girls Than One, Beautiful Brown Eyes, Walking in My Sleep, Love Letters in the Sand, Chittlin' Cookin' Time in Cheatham County,* and *Kilby Jail*. Kirk McGee used to joke: "For the longest time we couldn't get Arthur to sing or even open his mouth on-stage. Then when he did, we couldn't get him to stop singing."

By 1938, when the Delmores left the *Opry,* Smith played over WSM with Jack Shook and His Missouri Mountaineers, and then with Herald Goodman and his Tennessee Valley Boys. From 1940 to 1946, he rambled restlessly, appearing for short stints with Zeke Phillips in Birmingham, the Bailes Brothers in West Virginia, the York Brothers, and with the *Saddle Mountain Round Up* over KRLD in Dallas. The next few years he spent on the West Coast with cowboy singer Jimmy Wakely, where he appeared on network radio and in several Hollywood films. It was during this time that he introduced *Orange Blossom Special* in the clubs at Las Vegas and recorded it and several other sides for Capitol.

The early 1950's, though, saw hard times; his song *Beautiful Brown Eyes* became a Pop hit, but Arthur was cheated out of royalties. For a time he left music entirely, doing carpentry work and returning to Tennessee. In the 1960's he was rediscovered by Mike Seeger and did two new lps with the McGees, as well as several Folk festival dates. One of his protégés, Paul Warren, introduced him to Flatt & Scruggs, and Smith often jammed with them, producing an incredibly potent series of home tapes that younger Bluegrass pickers listened to avidly. A Starday lp followed in 1963, featuring Arthur and his son.

Health problems began to plague Arthur in the late 60's, the result of years of hard living and too much drinking. He made a last public appearance at Monroe's Bean Blossom Festival in 1969, and died in Louisville, of cancer, on February 28, 1971. He was buried near McEwen, Tennessee. A two-album retrospective of his best Bluebird work was issued by County in 1978 and an entire issue of the quarterly *The Devil's Box* was devoted to him about the same time (Vol. 11, No. 4). CKW

RECOMMENDED ALBUM:

"Fiddlin' Arthur Smith & His Dixieliners" (two albums) (County)(1978)

MARGO SMITH

(Singer, Songwriter, Yodeler, Actress)

Given Name:	**Betty Lou Miller**
Date of Birth:	**April 9, 1942**
Where Born:	**Dayton, Ohio**
Married:	**Richard Cammeron**

Children: **Holly**

A lady of great natural beauty, Margo Smith is one of Country music's superior performers. She is also a fine songwriter, who has written many of her hits and has gained the sobriquet of the Tennessee Yodeler for her great yodeling ability.

Margo was adopted into a large family and quickly gained an element of self-confidence. While still in high school, she and a friend won first prize in a talent contest, by dressing up as country bumpkins and calling themselves the Apple Sisters.

As a kindergarten teacher, Betty Lou Miller often used Folk and Country songs in the classroom. If she could not find a song to fit the subject matter, she wrote one herself. Eventually she pursued music full-time, developing a following in her home state of Ohio. She graduated from PTA performances to appearances on various radio stations.

In 1975, Margo was signed by 20th Century Fox Records and scored a Top 5 hit with her self-penned *There I Said It*. She followed her debut success with the Top 30 *Paper Lovin*. Margo completed an album for the label and then was devastated when they decided to close down their Nashville operation.

Margo's success had not gone unnoticed and she moved to Warner Brothers Records in 1976. Label executives put her with producer Norro Wilson and the results were three Top 10 singles: *Save Your Kisses for Me*, *Take My Breath Away* (both 1976) and *Love's Explosion* (1977). Her fourth single, *Don't Break the Heart That Loves You* (also 1977), shot to No.1 and stayed there for 2 weeks. Margo repeated her No.1 success, in 1978, with her next single, *It Only Hurts for a Little While,* and followed up with the Top 3 release *Little Things Mean a Lot*. She also teamed up with Norro Wilson, as Margo & Norro, for the 1977 Top 50 record *So Close Again*.

Margo toured heavily in the late 70's, with her band, Night Flight. She shared the bill with all the major stars of the era, including Conway Twitty, Tammy Wynette, the Statler Brothers, Kenny Rogers and Charley Pride. Margo was a popular guest on the national TV shows *Dinah!*, the *Mike Douglas Show, Pop Goes the Country, That Nashville Music* and *Hee Haw*. Her record success continued, in 1979, with *Still a Woman* and *If I Give My Heart to You*, both Top 10 successes.

In 1979, Margo Smith opted for a new sexier image. She appeared in a revealing satin robe on her ***Just Margo*** album cover. The following year she raised eyebrows when she lowered her neckline for the cover of ***Diamonds and Chills***. She added spandex to her wardrobe and created one of the most exciting stage shows in Country music. In 1979, Margo reached the Top 30 with *Baby My Baby*. At the end of 1979, the fans responded favorably to *The Shuffle Song* (Top 15 in 1980). In 1980, Margo recorded *Cup of Tea* with Rex Allen, Jr. and was nominated for "Top Duet of the Year" by both the ACM and *Music City News*. They repeated their chart success with the Top 30 duet *While the Feeling's Good*, in 1981.

The Tennessee Yodeler, ***Margo Smith***

In the early 80's, Margo returned to her hometown image. In 1982, she moved to AMI, without major success, and a year later, moved on to Moon Shine, with similar results. In 1985 she signed to Bermuda Dunes, where she had a low level duet with Tom Grant, *Everyday People*.

She paid homage to the 50's *Midwestern Hayride* yodeling star Bonnie Lou in 1985 with ***The Best of the Tennessee Yodeler***. The album, released on Bermuda Dunes, sold well via direct marketing on TV. To support the release, Margo did a music video for *I Want to Be Your Cowboy's Sweetheart*. It was distributed through MCA, in 1987. In the late 80's, Margo recorded for Cammeron Records (created by her banker husband, Richard, who is also her manager) in the U.S., MCA in Europe, and RCA in Canada. Margo had a low level single on Playback, in 1988, entitled *Echo Me*.

She also entered into acting when she made several appearances in TNN's *I-40 Paradise*. In 1991 Margo formed a Gospel duo with her daughter Holly, who received a degree in broadcasting and music from Belmont University in Nashville. Known as Margo Smith & Holly, the mother-daughter team records for Homeland Records. Calling their music Christian Country, the duo found success on Gospel radio. JIE

RECOMMENDED ALBUMS:

"Margo Smith" (20th Century)(1975)
"Songbird" (Warner Brothers)(1976)
"Happiness" (Warner Brothers)(1977)
"Don't Break the Heart That Loves You" (Warner Brothers)(1978)
"A Woman" (Warner Brothers)(1979)
"Just Margo" (Warner Brothers)(1979)
"Diamonds and Chills" (Warner Brothers)(1980)
"The Best of the Tennessee Yodeler" (Bermuda Dunes/MCA)(1985/1987)

SAMMI SMITH

(Singer, Songwriter)

Given Name: **Jewel Fay Smith**
Date of Birth: **August 5, 1943**
Where Born: **Orange, California**
Married: **Unknown**
Children: **four, plus three adopted**

Sammi Smith has made a career of selecting material that fitted into the "outlaw" concept—songs that speak of real life—written by writers such as Kris Kristofferson, John Hartford, John Sebastian, and of course songs from her own talented pen.

Although born in California, Sammi was raised in Oklahoma, Texas, Arizona and Colorado. She dropped out of school when age 11 and began singing nightly in a club when 12. Songwriter Gene Sullivan, who owned a recording studio in Oklahoma City, encouraged and helped her. She also received a lot of help from Marshall Grant, who played bass with the Tennessee Three. When she was 15, she got married and soon had four children. Sullivan encouraged her to move to Nashville, and when her marriage broke up, she did so, in 1967.

From singing at smoke-filled clubs, Sammi's voice soon developed a husky tonality which was to become her trademark. The same year as her arrival in Nashville, Sammi signed with Columbia, thanks to Grant's help. The following year, she had her first chart entry, *So Long, Charlie Brown, Don't Look for Me Around*, which made the Top 70. She had two more entries for that label but it was not until she moved to Mega Records that success came her way.

She had the first release on the label, *He's Everywhere*, which reached the Top 75, in 1970. However, it was her year-end single that launched her into stardom. Kristofferson's *Help Me Make It Through the Night* became a No.1 Country hit, staying at the top for 3 weeks. It also reached the Pop Top 10 and earned Sammi a Gold Record. In addition, she won a Grammy Award for "Best Country

Vocal Performance, Female" and the song won a Grammy for "Best Country Song." What made Sammi's version extra special was the sensual way in which she interpreted the song. This was probably the first time that a female Country singer had used her sexuality to such effect. It presaged singers such as Tanya Tucker, Reba McEntire and even Pop diva Madonna. That same year, Sammi's song *Cedartown, Georgia* was a big hit for Waylon Jennings.

She appeared with George Hamilton IV at the Royal Albert Hall, in London, England, as part of a package tour. She became friends with Jennings and Willie Nelson, and, in 1973, moved to Dallas, as she got interested in the outlaw movement. Sammi toured with Waylon and he nicknamed her Girl Hero. She also appeared at Willie's 4th of July Picnics.

Sammi stayed with Mega until 1975, and produced several major hits. Her Top 10 successes were *Then You Walk In* (1971) and *Today I Started Loving You Again* (1975), while she made the Top 20 with *I've Got to Have You* (1972) (also a Top 80 Pop hit) and *The Rainbow in Daddy's Eyes* (1974). Her other successes included *For the Kids* (1971), *Kentucky* and *Girl in New Orleans* (both 1972), *City of New Orleans* (1973), *Long Black Veil* (1974) and *Cover Me* (1975).

Sammi moved from Dallas to Globe, Arizona, in 1975, to live on the San Carlos Apache Reservation, and adopted three Apache children, to complement her four offspring. Sammi has crusaded for many years for the rights and condition of the Apache Indian. This stems from the fact that she is a direct descendant of the famed chief Cochise and is part Kiowa-Apache. She has organized benefits for a high school and scholarship fund for Apache children. At the school, they learn to read, write and speak the Apache language, which was in danger of dying out.

In 1975, Sammi switched labels to Elektra, just before Mega went out of business the following year and started off with the low level release *Huckleberry Pie*, in tandem with songwriter Even Stevens. She stayed on the label until 1978, during which time her most successful singles were *As Long As There's a Sunday* and *Sunday School to Broadway* (both 1976), *Loving Arms*, *I Can't Stop Loving You* and *Days That End in "Y"* (all 1977) and *It Just Won't Feel Like Cheating (with You)* (1978). Her final chart record for the label was the tribute to Marilyn Monroe, *Norma Jean*, which made the Top 75.

Moving back to an independent label seemed to resurrect her career. The label was Cyclone, and in 1979, she had a Top 20 single entitled *What a Lie*, and followed it with her version of the Box Tops' hit *The Letter*, which went Top 30. The following year, Sammi moved to Sound Factory, where she had a Top 40 release, *I Just Want to Be With You*. Her other major hits on the label were *Cheatin's a Two Way Street* (Top 20) and *Sometimes I Cry When I'm Alone* (both 1981).

Her outlaw image seemed to have gone by the time she released the album ***Better Than Ever***, on Step One Records. In fact, with her pictured on the cover in a sequined long dress, she looked positively "cabaret-ish." From this album, she had two low level chart singles, *You Just Hurt My Feeling* and *Love Me All Over*, in 1985 and 1986 respectively.

RECOMMENDED ALBUMS:

"Help Me Make It Through the Night" (Mega)(1970) [Originally titled "He's Everywhere"]
"The Best of Sammi Smith" (Mega)(1972)
"The Best of Sammi Smith" (double)(Trip)(1974)
"Today I Started Loving You Again" (Mega)(1975)
"New Winds—All Quadrants" (Elektra)(1978)
"Girl Hero" (Cyclone)(1979)
"Better Than Ever" (Step One)(1985)

HANK SNOW

(Singer, Songwriter, Guitar, Harmonica, Author)

Given Name:	**Clarence Eugene Snow**
Date of Birth:	**May 9, 1914**
Where Born:	**Brooklyn, Nova Scotia, Canada**
Married:	**Minnie Blanch Aalders**
Children:	**Jimmie Rodgers (Rev. Jimmie Rodgers Snow)**

With one of the most distinctive voices and styles in Country music, Hank Snow has enjoyed one of the most successful and long-running careers in the genre. He took the Folk songs of his native Canada, the "blue yodels" of his idol Jimmie Rodgers, the cowboy songs of the West, the older Pop standards of Tin Pan Alley, the best of the Nashville tunesmiths and his own considerable skills as a songwriter and forged from them a music that is almost a genre in itself—"Hank Snow music."

People who have little interest in most other forms of Country music are fascinated with the Snow sound and his long and rich career has spanned several generations of fans. His recordings, which began on Canadian Bluebird in 1936, number over 840 sides, including dozens of memorable albums and 20-odd Top 10 hits. His classic touring shows,

Country music legend Hank Snow

which often featured his pinto pony, Shawnee, and his own elaborate riding stunts, are still remembered by many who saw them in the 1950's.

His tenure on the *Grand Ole Opry* made him an equal favorite with radio fans and most deemed it highly appropriate when, in the early 1990's, he was the first artist honored in the *Grand Ole Opry* museum. His scrapbooks contain honors of all sorts, from proclamations for his work with abused children to an honorary doctorate. Hank is also renowned for his stage outfits which are extremely colorful.

Hank's career started in a remote fishing village on the Nova Scotia coast, Brooklyn, where Hank and his three sisters grew up. He led a reasonably normal life until he was 8; then his parents divorced, splitting up the family and plunging young Hank into a series of traumatic experiences. His new stepfather was a rough, violent fisherman who often beat Hank severely. To escape, the young teenager took jobs on local fishing schooners as a cabin boy in the Arctic area. Here Hank would entertain the crew by singing and playing the harmonica. When he could he listened to the old Victrola records of Vernon Dalhart and years later recalled and even performed many of Dalhart's repertoire such as *The Prisoner's Song*.

When Hank left the sea, after 4 years, he worked in a fish plant until he got side-lined by a ruptured appendix. He then worked in a stable and on a salt steamer for 11 days. By 1929, his mother got him some Jimmie Rodgers records and this had an even more profound effect on him. Within weeks, Hank had gotten a new mail-order guitar, a T Eaton Special, and was trying to copy Rodgers. That year, Hank signed on as a lumberjack.

In 1933 he brashly worked his way up to the nearest big town, Halifax, peddling housewares along the way to make his expenses; any customer who bought something got a free song by Hank as a bonus. He soon got his own radio show on CHNS, where he was billed as "Clarence Snow and his guitar" and then as "the Yodeling Ranger," but during the Depression this was far from enough to make a living with. He had to seek part-time jobs, and once found himself shoveling snow in front of the very station where he was a "radio star." About this time he met and married a Dutch-Irish native named Minnie Blanch Aalders. He also found a serious sponsor, Crazy Water Crystals, and changed his name to "Hank, the Singing Ranger." On October 10, 1936, in an old church in Montreal, he made his first records for Canadian Bluebird. During the next 10 years, he had a string of hits for this label, though they were not released in the U.S. They included *The Blue Velvet Band*, *Galveston Rose*, *My Blue River Rose* and *I'll Not Forget My Mother's Prayer*. Eventually he wound up doing some 90 sides in Canada. During 1942 and 1943, Hank broadcast over CBC in Montreal and Campbellton, New Brunswick. At the beginning of 1944, he was with CKCW Mocton, New Brunswick.

The next stage was obviously to crack the American market, but this was easier said than done, especially as WWII arrived. He initially worked on WCAU and WIP in Philadelphia. Then in 1945, Hank tried his luck at the WWVA *Wheeling Jamboree* in West Virginia, where he met Big Slim Aliff, one of his idols and a source for more than a few of his songs. There was an unsuccessful stay in Hollywood the following year and then he moved back to Canada, where he spent $2,000 on a silver saddle for Shawnee. By 1948, Hank was in Dallas, playing over *Big D Jamboree*. There he met Texas' most famous singer, Ernest Tubb, who took a liking to the young Canadian and eventually helped him get a job on the *Grand Ole Opry* in early 1950. He also finally persuaded Victor to release his records in the U.S. (fans had been smuggling them in for years), and by 1949, he was cutting his first American sides, in Chicago, on which he was backed by his Rainbow Ranch Boys, who played on all his recordings to the end of 1956.

At first, *Opry* audiences were lukewarm toward Hank. He first hit the Country chart with the Top 10 *Marriage Vow* in 1949, and then Hank's first big record, the self-penned *I'm Movin' On*, hit No.1, where it stayed for 21 weeks out of over 10 months on the charts. From then on, he could do no wrong. He ended 1950 with *Golden Rocket*, which went to No.1 the following year. It was followed by *The Rhumba Boogie*, which went to the top for 8 weeks.

Between 1951 and 1953, Hank's hits were: 1951: *Bluebird Island* (Top 5)/*Down the Trail of Achin' Hearts* (Top 3, with Anita Carter), *Unwanted Sign Upon Your Heart* (Top 10), *Music Makin' Mama from Memphis* (Top 5); 1952: *The Gold Rush Is Over* (Top 3), *Lady's Man* (Top 3)/*Married by the Bible, Divorced by the Law* (Top 10), *I Went to Your Wedding* (Top 3), *The Gal Who Invented Kissin'* (Top 5)/*(Now and Then, There's) A Fool Such As I* (Top 3); 1953: *Honeymoon on a Rocket Ship* (Top 10), *Spanish Fire Ball* (Top 3), *For Now and Always* (Top 10), *When Mexican Joe Met Jole Blon* (Top 10).

In 1954, Hank returned to the No.1 spot with *I Don't Hurt Anymore*, which stayed on top for 20 weeks out of 10 months on the charts. He followed that with *That Crazy Mambo Thing* and then another No.1, *Let Me Go, Lover!* Hank's other 50's hits were: 1955: *The Next Voice You Hear* (Top 15), *Silver Bell* (Top 15, an instrumental duet with Chet Atkins), the double-sided Top 3 hit *Yellow Roses/Would You Mind?*, the double-sided Top 10 hit *Cryin', Prayin', Waitin', Hopin'/I'm Glad I Got to See You Once Again*, the double-sided Top 5 hit, *Born to Be Happy/Mainliner (The Hawk with Silver Wings)*; 1956: *These Hands* (Top 5)/*I'm Moving In* (Top 15), the double-sided Top 5 hit *Conscience I'm Guilty/Hula Rock, Stolen Moments* (Top 10); 1957: *Tangled Mind* (Top 5)/*My Arms Are a House* (Top 10); 1958: *Whispering Rain* (Top 15), *Big Wheels* (Top 10), *A Woman Captured Me* (Top 20); 1959: *Doggone that Train* (Top 20), *Chasin' a Rainbow* (Top 10), *The Last Ride* (Top 3).

During the 60's, Hank's success was less consistent, yet this was a time when he crossed over to the Pop chart. He started 1960 with *Rockin' Rollin' Wave*, which only reached the Country Top 25, but it also reached the Pop Top 90. His other major successes were *Miller's Cave* (Top 10, 1960), *Beggar to a King* (Top 5) and *The Restless One* (Top 15 both 1961). He started 1962 with the Top 15 *You Take the Future (and I'll Take the Past)* and then Hank had the career single *I've Been Everywhere*, which reached No.1 on the Country chart and Top 70 Pop. The song was written by Australian Geoff Mack, mentioning Australian locations, and was adapted to the U.S. market.

He started 1963 with *The Man Who Robbed the Bank at Santa Fe* (Top 10) and followed with the Top 3 *Ninety Miles an Hour (Down a Dead End Street)*. During the remainder of the 60's, Hank's major successes were *Breakfast with the Blues* (Top 15, 1964), *The Wishing Well (Down in the Well)* (Top 10) and *I've Cried a Mile* (Top 20, both 1965) and *Down at the Pawn Shop* and *Learnin' a New Way of Life* (both Top 20, 1967), *The Late and Great Love (of My Heart)* and *The Name of the Game Was Love* (both Top 20, 1968). In 1974 came his biggest hit in years, *Hello, Love*, which gave him his first No.1 in 12 years, and from here on his chart singles increasingly occupied the basement level of the chart. He had his last chart single in 1980, a duet with Kelly Foxton entitled *Hasn't It Been Good Together*.

In addition to the chart hits, Hank pioneered the "concept" album, doing a number of thematic lps for RCA Victor, often averaging three albums a year in the 1960's. He also did a series of guitar albums, including a well-received pair with Chet Atkins, ***Reminiscing*** (1964) and ***C.B. Atkins & C.E. Snow, by Special Request*** (1970).

Through the 1970's, 80's and 90's, Hank held the line against diluting traditional Country music. He often went back into his own repertoire to rediscover old songs he could revive on the modern stage and often sang on the *Opry* stage some of the favorites from the Canadian days. He was an important figure in the growth of Nashville into Music City, by operating an important package tour organization (in which he signed a young Elvis Presley) as well as an influential music store. His Foundation for Child Abuse helped call attention to a major social problem. In 1994 he published a lengthy autobiography, *The Hank Snow Story*, and remained the most articulate and serious spokesman for classic Country music, as well as one of its leading performers. CKW

RECOMMENDED ALBUMS:

"Old Doc Brown & Other Narrations" (RCA Victor)(1955) [Re-issued by Stetson UK in the original sleeve (1988)]
"Country Classics" (RCA Victor)(1956) [Re-issued by Stetson UK in the original sleeve (1988)]
"Hank Snow's Country Guitar" (RCA Victor)(1957) [Originally released in 1954 as 10" album]
"Biggest Country Hits (Songs I Hadn't Recorded till Now)" (RCA Victor)(1961)
"The Guitar Stylings of Hank Snow" (RCA Victor)(1966)
"This Is My Story—Hank Snow" (double)(RCA Victor)(1966)
"The Jimmie Rodgers Story" (RCA Victor)(1972) [Re-issued 1977]
"The Living Legend" (double)(RCA Victor)(1978)
"I'm Movin' On" (double)(RCA Victor)(1982)
"20 of the Best" (RCA International UK)(1982)
Hank Snow & Chet Atkins:
"Reminiscing" (RCA Victor)(1964)
"C.B. Atkins & C.E. Snow, by Special Request" (RCA Victor)(1970)
Hank Snow & Anita Carter:
"Together Again" (RCA Victor)(1962)

VERNON SOLOMON
(Fiddle)

Given Name: Vernon Solomon
Date of Birth: December 23, 1924
Where Born: Forney, Texas
Married: Ruby
Children: Mike, Ricky, Terry, Steve
Date of Death: May 7, 1991

It was almost assumed that Vernon Solomon would become a fiddler because his father, Ervin, was considered one of the best fiddlers in Texas during the 20's and 30's. His skill came in useful because during the Depression, Ervin supported his family largely with money won at fiddling contests around the state. Inspired by his father and other players who frequently visited the Solomon home, Vernon started learning to play the fiddle at age 5. His first instrument was homemade from the wood of a bois d'arc tree and the first tune he learned to play was *Bully of the Town*. Vernon progressed quickly and at age 7 entered his first contest, coming in third. The following year, 1932, he beat his father in a contest held in Athens, Texas. For this feat he won a new suit of clothes, a welcome prize in Depression-era Texas. It was the first of many contests Vernon was to win. Probably his most important victory came in 1972 when he won the first Grand Masters Contest held in Nashville.

While serving in the South Pacific during WWII, Vernon kept playing music, primarily because he met another Texas fiddler, Carl Hazlewood. Even so, he made no attempt to earn his living playing music; it remained simply a very important avocation for the rest of his life. Solomon recorded albums for County and Davis Unlimited Records and for many years was a regular performer on the *Grapevine Opry* in Grapevine, Texas. WKM

RECOMMENDED ALBUMS:
"Texas Breakdown" (Davis Unlimited)
"Texas Hoedown" (County) [With Barstow Riley and Benny Thomasson]

JO-EL SONNIER
(Singer, Songwriter, French Accordion, Bass, Drums, Fiddle, Guitar, Harmonica, Actor)

Given Name: Joel Sonnier
Date of Birth: October 2, 1946
Where Born: Rayne, Louisiana
Married: 1. Jami Talbot (dec'd.)
2. Bobbye Weaver

*The great Cajun entertainer **Jo-el Sonnier***

Jo-el Sonnier has been one of the most successful Cajun performers to transcend the barrier to Country music, blending the two elements. He describes what he plays as Cajun-Country-Rock, and anyone who has seen him onstage can attest to the energy that he emits, and anyone who has met him will confirm what a nice guy he is.

He was born into a sharecropping family and attending to his chores meant rising at 4:00 a.m., milking cows, feeding pigs and picking cotton. He began playing accordion at age 5 and by the time he was age 6, he was so adept that he made his debut on radio KSIG Crowley, Louisiana. At age 11, he made his professional debut at the Triangle Club in nearby Scott.

He was early influenced by the great Cajun accordionist Iry LeJune. Jo-el, or as he still was, Joel, won a lot of accordion contests and then, when he was just 13, he recorded a watershed single, *Tes Yeux Bleu*, for Swallow. He became hailed as "the 13-year-old wonder," and was much in demand on live dates, which he played with the Pioneers.

Dominic Dupree of Ville Platte, Louisiana, formed the Dupree label to give Jo-el additional publicity. He was paired with Les Duson Playboys for the classic hunting-dog song, *Tayeaux Dog Tayeaux*, but the record was ruined by bad sound. When he left high school, Jo-el relocated to Lake Charles, Louisiana, where he joined Robert Bertrand's Louisiana Ramblers. With this group, he recorded for Goldband, and sang and played on *Memphis (Fais Do Do)* and sang duet with Robert on *My 50 Cents*.

He recorded for Goldband as a solo, and cut *Jump Little Frog* and *I'm Leaving You*. However, the recordings were swamped by bad recording gimmicks, and badly produced by Eddie Shuler. Also, Jo-el detracted from his ability as a musician by billing himself as "the Cajun Valentino," and wearing an Arabian headdress.

He was the winner of the first prize in the Mamou Mardi Gras Competition, in 1968. Although he had recorded four albums, including ***Cajun Valentino***, ***Hurricane Avory*** and ***Scene Today in Cajun Music*** and 12 singles, in 1972 Jo-el traveled to California to play a Folk festival and as a result, he and his wife Jami decided to move there. Jami played a major role in Jo-el's career, and was his rock. Jo-el began sitting in at the Palomino Club, and won $100 in a contest during his first visit. Up to now, Jo-el spoke and sang in French, but started to sing in English by listening to recordings by West Coast stars such as Buck Owens, Merle Haggard and Glen Campbell.

However, while in California, he hardly played accordion, concentrating on bass and drums. He toured with a group called Friends, which included Albert Lee, keyboardist Garth Hudson and multi-instrumentalist David Lindley. In 1974, Jo-el moved to Nashville and signed to Mercury Records. As Joel Sonnier, he had three Country chart entries, of which the most successful was the first, *I've Been Around Enough to Know*, which went Top 80. He stayed with the label until 1978, without further success. In 1976, he played on Asleep at the Wheel's ***Wheelin' and Dealin'*** album.

He returned to Louisiana in 1979, and the following year recorded ***Cajun Life*** for Rounder Records. This album features a blend of Cajun and Country musicians and includes songs such as *Tes Yeux Bleu*, Nathan Abshire's *Bayou Teche Waltz* and Iry LeJune's *Lacassine Special*. The following year, ***Cajun Life*** was nominated for a Grammy Award for "Best Ethnic Album."

Jo-el's career took off in 1987, when he signed to RCA and released his successful album ***Come on Joe***, which featured Steve Winwood on organ. The debut single, *Come on Joe*, reached the Top 40, and then the follow-up, in 1988, *No More One More Time*, climbed into the Top 10. It was followed by Richard Thompson's *Tear-Stained Letter*, which did the same. This latter was accompanied by his first video. He wrapped up the year with the Top 40 success *Rainin' in My Heart*. That year, he was voted "New Country Artist of the Year" in *Performance* magazine's Readers' Poll.

He opened his account in 1989 with the Top 50 single *(Blue, Blue, Blue) Blue, Blue* and followed it with the Top 25 release *If Your Heart Should Ever Roll This Way Again*. Jo-el released his second RCA album, ***Have a Little Faith***, in 1990 and it also sold well; however, he only had one single that charted that year, *The Scene of the Crime*, which only made it to the Top 70.

In 1991, Jo-el moved to Capitol (later Liberty) Records and released the album ***Tears of Joy***. Produced by James Stroud, the album failed to consolidate Jo-el's previous success. This album came hard on the heels of the untimely death of Jo-el's wife Jami, which totally shattered him and is reflected in the overall feel of the recordings. At the Evangeline Special, that year, he won the "French Song of the Year" award.

In August 1992, he married longtime friend Bobbye Weaver. His 1992 album ***Hello Happiness Again***, produced by Chips Moman, reflected his new marriage, however, it failed to ignite the charts. That didn't stop the South Louisiana Music Association from awarding him the "Lifetime Achievement Award."

As a songwriter, Jo-el has not only written for himself, but has also been covered by other artists, including Johnny Cash (*Cajun Born*), Fiddlin' Frenchie Burke (*Knock, Knock, Knock*), John Anderson (*One of Those Old Things We All Go Thru*), George Strait (*Blue is Not a Word*) and Mel McDaniel (*Inseparable*).

He is also a musician whose skills have been used by such diverse stars as Elvis Costello, Dolly Parton and Emmylou Harris. He has also appeared in four movies, *Mask*, *They All Laughed* (1981, which featured Dorothy Stratten, who was murdered before its release), *Wildfire* (which featured *Come on Joe* on the closing credits) and *A Thing Called Love*. In 1992, Mercury released the compilation ***The Complete Mercury Sessions***.

RECOMMENDED ALBUMS:

"Cajun Life" (Rounder)(1980)
"Come on Joe" (RCA)(1987)
"Have a Little Faith" (RCA)(1990)
"Tears of Joy" (Capitol)(1991)
"Hello Happiness Again" (Liberty)(1992)
"The Complete Mercury Sessions" (Mercury)(1992)

SONS OF THE PIONEERS

When Formed: **1934**

Members:

Len Slye	**Lead Vocals, Guitar (left 1937)**
Bob Nolan	**String Bass, Guitar, Baritone Vocals (left 1949)**
Hugh Farr	**Fiddle, Bass Vocals (left 1958)**
Karl Farr	**Guitar, Vocals (d. 1961)**
Tim Spencer	**Tenor Vocals (left 1936, rejoined 1942, left 1945)**
Lloyd Perryman	**Tenor Vocals, Guitar (joined 1936/d.1977)**
Pat Brady	**Stand-up Bass, Vocals, Comedy (joined 1938)**
Ken Carson	**Tenor Vocals (1942-47)**
Deuce Spriggens	**Stand-up Bass, Vocals, Comedy**
Shug Fisher	**Stand-up Bass, Vocals, Comedy**
Ken Curtis	**Baritone Vocals (joined 1945, left 1952)**
Tommy Doss	**Baritone Vocals, Fiddle (joined 1949)**
Dale Warren	**Vocals (joined 1952)**
Roy Lanham	**Guitar, Vocals (joined 1958)**
Luther Nallie	**Lead Vocals (joined 1968)**
Doye O'Dell	**Guitar, Vocals**
Rusty Richards	**Tenor Vocals**
Billy Armstrong	**Fiddle**
Billy Liebert	**Accordion**
Rome Johnson	**Vocals (joined 1977)**

The Sons of the Pioneer were the premier vocal and instrumental group within Western music. They sang, played and acted in numerous movies (see Movie Section), and their recordings remain the benchmark for all other groups. The impact of Bob Nolan's creation of the Western-style of three-part harmony singing is still felt in acts such as Riders in the Sky and Sons of the San Joaquin.

The origin of the group goes back to 1931, when Roy Rogers (then Len Slye) advertised for another singer to join the Rocky Mountaineers on radio KGFJ in California. Bob Nolan (b. Robert Clarence Nobles, April 1, 1908, New Brunswick, Canada), who had been living on the beach, answered the advertisement and joined the group. Shortly after, a friend of Bob's, Bill "Slumber" Nichols, was added on fiddle. Because money was short, Bob soon left the group and in response to another advertisement, Tim Spencer (b. Verne Spencer, July 7, 1908, Webb City, Missouri) came on board.

Rogers, Nichols and Spencer soon left the group and joined the International Cowboys, a group led by Bennie Nawahi. However, this didn't work and the trio formed O-Bar-O Cowboys and toured the Southwest, without success, except that Roy and Tim met their wives. Bill Nichols decided to call it a day and became a golf caddie in Beverly Hills. In the fall of 1933, Roy joined the Texas Outlaws, a group led by Jack Lefevre, playing on KFWB Hollywood and began to rehearse with Nolan and Spencer. However, they also joined the Texas Outlaws.

Bob had by now started to develop his now legendary songwriting skills and he would soon be joined by Tim Spencer. It became apparent to the radio station that the trio deserved their own slot and so the Pioneer Trio was created. Deciding to enlarge the group, they sought out fiddler and bass singer Hugh Farr (b. December 6, 1903, Llano, Texas), who insisted that they audition for him. When he heard them play some eight of Bob's songs, he quickly enrolled. Their name Sons of the Pioneers arose from a faux pas by announcer, Harry Hall, who introduced them as such on March 3, 1934. He explained that as they were too young to be pioneers, they could be rightly referred to as "sons of the pioneers."

That year, they recorded for the Standard Recording Company, under producer Jerry King. They recorded some 300 songs, and the transcriptions were issued on 12" discs that were sent to radio stations around the country. Even at this stage, the Sons of the Pioneers became an influence on budding musicians, both for their songs and their harmonies.

The group expanded to a quintet at the end of 1934, by the addition of Hugh Farr's brother, guitarist Karl (b. April 25, 1909, Rochelle, Texas). The following year, the group signed with Decca Records, being the third act to join the new label, after Stuart Hamblen and Bing Crosby. The same year, they signed with Columbia Pictures and they appeared with Charles Starrett in *The Old Homestead*. In all, they appeared in 31 movies with Starrett from 1935 through *Outlaws of the Panhandle*, in 1941.

In 1936, immediately after the Texas centennial, Tim left the group following an argument. He was replaced by Lloyd Perryman

The legendary **Sons of the Pioneers**

(b. January 29, 1917, Ruth, Arkansas), who was a baritone, but sang tenor in the group. In 1937, they signed with Columbia Records, with Art Satherley producing. They recorded in October of that year, but by the time of their December recording session, Roy was already on his way to a solo career.

The following year, Pat Brady replaced Roy as singer and became the group's funny man. While touring that year, they recorded in excess of 200 tracks for NBC's Orthacoustic Transcription series, which took place in Chicago. During 1941, Tim Spencer returned to the fold, and at the end of that year, the Sons of the Pioneers joined Roy at Republic Pictures. They stayed with Roy until 1948, and both Bob and Tim contributed many wonderful songs to these movies.

With the advent of WWII, Lloyd and Pat went on active duty to Europe and the South Pacific theaters respectively. During their absence, they were replaced by tenor Ken Carson (who stayed in the group until 1947) and stand-up bass player and singer Deuce Spriggens. Spriggens was later replaced by George "Shug" Fisher. He left in 1945, when Pat returned, but appeared for their December 14, 1949, recording session.

In 1945, they signed with RCA Victor and remained on the label until 1969. During the period 1945 through 1949, the Sons of the Pioneers made several appearances on the Country singles chart, and their hits were: *Stars and Stripes on Iwo Jima* (Top 5, 1945), *No One to Cry To* (Top 10, 1946), *Baby Doll* (Top 5), *Cool Water* (Top 5), *Cigareetes, Whuskey, Wild Wild Women* (Top 5) and *Tear Drops in My Heart* (Top 5, all 1947), *Tumbling Tumbleweeds* (Top 15) and *Cool Water* (Top 10, both 1948) and *My Best to You* (Top 15) and *Room Full of Roses* (Top 10, both 1949).

In 1949, Tim Spencer decided to leave the group after suffering problems with his voice, but continued his association with the Pioneers by becoming their manager and opened up a Gospel music publishing house. He was replaced by baritone Ken Curtis. In 1949, Bob Nolan also left, tired of performing, and was replaced by Tommy Doss (b. Lloyd Thomas Doss). His voice, so similar to Nolan's, ensured continuity of sound. In 1952, Ken Curtis decided to leave the group for a career in the movies. He in time became Festus in the long-running TV series *Gunsmoke*. Dale Warren replaced him, and it is often considered that the vocal trio of Perryman, Doss and Warren recorded the best sides made by the group.

In a fit of pique, Hugh Farr left the group in 1958, because he felt that his contribution to the success of the Pioneers was not acknowledged. Three years later, his brother Karl died suddenly (September 20, 1961, Springfield, Massachusetts). Karl was replaced by the good natured guitarist Roy Lanham. In 1968, Luther Nallie joined as lead singer, and six years later, Tim Spencer died (April 26, 1976, Apple Valley, California). When Lloyd Perryman died (May 31, 1977, Colorado Springs, Colorado), Dale Warren took over the leadership of the group. Both Hugh Farr and Bob Nolan passed away in 1980, on March 17 (Casper, Wyoming) and June 16 (Los Angeles), respectively.

In 1971, both Bob Nolan and Tim Spencer were elected to the Nashville Songwriters Hall of Fame. In 1976, the group was immortalized on the Hollywood Walk of Fame. In 1980, the Sons of the Pioneers were inducted into the Country Music Hall of Fame.

The songs of Bob Nolan and Tim Spencer, in particular, should be mentioned, because they have become the backbone of Western music. Bob wrote *Tumbling Tumbleweeds, Cool Water, Trail Herding Cowboy, A Cowboy Has to Sing, One More Ride, Way Out There* and *Song of the Bandit*, among many others, while Tim wrote *Cigareetes, Whuskey and Wild Wild Women, Careless Kisses* and *Room Full of Roses*, also among many others. For the movies, they often had to write on demand, as scripts were changed, and always came up with songs that have become Western classics.

The Pioneers still perform around the country and in 1993, they began work on an album, ***Johnny Western and the Sons of the Pioneers and Friends***, which was sidetracked by Johnny having to undergo quintuple heart bypass surgery and then Dale Warren had to contend with triple bypass surgery (he had already undergone quintuple surgery some years earlier).

RECOMMENDED ALBUMS:

"25 Favorite Cowboy Songs" (RCA Victor)(1956) [Re-released by Stetson UK in the original sleeve (1988)]
"The Sons of the Pioneers Sing Hymns of the Cowboy" (RCA Victor)(1963)
"The Original Pioneer Trio Sings Songs of the Hills & Plains (1934-1935)" (American Folk Music)
"Sons of the Pioneers (Lucky U Ranch Broadcasts 1951-1953)" (American Folk Music)
"The Sons of the Pioneers" (Columbia Historic Edition)(1982)
"20 of the Best" (RCA UK)(1985)
"Cool Water" (Bear Family Germany)
"Teardrops in My Heaven" (Bear Family Germany)(1987)
"A Hundred and Sixty Acres" (Bear Family Germany)(1987)
"Land Beyond the Sun" (Bear Family Germany)(1987)
Bear Family has also released two volumes of Standard Radio Transcriptions and three volumes of Radio Transcriptions.

SONS OF THE WEST

When Formed: **1936**
Members:

Son Lansford	**Fiddle**
Leonard Seago	**Fiddle**
Clifford Wells	**Banjo**
Freddie Dean	**Guitar, Vocals**
Jimmie Meek	**Bass, Lead Vocals**
Billy Briggs	**Steel Guitar**
Pat Trotter	**Fiddle, Vocals**
Jess Robertson	**Banjo**
Jess Williams	**Guitar, Vocals**
Loren Mitchell	**Piano**
Buck Buchanan	**Fiddle**

One of the numerous Western Swing bands established by a relative of Bob Wills, the Sons of the West were for most of their existence headquartered in Amarillo. Founder Son Lansford, one of Wills' cousins, left the Texas Playboys to start the group, which was based at Amarillo's Rainbow Gardens dance hall.

Shortly afterward, Lansford left to rejoin Wills, leaving Jimmie Meek in charge of the Sons of the West. Meek, a native of Oklahoma, came to Lansford's attention as a result of performances on WLS Chicago.

For a group with a relatively short life span the Sons of the West had a high personnel turnover rate, 11 people being members of the band at various times. An especially important addition came in 1938, when steel guitarist Billy Briggs joined. An admirer of Milton Brown's steel player, Bob Dunn, Briggs developed his own unique style of playing. He added a seventh string to his instrument and played three-string syncopated chords, innovations that made him one of the most individualistic of Western Swing instrumentalists. Briggs left the Sons of the West in 1939 to form his own group, Swinging Steel, but later returned for the band's final recording session.

Never a big name nationally, the Sons of the West nonetheless had a reputation as a quality unit. Indeed, they got their first recording session, for Decca, without even an audition. On this September 1938 date they cut a mix of Tin Pan Alley songs, like *Am I Blue*, and Pop standards like *Spanish Cavalier*. Although Dave Kapp of Decca was reportedly very enthusiastic about this band, they moved to Columbia for what proved to be their last session. In March 1941 they produced their most popular number, *Sally's Got a Wooden Leg*. The Sons of the West probably would have had a longer career had not WWII intervened. Their ranks were decimated by the draft and the band soon broke up. Briggs later helped form the XIT Boys with Jess Williams and Pat Trotter and in 1951 had his biggest hit with the novelty song *Chew Tobacco Rag*. Meek retired from playing music to run a music store in Amarillo.

RECOMMENDED ALBUM:

"Sons of the West" (Texas Rose)

SOUTHER, HILLMAN, FURAY BAND

When Formed: **1974**

Members:

J.D. Souther	**Guitars, Vocals**
Chris Hillman	**Bass Guitar, Guitars, Mandolin, Vocals**
Richie Furay	**Guitars, Vocals**

Other Musicians:

Paul Harris	**Keyboards**
Al Perkins	**Steel Guitar, Dobro, Bass Guitar**
Jim Gordon	**Drums**
Joe Lala	**Percussion**
Glenn Frey	**Vocals**
James Guercio	**Guitars**
Don Henley	**Vocals**
Ron Grinel	**Drums**

Although short-lived, the Souther, Hillman, Furay Band was probably the first Country-Rock supergroup. Every member of the group, not just the front trio of J.D. Souther, Chris Hillman and Richie Furay, had paid their musical dues in the cream of West Coast Country and Country-Rock bands.

J.D. (sometimes known as John David) Souther (b. November 3, 1945, Detroit, Michigan, and raised in Amarillo, Texas) started playing with Glenn Frey in Longbranch Pennywhistle, who recorded an album for Amos in 1970 and whose members included James Burton, Buddy Emmons, Ry Cooder and Doug Kershaw. He then played with Glenn as a duo and when Frey joined the Eagles, J.D. went solo. He became a prolific writer and co-wrote *Best of My Love* (the Eagles, 1974) and wrote *I Can Almost See It, Don't Cry Now* and *The Fast One* (all 1973), *Faithless Love* (1974) and *Prisoner in Disguise* and *Silver Blue* (both 1975) (all recorded by former girlfriend Linda Ronstadt). J.D. became a session player appearing on albums by Kate Taylor (James Taylor's sister) and Linda Ronstadt.

Chris Hillman (see separate entry and Desert Rose Band) had been a member of the Hillmen (with Vern & Rex Gosdin and Don Parmley), the Byrds, Flying Burrito Brothers and Stephen Stills' Manassas. Richie Furay (b. May 9, 1944, Yellow Springs, Ohio) was a founding member of Buffalo Springfield in 1966 and Poco in 1968.

For their first self-titled album, in 1974, the trio brought in session players Al Perkins, Paul Harris, Jim Gordon and Joe Lala. Perkins had played steel on sessions for the Flying Burrito Brothers, Alex Harvey, Rita Coolidge, Country Gazette and the Eagles. He was also featured on the Rolling Stones' ***Exile on Main Street***. Paul Harris, also a much-in-demand sessionman, had played on sessions for artists as diverse as Richie Havens and B.B. King. Gordon had formerly played with Derek & the Dominoes and had co-written with Eric Clapton the classic Rock number *Layla*. Joe Lala had played percussion for Joe Walsh and Dionne Warwick, among many others.

The first album on Asylum was produced by Richie Podolor, who had been the guitarist on Sandy Nelson's drum-based instrumentals in the late 50's and early 60's. The album yielded the Top 30 Pop hit *Fallin' in Love*. By the time of their second album in 1975, entitled ***Trouble in Paradise***, Ron Grinel had replaced Jim Gordon. Grinel had appeared on albums by Joe Walsh and Keith Moon. In addition, Eagles members Glenn Frey and Don Henley lent a hand on backup vocals and former Beach Boy associate James Guercio played guitar.

Following this album, J.D. Souther went on to be a much-in-demand session player and singer, appearing on albums by Bonnie Raitt, the Eagles, Rita Coolidge and Karla Bonoff (among many others) and a solo career. In 1979, J.D. had a Top 10 Pop hit with *You're Only Lonely*, on Columbia. The single gave him his first Country chart entry, reaching the Top 60. In 1981, J.D. teamed up with James Taylor for a Top 15 Pop hit, *Her Town Too*. The following year, J.D. had a duet with Linda Ronstadt, *Sometimes You Just Can't Win*, which went Top 30 on the Country chart. Since then J.D.'s career seems to be treading water and he still appears on records singing back-up. Chris Hillman eventually put together the Desert Rose Band, while Richie had a short-term solo career and in 1979 had a Top 40 hit with *I Still Have Dreams* on Asylum. In 1980, he appeared with Poco at their reunion concert.

RECOMMENDED ALBUMS:

"Souther, Hillman, Furay Band" (Asylum)(1974)
"Trouble in Paradise" (Asylum)(1975)

SOUTHERN PACIFIC

When Formed: **1985**

Members:

Stu Cook	**Bass Guitar, Vocals**
Kurt Howell	**Keyboards, Vocals**
Keith Knudsen	**Drums, Percussion, Vocals**
John McFee	**Guitar, Pedal Steel, Dobro, Violin, Vocals**
Tim Goodman	**Lead Vocals, Guitar, Synthesizer (left 1986)**
David Jenkins	**Guitar, Vocals (joined 1986)**

The major problem that Southern Pacific faced during their five-year existence was that they were too difficult to categorize. Although their roots were in Country-Rock, their attempts at being different from the then norm in Country music were not always accepted. In a way, it was also a matter of timing. If they had come along seven years later, it is almost certain that they could have become a major force. Listened to from the

Country-Rock group ***Southern Pacific***

perspective of the middle of the 1990's, they become a musical revelation.

The original members of the group had all paid their dues. When the Doobie Brothers ended in 1982, Keith Knudsen and John McFee turned to session work. Prior to their time with the Doobies, McFee had played in Clover with Huey Lewis, while Knudsen had been a short-term replacement for John Ware in Emmylou Harris' Hot Band. McFee met up withTim Goodman, who had played with New Grass Revival and produced the Goodman 1980 solo album ***Footsteps in the Night***. The three session players started to work together and appeared on albums by Johnny Cash, Nicolette Larsen, Karen Brooks and the Kendalls.

They decided to try to put a band together and recruited ex-Presley musicians Jerry Scheff (bass) and Glen D. Harden (keyboards), to record some demos. Jim Ed Norman, the head of Warner Brothers Records in Nashville, heard one of the demos and signed them to a record deal with the label. They had to come up with a name. They tried the Tex Pistols (they were warned off by Sex Pistols manager Malcolm McLaren), El Dorado, Rodeo Drive and the Adobe Brothers. They had a naming contest within Warner Brothers and Jeff Hanna from the Nitty Gritty Dirt Band came up with "Southern Pacific."

When Scheff and Harden left to return to session work, they were replaced by Kurt Howell, a Warner Brothers staff writer, and Stu Cook, who had been an integral part of Creedence Clearwater Revival and had been working as a studio engineer and had just returned to playing.

Their debut eponymous album was released in 1985, to great critical acclaim. In particular, Bob Oermann, the doyen of Country music journalists, raved about their performances. They opened for Hank Williams, Jr., the Oak Ridge Boys and Reba McEntire. They played on Willie Nelson's Farm Aid playing Bruce Springsteen's *Pink Cadillac*, with Emmylou Harris (this song should be re-mixed and re-released for the line-dancers!). The material came from various sources, but included songs written by John McFee and Bay Area writer Andre Pessis. Their first chart entry, *Somebody's Gonna Love Me Tonight*, reached the Top 60, but their next release, Tom Petty's *Thing About You*, with Emmylou guesting, made it to the Top 15. They ended the year with the Top 20 record *Perfect Stranger*.

The following year, they had their first Top 10 record, a slice of rock'n'roll called *Reno Bound*. They came up with their second album, ***Killbilly Hill***, which, like its predecessor, had a cover illustration by Lori Lohstoeter. On this album lead vocals were shared between Goodman, McFee and Howell. Two tracks were released from it during the year, *A Girl Like Emmylou* (Top 20) and the title track (Top 40). They were named "Top New Country Group" by *Billboard*, in October that year.

In January 1987, it was announced that Tim Goodman had decided to leave the group. He was replaced by David Jenkins, formerly with Pablo Cruise. The first single released from the third album, ***Zuma***, was *Midnight Highway*, which reached No.14, in 1988. They followed up with their most successful release, *New Shade of Blue*, which reached the Top 3, and the swingy *Honey I Dare You*, which made the Top 5. ***Zuma*** was to be the final album for David Jenkins and the group carried on as a four-piece, with McFee taking on lead vocal chores.

In 1989, the initial single, *All Is Lost*, which was co-written by Dave Gibson, now of the Gibson/Miller Band, reached the Top 20. This was followed by *Any Way the Wind Blows*, which was featured in the Clint Eastwood movie *Pink Cadillac*, and was another Top 5 record. Their final single of the year was *Time's Up*, on which they debuted with Carlene Carter. This and *Any Way the Wind Blows* came from their final album, ***County Line***. Their opening single, in 1990, was, surprisingly, Del Shannon's *I Go to Pieces*. Surprisingly, because it was sung a cappella, like the New York doo-wop vocal groups. This only reached in the Top 40 and was followed by their final chart single, *Reckless*, which also peaked in the Top 40. Sadly, the group is no more, having decided to call it a day, and the music world was deprived of their tight playing and superb harmonies. Kurt Howell has gone on to a solo career with Reprise.

RECOMMENDED ALBUMS:

"Southern Pacific" (Warner Brothers)(1985)
"Hillbilly Hill" (Warner Brothers)(1986)
"Zuma" (Warner Brothers)(1988)
"County Line" (Warner Brothers)(1989)
"Greatest Hits" (Warner Brothers)(1991) [Just for the live version of "Pink Cadillac"]

RED SOVINE

(Singer, Songwriter, Guitar)

Given Name:	**Woodrow Wilson Sovine**
Date of Birth:	**July 17, 1918**
Where Born:	**Charleston, West Virginia**
Married:	**Norma Searls (dec'd.)**
Children:	**Roger, Bill, Mike, Janet**
Date of Death:	**April 4, 1980**

Red Sovine gained fame for his sentimental recitations—especially those with truck driver themes—yet he exhibited a wide variety of vocal skills in a long musical career. His life in music also sustained a longer series of alternating high and low points.

Red grew up in a poor family with recording artist Billy Cox for a kinsman and Johnnie Bailes (of Bailes Brothers fame) as an adolescent companion. He also came under the influence, via local radio station WCHS, of Frank Welling and Buddy Starcher, two musicians who in their own individual ways had mastered the technique of delivering sentimental recitations.

In their late teens, Red and Johnnie attempted musical careers, first as members of a band known as Jim Pike's Carolina Tar Heels, and then as a duet in which they dubbed themselves "the Singing Sailors." After failing to make a living at either WCHS or WWVA Wheeling, Red opted for a factory job at the New Deal-organized industrial community of Eleanor, West Virginia. The business prospered during WWII and Sovine worked his way up to a mid-level management position. He never completely left music, however, as he still did a program on local radio.

Meanwhile, the Bailes Brothers, who had found commercial success first at the *Grand Ole Opry* and then at KWKH in Shreveport, Louisiana, kept urging Red to get back into music full-time. In 1948 he finally yielded to the temptation and resumed his show business career, but was placed in a time slot at KWKH so early in the morning that he attracted few listeners and even fewer show dates. Red became discouraged and nearly quit the business, but then Hank Williams offered to help him get a better spot at his old workplace, station WFSA Montgomery, Alabama.

Red Sovine not only found a warm reception for himself and his music in Alabama, but Williams also helped him secure a contract with MGM Records. He had his first session in January 1949 and remained with the company until 1953, having a total of 28 released sides. Although he had no real hits with MGM, he did record a solid body of Honky-Tonk material that enhanced his musical standing. Meanwhile, in mid-1949, he returned to Shreveport, now in a prime-time daily slot for sponsor Johnny Fair Syrup, as a star of the *Louisiana Hayride*. He replaced Hank Williams, who then advanced to WSM and the *Opry*.

In 1952 and 1953, another *Hayride* star, Webb Pierce, enjoyed a string of national Country hits and induced Red Sovine to come to Nashville to front his band. "The Wondering Boy" also persuaded Decca officials to sign his protégé to a contract and he initiated his new relationship with a January 12, 1954, session.

While none of Red's solo vocals on Decca made the charts, he scored with a duet of *Are You Mine?* with Goldie Hill which reached the Top 15 in the spring of 1955, and early 1956 duets with Webb Pierce, *Why Baby Why* (No.1) and *Little Rosa* (No.5). The flip-side of the latter was the solo *Hold Everything (Till I Get Home),* which went Top 5. This success also induced Red to strike out on his own and he joined the cast of the *Grand Ole Opry* briefly, only to drop

The immortal ***Red Sovine***

out when he received an opportunity to tour with the *Philip Morris Caravan*. He remained with Decca until 1959, having released nearly forty sides, which included a few numbers like *Juke Joint Johnny* that had a Rockabilly feel. In order to earn a living, Red toured heavily, often playing smaller clubs.

In the meantime, Sovine signed with Don Pierce's Starday Records and had several singles and two albums released on the label in 1961 and 1962. Finally, his 10th single release, *Dream House for Sale*, gave him his first solo hit for the label, in the early weeks of 1964. A year and a half later, Red had his first real superhit with *Giddy-up Go*, the first of his truck driver recitations, which was a No.1 for 6 weeks and crossed over to the Pop Top 90.

Red started out 1967 with the Top 20 hit *I Didn't Jump the Fence* and then went Top 10 with another recitation entitled *Phantom 309*. These seemed to indicate that this type of number was his key to success.

By this time, Starday had released 14 albums and 33 singles by the "Red Head," in addition to numerous cuts on mixed-artist albums and re-releases on the budget label Nashville. This ranked him with Carl Story and the Lewis Family as being among Starday's most prolific artists. Also in the later 60's, Red's son Roger Sovine recorded several numbers mostly on the Imperial label, including a couple that made the charts, the most successful of which was *Cullman, Alabam*, in 1968. Roger later opted for a career in the business end of the music industry.

In between his longer contract periods for Starday, Red did some additional recording. He cut an album for the Canadian label Arc, half an album for the budget label Somerset and even had a single released on RCA Victor and three on RIC. During an inactive period for Starday in the early 70's, Sovine switched to Chart Records and did two albums and had three singles reach the charts, of which the most successful was *It'll Come Back*, in 1974.

However, when Moe Lytle rejuvenated Starday as Starday Gusto in 1975, he soon came up with another number for Red that equaled and probably surpassed *Giddy-up Go* in popularity and impact. *Teddy Bear* told the story of a little invalid boy, his CB radio, and his trucker friends in a style that went counter to all the current Country trends. Sovine not only revived sentimentalism at a time when it seemed an anachronism, but provided for himself another No.1 hit that briefly made the Pop Top 40 and was Certified Gold (it later became a hit in the U.K.). A follow-up single, *Little Joe*, told the story of a trucker who had lost his sight in an accident and his faithful dog, but it only had modest success. Sovine continued recording, but had no more hits. One of his last recitations, *The Little Family Soldier*, in 1980, recounted the ageless Country music theme of the abused child and alcoholic parents.

On April 4, 1980, Red Sovine suffered a heart attack while driving his van through Nashville. That, combined with the injuries sustained in the subsequent accident, proved fatal. However, he left a legacy of more than 300 recordings that spanned five decades. Earlier in his career, he had been a highly capable if unexceptional singer who found more success in talking than in singing. As Mike Hanes, a Nashville deejay friend, wrote in 1976 of Red, "He milks every drop of meaning out of every song [*sic*] he records." He also deserves credit for the encouragement he gave Charley Pride in persuading him to come to Nashville to try to make it as a Country singer. This action and foresight displayed considerable courage and vision. IMT

RECOMMENDED ALBUMS:

"Red Sovine" (MGM)(1957) [Re-issued in reduced form on Metro]
"Gone But Not Forgotten" (Castle)(ca. 1981) [Contains 10 MGM and four Decca numbers not on other albums]
"The One and Only Red Sovine" (Starday and Official)(1961)
"Golden Country Ballads of the '60's" (Starday)(1962)
"Red Sovine" (Decca DL 74445)(1964) [Re-issued in reduced form on Vocalion]
"Little Rosa" (Starday)(1965)
"Giddy-Up Go" (Starday)(1965)
"Town and Country Action" (Starday)(1965)
"Phantom 309" (Starday and Power Pak)(1967)
"Sunday with Sovine" (Starday)(1968)
"Classic Narrations" (Starday)(1969)
"I Know You're Married but I Love You Still" (Starday 1970)
"The Greatest Grand Ole Opry" (Chart)(1972)
"It'll Come Back" (Chart)(1974)
"Teddy Bear" (Starday Gusto)(1976)
"Woodrow Wilson Sovine" (Starday Gusto)(1977)
"16 Greatest Hits" (Starday Gusto)(1977)

"16 All Time Favorites" (Starday Gusto)(1977)
"16 New Gospel Songs" (Gusto)(1978)
[Sovine Starday Gusto material has been issued and re-issued in a baffling array of releases too numerous to list; this compilation attempts to list mainly the first album release.]

LARRY SPARKS

(Singer, Songwriter, Guitar, Mandolin, Dobro)
Given Name: Larry Sparks
Date of Birth: September 15, 1947
Where Born: Lebanon, Ohio
Married: Unknown
Children: three

Larry Sparks has gained a deserved reputation as one of the best second-generation Bluegrass lead vocalists, guitarists and bandleaders.

Born and reared in Lebanon, Ohio, of Kentucky parentage, Larry began listening to Country radio and soon afterward initiated the process of seriously learning guitar. By his mid-teens, he was good enough to play lead in local Bluegrass, Country and Rock bands. Bluegrass, however, became his music of choice and in 1966, he cut a single for Jalyn and filled in as lead guitarist with the Stanley Brothers' Clinch Mountain Boys, on their trips to Ohio. Two months after Carter Stanley's death, Larry joined the Clinch Mountain Boys and recorded five albums with the group through 1969, three on King and two on Jalyn.

At the end of 1969, Larry left the Stanley band a seasoned professional and formed the Lonesome Ramblers. Early members included Joe Isaacs on banjo and sister Bernice Sparks on rhythm guitar. They recorded initially for the local Pine Tree label, beginning with an album which spotlighted Larry's skills on lead guitar, but soon moved on to Old Homestead and Starday. By this time, his group had acquired a pair of flashy sidemen in the personages of banjoist Mike Lilly and mandolinist Wendy Miller. They did not remain in the band for much over a year, but did help to mold its image as an exciting group.

Bluegrass great ***Larry Sparks***

Meanwhile, Larry developed a repertoire of songs through which the Bluegrass fan could readily identify him. These would come to include such numbers as *Brand New Broken Heart*, *Goodbye Little Darlin'*, *Green Pastures in the Sky* and *I Can't Go on Loving You*. Later he added other standards like *Don't Neglect the Rose*, *A Face in the Crowd*, *Girl at the Crossroads Bar* and *Love of the Mountains*; the latter of which came to be nearly as much identified with him as with the Lost and Found.

Larry did quite a bit of label hopping in the 70's and 80's. He recorded four albums for Robert Trout's King Bluegrass label, a Hank Williams tribute for County, one each for June Appal and Acoustic Revival, and two for his own Lesco Records. Old Homestead reissued some of his Pine Tree items as well as some more original material, and later the Lesco masters. By the mid-80's, however, his new recordings had become pretty much confined to periodic releases on David Freeman's Virginia-based Rebel firm, a company that bought the rights to King Bluegrass.

Meanwhile, Sparks relocated somewhat from his long-time residence in Ohio's Miami Valley to Richmond, Indiana. He continues as a popular figure on the Bluegrass festival circuit and probably ranks as the most influential among those traditionalists who has emerged from the "Stanley school" of Bluegrass while "manag[ing] yourself good" and as he told John Wright, "have something different to offer the people." IMT

RECOMMENDED ALBUMS:
"Ramblin' Guitar" (Pine Tree)(1970)
"New Gospel Songs" (Pine Tree)(1971) [Re-released as "Green Pastures in the Sky" (Old Homestead)(1982)]
"Ramblin Bluegrass" (Starday and Gusto)(1972)
"Bluegrass Old and New" (Old Homestead)(1972)
"Pickin' and Singin'" (Pine Tree)(1973) [Re-released as "Where the Dim Lights are the Dimmest" [Old Homestead)(1982)]
"Where the Sweet Waters Flow" (Old Homestead)(1973)
"The Lonesome Sounds" (Old Homestead)(1974)
"The Footsteps of Tradition" (King Bluegrass)(1974)
"Sparklin' Bluegrass" (King Bluegrass)(1975)
"You Could Have Called" (King Bluegrass)(1976)
"Christmas in the Hills" (King Bluegrass)(1976)
"Thank You Lord" (Old Homestead)(1976)
"Early and Essential, Volume I and II" (Old Homestead)(1980) [Note: Re-isssued from Jalyn and Pine Tree singles, plus a re-mastered "Bluegrass Old and New"]
"Larry Sparks Sings Hank Williams" (County)(1977)
"Kind'a Lonesome" (Lesco)(1979) [Re-released with added cuts as "A Face in the Crowd" on Old Homestead (1985)]
"John Deere Tractor" (Rebel)(1980)
"Live in Concert" (Lesco)(1980) [Re-released with added cuts on Old Homestead (1985)]
"It's Never Too Late" (June Appal)(1980)
"Ramblin' Letters" (Acoustic Revival)(1981)
"Dark Hollow" (Rebel)(1982)
"The Best of Larry Sparks" (Rebel)(1983) [From King Bluegrass and County masters)
"The Testing Times" (Rebel)(1983) [partly from King Bluegrass masters)
"Blue Sparks" (Rebel)(1983)
"Lonesome Guitar" (Rebel)(1985)
"Gonna Be Movin'" (Rebel)(1986)
"Silver Reflections" (Rebel REB)(1988)
"Classic Bluegrass" (Rebel)(1989) [Re-issued from earlier material]
"The Rock I Stand On" (Rebel)(1994)

BILLIE JO SPEARS

(Singer, Songwriter)
Given Name: Billie Jean Spears
Date of Birth: January 14, 1937
Where Born: Beaumont, Texas
Married: 1. Charles Wilson (div.)
2. Doug Walton (div.)
3. (Div.)
4. (Div.)
5. Terry

Although B.J. is not as big as she once was in the U.S., she still retains a loyal following in Europe, especially the U.K. and Ireland. She is one of the few Country singers to have crossed over to the U.K. Pop charts.

Billie Jo's professional career began in 1950, when, as a 13-year-old, she appeared at Keel Auditorium, Houston, with Arlie Duff, George Jones, Tommy Collins, Jean Shepard, Sonny Burns and Blackie Crawford and the Western Cherokees. A family friend was songwriter Jack Rhodes, who was instrumental in B.J. recording her debut side for Abbott Records, in 1953, at Rhodes' studio in Mineola. The track, *Too Old for Toys, Too Young for Boys*, was the flip-side of Mel Blanc's *I Dess I Dotta Doe* and was credited to Billie Jo Moore. She guested on the *Louisiana Hayride*, singing the song.

However, she was still at school and her career was severely curtailed until she graduated. She worked as a secretary and also became a drive-in bellhop (fender lizard). However, her music career beckoned and she became a singer at Yvonne's Night Club. She moved to Mineola, where she and Rhodes wrote songs and she sang. They made forays to Nashville with their songs without any success. The legendary producer Pete Drake was interested in what Billie Jean was doing and she recorded quite a few demos for him.

International favorite ***Billie Jo Spears***

In 1964, she moved to Nashville and signed with United Artists, where she was produced by Kelso Herston, without success. When he moved to Capitol, B.J. followed and at last success came her way. She hit the Top 50 with *He's Got More Love in His Little Finger*, her second release (her first being *Harper Valley P.T.A.*), but it was her next single, *Mr. Walker, It's All Over*, that did the trick. It reached the Top 5 and crossed over to the Pop Top 80. This resulted in her being named *Cash Box*'s "Most Promising Female Singer of the Year." However, this was not yet Billie Jo's time and her subsequent releases on the label had mixed responses, her most successful being *Marty Gray* and Tammy Wynette's song *I Stayed Long Enough* (both in 1970) and *It Could 'A Been Me*, the following year. Her 1969 single, *Stepchild*, although not a major hit, led to her calling her group the Stepchildren. They would later be renamed Owlkatraz (she collects owls!).

During 1970, B.J. was a part of the Capitol Caravan that visited Europe, and her album ***Country Girl*** was Certified Gold in the U.K. However, B.J. was starting to suffer with vocal problems, having a nodule on her cords. This affected her for about a year and she could not speak for six months. She then recorded for some minor labels including Brite Star and Cutlass. She was again ill in 1974, when she developed polyps on her cords and the doctors feared that she wouldn't sing again and she once more had a six-month-period of silence.

By the end of 1974, she returned to United Artists Records, where she was produced by Larry Butler. Although her debut single, *See the Funny Little Clown,* only made the Top 80, it was with her next release that B.J.'s time came. Roger Bowling's *Blanket on the Ground* (a song she didn't initially like) went to No.1 during early 1975 and crossed to the Pop Top 80. The single also went to the U.K. Pop Top 10. The two singles that year, *Stay Away from the Apple Tree* and *Silver Wings and Golden Rings*, both went Top 20.

The following year was highly successful for Billie Jo. It started with the Top 5 record, *What I've Got in Mind*, which was also a Top 5 single in the U.K., and was followed by *On the Rebound*, a Top 30 duet with Del Reeves. After this came another Top 5 solo hit, *Misty Blue,* and a Top 50 duet with Del Reeves, *Teardrops Will Kiss the Morning Dew*. She wrapped up the year with the Top 20 single *Never Did Like Whiskey*. In the U.K., *Sing Me an Old Fashioned Song* became a Top 40 record.

B.J. stayed with United Artists and its successor, Liberty Records, until 1981. Her most successful singles were: 1977: *I'm Not Easy* (Top 15), *If You Want Me* (Top 10) and *Too Much Is Not Enough* (Top 20); 1978: *Lonely Hearts Club* (Top 20), *I've Got to Go* (Top 20), *'57 Chevrolet* (Top 20) and *Love Ain't Gonna Wait for Us* (Top 25); 1979: *I Will Survive* (Top 25, Grammy-nominated and also a U.K. Top 50 success), *Livin' Our Love Together* (Top 25) and *Rainy Days and Stormy Nights* (Top 25); 1980: *Standing Tall* (Top 15), *Natural Attraction* (Top 40) and *Your Good Girl's Gonna Go Bad* (Top 15). In 1976, she became the ACM's "Most Promising Female Vocalist." She was named "Female Vocalist of the Year" in both 1980 and 1981, by *Texas Proud* magazine.

During this period, B.J. consolidated her fan base in the U.K. She appeared at the Wembley Festival in 1977 and then toured that year with Carl Perkins and the Dillards, as the Nashville Cavalcade. It was her appearance at Wembley that turned into a most important time personally, for she started to talk to the courtesy bus driver, Doug Walton, and when she appeared the following year, she again met Doug and they married in Nashville, in 1980. Following the success of *'57 Chevrolet*, B.J. did a 40-date tour of the U.K. with George Hamilton IV. When she did her London date on that tour, she was met by three Chevy owners. B.J. offered to buy the cars without success. That year, she also toured the U.K. with Ronnie Prophet, Vernon Oxford and Lloyd Green. She appeared at Wembley again, in 1979, and at Peterborough Festival, in 1985 and 1987.

On the recording front, she released the 1983 album ***B.J.—Billie Jo Spears Today***, which was recorded in Ireland and came out on the Irish Ritz label. She then had a double-sided minor hit with *Midnight Blue* (Top 40) and *Midnight Love* (Top 60), on the Parliament label, in 1984. That same year, she signed with the U.K. Premier label and released ***We Just Came Apart at the Dreams***. Two years later, Premier issued ***Midnight Blue***, which contained the 1984 Premier album tracks plus the two Parliament tracks.

In 1993, B.J., whose hobbies include roller skating, fishing and swimming, underwent heart bypass surgery, but she has now recovered and continues to perform.

RECOMMENDED ALBUMS:

"Country Girl" (Capitol)(1970)
"Blanket on the Ground" (United Artists)(1975)
"By Request: Del & Billie Jo" (United Artists)(1976) [With Del Reeves]
"The Best of Billie Jo Spears" (Capitol)(1979) [Released on Vine in U.K.]
"Billie Jo Singles Album" (United Artists)(1979)
"B.J.—Billie Jo Spears Today" (Ritz UK)(1983)
"Midnight Blue" (Premier UK)(1986)

G.T. "DAD" SPEER/ SPEER FAMILY, The

Given Name: George Thomas Speer
Date of Birth: 1891
Where Born: Fayetteville, Georgia
Married: Lena "Mom" Brock (d. 1967)
Children: Brock, Rosa Nell, Ben, Mary Tom
Date of Death: September 7, 1966
Members:
Pearl Claborn, Logan Claborn, Brock Speer, Rosa Nell Speer, Mary Tom Speer, Faye Speer, Joyce Black, Ben Speer, Anna Sanders Downing, Sue Chenault Dodge, Jeanne Johnson, Charles Yates, Sherrill "Sean" Neilsen, Harold Lane, Bill Itzel, Karen Apple, Daryl Williams, Susan Speer, Marc Speer, Brian Speer, Stephen Speer, Darin Speer, Tim Parton, David Gallagher

The Speer Family is America's First Family of Gospel Music. For over 70 years, they have been delighting audiences with a unique blend of traditional and middle-of-the-road Gospel.

G.T. Speer was born into a farming community and became a teacher at the Stamps-Baxter School of Music in Dallas and at the Vaughan School of Music, Lawrenceburg, Tennessee. In 1921, he formed the first Speer Quartet with his wife, Lena, who also played piano, and his sister and brother-in-law, Pearl and Logan Claborn. At the time, only quartets with male members were the norm. Dad thus broke down the barrier in Gospel music that had been dominated by male quartets.

At the time, it was also normal for radio programs to be a mix of Gospel and secular material, but the Speers sang only Gospel. They were told that it would not work but the Speers had faith that it would and soon they were playing Gospel music concerts and other

Gospel greats the ***Speer Family***

groups switched to all-Gospel programs. In 1925, the Claborns left the group and a new generation of Speers, Dad and Mom's children, filled the breach.

When Rosa Nell and Mary Tom left the group to get married, Brock's wife Faye joined the group but left to start a family, returning permanently when their children were grown. "Adopted" Speers joined the group, including Harold Lane, who was with the group for over 20 years. In 1946, the Speer Family cut their first commercial record. During the late 50's and early 60's, the group broadcast regularly on WLAC Nashville. Dad Speer died in 1966 and was the first inductee in the Deceased Category to the Gospel Music Hall of Fame. Mom died on October 6, 1967, and was the second inductee to the Hall of Fame in the same category, in 1972.

In 1969, the Speer Family received a Dove Award from the GMA as "Mixed Group of the Year." They were to repeat this honor in every year from then to 1977, except 1971 when there were no awards. Their other Dove Awards include "Album of the Year" in 1975 for ***I Just Feel Like Good Is About to Happen*** and in 1976 for ***Between the Cross and Heaven***. In addition, member Sue Chenault (from 1974, Chenault Dodge) won a Dove Award as "Female Vocalist of the Year" from 1972 through to 1974 and Jeanne Johnson did the same in 1975. The Speers, on Homeland Records since 1988, have also been nominated on five occasions for Grammy Awards, although to date, they have not taken home an award. In 1975, Brock Speer was inducted to the Gospel Music Hall of Fame in the Living Category.

The Speer Family's 60th anniversary, in 1981, was entered into the Congressional Record of the United States and SESAC honored them with a plaque that included the first commercial record recorded by the group. At the same time, the Benson Company released a commemorative anniversary album and produced a multi-media presentation that highlighted the 60-year history of the Speer Family in song. That year, Rosa Nell and Mary Tom rejoined the group on a part-time basis and when they participate in the group, they do a tribute to their parents, performing songs written or made famous by their father.

The current line-up of the Speer Family is Brock Speer, Faye Speer, Karen Apple, Tim Parton and David Gallagher.

RECOMMENDED ALBUMS:

"Masters of Gospel" (Benson)
"Love Grew Where the Blood Fell" (Benson)
"Saved to the Uttermost" (Homeland)(1988)
"He's Still in the Fire" (Homeland)(1989)
"Hallelujah Time" (Homeland)(1991)
"He Still Reigns" (Homeland)(1992)
"A Beautiful Day" (Homeland)(1993)

CARL T. SPRAGUE

(Singer, Songwriter, Guitar)

Given Name:	**Carl T. Sprague**
Date of Birth:	**May 10, 1895**
Where Born:	**near Houston, Texas**
Married:	**Lura Bess Mayo**
Children:	**Unknown**
Date of Death:	**1978**

Carl "Doc" Sprague is often referred to as the first cowboy singer on record. His August 1925 waxing of *When the Work's All Done This Fall* for Victor became a major success and paved the way for Jules Allen, the Cartwright Brothers, Harry McClintock and other authentic Western vocalists. Like some of the other pioneers in the music, Sprague never made a career of singing, but nonetheless emerged from retirement in his twilight years to make a few appearances at Folk festivals and cut some more records.

Sprague was born near Houston to a family that had extensive roots in farming and ranching and learned his cowboy songs as a youth around campfires. He had some authentic experiences as a ranch hand prior to entering Texas A & M College in 1915. His education was interrupted by two years of service with the U.S. Army Signal Corps during WWI. Back at Texas A & M, Carl resumed his studies, graduating in 1922. Although he originally intended to become a rancher, he joined the school's athletic department instead. Sprague spent the next 15 years as an assistant coach under the direction of the famed Dana X. Bible. He also worked with a band that appeared on the local college radio station for a 60-minute weekly show.

When Vernon Dalhart had a hit with *The Prisoner's Song*, Carl became inspired to attempt to record the cowboy songs he had learned in his youth. In the summer of 1925, he journeyed to Camden, New Jersey, with the intention of making phonograph discs. In early August, he waxed six numbers of which the coupling of *When the Work's All Done This Fall* and *Bad Companions* met with major success. Sprague's recordings consisted largely but not totally of traditional cowboy ballads.

Carl had another Victor session the following year, cutting six more songs, when he visited Camden while on his June honeymoon. He had two later recording opportunities in Savannah and Dallas in 1927 and 1929 respectively. His releases included some of the better-known cowboy ballads such as *Following the Cow Trail* (aka *Trail to Mexico*) and *Utah Carroll* as well as atypical ones like *The Last Longhorn* and *The Mormon Cowboy*. For the most part, his musical career was largely confined to his Victor offerings and occasional radio work.

After his last session in 1929, he remained inactive in music until after he had retired. Carl engaged in a variety of endeavors after departing from Texas A & M including operating a store, insurance sales, government employee, and serving in the U.S. Army again during WWII. He also participated in church activities in Bryan, Texas, where he continued to reside. In retirement, he appeared at some college concerts and Folk festivals including the University of Illinois and UCLA. In 1972 and 1974, he recorded albums for Bear Family which later appeared on compact disc. In addition, several of his old Victor sides have been released on anthologies of early cowboy songs. IMT

RECOMMENDED ALBUMS:

"The First Popular Singing Cowboy" (Bear Family Germany)(1973)
"Cowboy Songs from Texas" (Bear Family Germany) (1975)
"Classic Cowboy Songs" (Bear Family Germany)(1988)

JIM STAFFORD

(Singer, Songwriter, Guitar, Banjo, Harmonica, One-Man Band, Actor, Humorist)

Given Name:	**James Wayne Stafford**
Date of Birth:	**January 16, 1944**
Where Born:	**Eloise, Florida**
Married:	**1. (Div.)**
	2. Bobbie Gentry (m. 1978) (div.)
Children:	**Tyler**

When Jim Stafford became an international star in 1974 with *Spiders & Snakes*, he not only launched his own career but was also instrumental in helping launch the

Bellamy Brothers, because Jim had written the song with David Bellamy.

Jim's antecedents are rooted in Tennessee, where his forebears were Country musicians. His parents decided to relocate to Florida to pick citrus fruit, bringing their musical heritage with them. His father, Woody, who became a dry cleaner, played in a band called the Reelfoot Lake Stompers, while in Union City, Tennessee. By the time Jim was age 14, he was playing guitar in a rock'n'roll band in high school. He had wanted, at various times, to become a commercial artist and a preacher.

He decided to become a guitarist and when he graduated from high school, he headed straight for Nashville. He worked on the *Grand Ole Opry* backing Jumpin' Bill Carlisle and worked Kansas City with Carl Smith. While in Nashville, he met Kent Lavoie, who came to fame as Lobo, and Lavoie would play a major part in Jim's early career. While in Music City, Jim began playing with a drummer, but one day, the drummer quit, and Jim turned into a one-man band. In 1964, Jim entered *Ted Mack's Original Amateur Hour*, playing Chet Atkins' *Yankee Doodle and Dixie*, without success. He soon left Nashville and moved to Memphis and then Atlanta.

By now, Jim was writing his "off the wall" songs. He started writing these novelty songs because he felt he didn't have a good enough singing voice. Jim played go-go bars and was often called upon to provide humorous dialogue during the dancers' acts. While performing at the Shack Upon the Beach in Clearwater, Florida, he met up again with Lobo. Jim had written *Swamp Witch* and tried to pitch it at his friend, but Lobo felt that Jim should record it, and introduced him to producer Phil Gernhard. Mike Curb heard the song and liked what he heard and signed him to MGM Records, with Gernhard and Lobo producing.

In 1973, *Swamp Witch* became Jim's first Pop hit and reached the Top 40. However, it was the follow-up, *Spiders & Snakes*, that placed Jim in the international arena. It reached the Pop Top 3, Country Top 70, it was Certified Gold in 1974 and reached No.14 in the U.K. Jim followed up with the sexually ambiguous song *My Girl Bill*, which reached the Pop Top 15, the Country Top 70 and the U.K. Top 20. Next came another Top 10 Pop hit, *Wildwood Weed* (written by Jim and Don Bowman), which also went Top 60 on the Country chart. He ended the year with another novelty ditty, *Your Bulldog Drinks Champagne*, which went Top 25 on the Pop chart. That year, *Record World* listed Jim fourth in the "Top Male Vocalist" category, behind Elton John, Stevie Wonder and John Denver.

In 1975, Jim began the *Jim Stafford Show*, an ABC-TV summer series. The regulars on the show included Mel Blanc (the voice behind so many animated cartoon characters) and Deborah Allen (later a successful Nashville songwriter and singer). The show was produced by Stafford Entertainment, Inc./Fours Company. However, the series only ran for one season.

In such regard was Jim's guitar playing that in 1975, he was the subject of a feature in *Guitar Player* magazine, in which Jim related how he uses guitars made by Los Angeles-based guitar maker Arturo Valdez, who had also built Jim a revolutionary guitar banjo. In 1975, Jim had his last Pop hit for MGM and the last of his singles produced by Lobo and Phil Gernhard, entitled *I Got Stoned and I Missed It*. Around this time, Jim was based in Hollywood in an old Spanish villa once owned by the silent screen stars the Wayne Sisters. Jim's last two Pop entries were *Jasper* (Polydor, 1976) and *Turn Loose of My Leg* (Warner Brothers, 1977), but neither was very successful. In 1977, Jim won the *Esquire* magazine Lifestyle Award for Fashion, which proclaimed him as one of America's best-dressed men in the company of Bob Hope and Telly Savalas.

In 1978, Jim married singer Bobbie Gentry, but this marriage only survived for a couple of years. Jim, the consummate story-teller, had once said (before he and Bobbie married) that he couldn't understand Bobbie's *Ode to Billy Joe*. In 1980, Jim co-hosted *Those Amazing Animals* for ABC-TV with Burgess Meredith and Priscilla Presley and appeared in the Clint Eastwood movie *Any Which Way You Can*. From this came the wry *Cow Patti*, which gave Jim a Top 70 Country single the following year. In 1981, Jim co-hosted *Nashville on the Road* with Rex Allen, Jr., and Sue Powell. That year, Jim wrote three songs for the Walt Disney film *The Fox and the Hound*. Jim had two more Country chart entries, on Town House and Columbia, but neither made the Top 60.

The witty ***Jim Stafford***

In 1989, Jim moved back to Florida so as to be near his son, who had moved with his mother (Bobbie Gentry) to Georgia. Jim now plays Las Vegas rooms, concerts and state fairs. Among Jim's other accolades is honorary membership in the International Frisbee Association.

RECOMMENDED ALBUMS:

"Jim Stafford" (MGM)(1973) [Re-released on Polydor (1974) and again in 1987]
"Not Just Another Pretty Foot" (MGM)(1975)

JOE STAMPLEY

(Singer, Songwriter, Piano, Ukulele, Guitar)

Date of Birth: **June 6, 1943**
Where Born: **Springhill, Louisiana**
Married: **Jo Ann**
Children: **Terry**

For over 25 years, Joe Stampley has graced the Pop and Country charts. Yet despite that, he is still not the household name that his success and longevity should have ensured. In fact, he became known in the late 70's and early 80's as Joe in the double act of Moe & Joe, with Moe Bandy.

Joe was raised in Springhill and when he was age 7, he moved to Baytown, Texas (the family moved back seven years later). There he met Hank Williams at a local radio station and told him that he knew all of his songs. He proceeded to show his ability and was told by the great man to be himself, sing like himself, and later it might pay off for him. When he was 10, Joe won $10 as first prize in a talent contest. When age 15, he became friends with Merle Kilgore, who was then a local deejay in Springhill and who would play a major part in Joe's career. The other influence on Joe, at this time, was the music of Jerry Lee Lewis, the Everly Brothers and R & B groups like the Impalas.

Joe and Merle began writing together and Merle got Joe a record deal with Imperial, where, in 1959, he released a rock'n'roll record, *Glenda*. He followed up with *Heaven Dreams/Come a-Runnin'*, in 1960. The following year, he signed with R & B label Chess Records and released *Creation of Love/Teenage Picnic*, but this was not the label for him. That year, he joined a five-man Pop/rock'n'roll group, the Cutups, as singer. By 1963, the group had changed its name to the Uniques. He attended college and then, on leaving, married Jo Ann, his childhood sweetheart.

Joe Stampley, Frances Preston** (BMI President) and **Terry Stampley

While singing with the Uniques, Joe also wrote many of the group's songs. He also worked at various jobs, including selling encyclopedias, pumping gas, working in a soft-water department and working in a paper mill. The Uniques signed with Paula Records at the end of 1964, and had a Top 70 Pop record, *Not Too Long Ago* (written by Joe and Kilgore), in 1965. That year, the Uniques backed Nat Stuckey on his single *Don't You Believe Her/Round and Round.* A year later, *All These Things* made the Top 100 on the Pop chart. The group continued to release singles up to 1969, but only achieved regional success.

Joe then went on to Paramount Records, in 1970, and released *Quonette McGraw.* That same year, Al Gallico became his manager and Joe signed to Gallico Music. It was Gallico who arranged for Joe to be signed to Dot Records. Joe had started to write Country material and Gallico guided him in that direction. During his career, Joe would write many of the songs on his albums. Joe hit the charts with *Take Time to Know Her,* which made the Country Top 75.

Joe started out 1972 with another Top 75 record, *Hello Operator.* He followed this with his first big hit, *If You Touch Me (You've Got to Love Me),* which made the Top 10. He completed the year with his first No.1, *Soul Song,* which also became a Pop Top 40 single. He stayed with Dot until the end of 1974 and racked up further hits, namely, *Bring It on Home (to Your Woman), Too Far Gone* and the Top 3 record *I'm Still Loving You* (all 1973) and *How Lucky Can One Man Be* (Top 15) and *Take Me Home to Somewhere* (Top 5, both 1974). ABC/Dot continued to release singles after Joe had signed with Epic. The most successful of these were *Penny* (Top 10, 1975) and the No.1 *All These Things* (a re-recording of his Uniques hit) and the Top 20 releases *The Night Time and My Baby* and *Everything I Own* (all 1976).

At Epic, Joe was produced by Norro Wilson and Billy Sherrill. He struck immediately, in 1975, with the No.1 single *Roll on Big Mama,* but the follow-up singles, *Dear Woman* and *Billy, Get Me a Woman,* only made the Top 15. His final single of the year, *She's Helping Me Get Over You,* did worse, only reaching the Top 25. No doubt the flood of ABC/Dot material on the market confused the buying public, because in 1976, there were eight Stampley singles on the charts. Things didn't improve, however, the following year, when his Epic release *She's Long Legged* got to the Top 30. However, better things were ahead, when both *Baby, I Love You* and *Everyday I Have to Cry Some,* went Top 15.

In 1978, the renaissance of Joe Stampley began. His first two singles, *Red Wine and Blue Memories* and *If You've Got Ten Minutes (Let's Fall in Love),* both peaked in the Top 10, while *Do You Ever Fool Around* reached the Top 5. During the following year, Joe had four singles on the charts and it marked the arrival of those good ol' boys, Moe & Joe. Joe's solo record, *I Don't Lie,* got to the Top 15 and was followed by the Moe & Joe No.1 *Just Good Ol' Boys.* After this came Joe's solo Top 10 record, *Put Your Clothes Back On.* The year was closed out with another Top 10 duet, *Holding the Bag.* That year, he and Moe were named ACM "Vocal Duet of the Year," a feat they would repeat in 1980.

Then Joe's record career became less successful, in 1980. This was partly due to the fact that the public thought in terms of the duo rather than Joe as a solo. The first single of the year, *After Hours,* reached the Top 20; the second, *Haven't I Loved You Somewhere Before,* only got into the Top 40, and *There's Another Woman* made the Top 20. In addition, his single with Moe, *Tell Ole I Ain't Here, He Better Get on Home,* peaked in the Top 15. However, on the plus side, Moe & Joe won the CMA's "Vocal Duo of the Year" award.

1981 saw a reversal of fortunes with *I'm Gonna Love You Back to Loving Me Again* reaching the Top 10, and was followed by the Top 10 duet *Hey Moe (Hey Joe).* However, the other singles of the year fared less successfully, with *Whiskey Chasin'* going Top 20, the duet *Honky Tonk Queen* reaching the Top 15, and another re-recording of *All These Things,* backed by *Let's Get Together and Cry,* only reached the Top 70 and Top 50 respectively.

Matters didn't improve in 1982 and his three singles had mixed fortunes; they were *I'm Goin' Hurtin'* (Top 20), *I Didn't Know You Could Break a Broken Heart* (Top 30) and *Backslidin'* (Top 25). Joe's records were more successful in 1983, with *Finding You* going Top 25, *Poor Side of Town* reaching the Top 15 and *Double Shot (of My Baby's Love)* going Top 10.

In 1984, Joe and Moe teamed up again for the fun record *Where's the Dress.* The song, a spoof on Boy George and Culture Club, reached the Top 10 and landed them in trouble, when Culture Club's management sued them. This would be the last really successful year for Joe, with his recording of Van Morrison's *Brown Eyed Girl* reaching the Top 30 and his duet with Jessica Boucher of the title track of his 1983 album, *Memory Lane,* going Top 40. His other Top 40 record that year was the duet with Moe, *The Boy's Night Out.*

Joe left Epic in 1986 and for two years, he was in the record wilderness, then in 1988, he signed with Evergreen. He reached the Top 60 with *Cry Baby* that year and had two minor successes, in 1989, with *You Sure Got This Ol' Redneck Feelin' Blue* and *If You Don't Know Me by Now.* This was the end (so far) of his record successes, but Joe and his band, Double Shots, continue to entertain in venues around the country. When he's not playing, he's relaxing with his two pastimes, golf and fishing.

RECOMMENDED ALBUMS:

"Golden Hits" (Paula)(1970) [As the Uniques]
"Joe Stampley's Greatest Hits" (ABC/Dot)(1975) [Features Jessica Boucher]
"The Sheik of Chicago (Chuck Berry)" (Epic)(1976)
"The ABC Collection" (double)(ABC)(1977)
"Greatest Hits—Joe Stampley" (Epic)(1978)
"Just Good Ole Boys" (Columbia)(1979) [With Moe Bandy]
"Hey Moe—Hey Joe" (Columbia)(1979) [With Moe Bandy]
"Memory Lane" (Epic)(1983)
"The Good Ole Boys—Alive and Well" (Columbia)(1984) [With Moe Bandy]
"Live from Bad Bob's, Memphis" (Columbia)(1985) [With Moe Bandy]
"I'll Still Be Loving You" (Epic)(1985)

Ralph and Carter, the ***Stanley Brothers***

STANLEY BROTHERS, The (including RALPH STANLEY)

When Formed: 1946

CARTER STANLEY
(Singer, Songwriter, Guitar)

Given Name:	**Carter Glen Stanley**
Date of Birth:	**August 27, 1925**
Married:	**Mary Magdalene Kiser**
Children:	**Carter, William, Bobby, Doris, Jeannie**
Date of Death:	**December 1, 1966**

RALPH STANLEY
(Singer, Songwriter, Banjo)

Given Name:	**Ralph Edmund Stanley**
Date of Birth:	**December 1, 1966**
Married:	**1. Peggy (div.) 2. Jimmie Crabtree**
Children:	**Timothy, Lisa Joy, Tonya, Ralph II**

Both Born:	**Stratton, Virginia**

The Stanley Brothers rank as one of the four all-time greats of Bluegrass. They have often been termed the first band after that of Bill Monroe to adopt that style in 1946-47 and are also the most recorded among the early Bluegrass acts. Natives of the rugged Clinch Mountain county of Dickinson in Virginia, the Stanley boys had a singing father and an Old-Time banjo-picking mother. The latter took her children to the Primitive Baptist church. By the early 40's, Carter and Ralph had begun to entertain the neighborhood. WWII army service took both brothers right after they finished high school. Carter got his discharge first and began working in the radio band of a local musician named Roy Sykes. However, when Ralph got out of the Army in October 1946, the two soon combined to form the Stanley Brothers.

After two months at local WNVA in Norton, they moved on to brand-new WCYB in the border city of Bristol. The Stanleys soon attained considerable popularity on the *Farm and Fun Time* program. As Ralph later recalls, they came to Bristol in a 1937 Chevrolet, but within six months they bought a 1947 Cadillac. For the next dozen years, Carter and Ralph were in and out of Bristol several times, working in between at such varied locales as WPTF Raleigh, KWKH Shreveport, WSAZ-TV Huntington, and WVLK Versailles, Kentucky.

In the meantime, the Stanleys and their group, the Clinch Mountain Boys, initiated their recording career with Jim Stanton's Rich-R-Tone label of Johnson City, Tennessee, in the spring of 1947. Of their first 10 sides, *Little Glass of Wine*, a song of fairly recent origin with a more archaic sound, had the biggest impact. Columbia signed them in 1948, but couldn't do a session until the Petrillo ban ended. The Stanleys cut 22 sides for Columbia (1949-1952), had a final Rich-R-Tone session in 1952, and went with Mercury for five years beginning on August 9, 1953.

Several noted musicians served stints in the Clinch Mountain Boys, including Joe Meadows, Chubby Anthony, Curly Lambert, Pee Wee Lambert, Bill Napier and longtime stalwart George Shuffler. Briefly the brothers quit music during part of 1951 and Carter worked as a lead singer with Bill Monroe for a few months. Ralph got in a bad auto accident and spent several weeks recuperating.

In 1958, the Stanley Brothers made several moves. They switched their recording efforts to Starday and King—two different firms at that time—and in November transferred their base to Live Oak, Florida, and the *Suwannee River Jamboree*. For about four years, they did a circuit of TV shows for Jim Walter Homes throughout Florida, Georgia and Alabama and generally prospered. They recorded extensively for King—15 albums in seven years—but after 1961, the boys began to experience difficult times. Except for George Shuffler, they couldn't afford to keep a full band, and except for a few parks (e.g., Sunset) and club work, the opportunities for a hard-core Bluegrass group seemed to be waning. They did extensive recording for smaller companies including Wango and worked Carlton Haney's first Roanoke Bluegrass Festival. Club work around the Appalachian migrant centers of Dayton, Columbus, Middletown and Cincinnati along with trips to Baltimore were plentiful, but didn't pay much. Furthermore, Carter Stanley's health declined rapidly in 1966 and on December 1, he died at only 41.

After several weeks of indecision, Ralph Stanley decided to go ahead with a new Clinch Mountain Boys unit. He took former Lonesome Pine Fiddler Curly Ray Cline, who had worked a few months with the brothers, longtime stalwart Shuffler Melvin Goins, and a new lead vocalist, Larry Sparks, from Ohio and put together a solid traditional sound. Fortunately, Bluegrass festivals became increasingly popular and Ralph knew he had made the right decision to re-form the group. The band went through some personnel changes in the next 28 years, but remained remarkably stable. Curly Ray Cline remained Ralph's fiddler through May 1993 when he retired, giving way to Art Stamper. Jack Cooke became the regular bass player in mid-1970 and is now in his 25th year as a Clinch Mountain Boy.

After Melvin Goins left to re-form the Goins Brothers in the spring of 1969, Ralph thereafter often kept a lead guitarist, which over the years has included Ricky Lee, Renfro Profitt, Keith Whitley and Junior Blankenship. Several persons filled the lead vocal/rhythm guitar slot after the departure of Sparks, including the late Roy Lee Centers and Keith Whitley, Charlie Sizemore, Sammy Adkins, and Ernie Thacker. Beginning with a September 1959 King session, the Stanleys had usually favored a lead guitar over mandolin and the practice has persisted, although Ralph has had a scattering of mandolinists in his group over the years, including Ron Thomason, Ricky Skaggs, and Danny Marshall.

Like the Stanley Brothers, Ralph has been amazingly active in the record studios. In the earliest days of the late 60's, he cut three additional albums for King and a pair for the small Jalyn company of Dayton, Ohio. Beginning in 1970, Ralph initiated a long series of albums on the Rebel label that lasted for over 20 years and has resulted in 25 releases to date. However, the Clinch Mountain Boys did several albums for other companies, too, including King Bluegrass, Blue Jay, Jessup and his own (briefly) Stanleytone.

More recently, Ralph has recorded compact discs for Freeland (a new company owned by Dick Freeland, formerly of Rebel), which has included a double set featuring guest vocals by a host of Stanley admirers from both Country and Bluegrass ranks. In 1984, President Reagan honored him as a National Heritage Fellow and *Newsweek* recently labeled Ralph as "next to...Bill Monroe...he's the most revered [living] figure in the world of Bluegrass." Lincoln Memorial University awarded him an honorary doctorate, thus gaining him the title "Dr. Ralph Stanley," which is frequently used in stage introductions.

Many Stanley Brothers albums have remained in print in various forms and Copper Creek inaugurated a series of releases from their live shows. More recently, classics scholar John Wright authored the book *Traveling the High Way Home: Ralph Stanley and the World of Traditional Bluegrass Music* (1993). Only Bill Monroe, Lester Flatt and Earl Scruggs entered the Bluegrass Hall of Honor prior to the Stanley Brothers. IMT

RECOMMENDED ALBUMS:

Stanley Brothers recordings have been released in a sometimes baffling array of forms and albums; this listing will attempt to concentrate on original album releases and compact disc collections.

"Country Pickin' and Singin'"(Mercury)(1958)
"Mountain Song Favorites" (Starday)(1959)
"The Stanley Brothers" (King)(1959)
"In Person" (King and Power Pak)(1961)
"Sing the Songs They Like Best" (King)(1961)
"Mountain Music Sound of the Stanley Brothers" (Starday)(1962) [Not all cuts by the Stanley Brothers]
"Folk Song Festival" (King)(1962)
"Folk Concert" (King)(1963)
"Five String Banjo Hootenanny" (King)(1963)
"Bluegrass Songs for You" (King)(1964)
"Their First Recordings" (Melodeon)(ca. 1964)
"John's Gospel Quartet" (Wango/County)(1964)
"John's Country Quartet" (Wango/County)(1964)
"John's Gospel Quartet" (Wango/County)(1965)
"Songs of Mother and Home" (Wango/ County)(1965) [County releases from Wango masters as "The Stanley Brothers of Virginia"]
"Jacob's Vision" (Starday)(1966) [Some cuts from Rimrock masters]
"Collection of Gospel and Sacred Songs" (King)(1966)
"A Beautiful Life" (Rimrock/Old Homestead)(1966)
"Bluegrass Gospel Favorites" (Cabin Creek/Rebel 1966)
"Best Loved Sacred Songs of Carter Stanley" (King)(1967) [Taken from previously released albums]
"An Empty Mansion" (Rimrock/Old Homestead)(1967)
"How Far to Little Rock" (King)(1969) [Most taken from previously released albums]
"The Stanley Brothers on the Air" (Wango)(1976) [From radio shows]
"The Stanley Brothers on Radio, I and II" (County)(1983) [Both made in 1960]
"The Stanley Brothers...On Farm and Fun Time" (Rebel 1988) [Made in 1947]
"Stanley Brothers, 1949-1952" (Bear Family Germany)(1992) [Complete Columbia masters]
"Stanley Brothers, 1953-1959" (Bear Family Germany)(1993) [Complete Mercury and Blue Ridge masters]
"The Early Starday-King Years, 1958-1961" (King)(1993) [First of two projected four cd sets]
Stanley Brothers releases from live shows:
"Recorded Live, Vol. 1" (Rebel)(1970)
"Recorded Live, Vol. 2" (Rebel)(1971)
"Together for the Last Time" (Lisa Joy and Rebel)(1972)
"Live at Antioch College: 1960" (ZK)(ca. 1974)
"Shadows of the Past" (Copper Creek)(ca.1982)
"Stanley Series" (Copper Creek)(1984)
[This is a series of albums taken from live shows; there are at least 10 vinyl album releases in the series, and one or two releases on cd as well]
Ralph Stanley:
"Brand New Country Songs" (King)(1967)
"Old Time Music" (Jalyn)(1967)
"The Bluegrass Sound of Ralph Stanley" (Jalyn)(1968)
"Michigan Bluegrass" (Jessup)(1971)
"Ralph Stanley in Japan" (Seven Seas & Rebel)(1971)
"Cry from the Cross" (Rebel)(1971)
"Gospel Echoes of the Stanley Brothers" (Jessup)(1973)
"A Man and His Music" (Rebel)(1973)
"The Stanley Sound Around the World" (King Bluegrass/County)(1973) [County title is "On and On"]
"Live! At McClure, Virginia" (Rebel)(1975)
"Snow Covered Mound" (Stanleytone/Rebel)(1980)
"Hymn Time" (Blue Jay)(1980)
"The Stanley Sound Today" (Rebel)(1981)
"Live at the Old Home Place" (Rebel)(1983)
"I Can Tell You the Time" (Rebel REB 1637)(1985)
"Lonesome and Blue" (Rebel)(1986)
"I'll Answer the Call" (Rebel)(1987)
"Ralph Stanley & Raymond Fairchild" (Rebel)(1989) [Cassette only]
"Like Father, Like Son" (Copper Creek)(1990)
"Pray for the Boys" (Rebel)(1991)
"Almost Home" (Rebel)(1992)
"Back to the Cross" (Freeland)(1992)
"Saturday Night & Sunday Morning" (double)(Freeland)(1993)
"Hymns from the Heart" (1993) [Cassette only]

JACK STAPP

(Industry Executive)
Date of Birth: **December 8, 1912**
Where Born: **Nashville, Tennessee**
Date of Death: **December 20, 1980**

According to *Billboard* magazine, Tree Music is and has been since 1972 the most successful Country music publisher. Although it is now part of the Japanese Sony organization, the importance of the company alone is a testament to its founder, Jack Stapp.

Stapp moved with his family to Atlanta, Georgia, when age 9 and then he fell in love with radio. At age 16, he had his first job programming a radio station at the Weinkopf Hotel that was piped into the hotel's rooms. He then went to Georgia Tech and became involved with WGST, the college radio station. When it became a commercial station, Jack became the youngest ever Program Manager. It was here that he met Bert Parks, who he hired as an announcer, and they became life-long friends.

They both had a fascination with network radio and Parks went to New York, where he was hired by CBS. Stapp followed and was also retained and the two friends became roommates. Jack rose to become a senior executive for CBS while Parks achieved his fame on air. When WSM (Nashville) executive Jack Harris visited New York, Stapp was full of praise for the station and when Harris needed a Program Manager, he remembered the kind words of Jack Stapp and hired him.

Before he returned to Nashville, Stapp cemented a relationship with Phil Carlin, the Production Manager of NBC, and informed Carlin that he would like to network some programs from WSM. It was Stapp's intent to put together some first-rate groups for the station, but he had problems with the Musicians' Union over the musicians used. He felt that the musicians in town were not good enough but he found that some excellent musicians had left Nashville because of lack of work. He got some of them back and this led to the formation of the WSM Orchestra, Owen

Bradley's Orchestra, Beasley Smith's Orchestra and Francis Craig's Orchestra. He also helped create shows such as *Sunday Down South*, *Riverboat Rebels* and *Mr. Smith Goes to Town*, as well as the children's program *Wormwood Forest*. For the Country music fans, the *Prince Albert* portion of the *Grand Ole Opry*, which was hosted by Red Foley, was beamed over the network.

This was the start of the *Opry*'s dominance over the other barn dance shows. Up to then the premier show was WLS's *National Barn Dance* from Chicago. The *Opry*'s star at that time was Uncle Dave Macon. Jack Stapp was a major player in moving the emphasis on the *Opry* from string bands to a new breed of star that included Roy Acuff, who had joined in 1938, a year before Stapp came on board. Roy Acuff was followed by Ernest Tubb, Pee Wee King and, of course, Hank Williams.

Although initially not interested in Country music (Stapp preferring a more popular style), the *Opry* was part of his bailiwick. In 1939, the *Grand Ole Opry* was relocated from the old Dixie Tabernacle to the War Memorial Auditorium. During the fall, the *Opry* was broadcast on the NBC Red network. This network later became ABC. R.J. Reynolds Tobacco Company was the sponsor and Stapp was heavily involved in getting them for the *Prince Albert Show*.

With the arrival of WWII, Stapp had a deferment, as it was considered that his job was in the national interest. However, he went to New York to study psychological warfare and then moved to London, where he worked on preparing war effort propaganda. At the termination of hostilities, he returned to WSM. As Manager of the *Opry*, Stapp was instrumental in starting the annual D.J. Convention and *Opry* Birthday Celebration. He also persuaded Anita Kerr to form the Anita Kerr Singers.

In 1951, he was dining with wartime friend and WSM executive Lou Cowan, who urged Jack to form his own company. It was agreed that Cowan would put up the money and provide the personnel for Stapp to set up a music publishing company. For his part, Stapp agreed to bring in songwriters and songs. Jack himself had been listed as one of the writers of Red Foley's monster No.1 hit *Chattanoogie Shoe Shine Boy*. In reality, Fred Rose wrote the song, but Stapp came up with the original idea. Cowan's wife, also present at the dinner, who was an heiress of the Spiegel catalog company, started drawing a tree on the back of a menu and suggested that Tree Publishing should be the name for the new company.

In 1953, Stapp brought into the company former bass player Buddy Killen to listen to new songs. The first Tree song recorded was *By the Law of My Heart,* which was cut by Bluegrass star Benny Martin in 1954. The following year, Mae Boren Axton and Tommy Durden, both Tree writers, got together with Elvis Presley for Presley's hit *Heartbreak Hotel*. This laid the foundation for the success of Tree.

In 1957, Stapp left WSM and became General Manager and President of Rock station WKDA. Shortly after, Lou Cowan left Nashville and became President of CBS-TV and Killen became a partner in Tree. WKDA became the No.1 radio station in its market and stayed at the top until 1965. The previous year, Stapp moved to Tree full-time and appointed Killen Executive Vice-President.

Jack was one of the founders of the CMA and became a Director-at-Large and helped to arrange the TV broadcasting of its annual awards show. He was also a member of NARAS. In 1975 he became Board Chairman and Chief Executive Officer of Tree. Jack Stapp died at the end of 1980 and in 1989, he was inducted into the Country Music Hall of Fame. The final sentence of his Hall of Fame plaque says it all: "...Truly Stapp was a giant of his time."

(See also Buddy Killen)

BUDDY STARCHER

(Singer, Songwriter, Guitar, Banjo, Deejay)

Given Name: Oby Edgar Starcher
Date of Birth: March 16, 1906
Where Born: Nr. Ripley, Jackson County, West Virginia
Married: Mary Ann Vasas (Estes)

A radio entertainer who achieved tremendous popularity in his home state of West Virginia and selected other areas, Buddy Starcher enjoyed a long career in Country music. While having only one hit of national consequence, he nonetheless has managed to gain wide respect and influence among both fans and fellow artists.

Born near Ripley, West Virginia, Buddy's parents raised him in a remote section of Nicholas County where his Old-Time fiddler father taught his son to furnish rhythm accompaniment on guitar for square dances at an early age.

As a young adult somewhat given to wanderlust, Starcher first played guitar and sang on radio at WFBR Baltimore in the fall of 1928. In 1932, he was in Washington and wrote a parody of *Twenty-One Years* called *Bonus Blues*, which chronicled the plight of the Bonus Marchers. Somewhat later he also performed over WSOC in Gastonia, North Carolina. He first attracted a wide radio audience beginning in 1933 at WCHS Charleston and somewhat later at WMMN Fairmont, both in West Virginia. He returned to these locales frequently in his musical travels.

From 1937, Buddy generally associated himself with four or five other decent musicians who could provide audiences with a well-rounded variety of wholesome Country entertainment. Some of the more significant figures who worked with him over the next 20 years included guitarist/Dobroist Lee Moore, fiddlers Ted Grant and Georgia Slim Rutland, comedian and yodeler Smiley Sutter and the harmony duet of Budge and Fudge Mayse. Starcher's wife, Mary Ann Vasas (aka Estes), also worked in his show for several years as featured vocalist on both radio and television. Outside of West Virginia, Buddy did some of his more significant radio broadcasting from such stations as WSVA Harrisonburg, Virginia, KMA Shenandoah, Iowa, and WCAU Philadelphia. Along the way he gained a reputation as an outstanding radio pitchman (salesman) that rivaled his popularity as a singer and skill as a songwriter.

From the early 50's, Buddy Starcher often appeared on television, beginning in Miami, Florida, and later back in Harrisonburg. In January 1960, he returned to Charleston and for six years had a highly rated early morning program on WCHS-TV. In addition to Buddy and Mary Ann, key figures in the show's success included comedian-vocalist Sleepy Jeffers, the Davis Twins, guitarist Norm Chapman, lovely young Gospel singer Lori Lee Bowles, autoharpist Wick Craig, comedian–steel player Herman Yarbrough and two young singers, Darius Ray Parsons and Chester Lester. This broadcast further contributed to Buddy's near legendary status in West Virginia and won him a new generation of fans in adjacent states as well.

Although he had been popular on radio for many years, Starcher cut no records until 1946, when he did 16 sides for 4 Star (14 reissued on Cattle in 1984), including the best known of his early compositions, *I'll Still Write Your Name in the Sand*, a Top 10 hit in 1949. He did 10 more numbers for Columbia beginning in 1949, which included his own *Pale Welded Flower,* and had a session for Deluxe in 1954. Buddy had several releases on Starday from the later 50's and did an album for them in 1962.

Early in 1966, he did a recitation for the

small Boone Record Company entitled *History Repeats Itself*. It became something of a surprise hit on both the Country (Top 3) and Pop (Top 40) charts, leading Decca to buy the master and rush an entire Starcher album onto the market. It came as something of a shock to a 60 year old with nearly 40 years of media experience. Starcher followed this with another recitation album for Heart Warming and a fine album of his appealing but unadorned singing for Bluebonnet, but generally found his experience with national stardom to be otherwise brief and a bit troublesome.

By the end of 1967, Starcher returned to radio and managed stations in various locales, including KWBA Baytown, Texas, until he retired in 1976. He returned to Nicholas County and lived quietly for several years near the village of Craigsville, waxing an album for the German firm Bear Family and occasionally yielding to requests for a public appearance. With advancing age, he relocated in 1993 to Harrisonburg, Virginia, where better medical facilities existed.

Other than *History Repeats Itself*, a clever comparison of Presidents Lincoln and Kennedy, Buddy Starcher has several noted songs to his credit. *I'll Still Write Your Name in the Sand* and *Fire in My Heart* became Bluegrass classics through recordings by Mac Wiseman. Numerous artists have recorded Buddy's *Sweet Thing* since the Callahan Brothers first waxed it in 1941 and *Love Song of the Waterwheel* ranks as one of Slim Whitman's minor classics as does *A Faded Rose, A Broken Heart* for both Hank Snow and Doc Williams.

Starcher was also one of the first Country singers to write an autobiography (in his well-printed fan club journal, *Starcher's Buddies*, in 1944-1945), to have a published biography, *Bless Your Little Heart* in 1948, and at the age of 80 to have a second, *Buddy Starcher Biography* (by Robert Cagle) appear in print. Buddy was respected also for his help to aspiring newcomers. The late Keith Whitley praised him in one of his last public interviews for the help and encouragement Buddy provided him when he was only 8 years old. IMT

RECOMMENDED ALBUMS:

"The Boy from Down Home" (Cattle Germany)(1984) [4 Star Masters]
"Buddy Starcher and His Mountain Guitar" (Starday)(1962)
"History Repeats Itself" (Decca)(1966)
"Country Soul and Inspiration" (Heart Warming)(1967)
"Me and My Guitar" (Bluebonnet)(1968)
"Country Love Songs" (Bear Family, Germany)(1978)
"Pride of the West Virginia Hills" (Cattle, Germany)(1985) (From previously unissued material)

KENNY STARR

(Singer, Guitar)
Given Name: Kenneth Trebbe
Date of Birth: September 21, 1952
Where Born: Topeka, Kansas

Former Loretta Lynn Show member ***Kenny Starr***

Although by 1975 Kenny Starr had already enjoyed over 15 years' experience as a singer, his brief moment of stardom hinged on one single, Sterling Whipple's *The Blind Man in the Bleachers*.

Kenny's family moved to Burlingame, Kansas, where he was brought up and where his father worked in coal and construction. When only age 5, he visited the local Veterans of Foreign Wars hall, unplugged the jukebox and played and sang for small change. By the time he was 9 years old, he had formed his own band, the Rockin' Rebels. This was superseded by Kenny and the Imperials and a year later, the group toured the surrounding area.

He was still interested in Pop music as he reached his teens, but when he reached 16, he got interested in Country music, and formed Kenny Starr and the Country Showmen. He was encouraged by Bob Hampton, who was also a songwriter, and once Kenny had graduated from high school, Bob put him up for a talent contest sponsored by KFDI Wichita. Kenny submitted a demo of himself singing Ray Price's hit *I Won't Mention It Again*, which he performed on the final and was named the winner.

He was seen by famed promoter Hap Peebles, who gave Kenny a spot on a Conway Twitty-Loretta Lynn concert in Wichita, Kansas. He won a standing ovation and was congratulated by Loretta and her husband, Mooney. They offered help if he should move to Nashville. He did so and, in 1968, Kenny became a member of the Loretta Lynn Roadshow. Loretta also helped Kenny get a record deal with MCA. In 1973, he made his first chart entry with *That's a Whole Lotta Lovin' (You Give Me)*, which went Top 60.

However, it was not until the end of 1975 that *The Blind Man in the Bleachers* climbed to the Top 3 and crossed over to the Top 60 in the Pop chart. That year, Kenny decided to leave Loretta Lynn's show. He followed up with a Top 30 single, *Tonight I'll Face the Man (Who Made It Happen)*. Kenny stayed on the label until 1978, but the only reasonably successful releases were *Me and the Elephant* and *Hold Tight*, both in 1977.

After leaving MCA, nothing much happened for Kenny until 1982, when he recorded an eponymous album for SRO.

RECOMMENDED ALBUMS:

"The Blind Man in the Bleachers" (MCA)(1975)
"Kenny Starr" (SRO)(1982)

LUCILLE STARR

(Singer, Songwriter, Yodeler, Guitar, Bass, Mandolin)
Given Name: Lucille Marie Raymonde Savoie
Date of Birth: May 13
Where Born: St. Boniface, Manitoba, Canada
Married: 1. Bob Regan (div.)(dec'd.) 2. Bryan Cunningham
Children: Robert Frederickson; stepchildren: David, Shannon

Lucille Starr has long been one of the most successful Canadian Country acts.

She began her singing career in Maillardville, near Vancouver, British Columbia, as a member of the choir group Les Hirondelles. Lucille was trained in classical singing and knew at an early age she wanted to entertain. Later, Lucille became the female singer with the Keray Regan Band. Another member was guitarist/vocalist Bob Regan (b. March 13, 1931/d. March 5, 1990) and after several years of gaining experience and fans throughout Canada, Lucille and Bob left to start their own show.

They began recording and released several records which were Country/Pop successes on Canadian and U.S. radio, including *Eeny Meeny Miney Moe* and *No Help Wanted*. Lucille's powerful voice, unique style and energetic stage presence soon came to the attention of music industry people in Los Angeles, including Dorsey Burnette, "Uncle" Art Satherley and "Nudie, the Hollywood Tailor to the Stars," all of whom helped. The duo was given the name the Canadian Sweethearts by Ralph Hicks of the California Country Music Association.

Lucille and the duo appeared weekly on

four Country music TV shows out of L.A.: the *Spade Cooley Show*, *Country Music Time*, *The Country Music Hour* and ABC-TV's *Country America* show, on which they were the featured performers for two years. This exposure plus their continuing recordings led to appearances on the *Grand Ole Opry*, Disneyland's Theater, Knott's Berry Farm Stage in Los Angeles and numerous fairs and festivals in Canada and the U.S. They also toured with Hank Snow, Wilf Carter and Little Jimmy Dickens.

Lucille was introduced to Herb Alpert and Jerry Moss of A & M Records in Los Angeles and she and the Canadian Sweethearts were signed to recording contracts in 1963. The following year, the duo hit the Country Top 50 with the self-penned *Hootenanny Express* and won a BMI award. They also had Canadian hits with *Don't Knock on My Door* and *Looking Back to See*, reaching No.1 and No.2 respectively.

However, it was Lucille's first solo album, ***The French Cut***, produced by Herb Alpert and including the Tijuana Brass musicians, which brought Lucille acclaim. The title cut became a smash hit on music charts around the world, followed by numerous other hits from the same album and subsequent albums, including *Colinda*, *Crazy Arms*, *Jolie Jacqueline*, *Yours* and *Send Me No Roses*.

This success led to tours to Japan, Korea, the Philippines, Hong Kong, Guam, Taiwan, Okinawa, South Africa, Belgium, Mexico, coast-to-coast in the United States and Canada and to Holland, where, in recognition of her consistent successes as a recording artist, Lucille was awarded the very prestigious Golden Tulip Award. She was only the second artist to have earned the award, and the first female. Lucille was voted as the "Grande Vedette" (Grand Star) of the Grand Gala du Disques, the renowned annual international music awards ceremony and show in Amsterdam. The show's program for that year, which also featured the Everly Brothers and the Supremes, was entitled "Grand Gala Starr," in Lucille's honor.

Lucille was awarded membership in Phonogram's Gold Record Club and taped her own special for Dutch TV, the first Canadian artist to do so. Lucille taped a second TV special in Holland in 1982. *The French Song* reached No.1 on Holland's Top 40 charts and remained in the Top 40 for 19 weeks. *Colinda* and *Crazy Arms* both reached No.3 and remained in the Top 40 for 21 weeks.

Lucille was the top-selling artist in South Africa and at one point several of her recordings occupied positions on the South African charts at the same time. She headlined a five-week tour of international artists throughout South Africa and was awarded her first Gold Album there. So popular was Lucille in South Africa that the Prime Minister hosted a luncheon in her honor at the House of Parliament.

In the U.S. Lucille appeared on TV shows including *Shindig*, *Hullabaloo*, *Louisiana Hayride*, *Town Hall Party* and the *National Barn Dance*. Although not a widely-known fact, Lucille did the yodeling for Cousin Pearl on numerous segments of the hit TV series *The Beverly Hillbillies*.

In 1967, Lucille and the Canadian Sweethearts signed to Epic in Nashville and were produced by Billy Sherrill. Lucille reached the Top 75 with *Too Far Gone* and then at the beginning of 1968, the duo had *Let's Wait a Little Longer*, which went Top 60. This was followed by the Top 70 solo for Lucille, called *Is It Love?* They then moved to Dot in 1969 and charted with the Top 50 single *Dream Baby* as Bob Regan and Lucille Starr, the following year.

In 1977, the Canadian Sweethearts duet came to an end, and Lucille began a solo performing career. Lucille's first album after the break-up of the duet was ***The Sun Shines Again***, the title song having been co-written by Lucille. *The Sun Shines Again* and *Power in Your Love* did well on Canada's Country chart. Lucille's subsequent album, ***Back to You***, produced several Canadian hits, including a No.1 CanCountry hit, *The First Time I've Ever Been in Love*, written by Cyril Rawson, and a No.6 with the title song. A song which Lucille co-wrote and recorded with Sylvia Tyson in 1989 was *Pepere's Mill*, which reached No.5 on the Canadian Country chart.

Lucille's latest album includes re-makes of some of her classic hits, a number of Country standards and several new songs. Marketed throughout Europe, the album became a best-seller. The ***Back To You*** album, with two additional songs and re-titled ***Songs of Love***, is being marketed in Canada, Sweden, Norway and Australia.

A one-hour TV special, entitled *Lucille Starr Neige et Magie*, was taped in Canada in 1989, and was seen across Canada on the French network. In 1991, she did a two-month tour of Europe.

Lucille has earned Gold Albums and Gold Singles in several countries and was also awarded a Platinum Album in Canada, for sales of ***The French Song*** album. She is credited with being the first Canadian female artist to have a million-selling record and to earn Gold Records for sales of her recordings. In 1987, Lucille became the first female inducted into the Canadian Country Music Association's Hall of Honor. In 1988 Lucille was acknowledged for her accomplishments by the City of Coquitlam, B.C., which sponsored a "homecoming" celebration for Lucille and named a city street Lucille Starr Drive in her honor.

In 1989, Lucille was one of the inaugural inductees into the Canadian Country Music Hall of Fame.

In 1981 Herb Alpert wrote of Lucille, "To my ears Lucille Starr has one of the most naturally beautiful voices in the world. She sings with a unique ease and lyrical grace that makes her special."

RECOMMENDED ALBUMS:

"The French Song" (A & M)(1965)
"Lucille Starr" (double)(A & M)
"The Sun Shines Again" (SCR)
"Lonely Street" (Columbia)
"Back to You" (Quality Canada)
"Say You Love Me" (A & M)
"Side by Side" (Columbia)
"Songs of Love" (Intersound)
"Mississippi" (Koch International)

STATLER BROTHERS

When Formed:	**1960 as the Kingsmen/1963 as the Statler Brothers**
Current Members:	
Harold Reid	**Bass Vocals, Dobro**
Don Reid	**Lead Vocals, Piano**
Phil Balsley	**Baritone Vocals**
Jimmy Fortune	**Tenor Vocals, Guitar**
Former Member:	
Lew DeWitt	**Tenor Vocals**

There can be no argument that the Statler Brothers (or the Statlers) are the most successful and enduring vocal harmony group in Country music. Along with the Oak Ridge Boys, they have provided a constant and consistent outpouring of hit singles. Their fan base is totally loyal and in the 90's, they have garnered new admirers with their highly successful TNN *Statler Brothers Show*. Novelist Kurt Vonnegut referred to them as "America's Poets." However, they choose to call their music "Statlerized." They still live and base their business enterprises in Staunton, Virginia, and their offices are located in their old elementary school.

Growing up in the same rural area, it was natural for the four founding members of the Statlers—the Reid brothers, Phil Balsley and Lew DeWitt—to start singing together. Harold (b. Harold Wilson Reid, August 21, 1939, Augusta County, Virginia), Phil (b. Philip Elwood, August 8, 1939, Augusta County,

The Reid Brothers, Phil Balsley and Jimmy Fortune, the ***Statler Brothers***

Virginia) and Lew (b. Lewis Calvin DeWitt, March 8, 1938, Roanoke, Virginia; d. August 15, 1990, Crohn's disease), who were all contemporaries, first put their voices together in 1955 at the Lyndhurst Methodist Church in Staunton. However, it was not until 1960, when joined by Don (b. Donald Sydney Reid, June 5, 1945, Staunton, Virginia), that they formed the Kingsmen. They concentrated on Gospel material, but singing remained a part-time thing for them.

It was 1963 that marked a turning point for the group. Harold persuaded the promoter of a Johnny Cash show to let him talk to "the Man in Black." Although he hadn't heard them, Johnny invited them to sing on his show at nearby Berryville. He liked what he heard and Harold was tenacious and continued to contact Cash. At last, he agreed to take them on the road with him. They then decided to change their name. They saw a box of Statler tissues and decided to become the Statler Brothers. They toured with Cash for eight years and appeared on his TV show.

It was the connection with Johnny Cash that led to them signing with Columbia Records. From early on Lew and the Reid brothers revealed an ability to write excellent songs. This has now got to the point where they rarely record outside material. In fact, in Nashville, it's considered a major achievement for any songwriter to get a Statlers cut. Their first chart success came during the fall of 1965, when Lew's song *Flowers on the Wall* became a major cross-over hit. It reached the Top 3 on the Country charts and hung around for over 6 months and Top 5 on the Pop charts.

They didn't have another hit until the summer of the next year, when *The Right One* made the Top 30. This was followed, that year, by the Top 40 single *That'll Be the Day*. They had back-to-back Top 10 successes, in 1967, with *Ruthless* and the quirky *You Can't Have Your Kate and Edith Too*. They stayed with Columbia until 1969, but failed to have any further major hits.

When they moved to Mercury Records, they were about to embark on an association that has lasted over 20 years (and continues to date).

In 1970, their first chart record, *Bed of Roses*, went Top 10 and crossed over to the Top 60 on the Pop charts. That year, they inaugurated their 4th of July Picnic, which, in 1994, celebrated its 25th anniversary. The initial attendance was 3,000 and that has risen to 90,000. Their tally of hits through the early 70's was: 1971: *New York City* (Top 20), *Pictures* (Top 15) and *You Can't Go Home* (Top 25); 1972: *Do You Remember These* (Top 3) and the *Class of '57* (Top 10); 1973: *Monday Morning Secretary* (Top 20), *Woman Without a Home* (Top 30) and *Carry Me Back* (Top 30); 1974: *Whatever Happened to Randolph Scott* (Top 25), *Thank You World* and *Susan When She Tried* (Top 15). In 1973, they released the album ***Alive at the Johnny Mack Brown High School*** under the name of Lester "Roadhog" Moran & the Cadillac Cowboys.

With the arrival of 1975, their record success lifted up a gear. Their first single of the year, *All American Girl*, only reached the Top 40, however, following that came *I'll Go to My Grave Loving You*, which reached the Top 3. That year, they released their album ***The Best of the Statler Brothers***, which by 1977 had gone Gold and in 1991 was Certified Platinum and Double-Platinum in 1993. In 1976, they had a Top 40 record with *How Great Thou Art* and followed that with *Your Picture in the Paper*, which reached No.13. They wrapped up the year with the Top 10 single *Thank God I've Got You*. In 1977, they had two Top 10 entries with *The Movies* and *I Was There*. They followed with two Top 20 singles, *Silver Medals and Sweet Memories* and *Some I Wrote*.

They experienced their first No.1 single in 1978, with *Do You Know You Are My Sunshine*, a song written by the Reids. This was followed by two major hits, *Who Am I to Say* (Top 3) and *The Official Historian on Shirley Jean Berrell* (Top 5). Their classic album ***Entertainers...On and Off the Record*** was released that year and was Certified Gold, in 1978. In addition, their seasonal album that year, ***Statler Brothers' Christmas Card***, was at Gold standard by 1982 and Double Platinum in 1993. They also released a double Gospel album, in 1978, entitled ***Holy Bible (Old and New Testaments)***, which was Certified Gold in 1993. Their 1979 hits were *How to Be a Country Star* (Top 10), *Here We Are Again* (Top 15) and *Nothing As Original As You* (Top 10). That same year, the album ***The Originals*** was released and had gone Gold by 1981.

Mercury released the compilation ***The Best of the Statler Brothers Ride Again—Vol. II***, which became one of their most celebrated early albums when it was released in 1980, and the following year it was Certified Gold.

The 80's can be divided into two periods, the Statlers with Lew DeWitt and the Statlers with Jimmy Fortune. In the former period were these singles: 1980: *(I'll Even Love You) Better Than I Did Then* (Top 10), *Charlotte's Web* (from the movie *Smokey and the Bandit 2*, in which they appeared) (Top 5) and *Don't Forget Yourself* (Top 15); 1981: *In the Garden*, *Don't Wait on Me* (Top 5) and *Years Ago* (Top 15), and 1982: *You'll Be Back (Every Night in My Dreams)* (Top 3), *Whatever* (Top 10) and *A Child of the Fifties* (Top 20). The last two came from the album ***The Legend Lives On***, the final Statler album that Lew DeWitt recorded. Lew had been suffering from Crohn's disease and decided to leave the group and temporarily retire. Lew went on to record for Compleat Records, where he had a Top 80 single, *You'll Never Know,* and released an album. He died in 1990 from his ongoing illness, at age 52. He was replaced by Jimmy Fortune (b. Lester James Fortune, March 11,

1955, Newport News, Virginia), who, like Lew, soon revealed his songwriting ability.

Their 1983 album ***Today*** marked the first to feature Jimmy and gained Gold status in 1993. The first single from the album, *Oh Baby Mine (I Get So Lonely),* reached the Top 3. It was followed by the Top 10 record *Guilty* and their second No.1, Jimmy Fortune's *Elizabeth*. The following year saw the release of their excellent album ***Atlanta Blue***, with them credited as "The Statlers." The title track went Top 3 and was followed by Don Reid's *One Takes the Blame* and was ended by another No.1 from Jimmy Fortune, *My Only Love*. 1985 continued in the same way with *Hello Mary Lou* going Top 3 and yet another Jimmy Fortune song, *Too Much on My Heart*, going to No.1.

From 1986, the Statlers' success was irregular. In 1986, *Sweeter and Sweeter* went Top 10, *Count on Me* went Top 5, but *Only You* only reached the Top 40. However, the final single of the year, *Forever*, went Top 10. The last three singles came from the album ***Four for the Show***. They also released a very special album, ***Radio Gospel Favorites***, which garnered much interest and was Certified Gold in 1993. The most successful single of 1987 was the year's opener, *I'll Be the One*. This was followed by *Maple Street Mem'ries*, which only went Top 50. There were three chart entries in 1988 and they were *The Best I Know How* (Top 15), *Am I Crazy?* (Top 30) and *Let's Get Started If We're Gonna Break My Heart* (Top 15).

1989 was notable for the release of the live album ***Statler Brothers Live—Sold Out***, which was recorded live at Capitol Music Hall in Wheeling, West Virginia. The Statlers also had four chart records, *Moon Pretty Moon* (Top 40), *More Than a Name on a Wall* (Top 10) and two minor successes, *Don't Wait on Me* (a re-release) and *A Hurt I Can't Handle*. They had their final hit (so far), in 1990, with the Top 60 single *Small Small World*, which came from the album ***Music, Memories and You***.

Although the group's chart singles have since dried up, it is quite possible that they could still release another one of their successful modern-day nostalgia songs. Their TV series not only features their celebrated singing but also scripts written by the group. Initially, the pilot was written by outside writers, but since the public found the script to be less than convincing, the Statler Brothers now do their own writing.

One of the consistent parts of the Statler sound is producer Jerry Kennedy, who has worked with the group since their move to Mercury. However, the members of the Statlers have each got specific tasks within the organization and lead interesting outside lives. Harold designs the group's custom-tailored outfits and supervises their album covers and coordinates the bookings. Don is on the Board of Directors of the Staunton YMCA and is an Elder of Olivet Presbyterian Church and coaches a Little League team. He is also an avid reader. Phil looks after the Statlers' business and administrative affairs and is an expert at routing and town-to-town mileage. He also sings with the choir at Olivet Presbyterian Church, where over half of the members of the choir are members of his family. Jimmy is also a singer of Gospel songs. Many of the songs recorded by the Statlers have been written by Harold's daughters Kim and Kodi, who were prodigious prodigies and Don's equally talented son, Debo. As the Statlers' awards show, they have continuously reaped a harvest from their peers and fans alike. (See Statler Brothers Awards under Awards Section.) They are sure to be the recipients of many more. After all, they are "Entertainers...On and Off the Record."

RECOMMENDED ALBUMS:

"Flowers on the Wall" (Columbia)(1966)
"The World of the Statler Brothers" (double)(Columbia)(1972)
"Alive at the Johnny Mack Brown High School" (Mercury)(1974) [As Lester "Roadhog" Moran & the Cadillac Cowboys]
"The Best of the Statler Brothers" (Mercury)(1975)
"Entertainers...On and Off the Record" (Mercury)(1978)
"Holy Bible (Old and New Testaments)" (double)(Mercury)(1978)
"The Originals" (Mercury)(1979)
"The Best of the Statler Brothers Ride Again—Vol. II" (Mercury)(1980)
"The Legend Goes On" (Mercury)(1982)
"Today" (Mercury)(1983)
"Atlanta Blue" (Mercury)(1984)
"Radio Gospel Favorites" (Mercury)(1986)
"Four for the Show" (Mercury)(1986)
"Maple Street Memories" (Mercury)(1987)
"The Statlers Greatest Hits" (Mercury)(1988)
"Music, Memories and You" (Mercury)(1990)
"Home" (Mercury)(1993)
Lew DeWitt solo album:
"On My Own" (Compleat)(1985)

RED STEAGALL

(Singer, Songwriter, Guitar, Mandolin, Poet, Actor)
Given Name: **Russell Steagall**
Date of Birth: **December 22, 1937**
Where Born: **Gainesville, Texas**

Red Steagall was raised north of Amarillo, Texas, in the ranching community of Sanford. Growing up around the rodeos, Steagall starting riding bulls as a teenager. He was stricken with polio when he was 15 and took up the guitar and mandolin to help rehabilitate his arm.

He put together a Country band when he was a student at West Texas State University. His earnings playing music helped finance his education in animal science and agronomy (the science of soil management and crop production). He took a job selling agro-chemicals after he graduated and continued performing at night.

In the mid-60's, Red moved to California and performed at Folk clubs in the Los Angeles area. He found success in 1967 as a songwriter when Ray Charles charted *Here We Go Again*. The song was recorded two years later by Nancy Sinatra. After a stint working for United Artists Music publishing company, Red started his own music publishing company.

Dot Records signed him in 1969 and he moved to Capitol Records in 1971. In 1972, Steagall (as Stegall) scored his first Top 30 hit with *Party Dolls and Wine*. His next release, *Somewhere My Love*, made it into the Top 20. In 1973, he moved to Nashville and placed several more songs on the charts, including *True Love* and *If You've Got the Time*.

In 1974, Red discovered Reba McEntire when he was performing at the National Rodeo Finals in Oklahoma City. He was so impressed with her voice that he brought her to Nashville and helped her make her first demo tape. Red introduced Reba to his many friends in the music business and before long she signed with Mercury Records. That year, Red scored with *I Gave Up Good Mornin' Darling* and *Finer Things in Life* and then he had a Top 20 hit with *Someone Cares for You*.

In 1976, Red signed with ABC/Dot and had the biggest hit of his career when *Lone Star Beer and Bob Wills Music* reached the Top 15. Other hits followed later in the year with *Truck Drivin' Man* and *Rosie (Do You Wanna Talk It Over)*. In 1977 Steagall covered the Tony Bennett signature song *I Left My Heart in San Francisco,* and made the Top 60.

While Red continued writing and recording in the late 70's, many other artists recorded his songs. More than 200 of his songs have been recorded by such diverse artists as Dean Martin, Roy Clark, Johnny Duncan, and Del Reeves. In 1992, George Strait recorded Red's co-written song *Here We Go Again*.

In 1979, Red signed with Elektra and had a quartet of hits that all peaked in the 30s and 40s: *Goodtime Charlie's Got the Blues* (1979), *3 Chord Country Song*, *Dim the Lights and Pour the Wine* and *Hard Hat Days and Honky Tonk Nights* (all 1980).

As Red's association with the Nashville music business slowed after 1980, he returned to his small ranch west of Fort Worth, Texas.

He continued to maintain a heavy touring schedule and was in constant demand for rodeos, fairs, and concerts. Red also devoted his creative efforts to writing poetry and he gained a reputation as one of the best interpreters of the cowboy lifestyle.

The Texas state legislature named Red Steagall the Official Cowboy Poet of Texas in 1991, recognizing his "exceptional abilities and his influence in protecting his incomparable art form" and commending him for "keeping alive the music of the cowboy, a significant part of the culture and heritage of Texas and one of the many contributions that our state has made to the world." Among Steagall's most popular poems are *Ride for the Brand* and *Born to This Land.*

Red formed his own RS Records and sold his records by mail order. In addition to his solo work, he performed with his eight-piece Texas Swing band, the Coleman County Cowboys.

When Warner Brothers launched their Western label in 1992, Steagall was one of the label's debut artists. ***Born to this Land*** was released in the summer of 1993 and contained a mixture of music and cowboy poetry. In addition to his long career as a singer, songwriter, and performer, Red appeared in several motion pictures, including *Benji the Hunted, Dark Before the Dawn* and *Big Bad John.* He also worked on a variety of rodeo specials for the ESPN cable network. JIE

RECOMMENDED ALBUMS:

"Party Dolls & Wine" (Capitol)(1972)
"Somewhere My Love" (Capitol)(1973)
"If You've Got the Time" (Capitol)(1973)
"The Finer Things in Life" (Capitol)(1974)
"Texas Red" (ABC/Dot)(1976)
"Lone Star Beer and Bob Wills Music" (ABC/Dot)(1976)
"For All Our Cowboy Friends" (ABC/Dot)(1977) [Re-released on MCA]
"Hang on Feelin'" (ABC/Dot)(1978) [Re-released on MCA]
"Born to This Land" (Warner Western)(1993)

JUNE STEARNS

(Singer, Guitar)

Given Name:	**Agnes June Stearns**
Date of Birth:	**April 5, 1939**
Where Born:	**Albany, New York**
Married:	**James Edward Burdette**

During the late 60's and early 70's, June Stearns could be considered to be one of the ladies-in-waiting for the Country Queen crown. However, she had a career that went back much further.

Raised in Franklin, Indiana, in a prominent local musical family, June landed a job with WLW's *Midwestern Hayride* in Cincinnati, immediately on leaving high school in 1957. She stayed with the *Hayride* until 1958. In 1960, she wrote to Roy Acuff, enclosing a photograph with her sister, under which she wrote, "I'm the one with the guitar." Almost certainly, Roy would have heard about her work on the *Midwestern Hayride.* To June's surprise, she became a member of Mr. Roy's Smoky Mountain Gang. She stayed with the group until 1965, appearing on the *Grand Ole Opry* and on live dates.

While appearing with Roy Acuff, June also took time out to appear at the *Louisiana Hayride,* in 1963. In 1965, she broke her ankle in an auto crash in Roy Acuff's vehicle and never returned to the group. She can be considered the last regular Smoky Mountain Girl.

June released some singles on Starday from 1963 with Gene Martin and then she signed to Columbia in 1967, and after a couple of singles, got together with Lefty Frizzell as Agnes & Orville, in 1968, releasing one single, *Have I Ever Been Untrue/If You've Got the Money (I've Got the Time).* Her first solo single after this, *Empty House,* reached the Country Top 50. She followed up that year with *Where He Stops Nobody Knows,* which only went Top 60, and immediately, Columbia released *Jackson Ain't a Very Big Town,* a duet with Johnny Duncan, which just failed to reach the Top 20 at the end of 1968 and became her biggest hit. That year, she was voted third "Most Promising Female Artist" by *Cash Box.*

1969 was June's final year with Columbia; and although she charted four times, her most successful entrants were *Walking Midnight Road* and *Drifting Too Far (From Your Arms),* both of which went Top 60. The following year, June moved to Decca, where she scored with *Tyin' Strings* (Top 50, 1970) and *Sweet Baby on My Mind* and *Your Kind of Lovin'* (both Top 60, 1971). Since then, June has faded from the public limelight and the music scene.

RECOMMENDED ALBUMS:

"River of Regret" (Columbia)(1969)
"Back to Back" (Columbia)(1969) [With Johnny Duncan]

STEEL GUITAR
BY BUDDY EMMONS

In 1954, Webb Pierce recorded a song called *Slowly.* In place of the customary melodic intro, steel guitarist Bud Isaacs played a strange new sound completely unrelated to the melody of *Slowly*—or any other song. It was a three-note pitch-bending sound that seemed to sit still and move at the same time. The intro to *Slowly* was also the introduction of the pedal steel guitar to Country music.

The steel guitar evolved from the standard acoustic guitar. Long before acoustic steels such as Dobro and National were available, strings were raised above the standard guitar neck and played with a flat piece of metal, called a bar. A separate elevated nut and bar was included with many guitars for the purpose of having that option.

Bob Dunn, a pioneer of the acoustic and amplified steel, used a raised nut and Volutone pickup on a Martin guitar. Bob can be heard on the Milton Brown Swing albums of the mid-30's.

Patents for guitar tone changing devices date back to the 20's. Unfortunately, they were ahead of their time. It was only after a series of evolvements that a fragile musical instrument such as the guitar could withstand the physics involved in raising the pitch of a string.

With the introduction of pickups and amplifiers in the 30's, the need for an acoustic body was no longer a factor for the steel guitar. Playing a guitar in a horizontal position meant it could be placed on the lap, or on a stand. Since the body could be any size or shape, the next logical step was to build it to accommodate legs. With legs and a sturdy cabinet, the steel guitar was then capable of supporting a tone-changer mechanism. By the 40's, pedal steels with names such as Multichord and Electraharp were surfacing.

The first pedal steel guitar player I recall was Alvino Rey. Alvino was a popular artist who fronted his own orchestra in the 40's big band era. He was also the first steel player to use an electronic transducer called the Sonavox for talking guitar effects. Most of his solos consisted of chordal melodies played with an arpeggiated sound.

In the early 50's, the Bigsby guitar, made by Paul Bigsby of Downy, California, was becoming a popular choice among steel players. The Bigsby was a high-quality top-dollar steel, custom-built at a rate of one per month. At the time I ordered mine (1953), there was a two-year waiting period.

Two of Bigsby's first customers were Joaquin Murphy and Speedy West. Joaquin, one of the forerunners of Jazz-oriented single-note solos, spent the peak of his musical career with Spade Cooley. Speedy was a wonderful showman who integrated chords, wah-wah sounds and bar slams into his style. Speedy, now retired, ranks as one of the most recorded steel players of all time.

Other pedal steels of the 50's were the Wright Custom, Marlin, and Sho-Bud. Shot Jackson and I started the Sho-Bud company in 1957, working out of Shot's garage. Due to its Nashville-based operation, Sho-Bud became the popular choice of Nashville musicians. The MSA steel company was founded in 1962 by Tommy Morrell, Danny Shields, and Maurice Anderson.

The physics of a pedal steel are both fascinating and intimidating. The undercarriage consists of rods, levers, springs, and other paraphernalia requiring a barrage of adjustments. The standard double-neck guitar has eight pedals, five knee levers, and 10 strings per neck. Each string comprises 25 or more pounds pressure, depending upon string gauges. Multiply that stress by 20 strings, and you have in excess of 500 pounds pressure on the cabinet.

The heart of the pedal system is a mechanism at the bridge end. Each string is attached to separate pivotal devices called fingers. Beneath the guitar, rods are attached to the fingers and directed to cross shafts linked to each pedal. Levers, called bell cranks, are anchored to the cross shafts. When a pedal is depressed, the bell cranks pull the rods engaged at the string fingers and create the sound of bending notes.

The routing of mechanics, as well as choice of tunings and pedal arrangements, is up to the individual and can be changed at will. This custom feature makes the pedal steel the only instrument in the world that's not standardized. Pedal chords can be further modified by vertical and horizontal knee levers, which are accessible to both knees.

Around 1959, I felt the need for changes in the Sho-Bud guitar. I wanted a smaller, lighter body with a burn-resistant finish, aluminum necks, and a volume pedal that's attached to the pedal bar. Shot's philosophy of "if it ain't broke, don't fix it," prompted me to start integrating all the vetoed ideas into a new guitar. In two years, my Sho-Bud reject was on paper. Because of a road job and shopworn knuckles, I left Sho-Bud in search of someone to build a prototype. By 1963, my guitar was a reality, and in 1964, the Emmons Guitar Company was established.

In the last decade, the steel guitar market has expanded considerably. Counting the majors and independent builders, there are close to 100 brands available. A few of the more prominent brand names are Sierra, Franklin, JCH, Emmons, Derby, Mullins, and Carter.

Apart from the addition of two strings, the E9th pedal tuning has undergone three changes. In 1956, Jimmy Day placed an E note in the middle of the 8-string tuning. Around 1958, Ralph Mooney added a G# note at the first string position. In 1962, after steels had advanced to 10 strings per neck, I added a F# and D# note to the first and second string positions, giving the tuning a diatonic structure. The original three-note pedal sound is still intact, but the melodic capabilities have been greatly enhanced by the combined changes.

The inside neck, or C6th tuning, offers a wider range of chord combinations than the E9th. It has been shunned somewhat by the recording industry because of its modern sound. The irony of that theory is that, prior to the pedal revolution, most steel tunings were based off of the 6th chord.

Some of the better all-around players are Terry Crisp, Tommy White, Paul Franklin and Hal Rugg. Jay Dee Maness and Sneaky Pete Kleinow are two West Coast players that have been longtime favorites of mine.

Tom Brumley, a wonderful Country player, has a theater in Branson, Missouri, and can be heard on many of the Dwight Yoakam hits. John Hughey, who presently works for Vince Gill, enjoys the distinction of being able to play high on the neck where everyone else fears to tread. I refer to it as "Hugheyland."

Two steel players capable of kicking up some dust down the road are Joe Wright and Chris Templeton. There are no avenues Joe and Chris won't explore. Chris extends his abilities with a fretted guitar neck and his own tuning on which he uses the tapping technique.

My association with the Emmons Guitar Company ended in 1985. The company kept the Emmons name and, aside from the pedal mechanism, still manufactures a model cosmetically similar to my original design. I currently play a 1964 and 1967 Emmons Original, an EMCI, and a Sierra.

Sophisticated as it is, the pedal steel still has limits. Maurice Anderson believes the steel is a sleeping giant. Maybe so, but until you can make an instrument as smart as the person who plays it, the player will always lack for expression. From the time I first heard a Moog synthesizer in the late 60s, I've dreamed of electronic pitch transposing through pedals. My experience with a Midi steel makes me believe you could have one neck with unlimited tunings capable of raises and lowers up to an octave or more. With that kind of freedom, there would be no boundaries. At present, the technology is still lacking, but what I've heard is enough to stir the giant.

[For biographies on steel guitar players and recommended albums, see: Noel Boggs, Tom Brumley, Jerry Byrd, Cecil Campbell, B.J. Cole, Cousin Jody Jimmy Day, Pete Drake, Buddy Emmons, Lloyd Green, Gerry Hogan, Bud Isaacs, Shot Jackson, Sarah Jory, Leon McAuliffe, Joaquin Murphy, Herb Remington, Red Rhodes, Speedy West and Little Roy Wiggins.]

KEITH STEGALL

(Singer, Songwriter, Guitar, Drums, Piano, Actor, Record Producer, Music Publisher)

Given Name:	**Robert Keith Stegall**
Date of Birth:	**November 1, 1954**
Where Born:	**Wichita Falls, Texas**
Married:	**Diane**
Children:	**Jennifer, Erin**

The son of a steel guitar player who backed Country music legend Johnny Horton, also his third cousin, Keith Stegall comes from a rich musical heritage.

Keith was playing piano by age 4, made his performing debut at age 8 at a Country shindig in Tyler, Texas, and mastered the guitar and formed his first hillbilly band, the Pacesetters, by the time he was 12. When he was 13, he developed a love for Aretha Franklin's music and loves R & B to this day. Keith soon put down the guitar in favor of drums and began playing in a Rock group. He credits Shreveport's *Louisiana Hayride* radio and stage show as being among his earliest influences.

By the time Keith was 15, he was on the road as an acoustic guitarist and singer with the Folk act the Cheerful Givers. While in this group he met Diane and they married when Keith was 19, after they had toured Europe together as singers. After they married, the couple settled in Shreveport, Louisiana, where Stegall became a Methodist church music director on Sunday mornings and a lounge singer on Saturday nights. He received a B.A. in theology from Centenary College in Shreveport.

Keith met Kris Kristofferson while still in college and it was Kris who encouraged him to pursue his dream of becoming a songwriter and move to Nashville. Keith made the move in 1978. After arriving in Nashville, Charlie Monk recognized his talent immediately and became his manager and song publisher. He was signed to Capitol in 1979 and released the Top 60 single *The Fool Who Fooled Around*, in 1980. This was followed in 1981 by *Anything That Hurts You (Hurts Me)*, which also went Top 60. The same year, he had a Top 70 with *Won't You Be My Baby*. In 1982, Capitol switched to EMI and Keith had another Top 70 with *In Love with Loving You*, which was his final release on that label. Stegall says of his first three years in Nashville: "That first attempt at stardom fizzled. I was asking to get out of the deal, and they were ready to get rid of me too. I guess I 'went to school' on their money for three years and it was an invaluable experience."

In 1983, Keith signed with Epic and released his debut single the following year, *I Want to Go Somewhere*, which went Top 25, and *Whatever Turns You On*, which went Top 20. In 1985, he released *California*, which went Top 15, and followed this with his highest charting single to date, *Pretty Lady*, which made the Top 10. This was followed up the same year with his Top 50 *Feed the Fire*.

In 1986, he continued the roll he was on with his Top 40 *I Think I'm in Love* and his final chart entree to date, *Ole Rock and Roller (with a Country Heart)*, which went Top 60. In 1986, he toured Texas, Michigan and the Carolinas with his four-piece band. During the time Keith was vying for a career as an entertainer, he became known as one of Nashville's most prolific songwriters. A staff writer with CBS Music, he penned many of his own songs, including *I Want to Go Somewhere*, *California* and *Pretty Lady*. Other songs he has written or co-written include *Sexy Eyes* (Dr. Hook), *Lonely Nights* (Mickey Gilley), *We're in This Love Together* (Al Jarreau), *She's Playing Hard to Forget* (Eddie Raven), *Let's Get Over Them Together* (Moe Bandy/Becky Hobbs), *Simple* and *Touch by Touch* (Johnny Mathis), *Hurricane* (Leon Everette), *In Love with Loving You* (Jerry Reed and Eddy Arnold), *Looks Like Love* (Helen Reddy), *My Heart Will Know* (Con Hunley), *Texas Heartache* (Juice Newton), *Lonely Hotel* (Don King), *Down in Louisiana* (Charley Pride), *Hands* (Cynthia Clawson) and *I Think I'm in Love* (Ed Bruce and Conway Twitty).

Additionally, Keith performed as an actor in the movie *Killing at Hell's Gate* with Robert Urich (1981) and *Country Gold* with Loni Anderson (CBS-TV,1982). He has five BMI Songwriter Awards including *Sexy Eyes*, *We're in This Love Together*, *Hurricane* and *Lonely Nights*, and in 1985 was nominated for CMA's "New Male Vocalist" award.

In latter years Keith has worked as a Nashville record producer and music publisher. His principal production client is Country superstar Alan Jackson. In 1994, Keith signed as an artist with Mercury Records. Keith's hobbies include boating and waterskiing, and he currently lives in Nashville. LAP

JEFF STEVENS & THE BULLETS

When Formed: 1975
JEFF STEVENS
(Singer, Songwriter, Guitar)
Date of Birth: June 15, 1959

Jeff Stevens & the Bullets

Where Born: Charleston, West Virginia
Married: Sandy
Children: Jeremy, Jody, Melody

As a child growing up in Alum Creek, West Virginia, Jeff spent much of his time listening to his father's Johnny Cash record collection. His parents bought him a guitar one Christmas and Jeff learned to play by listening to records. When he was 9, Jeff entered a local talent contest with his brother Warren, playing bass guitar. His mother made them special stage outfits for the show and the Stevens Brothers took first place. Jeff recalls, "As soon as they handed me the $20 first prize I knew I wanted to be a Country singer."

Jeff and his brother continued performing through their school years and became local favorites in and around West Virginia. By 1975, they added cousin Terry Dotson on drums and formed Jeff Stevens & the Bullets. (Terry joined after the original drummer left, having preferred to play tennis. At the time, Terry didn't even own a drum-kit.) Their popularity grew and they opened concerts for many major stars including Conway Twitty, George Jones & Tammy Wynette and Johnny Cash. The group continued their heavy performance schedule in the 80's, working in Ohio, Pennsylvania and Kentucky opening shows for Alabama and Hank Williams, Jr.

Jeff and Terry tried their hand at songwriting and scored two Top 10 hits for the group Atlanta with *Atlanta Burned Again Last Night* (1983) and *Sweet Country Music* (1984). These successes helped to gain the interest of New York's Atlantic Records. The label had formed a Country division called Atlantic-America and signed Billy Joe Royal. Jeff Stevens & the Bullets landed a contract with the label and moved to Nashville in 1986. The group's first single release was the Bruce Springsteen song *Darlington County*. The song only reached the Top 70, but created enough interest for an album release. The group released their second album in 1987 and it produced the singles *You're in Love Alone* and the remake of Michael (Martin) Murphey's *Geronimo's Cadillac*. The latter was their most successful release, reaching just below the Top 50. The next few years the group struggled for a breakthrough single but radio acceptance evaded them. Their final chart single was *Johnny Lucky and Suzi 66*, which only reached the Top 70.

In 1990 Jeff Stevens & the Bullets decided to call it quits and Jeff's brother and cousin returned home to West Virginia. Atlantic Records gave Jeff one more shot in the studio with producer Keith Stegall. Jeff completed work on a solo album in 1991 but the label decided not to release it. Although disappointed that the record wasn't released, working on the album opened some new doors for Stevens. Jeff remembers, "Working on that album with Keith Stegall turned me around because Keith involved me in all aspects of making the record. I learned for the first time that year what a great song was and that changed my life. It gave me a career, because he set me up to write with major Nashville songwriters like Roger Murrah and Jim McBride." Jeff's investment in his songwriting began to pay big dividends within a few years. In 1993, Jeff and Jerry Salley wrote *I Fell in the Water,* with which John Anderson scored a Top 10 hit, and Alabama had a No.1 with *Reckless*, which Jeff wrote with Michael Clark.

RECOMMENDED ALBUM:

"Bolt Out of the Blue" (Atlantic-America)(1986)

RAY STEVENS

(Singer, Songwriter, Comedy, Piano, Drums)

Given Name: **Harold Ray Ragsdale**
Date of Birth: **January 24, 1939**
Where Born: **Clarksdale, Georgia**
Married: **Penny**
Children: **Timi, Suzi**

There can be no argument that Ray Stevens is the most successful funnyman in the history of recorded music. Yet as he told the writer in 1987, the view of the common man can be interpreted better through humor rather than through lofty views. His songs and those of his great friend C.W. "Buddy" Kalb, Jr., help make light of some of the stupidities of the world, in a way that Chaplin did by "pricking pomposity."

He first came to Country music via the songs of Ernest Tubb, Kitty Wells and Lefty Frizzell. By age 10, Ray had moved to Albany, Georgia, where he started to listen to Ray Charles and the Drifters. He was greatly influenced by the sounds the Coasters had produced in the 50's. While at high school, he formed his own band, the Barons. He attended Georgia State University, studying music theory and composition, and began his own recording career in 1957, signing to Capitol Records' Prep label, thanks to the help of publisher Bill Lowery. He initially released *Silver Bracelet*; then in 1959, he released the single *Sergeant Preston of the Yukon*, based on the cartoon character. However, he failed to get permission to use the name, and the single was withdrawn. During this time, Ray also acted as an arranger and producer for Patti Page, Brook Benton and Brenda Lee.

In 1961, Ray signed to Mercury Records and released *Jeremiah Peabody's Poly Unsaturated Quick Dissolving Fast Acting Pleasant Tasting Green and Purple Pills*, which reached the Pop Top 40. This was followed up by the single that would turn him into a star, *Ahab the Arab*, which reached the Top 5 on the Pop charts, in 1962. That year, Ray decided to make the move to Nashville. He stayed with Mercury until 1963, but his only major success on the label was the 1963 Top 20 hit *Harry the Hairy Ape*, although other charted singles would achieve greater acclaim later, like the 1962 Top 50 record

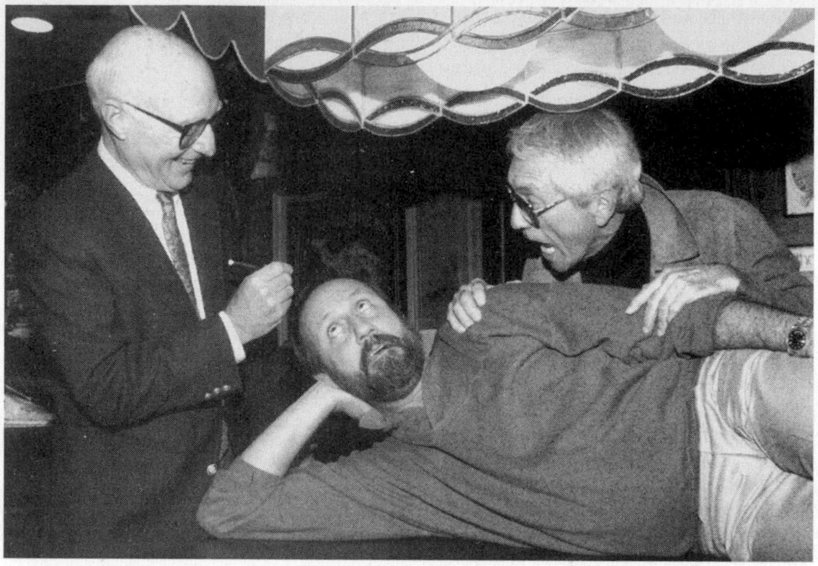

Curb Records sign on ***Ray Stevens***

Santa Claus Is Watching You. He spent some of his time as a session musician, and sang back-up, including sometimes subbing in the Jordanaires.

Ray moved over to Monument, where Fred Foster produced him. Here he recorded humor and some more conventional material. His biggest hits on the Pop charts were *Mr. Business Man* (1968, Top 30), *Gitarzan* (1969, Top 10) and *Along Came Jones* (1969, Top 30). *Gitarzan* earned Ray his first Gold Disc. He also made his debut on the Country charts in 1969, with Kristofferson's *Sunday Mornin' Comin' Down*, which went Top 60.

By the end of the 60's, Ray was managed by Andy Williams' brother Don and in 1969, Ray transferred to Andy's Barnaby label. He also appeared on Andy's TV show and got a summer TV show that replaced Andy's show. That year, his handclaps could be heard on the Archies' hit *Sugar Sugar*. The following year, Ray had his first international best-seller, *Everything Is Beautiful*. It went to No.1 on the Pop chart, Top 40 on the Country chart and Top 10 on the U.K. Pop chart. In the process, it earned Ray his second Gold Disc. The recording won for Ray a Grammy Award as "Best Contemporary Vocal Performance, Male."

In 1971, *Turn Your Radio On* became a Top 20 Country single. In the U.K., *Bridget the Midget* became a monster hit reaching No.2. Ray was featured on the *Music Country* TV show that ran from 1973 through 1974. His next big record came in 1974, when *The Streak* went to No.1 (going Gold), where it stayed for three weeks. It also went Top 3 on the Country charts, and gave him his first No.1 in the U.K. It sold in the region of 5 million copies. Ray played piano on the album ***Jerry Kennedy & Friends***, released on Mercury.

In 1975, he and some musicians were goofing around the old Jazz standard called *Misty*. Fortunately, the resultant adaptation was recorded and it became a Top 15 Pop single and went Top 3 on the Country chart. It also reached No.2 on the U.K. Pop chart. It won for Ray another Grammy Award for "Best Arrangement Accompanying Vocalists." The following year, Ray moved to Warner Brothers and scored with the Country Top 20 remake of *You Are So Beautiful*, which had been a No.1 for Joe Cocker. He followed up with the Top 30 record *Honky Tonk Waltz*.

During 1977, he had a hit with the mind-blowing version of *In the Mood*, under the name of Henhouse Five Plus Too, which had Ray making clucking noises to the famous Glenn Miller hit. His last Pop hit for Warner Brothers was *I Need Your Help Barry Manilow*, which came from his album ***The Feelin's Not Right Again***, in 1979.

Ray moved to RCA Victor the following year, and came up with another comedy classic, *Shriner's Convention*, which made the Country chart Top 10 (incidentally Ray and the Shriners have a mutual respect for one another and he does play their conventions!). It's at this point where the name C.W. Kalb, Jr. starts to appear. Cyrus William Kalb, Jr., a longtime friend of Ray's, was at one time signed to Lowery Music. A resident of Raytown, Missouri, he works for the Ford Motor Company. Often writing with wife,

Carlene, and Ray, "Buddy" Kalb is one of the funniest writers in popular music.

Ray's other RCA Country hits were *Night Games* (1980), *One More Last Chance* (1981) and *Written Down in My Heart* (1982). Ray moved back to Mercury in 1983 and in 1984, he signed with MCA. From here on in, it is his albums that become more important than his singles. His biggest hit single was the Top 20 *Mississippi Squirrel Revival.* Apart from that his highest placed records were *The Haircut Song* (1985), *The Ballad of the Blue Cyclone* (1986) and *Would Jesus Wear a Rolex* (1987), none of which got above the Top 50.

The albums released on MCA are worth buying for the sleeve photographs alone, in particular ***He Thinks He's Ray Stevens*** (1984) (which was Certified Gold in 1987), ***I Have Returned*** (1985) (which was Certified Gold in 1989), ***Surely You Joust*** (1986) and ***Crackin' Up*** (1987). Ray's 1988 album ***I Never Made a Record I Didn't Like*** is worth getting for Ray's version of Michael Jackson's *Bad.* On his 1989 album ***Beside Myself*** is the contemporary classic *I Saw Elvis in a U.F.O.* In 1990, he moved to Curb/Capitol, and continued with more of the same on ***Lend Me Your Ears***, which also has a great sleeve. His 1991 album ***#1 with a Bullet*** yielded the charted single *Working for the Japanese* and contains the delicious track *The Pirate Song (I Want to Sing & Dance).*

Ray has made the *Music City News* (now TNN/*Music City News*) Awards' "Comedian of the Year" title all his own, having won it 1986 through 1993. During 1988, Ray started his own label, Clyde Records, to which the first signing was his daughter, Suzi Ragsdale, a successful songwriter. It was on video that Ray became one of the most successful performers. His ***Ray Stevens: Comedy Video Classics*** had racked up sales of over 300,000, and was *Billboard*'s "Top Music Video of the Year," outselling Garth Brooks and Billy Ray Cyrus, as well as all the Rock performers.

RECOMMENDED ALBUMS:

"The Best of Ray Stevens" (Mercury)(1970)
"Ray Stevens' Greatest Hits" (Barnaby)(1972)
"The Best of Ray Stevens" (Barnaby)(1975)
"Ray Stevens' Greatest Hits" (RCA Victor)(1983)
"He Thinks He's Ray Stevens" (MCA)(1984)
"I Have Returned" (MCA)(1985)
"Surely You Joust" (MCA)(1986)
"Ray Stevens—Greatest Hits" (MCA)(1987)
"Crackin' Up" (MCA)(1987)
"Greatest Hits Vol. 2" (MCA)(1987)
"I Never Made a Record I Didn't Like" (MCA)(1988)
"Lend Me Your Ears" (Curb/Capitol)(1990)
"#1 with a Bullet" (Curb/Capitol)(1991)
Videos:
"Ray Stevens: Comedy Video Classics" (Curb Video)(1993)

CAL STEWART (a.k.a. UNCLE JOSH)

(Singer, Songwriter, Unknown Instruments, Comedy)

Given Name: **Calvin Edward Stewart**
Date of Birth: **ca. 1856**
Where Born: **Charlotte County, Virginia**
Married: **Rossini Waugh**
Children: **Unknown**
Date of Death: **December 7, 1919**

Although he died before the true era of recorded Country music even began, Cal Stewart with his rural comedy skits should be considered the true pioneer of Country humor to the same degree that Fiddlin' John Carson or Jimmie Rodgers ranks for picking and singing. From the late 1890's until his passing in 1919, Stewart in the role of Uncle Josh pioneered what would later become the staples for the generation of Rod Brasfield, Minnie Pearl, Archie Campbell and Jerry Clower. Ironically, although Stewart himself came from the South, his Uncle Weathersby character came from the fictional village of Pun'kin Center and was a Down East New Englander rather than a backwoods hick from the southern uplands.

Details on Cal Stewart's life are scant and it is difficult to separate fact from fiction on what is available. However, he was seemingly born to Scottish immigrant parents of modest means. Young Cal apparently wandered about the country for some years as an itinerant laborer, during which time he may have even been a Wells Fargo shotgun guard in the West. However, he seems to have gravitated toward entertainment, including the circus, minstrel shows and finally stage plays. His Uncle Josh character apparently was derived from Uncle Josh Whitcomb, a rustic New Hampshire farmer in the 1886 melodrama *The Old Homestead*, who rescued his son from a life of debauchery in New York City. Denman Thompson had been both playwright and actor in this production and Stewart reportedly served as his understudy.

Whatever the background, Cal began recording his Uncle Josh skits about 1898 and continued it for the rest of his life. He also wrote and performed a few songs, some of which would be covered by Country artists in the 20's. Many of the monologues concerned the bucolic rustic as he encountered various aspects of urban life or new, unfamiliar technology: *Uncle Josh's Arrival in New York, Uncle Josh on an Elevator*. Others dealt with his relations with the residents of Pun'kin Center such as Jim Lawson, Ezra Hoskins, and Deacon Witherspoon and bear such titles as *Train Time at Pun'kin Center, War Talk at Pun'kin Center*, and *Uncle Josh Takes the Census*. Joel Whitburn ranked forty-two of these skits as hit records between 1898 and 1921 in his book *Pop Memories*. Stewart recorded for all the major companies of that era including Columbia, Edison, and Victor. On some of the recordings Ada Jones (1873-1922), known for her various dialects and singing, played the role of Josh's wife, Aunt Nancy.

Cal Stewart also toured in vaudeville with both his actual wife and Ada Jones doing the Aunt Nancy role. In early December 1919, he suffered a stroke during a Chicago recording session and died in a hospital shortly afterward. At the time, Stewart and his wife resided on a farm near Tipton, Indiana. Byron Harlan (1861-1936) also played the role on a few recordings, but the Stewart originals continued to be popular on the market through the 20's. A measure of his early 20th-century popularity can be found in a newspaper editorial which once remarked that "half the people in insane asylums in this country got that way from listening to Uncle Josh records."

What little is known about Cal Stewart comes from the research of Jim Walsh, who wrote about him in *Hobbies* magazine. Walsh also edited an album reissue of Stewart's Edison offerings on Mark 56 Records in 1978. An example of Stewart's singing can be found on the John Edwards Memorial Foundation's anthology ***Minstrels and Tunesmiths***. IMT

RECOMMENDED ALBUM:

"Cal Stewart As Uncle Josh" (Mark 56)(1978)

GARY STEWART

(Singer, Songwriter, Piano, Bass Guitar, Guitar)

Date of Birth: **May 28, 1945**
Where Born: **Letcher County, Kentucky**
Married: **Mary Lou**

Over the years, Gary Stewart has acquired the reputation of being a bad boy and a wild man within Country music. This has overshadowed his obvious multi-faceted talent, and has meant that despite a sparkling start to his career in the early 70's, he has never been able to capitalize on this.

Gary, one of nine children, was named for Gary Cooper, his mother's favorite movie star. When he was 12, his family moved to Florida. He was initially influenced by both rock'n'roll and Country, and formed his first band, the Tomcats, while still in his teens. At age 16, he married Mary Lou and then went on the road as bass player with the Rock group the Amps.

He returned to Okeechobee, Florida, where he worked at an aircraft factory and also played at the Wagon Wheel club. There he met Mel Tillis, who advised him to write songs and go to Nashville. Gary recorded his first single for Cory, entitled *I Love You Truly*, in 1964. He began collaborating with Bill Eldridge, a policeman in Fort Pierce and former member of the Tomcats, and started making forays to Nashville, where Jerry Bradley signed them to his Forrest Hills publishing company.

Their first cover was Jimmy Griggs' recording of *Charlotte, North Carolina*, which didn't bother the charts. Their breakthrough song was *Poor Red Georgia*, which was a Top 50 success for Stonewall Jackson, in 1965. Eldridge became disillusioned with Nashville and returned to Florida. During 1968, Gary signed with Kapp Records and debuted with *Here Comes That Feeling Again/Merry Go Round*, without success. The following year, Cal Smith recorded a pair of Stewart-Eldridge songs, *It Takes All Night Long* and *You Can't Housebreak a Tomcat*, both of which peaked in the Top 60. Also in 1969, Nat Stuckey had a Top 10 hit with their song *Sweet Thang and Cisco*, which Gary had recorded that year as *Sweet Tater & Cisco*. By the end of the year, Gary was off the label.

During the period 1970 to 1971, Billy Walker recorded four Stewart-Eldridge songs, all of which were major successes. They were *When a Woman Loves a Man (The Way That I Love You)* and *She Goes Walking Through My Mind* (both 1970) and *It's Time to Love Her* and *Traces of a Woman* (both 1971). Gary signed with Decca Records in 1971 and released one single, *She's the Next Best Thing/Something to Believe In*, which also failed.

Gary returned to Fort Pierce, Florida, after hearing the Allman Brothers and developed a more Country-Rock style with shades of Honky-Tonk. Before he left, he had recorded some demos of Motown material while working in various jobs at Bradley's Barn studio. The tape fell into Roy Dea's lap. Dea had produced Jerry Lee Lewis and Charlie Rich and he was very impressed with Gary's tape. Two years after Gary had returned to Florida, Dea moved from Mercury to RCA, where he worked with Jerry Bradley. They immediately signed Gary to the label.

His first release, Wayne Carson's *Drinkin' Thing*, in 1973, did nothing chart-wise. By this time, Gary was playing piano in Nat's band, the Sweet Thangs. Also that year, Tony Booth had a chart hit with Gary's *When a Woman Loves a Man (The Way That I Love You)*. Strangely enough, Gary's initial successes were not his own compositions. At the end of the year, Gary's version of Dickie Betts' (of the Allman Brothers) *Ramblin' Man* made the Top 70. During 1974, Gary moved to Charley Pride's Plainsmen, as pianist/frontman. In the summer of that year, RCA decided to re-release *Drinkin' Thing* and this time, it reached the Country Top 10. The follow-up, Tom Jans/ Jeff Barry's *Out of Hand*, did even better and went Top 5.

The following year, Gary had his first No.1 with another Wayne Carson song, *She's Actin' Single (I'm Drinkin' Doubles)*. Both his other records that year, *You're Not the Woman You Used to Be* and his own *Flat Natural Born Good-Timin' Man*, went Top 20. During that year, he toured the U.K. as part of Charley Pride's entourage. Throughout 1976 to 1978, Gary continued to chart, mainly in the Top 20. His hits were *Oh, Sweet Temptation*, *In Some Room Above the Street* and the Top 15 placed *Your Place or Mine* (all 1976), *Ten Years of This* and *Quits* (both 1977) and *Whiskey Trip*, *Single Again* and *Stone Wall (Around Your Heart)* (all 1978).

From 1979 on, Gary's chart levels fell away, and his most successful releases were *Cactus and a Rose*, a Top 50 record in 1980, and *She's Got a Drinking Problem*, which went Top 40, the following year. During 1981, Gary teamed up with Dean Dillon in a writing and performing partnership and they had a Top 50 single the following year, with *Brotherly Love*, a song that would be reprised by Keith Whitley and Earl Thomas Conley and became a Top 3 hit, in 1991, two years after Keith's death. In 1983, the Stewart-Dillon pairing had a further Top 50 success with *Those Were the Days*.

By now, Gary was suffering from an excess of alcohol and he returned to Fort Pierce, where he stayed out of the limelight. In 1984, he had a pair of basement-level chart entries on the Red Ash label. During the next four years, he eschewed recording, but in 1988, he was reunited with Roy Dea, for a debut album, ***Brand New***, for the California-based Hightone label and was particularly noted for the great use of his famed vibrato. However, two singles, *Brand New Whiskey* and *Empty Glass*, only reached the Top 70. He continued to release albums on Hightone through the 90's, all of which were produced by Roy Dea. These were ***Battleground*** (1990), ***Out of Hand*** (1991), ***Gary's Greatest*** (1991) and ***I'm a Texan*** (1993).

RECOMMENDED ALBUMS:

"You're Not the Woman You Used to Be" (MCA)(1975)
"Your Place or Mine" (RCA Victor)(1977) [With Emmylou Harris, Rodney Crowell and Nicolette Larson] [Re-released in 1981]
"A Cactus & a Rose" (RCA Victor)(1980) [With Greg Allman, Dickie Betts and Bonnie Bramlett]
"Gary Stewart's Greatest Hits" (RCA Victor)(1982)
"Brotherly Love" (RCA Victor)(1982) [With Dean Dillon]
"Those Were the Days " (mini-album)(RCA Victor)(1983) [With Dean Dillon]
"Twenty of the Best" (RCA International UK)(1984)
"Collector's Series" (RCA Victor)(1985)
"Brand New" (Hightone)(1988)
"Battleground" (Hightone)(1990)
"Out of Hand" (Hightone)(1991)
"Gary's Greatest" (Hightone)(1991)
"I'm a Texan" (Hightone)(1993)

JOHN STEWART

(Singer, Songwriter, Guitar, Banjo)

Date of Birth:	**September 5, 1939**
Where Born:	**San Diego, California**
Married:	**Buffy Ford**
Children:	**one son**

John Stewart is one of the backbone performers in Folk and Country who have achieved cult status. As a songwriter, he has been covered by performers in a variety of musical styles from Pop to Bluegrass.

John, the son of a racehorse trainer, was early influenced by rock'n'roll and Folk music. Having learned to play guitar, he played in various garage bands and then formed John Stewart and the Furies, which recorded the single *Rocking Anna*, for the local Vita label. After high school, John attended Mount San Antonio Junior College, with vague ideas of entering music.

With the advent of the Folk boom, John felt himself drawn toward the music. By 1959, he had written a few songs and went backstage at a Kingston Trio concert. He played some songs to them, accompanying himself on banjo, and they immediately agreed to two of his songs, *Molly Dee* and *Green Grasses*. Their manager was very impressed with John and mentioned that the Roulette label was looking for a Folk group. He therefore put together a trio, the Cumberland Three. They released their first single, *Johnny Reb/Come Along Julie*, in 1960. They stayed with the label for two years, and released three albums.

When Dave Guard decided to leave the Kingston Trio in 1961, John was invited to replace him. John was in the group when they recorded *Where Have All the Flowers Gone* (1962), *Greenback Dollar* and *Reverend Mr. Black* (both 1963). By 1967, the group had decided to break up. John was by then feeling that the music of the group had become limited and he wanted to spread his solo wings.

John's songwriting skills now began to be noticed and during the late 60's, he had several songs cut. The most successful was *Daydream Believer*, which the Monkees took to No.1 on the Pop chart, in 1967. The song was demoed at a shared session with John Denver, during which Denver put down *Leaving on a Jet Plane*. Other minor successes were *Never*

Going Back by the Lovin' Spoonful (1968) and *July You're a Woman* by Pat Boone (1969).

After leaving the Kingston Trio, John joined up with Buffy Sainte-Marie and experimented with mixed media, utilizing themes and images from the painter Andrew Wyeth. These images of rural America would permeate John's work. Around 1967-1968, John worked on Robert Kennedy's election campaign and his experiences also came into his songs. In 1968, John signed with Capitol (which had released the Kingston Trio product) and that year debuted with the album ***Signals Through the Glass***. The following year, John released the album ***California Bloodlines***, which featured many of Nashville's session players "A Team". That year, John debuted on the Pop chart with *Armstrong*, which reached the Top 75.

In 1970, John had his last album on Capitol entitled ***Willard***. The following year, he moved to Warner Brothers Records, and issued ***Lonesome Picker Rides Again*** (1971) and ***Sunstorm*** (1972). John then moved to RCA, where he continued to produce critically acclaimed, albeit not high selling albums. In 1973, there was ***Cannons in the Rain*** and this was followed by ***Phoenix Concerts Live*** (John has always had a very big following in Phoenix) in 1974 and ***Wingless Angels*** in 1975, produced by Nik Venet. In 1974, two versions (Red, White & Blue(grass) and Ed Bruce) of *July You're a Woman* made the lower levels of the Country chart. John changed labels in 1977 and signed with Robert Stigwood's RSO label. The first album for this label was ***Fire in the Wind***, which was produced by John and Mentor Williams. In 1978, John was a member of the short-lived group Scarecrow, which released one eponymous album for the Spilt Milk label. John's 1979 album ***Bombs Away Dream Babies*** yielded John's biggest Pop hit *Gold*, which reached the Top 5, *Midnight Wind,* which went Top 30, and *Lost Her in the Sun*, which went Top 40. Also featured on the album were Lindsey Buckingham and Stevie Nicks (of Fleetwood Mac). In 1980, John released ***Dream Babies Go Hollywood***, which has a most entertaining sleeve of John dancing with a dress-store mannequin. Vocalists on the album include Phil Everly, Nicolette Larson, Linda Ronstadt and Wendy Waldman.

RCA re-released ***Phoenix Concerts Live*** as ***In Concert***, in 1980. That year, Anne Murray recorded *Daydream Believer*, and had a Top 3 Country and a Top 15 Pop hit with it. In 1984, John released the ***Trankus*** album on his own Sunstorm label. For most of the 80's, he turned his back on recording and then reverted to a more Folk-oriented style. John duetted with Nanci Griffith in 1987 on John's *Sweet Dreams Will Come*, which was on Nanci's ***Little Love Affairs,*** and the following year, Rosanne Cash had a No.1 Country hit with John's *Runaway Train*.

Most of John's early albums were re-released by the German Bear Family label. In 1990, John released ***Live '90, Neon Beach*** and in 1991 ***Live at McCabes***.

RECOMMENDED ALBUMS:

"Signals Through the Glass" (Capitol)(1968)
*"California Bloodlines" (Capitol)(1969) **
"Willard" (Capitol)(1970)
*"Lonesome Picker Rides Again" (Warner Brothers)(1971) **
*"Sunstorm" (Warner Brothers)(1972) **
*"Cannons in the Rain" (Warner Brothers)(1973) **
*"Phoenix Concerts Live" (RCA)(1974) **
*"Wingless Angels" (RCA)(1975) **
"Fire in the Wind" (RSO)(1977)
"Bombs Away Dream Babies" (RSO)(1979)
"Dream Babies Go Hollywood" (RSO)(1980)
"Trankus" (Sunstorm)(1984)
[Re-released on Bear Family Germany]*

REDD STEWART

(Singer, Songwriter, Piano, Guitar, Fiddle)
Given Name: Henry Stewart
Date of Birth: May 27, 1921
Where Born: Ashland City, Tennessee

The careers of Redd Stewart and Pee Wee King are interwoven, with Redd being vocalist for King's Golden West Cowboys and co-writer with King on such classics as *Tennessee Waltz* and *Slow Poke*.

Redd's family moved to Louisville, Kentucky, while he was still young. He started playing guitar and piano while still at school and began his career by writing a song for a car dealer's commercial, when 14. He then formed and played in various bands around Louisville, including the Prairie Riders. In 1937, Pee Wee came to Louisville to play on WHAS and signed Redd as a musician with the Golden West Cowboys. At the time, Eddy Arnold was the band's vocalist.

Following the attack on Pearl Harbor, Redd was drafted into the U.S. Army and sent to the South Pacific. While stationed there with the rank of sergeant, Redd wrote *A Soldier's Last Letter*, which Ernest Tubb worked on and recorded in 1944, making it a No.1 hit staying at the top for 4 weeks out of a 7-month stay on the Country charts and crossing over to the Pop chart Top 20.

When Redd returned to Pee Wee's Golden West Cowboys at the end of WWII, he became the band's vocalist, Arnold having gone solo. Now Redd started to take songwriting seriously. He appeared on the *Grand Ole Opry*

Redd Stewart *co-wrote "Tennessee Waltz"*

until 1947 and a year earlier, he and Pee Wee wrote their first major success, *Bonaparte's Retreat*, which was Kay Starr's launchpad to stardom.

In 1947, Pee Wee, Redd and the band moved to WAVE Louisville, Kentucky, where they had a weekly radio show and then later in the year, they transferred to WAVE-TV, where they had a television show until 1957. Redd and Pee Wee got together for another classic song, *Tennessee Waltz*, in 1948. Redd wrote the song on the back of a matchbox after seeing the success that Bill Monroe had with *Kentucky Waltz*.

Redd sang on Pee Wee King's 1948 version, which reached the Top 3 on the Country chart and crossed over to the Top 30 on the Pop charts, on RCA Victor. It was re-issued in 1951 and climbed to the Top 10. Other hit versions, in 1948, were by Cowboy Copas (Top 3) and Roy Acuff (Top 15).

The following year, Tennessee featured in the title of two other King hits on which Redd appeared, namely, *Tennessee Tears* and *Tennessee Polka*. Pee Wee King's version of *Bonaparte's Retreat* edged into the Top 10 during 1950. However, it was in 1951 that Pee Wee had a No.1 hit with the King-Stewart song *Slow Poke*, which also became a No.1 Pop success. That year, Patti Page took *The Tennessee Waltz* to No.1 on the Pop chart, which also became a Top 3 Country hit. It went on to sell over 6 million copies.

The following year, the song became a Top 10 hit for Hawkshaw Hawkins and *You Belong to Me* became a Pop hit for Jo Stafford. By now, Pee Wee had dropped his band's name and as Pee Wee King & His Band, he racked up *Silver and Gold* (Country Top 5/Pop

Top 20) and *Busybody* (Country Top 10/Pop Top 30).

Redd was still the featured vocalist on the 1954 Pee Wee King double-sided hit *Changing Partners/Bimbo*. Their final hit together was *Backward Turn Backward*. Redd toured with Pee Wee throughout the 50's and 60's, and during that time, their songs continued to be recorded. In 1959, Billy Grammar had a Pop success with *Bonaparte's Retreat* as did Bobby Comstock and Jerry Fuller with *Tennessee Waltz*. Other charted versions of Redd's songs were *Bonaparte's Retreat* by Carl Smith (1970) and Glen Campbell (1974) and *Tennessee Waltz* by Sam Cooke (1964) and Lacy J. Dalton (1980). On February 17, 1965, *Tennessee Waltz* was officially proclaimed by Governor Frank Clement as the Tennessee state song.

As well as recording with Pee Wee, Redd also recorded on his own, including the 1959 Audio Lab album ***Redd Stewart Sings Favorite Old Time Tunes***. He also appeared in several movies with Pee Wee King, including *Gold Mine in the Sky* (1938), *Ridin' the Outlaw Trail* (1951) and *The Rough, Tough West* (1952), the last two starring Charles Starrett as the Durango Kid. In 1961, Redd and Pee Wee appeared in the movie *Hoedown*. In 1970, Redd was inducted as a charter member of the Nashville Songwriters Hall of Fame.

RECOMMENDED ALBUMS:

"Redd Stewart Sings Favorite Old Time Tunes" (Audio Lab)(1959)
"Pee Wee King and Redd Stewart" (Starday)(1964)
"I Remember" (Hickory)(1974)
"The Best of Pee Wee King and Redd Stewart" (Starday)(1975)

WYNN STEWART

(Singer, Songwriter, Guitar)

Given Name: **Wynnford Lindsey Stewart**
Date of Birth: **June 7, 1934**
Where Born: **Morrisville, Missouri**
Married: **1. (Div.)**
2. Delores (div.)
3. (Div.)
Date of Death: **July 17, 1985**

It is highly possible that if Wynn Stewart's life had not been cut short, he would have re-emerged in the late 80's as an even greater Country music star. That, timing and a lack of drive on his own part ensured that today most people can't even remember his name. Yet, he was one performer who helped create the West Coast Country music sound that continued with Buck Owens, Merle Haggard and, currently, Dwight Yoakam. He also had a reputation for playing his music at high volume.

Wynn was raised with his sisters, Patty and Beverly, and because their father, Cleo, was a sharecropper, they moved around the country a lot. During WWII, they moved to California, where Cleo originated, but returned to Missouri after the war. In 1947, Wynn worked on KWTO Springfield, Missouri, and a year later returned to California. Wynn began singing in church, but his first love was baseball. He wanted to emulate his uncle, Ken Gables, who was a Major League pitcher. However, Wynn was not tall enough and also suffered with a hand disease. He therefore switched his attention to playing music.

While playing the clubs, he still maintained his academic studies. He got his first guitar when he was spotted by a member of the audience who sold Folgers Coffee on the road and was so impressed by Wynn's talent that he told him to go to the music store, where he paid for a Gibson guitar. Wynn was then 17.

It was meeting steel player Ralph Mooney that proved the first turning point in Wynn's career. At the time, Ralph was playing lead guitar on a show called *Squeakin Deacon's Amateur Hour*, and Wynn began winning the contest each Sunday and as a result was the proud owner of several wristwatches. Wynn began writing to Mooney when the latter's band moved to Las Vegas, and on his return, he joined Wynn, as steel player. His rolling chord style was one that trademarked Wynn's Challenge recordings.

Wynn cut his first recordings in 1954, for the Intro label, and released the single *I've Waited a Lifetime/After All*. His biggest influence at this time was Skeets McDonald and it was Skeets who set up an audition with Capitol's head of A & R, Ken Nelson. His first single, *Waltz of the Angels*, was later recorded by Lefty Frizzell and became a 1962 hit for George Jones and Margie Singleton. Wynn's version made a one-week chart visit in the Top 15. Despite other releases, he failed to register with any of his singles.

In 1958, Wynn moved on to Jackpot, a subsidiary of Joe Johnson's Challenge label. It was through the introduction of Harlan Howard that Wynn made the move. His initial recording for the label, *Come On*, was a Rockabilly number and *School Bus Love Affair* a teen ballad. The following year, he released a duet with Jan Howard, *Yankee Go Home/How the Other Half Lives*, which also failed to register. It was Wynn's interest that caused Jan Howard to sing, while his sister Beverly taught her to play guitar. At the end of the year, *Wishful Thinking*, on the parent Challenge label, gave Wynn a Top 5 single. The record featured Beverly on back-up vocals (she also co-wrote several songs with Wynn).

The following year, Wynn teamed up again with Jan for the Top 30 record *Wrong Company*. That year, he made his debut on the *Grand Ole Opry*. At the time, his session musicians included Mooney, Bobby Austin on bass guitar and vocals, Gordon Terry or Joe Maphis on Fiddle, and Dale Noe Tommy Collins or Bobby George on rhythm guitar.

Wynn had three further chart records while at Challenge, his self-penned *Big, Big Love* (later to be recorded by k.d. lang) (1961), *Another Day, Another Dollar* (1962) and *Half of This, Half of That* (1964). In 1960, Helen "Peaches" Price joined the Tourists (Wynn's backing band) as drummer and a year later, Roy Nichols, formerly with the Maddox Brothers and Rose, came on board as lead guitarist.

Until 1961, the band had been resident at a nightclub in Long Beach, California. During that year, the owners opened the Nashville Nevada Club in Las Vegas, and Wynn was given a third share of the venue and the band became the house act. He stayed here until 1963, during which time members of the band included Merle Haggard. Haggard's debut single for Talley, *Sing a Sad Song*, was a Wynn Stewart composition. The Vegas situation went wrong and left Wynn with financial problems and he returned to California.

Wynn re-signed to Capitol in 1965 and although *I Keep Forgettin' That I Forgot About You* made the Top 50, it took a while for him to establish himself. That happened in 1967, when *It's Such a Pretty World Today* made it to No.1. It stayed on the charts for over 5 months and was followed by the Top 10 record *'Cause I Have You*. The flip-side, *That's the Only Way to Cry*, also made it to the Top 70. He wrapped up the year with another Top 10 single *Love's Gonna Happen to Me*. He stayed with Capitol until 1971 where his principal hits were *Something Pretty* (Top 10), *In Love and Strings* (both 1968), *Let the Whole World Sing It with Me* and *World-Wide Travelin' Man* (both 1969) and *It's a Beautiful Day* (1970). Among musicians on his later sessions was the famed Clarence White. Around this time, Wynn lost his longtime band member Ralph Mooney, who was finding it difficult to make a living with Wynn being so apathetic about career.

In 1972, Wynn surfaced on RCA Victor, where he had three minor chart records, the most successful being *Paint Me a Rainbow*, that year. He moved over to the Playboy label in 1975, and the following year, had a Top 10 single, *After the Storm*, which was followed by a Top 20 record, his version of *Sing a Sad Song*. With California not being as active an area for Country music, Wynn moved to Nashville. However, he was getting a reputation for missing bookings and for his drinking. During 1976, Wynn released one single for Atlantic, without success. He returned to the charts, in 1978, on the WIN label, with the Top 40 single *Eyes Big As Dallas*, but his other chart entry on WIN, *Could I Talk You Into Loving Me Again* (1979), only reached the Top 60.

Wynn decided to make one more try for stardom, during the mid-80's. By this time, he was in ill health and suffering from high blood pressure. His new tour was scheduled to start at Twitty City, but Wynn didn't make it to the stage; he died at 6:00 p.m., from a heart attack. Following his death, his single *Wait Till I Get My Hands on You* made a one-week visit to the charts, on the Pretty World label.

Perhaps one day, Wynn Stewart's work, both as a singer and as a songwriter, will be greater appreciated and his song catalog will be trawled for material that is highly recordable in the 90's.

RECOMMENDED ALBUMS:

"Sweethearts of Country Music" (Challenge)(1961) [With Jan Howard]
"The Songs of Wynn Stewart" (Capitol)(1965) [Re-released by Stetson UK in the original sleeve (1989)]
"After the Storm" (Playboy)(1976)
"Wishful Thinking—Wynn Stewart—The Challenge Years 1958-1963" (double) (Bear Family Germany)(1988) [Challenge masters]

CLIFFIE STONE

(Singer, Songwriter, Bass, Comedy, Industry Executive)

Given Name: Clifford Gilpin Snyder
Date of Birth: March 1, 1917
Where Born: Burbank, California
Married: 1. Dorothy Darling (dec'd.) 2. Joan Carol
Children: Linda, Steven, Jonathan, Curtis

West Coast legend ***Cliffie Stone***

The man who probably did more than anyone else to popularize Country music in California during the post-WWII years began his musical career as a bassist in the big bands of Anson Weeks and Freddie Slack. He also had experience working at the Pasadena Community Playhouse and in Ken Murray's Hollywood Blackouts, playing bass in a comedy sketch with Gene Austin.

However, Cliffie soon got into Country radio, working as a deejay, emcee and performer on KFUD (*Covered Wagon Jubilee*) and KFWB (*Lucky Stars*) in the Los Angeles area. He also became a band leader and featured comedian on the *Hollywood Barn Dance*. From 1943 to 1947, Cliffie hosted twenty-eight radio shows each week.

In 1946, Cliffie moved into the executive branch of the music business with Capitol Records, remaining in A & R with the company for over two decades, during which time he guided the careers of Tennessee Ernie Ford, Hank Thompson, Mollie Bee and many others. He managed Tennessee Ernie from 1947 to 1957. Along the way he also recorded six albums of his own and co-wrote several songs, including *No Vacancy, Divorce Me C.O.D., New Steel Guitar Rag, So Round, So Firm, So Fully Packed* and *Sweet Temptation*.

However, from the standpoint of popularizing Country music, his most important activity was a daily variety show he hosted on KXLA Pasadena, the *Dinner Bell Roundup*. A large number of Country entertainers, including fiddler Red Murrell, banjo player/comedian Herman the Hermit (Stone's father), fiddler Harold Hensley, Tennessee Ernie Ford and the Armstrong Twins, appeared on this program. In 1944, the show changed locations, moving to the Legion Stadium in El Monte, California, and its name, to the *Hometown Jamboree*.

In 1947, Cliffie went Top 5 with *Silver Stars, Purple Sage, Eyes of Blue* (as Cliffie Stone and His Orchestra) and the following year he had hits with *Peepin' Through the Keyhole (Watching Jole Blon)* (as Cliffie Stone and His Barn Dance Band) and *When My Blue Moon Turns to Gold Again*. His last hit was in 1966, when the Cliffie Stone Group backed Kay Adams on *Little Pink Mack*. Cliffie also recorded for Capitol as Cliffie Stone's Country Hombres.

In the mid-1960's, Stone devoted most of his time to his publishing company, Central Songs, and to other music business enterprises. He eventually got back into the record business, heading up the Granite label for several years. In 1972, he was presented with the Pioneer Award by the ACM. In 1989, Cliffie was presented with his own star (the 1,887th) on the Hollywood Walk of Fame and he was elected to the Country Music Hall of Fame. In 1990, he was inducted into the Western Hall of Fame. Cliffie published his book *Everything You Always Wanted to Know About Songwriting but Didn't Know Who to Ask* in 1991. Cliffie has also been inducted into the Disc Jockey Country Music Hall of Fame. Cliffie's son Curtis plays with Highway 101. WKM

RECOMMENDED ALBUMS:

"The Party's on Me" (Capitol)(1958)
"Cool Cowboy" (Capitol)(1959)
"Square Dance Promenade" (Capitol)(1960)
"Original Cowboy Sing-a-Long" (Capitol)(1961)
"Together Again" (Tower)(1967)

DOUG STONE

(Singer, Songwriter, Guitar, Keyboards, Dobro, Bass Guitar, Drums, Actor)

Given Name: Douglas Jackson Brooks
Date of Birth: June 19, 1956
Where Born: Marietta, Georgia
Married: 1. Teresa (div.) 2. Carie
Children: 1. Michelle Beth, Daniel Jackson; 2. (Dustin) Chance, Kala Jade

If Doug Stone develops his songwriting skills, he has all the makings of being the heir apparent to the late Conway Twitty. He has the same ability to personalize the songs he sings and, like Conway, he is fast becoming a song's "best friend."

Doug's mother, Gail Menseer, was a singer and guitarist and taught him to play. She took him to her gigs and when he was age 7, his mother arranged for him to open for Loretta Lynn and he noticed he had the power to move an audience. When he was 12, his parents separated and Doug and his two brothers moved into a trailer with their father in Newnan. They did not have the comforts of home, but Doug's father instilled in his sons the value of happiness above money and "to be as good as your word." However, Doug ignored his father's advice not to be a musician.

Doug formed a band, Impact, with his best friend, Chet Hinesley, a nephew of Tony Joe White, and they played at skating rinks for the princely fee of $5 each. At the time, he had written a song called *Sugar* and he noticed that he still had this ability to move his audience. However, music took a backseat when he dropped out of school at age 16. He put to use the engineering skills that his father had imparted to him and worked on engines. His band, which also included another friend,

One of Country music's brightest stars, ***Doug Stone***

Steve Bledsoe, went through various name changes including Image and, finally, Main Street.

He moved into a trailer and set up his own studio. Eventually he would build nine of them in various domestic locations. However, according to Doug, he couldn't hold down a job, due to his infatuation with music, and he soon got into debt and lost his trailer. He then moved into a 12-foot-square well house that he, a brother and his father built (and which Doug gradually enlarged, after his first marriage), where he lived for seven years. Doug's mother still believed her son was star material and began getting dates for the band. It was at one such booking at the Veterans of Foreign Wars Club in Newnan, in 1987, that he was spotted by Phyllis Bennett and she became his manager a year later, sending a tape to producer Doug Johnson.

In 1988, Johnson produced three sides on Doug and he played the tape to the legendary Bob Montgomery of Epic Records, who wasn't looking for any new acts, but signed Doug, thereby breaking his life-long habit of never signing an act he hadn't seen perform live. At the time, Doug was working as a maintenance man at the Newnan Country Club.

His first single, *I'd Be Better Off (In a Pine Box),* climbed to the Top 5 in 1990 and stayed on the charts for just shy of six months and was nominated for a Grammy Award. This was swiftly followed by his debut self-titled album which made the Top 15 on the Country Albums chart and crossed over to middle order of the Pop Album chart and was Certified Gold in 1991 and Platinum in 1993. Doug had two more chart singles in 1990, *Fourteen Minutes Old* (Top 10) and *These Lips Don't Know How to Say Goodbye* (Top 5). That year, he named his back-up band Stone Age Band.

Doug opened up his 1991 account with his first No.1, *In a Different Light,* and followed up with the Top 5 hit *I Thought It Was You*, the title track of his second successful cross-over album (Certified Gold in 1992), and another No.1, the instant classic Honky-Tonk song *A Jukebox with a Country Song*. That year, he was nominated for the CMA's Horizon Award and the ACM's "Top New Male."

1992 was equally successful on the record front, with *Come in Out of the Pain* (Top 3), *Warning Labels* (Top 5) and his third No.1, *Too Busy Being in Love*. He released the album ***From the Heart,*** which was successful on both the Country and Album charts and went Gold in 1993. However, on the health front, all was not well and in April 1992, Doug had to undergo emergency quadruple bypass surgery. That year, he released the Christmas album ***The First Christmas***, which reached the Country Albums Top 60. He was nominated for the ACM's "Male Vocalist" award in 1992 and again in 1993.

More Love, Doug's fifth album released in 1993, marked a change of producers and James Stroud took over the reins, with Doug assisting. It also marked a greater input by Doug as a songwriter. Five of the songs were featured in the movie *Gordy*, in which he appeared in the role of Luke McAllister. He was named TNN/*Music City News*' "Star of Tomorrow," having already been nominated in 1991 and 1992. Doug's 1993 single successes were *Made for Lovin' You* (Top 10), *Why Didn't I Think of That* (No.1) and *I Never Knew Love* (Top 3 Country and Top 90 Pop). Doug's single *Addicted to a Dollar* went Top 5 in 1994.

RECOMMENDED ALBUMS:

"Doug Stone" (Epic)(1990)
"I Thought It Was You" (Epic)(1991)
"From the Heart" (Epic)(1992)
"More Love" (Epic)(1993)

ERNEST "POP" STONEMAN

(Singer, Songwriter, Guitar, Autoharp, Harmonica, Clawhammer Banjo, Jew's Harp)

Given Name:	**Ernest Van Stoneman**
Date of Birth:	**May 25, 1893**
Where Born:	**Monarat (Iron Ridge), Carroll County, Virginia**
Married:	**Hattie Frost**
Children:	**Eddie L., I. Grace, John C., Pattie I., J. William (dec'd.), A. Juanita (dec'd.), Jack M. (dec'd.), Gene A., Dean C. (dec.d.), C. Scott (dec'd.), Donna L., O. James, Reta V. (dec'd.), Veronica L., Van H.**
Date of Death:	**June 14, 1968**

Ernest Stoneman ranked among the more prominent recording artists from Country music's first commercial decade. His discs on OKeh, Edison, Victor, and other labels in the middle and late 20's helped give the music an identity along with his songs like *The Titanic*, *The Poor Tramp Has to Live*, *Two Little Orphans* and *In the Golden Bye and Bye*.

Ernest Stoneman was born a few miles from what later became the town of Galax, Virginia, a locale that would lay claim—with considerable justification—to being the Old-Time music capital of the nation. Left motherless at the age of 3, the youngster was reared by a stern old father with the help of three musically-inclined cousins (Burton, George and Bertha Stoneman) who would immerse him in the instrumental and vocal traditions of the Blue Ridge mountain culture.

When he married Hattie Frost (1900-1976) in November 1918, he entered into another family similarly involved in music. In early adulthood Ernest worked at a variety of laboring jobs, especially carpentry, and played music for his own and neighbor enjoyment, but after he heard the sound of a Henry Whitter record in the spring of 1924, he not only determined to better it but changed his own life as well.

Stoneman journeyed to New York in September 1924 and cut two songs for the OKeh label. His waxing of *The Titanic* initiated the start of a long career. Ralph Peer directed him through several sessions for OKeh and Victor. Later, by freelancing—in the Vernon Dalhart style—Stoneman also made records for Edison, Gennett, Paramount, and the Plaza and Pathé corporations as well. Initially Ernest accompanied himself on autoharp and harmonica but later used mostly guitar (in old age he returned to the autoharp). Beginning in 1926, he added other musicians to his group utilizing a full string band sound. These included in-laws and kin such as Bolen and Erma Frost, Hattie, George and Willie Stoneman, and neighbors such as the droll-voiced Uncle Eck Dunford, fiddle virtuoso Kahle Brewer, Walter Mooney, and Tom Leonard. Later he used Herbert and Earl Sweet, Frank and Oscar Jenkins, and Fields and Sampson Ward.

In July and August 1927, Stoneman helped Ralph Peer conduct the now legendary Bristol sessions that led to the discovery of the Carter Family and Jimmie Rodgers. This not only represented the zenith of his own career but inadvertently launched the success of those who would replace him as the top Country artists on the Victor roster. Nonetheless, Ernest would continue to be quite active as a recording artist through 1929 and had a final session for Vocalion in 1934, placing a total of more than 200 sides on disc. By that time, both he and the nation had fallen upon very difficult times.

Having lost their home and most of their possessions, the Stonemans, including their nine surviving children, moved to the Washington, D.C., area, in the fall of 1932, where they had four more children and endured several additional years of dire poverty. In that period, Ernest survived by whatever type of work he could find and struggled to revive his musical career.

In 1941, Ernest bought a lot in Carmody Hills, Maryland, and built a shack that provided shelter for the family and obtained more work in defense-related labor, which eventually led to a more or less regular job at the Naval Gun Factory. In 1947, the Stoneman Family won a talent contest at Constitution Hall, which gave them six months' exposure on local television, which in turn provided local Country fans with their musical abilities and opportunities to play for pay.

In 1956, "Pop" (as he now became known for obvious reasons) won $10,000 on NBC-TV's quiz program *The Big Surprise* and sang on the show as well. That same year, the Blue Grass Champs, composed largely of his children, emerged as a winner on the CBS-TV program *Arthur Godfrey's Talent Scouts*. Then Mike Seeger recorded Pop and Hattie for Folkways.

With Ernest's retirement from labor and the Champs going full-time they became the Stonemans. Pop sang on one side of a single for Blue Ridge about 1960. The entire group did albums for Starday in 1962 and 1963 with the venerable Ernest doing the lion's share of the lead vocals on both. In 1964, they went first to Texas and then to California in search of stardom, cutting an album for World Pacific, playing at Disneyland, on some network variety shows, and at several Folk festivals. In November 1965, they went to Nashville, where they contracted with MGM Records, started a syndicated TV show, and made a highly favorable impression, which landed them the CMA "Vocal Group of the Year" award in 1967.

Pop's health began to fail in the next few months and he played his last record session and shows in April 1968. Hospitalized for two months, he passed away in June. By that time Historical Records had started reissue projects devoted to some of his Edison sides and work with Fields Ward. Over the next several years, other collector labels such as Rounder, County, and Old Homestead produced albums of his originals. His first hit, *The Titanic*, was included on the Smithsonian Collection. Although nominated several times for the Country Music Hall of Fame, he has yet to be chosen. Other members of the Stoneman family have carried on with his musical legacy.

Garrison Keillor wrote the following poem about Pop Stoneman and the autoharp:

The autoharp is an instrument on which simple melody
Is obtained by pressing a Chord Bar, such as F or G
Felt dampers thereby deaden the strings that are not needed,
And strumming it makes music, it is generally conceded

It was invented by Charles F. Zimmerman in 1881
An event that he compared to the rising sun
"It is" he said, "the finest work of Man on Earth."
A statement that was greeted with some mirth.

Music can be played by anyone who hears,
Zimmerman believed and so did Sears
Which sold thousands of them yonder and hither,
But it was still known as the idiot Zither.

Until it was played by "Pop" Stoneman, a Virginian,
Who did his part to change public opinion
By recording many tunes that were fancier and harder
So did Kilby Snow and Maybelle Carter.

Many musicians otherwise liberal in their views
See an autoharp and ask to be excused,
But they've a surprise coming in that city bright and fair
They'll find no guitars only autoharps Up There.....

IMT

RECOMMENDED ALBUMS:

Pre-1935 recordings:

"Ernest V. Stoneman and His Dixie Mountaineers" (Historical)(1968)

"Ernest V. Stoneman and the Blue Ridge Corn Shuckers" (Rounder)(1975)

"Round the Heart of Old Galax, Vol. 1" (County)(1980)

"Ernest V. Stoneman with Family and Friends, Vol. 1" (Old Homestead)(1986)

"Ernest V. Stoneman with Family and Friends, Vol. 2" (Old Homestead)(1986)

"Sinking of the Titanic, Vol. III" (Old Homestead)(1991)

Post-1955 recordings:

"Old-Time Tunes of the South" (Folkways)(1957) [Side A by Ernest and Hattie Stoneman]

"Pop Stoneman Memorial Album" (MGM)(1969)

"A Rare Find!" (Stonehouse)(ca. 1982) [Recorded 1966; re-issued as "Me and My Autoharp" on Old Homestead (1993)]

(See also the Stonemans/Stoneman Family.)

RONI STONEMAN

(Singer, Banjo, Guitar, Bass, Fiddle, Comedy)

Given Name:	**Veronica Loretta Stoneman**
Date of Birth:	**May 5, 1938**
Where Born:	**Washington, D.C.**
Married:	**1. Eugene Cox (div./dec'd.)** **2. George Hemrick (div.)** **3. Richard Adams (div.)** **4. William Zimmerman (div.)** **5. Larry Corya (div.)**
Children:	**Eugene, Jr., Rebecca, Barbara, Bobby, Hattie Georgia**

Roni Stoneman is the one member of the second-generation Stoneman Family who has achieved a high degree of fame as a solo performer. Roni has gained renown as a banjo picker and has earned even greater laurels for her comedy work on *Hee Haw*. Her efforts as a straight Country vocalist, while adequate, have received less attention.

Like the other Stoneman children, Roni grew up in relative poverty, learning the basics of music at an early age, being particularly enamored with the banjo picking of Earl Scruggs in her youth. Since the older Stonemans worked in other bands in the early 50's, Pop Stoneman organized Roni and Van together with two other neighborhood youths—fiddler Zeke Dawson and bassist Larry King—as Pop Stoneman and His Little Pebbles. By the time the Little Pebbles won the band contest at Galax in August 1956, Roni had already married, and the group dissolved soon afterward.

After the birth of her first child, Roni worked on the Washington, D.C., club circuit scene playing bass for Johnnie Hopkins and banjo with Benny and Vallie Cain's Country Clan and the Al Jones group. About 1960, she joined the Bluegrass Champs following the departure of Porter Church. Roni had made her first instrumental recording for Folkways in 1956 when she and Eugene Cox each cut a banjo tune on the ***American Banjo Scruggs Style*** album. This represented the first Bluegrass banjo tune waxed by a female artist. Roni's initial vocal record occurred a little later when she sang *Won't You Come Home Bill Bailey* as part of a Stoneman Family session.

Roni worked with the Stonemans throughout the 60's in Washington, D.C., and California and after 1965, when they came to Nashville. She played a key role in their recording, touring, and syndicated television success, but left the group in February 1971, when she gave birth to her last child. By this time, she was living in Winston-Salem, North Carolina, with her second husband, George Hemrick. The following year she came back to Nashville and recorded a couple of singles for Dot.

Roni really found her forte in 1973 when she joined the cast of *Hee Haw*, with a voice and accent well fitted for many of their skits.

In her specialty, the Nagger segment, she portrayed the long-suffering housewife Ida Lee Nagger at the ironing board, usually engaged in disagreement with her ne'er-do-well husband Laverne (Gordie Tapp). She also did some banjo picking during her eighteen-year stint on the program. From time to time she also made special appearances with the Stoneman Family, especially in 1985 and 1989. Ironically, while delighting millions with her humor, Roni failed to secure long-term domestic happiness, accumulating a series of marriages and divorces.

Roni recorded relatively little during her *Hee Haw* years, a 1974 single on Chart and another on Spin-Chek being her only releases for more than a decade except for a CMH session with her family in 1981. In the fall of 1989, she cut two albums for her own Stone Ray label, one vocal and another highlighting her banjo work, which have been released on cassette only. Since the reorganization of *Hee Haw* in September 1991, Roni has toyed with several projects including an all-girl band and a pilot for a television program. In 1993, she re-issued her banjo album on sister Patsy's label. IMT

RECOMMENDED ALBUMS:

"First Lady of Banjo" (Stone Ray Records and Stonehouse)(1989) [Cassette only]
"Pure and Country" (Stone Ray Records)(1989)
(See also the Stonemans/Stoneman Family.)

STONEMANS, The (a.k.a. The STONEMAN FAMILY)

When Formed: 1956

PATSY STONEMAN
(Vocals, Guitar, Autoharp, Jew's Harp, Tipel)
Given Name: Pattie Inez Stoneman
Date of Birth: May 27, 1925
Where Born: Galax, Virginia
Married: 1. Charles Streeks (div.)
2. R.H. Caln (dlv.)
3. Donald Dixon (dec'd.)
4. John J. Murphy

SCOTTY STONEMAN
(Vocals, Fiddle, Banjo, Guitar)
Given Name: Calvin Scott Stoneman
Date of Birth: August 4, 1932
Where Born: Galax, Virginia
Married: 1. Cecile Phipps (div.)
2. Paula Brogan (div.)
3. Ann (div.)
4. Mary Madison
Children: Sandra, Ernest Scott, Faith Kerin
Date of Death: March 4, 1973

DONNA STONEMAN
(Vocals, Mandolin, Guitar, Fiddle)
Given Name: Donna LaVerne Stoneman
Date of Birth: February 7, 1934
Where Born: Alexandria, Virginia
Married: Robert Bean (div.)

JIMMY STONEMAN
(Vocals, Bass, Guitar, Fiddle)
Given Name: Oscar James Stoneman
Date of Birth: March 8, 1937
Where Born: Washington, D.C.
Married: 1. Peggy Brain (div.)
2. Mary Grubb Urich
Children: Jeanette

RONI STONEMAN
(Vocals, Banjo, Guitar, Bass)
Given Name: Veronica Loretta Stoneman
Date of Birth: May 5, 1937
Where Born: Washington, D.C.
Married: 1. Eugene Cox (div./dec'd.)
2. George Hemrick (div.)
3. Richard Adams (div.)
4. William Zimmerman (div.)
5. Larry Corya (div.)
Children: Eugene Jr., Rebecca, Barbara, Bobby, Hattie Georgia

VAN STONEMAN
(Vocals, Guitar, Bass, Clawhammer and Bluegrass Banjo, Dobro)
Given Name: Van Haden Stoneman
Date of Birth: December 31, 1940
Where Born: Washington, D.C.
Married: Helen Alvey (div.)
Children: Randy, Vicky

Non-family members have included Johnny Bellar, Jimmy Case, Porter Church, David Daugherty, Chuck Holcomb, Lew Houston (a.k.a. Lew Childre), Jerry Monday, Johnny Bellar and Eddie Mueller

Other than being the children of Country music pioneer Ernest "Pop" Stoneman and growing up with his traditional sounds, the Stoneman Family as a performing act evolved out of the Blue Grass Champs. This unit had been formed by Scotty Stoneman and Jimmy Case working nightly at the Famous, a club owned by Sam Bomstein in 1955.

Early members of the Blue Grass Champs included, in addition to Scotty and Case on respective fiddle and guitar, Jimmy Stoneman on bass fiddle and sister Donna on mandolin. By the time of their winning appearance on CBS-TV's *Arthur Godfrey's Talent Scouts* program in 1956, banjo picker Porter Church had joined them. Gradually they built up a following in the D.C. area and adjacent states northward to Pennsylvania. When non-family members Case, Church, and Lew Childre dropped out, Van, Roni and Pop Stoneman became regulars. In addition to their regular club and park work, the band performed on WTTG-TV with Don Owens and even had their own program for a while. Briefly, they also played the *New Dominion Barn Dance* in Richmond and recorded singles for Bakersfield and Blue Ridge labels.

The Stonemans aspired to the nationally acclaimed stature that Pop had enjoyed in the 20's, but found crashing the big time a major challenge. They guested on the *Opry* in the spring of 1962 under the management of artist/songwriter/promoter Billy Barton and recorded for his Gulf Reef label, but otherwise "starved out." They returned to Washington and subsequently cut a pair of albums for Don

The Stonemans gather around "Pop" Stoneman

Pierce's Starday Records. In May 1963, they worked a concert at the University of Illinois and in November worked some engagements in Las Vegas with Mac Wiseman.

Scott renewed an old friendship with Jack Clement, who had become a successful songwriter and record producer. Together they decided to try their luck in the far West. Although the Stoneman Family did not earn a great deal of money in California, they managed to guest on some TV network variety shows, made an album for World Pacific, appeared at Disneyland, and worked some prestigious club dates.

In November 1965, they landed a booking at The Black Poodle in Nashville and made a big hit. They signed with MGM Records and started a syndicated television program that would eventually be shown on about fifty stations (and notable not only for the music but the trendy miniskirts sported by the ladies). Jerry Monday joined their band, alternating on Dobro and drums and through April 1968 the Stonemans were a highly successful act. Scotty seldom worked with them from 1965, but Roni's comedy and banjo combined with "Dancing" Donna's mandolin, Pop's Old-Time songs, and the talents of Jim and Van made them highly appealing.

The Stonemans reached the Country chart with the Top 40 single *Tupelo County Jail* in 1966 and followed up that year with *The Five Little Johnson Girls*, which just failed to make the Top 20. In 1967, they had two singles on the Country chart, *Back to Nashville Tennessee* (Top 40) and *West Canterbury Subdivision Blues* (Top 50). Their overall charisma carried them to the CMA "Vocal Group of the Year" award that year. When Pop's hospitalization in April 1968 and subsequent death ended his participation in the band, older daughter Patsy replaced him. The Stonemans had their final chart single in July 1968, when *Christopher Robin* peaked just below the Top 40.

After five albums on MGM, the band switched to RCA Victor, but their singles failed to register and their three albums suggested that their producers were somewhat uncertain as to how to market them. From late 1970, the Stonemans also experienced personnel changes. Roni took time off to have a child and never returned.

Donna left in November 1972 and Scott returned, only to die a few months later. Finally, the band stabilized with Patsy, Van, Jim, David Daugherty on banjo and Johnny Bellar on Dobro, but by then their momentum had slipped. Furthermore, their only record release in a five-year period was a single for Million and an uncredited album, Disney's *Country Bear Jamboree* soundtrack. Eddie Mueller replaced Daugherty on banjo in 1977, and the group eventually had two album releases on CMH and another on RPA. Patsy took over management in 1977 and in 1981, she produced a fine two-album set anthology on CMH that included most of the extended family members who had been musically inactive for some years including Roni, who was a part of the *Hee Haw* cast, and Donna, who had become an evangelist and Gospel singer. Critics acclaimed it as their best effort in more than a decade.

During the 80's, the Stonemans, with Donna back on mandolin and sometimes Roni on banjo, continued to work on several shows per year and recorded albums on Rutabaga and Old Homestead. They also had several cuts on a live two-album set from the 1985 Galax Fiddlers Convention. Even with all five Stonemans in the band as it had been in late 1968, they found it hard to rekindle that spirit of youth which had made them so dynamic in that earlier era. Although all are now officially retired except Roni and Donna, they still make an occasional appearance. In 1989, the Stonemans appeared at the prestigious Wembley Festival in England. In 1993, the University of Illinois Press published Ivan M. Tribe's biography detailing their inter-generational story of struggle and survival in *The Stonemans: An Appalachian Family and the Music That Shaped Their Lives.* IMT

RECOMMENDED ALBUMS:

"Ernest V. Stoneman and the Stoneman Family" (Starday)(1962).
"The Great Old Timer at the Capitol" (Starday)(1964)
[This and the above album were subsequently repackaged and re-released on Starday and Nashville]
"Big Ball in Monterey" (World Pacific) [Re-released in shortened form on Sunset]
"Those Singin' Swingin' Stompin' Sensational Stonemans" (MGM)(1966)
"Stoneman's Country" (MGM)(1967)
"All in the Family (MGM)(1967)
"The Great Stonemans" (MGM)(1968)
"A Stoneman Christmas" (MGM)(1968)
"The Stonemans" (MGM)(1970)
"Dawn of the Stonemans' Age" (RCA Victor)(1970)
"In All Honesty" (RCA Victor)(1970)
"California Blues" (RCA Victor)(1970)
"Cuttin' the Grass" (CMH)(1976)
"On the Road" (CMH)(1977)
"Country Hospitality" (RPA)(1977)
"The First Family of Country Music" (double)(CMH)(1982)
"Family Bible" (Rutabaga)(1988)
"For God and Country" (Old Homestead)(1991)
Scott Stoneman:
"Mr. Country Fiddler" (Design and CML)(1967)
"Scotty Stoneman with the Kentucky Colonels" (Briar)(1976)
"The Lost Masters" (Old Homestead)(1991) [Cassette]
Donna Stoneman:
"Old Rugged Cross" (unlabeled cassette)(ca. 1985)
Donna Stoneman & Cathy Manzer:
"I'll Fly Away" (Temple)(1976)
(See also Ernest "Pop" Stoneman, Roni Stoneman)

CARL STORY

(Singer, Songwriter, Guitar, Fiddle)

Given Name:	**Carl Moore Story**
Date of Birth:	**May 29, 1916**
Where Born:	**Lenoir, North Carolina**
Married:	**1. Poy (div.) 2. Helen Anderson**
Children:	**Carl, Jr., Stewart, Jerry, James A., Linda, John Paul (dec'd.)**

Carl Story ranks among the pioneer figures in Bluegrass music although some of his earlier efforts straddled the fence between Bluegrass and Country. Still, his work has justly earned for him the sobriquet Father of Bluegrass Gospel. Eschewing Nashville, Carl has generally remained close to his home base in the mountain and Piedmont cities of Asheville, Charlotte and Knoxville.

Born in Lenoir, North Carolina, the son of a local Old-Time fiddler and rhythm guitarist, Carl Story started playing music himself at age 9. Although initially drawn to fiddle and square dance music by his parents, Story soon came under the influence of popular recording artists from the region such as the North Carolina Ramblers and the Carolina Tar Heels.

About 1933, Carl drifted northward to Lynchburg, Virginia, and soon acquired a program on the small local station, WLVA. By 1935, Carl had returned to Lenoir and played with other musicians including 14-year-old banjoist Johnnie Whisnant. In that year, the two went to WSPA Spartanburg, where they worked in a band called the Lonesome Mountaineers until they formed their own group, the Rambling Mountaineers.

At first they worked only part-time under the sponsorship of Scalf's Indian River Medicine, but eventually became full-time musicians working at WHKY Hickory and then at WWNC Asheville. Eventually, WWII broke up this band, but not before they made a few home recordings displaying their Bluegrass-like form of music. When Carl could no longer hold a band together, he joined Bill Monroe's Blue Grass Boys as a fiddler until he entered the U.S. Navy in 1943.

After the war, Carl reorganized the Rambling Mountaineers at WWNC Asheville and after a few months they moved over to WNOX Knoxville. Jack and Curley Shelton, Hoke Jenkins, and Claude Boone comprised his first group. Later members included Red Rector, Fred Smith, Tater Tate, Ray Atkins, the Brewster Brothers and Cotton Galyon. Several of these people rank as significant Bluegrass pioneers themselves although Carl never recorded with a Bluegrass banjo in his group until 1957.

***Carl Story** and the Rambling Mountaineers*

Carl remained at WNOX until late 1951, when he went to WCYB Bristol for a short time and to WAYS Charlotte for a longer stint. Then he returned to WNOX late in 1953 for another four years. From 1957 to 1960, the Rambling Mountaineers did daily TV at WLOS Asheville.

Carl had made his first commercial recordings with Mercury in 1947 and remained with the label through 1952, having several releases of both secular and sacred material. In 1953, he moved to Columbia and had fourteen sides released through 1955. In those days, the instrumentation varied somewhat although a mandolin usually played by Red Rector tended to be most prominent.

Carl did not actually have a full Bluegrass band until 1957, when with the aid of Claude Boone, Tater Tate and the Brewster Brothers, the Rambling Mountaineers cut their influential recording of *Mocking Banjo/Light at the River*. From then onward, all his recordings used this instrumentation, sometimes also with Dobro. His second Mercury period soon led to a long affiliation with Starday, when those labels separated again. Don Pierce produced a dozen Bluegrass-Gospel albums for Carl over a period of time, usually backed by the Brewster Brothers, Tater Tate and Claude Boone. Toward the end of the Starday era, Carl's band included C.E. Ward, Frank Hamilton and the Jones Brothers, who later went on their own. For a time, the Rambling Mountaineers had a weekly TV show at WCCB Charlotte, but increasingly were seen most often on the Bluegrass festival circuit.

In between his Starday contracts, Carl often cut albums for smaller companies such as Scripture, Sims, Songs of Faith, and Spar. After Starday ceased to function for a time, Story worked for other small companies, including Pine Tree, Atteiram, Jessup, and Mag, as well as the larger CMH, where Arthur Smith produced three albums for him including one double. Although sacred songs had usually been the band's mainstay, they also did some secular material on both live shows and recordings.

All this time, the Rambling Mountaineers stayed busy on the festival circuits with Carl using George Hazelwood's Tennessee Partners as a band for several of those years. Other noted musicians in Carl's band during the 70's included Harold Austin, Bill Millsaps, Randall Collins, Mitchell Moser and Mike Scott. By this time, he was recording less often, as many of his earlier efforts had been re-issued in both the domestic and foreign markets. During the slack season for live shows, Carl has often supplemented his income with deejay work at WSEC Greenville, South Carolina.

As of April 1994, Carl Story has nearly sixty years of show business experience. He reports that his current crop of Rambling Mountaineers—consisting of Danny Arms (mandolin), Brett Dalton (banjo) and Jim Clark (bass)—are looking forward to another season of festival activity. They have a new release on Pure White Dove, a Minnesota-based company. IMT

RECOMMENDED ALBUMS:

"Gospel Quartet Favorites" (Mercury)(1958) [Re-released on Stetson UK in the original sleeve (1988)]
"Carl Story and His Rambling Mountaineers" (Starday and Diplomat)(1959) [Diplomat, as by Carl Glass]
"More Gospel Quartet Favorites" (Mercury and BT)(1961)
"Gospel Revival" (Starday)(1961)
"Everybody Will Be Happy" (Starday and Nashville)(1961)
"Get Religion" (Starday and Power Pak)(1961)
"There's Nothing on Earth—That Heaven Can't Cure" (Starday)(1966)
"The Lewis Family Sings the Gospel with Carl Story" (Starday)(1966)
"Carl Story & the Brewster Brothers" (Rimrock and Old Homestead)(ca. 1967)
"From the Altar to Vietnam" (Scripture)(ca. 1967)
"The Best of Country Music" (Scripture)(ca. 1967)
"My Lord Keeps a Record" (Starday)(1968)
"Daddy Sang Bass" (Starday)(1969)
"The Best of Carl Story (Starday)(1970)
"'Neath the Tree of Life" (Pine Tree)(1971)
"Carl Story's Bluegrass Gospel Singing Convention" (Jessup)(1972)
"The Bluegrass Gospel Collection" (double)(CMH)(1976)
"16 Greatest Gospel Hits" (Starday)(1977)
"Live...At Hugo, Oklahoma" (Atteiram)(1977) [Recorded in 1971]
"Songs from the Blue Ridge" (Mag)(1979)
"The Early Days of Carl Story" (Cattle Germany)(1980) [Mercury Masters]
"Tennessee Border" (Cattle Germany)(1980) [Mercury Masters]
"Carl Story and his Rambling Mountaineers" (Collector's Classics)(1980) [Mercury and Columbia Masters]
"The Early Years (1953-1955)" (Old Homestead)(1982) [Columbia Masters]
"Thank the Lord for Everything" (Pure White Dove)(1994) [Cassette]

GEORGE STRAIT

(Singer, Songwriter, Guitar, Piano, Actor)

Date of Birth:	**May 18, 1952**
Where Born:	**Poteet, Texas**
Married:	**Norma**
Children:	**Jennifer (dec'd.), George, Jr. ("Bubba")**

George Strait, complete with his white (or sometimes black) Resistol hat, is probably single-handedly responsible for the re-emergence of straight-ahead Country that came about in the early 80's, and for over a decade, he has consolidated his position as one of the principal favorites of the public.

Born the son of a teacher and part-time farmer, George was taught to ride from an early age. He started out playing cornet for three years in the school band and then progressed to garage bands while at high school. However, George didn't consider a career in music until he was age 21. In 1972, he enlisted in the U.S. Army and was stationed at Schofield Barracks, in Hawaii. He bought a cheap guitar and some Hank Williams songbooks and put together a band in Hawaii, which survived for two months. The post commanding general decided to put some bands together from military personnel. George auditioned and, as a result, he spent the last year of service in a Country band.

He stayed on in Hawaii for six months after leaving the service, in 1975, and then moved back to San Marcos, Texas, with his wife and daughter. He returned to studies at Southwest Texas State University, where he had attended two semesters prior to his army duty. In 1975, he formed the Ace in the Hole Band. The members of the band were also students at the university and they had already formed a band and were looking for a lead singer. While playing at a club in San Marcos, George was befriended by the club owner, Erv Woolsey. George visited Nashville, where he recorded six songs written by Darrell Statler, but got no interest.

George majored in agricultural education and graduated in 1979. After leaving college, he managed a ranch during the day and played at night. He also took part in some rodeo riding. He was on the verge of quitting the entertainment business and moving to Uvalde, Texas, to design cattle facilities for an architect, but he decided to give music one more year. He contacted Erv, who was now Vice President of Promotion at MCA Records. Blake Mevis agreed to produce some sides on George, in Nashville. He came to Nashville for a third time, in 1980, and his recording of the Dean Dillon/Frank Dycus song *Unwound* ensured he had a deal with MCA.

This particular single charted in the spring of 1981 and reached the Top 10. The follow-up, *Down and Out*, in the fall, only reached the Top 20. His debut album, ***Strait Country***, was released in 1981 and by 1988 had gone Gold. That year, *Billboard* made him "New Male LP Artist of the Year" and *Record World* named him "New Male Artist of the Year." He began his meteoric rise to the top in 1982, when *If You're Thinking You Want a Stranger (There's One Coming Home)* reached the Top 3. This was followed by George's first No.1, *Fool Hearted Memory*, which came from the movie *The Soldier*, in which he appeared. The year was wrapped up by *Marina del Rey*, which went Top 10. During the year, he released his second album ***Strait from the Heart***, which had been Certified Gold by 1987.

George started out 1983 with *Amarillo by Morning*, which was a Top 5 single, and then he had a run of five No.1 records. In 1983, they were *A Fire I Can't Put Out* and *You Look So Good in Love* and, in 1984, he scored with *Right or Wrong*, *Let's Fall to Pieces Together* and *Does Fort Worth Ever Cross Your Mind.* During that period, George released two albums, ***Right or Wrong*** (1983), which was Certified Gold in 1984, and ***Does Fort Worth Ever Cross Your Mind*** (1984), which went Gold in 1985 and Platinum in 1992. The former was produced by Ray Baker, after George and Blake Mevis parted company over choice of material. The latter and all subsequent albums were produced by George and Jimmy Bowen. During 1985 George's successes were the Top 5 entries *The Cowboy Rides Away* and *The Fireman* and yet another No.1, *The Chair.* During the year, MCA released George's first volume of ***Greatest Hits*** and the same year it went Gold; by 1987 it was Platinum, and in 1991 it was Certified Double Platinum.

He received a slew of awards during 1983, 1984 and 1985 and these included *Billboard's* "Male Singles Artist of the Year," *Billboard*'s "Male Vocalist of the Year," and ACM's "Male Vocalist of the Year" in both 1984 and 1985. He was also named "Male Vocalist of the Year" by the CMA in 1985. ***Does Fort Worth Ever Cross Your Mind*** was made "Album of the Year" by both bodies.

His first hit of 1986 was the Top 5 record *You're Something Special to Me.* He then followed with 11 straight No.1's, taking him up to the end of 1989. These were *Nobody in His Right Mind Would've Left Her* and *It Ain't Cool to Be Crazy About You* (both 1986), *Ocean Front Property*, the classic *All My Ex's Live in Texas* and *Am I Blue* (all 1987), *Famous Last Words of a Fool*, *Baby Blue* and *If You Ain't Lovin' (You Ain't Livin')* (all 1988) and *Baby's Gotten Good at Goodbye*, *What's Going on in Your World* and *Ace in the Hole* (all 1989). It was not a good time for George, on a personal level, as in June 1986, his daughter, Jennifer, was killed in a highway accident and for eighteen months, he didn't do any interviews. His final single of 1989, *Overnight Success*, went Top 10.

His album successes during this period were ***Something Special*** and ***#7*** (both 1986), both of which went Gold the same year. His seasonal album ***Merry Christmas Strait to You*** was Certified Gold in 1990. His 1987 album ***Ocean Front Property*** went Gold and Platinum the same year and his second volume of ***Greatest Hits*** went Gold that year and Platinum the following year. His 1988 album ***If You Ain't Livin' (You Ain't Lovin')*** was Certified Gold the same year and reached Platinum status in 1991. George's 1989 album ***Beyond the Blue Neon*** reached the Gold standard in 1990 and Platinum in 1991. In addition, his 1988 video ***George Strait Live*** had sold over 50,000 copies that year and by 1989 had gone Platinum, selling over 100,000 units.

His awards during this period were CMA and *Music City News* "Male Vocalist of the Year," and *Billboard* "Overall Top Artist" and "Top Male Artist," all in 1986, ACM "Male Vocalist of the Year," 1988, and CMA and ACM "Entertainer of the Year," 1989.

Such was his popularity that in January 1990, the flip-side of *Overnight Success*, *Hollywood Squares*, went Top 70. He then had a big No.1, *Love Without End, Amen*, which stayed at the top for five weeks. This was followed by the Top 5 single *Drinking Champagne* and then he spent another five weeks at No.1, with *I've Come to Expect It*

Country music superstar ***George Strait***

from You. The public continued to buy his albums with relish and his album that year, ***Livin' It Up***, went Gold very shortly after release and Platinum the following year.

George's record success continued unabated in 1991, with back-to-back No.1 records, *If I Know Me* and *You Know Me Better Than This*, which stayed at the top for two and three weeks respectively. His close-out single of the year was the Top 3 success *The Chill of an Early Fall*. George had two album releases in 1991, ***Chill of an Early Fall***, which went Gold the same year and Platinum in 1992, and the compilation ***Ten Strait Hits***, which was Certified Gold, also in 1992.

The following year, George's recording of *Lovesick Blues* was his first "flop," only reaching the Top 25, even though it stayed in the charts for five months, but he came back strongly with *Gone As a Girl Can Get*, which went Top 5, and *So Much Like My Dad*, which got to the Top 3. In the fall of the year, he scored a No.1 with *I Cross My Heart*. This was the first single from his starring movie *Pure Country*, in which he played the role of Dusty. Radio created George's only real record failure when it lifted *Overnight Male*, also from the movie, and it only reached the Top 70. George's first album of the year, ***Holding My Own***, had gone Gold almost immediately, but the soundtrack from *Pure Country* was a runaway seller. Within two months of release it had been Certified Platinum, by 1993 it had gone Double Platinum, having shipped over 2 million and early in 1994 this rose to Triple Platinum. His 1993 album ***Easy Come, Easy Go*** was straight-ahead Country and the buying public responded by turning it Gold and Platinum almost simultaneously. During 1993, George had single success with *Heartland* (No.1), *When Did You Stop Loving Me* (Top 10), *Easy Come, Easy Go* (No.1 and Top 75 Pop) and *I'd Like to Have That One Back* (Top 3). In 1994, George charted with *I'd Love to Have That One Back* (Top 3) and *Love Bug* (Top 10). The latter had been a Top 10 hit for George Jones in 1965.

There is also another side to the multi-faceted George Strait. That is his love for riding and rodeos. In 1984, he instituted the George Strait Team Roping Classic, which is now in its 11th year and is held in Kingsville, Texas, every June. He incorporated his roping skills when filming *Pure Country* and he did all his own stunts.

RECOMMENDED ALBUMS:

"Strait Country" (MCA)(1981)
"Strait from the Heart" (MCA)(1982)
"Right or Wrong" (MCA)(1983)
"Does Fort Worth Ever Cross Your Mind" (MCA)(1984)
"George Strait's Greatest Hits" (MCA)(1985)
"Something Special" (MCA)(1986)
"#7" (MCA)(1987)
"Ocean Front Property" (MCA)(1987)
"Greatest Hits Volume Two" (MCA)(1987)
"If You Ain't Lovin' (You Ain't Livin')" (MCA)(1988)
"Beyond the Blue Neon" (MCA)(1989)
"Livin' It Up" (MCA)(1990)
"Chill of an Early Fall" (MCA)(1991)
"Ten Strait Hits" (MCA)(1991)
"Holding My Own" (MCA)(1992)
"Pure Country" (soundtrack)(MCA)(1992)
"Easy Come, Easy Go" (MCA)(1993)

MEL STREET

(Singer, Songwriter, Guitar)

Given Name:	**King Malachi Street**
Date of Birth:	**October 21, 1933**
Where Born:	**near Grundy, Virginia**
Married:	**Betty**
Children:	**Sherrie, Chester Malachi, David Allan, Jennie Carol**
Date of Death:	**October 21, 1978**

Mel Street ranks with Lefty Frizzell and George Jones as a master stylist whose vocal interpretation made every song he sang distinctively his own. There are many other artists who have a higher ranking of chart success, but few match the intensity and emotion of Street's delivery. In his far too brief six-year career, Mel made a major contribution to the art of Country music singing.

Choosing his name from the Old Testament, Mrs. Street named her son King Malachi when he was born near Grundy, Virginia, in 1933. Mel developed a love of music as a child and when he was 16, he was recruited by Bluefield, West Virginia, radio personality Cecil Surratt to sing on his radio shows on Welch, West Virginia, radio stations WELC and WBRW.

It was more than ten years before Mel performed publicly again. He married, started a family, and dedicated himself to his work. Street and new wife Betty lived in various Ohio towns, where he worked as an electrician on radio station power towers. In 1960, Mel and Betty moved to Niagara Falls, where he worked on the Niagara Power Project by day and in the clubs at night. Following completion of the Power Project, Street stayed in upstate New York and began working in an auto body shop while continuing his singing in the Niagara Falls nightclubs. A highlight of Street's time there was attending a concert of his favorite singer, George Jones.

Street moved his family back to West Virginia in 1963, settling in Bluefield. He opened his own body shop and was invited to perform on WHIS-TV's *Country Jamboree*. He chose Johnny Cash's *Ring of Fire* for his guest appearance and became so popular with the audience that he became a regular on the weekly show. Street starred in his own half-hour Saturday night show on WHIS-TV from 1968 to 1972. The station's signal in West Virginia reached into nearby Grundy, where Jim and Jean Prater saw the show. Prater, who owned a television cable company and electronics wholesale business, was so impressed with Street's performance that he and his wife got in their car and drove to the station to meet Mel. Although he knew nothing about the music business, Prater thought Mel had what it took to be a star and asked him if he'd like to make a record. Street was enthusiastic about the idea and in October 1970 traveled to Nashville to record his debut release for Tandem Records (a small independent label started by Prater's deejay friend Joe Deaton).

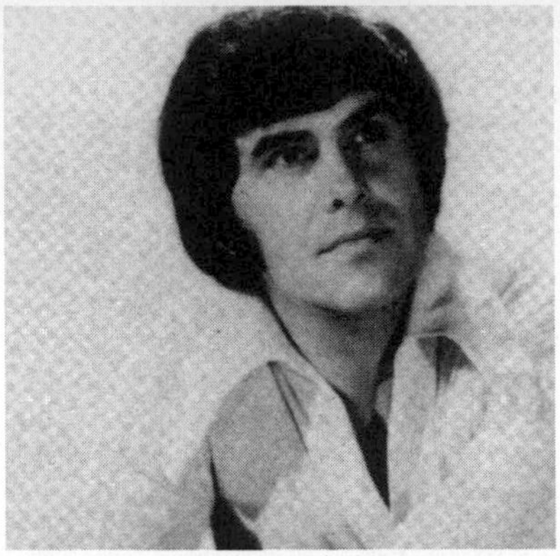

***Mel Street** had one of Country music's finest voices*

Mel recorded his self-penned *Borrowed Angel* backed by Nashville's finest musicians in RCA's Studio A. Prater promoted the record himself and never gave up his belief that the song was a hit, promoting the song for a year and a half on three different small labels. When the single made it to the Top 70 in the spring of 1972, it attracted the attention of Nashville-based Royal American Records, who licensed the master. The Music Row know-how combined with Street's powerful performance pushed the song to the Top 10 by the end of the summer.

Lovin' on Back Streets was Street's follow-up single and it became the highest charting single of his career, peaking in the Top 5. In early 1973 Street released the Dallas Frazier/Doodles Owens song *Walk Softly on the Bridges* and watched it climb to the Top 15. In the fall of that year Mel moved his family to

Nashville and ended the year with another song reaching the Top 15, *Lovin' on Borrowed Time*.

Mel switched to GRT Records in 1974 and he had two Top 20 hits that year with *You Make Me Feel More Like a Man* and *Forbidden Angel*. Street began 1975 with the release of *Smokey Mountain Memories*, a song penned by struggling songwriter and later star Earl Thomas Conley and producer Dick Heard (under the pseudonym Richmond Deveraux). Mel maintained a heavy touring schedule and was earning several thousand dollars per concert.

In 1976, Street returned to the Top 10 with *I Met a Friend of Yours Today*. The following year, Mel moved to Polydor and reached the Top 20 with *Barbara Don't Let Me Be the Last to Know*. He moved up a few spots to the Top 15, later in the year, with *Close Enough for Lonesome*.

Street had his last big hit early in 1978 with the Top 10 single *If I Had a Cheating Heart*. In the spring, Mel hit the Top 20 with *Shady Rest* and then moved to Mercury Records when Polydor decided to shut down their Nashville operation. The heavy demands of his career began taking their toll in the fall of 1978. Mel slipped into depression and was drinking heavily. On the day his debut single for Mercury, *Just Hangin' On*, was released Mel took his own life. He shot himself on his 45th birthday. At his funeral, George Jones paid tribute to his friend, singing *Amazing Grace*.

Mel would have been proud of the posthumous hits that his fans ensured he had. In 1979, there was the Top 20 single *The One Thing My Lady Never Puts into Words*, while 1980 had *Tonight Let's Sleep on It Baby* (Top 30) and *Who'll Turn Out the Lights* (Top 40). The last Mel Street chart single was the 1981 Top 50 record *Slip Away*, on which he was joined by Sandy Powell.

Street's continuing influence was evident fifteen years after his death in the career of 90's Country star Sammy Kershaw. Citing Street as a major influence, he pays tribute to the singer in his stage show by performing a medley of his hits. Country rocker Ricky Lynn Gregg broke into Country music with his version of Street's *If I Had a Cheating Heart*. A greatest hits package of Mel Street was released in 1994 and a book and home video on his life story are in production. JIE

RECOMMENDED ALBUMS:

"Borrowed Angel" (Metromedia Country)(1972)
"Mel Street's Greatest Hits" (GRT)(1976)
"Country Soul" (Polydor)(1978)
"The Many Moods of Mel" (Sunbird)(1980)
"The Very Best of Mel Street" (Sunbird)(1980)
"Some Special Moments" (Sunbird)(1980)

STRINGBEAN

(Singer, Banjo, Comedy)
Given Name: **David Akeman**
Date of Birth: **June 17, 1914**
Where Born: **Annville, Jackson County, Kentucky**
Married: **Estelle (d. 1973)**
Date of Death: **November 10, 1973**

One of the most colorful characters in Country music, David "Stringbean" Akeman parlayed his Old-Time eastern Kentucky frailing banjo style and comedy tunes into a successful career that extended from the stage of the *Grand Ole Opry* to the plush lounge stages of Las Vegas. At a time when the banjo was almost extinct in Country music, Stringbean helped keep it alive and in some ways paved the way for its re-discovery by Bluegrassers. "A man who plays the 5-string banjo has got it made," he often said onstage. "It never interferes with any of the pleasures of his life."

The Akeman family hailed from Annville, between Corbin and Richmond, in eastern Kentucky—a veritable nest of Old-Time banjo players, like Buell Kazee, Lily May Ledford, and B.F. Shelton. Stringbean was about midway in a family of eight, whose father farmed in the daytime and picked the banjo for dances at nights. String's first banjo was an old shoebox rigged up with some of his mother's thread but by the time he was 12, he had traded a banty hen and a rooster for a real banjo.

Stringbean grew up during the Depression and to find work, in 1935, he joined a Civilian Conservation Corps camp, where he planted trees and built roads. After a few months, he won a local talent contest held by radio star Asa Martin, and soon joined Martin's band. When Asa got ready to introduce his new banjo player, he forgot the youth's name. Looking over at the tall, skinny youth, he announced him as "String Beans" and the name stuck. At first, Stringbean was happy just playing banjo, but one night when Martin's comedian was sick, he asked Stringbean to go on and sing—in fact, he threatened to fire him if he didn't. Akeman was a success and impressed even himself.

For the last years of the 1930's, Stringbean worked with several different bands around the Lexington, Kentucky, area, often on station WLAP. He also played semi-pro baseball in his spare time, and became a reasonably good sandlot player. In fact, it was this ability, some

The late Grand Ole Opry star ***Stringbean***

say, that attracted the attention of Bluegrass star Bill Monroe, who hired him in 1942.

"As far as I know, Bill didn't even know he played the banjo when he hired him," recalled Doc Roberts. Stringbean stayed with Monroe three years, doing his delicate finger-picking on his classic Columbia sides like *Footprints in the Snow* and *True Life Blues*. After he left Monroe, Stringbean began a three-year partnership with Lew Childre, working the *Opry* and doing tent shows.

By now, Stringbean had devised his famous "short pants" costume, having adapted it from an older comedian he had seen. (Some have suggested he copied part of the costume from Slim Miller at Renfro Valley.) During this time, Stringbean also became a protégé of the *Opry*'s venerable Uncle Dave Macon. The older man shared his jokes, his banjo styles and his old songs with Stringbean. Eventually he gave Stringbean one of his banjos. By 1950, Stringbean was getting national recognition as a soloist, especially from Red Foley's network portion of the *Opry*, where he regularly appeared. He also developed a close friendship with Grandpa Jones, the other clawhammer player on the *Opry*.

It wasn't until 1960, after some 25 years in show business, that Stringbean started making his own solo records. His first effort was for Starday, and was an album called ***Old Time Banjo Pickin' and Singin'***. Other Starday sets followed, the most popular of which was a lovely tribute to Uncle Dave Macon. Later albums for Nugget and Cullman followed. Then, in the summer of 1968, he became a charter member of the new CBS television show *Hee Haw*. Along with Archie Campbell, Junior Samples, and Grandpa Jones, Stringbean brought a long tradition of Country comedy into living rooms. His droll, laconic wit and Chaplinesque figure added a lot to the barrage of one-liners that littered the show. His "cornfield crow" became one of the favorite parts of the show, along with his one-liners like, "Lord, I feel so unnecessary."

Stringbean's career was at its high point when he and his wife, Estelle, were murdered by burglars on the night of November 10, 1973, when they arrived home from the *Opry*. The crime horrified Nashville (Skeeter Davis' protest at crime in Nashville and police inactivity led to her being temporarily suspended from the *Opry*), and even the eventual capture and conviction of the murderers did little to assuage the loss felt by his friends and his fans. CKW

RECOMMENDED ALBUMS:

"Old Time Banjo Pickin' and Singin' with Stringbean" (Starday)(1961)

"Salute to Uncle Dave Macon" (Starday)(1963)

"Me and My Old Crow (Got a Good Thing Goin')" (Nugget)

STRIPLING BROTHERS, The

CHARLIE STRIPLING

(Vocals, Fiddle, Guitar)

Given Name: Charles Nevins Stripling
Date of Birth: August 8, 1896
Date of Death: January 19, 1966

IRA STRIPLING

(Vocals, Guitar, Fiddle)

Given Name: Ira Lee Stripling
Date of Birth: June 5, 1898
Date of Death: March 1967

Both Born: Pickens County, Alabama

The Stripling Brothers were one of the highest quality fiddle bands of the early years of Country music. Charlie Stripling's skills with the bow not only made the brothers well known throughout the hill country of northwest Alabama, but their recordings gave them a broader audience as well.

Natives of Pickens County, the Stripling boys took to music at an early age. Charlie later claimed to have won his first contest in January 1913 at a time when he had only been playing for less than a year and Ira for only three months. Be that as it may, Charlie Stripling went on to win many fiddling contests over the next four decades with Ira usually furnishing rhythm support. The Striplings developed a wide repertoire of tunes, many of them uncommon. Charlie also came up with innovative techniques in style, generally designed to impress audiences and contest judges.

The Striplings entertained from time to time on various radio stations in Alabama and Mississippi, especially WAPI Birmingham, and Charlie took second prize in the southern contest sponsored by Henry Ford in 1926. Two years later, they went to a field recording session held by Brunswick/Vocalion in Birmingham and cut two tunes, *The Lost Child* and *The Big Footed Nigger in the Sandy Lot*. Their 1929 waxing of *The Lost Child* has been identified as the forerunner of what later became known as *Black Mountain Blues* or *Black Mountain Rag*. These numbers made sufficient impact that they went to Chicago in August 1929 and cut sixteen more tunes, all released on Vocalion. Some years later, in 1934 and 1936, they journeyed to New York and New Orleans respectively to do two extensive sessions for Decca. In all, the Striplings recorded forty-six numbers of which forty-two were released.

Ira quit playing in the late 30's, but Charlie formed a band for local entertainment that included his two sons. They worked dances throughout their section of Alabama and eventually added more modern instruments such as an electric steel guitar to their unit. Charlie fiddled until 1958 when arthritis forced him to quit. In 1971, County Records released an album, mostly of their Vocalion sides.

IMT

RECOMMENDED ALBUM:

"The Lost Child & Other Original Fiddle Tunes" (County)(1971)

JUD STRUNK

(Singer, Songwriter, Tenor Banjo, Piano, Violin, Actor, Comedy)

Given Name: Justin Roderick Strunk, Jr.
Date of Birth: June 11, 1936
Where Born: Jamestown, New York
Married: 1. Martha (div.)
2. Martha (div.)
Children: Rory, Jeffrey, Joel
Date of Death: October 15, 1981

Jud Strunk was a singer/songwriter in the Jimmy Buffett vein, but whereas Buffett's songs and stories rotate around the Keys of south Florida, Jud's were instilled with the flavor of Maine. His material developed into political and ecological awareness and he sang in aid of FOIL, an organization trying to keep oil refineries out of Maine, often with singer/songwriter Marshall Dodge.

Although born in Jamestown, Jud was raised in Springville, near Buffalo, New York. In 1960, he moved to Farmington, Maine, where he played the Red Stallion Inn. Jud toured for a while as a one-man show for the U.S. Armed Forces. He made his base in Eustis, Maine, where he operated a farm, which was nearly self-sufficient. From there, he sortied to New York City and appeared in the Broadway musical *Beautiful Dreamer*. During the 70's, Jud appeared regularly on the *Rowan and Martin's Laugh-In* TV show.

In 1970, Jud signed with Columbia Records and released the album ***Downeast Viewpoint***. By the following year, he had moved to MGM, where he issued ***Jones' General Store***. At the beginning of 1973, Jud scored his biggest chart success with *Daisy a Day*, which went Top 15 on the Pop chart and Top 40 on the Country chart. He had one more basement Country chart entry before he moved to Capitol in 1974. Here he had a Top 60 Pop success with the spoken-word single *My Country*.

By 1975, he had moved labels again to Melodyland, where he had the Pop Top 50 novelty song *The Biggest Parakeets in Town*. The single fell just short of the Top 50 on the Country chart. Although he had one more basement Country chart record on the label the following year, by 1977 he was on MCA, where with his backing band, the Coplin Kitchen Band, he released ***A Semi-Reformed Tequila Crazed Gypsy Looks Back***. The album featured Glen Campbell on guitar and Jazz-Funk pianist Richard Tee. The most ironic track on the album is *Gordon Hall's Plane*, because in 1981, Jud met his end in a light plane crash in Maine. His youngest son is currently endeavoring to perpetuate Jud Strunk's name by writing a movie based on his life.

RECOMMENDED ALBUMS:

"Downeast Viewpoint" (Columbia)(1970)

"Jones' General Store" (MGM)(1971)

"Daisy a Day" (MGM)(1973)

"A Semi-Reformed Tequila Crazed Gypsy Looks Back" (MCA)(1977)

MARTY STUART

(Singer, Songwriter, Mandolin, Guitar, Fiddle, Photographer)

Given Name: John Marty Stuart
Date of Birth: September 30, 1958
Where Born: Philadelphia, Mississippi
Married: Cindy Cash (div.)

When Marty Stuart hit the Country chart in 1985, he was already a 20-year veteran of the music business, yet he was still only age 27. Marty is one of the most talented and likable people in Country music; an able musician, a talented writer and one of the best on-stage entertainers around. Sporting Manuel jackets and with a mane of black hair, Marty looks like a rock'n'roller of the 50's.

When he was age 12, Marty was already the boy wonder of the guitar in his town and had played with the Gospel group the Sullivans. His father took him to a Bluegrass festival in Indiana where Marty made friends with Roland White, also a child prodigy, who was then playing mandolin with Lester Flatt's Nashville Grass. When the group played Philadelphia, the following year, White was invited to Marty's home for dinner. By then, Marty had also started playing mandolin, and in January 1971 Jesse McReynolds (of Jim & Jesse), no slouch on the mandolin, introduced the 12-year-old Marty to Lester Flatt. Marty played *Rawhide* for Flatt on mandolin and astounded the veterans. He hung around with Roland and spent some time at Flatt's home, picking. Flatt decided to hire "Marny," as he called him, to join the band on guitar at half pay (because of his age), but the Musicians' Union negated this and so at full pay Marty joined the band for his first date in Glasgow, Delaware, over the Labor Day weekend, just 30 days short of his 13th birthday. He continued his education through correspondence classes, graduating two years ahead of time, in 1975.

For the first six months, Marty played rhythm guitar and then on March 15, 1973, Roland left and Marty stepped up front to become the mandolin player. He soon also did harmony and lead vocals. At Christmas 1978, Flatt wrapped up the group, due to ill health, and Marty moved on to working with Doc and Merle Watson, staying with them until 1979. That year, Johnny Cash, who would become his father-in-law, recognized Marty's talents and invited him to join his band. Marty stayed with Cash, who is still his favorite Country singer, until 1985, when Johnny cut down on road dates and Marty embarked on his own solo career.

Marty first recorded a solo project back in 1982, when Sugar Hill released his self-produced ***Busy Bee Cafe***. This was critically acclaimed and featured Cash, Earl Scruggs, Doc and Merle Watson, Carl Jackson, Jerry Douglas and T. Michael Coleman. Marty signed to Columbia Records in 1985 and recorded his eponymous album. Though it included pickers such as Duane Eddy, Mark O'Connor, Jody Maphis, Bobby Whitlock and Jim Horn, it did badly. However, from this, Marty hit the Country chart with the Top 20 single *Arlene*, that year. During 1986, three other tracks charted, two being by Steve Forbert, *Honky Tonker* (Top 60) and *All Because of You* (Top 40), and the Marty Stuart/Steve Goodman song *Do You Really Want My Lovin'* (Top 60).

At this point, Marty's marriage started to break up and then Columbia dropped him

Hillbilly Rocker ***Marty Stuart***

from the label. He returned home to Mississippi and sought the advice of his mother (he admits to being a "card-carrying momma's boy"). Then the Sullivans came back into his life and he contented himself playing Bluegrass-Gospel. In the interim, Columbia charted Marty's *Mirrors Don't Lie* (Top 60) and *Matches* (Top 70), both in 1988.

In 1989, Tony Brown signed Marty to MCA and this was the connection Marty needed. His first album with Brown and Richard Bennett producing was ***Hillbilly Rock*** and this clearly defined Marty's future style. The first two singles, Johnny Cash's *Cry, Cry, Cry* (Top 40) and *Don't Leave Her Lonely Too Long* (Top 50), which Marty had written with Kostas, paved the way for the album's title track. Written by Paul Kennerley, *Hillbilly Rock* gave Marty his first Top 10 hit in 1990. This was followed by *Western Girls* (Top 20), which Marty wrote with Kennerley. The same team wrote Marty's year-end Top 10 single *Little Things*. This came from the second album, ***Tempted***.

Marty started 1991 with *Till I Found You*, which went Top 15. This was followed by the album's title track, which went Top 5. At the end of the year, Travis Tritt invited Marty to join him on *The Whiskey Ain't Workin'*, which went Top 3. This led to the two hirsute stars touring together, in 1992, under the banner of the No Hats Tour, and the duo won the CMA "Vocal Event of the Year" award.

During 1992, CMH released an album of early Marty Stuart material, recorded while with Lester Flatt and Nashville Grass. That year, Marty hit the Top 10 with *Burn Me Down* and followed it with another duet with Travis, *This One's Gonna Hurt You (For a Long, Long Time)*, which also went Top 10. This came from the album ***This One's Gonna Hurt You*** (which went Gold in 1993), as did the next three singles: *Now That's Country* (from which the magazine *That's Country* took its name) went Top 20, *High on a Mountain Top*, which had been a big hit half a century earlier for Alex Campbell and Ola Belle, went Top 25 (both 1992) and *Hey Baby* reached the Top 40 in 1993.

During 1993, Marty became a member of the *Grand Ole Opry*. That year, Marty released his fourth album for MCA, ***Love and Luck,*** and the single *Kiss Me, I'm Gone* went Top 30 in 1994, indicating a revival of interest in Marty's releases.

Marty has two passions in his life. He is an avid record collector, having started when he was age 13. These records have helped shape his music and he still draws inspiration from them. He is also an excellent photographer and was responsible for the cover picture on Johnny Cash's ***The Adventures of Johnny Cash*** (1982). He has a collection of old photographs and old guitars. He has a great awareness of the history of Country music and has written articles on the music and its participants. He drives in the tour bus that belonged to Ernest Tubb and among his guitars are Clarence White's 1954 Telecaster, which has a B Bender, Hank Williams' Martin D-45 and Lester Flatt's Martin D-28.

The 13-year-old who told everyone he was really Eddie Munster has come a long way since those days, but he is still the same fun-loving guy.

RECOMMENDED ALBUMS:

"Busy Bee Cafe" (Sugar Hill)(1982)
"Marty Stuart" (Columbia)(1986)
"Hillbilly Rock" (MCA)(1989)
"Tempted" (MCA)(1991)
"This One's Gonna Hurt You" (MCA)(1992)
"Once Upon a Time" (CMH)(1992)
"Love and Luck" (MCA)(1993)

NAT STUCKEY

(Singer, Songwriter, Guitar)

Given Name:	**Nathaniel Wright Stuckey**
Date of Birth:	**December 17, 1934**
Where Born:	**Cass County, Texas**
Married:	**(Carolyn) Ann**
Date of Death:	**August 24, 1988**

It is possible that with the current trend of forgetting anyone in Country music before 1989, Nat Stuckey will become one of the casualties. However, for over a decade from the mid-60's, his name graced the Country charts as both singer and songwriter.

He attended Arlington State College, where he earned a degree in radio and television work and speech. He began working with KALT Atlanta, Texas, as a deejay. He remained at the radio station for two years and then joined the U.S. Army. While he was in the service, he did radio and TV work in New York and Korea. On his discharge, he went back to KALT and then he moved to KWKH Shreveport, Louisiana, where he was a deejay for some eight years.

Between 1957 and 1958, Nat worked with an eight-piece Jazz group, before turning to Country as a performer. He formed the Corn Huskers, which stayed together until the following year. About this time, he also started writing songs and these would later be powerful weapons in the Stuckey armory. In 1962, Nat moved back to KWKH, where he became leader of the Louisiana Hayriders. While at Shreveport, he met his future wife, Ann, at a New Year's Eve party and married her two months and nine days later. She later ran his fan club and was responsible for the badges bearing the legend "Stuck on Stuckey."

Nat cut his first single for Sims in 1964, entitled *Leave the Door Open*. In 1965, he moved on to Paula Records, and released *Hurtin' Together/Two Together*. On his second single *Don't You Believe Her/Round and Round*, he was backed by the Uniques, among whose members was Joe Stampley.

However, it was Nat's third single that did the trick. The self-penned *Sweet Thang* charted at the end of the summer of 1966, and reached the Top 5. It certainly was a sweet time for him. Buck Owens recorded the Stuckey song *Waitin' in the Welfare Line* and made it a seven weeks' No.1. This was a case of a song being written for an artist and that artist making it a hit. In addition, *Sound Format* named Nat "Star of Tomorrow" and he received a BMI award for *Sweet Thang*.

The following year, Jim Ed Brown recorded Nat's song *Pop-a-Top* and took it into the Top 3. That year, Nat received another BMI award, this time for *Waitin' in the Welfare Line*. In addition, Ernest Tubb and Loretta Lynn had a hit with *Sweet Thang*. Nat's own recording success was mixed. *Oh! Woman* reached the Top 20 and the follow-up, *All My Tomorrows*, made the Top 30, with the flip-side, *You're Puttin' Me On*, going Top 70. His other chart successes for Paula were *Adorable Women* and *My Can't Do Can't Keep Up with My Want To* (both 1967) and the low level *Leave This One Alone* (1968). His other song successes at this time included *Be True to Me*, which was recorded by both Ray Price and Ricky Nelson, and *Don't You Believe Her*, which was covered by both Ray Price and Conway Twitty. In 1967, Nat put together his backing group, the Sweet Thangs, among whose members, at one time, was Gary Stewart on piano.

Nat moved over to RCA Victor in 1968, and had a Top 10 hit with *Plastic Saddle*. This provided a springboard to his career. In 1969, he had three Top 20 hits with *Joe and Mabel's 12th Street Bar and Grill, Cut Across Shorty* and *Young Love*, the latter being a duet with Connie Smith. At the end of the year, he again had a Top 10 hit with *Sweet Thang and Cisco*.

With the arrival of the 70's, Nat maintained a chart run that varied in success level, but through to 1978, he didn't miss a year. The hits were *Sittin' in Atlanta Station* and another duet with Connie Smith, *If God Is Dead (Who's That Livin' in My Soul), Old Man Willis* and *Whiskey, Whiskey* and *She Wakes Me with a Kiss Every Morning (And She Loves Me to Sleep Every Night)* (Top 15) (all 1970), *Only a Woman Like You* (Top 25), *I'm Gonna Act Right* (Top 20) and *Forgive Me for Calling You Darling* (Top 20) (all 1971), *Is It Any Wonder That I Love You* (Top 30) and *Don't Pay the Ransom* (Top 20) (both 1972). 1973 was another watershed year for Nat, with *Take Time to Love Her* (Top 10), *I Used It All on You* (Top 3) and *Got Leaving on Her Mind* (Top 15). However, in 1974, his chart levels took a nosedive, and his most successful singles were the Top 40 entries, that year, *You Never Say You Love Me Anymore* and *You Don't Have to Go Home*.

In 1976, Nat moved from RCA to MCA and that year, he had the Top 20 hit *Sun Comin' Up*. Following that, his singles only reached the Top 50 or worse and then in 1978, he had his final chart hit *The Days of Sand and Shovels*, which made the Top 30. During the 80's, Nat became successful as a jingle singer, including his final TV commercial for Budweiser/Spuds McKenzie. Nat died in August 1988, in Nashville, from lung cancer.

RECOMMENDED ALBUMS:

"Nat Stuckey Really Sings" (Paula)(1966)
"Country Favorites—Stuckey Style" (Paula)(1967)
"Young Love" (RCA Victor)(1969) [With Connie Smith]
"Sunday Morning With" (RCA Victor)(1970) [With Connie Smith] [Religious album]
"Take Time to Love Her" (RCA Victor)(1973)
"The Best of Nat Stuckey" (RCA Victor)(1974)
"Independence" (MCA)(1976)

SULLIVAN FAMILY, The

When Formed: 1949

ENOCH SULLIVAN
(Singer, Fiddle, Guitar, Mandolin)
Given Name: Enoch Hugh Sullivan
Date of Birth: September 18, 1933
Where Born: St. Stephens, Alabama
Married: Margaret Louise Brewster

MARGIE SULLIVAN
(Singer, Guitar)
Given Name: Margie Louise Brewster ("Mrs. Enoch")
Date of Birth: January 22, 1933
Where Born: Winnsboro, Louisiana
Married: Enoch Hugh Sullivan
Children: DeWayne, Hugh, Sharon, Debbie, Lisa

EMMETT SULLIVAN
(Singer, Banjo, Bass, Guitar)
Given Name: Emmett Austin Sullivan
Date of Birth: July 23, 1936
Where Born: St. Stephens, Alabama
Married: Miriam Louise
Children: Renee (dec'd.), David, Zina, Shelley
Date of Death: April 10, 1993

Support Musicians:
Joy DeVille (Bass), James Phillips (Mandolin) or Joe Cook (Mandolin), Earn Steed (Banjo, Guitar)

Other Members: Arthur Sullivan, Jerry Sullivan, Lisa Sullivan, Aubrey Sullivan, Joe Stuart, Marty Stuart

For more than four decades, the Sullivan Family has carried the banner of Bluegrass-Gospel in the Deep South/Gulf Coast region. Active in both the Gospel and Bluegrass festival circuits, the Sullivans have long favored a hard-driving, traditional sound highlighted by the strong feminine lead voice of Margie Sullivan augmented by the fiddle of husband Enoch.

Enoch and Emmett Sullivan were the sons of the Rev. Arthur Sullivan of Washington County, in the Tombigbee Valley of south Alabama. Church music interested the Sullivans deeply and they also listened to the music of folks like Bill Monroe and Johnnie & Jack at the *Grand Ole Opry*. Likewise, from her childhood home in north Louisiana, Margie Brewster listened to KWKH and musicians like the Bailes Brothers as well as Johnnie & Jack and Kitty Wells during their stay in Shreveport. Margie was also attracted to Bill and Charlie Monroe's music as well as to recordings by strong-voiced females like Molly O'Day and Wilma Lee Cooper. Later as a teenager, Margie traveled with a lady evangelist named Hazel Chain. She married, in

1949, Enoch Sullivan, whom she had met at a revival in Sunflower, Alabama. They settled on a farm near St. Stephens.

The Sullivans played in churches initially and then started a weekly program in December 1949, at WRJW radio in Picayune, Mississippi. Later, they moved to a new station in nearby Jackson, Alabama, that had opened in June 1950, and in 1956 they went to Thomasville, Alabama. They did a daily show for several years live at 5:45 a.m. and an additional half hour on Sundays.

The Sullivans cut their first record, a 78 rpm disc, for the small Revival label. About 1959, they met evangelist Walter Bailes of the Bailes Brothers. Subsequently, they began recording for his Loyal Records, singles and EPs at first and eventually albums. Their version of *Walking My Lord up Calvary Hill* went over especially well. The Sullivans played mostly at Gospel sings in churches, but also continued to appear on radio and TV, where they guested frequently. To supplement their incomes, Emmett worked as a mechanic while Enoch farmed.

Thanks to their longtime friendship with Bill Monroe, the Sullivans began working on some Bluegrass festivals in 1968. This broadened their audience and they played at Bean Blossom and other Monroe festivals, plus others not managed by the Father of Bluegrass. The Sullivans also made a trip to the Netherlands.

Over the years, various other family members played in the group, including Enoch and Emmett's late father, Arthur, and uncle Jerry Sullivan. Enoch and Margie's youngest daughter, Lisa, worked with the Sullivans for four years and Aubrey Sullivan was another early member. Non-family musicians have also played with the Sullivans, including the late Bluegrass super-sideman Joe Stuart, who put in five years with them. Marty Stuart spent a year with the family before joining Lester Flatt. Joy DeVille has played bass for eleven years. James Phillips has picked mandolin for a long time and when he is not available, Joe Cook fills in for him. When Emmett Sullivan could no longer travel, former Blue Grass Boy Earn Sneed took his place.

After Loyal Records became inactive, the Sullivans cut albums for Atteiram and also the Country label in Canada. Some of their earlier releases appeared on the latter, too, as well as on Old Homestead in the U.S. More recently, they recorded for Pioneer, and have an album on Eddie Crook's Homeplace label with another expected out in June 1994. In 1989, the Sullivans also initiated a small quarterly tabloid paper to promote Bluegrass-Gospel music called *Bluegrass Gospel News*. The family has always remained close to their roots, see their mission as primarily one of praising God through music, make their home in the small community of St. Stephens, Alabama, and hope to continue their efforts for several more years. IMT

RECOMMENDED ALBUMS:

"Bluegrass Gospel" (Loyal)(ca. 1964)
"Old Brush Arbors" (Loyal)(ca. 1968)
"The Light in the Sky" (Loyal)(ca. 1969)
"Sing Daddy a Song" (Loyal)
"What a Wonderful Savior Is He" (Loyal)(ca. 1971)
"The Prettiest Flowers Will Be Blooming" (Atteiram)(1974)
"My Old Cottage Home" (Atteiram)(1977)
"Old and New" (double)(Country)(1978)
"Gospel Warmup" (Atteiram)(1979)
"Working on a Building" (Country)(1979)
"Life's Restless Sea" (Old Homestead)(1987)
"The Gospel Train Is Coming" (Old Homestead)(1987)
"The Sullivan Family Remembers the Louvin Brothers" (Pioneer)(ca. 1988) [Cassette only]
"Live in Philadelphia, Mississippi" (Pioneer)(ca. 1989) [Cassette only]
"I Have Found the Way" (Pioneer)(ca. 1990) [Cassette only]
"Pure & Simple" (Homeplace)(1991) [Cassette only]

Gene Sullivan refer WILEY & GENE

MARION SUMNER

(Fiddle, Guitar, Mandolin)

Given Name: Marion Sumner
Date of Birth: March 28, 1920
Where Born: Florida
Married: Mary
Children: Jess plus two others

Marion Sumner, an east Kentucky fiddler, worked as a sideman with various Country bands and became known as the Fiddle King of the South. His influence as a fiddler upon others of his generation was notable, particularly on Kenny Baker, who won wide acclaim as a sideman for Bill Monroe over a long period.

Although born in sunny Florida, Marion Sumner moved with his parents back to their Kentucky mountain homeland in 1921. His extended family contained numerous musicians and young Marion became something of a child prodigy. At age 10, he was especially captivated by the fiddling of the *Grand Ole Opry*'s Arthur Smith. At 16, Marion took his first radio job with the Haley Brothers at WCPO Cincinnati, Ohio. In 1937, he joined Cousin Emmy and her Kin Folks, remaining with them for several years. During WWII, Sumner worked briefly for Molly O'Day and Lynn Davis, and then with Eddie Hill and Johnny Wright (replacing Paul Warren, who was in the service).

In the post-war period, Marion worked as a sideman with many bands on the radio and at personal appearances. Some of his longer stints were with Don Gibson in Knoxville and Esco Hankins in Lexington. Marion spent briefer periods with Cowboy Copas, the York Brothers, Preston Ward, Archie Campbell and the then youthful duo of Jim & Jesse. Sumner also fiddled extensively on the nightclub circuits in Cincinnati, Columbus and Knoxville. Somewhat surprisingly, he recorded sparingly in his wide travels, doing a session with Preston Ward for King Records in 1947 and no more than two with Don Gibson.

Marion got off the road in 1965. For a time he worked in a band called the Payroll Boys, but mostly just honed his skills. In 1979, he cut a well-received album for June Appal. In the mid-80's, he waxed two more albums, both with the assistance of Jesse McReynolds, who always held Marion's fiddling in high regard. In recent years Sumner has lived in retirement in Isom, Kentucky, where he passed on his fiddle skills to his youngest son, Jess Sumner. IMT

RECOMMENDED ALBUMS:

"Road to Home" (June Appal)(1979)
"Old Friends" (Mag)(ca. 1985)
"Fiddle Fantastic" (Old Homestead)(1986)

JOE SUN

(Singer, Songwriter, Guitar, Harmonica, Actor, Deejay, Record Plugger, Cartoonist)

Given Name: James Joseph Paulsen
Date of Birth: September 25, 1943
Where Born: Rochester, Minnesota
Married: Inka

Occasionally a singer will come along who universally has the approbation of his peers and the media and yet doesn't become the star that his talent warrants. Such is the case with Joe Sun, who was described by Johnny Cash as the greatest talent he'd seen in 20 years.

While young, he listened to Country music in the form of Hank Williams and the *Grand Ole Opry*, R & B performers such as Ray Charles and Barrett Strong, Blues singers Lightning Hopkins and Howlin' Wolf and then Elvis Presley. When he reached his late teens, Joe became interested in the burgeoning Folk revival. All these influences helped mold Joe's style.

After graduation from high school, in 1961, he frequented Ten O'Clock Scholar, a coffeehouse in Dinkyland near the University of Minnesota. It was here that Joe first heard Bob Dylan, who then performed under his real name, Bob Zimmerman. The following year found Joe serving in the U.S. Air Force, where he remained until 1966, seeing active duty in Vietnam.

After he left the service, Joe worked in Los Angeles in a record shop and then went to the University of Minnesota, studying radio announcing, at their Minnesota Radio School. He had already started to play guitar and harmonica but after leaving college, he became a deejay in Minneapolis and then Key West in Florida. While in Florida, playing Rock records, Joe met Jimmy Buffett, who exposed Joe to the blend of Country and Island music and then Joe was bowled over by the songs of Mickey Newbury.

Joe made his first recording while he was in Los Angeles, in 1966. During early 1970, he worked for a computer research company in Chicago, and hung out at the Wells Street clubs, where he got to know Steve Goodman, Kris Kristofferson and John Prine and sang under the name of Jack Daniels.

Around 1971, he got a job on a Country radio station in Madison, Wisconsin, through the help of a fellow graduate from college. Joe formed a Honky-Tonk band, the Branded Men, playing his music with a heavy bluesy beat, around the area and the group traveled to Nashville to demo two of his songs, *Claxton County Jail* and *It's a Long Hard Road*.

In 1972, Joe moved to Nashville and became friends with songwriters Hugh Moffatt and Don Schlitz. He tried his hand at various music-based jobs, including drawing cartoons, some of which were published in the *Tennessean*. He began songwriting for the publishing company Lloyds of Nashville. Through a girlfriend, he met publisher Larry Rogers. At the time, the Shylo Boys were writing for Larry, and Joe demoed with the group, cutting among others, *Folsom Prison Blues*. Larry was working with the Bill Black Combo on Hi and got Joe to work for him as a promotion person. In 1975, Joe was persuaded to become the National Promotion Executive for Hi Records and then for London Records. In 1977, Joe appeared in the movie *Framed*, alongside Joe Don Baker.

At this point, Joe Sun was one of the most respected record promoters in the business, however, he was getting increasingly unhappy with the lack of support he was getting at London Records. It was then that he again met Brien Fisher, whom he had met initially in Chicago, and now Brien told him that he needed a promotion man at the new label, Ovation. The money he was offered was a tenth of what he had been getting, but he agreed with the proviso that if he could launch the Kendalls, then Brien would let Joe record. In the event, the Kendalls leapt to stardom with *Heaven's Just a Sin Away*, and Joe was taken into the studio. At the time, Joe was uncertain about his guitar playing ability, but Fisher went ahead.

Joe's first release, Hugh Moffatt's *Old Flames (Can't Hold a Candle to You)*, reached the Top 15 and became Joe's most successful single. However, during his stay with Ovation, he racked up other successful singles, namely, *High and Dry* (Top 20, 1978), *On Business for the King/Blue Ribbon Blues*, *I'd Rather Go on Hurtin'* (Top 20) and *Out of Your Mind* (all 1979). His first single of 1980 was a duet with Sheila Andrews, *What I Had with You*. He followed with *Shotgun Rider* (also a Pop Top 75 hit, after which his band, Shotgun, was named), *Bombed, Boozed and Busted* and *Ready for the Times to Get Better*.

By 1981, Ovation was bankrupt, but Joe was picked up by Elektra, where his biggest hit on the label was the Top 40 single *Holed Up in Some Honky Tonk*. In 1984, he moved to AMI, after he and Elektra had parted company, but although he had two minor chart entries, it marked the end of his singles success.

Joe continued to tour with his band, Solar System (1983-87), in the U.S., appearing on TV shows such as *Austin City Limits*, and touring Europe, often with the excellent British band Roger Humphries and Bite the Bullet. In 1985, Joe played the role of Thomas Prator in the movie *Marie*, based on Peter Mass' book about Marie Ragghianti and her fight against corruption in Tennessee prisons. The movie starred Sissy Spacek and was released in 1986.

Anglo-Swedish label Sonet released Joe's 1986 album ***The Sun Never Sets*** and he began a relationship with Europe that continues to date. In 1988, he released the album ***Twilight Zone*** on the French label Dixie Frog. Joe had his own 45-minute TV special in Germany, in 1989.

In 1989, he released a concept album, ***Hank and Bogart Still Live***, on Dixie Frog. The album is a tribute to Hank Williams and Humphrey Bogart, and the fondly remembered 50's. Two years later, the same label released ***Out on the Road***. In 1992, Austria's Crazy Music Records released Joe's ***Dixie and Me*** and then in 1993 issued ***Some Old Memories***, which is the best of Joe Sun, 1988-1993.A video was shot of the title track in Germany and Sweden.

Joe lives in Nashville, and still wows his audiences with his energy. Well remembered is his guest appearance on a Chili Shack Show at The Bluebird Cafe in October 1993, when he proved what a great singer/songwriter he is.

RECOMMENDED ALBUMS:

"Old Flames (Can't Hold a Candle to You)" (Ovation)(1979)
"Out of Your Mind" (Ovation)(1980)
"Livin' on Honky Tonkin' No More" (Elektra)(1981)
"The Best of Joe Sun" (Elektra)(1983)
"Joe Sun with Shotgun" (Intercord Germany)(1984)
"The Sun Never Sets" (Sonet Sweden)(1986)
"Twilight Zone" (Dixie Frog France)(1988)
"Hank and Bogart Still Live" (Dixie Frog France)(1989)
"Out on the Road" (Dixie Frog France)(1991)
"Dixie and Me" (Crazy Music Records Austria)(1992)
"Some Old Memories" (Crazy Music Records Austria)(1993)

DOUG SUPERNAW

(Singer, Songwriter, Guitar)
Date of Birth: September 26, 1960
Where Born: Houston, Texas

The son of a scientist and a coal miner's daughter, Doug Supernaw was raised in Houston, Texas, and influenced by Gene Watson, Vern Gosdin, Keith Whitley and George Jones. He attended college on a golf scholarship. He originally came to Nashville in 1987 after having played extensively throughout the Texas circuit with a series of house bands.

For four years after moving to Nashville, Supernaw attempted to secure a major record contract, but was always turned down. After many disappointments, however, his luck changed and he was signed as a staff writer at a music publishing company. It wasn't enough, though, and after finally getting inside those hard-to-open doors, Supernaw did a 180° turn and moved back to Texas, where he knew he could perform.

While in Texas he worked on an oil rig and and was an in-house promoter for a theater that booked artists such as Ricky Van Shelton, Reba McEntire and the Beastie Boys. While working there he learned more about the music business and began to hone his performance.

Soon he was garnering interest from major Country labels and signed with BNA. He quickly saw three singles hit the chart off his debut album ***Red and Rio Grande***, recorded in 1993. His first single, *Honky Tonkin' Fool* (also his nickname), reached the Top 50. The follow-up, *Reno* (1993), made it all the way to the Top 5. He hit pay dirt with *I Don't Call Him Daddy* (1994), which zoomed to No.1 and featured a touching music video as well. His final single to date, *Red and Rio Grande*, made the Top 30, as did the album on the Country album chart.

Despite his apparent successes, Doug was plagued by a list of catastrophes during the debuting of his album. In March 1993, he broke his neck in a surfing accident and just as he was getting the neck brace removed he was involved in a head-on car collision. He credits

***Doug Supernaw** getting to grips with a fan*

the car's air bag with saving him from more serious injury. Later, while with his band in Columbus, Ohio, his bus was broken into and all the band's musical equipment was stolen. Then, one morning in Richmond, Virginia, after doing a show, Supernaw came down with a serious case of food poisoning, collapsed on the sidewalk and had to be rushed to a local hospital.

Despite the catastrophes, Doug is blessed as a newcomer with his explosive musical career. He credits most of his success with just being persistent and never giving up no matter what comes along. With a little luck and fewer accidents, Doug should have a big career ahead of him. His hobbies include watching stock-car racing and he is known throughout the industry as a "downright nice guy." LAP

RECOMMENDED ALBUM:

"Red and Rio Grand" (BNA)(1993)

GLENN SUTTON

(Singer, Songwriter, Record Producer, Guitar, Mandolin, Piano, Trumpet, Bass, Steel Guitar, Drums)

Given Name:	**Royce Glenn Sutton**
Date of Birth:	**September 28, 1937**
Where Born:	**Hodge, Louisiana**
Married:	**1. Lynn Anderson (div.) 2. Pamela Tuggle (div.)**
Children:	**Lisa Lynn**

Although to most people outside of Country music, the name of Glenn Sutton is unknown, he is, in fact, one of the most successful songwriters and producers to have graced the Nashville scene over the last thirty years.

Glenn was raised in Henderson, Texas, and began writing songs at age 10. He graduated from high school after his family had moved to Mississippi. He soon became a very adept multi-instrumentalist and when he left school, Glenn sold insurance by day and played around the clubs in Jackson, Mississippi, with Murray Kellum, at night. In 1963, Glenn was on Murray's Pop hit *Long Tall Texan*, which was dropped by the radio stations following the death of President Kennedy (because of the subject matter).

The following year, Glenn moved to Nashville to become a songwriter, and that year, he had a hit when Hank Williams, Jr., scored with Glenn's *Guess What, That's Right, She's Gone*. In 1964, Glenn started an ongoing writing partnership with Billy Sherrill that was to create some of the finest and most popular Country songs of the 60's and 70's. That year, David Houston recorded the first of many Sherrill-Sutton songs and hit with *Livin' in a House Full of Love*, which went Top 3 on the Country chart. Glenn was also represented on the Pop chart that year when another co-written song, *Kiss Away*, became a hit for Ronnie Dove.

In 1966, Merle Kilgore signed Glenn to Al Gallico Music. Charlie Walker started off the year with the Top 40 single *He's a Jolly Good Fellow* and then David Houston provided Glenn with his first No.1, with *Almost Persuaded*. The song won for Glenn and Billy a Grammy Award as "Best Country & Western Song." Sheb Wooley in his Ben Colder guise recorded a parody version of the song which became a Top 10 hit. There was even a Top 50 "answer" version by Donna Harris.

Glenn's successes in 1967 were: *Where Could I Go? (But to Her)*, *A Loser's Cathedral*, *With One Exception* (No.1) and *You Mean the World to Me* (No.1) (all by David Houston) and *Your Good Girl's Gonna Go Bad* and the No.1 *I Don't Wanna Play House* (both by Tammy Wynette). The following year, Tammy had a No.1 with *Take Me to Your World* and David Houston provided a trio of hits with *Have a Little Faith* (No.1), *Already It's Heaven* (No.1) and *Where Love Used to Live*. Glenn began scoring with several of his solely penned songs, including *What's Made Milwaukee Famous (Has Made a Loser out of Me)* and *She Still Comes Around (to Love What's Left of Me)*, with which Jerry Lee Lewis had major hits. Glenn began producing for Epic, where one of his artists was Bob Luman, for whom he wrote *Ain't Got Time to Be Unhappy* and *I Like Trains*. In addition, Glenn wrote Bobby Barnett's hit *Love Me, Love Me*.

During 1969, Tammy Wynette had two chart-toppers with Sherrill-Sutton songs, *Singing My Song* and *The Ways to Love a Man*. David Houston had two further Top 5 hits with *My Woman's Good to Me* and *I'm Down to My Last "I Love You."* In addition, Johnny Duncan had a minor hit with Glenn's *I Live to Love You*, Jerry Lee Lewis scored with *To Make Love Sweeter for You* and Stonewall Jackson went Top 20 with *Ship in the Bottle*. *Almost Persuaded* also reappeared on the Pop chart with a version by Etta James.

In 1970, Glenn took over the production reins for his wife Lynn Anderson, and over the next few years, Lynn recorded many of Glenn's songs. That year, she charted with *He'd Still Love Me* and *Stay There 'Til I Get There*, and Glenn also wrote *I Found You Just in Time*, the flip-side of *No Love at All*. Other cuts that Glenn had that year included *The Gun* (Bob Luman), *Everything I Love* and *Blues Sells a Lot of Booze* (both Hugh X. Lewis), *A Woman Lives for Love* (Wanda Jackson), *Heavenly Sunshine* and *Your Sweet Love Lifted Me* (both Ferlin Husky), *Born That Way* (Stonewall Jackson) and *The Tears on Lincoln's Face* (Tommy Cash).

During 1971, Lynn Anderson had a No.1 with Glenn's *You're My Mind* and Tommy Cash went Top 30 with *I'm Gonna Write a Song*. The following year, Tammy Wynette opened Glenn's account with another No.1, *Bedtime Story*. The year continued with *We Can Make It* (George Jones), *The Day That Love Walked In* (David Houston), *You're Everything* (Tommy Cash), *There's a Party Goin' On* (Jody Miller) and *A Perfect Match* (David Houston and Barbara Mandrell). In

Songwriter and crazy man **Glenn Sutton**

the U.K., Rod Stewart took *What Made Milwaukee Famous (Has Made a Loser Out of Me)* and went to No.4 with it.

Glenn's principal cuts during the rest of the 70's were: 1973: *Keep Me in Mind* (No.1) and *Sing About Love* (Top 3) (both Lynn Anderson), *Kids Say the Darndest Things* (No.1, Tammy Wynette) and *It's a Man's World (If You Had a Man Like Mine)* (Top 20, Diana Trask); 1974: *I'm Still Loving You* (Top 3, Joe Stampley); 1975: *It's All Over Now* (Charlie Rich); 1976: *Rodeo Cowboy* (Lynn Anderson); 1977: *So Many Ways* (David Houston); *Hello Mexico (and Adios Baby to You)* (Top 5, Johnny Duncan).

Although Glenn's songs have not been cut with the same regularity since the end of the 70's, he still finds himself in the charts via such hits as *Your Good Girl's Gonna Go Bad* (Billie Jo Spears, 1981), *Almost Persuaded* (Merle Haggard, 1987), *Lighter Shade of Blue* (Andi & the Brown Sisters, 1989) and *Livin' in a House Full of Love* (Glen Campbell, 1991).

Glenn's recording career started out with Ace Records and went on to MGM and Epic without chart success. However, at the beginning of 1979, he charted with his Mercury label novelty single *The Football Card*. The song, about betting on football games, was not only a Country Top 60 hit, it also crossed over to the Pop Top 50. Anyone who knows Glenn (who is an avid toy collector) would not have been surprised by the humor; after all, he is one of the most off-the-wall characters in Country. It was he who started the pie-throwing craze in Nashville. When Webb Pierce's guitar-shaped pool was opened, Glenn swam the length in an Esther Williams swimsuit and cap. He followed up with another humorous record, *Red Neck Disco*, which was written by Lee Dresser. It was the story of what happens when a Country band's manager refuses to play Disco.

In 1986, Glenn's Mercury recording of *I'll Go Steppin' Too* went Top 75. Since his heady days, Glenn continues to write and has recorded some for Studio 16.

RECOMMENDED ALBUM:

"Close Encounters of the Sutton Kind" (Mercury)(1979)

BILLY SWAN

(Singer, Songwriter, Guitar, Drums, Piano)

Date of Birth: **May 12, 1942**
Where Born: **Cape Girardeau, Missouri**
Married: **Marlu**

Billy Swan had one desire and that was not to be a star. His dream was to own a pair of Elvis Presley's socks. He not only got the socks, the King also recorded Billy's song *I Can Help*.

As a youngster, Billy was influenced by Gene Autry and Hank Williams and later, Jerry Lee Lewis and Buddy Holly. He initially learned to play drums and then guitar and piano. When he was age 16, he wrote *Lover Please* for his band, Mirt Mirley and the Rhythm Steppers. The band went to Memphis to record for Bill Black's label and it became the flip-side of their single. However, the song was heard by a record producer and it wound up being recorded by Soul singer Clyde McPhatter, becoming a Top 10 Pop hit in 1962.

Billy moved to Memphis, to write for Bill Black, but he was still struggling to make ends meet. He got into conversation with Elvis' uncle, Travis Smith, who was the gatekeeper at Graceland, and began boarding at Smith's house and subbing for him as gatekeeper. However, he soon moved on to Nashville, becoming a roadie and gofer for Mel Tillis and the Masters of Music Festival (starring Chet Atkins, Boots Randolph and Floyd Cramer).

Billy got a job in a recording studio and then became a janitor at Columbia studios. When he left there after eighteen months, he was replaced by Kris Kristofferson. While at Columbia, he met Tony Joe White and this would become an important connection. In the late 60's, Billy worked as a record producer for Monument Records. He produced the first four albums by Tony Joe White, ***Black & White*** (1968), ***Continued*** (1969), ***Tony Joe*** (1970) and his Warner Brothers release ***Tony Joe White*** (1971). Sides produced by Billy included Tony Joe's 1969 hit single *Polk Salad Annie*.

In 1970, Billy traveled with Kristofferson to the Isle of Wight Festival in England. He went on to play with Kinky Friedman and Billy Joe Shaver. He began recording for Monument in 1973 and then, in 1974, his self-penned song *I Can Help* (inspired by his wife) became a monster hit. It topped both the Pop and Country charts and was Certified Gold. It also turned Billy into an international star when it reached No.6 on the U.K. charts. He followed up with an album of the same name, which fared very well and contained a mix of self-penned songs and rock'n'roll standards.

Although Billy never again achieved the heady heights, he continued to chart with fluctuating results. In 1975, he had a Top 20 Country hit with *Everything's the Same (Ain't Nothing Changed)*. That year, his classic slow version of *Don't Be Cruel* became a U.K. chart entry and it was rumored that Pop star David Essex played drums on it. He didn't, even though he appeared in the promo film; however, another British star, Leo Sayer, played harmonica on *You're OK, I'm OK* and *Lonely Avenue*. That year, Kris and Rita Coolidge bagged a Grammy Award for "Best Country Vocal Performance by a Duo or Group" for their single *Lover Please* (written by Billy), even though it didn't chart. In 1976, Billy had a Top 50 entry, *Just Want to Taste Your Wine*.

In 1978, Billy moved to A & M Records, where he had the Country Top 30 entry that year, *Hello! Remember Me*. He moved labels again in 1981, this time to Epic, and achieved three back-to-back Top 20 Country hits with *Do I Have to Draw a Picture*, *I'm Into Lovin' You* and *Stuck Right in the Middle of Your Love*. Billy stayed with Epic until 1983 and his other successful releases were *With Their Kind of Money* and *Our Kind of Love* (Top 40, 1982) and *Rainbows and Butterflies* (Top 40, 1983).

Billy signed with Mercury Records in 1986 and had a Top 50 release, *You Must Be Lookin' for Me*. That year, he joined up with former Eagles bassist Randy Meisner and formed

If you've got a problem, ***Billy Swan*** *can help*

Black Tie. However, before the year was out, he had returned to the Kristofferson fold and appeared on Kris' album ***Repossessed***, as one of the Border Lords, and was with Kris at the Peterborough Festival in England in 1987, playing his own spot.

RECOMMENDED ALBUMS:

"I Can Help" (Monument)(1975)
"Rock'n'Roll Moon" (Monument)(1976)
"Billy Swan" (Monument)(1976)
"Four" (Monument)(1977)
"You're OK, I'm OK" (A & M)(1978)
"I'm in to You" (Epic)(1981)

SWEETHEARTS OF THE RODEO

When Formed: **1974**
JANIS GILL
(Singer, Songwriter, Guitar)
Given Name: **Janis Oliver**
Date of Birth: **November 28, 1955**
Married: **Vince Gill**
Children: **Jennifer**
KRISTINE ARNOLD
(Singer)
Given Name: **Kristine Oliver**
Date of Birth: **March 1, 1957**
Married: **Leonard Arnold**
Children: **Mary Del, Annabelle Gray**

Both Born: **Manhattan Beach, California**

Back in 1986, when the Sweethearts were asked for a description of their music, Janis and Kristine's response was "Rockabilly definitely. When people ask, we ask them to imagine if the Everly Brothers were female and making records in 1986. That is what we are." Since then, their music has evolved into the Hillbilly Rock sound associated with Marty Stuart and the O'Kanes, while still retaining a Folk edge that is becoming de rigueur in Country music.

Raised in California of a Polish-Oklahoman background, they began their musical odyssey, aged 7 and 5, by miming, in front of a mirror, to Country hits such as *Wolverton Mountain*. When she was age 9, Janis started playing flat-picking style of guitar, and became a great fan of Bluegrass and Folk music. The two girls started to sing together, with Kristine instinctively taking lead and Janis naturally harmonizing.

They left school in 1973 and began calling themselves Sweethearts of the Rodeo, named for the Byrds' Gram Parsons-influenced album. Their music became more eclectic, with Janis being influenced by the Beatles as well as Country, Bluegrass and Folk, while Kristine was into Linda Ronstadt and Tracy Nelson.

They began playing at a shopping mall in Torrance, California, where they were originally known as the Sweethearts of the Rodeo and Their Handsome Band. Their band was made up of a Dobro player and a stand-up bass player, as well as Janis' guitar. Their music was a mixture of Bluegrass, Western Swing and Commander Cody Country-Rock.

They went on to win a talent competition at a Long Beach Bluegrass festival that was attended by Emmylou Harris. She came to see them perform at The Straw Hat Pizza Palace, and invited them to sing on a show she was doing at The Roxy in Los Angeles. They also played shows with Poco and Willie Nelson.

While the Sweethearts were playing a nightclub with Pure Prairie League, Janis met Vince Gill, then a member of the group. Janis also met guitarist, steel guitarist and singer Leonard Arnold and introduced him to Kristine (they share the same birthday), and soon both Oliver sisters were married. Both Janis and Kristine sang back-up vocals on Pure Prairie League's ***Firin' Up*** (1979) and ***Something in the Night*** (1980) and on Leonard's group, Blue Steel's ***Nothing But Time*** (1981).

Soon bookings dropped off as the interest in Country music waned and in 1980, Janis and Kristine took time out to start a family. In 1983, Janis and Vince moved to Nashville, where Vince initially did session work, and then signed to RCA. Janis was encouraged by producer Steve Buckingham. As soon as Kristine and Leonard moved to Nashville, a year later, the Sweethearts of Rodeo was reactivated. Hank DeVito, who had met them while he played with Emmylou Harris' Hot Band, was also helpful.

In 1985, the Sweethearts became national winners of the annual Wrangler Country Showdown. Longtime friend Mary Martin, an RCA executive, persuaded Bonnie Garner, at Columbia, to see them at a showcase, and as a result Columbia signed them (by the time they won the Wrangler contest, they were already signed to Columbia).

Their first Country chart hit came in 1986, and was a remake of the Coasters' hit *Hey Doll Baby*, which fell just short of the Top 20. This was followed by the Top 10 hit Foster and Lloyd's *Since I Found You*, and the year was wrapped up by their release *Midnight Girl/Sunset Town*, written by Don Schlitz, which reached the Top 5. These all came from their debut eight-song self-titled album, as did their next two hits in 1987, the Top 5 *Chains of Gold* and Janis' *Gotta Get Away*, which reached the Top 10. From the back sleeve of the album, the sisters can be seen in some very attractive clothes. Janis and Kristine design and make their stage outfits, and these became a highlight of their videos.

In 1988, they released their second album ***One Time, One Night***. The first single from this was *Satisfy You*, which was written by Janis and Don Schlitz, and went Top 5. The two of them went on to write several songs together. This was followed by another Top 5 release, *Blue to the Bone*, and the year was wrapped up by their version of Lennon-McCartney's *I Feel Fine*.

During 1989, their record success slipped and *If I Never See Midnight Again* only got to the Top 40. They improved slightly in 1990, when their opening single, *This Heart*, climbed into the Top 25. Their third album, ***Buffalo Zone***, with a sleeve that depicted the Sweethearts in a variant of the original Byrds' cover, reached the Country album chart Top 50. The following year, their two releases *Hard-Headed Man* and *Devil and Your Deep Blue Eyes* did not fare well, with the former going Top 70 and the latter Top 75. These both came from their fourth album, ***Sisters*** (1991), which was produced by Steve Buckingham and Wendy Waldman.

Nothing much happened until they signed to Sugar Hill Records, but their album ***Rodeo Waltz***, produced by Janis, is a disappointment. Like the curate's egg, it is good in parts, but their harmonies are not as tight as before and musically, there is a lack of direction. This is sad, as the Sweethearts of the Rodeo are a vibrant and talented duo, who benefited from the deft touch of Steve Buckingham's production and could still produce hit records.

RECOMMENDED ALBUMS:

"Sweethearts of the Rodeo" (Columbia)(1986)
"One Time, One Night" (Columbia)(1988)
"Buffalo Zone" (Columbia)(1990)
"Sisters" (Columbia)(1991)

SYLVIA

(Singer, Songwriter, Artist)
Given Name: **Sylvia Kirby**
Date of Birth: **December 9, 1956**
Where Born: **Kokomo, Indiana**
Married: **1. Mike Allen (div.)**
2. Tom Rutledge (div.)
3. Roy Hutton

Sylvia used her skill as a portrait artist to meet many of her favorite Country stars. Near her hometown of Kokomo, Indiana, was a popular stop for many performers in Nashville, Indiana. Sylvia's portraits were her backstage pass to the Little Nashville Opry and to the singers she loved. Dolly Parton was so impressed with her drawing skills that she invited the aspiring singer on her bus. Sylvia was inspired by Parton's encouragement to seek her dreams and she set her sights on Nashville.

Following high school graduation in 1976, Sylvia traveled to Nashville in hopes of a recording contract. She pitched her a cappella vocal demo tape all over town and her rendition of Patsy Cline's *Crazy* caught the ear of publisher and producer Tom Collins. He told her to keep in touch and that he might be able to use her to sing demos sometime. Sylvia returned home to Indiana but returned four months later and Collins hired her as a secretary.

Although her job was answering the phone and typing letters, Sylvia took advantage of the creative environment of the publishing company to learn about the music business. She developed friendships with the company songwriters and occasionally was called upon to sing a demo. Tom Collins and his writers taught her a lot about the process of creating a hit song.

Sylvia also learned about making hit records by spending time in the studio when Tom Collins was producing Barbara Mandrell. Her first major job in the studio was singing background vocals for the Country star. Mandrell was so impressed with Sylvia's vocal talents that she invited her to sing back-up for a series of concerts in Las Vegas.

Sylvia came to the attention of Jerry Bradley at RCA Records when she auditioned for the group Dave & Sugar. She wasn't hired to fill the vocalist position but later was signed to the label with the help of Tom Collins. Sylvia's debut single, *You Don't Miss a Thing*, was released in the fall of 1979 and made the Top 40. The success of the single earned Sylvia a spot as the opening act for Charley Pride on a two-week tour in Canada.

She started the following year with the Top 40 success *It Don't Hurt to Dream*. Sylvia then scored her first Top 10 single with the Western-influenced *Tumbleweed*. In 1981 she earned her first No.1 record with the title song from her ***Drifter*** album. Later in the year Sylvia placed two more songs in the Top 10, *The Matador* and *Heart on the Mend*.

Sylvia's ***Just Sylvia*** album in 1982 departed from the Western flavor of her early recordings in favor of a more Pop sound. The change produced the biggest song of her career when *Nobody* shot to No.1 on the Country charts and crossed over to the Pop chart Top 15. The single became one of the few to be Certified Gold to commemorate sales in excess of 500,000 copies. The performing rights agency BMI honored the hit as the "Most Performed Country Song of the Year."

Like Nothing Ever Happened certainly wasn't a commentary on Sylvia's success. It was her follow-up single later in 1982 and became a Top 3 hit. Sylvia then teamed up with Irish flautist James Galway for a reprise of *The Wayward Wind*, which went Top 60. Her chart reign continued in 1983 with *Snapshot* (Top 5), *The Boy Gets Around* (Top 20) and *I Never Quite Got Back (From Loving You)* (Top 3). Also in 1983, Sylvia was named "Female Vocalist of the Year" by the ACM.

In 1984, Sylvia reached the Top 30 with *Victims of Goodbye* and the Top 40 with *Love Over Old Times*. The following year she returned to the upper regions of the chart with *Fallin' in Love* (Top 3) and *Cry Just a Little Bit* (Top 10). Later in the year, Sylvia teamed up with Michael Johnson to record the Top 10 hit *I Love You by Heart*. Sylvia's album that year, ***One Step Closer***, found her with Brent Maher (who also produced the Judds) as her producer. In 1986, *Nothin' Ventured Nothin' Gained* reached the Top 40 and in 1987, *Straight from My Heart* (Top 70) marked Sylvia's last charted single for RCA Records.

Growing weary of the constant touring, Sylvia decided to take a break from the road to concentrate on her songwriting. She focused much of her attention on writing music for children and did limited performing in the Nashville area. In the late 80's, Sylvia was the regular guest host for Lorianne Crook on TNN's *Crook and Chase* TV show. Sylvia was also featured in her own series of cooking specials on TNN called the *Holiday Gourmet*. In 1992, as Sylvia Hutton, she returned to performing and could be found playing at songwriters' venues such as Nashville's Bluebird Cafe. JIE

RECOMMENDED ALBUMS:

"Drifter" (RCA Victor)(1981)
"Just Sylvia" (RCA Victor)(1982)
"Snapshot" (RCA Victor)(1983)
"Surprise" (RCA Victor)(1984)
"One Step Closer" (RCA Victor)(1985)

T

SHOJI TABUCHI

(Violin, Singer, Dancer)

Given Name: Shoji Tabuchi
Where Born: Daishoji, Ishikawa Prefecture, Japan
Married: Dorothy
Children: Christina and two others

Shoji grew up in the Japanese city of Osaka, one of three children. He attended government-sponsored schools, and was enrolled by his mother at the age of 7 as a violin student, in the Suzuki method. His father held a position as an executive with Japan Rayon Nylon and as a child it was expected that Shoji would follow his father into the corporate world. While his father later became president of Thia Nylon Corporation, Shoji had other dreams.

Shoji later attended St. Andrews College in Osaka, obtaining a degree in economics. Most of his elective courses, however, were in music. During his sophomore year at St. Andrews, *Grand Ole Opry* star Roy Acuff did a concert on campus. Shoji was completely taken by the music, particularly Howdy Forrester's version of *Listen to the Mockingbird*. He approached Acuff after the concert, who told him if he was ever in the U.S. to look him up. Shoji's love of American music never abated. While his father was away, Shoji convinced his mother to support him in his dream of becoming an entertainer and with $500 in his pocket and just another $100 hidden in his shoe he departed for the U.S.

At first, he settled in San Francisco, waited tables in Japanese restaurants and polished cars to make ends meet. Since he spoke little English, he wasn't taken seriously as a Country musician. He did, however, form the Osaka Okies with a couple of Japanese friends and performed several gigs at nightspots such as the Hungry Eye. He later moved to the Midwest, where his first steady job was playing fiddle in a Country band at the Starlite Club in Riverside, Missouri.

He ran into Roy Acuff again, who invited him to come to Nashville when he got a chance. "I'll put you on the *Opry*," Acuff told him. Shoji didn't wait to get the invitation twice and drove to Nashville that Friday night to appear at the Old Ryman Auditorium, where Country music fans gave him a standing ovation. Ultimately, Shoji would play the *Opry* 27 times. Instant success, however, was not to be had. He relocated to Wichita, where he worked in a hospital X-ray laboratory during the day, playing music at night.

His Nashville exposure finally paid off when he got to audition for David Houston's band. The audition was held in Shreveport; he got the job and immediately began six years of touring as a featured performer (1970-75).

By 1975, however, Shoji was ready to strike out on his own, playing with pick-up house bands around the country.

While returning from a concert date in Illinois, Shoji was asked to play a theater in Branson, Missouri. He fell in love with the area and after several sessions packed up and moved there. His new dream was to open his own theater in Branson. In 1989, the time was finally right. After spending one season in an existing theater, Shoji built a 2,000-seat theater, which opened in May 1990. His show consists of himself, his wife, Dorothy, who creates and produces the show, emcees, sings, dances and presents an electrifying family variety show. His daughter Christina, now 13, is a seasoned veteran of the music business and is a featured performer.

Being an avid fisherman himself, Shoji played fiddle for President George Bush during a fishing tournament in Pintlalla, Alabama. He has accompanied many of Country music's greats including Tammy Wynette, George Jones and Barbara Mandrell. He has been featured on *60 Minutes*, the *Home Show*, the *Today Show*, *CBS This Morning*, *Inside Edition*, *NBC Nightly News*, *USA Today*, *Nashville Now* and several TV broadcasts in Japan, including NHK-TV, as well as numerous newspaper and magazine stories.

Shoji was named "Entertainer of the Year" in 1984 by the Ozarks Music Awards, as well as "Instrumentalist of the Year" in 1984, 1985, 1986, and 1987. Shoji was also nominated "Instrumentalist of the Year" in 1991 and 1992, sponsored by TNN/*Music City News* Country Music Awards. Shoji's story proves that with a lot of inspiration and hard work, America is still a place where dreams can come true. LAP

RECOMMENDED ALBUMS:

For information on the following write Shoji Entertainment, Mail Order Dept-HCR 1, Box 755, Branson, MO 65616. Tel.: (417)334-5974. Video tapes also available.

"Shoji Tabuchi—Live at the Grapevine Opry" (cassette)
"Shoji—Fiddlin' Around" (cassette and cd)
"Shoji—After Dark" (cassette and cd)
"Live From Branson" (cassette and cd)
"Shoji—Songs for the Lord and Other Favorites" (cassette and cd)
"Shoji Tabuchi—In Concert" (cassette)
"Shoji—Classy" (cassette)
"Rove Retters from Shoji" (cassette)
"Christina Tabuchi—This Little Heart" (cassette)

GID TANNER/SKILLET LICKERS, The

(Singer, Songwriter, Fiddle, Banjo)
Given Name: James Gideon Tanner
Date of Birth: June 6, 1885
Where Born: Thomas Bridge, Georgia
Married: twice
Children: five
Date of Death: 1960
Skillet Lickers (formed 1926): Clayton McMichen (Fiddle), Fate Norris (Banjo, Harmonica), Riley Puckett (Guitar, Singer), Lowe Stokes (Fiddle), Bert Layne (Fiddle), Ted Hawkins (Mandolin, Fiddle), Arthur Tanner (Banjo, Guitar), Mike Whitten (Guitar), Hoke Rice (Guitar), Gordon Tanner (Fiddle), Hugh Cross (Guitar)

Gid Tanner was a big redheaded north Georgia chicken farmer who had a comic flair and a somewhat archaic Georgia fiddle style. The Skillet Lickers were an all-star string band that was formed around Tanner by a record company A & R man. Combined, they became the most popular of all the Old-Time string bands of the 1920's and one of the central acts of early Country music. Their superb musicianship, zany sense of humor and sense of showmanship combined the best of the old traditional southern dance music with the new world of records and radio.

Their complex arrangements, built around two or even three fiddles and the innovative guitar playing of Riley Puckett, combined the best of the old and the new. And though the original band was only together for a few years (roughly 1926 to 1931), they had an immense impact on the nature and image of Old-Time Country music. Other basic members included the fiddler Clayton McMichen, banjoist Fate Norris and blind guitarist-singer Riley Puckett. Later additions included fiddlers Lowe Stokes and Bert Layne.

Gid Tanner began playing the fiddle about 1900 and won his initial fame as a frequent winner in Atlanta's fiddlers conventions, which started about 1913. Like many older fiddlers, Tanner was also an entertainer; he sang comic songs like *I'm Satisfied*, dressed in outrageous hats that were fully three feet high and learned how to "turn his head around like an owl" in the middle of a tune. His fame in the contests led to his call to New York in early 1924, just a few months after Fiddlin' John Carson's first records, to record for Columbia. Accompanied by his friend and longtime contest partner, Riley Puckett, Tanner generated some of the first "southern fiddle and guitar records," with pieces like *Hen Cackle*, *Three Nights Drunk* and *Cumberland Gap*. Later, when Columbia's A & R man Frank Walker actually came to Atlanta to record, he remembered Tanner and his earlier records. With the new electrical recording process, though, Walker now wanted a fuller sound, and he asked Tanner and Puckett to join forces with Clayton McMichen and Fate Norris to form a sort of superband. Casting about for a name for the group, someone remembered that an Old-Time band that used to play at the fiddlers' contests was called the Lickskillet Band; reversing it, the group came up with the name Skillet Lickers.

The first Skillet Lickers records were recorded and issued in 1926 and they were instantly successful, knocking the work of citybilly Vernon Dalhart totally off the best-selling charts. *Bully of the Town* backed with *Pass Around the Bottle and We'll All Take a Drink* was their first giant double-sided hit followed closely by *Watermelon Hanging on the Vine* and *You*. The following year, 1927, saw the Skillet Lickers try another innovation: the comedy skit. These rustic dramas combined music with dialogue (often written by McMichen and Frank Walker) which portrayed the members of the band as back-country moonshiners, ones who were always "making a little brew, and drinking a little brew." *A Corn Licker Still in Georgia* (1927) was the first of these efforts to make it to records, followed shortly by a takeoff on the Atlanta contests, *A Fiddler's Convention in Georgia*. These skits sold more than the straight fiddle records, as did the discs which featured Puckett's singing; later on, McMichen gave Puckett's singing credit for really putting the band on the map.

Almost from the first, though, there was dissension in the band over billing. Original records read "Gid Tanner and His Skillet Lickers," but this upset McMichen and Puckett, who felt they carried more of the musical burden for the band, and soon the labels were changed to read "Gid Tanner and His Skillet Lickers with Clayton McMichen and Riley Puckett." Then the younger musicians, McMichen and his pals Stokes and Layne, who were interested in modern, even Swing, fiddling, began to chafe against the older, Folk-oriented styles of Tanner, Norris, and Puckett. McMichen began to work as a studio musician for Columbia, worked for a time with Jimmie Rodgers, and eventually organized a new "hot" band called the Georgia Wildcats. By 1931, at the time of their last Columbia session, the Skillet Lickers were together only in the studio.

Though Puckett and Layne worked for a time with bands called the Skillet Lickers, it was not until 1934 that Tanner decided to re-activate the band to record for Victor's Bluebird company. Drawing on some of his early Atlanta friends (Puckett, mandolin player Ted Hawkins) and the impressive skills of his 17-year-old son Gordon, Tanner traveled to San Antonio to record one final time—a marathon 30-plus-song session. It yielded one final mega-hit *Down Yonder*, which would stay in print well into the 1950's. In later years, Tanner retired from music and watched his friends McMichen and Puckett and Layne continue on in separate careers, making numerous solo records. Tanner died in Dacula, Georgia, in 1960. In later years, his son Gordon carried on with the fiddle tradition and in 1990 his grandson was still playing his music.

CKW

RECOMMENDED ALBUMS:

"Gid Tanner & His Skillet Lickers" (Rounder)(1973)
"Kikapoo Medicine Show" (Rounder)(1975)
"The Skillet Lickers" (County)
"Gid Tanner & the Skillet Lickers, Vol. 2" (County)
Gordon Tanner & the Junior Skillet Lickers:
"Down Yonder" (Folkways)

TATER TATE

(Fiddle, Guitar, Bass, Banjo, Mandolin)

Given Name: **Clarence E. Tate**
Date of Birth: **February 4, 1931**
Where Born: **Gate City, Virginia**
Married: **Lois**

Tater Tate has been one of Bluegrass music's most noted, albeit somewhat underrated, fiddlers. Over a 45-year period Tater has worked and recorded with many of the greats and near-greats of the genre: Carl Sauceman, Carl Butler, the Bailey Brothers, Bill Monroe, Jimmy Martin, Carl Story, Hylo Brown, Lester Flatt, Curly Sechler, Mac Wiseman, and Wilma Lee Cooper to name just a few.

A native of Gate City, Virginia, Clarence Tate grew up as the youngest child in a musical Appalachian family of nine. By the age of 4 he was displaying some serious interest in playing guitar and made his radio debut about 1940 on a live show broadcast from local station WKPT in nearby Kingsport, Tennessee. During the war years Tater played on a local jamboree show, the *Barrel of Fun*, in Elizabethton, Tennessee. About 1947, Tater began playing with Jim Smith and the Ridge Runners on a regular program at WKPT. Inspired by the fiddling of Art Wooten at WCYB Bristol, Tate got increasingly interested in that instrument. Archie Campbell hired the Ridge Runners to play at a Roy Acuff political rally in the fall of 1948. This resulted in his becoming a regular on the *Dinner Bell Show* at WROL Knoxville. The East Tennessee metropolis was a major center for the evolution of Bluegrass sounds in the 1948-1951 era with both the WNOX *Mid-Day Merry-Go-Round* and various Cas Walker-sponsored shows on WROL. These and other outlets provided opportunities for aspiring musicians. Walker gave young Tate his nickname of Tater in 1950 which remained with him.The young fiddler had early recording sessions with the Sauceman Brothers on Rich-R-Tone and with Carl Butler on Capitol.

Tater really began his career as a sideman with the Sauceman Brothers at WCYB Bristol in the summer of 1950 and then with the Bailey Brothers later that year at WPTF Raleigh. He subsequently moved with the Baileys to WDBJ Roanoke and WWVA Wheeling, working with them until June 1954, when he was drafted. He cut a few numbers with the Baileys on Canary, and Jamboree songstress Mabelle Sieger borrowed him for sessions on "X" Records. Out of the service two years later, Tate soon got a call to join Bill Monroe's band as a replacement for Bobby Hicks, who had gotten his draft notice. A recurring problem of migraine headaches forced Tate to give up heavy traveling and he went back to the Baileys, who were now in Knoxville. During the next few years Tater went successively with Carl Story (at least twice), the Brewster Brothers (on the *Cas Walker Show*), Hylo Brown, Bonnie Lou and Buster, Carl Sauceman, Jimmy Martin, and back again to the *Cas Walker Show*. He managed to get in at least one recording session with each of these folks except Sauceman.

In October 1965, Tater Tate joined Red Smiley's Bluegrass Cut-Ups at WDBJ-TV in Roanoke. This situation suited Tater's preferred musical circumstance, daily television with minimal traveling. It also provided an opportunity to record on his own as well as with Red's group. Tater did his first solo album on Rimrock at the same time Smiley made his and cut three on Uncle Jim O'Neal's Rural Rhythm Records.The Bluegrass Cut-Ups also served as back-up for other artists on the Rural Rhythm roster, including Jim Eanes, J.E. Mainer, and Lee Moore. Although the band did not travel extensively, they journeyed periodically to Wheeling for appearances on the WWVA *Jamboree* and worked a few early Bluegrass festivals. The happy circumstance at WDBJ came to a sudden end in March 1969 when the station's management canceled Red's *Top o' the Morning Show*. Red Smiley chose to retire rather than hit the road and travel extensively.

Tater and John Palmer decided to keep a band together with banjoist Billy Edwards, securing mandolinist Herschel Sizemore as the fourth member. They took the name Shenandoah Cut-Ups and worked the festival circuit by summer and the WWVA Jamboree in winter. At times they had a fifth member and recorded several albums on such labels as County, Rebel, Major, and especially Revonah. Tater remained with them until 1977, when Lester Flatt hired him to replace an ailing Paul Warren. His tenure with the Nashville Grass proved relatively short, only two years, but he cut a pair of albums in the studio and one live festival album in this brief tenure. He also did another fiddle effort, on Revonah, although it did not come out until 1981. In the meantime, Tater had been a member of Curly Sechler's group briefly and Wilma Lee Cooper's Clinch Mountain Clan somewhat longer, waxing an album with each.

By the mid-80's, Tater settled in for a second tenure with Bill Monroe's Blue Grass Boys. Ironically, he usually fiddled only for short stints or special occasions, preferring the physically more strenuous, but musically less stressful, bass fiddle.

IMT

RECOMMENDED ALBUMS:

"Fiddle & Banjo Instrumentals" (Rimrock)(1966)
"Fiddle Favorites of U.S.A. & Canada" (Rural Rhythm)(1967)
"Country Favorite Waltzes" (Rural Rhythm)(1968)
"More Favorite Waltzes" (Rural Rhythm)(1969)
"The Fiddler and His Lady" (Revonah)(1981)
(See also the Shenandoah Cut-Ups).

CARMOL TAYLOR

(Singer, Songwriter, Guitar)

Given Name: **Carmol Lee Taylor**
Date of Birth: **September 5, 1931**
Where Born: **Brilliant, Alabama**
Married: **Louise**
Children: **Carmol Gene, Bobby Junior**
Date of Death: **December 5, 1986**

Although Carmol Taylor was a performer, it was as a songwriter that he made his mark and it was as such that his own personal preference lay.

By the time he was 15, Carmol was already playing professionally at shows and square dances. It was around this time that he met Billy Sherrill and the two became friends. Carmol formed the group Carmol Taylor and the Country Pals (among whose members was Rick Hall, of Fame Recording Studio in Muscle Shoals) and between 1954 and 1974, they played various radio stations, including WERH Hamilton, Alabama, WCPC Houston, Mississippi, and WJBB Haleyville, Alabama. Although Carmol began his recording career in 1955, he started making his name when he recorded *Free as the Breeze* for the Timmy label in Memphis, also recording for the Crow label. In 1962, Carmol and the group began a

30-minute Channel 4 TV show from Columbus, Mississippi, where they stayed until 1971.

When Billy Sherrill became the main producer at Epic Records, he was instrumental in helping Carmol get his writing career off the ground, with Carmol becoming a staff writer for Al Gallico Music. Following the success of Carmol's *Wild as a Wildcat*, which Charlie Walker took into the Top 10 in 1965, Carmol began writing with Sherrill, George Richey and Norro Wilson.

This led to a string of hit songs such as *He Loves Me All the Way* (No.1, 1970) and *My Man* (No.1, 1972), both by Tammy Wynette, *Good Things* and *She's All Woman* (both Top 3, 1973) by David Houston, *If You Touch Me (You've Got to Love Me)* (Top 10, 1972) by Joe Stampley, *Get on My Love Train* (Top 3, 1974) by La Costa, *The Grand Tour* (No.1, 1974) by George Jones and *There's a Song on the Jukebox* (Top 10, 1975) by David Wills.

On the recording front, Carmol was less successful. Billy Sherrill signed him to Epic Records, but although several singles were released, Carmol failed to chart. In 1975, Mike Suttle signed Carmol to Elektra, and that year he hit the Top 50 with Chuck Berry's *Back in the U.S.A.* Although the next single failed, in 1976, he scored with *Play the Saddest Song on the Jukebox* (Top 40) and *I Really Had a Ball Last Night* (Top 25), ending the year with the Top 60 *That Little Difference*. 1977 was his last charting year with Elektra but none of the singles fared that well. However, of interest is his duet with Stella Parton, *Neon Women*. In 1980, Carmol signed with Country International Records, where he also became a producer.

In 1985, George Jones teamed up with Lacy J. Dalton for their Top 20 version of the Carmol Taylor-Gary Lumpkin song *Size Seven Round (Made of Gold)*. The following year, Carmol died from lung cancer. His songs continue to speak for him and, in 1993, Aaron Neville recorded *The Grand Tour* as the title track of an album, and the single of the song, accompanied by a music video, became a Top 40 Country hit and a Pop Top 90 success.

RECOMMENDED ALBUM:

"Song Writer" (Elektra)(1976)
"Honky Tonk Two Steppin' Beer Drinkin' Saturday Nite" (Password UK)(1987) [As the County Line Band (Featuring Carmol Taylor)]

EARL TAYLOR

(Singer, Songwriter, Mandolin, Harmonica, Guitar)

Given Name: Earl M. Taylor
Date of Birth: June 17, 1929
Where Born: Rose Hill, Lee County, Virginia
Married: Unknown
Children: Billy (dec'd.), others unknown
Date of Death: January 28, 1984

Earl Taylor led one of the more significant traditional Bluegrass bands off and on from the late 50's to the early 80's, although major stardom eluded him. Taylor and his Stoney Mountain Boys twice achieved major label contracts but Earl still did most of his personal appearances working bars and clubs first in Baltimore and then in Cincinnati.

A native of Lee County, Virginia, Earl Taylor grew up in the homes of older siblings after both parents had died in his early childhood. He heard the music of the Monroe Brothers in the late 30's, which inspired him to learn both guitar and mandolin. At age 12, Taylor took up the harmonica and carried one in his pocket, playing at every opportunity. He journeyed to Michigan when he turned 17 and joined a Country band called the Mountaineers which worked clubs in Monroe and the nearby city of Toledo.

After several months, Earl formed his initial version of the Stoney Mountain Boys, but by the end of 1948 they had disbanded and the youthful leader went back to Virginia. Taylor moved northward a few months later to Rockville, Maryland, where he took a job with a drywall firm and stayed out of the music scene for the next three years. Then he met Sam Hutchins and Charlie Waller, who were both 17 at the time. In 1953, they went to Baltimore, adding fiddler Louie Profitt to their entourage and successfully introducing Bluegrass to the Maryland metropolis. Profitt left to be replaced by Art Wooten, and Fred Keith took over for Charlie on guitar. Earl soon added bassist-comedian Vernon "Boatwhistle" McIntire to the Stoney Mountain Boys and Vernon remained a regular in Taylor bands for years.

In August 1955, this group dissolved. Hutchins and Taylor went to Detroit and joined Jimmy Martin's Sunny Mountain Boys. Earl helped Martin cut eight sides on Decca. Returning to Maryland in March 1957, the young mandolinist re-formed the Stoney Mountain Boys and soon added young banjo virtuoso Walter Hensley to the group. They continued working clubs in the Baltimore area and recorded a few numbers for Folkways. On April 3, 1959, the Stoney Mountain Boys became the first Bluegrass band to play Carnegie Hall and subsequently cut an entire album for United Artists. Back in Baltimore, Jim McCall, another key band member, joined the group. They cut a few sides for Rebel in March 1961.

Earl moved the entire entourage to Cincinnati, which thereafter became their main base for club work. They did some local TV at WKRC, spent a lengthy stint at the Ken-Mil and in 1963 cut another quality album, ***Bluegrass Taylor-Made*** for Capitol. Earl also did some session work at King studio, mostly assisting the Stanley Brothers. In June 1965, Earl rejoined Jimmy Martin briefly and then worked for Flatt & Scruggs from August 1965 to late 1966, playing a heavy road schedule and cutting four sessions with them on Columbia. Taylor then returned to Cincinnati and reorganized the Stoney Mountain Boys, recording an album with Jim McCall on Rural Rhythm. For several months in 1968-69, Earl took a band to California, but they eventually returned to the Queen City, where he and Jim McCall made two more albums for Rural Rhythm in 1971, both produced by Rusty York.

From 1972, Earl and yet another new crop of Stoney Mountain Boys worked sporadically in clubs in the Cincinnati and Columbus areas and also some festivals throughout the Midwest. During those years, Taylor cut a new album for Vetco and had another—recorded previously during his California sojourn—released on the same label.

Ill health plagued the Virginia born mandolin picker in his later years and he sometimes gave up playing for several months at a time. He also had to cope with the death of a 12-year-old son during a Florida trip in 1975. Earl worked only periodically in his last year of life with McIntyre, a band led by his late bass player's banjo-picking son, Vernon McIntyre. IMT

RECOMMENDED ALBUMS:

"Folk Songs from the Bluegrass" (United Artists)(1959)
"Bluegrass Taylor-Made" (Capitol)(1963) [Re-issued by Stetson UK in original packaging (1988)]
"Bluegrass Favorites" (Rural Rhythm)(1968)
"Bluegrass Favorites, Vol. 2" (Rural Rhythm)(1971)
"Bluegrass Favorites, Vol. 3" (Rural Rhythm)(1971) [Rural Rhythm albums credited to Earl Taylor and Jim McCall]
"The Bluegrass Touch" (Vetco)(1974) [Recorded in 1969]
"Body & Soul" (Vetco)(1976)

JOE TAYLOR

(Industry Executive)

Given Name: Joseph Daniel Taylor
Date of Birth: February 1, 1933
Where Born: McMinnville, Tennessee
Married: Jo Ann
Children: Lisa, Brent

In recent times, corporate booking agents have arrived in Nashville and the original artists agents have been to a large part ignored. Joe Taylor has survived through all the changes in Country to still be one of the most respected and admired industry executives.

When he was age 12, Joe moved with his family to Chattanooga, Tennessee, where he grew up. He wanted to be an actor and at school he appeared in plays. In his words, he was "stagestruck." He attended the University of Chattanooga (now called the University of Tennessee at Chattanooga), where he majored in social work, minored in psychology and graduated in June 1955. These disciplines would stand him in good stead in his future calling.

He started working in delinquent advertising accounts for the Chattanooga Publishing Company, which published the *Chattanooga Times* and the *Free Press*. Then in October that year, he went into the U.S. Army, with a commission as lieutenant. He was stationed in Japan as an armed forces courier at Tokyo International Airport. He was there for two years during which time his daughter was born. Japan also gave him a lifelong passion for Oriental art, which now bedecks his office.

He returned to the U.S. and became involved in outdoor advertising, which included billboards and street signs. Joe met the Wilburn Brothers, who were then managing Joe Dowell, who had a No.1 Pop hit with *Wooden Heart* (sung by Elvis Presley in the movie *G.I. Blues*) on Smash in 1961. The Wilburns had come to Chattanooga and Joe Taylor had set up the press for them. Joe remembers, "They said you ought to be in this business and I said, you know I always wanted to be. So I came to Nashville and talked to the Wilburn Brothers and Don Helms." The Wilburns and Don Helms ran the Wil-helm Agency, "so I became the first Director of Talent for the Wil-helm Agency."

Joe worked for them for a couple of years handling dates for Loretta Lynn. He was then offered the position of Advertising Manager of Martha White Mills (sponsor of the *Grand Ole Opry*). Here he was involved with Flatt & Scruggs and Jim & Jesse. In 1964, Joe set up the Joe Taylor Agency. His first artist was Ray Pillow and then he went on to represent Jim & Jesse (whom he still represents) and Bobby Lord. Over the years, he has worked with George Jones, Alabama and Mickey Gilley. For four and one-half years, Joe represented John Anderson during his highly successful "first go-round." He also handled many of the artists on *Hee Haw*, including Archie Campbell, Junior Samples, Stringbean and Grandpa Jones.

Joe currently represents Connie Smith, Grandpa Jones, Kitty Wells and Johnny Wright, Dave & Sugar, Johnny Paycheck, David Frizzell, Stella Parton, Sylvia, Ronnie Prophett and Billie Jo Spears. It was the connection with Billie Jo that led to Joe's ongoing relationship with Europe, where he still books many acts. Joe also manages singer/songwriter/funnyman Johnny Russell.

When asked why he had survived, he remarked that it was "either determination or stupidity."

JOE TAYLOR
(The Cowboy Auctioneer)

(Singer, Songwriter, Guitar)

Given Name: Joseph Carl Taylor
Date of Birth: May 11, 1921
Where Born: Portsmouth, Ohio
Married: Pauline Elizabeth Corbat
Children: Paula Jo, Daniel James

Although Joe Taylor, "the Cowboy Auctioneer," never became a major star, he is one of those artists who have been the backbone of Country music.

Joe's father was a horse trainer with Roger Selling Farms in Portsmouth, Ohio. When Joe was 15, his family moved to Fort Wayne, Indiana, where his father became chief horse trainer for the Berghoff Farms. In 1942, Joe began working for GE's Wire Mill (he stayed at the company for 40 years, retiring in 1982). In 1944, Joe started playing guitar, which his father won in a poker game several years earlier. He began playing floor shows and lodges as a single. At the same time, Joe decided to become an auctioneer and studied at Reppart School of Auctioneering in Decatur, Indiana.

In 1947, Joe began broadcasting from WFTW Fort Wayne, where he was sponsored by International Harvester. He was contacted by Elsie Byers, the owner of Red Bird Records, who had written some songs that she wanted Joe to record. For the recording, Joe put together a band that he called the Indiana Red Birds. The resulting single was Joe's self-penned song *He's a Cowboy Auctioneer*, which was backed with one of Elsie's numbers. After the recording was done, Joe returned to be a solo performer. The single sold well, particularly in Tyler, Texas.

Joe was approached to do a gig that required a band and, as a result, in 1948, he re-formed the Indiana Red Birds (or as they're now known, the Red Birds). One of the biggest supporters of the band was Randy Blake, a deejay at WJJD, who played *He's a Cowboy Auctioneer*. It was Blake that managed to persuade Tex Ritter to record the song. While the band was in Chicago, it recorded two sides for London Records, *My Girl's a Square Dance Caller/Tiger Rag*, but due to financial difficulties at the label, it was never released.

One of the specialties of the band is playing square dances and the calling is handled by Joe's sister-in-law, Patty, who started this skill back in 1949 at the Old Hayloft, when she was age 15. In 1950, the band started its own show on Saturdays on WGL Fort Wayne, which continued until 1967. During this time, Joe gave a teenage Buddy Emmons his first break. They also broadcast briefly over WOWO Fort Wayne. During 1957 and 1958, Joe produced and directed the *Hoosier Hayride*. In 1959-1960, he acted as President of the Association of Country Musicians & Entertainers.

In 1979, Joe Taylor met polka bandleader Joe Taylor from Minnesota and discovered that they had numerous things in common. They both had fathers called Joseph; they had both lost the same finger on their left hand by accident; they both had a daughter married to men named Dennis; Fort Wayne's Joe has a son called Daniel James, who is a drummer (in Joe's band), and Minneapolis Joe has two sons named Daniel and James, and James is also a drummer (and former member of his father's band); both are Catholic; both married in November and both drive Dodge maxi-vans.

Joe's daughter has also made her mark in Country music, playing bass and autoharp in her Country-Rock band, Goldrush. Over the years, Joe and the Red Birds have opened for many stars of Country music, including Pee Wee King, Porter Wagoner, Dolly Parton, Smiley Burnette, Jimmy Dean and Johnny Cash.

During 1988, Joe and the band recorded for Emerald Records and released *My Sweet Eleanor/My Gal's a Square Dance Caller*. The band is still active into the 90's and Joe is still as enthusiastic in 1994 as he was in 1944.

LES TAYLOR

(Singer, Songwriter, Guitar)

Date of Birth: December 27, 1948
Where Born: Oneida, Kentucky
Married: Lisa

Up to 1989, Les Taylor's claim to fame was as the rhythm guitarist with Exile. He decided to go the solo route, after 10 years with the group.

Les started playing music on weekends as

a way of picking up girls and with the hope of making some spare cash. It was not until he reached his early 30's that he decided to take music seriously. While with Exile, he often handled lead vocals and can be heard on their No.1 hits *It'll Be Me* (1986) and *She's Too Good to Be True* (1987).

When Epic Records signed Exile, they also signed the individual members, and although they could have not taken up the option on Les, they liked his solo material. Les' first single *Shoulda, Coulda, Woulda Loved You*, which he wrote with Lonnie Wilson and Ron Moore, went Top 50, in 1989. In 1990, Les had *Knowin' You Were Leavin'*, which reached the Top 60. That year, Les released his debut album ***That Old Desire***. In 1991, Les' solo recording career continued to be bogged down and both of his singles, *I Gotta Mind to Go Crazy* and *The Very First Lasting Love*, stuck in the Top 50; the last named was a duet with Shelby Lynne.

In 1991, Les released his second album ***Blue Kentucky Wind***, which was produced by James Stroud. Although Les has not yet succeeded on record, he and his band, the Rhythm Killers, have been well received around the clubs.

RECOMMENDED ALBUMS:

"That Old Desire" (Epic)(1990)
"Blue Kentucky Wind" (Epic)(1991)

TUT TAYLOR

(Dobro, Mandolin, Fiddle, Guitar, Dulcimer, Banjo, Composer, Instrument Builder, Sign Painter)

Given Name:	**Robert Arthur Taylor**
Date of Birth:	**November 20, 1923**
Where Born:	**Milledgeville, Georgia**
Married:	**Lee**
Children:	**Shirley, Robert, Jr., Mark, Lou Ellen, Lester, Barbara, David, Linda**

It is always surprising that where a relatively untalented performer will be acclaimed as a star because he has a few hit records under his belt, a performer of pure genius such as Tut Taylor will remain largely unknown to the general public, although he will be loudly lauded by his peer musicians.

Tut came from a musical family and by the time he was age 10, he could play banjo. Two years later, he had mandolin in his arsenal. When he was 14 he heard Pete Kirby, aka Brother Bashful Oswald, play Dobro and Tut knew he had to play it. However, he couldn't identify the instrument and so he wrote to Roy Acuff at the *Grand Ole Opry*. Tut got a response from Mildred Acuff and promptly went out and purchased a Dobro. Not knowing how to play it, he adopted a style similar to the mandolin, i.e. flat-picked it. He subsequently became a collector of the instrument and went on to run Tennessee Dulcimer Works.

During the 60's, Tut, Glen Campbell and the Dillards became members of the Folkswingers, and they released three albums for World Pacific, ***12 String Guitar*** and ***12 String Guitar, Vol. 2*** (both in 1963) and ***12 String Dobro!***, the following year. Also in 1964, Tut released the solo album ***Dobro Country***, which featured Roland and Clarence White, Billy Ray Lathum, Bill Keith, Chris Hillman and Victor Gaskin. The following year, he was featured on Porter Wagoner's album ***The Bluegrass Story***. During the late 60's, he became a member of the Dixie Gentlemen, alongside the legendary fiddler Vassar Clements. They recorded the album ***Blues & Bluegrass***, which was released on the Tune label, in 1967.

In 1970, Tut, instrument dealer George Gruhn and instrument repairer Randy Wood formed GTR, Inc. This was an instrument sales and repair shop, in Nashville, which specialized in selling and repairing acoustic instruments. The following year, Tut appeared on David Bromberg's self-titled album playing mandolin. He also joined forces with John Hartford. He appeared on the Hartford album ***Aero Plain*** and played in Hartford's band, which also included Vassar Clements and Norman Blake.

Tut recorded another solo album ***Friar Tut***, in 1972, for Rounder and he and Randy Wood split from George Gruhn and set up the Old Time Pickin' Parlor, along with Norman Blake and Ginger Boatwright (of Red, White & Blue(grass)). This was a combination nightclub and instrument shop. The following year, Tut was part of the Nashville ensemble backing Leon Russell on ***Hank Wilson's Back***.

During 1975, Tut appeared on Norman Blake's ***Norman Blake—Super Jam Session***, and recorded his own solo album ***The Old Post Office***, both on Flying Fish. It was the following year that Tut released his watershed album ***Dobrolic Plectoral Society***, with Norman Blake, for Takoma Records. Since then, Tut has operated Tut Taylor's General Store on Arlington Avenue, Nashville, until his retirement. He is now a resident of Merryville, Tennessee.

RECOMMENDED ALBUMS:

"Dobro Country" (World Pacific)(1964)
"Friar Tut" (Rounder)(1972)
"The Old Post Office" (Flying Fish)(1975)
"Dobrolic Plectoral Society" (Takoma)(1976)

TENNESSEE RAMBLERS, The

When Formed:	**1928**
Members:	
Dick Hartman	**Mandolin, Tenor Banjo**
Harry Blair	**Guitar, Vocals**
Cecil Campbell	**Tenor Banjo, Steel Guitar**
"Pappy" Wolfe	**Fiddle**
Fred "Happy" Morris	**String Bass**
Claude Casey	**Vocals, Guitar**
Garnet "Elmer" Warren	**Fiddle**
Jack Gillette	**Novelty Musician (Balloon, Tire Pump)**
Kelland "Kid" Clark	**Accordion**
Betty Lou DeMorrow	**Singer**
Roy Lear	**Guitar**
Tex Martin	**Guitar**
Don White	**String Bass, Guitar**

The Tennessee Ramblers were a Country band of the 30's and early 40's who fell into a musical category somewhere between Old-Time string bands, Western Swing novelty orchestras and what would emerge as modern Country.

Dick Hartman (b. Richard Arlington Hartman, June 12, 1898, Burlington, West Virginia/d. April 15, 1962) apparently organized the band at KDKA Pittsburgh about 1928. They evidently gained little in the way of a following until Harry Blair, a 16-year-old from New Martinsville, West Virginia, joined their ranks on guitar and vocals. Hartman had some musical skills, but was more of an emcee and "pitchman" than anything else. The band began to hit its stride about 1933 with Hartman, Blair, fiddler Kenneth "Pappy" Wolfe, and Cecil Campbell, who alternated on tenor banjo and steel guitar. Late that year the Ramblers went to WHEC Rochester, New York, sponsored by Crazy Water Crystals.

In 1934, the company sent them to WBT Charlotte, North Carolina, which thereafter became their main base except for occasional times when their sponsor sent them to such locales as Atlanta, Louisville, Cincinnati, and Pittsburgh for stints of several months each. Bass man Happy Morris, fiddler Elmer Warren, and novelty musician Jack Gillette joined the group in this era. They began recording for Bluebird in 1935 with their early releases credited to either Dick Hartman's Tennessee Ramblers, Hartman's Heart Breakers or the Washboard Wonders. The Heart Breaker sides featured a girl vocalist, Betty Lou DeMorrow, and contained lyrics of a risqué or double-entendre nature. The Ramblers made a pair of films with Gene Autry in 1936 and 1937, *Ride Ranger Ride* and *The Yodelin' Kid from Pine Ridge*.

Favorites in the 30's and 40's, the ***Tennessee Ramblers***

Hartman departed from the group about 1938 and Jack Gillette (b. ca. 1908) assumed leadership. Gillette, a Rhode Island native and one-time member of the Louis Prima band, played music on a variety of novelty items, including balloons and tire pumps, which attracted considerable attention. The band appeared in a Tex Ritter film, *The Pioneers*, in 1941, by which time the membership was Blair, Campbell, Gillette, and Kid Clark. When they did *Swing Your Partner* with Dale Evans, Blair had entered military service and Don White and Claude Casey accompanied Jack and Cecil. They made their final films in 1944, which starred Roy Acuff and Charles Starrett and featured the same personnel (see Movie Section). All this time they remained based with WBT except when touring theaters promoting the films.

By 1945, only Campbell and newly-returned-from-the-war "Horse Thief Harry" Blair remained of the old Tennessee Ramblers. Cecil took over the top position, although Harry remained until 1949, when he left show business. Campbell kept the name for his groups into the 80's. White and Warren worked extensively with the Briarhoppers in later years. Blair eventually retired to Murrell's Inlet, South Carolina, and Casey operated a radio station. Hartman, the original leader, went back to West Virginia and worked in a lumber mill at Luke, Maryland, until his death.

A couple of Washboard Wonder sides have been reissued on Western Swing anthologies, but the Hartman's Heart Breaker numbers were collected on an album on the Rambler label in 1981. The group founded by Dick Hartman was quite different from an East Tennessee string band of the same name led by fiddler Mack Sievers that had recorded for Brunswick in 1928. IMT

RECOMMENDED ALBUM:
"Hartman's Heart Breakers" (Rambler)(1981)

TENNEVA RAMBLERS, The

When Formed: 1927
Members:

Claude Grant	**Guitar, Vocals**
Jack Grant	**Mandolin**
Jack Pierce	**Fiddle**
Claude Slagle	**Banjo**

The Tenneva Ramblers, sometimes known as the Grant Brothers, are equally remembered for what they did not do as for what they did. They did not record as a band for Jimmie Rodgers although they worked with him. Fine musicians, the group worked out of the Bristol area for many years.

Claude (b. early 1900's, Bristol, Tennessee/d. 1976) and Jack Grant (b. early 1900's, Bristol, Tennessee/d. March 1968) began their musical careers in the early 20's when they were just coming of age. They soon added a Smyth County, Virginia, fiddler named Jack Pierce (b. early 1900's, Smyth County, Virginia/d. March 1950) to their group and the three entertained at parties and dances in Bristol and the surrounding territory in Tennessee and Virginia. In 1925, they began calling themselves the Tenneva Ramblers because of their state line location.

In March 1927, the Ramblers met a struggling, but ambitious, musician from Mississippi named Jimmie Rodgers. They combined forces and took the name Jimmie Rodgers Entertainers. They survived an unlucrative month at WWNC radio in Asheville, but did land a six-week stint at North Fork Mountain Resort at nearby Marion. Pierce and Rodgers went to Bristol and learned that Ralph Peer was conducting recording sessions there and made arrangements to cut some masters. The night before, however, the four had an argument as to how they would be billed on the discs. Rodgers subsequently recorded alone while the Ramblers got Claude Slagle (b. early 1900's, Bristol, Tennessee/d. March 1950), a local musician who had sometimes played with them, to take his place.

The boys did three numbers for Victor on August 4, 1927, and went to Atlanta the following February and cut six more. That October, the group recorded four masters for Columbia as the Grant Brothers and Their Music. Their songs included both traditional numbers and newer originals. One of their numbers, *Tell It to Me*, dealt with the atypical subject of cocaine addiction while a Civil War song, *The Johnson Boys*, later became a charted Bluegrass hit for Lester Flatt and Earl Scruggs. In addition, Pierce did a session for Victor in October 1927 as fiddler for the Smyth County Ramblers.

The Ramblers entertained full-time in their region until the Great Depression forced them to seek other employment. Jack Pierce went to western Kentucky, where he led a Western Swing-type band, the Oklahoma Cowboys, that recorded a few sides for Bluebird about 1936. Later he returned to the Bristol area and played again with the Grant Brothers, who had continued as part-time musicians. Slagle rarely played at all after 1930, but the others worked many dances and played sometimes on local radio until 1954.

Other musical associates of the Grants in later years included Red Vance, Paul Webb, and Ron Blevins. After 1954, the Grants played privately for their own amusement. Claude Grant served as a source of scholarly information concerning the band's relationship with Jimmie Rodgers. In the late 60's, a few of their recordings appeared in string band anthologies and, in 1972, Dave Samuelson collected their entire output in an album on his Puritan label. IMT

RECOMMENDED ALBUM:
"The Tenneva Ramblers" (Puritan)(1972)

AL TERRY

(Singer, Songwriter, Guitar, Clarinet)
Given Name: **Allison Joseph Theriot, Jr.**
Date of Birth: **January 14, 1922**
Where Born: **Kaplan, Louisiana**
Married: **Sandra Lee**

There have not been many Cajun artists who made the transition to Country music with any level of success. Jimmy C. Newman, Doug and Rusty Kershaw and Jo-el Sonnier spring to mind immediately, but it is important that Al Terry is not forgotten. It was, in particular, the advent of Rockabilly that launched Al into the Country Top 10, with his own co-written song, *Good Deal Lucille*.

Al was raised on a farm and came from a musical family. His maternal grandfather, Simeon Breaux, had been the leader of the only "Old Folks Band" in Vermilion Parish, Louisiana. It was a brass band whose members included Al's aunts, uncles and great-uncles. Simeon played numerous instruments, including cornet, trombone and his favorite, clarinet, and operated a dance hall until his death, in 1911.

Al started out playing clarinet, but once he began singing, he switched to guitar. Like a lot of Country singers, his first guitar was purchased from Sears Roebuck. A cousin gave him a windup phonograph and a stack of Country records by such artists as Jimmie Rodgers, Bradley Kincaid, Riley Puckett, the Carter Family and Vernon Dalhart, as well as Jazz greats like Django Reinhart. He began listening to Gene Autry and Jimmie Davis. Davis at the time was Public Service Commissioner in Shreveport. In 1944, Al met him during his first gubernatorial campaign and they became and remained close friends.

During his early days, Al was afflicted with illness that left him with a lame leg and when he had completed his 4th grade, the family doctor advised Al's parents to take him out of school. Al spent the next few years hunting and fishing and he became a sharpshooter with a .22 rifle, and spent a lot of time singing and playing and listening to WLS *Barn Dance* from Chicago. When he did return to school, he graduated and received the American Legion Award.

Al then formed a hillbilly band called the Drifting Cowboys (this was 15 years before Hank Williams created his band of the same name). The members were his brothers Floyd and Charles (known as Bobby Terry) and a local farm boy. They played dances and house parties and when KVOL Lafayette went on air, they got a 15-minute program, every Saturday morning at 10:00 a.m. A.B. Craft, the station's announcer, heard Al handling the announcing for the band, and got him to handle the five-minute newscast before their show.

Just prior to WWII, Al studied at Chenier Business College, Beaumont, Texas. During WWII, he continued on the radio with Doc Guidry's Sons of the Acadians, while Floyd and Bobby were in the service. In 1946, at the end of hostilities, the brothers got back together as the Southerners. They continued on KVOL with a daily show sponsored by Squirt Bottling Company of Sunset. In addition, they had a weekly show on KSIG Crowley and a three-times-a-week program on KSLO Opelousas for Red Chain Feeds. This led to the band being booked for eight engagements per week.

Al and the Southerners recorded *I'll Be Glad When I'm Free*, for Gold Star out of Houston, in 1946. He then had auditions for RCA Victor, Decca and 4 Star, but he was turned down, because his voice sounded too Pop. However, by 1947, he was recording for Feature, and sounded very much like the singing cowboys then so popular. By 1950, the line-up of Al Terry and the Southerners was Al, Bob Terry (steel guitar), Sexton Trahan (guitar), Danny Boulet (piano), Rufus Alleman (bass) and Alton Bernard (drums). The band survived through to 1952 and then he continued as a solo.

The turning point in Al's career occurred at the end of 1953. Fred Rose was in the midst of setting up Hickory Records when he took up Al's contract with Feature from owner Jay Miller. The following year, Miller produced the Terry single *Good Deal Lucille*, which was released on Hickory. The song had been written by Al, his brother "Bobby," and Miller's name also appears on the credits. It has similarities to Hank Williams' *Jambalaya*, in that it was written in a mix of English and French. Al found himself with a Top 10 single, and that year he formed his own unnamed band. He now joined the *Louisiana Hayride*, where he remained until 1956. He also appeared on the *Big D Jamboree* and toured with Red Foley.

The following year, Al was voted "No.1 New Singer" in a poll conducted by *Country & Western Jamboree* magazine, ahead of Sonny James and Elvis Presley. He had several releases for Hickory, but he didn't again get into the charts until 1960, when *Watch Dog* reached the Top 30. That year, he appeared on KSLO Opelousas, Louisiana, where he worked as a deejay. Through 1965-1966, Al appeared on KATC-TV, KXKW and KLFY-TV, all in Lafayette. In that city, he also operated Al Terry's Nightclub.

He was often tempted to record Cajun material, but never did. He kept true to Country, and although he never again hit the charts, he did record for a selection of labels, including Dot (1962-63), Jin and La Louisianne (1963), Index (1963-67), Crown (1967) (with Johnny Tyler) and Rice (late 60's). *Good Deal Lucille* became a Top 20 hit for Carl Smith, in 1969, and was also recorded by Werly Fairburn, Moon Mullican and Jack Scott.

By the early 80's, Al was working for the Louisiana State Employment Department and occasionally played around Lafayette. His early health problems reared their head later in life, when he initially walked using a cane and then was confined to a wheelchair. He has spent his later years helping other handicapped people by finding them jobs.

RECOMMENDED ALBUMS:
"Al Terry" (La Louisianne)(1963)
"This Is Al Terry" (Index)(1964)
"Al Terry Sings Country Classics" (Index)(1964)
"Country Music Stars" (Crown)(1967) [With Johnny Tyler]

GORDON TERRY

(Singer, Songwriter, Fiddle, Actor)
Given Name: **Gordon Terry**
Date of Birth: **October 7, 1931**
Where Born: **Decatur, Alabama**
Married: **Virginia Russell**
Children: **Rhonda Gail, Mitzi Dianne**

One of the premier Bluegrass fiddlers, Gordon Terry was on the *Grand Ole Opry* by age 19, remaining there for eight years. During this time he was a sideman with Bill Monroe's Blue Grass Boys and also recorded several sides on his own for Columbia, Cadence, RCA Victor and Liberty, including vocals. Of his many recordings he had the greatest commercial success in 1957 with *Wild Honey*.

The previous year, he appeared in *Hidden Guns*, the first of three movies in which he acted, the others being *Raiders of Old California* (1957) and *Buffalo Guns* (1958). Probably his activity in motion picture studios led him to move to Los Angeles in 1958. There he did a lot of solo work and also branched out into other areas of entertainment. He appeared on the TV shows *Country America* (1958-1959), *A Day in Court* and the *Sky King* series (both 1959) and was featured on the Country music show *Town Hall Party* (also 1959). Gordon also continued working as a sideman, most notably on an Elektra album ***New Dimensions in Banjo and Bluegrass***, featuring Eric Weissberg and Marshall Brickman. Clarence White also appeared on this 1963 album, which was, in retrospect, significant as much because of the sidemen as for the featured artists.

In the late 1960's, Gordon moved back to Tennessee, where he has remained active as a sideman, performing both Bluegrass and non-Bluegrass material. In 1977, Gordon released the album ***Disco Country*** for Plantation, on which he was backed by the Tennessee Guitars. Four years later, he issued ***Rockin' Fiddle***, which had the Tennessee Fiddles handling back-up. His most recent album, ***Fiddler on the Road***, is a non-Bluegrass offering.

During the 90's, Gordon, an officer of the Reunion of Professional Entertainers (R.O.P.E.), suffered with ill health, but has now recovered. WKM

RECOMMENDED ALBUMS:

"Liberty Square Dance Club" (Liberty)(1962) [With and without calls]
"Square Dance Party" (RCA Victor)(1962)
"Disco Country" (Plantation)(1977)
"Rockin' Fiddle" (Plantation)(1981)
"Fiddler on the Road" (Historical)

TEXAS PLAYBOYS, The

When Formed: 1935

Herman Arnspiger	1935-1940	Guitar
Jesse Ashlock	1935-1946	Fiddle
"Smokey" Dacus	1935-1940	Drums
Tommy Duncan	1935-1947	Vocal
Art Haines	1935	Fiddle, Tombone
"Sleepy" Johnson	1935-1938	Guitar, Banjo
Son Lansford	1935-1941	Bass
Leon McAuliffe	1935-1942	Steel Guitar
"Zeb" McNally	1935-1941	Saxophone
Ruth McMaster	1935	Fiddle
Al Stricklin	1935-1941	Piano
Johnnie Lee Wills	1935-1940	Banjo
Ray McGeer	1936-1937	Saxophone, Clarinet
Joe Ferguson	1936-1940	Bass, Saxophone
Everett Stover	1936-1940	Trumpet
Cecil Brower	1937	Fiddle
Tiny Mott	1937-1944	Saxophone
Charles Laughton	1938	Saxophone, Trumpet, Clarinet
Eldon Shamblin	1938-1954	Lead Guitar
Tubby Lewis	1940-1941	Saxophone
Wayne Johnson	1940-1941	Saxophone, Clarinet
Louis Tierney	1940-1947	Fiddle, Alto Saxophone
Don Harlan	1941-1942	Clarinet, Saxophone
Jamie MacIntosh	1941	Trumpet
Gene Tomlin	1941	Drums
Darrell Jones	1941-1942	Bass
Danny Alguire	1942	Trumpet
George Balay	1942	Clarinet, Saxophone
Morris Billington	1942	Piano
Alex Brashear	1942-1949	Trumpet
Neil Duer	1942	Trombone
Bob Fitzgerald	1942	Drums
Joe Holley	1942-1952	Fiddle
Leon Huff	1942	Guitar
Doyle Salathiel	1942	Electric Guitar
Benny Strickler	1942	Trumpet
Woodie Wood	1942	Clarinet, Alto Saxophone
Bob Lee	1942	Vocal
Howard Davis	1943-1944	Drums
Dick Hamilton	1943-1944	Electric Guitar
Laura Lee Owens (McBride)	1943-1944	Vocal
Buddy Ray	1943-1944	Fiddle
Les Anderson	1943-1945	Steel Guitar
Cameron Hill	1943-1945	Electric Guitar
Monte Mountjoy	1943-1947	Drums
Rip Ramsey	1943-1944	Bass
Jimmy Wyble	1943-1945	Electric Guitar
Millard Kelso	1943-1947	Piano
Ted Adams	1944-1945	Bass
Noel Boggs	1944-1947	Steel Guitar
Vic Davis	1944	Piano
Chuck Mackay	1944	Trumpet
Lester Barnard, Jr.	1945-1947	Electric Guitar
Johnny Edwards	1945-1947	Drums
Harley Huggins	1945	Guitar
Bill Mounce	1945	Banjo
Billy Jack Wills	1945-1950	Bass, Drums
Luke Wills	1945-1965	Vocal, Bass, Tenor Banjo
Leonard Seago	1945-1947	Fiddle
Jimmie Widener	1945-1950	Banjo, Tenor Banjo
Tommy "Spike" Doss	1945-1947	Vocal
Roy Honeycutt	1945-1947	Steel Guitar
Johnny Cuviello	1945-1947	Drums
Dean McKinney	1945-1947	Vocal
Evelyn McKinney	1945-1947	Vocal
Tiny Moore	1945-1950	Electric Mandolin, Fiddle
Herb Remington	1945-1949	Steel Guitar
Ocie Stockard	1945-1952	Banjo, Fiddle
Johnny Gimble	1947-1950	Fiddle, Electric Mandolin, Banjo
Doc Lewis	1949	Piano
Jack Loyd	1949-1955	Vocal, Bass
Hal Clampitt	1950	Steel Guitar
Keith Coleman	1950	Fiddle
Mancel Tierney	1950	Piano
Bob White	1950-1952	Fiddle, Steel Guitar

Billy Bowman	Steel Guitar	1950-1957
"Rusty" McDonald	Tenor Banjo	1950
Tommy Perkins	Drums	1950
Joe Andrews	Bass, Vocal	1951-1952
Billy Briggs	Saxophone	1951
Skeeter Elkins	Piano	1951-1955
Bobby Koeffer	Steel Guitar	1951
Paul Magee	Drums	1951-1952
Romona Reed	Vocal	1951-1952
Carolina Cotton	Vocal	1951
Cotton Whittington	Electric Guitar	1951
Darrell Glenn	Vocal	1952
V.O. "Shorty" Messer	Steel Guitar	1952
Jack Greenback	Drums	1953
Jay Roberts	Guitar	1953
Claude Fewell	Banjo	1954-1955
Johnny Megetto	Drums	1954
Lee Ross	Bass	1954
Darla Daret	Vocal	1955
Kenny Lowrey	Guitar	1955
Cotton Roberts	Fiddle	1955
Vance Terry	Steel Guitar	1955
Art McNulty	Piano	1955
Lee Ross	Bass	1955
Marvin Shaw	Trumpet	1955
Johnny Dalton	Drums	1955
Lew Walker	Electric Guitar	1955-1957
Jimmy Benjamin	Drums	1956-1957
Gary Cummings	Vocal	1956-1957
Tommy Jackson	Fiddle	1956
Lloyd Wheeler	Fiddle	1956
Jack Lloyd	Clarinet	1960
Wade Peeler	Drums	1960-1961
Leon Rausch	Electric Guitar, Vocal	1960-1966
Glenn Rhees	Saxophone	1960
Gene Crownover	Steel Guitar	1960-1965
George Clayborn	Fiddle	1961-1964
Gene "Tag" Lambert	Electric Guitar	1962-1969
Frank McWhorter	Fiddle	1962
Tommy Allsup	Rhythm Guitar, Bass	1963
Billy Armstrong	Fiddle	1963
Buzz Cason	Vocal	1963
Cliff Crofford	Vocal	1963
Casey Dickens	Drums	1963
Gene Garf	Piano	1963
Gene Gasaway	Fiddle	1963-1964
Billy Mize	Vocal	1963
Johnny Patterson	Electric Guitar	1963-1964
Billy Wright	Viola	1963
Benny Johnson	Piano	1964
Maurice Anderson	Steel Guitar	1964
Billy Carter	Electric Guitar	1964
Marvin Montgomery	Banjo	1964
Bob McBay	Drums	1964-1965
Harvey Gossman	Trumpet	1965
Walter Lyons	Electric Guitar	1965
Jim Belken	Fiddle	1965-1966
Harold Bradley	Electric Guitar, Banjo	1965-1968
"Buddy" Harman	Drums	1965-1968
Johnnie Manson	Fiddle	1965-1966
Bob Moore	Bass	1965-1967
Hargus "Pig" Robbins	Piano	1965-1967
Albert Talley	Steel Guitar	1965
Phil Sperbeck	Steel Guitar	1965
Jerry Case	Guitar	1966
Wayne Butler	Trombone	1966-1968
Bob Phillips	Trumpet	1966-1968
George Tidwell	Trumpet	1966-1968
Jerry Howard	Drums	1966
Pete Drake	Steel Guitar	1967-1968
Ray Edenton	Electric Guitar	1967
Rufus Long	Saxophone, Clarinet	1967-1968
Billy Sanford	Guitar	1967-1968
"Buddy" Spicher	Fiddle	1967
Fred Carter	Guitar	1967
Quitman Dennis	Saxophone	1967
Lloyd Green	Steel Guitar	1967
"Shorty" Lavender	Fiddle	1967
Don Tweedy	Saxophone	1967-1968
Jan Crutchfield	Vocal	1967
Jerry Crutchfield	Vocal	1967
Gordon Terry	Fiddle	1967
Henry "Tommy" Vaden	Fiddle	1967-1968
David Briggs	Piano	1968
Vassar Clements	Fiddle	1968
Kelton Herston	Guitar, Banjo	1968
Johnny Preston	Vocal	1968
Norbert Putnam	Bass	1968
Earl Dean Porter	Guitar	1968
Don Sheffield	Trumpet	1968

Johnny Duke 1968	**Saxophone**
Gene Mullins 1968	**Trombone**
Glynn Duncan 1971	**Vocal**
Hoyle Nix 1973	**Fiddle**
Jody Nix 1973	**Drums**

The above musicians played on Bob Wills and His Texas Playboys' recording sessions. Not all of them played on live dates. In addition, Merle Haggard played on sessions in 1971 and 1973. Some musicians came back to play for further short stints, including Tommy Duncan's reunion in 1960-1961. Dates shown above are musicians' principal time with Bob Wills.

(See also Bob Wills.)

Texas Ruby refer CURLY FOX & TEXAS RUBY

TEXAS TORNADOS

When Formed:	**1990**
Members:	
Freddy Fender	**Vocals, Guitar, Bass Guitar**
Augie Meyers	**Vocals, Keyboards, Accordion**
Doug Sahm	**Vocals, Guitar, Slide Guitar, Piano, Requinto, Vihuela**
Flaco Jimenez	**Vocals, Accordion**

When Tex-Mex group Texas Tornados got together, they proved that being young and a "hunk" was not necessary. All four members of the group had been around as soloists and session musicians for many years.

Probably the best known of the quartet, to the Country music buying public, was Freddy Fender, who seemed to grow in stature within this group environment. Doug Sahm had been the prime mover of the 60's-70's group Sir Douglas Quintet, and it was while operating that band that he had met and worked with Flaco Jimenez and Augie Meyers. Flaco Jimenez has become one of the most renowned players of the accordion in popular music.

Augie (b. May 31, 1940) had played with Sir Douglas Quintet and appeared on their albums ***Mendocino*** (1969) and ***1+1+1=4*** (1970). In 1973, he played on Doug Sahm's ***Doug Sahm & the Band*** and ***Rough Edges*** albums. When Sahm formed Doug Sahm & the Texas Tornados, in 1974, Augie appeared on two of their albums, ***Texas Rock for Country Rollers*** (1976) and ***Border Wave*** (1981). Augie also recorded several solo albums, namely ***You Ain't Rollin' Your Roll*** (Paramount) and ***Western Head Music Co.*** (Polydor) (both 1973), ***California Blues*** (Paramount, 1974), ***Live at the Longneck*** (Texas, 1976), ***Finally in Lights*** (Texas, 1977), ***Still Growing*** (Sonet, 1982) and ***August in New York*** (Sonet, 1984). In addition, he appeared on the 1979 album ***Joe King Carasco & the El Molino Band***.

Texas Tornados signed with Reprise Records, and one thing became apparent from their initial 1990 self-titled album, and that was that although they would perform together onstage, they would not necessarily all appear on every track they recorded. In fact, on this first album, only one track, Butch Hancock's *She Never Spoke Spanish to Me*, features all four members. Produced by themselves and Bill Halverson, who also engineered and mixed the sessions, the debut album, which was sung in Spanish and English, found favor with the fans, and reached No.25 on the Country album chart. Among the supporting musicians were Oscar Tellez (Bajo Sexto), Ernesto Saldana Durawa (percussion)and Louie Ortega (guitar), who would appear on later releases.

Their second album, ***Zone of Our Own***, was released in 1991. This also made the Top 50 on the Country album charts. For this release, Freddy Fender moved over to bass guitar for some of the tracks. On this album, the quartet appeared together on two tracks, *Is Anybody Goin' to San Antone* and *Oh Holy One*. They released their third album, ***Hangin' On By a Thread***, in 1992, and this was without doubt their best, even though it didn't chart. Less Country than its predecessors, it was more eclectic. It also marked the debut of Shawn Sahm and David Jimenez. The stand-out tracks are the title one, *Trying* (featuring classic Freddy Fender vocals, and tasty tenor sax playing from Jim Horn), and Shawn Sahm's *One and Only*. The latter, being musically a mix of John Lennon and Rock group Queen, features excellent guitar work from John Jorgenson. The foursome only play together on *To Ramona*.

The Texas Tornados have now called it a day and Freddy Fender has signed with Arista Texas, while Flaco Jimenez continues his solo career.

RECOMMENDED ALBUMS:

"Texas Tornados" (Reprise)(1990)
"Zone of Our Own" (Reprise)(1991)
"Hangin' on by a Thread" (Reprise)(1992)

B.J. THOMAS

(Singer, Songwriter)

Given Name:	**Billy Joe Thomas**
Date of Birth:	**August 7, 1942**
Where Born:	**Hugo, Oklahoma**
Married:	**Gloria Richardson (m. 1968)**
Children:	**Paige, Erin, Nora (adopted)**

It is a fact that B.J. Thomas has not become a bigger star because his musical stylistic changes have made fans vocally mad at him. Is he Country; is he Pop; is he Gospel, or is he just simply an MOR performer? Radio and fans alike want to have artists neatly labeled and pigeonholed. B.J. defies such categorization. Even as a successful Gospel singer, his long almost gypsy black curls and flamboyant attire antagonized evangelists who should have known better.

Although born in Oklahoma, he lived there for only two weeks. His family moved around and then settled in Rosenberg, Texas. He was musically influenced by Country greats Hank Williams, Ernest Tubb and Soul great Jackie Wilson. The first record B.J. had bought was Little Richard's *Miss Ann*. By the time he was 14, B.J. was a member of the church choir and a year later, while still in high school, he joined the Triumphs and they played around the Houston area.

As B.J. Thomas and the Triumphs, they recorded for the local Bragg label and had a local hit entitled *Lazy Man*. They then signed with Pacemaker Records in 1964 and released several singles as B.J. Thomas and as the Triumphs through 1964 and 1965. Scepter Records picked up these releases and in 1966, their single, a Hank Williams song, *I'm So Lonesome I Could Cry*, reached the Pop Top 10, but not the Country chart. This was followed by the Top 25 *Mama* and then Hickory Records had a Top 40 single *Billy and Sue*, which had originally been released on both Bragg and Warner Brothers Records. There then followed two more low level singles in 1966 (*Bring Back the Time* and *Tomorrow Never Comes*) and one more in 1967 (*I Can't Help It (If I'm Still in Love with You)*). All of these were credited to B.J. himself, without the group. In 1966, he was named "Most Promising Vocalist" by both *Cash Box* and *Billboard*.

His opening single for 1968 was first recorded for Scepter; it was the Top 30 release *The Eyes of a New York Woman*. He ended the year with the Top 5 single *Hooked on a Feeling*, which was Certified Gold in three months. B.J.'s two opening singles in 1969 did not fare so well. However, his year-end single *Raindrops Keep Fallin' on My Head* turned B.J. into a major star. Through fellow Scepter recording artist Dionne Warwick, songwriters Burt Bacharach and Hal David opted for B.J. to sing their song, which was featured in the 1969 movie *Butch Cassidy and the Sundance Kid.* The single stayed at No.1 on the Pop chart for 4 weeks and went Gold one month after release, going on to sell over 3 million. It also won an Oscar for "Best Song of the Year." In 1970, the album ***Raindrops Keep Falling on My Head*** was also Certified Gold.

B.J. began 1970 with the Top 30 release *Everybody's Out of Town* and the Top 10 *I Just Can't Help Believing*. Although B.J. did not achieve any further top entries while on Scepter, he still managed some big hits and others that didn't achieve major success, but were interesting. In the former group were *Most of All* (Top 40, 1970), *No Love at All* (Top 20) and *Mighty Clouds of Joy* (Top 40) (both 1971) and *Rock and Roll Lullaby* (Top 15, 1972). The last named featured Duane Eddy and R & B group the Blossoms. Among the other group were the two 1972 entries *That's What Friends Are For*, which featured singer/songwriter/actor Paul Williams, and Stevie Wonder's *Happier Than the Morning Sun*, which featured Stevie on harmonica.

The following year, B.J. signed with Paramount Records, but his stardom was costing a high price on him and he was relying heavily on drink, drugs and smoking, and suddenly success was eluding him. It took until the end of 1974 before B.J. climbed back on top when *(Hey Won't You Play) Another Somebody's Done Somebody Wrong Song*, a song written by master producers Larry Butler and Chips Moman. The single went to No.1 on both the Pop and Country charts, giving B.J. his first Country hit. The record was released on ABC, which had taken over Paramount. Many Country artists found that when their labels had been absorbed by ABC, unhappiness followed. This was the case with B.J., who also had managerial problems.

He ended 1975 with the cross-over minor hit *Help Me Make It (to My Rocking Chair)*. B.J. did not perform or record during 1976, as he got his life in order and became a born-again Christian. His first project on returning to recording, in 1977, was for the Gospel label Myrrh/Word, appropriately titled ***Home Is Where I Belong,*** and the title track just slipped into the basement area of the Country chart. The album earned B.J. his first Grammy Award for "Best Inspirational Performance." B.J. also won a Dove for this album as "Best Album by a Secular Recording Artist." That same year, B.J. signed to MCA (who would a year later absorb ABC), and during the summer, he had a Top 20 Pop hit with *Don't Worry Baby*.

Pop-Country star ***B.J. Thomas***

At the beginning of 1978, B.J. had a Top 25 Country hit with the Chips Moman-Mark James song *Everybody Loves a Rain Song*, which also crossed to the Pop Top 50. That year, B.J. won a second Grammy Award as "Best Inspirational Performance" for his Myrrh album ***Happy Man.*** During that year, he toured Taiwan and during the visit, B.J. and his wife, Gloria (who is also his manager), adopted Nora, a Korean orphan. He made it three straight years when B.J.'s 1979 Myrrh album ***You Gave Me Love (When Nobody Gave Me a Prayer)*** won a Grammy for "Best Inspirational Performance." During 1980, B.J. participated on ***The Lord's Prayer*** album for Light Records, alongside Reba Rambo, Dony McGuire, Andrae Crouch, the Archers, Walter & Tremaine Hawkins and Cynthia Clawson, and it won a Grammy for "Best Gospel Performance, Contemporary or Inspirational."

In 1981, he had two Top 30 successes for MCA, entitled *Some Love Songs Never Die* and *I Recall a Gypsy Woman*. B.J. also won another Grammy for "Best Inspirational Performance" for his Myrrh/Word album ***Amazing Grace***. B.J. also won a Dove for this album as "Best Album by a Secular Recording Artist." In 1983, B.J. signed with Steve Popovich's Cleveland International label, which was distributed by CBS. Then B.J. had back-to-back No.1 Country hits with *Whatever Happened to Old Fashioned Love* and the Gloria Thomas-Red Lane song *New Looks from an Old Lover*, both of which came from his Pete Drake-produced album ***New Looks***. The year ended with the Top 3 Country hit *Two Car Garage*, which came from B.J.'s next album ***The Great American Dream***, which also contained B.J.'s own song, *Beautiful World*.

He opened his 1984 account with the Top 10 single *The Whole World's in Love When You're Lonely*. B.J. then got together with Ray Charles on Ray's ***Friendship*** album for the Top 15 *Rock and Roll Shoes*. He closed out the year with the Top 20 Country success *The Girl Most Likely To*. That year, B.J.'s name was added to the Nashville Walkway of the Stars and became the 60th member of the *Grand Ole Opry* and B.J., a golf fanatic, also hosted his First Annual Golf Classic in New Orleans, which benefited the Arthritis Foundation.

In 1985, B.J. recorded his album ***Throwin' Rocks at the Moon*** in New York with Gary Kline producing and it contained *As Long as We've Got Each Other*, the theme song for the highly successful ABC-TV sitcom *Growing Pains*. B.J.'s final album for Columbia, ***Night Life***, was a collection of Country standards produced in Nashville by Steve Buckingham.

In 1989, B.J. got together with Dusty Springfield on a new version of *As Long as We've Got Each Other*, which did well on the Adult Contemporary chart. This started a relationship with Reprise and a connection with Steve Dorff and John Bettis, as writers and producers. By now, B.J. had moved more toward the Blue-Eyed Soul area that boasts Michael Bolton and Curtis Stigers and totally away from Country music.

RECOMMENDED ALBUMS:

"B.J. Thomas Sings Hank Williams & Other Favorites" (Buckboard) [Most Country of his albums]
"New Looks" (Cleveland International)(1983)
"The Great American Dream" (Cleveland International)(1983)
"Night Life" (Columbia)(1989)
"B.J. Golden Collection" (American Classics)(1990)
Gospel:
"Home Where I Belong" (Myrrh/Word)(1977)
"Happy Man" (Myrrh)(1978)
"You Gave Me Love (When Nobody Gave Me a Prayer)" (Myrrh)(1979)
"Amazing Grace" (Myrrh/Word)(1981)

ERNEST THOMPSON

(Singer, Guitar, Harmonica, Other String Instruments)

Given Name: **Ernest Errott Thompson**
Date of Birth: **1892**
Where Born: **Forsyth County, North Carolina**
Date of Death: **1961**

Ernest Thompson was one of the earliest Country singers on phonograph records, cutting some 34 sides for Columbia at two different sessions in 1924. A blind street singer, the man plied his trade in the area extending from Winston-Salem to Mount Airy, North Carolina, and eastward into Stokes County and sometimes into Virginia. Thompson's vocal was characterized by an unusual high pitch which could almost be termed a natural falsetto.

Thompson was born in Forsyth County, North Carolina, to a family that prided themselves on their singing skills. As a small child his clothing caught fire and he allegedly suffered from a "scorched throat and voice box" which affected his vocal abilities from that time onward. Then at age 18, tragedy struck the youth a second time when he totally lost his sight in a sawmill accident. Although he went to the State School for the Blind and learned some skills, including piano tuning, broom making and Braille reading and writing, Ernest became more interested in developing his musical talents, learning to play several instruments and even to perform as a one-man band.

According to researcher-writer Kirk Sutphin, who interviewed his sole surviving sister, Agnes, Thompson frequently played for dances, at schools and on the streets for at least three decades. His preferred instruments were the guitar and harmonica, which he could use to accompany his singing. Sometimes Ernest played in a string band which included some neighbors, sister Agnes and their niece Connie Faw Sides. The blind vocalist built up a large repertory of ballads, hymns, old popular songs and instrumental specialties. Old-timers still recall his singing on the streets of Winston-Salem, Mount Airy, Danbury and other communities.

Thompson journeyed to New York twice for recording sessions, in April and September 1924. His initial releases, *Are You from Dixie/Wreck of the Southern Old 97*, both went on to become standards. His version of the latter song—while a cover of Henry Whitter's original on OKeh—contained verses not found on the first release. Other Thompson favorites included the hymn *Yield Not to Temptation* and the Gussie Davis sentimental favorite from the 1890's, *The Baggage Coach Ahead.* Thompson also had a Prohibition protest titled *How Are You Going to Wet Your Whistle (When the Whole Wide World Goes Dry)?* in his repertory. On his second trip to the Columbia studio, Connie Sides went along and sang on a few numbers, making her one of the first Country girl vocalists to sing on record.

When Ernest died at age 69, he was buried in the Fraternity Church of the Brethren Cemetery near Winston-Salem. Since all his numbers were cut prior to the use of the electrical recording process, none have been reissued for the collector market. IMT

HANK THOMPSON

(Singer, Songwriter, Guitar, Harmonica)
Given Name: Henry William Thompson
Date of Birth: September 3, 1925
Where Born: Waco, Texas
Married: 1. Dorothy Jean Ray (div.)
2. Ann

Hank Thompson and his music bridged the gap between the Western Swing bands of the 30's and the new Honky-Tonk Country singers of the 40's except that his career peaked in the 50's and 60's, holding strong through the 70's as well. In fact, during a three-decade period—1952-1982—Thompson's name was missing from the charts only in 1962. Although many of his more memorable numbers dealt with beer drinking themes, Hank's repertoire ran the gamut of Country song subject matter.

Henry Thompson initially became a first-class harmonica player and, as such, won several talent contests. However, he drew his early inspiration from Hollywood film cowboy Gene Autry, whom he saw perform live at a fairly early age. This prompted the youngster to obtain a guitar and learn to play it for local entertainments. Soon he had a Saturday morning job at a local theater matinee. By 1942, he had a local flour company sponsoring a regular radio program on station WACO, as "Hank, the Hired Hand." When Hank finished high school in 1943, military service beckoned and he joined the U.S. Navy as a radio technician, for the duration of WWII.

On leaving the service, in 1945, Hank attended Princeton University in New Jersey and then went to Southern Methodist University in Dallas. The following year, he attended the University of Texas in Austin. Back in Waco, he secured a daily show on KWTX, which had newly opened on May 1. In August Hank did his initial record session in Dallas of *Whoa Sailor/Swing Wide Your Gate of Love*, on the small Globe label. A little later, Hank cut four sides for another local firm, Blue Bonnet, which led (through Tex Ritter's suggestion) to his signing a Capitol contract, with his first Dallas session, in late 1947, yielding a dual hit in *Humpty Dumpty Heart/Yesterday's Mail*. The former reached No.2, but couldn't dislodge Eddy Arnold from the top spot.

When the recording ban ended late in 1948, Capitol brought Hank to Hollywood for a second session where he cut another major hit, *Green Light*, which went Top 10. Hank had six more chartmakers in 1949, *What Are We Gonna Do About the Moonlight* (Top 10), *I Find You're Cheatin' on Me/You Broke My Heart* (double-sided, Top 15), a new version of *Whoa Sailor* (Top 10), *Soft Lips* (Top 10)/*The Grass Looks Greener Over Yonder* (Top 15).

Although Hank had no hits in 1950 or 1951, *The Wild Side of Life*, waxed on December 11, 1951, hit No.1 in May 1952 and remained there for 15 weeks of a 7-month stay on the charts. Hank followed it up with *Waiting in the Lobby of Your Heart* (Top 3) and *The New Wears Off Too Fast* (Top 10, both 1952). In 1953, he opened his account with the No.1 *Rub-a-Dub-Dub* and followed it with *Yesterday's Girl* (Top 10) and the No.1 *Wake Up Irene*. Between 1952 and 1954, Hank appeared on the Light Crust Doughboys' Southern Network.

In 1954, Hank's hits were back-to-back double-sided Top 10 singles *Breakin' the Rules/A Fooler, a Faker* and *Honky Tonk Girl/We've Gone Too Far*. Hank finished off the year with the Top 3 single *The New Green Light*. The flip-side, *If Lovin' You Is Wrong*, went Top 15, the following year. He followed it with the Top 15 *Annie Over*. In the summer, he and Merle Travis got together on the Top 5 instrumental *Wildwood Flower*, while Hank's solo flip-side, *Breakin' in Another Heart*, went Top 10. His other hits that year were *Most of All* (Top 10) and *Don't Take It Out on Me/Honey, Honey Bee Ball* (Top 5).

Unlike many Country stars of the era, Hank was never regularly affiliated with any noted radio barn dance although he guested on most with some regularity. Instead, he kept on the road with his Western Swing band, the Brazos Valley Boys, which he had formed in 1946, and which sometimes numbered as many as 11 regular members. From 1954 through 1957, Hank appeared on WKW-TV Oklahoma City.

In 1956, Hank had a Top 5 hit with *The Blackboard of My Heart*, with the flip-side, *I'm Not Mad, I'm Just Hurt*, going Top 15. The next year he had a mild success with a fling into Rockabilly sounds with *Rockin' in the Congo* and even more with the Top 3 revival of the Texas Jim Lewis song *Squaws Along the Yukon* in 1958. Hank's other chart singles during 1957 and 1958 were the flip of *Rockin' in the Congo*, *I Was the One* and *Tears Are Only Rain* (1957), then *How Do You Hold a Memory* (1958).

Hank had several other chartmakers in the late 50's, of which the most successful were *I've Run Out of Tomorrows* (Top 10, 1958) and *Anybody's Girl* (Top 15, 1959). *A Six Pack to Go* peaked in the Top 10 in 1960, and was probably Hank's second biggest number in terms of its standard status and longevity. He followed with the Top 15 *She's*

Just a Whole Lot Like You. Hank stayed with Capitol until 1965, and his principal hits were *Oklahoma Hills* (Top 10) and *Hangover Tavern* (both 1961). The Brazos Valley Boys also cut several albums of standard Western Swing songs and instrumentals. During 1965 through 1967, Hank and the band appeared on the WGN *Barn Dance*.

Leaving Capitol after 1965, Hank also broke up his larger band and gravitated more toward the Nashville Sound. Signed by Warner Brothers in 1966, he had a moderate hit with *Where Is the Circus* and a somewhat lesser one in *He's Got a Way with Women*. That year, Hank appeared in and sang the theme song for the movie *Smoky*, starring Fess Parker and Hoyt Axton. Switching to Dot, Hank had a pair of Top 10 hits with *On Tap, in the Can, or in the Bottle* and *Smokey the Bar*. A string of lesser hits followed that included *Next Time I Fall in Love (I Won't)*, *The Mark of a Heel* and *I've Come Awful Close* (all 1971) and *Cab Driver* (1972).

In 1974 Hank crashed the Top 10 twice more with *The Older the Violin, the Sweeter the Music* and *Who Left the Door to Heaven Open*. In the eight years from 1975, he had a dozen more chartmakers, of which *Mama Don't 'Low* (1975) and *I Hear the South Calling Me* (1979) both made the Top 30. Hank also did some interesting theme albums in those years, including a tribute to the Mills Brothers and a return to his earlier Swing sound titled ***Back in the Swing of Things***. His last two chart appearances came in the early 80's on Jim Halsey's Churchill Records, one of them a revival of *Rockin' in the Congo*.

In more recent years Thompson has continued as a respected figure in the genre. In 1987, Hank recorded for Step One Records and the following year, he appeared at Britain's Peterborough Festival. In 1989, Hank Thompson was elected to the Country Music Hall of Fame. A visit to the *Opry* in March 1994 illustrates that he can still belt out his standards like *A Six Pack to Go* with much of the old energy still intact. IMT

RECOMMENDED ALBUMS:

"All-Time Hits" (Capitol)(1956)
"Hank!" (Capitol)(1957)
"Dance Ranch" (Capitol)(1958) [Re-issued on Stetson UK in the original sleeve (1987)]
"Favorite Waltzes" (Capitol 1959)
"Songs for Rounders" (Capitol)(1959) [Re-issued on Stetson UK in the original sleeve (1987)]
"At the Golden Nugget" (Capitol)(1961) [Re-issued on Stetson UK in the original sleeve (1987)]
"The Number 1 Country & Western Band" (Capitol)(1962)
"Cheyenne Frontier Days" (Capitol)(1962)
"Best of Hank Thompson" (Capitol)(1963)
"At the State Fair of Texas" (Capitol)(1963)
"Golden Country Hits" (Capitol)(1964)
"Hank Thompson Salutes Oklahoma" (Dot)(1969)
"A Six Pack to Go" (double) (Dot)(1974)
"The Best of the Best of Hank Thompson" (Gusto)(1980)
"Take Me Back to Tulsa" (MCA)(1980)
"1000 and One Nighters" (Churchill)(1983)
"Hank Thompson Sings and Plays Bob Wills" (Waco)
"Greatest Hits/Volume I" (Step One)(1987)
"Greatest Hits/Volume II" (Step One)(1987)
"Here's to Country Music" (Step One)(1987)
"Hank Thompson & the Brazos Valley Boys" (Country Routes)(1990) [From 1952 radio shows]

SUE THOMPSON

(Singer, Guitar)

Given Name:	**Eva Sue McKee**
Date of Birth:	**July 19, 1926**
Where Born:	**Nevada, Missouri**
Married:	**1. (Div.)** **2. Dude Martin (div.)** **3. Herbert "Hank" Penny (div.)(dec'd.)** **4. Unknown**
Children:	**one daughter, one son**

Sue Thompson is a Country singer whose "little girl" voice gives her a degree of distinctiveness.

Sue's family encountered hard times in the Great Depression and went west from their western Missouri home, ultimately settling in San Jose, California, in 1937. Sue, inspired by Gene Autry movies, decided early that she wanted to be a cowgirl singer. During WWII, she worked in a defense plant, married, and gave birth to a daughter at 20. Prior to a divorce at 23, Sue had initiated a singing career at clubs in Oakland, San Francisco, San Jose and environs. Dude Martin had a popular Western band in Frisco and Sue became not only his vocalist but wife as well.

Her early waxings on Mercury, while not major hits, did fairly well, including *If You Want Some Lovin'*, *Tadpole* and *You Belong to Me*, which went on to become a major Pop hit for Jo Stafford. In the meantime, Martin moved his popular TV show from San Francisco to Los Angeles in 1951, where it proved at least as appealing as it had been in the Bay Area.

In 1952, Martin took singer-comedian Hank Penny into his entourage, which soon led to a romance between the newcomer and Sue. Marrying in 1953, Hank and Sue worked together for a decade. After a brief experience with their own show at KHJ-TV Los Angeles, the couple moved to Las Vegas in 1955, following the birth of a son. For the next several years, Hank and Sue worked the casino circuits in both Las Vegas and the Lake Tahoe-Reno areas, becoming two of the first Country musicians to have any real success in these markets. She and Hank recorded some singles and duets on Decca, but none made sufficient impact to propel her to national stardom. Then a combination of a contract with Hickory and a new focus on the teen market with John D. Loudermilk songs began to click. *Sad Movies* hit the Pop chart Top 5 in the fall of 1961 and the follow-up, *Norman*, shot up to the Top 3.

Sue Thompson *came to stardom with Sad Movies*

The following year, Sue charted with *Two of a Kind* (Top 50), *Have a Good Time* (Top 40) and another Loudermilk song, *James (Hold the Ladder Steady)* (Top 20). Her only chart record in 1963, *Willie Can*, only reached the Top 80. Sue divorced Hank Penny in 1963. Two years later, she had a final Pop hit with *Paper Tiger*, yet one more Loudermilk song.

After more than 20 years as a Country singer, Sue Thompson began to appear with some regularity on the Country charts in the early 70's with minor successes like *Candy and Roses* and *Big Mable Murphy*. Her nine charted duets with Don Gibson did better, especially *I Think They Call It Love* (1972), *Good Old Fashioned Country Love* (1974) and *Oh, How Love Changes* (1975), all Top 40 hits. Meanwhile, Sue returned to the Nevada casino circuit and also for a time hosted a show from the Palomino Club in North Hollywood.

In recent years, Sue Thompson could be described as either semi-retired or semi-active. A spokesman for her agency, Terry Hill and Associates, reports that she has remarried happily and resides in Las Vegas, but also spends a fair amount of time in the Los Angeles-San Fernando Valley area, where her grown children live. In between, the petite lady does some selected show dates. Whether her audiences realize and appreciate her role as a successful pioneer for Country girl vocalists on the Nevada club circuits is not certain. IMT

RECOMMENDED ALBUMS:

"Meet Sue Thompson" (Hickory)(1962)
"Two of a Kind" (Hickory)(1962)
"Sue Thompson's Golden Hits" (Hickory)(1963)

"Paper Tiger" (Hickory)(1965)
"The Country Side of Sue Thompson" (Mercury/Wing)(1966)
"Sue Thompson with Strings" (Hickory)(1966)
"This Is Sue Thompson" (Hickory)(1969)
"Sweet Memories" (Hickory/MGM)(1974)
"And Love Me" (Hickory/MGM)(1974)
"Big Mable Murphy" (Hickory/MGM)(1975)
Don Gibson & Sue Thompson:
"The 2 of Us Together" (Hickory)(1973)
"Warm Love" (Hickory)(1974)
"Oh, How Love Changes" (Hickory/MGM)(1975)

UNCLE JIMMY THOMPSON

(Fiddle)

Given Name:	**Jesse Donald Thompson**
Date of Birth:	**1848**
Where Born:	**Baxter, Smith County, Tennessee**
Married:	**1. Martha Elizabeth Montgomery (dec'd.) 2. Ella Manners**
Children:	**four**
Date of Death:	**February 17, 1931**

Known to generations as the white-bearded patriarch who accidentally started the show that became the *Grand Ole Opry*, Uncle Jimmy Thompson was far more than the colorful legend that *Opry* publicity likes to celebrate. He was one of the oldest musicians to survive into the age of mass media and early Country music, and one of the premier fiddlers of the late 19th and early 20th centuries.

Uncle Jimmy was born 12 years before the Civil War, in the rolling farmland of Smith County, halfway between Nashville and Knoxville, Tennessee. When he was a boy, his family moved to Texas, just before the Civil War. By now, he was starting to play the fiddle, for by 1860 he had learned the tune *Flying Clouds,* which would remain one of his favorites. Though he was too young to serve in the war, he continued to learn tunes from older musicians, some of whom had repertoires extending back to the Revolutionary War.

Though he primarily farmed for a living, young Thompson traveled widely and eventually returned to settle in Smith County. There he married Martha Elizabeth Montgomery in the 1880's and they had four children. In 1902, he took his family again to Texas, settling around Bonham, near the Oklahoma line. By now he was playing the fiddle more and more in a professional sense. In 1907, he defeated 100 other fiddlers in Dallas, winning "the nation's championship in his class."

Uncle Jimmy played a style that was in the 1920's called "fancy"; in fact, it was a variety of the so-called "long bow" Texas contest style seldom heard that early in the Southeast. By 1912, Uncle Jimmy, now 64 and with his family grown, returned again to Tennessee, buying a farm near Hendersonville. Here his wife died of cancer, but he remarried—to an Ella Manners of Wilson County—about 1916. Aunt Ella was as much a fun lover as was Uncle Jimmy and often traveled with him in a homemade camper truck, often buck dancing as he fiddled. For a time the two traveled around the country "busking" on street corners and courthouse lawns and picking up what a relative called a "right smart amount of money in donations."

In October 1925, WSM radio opened in Nashville, and the daughter of Uncle Jimmy's brother, Eva Thompson Jones, who was a music and voice teacher in Nashville, got a part-time job on the station. Through her, Station Director George D. Hay arranged an audition with Uncle Jimmy, and the following night—November 25, 1925—asked him to perform on the air. He was an immediate success—in part because he agreed to do requests—and in late December, 1925, the station announced that Thompson, along with Uncle Dave Macon, would do "an hour or two" of Old-Time tunes on a regular basis every Saturday night. With this announcement, the *Opry* was in a real sense born.

In the meantime, Uncle Jimmy won even more fame through his participation in a national round of fiddling contests sponsored by Henry Ford. He sent a challenge to Ford's champion—northeastern fiddler Mellie Dunham—asking him to come south and saying, "I'll lay with him like a bulldog." As it turned out, Uncle Jimmy didn't win the national contest, but his colorful personality helped endear him to radio listeners across the South.

In 1926, he made his first records, for Columbia: *Billy Wilson* and *Karo*. (Two others were never issued.) Later, in 1930, he recorded two other tunes in Knoxville for the Vocalion company. These were to be his total recorded output of a repertoire that supposedly numbered over 1,000.

As the *Opry* gained momentum and became better organized, Uncle Jimmy appeared on it less and less. One problem was his propensity to bring jugs of white lightning into the studio with him. Another was his difficulty in stopping with a time limit; he was from an older school of fiddlers who were used to playing a tune for 20 minutes for a rural dance. On February 17, 1931, Uncle Jimmy died at his home from pneumonia; Eva Thompson Jones was the only member of the *Opry* to attend his funeral service, in the hamlet of Laguardo.

For years, Uncle Jimmy lay in an unmarked grave. In 1975 the Tennessee Valley Old Time Fiddlers Association spearheaded a drive to erect a tombstone for him. This time, modern *Opry* stars like Roy Acuff, Brother Oswald, and Johnny Wright (who knew Uncle Jimmy when he was a boy) attended services.

CKW

RECOMMENDED ALBUMS:

"Grand Ole Opry Past and Present" (Hilltop) [Various artists including Uncle Jimmy Thompson and Eva Thompson Jones]
"Nashville, The Early String Bands, Vol. 2" (County) [Various artists including Uncle Jimmy Thompson performing "Karo"]

SONNY THROCKMORTON

(Songwriter, Singer, Guitar)

Given Name:	**James Fron Sonny Throckmorton**
Date of Birth:	**April 2, 1941**
Where Born:	**Carlsbad, New Mexico**
Married:	**1. Brenda (div.) 2. Cheryl**
Children:	**Fronda, Debbie, Jamie, Misty, Haley, Tillery, Austin Caleb**

After several failed attempts to find success in the music business in the 60's and early 70's, Sonny Throckmorton became one of Country music's premier songwriters. Between 1976 and 1980 Sonny had at least one song on the singles chart every week except for one three-week period. At one point he had seven songs he had written on the chart and in one six-month period he had nearly 100 of his songs recorded. During his career as a songwriter, Sonny has had more than 1,000 recordings of his songs.

Sonny was born in Carlsbad, New Mexico, but lived in many towns in the West and Southwest as a child. His father was a Pentecostal preacher who eventually settled in Wichita Falls, Texas, where Sonny graduated from high school and attended Midwestern State University.

Sonny's next stop was San Francisco, where his father was pastoring a church. Sonny played rock'n'roll in some of the city's clubs that his father warned church members to stay away from. When Sonny moved south to Los Angeles in 1962, he was offered a recording contract with an independent label. When things didn't work out with the label, Sonny returned to San Francisco.

With a growing interest in Country music, Sonny moved to Nashville, in 1964. He was encouraged to move to town by producer/steel guitar player/publisher Pete Drake. Drake helped Sonny get a job playing bass for Carl and Pearl Butler. After two years on the road with the Butlers, Sonny stayed in town to write for and manage Drake's publishing company. Several artists began to record his songs and in 1965 Sonny scored his first hit when Bobby Lewis reached the Top 5 with his *How Long Has It Been.*

Over the next several years, Sonny worked for several music publishers as a staff writer and song plugger. For a time he managed the publishing company of Hank Williams' widow, Audrey. Eventually, Sonny landed a job as a staff writer for the major Tree Publishing company, home of many of Nashville's top writers. One of those writers was Dave Kirby, who was instrumental in getting Sonny signed to Tree. Initially Tree executive Buddy Killen didn't want to sign Sonny to the company. Repeated appeals were rejected until Dave Kirby made Killen a promise. He told him if Sonny's songs didn't earn back the salary Tree paid him, the company could take the money out of his own earnings. Killen accepted the offer and signed Sonny as a staff writer. Before long several artists began to record his songs but none of them became hits. Eventually, Killen fired Sonny because he wasn't making the company money. Fortunately for Kirby, Killen didn't recoup the loss from his royalties.

After more than a decade in Nashville, Sonny returned home to central Texas in 1975. He kept a promise he made to himself that if he wasn't successful by the time he was 35 he'd give up the music business. However, his songwriting friends were convinced he had the potential to become a major writer.

Friends Don Gant and Curly Putman kept pitching Sonny's songs after he left town. They kept in touch with Sonny and encouraged him to give Nashville another try. After six months in Texas, Sonny heeded the call back to Nashville and eventually re-signed with Tree Publishing. This time he was more determined than ever to make his mark on Music City. "The first nine months back at Tree I had 150 songs cut," Sonny recalled. Sonny provided Johnny Duncan with his first No.1 single, *Thinkin' of a Rendezvous*, in 1976. His song *Knee Deep in Love with You* was recorded 13 times by, among others, Roy Drusky, Jim Mundy and Tanya Tucker, before Dave & Sugar took the song to No.1 in 1977. Merle Haggard went to Top 3, in 1977, with Sonny's now classic *If We're Not Back in Love by Monday.* The song was also a Top 30 Pop hit for Haggard and a Top 5 R & B hit for Millie Jackson, as *If You're Not Back in Love by Monday. Cash Box* magazine named Sonny "Songwriter of the Year" in 1977. Sonny's songs were in high demand and many artists proved he was a hit maker.

Jerry Lee Lewis had a 1978 Top 5 hit with *Middle Age Crazy*, which in 1980 become the subject of a movie starring Bruce Dern and Ann-Margret. The hits continued for Sonny in 1978 with *When Can We Do This Again* (T.G. Sheppard), *Smooth Sailin'* (Connie Smith) and *Fadin' in, Fadin' Out* (Tommy Overstreet). The Nashville Songwriters Association voted Sonny "Songwriter of the Year" in 1978, 1979 and 1980.

Sonny had tried his own hand at recording in 1976 for Starcrest Records. The singles *Rosie* and *Lovin' You, Lovin' Me* only reached the lower regions of the charts. With his incredible success as a songwriter in the late 70's, he got his chance with the major Mercury label. He placed *I Wish You Could Have Turned My Head (and Left My Heart Alone)* in the Top 60 (later a hit for the Oak Ridge Boys). In 1979, Sonny's versions of *Smooth Sailin'* and the flip, *Last Cheater's Waltz*, broke the Top 50 and *Can't You Hear That Whistle Blow* went Top 70.

Sonny continued his sojourn on the charts in 1979 with *I Had a Lovely Time* for The Kendalls, *It's a Cheatin' Situation* for Moe Bandy, *I Wish I Was Eighteen Again* for Jerry Lee Lewis and *Ain't No Way to Make a Bad Love Grow* by Johnny Russell. The following year the hits continued with Moe Bandy's recording of *One of a Kind*, George Burns' version of *I Wish I Was Eighteen Again*, Merle Haggard's recording of *The Way I Am*, Jeanne Pruett's *Temporarily Yours,* and the Oak Ridge Boys had a No.1 with *Trying to Love Two Women*. Sonny had his last chart entry for Mercury with the Top 90 *Friday Night Blues*. In 1980, Sonny was named BMI "Songwriter of the Year" along with Rhonda Kye Fleming, Merle Haggard, Bob McDill and Dennis Morgan.

In early 1981, Sonny celebrated another No.1 hit when T.G. Sheppard recorded his *I Feel Like Loving You Again.* That year, Sonny signed with MCA and had a Top 80 success with *A Girl Like You.* The chart-toppers continued in the 80's with the Grammy and CMA award-winning *Why Not Me* recorded by the Judds in 1984. Mel McDaniel scored big with *Stand Up* (1985) and George Strait took *The Cowboy Rides Away* into the Top 5, the same year. In 1987, Sonny Throckmorton was inducted into the Nashville Songwriters Hall of Fame.

Sonny recorded the album ***Southern Train*** for Warner Brothers before moving back to Texas in 1988. He decided to retire from the music business to spend time on his farm with his family. In 1993, Doug Stone took Sonny's *Made for Loving You* to the top of the charts.

JIE

RECOMMENDED ALBUMS:

"The Last Cheater's Waltz" (Mercury)(1978)
"Southern Train" (Warner Brothers)(1986)

BILLY THUNDERKLOUD & THE CHIEFTONES

When Formed: 1964

Members:

Billy Thunderkloud — **Lead Vocals**
Jack Wolf
Richard Grayowl
Barry Littlestar

Backing Band: **Some of Nashville's Finest**

Members:

Jerry Rivers (Fiddle), Ronnie Hughes (Bass), Warren Keith (Piano), George Edwards (Steel Guitar), Mike Hartgrove (Fiddle)

It is hard enough for a black male American to break into Country music; it is even harder for a black female American; however, if you are a band of Canadian Indians, then your chances are pretty much zero. Yet, Billy Thunderkloud & the Chieftones did just that.

Born in northwest British Columbia, into one of the world's proudest and most distinctive civilizations, the Tsimshian Indian nation, Billy, Jack, Richard and Barry were educated at an Indian Residential School in Edmonton, Alberta. The group formed in 1964 and worked hard for a decade trying to establish itself. In 1974, they signed with 20th Century Records. At the beginning of 1975, they added a back-up band, Some of Nashville's Finest, who had worked as the Cheatin' Hearts, behind Hank Williams, Jr. The following year, they debuted on the Country chart with *What Time of Day*, which went Top 20 and crossed over to the Pop Top 100. They followed this with *Pledging My Love*, which went Top 40. That year, Billy was named "Outstanding Indian for 1975" by the American Indian Exposition.

With the collapse of 20th Century Records, they signed with Polydor and had a Top 75 single, *Indian Nation (The Lament of the Cherokee Reservation Indian)*. Billy and the group closed out 1976 with the Top 50 *Try a Little Tenderness* and their final chart record, *It's Alright*, which went Top 80.

The group, complete with full Indian outfits, carried on for some while without further record success. When last heard of, Billy was working as a car salesman in Nashville.

RECOMMENDED ALBUMS:
"Off the Reservation" (20th Century)(1974)
"What Time of Day" (20th Century)(1975)

MEL TILLIS

(Singer, Songwriter, Guitar, Drums, Violin, Music Publisher, Actor, Author, Comedy)

Given Name: Lonnie Melvin Tillis
Date of Birth: August 8, 1932
Where Born: Tampa, Florida
Married: 1. Doris (div.)
2. Judy Edwards (m. 1979)
Children: Pam Tillis, Connie, Cindy, Mel. Jr. ("Sonny Boy"), Carrie, Hannah Elizabeth

M-M-M-Mel Tillis has made a career out of a stutter that would in anyone else be considered an impediment. Yet when he sings one of the many songs that have made him a star, the stutter disappears and the most mellifluous voice takes its place.

Mel's stutter goes back to when he was age 3 and caught malaria. It may have been the illness or it may have been his stuttering friend, LeRoy English, but one or the other left its mark on Mel. Brought up in Pahokee, Florida, Mel learned to play guitar and while at high school, he studied violin and also played drums in the school band. In 1948, Mel made his first public appearance at the local Prince Theatre, in a talent contest. However, he soon opted to play football. In 1951, Mel enlisted into the USAF and tried to get into flight school, but was told that the Air Force didn't need a pilot with a stutter. While serving in Okinawa, Japan, Mel formed the Westerners and entertained in local clubs.

He left the service in 1955 and for two semesters attended the University of Florida but then dropped out and worked as a truck driver for Harry's Cookies, fireman on the railroad, milkman, strawberry picker and baker. Mel had begun to write songs and came to Nashville in 1956 but was rejected as a recording artist.

Mel returned home to Dover, Florida. He wrote *So Tired* and at the end of the year, Webb Pierce recorded it and had a 1957 Top 3 hit with it. Also in 1956, Mel signed with Cedarwood Music, which was partly owned by Pierce. Mel joined the Duke of Paducah's band and went on to play with Minnie Pearl and Judy Lynn. During 1957, Mel and his family moved to Nashville. Mel began recording in 1957 for Columbia and recorded *It Takes a Worried Man to Sing a Worried Song*, but it was suggested that he look for original material. The flip-song of that debut record was *Honky Tonk Song*, which became a

*It's M-M-**Mel Tillis***

No.1 for Webb Pierce. Like a lot of Country singers at that time, Mel experimented with rock'n'roll with songs like *Hearts of Stone* and *Teen Age Wedding*. Mel didn't have *his* first chart entry until 1958, when *The Violet and the Rose* went Top 25. That year, Webb Pierce had a Top 10 success with a song he'd written with Mel, *Tupelo County Jail*.

In 1959, Mel made the Top 30 with *Finally* and then teamed up with Bill Phillips for another Top 30 success, *Sawmill*. That year Mel had two more of his songs on the chart when Webb Pierce had a monster hit with *I Ain't Never*, which would become a classic and which he and Mel had written. In addition, George Morgan went Top 20 with Mel's *Little Dutch Girl*. Mel and Bill Phillips got together again the following year for the Top 25 hit *Georgia Town Mills*.

During 1960, Mel was represented on the charts with *No Love Have I* (Webb Pierce), *Mary Don't You Weep* (Stonewall Jackson) and *One More Time* (Ray Price). Price also charted Mel's *Heart Over Mind* the following year.

Mel moved to Decca in 1962 and had covers on the charts by Webb Pierce (*Crazy Wild Desire*) and Little Jimmy Dickens (*The Violet and a Rose*). The following year, Mel teamed up with Webb Pierce for the co-written Top 25 release *How Come Your Dog Don't Bite Nobody But Me*. Pierce also had a Top 15 hit with Mel's *Sawmill*. This was the year that Mel's classic song *Detroit City*, written with Danny Dill, became a major hit for Bobby Bare on both the Country and Pop charts and a lesser hit for Billy Grammer. A parody version by Ben Colder (Sheb Wooley) reached the lower rungs of the Pop chart. In 1967, Tom Jones would have an international hit with the song.

Although Mel did not have any personal chart hits in 1964, he was well represented by his songs. These included *Burning Memories*, which Mel had written with Wayne Walker and became a Top 3 hit for Ray Price, and yet another version of *The Violet and the Rose*, this time by Wanda Jackson. In 1965, Mel turned up on the RIC label and went Top 15 with *Wine*. When Charley Pride signed with RCA Victor, his first single, in 1966, was a cover of a Mel Tillis song, *Snakes Crawl at Night*; although it didn't chart, it opened up the door to Charley's fine career. However, Faron Young went Top 10 with Mel's *Unmitigated Gall* and the Stonemans reached the Top 40 with their version of *Tupelo County Jail*.

1966 was an important year for Mel as he signed with Kapp Records and at last his recording career took flight. It started with *Stateside*, which went Top 20, and then in 1967, all his releases made the charts and were Harlan Howard's *Life Turned Her That Way* (Top 15), *Goodbye Wheeling* (Top 20) and the lowly *Survival of the Fittest*. In addition, Waylon Jennings took Mel's *Mental Revenge* into the chart and Johnny Darrell had the original hit with Mel's future classic *Ruby, Don't Take Your Love to Town*. During 1968, Mel charted with *All Right (I'll Sign the Papers)* (Top 30), *Something's Special* (Top 20), *Destroyed by Man* (Top 40) and Wayne Carson's *Who's Julie* (Top 10).

It was interesting to note that while Mel didn't always record his own songs, he was still a much covered writer including, in 1969, Kenny Rogers and the First Edition's international hit version of *Ruby, Don't Take Your Love to Town*. Mel stayed with Kapp until 1970 and charted with *Old Faithful* (Top 15) and *These Lonely Hands of Mine* (Top 10) (both 1969) and *She'll Be Hangin' Round Somewhere* (Top 10) and *Heart Over Mind* (Top 3) (both 1970).

Mel then moved to MGM Records and his recording status clicked up a notch. From *Heart Over Mind* until *Mental Revenge* in 1976, all his records were credited to Mel Tillis & the Statesiders. His backing group became one of the most noted and at one point included a three-fiddle line-up. Among alumni of the group were fiddler Rob Hajacos, steelie Paul Franklin and bassist Ernie Rowell. Mel's first hit for MGM was *Heaven Everyday*, which went Top 5. 1976 was completed by *Too Lonely, Too Long* (Kapp, Top 25) and his classic *Commercial Affection* (Top 10).

For the rest of his time at MGM, Mel split his recordings between his solo releases and duets with Sherry Bryce. His solo hits in 1971 were *The Arms of a Fool* (Top 5) and *Brand New Mister Me* (Top 10), while with Sherry, there were two Top 10 singles, *Take My Hand* and *Living and Learning*. That year, Mel was named "Comedy Act of the Year" by MCN and he took this title in 1973 through 1978.

He started off 1972 in a way that looked like record success was beginning to elude him. *Untouched* only made the Top 15, *Anything's Better Than Nothing* (with Sherry Bryce) went Top 40 and *Would You Want the World to End* also went Top 15. Then Mel released his version of *I Ain't Never* and it went to No.1. An interesting point of Mel's career was that when he put out a version of his own songs, his version mostly did better than the cover, even where the original cover was by a co-writer. Mel closed the year with the Top 3 *Neon Rose*.

Mel stayed with MGM until 1976 and his hits were: 1973: *Thank You for Being You* (Top 25), *Sawmill* (Top 3) and *Let's Go All the Way Tonight* (with Sherry Bryce, Top 30); 1974: *Midnight, Me and the Blues* (Top 3), *Don't Let Go* (with Sherry, Top 15), *Stomp Them Grapes* and *Memory Maker* (both Top 30); 1975: *You Are the One* (with Sherry, Top 15), *Best Way I Know How* (Top 10), *Mr. Right and Mrs. Wrong* (with Sherry, Top 40), *Woman in the Back of My Mind* (Top 5) and *Lookin' for Tomorrow (and Findin' Yesterdays)* (Top 20). Mel's final entrant for MGM was his version of *Mental Revenge*, which went Top 15, in 1976.

Although Mel had made his movie debut back in the 60's with *Cotton Pickin' Chicken Pickers,* he got involved with "real" acting in the 1975 movie *W.W. and the Dixie Dancekings,* which also starred Burt Reynolds, Jerry Reed, Conny Van Dyke and Don Williams. In 1976, Mel was inducted into the Nashville Songwriters Hall of Fame and also received the CMA's "Entertainer of the Year" Award.

His first entrant for his new label, MCA, was the Top 15 *Love Revival*, the title track of his debut album for the label. The album, which contained no Tillis songs, also yielded the No.1 single Ken McDuffie's *Good Woman Blues*, which closed out 1976. This was followed by another No.1, *Heart Healer*, in 1977. Mel's other hits that year were *Burning Memories* (Top 10), Gerry House's *I Got the Hoss* (Top 3) and *What Did I Promise Her Last Night* (Top 5). Mel started out 1978 with another No.1, *I Believe in You* and followed with the Top 5 *Ain't No California*.

During 1979, Mel could be seen in three movies, the TV movie *Murder in Music City* and the motion pictures *The Villain* with Kirk Douglas and Arnold Schwarzenegger, and Clint Eastwood's Every Which Way But Loose. From the last named Mel had two chart entries, the Top 3 Send Me Down to Tucson and the No.1 Coca Cola Cowboy.

Mel then moved labels again; this time to Elektra. He started off his account with the Top 10 *Blind in Love*. He stayed with Elektra through to 1982, and continued much as before. In 1980, he charted with *Lying Time Again* (Top 10), *Your Body Is an Outlaw* (Top 3), *Steppin' Out* (Top 10) and the No.1 *Southern Rains.* In 1980, Mel appeared in the Burt Reynolds-Jerry Reed movie *Smokey and the Bandit II.* He started 1981 with the Top 10 *A Million Old Goodbyes* and then he got together with Nancy Sinatra for the Top 25 release *Texas Cowboy Night.* He completed the year with the Top 10 *One-Night Fever* and another duet with Nancy, the Top 50 *Play Me or Trade Me/Where Would I Be.* That year, Mel appeared in the movie *Cannonball Run.* (He later appeared in *Cannonball Run II,* in 1984.)

From here on, Mel's recording career was somewhat less successful. His last successful record on Elektra was *Stay a Little Longer* (Top 20, 1982). He then returned to MCA, where his major successes were *In the Middle of the Night* (Top 10, 1983) and Tommy Collins' *New Patches* (Top 10, 1984). At the end of 1984, Mel teamed up with Glen Campbell for *Slow Nights*, but it only made the Top 50. That year, Ricky Skaggs had a No.1 hit with Mel's *Honey (Open That Door)*. Mel then recorded the 1985 album ***California Blues,*** for RCA Victor. The album contained a version of *Diggin' up Bones,* which the following year was a monster hit for Randy Travis. Of the two chart records from the album, *You Done Me Wrong* was the more successful, going Top 40.

Since the mid-60's, Mel had been operating his own Sawgrass Music Publishing (BMI) and Sabal Music, Inc. (ASCAP), both divisions of Mel's Musiplex Group, Inc. They were sold to MCA Music in 1987. For nearly three years, Mel's name was missing from the chart and then in 1988, he signed with Mercury and charted with *You'll Come Back (You Always Do)*, which reached the 30s. That year, Ricky Skaggs had a Top 20 hit with another of Mel's songs, *I'm Tired.* Mel had his last chart single in 1989 with *City Lights* on Radio Records, but it only reached the Top 70. That year, Mel's house on his 800-acre farm, 30 miles northwest of Nashville, caught fire. The 6,000-square-foot house was made of logs from old barns in Tennessee and Kentucky, all of which were over 250 years old and were hand-hewn to construct the house. In the house and destroyed was Tommy Jackson's 1923 Roth violin, heard on all the Webb Pierce records and on Ray Price's *Crazy Arms.* Also destroyed was Mel's Gibson guitar on which he wrote *Ruby, Don't Take Your Love to Town.*

During 1989, Mel's movie *Uphill All the Way*, with Roy Clark, was released on home video. In 1990, the Geezinslaws recorded yet another version of *Mental Revenge* and two years later, Holly Dunn had a minor hit with Mel's *No Love Have I.*

Mel calls himself the "Guru of Stutterers" and at one time had a King Air A-100 Beechcraft plane named "Stutter One." Mel has written his autobiography, entitled *Stutterin' Boy*.

RECOMMENDED ALBUMS:

"Mel Tillis' Greatest Hits" (Kapp)(1969)
"Heart Over Mind (& Other Big Country Hits)" (Columbia)(1970)
"Mel Tillis' Greatest Hits, Volume 2" (Kapp)(1971)
"Live at the Sam Houston Coliseum" (MGM)(1971) [Re-released in 1978]
"Mel Tillis' Greatest Hits" (MGM)(1974)
"Best of Mel Tillis" (double)(MCA)(1975)
"M-M-Mel Live" (MCA)(1980)
"Mel & Nancy" (Elektra)(1981)
"Greatest Hits" (Elektra)(1983)
"After All This Time" (MCA)(1983)
"New Patches" (MCA)(1984)
"California Road" (RCA Victor)(1985)
"Brand New Mister Me" (Polydor)(1988)

PAM TILLIS

(Singer, Songwriter, Guitar, Piano, Actress)

Date of Birth:	**July 24, 1958**
Where Born:	**Plant City, Florida**
Married:	**1. (Div.)**
	2. Bob DiPiero
Children:	**Ben**

Pam is a case of acorns not falling far from the tree. She is the daughter of Country music star Mel Tillis and has proven to everyone that she is her own person. Like her father, she is multi-talented and her songs have been recorded by artists outside of Country music.

As a child, growing up in Nashville, Pam did Judy Garland impressions and at age 8 appeared with her father and her family, on the *Grand Ole Opry*, singing *Tom Dooley*. She studied classical piano and bought her first guitar when she was 12. She learned to play from lessons on TV. She got her first gig on Talent Night at Nashville's Last Chance Saloon. Although she was still in her teens, she performed as a solo act at the Exit/In.

When she was 16, Pam was in a car crash that shattered her face in thirty places from her cheeks to her chin. Her nose was flattened and her eye sockets were damaged and it took five years of operations to get her fixed and she still has pain and requires surgical upkeep. She went to the University of Tennessee, where she started her first band, High Country Swing Band, which played jug-band music and Country-Rock, being influenced by Little Feat, Linda Ronstadt and the Eagles. She also sang solo and put together a Folk-type duo with Ashley Cleveland, who will appear later in the Tillis story.

Pam left college in 1976 and started working in Mel's publishing company, Sawgrass Music. She started songwriting and was encouraged by Jimmy Bowen. An early cut for her was *I'll Meet You on the Other Side of the Morning*, which was recorded by Barbara Fairchild. She then got together with some musicians and headed for San Francisco, performing as the Pam Tillis Band, which then became Freelight, playing "free-form Jazz/Rock/whatever" and they got a following around the Bay Area.

Pam returned to Nashville in 1978 and did a brief spell as a back-up singer in Mel's band and then fronted a white R & B band for a time. Around this time, Gloria Gaynor recorded Pam's *When I Get Around to It*, giving it a Disco feel. Pam recorded her debut album on Warner Brothers Records, in 1983, amusingly entitled ***Beyond the Doll of Cutey***, which was produced by Jolly Hills Productions and Dixie Gamble-Bowen, and on which Pam co-wrote all but one of the songs.

After the release of the album she went to England and spent several months there, observing and absorbing the music scene. She came back to Nashville and started writing again. In 1984, she had her first Country chart single, *Goodbye Highway*; it reached the Top 75. It was not until 1986 that she returned to the chart, when *Those Memories of You* made the Top 60 and then *I Thought I'd About Had It with Love* made the Top 70. Pam signed with Tree Publishing, as a staff writer. That same year, another Disco diva, Chaka Khan, recorded a Tillis song, *So Close* and the Forester Sisters cut *Drawn to the Fire*, which appeared on their debut album ***Perfume, Ribbons & Pearls***.

The following year, she had two low level singles, *I Wish She Wouldn't Treat You That Way* and *There Goes My Love*. That year, she was nominated for the ACM's "Best New Female" category and she appeared at the Landmark Hotel in Las Vegas. She also sang the title track for the pilot of Warner Brothers TV's *Too Many Cooks*, on which she duetted with Callee Adams, and sang on the soundtrack of Ryan O'Neal's *Tough Guys Don't Dance*. She also did jingle work, including a 1987 advertisement for Equal.

It was very much a return to her roots when Pam signed with Arista. After years of trying to be a Pop-Rock singer, Pam returned to contemporary Country. She had been building up a following around Nashville, as a member of Women in the Round, alongside Ashley Cleveland, Karen Staley and Tricia Walker. The group played acoustic songs that they had written and became one of the most sought-after attractions in clubs such as The Bluebird.

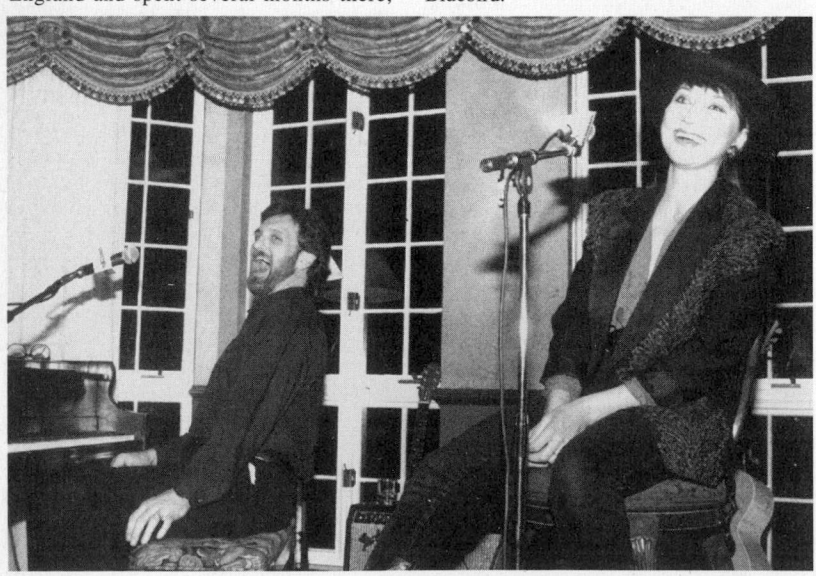

Pam Tillis** having fun with **Mike Reid

Pam hit the Top 5, in 1990, with *Don't Tell Me What to Do*, which was the lead-off single from her 1991 album ***Put Yourself in My Place***. The album, containing all but three songs co-written by Pam, made the Top 20 of the Country Album charts. By August, 1992, the album had been Certified Gold. In 1991, she followed up with another Top 10 single, *One of These Things*, a song she had written with Paul Overstreet and which had been recorded, initially, when Pam was on Warner Brothers. The second single, the title track, only reached the Top 15, but the final single of the year, *Maybe It Was Memphis*, reached the Top 3. During the year, she was nominated by the ACM as "Top Female Vocalist," by the CMA for "Single of the Year" for *Maybe It Was Memphis,* and for the coveted "Horizon Award" and by the American Music Awards for "Favorite New Artist—Country Category."

Her first single of 1992, *Blue Rose Is,* disappointed when it only climbed to the Top 25. 1992 also saw the release of her new album ***Homeward Looking Angel***, which also did well in the Country album charts, peaking in the Top 25 and going Gold, in June 1993. Pam co-wrote five of the ten tracks on the album and it was Chapin Hartford's *Shake the Sugar Tree* that followed and gave Pam a Top 3 hit. She started out 1993 with the Top 5 single Gretchen Peters' *Let That Pony Run*, but it was *Cleopatra, Queen of Denial* that caught the public imagination. A bit of fun written by Pam, Jan Buckingham and Pam's new husband (and super songwriter and ex-Billy Hill member) Bob DiPiero, it was accompanied with a really funny video that found favor on CMT. However, the single just failed to make the Top 10 and the follow-up, *Do You Know Where Your Man Is*, went Top 20. In 1994, *Spilled Perfume* went Top 5 and Pam's new album, ***Sweetheart's Dance***, reached the Country Albums Top 10. In 1994, Pam Tillis was named the CMA's "Female vocalist of the year."

RECOMMENDED ALBUMS:

"Beyond the Doll of Cutey" (Warner Brothers)(1983)
"Put Yourself in My Place" (Arista)(1991)
"Homeward Looking Angel" (Arista)(1992)
"Sweetheart's Dance" (Arista)(1994)

FLOYD TILLMAN

(Singer, Songwriter, Guitar, Mandolin, Banjo)

Date of Birth:	**December 8, 1914**
Where Born:	**Ryan, Oklahoma**
Married:	**Frances Inez**
Children:	**Larry Floyd, Donald Frank**

Although he is known as a Texas performer, Tillman was born in Oklahoma. In 1915, when he was less than a year old, his parents moved to Post, Texas. A few years later he began playing the guitar, perfecting his skills by backing up fiddlers at local dances in West Texas. He also became proficient on the mandolin and banjo. Even so, his first paying job, at age 13, was as a Western Union messenger.

In 1933, he was introduced to Honky-Tonk music when he became a member of Adolph and Emil Hofner's band playing at Gus's Palm Garden in San Antonio. At the time he was playing a single-string guitar style on an instrument amplified by a metal disc. In 1935, Floyd led the Blue Ridge Playboys with Ted Daffan and Moon Mullican. By 1936 Floyd had converted to an electric guitar with a Vol-U-Tone amplifier and homemade pickup supplied by Ted Daffan. During 1936 and 1937, Floyd was singer, guitar player, mandolinist and banjo player with Mark Clark Orchestra, frequently singing his own compositions. During the late 30's, Floyd recorded for Vocalion, Cimarron, Sims and Hilltop. In 1939 Tillman secured a recording contract with Decca Records, cutting, among other titles, *It Makes No Difference Now*. Although it was his own song, Tillman was beaten into the recording studio with it by Dickie McBride, the vocalist with Cliff Bruner's Texas Wanderers. Ironically, McBride, who had the biggest hit with the song, didn't like the number and only recorded it to fill a needed side.

During 1944, Floyd released such Country classics as the No.1 *They Took the Stars Out of Heaven* and the Top 5 double-sided hit *G.I. Blues/Each Night at Nine*, all as "Floyd Tillman and His Favorite Playboys." During WWII, Floyd was in the U.S. Army. In 1945, Floyd formed Floyd Tillman & All the Gang, a band he kept until 1950. In 1946, Floyd had a Top 3 hit with *Drivin' Nails in My Coffin*, for Columbia, with whom he stayed until 1954. In 1947, Floyd made his debut on the *Grand Ole Opry* and the following year, Floyd charted with *I Love You So Much It Hurts* (Top 5). In 1949, Floyd's hits were *Please Don't Pass Me By* (Top 15), *Slipping Around* (Top 5), its sequel, *I'll Never Slip Around Again* (Top 10) and *I Gotta Have My Baby Back* (Top 5).

Floyd's songs were covered frequently by Jimmy Wakely, who was at the top for 5 weeks in 1949 with *I Love You So Much It Hurts*. Later that year, Jimmy and Margaret Whiting had a 17-week Country chart-topper with Floyd's *Slipping Around*, which also went to No.1 on the Pop chart and was Certified Gold. The following year, they reached the Top 3 with *I'll Never Slip Around Again*. Floyd was active as a songwriter throughout the 1950's and 1960's.

He recorded for RCA Victor (1957-1958) and Liberty (1959-1960). His last real success was with the Top 30 1960 song, *It Just Tears Me Up*, on Liberty. In 1966, Floyd signed with Musicor. Floyd Tillman was a Charter inductee to the Nashville Songwriters Hall of Fame in 1970.

Floyd's singing has been described by historian Bill Malone as "a lazy, drawling baritone...replete with peculiar swoops and note bendings that was too irresistibly appealing to avoid imitation." His guitar style and songwriting were equally appealing and are at least partially responsible for his great success and induction into the Country Music Hall of Fame in 1984. WKM

RECOMMENDED ALBUMS:

"Floyd Tillman's Greatest" (RCA Victor)(1958)
"Floyd Tillman's Best" (Columbia)(1961)
"Let's Make Memories" (Cimarron)(1962) [Re-released on Starday in 1965]
"Floyd Tillman Sings His Greatest Hits of Love" (Pickwick/Hilltop)(1965)
"Floyd Tillman's Country" (Musicor)(1967)
"Portraits of Floyd Tillman" (Bagatelle)(1971)
"Golden Hits—Floyd Tillman" (Crazy Cajun)(1975)
"The Best of Floyd Tillman" (Columbia)(1976)
"Floyd Tillman & Friends" (Gilley's) [With Ernest Tubb, Merle Haggard, Willie Nelson and Johnny Lee]

AARON TIPPIN

(Singer, Songwriter, Guitar, Harmonica, Banjo)

Given Name:	**Aaron D. Tippin**
Date of Birth:	**July 3, 1958**
Where Born:	**Pensacola, Florida**
Married:	**(Div.)**
Children:	**Charla**

Aaron has been described as the working man's Country singer. His music is a blend of Honky-Tonk, Blues and no-nonsense hillbilly sounds. He also has a bravura that is not present in any other performer and is ideally suited for video.

He was raised in South Carolina, where his family owned a 120-acre farm. As a youngster, he showed hogs at county and state fairs. It was while plowing and bailing hay that he began singing. He reckons that the strength in his voice came from trying to sing over the noise of the tractor engine. He began playing guitar at age 10 and played in local Bluegrass and Country groups. He also played football and ran track while at school.

Aaron started to hang out at the airport that his father flew out of and he got the flying bug. By the age of 15, he had his own license and worked on airplanes. At age 20, he became a multi-engine instrument commercial pilot and flew as a freelance and corporate pilot. However, while studying for his Airline Transport Rating, the fuel shortage hit and he saw layoffs in the industry and decided to pursue a career in music.

He began weight lifting to trim down and after his divorce, he took it up again and was soon winning body building competitions. Although he no longer competes, he still trains six days a week and when he arrives in a town, he immediately seeks out the local gym.

After leaving South Carolina, Aaron headed for Kentucky, where he worked the graveyard shift in a factory, while driving to and from Nashville each day to write songs. He finally made the move to Nashville in 1986 and

Honky-Tonk Superman ***Aaron Tippin***

tried to get a record deal. He signed to Acuff-Rose Music as a staff writer, but, unable to land a record deal, he concentrated his singing efforts on his song demos. As luck would have it, his publisher sent some demos to RCA Records, who not only liked the songs but also liked Aaron's voice and signed him.

In 1990, *Something with a Ring on It*, a song written with Mark Collie, became Mark's debut chart single. This was followed by Aaron's debut release, *You've Got to Stand for Something*, a song he had written with Buddy Brock, who became a regular writing partner; it reached the Top 10 and hung around the Country charts for five months. This led to the release of his first album with the same title. All songs on the release were written or co-written by Aaron. This charted on the Country Album chart the following year and reached the Top 25. The two singles *I Wonder How Far It Is Over You* and *She Made a Memory Out of Me* only reached Top 40 and Top 60 respectively.

With the advent of 1992, Aaron had his first No.1 record, the fun-filled *There Ain't Nothing Wrong with the Radio*, which stayed at the top for 3 weeks. Aaron released his second album, ***Read Between the Lines***, which again contained totally co-written material by Aaron. It climbed to the Top 10 on the Country Album chart, reached the Pop Album chart Top 50, and four months after release, it was Certified Gold and in 1993, it went Platinum. The second single, *I Wouldn't Have It Any Other Way*, which reached the Top 5, was written by Aaron and another of his regular co-writers, Butch Curry. However, the final single of the year, *I Was Born with a Broken Heart*, only reached the Top 40.

Aaron started out 1993 with the wonderfully imaginative *My Blue Angel*, on which Aaron cleverly uses a variant on the yodel; this went Top 10. He followed with another Top 10 single, *Working Man's Ph.D.*, and wrapped up the year with *The Call of the Wild*, which went Top 20. For his 1993 album ***Call of the Wild***, he switched from producer Emory Gordy, Jr., to the highly successful Scott Hendricks. Four months after release, it was Certified Gold. That year, Capricorn's new act, Kenny Chesney, recorded the Tippin-Donny Kees song *In My Wildest Dreams* (also the title of his debut album). In 1994, Aaron charted with *Honky Tonk Superman* (Top 50) and *Whole Lotta Love on the Line* (Top 30). The former was accompanied by a very funny video that featured Reba McEntire.

RECOMMENDED ALBUMS:

"You've Got to Stand for Something" (RCA)(1990)
"Read Between the Lines" (RCA)(1992)
"Call of the Wild" (RCA)(1993

TNN (THE NASHVILLE NETWORK)

The Nashville Network is the No.1 source of Country music entertainment on TV. It was launched in March 1983, and in 1994 reached more than 59 million cable TV households. The 18-hours-a-day programming is produced by The Nashville Network of Nashville, Tennessee, supported by advertising, while marketing and distribution are handled by Group W Satellite Communications (GWSC) of Stamford, Connecticut. TNN was launched in Canada in September 1984, where a specialty service operates.

TNN is owned by Gaylord Entertainment Company (formerly WSM, Inc.) of Nashville, whose involvement in Country music goes back to 1925 when it created the *Grand Ole Opry*.

Seen through the U.S. and Canada, The Nashville Network shows a mix of programs that includes concerts, interviews, music videos, game shows, news and sports. TNN has achieved many milestones. In September, 1985, it made TV history with exclusive 12-hour coverage of Farm Aid, a concert featuring 57 Country and Rock artists organized by Willie Nelson to benefit the American farmer.

In 1988, TNN introduced the annual TNN Viewers' Choice Awards, which gave viewers the opportunity to vote in a major entertainment awards program for the first time. Two years later, the show merged with *Music City News* Cover Awards to become the annual TNN *Music City News* Country Awards.

In October 1991, the premiere telecast of *The Statler Brothers Show* became the highest-rated series debut in TNN's history, reaching 1.4 million households. The show, now in its third season, has become the highest-rated series on TNN.

In April 1986, TNN began *Sports Sunday*, an all-sports program featuring auto racing, motorcycling, fishing and rodeo. Its first telecast of live NASCAR Winston Cup auto racing in March 1991 reached approximately two million households. In 1994, the network offered 28 live NASCAR events and a selection of live ASA races, plus live coverage from seven NHRA Winston Drag Racing Series events.

TNN programming is produced at their state-of-the-art facility in Opryland. The Nashville Network produces over 2,400 hours of original programming each year, with TNN's remote Ku-Band truck, StarCatcher, journeying around the country feeding behind-the-scenes interviews with top performers to TNN's nightly primetime programs and to its music video series.

In March 1983, TNN had the largest cable network launch ever, with more than 7 million subscriber households on over 800 systems. In 1994, TNN is offered by 13,583 cable affiliates. It reaches over 59 million U.S. subscriber households, which is over 95% of all U.S. cable TV homes, according to A.C. Nielsen data.

In December 1988, TNN and Group W Satellite Communications launched the radio series *The Nashville Record Review*, which is now carried by over 300 stations. TNN and GWSC have also joined with Meredith Corporation to publish the magazine *Country America*. In January 1991, TNN and GWSC acquired Country Music Television. The four executives in charge of TNN are: Tom Griscom (President, Gaylord Communications Group), David Hall (Senior Vice President, Cable Networks, Opryland U.S.A., Inc.), Kevin Hale (Vice President, Opryland U.S.A., Inc. and General Manager, TNN Nashville) and Paul Corbin (Vice President, Music Industry Relations, The Gaylord Communications Group Nashville).

TOBACCO TAGS, The (a.k.a. THREE TOBACCO TAGS & FOUR TOBACCO TAGS)

When Formed: 1930

Members:

Luke Beaucom	**Mandolin**
Harvey Ellington	**Mandolin, Fiddle**
Sam Pridgin	**Guitar, Bass**
Reid Summey	**Guitar**
George Wade	**Mandolin**

Other members included:

Robert Hartsell, Harold Hensley

The Tobacco Tags gained considerable popularity in Virginia and the Carolinas during the 30's and 40's. Musically, the Tags featured twin mandolins and appear to have been a survival of the mandolin orchestras that were widely popular in the 1890-1910 era. Their repertoire included numerous Pop songs and comedy numbers in addition to those normally associated with Piedmont-based musicians of the Great Depression decade.

The original Three Tobacco Tags were mandolinists "Looney Luke" Beaucom (b. Henry Luther Beaucom, December 18, 1902, McDowell County, North Carolina/d. ca. 1968) and George Wade (b. ca. 1900, Gastonia, North Carolina/d. ca. 1958), together with guitarist Reid Summey (b. Edgar Reid

The Tobacco Tags were popular in the 1930's

Summey, June 9, 1903, Gaston County, North Carolina). Their group emerged from the cotton-mill culture in the industrial city of Gastonia about 1930. Wade had a prior recording experience for Columbia in a pair of duets with one Francom Braswell in 1929.

The Tags did regular radio programs at WSOC radio and had their first record sessions for Victor in May 1931 and Champion in July 1932. Because the national economy was so bad, few people bought the discs. However, when the group began to work the *Crazy Barn Dance* at WBT Charlotte in the mid-30's, their music and comedy skits soon made them quite popular over a much wider area. From 1936, their Bluebird recordings sold much better. Early in 1938, they moved to WPTF Raleigh and then to WRVA Richmond. George Wade left the group in 1938. Harvey Ellington (b. November 9, 1909, Berea, North Carolina), a veteran of the recently disbanded Swingbillies, replaced him. A man named Bob Hartsell also worked in the group briefly and the Three Tobacco Tags became the Four Tobacco Tags. When Hartsell left late in 1938, Sam Pridgin (b. Samuel Lee Pridgin, February 13, 1910, Henderson, North Carolina/d. August 27, 1989), a lifelong musical associate of Ellington, took over. In 1941, young fiddler Harold Hensley joined the Tags and worked on their last Bluebird session of December 1941.

WWII eventually took Hensley and Ellington to military service and Pridgin to a defense plant. Other musicians filled in with Luke and Reid during their absence. Sam came back after the war, but Hensley settled in California, where he continued his career as a Country fiddler. Ellington did a few shows with the Tags on a part-time basis. The Tobacco Tags broke up at the end of the 40's. Ellington and Pridgin continued to work together locally around Oxford, North Carolina, for many years afterward and even re-created their medicine show act for a documentary film before Sam became too ill to play anymore in 1986. Today, only Harvey Ellington survives of the pre-1940 group and at last report is in declining health. IMT

RECOMMENDED ALBUM:
"Songs of the Tobacco Tags" (Old Homestead)(1984)

TONY TOLLIVER

(Singer, Songwriter, Piano)
Where Born: Texas
Married: Debbie

As a 9-year-old growing up in Texas, Tony Tolliver fell in love with the music of Ray Charles and Merle Haggard. His father taught him to play the piano and he developed his skill accompanying the family Gospel group. He moved on to working in clubs with Country and Top 40 bands. Tony's aspirations of bigger things in music led him to Nashville.

Tony was hired by Dottie West to play piano and soon he became her band leader. Eventually she featured him in her shows and the crowds responded favorably. Working with Dottie gave Tony the opportunity to meet several other Country stars whom he developed friendships with. Larry Gatlin and Merle Haggard encouraged Tony to pursue his own career in Country music. He took their advice and began performing in local clubs.

A chance meeting with a powerful Nashville producer encouraged Tony. He had stopped at a fast-food restaurant and noticed James Stroud in the line next to him. Stroud's production credits include Clint Black, Tracy Lawrence and John Anderson. Tony introduced himself to Stroud and told him he was looking for a record deal. Stroud told him to drop off a demo tape and Tony did a few days later. The day he left the tape, he got a call from Stroud's office saying he wasn't interested.

That disappointment caused Tony to work even harder and he recorded more demos. This time he played the songs for friends Larry Gatlin and Dottie West, who both put in calls to Stroud. He agreed to meet with Tony in person and was impressed with his voice and the songs he'd written. Stroud agreed to produce Tony and helped him secure a contract with Curb Records.

Tony wrote or co-wrote seven of the ten songs on his self-titled debut album. He teamed with songwriting legend Hank Cochran to write *Freedom Ring* and wrote *Back in the Swing of Things* with former boss Dottie West. Merle Haggard offered his houseboat to Tony to write for the album and the result was *Bar Stool Fool.* Haggard joined Tolliver in the studio on a duet of his classic *Swinging Doors.* Tolliver's Curb debut was released in 1991. To date, Tony hasn't had any singles chart success, but provided he gets label support, he should soon achieve that. JIE

RECOMMENDED ALBUM:
"Tony Tolliver" (Curb/Capitol)(1991)

TOMPALL & THE GLASER BROTHERS

TOMPALL GLASER
(Lead Vocals, Songwriter, Guitar)
Given Name: Thomas Paul Glaser
Date of Birth: September 3, 1933
Married: 1. Rosemarie
2. Dorothy June

CHUCK GLASER
(Baritone Vocals, Songwriter, Guitar)
Given Name: Charles Glaser
Date of Birth: February 27, 1936
Married: Beverly Ann
Children: Michael Vernon, Kent, Louis, Bruce, Karen, Denise

JIM GLASER
(Tenor Vocals, Songwriter, Guitar)
Given Name: James William Glaser
Date of Birth: December 16, 1937
Married: Jane
Children: Jeffrey, James William II, Lynn, Connie

All Born: Spalding, Nebraska

Although the name of Tompall & the Glaser Brothers no longer appears on the Country chart, there was a time from the mid-60's through the mid-70's and then during the early 80's when the brothers were regular occupants.

The brothers were born and raised on a ranch in the non-Country music state of Nebraska. Their father, Louis, was an accomplished guitarist who taught his sons to play. While in their teens, they formed Tompall & the Glaser Brothers. They played local gigs and appeared in a 13-weeks series on KHAS-TV, Hastings, Nebraska. They also had a show on KHOL-TV Holdredge, Nebraska. In 1957, they managed to meet Marty Robbins at one of Marty's concerts; he was suitably impressed with their tight harmonies and as a result, they were signed to Marty's Robbins label. Their initial single for the label was *Five Penny Nickel*, written by Chuck. The following year, they appeared on the nationally televised *Arthur Godfrey Talent Scouts Show*.

They then moved to Nashville and in 1959 they signed with Decca, again without success. However, they started to work as session musicians, appearing on such memorable hits as Marty Robbins' *El Paso* and Claude King's

The Commancheros. The Glasers toured with Marty Robbins and also appeared with Johnny Cash at Carnegie Hall. When Cash invited them to be his backing vocal group, they declined, saying that they wanted their own identity. Cash agreed and for three years, while working with Johnny, they built up their act.

In 1960, the Glasers first appeared on the *Grand Ole Opry* and joined in 1962. However, it was joining up with Cowboy Jack Clement as their producer in 1965 that elevated their record career. In 1966, they signed to MGM Records and at the end of the year, they made their debut on the Country chart with the Top 25 single *Gone, on the Other Hand*. The following year, they made the chart once, with the Top 30 *Through the Eyes of Love*. During the mid-60's, Chuck Glaser was associated with Decca as a producer and produced Gordon Terry, Leon McAuliffe, Jimmy Payne and his own discovery, John Hartford. The Glasers became very popular in Britain through their several appearances at the Wembley Festival. At their first appearance, they received an unprecedented 5-minute standing ovation.

In 1968, they had two chart successes, *The Moods of Mary* (Top 50) and *One of These Days*. The elusive major hit came in 1969, when *California Girl (and the Tennessee Square)* just failed to reach the Country Top 10, but did cross over to the lower rungs of the Pop chart. They followed up with *Wicked California* (Top 25) and *Walk Unashamed* (Top 30). That year, the brothers opened their own recording studio at 916 19th Avenue South, Nashville, which became the unofficial headquarters for the burgeoning "outlaw" movement, and among those that hung out there were Waylon Jennings, Bobby Bare and Billy Joe Shaver. By this time, the Glasers also had their own group of music publishing companies.

Jim, Tompall and Chuck, the ***Glaser Brothers***

The Glasers opened their 1970 account with *All That Keeps Ya Goin'*, which went Top 40 and was featured in the movie *...tick...tick...tick*, starring Jim Brown and George Kennedy. They followed that with the Top 25 hit *Gone Girl*. That year, the CMA named Tompall & the Glaser Brothers "Vocal Group of the Year." The brothers started 1971 with the Top 25 reprise of Bob Wills' *Faded Love* and then had their first Top 10 single, *Rings*.

The following year, they started with *Sweet, Love Me Good Woman* (Top 25) and followed with *Ain't It All Worth Living For*, which went Top 15. On this last-named single they were "backed" by the London Symphony Orchestra.

1973 was to be their last year together for seven years. That year, they charted with two Top 50 singles, *A Girl Like You* and *Charlie*. Then they went their own ways until 1980, selling their publishing companies to Famous Music. In 1974, *Record World* named them "Vocal Group of the Decade." Chuck set up his own booking agency, Nova, and managed Kinky Freidman and the Texas Jewboys. He also had a solo chart entry on MGM with the lowly *Gypsy Queen*. In 1975, Chuck suffered a stroke from which, through his determination and rehabilitation, he had partially recovered by 1977.

The Glasers returned to Nebraska in 1978, to be with their father, Louis, who was seriously ill. By then Chuck could sing again and they reunited in 1980 and signed with Elektra Records. This time around they were even more successful than the first time, returning to Wembley Festival, where they were very well received. They started off with the Top 50 *Weight of My Chains* and the Top 40 *Sweet City Woman*. They then scored their biggest success with the 1971 Top 3 release, Kristofferson's *Lovin' Her Was Easier (Than Anything I'll Ever Do Again)*. They followed that with *Just One Time*, which went Top 20.

1982 was their last year together on record, and they hit the Top 20 with *It'll Be Her*, a new version of Tompall's 1977 Top 50 solo single. Their last two chart singles were *I Still Love You (After All These Years)* (Top 30) and *Maria Consuela* (Top 90).

This spelled the end of their joint career. Tompall continues with his studio, Jim still performs as a solo artist and Chuck still operates in management.

RECOMMENDED ALBUMS:

"This Land—Folk Songs by Tompall & the Glaser Brothers" (Decca)(1960)
"The Wonderful World of the Glaser Brothers" (MGM)(1968)
"Tompall & the Glaser Brothers Sing Great Hits from Two Decades" (MGM)(1973)
"Tompall & the Glaser Brothers' Greatest Hits" (MGM)(1974)
"Vocal Group of the Year" (MGM)(1975)
"Lovin' Her Was Easier" (Elektra)(1981)
"After All These Years" (Elektra)(1982)
"The Very Best of Tompall & the Glaser Brothers" (Country Store UK)(1986)

TOWN HALL PARTY

(Radio/TV Show, KFI Compton, California)

During the 1950s *Town Hall Party* was the most popular Country music show in Southern California. Starting in 1951 as a radio barn dance on KFI Compton, it became a television show in 1953. Soon KFI started feeding the one-hour show to the NBC network. Later, Armed Forces Television filmed it for overseas showing. Thirty-nine half-hour versions were filmed by Screen Gems for syndication showings around the world; these continued for several years after the show's demise. A "live" performance was recorded by Columbia Records and issued as an lp titled, not surprisingly, ***Town Hall Party***.

Town Hall Party proved to be the needed forum to launch several artists to stardom, including Freddie Hart and Buck Owens. A nucleus of established artists, such as Tex Ritter, Rex Allen, Johnny Bond, Tex Williams, Joe and Rose Lee Maphis, Eddie Dean, Lefty Frizzell, Merle Travis and others, headlined the show and were joined by well-known guests and regulars who were lesser-known talents. Like many such shows, *Town Hall Party* featured artists running the gamut from traditional Country, like Wayne Raney, to modern, like Tommy Sands and Larry and Lorrie, the Collins Kids. For several years, Johnny Bond was the show's writer, and another performer, Wesley Tuttle, was its Director. *Town Hall Party* was canceled in 1960. WKM

RECOMMENDED ALBUM:

"Town Hall Party" (Columbia)

DIANA TRASK

(Singer, Piano)

Date of Birth:	**June 23, 1940**
Where Born:	**Warburton, Nr. Melbourne, Australia**
Married:	**Tom Ewen**

Diana Trask is one of many performers who started out as a Pop and Jazz vocalist and switched over to Country, but is one of very few Australians to make it in Nashville.

Born in a lumber town, Diana grew up in a musical family. Her mother taught piano and singing and at age 16, Diana received national acclaim for her musical abilities when she won a talent contest that led to exposure on television. She toured for a while with a small group and quickly gained great popularity, opening for artists like Frank Sinatra and Sammy Davis, Jr., when they came to Australia. Davis was so impressed with her talent that he suggested she should try her luck in America. Diana took his advice and in 1959, came to the U.S.

At first her American stay was unsuccessful, and Diana was on the poverty line, but that changed as a result of appearing on TV for a week on Don McNeill's *Breakfast Club*. She signed a contract with Columbia Records, guested on the *Jack Benny Show*, became a regular on Mitch Miller's *Sing Along with Mitch* TV show and was even offered a movie contract by 20th Century Fox. She released two albums on Columbia, which were geared to the Pop market.

At this juncture, Diana got married and returned to Australia and began raising a family. In 1966 she came back to the U.S. with her American husband, initially moving to New York, and then she came to Nashville to attend the CMA D.J. Convention. She decided to switch from Pop to Country-Pop. Her first Country chart entry came in 1968 with *Lock, Stock and Teardrops*, which was released on the Dial label and reached the Top 70. Diana then signed to Dot Records, and at the end of the year had a Top 60 single, *Hold What You've Got*. Her first single of 1969, *Children*, fared about the same, but at year's end, *I Fall to Pieces* went Top 40 and crossed over to the lower rungs of the Pop chart. Diana began touring with Hank Williams, Jr., during this time. Although Diana released the album ***Miss Country Soul*** that year, the sobriquet actually belongs to Jeannie Seely.

She followed up in 1970 with the Top 40 *Beneath Still Waters*. She had her first Top 30 single in 1972 with *We've Got to Work It Out Between Us*, which was followed by the very feisty *It Meant Nothing to Me*. She opened her account in 1973 with the Top 15 release *Say When* and followed with *It's a Man's World (If You Had a Man Like Mine)* (Top 20). In 1974, she had her most successful single, *Lean on Me*, which reached the Top 15 and crossed over to the lower levels of the Pop chart. Diana had two more major successes on Dot with *(If You Wanna Hold On) Hold on to Your Man* (Top 40,1974) and *Oh Boy* (Top 25, 1975).

Although Diana achieved her greatest fame in the U.S. she did not forget her home country. After receiving several Gold Records in Australia, she returned, amid much fanfare, to Melbourne, where she first gained musical acclaim, giving a well-attended concert at the Myer Music Bowl. In 1979, Diana was inducted into Tamworth's Hands of Fame, the Australian equivalent of induction into Nashville's Country Music Hall of Fame.

In 1981, Diana returned to the U.S. and a pair of singles on the Kari label charted, of which the most successful was *This Must Be My Ship*, which almost went Top 70. During the 1980's, she spent several years in retirement, but recently she has been actively performing again. Country superstar Roy Clark, with whom Diana toured during the 70's, stated emphatically of her vocal abilities, "I'd give up my manhood if I could sing like that!" WKM

RECOMMENDED ALBUMS:

"Diana Trask's Greatest Hits" (ABC/Dot)(1974)
"The ABC Collection" (ABC)(1977)

MERLE TRAVIS

(Guitar, Singer, Songwriter)

Given Name:	**Merle Robert Travis**
Date of Birth:	**November 29, 1917**
Where Born:	**Rosewood, Muhlenberg County, Kentucky**
Married:	**1. Mary Elizabeth Johnson (div.)**
	2. Judy Hayden (div.)
	3. Betty Lou Morgan (div.)
	4. Dorothy Jean Ray Thompson
Children:	**Patricia, Cindy, Merlene, Thom Bresh**
Date of Death:	**October 20, 1983**

Merle Travis ranks as one of the greatest guitarists in the annals of Country music. He also sang a good song and made his mark as a lyric writer. In the decade following WWII, the Travis guitar style made a major impact upon Country pickers.

A native of the western Kentucky coal mining county of Muhlenberg, Merle Travis learned guitar in his youth and readily gave credit to other local pickers for teaching him what became known as the Travis style—Mose Rager and Ike Everly (who in turn owed their styles to Kennedy Jones and ultimately the same black player, Arnold Schultz, who also influenced Bill Monroe). Merle worked in the Civilian Conservation Corps for a while from 1933 and finally got his own guitar. In 1935, he began picking on radio at WGBF Evansville, Indiana, initially with the Knox County Knockabouts and later the Tennessee Tomcats.

He got a big break in 1937, when Clayton

*Legendary guitarist **Merle Travis***

McMichen recruited him for his Georgia Wildcats band. After that, Travis went to powerful WLW in Cincinnati as a member of a group called the Drifting Pioneers. This band built up a pretty big name for themselves until WWII forced them to disband. Travis also worked in a Gospel quartet with Grandpa Jones and the Delmores as the Brown's Ferry Four. Merle recorded with them and also cut a duet with Jones as the Shepherd Brothers for King Records.

After service with the U.S. Marines, Merle returned to WLW, but soon became restless for a California venture. By 1946, he was on the West Coast doing both session and solo recording for Capitol. Club work boomed and motion pictures with cowboy stars like Charles Starrett offered more employment opportunities (see Movie section). In this rich musical climate the young Kentuckian hit the Country chart with: 1946: *Cincinnati Lou/No Vacancy* (both Top 3), *Divorce Me C.O.D.* (a 14-week No.1 and a Top 30 Pop hit)/*Missouri* (Top 5); 1947: *So Round, So Firm, So Fully Packed* (another 14-week No.1 and a Top 30 Pop hit), *Steel Guitar Rag/ Three Times Seven* (both Top 5) and *Fat Gal* (Top 5)/*Merle's Boogie Woogie* (Top 10). He turned out hits for others, too, such as *Smoke, Smoke, Smoke (That Cigarette)* with Tex Williams (1947). He also composed such "Folk" songs as *Dark As a Dungeon, Sixteen Tons, Over by Number Nine* and what became the standard rendition of *Nine Pound Hammer*.

His instrumental work also gained its greatest notoriety in this period. He is generally credited with being the first Country musician to play a solid body electric guitar (a Bigsby model). In 1952, Merle sang the song *Re-Enlistment Blues* in the award-winning movie *From Here to Eternity*. Travis had few hits after 1950, but continued to record for Capitol.

In 1955, he paired up with Hank Thomson for the Top 5 instrumental hit *Wildwood Flower*. That year, Tennessee Ernie Ford had his phenomenal success with his rendition of *Sixteen Tons*, which topped the Country charts for 10 weeks and the Pop charts for 8 weeks. It also topped the U.K. charts for 4 weeks.

Merle turned out both guitar and vocal efforts, some built around themes such as his 1963 album of coal mining songs and recitations featuring his own spoken introductions. He also did some joint recording with Joe Maphis in 1964 and Johnny Bond in 1969. In 1974, Merle got together with Chet Atkins for the album ***The Atkins-Travis Traveling Show***, which that year won a Grammy Award as the "Best Country Instrumental Performance."

During the 60's, Merle was "discovered" by the college and urban Folk crowd and made occasional campus and festival appearances from then until his death. Travis eventually left California, spent some time in Nashville, and eventually settled in Tahlequah, Oklahoma, where he married Hank Thompson's former wife. He recorded several projects with CMH in his later years, including re-creations of his early standards, some new material, a tribute to Clayton McMichen with Mac Wiseman (1982) and Fiddlin' Red Herron, an Old-Time radio salute with the Grandpa Jones and Joe Maphis families and more guitar duets with Joe Maphis.

Merle had an intellectual bent and could also write quality prose and draw excellent cartoons, some of which appeared in Country music magazines. But he also had his moments of depression and despondency. An insightful look into his complex personality can be gleaned from his oldest daughter Patricia's book *In Search of My Father,* about her sometimes troubled albeit ultimately satisfying relationship with him. His son, multi-instrumentalist Thom Bresh, has received his father's genes and actively strives to keep his father's name alive. Bear Family Records has announced their intention of a box set re-issue of Merle's Capitol cuts with a booklet by the premier Travis expert, Rich Keinzle, having already released one on his coal mining songs.

IMT

RECOMMENDED ALBUMS:

"The Merle Travis Guitar" (Capitol)(1956) [Re-released on Stetson UK in the original sleeve (1988)]
"Back Home" (Capitol)(1957) [Re-released on Stetson UK in the original sleeve (1987)]
"Walkin' the Strings" (Capitol)(1960)
"Travis" (Capitol)(1962) [Re-released on Stetson UK in the original sleeve (1988)]
"Songs of the Coal Mines" (Capitol)(1963)
"The Best of Merle Travis" (Capitol)(1967)
"Strictly Guitar" (Capitol)(1969)
"The Guitar Player" (Shasta)(1975)
"The Merle Travis Story" (CMH)(1979)
"Guitar Standards" (CMH)(1980)
"Light Singin' & Heavy Pickin'" (CMH)(1980)
"Travis Pickin'" (CMH)(1981)
"The Radio Shows, 1945-1946" (Country Routes)(1990)
Merle Travis & Joe Maphis:
"Country Music's Two Guitar Greats" (Capitol)(1964)
"Country Guitar Giants" (double)(CMH)(1979)
Merle Travis & Johnny Bond:
"Great Songs of the Delmore Brothers" (Capitol)(1969) [Re-released on Stetson UK in the original sleeve (1988)]
Chet Atkins & Merle Travis:
"The Atkins-Travis Traveling Show" (RCA Victor)(1974)
Merle Travis & Mac Wiseman:
"The Clayton McMichen Story" (double)(CMH)(1982)

RANDY TRAVIS

(Singer, Songwriter, Guitar, Actor)

Given Name: Randy Bruce Traywick
Date of Birth: May 4, 1959
Where Born: Marshville, North Carolina
Married: Lib Hatcher (m. 1992)

There is no doubt that the advent of Randy Travis, in 1985, marked the arrival of the new breed of high-profile Country performers who would find cross-over appeal and herald in such contemporary stars as Clint Black, Travis Tritt and, most especially, Garth Brooks. Randy was among the first to sell Country albums in large numbers, which again led to the large market that Country music now enjoys.

Randy began singing and playing guitar at age 8. By the time he was 10, he and his brother Ricky had formed their own duo, playing local venues. His early influences were Hank Williams, Merle Haggard, Lefty Frizzell and Ernest Tubb. As a youth, he got into a lot of trouble with alcohol, drugs and fighting and landed in jail frequently. After a 135-mph car chase in his brother's car, which ended up with Randy losing control and crashing the car into a corn field, the police locked him up and he faced a five-year jail sentence. In fact the judge told him that next time Randy appeared before him, he should bring his toothbrush.

Moving to Charlotte at age 16, Randy came to a turning point in his life. He entered a talent contest at Lib Hatcher's Country City U.S.A. Club in Charlotte and as a result, Randy was offered a two-night-a-week booking at the club, which led to a full-time booking playing and working in the kitchen. After his last scrape, Randy was released into Lib's custody and she became his manager and mentor and this eventually led to the break-up of her own marriage.

In 1978, Joe Stampley, already an

*Country superstar **Randy Travis***

established Country star, helped the fledgling Randy and introduced him to Paula Records. Lib put up $10,000 and songwriter Joe South produced two singles of Randy (still called Randy Traywick), *I'll Take Any Willing Woman* and *She's My Woman*; the latter peaked in the Top 100 on the Country chart..

Lib so believed in Randy's ability that she sold her club and sold her house and in 1981, they moved to Nashville, where she took over the management of the famed Nashville Palace club. Randy continued two jobs, singing and working as a cook behind the grill. While at the Nashville Palace, Randy released an album under the name of Randy Ray entitled ***Randy Ray Live*** on the Randy Ray label.

In 1985, although Martha Sharp of Warner Brothers had turned Randy down three times for being "too Country," she now signed him to the label's roster and changed his name to Travis. Randy's first single, *Prairie Rose*, came from the soundtrack of the movie *Rustlers Rhapsody* and failed to make any impression on the charts. He followed with Don Schlitz-Paul Overstreet's *On the Other Hand*, and this reached the Top 70. However, it was the year-end single *1982* (originally called *1962* with T. Graham Brown singing the original demo) that propelled Randy into the Top 10. From then the Travis phenomenon was launched.

On the Other Hand was re-released in the spring of 1986 and this time it went to No.1 (originally Randy's producer, Kyle Lehning, had been pitched the song for Dan Seals). It was followed by another No.1, *Diggin' Up Bones*, which has in it what is described as a $20 word, "disinter" (so called because it's not a normal word in usage in Country songs). Randy released his debut album ***Storms of Life***, which went Gold in 1987 and by 1992 had sold over 3 million copies. At the end of

1986, Randy reached the Top 3 with *No Place Like Home*. That year, he became a member of the *Grand Ole Opry*.

In 1987, he began an unbroken run of seven No.1 hits. These were *Forever and Ever, Amen, I Won't Need You Anymore (Always and Forever)* and *Too Gone Too Long* (all 1987); *I Told You So, Honky Tonk Moon* and *Deeper Than the Holler* (all 1988) and *Is It Still Over?* (1989). In 1987, he released the album ***Always and Forever,*** which by the following year had sold 3 million copies and by 1990 had sold over 4 million copies. In 1988, Randy released his third album, ***Old 8 x 10***, which went Gold and Platinum the same year. The following year, the album ***No Holdin' Back*** went Gold and by 1990 had been Certified Platinum.

In the summer of 1989, Randy had his first relative "flop," *Promises*, which only reached the Top 20. However, he bounced back strongly with his No.1 remake of the Brook Benton classic *It's Just a Matter of Time*, which stayed on the chart for 6 months. He followed up with another No.1, in 1990, *Hard Rock Bottom of My Heart*. After this came *He Walked on Water* (Top 3) and *A Few Ole Country Boys* (Top 10). The last named was a duet with George Jones and came from the No.1 Country duet album ***Heroes and Friends***, on which Randy sang with Dolly Parton, Willie Nelson, Merle Haggard, Vern Gosdin, Loretta Lynn, B.B. King, Kris Kristofferson, Tammy Wynette, Clint Eastwood, Conway Twitty and Roy Rogers, and also features Chet Atkins. The album went Gold in 1990 and Platinum the year after.

Randy started out 1991 with back-to-back Top 3 singles, *Heroes and Friends* and *Point of Light*. The last named was written by Don Schlitz and Thom Schuyler for President Bush's Points of Light program, at the President's request. The program recognizes those who have done outstanding community service. Randy followed up with a duet with Tammy Wynette, *We're Strangers Again*, which came from Tammy's album ***Best Loved Hits*** and which reached the Top 50. Randy then bounded back with two hits that were written by Randy and Alan Jackson. They were the No.1 *Forever Together* and the Top 3 *Better Class of Losers*. Randy's album ***High Lonesome*** was Certified Gold that year. His seasonal album ***An Old Time Christmas*** went Gold in 1992. On May 31, 1992, Randy and Lib were married.

With the advent of the "new boys," Randy's album sales suffered and instead of going Platinum and Multi-Platinum, he had to content himself with Gold. He started off 1992 with another Travis-Jackson song, *I'd Surrender All* and once again Randy only made the Top 20. Then he came along with back-to-back No.1 hits with *If I Didn't Have You* and *Look Heart, No Hands*. That year, Warner Brothers released two volumes of ***Greatest Hits***, which were really greatest hits plus other tracks that became hits in 1992. ***Volume One*** went Gold the same year, while ***Volume Two*** was Certified Gold the following year. In 1992, Randy's video collection ***Forever and Ever*** was also Certified Gold. Randy could also claim another No.1 when Alan Jackson's recording of *She's Got the Rhythm (I've Got the Blues)*, which had been written by the two of them, topped the Country charts and produced a highly successful music video. Randy also appeared that year in an episode of the popular TV mystery series *Matlock*.

In 1993, Randy changed direction when he released the Western album ***Wind in the Wire***, which was produced by Steve Gibson. This led to the TV special spin-off of the same name, which also featured Burt Reynolds, Denver Pyle, Lou Diamond Phillips, Dale Robertson, Chuck Norris, Melanie Chartoff and the Sons of the San Joaquin. Randy also appeared in the made-for-TV movie *At Risk*.

His chart singles that year were *An Old Pair of Shoes*, *Cowboy Boogie* and *Wind in the Wire*, none of them achieving high status.

During 1994, Randy appeared in several acting roles. These were *Dead Man's Revenge* (for TV) and *Maverick*, *The Logic of O.B. Taggart* and *Frank and Jesse* (for TV). That year, Randy was reunited with producer Kyle Lehning for the album ***This Is Me***, which reached the Top 10 on the Country Album chart. The album's first single, *Before You Kill Us All*, went Top 10 and it was followed by Trey Bruce's *Whisper My Name*. (For Randy's awards see Awards section).

RECOMMENDED ALBUMS:

"Storms of Life" (Warner Brothers)(1986)
"Always and Forever" (Warner Brothers)(1987)
"Old 8 x 10" (Warner Brothers)(1988)
"No Holdin' Back" (Warner Brothers)(1989)
"Heroes and Friends" (Warner Brothers)(1990)
"High Lonesome" (Warner Brothers)(1991)
"Greatest Hits Volume One" (Warner Brothers)(1992)
"Greatest Hits Volume Two" (Warner Brothers)(1992)
"Wind in the Wire" (Warner Brothers)(1993)
"This Is Me" (Warner Brothers)(1994)

BUCK TRENT

(Electric 5-String Banjo, 5-String Banjo, Singer, Guitar, Dobro, Steel Guitar, Mandolin, Bass Guitar, Composer)

Given Name: **Charles Wilburn Trent**
Date of Birth: **February 17, 1938**
Where Born: **Spartanburg, South Carolina**
Married: **Unknown**
Children: **Charlie, Melissa**

Buck Trent is known as "Mr. Banjo" and is the inventor of the electric banjo. He is one of Country music's premier banjo players and entertainers. However, he is an adept musician on most string instruments.

Like so many Country musicians, he was in his pre-teens when he became an adept musician. He could play steel guitar by age 7 and he made his radio debut at age 10, when he broadcast on station WORD out of Spartanburg. He was age 17 when he made his professional debut on WLOS-TV Asheville, North Carolina. In 1959, he moved from South Carolina to California and Texas and then on to Nashville, where he joined the Bill Carlisle Show and debuted on the *Grand Ole Opry*.

However, it was when he became one of Porter Wagoner's Wagonmasters that his career moved upward. Joining in 1962, he was pushed by Porter to come up with a different sound on the banjo. As a result, Buck developed the electric banjo. It was built like a steel guitar and designed by steel guitarist Shot Jackson. It has a movable bridge that alters the pitch of the strings. While with the Wagonmasters, he appeared on Porter's TV show with both Norma Jean and Dolly Parton.

Buck left Porter in 1973 and joined Roy Clark. With Roy's help Buck became an entertainer and humorist, and for seven years he opened for Roy. From 1972 through 1981, Buck was nominated by the *Music City News* Awards as "Instrumentalist of the Year" and in 1975 and 1976, he won the prize. He and Roy also won the CMA "Instrumental Group of the Year" in 1975 and 1976. Buck's nominations in 1979 through 1981 for the *Music City News* Awards were in tandem with the late Wendy Holcomb. In 1976, Buck was named the "No.1 Instrumentalist" by *Record*

The creator of the electric banjo, ***Buck Trent***

World. While with Clark, Buck was also a featured musician on the TV series *Hee Haw*.

Buck is an avid golfer and in 1984, he was given golf's most prestigious award, the "Bogie Buster Award." After leaving Roy, Buck has been in great demand as a solo performer. He has appeared all over the world, with Wagoner, Clark and in his own right, including England, Belgium, Switzerland, France, Russia and Canada. He has also appeared on numerous TV shows including the *Tonight Show* and the *Mike Douglas Show*. He also did a commercial for Day's Work Chewing Tobacco.

Over the years, Buck has recorded for various labels. He started out in 1962 with Smash Records as Charles Trent, releasing *The Sound of a Bluegrass Banjo* and *The Sound of a Five String Banjo*. By 1966, he was with Boone Records, where he cut *Give Me Five* (1966) and *Five String General* (1967). He recorded for RCA Victor, while with Porter Wagoner, in 1972, and released *Sound of Now and Beyond*. When he moved to Roy Clark, he recorded several albums, both with Roy and on his own. In 1984, he released *Live from the Hee Haw Theatre*, on his own Buck Trent label, and it was picked up by the Run label. He was mentioned in the Bobby Braddock-Charles Williams song *The Night Porter Wagoner Came to Town*, which was recorded by T.C. Brown in 1985. Buck had a self-titled album released on MCA/Dot, in 1986.

For some time, Buck was the star of Music Village USA, in Nashville, but like many performers of his generation, Buck gravitated from Nashville toward Branson, Missouri. During 1992, he was temporarily sidelined by triple bypass heart surgery.

RECOMMENDED ALBUMS:

"The Sound of a Bluegrass Banjo" (Smash)(1962) [As Charles Trent]
"The Sound of a Five String Banjo" (Smash)(1962) [As Charles Trent]
"Give Me Five" (Boone)(1966)
"Five String General" (Boone)(1967)
"Sounds of Now & Beyond" (RCA Victor)(1972)
"A Pair of Fives (Banjos That Is)" (Dot)(1975) [With Roy Clark] [Re-released on MCA]
"Bionic Banjo" (ABC/Dot)(1976)
"Banjo Bandits (ABC)(1978) [With Roy Clark] [Re-released on MCA]
"Live from the Hee Haw Theatre" (Buck Trent)(1984) [Also on Run (1984)]
"Buck Trent" (MCA/Dot)(1986)

TONY TRISCHKA

(Banjo, Steel Guitar, Guitar, Composer, Writer)
Given Name: **Anthony Cattel Trischka**
Date of Birth: **January 16, 1949**
Where Born: **Syracuse, New York**
Married: **Assunta**
Children: **Sean Louis**

Tony Trischka is not only one of the most respected banjo players, he is also the leading teacher. His instructional books, workshops and audio and video tapes have helped many students and existing players to benefit from Tony's intimate knowledge of the instrument. His own style is a mix of Bluegrass, melodic and the experimental.

He began playing banjo in 1963 after hearing the Kingston Trio's *Charlie and the MTA*. He joined his first group, the Down City Ramblers, in 1965 and stayed with them until 1971. He attended Syracuse University from 1966 and graduated in 1970 with a BA degree in fine arts. In 1971, he joined two groups, Country Granola and Country Cooking and with the latter, recorded ***15 Bluegrass Instrumentals*** (1971), ***Frank Wakefield*** (1972) and ***Barrel of Fun*** (released in 1974) for Rounder.

In 1973, Tony joined Breakfast Special and stayed with them until 1975. During that time, he also recorded two solo albums for Rounder, ***Bluegrass Light*** (1974) and ***Heartlands*** (1975). In 1976, Tony released a third solo album for Rounder, ***Banjoland***. That year, he became musical leader of the Broadway show *The Robber Bridegroom*. He also went on tour with the show in 1978. During 1978, Tony was a member of Monroe Doctrine, but the group did not record during this time. That year, he, Peter Rowan and Richard Greene toured Japan and Hawaii. He also toured Australia and Hawaii with Stacy Phillips in 1978 and 1980.

Tony formed his own group, Skyline, in 1980, but they did not record until 1983. In the meanwhile, Tony recorded the 1981 album ***Fiddle Tunes for Banjo***, with fellow banjo stars Bill Keith and Béla Fleck. That year, Tony toured Finland as a solo artist and from then on, he was a constant visitor to Europe. He went to Germany in 1987, Finland, Czechoslovakia and Italy in 1989. In 1983, Tony and Skyline signed to Flying Fish (although his solo material still appeared on Rounder) and released ***Late to Work***. That year, Tony recorded the solo album ***Robot Plane Flies Over Arkansas***. In 1984, Skyline recorded ***Stranded in the Moonlight***. At this time the lineup of the group was Barry Mitterhoff (mandolin, vocals), Dede Wyland (guitars and vocals), Danny Weiss (guitars and vocals) and Larry Cohen (electric bass, piano, vocals). The material is a mix of original material and covers of songs by Vince Gill, Wynn Stewart and Richard Thompson. That year, Tony performed in *Foxfire*, which starred Jessica Tandy and Hume Cronyn, and when the play appeared on CBS-TV's *Hallmark Hall of Fame*, he also played the music. Also in 1984, Tony appeared on TNN's *Fire on the Mountain* and repeated it in 1986.

In 1985, Tony released the solo album ***Hill Country*** and in 1986, Skyline put out ***Skyline Drive***. That year, Tony was the guest soloist with Wichita Percussion Ensemble playing *The Void Beneath the Coffee Table*, a three-movement banjo concerto composed for Tony by Paul Elwood. Also in 1986, Tony was named "Banjo Player of the Year" by *Frets* magazine. He repeated the award in 1987 and 1988. Tony recorded the incidental music for Alfred Uhry's play *Driving Miss Daisy*, in 1987. In 1988, the solo album ***Dust on the Needle*** was released on cd. That year, Tony produced Belgian group Gold Rush's ***No More Angels***. Tony had two albums issued in 1989: the last album by Skyline, ***Fire of Grace,*** and a compilation of the material recorded with Country Cooking. During the year, Tony appeared on BBC-TV's *Voice of America—History of the Banjo*, from Britain. During 1990, Tony recorded the theme music for National Public Radio's *Books on Air*.

During the existence of Skyline, the group made five tours of Europe and went to Japan twice, in 1981 and 1989. With the demise of Skyline, Tony put together Big Dogs and in 1991 released ***Live at the Birchmere*** for Strictly Country Records. That year, he was the guest soloist with the National Radio Orchestra of Korea in Seoul for *The Slavery Documents*. The following year, Tony got together with Tony Furtado and Tom Adams (Johnson Mountain Boys), on ***Rounder Banjo Extravaganza***. He also did a duet album with Beppe Gambetta on Brambus Records, entitled ***Alone and Together***. Also in 1992, Tony played on the Cast Recording of Stephen Sondheim's *Assassins* and composed and performed the music for the national Ikea advertising campaign. He also appeared in the TV presentation *Where in the World is Carmen Sandiego*, on PBS. Tony toured as a solo artist to Croatia that year and returned to Germany in 1993.

During 1993, Tony released ***Solo Banjo Works*** with banjo star Béla Fleck and then he got together with Van Dyke Parks, Dudley Connell (Johnson Mountain Boys) and Alison Krauss and members of REM as World Turning and released an album of the same name. This project is a celebration of the banjo in music and narrative. That year, Tony played on ***American Dreamer***, an album of the songs of Stephen Foster, and recorded *Open Letter to Duke* for Hal Willner's ***Weird Nightmare—The Music of Charles Mingus***.

Tony has been in demand on National Public Radio, appearing on *Prairie Home Companion, Mountain Stage, The Flea Market* and *From Our Front Porch*. He has appeared on countless sessions, as diverse as Peter Rowan and Hazel Dickens to Alternative Rock group Violent Femmes.

Tony's instructional manuals have been issued on Oak Publications and are *Melodic Banjo* (1973), *The Banjo Songbook* (1975), *Teach Yourself Bluegrass Banjo* (1977), *Bill Keith* (1979), *Hot Licks for Bluegrass Banjo* (1983) and *Masters of the Five String Banjo* (co-written with "Dr. Banjo," Peter Wernick) (1987). He has also issued tablature for *Robot Plane Flies Over Arkansas* (1985) and *Hill Country* (1989). For Homespun Tapes, Tony has released the video ***Banjo-Tunes and Tips*** (1990) and the audio tapes ***Advanced Banjo*** (with Bill Keith) (1979), ***Hot Licks for Bluegrass Banjo*** (1986) and ***Easy Banjo Solos*** (1988). From 1971 to date, Tony has been a private tutor of the banjo, but he has also conducted five-day workshops; the Puget Sound Guitar Workshop (1977-1982, 1989-1990, 1992) and National Summer Guitar Workship in New Milford, Connecticut (1989-1993). Tony has also given one-day workshops in Australia, Japan and Europe, from 1978 to date. In 1993, Tony was inducted into the Syracuse Area Music Awards ("Sammy") Hall of Fame.

RECOMMENDED ALBUMS:

"Bluegrass Light" (Rounder)(1974)
"Heartlands" (Rounder)(1975)
"Banjoland" (Rounder)(1976)
"Fiddle Tunes for Banjo" (Rounder)(1981) [With Bill Keith and Béla Fleck]
"Robot Plane Flies Over Arkansas" (Rounder)(1983)
"Hill Country" (Rounder)(1985)
"Dust on the Needle" (Rounder)(1988)
"Rounder Banjo Extravaganza" (Rounder)(1992)
"Solo Banjo Works" (Rounder)(1993) [With Béla Fleck]
"World Turning" (Rounder)(1993) [With Van Dyke Parks, Dudley Connell and Alison Krauss]
Tony Trischka and Skyline:
"Late to Work" (Flying Fish)(1983)
"Stranded in the Moonlight" (Flying Fish)(1984)
"Skyline Drive" (Flying Fish)(1986)
"Fire of Grace" (Flying Fish)(1989)
Big Dogs:
"Live at Birchmere" (Strictly Country)(1991)
With Beppe Gambetta:
"Alone and Together" (Brambus)(1992)
Country Cooking:
"Country Cooking" (Rounder)(1989)

TRAVIS TRITT

(Singer, Songwriter, Guitar, Actor)
Given Name: **James Travis Tritt**
Date of Birth: **February 9, 1963**
Where Born: **Marietta, Georgia**

With the arrival of Travis Tritt, Honky-Tonk music and Southern Boogie finally blended in a way that it never had before. In addition, his good looks and winning smile made him instantly attractive to all aspects of the media and both male and female elements of the public.

Born and raised in Marietta, Georgia, Travis began singing as a soloist in the children's choir at his local church. By the time he was age 8, he had taught himself guitar and he wrote his first song six years later. Graduating in 1981, he worked at loading trucks and worked his way up to a management position. He left his job and started playing as a soloist.

In 1982, needing some demo tapes for the Marlborough Country Music Talent Round Up, which was coming through Marietta, Travis met Danny Davenport, who worked for Warner Brothers Records. Danny was building a recording studio and Travis cut guitar/vocal demos of three original songs. Danny asked him back to do some more. Eventually, after two years' work, they completed an album together and it was sent to Warner Brothers. The label was interested enough to send people to an Atlanta showcase that Travis was playing with his band and after six months, they signed him.

The label decided to release the single *Country Club* and then arranged for Ken Kragen to manage Travis. Kragen had become an industry legend as Kenny Rogers' manager and as the organizer of the *We Are the World* charity record. Although he hadn't worked with a newcomer in twenty years, he enthused over Travis and got him out playing with Dwight Yoakam, the Desert Rose Band and K.T. Oslin.

Country Club was released at the end of 1989 and reached the Top 10. Interestingly, the original demo for the song was sung by Alan Jackson. Travis started out 1990 with his own co-written *Help Me Hold On*, which went to No.1 and stayed on the chart for six months. In March of that year, his debut album ***Country Club*** was released and soared to the Top 3 on the Country Album charts and crossed over to the Pop Album chart Top 80. By August, it had been Certified Gold, going Platinum the following year. Travis' second single of the year, *I'm Gonna Be Somebody*, reached the Top 3, but his third single, another original, *Put Some Drive in Your Country*, only reached the Top 30. *Billboard* named him "Top New Male Country Artist."

*It's all about to change with **Travis Tritt***

Travis opened his account in 1991 with *Drift to a Dream*, which went Top 3. This was followed by the Tritt immediate classic *Here's a Quarter (Call Someone Who Cares)*, which climbed to the Top 3. This single came from his second album, ***It's All About to Change***, which went Gold two months after release, and by November had been Certified Platinum. The following year, sales had exceeded 2 million copies. It reached the Top 3 on the Country Album chart and fell just short of the Pop Albums Top 20. The third single of 1991, another original, *Anymore*, gave Travis his second No.1 and he finished off the year with *The Whiskey Ain't Workin'*, which featured Marty Stuart. Travis received the ultimate accolade for a new artist when he was awarded CMA's "Horizon Award."

Nothing Short of Dying, Travis' first single of 1992, reached the Top 5, while the flip-side, *Bible Belt*, which was featured in the movie *My Cousin Vinny*, peaked in the Top 75. He got together with Marty Stuart again for the Top 10 single *This One's Gonna Hurt You (For a Long, Long Time)*, which appeared on Marty's ***This One's Gonna Hurt You*** album. This was followed by *Lord Have Mercy on the Working Man*, on which Travis was joined by Little Texas, T. Graham Brown, Porter Wagoner, George Jones, Tanya Tucker, Brooks & Dunn and Dana McVicker; it went Top 5. During the year, Travis and Marty embarked on their "No Hats" tour. The two, among the most hirsute in Country music, formed a wonderfully compatible duo.

In September, Travis' third album, ***T-R-O-U-B-L-E***, was released and went Gold the following month. By 1993, this had also achieved Platinum status. It reached the Top 10 on the Country album chart and Top 30 on the Pop Album chart. He also released ***A Travis Tritt Christmas—Loving Time of the Year***, which reached the Top 25 in the Country Album chart and the Top 75 on the Pop album chart. His last single of the year was the album title track, which had been a hit for Elvis Presley. In Travis' hands it reached the Top 15. That year, Travis appeared in the Kenny Rogers movie *Rio Diablo*. Travis and Marty won CMA's "Vocal Event of the Year" and Travis was named by TNN/MCN as "Star of Tomorrow" (somewhat after the event!). In 1992, Travis was made a member of the *Grand Ole Opry*.

During 1993, Travis served as National Chairman for the Disabled American Veterans Association. Travis' hits during 1993 were *Looking Out for Number One* (Top 20) and *Worth Every Mile* (Top 30). His record *Take It Easy*, which was a cut from the chart-topping album ***Common Thread: The Songs of the Eagles***, went Top 25. His video ***It's All About to Change*** was Certified Gold for sales in excess of 50,000 units. In 1994, Travis released his fourth album, ***Ten Feet Tall and Bulletproof***, which again primarily contained self-penned songs. It soared into the Country album chart Top 3. Travis' single *Foolish Pride* reached the Top 5.

Although Travis has been called one of the "hunks"' of Country music and named by some of the media as the new macho man, he is in fact one of the finest songwriters and entertainers to have emerged in many a long time.

RECOMMENDED ALBUMS:

"Country Club" (Warner Brothers)(1990)
"It's All About to Change" (Warner Brothers)(1991)
"T-R-O-U-B-L-E" (Warner Brothers)(1992)
"Ten Feet Tall and Bulletproof" (Warner Brothers)(1994)

ERNEST TUBB

(Singer, Songwriter, Guitar, Actor)

Given Name:	**Ernest Dale Tubb**
Date of Birth:	**February 9, 1914**
Where Born:	**Crisp, Ellis County, Texas**
Married:	**1. Lois Elaine Cook (div.)**
	2. Olene Adams Carter (div.)
Children:	**Justin Wayne (Justin Tubb), Rodger Dale (dec'd.), Violet Elaine ("Scooter Bill"), Erlene Dale, Olene Gayle, Ernest Dale, Jr. ("Tinker"), Larry Dean, Karen Delene**
Date of Death:	**September 6, 1984**

Ernest Tubb, "the Texas Troubadour," was one of the Country music giants of the 40's and 50's who sustained a degree of popularity as long as his health permitted. Hank Williams may be a bigger legend, but for five years before Hank ever cut a master and for a decade after his death, Ernest Tubb ranked as the ultimate Honky-Tonk vocalist and stylist.

E.T. (as he was affectionately known) hailed from a tiny farm community in Ellis County, Texas, but later moved far westward to the community of Benjamin.

Ernest Tubb** (right) with **George Jones

In 1929, he heard a recording by Jimmie Rodgers, who quickly became his musical idol and inspiration. The youth got a guitar, learned to play it and with some friends got radio programs on local stations KMAC and KONO in San Antonio. Holding down a regular day job, Ernest married Elaine Cook, who became the inspiration for his first hit, *Blue Eyed Elaine*, in May 1934, and they became the parents of son Justin in August 1935.

Early in 1936, he journeyed to meet the widow of Jimmie Rodgers, who helped him land a pair of record sessions with Bluebird in October 1936 and March 1937. She also organized a theater tour for him. However, neither had much success, partly because Ernest still sang in a Jimmie Rodgers style for which he was not really well suited. However, Ernest did receive the guitar belonging to the late "Singing Brakeman."

In the next three years, Ernest worked at a variety of jobs, still playing music part-time on stations in Midland and San Angelo. Finally in April 1940 he landed another record deal with Decca, cutting four songs including *Blue Eyed Elaine*. This led to more sessions and a regular sponsored radio program on KGKO Fort Worth as the "Gold Chain [Flour] Troubadour."

In April 1941, Ernest recorded *Walking the Floor Over You*, which became one side of his seventh Decca release. This disc sold 400,000 copies in the next several months and the singer became a star, warbling in two Charles Starrett films (see Movie Section) and joining the *Grand Ole Opry* as a regular in January 1943. As had been the case with Roy Acuff and Pee Wee King, a managerial relationship with J.L. Frank from 1943 to 1947 also stimulated Ernest's career.

From 1944, Ernest (now known as "the Texas Troubadour") was a top Country star, touring heavily with his band, the Texas Troubadours, and working the Opry. That year, he had three singles on the Country chart, all of which crossed over to be major Pop hits. They were *Try Me One More Time* (Top 3), *Soldier's Last Letter* (No.1) and *Yesterday's Tears* (Top 5). The following year, Ernest had four sides on the charts: *Keep My Mem'ry in Your Heart* (Top 10)/*Tomorrow Never Comes* (Top 3), *Careless Darlin'* (Top 3) and *It's Been So Long Darling* (No.1 for 4 weeks).

In 1946, he had three records that made the Top 5: *Rainbow at Midnight* (No.1), *Filipino Baby* (Top 3)/*Drivin' Nails in My Coffin* (Top 5). The following year, E.T. scored with three Top 5 sides: *Don't Look Now (But Your Broken Heart Is Showing)*/*So Round, So Firm, So Fully Packed* and *I'll Step Aside*. In the meantime, Ernest starred in the film *Hollywood Barn Dance* (1947) and opened his famous Ernest Tubb Record Shop in Nashville. Norma Barthel started his fan club in 1945, which became one of the most successful and durable in the annals of such organizations. To get some idea of Ernest's impact in the latter half of the 40's, the premier Tubb scholar, Ronnie Pugh of the CMF Library, points out that one of his releases that failed to even make the charts from 1946 racked up sales of over 206,000 copies.

In 1948, Ernest started the year with *Seaman's Blues* (Top 5)/*You Nearly Lose Your Mind* (Top 15) and continued with *Forever Is Ending Today* (Top 5)/*That Wild and Wicked Look in Your Eye* (Top 10) and *Have You Ever Been Lonely (Have You Ever Been Blue)* (Top 3)/*Let's Say Goodbye Like We Said Hello* (Top 5).

In 1949 alone, Tubb had 13 sides on the charts, which in those days had only 15 on the list, and at least one side was placed every single week of the year! He started the year with *Till the End of the World* (Top 5)/*Daddy, When Is Mommy Coming Home* (Top 15). E.T. then got together with the Andrews Sisters for the double-sided *I'm Biting My Fingernails and Thinking of You* (Top 3 and Pop Top 30)/*Don't Rob Another Man's Castle* (Top 10). His other hits were *Mean Mama Blues*, *Slipping Around* (No.1 and Pop Top 20)/*My Tennessee Baby* (Top 10) and *My Filipino Rose/Warm Red Wine* (both Top 10). Ernest had one of the most successful of Christmas couplings, *Blue Christmas* (No.1 and Top 25 Pop)/*White Christmas* (Top 10). He ended the year with the first of his duets with Red Foley, *Tennessee Border No.2* (Top 3)/*Don't Be Ashamed of Your Age* (Top 10), the latter charting the following year.

In 1950, E.T. did almost as well with 11 sides on the charts. He started with back-to-back Top 3 records, *Letters Have No Arms* and *I Love You Because*. Then he had two Top 10 singles, *I'll Take a Back Seat for You* and *Unfaithful One*. He followed with *Throw Your Love My Way* (Top 3)/*Give Me a Little Old Fashioned Love* (Top 10). Ernest then got together again with Red Foley for *Goodnight Irene* (No.1)/*Hillbilly Fever No.2* (Top 10). E.T. finished off the year with *You Don't Have to Be a Baby to Cry* (Top 10), *(Remember Me) I'm the One Who Loves You* (Top 5) and a reprise of *Blue Christmas* (Top 10).

During the rest of the decade, Ernest racked up further major hits. In 1951, there were four Top 10 entries, *The Strange Little Girl* (with Red Foley), *Don't Stay Too Long*, *Hey La La* and *Driftwood on the River*. The following year, Ernest had another reprise of *Blue Christmas* (charting after Christmas), *Too Old to Cut the Mustard* (with Red Foley), *Missing in Action*, *Somebody's Stolen My Honey* and *Fortunes in Memories*.

During 1953, Ernest and Foley had their last success together with the Top 10 entry *No Help Wanted #2*. E.T.'s only other success that year was the Top 10 *Divorce Granted*. From here on, his hits peaked at a lower level. *Two Glasses, Joe* just failed to reach the Top 10, in 1954. The following year, he had back-to-back Top 10 singles, *The Yellow Rose of Texas* and *Thirty Days (To Come Back Home)* (the latter being a song written by Chuck Berry).

Between 1957 and 1963, E.T.'s Top 20 hits were *Mister Love* (Top 10, 1957), *House of Glass*, *Hey Mr. Bluebird* (Top 10, with the Wilburn Brothers) and *Half a Mind* (Top 10) (all 1958), *What Am I Living For*, *I Cried a Tear* and *Next Time* (1959), *Ev'rybody's Somebody's Fool* (1960), *Thoughts of a Fool* and *Through That Door* (both 1961), *I'm Looking High and Low for My Baby* (1962) and *Thanks a Lot* (Top 3).

Ironically, *Waltz Across Texas* (1964), one of his most popular numbers with fans and Ernest's own favorite, only reached the Top 40. However, *Pass the Booze*, that year, did make the Top 20. From 1964, Decca paired the veteran star with Loretta Lynn and they turned out three albums and four charted singles of which *Mr. and Mrs. Used to Be* (1964) and *Who's Gonna Take the Garbage Out* (1969) made the Top 20.

In 1966, physicians diagnosed Ernest as having emphysema, but for several years he continued to work a heavy road schedule. That same year, he returned to the Top 10 with *Another Story*. *I've Got All the Heartaches I Can Handle* was his last MCA chartmaker in 1973 although he remained with the Decca successor corporation through 1975.

He then went with Pete Drake's First Generation label and had two low level chart entries. In 1979, producer Pete Drake came out with a double album of his major songs featuring overdubbed vocal parts by guest stars ranging from Merle Haggard and Willie Nelson to son Justin, without informing E.T. of what he was doing. Two of the tracks were released on Cachet and were moderate successes: *Waltz Across Texas* with Willie Nelson and *Walkin' the Floor Over You*, with Merle Haggard, Chet Atkins and Charlie Daniels. The album proved a high-quality swan song for the veteran Texas Troubadour, who continued to work the road until late 1982.

However, by then, declining health forced his retirement. Emphysema took his life nearly two years later. Interest in his classic Honky-Tonk material has remained high for so much of it to be reissued on such labels as Rounder, Rhino and Stetson. Most significantly, Bear Family has released a pair of compact disc sets covering his entire output from 1947 through 1959. The Ernest Tubb Record Shop continues to be a Nashville institution, and has since expanded to six stores, including locations in Pigeon Forge, Branson, and Fort Worth. IMT

RECOMMENDED ALBUMS:

"Red and Ernie" (Decca)(1956) [Re-issued on Stetson UK in the original sleeve (1987)] [With Red Foley]
"Daddy of 'Em All" (Decca)(1956)
"The Ernest Tubb Story" (double)(Decca)(1958)
"The Importance of Being Ernest" (Decca)(1959) [Re-issued on Stetson UK in the original sleeve (1987)]
"The Ernest Tubb Record Shop" (Decca)(1960)
"Midnight Jamboree" (Decca)(1960)
"All Time Hits" (Decca)(1961)
"The Family Bible" (Decca)(1963)
"Thanks a Lot" (Decca)(1964)
"Blue Christmas" (Decca)(1964) [Re-issued on Stetson UK in the original sleeve (1987)]
"By Request" (Decca)(1966)
"Ernest Tubb Sings Hank Williams" (Decca)(1968)
"Ernest Tubb's Greatest Hits" (Decca)(1968)
"Ernest Tubb's Greatest Hits, Vol II" (Decca)(1970)
"Ernest Tubb" (MCA)(1975)
"The Living Legend" (First Generation)(1977)
"The Legend and the Legacy" (double)(First Generation)(1979) [Re-issued on Step One in 1989 on cd]
"Ernest Tubb Sings Jimmie Rodgers" (Golden Country)
"Early Radio Broadcasts" (Golden Country)
"Country Star of the Past" (Castle)(ca. 1985)
"Ernest Tubb & His Texas Troubadours" (Radiola)
"Live Transcripts" (Anthology of Country Music)(ca. 1985)
"Live Transcripts, Volume II" (Anthology of Country Music)(1989)
"Ernest Tubb: Live, 1965" (Rhino)(1989)
"Let's Say Goodbye Like We Said Hello" (Box Set)(Bear Family Germany) (1991)
"The Yellow Rose of Texas" (Box Set)(Bear Family Germany)(1993)

Ernest Tubb & Loretta Lynn:
"Mr. & Mrs. Used to Be" (Decca)(1965)
"Singing Again" (Decca)(1967)
"If We Put Our Heads Together" (Decca)(1969)
"The Ernest Tubb-Loretta Lynn Story" (double)(MCA)(1973)

JUSTIN TUBB

(Singer, Songwriter, Guitar)

Given Name:	**Justin Wayne Tubb**
Date of Birth:	**August 20, 1935**
Where Born:	**San Antonio, Texas**
Married:	**1. Bee (div.) 2. Carolyn (div.)**
Children:	**Leah-Lisa, Zachary Dale, Cary Justin**

Although Justin Tubb had some advantages in the business as the son of Ernest Tubb, he made a conscious effort to make it in Country music on his own. On the whole, he succeeded, although never quite to the degree that his father did. Justin always had his own style and has been a member of the *Grand Ole Opry* since 1955.

Justin was born in San Antonio, Texas, where his father had a radio program at the

Justin Tubb

time, and grew up in a Country music atmosphere. When his parents separated in 1948, Justin and his sister went back to Texas with their mother, "Blue Eyed Elaine." After high school, he attended the University of Texas for a year and began working some club dates in the Austin area, but aspired to get into the business full-time. Ernest suggested that he do some deejay work to gain microphone experience, which Justin did at WHIN Gallatin, Tennessee. Meanwhile the teenager had his initial Decca session on August 5, 1953, with *Ooh-La-La/The Story of My Life* being his first release.

Although Justin's early efforts were well received, his biggest numbers were novelty duets with rising female star Goldie Hill. Their cover of Jim Ed and Maxine Brown's *Looking Back to See* made the Top 5, in 1954, and their rendition of *Sure Fire Kisses*, the following year, just missed the Top 10. Justin's first solo chart entry, *I Gotta Go Get My Baby*, reached the Top 10 the following month. Justin joined the *Grand Ole Opry* in 1955, an affiliation he has retained to this day.

Justin stayed with Decca until 1960 and while he had no more hits he did release a fine album of Country standards. Afterward he joined the Starday roster and turned out a couple of albums. During the 60's, Justin toured extensively and at one point the *Opry* management dropped him briefly for not playing a sufficient number of broadcasts on the venerable program. Chart rejuvenation came in 1963 with *Take a Letter Miss Gray* on the RCA subsidiary Groove. This landed him a contract with the parent label, where he had a pair of successful duets with Lorene Mann in *Hurry Mr. Peters* and *We've Gone Too Far Again,* although his best solo single, *But Wait There's More*, peaked in the Top 70. In 1969, he joined Dot, without further chart success.

Although Justin stopped having hits by the 70's, he persisted as an *Opry* figure. His song *What's Wrong with the Way We're Doing It Now* became something of a cult song and a rallying cry for Country traditionalists. After the *Opry*, Justin often hosted the late-night *Ernest Tubb Midnight Jamboree*. After his father's death, he began singing more of his songs, but always in his own style. Always a good songwriter himself (e.g., *Lonesome 7-7203*, a 1963 No.1 for Hawkshaw Hawkins and *Be Glad*, a Top 5 single for Del Reeves, in 1969), Justin also came up with some tasteful Ernest Tubb tribute songs such as *Thanks, Troubadour, Thanks*, *Just You and Me, Daddy* and *Sing "Blue-Eyed Elaine" Again*, which came out on a new Dot album in 1985. Ironically, *Blue Eyed Elaine* on Ernest's ***The Legend and Legacy*** album (produced by Pete Drake) was the only number which the noted father and son ever recorded as a duet. IMT

RECOMMENDED ALBUMS:

"Country Boy in Love" (Decca)(1958) [Re-issued in reduced form as "That Country Style" on Vocalion in 1967]
"That Star of the Grand Ole Opry" (Starday)(1962)
"The Modern Country Music Sound" (Starday)(1962)
"Justin Tubb" (Vocalion)(1965)
"The Best of Justin Tubb" (Starday)(1965)
"Where You're Concerned" (RCA Victor)(1965)
"Country Style" (Vocalion)(1967)
"Things I Still Remember Very Well" (Dot)(1969)
"New Country Heard From" (Hilltop)(1974)
"Star of the Grand Ole Opry" (First Generation) (ca. 1980)
"Justin Tubb" (MCA/Dot)(1985)
Justin Tubb and Lorene Mann:
"Together and Alone" (RCA Victor)(1966)

LaCosta Tucker refer LA COSTA

TANYA TUCKER

(Singer, Songwriter, Guitar, Actress)

Given Name: Tanya Denise Tucker
Date of Birth: October 10, 1958
Where Born: Seminole, Texas
Children: Presley Tanita, Bo Grayson

It seems hard to believe that the sassy Tanya Tucker has been a star for over 20 years and she has still not reached her 40th birthday. This indefatigable lady has been at the top of the Country music tree since her first hit at age 13.

Tanya's parents, Beau (a construction worker) and Juanita, greatly encouraged her and her elder sister, LaCosta, when they showed an interest in music. In 1967, the family moved to Phoenix, Arizona, and when Tanya showed her liking for Country, Beau took her to watch touring Country stars. That year, she and LaCosta formed the Country Westerners with a couple of neighborhood kids, with brother Don preparing the posters.

Tanya began appearing on the *Lew King Show* on TV in 1969. They moved to St. George, Utah, and in 1971, when Sydney Pollack was shooting the movie *Jeremiah Johnson*, starring Robert Redford, her mother took her to audition for a part in it. She didn't get the part, but her horse did and she had a cameo role.

The family now moved to Las Vegas, and certain of Tanya's talent, Beau got together enough money for her to make a demo. Fortunately, this tape was heard by songwriter Dolores Fuller, who brought it to the attention of the famed Billy Sherrill, CBS's Nashville head of A & R. Tanya was signed to Columbia and was offered *The Happiest Girl in the Whole U.S.A.*, but turned it down in favor of

Pretty as a picture, ***Tanya Tucker***

the Alex Harvey-Larry Collins song *Delta Dawn*.

In the spring of 1972, *Delta Dawn* reached the Country Top 10 and crossed over to the Pop Top 75. The album of the same name also made its mark on the Country Album chart. Tanya followed up with a double-sided hit *Love's the Answer/The Jameson Ferry*, which did even better and got to the Top 5. The following year, *What's Your Mama's Name*, the title track of her second album, gave Tanya her first No.1 on the Country charts and crossed over to the Pop Top 90. That year, she was voted the ACM's "New Female Vocalist of the Year." She followed up with the 1973 No.1, *Blood Red and Goin' Down,* and was named MCN's "Most Promising Female Artist." David Allan Coe's *Would You Lay with Me (In a Field of Stone)* gave her another No.1 in 1974. She wrapped up that year with the Top 5 single *The Man That Turned My Mama On*.

Her first single of 1975, *I Believe the South's Gonna Rise Again*, only made the Top 20, but by then, Tanya was with MCA and her first release with them, *Lizzie and the Rainman*, not only went to No.1 but crossed over to the Pop Top 40. MCA's *Spring* followed and reached the Top 20. Tanya's next MCA single, the classic *San Antonio Stroll*, brought her another No.1. Columbia again caused confusion with the release of *Greener Than the Grass (We Laid Up)*, which climbed to the Top 25. She finished the year with the MCA release *Don't Believe My Heart Can Stand Another You*, which reached the Top 5.

Tanya started out 1976 with the Top 3 single *You've Got Me to Hold on To* and followed with another No.1, *Here's Some Love*, which crossed to the Pop Top 90. Her last single of the year, *Ridin' Rainbows*, just failed to reach the Top 10. The following year, she started out with the Top 10 hit *It's a Cowboy Lovin' Night*. This was followed by a final Columbia release, *You Are So Beautiful*, which went to Top 40. The year was completed by *Dancing the Night Away*, which went Top 20.

Her opening single of 1978, *Save Me*, was Tanya's first "disaster" and it only reached the Top 90. It was redeemed by the knowledge that it was used to publicize the "Save the Seals" campaign. However, the follow-up, *Texas (When I Do)*, reached the Top 5, while the flip-side, her version of Buddy Holly's *Not Fade Away*, reached the Pop chart Top 70. Tanya sang *Not Fade Away* on the *Grand Ole Opry* and was booed, because it was non-Country. She, the trouper she is, won the audience over with her personality. That year, she made her acting debut in the made-for-TV movie *Amateur Night*, with Dennis Quaid, Henry Gibson and Ed Begley, Jr. During the year, her 1975 album ***Tanya Tucker's Greatest Hits*** was Certified Gold. At MCA she underwent a change of image as the label turned her into a "sexpot" and the cover of her 1978 album, ***T.N.T.***, was far removed from the then-accepted image for a female Country singer. The year after its release this album was Certified Gold. Her only single to chart during 1979, *I'm the Singer, You're the Song,* peaked in the Top 20. During the year, Tanya appeared in the TV movie *The Rebels*, which starred Don Johnson. Although she had two major hits in 1980, *Pecos Promenade* (from the movie *Smokey and the Bandit II*)(Top 10) and the Top 5 release *Can I See You Tonight*, there were already cracks appearing in Tanya's success level, and her singles with Glen Campbell (with whom she was romantically involved), *Dream Lover* and *Why Don't We Just Sleep on It Tonight*, were only minor successes. During the year, Tanya appeared as a Rock singer in the TV movie *Georgia Peaches*.

She stayed with MCA until the end of 1981, but the only major success she had that year was *Love Knows We Tried*, which went Top 40. During the year, she appeared alongside Jan-Michael Vincent and Kim Basinger in the movie *Hard Country*. She briefly signed with Arista the following year, but only the flip-side of *Cry, Feel Right*, reached the Top 10, and her 1983 release *Baby I'm Yours* peaked in the Top 25.

Tanya was absent from the charts between 1983 and the end of 1985. She then signed with Capitol Records, with Jerry Crutchfield producing and her career took off into even higher gear than before. In 1986, her hits were *One Love at a Time* (Top 3), her first No.1 in 10 years, *Just Another Love,* and the Top 3 *I'll Come Back as Another Woman*.

She continued in 1987 with *It's Only You* (Top 10), *Love Me Like You Used To* (the title track of her 1987 album) (Top 3) and the No.1 *I Won't Take Less Than Your Love*, on which she was joined by Paul Davis and Paul Overstreet. That year, she appeared in the movie *Downtown*. The following year, she charted with back-to-back No.1 records, *If It Don't Easy* and the title track from her 1988 album ***Strong Enough to Bend***. She ended the year with *Highway Robbery*, which reached the Top 3. During the year, she checked into the Betty Ford Center for rehabilitation.

The following year, Tanya's two major hits were the Top 5 *Call Me* and the Top 3 *My Arms Stay All Night*. Her ***Greatest Hits*** package peaked in the Top 20 on the Country Album chart. In 1990, all three of her singles registered in the Top 10 and were *Walking Shoes* (Top 3), *Don't Go Out* (a duet with T. Graham Brown) and *It Won't Be Me*. Her album ***Tennessee Woman*** was also highly successful, reaching the Country Albums Top 20.

Tanya started out 1991 with *Oh What It Did to Me*, which charted Top 20 and was later in the year flipped as the "B" side of her year-end Top 3 hit *(Without You) What Do I Do with Me*. In between, she had a Top 3 hit with the infectious *Down to My Last Teardrop*. That year her album ***What Do I Do With Me*** reached the Top 10 on the Country Album chart and was Certified Gold and the following year went Platinum. The following year, all three of her chart entries, *Some Kind of Trouble*, *If Your Heart Ain't Busy Tonight* and the evocative *Two Sparrows in a Hurricane*, went Top 5. After several nominations, Tanya captured the CMA's "Female Vocalist of the Year" award. Her 1992 album ***Can't Run from Yourself*** reached the Top 15 on the Country Album chart and was Certified Gold. That year, the video of *Two Sparrows in a Hurricane* was made ACM's "Video of the Year." During 1992 and 1993, Tanya was the spokeswoman for Black Velvet Canadian Whiskey.

In 1993, her ***Greatest Hits 1990-1992*** was Certified Gold eight months after release. The title track of her album **Soon** was issued with an "R" rated video; however, there was nothing in it to shock even the most impressionable. During 1993, her single hits were *It's a Little Too Late* (Top 3), *Tell Me About It* (a Top 5 duet with Bluesman Delbert McClinton) and *Soon* (Top 3). She also had a Top 75 with *Already Gone*, a track from the chart-topping album ***Common Thread: The Songs of the Eagles***. In 1994, Tanya succeeded with *We Don't Have to Do This* (Top 20) while *Hangin' In* was still on the chart.

Tanya's passion is animals, and she used to show cutting horses; however, she sold her stock to Loretta Lynn. Tanya is her own person. Her past private life has always been good copy, but when she and her boyfriend, actor Ben Reed, decided to have children, they did and there was no public outcry. When Tanya gives one of her winning smiles, who could be upset at her? She is a lady with a heart of gold, and this was most evident when she organized a second "wedding" for her father (and manager) and mother, in 1993, in honor of their 50th wedding anniversary.

RECOMMENDED ALBUMS:

"Tanya Tucker's Greatest Hits" (Columbia)(1975)
"Tanya Tucker's Greatest Hits" (MCA)(1978)
"Live" (MCA)(1982)
"The Best of Tanya Tucker" (MCA)(1982)
"Girls Like Me" (Capitol)(1986)
"Love Me Like You Used To" (Capitol)(1987)
"Strong Enough to Bend" (Capitol)(1988)
"Greatest Hits" (Capitol)(1988)
"What Do I Do with Me" (Capitol)(1991)
"Can't Run from Yourself" (Liberty)(1992)
"Greatest Hits 1990-1992" (Liberty)(1993)
"Soon" (Liberty)(1993)

Video:
"Tanya Tucker" (Liberty)

TUNE WRANGLERS, The

When Formed:	**1935**
Members:	
Buster Coward	**Guitar, Vocal**
Tom Dickey	**Fiddle, Vocal**
Charlie Gregg	**Bass, Banjo**
Eddie Fielding	**Banjo**
Joe Barnes	**Banjo, Vocal**
Eddie Whitley	**Piano**
George Timberlake	**Piano**
Eddie Duncan	**Steel Guitar, Vocal**
Bill Dickey	**Banjo**
Cal Callison	**Accordion**
Curley Williams	**Bass**
Ben McKay	**Fiddle**
Neal Ruff	**Banjo**
Beal Ruff	**Saxophone, Clarinet**
Leonard Seago	**Fiddle**

Although very popular in San Antonio, the Tune Wranglers had little success outside their home city even though they had six recording sessions between 1936 and 1938.

Buster Coward formed the band in 1935 by joining forces with three friends, Tom Dickey, Charlie Gregg and Eddie Fielding. Later that year Fielding left and was replaced by Joe Barnes, who used the stage name Red Brown. By the time the Tune Wranglers made their first recordings, at San Antonio's Texas Hotel in February 1936, piano player Eddie Whitley had joined the group. Whitley later left to join Jimmie Revard's Oklahoma Playboys, San Antonio's most popular Western Swing band, and was replaced by George Timberlake. In a move characteristic of Western Swing groups, Whitley and Timberlake switched back and forth between Revard's band and the Tune Wranglers for the next several years.

Key personnel in the Tune Wranglers were Coward, who was important as much for his songwriting as for his playing, steel guitarist Eddie Duncan, who was both an excellent singer in the Pop vein and an instrumentalist, and the various fiddlers. Tom Dickey and Ben McKay were both hot Jazz-style performers, whereas Leonard Seago gave a more traditional sound to those recordings on which he appeared. Coward wrote *Texas Sand*, the band's longest lived hit—a number that was revised by Webb Pierce in the 1950's. The Tune Wranglers' repertoire, like that of most Western Swing bands, consisted of a mixture of Pop songs and traditional cowboy numbers.

Just why the Tune Wranglers did not become more widely popular is a matter for speculation. The most likely guess is that they did not aggressively pursue such a goal, preferring to think of themselves as cowboys with a musical avocation. Whatever the case, there is no doubt that they recorded some very enjoyable music. WKM

RECOMMENDED ALBUM:

"The Tune Wranglers" (Texas Rose)

GRANT TURNER

(Broadcaster, Singer, Ukulele, Tenor Banjo)

Given Name:	**Jesse Granderson Turner**
Date of Birth:	**May 17, 1912**
Where Born:	**Abilene, Callahan County, Texas**
Married:	**Lorene**
Children:	**Thomas, Nancy**
Date of Death:	**October 19, 1991**

Known to millions as the "Voice of the Grand Ole Opry" and the "Dean of the Grand Ole Opry," Grant Turner worked for WSM radio for nearly 50 years. The only radio announcer ever inducted into the Country Music Hall of Fame, Grant was also a member of the Country Music D.J. Hall of Fame.

The son of a Texas banker, Grant fell in love with the radio when his father purchased one of the new devices in the early 1920's. Turner was so fascinated with radio that he started building his own, as a teenager. While still a high school student, Turner got his first job in radio at KFYO in Abilene, Texas. He sang Pop songs and played ukulele and tenor guitar under the name of "Ike and his Guitar." Eventually, he took a steady job as a station announcer. Turner met the legendary Jimmie Rodgers when he came to the Abilene station for a live performance. The 18-year-old Turner was impressed with the $250 Rodgers was paid for his one-hour performance.

Grant earned a journalism degree from Hardin-Simmons College and worked at several newspapers including the *Dallas Morning News* and *The Shreveport Times*. He returned to his first love of radio in 1940 at KARO in Longview, Texas. His next stop was in Sherman, Texas, at KRRV and in 1942 he moved to Knoxville to WBIR. After two years in East Tennessee, Turner auditioned for WSM in Nashville. Grant Turner made his debut on the 50,000 watt powerhouse on June 6, 1944. His debut was overshadowed with the WWII D-Day invasion at Normandy. Turner's only duty that day was to do the station breaks in between the network news coverage.

Hosting a daily morning broadcast with Bill Monroe was his first regular show at the station. Later, Marty Robbins, Hank Williams and other singers became regulars on the program. Shortly after he began working at WSM, Turner was invited to be a *Grand Ole Opry* announcer by "The Solemn Old Judge," George D. Hay. Turner recalled, in an October 16, 1989, personal interview, the sponsor for the first half-hour show he announced. "The product was called 'Crazy Water Crystals.' It was crystals that went into mineral water and you put them in your drinking water and you made mineral water. The reason they were called 'crazy crystals' was the water came from Mineral Wells, Texas. The water was called 'crazy water' and they even had a hotel called the Crazy Water Hotel."

Turner soon became a favorite with the *Opry* stars and close friends with Roy Acuff, Little Jimmy Dickens and others. When Red Foley joined the *Opry*, Turner was the announcer on the *Prince Albert Show* and handled the hosting duties for more than a decade on the national NBC *Opry* show. Following WWII, Turner toured military bases in Europe as part of a *Grand Ole Opry* troupe that included Roy Acuff, Little Jimmy Dickens, Red Foley, Hank Williams and Minnie Pearl.

Grant remained a *Grand Ole Opry* announcer until his death in 1991. He had an excellent memory and was the unofficial historian of the *Opry*. In 1964, Grant had his sole Country chart single, when his Chart recording of *The Bible in Her Hand* made the Top 50.

He presided over the many decades of musical changes and was well loved by each new member of the *Opry*. Turner viewed his role as more than that of just an announcer. "I would like to be remembered more as the host of the *Opry* and not just the announcer who stands at the side of the stage. I want to be remembered along with such close personal friends as Roy Acuff as being dedicated to the *Grand Ole Opry* and to the future of the *Opry*." Grant Turner was inducted into the Country Music Hall of Fame in 1981. JIE

MARY LOU TURNER

(Singer)

Given Name:	**Mary Lou Turner**
Date of Birth:	**June 13, 1947**
Where Born:	**Hazard, Kentucky**
Married:	**David Byrd**
Children:	**Leslie, Tommy**

Like many natives of Hazard, Kentucky, Mary Lou's parents brought her from the mountains to the industrial city of Dayton, Ohio, while an infant. She went to Nashville and cut a record for Canary at 16, sang locally and guested a couple of times on the prestigious *Midwestern Hayride* at WLWT. Mary Lou sang in a contemporary Country vein and she landed a regular position on WWVA's *Jamboree, USA* in November 1965. During her Wheeling years, Mary and her musically talented husband, David Byrd, began their family while continuing their residence in Dayton.

Musical experiences in this era took her to New York, Chicago and a tour of NCO clubs at military bases. Jan Howard's departure from the Bill Anderson entourage indirectly led to the young lady's next career move. Although she hadn't actually applied for the position as replacement, Bill asked her to try out and she accepted in January 1973, after a trial excursion to Vero Beach, Florida. She stayed with the Anderson show through January 1980, spending some seven seasons with the *Grand Ole Opry* star's package unit.

Mary Lou had recorded with *Jamboree* in her pre-Anderson days, but she soon signed a solo contract with MCA.

Her first charted single, *All That Keeps Me Goin'*, just scraped into the Top 100 in the summer of 1974, but her duet with Anderson, *Sometimes*, climbed all the way to the top in February 1976 and was followed by another duet, *That's What Made Me Love You*, which went Top 10. As a result of this success,

Mary Lou's solo singles were more successful. In 1976, she charted with *It's Different with You* (Top 25) and *Love It Away* (Top 30).

In 1977, Mary Lou had a Top 40 single with *Cheatin' Overtime*. Mary Lou and Bill had a couple of moderate hits with *Where Are You Going, Billy Boy* (Top 20) and *I'm Way Ahead of You* (Top 25) in 1977 and 1978 respectively.

In 1980, Mary Lou went on her own. She contracted with Churchill and had four charted sides over the next two years. The strongest of these songs was *Yours and Mine*, which only went Top 80. The big hit that would propel her to top stardom never came, and after some efforts at Gospel, Mary and David moved to the emerging tourist Mecca of Branson, Missouri.

Mary Lou joined Boxcar Willie's show at his theater and is now in her eighth season. David plays piano in Boxie's band and they nearly always perform to packed houses. The pressure associated with the "rat race" in Nashville to turn out hits and the travel to show dates isn't a problem in Branson, so Mary Lou and David are quite happy with what they are doing. She hasn't cut any solo material in recent years, but has helped Boxie on some of his recent efforts with background vocals and some duets on his forthcoming album release. IMT

RECOMMENDED ALBUMS:

"Mary Lou Turner" (Jamboree)(1973)
Mary Lou Turner & Bill Anderson:
"Sometimes" (MCA)(1976)
"Billy Boy & Mary Lou" (MCA)(1977)
"Live in London" (MCA) [European release only]
(See also Boxcar Willie)

WESLEY TUTTLE

(Singer, Songwriter, Guitar)

Given Name: Wesley Tuttle
Date of Birth: December 30, 1917

West Coast star ***Wesley Tuttle***

Where Born: Lamar, Colorado
Married: Marilyn Myers
Children: Harva Lee, Wesley, Jr., Leslie Ann

Wesley Tuttle appeared in several musical Westerns during the 40's and recorded numerous songs for Capitol. Some of his numbers were duets with wife Marilyn, and his songs ran a gamut that extended from a hard "hillbilly" sound to a smooth Western vocal style.

Born in Colorado, Wesley moved to the San Fernando Valley of California at an early age and became part of the local Country music radio scene in the mid-30's, working in the bands of such Los Angeles-area music figures and groups as Stuart Hamblen and the Beverly Hill Billies respectively. Wesley played guitar left-handed and with a slight handicap, as he had only two fingers. Nonetheless, he had a fine rhythm and later did a lot of session work. He came east for a brief period in the early 40's and worked at WLW Cincinnati, meeting a young Merle Travis, then with the Drifting Pioneers. Later, Wesley also played with the Sons of the Pioneers himself.

From there, he returned west to appear in several "B" Westerns largely as a back-up musician in the films of singing cowpokes like Jimmy Wakely (see Movie Section), and at 6'4", Wesley looked every inch a cowboy. In 1944, he became the second Capitol contractee in the Country field, following Tex Ritter. Tuttle's first release, *Rainin' on the Mountain*, backed by *I Dreamed That My Daddy Came Home*, combined a number featuring an Old-Time string band sound with a soft ballad about an orphaned child. His second release, *With Tears in My Eyes*, went to the top of the Country charts in the fall of 1945 for four weeks.

Wesley had several other good numbers on Capitol. His cover of Jimmy Walker's *Detour* went Top 3 while the flip side, a cover of a Gene Autry hit, *I Wish I Had Never Met Sunshine*, peaked in the Top 5. Another popular hit for Wesley was *Tho' I Tried (I Can't Forget You)*, a Top 5 hit in 1946. While none of his next releases made the charts for several more years, he did turn out more singles of high quality, including some with Cold War themes such as *There's a Star Spangled Rainbow*, *A Heart Sick Soldier on Heartbreak Ridge* and *They Locked God Outside the Iron Curtain.*

He also did several duets with his wife, Marilyn. Marilyn had been a member of the Western back-up group the Sunshine Girls with, at various times, June Weidner, Vivian Earls and Colleen Summers (Mary Ford), who appeared in various Shirley Temple movies as well as Western movies. Leaving Capitol in 1949, Wesley cut four singles for Coral, but then returned to his original label, where he remained until 1957.

In addition to recording and touring, Wesley worked at many of the programs that popularized Country music in Southern California, including Cliffie Stone's *Hometown Jamboree* and the *Town Hall Party* in Compton. For a time, he also hosted the *Foreman Phillips Show* on KTLA-TV, which featured three hours of live programming five days a week. In the late 40's, Wesley led the house band at the Painted Post, a night club owned by old-time cowboy star Hoot Gibson. Although Tuttle remained with Capitol until 1957, his last hit came in 1954 with *Never*, a Terry Fell song which he and Marilyn did as a duet. Ironically, their best-known number together was a "Slippin' Around" type song titled *Our Love Isn't Legal.*

Wesley left his music career behind in 1957, when he entered the ministry. He and Marilyn did turn out some duet albums on the Sacred label. Today they still reside in the San Fernando Valley. Two album reissues exist of his early Capitol sides, one on the Canadian label Provincia and another from the German firm Cowgirlboy. IMT

RECOMMENDED ALBUMS:

"Tennessee Rose" (Provincia Canada)
"More Days of the Yodeling Cowboys" (Cowgirlboy Germany)

TWEEDY BROTHERS, The

When Formed: 1922

GEORGE TWEEDY
(Fiddle)
Given Name: George Tweedy
Date of Birth: 1898
Married: Unknown
Children: Unknown
Date of Death: Unknown

BIG RED TWEEDY
(Piano)
Given Name: Charles Tweedy
Date of Birth: 1902
Married: Unknown
Children: Unknown
Date of Death: ca. 1970

LITTLE RED TWEEDY
(Fiddle)
Given Name: Harry Tweedy
Date of Birth: June 18, 1906
Married: Cindy
Children: several
Date of Death: Unknown

All Born: Ohio County, West Virginia

The Tweedy Brothers were a fiddle band from the Northern Panhandle section of West Virginia who rank among the earliest professional Country musicians.

Sons of a country doctor in rural Richland Township near Wheeling, George and Harry Tweedy became accomplished fiddlers, while Charles played a fine ragtime-style piano. About 1922, the boys went professional although hillbilly commercialism tended toward the primitive in those early days. Actually, only Charles "Big Red" and Harry "Little Red" followed musical careers extensively, as George participated only occasionally in their traveling and playing. At one time or another, the Tweedys also worked the showboat circuit between Pittsburgh and Cincinnati.

After their first recording session for Gennett in June 1924, the company's parent firm, Starr Piano, provided "Big Red" a piano, which they bolted to their truck bed. Their radio work took them to WWVA Wheeling and WMMN Fairmont, southward to WSB Atlanta and westward to WLW Cincinnati and WAIU Columbus. They were among the original performers on the *Wheeling Jamboree* on January 7, 1933.

After 1930, the Tweedy Brothers made no more recordings but continued their touring and traveling for another decade or so. They added a girl singer named Cindy, who subsequently married "Little Red." The latter did a great deal of trick fiddling using various substitutes for his fiddle bow. In the 40's, Charles and Harry stayed increasingly in the Columbus area, working clubs, playing such spots as Hillbilly Park near Newark, or dances at Silver Moon Park near Oak Hill. Harry eventually took a day job as a city bus driver in Columbus. He and oldest brother George outlived Charles by more than a decade. Only one of their nineteen released sides has been reissued, significantly on an anthology of Old-Time songs from West Virginia. IMT

RECOMMENDED ALBUM:

"West Virginia Hills—Early Recordings from West Virginia" (Old Homestead)(1982) [Various Artists: credited as the Three Tweedy Brothers]

CONWAY TWITTY

(Singer, Songwriter, Guitar, Actor)

Given Name: **Harold Lloyd Jenkins**
Date of Birth: **September 1, 1933**
Where Born: **Friars Point, Mississippi**
Married: **1. Temple Maxine "Mickey" Jaco (div.)**
2. Temple Maxine "Mickey" Jaco (remarried)(div.)
3. Dee Henry
Children: **Michael Lloyd, Joni Lee, Kathy Ann, Jimmy Harold**
Date of Death: **June 6, 1993**

When the Roman general Germanicus died, the whole population of Rome personally mourned him as if the passing of a favorite son. So it was in 1993, when suddenly Conway Twitty, the man known as "the best friend a song ever had," passed away. In the early 70's, he was made an honorary chief of the Choctaw nation with the Indian title of Hatako-Chtokchito-A-Yakni-Toloa, which means Great Man of Country music. The Choctaws know a thing or two.

Conway's father, Floyd Dalton Jenkins, was a ferryboat captain, and he taught his son, then age 4, his first guitar chords (Conway got the instrument from his grandfather). Living next door was an old black man, Uncle Fred, who played guitar and harmonica, and taught Conway the Blues. The family moved to Helena, Arkansas, when Conway was 10 and that same year he began his first band, the Phillips County Ramblers (which included steel guitarist John Hughey). When Conway was 12, he had his own radio show on KFFA Helena, every Saturday morning.

However, his first love was baseball, and he received an offer to play for the Philadelphia Phillies while still a teenager, but in 1953, he was drafted into the U.S. Army. Although he could have joined the ball club when he left the service, by then he had heard Elvis Presley's *Mystery Train* and was hooked on music. He retained a love of sport, and was later instrumental in creating Nashville's minor league team, the Sounds. While in the service, Conway formed a group called the Cimarrons, who entertained at service shows in the Far East, ending up with a radio show out of Tokyo.

On leaving the Army, he joined the *Ozark Jubilee*, and began songwriting seriously. He decided to try his hand at recording and headed for Memphis and Sun Records. In 1956, he cut four sides for the label, as Harold Jenkins, none of which were released at the time and which did not see the light of day until 1970, when Birchmount Records of Canada released them. While with Sun, Conway's song *Rockhouse* was recorded by Roy Orbison.

The following year, he changed his name to Conway Twitty, being derived from Conway, Arkansas and Twitty, Texas. Under his new name, he signed with Mercury, releasing six singles, with only *I Need Your Lovin'* making any Pop chart impact (Top 100), although rock'n'roll aficionados consider them his best recordings. In 1958, he signed a five-year contract with MGM Records, and put together a new band made up of most of Sonny Burgess' Pacers, including drummer Jack Nance. With Nance, Conway wrote the song *It's Only Make Believe*, and it was with this that Conway finally launched his career. The single went to No.1 on the Pop charts, having two separate occupancies of the top spot of one week each. It also turned Conway into an international star by topping the U.K. charts for five weeks, leading to visits in 1959 and a tour in 1960.

However, he found it difficult to follow up with a major hit, and the most successful releases, *The Story of My Love* and *Mona Lisa* (a Top 5 hit in the U.K.), both in 1959, only made the Top 30. Then in the fall of that year, *Danny Boy* reached the Top 10, and was followed by *Lonely Blue Boy*, also a Top 10 entry. The last named was a variant on *Danny*, a song featured by Elvis Presley in the movie *King Creole*, and after which he initially named his band, the Lonely Blue Boys.

The following year, Conway made his movie debut in *Platinum High School* (which was retitled *Trouble at 16*) with Mickey Rooney. He followed up by appearing in *College Confidential* with Steve Allen, writing and singing the theme song for both. He went on to appear in *Rich, Young & Deadly* and *Sex Kittens Go to College*. The hit Broadway musical *Bye, Bye, Birdie* blatantly parodied Conway among all rock'n'roll singers.

Conway stayed with MGM until 1963, and his most successful singles were *What Am I Living For* (Top 30), *Is a Blue Bird Blue* (Top 40) and *C'est Si Bon (It's So Good)* (Top 30) (all 1960). He moved to ABC Paramount Records, but there he recorded only four titles, two of which were covers of Presley hits.

For some while, Conway had felt unhappy playing rock'n'roll and hankered after switching to Country. His opportunity came in 1965, when he stopped by radio WSM, where Ralph Emery was deejaying on his all-night show. Conway mentioned that he would like to play Country and Ralph called his bluff by handing him a guitar and saying, "Okay, show me you can sing Country." Conway responded by playing every Hank Williams song he could remember. A little later, Conway confided his aspirations to songwriter Harlan Howard, who told him to contact producer Owen Bradley at Decca. When Owen heard Conway sing, a five-year contract was produced and signed, and Conway Twitty, Country singer, was on his way.

His first Country hit came the following year, when *Guess My Eyes Were Bigger Than My Heart* reached the Top 20. He followed with minor successes, *Look Into My Teardrops* (1966), *I Don't Want to Be with Me* and *Don't Put Your Hurt in My Heart* (1967). Then in 1968, the superstar emerged. *The Image of Me* reached the Top 5, followed by the No.1 hit *Next in Line* and the Top 3 record *Darling, You Know I Wouldn't Lie*. Conway now decided to relocate to Nashville.

The following year, Conway had back-to-back No.1 singles, *I Love You More Today* and *To See My Angel Cry*. That year, he made his debut at the Wembley Festival in England. During the summer of that year, Conway renamed his band the Twitty Birds, with Joe E. Lewis on bass guitar, Tommy ("Pork Chop") Markham on drums and John Hughey on steel guitar. With the advent of a new decade, Conway consolidated his position in Country music. In 1970, *That's When He Started to Stop Loving You* reached the Top 5, and was followed by the No.1 hit that would always be associated with him, his wonderful self-penned *Hello Darlin'*, which stayed at the top of the Country charts for four weeks and crossed over to the Pop Top 60. He closed out the year with another No.1, *Fifteen Years Ago*, which was also a cross-over single. By now, Conway had set up the Twitty Bird Music Corporation, Conway Twitty Enterprises and a chain of drive-in eateries, called "Twittyburger" restaurants.

MGM re-released *What Am I Living For*, in 1971, and such was Conway's fan base that this reached the Top 60, even though it wasn't a regular release. The same day that charted, Conway's duet with Loretta Lynn, *After the Fire Is Gone*, also entered the Country chart and presented them with their first of five consecutive No.1 hits (it also crossed to the Pop Top 60), and for most of the 70's, they were Country music's top duo. The following month, he was back on the charts with *How Much More Can She Stand*, which also went to No.1. He followed this with Merle Haggard's *I Wonder What She'll Think About Me Leaving*, and then MGM had another re-release, *What a Dream*, which went Top 50. Conway then had his second No.1 duet with Loretta, *Lead Me On*. He finished the year with another one of his own songs, *I Can't See Me Without You*, which went Top 5.

He then had three-in-a-row No.1 singles through 1972, *(Lost Her Love) On Our Last Date*, *I Can't Stop Loving You* and *She Needs Someone to Hold Her (When She Cries)*. During the year, Conway's 1970 album ***Hello Darlin'*** was Certified Gold. In 1973, Decca became MCA, and Conway started out in fine fashion with the No.2 record *Baby's Gone*. This was followed by his third No.1 with Loretta, *Louisiana Woman, Mississippi Man*, and the big solo crossover hit *You've Never Been This Far Before*. Conway's penchant for writing "progressive" lyrics was epitomized in this memorable song of "first time" love. It went to No.1 for three weeks on the Country chart and also reached the Pop Top 30.

He got 1974 under way with yet one more No.1, *There's a Honky Tonk Angel (Who'll Take Me Back In)* and followed with *I'm Not Through Loving You Yet*, which peaked at No.3. He closed out the year with successive chart-toppers, *I See the Want to in Your Eyes* and the duet with Loretta, *As Soon as I Hang up the Phone*. He had back-to-back No.1s in 1975 with the classic *Linda on My Mind* (also a Pop Top 70 single) and *Touch the Hand*. The flip-side of the latter, *Don't Cry Joni*, on which he was accompanied by his daughter Joni Lee, also made it to the Top 5, and to the Pop Top 70. Sandwiched between the last two was *Feelin's*, a No.1 for Conway and Loretta. He ended the year with the No.1 hit *This Time I've Hurt Her More Than She Loves Me*.

All of his solo releases in 1976 went to No.1. They were *After All the Good Is Gone*, *The Games That Daddies Play* and *I Can't Believe She Gives It All to Me*. His only non-chart-topper was the duet with Loretta, *The Letter*, which reached the Top 3. During the year, Conway's 1973 album ***You've Never Been This Far Before*** was Certified Gold. The following year, he had back-to-back solo No.1s, *Play, Guitar Play* and *I've Already Loved You in My Mind*. In between them was the Top 3 duet *I Can't Love You Enough*. He ended the year with *Georgia Keeps Pulling on My Ring*, which climbed to the Top 3.

Conway had his first non-Top 10 record in 1978, when *The Grandest Lady of Them All* (which was dedicated to the opening of the new *Opry* House and was written by Mel McDaniel and Bob Morrison) only reached the Top 20. His other hits that year were *From Seven Till Ten/You're the Reason Our Kids Are Ugly*, a Top 10 duet with Loretta and two Top 3 solo singles, *Boogie Grass Band* and *Your Love Had Taken Me That High*.

In 1979, Conway underwent some changes. First, starting with the album ***Cross Winds***, he began producing himself and then he changed his image. Gone were his sideburns and slicked-back hair, and in came tight curls, making him look much younger. All of his 1979 solo singles went to No.1 and were *Don't Take It Away*, *I May Never Get to Heaven* and *Happy Birthday Darlin'*, the latter topping the charts for three weeks. His other success

The best friend a song ever had, ***Conway Twitty***

that year was *You Know Just What I'd Do/The Sadness of It All*, with Loretta. He stayed with MCA until 1981, and he racked up the following hits: 1980: *I'd Love to Lay You Down* (No.1), *It's True Love* (Top 5, with Loretta), *I've Never Seen the Likes of You* (Top 10) and *A Bridge That Just Won't Burn* (Top 3); 1981: *Lovin' What Your Lovin' Does to Me* (Top 10, with Loretta), *Rest Your Love on Me/I Am the Dreamer (You Are the Dream)* (No.1), *I Still Believe in Waltzes* (Top 3, with Loretta), and back-to-back No.1s, *Tight Fightin' Jeans* and *Red Neckin' Love Makin' Night*. During the year, Conway's 1974 ***Greatest Hits, Volume 1*** album and Conway's and Loretta's 1971 ***Lead Me On*** album both went Gold.

In 1982, Conway made a short-term move to Elektra and carried on as before, with his first two releases, *The Clown* and *Slow Hand*, going to No.1. These were followed by the Top 3 single *We Did But Now You Don't* and the chart-topper *The Rose*. These were interspersed by two low level MCA releases, *Over Thirty (Not Over the Hill)* and *We Had It All*. That year, Conway became the first Country artist to open his home to his fans, having invested over $3 million in Twitty City in Hendersonville, Tennessee.

The following year, Conway transferred to Warner Brothers, and that year had *Lost in the Feeling* (Top 3), *Heartache Tonight* (formerly a hit for the Eagles) and *Three Times a Lady* (formerly a hit for the Commodores), both of which made the Top 10. Also in 1983, Conway's 1978 ***The Very Best of*** was Certified Gold, and in 1990 reached Platinum status. He then had a run of four No.1 releases: *Somebody's Needin' Somebody*, *I Don't Know a Thing About Love (The Moon Song)* (accompanied by Joni Lee), *Ain't She*

Somethin' Else (all 1984) and *Don't Call Him a Cowboy* (1985). He wrapped up the year with *The Legend and the Man*, which only reached the Top 20.

1986 was his final year with Warner Brothers and he started off with *You'll Never Know How Much I Needed You Today*, which was his most unsuccessful legitimate release for many years, reaching only the Top 30. However, he came back strongly with the No.1 *Desperado Love* and the Top 3 *Fallin' for You for Years*.

He returned to MCA the following year, and despite the onslaught of new talent, the public and radio still clamored for Conway's recordings. That year he had consecutive Top 3 releases, *Julia* and *I Want to Know You Before We Make Love*, and then ended the year with the wonderful Gary Burr song *That's My Job*. That year, he signed a deal with Hanna-Barbera for the *Merry Twismas* animated special starring his longtime mascot, the Twitty Bird. This came out of the 1983 Christmas album ***Merry Twismas***, which at the time cost a reputed unheard-of $250,000. In 1988, *Goodbye Time* and *Saturday Night Special* (the latter had harmony vocals from Vince Gill) went Top 10 and *I Wish I Was Still in Your Dreams* climbed to the Top 5. That year, three of Conway's albums were Certified Gold, namely, ***Conway Twitty's Greatest Hits, Vol. II*** (1976), ***Number Ones*** (1982) and the duet album with Loretta, ***The Very Best of*** (1979).

During 1989, Conway started to feel the impact of radio's attention being diverted to the "new boys." His first single of the year, *She's Got a Single Thing in Mind*, reached the Top 3, but the follow-up releases, *House on Old Lonesome Road* and *Who's Gonna Know*, only reached the Top 20 and just under the Top 50 respectively. However, the public still wanted his records, and his album ***House on Old Lonesome Road*** got to the Top 40 of the Country Albums chart.

With the arrival of the 90's, Conway did better on the charts than most established performers. In 1990, *Fit to Be Tied Down* only got to the Top 30, but *Crazy in Love*, the title track from his Top 40 album, reached the Top 3 and stayed on the charts for five months. During the year, MCA honored him for his 25 years of Country hit making. He followed up in 1991 with *I Couldn't See You Leavin'*, which also went Top 3, but the others released that year fared less successfully and were *One Bridge I Didn't Burn* (Top 60) and *She's Got a Man on Her Mind* (Top 30). In 1992, *Who Did They Think He Was* reached the Top 60.

The whole world was saddened when without warning, Conway was gone, having completed a show in Branson. He died from an abdominal aneurysm. Close by him was his dearest friend and colleague, Loretta Lynn. Just before he died, he recorded a new album with Don Cook producing; it was released shortly after his death and was suitably called ***Final Touches***. That year, he had a posthumous Singles chart entry, *I'm the Only Thing (I'll Hold Against You)*, which made the Top 70. In 1994, MCA released ***Country, Rhythm and Blues***, an album that pairs Country and R & B artists, and was Conway's last project. He is teamed with Sam Moore (of Sam & Dave) on Tony Joe White's *Rainy Night in Georgia* and the result was one of the best records Conway ever released, capturing Conway's love of Country, Blues and Soul.

Of his children, Michael, Joni and Kathy have all recorded, with Kathy recording in the 70's as "Jesseca James." Joni Lee's most successful single, apart from her collaborations with her father, was the 1975 Top 20 record *I'm Sorry Charlie*, on MCA. Until Conway's death, they sang together as the Twitty Committee at Twitty City. Jimmy is a professional golfer.

During his career, Conway had more No.1 hits than any artist in popular music history, racking up 40 Country chart-toppers and 1 on the Pop lists, according to *Billboard* magazine; other music journals have made it as high as 54. This compares to 20 by the Beatles and 18 by Elvis. Only Merle Haggard (38) and Ronnie Milsap (34) get near that Country total.

Conway was responsible for writing 11 of his No.1 hits and in 1993, the Nashville Songwriters Hall of Fame elected him to their august body. No doubt election to the Country Music Hall of Fame will follow. For some reason, the CMA never gave him a solo award. However, for his legions of fans, his legacy is in his songs and his recordings. (For awards see Awards section.)

RECOMMENDED ALBUMS:

"Conway Twitty Sings" (MGM)(1959) [Re-released by Stetson UK in the original sleeve (1988)]
"Conway Twitty's Greatest Hits" (MGM)(1960) [Re-released in 1968]
"Lead Me On" (Decca)(1971) [With Loretta Lynn]
"Conway Twitty's Greatest Hits, Vol.1" (Decca)(1972) [Re-released on MCA (1974)]
"Conway Twitty's Greatest Hits, Vol.2" (MCA)(1976)
"Now and Then" (MCA)(1976)
"United Talent" (MCA)(1976) [With Loretta Lynn]
"The Very Best of Conway Twitty" (MCA)(1978)
"Lost in the Feeling" (Warner Brothers)(1983)
"Classic Conway" (MCA)(1983)
"The Beat Goes On" (Charly UK)(1985)
"Songwriter" (MCA)(1986)
"Greatest Hits Volume III" (MCA)(1990)
"Silver Anniversary Collection" (MCA)(1990)
"Crazy in Love" (MCA)(1990)
"Even Now" (MCA)(1991)
"Final Touches" (MCA)(1993)

T. TEXAS TYLER

(Singer, Songwriter, Guitar)

Given Name:	**David Luke Myrick**
Date of Birth:	**June 20, 1916**
Where Born:	**Mena, Arkansas**
Married:	**1. Claudia Louise (dec'd.)**
	2. Dorie Susan
Children:	**David L. Jr., Rodger**
Date of Death:	**January 23, 1972**

Known as the "Man with a Million Friends," T. Texas Tyler combined his ability to sing a pleasant song and a charismatic personality into a successful Country music career in the late 40's and early 50's.

Born in the same area of the Arkansas Ouachitas that gave America the "Lum and Abner" radio characters, T. Texas Tyler learned to play guitar at an early age and began aspiring to a show business career. Since his older brother was in the U.S. Navy and stationed in Rhode Island for a time, young Myrick stayed with him for a time in the early 30's and soon obtained a non-paying radio program on WMBA Newport.

For the next four or five years he worked around the country, spending short periods of time at a variety of radio stations. He also appeared on the famous *Amateur Hour* network radio program hosted by Major Bowes and then toured with one of his units for several weeks. Somewhere along the line, he began using the name "Tex Tyler" by combining the names of Tex Ritter and Tom Tyler, popular cowboy film stars, and always appearing in western clothing.

Early in 1939, Myrick came to WCHS Charleston, West Virginia, where he soon struck up a partnership with a young fiddler named Clarence "Slim" Clere (b. 1914). The duo of Slim and Tex worked together for three years, one in Charleston and nearly two for WSAZ Huntington, with a brief sojourn at Knoxville in between. While in Charleston, he began using his trademark good-natured "growl" during an appearance on the *Old Farm Hour*. While in Huntington, Tex met and married Claudia Foster.

In the spring of 1942 Slim and Tex split and Tex went to WMMN Fairmont, West Virginia. Here he worked both by himself and with Little Jimmy Dickens. Within a few months they moved to WIBC Indianapolis until Tex entered military service.

Discharged in California, Tyler joined the local musical scene, signed with 4 Star Records and obtained daily radio programs at KGER

Long Beach and KXLA Los Angeles. Successful recordings included *Filipino Baby* (a Country Top 5 success, in 1946), which he had picked up from Billy Cox in Charleston, *Remember Me* and *Oklahoma Hills*. However, it was the recitation *Deck of Cards* that provided Tex's biggest hit (charting Top 3) and ranked as one of the top songs of 1948. He followed up that year with the Mary Jean Shurtz recitation *Daddy Gave My Dog Away*, a Top 10 hit, and in the fall, he had the double-sided success *Memories of France/Honky Tonk Gal*. In 1949, he sang in the Durango Kid (Charles Starrett) film *Horsemen of the Sierras* and had a Top 5 hit with *My Bucket's Got a Hole in It*.

In 1953, Tex scored heavily with the Top 5 *Bumming Around* on Decca and the humorous Top 3 release *Courtin' in the Rain*, which had an atypical Bluegrass instrumentation, on 4 Star. Tex otherwise recorded with Western Swing accompaniment, using a studio band called the Oklahoma Melody Boys.

Tex experienced some personal and career problems in the mid-50's with the advent of rock'n'roll, but signed a management contract with Hank Snow Promotions in 1957 and joined the *Grand Ole Opry*. The following March, Tex had a conversion experience and turned to evangelism and Gospel music, becoming a licensed Assembly of God minister. In 1962, Tyler recorded a sacred album for Capitol and in the mid-60's cut a secular album for Starday. He also made three custom Gospel albums which he sold at church appearances. Through the 60's, he managed to

The man with a million friends, ***T. Texas Tyler***

balance his evangelistic work and Country singing, again based on the West Coast, where he was better known.

In April 1968, his wife, Claudia, died and Tyler later married a Canadian whom he described as "a wonderful Christian lady." They settled in Springfield, Missouri, in 1970, where he continued to speak at Assembly of God services and make occasional musical appearances. However, in March 1971, doctors diagnosed him as suffering from terminal stomach cancer. He died ten months later and his next of kin returned his remains to Huntington for interment.

Several of his 4 Star recordings had been released on King albums and a variety of budget labels. The German firm Castle also released an album of material from those sources and Radiola put a radio program from January 11, 1950, on the flip-side of an Ernest Tubb transcription album. IMT

RECOMMENDED ALBUMS:

"The Great Texan" (King)(1960)
"T. Texas Tyler" (King)(1961)
"Songs Along the Way" (King)(1961)
"T. Texas Tyler" (Wrangler)(1962)
"Salvation" (Capitol)(1962)
"The Hits of T. Texas Tyler" (Capitol)(1965)
"The Sensational New Hits" (Starday)(1966)
"Gone But Not Forgotten" (Castle Germany)(ca. 1981)
"Ernest Tubb and His Texas Troubadours/T. Texas Tyler and His Western Dance Band" (Radiola)(1983) [Tyler on side B]

IAN TYSON

(Singer, Songwriter, Guitar)

Given Name: Ian Dawson Tyson
Date of Birth: September 25, 1932
Where Born: Victoria, British Columbia, Canada
Married: 1. Sylvia Fricker (div.) 2. Twylla Boblow
Children: Adelita Rose, Clay

It took the Country music establishment an age to discover the honest "rodeo" songs of Chris LeDoux, and perhaps one day, it will discover the equally honest "cowboy" songs of Ian Tyson. In Canada, Ian has become a living legend for his music and recordings.

He started out in amateur rodeos, and it was while recovering in hospital from injuries that he learned to play guitar as therapy. In 1958, he moved to Toronto, where he worked as an industrial designer by day and sang in Folk clubs at night. While playing one of these clubs, in 1961, he met his future wife, Sylvia, also a singer/songwriter. They soon got together as Ian and Sylvia, and moved to New York, where within two months, they had signed to Vanguard Records and had Albert Grossman (who also managed Bob Dylan and Peter, Paul & Mary) as their manager. They became the first Canadian Folk act to break into the U.S. Folk scene, backed by their group, Great Speckled Bird.

In 1962, they released their debut eponymous album. The following year, they released ***Four Strong Winds***, which debuted Ian's song of the same name. This song went on to become one of Pop music's standards, with Country chart versions by Jim Lowe (1957) and Bobby Bare (1965). The duo greatly influenced other Canadian Folk and Rock acts such as Joni Mitchell, Gordon Lightfoot, Neil Young and Kate & Anna McGarrigle, who came in their wake. Ian also penned other classics while with the duo, including *Someday Soon* and *Summer Wages*, while Sylvia penned the song *You Were on My Mind* which was a Top 3 Pop hit for We Five in 1965 and British singer Crispian St. Peters the following year, in the U.K. The song appeared on the duo's 1964 album ***Northern Journey***. This was also the year that they married.

Their other albums for Vanguard were ***Early Morning Rain*** (1965), ***Play One More*** (1966), ***So Much Dreaming*** (1967) and ***Nashville*** (1968). They moved to MGM in 1968 and released the albums ***Full Circle*** and ***Lovin' Sound***. They then went on to record briefly for Columbia. In the 70's, they co-hosted their own weekly Canadian TV show, *Nashville North*. The duo stayed together until the mid-70's, when they parted personally and professionally, to embark on separate careers.

Nashville North then became the *Ian Tyson Show*. Ian went to A & M Records, where he released ***Ol'Oen***. In 1979, he moved to the foothills of Alberta and became a rancher and working cowboy. He continued writing songs and played local bars. In 1983, Ian returned to the public arena with the highly praised ***Old Corrals & Sagebrush***, which was released on Columbia. The following year, he released the ***Ian Tyson*** album and joined Ricky Skaggs on two major tours.

In 1986, the Canadian label Stony Plain released the third album in this "cowboy trilogy," the magnificent ***Cowboyography***, which was released the following year in the States by Sugar Hill. As a result, Ian won a slew of awards from the Canadian Country Music Association. He was named "Vocalist of the Year (Male)" and the Tyson-Tom Russell song *Navajo Rug* was made "Single of the Year" and ***Cowboyography*** became "Album of the Year." That same year, Ian was named "Country Male Vocalist of the

Year" at the Canadian Juno Awards. He also had hits with a remake of *Summer Wages* and a new song, *The Gift*. The following year, he retained the CCMA title of "Vocalist of the Year (Male)."

Ian released his fourth album, ***I Outgrew the Wagon***, on Stony Plain, in 1989. That same year, he was inducted by the CCMA to the Hall of Honour. The following year, he opened the Calgary Olympics accompanied by long-time friend Gordon Lightfoot. In 1991, Ian released another critically acclaimed album, ***And Stood There Amazed***, from which he had the Canadian hits *Springtime in Alberta* and *Black Nights*.

In 1992, Ian again became the CCMA's "Vocalist of the Year (Male)" and Ian and Sylvia were inducted to the Juno Awards Hall of Fame. (For the full list of Ian's awards see Awards Section.)

RECOMMENDED ALBUMS:

"Old Corrals & Sagebrush" (Stony Plain)(1983)
"Ian Tyson" (Stony Plain)(1984)
"Cowboyography" (Sugar Hill)(1987) [Stony Plain Canada (1986)]
"I Outgrew the Wagon" (Stony Plain)(1989)
"And Stood Amazed" (Stony Plain)(1991)
Ian and Sylvia:
"Greatest Hits, Vol. 1" (Vanguard)(1970)
"Greatest Hits, Vol. 2" (Vanguard)(1971)

U

UNCLE CYP AND AUNT SAP

UNCLE CYP

Given Name:	**Laurence Lemarr Brasfield**
Date of Birth:	**March 1, 1898**
Where Born:	**Smithville, Mississippi**
Date of Death:	**September 6, 1966**

AUNT SAP

Given Name:	**Neva Inez Fisher Greevi**
Date of Birth:	**March 14, 1889**
Where Born:	**Luther, Michigan**
Date of Death:	**March 19, 1980**
Children:	**Bonnie Inez**

This husband and wife team is primarily known for their tenure on the first successful Country music TV show, *Ozark Jubilee*, but they had decades of show business experience before joining the Springfield, Missouri, show in 1954.

Beginning in the early 20th century both worked numerous dramatic and comedy shows, both on the tent circuit and in vaudeville. For example, they were featured on one of the most famous tent shows, Bisbee Comedians. Laurence Lemarr played a comic character sometimes called "Boob," but most often known as "Cyprus." Later, he became "Uncle Cyp" and his wife, "Aunt Sap."

Although born in the North, Aunt Sap attended Quachita Baptist University in Arkadelphia, Arkansas, for three years beginning in 1902. She then worked as a cashier before marrying Brasfield. The couple then toured all over the United States for several years, playing essentially the same bucolic couple they portrayed on the *Ozark Jubilee*. They were among the few performers who were with the show for its entire run. When it closed in 1961, they retired from show business.

Cyp's younger brother, Rodney Leon Brasfield (Rod), followed him on the tent show circuit and ended on the *Grand Ole Opry* in 1944, a fortuitous time because the *Opry* then was heavily featuring comics. Both Uncle Cyp and Aunt Sap were Kentucky Colonels. They died in Raymondville, Texas, Uncle Cyp from lung cancer.

UNCLE HENRY'S ORIGINAL KENTUCKY MOUNTAINEERS

When Formed:	**1928**
Members:	
Henry Warren	**Emcee, Comedy**
Grady Warren	**Comedy**
Sally Warren	**Comedy**
Johnny Ford	**Fiddle**
Curly Bradshaw	**Harmonica**
Paul South	**Singer, Songwriter**
Casey Jones	**Fiddle**
Ballard Taylor	**Banjo**
Dell Remick	**Steel Guitar**
Jimmy Dale Warren	**Singer**

One of the most popular string bands in Louisville during the 30's was this group led by Henry Warren, a native of Taylor County, Kentucky. Born in 1903, Warren earned his living as a blacksmith, soldier, boxer, and dairyman before going into the music business. Some might have regarded the latter career move as courageous, or even foolhardy, because Warren played no instrument, but he had other talents that were useful in his chosen profession. He was a very astute manager, and a skillful emcee and comedian. Beginning in 1928, he led a band that broadcast over KFLV Rockford, Illinois, and performed throughout the Midwest as a combination modern dance band and string band.

In 1933, Warren modified the act, transforming his own persona by donning a long frock coat, a dark goatee, and wire-rimmed spectacles, a costume that gave him the appearance of a rube Abe Lincoln. Warren also renamed members of his band: his wife was now called "Sally, the Original Mountain Gal" and his brother, Grady Warren, became a character called the "Coonhunter." Other members of this band at the time included Johnny Ford on fiddle and Curly Bradshaw on harmonica. This version of the Kentucky Mountaineers spent time at WNOX Knoxville, WLAP Lexington, and WHIS Bluefield, West Virginia. Their greatest acclaim prior to WWII, though, came on WHAS Louisville, where they were headquartered during 1936-1940, appearing on both the *WHAS Morning Jamboree* and *Kentucky Play Party* programs.

In 1941, the band moved to WJJD Chicago, where for the next ten years they were featured on *Suppertime Frolic*. Singer and songwriter Paul South, fiddler Casey Jones, banjoist Ballard Taylor, who assumed the character of "Grandpa Nerit," steel guitarist Dell Remick, and singer Jimmy Dale Warren ("Uncle Henry" and Sally's son), all joined the band in Chicago. In the late 40's, they cut a large number of transcriptions for Capitol. Their repertoire was a mixture of old and new songs and tunes. Sally and the "Coonhunter" did older sentimental Country ballads while Jimmy Dale Warren performed modern Country heart songs. "Grandpa Nerit" did Old-Time "rapping" banjo numbers, and fiddle breakdowns and harmonica numbers rounded out the band's performances.

In 1952, after the Mountaineers broke up, Jimmy Dale Warren moved to the West Coast, where he became the lead singer for the Sons of the Pioneers. His father, Henry, died in 1968.

WKM

DICK UNTEED

(Singer, Songwriter, Guitar, Jew's Harp)

Given Name:	**Richard Alan Unteed**
Date of Birth:	**December 23, 1916**
Where Born:	**Trinway, Ohio**
Married:	**Linda Syler**
Children:	**Linda Lou, Diana Rose, Casey Renee**

Dick Unteed is best known to the wider Country music world through a series of Bluegrass and Old-Time-oriented albums he made for Rural Rhythm Records in the middle and late 60's. Yet his acquaintance with Country music goes back to the early days and he has a handful of anecdotal stories that extends from childhood encounters with Jimmie Rodgers and Uncle Dave Macon to Bluegrass legends such as the late Don Reno.

Dick hailed from a community near the town of Dresden, a place he describes as sixteen miles from every other significant spot in that part of east-central Ohio. He manifested interest in music and guitar as a child and made his first public appearance at age 12 in a theater in Cambridge, Ohio. He also managed to hear and get acquainted with many of the noted Country entertainers when they visited Cambridge. From age 20, he lived in Columbus, Ohio, a city that nearly every significant Country entertainer played or passed through at one time or another.

Dick sang or emceed at many shows in the region and became known as the "singing emcee." In the early 60's, he cut a few singles on Big Country and the Starday subsidiary, Nashville, but when Rural Rhythm got into the album business in a big way, Dick came into his own. He aided label boss Uncle Jim O'Neal in helping arrange for a studio in East Sparta, Ohio, where many of the company's eastern U.S. artists cut their material. In this capacity, he helped in the production of numerous albums by such people as Hylo Brown, Jim Greer, Red Smiley and especially J.E. Mainer. Along the way, Dick Unteed and his Pine Mountain Boys did five albums of their own. The group specialized in Old-Time songs, especially of a humorous nature. The Pine Mountain Boys provided Bluegrass instrumentation for Dick's straightforward vocals, with Dobroist Danny Milhon being the most accomplished player.

Dick's work for O'Neal soon prompted him and Jack Casey, a Bluegrass vocalist from Virgie, Kentucky, to start their own company, Rome Records. They cut an album by Don Reno and Red Smiley among others and recorded champion fiddlers like Kenny Sidle and Michelle Birkby (then Blizzard). The company is still in business today under Casey's direction, as Unteed left Columbus in 1978. Dick has resided in Nashville for the past sixteen years and is no longer involved in music. IMT

RECOMMENDED ALBUMS:

"Old Time Comedy Favorites" (Rural Rhythm)(ca. 1966)
"Dick Unteed and the Pine Mountain Boys" (Rural Rhythm)(ca. 1967)
"More Country Comedy Songs" (Rural Rhythm)(ca. 1968)
"The Pine Mountain Boys" (Rural Rhythm)(ca. 1968)
"Irish and Country Comedy" (Rural Rhythm)(ca. 1969)

V

VAGABONDS, The

When Formed: 1927
Members:
Curt Poulton
Dean Upson
Herald Goodman

The first vocal group to star on the *Grand Ole Opry*, the Vagabonds was a smooth-singing trio that specialized in sentimental songs, both old and new, and was one of the first fully professional acts on the show. Their publicity, which was better orchestrated than that of most other early pioneers on the *Opry*, insisted that the three were "all sons of ministers" and learned to sing as their fathers traveled "among the rural and mountain people of our great land."

Judge Hay of the *Opry* insisted that the group was the first non-southern act on the show, with all three members of the trio coming from the Midwest. Neither statement is really correct: only Curt Poulton's father was a minister, and Poulton himself was born not in the Midwest but in Dulaney, West Virginia, in 1907. The other two members, Dean Upson and Herald Goodman, were understandably vague about their background, not wishing to contradict their publicity.

The trio had its start in 1926 at Otterbein College in Westerville, Ohio, where Dean Upson, his brother Paul and childhood friend Poulton began singing in their spare time. After a stint with Bradley Kincaid over Chicago radio, Upson was encouraged enough to form his own trio in 1927, appearing over WLS Chicago. By 1928, he had wired Poulton to join them, getting not only a good baritone but an accomplished guitar player in the bargain.

For a time, they specialized in Pop songs and made their debut singing on a Brunswick record by bandleader Charlie Straight. Their next stop was KNOX in St. Louis, where Herald Goodman joined them. Their sophisticated booking and marketing techniques worked, and for a time they had a show called *The Vagabond Club* over a fifty-six station hookup with NBC.

In late 1931, WSM Nashville Manager Harry Stone invited the trio to join the station, not only appearing on the *Opry* but also serving as members of the WSM staff. They accepted and it was only after this that they began to emphasize the Old-Time and Folk element of their repertoire. They formed their own publishing and record company, Old Cabin, which became the first such Country organization in Nashville. By 1933, they were issuing their own songbook, sold by mail and at personal appearances, and were issuing their own records of their big hit, *When It's Lamp Lighting Time in the Valley*. Other favorites that came to be associated with the trio were *Little Mother of the Hills*, *Little Shoes* and a prison song, *99 Years*. A few months after they produced their Old Cabin record, they signed with Bluebird and began a discography with them that would eventually encompass some 32 sides.

The Vagabonds' attempt to sell Pop songs to a Country audience, though, eventually caused them trouble. In 1934, they decided to split. Herald Goodman went to Oklahoma, Dean Upson returned to Chicago and Curt stayed at WSM to work as a soloist and occasionally with the Delmore Brothers. WSM had a strong hold, though. By 1938, they were all three back at the station and the Vagabonds were briefly reactivated. Herald Goodman subsequently formed a Western Swing band, the Tennessee Valley Boys (they recorded for Bluebird). Upson eventually became WSM's Commercial Manager, and Poulton formed a band of West Virginia sidemen and worked briefly on the *Opry* and over Knoxville radio. Later, he worked as a single in the Midwest. He died in 1957. CKW

JOE VAL

(Singer, Songwriter, Mandolin, Banjo, Guitar)
Given Name: Joseph Valiante
Date of Birth: June 25, 1926
Where Born: Everett, Massachusetts
Date of Death: June 11, 1985

Despite his Italian background coupled with a New England accent and mannerisms, Joe Val led a very traditional-sounding Bluegrass band, the New England Bluegrass Boys, playing a high quality of music from the very beginning.

Joe was born in Everett, Massachusetts,

and became a convert to Country music at age 14, when he began playing guitar. By the late 40's, Joe took a serious interest in Bluegrass through the recordings of Bill Monroe and the local duos of Jerry and Sky and the Lane Brothers, both augmented at times by the exciting fiddle work of Texan-transplanted-to-M.I.T. graduate student Tex Logan. In fact, the latter gave Valiante his shortened stage name, "Joe Val." Moving from guitar to banjo and eventually mastering the mandolin, Val worked in a band called the Radio Rangers and later the Berkshire Mountain Boys. He also spent some time with the Lilly Brothers and Don Stover, who became the major Bluegrass influence in the Boston area from 1952.

When Bluegrass began to appeal to the intellectual audience, Joe mixed freely with the new enthusiasts and played mandolin on the Bill Keith-Jim Rooney album for Prestige-International. Later he also served as a key member of the Cambridge-Harvard aggregation, the Charles River Valley Boys, who also recorded for Prestige-International and did their most famous effort, an album of Beatles songs in Bluegrass style, for Elektra in 1967. Despite these ventures into progressive sounds, Val remained a staunch traditionalist with a particular affinity for the harmony duets of the past typified by the Bolicks, Monroes, Lillys, and Jerry and Sky.

In 1970, Joe put the New England Bluegrass Boys together with guitarist Herb Applin, banjoist Bob French, and bassist Bob Tidwell. They cut their initial Rounder album in the spring of 1971. Val's rendition of songs like *Sparkling Brown Eyes* with two-part harmony yodels could be a moving experience. Although the band went through the usual personnel changes, Joe managed to maintain a remarkable continuity in sound. Dave Dillon replaced Applin and later Dave Haney took his place. Paul Silvius and eventually Karl Lauber picked banjo instead of French, and Eric Levenson became their bass player in 1976. Over the years, the New England Bluegrass Boys cut a half-dozen albums for Rounder, all of excellent quality, and made a live album during the tour of the Netherlands, released on the Dutch label Strictly Country in January, 1981.

The band began reaching a wider live audience in the early 80's until Val's battle with cancer overtook him. The New England Bluegrass Boys played their last show at the Jekyll Island, Georgia, Bluegrass Festival in December 1984. Joe was hospitalized shortly afterward and died two weeks prior to his fifty-ninth birthday. IMT

RECOMMENDED ALBUMS:

"One Morning in May" (Rounder)(1972)
"Joe Val & the New England Bluegrass Boys" (Rounder)(1974)
"Not a Word from Home" (Rounder)(1977)
"Bound to Ride" (Rounder)(1979)
"Live in Holland" (Strictly Country Holland)(1981)
"Sparkling Brown Eyes" (Rounder)(1983)
"Cold Wind" (Rounder)(1983)

LEROY VAN DYKE

(Singer, Songwriter, Guitar)

Given Name: Leroy Frank Van Dyke
Date of Birth: October 4, 1929
Where Born: Spring Fork, Sedalia, Missouri
Married: Carole Sue Greathouse
Children: Lee Frank, Ray Leroy (dec'd.), Adam, Carla

Although Leroy Van Dyke will always be best remembered for his writing and recording of the novelty song *Auctioneer*, it was his infectious *Walk on By* that was by far the more successful.

Leroy, having been raised on a farm, originally had designs on a career in agriculture. He attended the University of Missouri at Columbia and gained a Bachelor of Science degree in agriculture, a major in animal husbandry and a minor in Spanish. While at university, he learned to play guitar and started listening to the music of Hank Snow, Red Foley and singing cowboys Roy Rogers and the Sons of the Pioneers and Gene Autry.

After leaving college, Leroy became farming journalist on a local newspaper and for a brief while, an auctioneer. In 1951, he enlisted in the U.S. Army and was attached to Military Intelligence, serving for a year in Korea. While in the service, he entertained the troops and wrote *Auctioneer*, as a dedication to his cousin Ray Sims, an auctioneer in Missouri. The first time Leroy sang the song was in 1953, during a 15-minute set on a show for the 160th Infantry Division, on which the star was Marilyn Monroe.

Leroy left the service later that year and on returning to the U.S., got a job in Chicago as a journalist on the Corn Belt Dailies, a group of livestock newspapers in the Midwest. He worked in the job for some three years, during which time he also auctioneered on a part-time basis and was involved in livestock advertising and promotion. Leroy had no thoughts about a professional career in music, although he occasionally entertained as an amateur.

Things changed in September 1956, when he entered an amateur talent contest, which was aired simultaneously on radio and TV via WGN Chicago. He sang *Auctioneer* and he was spotted by Bob Smith, who handled promotion for Dot Records. Buddy Black, the staff announcer and a deejay at WGN, also saw potential in Leroy and instructed the switchboard at the station that any inquiries regarding Van Dyke should be routed to him. By the time Black received a call from Smith, he had already signed Leroy to a management deal. Leroy was hurried to Universal Recording Studios in Chicago, and backed by his own guitar and Andy Nelson's electric guitar, Leroy cut *Auctioneer* and *I Fell in Love with a Pony Tail*, at a cost of $100. In all the rush, Leroy had signed various documents, including one that gave Black half the writing credits and thereby half the royalties for *Auctioneer*.

The single of *Auctioneer* debuted on the Pop charts in November 1956 and the Country charts during January 1957. It stayed on the Pop lists for nearly 4 months, reaching the Top 20, while it reached the Top 10 on the Country charts, but was present for only 2 weeks. Although Leroy had other releases on Dot, he didn't chart again for them. In 1958, Leroy joined Red Foley's *Ozark Jubilee* TV show. He moved to Nashville in 1961, and with the help of Shelby Singleton, signed to Mercury. During the summer, *Walk on By* entered the Country charts and after three weeks, it reached No.1 and stayed there for 19 weeks. In all, it was on the Country lists for 37 weeks. It also made the Pop charts and climbed to the Top 5. In addition, the single hit the U.K. Pop chart, reaching No.5.

Leroy made two visits to the Country charts in 1962, with the Top 3 release *If a Woman Answers (Hang Up the Phone)* (also a Top 40 Pop single) and *Black Cloud*, which went Top 40. In the U.K., his *Big Man in a Big House* reached the Top 40. That same year, he became a regular member of the *Grand Ole Opry*. While at Mercury, he failed to live up to his success and his three other chart entries, *Happy to Be Unhappy* and *Night People* (both 1964) and *Anne of a Thousand Days* (1965) peaked around the 40 to 50 mark.

Leroy moved on to Warner Brothers in 1965, and the following year, achieved a Top 40 hit with *Roses from a Stranger*. He made his film debut in 1967, in the auction-based *What Am I Bid?* That same year, he received the Connie B. Gay Award for "Outstanding Contributions to Furthering the Cause of Country Music." His next really successful single came with the 1968 charted release *Louisville*. That same year, he changed labels again, this time to Kapp, but again major success eluded him. The same held true when he moved on to Decca in 1970, and to ABC and ABC/Dot in 1975. His final chart entry came in 1977 and was the low-level *Texas Tea*. That same year, he was reunited with Shelby Singleton at Plantation Records and released the albums ***Gospel Greats*** and ***Rock Relics***. In 1982, Leroy moved over to the short-lived Audiograph Alive for a self-titled album. During the 80's, Leroy became active in the CMA and with UNICEF. He still is active as a live performer and occasionally appears on TV, singing one of his major hits.

RECOMMENDED ALBUMS:

"Leroy Van Dyke's Greatest Hits" (Mercury)(1964)
"The Leroy Van Dyke Show" (Mercury)(1965)
"Country Hits" (Warner Brothers)(1966)
"Just a Closer Walk with Thee" (Kapp)(1969) [Religious]
"Greatest Hits" (MCA)(1973)
"Gospel Greats" (Plantation)(1977) [Religious]
"Rock Relics" (Plantation)(1977)
"Leroy Van Dyke" (Audiograph Alive)(1982)
"Leroy Van Dyke—The Original Auctioneer" (Bear Family Germany)(1988)

TOWNES VAN ZANDT

(Singer, Songwriter, Guitar)

Given Name:	**John Townes Van Zandt**
Date of Birth:	**March 7, 1944**
Where Born:	**Fort Worth, Texas**
Married:	**1. Cindy (div.)**
	2. Jeanene
Children:	**William Vincent (Will), Katie, John Townes II**

It was Michael Martin Murphey, a genuine member of the Townes Van Zandt fan club, who made the profound statement "If you call Buddy Holly the father of Texas rock'n'roll, then Townes Van Zandt is the father of Texas Folk." Townes, in his raspy bluesy voice, has sung of trouble and pain in a way that perhaps only Hank Williams had been able to do.

Townes, of Dutch and British forebears, had a father who was in the oil business and took his family around from job to job. By the time he was age 21, Townes had lived in Fort Worth; Midland; Billings, Montana; Boulder, Colorado; Chicago; Minnesota; back to Colorado; and then he moved to Houston, when he was 19, from where he left home.

Townes wanted a guitar after seeing Elvis Presley and he asked his father for one for Christmas. His father made him write to Father Christmas for one. He learned his first chord at age 15 and his second one at age 21. The first song he learned was *Fraulein*. His education was somewhat fragmented due to the constant moves. He spent two years at a private military school, and then he went to the University of Colorado but dropped out in favor of being a Folk singer. Before going to college, he had intended to be a lawyer, as most members of his family were lawyers.

*The Father of Texas Folk, **Townes Van Zandt***

However, it was listening to Bob Dylan that made Townes realize that performers could write their own songs. Moving into Houston in 1966, he played a club called The Jester. There he met Don Sanders and they played a venue called Sand Mountain, where Townes became a regular attraction. It was Mickey Newbury who suggested that Townes try and get a record deal. Townes signed with the local Poppy label and recorded six albums for the label. These were ***For the Sake of the Song*** (1968), ***Our Mother the Mountain*** (1969), ***Townes Van Zandt*** (1970), ***Delta Mama Blues*** (1971), ***High, Low and In-Between*** (1972) and ***The Late, Great Townes Van Zandt*** (1973). The last named featured *Pancho and Lefty*, which would eventually be the song that introduced Townes to the world.

In 1976, Townes moved to Nashville and the following year, released the double album ***Live at the Old Quarter***, featuring recordings made in Houston. Townes' songs started to get recorded by other artists and these included *Tecumseh Valley* (by both Bobby Bare and the Stonemans) and *Pancho and Lefty* (by both Emmylou Harris and Hoyt Axton, during 1977). During 1978, Tomato released Townes' studio album ***Flyin' Shoes***. All the time, Townes' legendary status was growing among the public and his musical peers.

Townes left Nashville and returned to Texas. Although he didn't release another album again until 1987, his songs continued to be covered by other performers. These included *If I Needed You*, which was recorded by both Doc Watson and Marcia Routh. In 1981, Emmylou Harris and Don Williams got together and made the song a Top 3 Country hit. Two years later, Willie Nelson and Merle Haggard duetted on *Pancho and Lefty* and had a No.1 Country hit with it. Townes appeared in the video portraying a "federale." Other songs recorded included *No Place to Fall* by Steve Young and *None But the Rain* by Robin and Linda Williams.

In 1987, at his wife Jeanene's instigation, Townes moved back to Nashville and then released the Sugar Hill album ***At My Window***. On the sleeve Steve Earle made the statement "Townes Van Zandt is the best songwriter in the whole world and I'll stand on Bob Dylan's coffee table in my cowboy boots and say that." The album, produced by Jack Clement and Jim Rooney, featured his long-time musical associates Mickey White (acoustic, electric and slide guitar) and Donny Silverman (saxophone and flute), as well as Jack Clement, Jim Rooney, Mark O'Connor, Mickey Raphael, Joey Miskulin, Roy Huskey, Jr., and Kenny Malone. This represented the fourth time that Townes had recorded the title track. The following year, Richard Dobson included Townes' *White Freight Liner Blues* on his ***State of the Heart*** album.

Townes' next album release, ***Live and Obscure***, recorded in Nashville in 1985, was not initially released in the U.S., but was issued in the U.K. by Heartland Records. However, in 1989, Sugar Hill released it. Tracks included are *Pancho and Lefty*, *White Freight Liner Blues*, *Loretta* and *Talking Thunderbird Blues*.

The following year, Townes was touring with the Cowboy Junkies and wrote specifically for them *Cowboy Junkies Lament*, which was included on their ***Black Eyed Man*** album. They returned the compliment by writing *Townes Blues*, which is on the same album.

In 1991, Townes toured the U.K. with Guy Clark, John Stewart and Peter Rowan. This was not his first visit across the Atlantic, having played there in 1987 and at the Wembley Festival in 1988. Townes has appeared in concert many times with Guy Clark, who has been his buddy for over 20 years, and fellow spirits Robert Earl Keen and Mickey Newbury.

Townes had some interesting people as his advisors. John Lomax III was his manager and Pam Lewis, now Garth Brooks' manager, was his publicist. His hobbies include collecting Gideon Bibles, and at one time 50% of his mail was from inmates of mental hospitals who claimed that his music saved their lives.

RECOMMENDED ALBUMS:

"The Late Great Townes Van Zandt" (Poppy)(1973) [Released on United Artists UK (1973)]
"Live at the Old Quarter" (double)(Tomato)(1977)
"Flyin' Shoes" (Tomato)(1978)
"At My Window" (Sugar Hill)(1987)
"Live and Obscure" (Sugar Hill)(1989) [Released on Heartland UK (1987)]

LOWELL VARNEY

(Singer, Songwriter, Banjo)
Given Name: Lowell Varney
Date of Birth: September 21, 1936
Where Born: Crum, West Virginia
Married: Patricia (div.)
Children: Lowella Joan, Alva Denise

Lowell Varney, sometimes called "the banjo pickin' boy from West Virginia," had a varied career in Bluegrass and Country music. He enjoyed the advantage of a solid Scruggs-style talent on the five-string coupled with a voice not unlike that of Lester Flatt. While Lowell never quite achieved the level of stardom to which he aspired, he managed to rack up some noted accomplishments as a writer, singer, and picker, both by himself and with a couple of musical partners.

Lowell hailed from the Appalachian town of Crum in the Tug Fork section of the Big Sandy Valley. Near the Kentucky state line, this section of the mountains had produced such characters who entered the realm of folklore as Devil Anse Hatfield, other participants in the Hatfield-McCoy Feud, and the "King of the Bootleggers," John Fleming. The latter had two granddaughters who achieved fame—one as Country singer Molly O'Day and the other as Blaze Starr, who became a noted stripper. Lowell would later immortalize Fleming in his song *Twelve-Toed John.*

In the meantime, the youngster Varney would gain an appreciation for Flatt and Scruggs and came about as close as anyone could to emulating both of them. Lowell's preacher father bought him a banjo for his thirteenth birthday and he began making radio guest spots and playing local square dances about 1954. Concurrently, he learned the barbering trade and began a practice in Crum.

Around 1961, Lowell broadened his musical horizons when he went to Nashville and cut a session for Starday with a Bluegrass band. A little later he recorded *Twelve-Toed John* (patterned after *The Ballad of Jed Clampett*). Lowell and a vocalist from nearby Kermit named Landon Messer (b. 1940) worked part-time with Curly Ray and Ezra Cline in the Lonesome Pine Fiddlers during the mid-60's.

After Curly Ray joined the Stanley Brothers in 1966, the Fiddlers stopped performing and Lowell formed a team with Jim Horn (b. 1932), a blind lay preacher from Martin County, Kentucky, in a Bluegrass sacred group called the Gospel Pioneers. They had TV shows in Charleston and Oak Hill, West Virginia, for a time and cut a pair of albums for Rem and another for Tommy Crank's I.R.M.A. label. In the early 70's, Lowell cut three albums for Jessup Records. He also made an album with Hylo Brown on the Newland label, having played banjo with Brown intermittently during the 60's.

About 1973, Lowell Varney opened his Riverside Recording Studio in Crum and concentrated on the business end of music for some seven years. In early 1982, he got together with Landon Messer and they formed the Riverside Grass with Harold Brewer, Albun Clevenger, and Jim Horn. Later Lundy Fields also worked with them. That fall, they appeared in the movie *Kentucky Woman* starring Cheryl Ladd. They recorded three fine albums together and worked quite a number of festivals, but eventually Lowell dropped out and Landon carried on alone with the Riverside Grass, which featured his high lonesome lead voice.

In the early 90's, Lowell Varney experienced serious health problems, and as of March 1994 friends from Crum reported that the prematurely elderly banjoist had been confined to a wheelchair in a nursing home since 1993. IMT

RECOMMENDED ALBUMS:

Varney & Horn:
"A Place Called Heaven" (Rem)(1967)
"Lowell Varney & Jim Horn" (Rem)(1968)
"Sound of Blue Grass Gospel Style" (I.R.M.A.)(1969)
Lowell Varney:
"Banjo Pickin' Boy from West Virginia" (Jessup)(1973)
"Goin' Back to West Virginia" (Jessup)(1974)
"Instrumental Sounds" (Jessup)(1975)
Varney & Messer:
"Lowell Varney, Landon Messer & Riverside Grass" (Mountain)(1982)
"Going to a City" (Old Homestead)(1983)
"Hemlocks & Primroses" (Chain)(1984)

KENNY VERNON

(Singer, Songwriter, Guitar, Fiddle, Banjo, Mandolin, Drums)
Date of Birth: July 19, 1940
Where Born: Jackson, Tennessee

For a decade from the mid-60's to the mid-70's, the blond New Mexico resident Kenny Vernon was a constant occupant of the Country chart without ever scoring a major hit.

Kenny was born on a farm and by the time he was age 5, he had started playing guitar. At age 10, Kenny was playing on WDXI's *Uncle Tom Williams Farm Hour* with the then youthful Carl Perkins. Kenny began playing fiddle at 14, banjo at 15, mandolin at 16 and drums at 17. After leaving high school, Kenny served as gunner's mate 3rd Class in the U.S. Navy for two years. While in the service, he put a band together, winning an all-Navy talent contest. This led to him headlining a 45-day tour of the Orient, "Gobs of Fun." He also acted as the midday deejay on the service radio.

After leaving the Navy, Kenny won a car in a talent contest in San Diego, sold it for $120, and with the money joined the Musicians' Union. He then got a job playing at a San Diego nightclub.

After leaving San Diego, he moved to Las Vegas and talked his way into a week's trial at the Golden Nugget and ended up playing there with his band, Expression, on and off, for over a decade. Kenny cut an album for TWA Records without causing any major action. However, when he played The Caravan East, in Albuquerque, New Mexico, the owner, Bob Johnson, signed Kenny to a personal management deal and to his Caravan label.

It was on this label that Kenny had his first Country entry, when *It Makes You Happy (To Know You Make Me Blue)*, in 1966, reached the Top 50. At the end of 1968, Kenny signed with Chart Records and was teamed with LaWanda Lindsey. The following year, they had a Top 60 single, *Eye to Eye*. In 1970, they had his biggest hit, *Pickin' Wild Mountain Berries*, which went Top 30. They ended the year with *Let's Think About Where We're Going*, which fell just short of the Top 50. The following year, they had their final chart duet, *The Crawdad Song*, which went Top 50.

Then Kenny moved to Capitol Records, in 1972, where he was produced by Earl Ball, and he reached the Top 60 with a reprise of *That'll Be the Day*, which went Top 60. During 1973 and 1974, Kenny had three final chart records, *Feel So Fine* and *Lady* (1973) and *What Was Your Name Again* (1974), the most successful being the Top 60 *Feel So Fine*.

Kenny, who is a practical joker, raises quarter horses on his farm in Albuquerque and continues to entertain in Las Vegas.

RECOMMENDED ALBUMS:

"Pickin' Wild Mountain Berries" (Chart)(1970) [With LaWanda Lindsey]
"Nashville Union Station Depot" (Chart)(1971)

W

PORTER WAGONER

(Singer, Songwriter, Guitar, Record Producer, Television Host)

Given Name: Porter Wayne Wagoner
Date of Birth: August 12, 1927
Where Born: Howell County, Missouri
Married: 1. Velma Johnson (de facto annulled)
2. Ruth Olive Williams (div.)
Children: Richard, Debra, Denise

Porter Wagoner is one of the most conspicuous and memorable figures in Country music. His gaudy showmanship, his loyalty to the *Grand Ole Opry*, his TV leadership, plus his championing of Dolly Parton, have at times obscured his other talents, such as song-writing and, especially, record production.

Porter was born of Irish-German heritage in the Ozarks of Missouri, near the Arkansas border. His mother's family had lived in the area since the 1850's and his great-grandfather had been a school house fiddle player. Porter's father was a diligent farmer, crippled by arthritis, who provided inspiration for his son's poignant compositions on the 1974 album ***The Farmer***. Porter's older sister Lorraine taught him the old English ballad *Barbara Allen*. His talented brother Glenn Lee played fiddle and guitar, and Porter learned to fiddle *Sally Goodin'*. Glenn's teenage death devastated Porter and inspired him to carry on the musical tradition. Sister Lorraine began teaching him acoustic guitar.

Porter was graduated from eighth grade but couldn't enter high school due to family pressures. The Wagoners lost their farm and moved to the town of West Plains in 1943. Porter worked at menial jobs, attempted a fleeting teenage marriage—then in 1946 remarried. Earlier, he had met Roy Acuff in West Plains and confided to him his musical ambitions, and Acuff encouraged him. Porter's other big inspiration was Bill Monroe, and by the late 1940's, Porter was playing Bluegrass music all over Howell County and singing Gospel with the locally popular Hall Brothers. In 1949, Porter and his wife, Ruth, visited Nashville, and witnessed Hank Williams singing *Lovesick Blues* at the *Grand Ole Opry*. The song became Porter's favorite and he cut an acetate demo of it at Hopper's radio shop. By 1950, he was working in Vaughn's butcher shop on the town square, and singing (and reading commercials) on a 15-minute early morning show over local radio (KWPM).

Executives from Springfield, Missouri's KWTO radio station, Lou Black and E. E. "Si" Siman, heard Porter on KWPM and recruited him for their station in September 1951. So Porter became a salaried radio entertainer and moved his family to Springfield. In 1952, Porter's energetic and far-seeing manager, Si Siman, managed to have him signed to RCA Victor.

Steve Sholes began producing Porter's recording sessions at KWTO and then later in Nashville. Porter was typed as the next Hank Williams, since his audition version of *Lovesick Blues* had gotten him onto KWTO, then onto RCA. Porter's first release was Williams' *Settin' the Woods on Fire*, in 1952, but it ignited no flames—nor did any of his next seven singles. (Someone told Siman, "If Porter's going to succeed, someone's going to have to kill Hank!") However, a song Porter wrote with Gary Walker, *Trademark*, went Top 3 for Carl Smith in 1953 and won Porter an *Opry* guest appearance.

Siman founded a publishing company to handle Porter's songs, and Porter formed the Porter Wagoner Trio, with Don Warden (steel guitar) and Herschel "Speedy" Haworth (electric rhythm guitar). They played whatever small shows they could find, typically in schoolhouses for a percentage of the gate receipts. After expenses, Porter would keep 50% and share the other 50% with his band—a practice he never abandoned over the years. He became one of the few entertainers in any field whose side musicians worked for a piece of the profits, not for a fixed fee.

RCA ran out of patience and dropped Porter in 1954. Meanwhile, he had recorded two songs with his own money at KWTO, and these became his first two hits. He was off RCA when *Company's Comin'* went Top 10 in 1954—and an embarrassed but amused Steve Sholes re-signed Porter to the label. The other song, *A Satisfied Mind*, was also recorded after he was off the label. *A Satisfied Mind* wasn't released till 1955 and went to No.1 for 4 weeks, staying on the chart for over 8 months. Thanks to Porter's version, the song became a standard that was later recorded by the Byrds, Glen Campbell and Bob Dylan. Red Foley and Jean Shepard also recorded it in 1955, and their versions joined Porter's in the Top 10. All three were members of the *Ozark Jubilee*, founded by Si Siman. Publishing profits of *A Satisfied Mind* helped sustain and expand the influential Starday label.

The *Jubilee* gave Porter his first national exposure. The host was ex-*Opry* star Red Foley, and he became Porter's mentor. Foley had a superb voice, but Porter learned from Foley's example the difference between mere singing and entertaining. Probably the greatest lesson he gleaned from Foley was how to talk to audiences and how to graciously introduce other acts.

Elvis was breaking out at the time, and Porter had Rockabilly potential that was never realized. The breathless excitement of *Company's Comin'* anticipated that of Gene Vincent's *Be-Bop-A-Lula* two years later, and Porter co-wrote *Itchin' for My Baby*, the flipside of *A Satisfied Mind*, a sexy, shaking song that might have been written for Elvis. RCA even considered having Porter record *Bye, Bye Love*, then reneged.

Porter was invited to join the *Grand Ole Opry*, but his *Jubilee* obligation prevented this. Porter charted two more Top 10 records in 1956, *Eat, Drink and Be Merry (Tomorrow You'll Cry)* and *What Would You Do? (If Jesus Came to Your House)*. Then he followed with *Uncle Pen*, which only went Top 15, and both *Tryin' to Forget the Blues* (1956) and *I Thought I Heard You Call My Name* (1957) failed to make the Top 10.

By the time he joined the *Opry* (February 23, 1957), Porter's career had lost momentum. Not till 1961 did he re-enter the Top 10, with Johnny Bond's *Your Old Love Letters*. During those lean years, when rock'n'rollers like Carl Perkins were grossing $1,500 a night, the Porter Wagoner Trio was working for $50 a night. In 1959, Porter and Don Warden discovered and published Jimmy Driftwood's *The Battle of New Orleans*, which became a monster hit for Johnny Horton that year and was a prelude to Porter's co-publishing with Dolly Parton, a decade hence.

In 1960, the Chattanooga Medicine Company selected Porter to host a syndicated half-hour Country music TV show, to advertise its products like Black Draught Laxative (famous since the 19th century). Porter encouraged his musicians to develop TV-quality showmanship, and his band, the Wagonmasters, eventually included guitarist George McCormick, Mack ("Dancing fiddler") Magaha and Buck Trent, pioneer of the electric banjo. Porter wore rhinestone-studded costumes embroidered with wagonwheels and cacti, and his band members dressed similarly, in suits crafted by Nudie Cohen, the North Hollywood hillbilly (and Western) haberdasher to the stars.

Porter's producer in the late 50's was Chet Atkins. On the first occasion that Porter took over a session, the song (Jerry Reed's *Misery Loves Company*) went to No.1 in 1962 and was followed by *Cold, Dark Waters,* which went Top 10. At last, better songs were coming his way, thanks largely to the success of the TV show and the road show, and a live album, ***The Porter Wagoner Show***, was a Grammy nominee in 1963. Bill Anderson supplied Porter with *I've Enjoyed As Much of This As I Can Stand* (Top 10, 1963) and *I'll Go Down Swinging* (Top 15, 1964). Between those two, Porter had a Top 5 hit in 1964 with *Sorrow on the Rocks*.

In 1965, he helped create another Country and Pop standard, by charting the "death row" prison song *Green, Green Grass of Home*. There have been over 500 versions, but Porter's was the first hit. He especially liked strong, deep-cutting lyrics and *Skid Row Joe* (Top 3, 1966) signaled his late 60's move toward severe, uncompromising story-songs. The photograph of Porter (dressed as "Skid Row Joe") on the cover of the ***Confessions of a Broken Man*** album won a Grammy in 1966 as "Best Album Cover, Photography" for photographer Les Leverette and Art Director Robert Jones. That year, Porter in company with the Blackwood Brothers won a Grammy Award for "Best Sacred Recording (Musical)" for the album ***Grand Ole Gospel***.

Porter's prison album ***Soul of a Convict and Other Great Prison Songs*** (1967) revived Johnny Cash's *Folsom Prison Blues*. Bill Anderson wrote *The Cold, Hard Facts of Life*, which went Top 3 that year, earning three Grammy nominations. This was followed by Waylon Jennings' song *Julie*, which went Top 15. Porter also won a second Grammy with the Blackwood Brothers for "Best Gospel Performance" for ***More Grand Ole Gospel***.

In 1967, Norma Jean left Porter's road show to get married. Porter had produced many of Norma's hits and albums, and although he was separated from his wife, his love affair with Norma Jean had no future. In early September, he began featuring a fledgling female singer named Dolly Parton as Norma's replacement.

Porter went Top 20 in 1968 with *Be Proud of Your Man* and followed it with Bob Ferguson's *The Carroll County Accident*, which went Top 3 (peaking in 1969) and crossed to the Pop 100, earning Porter another Grammy nomination and winning CMA's "Song of the Year" Award, with Porter's company publishing it. During the year, Porter and Dolly began charting their duets and scored that year with the Top 10 *The Last Thing on My Mind* and *Holding on to Nothing* and the Top 5 *We'll Get Ahead Someday*. That year Porter and Dolly won the CMA's "Group of the Year" award. They also won the MCN "Duet of the Year" in 1968 through 1970.

Country music legend ***Porter Wagoner***

Porter's ***Bottom of the Bottle*** album (1968) was a further reminder that, unlike some Country singers, he loathed drunkenness. He had lost a brother, as well as Red Foley, to the bottle. Had Porter possessed a Jim Reeves or Faron Young crooner's voice, he would never have sought out such songs. Instead, his hometown, homemade style welcomed such searing, dramatic narratives, and his delivery made some of them immortal.

Porter's career was still on an upswing and *Big Wind* went Top 3 in 1969, and he won his third Grammy with the Blackwood Brothers that year for "Best Gospel Performance" for ***In Gospel Country***. His duet hits that year were *Yours Love* (Top 10), *Always, Always* (Top 20) and *Just Someone I Used to Know* (Top 5).

The *Porter Wagoner Show* was in close to one hundred markets (3.5 million viewers), and he was now producing not only his own records (officially with Bob Ferguson) but those of Dolly as well as their duets. With so many recordings under his control, he pursued both his songwriting (sometimes alone, sometimes with Dolly) and song publishing (with Dolly), and Dolly especially encouraged Porter's writing.

In this period, he charted occasional songs written by Dolly such as his next big hit, *The Last One to Touch Me*, which went Top 20 in 1971. Porter followed up with the Top 15 *Charley's Picture* and *Be a Little Quieter*. Between 1972 and 1974, he charted ten songs in a row he wrote himself, such as *What Ain't to Be, Just Might Happen* (Top 10, 1972). The song was the title cut from an "insanity-concept" album containing *The Rubber Room*, about a mental patient (which became a Rock cult classic thanks to Alex Chilton). His other 1972 hits were *A World Without Music* (Top 15) and *Katy Did* (Top 20). His composition *Highway Headin' South* (Top 15, 1974) is one of his *Grand Ole Opry* standards.

During this time, Porter and Dolly were continuing their success. In 1970, they had Top 10 hits with *Tomorrow Is Forever* and *Daddy Was an Old Time Preacher Man*. The following year, they scored with *Better Move It on Home* (Top 10) and *The Right Combination* (Top 15). In those two years, they received the CMA's "Vocal Duo of the Year" award. Their other hits were: 1972: *Burning the Midnight Oil* (Top 15), *Lost Forever in Your Kiss* (Top 10) and *Together Always* (Top 15); 1973: *If Teardrops Were Pennies* (Top 3); 1974: *Please Don't Stop Loving Me* (No.1).

Dolly split from Porter in 1974, but in 1975, RCA released their duet *Say Forever You'll Be Mine*, which went Top 5, and the following year, they repeated this with *Is Forever Longer Than Always*, which went Top 10.

Porter retired from the road in 1976, devoting himself to record production at his Fireside Studios. Porter produced a chart album for R & B singer Joe Simon in 1980, which included three chart singles as well. In 1979, Porter brought James Brown to the *Grand Ole Opry* as a showmanship spectacle, reaping national notoriety (and some consternation from the *Opry* purists).

Meanwhile, his contract with Dolly Parton had fallen into abeyance (though she thought he was still being paid, as she told *The Tennesseean*, October 12, 1978), so reluctantly he sued her in 1979. The dispute was amicably settled out of court—but RCA dropped him in 1980, squelching his guaranteed comeback recording of *The Rose* (Conway Twitty's version went Top 3 in 1982). However, they did release a Porter-Dolly duet, *Making Plans*, which went Top 3 in 1980, and the following year, they reached Top 15 with *If You Go, I'll Follow You*.

Porter sold his studio, sold his song

publishing (to Dolly!), lost his TV show in 1981 (its 20th year) and faced nearly half-a-million dollars in income tax debts. So he resumed his career as a touring act and landed a role in *Honkytonk Man* (with Clint Eastwood) in 1982 and scored two hits, *Turn the Pencil Over* (from the film) and in 1983, *This Cowboy's Hat* (later recorded by Chris Ledoux), both produced by Snuff Garrett. When he performed at the Lone Star Café in 1983, John Pareles of the *New York Times* noted his calm conversational baritone.

That same year, Porter created the all-girl band the Right Combination, which backed him for several years. (Its leader, Wanda Vick, went on to form the all-girl band Wild Rose). Gradually Porter became a familiar face on Ralph Emery's *Nashville Now* (TNN) and by 1992, Porter was co-hosting *Opry Backstage*, with Bill Anderson. Opryland named him its "Goodwill Ambassador," and today he personally greets tourists at the theme park, with all of the sincerity of an Ozarks schoolhouse musician from the 1940's.

Little about Porter Wagoner has changed. When he first met Roy Acuff in a West Plains drugstore, as a teenager, he lacked the money to even buy a soft drink, but he sat down and talked with Acuff anyway. At the Nashville Palace, on November 11, 1992, he performed a medley of Acuff songs—a few weeks later, Mr. Roy died, and Porter became the de facto leader of the *Opry*, a status he holds most modestly.

On September 26, 1993, the Reunion of Professional Entertainers (R.O.P.E.) awarded him their "Golden Eagle Achievement Award." However, his finest moment may have come in 1994, when Whitney Houston won the Grammy for her version of Dolly Parton's *I Will Always Love You*. Dolly began writing love songs at Porter's urging in 1973, and he predicted that *I Will Always Love You* would earn her more than anything she had written—and it has. SE

RECOMMENDED ALBUMS:

"Satisfied Mind" (RCA Victor)(1956)
"Porter Wagoner and Skeeter Davis Sing Duets" (RCA Victor)(1962)
"The Blue Grass Story" (RCA Victor)(1965)
"Grand Ole Gospel" (RCA Victor)(1966) [With the Blackwood Brothers]
"On the Road—The Porter Wagoner Show" (RCA Victor)(1966) [With Norma Jean, Speck Rhodes, et al.]
"Confessions of a Broken Man" (RCA Victor)(1966)
"Soul of a Convict and Other Great Prison Songs" (RCA Victor)(1967)
"The Cold, Hard Facts of Life" (RCA Victor)(1967)
"Green, Green Grass of Home" (RCA Victor)(1967)
"The Carroll County Accident" (RCA Victor)(1969)
"You Got-ta Have a License" (RCA Victor)(1970)
"What Ain't to Be, Just Might Happen" (RCA Victor)(1972)
"The Farmer" (RCA Victor)(1973)
"We Found It" (RCA Victor)(1973) [With Dolly Parton]
"Porter 'n' Dolly" (RCA Victor)(1974) [With Dolly Parton]
"Porter" (RCA Victor)(1977)
"Porter Wagoner Today" (RCA Victor)(1979)
"Viva Porter Wagoner" (Warner Brothers/Viva)(1983)
"Porter Wagoner" (MCA/Dot)(1986)
"Porter Wagoner: The Thin Man from the [sic] West Plains, 1952-1962" (Bear Family Germany)(1993) [With booklet by Dale Vinicur]

FRANK WAKEFIELD

(Mandolin, Singer, Songwriter, Guitar, Banjo, Fiddle, Bass, Autoharp, Harmonica, Dobro)

Given Name:	**Franklin Delano Wakefield**
Date of Birth:	**June 26, 1934**
Where Born:	**Emory Gap, Tennessee**
Married:	**Patricia**
Children:	**Pamela, Patricia, Gregory, Karen**

Frank Wakefield is a Bluegrass mandolin virtuoso who is one of the funniest men in music. He isn't a comedian, but his trick of "reverse" talking has most people either rolling around or infuriated. For example, if one rang him, he would pick up the telephone and say "Goodbye" and then follow with "You're glad I phoned me."

Frank's antecedents are Irish on his mother's side and Cherokee on his father's. His mother's family all played fiddle and she was a singer. He started playing harmonica at age 6 and guitar at 8 and bass from as early as he can remember. He initially played in church and did so until he was 16. Then in 1950, the family moved from Tennessee to Dayton, Ohio. That year, Frank began playing mandolin and with his guitar-playing brother, Ralph, formed the Wakefield Brothers, playing religious material. The following year they debuted on WHIO Dayton, Ohio.

Ralph began playing saxophone and the duo split up. Frank began working with evangelists who incorporated snake handling in their "presentation." They also included raising someone from the dead. Unfortunately, while in a tent show in Chillicothe, Ohio, in 1952, the man in the coffin started to suffocate and lifted the lid and freaked out the audience, who tore down the tent.

Later that year, while sitting on his front porch playing mandolin, Frank was approached by Red Allen and the two formed a partnership, as Red Allen and Frank Wakefield and the Kentuckians. This partnership would, with interruptions, go on until 1972. That year, Frank added playing banjo to his skills. In 1953, Frank wrote *New Camptown Races,* and this was the top-side of their first single for Detroit label Wayside that year, with another Wakefield song, *Leave Well Enough Alone*, on the flip. That year, Frank added yet another instrument to his arsenal when he began playing Dobro.

In 1957, Frank and Red recorded *Love and Wealth/You Will Always Be Untrue*, for BMC Records. That year, Frank played with Jimmy Martin in Detroit. It was about this time that Frank was failed for military service because at that point he couldn't read or write. These skills he would master when he was age 28.

Frank moved to Washington, D.C., in 1960, and Red followed. Among their musicians in D.C. was banjo genius Bill Keith. One of Frank's mandolin students was David Grisman, who at age 17 produced an album for Frank and Red for Folkways, in 1962. That year Frank and Red recorded an album with Scotty Stoneman of the Stoneman Family.

In 1965, Frank joined the Greenbriar Boys, who were by then recording for Vanguard. Frank had a hand in two of the songs they recorded. *Different Drum* was arranged by him, and he wrote *Up to My Neck in Muddy Water*. Both of these songs provided the initial charts singles for Linda Ronstadt with the Stone Poneys, in 1967.

Frank left the Greenbriar Boys in 1970 and formed Country Classics and Good Ol' Boys. In 1971, Frank recorded the album ***The Frank Wakefield Band*** for Rounder Records. In 1974, with Don Reno, Jerry Garcia, Dave Nelson and Chubby Wise, Frank recorded ***Pistol Packin' Mama***, for United Artists. The album was released the following year credited to Frank Wakefield and Dave Nelson & the Good Ol' Boys. However, it was soon withdrawn over a financial wrangle and was re-released in 1993 on the Grateful Dead label.

In 1975, Frank formed the Frank Wakefield Band, and this outfit still operates. Relic Records released some older tracks of Frank's in 1993 as ***She's No Angel***. As of 1994, Frank was playing and teaching, utilizing video as an educational tool. In June that year, he was playing occasional twin mandolins with Bill Monroe and "teaching Bill how to play." Frank's early ambition was to be "the world's greatest mandolin player," and he could just qualify, having played Beethoven with Leonard Bernstein and the New York Symphony at Carnegie Hall.

RECOMMENDED ALBUMS:

"Red Allen and Frank Wakefield—Bluegrass" (Folkways)(1964)
"The Frank Wakefield Band" (Rounder)(1971)
"Frank Wakefield & the Good Ol' Boys" (Flying Fish)(1978)
"She's No Angel" (Relic)(1993)
"Frank Wakefield and Dave Nelson & the Good Ol' Boys" (Grateful Dead)(1993)
"Blue Stay Away from Me" (Takoma)

JIMMY WAKELY

(Singer, Songwriter, Guitar, Piano, Bass, Harmonica, Actor)

Given Name: **James Clarence Wakely**
Date of Birth: **February 16, 1914**
Where Born: **Mineola, Arkansas**
Married: **Inez Miser**
Children: **Deanna, Carol, Linda, John**
Date of Death: **September 23, 1982**

Jimmy Wakely ranks as one of the best vocalists among the Hollywood singing cowboys. Wakely also had some of the earliest and most successful crossover hits in the post-WWII era. His duets with Pop songstress Margaret Whiting also started a brief trend in pairing Country and popular artists on record.

Born poor and raised in Arkansas and Oklahoma, Jimmy learned to love the music of Jimmie Rodgers and then Milton Brown. He developed both piano and guitar skills and sang both in Pop and Country styles. For some time in early adulthood, Wakely operated a service station and worked various part-time musical jobs in and around Oklahoma City. Finally, he landed a position at radio station WKY with the Bell Trio, ultimately composed of Johnny Bond, Scotty Harrell and himself.

In May 1940, Wakely, Bond and Dick Reinhart went to California, where they went to work on Gene Autry's *Melody Ranch* network radio show in September. Over the next five years, Wakely had some thirty-four sides released on the Decca label, including initial waxings of *I Wonder Where You Are Tonight*, *Cimarron (Roll On)*, a fine cover of Elton Bitt's *There's a Star Spangled Banner Waving Somewhere* and in 1944, his first record on the Country charts, *I'm Sending You Red Roses* (Top 3).

In the meantime, Wakely appeared in small film roles ranging from backup musician in various cowboy movies, starting with *Saga of Death Valley*, in 1939, with Roy Rogers, to a bigger one in Slim Summerville's low-budget hillbilly comedy *I'm from Arkansas*. He and his band appeared with Johnny Mack Brown and Charles Starrett as Jimmy Wakely's Rough Riders and with Brown, William Boys and Charles Starrett as the Jimmy Wakely Trio (with Johnny Bond and Dick Reinhart. Reinhart left in 1942 and was replaced by Scotty Harrell).

These bit parts paved the way for his own starring series at Monogram beginning with *Song of the Range* in January 1945. The Wakely Westerns ran to twenty-eight titles and lasted for five years. Former *Grand Ole Opry* and minstrel comedian Lee "Lasses" White served as sidekick in the first twelve,

Singing cowboy ***Jimmy Wakely***

and future *Hee Haw* funny man Dub Taylor in the remainder. Both critics and Wakely considered *Song of the Sierras*, in 1945, his strongest picture. He later believed that a misguided attempt to downplay the music and upgrade the action proved harmful to the series. Still, in the final count, only Autry, Rogers and Ritter starred in more musical westerns. (See Movie Section.)

In 1947, Jimmy Wakely switched over to Capitol for his recordings, and most of his hits came out on that label. He returned to the Top 10 with *Signed, Sealed and Delivered*, in 1948. He then followed up with two of the most successful records of the postwar decade. His version of Eddie Dean's *One Has My Name (The Other Has My Heart)* reached No.1 for 11 weeks out of 8 months on the Country chart and crossed over to the Pop Top 10. This was followed to the top by the Floyd Tillman song *I Love You So Much It Hurts,* which stayed in that position for 5 weeks and crossed to just below the Top 20 on the Pop lists. He closed the year with the Top 10 single *Mine All Mine*.

His solo hits in 1949 were the Top 10 singles *Forever More* and *Till the End of the World*, the Top 5 release *I Wish I Had a Nickel* and the flip-side, *Someday You'll Call My Name*, which went Top 10. A few months later his cover of Tillman's *Slipping Around*, done in duet with Margaret Whiting, spent 17 weeks at the top and became No.1 on the Pop lists as well. The flip-side, *Wedding Bells*, also went Top 10 on the Country chart and Top 30 on the Pop list. They finished the year with *I'll Never Slip Around Again*, which reached the Top 3 on the Country chart and Top 10 Pop.

Jimmy's solo successes in 1950 were *Peter Cottontail* and *Mona Lisa*, while his chart duets with Margaret Whiting were the double-sided Top 3 release *Broken Down Merry-Go-Round/The Gods Were Angry With Me* and the Top 3 *Let's Go to Church (Next Sunday Morning)*. Their other Top 10 single was *A Bushel and a Peck*.

Jimmy's final chart singles were in 1951 and were the Top 10 *My Heart Cries for You* and a composition by his movie fiddler, Arthur Smith, *Beautiful Brown Eyes*, on which he was joined by the Les Baxter Chorus and which went Top 5. Jimmy also had his final successes with Margaret Whiting, which were *When You and I Were Young Maggie Blues* (Top 10) and *I Don't Want to Be Free* (Top 5).

Jimmy Wakely signed with Coral Records in 1953 and in 1955 to its parent label, Decca. Although he had no more major hits, his material continued to do well, especially an excellent album of cowboy songs cut in 1956. Except for a pair of albums for Dot in 1966, he recorded for Decca through 1970. Wakely remained active in personal appearances throughout this period, even developing a fine night club act.

As his friend Wesley Tuttle once observed, Jimmy had a voice similar to Bing Crosby's, which made him appealing to a broad audience. From 1952 until 1958, he also had a CBS network radio program, one of the last of its type. In later years, Wakely started his own record company, Shasta. Although he cut some new material, the preserved tapes from his radio programs provided a valuable repository from which to draw.

In addition to several of his own albums, Shasta released material by other Western performers including Eddie Dean, Tex Ritter, Rex Allen, Johnny Bond, and Merle Travis. Jimmy also did some radio programming for foreign markets in his later years. His son, John Wakely, also had something of a singing career, cutting an album for Decca in 1969.

IMT

RECOMMENDED ALBUMS:

"Santa Fe Trail" (Decca)(1956)
"Enter, Rest and Pray" (Decca)(1957)
"Slipping Around" (Dot)(1966)
"I'll Never Slip Around Again" (Pickwick/Hilltop)(1967) [Capitol masters]
"Heartaches" (Decca)(1969)
"A Cowboy Serenade" (Tops)
"Now and Then" (Decca)(1970)
"Big Country Songs" (Vocalion)(1970)
"Jimmy Wakely Country" (Shasta)(1971)
"Blue Shadows" (Coral)(1973)
"Jimmy Wakely Family Show" (Shasta)(1973)

"Jimmy Wakely on Stage" (Shasta)(1974)
"The Jimmy Wakely CBS Radio Show" (Shasta)(1975)
"The Singing Cowboy" (Shasta)(1975)
"Western Swing and Pretty Things" (Shasta)(1975)
"The Early Transcriptions" (Danny)(ca. 1980)

CLIFF WALDRON

(Singer, Songwriter, Guitar)
Given Name: **Clifford Waldron**
Date of Birth: **April 4, 1941**
Where Born: **Jolo, West Virginia**
Married: **Brenda**
Children: **Beverly Arleen**

In the late 60's and early 70's, Cliff Waldron, first in partnership with banjo picker Bill Emerson and then as leader of the New Shades of Grass, ranked as a major innovative force in the evolution of progressive Bluegrass. As a powerful lead vocalist, Cliff pioneered in adapting both songs of contemporary Country and Rock origin, such as *Fox on the Run* and *Proud Mary,* into the idiom. Later he turned to Bluegrass-Gospel and recorded a pair of fine albums before going into other lines of work.

A native of Jolo, near the southern border of West Virginia, Cliff received his early musical training in a local band called the Southern Ramblers, which had a radio show at WNRG Grundy, Virginia. In 1963, Waldron came to Washington, D.C. to practice his barbering skills and soon became involved on the local Bluegrass scene with a group called the Page Valley Boys. He formed the Lee Highway Boys in 1966 with banjo picker Bill Emerson. Over the next four years the Lee Highway Boys cut three albums, with the first one titled ***New Shades of Grass***, an indicator of their direction. Their Bluegrass adaptation of the 1966 pop hit *If I Were a Carpenter* was the only real zinger, but their second album contained both *Fox on the Run* and *Proud Mary*, and had the most impact. By the time their third release hit the record shop, the group had dissolved, with Bill joining the Country Gentlemen in May 1970 and Cliff, the Shenandoah Cut-Ups.

Cliff Waldron and the New Shades of Grass

After only a few weeks, Cliff reformed the Lee Highway Boys as the New Shades of Grass, securing Ben Eldridge as banjo picker, taking Ed Ferris from the Country Gentlemen, and reclaiming Mike Auldridge on Dobro and fiddler Bill Poffinberger from his earlier band. Almost immediately, Cliff and his band became festival favorites and turned out a string of albums on Rebel that reflected the group's progressive focus while retaining a healthy respect for tradition. One album, ***Bluegrass Time***, contained strictly traditional numbers, half of them associated with the Stanley Brothers. Following the departure of Auldridge and Eldridge for the Seldom Scene in November 1971, several noted musicians loaned their talents to the New Shades of Grass, with the late tragic genius Jimmy Arnold and Japanese mandolin picker Akira Otsuka being among the best known.

Cliff Waldron had a conversion experience on January 12, 1975, and thereafter edged more in the direction of Gospel music, which made up the contents of his final two Rebel albums recorded in 1976 and 1977. In recent years, Cliff has been musically inactive, working as a park ranger, and still makes his home in the Virginia suburbs of Washington, D.C. The summer of 1994 found him recuperating from a recent illness. IMT

RECOMMENDED ALBUMS:
"Right On" (Rebel)(1971)
"Traveling Light" (Rebel)(1971)
"Just a Closer Walk with Thee" (Rebel)(1972)
"One More Step" (Rebel)(1972)
"One More Mile, One More Town, One More Time" (Rebel) (1973)
"Bluegrass Time" (Rebel)(1973)
"Cliff Waldron and the New Shades of Grass" (Rebel)(1974)
"Gospel" (Rebel)(1976)
"God Walks the Dark Hills" (Rebel)(1978)
Emerson and Waldron:
"New Shades of Grass" (Rebel)(1968)
"Bluegrass Country" (Rebel)(1969)
"Bluegrass Session" (Rebel)(1970)

BILLY WALKER

(Singer, Songwriter, Guitar)
Given Name: **Billy Marvin Walker**
Date of Birth: **January 14, 1929**
Where Born: **Ralls, Texas**
Married: **1. Kay ("Boots") (div.)**
2. Sylvia Dean Smith (div.)
3. Betty
Children: **Tina, Marie, Kelly (the Walker Sisters), Judy Deana, Lina, July**

Billy Walker, who was at one time known as "the Traveling Texan, the Masked Singer of Country Songs," has become one of Country music's most respected stars. Anyone who has met him will confirm that he is not only a gentleman but also a gentle man. This was never more in evidence than at 1989's Wembley Country Music Festival, in England. Having wowed the audience with his performance, he was unceremoniously called from the stage by an over-officious stage manager. The audience went mad, and Boxcar Willie informed promoter Mervyn Conn that unless Billy reappeared during his set, then he, Boxcar, would not go on. Billy, with the utmost dignity, sang an encore "not for Mervyn Conn, not for Boxcar Willie, but for you, the fans." He sang *The Old Rugged Cross.* For Billy is a deeply religious man, whose hand has been given, on many occasions, to those who need it. A born again Christian, Billy's "bus station" is the Rev. Eddie Cunningham.

Billy's early life was a series of moves from town to town, during the Great Depression. When he was age 13, his father gave him a dime to see a Gene Autry movie; Billy was hooked. He bought a cheap guitar and a 25-cent instruction book, from his earnings plucking chickens for his uncle. In 1944, Billy won a talent competition (winning a chocolate cake and $3.00), which led to an unpaid job on a show on KICA Clovis, New Mexico. He hitched 90 miles each way to play this gig, while also completing his school work. After leaving high school, Billy joined a Texas-based band and then formed his own trio.

In 1949, he joined the *Big D Jamboree* from KRLD Dallas, as the aforementioned Traveling Texan. From there, he went on to join the *Ranch Time Show*, out of Waco, later that year. He began his recording career when he signed with Capitol Records, where his first release was *Heading for Heartaches*, in 1949. He stayed with the label until 1951, but neither his debut single nor the subsequent three releases made the charts.

Things started happening for Billy when he was asked to join KWFT's *Barn Dance*, in 1951. He stayed with the show until 1952, when he became a member of the prestigious *Louisiana Hayride*, out of KWKH Shreveport. He remained on the show until 1955, during which time he toured with established hands such as Hank Thompson and Hank Williams and some of the newer boys, including Faron Young, Webb Pierce and the up-and-coming Elvis Presley. In fact, Billy headlined Elvis' first show in Memphis, at the Overton Band Shell. He was still with the Hayride when Elvis debuted on the show. Interestingly, he also shared studio time with another rock'n'roller, Buddy Holly.

Billy was signed to Columbia Records in 1954, and by the summer of that year, he had chalked up his first chart entry, *Thank You for Calling*, which reached the Top 10. Between 1955 and 1958, Billy was a member of Red Foley's *Ozark Jubilee*, out of Springfield, Missouri, and during that time, he failed to chart any of his releases, including a pair of duets with Jeanette Hicks. It was not until 1957 that he made his next trip to the charts, when *On My Mind Again* reached the Top 15. In 1960, Billy became a member of the *Grand Ole Opry* and that year, he again returned to the charts, with the Top 20 hit *I Wish You Love*. It would be another year before he would chart, this time with Willie Nelson's *Funny How Time Slips Away*, which just made the Top 25.

It was not until 1962 that Billy could really say he had arrived. His single *Charlie's Shoes* reached No.1, and hung around the charts for over five months. From then on, he was a constant occupier of a chart berth. He followed up with the Top 5 record *Willie the Weeper*, to wrap up the year. Both his chart records in 1963, *Heart, Be Careful* and *The Morning Paper*, finished in the Top 30. The following year, Billy had two major hits in *Circumstances/It's Lonesome* and a single that is still one of his most popular, the Western-flavored *Cross the Brazos at Waco* (Top 3), which crossed over to the lower regions of the Pop lists. 1965 was his final year with Columbia and he started out the year with the wonderful *Matamoros*, which went Top 10 and the Top 20 *If It Pleases You/I'm So Miserable Without You*.

During the mid-60's, Billy appeared on many major TV shows, including the *Jimmy Dean Show* and the *Tonight Show*. He also appeared in two movies, *Second Fiddle to a Steel Guitar* and *Red River Roundup*. In 1966, he changed labels and signed with Monument. That year, he had two Top 3 singles, *A Million and One*, which stayed at No.2 for 4 weeks, and *Bear with Me a Little Longer*. The following year, Billy had *Anything Your Heart Desires* (Top 10) and two Top 20 records, *In Del Rio* and *I Taught Her Everything She Knows*. He stayed with Monument until 1970 and racked up even more hits: 1968: *Sundown Mary* (Top 20), *Ramona* (Top 10) and *Age of Worry* (Top 20); 1969: *From the Bottle to the Bottom* (Top 20), *Smoky Places* (Top 15) and *Thinking 'Bout You Babe* (Top 10); 1970: *Darling Days* (Top 25).

Billy signed with MGM Records and his record success stepped up a gear. His first two

The gentle man from Texas, ***Billy Walker***

releases, *When a Man Loves a Woman (The Way That I Love You)* and *She Goes Walking Through My Mind*, both went Top 3. He stayed with MGM until 1974, and his major hits on the label were *I'm Gonna Keep on Keep on Lovin' You* (Top 3), *It's Time to Love Her, Don't Let Him Make a Memory Out of Me* and *Traces of a Woman* (all 1971), *Gone (Our Endless Love)* and the Top 3 single *Sing Me a Love Song to Baby* (both 1972). Billy was voted by *Billboard* as one of the Top 20 most played artists for 20 years, 1950-1970.

During the 70's, Billy, along with his backing group, the Tennessee Walkers, had their own syndicated show, *Country Music Carousel*. In 1975, Billy again changed labels, this time to RCA Victor. He remained on the label until the end of 1976 and chalked up some more big hits. In 1975, there was the Top 10 release *Word Games*, which was followed by *If I'm Losing You* and *Don't Stop in My World (If You Don't Mean to Stay)*, both in 1976. He did more label hopping in 1977, but his releases on Casino and MRC yielded no major hits, the most successful being his duet with Brenda Kaye Perry *Ringgold Georgia* (1977) and *Carlena and José Gomez* (1978). During 1978, he moved on to Scorpion and a year later, he moved on to Caprice, where he made the Top 50 with the 1980 single *You Turn My Love Light On*. That same year, Billy joined forces with Barbara Fairchild for the album ***It Takes Two***, from which they had two low-level chart singles.

From 1981 on, Billy appeared on several labels including Dimension, EMH (an album mainly written by Ray Pennington), Heritage Sound, his own Tall Texan, Erika and Dot/MCA. His last chart entry (to date) was in 1986, when the Tall Texan release *Wild Texas Rose* reached the Top 80. In 1988, k.d. lang had a hit with *Down to My Last Cigarette*, a song written by Billy and Harlan Howard.

Although the hits are no longer there, Billy remains very popular, especially in Europe, where he has appeared at all of the major festivals and where he has one of the finest fan club organizations in Country music. He has been a member of the *Grand Ole Opry* for over thirty years, and judging by the audience reaction, he will be there to entertain for many years to come. Billy once told the writer that "in Country music there are a lot of good singers, but not that many entertainers." Mr. Walker is both a good singer and an excellent entertainer.

RECOMMENDED ALBUMS:

"Billy Walker's Greatest Hits" (Columbia)(1963)
"Billy Walker's Greatest Hits, Vol. 2" (Columbia)(1969)
"Billy Walker's Greatest Hits" (Monument)(1972)
"The Billy Walker Show" (MGM)(1973)
"Lovin' and Losin'" (RCA Victor)(1975)
"It Takes Two" (Paid)(1980) [With Barbara Fairchild]
"How Great Thou Art" (Tall Texan)(1981) [Religious]
"Billy Walker" (Dot/MCA)(1986)

CHARLIE WALKER

(Singer, Songwriter, Guitar, Sports Broadcaster)

Date of Birth:	**November 2, 1926**
Where Born:	**Copeville, Collin County, Texas**
Married:	**Shirley**
Children:	**Art, Ronnie, Carrie Lucinda**

Charlie Walker is one of the few singers from the 50's whose voice is still as good forty years later as it was back then. It was with one song, Harlan Howard's *Pick Me Up on Your Way Down*, that Charlie entered Country music immortality. However, he is a man with other talents. He is an excellent golfer and a well-respected golfing broadcaster.

Charlie grew up on a cotton farm in Nevada, Texas, just north of Dallas. He found great support from his father, who encouraged him to play music. In 1943, while still at high school, Charlie played some bookings with the Western Swing group Bill Boyd & the Cowboy Ramblers, alongside Cousin Herald Goodman, Hal Horton and Gus Foster. That same year, he also became a deejay on KIOX Bay City, Texas.

In 1944, Charlie joined the service and served in Japan. He became a deejay on American Radio Forces Network and presented a Country music show. On release from the service, in 1946, he settled in San Antonio, Texas, and joined KMAC. For ten years, he was listed in *Billboard* as one of the Top 10 Country deejays in the U.S.

At the end of 1965, his singing came to the attention of Decca Records, and his 1966 single *Only You, Only You* reached the Top 10 on the Country chart. By the end of the year, he had switched to Columbia, and came up with his biggest hit, *Pick Me Up on Your Way Down*, which climbed to No.2, where it stayed for 4 weeks, kept off the top by Ray Price's monster *City Lights*. He stayed with Columbia until 1961, chalking up hits with *I'll Catch You When You Fall* (Top 20) *and When My Conscience Hurts the Most* (Top 25) (both 1959), *Who'll Buy the Wine* (Top 15, 1960) and *Facing the Wall* (Top 30, 1961).

He then moved over to Columbia's sister label, Epic, in 1964, and his biggest successes were *Close All the Honky Tonks* (Top 20, 1964), *Wild As a Wildcat* (Top 10) and *He's a Jolly Good Fellow* (both 1965), *The Man in the Little White Suit* (1966), *The Town That Never Sleeps, Don't Squeeze My Sharon* (Top 10) and *I Wouldn't Take Her to a Dogfight* (all 1967), *San Diego* (1968) and *Moffett, Oklahoma* (1969). In 1970, he had a minor hit with his version of the Rolling Stones' *Honky Tonk Women*. In 1967, he became a member of the *Grand Ole Opry*.

Charlie became very popular in Las Vegas, as a singer and emcee at the Golden Nugget, where he worked twenty-five weeks a year between 1965 and 1967. During 1966, he showed his prowess as a golfer when he won the Music City Pro-Celebrity Tournament in Nashville. He also showed his ability by being in the upper placings in the Sahara Invitational, held annually in Las Vegas. During the 60's, he was commentator on the Texas Open Golf Tournament for CBS-TV's *Wide World of Sports*, on four occasions. During the spring of 1970, he made his debut at the Wembley Festival in England.

Country singer and golfer ***Charlie Walker***

During 1972, Charlie moved on to RCA Victor, but only managed a pair of basement level singles, *I Don't Mind Goin' Under (If It'll Get Me Over You)* (1972) and *Soft Lips and Hard Liquor* (1974). By 1975, he had gone to Capitol, and had a final chart record with this label, entitled *Odds and Ends (Bits and Pieces)*. Like a lot of Country performers, Charlie appeared in one movie, his being Universal's *Country Music*.

Charlie, who headed the first hillbilly band in Japan, is still a crowd pleaser and always well received on the *Grand Ole Opry*, where his affability is a byword. In 1992, he threw his hat into the political arena, when he ran for the Senate primary as a Republican.

RECOMMENDED ALBUMS:

"Charlie Walker's Greatest Hits" (Columbia)(1961)
"Charlie Walker's Greatest Hits" (Epic)(1968)
"Charlie Walker Recorded 'Live' in Dallas, Texas" (Epic) (1969)
"Golden Hits—Charlie Walker" (Plantation)(1978)
"Texas Gold" (Plantation)(1979)

CINDY WALKER

(Songwriter, Singer, Guitar, Dancer)
Where Born: Mexia, Texas

It was master songwriter Harlan Howard who described Cindy Walker as "the greatest living songwriter of Country music." This was not idle flattery. Cindy Walker has for over 50 years been a writer whose songs not just Country artists want to record.

There was songwriting in her blood, as her grandfather, Prof. F.L. Eiland, was a famed hymnist whose credits include *Hold to God's Unchanging Hands*. Initially, Cindy's talent lay in other quarters. By the time she was age 7, she sang and danced in the *Toy Land Review*. She grew into her teens, dancing and playing guitar. By the time she was 16, she was dancing at Billy Rose's Casa De Mañana in Fort Worth. She had begun writing and she wrote *Casa De Mañana* as the theme for the show. It was then played by celebrated bandleader Paul Whiteman on a nationwide radio show.

In 1941, she traveled with her father, a cotton buyer, to Los Angeles on a business trip. Cindy had written a song called *Lone Star Trail* and was determined that she was going to pitch it while in L.A. They were about to drive past Bing Crosby's office when she marched in and against all odds saw Larry Crosby, Bing's brother. He listened to her sing the song, accompanied by her piano-playing mother, Oree (who was her loyal accompanist until her death, in 1991) and asked Cindy to demo it. As a result, Bing recorded the song. While demoing the song, Dave Kapp of Decca

One of Country music's finest writers, ***Cindy Walker***

Records (later of Kapp Records) heard Cindy singing and signed her to a recording contract.

Also in 1941, she made her first Soundie, of the song *Seven Beers With the Wrong Man*. She made a one-week visit to the Country charts at No.5, with the single *When My Blue Moon Turns to Gold Again*, strangely, not one of her songs. That same year, she started a close working relationship with Bob Wills. It was determination that got her together with Wills. She had seen his bus in Hollywood, and painstakingly contacted all the hotels in town to find the "King of Western Swing."

A week after meeting her, Wills recorded five of her songs, including *You're From Texas* (a 1944 Top 3 hit), *Cherokee Maiden*, *Don't Count Your Chickens* and *Dusty Skies*. Her relationship with Wills would go on for many years. In all she wrote some fifty songs for Wills, often with Wills himself, including thirty-nine for his movies. These included *Can It Be Wrong* (1946), *Sugar Moon* (1947), *Bubbles in My Beer* (1948, Top 5), *New Playboy Rag* (1948), *Warm Red Wine* (1949), *It's the Bottle Talkin'* and *So, Let's Rock* (both 1956), *Born to Love You* (1967) and *It's a Good World* (1969).

From the start, Cindy became a successful writer. She had a Top 5 hit in 1945, when Gene Autry recorded *Silver Spurs (On the Golden Stairs)*. That same year, both Al Dexter and Walt Shrum had major hits with Cindy's *Triflin' Gal*, Al's version going to No.2 and Walt's to No.3. In 1948, Johnny Bond had a Top 10 record with *Oklahoma Waltz*. The following year was busy, with both Margaret Whiting and Sammy Kaye recording *Dime a Dozen*, and Ernest Tubb and Red Foley cutting duets on *Don't Be Ashamed of Your Age* (Top 10) and *Texas vs. Kentucky*. In addition, George Morgan had a Top 5 hit with *I Love Everything About You*, and Ernest Tubb had a

Top 10 solo hit with *Warm Red Wine* (also recorded that year by Bob Wills).

During the 50's, Cindy continued at the same feverish level with one of her classic songs, *Take Me in Your Arms and Love Me*, which became a No.1 Country hit for Eddy Arnold. The song would later be recorded by many Country and Pop artists, including both Les Paul & Mary Ford and Tennessee Ernie Ford, Gladys Knight & the Pips (1967) and Jim Reeves, with overdubbed vocals from Deborah Allen (1980 Country Top 10). In 1952, Hank Snow recorded *The Gold Rush Is Over*, and the following year, Carl Smith had a Top 3 Country hit with *Trademark*.

During 1964, Cindy returned with her family to Mexia, where she based herself. She spent six months of each year in Nashville. That year, she also recorded an album for Monument Records entitled ***Words & Music***. Cindy's 1954 hits included *Thank You for Calling*, Billy Walker's first chart entry, which went Top 10; *Two Glasses, Joe* from Ernest Tubb; and Hank Snow's *The Next Voice You Hear*, which charted in 1955. That year, Ernest Tubb recorded another Cindy Walker song, this time *Answer the Phone*, and Webb Pierce had a No.1 success with *I Don't Care*. In 1956, both Eddy Arnold and Jerry Vale recorded the Walker song *You Don't Know Me*, and Arnold had a Top 10 Country hit with it. Cindy's hits during 1958 were Jim Reeves' recording of *Anna Marie*, which reached the Country Top 3, Ernest Tubb & the Wilburn Brothers' Top 10 get-together on *Hey Mr. Bluebird*, and Pat Boone's Top 5 Pop hit *Sugar Moon*.

Cindy's major covers during the 60's were: 1960: *China Doll* by the Ames Brothers (Top 40 Pop); 1961: Top 30 Country hit for *(Jim) I Wore a Tie Today;* a Top 30 Country hit from Eddy Arnold and Shirley Collie's *Dime a Dozen*; 1962: *China Doll* by George Hamilton IV (Top 30), *Leona* by Stonewall Jackson, *A Letter to My Heart* by Jim Reeves and *You Don't Know Me* by Ray Charles. In addition, Roy Orbison had a Top 5 Pop hit with another Cindy Walker song that would become a classic, *Dream Baby (How Long Must I Dream)*. Other successful versions of this song have included Glen Campbell in 1971, when it went Top 10 Country and reached No.31 on the Pop charts, and Lacy J. Dalton's 1983 Country Top 10 hit.

The other major covers of the 60's were *Flyin' South* (Hank Locklin) and *Not That I Care* (the Wilburn Brothers, both in 1963), Jerry Wallace's 1964 Top 20 Pop hit, *In the Misty Moonlight*, and *This Is It*, Jim Reeves' 1965 posthumous No.1. The following year, another Walker song, *Distant Drums*, became a further Reeves posthumous No.1, and crossed over to No.45 on the Pop charts. It also became a 5-week No.1 in the UK. Jerry Wallace also had a Country hit that year with *Not That I Care*.

Her 1967 covers included *Fifteen Days* from Wilma Burgess and *In the Misty Moonlight* by Dean Martin. The following year, Jimmy Newman had a Top 20 record in *Born to Love You*, Sonny James had a No.1 with *Heaven Says Hello*, as did Jack Green with *You Are My Treasure*, and both Tex Ritter and Wes Buchanan had basement hits with *T-E-X-A-S* and *Warm Red Wine*, respectively.

In 1970, she became a charter inductee to the Nashville Songwriters Hall of Fame. During the 70's she had further covers with *Flyin' South* from Hank Locklin (a re-recording by him) & Danny Davis and the Nashville Brass and *You Don't Know Me* by Ray Pennington (both 1970). Pennington recorded his version of *Bubbles in My Beer* the following year. George Morgan released his rendition of *In the Misty Moonlight* in 1975. Cindy returned to the No.1 slot when Merle Haggard charted the old Bob Wills hit *Cherokee Maiden*. That year, the Charlie Daniels Band had a Top 40 record with their version of *T-E-X-A-S*. Cindy had two other chart records that decade, with *Leona* by Johnny Russell (1978) and *Lorelei* by Sonny James (1979).

Mickey Gilley took *You Don't Know Me*, which had already had two chart versions, and turned it into a No.1 in 1981. The following year, Ricky Skaggs also topped the charts with *I Don't Care*, which had already enjoyed a No.1 slot through Webb Pierce. Karen Brooks took *Born to Love You* and had a Top 40 hit with it.

During her long career, Cindy has written a hymn book titled *Of Thee We Sing*. She also wrote the theme songs and music for the Billy Graham motion pictures *Mr. Texas* and *Oil Town, USA*. In 1990 and 1991, Cindy was inducted into the Western Swing Hall of Fame in Arizona, California and Texas. She is also the recipient of the "Golden Guitar Award" from the Texas Music Association. Cindy's song *You Don't Know Me* was performed by Meryl Streep in the movie *Postcards from the Edge*, in 1990. In addition, Cindy's song *Christian Cowboy* was featured in the production of *Smoke on the Water*, which was on Broadway in 1990 and 1991.

Cindy spent recent years looking after her mother, until Oree Walker died in 1991. Cindy is a very private person, and in recent years has suffered ill health. She is still very aware of what is happening in Country music and is complimentary about contemporary Country, especially the instrumentation aspect.

RECOMMENDED ALBUM:

"Words & Music" (Monument)(1964)

CLAY WALKER

(Singer, Songwriter, Guitar)

Where Born: Beaumont, Texas

A Beaumont, Texas, native, Clay Walker says he grew up playing the bars from the time he was 16. He was raised in a poor family, on a farm, surrounded with rice fields and woods. As a child, he fished in the bayou and rode bicycles. Walker admits to a certain amount of insecurity concerning his background. "When I reflect back on my childhood, those are things I remember and those are the things that can still make me emotional," he said. "When you become an adult there are less and less things that affect you in that way. When I can still get emotional about those days, it lets me know Clay hasn't changed."

Signed to Giant Records, he leapt into the Country music scene with his 1993 single *What's It to You*, which hit No.1 on the Country chart, crossing over to make the Top 75 on the Pop chart. The following year, he had his second No.1 with *Live Until I Die*. Both singles were from his self-titled Certified Gold debut album, which made the Top 10 Country Album Chart and the Top 60 Pop Album Chart.

His current single, *Where Do I Fit In* (1994), went Top 10. Walker considers himself

One of the hottest acts of the 90's, ***Clay Walker***

a loner and enjoys what he does. In an earlier interview, Walker said, "You can't find a person who enjoys living more than I do. For the most part I try to make everybody happy, and I'm trying to live life to its fullest like my song, *Live Until I Die*. That song fits me better than anything I've ever written or heard." Walker shares manager Erv Woolsey with singer George Strait and credits Strait's longevity to Woolsey's expertise. Walker has toured with Strait and expects to play more dates with him in the future. LAP

RECOMMENDED ALBUM:

"Clay Walker" (Giant)(1993)

JERRY JEFF WALKER

(Singer, Songwriter, Guitar)

Given Name:	**Ronald Clyde Crosby**
Date of Birth:	**March 16, 1942**
Where Born:	**Oneonta, New York**
Married:	**Susan**
Children:	**Jessie Jane, Django Cody**

Jerry Jeff Walker is one of the most important singer/songwriters in Country music. His influence on writers who followed in his wake is immeasurable.

Born in upstate New York, he adopted his performing name in 1966. As a teenager in the late 50's, he experimented with various musical styles as a member of several local bands. Following high school graduation, Jerry Jeff set out to discover America with guitar in hand, in the tradition of his musical heroes, Jimmie Rodgers, Woody Guthrie and Ramblin' Jack Elliott. Already an accomplished club performer, Jerry Jeff hitchhiked to Florida and then moved on to New Orleans. He paid for his travels by singing in bars and passing his hat.

While performing in New Orleans (using the stage name "Jerry Ferris"), he met street musician Babe Stovall. The veteran performer befriended Jerry Jeff and became an important musical influence. In the summer of 1965, Jerry Jeff was arrested in the city's French Quarter for public intoxication. He was jailed overnight and shared the accommodations with a street singer and dancer who called himself "Bojangles." The colorful character was later immortalized by Jerry Jeff in *Mr. Bojangles*.

After traveling to Texas, Jerry Jeff returned to the East, settling for a time in New York City. He formed the Lost Sea Dreamers, and they became the house band at the Electric Circus night club. After changing the name of the group to Circus Maximus, the band was signed to Vanguard Records in 1967. Following their self-titled debut album, the psychedelic Folk-Rock group released ***Neverland Revisited*** in 1968.

Later that year, Circus Maximus broke up and Jerry Jeff signed with Atco Records. His first solo album released in 1968 was titled ***Mr. Bojangles***. Jerry Jeff was invited to perform at the Newport Folk Festival, and his tale of the New Orleans street dancer began to attract the attention of other artists after repeated broadcasts on a Manhattan radio station. Although Jerry Jeff's version wasn't a major radio hit, only reaching the Top 80 on the Pop chart, it was a Top 10 Pop single for the Nitty Gritty Dirt Band in 1971. The song was eventually recorded by a wide range of artists, from Nilsson to Sammy Davis, Jr., and is considered one of popular music's classic compositions.

In 1969, Jerry Jeff released *Drifting Way of Life*, followed by the albums ***Five Years Gone*** and ***Bein' Free*** in 1970. He moved to Key West, Florida, in 1970 and took up residence in Austin, Texas, the following year. He quickly gained a loyal following and helped establish the city as the center of the emerging progressive Country movement in the mid-70's, with friends Michael Martin Murphey and Willie Nelson.

In 1972, Jerry Jeff began his long association with MCA Records with the release of his self-titled album. Recorded in a primitive Austin studio, the album contains Guy Clark's declaration of independence, *L.A. Freeway*. Jerry Jeff displayed his fine art of storytelling in Charlie Dunn, one of the Lone Star state's best known boot makers.

A dance hall in the tiny town of Luckenbach, Texas, was the location for his ***Viva Terlingua*** album. With accompaniment by the Lost Gonzo Band, the album included Ray Wiley Hubbard's bawdy Texas favorite *Up Against the Wall Redneck Mother*. It became Jerry Jeff's most successful album to date, selling more than 500,000 copies and earning a Gold Album.

Jerry Jeff performed at Willie Nelson's 4th of July Picnic in 1974 and married Susan Streit in December. He also released ***Walkers Collectables*** and in 1975 followed with ***Ridin' High***, his first album recorded partially in Nashville. ***It's a Good Night for Singing*** was released in 1976, and it was followed by the double album ***A Man Must Carry On*** (1977) and ***Contrary to Ordinary*** (1978).

He changed labels later that year and recorded ***Jerry Jeff*** (1978) and ***Too Old to Change*** (1979) for Elektra/Asylum. In 1980, Jerry Jeff returned to MCA and released a trio of albums over the next two years. 1982 marked the end of Jerry Jeff's major label releases with the eclectic ***Cowjazz***. In 1986, he and his wife formed the independent record label Tried & True Music and released ***Gypsy Songman***. The following year, they signed an international distribution agreement with the Rykodisc label.

Jerry Jeff recorded his 1989 ***Live at Gruene Hall*** in Texas' oldest dance hall in the small hill country town of Gruene. Three singles from the album charted Country: *I Feel Like Hank Williams Tonight*, *The Pickup Song* and *Trashy Women* (later a major hit for Confederate Railroad and written by Tried & True artist Chris Wall). Jerry Jeff transformed an Austin television studio into a recording studio for the making of ***Navajo Rug*** in 1990. The album was released in 1991 and MCA released a greatest hits collection entitled ***Great Gonzos***.

Also in 1991, Jerry Jeff hosted a weekly music show, *The Texas Connection* on TNN. The TV program was taped at KLRU-TV in Austin, and Kris Kristofferson and Willie Nelson were Jerry Jeff's guests for his premier show. He hosted a second season of the show in 1992, while working on his ***Hill Country Rain*** album. The album was well received by the critics, and *The Denver Post* suggested that ***Hill Country Rain*** just might be Jerry Jeff's finest album since 1973's live ***Viva Terlingua***. *The Washington Post* included Jerry Jeff Walker on their "In" list for 1993. JIE

RECOMMENDED ALBUMS:

"Viva Terlingua" (MCA)(1973)
"A Man Must Carry On" (double) (MCA)(1977)
"Cowjazz" (MCA)(1982)
"Gypsy Songman" (Rykodisc/Tried & True)(1987)
"Live at Gruene Hall" (Rykodisc/Tried & True)(1989)
"Great Gonzos" (MCA)(1991)
"Hill Country Rain" (Rykodisc/Tried & True)(1992)

JIMMY WALKER

(Singer, Songwriter, Guitar, Guitorgan)

Given Name:	**Earnest Earl Walker**
Date of Birth:	**December 18, 1915**
Where Born:	**Mason County, West Virginia**
Married:	**1. Lena (div.)** **2. Ellen (dec'd.)** **3. Betty (div.)**
Children:	**Richard, Lee, Clifford, Eddie(adopted), Nedra (adopted)**
Date of Death:	**June 27, 1990**

Jimmy Walker sang a fine Honky-Tonk song in a style that could best be described as a cross between Roy Acuff and Jack Guthrie. Today Jimmy is probably best known for introducing the Country standard *Detour* to the musical world.

Walker was born in West Virginia, a few

The Detour man, ***Jimmy Walker***

miles from the river town of Point Pleasant. He claimed descent from Thomas Walker, the legendary figure reputed to have discovered Cumberland Gap. Since his father was killed in WWI, Walker was partially raised by relatives in Pittsburgh. He worked as a riverboatman in the later 30's and entered military service during WWII. On return to civilian life in 1945, he went to the West Coast, where he became active on the local Country music scene.

He signed with the new Coast label and on December 3, 1945, recorded his first sides, *Detour* and *Sioux City Sue*. The former song had been written by Paul Westmoreland, who played steel and furnished the band for the session. It took off quickly and major label artists including Elton Britt, Spade Cooley and Wesley Tuttle covered it.

Walker continued recording on Coast and in 1946 joined the *Grand Ole Opry* for a year as a replacement for Roy Acuff. After that he alternately worked on the *Wheeling Jamboree* and *Midwestern Hayride* before returning to California at the end of the decade.

Back in the Far West, Jim cut a pair of singles for London, and then did a dozen sides for Intro at three sessions in 1951 and 1952. These latter included some of his finest numbers such as *Loving Country Heart, Out of Money, Out of Place and Out of Style* and *Heart Throb*. His recordings all had solid support from musicians like Joe Maphis, Tex Atchison, and Noel Boggs and typify the California Country sound of that era. Walker himself proved a popular figure on the club scene and also did some bit parts in Western films. He had a near brush with stardom when Monogram Pictures considered reviving their "Range Buster" series and cast Jim as one of the three headliners. After making two features, however, studio executives decided not to release them. In 1953, he returned east and after a brief stint with the *Louisiana Hayride* cut a single for MGM in Nashville with support from Chet Atkins, Don Helms and Jerry Rivers. The songs *God Was So Good/Look What Followed Me Home Tonight* probably ranked as his best-known numbers other than *Detour.*

Walker came back to Wheeling later that year and spent more than a decade as a *Jamboree* regular, touring through several states and also working part of that time as a deejay in Pittsburgh. His roving nature then took hold again and he returned to California, where he did more walk-ons and bit parts in such films as *Paint Your Wagon* and TV Westerns such as *Gunsmoke*, which qualified him for a pension.

For some years therafter he worked on the Holiday Inn circuit and other clubs. He did a final record session in 1965, from which a single appeared on his own Walker label. As work opportunities slowed, he retired to his old hometown of Point Pleasant. Old Homestead released a pair of albums containing most of his recordings in the mid-80's. Weakened by cancer in his last months, Jimmy died in the nearby Huntington V.A. Hospital, befriended by Leonard ("Toot") Sergent, a one-time radio musician who had worked with T. Texas Tyler and his wife. IMT

RECOMMENDED ALBUMS:

"Loving Country Heart" (Old Homestead)(1984)
"High Geared Daddy" (Old Homestead)(1986)

LAWRENCE WALKER

(Singer, Songwriter, Accordion)

Given Name:	**Lawrence Walker**
Date of Birth:	**September 1, 1907**
Where Born:	**Nr. Duson, Louisiana**
Married:	**Winnie**
Children:	**Alberta**
Date of Death:	**August 15, 1968**

Ironically, the "King of the Accordion Players," Lawrence Walker, who was one of the most important Cajun musicians during the 1950's, was not a full-bred Cajun. He did, however, speak perfect Cajun-French.

His father, Allen, was a well-known fiddle player. In 1915, Lawrence's family moved from Louisiana to Orange, Texas. While in his teens, he formed the Walker Brothers Band, with his brother Elton, who also played fiddle. This group featured accordion, fiddle and guitar and played both Cajun and hillbilly music. In 1929, this band recorded two numbers, *La Breakdown la Louisiane* and *La Vie Malheureuse*, for Bluebird.

In 1936, Walker appeared to great acclaim at the National Folk Festival, held that year in Dallas, Texas, to coincide with the Texas Centennial. His band won first place in the band contest there, the first of many such prizes Walker was to win. These victories led to his being known as "King of the Accordion Players." During 1936, Walker recorded *What's the Matter Now* and *Alberta* for Bluebird, both of which featured a bluesy, hillbilly quality that was unusual from previous Cajun recordings.

Although earning his living as a rice farmer, Walker kept busy playing music. After WWII he moved back to Louisiana and started performing at venues like the O.S.T. Club in Rayne, the Welcome Club in Crowley, Landry's Palladium near Lafayette and the Jolly Rogers Club in St. Martinville. Despite having an excellent band, the Wandering Aces (which from 1953 through 1958 included Johnny Allen), which featured mostly Cajun-French songs along with a small number of Country-Western numbers and was very popular, it was the early 1950's before he recorded again. These sides, including *Reno Waltz* (which was adapted from a Cajun tune sometimes known as *La Valse De Grand Chenier* and was named after the Reno Dance Hall between Kaplan and Gueydan), *Bosco Stomp* and *Evangeline Waltz*, were waxed for George Khoury's label, Khoury, headquartered in Lake Charles, Louisiana. Walker later recorded for La Louisiane, Vee-Pee and Swallow.

Some of Walker's popularity was due to his perfectionism. He insisted that everyone in his band keep their instruments perfectly tuned, and he gave his bandsmen strict instructions about how loud they should play, the style and general sound they should produce. Most of his popularity, however, was attributable to his good looks, which made him very appealing to women, as well as his expert musicianship and his songs. These were often sad, always melodic and although his favorite theme of lost love was commonplace he dealt with it in a unique way. Whereas other Cajun musicians just pulled lines from old songs, Walker used original imagery.

While painting his house southwest of Rayne, Louisiana, Walker suffered a heart attack while up on a ladder and fell dead to the ground. WKM

RECOMMENDED ALBUMS:

"A Tribute to the Late, Great, Lawrence Walker" (La Louisiane)
"Great Cajun Selections" (La Louisiane)
"A Legend at Last" (Swallow)

Wiley Walker refer WILEY AND GENE

JO WALKER-MEADOR

(Industry Executive)

Given Name: Edith Josephine Denning
Date of Birth: February 16, 1924
Where Born: Orlinda, Tennessee
Married: 1. Charles Walker (dec'd.)
2. Robert Huff Meador
Children: (Mary) Michelle

One of the most crucial events of the coming of age of Country music was the creation of the Country Music Association. Through such programs as the Country Music Hall of Fame the scope of Country music expanded from a small struggling industry with little centralized focus to the huge multi-billion-dollar industry of today that has saturated the far corners of the world. Jo Walker-Meador was a key individual in the direction of the CMA, serving as its Executive Director for some 33 years.

Born Edith Josephine Denning in Orlinda, Tennessee, the daughter of a tobacco farmer, her earliest career ambition was to be a coach. After high school she worked as a secretary at Vultee Aircraft Corporation in Nashville, Tennessee, from 1942-1945. After WWII ended, she attended Lambuth College (1946-48), then Peabody College (1947-48) in Nashville. In 1951, she worked for Crescent Amusement, as Executive Secretary, staying there until 1955. She also worked for the Goodhill Food Corporation and Tennessee gubernatorial candidate G. Edward Friar.

In October 1954 she married Charles Walker, President and General Manager of WKDA radio station in Nashville. Their happy union ended with the death of Walker in a motorcycle accident on Labor Day, 1967. They had one daughter, Michelle. Jo was recommended for the job of Office Manager to the newly formed CMA by close friend Betty Boles in 1958. Betty had also introduced her to her husband Charles Walker.

Jo began with CMA on December 8, 1958, when the organization was struggling to survive, with only 200 members and $2,000 in the bank account. Within a year she had moved up, assuming the title of Executive Director. Almost single-handedly, in those early days, she conducted daily business and helped coordinate plans for its growth. Thanks in part to Jo's persistence, the CMA weathered the depression that hit Country music in the mid-50's. During her years with CMA, and partly through her efforts, the organization established the Country Music Hall of Fame, the annual awards show, Fan Fair and a talent buyers' seminar.

Through the years she merited many awards and certificates for her efforts toward promotion of the music industry. Some of these include: the Metronome Award (1970), Mayoral Award presented to the person who has done the most to further the cause of Country music, Lady Executive of the Year (1981) presented by the Nashville Chapter of the National Association of Women Executives, SESAC Ambassador of Country Music (1981), the BMI Commendation of Excellence (1981), the international Hubert Long Award, the IFCO Tex Ritter Memorial Award, the Jim Reeves Memorial Award in recognition of her role in establishing CMA's London office (1983) and the Erving Waugh Award of Excellence, presented to her by the CMA.

Jo has also been active in local civics, belonging at one time or another to NARAS, the American Cancer Society, the Metropolitan Tourist Commission, the Nashville Chamber of Commerce Board of Governors, the Board of the National Music Council, the Arthritis Foundation, and Travelers Aid, and she was the first woman elected to the Board of Big Brothers of Nashville.

In 1981, Jo married Robert H. Meador, a Nashville businessman. Jo Walker-Meador retired in 1991, having seen the organization through numerous tough times, to what is considered today the world's most active trade organization. LAP

JERRY WALLACE

(Singer, Songwriter, Guitar, Actor)

Date of Birth: December 15, 1928
Where Born: Guilford, Missouri
Married: 1. (Div.)
2. (Div.)
Children: John, Wally

The easy style of ballad singer Jerry Wallace earned him the sobriquet of "Mr. Smooth" (given to him by Hal Atkinson of KWAM-FM Memphis), and for fifteen years his voice graced the Country and Pop charts on a selection of labels.

Jerry was raised in a town with a population of 96. When he was 11, his family moved to Los Angeles. He began to play guitar early on and after serving in the U.S. Navy, he began entering talent contests in the L.A. area. His early idol was Nat "King" Cole. In 1951, he recorded for Allied Records and then became involved in his other love, acting.

With the advent of the rock'n'roll era, Jerry tried his hand at recording again. In 1957, he was signed to Challenge Records and in 1958, he debuted on the Pop chart with *How the Time Flies*, which went Top 15. Although his next two singles bombed, he came back strongly in 1959 with his career single, *Primrose Lane*, which went Top 10. For this single the artist was credited as Jerry Wallace with the Jewels. The song was the theme for Henry Fonda's TV series, *The Smith Family*.

Although Jerry continued to have Pop chart singles on Challenge until 1964, not all of the entries were major hits. The most successful were *Little Coco Palm* (Top 40), *There She Goes* (Top 30) (both 1960), *Shutters and Boards*, which was written by Audie Murphy (Top 25, 1964) and Cindy Walker's *In the Misty Moonlight* (Top 20, 1964). In 1964, Jerry appeared in the movies *Flipper's New Adventure*, for which he wrote the music, and *Goodbye Charlie*, for which he wrote the title song.

In 1964, Jerry moved to Mercury Records and shifted his emphasis away from Pop to Country. He had his first Country hit in 1965 with *Life's Gone and Slipped Away*, which went Top 25. He had three other Country chart singles on the label, *Diamonds and Horseshoes*, *Wallpaper Roses* and *Not That I Care*, all of which made the Top 50. That year, Jerry wrote the introduction song for the movie *Johnny Reno*. In 1967, Jerry moved to Liberty, where his most successful singles were *This One's on the House* (Top 40, 1967) and *Sweet Child of Sunshine* (Top 25, 1968).

At the end of 1970, Jerry signed with Decca (MCA from 1973), and this was to be his golden period. He started with the Top 25 success *After You* in 1971 and that year followed with *The Morning After* (Top 20). He opened his account in 1972 with *To Get to You*, which went Top 15 Country and Top 50 Pop. This was followed by the No.1 Country hit *If You Leave Me Tonight I'll Cry*, which also went Top 40 Pop. The song came from "The Tune in Dan's Cafe," an episode of TV's *Night Gallery*. Jerry closed the year with *Do You Know What It's Like to be Lonesome*, which went Top 3.

Jerry stayed with MCA until 1974 and his major hits were *Sound of Goodbye/The Song Nobody Sings* (Top 25) and *Don't Give up on Me* (Top 3) (both 1973), *Guess Who* (Top 20), *My Wife's House* (Top 10) and *I Wonder Whose Baby (You Are Now)* (Top 20) (all 1974). At the end of 1974, Jerry moved to MGM Records and his principal hits were *Comin' Home to You* (Top 40) and *Wanted Man* (Top 50).

Then Jerry ran into contractual problems that stopped him recording until 1977. He then signed with BMA Records and immediately hit the Country chart with the Top 30 singles *I*

Miss You Already and *I'll Promise You Tomorrow*. In 1978, he had a Top 25 success with *At the End of the Rainbow*. These all came from the album ***I Miss You Already***, the cover of which shows Jerry with silver hair that could rival Charlie Rich as the "Silver Fox." Later that year, Jerry signed with 4 Star Records and had the Top 40 hit *I Wanna Go to Heaven*. The following year, he moved again to Gene Kennedy's Door Knob label and had three chart records, of which the most successful was the Top 60 *Cling to Me*.

As well as his recordings, Jerry has scripted the music for the TV series *Daniel Boone*, *Hec Ramsey* and *The Smith Family*. Jerry still continues to be a draw at the showrooms in Las Vegas. His act incorporates his skill at impersonating famous people.

RECOMMENDED ALBUMS:

"The Best of Jerry Wallace" (Mercury)(1966) [Re-issued on Mercury/Wing (1968)]
"Jerry Wallace" (double)(Challenge)(1972)
"To Get to You" (Decca)(1972) [Re-issued on MCA (1973)]
"Do You Know What It's Like to Be Lonesome" (MCA)(1973)
"Greatest Hits" (MGM)(1975)
"I Miss You Already" (BMA)(1977)
"The Golden Hits of Jerry Wallace" (4 Star)(1978)

FIELDS WARD

(Singer, Musician)

Given Name:	**Fields Mac Ward**
Date of Birth:	**January 23, 1911**
Where Born:	**Buck Mountain, Virginia**
Married:	**Naomi Elsie Todd**
Children:	**Frances and three others**
Date of Death:	**October 26, 1987**

Fields Ward is one of those Country musicians who was better known to folklorists and Folk-song collectors than to typical Country music audiences. Nevertheless, he was an important performer in the Old-Time Virginia style, who was significant as much for his repertoire as for his performances.

It was inevitable that he would be involved with music in some way because both parents, Davy Crockett and Perlina ("Linie") Ward, and his four siblings were musically inclined. Crockett was locally noted for his fiddling and Linie for her ballad singing. Indeed, one of Fields' earliest memories was of his mother's singing, her vocalizing helping to instill in him a lifelong love of such ballads as *Jesse James*. Other than his own family, Ward's two chief influences were Alec "Eck" Dunford and Riley Puckett. Dunford, a local musician primarily noted as a fiddler but also a good guitarist, taught Fields several finger-style guitar pieces and the rudiments of backup guitar. Ward knew Puckett only from his records, but he was nonetheless responsible for much of Fields' guitar technique. Ward listened to Puckett's 78s and assiduously practiced both his songs and guitar runs.

By the mid-1920's, a number of southwestern Virginia performers were making records. In 1927, Fields Ward became, at age 16, a recording artist as well. Along with his father and brothers Current and Sampson, Fields cut several sides for the OKeh label, of which four were released. Even so, most critics consider the OKeh sides unsatisfactory. Much better material was cut in 1929 for the Gennett Record Company. This band, called the Grayson County Railsplitters, consisted of Fields, his brother Sampson, "Eck" Dunford, and Ernest V. Stoneman. Although Ward considered this the best material he ever recorded, for some reason the record company decided not to release any of the sides. This decision was especially surprising because the band spent a week in the recording studio cutting the sixteen sides. The experience embittered Ward, who refused to have anything to do with any record company for almost forty years. The Gennett sides, which included three numbers, *Way Down in North Carolina, Ain't That Trouble in Mind* and *Those Cruel Slavery Days*, that Fields took writer's credits for, were eventually released in the 1960s by Historical Records, a New Jersey-based reissue label.

In the 1930s, Ward worked with the Buck Mountain String Band, which was led by his uncle, Wade Ward, and with a family band, the Bogtrotters, which eventually expanded to include non-family members. This group won numerous prizes at the fiddlers' convention held in Galax in 1935 and were a big hit at the Whitetop Folk Festival that same year. They also came to the attention of northern, urban audiences and between 1937 and 1942, various combinations of the Bogtrotters recorded, in Galax and Washington, D.C., a number of tunes for Alan Lomax at the Library of Congress. In 1940 the band also performed for national broadcast on the CBS *American School of the Air*. John Lair, head of the *Renfro Valley Barn Dance*, heard the broadcast and was sufficiently impressed that he offered Fields a contract, but made it clear that he didn't want the rest of the band. Fields refused to leave the "old fellows" that he was playing with, so that chance at stardom ended.

During WWII, the Bogtrotters broke up and, in 1947, Fields moved to Maryland to manage a dairy farm. After holding several other jobs, Ward became a painter, a trade he followed until retirement. He never completely gave up playing music, although usually just for his own pleasure. In the 1960's, he was "discovered" by the Folk revival audience and, as a result, subsequently recorded albums for Biograph and Rounder. He also found himself on one record unexpectedly. Portions of a show he and his uncle Wade did for a Virginia auction company turned up on a Folkways album. Folkways had not obtained Ward's permission and never offered him payment, an experience that did nothing to lessen his longstanding distrust of record companies.

Although during his years in Maryland he triumphed over early bouts with alcoholism, Ward's last years were beset with health problems, including hypertension, diabetes, ulcers, emphysema, and arthritis. Even so, he did not give up public performances until the 1980s. He also never completely lost his mistrust of record companies and various Folk-song collectors who he thought had not played fair with him and his music. In truth, many of the songs that he claimed as his own, such as *Deadheads and Suckers* and *Riley and Spencer*, were clever combinations of traditional lyrics with original verses. Most of the material he recorded was traditional.

WKM

RECOMMENDED ALBUMS:

"Fields Ward and His Buck Mountain Band" (Historical)
"Bury Me Not on the Prairie" (Rounder)

JACKY WARD

(Singer, Guitar, Impressionist, Deejay)

Date of Birth:	**November 18, 1946**
Where Born:	**Groveton, Texas**
Married:	**Tanya**
Children:	**Darrin, Vaness, Kay**

During the middle 70's through to the beginning of 1980, Jacky Ward looked like he would become a major recording star. However, like Roy Clark, Jerry Reed and Ronnie Prophet, Jacky's problem was that he was too versatile, being not just a singer but also a very talented impressionist and deejay. Among his impersonated "victims" are Elvis Presley, Gabby Hayes, Ernest Tubb, Johnny Cash, Chill Wills, Walter Brennan, John Wayne, the Diamonds and the Platters.

Jacky was born into a musical family and was singing in public by the time he was age 6, and two years later, he sang at a political rally. By the time he was 15, he was already a seasoned performer. When he reached his late teens, he joined the U.S. Army, rising to the rank of sergeant. After he left the service, he returned home and became a salesman by day and a deejay at night. Sometimes, he even played a live date after he had finished deejaying.

Jacky Ward pleasing his audience

The turning point in his career came in 1972, when a friend helped to finance his single *Big Blue Diamond*. It was released on Target and became a regional hit around the Houston area, before breaking out nationally and making the Country charts Top 40. A year later, he appeared on the Mega label with the low-level entry *Dream Weaver*.

Around this time, Jacky, with his electrifying stage act, was in demand playing casinos in Las Vegas, as well as clubs around the U.S. At the end of 1974, he signed with Mercury Records, and the following year, he had a Top 50 success with *Stealin'* and a Top 40 with *Dance Here By Me (One More Time)*. He was still looking for that elusive major hit and through the next two years, his successes were *I Never Said It Would Be Easy* (1976) and *Texas Angel* (1977). In the fall of 1977, he had his first Top 10 single, *Fools Fall in Love*.

His next release, in 1978, *A Lover's Question*, reached the Top 3 and crossed over to the lower regions of the Pop charts. Jacky then teamed up with relative newcomer Reba McEntire, for the Top 20 double-sided hit *Three Sheets in the Wind/I'd Really Love to See You Tonight*. He wrapped up the year with *I Want to Be in Love*, which went Top 25 and *Rhythm of the Rain*, which reached the Top 15.

Jacky started out 1979 with the Top 10 release *Wisdom of a Fool* and followed up with another duet with Reba, *That Makes Two of Us*, which went Top 30. He ended the year with the solo Top 20 single *You're My Kind of Woman*. He stayed with Mercury until 1981, and he had four further hits, *I'd Do Anything for You* and two Top 10 releases, *Save Your Heart for Me* and *That's the Way a Cowboy Rocks and Rolls*, in 1980, and *Somethin' on the Radio*, which peaked in the Top 15 the following year. In 1979, Jacky toured for three months with the circus family act the Flying Wallendas.

He then moved to the unlikely label Asylum. Unlikely, because the label always had a more Country-Rock image. Although he had a Top 40 success with *Travelin' Man*, a reprise of Ricky Nelson's 1961 No.1, his only other chart record for the label, *Take the Mem'ry When You Go*, only got to the Top 60. The following year, he surfaced on Warner Brothers but by now his recording career had run out of steam, even though he was hosting *Dancing U.S.A.* on TNN. It was not until 1988 that he had a lowly entry on the charts on the Electric label.

Jacky has put his stage presence to good use by appearing regularly on telethons and raising funds for the Arthritis Foundation and the March of Dimes.

RECOMMENDED ALBUMS:

"The Best of Jacky Ward...Up 'Til Now" (Mercury)(1979)
"More Jacky Ward" (Mercury)(1980)
"Big Blue Diamond" (Sunbird)(1980)
"Night After Night" (Asylum)(1982)

STEVE WARINER

(Singer, Songwriter, Guitar, Bass Guitar, Magician)

Given Name:	**Steven Noel Wariner**
Date of Birth:	**December 25, 1954**
Where Born:	**Noblesville, Indiana**
Married:	**Caryn**
Children:	**Ryan, Ross**

The word "magic" can be applied in two ways to Steve Wariner. As well as being a performer who has conjured up his fair share of hits, he is also an adept magician. He specializes in close-up card tricks, and what he calls the "disappearing bra." Steve has used his magic to good effect when he uses his sleight of hand to entertain disabled children in hospitals. He raised enough money at benefit concerts to build an educational wing for physically and mentally handicapped children at a local high school.

As a child, Steve made a cardboard bass, which he used to "play" in his bedroom. He began playing guitar at age 9 and when age 10, he played bass at his first gig with a Country band run by his father, Roy, and his uncle. By the time he was 17, Steve was performing during his summer vacation at the Nashville Country Club, near Indianapolis. Come 1972, he received a phone call from a friend to say that Dottie West would be at the club. Steve was singing on stage when Dottie joined him on harmonies. She offered him a job as bass player/singer with her band. He finished his school term and joined her, staying with the band for three years.

Steve then joined Bob Luman's band, doing more of the same, and during his three-year stint, he felt that he learned even more about stagecraft and presentation. In 1976, Luman recorded two of Steve's songs, *Labor of Love* (which charted) and *Blond Haired Woman*. The following year, Luman cut two more Wariner songs, *He'll Be the One* and *Give Someone You Love a Little Bit of Love This Year*. Luman was a major influence and his premature death, in 1978, greatly affected Steve. While recording with Luman, guitarist Paul Yandall heard a tape of Steve's and sent a copy to Chet Atkins at RCA Victor. Atkins signed Steve and in 1976 started to produce him. Shortly after, Steve joined Chet's band and recorded with him.

His debut release, in 1977, *I'm Already Taken*, made the Top 70 the following spring, but it was not until 1980 that his single *The Easy Part's Over* proved a turning point, when it reached the Top 50. By now, Steve was produced by Tom Collins, who was mega-hot as a producer and could call on the songs of Dennis Morgan, Kye Fleming and other writers, through his publishing company. It was the follow-up single at the end of that year, *Your Memory*, that signaled that Steve had arrived. This came from his debut self-titled 1981 album, as did the the next five chart entries. He started 1981 with another Top 10 record, *By Now*, and wrapped up the year with his first No.1, *All Roads Lead to You*, which also crossed to the lower regions of the Pop charts. That year, Conway Twitty recorded Steve's song *I'm Already Taken*.

In 1982, Steve's recording career started to get away from him when *Kansas City Lights* only reached the Top 15 and the next three singles, *Don't It Break Your Heart, Don't Plan on Sleepin' Tonight* (both 1982) and *Don't Your Mem'ry Ever Sleep at Night* (1983), only reached the Top 30. It was now time for Steve to change producers, and by the time his 1983 album ***Midnight Fire*** was released, Tom Collins had been replaced by Norro Wilson and Tony Brown. This marked a change of fortunes, and the title track, featuring a guitar solo from Steve, reached the Top 5. He followed up with his version of *Lonely Women Make Good Lovers*. The song had been a Top 5 single for his former mentor, Bob Luman, and now Steve took it to the same position. He had his last year with RCA in 1984, and his last two singles for the label

*No sleight of hands for **Steve Wariner**. Just pick and grin*

were *Why Goodbye*, which reached the Top 15, and *Don't You Give Up on Love*, which disappointingly only made the Top 50.

At the end of 1984, Steve signed with MCA, and Tony Brown continued as his producer with Jimmy Bowen. From here on in, Steve couldn't do wrong. His final single of the year, *What I Didn't Do*, reached the Top 3. He opened his 1985 account with the Top 10 record *Heart Trouble*. RCA, in an almost unprecedented move, released not only a ***Greatest Hits*** album but also an entirely new project, ***Down in Tennessee***. Steve also had his first album for his new label, ***One Good Night Deserves Another***.

He followed up with three straight No.1 records, *Some Fools Never Learn, You Can Dream on Me* (both 1985) and *Life's Highway* (1986), the last named being the title of Steve's second album for the label. This album was important because it marked the beginning of Steve's recording a lot more of his own material. Strangely, one of the best songs on the album, *The Heartland*, which he wrote with Wood Newton, never became a single. His other chart singles in 1986 were *Starting Over* (Top 5) and another No.1, *Small Town Girl*.

Steve started 1987 with his sixth No.1, *The Weekend,* and followed it with a duet with Glen Campbell, Ted Harris' *The Hand That Rocks the Cradle*, which came from Glen's album ***Still Within the Sound of My Voice***. The track was nominated the following year for a Grammy Award as "Best Country Performance by a Duo or Group with Vocal." Steve returned to the top spot in the fall with *Lynda*. During the year, MCA released a ***Greatest Hits*** package, and one of the tracks, *That's How You Know When Love's Right*, a duet with Nicolette Larson, was nominated for the CMA "Vocal Duo of the Year."

All three of his 1988 hits were written or co-written by Steve and came from the album ***I Should Be with You***, the first album on which he co-produced. *Baby I'm Yours*, which he co-wrote with Guy Clark, reached the Top 3, as did the title track, which Steve wrote. The final single of 1988, *Hold On (A Little Longer)*, made the Top 10.

He started 1989 with back-to-back No.1s, *Where Did I Go Wrong* and *I Got Dreams*, both from the ***I Got Dreams*** album and both written by Steve. In fact, all but one selection on the album were written or co-written by him. He finished the year with *When I Could Come Home to You*, which reached the Top 5 and stayed around the charts for 6 months. 1990 was Steve's final year with MCA and was a year of mixed fortunes. Both *The Domino Theory* and *Precious Thing* were Top 10 hits, but *There for a While* only reached the Top 20. His album that year, ***Laredo***, is notable for having three producers, Randy Scruggs, Tony Brown and Garth Fundis.

Steve's move to Arista, in 1991, brought him under the production baton of Scott Hendricks and Tim Dubois, and his debut album, ***I Am Ready***, was exquisite. Everything on it was in its right place. The production was tight, Steve's lead guitar playing was superb and the songs are all excellent. Yet, it was not with this album that Steve received recognition, initially, that year. He was a featured player on the Mark O'Connor and the New Nashville Cats' track *Restless*, alongside Ricky Skaggs and Vince Gill (on Warner Brothers Records). Although the record only reached the Top 25, it was the recipient of a Grammy Award, that year, for "Best Country Vocal Collaboration." It was also named, in 1992, as "Vocal Event of the Year" by the CMA and "Vocal Collaboration of the Year" by the TNN/*Music City News* Awards. It was followed into the charts by *Now It Belongs to You*, another track from the same album, which fell just short of the Top 70.

Steve's debut Arista single, *Leave Him Out of This*, climbed to the Top 10. In 1992, Steve reached the Top 3 with his version of the Bill Anderson Country classic *The Tips of My Fingers* (a long-time favorite of Steve's) and followed it with *A Woman Loves*, which went Top 10. His final single of the year, *Crash Course in the Blues*, was the amazing "live" track, which featured guitar work from Steve, Reggie Young and the legendary Albert Lee, plus classy fiddle playing from Mark O' Connor and frenetic harp playing by Terry McMillan. Why it only reached the Top 40 will remain one of the mysteries of radio programming.

His 1993 album ***Drive*** revealed a more aggressive Steve Wariner. His own image, which had taken on a more rugged look, continued to reveal a man with even more assurance. He had also learned to be more selective with what he did on a record, and the resulting recordings benefited by this added maturity. Steve's singles that year were *Like a River to the Sea* (Top 30), *If I Didn't Love You* (Top 10) and *Drivin' and Cryin'* (Top 25). In 1994, Steve's single *It Won't Be Over You* went Top 20.

"Stibbs," as Steve is known to his family and close friends, is, alongside Vince Gill, one of a rare breed who could succeed in any form of music he chose. A consummate guitar player, who is endorsed by Takamine Guitars and KMD Amps, he has played in projects alongside Rock heroes such as Mark Knopfler, Jon Bon Jovi, Richie Sambora, Lonnie Mack and Al DiMeola. Steve is one of Country music's nice guys, who has gained the respect of his peers by his ability as a singer, songwriter and musician. He was named, in 1992, as one of "Nashville's Ten Sexiest Men," by a poll of fans in *USA Today*.

RECOMMENDED ALBUMS:

"Greatest Hits" (RCA Victor)(1985)
"Greatest Hits" (MCA)(1987)
"Greatest Hits Volume II" (MCA)(1991)
"I Am Ready" (Arista)(1991)
"Drive" (Arista)(1993)

FIDDLIN' KATE WARREN

(Fiddle, Composer)

Given Name: Margie Ann DeVere
Date of Birth: January 19, 1922
Where Born: Grand Junction, Ohio
Married: Dale Warren (div.)
Children: Gayle Robin

For many years Fiddlin' Kate Warren was a mainstay of many of Country music's top bands. As a writer, her chief composition was *Katie Warren Breakdown*.

Kate studied music at the Hollywood Conservatory of Music between 1937 and 1938. During that period, she appeared on the *Stuart Hamblin Radio Show*. In 1940, she studied at Hartnell College in Salinas, California, and the following year, Kate formed the Fiddlin' Linvilles, a band she kept going until 1948.

Upon graduating in 1942, she joined Foreman Phillips' *Country Barn Dance* and while with Phillips, Kate appeared on the *Jimmy Wakely Show* during 1943 as a member of Wakely's band.

She left Phillips in 1944 and concentrated on her own band, while also playing in Paul Howard's Band on the WLS *Barn Dance* during 1947 to 1948. In 1948, Kate moved to the *Renfro Valley Barn Dance* with her group and also appeared that year on the *Grand Ole Opry*. She became a member of Merle Travis' Band in 1952 and appeared on *Ranch Party* from then until 1960. As a fiddle player for hire, Kate also played with Joe Maphis' Band (1954) and Tex Ritter's Band (1961).

Kate's recording career began in 1943 when she appeared on the King recording, *Linville Schottish*. However, from 1943 through 1956, she was associated with acts that recorded for Capitol, and she also cut solo material for the label, including *Green Grow the Lilacs* (1944). She went on to record for Windsor (1957), OKeh (1957) and Columbia (1957-60). While with Columbia, Kate recorded with Rose Lee Maphis and appeared on *Town Hall Party*.

Fiddlin' Kate Warren

It has been reported that this lady is still fiddling and is as feisty as ever, even though she is now in her 70's.

RECOMMENDED ALBUM:

"Fire on the Strings" (Columbia)(1958)

PAUL WARREN

(Fiddle)

Given Name: Dorris Paul Warren
Date of Birth: May 17, 1918
Where Born: Lyles, Hickman County, Tennessee
Married: Eloise
Children: Gary, Johnny, Debbie
Date of Death: January 12, 1978

Paul Warren was one of Country and Bluegrass music's all-time fiddle greats. Somewhat ironically, he never made a solo fiddle album in the studio in his lifetime. Paul spent over thirty-five years as a sideman and worked thousands of radio shows and personal appearances, hundreds of television programs, and many recording sessions.

Paul grew up in Hickman County, Tennessee, the son of an Old-Time fiddler and clawhammer banjo picker. Fiddlin' Arthur Smith, who worked regularly at the *Opry*, became his inspiration. Paul and Emory Martin played local school dances together in the mid-30's. After high school graduation, in 1936, he met Johnnie Wright and in 1938, became fiddler in Johnnie's group of aspiring musicians on their radio show at WSIX in Nashville. Johnnie also helped Paul get a job at the Davis Cabinet Company, where both worked until they became full-time professional musicians in 1940.

With the exception of WWII and a brief period when he spent a few months with Homer Briarhopper (Homer Drye) at WPTF Raleigh, North Carolina, Paul's tenure with the Tennessee Hillbillies/Tennessee Mountain Boys extended through difficult early years in Greensboro, Charleston, Bluefield, and Knoxville as well as their better days at KWKH Shreveport and WSM Nashville. Paul entered military service in September 1942 and was captured when an infantryman in North Africa, subsequently spending twenty-six months as a German P.O.W. According to some accounts, Paul's ability to fiddle *Under the Double Eagle* for one of his guards may have helped him survive.

Back in the entertainment business, Paul rejoined the band in Raleigh and moved with them to Nashville, Shreveport, and finally back to WSM and the *Grand Ole Opry*. As Johnnie & Jack began their recording career in March 1947 for Apollo, Paul was there. He participated on all their RCA Victor sessions through 1953, cutting seventy-six numbers with them as a band member, including some of their best-known songs like *Poison Love*, *Ashes of Love*, and *Let Your Conscience Be Your Guide*.

He also fiddled on all of Kitty Wells' recordings through January 1954, a total of thirty-seven songs on RCA Victor and Decca, including *It Wasn't God Who Made Honky-Tonk Angels*, *I Heard the Juke Box Playing*, and *Release Me*. In February 1954, Paul Warren traded places with Benny Martin and joined Lester Flatt & Earl Scruggs' Foggy Mountain Boys.

Paul Warren's tenure with the Flatt & Scruggs band and almost another decade with Lester Flatt's Nashville Grass lasted from February 16, 1954, until January 23, 1977, when he worked his last show in Lynchburg, Virginia. During that time, he worked on virtually all Flatt & Scruggs record sessions from May 1954 until the group dissolved early in 1969, appearing on more than 250 songs. He then recorded and toured with Flatt for nearly nine more years, including their early morning *Martha White* shows on WSM.

Ill health forced Paul to retire, and after his death, many of the numbers from these programs and live appearances were collected by Lance LeRoy in 1979 and released on a memorial tribute to Paul on CMH Records. Flatt generally did not permit band members to record on their own until Paul had passed his prime. So, unlike such contemporaries as Kenny Baker, Chubby Wise, Curly Ray Cline, Tater Tate and Howard Forrester, Paul never made a fiddle album in the studio. Paul's son Johnny carried on in his father's style with the Curly Sechler band. Nonetheless, Paul's many sessions with those in whose bands he played constitute an impressive legacy. IMT

RECOMMENDED ALBUM:

"America's Greatest Breakdown Fiddle Player" (CMH)(1979)

(See also Lester Flatt, Flatt & Scruggs, Johnnie & Jack, Kitty Wells)

DOC WATSON

(Singer, Songwriter, Guitar, Banjo)

Given Name: Arthel Watson
Date of Birth: March 2, 1923
Where Born: Deep Gap, North Carolina
Married: Rosa Lee Carlton
Children: Eddy Merle (dec'd.), Nancy

Doc Watson achieved national acclaim primarily as a result of his involvement in the Folk song revival of the 1960's. Nevertheless, he had been playing music for decades before coming to the attention of 60's urban audiences.

From birth, he was surrounded by music, his mother singing him to sleep with traditional ballads, such as *The House Carpenter* and *Omie Wise*. As he grew older, he would listen to her singing the younger children to sleep. His grandmother usually sang while churning, sewing, or cooking meals and his father sang a few hymns before bedtime each evening. Doc was blinded as an infant from a condition that restricted the flow of blood to his eyes. Each Christmas Doc received a new harmonica, and when he was 10, his father made him a fretless banjo, bending a piece of hickory for the hoop, stretching a groundhog hide over this for a head (although some stories relate it was made from the skin of his grandfather's cat!) and carving a neck and pegs out of maple. Around that time, Doc began attending the School for the Blind in Raleigh, North Carolina.

When Doc was thirteen, a cousin came by with a guitar and Watson became so taken with the instrument that his father purchased one for him. Within six months, Doc and his older brother, Linney, were performing together, singing on street corners, borrowing their repertoire largely from recordings by the Carter Family and the Monroe and Delmore Brothers.

At age 17, Doc played at a fiddlers' convention in Boone, North Carolina. Shortly before, a neighbor, Olin Miller, taught him the rudiments of finger-style guitar picking. In 1941, he joined a band that occasionally played for radio broadcasts on a station in Lenoir, North Carolina, where one of the announcers named him "Doc." In 1947, Doc married Rosa Lee Carlton, the daughter of fiddler Gaither W. Carlton. This proved both a happy and fortuitous union because his father-in-law supplied Doc with a vast body of traditional tunes. Even so, Doc did not generally perform traditional music publicly for more than a decade after his marriage; instead, he played mostly Country and Western music, reserving the traditional items he knew for his own amusement. He also earned money as a piano tuner.

In 1953, Doc played a Gibson Les Paul electric guitar in the band of Jack Williams, a local railroad worker and part-time pianist, performing in a variety of musical styles including Country and Western, Rock, Pop and traditional square dance tunes. He stayed with the band for eight years.

In 1960, Doc went to New York with the

The legendary ***Doc Watson***

Clarence Ashley String Band and appeared with them in concert at a "Friends of Old-Time Music" bill. (Clarence was a long-time neighbor and friend.) Doc made such an impact that he was booked into Gerde's Folk City in Greenwich Village. He began to attract a following among the young, and Ralph Rinzler and others involved in the Folk song revival persuaded Doc to switch exclusively to acoustic guitar. This change was soon followed by his ascendancy to national acclaim.

Doc recorded two albums with Clarence Ashley in 1961 and 1963 that catapulted Watson into the forefront of the 60's Folk movement. In 1962, Doc appeared with Clarence at the Ash Grove in Los Angeles. The following year, Doc appeared at the Newport Folk Festival and in 1964, Doc's talented son, Merle (b. February 8,1949/d. October 23, 1985), joined his father as accompanist. That year, Doc appeared at Newport with his father-in-law and members of his family. In 1972, Doc was one of the stars on the Nitty Gritty Dirt Band's ***Will the Circle Be Unbroken***. Unlike many of the stars of the Folk revival era, Doc's fame didn't wane when the revival declined, and he continues to the present as a recording star.

In 1973, Doc won a Grammy Award for "Best Ethnic or Traditional Recording" for the Poppy/United Artists album ***Then and Now***. The following year, Doc and Merle won the same award for the album ***Two Days in November***, also on Poppy/United Artists. They received another Grammy in 1979 for "Best Country Instrumental Performance" for the track *Big Sandy/Leather Britches*.

Doc received an Honorary Degree from Appalachian State University and in 1983, he received the third annual North Carolina Prize awarded by North Carolina newspapers owned by the New York Times Company.

In 1985, Merle was killed at age 36 in a tractor accident. His death marked the passing of a very talented guitarist and banjo player. He was content to perform in his preferred role as second guitarist to Doc's lead playing, hating to be in the spotlight. Jack Lawrence on guitar became Doc's accompanist, but Merle's playing was definitely missed. However, Doc still had the support of his long-time bass player and sometime producer, T. Michael Coleman (who joined Doc in 1974). The film *Doc and Merle*, dealing with the Watsons' careers, was released in 1986. That year, Doc received the North Carolina Award in Fine Arts for his "consummate artistry as a performer and interpreter of the traditional Folk music of the rural South." He also received a Grammy for "Best Traditional Folk Recording" for ***Riding the Midnight Train***, on Sugar Hill. Doc won the same award in 1990 for the Sugar Hill album ***On Praying Ground***.

Such is the love and esteem that Doc is held in that at one time, fans offered to provide corneas to Doc for transplant. Doc has said that if he hadn't become a musician, he would have been a carpenter or electrical engineer. To prove his point, he once re-wired his house.

WKM

RECOMMENDED ALBUMS:

"Old Time Music at Clarence Ashley's, Vol. I" (Folkways)(1961) [With Tom Ashley]
"Old Time Music at Clarence Ashley's, Vol.II" (Folkways)(1963) [With Tom Ashley]
"Doc Watson on Stage (Featuring Merle Watson)" (double)(Vanguard)(1970)
"The Best of Doc Watson" (double)(Vanguard)(1973)
"The Essential Doc Watson" (double)(Vanguard)(1973)
"Then and Now" (Poppy)(1973)
"Two Days in November" (Poppy)(1974)
"Doc Watson—Memories" (United Artists)(1975)
"Live and Pickin'" (United Artists)(1979)
"Red Rocking Chair" (Flying Fish)(1981)
"Favorites" (Liberty)(1983)
"Doc & Merle Watson's Guitar Album" (Flying Fish)(1983)
"Down South" (Sugar Hill)(1984)
"Riding the Midnight Train" (Sugar Hill)(1986)
"Portrait" (Sugar Hill)(1987)
"On Praying Ground" (Sugar Hill)(1990)
"Doc Watson Sings Songs for Little Pickers" (Sugar Hill)(1990)
"My Dear Old Southern Home" (Sugar Hill)(1991)
"Remembering Merle" (Sugar Hill)(1992) [As Doc & Merle Watson]
"Elementary Doctor Watson" (Sugar Hill)(1993)
The Watson family:
"Tradition" (Rounder) [Originally released on Topic (1977)]

Flatt & Scruggs and Doc Watson:
"Strictly Instrumental" (Columbia)(1967)
Chet Atkins & Doc Watson:
"Reflections" (RCA Victor)(1980)
Jean Ritchie & Doc Watson:
"Jean Ritchie & Doc Watson at Folk City" (Folkways)(1963)

GENE WATSON

(Singer, Songwriter, Guitar)

Given Name:	**Gary Gene Watson**
Date of Birth:	**October 11, 1943**
Where Born:	**Palestine, Texas**
Married:	**Mattie Louise (m. 1960)**
Children:	**Terri Lynn, Gary Wayne**

Gene Watson's hard Country vocal stylings are often credited as an influence by the new generation of Country stars, such as Doug Stone.

As a child, Gene Watson lived and traveled in a remodeled school bus with his parents and six brothers and sisters. The family eked out a living doing farm labor, moving from crop to crop. Watson's father also earned a living in various East Texas towns as a sawmill worker.

Gene's family eventually settled in Paris, Texas, where Gene attended school, until he dropped out in the ninth grade. He went to work full-time to help support the family in the auto salvage business. Gene learned to repair cars and developed a love for automobiles.

His early musical training came from singing in the local Pentecostal church and from the Blues his father played at home. Gene got his first taste of professional entertainment when he appeared on Fort Worth's *Cowtown Hoedown* with his steel guitar playing brother, Jesse.

Gene moved to Houston at 19 and found work as an auto body repairman and painter to support his wife and two children. To make some extra money, Gene formed a band with some brothers and cousins called Gene Watson and the Other Four; they became local club favorites, recording for the local Tonka label, in 1965.

While singing in the Dynasty Club, Gene came to the attention of two Houston businessmen: Russ Reeder, who was a record distributor, and Roy Stone, who owned a record store. They formed Wide World Records and took Gene to Nashville to record a song written by Gene's cousin Bill Watson, called *Autumn in June*. The single fizzled and so did the partnership of Reeder and Stone. Reeder's belief in Gene remained strong and he formed a new label for Gene. Reeder produced *Bad Water* and released it on his Resco label and Gene scored his first chart record in 1975.

Gene's next release on Resco was the

*Country stylist **Gene Watson***

provocative *Love in the Afternoon* (which initially had airplay problems over its subject matter). The single began receiving significant airplay and attracted the attention of Capitol Records, who signed Gene and took over the single, and it reached the Top 3 in 1975. Gene followed with the Top 5 *Where Love Begins*, later that year. He continued his string of hits in 1976 with *You Could Know As Much about a Stranger* (Top 10) and *Because You Believed in Me* (Top 20).

Although Gene's last single of 1976, *Her Body Couldn't Keep You off My Mind*, flopped, he came back strongly in 1977 with the Top 3 hit *Paper Rosie*, the story of a beggar woman, which actually reached No.1 in *Record World*. His other hits that year were *The Old Man and His Horn* and the Top 10 year-ender *I Don't Need a Thing at All*. 1978 brought the hits *Cowboys Don't Get Lucky All the Time* and the Top 10 success *One Sided Conversation*.

Gene had a stellar year in 1979, scoring three hits, starting with the Top 5 *Farewell Party*, a highly emotional suicide saga of unrequited love, which became his signature tune and after which he named his touring band. He followed this with *Pick the Wildwood Flower* (Top 5) and *Should I Go Home (Or Should I Go Crazy)* (Top 3). Celebrating five years with Capitol in 1980, Gene started with the Top 5 single *Nothing Sure Looked Good on You* and then followed with three Top 20 releases, *Bedroom Ballad*, *Raisin' Cane* and *No One Will Ever Know*.

Gene moved to MCA Records, in 1981, but before he got under way on the new label, *Any Way You Want Me*, from the Soundtrack of *Any Which Way You Can*, reached the Top 40. Gene's first release for MCA, *Between This Time and the Next Time*, reached the Top 20 and was followed by the Top 25 single *Maybe I Should Have Listened*. Gene closed out the year with his biggest record, the No.1 hit *Fourteen Carat Mind*. Gene's brand of pure Country singing produced three more hits in 1982 with *Speak Softly (You're Talking to My Heart)*, *This Dream's on Me* (both Top 10) and the anti-cheating lament *What She Don't Know Won't Hurt Her* (Top 5).

Gene's radio reign continued in 1983 and 1984 with six hit singles, *You're Out There Doing What I'm Here Doing Without* (Top 3), *Sometimes I Get Lucky and Forget* (Top 10) and *Drinkin' My Way Back Home* (Top 10) (all 1983), *Forever Again* (Top 10), *Little By Little* and *Got No Reason Now for Goin' Home* (Top 10) (all 1984). In 1985, Gene moved to Epic Records and returned to the Top 5 with the Western Swing-influenced *Memories to Burn*. However, although Gene maintained a heavy touring schedule, none of his other record releases got as high as the Top 20.

After a three-year absence from the Top 10, Gene's disillusionment with his career grew and he seriously considered retirement. It was Randy Travis' manager, Lib Hatcher, who convinced Gene to stay in the business. Lib began managing Gene and secured for him a contract with Warner Brothers Records that produced the 1988 Top 5 hit *Don't Waste It on the Blues*. Gene's revived career led to major tours with Randy Travis that introduced him to a new generation of Country fans.

In 1989, Gene hit the Top 20 with *Back in the Fire* and the Top 25 with *The Jukebox Played Along*, but subsequent releases on Warner Brothers failed to break the Top 40. In 1992, Gene recorded an album for the Canadian label Broadland International and then a year later signed with Step One, where a revival of his career looks distinctly possible. In 1993, Gene released his debut album for the label, ***Uncharted Mind***.

While major awards evaded Gene Watson, his soulful vocal interpretation was admired by many of his fellow singers. His fans include George Jones, George Strait and Randy Travis. Gene was a good friend of Marty Robbins and he was very proud of Marty's praise of his singing. Gene's Farewell Party Band includes former recording artist Tony Booth. JIE

RECOMMENDED ALBUMS:
"The Best of Gene Watson" (Capitol)(1978)
"The Best of Gene Watson, Vol. 2" (Capitol)(1981)
"Greatest Hits" (MCA)(1985)

"Texas Saturday Night" (MCA/Curb)(1986)
"Starting New Memories" (Epic)(1986)
"Honky Tonk Crazy" (Epic)(1987)
"Back in the Fire" (Warner Brothers)(1989)
"In Other Words" (Broadland International)(1992)
"Uncharted Mind" (Step One)(1993)

JAY LEE WEBB

(Singer, Songwriter, Guitar, Fiddle)
Given Name: Willie Lee Webb
Date of Birth: February 12, 1937
Where Born: Van Lear, Kentucky
Married: 1. Shirley Crandall (div.)
2. Louanne Hammons (div.)
Children: David Michael

Although Jay Lee Webb didn't achieve the fame of his siblings Loretta Lynn and Crystal Gayle or his distant cousin Patty Loveless, he has still managed to carve out a lengthy career in Country music.

When Jay Lee was born, his father's pet black snake curled up and went to sleep in his crib. At the age of 5, he traded his bicycle for a guitar. He then sold flower and garden seed to acquire his second instrument, a fiddle. He fiddled so long and hard that he wore out the hair on the bow and he repaired it using sea grass rope. By the time he was 13, he was playing on WSIP Paintsville, Kentucky, with the Sandy Valley Boys. Two years later, his family moved to Wabash, Indiana.

In 1959, Jay Lee and Loretta moved to Washington State and he began playing lead guitar and fiddle for the Trailblazers, which also included Loretta. Jay Lee played with the group for three years but also held down various jobs outside of music, including working in aircraft, woodwork, fiberglass, rock wool, an oil refinery, a fish cannery and a service station.

In 1962, he first came to Nashville and began backing a lot of the greats of Country music, including Buck Owens, Ferlin Husky and Slim Whitman. He went on to open for Loretta on personal appearances and on the *Grand Ole Opry*.

In 1966, Loretta recorded Jay Lee's songs *Today Has Been a Day,* on her album ***I Like 'em Country***, and *Christmas Without Daddy*, which appeared on her album ***Country Christmas***. Jay Lee began to make his own mark in 1967, when he signed to Decca Records. He first hit the Country chart with *I Come Home a-Drinkin' (To a Worn-Out Wife Like You)* which was an answer song to Loretta's hit *Don't Come Home a-Drinkin' (With Lovin' on Your Mind)*. The single, which reached the Top 40, was released under the name of "Jack Webb" and Jay Lee found himself in a lot of trouble from the actor of *Dragnet* fame. It was two years until Jay Lee had another chart record when *She's Lookin' Better* reached the Top 25. At the end of 1971, Jay Lee had his final chart record, *The Happiness of Having You*, which reached the Top 70.

He stayed with Decca through its transition to MCA and left in 1973. In 1978, he moved to Opryland Records without further success. He moved on to Palmer Records of Mississippi and although he had no chart records, of note was *The Birthmark Henry Thompson Talks About*, on which his sisters Crystal Gayle and Peggy Sue did harmony vocals. The following year, Jay Lee signed with O'Brien Records, where he stayed for two years and where he was produced by steelie Little Roy Wiggins. Jay Lee's second wife, Louanne, was also on the label at the same time.

Jay Lee is currently working for the Crystal Gayle organization and still does the occasional booking. His son, David, is proving to be a competent fiddle player. Jay Lee is currently putting a deal together with a Canadian label to start recording again.

RECOMMENDED ALBUMS:
"I Come Home a-Drinkin'" (Decca)(1967)
"She's Looking Better by the Moment" (Decca)(1969)

FREDDY WELLER

(Singer, Songwriter, Guitar, Bass, Banjo/Mandolin)
Given Name: Wilton Frederick Weller
Date of Birth: September 9, 1947
Where Born: Atlanta, Georgia
Married: Pippy
Children: Brandon

Freddy Weller's career can be divided into distinct areas. He has been a successful Pop-Rock musician, Country chart star and much covered songwriter of Pop and Country material.

He started out playing music when he was age 8, having discovered his father's banjo/mandolin. He soon learned to play the instrument and then went on to play guitar. Freddy's early writing style owed much to Hank Williams. While in high school, he began appearing on the *Georgia Jubilee* out of East Point, Georgia, alongside Jerry Reed, Ray Stevens, Joe South and Billy Joe Royal.

After graduation, Freddy got into music full-time. As a lead guitarist and bass guitarist, he became much in demand for studio work and he played on sessions for Joe South and could be heard on Billy Joe Royal's *Down in the Boondocks*, a hit in 1965. Freddy began playing in Billy Joe's band when he was spotted by Paul Revere and asked to join the Raiders as lead guitarist. Freddy debuted with the Raiders in April 1967, on the *Ed Sullivan Show*. While with the group, Freddy moved to Los Angeles and appeared on their network TV show.

*Singer and Songwriter **Freddy Weller***

In 1969, Tommy Roe had two No.1 Pop hits with *Dizzy* and *Jam Up Jelly Tight*, both of which Tommy and Freddy had co-written. Freddy got his opportunity to record as a solo performer when a recording session for the Raiders was canceled because not all of the group was available. Producer Mark Lindsay offered to record Freddy. They cut Joe South's *Games People Play* (a Top 10 hit for Joe in the U.K.), using a steel guitar on the recording. While Freddy was touring in Europe, the single charted in the U.S. and it gave Freddy his first Country hit, peaking in the Top 3. It was released on Columbia, and this label would be Freddy's home for the remainder of his hits, except for a pair of singles for ABC/Dot, in 1975. Freddy followed-up with *These Are Not My People*, which was a Top 5 hit, and ended 1969 with Freddy's Top 30 version of *Down in the Boondocks*. That year, Freddy was named the ACM's "Most Promising New Male Vocalist."

The following year, Freddy's version of Chuck Berry's *The Promised Land* gave him a Top 3 success. Although Freddy had stayed with the Raiders and toured with them as well as gigging as a solo, by 1971 this was proving too strenuous, and he left the Raiders. He now left Los Angeles and returned to Atlanta, and began recording in Nashville. During that year, Freddy had major hits with the Top 3 *Indian Lake* and the Top 5 *Another Night of Love*.

In 1972, Freddy received a BMI Award for his song *Lonely Women Make Good Lovers*, which gave Bob Luman a Top 5 hit. Eleven years later, Steve Wariner, Luman's former bass guitarist, took his recording of the song to the same position, and earned Freddy another BMI Award. During 1972, Freddy had three medium sized successes, *Ballad of a Hillbilly Singer* (Top 30), *The Roadmaster* (Top 20) and *She Loves Me (Right Out of My Mind)* (which just failed to reach the Top 10).

Freddy's 1973 single, another Chuck Berry song, *Too Much Monkey Business*, gave him his final Top 10 success. Between 1973 and 1974, Freddy scored with *The Perfect Stranger* and *I've Just Got to Know (How Loving You Would Be)*, both of which just failed to reach the Top 10, in 1973, and *Sexy Lady* and the Top 20 single *You're Not Getting Older (You're Getting Better)*.

Freddy left Columbia in 1975, and recorded an eponymous album, produced by Ron Chancy, from which two singles, *Love You Back to Georgia* and *Stone Crazy*, only reached the Top 70 and Top 60 respectively. The following year, Freddy was back with Columbia. However, although he charted fifteen more times, most of these peaked around the 40s. The most successful were *Bar Wars* (Top 40) and *Love Got in the Way* and *Fantasy Island* (both Top 30) (all in 1978) and *Nadine* and *Go for the Night* (both Top 40, 1979).

In 1984, he signed with BTB Records, where he was produced by Bob Montgomery, but without success. He also released a 20-song TV album ***Back on the Street***, on the North Carolina-based label, HMC. This album was released in 1987 on the U.K. Bulldog label. In recent years, Freddy has been a much covered songwriter in Nashville. Among his successes are *They Asked About You* (Reba McEntire), *She Don't Need a Band to Dance* (John Michael Montgomery), *She Never Cried When Old Yeller Died* (Confederate Railroad), *Big Heart* (Gibson/Miller Band), *Wrong's What I Do Best* (George Jones), *They Don't Make Years Like They Used To* (Doug Stone), *Writing on the Wall* (George Jones), *The Garden* (Vern Gosdin), *My Kinda Woman* (Pirates of the Mississippi) and *Play It Again Sam* (Wayne Newton). In 1992, Viv Reeves & the Wonderstuff had a U.K. No.1 with Freddy's *Dizzy*.

RECOMMENDED ALBUMS:

"Freddy Weller's Greatest Hits" (Columbia)(1975)
"Freddy Weller" (ABC/Dot)(1975)
"Love Got in the Way" (Columbia)(1978)
"Go for the Night" (Columbia)(1980)
"Back on the Street" (Bulldog UK)(1987)

FRANK WELLING AND JOHN McGHEE

When Formed: 1917

FRANK WELLING
(Hawaiian Guitar, Guitar, Ukulele)

Given Name: Benjamin Franklin Welling
Date of Birth: February 16, 1898
Where Born: Lawrence County, Ohio
Married: 1. Imogene Rippetoe (dec'd.) 2. Thelma Rippetoe
Children: Jean, Margie, Deanna
Date of Death: January 23, 1957

JOHN McGHEE
(Guitar, Harmonica, Organ, Calliope, etc.)

Given Name: John Leftridge McGhee
Date of Birth: April 9, 1882
Where Born: Griffithsville, West Virginia
Married: Sue Rankin Eskew
Children: Ernest, John Max, Julius, Ruth, Alma, Anna Lee
Date of Death: May 9, 1945

The team of Frank Welling and John McGhee recorded a considerable volume of over 250 sides of Old-Time and sacred music between 1927 and 1933, although most critics would describe it as being somewhat less than pure Country. On the other hand, most would also consider it more Country than anything else. Both the older McGhee and the younger Welling exhibited a wide range of musical influences extending from Gilbert and Sullivan operettas at one extreme to traditional Appalachian sounds at the other. Welling had earlier toured in vaudeville with a Hawaiian group and later sustained a radio career that included a wide variety of voice characterizations and announcing as well as music.

John McGhee came to Huntington, West Virginia, early in the century from rural Lincoln County while Frank Welling moved to that same river city about 1912 from Lawrence County, Ohio, where his father had been a traditional hill-country fiddler. The son became quite enamored with the steel guitar and toured with a Hawaiian unit called Domingo's Filipino [sic] Serenaders about the time of WWI. He and McGhee became acquainted about 1917, and for the next fifteen years were quite active on the local music scene. They worked alone, together, and in company with other musicians in a wide range of venues and styles, including private parties, church choirs, barbershop quartets, string bands, minstrel shows and even more elaborate stage productions such as *The Mikado*.

Beginning in 1927, William R. Callaway, a neighbor and talent scout who also lived in Huntington, West Virginia, recruited them to record for Gennett and over the next six years they had numerous sessions for that company as well as for Paramount, Brunswick, and the American Record Corporation. McGhee usually sang a bass part, which makes their duets sound rather unusual to those later accustomed to the tenor-oriented harmonies of the Monroe or Louvin Brothers. At times various Huntington associates accompanied them to the studios, including Miller Wikel, Ted Cogar, William Shannon, and Harry Sayre. John's daughter Alma McGhee (1913-1973) and Frank's wife Thelma Welling (b. 1907) also participated on some recordings. Welling and McGhee also accompanied Wikel on his solo recordings and backed fellow Huntingtonian Blind David Miller on his Paramount sides.

Frank and John had an extremely varied repertoire. It included sacred songs like *The Old Account Was Settled*, *Hallelujah Side*, and *In the Garden*, as well as comic parodies like *Sweet Adeline at the Still* and *Old Kentucky Dew*. They recorded minstrel songs such as *Hard Luck Jim*, topical ballads typified by *The Crime at Quiet Dell*, social commentary like *Bank Bustin' Blues*, and such turn of the century Pop fare as *Where Is My Mama?*, *Maple on the Hill* and *A Flower from My Angel Mother's Grave*. In addition McGhee recorded traditional fiddle tunes on harmonica such as *Beech Fork Special* and Welling introduced the sentimental recitation to Country music with his April 1928 Paramount waxing of *Too Many Parties* and *Too Many Pals*. Frank, in fact, is known to have directly influenced such later practitioners of recitation as Red Sovine, Buddy Starcher, and Red Foley.

After the mid-30's, the couple stopped working together as Welling moved to Charleston, where he worked as an announcer/entertainer for WCHS radio. He created a humorous oldster known as "Uncle Si," who engaged in downhome philosophy and comedy. Frank also had a big hand in Charleston's live jamboree show, the *Old Farm Hour*, as both emcee and director. He also worked for brief stints at WWVA Wheeling and WLW Cincinnati, and in his last years worked as an announcer at a station in Chattanooga, Tennessee. His last record session came in 1949 when he did a session for a small Ohio label called Red Robin, which included a cover of Jimmy Dickens' hit *Country Boy*.

After his death, his remains were returned to Huntington for burial. His first wife, Imogene, had died young in 1923 and he subsequently married her sister Thelma. The widow later relocated to Burbank, California, where two of her daughters resided. Like Lester McFarland and Robert Gardner (Mac and Bob), whose styles had some similarities, Welling and McGhee have been proportionately under-represented on re-issues. However, their work can be found on a few anthologies, and in 1987, Old Homestead released an album representative of their broad repertoire. IMT

RECOMMENDED ALBUM:

"Sacred, Sentimental and Silly Songs" (Old Homestead)(1987)

KITTY WELLS

(Singer, Songwriter, Guitar)

Given Name: Ellen Muriel Deason
Date of Birth: August 30, 1919
Where Born: Nashville, Tennessee
Married: Johnnie Robert Wright (Johnny Wright)
Children: Ruby, Bobby, Carol Sue

Kitty Wells, after a decade of performing experience spent in modest obscurity, emerged in 1952 as the first female Country vocalist to obtain and sustain major stardom, earning the unofficial title "Queen of Country Music." A real trouper, Kitty and husband Johnny Wright continued working about one hundred dates annually going into the 90's.

Muriel Deason was raised in Nashville and nearby McEwen, Tennessee. She grew up in a typical working class household and when she was 18, married Johnny Wright, who worked in a cabinet shop but aspired to a Country music career. He had a program on a smaller Nashville station, WSIX. Muriel and Louise Wright sang as the Harmony Girls. When the career of the Anglin Brothers ended in 1940, Jack Anglin, who married Louise Wright in 1938, teamed up with Johnny to form the duo of Johnnie & Jack.

At the beginning of 1941, their group, then known as the Tennessee Hillbillies, went full-time professional. The entourage included fiddler Paul Warren, banjoist Emory Martin, mandolinist Ernest Ferguson, and Louise and Muriel. Johnny gave Muriel the name "Kitty Wells" from the 19th-century sentimental ballad *Sweet Kitty Wells*. They worked out of such locales as Greensboro; Charleston, West Virginia; and Knoxville until late 1942 when the war caught up with them. Jack and Paul went into the service while Johnny and Ernest went into defense plants.

After some months out of radio, Wright reorganized the Tennessee Hillbillies with Smilin' Eddie Hill. Again, Kitty worked as a featured vocalist when not preoccupied with housework and child rearing. This situation continued through another sojourn at KNOX Knoxville and WPTF Raleigh (where Jack eventually returned), a year at WSM Nashville and the *Opry*, and a couple of years at KWKH Shreveport. Kitty had not participated in the group's early recordings for Apollo or King, but when they signed with RCA in 1949, she joined in on a few of their numbers and also cut eight sides on her own. None of these early numbers made much of an impact, although a later remake of *How Far Is Heaven* did quite well on Decca. Meanwhile the Tennessee Mountain Boys (as the group had now become) moved on to brief stints in Knoxville, Raleigh, WEAS Decatur, Georgia, and back to KWKH in June, 1951. In January, 1952, they returned to Nashville permanently and rejoined the *Opry*.

Kitty Wells** with **Johnny** and **Bobby Wright

In May, 1952, Kitty signed with Decca and recorded *It Wasn't God Who Made Honky Tonk Angels*. For the first time an "answer" song (to *The Wild Side of Life*) recorded by a girl vocalist did nearly as well as the original. She became the first female to have a No.1 (for 6 weeks). What's more, Kitty followed with more Top 10 hit songs in the next two years: 1953: *Paying for That Back Street Affair* and *Hey Joe*; 1954: *One By One* (No.1)/*I'm a Stranger in My House* (in duet with Red Foley), *Cheatin's a Sin* and *Release Me*; all of which proved she was not a one-hit fluke. In 1955, Kitty and Red got back together for the double-sided smash *As Long as I Live* (Top 3)/*Make Believe ('Til We Can Make It Come True)* (Top 10). Then her solo *Makin' Believe* reached the Top 3, staying there for 15 weeks out of 7 months on the chart. Other major hits (all Top 10, unless stated) in the later 50's included: 1955: *Whose Shoulder Will You Cry On* (the flip of *Makin' Believe*), *There's Poison in Your Heart/I'm in Love with You* (Top 15) 1956: *You and Me* (a Top 3 duet with Red Foley), *Lonely Side of Town/I've Kissed You My Last Time*, *How Far Is Heaven* (Top 15) and *Searching (For Someone Like You)/I'd Rather Stay Home* (Top 15); 1957: *Repenting/Oh, So Many Years* (the flip being a duet with Webb Pierce), *Three Ways (To Love You)* and *(I'll Always Be Your) Sweetheart*; 1958: *One Week Later* (a Top 15 duet with Webb Pierce), *I Can't Stop Loving You/She's No Angel* (Top 15), *Jealousy, Touch and Go Heart* (Top 20)/*He's Lost His Love for Me*; 1959: *Mommy for a Day/All the Time* (Top 20), *Your Wild Life's Gonna Get You Down* (Top 15). Even songs that didn't chart like *I Heard the Juke Box Playing*, *The Life They Live in Songs* and *I Don't Claim to Be an Angel* have gained a certain standard status. While urban critics might have scoffed at the nasal twang in her voice, Kitty and Johnnie cried all the way to the bank. Many, albeit by no means all, of her lyrics portrayed the narrator as an assertive victim of a faithless husband or lover.

The 60's may not have been as good to Kitty as the 50's, but still had plenty of high points. In 1960, both *Amigo's Guitar* and *Left to Right* went Top 5 and *Carmel by the Sea* reached the Top 20. 1961 started with the Top 20 *The Other Cheek*, then *Heartbreak U.S.A.* spent 4 weeks at No.1 and the flip, *There Must Be Another Way to Live*, went Top 20. The following year saw four singles make the Top 10: *Day into Night*; *Unloved, Unwanted* (Top 5), *Will Your Lawyer Talk to God* and *We Missed You*. In 1963, Kitty's only successful record was the Top 15 *Cold and Lonely (Is the Forecast for Tonight)*. The mid-60's saw six more songs in the Top 10, namely, *This White Circle on My Finger*, *Password* and the duet with Webb Pierce, *Finally* (1964) and *I'll Repossess My Heart*, *You Don't Hear* and *Meanwhile Down at Joe's* (all 1965). From 1965, a new wave of younger girl singers, Loretta Lynn, Connie Smith, and Norma Jean among them, began to compete more heavily but Miss Kitty continued charting regularly through 1972, the year before she left Decca/MCA, her most successful singles being *A Woman Half My Age* and *It's All Over (But the Crying)*, both Top 15 in 1966.

As well as recording with Red Foley and Webb Pierce, Kitty also recorded some other quality duets during her Decca years that did not achieve high chart placings, including *Goodbye Mr. Brown* with Roy Acuff, *I Can't Tell My Heart That* with Roy Drusky, *The Wild Side of Life* with Rayburn Anthony and in 1968 with husband Johnny Wright on their autobiographical *We'll Stick Together*.

Kitty and Johnny left the *Opry* after several

years and apparently—unlike some acts that have faded—have survived quite well without it. Kitty signed with Capricorn in 1975, but had only one lower ranking single, *Anybody Out There Wanna Be a Daddy*. Johnny thinks (correctly) that the Macon-based firm didn't know how to promote true Country acts. A Country Music Hall of Famer since 1976, Kitty did somewhat better on Johnny's Ruboca (for Ruby, Bobby, Carol) Records with *Thank You for the Roses* in 1979, the last time one of her solo numbers charted. Her final chart entry was later that year, when in tandem with Rayburn Anthony, their recording of *The Wild Side of Life* reached the Top 60.

Kitty has continued to record for Ruboca as well as Step One through 1989. Kitty and Johnny have a souvenir shop, Country Junction, in Nashville and they have continued touring with their son, Bobby Wright, up to the present. In recent years, companies such as Rounder, Stetson, and Bear Family continue to reissue "the Queen's" vintage recordings. In 1988, Kitty, Johnny and Bobby appeared at Britain's Peterborough Festival. In 1991, Kitty Wells won a Grammy Lifetime Achievement Award. IMT

RECOMMENDED ALBUMS:

"Country Hit Parade" (Decca)(1956) [Re-released on Stetson UK in the original sleeve (1987)]
"Kitty's Choice" (Decca)(1960) [Re-released on Stetson UK in the original sleeve (1987)]
"Golden Favorites" (Decca)(1961)
"Queen of Country Music" (Decca)(1962)
"Singing on a Sunday" (Decca)(1962)
"The Kitty Wells Story" (double)(Decca)(1963)
"Especially for You" (Decca)(1964)
"Kitty Wells Family Gospel Sing" (Decca)(1965)
"Songs Made Famous By Jim Reeves" (Decca)(1966) [Re-released on Stetson UK in the original sleeve (1987)]
"The Kitty Wells Show" (Decca)(1966)
"Queen of Honky Tonk Street" (Decca)(1967)
"Kitty Wells Showcase" (Decca)(1968)
"Greatest Hits" (Decca)(1968)
"We'll Stick Together" (Decca)(1968) [With Johnny Wright]
"Cream of Country Hits" (Decca)(1968)
"A Bouquet of Country Hits" (Decca)(1969)
"Singing 'Em Country" (Decca)(1970)
"Heartwarming Gospel Songs" (Decca)(1972) [With Johnny Wright]
"Yours Truly" (MCA)(1973)
"Kitty Wells Greatest Hits" (Capricorn)(1974)
"Forever Young" (Capricorn)(1974)
"Hall of Fame, Vol. I" (Ruboca)(1979)
"Hall of Fame, Vol. II" (Ruboca)(1981)
"The Golden Years" (Rounder)(1982)
"Early Classics" (Golden Country)(1982) [From Victor masters]
"The Golden Years, 1949-1957" (6 Album Box Set)(Bear Family Germany)(1987)
"Greatest Hits, Vol. I" (Step One)(1989)
"Greatest Hits, Vol. II" (Step One)(1989)
"Hall of Fame Series" (MCA)(1991)
(See also Johnnie & Jack, Johnny Wright)

DOTTIE WEST

(Singer, Songwriter, Guitar, Actress)

Given Name: Dorothy Marie Marsh
Date of Birth: October 11, 1932
Where Born: Frog Pond, McMinnville, Tennessee
Married: 1. Bill West (m. 1952)(div.)
2. Byron Allen Metcalf (m. 1972)(div.)
3. Allen ("Al") Winters (m. 1983)(div.)
Children: Dale, Kerry, William Morris III ("Mo"), Shelly West
Date of Death: September 4, 1991

When Dottie West died from injuries received in an auto crash in 1991, Country music lost one of its most glamorous and talented performers. She was renowned as one of the best dressed female performers to grace the live stage, often wearing Bob Mackie originals.

Dottie was raised and worked picking cotton on a farm outside McMinnville, the youngest of ten children. Her father, who played guitar, was a brutal alcoholic and when he left home, her mother, Pelina, opened a restaurant in McMinnville. It was her mother's strength of character that was passed on to Dottie, her eldest daughter. By the time she was age 12, Dottie had made her debut singing on WMMT McMinnville. She worked in her mother's restaurant and then attended Tennessee Tech in Cookeville, where she earned a degree in music.

While at college, she met Bill West, who was studying engineering, and they married in 1953. Bill was (and is) an adept steel player and he accompanied Dottie on broadcasts on WHUB Cookeville and at college concerts. They moved to Cleveland, Ohio, where Bill worked for a steel company. Dottie began to appear on the Cleveland TV show *Landmark Jamboree*, as one half of the duo, the Kay-Dots with Kathy Dee (1933-1968), remaining on the show for five years. However, it was Mother Maybelle Carter who became a great influence at this time on the fledgling star.

In 1959, while visiting Nashville, Dottie and Bill dropped by Starday Records, where Dottie auditioned live for the legendary Don Pierce. As a result she was signed to the label and although she released several singles, she had no success. Her output was later released by Starday on the 1964 album ***Country Girl Singing Sensation***. Dottie and Bill moved to Nashville, in 1961, and started songwriting and hanging around with other budding writers such as Willie Nelson, Hank Cochran, Roger Miller, and Red Lane, who would become one

Dottie West** with daughter **Shelly West

of her most frequent co-writers (she signed to Tree Publishing, where Lane also wrote).

In 1962, Dottie signed with Atlantic Records, but again success eluded her. In 1963, Jim Reeves had a Top 3 with Dottie's song *Is This Me?* It was Jim who made Chet Atkins aware of Dottie's talents and as a result, she was signed to RCA Victor that year and on this label, her "tear in her voice" style was heard to good effect. She made her Country chart debut with *Let Me Off at the Corner*, which went Top 30.

The following year, Dottie teamed up with Jim Reeves for the Top 10 single Justin Tubb's *Love Is No Excuse*. She ended the year with a song written by her and Bill, *Here Comes My Baby*, which went Top 10 and for which Dottie became the first recipient of a Grammy Award for "Best Country & Western Performance, Female" (a new category). That year, Dottie became a member of the *Grand Ole Opry*. The following year was not nearly as successful, with all singles peaking in the 20s and 30s, and the most successful being *Before the Ring on Your Finger Turns Green*. However, 1966 started out with another Dottie and Bill song, *Would You Hold It Against Me?*, which went Top 5. She ended the year with the Top 20 single *What's Come Over My Baby*, another West and West song.

The following year, Dottie had a Top 10 hit with the Ted Harris song *Paper Mansions*. She followed this with the Top 20 hit *Like a Fool*. During this time, she appeared in the movies *Second Fiddle to a Steel Guitar* and *There's a Still on the Hill*. In 1968, Dottie had two Top 20 singles, *Country Girl* and *Reno*, and then the following year, she teamed up with Don Gibson for two major hits, *Rings of Gold* (Top 3) and *There's a Story (Goin' 'Round)* (Top 10).

During 1970, Dottie was offered Kristofferson's *Help Me Make It Through the Night*, but Dottie refused to record it, because she felt it was too sexy. In 1970, her most successful release was *Forever Yours*, which just failed to reach the Top 20. She followed this, in 1971, with *Slowly*, a duet with Jimmy Dean, which went Top 30. Although the 1972 single *If It's All Right With You* only went Top 30, it did cross over to the Pop 100. Dottie's next major hit, *Country Sunshine*, happened in 1973. It reached the Top 3 on the Country chart and the Pop Top 50. This song was originally one of twelve jingles for Coca-Cola, and won the prestigious Clio advertising award and was nominated for two Grammy Awards. As a result of this song Dottie became known as "the Country Sunshine Girl." Dottie followed-up with the Top 10 single *Last Time I Saw Him*.

In 1972, Dottie married drummer Bryan Metcalf, who was twelve years her junior. On her own admission, she preferred younger men and around this time, a new-look Dottie started emerging. She stayed with RCA until 1976 and her major hit during this time was the 1974 Top 30 *House of Love*. By the time she left the label, she had become one very sexy lady and her glorious red hair and provocative outfits made her much sought after as a live act.

In 1976, Dottie moved to United Artists Records and from then until 1977, her main successes were *When It's Just for You and Me* (Top 20, 1976), *Every Word I Write* and *Tonight You Belong to Me* (both Top 30, 1977). At the end of the year, Dottie was in the studio recording *Every Time Two Fools Collide*, then according to songwriter Jeff Tweel, Kenny Rogers drifted into the studio and joined in. The result was that the duet went to No.1, the following year, on the Country chart and crossed over to just below the Top 100 on the Pop lists. Dottie followed with the solo Top 20 single *Come See Me and Come Lonely*. After this, Dottie and Kenny got together for the Top 3 release, *Anyone Who Isn't Me Tonight*. That year, the CMA named them "Vocal Duo of the Year," a feat they repeated the following year, 1979.

Dottie and Kenny had two monster hits in 1979, *All I Ever Need Is You* (No.1) and *Till I Can Make It on My Own* (Top 3), the latter having Tammy Wynette as one of its writers. Dottie's only solo hit was *You Pick Me Up (And Put Me Down)*, which just failed to make the Country Top 10. The following year, Dottie had her first solo No.1 single, *A Lesson in Leavin'*, which also went Top 75 on the Pop chart. This was followed by the Top 20 *Leavin's for Unbelievers* and another solo No.1, *Are You Happy Baby?*

She stayed with United Artists (renamed Liberty in 1981) and her major successes were the West-Rogers No.1 duet *What Are We Doin' in Love* and the solo Top 20 records *(I'm Gonna) Put You Back on the Rack* and *It's High Time* (all 1981), the Top 30 hits *You're Not Easy to Forget* and *She Can't Get My Love off the Bend* (both 1982) and the Top 20 duet with Kenny, *Together Again* (1984). During 1983, Dottie appeared in the touring production of *The Best Little Whorehouse in Texas*. Her visual image continued to reveal a lady who would not let age get in the way, appearing in a revealing photo spread in *Oui* magazine, and in 1983 she married her sound technician, Al Winters, twenty-three years her junior.

In 1984, Dottie appeared in the play *Bring It On Home*, which also starred Mary Martin and Shelley Duvall. That year, Dottie moved to Permian Records, but she failed to achieve major success, and the most successful release was *We Know Better Now*, a Top 60 single in 1985.

However, the bubble burst in 1990, when she divorced Winters. That same year her manager sued her and then the bank foreclosed on her house. Then she lost her car, declared bankruptcy and in June, 1991, the IRS held a public auction so they could recover $1 million. All her life's souvenirs were sold off and then in July that year, Dottie was involved in a car crash.

Her friends rallied round; Kenny Rogers loaned her a car and a new album with her old compadres was planned. This album was to have included a trio with Tanya Tucker and Tammy Wynette. She began writing her autobiography. Then, late for a Friday night appearance at the *Opry*, she got her 81-year-old neighbor to drive her, but approaching the Opry House, he lost control of the car and they crashed. Five days later, Dottie died from her injuries, which included a ruptured liver. Like her heroine, Patsy Cline, Dottie West was gone. In 1994, a movie about Dottie's life was filmed in Nashville.

Dottie's contribution to Country music extends far beyond her own career. She was also responsible for launching the careers of many songwriters and being among the first to record their material, in particular, Sandy Mason, Jessi Colter, Jeannie Seely and Toni Wine. Dottie also was responsible for getting the careers of many future stars off the ground. These included Steve Wariner, who played bass guitar in her band, the Heartbeats, during 1971 through 1974 and Larry Gatlin, who wrote for Dottie and who moved to Nashville in 1972, when Dottie paid his fare. She also assisted the career of her daughter, Shelly West (Dottie's sons Mo and Dale are both Rock drummers and Kerry is a sound engineer) and singer/pianist Tony Tolliver. Yes, Dottie was a great lady.

RECOMMENDED ALBUMS:

"Country Girl Singing Sensation" (Starday)(1964)
"Dottie & Don" (RCA Victor)(1969) [With Don Gibson]
"Country Boy & Country Girl" (RCA Victor)(1970) [With Jimmy Dean]
"The Best of Dottie West" (RCA Victor)(1972)
"Every Time Two Fools Collide" (United Artists)(1978)
"Classics" (United Artists)(1979) [With Kenny Rogers]
"New Horizons" (Liberty)(1983)
"The Best of Dottie West" (Liberty)(1984)
"Just Dottie" (Permian)(1984)
"20 of the Best" (RCA UK)(1986)

SHELLY WEST

(Singer, Songwriter, Guitar)

Date of Birth:	**May 23, 1958**
Where Born:	**Cleveland, Ohio**
Married:	**1. Allen Frizzell (div.)**
	2. Garry Hood
Children:	**Tess Marie**

During the early 80's, red-haired Shelly West was one of the hottest female singers in Country music, both as a solo, and as half of one of the most successful duos, with her then brother-in-law, David Frizzell.

Shelly was born the daughter of Country star Dottie West and steel guitarist Bill West. By 1975, she began singing harmony with her mother's touring show and after a while sang lead. She married Allen Frizzell, who was Dottie's lead guitarist and was the younger brother of Lefty and David Frizzell. In 1977 after marriage, they left the show and moved to Lindsay, California. At the time, David was resident at a night club in nearby Concord. Shelly and Allen became part of the house band until David organized a tour of Texas, Oklahoma, New Mexico and Southern California.

When they returned to Concord after about six months. David set about getting a record deal for himself and found interest from producer Snuff Garrett, who found the song *Lovin' on Borrowed Time*, which was a duet. David suggested that Shelly should sing on the demo. Garrett was knocked out by the result and fixed up a deal with Casablanca-West, the newly formed Country arm of the Disco label Casablanca. However, Polygram bought the company, axed the label and with it Shelly and David.

Finding no interest in Nashville, Garrett

resorted to using his connections in California. Having worked with Clint Eastwood on *Every Which Way But Loose*, and knowing that the star had formed Viva Records, he slipped a cassette into the player in Eastwood's car and hoped to providence. Eastwood didn't like the song, but did like another, *You're the Reason God Made Oklahoma,* and insisted that the song go into his new movie *Any Which Way You Can*.

The single, licensed to Warner Brothers Records, started to pick up airplay on KDEN Tulare, California, at the end of 1980. By January, 1981, it had hit the Country charts and in April reached the No.1 slot. The couple received a slew of awards that year. CMA made them "Duo of the Year," *Billboard* named them "New Group/Duo-Singles" and "New Group/Duo-Albums" (for their debut album ***Carryin' on the Family Name***) and "New Artists-Singles," *Cash Box* named them "New Duo-Singles" and "Duo of the Year," *Record World* made them "Top New Duo-Singles" and *Radio & Records* made them "Vocal Duo of the Year."

They followed up with *A Texas State of Mind*, which went Top 10, and wrapped up the year with the Top 20 single *Husbands and Wives*. The following year, they returned to the Top 10 with *Another Honky-Tonk Night on Broadway* and followed it with the Top 5 record *I Just Came Here to Dance*. The year was ended by a Top 50 single, *Please Surrender*, which came from the Clint Eastwood movie *Honkytonk Man*, in which they made a cameo appearance. They again scooped the pool with their awards that year. They were again CMA, *Billboard* and *Cash Box*'s "Duo of the Year." In addition, the ACM weighed in with "Duo of the Year" and they also made *You're the Reason God Made Oklahoma* "Song of the Year." *Music City News* Cover Awards made them "Duo of the Year." They repeated the ACM and MCN "Duo of the Year" the following year.

Shelly had her first solo hit, in 1983, with the fun-filled *Jose Cuervo*, which went to No.1. This was followed by a minor duet, *Cajun Invitation,* and then she had her second solo hit, the Top 5 *Flight 309 to Tennessee*, released on Viva. After this came the low level duet *Pleasure Island*. The year was wrapped up by the Top 10 solo single *Another Motel Memory*. In 1984, Shelly and David appeared at the International Country Music Festival at Wembley, England.

Shelly and David stayed together until 1985, and their other successful singles were the Top 20 entries *Silent Partners* and *It's a Be Together Night*, both in 1984. The reason for their split was due to the fact that they couldn't find good duet material, but was probably not helped by Shelly and Allen's divorce. Shelly's most successful solo hits between 1984 and 1986 were *Somebody Buy This Cowgirl a Beer* (1984), *Now There's You* and *Don't Make Me Wait on the Moon* (both 1985). She had her last chart entry in 1986, the Top 60 single *Love Don't Come Any Better Than This*.

Shelly has since remarried, and in 1988, she and David got back together for a series of show dates.

RECOMMENDED ALBUMS:

"Red Hot" (Viva)(1983)
"West By West" (Warner/Viva)(1983)
"Don't Make Me Wait on the Moon" (Warner/Viva)(1984)
With David Frizzell:
"Carryin' on the Family Name" (Warner Brothers)(1981)
"The David Frizzell and Shelly West Album" (Warner/Viva)(1982)
"Our Best to You" (Warner/Viva)(1983)
"In Session" (Viva)(1983)

SPEEDY WEST

(Steel Guitar, Composer)

Given Name:	**Wesley Webb West**
Date of Birth:	**January 25, 1924**
Where Born:	**Springfield, Missouri**
Married:	**1. Opal (div.)**
	2. Mary
Children:	**Donald Wesley, Gary Ernest, Tauni Dee**

The legendary Leo Fender, the creator of the Fender guitar, described Speedy West as the greatest steel guitarist in the world. The combination of Speedy West and guitarist Jimmy Bryant was one of the most famed on the West Coast.

Speedy became a member of Hank Penny's Band in 1946, leaving the following year to join the Spade Cooley Band, where he stayed for a year and then joined Cliffie Stone's Band, in 1948. He remained in situ until 1959, during which time he played out of Los Angeles. In 1949, Speedy appeared as part of Stone's band in the movie *House of the Sierras* and the following year appeared in *Singing Spurs*. Speedy's first recording with Cliffie was *Steel Strike*.

In 1951, Speedy signed to Capitol Records and also made his debut on the *Grand Ole Opry*. That year, he released his first single, *Stainless Steel/Railroadin'* and in 1954, Speedy released the album ***Two Guitars Country Style***, with Jimmy Bryant. In 1956, he and Jimmy Bryant received the "Best Instrumental Group of Less than 6" in the Annual D.J. Poll. Speedy continued releasing albums on Capitol, many of which were issued in Japan, France and Germany.

On leaving Cliffie Stone, in 1959, Speedy concentrated on session work and it is estimated that he played on more than 6,000 songs with 177 vocalists. These included sessions for Frank Sinatra, Bing Crosby, Phil Harris, Dinah Shore, Ernest Tubb, Tennessee Ernie Ford, Johnny Horton and Jim Reeves. Speedy produced Loretta Lynn's debut single, *I'm a Honky Tonk Angel*, on which he utilized double-tracking after hearing Patti Page's *Cross Over the Bridge*.

In 1975, Speedy got together with Jimmy Bryant after having not worked together for 16 years and recorded an album which was released in 1990 as ***For the Last Time***. When the movie *Coal Miner's Daughter* was released in 1980, guitarist Billy Strange played the part of Speedy West.

In 1981, Speedy was struck down by a stroke which made it impossible for him to play again. He contemplated suicide, but then considered all the positive things that had happened in his life and decided to put up with the pain. As of 1990, he was emceeing and talking on music, although in retirement in Broken Arrow, California. Speedy's son Gary works as Speedy West, Jr. and plays steel around the Oklahoma area. Speedy was quoted as saying "I used to get high, higher than a kite, just playing my guitar. You don't have to use drugs and drink if you love your instrument enough." Speedy was inducted into the Steel Guitar Hall of Fame in 1980. Speedy and his wife, Mary, live in Claremore, Oklahoma, and Speedy, despite his illness, remains chipper and is a font of information and remembers with affection his years in music.

RECOMMENDED ALBUMS:

"West of Hawaii" (Capitol)(1958)
"Steel Guitar" (Capitol)(1960) [Re-issued on Stetson UK in the original sleeve (1987)]
"Guitar Spectacular (The Incredible Stylings of Speedy West)" (Capitol)(1962) [Re-issued on Stetson UK in the original packaging (1989)]
Speedy West & Jimmy Bryant:
"Two Guitars Country Style" (Capitol)(1954)
"For the Last Time" (Step One)(1990)

JOHNNY WESTERN

(Singer, Songwriter, Guitar, Actor, Writer)

Date of Birth:	**October 28, 1934**
Where Born:	**Two Harbors, Minnesota**
Married:	**1. Louisa (div.)**
	2. Joenna
Children:	**1. Louisa, Leslie; 2. Brandi; stepchildren: Jami and Jana**

Although Johnny Western remains a shadowy figure on the Country landscape, his contribution to Western music is too great

Have guitar will travel, ***Johnny Western***

to be ignored. His predilection for the Old West was born out of the same love that Marty Robbins and Johnny Cash felt, and has subsequently led to the rebirth of the genre with the Warner Western label.

Johnny's family moved to Northfield, Minnesota, when he was quite young, where his father was Director of Physical Education. The town had become known because of the James Gang's abortive raid on the town's First National Bank in 1876 and this may have led to Johnny's interest.

When he was age 5, he became a lifetime fan of Gene Autry, after seeing the movie *Guns & Guitars*. By the time he was 15 and still at high school, Johnny was a deejay and singing cowboy on KDHL Northfield. *Billboard* named him as the youngest deejay and singer on commercial radio in the U.S. By the time he was 16, Johnny became a singing cowboy on KMMT-TV and gained a recording contract with Minneapolis-St. Paul label and publishing company J.O.C.O. He recorded two singles for the label, *The Violet & the Rose/Give Me More, More, More* and *Let Old Mother Nature Have Her Way/Little Buffalo Bill*, without success.

During the early 50's, he started to make his mark on TV, and then he began playing the rodeo circuit with the Sons of the Pioneers, but soon Hollywood beckoned, and in 1956, he arrived there to appear with Gene Autry. That year, he toured Canada with Autry and met Johnny Cash in Toronto. As well as appearing in some fifty movies (see Movie section), Johnny began his songwriting career

Johnny was asked to write the theme song for a new TV series to star Richard Boone, called *Have Gun Will Travel,* and Johnny sang the song *The Ballad of Paladin* at the beginning of each episode. The show ran from 1957 until 1962.

Because of the impact of the show, Johnny found himself signed to Columbia Records, by the legendary A & R man Mitch Miller. The following year, Johnny met Cash again, in California, and Cash asked him to join his show as emcee and singer, and that year, Cash also joined Columbia, where they were both produced by Don Law.

From August 1959 through April 1962, Johnny played on most of Cash's recordings. Johnny's singles for Columbia were *Ballad of Paladin* (1958), *Only the Lonely* (1959), *Della's Gone* (1960), *Darling Corey* and the re-issue of *Ballad of Paladin* (both 1961). He made his debut on the *Grand Ole Opry* in 1960. Two years later, Johnny recorded with the Tennessee Three when Cash became ill before a session, and Johnny took over the time. He recorded the self-penned songs *Gunfighter* and *Geronimo*. *Gunfighter* became his 1962 single and his final release on the label was *Kathy Come Home* (1963).

The following year, Johnny released *Light the Fuse/Tender Years*, which was released on Philips. He stayed with Cash for almost six years and then, in 1965, promoter Hap Peebles booked Johnny Western as a solo. He became very popular in Las Vegas, and four times a year, he appeared at the Golden Nugget. He also made a name for himself at the Cheyenne Frontier Days.

In 1967, Johnny went to the independent label Hep, and released *The Violet & the Rose/Ruby*. During 1970, Johnny recorded music for the movie *Dodge City, Kansas*, which starred Hugh O'Brian. A single was released on Boot Hill Records entitled *The Streets of Old Dodge City*, backed by his Columbia recording of *The Ballad of Paladin*.

In 1976, he wrote the music for the movie *Rodeo—A Matter of Style* and recorded the title song for the TV series *Mr. Rodeo Cowboy.* That year, Johnny was involved in a bad auto accident in Rawlings, and his life was saved by a passing trucker.

Through his career, Johnny was involved with the music for and appeared in the following TV series: *Have Gun Will Travel*, *Pony Express*, *Gunsmoke*, *Boots and Saddles*, *Wells Fargo* and *Bat Masterson*.

In 1986, Johnny signed with Great Empire Broadcasting and does a daily 4-hour show over KFDI Wichita, Kansas. In 1993, he commenced work on a new album, ***Johnny Western and the Sons of the Pioneers***, which swiftly became ***Johnny Western and the Sons of the Pioneers and Friends***, when they were joined by Rex Allen, Rex Allen, Jr., Sons of the San Joaquin, Red Stegall and Michael Martin Murphey. However, Johnny was temporarily sidelined by a quintuple heart bypass. That year, *Have Gun Will Travel* was inducted into the Television Music Archives Hall of Fame.

RECOMMENDED ALBUMS:

"Have Gun Will Travel" (Columbia)(1962)
"Johnny Western" (Bear Family Germany)(1980)
"The Gunfighter" (Bear Family Germany)(1981)
"Gunfight at the O.K. Corral" (Bear Family Germany)(1989)
"Heroes & Cowboys" (Bear Family Germany)(1993)

Westerners refer LOUISE MASSEY

BILLY EDD WHEELER

(Singer, Songwriter, Guitar, Author, Poet, Actor)

Given Name:	**Billy Edd Wheeler**
Date of Birth:	**December 9, 1932**
Where Born:	**Whitesville, West Virginia**
Married:	**Mary Mitchell Bannerman**
Children:	**Lucy, Travis**

Billy Edd Wheeler was once dubbed "the thinking man's hillbilly" by one historian; however, he could also be labeled Country music's "Renaissance Man."

Born in Boone County, West Virginia, the illegitimate son of a coal miner, Billy Edd had a typical mountain youth, first attending Warren Wilson College near Asheville, North Carolina, and then Berea College in Kentucky, receiving a B.A. degree in 1955. During 1955 and 1956, Billy Edd was editor of *Mountain Life and Work* magazine. During a hitch in the Navy in 1957 and 1958, Wheeler took pilot training.

On his departure from the service, Billy Edd returned to Berea College, where he became an instructor. In 1961, having left Berea, he appeared with the Lexington, Kentucky, Symphony Orchestra, playing his Folk songs in concert. His earliest recordings, which were Folk-flavored, appeared on the Monitor label and included the albums ***U.S.A.*** (1961) and ***Bluegrass Too*** (1962). He later studied at the Yale Drama School.

Following his year at Yale, Billy Edd spent four years as a New York resident where he wrote plays and gained his initial reputation as a songwriter with *The Reverend Mr. Black* and *Desert Pete*, both of them Pop hits for the Folk-oriented Kingston Trio, in 1963. After that Billy Edd cut an album of his own Folk numbers for Kapp Records.

Billy Edd scored a Country chart Top 3 success late in 1964 with his *Ode to the Little Brown Shack Out Back*, a tribute to that vanishing symbol of life in rural America, the outdoor toilet. He followed with several more recordings for Kapp, including four additional albums and some singles, but only *I Ain't the Worryin' Kind* in 1968 made the lower region of the chart. As a writer, he did better, turning out the major Country hit *Jackson* for June Carter and Johnny Cash in 1967 and having a couple of his numbers recorded by Elvis Presley.

In 1969, he switched over to United Artists, turning out an album along with two lesser hits in *West Virginia Woman* and *Fried Chicken and a Country Tune*. The most memorable cut on the album however, was the satirical look at the Great Society in Appalachia, not written by Billy Edd, titled *The Interstate Is Comin' Thru the Outhouse*. During this period, Wheeler moved first to North Carolina, then to Nashville and ultimately back to North Carolina, where he settled near Asheville.

More recorded efforts on both RCA Victor and Capitol won praise from critics, but had minimal impact on the charts, with *200 Lbs. o' Slingin' Hound* going Top 75 on RCA in 1972. He scraped into the chart with *Duel Under the Snow*, on Radio Cinema. He did have one more gigantic success as a writer, being co-author with Roger Bowling of Kenny Rogers' monster hit *Coward of the County*, in 1980. Billy Edd's last chart single was *Daddy*, a Top 60 duet with Rashell Richmond on NSD.

In the meantime, Billy Edd diversified his artistry, coming out with a book of poems, *Song of a Woods Colt*, in 1969 and authoring such outdoor dramas as *Hatfields & McCoys* and *Song of the Cumberland Gap*. Sometimes he acted and sang in them as well. He also continued to record his songs for such companies as Flying Fish and Sagittarius. More recently he has written (and sometimes co-written with Loyal Jones) several collections of humorous stories from the Appalachian Mountains.

He also continues to write songs and performs them at various festivals and workshops. One of his recent compositions, *Hormones*, takes a light-hearted look at recently alleged romantic entanglements involving such well-known figures as Bill Clinton, Gennifer Flowers and also the Duchess of York. IMT

RECOMMENDED ALBUMS:

"Billy Edd—U.S.A." (Monitor)(1961)
"Billy Edd & Bluegrass Too" (Monitor)(1962)
"Memories of America" (Kapp)(1965) [First released with title "A Brand New Bag of Songs"]
"The Wheeler Man" (Kapp)(1965)
"Goin' Town & Country" (Kapp)(1966)
"Paper Birds" (Kapp)(1967)
"I Ain't the Worryin' Kind" (Kapp)(1968)
"Nashville Zodiac" (United Artists)(1969)
"Love" (RCA Victor)(1971)
"My Mountains, My Music" (Sagittarius)(1975)
"Wild Mountain Flowers" (Flying Fish)(1979)
"Asheville" (Sagittarius)(1982)
"Gee-Haw Whimmy Diddle" (Sagittarius)(ca. 1984)

KAREN WHEELER

(Singer, Songwriter, Guitar, Banjo, Keyboards, Actress)

Given Name:	**Karen Deen Wheeler**
Date of Birth:	**March 12, 1947**
Where Born:	**Sikeston, Missouri**
Married:	**Glen Shoffner**
Children:	**Kevin, Stacia, Alicia, Jonathan, Danny, Donnell, Ben**

Karen Wheeler, the daughter of veteran performer Onie Wheeler, is a Country vocalist who while never quite attaining major stardom, established herself as a talented, dynamic, and durable performer.

Karen was born in Sikeston, Missouri. Her dad moved back and forth between there and Nashville in her early years as he endeavored to place his own career on a solid footing. Following in his footsteps, the youngster had her first single on K-Ark at 11, *Wait Till I'm Sixteen,* and signed with Columbia at age 14. As the decade progressed, she developed into a beautiful blonde with a dynamic vocal style. She signed with Boone Records and appeared as a more or less regular on such shows as the *Renfro Valley Barn Dance* and Wheeling's *Jamboree USA*. She also did a USO tour of Vietnam and Thailand with a Roy Acuff entourage.

When Arlene Harden dropped out of the Harden Trio in 1967, Karen filled in for her one weekend and ended up staying for nearly two years. She and another girl, Shirley Michaels, who replaced Robbie Harden, recorded an album on Starday with Bobby Harden, and Karen and Bobby had a successful single with *We Got Each Other*.

After going solo again in 1968, Karen signed first with Chart in 1972 and then RCA Victor in 1974 and had three numbers which landed on the Country chart. These were *The First Time for Us* (Chart, 1972, Top 70), *Born to Love and Satisfy* (Top 40) and *What Can I Do (To Make You Happy)* (both RCA, 1974). Meanwhile she guested frequently on the *Opry* and toured in package shows with such artists as Glenn Barber and Tommy Overstreet. Karen also made a pilot show as female lead for a TV drama with Jerry Reed and the late Claude Akins, about two Nashville detectives, but it never got sold as a series.

In 1974, she signed on as an opening act with Conway Twitty and also opened for Crash Craddock, Mickey Gilley, and Loretta Lynn. It was during this twelve-year period that her rousing arrangement of *Muleskinner Blues* became her virtual trademark. Dolly Parton

Karen Wheeler**, talented daughter of **Onie Wheeler

had a hit with the old Jimmie Rodgers number in 1970, but Karen's version was—if possible—even more dynamic and she continued performing the song long after Dolly dropped the number from her performing repertoire. Karen had some releases on Capitol in the later 70's, without success.

The mid-to-late 80's proved a difficult time for Karen Wheeler. She got over the shock of her father's sudden death on the *Opry* stage in May 1984 only to be diagnosed as having cancer in 1986. The next four years were tough ones but by the early 90's, she had beaten the illness and resumed her career with the aid of husband-manager Glen Shoffner and her family.

Bouncing back, Karen recorded three albums for Fox Fire and has gone back on the road again. Her new releases include not only *Muleskinner Blues* but also some of her father's classic sacred compositions (popularized in part through Lester Flatt and Earl Scruggs) such as *Mother Prays Loud in Her Sleep* and *I Saw [Dad] with God Last Night*. When not on tour Glen and Karen reside in Mount Juliet, Tennessee. IMT

RECOMMENDED ALBUMS:

"Special Delivery from Karen Wheeler" (Fox Fire)(ca. 1992) [Cassette only]
"Love Made" (Fox Fire)(ca. 1992) [Cassette only]
"A Country Christmas" (Fox Fire)(1992) [Cassette only]

ONIE WHEELER

(Singer, Songwriter, Harmonica, Guitar, Comedy)

Given Name:	**Onie Daniel Wheeler**
Date of Birth:	**November 10, 1921**
Where Born:	**Senath, Missouri**
Married:	**Betty Jean Crowe**
Children:	**Karen Deen (Karen Wheeler), Onia Jerene, Daniel Eugene**
Date of Death:	**May 26, 1984**

Onie Wheeler experienced a varied musicalcareer that endured for nearly four decades and produced some unusual and highly creative material. At times his stylings bordered on Rockabilly, Bluegrass and mainstream Country without conveniently fitting exactly into any category. While he never became a major star, his original songs and performances deserve to be honored and remembered for a long time.

A native of southeastern Missouri, Wheeler lost his mother at age 4, which may help to account for his later ability to produce some of the most original and excellent sentimental "mother" songs in the history of the genre. His farmer father later remarried and re-located the extended family to Morley, Missouri. Onie learned to play guitar and harmonica in his youth but seemingly never aspired to a career in music until after his five years in the U.S. Army during WWII. An injury to the index finger on his left hand limited his guitar playing abilities so the harmonica became his foremost instrument.

Onie began his musical endeavors in 1945, and spent the next several years on small radio stations where he often held down a day job in order to support himself and his family. These included stints in such locales as KWOC Poplar Bluff, Missouri; KBTM Jonesboro, Arkansas; WWOK Flint, Michigan; WKTM Mayfield, Kentucky and KSIM Sikeston, Missouri. In 1946, he married Betty Jean Crowe, who sometimes worked with him as "Little Jean." While in Michigan, the Wheelers cut their first record on the Agana label, one side of which was the old Jimmie Davis favorite *Shackles and Chains*. In Sikeston, in 1950, Onie met the brothers A. J. and Doyal Nelson, who, along with Ernest Thompson, would periodically work and tour with him as band members, under the name of the Ozark Cowboys. The Nelsons in particular remained associated with him off-and-on for the rest of his life. About 1952, the band journeyed to Texas and played clubs for several months. They met Little Jimmy Dickens, who suggested that they go to Nashville and attempt to land a record contract.

In Music City, Onie finally landed a deal with Columbia, through the help of Troy Martin, who took half ownership of some his client's songs in exchange for his aid. Onie's initial session on August, 1953 resulted in two of his most memorable originals, *Run 'Em Off* and *Mother Prays Loud in Her Sleep*, both released on OKeh and quickly covered by Lefty Frizzell and Flatt & Scruggs, respectively. Although his own versions didn't gain a place on the then limited *Billboard* charts, they did quite well. One of his songs from a May, 1954 OKeh recording, *I Saw Mother with God Last Night*, went on to also become a Flatt & Scruggs Bluegrass-Gospel classic.

Columbia renewed Onie's contract in 1955 and one of his 1956 numbers *Onie's Bop* (a song so personal that virtually no one else could do it), went on to become a Rockabilly classic. In this period, Wheeler made one extended tour with Elvis Presley and later worked as a featured vocalist with the Flatt & Scruggs band on their chain of live TV programs in the Appalachian region. In the fall of 1957, Onie signed with Sun and cut another of his minor classics, *Jump Right Out of This Jukebox*. During this period, he often worked package shows with other Sun artists such as Jerry Lee Lewis, Billy Lee Riley, and Carl Perkins.

Wheeler's career went through several phases in the next few years. He went to California briefly in late 1958 and then returned to Missouri and operated a Country music park until 1961 and then came back to Nashville. He had sessions for K-Ark, Epic, Starday, United Artists, JAB and Musicor in the 60's. Although none of his recordings became hits, at least one, *I'm Gonna Hang My Britches Up*, from 1965, reveals his flair for humor. For a time Onie fronted the George Jones Show, then worked with Roy Acuff's band as a regular from 1964 to 1967 and periodically thereafter. In between, the Missourian labored at the Sho-Bud factory and worked as a single. In 1973, he had a moderate hit on Royal American with *John's Been Shuckin' My Corn* and released an album on his own Onie label. In later years Wheeler moved to suburban Mt. Juliet, operated a guitar repair shop and worked the *Opry* with the Acuff unit. In the meantime, daughter Karen launched a musical career of her own, signing with Chart and RCA and having a trio of hits.

In January, 1984, Onie had an aneurysm and took some months to get back in action. On the night of May 25, 1984, he played the Friday night *Opry* with the Smoky Mountain Boys and then worked with the aid of the Nelsons on the Rev. Jimmie Snow's *Grand Ole Gospel Time* that followed. While singing *Mother Rang the Dinner Bell and Sang*, Onie collapsed and died on stage.

In 1991, Bear Family Records of Germany reissued all of his OKeh, Columbia, and Sun masters on a cd. IMT

RECOMMENDED ALBUMS:

"John's Been Shuckin' My Corn" (Onie)(ca. 1973)

"Onie's Bop" (Bear Family Germany)(1991)

CLARENCE WHITE

(Singer, Songwriter, Guitar, Mandolin)

Date of Birth: June 7, 1944

Where Born: Lewiston, Maine

Date of Death: July 14, 1973

Had Clarence White lived longer, he would probably have emerged as the single most important leader of the West Coast Country-Rock movement. Only Chris Hillman has similar background and pedigree, but Clarence had a schooling in Bluegrass and traditional Country music that even surpassed Hillman.

Although born in Maine, Clarence was raised in California. His early career was spent with the Country Boys, from age 10, and they evolved into the celebrated Kentucky Colonels. Following the attempts at "electrification," Clarence left the group and became a sessionman. He played with Cajun Gib & Gene, a duo comprising Gib Gilbeau and Gene Parsons, that worked a lot with the Gosdin Brothers (Rex and Vern). Around this time, Clarence recorded an album for Bakersfield International, which was unreleased. In 1967, he appeared on the ***Gene Clark and the Gosdin Brothers*** album.

The following year, Clarence joined forces with Gene Parsons, Gib Gilbeau, Wayne Moore, Sneaky Pete Kleinow and Glen D. Hardin as Nashville West and recorded the self-titled album, for Sierra, which was eventually released in 1978. He made his most significant move in September 1968, when he joined the Byrds' sixth configuration, as lead guitarist.

He moonlighted while with the band, and his external sessions included Joe Cocker's self-titled album (1969), Randy Newman's ***12 Songs*** (1970), Marc Benno's ***Minnows***, Delaney & Bonnie's ***Motel Shot***, Rita Coolidge's self-titled album (all 1971) and the Everly Brothers' ***Stories We Could Tell*** and Mother Hen's self-titled album (both 1972).

Clarence left the Byrds, on their demise, in 1973 and returned to session work. That year, he appeared on Skip Battin's ***Skip***, Country Gazette's ***Don't Give Up Your Day Job*** and Arlo Guthrie's ***Last of the Brooklyn Cowboys***. In addition, he joined Muleskinner with Richard Greene, John Guerin, Bill Keith, David Grisman, John Kahn and Peter Rowan. They released one eponymous album, that year.

Clarence also started work on a solo album and played some dates with the Kentucky

Colonels. Then on July 14, 1973, while loading equipment onto the band bus, after a gig, he was hit by a drunken woman driver and killed. Several posthumous albums were released of his work with the Kentucky Colonels and the Byrds, and in 1974, albums were released featuring his 1973 session work. These included Jackson Browne's ***Late for the Sky***, Terry Melcher and Maria Muldaur's self-titled albums and Gene Parsons' ***Kindling***.

In addition to the sessions mentioned, Clarence appeared on releases by Ricky Nelson, Wynn Stewart and the Flying Burrito Brothers. He was a consummate performer who was "done too soon."

RECOMMENDED ALBUMS:

"Muleskinner" (Warner Brothers)(1973) [As a member of Muleskinner]

"Nashville West" (Sierra)(1976) [As a member of Nashville West]

[See also, Country Boys, the, Kentucky Colonels, the, Byrds]

Roland White refer COUNTRY BOYS, KENTUCKY COLONELS, COUNTRY GAZETTE and NASHVILLE BLUEGRASS BAND

TONY JOE WHITE

(Singer, Songwriter, Guitar, Harmonica)

Given Name:	**Tony Joe White**
Date of Birth:	**July 23, 1943**
Where Born:	**Goodwill, Louisiana**
Married:	**Leann**
Children:	**Jim Bob, Jody, Michelle**

In the words of the guru of music critics, Robert K. Oermann, Tony Joe White is "the growling, sexy . . . bluesman who came steaming out of Louisiana with the red hot *Polk Salad Annie* in 1969." It was the French who named Tony Joe's music Swamp Rock and gave him the sobriquet of the "Swamp Fox," following the success of *Soul Francisco* in France.

Tony was the youngest of seven children born in a part-Cherokee background. He worked the clubs around Corpus Christi, Texas, during the mid-60's and he gravitated to Nashville in 1968, where he signed to Combine Music, the publishing wing of Monument Records. In 1969, Tony Joe released his debut album ***Black and White*** for Monument, which was produced by Billy Swan. In July that year, Tony Joe entered the Pop Singles chart with *Polk Salad Annie* and it rose to the Top 10. A week after it charted, Dusty Springfield entered the chart with Tony Joe's *Willie and Laura Mae Jones* and had a Top 80 hit with it. Tony ended up the year with his single of *Roosevelt and Ira Lee (Night of the Moccasin)*, which went Top 50 on the Pop chart. During 1969, Tony Joe released a second album, ***Continued***.

*Le Swamp Fox, **Tony Joe White***

At the beginning of 1970, Brook Benton had a Top 5 hit with Tony Joe's *Rainy Night in Georgia* and it was Certified Gold. The song has since been recorded by over 100 different artists. That year, Tony Joe appeared on the U.K. Pop chart with the Top 25 *Groupie Girl*. In the U.S., he had a low level entry with *Save Your Sugar for Me*. That year, Tony Joe released his album ***Tony Joe***.

In 1971, he moved to Warner Brothers Records and released his eponymous album. During the 70's, Tony Joe's more memorable cuts were *Polk Salad Annie* (Elvis Presley), *For Ole Times Sake* (Elvis Presley), *A Rainy Night in Georgia* (Hank Williams, Jr.) and *I've Got a Thing About You Baby* (Elvis Presley).

After recording *The Train I'm On* (1972), Tony Joe appeared on the 1973 soundtrack album of the musical adaptation of *Othello*, called *Catch My Soul*. That same year, he made his final album for Warner Brothers, entitled ***Homemade Ice Cream***. In 1976, Tony Joe recorded one album for 20th Century Fox Records entitled ***Eyes***.

It was four years until he recorded another album, ***The Real Thang***, for Casablanca. From this album Tony Joe had a Top 80 Pop hit, *I Can't Get Off on It* and a basement Country hit with his parody of *Mamas Don't Let Your Babies Grow Up to Be Cowboys*, entitled *Mama Don't Let Your Cowboys Grow Up to Be Babies*.

In 1983, Tony Joe released his album ***Dangerous*** for Columbia and from this Tony had two Country chart entries, *The Lady in My Life* (Top 60, 1983) and *We Belong Together* (Top 90, 1984). In 1989, Waylon Jennings had a Country hit with Tony Joe's *Trouble Man*. In all, Waylon recorded three of his songs, the others being *Up in Arkansas* and *Endangered Species*.

Tony Joe worked closely in 1989 with Tina Turner on her watershed album ***Foreign Affair***. He contributed four songs to the album (and also played guitar and harmonica on the album): *Steamy Windows*, *Foreign Affair*, *Undercover Agent for the Blues* and *You Know Who*. The following year, Tony Joe released his first album in eight years, ***Closer to the Truth***. It was released on Tony Joe's Swamp label in the U.S. and Remark in Europe. To date it has sold over 100,000 copies in France alone. During 1991 and 1992, Tony Joe toured throughout Europe and played some shows with Eric Clapton and Joe Cocker. Cocker has recorded several White songs including *Angeline*, *Let the Healing Begin* and *Out of the Rain*.

In 1993, Remark released a new album ***Path of a Decent Groove***, while Warner Brothers issued ***The Best of Tony Joe White***. In addition, Warner Brothers re-released Tony Joe's albums on that label in cd format. Kayenta Productions in Paris has just completed a documentary of Tony Joe's life.

Other recorded versions of songs written by Tony Joe are: *3/4 Time* (Ray Charles), *A Rainy Night in Georgia* (Randy Crawford), *Dream On* (George Jones), *Gospel Singer* (Tanya Tucker), *Love M.D.* (Hank Williams, Jr.), *Mississippi Moon* and *Steamy Windows* (both John Anderson), *Out of the Rain* (Etta James) and *Southern Man* (Roy Orbison).

In 1994, Conway Twitty and Sam Moore got together to record *Rainy Night in Georgia* as a part of the album ***Rhythm, Country & Blues***, which would be Conway's last recording. To pigeon-hole Tony Joe White is impossible. In his words, "They don't know if I'm black, white, Country or Rock."

RECOMMENDED ALBUMS:

"Black and White" (Monument)(1969)

"Continued" (Monument)(1969)

"Tony Joe" (Monument)(1970)

"Tony Joe White" (Warner Brothers)(1971)

"The Train I'm On" (Warner Brothers)(1972)

"Homemade Ice Cream" (Warner Brothers)(1973)

"Eyes" (20th Century Fox)(1976)

"The Real Thang" (Casablanca)(1980)

"Dangerous" (Columbia)(1983)

"Live in Europe (1971)" (Swamp)(1987)

"Closer to the Truth" (Swamp)(1991)

"Path of a Decent Groove" (Remark France)(1993)

"The Best of Tony Joe White" (Warner Brothers)(1993)

WHITES, The

When Formed: 1971

BUCK WHITE

(Vocals, Piano, Mandolin, Guitar, Harmonica, Fiddle, Banjo)

Given Name: H.S. White
Date of Birth: December 13, 1930
Where Born: Oklahoma
Married: Pat Goza
Children: Sharon, Cheryl, Melissa, Rosanne (Rosie)

SHARON WHITE

(Vocals, Guitar)

Given Name: Sharon White
Date of Birth: December 17, 1953
Where Born: Abilene, Texas
Married: 1. Jack Hicks (div.)
2. Ricky Skaggs
Children: Mandy, Andrew, Molly Kate

CHERYL WHITE

(Vocals, Bass Guitar)

Given Name: Cheryl White
Date of Birth: January 27, 1955
Where Born: Abilene, Texas
Married: David Warren

Supporting Musicians:

Jerry Douglas (Dobro), Ricky Skaggs (Fiddle, Guitar), Tim Crouch (Fiddle), Neil Worf (Drums), Rosie White, Pete Reiniger, Steve Thomas

During the first half of the 80's, the Whites were one of the top vocal groups in Country music. They became a sort of contemporary Carter Family. Their music, a blend of Country, Bluegrass and Gospel, is not currently in favor with radio deejays, but they still are in great demand on personal appearances.

Although born in Oklahoma, Buck grew up in Wichita Falls, Texas. He began playing piano in 1943, while still a boy and was totally besotted with music. He was initially influenced by the records of black Blues musicians including Pete Johnson and Albert Ammons and listened to the WLS *Barn Dance* and the *Grand Ole Opry*. While still in high school, he started playing mandolin and in 1947, formed a four-piece band. The band got a radio program in Vernon, Texas, fifty miles from Wichita Falls. Buck listened to the music of the Callahan Brothers, Karl and Harty and the Blue Sky Boys and became very interested in Bob Wills and Bill Monroe.

After leaving school, Buck worked as a pipefitter, while still playing various local bands. He soon came to specialize on mandolin and piano. In 1952, Buck began playing with the Blue Sage Boys. He also did quite a lot of session work. When Country stars like Lefty Frizzell, Floyd Tillman and Hank Snow played local dates, Buck was called in to play piano.

Buck, Sharon and Cheryl, the ***Whites***

Buck moved to Abilene and while playing in a band, he met his wife, whose brother was playing on the same show. They married in 1951 and settled down in Abilene.

In 1962, the White family, now augmented by daughters Sharon and Cheryl, moved to Fort Smith, Arkansas, where Buck and Pat (a fine singer), along with Arnold and Peggy Johnston, formed the Down Home Folks. In 1966, Sharon and Cheryl joined with Teddie and Eddie Johnston as the Down Home Kids. At that time, Sharon was playing bass, but soon Cheryl took over on that instrument and Sharon switched to guitar.

The family moved to Nashville in 1971, where Buck, Pat, Sharon and Cheryl became Buck and the Down Home Folks. The following year, they recorded an eponymous album for County Records on which they were assisted by Kenny Baker (fiddle) and Jack Hicks (who was with Bill Monroe's Blue Grass Boys). That same year they appeared with Doug Greene and Vic Jordan as the Buck White Family on the album ***Liza Jane & Sally Ann***, on Old Homestead. They later recorded a Gospel album with Doug and Vic for State Fair Records, titled ***In God's Eyes***. At this point, the group became full-time musicians and in 1973, Pat retired to concentrate on the rest of her family.

In 1977, County released a second album on the group, titled ***In Person/Live at the Old Time Picking Parlor***. Guests on the album were Norman Blake, Mark O'Connor, Jack Hicks and Terry Dearmore. That year, they also recorded the album ***That Down Home Feelin'*** for Ridge Runner, which featured Jerry Douglas, Roland White and Ricky Skaggs. The following year, they recorded ***Poor Folk's Pleasure*** for Sugar Hill. In 1979, while the family was playing in Japan, they recorded a live album ***Buck and Family Live, Trio*** for the Japan label, on which Jerry Douglas played Dobro. Following their work on Emmylou Harris' ***Blue Kentucky Girl***, the group opened for Emmylou on tour in 1979. That year, the Whites appeared on Ricky Skaggs' solo album ***Sweet Temptation***.

Buck released the 1980 solo album ***More Pretty Girls Than One***, for Sugar Hill, on which he was supported by David Grisman, Sam Bush, Tony Rice and, of course, Sharon, Cheryl, Jerry Douglas and Ricky Skaggs and which Skaggs produced. In 1981, Sharon and Ricky Skaggs married. That year, the Whites appeared on Capitol and made their debut on the Country chart with *Send Me the Pillow You Dream On*, but it peaked in the Top 70. The transition from the Buck White Family to the Whites marked Buck White moving to piano from mandolin.

In 1982, the Whites signed to Curb and started to make their mark on Elektra/Curb that year, having two Top 10 hits, *You Put the Blue in Me* and *Hangin' Around*. During that year, Cheryl was absent having a baby and sister Rosie stepped into the group and remained. In 1983, they switched to Warner/Curb and charted with *I Wonder Who's Holding My Baby Tonight* (Top 10), *When the New Wears Off Our Love* (Top 25) and *Give Me Back That Old Familiar Feeling* (Top 10).

The Whites moved to MCA/Curb in 1984 and that year, they chalked up two hits, *Forever You* (Top 15) and *Pins and Needles* (Top 10), both from their debut album on the label, ***Forever You***. The following year, the Whites charted with *If It Ain't Love (Let's Leave It Alone)* (Top 15), *Hometown Gossip* (Top 30) and *I Don't Want to Get Over You* (Top 40); all the tracks coming from the album ***Whole New World***, which also included *Daddy's Hands*, with which its writer, Holly Dunn, would have a hit in 1986.

In 1986, Ricky Skaggs handed over the production reins to veteran producer Larry Butler and it was the Butler-produced track *Love Won't Wait* that went Top 40. This came from the Whites' ***Greatest Hits*** album which was really a ***Greatest Hits*** plus. ***Ain't No Binds*** was the first full album produced by Butler and this yielded *It Shoulda Been Easy* (Top 30, 1986) and *There Ain't No Binds* (Top 60, 1987). One of the tracks, *Love Can't Ever Get Better Than This*, was really a duet between Sharon and Ricky Skaggs and was included on Ricky's album ***Love's Gonna Get Ya!*** It became a Top 10 hit and was the recipient of the CMA's 1987 "Vocal Duo of the Year" award.

That year, the Whites traveled to England to appear at the Wembley Festival. In 1989, the Whites recorded the Gospel album ***Doing It By the Book***, for the Canaan label. Although Ricky Skaggs was very busy, miraculously, time became available so that he could produce the album. As Sharon said, "The Lord's timing's really in it." The title track scraped into the lower regions of the Country chart. Since then, the Whites have not recorded, but are still greeted with great affection on the *Opry* and wherever they appear. In 1994, the Whites began working on a new album for Step One Records.

RECOMMENDED ALBUMS:

As Buck White and the Down Home Folks:
"Buck White and the Down Home Folks" (County)(1972)
"In Person/Live at the Old Time Pickin' Parlor" (County)(1977)
As the Whites:
"Old Familiar Feeling" (Warner/Curb)(1983)
"Forever You" (MCA/Curb)(1984)
"Whole New World" (MCA/Curb)(1985)
"Greatest Hits" (MCA/Curb)(1986)
"Ain't No Binds" (MCA/Curb)(1987)
"Doing it By the Book" (Canaan)(1989)
Buck White:
"More Pretty Girls Than One" (Sugar Hill)(1980)

KEITH WHITLEY

(Singer, Songwriter, Guitar)

Given Name:	**Jesse Keith Whitley**
Date of Birth:	**July 1, 1955**
Where Born:	**Sandy Hook, Kentucky**
Married:	**1. Kathy (div.)**
	2. Lorrie Morgan (m. 1986)
Children:	**Jesse**
Date of Death:	**May 9, 1989**

Keith Whitley came out of an Appalachian Kentucky Bluegrass background to emerge as one of the new Honky-Tonk vocalists of the late 80's.

From Bluegrass to Country star, ***Keith Whitley***

A native of Sandy Hook in the Big Sandy Valley of eastern Kentucky, Keith took an interest in Country music as his parents, Elmer and Faye Whitley, had a good collection of Country records, especially those of Hank Williams, George Jones, and Lefty Frizzell. Something of a local child star, Keith made his TV debut about 1962, guesting on Buddy Starcher's popular early morning show on WCHS in Charleston, West Virginia. A few years later, he met Ricky Skaggs from nearby Lawrence County and they formed the East Kentucky Mountain Boys, re-creating a sound not unlike the early efforts of the Stanley Brothers.

Ralph Stanley heard them early in 1970 and invited the adolescent singers to guest with him and the Clinch Mountain Boys on a few festivals. In 1971 and 1972, they worked all summer with him and sometimes in the off season, gaining valuable experience.

In those days, Keith sang lead and also played a fine lead guitar. In addition to several albums with Ralph, the young twosome cut a pair of duet albums, the first a Stanley tribute for Jalyn, and the second a traditional Bluegrass album of somewhat broader scope for Rebel. After the second summer with Ralph, Keith joined with Jimmy Gaudreau to form a short-lived band known variously as the New Tradition and the Country Store, while Ricky went on to work with other bands. When that group disbanded, Keith came back to Sandy Hook, but rejoined Ralph Stanley's band after the tragic death of Roy Lee Centers in May 1974, remaining with the Clinch Mountain Boys for three more years.

In 1978, Keith left the Stanley band for a stint with J.D. Crowe and the New South, who played a more progressive brand of Bluegrass. He recorded some with Crowe on Rounder, including a live album in Japan. By 1984, his one-time partner Ricky Skaggs had hit it big in Music City and Keith went to Nashville hoping to emulate his friend's success.

He secured a contract with RCA Victor, but initially had only modest success. His first appearance on the charts came in September 1984 when *Turn Me to Love*, on which Patty Loveless did harmony vocal, reached the Top 60. *A Hard Act to Follow*, his second effort and the title of his initial 6-selection mini-album, did less well, peaking in the Top 80. He followed-up with another Top 60 single, *I've Got the Heart for You.*

In late 1985, however, *Miami My Amy* did much better, reaching the Top 15 during 20 weeks on the listings. This came from his second album, ***L.A. to Miami***. At that time, RCA was issuing albums with only 8 selections on them and so when it was released in the U.K., two more selections were added to come up to the 10 selections expected there. Then Keith had three Top 10 singles in a row, *Ten Feet Away*, *Homecoming '83* (both 1986) and *Hard Livin'* (1987).

Keith had two moderate successes in 1987, *Would These Arms Be in Your Way* (Top 40) and *Some Old Side Road* (Top 20), before he had four No.1 hits in a row, starting with *Don't Close Your Eyes* in the spring of 1988. This was followed by *When You Say Nothing at All* (1988), *I'm No Stranger to the Rain* (CMA's 1989 "Single of the Year") and *I Wonder Do You Think of Me*, which could somewhat ironically be termed a posthumous goodbye.

Unfortunately, his recurring problem with alcohol abuse took his life at the age of 33. In public, Keith Whitley was the epitome of the polite and mannerly Country young man, but as one journalist termed it, privately a "binge drinker." Shortly after his death, a fifth No.1, *It Ain't Nothin'*, a song written by Tony Haselden, showed that his music was still in demand. Garth Fundis completed the album ***I Wonder Do You Think of Me*** after Keith's death, and the 1991 album ***Kentucky Bluebird*** includes interviews and demos. Keith recorded some duets with both his wife, Lorrie Morgan (*'Til a Tear Becomes a Rose*), and Earl Thomas Conley (*Brotherly Love*) in his last year. The last named reached the Top 3 in 1991. At the end of the year, Keith had a further posthumous hit with *Somebody's Doin' Me Right*. In 1990, the CMA voted Keith and Lorrie as "Vocal Event of the Year" and in 1991, they were named "Vocal Collaboration of the Year" by TNN/MCN. IMT

RECOMMENDED ALBUMS:

"A Hard Act to Follow" (RCA Victor)(1984)
"L.A. to Miami" (RCA Victor)(1985)
"Don't Close Your Eyes" (RCA Victor)(1988)
"I Wonder Do You Think of Me" (RCA)(1989)
"Kentucky Bluebird" (RCA)(1991)
Keith Whitley & Ricky Skaggs:
"Tribute to the Stanley Brothers" (Jalyn)(1971)
"Second Generation Bluegrass" (Rebel)(1972)

RAY WHITLEY

(Singer, Songwriter, Guitar, Ukulele, Actor)

Given Name:	**Raymond Otis Whitley**
Date of Birth:	**December 5, 1901**
Where Born:	**Atlanta, Georgia**
Married:	**Catherine "Kay" Johnson**
Children:	**Claire, Dolores, Judy Kay**
Date of Death:	**February 21, 1979**

Lovers of Western films often recall Ray Whitley as "RKO's Singing Cowboy." Unlike many others of this genre, Ray never fronted his own full series, but appeared in support of other stars, often in a featured role where he had the opportunity to sing a song or two.

A native of Atlanta, Ray Whitley grew up in Clay County, Alabama. Shortly after the end of WWI, he joined the U.S. Navy, where he served for three years and learned the electrician's trade. While stationed in Philadelphia he met his future wife, marrying and settling there after his discharge in 1923. Doing electrical work to support his wife and growing family, Ray remained in Philadelphia for a time and then moved to Nitro, West Virginia. By then he had begun to play and sing, mostly for community entertainments. The young southerner also developed a love for Jimmie Rodgers' music from 1927 onward. In 1929, Whitley moved to New York City, where he helped construct the Empire State Building. When the deepening Depression forced him into unemployment, friends suggested that he try show business. Soon he had a local radio program at WMCA with a small band he called the Range Ramblers. He also worked at the Stork Club, where he met such celebrities as Will Rogers and Wiley Post.

In 1932, Ray approached one Colonel Johnson, who directed the World Championship Rodeo, about furnishing the entertainment and was hired. Changing his band's name to the Six Bar Cowboys in honor of the Colonel's ranch in Texas, this arrangement provided Whitley and his group with several weeks of work yearly on the rodeo circuit well into the 60's.

In the meantime, Ray initiated his recording career with Melotone, in 1933. One of his early efforts was a topical ballad about a marine tragedy, *The Morro Castle Disaster*, while another focused on the gangster *Pretty Boy Floyd*. Otis Elder and Buck Nation assisted on some of his recordings. Whitley and his group also worked for a time on WHN *Barn Dance* in New York City until going to Texas in 1936 to play at the State Centennial celebration and a simultaneous program over WRR in Dallas. While there he met such luminaries as Bill Boyd, Art Linkletter, and future Pop singing great Kay Starr. Afterward Ray went to Hollywood, where he began working in movies, mostly "B" Westerns, beginning with a pair of movies for Educational Films, with the Frank Luther Trio. His first real Western was *Hopalong Cassidy Returns* (1936).

During a period when contracted by RKO, Ray made some of his most notable appearances in support of the likes of Tim Holt and George O'Brien. His composition *Back in the Saddle Again* was first heard in the O'Brien film *Border G-Men* (1938). Later Gene Autry reworked it slightly and his version elevated it to classic status, particularly as the theme for his long-running *Melody Ranch* radio series. Ray recorded it for Decca, in October 1938, a label on which he cut sixteen sides beginning in 1935. Whitley ultimately appeared in some fifty-four films (see Movie section), his last being *Giant* (1956). In between pictures he toured in rodeos and elsewhere. After WWII, he recorded again for Apollo, Cowboy, and Veejay.

In later years, Ray Whitley worked for a time for Gene Autry's Republic Records. He made occasional visits to old-timer events and Western film fairs in later years where fans marveled at his fine voice and sure-handed whip skills. Whitley died in 1979, while on a fishing vacation in Mexico, much admired by younger fans of Hollywood cowboy music, such as Doug Green of Riders in the Sky. Two of his original recordings have been issued on various anthologies, but the best collection of his recordings is available on cassette through Circle D Video of Memphis, Tennessee. IMT

RECOMMENDED ALBUM:

"Ray Whitley Sings His Favorite Songs" (Circle D Video)

SLIM WHITMAN

(Singer, Songwriter, Yodeler, Guitar)

Given Name:	**Ottis Dewey Whitman, Jr.**
Date of Birth:	**January 20, 1929**
Where Born:	**Tampa, Florida**
Married:	**Geraldine ("Jerry") Crist (m. 1941)**
Children:	**Byron Keith, Sharron Carlene**

Slim, who is known as "America's Favorite Folk Singer," is one of an elite group who has taken Country music and popularized it all around the world. He remains more popular and enduring outside of the States and is still pleasing crowds in Europe and Australia, long after he has reached his peak in the U.S.

Slim, known to his friends as "O.D.," had two loves as a child: baseball and fishing. He had no aspirations to be a singer, although he did listen to Montana Slim and Jimmie Rodgers, and could yodel like them. However, it was to be his faith that led him to his life-time love, his wife, Jerry. He was (and still is) a member of the Church of the Brethren. Here, at age 15, he met the preacher's daughter. By the time he was 17, they were married, and moved onto a 40-acre haven, south of Jacksonville, they call "Woodpecker Paradise."

Until the outbreak of WWII, Slim worked as a meat packer and then as a shipfitter and boilermaker in the Tampa shipyard. He joined the U.S. Navy and saw action in the South Pacific on board the *USS Chilton*. It was at this time that he took up boxing, and began playing guitar (left-handed, as he had lost two fingers in a meat packing factory accident). He joined a group and entertained his fellow seamen. During his service time, he had some lucky escapes. A ship that he was scheduled to be transferred to was sunk with the loss of all hands.

After the end of hostilities, in 1946, Slim returned to the shipyard and started playing baseball. He played with the Plant City Berries, a Class C team in the Orange Belt League. Standing some 6'2", Slim became a formidable batter with an average of .360, and he was also an adept left-handed pitcher, steering his team to a pennant in 1947, with an 11-1 count. He stopped playing in 1948 and started singing on WDAE, WHBO and WFLA, in Tampa. That same year, he put together his Variety Rhythm Boys, who were sponsored by a local supermarket.

Slim's singing on WFLA was heard by Colonel Tom Parker, who was then managing Eddy Arnold. Parker sent an acetate to RCA Victor and this led to Slim being signed to the label, in 1948. Parker didn't manage Slim, but his stepson, Bob Ross, did. The label didn't like Slim's real first name, and one day, according to one story, while he was off fishing, the label decided that Ottis should become "Slim"—he never has liked it!—although there is also a story that he was called "Slim" while in the Navy, because he was "as slim as a willow."

During the early part of his career, he was billed as "the Smilin' Starduster," because his soaring falsetto "could surely dust the stars." The musicians on his first recording session were Anita Kerr (keyboards), Chet Atkins (fiddle, guitar), Jerry Byrd (steel guitar) and Homer and Jethro on mandolin and guitar. The first single released was *I'm Casting My Lasso Towards the Sky*, which became Slim's theme song. In August, 1949, he made his radio debut on Mutual Network's *Smokey Mountain Hayride*, receiving many plaudits. Within two weeks, he was touring with the Light Crust Doughboys.

In the following May, he became a member of the *Louisiana Hayride*. At the time, Slim stuttered and hardly communicated with his audience. It was Hank Williams who encouraged him. As Slim only received $18 a week, he supplemented this by becoming a mailman. While on the *Hayride*, his trademark "singing guitar" sound was created. Like many fine things, it happened by accident. Slim's steel player, Hoot Rains, overshot a note, and Slim liked the resultant sound and this led to the "shooting arrows" now so popular with steel guitarists.

Slim's first single had been heard by Lew Chudd of Imperial Records and he signed Whitman to the label. At the end of 1951, Slim released a Bob Nolan song, *Love Song of the Waterfall*, which was a one-week Top 10 record the following year. However, it was the follow-up, *Indian Love Call*, that stated emphatically that Slim had arrived. It made the Top 3 on the Country charts, hanging around for nearly six months. In addition, it made the Top 10 of the Pop charts, and was Certified Gold. He ended the year with a double-sided monster, *Keep It a Secret* (Top 3)/*My Heart Is Broken in Three* (Top 10).

He had to wait until the end of 1953 for his next Country hit and it came in the shape of *North Wind*, another Top 10 record. He started out 1954 with his rendition of the Doris Day hit *Secret Love*. Slim's version went to the Top 3. He followed-up with another song from a Nelson Eddy-Jeanette MacDonald movie, *Rose Marie* (song title, *Rose-Marie*). This went Top 5 on the Country charts and Top 25 on the Pop lists, but, in addition, it opened up the U.K. to Slim's work. In 1955, it entered the U.K. Pop chart and went to No.1 within two weeks and stayed at the top for 11 straight weeks. Back in the States, Slim finished 1954 with another Top 5 record, *Singing Hills*.

Slim had a minor hit at the beginning of 1955 with *The Cattle Call* and then, in July, he became a member of the *Grand Ole Opry*. In the same month, *Indian Love Call* entered the British charts and reached the Top 10. The flip-side, *China Doll*, also made the Top 15. The following year, Slim played the London Palladium, being the first Country artist to do so. The shows were sold out nearly two months ahead of his two-week stint. About the time of his visit, he had another hit in the U.K., *Tumbling Tumbleweeds*, which went Top 20. While he was at the Palladium, he was filmed singing *Unchain My Heart* and his performance was included in the 1957 movie *Disc Jockey Jamboree*. He had other successful singles in Britain, most notably *Serenade* (1956) and *I'll Take You Home Again Kathleen* (1957), both Top 10 records.

During the latter part of the 50's and early 60's, rock'n'roll and the advent of the Beatles and other Pop icons spelled a lean time for Slim, as for other Country singers. He had a couple of minor Country successes, in 1961 and 1964, but it was the Top 10 hit *More Than Yesterday*, in 1965, that heralded his return. During the year, he toured South Africa and recorded some material in Afrikaans. He followed up, the next year, with his rendition of *The Twelfth of Never*, which became a Top 20 hit.

Between 1966 and 1969, Slim racked up another ten chart entries, of which the most successful were *Rainbows Are Back in Style* (Top 20) and *Happy Street* (Top 30), both in 1968. Slim was invited to play three concerts in the U.K., in 1970, and he played to packed houses. He had a Top 30 hit with *Tomorrow Never Comes*, and by the time he followed-up with another Top 30 success, *Shutters and Boards*, Imperial had ceased to be, absorbed into United Artists. At the end of the year, Slim returned to the Top 10 with *Guess Who*. He opened his account the next year with another Top 10 record, *Something Beautiful (To Remember)*.

Slim Whitman** with his son, **Byron

He stayed with United Artists until 1974, but although he had six more chart records, the biggest by far was the 1971 hit *It's a Sin to Tell a Lie*, which just fell short of the Top 20. During 1974, Slim returned to the British charts with *Happy Anniversary*, which reached No.14.

In 1979, Suffolk Marketing released a TV album of twenty of Slim's tracks. When he was asked to film a TV commercial, he wasn't keen, but his wife and son persuaded him to do it. The album, ***All My Best***, eventually sold 4 million copies, which made it the biggest selling TV album. Suffolk released a further TV album, ***Just for You***, in 1980, and the two albums were put together as a double package, in 1982, as ***The Best***. In 1980, Slim signed with Cleveland International Records and returned to the Top 15 with *When*. He followed up with the Top 70 record *That Silver-Haired Daddy of Mine*. The following year, he had a re-release of *I Remember You*, which he had first charted in 1966. This time it did better, reaching the Top 50. His final chart record came in the summer that year and was *Can't Help Falling in Love*, which peaked in the Top 60. In 1984, he recorded the Bob Montgomery-produced album ***Angeline***, which includes the duet *Four Walls* with son Byron. He had another TV album in 1989, when Heartland released ***Slim Whitman—Best Loved Favorites***. Progressive Music released a religious album via TV, in 1991, entitled ***20 Precious Memories***.

Throughout his career, Slim Whitman has recorded what he felt the public wanted and not what some record company executive felt they needed. He has never recorded drinking or cheating songs, but only ones that he would not be "ashamed to sing in church." Slim has admirers in many quarters of the music industry. They include(d) Elvis Presley, with whom Slim toured in the 50's, George Harrison of the Beatles and Michael Jackson (who is fond of Slim's version of *I Remember You*). One of his biggest fans was Audie Murphy, who listened to Slim's records to relax him, after his experiences in WWII.

Slim has received several awards over the years. He has a star on the Hollywood Walk of Fame. He has a rose and a tulip named after him in Holland and he has sold in excess of 65 million records throughout the world. His fan club commenced in 1970, and has branches in England, Holland, Australia and the U.S.

Slim is still a big draw in Britain and he is still able to fill big venues there. In March 1991, Slim and his son, Byron, came to England to headline the final Wembley Festival. Nowadays, Slim tours with Byron as the Slim and Byron Whitman Show. They are still backed by the Stardusters and although, now, Byron does a lot more of the show, it is still Slim who is the one the fans want to see. Which is a shame, because Byron is a good performer. Slim's fan club is now actively lobbying for greater recognition for his work in the States.

RECOMMENDED ALBUMS:

"Favorites" (Imperial)(1956) [Re-issued by Stetson UK in the original sleeve (1991)]
"Unchain My Heart" (Sunset)(1968)
"The Best of Slim Whitman" (United Artists)((1972) [Re-released in 1981]
"Ghost Riders in the Sky" (Liberty)(1981)
"Angeline" (Epic/Cleveland International)(1984)
"One of a Kind" (double) (Pair)(1984)
"The Very Best of Slim Whitman" (Country Store UK)(1985)
And if you can get it:
"America's Favorite Folk Artist" (Imperial)(1954) [10" album][Approximate cost $400]

WHITSTEIN BROTHERS, The

ROBERT WHITSTEIN
(Vocals, Guitar, Mandolin, Fiddle)

Given Name: Robert Carroll Whitstine
Date of Birth: March 16, 1944
Married: Sherry (div.)
Children: Robby, Marty, Shane, Daniel, Clint

CHARLES WHITSTEIN
(Vocals, Mandolin, Guitar, Tenor Guitar, Fiddle)

Given Name: Charles Edward Whitstine
Date of Birth: December 11, 1945
Married: Ida
Children: Chadwick (Chad)

Both Born: Pineville, Louisiana

Carrying on the classic duet singing tradition of the Louvins, the Blue Sky Boys and the Delmores, the Whitstein Brothers have carved out a niche of their own in the Country scene of the 1980's and 1990's. Their award-winning albums, appearances on shows like the *Grand Ole Opry* and work with figures like Charlie Louvin won them a wide audience and devoted following. Their repertoire ranges from classic chestnuts like *The Knoxville Girl* and *Nobody's Darling* to the more recent songs of Simon and Garfunkel, Porter Wagoner or Mel Street. "Even when we do an up-to-date song," says Charles, "we do it in our style."

The Whitstein story is actually a long and at times frustrating struggle that preceded their arrival in Nashville and recording contract with Rounder Records. It began in central Louisiana in the late 1940's, when Charles and Robert (two of a family of nine born to a farmer and logger named R.C. Whitstein, although their name was registered as "Whitstine") grew up listening to their father do a weekly radio show over a station in nearby Alexandria. A skilled guitarist and singer, R.C. fed his sons a steady diet of Hank Williams, Johnnie & Jack and Blue Sky Boys material.

By the time they were 11 and 12, Charles and Robert, armed with their Sears mail-order instruments, were winning local talent shows and appearing on a local TV show called *Country Time*. This led to their first record, a single on the J-Bo label, called *Louisiana Woman*. It was a regional hit in 1962, and it encouraged them to come to Nashville, where they called themselves the Whitt Brothers and took advantage of the current "Folk revival" craze to get shots on the *Opry* and tour dates with Faron Young, Porter Wagoner and Little Jimmy Dickens. A second single was cut for the Rik label, but before anything happened, the brothers were both drafted.

By the time they had done their service in the Marines, and returned home to get married, the brothers sensed a change in Nashville's music. A new slick sound was in vogue and they settled for cutting their first album at a local Alexandria studio: this was ***The Whitstein Brothers Sing Gospel Songs of the Louvin Brothers***. The Louvin Brothers had been the major influence on Robert and Charles for years, and this was their chance to pay homage. The album was sold at personal appearances in the area. Then, about 1980, veteran promoter Tillman Franks asked the pair to make a demo of some of his songs.

The brothers enjoyed this, and did a second demo of songs they themselves liked. A copy got to Bluegrass star Jesse McReynolds, who in turn passed it on to Ken Irwin at Rounder. Astounded that he had never heard of the brothers' singing, he soon signed them to a three-album contract. This yielded ***Rose of My Heart***, ***Trouble Ain't Nothing But the Blues***, as well as ***Old Time Duets***, a Grammy nominee. For a time in 1992, Charles took a job singing as a duet partner to Charlie Louvin, with whom he cut a good album for County. In May 1993, Charles recorded with Charlie Louvin ***Charlie Louvin Live in Holland, Louvin Brothers Music Celebration*** for Stricktly Country of Holland. That same year, Charles recorded three cds with Canadian banjo player Lesley Schatz for Bear Family of Germany. By 1994, the brothers were back together again, taking their music in new directions while maintaining their ties to the past.

CKW

RECOMMENDED ALBUMS:

"Rose of My Heart" (Rounder)(1984)
"Trouble Ain't NothingBut the Blues" (Rounder)(1986)
"Old Time Duets" (Rounder)(1989)
"Charlie Louvin and Charles Whitstein: Hoping That You're Hoping" (Copper Creek)(1992)

HENRY WHITTER

(Singer, Guitar, Harmonica, Other Stringed Instruments)

Given Name: William Henry Whitter
Date of Birth: April 6, 1892
Where Born: Grayson County, Virginia
Married: Hattie
Children: Paul
Date of Death: November 10, 1941

Henry Whitter was one of the earliest Country singers on phonograph records. While his musical talents and skills had limitations, his role as pioneer Country vocalist remains significant. He played a decent harmonica and introduced the railroad ballad *Wreck of the Old 97* to disc. Although Henry recorded over sixty sides solo or with a string band, the best material from a musical standpoint was those numbers made with the blind fiddler-vocalist G.B. Grayson, who contributed most of the quality and greatness to their sound.

Whitter was born in the New River Valley section of Grayson County, Virginia. When he was 10, the great textile mill at the new town of Fries was built, and after finishing the sixth grade, Henry went to work as a millhand. Interested in music from childhood, he learned to sing and play several instruments after a fashion and yearned for a better life. Listening to phonograph cylinders—particularly those of rural comic Uncle Josh (Cal Stewart)—fascinated him and Whitter aspired to put his own music on record.

Unaware that Eck Robertson had been cut by Victor in July 1922 or that Fiddlin' John Carson was in the process of being discovered by Polk Brockman and Ralph Peer, Whitter journeyed to New York and made audition tests for OKeh. After Carson's first releases did so well on the market, company officials called Henry back to New York for sessions. In addition to ballads and songs like *Old 97* and *Lonesome Road Blues*, he did some harmonica instrumentals, too. *Old 97* attracted considerable attention and inspired numerous covers, with that of Vernon Dalhart becoming one side of the first Country million seller.

Over the next three years, Henry Whitter had several more sessions for OKeh and one for Paramount. Although not of especially high musical quality, they had sufficient sales for the company to keep recalling him for more material. In July 1924, he took a fiddler and banjoist to the studio with him and Whitter's Virginia Breakdowners became the first mountain string band on record.

In 1925, Whitter accompanied Kelly Harrell, another hill-country vocalist, on a session. His thirty-four numbers with fiddler-balladeer G.B. Grayson between 1927 and 1929 represent the zenith of his musical career and Grayson's death in a 1930 freak auto-truck accident left him in a commercially weakened position. Henry did his last session for Victor in November 1930 at Memphis with banjoist Fisher Hendley and Marshall Small.

In 1934, Henry issued a songbook containing lyrics to many of his more familiar numbers and a few photographs. By the late 30's, his style was becoming outdated and as a diabetic, his health was in decline. He passed away in a hospital in Morganton, North Carolina, at age forty-nine.

Since most of his early solo recordings were done prior to the use of electrical equipment as well as of marginal musical quality, none have been reissued, although one or two of his later harmonica tunes have appeared on various anthologies. In addition, most of the Grayson and Whitter material has appeared on four long-play albums. IMT

RECOMMENDED ALBUMS:

(See Grayson & Whitter)

LITTLE ROY WIGGINS

(Steel Guitar)

Given Name:	**Ivan Leroy Wiggins**
Date of Birth:	**June 27, 1926**
Where Born:	**Nashville, Tennessee**
Married:	**1. Joyce (dec'd.)**
	2. Faye
Children:	**Barbara, Albert, Karen, Kristy**

Little Roy Wiggins is one of the great steel guitarists in Country music history. He gained this reputation largely as a result of a quarter century with Eddy Arnold. His years with "the Tennessee Plowboy," particularly the first decade, helped set the standard of Country steel guitar-playing for his generation.

A native of "Music City," Wiggins didn't care for either his first or middle names, so he shortened his second one to "Roy." At age 4, he saw Burt Hutcherson of the *Opry's* Gully Jumpers play a Martin guitar in the Hawaiian style with strings raised and from that point onward, mastery of the steel guitar became his consuming ambition. He studied until the age of 13, joined the *Opry* at 14 as a member of Paul Howard's Arkansas Cotton Pickers and then worked for a year with Pee Wee King and the Golden West Cowboys. Because of his youth, he earned the sobriquet "Little" Roy in those years.

When Eddy Arnold went on his own in the spring of 1943, Wiggins became a part of his entourage and so remained until 1968. Roy's steel played a big role in the RCA Victor sound that made Arnold a superstar on songs like *Anytime*, *Bouquet of Roses*, *I Couldn't Believe It Was True*, *There's No Wings on My Angel* and *Chained to a Memory*. Arnold didn't permit his band members to do session work or record by themselves for a long time, so Roy didn't do much playing with other artists or record solo (an exception seems to have been a session with George Morgan in the late 50's that produced his hit *I'm in Love Again*).

Roy Wiggins did do some steel guitar recordings for Starday in the 60's, turning out two albums of quality effort. After leaving Eddy Arnold's employ in 1968, which was an era when the Tennessee Plowboy moved toward an ultra-modern sound, Little Roy played most often with George Morgan, who ironically had once been Columbia's response to Arnold's success at RCA Victor. He worked on the "Candy Kid's" Starday, MCA and 4 Star sessions in this time and points out that all of Morgan's singles in this period proved to be moderate successes.

Roy also did two more steel albums. Already gaining legendary status for his steel stylings by the late 60's, with Morgan's untimely passing in 1975, Wiggins worked for the next decade with a variety of Country acts, including such *Opry* regulars as Ernest Ashworth and the Willis Brothers, in addition to doing some session work.

In 1987, Little Roy came to Pigeon Forge, Tennessee, where he worked during the tourist season at the Smoky Mountain Hayride with Bonnie Lou and Buster Moore. For three years from 1989, he also managed the Ernest Tubb Record Shop #4 in Pigeon Forge. In 1992, Roy opened the Little Roy Wiggins Music City guitar and instrument shop. He worked at the Hayride in Pigeon Forge until the fall of 1993. His two younger daughters often displayed their dancing skills on the program. A member of the Steel Guitar Hall of Fame, Roy has recorded several cassette tapes that showcase his talents.

For the past year he has concentrated on his business, although Roy does make special appearances such as furnishing the entertainment at the 1994 Knoxville Film Fair, where he had a reunion with former child star Tommy Ivo who had been in the Eddy Arnold motion pictures *Hoedown* and *Feudin' Rhythm* more than forty years earlier. Little Roy is also at work on what promises to be an exciting autobiography with Knoxville journalist Wayne Bledsoe. IMT

RECOMMENDED ALBUMS:

"Mister Steel Guitar" (Starday)(1962)
"18 All Time Hits" (Starday)(1968)
"Songs I Played for Eddy Arnold" (Diplomat)(1969)
"Memory Time" (Power Pak)(1974)
[Also several cassettes available from Little Roy Wiggins Music City, Pigeon Forge, Tennessee]
(See also Eddy Arnold)

WILBURN BROTHERS, The

When Formed:	**1938 Wilburn Family/ 1953 Wilburn Brothers**

DOYLE WILBURN

(Singer, Songwriter, Guitar, Music Publisher, Talent Agent)

Given Name:	**Virgil Doyle Wilburn**
Date of Birth:	**July 7, 1930**
Married:	**Margie Bowes**
Date of Death:	**October 16, 1982**

TEDDY WILBURN

(Singer, Songwriter, Guitar, Music Publisher, Talent Agent)

Given Name:	**Thurman Theodore Wilburn**
Date of Birth:	**November 30, 1931**
Both Born:	**Hardy, Missouri**

The importance of the Wilburn Brothers is not just as entertainers and songwriters but also as music publishers with their highly successful Sure-Fire Music and as booking agents with their Wil-Helm Talent Agency.

Originally Doyle and Teddy, then 8 and 7 respectively, performed with their elder brothers, Lester (b. May 19, 1924, Thayer, Missouri) and Leslie (b. October 13, 1925, Thayer, Missouri), sister, Vinita Geraldine ("Jerry") (b. June 5, 1927, Thayer, Missouri) and their parents as the Wilburn Family. They initially played on street corners in Thayer. The family broadcast on WBTM Jonesboro, Arkansas, during 1938 and then toured the South. In 1940, at Roy Acuff's behest they joined the *Grand Ole Opry*. They stayed on the

Country music's celebrated ***Wilburn Brothers***

show for six months, leaving because of the youth of some of the members and the strict child labor laws. Then WWII intervened and the act went into abeyance. From 1948 through 1951, the family (without Jerry, who had gotten married) appeared on the *Louisiana Hayride* out of Shreveport.

Then Doyle and Teddy entered the U.S. Army during the Korean War. They returned to the U.S. in 1953 and as a duo became cast members of the *Opry*. Initially, they toured with Webb Pierce and Faron Young. Pierce was instrumental in the brothers signing with Decca Records in 1954. They first hit the Country chart in tandem with Pierce on the Top 5 hit *Sparkling Brown Eyes*. The following year, they made the Top 15 with their first solo success, *I Wanna Wanna Wanna*. In 1956, they again reached the Top 15 with *You're Not Play Love*. They then entered the *Arthur Godfrey's Talent Scouts* televised show and they won. The brothers had two more Top 10 hits that year, *I'm So in Love with You* and *Go Away with Me*.

In 1957, the Wilburns got together with Ernest Tubb for the Top 10 *Mister Love* and the following year they repeated the combination for another Top 10 single, Cindy Walker's *Hey, Mr. Bluebird*. It was at this time that the four brothers set up Sure-Fire Music, so that Doyle and Teddy could control their own catalog and bring in outside material. Doyle was the one who did most of the business side while Teddy was the natural songwriter. They ended the decade with *Which One Is to Blame* (Top 5)/*The Knoxville Girl* (Top 20), their co-written *Somebody's Back in Town* (Top 10) and *A Woman's Intuition* (Top 10). They then went a year without a hit and at the end of 1960, they reached the Top 30 with *The Best of All My Heartaches*. Again, they did not have a speedy or particularly successful follow-up hit and they had to wait until July 1961 for the Top 15 *Blue Blue Day*.

In 1961, the Wilburns became involved in the career of Loretta Lynn. They took her into their Sure-Fire Studio and she recorded *Fool Number One* and took the demo to Owen Bradley at Decca. For many years, they managed Loretta and booked her through their Wil-Helm Talent Agency, which they owned with Smiley Wilson. The agency would later represent Jean Shepard, Jay Lee Webb, Martha Carson, Slim Whitman, the Osborne Brothers, Charlie Louvin and Harold Morrison.

By now, the brothers had their own TV show, which became one of the most important in Country music. In 1962, they came back strongly with the Top 5 single *Trouble's Back in Time*, which also crossed to the basement level of the Pop chart. They followed with the Top 25 release *The Sound of Your Footsteps*. Then in 1963, they had the Top 5 single *Roll Muddy River* and the Top 10 *Tell Her So*.

The Wilburn Brothers toured through the U.S. and went to Australia, where they appeared on TV in the 39-week *Roy Acuff Open House* show. In 1964, their two chart records did not fare so well, with *Hangin' Around* only reaching the Top 40 and *I'm Gonna Tie One on Tonight* going Top 20. Their opening single of 1965, *I Had One Too Many*, also only got to the Top 30 and then *It's Another World* climbed to the Top 5. Around this time, they received a lifetime recording contract from Decca. In 1966, they opened their account with *Someone Before Me* (Top 10), *I Can't Keep Away from You* (Top 15) and their biggest hit, the Top 3 *Hurt Her Once for Me*.

From then on, their records failed to register with the same success. Their bigger hits were *Roaring Again* (Top 15) and *Goody, Goody Gumdrop* (Top 25) (both 1967), *It Looks Like the Sun's Gonna Shine* (Top 40, 1969) and *Little Johnny from Down the Street* (Top 40, 1970). In 1967, the Wilburn Brothers were named "Duet of the Year" in the *Music City News* Cover Awards. They debuted at the Wembley Festival in London in 1970 and returned in 1978. During 1971, they were involved in a messy legal battle when Loretta Lynn sued the brothers' company over royalties, when she left them. The Wilburns continued with the *Opry* and were still popular on live dates. In 1973, a distant cousin of Loretta's, Patty Loveless, then only 15, joined the brothers' show and stayed with them for three years.

Doyle, who had been suffering from ill health for some while, died in 1982, leaving Teddy to carry on as a solo performer. Even while they had been duo, they had done solo numbers occasionally on albums. The two brothers, who looked and dressed on stage like twins, will always be remembered for their impeccable harmonies that were and are difficult to emulate.

RECOMMENDED ALBUMS:

"The Wilburn Brothers (Teddy-Doyle)" (Decca)(1957) [Re-issued by Stetson UK in the original sleeve (1987)]
"City Limits" (Decca)(1962)
"Country Gold" (Decca)(1964) [Re-issued by Stetson UK in the original sleeve (1987)]
"The Wilburn Brothers Show" (Decca)(1966) [Re-issued by Stetson UK in the original sleeve (1987)][With Loretta Lynn, Ernest Tubb and Harold Morrison]
"A Portrait" (double)(MCA)(1973)
"Retrospective" (MCA)(1990)

WILD ROSE

When Formed:	**1987**
Members:	
Wanda Vick	**Fiddle, Guitar, Steel Guitar, Dobro, Lap Steel, Mandolin**
Pam Gadd	**Vocals, Banjo, Guitar**
Pam Perry	**Vocals, Guitar, Mandolin**
Kathy Mac	**Vocals, Bass Guitar**
Nancy Given Prout	**Drums**

Wild Rose *teaching their record producers what to do with wild roses*

When Wild Rose appeared at Charlie Daniels' Chili Cook-Out, in Nashville, in 1988, it seemed like, at long last, here was an all-female group to take on the world. However, although they had the talent, stagecraft and entertainment ability, fate decided that other lesser talents would become stars.

The prime mover in getting the group together was Wanda Vick (b. 1961, Alabama), a multi-instrumentalist, who had won a fiddle contest at age 14 and played on an album by famed fiddler Buddy Spicher. She studied at Belmont College in Nashville and then became an active session player before joining Lynn Anderson's band. She recruited Nancy Given Prout (b. 1960, Pennsylvania), who is married to Diamond Rio's drummer Brian Prout. Nancy had developed her style from her professor at the University of South Carolina, Jim Hall. Wanda and Nancy had been playing together in Porter Wagoner's all-girl band, the Right Combination.

Pamela Gadd (b. 1960, Kentucky) and Pam Perry (b. 1960, Ohio) were members of the New Coon Creek Girls, with whom they both sang lead vocals. Pamela was about to leave, in 1987, to record a solo album. However, when she met the rest of the band, she decided to join. Kathy Mac, who hails from Kentucky, had also played in an all-girl group, Tina Carroll & the Nashville Satins.

Initially known as Miss Behavin', the group soon became Wild Rose. They were signed to Universal Records, in 1988, with James Stroud as their producer. However, the label was short-lived. There was time for Wild Rose to record their debut album, ***Breakin' New Ground***, from which they had the title track go Top 20, in 1989. During 1990, they became one of the few Country acts to appear on the spring network special *Night of 100 Stars*. That year, they moved with Jimmy Bowen when he took over Capitol Records and the label re-issued the debut album under its banner. It reached the Top 50 on the Country Album charts and the single *Go Down Swingin'* went Top 40. That year, Wild Rose released their second album, ***Straight and Narrow***. The video of *Everything He Touches* attracted a lot of attention. The title track reached the Top 75 the following year. They released their third and final album, ***Listen to Your Heart***, in 1991, but by then the dreams of Wild Rose had come to an end.

RECOMMENDED ALBUMS:

"Breakin' New Ground" (Capitol)(1989)
"Straight and Narrow" (Capitol)(1990)
"Listen to Your Heart" (Capitol)(1991)

WILEY & GENE

When Formed: 1939

WILEY
(Singer, Songwriter, Fiddle, Dancer)
Given Name: Wiley Walker
Date of Birth: November 17, 1911
Where Born: Laurel Hill, Florida
Married: Unknown
Children: Wiley, Jr. ("Chub")
Date of Death: May 17, 1966

GENE
(Singer, Songwriter, Instrumentalist)
Given Name: Gene Sullivan
Date of Birth: November 16, 1914
Where Born: Carbon Hill, Alabama
Date of Death: October 24, 1984

Although generally forgotten today, Wiley & Gene were one of Country music's most successful duets during the late 1930's and early 1940's. They also wrote two Country music standards, *Live and Let Live* and *When My Blue Moon Turns to Gold Again*. As well as their joint success, they both had successful careers of several years, standing prior to teaming up as a duet in 1939.

Wiley Walker grew up in Andalusia, Alabama, a town ninety miles southeast of Montgomery. An older brother taught him to play the fiddle and he also became a skilled buck-and-wing dancer. By 1925, he had left school and become a professional touring entertainer. Within six years, he was part of Harley Sadler's troupe, one of the most famous tent-show organizations. While with this show, he met Lew Childre and when the Sadler show broke up temporarily in 1932, Walker and Childre went to New Orleans, where they appeared on WWL as both the Alabama Boys and the Crazy Water Crystals Boys.

After nine months broadcasting daily in New Orleans and touring southern Louisiana on weekends, they moved to Birmingham. In 1937, Walker left Childre, moving to Memphis, where he was part of the Western Swing group the Swift Jewel Cowboys. Shortly afterward, he moved to KWKH Shreveport, Louisiana, where he became part of the Shelton Brothers band, one of the most popular acts in the Southwest. This is where he met Gene Sullivan.

Sullivan was born in Carbon Hill, Alabama, a town near Birmingham, in 1914. At first, those who knew Sullivan thought he would be a boxer, and he gained a good reputation as a flyweight and bantamweight in Birmingham. In 1932, however, he bought his first guitar and opted for a career in Country music. In early 1935 he traveled for three months with Happy Hal Burns' Tune Wranglers, but by June of that year he was a member of the Lone Star Cowboys on KWKH. The following year he joined the Shelton Brothers, who earlier had been part of the Lone Star Cowboys. He and Walker originally served as instrumentalists and comedians for the Sheltons. It was while riding one day near De Queen, Arkansas, that the two did some trial singing and considered the possibility of a duet act. Shortly thereafter, Wiley returned to the Sadler show and Gene moved to Dallas to work with pianist Roy Newman at WRR. It was April 1939 before Walker and Sullivan teamed up as a duet.

Wiley and Gene debuted on KXYZ in Fort Worth with a transcribed program two times a week for Comet Rice. Don Law of Columbia Records heard these programs and offered them a recording contract. Their first efforts were *Little Rubber Dolly* (their theme song) and *All Over Nothing at All*. By 1940, they had moved to Lubbock, Texas, for a year, and then to Oklahoma City, to appear on KOMA. They finished out their careers in Oklahoma, spending most of their time performing on KWXX, which they joined in the summer of 1941.

In 1941, their two most famous songs were written and recorded, initially as opposite sides of the same record. Originally, *Live and Let Live* was the most requested on Wiley & Gene's shows, but ultimately, *When My Blue Moon Turns to Gold Again* became the most popular. At first Wiley & Gene's recording of this song did not sell well, even though it was frequently requested on radio.

In 1943, that changed when Zeke Manners had a hit with it, then Wiley and Gene's record was re-issued successfully. The biggest selling recording came much later when Elvis Presley waxed the song.

In the late 1940's, Wiley and Gene gained TV exposure. Gene loved the new medium because it gave him a chance to expand his talents for comedy and mimicry. In 1946, their version of *Make Room in Your Heart for a Friend* reached the Top 3 on Columbia. Wiley's son, Wiley, Jr.—usually billed as "Chub"—started singing on their shows, but eventually left show business, opting instead for a career as a Minister of Music in Oklahoma City.

By the early 1950's, Wiley and Gene themselves had faded from prominence on the music scene. Gene did have one more fleeting bit of stardom, in 1957. He recorded his comic song/recitation *Please Pass the Biscuits* as a demo for Little Jimmy Dickens, but Don Law liked Gene's version and released it on the Columbia label. Thereafter, Gene was content to run a music store in Oklahoma City and, until the early 1960's, make occasional public appearances, both with Wiley and alone.

Wiley & Gene should equally be well regarded as excellent representatives of those Country performers who worked mainly in local settings, such as clubs and radio stations, where they built up loyal, adoring audiences.

WKM

RECOMMENDED ALBUM:

"Radio Favorites Volume 1" (Old Homestead)

MARIJOHN WILKIN

(Singer, Songwriter, Piano, Guitar)

Given Name:	**Marijohn Melson**
Date of Birth:	**1918**
Where Born:	**Kemp, Texas**
Married:	**1. Bedford E. Russell (dec'd.)**
	2. (Div.)
	3. Art Wilkin, Jr. (div.)
Children:	**John Buck ("Bucky")**

Marijohn Wilkin has become one of the most respected songwriters in Nashville. At one point in the mid-70's, she became known as "the Den Mother of Nashville" for her championing then unknown songwriters.

She grew up in a religious home, the daughter of a deacon. She began singing in church from age 5. Although she was a talented singer, Marijohn Wilkin originally had no interest in being a show business personality. In fact, she turned down a movie contract offered to her in the late 1930's by Monogram Studios.

Instead, she chose to complete her education at Hardin-Simmons University, marry her college sweetheart, Bedford E. Russell and begin teaching music at school. Unfortunately, not long after the marriage Russell, a member of the military during WWII, was killed when the Italian submarine in which he and other prisoners of war were being transported across the Mediterranean Sea was strafed by a British plane.

After his death, Marijohn entered into a brief, unhappy marriage that produced her only child, "Bucky"(b. April 26, 1946, Tulsa, Oklahoma). When this marriage dissolved, she wed Art Wilkin, a part-time choir director in Tulsa. It was after this marriage that she began writing songs.

In 1955, Marijohn's son, who was a skilled guitarist by the time he was 8 years old, was offered a contract to perform on the *Children's Ozark Jubilee*. As a result, the family moved to Springfield, Missouri, home of the *Ozark Jubilee*, were Marijohn got her first song recorded. This number, *Take This Heart*, was co-written by James P. Coleman and recorded by Mitchell Torok. Several other Jubilee artists recorded Marijohn's songs, of which *No Wedding Bells for Joe* by Wanda Jackson was the most successful commercially. Still, none of her songs earned much money and Wilkin sang in a Springfield piano bar to help her family financially. One night a local attorney, impressed by Marijohn's songs, suggested that she should be in Nashville. Shortly thereafter the family acted on the lawyer's suggestion and moved to Nashville in 1958.

At first Marijohn sang in the Voo-Doo Room in Nashville's Printer's Alley and had little success with her songwriting. When one of the customers was in a car wreck shortly after leaving the bar and was hospitalized for several weeks, Marijohn quit and took a job working for Jim Denny at Cedarwood Publishing for $50 a month. There she worked with Mel Tillis, Wayne Walker, Danny Dill and John D. Loudermilk, among others. She also wrote, or co-wrote, some of the biggest Country hits of the 1950's and 1960's, including *Waterloo* (Stonewall Jackson, 1959), *Long Black Veil* (Lefty Frizzell, 1959) and *P.T. 109* (Jimmy Dean, 1962).

Marijohn's songwriting wasn't just confined to Country material; she also wrote *Cut Across Shorty* for rock'n'roll singer Eddie Cochran and *Whip-Poor-Will* for Pop artist Teresa Brewer. She also appeared as a back-up singer on numerous hit records, working freelance, with the Jordanaires and Anita Kerr Singers as well as with her own Marijohn Singers, who were on the *Grand Ole Opry* for three years. She also recorded a pair of albums for Columbia: ***Country & Western Songs That Sold a Million*** (1960, as Marijohn & the Jacks) and ***Ballads of the Blue and Gray*** (1961).

In 1964, Marijohn's son, Bucky, wrote *G.T.O.*, which became a big Pop hit when recorded by his group, Ronny and the Daytonas (on Mala Records). It also was the first song published by Marijohn's company, Buckhorn Music. This organization specialized in promoting previously unproven writers, gaining successes with Johnny Duncan and Ed Bruce, among others. These others included Kris Kristofferson, who wrote *For the Good Times*, *Jody and the Kid* and several others for Buckhorn.

Despite her numerous successes, Marijohn was depressed and drinking heavily, especially after the breakup of her marriage in the mid-1960s, and attempted suicide twice. She turned to spiritualism and the supernatural without finding what she was looking for.

In 1970, Marijohn went to Europe and found on her return that Ray Price had given her company a No.1 Country hit (also a major Pop cut) with his rendition of Kristofferson's *For the Good Times*. After a dramatic religious conversion, she changed her songwriting emphasis to inspirational songs, penning *One Day at a Time* with Kristofferson as a cri de coeur. The song became a Top 20 hit for Marilyn Sellers that year and has since become a much recorded song around the world, including a No.1 version in the U.K. by Lena Martell in 1979 and a Country No.1 in 1980 by Cristy Lane. It has also twice won Golden Guitar Awards in Australia for versions by the Hawking Brothers (1979) and Suzanne Prentice (1983). In 1975, it was named "Song of the Year" by the GMA in their Dove Awards. Marijohn also wrote *The Scars in the Hands of Jesus* and numerous other Gospel songs.

In 1974, Marijohn recorded the Gospel album ***I Have Returned***, for the Word label, its success resulting in several other recordings. The following year, Marijohn was inducted into the Nashville Songwriters Hall of Fame. In 1978, she wrote her autobiography, *Lord, Let Me Leave a Song*, in conjunction with writer Darryl E. Hicks. For many years, Marijohn had an "autograph table" on which celebrated guests to her home etched their signatures with an electric needle.

WKM

RECOMMENDED ALBUMS:

"Ballads of the Blue & Gray" (Columbia)(1961)
"I Have Returned" (Word)(1975)
"One Day at a Time" (Word UK)(1980)

SLIM WILLET

(Singer, Songwriter)

Given Name:	**Winston Lee Moore**
Date of Birth:	**December 1, 1919**
Where Born:	**Nr. Dublin, Texas**
Married:	**Jimmie L. Crenshaw**
Children:	**Louis Ted, Tim Willet**
Date of Death:	**July 1, 1966**

Slim Willet is best remembered as the writer of the song *Don't Let the Stars Get in Your Eyes*. The song was a 1952 No.1 hit for Willet and Skeets McDonald, and a Top 5 hit for Ray Price, the same year. The following year, it became a Top 10 record for Red Foley and a No.1 Pop hit for Perry Como. An answer version, *I Let the Stars Get in Your Eyes,* became a No.1 hit for Goldie Hill, also in 1953.

Willet attended Hardin-Simmons University at Abilene, Texas, between 1946 and 1949, where he received a B.A. degree in journalism. He initially worked in the aircraft industry and then, later in 1949, he went to KRBC Abilene, where he stayed until 1956.

He formed his group, the Hired Hands, in 1950, released his first single, *Tool Pusher from Snyder,* on the Star Talent label, that year and joined the *Big D Jamboree* over WFAA in Dallas. He remained on the Jamboree until 1954.

In 1951, Slim and the band joined the *Louisiana Hayride* and stayed on the Hayride until the group folded, in 1955. The group moved on to 4 Star Records, in 1952, and released their original version of *Don't Let the Stars Get in Your Eyes.* They had three releases on the label during 1953, namely, *Red Rose,* Willet's own *Let Me Know* and *No Love Song to You.* That year, the group joined *Town Hall Party* in Compton, California. Slim stayed on the show until 1957.

In 1954, Slim and the Hired Hands appeared on the *Grand Ole Opry.* After the Hired Hands had disbanded, Slim moved on to KNIT Abilene, in 1956. He stayed on the station until 1964, and then made a final change of station to KCAD, also in Abilene, which he part owned. During 1954, Slim set up his own Winston label and released *Star Light Waltz* and *Leave Me Alone* (both 1954), *Abilene Waltz* (1959) and *You're the Only Woman* (1966). He remained at KCAD until his death in 1966, from a heart attack. He is buried in Victor, Texas.

RECOMMENDED ALBUM:

"Oil Patch Songs" (Winston)(1962)

AUDREY WILLIAMS

(Singer, Songwriter, Promoter)

Given Name:	**Audrey Mae Sheppard**
Date of Birth:	**February 28, 1923**
Where Born:	**Banks, Pike County, Alabama**
Married:	**1. Erskine Guy (div.) 2. Hiriam "Hank" Williams (div./dec'd.)**
Children:	**Lycrecia, Randall Hank (Hank Williams, Jr.)**
Date of Death:	**November 4, 1975**

Audrey Williams spent some three-fifths of her troubled life as either the wife or the ex-wife/"widow" of Country music's most legendary figure, Hank Williams. She also played a key role in the development of her son, Hank Williams, Jr., as a major Country star.

Born on a south-central Alabama farm, Audrey met Hank Williams in 1942, after an unsuccessful first marriage left her with a daughter. At the time, Hank was working in a medicine show during one of his absences from WFSA Montgomery, Alabama, and Audrey worked as a clerk in a drugstore. The pair quickly developed an infatuation for one

***Audrey Williams**, wife of Hank, mother of Hank, Jr.*

another and married in mid-December 1944. Their marriage had plenty of stormy moments from the start. Audrey had drive and ambition while Hank had singing talent and skill as a songwriter, but his irresponsible manner, particularly drinking, created problems.

Nonetheless, as Hank's star rose in the music industry from 1946 and the couple moved from Montgomery to Shreveport and ultimately Nashville, Audrey's did too as she sang some duets with him on MGM, and in 1950, had a couple of sessions on Decca from which three singles were released. None made much of an impact although the Hadacol-fad song *What Put the Pep in Grandma* and her own unreleased *Model T Love* could be classed as clever lyrics to say the least.

Hank and Audrey had several brief separations during their union, but the split of early January 1952 proved to be permanent, with their divorce being final on May 29. Audrey retained the couple's home on Franklin Road in Nashville and the rights to half Hank's songwriter royalties. On August 11, the *Grand Ole Opry* management dismissed Hank and he returned to Shreveport and the *Louisiana Hayride,* remarrying in October. Audrey contended, however, that he called her a few days before his death and that she and Hank agreed to a reconciliation. It all ended with Hank's death on New Year's Eve.

Audrey spent the next twenty-two years in the role of Hank Williams' "widow" with the tragic Country vocalist becoming even bigger in death and legend than he had been in life. She also continued to pursue musical activity herself. She cut two more sessions for Decca in 1953 and 1954, although none of the five masters were released for decades.

In 1955, Audrey went with MGM and had five single releases over a three-year period. None did especially well, but she could still draw crowds on the road, largely on the strength of name recognition. From 1958, she worked hard to promote the career of Hank Williams, Jr. and after he sang his dad's songs on the soundtrack of the motion picture *Your Cheatin' Heart,* in 1964, his show business rating shot rapidly upward, while repeating his father's success on MGM Records. As time went by, however, he came to resent her influence and control (although never her), much as his father had resented his own mother's efforts along that line.

Audrey found her role an increasingly difficult one with the passage of time and became a problem drinker, too. For a while in the late 60's, Audrey toured with her all-girl band, the Cold Cold Hearts, but disbanded in 1970. She also got increasingly in debt to the IRS. Many people believed that she blamed herself for Hank's demise and spent all those years wallowing in guilt. At any rate, this complex woman's health declined rapidly in 1975, particularly after Hank, Jr.'s near-fatal accident in August. Her story is probably told best in her daughter Lycrecia's sympathetic yet realistic portrayal (with Dale Vinicur), *Still in Love with You* (1989). Bear Family Records re-issued her complete Decca masters on album in 1988. IMT

RECOMMENDED ALBUM:

"Ramblin' Gal" (Bear Family Germany)(1988)

(See also Hank Williams, Hank Williams, Jr.)

BUDDY WILLIAMS

(Singer, Songwriter, Guitar, Bass Guitar)

Given Name:	**Harold Taylor**
Date of Birth:	**September 5, 1918**
Where Born:	**Sydney, New South Wales, Australia**
Married:	**1. Bernice Verl Perring (div.) 2. Grace Maldmen**
Children:	**Donita Carolyn (dec'd.), Harold George, Kaye Elizabeth, Karen Anne**
Date of Death:	**December 12, 1986**

Buddy Williams, known sometimes as "the Yodeling Jackaroo," became the second Australian Country music star, behind New Zealand-born Tex Morton. For some forty-five years, he traveled the length and breadth of the land "down under" entertaining the folks in the outback as well as the towns and cities. With a good mixture of traditional Country songs of American origin and Aussie compositions, Williams found favor with Australian fans until his death in 1986.

The first known information about the man music fans would know as Buddy Williams is that he entered an orphanage at an early age.

Later, at the age of 7, a dairy farm family near Dorrigo adopted him, but generally speaking, he suffered from poor treatment and hard labor. At 15, he ran away and thereafter worked as an itinerant laborer. During this time, he developed his singing and guitar skills and gained a great appreciation for the out of doors. Right after turning 21, on July 9, 1939, Buddy had his initial session for Regal-Zonophone, cutting six original songs, including *That Dappled Grey Bronco of Mine*, which became one of his all-time favorites. As the first native-born Australian star, Williams soon achieved considerable fame as an "outback" vocalist. As Australian historian/critic Eric Watson stated, Buddy's songs displayed a "first hand affinity with the bush itself that [Tex] Morton's own background did not make possible for him." While the latter mixed locally written songs and American songs, eleven of the first twelve Williams songs were his own.

WWII intruded into the Williams career, when he enlisted as a Bren gunner in the 2nd AIF. Some of his recording sessions took place during army leave, but he continued to turn out such classics as *Music in My Pony's Feet* and *Where the White Faced Cattle Roam*. He was one of the entertainers who formed 2/31st Battalion Concert Party. Buddy sustained a serious wound at the Battle of Balikpapan on the island of Borneo, but eventually healed after a long recovery and was recommended for a Military Medal. He returned to his musical career in 1946, owning and operating a traveling rodeo tent for about nine years. By then he had gained sufficient fame to have an exclusive musical variety show, the Country and Western Variety Show, which eventually included some of his own children. A stickler for tradition, his recordings for Regal-Zonophone, to 1951, and Columbia, from 1952, had only his own guitar for accompaniment until the late 50's.

After WWII, Williams began to record not only more songs of American origin but also his own and those of other Australian composers, including Shorty Ranger and Stan Coster. He did tribute albums to both Jimmie Rodgers and Hank Williams during the 60's. From 1965, his waxings appeared on the RCA (Australia) label. In 1977, he became the second elected member to the Australian Roll of Renown. Buddy continued his musical career, sometimes aided by various family members, although ill health plagued his last years. With Tex Morton and Slim Dusty, Buddy Williams ranks as one-third of a triumvirate of Australian Country greats.

IMT

RECOMMENDED ALBUMS:

(All Australian releases)
"Buddy Williams Sings Jimmie Rodgers" (Columbia)(1962)
"Buddy Williams Remembers, Vol. I" (RCA)(1965)
"Family Album" (RCA)(1966)
"Buddy Williams Remembers, Vol. II" (RCA)(1966)
"Williams Family" (RCA)
"Songs of the Australian Outback" (Reader's Digest)
"Buddy Sings Hank" (RCA)
"Family Affair" (RCA)
"Cowboy's Life Is Good Enough for Me" (RCA)
"Sentimental Buddy" (RCA)
"Buddy and Shorty" (RCA)
"Hard Times" (RCA)
"Along the Outback Tracks" (RCA)
"Aussie on My Mind" (RCA)(1972)
"35 Wonderful Years" (RCA)(1974)
"Ramblin' Around" (RCA)(1975)
"An Old Hillbilly from Wayback" (RCA)(1981)
"A Breath of Country Air" (RCA)(1982)
"Big Country Muster" (RCA)(1983)
"Our Buddy" (Axis)(1985) [Features Buddy with guest vocalists]
"The Immortal Buddy Williams" (EMI)(1987) [From Regal-Zonophone masters]
"Under Western Skies" (EMI)(1992) [From Regal-Zonophone masters]

CURLEY WILLIAMS

(Fiddle, Songwriter)
Given Name: Doc Williams
Date of Birth: 1913
Where Born: Georgia
Date of Death: September 5, 1970

Curley Williams is known primarily for his 1951 composition *Half As Much*, which was a hit for Hank Williams (no relation), and for having one of the earliest Western Swing units on the *Grand Ole Opry*. Williams and his Santa Fe Trail Riders came to the *Opry* in December 1942 from station WALD Albany, Georgia. Because there was already a Doc Williams and his Border Riders on WWVA Wheeling, West Virginia, George D. Hay decided it would be wise to change both the name of the band and the bandleader. Because Williams had curly hair the decision was made to call him "Curley." Choosing a new name for the band was equally easy. Williams was from Georgia, the Peach State, so Hay decided the band should be called Curley Williams and his Georgia Peach Pickers.

The Peach Pickers made their first appearance on a network *Opry* show in September 1943, performing *Smoke on the Water* and *When the Sun Goes Down*. In 1945 Williams signed a recording contract with Columbia, the band cutting its first sides on February 20 that year. During the next six years the Peach Pickers recorded thirty-six sides under their own name and did backup work for several others by Clyde Moody, Fred Rose, Johnny Bond and Zeke Clements. Their most successful releases were *Southern Belle (From Nashville, Tennessee)* and *Georgia Steel Guitar*.

In 1945 the Peach Pickers moved to the West Coast, where they played in dance halls operated by Foreman Phillips. They also appeared in the 1947 Charles Starrett "Durango Kid" movie *Riders of the Lone Star*. By 1948, they were part of the cast of Shreveport's *Louisiana Hayride*. The following year they were in Memphis but soon moved to Anniston, Alabama, station WHMA.

In 1951, at their last Columbia session, they recorded *Half As Much*. That same year they were part of a television show called the *Smoky Mountain Jamboree*. These programs were filmed at Toccoa, Georgia, and were popular for a brief time. By 1954 the Peach Pickers were doing a 30-minute show sponsored by the Jax Beer Company of New Orleans on WSFA Montgomery, Alabama. Thereafter, Williams drifted out of the music business, passing away sixteen years later at age 57.

WKM

DOC AND CHICKIE WILLIAMS

When Formed: 1946

DOC WILLIAMS
(Singer, Songwriter, Guitar, Harmonica)
Given Name: Andrew John Smik, Jr.
Date of Birth: June 26, 1914
Where Born: Cleveland, Ohio

CHICKIE WILLIAMS
(Singer, Songwriter, Bass Fiddle)
Given Name: Jessie Wanda Crupe
Date of Birth: February 13, 1919
Where Born: Bethany, West Virginia
Children: Barbara Diane, Madeline Dawn, Karen Dolores

Doc and Chickie Williams are one of traditional Country music's better-known husband-wife duets. Although major national stardom eluded them, the duo became long-time popular attractions throughout the northeastern states and eastern Canada. With their band, the Border Riders, the pair, sometimes known as "Country Music's Royal Couple," became a virtual institution in their region. They also illustrate the degree to which Country music, sometimes thought of as the cultural baggage of Celtic and Anglo-Saxon peoples, can be amalgamated into traditions of those of East European origins.

Andrew Smik was born in Cleveland but grew up in the mining town of Kittanning, Pennsylvania. In his youth he heard recordings of Vernon Dalhart and Riley Puckett as well as early day radio cowboys Jack and Jerry Foy at KDKA in nearby Pittsburgh. He also started playing guitar so that he could play at local dances; his younger brother Milo or "Cy" (b. 1918) began playing fiddle.

Doc soon joined a band called the Kansas Clodhoppers and in 1934 went to WJAY Cleveland, moving on to Pittsburgh's KQV the next year. After some name and personnel changes, this group eventually became the Border Riders, which included Cy on fiddle, Curley Sims on mandolin, Rawhide Fincher as bass player-comedian, and Cy's wife Mary "Sunflower" Calvas as featured vocalist.

In May, 1937, this group came to WWVA Wheeling, trading places with a group led by Joe Ray. Later Doc got a new comedian named Froggie Cortez and also brought Big Slim the Lone Cowboy (aka Harry McAuliffe) to play in his band for a time. Doc and his Border Riders quickly became one of the station's most popular acts and starred on the *Saturday Night Jamboree* as well.

With the exception of part of the WWII years and a brief period in 1957-1958, Doc remained a *Jamboree* regular and did daily shows for many years as well. His earlier bands had been built largely around a fiddle and mandolin sound, but after WWII, the accordion, played by Marion Martin (1919-1990), replaced the mandolin. Doc also kept his show moving with comedians like Hiram Hayseed (Shorty Godwin) and Smoky Pleacher. Doc had married in 1939 and in 1946, his wife, Chickie, joined as featured vocalist and remained with the group. Her "sweet voiced" singing style became quite popular and her 1947 waxing of *Beyond the Sunset* was quickly covered by numerous other artists on major labels.

Doc had started Wheeling Records that year and over the decades turned out numerous

Doc and Chickie Williams *with the Border Riders*

singles and albums mostly by Chickie and himself individually. They did a few duets as well and their three daughters, known on stage as Peeper, Poochie, and Punkin (Karen McKenzie), also made some recordings. While Doc had not made any hit records as such, he did have some well-known numbers closely associated with him, such as *Willie Roy the Crippled Boy*, *My Old Brown Coat and Me*, *Silver Bell* and *Polka Dots and Polka Dreams*. His guitar instruction course, sold via transcribed radio programs on several major stations in addition to WWVA, such as WCKY Cincinnati and KXEL Waterloo, Iowa, also helped spread Doc's reputation and sold a quarter of a million copies over a period of years.

Doc and Chickie continued touring well into the 70's, but as they grew older, they slowed their pace considerably. Doc opened a souvenir and western wear shop across from the *Jamboree*. Ironically, as his legendary status grew, his appearances on the venerable program decreased to one or two a year. He and Chickie continued to play an occasional show when the demand arose and each cut a new album in 1992 (released on cassette and combined on a single compact disc). Old Homestead reissued a few of his older albums and Doc kept most of the others available on cassette. As he approaches his eightieth birthday, Doc stays busy with his stores and organizing another annual Jamboree Old Timer Reunion. IMT

RECOMMENDED ALBUMS:

Doc Williams:

"25th Anniversary Album" (Wheeling)(1962)

"Wheeling Back to Wheeling" (Wheeling and Old Homestead)(1966)

"Favorites Old and New" (Wheeling)(1969)

"The Doc Williams Show" (Wheeling)(1972)

"Lonely" (Doxx)(1974)

"The Doc Williams Collection (1951-1957)" (Cattle Germany)(1978)

Chickie Williams:

"Chickie Williams Sings the Old Songs" (Wheeling and Old Homestead)(1959)

"Fireside Songs" (Wheeling)(1963)

"From Out of the Hills of West Virginia" (Wheeling and Old Homestead)(1968)

"Just a Melody" (Doxx)(1974)

Doc & Chickie et al.:

"Doc & Chickie Together" (Wheeling)(1966)

"The Doc Williams Family Sacred Album" (Wheeling)(1967)

"The Three of Us" (Wheeling)(1969)

"Encore: The Three of Us Again" (Wheeling)(ca. 1973)

"Full Circle: Doc & Chickie in England" (Wheeling)(1978)

"Anniversary" (Wheeling)(1984)

"The Famous Doc Williams Guitar Course" (Wheeling)(1986) [Three cassette set from radio transcriptions]

"Collector's Series #3" (Wheeling)(1990) [Cassette]

"The Golden Years Collection" (Wheeling cd)(1993) [Also issued as two cassettes, one each by Doc and Chickie]

DON WILLIAMS

(Singer, Songwriter, Guitar, Actor)

Date of Birth:	**May 27, 1939**
Where Born:	**Floydada, Texas**
Married:	**Joy Bucher**
Children:	**Gary, Timmy**

Don Williams is one of the rare performers who have become highly popular in the U.S. and has also achieved great fame overseas. In particular, he has been highly acclaimed in Europe. In addition, he has many fans among his peers in Rock music. Yet, with his light brown voice, he is still the consummate balladeer, which makes him acceptable to MOR audiences.

Raised near Corpus Christi, Texas, Don was age 3 when he sang in a local talent contest and won the first prize, an alarm clock. He learned to play guitar as a teenager and wrote his first song, *Walk It Off*, when 14. In 1957, he made his professional debut, while still in high school. With a group of friends, he played and sang for the opening of the Billings Service Station in Taft, Texas, for a group fee of $25. Don's early jobs included being a bill collector, driving a bread truck, working in the Texas oil fields, in a smelting plant and working for Pittsburgh Plate Glass.

He moved to Corpus Christi and formed the modern Folk trio the Pozo Seco Singers with Susan Taylor and Lofton Kline. In 1965, they signed to Edmark Records, and their single *Time* was picked up by Columbia and reached the Pop chart Top 50. They had two further singles that both reached the Top 40 on the Pop lists, in 1966, *I Can Make It with You* and *Look What You've Done*.

They moved to Nashville during 1967, but in 1971, the group disbanded. Don returned to Texas to work with his father-in-law in his furniture business. However, Susan Taylor embarked on a solo career and invited Don to return to Nashville and write songs for her. This he did and soon he was signed to Jack Clement as a staff writer and then (although, according to Cowboy Jack, Don never formally signed) he released his initial solo recordings through Clement's JMI label, where he was produced by Clement and Allen Reynolds and engineered by future star producer Garth Fundis.

Don's initial single was *Don't You Believe*, but he first hit the Country chart, at the end of 1972, with his second single *The Shelter of Your Eyes* (both written by Don) which made the Top 15. This was followed, the next year, with the double-sided hit *Come Early Morning/Amanda*, the former being the first concept music video by a Country performer

One of the most successful international Country singers, ***Don Williams***

and the latter becoming a No.1 for Waylon Jennings, both being written by Bob McDill. He and songwriter Wayland Holyfield found their songs in great demand by Don, whose easy, laid-back style perfectly suited their Country ballads. Don closed out 1973 with another Top 20 release, *Atta Way to Go*.

1974 was Don's last year with JMI and his opener for the year, Reynolds' *We Should Be Together*, was his most successful to date, going Top 5. His final single for JMI, *Down the Road I Go*, didn't fare too well, but by then he was already signed to Dot Records (it later became ABC/Dot, then ABC and finally MCA), where he was initially produced by Reynolds and then he and Fundis took over these duties. His debut single for the new affiliation, *I Wouldn't Want to Live if You Didn't Love Me*, presented him with his first No.1. He wrapped up the year with his version of Brook Benton's hit *The Ties That Bind*, which went Top 5.

With the advent of 1975, Don began a streak of four No.1 singles, *You're My Best Friend* and *(Turn Out the Lights And) Love Me Tonight* (both 1975) and *Till the Rivers All Run Dry* and *Say It Again* (both 1976). He ended 1976 with *She Never Knew Me*, which reached the Top 3 on the Country chart and crossed over to the lower levels of the Pop chart. Don made his movie debut in the Burt Reynolds movie *W.W. and the Dixie Dance-kings*, in 1975, and it was this movie that led to him wearing his trademark hat, which is now replaced by the Stetson company. This went well with his already established trademark Sedgefield jacket and denim pants.

During 1975, the British Country Music Society named him "Male Vocalist of the Year" and ***You're My Best Friend*** its "Album of the Year." The next year, he made his debut on the Wembley Festival in England and immediately consolidated his already successful career there. *I Recall a Gypsy Woman*, which reached No.13 on the U.K. Pop chart, was named the BCMA's 1976 "Single of the Year." He also charted in the U.K. with *You're My Best Friend*. Such was his European success that by the end of 1977, Don had six albums on the U.K. chart. That year, he was named "International Male Vocalist" at the British International Country Music Awards, and *Country Music People*/Radio 2, in the U.K., named *You're My Best Friend* "All-Time Favourite Country Record" and the BCMA made ***Visions*** their "Album of the Year" and two years later, the British Phonographic Industry (BPI) Certified that ***Visions*** had gone Double Platinum.

In 1977, Don had back-to-back No.1 records with *Some Broken Hearts Never Mend* and *I'm Just a Country Boy*, both of which were Pop basement successes. His success continued into 1978 with *I've Got a Winner in You* (Top 10), *Rake and Ramblin' Man* (Top 3) and the No.1, *Tulsa Time*. The latter's writer, Danny Flowers, a member of Don's band, once told Barry McCloud that when Don picked up the song from his table, it wasn't yet finished, and a close examination of it reveals that it only has two chords. That year, Don was invited back to Wembley Festival and the U.K.'s trade journal *Music Week* named him their "Top Record Sales." The decade ended with *Lay Down Beside Me* (Top 3) and successive No.1s, *It Must Be Love* and *Love Me Over Again*. During 1979, Don returned to the U.K. to tour and he played to full-houses. That year, the album ***The Best of Don Williams Volume II*** was Certified Gold in Canada.

The new decade started with *Could You Ever Really Love a Poor Boy*, on Phono, which made the Top 100. Then it was business as usual, when *Good Ole Boys Like Me* got to the Top 3. In the summer of 1980 came his most successful cross-over single, Roger Cook and Sam Hogin's *I Believe in You*, which went to No.1 on the Country chart and Top 30 on the Pop lists. British magazine *Country Music People* named Don "Country Music Artist of the Decade." ***The Best of Don Williams Volume II*** was Certified Gold and ***I Believe in You*** went Gold (it did the same in Canada, in 1982) and in 1990 was Certified Platinum. Don appeared in a second movie, *Smokey and the Bandit II*.

His 1981 hits were *Falling Again* (Top 10), *Miracles* (Top 5) and *If I Needed You*, a duet with Emmylou Harris, taken from her ***Cimarron*** album and his ***Especially for You*** album. Don ended the year with another No.1, *Lord, I Hope This Day Is Good*. The CMA named ***I Believe in You*** as their "Album of the Year" and *Radio & Records*' Country Radio Poll voted him "Male Vocalist." The following year, the British International Country Music Awards named Don "Male Vocalist of the Year."

Don stayed with MCA until the end of 1985, and his hits during this period were: 1982: *Listen to the Radio* and *Mistakes* (both Top 3) and *If Hollywood Don't Need You* (No.1); 1983: *Love Is on a Roll* (No.1), *Nobody But You* (Top 3) and another No.1, *Stay Young*; 1984: *That's the Thing About Love* (No.1) and *Maggie's Dream*, which only reached the Top 15; 1985: *Walkin' a Broken Heart* (Top 3) and the Top 20 entry, *It's Time for Love*. Don's 1983 ***Yellow Moon*** album reveals him with a luxuriant full beard. This was just the latest change in an ever developing image styling.

Don moved to Capitol Records and released his debut album for the label, ***New Moves***, in 1986. He and Garth Fundis still handled production chores, and quickly got into their stride with a Top 3 single, *We've Got a Good Fire Goin'*. This was followed by yet another No.1, *Heartbeat in the Darkness*. Don wrapped up the year with another Top 3 record, Dennis Linde's *Then It's Love*. During the year, he toured the U.K. with Barbara Fairchild.

In 1987, Don underwent surgery for a

ruptured disc. Some three years earlier, he had been forced to use a stool to sit on during his act, to ease the pain. He then had a rest for eighteen months, to recharge his batteries.

From 1987 through to 1989, his hits continued without let or hindrance, and were: 1987: *Senorita* (Top 10), *I'll Never Be in Love Again* (Top 5) and *I Wouldn't Be a Man* (Top 10); 1988: *Another Place, Another Time* (Top 5) and *Desperately* (Top 10); 1989: *Old Coyote Town* (Top 5).

In 1989, Don relocated to RCA, and enjoyed a continuation of his success, with his debut album on the label, ***One Good Well***, staying on the Country Album chart for 21 weeks. The title track reached the Top 5 of the Country Singles list, as did the follow-up, *I've Been Loved by the Best*.

The following year saw *Just As Long As I Have You* go Top 5, but *Maybe That's All It Takes* just failed to reach the Top 20. However, the last single of the year, *Back in My Younger Days*, got to the Top 3. Don's 1991 hits were the Top 5 single *True Love*, the title track of his second RCA album and *Lord Have Mercy on a Country Boy*, which went Top 10. His 1991 album ***Currents*** was produced by his old buddy Allen Reynolds. Then in 1992, the party was over, and both his chart singles, *Too Much Love* and *It's Who You Love*, only reached the Top 75.

"The Gentle Giant," as Don is known, has had a career that many would envy, and of course he is quite capable of having more hits. What often goes unnoticed is that he has also chalked up much success as a songwriter. As well as being responsible for many of his own hits, he has been recorded by Country performers such as Kenny Rogers and Jeannie Pruett (both cut *Lay Down Beside Me*), Charley Pride (*The Shelter of Your Eyes*), Johnny Cash (*Down the Road I Go*), Sonny James and Lefty Frizzell (both recorded *If She Just Helps Me Get Over You*), as well as Rock stars such as Pete Townshend (*Till the Rivers All Run Dry*).

He is also an adept producer, and as well as his own albums, he produced, with Allen Reynolds, Barbara Fairchild's releases for Capitol. Don's backing band, the Scratch Band, also had the benefit of Don's producing hand.

RECOMMENDED ALBUMS:

Although Don has achieved enormous success as a singles artist, all of his albums are worth getting, because there are never dead-weight tracks.

"Time" (Columbia)(1966) [As the Pozo Seco Singers]
"Don Williams Vol. 1" (JMI)(1972) [Re-released on ABC/Dot (1974)]
"Don Williams Vol. 2" (JMI)(1974) [Re-released on ABC/Dot (1974)]
"Don Williams Vol. 3" (ABC/Dot)(1974)
"The Very Best of Don Williams" (double)(MCA)(1980)
"Yellow Moon" (MCA)(1983)
"The Best of Don Williams Vol.3" (MCA)(1984)
"New Moves" (Capitol)(1986)
"Traces" (Capitol)(1987)
"Prime Cuts" (Capitol)(1989)
"One Good Well" (RCA)(1989)
"True Love" (RCA)(1990)
"Currents" (RCA)(1992)
(See also Scratch Band, the)

HANK WILLIAMS

(Singer, Songwriter, Guitar)

Given Name:	**Hiriam King Williams (first name misspelled on birth certificate)**
Date of Birth:	**September 17, 1923**
Where Born:	**Mt. Olive Community, near Garland in Butler County, Alabama**
Married:	**1. Audrey Mae Sheppard (div.) 2. Billie Jean Jones Eshlimar**
Children:	**Randall Hank (Hank Williams, Jr.), Lycrecia (stepdaughter), Antha Belle Jett (a.k.a. Cathy Stone/Jett Williams)**
Date of Death:	**December 31, 1952**

No other person, past or present, represents the heart and soul of Country music like the immortal singer/songwriter Hank Williams. Dead at 29 years of age from the ravages of alcoholism, Hank nevertheless wrote and recorded some of American popular music's most enduring standards, establishing himself as the model of soulful, simplistic expression that artists across all musical genres continue to emulate even today.

Born in rural Butler County, Alabama, Hank was fatherless by the age of 6 when an old WWI injury forced his father Lon's commitment to long-term care at the V.A. Hospital in Biloxi, Mississippi. Hank and his sister, Irene, were raised alone by their mother, the formidable Lillie Williams, in the Depression-era rural South, an experience that early on forged into Hank's character an independent spirit and feelings of compassion for society's less fortunate members.

They lived in Georgiana and then Greenville, Alabama, where Hank became acquainted with a black Blues street singer named Rufus Payne ("Tee Tot"), from whom he probably learned the basics of picking a guitar, singing the Blues, and entertaining a crowd. In 1937, Lillie moved her family to Montgomery, Alabama, where Hank formally began his musical career billed as "the Singing Kid" in 1941 on WSFA Montgomery, singing mostly Roy Acuff tunes and other popular songs of the day with his band, the Drifting Cowboys.

During 1943 Hank met Audrey Mae Sheppard, a farm girl from near Banks, Alabama (with a 2-year-old daughter from a previous brief marriage) and it was love at first sight. Audrey immediately began to manage Hank's career, a job that had been performed up to that time by Hank's mother, Lillie. She learned to play stand-up bass in the band, collected the admission at the door in the schoolhouses and roadside honky-tonks and searched the streets for Hank when he had wandered off drunk and they were scheduled to play an important gig. They lived

Hank Williams, *who wrote and recorded some of music's most popular songs*

in Lillie's boardinghouse along with the other members of the band, and Audrey's belief in Hank's talent and *her* ambition for *his* future success as a singer/songwriter possibly overshadowed his own. They were married on December 15, 1944, by a justice of the peace who ran a gas station in Andalusia, Alabama.

In 1946, the two traveled to Nashville to meet Tin Pan Alley songwriter and hillbilly music publisher Fred Rose (partners with Roy Acuff in Acuff-Rose Publishing). Fred was first impressed by Hank as a songwriter, but soon called upon him to record two sessions for Sterling Records, the first on December 11, 1946, and the second on February 13, 1947. These sessions led to a contract with MGM Records in early 1947, and Hank's first hit, *Move It on Over,* went Top 5 on the Country charts, later that year. Fred Rose would soon become a major influence in Hank's life, acting as both a professional mentor and father figure.

Hank was asked to join the *Louisiana Hayride* in Shreveport in the summer of 1948. His next releases for MGM, in 1948, were *Honky Tonkin'* (originally released on Sterling) and *I'm a Long Gone Daddy*, which reached the Top 15 and Top 10 respectively. Then, in early 1949, Hank recorded a 1922 Tin Pan Alley song called *Lovesick Blues,* which had already been winning him standing ovations at public appearances and on the Hayride. It soared to No.1 and remained there for 16 weeks out of over 10 months on the Country charts, crossed over to the Pop Top 25 and was Certified Gold. On June 11, 1949, Hank sang the song on the Warren Paint segment of the *Grand Ole Opry* and was called back for an unprecedented six encores. Almost instantaneously, Hank Williams was a star.

A son, Randall Hank, was born to Hank and Audrey that spring, and the family moved to Nashville. Hank put together the most famous version of his Drifting Cowboys band at this time. It consisted of steel guitarist Don Helms (who had been with the band off and on since 1943), fiddler Jerry Rivers, guitarist Bob McNett (who had played with Hank on the *Louisiana Hayride*), and bassist Hillous Butrum.

For the next three years, the hits kept coming. In 1949, Hank charted with *Mansion on the Hill* (Top 15), *Wedding Bells* (Top 3), *Never Again* (Top 10), which had also been released on Sterling, *Mind Your Own Business* (Top 5), *You're Gonna Change (or I'm Gonna Leave)* (Top 5) and the flip-side, Leon Payne's *Lost Highway* (Top 15) and *My Bucket's Got a Hole in It* (Top 3).

In 1950, he opened his account with *I Just Don't Like This Kind of Livin'*, which went Top 5. He followed up with *Long Gone Lonesome Blues*, which stayed at No.1 for 8 weeks with the flip-side, *My Son Calls Another Man Daddy*, reaching the Top 10. This was followed by *Why Don't You Love Me*, which topped the charts for 10 weeks out of nearly 6 months on the lists. His other 1950 successes were *They'll Never Take Her Love from Me* (Top 5) and the flip-side, *Why Should We Try Anymore* (Top 10), *Moanin' the Blues* (No.1), and the flip-side, *Nobody's Lonesome for Me* (Top 10).

In addition to these commercial recordings, Hank also began to record a series of spiritual/philosophic recitations, in 1950, including *The Funeral, Men with Broken Hearts,* and *Be Careful of Stones That You Throw*, under the name of "Luke the Drifter." There was never any secret about who Luke the Drifter was, but the pseudonym was agreed upon when Hank insisted to Fred Rose that he wanted to release these recitations, hoping to reach some of those whom he considered to be the lost souls of the world.

In 1951, Hank had a Top 10 hit with *Dear John*, but it was the flip-side, *Cold, Cold Heart*, that went to No.1, stayed on the charts for over 11 months and earned Hank his second Gold Record. He followed this with the double-sided Top 3 release *Howlin' at the Moon/I Can't Help It (If I'm Still in Love with You)*. Then came one of his finest singles, *Hey, Good Lookin'*, which stayed at No.1 for 8 weeks. He finished the year with *Crazy Heart* (Top 5), the flip-side, *Lonesome Whistle* (Top 10) and *Baby, We're Really in Love* (Top 5).

While Hank's career was on the rise, however, his personal life began to show signs of deterioration. The by-products of his fame, such as longer and longer absences from home, extreme demands on his time and the rapid accumulation of wealth, were not being handled well by either Hank or Audrey. One serious result was that Hank's drinking bouts, which had been more or less kept under control during the first couple of years of his ascent to stardom, became more pronounced, and his marriage, tempestuous from the beginning, began to crumble. It is one of the great tragedies of the story of the life of Hank Williams that just at the time when his opportunities for happiness were at their strongest, things began to fall apart.

In 1951, Tony Bennett recorded *Cold, Cold Heart,* elevating Hank's simple songwriting style to Pop market visibility; Bennett's recording was followed with covers of Hank's songs by popular artists such as Frankie Laine, Jo Stafford, Tennessee Ernie Ford, Helen O'Connell, Guy Mitchell, Kay Starr, Polly Bergen and Teresa Brewer. That same year, Hank appeared on Dudley LeBlanc's Hadacol Caravan traveling medicine show with Bob Hope, Jack Benny and Minnie Pearl and sang *Hey, Good Lookin'* on Perry Como's CBS television program. In 1951, he and Audrey also opened Hank and Audrey's Corral, Nashville's first western apparel store.

In the fall of 1951, Hank tripped and fell during a hunting excursion on a farm he had purchased in Franklin, Tennessee, aggravating a long-standing back condition and necessitating an operation which was scheduled for December. Then, in early January, 1952, he and Audrey separated. Hank first went back to Montgomery to continue to recuperate under the care of his mother, then returned to Nashville that spring to share a house with singer Ray Price.

Hank started 1952 with the Top 3 hits *Honky Tonk Blues* and Curley Williams' *Half As Much*. These were followed by the classic *Jambalaya (On the Bayou)*, which went to No.1 for 14 weeks out of 7 months on the Country charts, crossed over to the Pop Top 20 and went Gold. His other success was *Settin' the Woods on Fire* (Top 3) coupled with *You Win Again*, which went Top 10.

There is much evidence to support the claim that from the time he left home in early January 1952 until his death somewhere in the night of December 31, 1952, or the morning of January 1 1953, Hank Williams probably never drew another sober breath. Devastated by the loss of Audrey and his home and family, wracked with pain from the surgery that never was allowed to properly heal, Hank descended into a physical and psychological hell from which he never emerged.

In August, he was fired from the *Opry* for missing shows and appearing drunk on the stage. On October, 18, he married a red-headed beauty, Billie Jean Jones Eshlimar (his divorce from Audrey had been finalized in May) and also signed an agreement to support the baby of another of his girlfriends, Bobbie Jett. By December, he was suffering severe heart problems and was being regularly dosed on various prescription drugs by a bogus doctor, Toby Marshall, whom he and his mother had met in Oklahoma City.

Hank died either in the late night of December 31,1952 or the early morning hours of January 1, 1953, in the back seat of his new powder-blue Cadillac convertible. He was being driven by a teenage chauffeur to two shows scheduled for December 31 in

Charleston, West Virginia, and January 1 in Canton, Ohio. They tried to fly out of Knoxville on December 31 to Charleston, but the weather was bad and the plane was turned back. They spent several hours in a hotel in Knoxville, and then left for Canton, but not before a physician was called to the hotel and injected Hank, already very drunk, with two shots of vitamin B-12 laced with morphine (an addiction he had developed from his back pain). According to a report filed by the investigating police officer, Hank was probably already dead when he was carried out of the hotel late that night and laid in the back of the car for the trip to Canton. He was officially declared dead at 7:00 am on January 1, 1953, at the Oak Hill Hospital in Oak Hill, West Virginia.

At Hank's funeral on January 4 in Montgomery, Alabama, there had not been such a large gathering of people since Jefferson Davis had been sworn in as President of the Confederacy in 1861. In attendance were Audrey, Billie Jean and Bobbie Jett (who delivered a baby girl two days later). Red Foley sang *Peace in the Valley* and a choir of *Opry* stars, including Roy Acuff, Foley, Little Jimmy Dickens, Carl Smith, Webb Pierce, Johnny Wright and Jack Anglin sang Hank's own Gospel classic *I Saw the Light*.

Ironically, Hank's latest recording, which had entered the charts just before his death and which soon peaked at No.1, was titled *I'll Never Get Out of This World Alive*. This was followed by *Your Cheatin' Heart*, which stayed at the top for 6 weeks and the flip-side, *Kaw-Liga*, which also topped the charts for 13 weeks. Hank's other posthumous hits, in 1953, were the No.1 *Take These Chains from My Heart*, *I Won't Be Home No More* (Top 5) and *Weary Blues from Waiting* (Top 10). In 1955, *Please Don't Let Me Love You* went Top 10.

In 1961, Hank was one of the charter inductees to the Country Music Hall of Fame. After his death, there were at least two movie presentations about his life. One was *Your Cheatin' Heart*, in 1964, which featured Hank Williams, Jr. singing for his father behind George Hamilton's acting. The other, *Hank Williams: The Show He Never Gave*, with Snoozie Wilson, was an excellent portrayal. In 1966, Hank's recording of *I'm So Lonesome I Could Cry*, with new backing, made the Top 50.

In 1973, the ACM named Hank for its "Pioneer Award." In 1983, NARAS admitted *Your Cheatin' Heart* to its Hall of Fame and in 1987, presented a Lifetime Achievement Award to Hank as "A pioneering performer, who proudly sang his songs so honestly and openly, capturing completely the joys and sorrows and essence of country life and whose compositions helped create successful careers for various singers who followed him." That same year, he was inducted into the Rock and Roll Hall of Fame as a forefather of rock'n'roll.

In 1989, an obscure vinyl recording of *There's a Tear in My Beer* was discovered and Hank's vocals were dubbed onto a recording of the song by Hank Williams, Jr. and thirty-six years after his death, Hank was back in the Top 10. The recording won a Grammy Award that year as "Best Country Vocal Collaboration." The record also won the CMA's "Vocal Event of the Year" and the music video won their "Music Video of the Year" and the ACM's "Video of the Year." In 1990, the TNN/MCN Awards voted the recording "Vocal Collaboration of the Year" and the video, "Country Music Video of the Year."

Although the simplicity of his songs and manner and his lack of formal education might lead to the impression that Hank possessed an unsophisticated mind, he was in truth highly intelligent and quick-witted, as his legacy of timeless lyrics, his *Mother's Best Flour* live radio programs and the recollections of those who knew and loved him best can attest. DV

RECOMMENDED ALBUMS:

"Hank Williams as Luke the Drifter" (MGM)(1955) [Re-released in 1962]
"I Saw the Light" (MGM)(1956) [Re-issued 1959]
"The Last Picture Show" (MGM)(1971)
"40 Greatest Hits" (double)(MGM)(1978)
"On the Air" (Polydor)(1985)
"Let's Turn Back the Years July 1951-June 1952" (double)(Polydor)(1987)
"I Won't Be Home No More, June 1952-September 1952" (double)(Polydor)(1987)
"The Best of Hank & Hank" (Curb)(1992) [With Hank Williams, Jr.]
(See also Drifting Cowboys Band, Audrey Williams and Hank Williams, Jr.)

HANK WILLIAMS, JR.

(Singer, Songwriter, Guitar, Keyboards, Bass Guitar, Drums, Fiddle, Banjo, Harmonica, Steel Guitar)

Given Name:	**Randall Hank Williams**
Date of Birth:	**May 26, 1949**
Where Born:	**Shreveport, Louisiana**
Married:	**1. Sharon Martin (div.)**
	2. Gwen Yeargain (div.)
	3. Becky (div.)
	4. Mary Jane
Children:	**Shelton Hank Williams III, Hilary, Holly, Katherine Diana (Katie)**

When Red Foley said to an 8-year-old Hank, Jr., "You're a ghost, son, nothin' but a ghost of your daddy," the old redhead couldn't have been further from the truth. Hank, Jr., may not be the songwriter his daddy, Hank Williams, was (but then who is?), but as an entertainer, he is one of the finest and definitely his own man, having the knack of appealing to both Country and Southern Boogie rockers. His daddy nicknamed him "Bocephus" after Country comedy star Rod Brasfield's ventriloquist dummy, but Hank, Jr., was born to be a star and he has exceeded the early promise by a Country mile.

Hank, Jr. was first taken to Nashville when he was 3 months old and grew up there. When he was age 8, his mother, Audrey, became his manager and he made his professional debut in Swainsboro, Georgia, singing *Lovesick Blues*. He made his debut on the *Grand Ole Opry* when he was 11, singing the same song, and got seven encores. He also received what is a rarity at the *Opry*, his own curtain call. Initially the fans approached him with almost God-like reverence. Barely in his teens, he toured with his mother's Caravan of Stars show. He began by singing his father's songs, using his father's styling and generally being a "clone." He soon began an interest that has survived to date, that of collecting belt buckles. He would in time have Allan Hykes of Las Vegas make them, often to Hank, Jr.'s own designs.

By the end of 1963, he had signed to MGM, the label on which his daddy had had all his hits. Hank, Jr. scored his first Country hit in 1964 with *Long Gone Lonesome Blues*, which Hank had taken to No.1 in 1950. Hank, Jr. took it to the Top 5 and crossed it over to the Pop Top 70. That year, George Hamilton played the role of Hank Williams in the biopic *Your Cheatin' Heart* and Hank, Jr., then only 14, dubbed his father's vocals. The movie cost \$1.2 million and eventually grossed ten times that amount. He also appeared in the movie *Country Music on Broadway*. Although *Guess What, That's Right, She's Gone* and *Endless Sleep* both made the Top 50, Hank, Jr. didn't again achieve major Country chart success until 1966.

While at high school, Hank, Jr. excelled at swimming, football, basketball and boxing and became a health fanatic (he would later become an avid outdoorsman). At this time, he put a band together, calling himself Rockin' Randall. Already a guitar player, Hank, Jr. learned piano from another legend, Jerry Lee Lewis. In 1966, Hank, Jr. had a further Top 5 single in the autobiographical *Standing in the Shadows*, which had him giving a pointer for what was to come in his career.

In 1967, he appeared with Ed Begley in the movie *A Time to Sing*. It was another two years until he had another major hit when *It's*

All Over But the Crying went Top 3. He closed out the year with another autobiographical composition, *I Was with Red Foley (The Night He Passed Away)*. Based on that fateful night, the single went Top 40. During that year, Hank, Jr. assumed another of his father's mantles, rambling storyteller, when he released the album ***Luke the Drifter, Jr***. He went on to record two further albums of this ilk in 1969 and 1970. In 1968, he stopped fronting the Cheating Hearts, who had backed him since 1964, and stepped out in front of his father's band, the Drifting Cowboys, which was then made up of Jerry Rivers, Don Helms, Sammy Pruitt, Hillous Butrum and Cedric Rainwater.

In 1969, he and Johnny Cash got together at Detroit's Cobol Hall for what was then the largest grossing Country concert to date, bringing in $93,000. An album was released that year of Hank, Jr.'s performance. During the year, he racked up three major hits, *Custody* and *A Baby Again*, both of which went Top 20, and the Top 3 *Cajun Baby*, the latter a song bearing the composition names of Williams, father and son. He completed the year with another Top 5 single, *I'd Rather Be Gone*.

The following year, when Hank, Jr. re-signed to MGM, it was the biggest recording contract in MGM's history. However, he was getting increasingly unhappy with what he was playing and there were many who felt that his reliance on drink and drugs meant that he would be dead at a younger age than his father (Hank died at age 29).

Between 1970 and 1972, he continued to rack up a series of albums that increasingly contained less of his father's material and more of his own. His most successful singles were: 1970: *I Walked Out on Heaven*, *All for the Love of Sunshine*, his first No.1, which came from the movie *Kelly's Heroes*, and the Top 3 release *Rainin' in My Heart*; 1971: *I've Got a Right to Cry* (Top 10), *After All They All Used to Belong to Me* and *Ain't That a Shame* (Top 10); 1972: *Eleven Roses* (No.1) and *Pride's Not Hard to Swallow* (Top 3). He also did a series of duets with Lois Johnson, those charting being *Removing the Shadow* and *So Sad (To Watch Good Love Go Bad)* (both 1970) and *Send Me Some Lovin'* and *Whole Lotta Loving* (both 1972). In 1972, he appeared at the prestigious Wembley Festival in England and amazed the audience by playing every instrument on stage.

His 1973, Top 15 single *Hank* was an indicator of a recurring theme in Hank, Jr.'s recorded material; that of writing and singing about his parents, their relationship and how the Country establishment treated Hank Williams. His other hit singles over the next

That supreme entertainer ***Hank Williams, Jr.***

two years were, 1973: *The Last Love Song* (Top 5); 1974: *Rainy Night in Georgia* (Top 15), *I'll Think of Something* (Top 10) and *Angels Are Hard to Find* (Top 20).

Matters came to a head in Hank, Jr.'s life, in 1974, when he attempted suicide. However, this proved a turnaround point in his life and he wrote about it in his song *Getting Over You*. With the help of a psychiatrist and by moving away from Nashville to Cullman, Alabama, he began to reconstruct his life and do his own thing musically. This began with the album ***Hank Williams, Jr. & Friends***, released in 1975. The friends included Charlie Daniels, Marshall Tucker's Toy Caldwell and the Allman Brothers' Chuck Leavell. From this came the Top 20 single *Stoned at the Jukebox*.

On August 8, 1975, just as Hank, Jr. seemed to be on the mend, he had a near fatal accident while climbing Ajax Mountain, on the Montana-Idaho border. He fell 500 feet and split his head open, exposing his brain and shattering his face. He underwent massive facial reconstruction surgery and his new outlook on life helped him recover.

At the end of 1976, he changed labels and signed with Warner Brothers. However, success did not come immediately and between then and the end of 1978, his most successful single was the Top 15 version of *I Fought the Law*. By 1979, Hank, Jr. had moved to Curb Records and through their licensing arrangement, he was released on Elektra. This was the turning point in his career and his album ***Family Tradition*** was Certified Gold in 1983. His other album released in 1979, ***Whiskey Bent & Hell Bound***, went Gold in 1981. The title tracks of both were major singles hits that year, going Top 5 and Top 3 respectively.

As the new decade got under way, Hank, Jr. continued growing in popularity. In 1980, he scored with *Women I've Never Had* (Top 5), *Kaw-Liga* (Top 15) and *Old Habits* (Top 10). The following year, all three of his singles went to No.1; they were *Texas Women*, *Dixie on My Mind* and *All My Rowdy Friends (Have Settled Down)*. Hank, Jr.'s album ***Rowdy*** was Certified Gold in 1985, while his other album, ***The Pressure Is On***, went Gold in 1982 and Platinum in 1986.

In 1982, his hits were *A Country Boy Can Survive* (Top 3), his version of Hank's *Honky Tonkin'* (No.1) and *American Dream/If Heaven Ain't a Lot Like Dixie* (Top 5). His album ***High Notes*** went Gold in 1986 and his ***Greatest Hits*** package went Gold and Platinum in 1984 and had sold over 2 million by 1985. During 1983, Curb moved Hank, Jr. to Warner Brothers and he had Top 5 success with *Gonna Go Huntin' Tonight* (Top 5) and followed with *Leave Them Boys Alone*, on which he was joined by Waylon Jennings and Ernest Tubb and which was co-written by Hank, Jr., Dean Dillon, Gary Stewart and Tanya Tucker. He joined up with Waylon again for *The Conversation*, which came from Waylon's album ***Waylon & Co.*** Hank, Jr. finished off the year with the Top 5 single *Queen of My Heart*. His two albums ***Strong Stuff*** and ***Man of Steel*** went Gold in 1986 and 1985 respectively.

He had three more major successes in 1984, *Man of Steel* (Top 3), *Attitude Adjustment* (Top 5) and *All My Rowdy Friends Are Coming Over Tonight* (Top 10). His album ***Major Moves*** was a tour de force and featured Ray Charles, Dickie Betts (of the Allman Brothers) and John Lee Hooker on *The Blues Medley*. He started off 1985 with the title track of the album, which went Top 10. It was followed by another No.1, *I'm for Love*, and he wrapped up the year with the Top 5 *This Ain't Dallas*. The last two came from his album ***Five-O***, which went Gold that year. He also got together with Ray Charles on *Two Old Cats Like Us*, which came from Ray's ***Friendship*** album. Hank, Jr. released ***Greatest Hits Volume 2***, which went Gold in 1986 and Platinum in 1990.

Hank, Jr. started off 1986 with one of his finest singles, a remake of Fats Waller's *Ain't Misbehavin'*, which went to No.1. The single was also on the ***Five-O*** album, as was "Rockin' Randall's" version of New Orleans. His two other chart singles, *Country State of Mind* (Top 3) and *Mind Your Own Business*

(No.1), came from his album ***Montana Cafe***. *Mind Your Own Business* featured Willie Nelson, Reba McEntire, Tom Petty and Reverend Ike. During the year, Merle Kilgore took over Hank, Jr.'s management. ***Montana Cafe*** went Gold during the year.

During 1987, Steve Popovich at Mercury decided to re-release several of Hank, Jr.'s MGM albums on the Polydor label. Hank, Jr.'s initial single, *When Something Is Good (Why Does It Change)*, was his first relative failure for eight years and just failed to make the Top 30. This was followed by his "live" album ***Hank Live***, which, although exciting, suffered from bad sound quality. It did, however, show off Bocephus' backing band, the Bama Band, to fine effect. The album was Certified Gold the same year. On the singles front, he came back with a bang with the chart-topper *Born to Boogie*. This was the title track of his next album. This album went Gold the same year and Platinum the following year. He closed out the year with the Top 5 *Heaven Can't Be Found*. That year, Hank, Jr. at last received the recognition that had been due for many years, when both the CMA and ACM made him their "Entertainer of the Year."

Hank, Jr. opened 1988 with the Top 3 single *Young Country*. This is an acknowledgement to the new bloods emerging at the time and the "choir" featured the vocals of Butch Baker, T. Graham Brown, Jack Daniels, Paulette Carlson, Curtis Stone and Cactus Moser (Highway 101), Dana McVicker, Steve Earle, Keith Whitley and Marty Stuart. He followed with *If the South Woulda Won*, which came from the album ***Wild Streak***. Before year end, this album had been Certified Gold. He closed the year with *Early in the Morning and Late at Night*, which only went Top 15. He also guested on Doug Kershaw's album ***Hot Diggity Doug*** and they had the minor hit *Cajun Baby*. Hank, Jr. fared better with his duet with Johnny Cash, *That Old Wheel*, which came from Cash's ***Water from the Wells of Home*** and which reached just below the Top 20. That year, both the CMA and ACM named him "Entertainer of the Year" for the second straight year and the ACM made it three-in-a-row in 1989.

Through the magic of modern recording skills, Hank, Jr.'s voice was overdubbed on an obscure vinyl recording of his father's and the result was the Top 10 duet single *There's a Tear in My Beer*. He followed this with another Top 10 release, *Finders Are Keepers*. Hank, Jr.'s ***Greatest Hits III*** went Gold then Platinum in 1989. From 1990, Bocephus started to fall from favor with the radio stations and his most successful singles were *Ain't Nobody's Business* (Top 15), *Good Friends, Good Whiskey, Good Lovin'* (Top 10) and *Don't Give Us a Reason* (Top 30) (all 1990). The last named was a message to Saddam Hussein, just before the Gulf War. During the year, Bocephus' album ***Loan Wolf*** went Gold, as did his video ***Full Access***, which was Certified Platinum, the following year. In 1991, he went Top 30 with *If It Will It Will*.

In 1992, Curb moved Hank, Jr. to Phil Walden's legendary Capricorn label, which had opened up in Nashville. It was this label that had housed the Allman Brothers, Elvin Bishop and Wet Willie. Hank, Jr.'s first album with Capricorn, ***Maverick***, reached the Top 10 on the Country Albums chart and contained the duet with Clint Black *Hotel Whiskey* and the original version of *A Little Less Talk and a Lot More Action*. The compilation ***The Best of Hank and Hank***, with Hank Williams, reached the Top 50 on the Country Album chart. The following year, the album ***Out of Left Field*** was released, but the only single to chart, *Everything Comes Down to Money and Love*, peaked in the 60s. Also noticeable was the fact that only three songs on the album were written by Hank, Jr. This followed a trend that had started with ***Maverick***. The 1994 album ***The Real Deal*** was released on Curb.

Although his records are not as much in demand as during the late 80's, Bocephus is still one of the most sought-after live performers in Country music. (For a full list of Hank, Jr.'s awards, see Awards section.)

RECOMMENDED ALBUMS:

"Your Cheatin' Heart" (MGM)(1964) [Soundtrack]
"Luke the Drifter, Jr." (MGM) Volume 1 (1968), Volume 2 (1969), Volume 3 (1970)
"Hank Williams, Jr., Live at Cobol Hall, Detroit" (MGM)(1969)
"Hank Williams, Jr. & Friends" (MGM)(1976)
"Fourteen Greatest Hits" (MGM)(1976)
"Hank Williams, Jr.'s Greatest Hits" (Elektra/Curb)(1982)
"Major Moves" (Warner/Curb)(1984)
"Greatest Hits, Vol. 2" (Warner/Curb)(1985)
"Hank Live" (Warner/Curb)(1987)
"Greatest Hits III" (Warner/Curb)(1989)
"Maverick" (Capricorn/Curb)(1992)
"Out of Left Field" (Capricorn/Curb)(1993)
"The Real Deal" (Curb)(1994)

JIMMY WILLIAMS

(Singer, Mandolin, Guitar, Fiddle)

Given Name:	**James Williams**
Date of Birth:	**February 29, 1932**
Where Born:	**Wythe County, Virginia**
Married:	**Phyllis**
Children:	**Virgil, Valorie**

In the early years of Bluegrass music, Jimmy Williams emerged as a significant early-day sideman with his quality mandolin picking and piercing high lonesome voice that adapted well to either high leads or tenors.

Jimmy hailed from the New River Valley of Wythe County, Virginia, where he listened to traditional tunes and songs as a child, learning to fiddle at age 10, and then followed with guitar and his favorite instrument, the mandolin. In his later teens, Jimmy teamed up with a cousin, Paul Humphrey, and they began calling themselves the Williams Brothers. They entertained locally and on radio in Pulaski, Virginia, and Pineville, West Virginia.

About 1951, they joined Cousin Ezra Cline's Lonesome Pine Fiddlers for several months. While Paul remained with this band and cut three sessions on RCA Victor for them, Jimmy soon went with Mac Wiseman's Country Boys at WMAQ Mount Airy, North Carolina, and subsequently recorded with them on Dot, having one of the few tenor voices that blended well with that of the leader. After that Jimmy signed on with the Stanley Brothers, worked with them at WCYB Bristol and cut one session with them on Rich-R-Tone and three for Mercury. For a time, Jimmy also led his own Shady Valley Boys on Bluefield and Bristol radio, a band that included Udell McPeek, Ted Lundy, and fiddler Wayburn Johnson.

In the meantime, Jimmy, whose personal life and health had been in a deteriorating state, moved to Michigan and got saved. He got a job at General Motors and heard Red Ellis on radio one day. He went out to meet him and the twosome soon formed a team. They worked a lot of Gospel sings and recorded several extended play records and one album for Starday, and a single for Happy Hearts. All ranked among the true classics of Bluegrass-Gospel. Jimmy longed to return southward and eventually went back to Virginia, where he again formed a Bluegrass-Gospel combo that included Dewey and Udell McPeek. Then he went back to being a sideman again, working a stint with Charlie Moore and Bill Napier's Dixie Partners on WJHG-TV in Panama City, Florida, and helping them do their first album for King in 1962.

For the past three decades, Jimmy Williams has been primarily engaged in evangelistic endeavors. This has included mission work in Haiti and Jamaica as well as some television programming on such local stations as WDHN in Dothan, Alabama. However, he has never abandoned his love for Bluegrass-Gospel music and has sometimes had onstage reunions with former employers like Mac Wiseman. He and Red Ellis also get together about once a year and jam a bit. Red and Jimmy did two reunion albums for Jessup in the early 70's and the latter did a solo effort for the same firm.

Jimmy Williams and his Gospel Grass, which includes wife Phyllis and son Virgil, have also done some recording on their own. When not on the road with his ministry of word and music, Williams makes his home in Florida. IMT

RECOMMENDED ALBUMS:

"Summers Gone" (Jessup)(ca. 1973)
"Oh Yes, Lord" (Gospel Grass)(ca. 1976)
Williams & Ellis:
"Holy Cry from the Hills" (Starday)(1961)
"God Brings Bluegrass Back Together" (Jessup)(ca. 1971)
"Little David's Harp" (Jessup)(ca. 1975)
(See also Red Ellis, the Stanley Brothers, Mac Wiseman)

LEONA WILLIAMS

(Singer, Songwriter, Guitar, Bass, Fiddle, Drums, Mandolin)

Given Name:	**Leona Belle Helton**
Date of Birth:	**January 7, 1943**
Where Born:	**Vienna, Missouri**
Married:	**1. Ray Williams (m. 1959)(div.)**
	2. Merle Haggard (m. 1978)(div.)
	3. Dave Kirby (m. 1985)
Children:	**Cathy, Ron, Brady**

Although Leona Williams has only had one Top 10 single during her recording career, she has been responsible for writing many hits for other artists. She and her songwriting husband Dave Kirby have eschewed the politics of Nashville to make their home in Missouri.

Leona came from a musical family. Her father, a road construction worker, played fiddle, her mother played banjo, and all her siblings played (4 brothers and seven sisters, of which she was ninth). She became part of the Helton Family Band at an early age. When Leona was 15, she got her own radio show on KWOS Jefferson City, Missouri. Getting the show was dependent upon her getting sponsors and she got them by walking through town and visiting every business until she received enough sponsorship.

A year later, she married drummer Ron Williams and they moved to St. Louis, where Leona attended beautician school. In 1966, the twosome became members of Loretta Lynn's backup band, the Blue Kentuckians, with Leona on bass and vocals and Ron on drums. The following year, Loretta recorded Leona's song *Get Whatcha Got and Go*. In Loretta's autobiography, *Coal Miner's Daughter* (1976), she is highly complimentary towards Leona.

As a result of a guest appearance on the *Grand Ole Opry*, Leona cut a demo recording, which was paid for by Lonzo and Oscar. This resulted in Leona signing a recording contract with Hickory, in January 1968. That year, Tammy Wynette recorded Leona's song *Broadminded* and Leona toured in Vietnam. The following year, Leona made her Country chart debut with the Top 70 single *Once More*. Although she had other releases on Hickory, she did not chart again until the summer of 1971, when *Country Girl with Hot Pants On* just failed to reach the Top 50. Hickory continued to release singles, but Leona's only chart record for the label was *Your Shoeshine Girl*, in 1993, which only went Top 100.

By the time Leona met Merle Haggard, in 1974, she and Ron had divorced. During 1975, Leona joined Merle's touring show and the two were traditional Country magic. The next year, Merle was by Leona's side as she became the first female Country singer to record an album in a prison. The album was ***San Quentin's First Lady*** and was released on MCA. In 1977, Merle recorded their co-written *I Think It's Gone Forever*. Leona and Merle married in 1978 and that same year the couple had a Top 10 hit with their self-penned *The Bull and the Beaver*. Merle also recorded Leona's song *Mama, I've Gotta Go to Memphis*. The following year, Leona had a basement level solo hit *The Baby Song/Call Me Crazy Lady*.

At the end of 1980, Leona signed with Elektra Records, and the following year had two medium to low chart entries, *I'm Almost Ready* and *Always Late with Your Kisses*. During 1982, Merle recorded their co-written song *Someday You're Gonna Need Your Friends Again*. In 1983, Leona and Merle got together for the Mercury album ***Heart to Heart***, but by now their Top 50 single—a joint composition, *We're Strangers Again*—seemed more realistic than the title track, as by the time the album hit the streets, they had gone their separate ways. During the year, Merle had a No.1 with Leona's song *You Take Me for Granted* (recording in 1982) and repeated this the following year with *Someday When Things Are Good*. In 1984, Leona duetted with George Jones on *Best Friends*, which she had written with Hank Cochran, and which appeared on the Jones album ***Ladies Choice***.

She released one more album for Mercury, ***Some Days When Things Are Good***, in 1984, but since then has been without a major label. In 1985, Leona married hit songwriter Dave Kirby and they returned to Missouri.She has released two cassettes, which are marketed through Ernest Tubb Record Shops, on the Loveshine label, entitled ***The Way It Was*** and ***Once More***. These she sells at gigs. Leona and Dave run a demo studio in Vienna, Missouri, while still making sorties to Nashville once a month. In 1991, Tammy Wynette and Randy Travis duetted on the

Leona Williams** with **George Jones

Williams-Haggard song *We're Strangers Again*, which went Top 50.

RECOMMENDED ALBUMS:

"The Best of Leona Williams" (Hickory)(1972)
"San Quentin's First Lady" (MCA)(1978)
"Heart to Heart" (Mercury)(1983) [With Merle Haggard]
"Someday When Things Are Good" (Mercury)(1984)
"The Way It Was" (Loveshine) [Cassette]
"Once More" (Loveshine) [Cassette]

ROBIN AND LINDA WILLIAMS & THEIR FINE GROUP

When Formed: 1973

ROBIN WILLIAMS
(Singer, Songwriter, Guitar, Harmonica)
Given Name: Robin Williams Murphy III
Date of Birth: March 16, 1949

LINDA WILLIAMS
(Singer, Songwriter, Guitar, Banjo)
Given Name: Linda Hill
Date of Birth: July 7, 1949
Where Born: Anniston, Alabama

Robin and Linda Williams are Country music's best kept secret. Yet, for over 20 years, they've been delighting audiences on radio, TV and in concert, bridging the straits of Country and Folk music and earning the approbation of their peers.

They made their mark on November 1, 1975, when they debuted on American Public Radio's *Prairie Home Companion* (NPR). They guested regularly on the show including three TV performances on the Disney Channel. Every season from 1982 to 1991 they toured throughout the U.S. performing on the Columbia Arts Community Concerts.

Robin and Linda met some 21 years ago while she was visiting her parents in South Carolina. They were both at a local bar that had an "open stage," and hit it off both personally and professionally. Linda moved to Nashville and got a job in state government, playing music on the side. Within two years, Robin followed, the two got married in June 1973, and they started singing together at Bishop's Pub.

They first started playing the college and coffee house circuits. Robin made some musical contacts in Minneapolis, including Peter Ostroushko, who played on their first record. Afterward, Peter joined them as a trio and the three went out on the road. That was 1975. Peter had met Garrison Keillor, who had a morning show at the time on Minnesota Public Radio. They called and asked to be on his show. That week Keillor drove 60 miles to hear them perform and after seeing them play invited them on. When *Prairie Home Companion* went national, Garrison made the decision to use them on a more regular basis. They began doing 10 to 12 shows a year and continued to work with him some 20-odd years later. Soon, they began writing songs together, and over the years some of their hits included Emmylou Harris' *Rollin & Ramblin'*, and Tom T. Hall's *Famous in Mississippi*, among many others. The many years of working with Garrison Keillor led to the 1992 release of ***Garrison Keillor and the Hopeful Gospel Quartet*** on Sony/Epic. Robin and Linda joined Garrison and Kate MacKenzie for the recording as well as many Hopeful Gospel Quartet concert dates.

The band appeared on *Austin City Limits* and PBS in March 1993 and December 1993. They have toured in the U.S., London and Norwich, England, Edinburgh, Scotland and Tonder, Denmark. NPR produced a tour in the Southeast in Febuary, 1994 to include live radio broadcasts of *A Prairie Home Companion* as well as the Hopeful Gospel Quartet.

Robin and Linda have written the lyrics and music for two musicals performed at the Lime Kiln Theatre in Lexington, Virginia. *Stonewall Jackson* is about General Stonewall Jackson and includes 14 original Williams songs, and *Virgil Powers, The Black Life*, includes another 10. The couple are currently working on their third musical with the Circle Repertoire Company in New York, titled *Streets of Gold*. It is expected to begin regional touring in 1995. Additionally, Robin and Linda Williams & Their Fine Group have opened concert dates across the country for Mary-Chapin Carpenter. Their band is joined on bass and harmony by Jim Watson, a founding member of the Red Clay Ramblers, and Kevin Maul on Dobro and vocal harmonics rounding out Their Fine Group. Robin and Linda have released eleven albums since their partnership began. Recent album releases are ***Live in Holland*** (1993) on the Striktly Country label and their final record to date, a studio album, ***Turn Toward Tomorrow*** (1993) on Sugar Hill Records. Within their basically acoustic framework, the Williamses combine the hardiest strands of Folk, Country and Bluegrass. They are some of the hardiest writers in the business. It is rare for any collaboration to last more than 20 years but Robin and Linda are still going strong. There seems to be little standing in their way toward becoming legends in American music. LAP

RECOMMENDED ALBUMS:

"Close as We Can Get" (Flying Fish)(1984)
"The Rhythm of Love" (Sugar Hill)(1990)
"Live in Holland" (Striktly Country Holland)(1993)
"Turn Toward Tomorrow" (Sugar Hill)(1993)

TEX WILLIAMS

(Singer, Songwriter, Guitar, Banjo, Harmonica, Actor)
Given Name: Sollie Paul Williams
Date of Birth: August 23, 1917
Where Born: Ramsey, Fayette County, Illinois
Married: Dallas Orr
Date of Death: October 11, 1985

Tex Williams' name will forever be associated with the classic song *Smoke! Smoke! Smoke! (That Cigarette)*, which became Capitol Records' first million-selling single. However, he had many strings to his bow, and among his credits were appearances in several "B" Westerns, despite having polio while in his infancy, which left him with a slight limp.

Tex learned guitar at age 5, and had his own one-man band and vocal show, playing banjo and harmonica, on station WJBL Decatur, Illinois, when he was age 13. By the time he was 14, Tex had moved on to WDZ Tuscola, Illinois. He toured through Canada, the U.S. and Mexico with various hillbilly and Western groups, including the six-piece Reno Racketeers, whom he joined in Washington, D.C., and they became his back-up band when he moved to San Francisco, where they worked on KNBC. During the 30's, he was based in Hollywood, where he became a friend of Tex Ritter and appeared on radio KFWB.

By 1940, Williams had become a member of Cal Shrum's Rhythm Rangers, under the name of "Jack Williams," and while with this group, he appeared in Tex Ritter's Monogram movie *Rollin' Home to Texas*. By 1943, Tex had joined Spade Cooley's band, replacing Red River Dave, and sang on Cooley's hit recording of *Shame on You*, which went to No.1 in 1945. That same year, he appeared with Cooley's band in Charles Starrett's movie *Outlaws of the Rockies*, which was part of the Durango Kid series. He also did the vocals on Cooley's 1947 release *Crazy 'Cause I Love You*.

In 1946, Tex formed his own twelve-piece group, Western Caravan, and the following year, now Tex Williams, he was contracted by Will Cowan at Universal-International, to make a series of musical shorts. Tex was utilized as the replacement for Red River Dave at U-I, when it was realized that filming Westerns in upstate New York didn't work. The first was called *Tex Williams and His Western Caravan* and was a two reeler. Utilizing footage from the Bob Baker features, Tex's shorts were extended to three reelers, running for some 20 minutes each. In all,

Tex Williams charms a leading lady

fifteen shorts were made, and two of them were spliced together to make the 1950 feature *Tales of the West*. Three more such pairings were made and released in 1951.

While he was enjoying a movie career, Tex and his Western Caravan also had a very fruitful recording career. He signed to Capitol, then in its infancy, in 1946. His initial release, *The Rose of the Alamo*, did well and at the end of the year, he reached No.4 on the Country charts with *California Polka*. The following year, Capitol became Capitol America and it was during the summer of 1947 that *Smoke! Smoke! Smoke! (That Cigarette)* became a monster hit. The song, written by Tex and Merle Travis, went to No.1 on both the Country and Pop charts. It remained on top of the Country charts for 16 weeks out of a total of 23 weeks on the charts. The song featured Tex's deep brown voice half talking and half singing in a way that is associated with Phil Harris and would be utilized by Jerry Reed. Tex had two Top 5 hits that year, *That's What I Like About the West* and *Never Trust a Woman*. The latter reached No.2 and stayed there for 8 weeks, being held from the top by Eddy Arnold's *I'll Hold You in My Heart (Till I Can Hold You in My Arms)*, which was in the midst of a 21-week residency at No.1.

In 1948, his success continued unabated. *Don't Telephone, Don't Telegraph, Tell a Woman* (wouldn't that have the feminists climbing walls today!) also reached the Top 3, being held off from the top by the same song of Arnold's. Tex's single also crossed-over to the Pop Top 30, as did the follow-up, *Suspicion*, which reached the Top 5 on the Country charts. His other hits during the year were *Banjo Polka, Who? Me?/Foolish Tears* and *Talking Boogie/Just a Pair of Blue Eyes*. Then at the end of the year, he had another career monster, *Life Gits Tee-Jus, Don't It?*, which made the Top 5, and crossed over to the Pop Top 30. The song became very popular in the U.K. on the BBC Armed Forces request show, *Family Favourites*, though the original version by Carson Robison was a Top 3 Country hit, the same year. Tex had his final hit for Capitol, in 1949, with *Bluebird on Your Windowsill*.

With this string of hits, Tex and his band became great crowd pleasers, and played to capacity audiences in ballrooms around the country. In the late 40's and early 50's, they could be found five nights a week at the Riverside Rancho or at Tex's own club, Tex Williams Village in Newhall. They also guested with stars such as Dinah Shore, Tennessee Ernie Ford and Jo Stafford, and appeared on the principal TV and radio shows, including the *Grand Ole Opry, Gene Autry's Melody Ranch, National Barn Dance* and the *Midwestern Hayride*, as well as shows that had a wider audience appeal such as the *Spike Jones Show*.

In the 50's, he recorded for Decca, which released the 10" album ***Dance-O-Rama—Tex Williams***. In 1962, the label issued ***Country Music Time***. During the 60's he had his own TV show, *Riverside Rancho*, over NBC. During 1963, Liberty recorded a live album in Las Vegas that was later released by the U.K. label, Stetson. Then in 1965, he wound up his Western Caravan, as he was no longer able or interested to keep working nearly every night.

It was in 1965 that Tex signed with the Kentucky label Boone and found himself back in the charts with a string of medium sized hits. That same year, he had two Top 30 hits, *Too Many Tigers* and *Big Tennessee*. His other major hits on the label were *Bottom of a Mountain* (1966) and *Smoke, Smoke, Smoke '68*, a new version of his 1947 No.1. By 1970, he had moved over to Monument, and the following year, he had a Top 30 hit, with *The Night Miss Nancy Ann's Hotel for Single Girls Burned Down*.

He signed with Granite Records in Los Angeles and was reunited with Cliffie Stone, who had originally signed Tex back in the Capitol days. With this label, he had his last chart entry with *Those Lazy, Hazy, Crazy Days of Summer*, a hit for Nat "King" Cole in 1963. He recorded one album for Garu, in 1981, when he teamed up with California Express. Tex was a man with a lot of friends, and many people were saddened by his death in 1985, from lung cancer.

RECOMMENDED ALBUMS:

"Smoke! Smoke! Smoke!" (Capitol)(1960) [Re-released by Stetson U.K. in the original sleeve (1987)] [Read those really funny liner notes!!]
"Tex Williams in Las Vegas" (Liberty)(1963) [Re-released by Stetson UK in the original sleeve (1989)]
"Two Sides of Tex Williams" (Boone)(1966)
"A Man Called Tex" (Monument)(1971)
"Those Lazy Hazy Days" (Granite)(1974)
"Tex Williams & California Express" (Garu)(1981)
[Listen also to Spade Cooley albums]

FIDDLIN' SKEETS WILLIAMSON

(Fiddle)

Given Name:	**Cecil James Williamson**
Date of Birth:	**September 3, 1920**
Where Born:	**McVeigh, Pike County, Kentucky**
Married:	**Sylvia**
Children:	**Mary Ruth**
Date of Death:	**ca. 1984**

During the 1940s "Skeets" Williamson was one of Country music's premier fiddlers. Since he worked primarily as a sideman, Skeets gained only minimal fame. However, such traditionally oriented Country musicians as the Bailes Brothers, Everett Lilly, Mac Wiseman, and his more famous sister, Molly O'Day, all hailed Skeets as being one of the best fiddlers in his day.

Skeets grew up in a musically rich environment where folks treasured records by the duo of Burnett and Rutherford and looked forward to visits by Blind Ed Haley, the most famous traditional fiddler of that time and place. As Skeets and his sister, LaVerne (Molly O'Day), and brother Joe grew into teenagers, they formed a string band. At 18, Skeets journeyed to Charleston, West Virginia, to play with Ervin Staggs and His Radio Ramblers at WCHS.

Later Skeets and another member, Johnnie Bailes, organized their own Happy Valley Boys, which included both Molly and Little Jimmy Dickens. They worked on radio at both Beckley and Bluefield, West Virginia. After Molly married Lynn Davis, Skeets went with the Holden Brothers and played on the *Texas Roundup* at KRLD Dallas, Texas and back in Alabama with his brother-in-law and sister. He also served with the U.S. Navy during WWII.

After the conflict, Williamson came to Knoxville, where he played in the Cumberland Mountain Folks band during their best days. He worked on Molly's first and third Columbia sessions in 1946 and 1949 respectively. In between, he worked in a band that included Carl Smith and Hoke Jenkins. He also played with Fairly Holden on WIBW Topeka, Kansas, and briefly for the Bailes Brothers at KWKH Shreveport.

When the Korean War broke out, Williamson joined the U.S. Air Force and never returned to a musical performing career. He spent the remainder of his life in Brighton, Michigan, engaged in industrial work. Skeets did manage to record one album of his fiddle music in later life with some instrumental support from his famous sister and brother-in-law. IMT

RECOMMENDED ALBUM:

"Fiddlin' Skeets Williamson" (Old Homestead)(1977)
(See also Molly O'Day)

GEORGE & MARY WILLIAMSON (a.k.a. THE OLD KENTUCKY STRING BAND)

When Formed: 1948
GEORGE WILLIAMSON
(Vocals, Fiddle, Guitar, Dulcimer, Autoharp, Mandolin)
Given Name: George Williamson
Date of Birth: 1927
MARY WILLIAMSON
(Vocals, Guitar, Banjo, Dulcimer)
Given Name: Mary Thacker
Date of Birth: 1932
Date of Death: ca. 1980

Both Born: Pike County, Kentucky

George & Mary Williamson were a Kentucky husband-wife team who took their musical culture with them when they migrated to Michigan.

George and Mary both came from the rich musical culture of Pike County, Kentucky, in the heart of Appalachia. As a youth, George and his brothers won a talent contest and appeared on WBTH radio in Williamson, West Virginia, with Budge and Fudge Mayse. In 1948, he married Mary Thacker and the two sang on WLSI Pikeville. After their move to Michigan, George worked in the auto plants but fiddled in a variety of Bluegrass bands, on a part-time basis, including those of Curly Dan and Wilma Ann (Holcomb), John Hunley, Wendy Smith and especially Roy McGinnis and the Sunnysiders. Mary, an individual of keen intellect, completed her education, including two college degrees, and became a junior high school English teacher in Wyandotte.

While George continued Bluegrass fiddling, he and Mary also put together a variety of Old-Time groups who played mostly for their own pleasure and satisfaction, beginning with the Southern Michigan String Band, which consisted of themselves; a transplanted Tennessee clawhammer banjo picker, Joe Lomax; a local blind guitarist, Jim Childress; and Roy McGinnis, who sang on certain numbers.

They cut a fine album for Ozzie Thorpe's Pine Tree Records, but with the growth of the Old Homestead label, they did their remaining albums for that firm. Their first featured twin dulcimers and the second returned to a string band sound by the now renamed Old Kentucky String Band (essentially the same group minus McGinnis). Their likely masterpiece album, ***Our Mountain Heritage***, paid tribute to the great Country duets of the 30's and 40's, including the Bailes and Delmore Brothers. By that time, Mable Damron had replaced Lomax on banjo. Mable, a spirited picker and vocalist in the tradition of Cousin Emmy and Lily May Ledford, held center stage on what was destined to be the group's final album in 1977. The previous year, George, Mary, and Mable had performed at the Smithsonian Institutution's Festival of American Folklife, which was probably the highlight of their musical presentations.

Not long afterward, Mary contracted cancer and after her passing, was returned to Kentucky for burial. As George grew older, he developed hearing problems which hampered his playing abilities. Fay McGinnis reports in May 1994 that George Williamson continues to reside in Wyandotte, but no longer plays in public because of his auditory difficulties. IMT

RECOMMENDED ALBUMS:

"Appalachian Echoes by George and Mary Williamson" (Old Homestead)(1975)
"Our Mountain Heritage" (Old Homestead)(1976)
Southern Michigan String Band/Old Kentucky String Band: "Transplanted Old Timy [sic] Music" (Pine Tree)(ca. 1973)
"Twilight Is Stealing" (Old Homestead)(1976)
"Banjo Pickin' Girl" (Old Homestead)(1977) [Features Mable Damron]

FOY WILLING AND THE RIDERS OF THE PURPLE SAGE

FOY WILLING
(Singer, Songwriter, Guitar, Actor)
Given Name: Foy Willingham
Date of Birth: 1915
Where Born: Bosque County, Texas
Date of Death: July 24, 1978
RIDERS OF THE PURPLE SAGE, The
Formed: 1942
Original Members:

Al Sloey	**Vocals**
Jimmy Dean	**Vocals**

Later Members:

Scotty Harrell	**Vocals**
Johnny Paul	**Fiddle**
Bud Sievert	**Accordion, Arranger**
Jerry Vaughn	**Guitar**
Paul Sells	**Accordion**
Fred Taveres	**Steel Guitar**
Neely Plumb	**Clarinet**
Maury Stein	**Clarinet**
Irving Edelman	**String Bass**
Larry Breen	**String Bass**
Mike Rubin	**String Bass**

For the decade following 1942, Foy Willing and the Riders of the Purple Sage were almost as important to the singing cowboy genre as the Sons of the Pioneers. Their importance lay in their ability to harmonize and musically back the "star" as well as to contribute musically as performers, as well as actors, in the "B" Westerns that proliferated in the 40's and 50's.

Foy knew that he wanted a musical career while still in high school and appeared on radio, as a soloist and with a Gospel quartet. From 1933 through 1935, he was in New York City, appearing on a radio show sponsored by Crazy Water Crystals. He then returned to Texas and was employed as an executive and announcer in radio. Foy moved to California in 1940 and two years later, formed the Riders of the Purple Sage, as cast members of the *Hollywood Barn Dance*, with high tenor Al Sloey and Eddie Dean's brother, Jimmy Dean. With the arrival of Johnny Paul and Bud Sievert, the group acquired a reputation for fine musical harmonies. Among the members was Scotty Harrell, who had been a part of the Jimmy Wakely Trio.

Throughout the 40's, they appeared in many radio shows and began to make their mark in the movie world. They appeared in two Charles Starrett movies, in 1944, *Cowboy from Lonesome River* and *Cyclone Prairie Ramblers*. In 1945, they became regulars on the *All-Star Western Theater*, on which they sang a couple of songs and then backed the guest and appeared in a dramatic sketch. The show ran until 1947. Toward the end of its run, Foy came up with the idea of recording the Riders' performances, and these were transcribed as the ***Teleways Transcriptions***, with new introductions by Willing, Sloey and Paul. In two separate "series," 152 shows of 15 minutes' duration were compiled, complete with the Riders' theme song, *Sing Me a Song of the Sage*.

Other movies having Foy and the boys were Tom Tyler's *Sing Me a Song of Texas* (1945) and Monte Hale's *Out California Way* (1946) and *Along the Oregon Trail* (1947). In 1948, Foy and the Riders replaced the Sons of the Pioneers as Roy Rogers' movie group and their first movie together was *Grand Canyon Trail*. Their final movie together was the 1951 production, *Heart of the Rockies* (see Movie section).

The group was signed to various labels over the years. In 1944, they recorded one of Willing's many compositions, *Texas Blues*, for Capitol, which became a Top 3 Country hit. During 1946, they again charted with *Detour*, on Decca. The same year, they made the Top 5 with their Majestic recording of *Have I Told You Lately That I Love You*. Other sides recorded for Majestic included *No One to Cry To* and *Cool Water*. In 1948, they cut *Anytime* for Capitol American, and that reached the Top 15. The following year, *Brush Those Tears from Your Eyes*, for Capitol, had a one-week stay at No.15. In 1950, Willing went on to record for Columbia.

The group called it a day, in 1952, when Willing left active performing. They have regrouped over the years, most notably in 1958, to record an album for Roulette, in 1959, when they toured with Gene Autry and again, in 1962, to record for Jubilee. During the 70's, Foy appeared at Western festivals and did some writing and recording. Foy Willing died on July 24, 1978.

RECOMMENDED ALBUMS:

"Cowboy" (Roulette)(1958)

"The New Sound of American Folk" (Jubilee)(1962)

WILLIS BROTHERS, The

When Formed: 1932

GUY WILLIS

(Guitar, Vocals, Emcee)

Given Name: James Ulysis Willis
Date of Birth: July 5, 1915
Where Born: Alex, Arkansas
Married: Elva
Children: James
Date of Death: April 13, 1981

SKEETER WILLIS

(Fiddle, Vocals)

Given Name: Charles Ray Willis
Date of Birth: December 20, 1917
Where Born: Coalton, Oklahoma
Married: Lois
Children: Phyllis Jean
Date of Death: 1976

VIC WILLIS

(Accordion, Piano, Vocals)

Given Name: John Victor Willis
Date of Birth: May 31, 1922
Where Born: Schulter, Oklahoma
Married: Joycelyn (div.)
Children: Victoria Lynn, Peggy Del (twins)
Date of Death: January 15, 1995

Also known as the Oklahoma Wranglers, the Willis Brothers, either as a trio or after Skeeter Willis' death, as a duo, were one of the foremost Country groups and a mainstay on the *Grand Ole Opry* for many years. Their music was a blend of Western Swing and Western.

The Willis family moved from Arkansas a short while after the birth of Guy and in time all five brothers grew up on a farm (including eldest brother Joe and younger brothers Harold and Eugene) doing their chores and living in a musical environment. They took part in evening sings long before they reached their teens and soon became proficient on several instruments, Eugene being the only non-musical member of the family. In 1932, with the Depression starting to bite, Joe, Guy and Skeeter left the farm and worked on radio station KGEF Shawnee, Oklahoma, as the Oklahoma Wranglers. This was about the same time as Guy began songwriting. The brothers went on to work at various stations in Oklahoma including KTUL Tulsa (1933-34) and then by 1935 they were broadcasting over a station in Gallup, New Mexico.

In 1939, Joe got married and left the group and Vic joined. In addition, accordionist Webb Cardwell played occasional dates with the band. Cardwell taught Vic how to play accordion. The group began appearing on KITE Kansas City, Missouri, and the following year, they joined that city's *Brush Creek Follies* on KMBC. In 1942, the group broke up temporarily as they were each called to active duty in WWII. They got back together in 1946 and joined the *Grand Ole Opry*. In December 1946, they started recording for Sterling Records and at the same session backed Hank Williams on his debut recordings, as the Drifting Cowboys had been left at home. Still styled the Oklahoma Wranglers, they left the *Opry* in 1949 and became an integral part of Eddy Arnold's touring show and his radio show. That year, they appeared in two movies, *Feuding Rhythm* and *Hoe Down*. It was Arnold who suggested, in 1950, that they change their name to the Willis Brothers to avoid being labeled a Western group.

They moved labels quite frequently, recording for Mercury in 1948, RCA in 1950, Coral 1954 and then on to Starday. Although Guy provided them with a string of fine songs such as *I Miss Old Oklahoma*, *Drive My Blues Away*, *You Don't Have to Worry*, *My Pillow Talks* and *Long Gone*, chart success was still some years off.

In 1953, the Willis Brothers left Arnold's show and the following year became members of the *Ozark Jubilee* in Springfield, Missouri. They toured around the U.S. and became in demand as session players. In 1956, they joined the televised WLW *Midwestern Hayride* and over the next few years appeared on WRCP-TV Chattanooga, Tennessee (1956-1957), WABT-TV Birmingham, Alabama (1957-1958) and WTVC-TV Chattanooga (1958-1959). The Willis Brothers rejoined the *Grand Ole Opry* in 1960 and remained on the show until Guy's death in 1981.

The brothers hit the Country chart in 1964 with the Top 10 trucker single *Give Me Forty Acres (To Turn This Rig Around)*, on Starday. They followed this, the following year, with the novelty number *A Six Foot Two by Four*, which went Top 50. In 1967, they had their final two chart singles, *Bob* (Top 15) and *Somebody Knows My Dog* (Top 70).

Unlike other groups before and after, the Willis Brothers owed a lot of their success to the fact that they all could take lead vocals. In addition, with Guy acting as emcee for the group and each of the brothers excelling on their instruments, they were also brilliant at impersonating other Country artists and groups. Their popularity extended beyond the U.S. and they had fans throughout Europe and Central America, where they had toured as part of USO tours.

In 1976, Skeeter died from lymph cancer and Guy and Vic continued as a duo. Guy died in 1981 and Vic became the Secretary/Treasurer and a Trustee of the American Federation of Musicians, AFM Local 257, in Nashville. He also moonlighted as Chief Photographer of *Nashville Musician*, the union's newspaper. Vic was tragically killed on Natchez Trace, Nashville, around 1:00 a.m. on January 15, 1995. His car went out of control following either a heart attack or him falling asleep.

RECOMMENDED ALBUMS:

"Code of the West" (Starday)(1963)

"Road Stops—Juke Box Hits" (Starday)(1965)

"The Willis Brothers Goin' to Town" (Starday)(1966)

"The Best of the Willis Brothers" (Starday)(1975)

Johnny Bond & the Willis Brothers:

"The Singing Cowboy Rides Again" (CMH)(1977)

"The Return of the Singing Cowboy" (CMH)(1977)

BILLY JACK WILLS

(Singer, Songwriter, Bass, Drums, Guitar)

Given Name: Billy Jack Wills
Date of Birth: February 1926
Where Born: Memphis, Texas
Date of Death: March 2, 1991

The ninth of ten children, Billy Jack Wills was the youngest brother of Bob Wills. Considering his family's interest in music, it is hardly surprising that Billy Jack grew up listening to plenty of it.

At a very young age, he started playing guitar around the house, frequently backing up his father's fiddling. Subsequently, he became more interested in rhythm instruments like bass and drums. While still a teenager, he gained his first band experience in the early 1940's as a member of brother Johnnie Lee's organization. After WWII, Billy Jack became a member of Bob's Texas Playboys and for the next six years, he worked as the bassist or drummer and after 1948, as a vocalist.

During these years, Billy Jack also contributed a number of his songs to the band's record dates, including *A King Without a Queen*, *Pastime Blues*, *Cadillac in Model A* and *Rock-A-Bye Baby Blues*. The latter was a 1950 hit recording featuring Billy Jack's vocalizing. However, the most famous songs associated with him were *Faded Love* and *Lily Dale*. Billy Jack penned the lyrics for the former, whose melody was an inverted form of Benjamin Russell Hanby's 1856 *Darling Nellie Gray*. The version of the tune utilized for the copyrighted song had been used as a fiddle tune in the Wills family for several decades prior to the 1950's. In 1988, the song was made Oklahoma's official Country song and the Wills family successfully petitioned the Oklahoma State Senate that not only should Bob Wills' name be on the copyright, but also Billy Jack's. Billy Jack and mandolinist Tiny Moore were credited with *Lily Dale*, but it was actually a re-write of H.S. Thompson's 1852 tearjerker of the same name.

In 1952, Billy Jack started his own band, performing at the Wills Point Ballroom near Sacramento and broadcasting over radio station KFBK. Tiny Moore, manager of the ballroom, was responsible for the band's existence. After Moore became manager, a local band was used, but he felt the Wills identity should be emphasized. Therefore, he talked to Bob about sending his youngest brother to head up a band. The group that resulted included Moore on mandolin, fiddle, and vocals, Wills on drums and vocals, Dick McComb on trumpet and bass, Cotton Roberts on bass and fiddle, Kenny Lowery on rhythm guitar and Tommy Varner on steel guitar. Varner was later replaced by Vance Terry, a disciple of Noel Boggs and a student of Herb Remington. During the years 1952-1954, this band recorded a large number of transcriptions which accurately reflected their repertoire of Western Swing standards, current Country and Western hits, Jazz, and Blues numbers. Billy Jack was greatly impressed with black Rhythm and Blues, counting B.B. King as one of his favorite artists.

In 1954, the band's fortunes began to decline. The growing popularity of television reduced the size of their crowds at Wills Point. Then Bob Wills moved to Wills Point in an effort to boost the ballroom's business. This attempt didn't work and soon Bob went back on the road, taking most of the band members with him. That situation really marked the end of Billy Jack's music career. For a time, he once again became a Texas Playboy, then briefly tried to keep in the music business, first in Sacramento, then Redding, California. By 1960 he was retired, coming out of retirement in 1967, when he worked for a short time with brother Bob. WKM

RECOMMENDED ALBUMS:

"Billy Jack Wills and His Western Swing Band (Sacramento 1952-1954)" (Western) [With Tiny Moore]
"Crazy, Man Crazy" (Western) [With Tiny Moore]

BOB WILLS

(Singer, Songwriter, Fiddle, Mandolin, Bandleader)

Given Name:	**James Robert Wills**
Date of Birth:	**March 6, 1905**
Where Born:	**Nr. Kosse, Limestone County, Texas**
Married:	**1. Edna Posey (div.) 2. Ruth McMaster (div.) 3. Mary Helen Brown (div.) 4. Mary Helen Brown (remarried)(div.) 5. Mary-Louise Parker (div.) 6. Betty Anderson**
Children:	**Robbie, Rosetta, James Robert II, Carolyn, Diane, Cindy**
Date of Death:	**May 13, 1975**

The importance of Bob Wills to both Country music and popular music, in general, cannot be underestimated. Known as "The King of Western Swing," Bob blended Country, string band music, Jazz, Blues and Tin Pan Alley, to achieve the form of music known as Western Swing. He has influenced later performers such as Merle Haggard, George Strait and of course, Asleep at the Wheel.

Jim Rob, as he was initially known, was the eldest of ten children, among them Johnny Lee and Billy Jack, both of whom carved out careers in music. He came from a fiddling tradition on both sides of his family, the Willses and the Foleys. In 1913, the family moved to a farm in Memphis, Hall County, west Texas, where Bob began playing fiddle at square dances, although he had started out playing mandolin. He began playing professionally at age 10, when his father, John, was too drunk to perform at a ranch dance.

He moved to Fort Worth, and joined a medicine show as singer, musician and black-face comic, and changed to being "Bob" as there was more than one "Jim." After the show had become bankrupt, Bob worked as a barber in Alvarado and Fort Worth. It was in Fort Worth that he formed a duo, the Willis Fiddle Band, with guitarist Herman Arnspiger, during the summer of 1929. Toward the end of the year, the pair recorded *Gulf Coast Blues* and *Wills Breakdown*, in Dallas, for Brunswick.

The following year, Bob added vocalist Milton Brown, Milton's brother Durwood on guitar and Clifton "Sleepy" Johnson on tenor banjo. As such, they became Aladdin's Laddies, and performed over KTAT, KFJZ and WBAP in Fort Worth.

It was during this time that Bob developed what they played from Folk music to a style that took in all the other influences and led to a more danceable type of music. Early in January 1931, the band began advertising Light Crust Flour over KFJZ and they began calling themselves the Light Crust Doughboys. W. Lee O'Daniel, the President and General Manager of Burrus Mill, which made Light Crust, became the announcer and manager for the group, and got the program put out on WBAP. By year's end, they had moved to WOAI San Antonio and KPRC and then over the Southwest Quality Network, which encompassed KTAT Fort Worth and KOMA Oklahoma City.

The following February (1932), the band traveled to Dallas to record *Nancy Jane* and *Sunbonnet Sue*, for Victor. Following O'Daniel's instruction to the band to stop playing dances, he and Wills became adversaries. Milton Brown then quit the group, and after auditioning sixty-seven singers, Tommy Duncan was chosen to replace him. The band became unsettled by band members being fired by O'Daniel and by Bob's alcohol problem. By August, 1933, Bob had missed one too many broadcasts, and he was fired from the group.

Bob moved to station WACO Waco, and most of the former Doughboys followed. He named his band Bob Wills and His Playboys, with Tommy Duncan on vocals and piano, Kermit Whalin on bass and steel guitar, Johnny Lee Wills on tenor banjo and June Whalin on rhythm guitar. While they were at the station, they were sued by Burrus and O'Daniel for $10,000 to prevent them using "formerly the Light Crust Doughboys." Wills won the case and moved to Oklahoma, in January 1934.

As "Bob Wills and His Texas Playboys," they broadcast over WKY Oklahoma City; however, O'Daniel got them canned. Then on February 9, 1934, they joined KVOO Tulsa, advertising Play Boy Flour for General Mills, and despite O'Daniel's efforts, they (or Johnny Lee Wills' band) remained on air until 1958.

In September 1935, Bob and a dozen musicians went to Dallas to record again for Brunswick/ARC (released on Vocalion).

These were Tommy Duncan, Johnny Lee Wills, bassist Son Lansford, Everett Stover on trumpet, reeds player Zeb McNally, the returning Herman Arnspiger, Art Haines on trumpet and fiddle, drummer Smokey Dacus, Jesse Ashlock on fiddle, Clifton Johnson, steelie Leon McAuliffe and pianist Al Stricklin.

This combination of reeds, brass and twin fiddles increased in number to an 18-piece by 1940 and had them pulling record-breaking throngs to Cain's Academy in Tulsa and Venice Pier in California, where they were advertised as "America's Most Versatile Dance Band." They had recorded an instrumental version of the Wills melody *New San Antonio Rose*, and in 1940, this was re-recorded as a vocal and made Bob and the band nationally known. That same year, they made their movie debut in Tex Ritter's Western *Take Me Back to Oklahoma* (see Movie section).

The following year, they appeared in *Go West Young Lady*. 1941 would be a crucial year for the Playboys, as Tommy Duncan enlisted in the service a few days after the Japanese bombed Pearl Harbor. Other members followed and the band started to disintegrate. Bob himself joined the Army by Christmas the following year. However, on July 27, 1943, he was discharged as not being fit for service. Bob moved to the San Fernando Valley in California, two months later and began to broadcast on KMTR.

With Art Satherley heading A & R, Bob's recordings were now released on OKeh. *New San Antonio Rose* became a million seller in early 1944, reaching the Top 3 on the Country charts and Top 15 on the Pop lists. This was followed by the double-sided smash hit *We Might As Well Forget It/You're from Texas*, with both sides going Top 3 on the Country charts and also going Top 15 Pop. From 1944 through the mid-50's, the band was booked by the Music Corporation of America. Bob and the Playboys outsold the top Swing bands such as those of Tommy Dorsey and Benny Goodman. Following the war, Bob opted for a smaller, more fiddle-driven band.

The following year, *Smoke on the Water* went to No.1 and the flip-side, *Hang Your Head in Shame*, made the Top 3. This was followed by another No.1, *Stars and Stripes in Iwo Jima*, with the "B" side, *You Don't Care What Happens to Me*, reaching the Top 5. As OKeh was absorbed into Columbia, the instrumental *Texas Playboy Rag* gave the label a Top 3 hit and then the flip-side,

The King of Western Swing, ***Bob Wills***

Silver Dew on the Blue Grass Tonight, stayed at No.1 for three weeks. The year was wrapped up by another No.1, *White Cross on Okinawa*. Bob and the band appeared in two Charles Starrett movies during the year, *Blazing the Western Trail* and *Lawless Empire*.

Bob's 1946 version of *New Spanish Two Step*, a vocal version of his 1935 recording, became a No.1 hit, stayed at the top of the Country charts for 16 weeks and crossed over to the Top 20 of the Pop charts. The flip-side, *Roly-Poly*, also reached the Top 3. This was followed by the double-sided smash *Stay a Little Longer/I Can't Go on This Way*. During the year, Universal-International released *Frontier Frolic*, the first of a series of movies starring Bob and the band. The next year, he had a Top 5 single, *I'm Gonna Be Boss from Now On*, followed it with another No.1, *Sugar Moon* and closed out the year with the instrumental, *Bob Wills Boogie*.

During 1948, two releases on MGM, *Bubbles in My Beer* and *Keeper of My Heart*, made the Top 10 and were followed by the Top 20 entry *Texarkana Baby* on Columbia and the MGM Top 10 single, *Thorn in My Heart*. The band appeared in the movie *Echo Ranch*. During the year, Tommy Duncan decided to leave the Wills fold to form his own band. In 1949, Bob decided to move back to Oklahoma City, but over the next fifteen years, he moved nearly as many times. These moves often cost Bob a lot of money, and included properties at Wills Point near Sacramento and Bob Wills Ranch House in Dallas. During 1950, Bob hit the Country charts Top 10 with two more MGM releases, *Ida Red Likes the Boogie* and *Faded Love*.

During the 50's, Bob suffered ill health, but he still soldiered on. When Western Swing also started to suffer, with the onset of rock'n'roll and TV, Bob was not daunted, and brought rock'n'roll numbers into the act. In 1954, the band appeared in the movie *Corral Cuties*. By the end of the 50's, he had once more extended the band, and in 1960, Tommy Duncan returned to the fold. They set to recording several memorable albums for Liberty Records, and once more, the band was in the Country charts with the Top 5 single *Heart to Heart Talk*. The following year, they scored a Top 30 success with *Image of Me*.

Bob suffered the first of his heart attacks in 1962, but the following year, he was in Nashville recording an album, ***From the Heart of Texas***, for Kapp, with Leon Rausch handling vocals and including the Leiber and Stoller Blues rocker *Kansas City*. By the end of the year, he moved to Fort Worth. He recorded the album ***Time Changes Everything***, which features Johnny Preston and Tag Lambert handling vocals. Preston serves up a version of his hit *Running Bear*. By the end of the year, Bob had suffered another heart attack, and gave up the running of the band. After recuperating, he was booked out as a solo act, for more money than he and the band had gotten combined.

In 1968, Bob was inducted into the Country Music Hall of Fame, and at the induction, he did something that he had never done before: he doffed his famed white hat to the audience. Following a successful tour of California and further recording, Bob was honored by Governor Preston Smith and the State of Texas, appearing in front of the two Houses and receiving acknowledgment for his contribution to American music. The next day, Bob suffered a stroke. Although partially paralyzed, by the following year he had returned to public appearances and in 1973, he set himself three targets. First he played fiddle (with Hoyle Nix of Hoyle Nix and His West Texas Playboys) bowing, and also sang. He then traveled to Nashville to receive a citation from ASCAP, although confined to a wheelchair. He even managed to make an acceptance speech.

Bob had his final recording session on December 3, 1973, in Dallas and it featured Smokey Dacus, Leon McAuliffe, Eldon Shamblin, Johnny Gimble, Keith Coleman,

Al Stricklin and Leon Rausch, as well as the foremost Wills fan, Merle Haggard, who played fiddle on the final sessions. During the night, Bob suffered another stroke, and never regained consciousness. On May 13, 1975, he died, some seventeen months later. Although "the old man" (as he was lovingly called by the musicians) was not able to take part, the Texas Playboys finished the final sessions on December 4, 1973. Merle received as a gift Bob's fiddle, which he still plays on stage.

Although his familiar encouragement to Leon McAuliffe, "Take it away Leon," is no longer heard, Bob's influence has continued unabated, and in 1982, Merle Haggard recorded ***Tribute to the Best Damn Fiddle Player in the World (Or My Salute to Bob Wills)*** and in 1994, Asleep at the Wheel's tribute to Bob and His Texas Playboys refocused the importance of Western Swing within Country music.

RECOMMENDED ALBUMS:

"Together Again—Bob Wills & Tommy Duncan" (Liberty)(1960)
"Mr. Words & Mr. Music" (Liberty)(1961)
"From the Heart of Texas" (Kapp)(1963) [Re-released on Stetson UK in the original sleeve (1987)]
"Time Changes Everything" (Kapp)(1964) [re-released on Stetson UK in the original sleeve (1987)]
"King of Western Swing" (Kapp)(1967) [With Mel Tillis]
"The Legendary Masters—Bob Wills & Tommy Duncan" (double)(United Artists)(1971)
"San Antonio Rose" (Vocalion)(1971) [Previously unreleased material]
"The History of Bob Wills & the Texas Playboys" (MGM)(1973)
"Bob Wills and His Texas Playboys—For the Last Time" (double box-set)(United Artists)(1974)
"The Tiffany Transcriptions Volumes 1 and 2" (Kaleidoscope)(1983)
"The Tiffany Transcriptions Volume 3" (Cattle Germany)(1983)
"The King of Western Swing" (Charly UK)(1983)
"The Very Best of Bob Wills and the Texas Playboys Featuring Tommy Duncan" (Liberty) (1984)
"The Golden Era" (Columbia Historic Edition)(1987)
[See also, Light Crust Doughboys, the, Texas Playboys, the]

DAVID WILLS

(Singer, Songwriter, Guitar)

Date of Birth:	**October 23, 1951**
Where Born:	**Pulaski, Tennessee**
Married:	**Deborah**
Children:	**Jordan**

At the age of 23, David found his initial mentor in Charlie Rich, who also became his first record producer at Epic Records. At the end of 1974, David had a Top 10 success with *There's a Song on the Jukebox*. He then followed up, in the spring of the following year, with another Top 10 record, his own song *From Barrooms to Bedrooms*. Then record success fell away and his most successful releases on Epic were *The Barmaid* and *She Deserves My Very Best* (both 1975) and *Queen of the Starlight Ballroom* (1976).

In 1977, David moved to United Artists Records, but still success eluded and his most successful record was *The Best Part of My Days (Are My Nights with You)*, which only made it to just below the Top 50, in 1977 and the Top 50 single *I'm Being Good* (1979). David now decided to concentrate on his songwriting and signed with Charley Pride's Pride Music Group and began co-writing with Bill Shore. Con Hunley had a Top 20 hit, in 1980, with David's song *They Never Lost You*. In 1982, George Strait had a Top 3 hit with *If You're Thinking You Want a Stranger (There's One Coming Home)*, which he had written with Blake Mevis.

The following year, David linked with producer Blake Mevis on the release of his mini-album ***New Beginnings***, on RCA. During the summer of that year, he had a Top 20 hit with Steve Davis' *The Eyes of a Stranger*. He closed out the year with another of his co-written songs, *Miss Understanding*, which went Top 30. His only other successful single for the label was the Wills-Shore song *Lady in Waiting*, which reached the Top 40, in 1984. He signed with Epic again, in 1988, but he only managed one basement entry, *Paper Thin Walls*. David continues his career as a songwriter into the 90's.

RECOMMENDED ALBUMS:

"Barrooms to Bedrooms" (Epic)(1975)
"Everybody's Country" (Epic)(1975)
"New Beginnings" (RCA Victor)(1984) [Mini-album]

JOHNNIE LEE WILLS

(Tenor Banjo, Fiddle, Bandleader)

Given Name:	**Johnnie Lee Wills**
Date of Birth:	**September 2, 1912**
Where Born:	**Jewett, Texas**
Married:	**Irene**
Children:	**John T., Millie**
Date of Death:	**October 25, 1984**

Johnnie Lee Wills is the second of four Wills brothers who had a career in Western Swing music and also the second most significant.

The son of a Texas fiddler, Johnnie Lee learned the rudiments of music from his father, John Wills, as had brother Bob before him. Johnnie's first professional instrument was tenor banjo, of which he learned the fundamentals when the Texas Playboys first went to Tulsa and KVOO radio about 1933. The brother worked in Bob's band for about six years, making a brief unsuccessful effort on his own about 1939 with a group called the Rhythmairs.

About 1940, Bob split his band into two groups for a few months with Johnnie Lee leading the second band, which also included a third brother, Luther Jay (b. 1920), on bass fiddle. After a few months, Bob took the Texas Playboys to Hollywood, leaving KVOO and Tulsa to Johnnie Lee Wills and His Boys. The two brothers remained close, exchanged band members from time to time, and on occasions when Bob was absent, Johnnie Lee would take over for brief periods. Johnnie also took up the fiddle about this time and became leader of his own unit. He also contracted with Decca, cutting ten sides in 1941. After WWII, the band recorded eight more numbers for Decca. His most memorable effort on this label, *Milk Cow Blues*, was a 1941 Western Swing adaptation of a Kokomo Arnold Blues song.

With the exception of a few brief periods, Johnnie Lee Wills and His Boys dominated the Western Swing scene in Oklahoma, Kansas, Arkansas and Missouri from their base at Tulsa (at KVOO until 1958) through 1964 when he dissolved his band. Like the Playboys before them, the Boys played more or less regularly at Cain's Dancing Academy. Among the better known musicians who worked in the Boys were fiddler-vocalist Guy "Cotton" Thompson, pianist Millard Kelso, guitarist-vocalist Harley Hubbard and electric guitarist Lester Bernard. Vocalist Leon Huff, along with Curley Lewis and steel guitar specialists Gene Pooler and Gene Crownover, also put in many years of service with the Boys.

After a post-war Decca session, Wills went with the independent Bullet label around 1949 and subsequently cut twenty two-sides for them, including, in 1950, his biggest record hits. *Rag Mop*, a novelty song, went Top 3 on the Country charts and Top 10 on the Pop listings, where a cover by the Ames Brothers did even better. His other hit was the Easter bunny song, *Peter Cotton Tail* (Top 10), which also scored big for Gene Autry and Merv Shiner.

Wills signed with RCA Victor in 1952, but none of his seven single releases sold especially well. Their quality remained high, but Western Swing seemed to be losing much of the broad public that once supported it. Nonetheless, the Wills magic never faded away in the Tulsa area and Johnnie Lee continued to earn his living playing dances in that region, with occasional national tours. In

1962, he cut two albums for Sims, and attracted some attention with a tune called *Blub Twist*, but no chart action.

Although no longer keeping a band, Wills still worked some show dates, dances and rodeos throughout the region. He and his son, John Thomas Wills, also opened a thriving western wear store on Memorial Drive in Tulsa. After Bob's death, Johnnie Lee began to get more recognition as a Western Swing pioneer in his own right. Four of his numbers appeared on anthology albums and Rounder released an album from 1950-51 radio transcriptions while Bear Family re-issued his entire RCA Victor output. He also recorded reunion albums for Flying Fish and Delta with former band members (many of whom were also former Texas Playboys). Wills also made numerous appearances himself in the years prior to his passing. IMT

RECOMMENDED ALBUMS:

"Where There's a Wills There's a Way" (Sims)(ca. 1962)
"At the Tulsa Stampede" (Sims)(ca. 1963)
"The Best of Johnny [sic] Lee Wills" (Crown)(ca. 1965) [Sims masters]
"Reunion" (Flying Fish)(1978)
"Tulsa Swing" (Rounder)(1978) [From radio transcriptions]
"Dance All Night" (Delta)(ca. 1980)
"Rompin' Stompin' Singin' Swingin'" (Bear Family Germany)(1983) [RCA Victor masters]
(See also Bob Wills)

CHUBBY WISE

(Fiddle, Guitar, Songwriter, Composer)

Given Name:	**Robert Russell Wise**
Date of Birth:	**October 2, 1915**
Where Born:	**Lake City, Florida**
Married:	**Rossi**
Children:	**Marvalene (dec'd.)**

Chubby Wise is one of Country music's great fiddlers. Originally oriented more toward Western Swing sounds, he could in a sense be considered the original Bluegrass fiddler, especially for his work with Bill Monroe.

Chubby's father had some local renown as an Old-Time fiddler. The youngster learned some banjo chords and guitar first before taking up fiddle in his mid-teens. In addition to his dad and a state champ named Bryan Purcell, Wise drew his inspiration from early professionals like Curly Fox, Clayton McMichen and Arthur Smith. By 1936, Chubby resided in Jacksonville, where he drove a taxi by day and fiddled in clubs at night.

An early associate, North Carolinian Ervin Rouse, composed the classic tune *Orange Blossom Special*, perhaps with some assists from Chubby. In 1938, Chubby landed a full-time position with a Gainesville-based Country band, the Jubilee Hillbillies, with whom he played in a variety of styles, especially Western Swing.

American entry into WWII took a heavy toll on the band, and Chubby took advantage of an opportunity to join Bill Monroe's Blue Grass Boys at the *Grand Ole Opry* in 1942. Chubby remained with the band until 1948, recording many sides with the original full Bluegrass group consisting of Monroe, Flatt, Scruggs, Howard Watts, and himself. He worked on all of the Monroe numbers except those vocal quartets which did not use a fiddle. He also did a few sessions with other artists including one-time Blue Grass Boy Clyde Moody, who collaborated with him on composing Moody's hit recording of the *Shenandoah Waltz*. In January 1948, Chubby went with Clyde to the Washington, D.C., area where for a time, they worked for Connie B. Gay. However, by the fall of 1949, he had returned to the Monroe band for a second time that lasted until early 1950.

Chubby spent brief stints with the York Brothers, Flatt & Scruggs, and back in Washington with another Connie B. Gay musical aggregation until 1954, when he returned to Nashville and the *Opry* as a fiddler for Hank Snow's Rainbow Ranch Boys. Except for an eighteen-month stretch extending from late 1963 until early 1965, this tenure with the Rainbow Ranch Boys lasted until March 1970.

In addition to tours, the *Opry* and numerous Snow recordings with RCA Victor, Wise did some session work for such Bluegrass vocalists as Mac Wiseman, Red Allen and Hylo Brown and cut a fiddle album on a budget label. In 1969 he began making some fiddle records for Stoneway, the Houston, Texas, label. This subsequently led to him leaving the Snow band the following March and relocating in Texas.

Fiddle wizard ***Chubby Wise***

In Texas, Chubby found that he could earn a comfortable living as a guest fiddler at special dances, club appearances, and occasional Bluegrass festivals. From his home in Livingston, Texas, Chubby traveled both east and west cutting numerous albums for Stoneway in between times. He still did some session work with various Bluegrass groups, including Charlie Moore, Mac Wiseman, Raymond Fairchild, Frank Wakefield and the Boys from Indiana. Chubby also did two twin fiddle albums with another legendary figure, Howdy Forrester. By the 80's, however, he had slowed down somewhat and in 1984, relocated to Mary, Florida. However, he continued to work weekend festivals regularly and cut a session with the Bass Mountain Boys in 1992.

In December 1993, Chubby recorded his first compact disc for release on Pinecastle. As of March 1994, the legendary fiddler reports that he is booked "solid," and he thanks "the good Lord" for his health and capacity to keep fiddling for as long as he has. IMT

RECOMMENDED ALBUMS:

"Chubby Wise & the Rainbow Ranch Boys" (Starday)(1961)
"Chubby Plays Bluegrass" (Stoneway)(1970)
"Chubby Plays Bob Wills" (Stoneway)(1970)
"Grassy Fiddle" (Stoneway)(1975)
"Million Dollar Fiddle" (Stoneway)(1976)
"Chubby Plays Hank Williams" (Stoneway)(1977)
Chubby Wise & Howdy Forrester:
"Sincerely Yours" (Stoneway)(1975)
"Fiddle Tradition" (Stoneway)(1975)
Chubby Wise & Mac Wiseman:
"Give Me My Smokies & the Tennessee Waltz" (double)(Gilly's)(1982)
Chubby Wise & Raymond Fairchild:
"Cherokee Tunes & Seminole Swing" (Rebel)(1990) [Cassette]

MAC WISEMAN

(Singer, Songwriter, Guitar, Banjo, Bass)

Given Name:	**Malcolm B. Wiseman**
Date of Birth:	**May 23, 1925**
Where Born:	**Cremora, Virginia**
Married:	**Margie**
Children:	**Malcolm Scott, others unknown**

Mac Wiseman, often called "the Voice with a Heart," has enjoyed a long and durable career in Country and Bluegrass music. He has continued to record in both styles, but has seldom endeavored to mix them.

Born in a small town in the Shenandoah Valley, Mac listened to the traditional and church music of his region where he also heard radio balladeers ranging from Bradley Kincaid to Wilf "Montana Slim" Carter. After taking a course in radio at Shenandoah College, he

Bluegrass and Country star ***Mac Wiseman***

went to work as an announcer in 1944 at WSVA Harrisonburg, where he also began singing in Buddy Starcher's group. Later, he had his own band briefly at WFMD Frederick, Maryland, but then went to WNOX Knoxville as bass player and featured vocalist in Molly O'Day's Cumberland Mountain Folks.

In December 1946, he played bass on her first Columbia session. The next year found Mac working on his own again at WCYB Bristol and then as a sideman for Lester Flatt & Earl Scruggs, with whom he cut a session on Mercury. After another brief sojourn at WSB Atlanta, he went to Nashville as a sideman for Bill Monroe, helping him do his October 1949 Columbia session, one on which Mac did a solo lead on *Travelin' Down This Lonesome Road.*

Back on his own again in the early 50's, Mac worked at KWKH Shreveport and began recording for Dot. He used the same instrumentation that Flatt & Scruggs and Monroe had used, but soon favored the use of twin fiddles and generally also did solo vocals with very little harmony singing. Mac had very few original songs, but dug out some forgotten oldies that he virtually remade into his own, such as Mac and Bob's *'Tis Sweet to Be Remembered*, the Carters' *Wonder How the Old Folks Are at Home* and Buddy Starcher's *I'll Still Write Your Name in the Sand.* He also utilized some new material by writers like Dobro player Speedy Krise, who penned *Goin' Like Wildfire* and *You're Sweeter Than Honey*. Mac's clear, natural high-tenor voice quickly made him a favorite with Bluegrass fans.

After he moved to WRVA Richmond, he maintained a quality band, the Country Boys, which at times contained such fine musicians as Eddie Adcock, Scott Stoneman, Buck Graves and Jimmy Williams. Although Mac's recordings were popular and sold well, none really made the national charts until mid-1955 when his cover of *The Ballad of Davy Crockett* hit the Top 10. After this, most of Mac's recording arrangements moved in the direction of more contemporary Country and Pop.

In 1957, Mac took a job as an A & R man for Dot Records and moved to California for a time. He continued to cut sessions for them and had his biggest chart success in 1959 when his folksy arrangement of the old Will S. Hays ballad via the Carter Family of *Jimmy Brown the Newsboy* reached the Top 5. In 1962, Mac left Dot for Capitol, where he cut both Bluegrass and Country material, having a fine album of traditional songs as well as a Top 15 Country hit in 1963 with *Your Best Friend and Me*.

From 1965 onward, Mac spent about five years at Wheeling and the WWVA *Jamboree*. During this time, he cut a Bluegrass album for Dot with the Osborne Brothers backing and another one for Uncle Jim O'Neal's Rural Rhythm Records. In this period, Mac also began to play his first Bluegrass festivals, where he was well received. At the same time, he kept his foot in the Country door, too, having modest success with a single on MGM of *Got Leavin' on Her Mind* in 1968.

In 1969, Mac settled in Nashville after signing with RCA Victor. He had two albums—one in Country style and the other a watered-down brand of Bluegrass. His novelty Country single *Johnny's Cash & Charley's Pride* reached the Top 40, but a follow-up, *On Susan's Floor*, had little impact. More endearing to traditionalists from Mac's stay at RCA Victor were his three albums with Bluegrass legend Lester Flatt.

In the mid-70's, Mac did two straight traditional Bluegrass albums for the Cincinnati-based Vetco Records and a double one to inaugurate CMH Records' 9000 series. Both used the Shenandoah Cut-Ups for a support band and included new renditions of some of his classic numbers from Dot, as well as some other old standards. He also did some Country sessions for CMH, including an album of Gordon Lightfoot compositions and another double of Honky-Tonk standards. He also showed on the chart with some single cuts on Churchill. Then, converting to traditional Bluegrass, Mac did a double album with the Osborne Brothers, one cut of which even hit the lower rungs of the Country chart.

In the last decade, Mac Wiseman has continued to be a Bluegrass festival favorite while still dabbling in Country from time to time. He has gained some status as an elder statesman in the industry, being active in R.O.P.E. and serving as narrator for the Bluegrass documentary film *High Lonesome* (1992). He has recorded for Gusto, CMH, and 51 West while some of his earlier material continues to be reissued. County re-issued many of the early Dot Bluegrass cuts while Stetson did the same with his Capitol album and Rebel put out a compact disc from Vetco masters. The most unusual offering came from Bear Family, where Richard Weize assembled some scattered singles from the late 50's originally aimed at the teen market. In 1993, Mac Wiseman was inducted into the Bluegrass Hall of Fame. IMT

RECOMMENDED ALBUMS:

"Great Folk Ballads" (Dot)(1959)
"12 Great Hits" (Dot)(1960)
"Bluegrass Favorites" (Capitol)(1962)
"At the Golden Horseshoe" (Wise)(ca. 1964) [Canadian release only]
"Mac Wiseman" (Rural Rhythm)(ca. 1965)
"Bluegrass" (Dot)(1966)
"Golden Hits" (Dot)(1968)
"Johnny's Cash & Charlie's Pride" (RCA Victor)(1970)
"Concert Favorites" (RCA Victor)(1973)
"New Traditions, Vol. 1" (Vetco)(1975)
"New Traditions, Vol. 2" (Vetco)(1975)
"The Mac Wiseman Story" (double)(CMH)(1976)
"Country Music Memories" (CMH)(1976)
"Mac Wiseman Sings Gordon Lightfoot" (CMH)(1977)
"Songs That Made the Juke Box Play" (double)(CMH)(1980)
"Early Dot Recordings, Volume One" (County)(1985)
"Early Dot Recordings, Volume Two" (Rebel)(1988)
"Classic Bluegrass" (Rebel)(1989) [Vetco masters]
"Grassroots to Bluegrass" (CMH)(1990)
"The Rare Singles and Radio Transcriptions" (Cowgirlboy Germany)(1992)
"Early Dot Recordings, Volume Three" (County)(1992)
"Teenage Hangout" (Bear Family Germany)(1993) [Dot masters]
Mac Wiseman & Lester Flatt:
"Lester & Mac" (RCA Victor)(1971)
"On the Southbound" (RCA Victor)(1972)
"Over the Hills to the Poorhouse" (RCA Victor)(1973)
Mac Wiseman & the Osborne Brothers:
"The Essential Bluegrass Album" (double)(CMH)(1979)
Mac Wiseman & Chubby Wise:
"Give Me My Smokies & the Tennessee Waltz" (Gilley's)(1982)

KATE WOLF

(Singer, Songwriter, Guitar, Piano)

Date of Birth:	**1942**
Where Born:	**Sonoma County, California**
Married:	**Terry Fowler**
Date of Death:	**December 10, 1986**

Kate Wolf could be summed up as a family woman, Country music deejay, bar-singer and promoter, who helped run the Santa Rosa Folk Festival. However, that is too simplistic, and preferable is the description of Kate by

David Deverson of *Detour* magazine as "a weaver of visions." Although perhaps more of a Folk singer and writer, she had that rare ability to take her music into areas of music that could be Country, could be Bluegrass, but was always blessed with lyrics that were pure poetry.

Kate first came to notice with her band, the Wildwood Flower, and some friends when she recorded ***Back Roads*** in 1976. The album was cut in a living room and released on Owl Records. It contained eight original tracks and also included a tribute to Gram Parsons, *Legend in His Time*, written by Cyrus Clarke and David West. For her second album, ***Lines on the Paper*** (1977), Kate again recorded in a living room. On this album, she was joined by four members of the Cache Valley Drifters.

By 1979, Kate had attracted the attention of California-based Kaleidoscope Records. The label released the first two albums and then released the new album, ***Safe at Anchor***, her first studio album. During the first seven months of 1981, Kate recorded ***Close to You***, which like its predecessors contained Kate's expressive and impressive songs.

During 1982 and 1983, Kate recorded the live double-album ***Give Yourself to Love***, which was cut at various locations in Davis, Nevada City, San Francisco and Berkeley. As well as her own material, this project contains Kate's version of *Peaceful Easy Feeling* (a hit for the Eagles). In 1985, Kate recorded ***Poet's Heart***, which included the track *Carolina Pines*, which was recorded at the 1985 Kerrville Folk Festival. By now, she was starting to become ill with leukemia. She continued to work on recording material, but no further albums were released during her lifetime.

Kaleidoscope released two albums after her death, the double ***Gold in California*** and ***The Wind Blows Wild*** and the video ***An Evening in Austin***. The title track of ***The Wind Blows Wild*** was recorded by Kate from her hospital bed.

RECOMMENDED ALBUMS:

"Back Roads" (Kaleidoscope)(1976)
"Lines on Paper" (Kaleidoscope)(1977)
"Safe at Anchor" (Kaleidoscope)(1979)
"Close to You" (Kaleidoscope)(1981)
"Give Yourself to Love" (double)(Kaleidoscope)(1983)
"Poet's Heart" (Kaleidoscope)(1985)
"Gold in California" (double)(Kaleidoscope)(1986)
"The Wind Blows Wild" (Kaleidoscope)(1988)
Video:
"An Evening in Austin" (Kaleidoscope)(1989)

DEL WOOD

(Piano)

Given Name:	**Polly Adelaide Hendricks**
Date of Birth:	**February 22, 1920**
Where Born:	**Nashville, Tennessee**
Married:	**Carson Hazelwood (div./dec'd.)**
Children:	**Wesley (adopted)**
Date of Death:	**October 3, 1989**

Del Wood was probably the foremost female instrumentalist in Country music. Del spent thirty-six years as a member of the *Grand Ole Opry*, from 1953 until her death. Prior to the rise of Floyd Cramer in the 60's, she was probably the most significant Country instrumentalist on the keys other than those associated with Western Swing bands like Moon Mullican.

Del began playing piano at the age of 5 and became quite skilled by the time she reached her teens. She took her stage name by contracting her middle and married names. As a substitute staff pianist in 1950 at WLBJ Bowling Green, Kentucky, she began playing *Down Yonder*, subsequently recording it for the Tennessee label. It became a surprise hit, peaking in the Top 5 on the Country and Pop charts, in 1951, going Gold in the process. Del guested on the *Opry* for the first time in 1952 and became a cast member the next year.

Del recorded many instrumental albums for major record labels although *Down Yonder* was her only hit. She worked many package shows over the years including a six-week tour of Vietnam in 1968. She became known as "Queen of the Ivories." Like many *Opry* regulars of the older generation, she became somewhat disgruntled in her later years over reduced air-time. She was a long-time active member of AFTRA, the AFM and later R.O.P.E. A divorcee, Del, according to close friend Patsy Stoneman, took a great deal of pride in her adopted son Wesley and was quite thankful that she had raised, educated and settled him before her death at the age of sixty-nine. IMT

RECOMMENDED ALBUMS:

"Down Yonder" (RCA Victor)(1955)
"Hot, Happy & Honky" (RCA Victor)(1957)
"Rags to Riches" (RCA Victor)(1957)
"Mississippi Showboat" (RCA Victor)(1959)
"Flowers, Flappers & Fox Trots" (RCA Victor)(1960)
"Buggies, Bustles & Barrelhouse" (RCA Victor)(1960)
"Ragtime Goes International" (Mercury)(1961)
"Ragtime Goes South of the Border" (Mercury)(1962)
"Piano Roll Blues" (Mercury)(1963)
"Roll Out the Piano" (Mercury)(1964)
"Upright, Low Down & Honky Tonk" (Columbia)(1966)
"Best of Del Wood" (RCA Victor)(1968)
"Del Wood Favorites" (Republic LP 900)
"Ragtime Favorites" (Republic)
"Encore Del Wood" (Republic)

SHEB WOOLEY/BEN COLDER

(Singer, Songwriter, Guitar, Comedy, Actor)

Given Name:	**Shelby F. Wooley**
Date of Birth:	**April 10, 1921**
Where Born:	**Nr. Erick, Oklahoma**
Married:	**Beverly**
Children:	**Christi Lynn**

One of the most versatile performers in Country music, Sheb has won great acclaim for his accomplishments as a performer, writer and comedian as himself and his alter ego, drunken parodist Ben Colder. He has also appeared in over fifty movies (see Movie section).

This talented artist spent his early years on his father's farm near Erick, Oklahoma. By the age of 4, he was a competent horseman and during his teen years he worked as a rodeo rider. All his time wasn't devoted to horses, though, because while he was in high school at Plainview, Oklahoma, Sheb formed his own band. During 1945 and 1946, he appeared on WLAC Nashville and in 1946-50, he had his own show on the Calumet Radio Network. Then, in 1948, he got a recording contract with MGM, remaining with the label for more than two decades.

Shortly after signing with MGM, Sheb, who had been studying at the Jack Koslyn School of Acting, moved to California and in 1950 began working on *Rocky Mountain*, a Warner Brothers movie starring Errol Flynn. Two years later, Sheb gained considerable notice for his performance as the whiskey-drinking killer "Ben Miller," in the classic film *High Noon*. In the same decade he entered TV, appearing on *Cheyenne*, *Lassie*, *Range Rider* and *The Lone Ranger*, among others. Then, in 1959, he began a seven-year run as "Pete Nolan" on the TV series *Rawhide*.

Although Sheb had debuted on the Pop chart with *Are You Satisfied?*, it was the 1958 novelty hit *The Purple People Eater* that turned him into an international star. The single stayed at the Top of the Pop chart for 6 weeks and reached No.12 in the U.K. His next big hit came in 1962, when *That's My Pa* became a No.1 Country hit. During the 60's and 70's he also scored with several comedy songs as Ben Colder; the most successful were *Don't Go Near the Eskimos* (Top 20, 1962), *Hello Wall No.2* (Top 30, 1963), *Almost Persuaded No.2* (Top 10, 1966), *Harper Valley P.T.A. (Later That Same Day)* (Top 25, 1968) and *Fifteen Beers Ago* (Top 50, 1971). Sheb also turned out some hits under his own name, including *Blue Guitar* (Top 40, 1964) and *Tie a Tiger Down* (Top 25, 1968).

In 1964, *Cash Box* magazine gave Sheb a special award for his contributions to Country and popular music as a writer, recording artist and entertainer. In 1968, Sheb was selected as CMA "Comedian of the Year" for Ben Colder. Sheb brought Ben Colder to TV's *Hee Haw* and was responsible for writing the show's theme music.

He currently lives in Nashville and is an active member of R.O.P.E. WKM

RECOMMENDED ALBUMS:

"That's My Ma & That's My Pa" (MGM)(1962)
"The Very Best of Sheb Wooley" (MGM)(1965)
"Warm & Wooley" (MGM)(1969)
Ben Colder:
"Spoofing the Big Ones" (MGM)(1963)
"The Best of Ben Colder" (MGM)(1968)
"Ben Colder Live & Loaded at the Sam Houston Coliseum" (MGM)(1971)
Both:
"Greatest Hits of Sheb Wooley or Do You Say Ben Colder" (Gusto)(1979)

TOM WOPAT

(Singer, Songwriter, Trombone, Actor)
Date of Birth: September 9, 1951
Where Born: Lodi, Wisconsin

Like his fellow "Duke," John Schneider, Tom Wopat has established himself as both an actor and a Country singer. Although not as successful chartwise or as "Country" as John, he has nonetheless produced some memorable releases.

Tom grew up on a dairy farm and began singing and acting in school musicals. After high school, Tom attended the University of Wisconsin in Madison, studying music. However, he soon began working full-time as a member of a Rock group, handling lead vocals and playing trombone. After eighteen months with the group, he returned to his college studies, and appeared in civic productions of *West Side Story*, *Jesus Christ Superstar* and *South Pacific*.

*Singer and Actor **Tom Wopat***

He went into summer stock in Michigan, where he stayed for two full seasons and then, in the fall of 1977, he moved to New York City. Within a few weeks, he was cast in the off-Broadway production of the musical *A Bistro Car*. He then traveled to appear in the title role of *The Robber Bridegroom*, which ran for four weeks at Ford's Theatre in Washington, D.C. While he was in this production, Tom flew back to New York to audition for Cy Coleman's *I Love My Wife*, and was in the three-month run on Broadway. He followed this by appearing as "Curly" in an off-Broadway production of *Oklahoma!*

In 1978, he flew to Los Angeles and was cast in the role of "Luke Duke" in the soon to be highly successful CBS-TV series *The Dukes of Hazzard*. In 1982, after four seasons of the show, they experienced contractual problems. While these were being resolved, Tom went back to singing with his band, the North Hollywood All-Stars, whose members went on to be members of the Desert Rose Band and Bruce Hornsby's Range. The "Dukes" returned in 1983, with even better ratings, and Tom got his opportunity to direct. That year, he released his first eponymous Country album for Columbia, which was produced by Mike Post.

The Dukes of Hazzard ceased in 1985 and, the following year, Tom went on to star in *Carousel*, at the Kennedy Center for the Performing Arts in Washington, D.C. Later in the year, he returned to New York and appeared in the off-Broadway production of *Olympus on My Mind*, and then starred in the TV pilot *Blue Skies*, with Season Hubley and Pat Hingle.

That year, Tom signed with EMI America Records, and had his debut Country Top 40 single *True Love (Never Did Run Smooth)*, and followed it with *I Won't Let You Down*, which peaked in the Top 50. He started out 1987 with the Bob McDill-Charlie Black song, *The Rock and Roll of Love*, which reached the Top 20. This was followed by *Put Me Out of Your Misery* (Top 30) and *Susannah* (Top 20). All of these singles came from Tom's 1987 album ***A Little Bit Closer***. That year, Tom appeared in the made-for-TV movies *Burning Rage* with Barbara Mandrell and *Christmas Comes to Willow Creek* with John Schneider.

In 1988, Tom had a Top 20 entry with the title track of the 1987 album and it was followed by *Hey Little Sister* (Top 40) and *Not Enough Love* (Top 30), both of which came from the album ***Don't Look Back***. To support his two albums, Tom had put together a touring band, the Full Moon Band.

During 1988, Tom had a six-month run in the Tony Award-winning musical *City of Angels*. In 1989, Tom starred in the CBS movie *A Peaceable Kingdom* with Lindsay Wagner. Tom signed with Epic, in 1991, and returned to the singles chart with the very Country *Too Many Honky Tonks (On My Way Home)*, which made the Top 50. He followed with *Back to the Well*, a song that sounds like Don Williams meets Paul Simon, and reveals Tom in a delicate "Folky"mood, and then in 1992, he released the excellent Rick Hall-produced album ***Learning to Love***, the title track of which was co-written by Tom.

RECOMMENDED ALBUMS:

"Tom Wopat" (Columbia)(1983)
"A Little Bit Closer" (EMI America)(1987)
"Don't Look Back" (EMI America)(1988)
"Learning to Love" (Epic)(1992)

JIMMY WORK

(Singer, Songwriter, Guitar)
Date of Birth: March 29, 1924
Where Born: Akron, Ohio

It is on the strength of one composition that Jimmy Work has achieved immortality. *Makin' Believe* was published in 1954, by Acuff-Rose, and has since become one of the classic songs of Country music.

When he was age 2, his family bought a farm near Dukedom on the Kentucky-Tennessee border. He began playing guitar at age 7 and within four years, he was playing publicly. His early influences were Gene Autry and Roy Acuff, but he did not contemplate a career in music and was initially a millwright.

He began songwriting in his late teens and in 1945 moved to Pontiac near Detroit, Michigan and worked at WCAR, where he soon gained a following. He made his initial recordings, in 1947, for the local label, Trophy, most notably *These Kentucky Bluegrass Hills*.

In 1948, Jimmy wrote a song called *Tennessee Border*, which he recorded for the Alben label, also out of Detroit. He later recorded the song for the Nashville-based Bullett label and although it didn't sell, it was recorded by Red Foley as the flip-side of his version of *Candy Kisses*, in 1949. As part of a double-sided success, it outdid the top side and rose to the Top 3. Other charted versions of the song, that year, were by Tennessee Ernie Ford (Top 10), Bob Atcher and Jimmie Skinner (both Top 15). In addition, Homer & Jethro had a Top 15 parody version that year. The following year, Ernest Tubb & Foley took an "answer"version to the Top 3. Other versions include that by Hank Williams.

As a result of this song, Jimmy was signed to Decca and the label brought him to Nashville, where he began recording, in 1949. However, this came to nothing, and despite exposure on the *Grand Ole Opry* and Ernest Tubb's *Midnight Jamboree*, Jimmy was off the label the following year, after three singles. His back-up musicians on four of the tracks recorded were Red Foley's Pleasant Valley Boys and all tracks were produced by Paul Cohen. By 1951, Jimmy was back on Bullett, for the single *Hospitality/Mr. & Mrs. Cloud*, being backed by the Tennessee Border Boys.

He signed to Capitol, in 1952, but between then and 1954, he failed to score with his releases. In 1953, he signed to Acuff-Rose, who promoted his material, while he returned to perform in Detroit. The following year, he signed to Dot Records and in 1955 released his version of *Makin' Believe*. Although his version reached the Top 5, it was overshadowed by that of Kitty Wells, which quickly rose to No.2, where it stayed for fifteen weeks (out of a total of 28 weeks on the chart), being kept off the top by Webb Pierce's *In the Jailhouse Now*. The song has subsequently charted by five other artists, namely, Debi Hawkins (1975), Emmylou Harris (Top 10, 1977), the Kendalls (1977), Merle Haggard (1978) and Paul Williams (1981).

Jimmy followed up with another Top 10 song of his, *That's What Makes the Juke Box Play*. In 1978, Moe Bandy took the song to the Top 15. Although Jimmy continued to perform, he never again had success. His songs stand as a testament of his ability. The regret is that as a performer, he has never achieved the acclaim that his obvious talent deserved.

RECOMMENDED ALBUMS:

"Making Believe" (Bear Family Germany)(1986)
"Crazy Moon" (Bear Family Germany)(1988)

MARION WORTH

(Singer, Songwriter, Guitar, Piano)
Given Name: **Mary Ann Ward**
Date of Birth: **July 4, 1930**
Where Born: **Birmingham, Alabama**
Married: **Eugene "Happy" Wilson**
Children: **Joyce Lee**

For a decade from the end of the 50's through the end of the 60's, the blonde, green-eyed Marion Worth was a highly vaunted chart artist, who was a favorite on the *Grand Ole Opry* as well as the music rooms in Las Vegas. She was also one of the first Country performers to play New York's Carnegie Hall.

Marion's father was a railroad worker who taught her to play piano. When she was age 10, she won a local talent contest for 5 straight weeks. However, she had her sights on being a nurse and after high school and Paul Heynes, Jr. Business College, she began medical training, but decided against nursing and utilized her business studies to become bookkeeper for a record company. Then Marion and her sister won another talent contest and this was the catalyst that Marion needed to make up her mind on a musical career.

She made her radio debut on KLIF Dallas and then she worked on WVOK, WAPI and WAPI-TV, all in Birmingham. It was Happy Wilson (later her husband) who was so impressed with Marion that he began recording her. At the end of 1959, Marion's recording of *Are You Willing, Willie*, on Cherokee, went Top 15. The following year, at a time when independent labels could still get high chart placings, Marion had a Top 5 hit with her Guyden recording of her self-penned song *That's My Kind of Love*, which would be her most successful single.

Jack Stapp signed her to WSM's *Friday Night Follies*. As a result of the Guyden record, Marion was signed to Columbia Records, where she came under the production skills of Don Law and Frank Jones. With her new label, Marion scored a Top 10 single with *I Think I Know*. In 1961, she reached the Top 25, with *There'll Always Be Sadness*. Then for nearly two years, she was absent from the chart. Then her 1963 recording of *Shake Me I Rattle (Squeeze Me I Cry)* reached the Country Top 15 and crossed-over to the Pop Top 50. She followed up with her Top 20 version of *Crazy Arms*. That year, she became a member of the *Grand Ole Opry*.

1964 opened with the Top 40 hit *You Took Him Off My Hands (Now Please Take Him Off My Mind)* and followed with the Top 25 duet with George Morgan *Slippin' Around*. She finished the year with *The French Song*, which also went Top 25. It was another year before Marion was back in the charts, when *I Will Blow Out the Light* was a Top 40 record.

Then Marion moved labels and went to Decca, but by now her recording career was coming to an end and although she charted twice more for her new label with *A Woman Needs Love* (1967) and *Mama Sez* (1968), neither rose up the middle level of the chart.

Although Marion, whose hobby is the study of world history, has not graced the charts for years, she continues to be a much-in-demand live performer in the U.S. and Canada, appearing in Vegas at the New Frontier Hotel.

RECOMMENDED ALBUMS:

"Marion Worth's Greatest Hits" (Columbia)(1963)
"Slippin' Around" (Columbia)(1964) [With George Morgan]
"Marion Worth Sings Marty Robbins" (Columbia)(1964)
"A Woman Needs Love" (Columbia)(1967)

BOBBY WRIGHT

(Singer, Songwriter, Actor, Guitar, Drums, Trumpet)
Given Name: **John Robert Wright, Jr.**
Date of Birth: **March 30, 1942**
Where Born: **Charleston, West Virginia**
Married: **Brenda Kay Davis**
Children: **Theresa LeAnn, Kamela Lynn**

Although Bobby Wright has never had the really major hit that turns stars into superstars, he chalked up twenty-one chart records during the decade from the late 60's through the late 70's. Born the son of Country music legends Johnny Wright and Kitty Wells, he was exposed to music at an early age, but initially opted for acting as his chosen field.

When he was born, Johnny and Kitty were stars on the WWVA *Wheeling Jamboree*. Briefly, they moved to Nashville, but most of Bobby's early years were spent in Louisiana, where his parents starred on the *Louisiana Hayride*, in Shreveport. In 1958, the family moved back to Nashville, as his parents headlined at the *Grand Ole Opry*. Bobby still shunned the music business, except for two brief flirtations when he was age 8, when he appeared on the *Louisiana Hayride*, and in 1954, when he first recorded for Decca, cutting *My Mama Didn't Raise No Foolish Children/You'd Better Not Do That*.

His main interests at this stage were basketball and football, and during a dance following a basketball game, he met his future wife. They married after he had completed studies at Middle Tennessee State University, in 1962. However, it was his ability to play guitar that led to the development of his acting skills. He heard from Ott Devine, the Manager of the *Grand Ole Opry*, that Hollywood producer Peter Tewkesbury was looking for a guitar-playing southern lad for a drama entitled *It's a Man's World*. Bobby traveled to California, and although the project came to nothing, his screen test was seen by the producer of the TV series *McHale's Navy*, and in 1962, he began playing the role of "Willie," the radio operator. He played the part until 1966, and this led to appearances in *Pistols and Petticoats* and *The Road West*.

Before *McHale's Navy* had ended, Bobby had tried his hand at singing and appeared on the ***Kitty Wells Family Gospel Sing*** album, in 1965. He moved back to Nashville, in 1966, joined the Kitty Wells-Johnny Wright Family Show and began recording again with Decca. He made his debut on the Country charts, the following year, with the Top 50 record *Lay Some Happiness on Me*. His next sizable hit was the 1969 single *Upstairs in the Bedroom*, which made the Top 40. The following year, he again reached the Top 50, with *Hurry Home to Me*. During 1970-71, he appeared with the family on their syndicated TV show. He achieved his biggest success in 1971, when *Here I Go Again* climbed to the Top 15.

Bobby changed labels in 1973, and moved to ABC. That year, he achieved Top 40 status with *Lovin' Someone on My Mind* and followed it, the following year, with his version of *Seasons in the Sun* peaking in the Top 25. He stayed with ABC until 1975, and then two years later, charted on United Artists (where he was produced by Larry Butler) with *Neon Lady*, a Top 75 single, and although he had three more chart records, none of them climbed above the basement level.

Bobby found approbation overseas, and his appearances in the family shows were extremely well received in Europe. In 1977, he recorded an album for Starday of Johnnie & Jack material, as a tribute to his father and the late Jack Anglin. Bobby continues to be a part of the family show.

RECOMMENDED ALBUM:
"Here I Go Again" (Decca)(1971)

JOHNNY WRIGHT

(Singer, Songwriter, Guitar, Bass Fiddle)

Given Name:	**Johnnie Robert Wright, Jr.**
Date of Birth:	**May 13, 1914**
Where Born:	**Mount Juliet, Tennessee**
Married:	**Ellen Muriel Deason (Kitty Wells)**
Children:	**Ruby, Bobby, Carol Sue**

Johnny Wright is best known for his role as half of the Johnnie & Jack duo. However, after Jack Anglin's tragic death in 1963, Johnny went solo.

Johnny grew up near Nashville, met Jack and worked locally with him as early as 1936. Following the relatively brief career of the Anglin Brothers in 1940, Wright and Anglin teamed up and worked together as a "brother-in-law" duet for some twenty-three years with a break for Jack's military service in WWII. During their last decade together, the success of the duo was somewhat overshadowed by that of Kitty's phenomenal rise to stardom.

From the early 60's, Johnny also toured heavily with the Kitty Wells-Johnny Wright Family Show, a package unit, which included at various times Johnny, wife and superstar Kitty Wells, vocalist Bill Phillips, and various of the Wright children: Ruby (b. 1939), Bobby (b. 1942), and Carol Sue (b. 1945).

Johnny continued to record for Decca solo after Jack's death. An early release, *Walkin', Talkin', Cryin', Barely Beatin' Broken Heart*, reached the Top 25 in the spring of 1964, being credited to Johnny Wright and the Tennessee Mountain Boys. The song became a hit in 1990 for Highway 101. After a pair of lesser chartmakers, *Don't Give Up the Ship* and *Blame It on the Moonlight*, in 1965, Johnny's recording of Tom T. Hall's *Hello Vietnam* spent 5 months on the chart including 3 weeks at No.1. Johnny had seven more entries over the next three years of which *Keep the Flag Flying* and *Nickels, Quarters and Dimes*, in 1966, did best. Johnny's duet with Kitty, the autobiographical *We'll Stick Together*, in 1968, only reached the Top 60, but became a long-time favorite with their many fans.

Although Kitty's name also dropped from the charts after 1979, the duo could still draw moderate crowds. Bill Phillips, Ruby, and Carol dropped out of music after a time, but Johnnie, Kitty, and Bobby continued to work. They practically stopped touring for a time, concentrating on their souvenir shop, Country Junction, but becoming restless they went back on the road. As of mid-1992, the threesome continue to play about one hundred dates a year. An astute manager, Johnny has demonstrated a thorough understanding of both the music and the business in a career that spans nearly six decades. IMT

RECOMMENDED ALBUMS:
"Hello Vietnam" (Decca)(1965)
"Country Music Special" (Decca)(1966)
"Country, the Wright Way" (Decca)(1967)
"Country Favorites" (Decca)(1968)
(See also Johnnie & Jack, Kitty Wells)

MICHELLE WRIGHT

(Singer, Guitar, Drums)

Date of Birth:	**July 1, 1961**
Where Born:	**Morpeth, Ontario, Canada**

Canada has provided many a Country talent for Nashville's voracious music machine. Michelle Wright is one of the latest entrants in the arena, bringing a powerful soulful voice to the public with a style she dubs "cruise music," a rich blend of Country and Rhythm & Blues.

Both her mother and father were involved with Country music while she was growing up in Canada. The family was always traveling and some of Michelle's earliest memories were of singing in the car and watching her father perform in a rhinestone-studded suit after her parents were separated. While her parents were performing, Michelle was growing up across the Canadian border from

Superb Canadian talent ***Michelle Wright***

Detroit. Because of this she was exposed to Motown music at an early age and became a great fan of Diana Ross and Otis Redding.

When she was 9, Michelle's family settled in Merlin, Ontario, and by the time she was 12, the family had accumulated a garage full of musical equipment. Her mother remarried a grain farmer and after putting in time on a tractor, she and her brother used to perform in the garage. She would play drums and he guitar. Michelle began playing acoustic guitar when she was 13, playing weddings and local dances.

Throughout high school she participated in athletics, developing a competitive edge that would serve her well later. Her first job came about as a result of a phone call for her mother, who was away selling real estate. So Michelle took the job herself.

Later, during her first year of college, she was performing with a local band in Chatham when she attracted the attention of an American booking agent who offered her a job singing on the road. Although she was thinking about getting married and living on a farm, she took the job, which was the end of her previous plans and the beginning of eight years on the road.

After three years of touring with bands throughout the U.S. and Canada, Michelle started her own band and came to the attention of Brian Ferriman, of Canada's Savannah Music Group. Brian gave her direction and helped her surround herself with the right kind of people. A year later, Michelle's band was called in to replace another band that had canceled at an outdoor performance outside Ottawa. There wasn't a very good turnout, but one member of the audience that night was Nashville songwriter Rick Giles. He heard her voice and thought she was a man—but when he found out she wasn't, he became interested enough to meet the face behind the voice.

Giles and his songwriting partner, Steve Bogard, brought Michelle to Nashville in January 1986 and began working on songs for her to record. In February of the same year, Michelle won the CJBX-FM Country Roads Talent contest in London, Ontario, and used the prize money she had won to go into the studio and record the first of three Giles-Bogard songs. Michelle was nominated as "Vista (Rising Star)" in 1986 in the Canadian Country Music Association awards. Following the success of her initial singles in Canada, Michelle received a 1987 nomination as CCMA "Vocalist of the Year." Her first Canadian album, ***Do Right By Me***, was released in 1988.

The following year brought Michelle two nominations for Juno Awards from the Canadian Academy of Recording Arts and Sciences (CARAS) and five nominations from the CCMA. The subscribers of *RPM* magazine presented her with her first industry award, voting Michelle the Big Country Award as Canada's 1989 "Top Country Female Vocalist." During the same time, she was chosen as the opening act for Randy Travis' tour of western Canada.

In the U.S., Rick Giles had heard that Tim Dubois was heading up a new Country Division of Arista Records in Nashville. He presented Tim with a tape of Michelle. Tim went to Toronto to see her perform and offered her a recording contract, making her Arista's third Country artist. Her first Arista release, *New Kind of Love* (1990), went Top 40 in the U.S. This was followed by *Woman's Intuition*, the same year, which went Top 75. During the year, Michelle was named CCMA "Female Vocalist of the Year." She also received CCMA nominations for "Video of the Year" for *New Kind of Love*, and "Entertainer of the Year."

1991 produced the Top 75 *All You Really Wanna Do*. Michelle retained the CCMA "Female Vocalist of the Year" Award and the album ***Michelle Wright*** was named CCMA's "Album of the Year." In addition, the album earned the CCMA's "Album Graphics of the Year" Award for designer Susan Mendola (Michelle's shoulder-length hair had now become fashionably close-cropped) and the single *New Kind of Love* was named "Single of the Year." The Michelle Wright Band was named by the CCMA as "Back Up Band of the Year." Michelle received the Big Country Award as "Top Female Vocalist" and "Artist of the Year." Michelle also received a CCMA nomination as "Entertainer of the Year" and Big Country Award nomination for *All You Really Want to Do* as " Single of the Year" and from the CCMA as "Video of the Year."

In 1992, Michelle had her first U.S. Top 10 single with *Take It Like a Man* (the song was also her first No.1 hit in Canada) which was followed by the Top 50 *One Time Around*. She completed the year with the song about teenage death, *He Would Be Sixteen*, which went Top 40. That year, Michelle's second album, ***Now & Then***, was Certified Gold in Canada and went on to Platinum status in 1993. During 1992, Michelle was again named CCMA's "Female Vocalist of the Year" and she also won CCMA's "Country Music Person of the Year" award and *Take It Like a Man* was named "Single of the Year." Once again, the Michelle Wright Band was named "Back Up Band of the Year."

In 1993 Arista released *The Change*, which went Top 60 and was her last U.S. chart entry to date. During 1993, Michelle's eponymous U.S. debut album was Certified Gold in Canada.

Michelle Wright has emerged as one of Canada's strongest female artists over the past few years, and it looks like she is in for a very successful run in the U.S. as well. LAP

RECOMMENDED ALBUMS:

"Do Right By Me" (Savannah) (1988)
"Michelle Wright" (Arista)(1990)
"Now and Then" (Arista) (1992)

TAMMY WYNETTE

(Singer, Songwriter, Guitar, Accordion, Piano, Actress)

Given Name:	**Virginia Wynette Pugh**
Date of Birth:	**May 5, 1942**
Where Born:	**Itawamba County, Mississippi**
Married:	**1. Euple Byrd (div.)** **2. Don Chapel (div.)** **3. George Jones (m. 1969/div.1975)** **4. Michael Tomlin (m. 1976)(div.)** **5. George Richey (m. 1978)**
Children:	**Gwendolyn Lee (Gwen), Jacqueline Fay (Jackie), Denise Tina, Tamela Georgette; stepdaughter Georgie**

Although Tammy may no longer be considered the Queen of Country music, in the eyes of her fans she will always reign supreme as the "First Lady of Country Music." She remains the third most successful female Country recording artist of all time, behind Dolly Parton and Loretta Lynn.

Tammy was born on her grandfather's farm, a property which crossed the Mississippi and Alabama state lines. Her father, William Hollis Pugh, a local musician and singer who could play any instrument he picked up, recorded in 1939 and 1940 (records which Tammy has framed). When Tammy was 8 months old, her father died from a brain tumor and the family moved to Red Bay, near Birmingham, Alabama. During WWII, her mother was employed in war work in an aircraft factory and she was left in the care of her grandparents for the duration of the war.

Brought up on their farm in Mississippi, Tammy learned to play the collection of instruments formerly owned by her father. By the time she was age 8, she worked in the cotton fields. She took five years of music lessons with the intent of going into the music business. She also began singing Sacred Harp religious songs, which emphasized the musical note rather than the lyrics. She formed a trio while in her teens and they broadcast on local radio.

However, when she was age 17, she got married and settled in Tupelo, Mississippi. She enrolled in a beauty college and became a beautician and hairdresser (she still holds a license) and also worked as a chiropractor's receptionist. Within three years, she had three children, but before the birth of her third child, the marriage broke up, and when the baby developed spinal meningitis, Tammy had to find ways to boost her income to pay $6,000 in medical bills. She managed to get the occasional singing engagement, and in 1965, she began appearing on the *Country Boy Eddie Show* on WBRC-TV out of Birmingham.

She sang in various clubs as far afield as Memphis and began songwriting with Fred Lehner, who was with WYAM Birmingham. She also appeared on Porter Wagoner's road show, and then in 1966, she came to Nashville and started shopping for a record label. Tammy was turned down by five labels including United Artists and Hickory. Kapp showed some interest, but after she returned to Birmingham, nothing further happened. She returned again to Nashville to pitch some of a friend's songs to Epic, and as a result the label's Head of A & R, Billy Sherrill, signed her and began a relationship that would last until 1981.

At the end of 1966, her first single, *Apartment #9*, reached the Top 50 and was named the ACM's "Song of the Year." However, it was the follow-up, *Your Good Girl's Gonna Go Bad*, in 1967, that started the Wynette career in earnest. It reached the Top 3 and was followed by her first No.1, *My Elusive Dreams*, a duet with David Houston, which was also a Top 90 Pop hit. The year ended with her first solo No.1, *I Don't Wanna Play House*. For her rendition of the song, Tammy won a Grammy Award as "Best Country & Western Solo Vocal Performance, Female."

She started 1968 with another No.1, *Take Me to Your World*, and although the follow-up, another duet with Houston, *It's All Over*, just failed to make the Top 10, Tammy then had four-in-a-row No.1 hits, *D-I-V-O-R-C-E* and her co-written *Stand By Your Man* (both 1968) and *Singing My Song* and *The Ways to Love a Man* (both 1969). All of these singles crossed-over to the Pop charts, the most successful being *Stand By Your Man*, which went Top 20. In 1968 she was voted the CMA's "Female Vocalist of the Year," a crown she retained in 1969 and 1970. In 1969, she released ***Tammy's Greatest Hits***, which was Certified Gold in 1970 and Platinum in 1989. Also in 1970, she was named the ACM's "Female of the Year" and also received a Grammy Award for "Best Country Vocal Performance, Female" for *Stand By Your Man*.

As well as her hitmaking talent, it was also being revealed that she was a songwriter to be reckoned with, often writing with Billy Sherrill. That year, she married Country superstar George Jones, and began a partnership that was musically rewarding but often personally stormy. It was also a very successful period for her as a solo artist.

She started off 1970 with the Top 3 record *I'll See Him Through* and followed by back-to-back No.1s, *He Loves Me All the Way* and *Run, Woman, Run*. She closed out the year with the Top 5 release *The Wonders You Perform*. She opened her account in 1971 with the Top 3 single *We Sure Can Love Each Other* and followed up with the No.1 *Good Lovin' (Makes It Right)*. She ended the year with her first duet success with George Jones, *Take Me*, a Top 10 hit. *Bedtime Stories* opened up 1972, and also went to No.1. Including the last named, Tammy had had an unbroken run of 11 solo Pop crossover hits. She followed with the Top 3 single *Reach Out Your Hand* and then had the Top 10 duet with George, *The Ceremony*. Tammy then had a run of four No.1 solo hits, *My Man* and *'Til I Get It Right* (both 1972) and *Kids Say the Darndest Things* and *Another Lonely Song* (both 1973). During this time she also racked up hits with George,

Tammy Wynette** (right) with her fellow Honky Tonk Angels, **Loretta Lynn** and **Dolly Parton

namely, the Top 40 *Old Fashioned Singing* (1972) and *Let's Build a World Together* (1973) and the No.1 *We're Gonna Hold On*.

In 1974, she had the Top 5 *Woman to Woman* and two duets with George, *(We're Not) The Jet Set* (Top 20) and *We Loved It Anyway* (Top 10). That year, Tammy and George went to England to appear at the Wembley Festival, but were called home by the death of George's mother. She did play the festival in 1975 and again in 1976, 1979 and 1988. During the 1988 show, she came on stage during Merle Haggard's set and duetted with him. By now, storm clouds were on the horizon for the two stars, and in 1975, they divorced. This did not stop the hits coming from both Tammy and the duo. She started out with the Top 5 release, *(You Make Me Want to Be) A Mother* and the ironically titled *I Still Believe in Fairy Tales*. Her duet hit was the Top 25 *God's Gonna Get'cha (For That)*. In the U.K., *Stand By Your Man* became a No.1 hit after having been released five times before it charted. She also charted later that year, in Britain, with *D-I-V-O-R-C-E* (also a No.1 for Scottish comedian Billy Connelly, in parody form).

All of her releases in 1976 went to No.1. These were *'Til I Can't Make It on My Own*, *Golden Ring* (with George), the solo *You and Me* and *Near You* (with George). That year, Tammy was named "No.1 Female Vocalist" in the U.K. That year, she married Nashville realtor Michael Tomlin, but within six weeks of their marriage it was all over and Tammy was saddled with Tomlin's bills. In 1977, all her singles went Top 10 and were *(Let's Get Together) One Last Time*, *Southern California* (with Jones) and *One of a Kind*. Although her first single in 1978, *I'd Like to See Jesus (On the Midnight Special)*, only peaked in the Top 30, Tammy was back on track when *Womanhood* reached the Top 3. That year, she married George Richey, who had been Musical Director on *Hee Haw*. He now began to assume an increasingly major role in Tammy's career, including managing her. In September that year, she was kidnapped in a Nashville shopping plaza and henceforth, she hired fifty bodyguards for subsequent tours.

Both her 1979 singles, *They Call It Making Love* and *No One Else in the World*, climbed into the Top 10. However, from here on in, her record success was less predictable. That year, Tammy wrote her autobiography, *Stand By Your Man* (Simon & Schuster), which was issued in paperback by Pocket Books in 1980. That same year, RTE, Eire's radio and TV station, held a public poll and Tammy was named "Country Female Vocalist of the Year."

She teamed up again with Jones under happier circumstances, in 1980, and they cracked the charts with the Top 3 smash *Two Story House*. Then both her solo entries, *He Was There (When I Needed You)* and *Starting Over*, went Top 20, as did her final chart duet with George, *A Pair of Old Sneakers*, a record that deserved to do better. In 1981, Annette O'Toole portrayed Tammy in the CBS-TV biopic, *Stand By Your Man,* which aired in May that year.

Now that Tammy was not produced by Sherrill, various people replaced him, including Chips Moman and George Richey. From 1981 through 1986, Tammy's most successful singles were *Cowboys Don't Shoot Straight (Like They*

Used To) and *Crying in the Rain* (Top 20) (both 1981), *Another Chance* (Top 10), *You Still Get to Me* (Top 20) and *A Good Night's Love* (Top 20) (all 1982), *Sometimes When We Touch* (Top 10, with Mark Gray) (1985). During 1984, Tammy appeared in the movie *Stick*, starring and directed by Burt Reynolds. Although this was her first movie role, her songs had been featured on the soundtracks of *Run, Angel, Run* and *Five Easy Pieces*. That year, Tammy and Richey filed for bankruptcy following the collapse of a Florida bank that financed their investment in two shopping centers. They later that year paid $450,000 to settle the claim. During this time, Tammy became dependent on painkillers, following seventeen operations, and entered the Betty Ford Center. She had almost completed the course when she collapsed and had to have further major surgery; she then completed the course.

In 1987, Tammy teamed up with master producer Steve Buckingham, and the result was the album that many, including "Buck," consider Tammy's finest, ***Higher Ground***. She is joined on harmonies on this album by Ricky Skaggs, Gene Watson, Vern Gosdin, Emmylou Harris, Vince Gill, the Gatlin Brothers, the O'Kanes, John Wesley Riles, Ricky Van Shelton and Paul Overstreet, among others. Up to then Tammy had a reputation of singing material that epitomized the acceptable face of Country conservatism. With this album she became the Tammy Wynette of the 90's. Three tracks were sizable hits without achieving the airplay they warranted. They were *Your Love* (with Ricky Skaggs) and *Talkin' to Myself Again* (with the O'Kanes) (both 1987) and *Beneath a Painted Sky* (with Emmylou Harris) (1988).

Her 1989 album ***Next to You*** was produced by Norro Wilson and contained much good material, but the most successful single, the title track, just failed to make the Top 50. Even her duet with Wayne Newton, *While the Feeling's Good*, on Curb, only reached the Top 70. The following year, Bob Montgomery was her producer for ***Heart Over Mind***. The album has Tammy singing material by a lot of happening writers, including Tim Mensy, Lari White and Dave Gibson as well as songwriting giants Curly Putman, Sonny Throckmorton and Max D. Barnes.

Tammy's most successful single in 1990 came from her ***Best Loved Hits*** album and was the Merle Haggard-Leona Williams song *We're Strangers Again*, which teamed her with Randy Travis, with Kyle Lehning producing. The following year, *Music City News* honored her with the prestigious "Living Legend" Award.

In 1992, Tammy was not to be found on the Country charts; however, a new Tammy did chart. This was Tammy Wynette, Disco diva. In company with British Funk duo Bill Drummond and Jimmy Cauty, known as the KLF, and a cast of thousands, she reached the Top 15 on the Pop charts with *Justified & Ancient,* becoming a Pop chart topper in the U.K.

In 1993, Tammy enjoyed a resurgence in her recording career when she appeared with Dolly Parton and Loretta Lynn on the album ***Honky Tonk Angels*** (also produced by Steve Buckingham). Before year end, the album was Certified Gold and the single *Silver Threads and Golden Needles*, which was accompanied by an amusing promotional video, was a minor success. Again, in 1994, she was taken seriously ill, but has now happily recovered.

RECOMMENDED ALBUMS:

"Tammy's Greatest Hits" (Epic)(1969)
"Tammy's Greatest Hits Vol. 2" (Epic)(1971)
"We Go Together"/"Me and the First Lady" (double)(Epic)(1975) [With George Jones]
"Greatest Hits—George Jones & Tammy Wynette" (Epic)(1977)
"Tammy Wynette: The Classic Collection" (Epic)(1979)
"George Jones & Tammy Wynette Together Again" (Epic)(1980)
"The President & the First Lady" (Columbia Special Products)(1981)
"I Love Country" (CBS UK)(1986)
"Higher Ground" (Epic)(1987)
"Anniversary: Twenty Years of Hits" (Epic)(1987)
"Next to You" (Epic)(1989)
"Heart Over Mind" (Epic)(1990)
"Best Loved Hits" (Epic)(1991)
"Honky Tonk Angels" (Columbia)(1993) [With Dolly Parton and Loretta Lynn]

WYNONNA

(Singer, Songwriter, Guitar, Actress)
Given Name: Christina Ciminella
Date of Birth: May 30, 1964
Where Born: Ashland, Kentucky
Children: Elijah

After the much publicized break-up of the Judds, in 1991, Wynonna's first year as a solo artist began with a bang. With her powerful Country-R & B style Wynonna left no questions about her ability to make it alone. Her first three singles, recorded on Curb/MCA, went straight to No.1. She started the roll with 1992's *She Is His Only Need*, followed by *I Saw the Light* (3 weeks at the top) and *No One Else on Earth* (4 weeks at No.1). The latter crossed over to the Pop chart, making the Top 90. Wynonna concluded her first year with *My Strongest Weakness*, which went Top 5.

1993 brought *Tell Me Why*, which went Top 3, once again crossing over, making it to the Top 80 on the Pop chart. A duet with Clint Black followed, *A Bad Goodbye*, that went Top 3 and again went Top 50 on the Pop chart. This single was recorded on her ***No Time to Kill*** album, released on RCA. Wynonna's next single, *Only Love*, reached the Top 3, followed by *Is it Over Yet*, making the Top 10.

In 1994, radio deejays decided to play *Let's Make a Baby King*, but quickly lost interest, breaking Wynonna's established chart pattern. The track made it into the Top 70 but it was only on the chart for one week. Wynonna bounced back, however, with *Rock Bottom*, her latest single to date, which made the Top 3.

Her two albums with Curb/MCA have also been very successful. ***Wynonna***, released in 1992, went Triple Platinum in 1994 and ***Tell Me Why***, her latest cd, went Platinum in 1993. With Wynonna's track record of hits, there is no reason to believe fans won't be hearing a lot more from her in the future. On December 23, 1994, Wynonna and her boyfriend, Arch Kelley, had a son, Elijah. LAP

RECOMMENDED ALBUMS:

"Wynonna" (Curb/MCA)(1992)
"Tell Me Why" (Curb/MCA)(1993)
(See also Judds, the)

Y

SKEETS YANEY

(Singer, Songwriter, Guitar, Harmonica)
Given Name: Clyde A. Yaney
Date of Birth: June 16, 1912
Where Born: Mitchell, Indiana
Married: Unknown
Children: Joan

One of the great regional stars, Skeets Yaney has largely been overlooked because he had no big selling records. He did, however, make a number of 78s for the MGM, Columbia and Town and Country labels.

He was given the nickname "Skeets" by his older brother, Jim. For his harmonica and singing act, he was awarded the title of "Best Entertainer in Southern Indiana," when he was only age 6. Skeets was given a shotgun by his father and he traded it for a guitar. One day, a group passed through Mitchell and Skeets sang with them. A few weeks later, they wired him to join them in Louisville, Kentucky. He stayed with them until they reached St. Louis and there he joined KMOX.

A few years later he teamed up with accordion player Frankie Taylor, as Skeets and Frankie. They were partners for more than two decades. This talented duo became one of the most popular acts on KMOX, being particularly noted for Skeets' spectacular yodeling. He was named "National Champion Yodeler" seven times.

During the 1930's and 1940's, they were featured on *Slack's Big Old Fashioned Barn Dance* and *Slack's Ozark Varieties*, on KMOX, drawing over 90% of the station's fan mail. Both programs were sponsored by Uncle Dick Slack. For live dates, Skeets was backed by the National Champion Hillbillies. Skeets was noted for his wardrobe of Western costumes, which were specially designed and tailored. Skeets recorded for MGM and Town & Country and among the sides released were *I'm Not Alone*, *Just Lonesome*, *You Count All My Mistakes*, *Another World Ago*, *Feeling Sorry*, *Forever and Always*, *Candy Coated Lies*, *Train Track Shuffle*, *Don't Tell a Lie*, *Time and Time Again* and *Who's Taking Over*. Once the heyday of live radio ended, Skeets moved as a deejay to station WEW (later KSTL-690), St. Louis. He was also named by WSM Nashville, in 1964, as a finalist for the title "Mr. Opry D.J.," having appeared on the *Grand Ole Opry* on several occasions. In 1966, Skeets appeared in the movie *Country Music on Broadway*. In 1972 and 1973, he was named "Mr. Deejay U.S.A." In the late 70's, Skeets retired to St. Louis.

WKM

FRANK YANKOVIC

(Piano Accordion, Composer, Songwriter, Singer)

Given Name:	**Frank John Yankovic**
Date of Birth:	**July 28, 1915**
Where Born:	**Davis, West Virginia**
Married:	**1. June (div.)**
	2. Pat (div.)
	3. Ida
Children:	**1. Linda, Frankie, Jr., Richard, Andrea, Gerald, Mark, John, Robert**
	2. Teresa, Tricia

Frank Yankovic, dubbed "America's Polka King," has been unique in making the polka more than just an ethnic form of music. He has made it acceptable to Country music buyers, in a way that only Cajun music has

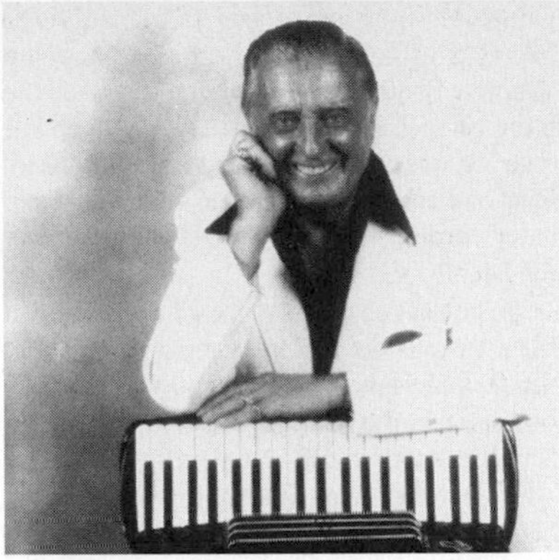

Frank Yankovic, the Polka King

achieved. It was in the wake of WWII that G.I.s returning from Europe discovered the dance music of Slovenia and on their return to the U.S., elevated Frank to stardom, outside of his own immigrant community.

Born of Slovenian parents and raised in Cleveland, Frank was taught to play the button-box accordion by a family boarder, Max Zelodec. By the time he was age 15, Frank had mastered the instrument. He wanted to learn the piano accordion, but found some opposition from his father, Andy. However, his mother, Rose, bought him one for $500, out of her savings and as a result, Frank learned the instrument in secret. When he had mastered it, his father became enthusiastic.

Frank performed professionally at age 16 and soon he was recording with his band on his own Yankee label, using various names, including, in 1932, Slovene Folk Orchestra. He translated the Folk songs he had learned into English. He very quickly made this blend of the old and the new into a popular music style. However, he always played at least one polka using his native language.

On December 6, 1941, a day before the bombing of Pearl Harbor, Frank opened the Yankovic Bar in Cleveland. However, soon he was participating in the hostilities, when he joined the U.S. Army. Some three years later, he nearly lost his hands from the freezing conditions during the Battle of the Bulge. However, his strength of mind meant that he didn't have to undergo an operation.

Frank (or as he was billed, Frankie) and His Yanks signed with Columbia Records, in 1946, and remained with them for some twenty-seven years. In 1948, he had a million-seller with *Just Because*, which reached the Top 10 on the Country and Pop charts and featured the vocals of Johnny Pecon. The following year, *Iron Range* reached the Top 15 on the Country charts, and was followed by another million-seller, *Blue Skirt Waltz*. The single, featuring the Marlin Sisters, got to the Country Top 10 and Top 15 on the Pop chart.

He continued releasing singles for Columbia through to the late 60's and became an institution within the entertainment industry. He then went on to cut an album for Dyno, before signing with RCA Victor. At that label, he released five albums, three of which were produced by Danny Davis. In 1969, Frank was charter inductee into the International Polka Hall of Fame.

During 1970, Frank and Bob Dolgon wrote the book *The Polka King*, a biography (so far) of Yankovic. He left RCA during the 70's and cut an album for Helidon, which was only available in Europe. From there, he went on to Western World Music. During 1983, Frank was temporarily side-tracked by a long hospital stay, but the following year, he signed with Cleveland International and released ***I Wish I Was 18 Again***, which was produced by Joey Miskulin, his friend, associate and co-writer of some 25 years, who has now become one of the leading lights behind the Warner Western label.

In 1985, Frank became the first recipient of a Polka Grammy for his album ***70 Years of Hits***. The following year, he signed with Smash Records and released ***America's Favorites***, which contained previously unreleased recordings. One of his finest albums, entitled ***Frank Yankovic—Live in Nashville***, was issued in 1987, and was produced by Jack Clement and Joey Miskulin. Among the "drunken louts" vocalizing on the classic polka song *Who Stole the Keeshka* were Marty Stuart, Sandy Mason and Roger Cook. The album was recorded at the now defunct Music Row venue.

An interesting aside on Frank is the fact that whenever he plays a town, he never stays in a hotel; fans always insist that he be made welcome in one of their homes. Frank is still active in the 90's and shows no sign of slowing down. In 1994, PBS aired a documentary on "America's Polka King."

RECOMMENDED ALBUMS:

"All-Stars of Polkaland U.S.A." (King)(1963) [Re-released 1976] [Features Frank Yankovic]

All feature Joey Miskulin:

"70 Years of Hits" (Cleveland International)(1985) [Re-released on Smash]

"I Wish I Was 18 Again" (Cleveland International)(1986) [Re-released on Smash]

"Frank Yankovic—Live in Nashville" (Smash)(1987)

RUAL YARBROUGH

(Banjo)
Given Name: **Rual Yarbrough**
Date of Birth: **January 13, 1930**
Where Born: **Lawrence County, Tennessee**
Married: **Unknown**
Children: **Unknown but includes a stepdaughter, Julie**

Rual Yarbrough has established himself as one of the Deep South's finer banjo pickers.

Born and reared in Lawrenceburg, Tennessee, Rual Yarbrough listened to the *Grand Ole Opry* in his formative years, but didn't realistically imagine that he might play there some day. He fooled around with different instruments, but never made much headway with mastering any of them until 1956. In that year, he opened a barber shop in Muscle Shoals, Alabama, and also took up the banjo seriously. Shortly afterward, Rual, Herschel Sizemore and Jake Landers formed the Country Gentlemen, but soon changed that to Dixie Gentlemen when they learned that a group in Washington, D.C., already had that name.

This band remained together for a decade recording four albums, including one on the United Artists label and a fifth as a backup for Tommy Jackson on Dot. Rual closed his barbershop in 1966 about the time that he and Herschel went to work for Jimmy Martin as sidemen. Rual also worked for a time with Bobby Smith and the Boys from Shiloh. He then joined Bill Monroe's Blue Grass Boys and played in his band for a couple of years from 1969, when Bluegrass festivals first began to boom.

When Yarbrough left Monroe's employ, he got back with Jake Landers in a band called the Dixiemen. He kept this unit together for several years although except for himself and Jake, the personnel shifted often. James Bryan, who later became a top fiddler in Nashville, gained his first notice as a Dixieman while James Smith, John Montgomery and the Whitten Brothers all served stints with the band. The Dixiemen cut five albums all together, released on Tune and Old Homestead. Rual had earlier done a banjo album on Tune and recorded two more for Old Homestead in the later 70's.

Rual Yarbrough** and his Dixiemen with **Jake Landers

When not on the road, the genial Alabaman ran a music store and instrument repair shop. Since some noted non-Bluegrass musicians occasionally did recording sessions in Muscle Shoals, Rual could usually be available whenever they needed a banjo picker and he helped vocalists as diverse as Mac Davis and Hank Williams, Jr., at one time or another.

Rual became less active musically in the 80's. He did a Gospel album with his stepdaughter, Julie Donahue York, for Old Homestead and continued to operate Rual's Music Service. Rual reports in May 1994 that he is still operating his instruments repair, but is trying to retire. He has also done some Gospel music which has been released on cassettes. Otherwise his most recent recording studio visit came with a 1992 Dixie Gentlemen reunion session of old stalwarts from a generation earlier—Jake Landers, Herschel Sizemore, and Vassar Clements. IMT

RECOMMENDED ALBUMS:

"5 String Banjo by Rual Yarbrough" (Tune)(1969) [Re-released as "Blue Grass from Dixieland" on Old Homestead in 1978)]
"Just Me" (Old Homestead)(1976)
"Banjo Gentleman" (Old Homestead)(1980)
Rual Yarbrough & the Dixiemen:
"The Dixiemen Sing Gospel" (Tune)(1971) [Re-released as "The Greatest Day of My Life" (Old Homestead)(1973)]
"Secret of the Waterfall" (Old Homestead)(1972)
"Rual Yarbrough & the Dixiemen Featuring James Bryan on Fiddle" (Old Homestead)(1972)
"California Cotton Fields" (Old Homestead)(1973)
"Rual Yarbrough & the Dixiemen" (Old Homestead)(1974)
Rual Yarbrough & Julie York:
"Old Time Revival" (Old Homestead)(1982)
(See also Dixie Gentlemen, the)

TRISHA YEARWOOD

(Singer, Songwriter, Guitar)
Given Name: **Patricia Lynn Yearwood**
Date of Birth: **September 19, 1964**
Where Born: **Monticello, Georgia**
Married: **1. Chris (div. 1991)**
2. Robert Reynolds (m. 1994)

With one single, *She's in Love with the Boy*, Trisha Yearwood leapt from relative obscurity to No.1 on the charts and stardom. However, because she has genuine talent, she has stayed at the top, without losing her "girl next door" appeal.

Trisha was born the younger daughter of a banker father (Vice President of the Bank of Monticello) and a schoolteacher mother (teaches third grade at Piedmont Academy). Around the time Trisha was a 6-year-old, her family moved to a 30-acre farm, where the budding tomboy could have fun, often ending up at the hospital receiving stitches. Having set her sights on a music career (she had a crush on Elvis Presley), she began playing guitar at age 14. She became "Trisha" while in high school and in 1985, progressed to Nashville's Belmont College (now University) to study music business.

***Trisha Yearwood** with her sights on superstardom*

As with many students at Belmont, she landed an internship on Music Row; in her case with the now defunct MTM Records. In addition, she became in demand as a demo singer, which after graduation became her trade. As a result she sang on fellow demo singer Garth Brooks' 1990 album ***No Fences*** and Kathy Mattea's 1991 album ***Time Passes By***.

In 1987, Trisha married Chris, a fellow classmate at Belmont, and graduated with a degree in music business. During 1989, she worked with the Gatlin Brothers Music Resources, writing and cutting demos to shop around, produced by Randy Hauser and Michael G. Smith, and playing with a small back-up unit. Then her career came under the guidance of Garth Brooks' management, Doyle-Lewis. In 1990, she did a showcase in Nashville and as a result, Buzz Stone at MCA signed her to the label and veteran producer Garth Fundis (who had worked with Don Williams) was assigned to her.

Garth Brooks had promised Trisha that if

he got his own career going he would help her, and he kept to his word. That year, Trisha opened for him on his 1991 tour and she began by playing to 6,000 people at the Universal Amphitheatre in Los Angeles. After *She's in Love with the Boy* had climbed to the top (the first time a debut single by a female Country artist had achieved this), she released her first, eponymous album and proved that the public and the radio programmers were in agreement. It climbed to the Top 3 on the Country Album chart and was Certified Gold just three months after release and by March 1992, it had gone Platinum. Trisha followed up her debut single with back-to-back Top 10 releases, *Like We Never Had a Broken Heart*, a Top 5 achiever co-written by Garth, and *That's What I Like About You*.

In 1992, Trisha continued her success with the Top 5 singles *The Woman Before Me* and *Wrong Side of Memphis*. She followed with her second album ***Hearts in Armor***, which went Gold two months after release and Platinum in 1993. She closed out 1992 with *Walkaway Joe*, a duet with former Eagle Don Henley, which went Top 3.

1993 was even more of a landmark year for Trisha with the release of Lisa Gubernick's biography, *Get Hot or Go Home*, and a TV ad campaign for a Trisha Yearwood perfume for Revlon. Her third album, ***The Song Remembers When***, went Gold two months after release, and Disney filmed a one-hour special of the same name at the Tennessee Performing Arts Center. This concert was later released as a home video. During the year she appeared as herself in the Peter Bogdanovich movie *The Thing Called Love*. Trisha's 1993 chart singles were *You Say You Will* and *Down on My Knees*, both Top 20, and in 1994 she reached the Top 10 with *The Song Remembers When*, which also crossed over to the Pop Top 90. Trisha married Robert Reynolds, the bass guitarist of the Mavericks, at the Ryman Auditorium, Nashville, in 1994.

RECOMMENDED ALBUMS:

"Trisha Yearwood" (MCA)(1991)
"Hearts in Armor" (MCA)(1992)
"The Song Remembers When" (MCA)(1993)

DWIGHT YOAKAM

(Singer, Songwriter, Guitar, Actor)
Date of Birth: October 23, 1956
Where Born: Pikeville, Kentucky

The uniqueness of Dwight Yoakam lies in the fact that ostensibly he plays straight-ahead Honky-Tonk songs. However, wrapped up in a persona that is part Country and part Rock and an instrumentation that is the same, Dwight has managed to make himself attractive to both Country fans and rockers.

The heir to Bakersfield, ***Dwight Yoakam***

Born in a coal mining area of Kentucky, Dwight was raised in Columbus, Ohio, and grew up listening to Johnny Horton, Elvis Presley, Hank Williams and Johnny Cash's early material. He knew from an early age that he wanted to be a musician and had started to write Country songs from age 8. In high school, he had a Rockabilly band, but he soon returned to Country.

After graduation in 1974, he tried his luck in Nashville without success. By 1977, he decided to try Los Angeles, where Emmylou Harris was a major inspiration. Playing in the San Fernando Valley, Dwight soon found he had an audience in the honky tonks among the heirs of the Oklahoma and Texas Dust Bowl transplants. By 1982, he found favor on the "cow punk" scene, which has given birth to several Country-Hard Rock acts. However, this didn't help his aspirations of signing a record deal, because the West Coast record company executives felt that Country acts got signed by Nashville and Nashville felt he was "too Rock."

In 1984, Pete Anderson, who is now his producer, but at the time was Dwight's lead guitarist, produced an EP, ***A Town South of Bakersfield***, that was released on Oak Records, an independent label. This eventually led to Dwight being signed to Warner Brothers' sister label, Reprise. He debuted with his critically acclaimed 1986 album ***Guitars, Cadillacs, Etc. Etc.***, which went Gold in 1987 and Platinum in 1989. He released his version of the Johnny Horton 1956 hit *Honky Tonk Man*, which reached the Top 3, staying on the Country charts for nearly six months. The powers that be at Reprise felt that the word "hillbilly" in the song should be removed, as it was derogatory, but Dwight refused and was proven right. The single reached the Top 5; however, his final single of the year, *It Won't Hurt*, fell just short of the Top 30. That year, the ACM named Dwight "New Male Vocalist of the Year."

In 1987, he released *Little Sister*, which had been a hit for Elvis in 1961 and came from Dwight's second album ***Hillbilly Deluxe*** (which went Gold that year). This went Top 10 as did both the follow-up, *Little Ways*, and the final single of the year, *Please, Please Baby*. In 1988, he opened his account with *Always Late with Your Kisses*, which had been a big No.1 for Lefty Frizzell in 1951. Dwight had a Top 10 hit with it and followed up with his first No.1, *Streets of Bakersfield*. He was joined on this single by his idol and mentor, Buck Owens, and the track could be found on Dwight's third album ***Buenas Noches from a Lonely Room***, which went Gold the following year. The album, which also featured the duet with Maria McKee *Send Me the Pillow*, was indicative of the balance between his own well-crafted material and his versions of established songs that marks Dwight's repertoire. He ended the year with another No.1, *I Sang Dixie*.

He opened his 1989 account with the Top 5 hit *I Got You* and then his singles dropped from favor with the radio stations, with *Buenas Noches from a Lonely Room (She Wore Red Dresses)* only reaching the Top 50 and *Long White Cadillac* going Top 40. However, the public responded and his "greatest hits" package, ***Just Lookin' for a Hit,*** reached the Top 3 on the Country Album chart and Top 70 on the Pop Album chart and went Gold in 1991. *Music City News* voted Dwight and Buck its "Vocal Collaboration of the Year."

He still didn't return to radio favor in 1990 when his only single hit of the year, *Turn It On, Turn It Up, Turn Me Loose*, peaked in the Top 15; however, the public still responded well and Dwight's album ***If There Was a Way*** went Top 10. It went Gold that year and Platinum in 1993. This album marked the first time that Dwight had recorded new songs by outside writers. Then just as suddenly as he was out of favor with radio, so he was back in and in 1991, his opening single, *You're the One*, went Top 5. Both the other singles of the year, *Nothing's Changed Here* and *It Only Hurts When I Cry* (the first time that either

Dwight or songwriting legend Roger Miller had ever co-written), just failed to make the Top 10.

Dwight had mixed success in 1992, with *The Heart That You Own* going Top 20, but his duet single with Patty Loveless, *Send a Message to My Heart*, only reached the Top 50. He closed out the year with the Top 40 *Suspicious Minds*, which was featured in the movie *Honeymoon in Vegas* and had been a major success for both Elvis in 1969 and Waylon Jennings & Jessi Colter in 1976. To make matters worse, his album ***La Croix D'Amour***, failed to make the charts. That year, he made his movie debut in *Red Rock West* with Dennis Hopper and Nicholas Cage.

In 1993, Dwight released his ***This Time*** album and again this marked a development of the Yoakam skills; for the first time he was actively co-writing, this time with another songwriting giant, Kostas. It was without doubt his best album to date and it reached the Top 5 of the Country Album chart. The exquisite track *Try Not to Look So Pretty* is so Country, that at times the listener may think that he's playing a Merle Haggard track, while *Wild Ride* is straight out of the Rolling Stones/ZZ Top top drawer. The public responded and two months after release, it was Certified Gold and five months later, it went Platinum. All three of his singles in 1993, *Ain't That Lonely Yet*, *A Thousand Miles from Nowhere* and *Fast as You*, went Top 3, with *Ain't That Lonely Yet* and *Fast as You* crossing over to the Pop chart. In 1994, *Try Not to Look So Pretty* reached the Top 20.

Dwight has been accused of being arrogant, but the truth is that he hasn't hesitated in speaking his mind to people who would make a saint curse. At one time, the media seemed to be more preoccupied with Dwight's ripped-at-the-knees denims than his music and more engrossed in his love life than in the finely crafted songs that he has recorded. Based in California, Dwight refuses to relocate to Nashville.

RECOMMENDED ALBUMS:

"Guitars, Cadillacs, Etc., Etc." (Reprise)(1986)
"Hillbilly Deluxe" (Reprise)(1987)
"Buenas Noches from a Lonely Room" (Reprise)(1988)
"Just Lookin' for a Hit" (Reprise)(1989)
"If There Was a Way" (Reprise)(1990)
"La Croix D'Amour" (Reprise)(1991)
"This Time" (Reprise)(1993)

YORK BROTHERS, The

GEORGE YORK
(Vocals, Songwriter, Guitar, Harmonica)
Date of Birth: February 17, 1910
Married: Roberta
Children: Alan
Date of Death: July 1974

LESLIE YORK
(Vocals, Guitar)
Date of Birth: August 23, 1917
Married: Hannah
Children: two daughters
Date of Death: February 21, 1984

Both Born: Louisa, Kentucky

The York Brothers moved from a traditional harmony duet toward a more contemporary type of Country music during their twenty-plus years in the business.

They hailed from Lawrence County, Kentucky, the same area that would spawn recent Bluegrass-Country great Ricky Skaggs. As they grew to adulthood, their music showed a considerable Delmore Brothers influence. George, the elder brother, went southward into the coal country, where he labored in the mines at Benham, Jenkins, and Wheelwright. Later, he moved west and lived in Denver for a time, where he played music in night clubs and over local radio.

In the meantime, Leslie won a talent contest in Lexington. At that point the brothers teamed up at WPAY radio in Portsmouth, Ohio. Soon, however, they caught a larger, more concentrated audience in the city of Detroit, where many rural folk had already found work in the auto factories. Their first recording in 1939, on the local Universal label, featured the nostalgic *Going Home* (usually known as *The Little White Washed Chimney*) backed with a "red hot" female lyric, *Hamtramck Mama*. The latter attracted a wide local audience, allegedly sold some 300,000 copies, and was said to have been banned in Hamtramck, Michigan (whether because of its being offensive to the natives, nearly all Polish-Americans, or its mildly risqué content, cannot be determined).

At any rate, it helped George and Leslie land a Decca contract, where they cut six numbers on February 26, 1941, most notably a "dead lover" song, *Speak to Me Little Darling*. Then WWII interrupted their careers and both brothers served long stints in the U.S. Navy. This break undoubtedly hurt them career-wise, for they were just beginning to hit their stride.

After the war, George and Leslie York went to WSM Nashville and joined the *Grand Ole Opry*. In 1947, they began recording for King, a label with which they retained an affiliation for nearly a decade. One of their earliest cuts for Syd Nathan's company was a topical anti-isolationist effort titled *Let's Not Sleep Again*, while another, *Mountain Rosa Lee*, looked at the images of women in Country songs. Most of their recordings, however, took on a modern flavor and could be described as somewhat ahead of their time with piano accompaniment and sounds influenced by the Rhythm and Blues music being produced by King's black artists. *Tennessee Tango* and the original *River of Tears* were among the more memorable of their later King sides.

From Kentucky, the ***York Brothers***

In 1950, the York Brothers left the *Opry* and went back to Detroit. Three years later they traveled to Dallas and stayed, working on local TV at the *Big D Jamboree* over KRLD and at WFAA's *Saturday Nite Shindig*. They remained with King through 1956, but turned out later efforts on their own York label. According to nephew George E. York, Leslie told him that from just before the brothers left Nashville, George began experiencing periodic problems with his voice, which accounted for some of their later King efforts being solos by Leslie. At any rate, both brothers continued to sing, but George did cut back some on his vocals.

George, in later years, owned a night club in Dallas and Leslie worked at various jobs. King released three albums of York recordings while Old Homestead reissued an album of singles from the later years, which showed that they retained a few older songs in their repertoire along with newer numbers and originals. IMT

RECOMMENDED ALBUMS:

"The York Brothers, Vol. 1" (King)(1958)
"The York Brothers, Vol. 2" (King)(1958)
"16 Great Country Songs" (King)(1963)
"Early Favorites" (Old Homestead)(1987)

RUSTY YORK

(Guitar, Banjo, Dobro, Harmonica, Bass)
Given Name: Charles Edward York
Date of Birth: May 24, 1935
Where Born: Harlan County, Kentucky
Married: Linda Jean
Children: Charles A., Virginia, Elizabeth, John

Rusty York holds a unique distinction of being a minor legend in both Rockabilly and Bluegrass. As a young Appalachian migrant to Cincinnati, Rusty became an early convert to the Scruggs banjo and then went on to play Rockabilly.

Born in rugged Harlan County, Kentucky, young Charles York grew up with the usual Appalachian musical influences, but became especially enamored with the banjo picking of Earl Scruggs when he saw the Foggy Mountain Boys in person about 1951. He soon converted an old tenor banjo to a 5-string and by the time he moved to Cincinnati after turning 17, he had obtained a regular banjo. He met another Kentucky mountain boy named Willard Hale and they teamed up for club work in the area and worked with established artists such as Jimmie Skinner and from 1954, Hylo Brown. Rusty and Willard soon recorded some material for Starday, which found its way onto the Mercury label—*Don't Do It* and the instrumentals *Dixie Strut* and *Banjo Breakdown.*

Meanwhile the Presley phenomenon had hit and York and Hale began modernizing, for as Rusty told Country music historian Neil Rosenberg, "Even country boys started liking Elvis." Late in 1957, they did a cover of *Peggy Sue* for King and label boss Syd Nathan teamed Rusty with popular *Midwestern Hayride* cowgirl Bonnie Lou on a Rockabilly session where they recorded such numbers as *Lah De Dah* and *Let the School Bell Ring Ding a Ling.* However, Rusty's best Rockabilly numbers were *Red Rooster* and *Sugaree*, the latter originally appearing on P.J. and Note in 1959, before being picked up that year by Chess and reaching the Top 80 on the Pop chart. It got the Kentucky-born youngster an appearance on *American Bandstand* and on August 30, 1959, the honor of being the first Rockabilly artist to appear at the Hollywood Bowl. Lacking a follow-up, however, York soon found himself back in his old haunts.

In the 60's, Rusty returned to Bluegrass and mainstream Country. In 1960, he cut a six-song EP, which was marketed by Jimmie Skinner and WCKY radio, credited to Rusty York and the Kentucky Mountain Boys. He also had Country singles on such labels as Monument and Capitol. For a time Rusty toured with Bobby Bare. Rusty shared a Bluegrass-Gospel album with his friend J.D. Jarvis on Uncle Jim O'Neal's Rural Rhythm Records. As a sideman with Jimmie Skinner, he played steel guitar on a memorable Jimmie Rodgers tribute album released on Mercury in 1962.

Increasingly, however, York's musical interests turned toward the business side of the industry. As early as 1961, he began developing a studio in his garage which eventually grew into Jewel Records. Over the years a number of significant artists such as J.D. Jarvis, Esco Hankins, Claude Ely, and Jimmie Logsdon cut sessions for Jewel as well as local Rockabillies like Ronnie Whetstone. Rusty pretty well gave up performing after 1971 although he did a Bluegrass banjo album for Q.C.A. in 1973 (with Lonnie Mack on guitar) and a Country single for Starday-King, *This Could Go on Forever.* As of 1994, he remains at the helm of Jewel Records on Kinney Avenue in Cincinnati and as a quick conversation reveals, Rusty York is a virtual gold mine of information on the forty years of Country music in the Queen City through which he has lived. IMT

RECOMMENDED ALBUMS:

"Rusty York and the Kentucky Mountain Boys" (Blue Grass Special)(1960) [Six-song EP]
"Bluegrass Gospel Songs" (Rural Rhythm)(1968) [Half of album credited to J.D. Jarvis]
"Dueling Banjos" (Q.C.A.)(1973)

FARON YOUNG

(Singer, Songwriter, Guitar, Actor)
Date of Birth: February 25, 1932
Where Born: Shreveport, Louisiana
Married: Hilda Margo Macon (div.)
Children: Damion Ray, Robin Farrell, Kevin Robert, Alana

To experience Faron Young at his very best, don't just listen to his records, go and see him on stage. His is still one of the consummate showmen. In 1993, he was in the audience at the Annual Fish Fry at Gabe's club in Nashville, when he was (easily) persuaded to come on stage to sing. Within minutes, he had the audience in the palm of his hand. In a "you had to be there" moment, singer Jimmy Snyder came on stage doing his famed impersonation of Faron and the two sang together *Sweet Dreams.*

Faron was raised on a farm outside Shreveport where he spent his early days playing guitar while tending the cattle. He formed his first band while still at school and played local hoedowns. While attending the local Centenary College, Faron was invited in 1951 to join the *Louisiana Hayride* out of Shreveport. There he worked with Webb Pierce as a featured vocalist. Faron first recorded with Tillman Franks & His Rainbow Boys, the following year, for Gotham.

In 1952, Faron became a solo performer and signed with Capitol Records, where he was produced by Ken Nelson. That same year, Faron was sent for by Uncle Sam and as part of the Entertainments Unit, he sang to the troops in Korea. During his time in the service, 1952-1954, Capitol started to get Faron's recording career under way. Faron's name first appeared on the chart in 1953 when the self-penned *Goin' Steady* reached the Top 3. This was followed by the Top 5 release *I Can't Wait (For the Sun to Go Down).* In 1954, he went Top 10 with *A Place for Girls Like You*, then he charted with Tommy Collins' infectious *If You Ain't Lovin'*, which went Top 3.

On his release from the service, Faron's career took off like a rocket. His first hit of 1955 was also his first No.1, *Live Fast, Love Hard, Die Young/Forgive Me Dear.* The top side is still just about the most danceable Honky-Tonk song around. When the follow-up was released, it was initially the "A" side, *Go Back You Fool*, that found favor and then the flip-side, *All Right*, took over and went Top 3. Faron completed the year with the Top 5 *It's a Great Life (If You Don't Weaken).* That year, Faron made his movie debut in the Republic Western *Hidden Guns.* From this movie Faron got his nickname, "The Young Sheriff," and his backing band became "His Country Deputies."

Faron got 1956 under way with the double-sided Top 5 smash *I've Got Five Dollars and It's Saturday Night/You're Still Mine.* This was followed by Faron's version of Don Gibson's *Sweet Dreams*, which went Top 3 and stayed on the charts for over 8 months. Faron closed out the year with *Turn Her Down*, which went Top 10. That year, Faron appeared in two Republic movies, *Daniel Boone* and *Raiders of Old California.* With the advent of the rock'n'roll era, Faron, like many Country singers, suffered but not as much as some. He started off 1957 with *I Miss You Already (and You're Not Even Gone)*, a song written by Faron and Marvin Rainwater, which went Top 5. His next two releases, *The Shrine of St. Cecilia* and *Love Has Finally Come My Way*, just made the Top 15, but the former did cross-over to the Pop Top 100.

Then in the summer of 1958, Faron went to No.1 with *Alone with You.* The song, written by Roy Drusky and Lester Vanadore, stayed at the top for 13 weeks and crossed to the Pop Top 60. The flip-side, *Every Time I'm Kissing*

Faron Young, the supreme entertainer

You, also went Top 10. Faron closed the year with *That's the Way I Feel* (Top 10)/*I Hate Myself* (Top 25). During the year, Faron appeared in the movie *Country Music Holiday* along with Ferlin Husky and June Carter. The final year of the decade was good in parts. It started with the double-sided Top 20 releases *Last Night at a Party/A Long Time Ago* and then the Top 15 *That's the Way It's Gotta Be*. He then resurfaced with the No.1 *Country Girl*, written by Roy Drusky. It stayed at the top for 4 weeks out of nearly 8 months on the chart and the flip, *I Hear You Talkin'*, also went Top 30. Faron wrapped up the year with *Riverboat* (Top 5)/*Face to the Wall* (Top 10), with the former crossing to the Pop Top 90.

Faron started out the new decade with the Top 5 *Your Old Used to Be* and then his next two releases, *There's Not Any Like You Left* and *Forget the Past/A World So Full of Love*, only peaked in the 20s. In the spring of 1961, Faron released a single with both sides written by "new boy" Willie Nelson, *Hello Walls* and *Congratulations*. The former went to No.1 for 9 weeks and made the Pop Top 15, while the flip went Top 30. Faron's delivery on these sides is remarkably like Willie's. Faron finished the year with *Backtrack*, which went Top 10 and crossed to the Pop Top 90. 1962 was Faron's last year with Capitol and his hits were *Three Days*, written by Faron and Willie (Top 10), *The Comeback* (Top 5) and *Down by the River* (Top 10).

In 1963, Faron moved to Mercury and his time at this label can be divided into two definable sections, 1963-1969 and 1969-1978, with the second section being easily the more successful. His major hits in the first period were: 1963: *The Yellow Bandana* (Top 5), *Nightmare* (Top 15), *We've Got Something in Common* (Top 15) and *You'll Drive Me Back (Into Her Arms Again)* (Top 10); 1964: *Keeping up with the Joneses* (with Margie Singleton, Top 5), *Rhinestones* (Top 25) and *My Friend on the Right* (Top 15); 1965: *Walk Tall* (Top 10) and *My Dreams* (Top 15); 1966: *Unmitigated Gall* (Top 10); 1967: *Wonderful World of Women* (Top 15); 1968: *She Went a Little Bit Farther* (Top 15), *I Just Came to Get My Baby* (Top 10); 1969: *I've Got Precious Memories* (Top 25). In 1966, Faron appeared in the movie *Nashville Rebel* alongside Waylon Jennings and in 1967 in the Leroy Van Dyke movie *What Am I Bid?* and *Road to Nashville* with Marty Robbins and Connie Smith.

After six years of getting less than satisfactory chart placings on excellent material, Faron just as suddenly found himself in a golden period. It started with *Wine Me Up*, a song written by Faron and his manager, the legendary Billy Deaton (the song would be reprised two decades later by Larry Boone and become a Top 20 hit). Faron followed with the Top 5 *Your Time's Comin'* and then in 1970, all his releases were major successes; *Occasional Wife* (Top 10), Tom T. Hall's *If I Ever Fall in Love (With a Honky Tonk Girl)* (Top 5) and a re-recording of his first hit *Goin' Steady*, which this time around went Top 5. That year, Faron's career nearly came to an end when a head-on collision in his car nearly ripped out his tongue and after four operations, left him with a lisp on "s" words.

He started 1971 with two Top 10 singles, *Step Aside* and *Leavin' and Sayin' Goodbye* and then had another career single, Jerry Chesnut's *It's Four in the Morning*, which went to No.1. During the remainder of Faron's time at Mercury, his major successes were: 1972: *This Little Girl of Mine* (Top 5); 1973: *She Fights That Lovin' Feeling* (Top 15) and *Just What I Had in Mind* (Top 10); 1974: *Some Kind of Woman* (Top 10), *The Wrong in Loving You* (Top 20) and *Another You* (Top 25); 1975: *Here I Am in Dallas* (Top 20) and *Feel Again* (Top 25); 1977: *Crutches* (Top 25). In 1976, Faron received the "Founders Award" from *Music City News*.

In 1979, Faron signed with MCA but his two-year stint with the label failed to ignite his recording career and the most successful single was *(If I'd Only Known) It Was the Last Time*, which went Top 60. During 1982 through 1987, Faron's name was missing from the chart and then in 1988 he had two basement entries through his new affiliation with Step One Records. He had his final chart record, *Here's to You*, in 1989.

Over the years, Faron has built a healthy portfolio of investments in Nashville including the Young Executive Building on Division Street, which now houses Billy Deaton's offices and those of Step One Records. He was also the owner and publisher of *Music City News* and owned a booking agency, book publishing and music publishing concerns.

Faron has a great reputation for helping new talent, who have included Roger Miller, whom he engaged while Roger was still a bellhop at the Andrew Jackson Hotel. Faron needed a drummer and took on Roger even though he'd never played drums before. In any event, Roger stayed with the Country Deputies for two years.

"The King of Country Music Fairs," as he was known, is definitely a "man's man" and more than one female singer has bemoaned his earthiness while on tour. However, as he has gotten older, on the occasions that he is "in his cups," he is affability itself. More importantly, with a song range from Honky-Tonk to Pop croonin', instead of becoming a Pop star, Faron has shown that he cares about Country music and whether on the *Grand Ole Opry*, where he has been a member since 1952, or on live dates, he gives to his audience 150%. When he walks up to you and puts his arm around your shoulders, he makes you believe that you are the only fan that matters.

RECOMMENDED ALBUMS:

"The Young Sheriff (1955-1958 Radio Broadcasts)" (Castle)
"Sweethearts or Strangers" (Capitol)(1957) [Re-released by Stetson UK in the original sleeve (1987)]
"Talk About Hits" (Capitol)(1959) [Re-released by Stetson UK in the original sleeve (1987)]
"Faron Young Sings the Best of Faron Young" (Capitol)(1960)
"Faron Young's Greatest Hits" (Mercury)(1965)
"Faron Young's Greatest Hits, Vol.2" (Mercury)(1968)
"The Best of Faron Young" (Mercury)(1970)
"The Best of Faron Young, Vol.2" (Mercury)(1977)
"That Young Feelin'" (Mercury)(1977)
"Chapter Two" (MCA)(1979)
"The Sheriff" (Allegiance)(1984)
"Greatest Hits, Vol. I, II & III" (double-cd)(Step One)(1989)
"Memories That Last" (Step One)(1991) [With Ray Price]

JESS YOUNG

(Fiddle, Guitar)
Given Name: **Jess Young**
Date of Birth: **October 23, 1883**
Where Born: **Flat Rock, Alabama**
Date of Death: **December 31, 1938**

Jess Young was one of the best-known fiddlers from Tennessee, a fixture at regional fiddling contests and a popular recording artist for both Columbia and Gennett. He was an important conduit for moving the Folk music of the Sequatchie Valley and Chattanooga area into the world of commercial Country music of the 1920's. He knew and worked with a number of black string band players in the area and codified a number of fiddle tunes that are still featured today.

His influence is heard in the work of Curly Fox, Bert Layne, Bob Douglas and others. The banjo player in his band, Homer Davenport, was one of the pioneers of the three-finger style later popularized by Earl Scruggs. At times, Young himself defeated, in contests, some of the biggest names in southern fiddling, including Gid Tanner, Clayton McMichen and A.A. Gray.

Though he was born in Alabama, Young's family moved north in 1897 to the mining town of Whitewell, Tennessee, a few miles north of Chattanooga. Jess was to work in the mines off and on for the next twenty years, until black lung cut short his career. This became bad enough that by 1920, he decided to give up mining and try to make a living with his fiddle. His family had been musical and he had learned the fiddle as a boy.

Now he organized a band, using his nephew, Alvin, who was a guitarist (and admirer of Riley Puckett) and Homer Davenport, a banjo player from nearby Pikeville. It was this trio that journeyed to the Gennett studios at Richmond, Indiana, on April 22, 1925. The ten sides they cut are probably the earliest records of a regular working southern string band. Among the hits from the session was *Maybelle Rag*, learned from a black riverboat guitarist, and *Smoke Behind the Clouds*, a local dance tune. Some of Young's best tunes, such as *Sequatchie Valley* and *Young's Hornpipe*, were released on "private issue" for Young himself to sell—another first for Country music.

Young continued to perform around Chattanooga in the later 1920's and became the most often recorded of a number of area musicians who made their mark on records during this time. (These included Bob Douglas, the Allen Brothers, the Gibbs Brothers, Claude Davis, Otis Elder, Grover Rann, Bill Jackson and Allen Sissom.) A local furniture dealer got them a session with Columbia and in 1926, they reported to Atlanta to do their first of three sessions. Dan Hornsby, young Columbia A & R assistant for the sessions, felt the records would sell better with vocals and proceeded to add such himself—much to Young's protests. The first session yielded *Bill Bailey* and *Are You from Dixie*, with Hornsby doing the vocals. This record sold over 30,000 copies and brought the band back to the studio. Later favorites included a piece Young called *Fiddle Up*, but which was actually a version of Irving Berlin's *Ragtime Violin*, Young's signature song, *Sweet Bunch of Daisies,* and old 19th-century band favorites like *Lovin' Henry* and *Silver Bell*.

Young's recording career ended in 1929, but he continued to work as the best-known fiddler in Chattanooga. He routinely won the championship fiddle contests held in the area, played for numerous dances and played on a regular radio show over WDOD. In 1937, *Grand Ole Opry* Manager Harry Stone was having trouble with his lead fiddler, Arthur Smith, and sought to replace him with Jess Young—even to the point of mailing him a contract. However, by then Young's health was seriously failing. He made a last trip home to the Valley in late 1938 and died shortly before the new year on December 31, 1938.

CKW

RECOMMENDED ALBUM:

"Ragtime 2: The Country" (Folkways) [Various Artists: One track, Old Weary Blues, credited to Jess Young's Tennessee Band]

ACADEMY OF COUNTRY MUSIC HAT AWARDS

ENTERTAINER

1973	Roy Clark
1974	Mac Davis
1975	Loretta Lynn
1976	Mickey Gilley
1977	Dolly Parton
1978	Kenny Rogers
1979	Willie Nelson
1980	Barbara Mandrell
1981	Alabama
1982	Alabama
1983	Alabama
1984	Alabama
1985	Alabama
1986	Hank Williams, Jr.
1987	Hank Williams, Jr.
1988	Hank Williams, Jr.
1989	George Strait
1990	Garth Brooks
1991	Garth Brooks
1992	Garth Brooks
1993	Garth Brooks

MALE VOCALIST

1965	Buck Owens
1966	Merle Haggard
1967	Glen Campbell
1968	Glen Campbell
1969	Merle Haggard
1970	Merle Haggard
1971	Freddie Hart
1972	Merle Haggard
1973	Charlie Rich
1974	Merle Haggard
1975	Conway Twitty
1976	Mickey Gilley
1977	Kenny Rogers
1978	Kenny Rogers
1979	Larry Gatlin
1980	George Jones
1981	Merle Haggard
1982	Ronnie Milsap
1983	Lee Greenwood
1984	George Strait
1985	George Strait
1986	Randy Travis
1987	Randy Travis
1988	George Strait
1989	Clint Black
1990	Garth Brooks
1991	Garth Brooks
1992	Vince Gill
1993	Vince Gill

FEMALE VOCALIST

1965	Bonnie Owens
1966	Bonnie Guitar
1967	Lynn Anderson
1968	Cathie Taylor
1969	Tammy Wynette
1970	Lynn Anderson
1971	Loretta Lynn
1972	Donna Fargo
1973	Loretta Lynn
1974	Loretta Lynn
1975	Loretta Lynn
1976	Crystal Gayle
1977	Crystal Gayle
1978	Barbara Mandrell
1979	Crystal Gayle
1980	Dolly Parton
1981	Barbara Mandrell
1982	Sylvia
1983	Janie Fricke
1984	Reba McEntire
1985	Reba McEntire
1986	Reba McEntire
1987	Reba McEntire
1988	K.T. Oslin
1989	Kathy Mattea
1990	Reba McEntire
1991	Reba McEntire
1992	Mary-Chapin Carpenter
1993	Wynonna

VOCAL GROUP

1967	Sons of the Pioneers
1969	Kimberleys
1970	Kimberleys
1972	Statler Brothers
1973	Brush Arbor
1974	Loretta Lynn/Conway Twitty
1975	Conway Twitty/Loretta Lynn
1976	Conway Twitty/Loretta Lynn
1977	Statler Brothers
1978	Oak Ridge Boys
1981	Alabama

1982 Alabama
1983 Alabama
1984 Alabama
1985 Alabama
1986 Forester Sisters
1987 Highway 101
1988 Highway 101
1989 Restless Heart
1990 Shenandoah
1991 Diamond Rio
1992 Diamond Rio
1993 Little Texas

VOCAL DUET

1965 Merle Haggard/Bonnie Owens
1966 Merle Haggard/Bonnie Owens
1967 Merle Haggard/Bonnie Owens
1968 Johnny and Jonie Mosby
1969 No Awards
1970 No Awards
1971 Loretta Lynn/Conway Twitty
1972 No Awards
1973 No Awards
1974 Loretta Lynn/Conway Twitty
1975 Loretta Lynn/Conway Twitty
1976 Loretta Lynn/Conway Twitty
1977 No Awards
1978 No Awards
1979 Joe Stampley/Moe Bandy
1980 Moe Bandy/Joe Stampley
1981 Shelly West/David Frizzell
1982 David Frizzell/Shelly West
1983 Dolly Parton/Kenny Rogers
1984 The Judds
1985 The Judds
1986 The Judds
1987 The Judds
1988 The Judds
1989 The Judds
1990 The Judds
1991 Brooks & Dunn
1992 Brooks & Dunn
1993 Brooks & Dunn

NEW MALE VOCALIST (MOST PROMISING)

1965 Merle Haggard
1966 Billy Mize
1967 Jerry Inman
1968 Ray Sanders
1969 Freddy Weller
1970 Buddy Alan
1971 Tony Booth
1972 Johnny Rodriguez
1973 Dorsey Burnette
1974 Mickey Gilley
1975 Freddy Fender
1976 Moe Bandy
1977 Eddie Rabbitt
1978 John Conlee
1979 R.C. Bannon
1980 Johnny Lee
1981 Ricky Skaggs
1982 Michael Martin Murphey
1983 Jim Glaser
1984 Vince Gill
1985 Randy Travis
1986 Dwight Yoakam
1987 Ricky Van Shelton
1988 Rodney Crowell
1989 Clint Black
1990 Alan Jackson
1991 Billy Dean
1992 Tracy Lawrence
1993 John Michael Montgomery

NEW FEMALE VOCALIST (MOST PROMISING)

1965 Kaye Adams
1966 Cathie Taylor
1967 Bobbie Gentry
1968 Cheryl Poole
1969 Donna Fargo
1970 Sammi Smith
1971 Barbara Mandrell
1972 Tanya Tucker
1973 Olivia Newton-John
1974 Linda Ronstadt
1975 Crystal Gayle
1976 Billie Jo Spears
1977 Debby Boone
1978 Christy Lane
1979 Lacy J. Dalton
1980 Terri Gibbs
1981 Juice Newton
1982 Karen Brooks
1983 Gus Hardin
1984 Nicolette Larson
1985 Judy Rodman
1986 Holly Dunn
1987 K.T. Oslin

1988 Suzy Bogguss
1989 Mary-Chapin Carpenter
1990 Shelby Lynne
1991 Trisha Yearwood
1992 Michelle Wright
1993 Faith Hill

NEW VOCAL DUET/GROUP

1966 Fay Hardin/Bob Morris
1966 Bob Morris/Fay Hardin
1989 Kentucky Headhunters
1990 Pirates of the Mississippi
1991 Brooks & Dunn
1992 Confederate Railroad
1993 Gibson/Miller Band

SONG OF THE YEAR

1966 "Apartment #9"
Tammy Wynette
(Songwriter: Bobby Austin)

1967 "It's Such a Pretty World Today"
Wynn Stewart
(Songwriter: Dale Noe)

1968 "Wichita Lineman"
Glen Campbell
(Songwriter: Jimmy Webb)

1969 "Okie From Muskogee"
Merle Haggard
(Songwriters: Merle Haggard, Roy Edward Burris)

1970 "For the Good Times"
Ray Price
(Songwriter: Kris Kristofferson)

1971 "Easy Loving"
Freddie Hart
(Songwriter: Freddie Hart)

1972 "Happiest Girl in the Whole U.S.A."
Donna Fargo
(Songwriter: Donna Fargo

1973 "Behind Closed Doors"
Charlie Rich
(Songwriter: Kenny O'Dell)

1974 "Country Bumpkin"
Cal Smith
(Songwriter: Don Wayne)

1975 "Rhinestone Cowboy"
Glen Campbell
(Songwriter: Larry Weiss)

1976 "Don't the Girls Get Prettier at Closing Time"
Mickey Gilley
(Songwriter: Baker Knight)

1977 "Lucille"
Kenny Rogers
(Songwriters: Roger Bowling, Hal Bynum)

1978 "You Needed Me"
Anne Murray
(Songwriter: Randy Goodrum)

1979 "It's a Cheatin' Situation"
Moe Bandy
(Songwriters: Sonny Throckmorton, Curly Putman)

1980 "He Stopped Loving Her Today"
George Jones
(Songwriters: Bobby Braddock, Curly Putman)

1981 "You're the Reason God Made Oklahoma"
David Frizzell/Shelley West
(Songwriters: Sandy Pinkard, Larry Collins)

1982 "Are the Good Times Really Over"
Merle Haggard
(Songwriter: Merle Haggard)

1983 "The Wind Beneath My Wings"
Gary Morris
(Songwriters: Larry Henley, Jeff Silbar)

1984 "Why Not Me"
The Judds
(Songwriters: Harlan Howard, Sonny Throckmorton, Brent Maher)

1985 "Lost in the Fifties (in the Still of the Night)"
Ronnie Milsap
(Songwriters: Mike Reid, Troy Seals, Fred Parris)

1986 "On the Other Hand"
Randy Travis
(Songwriters: Don Schlitz, Paul Overstreet)

1987 "Forever and Ever Amen"
Randy Travis
(Songwriters: Don Schlitz, Paul Overstreet)

1988 "Eighteen Wheels and a Dozen Roses"
Kathy Mattea
(Songwriters: Paul Nelson, Gene Nelson)

1989 "Where've You Been"
Kathy Mattea
(Songwriters: Jon Vezner, Don Henry)

1990 "The Dance"
Garth Brooks
(Songwriter: Tony Arata)

1991 "Somewhere in My Broken Heart"
Billy Dean
(Songwriters: Billy Dean, Richard Leigh)

1992 "I Still Believe in You"
Vince Gill
(Songwriters: John Jarvis, Vince Gill)

1993 "I Love the Way You Love Me"
John Michael Montgomery
(Songwritérs: Victoria Shaw, Chuck Cannon)

SINGLE RECORD OF THE YEAR

1967 "Gentle on My Mind"
Glen Campbell

1968 "Little Green Apples"
Roger Miller

1969 "Okie From Muskogee"
Merle Haggard

1970 "For the Good Times"
Ray Price

1971 "Easy Loving"
Freddie Hart

1972 "Happiest Girl in the Whole U.S.A"
Donna Fargo

1973 "Behind Closed Doors"
Charlie Rich

1974 "Country Bumpkin"
Cal Smith

1975 "Rhinestone Cowboy"
Glen Campbell

1976 "Bring It on Home"
Mickey Gilley

1977 "Lucille"
Kenny Rogers

1978 "Tulsa Time"
Don Williams

1979 "All the Gold in California"
Larry Gatlin & The Gatlin Brothers

1980 "He Stopped Loving Her Today"
George Jones

1981 "Elvira"
Oak Ridge Boys

1982 "Always on My Mind"
Willie Nelson

1983 "Islands in the Stream"
Kenny Rogers/Dolly Parton

1984 "To All the Girls I've Loved Before"
Willie Nelson/Julio Iglesias

1985 "Highwayman"
Willie Nelson/Waylon Jennings/Kris Kristofferson/Johnny Cash

1986 "On the Other Hand"
Randy Travis

1987 "Forever and Ever Amen"
Randy Travis

1988 "Eighteen Wheels and a Dozen Roses"
Kathy Mattea

1989 "Better Man"
Clint Black

1990 "Friends in Low Places"
Garth Brooks

1991 "Don't Rock the Jukebox"
Alan Jackson

1992 "Boot Scootin' Boogie"
Brooks & Dunn

1993 "Chattahoochie"
Alan Jackson

ALBUM OF THE YEAR

1967 "Gentle on My Mind"
Glen Campbell

1968 "Glen Campbell & Bobbie Gentry"
Glen Campbell & Bobbie Gentry

1969 "Okie From Muskogee"
Merle Haggard

1970 "For the Good Times"
Ray Price

1971 "Easy Loving"
Freddie Hart

1972 "Happiest Girl in the Whole U.S.A."
Donna Fargo

1973 "Behind Closed Doors"
Charlie Rich

1974 "Back Home Again"
John Denver

1975 "Feelin's"
Conway Twitty/Loretta Lynn

1976 "Gilley's Smoking"
Mickey Gilley

1977 "Kenny Rogers"
Kenny Rogers

1978 "Ya'll Come Back Saloon"
Oak Ridge Boys

1979 "Straight Ahead"
Larry Gatlin & The Gatlin Brothers

1980 "Urban Cowboy Soundtrack"

1981 "Feels So Right"
Alabama

1982 "Always on My Mind"
Willie Nelson

1983 "The Closer You Get"
Alabama

1984	"Roll On"
	Alabama
1985	"Does Ft. Worth Ever Cross Your Mind"
	George Strait
1986	"Storms of Life"
	Randy Travis
1987	"Trio"
	Dolly Parton/Emmylou Harris/Linda Ronstadt
1988	"This Woman"
	K.T. Oslin
1989	"Killin' Time"
	Clint Black
1990	"No Fences"
	Garth Brooks
1991	"Don't Rock the Jukebox"
	Alan Jackson
1992	"Brand New Man"
	Brooks & Dunn
1993	"A Lot About Livin' (and a Little 'Bout Love)"
	Alan Jackson

NIGHT CLUB

1965	Palomino Club
1966	Palomino Club
1967	Palomino Club
1968	Palomino Club/Golden Nugget
1969	Palomino Club
1970	Palomino Club
1971	Palomino Club
1972	Palomino Club
1973	Palomino Club
1974	Palomino Club
1975	Palomino Club
1976	Palomino Club
1977	Palomino Club
1978	Palomino Club
1979	Gilley's
1980	Gilley's/Palomino Club
1981	Billy Bob's, Fort Worth, TX
1982	Gilley's
1983	Gilley's
1984	Gilley's
1985	Billy Bob's, Fort Worth, TX
1986	Crazy Horse Steak House & Saloon, Santa Ana, CA
1987	Crazy Horse Steak House & Saloon, Santa Ana, CA
1988	Crazy Horse Steak House & Saloon, Santa Ana, CA
1989	Crazy Horse Steak House & Saloon, Santa Ana, CA
1990	Crazy Horse Steak House & Saloon, Santa Ana, CA
1991	Crazy Horse Steak House & Saloon, Santa Ana, CA
1992	Billy Bob's, Fort Worth, TX
1993	Coolies, Phoenix, AZ

DISC JOCKEY

1965	Biff Collie
1966	Bob Kingsley/Biff Collie
1967	Bob Kingsley
1968	Tex Williams/Larry Scott
1969	Dick Haynes
1970	Corky Mayberry
1971	Larry Scott
1972	Larry Scott
1973	Craig Scott
1974	Larry Scott
1975	Billy Parker
1976	Charlie Douglas
1977	Billy Parker
1978	Billy Parker
1979	King Edward IV
1980	Sammy Jackson
1981	Arch Yancey
1982	Lee Arnold
1983	Rhubarb Jones
1984	Coyote Calhoun/Large Market
1984	Billy Parker/Medium Market
1984	Don Hollander/Small Market
1985	Eddie Edwards
1986	Chris Taylor
1987	Jim Tabor/WMC Memphis, TN
1988	Jon Conlon/Dandalion
1988	Dandalion/Jon Conlon
1989	Jon Conlon
1990	Gerry House
1991	Gerry House, WSIX, Nashville, TN
1992	Jon Conlon, WGKX, Memphis, TN
1993	Tim Hattrick & Wally D. Loon
1993	Wally D. Loon & Tim Hattrick

FIDDLE

1965	Billy Armstrong
1966	Billy Armstrong
1967	Billy Armstrong
1968	Billy Armstrong
1969	Billy Armstrong
1970	Billy Armstrong
1971	Billy Armstrong
1972	Billy Armstrong
1973	Billy Armstrong
1974	Billy Armstrong
1975	Billy Armstrong

1976 Billy Armstrong
1977 Billy Armstrong
1978 Johnny Gimble
1979 Johnny Gimble
1980 Johnny Gimble
1981 Johnny Gimble
1982 Johnny Gimble
1983 Johnny Gimble
1984 Johnny Gimble
1985 Johnny Gimble
1986 Mark O'Connor
1987 Johnny Gimble
1988 Mark O'Connor
1989 Mark O'Connor
1990 Mark O'Connor
1991 Mark O'Connor
1992 Mark O'Connor
1993 Mark O'Connor

STEEL GUITAR

1965 Red Rhodes
1966 Red Rhodes/Tom Brumley
1966 Tom Brumley/Red Rhodes
1967 Red Rhodes
1968 Red Rhodes
1969 Buddy Emmons
1970 J.D. Maness
1971 J.D. Maness
1972 Buddy Emmons
1973 Red Rhodes
1974 J.D. Maness
1975 J.D. Maness
1976 J.D. Maness
1977 Buddy Emmons
1978 Buddy Emmons
1979 Buddy Emmons
1980 J.D. Maness/Buddy Emmons
1980 Buddy Emmons/J.D. Maness
1981 Buddy Emmons
1982 J.D. Maness
1983 J.D. Maness
1984 Buddy Emmons
1985 Buddy Emmons
1986 J.D. Maness
1987 J.D. Maness
1988 J.D. Maness
1989 J.D. Maness
1990 J.D. Maness
1991 Paul Franklin
1992 J. D. Maness
1993 J. D. Maness

KEYBOARD

1965 Billy Liebert
1966 Billy Liebert
1967 Earl Ball
1968 Earl Ball
1969 Floyd Cramer
1970 Floyd Cramer
1971 Floyd Cramer
1972 Floyd Cramer
1973 Floyd Cramer
1974 Floyd Cramer
1975 Jerry Lee Lewis
1976 Hargus "Pig" Robbins
1977 Hargus "Pig" Robbins
1978 Jimmy Pruett
1979 Hargus "Pig" Robbins
1980 Hargus "Pig" Robbins
1981 Hargus "Pig" Robbins
1982 Hargus "Pig" Robbins
1983 Floyd Cramer
1984 Hargus "Pig" Robbins
1985 Glen Hardin
1986 John Hobbs
1987 Ronnie Milsap/John Hobbs
1987 John Hobbs/Ronnie Milsap
1988 John Hobbs
1989 Skip Edwards
1990 John Hobbs
1991 Matt Rollings
1992 Matt Rollings
1993 Matt Rollings

BASS

1965 Bob Morris
1966 Bob Morris
1967 Red Wooten
1968 Red Wooten
1969 Billy Graham
1970 Doyle Holly/ Billy Graham
1970 Billy Graham/Doyle Holly
1971 Larry Booth
1972 Larry Booth
1973 Larry Booth
1974 Billy Graham
1975 Billy Graham
1976 Curtis Stone
1977 Larry Booth

1978 Rod Culpepper
1979 Billy Graham
1980 Curtis Stone
1981 Curtis Stone/Joe Osborn
1981 Joe Osborn/Curtis Stone
1982 Red Wooten
1983 Joe Osborn
1984 Joe Osborn
1985 Joe Osborn
1986 Emory Gordy, Jr.
1987 Emory Gordy, Jr./David Hungate
1987 David Hungate/Emory Gordy Jr
1988 Curtis Stone
1989 Michael Rhodes
1990 Bill Bryson
1991 Roy Huskey, Jr.
1992 Glen Worf
1993 Glen Worf

GUITAR

1965 Phil Baugh
1966 Jimmy Bryant
1967 Jimmy Bryant
1968 Jimmy Bryant
1969 Al Bruno/Jerry Inman
1969 Jerry Inman/Al Bruno
1970 Al Bruno
1971 Al Bruno
1972 Al Bruno
1973 Al Bruno
1974 Al Bruno
1975 Jerry Inman (rhythm)
1975 Russ Hansen (lead)
1976 Danny Michaels
1977 Roy Clark
1978 James Burton
1979 Al Bruno
1980 Al Bruno
1981 James Burton
1982 Al Bruno
1983 Reggie Young
1984 James Burton
1985 James Burton
1986 Chet Atkins
1987 Chet Atkins
1988 Al Bruno
1989 Brent Rowan
1990 John Jorgenson
1991 John Jorgenson
1992 John Jorgenson
1993 Brent Mason

DRUMS

1965 Muddy Berry
1966 Jerry Wiggins
1967 Pee Wee Adams
1968 Jerry Wiggins
1969 Jerry Wiggins
1970 Archie Francis
1971 Jerry Wiggins
1972 Jerry Wiggins
1973 Jerry Wiggins
1974 Jerry Wiggins
1975 Archie Francis
1976 Archie Francis
1977 Archie Francis/George Manz
1977 George Manz/Archie Francis
1978 Archie Francis
1979 Archie Francis
1980 Archie Francis
1981 Buddy Harmon
1982 Archie Francis
1983 Archie Francis
1984 Larrie Londin
1985 Archie Francis
1986 Larrie Londin
1987 Archie Francis
1988 Steve Duncan
1989 Steve Duncan
1990 Steve Duncan
1991 Eddie Bayers
1992 Eddie Bayers
1993 Eddie Bayers

TOURING BAND

1965 Buckaroos/Buck Owens
1966 Buckaroos/Buck Owens
1967 Buckaroos/Buck Owens
1968 Buckaroos/Buck Owens
1969 The Strangers
1970 The Strangers
1971 The Strangers
1972 The Strangers
1973 Brush Arbor
1974 The Strangers
1975 The Strangers
1976 Red Rose Express
1977 Asleep at the Wheel/Sons of the Pioneers
1977 Sons of the Pioneers/Asleep at the Wheel

1978	Original Texas Playboys
1979	Charlie Daniels Band
1980	Charlie Daniels Band
1981	The Strangers
1982	Ricky Skaggs Band
1983	Ricky Skaggs Band
1984	Ricky Skaggs Band
1985	Ricky Skaggs Band
1986	Ricky Skaggs Band
1987	The Strangers
1988	Desert Rose Band
1989	Desert Rose Band
1990	Desert Rose Band

INDIVIDUAL AWARD

1965	Roger Miller/Songwriter
1965	Roger Miller/Man of the Year
1965	Ken Nelson/Producer-A&R Man
1965	Jack McFadden/Talent Manager
1965	Central Songs/Publisher
1965	Billy Mize/TV Personality
1965	Billboard/Publication
1966	Ken Nelson/Producer-A&R Man
1966	Jack McFadden/Talent Manager
1966	Dean Martin/Man of the Year
1966	Central Songs/Publisher
1966	Billy Mize/TV Personality
1967	Billy Mize/TV Personality
1967	Joey Bishop/Man of the Year
1968	Tom Smothers/Man of the Year
1968	Nudie/Director's Award
1968	Glen Campbell/TV Personality
1969	Roy Clark/Comedy Act
1969	Johnny Cash/TV Personality
1969	John Aylesworth/Frank Peppiatt/Man of the Year
1969	Frank Peppiatt/John Aylesworth/Man of the Year
1970	Roy Clark/Comedy Act
1970	Johnny Cash/TV Personality
1970	Billboard/Publication
1970	Hugh Cherry/Man of the Year
1971	Walter Knott/ Man of the Year
1971	Roy Clark/Comedy Act
1971	Glen Campbell/TV Personality
1972	Roy Clark/TV Personality
1972	Lawrence Welk/Man of the Year
1977	Johnny Paycheck/Career Achievement
1980	George Burns/Social Achievement
1986	Carl Perkins/Career Achievement
1993	John Anderson/Career Achievement
1993	Bill Banchand-Mr. Bill Presents (Phoenix, AZ) Talent Buyer/Promoter of the Year

PIONEER AWARD

1968	Uncle Art Satherley
1969	Bob Wills
1970	Tex Ritter
1970	Patsy Montana
1971	Tex Williams
1971	Bob Nolan
1971	Stuart Hamblen
1972	Gene Autry
1972	Cliffie Stone
1973	Hank Williams
1974	Johnny Bond
1974	Merle Travis
1974	Tennessee Ernie Ford
1975	Roy Rogers
1976	Owen Bradley
1977	Sons of the Pioneers
1978	Eddie Dean
1979	Patti Page
1980	Ernest Tubb
1981	Leo Fender
1982	Chet Atkins
1983	Eddy Arnold
1984	Roy Acuff
1985	Kitty Wells
1986	Minnie Pearl
1987	Roger Miller
1988	Buck Owens
1990	Johnny Cash
1991	Willie Nelson
1992	George Jones
1993	Charley Pride

NON-TOURING BAND

1968	Billy Mize's Tennesseans
1970	Tony Booth Band
1971	Tony Booth Band
1972	Tony Booth Band
1973	Sound Company
1974	Palomino Riders
1975	Palomino Riders
1976	Possum Holler Band
1977	Palomino Riders
1978	Rebel Playboys
1979	Midnight Riders
1980	Palomino Riders
1981	Desperados

1982 Desperados
1983 The Tennesseans
1984 The Tennesseans
1985 Nashville Now Band
1986 Nashville Now Band
1987 Nashville Now Band
1988 Nashville Now Band
1989 Nashville Now Band
1990 Boy Howdy Band

SPECIALITY INSTRUMENT

1969 John Hartford/Banjo
1977 Charlie McCoy/Harmonica
1978 Charlie McCoy/Harmonica
1979 Charlie McCoy/Harmonica
1980 Charlie McCoy/Harmonica
1981 Charlie McCoy/Harmonica
1982 James Burton/Dobro
1983 Charlie McCoy/Harmonica
1984 Ricky Skaggs/Mandolin
1985 James Burton/Dobro
1986 James Burton/Dobro
1987 Ricky Skaggs/Mandolin
1987 Jerry Douglas/Dobro
1988 Charlie McCoy/Harmonica
1989 Jerry Douglas/Dobro
1990 Jerry Douglas/Dobro
1991 Jerry Douglas/Dobro
1992 Jerry Douglas/Dobro
1993 Terry McMillan/Percussion/Harmonica

ARTIST OF THE DECADE

1960-69 Marty Robbins
1970-79 Loretta Lynn
1980-89 Alabama

JIM REEVES MEMORIAL AWARD

1969 Joe Allison
1970 Bill Boyd
1971 Roy Rogers
1972 Thurston Moore
1973 Sam Lovullo
1974 Merv Griffin
1975 Dinah Shore
1976 Roy Clark
1977 Jim Halsey
1978 Joe Cates
1979 Bill Ward
1980 Ken Kragen
1981 Al Gallico
1982 Jo Walker-Meader

RADIO STATION

1970 KLAC (Los Angeles, CA)
1971 KLAC (Los Angeles, CA)
1972 KLAC (Los Angeles, CA)
1973 KLAC (Los Angeles, CA)
1974 KLAC (Los Angeles, CA)
1975 KLAC (Los Angeles, CA)
1976 KLAC (Los Angeles, CA)
1977 KGBS (Los Angeles, CA)
1978 KVOO (Tulsa, OK)
1979 KFDI (Wichita, KS)
1980 KLAC (Los Angeles, CA)
1981 WPLO (Atlanta, GA)
1982 KIKK (Houston, TX)
1983 KRMD (Shreveport, LA)
1984 WCM (Memphis, TN) large
1984 KVOO (Tulsa, OK) medium
1984 WLWI (Montgomery, AL) small
1985 WAMZ (Louisville, KY)
1986 KNIX (Tempe, AZ)
1987 KNIX (Tempe, AZ)
1988 WSIX (Nashville, TN)
1989 WSIX (Nashville, TN)
1990 WSIX (Nashville, TN)
1991 WAMZ (Louisville, KY)
1992 KNIX (Phoenix, AZ)
1993 KNIX (Phoenix, AZ)

TEX RITTER AWARD

1970 "Electric Horseman"
1980 "Coal Miner's Daughter"
1981 "Any Which Way You Can"
1982 "The Best Little Whorehouse in Texas"
1983 "Tender Mercies"
1984 "Songwriter"
1985 "Sweet Dreams"
1992 "Pure Country"

VIDEO OF THE YEAR

1984 "All My Rowdy Friends Are Comin' Over Tonight"
Hank Williams, Jr.
1985 "Who's Gonna Fill Their Shoes"
George Jones
1986 "Whoever's in New England"
Reba McEntire
1987 "80's Ladies"
K.T. Oslin
1988 "Young Country"
Hank Williams, Jr.

1989 "There's a Tear in My Beer"
Hank Williams and Hank Williams, Jr.

1990 "The Dance"
Garth Brooks

1992 "Two Sparrows in a Hurricane"
Tanya Tucker

1993 "We Shall Be Free"
Garth Brooks

AMERICAN MUSIC AWARDS

The winners of these awards are decided by votes cast by a cross-section of the American record-buying public. To determine the public's selection of competitive "American Music Awards," Dick Clark Productions, Inc., through the National Family Opinion, Inc. firm under the supervision of Broadcast Research and Consulting, Inc., sends ballots to a national sampling of approximately 20,000 record buyers. The sampling takes into account geographic location, age, sex and ethnic origin of those polled. Names of the nominees appearing on the ballot are compiled from data supplied by the music industry trade publication Radio & Records and the SoundScan, Inc., management information system. Results of the voting, tabulated by the KPMG Peat Marwick accounting firm, are kept secret until the envelopes are opened during the evening's live presentation ceremonies. (Listed are Country artists only.)

POP/ROCK CATEGORY

FAVORITE MALE ARTIST

1975 John Denver
1976 John Denver
1981 Kenny Rogers
1982 Kenny Rogers
1983 John Cougar (Mellencamp)
(Tied with Rick Springfield)

FAVORITE FEMALE ARTIST

1975 Olivia Newton-John
1976 Olivia Newton-John
1977 Olivia Newton-John
1978 Linda Ronstadt
1979 Linda Ronstadt
1983 Olivia Newton-John

FAVORITE BAND, DUO OR GROUP

1981 The Eagles

FAVORITE ALBUM

1975 "Behind Closed Doors"
Charlie Rich

1976 "Have You Never Been Mellow"
Olivia Newton-John

1977 "Eagles' Greatest Hits"
The Eagles

1982 "Greatest Hits"
Kenny Rogers

1983 "Always on My Mind"
Willie Nelson

FAVORITE SINGLE

1975 "I Honestly Love You"
Olivia Newton-John

1976 "Rhinestone Cowboy"
Glen Campbell

1978 "You Light Up My Life"
Debby Boone

1994 "I Will Always Love You"
Whitney Houston
(Written by Dolly Parton)

COUNTRY CATEGORY

FAVORITE MALE ARTIST

1974 Charley Pride
1975 Charlie Rich
1976 John Denver
1977 Charley Pride
1978 Conway Twitty
1979 Kenny Rogers
1980 Kenny Rogers
1981 Kenny Rogers
1982 Willie Nelson
1983 Kenny Rogers
1984 Willie Nelson
1985 Kenny Rogers
1986 Willie Nelson
1987 Willie Nelson
1988 Randy Travis
1989 Randy Travis
1990 Randy Travis
1991 George Strait
1992 Garth Brooks
1993 Garth Brooks
1994 Garth Brooks

FAVORITE FEMALE ARTIST

1974 Lynn Anderson
1975 Olivia Newton-John
1976 Olivia Newton-John
1977 Loretta Lynn
1978 Loretta Lynn
1979 Crystal Gayle
1980 Crystal Gayle
1981 Barbara Mandrell
1982 Barbara Mandrell

1983 Barbara Mandrell
1984 Barbara Mandrell
1985 Barbara Mandrell
1986 Crystal Gayle
1987 Barbara Mandrell
1988 Reba McEntire
1989 Reba McEntire
1990 Reba McEntire
1991 Reba McEntire
1992 Reba McEntire
1993 Reba McEntire
1994 Reba McEntire

FAVORITE BAND, DUO OR GROUP

1974 The Carter Family
1975 Conway Twitty & Loretta Lynn
1976 Donny & Marie Osmond
1977 Conway Twitty & Loretta Lynn
1978 Conway Twitty & Loretta Lynn
1979 The Statler Brothers
1980 The Statler Brothers
1981 The Statler Brothers
1982 The Oak Ridge Boys
1983 Alabama
1984 Alabama
1985 Alabama
1986 Alabama
1987 Alabama
1988 Alabama
1989 Alabama
1990 Alabama
1991 Alabama
1992 Alabama
1993 Alabama
1994 Alabama

FAVORITE ALBUM

1974 "A Sun Shiny Day"
Charley Pride
1975 "Let Me Be There"
Olivia Newton-John
1976 "Back Home Again"
John Denver
1977 "Rhinestone Cowboy"
Glen Campbell
1978 "New Harvest, First Gathering"
Dolly Parton
1979 "Ten Years of Gold"
Kenny Rogers
1980 "The Gambler"
Kenny Rogers
1981 "The Gambler"
Kenny Rogers
1982 "Greatest Hits"
Kenny Rogers
1983 "Always on My Mind"
Willie Nelson
1984 "The Closer You Get"
Alabama
1985 "Eyes That See in the Dark"
Kenny Rogers
1986 "40 Hour Week"
Alabama
1987 "Greatest Hits"
Alabama
1988 "Always & Forever"
Randy Travis
1989 "Always & Forever"
Randy Travis
1990 "Old 8 x 10"
Randy Travis
1991 "Reba Live"
Reba McEntire
1992 "No Fences"
Garth Brooks
1993 "For My Broken Heart"
Reba McEntire
1994 "A Lot About Livin' (and a Little 'Bout Love)"
Alan Jackson

FAVORITE SINGLE

1974 "Behind Closed Doors"
Charlie Rich
1975 "The Most Beautiful Girl"
Charlie Rich
1976 "Rhinestone Cowboy"
Glen Campbell
1977 "Blue Eyes Cryin' in the Rain"
Willie Nelson
1978 "Lucille"
Kenny Rogers
1979 "Blue Bayou"
Linda Ronstadt
1980 "Sleeping Single in a Double Bed"
Barbara Mandrell
1981 "Coward of the County"
Kenny Rogers
1982 "Could I Have This Dance"
Anne Murray

1982 "On the Road Again"
Willie Nelson
(Tie in 1982)
1983 "Love Will Turn You Around"
Kenny Rogers
1984 "Islands in the Stream"
Kenny Rogers & Dolly Parton
1985 "Islands in the Stream"
Kenny Rogers & Dolly Parton
1986 "Forgiving You Was Easy"
Willie Nelson
1987 "Grandpa"
The Judds
1988 "Forever and Ever Amen"
Randy Travis
1989 "I Told You So"
Randy Travis
1990 "Deeper Than the Holler"
Randy Travis
1991 "If Tomorrow Never Comes"
Garth Brooks
1992 "The Thunder Rolls"
Garth Brooks
1993 "Achy Breaky Heart"
Billy Ray Cyrus
1994 "Chattahoochee"
Alan Jackson

FAVORITE NEW ARTIST

1989 Patty Loveless
1990 Clint Black
1991 Kentucky Headhunters
1992 Trisha Yearwood
1993 Billy Ray Cyrus
1994 John Michael Montgomery

FAVORITE VIDEO

1984 "Dixieland Delight"
Alabama
1988 "Forever and Ever Amen"
Randy Travis

FAVORITE MALE VIDEO ARTIST

1985 Willie Nelson
1986 Hank Williams, Jr.
1987 George Jones

FAVORITE FEMALE VIDEO ARTIST

1985 Anne Murray
1986 Crystal Gayle
1987 Reba McEntire

FAVORITE VIDEO DUO OR GROUP

1985 The Oak Ridge Boys
1986 Highwayman (Willie Nelson, Waylon Jennings, Kris Kristofferson, Johnny Cash)
1987 Alabama

FAVORITE VIDEO SINGLE

1985 "A Little Good News"
Anne Murray
1986 "Highwayman"
Willie Nelson, Waylon Jennings,
Kris Kristofferson, Johnny Cash
1987 "Grandpa"
The Judds

ADULT CONTEMPORARY SECTION

FAVORITE NEW ARTIST

1992 Michael W. Smith
1993 k.d. lang

SOUL/RHYTHM & BLUES CATEGORY

FAVORITE SINGLE

1994 "I Will Always Love You"
Whitney Houston
(Written by Dolly Parton)

SPECIAL AWARD OF MERIT

1977 Johnny Cash
1983 Kenny Rogers
1985 Loretta Lynn
1987 Elvis Presley (posthumously)
1989 Willie Nelson
1991 Merle Haggard

AWARD OF APPRECIATION

1986 Willie Nelson
(Also Harry Belafonte and Bob Geldof)

ASCAP

SONGWRITER OF THE YEAR

1982 Bob Morrison
1983 Charlie Black, Rory Bourke, Wayland Holyfield
1984 Charlie Black, Tommy Rocco
1985 Mike Reid
1986 Troy Seals
1987 Dave Loggins
1988 Don Schlitz
1989 Don Schlitz
1990 Don Schlitz
1991 Don Schlitz
1992 Pat Alger
1993 Garth Brooks, Alan Jackson
1994 Garth Brooks, Alan Jackson, Bob McDill, Kim Williams

SONG OF THE YEAR

1982 "(There's) No Getting Over Me"
Walt Aldridge, Tommy Brasfield
1983 "Love Will Turn You Around"
Kenny Rogers
1984 "We've Got Tonight"
Bob Seger
1985 "To All the Girls I've Loved Before"
Hal David, Albert Hammond
1986 "Lost in the Fifties Tonight (In the Still of the Night)"
Mike Reid, Troy Seals
1987 "Now and Forever (You and Me)"
Randy Goodrum
1988 "I'll Still Be Loving You"
Todd Cerney
1989 "Too Gone, Too Long"
Gene Pistilli
1990 "What's Going on in Your World"
David Chamberlain, Royce Porter
1991 "Friends in Low Places"
Earl Bud Lee
1992 "Don't Rock the Jukebox"
Alan Jackson
1993 "When She Cries"
Marc Beeson
1994 "Chattahoochie"
Alan Jackson, Jim McBride

BRITISH COUNTRY MUSIC ASSOCIATION AWARDS

GROUP OF THE YEAR

1980 Poacher
1981 Colorado
1982 Colorado
1983 Colorado
1984 Colorado
1985 Colorado
1986 Colorado
1987 Colorado
1988 Colorado
1989 Colorado
1990 Stu Page Band
1991 Brazil Band
1992 Stu Page Band
1993 Stu Page Band

DUO OF THE YEAR

1980 Miki & Griff
1981 Miki & Griff
1982 Duffy Brothers
1983 Duffy Brothers
1984 Duffy Brothers
1985 Duffy Brothers
1986 Ray Lynam & Philomena Begley
1987 Bob Newman & Carole Gordon
1988 Bob Newman & Carole Gordon
1989 Bob Newman & Carole Gordon
1990 West 'N' Elliott
1991 West 'N' Elliott
1992 Haley Sisters
1993 Haley Sisters

SOLO PERFORMER

1980 Stu Stevens
1991 Nicky James
1992 Charlie Landsborough
1993 Dave Sheriff

MALE VOCALIST

1981 Stu Stevens
1982 Tony Goodacre
1983 Tony Goodacre
1984 Tony Goodacre
1985 Raymond Froggatt
1986 Raymond Froggatt
1987 Raymond Froggatt
1988 Raymond Froggatt
1989 Raymond Froggatt
1990 Raymond Froggatt
1991 Raymond Froggatt
1992 Raymond Froggatt
1993 Kenny Johnson

FEMALE VOCALIST

1981 Tammy Cline
1982 Tammy Cline
1983 Tammy Cline
1984 Tammy Cline
1985 Philomena Begley
1986 Philomena Begley
1987 Tammy Cline
1988 Philomena Begley
1989 Philomena Begley
1990 Sarah Jory
1991 Sarah Jory
1992 Sarah Jory
1993 Sarah Jory

MOST PROMISING NEW ACT

1980 Country Shack

1981 Billy Finnegan & Stagecoach
1982 Roxon Roadshow
1983 Indigo Lady
1984 West Coast
1985 Sarah Jory
1986 Stu Page & Remuda
1987 Spill the Beans
1988 Lindsey St. John Band
1989 Medicine Bow
1990 Haley Sisters
1991 New Dawn Trio
1992 Texas Gun
1993 John Douglas & Southern Star

INTERNATIONAL ACT

1988 Randy Travis
1989 Randy Travis
1990 George Strait
1991 Daniel O'Donnell
1992 Daniel O'Donnell
1993 Vince Gill

BCMA COMMITTEE AWARD

1988 Bob Powel
1989 Hillsiders
1990 Wally Whyton
1991 Ginny Brown
1992 Philomena Begley
1993 Brian Golbey

BMI AWARDS

SONGWRITER OF THE YEAR

1967 Don Gibson
1968 Billy Sherrill
1969 John D. Loudermilk
1970 Billy Sherrill
1971 Kris Kristofferson, Billy Sherrill
1972 Kris Kristofferson, Billy Sherrill
1973 Norro Wilson
1974 Kris Kristofferson, Billy Sherrill, Norro Wilson
1975 Norro Wilson
1976 Merle Haggard
1977 Bobby Braddock, Bob McDill, Billy Sherrill
1978 Billy Sherrill
1979 Billy Sherrill
1980 Rhonda Kye Fleming, Merle Haggard, Bob McDill, Dennis Morgan, Sonny Throckmorton
1981 Snuff Garrett
1982 Rhonda Kye Fleming, Dennis Morgan
1983 Bobby Braddock, Rhonda Kye Fleming, Dennis Morgan
1984 Lewis Anderson
1985 Bob McDill
1986 Sonny Lemaire, Dennis Morgan, J.P. Pennington
1987 Paul Overstreet
1988 Holly Dunn, Roger Murrah, Paul Overstreet, Dan Seals
1989 Mike Geiger, Paul Kennerley, Paul Overstreet
1990 Paul Overstreet
1991 Paul Overstreet
1992 Vince Gill
1993 Tom Shapiro
1994 Dennis Linde

ROBERT J. BURTON AWARD

(Presented as a special honor to the writer and the publisher of the Country song most performed from April 1, previous year, to March 31, current year)

1967 "Almost Persuaded" (Glenn Sutton/Billy Sherrill)
1968 "Release Me" (Eddie Miller/W.S. Stevenson)
1969 "Gentle on My Mind" (John Hartford)
1970 "Gentle on My Mind" (John Hartford)
1971 "(I Never Promised You a) Rose Garden" (Joe South)
1972 "Help Me Make It Through the Night" (Kris Kristofferson)
1973 "The Happiest Girl in the Whole U.S.A." (Donna Fargo)
1974 "Let Me Be There" (John Rostill)
1975 "If You Love Me (Let Me Know)" (John Rostill)
1976 "When Will I Be Loved" (Phil Everly)
1977 "Misty Blue" (Bob Montgomery)
1978 "Here You Come Again" (Barry Mann/Cynthia Weil)
1979 "Talkin' in Your Sleep" (Roger Cook (PRS)/Bobby Wood)

1980 "Suspicions"
(David Malloy/Randy McCormick/Eddie Rabbitt/Even Stevens)

1981 "9 to 5"
(Dolly Parton)

1982 "Elvira"
(Dallas Frazier)

1983 "Nobody"
(Rhonda Fleming/Gill/Dennis Morgan)

1984 "Islands in the Stream"
(Barry Gibb/Maurice Gibb/Robin Gibb)

1985 "Mama He's Crazy"
(Kenny O'Dell)

1986 "Don't Call It Love"
(Dean Pitchford/Tom Snow)

1987 "Hold On"
(Rosanne Cash)

1988 "To Know Him Is to Love Him"
(Phil Spector)

1989 "Fallin' Again"
(Greg Fowler/Teddy Gentry/Randy Owen)

1990 "Cathy's Clown"
(Don Everly)

1991 "Hard Rock Bottom of Your Heart"
(Hugh Prestwood)

1992 "She's in Love With the Boy"
(Jon Ims)

1993 "Achy Breaky Heart"
(Don Von Tress)

1994 "Blame It on Your Heart"
(Harlan Howard, Kostas)

CANADIAN COUNTRY MUSIC ASSOCIATION AWARDS

HALL OF HONOUR INDUCTEES

1985 Hank Snow, Don Messer
1986 Papa Joe Brown
1987 Lucille Starr
1988 Jack Feeney
1989 Ian Tyson, Don Grashey
1990 Gordie Tapp, Ron Sparling
1991 The Rhythm Pals, Hugh Joseph
1992 Carroll Baker, Gordon Burnett
1993 Bob Nolan, Frank Jones

C.F. MARTIN AWARD

(Presented to the person in Country music who contributes the most to the advancement and promotion of Country music in Canada in that year)

1981 Wilf Carter
1982 Dick Damron
1983 Barry Brown
1984 Papa Joe Brown
1985 Tommy Hunter
1986 No Recipient
1987 The Mercey Brothers
1988 Ronnie Prophet
1989 Carroll Baker
1990 Jack Feeney

TMI FENDER GUITAR HUMANITARIAN AWARD

1989 Wayne Rostad
1990 Gary Fjellgaard

C.F. MARTIN HUMANITARIAN AWARD

1991 Carroll Baker
1992 John Allan Cameron
1993 "A Song for Brent"

OUTSTANDING INTERNATIONAL SUPPORT AWARD

1988 Jo Walker-Meader
1989 George Hamilton IV
1990 Kees de Haan
1991 Bart Barton, Tony Migliori
1992 Tim Dubois
1993 CTV Television Network

ENTERTAINER OF THE YEAR

1982 Family Brown
1983 Family Brown
1984 Ronnie Prophet
1985 Dick Damron
1986 Family Brown
1987 k.d. lang
1988 k.d. lang
1989 k.d. lang

BUD COUNTRY FAN CHOICE ENTERTAINER OF THE YEAR

1990 k.d. lang
1991 Rita MacNeil
1992 Rita MacNeil
1993 Michelle Wright

VOCALIST OF THE YEAR (MALE)

1982 Terry Carisse
1983 Dick Damron
1984 Terry Carisse
1985 Terry Carisse
1986 Terry Carisse
1987 Ian Tyson
1988 Ian Tyson

1989 Gary Fjellgaard
1990 George Fox
1991 George Fox
1992 Ian Tyson
1993 George Fox

VOCALIST OF THE YEAR (FEMALE)

1982 Carroll Baker
1983 Marie Bottrell
1984 Marie Bottrell
1985 Carroll Baker
1986 Anita Perras
1987 Anita Perras
1988 k.d. lang
1989 k.d. lang
1990 Michelle Wright
1991 Michelle Wright
1992 Michelle Wright
1993 Michelle Wright

DUO OF THE YEAR

1983 Donna/Leroy Anderson
1984 Glory Anne Carriere/Ronnie Prophet
1985 Anita Perras/Tim Taylor
1986 Anita Perras/Tim Taylor
1987 Anita Perras/Tim Taylor
1988 Anita Perras/Tim Taylor
1989 Gary Fjellgaard/Linda Kidder
1990 Gary Fjellgaard/Linda Kidder
1991 The Johner Brothers

VOCAL COLLABORATION OF THE YEAR

1992 Gary Fjellgaard/Linda Kidder
1993 Cassandra Vasik/Russelle deCarle

GROUP OF THE YEAR

1982 Family Brown
1983 Family Brown
1984 Family Brown
1985 The Mercey Brothers
1986 Family Brown
1987 Family Brown
1988 Family Brown
1989 Family Brown
1990 Prairie Oyster
1991 Prairie Oyster

VOCAL DUO OR GROUP OF THE YEAR

1992 Prairie Oyster
1993 The Rankin Family

VISTA (RISING STAR)

1982 Ruth Ann
1983 Kelita Haverland
1984 Roni Sommers
1985 Ginny Mitchell
1986 J.K. Gulley
1987 k.d. lang
1988 Blue Rodeo
1989 George Fox
1990 Patricia Conroy
1991 South Mountain
1992 Cassandra Vasik
1993 The Rankin Family

SINGLE OF THE YEAR

1982 "Some Never Stand a Chance"
Family Brown
1983 "Raised on Country Music"
Family Brown
1984 "A Little Good News"
Anne Murray
1985 "Riding on the Wind"
Gary Fjellgaard
1986 "Now and Forever (You and Me)"
Anne Murray
1987 "Navajo Rug"
Ian Tyson
1988 "One Smokey Rose"
Anita Perras
1989 "Town of Tears"
Family Brown
1990 "Goodbye, So Long, Hello"
Prairie Oyster
1991 "New Kind of Love"
Michelle Wright
1992 "Take It Like a Man"
Michelle Wright
1993 "He Would Be Sixteen"
Michelle Wright

ALBUM OF THE YEAR

1982 "Raised on Country Music"
Family Brown
1983 "Raised on Country Music"
Family Brown
1984 "Repeat After Me"
Family Brown
1985 "Closest Thing to Me"
Terry Carisse
1986 "Feel the Fire"
Family Brown
1987 "Cowboyography"
Ian Tyson

1988 "Shadowland"
k.d. lang
1989 "Shadowland"
k.d. lang
1990 "Absolute Torch and Twang"
k.d. lang
1991 "Michelle Wright"
Michelle Wright
1992 "Everybody Knows"
Prairie Oyster
1993 "Bad Day for Trains"
Patricia Conroy

SONG OF THE YEAR

1982 "Some Never Stand a Chance"
Family Brown
1983 "Raised on Country Music"
Family Brown
1984 "Jesus It's Me Again"
Dick Damron
1985 "Counting the I Love Yous"
Terry Carisse/Bruce Rawlins
1986 "Now and Forever (You and Me)"
David Foster/Jim Vallance/Charles Goodrum
1987 "Heroes"
Gary Fjellgaard MBS
1988 "One Smokey Rose"
Tim Taylor
1989 "Town of Tears"
Barry Brown/Randall Prescott/Bruce Campbell
1990 "Pioneers"
Barry Brown
1991 "Lonely You, Lonely Me"
Joan Besen
1992 "Did You Fall in Love With Me"
Joan Besen
1993 "Backroads"
Charlie Major

VIDEO OF THE YEAR

1990 "Pioneers"
Bob Holbrook
1991 "Springtime in Alberta"
Michael Watt
1992 "Take It Like a Man"
Steven Goldmann
1993 "He Would Be Sixteen"
Steven Goldmann

TOP SELLING ALBUM (FOREIGN OR DOMESTIC)

1984 "Eyes That See in the Dark"
Kenny Rogers
1985 "Once Upon a Christmas"
Dolly Parton/Kenny Rogers
1986 "Hymns of Gold"
Carroll Baker
1987 "Storms of Life"
Randy Travis
1988 "Always & Forever"
Randy Travis
1989 "Old 8 x 10"
Randy Travis
1990 "Rita"
Rita MacNeil
1991 "Home I'll Be"
Rita MacNeil
1992 "Ropin' the Wind"
Garth Brooks
1993 "Some Gave All"
Billy Ray Cyrus

BACK-UP BAND OF THE YEAR

1982 Baker Street
1983 Baker Street
1984 Baker Street
1985 Tracks
1986 The Bobby Lalonde Band
1987 The Bobby Lalonde Band
1988 the reclines
1989 the reclines
1990 the reclines
1991 The Michelle Wright Band
1992 The Michelle Wright Band
1993 The Michelle Wright Band

INSTRUMENTALIST OF THE YEAR

1984 Bobby Lalonde
1985 Steve Piticco
1986 Bobby Lalonde
1987 Bobby Lalonde
1988 Randall Prescott
1989 Dick Damron
1990 Steve Piticco
1991 Steve Piticco

ALL-STAR BAND OF THE YEAR

1990
Drums Bill Carruthers
Bass John Dymond

Guitar Steve Piticco
K/bds Joan Besen
Special Bobby Lalonde (Fiddle), Ben Mink (Fiddle)

1991
Drums Bill Carruthers
Bass Russell deCarle
Guitar Steve Piticco
K/bds Joan Besen
Fiddle John P. Allen
S. Gtr. Dennis Delorme
Special Leroy Anderson (Banjo), Randall Prescott (Harmonica), Ben Fink (Fiddle)

1992
Drums Bill Carruthers
Bass Russell deCarle
Guitar Steve Piticco
K/bds Joan Besen
Fiddle John P. Allen
S. Gtr. Dennis Delorme
Special Randall Prescott (Harmonica)

1993
Drums Bill Carruthers
Bass Russell deCarle
Guitar Steve Piticco
K/bds Joan Besen
Fiddle John P. Allen
S. Gtr. Dennis Delorme
Special Randall Prescott (Harmonica)

MANAGER OF THE YEAR

1982 Ron Sparling
1983 Ron Sparling
1984 Ron Sparling
1985 Brian Ferriman
1986 Brian Ferriman
1987 Brian Ferriman
1988 Brian Ferriman
1989 Leonard Rambeau
1990 Leonard Rambeau
1991 Brian Ferriman
1992 Brian Ferriman
1993 Brian Ferriman

TALENT BUYER OR PROMOTER OF THE YEAR

1993 Ron Sakamoto

BOOKING AGENT OF THE YEAR

1982 Laurie Ann Entertainment Agency
1983 Ron Sparling
1984 Ron Sparling
1985 Ron Sparling
1986 Paul Mascioli
1987 Ron Sparling
1988 Tinti Moffat
1989 Tinti Moffat
1990 Tinti Moffat
1991 Ron Sparling
1992 Brian Edwards
1993 Allan Askew

COUNTRY CLUB OF THE YEAR

1982 Golden Rail, Lafontaine Hotel, Ottawa
1983 Urban Corral, Moncton
1984 Urban Corral, Moncton
1985 Cook County Saloon, Edmonton
1986 Urban Corral, Moncton
1987 Rodeo Roadhouse, Kingston
1988 Rodeo Roadhouse, Kingston
1989 Rodeo Roadhouse, Kingston
1990 Cook County Saloon, Edmonton
1991 Cook County Saloon, Edmonton
1992 Cook County Saloon, Edmonton
1993 Cook County Saloon, Edmonton

ALBUM GRAPHICS OF THE YEAR

1990 "Absolute Torch & Twang"
Jeri Helden/k.d. lang
1991 "Michelle Wright"
Susan Mendola
1992 "Bad Day for Trains"
Rosamund Norbury
1993 "Feels Like Home"
Kathi Prosser

RECORD COMPANY OF THE YEAR

1982 RCA Ltd.
1983 RCA Ltd.
1984 RCA Ltd.
1985 RCA Ltd.
1986 RCA Ltd./Ariola
1987 Savannah Music
1988 BMG Music Canada Inc.
1989 WEA Music of Canada Ltd.
1990 WEA Music of Canada Ltd.
1991 Stony Plain Recording Co. Ltd.
1992 BMG Music Canada Inc.
1993 BMG Music Canada Inc

RECORD INDUSTRY PERSON OF THE YEAR

1982	Barry Haugen	RCA Records
1983	Ed Preston	Tembo Music
1984	Dallas Harms	
1985	Barry Haugen	RCA Records

1986	Brian Ferriman	Savannah Music
1987	Brian Ferriman	Savannah Music
1988	Ron Solleveld	BMG Music
1989	Holger Petersen	Stony Plain
1990	Gilles Godard	Bookshop
1991	Brian Ferriman	Savannah Music
1992	Brian Ferriman	Savannah Music
1993	Ken Bain	BMG Music

RECORD PRODUCER OF THE YEAR

1982	Jack Feeney
1983	Dallas Harms
1984	Dallas Harms/Mike Francis
1985	Terry Carisse
1986	Mike Francis
1987	Mike Francis
1988	Randall Prescott
1989	Randall Prescott
1990	Randall Prescott
1991	Randall Prescott
1992	Randall Prescott
1993	Randall Prescott

MUSIC PUBLISHING COMPANY OF THE YEAR

1982	Sunbury/Dunbar Music
1983	Sunbury/Dunbar Music
1984	Carisse-Rawlins
1985	The Mercey Brothers Publishing Company
1986	Sunbury/Dunbar Music
1987	Sunbury/Dunbar Music
1988	Sunbury/Dunbar Music
1989	BMG Music Publishing Canada Inc.
1990	Savannah Music Group
1991	BMG Music Publishing Canada Inc.
1992	Stony Plain Music
1993	BMG Music Publishing Canada Inc.

BROADCASTER OF THE YEAR

1982	Bill Andersen	CFRB, Toronto
1983	Fred King	CKRM, Regina
1984	Bill Andersen	CFRB, Toronto
1985	Robin Ingram	CFAC, Calgary
1986	Paul Kennedy	CHFX, Halifax
1987	Paul Kennedy	CHFX, Halifax

ON-AIR PERSONALITY (MAJOR MARKET)

1988	Randy Owen	CKGL, Kitchener
1989	Paul Kennedy	CHFX, Halifax
1990	Cliff Dumas	CHAM, Hamilton
1991	Cliff Dumas	CHAM, Hamilton
1992	Cliff Dumas	CHAM, Hamilton
1993	Ray & Robyn	CKRY-FM, Calgary

ON-AIR PERSONALITY (SECONDARY MARKET)

1988	Fred King	CKRM, Regina
1989	Fred King	CKRM, Regina
1990	Fred King	CKRM, Regina
1991	Ken Kilcullen	CKGY, Red Deer
1992	Mark Cartland	CKTY, Sarnia
1993	Mark Cartland	CKTY, Sarnia

MAJOR DIRECTOR OR PROGRAM DIRECTOR (MAJOR MARKET)

1988	Paul Kennedy	CHFX, Halifax
1989	Paul Kennedy	CHFX, Halifax
1990	Paul Kennedy	CHFX, Halifax

MUSIC DIRECTOR OR PROGRAM DIRECTOR (SECONDARY MARKET)

1988	Gord Ambrose	CFMK, Kingston
1989	Gord Ambrose	CFMK, Kingston
1990	Gord Ambrose	CFMK, Kingston

PROGRAM DIRECTOR OF THE YEAR (MAJOR MARKET)

1991	Vic Folliott	CKGL, Kitchener

PROGRAM DIRECTOR OF THE YEAR (SECONDARY MARKET)

1991	Bob Mills	CKGY, Red Deer

MUSIC DIRECTOR OF THE YEAR (MAJOR MARKET)

1991	Joel Christie	CHAM, Hamilton
1992	Paul Kennedy	CHFX-FM, Halifax
1993	Phill Kallsen	CKRY-FM, Calgary

MUSIC DIRECTOR OF THE YEAR (SECONDARY MARKET)

1991	Ritch Nichol	CKGY, Red Deer
1992	Ritch Nichol	CKGY, Red Deer
1993	Ritch Nichol	CKGY, Red Deer

RADIO STATION OF THE YEAR (MAJOR MARKET)

1988	CHAM, Hamilton
1989	CHAM, Hamilton
1990	CHAM, Hamilton
1991	CKRY, Calgary
1992	CHAM, Hamilton
1993	CKRY-FM, Calgary

RADIO STATION OF THE YEAR (SECONDARY MARKET)

1988	CJWW, Saskatoon
1989	CFMK, Kingston
1990	CHOO, Ajax
1991	CJWW, Saskatoon

1992 CJWW, Saskatoon
1993 CKQM-FM, Peterborough

COUNTRY MUSIC PERSON OF THE YEAR

1982 Ron Sparling
1983 Gordon Burnett
1984 Neville Watts
1985 No Award
1986 Joe Brown
1987 Larry Delaney
1988 Larry Delaney
1989 Larry Delaney
1990 Larry Delaney
1991 Larry Delaney
1992 Michelle Wright
1993 Larry Delaney

RETAIL STORE OF THE YEAR

1982 Country Music Store, Toronto
1983 Country Music Store, Toronto
1984 Country Music Store, Toronto
1985 Country Music Store, Toronto
1986 Country Music Store, Toronto
1987 Country Music Store, Toronto
1988 Roundelay Records, Ottawa
1989 Sam The Record Man, Toronto
1990 Country Music Store, Toronto
1991 Sam the Record Man, Toronto
1992 Sam the Record Man, Calgary
1993 Sam the Record Man, Calgary

RACK JOBBER OR SUB-DISTRIBUTOR OF THE YEAR

1993 Sunrise Records, Toronto

COUNTRY MUSIC HALL OF FAME MEMBERS ELECTED

1961 Jimmie Rodgers
1961 Fred Rose
1961 Hank Williams
1962 Roy Acuff
1964 Tex Ritter
1965 Ernest Tubb
1966 Eddy Arnold
1966 James R. Denny
1966 George D. Hay
1966 Uncle Dave Macon
1967 Red Foley
1967 J.L. (Joe) Frank
1967 Jim Reeves
1967 Stephen H. Sholes
1968 Bob Wills
1969 Gene Autry
1970 Bill Monroe
1970 Original Carter Family
1971 Arthur Edward Satherley
1972 Jimmie H. Davis
1973 Chet Atkins
1973 Patsy Cline
1974 Owen Bradley
1974 Frank “Pee Wee” King
1975 Minnie Pearl
1976 Paul Cohen
1976 Kitty Wells
1977 Merle Travis
1978 Grandpa Jones
1979 Hank Snow
1979 Hubert Long
1980 Johnny Cash
1980 Connie B. Gay
1980 Original Sons of the Pioneers
1981 Vernon Dalhart
1981 Grant Turner
1982 Lefty Frizzell
1982 Roy Horton
1982 Marty Robbins
1983 Little Jimmy Dickens
1984 Ralph Sylvester Peer
1984 Floyd Tillman
1985 Flatt & Scruggs
1986 Benjamin F. Ford
1986 Wesley H. Rose
1987 Rod Brasfield
1988 Loretta Lynn
1988 Roy Rogers
1989 Jack Stapp
1989 Cliffie Stone
1989 Hank Thompson
1990 Tennessee Ernie Ford
1991 Boudleaux & Felice Bryant
1992 George Jones
1992 Frances Williams Preston
1993 Willie Nelson
1994 Merle Haggard

COUNTRY MUSIC ASSOCIATION AWARDS

ENTERTAINER OF THE YEAR

1967 Eddie Arnold
1968 Glen Campbell

1969 Johnny Cash
1970 Merle Haggard
1971 Charley Pride
1972 Loretta Lynn
1973 Roy Clark
1974 Charlie Rich
1975 John Denver
1976 Mel Tillis
1977 Ronnie Milsap
1978 Dolly Parton
1979 Willie Nelson
1980 Barbara Mandrell
1981 Barbara Mandrell
1982 Alabama
1983 Alabama
1984 Alabama
1985 Ricky Skaggs
1986 Reba McEntire
1987 Hank Williams, Jr.
1988 Hank Williams, Jr.
1989 George Strait
1990 George Strait
1991 Garth Brooks
1992 Garth Brooks
1993 Vince Gill
1994 Vince Gill

SONG OF THE YEAR

1967 "There Goes My Everything"
Dallas Frazier
1968 "Honey"
Bobby Russell
1969 "Carroll County Accident"
Bob Ferguson
1970 "Sunday Morning Coming Down"
Kris Kristofferson
1971 "Easy Loving"
Freddie Hart
1972 "Easy Loving"
Freddie Hart
1973 "Behind Closed Doors"
Kenny O'Dell
1974 "Country Bumpkin"
Don Wayne
1975 "Back Home Again"
John Denver
1976 "Rhinestone Cowboy"
Larry Weiss
1977 "Lucille"
Roger Bowling, Hal Bynum
1978 "Don't It Make My Brown Eyes Blue"
Richard Leigh
1980 "He Stopped Loving Her Today"
Bobby Braddock, Curly Putman
1981 "He Stopped Loving Her Today"
Bobby Braddock, Curly Putman
1982 "Always on My Mind"
Johnny Christopher, Wayne Carson, Mark James
1983 "Always on My Mind"
Johnny Christopher, Wayne Carson, Mark James
1984 "The Wind Beneath My Wings"
Larry Henley, Jeff Silbar
1985 "God Bless the USA"
Lee Greenwood
1986 "On the Other Hand"
Paul Overstreet, Don Schlitz
1987 "Forever and Ever Amen"
Paul Overstreet, Don Schlitz
1988 "80's Ladies"
K.T. Oslin
1989 "Chiseled in Stone"
Max D. Barnes, Vern Gosdin
1990 "Where've You Been"
Jon Vezner, Don Henry
1991 "When I Call Your Name"
Vince Gill, Tim DuBois
1992 "Look at Us"
Vince Gill, Max D. Barnes
1993 "I Still Believe in You"
Vince Gill, John Barlow Jarvis
1994 "Chattahoochie"
Alan Jackson, Jim McBride

FEMALE VOCALIST OF THE YEAR

1967 Loretta Lynn
1968 Tammy Wynette
1969 Tammy Wynette
1970 Tammy Wynette
1971 Lynn Anderson
1972 Loretta Lynn
1973 Loretta Lynn
1974 Olivia Newton-John
1975 Dolly Parton
1976 Dolly Parton
1977 Crystal Gayle
1978 Crystal Gayle
1979 Barbara Mandrell

1980 Emmylou Harris
1981 Barbara Mandrell
1982 Janie Fricke
1983 Janie Fricke
1984 Reba McEntire
1985 Reba McEntire
1986 Reba McEntire
1987 Reba McEntire
1988 K.T. Oslin
1989 Kathy Mattea
1990 Kathy Mattea
1991 Tanya Tucker
1992 Mary-Chapin Carpenter
1993 Mary-Chapin Carpenter
1994 Pam Tillis

MALE VOCALIST OF THE YEAR

1967 Jack Greene
1968 Glen Campbell
1969 Johnny Cash
1970 Merle Haggard
1971 Charley Pride
1972 Charley Pride
1973 Charlie Rich
1974 Ronnie Milsap
1975 Waylon Jennings
1976 Ronnie Milsap
1977 Ronnie Milsap
1978 Don Williams
1979 Kenny Rogers
1980 George Jones
1981 George Jones
1982 Ricky Skaggs
1983 Lee Greenwood
1984 Lee Greenwood
1985 George Strait
1986 George Strait
1987 Randy Travis
1988 Randy Travis
1989 Ricky Van Shelton
1990 Clint Black
1991 Vince Gill
1992 Vince Gill
1993 Vince Gill
1994 Vince Gill

ALBUM OF THE YEAR

1967 "There Goes My Everything"
Jack Greene/Decca
1968 "Johnny Cash at Folsom Prison"
Johnny Cash/Columbia
1969 "Johnny Cash at San Quentin Prison"
Johnny Cash/Columbia
1970 "Okie From Muskogee"
Merle Haggard
1971 "I Won't Mention It Again"
Ray Price/Columbia
1972 "Let Me Tell You About a Song"
Merle Haggard/Capitol
1973 "Behind Closed Doors"
Charlie Rich/Epic
1974 "A Very Special Love Song"
Charlie Rich/Epic
1975 "A Legend in My Time"
Ronnie Milsap
1976 "Wanted!—The Outlaws"
Waylon Jennings, Willie Nelson, Tompall Glaser, Jessi Colter/RCA
1977 "Ronnie Milsap Live"
Ronnie Milsap/RCA
1978 "It Was Almost Like a Song"
Ronnie Milsap/RCA
1979 "The Gambler"
Kenny Rogers/United Artists
1980 "Coal Miner's Daughter"
Original Motion Picture Soundtrack/MCA
1981 "I Believe in You"
Don Williams/MCA
1982 "Always on My Mind"
Willie Nelson/Columbia
1983 "The Closer You Get"
Alabama/RCA
1984 "A Little Good News"
Anne Murray/Capitol
1985 "Does Fort Worth Ever Cross Your Mind"
George Strait/MCA
1986 "Lost in the Fifties Tonight"
Ronnie Milsap/RCA
1987 "Always and Forever"
Randy Travis/Warner Bros.
1988 "Born to Boogie"
Hank Williams, Jr./Warner Bros.
1989 "Will the Circle Be Unbroken 2"
Nitty Gritty Dirt Band/Universal
1990 "Pickin' on Nashville"
Kentucky Headhunters/Mercury

1991 "No Fences"
Garth Brooks/Liberty

1992 "Ropin' the Wind"
Garth Brooks/Liberty

1993 "I Still Believe in You"
Vince Gill/MCA

1994 "Common Thread: The Songs of the Eagles"
Various Artists

SINGLE OF THE YEAR

1967 "There Goes My Everything"
Jack Greene/Decca

1968 "Harper Valley P.T.A."
Jeannie C. Riley/Plantation

1969 "A Boy Named Sue"
Johnny Cash/Columbia

1970 "Okie From Muskogee"
Merle Haggard/Capitol

1971 "Help Me Make It Through the Night"
Sammi Smith/Mega

1972 "The Happiest Girl in the Whole U.S.A."
Donna Fargo/Dot

1973 "Behind Closed Doors"
Charie Rich/Epic

1974 "Country Bumpkin"
Cal Smith/MCA

1975 "Before the Next Teardrop Falls"
Freddy Fender/ABC-Dot

1976 "Good Hearted Woman"
Waylon Jennings & Willie Nelson/RCA

1977 "Lucille"
Kenny Rogers/United Artists

1978 "Heaven's Just a Sin Away"
The Kendalls/Ovation

1979 "The Devil Went Down to Georgia"
Charlie Daniels Band/Epic

1980 "He Stopped Loving Her Today"
George Jones/Epic

1981 "Elvira"
Oak Ridge Boys/MCA

1982 "Always on My Mind"
Willie Nelson/Columbia

1983 "Swingin'"
John Anderson/Warner Bros.

1984 "A Little Good News"
Anne Murray/Capitol

1985 "Why Not Me"
The Judds/RCA

1986 "Bop"
Dan Seals/EMI-America

1987 "Forever and Ever Amen"
Randy Travis/Warner Bros.

1988 "Eighteen Wheels and a Dozen Roses"
Kathy Mattea/PolyGram

1989 "I'm No Stranger to the Rain"
Keith Whitley/RCA

1990 "When I Call Your Name"
Vince Gill/MCA

1991 "Friends in Low Places"
Garth Brooks/Capitol Nashville

1992 "Achy Breaky Heart"
Billy Ray Cyrus/Mercury

1993 "Chattahoochee"
Alan Jackson/Arista

1994 "I Swear"
John Michael Montgomery/Atlantic

VOCAL GROUP OF THE YEAR

1967 The Stonemen Family
1968 Porter Wagoner and Dolly Parton
1969 Johnny Cash and June Carter
1970 The Glaser Brothers
1971 The Osborne Brothers
1972 The Statler Brothers
1973 The Statler Brothers
1974 The Statler Brothers
1975 The Statler Brothers
1976 The Statler Brothers
1977 The Statler Brothers
1978 The Oak Ridge Boys
1979 The Statler Brothers
1980 The Statler Brothers
1981 Alabama
1982 Alabama
1983 Alabama
1984 The Statler Brothers
1985 The Judds
1986 The Judds
1987 The Judds
1988 Highway 101
1989 Highway 101
1990 Kentucky Headhunters
1991 Kentucky Headhunters
1992 Diamond Rio
1993 Diamond Rio
1994 Diamond Rio

VOCAL EVENT OF THE YEAR

1988	Trio—Dolly Parton/Emmylou Harris/Linda Ronstadt
1989	Hank Williams, Jr./Hank Williams
1990	Lorrie Morgan/Keith Whitley
1991	Mark O'Connor & The New Nashville Cats (Featuring Vince Gill, Ricky Skaggs and Steve Wariner)
1992	Marty Stuart/Travis Tritt
1993	"I Don't Need Your Rockin' Chair" George Jones with Vince Gill, Mark Chesnutt, Garth Brooks, Travis Tritt, Joe Diffie, Alan Jackson, Pam Tillis, T. Graham Brown, Patty Loveless, Clint Black
1994	"Does He Love You" Reba McEntire with Linda Davis

HORIZON AWARD

1981	Terri Gibbs
1982	Ricky Skaggs
1983	John Anderson
1984	The Judds
1985	Sawyer Brown
1986	Randy Travis
1987	Holly Dunn
1988	Ricky Van Shelton
1989	Clint Black
1990	Garth Brooks
1991	Travis Tritt
1992	Suzy Bogguss
1993	Mark Chesnutt
1994	John Michael Montgomery

VOCAL DUO OF THE YEAR

1970	Porter Wagoner and Dolly Parton
1971	Porter Wagoner and Dolly Parton
1972	Conway Twitty and Loretta Lynn
1973	Conway Twitty and Loretta Lynn
1974	Conway Twitty and Loretta Lynn
1975	Conway Twitty and Loretta Lynn
1976	Waylon Jennings and Willie Nelson
1977	Jim Ed Brown and Helen Cornelius
1978	Kenny Rogers and Dottie West
1979	Kenny Rogers and Dottie West
1980	Moe Bandy and Joe Stampley
1981	David Frizzell and Shelly West
1982	David Frizzell and Shelly West
1983	Merle Haggard and Willie Nelson
1984	Willie Nelson and Julio Iglesias
1985	Anne Murray and Dave Loggins
1986	Dan Seals and Marie Osmond
1987	Ricky Skaggs and Sharon White
1988	The Judds
1989	The Judds
1990	The Judds
1991	The Judds
1992	Brooks & Dunn
1993	Brooks & Dunn
1994	Brooks & Dunn

MUSICIAN OF THE YEAR

1967	Chet Atkins
1968	Chet Atkins
1969	Chet Atkins
1970	Jerry Reed
1971	Jerry Reed
1972	Charlie McCoy
1973	Charlie McCoy
1974	Don Rich
1975	Johnnie Gimble
1976	Hargus "Pig" Robbins
1977	Roy Clark
1978	Roy Clark
1979	Chet Atkins
1980	Chet Atkins
1981	Chet Atkins
1982	Chet Atkins
1983	Chet Atkins
1984	Chet Atkins
1985	Chet Atkins
1986	Johnny Gimble
1987	Johnny Gimble
1988	Chet Atkins
1989	Johnny Gimble
1990	Johnny Gimble
1991	Mark O'Connor
1992	Mark O'Connor
1993	Mark O'Connor
1994	Mark O'Connor

MUSIC VIDEO OF THE YEAR

1985	"All My Rowdy Friends Are Comin' Over Tonight" Hank Williams, Jr./Warner Bros. Records
1986	"Who's Gonna Fill Their Shoes" George Jones/Epic Records
1987	"My Name Is Bocephus" Hank Williams, Jr./Warner Bros. Records
1989	"There's a Tear in My Beer" Hank Williams, Jr./Hank Williams Directed by Ethan Russell/ Warner Bros. Records
1990	"The Dance" Garth Brooks Directed by John Lloyd Miller/Capitol Nashville

1991 "The Thunder Rolls"
Garth Brooks
Directed by Bud Schaetzle/Capitol Nashville

1992 "Midnight in Montgomery"
Alan Jackson
Directed by Jim Shea/Arista

1993 "Chattahoochee"
Alan Jackson
Directed by Martin Kahan/Arista

1994 "Independence Day"
Martina McBride
Directed by Robert Deaton, George J. Flanigen IV

INSTRUMENTAL GROUP OF THE YEAR

1967 The Buckaroos
1968 The Buckaroos
1969 Danny Davis & the Nashville Brass
1970 Danny Davis & the Nashville Brass
1971 Danny Davis & the Nashville Brass
1972 Danny Davis & the Nashville Brass
1973 Danny Davis & the Nashville Brass
1974 Danny Davis & the Nashville Brass
1975 Roy Clark and Buck Trent
1976 Roy Clark and Buck Trent
1977 The Original Texas Playboys
1978 The Oak Ridge Boys Band
1979 The Charlie Daniels Band
1980 The Charlie Daniels Band
1981 Alabama
1982 Alabama
1983 The Ricky Skaggs Band
1984 The Ricky Skaggs Band
1985 The Ricky Skaggs Band
1986 The Oak Ridge Boys Band

COMEDIAN OF THE YEAR

1967 Don Bowman
1968 Ben Colder
1969 Archie Campbell
1970 Roy Clark

COUNTRY MUSIC ASSOCIATION OF AUSTRALIA

"GOLDEN GUITAR AWARDS"

The Australian Country Awards were first presented in January 1973 by Radio Station 2TM for records released in Australia and New Zealand during the previous year. Judging is undertaken by 11 invited individuals, representing all aspects of the Country Music community. The award presented is a 23cm solid bronze golden guitar mounted on Tasmanian Blackwood. Changes have been made in 1974, 1976, 1977, 1980 and 1990. In 1981, finalists were standardized to five for each of the judged categories. Since 1993, the awards have been organized by the Country Music Association of Australia.

ROLL OF RENOWN

1976 Tex Morton
1977 Buddy Williams
1978 Smoky Dawson
1979 Slim Dusty
1980 Shirley Thoms
1981 Tim McNamara
1982 Gordon Parsons
1983 The McKean Sisters (Joy & Heather)
1984 Reg Lindsay
1985 Rick & Thel Carey
1986 Johnny Ashcroft
1987 Chad Morgan
1988 John Minson
1989 The Hawking Brothers
1990 Stan Coster
1991 Barry Thornton
1992 Nev Nicholls
1993 Shorty Ranger
1994 Jimmy Little

MALE VOCALIST

1974 Reg Lindsay
"July, You're a Woman" (Festival)

1975 Slim Dusty
"Biggest Disappointment" (EMI)

1976 Rex Dallas
"My Lancashire Yodelling Lass" (Hadley)

1977 Slim Dusty
"Angel of Goulburn Hill" (EMI)

1978 Reg Lindsay
"Silence on the Line" (EMI)

1979 Slim Dusty
"Marty" (EMI)

1980 Reg Lindsay
"The Empty Arms Hotel" (7 Records)

1981 Johnny Chester
"I Love You So Rebecca" (WEA)

1982 Johnny Chester
"Rough Around the Edges" (WEA)

1983 Johnny Chester
"Ad in the Weekly Times" (WEA)

1984 Arthur Blanch
"I've Come a Long Way" (Reflection)

1985 Arthur Blanch
"What Do Lonely People Do" (EMI)

1986 John Williamson
"You and My Guitar" (Emusic)

1987 John Williamson
"True Blue" (Festival)

1988 Alan Caswell
"Black Jack Blues Again" (EMI)

1989 James Blundell
"Cloncurry Cattle Song" (EMI)

1990 James Blundell
"Kimberley Moon" (EMI)

1991 James Blundell
"Age of Grace" (EMI)

1992 Keith Urban
"The River" (EMI)

1993 Lee Kernaghan
"Boys From the Bush" (ABC Music)

1994 Lee Kernaghan
"Three Chain Road"
(ABC Music/Phonogram)

FEMALE VOCALIST

1974 Suzanne Prentice
"Dust on Mother's Bible" (Master)

1975 Jean Stafford
"What Kind of Girl Do You Think I Am" (Hadley)

1976 Heather McKean
"I Can Feel Love" (Festival)

1977 Suzanne Prentice
"Sweet Country Music" (Music World)

1978 Suzanne Prentice
"How Sweet Thou Art" (Music World)

1979 Anne Kirkpatrick
"Grievous Angel" (EMI)

1980 Jean Stafford
"Hello Love" (Hadley)

1981 Jean Stafford
"That Glory Bound Train" (Hadley)

1982 Jewel Blanch
"I Can Love You" (CBS)

1983 Jewel Blanch
"Send All the Ghosts Away" (CBS)

1984 Patsy Riggir
"Beautiful Lady" (CBS (NZ))

1985 Patsy Riggir
"You'll Never Take the Country Out of Me" (CBS (NZ))

1986 Patsy Riggir
"You Remind Me of a Love Song"
(Epic (NZ))

1987 Deniese Morrison
"Now I'm Easy"
(Country City Entertainment)

1988 Evelyn Bury
"I'm Stronger Than I Look" (Selection)

1989 Deniese Morrison
"Battle Hymn of Love"
(Country City Entertainment)

1990 Deniese Morrison
"You've Gotta Learn to Dance"
(Country City Entertainment)

1991 Norma Murphy
"Sarah's Memory" (Festival)

1992 Anne Kirkpatrick
"I Guess We've Been Together for Too Long" (ABC)

1993 Norma O'Hara Murphy
"Tamworth" (Festival)

1994 Gina Jeffreys
"Two Stars Fell"
(ABC Music/Phonogram)

GROUP (From 1976, VOCAL GROUP) (From 1985, VOCAL GROUP OR DUO)

1974 Hawking Brothers
"Catfish John" (Fable)

1975 Hawking Brothers
"Julianna" (Fable)

1976 Webb Brothers
"Palmer River Songs" (Festival)

1977 Hawking Brothers
"This House Runs on Sunshine" (Crest)

1978 Hawking Brothers
"Silver Wings" (RCA)

1979 Saltbush
"Stranger" (EMI)

1980 1901
"On the Road to Gundagal" (Bullet)

1981 Grand Junction
"Married Women" (RCA)

1982 1901
"Lifting Me Up, Letting Me Down"
(Omega)

1983 Bullamakanka
"Home Among the Gum Trees"
(Mercury)

1984 Bullamakanka
"Gaylene" (RCA)
1985 Bullamakanka
"G'Day" (EMI)
1986 The Flying Emus
"Diamond Creek" (Larrikin)
1987 Three Chord Wonders
"Losin' My Blues Tonight" (EMI)
1988 The Flying Emus
"Auctioneer" (Festival)
1989 Smoky Dawson/Trevor Knight
"High Country" (EMI)
1990 Bullamakanka
"Ride These Roads" (True Blue)
1991 Bullamakanka
"Dust" (True Blue)
1992 Jan Cooper/Michael Roycroft
"As Far as This Feelin' Will Take Us" (RCA)
1993 James Blundell/James Rayne
"Way Out West" (EMI Music)
1994 Lee Kernaghan & Slim Dusty
"Leave Him in the Longyard" (ABC Music/Phonogram)

NEW TALENT

1974 Reg Poole
"Country Music Hall of Fame" (W & G)
1975 Rob Brown
"Beautiful World" (WEA/Angelwood)
1976 Bob Purtell
"Motivation Day" (ATA)
1977 Saltbush
"Sassafras Gap" (Rainbird)
1978 Mike Fox
"If Nobody Loves Me" (Bunyip)
1979 1901
"House Where the Wind Blows Cold" (EMI)
1980 Allan Caswell
"King of the Rodeo" (Mercury)
1981 Patsy Riggir
"It's Not Love" (EMI (NZ))
1982 Paul Wookey
"Roll Along" (Troubador)
1983 Leanne Douglas (RCA)
"Don't It Make You Wanna Cry" (RCA)
1984 Natalie Wood
"Who Were You Thinking Of" (Hadley)
1985 Vic Lanyon
"Here's to You" (EMI)
1986 Great Divide
"Landed on My Feet" (RCA)
1987 Jane Maddick
"Rainbow Chaser" (RCA/Ariola)
1988 James Blundell
"Song for Louise" (RCA)
1989 Jenine Vaughan
"Gypsy Man" (RCA)
1990 Happening Thang
"I Don't Wanna Go to Work" (WEA)
1991 Keith Urban
"I Never Work on Sunday" (EMI)
1992 Colin Buchanan
"Galahs in the Gidgee" (ABC)
1993 Brent Parlane
"Save a Little Love" (ABC Music)
1994 Beccy Cole
"Foolin' Around" (Outback Music)

RADIO LISTENER AWARD

1973 Col Hardy (Opal)

WRANGLER SPECIAL AWARD

1977 Eric Watson

COUNTRY MUSIC CAPITAL AWARD

1978 John Minson
1979 Nick Erby
1980 Eric Scott
1981 Arch Kerr
1982 Don McGuire
1983 Rocky Page
1984 Bill Robertson
1985 Ron Willis
1986 Wally Bishop
1987 Jazzer Smith
1988 Barry Forrester
1989 Kevin Knapp
1990 Tex Banes
1991 Ross Murphy
1992 Cal Phillips

SONG OF THE YEAR (From 1985, APRA SONG OF THE YEAR)

1973 "Light on the Hill"
(Joy McKean) (EMI)
1974 "Goondiwindi Grey"
(Wallace/Hauritz) (Essex)

1975 "Biggest Disappointment" (Joy McKean) (EMI)

1976 "Santa Never Made It Into Darwin" (Bill Cate) (Fable)

1977 "Three Rivers Hotel" (Stan Coster) (EMI)

1978 "Indian Pacific" (Joy McKean) (EMI)

1979 "Best of the Government Stroke" (Oliver/McKean) (EMI)

1980 "Three Empty Bottles" (Dave Pincombe) (Astor)

1981 "One Armed Bandit" (Allan & Brian Caswell) (7 Records)

1982 "His Spurs Are Rusty Now" (Rex & Collin Dallas) (Hadley)

1983 "Used to Be a Gold Song" (Allan Caswell/Keith Potger) (Country Man)

1984 "I Was Only 19" (John Schumann) (CBS)

1985 "Queen in the Sport of Kings" (John Williamson) (Festival)

1986 "The Garden" (Allan Caswell) (Albert Productions)

1987 "He's a Good Bloke When He's Sober" (Stan Coster) (EMI)

1988 "The Old Time Tent Shows" (Barry Forrester) (RCA Records)

1989 "We've Done Us Proud" (Graeme Connors) (EMI Records)

1990 "Kimberley Moon" (James Blundell/Doug Trevor) (EMI Records)

1991 "Blue Heeler" (James Blundell) (EMI Records)

1992 "Things Are Not the Same on the Land" (Bill Chambers) (EMI Records)

1993 "Boys From the Bush" (Garth Porter/Lee Kernaghan) (ABC Music)

1994 "Three Chain Road" (Garth Porter/Lee Kernaghan) (ABC Music/Phonogram)

HERITAGE AWARD

1980 Buddy Williams "What a Dreary Old World It Would Be" (RCA)

1981 Reg Poole "The Warrumbungle Mare" (Selection)

1982 Slim Dusty "Where Country Is" (EMI/Columbia)

1983 Slim Dusty "Banjo's Man" (EMI/Columbia)

1984 Slim Dusty "Australia's on the Wallaby" (EMI)

1985 Reg Poole "When the Big Mobs Came to Bourke" (Selection)

1986 Norma Murphy "How the Fire Queen Crossed the Swamp" (Selection)

1987 Slim Dusty "Mount Buckaroo" (EMI)

1988 Smoky Dawson/Trevor Knight's Newport Trio "The Days of Old Khan Coban" (Jane)

1989 Slim Dusty "We've Done Us Proud" (EMI)

1990 John Williamson "Drover's Boy" (Emusic/Festival)

1991 Brian Young "Thistles on the Millside" (CBS)

1992 Rex Dallas "The Western Man" (Enrec)

1993 Colin Buchanan "A Drover's Wife" (ABC Music)

HERITAGE SONG OF THE YEAR

1994 Kev Carmody "From Little Things Big Things Grow" (Paul Kelly-Kev Carmody) (Festival Records)

TOP SELLING TRACK (From 1977, TOP SELLING RECORD)

1973 "Redback on the Toilet Seat" (Slim Newton) (Hadley)

1974 "Heaven Is My Woman's Love" (Col Joye) (ATA)

1975 "My Kind of Woman" (Johnny Chester) (Fable)

1976 "Worst in the World" (Slim Dusty) (EMI)

1977 "Things I See Around Me" (Slim Dusty) (EMI)

1978 "Indian Pacific" (Slim Dusty) (EMI)

1979 "One Day at a Time"
(Hawking Brothers) (RCA)

1980 "Walk a Country Mile"
(Slim Dusty) (EMI)

1981 "The Man Who Steadies the Lead"
(Slim Dusty) (EMI)

1982 "Who Put the Roo in the Stew"
(Webb Brothers) (RCA)

1983 "One Day at a Time"
(Suzanne Prentice) (Music World)

1984 "I Was Only 19"
(Redgum) (CBS)

1985 "Trucks on the Track"
(Slim Dusty) (EMI)

1986 "Yodelling Man—Roger Tibbs"
(Roger Tibbs) (Music World)

1987 "Patsy Riggir Country"
(Patsy Riggir) (CBS (NZ))

1988 "Mallee Boy"
(John Williamson) (Emusic/Festival)

1989 "Boomerang Cafe"
(John Williamson) (Emusic)

1990 "Warrangul"
(John Williamson) (Emusic/Festival)

1991 "Two Singers/One Song"
(Slim Dusty/Ann Kirkpatrick)
(EMI Records)

1992 "JW's Family Album"
(John Williamson) (Gumleaf Recordings)

1993 "This Road"
(James Blundell) (EMI Music)

ALBUM

1973 "Me & My Guitar"
(Slim Dusty) (EMI)

1974 "Live at Tamworth"
(Slim Dusty) (EMI)

1975 "Australiana"
(Slim Dusty) (EMI)

1976 "Lights on the Hill"
(Slim Dusty) (EMI)

1977 "Things I See Around Me"
(Slim Dusty) (EMI)

1978 "Country Travellin'"
(Hawking Brothers) (RCA)

1979 "One Day at a Time"
(Hawking Brothers) (RCA)

1980 "Walk a Country Mile"
(Slim Dusty) (EMI)

1981 "The Man Who Steadies the Lead"
(Slim Dusty) (EMI)

1982 "The Lady & The Cowboy"
(Jewel & Arthur Blanch) (CBS)

1983 "Too Late for Regrets"
(Arthur Blanch) (CBS)

1984 "On the Wallaby"
(Slim Dusty) (EMI)

1985 "Trucks on the Track"
(Slim Dusty) (EMI)

1986 "Road Thru the Heart"
(John Williamson) (Emusic)

1987 "Mallee Boy"
(John Williamson) (Festival)

1988 "Neon City"
(Slim Dusty) (EMI)

1989 "Boomerang Cafe"
(John Williamson) (Emusic)

1990 "Warrangul"
(John Williamson) (Emusic/Festival)

1991 "Coming Home"
(Slim Dusty) (EMI Records)

1992 "Out of the Blue"
(Ann Kirkpatrick) (ABC Records)

1993 "The Outback Club"
(Lee Kernaghan) (ABC Music)

ALBUM OF THE YEAR

1994 "Three Chain Road"
(Lee Kernaghan)
(ABC Music/Phonogram)

TOP SELLING ALBUM

1994 "Touch of Water"
(James Blundell) (EMI Music)

EP OR SINGLE (From 1974, EP)

1973 "Lights on the Hill"
(Slim Dusty) (EMI)

1974 "Live at Tamworth"
(Hamilton County Bluegrass Band)
(EMI)

1975 "Old Wallerawang"
(Rex Dallas) (Hadley)

INSTRUMENTAL

1973 "Ring-a-Ding"
(Hamilton County Bluegrass Band)
(EMI)

1974 "Yakity Axe"
(Hawking Brothers) (Fable)

1975	"Nashville Express" (Nev Nicholls' Country Playboys) (RCA)
1976	"Orange Blossom Special" (Paul & Colleen Trenwith) (EMI)
1977	"Closest Thing to Freedom" (Lindsay Butler) (Opal)
1978	"Fender Bender" (Norm Bodkin) (Hadley)
1979	"Fiddle in the Gorge" (Trev & Dennis) (Nationwide)
1980	"Panning for Gold" (Buckskin) (Festival)
1981	"Flying Pieman" (The Bushwackers) (Avenue)
1982	"Brian's Tune" (Brian Thornton) (Selection)
1983	"Back to Those Rolling Plains" (Alan Hawking) (Country Man)
1984	"Moonjbah Mull" (Hired Hands) (Country)
1985	"Gospel Train" (Alan Hawking) (RCA)
1986	"Look Out Below" (The Flying Emus) (Larrikin)
1987	"Emu Strut" (The Flying Emus) (Flying Emu Productions through Festival Records)
1988	"Jackaroo" (The Flying Emus) (Infinity)
1989	"Bullebounce" (Bullamakanka) (True Blue)
1990	"Wild River" (Lawrie Minson) (EMI)
1991	"Dixie Breakdown" (The Flying Emus) (Festival)
1992	"Clutterbilly" (Keith Urban) (EMI)
1993	"Kanga" (Pixie Jenkins) (EMI Music)
1994	"Kindee" (Pixie) (EMI Music)

RECORD PRODUCER OF THE YEAR

1990	Rod Coe
1991	Lindsay Butler
1992	Lindsay Butler
1993	Garth Porter

VIDEO TRACK OF THE YEAR

1994	"May Your Fridge Be Full of Coldies" (Directed by Cathy Philips) (Artist: Greg Champion) (ABC Music/Phonogram)

NATIONAL COWBOY HALL OF FAME

The National Cowboy Hall of Fame in Oklahoma City, Oklahoma, was the idea of Kansas City businessman Chester A. Reynolds. During a visit to the Will Rogers Memorial in Claremore, Oklahoma, in 1954, he thought it would be a wonderful idea to have a national memorial paying homage to all the men and women who made lasting contributions to the history and legacy of the American West. The resultant National Cowboy Hall of Fame and Western Heritage Center was declared a national memorial in 1958 and opened to the public in June 1965. It is a private, non-profit organization that represents the seventeen western states.

HALL OF GREAT WESTERN PERFORMERS

1958	Tom Mix
1966	Gary Cooper
1968	Amanda Blake
1969	Joel McCrea
1970	Walter Brennan
1970	Robert Taylor
1972	Gene Autry
1972	James Stewart
1973	Tim McCoy
1973	Barbara Stanwick
1973	Buck Jones
1974	John Wayne
1975	William S. Hart
1975	Randolph Scott
1976	Harry Carey
1976	Roy Rogers & Dale Evans
1978	Glenn Ford
1979	Hoot Gibson
1979	Gregory Peck
1980	Tex Ritter
1981	James Arness
1981	Ken Curtis
1981	Dennis Weaver
1982	Ben Johnson
1982	Slim Pickens
1983	Rex Allen
1984	Kirk Douglas
1984	Dale Robertson
1989	Ronald Reagan

1990	Clayton Moore
1990	James Garner
1991	James Drury
1991	Chuck Connors
1991	Tim Holt
1992	Hugh O'Brian
1992	Jack Pallance
1993	Maureen O'Hara
1993	Jay Silverheels
1994	Jack Elam
1994	"Texas" Jack Omohundra

DOVE AWARDS

These awards recognize outstanding achievement in the Gospel music field and are given by the **Gospel Music Association**. Please see the Gospel Music Association's entry in the main body of this work.

ARTIST OF THE YEAR

1981	The Imperials
1982	Sandi Patti
1983	Amy Grant
1984	Sandi Patti
1985	Sandi Patti
1986	Amy Grant
1987	Sandi Patti
1988	Sandi Patti
1989	Amy Grant
1990	Steven Curtis Chapman
1991	Steven Curtis Chapman
1992	Amy Grant
1993	Steven Curtis Chapman
1994	Michael English

MALE VOCALIST OF THE YEAR

1969	James Blackwood
1970	James Blackwood
1971	No Awards
1972	James Blackwood
1973	James Blackwood
1974	James Blackwood
1975	James Blackwood
1976	Johnny Cook
1977	James Blackwood
1978	Dallas Holm
1979	No Awards
1980	Dallas Holm
1981	Russ Taff
1982	Russ Taff
1983	Larnelle Harris
1984	Russ Taff
1985	Steve Green
1986	Larnelle Harris
1987	Steve Green
1988	Larnelle Harris
1989	Wayne Watson
1990	Steven Curtis Chapman
1991	Steven Curtis Chapman
1992	Michael English
1993	Michael English
1994	Michael English

FEMALE VOCALIST OF THE YEAR

1969	Vestal Goodman
1970	Ann Downing
1971	No Awards
1972	Sue Chenault
1973	Sue Chenault
1974	Sue Chenault Dodge
1975	Jeanne Johnson
1976	Joy McQuire
1977	Evie Tornquist
1978	Evie Tornquist
1979	No Awards
1980	Cynthia Clawson
1981	Cynthia Clawson
1982	Cynthia Clawson
1983	Larnelle Harris
1984	Sandi Patti
1985	Sandi Patti
1986	Sandi Patti
1987	Sandi Patti
1988	Sandi Patti
1989	Sandi Patti
1990	Sandi Patti
1991	Sandi Patti
1992	Sandi Patti
1993	Twila Paris
1994	Twila Paris

MALE GROUP OF THE YEAR

1969	Imperials
1970	Oak Ridge Boys
1971	No Awards
1972	Oak Ridge Boys
1973	Blackwood Brothers
1974	Blackwood Brothers
1975	Imperials
1976	Imperials
1977	Cathedral Quartet

1978 Imperials
1979 No Awards
1980 Imperials

MIXED GROUP OF THE YEAR

1969 Speer Family
1970 Speer Family
1971 No Awards
1972 Speer Family
1973 Speer Family
1974 Speer Family
1975 Speer Family
1976 Speer Family
1977 Speer Family
1978 Dallas Holm And Praise
1979 No Awards
1980 Bill Gaither Trio

GROUP OF THE YEAR

1981 Imperials
1982 Imperials
1983 Imperials
1984 No Awards
1985 No Awards
1986 No Awards
1987 First Call
1988 First Call
1989 Take 6
1990 BeBe & CeCe Winans
1991 Petra
1992 BeBe & CeCe Winans
1993 4Him
1994 4Him

NEW ARTIST OF THE YEAR

1988 BeBe & CeCe Winans
1989 Take 6
1990 David Mullen
1991 4 Him
1992 Michael English
1993 Cindy Morgan
1994 Point Of Grace

SONGWRITER OF THE YEAR

1969 Bill Gaither
1970 Bill Gaither
1971 No Awards
1972 Bill Gaither
1973 Bill Gaither
1974 Bill Gaither
1975 Bill Gaither
1976 Bill Gaither
1977 Bill Gaither
1978 Dallas Holm
1979 No Awards
1980 Don Francisco
1981 Gary Chapman
1982 Dottie Rambo
1983 Michael Card
1984 Lanny Wolfe
1985 Michael W. Smith
1986 Gloria Gaither
1987 Dick & Melodie Tunney
1988 Larnelle Harris
1989 Steven Curtis Chapman
1990 Steven Curtis Chapman
1991 Steven Curtis Chapman
1992 Steven Curtis Chapman
1993 Steven Curtis Chapman
1994 Steven Curtis Chapman

SONG OF THE YEAR

1969 R.E. Winsett
"Jesus Is Coming Soon"
1970 Don Summer, Dwayne Friend
"The Night Before Easter"
1971 No Awards
1972 Ron Hinson
"The Lighthouse"
1973 Kris Kristofferson
"Why Me Lord?"
1974 Bill Gaither
"Because He Lives"
1975 Marijohn Wilkin, Kris Kristofferson
"One Day at a Time"
1976 Neil Enloe
"Statue of Liberty"
1977 John Stallings
"Learning to Live"
1978 Dallas Holm
"Rise Again"
1979 No Awards
1980 Don Francisco
"He's Alive"
1981 Brown Bannister, Mike Hudson
"Praise the Lord"
1982 Dottie Rambo
"We Shall Behold Him"
1983 Michael Card, John Thompson
"El Shaddai"

1984 Lanny Wolfe
"More Than Wonderful"
1985 Gloria Gaither, Dony McGuire
"Upon This Rock"
1986 Billy Sprague, Niles Borop
"Via Dolorosa"
1987 Dick & Melodie Tunney, Paul Smith
"How Excellent Is Thy Name"
1988 Phil McHugh, Gloria Gaither, Sandi Patti Helvering
"In the Name of the Lord"
1989 Wayne Watson, Claire Cloninger
"Friend of a Wounded Heart"
1990 Ray Boltz
"Thank You"
1991 Gary Driskell
"Another Time, Another Place"
1992 Amy Grant, Michael W. Smith
"Place in this World"
1993 Steven Curtis Chapman, Geoff Moore
"The Great Adventure"
1994 Shawn Craig, Don Koch
"In Christ Alone"

ASSOCIATE MEMBERSHIP AWARD

1974 Blackwood Brothers
1975 "Statue of Liberty"
Neil Ensloe
1976 Blackwood Brothers
1977 Blackwood Brothers
1978 "Rise Again"
Dallas Holm

INSTRUMENTALIST

1969 Dwayne Friend
1970 Dwayne Friend
1971 No Awards
1972 Tony Brown
1973 Henry Slaughter
1974 Henry Slaughter
1975 Henry Slaughter
1976 Henry Slaughter
1977 Henry Slaughter
1978 Dino Kartsonakis
1979 No Awards
1980 Dino Kartsonakis
1981 Dino Kartsonakis
1982 Dino Kartsonakis
1983 Dino Kartsonakis
1984 Phil Driscoll
1985 Phil Driscoll
1986 Dino Kartsonakis

TELEVISION PROGRAM

1969 Gospel Singing Jubilee
Florida Boys
1970 Gospel Singing Jubilee
Florida Boys
1971 No Awards
1972 Gospel Singing Jubilee
Florida Boys
1973 Gospel Singing Jubilee
Florida Boys
1974 Gospel Singing Jubilee
Florida Boys
1975 Gospel Singing Jubilee
Florida Boys
1976 No Awards
1977 PTL Club
Jim Bakker
1978 Gospel Singing Jubilee
Florida Boys
1979 No Awards
1980 Hemphill Family Time
Hemphill Family

BACKLINER NOTES

1970 "Ain't That Beautiful"
Jake Hess
Annotator: Mrs. Jake Hess
1971 No Awards
1972 "Light"
Oak Ridge Boys
Annotator: Johnny Cash
1973 "Release Me"
Blackwood Brothers
Annotator: Eddie Miller
1974 "On Stage"
Blackwood Brothers
Annotator: Don Butler
1975 "Bust Out Laffin'"
Wendy Bagwell and The Sunliters
Annotator: Wendy Bagwell
1976 "Just a Little Talk With Jesus"
Cleavant Derricks Family
Annotator: Sylvia Mays
1977 "Cornerstone"
Speers Family
Annotator: Joe Huffman

1978 "Transformation"
Joe and Nancy Cruse
Annotator: Joe and Nancy Cruse

1979 No Awards

1980 "Breakout"
Mercy River Boys
Annotator: Merlin Littlefield

SOUTHERN GOSPEL ALBUM OF THE YEAR

1969 "It's Happening"
Oak Ridge Boys
Producer: Bob MacKenzie
HeartWarming

1970 "Fill My Cup, Lord"
Blackwood Brothers
Producer: Darol Rice
RCA Victor

1971 No Awards

1972 "Light"
Oak Ridge Boys
Producer: Bob MacKenzie
HeartWarming

1973 "Street Gospel"
Oak Ridge Boys
Producer: Bob MacKenzie
HeartWarming

1974 "Big and Live"
Kingsmen Quartet
Producer: Marvin Norcross
Canaan

1975 "I Just Feel Like Something Good Is About to Happen"
Speer Family
Producer: Bob MacKenzie
HeartWarming

1976 "Between the Cross and Heaven"
Speer Family
Producer: Joe Huffman
HeartWarming

1977 "Then and Now"
Cathedral Quartet
Producer: Ken Harding
Canaan

1978 "Kingsmen Live in Chattanooga"
Kingsmen
Producer: Joe Huffman/Eldridge Fox
HeartWarming

1979 No Awards

1980 "From Out of the Past"
Kingsmen
Producer: Joe Huffman/Eldridge Fox
HeartWarming

1981 "Workin'"
Hemphills
Producer: Jerry Crutchfield
HeartWarming

1982 "One Step Closer"
Rex Nelon Singers
Producer: Ken Harding
Canaan

1983 "Feeling at Home"
Rex Nelon Singers
Producer: Ken Harding
Canaan

1984 "We Shall Behold the King"
Rex Nelon Singers
Producer: Ken Harding
Canaan

1985 "The Best of and a Whole Lot More"
Rex Nelon Singers
Producer: Ken Harding
Canaan

1986 "Excited"
Hemphills
Producer: Wayne Hilton/Trent Hemphill
HeartWarming

1987 "The Master Builder"
The Cathedrals
Producer: William Gaither/Gary McSpadden
RiverSong

1988 "Symphony of Praise"
The Cathedrals
Producer: Lari Goss
RiverSong

1989 "Goin' in Style"
The Cathedrals
Producer: Lari Goss
Homeland

1990 "I Just Started Living"
The Cathedrals
Producer: Lari Goss
Homeland

1991 "Climbing High & Higher"
The Cathedrals
Producer: Bill Gaither/Mark Trammel/Lari Goss
Homeland

1992 "Homecoming"
The Gaither Vocal Band
Producer: Ken Mansfield/The Gaither Vocal Band
Star Song

1993 "Reunion: A Gospel Homecoming Celebration"
Bill & Gloria Gaither
Producer: Bill Gaither
Star Song

1994 "Southern Classics"
The Gaither Vocal Band
Producer: Bill Gaither, Michael Sykes, Michael English
Benson

INSPIRATIONAL ALBUM

1976 "Jesus, We Just Want to Thank You"
Bill Gaither Trio
Producer: Bob MacKenzie
HeartWarming

1977 "Ovation"
Couriers
Producer: Jesse Peterson
Tempo

1978 "Pilgrim's Progress"
Bill Gaither Trio
Producers: Bob MacKenzie/John W. Thompson
Impact

1979 No Awards

1980 "Special Delivery"
Doug Oldham
Producer: Joe Huffman
Impact

1981 "You're Welcome Here"
Cynthia Clawson
Producer: JEN Productions
Triangle

1982 "Joni's Song"
Joni Eareckson
Producer: Kurt Kaiser
Word

1983 "Lift Up the Lord"
Sandi Patti
Producer: Greg Nelson
Impact

1984 "More Than Wonderful"
Sandi Patti
Producers: David Clydesdale/Sandi Patti Helvering
Impact

1985 "Songs From the Heart"
Sandi Patti
Producer: David Clydesdale/Sandi Patti Helvering
Impact

1986 "I've Seen Jesus"
Larnelle Harris
Producer: Greg Nelson
Impact

1987 "Morning Like This"
Sandi Patti
Producer: Greg Nelson/Sandi Patti Helvering
Word

1988 "The Father Hath Provided"
Larnelle Harris
Producer: Greg Nelson
Benson

1989 "Make His Praise Glorious"
Sandi Patti
Producers: Greg Nelson/Sandi Patti Helvering
Word

1990 "The Mission"
Steve Green
Producer: Greg Nelson
Sparrow

1991 "Another Time, Another Place"
Sandi Patti
Producer: Greg Nelson
Word

1992 "Larnelle Live...Psalms, Hymns & Spiritual Songs"
Larnelle Harris
Producer: Lari Goss
Benson

1993 "Generation 2 Generation"
Benson artists and their families
Producers: Don Koch, Ed Nalle, Fred Hammond, Joe Hogue, Dana Key
Benson

1994 "The Season of Love"
4Him
Producer: Don Koch
Benson

CONTEMPORARY ALBUM

1976 "No Shortage"
Imperials
Producer: Bob MacKenzie/Gary Paxton
Impact

1977 "Reba...Lady"
Reba Rambo Gardner
Producer: Phil Johnson
Greentree

1978 "Transformation"
Cruse Family
Producer: Ken Harding
Canaan

1979 No Awards

1980 "All That Matters"
Dallas Holm And Praise
Producer: Phil Johnson
Greentree

1981 "One More Song for You"
Imperials
Producer: Michael Omartian
DaySpring

1982 "Priority"
Imperials
Producer: Michael Omartian
DaySpring

1983 "Age to Age"
Amy Grant
Producer: Brown Bannister
Myrrh

1984 "Side by Side"
Imperials
Producers: Keith Thomas/Neal Joseph
DaySpring

1985 "Straight Ahead"
Amy Grant
Producer: Brown Bannister
Myrrh

1986 "Medals"
Russ Taff
Producers: Russ Taff/Jack Pulg
Myrrh

1987 "The Big Picture"
Michael W. Smith
Producers: Michael W. Smith/John Potoker
Reunion

1988 "Watercolour Ponies"
Wayne Watson
Producers: Wayne Watson/Paul Mills
DaySpring

1989 "Lead Me On"
Amy Grant
Producer: Brown Bannister
Myrrh

1990 "Heaven"
BeBe And CeCe Winans
Producer: Keith Thomas
Sparrow

1991 "Go West Young Man"
Michael W. Smith
Producers: Michael W. Smith/Brian Lenox

1992 "For the Sake of the Call"
Steven Curtis Chapman
Producer: Phil Naish
Sparrow

1993 "The Great Adventure"
Steven Curtis Chapman
Producer: Phil Naish
Sparrow

1994 "Hope"
Michael English
Producer: Brown Bannister
Warner Alliance

COUNTRY ALBUM

1988 "An Evening Together"
Steve & Annie Chapman
Producers: Ron Griffin/Steve Chapman
Star Song

1989 "Richest Man in Town"
Bruce Carroll
Producer: Bubba Smith
New Canaan

1990 "Heirloom"
Heirloom
Producers: Michael Sykes/Trent Hemphill
Benson

1991 "Sojourner's Song"
Buddy Greene
Producer: Bubba Smith
Word

1992 "Sometimes Miracles Hide"
Bruce Carroll
Producers: Brown Bannister/Tom Hemby
Word

1993 "Love Is Strong"
Paul Overstreet
Producer: Brown Bannister
Word

1994 "Walk On"
Bruce Carroll
Producer: Brown Bannister
Word

ALBUM BY A SECULAR RECORDING ARTIST

1975 "Sunday Morning With Charley Pride"
Charley Pride
Producer: Jerry Bradley
RCA Victor

1976 No Awards

1977 "Home Where I Belong"
B.J. Thomas
Myrrh

1978 "First Class"
The Boones
Producer: Chris Christian
Lamb & Lion

1979 No Awards

1980 "Slow Train Coming"
Bob Dylan
Producers: Jerry Wexler/Barry Beckett
Columbia

1981 "With My Song"
Debby Boone
Producer: Brown Bannister
Lamb & Lion

1982 "Amazing Grace"
B.J. Thomas
Producer: Pete Drake
Myrrh

1983 "He Set My Life to Music"
Barbara Mandrell
Producer: Tom Collins
MCA

1984 "Surrender"
Debby Boone
Producer: Brown Bannister
Lamb & Lion

1985 "You Were Loving Me"
Lulu Roman Smith
Producer: Gary McSpadden
Canaan

1986 "No More Night"
Glen Campbell
Producer: Glen Campbell/Ken Harding
Word

COUNTRY RECORDED SONG OF THE YEAR

1989 "Above and Beyond"
Bruce Carroll
(Bruce Carroll/Paul Smith)
Word

1990 "Tis So Sweet to Trust in Jesus" (PD)
Amy Grant

1991 "Seein' My Father in Me"
Paul Overstreet
(Paul Overstreet)
RCA

1992 "Sometimes Miracles Hide"
Bruce Carroll
(Bruce Carroll/C. Aaron Wilburn)
Word

1993 "If We Only Had the Heart"
Bruce Carroll
(Bruce Carroll/Michael Puyear-Dwight Liles)
Word

1994 "There but for the Grace of God"
Paul Overstreet
(Paul Overstreet/Taylor Dunn)
Word

CONTEMPORARY RECORDED SONG OF THE YEAR

1989 "His Eyes"
Steven Curtis Chapman
(Steven Curtis Chapman)
Sparrow

1990 "Heaven"
BeBe & CeCe Winans
(Keith Thomas/Benjamin Winans)
Sparrow

1991 "Another Time, Another Place"
Sandi Patti
(Gary Driskell)
Word

1992 "Home Free"
Wayne Watson
(Wayne Watson)
DaySpring

1993 "The Great Adventure"
Steven Curtis Chapman
(Steven Curtis Chapman/Geoff Moore)
Sparrow

1994 "Go There With You"
Steven Curtis Chapman
(Steven Curtis Chapman)
Sparrow

INSPIRATIONAL RECORDED SONG OF THE YEAR

1989 "In Heaven's Eyes"
Sandi Patti
Producer: Phil McHugh
Word

1990 "His Strength Is Perfect"
Steven Curtis Chapman
(Steven Curtis Chapman/Jerry Salley)
Sparrow

1991 "Who Will Be Jesus"
Bruce Carroll
(Bruce Carroll/C. Aaron Wilburn)
Word

1992 "For All the World"
Sandi Patti
(Greg Nelson/Bob Farrell)
Word

1993 "In Christ Alone"
Michael English
(Shawn Craig/Don Koch)
Warner Alliance

1994 "Holding Out Hope to You"
Hope
(Michael English/Joe Beck/Brian White/David Wills)
Warner Alliance

SOUTHERN GOSPEL RECORDED SONG OF THE YEAR

1989 "Champion of Love"
The Cathedrals
(Phil Cross/Carolyn Cross)
RiverSong

1990 "I Can See the Hand of God"
The Cathedrals
(Steven Curtis Chapman/Jim Chapman III)

1991 "He Is Here"
The Talleys
(Kirk Talley)
Word

1992 "Where Shadows Never Fall"
Glen Campbell
(Carl Jackson/Jim Weatherly)
New Haven

1993 "There Rose a Lamb"
Gold City
(Kyla Rowland)
RiverSong

1994 "Satisfied"
The Gaither Vocal Band
(PD)
Benson

SHORT FORM MUSIC VIDEO

1987 "Famine in Their Land"
The Nelons
George J. Flanigen (Director)
Word

1988 "Stay for a While"
Amy Grant
Marc Ball (Producer)/Jack Cole for Scene Three
Myrrh

1989 "Lead Me On"
Amy Grant
Tina Silvey (Producer)/Andrew Doucette
Myrrh

1990 "I Miss the Way"
Michael W. Smith
Steve Yake (Producer)
Reunion

1991 "Revival in the Land"
Carman
Stephen Yake/Video Impact Productions
Benson

1992 "Another Time. . . Another Place"
Sandi Patti
Sandi Patti/Wayne Watson/Stephen Yake Productions
Word

1993 "The Great Adventure"
Steven Curtis Chapman
Nancy Cox (Producer)/Greg Crutcher (Director)
Sparrow

1994 "Hand on My Shoulder"
Sandi Patti
Jack Clark, Stephen Yake
Word

LONG FORM MUSIC VIDEO

1987 "Limelight"
Steve Taylor
John Anneman/Steve Taylor
Sparrow

1988 "The Big Picture Tour Video"
Michael W. Smith
Brian Shipley (Producer)/Stephen Bowlby
Reunion

1989 "Carman Live...Radically Saved"
Carman
Cindy Dupree (Producer)/George J. Flanigen and Robert Deaton

1990 "On Fire"
Petra
Stephen Yake
DaySpring

1991 "Revival in the Land"
Carman
Stephen Yake/Video Impact Productions
Benson

1992 "Rap, Rock & Soul"
DC Talk
Robert Deaton/George J. Flanigen
ForeFront

1993 "Addicted to Jesus"
Carman
Stephen Yake
Benson

1994 "The Live Adventure"
Steven Curtis Chapman
Bret Wolcott/Douglas C. Forbes/Michael Solomon
Sparrow

GRAPHIC LAYOUT AND DESIGN

1970 "Trasher Brothers at Fantastic Caverns"
Trasher Brothers
Jeff Goff

1971 No Awards

1972 "L-O-V-E Love"
Blackwood Brothers
Ace Lehman

1973 "Street Gospel"
Oak Ridge Boys
Bob McConnell

1974 "On Stage Volume I"
Blackwood Brothers
Charles Hooper

1975 "Praise Him...Live"
Downings
Bob McConnell

1976 "No Shortage"
Imperials
Bob McConnell

1977 "Then...and Now"
Cathedral Quartet
Dennis Hill

1978 "Grand Opening"
Andrus, Blackwood & Co.
Bob McConnell

1979 No Awards

1980 "Special Delivery"
Doug Oldham
Bob McConnell

COVER PHOTO OR COVER ART

1970 "This Is My Valley"
Rambos
Bill Grine

1971 No Awards

1972 "Street Gospel"
Oak Ridge Boys
Bill Grine

1973 No Award

1974 "On Stage Volume I"
Blackwood Brothers
Hope Powell

1975 "There He Goes"
Blackwood Brothers
Spears Photo

1976 "Old Fashion, Down Home, Hand Clappin', Foot Stomping, Southern Style, Gospel Quartet"
Oak Ridge Boys
Bill Barnes

1977 "Then...and Now"
Cathedral Quartet
Roy Tremble

1978 "Live in London"
Andrae Crouch & The Disciples
Robert August

1979 No Awards

1980 "You Make It Rain for Me"
Rusty Goodman
Mike Borum

RECORDED MUSIC PACKAGING

1981 "You're Welcome Here"
Cynthia Clawson
Bill Barnes/Clark Thomas

1982 "Finest Hour"
Cynthia Clawson
Bill Barnes/Matt Barnes/Pat Barnes

1983 "Age to Age"
Amy Grant
Dennis Hill/Michael Borum

1984 "A Christmas Album"
Amy Grant
Dennis Hill/Bill Farrell/Michael Borum

1985 "Kingdom of Love"
Scott Wesley Brown
Eddie Yip/Stan Evenson/Don Putnam

1986 "Unguarded"
Amy Grant
Thomas Ryan/Kent Hunter/Mark Tucker

1987 "Don't Wait for the Movie"
White Heart
Buddy Jackson/Mark Tucker

1988 "Peaceful Meditation"
Greg Buchanan
John Summers/Erik Neuhaus

1989 "Russ Taff"
Russ Taff
Patrick Pollei/Joan Tankersley/Phillip Dixon

1990 "Petra Praise"
Petra
Buddy Jackson/Mark Tucker

1991 "Beyond Belief"
Petra
Buddy Jackson/Mark Tucker

1992 "Brave Heart"
Kim Hill
Mark Tucker/Buddy Jackson/Beth Middleworth

1993 "Coram Deo"
Susan Ashton/Michael Card/Michael English
Out of the Grey/Charlie Peacock
Larry Vigon/Denise Milford

1994 "The Wonder Years 1983-1993"
Michael W. Smith
D. Rhodes/Buddy Jackson/Beth Middleworth/
Mark Tucker
Roun

GOSPEL MUSIC HALL OF FAME

LIVING CATEGORY

1971 "Pappy" Jim Waites
1972 Albert E. Brumley
1973 Lee Roy Abernathy
1974 James Blackwood, Sr.
1975 Brock Speer
1976 Mosie Lister
1977 Eva Mae LeFevre
1978 George Beverly Shea
1979-80 Conor B. Hall
1981 John T. Benson, Jr.
Ira Stamphill
1982 Thomas A. Dorsey
1983 William "Bill" Gaither
1984 Hovie Lister
Rev. James Cleveland
John Wallace "Wally" Fowler
W.B. Nowlin
J.D. Sumner
P. J. Zondervan
1985 Ralph Carmichael
1986 John W. Peterson
1987 W.J. Jake Hess
1988 Cliff Barrows
1989 Les Beasley
1990 J.G. Whitfield
1991 Dottie Rambo

DECEASED CATEGORY

1971 G.T. "Dad" Speer
1972 Lena Brock Speer
James D. Vaughn
1973 Denver Crumpler
J.R. Baxter, Jr.
E.M. Bartlett
John Daniel
Adger M. Pace
Homer Rodeheaver
A.J. Showalter
V.O. Stamps
Frank Stamps
W.B. Walbert
R.E. Winsett
1974 G. Kieffer Vaughan
1975 Fanny Crosby
1976 George Bernard
1977 James "Big Chief" Wetherington
1978 Mahalia Jackson
1979-80 Ira Sanky (award date changed)
1981 Clarice Baxter
1982 John T. Benson, Sr.
Charles Gabriel
Haldor Lillenas
B.B. McKinney
Lowell Mason
John Newton
1983 Marvin Norcross
1984 Cleavant Derriks
D.P. "Dad" Carter
Paul Heinecke
Lloyd Orrell
Clara Ward
Ethel Waters
1985 Tim Spencer
1986 Urias LeFevre
1989 P.P. Bliss

In 1991, a "Special Slate" of five inductees was introduced

1991 Robert "Bob" Benson
B.D. Ackley

Charles M. Alexander
Sallie Martin
William Morgan Ramsey
Charles Weigle (Special Slate)

In 1992, the "Living" and "Deceased" categories were replaced by "Performing" and "Non-Performing" categories. The "Special Slate" continued.

1992 Jarrell McCracken (Non-Performing)
W.F. "Jim" Myers (Performing)
Samuel Beazley (Special Slate)
J.B. Coats (Special Slate)
W. Oliver Cooper (Special Slate)
J.A. McClung (Special Slate)
O.A. Parris (Special Slate)

1993 Stuart Hamblen (Non-Performing)
Stuart Hine (Non-Performing)
Jimmie Davis (Performing)
Tennessee Ernie Ford (Performing)
James Marsh (Special Slate)
Asa Brook Everett (Special Slate)
James Rowe (Special Slate)
Charlie Tillman (Special Slate)
C.H. Tindley (Special Slate)

GRAMMY AWARDS

NATIONAL ACADEMY OF RECORDING ARTS & SCIENCES, INC. (NARAS)

The awards listed below are the part of the Grammy Awards that have been presented to Country music acts, songwriters and songs.

1958

BEST COUNTRY & WESTERN PERFORMANCE

"Tom Dooley"
The Kingston Trio
(Capitol)

1959

SONG OF THE YEAR

"The Battle of New Orleans"
Writer: Jimmy Driftwood

BEST COMEDY PERFORMANCE—MUSICAL

"The Battle of Kookamonga"
Homer & Jethro
(RCA Victor)

BEST COUNTRY & WESTERN PERFORMANCE

"The Battle of New Orleans"
Johnny Horton
(Columbia)

1960

BEST COUNTRY & WESTERN PERFORMANCE

"El Paso"
Marty Robbins
(Columbia)

1961

BEST COUNTRY & WESTERN RECORDING

"Big Bad John"
Jimmy Dean
(Columbia)

1962

BEST COUNTRY & WESTERN RECORDING

"Funny Way of Laughin'"
Burl Ives
(Decca)

BEST RHYTHM AND BLUES RECORDING

"I Can't Stop Loving You"
Ray Charles
(ABC)

1963

BEST INSTRUMENTAL ARRANGEMENT

"I Can't Stop Loving You"
Count Basie
Arranger: Quincy Jones
(Reprise)

BEST COUNTRY & WESTERN RECORDING

"Detroit City"
Bobby Bare
(Columbia)

BEST RHYTHM AND BLUES RECORDING

"Busted"
Ray Charles
(Columbia)

1964

BEST GOSPEL OR OTHER RELIGIOUS RECORDING (MUSICAL)

"Great Gospel Songs"
Tennessee Ernie Ford
(Capitol)

BEST COUNTRY & WESTERN SINGLE

"Dang Me"
Roger Miller
(Smash)

BEST COUNTRY & WESTERN ALBUM

"Dang Me/Chug-A-Lug"
Roger Miller
(Smash)

BEST COUNTRY & WESTERN VOCAL PERFORMANCE, FEMALE
"Here Comes My Baby"
Dottie West
(RCA)

BEST COUNTRY & WESTERN VOCAL PERFORMANCE, MALE
"Dang Me" (Single)
Roger Miller
(Smash)

BEST COUNTRY & WESTERN SONG
"Dang Me"
Composer: Roger Miller
(Smash)

BEST NEW COUNTRY & WESTERN ARTIST OF 1964
Roger Miller
(Smash)

1965

BEST NEW ARTIST
Tom Jones
(Parrot)

BEST CONTEMPORARY (R&R) SINGLE
"King of the Road"
Roger Miller
(Smash)

BEST CONTEMPORARY (R&R) VOCAL PERFORMANCE, MALE
"King of the Road"
Roger Miller
(Smash)

BEST CONTEMPORARY (R&R) PERFORMANCE, GROUP (VOCAL OR INSTRUMENTAL)
"Flowers on the Wall" (Single)
The Statler Brothers
(Columbia)

BEST COUNTRY & WESTERN SINGLE
"King of the Road"
Roger Miller
(Smash)

BEST COUNTRY & WESTERN ALBUM
"The Return of Roger Miller"
Roger Miller
(Smash)

BEST COUNTRY & WESTERN VOCAL PERFORMANCE, FEMALE
"Queen of the House"
Jody Miller
(Capitol)

BEST COUNTRY & WESTERN VOCAL PERFORMANCE, MALE
"King of the Road"
Roger Miller
(Smash)

BEST COUNTRY & WESTERN SONG
"King of the Road"
Songwriter: Roger Miller
(Smash)

BEST NEW COUNTRY & WESTERN ARTIST
Statler Brothers
(Columbia)

1966

BEST PERFORMANCE BY A VOCAL GROUP
"A Man and a Woman"
Anita Kerr Singers
(Warner Bros.)

BEST RHYTHM & BLUES RECORDING
"Crying Time"
Ray Charles
(ABC-Paramount)

BEST RHYTHM & BLUES SOLO VOCAL PERFORMANCE, MALE OR FEMALE
"Crying Time"
Ray Charles
(ABC-Paramount)

BEST SACRED RECORDING (MUSICAL)
"Grand Old Gospel"
Porter Wagoner & The Blackwood Bros.
(RCA Victor)

BEST COUNTRY & WESTERN RECORDING
"Almost Persuaded"
David Houston
(Epic)

BEST COUNTRY & WESTERN VOCAL PERFORMANCE, FEMALE
"Don't Touch Me"
Jeannie Seely
(Monument)

BEST COUNTRY & WESTERN VOCAL PERFORMANCE, MALE
"Almost Persuaded"
David Houston
(Epic)

BEST COUNTRY & WESTERN SONG
"Almost Persuaded"
Songwriters: Billy Sherrill, Glenn Sutton

BEST ALBUM COVER, PHOTOGRAPHY
"Confessions of a Broken Man"
Porter Wagoner
Art Direction: Robert Jones
Photographer: Les Leverette
(RCA Victor)

1967

BEST VOCAL PERFORMANCE, FEMALE
"Ode to Billie Joe"
Bobbie Gentry
(Capitol)

BEST VOCAL PERFORMANCE, MALE
"By the Time I Get to Phoenix"
Glen Campbell
(Capitol)

BEST INSTRUMENTAL PERFORMANCE
"Chet Atkins Picks the Best"
Chet Atkins
(RCA Victor)

BEST NEW ARTIST
Bobbie Gentry
(Capitol)

BEST CONTEMPORARY FEMALE SOLO VOCAL PERFORMANCE
"Ode to Billie Joe"
Bobbie Gentry
(Capitol)

BEST CONTEMPORARY MALE SOLO VOCAL PERFORMANCE
"By the Time I Get to Phoenix"
Glen Campbell
(Capitol)

BEST SACRED PERFORMANCE
"How Great Thou Art"
Elvis Presley
(RCA Victor)

BEST GOSPEL PERFORMANCE
"More Grand Old Gospel"
Porter Wagoner & The Blackwood Bros.
(RCA Victor)

BEST FOLK PERFORMANCE
"Gentle on My Mind"
John Hartford
(RCA Victor)

BEST COUNTRY & WESTERN RECORDING
"Gentle on My Mind"
Glen Campbell
A & R Producer: Al de Lory
(Capitol)

BEST COUNTRY & WESTERN SOLO VOCAL PERFORMANCE, FEMALE
"I Don't Wanna Play House"
Tammy Wynette
(Epic)

BEST COUNTRY & WESTERN SOLO VOCAL PERFORMANCE, MALE
"Gentle on My Mind"
Glen Campbell
(Capitol)

BEST COUNTRY & WESTERN PERFORMANCE, DUET, TRIO OR GROUP (VOCAL OR INSTRUMENTAL)
"Jackson"
Johnny Cash & June Carter
(Columbia)

BEST COUNTRY & WESTERN SONG
"Gentle on My Mind"
Songwriter: John Hartford

1968

ALBUM OF THE YEAR
"By the Time I Get to Phoenix"
Glen Campbell
A & R Producer: Al de Lory
(Capitol)

SONG OF THE YEAR
"Little Green Apples"
Songwriter: Bobby Russell
(Columbia)

BEST INSTRUMENTAL ARRANGEMENT
"Classical Gas"
Mason Williams
Arranger: Mike Post
(Warner Bros./7 Arts)

BEST ENGINEERED RECORDING
"Wichita Lineman"
Glen Campbell
Engineers: Joe Polito, Hugh Davies
(Capitol)

BEST ALBUM NOTES
"Johnny Cash at Folsom Prison"
Annotator: Johnny Cash
(Columbia)

BEST CONTEMPORARY-POP PERFORMANCE, INSTRUMENTAL
"Classical Gas"
Mason Williams
(Warner Bros./7 Arts)

BEST COUNTRY VOCAL PERFORMANCE, FEMALE
"Harper Valley P.T.A." (Single)
Jeannie C. Riley
(Plantation)
BEST COUNTRY VOCAL PERFORMANCE, MALE
"Folsom Prison Blues" (Single)
Johnny Cash
(Columbia)
BEST COUNTRY PERFORMANCE, DUO OR GROUP (VOCAL OR INSTRUMENTAL)
"Foggy Mountain Breakdown"
Flatt & Scruggs
(Columbia)
BEST COUNTRY SONG
"Little Green Apples"
Songwriter: Bobby Russell
BEST GOSPEL PERFORMANCE
"The Happy Gospel of the Happy Goodmans"
Happy Goodman Family
(Word)
BEST FOLK PERFORMANCE
"Both Sides Now"
Judy Collins
(Elektra)
BEST INSTRUMENTAL THEME
"Classical Gas"
Composer: Mason Williams
(Warner Bros./7 Arts)
1969
SONG OF THE YEAR
"Games People Play"
Songwriter: Joe South
BEST ALBUM NOTES
"Nashville Skyline"
Bob Dylan
Annotator: Johnny Cash
(Columbia)
BEST CONTEMPORARY SONG
"Games People Play"
Songwriter: Joe South
(Capitol)
BEST COUNTRY VOCAL PERFORMANCE, FEMALE
"Stand by Your Man" (Album)
Tammy Wynette
(Epic)
BEST COUNTRY VOCAL PERFORMANCE, MALE
"A Boy Named Sue" (Single)
Johnny Cash
(Columbia)
BEST COUNTRY PERFORMANCE BY A DUO OR GROUP
"Macarthur Park"
Waylon Jennings & The Kimberleys
(RCA Victor)
BEST COUNTRY INSTRUMENTAL PERFORMANCE
"The Nashville Brass Featuring Danny Davis Play More Nashville Sounds"
Danny Davis & The Nashville Brass
(RCA Victor)
BEST COUNTRY SONG
"A Boy Named Sue"
Songwriter: Shel Silverstein
BEST GOSPEL PERFORMANCE
"In Gospel Country"
Porter Wagoner & The Blackwood Bros.
(RCA Victor)
1970
BEST CONTEMPORARY VOCAL PERFORMANCE, MALE
"Everything Is Beautiful" (Single)
Ray Stevens
(Barnaby)
BEST COUNTRY VOCAL PERFORMANCE, FEMALE
"Rose Garden"
Lynn Anderson
(Columbia)
BEST COUNTRY VOCAL PERFORMANCE, MALE
"For the Good Times"
Ray Price
(Columbia)
BEST COUNTRY VOCAL PERFORMANCE BY DUO OR GROUP
"If I Were a Carpenter"
Johnny Cash & June Carter
(Columbia)
BEST COUNTRY INSTRUMENTAL PERFORMANCE
"Me & Jerry"
Chet Atkins & Jerry Reed
(RCA Victor)
BEST COUNTRY SONG
"My Woman, My Woman, My Wife"
Songwriter: Marty Robbins
BEST GOSPEL PERFORMANCE (OTHER THAN SOUL GOSPEL)
"Talk About the Good Times"
Oak Ridge Boys
(Heartwarming)

1971

BEST POP VOCAL PERFORMANCE, MALE

"You've Got a Friend" (Single)
James Taylor
(Warner Bros.)

BEST COUNTRY VOCAL PERFORMANCE, FEMALE

"Help Me Make It Through the Night"
Sammi Smith
(Mega)

BEST COUNTRY VOCAL PERFORMANCE, MALE

"When You're Hot, You're Hot"
Jerry Reed
(RCA Victor)

BEST COUNTRY VOCAL PERFORMANCE BY A GROUP

"After the Fire Is Gone" (Single)
Conway Twitty and Loretta Lynn
(Decca)

BEST COUNTRY INSTRUMENTAL PERFORMANCE

"Snowbird" (Single)
Chet Atkins
(RCA Victor)

BEST COUNTRY SONG

"Help Me Make It Through the Night"
Songwriter: Kris Kristofferson

BEST SACRED PERFORMANCE

"Did You Think to Pray"
Charley Pride
(RCA Victor)

BEST GOSPEL PERFORMANCE (OTHER THAN SOUL GOSPEL)

"Let Me Live"
Charley Pride
(RCA Victor)

1972

BEST ALBUM NOTES

"Tom T. Hall's Greatest Hits"
Annotator: Tom T. Hall
(Mercury)

BEST COUNTRY VOCAL PERFORMANCE, FEMALE

"Happiest Girl in the Whole U.S.A." (Single)
Donna Fargo
(Dot)

BEST COUNTRY VOCAL PERFORMANCE, MALE

"Charley Pride Sings Heart Songs" (Album)
Charley Pride
(RCA Victor)

BEST COUNTRY VOCAL PERFORMANCE BY A DUO OR GROUP

"Class of '57"
The Statler Bros.
(Mercury)

BEST COUNTRY INSTRUMENTAL PERFORMANCE

"Charlie McCoy/The Real McCoy"
Charlie McCoy
(Monument)

BEST COUNTRY SONG

"Kiss an Angel Good Mornin'"
Songwriter: Ben Peters

BEST INSPIRATIONAL PERFORMANCE

"He Touched Me"
Elvis Presley
(RCA Victor)

BEST GOSPEL PERFORMANCE

"Love"
Blackwood Bros.
(RCA Victor)

1973

BEST RHYTHM & BLUES VOCAL PERFORMANCE BY A DUO, GROUP OR CHORUS

"Midnight Train to Georgia" (Single)
Gladys Knight & The Pips
(Buddah)

BEST COUNTRY VOCAL PERFORMANCE, FEMALE

"Let Me Be There" (single)
Olivia Newton-John
(MCA)

BEST COUNTRY VOCAL PERFORMANCE, MALE

"Behind Closed Doors"
Charlie Rich
(Epic)

BEST COUNTRY VOCAL PERFORMANCE BY A DUO OR GROUP

"From the Bottle to the Bottom"
Kris Kristofferson & Rita Coolidge
(A & M)

BEST COUNTRY INSTRUMENTAL PERFORMANCE

"Duelling Banjos" (Track)
Eric Weissberg & Steve Mandell
(Warner Bros.)

BEST COUNTRY SONG

"Behind Closed Doors"
Songwriter: Kenny O'Dell

BEST GOSPEL PERFORMANCE
"Release Me (From My Sin)" (Album)
The Blackwood Bros.
(Skylite)
BEST ETHNIC OR TRADITIONAL RECORDING
"Then and Now" (Album)
Doc Watson
(United Artists)
1974
RECORD OF THE YEAR
"I Honestly Love You"
Olivia Newton-John
(MCA)
BEST ALBUM NOTES (A TIE)
"For the Last Time"
Bob Wills and His Texas Playboys
(United Artists)
Annotator: Charles R. Townsend
BEST POP VOCAL PERFORMANCE, FEMALE
"I Honestly Love You"
Olivia Newton-John
(MCA)
BEST COUNTRY VOCAL PERFORMANCE, FEMALE
"Love Song"
Anne Murray
(Capitol)
BEST COUNTRY VOCAL PERFORMANCE, MALE
"Please Don't Tell Me How the Story Ends"
Ronnie Milsap
(RCA Victor)
BEST COUNTRY VOCAL PERFORMANCE BY A DUO OR GROUP
"Fairytale" (Track)
The Pointer Sisters
(Blue Thumb)
BEST COUNTRY INSTRUMENTAL PERFORMANCE
"The Atkins-Travis Traveling Show"
Chet Atkins & Merle Travis
(RCA Victor)
BEST COUNTRY SONG
"A Very Special Love Song"
Songwriters: Norris Wilson & Billy Sherrill
BEST INSPIRATIONAL PERFORMANCE
"How Great Thou Art" (Track)
Elvis Presley
(RCA Victor)
BEST GOSPEL PERFORMANCE
"The Baptism of Jesse Taylor" (Single)
Oak Ridge Boys
(Columbia)
BEST ETHNIC OR TRADITIONAL RECORDING
"Two Days in November" (Album)
Doc & Merle Watson
(United Artists)
1975
BEST ARRANGEMENT ACCOMPANYING VOCALISTS
"Misty"
Ray Stevens
Arranger: Ray Stevens
(Barnaby)
BEST ENGINEERED RECORDING (NON-CLASSICAL)
"Between the Lines"
Janis Ian
(Columbia)
Engineers: Brooks Arthur, Larry Alexander & Russ Payne
BEST POP VOCAL PERFORMANCE, FEMALE
"At Seventeen"
Janis Ian
(Columbia)
BEST POP VOCAL PERFORMANCE BY A DUO, GROUP OR CHORUS
"Lyin' Eyes" (Single)
Eagles
(Asylum)
BEST COUNTRY VOCAL PERFORMANCE, FEMALE
"I Can't Help It (If I'm Still in Love With You)" (Single)
Linda Ronstadt
(Capitol)
BEST COUNTRY VOCAL PERFORMANCE, MALE
"Blue Eyes Crying in the Rain" (Single)
Willie Nelson
(Columbia)
BEST COUNTRY VOCAL PERFORMANCE BY A DUO OR GROUP
"Lover Please"
Kris Kristofferson & Rita Coolidge
(Monument)
BEST COUNTRY INSTRUMENTAL PERFORMANCE
"The Entertainer" (Track)
Chet Atkins
(RCA Victor)

BEST COUNTRY SONG
"(Hey Won't You Play) Another Somebody Done Somebody Wrong Song"
Songwriters: Chips Moman & Larry Butler

1976

BEST NEW ARTIST OF THE YEAR
Starland Vocal Band
(Windsong/RCA Victor)

BEST ARRANGEMENT FOR VOICES
"Afternoon Delight"
Starland Vocal Band
(Windsong/RCA Victor)
Arranger: Starland Vocal Band

BEST POP VOCAL PERFORMANCE, FEMALE
"Hasten Down the Wind" (Album)
Linda Ronstadt
(Asylum)

BEST COUNTRY VOCAL PERFORMANCE, FEMALE
"Elite Hotel" (Album)
Emmylou Harris
(Reprise)

BEST COUNTRY VOCAL PERFORMANCE, MALE
"(I'm a) Stand by My Woman Man" (Single)
Ronnie Milsap
(RCA Victor)

BEST COUNTRY VOCAL PERFORMANCE BY A DUO OR GROUP
"The End Is Not in Sight (The Cowboy Tune)" (Single)
Amazing Rhythm Aces
(ABC)

BEST COUNTRY INSTRUMENTAL PERFORMANCE
"Chester & Lester"
Chet Atkins & Les Paul
(RCA Victor)

BEST COUNTRY SONG
"Broken Lady"
Songwriter: Larry Gatlin

BEST INSPIRATIONAL PERFORMANCE
"The Astonishing, Outrageous, Amazing, Incredible, Unbelievable, Different World of Gary S. Paxton" (Album)
Gary S. Paxton
(Newpax)

BEST GOSPEL PERFORMANCE
"Where the Soul Never Dies" (Single)
Oak Ridge Boys
(Columbia)

BEST ETHNIC OR TRADITIONAL RECORDING
"Mark Twang" (Album)
John Hartford
(Flying Fish)

1977

RECORD OF THE YEAR
"Hotel California"
Eagles
(Asylum)
Producer: Bill Szymczyk

BEST NEW ARTIST OF THE YEAR
Debby Boone
(Warner Bros./Curb)

BEST ARRANGEMENTS FOR VOICES
"New Kid in Town"
Eagles
Arrangers: Eagles
(Asylum)

BEST ALBUM PACKAGE
"Simple Dreams"
Linda Ronstadt
Art Director: Kosh
(Asylum)

BEST POP VOCAL PERFORMANCE, MAN
"Handy Man" (Single)
James Taylor
(Columbia)

BEST GOSPEL PERFORMANCE, TRADITIONAL
"Just a Little Talk With Jesus" (Track)
Oak Ridge Boys
(Rockland Road)

BEST INSPIRATIONAL PERFORMANCE
"Home Where I Belong" (Album)
B.J. Thomas
(Myrrh/Word)

BEST COUNTRY VOCAL PERFORMANCE, FEMALE
"Don't It Make My Brown Eyes Blue" (Single)
Crystal Gayle
(United Artists)

BEST COUNTRY VOCAL PERFORMANCE, MALE
"Lucille" (Single)
Kenny Rogers
(United Artists)

BEST COUNTRY VOCAL PERFORMANCE BY A DUO OR GROUP
"Heaven's Just a Sin Away" (Single)
The Kendalls
(Ovation)

BEST COUNTRY INSTRUMENTAL PERFORMANCE
"Country Instrumentalist of the Year"
Hargus "Pig" Robbins
(Elektra)
BEST COUNTRY SONG
"Don't It Make My Brown Eyes Blue"
Songwriter: Richard Leigh
1978
BEST POP VOCAL PERFORMANCE, FEMALE
"You Needed Me" (Single)
Anne Murray
(Capitol)
BEST COUNTRY VOCAL PERFORMANCE, FEMALE
"Here You Come Again" (Album)
Dolly Parton
(RCA Victor)
BEST COUNTRY VOCAL PERFORMANCE, MALE
"Georgia on My Mind" (Single)
Willie Nelson
(Columbia)
BEST COUNTRY VOCAL PERFORMANCE BY A DUO OR GROUP
"Mamas Don't Let Your Babies Grow Up to Be Cowboys" (Single)
Waylon Jennings & Willie Nelson
(RCA Victor)
BEST COUNTRY INSTRUMENTAL PERFORMANCE
"One O'Clock Jump" (Track)
Asleep at the Wheel
(Capitol)
BEST COUNTRY SONG
"The Gambler"
Songwriter: Don Schlitz
BEST GOSPEL PERFORMANCE, TRADITIONAL
"Refreshing" (Album)
The Happy Goodman Family
(Canaan)
BEST INSPIRATIONAL PERFORMANCE
"Happy Man" (Album)
B.J. Thomas
(Myrrh)
1979
SONG OF THE YEAR
"What a Fool Believes"
Songwriters: Kenny Loggins, Michael McDonald
BEST ROCK VOCAL PERFORMANCE BY A DUO OR GROUP
"Heartache Tonight" (Single)
Eagles
(Asylum)
BEST COUNTRY VOCAL PERFORMANCE, FEMALE
"Blue Kentucky Girl" (Album)
Emmylou Harris
(Warner Bros.)
BEST COUNTRY VOCAL PERFORMANCE, MALE
"The Gambler" (Single)
Kenny Rogers
(United Artists)
BEST COUNTRY VOCAL PERFORMANCE BY A DUO OR GROUP
"The Devil Went Down to Georgia" (Single)
Charlie Daniels Band
(Epic)
BEST COUNTRY INSTRUMENTAL PERFORMANCE
"Big Sandy/Leather Britches" (Track)
Doc & Merle Watson
(United Artists)
BEST COUNTRY SONG
"You Decorated My Life"
Songwriters: Debbie Hupp, Bob Morrison
BEST GOSPEL PERFORMANCE CONTEMPORARY OR INSPIRATIONAL
"Heed the Call" (Album)
Imperials
(Dayspring)
BEST GOSPEL PERFORMANCE, TRADITIONAL
"Lift Up the Name of Jesus" (Album)
The Blackwood Brothers
(Skylite)
BEST INSPIRATIONAL PERFORMANCE
"You Gave Me Love (When Nobody Gave Me a Prayer)" (Album)
B.J. Thomas
(Myrrh)
PRODUCER OF THE YEAR (NON-CLASSICAL)
Larry Butler
1980
BEST POP PERFORMANCE, MALE
"This Is It" (Track)
Kenny Loggins
(Columbia)
BEST COUNTRY VOCAL PERFORMANCE, FEMALE
"Could I Have This Dance" (Single)
Anne Murray
(Capitol)
BEST COUNTRY VOCAL PERFORMANCE, MALE
"He Stopped Loving Her Today" (Single)
George Jones
(Epic)

BEST COUNTRY PERFORMANCE BY A DUO OR GROUP WITH VOCAL
"That Lovin' You Feelin' Again" (Single)
Roy Orbison and Emmylou Harris
(Warner Bros.)
BEST COUNTRY INSTRUMENTAL PERFORMANCE
"Orange Blossom Special/Hoedown" (Track)
Gilley's "Urban Cowboy" Band
(Full Moon/Asylum)
BEST COUNTRY SONG
"On the Road Again"
Songwriter: Willie Nelson
BEST GOSPEL PERFORMANCE, CONTEMPORARY OR INSPIRATIONAL
"The Lord's Prayer" (Album)
Reba Rambo, Dony McGuire, B.J. Thomas, Andrea Crouch, The Archers, Walter & Traimaine Hawkins, Cynthia Clawson
(Light)
BEST GOSPEL PERFORMANCE, TRADITIONAL
"Welcome to Worship" (Album)
Blackwood Brothers
(Voice Box)
BEST INSPIRATIONAL PERFORMANCE
"With My Song I Will Praise Him" (Album)
Debby Boone
(Lamb & Lion)
1981
BEST COUNTRY VOCAL PERFORMANCE, FEMALE
"9 to 5" (Single)
Dolly Parton
(RCA Victor)
BEST COUNTRY VOCAL PERFORMANCE, MALE
"(There's) No Gettin' Over Me" (Single)
Ronnie Milsap
(RCA Victor)
BEST COUNTRY PERFORMANCE BY A DUO OR GROUP WITH VOCAL
"Elvira" (Single)
Oak Ridge Boys
(MCA)
BEST COUNTRY INSTRUMENTAL PERFORMANCE
"After All These Years"
Chet Atkins
(RCA Victor)
BEST COUNTRY SONG
"9 to 5"
Songwriter: Dolly Parton
BEST GOSPEL PERFORMANCE, CONTEMPORARY OR INSPIRATIONAL
"Priority" (Album)
Imperials
(Dayspring/Word)
BEST GOSPEL PERFORMANCE, TRADITIONAL
"The Masters V" (Album)
J.D. Sumner, James Blackwood, Hovie Lister, Rosie Rozell, Jake Hess
(Skylite)
BEST INSPIRATIONAL PERFORMANCE
"Amazing Grace" (Album)
B.J. Thomas
(Myrrh/Word)
VIDEO OF THE YEAR
"Michael Nesmith in Elephant Parts"
Michael Nesmith
(Pacific Arts Video)
1982
SONG OF THE YEAR
"Always on My Mind"
Songwriters: Johnny Christopher, Mark James & Wayne Carson
BEST COUNTRY VOCAL PERFORMANCE, FEMALE
"Break It to Me Gently" (Single)
Juice Newton
(Capitol)
BEST COUNTRY VOCAL PERFORMANCE, MALE
"Always on My Mind" (Single)
Willie Nelson
(Columbia)
BEST COUNTRY PERFORMANCE BY A DUO OR GROUP WITH VOCAL
"Mountain Music" (Album)
Alabama
(RCA Victor)
BEST COUNTRY INSTRUMENTAL PERFORMANCE
"Alabama Jubilee" (Track)
Roy Clark
(Churchill)
BEST COUNTRY SONG
"Always on My Mind"
Songwriters: Johnny Christopher, Mark James & Wayne Carson
BEST GOSPEL PERFORMANCE, CONTEMPORARY
"Age to Age" (Album)
Amy Grant
(Myrrh/Word)

BEST GOSPEL PERFORMANCE, TRADITIONAL
"I'm Following You" (Album)
Blackwood Brothers
(Voice Box)
BEST INSPIRATIONAL PERFORMANCE
"He Set My Life to Music" (Album)
Barbara Mandrell
(Songbird/MCA)
BEST ETHNIC OR TRADITIONAL FOLK RECORDING
"Queen Ida and the Bon Temps Zydeco Band on Tour" (Album)
Queen Ida
(GNR/Crescendo)
BEST ALBUM PACKAGE
"Get Closer"
Linda Ronstadt
Art Directors: Kosh with Ron Larson
(Elektra/Asylum)
1983
BEST COUNTRY VOCAL PERFORMANCE, FEMALE
"A Little Good News" (Single)
Anne Murray
(Capitol)
BEST COUNTRY VOCAL PERFORMANCE, MALE
"I.O.U." (Single)
Lee Greenwood
(MCA)
BEST COUNTRY PERFORMANCE BY A DUO OR GROUP WITHVOCAL
"The Closer You Get" (Album)
Alabama
(RCA Victor)
BEST COUNTRY INSTRUMENTAL PERFORMANCE
"Fireball" (Track)
The New South (Ricky Skaggs, Jerry Douglas, Tony Rice, J.D. Crowe, Todd Phillips)
(Sugar Hill)
BEST NEW COUNTRY SONG
"Stranger in My House"
Songwriter: Mike Reid
BEST GOSPEL PERFORMANCE, FEMALE
"Ageless Medley" (Single)
Amy Grant
(Myrrh/Word)
BEST GOSPEL PERFORMANCE BY A DUO OR GROUP
"More Than Wonderful" (Track)
Sandi Patti & Larnelle Harris
(Impact/Benson)
BEST SOUL GOSPEL PERFORMANCE BY A DUO OR GROUP
"I'm So Glad I'm Standing Here Today" (Track)
Bobby Jones with Barbara Mandrell
(Myrrh/Word)
1984
BEST COUNTRY VOCAL PERFORMANCE, FEMALE
"In My Dreams" (Single)
Emmylou Harris
(Warner Bros.)
BEST COUNTRY VOCAL PERFORMANCE, MALE
"That's the Way Love Goes" (Single)
Merle Haggard
(Epic)
BEST COUNTRY PERFORMANCE BY A DUO OR GROUP WITH VOCAL
"Mama He's Crazy" (Single)
The Judds
(RCA Victor)
BEST COUNTRY INSTRUMENTAL PERFORMANCE
"Wheel Hoss" (Track from "Country Boy")
Ricky Skaggs
(Epic)
BEST COUNTRY SONG
"City of New Orleans"
Songwriter: Steve Goodman
BEST GOSPEL PERFORMANCE, FEMALE
"Angels" (Track from "Straight Ahead")
Amy Grant
(Myrrh/Word)
BEST GOSPEL PERFORMANCE BY A DUO OR GROUP
"Keep the Flame Burning" (Track from Debby Boone Album "Surrender")
Debby Boone & Phil Driscoll
(Lamb & Lion/Sparrow)
BEST RECORDING FOR CHILDREN
"Where the Sidewalk Ends" (Album)
Shel Silverstein
Producer: Ron Haffkine
(Columbia)
1985
BEST ROCK VOCAL PERFORMANCE, MALE
"The Boys of Summer" (Single)
Don Henley
(Geffen)
BEST COUNTRY VOCAL PERFORMANCE, FEMALE
"I Don't Know Why You Don't Want Me" (Single)
Rosanne Cash
(Columbia)

BEST COUNTRY VOCAL PERFORMANCE, MALE
"Lost in the Fifties Tonight (In the Still of the Night)" (Single)
Ronnie Milsap
(RCA Victor)
BEST COUNTRY PERFORMANCE BY A DUO OR GROUP WITH VOCAL
"Why Not Me" (Album)
The Judds
(RCA Victor)
BEST COUNTRY INSTRUMENTAL PERFORMANCE
"Cosmic Square Dance" (Track from Chet Atkins Album "Stay Tuned")
Chet Atkins & Mark Knopfler
(Columbia)
BEST COUNTRY SONG
"Highwayman"
Songwriter: Jimmy L. Webb
BEST GOSPEL PERFORMANCE, FEMALE
"Unguarded" (Album)
Amy Grant
(Myrrh/Word)
BEST GOSPEL PERFORMANCE BY A DUO OR GROUP
"I've Just Seen Jesus" (Track from "I've Just Seen Jesus")
Larnelle Harris & Sandi Patti
(Impact/Benson)
BEST ETHNIC OR TRADITIONAL FOLK RECORDING
"My Toot Toot" (Single)
Rockin' Sidney
(Maison De Soul)
BEST POLKA RECORDING
"70 Years of Hits" (Album)
Frank Yankovic
(Cleveland International)
BEST INSTRUMENTAL ARRANGEMENT ACCOMPANYING VOCAL(S)
"Lush Life" (Track from "Lush Life")
Linda Ronstadt
Arranger: Nelson Riddle
(Asylum)
BEST ALBUM PACKAGE
"Lush Life"
Linda Ronstadt
Art Director: Kosh & Ron Larson
(Asylum)

1986
BEST COUNTRY VOCAL PERFORMANCE, FEMALE
"Whoever's in New England" (Single)
Reba McEntire
(MCA)
BEST COUNTRY VOCAL PERFORMANCE, MALE
"Lost in the Fifties Tonight" (Album)
Ronnie Milsap
(RCA Victor)
BEST COUNTRY PERFORMANCE BY A DUO OR GROUP WITH VOCAL
"Grandpa (Tell Me 'Bout the Good Old Days)" (Single)
The Judds
(RCA Victor)
BEST COUNTRY INSTRUMENTAL PERFORMANCE (ORCHESTRA, GROUP OR SOLOIST)
"Raisin' the Dickens" (Track from "Love's Gonna Get Ya")
Ricky Skaggs
(Epic)
BEST COUNTRY SONG
"Grandpa (Tell Me 'Bout the Good Old Days)"
Songwriter: Jamie O'Hara
BEST GOSPEL PERFORMANCE, FEMALE
"Morning Like This" (Album)
Sandi Patti
(Word)
BEST GOSPEL PERFORMANCE BY A DUO OR GROUP, CHOIR OR CHORUS
"They Say" (Track from "So Glad I Know")
Sandi Patti & Deniece Williams
(Sparrow)
BEST MEXICAN/AMERICAN PERFORMANCE
"Ay Te Dejo En San Antonio" (Album)
Flaco Jiminez
(Arhoolie)
BEST TRADITIONAL FOLK RECORDING
"Riding the Midnight Train" (Album)
Doc Watson
(Sugar Hill)
BEST CONTEMPORARY FOLK RECORDING
"Tribute to Steve Goodman" (Album)
(Arlo Guthrie, John Hartford, Richie Havens, Bonnie Koloc, Nitty Gritty Dirt Band, John Prine & Others)
Album Producers: Hank Neuberger, Al Burnetta & Dan Einstein
(Red Pajamas)

BEST SPOKEN WORD OR NON-MUSICAL RECORDING
Interviews From "The Class of '55" Recording Sessions (Album)
Carl Perkins, Jerry Lee Lewis, Roy Orbison, Johnny Cash, Sam Phillips, Rick Nelson and Chips Moman
(American Record Corp.)

1987

SONG OF THE YEAR
"Somewhere Out There" (Single)
Linda Ronstadt & James Ingram
Songwriters: James Horner, Barry Mann & Cynthia Weil
(MCA)

BEST POP PERFORMANCE BY A DUO OR GROUP WITH VOCAL
"(I've Had) The Time of My Life" (Track from "Dirty Dancing" Original Soundtrack)
Bill Medley & Jennifer Warnes
(BMG Music/RCA Victor)

BEST COUNTRY VOCAL PERFORMANCE, FEMALE
"80's Ladies" (Track from "80's Ladies")
K.T. Oslin
(RCA Victor)

BEST COUNTRY VOCAL PERFORMANCE, MALE
"Always & Forever" (Album)
Randy Travis
(Warner Bros.)

BEST COUNTRY PERFORMANCE BY A DUO OR GROUP WITH VOCAL
"Trio" (Album)
Dolly Parton, Linda Ronstadt & Emmylou Harris
(Warner Bros.)

BEST COUNTRY VOCAL PERFORMANCE, DUET
"Make No Mistake, She's Mine" (Single)
Ronnie Milsap & Kenny Rogers
(BMG Music/RCA Victor)

BEST COUNTRY INSTRUMENTAL PERFORMANCE (ORCHESTRA, GROUP OR SOLOIST)
"String of Pars" (Track from "Asleep at the Wheel")
Asleep at the Wheel
(Epic)

BEST COUNTRY SONG
"Forever and Ever Amen"
Randy Travis
Songwriters: Paul Overstreet & Don Schlitz
(Warner Bros.)

BEST GOSPEL PERFORMANCE BY A DUO, GROUP, CHOIR OR CHORUS
"Crack the Sky" (Album)
Mylon LeFevre & Broken Heart
(Myrrh/Word)

BEST CONTEMPORARY FOLK RECORDING
"Unfinished Business" (Album)
Steve Goodman
(Red Pajamas)

BEST SONG WRITTEN SPECIFICALLY FOR A MOTION PICTURE OR TELEVISION
"Somewhere Out There"
Linda Ronstadt & James Ingram
Songwriters: James Horner, Barry Mann & Cynthia Weil
(MCA)

BEST ALBUM PACKAGE
"King's Record Shop" (Album)
Rosanne Cash
Art Director: Bill Johnson
(Columbia)

1988

BEST COUNTRY VOCAL PERFORMANCE, FEMALE
"Hold Me" (Track from "This Woman")
K.T. Oslin
(RCA Victor)

BEST COUNTRY VOCAL PERFORMANCE, MALE
"Old 8 X 10" (Album)
Randy Travis
(Warner Bros.)

BEST COUNTRY PERFORMANCE BY A DUO OR GROUP WITH VOCAL
"Give a Little Love" (Track from "Greatest Hits")
The Judds
(RCA Victor)

BEST COUNTRY VOCAL PERFORMANCE
"Crying" (Single)
Roy Orbison & k.d. lang
(Virgin)

BEST COUNTRY INSTRUMENTAL PERFORMANCE (ORCHESTRA, GROUP OR SOLOIST)
"Sugarfoot Rag" (Track from "Western Standard Time")
Asleep at the Wheel
(Epic)

BEST BLUEGRASS RECORDING (VOCAL OR INSTRUMENTAL)
"Southern Flavor" (Album)
Bill Monroe
(MCA)

BEST COUNTRY SONG
"Hold Me"
K.T. Oslin
Songwriter: K.T. Oslin
BEST GOSPEL PERFORMANCE, FEMALE
"Lead Me On" (Album)
Amy Grant
(A & M)
BEST MEXICAN/AMERICAN PERFORMANCE
"Canciones De Mi Padre" (Album)
Linda Ronstadt
(Elektra)
BEST TRADITIONAL FOLK RECORDING
"Folkways: A Vision Shared—A Tribute to Woody Guthrie And Leadbelly" (Album)
Producers: Don DeVito, Joe McEwen, Harold Leventhal and Ralph Rinzler
(Columbia)
BEST ALBUM PACKAGE
"Tired of Runnin' "
O'Kanes
Art Director: Bill Johnson
1989
RECORD OF THE YEAR
"Wind Beneath My Wings"
Bette Midler
Producer: Arif Mardin
(Atlantic)
SONG OF THE YEAR
"Wind Beneath My Wings"
Bette Midler
Songwriters: Larry Henley & Jeff Silbar
(Atlantic)
BEST POP PERFORMANCE BY A DUO OR GROUP WITH VOCAL
"Don't Know Much" (Single)
Linda Ronstadt & Aaron Neville
(Elektra)
BEST ROCK VOCAL PERFORMANCE, MALE
"The End of the Innocence" (Album)
Don Henley
(Geffen)
BEST ROCK PERFORMANCE BY A DUO OR GROUP WITH VOCALS
"Traveling Wilburys Volume One" (Album)
Traveling Wilburys
(Wilbury/Warner Bros.)
BEST COUNTRY VOCAL PERFORMANCE, FEMALE
"Absolute Torch and Twang" (Album)
k.d. lang
(Sire)
BEST COUNTRY VOCAL PERFORMANCE, MALE
"Lyle Lovett and His Large Band" (Album)
Lyle Lovett
(MCA)
BEST COUNTRY PERFORMANCE BY A DUO OR GROUP WITH VOCAL
"Will the Circle Be Unbroken Volume 2" (Album)
The Nitty Gritty Dirt Band
(Universal)
BEST COUNTRY VOCAL COLLABORATION
"There's a Tear in My Beer" (Single)
Hank Williams, Jr. & Hank Williams
(Curb)
BEST COUNTRY INSTRUMENTAL PERFORMANCE
"Amazing Grace" (Track from "Will the Circle Be Unbroken Vol. 2")
Randy Scruggs
(Universal)
BEST BLUEGRASS RECORDING
"The Valley Road" (Track from "Will the Circle Be Unbroken Vol. 2)
Bruce Hornsby & The Nitty Gritty Dirt Band
(Universal)
BEST COUNTRY SONG
"After All This Time"
Rodney Crowell
Songwriter: Rodney Crowell
(Columbia)
BEST CONTEMPORARY FOLK RECORDING
"Indigo Girls" (Album)
Indigo Girls
(Epic)
BEST ENGINEERED RECORDING (NON-CLASSICAL)
"Cry Like a Rainstorm, Howl Like the Wind" (Album)
Linda Ronstadt
Album Engineer: George Massenburg
(Elektra)
1990
BEST POP VOCAL PERFORMANCE, MALE
"Oh Pretty Woman" (Track from "A Black & White Night Live") (Single)
Roy Orbison
(Virgin)

BEST POP PERFORMANCE BY A DUO OR GROUP WITH VOCAL
"All My Life" (Single)
Linda Ronstadt with Aaron Neville
(Elektra Entertainment)

BEST COUNTRY VOCAL PERFORMANCE, FEMALE
"Where've You Been" (Single)
Kathy Mattea
(Mercury)

BEST COUNTRY VOCAL PERFORMANCE, MALE
"When I Call Your Name" (Single)
Vince Gill
(MCA)

BEST COUNTRY PERFORMANCE BY A DUO OR GROUP WITH VOCAL
"Pickin' on Nashville" (Album)
The Kentucky Headhunters
(Mercury)

BEST COUNTRY VOCAL COLLABORATION
"Poor Boy Blues" (Single)
Chet Atkins & Mark Knopfler
(Columbia)

BEST COUNTRY INSTRUMENTAL PERFORMANCE
"So Soft, Your Goodbye" (Track from "Neck and Neck")
Chet Atkins & Mark Knopfler
(Columbia)

BEST BLUEGRASS RECORDING
"I've Got That Old Feeling" (Album)
Alison Krauss
(Rounder)

BEST COUNTRY SONG
"Where've You Been"
Kathy Mattea
Songwriters: Jon Vezner & Don Henry

BEST POP GOSPEL ALBUM
"Another Time....Another Place" (Album)
Sandi Patti
(A & M/Word)

BEST MEXICAN/AMERICAN PERFORMANCE
"Soy De San Luis" (Track from "Texas Tornados")
Texas Tornados
(Reprise)

BEST TRADITIONAL FOLK RECORDING
"On Praying Ground" (Album)
Doc Watson
(Sugar Hill)

1991

BEST COUNTRY VOCAL PERFORMANCE, FEMALE
"Down at the Twist and Shout" (Single)
Mary-Chapin Carpenter
(Columbia)

BEST COUNTRY VOCAL PERFORMANCE, MALE
"Ropin' the Wind" (Album)
Garth Brooks
(Capitol)

BEST COUNTRY PERFORMANCE BY A DUO OR GROUP WITH VOCAL
"Love Can Build a Bridge" (Single)
The Judds
(Curb/RCA)

BEST COUNTRY VOCAL COLLABORATION
"Restless" (Single)
Steve Wariner, Ricky Skaggs & Vince Gill (From the "Mark O'Connor & The New Nashville Cats" album)
(Warner Bros.)

BEST COUNTRY INSTRUMENTAL PERFORMANCE
"The New Nashville Cats" (Album)
Mark O'Connor
(Warner Bros.)

BEST BLUEGRASS ALBUM
"Spring Training"
Carl Jackson & John Starling (& The Nash Ramblers)
(Sugar Hill)

BEST COUNTRY SONG
"Love Can Build a Bridge"
The Judds
Songwriters: Naomi Judd, John Jarvis & Paul Overstreet
(Curb/RCA)

BEST CONTEMPORARY FOLK ALBUM
"The Missing Years" (Album)
John Prine
(Oh Boy)

1992

BEST POP VOCAL PERFORMANCE, FEMALE
"Constant Craving" (Single)
k.d. lang
(Capitol)

BEST COUNTRY VOCAL PERFORMANCE, FEMALE
"I Feel Lucky"
Mary-Chapin Carpenter
(Columbia)

BEST COUNTRY VOCAL PERFORMANCE, MALE
"I Still Believe in You" (Album)
Vince Gill
(MCA)

BEST COUNTRY PERFORMANCE BY A DUO OR GROUP WITH VOCAL
"Emmylou Harris & The Nash Ramblers at The Ramblers" (Album)
Emmylou Harris & The Nash Ramblers
(Reprise)
BEST COUNTRY VOCAL COLLABORATION
"The Whiskey Ain't Workin'" (Single)
Travis Tritt & Marty Stuart
(Warner Bros.)
BEST COUNTRY INSTRUMENTAL PERFORMANCE
"Sneakin' Around" (Album)
Chet Atkins & Jerry Reed
(Columbia)
BEST BLUEGRASS ALBUM
"Every Time You Say Goodbye"
Alison Krauss & Union Station
(Rounder)
BEST COUNTRY SONG
"I Still Believe in You" (Album)
Songwriters: Vince Gill & John Barlow
BEST ROCK/CONTEMPORARY GOSPEL ALBUM
"Unseen Power" (Album)
Petra
(DaySpring)
BEST POP GOSPEL ALBUM
"The Great Adventure" (Album)
Steven Curtis Chapman
(Sparrow)
BEST SOUTHERN GOSPEL ALBUM
"Sometimes Miracles Hide" (Album)
Bruce Carroll
(Word)
BEST TROPICAL LATIN ALBUM
"Frenesi" (Album)
Linda Ronstadt
(Elektra Entertainment)
BEST MEXICAN/AMERICAN ALBUM
"Mas Canciones" (Album)
Linda Ronstadt
(Elektra Entertainment)

1993

BEST COUNTRY VOCAL PERFORMANCE, FEMALE
"Passionate Kisses" (Single)
Mary-Chapin Carpenter
(Columbia)
BEST COUNTRY VOCAL PERFORMANCE, MALE
"Ain't That Lonely Yet" (Single)
Dwight Yoakam
(Reprise)
BEST COUNTRY PERFORMANCE BY A DUO OR GROUP WITH VOCAL
"Hard Workin' Man" (Single)
Brooks & Dunn
(Arista)
BEST COUNTRY VOCAL COLLABORATION
"Does He Love You" (Single)
Reba McEntire & Linda Davis
(MCA)
BEST COUNTRY INSTRUMENTAL PERFORMANCE
"Red Wing" (Single)
Asleep at the Wheel, featuring Eldon Shamblin, Johnny Gimble, Chet Atkins, Vince Gill, Marty Stuart & Reuben "Lucky Oceans" Gosfield
(Liberty)
BEST BLUEGRASS ALBUM
"Waitin' for the Hard Times to Go"
Nashville Bluegrass Band
(Sugar Hill)
BEST COUNTRY SONG
"Passionate Kisses"
Songwriters: Lucinda Williams, Mary-Chapin Carpenter
BEST POP/CONTEMPORARY GOSPEL ALBUM
"The Live Adventure"
Steven Curtis Chapman
(Sparrow)
BEST SOUTHERN GOSPEL, COUNTRY GOSPEL OR BLUEGRASS GOSPEL ALBUM
"Good News"
Kathy Mattea
(Mercury)
BEST CONTEMPORARY FOLK ALBUM
"Other Voices/Other Rooms"
Nanci Griffith
(Elektra)
LIFETIME ACHIEVEMENT AWARDS
1971 Elvis Presley
1987 Roy Acuff
1987 Hank Williams
1991 Kitty Wells
1993 Chet Atkins
TRUSTEES AWARDS
1992 Thomas A. Dorsey

GRAMMY LEGENDS AWARDS

1989 Willie Nelson
1990 Johnny Cash

HALL OF FAME AWARDS

1979 "How High the Moon"
Les Paul & Mary Ford
(Capitol)
(Released in 1951)
1982 "Rock Around the Clock"
Bill Haley & The Comets
(Decca)
(Released in 1955)
1983 "Your Cheating Heart"
Hank Williams
(MGM)
(Released in 1953)
1985 "Blue Yodel (T for Texas)"
Jimmie Rodgers
(Victor)
(Released in 1944)
1986 "Blue Suede Shoes"
Carl Perkins
(Sun)
(Released in 1956)
1986 "Cool Water"
Sons of the Pioneers
(Decca)
(Released in 1946)
1988 "Hound Dog"
Elvis Presley
(RCA Victor)
(Released in 1956)
1989 "This Land Is Your Land"
Woody Guthrie
(Asch)
(Released in 1947)
1992 "Crazy"
Patsy Cline
(Decca)
(Released in 1961)

INTERNATIONAL BLUEGRASS MUSIC AWARDS

Each of the International Bluegrass Music Awards is voted on by the professional membership of IBMA in accordance with strict multi-stage balloting procedures established by the organization's Awards Committee and approved by the IBMA Board of Directors. Tabulations and final results come under the careful scrutiny and confidentiality of the accounting firm of Riney, Hancock & Company of Owensboro, KY. Winners are announced annually during the broadcast production of the awards show in late September.

HALL OF HONOR INDUCTEES

1991 Bill Monroe
1991 Earl Scruggs
1992 Lester Flatt
1992 The Stanley Brothers, Carter & Ralph
1992 Don Reno & Arthur Lee "Red" Smiley
1993 Mac Wiseman
1993 Jim & Jesse McReynolds
1994 The Osborne Brothers

ENTERTAINER OF THE YEAR

1990 Hot Rize
1991 Alison Krauss & Union Station
1992 The Nashville Bluegrass Band
1993 The Nashville Bluegrass Band
1994 The Del McCoury Band

VOCAL GROUP OF THE YEAR

1990 The Nashville Bluegrass Band
1991 The Nashville Bluegrass Band
1992 The Nashville Bluegrass Band
1993 The Nashville Bluegrass Band
1994 IIIrd Tyme Out

INSTRUMENTAL GROUP OF THE YEAR

1990 The Bluegrass Album Band
1991 The Tony Rice Unit
1992 California
1993 California
1994 California

FEMALE VOCALIST OF THE YEAR

1990 Alison Krauss
1991 Alison Krauss
1992 Laurie Lewis
1993 Alison Krauss
1994 Laurie Lewis

MALE VOCALIST OF THE YEAR

1990 Del McCoury
1991 Del McCoury
1992 Del McCoury
1993 Tim O'Brien
1994 Russell Moore

EMERGING ARTIST

1994 Lou Reid, Terry Baucom & Carolina

SONG OF THE YEAR

1990 "Little Mountain Church"
(Jim Rushing/Carl Jackson)

1991 "Colleen Malone"
(Pete Goble/Leroy Drumm)
1992 "Blue Train"
(Dave Allen)
1993 "Lonesome Standard Time"
(Larry Cordle/Jim Rushing)
1994 "Who Will Watch the Home Place?"
(Kate Long)

ALBUM OF THE YEAR

1990 "At the Old Schoolhouse"
The Johnson Mountain Boys
(Rounder)
1991 "I've Got That Old Feeling"
Alison Krauss & Union Station
(Rounder)
1992 "Carrying the Tradition"
The Lonesome River Band
(Rebel)
1993 "Every Time You Say Goodbye"
Alison Krauss & Union Station
(Rounder)
1994 "A Deeper Shade of Blue"
Del McCoury
(Rounder)

INSTRUMENTAL RECORDING OF THE YEAR

1990 "The Masters"
Adcock, Baker, Graves & McReynolds
(CMH)
1991 "Norman Blake & Tony Rice 2"
Norman Blake & Tony Rice
(Rounder)
1992 "Slide Rule"
Jerry Douglas
(Sugar Hill)
1993 "Stuart Duncan"
Stuart Duncan
(Rounder)
1994 "Skip, Hop & Wobble"
Jerry Douglas, Russ Barenberg & Edgar Meyer
(Sugar Hill)

RECORDED EVENT OF THE YEAR

1990 "Classic Country Gents Reunion"
Duffey, Waller, Adcock & Gray
(Sugar Hill)
1991 "Families of Tradition"
Parmley & McCoury
(BGC)
1992 "Slide Rule"
Jerry Douglas
(Sugar Hill)
1993 "Saturday Night & Sunday Morning"
Ralph Stanley & Special Guests
(Freeland Recordings)
1994 "A Touch of the Past"
Larry Perkins & Friends
(Pinecastle)

INSTRUMENTAL PERFORMANCES OF THE YEAR

BANJO

1990 Béla Fleck
1991 Alison Brown
1992 Tom Adams
1993 Tom Adams
1994 J. D. Crowe

GUITAR

1990 Tony Rice
1991 Tony Rice
1992 David Grier
1993 David Grier
1994 Tony Rice

FIDDLE

1990 Stuart Duncan
1991 Stuart Duncan
1992 Stuart Duncan
1993 Stuart Duncan
1994 Stuart Duncan

BASS

1990 Roy Huskey, Jr.
1991 Roy Huskey, Jr.
1992 Roy Huskey, Jr.
1993 Roy Huskey, Jr.
1994 Mark Schatz

DOBRO

1990 Jerry Douglas
1991 Jerry Douglas
1992 Jerry Douglas
1993 Jerry Douglas
1994 Jerry Douglas

MANDOLIN

1990 Sam Bush
1991 Sam Bush
1992 Sam Bush
1993 Ronnie McCoury
1994 Ronnie McCoury

THE AWARD OF MERIT

1994 Wilma Lee Cooper
Johnnie Wright & Jack Anglin
Ken Irwin
Lance LeRoy

BEST GRAPHIC DESIGN—ALBUM PROJECT

1994 "I Got a Bullfrog: Folksongs for the Fun of It"
David Holt
(High Windy Audio)
Graphic Designer: Bob Boeberitz
Cover Designer: Alex Murawski

BEST LINER NOTES—ALBUM PROJECT

1994 "Don Reno & Red Smiley: 1951-1959"
(King/IMG)
Annotators: Gary B. Reid & Bill Vernon

PRINT MEDIA PERSONALITY

1994 John Wright

BROADCASTER OF THE YEAR

1994 Frank L. Javorsek
(KCSN-FM, Northridge, CA)

JUNO AWARDS

These awards are given by the Canadian Academy of Recording Arts and Sciences. Please see their entry in the main body of this work.

1974

Country Female Vocalist of the Year
Anne Murray
Country Male Vocalist of the Year
Stompin' Tom Connors
Country Group or Duo of the Year
Carlton Showband
Folksinger/Folk artist of the Year
Gordon Lightfoot
Female Vocalist of the Year
Anne Murray
Male Vocalist of the Year
Gordon Lightfoot

1975

Composer of the Year
Hagood Hardy
Country Female Vocalist of the Year
Anne Murray
Country Male Vocalist of the Year
Murray McLaughlan
Country Group or Duo of the Year
Mercey Brothers
Instrumental Artist of the Year
Hagood Hardy
Folksinger/Folk artist of the Year
Gordon Lightfoot

1976

Male Vocalist of the Year
Burton Cummings
Composer of the Year
Gordon Lightfoot
Country Female Vocalist of the Year
Carroll Baker
Country Male Vocalist of the Year
Murray McLaughlan
Country Group or Duo of the Year
The Good Brothers
Most Promising Female Vocalist of the Year
Colleen Peterson
Most Promising Male Vocalist of the Year
Burton Cummings
Instrumental Artist of the Year
Hagood Hardy
Folksinger/Folk artist of the Year
Gordon Lightfoot

1977

Country Female Vocalist of the Year
Carroll Baker
Country Male Vocalist of the Year
Ronnie Prophet
Country Group or Duo of the Year
The Good Brothers
Folksinger/Folk artist of the Year
Gordon Lightfoot

1978

Album of the Year
Burton Cummings
Female Vocalist of the Year
Anne Murray
Country Female Vocalist of the Year
Carroll Baker
Country Male Vocalist of the Year
Ronnie Prophet
Country Group or Duo of the Year
The Good Brothers
Folksinger/Folk artist of the Year
Murray McLaughlan
Best Children's Album
Anne Murray

1979
Album of the Year
Anne Murray
Single of the Year
Anne Murray
Female Vocalist of the Year
Anne Murray
Country Female Vocalist of the Year
Anne Murray
Country Male Vocalist of the Year
Murray McLaughlan
Country Group or Duo of the Year
The Good Brothers
The Hall of Fame Award
Hank Snow

1980
Album of the Year
Anne Murray
Single of the Year
Anne Murray
Female Vocalist of the Year
Anne Murray
Country Female Vocalist of the Year
Anne Murray
Country Male Vocalist of the Year
Eddie Eastman
Country Group or Duo of the Year
The Good Brothers

1981
Female Vocalist of the Year
Anne Murray
Country Female Vocalist of the Year
Anne Murray
Country Male Vocalist of the Year
Ronnie Hawkins
Country Group or Duo of the Year
The Good Brothers

1982
Country Female Vocalist of the Year
Anne Murray
Country Male Vocalist of the Year
Eddie Eastman
Country Group or Duo of the Year
The Good Brothers

1983/1984
Country Female Vocalist of the Year
Anne Murray
Country Male Vocalist of the Year
Murray McLaughlan
Country Group or Duo of the Year
The Good Brothers

1985
Country Female Vocalist of the Year
Anne Murray
Country Male Vocalist of the Year
Murray McLaughlan
Country Group or Duo of the Year
The Family Brown
Most Promising Female Vocalist of the Year
k.d. lang
The Hall of Fame Award
Wilf Carter

1986
Country Female Vocalist of the Year
Anne Murray
Country Male Vocalist of the Year
Murray McLaughlan
Country Group or Duo of the Year
Prairie Oyster
The Hall of Fame Award
Gordon Lightfoot

1987
Country Female Vocalist of the Year
k.d. lang
Country Male Vocalist of the Year
Ian Tyson
Country Group or Duo of the Year
Prairie Oyster
Most Promising Female Vocalist of the Year
Rita MacNeil

1988
No Awards

1989
Single of the Year
Blue Rodeo
Female Vocalist of the Year
k.d. lang
Group of the Year
Blue Rodeo
Country Female Vocalist of the Year
Rita MacNeil/k.d. lang
Country Male Vocalist of the Year
Murray McLaughlan
Country Group or Duo of the Year
The Family Brown

Most Promising Male Vocalist of the Year
Colin James
Best Video
Michael Buckley (Director)/Blue Rodeo (Artist)
1990
Female Vocalist of the Year
Rita MacNeil
Group of the Year
Blue Rodeo
Country Female Vocalist of the Year
k.d. lang
Country Male Vocalist of the Year
George Fox
Country Group or Duo of the Year
The Family Brown
1991
Single of the Year
Colin James "Just Come Back"
Male Vocalist of the Year
Colin James
Group of the Year
Blue Rodeo
Country Female Vocalist of the Year
Rita MacNeil
Country Male Vocalist of the Year
George Fox
Country Group or Duo of the Year
Prairie Oyster
1992
Foreign Entertainer of the Year
Garth Brooks
Country Female Vocalist of the Year
Cassandra Vasik
Country Male Vocalist of the Year
George Fox
Country Group or Duo of the Year
Prairie Oyster
The Hall of Fame Award
Ian & Sylvia (Tyson)1993
Album of the Year
k.d. lang
Songwriter of the Year
k.d. lang
Country Female Vocalist of the Year
Michelle Wright
Country Male Vocalist of the Year
Gary Fjellgard
Country Group or Duo of the Year
Tracey Prescott & Lonesome Daddy
Producer of the Year
k.d. lang
The Hall of Fame Award
Anne Murray
Best Selling Single (Foreign or Domestic)
Billy Ray Cyrus
1993
Single of the Year
The Rankin Family
Group of the Year
The Rankin Family
Country Female Vocalist of the Year
Cassandra Vasik
Country Male Vocalist of the Year
Charlie Major
Country Group or Duo of the Year
The Rankin Family
Canadian Entertainer of the Year
The Rankin Family

NASHVILLE SONGWRITERS ASSOCIATION INTERNATIONAL

SONGWRITER OF THE YEAR & SONGWRITER/ARTIST OF THE YEAR AWARD

1967 Dallas Frazier
"There Goes My Everything"
1968 Bobby Russell
"Honey"
1969 Merle Haggard
"Okie from Muskogie"
1970 Kris Kristofferson
"For the Good Times"
1971 Kris Kristofferson
"Sunday Morning Coming Down"
1972 Tom T. Hall
"Old Dogs, Children and Watermelon Wine"
1973 Kris Kristofferson
"Why Me, Lord?"
1974 Don Wayne
"Country Bumpkin"
1975 Ben Peters
"Before the Next Teardrop Falls"
1976 Bob McDill
"Amanda"

1977 Roger Bowling, Hal Bynum
"Lucille"
1978 Sonny Throckmorton
1979 Sonny Throckmorton
1980 Bob Morrison
1981 Kye Fleming, Dennis Morgan
1982 Kye Fleming, Dennis Morgan
1983 Jeff Silbar, Larry Henley
1984 Kenny O'Dell
1985 Bob McDill
1986 Paul Overstreet
1987 Don Schlitz
1988 Bob McDill
1989 Kostas—Songwriter of the Year
1989 Clint Black—Songwriter/Artist of the Year
1990 Jon Vezner—Songwriter of the Year
1990 Vince Gill—Songwriter/Artist of the Year
1991 Pat Alger—Songwriter of the Year
1991 Alan Jackson—Songwriter/Artist of the Year
1992 Gary Burr/Susan Longacre (Tie)—
Songwriter of the Year
1992 Garth Brooks/Alana Jackson (Tie)—
Songwriter/Artist of the Year
1993 Dennis Linde—Songwriter of the Year
1994 Clint Black—Songwriter/Performer of the Year

SONG OF THE YEAR AWARD

1978 "You Needed Me"
Randy Goodrum
1979 "She Believes in Me"
Steve Gibb
1980 "He Stopped Loving Her Today"
Bobby Braddock, Curly Putman
1981 "You're the Reason God Made Oklahoma"
Larry Collins, Sandy Pinkard
1982 "Always on My Mind"
Johnny Christopher, Wayne Carson (Thompson), Mark James
1983 "Holding Her and Loving You"
Walt Aldridge, Tommy Brasfield
1984 "Mama He's Crazy"
Kenny O'Dell
1985 "Baby's Got Her Blue Jeans On"
Bob McDill
1986 "On the Other Hand"
Don Schlitz, Paul Overstreet
1987 "Forever and Ever Amen"
Don Schlitz, Paul Overstreet
1988 "Chiseled in Stone"
Max D. Barnes, Vern Gosdin
1989 "If Tomorrow Never Comes"
Garth Brooks, Kent Blazy
1990 "Where've You Been"
Jon Vezner, Don Henry
1991 "Somewhere in My Broken Heart"
Richard Leigh, Billy Dean
1992 "Achy Breaky Heart"
Don Von Tress
1993 "The Song Remembers When"
Hugh Prestwood
1994 "The Song Remembers When"
Hugh Prestwood

NASHVILLE SONGWRITERS HALL OF FAME INDUCTEES

1970

Gene Autry
Johnny Bond
Albert Brumley
A.P. Carter
Ted Daffan
Vernon Dalhart
Rex Griffin
Stuart Hamblen
Pee Wee King
Vic McAlpin
Bob Miller
Leon Payne
Jimmie Rodgers
Fred Rose
Redd Stewart
Floyd Tillman
Merle Travis
Ernest Tubb
Cindy Walker
Hank Williams
Bob Wills

1971

Smiley Burnette
Jenny Lou Carson
Wilf Carter
Zeke Clements
Jimmie Davis
Alton and Rabon Delmore
Al Dexter
Vaughan Horton

Bradley Kincaid
Bill Monroe
Bob Nolan
Tex Owens
Tex Ritter
Carson J. Robinson
Tim Spencer
Gene Sullivan
Jimmy Wakely
Wiley Walker
Scotty Wiseman

1972
Boudleaux and Felice Bryant
Lefty Frizzell
Jack Rhodes
Don Robertson

1973
Jack Clements
Don Gibson
Harlan Howard
Roger Miller
Steve and Ed Nelson
Willie Nelson

1974
Hank Cochran

1975
Bill Anderson
Danny Dill
Eddie Miller
Marty Robbins
Wayne Walker
Marijohn Wilkin

1976
Carl Belew
Dallas Frazier
John D. Loudermilk
Moon Mulican
Curly Putman
Mel Tillis

1977
Johnny Cash
Woody Guthrie
Merle Haggard
Kris Kristofferson

1978
Joe Allison
Tom T. Hall
Hank Snow
Don Wayne

1979
The Rev. Thomas A. Dorsey
Charles and Ira Louvin
Elsie McWilliams
Joe South

1980
Huddie "Ledbelly" Ledbetter
Mickey Newbury
Ben Peters
Ray Stevens

1981
Bobby Braddock
Ray Whitley

1982
Chuck Berry
William J. "Billy" Hill

1983
W.C. Handy
Loretta Lynn
Beasley Smith

1984
Hal David
Billy Sherrill

1985
Bob McDill
Carl Perkins

1986
Otis Blackwell
Dolly Parton

1987
Roy Orbison
Sonny Throckmorton

1988
Hoagey Carmichael
Troy Seals

1989
Rory Michael Bourke
Maggie Cavender
Sanger D. "Whitey" Shafer

1990
Sue Brewer
Ted Harris
Jimmy Webb

1991
Charlie Black
Sonny Curtis

1992
Max D. Barnes
Wayland Holyfield

1993
Conway Twitty
Don Sclitz
Red Lane

1994
Bobby Russell
Jerry Foster & Bill Rice
Buddy Holly

MUSIC CITY NEWS AWARDS TNN/MUSIC CITY NEWS AWARDS (MUSIC CITY AWARDS ONLY UP TO 1989, COMBINED FROM 1990)

MALE VOCALIST OF THE YEAR

1967 Merle Haggard
1968 Merle Haggard
1969 Charley Pride
1970 Charley Pride
1971 Charley Pride
1972 Charley Pride
1973 Charley Pride
1974 Conway Twitty
1975 Conway Twitty
1976 Conway Twitty
1977 Conway Twitty
1978 Larry Gatlin
1979 Kenny Rogers
1980 Marty Robbins
1981 George Jones
1982 Marty Robbins
1983 Marty Robbins
1984 Lee Greenwood
1985 Lee Greenwood
1986 George Strait
1987 Randy Travis
1988 Randy Travis
1989 Ricky Van Shelton
1990 Ricky Van Shelton
1991 Ricky Van Shelton
1992 Alan Jackson
1993 Alan Jackson
1994 Alan Jackson

MOST PROMISING MALE ARTIST

1967 Tom T. Hall
1968 Cal Smith
1969 Johnny Bush
1970 Tommy Cash
1971 Tommy Overstreet
1972 Billy "Crash" Craddock
1973 Johnny Rodriguez
1974 Johnny Rodriguez
1975 Ronnie Milsap
1976 Mickey Gilley
1977 Larry Gatlin
1978 Don Williams
1979 Rex Allen, Jr.
1980 Hank Williams, Jr.
1981 Boxcar Willie
1982 T.G. Sheppard

FEMALE VOCALIST OF THE YEAR

1967 Loretta Lynn
1968 Loretta Lynn
1969 Loretta Lynn
1970 Loretta Lynn
1971 Loretta Lynn
1972 Loretta Lynn
1973 Loretta Lynn
1974 Loretta Lynn
1975 Loretta Lynn
1976 Loretta Lynn
1977 Loretta Lynn
1978 Loretta Lynn
1979 Barbara Mandrell
1980 Loretta Lynn
1981 Barbara Mandrell
1982 Barbara Mandrell
1983 Janie Fricke
1984 Janie Fricke
1985 Reba McEntire

1986 Reba McEntire
1987 Reba McEntire
1988 Reba McEntire
1989 Reba McEntire
1990 Patty Loveless
1991 Reba McEntire
1992 Reba McEntire
1993 Reba McEntire
1994 Lorrie Morgan

MOST PROMISING FEMALE ARTIST

1967 Tammy Wynette
1968 Dolly Parton
1969 Peggy Sue
1970 Susan Raye
1971 Susan Raye
1972 Donna Fargo
1973 Tanya Tucker
1974 Olivia Newton-John
1975 Crystal Gayle
1976 Barbara Mandrell
1977 Helen Cornelius
1978 Debby Boone
1979 Janie Fricke
1980 Charlie McClain
1981 Louise Mandrell
1982 Shelly West

VOCAL GROUP OF THE YEAR

1967 Tompall and the Glasers
1968 Tompall and the Glasers
1969 Tompall and the Glasers
1970 Tompall and the Glasers
1971 The Statler Brothers
1972 The Statler Brothers
1973 The Statler Brothers
1974 The Statler Brothers
1975 The Statler Brothers
1976 The Statler Brothers
1977 The Statler Brothers
1978 The Statler Brothers
1979 The Statler Brothers
1980 The Statler Brothers
1981 The Statler Brothers
1982 The Statler Brothers
1983 Alabama
1984 The Statler Brothers
1985 The Statler Brothers
1986 The Statler Brothers
1987 The Statler Brothers
1988 The Statler Brothers
1989 The Statler Brothers
1990 The Statler Brothers
1991 The Statler Brothers
1992 The Statler Brothers
1993 The Statler Brothers
1994 The Statler Brothers

ALBUM OF THE YEAR

1976 "When a Tingle Becomes a Chill"
Loretta Lynn/MCA
1977 "I Don't Want to Have to Marry You"
Jim Ed Brown and Helen Cornelius/RCA
1978 "Moody Blues"
Elvis Presley/RCA
1979 "Entertainers . . . On and Off the Record"
The Statler Brothers/Mercury
1980 "The Originals"
The Statler Brothers/Mercury
1981 "Tenth Anniversary"
The Statler Brothers/Mercury
1982 "Feels So Right"
Alabama/RCA
1983 "Come Back to Me"
Marty Robbins/Columbia
1984 "The Closer You Get"
Alabama/RCA
1985 "Atlanta Blues"
The Statler Brothers/Mercury
1986 "Pardners in Rhyme"
The Statler Brothers/Mercury
1987 "Storms of Life"
Randy Travis/Warner Bros.
1988 "Always and Forever"
Randy Travis/Warner Bros.
1989 "Old 8 x 10"
Randy Travis/Warner Bros./TNN
1989 "Loving Proof"
Ricky Van Shelton/MCN
1990 "Killin' Time"
Clint Black/RCA
1991 "Here in the Real World"
Alan Jackson/Arista
1992 "Don't Rock the Jukebox"
Alan Jackson/Arista
1993 "I Still Believe in You"
Vince Gill/MCA
1994 "A Lot About Livin' (And a Little 'Bout Love)"
Alan Jackson/Arista

SONGWRITER OF THE YEAR

1967 Bill Anderson
1968 Bill Anderson
1969 Bill Anderson
1970 Merle Haggard
1971 Kris Kristofferson
1972 Kris Kristofferson
1973 Kris Kristofferson
1974 Bill Anderson
1975 Bill Anderson
1976 Bill Anderson
1977 Larry Garlin
1978 Larry Gatlin
1979 Eddie Rabbitt
1980 Marty Robbins

SONG OF THE YEAR

1967 "There Goes My Everything"
Writer: Dallas Frazier
1969 "All I Have to Offer You Is Me"
Writer: Dallas Frazier & A.L. "Doodle" Owens
1970 "Hello Darlin'"
Writer: Conway Twitty
1971 "Help Me Make It Through the Night"
Writer: Kris Kristofferson
1972 "Kiss an Angel Good Mornin'"
Writer: Ben Peters
1973 "Why Me Lord"
Writer: Kris Kristofferson
1974 "You've Never Been This Far Before"
Writer: Conway Twitty
1975 "Country Bumpkin"
Writer: Don Wayne
1976 "Blue Eyes Crying in the Rain"
Writer: Fred Rose
1977 "I Don't Want to Have to Marry You"
Writers: Fred Imus & Phil Sweet

SINGLE OF THE YEAR

1978 "Heaven's Just a Sin Away"
The Kendalls
Writer: Jerry Gillespie
1979 "The Gambler"
Kenny Rogers
Writer: Don Schlitz
1980 "Coward of the County"
Kenny Rogers
Writers: Roger Bowling & Billy Ed Wheeler
1981 "He Stopped Loving Her Today"
George Jones
Writers: Curly Putman & Bobby Braddock
1982 "Elvira"
The Oak Ridge Boys
Writer: Dallas Frazier
1983 "Some Memories Just Won't Die"
Marty Robbins
Writer: Bobby Lee Springfield
1984 "Elizabeth"
The Statlers
Writer: Jimmy Fortune
1985 "God Bless the USA"
Lee Greenwood
Writer: Lee Greenwood
1986 "My Only Love"
The Statlers
Writer: Jimmy Fortune
1987 "On the Other Hand"
Randy Travis
Writers: Don Schlitz & Paul Overstreet
1988 "Forever and Ever Amen"
Randy Travis
Writers: Don Schlitz & Paul Overstreet
1989 "I'll Leave This World Loving You"
Ricky Van Shelton
1990 "More Than a Name on the Wall"
The Statler Brothers
1991 "When I Call Your Name"
Vince Gill
1992 "Don't Rock the Jukebox"
Alan Jackson
1993 "I Still Believe in You"
Vince Gill
1994 "Chattahoochie"
Alan Jackson

DUET OF THE YEAR

1967 The Wilburn Brothers
1968 Porter Wagoner/Dolly Parton
1969 Porter Wagoner/Dolly Parton
1970 Porter Wagoner/Dolly Parton
1971 Conway Twitty/Loretta Lynn
1972 Conway Twitty/Loretta Lynn
1973 Conway Twitty/Loretta Lynn
1974 Conway Twitty/Loretta Lynn
1975 Conway Twitty/Loretta Lynn
1976 Conway Twitty/Loretta Lynn
1977 Conway Twitty/Loretta Lynn
1978 Conway Twitty/Loretta Lynn
1979 Kenny Rogers/Dottie West
1980 Conway Twitty/Loretta Lynn

1981 Conway Twitty/Loretta Lynn
1982 David Frizzell/Shelly West
1983 David Frizzell/Shelly West
1984 Kenny Rogers/Dolly Parton
1985 The Judds
1986 The Judds
1987 The Judds
1988 The Judds
1989 The Judds
1990 The Judds
1991 The Judds
1992 The Judds

VOCAL DUO

1993 Brooks & Dunn
1994 Brooks & Dunn

VOCAL BAND

1993 Sawyer Brown
1994 Sawyer Brown

INSTRUMENTAL ENTERTAINER OF THE YEAR

1974 Charlie McCoy
1975 Roy Clark
1976 Roy Clark
1977 Roy Clark

INSTRUMENTALIST OF THE YEAR

1969 Roy Clark
1970 Roy Clark
1971 Roy Clark
1972 Roy Clark
1973 Charlie McCoy
1974 Roy Clark
1975 Buck Trent
1976 Buck Trent
1977 Johnny Gimble
1978 Roy Clark

MUSICIAN OF THE YEAR

1979 Roy Clark
1980 Roy Clark
1981 Barbara Mandrell
1982 Barbara Mandrell

INSTRUMENTAL ARTIST OF THE YEAR

1988 Ricky Skaggs
1989 Ricky Skaggs
1990 Ricky Skaggs
1991 Vince Gill
1992 Vince Gill

INSTRUMENTALIST OF THE YEAR

1993 Vince Gill
1994 Vince Gill

GOSPEL ARTIST OR GROUP OF THE YEAR

1979 Connie Smith
1980 The Carter Family
1980 Hee Haw Gospel Quartet
1981 Hee Haw Gospel Quartet
1982 Hee Haw Gospel Quartet
1983 Hee Haw Gospel Quartet
1984 Hee Haw Gospel Quartet
1985 Hee Haw Gospel Quartet
1986 Hee Haw Gospel Quartet
1987 Hee Haw Gospel Quartet
1988 The Chuck Wagon Gang
1989 The Chuck Wagon Gang
1990 The Chuck Wagon Gang
1991 The Chuck Wagon Gang
1992 The Chuck Wagon Gang
1993 The Chuck Wagon Gang

CHRISTIAN COUNTRY ARTIST

1994 Paul Overstreet

COUNTRY MUSIC VIDEO

1985 "Elizabeth"
The Statlers
1986 "My Only Love"
The Statlers
1987 "Whoever's in New England"
Reba McEntire
1988 "Maple Street Memories"
The Statlers
1988 "Forever and Ever Amen"
Randy Travis
1989 "I'll Leave This World Loving You"
Ricky Van Shelton
1990 "Tear in My Beer"
Hank Williams & Hank Williams, Jr.
1991 "The Dance"
Garth Brooks
1992 "Rockin' Years"
Dolly Parton with Ricky Van Shelton
1993 "Midnight in Montgomery"
Alan Jackson
1994 "Chattahoochie"
Alan Jackson

COMEDY ACT OF THE YEAR

1971 Mel Tillis
1972 Archie Campbell
1973 Mel Tillis
1974 Mel Tillis
1975 Mel Tillis

1976 Mel Tillis
1977 Mel Tillis
1978 Mel Tillis
1979 Jerry Clower
1980 The Statlers
1981 The Mandrell Sisters
1982 The Statlers
1983 The Statlers
1984 The Statlers
1985 The Statlers

COMEDIAN OF THE YEAR

1986 Ray Stevens
1987 Ray Stevens
1988 Ray Stevens
1989 Ray Stevens
1990 Ray Stevens
1991 Ray Stevens
1992 Ray Stevens
1993 Ray Stevens
1994 Ray Stevens

FOUNDERS AWARD

1976 Faron Young
1977 Ralph Emery
1978 Ernest Tubb
1979 Pee Wee King
1980 Buck Owens
1981 Betty Cox Adler

MINNIE PEARL AWARD

1987 Roy Acuff
1988 Minnie Pearl
1990 Tennessee Ernie Ford
1991 Barbara Mandrell
1992 Emmylou Harris
1993 Vince Gill
1994 Dolly Parton

VOCAL COLLABORATION OF THE YEAR

1988 Emmylou Harris, Dolly Parton & Linda Ronstadt
1989 Dwight Yoakam & Buck Owens
1990 Hank Williams & Hank Williams, Jr.
1991 Keith Whitley & Lorrie Morgan
1992 Dolly Parton & Ricky Scaggs
1993 Travis Tritt & Marty Stuart
1994 Reba McEntire & Linda Davis

ENTERTAINER OF THE YEAR

1985 The Statlers
1986 The Statlers
1987 The Statlers
1988 Randy Travis
1989 Randy Travis
1990 Ricky Van Shelton
1991 Ricky Van Shelton
1992 Garth Brooks
1993 Alan Jackson
1994 Alan Jackson

LIVING LEGEND AWARD

1983 Roy Acuff
1984 Ernest Tubb
1985 Barbara Mandrell
1986 Loretta Lynn
1987 George Jones
1988 Conway Twitty
1989 Johnny Cash
1990 Merle Haggard
1991 Tammy Wynette
1992 Roy Rogers
1993 Kitty Wells
1994 Dolly Parton

STAR OF TOMORROW

1983 Ricky Skaggs
1984 Ronny Robbins
1985 The Judds
1986 John Schneider
1987 Randy Travis
1988 Ricky Van Shelton
1989 Patty Loveless
1990 Clint Black
1991 Alan Jackson
1992 Travis Tritt
1993 Doug Stone
1994 John Michael Montgomery

BAND OF THE YEAR

1967 The Buckaroos
1968 The Buckaroos
1969 The Buckaroos
1970 The Buckaroos
1971 The Strangers
1972 The Strangers
1973 The Po' Boys
1974 The Buckaroos
1975 The Coalminers
1976 The Coalminers
1977 The Coalminers
1978 Larry Gatlin, Family and Friends
1979 The Oak Ridge Boys' Band
1980 Charlie Daniels Band
1981 Marty Robbins Band

1982 Alabama
1983 Alabama
1984 Alabama

COUNTRY MUSIC TV SHOW

1969 Johnny Cash Show
1969 Hee Haw
1970 Hee Haw
1971 Hee Haw
1972 Hee Haw
1973 Hee Haw
1974 Hee Haw
1975 Hee Haw
1976 Hee Haw
1977 Hee Haw
1978 Fifty Years Of Country Music
1979 PBS Live From The Grand Ole Opry
1980 PBS Live From The Grand Ole Opry
1981 Barbara Mandrell and the Mandrell Sisters
1982 Barbara Mandrell and the Mandrell Sisters

COUNTRY MUSIC TV SERIES

1983 Hee Haw
1984 Hee Haw
1985 Nashville Now
1986 Nashville Now
1987 Nashville Now
1988 Nashville Now

COUNTRY MUSIC TV SPECIAL

1983 Conway Twitty on the Mississippi
1984 Another Evening With The Statler Brothers
1985 Another Evening With The Statler Brothers (Heroes, Legends and Friends)
1986 Farm Aid
1987 The Statlers' Christmas Present
1988 Grand Ole Opry Live

BLUEGRASS GROUP OF THE YEAR

1971 The Osborne Bros.
1972 The Osborne Bros.
1973 The Osborne Bros.
1974 The Osborne Bros.
1975 The Osborne Bros.
1976 The Osborne Bros.
1977 The Osborne Bros.
1978 The Osborne Bros.
1979 The Osborne Bros.
1980 Bill Monroe and The Bluegrass Boys
1981 Bill Monroe and The Bluegrass Boys
1982 Ricky Skaggs
1983 Ricky Skaggs
1984 Ricky Skaggs

TOURING ROAD SHOW

1974 Loretta Lynn/The Coalminers & Kenny Starr

FAVORITE GROUP

1988 The Oak Ridge Boys
1989 The Oak Ridge Boys

FAVORITE NEWCOMER

1988 Ricky Van Shelton

RPM BIG COUNTRY AWARDS

On September 22-23, 1973, RPM Publications staged the first Big Country Conference at the Holiday Inn, Don Mills, Ontario. In 1975, RPM announced formation of CACMA (Canadian Academy of Country Music Advancement) to raise funds to start an academy. As a result of a ballot, ACME (Academy of Country Music Entertainers) held separate awards. RPM returned with the Big Country Awards in 1985.

CANADIAN COUNTRY ARTIST OF THE YEAR

1978 Carroll Baker
1979 Anne Murray
1980 Carroll Baker
1981 Family Brown
1982 No Awards
1983 No Awards
1984 No Awards
1985 No Awards

ARTIST OF THE YEAR

1986 The Family Brown

CANADIAN COUNTRY ARTIST OF THE YEAR

1987 Anne Murray
1988 Ian Tyson
1989 George Fox
1990 k.d. lang
1991 Michelle Wright
1992 Prairie Oyster
1993 Michelle Wright
1994 Charlie Major

TOP COUNTRY FEMALE SINGER

1975 Carroll Baker
1976 Carroll Baker
1977 Carroll Baker
1978 Carroll Baker
1979 Anne Murray
1980 Carroll Baker
1981 Carroll Baker
1982 No Awards

1983 No Awards
1984 No Awards

TOP COUNTRY FEMALE VOCALIST

1985 Anne Murray
1986 Anne Murray
1987 Carroll Baker
1988 Anne Murray

TOP FEMALE VOCALIST

1989 Michelle Wright
1990 k.d. lang
1991 Michelle Wright
1992 Michelle Wright

FEMALE VOCALIST

1993 Michelle Wright
1994 Michelle Wright

TOP COUNTRY MALE SINGER

1975 Gary Buck
1976 Dick Damron
1977 Dick Damron
1978 Dick Damron
1979 Eddie Eastman
1980 Terry Carisse
1981 Terry Carisse
1982 No Awards
1983 No Awards
1984 No Awards

TOP COUNTRY MALE VOCALIST

1985 Murray McLaughlan
1986 Murray McLaughlan
1987 Terry Carisse
1988 Ian Tyson

TOP MALE VOCALIST

1989 George Fox
1990 George Fox
1991 George Fox
1992 George Fox

MALE VOCALIST

1993 George Fox
1994 Charlie Major

TOP COUNTRY GROUP

1975 Eastwind
1976 The Family Brown
1977 The Family Brown
1978 The Family Brown

TOP GROUP

1979 The Family Brown
1980 The Family Brown
1981 The Family Brown
1982 No Awards
1983 No Awards
1984 No Awards

TOP COUNTRY DUO OR GROUP

1985 The Family Brown

TOP COUNTRY GROUP

1986 The Mercey Brothers
1987 The Family Brown
1988 Blue Rodeo

TOP GROUP OR DUO

1989 The Family Brown

TOP GROUP

1990 The Family Brown
1991 Prairie Oyster
1992 Prairie Oyster

GROUP OR DUO

1993 The Rankin Family
1994 Prairie Oyster

OUTSTANDING PERFORMER, FEMALE

1975 Sylvia Tyson
1976 Sylvia Tyson
1977 Myrna Lorrie
1978 Glory-Anne Carriere
1979 Marie Bottrell
1980 Glory-Anne Carriere

OUTSTANDING PERFORMER COUNTRY FEMALE SINGER

1981 Chris Nielsen
1982 No Awards
1983 No Awards
1984 No Awards

OUTSTANDING PERFORMER, MALE

1975 Ian Tyson
1976 Ronnie Prophet
1977 Barry Brown
1978 Orval Prophet
1979 Wayne Rostad
1980 Ronnie Prophet
1981 Eddie Eastman
1982 No Awards
1983 No Awards
1984 No Awards

OUTSTANDING PERFORMER, GROUP

1975 Bob Murphy & Big Buffalo
1976 The Good Brothers
1977 The Carlton Showband
1978 Terry Carisse & Tenderfoot
1979 Ralph Carlson & Country Mile
1980 The Good Brothers

OUTSTANDING PERFORMER COUNTRY DUO OR GROUP

1981 Ralph Carlson & Country Mile
1982 No Awards
1983 No Awards
1984 No Awards

OUTSTANDING NEW ARTIST

1978 Eddie Eastman
1979 Larry Mattson
1980 Wilf Ingersoll
1981 Harold Macintyre
1982 No Awards
1983 No Awards
1984 No Awards
1985 Jamie Warren
1986 The Haggertys
1987 Double Eagle Band
1988 Blue Rodeo
1989 Carmen Westfall
1990 Great Western Orchestra
1991 Patricia Conroy
1992 Joel Feeney
1993 The Rankin Family
1994 Jim Witter

BEST COUNTRY SINGLE

1975 "Paper Rosie"
Dallas Harms
1976 "Georgia I'm Cheating on You Tonight"
Dallas Harms
1977 "Susan Flowers"
Dick Damron
1978 "Wild Honey"
Johnny Burke & Eastwind
1979 "Stay With Me"
The Family Brown
1980 "The Star"
Marie Bottrell
1981 "Windship"
Terry Carisse
1982 No Awards
1983 No Awards
1984 No Awards
1985 "Nobody Loves Me Like You Do"
Anne Murray and Dave Loggins
1986 "Nobody Loves Me Like You Do"
Anne Murray and Dave Loggins
1987 "Now and Forever (You and Me)"
Anne Murray
1988 "Try"
Blue Rodeo
1989 "Angelina"
George Fox
1990 "Full Moon of Love"
k.d. lang and the reclines
1991 "Goodbye, So Long, Hello"
Prairie Oyster
1992 "Something to Remember You By"
Prairie Oyster
1993 "He Would Be Sixteen"
Michelle Wright
1994 "I'm Gonna Drive You Out of My Mind"
Charlie Major

BEST COUNTRY ALBUM

1975 "Ol Eon"
Ian Tyson
1976 "Carroll Baker"
Carroll Baker
1977 "Here Comes Yesterday"
R. Harlan Smith
1978 "The Fastest Gun"
Dallas Harms
1979 "Familiar Faces, Familiar Places"
The Family Brown
1980 "I'll Always Love You"
Anne Murray
1981 "We Can Make Beautiful Music Together"
Terry Carisse
1982 No Awards
1983 No Awards
1984 No Awards
1985 "Great Western Orchestra"
Great Western Orchestra
1986 "Feel the Fire"
The Family Brown
1987 "None of the Feeling Is Gone"
Terry Carisse
1988 "Cowboyography"
Ian Tyson
1989 "These Days"
The Family Brown
1990 "Absolute Torch and Twang"
k.d. lang and the reclines
1991 "With All My Might"
George Fox

1992 "Everybody Knows"
Prairie Oyster

1993 "Now and Then"
Michelle Wright

1994 "The Other Side"
Charlie Major

TOP COUNTRY COMPOSER

1975 Dallas Harms
1976 Dick Damron
1977 Dallas Harms
1978 Dallas Harms
1979 Dallas Harms
1980 Barry Brown

TOP COUNTRY COMPOSITION

1981 Terry Carisse and Bruce Rawlins for "Windship"
1982 No Awards
1983 No Awards
1984 No Awards

TOP COUNTRY COMPOSER

1985 Barry Brown
1986 Terry Carisse and Bruce Rawlins for "Counting the I Love Yous"
1987 Terry Carisse and Bruce Rawlins for "Love Sweet Love"
1988 Greg Keelor and Jim Cuddy for "Try"
1989 George Fox for "Angelina"
1990 Gary Fjellgard for "Cowboy in Your Heart"
1991 Gary Fjellgard for "Somewhere on the Island"
1992 Keith Glass and Joan Besen for "Something to Remember You By"
1993 Joan Besen for "One Time Around"
1994 Charlie Major and Barry Brown for "I'm Gonna Drive You Out of My Mind"

TOP COUNTRY PRODUCER

1975 Gary Buck
1976 R. Harlan Smith
1977 Jack Feeney
1978 Dallas Harms
1979 Dallas Harms
1980 R. Harlan Smith
1981 Larry Mercey, Lloyd Mercey and Ray Mercey for "Windship"
1982 No Awards
1983 No Awards
1984 No Awards
1985 Randall Prescott for "Let's Build a Life Together"
1986 Gilles Godard for "We Won't Ever Say Goodbye"
1987 David Foster for "Now and Forever (You and Me)"
1988 Terry Brown for "Try"
1989 Randall Prescott for "Til I Find My Love"
1990 Randall Prescott for "Let's Build a Life Together"
1991 Howie Vickers for "Somewhere on the Island"
1992 Randall Prescott for "Take Me With You"
1993 Chad Irschuck for "Orangedale Whistle"
1994 Chad Irschuck for "Gillis Mountain"

TOP COUNTRY D.J.

1975 Charlie Russell (CJCJ Woodstock, New Brunswick)
1976 Johnny Murphy (CHML Hamilton, Ontario)
1977 Ted Daigle (CKBY-FM Ottawa, Ontario)
1978 Bill Anderson (CFRB Toronto, Ontario)
1979 Stan Campbell (CFGM Toronto, Ontario)
1980 Bill Anderson (CFRB Toronto, Ontario)
1981 Bill Anderson (CFRB Toronto, Ontario)
1982 No Awards
1983 No Awards
1984 No Awards
1985 No Awards

TOP RADIO PERSONALITY

1986 Robin Ingram (CFAC Calgary, Alberta)

TOP COUNTRY RADIO PERSONALITY

1987 Cliff Dumas (CHAM Hamilton, Ontario)
1988 Randy Owen (CKGL Kitchener, Ontario)
1989 Cliff Dumas (CHAM Hamilton, Ontario)
1990 Paul Kennedy (CHFX-FM Halifax, Nova Scotia)
1991 Cliff Dumas (CHAM Hamilton, Ontario)
1992 Cliff Dumas (820 CHAM Hamilton, Ontario)

TOP RADIO STATION

1986 CHAM Hamilton, Ontario
1987 CHAM Hamilton, Ontario
1988 CHAM Hamilton, Ontario
1989 820 CHAM Hamilton, Ontario
1990 820 CHAM Hamilton, Ontario
1991 820 CHAM Hamilton, Ontario
1992 820 CHAM Hamilton, Ontario

TOP RECORD COMPANY

1975 Broadland Records
1976 RCA Ltd.
1977 RCA Ltd.
1978 RCA Ltd.

TOP COUNTRY RECORD COMPANY

1979 RCA Ltd.

TOP RECORD COMPANY

1980 RCA Ltd.
1981 RCA

1982 No Awards
1983 No Awards
1984 No Awards
1985 No Awards
1986 RCA
1987 BMG Music Canada
1988 BMG/RCA Canada
1989 WEA Music Canada
1990 Savannah Records
1991 Warner Music Canada
1992 BMG Music Canada

MAJOR RECORD COMPANY

1993 BMG Music Canada
1994 BMG Music Canada

INDEPENDENT LABEL

1993 Savannah Records
1994 Savannah Records

TOP CANADIAN COUNTRY TELEVISION SHOW

1975 "Ian Tyson" from Glen Warren Productions
1976 "Grand Old Country with Ronnie Prophet" from Glen Warren Productions
1977 "Grand Old Country with Ronnie Prophet" from Glen Warren Productions
1978 "Tommy Hunter Country" from the CBS-TV Network
1979 "Grand Old Country with Ronnie Prophet" from Glen Warren Productions
1980 "Grand Old Country with Ronnie Prophet" from Glen Warren Productions

TOP COUNTRY TELEVISION SHOW

1981 "Family Brown Country" from CJOH-TV Ottawa
1982 No Awards
1983 No Awards
1984 No Awards

SESAC

WRITER OF THE YEAR

1969 Ted Harris
1970 Ted Harris
1971 Ted Harris
1972 Ted Harris
1973 Raymond Smith
1974 Ricci Mareno
1975 Chip Dabis & William Fries
1976 Ted Harris
1977 Jerry Gillespie
1978 Peggy Forman
1979 Charlie Black
1980 Shirl Milette
1981 Jerry Gillespie
1982 Glenn Ray
1983 Jerry Gillespie
1984 Randy Brooks
1985 No Awards
1986 Kendal Franceschi
1987 Ted Harris
1988 K.T. Oslin
1989 K.T. Oslin
1990 Susan Longacre
1991 K.T. Oslin
1992 Susan Longacre
1993 Susan Longacre
1994 Karen Taylor-Good, Amanda Hunt-Taylor

PUBLISHER OF THE YEAR

1991 W.B.M. Music Corp.
1992 W.B.M. Music Corp.
1993 W.B.M. Music Corp.
1994 W.B.M. Music Corp.

INDIVIDUAL ARTIST AWARDS
ALABAMA

YEAR	BODY	AWARD
1980	Cash Box	New Vocal Group of the Year—Albums
1980	Cash Box	New Vocal Group of the Year—Singles
1981	ACM	Vocal Group of the Year
1981	Billboard	New Group of the Year
1981	Cash Box	Top Vocal Group of the Year—Albums
1981	Cash Box	Top Vocal Group of the Year—Singles
1981	CMA	Instrumental Group of the Year
1981	CMA	Vocal Group of the Year
1981	NARM Gift of Music Award	Best Selling Country Album by Group—"Feels So Right"
1981	Radio & Records	Album of the Year—"Feels So Right"
1981	Radio & Records	Group of the Year
1982	ACM	Album of the Year—"Feels So Right"
1982	ACM	Entertainer of the Year
1982	ACM	Vocal Group of the Year
1982	Amusement & Music Operators of America	Most Popular Artist of the Year
1982	Billboard	Top Album—"Feels So Right"
1982	Billboard	Top Album Artist
1982	Billboard	Top Artists of the Year—Albums and Singles
1982	Billboard	Top Group of the Year—Albums and Singles
1982	Billboard	Top Singles Group
1982	Billboard	Breakthrough Award—Country to Pop
1982	Cash Box	Male Entertainer of the Year
1982	Cash Box	Top Group of the Year—Albums
1982	Cash Box	Top Group of the Year—Singles
1982	Cash Box Programmers Choice Awards	Album of the Year
1982	Cash Box Programmers Choice Awards	Vocal Group of the Year
1982	CMA	Entertainer of the Year
1982	CMA	Instrumental Group of the Year
1982	CMA	Vocal Group of the Year
1982	Grammy Award	Best Country Performance by a Duo or Group With Vocal—"Mountain Music" (album)
1982	MCN	Album of the Year—"Feels So Right"
1982	MCN	Band of the Year
1982	NARM Gift of Music Award	Best Selling Country Album by Group—"Mountain Music"
1982	Radio & Records	Album of the Year—"Mountain Music"
1982	Radio & Records	Group of the Year
1982	Radio & Records	Performers of the Year
1982	US Magazine Award	Favorite Country Group
1983	ACM	Entertainer of the Year
1983	ACM	Vocal Group of the Year
1983	American Music Award	Favorite Country Group
1983	Billboard	Overall Top Artist
1983	Billboard	Overall Top Group
1983	Billboard	Top Album—"Mountain Music"
1983	Billboard	Top Album Artist
1983	Billboard	Top Album Group
1983	Cash Box	Group of the Year
1983	Cash Box	Single of the Year
1983	Cash Box	Vocal Group of the Year—Albums

1983	Cash Box	Vocal Group of the Year—Singles
1983	Cash Box Programmers Choice Awards	Album of the Year
1983	Cash Box Programmers Choice Awards	Group of the Year
1983	CMA	Album of the Year—"The Closer You Get"
1983	CMA	Entertainer of the Year
1983	CMA	Vocal Group of the Year
1983	Grammy Award	Best Country Performance by a Duo or Group With Vocal—"The Closer You Get" (album)
1983	MCN	Band of the Year
1983	MCN	Vocal Group of the Year
1983	NARM Gift of Music Award	Best Selling Country Album by Group—"The Closer You Get"
1983	Radio & Records	Album of the Year—"The Closer You Get"
1983	Radio & Records	Group of the Year
1983	Radio & Records	Performers of the Year
1983	US Magazine Award	Favorite Country Group
1984	ACM	Album of the Year—"The Closer You Get"
1984	ACM	Entertainer of the Year
1984	ACM	Vocal Group of the Year
1984	American Music Award	Country Album of the Year—"The Closer You Get"
1984	American Music Award	Group of the Year
1984	American Music Award	Favorite Video—"Dixieland Delight"
1984	Billboard	Artist of the Year
1984	Billboard	Overall Top Country Artist—Albums and Singles
1984	Billboard	Overall Top Country Group—Albums and Singles
1984	Billboard	Top Album Artist
1984	Billboard	Top Album Group
1984	Billboard	Top Singles Group
1984	Cash Box	Country Singles Award—Vocal Group
1984	Cash Box	Top 50 Country Album-#1—"Roll On"
1984	CMA	Entertainer of the Year
1984	MCN	Album of the Year—"The Closer You Get"
1984	MCN	Band of the Year
1984	NARM Gift of Music Award	Best Selling Country Album by Group—"Roll On"
1984	Radio & Records	Album of the Year—"Roll On"
1984	Radio & Records	Performers of the Year
1985	ACM	Album of the Year—"Roll On"
1985	ACM	Entertainer of the Year
1985	ACM	Vocal Group of the Year
1985	Alabama Music Hall of Fame	Country Group
1985	American Music Award	Country Group of the Year
1985	Billboard	Top Artist for Singles and Albums
1985	Billboard	Top Group for Albums
1985	Billboard	Top Group for Singles
1985	Billboard	Top Group for Singles and Albums
1985	Billboard	Top Singles Artist
1985	Cash Box	#1 Album
1985	Cash Box	#1 Group
1985	Cash Box	Programmers Choice Award
1985	MCN Songwriter Awards	"Lady Down on Love"
1985	NARM Gift of Music Award	Best Selling Country Album by Group—"40 Hour Week"
1985	Radio & Records	Album of the Year—"Roll On"
1985	Radio & Records	Best Album
1985	Radio & Records	Best Group

1985	Radio & Records	Group of the Year
1985	Radio & Records	Performer of the Year (readers)
1985	Radio & Records	Performers of the Year
1986	ACM	Entertainer of the Year
1986	ACM	Vocal Group of the Year
1986	American Music Award	Country Album of the Year—"40 Hour Week"
1986	American Music Award	Country Group of the Year
1986	Billboard	Top Overall Album Artist
1986	Billboard	Top Overall Album Group
1986	Billboard	Top Overall Vocal Group—Singles and Albums
1986	Cash Box	Album—Group of the Year
1986	Cash Box	Entertainer of the Year
1986	NARM Gift of Music Award	Best Selling Country Album by Group—"Greatest Hits"
1987	Alabama Music Hall of Fame	Governor's Sustaining Achievement Award for Popular Music
1987	American Music Award	Best Country Album— "Greatest Hits"
1987	American Music Award	Best Country Group
1987	American Music Award	Best Country Video
1987	Ampex Golden Reel Award	"The Touch"
1987	Bob Hope Humanitary Award	For Public Service Work and Contributions Involving Children
1987	Cash Box	Country Vocal Group of the Year
1987	National Association for Campus Activities	Favorite Country Music Performer
1987	People's Choice Awards	Favorite Musical Group
1988	Alabama Music Hall of Fame	Distinguished Service Award
1988	American Music Award	Favorite Country Group
1988	Ampex Golden Reel Award	"Just Us"
1988	National Association for Campus Activities	Vocal Group of the Year
1989	ACM	Artist of the Decade
1989	American Music Award	Favorite Country Group
1989	Billboard	Country Artist of the 80's
1989	BMG	Global Achievement Award
1989	Broadcast Music, Inc. (BMI)	Song of the Year—"Fallin' Again"
1989	Cash Box	Artist of the Decade
1989	Cash Box	Entertainer of the Year
1990	Alabama Music Hall of Fame	Service Award
1990	American Music Award	Country Group of the Year
1990	Country Radio Broadcasters	Humanitarian Award
1990	Playboy	Country Album of the Year—"Southern Star"
1990	Playboy	Top Group/Country Award
1990	Prince Matchabelli National Hero Award	Music
1991	American Music Awards	Favorite Country Group
1991	Playboy	Top Country Group

GARTH BROOKS

YEAR	BODY	AWARD
1990	CMA	Horizon Award
1990	CMA	Video of the Year—"The Dance"
1990	Country Music People Magazine (UK)	International Single of the Year—"If Tomorrow Never Comes"
1990	NSAI	Song of the Year—"If Tomorrow Never Comes" (writers: Garth Brooks/Kent Blazy)
1991	ACM	Album of the Year—"No Fences"
1991	ACM	Entertainer of the Year
1991	ACM	Male Vocalist of the Year

1991	ACM	Single Record of the Year—"Friends in Low Places"
1991	ACM	Song of the Year—"The Dance"
1991	ACM	Video of the Year—"The Dance"
1991	AMA	Country Category—Favorite Single—"If Tomorrow Never Comes"
1991	Billboard Music Awards	Top Country Album Artist
1991	Billboard Music Awards	Top Country Artist
1991	Billboard Music Awards	Top Country Singles Artist
1991	Billboard Music Awards	Top Pop Album Artist
1991	CMA	Video of the Year—"The Thunder Rolls"
1991	CMA	Album of the Year—"No Fences"
1991	CMA	Entertainer of the Year
1991	CMA	Single of the Year—"Friends in Low Places"
1991	Juno Award (Canada)	Foreign Entertainer of the Year
1991	MCN—Songwriters Awards	"If Tomorrow Never Comes" voted one of the Top 10 songs of the year
1991	MCN/TNN Viewers' Choice Awards	Video of the Year—"The Dance"
1991	NARM Best Seller Awards	Best selling Country Music Recording by a Male Artist—"Ropin' the Wind"
1991	NARM Best Seller Awards	Best Selling Music Video—"Garth Brooks" (the long-form video)
1991	NARM Best Seller Awards	Best Selling Recording by a Male Artist—"Ropin' the Wind"
1991	NARM Best Seller Awards	Best Selling Recording of the Year—"Ropin' the Wind"
1991	Radio and Records Readers Poll	Best Album—"No Fences"
1991	Radio and Records Readers Poll	Best Single—"Friends in Low Places"
1991	Radio and Records Readers Poll	Male Vocalist of the Year
1991	Radio and Records Readers Poll	Performer of the Year
1992	ACM	Entertainer of the Year
1992	ACM	Male Vocalist of the Year
1992	ACM	Special Achievement Award
1992	AMA	Country Category—Favorite Single—"The Thunder Rolls"
1992	AMA	Country Category—Favorite Album—"No Fences"
1992	AMA	Country Category—Favorite Male Artist
1992	ASCAP	Voice of Music Award (first ever given)
1992	Country Music People magazine (UK)	International Album of the Year—"Ropin' the Wind"
1992	Country Music People magazine (UK)	International Male Vocalist
1992	Dutch Country Music Awards (Gram Awards)	Male Vocalist of the Year
1992	Entertainment Weekly's Readers' Poll	In July 1992, named Garth Top Male Singer (Runners-up included Michael Bolton, Axel Rose, Bruce Springsteen)
1992	Grammy Award	Best Country Vocal Performance, Male—"Ropin' the Wind" (album)
1992	MCN/TNN Viewers' Choice Awards	Entertainer of the Year
1992	People's Choice Awards	Best Male Country Performer
1992	People's Choice Awards	Best Male Musical Performer
1992	Performance magazine	Country Artist of the Year
1992	Radio and Records Readers Poll	Album of the Year—"Ropin' the Wind"
1992	Radio and Records Readers Poll	Single of the Year—"Shameless"
1992	Radio and Records Readers Poll	Male Vocalist of the Year
1992	Radio and Records Readers Poll	Performer of the Year
1992	Rolling Stone Readers' Choice Awards	Country Artist of the Year
1993	AMA	Country Category—Favorite Male Artist
1994	AMA	Country Category—Favorite Male Artist
1994	ASCAP	Songwriter of the Year

JOHNNY CASH

YEAR	BODY	AWARD
1967	Grammy Award	Best Country & Western Performance, Duo, Trio or Group (Vocal or Instrumental)—"Jackson" (Single)—Johnny Cash and June Carter
1968	CMA	Album of the Year—"Johnny Cash at Folsom Prison"
1968	Grammy Award	Best Album Notes—"Johnny Cash at Folsom Prison"/Annotator: Johnny Cash
1968	Grammy Award	Best Country Vocal Performance, Male—"Folsom Prison Blues" (Single)
1969	ACM	TV Personality
1969	CMA	Album of the Year—"Johnny Cash at San Quentin"
1969	CMA	Entertainer of the Year
1969	CMA	Male Vocalist of the Year
1969	CMA	Single of the Year—"A Boy Named Sue"
1969	CMA	Vocal Group of the Year—Johnny Cash and June Carter
1969	Grammy Award	Best Album Notes—"Nashville Skyline" by Bob Dylan/Annotator: Johnny Cash
1969	Grammy Award	Best Country Vocal Performance, Male—"A Boy Named Sue" (Single)
1969	MCN	Country Music TV Show—"The Johnny Cash Show"
1970	Grammy Award	Best Country Vocal Performance by Duo or Group—"If I Were a Carpenter" (Single)—Johnny Cash and June Carter
1972	Dove Award	Backliner Notes—"Light" by the Oak Ridge Boys/Annotator: Johnny Cash
1977	AMA	Special Award of Merit
1977	NSAI	Induction to Nashville Songwriters' Hall of Fame
1980	Country Music Hall of Fame	Induction
1985	ACM	Single Record of the Year—"Highwayman" (with Waylon Jennings, Willie Nelson & Kris Kristofferson)
1986	AMA	Country Category—Favorite Video Duo or Group—"Highwayman" (with Waylon Jennings, Willie Nelson & Kristofferson)
Kris		
1986	AMA	Country Category—Favorite Video Single—"Highwayman" (with Waylon Jennings, Willie Nelson & Kris Kristofferson)
1986	Grammy Award	Best Spoken or Non-Music Recording—"Interviews from the Class Of '55"—Johnny among several people
1989	TNN/MCN	Living Legend Award
1990	ACM	Pioneer Award
1990	Grammy Award	Grammy Legend Award

SLIM DUSTY AND FAMILY

YEAR	BODY	AWARD
1973	2TM—Golden Guitar Awards	Album—"Me & My Guitar"
1973	2TM—Golden Guitar Awards	EP or Single—"Lights on the Hill"
1974	2TM—Golden Guitar Awards	Album—"Live at Tamworth"
1975	2TM—Golden Guitar Awards	Album—"Australiana"
1975	CMAA—Golden Guitar Awards	Male Vocalist—"Biggest Disappointment"
1976	CMAA—Golden Guitar Awards	Top Selling Track—"Worst in the World"
1976	CMAA—Golden Guitar Awards	Album—"Lights on the Hill"
1977	CMAA—Golden Guitar Awards	Male Vocalist—"Angel of Goulburn Hill"

1977	CMAA—Golden Guitar Awards	Top Selling Record— "Things I See Around Me"
1977	CMAA— Golden Guitar Awards	Album—"Things I See Around Me"
1979	CMAA— Golden Guitar Awards	Roll of Renown
1979	CMAA— Golden Guitar Awards	Male Vocalist—"Marty"
1980	CMAA— Golden Guitar Awards	Top Selling Record—"Walk a Country Mile"
1980	CMAA— Golden Guitar Awards	Album—"Walk a Country Mile"
1981	CMAA— Golden Guitar Awards	Top Selling Record—"The Man Who Steadies the Lead"
1981	CMAA— Golden Guitar Awards	Album—"The Man Who Steadies the Lead"
1982	CMAA— Golden Guitar Awards	Heritage Award—"Where Country Is"
1983	CMAA— Golden Guitar Awards	Heritage Award—"Banjo's Man"
1984	CMAA— Golden Guitar Awards	Heritage Award—"Australia's on the Wallaby"
1984	CMAA— Golden Guitar Awards	Album—"On the Wallaby"
1985	CMAA— Golden Guitar Awards	Top Selling Record—"Trucks on the Track"
1985	CMAA— Golden Guitar Awards	Album—"Trucks on the Track"
1987	CMAA— Golden Guitar Awards	Heritage Award—"Mount Buckaroo"
1988	CMAA— Golden Guitar Awards	Album—"Neon City"
1989	CMAA— Golden Guitar Awards	Heritage Award—"We've Done Us Proud"
1991	CMAA— Golden Guitar Awards	Top Selling Record—"Two Singers/One Song" (with Ann Kirkpatrick)
1991	CMAA— Golden Guitar Awards	Album—"Coming Home"

JOY McKEAN (Writing Awards)

1973	2TM— Golden Guitar Awards	Song of the Year—"Lights on the Hill"
1975	2TM— Golden Guitar Awards	Song of the Year—"Biggest Disappointment"
1978	CMAA— Golden Guitar Awards	Song of the Year—"Indian Pacific"

ANNE KIRKPATRICK

1979	CMAA— Golden Guitar Awards	Female Vocalist—"Grievous Angel"
1992	CMAA— Golden Guitar Awards	Female Vocalist

MERLE HAGGARD

YEAR	BODY	AWARD
1965	ACM	Best Vocal Group (with Bonnie Owens)
1965	ACM	Most Promising Male Vocalist
1966	ACM	Best Vocal Group (with Bonnie Owens)
1966	ACM	Top Male Vocalist
1966	Cash Box	Top Album
1966	Cash Box	Top Vocal Group (with Bonnie Owens)
1966	Record World	Fastest Climbing Male Vocalist
1967	ACM	Best Vocal Group/Duet (with Bonnie Owens)
1967	MCN	Male Artist of the Year
1968	Cash Box	Male Vocalist of the Year
1968	MCN	Male Artist of the Year
1969	ACM	Album of the Year—"Okie From Muskogee"
1969	ACM	Band of the Year (The Strangers)
1969	ACM	Single of the Year—"Okie From Muskogee"
1969	ACM	Top Male Vocalist
1969		Awarded a spot on Hollywood's Walkway of the Stars
1970	ACM	Entertainer of the Year
1970	ACM	Songwriter of the Year

1970	ACM	Top Male Vocalist
1970	ACM	Touring Band of the Year (The Strangers)
1970	CMA	Album of the Year—"Okie From Muskogee"
1970	CMA	Entertainer of the Year
1970	CMA	Male Vocalist of the Year
1970	CMA	Single of the Year—"Okie From Muskogee"
1971	ACM	Touring Band of the Year (The Strangers)
1971	Cash Box	Instrumental Group of the Year (The Strangers)
1971	MCN	Band of the Year (The Strangers)
1972	ACM	Top Male Vocalist
1972	ACM	Touring Band of the Year (The Strangers)
1972	CMA	Album of the Year—"Let Me Tell You About a Song"
1972	MCN	Band of the Year (The Strangers)
1973	Cash Box	Male Vocalist of the Year—Album Charts
1973	Cash Box	Male Vocalist of the Year—Single Charts
1973	Record World	Male Vocalist of the Year—Single Charts
1974	ACM	Top Male Vocalist
1974	ACM	Touring Band of the Year (The Strangers)
1975	ACM	Touring Band of the Year (The Strangers)
1975	Record World	Male Vocalist of the Year—Single Charts
1978	Billboard	Male Vocalist of the Year (6 singles)
1978	Record World	Male Vocalist of the Year (tied with Willie Nelson)
1981	ACM	Top Male Vocalist
1981	ACM	Touring Band of the Year (The Strangers)
1982	ACM	Entertainer of the Year
1982	ACM	Song of the Year—"Are the Good Times Really Over"
1982	Cash Box	Composer/Performer of the Year
1983	American Video Award	Best Country Video—"Are the Good Times Really Over"
1983	Cashbox	Vocal Duet of the Year (with Willie Nelson)
1983	CMA	Vocal Duo of the Year (with Willie Nelson)
1984	ACM	Top Vocal Duet of the Year (with Willie Nelson)
1984	Cashbox	Vocal Duet of the Year (with Willie Nelson)
1984	Grammy Award	Best Country Vocal Performance, Male—"That's the Way Love Goes" (single)
1991	AMA	Special Award of Merit
1994	Country Music Hall of Fame	Induction

GEORGE JONES

YEAR	BODY	AWARD
1980	ACM	Male Vocalist of the Year
1980	ACM	Song of the Year—"He Stopped Loving Her Today"
1980	ACM	Single of the Year—"He Stopped Loving Her Today"
1980	CMA	Male Vocalist of the Year
1980	CMA	Single of the Year—"He Stopped Loving Her Today"
1980	Grammy Award	Best Country Vocal Performance Male—"He Stopped Loving Her Today" (single)
1981	CMA	Male Vocalist of the Year
1981	MCN	Male Vocalist of the Year
1981	MCN	Single of the Year—"He Stopped Loving Her Today"
1985	ACM	Video of the Year—"Who's Gonna Fill Their Shoes"
1986	CMA	Music Video of the Year—"Who's Gonna Fill Their Shoes"
1987	AMA	Country Category—Favorite Male Video Artist
1987	MCN	Living Legend Award

1992	ACM	Pioneer Award
1992	CMA	Country Music Hall of Fame
1993	Entertainment Weekly	Cool Hall of Fame
1993	Country America	#1 Country Song of All Time—"He Stopped Loving Her Today"
1993	BBC	#1 Country Song of All Time—"He Stopped Loving Her Today"

LORETTA LYNN

YEAR	BODY	AWARD
1967	CMA	Female Vocalist of the Year
1971	Grammy Award	Best Country Vocal Performance by a Group (with Conway Twitty)—"After the Fire Is Gone" (Single)(Decca)
1971	ACM	Top Female Vocalist
1971	ACM	Top Vocal Group (with Conway Twitty)
1972	CMA	Female Vocalist of the Year
1972	CMA	Entertainer of the Year (First Female Recipient)
1973	CMA	Female Vocalist of the Year
1973	ACM	Top Female Vocalist
1974	MCN Cover Awards	Turing Band of the Year: Loretta Lynn/The Coalminers/Kenny Starr
1975	ACM	Entertainer of the Year (First Female Recipient)
1975	ACM	Album of the Year—"Feelin's" (with Conway Twitty)
1976	MCN Cover Awards	Album of the Year—"When a Tingle Becomes a Chill"
1979	ACM	Artist of the Decade (1969-79)
1980	CMA	Album of the Year—"Coal Miner's Daughter" (Soundtrack)
1980	ACM	Country Music Movie of the Year—"Coal Miner's Daughter"
1986	MCN Cover Awards	Living Legend Award
1967-78	MCN Cover Awards	Female Artist of the Year
1971-78	MCN Cover Awards	Duet of the Year (with Conway Twitty)
1972-75	CMA	Vocal Duo of the Year (with Conway Twitty)
1974-75	ACM	Female Vocalist of the Year
1974-76	ACM	Top Vocal Group (with Conway Twitty)
1975-77	MCN Cover Awards	Band of the Year: The Coalminers
1980-81	MCN Cover Awards	Duet of the Year (with Conway Twitty)
1980-81	MCN Cover Awards	Female Artist of the Year

REBA McENTIRE

YEAR	BODY	AWARD
1984	CMA	Female Vocalist of the Year
1985	ACM	Top Female Vocalist
1985	CMA	Female Vocalist of the Year
1985	Music City News	Female Artist of the Year
1985	Rolling Stone	Critics Choice Poll: Top Five Country Artists
1986	ACM	Top Female Vocalist
1986	CMA	Entertainer of the Year
1986	CMA	Female Vocalist of the Year
1986	Grammy Award	Best Country Vocal Performance, Female "Whoever's in New England"
1986	Music City News	Female Artist of the Year

1987	ACM	Top Female Vocalist
1987	ACM	Video of the Year—"Whoever's in New England"
1987	American Music Award	Favorite Female Video Artist, Country Category
1987	CMA	Female Vocalist of the Year
1987	Music City News	Female Artist of the Year
1987	Music City News	Country Music Video of the Year "Whoever's in New England"
1987	NARM	Best Selling Country Album by a Female Artist
1988	ACM	Top Female Vocalist
1988	American Music Award	Favorite Female Vocalist, Country Category
1988	Gallup Youth Survey	Top 10 Female Vocalists
1988	Music City News	Female Artist of the Year
1988	People Magazine	Top Three Female Vocalists
1988	TNN Viewers' Choice	Favorite Female Vocalist
1989	American Music Award	Favorite Female Vocalist, Country Category
1989	Music City News	Female Artist of the Year
1989	TNN Viewers' Choice	Favorite Female Vocalist
1990	American Music Award	Favorite Female Vocalist, Country Category
1991	ACM	Top Female Vocalist
1991	American Music Award	Favorite Female Vocalist, Country Category
1991	American Music Award	Favorite Album, Country Category
1992	American Music Award	Favorite Female Vocalist, Country Category
1993	Grammy Award	Best Country Vocal Collaboration (with Linda Davis) "Does He Love You"

RONNIE MILSAP

YEAR	BODY	AWARD
1974	Grammy Award	Best Country Vocal Performance, Male—"Please Don't Tell Me How the Story Ends" (Single)
1974	CMA	Male Vocalist of the Year
1975	MCN Cover Awards	Most Promising Male Artist
1975	CMA	Album of the Year—"A Legend in My Time"
1976	Grammy Award	Best Country Vocal Performance, Male—"(I'm a) Stand by My Woman Man" (Single)
1976	CMA	Male Vocalist of the Year
1977	CMA	Male Vocalist of the Year
1977	CMA	Album of the Year—"Ronnie Milsap Live"
1977	CMA	Entertainer of the Year
1978	CMA	Album of the Year—"It Was Almost Like a Song"
1981	Grammy Award	Best Country Vocal Performance, Male—"(There's) No Gettin' Over Me" (Single)
1982	ACM	Top Male Vocalist
1985	Grammy Award	Best Country Vocal Performance, Male—"Lost in the Fifties Tonight (In the Still of the Night)" (Single)
1985	ACM	Song of the Year—"Lost in the Fifties Tonight (In the Still of the Night)" by Mike Reid-Troy Seals/Fred Paris (Award to writers)
1986	Grammy Award	Best Country Vocal Performance, Male—"Lost in the Fifties Tonight" (Album)

1986	CMA	Album of the Year—"Lost in the Fifties Tonight"
1987	Grammy Award	Best Country Vocal Performance, Duet (with Kenny Rogers)—"Make No Mistake, She's Mine"

ANNE MURRAY

YEAR	BODY	AWARD
1974	Juno	Country Female Vocalist of the Year
1974	Juno	Female Vocalist of the Year
1975	Juno	Country Female Vocalist of the Year
1978	Juno	Female Vocalist of the Year
1978	Juno	Best Children's Album—"There's a Hippo in My Tub"
1979	Juno	Album of the Year
1979	Juno	Single of the Year
1979	Juno	Female Vocalist of the Year
1979	Juno	Country Female Vocalist of the Year
1980	Juno	Album of the Year
1980	Juno	Single of the Year
1980	Juno	Female Vocalist of the Year
1980	Juno	Country Female Vocalist of the Year
1981	Juno	Female Vocalist of the Year
1981	Juno	Country Female Vocalist of the Year
1982	AMA	Country Category—Favorite Single—"Could I Have This Dance"
1982	Juno	Country Female Vocalist of the Year
1984	CCMA	Single of the Year—"A Little Good News"
1984	CMA	Album of the Year—"A Little Good News"
1984	CMA	Single of the Year—"A Little Good News"
1985	AMA	Country Category—Favorite Video Single—"A Little Good News"
1985	AMA	Country Category—Favorite Female Video Artist
1985	CMA	Vocal Duo of the Year—Anne Murray and Dave Loggins
1985	Juno	Country Female Vocalist of the Year
1986	CCMA	Single of the Year—"Now and Forever (You and Me)"
1986	CCMA	Song of the Year—"Now and Forever (You and Me)" to writers: David Foster/Jim Vallance/Charles Goodrum
1986	Juno	Country Female Vocalist of the Year
1983-84	Juno	Country Female Vocalist of the Year

OLIVIA NEWTON-JOHN

YEAR	BODY	AWARD
1973	Grammy Award	Best Country Vocal Performance, Female—"Let Me Be There"
1974	Grammy Award	Record of the Year—"I Honestly Love You"
1974	Grammy Award	Best Pop Vocal Performance, Female—"I Honestly Love You"
1974	CMA	Female Vocalist of the Year
1974	ACM	Most Promising Female Vocalist
1974	CMA (GB)	Top British Female Country Vocalist
1974	Billboard	No.1 Awards for LPs and Singles
1974	Cash Box	No.1 New Female Vocalist, Singles
1974	Cash Box	No.1 New Female Vocalist, Albums
1975	CMA (GB)	Top British Female Country Vocalist

1975	AMA	Rock/Pop Category—Favorite Female Artist
1975	AMA	Rock/Pop Category—Favorite Single—"I Honestly Love You"
1975	AMA	Country Category—Favorite Female Artist
1975	AMA	Country Category—Favorite Album—"Let Me Be There"
1976	AMA	Rock/Pop Category—Favorite Female Artist
1976	AMA	Rock/Pop Category—Favorite Album—"Have You Never Been Mellow"
1976	AMA	Country Category—Favorite Female Artist
1977	AMA	Rock/Pop Category—Favorite Female Artist
1983	AMA	Rock/Pop Category—Favorite Female Artist

DOLLY PARTON

YEAR	BODY	AWARD
1968	CMA	Vocal Group of the Year (With Porter Wagoner)
1968	MCN	Most Promising Female Singer
1968	MCN	Duet of the Year (With Porter Wagoner)
1969	MCN	Duet of the Year (With Porter Wagoner)
1970	CMA	Vocal Duo of the Year (With Porter Wagoner)
1970	MCN	Duet of the Year (With Porter Wagoner)
1971	ACM	Entertainer of the Year
1971	CMA	Vocal Duo of the Year (With Porter Wagoner)
1975	CMA	Female Vocalist of the Year
1976	CMA	Female Vocalist of the Year
1978	AMA	Favorite Album (Country Category)—"New Harvest, First Gathering"
1978	CMA	Entertainer of the Year
1980	ACM	Female Vocalist of the Year
1983	ACM	Vocal Duet of the Year (With Kenny Rogers)—"Islands in the Stream"
1983	ACM	Single Record of the Year—(With Kenny Rogers)—"Islands in the Stream"
1984	AMA	Favorite Single (Country Category) (With Kenny Rogers)—"Islands in the Stream"
1984	MCN	Duet of the Year (With Kenny Rogers)
1985	AMA	Favorite Single (Country Category) (With Kenny Rogers)—"Islands in the Stream"
1986	NSAI	Induction to the Nashville Songwriters Hall of Fame
1987	ACM	Album of the Year (With Linda Ronstadt & Emmylou Harris)—"Trio"
1988	TNN/MCN	Vocal Collaboration (With Linda Ronstadt & Emmylou Harris)—"Trio"
1992	TNN/MCN	Country Music Video (With Ricky Van Shelton)—"Rockin' Years"
1992	TNN/MCN	Vocal Collaboration (With Ricky Skaggs)—"More Where That Came From"

RAY PRICE

YEAR	BODY	AWARD
1954	Down Beat	Best New Big Band—C & W DJ Poll
1956	Billboard Awards	Most Played and Voted Favorite C & W Record by D.J. Poll—"Crazy Arms"

1956	Cash Box Awards	Best Country Record by the Automatic Music Industry of America —"Crazy Arms"
1957	Billboard Awards	Favorite C & W Album—"Ray Price Sings Heart Songs"
1958	Music Reporter Hit Award	"City Lights"
1959	Billboard Awards	Most Played and Voted Favorite C & W Record by D.J. Poll— "Heartaches by the Number"
1959	Billboard Awards	Favorite C & W Artist—Voted by America's C & W DJs
1959	Cash Box Awards	Best Country Male Vocalist of the Year—Cash Box Operator Poll
1959	Music Reporter Hit Award	"Heartaches by the Number"
1960	Cash Box Awards	Best Country Male Vocalist of the Year—Cash Box Operator Poll
1960	Music Reporter Hit Award	"Same Ole Me"
1960	Music Reporter Hit Award	"One More Time"
1961	WMBD Baltimore, Maryland	No.1 Male Vocalist
1961	Columbia Records	Ten Year Club—Appreciation of 10 Successful Years of Outstanding Product, November 4
1962	Billboard Awards	Favorite C & W Album—"San Antonio Rose"
1963	Billboard Awards	Favorite C & W Album—"Night Life"
1963	Music Reporter Hit Award	"You Took Her Off My Hands (Now Please Take Her Off My Mind)"
1964	Billboard Awards	Favorite C & W Album—"Night Life"
1964	Billboard Awards	Favorite C & W Single—"Crazy Arms"
1966	Billboard Awards	Hot Country Album—"Another Bridge to Burn"
1967	ASCAP Chart Buster Awards	"Danny Boy"
1967	Billboard Awards	Hot Country Album—"Touch My Heart"
1967	ASCAP	Award of Merit—"Danny Boy"
1967	Western Apparel Clothing Designers	Pioneer Award
1969	State of Texas	Honorary Colonel on the Governor's Staff—Preston Smith, Governor, January 21
1970	Grammy Award	Best Country Vocal Performance, Male—"For the Good Times"
1970	Del Rio, TX	Honorary Mayor, March 28
1971	Billboard Awards	Hot Country LPs #1 in the Nation
1971	USAF	Assisting the USAF Recruiting Service, February 1971
1971	State of Texas	"A Special Citation for Your Contribution to Country Music"— Preston Smith, Governor, January, 19
1971	State of Texas	Honorary Legislator of the State of Texas, October 23
1971-72	Billboard Awards	Country Music Award—"For the Good Times"
1972	ASCAP Chart Buster Awards	"She's Got to Be a Saint"
1972	U. of Texas at Arlington Alumni Association	For Outstanding Achievement
1972	CMA	Album of the Year—"I Won't Mention It Again"
1972	SRAA	Silver Record Achievement Award
1972	Press Club of Dallas	Dallastar Award—Distinguished Contributions
1972-73	Worldwide Friends of Country Music	1st Annual Awards
1973	ASCAP Chart Buster Awards	"You're the Best Thing That Ever Happened to Me"
1973	Billboard Awards	Most Programmed Artist
1973	Knights of Ak-Sar-Ben, Omaha, Nebraska	Award of Merit
1974	ASCAP Chart Buster Awards	"Storms of Troubled Times"
1974	ASCAP Chart Buster Awards	"Like Old Times Again"
1975	ASCAP Chart Buster Awards	"Roses and Love Songs"
1981	BMI	Country Citation of Achievement—"I'll Be There (If You Ever Want Me)"

MARTY ROBBINS

YEAR	BODY	AWARD
1956	Billboard	Triple Crown Award—"Singing the Blues"
1956	NSAI Hall of Fame Top 10 Country Songs	"Singing the Blues"
1957	Billboard	Favorite Country & Western Artist
1957	BMI Awards	"A White Sport Coat (and a Pink Carnation)"
1957	BMI Awards	"I Can't Quit"
1957	C & W Jamboree D.J. Poll (Radio)	Best Male Singer
1957	Cash Box	Most Programmed Male Country Vocalist
1957	Cash Box	Most Programmed Country Record—"Singing the Blues"
1957	Gold Guitar*	"Singing the Blues"
1957	NSAI Hall of Fame Top 10 Country Songs	"A White Sport Coat (and a Pink Carnation)"
1957	NSAI Hall of Fame Top 10 Country Songs	"The Story of My Life"
1958	NSAI Hall of Fame Top 10 Country Songs	"El Paso"
1959	BMI Awards	"El Paso"
1960	Billboard	Favorite Country & Western Album—"Gunfighter Ballads and Trail Songs"
1960	BMI Awards	"Big Iron"
1960	BMI Awards	"El Paso"
1960	Cash Box	Most Programmed Country Record—"El Paso"
1960	Cash Box	Most Programmed Male Country Vocalist
1960	Gold Guitar*	"El Paso"
1960	Gold Guitar*	"Big Iron"
1960	Grammy Awards	Best Country & Western Performance—"El Paso" (first recipient)
1960	Music Reporter Hit Awards	"El Paso"
1960	Music Vendor	Award of Distinction—"Gunfighter Ballads and Trail Songs"
1960	Music Vendor	Award of Distinction—"More Gunfighter Ballads and Trail Songs"
1961	BMI Awards	"Don't Worry"
1961	Cash Box	Most Programmed Male Country Vocalist
1961	Cash Box	Most Programmed Country Album—"Gunfighter Ballads and Trail Songs"
1961	Gold Guitar*	"Don't Worry"
1961	Music Reporter Hit Awards	"Don't Worry"
1961	NSAI Hall of Fame Top 10 Country Songs	"Don't Worry"
1962	BMI Awards	"It's Your World"
1962	BMI Awards	"Devil Woman"
1962	Gold Guitar*	"Devil Woman"
1962	Gold Guitar*	"Ruby Ann"
1962	Music Reporter Hit Awards	"Devil Woman"
1962	NSAI Hall of Fame Top 10 Country Songs	"Ruby Ann"
1963	Billboard	All-Time Favorite Country Album—"Gunfighter Ballads and Trail Songs"
1963	BMI Awards	"Ruby Ann"
1963	NSAI Hall of Fame Top 10 Country Songs	"Begging to You"
1963	WBMD, Baltimore, MD (Radio)	#1 Recording Artist
1963	WOKY, Milwaukee, WI (Radio)	Golden Mike Award
1964	BMI Awards	"The Cowboy in the Continental Suit"
1964	BMI Awards	"Begging to You"
1964	Gallup Poll	One of the Most Admired Men

1965	BMI Awards	"I Washed My Hands in Muddy Water"
1966	Sportsmanship Award, Nashville Speedway	
1967	BMI Awards	"The Shoe Goes on the Other Foot Tonight"
1967	Sportsmanship Award, Nashville Speedway	
1969	BMI Awards	"You Gave Me a Mountain"
1969	WSM, Nashville, TN (Radio)	Opry Star Spotlight's Top Male Vocalist
1970	ACM (then ACWM)	Man of the Decade
1970	BMI Awards	"Camelia"
1970	BMI Awards	"You Gave Me a Mountain"
1970	BMI Awards	"My Woman, My Woman, My Wife"
1970	CMA	Citation of Merit as Finalist, Song of the Year—"My Woman, My Woman, My Wife"
1970	CMA	Citation of Merit as Finalist, Single of the Year—"My Woman, My Woman, My Wife"
1970	Grammy Awards	Best Country Song—"My Woman, My Woman, My Wife"
1970	NSAI Hall of Fame Top 10 Country Songs	"My Woman, My Woman, My Wife"
1971	ASCAP Award of Merit	"Padre"
1971	ASCAP Award of Merit	"Jolie Girl"
1971	BMI Awards	"My Woman, My Woman, My Wife"
1971	Southern 500, Darlington, SC	Rookie of the Race (September 6)
1972	BMI Awards	"The Best Part of Living"
1972	BMI Awards	"The Chair"
1972	BMI Awards	"Early Morning Sunshine"
1972	Miller High Life 500, Ontario, CA	Sportsman of the Race (March 5)
1973	BMI Awards	"Kate"
1973	BMI Awards	"This Much a Man"
1973	Franklin, TN	Marty Robbins Day
1974	Appreciation Award	For efforts on the NASCAR Winston Cup Circuit, Nashville Speedway—Lifetime Pass
1974	Nashville Speedway	Marty Robbins Appreciation Night (July 20)
1975	CMA GB	Entertainer of the Year
1975	Nashville magazine	One of the 9 Most Imaginative Dressers in Nashville
1975	NSAI	Inducted to Nashville Songwriters Hall of Fame
1976	Appreciation Plaque	For Indy Pace Car Driver
1976	Country Music People/CMA GB/BBC	Best International Male Vocalist
1976	NSAI Hall of Fame Top 10 Country Songs	"El Paso City"
1976	WBAP, Ft. Worth-Dallas, TX	Billy Mack Show (Radio)—Favorite Song—"El Paso City"
1976	WBAP, Ft. Worth-Dallas, TX	Billy Mack Show (Radio)—Favorite Male Country Vocalist
1976	WHNE, Cumming, GA (Radio)	Listener's Choice Award/Most Popular Song—"El Paso City"
1977	ASCAP Award of Merit	"Among My Souvenirs"
1977	ASCAP Award of Merit	"I Don't Know Why (I Just Do)"
1977	BMI Awards	"El Paso City"
1977	CBS Australia	Platinum Album—"Gunfighter Ballads and Trail Songs"
1977	George D. Hay Award	Given for Outstanding Contribution to Country Music
1977	Terre Haute, IN	Marty Robbins Day (November 20)
1978	ASCAP Award of Merit	"Return to Me"
1978	BMI Awards	"Don't Let Me Touch You"
1978	Pittsburg, KS	Marty Robbins Day (April 22)
1978	Shelby County, TN	Honorary Deputy Sheriff
1979	Arizona Rangers	Honorary Member
1979	Cincinnati, OH, Local 100 Teamsters Award	For 25 years and 2 million miles of safe driving
1979	Western Heritage Awards	Golden Trustee Award (Presented by Gene Autry at National Cowboy Hall of Fame, Oklahoma)

1980	ASCAP Award of Merit	"Buenos Dias Argentina"
1980	Lafayette, LA	Honorary Cajun Award
1980	MCN Awards	Songwriter of the Year
1980	MCN Awards	Male Artist of thc Year
1980	SESAC	Best Country Song—"The Patriot" (performed by Johnny Cash/written by Marty Robbins)
1980	WBAP, Ft. Worth-Dallas, TX	Billy Mack Show (Radio)—Male Vocalist of the Year
1981	MCN Awards	Band of the Year—Marty Robbins Band
1981	Ocean Opry, Panama City, FL	Entertainer of the Year
1981	Panama City, FL	Bay County Honorary Deputy Sheriff and Certificate of Appreciation
1982	CMA	Inducted into Country Music Hall of Fame
1982	MCN Awards	Male Artist of the Year
1983	BMI Million-air Award	"A White Sport Coat (and a Pink Carnation)"
1983	BMI Million-air Award	"El Paso"
1983	MCN Awards	Single of the Year—"Some Memories Just Won't Die"
1983	MCN Awards	Album of the Year—"Come Back to Me"
1983	MCN Awards	Male Artist of the Year

*Presented for sales of 250,000 copies. He received more Gold Awards from 1957-1963 than any other artist.

KENNY ROGERS

YEAR	BODY	AWARD
1977	ACM	Song of the Year—"Lucille"
1977	ACM	Single Record of the Year—"Lucille"
1977	ACM	Album of the Year—"Kenny Rogers"
1977	ACM	Male Vocalist of the Year
1977	CMA	Single of the Year—"Lucille"
1977	Grammy Award	Best Country Vocal Performance, Male—"Lucille" (Single)
1978	ACM	Entertainer of the Year
1978	ACM	Male Vocalist of the Year
1978	AMA	Country Category—Favorite Single—"Lucille"
1978	CMA	Vocal Duo of the Year (with Dottie West)
1979	AMA	Country Category—Favorite Male Artist
1979	AMA	Country Category—Favorite Album—"Ten Years of Gold"
1979	CMA	Vocal Duo of the Year (with Dottie West)
1979	CMA	Male Vocalist of the Year
1979	CMA	Album of the Year—"The Gambler"
1979	Grammy Award	Best Country Vocal Performance, Male—"The Gambler" (Single)
1979	MCN	Male Vocalist of the Year
1979	MCN	Single of the Year—"The Gambler"
1979	MCN	Duet of the Year—Kenny Rogers and Dottie West
1979	People Magazine	Readers' Poll—Favorite Male Vocalist
1980	AMA	Country Category—Favorite Male Artist
1980	AMA	Country Category—Favorite Album—"The Gambler"
1980	MCN	Single of the Year—"Coward of the County"
1981	AMA	Country Category—Favorite Male Artist
1981	AMA	Country Category—Favorite Album—"The Gambler"
1981	AMA	Country Category—Favorite Single—"Coward of the County"
1981	AMA	Pop/Rock Category—Favorite Male Artist
1982	AMA	Country Category—Favorite Album—"Greatest Hits"
1982	AMA	Pop/Rock Category—Favorite Male Artist

1982	AMA	Pop/Rock Category—Favorite Album—"Greatest Hits"
1983	ACM	Vocal Duet of the Year (with Dolly Parton)
1983	ACM	Single Record of the Year—"Island in the Stream" (with Dolly Parton
1983	AMA	Country Category—Favorite Male Artist
1983	AMA	Special Award of Merit
1984	AMA	Country Category—Favorite Single—"Islands in the Stream" (with Dolly Parton)
1984	MCN	Duet of the Year (with Dolly Parton)
1984	NARM	Best Selling Country Album by a Male Artist—"Eyes That See in the Dark"
1985	AMA	Country Category—Favorite Male Artist
1985	AMA	Country Category—Favorite Album—"Eyes That See in the Dark"
1985	AMA	Country Category—Favorite Single—"Islands in the Stream" (with Dolly Parton)
1985	High Hopes Award	Presented to Kenny & Marianne Rogers at the Carousel Ball
1986	People's Choice Awards	Favorite Country Music Performer
1986	P.M. Magazine/U.S. Today	Favorite Singer of All Time
1987	Grammy Award	Best Country Vocal Performance, Duet—"Make No Mistake, She's Mine" (Single) (with Ronnie Milsap)
1990	Horatio Alger Award	To select people who have risen from humble beginnings

STATLER BROTHERS

YEAR	BODY	AWARD
1965	Grammy Award	Best New Country & Western Artist
1965	Grammy Award	Best Contemporary (R&R) Performance Group (Vocal or Instrumental)—"Flowers on the Wall" (Single)
1971	MCN Cover Awards	Vocal Group of the Year
1972	ACM	Group of the Year
1972	CMA	Vocal Group of the Year
1972	Grammy Award	Best Country Vocal Performance by a Duo or Group—"Class of '57" (Single)
1972	MCN Cover Awards	Vocal Group of the Year
1973	CMA	Vocal Group of the Year
1973	MCN Cover Awards	Vocal Group of the Year
1974	CMA	Vocal Group of the Year
1974	MCN Cover Awards	Vocal Group of the Year
1975	CMA	Vocal Group of the Year
1975	MCN Cover Awards	Vocal Group of the Year
1975	Truck Driver's Country Music Award	Best Country Vocal Group
1976	CMA	Vocal Group of the Year
1976	International Country Music Awards	Best International Group
1976	MCN Cover Awards	Vocal Group of the Year
1976	Truck Driver's Country Music Award	Best Country Vocal Group
1977	CMA	Vocal Group of the Year
1977	International Country Music Awards	Best International Group
1977	MCN Cover Awards	Vocal Group of the Year
1977	Truck Driver's Country Music Award	Best Country Vocal Group
1978	ACM	Group of the Year
1978	CMA	Vocal Group of the Year

1978	International Country Music Awards	Best International Group
1978	MCN Cover Awards	Vocal Group of the Year
1978	NARM Awards	Best Selling Album by a Country Group
1978	Truck Driver's Country Music Award	Best Country Vocal Group
1979	AMA	Country Category—Favorite Band, Duo or Group
1979	CMA	Vocal Group of the Year
1979	International Country Music Awards	Best International Group
1979	MCN Cover Awards	Album of the Year—"Entertainers...On and Off the Record"
1979	MCN Cover Awards	Vocal Group of the Year
1979	Truck Driver's Country Music Award	Best Country Vocal Group
1980	AMA	Country Category—Favorite Band, Duo or Group
1980	CMA	Vocal Group of the Year
1980	International Country Music Awards	Best International Group
1980	MCN Cover Awards	Album of the Year—"The Originals"
1980	MCN Cover Awards	Vocal Group of the Year
1981	AMA	Country Category—Favorite Band, Duo or Group
1981	International Country Music Awards	Best International Group
1981	MCN Cover Awards	Album of the Year—"Tenth Anniversary"
1981	MCNCover Awards	Vocal Group of the Year
1982	A.C. Nielsen—Best Syndicated TV Special	"An Evening With The Statler Brothers"
1982	MCN Cover Awards	Comedy Act of the Year
1982	MCN Cover Awards	Vocal Group of the Year
1982	MCN Songwriter Awards	"Don't Wait on Me"—Harold Reid/Don Reid
1983	MCN Cover Awards	Comedy Act of the Year
1984	CMA	Vocal Group of the Year
1984	MCN Cover Awards	Country TV Special of the Year—"An Evening With The Statler Brothers"
1984	MCN Cover Awards	Single of the Year—"Elizabeth"
1985	MCN Cover Awards	Album of the Year—"Atlanta Blue"
1985	MCN News Cover Awards	Comedy Act of the Year
1985	MCN Cover Awards	Country Music Video of the Year—"Elizabeth"
1985	MCN Cover Awards	Country TV Special of the Year—"Another Evening With The Statler Brothers (Heroes, Legends & Friends)"
1985	MCN Cover Awards	Entertainer of the Year
1985	MCN Cover Awards	Vocal Group of the Year
1985	MCN Songwriter Awards	"Elizabeth"—Jimmy Fortune
1986	MCN Cover Awards	Album of the Year—"Pardners in Rhyme"
1986	MCN Cover Awards	Country Music Video of the Year—"My Only Love"
1986	MCN Cover Awards	Entertainer of the Year
1986	MCN Cover Awards	Single of the Year—"My Only Love"
1986	MCN Cover Awards	Vocal Group of the Year
1986	MCN Songwriter Awards	"My Only Love"—Jimmy Fortune
1986	Virginia Broadcasters Association	Distinguished Virginian Award
1987	MCN Cover Awards	Country TV Special of the Year—"Christmas Present"
1987	MCN Cover Awards	Entertainer of the Year
1987	MCN Cover Awards	Single of the Year—"Too Much on My Heart"
1987	MCN Cover Awards	Vocal Group of the Year
1987	MCN Songwriter Awards	"Too Much on My Heart"—Jimmy Fortune
1987	People's Choice Awards	Top Three Finalists
1988	MCN Cover Awards	Country Music Video of the Year—"Maple Street Memories"
1988	MCN Cover Awards	Vocal Group of the Year
1989	MCN Cover Awards	Vocal Group of the Year
1990	MCN Cover Awards	Single of the Year—"More Than a Name on a Wall"

1990	MCN Cover Awards	Vocal Group of the Year
1990	People's Choice Awards	American Spirit U.S. Air Force Award
1991	MCN Cover Awards	Vocal Group of the Year
1991	People's Choice Awards	Virginia—House of Delegates Resolution
1991	People's Choice Awards	Virginia—State Senate Resolution
1992	MCN Cover Awards	Vocal Group of the Year
1993	MCN Cover Awards	Vocal Group of the Year
1993	People's Choice Awards	Top Three Finalists—Favorite Group

RANDY TRAVIS

YEAR	BODY	AWARD
1985	ACM	Top Ten Male Artist
1986	ACM	Top Male Vocalist
1986	ACM	Album of the Year—"Storms of Life"
1986	ACM	Song of the Year—"On the Other Hand"
1986	ACM	Single Record of the Year—"On the Other Hand"
1986	CMA	Horizon Award
1987	ACM	Male Vocalist
1987	ACM	Single of the Year—"Forever & Ever Amen"
1987	ACM	Song of the Year—"Forever & Ever Amen"
1987	CMA	Male Vocalist of the Year
1987	CMA	Album of the Year—"Always and Forever"
1987	CMA	Single of the Year—"Forever & Ever Amen"
1987	MCN	Male Artist of the Year
1987	MCN	Star of Tomorrow
1987	MCN	Album of the Year—"Storms of Life"
1987	MCN	Single of the Year—"On the Other Hand"
1987	AMOA	Jukebox Best Country Record—"Forever & Ever Amen"
1987	Country Music Roundup	International Male Vocalist
1987	Grammy Award	Best Country Vocal Performance, Male—"Always & Forever" (Album)
1988	CMA	Male Vocalist of the Year
1988	MCN	Entertainer of the Year
1988	MCN	Single of the Year—"Forever & Ever Amen"
1988	MCN	Male Artist of the Year
1988	MCN	Album of the Year—"Always and Forever"
1988	AMOA	Jukebox Artist of the Year
1988	Grammy Award	Best Country Vocal Performance, Male—"Old 8 x 10" (Album)
1988	AMA	Country Category—Favorite Male Artist
1988	AMA	Country Category—Favorite Album—"Always & Forever"
1988	AMA	Country Category—Favorite Single—"Forever and Ever Amen"
1988	AMA	Country Category—Favorite Single—"I Told You So"
1988	AMA	Country Category—Favorite Single—"Deeper Than the Holler"
1988	AMA	Country Category—Favorite Video—"Forever and Ever Amen"
1988	AMA	Video/Country—"Forever & Ever Amen"
1988	AMA	Album/Country—"Always and Forever"
1988	AMA	Single/Country—"Forever & Ever Amen"
1988	TNN Viewers Choice	Favorite Male Vocalist
1988	TNN Viewers Choice	Favorite Entertainer
1988	TNN Viewers Choice	Favorite Album—"Always and Forever"
1988	TNN Viewers Choice	Favorite Video—"Forever & Ever Amen"

1988	TNN Viewers Choice	Favorite Song—"Forever & Ever Amen"
1988	World Music Award	Favorite Country LP—"Always and Forever"
1989	MCN	Entertainer of the Year
1989	AMOA	Jukebox Artist of the Year
1989	Country Music Roundup	International Country Music Award
1989	AMA	Country Category—Favorite Male Artist
1989	AMA	Country Category—Favorite Album—"Always & Forever"
1989	TNN Viewers Choice	Favorite Album—"Old 8 x 10"
1989	TNN Viewers Choice	Favorite Entertainer
1989	People's Choice Awards	Best Male Musical Performer
1989	Rolling Stone Annual Readers' Poll	Best Country Artist
1990	AMA	Country Category—Favorite Male Artist
1990	AMA	Country Category—Favorite Album—"Old 8 x 10"
1990	World Music Award	Favorite Country Artist
1990	Jukebox	Country Record of the Year—"Just a Matter of Time"
1990	Billboard Music Award	#1 Country Albums Artist
1990	Billboard Music Award	#1 Country Artist
1990	Amusement Business	Top Grossing Country Tour
1990	Performance	Country Tour of the Year
1990	Golden Angel Award	For Excellence in Media
1990	Playboy Music Poll	Male Vocalist/Country
1991	Rolling Stone Annual Readers' Poll	Best Country Artist
1991	Playboy Music Poll	Male Vocalist/Country

CONWAY TWITTY

YEAR	BODY	AWARD
1970	MCN	Song of the Year—"Hello Darlin'"
1971	ACM	Vocal Duet of the Year (with Loretta Lynn)
1971	Grammy Award	Best Country Vocal Performance by Group—"After the Fire Is Gone" (Single) (with Loretta Lynn)
1971	MCN	Duet of the Year (with Loretta Lynn)
1972	CMA	Vocal Duo of the Year (with Loretta Lynn)
1972	MCN	Duet of the Year (with Loretta Lynn)
1973	CMA	Vocal Duo of the Year (with Loretta Lynn)
1973	MCN	Duet of the Year (with Loretta Lynn)
1974	ACM	Vocal Duet of the Year (with Loretta Lynn)
1974	CMA	Vocal Duo of the Year (with Loretta Lynn)
1974	MCN	Male Vocalist of the Year
1974	MCN	Song of the Year—"You've Never Been This Far Before"
1974	MCN	Duet of the Year (with Loretta Lynn)
1975	ACM	Album of the Year—"Feelin's" (with Loretta Lynn)
1975	ACM	Male Vocalist of the Year
1975	ACM	Vocal Duet of the Year (with Loretta Lynn)
1975	AMA	Country Category—Favorite Band, Duo or Group (with Loretta Lynn)
1975	CMA	Vocal Duo of the Year (with Loretta Lynn)
1975	MCN	Male Vocalist of the Year
1975	MCN	Duet of the Year (with Loretta Lynn)
1976	ACM	Vocal Duet of the Year (with Loretta Lynn)
1976	MCN	Male Vocalist of the Year
1976	MCN	Duet of the Year (with Loretta Lynn)
1977	AMA	Country Category—Favorite Band, Duo or Group (with Loretta Lynn)

1977	MCN	Male Vocalist of the Year
1977	MCN	Duet of the Year (with Loretta Lynn)
1978	AMA	Country Category—Favorite Male Artist
1978	AMA	Country Category—Favorite Band, Duo or Group (with Loretta Lynn)
1978	MCN	Duet of the Year (with Loretta Lynn)
1980	MCN	Duet of the Year (with Loretta Lynn)
1981	MCN	Duet of the Year (with Loretta Lynn)
1983	MCN	Country Music TV Spectacular—"Conway Twitty on the Mississippi"
1988	MCN	Living Legend Award

IAN TYSON

YEAR	BODY	AWARD
1975	Big Country (RPM Magazine)	Outstanding Performance (Male)
1975	Big Country (RPM Magazine)	Best Country Album—"Ol' Eon"
1975	Big Country (RPM Magazine)	Top Canandian Country TV Show
1987	Canadian Country Music Association (CCMA)	Album of the Year—"Cowboyography"
1987	Canadian Country Music Association (CCMA)	Male Vocalist of the Year
1987	Canadian Country Music Association (CCMA)	Single of the Year—"Navajo Rug"
1987	Juno Awards	Male Vocalist of the Year
1987	Alberta Recording Industry Association (ARIA)	"Album of the Year—"Cowboyography"
1987	Alberta Recording Industry Association (ARIA)	Country Artist of the Year
1987	Alberta Recording Industry Association (ARIA)	Male Performer of the Year
1987	Alberta Recording Industry Association (ARIA)	Single of the Year—"Navajo Rug"
1988	Canadian Country Music Association (CCMA)	Male Vocalist of the Year
1988	Big Country (RPM Magazine)	Artist of the Year
1988	Big Country (RPM Magazine)	Top Male Vocalist
1988	Big Country (RPM Magazine)	Best Album—"Cowboyography"
1988	Alberta Recording Industry Association (ARIA)	Best Country Artist on Record
1988	Alberta Recording Industry Association (ARIA)	Male Vocalist of the Year
1988	Alberta Recording Industry Association (ARIA)	Performer of the Year
1988	Alberta Recording Industry Association (ARIA)	Single of the Year—"Fifty Years Ago"
1988	Alberta Recording Industry Association (ARIA)	Song of the Year—"Fifty Years Ago"
1988	Country Music News—Readers' Poll	"Four Strong Winds" named All Time Favourite Can-Country Song
1989	Canadian Country Music Association (CCMA)	Induction—Canadian Country Music Hall of Honour
1989	Alberta Recording Industry Association (ARIA)	Album of the Year—"I Outgrew the Wagon"
1989	Alberta Recording Industry Association (ARIA)	Best Country Artist on Record
1989	Alberta Recording Industry Association (ARIA)	Composer of the Year
1989	Alberta Recording Industry Association (ARIA)	Performer of the Year
1989	Alberta Recording Industry Association (ARIA)	Single of the Year—"Cowboys Don't Cry"
1989	Country Music Association of Calgary	Top Alberta Male Vocalist of the Year
1989	Country Music Association of Calgary	Top Alberta Single of the Year—"Fifty Years Ago"
1989	Country Music Association of Calgary	Top Alberta Song of the Year—"Fifty Years Ago"
1989	Country Music Association of Calgary	Favourite Calgary and Area Country Entertainer
1989	World Championship Cutting Horse Futurity	Finalist, Fort Worth, Texas
1989	Canadian Country Music Hall of Fame	Induction
1989	C.R.I.A.	Certified Gold—"Cowboyography"
1991	Canadian Country Music Association (CCMA)	Video of the Year—"Springtime in Alberta"
1992	Canadian Country Music Association (CCMA)	Male Vocalist of the Year

1992	Juno Awards	Induction—Juno Hall of Fame
1992	Alberta Recording Industry Association (ARIA)	Album of the Year—"And Stood There Amazed"
1992	Alberta Recording Industry Association (ARIA)	Best Music Video of the Year—"Springtime in Alberta"
1992	Alberta Recording Industry Association (ARIA)	Male Vocalist of the Year
1992	ASCAP	Country Award—"Someday Soon"
1992	C.R.I.A.	Certified Gold—"I Outgrew the Wagon"
1993	Alberta Recording Industry Association (ARIA)	Performer of the Year

HANK WILLIAMS, JR.

YEAR	BODY	AWARD
1966	BMI	Writer's Award—"Standing in the Shadows"
1970	BMI	Writer's Award—"Cajun Baby"
1971	Country Music Association of Britain	Entertainer of the Year
1972	Billboard	Best Country Single—"Eleven Roses"
1972	Billboard	Top Male Country Artist
1972	Billboard	Duo of the Year—"Whole Lot of Lovin" (with Lois Johnson)
1974	BMI	Writer's Award—"The Last Love Song"
1980	BMI	Writer's Award—"Family Tradition"
1981	BMI	Writer's Award—"Old Habits"
1982	Billboard	Top Male Artist
1982	Billboard	Top Album
1982	Billboard	Top Album Artist
1982	BMI	Writer's Award—"All My Rowdy Friends (Have Settled Down)"
1982	BMI	Writer's Award—"Texas Women"
1982	BMI	Writer's Award—"Dixie on My Mind"
1983	BMI	Writer's Award—"A Country Boy Can Survive"
1984	BMI	Writer's Award—"Gonna Go Huntin' Tonight"
1984	BMI	Writer's Award—"Leave Them Boys Alone"
1985	ACM	Video of the Year—"All My Rowdy Friends Are Coming Over Tonight"
1985	AMA	Country Category—Favorite Male Video Artist
1985	BMI	Writer's Award—"Attitude Adjustment"
1985	BMI	Writer's Award—"Man of Steel"
1986	Cash Box	Composer/Performer of the Year
1987	ACM	Entertainer of the Year
1987	CMA	Entertainer of the Year
1987	CMA	Video of the Year—"My Name Is Bocephus"
1988	ACM	Entertainer of the Year
1988	BMI	Writer's Award—"Born to Boogie"
1988	BMI	Writer's Award—"Heaven Can't Be Found"
1988	CMA	Entertainer of the Year
1988	Radio & Records Reader's Poll	Performer of the Year
1989	ACM	Video of the Year—"There's a Tear in My Beer"
1989	CMA	Video of the Year—"There's a Tear in My Beer"
1989	CMA	Vocal Event of the Year—"There's a Tear in My Beer" (with Hank Williams)
1989	Grammy Award	Best Country Vocal Collaboration—"There's a Tear in My Beer" (Single) (with Hank Williams)
1989	Music Operators of America	Record of the Year—"There's a Tear in My Beer"
1989	National Association of Campus Activities	Hall of Fame Award
1990	ACM	Video of the Year—"There's a Tear in My Beer"
1990	International Film & TV Festival of New York	Gold Medal for Best Commercial Video—"All My Rowdy Friends Are Coming Over Tonight"—ABC Monday Night Football

1990	MCN/TNN	Video of the Year—"There's a Tear in My Beer"
1990	MCN/TNN	Vocal Collaboration of the Year—"There's a Tear in My Beer" (with Hank Williams)
1990	Music Operators of America	cd of the Year—"Greatest Hits III"
1990	Sports Emmy	ABC Monday Night Football—"All My Rowdy Friends Are Coming Over Tonight"
1991	Playboy Music Poll	Best Country Album—"Lone Wolf"
1991	Sports Emmy	ABC Monday Night Football—"All My Rowdy Friends Are Coming Over Tonight II"
1992	Sports Emmy	ABC Monday Night Football—"ABC Monday Night Football Boogie"

RECORDING INDUSTRY ASSOCIATION OF AMERICA, INC. (R.I.A.A.)

R.I.A.A. is the body that issues Gold, Platinum and Multi-Platinum Records for sales of records in the U.S.A. The records listed are by Country artists or are of Country material recorded by non-Country acts.

Award Date	Artist	Title	Record Label	Award Level	Type
1958					
Aug. 11	Elvis Presley	Hard Headed Woman	RCA Victor	Gold	Single
1959					
Feb. 20	Tennessee Ernie Ford	Hymns	Capitol	Gold	Album
1960					
Feb. 12	Pat Boone	Pat's Greatest Hits	Dot	Gold	Album
Feb.17	Elvis Presley	Elvis	RCA Victor	Gold	Album
1961					
Oct. 10	Tennessee Ernie Ford	Spirituals	Capitol	Gold	Album
Oct. 17	Elvis Presley	Elvis' Golden Records	RCA Victor	Gold	Album
Dec. 14	Jimmy Dean	Big Bad John	Columbia	Gold	Single
Dec. 21	Elvis Presley	Blue Hawaii	RCA Victor	Gold	Album
1962					
Mar. 12	Tennessee Ernie Ford	Star Carol	Capitol	Gold	Album
Mar. 22	Tennessee Ernie Ford	Nearer the Cross	Capitol	Gold	Album
Mar. 30	Elvis Presley	Can't Help Falling in Love	RCAVictor	Gold	Single
Jul. 19	Ray Charles	I Can't Stop Loving You	ABC-Paramount	Gold	Single
Jul. 19	Ray Charles	Modern Sounds in Country & Western Music	ABC-Paramount	Gold	Album
Aug. 13	Bobby Vinton	Roses Are Red	Epic	Gold	Single
1963					
Mar. 12	Elvis Presley	G.I. Blues	RCA Victor	Gold	Album
Aug. 13	Elvis Presley	Elvis' Christmas Album	RCA Victor	Gold	Album
Aug. 13	Elvis Presley	Girls, Girls, Girls	RCA Victor	Gold	Album
1964					
Oct. 30	Roy Orbison	Oh, Pretty Woman	Monument	Gold	Single
Nov. 02	Johnny Horton	Johnny Horton's Greatest Hits	Columbia	Gold	Album

1965					
Feb. 11	Johnny Cash	Ring of Fire	Columbia	Gold	Album
May 19	Roger Miller	King of the Road	Smash	Gold	Single
Sep. 01	Roger Miller	Return of Roger Miller	Smash	Gold	Album
Sep. 21	Marty Robbins	Gunfighter Ballads & Trail Songs	Columbia	Gold	Album
1966					
Feb. 11	Roger Miller	Golden Hits	Smash	Gold	Album
Mar. 24	Roy Orbison	Roy Orbison's Greatest Hits	Monument	Gold	Album
May 09	Righteous Brothers	Soul & Inspiration	Verve	Gold	Single
May 12	Eddy Arnold	My World	RCA Victor	Gold	Album
Jul. 20	Jim Reeves	The Best of Jim Reeves	RCA Victor	Gold	Album
Aug. 04	Roger Miller	Dang Me	Smash	Gold	Album
Nov. 01	Elvis Presley	Elvis Presley	RCA Victor	Gold	Album
Nov. 01	Elvis Presley	Elvis' Golden Records, Volume 2	RCA Victor	Gold	Album
Nov. 01	Elvis Presley	Elvis' Golden Records, Volume 3	RCA Victor	Gold	Album
Nov. 28	Righteous Brothers	Soul & Inspiration	Verve	Gold	Album
Dec. 12	Bobby Vinton	Bobby Vinton's Greatest Hits	Epic	Gold	Album
Dec. 20	Johnny Horton	Battle of New Orleans	Columbia	Gold	Single
1967					
Feb. 07	Boots Randolph	Yakety Sax	Monument	Gold	Album
Jul. 14	Johnny Cash	I Walk the Line	Columbia	Gold	Album
Sep. 11	Bobbie Gentry	Ode to Billy Joe	Capitol	Gold	Single
Oct. 09	Bobbie Gentry	Ode to Billy Joe	Capitol	Gold	Album
Dec. 06	Engelbert Humperdinck	Release Me	Parrot	Gold	Album
1968					
Jan. 05	Jim Nabors	Jim Nabors Sings	Columbia	Gold	Album
Feb. 16	Elvis Presley	How Great Thou Art	RCA Victor	Gold	Album
Feb. 26	Jim Reeves	Distant Drums	RCA Victor	Gold	Album
Mar. 06	Buck Owens	Best of Buck Owens	Capitol	Gold	Album
Mar. 13	The Byrds	The Byrds' Greatest Hits	Columbia	Gold	Album
Mar. 19	Bob Dylan	John Wesley Harding	Columbia	Gold	Album
Mar. 28	Eddy Arnold	The Best of Eddy Arnold	RCA Victor	Gold	Album
Apr. 04	Bobby Goldsboro	Honey	United Artists	Gold	Single
Apr. 06	Ray Charles	Modern Sounds in Country & Western Music, Vol. 2	Columbia	Gold	Album
Apr. 09	Elvis Presley	Loving You	RCA Victor	Gold	Album
Aug. 26	Jeannie C. Riley	Harper Valley P.T.A.	Plantation	Gold	Single
Oct. 17	Glen Campbell	By the Time I Get to Phoenix	Capitol	Gold	Album
Oct. 17	Glen Campbell	Gentle on My Mind	Capitol	Gold	Album
Oct. 30	Johnny Cash	Johnny Cash at Folsom Prison	Columbia	Gold	Album
Nov. 18	Glen Campbell	Wichita Lineman	Capitol	Gold	Album
Nov. 27	Bobby Goldsboro	Honey	United Artists	Gold	Album
Dec. 19	Bobby Vinton	I Love How You Love Me	Epic	Gold	Single
Dec. 20	Jeannie C. Riley	Harper Valley P.T.A.	Plantation	Gold	Album
1969					
Jan. 01	Judy Collins	Wildflowers	Elektra	Gold	Album
Jan. 10	Glen Campbell	Hey Little One	Capitol	Gold	Album
Jan. 22	Glen Campbell	Wichita Lineman	Capitol	Gold	Single

Jan. 29	Bobbie Gentry & Glen Campbell	Gentry/Campbell	Capitol	Gold	Album
Feb. 18	Boots Randolph	Boots With Strings	Monument	Gold	Album
Feb. 24	B.J. Thomas	Hooked on a Feeling	Scepter	Gold	Single
Feb. 27	Engelbert Humperdinck	A Man Without Love	Parrot	Gold	Album
Feb. 27	Engelbert Humperdinck	The Last Waltz	Parrot	Gold	Single
Mar. 07	Tommy Roe	Dizzy	ABC	Gold	Single
Mar. 25	Tommy Roe	Sheila	ABC	Gold	Single
Mar. 25	Tommy Roe	Sweet Pea	ABC	Gold	Single
Apr. 09	Elvis Presley	His Hand in Mine	RCA Victor	Gold	Album
Apr. 16	Glen Campbell	Galveston	Capitol	Gold	Album
May 07	Bob Dylan	Nashville Skyline	Columbia	Gold	Album
May 07	Tom Jones	Fever Zone	Parrot	Gold	Album
May 07	Tom Jones	Help Yourself	Parrot	Gold	Album
May 29	The Righteous Brothers	The Righteous Brothers' Greatest Hits	Verve	Gold	Album
Jun. 04	Tom Jones	This Is Tom Jones	Parrot	Gold	Album
Jun. 11	Connie Francis	The Very Best of Connie Francis	MGM	Gold	Album
Jun. 11	Soundtrack	How the West Was Won	MGM	Gold	Album
Jun. 11	Hank Williams	Hank Williams' Greatest Hits	MGM	Gold	Album
Jun. 11	Hank Williams	Your Cheatin' Heart	MGM	Gold	Album
Jun. 16	Ray Stevens	Gitarzan	Monument	Gold	Single
Jun. 25	Elvis Presley	In the Ghetto	RCA Victor	Gold	Single
Jul. 03	Tom Jones	Tom Jones Live	Parrot	Gold	Album
Jul. 22	Elvis Presley	Elvis TV Special	RCA Victor	Gold	Album
Jul. 24	Johnny Cash	Johnny Cash's Greatest Hits	Columbia	Gold	Album
Aug. 12	Johnny Cash	Johnny Cash at San Quentin	Columbia	Gold	Album
Aug. 14	Johnny Cash	A Boy Named Sue	Columbia	Gold	Single
Aug. 30	Dean Martin	Gentle on My Mind	Reprise	Gold	Album
Sep. 19	Glen Campbell	Glen Campbell—"Live"	Capitol	Gold	Album
Sep. 29	Arlo Guthrie	Alice's Restaurant	Reprise	Gold	Album
Sep. 29	Johnny Rivers	Realization	Imperial	Gold	Album
Oct. 03	Tom Jones	I'll Never Fall in Love Again	Parrot	Gold	Single
Oct. 08	Judy Collins	Who Knows Where the Time Goes	Elektra	Gold	Album
Oct. 14	Glen Campbell	Galveston	Capitol	Gold	Single
Oct. 27	Tom Jones	Tom Jones—Live at Las Vegas	Parrot	Gold	Album
Oct. 28	Elvis Presley	Suspicious Minds	RCA Victor	Gold	Single
Nov. 10	Gene Autry	Rudolph, the Red Nosed Reindeer	Columbia	Gold	Single
Nov. 24	Tom Jones	Green Green Grass	Parrot	Gold	Album
Nov. 26	The Band	The Band	Capitol	Gold	Album
Dec. 12	Elvis Presley	From Vegas to Memphis	RCA Victor	Gold	Album
Dec. 23	B.J. Thomas	Raindrops Keep Falling on My Head	Scepter	Gold	Single
Dec. 24	Buddy Holly & the Crickets	Buddy Holly Story	Decca	Gold	Album
Dec. 30	Buddy Holly & the Crickets	That'll Be the Day	Coral	Gold	Single

1970

Jan. 14	Engelbert Humperdinck	Engelbert Humperdinck	Parrot	Gold	Album
Jan. 14	Engelbert Humperdinck	Engelbert	Parrot	Gold	Album
Jan. 19	Charley Pride	The Best of Charley Pride	RCA Victor	Gold	Album
Jan. 19	Tommy Roe	Jam Up & Jelly Tight	ABC	Gold	Single
Jan. 21	Elvis Presley	Don't Cry Daddy	RCA Victor	Gold	Single
Jan. 28	Elvis Presley	From Elvis in Memphis	RCA Victor	Gold	Album
Jan. 29	Johnny Cash	Hello, I'm Johnny Cash	Columbia	Gold	Album
Feb. 18	Tom Jones	Without Love	Parrot	Gold	Single

Feb. 19	Glen Campbell	Try a Little Kindness	Capitol	Gold	Album
Apr. 13	Loretta Lynn	Don't Come Home a Drinkin'	Decca	Gold	Album
Apr. 16	Tammy Wynette	Tammy's Greatest Hits	Epic	Gold	Album
Apr. 24	Tom Jones	Tom	Parrot	Gold	Album
Jun. 26	Ray Stevens	Everything Is Beautiful	Barnaby	Gold	Single
Jul. 22	B.J. Thomas	Raindrops Keep Falling on My Head	Scepter	Gold	Album
Aug. 14	Elvis Presley	The Wonder of You	RCA Victor	Gold	Single
Oct. 02	Merle Haggard	Okie From Muskogee	Capitol	Gold	Album
Oct. 16	James Taylor	Sweet Baby James	Warner Bros.	Gold	Album
Nov. 16	Anne Murray	Snowbird	Capitol	Gold	Single
Dec. 04	Jim Nabors	Jim Nabor's Chistmas Album	Columbia	Gold	Album
Dec. 18	Engelbert Humperdinck	We Made It Happen	Parrot	Gold	Album
Dec. 21	Judy Collins	In My Life	Elektra	Gold	Album
1971					
Jan. 15	Tom Jones	I Who Have Nothing	Parrot	Gold	Album
Feb. 03	Lynn Anderson	Rose Garden	Columbia	Gold	Single
Feb. 23	Elvis Presley	On Stage 1970	RCA Victor	Gold	Album
Feb. 23	Charley Pride	Charley Pride's 10th Album	RCA Victor	Gold	Album
Feb. 23	Charley Pride	Charley Pride in Person	RCA Victor	Gold	Album
Feb. 23	Charley Pride	Just Plain Charley	RCA Victor	Gold	Album
Mar. 03	Ray Price	For the Good Times	Columbia	Gold	Album
Mar. 11	Merle Haggard	The Fightin' Side of Me	Capitol	Gold	Album
Mar. 25	Lynn Anderson	Rose Garden	Columbia	Gold	Album
Mar. 25	Tom Jones	She's a Lady	Parrot	Gold	Single
Mar. 29	Jerry Reed	Amos Moses	RCA Victor	Gold	Single
Apr. 06	Judy Collins	Whales & Nightingales	Elektra	Gold	Album
Apr. 15	Tracy Nelson	The Battle Hymn of Lt. Calley	Plantation	Gold	Single
Apr. 26	Sammi Smith	Help Me Make It Through the Night	Mega	Gold	Single
Apr. 30	James Taylor	Mud Slide Slim & the Blue Horizon	Warner Bros.	Gold	Album
May 13	Engelbert Humperdinck	Sweetheart	Parrot	Gold	Album
Jun. 14	Gordon Lightfoot	If You Could Read My Mind	Reprise	Gold	Album
Aug. 18	John Denver	Take Me Home, Country Roads	RCA Victor	Gold	Single
Sep. 13	James Taylor	You've Got a Friend	Warner Bros.	Gold	Single
Sep. 15	John Denver	Poems, Prayers & Promises	RCA Victor	Gold	Album
Nov. 29	Freddie Hart	Easy Loving	Capitol	Gold	Single
Dec. 23	Johnny Cash	The World of Johnny Cash	Columbia	Gold	Album
1972					
Jan. 03	Don McLean	American Pie	United Artists	Gold	Single
Jan. 03	Don McLean	American Pie	United Artists	Gold	Album
Jan. 05	John Denver	Aerie	RCA Victor	Gold	Album
Jan. 12	Tom Jones	She's a Lady	Parrot	Gold	Album
Jan. 17	Jonathan Edwards	Sunshine	Capricorn	Gold	Single
Jan. 18	Loretta Lynn	Loretta Lynn's Greatest Hits	Decca	Gold	Album
Feb. 15	Charley Pride	Charley Pride Sings Heart Songs	RCA Victor	Gold	Album
Mar. 08	Charley Pride	Kiss An Angel Good Mornin'	RCA Victor	Gold	Single
Mar. 31	Engelbert Humperdinck	Another Time, Another Place	Parrot	Gold	Album
Mar. 31	Tom Jones	Tom Jones Live at Caesars Palace	Parrot	Gold	Album
May 15	Glen Campbell	Glen Campbell's Greatest Hits	Capitol	Gold	Album
May 15	Conway Twitty	Hello Darlin'	Decca	Gold	Album
Aug. 02	Dr. Hook & the Medicine Show	Sylvia's Mother	Columbia	Gold	Single

Aug. 04	Elvis Presley	Elvis As Recorded at Madison Square Garden	RCA Victor	Gold	Album
Aug. 23	Donna Fargo	Happiest Girl in the Whole U.S.A.	Dot	Gold	Single
Sep. 20	Mac Davis	Baby, Don't Get Hooked on Me	Columbia	Gold	Single
Oct. 19	Charley Pride	The Best of Charley Pride, Vol. II	RCA Victor	Gold	Album
Oct. 23	Freddie Hart	Easy Loving	Capitol	Gold	Album
Oct. 27	Elvis Presley	Burning Love	RCA Victor	Gold	Single
Nov. 02	The Band	Rock of Ages	Capitol	Gold	Album
Nov. 02	Merle Haggard	The Best of Merle Haggard	Capitol	Gold	Album
Nov. 24	Rick Nelson	Garden Party	Decca	Gold	Single
Nov. 29	Lobo	I'd Love You to Want Me	Big Tree	Gold	Single
Dec. 18	James Taylor	One Man Dog	Warner Bros.	Gold	Album
Dec. 30	John Denver	Rocky Mountain High	RCA Victor	Gold	Album
1973					
Jan. 04	Donna Fargo	Funny Face	Dot	Gold	Single
Jan. 29	Donna Fargo	The Happiest Girl in the Whole U.S.A.	Dot	Gold	Album
Jan. 29	Johnny Rivers	Rockin' Pneumonia & the Boogie Woogie Flu	United Artists	Gold	Single
Feb. 02	Loggins & Messina	Loggins & Messina	Columbia	Gold	Album
Feb. 13	Elvis Presley	Elvis—Aloha From Hawaii Via Satellite	RCA Victor	Gold	Album
Feb. 13	Elvis Presley	World Wide 50 Gold Award Hits, Volume 1	RCA Victor	Gold	Album
Mar. 07	Mac Davis	Baby, Don't Get Hooked on Me	Columbia	Gold	Album
Mar. 07	Loggins & Messina	Your Mama Don't Dance	Columbia	Gold	Single
Mar. 07	Soundtrack	Dueling Banjos/Deliverance	Warner Bros.	Gold	Album
Mar. 07	Eric Weissberg	Dueling Banjos	Warner Bros.	Gold	Single
Mar. 27	Kenny Rogers & the First Edition	Kenny Rogers & the First Edition Greatest Hits	Reprise	Gold	Album
Apr. 04	Dr. Hook & the Medicine Show	The Cover of "Rolling Stone"	Columbia	Gold	Single
May 11	Loggins & Messina	Sittin' In	Columbia	Gold	Album
May 25	The Nitty Gritty Dirt Band	William E. McEuen Presents Will the Circle Be Unbroken	United Artists	Gold	Album
Jun. 14	Charley Pride	From Me to You	RCA Victor	Gold	Album
Jun. 14	Charley Pride	The Country Way	RCA Victor	Gold	Album
Jun. 14	Charley Pride	The Sensational Charley Pride	RCA Victor	Gold	Album
Jun. 28	Elvis Presley	Elvis—That's the Way It Is	RCA Victor	Gold	Album
Jul. 03	Clint Holmes	Playground in My Mind	Epic	Gold	Single
Aug. 27	John Denver	Farewell Andromeda	RCA Victor	Gold	Album
Sep. 04	Charlie Rich	Behind Closed Doors	Epic	Gold	Single
Nov. 08	Kris Kristofferson	Why Me	Monument	Gold	Single
Nov. 09	Kris Kristofferson	The Silver Tongued Devil & I	Monument	Gold	Album
Nov. 27	Charlie Rich	Behind Closed Doors	Epic	Gold	Album
Nov. 29	Kris Kristofferson	Jesus Was a Capricorn	Monument	Gold	Album
Dec. 10	Charlie Rich	The Most Beautiful Girl	Epic	Gold	Single
Dec. 11	John Denver	John Denver's Greatest Hits	RCA Victor	Gold	Album
Dec. 12	Loggins & Messina	Full Sail	Columbia	Gold	Album
Dec. 21	Anne Murray	Snowbird	Capitol	Gold	Album
1974					
Jan. 15	Jim Nabors	The Lord's Prayer	Columbia	Gold	Album
Jan. 22	Eagles	Eagles	Asylum	Gold	Album
Jan. 24	Judy Collins	Colors of the Day	Elektra	Gold	Album
Feb. 08	Olivia Newton-John	Let Me Be There	MCA	Gold	Single
Mar. 06	Jim Stafford	Spiders & Snakes	MGM	Gold	Single
Mar. 28	John Denver	Sunshine on My Shoulder	RCA Victor	Gold	Single

Apr. 22	Charlie Rich	Very Special Love Songs	Epic	Gold	Album
Apr. 30	Merle Haggard	The Best of the Best of Merle Haggard	Capitol	Gold	Album
May 14	James Taylor & Carly Simon	Mockingbird	Elektra	Gold	Single
May 31	Gordon Lightfoot	Sundown	Reprise	Gold	Album
Jun. 06	Eagles	On the Border	Asylum	Gold	Album
Jun. 18	Gordon Lightfoot	Sundown	Reprise	Gold	Single
Jun. 18	Loggins & Messina	On Stage	Columbia	Gold	Album
Jun. 24	John Denver	Back Home Again	RCA Victor	Gold	Album
Jun. 26	Olivia Newton-John	If You Love Me (Let Me Know)	MCA	Gold	Single
Jul. 26	John Denver	Annie's Song	RCA Victor	Gold	Single
Aug. 24	Ray Stevens	The Streak	Barnaby	Gold	Single
Sep. 09	Olivia Newton-John	If You Love Me (Let Me Know)	MCA	Gold	Album
Sep. 23	Mac Davis	Stop & Smell the Roses	Columbia	Gold	Album
Sep. 23	Eagles	Desperado	Asylum	Gold	Album
Sep. 23	The Souther-Hillman-Furay Band	The Souther-Hillman-Furay Band	Asylum	Gold	Album
Oct. 09	Olivia Newton-John	I Honestly Love You	MCA	Gold	Single
Oct. 14	Olivia Newton-John	Let Me Be There	MCA	Gold	Album
Oct. 23	Charlie Rich	There Won't Be Anymore	RCA	Gold	Album
Nov. 25	Loggins & Messina	Mother Lode	Columbia	Gold	Album
Dec. 02	Billy Swan	I Can Help	Monument	Gold	Single
Dec. 05	Bobby Vinton	Melodies of Love	ABC	Gold	Album
Dec. 05	Bobby Vinton	Melodies of Love	ABC	Gold	Single
Dec. 18	Kris Kristofferson	Me & Bobby McGee	Monument	Gold	Album
Dec. 24	Jackson Browne	Late for the Sky	Asylum	Gold	Album
1975					
Jan. 03	John Denver	Back Home Again	RCA Victor	Gold	Single
Jan. 08	Elvis Presley	Elvis—A Legendary Performer, Volume I	RCA Victor	Gold	Album
Jan. 09	Charley Pride	(Country) Charley Pride	RCA Victor	Gold	Album
Jan. 09	Charley Pride	Did You Think to Pray	RCA Victor	Gold	Album
Jan. 31	Linda Ronstadt	Heart Like a Wheel	Capitol	Gold	Album
Feb. 19	John Denver	An Evening With John Denver	RCA Victor	Gold	Album
Feb. 26	Olivia Newton-John	Have You Never Been Mellow	MCA	Gold	Album
Mar. 05	Olivia Newton-John	Have You Never Been Mellow	MCA	Gold	Single
Mar. 06	Johnny Rivers	A Touch of Gold Volume II	Imperial	Gold	Album
Mar. 06	Johnny Rivers	Johnny Rivers' Golden Hits	Imperial	Gold	Album
May 22	Freddy Fender	Before the Next Teardrop Falls	Dot	Gold	Single
May 23	B.J. Thomas	(Hey Won't You Play) Another Somebody Done Somebody Wrong Song	ABC	Gold	Single
Jun. 26	John Denver	Thank God I'm a Country Boy	RCA Victor	Gold	Single
Jun. 30	Eagles	One of These Nights	Asylum	Gold	Album
Jul. 21	Michael Murphey	Wildfire	Epic	Gold	Single
Aug. 14	The Marshall Tucker Band	The Marshall Tucker Band	Capricorn	Gold	Album
Aug. 25	Linda Ronstadt	Don't Cry Now	Asylum	Gold	Album
Aug. 29	Freddy Fender	Before the Next Teardrop Falls	Dot	Gold	Album
Sep. 05	Glen Campbell	Rhinestone Cowboy	Capitol	Gold	Single
Sep. 11	Janis Ian	Between the Lines	Columbia	Gold	Album
Sep. 12	James Taylor	Gorilla	Warner Bros.	Gold	Album
Sep. 16	Olivia Newton-John	Please Mister Please	MCA	Gold	Single
Sep. 18	Freddy Fender	Wasted Days & Wasted Nights	Dot	Gold	Single
Sep. 19	John Denver	Windsong	RCA Victor	Gold	Album
Sep. 29	Olivia Newton-John	Clearly Love	MCA	Gold	Album

Oct. 08	Jackson Browne	For Everyman	Asylum	Gold	Album
Oct. 08	Linda Ronstadt	Prisoner in Disguise	Asylum	Gold	Album
Oct. 20	Kris Kristofferson/Rita Coolidge	Full Moon	A & M	Gold	Album
Oct. 24	John Denver	Rocky Mountain Christmas	RCA Victor	Gold	Album
Nov. 07	The Marshall Tucker Band	Where We All Belong	Capricorn	Gold	Album
Nov. 11	Judy Collins	Judith	Elektra	Gold	Album
Nov. 17	Michael Murphey	Blue Sky—Night Thunder	Epic	Gold	Album
Nov. 18	John Denver	I'm Sorry	RCA Victor	Gold	Single
Dec. 19	C.W. McCall	Convoy	MGM	Gold	Single
Dec. 31	Glen Campbell	Rhinestone Cowboy	Capitol	Gold	Album

1976

Jan. 29	C.W. McCall	Black Bear Road	MGM	Gold	Album
Feb. 04	The Marshall Tucker Band	Searchin' for a Rainbow	Capricorn	Gold	Album
Feb. 2	Eagles	Eagles—Their Greatest Hits 1971-1975	Asylum	Gold	Album
Feb. 24	Eagles	Eagles—Their Greatest Hits 1971-1975	Asylum	Platinum	Album
Mar. 11	Willie Nelson	Red Headed Stranger	Columbia	Gold	Album
Mar. 16	Pure Prairie League	Bustin' Out	RCA Victor	Gold	Album
Mar. 30	Waylon Jennings, Willie Nelson, Jessi Colter, Tompall Glaser	Wanted! the Outlaws	RCA Victor	Gold	Album
Apr. 27	Olivia Newton-John	Come on Over	MCA	Gold	Album
Apr. 29	Conway Twitty	You've Never Been This Far Before	MCA	Gold	Album
May 17	Dr. Hook	Only Sixteen	Capitol	Gold	Single
May 19	John Sebastian	Welcome Back	Reprise	Gold	Single
May 20	Jimmy Dean	I.O.U.	GRT	Gold	Single
May 21	Mac Davis	All the Love in the World	Columbia	Gold	Album
May 21	Dan Fogelberg	Souvenirs	Epic	Gold	Album
Jul. 15	Starland Vocal Band	Afternoon Delight	Windsong	Gold	Single
Aug. 17	John Denver	Spirit	RCA Victor	Gold	Album
Aug. 19	Loggins & Messina	Native Sons	Columbia	Gold	Album
Aug. 30	Linda Ronstadt	Hasten Down the Wind	Asylum	Gold	Album
Oct. 06	John Denver	Spirit	RCA Victor	Platinum	Album
Oct. 12	England Dan & John Ford Coley	I'd Really Love to See You Tonight	Big Tree	Gold	Single
Oct. 19	James Taylor	In the Pocket	Warner Bros.	Gold	Album
Oct. 26	Gordon Lightfoot	Summertime Dream	Reprise	Gold	Album
Oct. 28	Linda Ronstadt	Hasten Down the Wind	Asylum	Platinum	Album
Nov. 15	Jackson Browne	The Pretender	Asylum	Gold	Album
Nov. 16	Jackson Browne	Jackson Browne	Asylum	Gold	Album
Nov. 16	Red Sovine	Teddy Bear	Gusto	Gold	Single
Nov. 24	Waylon Jennings, Willie Nelson, Jessi Colter, Tompall Glaser	Wanted! the Outlaws	RCA Victor	Platinum	Album
Dec. 01	England Dan & John Ford Coley	Nights Are Forever	Big Tree	Gold	Album
Dec. 08	Linda Ronstadt	Greatest Hits	Asylum	Gold	Album
Dec. 10	Glen Campbell	That Christmas Feeling	Capitol	Gold	Album
Dec. 12	Eagles	Hotel California	Asylum	Gold	Album
Dec. 12	Olivia Newton-John	Don't Stop Believin'	MCA	Gold	Album
Dec. 15	Eagles	Hotel California	Asylum	Platinum	Album
Dec. 22	James Taylor	James Taylor's Greatest Hits	Warner Bros.	Gold	Album
Dec. 23	Barbra Streisand/Kris Kristofferson	A Star Is Born	Columbia	Gold	Album

1977

Jan. 01	Engelbert Humperdinck	After the Lovin'	Epic	Gold	Album
Jan. 19	Linda Ronstadt	Greatest Hits	Asylum	Platinum	Album
Jan. 21	Burton Cummings	Stand Tall	Portrait	Gold	Single
Jan. 21	Barbra Streisand/Kris Kristofferson	A Star Is Born	Columbia	Platinum	Album
Feb. 15	Engelbert Humperdinck	After the Lovin'	Epic	Gold	Single
Mar. 01	Hank Williams	24 Greatest Hits	MGM	Gold	Album
Mar. 10	Statler Brothers	The Best of the Statler Brothers	Mercury	Gold	Album
Mar. 21	Eagles	New Kid in Town	Asylum	Gold	Single
Mar. 24	Waylon Jennings	Dreaming My Dreams	RCA Victor	Gold	Album
Mar. 30	John Denver	John Denver's Greatest Hits, Volume II	RCA Victor	Gold	Album
Apr. 12	Jackson Browne	The Pretender	Asylum	Platinum	Album
Apr. 19	Gordon Lightfoot	Gord's Gold	Reprise	Gold	Album
Apr. 20	Glen Campbell	Southern Nights	Capitol	Gold	Single
May 10	Loggins & Messina	Best of Friends	Columbia	Gold	Album
May 12	Eagles	Hotel California	Asylum	Gold	Single
May 23	Engelbert Humperdinck	After the Lovin'	Epic	Platinum	Album
Jun. 02	The Marshall Tucker Band	Carolina Dreams	Reprise	Gold	Album
Jun. 14	Waylon Jennings	Ol' Waylon	RCA Victor	Gold	Album
Jun. 20	Jimmy Buffett	Changes in Latitudes, Changes in Attitudes	ABC	Gold	Album
Jun. 22	Kenny Rogers	Lucille	United Artists	Gold	Single
Jul. 05	James Taylor	J.T.	Columbia	Gold	Album
Aug. 01	Waylon Jennings	Are You Ready for the Country	RCA Victor	Gold	Album
Aug. 09	Dan Fogelberg	Nether Lands	Epic	Gold	Album
Aug. 10	Ricky Nelson	Travelin' Man	Imperial	Gold	Single
Aug. 10	Kenny Rogers	Kenny Rogers	United Artists	Gold	Album
Aug. 16	The Marshall Tucker Band	A New Life	Warner Bros.	Gold	Album
Aug. 18	Rita Coolidge	Anytime...Anywhere	A & M	Gold	Album
Aug. 30	Rita Coolidge	(Your Love Has Lifted Me) Higher & Higher	A & M	Gold	Single
Sep. 01	James Taylor	J.T.	Columbia	Platinum	Album
Sep. 06	Ozark Mountain Daredevils	Ozark Mountain Daredevils	A & M	Gold	Album
Sep. 08	Ronnie McDowell	The King Is Gone	GRT	Gold	Single
Sep. 12	Elvis Presley	Moody Blue	RCA Victor	Gold	Album
Sep. 12	Elvis Presley	Moody Blue	RCA Victor	Platinum	Album
Sep. 12	Elvis Presley	Pure Gold	RCA Victor	Gold	Album
Sep. 12	Elvis Presley	Way Down	RCA Victor	Gold	Single
Sep. 19	Linda Ronstadt	Simple Dreams	Asylum	Gold	Album
Sep. 20	Loggins & Messina	Celebrate Me Home	Columbia	Gold	Album
Sep. 20	The Outlaws	The Outlaws	Arista	Gold	Album
Sep. 30	Elvis Presley	Welcome to My World	RCA Victor	Gold	Album
Oct. 05	Glen Campbell	Southern Nights	Capitol	Gold	Album
Oct. 07	Waylon Jennings	Ol' Waylon	RCA Victor	Platinum	Album
Oct. 07	Elvis Presley	From Elvis Presley Blvd., Memphis, Tennessee	RCA Victor	Gold	Album
Oct. 12	Linda Ronstadt	Simple Dreams	Asylum	Platinum	Album
Oct. 14	Elvis Presley	In Concert	RCA Victor	Gold	Album
Oct. 14	Elvis Presley	In Concert	RCA Victor	Platinum	Album
Oct. 19	Debby Boone	You Light Up My Life	Warner Bros.	Gold	Single
Oct. 19	Rita Coolidge	Anytime...Anywhere	A & M	Platinum	Album
Oct. 21	Olivia Newton-John	Greatest Hits	MCA	Gold	Album
Oct. 25	Debby Boone	You Light Up My Life	Warner Bros.	Gold	Album

Oct. 25	Johnny Cash	The Johnny Cash Portrait/His Greatest Hits, Vol. 2	Columbia	Gold	Album
Oct. 25	Elvis Presley	Elvis—The Legendary Performer, Volume II	RCA Victor	Gold	Album
Nov. 01	Dan Fogelberg	Captured Angel	Epic	Gold	Album
Nov. 04	Elvis Presley	Elvis Sings the World of Christmas	RCA Victor	Gold	Album
Nov. 14	Crystal Gayle	Don't It Make My Brown Eyes Blue	United Artists	Gold	Single
Nov. 14	Crystal Gayle	We Must Believe in Magic	United Artists	Gold	Album
Nov. 21	James Taylor	James Taylor's Greatest Hits	Warner Bros.	Platinum	Album
Nov. 22	Debby Boone	You Light Up My Life	Warner Bros.	Platinum	Single
Nov. 29	Johnny Rivers	Swayin' to the Music	Big Tree	Gold	Single
Dec. 01	John Denver	I Want to Live	RCA Victor	Gold	Album
Dec. 01	Elvis Presley	Elvis Country	RCA Victor	Gold	Album
Dec. 01	Elvis Presley	His Hand in Mine	RCA Victor	Gold	Album
Dec. 12	Elvis Presley	Elvis—The Legendary Performer, Volume II	RCA Victor	Platinum	Album
Dec. 13	Debby Boone	You Light Up My Life	Warner Bros.	Platinum	Album
Dec. 14	Jimmy Buffett	Changes in Latitudes, Changes in Attitudes	ABC	Platinum	Album
Dec. 15	Olivia Newton-John	Greatest Hits	MCA	Platinum	Album
Dec. 15	Kenny Rogers	Daytime Friends	United Artists	Gold	Album
Dec. 27	Dolly Parton	Here You Come Again	RCA Victor	Gold	Album
Dec. 28	Jackson Browne	Running on Empty	Asylum	Gold	Album
1978					
Jan. 09	Little River Band	Diamantina Cocktail	Capitol	Gold	Album
Jan. 13	Waylon Jennings	Waylon Live	RCA Victor	Gold	Album
Jan. 13	Elvis Presley	My Way	RCA Victor	Gold	Single
Jan. 23	Linda Ronstadt	Blue Bayou	Asylum	Gold	Single
Feb. 01	Dolly Parton	Here You Come Again	RCA Victor	Gold	Single
Feb. 02	Rita Coolidge	We're All Alone	A & M	Gold	Single
Feb. 03	Waylon Jennings/ Willie Nelson	Waylon & Willie	RCA Victor	Gold	Album
Feb. 10	Ronnie Milsap	It Was Almost Like a Song	RCA Victor	Gold	Album
Feb. 15	Crystal Gayle	We Must Believe in Magic	United Artists	Platinum	Album
Feb. 15	Kenny Rogers	Ten Years of Gold	United Artists	Gold	Album
Apr. 05	Jimmy Buffett	Son of a Son of a Sailor	ABC	Gold	Album
Apr. 11	Waylon Jennings/ Willie Nelson	Waylon & Willie	RCA Victor	Platinum	Album
Apr. 25	Gordon Lightfoot	Endless Wire	Warner Bros.	Gold	Album
Apr. 28	Dolly Parton	Here You Come Again	RCA Victor	Platinum	Album
May 02	The Marshall Tucker Band	Together Forever	Capricorn	Gold	Album
May 05	Willie Nelson	The Sound in Your Mind	Columbia	Gold	Album
May 10	Jimmy Buffett	Son of a Son of a Sailor	ABC	Platinum	Album
May 12	John Denver	I Want to Live	RCA Victor	Platinum	Album
May 23	The Marshall Tucker Band	Carolina Dreams	Capricorn	Platinum	Album
Jun. 12	Dolly Parton	The Best of Dolly Parton	RCA Victor	Gold	Album
Jun. 16	Bonnie Tyler	It's a Heartache	RCA Victor	Gold	Single
Jun. 21	Rita Coolidge	Love Me Again	A & M	Gold	Album
Jun. 27	Bonnie Tyler	It's a Heartache	RCA Victor	Gold	Album
Jul. 20	Kenny Rogers	Ten Years of Gold	United Artists	Platinum	Album
Jul. 21	Willie Nelson	Stardust	Columbia	Gold	Album
Jul. 27	Emmylou Harris	Elite Hotel	Reprise	Gold	Album
Aug. 16	Dolly Parton	Heartbreaker	RCA Victor	Gold	Album
Aug. 25	Jackson Browne	Running on Empty	Asylum	Platinum	Album

Aug. 29	Little River Band	Sleep Catcher	Capitol	Gold	Album
Aug. 31	Olivia Newton-John	Hopelessly Devoted to You	MCA	Gold	Single
Sep. 14	Kenny Loggins	Nightwatch	Columbia	Gold	Album
Sep. 15	Crystal Gayle	When I Dream	United Artists	Gold	Album
Sep. 15	Kenny Rogers	Love or Something Like It	United Artists	Gold	Album
Sep. 22	Linda Ronstadt	Living in the U.S.A.	Asylum	Gold	Album
Sep. 22	Linda Ronstadt	Living in the U.S.A.	Asylum	Platinum	Album
Sep. 26	Waylon Jennings	I've Always Been Crazy	RCA Victor	Gold	Album
Sep. 29	Dan Fogelberg & Tim Weisberg	Twin Sons of Different Mothers	Full Moon	Gold	Album
Oct. 04	Exile	Kiss You All Over	Curb	Gold	Single
Oct. 10	Exile	Mixed Emotions	Warner Bros.	Gold	Album
Oct. 12	Anne Murray	Let's Keep It That Way	Capitol	Gold	Album
Oct. 13	Kenny Loggins	Nightwatch	Columbia	Platinum	Album
Oct. 13	Ronnie Milsap	Only One Love in My Life	RCA Victor	Gold	Album
Oct. 26	Anne Murray	You Needed Me	Capitol	Gold	Single
Oct. 30	The Marshall Tucker Band	Greatest Hits	Capricorn	Gold	Album
Nov. 09	Kris Kristofferson	Songs of Kristofferson	Columbia	Gold	Album
Nov. 10	Jimmy Buffett	You Had to Be There	ABC	Gold	Album
Nov. 13	Linda Ronstadt	A Retrospective	Capitol	Gold	Album
Nov. 15	Olivia Newton-John	Totally Hot	MCA	Gold	Album
Nov. 30	Kenny Rogers	The Gambler	United Artists	Gold	Album
Dec. 05	Olivia Newton-John	Totally Hot	MCA	Platinum	Album
Dec. 12	Dan Fogelberg & Tim Weisberg	Twin Sons of Different Mothers	Full Moon	Platinum	Album
Dec. 14	Tanya Tucker	Tanya Tucker's Greatest Hits	Columbia	Gold	Album
Dec. 18	Elvis Presley	Elvis—The Legendary Performer, Volume III	RCA Victor	Gold	Album
Dec. 19	Anne Murray	Let's Keep It That Way	Capitol	Platinum	Album
Dec. 19	Statler Brothers	Entertainers...On and Off the Record	Mercury	Gold	Album
Dec. 26	Dr. Hook	Sharing the Night Together	Capitol	Gold	Single
Dec. 26	Willie Nelson	Stardust	Columbia	Platinum	Album
Dec. 29	Roger Whittaker	The Last Farewell & Other Hits	RCA Victor	Gold	Album

1979

Jan. 19	John Denver	John Denver	RCA Victor	Gold	Album
Feb. 05	Anne Murray	New Kind of Feeling	Capitol	Gold	Album
Feb. 12	Olivia Newton-John	A Little More Love	MCA	Gold	Single
Feb. 13	Willie Nelson	Willie & Family Live	Columbia	Gold	Album
Feb. 23	Tanya Tucker	TNT	MCA	Gold	Album
Feb. 27	Nicolette Larson	Nicolette	Warner Bros.	Gold	Album
Feb. 27	Kenny Rogers	The Gambler	United Artists	Platinum	Album
Apr. 12	Poco	Legend	MCA	Gold	Album
May 09	Little River Band	Sleep Catcher	Harvest	Platinum	Album
May 16	Waylon Jennings	Greatest Hits	RCA Victor	Gold	Album
Jun. 13	Little Feat	Waiting for Columbus	Warner Bros.	Gold	Album
Jun. 28	Charlie Daniels Band	Million Mile Reflection	Epic	Gold	Album
Jul. 02	Kenny Rogers & Dottie West	Classics	United Artists	Gold	Album
Aug. 02	Willie Nelson & Leon Russell	One for the Road	Columbia	Gold	Album
Aug. 06	Kenny Rogers	She Believes in Me	United Artists	Gold	Single
Aug. 16	Charlie Daniels Band	Million Mile Reflection	Epic	Platinum	Album
Aug. 21	Charlie Daniels Band	The Devil Went Down to Georgia	Epic	Gold	Single

Aug. 22	Dr. Hook	When You're in Love With a Beautiful Woman	Capitol	Gold	Single
Sep. 09	Waylon Jennings	Greatest Hits	RCA Victor	Platinum	Album
Sep. 11	Dr. Hook	Pleasure & Pain	Capitol	Gold	Album
Sep. 14	The Outlaws	Bring It Back Alive	Arista	Gold	Album
Oct. 16	Ronnie Milsap	Ronnie Milsap Live	RCA Victor	Gold	Album
Nov. 13	Dolly Parton	Great Balls of Fire	RCA Victor	Gold	Album
Nov. 19	New Riders of the Purple Sage	Adventures of Panama Red	Columbia	Gold	Album
Nov. 20	Little River Band	First Under the Wire	Capitol	Gold	Album
Nov. 20	Little River Band	First Under the Wire	Capitol	Platinum	Album
Dec. 26	Dan Fogelberg	Home Free	Columbia	Gold	Album
Dec. 26	Dan Fogelberg	Nether Lands	Epic	Platinum	Album
Dec. 27	Jimmy Buffett	Volcano	MCA	Gold	Album
1980					
Jan. 10	Crystal Gayle	Miss the Mississippi	Columbia	Gold	Album
Jan. 16	Kenny Rogers	Kenny	Capitol	Gold	Album
Jan. 16	Kenny Rogers	Kenny	Capitol	Platinum	Album
Feb. 01	John Denver & the Muppets	A Christmas Together	RCA Victor	Gold	Album
Feb. 01	John Denver & the Muppets	A Christmas Together	RCA Victor	Platinum	Album
Feb. 01	Eagles	Heartache Tonight	Asylum	Gold	Single
Feb. 01	Eagles	The Long Run	Asylum	Gold	Album
Feb. 01	Eagles	The Long Run	Asylum	Platinum	Album
Feb. 06	Kenny Loggins	Keep the Fire	Columbia	Gold	Album
Feb. 07	Gordon Lightfoot	Summertime Dream	Reprise	Platinum	Album
Feb. 07	Anne Murray	I'll Always Love You	Capitol	Gold	Album
Mar. 03	Waylon Jennings	What Goes Around	RCA Victor	Gold	Album
Mar. 06	Willie Nelson	Willie Nelson Sings Kristofferson	Columbia	Gold	Album
Mar. 06	Willie Nelson	Willie Nelson & Family Live	Columbia	Platinum	Album
Mar. 07	Crystal Gayle	Classic Crystal	United Artists	Gold	Album
Mar. 07	Kenny Rogers	Coward of the County	United Artists	Gold	Single
Mar. 13	Dan Fogelberg	Phoenix	Epic	Gold	Album
Mar. 13	Dan Fogelberg	Phoenix	Epic	Platinum	Album
May 12	Linda Ronstadt	Made Love	Asylum	Gold	Album
May 12	Linda Ronstadt	Made Love	Asylum	Platinum	Album
May 28	Kenny Rogers	Gideon	United Artists	Gold	Album
May 28	Kenny Rogers	Gideon	United Artists	Platinum	Album
Jun. 06	Larry Gatlin	Straight Ahead	Columbia	Gold	Album
Jul. 10	Dr. Hook	Sexy Eyes	Capitol	Gold	Single
Jul. 14	Soundtrack	Urban Cowboy	Asylum	Gold	Album
Jul. 14	Roger Whittaker	Best of Roger Whittaker	RCA Victor	Gold	Album
Jul. 24	Soundtrack	Urban Cowboy	Asylum	Platinum	Album
Aug. 22	Waylon Jennings	Music Man	RCA Victor	Gold	Album
Sep. 15	Jackson Browne	Hold Out	Elektra	Gold	Album
Sep. 15	Jackson Browne	Hold Out	Elektra	Platinum	Album
Sep. 29	Charlie Daniels Band	Full Moon	Epic	Gold	Album
Oct. 07	Don Williams	Best of Don Williams Volume II	MCA	Gold	Album
Oct. 15	Willie Nelson & Family	Honeysuckle Rose (Soundtrack)	Columbia	Gold	Album
Oct. 24	Eddie Rabbitt	Horizon	Elektra	Gold	Album
Oct. 24	Eddie Rabbitt	The Best of Eddie Rabbitt	Elektra	Gold	Album
Nov. 07	Charlie Daniels Band	Full Moon	Epic	Platinum	Album

Nov. 10	Anne Murray	Greatest Hits	Capitol	Gold	Album
Nov. 12	Willie Nelson & Family	Honeysuckle Rose (Soundtrack)	Columbia	Platinum	Album
Nov. 14	Kenny Loggins	Alive	Columbia	Gold	Album
Nov. 25	Kenny Rogers	Lady	United Artists	Gold	Single
Nov. 26	Anne Murray	Greatest Hits	Capitol	Platinum	Album
Dec. 02	Kenny Rogers	Greatest Hits	Liberty	Gold	Album
Dec. 02	Kenny Rogers	Greatest Hits	Liberty	Platinum	Album
Dec. 02	Don Williams	I Believe in You	MCA	Gold	Album
Dec. 05	Linda Ronstadt	Linda Ronstadt's Greatest Hits, Volume II	Asylum	Gold	Album
Dec. 09	Waylon Jennings	Theme From "Dukes of Hazzard"	RCA Victor	Gold	Single
Dec. 22	Kenny Loggins	Celebrate Me Home	Columbia	Platinum	Album
1981					
Jan. 07	Eagles	Live	Asylum	Gold	Album
Jan. 07	Eagles	Live	Asylum	Platinum	Album
Jan. 26	Barbara Mandrell	The Best of Barbara Mandrell	ABC	Gold	Album
Feb. 11	Emmylou Harris	Luxury Liner	Warner Bros.	Gold	Album
Feb. 12	Ronnie Milsap	Greatest Hits	RCA Victor	Gold	Album
Feb. 18	Emmylou Harris	Blue Kentucky Girl	Warner Bros.	Gold	Album
Feb. 18	Emmylou Harris	Profile—Best of Emmylou Harris	Warner Bros.	Gold	Album
Feb. 19	Dolly Parton	9 to 5	RCA Victor	Gold	Single
Feb. 23	Eddie Rabbitt	Horizon	Elektra	Platinum	Album
Feb. 25	Statler Brothers	The Best of the Statler Brothers Rides Again, Vol. 2	Mercury	Gold	Album
Mar. 04	Mac Davis	It's Hard to Be Humble	Casablanca	Gold	Album
Mar. 06	Dolly Parton	9 to 5 and Odd Jobs	RCA Victor	Gold	Album
Mar. 10	Eddie Rabbitt	I Love a Rainy Night	Elektra	Gold	Single
Mar. 25	Eddie Rabbitt	Drivin' My Life Away	Elektra	Gold	Single
Apr. 01	Emmylou Harris	Roses in the Snow	Warner Bros.	Gold	Album
May 05	Willie Nelson	Somewhere Over the Rainbow	Columbia	Gold	Album
May 05	James Taylor	Dad Loves His Work	Columbia	Gold	Album
May 27	Alabama	Feels So Right	RCA Victor	Gold	Album
Jun. 05	John Denver	John Denver's Greatest Hits Volume II	RCA Victor	Platinum	Album
Jun. 16	Oak Ridge Boys	Elvira	MCA	Gold	Single
Jun. 26	Statler Brothers	The Originals	Mercury	Gold	Album
Jun. 29	Anne Murray	Where Do You Go When You Dream	Capitol	Gold	Album
Jul. 01	Juice Newton	Angel of the Morning	Capitol	Gold	Single
Jul. 14	Alabama	My Home's in Alabama	RCA Victor	Gold	Album
Jul. 14	Ronnie Milsap	Greatest Hits	RCA Victor	Platinum	Album
Jul. 20	The Outlaws	Ghost Riders	Arista	Gold	Album
Jul. 21	Ronnie Milsap	There's No Gettin' Over Me	RCA Victor	Gold	Album
Jul. 23	Oak Ridge Boys	Fancy Free	MCA	Gold	Album
Aug. 11	Joey Scarbury	Theme From "Greatest American Hero"	Elektra	Gold	Single
Aug. 13	Willie Nelson	Somewhere Over the Rainbow	Columbia	Platinum	Album
Aug. 13	Juice Newton	Juice	Capitol	Gold	Album
Aug. 28	Kenny Rogers	Share Your Love	Liberty	Gold	Album
Aug. 28	Kenny Rogers	Share Your Love	Liberty	Platinum	Album
Sep. 02	Juice Newton	Queen of Hearts	Capitol	Gold	Single
Sep. 04	Charlie Daniels Band	Saddle Tramp	Epic	Gold	Album
Sep. 09	Larry Gatlin	Greatest Hits	Columbia	Gold	Album
Sep. 15	Alabama	Feels So Right	RCA Victor	Platinum	Album
Sep. 15	Waylon Jennings/ Jessi Colter	Leather & Lace	RCA Victor	Gold	Album

Sep. 18	George Jones	I Am What I Am	Epic	Gold	Album
Oct. 05	Eddie Rabbitt	Step by Step	Elektra	Gold	Album
Oct. 09	Emmylou Harris	Evangeline	Warner Bros.	Gold	Album
Oct. 29	Loretta Lynn	Greatest Hits Volume II	MCA	Gold	Album
Oct. 29	Conway Twitty	Greatest Hits Volume I	Decca	Gold	Album
Oct. 29	Conway Twitty & Loretta Lynn	Lead Me On	Decca	Gold	Album
Nov. 02	Hank Williams, Jr.	Whiskey Bent & Hell Bound	Elektra/Curb	Gold	Album
Nov. 03	Dan Fogelberg	The Innocent Age	Full Moon	Gold	Album
Nov. 03	Willie Nelson	Willie Nelson's Greatest Hits (& Some That Will Be)	Columbia	Gold	Album
Nov. 11	Dan Fogelberg	The Innocent Age	Full Moon	Platinum	Album
Nov. 18	Little River Band	Time Exposure	Capitol	Gold	Album
Dec. 08	Ronnie Milsap	There's No Gettin' Over Me	RCA Victor	Gold	Album
Dec. 23	Engelbert Humperdinck	Christmas Tyme	Epic	Gold	Album
Dec. 30	John Denver	Some Days Are Diamonds	RCA Victor	Gold	Album
Dec. 30	Loggins & Messina	Best of Friends	Columbia	Platinum	Album

1982

Jan. 01	Juice Newton	Juice	Capitol	Platinum	Album
Jan. 05	Kenny Rogers	Christmas	Liberty	Gold	Album
Jan. 05	Kenny Rogers	Christmas	Liberty	Platinum	Album
Jan. 11	Soundtrack	Coal Miner's Daughter	MCA	Gold	Album
Feb. 22	Barbara Mandrell	Live	MCA	Gold	Album
Mar. 08	Oak Ridge Boys	Elvira	MCA	Platinum	Single
Apr. 06	Oak Ridge Boys	Bobby Sue	MCA	Gold	Album
Apr. 13	Hank Williams, Jr.	The Pressure Is On	Elektra/Curb	Gold	Album
Apr. 29	Alabama	Mountain Music	RCA Victor	Gold	Album
Apr. 29	Alabama	Mountain Music	RCA Victor	Platinum	Album
Apr. 30	Willie Nelson	Always on My Mind	Columbia	Gold	Album
May 12	Johnny Lee	Lookin' for Love	Full Moon	Gold	Album
Jun. 15	Willie Nelson	Always on My Mind	Columbia	Platinum	Album
Jun. 15	Willie Nelson	Willie Nelson's Greatest Hits (& Some That Will Be)	Columbia	Platinum	Album
Jun. 30	Alabama	My Home's in Alabama	RCA Victor	Platinum	Album
Jul. 07	Juice Newton	Quiet Lies	Capitol	Gold	Album
Aug. 30	Kenny Rogers	Love Will Turn You Around	Liberty	Gold	Album
Oct. 20	Statler Brothers	Christmas Card	Mercury	Gold	Album
Oct. 25	Anne Murray	Christmas Wishes	Capitol	Gold	Album
Nov. 11	Crystal Gayle	When I Dream	Liberty	Platinum	Album
Nov. 15	Olivia Newton-John	Greatest Hits Volume II	MCA	Gold	Album
Nov. 19	Charlie Daniels Band	Windows	Epic	Gold	Album
Nov. 22	Kenny Loggins	High Adventure	Columbia	Gold	Album
Nov. 22	Willie Nelson	Pretty Paper	Columbia	Gold	Album
Nov. 23	Linda Ronstadt	Get Closer	Asylum	Gold	Album
Nov. 29	Olivia Newton-John	Greatest Hits Volume II	MCA	Platinum	Album
Nov. 30	The Kendalls	Heaven's Just a Sin Away	Churchill	Gold	Album
Dec. 08	Don Henley	I Can't Stand Still	Asylum	Gold	Album
Dec. 18	Glenn Frey	No Fun Aloud	Asylum	Gold	Album
Dec. 21	Sylvia	Nobody	RCA Victor	Gold	Single
Dec. 27	Dan Fogelberg	Greatest Hits	Epic	Gold	Album
Dec. 27	Oak Ridge Boys	Christmas	MCA	Gold	Album
Dec. 28	Ray Price	All Time Greatest Hits	Columbia	Gold	Album
Dec. 28	Marty Robbins	All Time Greatest Hits	Columbia	Gold	Album

1983

Jan. 06	Rosanne Cash	Seven Year Ache	Columbia	Gold	Album
Jan. 07	Eagles	Eagles Greatest Hits Volume II	Asylum	Gold	Album
Jan. 14	Elvis Presley	Welcome to My World	RCA Victor	Platinum	Album
Feb. 15	Sylvia	Just Sylvia	RCA Victor	Gold	Album
Mar. 07	Ricky Skaggs	Waitin' for the Sun to Shine	Epic	Gold	Album
Mar. 21	Waylon Jennings/ Willie Nelson	WWII	RCA Victor	Gold	Album
Mar. 28	Don Henley	Dirty Laundry	Asylum	Gold	Single
Apr. 03	Oak Ridge Boys	American Made	MCA	Gold	Album
Apr. 14	Kenny Rogers	We've Got Tonight	Liberty	Gold	Album
Apr. 15	Elvis Presley	Are You Lonesome Tonight	RCA Victor	Gold	Single
Apr. 15	Elvis Presley	Don't	RCA Victor	Gold	Single
Apr. 15	Elvis Presley	I Got Stung	RCA Victor	Gold	Single
Apr. 15	Elvis Presley	It's Now or Never	RCA Victor	Gold	Single
Apr. 15	Elvis Presley	Return to Sender	RCA Victor	Gold	Single
May 03	Alabama	The Closer You Get	RCA Victor	Gold	Album
May 03	Alabama	The Closer You Get	RCA Victor	Platinum	Album
Jun. 14	John Anderson	Swingin'	Warner Bros.	Gold	Single
Jun. 15	Loretta Lynn	Coal Miner's Daughter	MCA	Gold	Album
Jul. 11	Merle Haggard	Big City	Epic	Gold	Album
Jul. 11	Merle Haggard & Willie Nelson	Pancho & Lefty	Epic	Gold	Album
Aug. 03	Elvis Presley	A Fool Such As I	RCA Victor	Gold	Single
Aug. 03	Elvis Presley	Wear My Ring Around Your Neck	RCA Victor	Gold	Single
Oct. 03	Willie Nelson & Ray Price	San Antonio Rose	Columbia	Gold	Album
Oct. 03	Ricky Skaggs	Highways & Heartaches	Epic	Gold	Album
Oct. 03	Bonnie Tyler	Faster Than the Speed of Night	Columbia	Gold	Album
Oct. 03	Bonnie Tyler	Total Eclipse of the Heart	Columbia	Gold	Single
Oct. 18	Kenny Rogers & Dolly Parton	Islands in the Stream	RCA Victor	Gold	Single
Oct. 19	Little River Band	Little River Band Greatest Hits	Capitol	Gold	Album
Oct. 31	Dolly Parton	Greatest Hits	RCA Victor	Gold	Album
Oct. 31	Kenny Rogers	Eyes That See in the Dark	RCA Victor	Gold	Album
Oct. 31	Kenny Rogers	Eyes That See in the Dark	RCA Victor	Liberty	Album
Nov. 07	David Allan Coe	Greatest Hits	Columbia	Gold	Album
Nov. 07	Bonnie Tyler	Faster Than the Speed of Night	Columbia	Platinum	Album
Nov. 08	Jackson Browne	Lawyers in Love	Asylum	Gold	Album
Nov. 14	Buddy Holly & the Crickets	20 Golden Greats	MCA	Gold	Album
Nov. 17	Linda Ronstadt	What's New	Asylum	Gold	Album
Nov. 21	Amy Grant	Age to Age	Myrrh	Gold	Album
Dec. 07	John Denver	Seasons of the Heart	RCA Victor	Gold	Album
Dec. 07	Kenny Rogers & Dolly Parton	Islands in the Stream	RCA Victor	Platinum	Single
Dec. 08	Conway Twitty	The Very Best of	MCA	Gold	Album
Dec. 14	Linda Ronstadt	What's New	Asylum	Platinum	Album
Dec. 21	Kenny Rogers	20 Greatest Hits	Liberty	Gold	Album
Dec. 21	Kenny Rogers	20 Greatest Hits	Liberty	Platinum	Album
Dec. 23	Hank Williams, Jr.	Family Tradition	Elektra/Curb	Gold	Album

1984

Jan. 09	Willie Nelson	Without a Song	Columbia	Gold	Album
Feb. 24	Lee Greenwood	Somebody's Gonna Love You	MCA	Gold	Album

Mar. 27	Dallas Holm & Praise	Dallas Holm & Praise Live	Benson	Gold	Album
Apr. 02	Alabama	Roll On	RCA Victor	Gold	Album
Apr. 02	Alabama	Roll On	RCA Victor	Platinum	Album
Apr. 02	Dan Fogelberg	Windows and Walls	Epic	Gold	Album
Apr. 09	Kenny Loggins	Footloose	Columbia	Gold	Single
May 14	Julio Iglesias/Willie Nelson	To All the Girls I've Loved Before	Columbia	Gold	Single
May 15	John Anderson	Wild & Blue	Warner Bros.	Gold	Album
Jun. 15	Oak Ridge Boys	Deliver	MCA	Gold	Album
Aug. 07	Merle Haggard & Willie Nelson	Pancho & Lefty	Epic	Platinum	Album
Aug. 21	Hank Williams, Jr.	Hank Williams, Jr.'s Greatest Hits	Curb	Gold	Album
Aug. 21	Hank Williams, Jr.	Hank Williams, Jr.'s Greatest Hits	Curb	Platinum	Album
Oct. 05	Ricky Skaggs	Don't Cheat in Our Hometown	Epic	Gold	Album
Oct. 12	Olivia Newton-John	Greatest Hits	MCA	2 Plat.	Album
Oct. 12	Olivia Newton-John	Greatest Hits, Vol. 2	MCA	2 Plat.	Album
Oct. 19	Willie Nelson	Always on My Mind	Columbia	3 Plat.	Album
Oct. 19	Willie Nelson	Stardust	Columbia	3 Plat.	Album
Oct. 22	James Taylor	Greatest Hits	Warner Bros.	2 Plat.	Album
Oct. 25	Alabama	Feels So Right	RCA Victor	3 Plat.	Album
Oct. 25	Alabama	Mountain Music	RCA Victor	3 Plat.	Album
Oct. 25	Alabama	Roll On	RCA Victor	2 Plat.	Album
Oct. 25	Alabama	The Closer You Get	RCA Victor	2 Plat.	Album
Oct. 26	Barbra Streisand/Kris Kristofferson	A Star Is Born	Columbia	4 Plat.	Album
Oct. 30	Linda Ronstadt	What's New	Asylum	2 Plat.	Album
Nov. 16	George Strait	Right or Wrong	MCA	Gold	Album
Dec. 03	Kenny Rogers	What About Me	RCA Victor	Gold	Album
Dec. 03	Kenny Rogers	What About Me	RCA Victor	Platinum	Album
Dec. 03	Kenny Rogers & Dolly Parton	Once Upon a Christmas	RCA Victor	Gold	Album
Dec. 03	Kenny Rogers & Dolly Parton	Once Upon a Christmas	RCA Victor	Platinum	Album
Dec. 18	Willie Nelson	City of New Orleans	Columbia	Gold	Album

1985

Jan. 10	Hank Williams, Jr.	Major Moves	Warner/Curb	Gold	Album
Jan. 17	Linda Ronstadt	Lush Life	Asylum	Gold	Album
Jan. 17	Linda Ronstadt	Lush Life	Asylum	Platinum	Album
Jan. 21	Waylon Jennings/ Willie Nelson	Waylon & Willie	RCA Victor	2 Plat.	Album
Jan. 21	Waylon Jennings	Greatest Hits	RCA Victor	3 Plat.	Album
Jan. 21	Waylon Jennings, Willie Nelson, Jessi Colter, Tompall Glaser	Wanted! the Outlaws	RCA Victor	2 Plat.	Album
Jan. 29	Don Henley	Building the Perfect Beast	Geffen	Gold	Album
Jan. 29	Hank Williams, Jr.	Man of Steel	Warner/Curb	Gold	Album
Feb. 15	Lee Greenwood	You've Got a Good Love Comin'	MCA	Gold	Album
Mar. 15	Anne Murray	A Little Good News	Capitol	Gold	Album
Apr. 01	Alabama	40 Hour Week	RCA Victor	Gold	Album
Apr. 01	Alabama	40 Hour Week	RCA Victor	Platinum	Album
Apr. 04	The Judds	Why Not Me	RCA/Curb	Gold	Album
Apr. 08	George Strait	Does Fort Worth Ever Cross Your Mind	MCA	Gold	Album
Apr. 19	Don Henley	Building the Perfect Beast	Geffen	Platinum	Album

May 02	Amy Grant	Straight Ahead	Myrrh	Gold	Album
May 31	Hank Williams, Jr.	Rowdy	Elektra/Curb	Gold	Album
Jun. 11	Anne Murray	Heart Over Mind	Capitol	Gold	Album
Jun. 24	Amy Grant	Age to Age	Myrrh	Platinum	Album
Jun. 25	Sandi Patti	More Than Wonderful	Impact	Gold	Album
Jul. 30	Alabama	Feels So Right	RCA Victor	4 Plat.	Album
Jul. 30	Alabama	Mountain Music	RCA Victor	4 Plat.	Album
Jul. 30	Alabama	The Closer You Get	RCA Victor	3 Plat.	Album
Jul. 31	Patsy Cline	Greatest Hits	MCA	Gold	Album
Aug. 06	Glenn Frey	The Allnighter	MCA	Gold	Album
Sep. 05	Amy Grant	Unguarded	Myrrh	Gold	Album
Oct. 02	Ronnie Milsap	Greatest Hits, Volume 2	RCA Victor	Gold	Album
Oct. 29	Hank Williams, Jr.	Five-O	Warner/Curb	Gold	Album
Nov. 01	Charlie Daniels Band	A Decade of Hits	Epic	Gold	Album
Nov. 01	Kenny Loggins	Keep the Fire	Columbia	Platinum	Album
Nov. 07	Lee Greenwood	Greatest Hits	MCA	Gold	Album
Nov. 15	Alabama	Alabama Christmas	RCA Victor	Gold	Album
Nov. 15	Alabama	Alabama Christmas	RCA Victor	Platinum	Album
Nov. 22	George Strait	George Strait's Greatest Hits	MCA	Gold	Album
Nov. 25	Amy Grant	A Christmas Album	Myrrh	Gold	Album
Dec. 05	Kenny Rogers	Heart of the Matter	RCA Victor	Gold	Album
Dec. 23	James Taylor	That's Why I'm Here	Columbia	Gold	Album
1986					
Jan. 22	Hank Williams, Jr.	Strong Stuff	Warner/Curb	Gold	Album
Feb. 04	George Strait	Something Special	MCA	Gold	Album
Feb. 10	Waylon Jennings, Willie Nelson, Johnny Cash, Kris Kristofferson	Highwayman	Columbia	Gold	Album
Feb. 12	The Judds	Rockin' With the Rhythm	RCA/Curb	Gold	Album
Mar. 31	Alabama	Alabama's Greatest Hits	RCA Victor	Gold	Album
Mar. 31	Alabama	Alabama's Greatest Hits	RCA Victor	Platinum	Album
Mar. 31	Elvis Presley	Crying in the Chapel	RCA Victor	Gold	Single
Apr. 07	Hank Williams, Jr.	High Notes	Warner/Curb	Gold	Album
Apr. 07	Hank Williams, Jr.	The Pressure Is On	Warner/Curb	Platinum	Album
Apr. 17	The Everly Brothers	The Very Best of the Everly Brothers	Warner Bros.	Gold	Album
Apr. 17	Little Feat	Feats Don't Fail Me	Warner Bros.	Gold	Album
Apr. 25	Ronnie Milsap	Greatest Hits	RCA Victor	2 Plat.	Album
May 13	Hank Williams, Jr.	Greatest Hits—Volume 2	Warner/Curb	Gold	Album
Jun. 16	Amy Grant	Unguarded	Myrrh	Platinum	Album
Jul. 08	Jackson Browne	Lives in the Balance	Asylum	Gold	Album
Aug. 20	Alabama	My Home's in Alabama	RCA Victor	2 Plat.	Album
Sep. 18	George Strait	#7	MCA	Gold	Album
Oct. 07	The Judds	Rockin' With the Rhythm	RCA/Curb	Platinum	Album
Oct. 07	Dolly Parton	Greatest Hits	RCA Victor	Platinum	Album
Oct. 10	The Bellamy Brothers	The Bellamy Brothers Greatest Hits	MCA	Gold	Album
Oct. 10	Randy Travis	Storms of Life	Warner Bros.	Gold	Album
Oct. 13	Arlo Guthrie	Alice's Restaurant	Reprise	Platinum	Album
Oct. 13	Gordon Lightfoot	Gord's Gold	Reprise	Platinum	Album
Oct. 13	Gordon Lightfoot	Sundown	Reprise	Platinum	Album
Oct. 13	James Taylor	Mud Slide Slim & the Blue Horizon	Warner Bros.	Platinum	Album
Oct. 13	James Taylor	Sweet Baby James	Warner Bros.	Platinum	Album
Oct. 13	James Taylor	Sweet Baby James	Warner Bros.	3 Plat.	Album

Oct. 15	The Judds	Why Not Me	RCA/Curb	Platinum	Album
Nov. 06	John Conlee	John Conlee's Greatest Hits	MCA	Gold	Album
Nov. 06	Lee Greenwood	Inside Out	MCA	Gold	Album
Nov. 21	Lynn Anderson	Rose Garden	Columbia	Platinum	Album
Nov. 21	Byrds	The Byrds' Greatest Hits	Columbia	Platinum	Album
Nov. 21	Johnny Cash	Johnny Cash's Greatest Hits	Columbia	Platinum	Album
Nov. 21	Johnny Cash	Johnny Cash's Greatest Hits	Columbia	2 Plat.	Album
Nov. 21	Johnny Cash	Johnny Cash at San Quentin	Columbia	Platinum	Album
Nov. 21	Johnny Cash	Johnny Cash at San Quentin	Columbia	2 Plat.	Album
Nov. 21	Johnny Cash	Johnny Cash at Folsom Prison	Columbia	Platinum	Album
Nov. 21	Johnny Cash	Johnny Cash at Folsom Prison	Columbia	2 Plat.	Album
Nov. 21	Mac Davis	Baby, Don't Get Hooked on Me	Columbia	Platinum	Album
Nov. 21	Bob Dylan	Nashville Skyline	Columbia	Platinum	Album
Nov. 21	Dan Fogelberg	Souvenirs	Epic	Platinum	Album
Nov. 21	Dan Fogelberg	Souvenirs	Epic	2 Plat.	Album
Nov. 21	Johnny Horton	Johnny Horton's Greatest Hits	Columbia	Platinum	Album
Nov. 21	Janis Ian	Between the Lines	Columbia	Platinum	Album
Nov. 21	Loggins & Messina	Full Sail	Columbia	Platinum	Album
Nov. 21	Loggins & Messina	Loggins & Messina	Columbia	Platinum	Album
Nov. 21	Willie Nelson	Red Headed Stranger	Columbia	Platinum	Album
Nov. 21	Willie Nelson	Red Headed Stranger	Columbia	2 Plat.	Album
Nov. 21	Marty Robbins	Gunfighter Ballads and Trail Songs	Columbia	Platinum	Album
Nov. 24	Charlie Daniels Band	Million Mile Reflections	Epic	2 Plat.	Album
Dec. 08	Willie Nelson	Willie Nelson's Greatest Hits (& Some That Will Be)	Columbia	2 Plat.	Album
Dec. 08	Linda Ronstadt	For Sentimental Reasons	Asylum	Gold	Album
Dec. 16	Willie Nelson	The Troublemaker	Columbia	Gold	Album
Dec. 18	Sandi Patti	Hymns Just for You	Impact	Gold	Album
Dec. 22	Hank Williams, Jr.	Montana Cafe	Warner/Curb	Gold	Album

VIDEO

Apr. 14	Alabama	Alabama's Greatest Video Hits	RCA Video Prods.	Gold	Video
Jul. 15	Alabama	Alabama's Greatest Video Hits	RCA Video Prods.	Platinum	Video
Jul. 16	Elvis Presley	68 Comeback Special	RCA Video Prods.	Gold	Video
Jul. 16	Elvis Presley	Aloha From Hawaii	RCA Video Prods.	Gold	Video
Jul. 16	Elvis Presley	Aloha From Hawaii	RCA Video Prods.	Platinum	Video

1987

Jan. 06	Alabama	The Touch	RCA Victor	Gold	Album
Jan. 06	Alabama	The Touch	RCA Victor	Platinum	Album
Jan. 21	Dwight Yoakam	Guitars, Cadillacs, Etc., Etc.	Reprise	Gold	Album
Jan. 23	Reba McEntire	Whoever's in New England	MCA	Gold	Album
Feb. 05	Dan Seals	Won't Be Blue Anymore	EMI America	Gold	Album
Feb. 10	Amy Grant	The Collection	Myrrh	Gold	Album
Feb. 10	Sandi Patti	Morning Like This	Myrrh	Gold	Album
Feb. 10	Randy Travis	Storms of Life	Warner Bros.	Platinum	Album
Feb. 26	Ray Stevens	He Thinks He's Ray Stevens	MCA	Gold	Album
Feb. 26	George Strait	George Strait's Greatest Hits	MCA	Platinum	Album
Feb. 26	George Strait	Strait From the Heart	MCA	Gold	Album
Mar. 16	George Strait	Ocean Front Property	MCA	Gold	Album
Mar. 17	Anne Murray	Country	Capitol	Gold	Album
Mar. 30	Sandi Patti	Songs From the Heart	Benson	Gold	Album
Apr. 02	Patsy Cline	Sweet Dreams (Soundtrack)	MCA	Gold	Album

Apr. 06	Willie Nelson	Half Nelson	Columbia	Gold	Album
Apr. 09	The Judds	Heartland	RCA/Curb	Gold	Album
Apr. 21	Amy Grant	My Father's Eyes	Myrrh	Gold	Album
Apr. 21	Reba McEntire	What Am I Gonna Do About You	MCA	Gold	Album
Jul. 14	Dolly Parton, Linda Ronstadt, Emmylou Harris	Trio	Warner Bros.	Gold	Album
Jul. 14	Dolly Parton, Linda Ronstadt, Emmylou Harris	Trio	Warner Bros.	Platinum	Album
Jul. 14	Randy Travis	Always & Forever	Warner Bros.	Gold	Album
Jul. 14	Randy Travis	Always & Forever	Warner Bros.	Platinum	Album
Aug. 08	Hank Williams, Jr.	Hank Live	Warner/Curb	Gold	Album
Aug. 19	Anne Murray	Christmas Wishes	Capitol	Platinum	Album
Aug. 19	Anne Murray	New Kind of Feeling	Capitol	Platinum	Album
Sep. 15	Hank Williams, Jr.	Born to Boogie	Warner/Curb	Gold	Album
Sep. 23	Anne Murray	Something to Talk About	Capitol	Gold	Album
Oct. 16	Anne Murray	Greatest Hits	Capitol	2 Plat.	Album
Oct. 21	Dwight Yoakam	Hillbilly Deluxe	Reprise	Gold	Album
Nov. 13	Patsy Cline	Greatest Hits	MCA	Platinum	Album
Nov. 16	George Strait	Greatest Hits Volume II	MCA	Gold	Album
Dec. 01	George Strait	Ocean Front Property	MCA	Platinum	Album
Dec. 09	Reba McEntire	Greatest Hits	MCA	Gold	Album
1988					
Jan. 29	Randy Travis	Always & Forever	Warner Bros.	2 Plat.	Album
Feb. 17	Linda Ronstadt	Canciones de Mi Padre	Asylum	Gold	Album
Feb. 23	Hank Williams, Jr.	Born to Boogie	Warner/Curb	Platinum	Album
Mar. 22	K.T. Oslin	80's Ladies	RCA Victor	Gold	Album
Mar. 22	Restless Heart	Wheels	RCA Victor	Gold	Album
Mar. 23	Emmylou Harris	Quarter Moon in a Ten Cent Town	Warner Bros.	Gold	Album
Apr. 08	Randy Travis	Storms of Life	Warner Bros.	2 Plat.	Album
Apr. 11	Ricky Van Shelton	Wild-Eyed Dream	Columbia	Gold	Album
Apr. 11	James Taylor	Never Die Young	Columbia	Gold	Album
Apr. 19	George Strait	Strait Country	MCA	Gold	Album
Apr. 20	Reba McEntire	The Last One to Know	MCA	Gold	Album
Apr. 22	George Strait	If You Ain't Lovin' (You Ain't Livin')	MCA	Gold	Album
May 20	Elvis Presley	Aloha From Hawaii Via Satellite	RCA Victor	Platinum	Album
May 20	Elvis Presley	Aloha From Hawaii Via Satellite	RCA Victor	2 Plat.	Album
May 20	Elvis Presley	Elvis Sings the Wonderful World of Christmas	RCA Victor	Platinum	Album
May 20	Elvis Presley	Elvis As Recorded at Madison Square Garden	RCA Victor	2 Plat.	Album
May 20	Elvis Presley	Elvis' Golden Records	RCA Victor	Platinum	Album
May 20	Elvis Presley	Pure Gold	RCA Victor	Platinum	Album
May 20	Elvis Presley	Roustabout	RCA Victor	Gold	Album
Jun. 23	George Strait	Greatest Hits Volume II	MCA	Platinum	Album
Aug. 11	Alabama	Alabama Live	RCA Victor	Gold	Album
Aug. 23	Hank Williams, Jr.	Wild Streak	Warner/Curb	Gold	Album
Aug. 30	Randy Travis	Always & Forever	Warner Bros.	3 Plat.	Album
Sep. 09	Alabama	Just Us	RCA Victor	Gold	Album
Sep. 13	Randy Travis	Old 8 x 10	Warner Bros.	Gold	Album
Sep. 13	Randy Travis	Old 8 x 10	Warner Bros.	Platinum	Album
Oct. 05	The Judds	The Judds Greatest Hits	RCA/Curb	Gold	Album
Oct. 18	Hank Williams, Jr.	Hank Williams, Jr.'s Greatest Hits	Warner/Curb	2 Plat.	Album

Nov. 29	Conway Twitty	Conway Twitty's Greatest Hits Vol. II	MCA	Gold	Album
Nov. 29	Conway Twitty	Number Ones	MCA	Gold	Album
Nov. 29	Conway Twitty & Loretta Lynn	The Very Best Of	MCA	Gold	Album
Nov. 29	Conway Twitty & Loretta Lynn	We Only Make Believe	MCA	Gold	Album
Dec. 02	Ricky Van Shelton	Loving Proof	Columbia	Gold	Album
Dec. 13	Reba McEntire	Reba	MCA	Gold	Album
Dec. 14	Sandi Patti	The Gift Goes On	Word	Gold	Album
Dec. 21	K.T. Oslin	This Woman	RCA Victor	Gold	Album
Dec. 22	Amy Grant	Lead Me On	A & M	Gold	Album

VIDEO

Jul. 20	George Strait	George Strait Live	MCA Records	Gold	Video

1989

Jan. 01	Dwight Yoakam	Buenas Noches From a Lonely Room	Reprise	Gold	Album
Jan. 04	Traveling Wilburys	Traveling Wilburys	Warner Bros.	Gold	Album
Jan. 04	Traveling Wilburys	Traveling Wilburys	Warner Bros.	Platinum	Album
Jan. 23	Charlie Daniels Band	A Decade of Hits	Epic	Platinum	Album
Jan. 25	The Judds	Heartland	RCA/Curb	Platinum	Album
Feb. 06	Billy Vera & the Beaters	At This Moment	Capitol	Gold	Single
Feb. 14	Little Feat	Let It Roll	Warner Bros.	Gold	Album
Feb. 24	Bill Medley & Jennifer Warnes	(I've Had) the Time of My Life	RCA Victor	Gold	Single
Mar. 01	Traveling Wilburys	Traveling Wilburys	Warner Bros.	2 Plat.	Album
Mar. 29	Roy Orbison	Mystery Girl	Virgin	Gold	Album
Mar. 29	Roy Orbison	Mystery Girl	Virgin	Platinum	Album
Apr. 04	Alabama	Southern Star	RCA	Gold	Album
Apr. 11	Don Henley	Building the Perfect Beast	Geffen	2 Plat.	Album
Apr. 11	Hank Williams, Jr.	Greatest Hits III	Warner/Curb	Gold	Album
May 05	Ronnie Milsap	Greatest Hits Volume 2	RCA Victor	Platinum	Album
May 10	Dwight Yoakam	Guitars, Cadillacs, Etc., Etc.	Reprise	Platinum	Album
May 16	Jackson Browne	For Everyman	Elektra	Platinum	Album
May 16	Jackson Browne	Late for the Sky	Elektra	Platinum	Album
May 16	Reba McEntire	Greatest Hits	MCA	Platinum	Album
May 23	The Judds	The Judds Greatest Hits	RCA/Curb	Platinum	Album
May 23	K.T. Oslin	80's Ladies	RCA Victor	Platinum	Album
Jun. 01	James Taylor	James Taylor's Greatest Hits	Warner Bros.	3 Plat.	Album
Jun. 09	The Judds	Rivers of Time	RCA/Curb	Gold	Album
Jun. 09	Tammy Wynette	Tammy's Greatest Hits	Epic	Platinum	Album
Jul. 05	Sandi Patti	Hymns Just for You	Impact	Platinum	Album
Jul. 06	James Taylor	J.T.	Columbia	2 Plat.	Album
Jul. 09	Ray Stevens	I Have Returned	MCA	Gold	Album
Jul. 11	Roy Orbison	In Dreams: Greatest Hits	Virgin	Gold	Album
Jul. 24	Patsy Cline	Greatest Hits	MCA	2 Plat.	Album
Jul. 24	Ricky Van Shelton	Wild-Eyed Dream	Columbia	Platinum	Album
Jul. 25	Keith Whitley	Don't Close Your Eyes	RCA Victor	Gold	Album
Aug. 07	Merle Haggard	His Epic—The First Eleven—To Be Continued	Epic	Gold	Album
Aug. 22	Reba McEntire	Sweet Sixteen	MCA	Gold	Album
Aug. 23	Amy Grant	The Collection	Myrrh	Platinum	Album
Aug. 23	Sandi Patti	Make His Praise Glorious	Word	Gold	Album
Sep. 06	Don Henley	The End of the Innocence	Geffen	Gold	Album

Sep. 11	George Jones	Anniversary—Ten Years of Hits	Epic	Gold	Album
Sep. 11	Johnny Paycheck	Greatest Hits Vol. II	Epic	Gold	Album
Sep. 13	Linda Ronstadt	Greatest Hits Vol. I	Asylum	4 Plat.	Album
Sep. 13	Linda Ronstadt	Greatest Hits Vol. II	Asylum	Platinum	Album
Sep. 13	Linda Ronstadt	Prisoner in Disguise	Asylum	Platinum	Album
Sep. 18	David Allan Coe	Greatest Hits	Columbia	Platinum	Album
Sep. 18	Willie Nelson	Pretty Paper	Columbia	Platinum	Album
Sep. 18	Willie Nelson	Take It to the Limit	Columbia	Gold	Album
Sep. 24	Clint Black	Killin' Time	RCA	Gold	Album
Sep. 24	The Judds	Christmas Time With the Judds	RCA/Curb	Gold	Album
Oct. 03	K.T. Oslin	This Woman	RCA Victor	Platinum	Album
Oct. 25	Alabama	40 Hour Week	RCA Victor	2 Plat.	Album
Oct. 25	Alabama	Alabama's Greatest Hits	RCA Victor	3 Plat.	Album
Oct. 25	Alabama	Roll On	RCA Victor	3 Plat.	Album
Oct. 25	Kenny Rogers & Dolly Parton	Once Upon a Christmas	RCA Victor	2 Plat.	Album
Nov. 08	Don Henley	The End of the Innocence	Geffen	Platinum	Album
Nov. 08	Little Feat	Dixie Chicken	Warner Bros.	Gold	Album
Nov. 08	Little Feat	Time Loves a Hero	Warner Bros.	Gold	Album
Nov. 08	Little Feat	Waiting for Columbus	Warner Bros.	Platinum	Album
Nov. 13	Billy Joe Royal	The Royal Treatment	Atlantic	Gold	Album
Nov. 17	Amy Grant	A Christmas Album	Myrrh	Platinum	Album
Nov. 21	Linda Ronstadt	Cry Like a Rainstorm—Howl Like the Wind	Asylum	Gold	Album
Nov. 29	Randy Travis	No Holdin' Back	Warner Bros.	Gold	Album
Nov. 29	Hank Williams, Jr.	Greatest Hits III	Warner/Curb	Platinum	Album
Dec. 06	Linda Ronstadt	Cry Like a Rainstorm—Howl Like the Wind	Asylum	Platinum	Album
Dec. 06	Linda Ronstadt	Don't Know Much	Asylum	Gold	Single
Dec. 12	Jimmy Buffett	Songs You Know by Heart	MCA	Gold	Album
Dec. 12	Jimmy Buffett	Songs You Know by Heart	MCA	Platinum	Album
Dec. 20	Charlie Daniels Band	The Devil Went Down to Georgia	Epic	Platinum	Single
Dec. 20	Ricky Van Shelton	Loving Proof	Columbia	Platinum	Album
Dec. 27	Elmo 'n' Patsy	Grandma Got Run Over by a Reindeer	Epic	Gold	Single
Dec. 27	Elmo 'n' Patsy	Grandma Got Run Over by a Reindeer	Epic	Gold	Album

VIDEO

Jan. 10	George Strait	George Strait Live	MCA Records	Platinum	Video
Aug. 23	Sandi Patti	Let There Be Praise	Word, Inc.	Gold	Video
Dec. 27	The Judds	Heartland	MPI Home Video	Gold	Video

1990

Jan. 09	Willie Nelson	Stardust	Columbia	4 Plat.	Album
Jan. 17	Kenny Loggins	Footloose	Columbia	Platinum	Single
Jan. 17	Randy Travis	No Holdin' Back	Warner Bros.	Platinum	Album
Jan. 23	Clint Black	Killin' Time	RCA	Platinum	Album
Jan. 23	Highway 101	Highway 101	Warner Bros.	Gold	Album
Mar. 07	Hank Williams, Jr.	Greatest Hits—Volume 2	Warner/Curb	Platinum	Album
Mar. 12	Vern Gosdin	Chiseled in Stone	Columbia	Gold	Album
Mar. 14	Ricky Van Shelton	RVS III	Columbia	Gold	Album
Mar. 26	Rodney Crowell	Diamonds & Dirt	Columbia	Gold	Album
Mar. 27	k.d. lang & the reclines	Absolute Torch & Twang	Sire	Gold	Album
Mar. 27	Kenny Rogers	Something Inside So Strong	Reprise	Gold	Album
Apr. 03	Hank Williams, Jr.	Loan Wolf	Warner/Curb	Gold	Album
Apr. 19	Ronnie Milsap	Lost in the Fifties	RCA Victor	Gold	Album

Apr. 19	Lorrie Morgan	Leave the Light On	RCA	Gold	Album
Apr. 20	Kentucky Headhunters	Pickin' on Nashville	Mercury	Gold	Album
Apr. 28	George Strait	Beyond the Blue Neon	MCA	Gold	Album
May 14	Conway Twitty	The Very Best Of	MCA	Platinum	Album
May 15	Don Henley	The End of the Innocence	Geffen	2 Plat.	Album
Jun. 29	Charlie Daniels Band	Simple Man	Epic	Gold	Album
Jul. 11	Reba McEntire	Live	MCA	Gold	Album
Jul. 13	Roy Orbison	All Time Greatest Hits of Roy Orbison—Vol. I	CBS	Gold	Album
Jul. 20	Keith Whitley	I Wonder Do You Think of Me	RCA	Gold	Alum
Jul. 23	George Strait	Livin' It Up	MCA	Gold	Album
Jul. 24	Kathy Mattea	Willow in the Wind	Mercury	Gold	Album
Jul. 26	Alabama	Pass It on Down	RCA	Gold	Album
Jul. 30	Randy Travis	Always & Forever	Warner Bros.	4 Plat.	Album
Aug. 02	Garth Brooks	Garth Brooks	Capitol	Gold	Album
Aug. 02	Restless Heart	Big Dreams in a Small Town	RCA	Gold	Album
Aug. 14	Eagles	Hotel California	Asylum	9 Plat.	Album
Aug. 14	Eagles	The Long Run	Asylum	4 Plat.	Album
Aug. 21	Eagles	Eagles—Their Greatest Hits 1971-1975	Asylum	12 Plat.	Album
Aug. 22	Willie Nelson	Willie & Family Live	Columbia	2 Plat.	Album
Sep. 12	Alan Jackson	Here in the Real World	Arista	Gold	Album
Sep. 19	Travis Tritt	Country Club	Warner Bros.	Gold	Album
Oct. 01	Garth Brooks	Garth Brooks	Capitol	Platinum	Album
Oct. 17	Kentucky Headhunters	Pickin' on Nashville	Mercury	Platinum	Album
Oct. 22	Sandi Patti	More Than Wonderful	Impact	Platinum	Album
Oct. 29	Clint Black	Killin' Time	RCA	2 Plat.	Album
Oct. 29	Vince Gill	When I Call Your Name	MCA	Gold	Album
Oct. 30	Garth Brooks	No Fences	Capitol	Gold	Album
Oct. 30	Garth Brooks	No Fences	Capitol	Platinum	Album
Nov. 05	Reba McEntire	Rumor Has It	MCA	Gold	Album
Nov. 07	Keith Whitley	Greatest Hits	RCA	Gold	Album
Nov. 27	Linda Ronstadt	Blue Bayou	Asylum	Platinum	Single
Nov. 27	Linda Ronstadt	Cry Like a Rainstorm—Howl Like the Wind	Asylum	2 Plat.	Album
Nov. 27	Linda Ronstadt	Simple Dreams	Asylum	3 Plat.	Album
Nov. 27	Don Williams	Best of Don Williams, Volume III	MCA	Gold	Album
Nov. 27	Don Williams	I Believe in You	MCA	Platinum	Album
Nov. 30	Garth Brooks	No Fences	Capitol	2 Plat.	Album
Nov. 30	Randy Travis	Heroes & Friends	Warner Bros.	Gold	Album
Dec. 14	George Strait	Merry Christmas Strait to You	MCA	Gold	Album

VIDEO

Mar. 02	Keith Whitley	I Wonder Do You Think of Me	RCA Records	Gold	Video
Mar. 09	Reba McEntire	Reba	MCA Music Video	Gold	Video
Jun. 15	Hank Williams, Jr.	Full Access	Cabin Fever Ent. Jr. Enterprises	Gold	Video
Jun. 26	The Judds	Great Video Hits	RCA Records	Gold	Video
Jun. 26	Kenny Rogers	Great Video Hits	RCA Records	Gold	Video
Jul. 26	Alabama	Pass It on Down	RCA Records	Gold	Video
Jul. 26	Alabama	Pass It on Down	RCA Records	Platinum	Video
Jul. 26	Alabama	Pass It on Down	RCA Records	2 Plat.	Video
Jul. 26	Ronnie Milsap	Great Video Hits	RCA Records	Gold	Video
Jul. 26	Don Williams	Don Williams Live	RCA Records	Gold	Video
Nov. 06	Elvis Presley	Great Performances Vol. I: Center Stage	Buena Vista Home Video	Gold	Video

Nov. 06	Elvis Presley	Great Performances Vol. I: Center Stage	Buena Vista Home Video	Platinum	Video
Nov. 06	Elvis Presley	Great Performances Vol. I: Center Stage	Buena Vista Home Video	3 Plat.	Video
Nov. 06	Elvis Presley	Great Performances Vol. II: Man & Music	Buena Vista Home Video	Gold	Video
Nov. 06	Elvis Presley	Great Performances Vol. II: Man & Music	Buena Vista Home Video	Platinum	Video
Nov. 06	Elvis Presley	Great Performances Vol. II: Man & Music	Buena Vista Home Video	3 Plat.	Video

1991

Jan. 01	George Strait	Livin' It Up	MCA	Platinum	Album
Jan. 08	Clint Black	Put Yourself in My Shoes	RCA	Gold	Album
Jan. 08	Clint Black	Put Yourself in My Shoes	RCA	Platinum	Album
Jan. 10	Righteous Brothers	Unchained Melody	Curb	Gold	Single
Jan. 10	Righteous Brothers	Unchained Melody	Curb	Platinum	Single
Jan. 22	Shenandoah	The Road Not Taken	Columbia	Gold	Album
Feb. 25	K.T. Oslin	Love in a Small Town	RCA	Gold	Album
Mar. 08	The Judds	Love Can Build a Bridge	RCA/Curb	Gold	Album
Mar. 12	Alan Jackson	Here in the Real World	Arista	Platinum	Album
Apr. 01	Reba McEntire	Rumor Has It	MCA	Gold	Album
Apr. 02	Garth Brooks	No Fences	Capitol	3 Plat.	Album
Apr. 08	Ricky Van Shelton	RVS III	Columbia	Platinum	Album
Apr. 09	Patty Loveless	Honky Tonk Angel	MCA	Gold	Album
Apr. 10	Trisha Yearwood	Trisha Yearwood	MCA	Gold	Album
Apr. 11	Lee Greenwood	Greatest Hits	MCA	Platinum	Album
May 21	Amy Grant	Heart in Motion	A & M	Gold	Album
May 21	George Strait	Chill of an Early Fall	MCA	Gold	Album
May 29	Garth Brooks	Garth Brooks	Capitol	2 Plat.	Album
May 30	Anne Murray	Greatest Hits	Capitol	4 Plat.	Album
May 30	Dan Seals	The Best Of	Capitol	Gold	Album
Jun. 05	Kentucky Headhunters	Electric Barnyard	Mercury	Gold	Album
Jun. 07	Dwight Yoakam	Just Lookin' for a Hit	Reprise	Gold	Album
Jun. 11	Restless Heart	Fast Movin' Train	RCA	Gold	Album
Jun. 17	Amy Grant	Heart in Motion	A & M	Platinum	Album
Jun. 19	Righteous Brothers	Unchained Melody—Best of the Righteous Brothers	Curb	Gold	Album
Jun. 20	Mickey Gilley	Encore	Epic	Gold	Album
Jun. 21	Juice Newton	Juice Newton—Greatest Hits	Capitol	Gold	Album
Jul. 02	Dolly Parton	Eagle When She Flies	Columbia	Gold	Album
Jul. 03	Garth Brooks	No Fences	Capitol	4 Plat.	Album
Jul. 16	Roy Orbison	All Time Greatest Hits of Roy Orbison—Vol. II	Columbia	Gold	Album
Jul. 16	Ricky Van Shelton	Backroads	Columbia	Gold	Album
Jul. 19	Alan Jackson	Don't Rock the Jukebox	Arista	Gold	Album
Jul. 22	Loggins & Messina	On Stage	Columbia	Platinum	Album
Jul. 22	Loggins & Messina	Sittin' In	Columbia	Platinum	Album
Jul. 24	Randy Travis	Heroes & Friends	Warner Bros.	Platinum	Album
Jul. 30	Travis Tritt	Country Club	Warner Bros.	Platinum	Album
Aug. 01	Traveling Wilburys	Volume 3	Warner Bros.	Gold	Album
Aug. 01	Traveling Wilburys	Volume 3	Warner Bros.	Platinum	Album
Aug. 02	George Strait	Beyond the Blue Neon	MCA	Platinum	Album
Aug. 07	Vince Gill	Pocket Full of Gold	MCA	Gold	Album

Aug. 07	Travis Tritt	It's All About to Change	Warner Bros.	Gold	Album
Aug. 07	Reba McEntire	My Kind of Country	MCA	Gold	Album
Aug. 09	Mac Davis	Greatest Hits	Columbia	Gold	Album
Aug. 21	Kathy Mattea	A Collection of Hits	Mercury	Gold	Album
Aug. 27	Linda Ronstadt	Canciones De Mi Padre	Asylum	Platinum	Album
Aug. 27	George Strait	If You Ain't Lovin' (You Ain't Livin')	MCA	Platinum	Album
Sep. 12	Dwight Yoakam	If There Was a Way	Reprise	Gold	Album
Sep. 13	Patsy Cline	Greatest Hits	MCA	3 Plat.	Album
Sep. 13	Doug Stone	Doug Stone	Epic	Gold	Album
Sep. 19	George Strait	Greatest Hits	MCA	2 Plat.	Album
Sep. 24	Mark Chesnutt	Too Cold at Home	MCA	Gold	Album
Oct. 01	Clint Black	Put Yourself in My Shoes	RCA	2 Plat.	Album
Oct. 04	Vince Gill	When I Call Your Name	MCA	Platinum	Album
Oct. 07	Willie Nelson	Always on My Mind	Columbia	Gold	Single
Oct. 07	Willie Nelson	Always on My Mind	Columbia	Platinum	Single
Oct. 23	James Taylor	James Taylor's Greatest Hits	Warner Bros.	4 Plat.	Album
Oct. 24	Garth Brooks	No Fences	Capitol	5 Plat.	Album
Oct. 25	Alan Jackson	Don't Rock the Jukebox	Arista	Platinum	Album
Oct. 28	Statler Brothers	The Best of the Statler Brothers	Mercury	Platinum	Album
Oct. 31	Randy Travis	High Lonesome	Warner Bros.	Gold	Album
Nov. 08	Garth Brooks	Ropin' the Wind	Capitol	Gold	Album
Nov. 08	Garth Brooks	Ropin' the Wind	Capitol	Platinum	Album
Nov. 08	Garth Brooks	Ropin' the Wind	Capitol	4 Plat.	Album
Nov. 13	Travis Tritt	It's All About to Change	Warner Bros.	Platinum	Album
Nov. 18	Amy Grant	Heart in Motion	A & M	2 Plat.	Album
Nov. 22	Anne Murray	Christmas Wishes	Capitol	2 Plat.	Album
Nov. 27	Linda Ronstadt	Heart Like a Wheel	Capitol	Platinum	Album
Nov. 27	Linda Ronstadt	Heart Like a Wheel	Capitol	2 Plat.	Album
Dec. 02	The Band	The Band	Capitol	Platinum	Album
Dec. 02	Glen Campbell	Glen Campbell's Greatest Hits	Capitol	Platinum	Album
Dec. 03	Merle Haggard	Okie From Muskogee	Capitol	Platinum	Album
Dec. 03	Merle Haggard	The Best of the Best of Merle Haggard	Capitol	Platinum	Album
Dec. 04	Reba McEntire	For My Broken Heart	MCA	Gold	Album
Dec. 04	Reba McEntire	For My Broken Heart	MCA	Platinum	Album
Dec. 06	Lorrie Morgan	Something in Red	RCA	Gold	Album
Dec. 06	Dolly Parton	White Limozeen	Columbia	Gold	Album
Dec. 06	Elvis Presley	Memories at Christmas	RCA Victor	Gold	Album
Dec. 06	Ricky Van Shelton	Backroads	Columbia	Platinum	Album
Dec. 16	James Taylor	New Moon Shine	Columbia	Gold	Album
Dec. 19	Garth Brooks	Ropin' the Wind	Capitol	5 Plat.	Album
Dec. 19	The Judds	Greatest Hits, Volume 2	RCA/Curb	Gold	Album
Dec. 20	Tanya Tucker	What Do I Do With Me	Capitol	Gold	Album
Dec. 26	Glen Campbell	Galveston	Capitol	Platinum	Album
Dec. 26	Glen Campbell	Gentle on My Mind	Capitol	Platinum	Album

VIDEO

Jan. 08	Ricky Van Shelton	To Be Continued	Sony Music Video	Gold	Video
Feb. 07	The Judds	Love Can Build a Bridge	MPI Home Video	Gold	Video
Feb. 07	The Judds	Love Can Build a Bridge	MPI Home Video	Platinum	Video
Feb. 25	Clint Black	Put Yourself in My Shoes	RCA Records	Gold	Video
Mar. 01	Patsy Cline	The Real Patsy Cline	Cabin Fever Ent.	Gold	Video
Mar. 01	Hank Williams, Jr.	Full Access	Cabin Fever Ent.	Platinum	Video
Mar. 20	K.T. Oslin	Love in a Small Town	RCA Records	Gold	Video

Mar. 25	Charlie Daniels	Homefolks and Highways	Cabin Fever Ent.	Gold	Video
Mar. 26	Alan Jackson	Here in the Real World	Arista	Gold	Video
Mar. 29	Kentucky Headhunters	Pickin' on Nashville	Polygram	Gold	Video
May 21	Lee Greenwood	God Bless the U.S.A.	MCA Music Video	Gold	Video
May 21	Lee Greenwood	God Bless the U.S.A.	MCA Music Video	Platinum	Video
Oct. 02	Garth Brooks	Garth Brooks	Capitol Nashville	Gold	Video
Oct. 02	Garth Brooks	Garth Brooks	Capitol Nashville	Platinum	Video
Oct. 02	Garth Brooks	Garth Brooks	Capitol Nashville	2 Plat.	Video
1992					
Jan. 03	Ricky Skaggs	Highways & Heartaches	Epic	Platinum	Album
Jan. 08	Glen Campbell	By the Time I Get to Phoenix	Capitol	Platinum	Album
Jan. 08	Vince Gill	Pocket Full of Gold	MCA	Platinum	Album
Jan. 13	George Strait	Does Fort Worth Ever Cross Your Mind	MCA	Platinum	Album
Jan. 15	Garth Brooks	Garth Brooks	Capitol	3 Plat.	Album
Jan. 15	Garth Brooks	No Fences	Capitol	6 Plat.	Album
Jan. 15	Garth Brooks	Ropin' the Wind	Liberty	6 Plat.	Album
Jan. 15	The Judds	The Judds Greatest Hits	RCA/Curb	2 Plat.	Album
Jan. 16	k.d. lang	Shadowland	Sire	Gold	Album
Jan. 16	Gary Morris	Why Lady Why	Warner Bros.	Gold	Album
Jan. 16	Linda Ronstadt & James Ingram	Somewhere Out There	MCA	Gold	Single
Jan. 16	George Strait	Chill of an Early Fall	MCA	Platinum	Album
Jan. 22	Charlie Daniels Band	Fire on the Mountain	Epic	Platinum	Album
Jan. 22	Dan Fogelberg	Captured Angel	Epic	Platinum	Album
Feb. 05	Tennessee Ernie Ford	Hymns	Capitol	Platinum	Album
Feb. 12	Glen Campbell	Wichita Lineman	Capitol	Platinum	Album
Feb. 12	Glen Campbell	Wichita Lineman	Capitol	2 Plat.	Album
Feb. 13	George Jones	Super Hits	Epic	Gold	Album
Feb. 18	Randy Travis	An Old Time Christmas	Warner Bros.	Gold	Album
Feb. 18	Randy Travis	Storms of Life	Warner Bros.	3 Plat.	Album
Mar. 10	Willie Nelson	Willie Nelson's Greatest Hits (& Some That Will Be)	Columbia	3 Plat.	Album
Mar. 10	Willie Nelson	Willie Nelson Sings Kristofferson	Columbia	Platinum	Album
Mar. 11	Garth Brooks	No Fences	Capitol	7 Plat.	Album
Mar. 24	Diamond Rio	Diamond Rio	Arista	Gold	Album
Mar. 26	Trisha Yearwood	Trisha Yearwood	MCA	Platinum	Album
Mar. 27	Alabama	Greatest Hits Volume II	RCA	Gold	Album
Mar. 27	Elvis Presley	(Marie's the Name) His Latest Flame	RCA Victor	Gold	Single
Mar. 27	Elvis Presley	A Big Hunk o' Love	RCA Victor	Gold	Single
Mar. 27	Elvis Presley	A Fool Such As I	RCA Victor	Platinum	Single
Mar. 27	Elvis Presley	Ain't That Loving You Babe	RCA Victor	Gold	Single
Mar. 27	Elvis Presley	All Shook Up	RCA Victor	Gold	Single
Mar. 27	Elvis Presley	All Shook Up	RCA Victor	Platinum	Single
Mar. 27	Elvis Presley	All Shook Up	RCA Victor	2 Plat.	Single
Mar. 27	Elvis Presley	Are You Lonesome Tonight	RCA Victor	Platinum	Single
Mar. 27	Elvis Presley	Are You Lonesome Tonight	RCA Victor	2 Plat.	Single
Mar. 27	Elvis Presley	Blue Christmas	RCA Victor	Gold	Single
Mar. 27	Elvis Presley	Blue Hawaii	RCA Victor	Platinum	Album
Mar. 27	Elvis Presley	Blue Hawaii	RCA Victor	2 Plat.	Album
Mar. 27	Elvis Presley	Bossa Nova Baby	RCA Victor	Gold	Single
Mar. 27	Elvis Presley	Burning Love and Hits From His Movies, Volume 2	RCA Victor	Gold	Album

Mar. 27	Elvis Presley	Burning Love	RCA Victor	Platinum	Single
Mar. 27	Elvis Presley	Can't Help Falling in Love	RCA Victor	Platinum	Single
Mar. 27	Elvis Presley	Clean Up Your Backyard	RCA Victor	Gold	Single
Mar. 27	Elvis Presley	Crying in the Chapel	RCA Victor	Platinum	Single
Mar. 27	Elvis Presley	Devil in Disguise	RCA Victor	Gold	Single
Mar. 27	Elvis Presley	Don't	RCA Victor	Platinum	Single
Mar. 27	Elvis Presley	Don't Cry Daddy	RCA Victor	Platinum	Single
Mar. 27	Elvis Presley	Elvis Aaron Presley	RCA Victor	Gold	EP
Mar. 27	Elvis Presley	Elvis Aaron Presley	RCA Victor	Platinum	EP
Mar. 27	Elvis Presley	Elvis As Recorded at Madison Square Garden	RCA Victor	2 Plat.	Album
Mar. 27	Elvis Presley	Elvis in Person	RCA Victor	Gold	Album
Mar. 27	Elvis Presley	Elvis Now	RCA Victor	Gold	Album
Mar. 27	Elvis Presley	Elvis Presley	RCA Victor	Gold	B/ Set
Mar. 27	Elvis Presley	Elvis Presley	RCA Victor	Gold	B/Set
Mar. 27	Elvis Presley	Elvis Sings Christmas Songs	RCA Victor	Gold	EP
Mar. 27	Elvis Presley	Elvis Sings Christmas Songs	RCA Victor	Gold	EP
Mar. 27	Elvis Presley	Elvis Volume 1	RCA Victor	Gold	EP
Mar. 27	Elvis Presley	Elvis Volume 1	RCA Victor	Platinum	EP
Mar. 27	Elvis Presley	Elvis Volume 1	RCA Victor	2 Plat.	EP
Mar. 27	Elvis Presley	Elvis Volume 2	RCA Victor	Gold	EP
Mar. 27	Elvis Presley	Elvis' Golden Records, Volume 1	RCA Victor	5 Plat.	Album
Mar. 27	Elvis Presley	Elvis' Christmas Album	RCA Victor	Platinum	Album
Mar. 27	Elvis Presley	Elvis' Christmas Album	RCA Victor	2 Plat.	Album
Mar. 27	Elvis Presley	Elvis' Golden Records, Volume 3	RCA Victor	Platinum	Album
Mar. 27	Elvis Presley	Elvis' Golden Records, Volume 2	RCA Victor	Platinum	Album
Mar. 27	Elvis Presley	Elvis' Christmas Album	RCA Victor	Gold	Album
Mar. 27	Elvis Presley	Elvis' Christmas Album	RCA Victor	Platinum	Album
Mar. 27	Elvis Presley	Elvis' Golden Records, Volume 4	RCA Victor	Gold	Album
Mar. 27	Elvis Presley	Follow That Dream	RCA Victor	Gold	EP
Mar. 27	Elvis Presley	Follow That Dream	RCA Victor	Platinum	EP
Mar. 27	Elvis Presley	Frankie and Johnny	RCA Victor	Gold	Single
Mar. 27	Elvis Presley	G.I. Blues	RCA Victor	Platinum	Album
Mar. 27	Elvis Presley	Good Luck Charm	RCA Victor	Gold	Single
Mar. 27	Elvis Presley	Good Luck Charm	RCA Victor	Platinum	Single
Mar. 27	Elvis Presley	Hard Headed Woman	RCA Victor	Platinum	Single
Mar. 27	Elvis Presley	He Touched Me	RCA Victor	Gold	Album
Mar. 27	Elvis Presley	He Walks Beside Me—Favorite Songs of Faith & Inspiration	RCA Victor	Gold	Album
Mar. 27	Elvis Presley	Heartbreak Hotel	RCA Victor	Gold	EP
Mar. 27	Elvis Presley	Heartbreak Hotel	RCA Victor	Gold	Single
Mar. 27	Elvis Presley	Heartbreak Hotel	RCA Victor	Platinum	Single
Mar. 27	Elvis Presley	His Hand in Mine	RCA Victor	Platinum	Album
Mar. 27	Elvis Presley	Hound Dog	RCA Victor	Gold	Single
Mar. 27	Elvis Presley	Hound Dog	RCA Victor	Platinum	Single
Mar. 27	Elvis Presley	Hound Dog	RCA Victor	3 Plat.	Single
Mar. 27	Elvis Presley	How Great Thou Art	RCA Victor	Platinum	Album
Mar. 27	Elvis Presley	How Great Thou Art	RCA Victor	2 Plat.	Album
Mar. 27	Elvis Presley	I Feel So Bad	RCA Victor	Gold	Single
Mar. 27	Elvis Presley	I Got Stung	RCA Victor	Platinum	Single
Mar. 27	Elvis Presley	I Want You, I Need You, I Love You	RCA Victor	Gold	Single
Mar. 27	Elvis Presley	I Want You, I Need You, I Love You	RCA Victor	Platinum	Single
Mar. 27	Elvis Presley	I'm Yours	RCA Victor	Gold	Single
Mar. 27	Elvis Presley	I've Lost You	RCA Victor	Gold	Single

Mar. 27	Elvis Presley	If I Can Dream	RCA Victor	Gold	Single
Mar. 27	Elvis Presley	In the Ghetto	RCA Victor	Platinum	Single
Mar. 27	Elvis Presley	It's Now or Never	RCA Victor	Platinum	Single
Mar. 27	Elvis Presley	Jailhouse Rock	RCA Victor	Gold	EP
Mar. 27	Elvis Presley	Jailhouse Rock	RCA Victor	Platinum	EP
Mar. 27	Elvis Presley	Jailhouse Rock	RCA Victor	2 Plat.	EP
Mar. 27	Elvis Presley	Jailhouse Rock	RCA Victor	Gold	Single
Mar. 27	Elvis Presley	Jailhouse Rock	RCA Victor	Platinum	Single
Mar. 27	Elvis Presley	Jailhouse Rock	RCA Victor	2 Plat.	Single
Mar. 27	Elvis Presley	Kentucky Rain	RCA Victor	Gold	Single
Mar. 27	Elvis Presley	Kid Galahad	RCA Victor	Gold	EP
Mar. 27	Elvis Presley	King Creole Volume 1	RCA Victor	Gold	EP
Mar. 27	Elvis Presley	King Creole Volume 1	RCA Victor	Platinum	EP
Mar. 27	Elvis Presley	King Creole Volume 2	RCA Victor	Gold	EP
Mar. 27	Elvis Presley	King Creole Volume 2	RCA Victor	Platinum	EP
Mar. 27	Elvis Presley	Kissin' Cousins	RCA Victor	Gold	Single
Mar. 27	Elvis Presley	Love Me Tender	RCA Victor	Gold	EP
Mar. 27	Elvis Presley	Love Me Tender	RCA Victor	Platinum	EP
Mar. 27	Elvis Presley	Love Me Tender	RCA Victor	Gold	Single
Mar. 27	Elvis Presley	Love Me Tender	RCA Victor	Platinum	Single
Mar. 27	Elvis Presley	Love Me Tender	RCA Victor	2 Plat.	Single
Mar. 27	Elvis Presley	Loving You, Volume 2	RCA Victor	Gold	EP
Mar. 27	Elvis Presley	Loving You, Volume 2	RCA Victor	Platinum	EP
Mar. 27	Elvis Presley	Loving You, Volume 1	RCA Victor	Gold	EP
Mar. 27	Elvis Presley	Moody Blues	RCA Victor	2 Plat.	Album
Mar. 27	Elvis Presley	One Broken Heart	RCA Victor	Gold	Single
Mar. 27	Elvis Presley	Peace in the Valley	RCA Victor	Gold	EP
Mar. 27	Elvis Presley	Peace in the Valley	RCA Victor	Platinum	EP
Mar. 27	Elvis Presley	Puppet on a String	RCA Victor	Gold	Single
Mar. 27	Elvis Presley	Pure Gold	RCA Victor	Platinum	Album
Mar. 27	Elvis Presley	Pure Gold	RCA Victor	2 Plat.	Album
Mar. 27	Elvis Presley	Really Don't Want to Know	RCA Victor	Gold	Single
Mar. 27	Elvis Presley	Return to Sender	RCA Victor	Platinum	Single
Mar. 27	Elvis Presley	Separate Ways	RCA Victor	Gold	Single
Mar. 27	Elvis Presley	She's Not You	RCA Victor	Gold	Single
Mar. 27	Elvis Presley	Stuck on You	RCA Victor	Gold	Single
Mar. 27	Elvis Presley	Stuck on You	RCA Victor	Platinum	Single
Mar. 27	Elvis Presley	Surrender	RCA Victor	Gold	Single
Mar. 27	Elvis Presley	Surrender	RCA Victor	Platinum	Single
Mar. 27	Elvis Presley	Suspicious Minds	RCA Victor	Platinum	Single
Mar. 27	Elvis Presley	Teddy Bear	RCA Victor	Gold	Single
Mar. 27	Elvis Presley	Teddy Bear	RCA Victor	Platinum	Single
Mar. 27	Elvis Presley	Tell Me Why	RCA Victor	Gold	Single
Mar. 27	Elvis Presley	The Complete 50's Masters	RCA Victor	Gold	B/Set
Mar. 27	Elvis Presley	The Complete 50's Masters	RCA Victor	Platinum	B/Set
Mar. 27	Elvis Presley	The Number One Hits	RCA Victor	Gold	Album
Mar. 27	Elvis Presley	The Real Elvis	RCA Victor	Gold	EP
Mar. 27	Elvis Presley	The Real Elvis	RCA Victor	Platinum	EP
Mar. 27	Elvis Presley	The Top Ten Hits	RCA Victor	Gold	Album
Mar. 27	Elvis Presley	Too Much	RCA Victor	Gold	Single
Mar. 27	Elvis Presley	Too Much	RCA Victor	Platinum	Single
Mar. 27	Elvis Presley	Viva Las Vegas	RCA Victor	Gold	Single
Mar. 27	Elvis Presley	Wear My Ring Around Your Neck	RCA Victor	Platinum	Single

Mar. 27	Elvis Presley	World Wide 50 Gold Award Hits, Volume 1	RCA Victor	Platinum	Album
Mar. 27	Elvis Presley	World Wide 50 Gold Award Hits, Volume 1	RCA Victor	2 Plat.	Album
Mar. 27	Elvis Presley	You Don't Have to Say You Love Me	RCA Victor	Gold	Single
Mar. 27	Elvis Presley	You'll Never Walk Alone	RCA Victor	Gold	Album
Mar. 30	Garth Brooks	Ropin' the Wind	Liberty	7Plat.	Album
Apr. 01	Tennessee Ernie Ford	Star Carol	Capitol	Platinum	Album
Apr. 01	Amy Grant	Heart in Motion	A & M	3 Plat.	Album
Apr. 08	Mary-Chapin Carpenter	Shooting Straight in the Dark	Columbia	Gold	Album
May 11	Willie Nelson & Family	Honeysuckle Rose (Soundtrack)	Columbia	2 Plat.	Album
May 26	Brooks & Dunn	Brand New Man	Arista	Gold	Album
Jun. 02	Hal Ketchum	Past the Point of Rescue	Curb	Gold	Album
Jun. 05	Jimmy Buffett	Songs You Know by Heart	MCA	2 Plat.	Album
Jun. 05	Wynonna	Wynonna	MCA/Curb	Gold	Album
Jun. 05	Wynonna	Wynonna	MCA/Curb	Platinum	Album
Jun. 09	Doug Stone	I Thought It Was You	Epic	Gold	Album
Jun. 16	Pam Tillis	Put Yourself in My Place	Arista	Gold	Album
Jun. 17	Garth Brooks	No Fences	Capitol	8 Plat.	Album
Jun. 23	George Strait	Holding My Own	MCA	Gold	Album
Jul. 07	Billy Ray Cyrus	Achy Breaky Heart	Mercury	Gold	Single
Jul. 07	Billy Ray Cyrus	Achy Breaky Heart	Mercury	Platinum	Single
Jul. 15	Travis Tritt	It's All About to Change	Warner Bros.	2 Plat.	Album
Jul. 20	Billy Ray Cyrus	Some Gave All	Mercury	Gold	Album
Jul. 20	Billy Ray Cyrus	Some Gave All	Mercury	Platinum	Album
Jul. 20	Billy Ray Cyrus	Some Gave All	Mercury	2 Plat.	Album
Jul. 20	Little River Band	Little River Band Greatest Hits	Capitol	Platinum	Album
Jul. 20	Little River Band	Little River Band Greatest Hits	Capitol	2 Plat.	Album
Jul. 20	Reba McEntire	For My Broken Heart	MCA	2 Plat.	Album
Jul. 20	George Strait	Ten Strait Hits	MCA	Gold	Album
Jul. 22	Jimmy Buffett	Boats, Beaches, Bars & Ballads	MCA	Gold	B/Set
Jul. 22	Patsy Cline	Greatest Hits	MCA	4 Plat.	Album
Jul. 22	The Judds	Why Not Me	RCA/Curb	2 Plat.	Album
Jul. 22	Aaron Tippin	Read Between the Lines	RCA	Gold	Album
Jul. 24	Billy Ray Cyrus	Some Gave All	Mercury	3 Plat.	Album
Jul. 27	Sandi Patti	Another Time...Another Place	Word	Gold	Album
Jul. 29	Garth Brooks	Garth Brooks	Capitol	4 Plat.	Album
Jul. 29	Garth Brooks	Ropin' the Wind	Liberty	8 Plat.	Album
Aug. 03	Lyle Lovett	Lyle Lovett and His Large Band	MCA/Curb	Gold	Album
Aug. 04	Dolly Parton	Eagle When She Flies	Columbia	Platinum	Album
Aug. 11	Charlie Daniels Band	A Decade of Hits	Epic	2 Plat.	Album
Aug. 17	Brooks & Dunn	Brand New Man	Arista	Platinum	Album
Aug. 25	Sammy Kershaw	Don't Go Near the Water	Mercury	Gold	Album
Aug. 26	Alan Jackson	Don't Rock the Jukebox	Arista	2 Plat.	Album
Aug. 28	Lorrie Morgan	Something in Red	RCA	Platinum	Album
Sep. 01	John Anderson	Seminole Wind	BNA	Gold	Album
Sep. 01	Mary-Chapin Carpenter	Come On, Come On	Columbia	Gold	Album
Sep. 10	k.d. lang	Ingenue	Sire	Gold	Album
Sep. 14	Suzy Bogguss	Aces	Liberty	Gold	Album
Sep. 16	Jimmy Buffett	Feeding Frenzy	MCA	Gold	Album
Sep. 16	Ray Stevens	Greatest Hits	MCA	Gold	Album
Sep. 16	Tanya Tucker	What Do I Do With Me	Liberty	Platinum	Album
Sep. 18	Clint Black	The Hard Way	RCA	Gold	Album
Sep. 18	Clint Black	The Hard Way	RCA	Platinum	Album
Sep. 22	Billy Ray Cyrus	Some Gave All	Mercury	4 Plat.	Album

Sep. 23	Garth Brooks	No Fences	Capitol	9 Plat.	Album
Oct. 06	Soundtrack	Hollywood in Vegas	Epic	Gold	Album
Oct. 20	Travis Tritt	T-R-O-U-B-L-E	Warner Bros.	Gold	Album
Oct. 22	Mark Chesnutt	Longnecks and Short Stories	MCA	Gold	Album
Oct. 22	Wynonna	Wynonna	MCA/Curb	2 Plat.	Album
Nov. 04	Vince Gill	I Still Believe in You	MCA	Gold	Album
Nov. 04	Trisha Yearwood	Hearts in Armor	MCA	Gold	Album
Nov. 06	Alabama	American Pride	RCA	Gold	Album
Nov. 06	Jimmy Buffett	Boats, Beaches, Bars & Ballads	MCA	Platinum	B/Set
Nov. 06	Vince Gill	I Still Believe in You	MCA	Platinum	Album
Nov. 06	Ricky Van Shelton	Greatest Hits Plus	Columbia	Gold	Album
Nov. 09	Garth Brooks	Beyond the Season	Liberty	Gold	Album
Nov. 09	Garth Brooks	Beyond the Season	Liberty	Platinum	Album
Nov. 09	Garth Brooks	Beyond the Season	Liberty	2 Plat.	Album
Nov. 12	Billy Ray Cyrus	Some Gave All	Mercury	5 Plat.	Album
Nov. 16	Jerry Clower	Greatest Hits	MCA	Gold	Album
Nov. 16	Kenny Loggins	Leap of Faith	Columbia	Gold	Album
Nov. 18	George Strait	Pure Country (Soundtrack)	MCA	Gold	Album
Nov. 18	George Strait	Pure Country (Soundtrack)	MCA	Platinum	Album
Nov. 19	Garth Brooks	The Chase	Liberty	Gold	Album
Nov. 19	Garth Brooks	The Chase	Liberty	Platinum	Album
Nov. 19	Garth Brooks	The Chase	Liberty	5 Plat.	Album
Nov. 30	Righteous Brothers	Anthology (1962-1974)	Rhino	Gold	B/Set
Dec. 01	Brooks & Dunn	Brand New Man	Arista	2 Plat.	Album
Dec. 01	Alan Jackson	A Lot About Livin' (and a Little 'Bout Love)	Arista	Gold	Album
Dec. 02	Billy Dean	Billy Dean	Liberty	Gold	Album
Dec. 03	Alan Jackson	A Lot About Livin' (and a Little 'Bout Love)	Arista	Platinum	Album
Dec. 07	John Anderson	Seminole Wind	BNA	Platinum	Album
Dec. 07	Chipmunks	Chipmunks in Low Places	Epic	Gold	Album
Dec. 09	Tanya Tucker	Can't Run From Myself	Liberty	Gold	Album
Dec. 14	Amy Grant	Home for Christmas	A & M	Gold	Album
Dec. 14	Amy Grant	Home for Christmas	A & M	Platinum	Album
Dec. 16	Garth Brooks	Ropin' the Wind	Liberty	9 Plat.	Album
Dec. 17	Randy Travis	Greatest Hits Volume I	Warner Bros.	Gold	Album

VIDEO

Jan. 06	Reba McEntire	Reba in Concert	MCA Music Video	Gold	Video
Jan. 15	Garth Brooks	Garth Brooks	Liberty Records	3 Plat.	Video
Jan. 22	Alan Jackson	Here in the Reel World	Arista	Platinum	Video
Jan. 28	Amy Grant	Heart in Motion Video Collection	A & M Video	Gold	Video
Apr. 02	Randy Travis	Forever and Ever	Warner Reprise Video	Gold	Video
Apr. 15	Reba McEntire	For My Broken Heart	MCA Music Video	Gold	Video
Apr. 24	Garth Brooks	Garth Brooks	Liberty Records	4 Plat.	Video
Aug. 03	The Judds	Their Final Concert	MPI Home Video	Gold	Video
Aug. 03	The Judds	Their Final Concert	MPI Home Video	Platinum	Video
Aug. 18	Garth Brooks	This Is Garth Brooks	Liberty Records	Gold	Video
Aug. 18	Garth Brooks	This Is Garth Brooks	Liberty Records	Platinum	Video
Aug. 18	Garth Brooks	This Is Garth Brooks	Liberty Records	4 Plat.	Video
Oct. 05	Billy Ray Cyrus	Billy Ray Cyrus	Polygram Music Video	Gold	Video
Oct. 05	Billy Ray Cyrus	Billy Ray Cyrus	Polygram Music Video	Platinum	Video

Oct. 05	Billy Ray Cyrus	Billy Ray Cyrus	Polygram Music Video	2 Plat.	Video
Nov. 02	Billy Ray Cyrus	Billy Ray Cyrus	Polygram Music Video	3 Plat.	Video
Nov. 16	Reba McEntire	For My Broken Heart	MCA Music Video	Platinum	Video
Nov. 30	Various Artists	NFL Country	Polygram Music Video	Gold	Video
Dec. 29	Amy Grant	Old Fashioned Christmas	A & M Video	Gold	Video
1993					
Jan. 06	Sawyer Brown	The Dirt Road	Curb	Gold	Album
Jan. 06	Kenny Rogers	Christmas in America	Reprise	Gold	Album
Jan. 06	Dwight Yoakam	If There Was a Way	Reprise	Platinum	Album
Jan. 07	Exile	Greatest Hits	Epic	Gold	Album
Jan. 07	Reba McEntire	Sweet Sixteen	MCA	Platinum	Album
Jan. 12	Marty Stuart	This One's Gonna Hurt You	MCA	Gold	Album
Jan. 14	Lorrie Morgan	Watch Me	BNA	Gold	Album
Jan. 15	Billy Ray Cyrus	Some Gave All	Mercury	6 Plat.	Album
Jan. 19	Mary-Chapin Carpenter	Come On, Come On	Columbia	Platinum	Album
Jan. 26	John Prine	The Best of John Prine	Atlantic	Gold	Album
Jan. 27	Randy Travis	Greatest Hits Volume Two	Warner Bros.	Gold	Album
Feb. 01	Amy Grant	Heart in Motion	A & M	4 Plat.	Album
Feb. 02	George Strait	Pure Country	MCA	2 Plat.	Album
Feb. 09	Reba McEntire	Reba	MCA	Platinum	Album
Feb. 10	Ray Stevens	Greatest Hits	MCA	Platinum	Album
Feb. 18	Collin Raye	In This Life	Epic	Gold	Album
Feb. 19	Reba McEntire	It's Your Call	MCA	Gold	Album
Feb. 19	Reba McEntire	It's Your Call	MCA	Platinum	Album
Mar. 01	Doug Stone	Doug Stone	Epic	Platinum	Album
Mar. 08	Vince Gill	Best of Vince Gill	RCA Victor	Gold	Album
Mar. 10	Travis Tritt	T-R-O-U-B-L-E	Warner Bros.	Platinum	Album
Mar.11	Sandi Patti	Morning Like This	Word	Platinum	Album
Mar. 24	Diamond Rio	Diamond Rio	Arista	Platinum	Album
Mar. 25	Lyle Lovett	Joshua Judges Ruth	MCA/Curb	Gold	Album
Apr. 15	Trisha Yearwood	Hearts in Armor	MCA	Platinum	Album
Apr. 19	Dolly Parton	Slow Dancing With the Moon	Columbia	Gold	Album
Apr. 20	Tracy Lawrence	Alibis	Atlantic	Gold	Album
Apr. 23	Reba McEntire	Rumor Has it	MCA	Platinum	Album
Apr. 27	Brooks & Dunn	Hard Workin' Man	Arista	Gold	Album
Apr. 27	Brooks & Dunn	Hard Workin' Man	Arista	Platinum	Album
Apr. 28	John Michael Montgomery	Life's a Dance	Atlantic	Gold	Album
May 03	Billy Ray Cyrus	Some Gave All	Mercury	7 Plat.	Album
May 04	Garth Brooks	No Fences	Liberty	10 Plat.	Album
May 25	Dwight Yoakam	This Time	Reprise	Gold	Album
May 27	Patsy Cline	The Patsy Cline Collection	MCA	Gold	B/Set
May 28	Confederate Railroad	Confederate Railroad	Atlantic	Gold	Album
May 28	Confederate Railroad	Confederate Railroad	Atlantic	Platinum	Album
May 28	Linda Ronstadt	What's New	Elektra/Asylum	3 Plat.	Album
Jun. 01	Judds	Collector's Series	RCA	Gold	Album
Jun. 01	Judds	Wynonna & Naomi	RCA Victor	Gold	Album
Jun. 06	Pam Tillis	Homeward Looking Angel	Arista	Gold	Album
Jun. 15	Steven Curtis Chapman	The Great Adventure	Sparrow	Gold	Album
Jun. 16	Reba McEntire	It's Your Call	MCA	2 Plat.	Album

Jun. 23	Brooks & Dunn	Brand New Man	Arista	3 Plat.	Album
Jun. 24	Alabama	American Pride	RCA	Platinum	Album
Jun. 24	Alabama	Pass It on Down	RCA	Platinum	Album
Jun. 24	Alabama	Southern Star	RCA Victor	Platinum	Album
Jun. 24	Keith Whitley	Greatest Hits	RCA	Platinum	Album
Jul. 06	Reba McEntire	Whoever's in New England	MCA	Platinum	Album
Jul. 08	Reba McEntire	Merry Christmas to You	MCA	Gold	Album
Jul. 13	Statler Brothers	Christmas Card	Mercury	Platinum	Album
Jul. 13	Statler Brothers	Holy Bible-New Testament	Mercury	Gold	Album
Jul. 13	Statler Brothers	The Best of the Statler Brothers	Mercury	2 Plat.	Album
Jul. 13	Statler Brothers	Today	Mercury	Gold	Album
Jul. 16	Wynonna	Tell Me Why	MCA/Curb	Gold	Album
Jul. 16	Wynonna	Tell Me Why	MCA/Curb	Platinum	Album
Jul. 19	Judds	Love Can Build a Bridge	RCA	Platinum	Album
Jul. 19	Aaron Tippin	Read Between the Lines	RCA	Platinum	Album
Aug. 06	Wynonna Judd	Wynonna	MCA/Curb	3 Plat.	Album
Aug. 11	Alan Jackson	A Lot About Livin' (and a Little 'Bout Love)	Arista	2 Plat.	Album
Aug. 27	John Michael Montgomery	Life's a Dance	Atlantic	Platinum	Album
Aug. 31	Tracy Lawrence	Alibis	Atlantic	Platinum	Album
Sep. 01	Lorrie Morgan	Leave the Light On	RCA	Platinum	Album
Sep. 13	Billy Ray Cyrus	It Won't Be the Last	Mercury	Gold	Album
Sep. 13	Billy Ray Cyrus	It Won't Be the Last	Mercury	Gold	Album
Sep. 21	Garth Brooks	Garth Brooks	Liberty	5 Plat.	Album
Sep. 29	Vince Gill	I Still Believe in You	MCA	2 Plat.	Album
Oct. 05	Dolly Parton	Slow Dancing With the Moon	Columbia	Platinum	Album
Oct. 11	Judds	Christmas Time With the Judds	RCA Victor	Platinum	Album
Oct. 12	Suzy Bogguss	Voices in the Wind	Liberty	Gold	Album
Oct. 12	Billy Dean	Fire in the Dark	Liberty	Gold	Album
Oct. 13	Sammy Kershaw	Haunted Heart	Mercury	Gold	Album
Oct. 19	Patty Loveless	Only What I Feel	Epic	Gold	Album
Oct. 20	Mark Chesnutt	Almost Goodbye	MCA	Gold	B/Set
Oct. 25	James Taylor	Live (2 CD Box Set)	Columbia	Gold	Album
Oct. 26	Sandi Patti	The Finest Moments	Word	Gold	Album
Oct. 26	Dwight Yoakam	This Time	Reprise	Platinum	Album
Oct. 28	Garth Brooks	In Pieces	Liberty	Gold	Album
Oct. 28	Garth Brooks	In Pieces	Liberty	Platinum	Album
Oct. 28	Garth Brooks	In Pieces	Liberty	3 Plat.	Album
Nov. 02	Waylon Jennings	Greatest Hits	RCA Victor	4 Plat.	Album
Nov. 03	Alabama	Live	RCA Victor	Platinum	Album
Nov. 15	Lyle Lovett	Pontiac	MCA/Curb	Gold	Album
Nov. 16	Vince Gill	Let There Be Peace on Earth	MCA	Gold	Album
Nov. 16	James Taylor	Live (2 CD Box Set)	Columbia	Platinum	B/Set
Nov. 30	Elvis Presley	From Nashville to Memphis (5 CD Set)	RCA	Gold	B/Set
Dec. 01	Alan Jackson	A Lot About Livin' (and a Little 'Bout Love)	Arista	3 Plat.	Album
Dec. 01	Alan Jackson	Chattahoochie	Arista	Gold	Single
Dec. 01	Little Texas	Big Time	Warner Bros.	Gold	Album
Dec. 01	Reba McEntire	Greatest Hits, Volume II	MCA	Gold	Album
Dec. 01	Reba McEntire	Greatest Hits, Volume II	MCA	Platinum	Album
Dec. 01	George Strait	Easy Come, Easy Go	MCA	Gold	Album
Dec. 01	George Strait	Easy Come, Easy Go	MCA	Platinum	Album
Dec. 03	Nitty Gritty Dirt Band	20 Years of Dirt: Best of Nitty Gritty Dirt Band	Warner Bros.	Gold	Album
Dec. 07	Lorrie Morgan	Watch Me	BNA	Platinum	Album
Dec. 14	Eagles	Greatest Hits 1971-1975	Elektra/Asylum	14 Plat.	Album

Dec. 14	Toby Keith	Toby Keith	Mercury	Gold	Album
Dec. 15	Brooks & Dunn	Hard Workin' Man	Arista	2 Plat.	Album
Dec. 15	Reba McEntire	Greatest Hits, Volume II	MCA	2 Plat.	Album
Dec. 17	Doug Stone	From the Heart	Epic	Gold	Album
Dec. 17	Aaron Tippin	Call of the Wild	RCA	Gold	Album
Dec. 17	Tanya Tucker	Greatest Hits 1990-1992	Liberty	Gold	Album
Dec. 17	Various Artists	Common Thread: Songs of the Eagles	Giant	Gold	Album
Dec. 17	Various Artists	Common Thread: Songs of the Eagles	Giant	Platinum	Album
Dec. 17	Various Artists	Common Thread: Songs of the Eagles	Giant	2 Plat.	Album
Dec. 17	Clay Walker	Clay Walker	Giant	Gold	Album
Dec. 28	Joe Diffie	Honky Tonk Attitude	Epic	Gold	Album
Dec. 29	Trisha Yearwood	The Heart Remembers When	MCA	Gold	Album

VIDEO

Jan. 07	Garth Brooks	This Is Garth Brooks	Liberty Records	5 Plat.	Video
Jan. 12	Reba McEntire	Reba in Concert	MCA Music Video	Platinum	Album
Jan. 15	Billy Ray Cyrus	Live on Tour	Polygram Music Video	Gold	Video
Jan. 15	Billy Ray Cyrus	Live on Tour	Polygram Music Video	Platinum	Video
Jan. 17	Billy Ray Cyrus	Live on Tour	Polygram Music Video	2 Plat.	Video
Feb. 08	Elvis Presley	The Lost Performances	MGM/UA Home Video	Gold	Video
Apr. 21	Vince Gill	I Still Believe in You	MCA Music Video	Platinum	Video
Jun. 07	Travis Tritt	It's All About to Change	Warner Music Video	Gold	Video
Dec. 01	Gaither Vocal Band	Homecoming Video Album	Star Song Communications	Gold	Video
Dec. 01	Bill Gaither and Friends	Reunion: a Gospel Homecoming Celebration	Star Song Communications	Gold	Video
Dec. 15	Reba McEntire	Greatest Hits	MCA Music Video	Gold	Video
Dec. 23	Ray Stevens	Comedy Video Classics	Curb Home Video	Gold	Video
Dec. 23	Ray Stevens	Comedy Video Classics	Curb Home Video	Platinum	Video
Dec. 23	Ray Stevens	Comedy Video Classics	Curb Home Video	2 Plat.	Video

CANADIAN RECORDING INDUSTRY ASSOCIATION (C.R.I.A.)

C.R.I.A. is the body that issues Gold, Platinum and Multi-Platinum Records for sales of records in Canada. The records listed are by Country artists or are of Country matetrial recorded by non-Country acts.

Award Date	Artist	Title	Record Label	Award Level	Type
1975					
Aug.	John Denver	Evening With John Denver	RCA	Gold	Album
Aug.	John Denver	Back Home Again	RCA	Gold	Album
Nov.	Roger Whittaker	Travellin'	RCA	Gold	Album
Dec.	Freddy Fender	Before the Next Teardrop Falls	Quality	Gold	Album
Dec.	Freddy Fender	Wasted Days and Wasted Nights	Quality	Gold	Single
Dec.	Roger Whittaker	Roger Whittaker's Greatest Hits	RCA	Gold	Album
1976					
Mar.	Olivia Newton-John	Clearly Love	MCA	Gold	Album
Mar.	Olivia Newton-John	Clearly Love	MCA	Platinum	Album
May	Olivia Newton-John	Come on Over	MCA	Gold	Album
Jun.	Tom Jones	10th Anniversary Album	Tee Vee	Platinum	Album
Jun.	John Denver	Rocky Mountain Christmas	RCA	Gold	Album
Jun.	John Denver	Windsong	RCA	Platinum	Album
Jun.	C.W. McCall	Black Bear Road	Polydor	Gold	Album
Jul.	Eagles	One of These Nights	WEA Music	Platinum	Album
Jul.	Eagles	Their Greatest Hits	WEA Music	Platinum	Album
Aug.	Kris Kristofferson	Jesus Was a Capricorn	CBS	Gold	Album
Oct.	Charley Pride	Charley's Best	Tee Vee	Platinum	Album
Nov.	Burton Cummings	Burton Cummings	CBS	Gold	Album
Nov.	Conway Twitty	High Priest of Country Music	MCA	Gold	Album
1977					
Jan.	Roger Whittaker	Roger Whittaker's Greatest Hits	RCA	Platinum	Album
Jan.	Burton Cummings	Stand Tall	CBS	Gold	Single
Feb.	Gordon Lightfoot	Summertime	WEA Music	Platinum	Album
Feb.	Eagles	Hotel California	WEA Music	Gold	Album
Feb.	Eagles	Hotel California	WEA Music	Platinum	Album
Feb.	Conway Twitty	Greatest Hits Vol. 2	MCA	Gold	Album
Feb.	Engelbert Humperdinck	After the Lovin'	CBS	Gold	Album
Feb.	Olivia Newton-John	Don't Stop Believin'	MCA	Gold	Album
Mar.	Roger Whittaker	All My Best	Tee Vee	Platinum	Album
Mar.	Murray McLaughlan	Boulevard	CBS	Gold	Album
Mar.	Burton Cummings	Burton Cummings	CBS	Platinum	Album
Apr.	Charley Pride	Best of Charley Pride Vol. III	RCA	Gold	Album
May	Tom Jones	Say You'll Stay Until Tomorrow	CBS	Gold	Album
Jun.	Carroll Baker	Carroll Baker	RCA	Gold	Album
Jun.	Red Sovine	Teddy Bear	Quality	Gold	Album
Jun.	Freddy Fender	Before the Next Teardrop Falls	GRT	Gold	Album
Jun.	Glen Campbell	Southern Comfort	Capitol	Gold	Single
Jul.	Kenny Rogers	Kenny Rogers	United Artists	Gold	Album

Jul.	Burton Cummings	My Own Way to Rock	CBS	Gold	Album
Jul.	Kenny Rogers	Lucille	United Artists	Gold	Single
Aug.	Engelbert Humperdinck	After the Lovin'	CBS	Platinum	Album
Aug.	Engelbert Humperdinck	After the Lovin'	CBS	Platinum	Single
Aug.	Merle Haggard	Merle Haggard 20 Greatest Hits	Tee Vee	Platinum	Album
Aug.	Kris Kristofferson	Songs of Kristofferson	CBS	Gold	Album
Sep.	James Taylor	J.T.	CBS	Gold	Album
Oct.	Elvis Presley	Moody Blue	RCA	Platinum	Album
Oct.	Kenny Rogers	Kenny Rogers	United Artists	Platinum	Album
Oct.	Buck Owens	Buck Owens 20 Greatest Hits	Tee Vee	Gold	Album
Oct.	Kenny Rogers	Daytime Friends	United Artists	Gold	Album
Oct.	Dr. Hook	A Little Bit More	Capitol	Gold	Album
Oct.	Olivia Newton-John	Making a Good Thing Better	MCA	Gold	Album
Nov.	Elvis Presley	Elvis in Concert	RCA	Platinum	Album
Nov.	Olivia Newton-John	Greatest Hits	MCA	Platinum	Album
Nov.	Olivia Newton-John	Let Me Be There	MCA	Platinum	Album
Nov.	Olivia Newton-John	Come on Over	MCA	Platinum	Album
Nov.	James Taylor	J.T.	CBS	Platinum	Album
Nov.	Burton Cummings	My Own Way to Rock	CBS	Platinum	Album
Nov.	Bobby Vinton	Bobby Vinton Party Music	Ahed	Platinum	Album
Nov.	Olivia Newton-John	Greatest Hits	MCA	Gold	Album
Nov.	Little River Band	Diamantina Cocktail	Capitol	Gold	Album
Nov.	Engelbert Humperdinck	Christmas Tyme	CBS	Gold	Album
Nov.	Ronnie McDowell	The King Is Gone	GRT	Gold	Single
Dec.	Rita Coolidge	Anytime Anywhere	A & M	Platinum	Album
Dec.	Crystal Gayle	We Must Believe in Magic	United Artists	Gold	Album
Dec.	John Denver	Greatest Hits Vol. 2	RCA	Gold	Album
Dec.	Waylon Jennings	Ol' Waylon	RCA	Gold	Album
Dec.	Debby Boone	You Light Up My Life	WEA Music	Platinum	Single
Dec.	Crystal Gayle	Don't It Make My Brown Eyes Blue	United Artists	Gold	Single
Dec	Barbra Streisand & Kris Kristofferson	A Star Is Born	CBS	3 Plat.	Album
1978					
Feb.	The Irish Rovers	The Unicorn	MCA	Platinum	Album
Feb.	The Irish Rovers	The Unicorn	MCA	Platinum	Single
Feb.	Elvis Presley	Blue Christmas	RCA	Platinum	Album
Feb.	Elvis Presley	My Way	RCA	Platinum	Single
Feb.	Elvis Presley	Way Down	RCA	Gold	Single
Mar.	Roger Whittaker	Roger Whittaker's Greatest Hits	RCA	2 Plat.	Album
Mar.	Dolly Parton	Here You Come Again	RCA	Gold	Album
Apr.	Charlie Rich	Behind Closed Doors	CBS	2 Plat.	Album
Apr.	Jimmy Buffett	Son of a Son of a Sailor	GRT	Gold	Album
Apr.	Dr. Hook	Best of Dr. Hook and the Medicine Show	CBS	Gold	Album
Apr.	Loggins & Messina	On Stage	CBS	Gold	Album
May	Olivia Newton-John	If You Love Me	MCA	2 Plat.	Album
May	Olivia Newton-John	Have You Never Been Mellow	MCA	2 Plat.	Album
May	Elvis Presley	Moody Blue	RCA	2 Plat.	Album

May	Carroll Baker	20 Country Classics	RCA	Platinum	Album
May	Waylon Jennings & Willie Nelson	Waylon & Willie	RCA	Gold	Album
Jun.	Little River Band	Diamantina Cocktail	Capitol	Platinum	Album
Jun.	Jackson Browne	Running on Empty	WEA Music	Platinum	Album
Jun.	Little River Band	Sleep Catcher	Capitol	Gold	Album
Jun.	Johnny Cash	Greatest Hits	CBS	Platinum	Album
Jul.	Linda Ronstadt	Simple Dreams	WEA Music	2 Plat.	Album
Jul.	Engelbert Humperdinck	Release Me	London	2 Plat.	Album
Jul.	Engelbert Humperdinck	A Man Without Love	London	2 Plat.	Album
Jul.	Engelbert Humperdinck	Greatest Hits	London	2 Plat.	Album
Jul.	Tom Jones	Live in Las Vegas	London	2 Plat.	Album
Jul.	Linda Ronstadt	Greatest Hits	WEA Music	Platinum	Album
Jul.	Engelbert Humperdinck	The Last Waltz	London	Platinum	Album
Jul.	Bonnie Tyler	It's a Heartache	RCA	Platinum	Single
Aug.	Bonnie Tyler	It's a Heartache	RCA	Platinum	Album
Aug.	Linda Ronstadt	Greatest Hits	WEA Music	Platinum	Album
Aug.	Conway Twitty	20 Certified #1 Hits	Tee Vee	Platinum	Album
Aug.	The Kendalls	Heaven's Just a Sin Away	RCA	Gold	Album
Aug.	Charley Pride	Someone Loves You Honey	RCA	Gold	Album
Aug.	Rita Coolidge	Love Me Again	A & M	Gold	Album
Aug.	Roger Whittaker	Live in Canada	Tembo Music	Gold	Album
Aug.	Burton Cummings	Dream of a Child	CBS	Gold	Album
Aug.	Anne Murray	Let's Keep It That Way	Capitol	Gold	Album
Aug.	Ronnie Milsap	Night Things	RCA	Gold	Album
Sep.	Burton Cummings	Dream of a Child	CBS	Platinum	Album
Sep.	The Band	The Last Waltz	WEA Music	Gold	Album
Sep.	Zachary Richard	L'Arbre Es Dans Ses Feuilles	CBS	Gold	Single
Oct.	Elvis Presley	Elvis—A Canadian Tribute	RCA	2 Plat.	Album
Oct.	Buddy Holly, the Crickets	20 Golden Greats	MCA	Gold	Album
Oct.	Olivia Newton-John	Summer Nights	Polygram	Gold	Single
Oct.	Olivia Newton-John	Hopelessly Devoted to You	Polygram	Gold	Single
Nov.	Burton Cummings	Dream of a Child	CBS	2 Plat.	Album
Nov.	Kenny Loggins	Night Watch	CBS	Gold	Album
Dec.	Lynn Anderson	Rose Garden	CBS	Platinum	Album
Dec.	Loggins & Messina	Full Sail	CBS	Gold	Album
Dec.	Lynn Anderson	Rose Garden	CBS	Gold	Album
Dec.	Dolly Parton	Heartbreaker	RCA	Gold	Album
Dec.	Roger Whittaker	A Time for Peace	Tembo Music	Gold	Album
Dec.	Roger Whittaker	Imagine	Tembo Music	Gold	Album

1979

Jan.	Dan Fogelberg/ Tim Weisberg	Twin Sons of Different Mothers	CBS	Gold	Album
Jan.	Willie Nelson	Stardust	CBS	Gold	Album
Jan.	Bob Dylan	Nashville Skyline	CBS	Gold	Album
Feb.	Anne Murray	Let's Keep It That Way	Capitol	Platinum	Album
Feb.	Little River Band	Sleep Catcher	Capitol	Platinum	Album

Feb.	Kenny Rogers	Love or Something Like It	Capitol	Gold	Album
Feb.	Kenny Rogers	Ten Years of Gold	Capitol	Gold	Album
Feb.	Kenny Rogers	The Gambler	Capitol	Gold	Album
Feb.	Dr. Hook	Pleasure and Pain	Capitol	Gold	Album
Feb.	Anne Murray	New Kind of Feeling	Capitol	Gold	Album
Feb.	Anne Murray	You Needed Me	Capitol	Gold	Single
Feb.	Dr. Hook	Sharing the Night Together	Capitol	Gold	Single
Mar.	Kenny Rogers	The Gambler	Capitol	Platinum	Album
Mar.	Carlton Showband	Gospel Favorites	RCA	Platinum	Album
Mar.	Elvis Presley	Elvis Vol. 3—A Legendary Performer	RCA	Gold	Album
Mar.	Tanya Tucker	TNT	MCA	Gold	Album
Apr.	Kenny Rogers	Ten Years of Gold	Capitol	Platinum	Album
Apr.	Zachary Richard	Migration	CBS	Gold	Album
Apr.	Poco	Legend	GRT	Gold	Album
May	Johnny Cash	Greatest Hits	CBS	Gold	Album
May	Johnny Cash	Greatest Hits	CBS	Platinum	Album
May	Tammy Wynette	Greatest Hits	CBS	Gold	Album
May	Tammy Wynette	Greatest Hits	CBS	Platinum	Album
May	Johnny Cash	At San Quentin	CBS	Gold	Album
May	Johnny Cash	At San Quentin	CBS	Platinum	Album
May	Johnny Cash	Folsom Prison Blues	CBS	Gold	Album
May	Johnny Cash	Folsom Prison Blues	CBS	Platinum	Album
May	Johnny Horton	Greatest Hits	CBS	Gold	Album
May	Kris Kristofferson	The Silver Tongued Devil and I	CBS	Gold	Album
May	Kris Kristofferson	Jesus Was a Capricorn	CBS	Gold	Album
May	Kris Kristofferson	Me and Bobby McGee	CBS	Gold	Album
May	Jim Nabors	Sacred Songs	CBS	Gold	Album
May	Tanya Tucker	Greatest Hits	CBS	Gold	Album
May	Mercy Brothers	Comin' on Stronger	CBS	Gold	Album
May	Ronnie Prophet	Just for You	Cachet	Gold	Album
May	Olivia Newton-John	A Little More Love	MCA	Gold	Single
Jun.	Anne Murray	New Kind of Feeling	Capitol	Platinum	Album
Jun.	Nicolette Larson	Nicolette	WEA Music	Gold	Album
Jun.	Waylon Jennings	Greatest Hits	RCA	Gold	Album
Aug.	Kenny Rogers	The Gambler	Capitol	2 Plat.	Album
Aug.	Carroll Baker	Carroll Baker	RCA	Platinum	Album
Aug.	Little River Band	First Under the Wire	Capitol	Gold	Album
Aug.	Anne Murray	There's a Hippo in My Tub	Capitol	Gold	Album
Aug.	John Stewart	Bombs Away Dream Babies	Polygram	Gold	Album
Sep.	Burton Cummings	Dream of a Child	CBS	2 Plat.	Album
Sep.	Kris Kristofferson	Me and Bobby McGee	CBS	Platinum	Album
Sep.	Ernest Tubb	The Legend and the Legacy	Cachet	Gold	Album
Sep.	Don Williams	Best of Don Williams, Vol. II	MCA	Gold	Album
Oct.	Kenny Rogers	The Gambler	Capitol	3 Plat.	Album
Oct.	Dr. Hook	Pleasure and Pain	Capitol	Platinum	Album
Oct.	Willie Nelson	Stardust	CBS	Platinum	Album
Oct.	Charlie Daniels Band	Million Mile Reflections	CBS	Gold	Album
Oct.	Dr. Hook	When You're in Love With a Beautiful Woman	Capitol	Gold	Single

Nov.	Waylon Jennings	Waylon's Greatest Hits	RCA	Platinum	Album
Nov.	Loretta Lynn	All My Best	Tee Vee	Platinum	Album
Nov.	Charlie Daniels Band	Million Mile Reflections	CBS	Platinum	Album
Nov.	Kris Kristofferson	Songs of Kristofferson	CBS	Platinum	Album
Nov.	Rita Coolidge	Satisfied	A & M	Gold	Album
Nov.	Jimmy Buffett	Volcano	MCA	Gold	Album
Nov.	Hagood Hardy	The Homecoming	Attic	2 Plat.	Album
Dec.	Willie Nelson	Willie Nelson Sings Kristofferson	CBS	Gold	Album
Dec.	Willie Nelson	One for the Road	CBS	Gold	Album
1980					
Jan.	Little River Band	First Under the Wire	Capitol	Platinum	Album
Jan.	Little River Band	First Under the Wire	Capitol	2 Plat.	Album
Jan.	Anne Murray	I'll Always Love You	Capitol	Gold	Album
Jan.	Anne Murray	I'll Always Love You	Capitol	Platinum	Album
Jan.	Anne Murray	Let's Keep It That Way	Capitol	2 Plat.	Album
Jan.	Kenny Rogers	Kenny	Capitol	Gold	Album
Jan.	Kenny Rogers	Kenny	Capitol	Platinum	Album
Jan.	Kenny Rogers	Kenny	Capitol	2 Plat.	Album
Jan.	Dr. Hook	Somctimes You Win	Capitol	Gold	Album
Jan.	Zachary Richard	Migration	CBS	Gold	Album
Jan.	Crystal Gayle	Classic Crystal	Capitol	Gold	Album
Feb.	Engelbert Humperdinck	Especially for You	CBS	Platinum	Album
Mar.	Kenny Rogers	Kenny	Capitol	3 Plat.	Album
Mar.	Kenny Rogers	Kenny	Capitol	4 Plat.	Album
Mar.	Kenny Rogers	The Gambler	Capitol	4 Plat.	Album
Mar.	John Denver and The Muppets	A Christmas Together	RCA	Gold	Album
Mar.	Steve Forbert	Jack Rabbit Slim	CBS	Gold	Album
Mar.	The Kendalls	Old Fashioned Love	RCA	Gold	Album
Mar.	Kenny Rogers	Coward of the County	Capitol	Gold	Single
Jun.	Willie Nelson	Stardust	CBS	Platinum	Album
Jun.	Willie Nelson	Red Headed Stranger	CBS	Gold	Album
Jun.	Willie Nelson	His Very Best	CBS	Gold	Album
Jun.	Kris Kristofferson	The Man and His Songs	CBS	Gold	Album
Jul.	Kenny Rogers	Gideon	Capitol	2 Plat.	Album
Jul.	Anne Murray	Somebody's Waiting	Capitol	Gold	Album
Aug.	Mac Davis	It's Hard to Be Humble	Polygram	Gold	Album
Sep.	Burton Cummings	Woman Love	CBS	Platinum	Album
Sep.	Dr. Hook	Sometimes You Win	Capitol	Platinum	Album
Oct.	Waylon Jennings	Greatest Hits	RCA	2 Plat.	Album
Oct.	Mac Davis	It's Hard to Be Humble	Polygram	Gold	Single
Nov.	Burton Cummings	Burton Cummings	CBS	2 Plat.	Album
Nov.	Rocky Burnette	Son of Rock'n'Roll	Capitol	Gold	Album
Nov.	Rocky Burnette	Tired of Toein' the Line	Capitol	Gold	Single
Dec.	Anne Murray	Anne Murray's Greatest Hits	Capitol	3 Plat.	Album
Dec.	Anne Murray	There's a Hippo in My Tub	Capitol	Platinum	Album
Dec.	Minglewood Band	Minglewood Band	RCA	Gold	Album

1981

Jan.	The Rovers	Rovers	Attic	Gold	Album
Jan.	The Rovers	Wasn't That a Party	Attic	Gold	Single
Feb.	Burton Cummings	Best of Burton Cummings	CBS	2 Plat.	Album
Feb.	The Rovers	The Rovers	Attic	Platinum	Album
Feb.	The Rovers	Wasn't That a Party	Attic	Platinum	Single
Mar.	Kenny Rogers	Kenny Rogers' Greatest Hits	Capitol	Gold	Album
Mar.	Kenny Rogers	Kenny Rogers' Greatest Hits	Capitol	Platinum	Album
Mar.	Kenny Rogers	Kenny Rogers' Greatest Hits	Capitol	2 Plat.	Album
Mar.	Kenny Rogers	Kenny Rogers' Greatest Hits	Capitol	3 Plat.	Album
Mar.	Kenny Rogers	Kenny Rogers' Greatest Hits	Capitol	4 Plat.	Album
Mar.	Kenny Rogers	Kenny Rogers' Greatest Hits	Capitol	5 Plat.	Album
Apr.	Anne Murray	Anne Murray's Greatest Hits	Capitol	4 Plat.	Album
Apr.	Dolly Parton	9 to 5 and Odd Jobs	RCA	Gold	Album
Apr.	Dolly Parton	9 to 5	RCA	Gold	Single
Apr.	Kenny Rogers	Lady	Capitol	Gold	Single
May	Eddie Rabbitt	Horizon	WEA	Platinum	Album
Jun.	Kenny Rogers	Kenny Rogers' Greatest Hits	Capitol	Million	Album
Jun.	Showdown	Welcome to the Rodeo	World	Platinum	Album
Jun.	Ronnie Milsap	Ronnie Milsap's Greatest Hits	RCA	Gold	Album
Jun.	Juice Newton	Juice	Capitol	Gold	Album
Jun.	Jim Nabors	Magic Moods	CBS	Gold	Album
Jul.	Juice Newton	Juice	Capitol	Platinum	Album
Jul.	Anne Murray	Where Do You Go When You Dream	Capitol	Platinum	Album
Aug.	The Outlaws	Ghost Riders	Capitol	Gold	Album
Aug.	Waylon Jennings & Jessi Colter	Leather & Lace	RCA	Gold	Album
Aug.	Juice Newton	Angel of the Morning	Capitol	Gold	Single
Sep.	Charley Pride	The Best of Charley Pride Vol. 3	RCA	Platinum	Album
Sep.	Charley Pride	There's a Little Bit of Hank in Me	RCA	Gold	Album
Nov.	Waylon Jennings	Greatest Hits	RCA	3 Plat.	Album
Nov.	The Good Brothers	The Good Brothers Live	Solid Gold	Gold	Album
Nov.	Hagood Hardy	The Hagood Hardy Collection	Attic	Gold	Album
Nov.	The Emeralds	Just for You	Boot	Gold	Album
Nov.	Minglewood Band	Movin'	RCA	Gold	Album
Nov.	Oak Ridge Boys	Fancy Free	MCA	Gold	Album
Dec.	Anne Murray	Anne Murray's Greatest Hits	Capitol	5 Plat.	Album
Dec.	Kenny Rogers	Share Your Love	Capitol	2 Plat.	Album
Dec.	Juice Newton	Juice	Capitol	2 Plat.	Album
Dec.	Juice Newton	Queen of Hearts	Capitol	Gold	Single
Dec.	Kenny Rogers	Share Your Love	Capitol	Gold	Album
Dec.	Kenny Rogers	Share Your Love	Capitol	Platinum	Album
Dec.	Little River Band	Time Exposure	Capitol	Gold	Album

1982

Jan.	Boxcar Willie	King of the Road	CBS	Platinum	Album
Feb.	The Statler Brothers	The Best of the Statler Brothers	Polygram	Gold	Album
Feb.	George Jones	I Am What I Am	CBS	Gold	Album

Mar.	Oak Ridge Boys	Fancy Free	MCA	Platinum	Album
Mar.	Burton Cummings	Sweet, Sweet	CBS	Gold	Album
Mar.	Oak Ridge Boys	Greatest Hits	MCA	Gold	Album
Mar.	Dan Fogelberg	The Innocent Age	CBS	Gold	Album
Jun.	Oak Ridge Boys	Bobby Sue	MCA	Gold	Album
Jun.	Alabama	Feels So Right	RCA	Gold	Album
Jun.	Alabama	Mountain Music	RCA	Gold	Album
Jun.	Don Williams	I Believe in You	MCA	Gold	Album
Jun.	Juice Newton	Queen of Hearts	Capitol	Platinum	Single
Jul.	Kenny Rogers	Christmas	Capitol	Gold	Album
Jul.	Kenny Rogers	Christmas	Capitol	Platinum	Album
Aug.	John Cougar	American Fool	Polygram	Gold	Album
Aug.	John Cougar	American Fool	Polygram	Platinum	Album
Aug.	John Cougar	Hurt So Good	Polygram	Gold	Single
Sep.	The Emeralds	Bird Dance	Boot	Platinum	Album
Sep.	Kenny Rogers	Love Will Turn You Around	Capitol	Gold	Album
Sep.	Kenny Rogers	Love Will Turn You Around	Capitol	Platinum	Album
Sep.	Juice Newton	Juice	Capitol	3 Plat.	Album
Sep.	Juice Newton	Quiet Lies	Capitol	Gold	Album
Oct.	Anne Murray	Christmas Wishes	Capitol	Gold	Album
Oct.	Anne Murray	Christmas Wishes	Capitol	Platinum	Album
Oct.	Anne Murray	Christmas Wishes	Capitol	2 Plat.	Album
Oct.	Anne Murray	Hottest Night of the Year	Capitol	Gold	Album
Oct.	Willie Nelson	Always on My Mind	CBS	Platinum	Album
Oct.	Charley Pride	Christmas in My Home Town	RCA	Gold	Album
Oct.	Ricky Skaggs	Waitin' for the Sun to Shine	CBS	Gold	Album
Nov.	Roger Whittaker	A Time for Peace	Tembo Music	Platinum	Album
Nov.	Emmylou Harris	Profile: Best of Emmylou Harris	WEA	Gold	Album
Dec.	Olivia Newton-John	Greatest Hits Volume II	MCA	Gold	Album
Dec.	Olivia Newton-John	Greatest Hits Volume II	MCA	Platinum	Album
Dec.	Olivia Newton-John	Greatest Hits Volume II	MCA	2 Plat.	Album
1983					
Jan.	Sylvia	Nobody	RCA	Gold	Single
Jan.	John Cougar	American Fool	Polygram	4 Plat.	Album
Jan.	Sylvia	Nobody	RCA	Gold	Single
Feb.	Little River Band	Greatest Hits	Capitol	Gold	Album
Feb.	Sylvia	Just Sylvia	RCA	Gold	Album
Mar.	Gordon Lightfoot	Gord's Gold	WEA	Gold	Album
Mar.	Gordon Lightfoot	Gord's Gold	WEA	Platinum	Album
Mar.	Gordon Lightfoot	Gord's Gold	WEA	2 Plat.	Album
Mar.	Jim Nabors	Precious Memories	CBS	Gold	Album
Apr.	Kenny Rogers	We've Got Tonight	Capitol	Gold	Album
Apr.	Kenny Rogers	We've Got Tonight	Capitol	Platinum	Album
Apr.	Alabama	Mountain Music	RCA	Platinum	Album
May	Alabama	The Closer You Get	RCA	Gold	Album
May	Ricky Skaggs	Highways and Heartaches	CBS	Gold	Album
May	Kenny Rogers	We've Got Tonight	Capitol	Gold	Single

Jul.	Olivia Newton-John	Greatest Hits Volume II	MCA	3 Plat.	Album
Jul.	Alabama	Feels So Right	RCA	Platinum	Album
Jul.	Roger Whittaker	The Best of Roger Whittaker	Tembo Music	Gold	Album
Jul.	Roger Whittaker	The Best of Roger Whittaker	Tembo Music	Platinum	Album
Jul.	Bonnie Tyler	Faster Than the Speed of Night	CBS	Gold	Album
Sep.	Charley Pride	The Best of Charley Pride	RCA	4 Plat.	Album
Sep.	Willie Nelson	Always on My Mind	CBS	2 Plat.	Album
Sep.	Bonnie Tyler	Faster Than the Speed of Night	CBS	Platinum	Album
Sep.	Kenny Rogers	Eyes That See in the Dark	RCA	Gold	Album
Sep.	Kenny Rogers	Eyes That See in the Dark	RCA	Platinum	Album
Sep.	Waylon Jennings & Willie Nelson	Waylon & Willie	RCA	Platinum	Album
Sep.	Waylon Jennings, Willie Nelson, Jessi Colter & Tompall Glaser	The Outlaws	RCA	Gold	Album
Sep.	Waylon Jennings, Willie Nelson, Jessi Colter & Tompall Glaser	The Outlaws	RCA	Platinum	Album
Oct.	Juice Newton	Dirty Looks	Capitol	Gold	Album
Nov.	Alabama	The Closer You Get	RCA	Platinum	Album
Nov.	Dan Fogelberg	Greatest Hits	CBS	Gold	Album
Nov.	Anne Murray	A Little Good News	Capitol	Gold	Album
Nov.	Kenny Rogers & Dolly Parton	Islands in the Stream	RCA	Gold	Single
Dec.	Kenny Rogers	Eyes That See in the Dark	RCA	2 Plat.	Album
Dec.	The Emeralds	Dance, Dance, Dance	K-Tel Music	Gold	Album
1984					
Jan.	Kenny Rogers	Eyes That See in the Dark	RCA	3 Plat.	Album
Jan.	Kenny Rogers	Islands in the Stream	RCA	Platinum	Single
Jan.	Bonnie Tyler	Total Eclipse of the Heart	CBS	Platinum	Single
Feb.	Kenny Rogers	Twenty Greatest Hits	Capitol	Gold	Album
Feb.	Kenny Rogers	Twenty Greatest Hits	Capitol	Platinum	Album
Feb.	Kenny Rogers	Twenty Greatest Hits	Capitol	2 Plat.	Album
Feb.	Willie Nelson	Without a Song	CBS	Gold	Album
Mar.	Olivia Newton-John	Greatest Hits Volume II	MCA	5 Plat.	Album
Mar.	Ricky Skaggs	Waitin' for the Sun to Shine	CBS	Platinum	Album
Mar.	Alabama	Roll On	RCA	Gold	Album
Mar.	Ricky Skaggs	Don't Cheat in Our Hometown	CBS	Gold	Album
May	Alabama	Roll On	RCA	Platinum	Album
May	Merle Haggard & Willie Nelson	Pancho & Lefty	CBS	Gold	Album
Jun.	Roger Whittaker	Roger Whittaker's Greatest Hits	RCA	3 Plat.	Album
Jul.	Kenny Rogers	Duets	Capitol	Gold	Album
Jul.	Julio Iglesias & Willie Nelson	To All the Girls I've Loved Before	CBS	Gold	Single
Aug.	Willie Nelson	Stardust	CBS	2 Plat.	Album
Aug.	Willie Nelson	His Very Best	CBS	2 Plat.	Album
Aug.	Willie Nelson	Greatest Hits (& Some That Will Be)	CBS	Gold	Album

Aug.	Willie Nelson	Willie & Family Live	CBS	Gold	Album
Aug.	Kenny Loggins	Footloose	CBS	Platinum	Single
Sep.	Roger Whittaker	Roger Whittaker's Greatest Hits	RCA	4 Plat.	Album
Sep.	Carroll Baker	Carroll Baker's Greatest Hits	K-Tel Music	Gold	Album
Nov.	Anne Murray	Anne Murray's Greatest Hits	Capitol	6 Plat.	Album
Nov.	Anne Murray	Christmas Wishes	Capitol	3 Plat.	Album
Nov.	Linda Ronstadt	What's New	WEA	Platinum	Album
Nov.	Anne Murray	Heart Over Mind	Capitol	Gold	Album
Nov.	Anne Murray	You Needed Me	Capitol	Platinum	Single
Dec.	Kenny Rogers	What About Me	RCA	Gold	Album
Dec.	Kenny Rogers	What About Me	RCA	Platinum	Album
Dec.	Kenny Rogers Dolly Parton	Once Upon a Christmas	RCA	Gold	Album
Dec.	Kenny Rogers & Dolly Parton	Once Upon a Christmas	RCA	Platinum	Album
Dec.	The Emeralds	The Best of the Emeralds	K-Tel	Gold	Album
Dec.	Willie Nelson	City of New Orleans	CBS	Gold	Album
1985					
Jan.	Ronnie Milsap	Greatest Hits	RCA	Platinum	Album
Jan.	Dolly Parton	Dolly Parton's Greatest Hits	RCA	Gold	Album
Mar.	Alabama	40 Hour Week	RCA	Gold	Album
Mar.	Amy Grant	Age to Age	Word	Gold	Album
Mar.	The Judds	Why Not Me	RCA	Gold	Album
Apr.	John Conlee	Greatest Hits	MCA	Gold	Album
Jun.	Ricky Skaggs	Highways and Heartaches	CBS	Platinum	Album
Jun.	Glenn Frey	The Heat Is On	MCA	Gold	Single
Aug.	Alabama	40 Hour Week	RCA	Platinum	Album
Sep.	Ricky Skaggs	Country Boy	CBS	Gold	Album
Nov.	Kenny Rogers & Dolly Parton	Once Upon a Christmas	RCA	3 Plat.	Album
Nov.	Alabama	Alabama Christmas	RCA	Platinum	Album
Nov.	Kenny Rogers	The Heart of the Matter	RCA	Gold	Album
Nov.	Amy Grant	Unguarded	Word	Gold	Album
Dec.	Elvis Presley	Blue Christmas	RCA	3 Plat.	Album
1986					
Jan.	The Rovers	The Rovers' 20th Anniversary	CBS	Gold	Album
Jan.	The Rovers	The Rovers' 20th Anniversary	CBS	Platinum	Album
Jan.	The Judds	Rockin' With the Rhythm	RCA	Gold	Album
Feb.	Johnny Cash, Waylon Jennings, Willie Nelson & Kris Kristofferson	Highwayman	CBS	Gold	Album
Mar.	Alabama	Greatest Hits	RCA/Ariola	Gold	Album
Apr.	Dan Seals	Won't Be Blue	Capitol	Gold	Album
Apr.	Anne Murray	Something to Talk About	Capitol	Gold	Album
Apr.	Dan Seals	Bop	Capitol	Gold	Single

May	George Strait	Greatest Hits	MCA	Gold	Album
May	John Denver	John Denver's Greatest Hits	RCA/Ariola	5 Plat.	Album
May	Carroll Baker	Hymns of Gold	Quality Special Products	Platinum	Album
Jul.	Kenny Rogers	Eyes That See in the Dark	RCA/Ariola	5 Plat.	Album
Jul.	Roger Whittaker	Roger Whittaker Songs From the Heart	CBS	Gold	Album
Jul.	Elvis Presley	Unchained Melody	RCA/Ariola	Gold	Single
Aug.	The Judds	Why Not Me	RCA/Ariola	Platinum	Album
Oct.	Alabama	Greatest Hits	RCA/Ariola	Platinum	Album
Nov.	Dan Seals	Won't Be Blue	Capitol	Platinum	Album
Nov.	Ricky Skaggs	Don't Cheat in Our Hometown	CBS	Platinum	Album
Nov.	Willie Nelson	Greatest Hits (& Some That Will Be)	CBS	Platinum	Album
1987					
Jan.	Kenny Rogers & Dolly Parton	Once Upon a Christmas	RCA/Ariola	4 Plat.	Album
Jan.	Alabama	Roll On	RCA/Ariola	2 Plat.	Album
Jan.	Alabama	The Touch	RCA/Ariola	Gold	Album
Feb.	Connie Francis	A Sentimental Treasury	PolyTel	Gold	Album
Apr.	The Judds	Heartland	BMG	Gold	Album
May	Rita MacNeil	Flying on Your Own	MCA	Gold	Album
May	Billy Vera and the Beaters	At This Moment	Trend	Gold	Single
Jun.	Tom Jones	The Golden Hits of Tom Jones	Polygram	Gold	Album
Jun.	Hank Williams	The Very Best of Hank Williams	Polygram	Gold	Album
Jul.	Eagles	Greatest Hits 1971-1975	WEA	Gold	Album
Jul.	Eagles	Greatest Hits 1971-1975	WEA	Platinum	Album
Jul.	Eagles	Greatest Hits 1971-1975	WEA	2 Plat.	Album
Jul.	Eagles	Greatest Hits 1971-1975	WEA	3 Plat.	Album
Jul.	Eagles	Greatest Hits 1971-1975	WEA	4 Plat.	Album
Jul.	Eagles	Greatest Hits 1971-1975	WEA	5 Plat.	Album
Jul.	Eagles	Greatest Hits 1971-1975	WEA	6 Plat.	Album
Jul.	Eagles	Greatest Hits 1971-1975	WEA	7 Plat.	Album
Jul.	Eagles	Greatest Hits 1971-1975	WEA	8 Plat.	Album
Jul.	Eagles	Greatest Hits 1971-1975	WEA	9 Plat.	Album
Jul.	Eagles	Greatest Hits 1971-1975	WEA	10 Plat.	Album
Jul.	Willie Nelson	Pretty Paper	CBS	Gold	Album
Jul.	Anne Murray	Harmony	Capitol	Gold	Album
Aug.	Steve Earle	Exit O	MCA	Gold	Album
Oct.	k.d. lang and the reclines	Angel With a Lariat	WEA	Gold	Album
Nov.	John Cougar Mellencamp	The Lonesome Jubilee	Polygram	3 Plat.	Album
Nov.	Reba McEntire	Greatest Hits	MCA	Gold	Album
Nov.	George Strait	Ocean Front Property	MCA	Gold	Album
Dec.	Rita MacNeil	Flying on Your Own	Virgin	Platinum	Album
Dec.	The Judds	Christmas With the Judds	BMG	Gold	Album
1988					
Jan.	Eagles	Hotel California	WEA	10 Plat.	Album
Jan.	Blue Rodeo	Outskirts	WEA	Gold	Album

Jan.	Bill Medley & Jennifer Warnes	I've Had the Time of My Life	BMG	Gold	Single
Jan.	Blue Rodeo	Try	BMG	Gold	Single
Mar.	Roger Whittaker	Tidings of Comfort and Joy	BMG	Gold	Album
Mar.	Roger Whittaker	Tidings of Comfort and Joy	BMG	Platinum	Album
Mar.	Amy Grant	A Christmas Album	Word	Gold	Album
Mar.	Amy Grant	Straight Ahead	Word	Gold	Album
Mar.	Rosanne Cash	King's Record Shop	CBS	Gold	Album
Apr.	Kenny Rogers & Dolly Parton	Once Upon a Christmas	RCA/Ariola	5 Plat.	Album
Apr.	Blue Rodeo	Outskirts	WEA	Platinum	Album
Jun.	Randy Travis	Always and Forever	WEA	Gold	Album
Jun.	Randy Travis	Always and Forever	WEA	Platinum	Album
Jun.	Randy Travis	Always and Forever	WEA	2 Plat.	Album
Jun.	Randy Travis	Always and Forever	WEA	3 Plat.	Album
Jun.	Randy Travis	Always and Forever	WEA	4 Plat.	Album
Jun.	Engelbert Humperdinck	With Love	BMG	Gold	Album
Jul.	Ricky Van Shelton	Wild-Eyed Dream	CBS	Gold	Album
Aug.	Steve Earle	Guitar Town	MCA	Platinum	Album
Oct.	The Judds	Christmas With the Judds	BMG	Platinum	Album
Oct.	k.d. lang	Shadowland	WEA	Gold	Album
Oct.	The Judds	Greatest Hits	BMG	Gold	Album
Oct.	Colin James	Colin James	Virgin	Gold	Album
Oct.	Rita MacNeil	Now the Bells Ring	Virgin	Gold	Album
Oct.	Rita MacNeil	Reason to Believe	Virgin	Gold	Album
Nov.	Rita MacNeil	Now the Bells Ring	Virgin	Platinum	Album
Nov.	Colin James	Colin James	Virgin	Platinum	Album
Nov.	Rita MacNeil	Reason to Believe	Virgin	Platinum	Album
1989					
Jan.	Randy Travis	Always and Forever	WEA	5 Plat.	Album
Jan.	Randy Travis	Old 8 x 10	WEA	Gold	Album
Jan.	Randy Travis	Old 8 x 10	WEA	Platinum	Album
Jan.	Randy Travis	Old 8 x 10	WEA	2 Plat.	Album
Jan.	Steve Earle	Copperhead Road	MCA	Gold	Album
Jan.	Steve Earle	Copperhead Road	MCA	Platinum	Album
Jan.	Glenn Frey	Soul Searchin'	MCA	Gold	Album
Feb.	Roy Orbison	Mystery Girl	Virgin	Gold	Album
Feb.	Roy Orbison	Mystery Girl	Virgin	Platinum	Album
Feb.	k.d. lang	Shadowland	WEA	Platinum	Album
Feb.	Ricky Van Shelton	Loving Proof	CBS	Gold	Album
Mar.	Steve Earle	Copperhead Road	MCA	2 Plat.	Album
Mar.	Michelle Shocked	Short, Sharp, Shocked	Polygram	Gold	Album
Mar.	Ian Tyson	Cowboyography	Stony Plain	Gold	Album
Apr.	Roy Orbison	Mystery Girl	Virgin	2 Plat.	Album
Apr.	Roy Orbison	The Legendary Roy Orbison	PolyTel	Gold	Album
Apr.	Roy Orbison	The Legendary Roy Orbison	PolyTel	Platinum	Album
Jun.	K.T. Oslin	This Woman	BMG	Gold	Album
Jun.	Roy Orbison	You Got It	Virgin	Gold	Single

Aug.	Roy Orbison	Mystery Girl	Virgin	3 Plat.	Album
Sep.	K.T. Oslin	80's Ladies	BMG	Gold	Album
Oct.	Rodney Crowell	Diamonds and Dirt	CBS	Gold	Album
Nov.	Anne Murray	Greatest Hits—Volume II	Capitol	Gold	Album
Nov.	Linda Ronstadt	Cry Like a Rainstorm—Howl Like the Wind	WEA	Gold	Album
Dec.	Steve Earle	Copperhead Road	MCA	3 Plat.	Album
Dec.	Rita MacNeil	Now the Bells Ring	Virgin	2 Plat.	Album
Dec.	Rita MacNeil	Rita	Virgin	Platinum	Album
Dec.	Various Artists	Hits of the 70's Volume 1	Attic	Gold	Album
Dec.	Various Artists	Hits of the 70's Volume 1	Attic	Platinum	Album
Dec.	Various Artists	Hits of the 70's Volume 2	Attic	Gold	Album
Dec.	Various Artists	Hits of the 70's Volume 2	Attic	Platinum	Album
Dec.	Various Artists	Hits of the 80's Volume 1	Attic	Gold	Album
Dec.	Various Artists	Hits of the 80's Volume 1	Attic	Platinum	Album
Dec.	Various Artists	Hits of the 80's Volume 2	Attic	Gold	Album
Dec.	Various Artists	Hits of the 80's Volume 2	Attic	Platinum	Album
Dec.	Rita MacNeil	Rita	Virgin	Gold	Album
Dec.	Nitty Gritty Dirt Band	Will the Circle Be Unbroken Volume II	MCA	Gold	Album
Dec.	Anne Murray	Christmas	Capitol	Gold	Album
Dec.	Clint Black	Killin' Time	BMG	Gold	Album
1990					
Jan.	Linda Ronstadt	Cry Like a Rainstorm—Howl Like the Wind	WEA	Platinum	Album
Jan.	Sawyer Brown	The Boys Are Back	Capitol	Gold	Album
Mar.	Don Henley	The End of the Innocence	WEA	Gold	Album
Mar.	Don Henley	The End of the Innocence	WEA	Platinum	Album
Mar.	Don Henley	The End of the Innocence	WEA	2 Plat.	Album
Mar.	Rita MacNeil	Rita	Virgin	2 Plat.	Album
Mar.	Rita MacNeil	Reason to Believe	Virgin	2 Plat.	Album
Mar.	k.d. lang and the reclines	Absolute Torch & Twang	WEA	Gold	Album
Mar.	k.d. lang and the reclines	Absolute Torch & Twang	WEA	Platinum	Album
Apr.	Hank Williams, Jr.	Greatest Hits Volume 3	WEA	Gold	Album
Apr.	Hank Williams, Jr.	Greatest Hits Volume 3	WEA	Platinum	Album
Apr.	Burton Cummings	Plus Signs	Capitol	Gold	Album
May	Blue Rodeo	Diamond Mine	WEA	Platinum	Album
May	Blue Rodeo	Diamond Mine	WEA	2 Plat.	Album
May	Kentucky Headhunters	Pickin' on Nashville	Polygram	Gold	Album
May	Blue Rodeo	Diamond Mine	WEA	Gold	Album
Jun.	George Strait	Beyond the Blue Neon	MCA	Gold	Album
Jun.	Notting Hillbillies	Missing...Presumed Having a Good Time	WEA	Gold	Album
Jul.	Colin James	Sudden Stop	Virgin	Gold	Album
Jul.	Colin James	Sudden Stop	Virgin	Platinum	Album
Aug.	Kentucky Headhunters	Pickin' on Nashville	Polygram	Platinum	Album
Aug.	Clint Black	Killin' Time	BMG	Platinum	Album
Sep.	Steve Earle	The Hard Way	MCA	Gold	Album
Sep.	Steve Earle	The Hard Way	MCA	Platinum	Album
Sep.	The Righteous Brothers	Greatest Hits	Polygram	Gold	Album
Sep.	Patty Loveless	Honky Tonk Angel	MCA	Gold	Album

Sep.	Alan Jackson	Here in the Real World	BMG	Gold	Album
Oct.	Rita MacNeil	Flying on Your Own	Virgin	2 Plat.	Album
Oct.	Blue Rodeo	Outskirts	Warner	2 Plat.	Album
Oct.	George Fox	With All My Might	Warner	Gold	Album
Oct.	George Strait	If You Ain't Lovin' You Ain't Livin'	MCA	Gold	Album
Nov.	Rita MacNeil	Home I'll Be	Virgin	Gold	Album
Nov.	Rita MacNeil	Home I'll Be	Virgin	Platinum	Album
Dec.	Garth Brooks	No Fences	Capitol	Gold	Album
1991					
Jan.	Dan Seals	Best Of...	Capitol	Gold	Album
Jan.	Garth Brooks	Garth Brooks	Capitol	Gold	Album
Jan.	Dwight Yoakam	If There Was a Way	Warner	Gold	Album
Jan.	Clint Black	Put Yourself in My Shoes	BMG	Gold	Album
Feb.	Blue Rodeo	Casino	Warner	Gold	Album
Feb.	Blue Rodeo	Casino	Warner	Platinum	Album
Feb.	The Judds	Greatest Hits Album	BMG	Platinum	Album
Feb.	Keith Whitley	Greatest Hits Album	BMG	Gold	Album
Mar.	Garth Brooks	No Fences	Capitol	Platinum	Album
Mar.	Randy Travis	Heroes and Friends	Warner	Gold	Album
Mar.	Randy Travis	Heroes and Friends	Warner	Platinum	Album
Mar.	Reba McEntire	Rumor Has It	MCA	Gold	Album
Mar.	Vince Gill	When I Call Your Name	MCA	Gold	Album
Apr.	Kentucky Headhunters	Pickin' on Nashville	Polygram	2 Plat.	Album
May	Alan Jackson	Here in the Real World	BMG	Platinum	Album
May	Amy Grant	Heart in Motion	A & M	Gold	Album
May	Amy Grant	Lead Me On	Word	Gold	Album
Jun.	Garth Brooks	Garth Brooks	Capitol	Platinum	Album
Jun.	Kentucky Headhunters	Electric Barnyard	Polygram	Gold	Album
Jul.	Dwight Yoakam	If There Was a Way	Warner	Platinum	Album
Jul.	Anne Murray	Danny's Song	Capitol	Gold	Album
Aug.	Alan Jackson	Don't Rock the Jukebox	BMG	Gold	Album
Sep.	Garth Brooks	No Fences	Capitol	2 Plat.	Album
Sep.	Reba McEntire	Rumor Has It	MCA	Platinum	Album
Sep.	Garth Brooks	Ropin' the Wind	Capitol	Gold	Album
Sep.	Garth Brooks	Ropin' the Wind	Capitol	Platinum	Album
Sep.	Travis Tritt	Country Club	Warner	Gold	Album
Sep.	Ricky Van Shelton	His Very Best	Sony	Gold	Album
Oct.	Clint Black	Put Yourself in My Shoes	BMG	Platinum	Album
Oct.	Ricky Van Shelton	Loving Proof	Sony	Platinum	Album
Oct.	Ricky Van Shelton	Wild-Eyed Dream	Sony	Platinum	Album
Oct.	Amy Grant	Heart in Motion	A & M	Platinum	Album
Oct.	The Judds	Love Can Build a Bridge	BMG	Gold	Album
Oct.	Ricky Van Shelton	Backroads	Sony	Gold	Album
Oct.	Ricky Van Shelton	RVS III	Sony	Gold	Album
Oct.	Vince Gill	Pocket Full of Gold	MCA	Gold	Album
Oct.	Mark Chestnutt	Too Cold at Home	MCA	Gold	Album
Nov.	Dolly Parton	Eagle When She Flies	Sony	Gold	Album

Nov.	Carlene Carter	I Fell in Love	Warner	Gold	Album
Dec.	Various Artists	Country Heat	BMG	Gold	Album
Dec.	Reba McEntire	For My Broken Heart	MCA	Gold	Album
Dec.	Travis Tritt	It's All About to Change	Warner	Gold	Album
Dec.	Randy Travis	High Lonesome	Warner	Gold	Album
1992					
Feb.	Vince Gill	Pocket Full of Gold	MCA	Platinum	Album
Feb.	Vince Gill	When I Call Your Name	MCA	Platinum	Album
Feb.	Prairie Oyster	Everybody Knows	BMG	Gold	Album
Feb.	Trisha Yearwood	Trisha Yearwood	MCA	Gold	Album
Apr.	Garth Brooks	No Fences	Capitol	3 Plat.	Album
Apr.	Garth Brooks	Ropin' the Wind	Capitol	2 Plat.	Album
Apr.	Wynonna	Wynonna	MCA	Gold	Album
Apr.	k.d. lang	Ingenue	Warner	Gold	Album
May	Travis Tritt	It's All About to Change	Warner	Platinum	Album
May	Kathy Mattea	A Collection of Hits	Polygram	Gold	Album
May	The Judds	From the Heart	BMG	Gold	Album
May	Ian Tyson	I Outgrew the Wagon	Stony Plain	Gold	Album
Jun.	Billy Ray Cyrus	Some Gave All	Polygram	Gold	Album
Jun.	Billy Ray Cyrus	Some Gave All	Polygram	Platinum	Album
Jun.	Marty Stuart	Tempted	MCA	Gold	Album
Jul.	k.d. lang	Ingenue	Warner	Platinum	Album
Aug.	Billy Ray Cyrus	Some Gave All	Polygram	2 Plat.	Album
Aug.	Billy Ray Cyrus	Some Gave All	Polygram	3 Plat.	Album
Aug.	Blue Rodeo	Outskirts	Warner	3 Plat.	Album
Aug.	Alan Jackson	Don't Rock the Jukebox	BMG	Platinum	Album
Aug.	Blue Rodeo	Lost Together	Warner	Gold	Album
Aug.	Blue Rodeo	Lost Together	Warner	Platinum	Album
Aug.	Lorrie Morgan	Something in Red	BMG	Gold	Album
Sep.	Roger Whittaker	Greatest Hits	BMG	5 Plat.	Album
Sep.	Garth Brooks	No Fences	Capitol	4 Plat.	Album
Sep.	Garth Brooks	Ropin' the Wind	Capitol	3 Plat.	Album
Sep.	Garth Brooks	Garth Brooks	Capitol	2 Plat.	Album
Sep.	Garth Brooks	The Chase	Capitol	Gold	Album
Sep.	Garth Brooks	The Chase	Capitol	Platinum	Album
Sep.	Garth Brooks	The Chase	Capitol	2 Plat.	Album
Sep.	Reba McEntire	For My Broken Heart	MCA	Platinum	Album
Sep.	Garth Brooks	Beyond the Season	Capitol	Gold	Album
Sep.	Garth Brooks	Beyond the Season	Capitol	Platinum	Album
Sep.	Michelle Wright	Now and Then	BMG	Gold	Album
Sep.	Brooks & Dunn	Brand New Man	BMG	Gold	Album
Sep.	Clint Black	The Hard Way	BMG	Gold	Album
Sep.	Marty Stuart	Hillbilly Rock	MCA	Gold	Album
Sep.	Marty Stuart	This One's Gonna Hurt You	MCA	Gold	Album
Sep.	Travis Tritt	T-R-O-U-B-L-E	Warner	Gold	Album
Oct.	Billy Ray Cyrus	Some Gave All	Polygram	4 Plat.	Album
Oct.	Billy Ray Cyrus	Some Gave All	Polygram	5 Plat.	Album

Oct.	Wynonna	Wynonna	MCA	Platinum	Album
Oct.	Vince Gill	I Still Believe in You	MCA	Gold	Album
Oct.	Various Artists	Honeymoon in Vegas/Original Motion Picture Soundtrack	Sony	Gold	Album
Oct.	Various Artists	More Country Heat	BMG	Gold	Album
Nov.	Elvis Presley	Elvis the King of Rock 'n' Roll—The Complete 50's Masters	BMG	Gold	Album
Nov.	Elvis Presley	Elvis the King of Rock 'n' Roll—The Complete 50's Masters	BMG	Platinum	Album
Nov.	The Rankin Family	Fare Thee Well	Capitol	Gold	Album
Nov.	Trisha Yearwood	Hearts in Armor	MCA	Gold	Album
Nov.	Sammy Kershaw	Don't Go Near the Water	Polygram	Gold	Album
Dec.	Kenny Rogers	His Greatest Hits & Finest Performances	Capitol	Gold	B/Set
Dec.	Kenny Rogers	His Greatest Hits & Finest Performances	Capitol	Platinum	B/Set
Dec.	Kenny Rogers	His Greatest Hits & Finest Performances	Capitol	2 Plat.	B/Set
Dec.	Billy Ray Cyrus	Some Gave All	Polygram	6 Plat.	Album
Dec.	Prairie Oyster	Everybody Knows	BMG	Platinum	Album
Dec.	Anne Murray	Her Greatest Hits & Finest Performances	Capitol	Gold	B/Set
Dec.	Anne Murray	Her Greatest Hits & Finest Performances	Capitol	Platinum	B/Set
Dec.	Various Artists	Honeymoon in Vegas/Original Motion Picture Soundtrack	Sony	Platinum	Album
Dec.	Alvin & the Chipmunks	Chipmunks in Low Places	Sony	Gold	Album
Dec.	Alvin & the Chipmunks	Chipmunks in Low Places	Sony	Platinum	Album
Dec.	George Strait	Pure Country	MCA	Gold	Album
Dec.	Alan Jackson	A Lot About Livin' (and a Little 'Bout Love)	BMG	Gold	Album
Dec.	Amy Grant	Home for Christmas	A & M	Gold	Album
Dec.	Reba McEntire	It's Your Call	MCA	Gold	Album
1993					
Jan.	The Rankin Family	Fare Thee Well	Capitol	Platinum	Album
Jan.	Vince Gill	I Still Believe in You	MCA	Platinum	Album
Jan.	George Fox	George Fox	Warner Music	Gold	Album
Jan.	Mark Chesnutt	Longnecks & Short Stories	MCA	Gold	Album
Jan.	Alabama	American Pride	BMG Music	Gold	Album
Feb.	Rita MacNeil	Now the Bell Rings	Virgin	3 Plat.	Album
Feb.	Rita MacNeil	Home I'll Be	Virgin	2 Plat.	Album
Feb.	Sawyer Brown	The Boys Are Back	Capitol	Platinum	Album
Feb.	Sawyer Brown	Greatest Hits	Capitol	Gold	Album
Feb.	Reba McEntire	Greatest Hits	MCA	Platinum	Album
Feb.	Rita MacNeil	Thinking of You	Virgin Music	Gold	Album
Feb.	Rita MacNeil	Thinking of You	Virgin Music	Platinum	Album
Mar.	Brooks & Dunn	Brand New Man	BMG Music	Platinum	Album
Mar.	Michelle Wright	Now and Then	BMG Music	Platinum	Album
Mar.	Rosanne Cash	King's Record Shop	Sony Music	Platinum	Album
Mar.	Elvis Presley	The Number 1 Hits	BMG Music	Gold	Album
Mar.	Lorrie Morgan	Watch Me	BMG Music	Gold	Album
Mar.	John Anderson	Seminole Wind	BMG Music	Gold	Album
Mar.	Rosanne Cash	Seven Year	Sony Music	Gold	Album

Mar.	Rosanne Cash	Hits 1979-1989	Sony Music	Gold	Album
Apr.	Billy Ray Cyrus	Some Gave All	Polygram	7 Plat.	Album
Apr.	k.d. lang	Ingenue	Warner Music	2 Plat.	Album
Apr.	The Rankin Family	Fare Thee Well	Capitol	2 Plat.	Album
Apr.	Reba McEntire	It's Your Call	MCA	Platinum	Album
Apr.	Dwight Yoakam	This Time	Warner Music	Gold	Album
Apr.	Michael W. Smith	Go West Young Man	Word Communications	Gold	Album
Apr.	The Rankin Family	The Rankin Family	EMI Music	Gold	Album
Apr.	Mary-Chapin Carpenter	Come On, Come On	Sony Music	Gold	Album
Jun.	Brooks & Dunn	Hard Workin' Man	BMG Music	Gold	Album
Jun.	Various Artists	Country Heat 3	BMG Music	Gold	Album
Jul.	Blue Rodeo	Diamond Mine	Warner Music	3 Plat.	Album
Jul.	Wynonna	Wynonna	MCA	2 Plat.	Album
Jul.	Brooks & Dunn	Hard Workin' Man	BMG Music	Platinum	Album
Jul.	Michelle Wright	Michelle Wright	BMG Music	Gold	Album
Jul.	Pirates of the Mississippi	Pirates of the Mississippi	EMI Music	Gold	Album
Jul.	Tanya Tucker	What Do I Do With Me	EMI Music	Gold	Album
Jul.	Tanya Tucker	What Do I Do With Me	EMI Music	Platinum	Album
Jul.	Various Artists	Kickin' Country	Sony Music	Gold	Album
Aug.	The Rankin Family	Fare Thee Well	EMI Music	3 Plat.	Album
Aug.	Dwight Yoakam	This Time	Warner Music	Platinum	Album
Aug.	Various Artists	Country Heat	BMG Music	Platinum	Album
Aug.	Alan Jackson	A Lot About Livin' (and a Little 'Bout Love)	BMG Music	Platinum	Album
Aug.	Wynonna	Tell Me Why	MCA	Platinum	Album
Sep.	Garth Brooks	No Fences	EMI Music	5 Plat.	Album
Sep.	Garth Brooks	The Chase	EMI Music	3 Plat.	Album
Sep.	Garth Brooks	The Chase	EMI Music	4 Plat.	Album
Sep.	Vince Gill	I Still Believe in You	MCA	2 Plat.	Album
Sep.	Tanya Tucker	Can't Run From Yourself	EMI Music	Gold	Album
Sep.	Tanya Tucker	Can't Run From Yourself	EMI Music	Platinum	Album
Sep.	George Strait	Pure Country	MCA	Platinum	Album
Sep.	The Rankin Family	North Country	EMI Music	Platinum	Album
Sep.	Mary-Chapin Carpenter	Come On, Come On	Sony Music	Platinum	Album
Sep.	Trisha Yearwood	Hearts in Armor	MCA	Platinum	Album
Sep.	Marty Stuart	This One's Gonna Hurt	MCA	Platinum	Album
Sep.	John Michael Montgomery	Life's a Dance	Warner Music	Gold	Album
Sep.	Tracy Lawrence	Alibis	Warner Music	Gold	Album
Sep.	Dolly Parton	Dancing With the Moon	Sony Music	Gold	Album
Sep.	Reba McEntire	Greatest Hits, Vol. II	MCA	Gold	Album
Sep.	Garth Brooks	In Pieces	EMI Music	Gold	Album
Sep.	Garth Brooks	In Pieces	EMI Music	Platinum	Album
Sep.	Garth Brooks	In Pieces	EMI Music	2 Plat.	Album
Sep.	Anne Murray	Croonin'	EMI Music	Gold	Album
Oct.	Roger Whittaker	Celebration	BMG Music	Gold	Album
Nov.	Various Artists	Kickin' Country	Sony Music	Platinum	Album
Nov.	Anne Murray	Croonin'	EMI Music	Platinum	Album
Nov.	Bruce Cockburn	Waiting for a Miracle	Sony Music	Platinum	Album

Nov.	Billy Dean	Fire in the Dark	EMI Music	Gold	Album
Nov.	Alabama	For Our Fans	BMG Music	Gold	Album
Nov.	Elvis Presley	The Essential 60's Masters	BMG Music	Gold	Album
Nov.	Vince Gill	Let There Be Peace on Earth	MCA	Gold	Album
Nov.	Patty Loveless	Only What I Feel	Sony Music	Gold	Album
Nov.	Mark Chesnutt	Almost Goodbye	MCA	Gold	Album
Dec.	Alan Jackson	A Lot About Livin' (and a Little 'Bout Love)	BMG Music	2 Plat.	Album
Dec.	Reba McEntire	Greatest Hits, Vol.II	MCA	Platinum	Album
Dec.	Clay Walker	Clay Walker	Warner Music	Gold	Album
Dec.	Carlene Carter	Little Love Letters	Warner Music	Gold	Album
Dec.	Pam Tillis	Put Yourself in My Place	BMG Music	Gold	Album
Dec.	Pam Tillis	Homeward Looking Angel	BMG Music	Gold	Album
Dec.	Rita MacNeil	Once Upon a Christmas	Virgin Music	Gold	Album
Dec.	Rita MacNeil	Once Upon a Christmas	Virgin Music	Platinum	Album
Dec.	Colin James	Colin James and the Little Big Band	Virgin Music	Gold	Album
Dec.	Blue Rodeo	5 Days in July	Warner Music	Gold	Album
Dec.	Blue Rodeo	5 Days in July	Warner Music	Platinum	Album
Dec.	Various Artists	Common Thread: The Songs of the Eagles	Warner Music	Gold	Album
Dec.	Various Artists	Common Thread: The Songs of the Eagles	Warner Music	Platinum	Album
1994					
Jan.	The Rankin Family	Fare Thee Well	EMI Music	4 Plat.	Album
Jan.	Dwight Yoakam	This Time	Warner Music	2 Plat.	Album
Jan.	Tanya Tucker	Greatest Hits Vol. 2	EMI Music	Gold	Album
Jan.	Sawyer Brown	Outskirts of Town	EMI Music	Gold	Album
Jan.	George Strait	Easy Come, Easy Go	MCA	Gold	Album
Jan.	Trisha Yearwood	The Song Remembers When	MCA	Gold	Album
Jan.	Collin Raye	All I Can Be	Sony Music	Gold	Album
Feb.	Colin James	Colin James	Virgin Music	2 Plat.	Album
Mar.	Vince Gill	I Still Believe in You	MCA	3 Plat.	Album
Mar.	Lorrie Morgan	Watch Me	BMG Music	Platinum	Album
Mar.	Various Artists	Rhythm Country & Blues	MCA	Gold	Album
Mar.	John Michael Montgomery	Kickin' It Up	Warner Music	Gold	Album
Apr.	Alan Jackson	A Lot About Livin' (and a Little 'Bout Love)	BMG Music	3 Plat.	Album
Apr.	Various Artists	The Sound New Country	Warner Music	Platinum	Album
Apr.	Ricky Van Shelton	A Bridge I Didn't Burn	Sony Music	Gold	Album
Apr.	Dolly Parton, Tammy Wynette, & Loretta Lynn	Honky Tonk Angels	Sony Music	Gold	Album
Apr.	Reba McEntire	Read My Mind	MCA	Gold	Album
May	Alan Jackson	Here in the Real World	BMG Music	2 Plat.	Album
May	Colin James	Colin James and the Little Big Band	EMI Music	Platinum	Album
May	Faith Hill	Take Me As I Am	Warner Music	Gold	Album
May	Clint Black	No Time to Kill	BMG Music	Gold	Album
May	Sammy Kershaw	Haunted Heart	Polygram	Gold	Album
May	Various Artists	Country Heat 4	BMG Music	Gold	Album
Jun.	The Rankin Family	North Country	EMI Music	3 Plat.	Album
Jun.	Garth Brooks	In Pieces	EMI Music	3 Plat.	Album

Jun.	Clay Walker	Clay Walker	Warner Music	Platinum	Album
Jun.	Vince Gill	When Love Finds You	MCA	Gold	Album
Jun.	Spirit of the West	Go Figure	Warner Music	Gold	Album
Jun.	Tim McGraw	Not a Moment Too Soon	EMI Music	Gold	Album
Jun.	Tanya Tucker	Soon	EMI Music	Gold	Album
Jul.	Tim McGraw	Not a Moment Too Soon	EMI Music	Platinum	Album
Jul.	Alabama	The Cheap Seats	BMG Music	Gold	Album
Jul.	Alan Jackson	Who I Am	BMG Music	Gold	Album
Jul.	Prairie Oyster	Only One Moon	BMG Music	Gold	Album
Aug.	John Michael Montgomery	Kickin' It Up	Warner Music	Platinum	Album
Aug.	Tracy Lawrence	Sticks and Stones	Warner Music	Gold	Album
Aug.	Doug Stone	More Love	Sony Music	Gold	Album
Aug.	Little Texas	Big Time	Warner Music	Gold	Album
Aug.	Collin Raye	Extremes	Sony Music	Gold	Album
Sep.	Alan Jackson	Who I Am	BMG Music	Platinum	Album
Sep.	Various Artists	Rhythm, Country & Blues	MCA	Platinum	Album
Sep.	Joe Diffie	Honky Tonk Attitude	Sony Music	Gold	Album
Sep.	Amy Grant	House of Love	A & M	Gold	Album
Sep.	The Mavericks	What a Crying Shame	MCA	Gold	Album
Sep.	Lorrie Morgan	War Paint	BMG Music	Gold	Album
Sep.	Bruce Cockburn	Inner City Front	Sony Music	Gold	Album
Oct.	Billy Ray Cyrus	It Won't Be the Last	Polygram	2 Plat.	Album
Oct.	Sammy Kershaw	Don't Go Near the Water	Polygram	Platinum	Album
Oct.	Righteous Brothers	Best Of	EMI Music	Platinum	Album
Oct.	Michelle Wright	The Reasons Why	BMG Music	Gold	Album
Oct.	David Ball	Thinkin' Problem	Warner Music	Gold	Album
Oct.	Charlie Major	The Other Side	BMG Music	Gold	Album
Oct.	Neal McCoy	No Doubt About It	Warner Music	Gold	Album
Oct.	Barney Bentall & the Legendary Hearts	Ain't Life Strange	Sony Music	Gold	Album
Oct.	Anne Murray	Best of the Season	EMI Music	Gold	Album
Oct.	Ray Stevens	Ray Stevens Comedy Classics	EMI Music	4 Plat.	Video
Oct.	Alan Jackson	Livin', Lovin' and Rockin' the Jukebox	BMG Music	Gold	Video
Oct.	Ray Stevens	Live	EMI Music	Gold	Video
Nov.	Blue Rodeo	5 Days in July	Warner Music	2 Plat.	Album
Nov.	Eagles	Hell Freezes Over	MCA	Platinum	Album
Nov.	Eagles	Hell Freezes Over	MCA	2 Plat.	Album
Nov.	Rita MacNeil	Collection	Virgin Music	Platinum	Album
Nov.	Reba McEntire	Read My Mind	MCA	Platinum	Album
Nov.	Mary-Chapin Carpenter	Stones on the Road	Sony Music	Gold	Album
Nov.	Anne Murray	The Best . . . So Far	EMI Music	Gold	Album
Nov.	Lyle Lovett	And His Big Band	MCA	Gold	Album

ADDRESSES

AGENTS

Ace Productions
4825 Shasta Drive
Old Hickory, TN 37138-4124
Tel.: (615) 889-1147
Contact: Jimmy Case

Agency for the Performing Arts
9000 Sunset Blvd., Suite 1200
Los Angeles, CA 90069
Tel.: (213) 273-0744
Contact: Bonnie Sugarman

All Star Talent
1824 Acacia Drive
Laplace, LA 70068
Tel.: (504) 652-3061
Contact: Jeff Whitlow

Rex Allen, Sr.
PO Box 1111
Sonita, AZ 85637
Tel.: (602) 455-5805
Contact: Rex Allen, Sr.

American Concert & Touring
PO Box 24599
Nashville, TN 37202
Tel.: (615) 244-2290
Contact: Jesse Garon

American Management, Inc.
17530 Ventura Blvd., Suite 108
Encino, CA 91316
Tel.: (818) 981-6500
Contact: Jim Wagner

The Beacham Agency
PO Box 125
Nashville, TN 37202
Tel.: (615) 327-0777
Contact: Richard Beacham

The Blade Agency
PO Box 1556
Gainesville, FL 32602
Tel.: (904) 372-8158
Contact: Charles Stedham

The Box Office, Inc.
1010 16th Avenue South
Nashville, TN 37212
Tel.: (615) 321-0001

Keith Case & Associates
59 Music Square West
Nashville, TN 37203
Tel.: (615) 327-4646
Contact: Keith Case

Center Stage Attractions
PO Box 23795
Nashville, TN 37202
Tel.: (615) 254-7844
Contact: Clyde Masters

Chardon, Inc.
3198 Royal Lane, Suite 204
Dallas, TX 75229
Tel.: (214) 350-4650
Contact: Daniel Hexter

Chief Talent Corporation
33 Music Square West, Suite 110
Nashville, TN 37203
Tel.: (615) 256-7101
Contact: James Yelich

Circuit Riders Talent
123 Walton Ferry Road, 2nd Floor
Hendersonville, TN 37075
Tel.: (615) 824-1947
Contact: Linda Dotson

Creative Artists Agency, Inc.
3310 West End Avenue, 5th Floor
Nashville, TN 37203
Tel.: (615) 383-8787
Contact: Ron Baird

Creative Artists Agency
9830 Wilshire Blvd.
Beverly Hills, CA 90212
Tel.: (310) 277-4545

Billy Deaton Enterprises
1300 Division Street, Suite 103
Nashville, TN 37203
Tel.: (615) 244-4259
Contact: Billy Deaton

E & R Music
PO Box 546
Kirkland Lake, Ont., P2N 3LA
Canada
Tel.: (705) 567-5351
Contact: Mary Bailey

Al Embry International
PO Box 23162
Nashville, TN 37202
Tel.: (615) 327-4074
Contact: Alton Embry

Encore Talent, Inc.
2137 Zercher Road
San Antonio, TX 78209
Tel.: (512) 822-2655

Entertainment Artists
819 18th Avenue South
Nashville, TN 37203
Tel.: (615) 320-7041
Contact: Dan Wojcik

Scott Faragher
123 Taggart
Nashville, TN 37205
Tel.: (615) 353-0573
Contact: Scott Faragher

Folklore Productions
1671 Appian Way
Santa Monica, CA 90401
Tel.: (213) 451-0767

Don Fowler & Associates
50 Music Square West
UA Tower, Suite 205
Nashville, TN 37203
Tel.: (615) 321-5323
Contact: Don Fowler

Janie Fricke Concerts
PO Box 798
Lancaster, TX 75146
Tel.: (817) 572-2074

Kathy Gangwisch & Associates
207 Westport Road
Kansas City, MO 64111
Tel.: (816) 931-8000
Contact: Kathy Gangwisch

Harp Agency
1018 17th Avenue South, Suite 3
Nashville, TN 37212
Tel.: (615) 321-5223
Contact: David Harp

Lib Hatcher Agency
1610 16th Avenue South
Nashville, TN 37212
Tel.: (615) 383-7258
Contact: Lib Hatcher

David Hickey Agency
PO Box 330160
Fort Worth, TX 76163
Tel.: (817) 346-6666
Contact: David Hickey

Horizon Talent
2500 Hillsboro Road, Suite 200
Nashville, TN 37212
Tel.: (615) 269-5518
Contact: Tom Laffey

ICM
8899 Beverly Blvd.
Los Angeles, CA 90048
Tel.: (213) 550-4000

International Management
818 19th Avenue South
Nashville, TN 37203
Tel.: (615) 321-5025
Contact: Eddie Rhines

ITG
729 7th Avenue
New York, NY 10019
Tel.: (212) 221-7878

Buddy Lee Attractions, Inc.
38 Music Square East, Suite 300
Nashville, TN 37203
Tel.: (615) 244-4336
Contact: Tony Conway

Mandrell Management
PO Box 800
Hendersonville, TN 37203-3219
Tel.: (615) 822-7200

McFadden Artists Corp.
818 18th Avenue South
Nashville, TN 37203
Tel.: (615) 242-1500
Contact: Jack McFadden

Larry McFaden Enterprises
48 Music Square East
Nashville, TN 37203
Tel.: (615) 255-4600

Monterey Artists
33 Music Square West
Nashville, TN 37203
Tel.: (615) 726-0950
Contact: Steve Dahl

Dale Morris & Associates
818 19th Avenue South
Nashville, TN 37203
Tel.: (615) 327-3400
Contact: Dale Morris

William Morris Agency
PO Box 150245
Nashville, TN 37215
Tel.: (615) 385-0310
Contact: Paul Moore/Rick Shipp

MTE, Inc.
PO Box 687
Bullard, TX 75757
Tel.: (903) 825-6957
Contact: Sharon Dengler

Music Square Talent
11 Music Square East, Suite 204
Nashville, TN 37203
Tel.: (615) 742-8845
Contact: Allen Whitcomb

North American Tours
128 Volunteer Drive
Hendersonville, TN 37075
Tel.: (615) 822-1401
Contact: C.K. Spurlock

Scott O'Malley & Associates
PO Box 9188
Colorado Springs, CO 80932
Tel.: (719) 635-7776

Pro Tours, Inc.
1321 Murfreesboro Road, Suite 100
Nashville, TN 37217
Tel.: (615) 361-5200
Contact: Steven Pritchard

Gerard W. Purcell & Assoc. Ltd.
964 2nd Avenue, 3rd Floor
New York, NY 10022
Tel.: (212) 421-2670
Contact: Gerard Purcell

Bobby Roberts Entertainment
PO Box 3007
Hendersonville, TN 37077
Tel.: (615) 859-8899
Contact: Bobby Roberts

Santa Fe World Music Agency
609 Onate Place
Santa Fe, NM 87501
Tel.: (505) 988-8037

StarStruck Talent
PO Box 121996
Nashville, TN 37212-1996
Tel.: (615) 742-8835
Contact: Narvel Blackstock

Statlers Productions
PO Box 2703
Staunton, VA 24401
Tel.: (703) 885-7297
Contact: Marshall Grant

The Talent Agency
PO Box 1040
Hendersonville, TN 37077-1040
Tel.: (615) 822-1143
Contact: Jimmie Jay

Joe Taylor Artist Agency
48 Music Square East
Nashville, TN 37203
Tel.: (615) 242-5588
Contact: Joe Taylor

Tessier-Marsh Talent, Inc.
505 Canton Pass
Madison, TN 37115
Tel.: (615) 868-3440
Contact: Roy Tessier/Rena Marsh

Titley Quinn
706 18th Avenue South
Nashville, TN 37203
Tel.: (615) 255-1326
Contact: Bob Titley/Walt Quinn

Top Billing International
PO Box 121089
Nashville, TN 37212
Tel.: (615) 327-1133
Contact: Tandy Rice

Tim Tye
1808 West End Avenue, Suite 1009
Nashville, TN 37203
Tel.: (615) 320-5320

Variety Artists
2980 Beverly Glen Circle, #302
Los Angeles, CA 90077
Tel.: (310) 475-8900

The Wintersett Agency
890 Everett Street
Lakewood, CO 80215
Tel.: (303) 234-1144

The Erv Woolsey Co.
1000 18th Avenue South
Nashville, TN 37212
Tel.: (615) 329-2402
Contact: Erv Woolsey

World Class Talent
48 Music Square East
Nashville, TN 37203
Tel.: (615) 244-1964
Contact: Joann Berry

ARTISTS' MANAGERS

Ritchie Albright
5810 Peach Hollow Road
Franklin, TN 37064
Tel.: (615) 794-2172

Bruce Allen
406-68 Water Street
Vancouver, B.C. V6B 4E9
Canada
Tel.: (604) 688-7274

Rick Alter
Rick Alter Management, Inc.
PO Box 150973
Nashville, TN 37215-1702
Tel.: (615) 292-6313

Mieke Appel
3124B Long Road
Nashville, TN 37203

Mae Boren Axton
Mae Boren Axton Public Relations
PO Box 976
Hendersonville, TN 37075
Tel.: (615) 822-6033

Mary Bailey
Mary Bailey Management
One Music Circle South, Suite 3
Nashville, TN 37203
Tel.: (615) 259-9272

Mickey Baker
128 Volunteer Drive
Hendersonville, TN 37075
Tel.: (615) 822-0991

Bobby Bare
PO Box 2422
Hendersonville, TN 37075
Tel.: (615) 824-9372

Miles Bell Williams
Bell & Associates
707 18th Avenue South
Nashville, TN 37203
Tel.: (615) 327-8008

Frances Bellamy
Bellamy Brothers Ents.
201 Restless Lane
Dade City, FL 33525
Tel.: (904) 588-3628

Al Beneta
Oh Boy Records
4121 Wilshire Blvd., Suite 204
Los Angeles, CA 90010
Tel.: (213) 385-0882

Phyllis Bennett
Take Three Entertainment
815 18th Avenue South
Nashville, TN 37203
Tel.: (615) 327-8060

Ray Benson
Bismeaux Productions
PO Box 463
Austin, TX 78767
Tel.: (512) 444-9944

Jerry Bentley
1311 Elm Hill Pike
Nashville, TN 37210
Tel.: (615) 242-2166

Geoff Berne
American Arts Prodns., Inc.
1650 N.W. Washington Blvd.
Hamilton, OH 45013
Tel.: (513) 895-7300

Narvel Blackstock
StarStruck Talent
PO Box 121996
Nashville, TN 37212-1996
Tel.: (615) 742-8835

Gary Borman
Borman Entertainment
9220 Sunset Blvd., Suite 320
Los Angeles, CA 90069
Tel.: (213) 859-9292

Will Botwin
Side One Management
1775 Broadway, 7th Floor
New York, NY 10019
Tel.: (212) 307-1015

Woody Bowles
The Woody Bowles Company
5420 Camelot Road
Brentwood, TN 37027
Tel.: (615) 370-4848

Gloria Boyce
Peter Asher & Associates
644 North Doheny
Los Angeles, CA 90069
Tel.: (310) 273-9433

Robert Bradley
Bradley Artists
5880 South Quebec
Tulsa, OK 74135
Tel.: (918) 448-0335

D.D. Bray
Celebrity Country Artists
5 Rushing Creek Court
Roanoke, TX 76262
Tel.: (817) 491-3651

Bobby Brenner
Bill Anderson Enterprises
31 Amhearst Drive
New Rochelle, NY 10804

David Brokaw
The Brokaw Company
9255 Sunset Blvd., Suite 706
Los Angeles, CA 90069
Tel.: (310) 273-2060

Allen Brown
Plan A. Inc.
1900 Church Street, Suite 102
Nashville, TN 37203
Tel.: (615) 321-1040

Teri Brown
TBA Management
147 Bell Canyon Road
Bell Canyon, CA 91301
Tel.: (818) 712-0311

Jackson Brumley
Jackson Brumley Management
128 Pin Oak Drive
Hendersonville, TN 37075
Tel.: (615) 352-3770

John Bumgardner
Sportsman Music Ent. Group
1207 17th Avenue South, Suite 301
Nashville, TN 37212
Tel: (615) 320-1900

Bob Burwell
818 18th Avenue South
Nashville, TN 37203
Tel.: (615) 321-5656

Stan Byrd
1106 16th Avenue South
Nashville, TN 37212
Tel.: (615) 244-7445

Will Byrd/Rich Schwan
1306 South Street
Nashville, TN 37212
Tel.: (615) 242-4400

Frank Callari
TCA Group
PO Box 23329
Nashville, TN 37201
Tel.: (615) 251-0007

Alie Campbell
Creative Directions
713 18th Avenue South
Nashville, TN 37203
Tel.: (615) 329-4939

Michael Campbell
Michael Campbell & Associates
PO Box 121754
Nashville, TN 37212-1754
Tel.: (615) 259-4985

Kathleen Capper
High Time Management
39 East Field Drive
Rolling Hills, CA 90274
Tel.: (213) 541-8493

Tom Carrico
Studio I Artists, Inc.
7003 Carroll Avenue
Takoma Park, MD 20912
Tel.: (301) 891-0700

Bill Carter
1114 17th Avenue South, Suite 204
Nashville, TN 37203
Tel.: (615) 327-1270

Jeff Carver
Music Matters Management
11 Music Square East, Suite 103
Nashville, TN 37203
Tel.: (615) 259-2415

Keith Case
Keith Case & Associates
59 Music Square West
Nashville, TN 37203
Tel.: (615) 327-4646

Kathy Chrestman
Monroe Enterprises
3819 Dickerson Road
Nashville, TN 37207
Tel.: (615) 868-3333

Barry Coburn
Ten Ten Management
33 Music Square West, Suite 110
Nashville, TN 37203
Tel.: (615) 255-9955

Bruce Cohn
Bruce Cohn Management
15140 Sonoma Highway
Glen Ellen, CA 95442
Tel.: (707) 938-4060

Fred Conley
2809 Glen Oaks Drive
Nashville, TN 37214
Tel.: (615) 391-0574

Mike Cook
Network Entertainment
1280 Winchester Parkway, Suite 245
Altanta, GA 30080
Tel.: (404) 319-8822

Maria Cooper-Brunner
Insight Management
1209 16th Avenue South, Suite 401
Nashville, TN 37212
Tel.: (615) 329-8090

David Corlew
The Charlie Daniels Band
17060 Central Pike
Lebanon, TN 37087
Tel.: (615) 443-2112

Tony Cornell
Crash Craddock Enterprises
PO Box 16426
Greensboro, NC 27416-0426
Tel.: (615) 889-1147

Fred Cortez
621 S.W. 111th Street
Oklahoma, OK 73170
Tel.: (405) 692-0346

Ronald Cotton
C & M Productions
5114 Albert Drive
Brentwood, TN 37027
Tel.: (615) 371-5098

Steve Cox
Scott Dean Agency
612 Humbolt Street
Reno, NV 89509
Tel.: (702) 322-9426

Floyd Cramer
Floyd Cramer Enterprises
110 Glancy Street
Goodlettsville, TN 37072
Tel.: (615) 255-8578

Tanja Crouch
Turn Key Management
PO Box 121972,
Nashville, TN 37212
Tel.: (615) 321-2833

Jerry Crowe
Crowe Enterprises, Inc.
44 Music Square East, Suite 711
Nashville, TN 37203
Tel.: (615) 832-1835

Mike Crowley
Mike Crowley Artist Management
122 Longwood Avenue
Austin, TX 78734
Tel.: (512) 261-7755

Jeff Davis
Sum Management, Inc.
PO Box 1020
Hendersonville, TN 37077
Tel.: (615) 822-8184

Richard Davis
Tater-Patch Records
PO Box 11276
Kansas City, MO 64119
Tel.: (816) 452-5412

Roy Dey
620 Templewood Court
Nashville, TN 37214
Tel.: (615) 885-7497

Stuart Dill
Refugee Management, Inc.
1025 16th Avenue South, Suite 300
Nashville, TN 37217
Tel.: (615) 329-1546

Christy Dinapoli
Square West Entertainments
PO Box 120053
Nashville, TN 37212
Tel.: (615) 329-0851

John Dorris
Hallmark Direction Company
1819 Broadway
Nashville, TN 37203
Tel.: (615) 320-7714

John Dotson
International Management
818 19th Avenue South
Nashville, TN 37203
Tel.: (615) 321-5025

Linda Dotson
123 Walton Ferry Road, 2nd Floor
Hendersonville, TN 37075
Tel.: (615) 321-0140

John Doumanian
John Doumanian Management
201 E. 77th Street, Suite 12A
New York, NY 10021
Tel.: (212) 535-7911

James Dowell
James Dowell Management
50 Music Square West, Suite 207
Nashville, TN 37203
Tel.: (615) 320-5629

Bob Doyle
Doyle/Lawson Management
1109 17th Avenue South
Nashville, TN 37212
Tel.: (615) 329-4150

Sharon Eaves
Sharon Eaves Management
PO Box 121551
Nashville, TN 37212
Tel.: (615) 320-0741

Wayne Edwards
Tracy Lawrence Enterprises
1214 16th Avenue South
Nashville, TN 37212
Tel.: (615) 329-0900

Karl Engemann
United Management
3325 N. University Avenue, Suite 150
Provo, UT 84604
Tel.: (801) 373-3600

Barbara Fairchild
15 Music Square West
Nashville, TN 37203
Tel.: (615) 794-9064

Scott Faragher
123 Taggart
Nashville, TN 37205
Tel.: (615) 353-0573

Brian Ferriman
Savannah Music Group
1207 17th Avenue South, Suite 305
Nashville, TN 37212
Tel.: (615) 329-4747

Larry Fitzgerald
The Fitzgerald Hartley Company
50 West Main Street
Ventura, CA 93001
Tel.: (805) 641-6441

Chuck Flood
Chuck Flood & Associates
PO Box 121885
Nashville, TN 37212
Tel.: (615) 329-9902

D. Noel Fox
PO Box 120551
Nashville, TN 37212
Tel.: (615) 329-1620

Mitchell Fox
The Kentucky Headhunters
447 East 65th Street, Suite 3-CC
New York, NY 10021
Tel.: (212) 472-9888

Ted Fuller
Music Park Talent, Inc.
116 17th Avenue South
Nashville, TN 37203
Tel.: (615) 242-5044

Kathy Gangwisch
Kathy Gangwisch & Associates
207 Westport Road
Kansas City, MO 64111
Tel.: (816) 931-8000

Bonnie Garner
Rothbaum and Garner
38 Music Square East, Suite 218
Nashville, TN 37203
Tel.: (615) 259-9050

Bill Gatzimos
Gayle Enterprises, Inc.
51 Music Square East
Nashville, TN 37203
Tel.: (615) 327-2651

Tracy Gershon
Sony Tree
8 Music Square West
Nashville, TN 37203
Tel.: (615) 726-0890

Steve Goetzman
Renaissance Management
PO Box 1647
Franklin, TN 37065-1647
Tel.: (615) 591-8930

Ron Golden
Golden Eagle Management
168 Hickory Heights Drive, Suite F-88
Hendersonville, TN 37075
Tel.: (615) 832-0337

Dan Goodman
Vector Management
1500 17th Avenue South
Nashville, TN 37212-8037
Tel.: (615) 386-9090

Tony Gottlieb
Morningstar Management
PO Box 1770
Hendersonville, TN 37077
Tel.: (615) 824-9439

Marshall Grant
Statlers Productions
PO Box 2703
Staunton, VA 24401
Tel.: (703) 885-7297

Mitch Greenhill
1671 Appian Way
Santa Monica, CA 90401
Tel.: (213) 451-0767

Ted Hacker
International Artist Management
1105 16th Avenue South, Suite D
Nashville, TN 37212
Tel.: (615) 329-9394

Susan Hackney
Susan Hackney Associates
33 Music Square West, Suite 104B
Nashville, TN 37203
Tel.: (615) 244-7976

Ron Haffkine
Ron Haffkine Enterprises
PO Box 121017
Nashville, TN 37221
Tel.: (615) 662-2727

Lib Hatcher
Lib Hatcher Agency
1610 16th Avenue South
Nashville, TN 37212
Tel.: (615) 383-7258

Kenneth Hatley
Ken Hatley & Associates, Inc.
486 Osceola Street
Clermont, FL 34711
Tel.: (305) 834-0920

Eloise Jones Hawkins
116 Allen Road
Hendersonville, TN 37075
Tel.: (615) 824-1484

Bobby Heller
Hazel & Heller
900 19th Avenue South
Nashville, TN 37212
Tel.: (615) 327-8741

Richard Helm
Warner Bros.
PO Box 120897
Nashville, TN 37212
Tel.: (615) 320-7525

Scott Heuerman
Warner Bros. Records
1815 Division Street
Nashville, TN 37203
Tel.: (615) 320-7525

Daniel Hexter
Management Associates
10620 Marquis Lane
Dallas, TX 75229
Tel.: (214) 350-4650

Raymond Hicks
The Entertainment Group
1025 16th Avenue South, Suite 401
Nashville, TN 37212
Tel.: (615) 327-3900

Peter Himberger
Dream Street Management
1460 4th Street, Suite 205
Santa Monica, CA 90401
Tel.: (310) 395-6550

Monty Hitchcock
PO Box 159007
Nashville, TN 37215
Tel.: (615) 292-2896

John Hitt
Roy Clark Productions
3225 S. Norwood
Tulsa, OK 74135
Tel.: (918) 663-3883

Gary Hood
Shelly West, Inc.
PO Box 158718
Nashville, TN 37215
Tel.: (615) 244-2344

Alan Hopper
Boy Hopper Management
2350 Rodney Drive
Reno, NV 89509-3845
Tel.: (702) 322-1570

Marylou Hyatt
1117 17th Avenue South
Nashville, TN 37212
Tel.: (615) 329-9180

Joe Infuso
Joe Infuso Management
13063 Ventura Blvd., Suite 201
Studio City, CA 91604
Tel.: (818) 992-3481

Nancy Jones
48 Music Square East
Nashville, TN 37203
Tel.: (615) 373-5699

R. Kaltenbach
PO Box 510
Dundee, IL 60118-0510
Tel.: (708) 428-4777

Alan Kates
AMK Management
9 New Street, 2nd Floor
Toronto, Ont. M54 1P7
Canada
Tel.: (416) 531-0726

Gene Kennedy
Gene Kennedy Enterprises
3950 N. Mt. Juliet Road
Mt. Juliet, TN 37122
Tel.: (615) 754-0417

Mark Ketchem
Billy Joe Royal Enterprises
48 Music Square East
Nashville, TN 37203
Tel.: (615) 254-1272

Fred Kewley
Fred Kewley Management
1711 18th Avenue South, Suite D3
Nashville, TN 37212
Tel.: (615) 292-9876

Merle Kilgore
Hank Williams, Jr. Enterprises
PO Box 850
Paris, TN 38242
Tel.: (901) 642-7455

T.K. Kimbrell
TKO Management
4205 Hillsboro Road, Suite 208
Nashville, TN 37215-3339
Tel.: (615) 383-5017

King Enterprises
240 W. Jefferson Street
Louisville, KY 40202
Tel.: (502) 584-5535

Kenn Kingsbury
Black Stallion Country
PO Box 368
Tujunga, CA 91043-0368
Tel.: (818) 352-8142

Steve Knill
Impresario Ltd.
16535 West Blue Mound Road, Suite 230
Brookfield, WI 53005
Tel.: (414) 786-5600

Ken Kragen
Kragen & Co.
1112 N. Sherbourne Drive
Los Angeles, CA 90069
Tel.: (310) 854-4400

Tom Laffey
Horizon Talent
2500 Hillsboro Road, Suite 200
Nashville, TN 37212
Tel.: (615) 269-5518

Buddy Lee
Buddy Lee Attractions
38 Music Square East
Nashville, TN 37203
Tel.: (615) 244-4336

Ken Levitan
Vector Management
PO Box 128037
Nashville, TN 37212
Tel.: (615) 386-9090

Don Light
Don Light Talent
PO Box 120308
Nashville, TN 37212
Tel.: (615) 298-9944

Mick Lloyd
Advantage Records
1018 17th Avenue South, Suite 11
Nashville, TN 37212
Tel.: (615) 329-9093

John Lomax III
PO Box 120316
Nashville, TN 37212
Tel.: (615) 356-4684

Carlyne Majer
8306 Appalachian
Austin, TX 78759-8413
Tel.: (512) 338-1991

Irby Mandrell
Mandrell Management
PO Box 800
Hendersonville, TN 37077-0800
Tel.: (615) 822-7200

Becky Mares
Michael Martin Murphey Office
207K Paseo del Pueblo Sur
Taos, NM 87571
Tel.: (505) 758-1873

Judi Marshall
Tom T. Hall Enterprises
PO Box 1246
Franklin, TN 37065
Tel.: (615) 371-8767

Lee Marshall
Tangerine Management
1101 17th Avenue South
Nashville, TN 37212
Tel.: (615) 329-0759

Debra McCloud
Mel Tillis Enterprises
809 18th Avenue South
Nashville, TN 37203
Tel.: (615) 255-2300

Jack McFadden
McFadden Artists Corp.
818 18th Avenue South
Nashville, TN 37203
Tel.: (615) 242-1500

Jim McReynolds
PO Box 304
Gallatin, TN 37066
Tel.: (615) 452-6994

Joe Meador
Ronnie McDowell Enterprises
146 Lake Terrace Drive
Hendersonville, TN 37075
Tel.: (615) 824-1946

Blake Mevis
Blake Mevis Music
811 18th Avenue South
Nashville, TN 37203
Tel.: (615) 329-9186

Craig Miller
C.M. Management
7957 Nita Avenue
Kanoga Park, CA 91304
Tel.: (818) 704-7800

Ronnie Milsap
12 Music Circle South
Nashville, TN 37203
Tel.: (615) 256-7575

Tinti Moffat
Balmur Ltd.
Madison Centre
4950 Yonge Street, Suite 2400
Toronto, Ont. M2N 6K1
Canada
Tel.: (416) 223-7700

Stan Moress
Moress, Nanas, Shea Entertainment
1209 16th Avenue South
Nashville, TN 37212
Tel.: (615) 329-9945

Jim Morey
Gallin Morey Associates
8730 Sunset Blvd., Penthouse W
Los Angeles, CA 90069
Tel.: (310) 659-5593

Carolyn Morgan
Everly Bros.
277 Comroe Road
Nashville, TN 37211
Tel.: (615) 831-0242

Chuck Morris
Chuck Morris Ent.
4155 East Jewell Avenue, Suite 412
Denver, CO 80222
Tel.: (303) 782-9292

Dale Morris
Dale Morris & Associates
818 19th Avenue South
Nashville, TN 37203
Tel.: (615) 327-3400

Danny Morrison
Image Management Group, Inc.
11 Music Square East
Nashville, TN 37203
Tel.: (615) 256-9850

Kelly Newby
Guber-Peters Entertainment Company
1990 South Bundy Drive, Penthouse
Los Angeles, CA 90025
Tel.: (310) 820-2100

Paul Overstreet
Paul Overstreet, Inc.
7087 Old Harding Road
Nashville, TN 37211
Tel.: (615) 662-1313

Charles Owen
Fuzzy Owen, Inc.
Box 842
Bakersfield, CA 93302
Tel.: (805) 871-5490

Ben Payne, Jr.
No Payne No Gain Artist Management
PO Box 120331
Nashville, TN 37212-0331
Tel.: (615) 298-3625

Chip Peay
2132 Sharondale Drive
Nashville, TN 37215
Tel.: (615) 298-9260

Ray Pennington
Rt. 1, New Hope Road
Hendersonville, TN 37075
Tel.: (615) 255-3009

Robert Porter
9 Music Square East
Nashville, TN 37203
Tel.: (615) 254-9000

Jim Prater
Hands on Management
42 Music Square West, Suite 335
Nashville, TN 37203
Tel.: (615) 726-1780

Ronnie Prophet
Prophet Records
1030 17th Avenue South
Nashville, TN 37212
Tel.: (615) 321-0539

Gerard Purcell
Gerard W. Purcell & Associates Ltd.
964 2nd Avenue, 3rd Floor
New York, NY 10022
Tel.: (212) 421-2670

Walt Quinn/Bob Titley
Titley Quinn
706 18th Avenue South
Nashville, TN 37203
Tel.: (615) 255-1326

Leonard Rambeau
Balmur Ltd.
Madison Centre
4950 Yonge Street, Suite 2400
Toronto, Ont. M2N 6K1
Canada
Tel.: (416) 223-7700

Tim Rand
Tim Rand Management
PO Box 459
Paragould, AR 72451
Tel.: (615) 327-2251

Norman Ratner
Platinum International Music
2203 Westview Drive
Nashville, TN 37212-4123
Tel.: (615) 292-6002

Suzi Reed
Mountain Magic Talent
285 Burning Tree Drive
Hermitage, TN 37076
Tel.: (615) 885-4679

Simon Renshaw
Senior Management
1025 16th Avenue South, Suite 200
Nashville, TN 37212
Tel.: (615) 321-5200
Fax.: (615) 321-5227

Tandy Rice
Top Billing, Inc.
PO Box 121089
Nashville, TN 37212
Tel.: (615) 327-1133

George Richey
c/o Tammy Wynette Enterprises
1222 16th Avenue South, 2nd Flr.
Nashville, TN 37212-2926

Mitchell Riley
Jeannie C. Riley Enterprises
PO Box 254
Brentwood, TN 37027
Tel.: (615) 791-0022

Ken Ritter
Ritter-Carter Managememt
4345 Thomas Lane
Beaumont, TX 77706
Tel.: (409) 892-3999

Bobby Roberts
Bobby Roberts Entertainment
PO Box 2977
Hendersonville, TN 37077
Tel.: (615) 859-8899

Dave Roberts
John Conlee Enterprises
38 Music Square East, Suite 117
Nashville, TN 37203
Tel.: (615) 726-2676

Mike Robertson
Mike Robertson Management
1232 17th Avenue South
Nashville, TN 37212
Tel.: (615) 383-4299

Lou Robin
Artist Consultants Productions
11777 San Vincente Blvd.
Los Angeles, CA 90049
Tel.: (213) 826-5002

Gaynell Rogers
Gaynell Rogers & Associates
1683 Novato Blvd.
Novato, CA 94947
Tel.: (415) 898-6840

Mark Rothbaum
Mark Rothbaum & Associates
PO Box 2689
Danbury, CT 06813
Tel.: (203) 792-2400

Stan Schneider
Gursey Schneider
10351 Santa Monica Blvd, Suite 300
Santa Monica, CA 90025-5007
Tel.: (213) 552-0960

Louise Scruggs
Scruggs Talent Agency
PO Box 66
Madison, TN 37115
Tel.: (615) 868-2254

Judy Seale
Refugee Management, Inc.
1025 16th Avenue South, Suite 300
Nashville, TN 37212
Tel.: (615) 329-1546

Ronnie Shacklett
Brenda Lee Enterprises
PO Box 101188
Nashville, TN 37210-1188
Tel.: (615) 256-3054

Lisa Shively
The Press Network
Crossroads of the World
6671 Sunset Blvd., Suite 1574
Los Angeles, CA 90028
Tel.: (213) 466-6277

Evelyn Shriver
Shriver Public Relations
1313 16th Avenue South
Nashville, TN 37212
Tel.: (615) 383-1000

Stan Silver
The Silver Organization
PO Box 150527
Nashville, TN 37215
Tel.: (615) 794-0606

Bill Simmons
Fitzgerald Hartey Company
1212 16th Avenue South
Nashville, TN 37212
Tel.: (615) 322-9493

Ricky Skaggs
Ricky Skaggs Enterprises
PO Box 150871
Nashville, TN 37215
Tel.: (615) 255-4563

Tom Skeeter
Carman Productions
15456 Cabrito Road
Van Nuys, CA 91406
Tel.: (213) 873-7370

David Skepner
Buckskin Corporation
7 Music Circle North
Nashville, TN 37203
Tel.: (615) 259-2599

Bobbi Smith
Country Music Parade
PO Box 23771
Nashville, TN 37202
Tel.: (615) 383-8283

Mike Smith
1110 Brentwood Point
Brentwood, TN 37027-7968
Tel.: (615) 790-8270

Robert Smith
First Image
2141 Thompson Road
Murfreesboro, TN 37129
Tel.: (615) 849-9600

Donna Spangler
4316 Glen Eden Drive
Nashville, TN 37205
Tel.: (615) 385-4045

C.K. Spurlock
North American Tours/Starbound
128 Volunteer Drive
Hendersonville, TN 37075
Tel.: (615) 822-1401

Charles Steadham
Blade Agency
PO Box 1556
Gainesville, FL 32602
Tel.: (904) 372-8158

Harriet Sternberg
15260 Ventura Blvd., Suite 110
Sherman Oaks, CA 91403
Tel.: (818) 906-9600

Ken Stilts
Ken Stilts Company, Inc.
PO Box 17087
Nashville, TN 37217
Tel.: (615) 754-6100

Sheri Stokes
Bixmeaux Productions
PO Box 463
Austin, TX 78767
Tel.: (512) 444-9885

Larry Strickland
StarStruck
PO Box 121996
Nashville, TN 37212
Tel.: (615) 742-8835

Roy Tessier/Rena Marsh
Tessier-Marsh Talent, Inc.
505 Canton Pass
Madison, TN 37115
Tel.: (615) 868-3440

Jerry Thompson
Jerry Thompson Management
1100 Broadway
Nashville, TN 37202
Tel.: (615) 384-2102

Bob Titley/Walt Quinn
Titley Quinn
706 18th Avenue South
Nashville, TN 37203
Tel.: (615) 255-1326

David Trask
1117 17th Avenue South
Nashville, TN 37212
Tel.: (615) 329-9180

Beau Tucker
Tanya Tucker Enterprises
Chapple Building
5200 Maryland Way, Suite 103
Brentwood, TN 37027
Tel.: (615) 371-8262

Trey Turner
StarStruck Entertainment
PO Box 121996
Nashville, TN 37212-1996
Tel.: (615) 742-8835

Gladys Van Dyke
Leroy Van Dyke Enterprises
Route 1, Box 271
Smithton, MO 65350
Tel.: (816) 343-5373

Porter Wagoner
PO Box 290785
Nashville, TN 37229-0785
Tel.: (615) 885-8045

Susan Walker
Route 6, Box 41L
Austin, TX 78737
Tel.: (512) 288-1695

Larry Wanagas
Bumstead Productions
1616 W. 3rd Avenue
Vancouver, B.C. V6J 1KU
Canada
Tel.: (604) 736-3512

Drew Weeks
Trailblazer Management
248 Freyer Drive
Marietta, GA 30060
Tel.: (404) 423-1336

Jeff Whitlow
8717 Gary Jim Gray Way
Louisville, KY 40118
Tel.: (502) 635-6613

Donald Williams
c/o Ray Stevens Theatre
3815 West Highway 76
Branson, MO 65616

Erv Woolsey
The Erv Woolsey Co.
1000 18th Avenue South
Nashville, TN 37212
Tel.: (615) 329-2402

RECORD COMPANIES

A & R Records
900 19th Avenue South, Suite 207
Nashville, TN 37212
Tel.: (615) 329-9127
CEO: Ruthie Steele

Affinity Music
749 Appleyard Court
Port Moody, B.C. V3H 3X1
Canada
Contact: John F. Higgins

Altair Four
PO Box 233
Lanark, Ont. K0G 1KO
Canada
Tel.: (613) 259-2085
Contact: Nancy Markle

Arista Records, Inc.
7 Music Circle North
Nashville, TN 37203
Tel.: (615) 780-9100
CEO (Country): Tim DuBois
A & R: Joe Tassi

Art Prorecords
1015 16th Avenue South
Nashville, TN 37212
Tel.: (615) 321-5508

Asylum Records, Inc.
1906 Acklen Avenue
Nashville, TN 37212
Tel.: (615) 292-7990
CEO (Country): Kyle Lehning
A & R: John Condon

ATI Access to Industry
75 Parkway Avenue
Markham, Ont. L3P 2H1
Canada
Tel.: (416) 294-5538
Contact: Scoot Irwin

Atlantic Records
1812 Broadway
Nashville, TN 37203
Tel.: (615) 327-9394
CEO (Country): Rick Blackburn
A & R: Al Cooley

Atlantica Music
1800 Argyle Street, Suite 507
Halifax, N.S. B3J 2N8
Canada
Tel.: (902) 422-7000

Bear Family Records
PO Box 1154
2864 Vollersode
Germany
Tel.: 011-49-04794-1399
CEO: Richard Weize

B.E.I.
2145 Avenue Road
Toronto, Ont. K9V 4S3
Canada
Tel.: (416) 482-6535
Contact: Dale Murray

Benwa Music
Box 357
Lindsay, Ont. K9V 4S3
Canada
Tel.: (416) 274-8874
Contact: Reg Benoit

BGM Records
10452 Sentinel
San Antonio, TX 78217
Tel.: (512) 654-8773

Blue Eye/Sony Music
PO Box 159159
Nashville, TN 37215
Tel.: (615) 297-2588
Contact: Steve Buckingham

Blue Heron Music
310 Queen Street
Charlottetown, P.E.I. C1A 4C2
Canada

BMG Music Canada, Inc.
3640A McNicoll Avenue
Scarborough, Ont. M1X 1G1
Canada
Tel.: (416) 299-9000
Contact: Terry Carson

BMG Music Canada, Inc.
151 John Street, Suite 309
Toronto, Ont. M5V 2T2
Canada
Tel.: (416) 586-0022
Contact: Ken Bain

BMG Music Canada, Inc.
1535 Birmingham Street, 3rd Floor
Halifax, N.S. B3J 2J6
Canada
Tel.: (902) 455-0409
Contact: Chris Jangaard

BMG Music Canada, Inc.
1625 Dublin Avenue, Suite 120
Winnipeg, Man. R3H 0W3
Canada
Tel.: (204) 774-4812
Contact: Robert Tait

BMG Music Canada, Inc.
#145 - 2880 Glenmore Trail S.E.
Glenmore Commerce Court
Calgary, Alta. T2C 2E7
Canada
Tel.: (403) 236-2415
Contact: Doug Kinaschuk

BMG Music Canada, Inc.
10215 178 Street
Edmonton, Alta. T5S 1M3
Canada
Tel.: (403) 489-1059
Contact: Michelle Smith

BMG Music Canada, Inc.
5500 Royalmount Avenue
Suite 330
Montreal, Que. H4P 1H7
Canada
Tel.: (514) 735-6523
Contact: Michel Turcot

BMG Music Canada, Inc.
207 - 1050 Kingsway
Vancouver, B.C. V5V 3C7
Canada
Tel.: (604) 872-5471
Contact: Bryan Boyce

BNA Entertainment
1 Music Circle North
Nashville, TN 37203
Tel.: (615) 780-4400
CEO (Country): Ric Pepin
A & R: Richard Landis

Bookshop Records
1030 17th Avenue South
Nashville, TN 37212
Tel.: (615) 321-4166
Contact: Gilles Godard

Bovine International Record Co.
593 Kildare Road
London, Ont. N6H 3H8
Canada
Tel.: (519) 472-7170

Brainchild Music
1140 East 24th Avenue
Vancouver, B.C. V5V 2B2
Canada
Tel.: (519) 472-7170
Contact: Larry W. Clark

Brewster Records
3722 Manor Street
Burnaby, B.C. V5G 1A6
Canada
Tel.: (604) 430-9223
Contact: Cori Brewster

Broadland International
50 Music Square West, Suite 607
Nashville, TN 37203
Tel.: (615) 327 0535
Contact: Gary Buck

Brunetunes Records & Publishing
Box 391
Aylmer, Que. J9H 5E7
Canada
Tel.: (819) 684-3417
Contact: Bob Brunet

Burco Records
1716 Main Street West, Suite 317
Hamilton, Ont. L8S 1G9
Canada
Tel.: (416) 529-4127
Contact: Larry Coad

Canyon Creek Records
Box 671008
Dallas, TX 75367-8008
Tel.: (214) 750-0720
CEO: Bart Barton

Capitol Records-EMI of Canada
10330 Cote de Liesse
Lachine, Que. H8T 1A3
Canada
Tel.: (514) 631-9072
Contact: Val D'Amico

Capitol Records-EMI of Canada
18 Savona Court
Dartmouth, N.S. B2W 4R1
Canada
Tel.: (902) 434-9520
Contact: Barry Kent

Capitol Records-EMI of Canada
4240 Manor Street, Suite 213
Burnaby, B.C. V5G 1B2
Canada
Tel.: (604) 431-0177
Contact: Ralph Schmidtke

Capitol Records-EMI of Canada
HMV Southgate Shopping Centre
343 51st Avenue/111th Street
Edmonton, Alta. T5H 4M6
Canada
Tel.: (403) 439-5536
Contact: Kelly Zamiski

Capitol Records-EMI of Canada
15 Tralee Place
Winnipeg, Man. R2N 1P6
Canada
Tel.: (204) 677-5050
Contact: Jim Maxwell

Capitol Records-EMI of Canada
3109 American Drive
Mississauga, Ont. L4V 1B2
Canada
Contact: John Toews

Capitol Records-EMI of Canada
175 1209 59th Avenue S.E.
Calgary, Alta. T2H 2P6
Canada
Tel.: (403) 258-2336
Contact: Brad Morrisey

Capitol Records-EMI of Canada
3212 Yorks Corners Road
Kenmore, Ont. K0A 2GO
Canada
Tel.: (613) 821-0329
Contact: John Foliot

Capricorn Records
120 30th Avenue North
Nashville, TN 37203
Tel.: (615) 320-8470
CEO: Phil Walden
A & R: Gene Amonette

Cardinal Records
7118 Peach Court
Brentwood, TN 37027
Tel.: (615) 373-5223
Contact: Tony Migliore

Carousel Records
50 Music Square West, Suite 607
Nashville, TN 37203
Tel.: (615) 327-0535

Challenger Records
35 Kirby Crescent
Newmarket, Ont. L3X 1G7
Canada
Contact: Frank Rogers

Chokecherry Records & Tapes
215 6th Avenue S.E.
High River, Alta. T0L 1B0
Canada
Tel.: (403) 652-7818
Contact: Lewis Martin Pederson

Citation Records
191A Wolseley Street, Suite 200
Thunder Bay, Ont. P7A 3G5
Canada
Tel: (416) 345-2448
Contact: Chuck Williams

Claymar Records Sales
PO Box 112
Weymouth, N.S. B0W 3T0
Canada
Tel.: (902) 837-4338

Columbia Records
(Div. of Sony)
34 Music Square East
Nashville, TN 37203
Tel.: (615) 742-4321
CEO (Country): Roy Wunsch
A & R: Steve Buckingham

Comstock Records
10603 N. Hayden Street, Suite 114
Scottsdale, AZ 85260
Tel.: (602) 951-3115
CEO: Frank Fara

Country Style Records
36 Erickson Drive
Red Deer, Alta. T4R 1Z8
Canada
Tel.: (403) 342-4246

Curb Records
47 Music Square East
Nashville, TN 37203
Tel.: (615) 321-5080
CEO (Country): Mike Borchetta

Curb Records
3907 W. Alameda Avenue
Burbank, CA 91505
Tel.: (818) 843-2872
CEO: Mike Curb

Custer Music, Inc.
643 Queen Street East, 2nd Floor
Toronto, Ont. M4M 1G4
Canada
Tel.: (416) 462-0860
Contact: Chris Hughes

Dark Light Music Ltd.
686 Richmond Street West
Toronto, Ont. M6J 1C3
Canada
Tel.: (416) 363-9466

Decca Records
60 Music Square East
Nashville, TN 37203
Tel.: (615) 880-7475
CEO: Sheila ShipleyBiddy
A & R: Mark Wright

Denon Canada, Inc.
17 Denison Street
Markham, Ont. L3R 1B5
Canada
Tel.: (416) 475-4085
Contact: Kelly Mulvey

Destiny Records
358 Dunlop Crescent
Burlington, Ont. L7L 3N7
Canada
Contact: Jeff Johnston

D.M.G. Record Company
c/o 1969 Pandora Street
Vancouver, B.C. V5L 5B2
Canada
Contact: Vanni Barbon

DMT Records
11714 113th Avenue
Edmonton, Alta. T5G 0J8
Canada
Contact: Danny Makarus

Door Knob Records
315 Mount Juliet Road
Mount Juliet, TN 37122
Tel.: (615) 754-0417
CEO: Gene Kennedy

Duke Street Records
121 Logan Avenue
Toronto, Ont. M4M 2M9
Canada
Tel.: (416) 406-4121

Ebony Records Publications
PO Box 206
Kingston, Ont. K7L 4V8
Canada
Tel.: (613) 547-5727
Contact: Kevin M. Simpson

Einstein Brothers Record Label
49 Ontario Street, 2nd Flr.
Toronto, Ont. M5A 2V1
Canada
Tel.: (416) 364-8851
Contact: Alan Kates

EMC Records of Canada
189 Scugog Street
Bowmanville, Ont. L1C 3J9
Canada
Tel.: (416) 723-8916
Contact: Paul Andrew Smith

EMCI
15 John Street, Suite 508
Toronto, Ont. M5V 2T2
Canada
Contact: Olie Kornelson

Epic Records
(Div. of Sony)
34 Music Square East
Nashville, TN 37203
Tel.: (615) 742-4321
CEO (Country): Roy Wunsch
A & R: Doug Johnson

Epic Records
1121 Leslie Street
Don Mills, Ont. M3C 2J9
Canada
Tel.: (416) 391-3311

Evergreen Records
1021 16th Avenue South
Nashville, TN 37203
Tel.: (615) 320-5641
CEO: Johnny Morris

Flat Top Recording Co.
PO Box 24051
301 Oxford Street West
London, Ont. N6H 5C4
Canada
Tel.: (519) 659-1256

Flying Fish Records
1304 W. Schubert
Chicago, IL 60614
Tel.: (312) 528-5455

Flying High Records
R.R. 2
Odessa, Ont. K0H 2H0
Canada
Tel.: (613) 386-3582
Contact: Anita Boehme

fre Records
2181 Dunwin Drive
Mississauga, Ont. L5L 3S3
Canada
Tel.: (416) 828-6121
Contact: Terry Flood

Galahad Records, Inc.
Stokes Building
39 James Street, Box 10
St. Catharines, Ont. L2R 6R6
Canada
Contact: John F. Gale

GB Records
50 Music Square West, Suite 607
Nashville, TN 37203
Tel.: (615) 327-0535
Contact: Gary Buck

GBS Records
38 Music Square East
Nashville, TN 37203
Tel.: (615) 242-5001
CEO: Ernie Bivens

Gemini Records
R.R. 2
New Germany, N.S. B0R 1E0
Canada
Tel.: (902) 543-5053
Contact: Gerald Seamone

Giant Records
45 Music Square West
Nashville, TN 37203
Tel.: (615) 256-3110
CEO (Country): James Stroud
A & R: James Stroud

Golden Eagle Records
55 S. Cumberland Street
Thunder Bay, Ont. P7B 2T6
Canada
Tel.: (807) 344-1511
Contact: Don Grashey

Grizzly Production
3220 Universite
St. Hubert, Que. J3Y 5R1
Canada
Tel.: (514) 676-8606
Contact: Gerard Pesant

Gun Records, Inc.
PO Box 8391, Station A
Halifax, N.S. B3K 5M1
Canada
Tel.: (902) 423-8434
Contact: Tony Kelly

Harvestholm
PO Box 37
Novel, Ont. P0G 1G0
Canada
Tel.: (705) 342-9304

Heritage Music
41 Antrim Crescent, Suite 311
Scarborough, Ont. M1P 4T1
Canada
Tel.: (416) 292-4724
Contact: Jack Boswell

HI 5 Music
1041 Avenue Road, Suite 4
Toronto, Ont. M5N 2C5
Canada
Tel.: (416) 481-4184
Contact: David McLachlan

Homestead
14522 118th Avenue
Edmonton, Alta. T5L 2M8
Canada
Tel.: (403) 454-8434

Image VII
10551 Shellbridge Way, Suite 35
Richmond, B.C. V6X 2W9
Canada
Tel.: (604) 270-2707

Intermodel Productions
PO Box 2199
Vancouver, B.C. V6B 3V7
Canada
Tel.: (604) 669-4399

International Talent Services
1177 W. 8th Avenue
Vancouver, B.C. V6H 1C5
Canada
Tel.: (604) 739-7077
Contact: Diana Kelly

Intersound International
1 Select Avenue, Unit 10
Scarborough, Ont. M1V 5J3
Canada
Tel.: (416) 609-9718
Contact: Ray Rosenberg

J-Bash Records
PO Box 490
Angus, Ont. L0M 1B0
Canada
Tel.: (705) 424-1753
Contact: Brent Williams

Jay-Dee Records
78 Ottawa Street South
Hamilton, Ont. L8K 2E3
Canada
Tel.: (416) 544-6807
Contact: John Mac, Sr.

Jennie Records
PO Box 421
Schomberg, Ont. L0G 1T0
Canada
Tel.: (416) 939-7900

John Bull Records
Box 48204
Midlake P.O.
Calgary, Alta. T2X 3C9
Canada
Tel.: (403) 254-2096
Contact: Glenn Neale

K-Ark Records
6005 Port Jamaica Drive
Hermitage, TN 37076
Tel.: (615) 883-5349

Kadajuke Records
250 Harding Blvd. West, Suite 209
Richmond Hill, Ont. L4C 9M7
Canada
Tel.: (416) 930-2571

Kansa Records
PO Box 1014
Lebanon, TN 37088
Tel.: (615) 444-3865
CEO: Kit Johnson

Kappa Records
86 Cote Ste.-Catharine
Outremont, Que. H2V 2A3
Canada
Tel.: (514) 270-9556
Contact: Lise Aubut

Kate & Becca Records
7454 Northcote Street
Mission, B.C. V2V 4G8
Canada
Tel.: (604) 826-6112

Key Records of Canada
PO Box 1085
569 Lynwood Drive
Cornwall, Ont. K6H 5V2
Canada
Tel.: (613) 938-1532

LCDM Consultants/Ent.
19 Victoria Avenue West, Suite 2
Weston, Ont. M9N 1E3
Canada
Tel.: (416) 242-7391
Contact: Lee

Les Disques Jouflu
2379 Guenette
Ville St.-Laurent, Que. H4R 2E9
Canada
Tel.: (514) 745-3223

Liberty Records
3322 West End Avenue, 11th Floor
Nashville, TN 37203
Tel.: (615) 269-2000
CEO (Country): Jimmy Bowen
A & R: Janie West

Libre Music
7101C 120th Street
Delta, B.C. V4E 2A0
Canada
Tel.: (604) 594-1103

Longmeadow Records
R.R. 1
Site 13, Box 6
Charlottetown, P.E.I. C1A 7J6
Canada
Tel.: (902) 569-3745
Contact: Garth Matthews

Lupins Records
PO Box 183
Sydney, N.S. B1P 1B5
Canada
Tel.: (902) 562-7482
Contact: Wade Langham

Magnum Records
8607 128th Avenue
Edmonton, Alta. T5E 0G3
Canada
Tel.: (403) 476-8230
Contact: Bill Maxim

Major Label Records
R.R. 2
Stirling, Ont. K0K 3E0
Canada
Tel.: (613) 395-5115

Manville Records
127 Manville Road, Unit 9
Scarborough, Ont. M1L 4J7
Canada
Tel.: (416) 288-9967

Margaree Sound
225 Lake Driveway West
Ajax, Ont. L1S 5A3
Canada
Tel.: (416) 683-5680
Contact: Russel Daigle

Marigold Records
1712 Avenue Road, Box 54552
Toronto, Ont. M5M 4N5
Canada
Tel.: (416) 484-8789

Maritime Express
157 Sussex Avenue
Riverview, N.B. E1B 3A8
Canada
Tel.: (506) 386-2996
Contact: Ivan Hicks

MBS Records
590 Hunters Place
Waterloo, Ont. N2K 3L1
Canada
Tel.: (519) 746-8488
Contact: Larry Mercey

MCA Records
60 Music Square East
Nashville, TN 37203
Tel.: (615) 244-8944
CEO (Country): Bruce Hinton
A & R: Tony Brown

MCA Canada Ltd.
364 Smith Street
Winnipeg, Man. R3B 2H2
Tel.: (416) 491-3000
Contact: Stephen Tennant

MCA Canada Ltd.
2450 Victoria Park Avenue
Willowdale, Ont. M2J 4A2
Tel.: (204) 943-3323
Contact: Jack Skelly

MCA Canada Ltd.
10500 Cote de Liesse, Suite 110
Lachine, Que. H8T 1A4
Tel.: (514) 636-6059
Contact: Frank Iacovella

MCA Canada Ltd.
3031 Viking Way, Suite 103
Richmond, B.C. V6V 1W1
Tel.: (604) 273-7797
Contact: Bill Tait

MCA Canada Ltd.
1209 59th Avenue S.E., Suite 160
Calgary, Alta. T2H 2P6
Tel.: (403) 640-4700
Contact: Ed Harris

MCA Canada Ltd.
13 Ruth Street
Moncton, N.B. E1A 4B3
Tel.: (506) 856-6833
Contact: Kevin Frennette

Mercury Nashville
66 Music Square West
Nashville, TN 37203
Tel.: (615) 320-0110
CEOs (Country): Luke Lewis/Harold Shedd
A & R: Harold Shedd/Buddy Cannon

Metratron Productions
Box 103
Inglewood, Ont. L0N 1K0
Tel.: (416) 838-3274
Contact: Jim Matt

Moon Tan Music
PO Box 31581
Pitt Meadows, B.C. V3Y 2G7
Tel.: (604) 465-4727

MRV Records
PO Box 224
Allan, Sask. S0K 0C0
Tel.: (306) 257-3588

MSR Records
42 Music Square West, # 347
Nashville, TN 37203
Tel.: (615) 252-8207
CEO: L.C. Parsons

Mur-Pat Enterprises
PO Box 89
Redvers, Sask. S0C 2H0
Canada
Tel.: (306) 739-2724
CEO: Murray Patron

Music Machine Records
Box 541
Regina, Sask. S4P 3A2
Canada
Tel.: (306) 634-4995
Contact: Don Leblanc

Music World Creations
2 Doerr Road
Scarborough, Ont. M1P 4M6
Canada
Contact: Mel Shaw

Music World Creations America
1710 Grand Avenue
Nashville, TN 37212
Tel.: (615) 329-3323
Contact: Mel Shaw

Newsflash Sounds
PO Box 333
Grand Falls
Newfoundland, A2A 2J7
Canada
Tel.: (709) 489-9496

Oh Boy Records
4121 Wilshire Blvd., Suite 204
Los Angeles, CA 90010
Tel.: (213) 385-0882
CEO: Al Beneta

Old Homestead Records
Box 100
Brighton, MI 48116
Tel.: (313) 227-1997
CEO: John Morris

Palamino Records
21-10405 Jasper Avenue, Suite 561
Edmonton, Alta. T5J 3S2
Canada
Tel.: (403) 482-7080
Contact: Ruth Blakely

Panio Bros. Label
Box 99
Montmartre, Sask. S0G 3M0
Tel.: (306) 424-2258
Canada
Contact: John Panio

Patriot Records
3322 West End Avenue, 11th Floor
Nashville, TN 37203
Tel.: (615) 383-1800
CEO: Jimmy Bowen

PB Records
Box 99
Montmartre, Sask. S0G 3M0
Canada
Tel.: (306) 424-2258
Contact: John Panio

Playback Records
Box 630755
Miami, FL 33163
CEO: Jack Gale

Pleasure Records
Rt. 1, Box 187-A
Whitney, TX 76692
Tel.: (817) 694-4047

Polygram Records
1345 Denison Street
Markham, Ont. L3R 5V2
Canada
Tel.: (416) 415-9900
Contact: Bob Ansell

Premiere Records
185 Oshawa Blvd. South
Oshawa, Ont. L1H 5R6
Canada
Tel.: (416) 579-7476

Pure Pacific Music
319-5 Woodcock Crescent
Mission, B.C. V2V 4K2
Canada
Tel.: (604) 826-4946
Contact: Laurie Thain

Quality Special Products
480 Tapscott Road, Unit 1
Scarborough, Ont. M1B 1W3
Canada
Tel.: (416) 291-5590
Contact: Bernie Willock

Raeni Music
21 Bamboo Crescent
Whitehorse, Yukon Y1A 4V4
Canada
Tel.: (403) 633-2982

Raincoat Music
530 4th Street
Nanaimo, B.C. V9R 1T7
Canada
Contact: Susan Sullivan

Rana Records
2475 Dunbar Street
Vancouver, B.C. V6R 3N2
Canada

Randon Records
209A Madison Avenue
Toronto, Ont. M5R 2S6
Canada
Tel.: (416) 538-2666
Contact: Peter Randall

Rarerabit Records
3590 Nablus Gate
Mississauga, Ont. L5B 3K1
Canada
Tel.: (416) 276-4040
Contact: Dorothy Rainville

RCA Records
1 Music Circle North
Nashville, TN 37203
Tel.: (615) 664-1200
CEO (Country): Thom Schuyler/Jack Weston
A & R: Thom Schuyler

RDR Promotions
7370 Woodbine Avenue, Suite 12
Markham, Ont. L3R 1A5
Canada
Tel.: (416) 477-8050
Contact: Joe Wood

Reba Records
PO Box 56, Station N
Toronto, Ont. M8V 3T2
Canada
Tel.: (416) 255-7423
Contact: Jerry Knight

Renaissance Records
40 Carisbrooke Court
Brampton, Ont. L6S 3K1
Canada
Contact: George Cattapan

Reptile Records
PO Box 121213
Nashville, TN 37212
Tel.: (615) 331-7400
Canada
CEO: Scott Tutt

Ridge Records
R.R. 11
1490 Goods Road
Thunder Bay, Ont. P7B 5E2
Canada
Tel.: (807) 767-9079
Contact: Michael McFarlane

RMS Recordings
41 Dahlia Street
Dartmouth, N.S. B3A 2S1
Canada
Tel.: (902) 469-5992
Contact: Rick Gautreau

Rockin' Horse Music
940 Brunette Avenue
Coquitlam, B.C. V3K 1C9
Canada
Tel.: (604) 521-1558

Roto Noto Music
148 Erin Avenue
Hamilton, Ont. L8K 4W3
Canada
Tel.: (416) 796-8236
Contact: Randall Cousins

Royalty Records, Inc.
PO Box 8768
Edmonton, Alta. T6C 4J5
Canada
Tel.: (403) 449-4372
Contact: R. Harlan Smith

Rumental Records of Canada
PO Box 730, Station C
Toronto, Ont. M6J 3S1
Canada
Tel.: (416) 367-0925
Contact: J.M. Pedrow

Saddlestone Records
8821 Dellwood Drive
Delta, B.C. V4C 4A1
Canada
Tel.: (604) 582-7117
Contact: Candice James

Sam Cat Records
8 Woodlands Road
St. Albert, Alta. T8N 3L9
Canada
Tel.: (403) 460-7460
Contact: Peter Jansen

Savannah Music Group
5409 Eglinton Avenue West, Suite 104
Etobicoke, Ont. M9C 5K6
Canada
Tel.: (416) 620-0396
Contact: Allen Zarnett

Savannah Music Group
1207 17th Avenue South, 3rd Floor
Nashville, TN 37212
Tel.: (615) 329-4747
CEO: Brian Ferriman

Sceptre Records
Box 182
Midale, Sask. S0C 1S0
Canada
Tel.: (306) 458-2659

Service De Musique B.M.
3465 Ontario East
Montreal, Que. H1W 1R4
Canada
Tel.: (514) 526-2464

Sha-Nor Music
213 Mohawk Road
Oakville, Ont. L6L 2Z1
Canada
Tel.: (416) 827-8278
Contact: Pat McCrossan

Shadow Records
Box 1682
Campbellford, Ont. K0L 1L0
Canada
Tel.: (705) 653-4635
Contact: Ron Demmans

Sibley Records of Canada
540 Oliver Road, Suite 207
Thunder Bay, Ont. P7A 3K4
Canada
Tel.: (807) 344-8233
Contact: David F. Petrunka

Signature Records
500 Newbold Street
London, Ont. N6E 1K6
Canada
Tel.: (519) 686-5060
Contact: Geoff Kymer

Silver City Records
PO Box 463
Mountainhome, PA 18342

Silver Spur Music
1969 Pandora Street
Vancouver, B.C. V5L 5B2
Canada
Tel.: (604) 255-3536
Contact: Brian Wadsworth

Snocan Enterprises Ltd.
5298 Driscoll Drive
Manotick, Ont. K0A 2N0
Canada
Tel.: (613) 692-6137

Sony Music Canada, Inc.
1121 Leslie Street
Don Mills, Ont. M3C 2J9
Canada
Tel.: (416) 391-3311
Contact: Bill Bannon

Sony Music Canada, Inc.
602 Blythwood Avenue
Riverview, N.B. E1B 2H5
Canada
Tel.: (506) 388-1515
Contact: Jim Bradley

Sony Music Canada, Inc.
1525 Dublin Avenue
Winnipeg, Man. R3H 0W8
Canada
Tel.: (204) 786-1096
Contact: Mark Abson

Sony Music Canada, Inc.
610G 70th Avenue S.E.
Calgary, Alta. T2H 2G2
Canada
Tel.: (403) 253-8719
Contact: Gary McLeish

Sony Music Canada, Inc.
1847 W. Broadway, Suite 101
Vancouver, B.C. V6K 1Y6
Canada
Tel.: (604) 734-5151
Contact: Don Gunter

Sony Musique Canada, Inc.
333 Boul, Graham, Suite 602
Ville Mont-Royal, Que. H3R 3L5
Canada
Tel.: (514) 737-6896
Contact: Bill Rotari

Soundwaves/NSD
1012 18th Avenue South
Nashville, TN 37212
Tel.: (615) 327-7988
CEO: Joe Gibson

Spider Records
49-49 Cedarwoods Crescent
Kitchener, Ont. N2C 2L1
Canada
Tel.: (519) 893-0746
Contact: Darlene De Haw

Spin Records
9-300 Trillium Drive
Kitchener, Ont. N2E 2K6
Canada
Tel.: (519) 893-1172

Stardust Records
1731 Centennial Crescent
North Battleford, Sask. S9A 3J2
Canada
Tel.: (306) 445-2002

Starway Records, Inc.
7600-B Leeburg Pike, Suite 400
Falls Church, VA 22043
Tel.: (703) 821-0500

Step One Records
1300 Division Street
Nashville, TN 37203
Tel.: (615) 255-3009
A & R: Ray Pennington

Stereotype Music International
1831 151st Avenue
Edmonton, Alta. T5Y 1W1
Canada
Tel.: (403) 478-2265
Contact: Fred LaRose

Stereotype Music International
R.R. 6, Site 7, Box 6
Edmonton, Alta. T5B 4K3
Canada
Tel.: (403) 478-9252
Contact: Roy Powell

Stony Plain Records
PO Box 861
Edmonton, Alta. T5J 2L8
Canada
Tel.: (403) 478-9252
Contact: Holger Petersen

Stop Hunger Records
1300 Division Street
Nashville, TN 37203
Tel.: (615) 242-4722
CEO: Robert Metzgar
A & R: Robert Metzgar

Sugar Hill Records
Box 4040, Duke Station
Durham, NC 27706
Tel.: (919) 489-4349
CEO: Barry Poss

Sunshine Records Ltd.
228 Selkirk Avenue
Winnipeg, Man. R2W 2L6
Canada
Tel.: (204) 586-8057
Contact: Ness Michaels

Tembo Music Canada, Inc.
284 Church Street, Suite 201
Oakville, Ont. L6J 7N2
Canada
Tel.: (416) 338-0896
Contact: J. Edward (Ed) Preston

The Label
PO Box 1234
Calgary, Alta. T2P 2C2
Canada
Tel.: (403) 230-5334

The Music Connection
14 Rovers Avenue
Red Deer, Alta. T4P 3K4
Canada
Tel.: (403) 347-6593

Three Flamingos Music
PO Box 282, Station U
Toronto, Ont. L5A 2E9
Canada
Tel.: (416) 897-0683
Contact: Wayne Marshall

Thunder Records, Inc.
444 St. Mary Avenue, Suite 1212
Winnipeg, Man. R3C 3T1
Canada
Tel.: (204) 956-4410
Contact: Dyan Starr

Trailstar Records
206 Thornton Avenue
Thornton, Ont. L0L 2N0
Canada
Tel.: (705) 458-4255
Contact: Sue Bourne

Trilogy Records
3015 Kennedy Road, Suite 1
Scarborough, Ont. M1V 1E7
Canada
Tel.: (416) 291-4913

True North Records
151 John Street, Suite 301
Toronto, Ont. M5V 2T2
Canada
Tel.: (416) 596-8696

2M Records
R.R. 12, Box 24, Site 38,
Calgary, Alta. T3E 6WE
Canada
Tel.: (403) 242-8849
CEO: Molly Hamilton

Uptown Records
10751 63rd Street
Edmonton, Alta. T6A 2N2
Canada
Contact: Glen A. Fraser

Virgin Records Canada, Inc.
Runde House
514 Jarvis Street
Toronto, Ont. M4Y 2H6
Canada
Tel.: (416) 961-8863
Contact: Doug Chappell

Walters Family Studios
R.R. 3
Bright, Ont. N0J 1B0
Canada
Tel.: (519) 463-5559
Contact: Darren Walters

Warner Bros. Records
20 Music Square East
Nashville, TN 37203
Tel.: (615) 320-7525
CEO (Country): Jim Ed Norman
A & R: Martha Sharp

Warner Music Canada Ltd.
1810 Birchmount Road
Scarborough, Ont. M1P 2J1
Canada
Tel.: (416) 291-2515
Contact: Randy Stark

Warner Music Canada Ltd.
75 Ontario Avenue
Hamilton, Ont. L8N 2X1
Canada
Tel.: (416) 522-3663
Contact: Grant Rorabeck

Warner Music Canada Ltd.
11 Robinson Crescent
Regina, Sask. S4R 3R1
Canada
Tel.: (306) 545-5905
Contact: Kevin Korchinski

Warner Music Canada Ltd.
111 Colonnade Road, Suite 205
Nepean, Ont. K2E 7ME
Canada
Tel.: (613) 723-8201
Contact: Mary Armstrong

Warner Music Canada Ltd.
145 Rue Barr, Unit 1
Ville St. Laurent, Que. H4T 1W6
Canada
Tel.: (514) 731-6402
Contact: Ken Dion

Warner Music Canada Ltd.
24 Northview Avenue
Moncton, N.B. E1E 3Z4
Canada
Tel.: (506) 389-2538
Contact: John Poirier

Warner Music Canada Ltd.
548 Curlew Drive
Kelowna, B.C. V1Y 7R3
Canada
Tel.: (604) 764-0064
Contact: Ralph Hass

Warner Music Canada Ltd.
7272 Rue des Grebes
Charny, Que. G6W 5H6
Canada
Tel.: (418) 832-7011
Contact: Luc Laroche

Warner Music Canada Ltd.
68 Water Street, Suite 1400
Vancouver, B.C. V6B 1A4
Canada
Tel.: (604) 684-4717
Contact: Peter Moser

Warner Music Canada Ltd.
6325 21st Street S.E., Unit 12
Calgary, Alta. T2H 2K1
Canada
Tel.: (403) 259-3000
Contact: Alex Clark

Warner Music Canada Ltd.
10215 178th Street
Edmonton, Alta. T2H 2K1
Canada
Tel.: (403) 489-0024
Contact: Marilyn Brodeur

Warner Music Canada Ltd.
1265 Dublin Avenue, Suite 124
Winnipeg, Man. R3H 0W3
Canada
Tel.: (204) 783-2346
Contact: Jeff Storry

Warner Music Canada Ltd.
465 Castlegrove Blvd., Suite 402
London, Ont. N6G 3R8
Canada
Tel.: (519) 473-1456
Contact: Ken Berry

Warose Records
320 Niska Road, Suite 202
Downsview, Ont. M3N 2W1
Canada
Tel.: (416) 661-0806
Contact: Walter Baye

Wellcraft Music Group
1890 Valley Farm Road, Suite 1509
Pickering, Ont. L1V 6B4
Canada
Tel.: (416) 839-7309
Contact: James H. Hopson

WES Productions
R.R. 3
Bright, Ont. N0J 1B0
Canada
Tel.: (519) 463-5559
Contact: Darren Walters

Westar Records
624 Beaver Dam Road N.E., D1
Calgary, Alta. T2K 4W6
Canada
Tel.: (403) 275-4455
Contact: Blaine Wikins

World Records
Baseline Road West
PO Box 2000
Bowmanville, Ont. L1C 3Z3
Canada

Yonge Street Records
26 Sloane Avenue, Suite 313
North York, Ont. M4A 2A4
Canada
Tel.: (416) 759-1393
Contact: Bob Johnston

MUSIC PUBLISHERS

Acuff-Rose Music, Inc.
65 Music Square West
Nashville, TN 37203
Tel.: (615) 321-5000

Affiliated Publishers, Inc.
27 Music Square East
Nashville, TN 37203
Tel.: (615) 256-9850

Ahab Music Co., Inc.
1707 Grand Avenue
Nashville, TN 37212
Tel.: (615) 327-4629

Almo-Irving Music
1904 Adelicia Avenue
Nashville, TN 37212
Tel.: (615) 321-0820

Amanda-Lin
PO Box 15871
Nashville, TN 37215

AMR Publications, Inc.
54 Music Square East
Nashville, TN 37203
Tel.: (615) 256-9353

Andite Invasion
3615 Hoods Hill Road
Nashville, TN 37215

Bait & Beer
PO Box 121681
Nashville, TN 37212

Bellamy Bros. Music
1102 17th Avenue South, Suite 401
Nashville, TN 37212

Bluewater Music Corporation
1114 17th Avenue South
Nashville, TN 37212
Tel.: (615) 329-0777

BMG Songs
1 Music Circle North
Nashville, TN 37203
Tel.: (615) 780-5420

Bocephus Music, Inc.
PO Box 40929
Nashville, TN 37204
Tel.: (615) 370-3002

Brentwood Music
1 Maryland Farms Blvd.
Brentwood, TN 37027
Tel.: (615) 373-9850

Buckhorn Music, Inc.
1009 17th Avenue South
Nashville, TN 37212
Tel.: (615) 327-4590

Bug Music
1026 16th Avenue South
Nashville, TN 37212
Tel.: (615) 726-0782

Bugle Publishing Group
27 Music Square East
Nashville, TN 37203
Tel.: (615) 259-2485

Bulls Creek Music Group
11 Music Circle South
Nashville, TN 37203
Tel.: (615) 242-7410

Cabin Fever Entertainment
803 18th Avenue South
Nashville, TN 37203

Cholampy Music
40 Music Square East
Nashville, TN 37203

Co-Heart Music Group
1103 17th Avenue South
Nashville, TN 37212
Tel.: (615) 327-0031

Debarris Music
1107 17th Avenue South
Nashville, TN 37212

Edge O'Woods
1214 16th Avenue South
Nashville, TN 37212

Emerald River
1025 16th Avenue South, Suite 202
Nashville, TN 37212

EMI Music Publishing
35 Music Square East
Nashville, TN 37203
Tel.: (615) 742-8081

End of August
1102 17th Avenue South, Suite 400
Nashville, TN 37212

Endless Frogs
PO Box 7072
Corte Madera, CA 94925

Evanlee
1705 Warfield
Nashville, TN 37215

Famous Music Group
65 Music Square East
Nashville, TN 37203
Tel.: (615) 329-0500

Forerunner Music, Inc.
1308 16th Avenue South
Nashville, TN 37212

Forrest Hills Music
PO Box 120838
Nashville, TN 37212

Front Burner
1203 16th Avenue South
Nashville, TN 37212

Gehl Force Music Group
1106 18th Avenue South
Nashville, TN 37212
Tel.: (615) 321-4465

James Griffin Music
801 Hillmeade Drive
Nashville, TN 37221

Rick Hall Music
PO Box 2527
Muscle Shoals, AL 35662

Hannah's Eyes Music, Inc.
1116 Frances Avenue
Nashville, TN 37204

Hayes Street Music
1700 Hayes Street, Suite 203
Nashville, TN 37203
Tel.: (615) 327-1991

Hidden Harbor Music
811 18th Avenue South
Nashville, TN 37203

Hiriam Music
9000 Sunset Blvd.
Los Angeles, CA 90069

Hookem Music
217 E. 86th Street, Suite 384
New York, NY 10028

Howlin Hits Music
PO Box 19647
Houston, TX 77224

Ides of March
1136 Gateway Lane
Nashville, TN 37220

Inorbit Music
8857 W. Olympic Blvd., Suite 200
Beverly Hills, CA 90211

Intersong
21 Music Square East
Nashville, TN 37203

Kentucky Sweetheart Music
PO Box 17087
Nashville, TN 37217

Kinetic Diamond
513 Hill Road
Nashville, TN 37220

Kristoshua Music
1102 17th Avenue South, Suite 401
Nashville, TN 37212

Lillybilly Music
6777 Hollywood Blvd., 9th Flr.
Hollywood, CA 90028

Little Beagle
59 Music Square West
Nashville, TN 37203

Little Big Town
803 18th Avenue South
Nashville, TN 37203
Tel.: (615) 321-5286

Littlemarch
1358 La Brea Blvd.
Hollywood, CA 90028

Lodge Hall
12 Music Circle South
Nashville, TN 37212

Long Run Music
30 Music Square West
Nashville, TN 37203
Tel.: (615) 251-3044

Loose Ends
5109 Hilson Road
Nashville, TN 37211

Macy Place
228 Bermuda
Nashville, TN 37214

Major Bob Music
1109 17th Avenue South
Nashville, TN 37212
Tel.: (615) 329-4150

Makin' Music
1230 17th Avenue South
Nashville, TN 37212
Tel.: (615) 269-6770

Malaco Music Group
47 Music Square East
Nashville, TN 37203

Mariposa Music, Inc.
713 18th Avenue South
Nashville, TN 37203
Tel.: (615) 327-3752

Maypop Music
702 18th Avenue South
Nashville, TN 37203
Tel.: (615) 254-8800

MCA Music
1114 17th Avenue South
Nashville, TN 37212
Tel.: (615) 327-4622

Merit Music
66 Music Square West
Nashville, TN 37202

Blake Mevis Music
811 18th Avenue South
Nashville, TN 37203
Tel.: (615) 329-9186

Mid-Summer Music
1109 17th Avenue South
Nashville, TN 37212

Moody Blue Music
13 Music Square East
Nashville, TN 37203
Tel.: (615) 321-9029

Morgan Music Group, Inc.
1800 Grand Avenue
Nashville, TN 37212

Muckleroy
PO Box 121994
Nashville, TN 37212

Murrah Music Corporation
1025 16th Avenue South, Suite 102
Nashville, TN 37212
Tel.: (615) 329-4236

Music Ridge
2702 Larmon Drive
Nashville, TN 37204

New Clarion Music Group
1233 17th Avenue South
Nashville, TN 37212
Tel.: (615) 321-4422

New Haven Music
1221 16th Avenue South, Suite 101
Nashville, TN 37212

Opryland Music Group, Inc.
PO Box 121900
Nashville, TN 37212
Tel.: (615) 321-5000

O-Tex Music
1000 18th Avenue South
Nashville, TN 37212

Patrick-Joseph Music, Inc.
119 17th Avenue South
Nashville, TN 37212
Tel.: (615) 242-1681

Peer/Talbot Publishing
2 Music Circle South
Nashville, TN 37203
Tel.: (615) 244-6200

Polygram Music Publishing Group
54 Music Square East
Nashville, TN 37203
Tel.: (615) 256-7648

Pookie Bear Music
PO Box 121242
Nashville, TN 37212

Rancho Bogardo
825 W. Hillwood Drive
Nashville, TN 37205

RavenSong
PO Box 1402
Hendersonville, TN 37077

Scarlet Moon Music
7087 Old Harding Pike
Nashville, TN 37212
Tel.: (615) 383-5007

Serenity Manor
1470 Old Hillsboro Road
Nashville, TN 37115

Seventh Son
4206 Kirtland Road
Nashville, TN 37064

Sheddhouse Music
1710 Roy Acuff Place
Nashville, TN 37203
Tel.: (615) 255-0428

Songpainter Music
10960 Wilshire Blvd., Suite 938
Los Angeles, CA 90024

Sony/Tree Music
1111 16th Avenue South
Nashville, TN 37212
Tel.: (615) 726-0890

Billy Strange Music Group
7118 Peach Court
Brentwood, TN 37027
Tel.: (615) 373-0600

Sun Mare Music Publishing
50 Music Square West
Nashville, TN 37203

Sure-Fire Music Co., Inc.
60 Music Square West
Nashville, TN 37203
Tel.: (615) 244-1401

Swallowfork
1708 Grand Avenue
Nashville, TN 37203

Ten Ten Music
33 Music Square West
Nashville, TN 37203
Tel.: (615) 255-9955

Terrace
217 E. 86th Street, Suite 384
New York, NY 10028

Texas Wedge
11 Music Square East
Nashville, TN 37203
Tel.: (615) 256-9850

Tillis Tunes
48 Music Square East
Nashville, TN 37203

Trio Music Co.
9000 Sunset Blvd.
Los Angeles, CA 90069

Triumvirate Music, Inc.
1013 16th Avenue South
Nashville, TN 37212

2Kids
1002 Natchez Trace Road
Franklin, TN 37064

Warner/Chappell Music
21 Music Square East
Nashville, TN 37203
Tel.: (615) 254-8777

Willin' David Music
PO Box 120009
Nashville, TN 37212

Willowcreek Music
19 Music Square West
Nashville, TN 37203
Tel.: (615) 256-1629

Word Record & Music Group
3319 West End Avenue
Nashville, TN 37212
Tel: (615) 385-9673

Wrensong Music
1229 17th Avenue South
Nashville, TN 37212
Tel.: (615) 321-4487

Zomba Music
916 19th Avenue South
Nashville, TN 37212
Tel.: (615) 321-4850

PUBLICISTS

Aristo Media
PO Box 22765
Nashville, TN 37202
Tel.: (615) 269-7071

Representing:
Canadian Country Music Association
Cimmaron
Country Radio Seminar
Chris LeDoux
River North Nashville Records
Lari White
BNA Records

The Brokaw Company
9255 Sunset Blvd., Suite 804
Los Angeles, CA 90069
Tel.: (310) 273-2060
Representing:
Glen Campbell
Mark Chesnutt
Roy Clark
Vince Gill
Mickey Gilley
Merle Haggard
Loretta Lynn
Reba McEntire
Riders in the Sky
The Statler Brothers
Doug Stone
Aaron Tippin
Tom Wopat

Creative Media Services
1024 17th Avenue South
Nashville, TN 37212
Tel.: (615) 320-5495
Representing:
Chet Atkins
Banjo Mania
Cleve Francis
Becky Hobbs
Intersound Branson Entertainment
Eddy Raven
Dan Seals

Doyle/Lewis Management
1109 17th Avenue South
Nashville, TN 37212
Tel.: (615) 329-9447
Representing:
Garth Brooks
Stephanie Davis
Hank Flamingo
Great Plains
Buddy Mondlock

Greg Fowler Promotions
201 Glenn Ave. S.W.
Fort Payne, AL 35967
Tel.: (205) 845-4283
Representing:
Alabama

Kathy Gangwisch & Associates
207 Westport Rd.
Kansas City, MO 64111
Tel.: (816) 931-8000
and
1706 Grand Ave.
Nashville, TN 37212
Tel.: (615) 327-8000
Fax: 615-329-2445
Representing:
Darryl & Don Ellis
Ralph Emery
Gatlin Brothers
Nicolette Larson
Wayne Newton
The Oak Ridge Boys
Marie Osmond
Osmond Brothers
Don Williams
Hank Williams, Jr.
Wylie & Wild West Show

Hot Schatz Productions
PO Box 50221
Nashville, TN 37205
Tel.: (615) 356-6614
Representing:
Waylon Jennings
Lari White

Levine/Schneider Public Relations
8730 Sunset Blvd., 6th Flr.
Los Angeles, CA 90069
Tel.: (310) 659-6440
Representing:
Stacy Dean Campbell
Dwight Yoakam

Mandrell Incorporated
PO Box 800
Hendersonville, TN 37077
Tel.: (615) 822-7200
Representing:
Barbara Mandrell
Irlene Mandrell
Louise Mandrell

Mercer & Associates
8447 Stults Avenue
Dallas, TX 75243
Tel.: (214) 340 7844
Representing:
Asleep at the Wheel
Janie Fricke
Penny Gilley
Ricky Lynn Gregg
Chris LeDoux
Rich Lloyd
Charley Pride

Myers Media
310 E. 46th Street, Suite 9-V
New York, NY 10017
Tel.: (212) 682-6767
and
1301 16th Avenue South
Nashville, TN 37212
Tel.: (615) 320-1914
Representing:
Béla Fleck and the Flecktones
Junior Brown
David Gates
Alison Krauss
Jamie O'Hara
Mike Reid
Rounder Records
Cheryl Wheeler

Network Ink, Inc.
1101 18th Avenue South
Nashville, TN 37212
Tel.: (615) 320-5727
Representing:
Americana Television
The Blues Foundation
Nashville Country Club
Country Music Foundation
Country Music Foundation Records
Country Music Foundation Press
Country Music Hall of Fame
Gibson-Miller Band
Hatch Show Print
Naomi Judd
RCA's Historic Studio B
Sammy Kershaw
Marlboro Music
John Michael Montgomery
Mark O'Connor
Red Hot & Country/Mercury
Ray Stevens
Wynonna

PLA Media
1303 16th Avenue South
Nashville, TN 37212
Tel.: (615) 327-0100
Representing:
John Anderson
Boy Howdy
Diamond Rio
William Lee Golden
Rebecca Holden
Pearl River
Charley Pride
Jim Wise
Michelle Wright

The Press Network
1018 17th Avenue South, Suite I
Nashville, TN 37212
Tel.: (615) 322-5445
Representing:
Evangeline
The Mavericks
Marty Stuart
lan Tyson

Thc Press Office
1229 17th Avenue South
Nashville, TN 37212
Tel.: (615) 320-5153
Representing:
John Anderson
Lynn Anderson

Arista/Nashville
Arista/Texas
Radney Foster
Run C&W
Sony Music/Nashville
Steve Wariner
Bob Woodruff

Rogers & Cowan
10000 Santa Monica Blvd., Suite 440
Los Angeles, CA 90067-7007
Tel: (310) 201 8800
Representing:
ASCAP
Clint Black
Curb Records
Billy Ray Cyrus
Billy Dean
Toby Keith
Tracy Lawrence
Tim McGraw
Kenny Rogers
Six Shooter
Marty Stuart

Rubin Media
PO Box I58161
Nashville, TN 37215
Tel.: (615) 269-5824
Fax: 615-269-5825
Representing:
Maura O'Connell
Jason Ringenberg
Sawyer Brown
Pam Tillis

Shock Ink
629 5th Avenue
Pelham, NY 10803
Tel.: (914) 738-2820
and
1108 16th Avenue South
Nashville, TN 37212
Tel.: (615) 251-8077
Representing:
Blackhawk
Brooks & Dunn
Lynyrd Skynyrd
Kathy Mattea
Lee Roy Parnell
Southern Spirit Tour
Travis Tritt
Trisha Yearwood

Evelyn Shriver Public Relations
1313 16th Avenue South
Nashville, TN 37212
Tel.: (615) 383-1000
Representing:
Deborah Allen
John Berry
T. Graham Brown
Tracy Byrd
Carlene Carter
Country Weekly
Bobbie Cryner
Holly Dunn
The Eagles Tour
Farm Aid
Hank Flamingo
Alexander Gudunov
Giant Records
Emmylou Harris
James House
Janis Ian
George Jones
Hal Ketchum
Kris Kristofferson
Shelby Lynne
Kevin Montgomery
Lorrie Morgan
Willie Nelson
Daron Norwood
Orrall & Wright
K.T. Oslin
River North Records
Dennis Robbins
Ricky Van Shelton
Sweethearts of the Rodeo
Randy Travis
Rhonda Vincent
Clay Walker
Monte Warden
Joy Lynn White
Tammy Wynette

StarStruck Entertainment
PO Box 121996
Nashville, TN 37212
Tel.: (615) 742-8835
Representing:
Brother Phelps
Linda Davis
Joe Diffie
Reba McEntire
Ruth McGinnis
Aaron Tippin
The Tractors

The Ken Stilts Company
PO Box 17087
Nashville, TN 37217
Tel.: (615) 754-6100
Representing:
Jon Brennan
McBride & The Ride
Pirates of the Mississippi
Orrall & Wright

Turner & Co.
1018 17th Avenue South, Suite 6
Nashville, TN 37212
Tel.: (615) 327-1274
Representing:
Harlan Howard Songs
Maypop Music
The Nitty Gritty Dirt Band
Shenandoah
Lisa Stewart

K. West Company
PO Box 24545
Nashville, TN 37202
Tel.: (615) 383-9388
Representing:
George Strait

VIDEO PRODUCTION COMPANIES

Ace Pictures Inc.
1016 17th Avenue South
Nashville, TN 37212
Tel.: (615) 327-3377

Alpha Video Productions
915 West Main
Hendersonville, TN 37075
Tel.: (615) 822-6187

Atlas Productions
PO Box 50
Goodlettsville, TN 37072
Tel.: (615) 859-1343

Caluger & Associates
237 French Landing, Suite 100
Nashville, TN 37228
Tel.: (615) 824-9191

Century City Artists Colony
2 Music Square West
Nashville, TN 37203
Tel.: (615) 244-7900

Churchill Video
3225 South Norwood
Tulsa, OK 74135
Tel.: (910) 503-3883

Citation Film Tape Support
2602-A Westwood Drive
Nashville, TN 37204
Tel.: (615) 298-5252

Dixie Moose Productions
113 Winding Way Drive
Hendersonville, TN 37075
Tel.: (615) 264-3166

Evans-Hale Company
1 Maryland Farms Blvd.
Brentwood, TN 37027
Tel.: (615) 313-5936

Film House, Inc.
230 Cumberland Bend
Nashville, TN 37228
Tel.: (615) 255-4000

Kingswood Productions
810 12th Avenue South
Nashvllle, TN 37203
Tel.: (615) 742-5433

Kenny Kiper Productions
1451 Elm Hill Pike, Suite 162
Nashville, TN 37210
Tel.: (615) 367-0126

Media Productions
PO Box 210143
Nashville, TN 37221
Tel.: (615) 646-0382

Multi Media
3401 West End Avenue, #185 West
Nashville, TN 37203
Tel.: (615) 298-1425

The Music Machine TV Corp.
PO Box 22653
Nashville, TN 37202
Tel.: (615) 822-6199

The Nashville Network
2806 Opryland Drive
Nashville, TN 37214
Tel.: (615) 871-6987

Jim Owens & Associates., Inc.
1525 McGavock Street
Nashville, TN 37203
Tel.: (615) 256-7700

Dyann Rivkin Productions
1406 Sigler
Music Circle North
Nashville, TN 37203
Tel.: (615) 726-2774

Roxy Production Center
827 Meridian Street
Nashville, TN 37207
Tel.: (615) 226-1122

Scene Three Video
1811 8th Avenue South
Nashville, TN 37203
Tel.: 615-385-2820

Soundshop
1307 Division St.
Nashville, TN 37203
Tel.: (615) 244-4149

Studio Productions
145 12th Avenue North
Nashville, TN 37203
Tel.: (615) 256-4960

Thirtys Film & Tape
2831 Columbine Place
Nashville, TN 37204
Tel.: (615) 385-2277

TSC Video
1107 18th Avenue South
Nashville, TN 37212
Tel.: (615) 320-1591

Video Productions Unlimited
PO Box 121626
Nashville, TN 37212
Tel.: (615) 726-1556

World Wide Sound Productions
202 West Plaza Street
Robinson, IL 62454
Tel.: (613) 544-7898

FAN CLUBS

Alabama
PO Box 529
Fort Wayne, AL 35967

Rex Allen, Jr.
PO Box 7672
Texarkana, TX 75505

Bill Anderson
PO Box 85
Watervliet, MI 49098

Lynn Anderson
PO Box 90454
Charleston, SC 29410

Darlene Austin
PO Box 120375
Nashville, TN 37212

Hoyt Axton
2485 Canabury Drive, #219
St. Paul, MN 55117

Razzy Bailey
PO Box 2196
Hendersonville, TN 37075

Butch Baker
PO Box 1423
Antioch, TN 37075

Joe Barnhill
2607 Westwood Drive
Nashville, TN 37204

Susi Beatty
PO Box 292866
Nashville, TN 37229

Bellamy Brothers
PO Box 801
San Antonio, FL 34266-0801

Vicki Bird
PO Box 1368
Hendersonville, TN 37077

Clint Black
PO Box 299386
Houston, TX 77299-0386

Suzy Bogguss
PO Box 7535
Marietta, GA 30065

Larry Boone
815 East 95th
Hutchinson, KS 67502

Lane Brody
PO Box 24775
Nashville, TN 37202

T. Graham Brown
1516 16th Avenue South
Nashville, TN 37212

Jann Browne
PO Box 3481
Laguna Hills, CA 92654-3481

Ed Bruce
PO Box 120428
Nashville, TN 37212

Canyon
607 West Church Drive
Sugarland, TX 77478

Paulette Carlson
PO Box 1144
Arvada, CO 80001-1144

Lionel Cartwright
27 Music Square East, #182
Nashville, TN 37203

Johnny Cash
Rt. 12, Box 350
Winston-Salem, NC 27107

Mark Chesnutt
PO Box 128031
Nashville, TN 37212

Chuck Wagon Gang
PO Box 140215
Nashville, TN 37214-0215

Roy Clark
PO Box 470304
Tulsa, OK 74147

David Allan Coe
PO Box 509
Branson, MO 65616

Mark Collie
PO Box 90132
Nashville, TN 37209

Earl Thomas Conley
PO Box 23552
Nashville, TN 37202

Helen Cornelius
R.R. 4, 9 Sunset Drive
East Hampton, CT 06424

Billy "Crash" Craddock
PO Box 1585
Mt. Vernon, IL 62864

Rodney Crowell
PO Box 120576
Nashville, TN 37212

Lacy J. Dalton
PO Box 1109
Mt. Juliet, TN 37122

Davis Daniel
1500 W. Littleton, Box C-15
Littleton, CO 80120

Charlie Daniels Band
17060 Central Pike
Lebanon, TN 37087

Linda Davis
PO Box 121996
Nashville, TN 37212-1996

Billy Dean
PO Box 23362
Nashville, TN 37202

Desert Rose Band
PO Box 1053
Arvada, CO 80001

Suzi Deveraux
201 Waters Avenue
Watertown, TN 37184

Joe Diffie
PO Box 479
Velma, OK 73081

Dean Dillon
PO Box 40523
Nashville, TN 37204

Steve Douglas
PO Box 2866
Conroe, TX 77305

Exile
PO Box 180753
Utica, MI 48318

Donna Fargo
PO Box 233
Crescent, GA 31304

The Forester Sisters
PO Box 1456
Trenton, GA 30752

Four Guys
PO Box 615
Antioch, TN 37013

Janie Fricke
PO Box 80785
San Antonio, TX 78268-0785

Vince Gill
27 Music Square East, #107
Nashville, TN 37203

Mickey Gilley
PO Box 1242
Pasadena, TX 77504

Vern Gosdin
2509 W. Marquette Avenue
Tampa, FL 33614

Merle Haggard
PO Box 2065
Pinellas Park, FL 34664

Tom T. Hall
Fox Hollow
Berry Chappel Road
Franklin, TN 37064
and
Highway 101
PO Box 120875
Nashville, TN 37212

Hee Haw
PO Box 140400
Nashville, TN 37214

Highway 101
PO Box 120875
Nashville, TN 37212

Becky Hobbs
PO Box 12197
Nashville, TN 37212

Alan Jackson
PO Box 121945
Nashville, TN 37212

Jim & Jesse
404 Shoreline Drive
Tallahassee, FL 32311

George Jones
Rt. 3, Box 150
Murphy, NC 28906

The Kentucky Headhunters
301 Ridgecrest Drive
Goodlettsville, TN 37072

Doug Kershaw
PO Box 24762
San Jose, CA 95154

Hal Ketchum
PO Box 120205
Nashville, TN 37212

Alison Krauss & Union Station
PO Box 2179
Johnson City, TN 37605

Kris Kristofferson
313 Lakeshore Drive
Marietta, GA 30067

Jim Lauderdale
PO Box 2163
Silverthorne, CO 80498

Chris LeDoux
PO Box 253
Sumner, IA 50674

Brenda Lee
2126 N. North Street
Peoria, IL 61604

Robin Lee
PO Box 22067
Nashville, TN 37202

Patty Loveless
PO Box 363
Groveport, OH 43125-0363

Loretta Lynn
PO Box 40328
Nashville, TN 37204-0328

Shelby Lynne
PO Box 190
Monroeville, AL 36461

Barbara Mandrell
PO Box 620
Hendersonville, TN 37077

Marcy Brothers
PO Box 2502
Oroville, CA 95965

Kathy Mattea
PO Box 158482
Nashville, TN 37215

McBride & The Ride
PO Box 17617
Nashville, TN 37217

The McCarters
PO Box 41455
Nashville, TN 37204

Neal McCoy
PO Box 662
Poteau, OK 74953

Mel McDaniel
PO Box 680445
Orlando, FL 32868

Ronnie McDowell
PO Box 82
Gallatin, TN 37066

Reba McEntire
PO Box 121996
Nashville, TN 37212-1996

Ronnie Milsap
PO Box 23109
Nashville, TN 37202

Lorrie Morgan
PO Box 2204
Brentwood, TN 37027

Gary Morris
607 W. Church Drive
Sugar Land, TX 77478

Willie Nelson
PO Box 7104
Lancaster, PA 17604-7104

Nitty Gritty Dirt Band
PO Box 6106
Branson, MO 65616

Oak Ridge Boys
329 Rockland Road
Hendersonville, TN 37075

K.T. Oslin
27 Music Square East, #180
Nashville, TN 37203

Marie Osmond
3325 N. University Avenue, #150
Provo, UT 84604

Paul Overstreet
PO Box 121975
Nashville, TN 37212

Dolly Parton
700 Dollywood Lane
Pigeon Forge, TN 37863

Johnny Paycheck
PO Box 2474
Huntington, WV 25725-2474

Pirates of the Mississippi
PO Box 17617
Nashville, TN 37217

Ray Price
PO Box 61
Harrisburg, PA 17108

Charley Pride
PO Box 670507
Dallas, TX 75367-0507

Jeanne Pruett
7117 Sutton Place
Fairview, TN 37062

Eddie Rabbitt
PO Box 125
Lewistown, OH 43333

Eddy Raven
PO Box 2476
Hendersonville, TN 37077

Collin Raye
PO Box 530
Reno, NV 89504

Jerry Reed
45 Music Square West
Nashville, TN 37203

Ronna Reeves
PO Box 80424
Midland, TX 79709

Restless Heart
PO Box 35453
Des Moines, IA 50315-5453

Riders in the Sky
Rt. 3, Box 76
Fairview, TN 37062

Jeannie C. Riley
PO Box 454
Brentwood, TN 37027

Johnny Rodriguez
PO Box 488
Sabinal, TX 78881

Kenny Rogers
1516 16th Avenue South
Nashville, TN 37212

Billy Joe Royal
PO Box 121862
Nashville, TN 37212

Johnny Russell
PO Box Drawer 37
Hendersonville, TN 37077

Sawyer Brown
4205 Hillsboro Road, #208
Nashville, TN 37215

Ricky Van Shelton
PO Box 120548
Nashville, TN 37212

Shenandoah
PO Box 2442
Muscle Shoals, AL 35662

T.G. Sheppard
916 South Byrne, #2
Toledo, OH 43609

Shotgun Red
HCR 1, Box 420A
Hollister, MO 65672

Ricky Skaggs
PO Box 121799
Nashville, TN 37212-1799

Margo Smith
1802 Williamson Court, #200
Brentwood, TN 37027

Jo-EI Sonnier
PO Box 120845
Nashville, TN 37212

Billie Jo Spears
28 Starlane Road
Rome, NY 13440

George Strait
PO Box 2119
Hendersonville, TN 37077

The Statler Brothers
PO Box 2703
Staunton, VA 24401

Ray Stevens
1707 Grand Avenue
Nashville, TN 37212

Doug Stone
PO Box 40465
Nashville, TN 37204

Sweethearts of the Rodeo
PO Box 1600077
Nashville, TN 37216

Les Taylor
177 Northwood Drive
Lexington, KY 40505

Marsha Thornton
Rt. 7, Box 19
Florence, AL 35630

Mel Tillis
809 18th Avenue South
Nashville, TN 37203

Pam Tillis
PO Box 25304
Nashville, TN 37202

Aaron Tippin
PO Box 121709
Nashville, TN 37212

Randy Travis
1604 16th Avenue South
Nashville, TN 37212

Travis Tritt's Country Club
PO Box 440099
Kennesaw, GA 30144

Billy Walker
21 Gt. Stone Road
Northfield
Birmingham, B31 2LR
England

Steve Wariner
PO Box 1209
Nolensville, TN 37135-1209

Kevin Welch
PO Box 27125
Tulsa, OK 74149

Kitty Wells
240 Old Hickory Blvd. East
Madison, TN 37115

The Whites
PO Box 2158
Hendersonville, TN 37075

Hank Williams, Jr.
PO Box 1350
Paris, TN 38242

Jason D. Williams
240 Valley Loop
Heber Springs, AR 72543

Tom Wopat
PO Box 128031
Nashville, TN 37212

Tammy Wynette
PO Box 753
Richboro, PA 18954

Dwight Yoakam
4915840 Ventura Blvd., #65
Encino, CA 91436

FAIRS AND FESTIVALS

BLUEGRASS

Alabama
Cullman
Bluegrass Superjam
March and November
Tel.: (205) 747-1650

Arizona
Wickenburg
Four Corner States Bluegrass
November
Tel.: (602) 684-5479

California
Barstow
Calico Spring Festival, Calico Ghost Town
May
Tel.: (714) 533-9910

Blythe
Colorado River Country Music Festival
January
Tel.: (619) 922-8166

Grass Valley
California Bluegrass Association's Annual Father's Day
Weekend Bluegrass Festival
June (mid)
Tel.: (209) 464-5324

Santa Barbara
Live Oak Music Festival
June
Tel.: (805) 544-5229

Yosemite
Strawberry Spring Music Festival
May (late)
Tel.: (203) 533-0191

Yosemite
Strawberry Fall Music Festival
September
Tel.: (203) 533-0191

Yucaipa
Ol' Time Farmer's Fair and Bluegrass Festival
Yucaipa Regional Park
Labor Day
Tel.: (714) 790-3125/(714) 790-3126

Colorado
Central City
Central City Bluegrass Festival
May (mid)
Tel.: (303) 583-5915

Loveland
Rocky Mountain Bluegrass Festival
August (late)
Tel.: (303) 364-GRAS

Telluride
Telluride Bluegrass Festival
June (mid)
Tel.: (303) 449-6007/(800) 624-2442

Florida
Dunnellon
Withlacoochie Bluegrass Jamboree
March (late)
Tel.: (904) 489-8330

Kissimmee
Kissimmee Bluegrass Festival
March
Tel.: (407) 856-0245

Live Oak
Spring Bluegrass Festival
April
Tel.: (904) 364-1683

Georgia
Augusta
Free Riverwalk/Augusta Bluegrass Festival
May
Tel.: (404) 592-4302

Dahlonega
Dahlonega Bluegrass Festival
June (late)
Tel.: (404) 864-7203

Jekyll Island
New Year's Bluegrass Festival
December 31
Tel.: (404) 864-7203

Lawrenceville
Peach State Classic
July (end)
Tel.: (404) 781-4542

Lincolnton
Lewis Family Homecoming and Bluegrass Festival
April (end)
Tel.: (404) 864-7203

Idaho
Sandpoint
Great Northern Bluegrass Festival
July (late)
Tel.: (208) 263-2161

Illinois
Havana
Mason County Summer Festival of Bluegrass Music
July
Tel.: (217) 243-3159

Indiana
Westfield
Little Eagle Creek Bluegrass Invitational
July
Tel.: (317) 896-2985

Iowa
Guthrie Center
Guthrie Center Bluegrass Music Festival
July
Tel.: (816) 665-7172

Kansas
Winfield
International Guitar Flat-Picking Championships
September (mid)
Tel.: (316) 221-3250

Kentucky
Lexington
Festival of the Bluegrass
June (mid)
Tel.: (904) 364-1683

Owensboro
IBMA World of Bluegrass Trade Show and Fan Fest
September (late)
Tel.: (502) 684-9025

Renfro Valley
Renfro Valley Bluegrass Festival
September
Tel.: (606) 986-1269/(800) 765-7464

Maryland
Hyattstown
Hyattstown Volunteer Fire Department Bluegrass Festival
June
Tel.: (301) 831-8118

Michigan
Charlotte
Charlotte Bluegrass Festival
June
Tel.: (313) 227-1997

Ypsilanti
E & W Productions and Wiard's Orchards Annual Bluegrass Festival
August
Tel.: (419) 726-5089

Minnesota
Princeton
Minnesota Bluegrass and Old-Time Music Festival
July (end)
Tel.: (715) 635-2479

Missouri
Branson
American Folk Music Festival
June
Tel.: (417) 338-8281

St. Louis
Gateway City Indoor Bluegrass Festival and Instrument Dealer Trade Show
February (end)
Tel.: (417) 243-3159

Montana
Hamilton
Bitterroot Valley Bluegrass Festival
July (mid)
Tel.: (406) 363-2400

Nevada
Fallon
Desert Oasis Bluegrass Festival
April (late)
Tel.: (702) 432-7733

New Jersey
Woodstown
Brandywine Mountain Music Convention
June
Tel.: (505) 257-3131

New Mexico
Angel Fire
Angel Fire Bluegrass Festival
August (early)
Tel.: (800) 446-8117

Ruidoso
Springtime in the Rockies Bluegrass Festival
June
Tel.: (505) 257-3131

New York
Hillsdale
Winterhawk Bluegrass Festival
July (mid)
Tel.: (513) 390-6211

New York
NYC Bluegrass Band and Banjo Contest
Tel.: (212) 427-3221

Shinhopple
Peaceful Valley Bluegrass Festival
July
Tel.: (607) 363-2211

North Carolina
Asheville
Doyle Lawson and Quicksilver's Family-Style Bluegrass Festival
July (early)
Tel.: (704) 274-5942

Black Mountain
Fiddlehead Fall Festival
September
Tel.: (704) 253-3917

Burlington
Bass Mountain Music Park Memorial Day Weekend Bluegrass Festival
May
Tel.: (919) 228-7344

Burlington
Bass Mountain Music Park Labor Day Weekend Bluegrass Festival
September
Tel.: (919) 228-7344

Cherokee
Cherokee Bluegrass Festival
August
Tel.: (404) 864-7203

Wilkesboro
Merle Watson Memorial Festival
April (late)
Tel.: (919) 651-8691

Ohio
Columbus
Bluegrass Classic at Frontier Ranch
July (late)
Tel.: (614) 548-4199

Oklahoma
Hugo
Grant's Annual Bluegrass Festival
August (early)
Tel.: (405) 326-5598

Langley
Langley Bluegrass Festival
August (late) through Labor Day
Tel.: (918) 782-9850

McAlester
Sanders Family Bluegrass Festival
June
Tel.: (918) 423-4891

Tulsa
Bluegrass and Chili Festival
September (mid)
Tel.: (918) 583-2617

Pennsylvania
Gettysburg
Gettysburg Bluegrass Camporee
May and September
Tel.: (717) 642-8749
Wind Gap
Wind Gap Bluegrass Festival
June
Tel.: (201) 584-2324

South Carolina
Myrtle Beach
South Carolina State Bluegrass Festival
November
Tel.: (404) 864-7203

South Dakota
The Black Hills Bluegrass Festival
June (late)
Tel.: (605) 394-4101

Tennessee
Elizabethton
Jim and Jesse's Annual Bluegrass Festival
June
Tel.: (615) 323-4352

Nashville
SPBGMA's Annual Bluegrass Music Awards National Convention
January (late)
Tel.: (816) 665-7172

Texas
Canton
Texas State Bluegrass Festival
June (late)
Tel.: (903) 567-2857

Utah
Snowbird Ski Resort
Snowbird Annual Bluegrass Festival
July (mid)
Tel.: (801) 521-2822

Virginia
Amelia
Central Virginia Family Bluegrass Music Festival
May and August
Tel.: (804) 561-3011

Stuart
Dominion Valley Park Gospel Festival
May
Tel.: (703) 694-7009

Stuart
July 4 Bluegrass Festival
July
Tel.: (703) 694-7009

Virginia Beach
Bluegrass Kickoff
May
Tel.: (804) 539-5063

Washington
Sedro-Woolley
Bluegrass and Country Music Jam
Cascade Middle School
First Sunday (monthly)
Tel.: (206) 856-1058

West Virginia
Summersville
Summersville Bluegrass Country Music
June (late)
Tel.: (304) 872-3145

Wyoming
Grand Targhee Resort
Bluegrass Festival
August (early)
Tel.: (307) 353-2304

GOSPEL

Alabama
Glencoe
Gold City Homecoming
Gold City Music Park
July (mid)
Tel.: (205) 492-0942

Arkansas
Springdale
Albert E. Brumley Sun-down to Sun-up Sing
Rodeo Arena
August (early)
Tel.: (417) 235-8312

California
Carlsbad
American Music Conference
Tel.: (619) 431-9124

San Diego
Music California
April (mid)
Tel.: (818) 993-8378

Colorado
Denver
DC
Tel.: (800) 729-3294

Estes Park
Christian Artists' Music Seminar
August
Tel.: (303) 452-1313/(303) 452-3411

Florida
Jacksonville
Gospel Explosion
First Baptist Church
Tel.: (407) 831-0333

Live Oak
Suwannee River Jubilee
Spirit of Suwannee Music Park and Campground
June (late)
Tel.: (904) 477-6391

Longwood
Music Florida
Tel.: (407) 831-0333

Orlando
Jesus
Sea World
June (mid)
Tel.: (704) 376-4388

Orlando
Kingdom Youth Conference
Hyatt
July (end)
Tel.: (704) 739-3838

Taylor
Taylor Campmeeting
Taylor Church
June (late)
Tel.: (904) 259-4308/(800) 874-8465

Georgia
Atlanta
Southern Gospel Music Weekend at Six Flags Over Georgia
May (late)
Tel.: (404) 424-8839

Atlanta
Atlanta Fest
Six Flags Over Georgia
June (mid)
Tel.: (404) 424-8839/(404) 424-7958

Atlanta
Christian Booksellers Association Convention
July
Tel.: (719) 576-7880

Atlanta
IS Fest
July
Tel.: (404) 319-7064/(404) 434-2068

Dahlonega
Gospel Gold Festival
Blackburn Park
July (late)-August (early)
Tel.: (404) 265-1980

Gainesville
New Year's Sing
Georgia Mountain Center
December (late)
Tel.: (800) 654-0810

Illinois
Greenville
Agape Music Festival
Bond County Fairgrounds
May
Tel.: (618) 664-1806

Indiana
Indianapolis
Gospel Music Workshop of America
Indianapolis Hoosier Dome
August
Tel.: (313) 898-2340

Iowa
Des Moines
Southern Gospel Music Jubilee
September (middle)
Tel.: (515) 255-2122/(515) 255-0052

Kentucky
Louisville
Covenant Festival
June
Tel.: (502) 448-8526/(502) 231-0387

Red Lick
Bishop's Annual Homecoming
July (mid)
Tel.: (606) 369-3635

Mississippi
Jackson
JaxFest
September (end)
Tel.: (601) 925-5112/(601) 992-3729

Missouri
Stanton
Merimac Caverns Sing
Merimac Cavern
October (mid)
Tel.: (314) 771-4432

New Mexico
Glorieta
Church Music Week
July (mid)
Tel.: (615) 251-2292

New York
Darien Lake
Kingdom Bound
August (end)
Tel.: (716) 633-1117

Tarrytown
Harrogate International Youth Music Festival
Tel.: (914) 631-9100

Tarrytown
Shrewsbury International Music Festival
Tel.: (914) 631-9100

North Carolina
Boone
Greene's Annual Singing Jubilee
High Country Fairgrounds
August (mid)
Tel.: (704) 297-3030

Bryson City
Inspirations' Annual Singing in the Smokies
Inspirations Park
June (late)-July (early)
Tel.: (704) 488-2865

Bryson City
Singing in the Smokies
Inspirations Park
July (late)-August (early)
Tel.: (704) 488-2865

Bryson City
Inspirations' Labor Day Festival
Inspirations Park
September (early)
Tel.: (704) 488-2865

Bryson City
Singing in the Smokies Fall Color Festival
Inspirations Park
October (mid)
Tel.: (704) 488-2865

Candler
Singing in Hominey Valley
Hominy Valley Music Park
June (late)-July (early)
Tel.: (704) 667-8502

Candler
Hominy Valley Fall Color Sing
Hominy Valley Music Park
October (mid)
Tel.: (704) 667-8502

Charlotte
North Carolina Song Festival
Owens Auditorium
April (mid)
Tel.: (704) 372-3600/(704) 428-2640

Greensboro
Hoppers' Annual North Carolina Singing Convention and Campmeeting
North Carolina Pentecostal Holiness Campground
July (late)
Tel.: (919) 548-2526

Kinston
Heaven Bound Anniversary Sing
Lenoir Community College
May (early)
Tel.: (919) 522-3127

Ridgecrest
Church Music Week
June (mid-end)
Tel.: (615) 251-2292

Ohio
Canton
Choral Music Celebration
August
Tel.: (216) 492-7990/(800) 423-1232

Westerville
Hosanna
Grace Brethren Worship Center
April (end)
Tel.: (614) 431-8223

Pennsylvania
Kempton
Garden Spot Promotions' Blue Mountain Gospel Music Festival
Community Grounds
August (late)-September (early)
Tel.: (717) 872-5615

Mt. Union
Creation Festival
Agape Farm
June (end)
Tel.: (800) 327-6921

Philadelphia
Praise in the Park
July (mid)
Tel.: (215) 887-5287

Rehrersburg
Celebrate
Teen Challenge Training Center
August'
Tel.: (803) 585-5436

South Carolina

Greenville
Grand Ole Gospel Reunion
Greenville Memorial Auditorium
August (early)
Tel.: (803) 877-6923

Greenville
America's Biggest Thanksgiving Sing
November (late)
Tel.: (803) 877-6923

Spartanburg
Choral Festival
August
Tel.: (803) 585-5436

South Dakota

South Dakota
The Black Hills Bluegrass Festival
Includes free Gospel concert
June (late)
Tel.: (605) 394-4101

Tennessee

Carthage
Wilburns' Homecoming
October (late)
Tel.: (615) 735-2650

Cleveland
Singing Echoes Blue Springs Valley Sing
Blue Springs Valley
July (mid)
Tel.: (615) 476-4254

Clinton
McKameys Anniversary Sing
Anderson County High School Gymnasium
June (late)
Tel.: (615) 457-3678

Gatlinburg
Church Music in the Smokies
July
Tel.: (800) 456-4966

Kingsport
Greenland Park Gospel Sing
August (late)
Tel.: (615) 246-8229

Memphis
Music Memphis
Tel.: (407) 831-0333

Nashville
Gospel Music
March (end)-April (early)
Tel.: (615) 242-0303

Nashville
Industry Summit Music Row
May
Tel.: (615) 269-7056/(615) 269-0131

Nashville
Gospel Jubilee at Opryland
May (late)
Tel.: (615) 889-6611

Nashville
National Quartet Convention
Municipal Auditorium
September (late)-October (early)
Tel.: (615) 320-7000/(615) 327-1518

Nashville
"Singin' News" Fan Awards
Municipal Auditorium
October (early)
Tel.: (615) 320-7000

Nashville
Doulos Training Schools
Tel.: (615) 227-4051

Texas
Dallas
Music Texas
Tel.: (407) 831-0333

Fort Worth
Church Music Workshop
Southwestern Baptist Theological Seminary

Houston
Church Music USA
January
Tel.: (800) 456-4966

Lindale
Jesus Go Fest
April (mid)
Tel.: (214) 882-5591

Virginia
Front Royal
Fishnet
July
Tel.: (703) 636-2961

Virginia Beach
Church Music USA
January (mid)
Tel.: (800) 456-4966

Washington
Bellevue
Church Music NW
May (mid)
Tel.: (206) 823-9099

Vancouver
Jesus Northwest Festival
Clark County Fair
July (end)
Tel.: (503) 393-1613

West Virginia
Charleston
World's Largest New Year's Eve Sing
Municipal Auditorium
December 31
Tel.: (304) 345-7469/(304) 342-5757

COUNTRY MUSIC

Arkansas
Phoenix
Fourth of July Country Music Festival
KMLE-FM
July 4
Tel.: (602) 264-0108

Prairie Grove
Prairie Grove Clothesline Fair
September (early)
Tel.: (501) 846-2990

Tucson
Sons of the Pioneers Westfest
Tel.: (602) 323-3311

California
Auburn
Auburn Wild West Stampede
April
Tel.: (916) 889-BUCK

Banning
Stagecoach Days
A.C. Dysart Equestrian Park
September (late)
Tel.: (714) 849-4695

Bishop
Mule Days Celebration
Tri-County Fairgrounds
Memorial Day weekend
Tel.: (619) 873-8405

Blythe
Colorado River Country Music Festival
January (early)
Tel.: (619) 922-7577/(800) 443-5513

Fortuna
Fortuna Rodeo
Rohnert Park
July
Tel.: (707) 445-9211

Pismo Beach
Rancho El Pismo Western Days Celebration
September (mid)
Tel.: (805) 773-4382

Red Bluff
Round-Up Rodeo and Parade
Sun Country Fairgrounds
April
Tel.: (916) 527-6220

Redding
Redding Rodeo Week
May
Tel.: (916) 241-3215

Tehachapi
Mountain Festival
Rodeo Grounds
August
Tel.: (805) 822-4180

Victorville
Huck Finn's Jubilee
Mojave Narrows
Father's Day Weekend
Tel.: (714) 780-8810

Yermo
Calico Ghost Town
Throughout year
Tel.: (619) 254-2122

Yucaipa
Ol' Time Farmer's Fair and Bluegrass Festival
Yucaipa Regional Park
Labor Day
Tel.: (714) 790-3125/(714) 790-3126

Colorado
Copper Mountain
Michael Martin Murphey's West Fest
Labor Day weekend
Tel.: (303) 968-2882

Durango
Durango Cowboy Poetry Gathering
October (early)
Tel.: (303) 259-1388

Manitou Springs
Mountain Music Festival
August (mid)
Tel.: (800) 642-2567

Winter Park
Winter Park American Music Festival
July (mid)
Tel.: (303) 726-4118

Woodland Park
Cowboys With Culture
September (late)
Tel.: (719) 687-9975

Florida
Wauchula
Pioneer Park Days
March (early)
Tel.: (813) 773-2161

Zellwood
Zellwood Sweet Corn Festival
May (end)
Tel.: (407) 886-0014

Georgia
Atlanta
Georgia Music Festival
September (mid)
Tel.: (404) 656-3551

Calhoun
Concerts in the Country
May through October
Tel.: (404) 291-3819

Gainesville
Concerts in the Country
May through October
Tel.: (404) 291-3819

Rome
Heritage Holidays
October (late)
Tel.: (401) 291-3819

Smyrna
Buckboard Country Music Showcase
Tel.: (404) 955-7340

Idaho
Athol
Silverwood
Throughout year
Tel.: (208) 772-0515

Nampa
Snake River Stampede
July (mid)
Tel.: (208) 466-8497

Sun Falls
Ketchum Wagon Days Celebration
Labor Day
Tel.: (800) 634-3347

Twin Falls
Western Days
May (late)
Tel.: (208) 733-3974

Illinois
Chicago
Country Music Festival
July (end)
Tel.: (312) 744-3315

Kansas
Independence
Neewollah
October (late)-November (early)
Tel.: (316) 331-6090

Kentucky
Berea
Traditional Music Festival
Berea College
October (late)
Tel.: (606) 986-9341 x5140

Paintsville
Butcher Hollow
Red Caboose
All year
Tel.: (606) 789-5688

Michigan
Detroit
W4 Country Music Weekend
WWWW-FM
May
Tel.: (313) 259-4323

Mississippi
Amory
Amory Railroad Festival
April (mid)
Tel.: (601) 256-7194

Meridian
Jimmie Rodgers Museum
All year
Tel.: (601) 485-1808

Montana
Conrad
Whoop-Up Parade and Rodeo
May (mid)
Tel.: (406) 278-7791

Great Falls
Montana Roundup Days
June (late)
Tel.: (406) 727-8787

Lewistown
Cowboy Poetry Gathering
August (mid)
Tel.: (406) 538-8721/(406) 538-5436

Miles City
Miles City Jaycee Bucking Horse Sale
May (mid)
Tel.: (406) 232-2890

Miles City
Range Riders Fiddler's Festival
September (late)
Tel.: (406) 232-2890

Reedpoint
Running of the Sheep and Sheep Drive
September (early)
Tel.: (406) 326-2288

Nebraska

Firth
Prairieland CountryFest
Prairieland Park
May (end)
Tel.: (402) 791-2029

North Platte
NEBRASKAland Days
June (mid)
Tel.: (308) 532-7939

Nevada

Elko
Cowboy Poetry Gathering
Western Folklife Center
January (end)
Tel.: (702) 738-7508

Reno
KBUL-FM Listener Appreciation Concert
Fall
Tel.: (702) 827-0980

New Mexico

Albuquerque
KOLT 106 FM Countryfest
Tel.: (505) 247-2381

Capitan
Smokey Bear Stampede
July (early)
Tel.: (505) 354-2224

Carlsbad
AJAR Rodeo and Western Days
July (early)
Tel.: (505) 887-6516

Carlsbad
American West Celebration
Washington Ranch
April (early)

Carlsbad
The Flying X Chuckwagon
During Summer
Tel.: (505) 885-6789

Clayton
Old Western Dance
American Legion Hall
April (late)
Tel.: (505) 374-8344

Clovis
Pioneer Days and Rodeo
June (late)
Tel.: (505) 763-3425

Cloudcroft
Western Roundup
June
Tel.: (505) 682-2733

Crownpoint
Eastern Navajo Fair
July (late)
Tel.: (505) 786-5841

Des Moines
Cowboy Camp Meeting
Waverly Lodge
July (mid)
Tel.: (505) 278-2683

Farmington
The San Juan County Fair
August (late)
Tel.: (505) 334-2688

Grants
Wild West Days
July
Tel.: (505) 287-4802

Gallup
Lions Club Western Jubilee Week
Red Rock State Park
June (mid)
Tel.: (505) 863-5152

Hobbs
Hobbs Hoedown Days
September (late)
Tel.: (505) 397-3202

Hobbs
Staked Plains Roundup
September (late)
Tel.: (505) 392-4510

Lovington
Country Caravan Music Festival
Lea County Courthouse
June (late)
Tel.: (505) 361-5311

Raton
PRCA and WRPA Rodeo
Rodeo Arena
June (late)
Tel.: (505) 445-3689

Ruidoso
Southwestern Pickers Reunion Festival
July (late)
Tel.: (505) 257-7395

Silver City
Frontier Days
Gough Park
July 4
Tel.: (800) 548-9378

Truth or Consequences
Union Mill Opry
February
Tel.: (505) 894-9066

North Carolina
Agnos
Annual String Band
Fiddle and Jig Dance Contests
June (mid)
Tel.: (714) 895-2286

Monroe
WSOC Family Reunion
September (late)
Tel.: (704) 335-4848

North Dakota
Dickinson
Roughrider Days
June (late)-July (early)
Tel.: (701) 225-5115

Medora
The Medora Musical
June through September
Tel.: (701) 623-4444

Oklahoma
Anadarko
Western Day Celebration
Tel.: (405) 247-6651

Hartshorne
Blue Mountain Western Festival and Rodeo
June (late)
Tel.: (918) 297-2620

Oklahoma City
The National Cowboy Hall of Fame
Memorial Day through Labor Day
Tel.: (415) 478-2250

Tulsa
KVOO Big Country Picnic and Country Music Show
August
Tel.: (918) 743-7814

Oregon
Pendleton
Pendleton Round-Up and Happy Canyon Indian Pageant
September (mid)
Tel.: (800) 524-2984

Pennsylvania

Bethlehem
Musikfest
August (mid)
Tel.: (215) 861-0678

Chambersburg
Appalachian Jubilee
Capitol Theatre
50 Saturdays of the year
Tel.: (717) 264-8349

Coudersport
Laurelwood Jamboree
September (early)
Tel.: (814) 274-9220

Du Bois
Tom Mix Festival
September (early)
Tel.: (814) 371-5010/(814) 546-2628

Lewistown
Mifflin-Juniata Arts Festival
May (mid)
Tel.: (717) 242-3028/(717) 248-6713

Meyersdale
Pennsylvania Maple Festival
April (early)
Tel.: (814) 634-0213

New Holland
Spring Gulch Folk Festival
May (mid)
Tel.: (800) 255-5744/(717) 354-3100

Shade Gap
Shade Gap Picnic
July (late)-August (early)
Tel.: (814) 259-3279

West Chester
Turk's Head Music Festival
July (late)
Tel.: (215) 436-9010

South Dakota

Custer
The Mountain Music Show
May (late) through Labor Day
Tel.: (605) 673-2405

Custer
Buffalo Wallow Chili Cook-Off
September (late)
Tel.: (605) 673-2244

Deadwood
Days of '76
August (early)

Huron
The South Dakota State Fair
August (late)-September (early)
Tel.: (605) 352-8775

Keystone
The Miners Music Show
May (late) through Labor Day
Tel.: (605) 673-3454

Lake Norden
The Hee Haw Show
November (mid)
Tel.: (605) 785-3115

Nisland
Butte-Lawrence County Fair
August (mid)
Tel.: (605) 892-3139

St. Onge
St. Onge Rodeo
June (mid)
Tel.: (605) 578-1655

Spearfish
Mathews Opera House
May (late) through September (mid)
Tel.: (605) 642-7973

Tennessee

Erwin
Unicol County Apple Festival
October (early)
Tel.: (615) 743-3000

Nashville
Country Music Fan Fair
Tennesse State Fair Ground
June (mid)
Tel.: (615) 259-3900

Nashville
Midnight Jamboree
Ernest Tubb Record Shop, Music Valley Drive
Every Saturday at 11:30 p.m. (after the Grand Ole Opry)
Tel.: (615) 889-2474

Smithville
Old-Time Fiddlers Jamboree and Crafts Festival
The National Championship for Country Musician Beginners
July (early)
Tel.: (615) 597-4163

Texas

Amarillo
Cowboy Breakfasts and Dinners
April (mid) through October (mid)
Tel.: (806) 374-1497

Aransas Pass
Shrimporee
September (late)
Tel.: (512) 758-2750

Austin
Austin City Limits
KLRU-TV
August through December
Tel.: (512) 471-4811

Austin
The Texas Connection
KLRU-TV
January through April
Tel.: (512) 471-4811

Austin
The Jerry Jeff Walker Birthday Fest
March (mid)
Tel.: (512) 288-6170

Gilmer
East Texas Yamboree
October (mid)
Tel.: (915) 772-4327

Hereford
The National Cowgirl Hall of Fame
Western Heritage Center
Late Summer
Tel.: (808) 364-5252

Houston
KIKK Country Concerts
Miller Park
May and October
Tel.: (713) 772-4433

Kerrville
Kerrville Folk Festival
May (late)-June (late)
Tel.: (512) 257-3600

Rosenberg
The Ford Bend Country Czech Fest
May (early)
Tel.: (713) 342-5464

Utah

Cedar City
Mountain Man Rendezvous
August (early)
Tel.: (801) 677-2029

Cedar City
Calling All Cowboys
August (mid)
Tel.: (801) 677-2029

Logan
Festival of the American West
Utah State University
July (late)
Tel.: (801) 752-2161

Parowan
Iron County Cowboy Days
March (late)
Tel.: (801) 477-3331

Salt Lake City
Utah State Fair
September (early)
Tel.: (801) 538-8440

Virginia
Hilton
Carter Family Folk Music Concerts
Every Saturday night
Tel.: (800) VA-BYWAY

West Virginia
Glenville
West Virginia State Folk Festival
June (late)
Tel.: (304) 462-7361

Wheeling
Jamboree in the Hills
WWVA
July (mid)
Tel.: (800) 624-5456/(304) 234-0050

Wheeling
Jamboree USA [TV/Radio Show]
Capitol Music Hall
WWVA
Every Saturday night
Tel.: (304) 232-1170/(800) 624-5456

Washington
Omak
Omak Stampede and Suicide Race
Tel.: (800) 933-6625

Wisconsin
Rhinelander
Hodag Country Festival
July
Tel.: (715) 369-1300

Wyoming
Alta
High Country Cowboy Festival
Tel.: (307) 353-2304

Cheyenne
Cheyenne Frontier Days
July (last week)
Tel.: (307) 778-7200/(800) 227-6336

Laramie
KCGY-FM Country Showdown
Albany County Fairground
July (early)
Tel.: (307) 745-9242

Sheridan
Wyoming Country Music Festival
June (late)
Tel.: (307) 868-2374

Wilson
Bar-J Chuckwagon Suppers and Western Show
June through Labor Day
Tel.: (307) 733-7370

PRINCIPAL RADIO STATIONS

ALABAMA

WQSB-FM	ALBERTVILLE
WHMA-FM	ANNISTON
WHVK-FM	ATHENS
WIKX-FM	BIRMINGHAM
WZZK-FM	BIRMINGHAM
WDRM-FM	DECATUR
WTVY-FM	DOTHAN
WKSJ-FM	MOBILE
WZBA-FM	MOBILE
WLWI-FM	MONTGOMERY
WELR-FM	ROANOKE
WDXX-FM	SELMA
WTXT-FM	TUSCALOOSA

ALASKA

KASH-FM	ANCHORAGE
KYAK	ANCHORAGE

KIAK-FM	FAIRBANKS
KPEN-FM	HOMER

ARIZONA

KFLG-FM	BULLHEAD CITY
KAFF-FM	FLAGSTAFF
KGMN-FM	KINGMAN
KMLE-FM	PHOENIX
KFMM-FM	SAFFORD
KXKQ-FM	SAFFORD
KCWW	TEMPE
KNIX-FM	TEMPE
KIIM-FM	TUCSON
KTNN	WINDOW ROCK
KTTI-FM	YUMA

ARKANSAS

KWOZ-FM	BATESVILLE
KHLS-FM	BLYTHEVILLE
KWEH-FM	CAMDEN
KKIX-FM	FAYETTEVILLE
KBFC-FM	FORREST CITY
KMAG-FM	FORT SMITH
KTCS-FM	FORT SMITH
KCWD-FM	HARRISON
KHOZ-FM	HARRISON
KQUS-FM	HOT SPRINGS
KFIN-FM	JONESBORO
KSSN-FM	LITTLE ROCK
KXIX-FM	LITTLE ROCK
KZHE-FM	MAGNOLIA
KAMS-FM	MAMMOTH SPRING
KPFM-FM	MOUNTAIN HOME
KPBQ-FM	PINE BLUFF
KAMO-FM	ROGERS
KWCK-FM	SEARCY
KKYR-FM	TEXARKANA

CALIFORNIA

KYAK-FM	ALTURAS
KZLA-FM	BURBANK
KFRG-FM	COLTON
KWST-FM	EL CENTRO
KEKA-FM	EUREKA
KFRE-FM	FRESNO
KNAX-FM	FRESNO
KSKS-FM	FRESNO
KUBB-FM	MERCED
KTRB	MODESTO
KNCQ-FM	REDDING
KNCI-FM	SACRAMENTO
KRAK	SACRAMENTO
KRAK-FM	SACRAMENTO
KTOM-FM	SALINAS
KSON-FM	SAN DIEGO
KSAN-FM	SAN FRANCISCO
KEEN	SAN JOSE
KSUE-FM	SUSANVILLE
KJUG-FM	TULARE
KUKI-FM	UKIAH
KHAY-FM	VENTURA

COLORADO

KHII-FM	COLORADO SPRINGS
KKCS-FM	COLORADO SPRINGS
KRTZ-FM	CORTEZ
KDHT-FM	DENVER
KYGO-FM	DENVER
KRSJ-FM	DURANGO
KGLL-FM	FORT COLLINS
KEKB-FM	GRAND JUNCTION
KSEC-FM	LAMAR
KVAY-FM	LAMAR
KCCY-FM	PUEBLO
KSPK-FM	WALSENBURG
KUAD-FM	WINDSOR

CONNECTICUT

WWYZ-FM	WATERBURY

DELAWARE

WDSD-FM	DOVER

FLORIDA

WGNE-FM	DAYTONA BEACH
WCKT-FM	FORT MYERS
WHEW-FM	FORT MYERS

WKIS-FM	HOLLYWOOD
WQIK-FM	JACKSONVILLE
WROO-FM	JACKSONVILLE
WQLC-FM	LAKE CITY
WPCV-FM	LAKELAND
WQHL-FM	LIVE OAK
WTRS-FM	OCALA
WWKA-FM	ORLANDO
WXBM-FM	PACE
WJST-FM	PANAMA CITY
WPAP-FM	PANAMA CITY
WOWW-FM	PENSACOLA
WQYK	SAINT PETERSBURG
WQYK-FM	SAINT PETERSBURG
WHKX-FM	TALLAHASSEE
WTNT-FM	TALLAHASSEE
WIRK-FM	WEST PALM BEACH

GEORGIA

WNGC-FM	ATHENS
WKHX-FM	ATLANTA
WYAI-FM	ATLANTA
WYAY-FM	ATLANTA
WBYZ-FM	BAXLEY
WKUB-FM	BLACKSHEAR
WBGA-FM	BRUNSWICK
WCHK-FM	CANTON
WSTH-FM	COLUMBUS
WCON-FM	CORNELIA
WOKA-FM	DOUGLAS
WDEN-FM	MACON
WMAZ	MACON
WMTM-FM	MOULTRIE
WSTH-FM	ROME
WCHY-FM	SAVANNAH
WZLI-FM	TOCCOA
WAAC-FM	VALDOSTA

IDAHO

KIZN-FM	BOISE
KQFC-FM	BOISE
KCDA-FM	COEUR D'ALENE
KUPI-FM	IDAHO FALLS
KZBQ-FM	POCATELLO
KEZJ-FM	TWIN FALLS

ILLINOIS

WRUL-FM	CARMI
WUSN-FM	CHICAGO
WIAI-FM	DANVILLE
WDZQ-FM	DECATUR
WCRC-FM	EFFINGHAM
WAAG-FM	GALESBURG
WDDD-FM	MARION
WMIX-FM	MOUNT VERNON
WACF-FM	PARIS
WGEM-FM	QUINCY
WXXG-FM	ROCKFORD
WCCI-FM	SAVANNA
WFMB-FM	SPRINGIELD

INDIANA

WKKG-FM	COLUMBUS
WCNB-FM	CONNERSVILLE
WYNG-FM	EVANSVILLE
WBTU-FM	FORT WAYNE
WFMS-FM	INDIANAPOLIS
WWKI-FM	KOKOMO
WASK-FM	LAFAYETTE
WMDH-FM	MUNCIE
WTHI-FM	TERRE HAUTE

IOWA

KHAK-FM	CEDAR RAPIDS
KMGO-FM	CENTERVILLE
KITR-FM	CRESTON
WLLR-FM	DAVENPORT
KJJY-FM	DES MOINES
KDMI-FM	DES MOINES
KXIA-FM	MARSHALLTOWN
KIAI-FM	MASON CITY
KOEL-FM	OELWEIN
KJJC-FM	OSCEOLA
KBOE-FM	OSKALOOSA
KTLB-FM	ROCKWELL CITY
KSUX-FM	SIOUX CITY
KICD-FM	SPENCER CITY
KXEL	WATERLOO
KQWC-FM	WEBSTER CITY

KANSAS

KKJQ-FM	GARDEN CITY
KBUF	GARDEN CITY
KVGB-FM	GREAT BEND
KHAZ-FM	HAYS
KGLS-FM	HUTCHINSON
KHUT-FM	HUTCHINSON
KSLS-FM	LIBERAL
KFNF-FM	OBERLIN
KZOC-FM	OSAGE CITY
KKOW-FM	PITTSBURG
KYEZ-FM	SALINA
KTPK-FM	TOPEKA
WIBW-FM	TOPEKA
KFDI-FM	WICHITA
KZSN-FM	WICHITA

KENTUCKY

WKYA-FM	CENTRAL CITY
WKDP-FM	CORBIN
WPRX-FM	GLASGOW
WLGC-FM	GREENUP
WSGS-FM	HAZARD
WHOP-FM	HOPKINSVILLE
WVLK-FM	LEXINGTON
WAMZ-FM	LOUISVILLE
WXID-FM	MAYFIELD
WBKR-FM	OWENSBORO
WKYQ-FM	PADUCAH
WSIP-FM	PAINTSVILLE
WBVR-FM	RUSSELLVILLE
WSEK-FM	SOMERSET

LOUISIANA

KRRV-FM	ALEXANDRIA
WKJN-FM	BATON ROUGE
WYNK-FM	BATON ROUGE
KCIL-FM	HOUMA
KJEF	JENNINGS
KJEF-FM	JENNINGS
KMDL-FM	LAFAYETTE
KYKZ-FM	LAKE CHARLES
KWLV-FM	MANY
KJLO-FM	MONROE
WNOE	NEW ORLEANS
WNOE-FM	NEW ORLEANS
WWL	NEW ORLEANS
KLAA-FM	PINEVILLE
KXKZ-FM	RUSTON
KRMD-FM	SHREVEPORT
KWKH	SHREVEPORT
KWKH-FM	SHREVEPORT

MAINE

WKCG-FM	AUGUSTA
WYOU-FM	BANGOR
WQCB-FM	BREWER
WPOR-FM	PORTLAND
WMCM-FM	ROCKLAND
WCME-FM	YARMOUTH

MARYLAND

WROG-FM	CUMBERLAND
WXCY-FM	HAVRE DE GRACE

MASSACHUSETTS

WPKK-FM	SPRINGFIELD

MICHIGAN

WATZ-FM	ALPENA
WCXI	DETROIT
WWWW-FM	DETROIT
WYKX-FM	ESCANABA
WCUZ-FM	GRAND RAPIDS
WLTO-FM	HARBOR SPRINGS
WJPD-FM	ISHPEMING
WNWM-FM	KALAMAZOO
WITL-FM	LANSING
WCEN-FM	MOUNT PLEASANT
WHCH-FM	MUNISING
WMUS-FM	MUSKEGON
WUPY-FM	ONTONAGON
WKCQ-FM	SAGINAW
WIDN	SAINT IGNACE
WMKC-FM	SAINT IGNACE
WKJC-FM	TAWAS CITY
WTCM-FM	TRAVERSE CITY

MINNESOTA

KIKV-FM	ALEXANDRIA
KAUS-FM	AUSTIN
KBHP-FM	BEMIDJI
WAVC-FM	DULUTH
WLKX-FM	FERGUS FALLS
KLQL-FM	LUVERNE
KVOX-FM	MOORHEAD
KYSM-FM	NORTH MANKATO
KPRM	PARK RAPIDS
KWWK-FM	ROCHESTER
WWJO-FM	SAINT CLOUD
KEEY-FM	SAINT PAUL
KQYB-FM	SPRING GROVE
KSRQ-FM	THIEF RIVER FALLS
WCDK-FM	VIRGINIA
KKWS-FM	WADENA
KKWQ-FM	WARROAD

MISSISSIPPI

WBLE-FM	BATESVILLE
WKNN-FM	BILOXI
WMBC-FM	COLUMBUS
WQST-FM	FOREST
WDMS-FM	GREENVILLE
WHER-FM	HATTIESBURG
WCPC	HOUSTON
WIIN-FM	JACKSON
WMSI-FM	JACKSON
WBKJ-FM	KOSCIUSKO
WBBN-FM	LAUREL
WAKH-FM	McCOMB
WOKK-FM	MERIDIAN
WZMP-FM	MERIDIAN
WQNZ-FM	NATCHEZ
WWMS-FM	OXFORD
WZRH-FM	PICAYUNE
WKOR-FM	STARKVILLE
WWZD-FM	TUPELO

MISSOURI

KAAN-FM	BETHANY
KPCR-FM	BOWLING GREEN
KRZK-FM	BRANSON
KEZS-FM	CAPE GIRARDEAU
KMZU-FM	CARROLLTON
KCLR-FM	COLUMBIA
KOEA-FM	DONIPHAN
KTJJ-FM	FARMINGTON
KICK-FM	HANNIBAL
KIXQ-FM	JOPLIN
KFKF-FM	KANSAS CITY
KTMO-FM	KENNETT
KMMO-FM	MARSHALL
KWWR-FM	MEXICO
KRES-FM	MOBERLY
KKLR-FM	POPLAR BLUFF
KZNN-FM	ROLLA
KSJQ-FM	SAINT JOSEPH
WIL-FM	SAINT LOUIS
WKKX-FM	SAINT LOUIS
KLTQ-FM	SPRINGFIELD
KTTS-FM	SPRINGFIELD
KUKU-FM	WILLOW SPRINGS

MONTANA

KGLM-FM	ANACONDA
KCTR-FM	BILLINGS
KYBS-FM	BOZEMAN
KIKC-FM	FORSYTH
KLFM-FM	GREAT FALLS
KMON-FM	GREAT FALLS
KPQX-FM	HAVRE
KBLL-FM	HELENA
KOFI-FM	KALISPELL
KERR	POLSON
KCGM-FM	SCOBEY
KCGH-FM	SIDNEY

NEBRASKA

KQSK-FM	ALLIANCE
KZEN-FM	CENTRAL CITY
KAMI-FM	COZAD
KSDZ-FM	GORDON
KRGI-FM	GRAND ISLAND
KEZH-FM	HASTINGS
KRVN	LEXINGTON
KZKX-FM	LINCOLN
KNCY-FM	NEBRASKA CITY
KXNP-FM	NORTH PLATTE
KRBX-FM	O'NEILL

KMCX-FM	OGALLALA
WOW-FM	OMAHA
KNLV-FM	ORD
KNEB-FM	SCOTTSBLUFF

NEVADA

KFMS-FM	LAS VEGAS
KBUL-FM	RENO
KHIT-FM	RENO
KROW	RENO

NEW HAMPSHIRE

WOKQ-FM	DOVER

NEW JERSEY

WLQE-FM	RIO GRANDE

NEW MEXICO

KOLT-FM	ALBUQUERQUE
KRST-FM	ALBUQUERQUE
KUCU-FM	ALBUQUERQUE
KTZA-FM	ARTESIA
KCEM-FM	AZTEC
KCLV-FM	CLOVIS
KTRA-FM	FARMINGTON
KGLX-FM	GALLUP
KXTC-FM	GALLUP
KPER-FM	HOBBS
KCKN	ROSWELL
KWES-FM	RUIDOSO
KNYN-FM	SANTA FE
KNFT-FM	SILVER CITY

NEW YORK

WGNA-FM	ALBANY
WPCX-FM	AUBURN
WYRK-FM	BUFFALO
WPIG-FM	OLEAN
WBEE-FM	ROCHESTER
WFRG-FM	ROME

NORTH CAROLINA

WPCM-FM	BURLINGTON
WSOC-FM	CHARLOTTE
WTDR-FM	CHARLOTTE
WKML-FM	FAYETTEVILLE
WKTC-FM	GOLDSBORO
WRNS-FM	KINSTON
WQDR-FM	RALEIGH
WFMX-FM	STATESVILLE
WTQR-FM	WINSTON-SALEM

NORTH DAKOTA

KBMR	BISMARCK
KQDY-FM	BISMARCK
KBTO-FM	BOTTINEAU
KZZY-FM	DEVILS LAKE
KFGO-FM	FARGO
KNOX-FM	GRAND FORKS
KYCK-FM	GRAND FORKS
KQDJ-FM	JAMESTOWN
KQLX-FM	LISBON
KZPR-FM	MINOT
KDSR-FM	WILLISTON
KDRQ-FM	WISHEK

OHIO

WNCO-FM	ASHLAND
WKKJ-FM	CHILLICOTHE
WLW	CINCINNATI
WGAR-FM	CLEVELAND
WHKO-FM	CHUCK BROWNING
WELA-FM	EAST LIVERPOOL
WSRW-FM	HILLSBORO
WHOK-FM	LANCASTER
WIMT-FM	LIMA
WMRN-FM	MARION
WPFB-FM	MIDDLETON
WCLT-FM	NEWARK
WPAY-FM	PORTSMOUTH
WQXK-FM	SALEM
WKKO-FM	TOLEDO
WQKT-FM	WOOSTER

OKLAHOMA

KRPT-FM	ANADARKO
KICM-FM	ARDMORE

KKAJ-FM	ARDMORE
KSWR-FM	CLINTON
KECO-FM	ELK CITY
KNID-FM	ENID
KKBS-FM	GUYMON
KGYN	GUYMON
KITX-FM	HUGO
KLAW-FM	LAWTON
KFXI-FM	MARLOW
KMCO-FM	McALESTER
KMMY-FM	MUSKOGEE
KEBC-FM	OKLAHOMA CITY
KXXY-FM	OKLAHOMA CITY
KTFX-FM	TULSA
KVOO	TULSA
KVOO-FM	TULSA
KWEN-FM	TULSA
KITO-FM	VINITA
KWEY-FM	WEATHERFORD
KWOX-FM	WOODWARD

OREGON

KRKT-FM	ALBANY
KICE-FM	BEND
KOOS-FM	COOS BAY
KFAT-FM	CORVALLIS
KUGN-FM	EUGENE
KRWQ-FM	GOLD HILL
KLAD-FM	KLAMATH FALLS
KCMB-FM	LA GRANDE
KTEL-FM	MILTON-FREEWATER
KSRV-FM	ONTARIO
KWHT-FM	PENDLETON
KUPL-FM	PORTLAND
KWJJ	PORTLAND
KWJJ-FM	PORTLAND
KSJJ-FM	REDMOND

PENNSYLVANIA

WXTU	BALA-CYNWYD
WOWQ-FM	DUBOIS
WIOV-FM	EPHRATA
WXTA-FM	ERIE
WGTY-FM	GETTYSBURG
WRKZ-FM	HERSHEY
WZPR-FM	MEADVILLE
WRJS-FM	OIL CITY
WDSY-FM	PITTSBURGH
WFGY-FM	STATE COLLEGE
WGMR-FM	STATE COLLEGE
WHGL-FM	TROY
WAYZ-FM	WAYNESBORO

RHODE ISLAND

WCTK-FM	EAST PROVIDENCE

SOUTH CAROLINA

WEZL-FM	CHARLESTON
WCOS-FM	COLUMBIA
WAGI-FM	GAFFNEY
WESC	GREENVILLE
WESC-FM	GREENVILLE
WSSL-FM	GREENVILLE
WAGL	LANCASTER
WHLZ-FM	MANNING
WKXC-FM	NORTH AUGUSTA

SOUTH DAKOTA

KBWS-FM	EDEN
KMIT-FM	MITCHELL
KOLY	MOBRIDGE
KIQK-FM	RAPID CITY
KQKD-FM	REDFIELD
KDLO-FM	SIOUX FALLS
KPLO-FM	SIOUX FALLS
KTWB-FM	SIOUX FALLS
KBHB	STURGIS
KRCS-FM	STURGIS
KSDR-FM	WATERTOWN
KKYA-FM	YANKTON

TENNESSEE

WDOD-FM	CHATTANOOGA
WUSY-FM	CHATTANOOGA
WGSQ-FM	COOKEVILLE
WTNV-FM	JACKSON
WWYN-FM	JACKSON
WUSJ-FM	JOHNSON CITY
WIVK-FM	KNOXVILLE
WGFX-FM	MEMPHIS
WSIX-FM	NASHVILLE
WSM	NASHVILLE

WSM-FM	NASHVILLE
WYCQ-FM	NASHVILLE

TEXAS

KBCY-FM	ABILENE
KEAN-FM	ABILENE
KBUY-FM	AMARILLO
KMML-FM	AMARILLO
KASE-FM	AUSTIN
KVET-FM	AUSTIN
KIOX-FM	BAY CITY
KAYD-FM	BEAUMONT
KYKR-FM	BEAUMONT
KWHI-FM	BRENHAM
KOXE-FM	BROWNWOOD
KYWL-FM	BROWNWOOD
KAGG-FM	BRYAN COLLEGE ST.
KSRW-FM	CHILDRESS
KOUL-FM	CORPUS CHRISTI
KRYS-FM	CORPUS CHRISTI
KAND-FM	CORSICANA
KIVY-FM	CROCKETT
KPLX-FM	DALLAS
KRSR-FM	DALLAS
KHEY-FM	EL PASO
KSCS-FM	FORT WORTH
WBAP	FORT WORTH
KTEX-FM	HARLINGEN
KVRP-FM	HASKELL
KIKK-FM	HOUSTON
KILT-FM	HOUSTON
KKBQ-FM	HOUSTON
KRVL-FM	KERRVILLE
KETX-FM	LIVINGSTON
KYKX-FM	LONGVIEW
KLLL-FM	LUBBOCK
KYKS-FM	LUFKIN
KATG-FM	LULING
KLSR-FM	MEMPHIS
KCRS-FM	MIDLAND
KNFM-FM	MIDLAND
KYXS-FM	MINERAL WELLS
KPXI-FM	MOUNT PLEASANT
KJCS-FM	NACOGDOCHES
KGEE-FM	ODESSA
KYYK-FM	PALESTINE
KOMX-FM	PAMPA
KOYN-FM	PARIS
KPOS-FM	POST
KGKL-FM	SAN ANGELO
KAJA-FM	SAN ANTONIO
KCYY-FM	SAN ANTONIO
KKYK	SAN ANTONIO
KSTV	STEPHENVILLE
KPLE-FM	TEMPLE
KNUE-FM	TYLER
KIXS-FM	VICTORIA
KPLV-FM	VICTORIA
KJNE-FM	WACO
KNFO-FM	WACO
WACO-FM	WACO
KLUR-FM	WICHITA FALLS
KYYI-FM	WICHITA FALLS

UTAH

KSSD-FM	CEDAR CITY
KKWZ-FM	RICHFIELD
KSGI-FM	SAINT GEORGE
KKAT-FM	SALT LAKE CITY
KSOP-FM	SALT LAKE CITY

VERMONT

WOKO-FM	NEWPORT

VIRGINIA

WAXM-FM	BIG STONE GAP
WXBQ-FM	BRISTOL
WSVS	CREWE
WSVS-FM	CREWE
WAKG-FM	DANVILLE
WPKZ-FM	ELKTON
WFLS-FM	FREDERICKSBURG
WBRF-FM	GALAX
WKCY-FM	HARRISONBURG
WYYD-FM	LYNCHBURG
WMEV-FM	MARION
WPSK-FM	PULASKI
WFHK-FM	RICHMOND
WRVA	RICHMOND
WCMS-FM	VIRGINIA BEACH
WGH-FM	VIRGINIA BEACH
WUSQ	WINCHESTER

WASHINGTON

KRPM-FM	BELLEVUE
KMNT-FM	CENTRALIA
KCLK-FM	CLARKSTON
KZZL-FM	COLFAX
KEYF-FM	GRAND COULEE
KOTY-FM	KENNEWICK
KWIQ-FM	MOSES LAKE
KMPS-FM	SEATTLE
KDRK-FM	SPOKANE
KORD-FM	TRI-CITIES
KXDD-FM	YAKIMA

WEST VIRGINIA

WJLS-FM	BECKLEY
WTNJ-FM	BECKLEY
WBUC-FM	BUCKHANNON
WQBE-FM	CHARLESTON
WKKW-FM	CLARKSBURG
WTCR-FM	HUNTINGTON
WHCM-FM	PARKERSBURG
WCKA-FM	SUTTON
WOVK-FM	WHEELING
WWVA	WHEELING
WXCC-FM	WILLIAMSON

WISCONSIN

WJLW-FM	DE PERE
WRJO-FM	EAGLE RIVER
WIGN-FM	MEDFORD
WMIL	MILWAUKEE
WPKR-FM	OSHKOSH
WPRE-FM	PRAIRIE DU CHIEN
WJMC-FM	RICE LAKE
WCOW-FM	SPARTA
WYTE-FM	STEVENS POINT
WJJQ-FM	TOMAHAWK
WEGZ-FM	WASHBURN
WDEZ-FM	WAUSAU
WBWI-FM	WEST BEND

WYOMING

KTWO	CASPER
KMUS-FM	CHEYENNE
KOTB-FM	EVANSTON
KZMQ-FM	GREYBULL
KCGY-FM	LARAMIE
KQSW-FM	ROCK SPRINGS

DISTRICT OF COLUMBIA

WMZQ-FM	WASHINGTON, D.C.

CANADA

ALBERTA

CFAC	CALGARY
CKRY-FM	CALGARY
CKDQ	DRUMHELLER
CFCW	EDMONTON
CISN-FM	EDMONTON
CKGY	RED DEER

BRITISH COLUMBIA

CFJC	KAMLOOPS
CJJR-FM	VANCOUVER
CKWX	VANCOUVER
CFFM-FM	WILLIAMS LAKE

MANITOBA

CFRY	PORT LA PRAIRIE
CFQK-FM	SELKIRK

NEW BRUNSWICK

CHHJ-FM	FREDERICTON
CFQM-FM	MONCTON

NEWFOUNDLAND

CKIX-FM	SAINT JOHN'S

NOVA SCOTIA

CJFX	ANTIGONISH
CHFX-FM	HALIFAX
CKEC	NEW GLASGOW
CKPE-FM	SYDNEY

ONTARIO

CHAM	HAMILTON
CFMK-FM	KINGSTON
CKGL-FM	KITCHENER
CJBX-FM	LONDON
CKAT-FM	NORTH BAY
CKBY-FM	OTTAWA
CKQM-FM	PETERBOROUGH
CJQM-FM	SAULT STE. MARIE
CHEQ-FM	SMITHS FALLS
CIGM	SUDBURY
CKYC	TORONTO

PRINCE EDWARD ISLAND

CHLQ-FM	CHARLOTTETOWN

QUEBEC

CIRO-FM	VILLE ST. GEORGES

MOVIES IN WHICH COUNTRY MUSIC PERFORMERS HAVE APPEARED

(For contemporary performers see their biographical entries. We regret that the year of release was not available for some of the movies listed here.)

ROY ACUFF AND HIS SMOKEY MOUNTAIN BOYS
1940 Grand Ole Opry
1940 Hi Neighbor
1944 Oh My Darling Clementine
1944 Cowboy Canteen
1947 "Sing, Neighbor, Sing"
1948 Smoky Mountain Melody
1949 San Antonio Rose
The Night Train to Memphis

REX ALLEN
1950 Trail of Robin Hood
1950 The Arizona Cowboy
1950 Under Mexicali Rose
1951 Silver City Bonanza
1951 Rodeo King and the Senorita
1951 Utah Wagon Train
1952 Old Oklahoma Plains
1953 Iron Mountain Trail
1953 Down Laredo Way
1954 Phantom Stallion
Frontier Doctor

1960 For the Love of Mike
1960 Tomboy and the Champ

BILL ANDERSON
1964 Country Music on Broadway
1966 Forty Acre Feud
1966 The Road to Nashville
1967 Las Vegas Hillbillies

JOHNNIE ARIZONA
1945 Kid from Arizona
1947 I Shot Jesse James
1947 El Paso
1948 Red Rock Outlaw
1948 Gun Shot Pass
1949 Silver Bandit
1950 Kansas

ARKIE THE ARKANSAS WOODCHOPPER
1945 National Barn Dance

RED ARNALL AND THE WESTERN ACES
1948 Blazing Across the Pecos

EDDIE ARNOLD
1949 Feudin' Rhythm
1950 Hoedown

ERNEST ASHWORTH
1964 The Farmer's Other Daughter

BOB ATCHER
1941 Panhandle Trail
1943 Hail to the Rangers

TEX ATCHISON
1943-47 33 movies

GENE AUTRY
1934 In Old Santa Fe
1934 Mystery Mountain
The Rattler
The Man Nobody Knows
The Eye That Never Sleeps
The Human Target
Phantom Outlaws
The Perfect Crime
Tarzan the Cunning
The Enemy's Stronghold
The Fatal Warning
The Secret of the Mountain
Behind the Mask
The Judgement of Tarzan

1935	The Phantom Empire
	The Singing Cowboy
	The Thunder Riders
	The Lightning Chamber
	The Phantom Broadcast
	Beneath the Earth
	Disaster from the Skies
	Jaws of Jeapardy
	From Death to Life
	Prisoners of the Ray
	The Rebellion
	A Queen in Chains
	The End of Murania
1935	Tumbling Tumbleweeds
1935	Melody Trail
1935	The Sagebrush Troubadour
1935	The Singing Vagabond
1936	Red River Valley
1936	Comin' Round the Mountain
1936	The Singing Cowboy
1936	Guns and Guitars
1936	Oh, Susanna!
1936	Ride, Ranger, Ride
1936	The Big Show
1936	The Old Corral
1937	Round-Up Time in Texas
1937	Git Along Little Dogies
1937	Rootin' Tootin' Rhythm
1937	Yodelin' Kid from Pine Ridge
1937	Public Cowboy No. 1
1937	Boots and Saddles
1937	Manhattan Merry-Go-Round
1937	Springtime in the Rockies
1938	The Old Barn Dance
1938	Gold Mine in the Sky
1938	Man from Music Mountain
1938	Prairie Moon
1938	Rhythm of the Saddle
1938	Rodeo Dough
1938	Western Jamboree
1939	Home on the Prairie
1939	Mexicali Rose
1939	Blue Montana Skies
1939	Mountain Rhythm
1939	Colorado Sunset
1939	In Old Monterey
1939	Rovin' Tumbleweeds
1939	South of the Border
1940	Rancho Grande
1940	Shooting High
1940	Gaucho Serenade
1940	Carolina Moon
1940	Ride, Tenderfoot, Ride
1940	Melody Ranch
1941	Ridin' on a Rainbow
1941	Back in the Saddle
1941	The Singing Hills
1941	Meet Roy Rogers
1941	Sunset in Wyoming
1941	Under Fiesta Stars
1941	Down Mexico Way
1941	Sierra Sue
1942	Cowboy Serenade
1942	Heart of the Rio Grande
1942	Home in Wyomin'
1942	Stardust on the Sage
1942	Call of the Canyon
1942	Bells of Capistrano
1946	Sioux City Sue
1947	Trail to San Antone
1947	Twilight on the Rio Grande
1947	Saddle Pals
1947	Screen Snapshots
1947	Robin Hood of Texas
1947	The Last Roundup
1948	The Strawberry Roan
1949	Loaded Pistols
1949	The Big Sombrero
1949	Riders of the Whistling Pines
1949	Rim of the Canyon
1949	The Cowboy and the Indians
1949	Riders in the Sky
1950	Sons of New Mexico
1950	Mule Train
1950	Cow Town
1950	Beyond the Purple Hills
1950	Indian Territory
1950	The Blazing Hills
1951	Gene Autry and the Mounties
1951	Texans Never Cry
1951	Whirlwind
1951	Silver Canyon
1951	The Hills of Utah
1951	Valley of Fire
1952	The Old West
1952	Night Stage to Galveston
1952	Apache Country
1952	Barbed Wire
1952	Wagon Team
1952	Blue Canadian Rockies
1953	The Winning of the West
1953	On Top of Old Smokey
1953	Gold Town Ghost Riders
1953	Pack Train
1953	Saginaw Trail
1953	The Last of the Pony Riders

1956 Hollywood Bronc Busters
1973 Ken Murray's Hometown Hollywood
1976 It's Showtime
1977 Semi Tough
1982 Some Kind of Hero
1989 Great Balls of Fire

BOB BAKER
1937 Courage of the West
1938 The Black Bandit
1938 Outlaw Express
1938 Western Trails
1939 Honor of the West
1939 Ghost Town Raiders
1939 Desperate Trails
1939 Oklahoma Frontier
1939 Chip of the Flying U
1940 Riders of Pasco Basin
1940 West of Carson City
1940 Badman of Red Butte
1941 Meet Roy Rogers
1942 Ride 'Em Cowboy
1943 Wild Horse Stampede
1944 Mystery Man

SMITH BALLEW
1936 Palm Springs
1937 Western Gold
1937 Roll Along, Cowboy
1937 Hawaiian Buckaroo
1938 Rawhide
1938 Panamint's Bad Man
1946 Under Arizona Skies
1950 The Cariboo Trail

BOBBY BARE
1964 A Distant Trumpet

CURT BARRETT AND THE TRAILSMEN
1946 Drifting Along
1946 Gunning for Vengeance
1946 The Gentleman from Texas
1947 Raiders of the South

MOLLY BEE
1954 Corral Cuties

BILL BLACK
1957 Loving You
1957 Jailhouse Rock
1958 King Creole

NOEL BOGGS
1950 Everybody's Dancin'
1950 Out West Teenagers

JOHNNY BOND
1939 Saga of Death Valley
1940 The Tulsa Kid
1940 Pony Post
1940 Trailing Double Trouble
1940 Give Us Wings
1941 Twilight on the Trail
1941 Stick to Your Guns
1942 Deep in the Heart of Texas
1942 Little Joe the Wrangler
1942 The Old Chisholm Trail
1943 Tenting Tonight on the Old Camp Ground
1943 Cheyenne Roundup
1943 Raiders of San Joaquin
1943 Robin Hood of the Range
1943 The Lone Star Trail
1943 Frontier Jury
1944 Riding West
1947 Duel in the Sun
Kansas City Kitty
Gallant Bess
Six Lessons
Wilson
Cowboy Commandos

DON BOWMAN
Hillbillies in a Haunted House
Hillbillies in Las Vegas

BILL (COWBOY RAMBLER) BOYD
1942 Prairie Pals

ROD BRASFIELD
1956 Face in the Crowd
Country Music Holiday

ELTON BRITT
1949 Laramie
The Last Doggie
The Prodigal Son

THE BROWN BROTHERS
1949 Square Dance Jubilee

SMILEY BURNETTE
Under Sea Kingdom
Rex and Rinty
1935 The Phantom Empire
1935 Tumbling Tumbleweeds

1936 The Big Show
1936 The Old Corral
1937 Dick Tracy
1938 The Old Barn Dance
1938 Gold Mine the Sky
1938 Under Western Stars
1938 Billy the Kid Returns
1938 Western Jamboree
1939 Mexicali Rose
1939 Blue Montana Skies
1939 Colorado Sunset
1939 South of the Border
1940 Carolina Moon
1941 Back in the Saddle
1941 Sierra Sue
1941 Heart of the Golden West
1942 Home in Wyomin'
1942 Call of the Canyon
1943 Idaho
1943 King of the Cowboys
1943 Silver Spurs
1943 Beyond the Last Frontier
1944 Call of the Rockies
1944 Firebrands of Arizona
1946 Roaring Rangers
1946 Gunning for Vengeance
1946 Galloping Thunder
1946 Two-Fisted Stranger
1946 The Desert Horseman
1946 Heading West
1946 Landrush
1946 The Fighting Frontiersman
1947 South of the Chisholm Trail
1947 The Lone Hand Texan
1947 West of Dodge City
1947 Law of the Canyon
1947 Prairie Rangers
1947 The Stranger from Ponca City
1947 Riders of the Lone Star
1947 Buckaroo from Powder River
1947 Last Days of Boot Hill
1947 My Pal Ringeye
1948 Six Gun Law
1948 Phantom Valley
1948 West of Sonora
1948 Whirlwind Raiders
1948 Blazing Across the Pecos
1948 Trail to Laredo
1948 El Dorado Pass
1948 Quick on the Trigger
1949 Challenge of the Range
1949 Laramie
1949 The Blazing Trail
1949 South of Death Valley
1949 Bandits of El Dorado
1949 Desert Vigilante
1949 Horseman of the Sierras
1949 Renegades of the Sage
1950 Trail of the Rustlers
1950 Outcasts of Black Mesa
1950 Texas Dynamo
1950 Streets of Ghost Town
1950 Across the Badlands
1950 Raiders of Tomahawk Creek
1950 Lightning Guns
1951 Frontier Outpost
1951 Prairie Roundup
1951 Ridin' the Outlaw Trail
1951 Fort Savage Raiders
1951 Snake River Desperadoes
1951 Bonanza Town
1951 Cyclone Fury
1951 The Kid from Amarillo
1951 Pecos River
1952 Smoky Canyon
1952 The Hawk of Wild River
1952 Laramie Mountains
1952 The Rough, Tough West
1952 Junction City
1952 The Kid from Broken Gun
1953 Pack Train

JERRY BYRD
1947 Hollywood Barn Dance

GLEN CAMPBELL
1969 True Grit
1970 Norwood
Baby the Rain Must Fall
The Cool Ones
1974 Strange Homecoming

JUDY CANOVA
1937 Thrill of a Lifetime

CLAUDE CASEY
1949 Square Dance Jubilee

TOMMY CASH
1968 Still on the Hill

THE CASS COUNTY BOYS
1947 Trail to San Antone
1947 Twilight on the Rio Grande
1947 Buckaroo from Powder River
1948 Trail to Laredo
1951 The Kid from Amarillo

CHICKIE AND BUCK
1944 Cowboy Canteen

CURLY CLEMENTS AND HIS RODEO RANGERS
1948 Six Gun Law

ZEKE CLEMENTS
1937 Snow White & the Seven Dwarfs
1938 Code of the Rangers
1946 Two-Fisted Stranger

EDDIE CLETRO AND HIS ROUNDUP BOYS
1950 Trail of the Rustlers

SPADE COOLEY
Redskins and Redheads
1939 Marshall of Mesa City
1942 Home in Wyomin'
1945 Outlaws of the Rockies
1945 Texas Panhandle
1949 Square Dance Jubilee
1949 The Silver Bandit
1950 Border Outlaws

COWBOY COPAS
1949 Square Dance Jubilee

CARL COTNER
1939-48 40 Gene Autry movies

COUSIN EMMY
1944 Swing in the Saddle
1955 The Second Greatest Sex

COUSIN HERB
In Ranch Party TV films

KEN CURTIS
1945 Song of the Prairie
1947 Over the Santa Fe Trail
1949 Stallion Canyon
1949 Riders of the Pony Express
Ripcord
Have Gun, Will Travel
Gunsmoke

T. TOMMY CUTRER
1966 Music City, U.S.A.

ART DAVIS
1938 Code of the Cactus
1941 The Texas Marshall
1942 Texas Manhunt
1942 Along the Sundown

GAIL DAVIS
1946 The Romance of Rosy Ridge
If You Knew Susie
1948 The Far Frontier
1950 Trail of the Rustlers
1950 Six Gun Mesa
1951 Silver Canyon
1952 The Old West
1959 Alias Jesse James
Cow Town
Annie Oakley

JIMMIE DAVIS
1942 Riding Through Nevada
1943 Frontier Fury
1944 Cyclone Prairie Rangers
1947 Louisiana

EDDIE DEAN
1938 Western Jamboree
1939 Renegade Trail
1939 Range War
1939 Law of the Pampas
1940 Santa Fe Marshal
1940 The Showdown
1940 The Light of Western Stars
1940 Hidden Gold
1940 Stagecoach War
1941 Trail of the Silver Spurs
1941 Gauchos of Eldorado
1941 Sierra Sue
1941 Fighting Bill Fargo
1945 Wildfire
1945 Song of Old Wyoming
1946 Tumbleweed Trail
1946 The Caravan Trail
1946 Colorado Serenade
1946 Stars Over Texas
1946 Wild West
1947 West to Glory
1947 Black Hills
1948 The Hawk of Powder River
1948 Prairie Outlaws

TOMMY DUNCAN AND HIS WESTERN ALL STARS
1941 Go West Young Lady
1949 South of Death Valley

CLIFF "UKELELE IKE" EDWARDS
1940 Pinnochio
1941 Thunder Over the Prairie
1941 Prairie Stranger
1941 Riders of the Badland

1941 West of Tombstone
1941 Lawless Plainmen
1942 Riders of the Northland
1942 Bad Men of the Hills
1942 Overland to Deadwood

DALE EVANS
Swing Your Partner
West Side Kid
Here Comes Elmer
Hoosier Holiday
In Old Oklahoma
1944 The Cowboy and the Senorita
1944 Yellow Rose of Texas
1944 Song of Nevada
1944 San Fernando Valley
1944 Lights of Old Santa Fe
1945 Utah
1945 Bells of Rosarita
1945 The Man From Oklahoma
1945 Sunset in El Dorado
1945 Don't Fence Me In
1945 Along the Navajo Trail
1946 Song of Arizona
1946 Rainbow of Texas
1946 My Pal Trigger
1946 Under Nevada Skies
1946 Roll on Texas Moon
1946 Home in Oklahoma
1946 Out California Way
1947 Heldorado
1947 Apache Rose
1947 Bells of San Angelo
1949 Susanna Pass
1949 Down Dakota Way
1949 The Golden Stallion
1950 Bells of Coronado
1950 Twilight in the Sierras
1950 Trigger, Jr.
1951 South of Caliente
1951 Pals of the Golden West

RITA FAYE
1966 Girl from Tobacco Row

SHUG FISHER
1941 Don't Fence Me In
1962 The Man Who Shot Liberty Vallance
1964 Cheyenne Autumn

TEX FLETCHER
1939 Six Gun Rhythm

RED FOLEY
1941 The Pioneers
1946 Over the Trail

D.J. FONTANA
1957 Loving You
1957 Jailhouse Rock
1958 King Creole

DICK FORAN
1934 Stand Up and Cheer
1935 Moonlight on the Prairie
1936 Treachery Rides the Range
1936 Song of the Saddle
1936 Rhythm of the Range
1936 Trailin' West
1936 The California Mail
1937 Guns of the Pecos
1937 Land Beyond the Law
1937 Cherokee Strip
1937 Blazing Sixes
1937 Empty Holsters
1937 The Devil's Saddle Legion
1937 Prairie Thunder
1937 Vitaphone Pictorial Revue, New Series No. 3
1938 Heart of the North
1940 The Mummy's Hand
1941 Road Agent
1942 Ride 'Em Cowboy
1945 Guest Wife
1948 Fort Apache
1964 Taggart

TENNESSEE ERNIE FORD
1954 Corral Cuties
River of No Return

JIMMY GATELY
1966 Forty Acre Feud
1966 Road to Nashville
Las Vegas Hillbillies

TERRY GILKYSON
1956 Star in the Dust

TOMPALL GLASER
1966 Country Boy

GEORGE GOBEL
1956 The Birds and the Bees
1957 I Married a Woman

MONTE HALE
1944 Stepping in Society
1944 Big Bonanza
1946 Home on the Range
1946 Out California Way
1947 Along the Oregon Trail
1949 Pioneer Marshal
1950 Trail of Robin Hood
1950 Vanishing Westerner
1956 Giant
1973 Guns of a Stranger
1974 The Chase

STUART HAMBLEN
1939 The Arizona Kid
1941 King of the Cowboys
1950 The Savage Horde

TEX HARDING
1945 Return of the Durango Kid
1945 Both Barrels Blazing
1945 Rustlers of the Badlands
1945 Blazing the Western Trail
1945 Outlaws of the Rockies
1945 Lawless Empire
1945 Texas Panhandle
1946 Frontier Gunlaw

REDD HARPER
1948 Strawberry Roan
1951 Mr. Texas
1952 Oil Town, U.S.A.
1954 Letter from Green Oaks
1963 Mr. T. at Teen Ranch

GEORGE D. HAY
1940 Grand Ole Opry
Hoosier Holiday

BOBBY HELMS
1958 Case Against Brooklyn

HAROLD HENSLEY
1946 Headin' West
1948 West of the Alamo
1949 Copper Canyon
1959 The Philadelphians
1960 Oceans Eleven
1961 Spartacus
1961 Inherit the Wind
1966 The Pad & How to Use It
1966 The Hank Williams Story

HERMAN THE HERMIT
1949 Square Dance Jubilee

BILLY HILL
1934 The Last Roundup
1934 The Old Spinning Wheel
1934 Wagon Wheels
1936 Empty Saddles

SALTY HOLMES
1944 Saddle Leather Law

THE HOOSIER HOTSHOTS
1939 Mountain Rhythm
1945 Sing Me a Song of Texas

GEORGE HOUSTON
1934 The Melody Lingers On
1938 Frontier Scout
1941 The Lone Rider Rides On
1942 Outlaws of Boulder Pass

FERLIN HUSKY
Mr. Rock and Roll
Country Music Holiday
Hillbillies in a Haunted House
Las Vegas Hillbillies

AUTRY INMAN
Face in the Crowd
Music City U.S.A.

STONEWALL JACKSON
1964 Country Music on Broadway

SONNY JAMES
Second Fiddle to a Steel Guitar
1966 Nashville Rebel
1967 Las Vegas Hillbillies

WAYLON JENNINGS
1966 Nashville Rebel

JORDANAIRES
1957 Loving You
1957 Jailhouse Rock
1958 Sing, Boy, Sing
1958 Country Music Holiday
1958 King Creole
1960 G.I. Blues

PEE WEE KING AND HIS GOLDEN WEST COWBOYS
1938 Gold Mine in the Sky
1951 Ridin' the Outlaw Trail
1952 The Rough, Tough West
1961 Hoedown

LA DELL SISTERS
Country Music Holiday

JOHN LAIR
1966 Renfro Valley Barn Dance

LILY MAY LEDFORD
1966 Renfro Valley Barn Dance

HUGH X. LEWIS
1966 Forty Acre Feud
1967 Gold Guitar
1967 Cotton-Pickin' Chicken-Pickers

JERRY LEE LEWIS
1957 Jamboree
1958 High School Confidential
1960 Young and Deadly

TEXAS JIM LEWIS AND HIS LONE STAR COWBOYS
1940 Badmen from Red Butte
1942 Pardon My Gun
1947 Law of the Canyon
1947 The Stranger from Ponca City

RONNY LIGHT
Second Fiddle to a Steel Guitar

LONZO & OSCAR
Country Music Holiday

LULU BELLE AND SCOTTY
1938 Shine on Harvest Moon
1939 Village Barn Dance
1940 Hi Neighbor
1941 Country Fair
1944 National Barn Dance
1947 Sing, Neighbor, Sing

BOB LUMAN
1967 Carnival Rock

LORETTA LYNN
1966 Nashville Rebel
1966 Forty Acre Feud
1966 Music City U.S.A.

UNCLE DAVE MACON
1940 Grand Ole Opry

DORRIS MACON
1940 Grand Ole Opry

LORENE MANN
1966 Music City U.S.A.

THE MAPLE CITY FOUR
1938 The Old Barn Dance
1938 Under Western Stars

FRANKIE MARVIN
1938 Gold Mine in the Sky
1938 The Old Barn Dance
1939 Colorado Sunset
1939 Saga of Death Valley
1941 Sierra Sue
1951 Silver Canyon

KEN MAYNARD
1923 The Man Who Won
1929 In Old Arizona
1929/30 Mountain Justice
1929/30 Song of the Caballero
1929/30 Sons of the Saddle
1930 Roarin' Ranch
1930 Trigger Tricks
1931 Range Law
1932 Dynamite Ranch
1932 Between Fighting Men
Arizona Terror
Branded Men
Alias—The Bad Men
1932 Hell-Fire Austin
1932 Come On, Tarzan
1932 Fargo Express
1932 Tombstone Canyon
1933 Drum Taps
1933 King of the Arena
1933 Fiddlin' Buckaroo
1933 Strawberry Roan
1933 Trail Drive
1934 Gun Justice
1934 Wheels of Destiny
1934 Smoking Guns
1934 In Old Santa Fe
1934 Mystery Mountain
1935 Western Frontier
1935 Western Courage
1937 Boots of Destiny
1937 Trailin' Trouble
1938 Whirlwind Horseman

1938 Shootin' Sheriff
1939 Flaming Lead
1940 Death Rides the Range
1943 Death Valley Rangers
1943 Wild Horse Stampede
1944 Arizona Whirlwind
1944 Harmony Trail

LEON McAULIFE
1940 Take Me Back to Oklahoma
1940 Northwest Mounted Police
1941 Go West, Young Lady
1942 Saddles & Sage Brush
1942 Silver City Raider
1942 Tornado in the Saddle

SKEETS McDONALD
Ma & Pa Kettle
1954 The Glenn Miller Story

BIG RED McPEAKE
1964 Country Music on Broadway
1966 Forty Acre Feud

MINNIE PEARL
1966 Forty Acre Feud
1966 Nashville Beat

PATSY MONTANA
1939 Colorado Sunset

SCOTTY MOORE
1957 Loving You
1957 Jailhouse Rock
1958 King Creole

MOON MULLICAN
1939 Village Barn Dance

MUSTARD AND GRAVY
1947 The Lone Hand Texan
1947 West of Dodge City
1949 Bandits of El Dorado

WELDON MYRICK
1966 Forty Acre Feud
1967 Nashville Rebel
1967 Hell on Wheels
1967 Las Vegas Hillbillies

RICKY (RICK) NELSON
1959 Rio Bravo

HANK NEWMAN AND THE GEORGIA CRACKERS
1946 The Fighting Frontiersman
1947 South of the Chisholm Trail
1949 Desert Vigilante

THE NOTABLES QUARTET
1940 West of Carson City
1940 Law and Order

DOYE O'DELL AND THE RADIO RANGERS
1946 Heldorado
1948 Whirlwind Rangers

OSBORNE BROTHERS
1966 Music City U.S.A.
1966 Road to Nashville

BUCK OWENS
1964 Country Music on Broadway
1967 Buck Owens on Tour

DOROTHY PAGE
Manhattan Moon
King Solomon of Broadway
Mama Runs Wild
1938 Ride 'Em Cowgirl
1938 The Singing Cowgirl
1938 Water Rustlers

PALS OF THE GOLDEN WEST
1942 The Silver Bullet
1942 Boss of Hangtown Mesa

ANDY PARKER AND THE PLAINSMEN
1947 Black Hills

HANK PENNY AND HIS PLANTATION BOYS
1946 Heading West
1947 The Blazing Trail
1950 Frontier Outpost

CARL PERKINS
1956 Jamboree
1958 Hawaiian Boy

WEBB PIERCE
1958 Buffalo Guns

RAY PILLOW
1966 Country Boy

ELVIS PRESLEY
1956 Love Me Tender
1957 Loving You

1957 Jailhouse Rock
1958 King Creole
1960 G.I. Blues
1960 Flaming Star
1961 Wild in the Country
1961 Blue Hawaii
1962 Follow That Dream
1962 Kid Gallahad
1962 Girls! Girls! Girls!
1963 It Happened at the World's Fair
1963 Fun in Acapulco
1964 Kissin' Cousins
1964 Viva Las Vegas
1964 Roustabout
1965 Girl Happy
1965 Tickle Me
1965 Harum Scarum
1966 Paradise—Hawaiian Style
1966 Frankie and Johnnie
1966 Spinout
1967 Double Trouble
1967 Easy Come, Easy Go
1967 Clambake
1968 Stay Away, Joe
1968 Speedway
1968 Live a Little, Love a Little
1969 Charro!
1969 The Trouble with Girls
1969 Change of Habit
1970 Elvis, That's the Way It Is
1971 Warnung Vor Einer Heiligen Nutte
1973 Elvis on Tour
1981 This Is Elvis

LEW PRESTON AND HIS RANCH HANDS
1941 Prairie Stranger

JACK RANDALL
1935 His Family Tree
1937 Riders in the Dawn
1937 Danger Valley
1937 Stars Over Arizona
1938 Where the West Begins
1938 Land of Fighting Men
1938 The Mexicali Kid
1939 Drifting Westward
1939 Trigger Smith
1940 Wild Horse Range
1940 Riders from Nowhere
1940 The Cheyenne Kid
1940 Covered Wagon Trails
1945 The Royal Mounted Rides Again

RED RIVER DAVE
1948 Swing in the Saddle
1948 Hidden Valley Days
1948 Echo Ranch

DEL REEVES
Second Fiddle to a Steel Guitar
1966 Forty Acre Feud
1967 Gold Guitar
1967 Cotton-Pickin' Chicken-Pickers
Whiskey's Renegades

JIM REEVES
1964 Kimberly Jim

AL RICE
1938 The Old Barn Dance
1938 Under Western Stars
Get Along Little Dogies

JERRY RICHARDS
1946 Musical Shipmates

ACE RICHMAN (See also SUNSHINE BOYS)
1951 Prairie Roundup

JIMMY RIDDLE
1944 Oh My Darling Clemetine
1945 Cowboy Canteen
1947 Sing, Neighbor, Sing
1948 Smoky Mountain Melody
1949 San Antonio Rose

TEX RITTER
1936 Song of the Gringo
1936 Headin' for the Rio Grande
1937 Arizona Days
1937 Trouble in Texas
1937 Riders of the Rockies
1937 The Mystery of the Hooded Horsemen
1937 Tex Rides with the Boy Scouts
1937 Hittin' the Trail
1938 Frontier Town
1938 Rollin' Plains
1938 Utah Trail
1938 Starlight over Texas
1938 Where the Buffalo Roam
1938 Song of the Buckaroo
1939 Down the Wyoming Trail
1939 The Man from Texas
1939 Riders of the Frontier
1939 Sundown on the Prairie
1940 Rhythm of the Rio Grande
1940 Arizona Frontier

1941	The Pioneers
1942	Deep in the Heart of Texas
1942	Little Joe the Wrangler
1942	The Old Chisholm Trail
1943	Tenting Tonight on the Old Camp Ground
1943	Cheyenne Roundup
1943	Raiders of San Joaquin
1943	The Lone Star Trail
1943	Arizona Trail
1943	Marshal of Gunsmoke
1944	Oklahoma Raiders
1944	Cowboy Canteen
1945	Marked for Murder
1945	Enemy of the Law
1945	Flaming Bullets
1953	Wichita
1955	Apache Ambush
1966	Girl from Tobacco Row
1967	Nashville Rebel
	What Am I Bid
	The Cowboy
	The First Badman
	What's This Country Coming To
1952	High Noon
1953	The Marshall's Daughter
1955	Wichita
1957	Trooper Hook

MARTY ROBBINS

1958	Buffalo Guns
	The Gun & the Gavel
	The Badge of Marshall Breman
1966	Road to Nashville
1967	Hell on Wheels

JIMMIE RODGERS

	Movie short

ROY ROGERS

1935	Slightly Static
1935	The Old Homestead
1935	Way Up Thar
1935	Tumbling Tumbleweeds
1935	Gallant Defender
1936	The Mysterious Avenger
1936	Song of the Saddle
1936	Rhythm of the Range
1936	The California Mail
1936	The Big Show
1936	The Old Corral
1937	The Old Wyoming Trail
1937	Wild Horse Rodeo
1938	The Old Barn Dance
1938	Under Western Stars
1938	Billy the Kid Returns
1938	Come on, Rangers!
1938	Shine on Harvest Moon
1939	Rough Riders Round-Up
1939	Frontier Pony Express
1939	Southward Ho!
1939	In Old Caliente
1939	Wall Street Cowboy
1939	The Arizona Kid
1939	Jeepers Creepers
1939	Saga of Death Valley
1939	Days of Jesse James
1940	Dark Command
1940	Young Buffalo Bill
1940	The Carson City Kid
1940	The Ranger and the Lady
1940	Colorado
1940	Young Bill Hickok
1940	Rodeo Dough
1940	The Border Legion
1941	Robin Hood of the Pecos
1941	Arkansas Judge
1941	In Old Cheyenne
1941	Sheriff of Tombstone
1941	Nevada City
1941	Meet Roy Rogers
1941	Bad Men of Deadwood
1941	Jesse James at Bay
1941	Red River Valley
1942	Man From Cheyenne
1942	South of Santa Fe
1942	Sunset on the Desert
1942	Romance of the Range
1942	Son of the Pioneers
1942	Sunset Serenade
1942	Heart of the Golden West
1942	Ridin' Down the Canyon
1943	Idaho
1943	King of the Cowboys
1943	Song of Texas
1943	Silver Spurs
1943	Man from Music Mountain
1944	Hands Across the Border
1944	The Cowboy and the Senorita
1944	Yellow Rose of Texas
1944	Song of Nevada
1944	San Fernando Valley
1944	Lights of Old Santa Fe
1944	Brazil
1944	Lake Placid Serenade
1944	Hollywood Canteen
1945	Utah

1945 Bells of Rosarita
1945 The Man From Oklahoma
1945 Sunset in El Dorado
1945 Don't Fence Me In
1945 Along the Navajo Trail
1946 Song of Arizona
1946 Rainbow of Texas
1946 My Pal Trigger
1946 Under Nevada Skies
1946 Roll on Texas Moon
1946 Home in Oklahoma
1946 Out California Way
1947 Heldorado
1947 Apache Rose
1947 Hit Parade of 1947
1947 Bells of San Angelo
1947 Springtime in the Sierras
1947 Screen Snapshots
1947 On the Old Spanish Trail
1948 The Gay Ranchero
1948 Under California Stars
1948 Eyes of Texas
1948 Melody Time
1948 Night Time in Nevada
1948 Grand Canyon Trail
1948 The Far Frontier
1949 Susanna Pass
1949 Down Dakota Way
1949 The Golden Stallion
1950 Bells of Coronado
1950 Twilight in the Sierra
1950 Trigger, Jr.
1950 Sunset in the West
1950 North of the Great Divide
1950 Trail of Robin Hood
1950 Spoilers of the Plains
1950 Heart of the Rockies
1951 In Old Amarillo
1951 South of Caliente
1951 Pals of the Golden West
1952 Son of Palceface
1956 Hollywood Bronc Busters
1959 Alias Jesse James
1973 Ken Murray's Hometown Hollywood
1976 Macintosh & T.J.

FRED SCOTT
1936 The Last Outlaw
1936 Romance Rides the Range
1936 The Singing Buckaroo
1937 Melody of the Plains
1937 Rangers' Roundup
1939 Code of the Fearless
1939 In Old Montana
1939 Two Gun Troubadour
1942 Ridin' the Trail
1942 Rodeo Rhythm
Songs and Bullets

CARL (CAL) SHRUM AND HIS RHYTHM RANGERS
1940 Rollin' Home to Texas
1941 Thunder Over the Prairie
1945 The Lost Trail

WALT SHRUM AND HIS COLORADO HILLBILLIES
1938 The Old Barn Dance
1939 Blue Montana Skies
1946 The Desert Horseman

JIMMY SIMPSON
1960 The Alamo

BEN SMATHERS
1964 Country Music on Broadway
1965 Tennessee Beat
1966 Country Boy

SMILEY & KITTY
1949 Square Dance Jubilee

CARL SMITH
1958 Buffalo Guns
The Badge of Marshall Breman

SONS OF THE PIONEERS
1935 Slightly Static
1935 The Old Homestead
1935 Way Up Thar
1935 Gallant Defender
1936 The Mysterious Avenger
1936 Song of the Saddle
1936 Rhythm of the Range
1936 The California Mail
1936 The Big Show
1936 The Old Corral
1937 The Old Wyoming Trail
1937 Outlaws of the Prairie
1938 Cattle Raiders
1938 Call of the Rockies
1938 Law of the Plains
1938 West of Cheyenne
1938 South of Arizona
1938 The Colorado Trail
1938 West of the Santa Fe
1938 Rio Grande

1939 The Thundering West
1939 Texas Stampede
1939 North of the Yukon
1939 Spoilers of the Range
1939 Western Caravans
1939 The Man From Sundown
1939 Riders of Black River
1939 Outpost of the Mounties
1939 The Stranger from Texas
1940 Two-Fisted Rangers
1940 Bullets for Rustlers
1940 Blazing Six Shooters
1940 Texas Stagecoach
1940 The Durango Kid
1940 West of Abilene
1940 Thundering Frontier
1941 The Pinto Kid
1941 Outlaws of the Panhandle
1941 Red River Valley
1942 Call of the Canyon
1942 Man from Cheyenne
1942 South of Santa Fe
1942 Sunset on the Desert
1942 Romance of the Range
1942 Sons of the Pioneers
1942 Sunset Serenade
1942 Heart of the Golden West
1942 Ridin' Down the Canyon
1943 Idaho
1943 King of the Cowboys
1943 Song of Texas
1943 Silver Spurs
1943 Man from Music Mountain
1944 Hands Across the Border
1944 The Cowboy and the Senorita
1944 Yellow Rose of Texas
1944 Song of Nevada
1944 San Fernando Valley
1944 Lights of Old Santa Fe
1944 Hollywood Canteen
1945 Utah
1945 Bells of Rosarita
1945 The Man from Oklahoma
1945 Sunset in El Dorado
1945 Don't Fence Me In
1945 Along the Navajo Trail
1946 Song of Arizona
1946 Rainbow of Texas
1946 My Pal Trigger
1946 Under Nevada Skies
1946 Roll on Texas Moon
1946 Home in Oklahoma
1946 Heldorado
1947 Apache Rose
1947 Hit Parade of 1947
1947 Bells of San Angelo
1947 Springtime in the Sierras
1947 On the Old Spanish Trail
1948 The Gay Ranchero
1948 Under California Stars
1948 Eyes of Texas
1948 Melody Time
1948 Night Time in Nevada

BILLY STRANGE
1964 The Jet Set
1965 Baby, the Rain Must Fall
1980 Coal Miner's Daughter

THE SUNSHINE BOYS
1948 West of Sonora
1948 Quick on the Trigger
1949 Challenge of the Range
1951 Prairie Roundup

DOTTIE SWAN
1947 Hollywood Barn Dance

THE TAILOR MAIDS
1944 Cowboy Canteen

TOM TALL
1951 Kidnapper's Foil

THE TENNESEE RAMBLERS
1944 Sundown Valley

GORDON TERRY
1956 Hidden Guns
1957 Raiders of Old California
1958 Buffalo Guns

THE TEXAS RANGERS
1939 Colorado Sunset
1939 Oklahoma Frontier
1940 Son of Roaring Dan
1940 Ragtime Cowboy Joe
1941 Law of the Range
1941 Rawhide Ranger

HANK THOMPSON
1966 Smokey

SHORTY THOMPSON AND HIS SADDLE ROCKIN' RHYTHM
1948 El Dorado Pass

MEL TILLIS
1967 Cotton-Pickin' Chicken-Pickers

MERLE TRAVIS
1946 Roaring Rangers
1946 Galloping Thunder
1951 Cyclone Fury
1953 From Here to Eternity

ERNEST TUBB
1943 The Fighting Buckaroo
1944 Riding West
1944 Jamboree
1947 Hollywood Barn Dance

T. TEXAS TYLER
1949 Horsemen of the Sierras

LEROY VAN DYKE
Bartholomew
1967 What Am I Bid
Can You See the Rainbow

JIMMY WAKELY
1939 Saga of Death Valley
1940 Pony Post
1941 Bury Me Not on the Lone Prairie
1941 Heart of the Rio Grande
1941 The Silver Bullet
1941 Twilight on the Trail
1942 Deep in the Heart of Texas
1942 Little Joe the Wrangler
1942 The Old Chisholm Trail
1943 Tenting Tonight on the Old Camp Ground
1943 Cheyenne Roundup
1943 Raiders of San Joaquin
1943 Robin Hood of the Range
1943 The Lone Star Trail
1943 Cowboy in the Clouds
1944 Cowboy Canteen
1944 Sundown Valley
1944 Cowboy from Lonesome River
1944 Cyclone Prairie Ramblers
1944 Saddle Leather Law
1944 Song of the Range
1945 Springtime in Texas
1945 Saddle Serenade
Song of the Sierras
1945 Sagebrush Heroes
1945 Rough Ridin' Justice
1947 Ridin' Down the Trail
1947 Song of the Wasteland
1948 Oklahoma Blues
1948 Silver Trails
1948 Swing in the Saddle
1949 Lawless Code
1953 The Marshal's Daughter
1954 Arrow in the Dust
Brand of Fear
Moon Over Montana
Riders of the Swan
Lonesome Trail

OZIE WATERS AND HIS COLORADO RANGERS
1944 Mystery Man
1946 Landrush
1946 Terror Trail
1947 Prairie Raiders
1948 Phantom Valley
1950 Outcasts of Black Mesa
1950 Streets of Ghost Town

DENNIS WEAVER
1952 The Redhead from Wyoming
1952 Law and Order
1953 Column South

KITTY WELLS
Second Fiddle to a Steel Guitar

DOTTIE WEST
There's a Still on the Hill

JOHNNY WESTERN
Have Gun, Will Travel
Pony Express
Gunsmoke
Boots and Saddles
Wells Fargo
Bat Masterson

RAY WHITLEY
1934 Educational Pictures
1935 Educational Pictures
1936 Hopalong Cassidy Returns
1937 The Old Wyoming Trail
1938 Gun Law
1938 Border G-Man
1938 The Painted Desert
1938 The Renegade Ranger
1939 Trouble in Sundown
1939 Racketeers of the Range
1939 Cupid Rides the Range
1940 Prairie Papas
1940 Molly Cures a Cowboy

1940 Wagon Train
1940 The Fargo Kid
1941 Along the Rio Grande
1941 Robbers of the Range
1941 Cyclone on Horseback
1941 Six Gun Gold
1941 The Bandit Trail
1941 Dude Cowboy
1942 Riding the Wind
1942 Land of the Open Range
1942 Come on, Danger!
1942 Thudering Hoofs
1944 Boss of Boomtown
1944 Trigger Trail
1944 Riders of the Santa Fe
1944 The Old Texas Trail
1945 Beyond the Pecos
1945 Renegades of the Rio Grande
1951 California or Bust
1956 Giant

AUDREY WILLIAMS
1964 Country Music on Broadway

CURLY WILLIAMS AND HIS GEORGIA PEACH PICKERS
1947 Riders of the Lone Star

GARY WILLIAMS
Western Ranch Party

HANK WILLIAMS, JR.
1964 Country Music on Broadway

TEX WILLIAMS
1945 Outlaws of the Rockies
1947 Tex Williams and His Western Caravan
1950 Tales of the West

FOY WILLING AND THE RIDERS OF THE PURPLE SAGE
1944 Cowboy from Lonesome River
1944 Cyclone Prairie Rangers
1945 Sing Me a Song of Texas
1946 Out California Way
1947 Along the Oregon Trail
1948 Grand Canyon Trail
1948 The Far Frontier
1949 Susanna Pass
1949 Down Dakota Way
1949 The Golden Stallion
1950 Bells of Coronado
1950 Twilight in the Sierras
1950 Trigger, Jr.
1950 Sunset in the West
1950 North of the Great Divide
1950 Trail of Robin Hood
1951 Spoilers of the Plains
1951 Heart of the Rockies

WILLIS BROTHERS
1949 Feuding Rhythm
1949 Hoe Down

BOB WILLS AND HIS TEXAS PLAYBOYS
1940 Take Me Back to Oklahoma
1941 Go West Young Lady
1945 Blazing the Western Trail
1945 Lawless Empire
1946 Frontier Frolic
1948 Echo Ranch
1954 Corral Cuties

CHILL WILLS AND HIS AVALON BOYS
1935 Bar 20 Rides Again
1936 Call of the Prairie
1960 The Alamo

SMILEY WILSON (see SMILEY & KITTY)
1952 The Black Lash

SHEB WOOLEY
1950 Rocky Mountain
1952 Hellgate
1952 High Noon
1952 Distant Drums
Little Big Horn
1954 Man Without a Star
1956 Giant
1968 War Wagon

JOHNNY WRIGHT
Second Fiddle to a Steel Guitar
1964 Country Music on Broadway
1966 The Road to Nashville

FARON YOUNG
1955 Hidden Guns
1956 Raiders of Old California
1956 Daniel Boone
1957 Country Music Holiday
1966 Nashville Rebel
1967 What Am I Bid

BIBLIOGRAPHY/RECOMMENDED FURTHER READING

"San Antonio Rose (The Life and Music of Wills)"
Charles R. Townsend (University of Illinois)
"The Oak Ridge Boys: Our Story"
With Ellis Widner and Walter Carter (Contemporary)
"A Satisfied Mind: The Music Life of Porter Wagoner"
Steve Eng (Rutledge Hill Press)
"Heroes of the Range: Yesteryear's Saturday Matinee Movie Cowboys"
Buck Rainey (Scarecrow Press)
"Finding Her Voice: The Saga of Women in Country Music"
Mary A. Bufwack and Robert Oermann (Crown Publishers)
"Country Music U.S.A."
Bill C. Malone (University of Texas)
"Nashville: Music City U.S.A."
John Lomax III (Harry N. Abrams)
"Hollywood Corral"
Don Miller (Riverwood Press)
"New Life in Country Music"
Paul Davis (Walter UK)
"Heart Worn Memories"
Susie Nelson (Eakin Press)
"One Day at a Time"
Cristy Lane (St. Martin's Press/LS)
"Roy Acuff's Nashville: The Life and Good Times of Country Music"
Roy Acuff with William Neely (Perigee)
"Country Music Buyers/Sellers Reference Book and Price Guide"
Jerry Osborne (Osborne Enterprises)
"Box-Office Buckaroos: The Cowboy Hero from the Wild West Show to the Silver Screen"
Robert Heide & John Gilman (Abbeville Press)
"Sunshine and Shadow"
Jan Howard (Richardson & Steirman)
"Coal Miner's Daughter"
Loretta Lynn (Contemporary Books)
"Bluegrass: A History"
Neil Rosenberg (University of Illinois Press)
"South to Louisiana: The Music of the Cajun Bayous"
John Broven (Pelican)
"Tears, Love and Laughter: The Story of the Cajuns and Their Music"
Pierre V. Dagle (Swallow Publications)
"Stars of Country Music"
Edited by Bill C. Malone and Judith McCulloh (University of Illinois Press)
"New Rock Record"
Terry Hounsome (Blandford Press UK)
"Sing Your Heart Out Country Boy"
Dorothy Horstman (Country Music Foundation)
"Rock and Pop Day by Day"
Frank Laufenberg (Blandford UK)
"Still in Love with You: The Story of Hank & Audrey Williams"
Lycrecia Williams and Dale Vinicur (Rutledge Hill)
"The Stonemans"
Ivan M. Tribe (University of Illinois Press)